# EMPLOYMENT, HOURS, AND EARNINGS

## STATES AND AREAS

**Fifteenth Edition**
**2020**

# EMPLOYMENT, HOURS, AND EARNINGS

## STATES AND AREAS

**Fifteenth Edition**
**2020**

**Edited by Mary Meghan Ryan**

Lanham, MD

Published by Bernan Press
An imprint of The Rowman & Littlefield Publishing Group, Inc.
4501 Forbes Boulevard, Suite 200, Lanham, Maryland 20706
www.rowman.com
800-865-3457

6 Tinworth Street, London SE11 5AL, United Kingdom

ISBN:   978-1-64143-433-1
e-ISBN: 978-1-64143-434-8

∞™ The paper used in this publication meets the minimum requirements of
American National Standard for Information Sciences—Permanence of
Paper for Printed Library Materials, ANSI/NISO Z39.48-1992.

# CONTENTS

## PART B: METROPOLITAN STATISTICAL AREA (MSA) DATA

**APPENDIX**

# PREFACE

Bernan Press proudly presents the fifteenth edition of *Employment, Hours, and Earnings: States and Areas, 2020.* A special addition to Bernan Press's *Handbook of U.S. Labor Statistics: Employment, Earnings, Prices, Productivity, and Other Labor Data*, this reference is a consolidated wealth of employment information, providing monthly and annual data on hours worked and earnings made by industry across America for the years 2011 through 2019, including figures and summary information spanning years the same time period. These data, compiled by the Bureau of Labor Statistics, are presented for states and metropolitan statistical areas.

This edition features:

- Nearly 300 tables with data on employment for each state, the District of Columbia, and the nation's 75 largest metropolitan statistical areas (MSAs)

- Detailed, non-seasonally adjusted, industry data organized by month and year

- Hours and earnings data for each state, by industry

- An introduction for each state and the District of Columbia that denotes salient data and noteworthy trends, including changes in population and the civilian labor force, industry increases and declines, employment and unemployment statistics, and a chart detailing employment percentages, by industry

- Ranking of the 75 largest MSAs, including Census population estimates for 2019, unemployment rates for 2010 and 2019, and the percent change in total non-farm employment from 2011 through 2019

- Concise technical notes that explain pertinent facts about the data, including sources, definitions, and significant changes; and provides references for further guidance

- A comprehensive appendix that details the geographical components of the 75 largest MSAs

The employment, hours, and earnings data in this publication provide a detailed and timely picture of the 50 states, the District of Columbia, and the nation's 75 largest MSAs. These data can be used to analyze key factors affecting state and local economies and to compare national cyclical trends to local-level economic activity.

This reference is an excellent source of information for analysts in both the public and private sectors. Readers who are involved in public policy can use these data to determine the health of the economy, to clearly identify which sectors are growing and which are declining, and to determine the need for federal assistance. State and local jurisdictions can use the data to determine the need for services, including training and unemployment assistance, and for planning and budgetary purposes. In addition, the data can be used to forecast tax revenue. In private industry, the data can be used by business owners to compare their business to the economy as a whole; and to identify suitable areas when making decisions about plant locations, wholesale and retail trade outlets, and for locating a particular sector base.

In this fifteenth edition, *Employment, Hours, and Earnings: States and Areas* presents monthly and annual average data on employment for each state, the District of Columbia, and the nation's 75 largest metropolitan statistical areas (MSAs). In addition, hours and earnings data are provided, where available, for each state. The industry data are based on the North American Industry Classification System (NAICS), which is discussed in greater detail later in these notes. The employment data are presented on a monthly and annual basis for 2011 through 2019. The hours and earnings data are available from 2015 through 2019.

The Bureau of Labor Statistics (BLS), the statistical agency within the U.S. Department of Labor, conducts the Current Employment Statistics (CES) survey to provide industry data on the employment, hours, and earnings of workers on nonfarm payrolls. The unemployment data and the civilian labor force estimates in this publication were obtained from the Local Area Unemployment Statistics (LAUS) program, which provides monthly employment and unemployment data for over 7,500 geographic areas including Census regions and divisions, states, counties, metropolitan areas, and many cities and towns.

The data from both the CES and LAUS are derived from federal and state cooperative collection efforts in which state employment security agencies prepare data using concepts, definitions, and technical procedures prescribed by the BLS. Although the estimation of the two data sets are based on differing methodologies (described in more detail later in this section), their inclusion together in this reference is intended to provide a broad overview of state and local labor market conditions.

## THE CURRENT EMPLOYMENT STATISTICS (CES) SURVEY—EMPLOYMENT, HOURS, AND EARNINGS DATA

The CES survey is a monthly survey commonly referred to as the establishment or payroll survey that provides estimates of employment, hours, and earnings data by industry. Its estimates are derived from a sample of about 145,000 private nonfarm businesses and federal, state, and local government entities, which cover approximately 697,000 individual worksites in all 50 states, the District of Columbia, Puerto Rico, the U.S. Virgin Islands, and more than 350 metropolitan areas and divisions. These establishments are classified on the basis of their primary activity by major industry groupings in accordance with NAICS. For an establishment engaging in more than one activity, the entire establishment is included under the industry indicated as the principal activity.

More information on the exact methodology used to obtain data for employment, hours, and earnings was originally detailed in the *BLS Handbook of Methods*. The *Handbook* is updated online and can be found at www.bls.gov/opub/hom. Information on the CES survey can also be found on the BLS website at www.bls.gov/ces/cesprog.htm.

## CONCEPTS

*Employment* is the total number of persons employed either full or part-time in nonfarm business establishments during a specific payroll period. Temporary employees are included as well as civilian government employees. Unpaid family members working in a family-owned business, domestic workers in private homes, farm employees, and self-employed persons are excluded from the CES, as well as military personnel and employees of the Central Intelligence Agency, the National Security Agency, the National Imagery and Mapping Agency, and the Defense Intelligence Agency. In addition, employees on layoff, on leave without pay, on strike for the entire pay period, or who had been hired but did not start work during the pay period are also excluded.

The reference period includes all persons who worked during or received pay for any part of the pay period that includes the 12th of the month, a standard for all federal agencies collecting employment data from business establishments. Workers who are on paid sick leave (when pay is received directly from the employer) or paid holiday or vacation, or who worked during only part of the specified pay period (because of unemployment or strike during the rest of the pay period) are counted as employed. Employees on the payroll of more than one establishment during the pay period are counted in each establishment that reports them, whether the duplication is due to turnover or dual jobholding.

*Nonfarm employment* includes employment in all goods-producing and service-providing industries. The goods-producing sector includes mining and logging, construction, and manufacturing, the last of which is made up of durable and nondurable goods (these breakdowns are not provided in this publication). The service-providing sector includes both private service-providing and government employment. Private service sector employment includes trade, transportation, and utilities (which is comprised of wholesale trade, retail trade, and transportation and utilities); information; financial activities; professional and business services; educational and health services; leisure and hospitality; and other services. Government employment encompasses federal-, state-, and local-level civilian employees. Subcategories of these industries are available on the BLS website at www.bls.gov/sae.

*Unemployment* consists of those who were not employed during the reference week but were available for work, except for temporary illness, and had made specific efforts to find employment some time during the 4-week period ending with the reference week. Persons who were waiting to be recalled to a job from which they had been laid off are classified as unemployed even if they have not been looking for another job.

The *unemployment rate* is the number of unemployed persons as a percent of the civilian labor force.

The *civilian labor force* consists of all persons classified as employed or unemployed as described above.

*Hours and earnings* data for each state are based on reports from industry payrolls and the corresponding hours paid for construction workers, production workers, and nonsupervisory workers. The data include workers who received pay for any part of the pay period that includes the 12th day of the month. Because not all sample respondents report production worker hours and earnings data, insufficient sample sizes preclude hours and earnings data from many sectors in many states. Therefore, the data available, and thus published, vary from state to state.

The payroll for these workers is reported before deductions of any kind, including Social Security, unemployment insurance, group health insurance, withholding taxes, retirement plans, or union dues.

Included in the payroll report of earnings is pay for all hours worked, including overtime, shift premiums, vacations, holiday, and sick-leave pay. Bonuses and commissions are excluded unless they are earned and paid regularly each pay period. Benefits, such as health insurance and contribution to a retirement fund, are also excluded.

*Hours* include all hours worked (including overtime hours) and hours paid for holidays, vacations, and sick leave during the pay period that includes the 12th day of the month. Average weekly hours differ from the concept of scheduled hours worked because of factors such as unpaid absenteeism, labor turnover, part-time work, and strikes, as well as fluctuations in work schedules. Average weekly hours are typically lower than scheduled hours of work.

*Average hourly earnings* are derived by dividing gross payrolls by total hours, reflecting the actual earnings of workers (including premium pay). They differ from wage rates, which are the amounts stipulated for a given unit of work or time. Average hourly earnings do not represent total labor costs per hour because they exclude retroactive payments and irregular bonuses, employee benefits,

and the employer's share of payroll taxes. Earnings for employees not included in the production worker or non-supervisory categories are not reflected in the estimates in this publication.

*Average weekly earnings* are derived by multiplying average weekly hours by average hourly earnings.

Users should note that in the context of historical data, long-term trends in hours and earnings data also reflect structural changes, such as the changing mixes of full-time and part-time employees and highly paid and lower-wage workers within businesses and across industries.

## METROPOLITAN STATISTICAL AREAS (MSAS) AND NEW ENGLAND CITY AND TOWN AREAS (NECTAS)

A metropolitan statistical area (MSA) is a core area with a large population nucleus, combined with adjacent communities that have high degrees of economic and social integration with the core area. The standard definition of a MSA is determined by the Office of Management and Budget (OMB), which updates the definition based on the decennial census and updated information provided by the Census Bureau between the censuses. Each MSA must have at least one urbanized area of 50,000 inhabitants or more.

New England city and town areas (NECTAs) are similar to MSAs, but are defined using cities and towns instead of counties in the six New England states. BLS only provides employment data on NECTAs in the New England region. Employment and Unemployment data are provided for the following NECTAs in this publication: Boston-Cambridge-Newton, MA-NH; Hartford-East Hartford-Middletown, CT; Providence-Warwick, RI-MA; New Haven, CT; and Worcester, MA-CT. All other areas are MSAs.

The appendix details the geographic components for each MSA and NECTA.

## REVISIONS TO THE DATA

### *North American Industry Classification System (NAICS)*

The most far-reaching revision of the CES data occurred when the industrial classification system was changed from the 60-year-old Standard Industrial Classification (SIC) system to the North American Industry Classification System (NAICS) in January 2003. The revision changed the way establishments were classified into industries in order to more accurately reflect the current composition of U.S. businesses. In March 2008, the CES state and area nonfarm payroll series was converted to the 2007 NAICS series. This resulted in relatively minor changes. In February

2012, CES updated the national payroll series to NAICS 2012 from NAICS 2007. This resulted in minor content changes within the Manufacturing and Retail trade sectors as well as minor coding changes within the Utilities and Leisure and hospitality sectors. Several industry titles and descriptions were updated as well.

The CES program updated to the 2017 North American Industry Classification System from the NAICS 2012 System with the February 2, 2018 Employment Situation release. For more information on the NAICS 2012 and 2017 classifications, see www.census.gov/epcd/www/naics.html.

NAICS was adopted as the standard measure of industry classification by statistical agencies in the United States, Canada, and Mexico to enhance the comparability of economic data across the North American Free Trade Association (NAFTA) trade area. Comparison between the NAICS and the old SIC are limited, however, the historical industry series from April 1995 through 2001 are available on both SIC and NAICS bases. The BLS has not updated the SIC data nor (for the most part) linked the historical SIC data with the current NAICS data.

### Benchmark Revisions

Employment estimates are adjusted annually to a complete count of jobs—called benchmarks—which are primarily derived from tax reports submitted by employers covered by state unemployment laws (which cover most establishments). In this re-anchoring of sample-based employment estimates to full population counts, the original sample-based estimates are replaced with the benchmark data from the previous year. The benchmark information is used to adjust monthly estimates between the new benchmark and the preceding benchmark, thereby preserving the continuity of the series and establishing the level of employment for the new benchmark month.

### Seasonal Adjustment

Over the course of a year, the size of a state's employment level undergoes sharp fluctuations because of changes in the weather, reduced or expanded production, harvests, major holidays, and the like. Because these seasonal events follow a more or less regular pattern each year, adjusting the data on a month-to-month basis may eliminate their influence on data trends. These adjustments make it easier for users to observe the cyclical and other nonseasonal movements in the data series, but it must be noted that the seasonally adjusted series are only an approximation based on past experience. The seasonally adjusted data have a broader margin of error than the unadjusted data because they are subject to both sampling and other errors in the seasonal adjustment process. The data presented in this publication are not seasonally adjusted; therefore, the month-to-month variations in the data contain seasonal variations that may distort month-to-month comparisons. Data for the MSAs are also not seasonally adjusted, as the sample sizes do not allow for reliable estimates for seasonal adjustment factors.

## THE LOCAL AREA UNEMPLOYMENT STATISTICS (LAUS) PROGRAM

The Local Area Unemployment Statistics (LAUS) program provides monthly and annual estimates on several labor force concepts, including employment, unemployment, labor force totals, and the employment-population ratio. The unemployment data as well as the civilian labor force estimates presented in this publication are from the LAUS program. The unemployment rate is shown for each state in 2010 and 2019 along with the rank for each state. The rankings are from highest to lowest—a change from earlier editions of *Employment, Hours, and Earnings* but consistent with recent editions. In 2019, unemployment ranged from a low of 2.4 percent in North Dakota and Vermont to a high of 6.1 percent in Alaska. Therefore, North Dakota and Vermont are tied for last and Alaska is ranked first. Unemployment data are not available by industry.

The concepts and definitions underlying the LAUS program come from the Current Population Survey (CPS), the household survey conducted by the Census Bureau for the BLS. The LAUS models combine current and historical data from the CPS, Current Employment Statistics (CES), and the State Unemployment Insurance (UI) Systems. Numerous conceptual and technical differences exist between the household and establishment surveys, and estimates of monthly employment changes from these two surveys usually do not match in size or even direction. As a result, the unemployment data and the civilian labor force estimates on each state header page presented in this edition are not directly comparable to the employment data. However, this publication includes this information to provide complementary information on labor market conditions in each state and the District of Columbia. Monthly and annual data are available from the BLS on their website at www.bls.gov/lau. More information on the differences between the surveys, as well as guidance on the complex methods used to obtain the LAUS data, is provided on the BLS website at www.bls.gov/lau/laufaq.htm.

# PART A

# STATE DATA

# ALABAMA
## At a Glance

Population:
  2010 census: 4,779,736
  2019 estimate: 4,903,185

Percent change in population:
  2010–2019: 2.6%

Percent change in total nonfarm employment:
  2011–2019: 9.7%

Industry with the largest growth in employment, 2011–2019 (percent):
  Leisure and hospitality, 23.4%

Industry with the largest decline or smallest growth in employment, 2011–2019 (percent):
  Mining and logging, -18.5%

Civilian labor force:
  2010: 2,196,042
  2019: 2,241,747

Unemployment rate and rank among states (highest to lowest):
  2010: 10.5%, 9th
  2019: 3.0%, 38nd

Over-the-year change in unemployment rates:
  2017–2018: -0.5%
  2018–2019: -0.9%

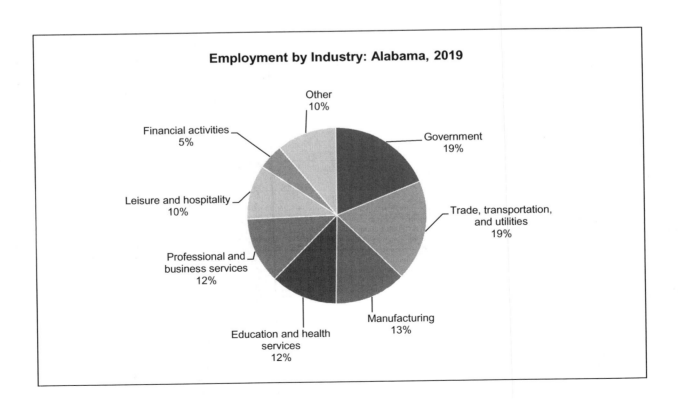

**Employment by Industry: Alabama, 2019**

Other 10%
Financial activities 5%
Government 19%
Leisure and hospitality 10%
Trade, transportation, and utilities 19%
Professional and business services 12%
Education and health services 12%
Manufacturing 13%

## 1. Employment by Industry: Alabama, 2011–2019

| Industry and yea | January | February | March | April | May | June | July | August | September | October | November | December | Annual average |
|---|---|---|---|---|---|---|---|---|---|---|---|---|---|
| **Total Nonfarm** | | | | | | | | | | | | | |
| 2011 | 1,858.7 | 1,873.6 | 1,886.2 | 1,894.6 | 1,897.3 | 1,896.9 | 1,881.7 | 1,886.9 | 1,899.9 | 1,894.4 | 1,905.3 | 1,904.7 | 1,890.0 |
| 2012 | 1,870.4 | 1,882.8 | 1,901.5 | 1,909.6 | 1,912.5 | 1,916.7 | 1,892.7 | 1,903.4 | 1,911.2 | 1,914.0 | 1,927.5 | 1,926.2 | 1,905.7 |
| 2013 | 1,885.5 | 1,903.4 | 1,917.8 | 1,926.4 | 1,934.2 | 1,935.2 | 1,915.2 | 1,923.2 | 1,927.4 | 1,929.6 | 1,942.6 | 1,947.2 | 1,924.0 |
| 2014 | 1,905.7 | 1,915.4 | 1,930.0 | 1,944.1 | 1,950.5 | 1,953.2 | 1,934.1 | 1,945.0 | 1,953.0 | 1,959.0 | 1,966.3 | 1,974.0 | 1,944.2 |
| 2015 | 1,932.5 | 1,945.0 | 1,953.7 | 1,969.1 | 1,978.2 | 1,979.7 | 1,965.9 | 1,972.4 | 1,977.6 | 1,985.9 | 1,993.7 | 2,000.1 | 1,971.2 |
| 2016 | 1,962.9 | 1,974.7 | 1,984.8 | 2,001.5 | 2,003.7 | 2,003.9 | 1,991.6 | 1,998.0 | 2,007.0 | 2,005.7 | 2,013.5 | 2,016.2 | 1,997.0 |
| 2017 | 1,984.4 | 1,999.0 | 2,010.7 | 2,016.6 | 2,023.0 | 2,028.2 | 2,011.3 | 2,019.6 | 2,024.6 | 2,030.7 | 2,039.3 | 2,037.2 | 2,018.7 |
| 2018 | 2,002.0 | 2,018.7 | 2,030.1 | 2,040.7 | 2,044.9 | 2,054.2 | 2,039.8 | 2,048.0 | 2,050.4 | 2,060.8 | 2,073.2 | 2,071.6 | 2,044.5 |
| 2019 | 2,040.0 | 2,053.7 | 2,061.4 | 2,071.3 | 2,075.9 | 2,076.7 | 2,069.2 | 2,076.8 | 2,073.8 | 2,085.7 | 2,093.1 | 2,093.2 | 2,072.6 |
| **Total Private** | | | | | | | | | | | | | |
| 2011 | 1,471.5 | 1,483.0 | 1,494.6 | 1,503.6 | 1,506.8 | 1,510.2 | 1,507.6 | 1,512.9 | 1,516.1 | 1,508.3 | 1,517.6 | 1,518.8 | 1,504.3 |
| 2012 | 1,489.3 | 1,497.6 | 1,514.1 | 1,523.8 | 1,527.5 | 1,534.9 | 1,524.6 | 1,534.4 | 1,533.2 | 1,529.9 | 1,542.1 | 1,541.1 | 1,524.4 |
| 2013 | 1,506.3 | 1,519.4 | 1,531.4 | 1,540.9 | 1,549.4 | 1,554.7 | 1,543.6 | 1,551.4 | 1,549.4 | 1,546.6 | 1,558.0 | 1,563.5 | 1,542.9 |
| 2014 | 1,526.8 | 1,532.6 | 1,545.9 | 1,559.4 | 1,564.6 | 1,569.9 | 1,564.2 | 1,572.6 | 1,571.9 | 1,574.1 | 1,580.3 | 1,587.3 | 1,562.5 |
| 2015 | 1,553.7 | 1,563.0 | 1,570.7 | 1,585.3 | 1,593.0 | 1,597.0 | 1,595.3 | 1,598.8 | 1,597.8 | 1,603.3 | 1,610.1 | 1,616.0 | 1,590.3 |
| 2016 | 1,584.4 | 1,593.0 | 1,601.8 | 1,618.0 | 1,619.1 | 1,620.3 | 1,618.9 | 1,621.6 | 1,623.5 | 1,620.4 | 1,627.0 | 1,629.0 | 1,614.8 |
| 2017 | 1,602.8 | 1,614.2 | 1,624.4 | 1,630.1 | 1,635.3 | 1,641.4 | 1,635.9 | 1,641.5 | 1,639.5 | 1,643.4 | 1,651.1 | 1,649.5 | 1,634.1 |
| 2018 | 1,620.3 | 1,633.4 | 1,643.2 | 1,652.4 | 1,655.0 | 1,664.1 | 1,661.7 | 1,666.5 | 1,662.8 | 1,671.1 | 1,682.4 | 1,680.1 | 1,657.8 |
| 2019 | 1,653.7 | 1,663.9 | 1,670.2 | 1,679.3 | 1,682.6 | 1,683.7 | 1,685.7 | 1,689.7 | 1,680.9 | 1,689.3 | 1,694.3 | 1,696.7 | 1,680.8 |
| **Goods Producing** | | | | | | | | | | | | | |
| 2011 | 322.5 | 326.3 | 329.0 | 330.0 | 331.7 | 332.5 | 331.3 | 332.7 | 332.7 | 331.4 | 332.5 | 334.0 | 330.6 |
| 2012 | 328.6 | 329.9 | 333.3 | 335.1 | 335.5 | 337.0 | 336.7 | 338.2 | 337.9 | 339.0 | 339.1 | 339.7 | 335.8 |
| 2013 | 334.7 | 336.3 | 340.6 | 341.1 | 341.1 | 342.6 | 340.8 | 342.4 | 341.8 | 342.1 | 341.8 | 343.2 | 340.7 |
| 2014 | 338.5 | 339.3 | 341.7 | 342.6 | 344.0 | 345.7 | 345.4 | 346.6 | 347.6 | 348.6 | 348.5 | 349.5 | 344.8 |
| 2015 | 345.6 | 346.8 | 347.6 | 348.8 | 350.0 | 351.8 | 351.2 | 351.6 | 352.2 | 353.0 | 352.9 | 354.4 | 350.5 |
| 2016 | 351.4 | 351.2 | 352.9 | 354.8 | 353.8 | 354.6 | 355.2 | 354.3 | 356.6 | 355.0 | 354.6 | 356.3 | 354.2 |
| 2017 | 354.4 | 356.6 | 358.0 | 356.8 | 357.7 | 358.5 | 358.1 | 358.8 | 360.0 | 361.8 | 361.2 | 362.4 | 358.7 |
| 2018 | 358.3 | 361.8 | 363.4 | 363.4 | 364.2 | 366.2 | 366.8 | 368.2 | 368.9 | 369.9 | 370.7 | 371.7 | 366.1 |
| 2019 | 367.5 | 369.5 | 371.8 | 371.1 | 371.9 | 372.5 | 373.3 | 373.9 | 373.3 | 374.4 | 373.8 | 374.0 | 372.3 |
| **Service-Providing** | | | | | | | | | | | | | |
| 2011 | 1,536.2 | 1,547.3 | 1,557.2 | 1,564.6 | 1,565.6 | 1,564.4 | 1,550.4 | 1,554.2 | 1,567.2 | 1,563.0 | 1,572.8 | 1,570.7 | 1,559.5 |
| 2012 | 1,541.8 | 1,552.9 | 1,568.2 | 1,574.5 | 1,577.0 | 1,579.7 | 1,556.0 | 1,565.2 | 1,573.3 | 1,575.0 | 1,588.4 | 1,586.5 | 1,569.9 |
| 2013 | 1,550.8 | 1,567.1 | 1,577.2 | 1,585.3 | 1,593.1 | 1,592.6 | 1,574.4 | 1,580.8 | 1,585.6 | 1,587.5 | 1,600.8 | 1,604.0 | 1,583.3 |
| 2014 | 1,567.2 | 1,576.1 | 1,588.3 | 1,601.5 | 1,606.5 | 1,607.5 | 1,588.7 | 1,598.4 | 1,605.4 | 1,610.4 | 1,617.8 | 1,624.5 | 1,599.4 |
| 2015 | 1,586.9 | 1,598.2 | 1,606.1 | 1,620.3 | 1,628.2 | 1,627.9 | 1,614.7 | 1,620.8 | 1,625.4 | 1,632.9 | 1,640.8 | 1,645.7 | 1,620.7 |
| 2016 | 1,611.5 | 1,623.5 | 1,631.9 | 1,646.7 | 1,649.9 | 1,649.3 | 1,636.4 | 1,643.7 | 1,650.4 | 1,650.7 | 1,658.9 | 1,659.9 | 1,642.7 |
| 2017 | 1,630.0 | 1,642.4 | 1,652.7 | 1,659.8 | 1,665.3 | 1,669.7 | 1,653.2 | 1,660.8 | 1,664.6 | 1,668.9 | 1,678.1 | 1,674.8 | 1,660.0 |
| 2018 | 1,643.7 | 1,656.9 | 1,666.7 | 1,677.3 | 1,680.7 | 1,688.0 | 1,673.0 | 1,679.8 | 1,681.5 | 1,690.9 | 1,702.5 | 1,699.9 | 1,678.4 |
| 2019 | 1,672.5 | 1,684.2 | 1,689.6 | 1,700.2 | 1,704.0 | 1,704.2 | 1,695.9 | 1,702.9 | 1,700.5 | 1,711.3 | 1,719.3 | 1,719.2 | 1,700.3 |
| **Mining and Logging** | | | | | | | | | | | | | |
| 2011 | 12.1 | 12.1 | 12.1 | 12.3 | 12.4 | 12.5 | 12.3 | 12.5 | 12.6 | 12.5 | 12.5 | 12.6 | 12.4 |
| 2012 | 12.7 | 12.6 | 12.5 | 12.5 | 12.5 | 12.6 | 12.8 | 12.8 | 12.7 | 12.6 | 12.6 | 12.6 | 12.6 |
| 2013 | 12.3 | 12.3 | 12.4 | 12.1 | 12.2 | 12.3 | 11.9 | 12.0 | 12.0 | 11.9 | 11.9 | 11.9 | 12.1 |
| 2014 | 11.8 | 11.6 | 11.7 | 11.7 | 11.6 | 11.7 | 11.8 | 11.8 | 11.8 | 11.7 | 11.6 | 11.5 | 11.7 |
| 2015 | 11.5 | 11.4 | 11.3 | 11.1 | 11.1 | 11.1 | 11.2 | 11.0 | 10.9 | 10.8 | 10.3 | 10.2 | 11.0 |
| 2016 | 9.9 | 9.5 | 9.5 | 9.3 | 9.2 | 9.2 | 9.3 | 9.2 | 9.4 | 9.1 | 9.3 | 9.3 | 9.4 |
| 2017 | 9.6 | 9.7 | 9.7 | 9.7 | 9.7 | 9.7 | 9.8 | 9.9 | 10.0 | 9.9 | 10.0 | 10.0 | 9.8 |
| 2018 | 9.9 | 9.9 | 9.9 | 9.9 | 9.9 | 9.9 | 10.1 | 10.1 | 10.1 | 10.1 | 10.0 | 10.2 | 10.0 |
| 2019 | 10.2 | 10.2 | 10.2 | 10.0 | 10.1 | 10.2 | 10.3 | 10.3 | 10.2 | 10.1 | 10.0 | 9.8 | 10.1 |
| **Construction** | | | | | | | | | | | | | |
| 2011 | 77.2 | 79.2 | 81.1 | 80.8 | 82.0 | 81.8 | 81.2 | 81.1 | 81.9 | 81.0 | 80.7 | 80.6 | 80.7 |
| 2012 | 76.7 | 77.7 | 79.9 | 80.3 | 79.9 | 80.0 | 79.7 | 80.2 | 80.2 | 80.7 | 80.0 | 79.3 | 79.6 |
| 2013 | 76.5 | 76.9 | 79.9 | 80.4 | 79.9 | 80.1 | 79.5 | 80.1 | 79.5 | 80.0 | 78.7 | 79.3 | 79.2 |
| 2014 | 76.2 | 77.4 | 79.0 | 79.4 | 79.9 | 80.3 | 80.4 | 80.9 | 81.1 | 82.0 | 81.2 | 81.0 | 79.9 |
| 2015 | 78.5 | 79.1 | 79.6 | 80.9 | 81.2 | 82.3 | 81.9 | 82.2 | 82.7 | 83.4 | 83.5 | 84.2 | 81.6 |
| 2016 | 82.9 | 82.8 | 84.6 | 85.6 | 84.7 | 84.4 | 84.3 | 83.5 | 84.9 | 84.5 | 83.7 | 84.7 | 84.2 |
| 2017 | 83.2 | 84.1 | 85.5 | 84.2 | 85.1 | 84.9 | 84.8 | 85.2 | 86.3 | 87.8 | 86.6 | 86.5 | 85.4 |
| 2018 | 84.2 | 86.5 | 88.2 | 88.5 | 88.7 | 89.3 | 89.3 | 90.1 | 90.8 | 91.8 | 91.3 | 91.2 | 89.2 |
| 2019 | 89.0 | 90.4 | 93.0 | 93.6 | 93.8 | 93.7 | 93.9 | 94.9 | 95.1 | 95.2 | 94.6 | 94.6 | 93.5 |

## 1. Employment by Industry: Alabama, 2011–2019—*Continued*

| Industry and yea | January | February | March | April | May | June | July | August | September | October | November | December | Annual average |
|---|---|---|---|---|---|---|---|---|---|---|---|---|---|
| **Manufacturing** | | | | | | | | | | | | | |
| 2011 | 233.2 | 235.0 | 235.8 | 236.9 | 237.3 | 238.2 | 237.8 | 239.1 | 238.2 | 237.9 | 239.3 | 240.8 | 237.5 |
| 2012 | 239.2 | 239.6 | 240.9 | 242.3 | 243.1 | 244.4 | 244.2 | 245.2 | 245.0 | 245.7 | 246.5 | 247.8 | 243.7 |
| 2013 | 245.9 | 247.1 | 248.3 | 248.6 | 249.0 | 250.2 | 249.4 | 250.3 | 250.3 | 250.2 | 251.2 | 252.0 | 249.4 |
| 2014 | 250.5 | 250.3 | 251.0 | 251.5 | 252.5 | 253.7 | 253.2 | 253.9 | 254.7 | 254.9 | 255.7 | 257.0 | 253.2 |
| 2015 | 255.6 | 256.3 | 256.7 | 256.8 | 257.7 | 258.4 | 258.1 | 258.4 | 258.6 | 258.8 | 259.1 | 260.0 | 257.9 |
| 2016 | 258.6 | 258.9 | 258.8 | 259.9 | 259.9 | 261.0 | 261.6 | 261.6 | 262.3 | 261.4 | 261.6 | 262.3 | 260.7 |
| 2017 | 261.6 | 262.8 | 262.8 | 262.9 | 262.9 | 263.9 | 263.5 | 263.7 | 263.7 | 264.1 | 264.6 | 265.9 | 263.5 |
| 2018 | 264.2 | 265.4 | 265.3 | 265.0 | 265.6 | 267.0 | 267.4 | 268.0 | 268.0 | 268.0 | 269.4 | 270.3 | 267.0 |
| 2019 | 268.3 | 268.9 | 268.6 | 267.5 | 268.0 | 268.6 | 269.1 | 268.7 | 268.0 | 269.1 | 269.2 | 269.6 | 268.6 |
| **Trade, Transportation, and Utilities** | | | | | | | | | | | | | |
| 2011 | 358.5 | 358.6 | 360.2 | 361.7 | 362.0 | 363.6 | 363.9 | 364.5 | 363.9 | 364.7 | 371.2 | 374.0 | 363.9 |
| 2012 | 361.6 | 360.1 | 363.2 | 363.4 | 365.2 | 366.1 | 364.0 | 364.4 | 364.0 | 365.9 | 374.6 | 376.3 | 365.7 |
| 2013 | 361.2 | 361.6 | 363.8 | 364.7 | 366.8 | 368.8 | 367.9 | 368.7 | 367.6 | 368.7 | 376.9 | 381.2 | 368.2 |
| 2014 | 366.9 | 365.5 | 368.7 | 369.9 | 370.6 | 372.0 | 372.1 | 371.9 | 371.5 | 372.7 | 381.6 | 385.4 | 372.4 |
| 2015 | 370.8 | 369.9 | 372.6 | 375.0 | 376.9 | 377.8 | 377.8 | 378.0 | 376.8 | 379.2 | 387.1 | 390.1 | 377.7 |
| 2016 | 376.4 | 375.8 | 377.3 | 379.2 | 379.7 | 379.8 | 379.6 | 378.8 | 378.7 | 379.8 | 386.8 | 388.7 | 380.1 |
| 2017 | 376.8 | 375.3 | 376.4 | 377.1 | 377.6 | 378.8 | 377.5 | 377.8 | 376.8 | 378.6 | 386.0 | 388.1 | 378.9 |
| 2018 | 376.5 | 375.4 | 378.0 | 378.7 | 379.8 | 380.1 | 380.3 | 380.1 | 379.0 | 381.2 | 390.3 | 392.0 | 381.0 |
| 2019 | 381.8 | 379.7 | 380.2 | 380.9 | 381.5 | 381.6 | 381.7 | 381.4 | 380.9 | 384.1 | 389.7 | 394.4 | 383.2 |
| **Wholesale Trade** | | | | | | | | | | | | | |
| 2011 | 70.7 | 71.2 | 71.2 | 71.6 | 71.6 | 71.7 | 72.1 | 72.2 | 72.3 | 72.6 | 72.5 | 72.8 | 71.9 |
| 2012 | 71.7 | 71.9 | 72.3 | 72.4 | 72.7 | 72.8 | 72.4 | 72.4 | 72.4 | 72.8 | 72.8 | 72.8 | 72.5 |
| 2013 | 71.7 | 72.1 | 72.3 | 72.7 | 72.9 | 72.8 | 72.8 | 72.9 | 72.9 | 73.0 | 73.2 | 73.1 | 72.7 |
| 2014 | 72.0 | 72.1 | 72.3 | 72.6 | 72.9 | 73.0 | 73.0 | 73.2 | 73.2 | 73.4 | 73.6 | 73.8 | 72.9 |
| 2015 | 72.6 | 72.9 | 73.1 | 73.6 | 73.7 | 73.6 | 73.9 | 73.8 | 73.7 | 74.0 | 73.9 | 73.8 | 73.6 |
| 2016 | 72.7 | 73.0 | 73.1 | 73.7 | 73.7 | 73.7 | 73.7 | 73.5 | 73.6 | 73.7 | 73.5 | 73.5 | 73.5 |
| 2017 | 72.6 | 72.8 | 72.9 | 73.3 | 73.5 | 73.8 | 73.6 | 73.5 | 73.5 | 74.0 | 74.0 | 74.0 | 73.5 |
| 2018 | 73.1 | 73.3 | 73.6 | 73.8 | 73.8 | 74.1 | 74.1 | 74.1 | 73.9 | 74.2 | 74.2 | 74.3 | 73.9 |
| 2019 | 73.5 | 73.9 | 73.9 | 74.3 | 74.3 | 74.8 | 74.5 | ˙74.5 | 74.5 | 75.0 | 74.2 | 75.1 | 74.4 |
| **Retail Trade** | | | | | | | | | | | | | |
| 2011 | 221.4 | 220.6 | 221.9 | 223.2 | 223.1 | 224.3 | 224.3 | 224.4 | 223.6 | 224.5 | 231.0 | 232.7 | 224.6 |
| 2012 | 222.4 | 220.1 | 222.1 | 222.1 | 223.5 | 223.9 | 222.5 | 222.4 | 221.8 | 223.4 | 231.8 | 232.7 | 224.1 |
| 2013 | 219.4 | 219.2 | 220.9 | 221.6 | 223.1 | 224.8 | 224.2 | 224.7 | 223.5 | 224.4 | 232.0 | 235.2 | 224.4 |
| 2014 | 223.3 | 222.1 | 224.4 | 225.3 | 225.7 | 226.6 | 226.7 | 226.2 | 225.6 | 226.9 | 235.1 | 237.5 | 227.1 |
| 2015 | 225.1 | 224.7 | 226.7 | 228.5 | 229.9 | 230.7 | 230.4 | 230.6 | 229.8 | 231.8 | 239.5 | 241.3 | 230.8 |
| 2016 | 229.7 | 229.4 | 230.8 | 232.2 | 232.5 | 232.5 | 232.3 | 231.7 | 231.3 | 232.7 | 239.7 | 240.1 | 232.9 |
| 2017 | 230.6 | 229.1 | 229.7 | 230.7 | 230.8 | 231.7 | 231.0 | 230.6 | 229.5 | 230.7 | 237.2 | 237.2 | 231.6 |
| 2018 | 228.6 | 227.8 | 229.7 | 230.1 | 230.8 | 230.7 | 230.3 | 229.6 | 228.9 | 230.2 | 237.9 | 237.5 | 231.0 |
| 2019 | 230.1 | 228.5 | 229.1 | 229.7 | 230.1 | 229.7 | 229.4 | 228.8 | 228.6 | 230.5 | 235.9 | 236.6 | 230.6 |
| **Transportation and Utilities** | | | | | | | | | | | | | |
| 2011 | 66.4 | 66.8 | 67.1 | 66.9 | 67.3 | 67.6 | 67.5 | 67.9 | 68.0 | 67.6 | 67.7 | 68.5 | 67.4 |
| 2012 | 67.5 | 68.1 | 68.8 | 68.9 | 69.0 | 69.4 | 69.1 | 69.6 | 69.8 | 69.7 | 70.0 | 70.8 | 69.2 |
| 2013 | 70.1 | 70.3 | 70.6 | 70.4 | 70.8 | 71.2 | 70.9 | 71.1 | 71.2 | 71.3 | 71.7 | 72.9 | 71.0 |
| 2014 | 71.6 | 71.3 | 72.0 | 72.0 | 72.0 | 72.4 | 72.4 | 72.5 | 72.7 | 72.4 | 72.9 | 74.1 | 72.4 |
| 2015 | 73.1 | 72.3 | 72.8 | 72.9 | 73.3 | 73.5 | 73.5 | 73.6 | 73.3 | 73.4 | 73.7 | 75.0 | 73.4 |
| 2016 | 74.0 | 73.4 | 73.4 | 73.3 | 73.5 | 73.6 | 73.6 | 73.6 | 73.8 | 73.4 | 73.6 | 75.1 | 73.7 |
| 2017 | 73.6 | 73.4 | 73.8 | 73.1 | 73.3 | 73.3 | 72.9 | 73.7 | 73.8 | 73.9 | 74.8 | 76.9 | 73.9 |
| 2018 | 74.8 | 74.3 | 74.7 | 74.8 | 75.2 | 75.3 | 75.9 | 76.4 | 76.2 | 76.8 | 78.2 | 80.2 | 76.1 |
| 2019 | 78.2 | 77.3 | 77.2 | 76.9 | 77.1 | 77.1 | 77.8 | 78.1 | 77.8 | 78.6 | 79.6 | 82.7 | 78.2 |
| **Information** | | | | | | | | | | | | | |
| 2011 | 23.5 | 23.4 | 23.3 | 23.1 | 23.3 | 23.3 | 23.2 | 23.1 | 23.1 | 22.7 | 22.8 | 22.8 | 23.1 |
| 2012 | 22.9 | 22.9 | 23.0 | 22.8 | 22.8 | 22.8 | 22.7 | 22.6 | 22.5 | 22.2 | 22.4 | 22.4 | 22.7 |
| 2013 | 22.4 | 22.4 | 22.3 | 22.4 | 22.8 | 22.9 | 22.9 | 22.7 | 22.5 | 22.6 | 22.8 | 22.9 | 22.6 |
| 2014 | 22.2 | 22.1 | 22.1 | 22.1 | 22.1 | 22.0 | 22.0 | 21.9 | 21.8 | 21.7 | 21.9 | 21.9 | 22.0 |
| 2015 | 21.6 | 21.9 | 21.8 | 21.6 | 22.0 | 21.4 | 21.5 | 21.3 | 21.0 | 21.0 | 21.1 | 21.2 | 21.5 |
| 2016 | 20.8 | 20.7 | 20.6 | 20.8 | 21.0 | 21.0 | 20.8 | 20.7 | 20.5 | 20.7 | 20.9 | 20.9 | 20.8 |
| 2017 | 20.5 | 20.7 | 20.9 | 20.7 | 21.1 | 21.0 | 21.0 | 20.7 | 20.6 | 20.8 | 20.9 | 20.9 | 20.8 |
| 2018 | 20.7 | 21.0 | 21.1 | 21.1 | 21.3 | 21.2 | 21.1 | 21.0 | 21.1 | 21.0 | 21.2 | 21.2 | 21.1 |
| 2019 | 21.2 | 21.4 | 21.9 | 21.8 | 21.6 | 21.4 | 21.1 | 21.0 | 20.6 | 20.7 | 20.9 | 20.8 | 21.2 |

## 1. Employment by Industry: Alabama, 2011–2019—*Continued*

| Industry and year | January | February | March | April | May | June | July | August | September | October | November | December | Annual average |
|---|---|---|---|---|---|---|---|---|---|---|---|---|---|
| **Financial Activities** | | | | | | | | | | | | | |
| 2011 | 91.1 | 91.5 | 91.6 | 92.4 | 93.8 | 93.0 | 93.2 | 92.5 | 93.3 | 92.1 | 92.0 | 91.8 | 92.4 |
| 2012 | 90.6 | 91.1 | 91.5 | 91.7 | 92.2 | 92.7 | 93.5 | 93.4 | 93.6 | 93.5 | 94.0 | 93.9 | 92.6 |
| 2013 | 93.2 | 93.3 | 93.8 | 93.7 | 94.0 | 94.5 | 94.7 | 94.9 | 94.2 | 94.6 | 94.8 | 95.0 | 94.2 |
| 2014 | 93.8 | 93.9 | 94.2 | 94.6 | 95.1 | 95.5 | 95.4 | 95.4 | 94.4 | 94.7 | 94.8 | 95.2 | 94.8 |
| 2015 | 94.2 | 94.3 | 94.8 | 95.3 | 95.8 | 96.1 | 96.2 | 95.9 | 95.4 | 95.6 | 95.6 | 95.7 | 95.4 |
| 2016 | 95.1 | 95.3 | 95.5 | 95.9 | 96.1 | 96.2 | 96.4 | 96.6 | 96.6 | 96.6 | 96.6 | 96.6 | 96.1 |
| 2017 | 95.5 | 95.7 | 96.0 | 95.7 | 96.1 | 96.3 | 97.0 | 97.1 | 97.5 | 98.4 | 97.7 | 96.5 | 96.6 |
| 2018 | 95.4 | 95.5 | 95.6 | 95.6 | 95.9 | 96.6 | 96.7 | 96.8 | 96.9 | 97.4 | 96.7 | 96.1 | 96.3 |
| 2019 | 94.8 | 95.1 | 95.1 | 95.5 | 96.0 | 96.5 | 97.2 | 97.2 | 97.6 | 97.0 | 96.8 | 96.8 | 96.3 |
| **Professional and Business Services** | | | | | | | | | | | | | |
| 2011 | 208.9 | 211.9 | 212.7 | 213.6 | 213.0 | 213.9 | 213.1 | 215.3 | 217.6 | 216.1 | 216.0 | 216.4 | 214.0 |
| 2012 | 211.0 | 214.4 | 216.7 | 218.1 | 218.9 | 220.2 | 218.1 | 222.4 | 221.7 | 220.3 | 220.6 | 219.0 | 218.5 |
| 2013 | 213.5 | 217.0 | 219.0 | 220.4 | 220.4 | 221.8 | 219.3 | 221.0 | 219.7 | 220.2 | 220.1 | 221.6 | 219.5 |
| 2014 | 216.6 | 217.4 | 219.4 | 222.6 | 223.4 | 224.4 | 224.3 | 227.5 | 226.7 | 228.4 | 228.2 | 228.5 | 224.0 |
| 2015 | 222.5 | 224.2 | 225.7 | 227.8 | 228.8 | 228.6 | 229.5 | 231.0 | 230.4 | 233.3 | 233.5 | 234.1 | 229.1 |
| 2016 | 229.1 | 230.7 | 231.9 | 235.4 | 234.9 | 234.3 | 232.7 | 234.6 | 234.1 | 234.9 | 235.5 | 234.9 | 233.6 |
| 2017 | 231.6 | 234.3 | 237.0 | 237.7 | 239.0 | 241.3 | 238.9 | 242.1 | 240.7 | 242.4 | 242.6 | 242.1 | 239.1 |
| 2018 | 237.5 | 240.8 | 242.7 | 244.5 | 242.8 | 245.4 | 244.9 | 245.9 | 245.3 | 250.4 | 251.6 | 249.4 | 245.1 |
| 2019 | 246.0 | 248.0 | 248.9 | 250.4 | 250.7 | 251.1 | 251.4 | 253.1 | 248.8 | 252.5 | 252.4 | 252.2 | 250.5 |
| **Education and Health Services** | | | | | | | | | | | | | |
| 2011 | 218.7 | 219.6 | 221.6 | 221.2 | 221.0 | 219.1 | 218.9 | 220.1 | 223.2 | 222.9 | 224.7 | 223.1 | 221.2 |
| 2012 | 221.5 | 222.2 | 223.8 | 224.9 | 222.9 | 222.8 | 219.7 | 222.9 | 225.8 | 225.0 | 228.1 | 228.3 | 224.0 |
| 2013 | 223.4 | 228.0 | 225.8 | 226.9 | 229.3 | 226.4 | 222.6 | 225.9 | 229.5 | 228.4 | 231.6 | 231.8 | 227.5 |
| 2014 | 225.1 | 228.6 | 227.4 | 229.8 | 228.9 | 226.9 | 224.1 | 227.3 | 230.8 | 232.5 | 231.3 | 233.8 | 228.9 |
| 2015 | 228.6 | 232.1 | 229.8 | 232.6 | 232.0 | 231.5 | 230.8 | 233.0 | 235.6 | 237.3 | 236.4 | 238.6 | 233.2 |
| 2016 | 233.2 | 236.7 | 235.6 | 237.9 | 237.3 | 236.4 | 237.0 | 239.2 | 241.6 | 241.5 | 240.8 | 242.4 | 238.3 |
| 2017 | 237.2 | 240.8 | 240.2 | 241.9 | 241.0 | 241.0 | 239.3 | 240.9 | 243.3 | 243.1 | 245.1 | 245.0 | 241.6 |
| 2018 | 240.8 | 244.0 | 243.0 | 245.3 | 244.2 | 245.0 | 243.2 | 245.1 | 246.8 | 247.0 | 248.8 | 248.6 | 245.2 |
| 2019 | 245.1 | 248.2 | 246.9 | 248.2 | 247.9 | 246.9 | 248.9 | 250.7 | 252.3 | 252.6 | 254.0 | 253.4 | 249.6 |
| **Leisure and Hospitality** | | | | | | | | | | | | | |
| 2011 | 159.5 | 162.3 | 166.5 | 171.5 | 171.8 | 174.1 | 173.7 | 174.7 | 172.4 | 168.5 | 168.0 | 166.7 | 169.1 |
| 2012 | 163.1 | 166.3 | 170.9 | 176.1 | 178.2 | 180.6 | 177.7 | 178.8 | 176.6 | 172.7 | 172.7 | 171.0 | 173.7 |
| 2013 | 167.9 | 170.4 | 174.8 | 180.3 | 183.4 | 185.4 | 183.6 | 184.0 | 182.5 | 178.7 | 179.0 | 176.8 | 178.9 |
| 2014 | 173.1 | 174.8 | 180.4 | 185.6 | 187.9 | 190.4 | 188.3 | 189.6 | 187.0 | 183.6 | 182.3 | 181.4 | 183.7 |
| 2015 | 178.8 | 182.1 | 186.1 | 191.1 | 194.0 | 196.0 | 195.1 | 195.1 | 193.6 | 191.3 | 191.0 | 189.6 | 190.3 |
| 2016 | 186.2 | 190.0 | 194.6 | 199.7 | 202.2 | 203.2 | 202.2 | 202.6 | 200.5 | 197.4 | 197.2 | 194.4 | 197.5 |
| 2017 | 192.2 | 195.7 | 200.1 | 204.2 | 206.5 | 208.0 | 207.7 | 207.9 | 204.2 | 202.2 | 201.4 | 198.6 | 202.4 |
| 2018 | 195.8 | 199.2 | 203.1 | 207.2 | 209.7 | 211.9 | 211.4 | 211.8 | 207.0 | 206.4 | 205.0 | 203.1 | 206.0 |
| 2019 | 199.3 | 203.3 | 206.4 | 211.9 | 213.6 | 213.9 | 212.9 | 213.1 | 208.1 | 208.3 | 206.7 | 205.6 | 208.6 |
| **Other Services** | | | | | | | | | | | | | |
| 2011 | 88.8 | 89.4 | 89.7 | 90.1 | 90.2 | 90.7 | 90.3 | 90.0 | 89.9 | 89.9 | 90.4 | 90.0 | 90.0 |
| 2012 | 90.0 | 90.7 | 91.7 | 91.7 | 91.8 | 92.7 | 92.2 | 91.7 | 91.1 | 91.3 | 90.6 | 90.5 | 91.3 |
| 2013 | 90.0 | 90.4 | 91.3 | 91.4 | 91.6 | 92.3 | 91.8 | 91.8 | 91.6 | 91.3 | 91.0 | 91.0 | 91.3 |
| 2014 | 90.6 | 91.0 | 92.0 | 92.2 | 92.6 | 93.0 | 92.6 | 92.4 | 92.1 | 91.9 | 91.7 | 91.6 | 92.0 |
| 2015 | 91.6 | 91.7 | 92.3 | 93.1 | 93.5 | 93.8 | 93.2 | 92.9 | 92.8 | 92.6 | 92.5 | 92.3 | 92.7 |
| 2016 | 92.2 | 92.6 | 93.4 | 94.3 | 94.1 | 94.8 | 95.0 | 94.8 | 94.9 | 94.5 | 94.6 | 94.8 | 94.2 |
| 2017 | 94.6 | 95.1 | 95.8 | 96.0 | 96.3 | 96.5 | 96.4 | 96.2 | 96.4 | 96.1 | 96.2 | 95.9 | 96.0 |
| 2018 | 95.3 | 95.7 | 96.3 | 96.6 | 97.1 | 97.7 | 97.3 | 97.6 | 97.8 | 97.8 | 98.1 | 98.0 | 97.1 |
| 2019 | 98.0 | 98.7 | 99.0 | 99.5 | 99.4 | 99.8 | 99.2 | 99.3 | 99.3 | 99.7 | 100.0 | 99.5 | 99.3 |
| **Government** | | | | | | | | | | | | | |
| 2011 | 387.2 | 390.6 | 391.6 | 391.0 | 390.5 | 386.7 | 374.1 | 374.0 | 383.8 | 386.1 | 387.7 | 385.9 | 385.8 |
| 2012 | 381.1 | 385.2 | 387.4 | 385.8 | 385.0 | 381.8 | 368.1 | 369.0 | 378.0 | 384.1 | 385.4 | 385.1 | 381.3 |
| 2013 | 379.2 | 384.0 | 386.4 | 385.5 | 384.8 | 380.5 | 371.6 | 371.8 | 378.0 | 383.0 | 384.6 | 385.1 | 381.3 |
| 2014 | 378.9 | 382.8 | 384.1 | 384.7 | 385.9 | 383.3 | 369.9 | 372.4 | 381.1 | 384.9 | 386.0 | 386.7 | 381.7 |
| 2015 | 378.8 | 382.0 | 383.0 | 383.8 | 385.2 | 382.7 | 370.6 | 373.6 | 379.8 | 382.6 | 383.6 | 384.1 | 380.8 |
| 2016 | 378.5 | 381.7 | 383.0 | 383.5 | 384.6 | 383.6 | 372.7 | 376.4 | 383.5 | 385.3 | 386.5 | 387.2 | 382.2 |
| 2017 | 381.6 | 384.8 | 386.3 | 386.5 | 387.7 | 386.8 | 375.4 | 378.1 | 385.1 | 387.3 | 388.2 | 387.7 | 384.6 |
| 2018 | 381.7 | 385.3 | 386.9 | 388.3 | 389.9 | 390.1 | 378.1 | 381.5 | 387.6 | 389.7 | 390.8 | 391.5 | 386.8 |
| 2019 | 386.3 | 389.8 | 391.2 | 392.0 | 393.3 | 393.0 | 383.5 | 387.1 | 392.9 | 396.4 | 398.8 | 396.5 | 391.7 |

## 2. Average Weekly Hours by Selected Industry: Alabama, 2015–2019

(Not seasonally adjusted)

| Industry and year | January | February | March | April | May | June | July | August | September | October | November | December | Annual average |
|---|---|---|---|---|---|---|---|---|---|---|---|---|---|
| **Total Private** | | | | | | | | | | | | | |
| 2015 | 34.9 | 35.4 | 35.4 | 35.2 | 35.5 | 35.5 | 35.4 | 35.9 | 35.4 | 35.8 | 35.9 | 35.6 | 35.5 |
| 2016 | 35.5 | 35.6 | 35.5 | 35.5 | 35.8 | 35.6 | 35.6 | 35.4 | 35.6 | 36.0 | 35.3 | 35.4 | 35.6 |
| 2017 | 35.3 | 35.2 | 35.2 | 35.2 | 35.2 | 35.3 | 35.4 | 35.3 | 34.9 | 35.6 | 35.3 | 35.2 | 35.3 |
| 2018 | 34.3 | 35.0 | 35.3 | 35.5 | 35.2 | 35.4 | 35.5 | 35.4 | 35.8 | 35.3 | 35.3 | 35.9 | 35.3 |
| 2019 | 34.9 | 35.1 | 35.1 | 35.1 | 35.2 | 35.7 | 35.0 | 35.3 | 35.4 | 35.3 | 35.2 | 35.5 | 35.2 |
| **Goods-Producing** | | | | | | | | | | | | | |
| 2015 | 41.2 | 41.2 | 41.3 | 41.2 | 41.7 | 41.7 | 41.6 | 41.9 | 40.8 | 42.2 | 41.7 | 42.2 | 41.6 |
| 2016 | 41.5 | 41.5 | 41.4 | 41.4 | 42.1 | 42.2 | 41.5 | 41.5 | 42.1 | 42.3 | 41.2 | 41.3 | 41.7 |
| 2017 | 40.8 | 41.0 | 41.0 | 40.8 | 41.8 | 42.0 | 41.5 | 42.3 | 41.4 | 42.0 | 42.4 | 41.8 | 41.6 |
| 2018 | 40.0 | 41.5 | 42.0 | 41.7 | 42.1 | 41.9 | 41.0 | 42.1 | 42.0 | 41.6 | 41.8 | 42.4 | 41.7 |
| 2019 | 41.6 | 41.4 | 41.6 | 41.5 | 41.7 | 42.2 | 41.1 | 41.9 | 41.9 | 42.4 | 41.8 | 41.7 | 41.7 |
| **Construction** | | | | | | | | | | | | | |
| 2015 | 38.6 | 39.7 | 39.6 | 39.5 | 41.4 | 41.5 | 41.7 | 41.6 | 40.1 | 41.8 | 41.7 | 42.4 | 40.8 |
| 2016 | 41.7 | 41.3 | 40.1 | 41.2 | 41.6 | 41.7 | 41.4 | 40.5 | 41.0 | 41.5 | 40.3 | 39.8 | 41.0 |
| 2017 | 39.6 | 39.9 | 39.8 | 39.8 | 41.4 | 40.5 | 41.2 | 40.0 | 39.9 | 40.7 | 41.2 | 40.1 | 40.4 |
| 2018 | 37.7 | 39.5 | 40.5 | 40.9 | 42.0 | 40.3 | 40.0 | 40.0 | 39.7 | 40.2 | 40.1 | 40.3 | 40.1 |
| 2019 | 39.5 | 39.6 | 41.2 | 41.0 | 40.8 | 40.6 | 39.7 | 40.6 | 40.7 | 41.7 | 40.0 | 39.6 | 40.4 |
| **Manufacturing** | | | | | | | | | | | | | |
| 2015 | 41.8 | 41.6 | 41.7 | 41.7 | 41.4 | 41.4 | 41.2 | 41.8 | 41.4 | 42.4 | 41.8 | 42.0 | 41.7 |
| 2016 | 41.5 | 41.5 | 41.7 | 41.4 | 42.2 | 42.2 | 41.3 | 41.7 | 42.4 | 42.5 | 41.5 | 41.9 | 41.8 |
| 2017 | 41.3 | 41.4 | 41.5 | 41.2 | 42.1 | 42.8 | 41.7 | 43.4 | 42.2 | 42.7 | 43.0 | 42.7 | 42.2 |
| 2018 | 41.3 | 42.5 | 42.9 | 42.3 | 42.3 | 42.8 | 41.5 | 42.1 | 42.3 | 41.6 | 42.1 | 42.9 | 42.2 |
| 2019 | 42.1 | 41.8 | 41.3 | 41.3 | 41.7 | 42.6 | 41.2 | 42.1 | 42.2 | 42.3 | 42.5 | 42.8 | 42.0 |
| **Trade, Transportation, and Utilities** | | | | | | | | | | | | | |
| 2015 | 34.2 | 34.6 | 34.3 | 34.5 | 34.6 | 34.7 | 34.7 | 34.9 | 34.4 | 34.5 | 34.5 | 34.4 | 34.5 |
| 2016 | 34.1 | 34.3 | 33.9 | 34.0 | 34.0 | 34.1 | 34.3 | 34.0 | 33.7 | 33.8 | 33.5 | 33.9 | 34.0 |
| 2017 | 33.5 | 33.4 | 33.4 | 34.0 | 33.5 | 33.6 | 33.9 | 33.7 | 33.2 | 33.5 | 33.2 | 33.5 | 33.5 |
| 2018 | 32.7 | 32.8 | 32.8 | 33.2 | 33.0 | 33.2 | 33.6 | 33.3 | 33.3 | 33.0 | 32.9 | 33.2 | 33.1 |
| 2019 | 32.5 | 32.8 | 32.7 | 33.1 | 33.0 | 33.2 | 33.1 | 33.2 | 33.2 | 33.0 | 33.3 | 33.6 | 33.1 |
| **Financial Activities** | | | | | | | | | | | | | |
| 2015 | 37.0 | 38.1 | 38.4 | 36.8 | 37.2 | 37.2 | 36.9 | 38.3 | 37.2 | 36.9 | 38.6 | 37.3 | 37.5 |
| 2016 | 37.9 | 37.9 | 37.2 | 37.5 | 38.5 | 37.9 | 37.7 | 37.1 | 38.3 | 38.0 | 37.8 | 37.3 | 37.8 |
| 2017 | 39.0 | 38.4 | 38.5 | 38.7 | 38.2 | 38.1 | 38.2 | 38.0 | 37.5 | 38.5 | 37.9 | 38.1 | 38.3 |
| 2018 | 37.6 | 37.6 | 37.5 | 38.1 | 37.4 | 37.6 | 38.4 | 37.5 | 38.8 | 37.7 | 38.4 | 39.4 | 38.0 |
| 2019 | 38.1 | 38.4 | 37.5 | 37.3 | 37.1 | 38.3 | 37.4 | 36.9 | 38.2 | 37.2 | 37.1 | 38.0 | 37.6 |
| **Professional and Business Services** | | | | | | | | | | | | | |
| 2015 | 36.3 | 37.0 | 36.7 | 36.5 | 36.7 | 36.6 | 36.7 | 37.3 | 36.7 | 36.7 | 36.9 | 36.0 | 36.7 |
| 2016 | 36.3 | 36.4 | 36.5 | 36.7 | 37.0 | 36.5 | 37.0 | 37.1 | 37.1 | 37.7 | 37.0 | 37.0 | 36.9 |
| 2017 | 37.0 | 36.6 | 37.0 | 36.7 | 36.8 | 36.7 | 37.2 | 36.9 | 36.6 | 37.7 | 37.0 | 37.1 | 36.9 |
| 2018 | 35.8 | 36.9 | 37.5 | 37.4 | 36.6 | 37.0 | 36.9 | 36.5 | 37.4 | 36.7 | 36.5 | 37.4 | 36.9 |
| 2019 | 36.0 | 36.3 | 36.2 | 36.4 | 36.7 | 37.3 | 36.0 | 37.0 | 37.2 | 36.8 | 36.8 | 37.3 | 36.7 |
| **Education and Health Services** | | | | | | | | | | | | | |
| 2015 | 32.5 | 33.4 | 33.2 | 33.1 | 33.3 | 33.3 | 33.3 | 33.8 | 33.4 | 33.8 | 34.6 | 33.3 | 33.4 |
| 2016 | 34.0 | 34.0 | 33.8 | 34.0 | 34.2 | 33.9 | 33.9 | 34.2 | 34.4 | 34.8 | 34.5 | 34.2 | 34.2 |
| 2017 | 34.5 | 34.1 | 33.8 | 33.2 | 32.9 | 33.1 | 33.6 | 33.1 | 33.5 | 34.0 | 33.5 | 33.5 | 33.6 |
| 2018 | 32.8 | 33.4 | 33.5 | 34.1 | 33.2 | 33.5 | 33.9 | 33.5 | 34.5 | 33.4 | 33.5 | 34.3 | 33.6 |
| 2019 | 33.4 | 33.7 | 33.4 | 33.1 | 33.2 | 33.8 | 33.5 | 33.3 | 33.6 | 33.0 | 33.3 | 33.5 | 33.4 |
| **Leisure and Hospitality** | | | | | | | | | | | | | |
| 2015 | 25.7 | 26.5 | 26.6 | 26.9 | 26.9 | 27.3 | 27.1 | 26.7 | 26.0 | 26.2 | 25.8 | 26.1 | 26.5 |
| 2016 | 25.4 | 25.5 | 26.3 | 26.0 | 26.1 | 26.5 | 26.3 | 25.8 | 25.5 | 26.1 | 25.8 | 25.9 | 25.9 |
| 2017 | 25.3 | 25.8 | 26.0 | 25.9 | 25.8 | 26.2 | 26.2 | 25.6 | 25.4 | 25.9 | 25.7 | 25.3 | 25.8 |
| 2018 | 25.4 | 26.2 | 26.5 | 26.4 | 26.5 | 27.2 | 27.1 | 26.7 | 26.9 | 27.1 | 26.4 | 26.6 | 26.6 |
| 2019 | 25.8 | 26.2 | 26.5 | 26.4 | 26.3 | 27.2 | 26.2 | 26.1 | 26.1 | 26.5 | 26.0 | 26.2 | 26.3 |
| **Other Services** | | | | | | | | | | | | | |
| 2015 | 32.0 | 32.9 | 33.5 | 33.1 | 33.9 | 33.2 | 32.1 | 33.6 | 32.6 | 33.8 | 34.5 | 34.5 | 33.3 |
| 2016 | 34.1 | 34.5 | 35.2 | 34.9 | 34.6 | 33.9 | 34.2 | 33.8 | 34.1 | 35.0 | 33.5 | 33.5 | 34.3 |
| 2017 | 32.2 | 33.1 | 33.0 | 33.0 | 32.6 | 33.1 | 33.4 | 32.4 | 32.8 | 33.2 | 32.9 | 32.6 | 32.9 |
| 2018 | 32.3 | 32.9 | 33.0 | 32.8 | 32.4 | 32.4 | 32.9 | 33.0 | 33.4 | 33.6 | 32.6 | 32.7 | 32.8 |
| 2019 | 31.2 | 31.7 | 31.7 | 32.2 | 31.4 | 32.1 | 31.4 | 33.2 | 31.9 | 31.8 | 31.9 | 32.7 | 31.9 |

## 3. Average Hourly Earnings by Selected Industry: Alabama, 2015–2019

(Dollars, not seasonally adjusted)

| Industry and year | January | February | March | April | May | June | July | August | September | October | November | December | Annual average |
|---|---|---|---|---|---|---|---|---|---|---|---|---|---|
| **Total Private** | | | | | | | | | | | | | |
| 2015 | 21.13 | 21.32 | 21.23 | 21.18 | 21.10 | 21.16 | 21.23 | 21.41 | 21.50 | 21.56 | 21.72 | 21.72 | 21.36 |
| 2016 | 21.97 | 21.89 | 21.69 | 22.07 | 22.10 | 21.97 | 22.22 | 22.01 | 22.03 | 22.41 | 22.22 | 22.21 | 22.07 |
| 2017 | 22.61 | 22.45 | 22.36 | 22.78 | 22.47 | 22.22 | 22.70 | 22.58 | 22.98 | 23.03 | 22.81 | 23.08 | 22.67 |
| 2018 | 23.14 | 23.12 | 23.16 | 23.39 | 23.16 | 23.15 | 23.43 | 23.27 | 23.84 | 23.78 | 23.92 | 24.20 | 23.47 |
| 2019 | 23.79 | 24.01 | 24.04 | 24.03 | 23.83 | 24.14 | 24.03 | 24.10 | 24.50 | 24.54 | 24.54 | 24.89 | 24.21 |
| **Goods-Producing** | | | | | | | | | | | | | |
| 2015 | 22.55 | 22.78 | 22.60 | 22.58 | 22.44 | 22.46 | 22.47 | 22.61 | 22.90 | 22.86 | 23.14 | 23.12 | 22.71 |
| 2016 | 23.16 | 23.32 | 22.92 | 23.28 | 23.27 | 23.15 | 23.36 | 23.22 | 23.00 | 23.29 | 23.23 | 23.47 | 23.22 |
| 2017 | 23.60 | 23.42 | 23.51 | 24.06 | 23.81 | 23.59 | 23.83 | 23.59 | 24.19 | 24.30 | 24.22 | 24.36 | 23.88 |
| 2018 | 24.26 | 24.15 | 24.46 | 24.60 | 24.35 | 24.25 | 24.38 | 24.38 | 24.95 | 24.96 | 25.18 | 25.12 | 24.59 |
| 2019 | 24.64 | 24.84 | 25.35 | 25.21 | 25.21 | 25.19 | 25.28 | 25.08 | 25.39 | 25.65 | 25.59 | 25.90 | 25.28 |
| **Construction** | | | | | | | | | | | | | |
| 2015 | 23.05 | 22.82 | 22.55 | 22.51 | 22.06 | 22.22 | 22.11 | 22.32 | 22.70 | 22.97 | 23.08 | 22.86 | 22.60 |
| 2016 | 22.75 | 22.40 | 22.27 | 22.58 | 22.25 | 22.43 | 22.21 | 21.98 | 21.95 | 22.10 | 22.09 | 22.30 | 22.28 |
| 2017 | 22.14 | 22.56 | 22.30 | 22.13 | 22.40 | 22.27 | 22.39 | 22.69 | 23.05 | 23.23 | 23.47 | 23.54 | 22.69 |
| 2018 | 23.06 | 23.07 | 23.87 | 23.56 | 23.31 | 23.00 | 23.03 | 23.48 | 24.39 | 24.53 | 24.65 | 24.32 | 23.70 |
| 2019 | 23.75 | 23.96 | 24.96 | 24.47 | 24.46 | 24.26 | 24.45 | 24.51 | 24.41 | 25.37 | 25.22 | 25.55 | 24.62 |
| **Manufacturing** | | | | | | | | | | | | | |
| 2015 | 22.36 | 22.74 | 22.60 | 22.53 | 22.56 | 22.57 | 22.62 | 22.72 | 23.00 | 22.85 | 23.19 | 23.29 | 22.75 |
| 2016 | 23.36 | 23.71 | 23.18 | 23.57 | 23.64 | 23.44 | 23.86 | 23.72 | 23.41 | 23.82 | 23.74 | 23.97 | 23.62 |
| 2017 | 24.27 | 23.81 | 24.02 | 24.46 | 24.08 | 23.81 | 24.19 | 23.70 | 24.44 | 24.54 | 24.30 | 24.48 | 24.17 |
| 2018 | 24.52 | 24.38 | 24.44 | 24.77 | 24.54 | 24.51 | 24.72 | 24.74 | 25.17 | 25.13 | 25.35 | 25.42 | 24.81 |
| 2019 | 24.94 | 25.13 | 25.18 | 25.21 | 25.22 | 25.34 | 25.43 | 25.08 | 25.59 | 25.44 | 25.44 | 25.83 | 25.32 |
| **Trade, Transportation, and Utilities** | | | | | | | | | | | | | |
| 2015 | 18.92 | 19.09 | 18.99 | 19.13 | 19.04 | 18.88 | 18.99 | 19.16 | 19.32 | 19.17 | 19.17 | 18.87 | 19.06 |
| 2016 | 19.50 | 19.37 | 19.46 | 19.88 | 19.71 | 19.75 | 19.77 | 19.51 | 19.64 | 19.89 | 19.56 | 19.23 | 19.61 |
| 2017 | 19.88 | 19.67 | 19.51 | 19.94 | 19.58 | 19.63 | 19.76 | 19.81 | 20.11 | 20.19 | 19.87 | 19.93 | 19.82 |
| 2018 | 20.05 | 19.59 | 19.61 | 19.79 | 19.68 | 19.85 | 20.09 | 20.13 | 20.66 | 20.86 | 20.50 | 20.53 | 20.12 |
| 2019 | 20.22 | 20.51 | 20.53 | 20.64 | 20.64 | 21.20 | 21.27 | 21.27 | 21.21 | 21.22 | 21.00 | 21.04 | 20.90 |
| **Financial Activities** | | | | | | | | | | | | | |
| 2015 | 21.67 | 22.12 | 22.14 | 22.45 | 22.23 | 22.89 | 23.00 | 22.65 | 23.08 | 23.59 | 23.64 | 24.14 | 22.80 |
| 2016 | 24.04 | 23.63 | 24.27 | 25.21 | 25.62 | 24.84 | 25.19 | 24.93 | 25.52 | 26.36 | 25.87 | 25.86 | 25.12 |
| 2017 | 26.52 | 25.92 | 25.27 | 25.80 | 25.51 | 25.01 | 25.40 | 25.53 | 25.84 | 25.93 | 25.50 | 25.77 | 25.67 |
| 2018 | 26.01 | 26.12 | 26.55 | 27.22 | 27.31 | 26.89 | 27.60 | 27.32 | 28.16 | 27.59 | 27.66 | 27.77 | 27.19 |
| 2019 | 27.19 | 27.18 | 26.91 | 27.22 | 27.49 | 27.97 | 27.71 | 28.52 | 29.23 | 29.24 | 29.39 | 30.07 | 28.18 |
| **Professional and Business Services** | | | | | | | | | | | | | |
| 2015 | 24.90 | 25.35 | 25.44 | 25.21 | 25.25 | 25.50 | 25.32 | 25.91 | 25.83 | 25.71 | 25.96 | 26.20 | 25.55 |
| 2016 | 26.77 | 26.21 | 25.89 | 25.77 | 26.29 | 25.92 | 26.19 | 25.97 | 26.13 | 26.31 | 26.38 | 26.51 | 26.19 |
| 2017 | 26.95 | 26.74 | 26.50 | 27.08 | 26.68 | 26.45 | 27.36 | 26.79 | 27.17 | 27.06 | 26.91 | 27.93 | 26.97 |
| 2018 | 28.32 | 28.39 | 28.01 | 28.34 | 27.99 | 28.14 | 28.67 | 27.68 | 28.55 | 28.24 | 28.60 | 28.92 | 28.32 |
| 2019 | 29.01 | 29.14 | 29.19 | 29.12 | 28.48 | 29.25 | 28.86 | 28.56 | 29.30 | 28.73 | 29.10 | 29.81 | 29.05 |
| **Education and Health Services** | | | | | | | | | | | | | |
| 2015 | 22.16 | 22.14 | 21.83 | 22.04 | 21.91 | 22.06 | 22.17 | 22.16 | 22.19 | 22.32 | 22.54 | 22.58 | 22.18 |
| 2016 | 22.46 | 22.56 | 22.33 | 22.90 | 22.37 | 22.88 | 23.46 | 22.91 | 22.88 | 22.90 | 22.81 | 22.74 | 22.77 |
| 2017 | 22.90 | 22.94 | 22.91 | 23.14 | 23.14 | 22.98 | 23.33 | 23.22 | 23.39 | 23.37 | 23.60 | 23.51 | 23.20 |
| 2018 | 23.66 | 23.61 | 23.68 | 23.54 | 23.13 | 23.24 | 23.30 | 23.24 | 23.20 | 23.00 | 23.31 | 23.27 | 23.35 |
| 2019 | 23.23 | 23.72 | 23.49 | 23.61 | 23.46 | 23.53 | 23.39 | 23.62 | 23.88 | 24.18 | 24.14 | 24.29 | 23.71 |
| **Leisure and Hospitality** | | | | | | | | | | | | | |
| 2015 | 10.93 | 11.16 | 11.05 | 11.04 | 11.00 | 10.88 | 10.84 | 10.97 | 11.03 | 10.99 | 11.08 | 11.28 | 11.02 |
| 2016 | 11.23 | 11.47 | 11.24 | 11.18 | 11.25 | 11.31 | 11.30 | 11.44 | 11.55 | 11.72 | 11.73 | 11.94 | 11.45 |
| 2017 | 11.80 | 11.92 | 11.83 | 11.89 | 11.84 | 11.76 | 11.89 | 11.97 | 12.08 | 12.06 | 12.09 | 12.25 | 11.95 |
| 2018 | 12.12 | 12.27 | 12.24 | 12.18 | 12.30 | 12.08 | 12.12 | 12.20 | 12.15 | 12.34 | 12.21 | 12.51 | 12.23 |
| 2019 | 12.30 | 12.40 | 12.56 | 12.44 | 12.30 | 12.27 | 12.42 | 12.52 | 12.59 | 12.58 | 12.61 | 12.80 | 12.48 |
| **Other Services** | | | | | | | | | | | | | |
| 2015 | 20.87 | 21.18 | 21.52 | 19.99 | 20.06 | 20.23 | 20.05 | 20.28 | 19.72 | 19.54 | 19.25 | 19.12 | 20.14 |
| 2016 | 19.23 | 19.17 | 19.22 | 19.10 | 19.00 | 19.04 | 18.91 | 19.11 | 19.15 | 19.81 | 19.56 | 19.55 | 19.24 |
| 2017 | 20.63 | 20.86 | 20.05 | 20.40 | 19.99 | 19.68 | 19.62 | 19.60 | 20.56 | 21.13 | 21.52 | 21.73 | 20.48 |
| 2018 | 21.02 | 21.69 | 21.97 | 22.47 | 22.57 | 22.68 | 22.75 | 22.85 | 23.43 | 23.10 | 23.17 | 22.68 | 22.54 |
| 2019 | 23.45 | 23.32 | 23.55 | 23.23 | 23.08 | 23.08 | 23.34 | 23.14 | 23.09 | 23.27 | 23.27 | 23.71 | 23.29 |

## 4. Average Weekly Earnings by Selected Industry: Alabama, 2015–2019

(Dollars, not seasonally adjusted)

| Industry and year | January | February | March | April | May | June | July | August | September | October | November | December | Annual average |
|---|---|---|---|---|---|---|---|---|---|---|---|---|---|
| **Total Private** | | | | | | | | | | | | | |
| 2015 | 737.44 | 754.73 | 751.54 | 745.54 | 749.05 | 751.18 | 751.54 | 768.62 | 761.10 | 771.85 | 779.75 | 773.23 | 758.28 |
| 2016 | 779.94 | 779.28 | 770.00 | 783.49 | 791.18 | 782.13 | 791.03 | 779.15 | 784.27 | 806.76 | 784.37 | 786.23 | 785.69 |
| 2017 | 798.13 | 790.24 | 787.07 | 801.86 | 790.94 | 784.37 | 803.58 | 797.07 | 802.00 | 819.87 | 805.19 | 812.42 | 800.25 |
| 2018 | 793.70 | 809.20 | 817.55 | 830.35 | 815.23 | 819.51 | 831.77 | 823.76 | 853.47 | 839.43 | 844.38 | 868.78 | 828.49 |
| 2019 | 830.27 | 842.75 | 843.80 | 843.45 | 838.82 | 861.80 | 841.05 | 850.73 | 867.30 | 866.26 | 863.81 | 883.60 | 852.19 |
| **Goods-Producing** | | | | | | | | | | | | | |
| 2015 | 929.06 | 938.54 | 933.38 | 930.30 | 935.75 | 936.58 | 934.75 | 947.36 | 934.32 | 964.69 | 964.94 | 975.66 | 944.74 |
| 2016 | 961.14 | 967.78 | 948.89 | 963.79 | 979.67 | 976.93 | 969.44 | 963.63 | 968.30 | 985.17 | 957.08 | 969.31 | 968.27 |
| 2017 | 962.88 | 960.22 | 963.91 | 981.65 | 995.26 | 990.78 | 988.95 | 997.86 | 1,001.47 | 1,020.60 | 1,026.93 | 1,018.25 | 993.41 |
| 2018 | 970.40 | 1,002.23 | 1,027.32 | 1,025.82 | 1,025.14 | 1,016.08 | 999.58 | 1,026.40 | 1,047.90 | 1,038.34 | 1,052.52 | 1,065.09 | 1,025.40 |
| 2019 | 1,025.02 | 1,028.38 | 1,054.56 | 1,046.22 | 1,051.26 | 1,063.02 | 1,039.01 | 1,050.85 | 1,063.84 | 1,087.56 | 1,069.66 | 1,080.03 | 1,054.18 |
| **Construction** | | | | | | | | | | | | | |
| 2015 | 889.73 | 905.95 | 892.98 | 889.15 | 913.28 | 922.13 | 921.99 | 928.51 | 910.27 | 960.15 | 962.44 | 969.26 | 922.08 |
| 2016 | 948.68 | 925.12 | 893.03 | 930.30 | 925.60 | 935.33 | 919.49 | 890.19 | 899.95 | 917.15 | 890.23 | 887.54 | 913.48 |
| 2017 | 876.74 | 900.14 | 887.54 | 880.77 | 927.36 | 901.94 | 922.47 | 907.60 | 919.70 | 945.46 | 966.96 | 943.95 | 916.68 |
| 2018 | 869.36 | 911.27 | 966.74 | 963.60 | 979.02 | 926.90 | 921.20 | 939.20 | 968.28 | 986.11 | 988.47 | 980.10 | 950.37 |
| 2019 | 938.13 | 948.82 | 1,028.35 | 1,003.27 | 997.97 | 984.96 | 970.67 | 995.11 | 993.49 | 1,057.93 | 1,008.80 | 1,011.78 | 994.65 |
| **Manufacturing** | | | | | | | | | | | | | |
| 2015 | 934.65 | 945.98 | 942.42 | 939.50 | 933.98 | 934.40 | 931.94 | 949.70 | 952.20 | 968.84 | 969.34 | 978.18 | 948.68 |
| 2016 | 969.44 | 983.97 | 966.61 | 975.80 | 997.61 | 989.17 | 985.42 | 989.12 | 992.58 | 1,012.35 | 985.21 | 1,004.34 | 987.32 |
| 2017 | 1,002.35 | 985.73 | 996.83 | 1,007.75 | 1,013.77 | 1,019.07 | 1,008.72 | 1,028.58 | 1,031.37 | 1,047.86 | 1,044.90 | 1,045.30 | 1,019.97 |
| 2018 | 1,012.68 | 1,036.15 | 1,048.48 | 1,047.77 | 1,038.04 | 1,049.03 | 1,025.88 | 1,041.55 | 1,064.69 | 1,045.41 | 1,067.24 | 1,090.52 | 1,046.98 |
| 2019 | 1,049.97 | 1,050.43 | 1,039.93 | 1,041.17 | 1,051.67 | 1,079.48 | 1,047.72 | 1,055.87 | 1,079.90 | 1,076.11 | 1,081.20 | 1,105.52 | 1,063.44 |
| **Trade, Transportation, and Utilities** | | | | | | | | | | | | | |
| 2015 | 647.06 | 660.51 | 651.36 | 659.99 | 658.78 | 655.14 | 658.95 | 668.68 | 664.61 | 661.37 | 661.37 | 649.13 | 657.57 |
| 2016 | 664.95 | 664.39 | 659.69 | 675.92 | 670.14 | 673.48 | 678.11 | 663.34 | 661.87 | 672.28 | 655.26 | 651.90 | 666.74 |
| 2017 | 665.98 | 656.98 | 651.63 | 677.96 | 655.93 | 659.57 | 669.86 | 667.60 | 667.65 | 676.37 | 659.68 | 667.66 | 663.97 |
| 2018 | 655.64 | 642.55 | 643.21 | 657.03 | 649.44 | 659.02 | 675.02 | 670.33 | 687.98 | 688.38 | 674.45 | 681.60 | 665.97 |
| 2019 | 657.15 | 672.73 | 671.33 | 683.18 | 681.12 | 703.84 | 704.04 | 706.16 | 704.17 | 700.26 | 699.30 | 706.94 | 691.79 |
| **Financial Activities** | | | | | | | | | | | | | |
| 2015 | 801.79 | 842.77 | 850.18 | 826.16 | 826.96 | 851.51 | 848.70 | 867.50 | 858.58 | 870.47 | 912.50 | 900.42 | 855.00 |
| 2016 | 911.12 | 895.58 | 902.84 | 945.38 | 986.37 | 941.44 | 949.66 | 924.90 | 977.42 | 1,001.68 | 977.89 | 964.58 | 949.54 |
| 2017 | 1,034.28 | 995.33 | 972.90 | 998.46 | 974.48 | 952.88 | 970.28 | 970.14 | 969.00 | 998.31 | 966.45 | 981.84 | 983.16 |
| 2018 | 977.98 | 982.11 | 995.63 | 1,037.08 | 1,021.39 | 1,011.06 | 1,059.84 | 1,024.50 | 1,092.61 | 1,040.14 | 1,062.14 | 1,094.14 | 1,033.22 |
| 2019 | 1,035.94 | 1,043.71 | 1,009.13 | 1,015.31 | 1,019.88 | 1,071.25 | 1,036.35 | 1,052.39 | 1,116.59 | 1,087.73 | 1,090.37 | 1,142.66 | 1,059.57 |
| **Professional and Business Services** | | | | | | | | | | | | | |
| 2015 | 903.87 | 937.95 | 933.65 | 920.17 | 926.68 | 933.30 | 929.24 | 966.44 | 947.96 | 943.56 | 957.92 | 943.20 | 937.69 |
| 2016 | 971.75 | 954.04 | 944.99 | 945.76 | 972.73 | 946.08 | 969.03 | 963.49 | 969.42 | 991.89 | 976.06 | 980.87 | 966.41 |
| 2017 | 997.15 | 978.68 | 980.50 | 993.84 | 981.82 | 970.72 | 1,017.79 | 988.55 | 994.42 | 1,020.16 | 995.67 | 1,036.20 | 995.19 |
| 2018 | 1,013.86 | 1,047.59 | 1,050.38 | 1,059.92 | 1,024.43 | 1,041.18 | 1,057.92 | 1,010.32 | 1,067.77 | 1,036.41 | 1,043.90 | 1,081.61 | 1,045.01 |
| 2019 | 1,044.36 | 1,057.78 | 1,056.68 | 1,059.97 | 1,045.22 | 1,091.03 | 1,038.96 | 1,056.72 | 1,089.96 | 1,057.26 | 1,070.88 | 1,111.91 | 1,066.14 |
| **Education and Health Services** | | | | | | | | | | | | | |
| 2015 | 720.20 | 739.48 | 724.76 | 729.52 | 729.60 | 734.60 | 738.26 | 749.01 | 741.15 | 754.42 | 779.88 | 751.91 | 740.81 |
| 2016 | 763.64 | 767.04 | 754.75 | 778.60 | 765.05 | 775.63 | 795.29 | 783.52 | 787.07 | 796.92 | 786.95 | 777.71 | 778.73 |
| 2017 | 790.05 | 782.25 | 774.36 | 768.25 | 761.31 | 760.64 | 783.89 | 768.58 | 783.57 | 794.58 | 790.60 | 787.59 | 779.52 |
| 2018 | 776.05 | 788.57 | 793.28 | 802.71 | 767.92 | 778.54 | 789.87 | 778.54 | 800.40 | 768.20 | 780.89 | 798.16 | 784.56 |
| 2019 | 775.88 | 799.36 | 784.57 | 781.49 | 778.87 | 795.31 | 783.57 | 786.55 | 802.37 | 797.94 | 803.86 | 813.72 | 791.91 |
| **Leisure and Hospitality** | | | | | | | | | | | | | |
| 2015 | 280.90 | 295.74 | 293.93 | 296.98 | 295.90 | 297.02 | 293.76 | 292.90 | 286.78 | 287.94 | 285.86 | 294.41 | 292.03 |
| 2016 | 285.24 | 292.49 | 295.61 | 290.68 | 293.63 | 299.72 | 297.19 | 295.15 | 294.53 | 305.89 | 302.63 | 309.25 | 296.56 |
| 2017 | 298.54 | 307.54 | 307.58 | 307.95 | 305.47 | 308.11 | 311.52 | 306.43 | 306.83 | 312.35 | 310.71 | 309.93 | 308.31 |
| 2018 | 307.85 | 321.47 | 324.36 | 321.55 | 325.95 | 328.58 | 328.45 | 325.74 | 326.84 | 334.41 | 322.34 | 332.77 | 325.32 |
| 2019 | 317.34 | 324.88 | 332.84 | 328.42 | 323.49 | 333.74 | 325.40 | 326.77 | 328.60 | 333.37 | 327.86 | 335.36 | 328.22 |
| **Other Services** | | | | | | | | | | | | | |
| 2015 | 667.84 | 696.82 | 720.92 | 661.67 | 680.03 | 671.64 | 643.61 | 681.41 | 642.87 | 660.45 | 664.13 | 659.64 | 670.66 |
| 2016 | 655.74 | 661.37 | 676.54 | 666.59 | 657.40 | 645.46 | 646.72 | 645.92 | 653.02 | 693.35 | 655.26 | 654.93 | 659.93 |
| 2017 | 664.29 | 690.47 | 661.65 | 673.20 | 651.67 | 651.41 | 655.31 | 635.04 | 674.37 | 701.52 | 708.01 | 708.40 | 673.79 |
| 2018 | 678.95 | 713.60 | 725.01 | 737.02 | 731.27 | 734.83 | 748.48 | 754.05 | 782.56 | 776.16 | 755.34 | 741.64 | 739.31 |
| 2019 | 731.64 | 739.24 | 746.54 | 748.01 | 724.71 | 740.87 | 732.88 | 768.25 | 736.57 | 739.99 | 742.31 | 775.32 | 742.95 |

# ALASKA
## *At a Glance*

Population:
  2010 census: 710,231
  2019 estimate: 731,545

Percent change in population:
  2010–2019: 3.0%

Percent change in total nonfarm employment:
2011–2019: -0.2%

Industry with the largest growth in employment, 2011–2019 (percent):
  Education and health services, 11.6%

Industry with the largest decline or smallest growth in employment, 2011–2019 (percent):
  Information, -15.9%

Civilian labor force:
  2010: 361,913
  2019: 347,779

Unemployment rate and rank among states (highest to lowest):
  2010: 7.9%, 36th
  2019: 6.1%, 1st

Over-the-year change in unemployment rates:
  2017–2018: -0.4%
  2018–2019: -0.4%

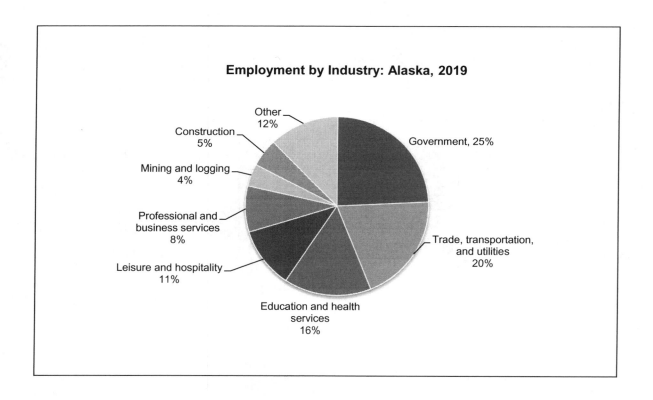

**Employment by Industry: Alaska, 2019**

Other 12%
Construction 5%
Mining and logging 4%
Professional and business services 8%
Leisure and hospitality 11%
Education and health services 16%
Government, 25%
Trade, transportation, and utilities 20%

# 1. Employment by Industry: Alaska, 2011–2019

(Numbers in thousands, not seasonally adjusted)

| Industry and year | January | February | March | April | May | June | July | August | September | October | November | December | Annual average |
|---|---|---|---|---|---|---|---|---|---|---|---|---|---|
| **Total Nonfarm** | | | | | | | | | | | | | |
| 2011 | 308.6 | 314.2 | 316.4 | 321.2 | 330.5 | 348.8 | 354.0 | 352.6 | 347.2 | 329.4 | 321.3 | 318.0 | 330.2 |
| 2012 | 312.6 | 320.2 | 322.9 | 326.7 | 337.9 | 354.5 | 358.1 | 357.3 | 349.0 | 336.4 | 325.5 | 321.8 | 335.2 |
| 2013 | 314.7 | 322.3 | 324.7 | 329.3 | 340.1 | 355.3 | 360.2 | 359.8 | 351.3 | 333.5 | 325.1 | 322.1 | 336.5 |
| 2014 | 318.6 | 322.9 | 325.5 | 331.2 | 344.0 | 356.4 | 362.4 | 360.3 | 350.6 | 335.1 | 326.3 | 324.2 | 338.1 |
| 2015 | 321.9 | 326.2 | 328.4 | 332.8 | 345.1 | 358.0 | 365.0 | 360.3 | 351.1 | 334.2 | 324.2 | 321.4 | 339.1 |
| 2016 | 317.7 | 322.1 | 323.7 | 330.0 | 340.2 | 351.8 | 358.1 | 354.0 | 342.5 | 328.1 | 318.0 | 316.0 | 333.5 |
| 2017 | 310.5 | 317.2 | 318.2 | 321.9 | 335.3 | 349.7 | 353.6 | 351.2 | 340.5 | 325.2 | 314.7 | 312.1 | 329.2 |
| 2018 | 308.0 | 314.7 | 316.3 | 319.5 | 332.8 | 347.3 | 351.4 | 349.3 | 338.5 | 326.1 | 315.8 | 313.2 | 327.7 |
| 2019 | 309.5 | 316.4 | 317.9 | 322.5 | 334.5 | 349.3 | 355.4 | 351.6 | 342.6 | 324.3 | 315.1 | 313.8 | 329.4 |
| **Total Private** | | | | | | | | | | | | | |
| 2011 | 224.4 | 228.3 | 230.9 | 234.7 | 245.6 | 263.1 | 274.0 | 272.5 | 261.0 | 242.7 | 235.4 | 232.1 | 245.4 |
| 2012 | 230.7 | 234.8 | 237.0 | 240.7 | 253.1 | 270.2 | 279.0 | 276.8 | 263.4 | 250.8 | 240.3 | 236.8 | 251.1 |
| 2013 | 233.5 | 238.2 | 240.4 | 244.4 | 255.9 | 271.9 | 282.3 | 281.0 | 267.9 | 250.2 | 241.7 | 239.2 | 253.9 |
| 2014 | 237.2 | 240.1 | 242.4 | 247.2 | 260.0 | 273.7 | 284.5 | 281.7 | 267.7 | 252.2 | 243.1 | 241.1 | 255.9 |
| 2015 | 240.4 | 243.3 | 245.3 | 248.8 | 261.1 | 275.5 | 287.3 | 282.1 | 268.3 | 251.6 | 241.6 | 238.9 | 257.0 |
| 2016 | 236.6 | 239.9 | 241.3 | 246.1 | 256.5 | 269.3 | 281.4 | 276.3 | 260.2 | 245.2 | 235.2 | 233.9 | 251.8 |
| 2017 | 229.6 | 235.0 | 235.9 | 239.2 | 251.6 | 267.9 | 277.9 | 274.4 | 259.0 | 243.5 | 233.2 | 230.7 | 248.2 |
| 2018 | 228.1 | 233.3 | 234.8 | 237.4 | 250.1 | 266.3 | 275.9 | 272.4 | 257.6 | 244.9 | 234.7 | 232.7 | 247.4 |
| 2019 | 229.7 | 235.2 | 236.6 | 240.8 | 253.1 | 268.4 | 280.1 | 275.7 | 262.5 | 244.2 | 235.1 | 233.9 | 249.6 |
| **Goods Producing** | | | | | | | | | | | | | |
| 2011 | 37.8 | 40.0 | 40.9 | 41.1 | 42.8 | 51.6 | 60.0 | 58.3 | 52.5 | 45.4 | 40.5 | 37.1 | 45.7 |
| 2012 | 39.7 | 42.2 | 43.4 | 43.6 | 45.6 | 54.2 | 61.3 | 59.3 | 52.3 | 47.4 | 42.2 | 38.7 | 47.5 |
| 2013 | 40.4 | 43.2 | 44.4 | 44.7 | 45.9 | 54.1 | 62.3 | 60.4 | 54.6 | 47.3 | 42.5 | 40.3 | 48.3 |
| 2014 | 43.0 | 44.8 | 45.7 | 47.3 | 47.7 | 55.9 | 63.8 | 60.8 | 53.8 | 47.7 | 43.7 | 41.5 | 49.6 |
| 2015 | 44.2 | 45.9 | 46.9 | 47.3 | 47.8 | 55.2 | 64.4 | 60.5 | 52.9 | 46.5 | 41.2 | 39.0 | 49.3 |
| 2016 | 41.0 | 43.2 | 43.7 | 43.2 | 43.0 | 49.7 | 59.0 | 54.1 | 45.5 | 41.3 | 36.4 | 34.4 | 44.5 |
| 2017 | 34.9 | 38.6 | 39.0 | 38.5 | 39.1 | 47.4 | 55.5 | 52.5 | 44.8 | 39.9 | 34.6 | 32.6 | 41.5 |
| 2018 | 33.8 | 37.4 | 37.8 | 38.1 | 38.9 | 46.9 | 54.9 | 51.0 | 44.4 | 40.5 | 35.6 | 34.2 | 41.1 |
| 2019 | 35.1 | 38.9 | 39.0 | 40.1 | 40.6 | 48.5 | 57.1 | 53.2 | 47.8 | 40.5 | 35.1 | 34.2 | 42.5 |
| **Service-Providing** | | | | | | | | | | | | | |
| 2011 | 270.8 | 274.2 | 275.5 | 280.1 | 287.7 | 297.2 | 294.0 | 294.3 | 294.7 | 284.0 | 280.8 | 280.9 | 284.5 |
| 2012 | 272.9 | 278.0 | 279.5 | 283.1 | 292.3 | 300.3 | 296.8 | 298.0 | 296.7 | 289.0 | 283.3 | 283.1 | 287.8 |
| 2013 | 274.3 | 279.1 | 280.3 | 284.6 | 294.2 | 301.2 | 297.9 | 299.4 | 296.7 | 286.2 | 282.6 | 281.8 | 288.2 |
| 2014 | 275.6 | 278.1 | 279.8 | 283.9 | 296.3 | 300.5 | 298.6 | 299.5 | 296.8 | 287.4 | 282.6 | 282.7 | 288.5 |
| 2015 | 277.7 | 280.3 | 281.5 | 285.5 | 297.3 | 302.8 | 300.6 | 299.8 | 298.2 | 287.7 | 283.0 | 282.4 | 289.7 |
| 2016 | 276.7 | 278.9 | 280.0 | 286.8 | 297.2 | 302.1 | 299.1 | 299.9 | 297.0 | 286.8 | 281.6 | 281.6 | 289.0 |
| 2017 | 275.6 | 278.6 | 279.2 | 283.4 | 296.2 | 302.3 | 298.1 | 298.7 | 295.7 | 285.3 | 280.1 | 279.5 | 287.7 |
| 2018 | 274.2 | 277.3 | 278.5 | 281.4 | 293.9 | 300.4 | 296.5 | 298.3 | 294.1 | 285.6 | 280.2 | 279.0 | 286.6 |
| 2019 | 274.4 | 277.5 | 278.9 | 282.4 | 293.9 | 300.8 | 298.3 | 298.4 | 294.8 | 283.8 | 280.0 | 279.6 | 286.9 |
| **Mining and Logging** | | | | | | | | | | | | | |
| 2011 | 14.4 | 14.6 | 14.8 | 15.0 | 15.2 | 15.8 | 16.2 | 16.2 | 16.1 | 15.9 | 15.6 | 15.8 | 15.5 |
| 2012 | 15.1 | 15.3 | 15.5 | 16.0 | 16.4 | 16.9 | 17.2 | 17.4 | 16.9 | 16.7 | 16.4 | 16.2 | 16.3 |
| 2013 | 15.8 | 16.3 | 16.7 | 16.6 | 16.8 | 17.3 | 17.3 | 17.4 | 17.1 | 16.5 | 16.4 | 16.5 | 16.7 |
| 2014 | 16.2 | 16.5 | 16.7 | 17.1 | 17.2 | 17.6 | 17.9 | 17.9 | 17.7 | 17.6 | 17.7 | 17.8 | 17.3 |
| 2015 | 17.5 | 17.5 | 17.7 | 17.8 | 17.6 | 17.8 | 17.8 | 17.8 | 17.6 | 17.1 | 16.4 | 16.3 | 17.4 |
| 2016 | 15.7 | 15.6 | 15.6 | 15.1 | 15.0 | 14.6 | 14.3 | 14.2 | 13.9 | 13.7 | 13.5 | 13.7 | 14.6 |
| 2017 | 13.1 | 13.1 | 13.1 | 13.0 | 13.1 | 13.4 | 13.5 | 13.5 | 13.2 | 12.8 | 12.3 | 12.4 | 13.0 |
| 2018 | 12.2 | 12.3 | 12.5 | 12.4 | 12.7 | 12.9 | 12.9 | 13.0 | 12.9 | 12.8 | 12.5 | 12.8 | 12.7 |
| 2019 | 12.6 | 12.9 | 13.1 | 13.2 | 13.3 | 13.7 | 13.7 | 13.9 | 13.6 | 13.4 | 13.1 | 13.1 | 13.3 |
| **Construction** | | | | | | | | | | | | | |
| 2011 | 12.8 | 13.0 | 13.2 | 14.5 | 16.6 | 18.8 | 19.5 | 19.9 | 19.2 | 18.2 | 15.7 | 14.5 | 16.3 |
| 2012 | 13.5 | 13.7 | 14.1 | 15.0 | 17.1 | 19.6 | 20.5 | 21.0 | 20.0 | 19.1 | 16.2 | 15.1 | 17.1 |
| 2013 | 13.4 | 13.9 | 14.5 | 15.1 | 16.9 | 19.5 | 20.4 | 21.4 | 20.4 | 18.9 | 16.6 | 15.8 | 17.2 |
| 2014 | 14.5 | 14.8 | 15.4 | 16.1 | 18.2 | 20.2 | 20.9 | 21.6 | 20.6 | 18.7 | 16.6 | 15.8 | 17.8 |
| 2015 | 14.9 | 15.3 | 15.9 | 16.9 | 18.5 | 20.2 | 20.9 | 20.8 | 19.5 | 17.9 | 15.9 | 15.0 | 17.6 |
| 2016 | 13.9 | 14.2 | 14.3 | 15.5 | 17.3 | 18.6 | 19.5 | 19.2 | 18.0 | 16.7 | 14.6 | 13.5 | 16.3 |
| 2017 | 12.2 | 12.8 | 13.0 | 13.9 | 15.5 | 17.5 | 18.0 | 18.1 | 17.4 | 16.3 | 14.2 | 13.3 | 15.2 |
| 2018 | 12.6 | 13.0 | 13.5 | 14.2 | 16.0 | 17.9 | 18.4 | 18.7 | 18.1 | 17.4 | 15.5 | 14.8 | 15.8 |
| 2019 | 13.4 | 13.8 | 14.2 | 15.3 | 17.1 | 18.5 | 18.9 | 19.2 | 18.4 | 17.5 | 15.1 | 15.2 | 16.4 |

## 1. Employment by Industry: Alaska, 2011–2019—*Continued*

(Numbers in thousands, not seasonally adjusted)

| Industry and year | January | February | March | April | May | June | July | August | September | October | November | December | Annual average |
|---|---|---|---|---|---|---|---|---|---|---|---|---|---|
| **Manufacturing** | | | | | | | | | | | | | |
| 2011 | 10.6 | 12.4 | 12.9 | 11.6 | 11.0 | 17.0 | 24.3 | 22.2 | 17.2 | 11.3 | 9.2 | 6.8 | 13.9 |
| 2012 | 11.1 | 13.2 | 13.8 | 12.6 | 12.1 | 17.7 | 23.6 | 20.9 | 15.4 | 11.6 | 9.6 | 7.4 | 14.1 |
| 2013 | 11.2 | 13.0 | 13.2 | 13.0 | 12.2 | 17.3 | 24.6 | 21.6 | 17.1 | 11.9 | 9.5 | 8.0 | 14.4 |
| 2014 | 12.3 | 13.5 | 13.6 | 14.1 | 12.3 | 18.1 | 25.0 | 21.3 | 15.5 | 11.4 | 9.4 | 7.9 | 14.5 |
| 2015 | 11.8 | 13.1 | 13.3 | 12.6 | 11.7 | 17.2 | 25.7 | 21.9 | 15.8 | 11.5 | 8.9 | 7.7 | 14.3 |
| 2016 | 11.4 | 13.4 | 13.8 | 12.6 | 10.7 | 16.5 | 25.2 | 20.7 | 13.6 | 10.9 | 8.3 | 7.2 | 13.7 |
| 2017 | 9.6 | 12.7 | 12.9 | 11.6 | 10.5 | 16.5 | 24.0 | 20.9 | 14.2 | 10.8 | 8.1 | 6.9 | 13.2 |
| 2018 | 9.0 | 12.1 | 11.8 | 11.5 | 10.2 | 16.1 | 23.6 | 19.3 | 13.4 | 10.3 | 7.6 | 6.6 | 12.6 |
| 2019 | 9.1 | 12.2 | 11.7 | 11.6 | 10.2 | 16.3 | 24.5 | 20.1 | 15.8 | 9.6 | 6.9 | 5.9 | 12.8 |
| **Trade, Transportation, and Utilities** | | | | | | | | | | | | | |
| 2011 | 58.8 | 58.8 | 59.6 | 60.9 | 64.7 | 67.1 | 68.1 | 68.5 | 66.4 | 62.3 | 61.6 | 61.5 | 63.2 |
| 2012 | 59.7 | 59.5 | 59.7 | 61.3 | 65.2 | 67.5 | 68.4 | 68.5 | 66.7 | 64.0 | 61.9 | 62.0 | 63.7 |
| 2013 | 59.9 | 59.6 | 59.9 | 61.4 | 65.6 | 67.7 | 68.4 | 69.2 | 67.2 | 63.1 | 62.3 | 62.4 | 63.9 |
| 2014 | 60.0 | 60.3 | 60.3 | 62.2 | 67.0 | 68.4 | 69.4 | 69.8 | 67.5 | 64.3 | 62.8 | 63.0 | 64.6 |
| 2015 | 61.1 | 61.2 | 61.5 | 63.2 | 67.5 | 69.3 | 70.4 | 70.6 | 68.7 | 65.5 | 63.9 | 63.8 | 65.6 |
| 2016 | 61.6 | 61.6 | 61.7 | 63.9 | 67.8 | 69.2 | 70.0 | 70.1 | 67.7 | 64.9 | 63.2 | 63.0 | 65.4 |
| 2017 | 60.9 | 60.9 | 60.9 | 62.6 | 66.5 | 68.5 | 69.5 | 69.5 | 66.9 | 63.9 | 62.5 | 62.2 | 64.6 |
| 2018 | 60.5 | 60.3 | 60.7 | 62.2 | 66.5 | 68.6 | 69.1 | 69.4 | 67.0 | 64.2 | 62.5 | 62.2 | 64.4 |
| 2019 | 60.5 | 60.4 | 61.1 | 62.4 | 66.6 | 68.4 | 69.8 | 69.5 | 67.3 | 63.7 | 63.0 | 63.1 | 64.7 |
| **Wholesale Trade** | | | | | | | | | | | | | |
| 2011 | 6.0 | 6.0 | 6.0 | 6.1 | 6.2 | 6.4 | 6.7 | 6.7 | 6.4 | 6.3 | 6.1 | 6.1 | 6.3 |
| 2012 | 6.0 | 6.0 | 6.0 | 6.1 | 6.3 | 6.4 | 6.6 | 6.6 | 6.5 | 6.4 | 6.4 | 6.4 | 6.3 |
| 2013 | 6.3 | 6.3 | 6.4 | 6.5 | 6.6 | 6.7 | 6.7 | 6.7 | 6.6 | 6.5 | 6.5 | 6.5 | 6.5 |
| 2014 | 6.3 | 6.3 | 6.3 | 6.4 | 6.5 | 6.6 | 6.6 | 6.6 | 6.5 | 6.4 | 6.3 | 6.4 | 6.4 |
| 2015 | 6.3 | 6.4 | 6.4 | 6.5 | 6.5 | 6.6 | 6.7 | 6.6 | 6.5 | 6.5 | 6.4 | 6.4 | 6.5 |
| 2016 | 6.4 | 6.3 | 6.3 | 6.4 | 6.4 | 6.5 | 6.5 | 6.5 | 6.4 | 6.3 | 6.3 | 6.2 | 6.4 |
| 2017 | 6.1 | 6.2 | 6.2 | 6.2 | 6.4 | 6.5 | 6.5 | 6.5 | 6.4 | 6.3 | 6.3 | 6.3 | 6.3 |
| 2018 | 6.3 | 6.3 | 6.3 | 6.4 | 6.5 | 6.6 | 6.6 | 6.6 | 6.5 | 6.4 | 6.4 | 6.4 | 6.4 |
| 2019 | 6.5 | 6.6 | 6.6 | 6.5 | 6.5 | 6.6 | 6.7 | 6.7 | 6.6 | 6.5 | 6.8 | 6.9 | 6.6 |
| **Retail Trade** | | | | | | | | | | | | | |
| 2011 | 33.9 | 33.6 | 33.8 | 34.5 | 35.9 | 37.1 | 37.4 | 37.4 | 36.6 | 35.6 | 35.8 | 35.8 | 35.6 |
| 2012 | 34.4 | 33.9 | 33.9 | 34.6 | 36.1 | 37.2 | 37.3 | 37.2 | 36.4 | 35.7 | 35.6 | 35.6 | 35.7 |
| 2013 | 34.2 | 33.7 | 33.8 | 34.5 | 36.0 | 37.2 | 37.5 | 37.9 | 37.1 | 36.0 | 36.1 | 36.2 | 35.9 |
| 2014 | 34.7 | 34.6 | 34.6 | 35.5 | 37.2 | 38.2 | 38.6 | 38.7 | 37.6 | 36.8 | 36.9 | 36.9 | 36.7 |
| 2015 | 35.5 | 35.2 | 35.4 | 36.1 | 37.7 | 38.8 | 39.2 | 39.2 | 38.4 | 37.4 | 37.5 | 37.4 | 37.3 |
| 2016 | 35.8 | 35.6 | 35.6 | 36.5 | 37.8 | 38.6 | 38.8 | 38.5 | 37.7 | 37.0 | 36.9 | 36.7 | 37.1 |
| 2017 | 35.4 | 35.1 | 35.0 | 35.7 | 36.8 | 37.9 | 38.2 | 37.9 | 36.9 | 36.0 | 36.1 | 35.8 | 36.4 |
| 2018 | 34.8 | 34.3 | 34.3 | 34.8 | 36.2 | 37.2 | 37.4 | 37.2 | 36.4 | 35.6 | 35.8 | 35.7 | 35.8 |
| 2019 | 34.6 | 34.1 | 34.4 | 34.9 | 36.0 | 36.9 | 37.3 | 36.9 | 36.1 | 35.4 | 35.1 | 35.1 | 35.6 |
| **Transportation and Utilities** | | | | | | | | | | | | | |
| 2011 | 18.9 | 19.2 | 19.8 | 20.3 | 22.6 | 23.6 | 24.0 | 24.4 | 23.4 | 20.4 | 19.7 | 19.6 | 21.3 |
| 2012 | 19.3 | 19.6 | 19.8 | 20.6 | 22.8 | 23.9 | 24.5 | 24.7 | 23.8 | 21.9 | 19.9 | 20.0 | 21.7 |
| 2013 | 19.4 | 19.6 | 19.7 | 20.4 | 23.0 | 23.8 | 24.2 | 24.6 | 23.5 | 20.6 | 19.7 | 19.7 | 21.5 |
| 2014 | 19.0 | 19.4 | 19.4 | 20.3 | 23.3 | 23.6 | 24.2 | 24.5 | 23.4 | 21.1 | 19.6 | 19.7 | 21.5 |
| 2015 | 19.3 | 19.6 | 19.7 | 20.6 | 23.3 | 23.9 | 24.5 | 24.8 | 23.8 | 21.6 | 20.0 | 20.0 | 21.8 |
| 2016 | 19.4 | 19.7 | 19.8 | 21.0 | 23.6 | 24.1 | 24.7 | 25.1 | 23.6 | 21.6 | 20.0 | 20.1 | 21.9 |
| 2017 | 19.4 | 19.6 | 19.7 | 20.7 | 23.3 | 24.1 | 24.8 | 25.1 | 23.6 | 21.6 | 20.1 | 20.1 | 21.8 |
| 2018 | 19.4 | 19.7 | 20.1 | 21.0 | 23.8 | 24.8 | 25.1 | 25.6 | 24.1 | 22.2 | 20.3 | 20.1 | 22.2 |
| 2019 | 19.4 | 19.7 | 20.1 | 21.0 | 24.1 | 24.9 | 25.8 | 25.9 | 24.6 | 21.8 | 21.1 | 21.1 | 22.5 |
| **Information** | | | | | | | | | | | | | |
| 2011 | 6.3 | 6.3 | 6.4 | 6.4 | 6.3 | 6.4 | 6.4 | 6.3 | 6.2 | 6.3 | 6.3 | 6.3 | 6.3 |
| 2012 | 6.2 | 6.2 | 6.2 | 6.2 | 6.3 | 6.3 | 6.3 | 6.2 | 6.1 | 6.2 | 6.1 | 6.2 | 6.2 |
| 2013 | 6.0 | 6.0 | 6.0 | 6.1 | 6.2 | 6.2 | 6.2 | 6.2 | 6.2 | 6.2 | 6.3 | 6.3 | 6.2 |
| 2014 | 6.2 | 6.2 | 6.2 | 6.2 | 6.3 | 6.2 | 6.3 | 6.3 | 6.2 | 6.3 | 6.3 | 6.3 | 6.3 |
| 2015 | 6.3 | 6.3 | 6.4 | 6.4 | 6.3 | 6.3 | 6.3 | 6.3 | 6.3 | 6.3 | 6.3 | 6.3 | 6.3 |
| 2016 | 6.2 | 6.3 | 6.2 | 6.4 | 6.4 | 6.4 | 6.4 | 6.3 | 6.3 | 6.1 | 6.1 | 6.1 | 6.3 |
| 2017 | 6.1 | 6.1 | 6.1 | 6.0 | 6.0 | 6.0 | 6.0 | 5.9 | 5.9 | 5.8 | 5.8 | 5.8 | 6.0 |
| 2018 | 5.7 | 5.7 | 5.7 | 5.7 | 5.7 | 5.7 | 5.7 | 5.6 | 5.5 | 5.5 | 5.5 | 5.5 | 5.6 |
| 2019 | 5.4 | 5.4 | 5.4 | 5.3 | 5.4 | 5.4 | 5.4 | 5.3 | 5.3 | 5.3 | 5.2 | 5.3 | 5.3 |

# 1. Employment by Industry: Alaska, 2011–2019—*Continued*

(Numbers in thousands, not seasonally adjusted)

| Industry and year | January | February | March | April | May | June | July | August | September | October | November | December | Annual average |
|---|---|---|---|---|---|---|---|---|---|---|---|---|---|
| **Financial Activities** | | | | | | | | | | | | | |
| 2011 | 11.9 | 12.0 | 12.0 | 12.0 | 12.1 | 12.5 | 12.7 | 12.7 | 12.3 | 12.1 | 12.0 | 11.9 | 12.2 |
| 2012 | 11.9 | 11.9 | 11.8 | 11.9 | 12.2 | 12.5 | 12.7 | 12.7 | 12.2 | 12.3 | 12.1 | 12.1 | 12.2 |
| 2013 | 11.8 | 11.9 | 11.8 | 12.0 | 12.1 | 12.7 | 12.9 | 12.8 | 12.2 | 12.2 | 12.0 | 12.0 | 12.2 |
| 2014 | 11.9 | 11.9 | 11.8 | 11.9 | 12.2 | 12.6 | 12.7 | 12.5 | 12.1 | 12.0 | 11.8 | 11.8 | 12.1 |
| 2015 | 11.6 | 11.6 | 11.6 | 11.7 | 12.1 | 12.8 | 13.1 | 12.7 | 12.3 | 12.0 | 12.0 | 11.7 | 12.1 |
| 2016 | 11.7 | 11.6 | 11.7 | 11.8 | 12.0 | 12.4 | 12.9 | 12.8 | 12.1 | 11.9 | 11.9 | 11.9 | 12.1 |
| 2017 | 11.5 | 11.7 | 11.6 | 11.8 | 12.0 | 12.5 | 12.6 | 12.6 | 11.9 | 11.8 | 11.7 | 11.7 | 12.0 |
| 2018 | 11.4 | 11.5 | 11.5 | 11.6 | 11.7 | 12.4 | 12.4 | 12.3 | 11.7 | 11.6 | 11.5 | 11.4 | 11.8 |
| 2019 | 11.4 | 11.3 | 11.3 | 11.4 | 11.7 | 12.5 | 12.3 | 12.3 | 11.6 | 11.6 | 11.5 | 11.6 | 11.7 |
| **Professional and Business Services** | | | | | | | | | | | | | |
| 2011 | 26.9 | 27.5 | 27.5 | 28.2 | 29.1 | 30.3 | 30.2 | 29.9 | 30.0 | 29.0 | 28.6 | 28.6 | 28.8 |
| 2012 | 28.0 | 28.6 | 28.8 | 29.1 | 30.3 | 31.4 | 31.5 | 31.5 | 31.2 | 30.1 | 29.4 | 29.3 | 29.9 |
| 2013 | 28.6 | 29.4 | 29.3 | 29.8 | 30.7 | 31.7 | 31.8 | 32.1 | 31.1 | 29.9 | 29.7 | 29.6 | 30.3 |
| 2014 | 28.8 | 28.7 | 29.3 | 29.3 | 30.7 | 31.2 | 31.5 | 31.7 | 31.1 | 30.3 | 29.2 | 29.5 | 30.1 |
| 2015 | 29.0 | 29.3 | 29.3 | 29.9 | 31.0 | 31.7 | 31.6 | 31.5 | 30.8 | 29.7 | 29.1 | 28.5 | 30.1 |
| 2016 | 27.6 | 27.8 | 27.8 | 28.8 | 29.3 | 30.0 | 29.8 | 29.9 | 29.2 | 28.0 | 26.9 | 27.5 | 28.6 |
| 2017 | 26.7 | 27.4 | 26.9 | 27.3 | 28.5 | 29.4 | 29.6 | 29.5 | 28.7 | 27.5 | 27.0 | 26.6 | 27.9 |
| 2018 | 26.1 | 26.7 | 26.7 | 26.2 | 27.5 | 28.5 | 28.5 | 28.8 | 28.1 | 27.4 | 26.8 | 26.7 | 27.3 |
| 2019 | 26.1 | 26.8 | 26.6 | 27.2 | 28.1 | 28.7 | 29.2 | 29.4 | 28.3 | 26.9 | 26.3 | 26.0 | 27.5 |
| **Education and Health Services** | | | | | | | | | | | | | |
| 2011 | 44.3 | 44.7 | 44.8 | 45.3 | 45.5 | 45.5 | 45.5 | 45.8 | 45.8 | 46.0 | 46.2 | 46.6 | 45.5 |
| 2012 | 46.2 | 46.9 | 46.9 | 47.0 | 47.3 | 47.3 | 46.5 | 46.6 | 46.3 | 47.4 | 47.6 | 47.7 | 47.0 |
| 2013 | 47.3 | 47.8 | 47.9 | 48.2 | 48.3 | 48.0 | 47.9 | 47.9 | 47.8 | 47.9 | 48.0 | 48.0 | 47.9 |
| 2014 | 47.4 | 47.7 | 47.8 | 47.9 | 47.8 | 47.6 | 47.6 | 47.6 | 47.4 | 47.6 | 47.6 | 47.6 | 47.6 |
| 2015 | 47.6 | 47.9 | 47.9 | 47.3 | 47.3 | 47.4 | 47.5 | 47.2 | 47.0 | 47.4 | 47.5 | 47.9 | 47.5 |
| 2016 | 47.8 | 48.3 | 48.5 | 48.8 | 48.7 | 48.3 | 48.8 | 48.8 | 48.7 | 48.8 | 48.9 | 49.2 | 48.6 |
| 2017 | 49.0 | 49.4 | 49.7 | 49.8 | 50.0 | 50.1 | 49.8 | 49.9 | 49.6 | 49.9 | 50.1 | 50.2 | 49.8 |
| 2018 | 50.0 | 50.4 | 50.6 | 50.4 | 50.5 | 50.5 | 50.2 | 50.2 | 50.1 | 50.5 | 50.8 | 50.9 | 50.4 |
| 2019 | 50.3 | 50.6 | 50.8 | 51.1 | 51.0 | 50.9 | 50.6 | 50.6 | 50.5 | 51.2 | 51.2 | 51.0 | 50.8 |
| **Leisure and Hospitality** | | | | | | | | | | | | | |
| 2011 | 27.5 | 28.0 | 28.6 | 29.7 | 33.9 | 38.3 | 39.8 | 39.7 | 36.5 | 30.2 | 29.0 | 28.9 | 32.5 |
| 2012 | 27.9 | 28.4 | 29.1 | 30.4 | 34.7 | 39.4 | 40.7 | 40.5 | 37.2 | 32.1 | 29.7 | 29.6 | 33.3 |
| 2013 | 28.4 | 29.1 | 29.8 | 30.8 | 35.6 | 39.9 | 41.2 | 41.0 | 37.5 | 32.4 | 29.7 | 29.5 | 33.7 |
| 2014 | 28.8 | 29.4 | 30.3 | 31.1 | 36.8 | 40.3 | 41.5 | 41.4 | 38.1 | 32.4 | 30.3 | 30.3 | 34.2 |
| 2015 | 29.7 | 30.2 | 30.8 | 31.8 | 37.7 | 41.3 | 42.7 | 42.3 | 39.3 | 33.2 | 30.6 | 30.7 | 35.0 |
| 2016 | 29.9 | 30.3 | 30.8 | 32.1 | 38.0 | 42.0 | 43.2 | 43.2 | 39.6 | 33.2 | 30.8 | 31.0 | 35.3 |
| 2017 | 29.8 | 30.1 | 30.9 | 32.0 | 38.1 | 42.4 | 43.5 | 43.2 | 39.9 | 33.6 | 30.5 | 30.7 | 35.4 |
| 2018 | 29.8 | 30.5 | 31.0 | 32.1 | 38.0 | 42.2 | 43.8 | 43.9 | 39.9 | 34.2 | 31.1 | 31.0 | 35.6 |
| 2019 | 30.3 | 31.1 | 31.6 | 32.4 | 38.5 | 42.6 | 44.3 | 44.2 | 40.6 | 34.0 | 32.0 | 31.8 | 36.1 |
| **Other Services** | | | | | | | | | | | | | |
| 2011 | 10.9 | 11.0 | 11.1 | 11.1 | 11.2 | 11.4 | 11.3 | 11.3 | 11.3 | 11.4 | 11.2 | 11.2 | 11.2 |
| 2012 | 11.1 | 11.1 | 11.1 | 11.2 | 11.5 | 11.6 | 11.6 | 11.5 | 11.4 | 11.3 | 11.3 | 11.2 | 11.3 |
| 2013 | 11.1 | 11.2 | 11.3 | 11.4 | 11.5 | 11.6 | 11.6 | 11.4 | 11.3 | 11.2 | 11.2 | 11.1 | 11.3 |
| 2014 | 11.1 | 11.1 | 11.0 | 11.3 | 11.5 | 11.5 | 11.7 | 11.6 | 11.5 | 11.6 | 11.4 | 11.1 | 11.4 |
| 2015 | 10.9 | 10.9 | 10.9 | 11.2 | 11.4 | 11.5 | 11.3 | 11.0 | 11.0 | 11.0 | 11.0 | 11.0 | 11.1 |
| 2016 | 10.8 | 10.8 | 10.9 | 11.1 | 11.3 | 11.3 | 11.3 | 11.1 | 11.1 | 11.0 | 11.0 | 10.8 | 11.0 |
| 2017 | 10.7 | 10.8 | 10.8 | 11.2 | 11.4 | 11.6 | 11.4 | 11.3 | 11.3 | 11.1 | 11.0 | 10.9 | 11.1 |
| 2018 | 10.8 | 10.8 | 10.8 | 11.1 | 11.3 | 11.5 | 11.3 | 11.2 | 10.9 | 11.0 | 10.9 | 10.8 | 11.0 |
| 2019 | 10.6 | 10.7 | 10.8 | 10.9 | 11.2 | 11.4 | 11.4 | 11.2 | 11.1 | 11.0 | 10.8 | 10.9 | 11.0 |
| **Government** | | | | | | | | | | | | | |
| 2011 | 84.2 | 85.9 | 85.5 | 86.5 | 84.9 | 85.7 | 80.0 | 80.1 | 86.2 | 86.7 | 85.9 | 85.9 | 84.8 |
| 2012 | 81.9 | 85.4 | 85.9 | 86.0 | 84.8 | 84.3 | 79.1 | 80.5 | 85.6 | 85.6 | 85.2 | 85.0 | 84.1 |
| 2013 | 81.2 | 84.1 | 84.3 | 84.9 | 84.2 | 83.4 | 77.9 | 78.8 | 83.4 | 83.3 | 83.4 | 82.9 | 82.7 |
| 2014 | 81.4 | 82.8 | 83.1 | 84.0 | 84.0 | 82.7 | 77.9 | 78.6 | 82.9 | 82.9 | 83.2 | 83.1 | 82.2 |
| 2015 | 81.5 | 82.9 | 83.1 | 84.0 | 84.0 | 82.5 | 77.7 | 78.2 | 82.8 | 82.6 | 82.6 | 82.5 | 82.0 |
| 2016 | 81.1 | 82.2 | 82.4 | 83.9 | 83.7 | 82.5 | 76.7 | 77.7 | 82.3 | 82.9 | 82.8 | 82.1 | 81.7 |
| 2017 | 80.9 | 82.2 | 82.3 | 82.7 | 83.7 | 81.8 | 75.7 | 76.8 | 81.5 | 81.7 | 81.5 | 81.4 | 81.0 |
| 2018 | 79.9 | 81.4 | 81.5 | 82.1 | 82.7 | 81.0 | 75.5 | 76.9 | 80.9 | 81.2 | 81.1 | 80.5 | 80.4 |
| 2019 | 79.8 | 81.2 | 81.3 | 81.7 | 81.4 | 80.9 | 75.3 | 75.9 | 80.1 | 80.1 | 80.0 | 79.9 | 79.8 |

## 2. Average Weekly Hours by Selected Industry: Alaska, 2015–2019

(Not seasonally adjusted)

| Industry and year | January | February | March | April | May | June | July | August | September | October | November | December | Annual average |
|---|---|---|---|---|---|---|---|---|---|---|---|---|---|
| **Total Private** | | | | | | | | | | | | | |
| 2015 | 34.1 | 34.9 | 35.0 | 34.0 | 34.7 | 35.2 | 35.8 | 36.1 | 34.7 | 34.2 | 34.1 | 33.4 | 34.7 |
| 2016 | 33.5 | 34.3 | 34.2 | 33.9 | 34.0 | 34.5 | 35.8 | 35.4 | 34.5 | 34.7 | 34.0 | 33.6 | 34.4 |
| 2017 | 34.7 | 35.1 | 35.1 | 34.7 | 34.6 | 35.7 | 36.7 | 36.3 | 34.8 | 34.7 | 34.2 | 34.1 | 35.1 |
| 2018 | 34.0 | 34.7 | 34.8 | 34.4 | 34.4 | 35.4 | 36.7 | 36.3 | 35.7 | 35.0 | 34.6 | 34.9 | 35.1 |
| 2019 | 34.5 | 35.1 | 35.3 | 34.8 | 34.8 | 36.0 | 36.2 | 36.6 | 35.6 | 34.3 | 34.0 | 34.6 | 35.2 |
| **Goods-Producing** | | | | | | | | | | | | | |
| 2015 | 38.3 | 39.0 | 39.7 | 35.0 | 37.9 | 37.8 | 39.2 | 39.5 | 35.6 | 35.7 | 34.0 | 34.5 | 37.4 |
| 2016 | 35.0 | 39.1 | 38.9 | 35.7 | 37.3 | 39.2 | 43.6 | 41.3 | 39.3 | 37.0 | 35.3 | 34.0 | 38.3 |
| 2017 | 36.6 | 40.9 | 40.4 | 36.2 | 37.3 | 38.8 | 41.2 | 40.0 | 35.9 | 36.0 | 34.6 | 34.0 | 37.9 |
| 2018 | 34.2 | 37.7 | 37.3 | 34.5 | 35.6 | 37.6 | 40.9 | 40.8 | 41.0 | 39.0 | 37.6 | 38.4 | 38.1 |
| 2019 | 36.9 | 40.8 | 42.1 | 38.9 | 39.2 | 39.1 | 42.2 | 44.3 | 39.8 | 37.4 | 35.1 | 36.8 | 39.7 |
| **Construction** | | | | | | | | | | | | | |
| 2015 | 36.2 | 35.5 | 35.7 | 38.0 | 38.4 | 40.5 | 40.2 | 40.4 | 36.4 | 38.1 | 35.5 | 35.2 | 37.7 |
| 2016 | 35.3 | 37.1 | 36.8 | 36.9 | 38.3 | 40.5 | 41.7 | 41.7 | 39.8 | 39.3 | 37.6 | 35.6 | 38.6 |
| 2017 | 36.1 | 36.5 | 37.7 | 39.1 | 40.0 | 42.7 | 43.7 | 44.4 | 42.7 | 42.2 | 39.0 | 38.4 | 40.6 |
| 2018 | 37.5 | 38.1 | 38.4 | 38.4 | 37.1 | 40.0 | 40.2 | 40.7 | 41.1 | 39.1 | 36.7 | 37.4 | 38.8 |
| 2019 | 33.8 | 36.2 | 37.1 | 37.8 | 39.5 | 39.7 | 39.4 | 40.2 | 40.2 | 40.1 | 36.9 | 38.7 | 38.5 |
| **Manufacturing** | | | | | | | | | | | | | |
| 2015 | 41.0 | 44.5 | 45.8 | 35.0 | 44.3 | 37.3 | 47.1 | 45.0 | 38.2 | 34.0 | 31.5 | 31.8 | 40.8 |
| 2016 | 33.4 | 40.7 | 41.1 | 32.1 | 33.7 | 36.6 | 47.2 | 40.4 | 37.8 | 29.7 | 26.5 | 25.6 | 37.3 |
| 2017 | 34.2 | 46.7 | 42.2 | 29.4 | 30.8 | 32.7 | 37.0 | 34.0 | 22.5 | 21.1 | 24.0 | 22.5 | 32.6 |
| 2018 | 25.0 | 35.9 | 33.9 | 24.0 | 29.7 | 30.9 | 42.0 | 41.7 | 39.7 | 35.8 | 32.7 | 32.4 | 35.0 |
| 2019 | 34.5 | 41.2 | 43.4 | 35.8 | 34.7 | 34.7 | 44.4 | 49.1 | 37.1 | 31.3 | 30.3 | 30.2 | 39.0 |
| **Trade, Transportation, and Utilities** | | | | | | | | | | | | | |
| 2015 | 33.0 | 34.1 | 34.0 | 33.7 | 34.4 | 34.9 | 35.3 | 35.5 | 35.0 | 33.3 | 34.1 | 33.4 | 34.3 |
| 2016 | 33.4 | 33.0 | 33.0 | 33.2 | 34.1 | 34.6 | 35.1 | 35.1 | 33.7 | 34.0 | 33.5 | 33.9 | 33.9 |
| 2017 | 34.0 | 33.5 | 33.4 | 34.5 | 34.1 | 35.5 | 35.7 | 35.1 | 34.2 | 33.9 | 33.8 | 33.8 | 34.3 |
| 2018 | 33.9 | 34.2 | 34.0 | 34.4 | 34.3 | 35.9 | 36.5 | 35.8 | 34.9 | 34.3 | 34.7 | 34.6 | 34.8 |
| 2019 | 33.5 | 33.4 | 33.5 | 33.2 | 33.6 | 35.5 | 34.7 | 34.3 | 33.8 | 32.8 | 33.4 | 34.0 | 33.8 |
| **Professional and Business Services** | | | | | | | | | | | | | |
| 2015 | 34.8 | 36.6 | 36.9 | 36.9 | 36.6 | 37.9 | 37.8 | 38.7 | 37.6 | 37.6 | 37.3 | 35.0 | 37.0 |
| 2016 | 34.9 | 36.9 | 36.8 | 35.9 | 35.4 | 35.0 | 34.8 | 35.4 | 34.8 | 36.4 | 34.9 | 33.7 | 35.4 |
| 2017 | 35.4 | 36.2 | 36.4 | 36.2 | 35.1 | 35.9 | 36.9 | 36.7 | 34.8 | 35.5 | 34.4 | 34.0 | 35.6 |
| 2018 | 34.2 | 35.4 | 35.2 | 35.2 | 34.2 | 36.2 | 36.6 | 36.9 | 36.2 | 35.1 | 34.4 | 35.0 | 35.4 |
| 2019 | 33.7 | 34.5 | 34.8 | 35.8 | 34.6 | 37.0 | 35.8 | 36.2 | 36.2 | 35.4 | 34.2 | 35.1 | 35.3 |
| **Leisure and Hospitality** | | | | | | | | | | | | | |
| 2015 | 26.8 | 27.3 | 27.6 | 27.3 | 27.4 | 28.6 | 29.0 | 29.7 | 28.5 | 26.9 | 26.6 | 25.9 | 27.7 |
| 2016 | 25.4 | 25.3 | 25.8 | 25.8 | 26.4 | 27.3 | 28.1 | 28.3 | 25.9 | 25.6 | 24.4 | 24.0 | 26.2 |
| 2017 | 24.1 | 24.0 | 24.6 | 24.8 | 26.4 | 29.0 | 29.5 | 29.6 | 27.6 | 25.6 | 25.5 | 25.5 | 26.7 |
| 2018 | 24.7 | 25.1 | 26.1 | 25.6 | 27.6 | 29.1 | 30.4 | 29.3 | 27.1 | 25.8 | 25.4 | 25.6 | 27.1 |
| 2019 | 24.3 | 24.8 | 25.6 | 25.1 | 26.4 | 29.2 | 28.8 | 29.0 | 27.2 | 25.5 | 25.2 | 26.3 | 26.7 |

## 3. Average Hourly Earnings by Selected Industry: Alaska, 2015–2019

(Dollars, not seasonally adjusted)

| Industry and year | January | February | March | April | May | June | July | August | September | October | November | December | Annual average |
|---|---|---|---|---|---|---|---|---|---|---|---|---|---|
| **Total Private** | | | | | | | | | | | | | |
| 2015 | 26.93 | 27.02 | 27.41 | 28.11 | 27.87 | 27.75 | 27.85 | 28.09 | 27.90 | 28.51 | 28.63 | 28.60 | 27.89 |
| 2016 | 27.92 | 27.73 | 27.96 | 28.41 | 28.48 | 27.77 | 27.66 | 27.89 | 28.24 | 28.99 | 28.81 | 28.99 | 28.22 |
| 2017 | 28.13 | 27.56 | 27.92 | 28.47 | 27.98 | 27.69 | 27.57 | 27.90 | 28.65 | 29.43 | 29.10 | 29.39 | 28.28 |
| 2018 | 29.21 | 29.06 | 29.06 | 29.16 | 28.24 | 28.13 | 28.13 | 28.14 | 28.77 | 29.26 | 29.19 | 29.39 | 28.78 |
| 2019 | 28.77 | 28.87 | 28.94 | 29.22 | 29.07 | 28.45 | 27.96 | 28.32 | 29.11 | 30.09 | 29.71 | 30.18 | 29.02 |
| **Goods-Producing** | | | | | | | | | | | | | |
| 2015 | 30.93 | 30.60 | 31.60 | 36.26 | 35.57 | 35.51 | 34.62 | 35.39 | 35.55 | 36.91 | 38.16 | 38.18 | 34.82 |
| 2016 | 32.70 | 32.13 | 32.62 | 35.98 | 37.12 | 33.51 | 31.61 | 33.23 | 34.85 | 37.81 | 37.67 | 38.44 | 34.44 |
| 2017 | 34.22 | 31.58 | 33.10 | 35.83 | 36.90 | 35.05 | 32.51 | 33.83 | 37.28 | 39.42 | 38.86 | 39.87 | 35.35 |
| 2018 | 37.07 | 36.23 | 36.29 | 36.96 | 35.73 | 35.04 | 33.42 | 34.03 | 35.69 | 37.00 | 38.37 | 39.15 | 35.98 |
| 2019 | 34.73 | 33.12 | 33.33 | 34.43 | 36.76 | 34.22 | 30.98 | 31.32 | 35.46 | 38.67 | 39.29 | 38.79 | 34.63 |
| **Construction** | | | | | | | | | | | | | |
| 2015 | 35.94 | 36.05 | 37.31 | 38.72 | 38.34 | 39.44 | 39.05 | 39.07 | 38.19 | 37.49 | 37.25 | 37.06 | 38.00 |
| 2016 | 36.67 | 37.65 | 37.51 | 38.06 | 38.91 | 40.09 | 40.57 | 40.35 | 39.51 | 38.99 | 38.35 | 37.93 | 38.92 |
| 2017 | 37.81 | 37.30 | 38.44 | 38.17 | 37.86 | 38.66 | 38.26 | 38.89 | 37.80 | 37.43 | 37.10 | 37.02 | 37.96 |
| 2018 | 35.97 | 37.01 | 37.80 | 37.93 | 37.64 | 38.26 | 39.01 | 39.54 | 38.25 | 38.04 | 37.80 | 37.24 | 38.00 |
| 2019 | 35.52 | 35.99 | 36.27 | 36.94 | 37.34 | 37.50 | 38.11 | 38.36 | 38.86 | 37.26 | 37.77 | 36.98 | 37.38 |
| **Manufacturing** | | | | | | | | | | | | | |
| 2015 | 17.54 | 16.30 | 17.24 | 20.08 | 20.58 | 19.21 | 17.18 | 19.41 | 20.32 | 23.66 | 25.93 | 26.96 | 19.40 |
| 2016 | 20.21 | 19.17 | 19.72 | 23.38 | 26.47 | 20.03 | 17.45 | 19.12 | 21.56 | 24.39 | 26.64 | 29.76 | 20.80 |
| 2017 | 21.15 | 18.40 | 19.52 | 22.61 | 25.34 | 21.84 | 19.83 | 20.10 | 24.45 | 27.80 | 27.59 | 30.11 | 21.73 |
| 2018 | 25.02 | 22.35 | 22.70 | 23.22 | 25.61 | 23.58 | 20.04 | 21.70 | 27.16 | 31.87 | 36.13 | 39.13 | 24.78 |
| 2019 | 31.32 | 28.18 | 27.94 | 28.24 | 30.80 | 27.21 | 23.95 | 24.53 | 26.54 | 30.12 | 31.46 | 32.58 | 27.21 |
| **Trade, Transportation, and Utilities** | | | | | | | | | | | | | |
| 2015 | 23.19 | 22.97 | 23.27 | 22.85 | 22.63 | 22.26 | 22.51 | 22.64 | 22.60 | 23.41 | 23.16 | 23.42 | 22.89 |
| 2016 | 23.44 | 22.90 | 23.79 | 23.53 | 22.98 | 22.53 | 22.59 | 22.56 | 23.56 | 23.81 | 23.74 | 24.13 | 23.27 |
| 2017 | 24.06 | 23.63 | 23.94 | 23.99 | 23.31 | 23.28 | 23.52 | 23.54 | 24.00 | 24.36 | 24.12 | 24.57 | 23.84 |
| 2018 | 24.10 | 23.97 | 24.50 | 24.74 | 24.25 | 24.10 | 24.16 | 24.44 | 25.37 | 26.06 | 25.63 | 25.75 | 24.75 |
| 2019 | 25.61 | 25.48 | 25.71 | 25.59 | 25.08 | 25.04 | 24.83 | 25.62 | 26.45 | 27.40 | 26.42 | 27.43 | 25.87 |
| **Professional and Business Services** | | | | | | | | | | | | | |
| 2015 | 34.16 | 33.82 | 33.95 | 34.08 | 34.26 | 33.57 | 33.65 | 34.34 | 33.60 | 34.01 | 34.33 | 34.26 | 34.00 |
| 2016 | 33.91 | 33.28 | 32.66 | 33.18 | 33.48 | 34.32 | 34.96 | 34.46 | 34.91 | 35.74 | 36.26 | 36.48 | 34.44 |
| 2017 | 35.25 | 33.88 | 34.19 | 35.07 | 34.14 | 33.22 | 33.58 | 33.44 | 35.02 | 35.31 | 35.55 | 35.92 | 34.50 |
| 2018 | 35.38 | 35.07 | 34.81 | 34.89 | 33.74 | 33.50 | 33.98 | 33.20 | 32.98 | 33.24 | 33.43 | 33.69 | 33.97 |
| 2019 | 33.42 | 33.79 | 33.96 | 33.87 | 34.10 | 33.90 | 33.34 | 33.74 | 34.44 | 35.01 | 35.20 | 35.58 | 34.18 |
| **Leisure and Hospitality** | | | | | | | | | | | | | |
| 2015 | 16.96 | 17.15 | 17.13 | 17.19 | 17.01 | 16.81 | 16.79 | 16.80 | 16.87 | 17.58 | 17.60 | 18.04 | 17.11 |
| 2016 | 17.94 | 17.80 | 17.56 | 17.45 | 17.46 | 17.29 | 17.45 | 17.36 | 17.31 | 17.52 | 17.67 | 17.79 | 17.52 |
| 2017 | 17.93 | 17.61 | 17.62 | 17.61 | 16.77 | 16.65 | 16.67 | 16.76 | 16.88 | 17.84 | 17.65 | 18.31 | 17.25 |
| 2018 | 18.25 | 17.92 | 18.01 | 17.96 | 16.95 | 16.69 | 16.65 | 16.53 | 16.96 | 17.33 | 17.42 | 17.53 | 17.24 |
| 2019 | 17.29 | 17.76 | 17.51 | 17.49 | 17.27 | 16.84 | 17.00 | 17.17 | 17.41 | 17.64 | 17.60 | 17.90 | 17.36 |

## 4. Average Weekly Earnings by Selected Industry: Alaska, 2015–2019

(Dollars, not seasonally adjusted)

| Industry and year | January | February | March | April | May | June | July | August | September | October | November | December | Annual average |
|---|---|---|---|---|---|---|---|---|---|---|---|---|---|
| **Total Private** | | | | | | | | | | | | | |
| 2015 | 918.31 | 943.00 | 959.35 | 955.74 | 967.09 | 976.80 | 997.03 | 1,014.05 | 968.13 | 975.04 | 976.28 | 955.24 | 967.78 |
| 2016 | 935.32 | 951.14 | 956.23 | 963.10 | 968.32 | 958.07 | 990.23 | 987.31 | 974.28 | 1,005.95 | 979.54 | 974.06 | 970.77 |
| 2017 | 976.11 | 967.36 | 979.99 | 987.91 | 968.11 | 988.53 | 1,011.82 | 1,012.77 | 997.02 | 1,021.22 | 995.22 | 1,002.20 | 992.63 |
| 2018 | 993.14 | 1,008.38 | 1,011.29 | 1,003.10 | 971.46 | 995.80 | 1,032.37 | 1,021.48 | 1,027.09 | 1,024.10 | 1,009.97 | 1,025.71 | 1,010.18 |
| 2019 | 992.57 | 1,013.34 | 1,021.58 | 1,016.86 | 1,011.64 | 1,024.20 | 1,012.15 | 1,036.51 | 1,036.32 | 1,032.09 | 1,010.14 | 1,044.23 | 1,021.50 |
| **Goods-Producing** | | | | | | | | | | | | | |
| 2015 | 1,184.62 | 1,193.40 | 1,254.52 | 1,269.10 | 1,348.10 | 1,342.28 | 1,357.10 | 1,397.91 | 1,265.58 | 1,317.69 | 1,297.44 | 1,317.21 | 1,302.27 |
| 2016 | 1,144.50 | 1,256.28 | 1,268.92 | 1,284.49 | 1,384.58 | 1,313.59 | 1,378.20 | 1,372.40 | 1,369.61 | 1,398.97 | 1,329.75 | 1,306.96 | 1,319.05 |
| 2017 | 1,252.45 | 1,291.62 | 1,337.24 | 1,297.05 | 1,376.37 | 1,359.94 | 1,339.41 | 1,353.20 | 1,338.35 | 1,419.12 | 1,344.56 | 1,355.58 | 1,339.77 |
| 2018 | 1,267.79 | 1,365.87 | 1,353.62 | 1,275.12 | 1,271.99 | 1,317.50 | 1,366.88 | 1,388.42 | 1,463.29 | 1,443.00 | 1,442.71 | 1,503.36 | 1,370.84 |
| 2019 | 1,281.54 | 1,351.30 | 1,403.19 | 1,339.33 | 1,440.99 | 1,338.00 | 1,307.36 | 1,387.48 | 1,411.31 | 1,446.26 | 1,379.08 | 1,427.47 | 1,374.81 |
| **Construction** | | | | | | | | | | | | | |
| 2015 | 1,301.03 | 1,279.78 | 1,331.97 | 1,471.36 | 1,472.26 | 1,597.32 | 1,569.81 | 1,578.43 | 1,390.12 | 1,428.37 | 1,322.38 | 1,304.51 | 1,432.60 |
| 2016 | 1,294.45 | 1,396.82 | 1,380.37 | 1,404.41 | 1,490.25 | 1,623.65 | 1,691.77 | 1,682.60 | 1,572.50 | 1,532.31 | 1,441.96 | 1,350.31 | 1,502.31 |
| 2017 | 1,364.94 | 1,361.45 | 1,449.19 | 1,492.45 | 1,514.40 | 1,650.78 | 1,671.96 | 1,726.72 | 1,614.06 | 1,579.55 | 1,446.90 | 1,421.57 | 1,541.18 |
| 2018 | 1,348.88 | 1,410.08 | 1,451.52 | 1,456.51 | 1,396.44 | 1,530.40 | 1,568.20 | 1,609.28 | 1,572.08 | 1,487.36 | 1,387.26 | 1,392.78 | 1,474.40 |
| 2019 | 1,200.58 | 1,302.84 | 1,345.62 | 1,396.33 | 1,474.93 | 1,488.75 | 1,501.53 | 1,542.07 | 1,562.17 | 1,494.13 | 1,393.71 | 1,431.13 | 1,439.13 |
| **Manufacturing** | | | | | | | | | | | | | |
| 2015 | 719.14 | 725.35 | 789.59 | 702.80 | 911.69 | 716.53 | 809.18 | 873.45 | 776.22 | 804.44 | 816.80 | 857.33 | 791.52 |
| 2016 | 675.01 | 780.22 | 810.49 | 750.50 | 892.04 | 733.10 | 823.64 | 772.45 | 814.97 | 724.38 | 705.96 | 761.86 | 775.84 |
| 2017 | 723.33 | 859.28 | 823.74 | 664.73 | 780.47 | 714.17 | 733.71 | 683.40 | 550.13 | 586.58 | 662.16 | 677.48 | 708.40 |
| 2018 | 625.50 | 802.37 | 769.53 | 557.28 | 760.62 | 728.62 | 841.68 | 904.89 | 1,078.25 | 1,140.95 | 1,181.45 | 1,267.81 | 867.30 |
| 2019 | 1,080.54 | 1,161.02 | 1,212.60 | 1,010.99 | 1,068.76 | 944.19 | 1,063.38 | 1,204.42 | 984.63 | 942.76 | 953.24 | 983.92 | 1,061.19 |
| **Trade, Transportation, and Utilities** | | | | | | | | | | | | | |
| 2015 | 765.27 | 783.28 | 791.18 | 770.05 | 778.47 | 776.87 | 794.60 | 803.72 | 791.00 | 779.55 | 789.76 | 782.23 | 785.13 |
| 2016 | 782.90 | 755.70 | 785.07 | 781.20 | 783.62 | 779.54 | 792.91 | 791.86 | 793.97 | 809.54 | 795.29 | 818.01 | 788.85 |
| 2017 | 818.04 | 791.61 | 799.60 | 827.66 | 794.87 | 826.44 | 839.66 | 826.25 | 820.80 | 825.80 | 815.26 | 830.47 | 817.71 |
| 2018 | 816.99 | 819.77 | 833.00 | 851.06 | 831.78 | 865.19 | 881.84 | 874.95 | 885.41 | 893.86 | 889.36 | 890.95 | 861.30 |
| 2019 | 857.94 | 851.03 | 861.29 | 849.59 | 842.69 | 888.92 | 861.60 | 878.77 | 894.01 | 898.72 | 882.43 | 932.62 | 874.41 |
| **Professional and Business Services** | | | | | | | | | | | | | |
| 2015 | 1,188.77 | 1,237.81 | 1,252.76 | 1,257.55 | 1,253.92 | 1,272.30 | 1,271.97 | 1,328.96 | 1,263.36 | 1,278.78 | 1,280.51 | 1,199.10 | 1,258.00 |
| 2016 | 1,183.46 | 1,228.03 | 1,201.89 | 1,191.16 | 1,185.19 | 1,201.20 | 1,216.61 | 1,219.88 | 1,214.87 | 1,300.94 | 1,265.47 | 1,229.38 | 1,219.18 |
| 2017 | 1,247.85 | 1,226.46 | 1,244.52 | 1,269.53 | 1,198.31 | 1,192.60 | 1,239.10 | 1,227.25 | 1,218.70 | 1,253.51 | 1,222.92 | 1,221.28 | 1,228.20 |
| 2018 | 1,210.00 | 1,241.48 | 1,225.31 | 1,228.13 | 1,153.91 | 1,212.70 | 1,243.67 | 1,225.08 | 1,193.88 | 1,166.72 | 1,149.99 | 1,179.15 | 1,202.54 |
| 2019 | 1,126.25 | 1,165.76 | 1,181.81 | 1,212.55 | 1,179.86 | 1,254.30 | 1,193.57 | 1,221.39 | 1,246.73 | 1,239.35 | 1,203.84 | 1,248.86 | 1,206.55 |
| **Leisure and Hospitality** | | | | | | | | | | | | | |
| 2015 | 454.53 | 468.20 | 472.79 | 469.29 | 466.07 | 480.77 | 486.91 | 498.96 | 480.80 | 472.90 | 468.16 | 467.24 | 473.95 |
| 2016 | 455.68 | 450.34 | 453.05 | 450.21 | 460.94 | 472.02 | 490.35 | 491.29 | 448.33 | 448.51 | 431.15 | 426.96 | 459.02 |
| 2017 | 432.11 | 422.64 | 433.45 | 436.73 | 442.73 | 482.85 | 491.77 | 496.10 | 465.89 | 456.70 | 450.08 | 466.91 | 460.58 |
| 2018 | 450.78 | 449.79 | 470.06 | 459.78 | 467.82 | 485.68 | 506.16 | 484.33 | 459.62 | 447.11 | 442.47 | 448.77 | 467.20 |
| 2019 | 420.15 | 440.45 | 448.26 | 439.00 | 455.93 | 491.73 | 489.60 | 497.93 | 473.55 | 449.82 | 443.52 | 470.77 | 463.51 |

# ARIZONA
*At a Glance*

Population:
  2010 census: 6,392,017
  2019 estimate: 7,278,717

Percent change in population:
  2010–2019: 13.9%

Percent change in total nonfarm employment:
  2011–2019: 21.8%

Industry with the largest growth in employment, 2011–2019 (percent):
  Construction, 53.9%

Industry with the largest decline or smallest growth in employment, 2011–2019 (percent):
  Government, 3.7%

Civilian labor force:
  2010: 3,089,705
  2019: 3,551,260

Unemployment rate and rank among states (highest to lowest):
  2010: 10.4%, 11th
  2019: 4.7%, 7th

Over-the-year change in unemployment rates:
  2017–2018: -0.2%
  2018–2019: 0.0%

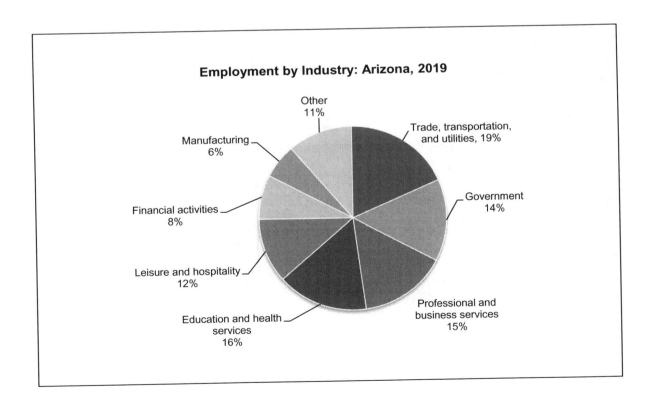

**Employment by Industry: Arizona, 2019**

- Other 11%
- Trade, transportation, and utilities, 19%
- Manufacturing 6%
- Government 14%
- Financial activities 8%
- Leisure and hospitality 12%
- Professional and business services 15%
- Education and health services 16%

## 1. Employment by Industry: Arizona, 2011–2019

(Numbers in thousands, not seasonally adjusted)

| Industry and year | January | February | March | April | May | June | July | August | September | October | November | December | Annual average |
|---|---|---|---|---|---|---|---|---|---|---|---|---|---|
| **Total Nonfarm** | | | | | | | | | | | | | |
| 2011 | 2,379.2 | 2,402.4 | 2,414.8 | 2,426.6 | 2,425.8 | 2,361.7 | 2,337.8 | 2,392.9 | 2,422.6 | 2,440.5 | 2,464.5 | 2,467.7 | 2,411.4 |
| 2012 | 2,425.2 | 2,448.3 | 2,466.3 | 2,467.9 | 2,464.2 | 2,420.2 | 2,387.7 | 2,445.3 | 2,474.9 | 2,494.2 | 2,523.0 | 2,531.1 | 2,462.4 |
| 2013 | 2,478.4 | 2,505.1 | 2,517.8 | 2,527.0 | 2,524.2 | 2,472.5 | 2,451.0 | 2,502.1 | 2,530.4 | 2,553.8 | 2,585.9 | 2,592.2 | 2,520.0 |
| 2014 | 2,536.3 | 2,558.1 | 2,566.5 | 2,577.7 | 2,565.0 | 2,520.1 | 2,497.0 | 2,547.8 | 2,576.0 | 2,610.1 | 2,639.3 | 2,649.6 | 2,570.3 |
| 2015 | 2,596.4 | 2,621.5 | 2,628.7 | 2,639.6 | 2,630.0 | 2,576.7 | 2,563.4 | 2,614.5 | 2,646.4 | 2,686.0 | 2,715.0 | 2,718.0 | 2,636.4 |
| 2016 | 2,663.7 | 2,693.1 | 2,701.8 | 2,717.4 | 2,704.0 | 2,647.4 | 2,641.9 | 2,690.8 | 2,730.4 | 2,754.7 | 2,778.6 | 2,782.6 | 2,708.9 |
| 2017 | 2,731.3 | 2,758.9 | 2,769.3 | 2,782.4 | 2,769.1 | 2,726.8 | 2,703.8 | 2,758.3 | 2,794.5 | 2,823.3 | 2,852.1 | 2,857.1 | 2,777.2 |
| 2018 | 2,807.6 | 2,839.5 | 2,850.5 | 2,853.3 | 2,845.2 | 2,797.8 | 2,783.5 | 2,846.3 | 2,876.5 | 2,906.6 | 2,941.8 | 2,943.8 | 2,857.7 |
| 2019 | 2,899.7 | 2,922.7 | 2,929.6 | 2,930.1 | 2,919.6 | 2,869.8 | 2,860.2 | 2,936.4 | 2,953.4 | 2,982.3 | 3,019.3 | 3,025.6 | 2,937.4 |
| **Total Private** | | | | | | | | | | | | | |
| 2011 | 1,968.8 | 1,980.3 | 1,993.8 | 2,003.9 | 2,004.8 | 1,993.0 | 1,984.2 | 1,998.2 | 2,005.8 | 2,020.3 | 2,042.6 | 2,052.6 | 2,004.0 |
| 2012 | 2,016.8 | 2,027.7 | 2,045.0 | 2,045.7 | 2,048.8 | 2,044.0 | 2,029.6 | 2,048.5 | 2,054.6 | 2,072.3 | 2,099.1 | 2,109.7 | 2,053.5 |
| 2013 | 2,066.2 | 2,082.5 | 2,096.1 | 2,103.8 | 2,105.8 | 2,098.9 | 2,090.6 | 2,108.8 | 2,111.4 | 2,131.3 | 2,163.0 | 2,172.5 | 2,110.9 |
| 2014 | 2,122.9 | 2,135.8 | 2,145.7 | 2,155.4 | 2,154.4 | 2,144.5 | 2,133.3 | 2,152.9 | 2,154.8 | 2,183.6 | 2,211.9 | 2,226.1 | 2,160.1 |
| 2015 | 2,184.3 | 2,197.3 | 2,205.3 | 2,216.1 | 2,215.3 | 2,206.2 | 2,205.2 | 2,222.3 | 2,227.3 | 2,260.2 | 2,286.5 | 2,295.5 | 2,226.8 |
| 2016 | 2,253.0 | 2,269.4 | 2,277.3 | 2,292.9 | 2,289.2 | 2,273.6 | 2,278.1 | 2,295.6 | 2,306.4 | 2,328.0 | 2,349.7 | 2,357.6 | 2,297.6 |
| 2017 | 2,318.3 | 2,333.0 | 2,343.2 | 2,355.7 | 2,353.0 | 2,348.4 | 2,337.9 | 2,357.4 | 2,368.5 | 2,395.1 | 2,422.7 | 2,432.6 | 2,363.8 |
| 2018 | 2,393.3 | 2,413.2 | 2,424.7 | 2,427.3 | 2,425.7 | 2,417.2 | 2,415.4 | 2,438.4 | 2,447.8 | 2,474.8 | 2,509.0 | 2,515.5 | 2,441.9 |
| 2019 | 2,476.2 | 2,491.4 | 2,498.1 | 2,499.0 | 2,494.3 | 2,485.4 | 2,487.8 | 2,514.3 | 2,518.6 | 2,545.2 | 2,580.8 | 2,587.8 | 2,514.9 |
| **Goods Producing** | | | | | | | | | | | | | |
| 2011 | 267.2 | 267.1 | 269.0 | 270.6 | 272.6 | 275.4 | 276.9 | 277.4 | 277.4 | 277.6 | 277.0 | 277.4 | 273.8 |
| 2012 | 274.6 | 275.8 | 279.4 | 280.5 | 282.7 | 286.8 | 288.0 | 289.9 | 289.7 | 290.2 | 290.1 | 289.8 | 284.8 |
| 2013 | 284.9 | 286.9 | 289.2 | 290.1 | 292.6 | 296.5 | 297.3 | 297.6 | 295.8 | 296.7 | 296.2 | 295.6 | 293.3 |
| 2014 | 293.3 | 295.2 | 295.3 | 296.2 | 296.5 | 297.4 | 296.7 | 296.8 | 294.6 | 296.5 | 296.1 | 296.6 | 295.9 |
| 2015 | 292.3 | 294.3 | 295.0 | 297.4 | 298.8 | 301.2 | 302.6 | 302.9 | 301.4 | 304.0 | 303.9 | 305.0 | 299.9 |
| 2016 | 301.2 | 304.3 | 305.1 | 306.2 | 306.8 | 310.1 | 311.4 | 311.7 | 310.6 | 310.3 | 310.3 | 312.4 | 308.4 |
| 2017 | 310.3 | 313.3 | 315.0 | 317.0 | 319.7 | 324.8 | 326.1 | 327.1 | 327.6 | 330.4 | 331.9 | 333.7 | 323.1 |
| 2018 | 330.3 | 334.3 | 337.0 | 337.7 | 338.7 | 344.1 | 345.8 | 346.9 | 347.7 | 348.9 | 351.7 | 353.8 | 343.1 |
| 2019 | 351.5 | 354.6 | 356.3 | 357.9 | 359.7 | 363.5 | 365.3 | 365.8 | 365.3 | 365.8 | 365.5 | 366.1 | 361.4 |
| **Service-Providing** | | | | | | | | | | | | | |
| 2011 | 2,112.0 | 2,135.3 | 2,145.8 | 2,156.0 | 2,153.2 | 2,086.3 | 2,060.9 | 2,115.5 | 2,145.2 | 2,162.9 | 2,187.5 | 2,190.3 | 2,137.6 |
| 2012 | 2,150.6 | 2,172.5 | 2,186.9 | 2,187.4 | 2,181.5 | 2,133.4 | 2,099.7 | 2,155.4 | 2,185.2 | 2,204.0 | 2,232.9 | 2,241.3 | 2,177.6 |
| 2013 | 2,193.5 | 2,218.2 | 2,228.6 | 2,236.9 | 2,231.6 | 2,176.0 | 2,153.7 | 2,204.5 | 2,234.6 | 2,257.1 | 2,289.7 | 2,296.6 | 2,226.8 |
| 2014 | 2,243.0 | 2,262.9 | 2,271.2 | 2,281.5 | 2,268.5 | 2,222.7 | 2,200.3 | 2,251.0 | 2,281.4 | 2,313.6 | 2,343.2 | 2,353.0 | 2,274.4 |
| 2015 | 2,304.1 | 2,327.2 | 2,333.7 | 2,342.2 | 2,331.2 | 2,275.5 | 2,260.8 | 2,311.6 | 2,345.0 | 2,382.0 | 2,411.1 | 2,413.0 | 2,336.5 |
| 2016 | 2,362.5 | 2,388.8 | 2,396.7 | 2,411.2 | 2,397.2 | 2,337.3 | 2,330.5 | 2,379.1 | 2,419.8 | 2,444.4 | 2,468.3 | 2,470.2 | 2,400.5 |
| 2017 | 2,421.0 | 2,445.6 | 2,454.3 | 2,465.4 | 2,449.4 | 2,402.0 | 2,377.7 | 2,431.2 | 2,466.9 | 2,492.9 | 2,520.2 | 2,523.4 | 2,454.2 |
| 2018 | 2,477.3 | 2,505.2 | 2,513.5 | 2,515.6 | 2,506.5 | 2,453.7 | 2,437.7 | 2,499.4 | 2,528.8 | 2,557.7 | 2,590.1 | 2,590.0 | 2,514.6 |
| 2019 | 2,548.2 | 2,568.1 | 2,573.3 | 2,572.2 | 2,559.9 | 2,506.3 | 2,494.9 | 2,570.6 | 2,588.1 | 2,616.5 | 2,653.8 | 2,659.5 | 2,576.0 |
| **Mining and Logging** | | | | | | | | | | | | | |
| 2011 | 11.3 | 11.4 | 11.5 | 11.2 | 11.4 | 11.6 | 11.2 | 11.3 | 11.4 | 12.1 | 12.1 | 12.2 | 11.6 |
| 2012 | 12.2 | 12.3 | 12.4 | 12.5 | 12.6 | 12.7 | 12.9 | 12.9 | 12.9 | 12.8 | 12.9 | 13.0 | 12.7 |
| 2013 | 13.0 | 13.1 | 13.1 | 13.3 | 13.3 | 13.6 | 13.6 | 13.5 | 13.2 | 13.2 | 13.0 | 13.0 | 13.2 |
| 2014 | 13.0 | 13.0 | 13.0 | 13.1 | 13.0 | 13.3 | 13.3 | 13.2 | 13.1 | 13.2 | 13.2 | 13.2 | 13.1 |
| 2015 | 12.6 | 12.7 | 12.6 | 12.5 | 12.6 | 12.9 | 12.9 | 12.7 | 12.5 | 12.3 | 12.2 | 12.1 | 12.6 |
| 2016 | 11.8 | 12.0 | 11.5 | 11.5 | 11.4 | 11.6 | 11.6 | 11.5 | 11.4 | 11.4 | 11.4 | 11.5 | 11.6 |
| 2017 | 11.3 | 11.4 | 11.4 | 11.6 | 11.6 | 11.9 | 12.1 | 12.1 | 12.0 | 12.2 | 12.2 | 12.3 | 11.8 |
| 2018 | 12.3 | 12.5 | 12.7 | 13.0 | 13.0 | 13.3 | 13.3 | 13.4 | 13.3 | 13.3 | 13.2 | 13.3 | 13.1 |
| 2019 | 13.3 | 13.3 | 13.3 | 13.3 | 13.3 | 13.6 | 13.7 | 13.7 | 13.6 | 13.6 | 13.6 | 13.5 | 13.5 |
| **Construction** | | | | | | | | | | | | | |
| 2011 | 106.6 | 106.4 | 107.9 | 109.4 | 110.1 | 112.4 | 113.7 | 113.9 | 113.9 | 113.1 | 112.1 | 111.2 | 110.9 |
| 2012 | 108.8 | 109.3 | 112.0 | 112.6 | 114.1 | 117.0 | 118.1 | 119.8 | 120.1 | 120.7 | 120.5 | 119.5 | 116.0 |
| 2013 | 116.2 | 117.6 | 120.0 | 120.9 | 123.1 | 126.1 | 126.5 | 127.4 | 126.4 | 127.2 | 126.9 | 125.9 | 123.7 |
| 2014 | 123.7 | 124.8 | 124.8 | 125.9 | 125.8 | 125.8 | 125.4 | 125.4 | 124.1 | 125.9 | 125.2 | 124.4 | 125.1 |
| 2015 | 122.5 | 123.8 | 124.7 | 126.8 | 127.6 | 128.5 | 129.3 | 129.6 | 129.0 | 131.0 | 130.8 | 130.9 | 127.9 |
| 2016 | 128.6 | 130.9 | 132.6 | 133.7 | 134.2 | 136.4 | 138.2 | 138.5 | 137.9 | 138.2 | 137.5 | 137.7 | 135.4 |
| 2017 | 136.8 | 138.5 | 140.8 | 142.5 | 144.4 | 147.3 | 148.0 | 148.7 | 149.1 | 151.4 | 151.8 | 152.3 | 146.0 |
| 2018 | 150.3 | 152.6 | 154.5 | 155.4 | 156.5 | 159.2 | 160.2 | 161.0 | 161.5 | 162.7 | 164.2 | 165.2 | 158.6 |
| 2019 | 163.4 | 165.6 | 167.0 | 168.8 | 170.2 | 172.1 | 173.0 | 173.1 | 173.2 | 173.7 | 173.6 | 174.2 | 170.7 |

# 1. Employment by Industry: Arizona, 2011–2019—*Continued*

(Numbers in thousands, not seasonally adjusted)

| Industry and year | January | February | March | April | May | June | July | August | September | October | November | December | Annual average |
|---|---|---|---|---|---|---|---|---|---|---|---|---|---|
| **Manufacturing** | | | | | | | | | | | | | |
| 2011 | 149.3 | 149.3 | 149.6 | 150.0 | 151.1 | 151.4 | 152.0 | 152.2 | 152.1 | 152.4 | 152.8 | 154.0 | 151.4 |
| 2012 | 153.6 | 154.2 | 155.0 | 155.4 | 156.0 | 157.1 | 157.0 | 157.2 | 156.7 | 156.7 | 156.7 | 157.3 | 156.1 |
| 2013 | 155.7 | 156.2 | 156.1 | 155.9 | 156.2 | 156.8 | 157.2 | 156.7 | 156.2 | 156.3 | 156.3 | 156.7 | 156.4 |
| 2014 | 156.6 | 157.4 | 157.5 | 157.2 | 157.7 | 158.3 | 158.0 | 158.2 | 157.4 | 157.4 | 157.7 | 159.0 | 157.7 |
| 2015 | 157.2 | 157.8 | 157.7 | 158.1 | 158.6 | 159.8 | 160.4 | 160.6 | 159.9 | 160.7 | 160.9 | 162.0 | 159.5 |
| 2016 | 160.8 | 161.4 | 161.0 | 161.0 | 161.2 | 162.1 | 161.6 | 161.7 | 161.3 | 160.7 | 161.4 | 163.2 | 161.5 |
| 2017 | 162.2 | 163.4 | 162.8 | 162.9 | 163.7 | 165.6 | 166.0 | 166.3 | 166.5 | 166.8 | 167.9 | 169.1 | 165.3 |
| 2018 | 167.7 | 169.2 | 169.8 | 169.3 | 169.2 | 171.6 | 172.3 | 172.5 | 172.9 | 172.9 | 174.3 | 175.3 | 171.4 |
| 2019 | 174.8 | 175.7 | 176.0 | 175.8 | 176.2 | 177.8 | 178.6 | 179.0 | 178.5 | 178.5 | 178.3 | 178.4 | 177.3 |
| **Trade, Transportation, and Utilities** | | | | | | | | | | | | | |
| 2011 | 466.0 | 465.6 | 466.8 | 468.8 | 468.8 | 467.9 | 466.5 | 467.6 | 466.5 | 472.9 | 486.0 | 489.5 | 471.1 |
| 2012 | 473.9 | 470.8 | 472.4 | 471.3 | 471.9 | 470.5 | 468.6 | 468.8 | 469.5 | 474.6 | 489.6 | 493.9 | 474.7 |
| 2013 | 473.3 | 471.7 | 471.8 | 473.1 | 474.2 | 474.2 | 474.4 | 476.5 | 477.4 | 482.8 | 497.7 | 504.9 | 479.3 |
| 2014 | 486.9 | 485.3 | 485.8 | 486.2 | 486.1 | 486.2 | 485.1 | 487.5 | 487.4 | 494.0 | 508.3 | 515.7 | 491.2 |
| 2015 | 497.3 | 496.0 | 496.9 | 497.7 | 498.4 | 499.1 | 499.4 | 502.3 | 504.0 | 511.5 | 525.5 | 528.6 | 504.7 |
| 2016 | 508.9 | 508.2 | 509.0 | 510.7 | 510.7 | 508.5 | 510.1 | 511.4 | 511.1 | 520.1 | 534.4 | 538.7 | 515.2 |
| 2017 | 520.1 | 517.6 | 516.6 | 517.5 | 517.4 | 517.7 | 517.8 | 519.4 | 519.5 | 526.6 | 544.1 | 546.0 | 523.4 |
| 2018 | 530.3 | 526.8 | 527.2 | 526.5 | 528.1 | 527.7 | 528.8 | 530.1 | 532.1 | 539.2 | 558.1 | 560.4 | 534.6 |
| 2019 | 543.4 | 538.5 | 537.8 | 536.2 | 535.2 | 535.7 | 535.8 | 537.4 | 538.5 | 544.8 | 562.8 | 567.4 | 542.8 |
| **Wholesale Trade** | | | | | | | | | | | | | |
| 2011 | 92.8 | 93.5 | 93.5 | 93.8 | 93.8 | 93.7 | 93.1 | 92.7 | 92.5 | 92.9 | 93.3 | 93.4 | 93.3 |
| 2012 | 92.4 | 92.9 | 93.4 | 93.2 | 93.2 | 93.4 | 93.1 | 92.9 | 93.0 | 93.3 | 93.7 | 94.0 | 93.2 |
| 2013 | 92.6 | 93.4 | 93.3 | 93.5 | 93.0 | 93.4 | 92.8 | 92.8 | 92.6 | 93.5 | 93.9 | 94.4 | 93.3 |
| 2014 | 92.9 | 93.2 | 93.5 | 93.1 | 93.3 | 92.9 | 92.8 | 92.7 | 92.6 | 92.6 | 92.9 | 93.6 | 93.0 |
| 2015 | 92.2 | 92.4 | 92.4 | 92.7 | 92.9 | 92.8 | 92.4 | 92.5 | 92.6 | 93.1 | 93.6 | 93.8 | 92.8 |
| 2016 | 93.4 | 93.7 | 93.3 | 93.5 | 93.6 | 93.3 | 93.5 | 93.1 | 93.0 | 94.3 | 94.5 | 94.9 | 93.7 |
| 2017 | 94.0 | 94.4 | 94.4 | 94.4 | 94.5 | 94.5 | 94.1 | 94.1 | 94.2 | 95.0 | 95.5 | 95.8 | 94.6 |
| 2018 | 95.3 | 95.7 | 96.0 | 96.4 | 96.8 | 96.7 | 96.9 | 96.9 | 97.2 | 97.7 | 98.4 | 98.8 | 96.9 |
| 2019 | 97.7 | 98.4 | 98.1 | 98.2 | 98.3 | 98.6 | 98.3 | 98.1 | 98.1 | 99.1 | 100.5 | 101.5 | 98.7 |
| **Retail Trade** | | | | | | | | | | | | | |
| 2011 | 290.1 | 288.7 | 289.7 | 291.1 | 290.8 | 289.4 | 289.1 | 290.3 | 289.0 | 294.1 | 306.1 | 307.7 | 293.0 |
| 2012 | 295.6 | 291.9 | 292.6 | 292.1 | 292.7 | 291.0 | 289.3 | 289.5 | 290.2 | 294.6 | 308.7 | 310.8 | 294.9 |
| 2013 | 293.4 | 291.0 | 291.8 | 293.6 | 294.2 | 294.0 | 295.0 | 296.8 | 297.4 | 300.8 | 314.2 | 318.9 | 298.4 |
| 2014 | 304.2 | 302.5 | 302.4 | 304.0 | 303.2 | 303.4 | 303.1 | 304.7 | 304.6 | 309.7 | 322.4 | 326.8 | 307.6 |
| 2015 | 311.4 | 309.2 | 309.7 | 311.3 | 311.5 | 312.2 | 311.7 | 313.3 | 314.2 | 319.9 | 331.0 | 332.3 | 315.6 |
| 2016 | 316.8 | 315.8 | 315.9 | 316.8 | 316.7 | 315.6 | 316.2 | 317.5 | 317.3 | 323.7 | 335.5 | 336.9 | 320.4 |
| 2017 | 322.8 | 320.4 | 320.3 | 321.0 | 320.8 | 320.8 | 321.6 | 322.3 | 321.6 | 325.7 | 339.3 | 338.4 | 324.6 |
| 2018 | 326.2 | 323.0 | 323.1 | 321.5 | 322.3 | 321.5 | 322.3 | 323.2 | 323.9 | 328.8 | 342.8 | 342.6 | 326.8 |
| 2019 | 327.7 | 323.8 | 323.2 | 322.4 | 321.3 | 320.7 | 320.9 | 321.8 | 322.3 | 326.1 | 338.9 | 339.6 | 325.7 |
| **Transportation and Utilities** | | | | | | | | | | | | | |
| 2011 | 83.1 | 83.4 | 83.6 | 83.9 | 84.2 | 84.8 | 84.3 | 84.6 | 85.0 | 85.9 | 86.6 | 88.4 | 84.8 |
| 2012 | 85.9 | 86.0 | 86.4 | 86.0 | 86.0 | 86.1 | 86.2 | 86.4 | 86.3 | 86.7 | 87.2 | 89.1 | 86.5 |
| 2013 | 87.3 | 87.3 | 86.7 | 86.0 | 87.0 | 86.8 | 86.6 | 86.9 | 87.4 | 88.5 | 89.6 | 91.6 | 87.6 |
| 2014 | 89.8 | 89.6 | 89.9 | 89.1 | 89.6 | 89.9 | 89.2 | 90.1 | 90.2 | 91.7 | 93.0 | 95.3 | 90.6 |
| 2015 | 93.7 | 94.4 | 94.8 | 93.7 | 94.0 | 94.1 | 95.3 | 96.5 | 97.2 | 98.5 | 100.9 | 102.5 | 96.3 |
| 2016 | 98.7 | 98.7 | 99.8 | 100.4 | 100.4 | 99.6 | 100.4 | 100.8 | 100.8 | 102.1 | 104.4 | 106.9 | 101.1 |
| 2017 | 103.3 | 102.8 | 101.9 | 102.1 | 102.1 | 102.4 | 102.1 | 103.0 | 103.7 | 105.9 | 109.3 | 111.8 | 104.2 |
| 2018 | 108.8 | 108.1 | 108.1 | 108.6 | 109.0 | 109.5 | 109.6 | 110.0 | 111.0 | 112.7 | 116.9 | 119.0 | 110.9 |
| 2019 | 118.0 | 116.3 | 116.5 | 115.6 | 115.6 | 116.4 | 116.6 | 117.5 | 118.1 | 119.6 | 123.4 | 126.3 | 118.3 |
| **Information** | | | | | | | | | | | | | |
| 2011 | 37.7 | 37.6 | 37.7 | 38.0 | 38.1 | 38.2 | 38.6 | 38.6 | 38.3 | 38.7 | 39.6 | 39.7 | 38.4 |
| 2012 | 39.5 | 40.0 | 40.2 | 40.5 | 41.1 | 41.0 | 41.1 | 41.4 | 40.8 | 40.9 | 42.1 | 42.2 | 40.9 |
| 2013 | 42.0 | 42.6 | 42.8 | 42.9 | 43.9 | 43.2 | 43.4 | 43.6 | 42.9 | 43.1 | 44.0 | 43.9 | 43.2 |
| 2014 | 43.7 | 43.7 | 44.0 | 44.4 | 44.9 | 45.2 | 45.6 | 45.5 | 44.5 | 44.9 | 45.3 | 45.6 | 44.8 |
| 2015 | 45.3 | 46.7 | 45.6 | 46.1 | 46.5 | 46.1 | 46.1 | 45.5 | 44.8 | 45.0 | 45.9 | 45.8 | 45.8 |
| 2016 | 46.1 | 46.9 | 46.3 | 46.9 | 47.3 | 46.9 | 46.6 | 46.0 | 45.5 | 46.0 | 46.1 | 46.2 | 46.4 |
| 2017 | 46.0 | 46.7 | 46.8 | 47.4 | 47.5 | 47.4 | 47.0 | 46.9 | 46.1 | 46.6 | 47.0 | 47.3 | 46.9 |
| 2018 | 47.1 | 48.1 | 47.2 | 47.5 | 47.7 | 47.5 | 47.4 | 47.2 | 46.7 | 47.5 | 48.4 | 48.7 | 47.6 |
| 2019 | 48.1 | 48.7 | 48.6 | 48.4 | 48.8 | 48.5 | 49.0 | 49.4 | 48.5 | 49.1 | 49.1 | 49.1 | 48.8 |

## 1. Employment by Industry: Arizona, 2011–2019—*Continued*

(Numbers in thousands, not seasonally adjusted)

| Industry and year | January | February | March | April | May | June | July | August | September | October | November | December | Annual average |
|---|---|---|---|---|---|---|---|---|---|---|---|---|---|
| **Financial Activities** | | | | | | | | | | | | | |
| 2011 | 168.3 | 169.2 | 169.9 | 170.5 | 170.4 | 170.9 | 171.5 | 172.1 | 172.0 | 172.7 | 173.4 | 175.4 | 171.4 |
| 2012 | 173.5 | 175.3 | 175.5 | 175.2 | 175.5 | 175.5 | 175.6 | 176.4 | 176.7 | 178.9 | 180.1 | 181.4 | 176.6 |
| 2013 | 179.5 | 182.2 | 182.2 | 183.3 | 184.0 | 184.6 | 184.8 | 185.3 | 185.4 | 188.1 | 189.4 | 190.0 | 184.9 |
| 2014 | 187.2 | 188.1 | 187.7 | 189.9 | 190.0 | 189.7 | 189.5 | 189.8 | 189.4 | 191.3 | 192.5 | 192.7 | 189.8 |
| 2015 | 190.7 | 191.9 | 192.4 | 192.4 | 193.1 | 193.4 | 194.5 | 195.4 | 195.6 | 198.0 | 199.3 | 200.8 | 194.8 |
| 2016 | 199.2 | 200.8 | 201.2 | 202.8 | 202.8 | 203.1 | 204.7 | 205.7 | 206.7 | 208.6 | 210.2 | 211.2 | 204.8 |
| 2017 | 210.1 | 210.8 | 211.6 | 212.0 | 212.2 | 213.6 | 214.6 | 215.5 | 216.2 | 218.0 | 219.0 | 219.6 | 214.4 |
| 2018 | 218.1 | 219.6 | 219.5 | 220.4 | 220.5 | 221.1 | 221.7 | 222.7 | 223.0 | 225.0 | 226.3 | 226.9 | 222.1 |
| 2019 | 224.9 | 226.3 | 227.2 | 228.1 | 228.2 | 229.2 | 230.1 | 231.5 | 231.6 | 234.0 | 233.9 | 233.4 | 229.9 |
| **Professional and Business Services** | | | | | | | | | | | | | |
| 2011 | 338.7 | 342.0 | 344.0 | 345.5 | 341.8 | 340.8 | 340.8 | 342.5 | 344.3 | 348.5 | 351.4 | 356.0 | 344.7 |
| 2012 | 346.1 | 348.0 | 351.1 | 351.3 | 350.7 | 352.9 | 351.8 | 355.5 | 355.6 | 361.0 | 367.1 | 370.4 | 355.1 |
| 2013 | 364.4 | 364.6 | 367.6 | 369.7 | 369.3 | 370.6 | 369.0 | 371.2 | 370.7 | 376.9 | 386.2 | 388.0 | 372.4 |
| 2014 | 371.7 | 371.6 | 373.6 | 376.5 | 376.7 | 377.0 | 375.9 | 379.9 | 380.8 | 389.1 | 396.3 | 400.0 | 380.8 |
| 2015 | 388.6 | 388.2 | 387.7 | 391.1 | 389.7 | 389.6 | 391.2 | 393.8 | 395.7 | 404.6 | 411.2 | 414.1 | 395.5 |
| 2016 | 402.2 | 403.0 | 403.5 | 408.5 | 405.5 | 402.5 | 408.3 | 410.8 | 414.1 | 417.4 | 419.7 | 420.5 | 409.7 |
| 2017 | 412.6 | 412.7 | 412.8 | 414.8 | 413.1 | 412.7 | 410.5 | 413.2 | 416.4 | 422.2 | 426.5 | 429.9 | 416.5 |
| 2018 | 420.7 | 424.0 | 424.9 | 425.3 | 423.8 | 425.4 | 427.3 | 431.5 | 432.6 | 440.0 | 445.0 | 447.3 | 430.7 |
| 2019 | 436.6 | 439.4 | 439.0 | 439.0 | 436.3 | 438.1 | 443.4 | 445.7 | 445.5 | 451.2 | 462.8 | 458.7 | 444.6 |
| **Education and Health Services** | | | | | | | | | | | | | |
| 2011 | 350.9 | 353.3 | 354.2 | 356.0 | 359.2 | 351.6 | 349.3 | 357.3 | 361.3 | 363.5 | 365.9 | 367.1 | 357.5 |
| 2012 | 364.1 | 367.2 | 368.0 | 368.2 | 368.4 | 363.6 | 359.1 | 367.4 | 370.5 | 372.7 | 374.9 | 376.4 | 368.4 |
| 2013 | 369.8 | 373.2 | 375.7 | 376.2 | 375.0 | 368.8 | 366.4 | 375.0 | 377.5 | 378.2 | 381.3 | 381.8 | 374.9 |
| 2014 | 377.0 | 379.7 | 380.1 | 381.6 | 381.8 | 376.7 | 375.1 | 383.7 | 386.2 | 391.2 | 393.9 | 396.1 | 383.6 |
| 2015 | 390.8 | 394.7 | 395.6 | 397.8 | 397.8 | 392.3 | 392.5 | 400.6 | 402.3 | 408.3 | 410.3 | 411.2 | 399.5 |
| 2016 | 407.7 | 410.5 | 411.1 | 413.7 | 412.7 | 406.5 | 406.3 | 415.2 | 420.0 | 422.8 | 425.7 | 427.7 | 415.0 |
| 2017 | 422.4 | 426.9 | 427.8 | 429.6 | 428.7 | 423.5 | 420.4 | 429.8 | 434.1 | 438.1 | 440.5 | 442.7 | 430.4 |
| 2018 | 437.7 | 442.7 | 443.9 | 444.5 | 443.3 | 434.1 | 433.9 | 445.7 | 449.8 | 454.1 | 457.5 | 458.3 | 445.5 |
| 2019 | 453.6 | 458.9 | 458.2 | 459.1 | 458.2 | 448.9 | 448.2 | 462.7 | 466.3 | 470.9 | 476.6 | 479.7 | 461.8 |
| **Leisure and Hospitality** | | | | | | | | | | | | | |
| 2011 | 252.1 | 256.5 | 263.0 | 265.3 | 264.6 | 259.0 | 252.7 | 255.5 | 259.2 | 259.8 | 262.7 | 261.5 | 259.3 |
| 2012 | 259.9 | 265.0 | 272.2 | 272.6 | 271.8 | 266.5 | 259.4 | 263.5 | 266.0 | 267.8 | 268.4 | 268.8 | 266.8 |
| 2013 | 266.7 | 273.6 | 279.4 | 280.9 | 279.2 | 273.4 | 268.6 | 273.3 | 275.3 | 278.3 | 280.7 | 280.8 | 275.9 |
| 2014 | 277.0 | 285.0 | 291.4 | 292.6 | 290.5 | 284.4 | 278.3 | 282.9 | 284.9 | 288.6 | 291.2 | 291.1 | 286.5 |
| 2015 | 292.1 | 297.2 | 303.6 | 306.0 | 303.0 | 296.7 | 292.0 | 295.4 | 296.9 | 301.6 | 302.7 | 302.6 | 299.2 |
| 2016 | 300.3 | 307.3 | 312.4 | 315.5 | 313.9 | 307.0 | 302.7 | 307.2 | 310.2 | 314.0 | 314.2 | 312.6 | 309.8 |
| 2017 | 309.5 | 316.8 | 324.0 | 327.7 | 324.2 | 318.5 | 312.4 | 316.7 | 319.6 | 323.2 | 323.0 | 322.8 | 319.9 |
| 2018 | 319.1 | 326.7 | 333.5 | 332.6 | 330.5 | 324.1 | 318.0 | 322.0 | 323.1 | 326.6 | 328.1 | 327.4 | 326.0 |
| 2019 | 324.8 | 330.8 | 336.9 | 336.1 | 333.0 | 326.7 | 321.6 | 327.3 | 328.2 | 333.4 | 333.3 | 336.6 | 330.7 |
| **Other Services** | | | | | | | | | | | | | |
| 2011 | 87.9 | 89.0 | 89.2 | 89.2 | 89.3 | 89.2 | 87.9 | 87.2 | 86.8 | 86.6 | 86.6 | 86.0 | 87.9 |
| 2012 | 85.2 | 85.6 | 86.2 | 86.1 | 86.7 | 87.2 | 86.0 | 85.6 | 85.8 | 86.2 | 86.8 | 86.8 | 86.2 |
| 2013 | 85.6 | 87.7 | 87.4 | 87.6 | 87.6 | 87.6 | 86.7 | 86.3 | 86.4 | 87.2 | 87.5 | 87.5 | 87.1 |
| 2014 | 86.1 | 87.2 | 87.8 | 88.0 | 87.9 | 87.9 | 87.1 | 86.8 | 87.0 | 88.0 | 88.3 | 88.3 | 87.5 |
| 2015 | 87.2 | 88.3 | 88.5 | 87.6 | 88.0 | 87.8 | 86.9 | 86.4 | 86.6 | 87.2 | 87.7 | 87.4 | 87.5 |
| 2016 | 87.4 | 88.4 | 88.7 | 88.6 | 89.5 | 89.0 | 88.0 | 87.6 | 88.2 | 88.8 | 89.1 | 88.3 | 88.5 |
| 2017 | 87.3 | 88.2 | 88.6 | 89.7 | 90.2 | 90.2 | 89.1 | 88.8 | 89.0 | 90.0 | 90.7 | 90.6 | 89.4 |
| 2018 | 90.0 | 91.0 | 91.5 | 92.8 | 93.1 | 93.2 | 92.5 | 92.3 | 92.8 | 93.5 | 93.9 | 92.7 | 92.4 |
| 2019 | 93.3 | 94.2 | 94.1 | 94.2 | 94.9 | 94.8 | 94.4 | 94.5 | 94.7 | 96.0 | 96.8 | 96.8 | 94.9 |
| **Government** | | | | | | | | | | | | | |
| 2011 | 410.4 | 422.1 | 421.0 | 422.7 | 421.0 | 368.7 | 353.6 | 394.7 | 416.8 | 420.2 | 421.9 | 415.1 | 407.4 |
| 2012 | 408.4 | 420.6 | 421.3 | 422.2 | 415.4 | 376.2 | 358.1 | 396.8 | 420.3 | 421.9 | 423.9 | 421.4 | 408.9 |
| 2013 | 412.2 | 422.6 | 421.7 | 423.2 | 418.4 | 373.6 | 360.4 | 393.3 | 419.0 | 422.5 | 422.9 | 419.7 | 409.1 |
| 2014 | 413.4 | 422.3 | 420.8 | 422.3 | 410.6 | 375.6 | 363.7 | 394.9 | 421.2 | 426.5 | 427.4 | 423.5 | 410.2 |
| 2015 | 412.1 | 424.2 | 423.4 | 423.5 | 414.7 | 370.5 | 358.2 | 392.2 | 419.1 | 425.8 | 428.5 | 422.5 | 409.6 |
| 2016 | 410.7 | 423.7 | 424.5 | 424.5 | 414.8 | 373.8 | 363.8 | 395.2 | 424.0 | 426.7 | 428.9 | 425.0 | 411.3 |
| 2017 | 413.0 | 425.9 | 426.1 | 426.7 | 416.1 | 378.4 | 365.9 | 400.9 | 426.0 | 428.2 | 429.4 | 424.5 | 413.4 |
| 2018 | 414.3 | 426.3 | 425.8 | 426.0 | 419.5 | 380.6 | 368.1 | 407.9 | 428.7 | 431.8 | 432.8 | 428.3 | 415.8 |
| 2019 | 423.5 | 431.3 | 431.5 | 431.1 | 425.3 | 384.4 | 372.4 | 422.1 | 434.8 | 437.1 | 438.5 | 437.8 | 422.5 |

## 2. Average Weekly Hours by Selected Industry: Arizona, 2015–2019

(Not seasonally adjusted)

| Industry and year | January | February | March | April | May | June | July | August | September | October | November | December | Annual average |
|---|---|---|---|---|---|---|---|---|---|---|---|---|---|
| **Total Private** | | | | | | | | | | | | | |
| 2015 | 34.6 | 35.2 | 35.0 | 34.8 | 34.7 | 34.9 | 34.6 | 35.2 | 34.5 | 34.5 | 34.7 | 34.5 | 34.8 |
| 2016 | 34.3 | 34.3 | 34.5 | 34.5 | 34.8 | 34.5 | 34.4 | 34.4 | 34.3 | 34.9 | 34.4 | 34.5 | 34.5 |
| 2017 | 34.8 | 34.3 | 34.5 | 35.1 | 34.6 | 34.8 | 35.4 | 34.7 | 34.8 | 35.3 | 35.0 | 35.0 | 34.9 |
| 2018 | 34.9 | 34.9 | 35.0 | 35.5 | 34.9 | 35.0 | 35.3 | 34.9 | 35.2 | 34.6 | 34.6 | 35.1 | 35.0 |
| 2019 | 34.5 | 34.5 | 34.5 | 35.0 | 34.7 | 35.4 | 34.6 | 34.7 | 35.2 | 34.8 | 34.7 | 35.2 | 34.8 |
| **Goods-Producing** | | | | | | | | | | | | | |
| 2015 | 37.8 | 38.1 | 38.2 | 38.6 | 38.7 | 39.2 | 38.6 | 38.5 | 37.9 | 38.2 | 38.2 | 38.3 | 38.4 |
| 2016 | 37.8 | 37.8 | 38.3 | 38.3 | 39.0 | 38.8 | 38.4 | 38.6 | 38.3 | 38.5 | 37.6 | 38.3 | 38.3 |
| 2017 | 37.8 | 37.5 | 37.8 | 38.2 | 38.1 | 38.9 | 38.4 | 38.7 | 39.2 | 39.2 | 39.3 | 39.5 | 38.6 |
| 2018 | 38.9 | 38.1 | 38.6 | 39.5 | 38.8 | 39.2 | 39.3 | 39.5 | 39.7 | 39.8 | 39.7 | 40.3 | 39.3 |
| 2019 | 39.1 | 39.1 | 39.0 | 40.5 | 40.1 | 40.6 | 39.7 | 40.1 | 39.8 | 39.7 | 39.4 | 39.5 | 39.7 |
| **Construction** | | | | | | | | | | | | | |
| 2015 | 35.9 | 36.6 | 37.0 | 37.7 | 38.0 | 38.2 | 37.8 | 37.2 | 35.9 | 37.1 | 36.9 | 36.8 | 37.1 |
| 2016 | 36.0 | 36.4 | 36.9 | 37.5 | 38.1 | 38.3 | 37.7 | 37.6 | 37.3 | 37.5 | 36.2 | 36.8 | 37.2 |
| 2017 | 36.0 | 35.9 | 36.6 | 37.3 | 36.4 | 38.0 | 37.4 | 37.7 | 38.6 | 38.6 | 38.6 | 38.6 | 37.5 |
| 2018 | 37.7 | 36.8 | 37.4 | 38.4 | 37.4 | 37.6 | 37.9 | 38.4 | 38.6 | 38.7 | 38.7 | 38.8 | 38.0 |
| 2019 | 37.7 | 37.4 | 36.8 | 38.6 | 37.9 | 38.6 | 37.7 | 38.3 | 38.4 | 38.4 | 38.2 | 38.0 | 38.0 |
| **Manufacturing** | | | | | | | | | | | | | |
| 2015 | 39.7 | 39.3 | 39.2 | 39.5 | 39.4 | 40.4 | 39.5 | 39.7 | 39.9 | 39.4 | 39.4 | 39.6 | 39.6 |
| 2016 | 39.7 | 39.2 | 39.8 | 39.3 | 40.2 | 39.6 | 39.6 | 40.3 | 40.0 | 40.1 | 39.2 | 40.0 | 39.8 |
| 2017 | 39.9 | 39.3 | 39.2 | 39.2 | 39.9 | 39.8 | 39.5 | 39.8 | 39.8 | 39.8 | 40.1 | 40.6 | 39.7 |
| 2018 | 40.2 | 39.5 | 39.7 | 40.6 | 40.4 | 41.2 | 41.0 | 40.8 | 41.1 | 41.2 | 41.1 | 42.1 | 40.8 |
| 2019 | 40.7 | 41.0 | 41.5 | 41.5 | 41.7 | 42.1 | 41.2 | 41.6 | 41.0 | 41.2 | 41.2 | 41.6 | 41.4 |
| **Trade, Transportation, and Utilities** | | | | | | | | | | | | | |
| 2015 | 34.8 | 35.5 | 35.4 | 35.4 | 35.2 | 35.2 | 35.3 | 35.4 | 35.3 | 34.9 | 35.4 | 34.9 | 35.2 |
| 2016 | 34.7 | 35.0 | 35.0 | 35.1 | 35.2 | 35.0 | 35.0 | 34.7 | 35.0 | 35.4 | 35.1 | 35.2 | 35.0 |
| 2017 | 35.1 | 34.8 | 35.2 | 35.7 | 35.2 | 35.4 | 36.2 | 35.5 | 35.4 | 35.6 | 35.0 | 35.5 | 35.4 |
| 2018 | 35.7 | 35.1 | 35.0 | 35.5 | 35.2 | 35.3 | 35.5 | 35.0 | 35.4 | 34.8 | 34.4 | 35.0 | 35.2 |
| 2019 | 34.6 | 34.2 | 34.4 | 34.4 | 34.3 | 34.6 | 34.4 | 34.5 | 35.1 | 34.5 | 34.1 | 35.2 | 34.5 |
| **Financial Activities** | | | | | | | | | | | | | |
| 2015 | 38.2 | 38.6 | 38.6 | 38.5 | 38.0 | 38.2 | 38.3 | 39.8 | 38.8 | 38.4 | 39.0 | 38.9 | 38.6 |
| 2016 | 38.5 | 37.8 | 38.1 | 38.0 | 38.8 | 38.6 | 38.5 | 39.2 | 38.8 | 39.6 | 39.2 | 39.0 | 38.7 |
| 2017 | 39.8 | 38.6 | 38.9 | 39.2 | 38.7 | 39.2 | 39.8 | 39.0 | 38.8 | 39.1 | 38.7 | 38.5 | 39.0 |
| 2018 | 38.9 | 38.8 | 38.8 | 39.5 | 38.8 | 39.0 | 39.6 | 38.6 | 39.2 | 38.2 | 38.2 | 38.4 | 38.8 |
| 2019 | 37.5 | 37.9 | 37.6 | 37.7 | 37.6 | 38.9 | 37.4 | 37.7 | 38.8 | 37.8 | 38.4 | 39.1 | 38.0 |
| **Professional and Business Services** | | | | | | | | | | | | | |
| 2015 | 36.0 | 36.9 | 36.8 | 36.3 | 36.1 | 36.5 | 36.3 | 37.6 | 36.4 | 36.4 | 37.0 | 36.7 | 36.6 |
| 2016 | 36.5 | 36.7 | 37.0 | 37.0 | 37.6 | 37.0 | 36.8 | 36.9 | 36.7 | 37.4 | 36.4 | 36.5 | 36.9 |
| 2017 | 36.9 | 36.6 | 36.5 | 37.7 | 36.7 | 36.5 | 37.5 | 36.9 | 36.8 | 37.8 | 37.3 | 37.3 | 37.0 |
| 2018 | 36.9 | 37.0 | 37.2 | 37.9 | 36.9 | 36.8 | 37.7 | 37.2 | 37.0 | 36.2 | 36.4 | 36.6 | 37.0 |
| 2019 | 35.9 | 35.9 | 35.6 | 36.2 | 35.8 | 36.5 | 35.3 | 36.0 | 36.2 | 36.0 | 35.6 | 36.1 | 35.9 |
| **Education and Health Services** | | | | | | | | | | | | | |
| 2015 | 33.8 | 34.4 | 34.1 | 33.9 | 33.8 | 33.6 | 33.7 | 33.9 | 33.7 | 33.5 | 33.8 | 33.3 | 33.8 |
| 2016 | 33.4 | 33.5 | 33.3 | 33.0 | 33.4 | 32.8 | 33.0 | 33.2 | 33.2 | 33.5 | 33.6 | 33.4 | 33.3 |
| 2017 | 34.4 | 33.7 | 33.5 | 34.1 | 33.5 | 34.0 | 34.5 | 34.0 | 33.8 | 34.2 | 34.0 | 33.8 | 34.0 |
| 2018 | 33.8 | 34.0 | 33.7 | 34.2 | 33.7 | 33.7 | 34.2 | 33.7 | 34.3 | 33.4 | 33.3 | 33.7 | 33.8 |
| 2019 | 32.9 | 32.7 | 32.6 | 33.3 | 33.3 | 34.1 | 33.4 | 33.8 | 34.7 | 33.8 | 34.3 | 34.6 | 33.6 |
| **Leisure and Hospitality** | | | | | | | | | | | | | |
| 2015 | 26.9 | 28.0 | 28.1 | 27.1 | 27.1 | 26.8 | 26.3 | 26.6 | 25.9 | 26.1 | 26.4 | 26.0 | 26.8 |
| 2016 | 26.0 | 26.5 | 26.7 | 26.3 | 26.7 | 26.1 | 26.0 | 25.4 | 25.7 | 26.3 | 25.9 | 25.8 | 26.1 |
| 2017 | 26.0 | 25.9 | 26.5 | 26.9 | 26.1 | 25.6 | 26.4 | 25.1 | 25.4 | 25.9 | 26.1 | 26.1 | 26.0 |
| 2018 | 26.1 | 26.8 | 27.3 | 27.2 | 26.6 | 26.5 | 25.9 | 25.6 | 26.1 | 25.6 | 26.2 | 26.5 | 26.4 |
| 2019 | 25.9 | 26.6 | 27.3 | 27.2 | 26.8 | 27.0 | 26.0 | 25.7 | 25.8 | 25.5 | 25.6 | 26.1 | 26.3 |
| **Other Services** | | | | | | | | | | | | | |
| 2015 | 32.8 | 33.6 | 33.1 | 33.6 | 32.6 | 33.8 | 33.0 | 34.3 | 32.3 | 32.9 | 33.5 | 33.2 | 33.2 |
| 2016 | 33.3 | 33.3 | 33.8 | 33.7 | 33.6 | 33.3 | 32.9 | 33.5 | 33.4 | 34.9 | 34.4 | 34.3 | 33.7 |
| 2017 | 34.2 | 34.1 | 34.5 | 34.4 | 33.8 | 34.6 | 34.3 | 33.6 | 34.2 | 35.1 | 35.0 | 36.1 | 34.5 |
| 2018 | 35.4 | 35.4 | 35.4 | 36.0 | 35.1 | 35.9 | 34.1 | 34.4 | 35.4 | 34.7 | 36.0 | 34.9 | 35.2 |
| 2019 | 35.2 | 35.5 | 35.8 | 35.1 | 33.9 | 35.4 | 34.5 | 34.0 | 35.0 | 34.4 | 34.9 | 35.3 | 34.9 |

## 3. Average Hourly Earnings by Selected Industry: Arizona, 2015–2019

(Not seasonally adjusted)

| Industry and year | January | February | March | April | May | June | July | August | September | October | November | December | Annual average |
|---|---|---|---|---|---|---|---|---|---|---|---|---|---|
| **Total Private** | | | | | | | | | | | | | |
| 2015 | 22.98 | 23.07 | 23.09 | 23.13 | 23.02 | 22.99 | 23.05 | 23.39 | 23.29 | 23.33 | 23.45 | 23.23 | 23.17 |
| 2016 | 23.41 | 23.48 | 23.60 | 23.81 | 24.01 | 23.63 | 23.78 | 24.28 | 24.25 | 24.46 | 24.34 | 24.08 | 23.93 |
| 2017 | 24.77 | 24.93 | 24.80 | 25.28 | 25.01 | 24.92 | 25.41 | 25.43 | 25.44 | 25.66 | 25.42 | 25.42 | 25.21 |
| 2018 | 25.41 | 25.48 | 25.27 | 25.41 | 25.45 | 25.44 | 25.72 | 25.68 | 25.73 | 25.73 | 25.59 | 25.86 | 25.57 |
| 2019 | 25.94 | 26.00 | 25.89 | 26.22 | 26.15 | 26.26 | 26.44 | 26.65 | 26.93 | 26.80 | 26.90 | 26.92 | 26.43 |
| **Goods-Producing** | | | | | | | | | | | | | |
| 2015 | 24.12 | 23.94 | 23.92 | 24.15 | 23.61 | 23.42 | 23.72 | 23.73 | 23.73 | 23.81 | 24.28 | 24.15 | 23.88 |
| 2016 | 24.25 | 24.13 | 24.49 | 24.43 | 24.44 | 24.63 | 24.74 | 24.88 | 24.90 | 24.78 | 24.72 | 24.80 | 24.60 |
| 2017 | 25.15 | 25.34 | 25.04 | 24.94 | 24.87 | 24.89 | 25.15 | 24.65 | 25.15 | 25.10 | 24.95 | 24.92 | 25.01 |
| 2018 | 25.02 | 25.06 | 25.60 | 25.67 | 25.89 | 25.80 | 26.21 | 26.24 | 26.18 | 26.55 | 26.23 | 26.94 | 25.97 |
| 2019 | 27.02 | 26.74 | 26.95 | 27.40 | 26.96 | 27.16 | 27.44 | 27.53 | 27.65 | 27.77 | 28.15 | 28.45 | 27.44 |
| **Construction** | | | | | | | | | | | | | |
| 2015 | 23.67 | 23.14 | 23.14 | 23.49 | 22.64 | 22.69 | 22.94 | 22.89 | 23.17 | 23.01 | 23.45 | 23.86 | 23.17 |
| 2016 | 24.39 | 24.05 | 24.51 | 24.44 | 24.60 | 24.73 | 25.10 | 25.65 | 25.55 | 25.26 | 25.47 | 25.72 | 24.97 |
| 2017 | 25.82 | 26.27 | 25.82 | 25.46 | 25.27 | 25.60 | 25.82 | 25.48 | 26.29 | 25.90 | 25.48 | 25.69 | 25.74 |
| 2018 | 25.76 | 25.81 | 26.04 | 26.09 | 26.39 | 25.93 | 26.38 | 26.03 | 26.13 | 26.34 | 26.15 | 26.44 | 26.13 |
| 2019 | 26.12 | 25.59 | 26.33 | 26.87 | 26.39 | 26.42 | 26.72 | 26.75 | 26.82 | 27.16 | 27.25 | 27.70 | 26.69 |
| **Manufacturing** | | | | | | | | | | | | | |
| 2015 | 24.38 | 24.62 | 24.60 | 24.67 | 24.59 | 24.13 | 24.50 | 24.57 | 24.28 | 24.57 | 25.06 | 24.38 | 24.53 |
| 2016 | 24.01 | 24.12 | 24.34 | 24.32 | 24.17 | 24.42 | 24.22 | 23.87 | 24.02 | 24.11 | 23.73 | 23.65 | 24.08 |
| 2017 | 24.30 | 24.26 | 24.03 | 24.24 | 24.38 | 24.06 | 24.38 | 23.68 | 23.76 | 24.12 | 24.28 | 24.04 | 24.13 |
| 2018 | 24.16 | 24.20 | 24.94 | 24.99 | 25.12 | 25.46 | 25.87 | 26.35 | 26.05 | 26.00 | 26.13 | 26.99 | 25.54 |
| 2019 | 27.71 | 27.72 | 27.41 | 27.79 | 27.40 | 27.81 | 28.10 | 28.25 | 28.53 | 27.93 | 28.71 | 28.66 | 28.00 |
| **Trade, Transportation, and Utilities** | | | | | | | | | | | | | |
| 2015 | 21.27 | 21.20 | 21.27 | 21.40 | 21.65 | 21.28 | 21.18 | 21.41 | 21.35 | 21.53 | 21.87 | 22.06 | 21.46 |
| 2016 | 22.64 | 22.50 | 22.56 | 22.66 | 22.96 | 23.12 | 23.06 | 23.90 | 23.88 | 24.14 | 23.73 | 23.08 | 23.19 |
| 2017 | 24.36 | 24.97 | 24.62 | 25.57 | 24.72 | 24.71 | 25.12 | 24.70 | 24.60 | 24.93 | 24.18 | 24.41 | 24.74 |
| 2018 | 25.22 | 25.26 | 24.55 | 25.09 | 24.47 | 24.53 | 24.71 | 24.33 | 24.51 | 24.50 | 23.87 | 23.98 | 24.58 |
| 2019 | 24.38 | 24.00 | 23.89 | 24.34 | 24.29 | 24.30 | 24.29 | 24.35 | 24.68 | 25.67 | 25.45 | 25.48 | 24.60 |
| **Financial Activities** | | | | | | | | | | | | | |
| 2015 | 25.05 | 25.48 | 25.94 | 25.98 | 25.99 | 26.27 | 26.34 | 27.73 | 27.34 | 27.66 | 27.57 | 27.33 | 26.58 |
| 2016 | 26.98 | 27.97 | 27.80 | 27.61 | 27.97 | 27.16 | 27.47 | 28.06 | 28.04 | 28.72 | 28.71 | 28.42 | 27.92 |
| 2017 | 29.09 | 28.90 | 28.47 | 29.23 | 29.11 | 29.10 | 29.68 | 29.79 | 29.45 | 30.00 | 29.86 | 30.15 | 29.41 |
| 2018 | 29.27 | 29.73 | 29.64 | 29.70 | 29.96 | 29.74 | 30.09 | 31.14 | 30.29 | 30.40 | 31.06 | 31.09 | 30.18 |
| 2019 | 29.80 | 29.66 | 29.72 | 30.04 | 30.48 | 30.91 | 30.69 | 31.98 | 31.88 | 31.89 | 31.50 | 31.73 | 30.87 |
| **Professional and Business Services** | | | | | | | | | | | | | |
| 2015 | 25.96 | 26.37 | 26.72 | 26.59 | 26.53 | 26.74 | 26.46 | 27.06 | 26.88 | 26.85 | 26.84 | 26.06 | 26.59 |
| 2016 | 25.98 | 25.97 | 26.16 | 26.65 | 27.09 | 26.67 | 26.92 | 26.97 | 27.06 | 27.26 | 26.84 | 26.96 | 26.72 |
| 2017 | 27.57 | 27.55 | 27.69 | 28.19 | 27.79 | 27.69 | 28.07 | 27.98 | 28.01 | 28.16 | 27.79 | 27.82 | 27.86 |
| 2018 | 27.45 | 27.09 | 27.04 | 27.24 | 26.92 | 27.13 | 27.32 | 27.17 | 27.63 | 27.52 | 27.73 | 28.18 | 27.37 |
| 2019 | 28.37 | 28.12 | 28.21 | 28.37 | 28.04 | 28.62 | 29.16 | 29.43 | 30.14 | 29.79 | 29.52 | 30.38 | 29.03 |
| **Education and Health Services** | | | | | | | | | | | | | |
| 2015 | 24.79 | 24.83 | 24.80 | 24.68 | 24.60 | 24.72 | 24.83 | 25.03 | 25.14 | 25.12 | 25.29 | 25.22 | 24.92 |
| 2016 | 25.28 | 25.16 | 25.44 | 25.66 | 25.35 | 25.24 | 25.21 | 25.23 | 25.52 | 25.55 | 25.49 | 26.25 | 25.45 |
| 2017 | 25.73 | 25.71 | 26.18 | 26.25 | 26.27 | 26.22 | 26.67 | 26.67 | 26.72 | 26.74 | 26.94 | 26.95 | 26.43 |
| 2018 | 26.74 | 26.53 | 26.74 | 26.60 | 26.47 | 26.47 | 26.54 | 26.28 | 26.58 | 26.50 | 26.38 | 26.63 | 26.54 |
| 2019 | 27.16 | 27.44 | 27.13 | 26.98 | 26.76 | 26.61 | 26.97 | 26.67 | 27.05 | 26.91 | 26.74 | 26.55 | 26.91 |
| **Leisure and Hospitality** | | | | | | | | | | | | | |
| 2015 | 13.95 | 14.01 | 13.89 | 13.93 | 14.00 | 13.80 | 13.91 | 13.99 | 14.07 | 14.12 | 14.28 | 14.24 | 14.01 |
| 2016 | 14.32 | 14.14 | 13.92 | 14.23 | 14.32 | 14.09 | 14.10 | 14.04 | 14.06 | 14.23 | 14.36 | 14.26 | 14.17 |
| 2017 | 15.05 | 15.15 | 15.00 | 15.05 | 15.18 | 14.86 | 14.73 | 14.86 | 14.79 | 15.05 | 15.13 | 15.22 | 15.01 |
| 2018 | 15.47 | 15.55 | 15.60 | 15.58 | 15.57 | 15.40 | 15.47 | 15.50 | 15.46 | 15.80 | 16.11 | 16.31 | 15.65 |
| 2019 | 16.42 | 16.52 | 16.74 | 16.76 | 16.65 | 16.69 | 16.67 | 16.69 | 16.85 | 17.13 | 17.13 | 17.21 | 16.79 |
| **Other Services** | | | | | | | | | | | | | |
| 2015 | 20.10 | 20.37 | 20.09 | 20.07 | 20.41 | 20.25 | 20.96 | 21.27 | 21.18 | 21.01 | 21.05 | 20.98 | 20.64 |
| 2016 | 21.12 | 21.38 | 21.65 | 21.58 | 21.42 | 21.34 | 21.52 | 22.34 | 22.56 | 22.63 | 22.91 | 22.76 | 21.94 |
| 2017 | 23.54 | 23.45 | 23.13 | 23.51 | 23.37 | 23.50 | 23.58 | 23.63 | 23.93 | 23.95 | 23.42 | 23.24 | 23.52 |
| 2018 | 22.57 | 22.38 | 22.02 | 21.66 | 22.01 | 21.82 | 22.70 | 22.72 | 22.41 | 22.08 | 21.76 | 22.67 | 22.23 |
| 2019 | 22.38 | 21.44 | 21.38 | 21.25 | 21.69 | 21.26 | 21.62 | 21.68 | 21.88 | 21.62 | 21.80 | 22.70 | 21.73 |

# 4. Average Weekly Earnings by Selected Industry: Arizona, 2015–2019

(Dollars, not seasonally adjusted)

| | January | February | March | April | May | June | July | August | September | October | November | December | Annual average |
|---|---|---|---|---|---|---|---|---|---|---|---|---|---|
| **Total Private** | | | | | | | | | | | | | |
| 2015 | 795.11 | 812.06 | 808.15 | 804.92 | 798.79 | 802.35 | 797.53 | 823.33 | 803.51 | 804.89 | 813.72 | 801.44 | 806.32 |
| 2016 | 802.96 | 805.36 | 814.20 | 821.45 | 835.55 | 815.24 | 818.03 | 835.23 | 831.78 | 853.65 | 837.30 | 830.76 | 825.59 |
| 2017 | 862.00 | 855.10 | 855.60 | 887.33 | 865.35 | 867.22 | 899.51 | 882.42 | 885.31 | 905.80 | 889.70 | 889.70 | 879.83 |
| 2018 | 886.81 | 889.25 | 884.45 | 902.06 | 888.21 | 890.40 | 907.92 | 896.23 | 905.70 | 890.26 | 885.41 | 907.69 | 894.95 |
| 2019 | 894.93 | 897.00 | 893.21 | 917.70 | 907.41 | 929.60 | 914.82 | 924.76 | 947.94 | 932.64 | 933.43 | 947.58 | 919.76 |
| **Goods-Producing** | | | | | | | | | | | | | |
| 2015 | 911.74 | 912.11 | 913.74 | 932.19 | 913.71 | 918.06 | 915.59 | 913.61 | 899.37 | 909.54 | 927.50 | 924.95 | 916.99 |
| 2016 | 916.65 | 912.11 | 937.97 | 935.67 | 953.16 | 955.64 | 950.02 | 960.37 | 953.67 | 954.03 | 929.47 | 949.84 | 942.18 |
| 2017 | 950.67 | 950.25 | 946.51 | 952.71 | 947.55 | 968.22 | 965.76 | 953.96 | 985.88 | 983.92 | 980.54 | 984.34 | 965.39 |
| 2018 | 973.28 | 954.79 | 988.16 | 1,013.97 | 1,004.53 | 1,011.36 | 1,030.05 | 1,036.48 | 1,039.35 | 1,056.69 | 1,041.33 | 1,085.68 | 1,020.62 |
| 2019 | 1,056.48 | 1,045.53 | 1,051.05 | 1,109.70 | 1,081.10 | 1,102.70 | 1,089.37 | 1,103.95 | 1,100.47 | 1,102.47 | 1,109.11 | 1,123.78 | 1,089.37 |
| **Construction** | | | | | | | | | | | | | |
| 2015 | 849.75 | 846.92 | 856.18 | 885.57 | 860.32 | 866.76 | 867.13 | 851.51 | 831.80 | 853.67 | 865.31 | 878.05 | 859.61 |
| 2016 | 878.04 | 875.42 | 904.42 | 916.50 | 937.26 | 947.16 | 946.27 | 964.44 | 953.02 | 947.25 | 922.01 | 946.50 | 928.88 |
| 2017 | 929.52 | 943.09 | 945.01 | 949.66 | 919.83 | 972.80 | 965.67 | 960.60 | 1,014.79 | 999.74 | 983.53 | 991.63 | 965.25 |
| 2018 | 971.15 | 949.81 | 973.90 | 1,001.86 | 986.99 | 974.97 | 999.80 | 999.55 | 1,008.62 | 1,019.36 | 1,012.01 | 1,025.87 | 992.94 |
| 2019 | 984.72 | 957.07 | 968.94 | 1,037.18 | 1,000.18 | 1,019.81 | 1,007.34 | 1,024.53 | 1,029.89 | 1,042.94 | 1,040.95 | 1,052.60 | 1,014.22 |
| **Manufacturing** | | | | | | | | | | | | | |
| 2015 | 967.89 | 967.57 | 964.32 | 974.47 | 968.85 | 974.85 | 967.75 | 975.43 | 968.77 | 968.06 | 987.36 | 965.45 | 971.39 |
| 2016 | 953.20 | 945.50 | 968.73 | 955.78 | 971.63 | 967.03 | 959.11 | 961.96 | 960.80 | 966.81 | 930.22 | 946.00 | 958.38 |
| 2017 | 969.57 | 953.42 | 941.98 | 950.21 | 972.76 | 957.59 | 963.01 | 942.46 | 945.65 | 959.98 | 973.63 | 976.02 | 957.96 |
| 2018 | 971.23 | 955.90 | 990.12 | 1,014.59 | 1,014.85 | 1,048.95 | 1,060.67 | 1,075.08 | 1,070.66 | 1,071.20 | 1,073.94 | 1,136.28 | 1,042.03 |
| 2019 | 1,127.80 | 1,136.52 | 1,137.52 | 1,153.29 | 1,142.58 | 1,170.80 | 1,157.72 | 1,175.20 | 1,169.73 | 1,150.72 | 1,182.85 | 1,192.26 | 1,159.20 |
| **Trade, Transportation, and Utilities** | | | | | | | | | | | | | |
| 2015 | 740.20 | 752.60 | 752.96 | 757.56 | 762.08 | 749.06 | 747.65 | 757.91 | 753.66 | 751.40 | 774.20 | 769.89 | 755.39 |
| 2016 | 785.61 | 787.50 | 789.25 | 795.37 | 808.19 | 809.20 | 807.10 | 829.33 | 835.80 | 854.56 | 832.92 | 812.42 | 811.65 |
| 2017 | 855.04 | 868.96 | 866.62 | 912.85 | 870.14 | 874.73 | 909.34 | 876.85 | 870.84 | 887.51 | 846.30 | 866.56 | 875.80 |
| 2018 | 900.35 | 886.63 | 859.25 | 890.70 | 861.34 | 865.91 | 877.21 | 851.55 | 867.65 | 852.60 | 821.13 | 839.30 | 865.22 |
| 2019 | 843.55 | 820.80 | 821.82 | 837.30 | 833.15 | 840.78 | 835.58 | 840.08 | 866.27 | 885.62 | 867.85 | 896.90 | 848.70 |
| **Financial Activities** | | | | | | | | | | | | | |
| 2015 | 956.91 | 983.53 | 1,001.28 | 1,000.23 | 987.62 | 1,003.51 | 1,008.82 | 1,103.65 | 1,060.79 | 1,062.14 | 1,075.23 | 1,063.14 | 1,025.99 |
| 2016 | 1,038.73 | 1,057.27 | 1,059.18 | 1,049.18 | 1,085.24 | 1,048.38 | 1,057.60 | 1,099.95 | 1,087.95 | 1,137.31 | 1,125.43 | 1,108.38 | 1,080.50 |
| 2017 | 1,157.78 | 1,115.54 | 1,107.48 | 1,145.82 | 1,126.56 | 1,140.72 | 1,181.26 | 1,161.81 | 1,142.66 | 1,173.00 | 1,155.58 | 1,160.78 | 1,146.99 |
| 2018 | 1,138.60 | 1,153.91 | 1,150.03 | 1,173.15 | 1,162.45 | 1,159.86 | 1,191.56 | 1,202.00 | 1,187.37 | 1,161.28 | 1,186.49 | 1,193.86 | 1,170.98 |
| 2019 | 1,117.50 | 1,124.11 | 1,117.47 | 1,132.51 | 1,146.05 | 1,202.40 | 1,147.81 | 1,205.65 | 1,236.94 | 1,205.44 | 1,209.60 | 1,240.64 | 1,173.06 |
| **Professional and Business Services** | | | | | | | | | | | | | |
| 2015 | 934.56 | 973.05 | 983.30 | 965.22 | 957.73 | 976.01 | 960.50 | 1,017.46 | 978.43 | 977.34 | 993.08 | 956.40 | 973.19 |
| 2016 | 948.27 | 953.10 | 967.92 | 986.05 | 1,018.58 | 986.79 | 990.66 | 995.19 | 993.10 | 1,019.52 | 976.98 | 984.04 | 985.97 |
| 2017 | 1,017.33 | 1,008.33 | 1,010.69 | 1,062.76 | 1,019.89 | 1,010.69 | 1,052.63 | 1,032.46 | 1,030.77 | 1,064.45 | 1,036.57 | 1,037.69 | 1,030.82 |
| 2018 | 1,012.91 | 1,002.33 | 1,005.89 | 1,032.40 | 993.35 | 998.38 | 1,029.96 | 1,010.72 | 1,022.31 | 996.22 | 1,009.37 | 1,031.39 | 1,012.69 |
| 2019 | 1,018.48 | 1,009.51 | 1,004.28 | 1,026.99 | 1,003.83 | 1,044.63 | 1,029.35 | 1,059.48 | 1,091.07 | 1,072.44 | 1,050.91 | 1,096.72 | 1,042.18 |
| **Education and Health Services** | | | | | | | | | | | | | |
| 2015 | 837.90 | 854.15 | 845.68 | 836.65 | 831.48 | 830.59 | 836.77 | 848.52 | 847.22 | 841.52 | 854.80 | 839.83 | 842.30 |
| 2016 | 844.35 | 842.86 | 847.15 | 846.78 | 846.69 | 827.87 | 831.93 | 837.64 | 847.26 | 855.93 | 856.46 | 876.75 | 847.49 |
| 2017 | 885.11 | 866.43 | 877.03 | 895.13 | 880.05 | 891.48 | 920.12 | 906.78 | 903.14 | 914.51 | 915.96 | 910.91 | 898.62 |
| 2018 | 903.81 | 902.02 | 901.14 | 909.72 | 892.04 | 892.04 | 907.67 | 885.64 | 911.69 | 885.10 | 878.45 | 897.43 | 897.05 |
| 2019 | 893.56 | 897.29 | 884.44 | 898.43 | 891.11 | 907.40 | 900.80 | 901.45 | 938.64 | 909.56 | 917.18 | 918.63 | 904.18 |
| **Leisure and Hospitality** | | | | | | | | | | | | | |
| 2015 | 375.26 | 392.28 | 390.31 | 377.50 | 379.40 | 369.84 | 365.83 | 372.13 | 364.41 | 368.53 | 376.99 | 370.24 | 375.47 |
| 2016 | 372.32 | 374.71 | 371.66 | 373.99 | 382.34 | 367.75 | 366.60 | 356.62 | 361.34 | 374.25 | 371.92 | 367.91 | 369.84 |
| 2017 | 391.30 | 392.39 | 397.50 | 404.85 | 396.20 | 380.42 | 388.87 | 372.99 | 375.67 | 389.80 | 394.89 | 397.24 | 390.26 |
| 2018 | 403.77 | 416.74 | 425.88 | 423.78 | 414.16 | 408.10 | 400.67 | 396.80 | 403.51 | 404.48 | 422.08 | 432.22 | 413.16 |
| 2019 | 425.28 | 439.43 | 457.00 | 455.87 | 446.22 | 450.63 | 433.42 | 428.93 | 434.73 | 436.82 | 438.53 | 449.18 | 441.58 |
| **Other Services** | | | | | | | | | | | | | |
| 2015 | 659.28 | 684.43 | 664.98 | 674.35 | 665.37 | 684.45 | 691.68 | 729.56 | 684.11 | 691.23 | 705.18 | 696.54 | 685.25 |
| 2016 | 703.30 | 711.95 | 731.77 | 727.25 | 719.71 | 710.62 | 708.01 | 748.39 | 753.50 | 789.79 | 788.10 | 780.67 | 739.38 |
| 2017 | 805.07 | 799.65 | 797.99 | 808.74 | 789.91 | 813.10 | 808.79 | 793.97 | 818.41 | 840.65 | 819.70 | 838.96 | 811.44 |
| 2018 | 798.98 | 792.25 | 779.51 | 779.76 | 772.55 | 783.34 | 774.07 | 781.57 | 793.31 | 766.18 | 783.36 | 791.18 | 782.50 |
| 2019 | 787.78 | 761.12 | 765.40 | 745.88 | 735.29 | 752.60 | 745.89 | 737.12 | 765.45 | 743.73 | 760.82 | 801.31 | 758.38 |

# ARKANSAS
## *At a Glance*

Population:
  2010 census: 2,915,918
  2019 estimate: 3,017,804

Percent change in population:
  2010–2019: 3.5%

Percent change in total nonfarm employment:
  2011–2019: 9.1%

Industry with the largest growth in employment, 2011–2019 (percent):
  Other services, 37.2%

Industry with the largest decline or smallest growth in employment, 2011–2019 (percent):
  Mining and logging, -47.3%

Civilian labor force:
  2010: 1,353,338
  2019: 1,362,642

Unemployment rate and rank among states (highest to lowest):
  2010: 8.2%, 31st
  2019: 3.5%, 25th

Over-the-year change in unemployment rates:
  2017–2018: -0.1%
  2018–2019: -0.1%

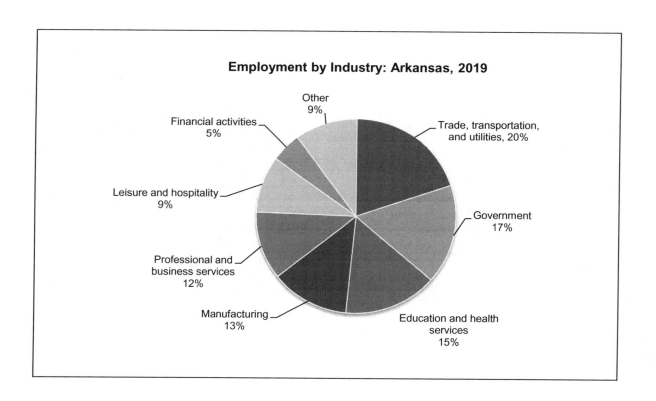

**Employment by Industry: Arkansas, 2019**

- Other 9%
- Financial activities 5%
- Trade, transportation, and utilities, 20%
- Leisure and hospitality 9%
- Government 17%
- Professional and business services 12%
- Manufacturing 13%
- Education and health services 15%

# 1. Employment by Industry: Arkansas, 2011–2019

(Numbers in thousands, not seasonally adjusted)

| Industry and year | January | February | March | April | May | June | July | August | September | October | November | December | Annual average |
|---|---|---|---|---|---|---|---|---|---|---|---|---|---|
| **Total Nonfarm** | | | | | | | | | | | | | |
| 2011 | 1,148.3 | 1,148.2 | 1,162.0 | 1,177.9 | 1,173.9 | 1,166.3 | 1,159.7 | 1,166.4 | 1,178.3 | 1,184.0 | 1,184.6 | 1,183.8 | 1,169.5 |
| 2012 | 1,160.4 | 1,166.2 | 1,177.7 | 1,182.9 | 1,188.1 | 1,181.8 | 1,161.9 | 1,170.9 | 1,181.0 | 1,182.8 | 1,184.9 | 1,187.1 | 1,177.1 |
| 2013 | 1,161.7 | 1,170.6 | 1,177.3 | 1,182.9 | 1,186.5 | 1,176.7 | 1,162.2 | 1,169.2 | 1,183.6 | 1,186.4 | 1,189.8 | 1,184.8 | 1,177.6 |
| 2014 | 1,164.4 | 1,173.0 | 1,182.0 | 1,190.5 | 1,198.3 | 1,190.1 | 1,173.7 | 1,183.9 | 1,200.1 | 1,203.1 | 1,208.5 | 1,212.1 | 1,190.0 |
| 2015 | 1,187.0 | 1,196.6 | 1,198.1 | 1,209.6 | 1,219.1 | 1,212.2 | 1,198.9 | 1,210.0 | 1,227.3 | 1,228.8 | 1,233.9 | 1,237.1 | 1,213.2 |
| 2016 | 1,210.5 | 1,220.2 | 1,227.9 | 1,235.9 | 1,239.0 | 1,231.8 | 1,218.2 | 1,227.0 | 1,245.3 | 1,245.3 | 1,247.7 | 1,247.5 | 1,233.0 |
| 2017 | 1,224.5 | 1,235.6 | 1,243.1 | 1,251.2 | 1,254.5 | 1,248.7 | 1,232.0 | 1,241.3 | 1,259.3 | 1,262.0 | 1,266.6 | 1,265.8 | 1,248.7 |
| 2018 | 1,242.8 | 1,253.1 | 1,260.2 | 1,266.2 | 1,271.7 | 1,262.4 | 1,249.9 | 1,259.6 | 1,276.1 | 1,280.4 | 1,285.0 | 1,284.1 | 1,266.0 |
| 2019 | 1,265.3 | 1,273.1 | 1,277.2 | 1,283.2 | 1,284.0 | 1,272.4 | 1,257.2 | 1,265.8 | 1,279.2 | 1,286.5 | 1,286.4 | 1,286.8 | 1,276.4 |
| **Total Private** | | | | | | | | | | | | | |
| 2011 | 931.6 | 929.5 | 941.9 | 957.0 | 953.1 | 952.5 | 960.6 | 960.3 | 961.5 | 963.1 | 963.0 | 963.7 | 953.2 |
| 2012 | 944.4 | 946.9 | 957.7 | 962.6 | 966.6 | 967.6 | 960.5 | 965.6 | 964.6 | 962.6 | 963.1 | 966.2 | 960.7 |
| 2013 | 946.1 | 951.4 | 958.0 | 963.4 | 967.1 | 964.6 | 962.8 | 965.5 | 968.1 | 969.2 | 972.3 | 967.8 | 963.0 |
| 2014 | 952.1 | 957.2 | 965.6 | 974.0 | 980.8 | 979.5 | 975.3 | 981.3 | 985.9 | 987.7 | 991.0 | 994.9 | 977.1 |
| 2015 | 973.8 | 981.2 | 982.3 | 993.8 | 1,002.3 | 1,002.1 | 1,000.7 | 1,007.4 | 1,013.6 | 1,014.2 | 1,018.2 | 1,020.9 | 1,000.9 |
| 2016 | 998.3 | 1,005.4 | 1,011.6 | 1,019.4 | 1,022.1 | 1,021.2 | 1,020.3 | 1,024.4 | 1,032.0 | 1,032.2 | 1,033.7 | 1,033.3 | 1,021.2 |
| 2017 | 1,014.6 | 1,022.8 | 1,029.9 | 1,035.7 | 1,039.8 | 1,039.1 | 1,034.4 | 1,040.1 | 1,045.5 | 1,046.7 | 1,050.6 | 1,050.7 | 1,037.5 |
| 2018 | 1,031.3 | 1,038.7 | 1,044.7 | 1,050.3 | 1,056.6 | 1,052.2 | 1,051.8 | 1,058.0 | 1,061.7 | 1,064.6 | 1,068.0 | 1,068.3 | 1,053.9 |
| 2019 | 1,053.2 | 1,058.5 | 1,062.1 | 1,067.2 | 1,068.8 | 1,064.0 | 1,060.3 | 1,065.4 | 1,066.2 | 1,072.6 | 1,071.6 | 1,072.9 | 1,065.2 |
| **Goods Producing** | | | | | | | | | | | | | |
| 2011 | 214.1 | 213.9 | 216.6 | 218.7 | 218.1 | 217.9 | 220.3 | 219.1 | 219.3 | 217.8 | 216.7 | 216.2 | 217.4 |
| 2012 | 212.7 | 212.8 | 214.9 | 214.7 | 216.1 | 216.7 | 215.0 | 214.8 | 213.9 | 211.3 | 209.7 | 210.2 | 213.6 |
| 2013 | 206.7 | 206.9 | 208.0 | 207.3 | 208.6 | 208.9 | 208.5 | 208.6 | 208.4 | 207.8 | 207.3 | 206.2 | 207.8 |
| 2014 | 205.1 | 204.4 | 205.3 | 207.2 | 209.2 | 210.1 | 210.8 | 211.3 | 212.1 | 212.2 | 211.4 | 212.6 | 209.3 |
| 2015 | 210.8 | 210.7 | 209.8 | 210.5 | 211.1 | 212.7 | 214.0 | 214.2 | 215.3 | 213.8 | 213.0 | 213.2 | 212.4 |
| 2016 | 209.7 | 209.8 | 209.9 | 210.3 | 210.7 | 212.7 | 213.2 | 212.7 | 213.4 | 212.6 | 211.7 | 211.8 | 211.5 |
| 2017 | 210.4 | 211.6 | 213.2 | 213.0 | 213.8 | 215.8 | 215.6 | 215.8 | 216.5 | 215.9 | 216.4 | 216.4 | 214.5 |
| 2018 | 213.2 | 214.9 | 215.5 | 215.3 | 216.7 | 218.2 | 218.7 | 218.8 | 219.4 | 219.6 | 219.5 | 220.3 | 217.5 |
| 2019 | 218.3 | 219.2 | 219.7 | 220.1 | 220.6 | 221.8 | 221.1 | 221.7 | 221.1 | 223.2 | 221.3 | 219.9 | 220.7 |
| **Service-Providing** | | | | | | | | | | | | | |
| 2011 | 934.2 | 934.3 | 945.4 | 959.2 | 955.8 | 948.4 | 939.4 | 947.3 | 959.0 | 966.2 | 967.9 | 967.6 | 952.1 |
| 2012 | 947.7 | 953.4 | 962.8 | 968.2 | 972.0 | 965.1 | 946.9 | 956.1 | 967.1 | 971.5 | 975.2 | 976.9 | 963.6 |
| 2013 | 955.0 | 963.7 | 969.3 | 975.6 | 977.9 | 967.8 | 953.7 | 960.6 | 975.2 | 978.6 | 982.5 | 978.6 | 969.9 |
| 2014 | 959.3 | 968.6 | 976.7 | 983.3 | 989.1 | 980.0 | 962.9 | 972.6 | 988.0 | 990.9 | 997.1 | 999.5 | 980.7 |
| 2015 | 976.2 | 985.9 | 988.3 | 999.1 | 1,008.0 | 999.5 | 984.9 | 995.8 | 1,012.0 | 1,015.0 | 1,020.9 | 1,023.9 | 1,000.8 |
| 2016 | 1,000.8 | 1,010.4 | 1,018.0 | 1,025.6 | 1,028.3 | 1,019.1 | 1,005.0 | 1,014.3 | 1,031.9 | 1,032.7 | 1,036.0 | 1,035.7 | 1,021.5 |
| 2017 | 1,014.1 | 1,024.0 | 1,029.9 | 1,038.2 | 1,040.7 | 1,032.9 | 1,016.4 | 1,025.5 | 1,042.8 | 1,046.1 | 1,050.2 | 1,049.4 | 1,034.2 |
| 2018 | 1,029.6 | 1,038.2 | 1,044.7 | 1,050.9 | 1,055.0 | 1,044.2 | 1,031.2 | 1,040.8 | 1,056.7 | 1,060.8 | 1,065.5 | 1,063.8 | 1,048.5 |
| 2019 | 1,047.0 | 1,053.9 | 1,057.5 | 1,063.1 | 1,063.4 | 1,050.6 | 1,036.1 | 1,044.1 | 1,058.1 | 1,063.3 | 1,065.1 | 1,066.9 | 1,055.8 |
| **Mining and Logging** | | | | | | | | | | | | | |
| 2011 | 10.7 | 10.6 | 10.8 | 11.0 | 10.8 | 11.0 | 11.5 | 11.4 | 11.5 | 11.7 | 11.6 | 11.6 | 11.2 |
| 2012 | 11.3 | 11.3 | 11.3 | 11.1 | 11.1 | 11.1 | 10.7 | 10.5 | 10.3 | 10.2 | 10.1 | 10.0 | 10.8 |
| 2013 | 9.6 | 9.6 | 9.7 | 9.5 | 9.6 | 9.6 | 9.7 | 9.6 | 9.5 | 9.3 | 9.2 | 9.1 | 9.5 |
| 2014 | 8.8 | 8.7 | 8.7 | 8.8 | 9.0 | 8.9 | 9.0 | 9.0 | 9.1 | 9.0 | 9.1 | 9.1 | 8.9 |
| 2015 | 8.8 | 8.7 | 8.4 | 8.3 | 8.1 | 8.0 | 8.0 | 7.9 | 7.8 | 7.7 | 7.6 | 7.5 | 8.1 |
| 2016 | 7.1 | 6.9 | 6.7 | 6.3 | 6.3 | 6.3 | 6.2 | 6.2 | 6.2 | 6.0 | 6.0 | 6.0 | 6.4 |
| 2017 | 5.9 | 5.9 | 5.9 | 5.9 | 6.0 | 6.1 | 6.1 | 6.0 | 6.0 | 6.0 | 6.0 | 5.9 | 6.0 |
| 2018 | 5.8 | 5.9 | 5.9 | 5.9 | 6.0 | 6.1 | 6.0 | 6.0 | 6.0 | 5.9 | 5.8 | 5.8 | 5.9 |
| 2019 | 5.7 | 5.7 | 5.8 | 5.8 | 5.9 | 6.0 | 5.9 | 6.0 | 6.0 | 5.9 | 5.9 | 5.8 | 5.9 |
| **Construction** | | | | | | | | | | | | | |
| 2011 | 43.6 | 43.6 | 45.5 | 47.3 | 47.2 | 48.3 | 49.3 | 48.8 | 49.2 | 48.7 | 48.1 | 47.8 | 47.3 |
| 2012 | 45.6 | 46.1 | 47.5 | 47.6 | 48.6 | 49.4 | 47.7 | 48.3 | 48.5 | 47.3 | 46.1 | 46.0 | 47.4 |
| 2013 | 43.9 | 44.4 | 45.3 | 45.4 | 46.4 | 46.5 | 46.3 | 46.3 | 46.0 | 45.4 | 45.2 | 44.3 | 45.5 |
| 2014 | 43.9 | 43.2 | 43.7 | 45.0 | 46.2 | 46.6 | 46.8 | 47.2 | 47.6 | 47.6 | 47.4 | 47.7 | 46.1 |
| 2015 | 45.9 | 46.2 | 46.0 | 47.3 | 48.5 | 49.5 | 50.7 | 51.2 | 52.2 | 51.4 | 50.8 | 50.4 | 49.2 |
| 2016 | 48.3 | 48.6 | 49.2 | 50.3 | 50.5 | 51.5 | 51.6 | 51.1 | 51.5 | 51.1 | 50.1 | 49.6 | 50.3 |
| 2017 | 48.7 | 49.5 | 50.8 | 51.1 | 51.6 | 52.6 | 52.0 | 51.9 | 52.4 | 51.4 | 51.4 | 50.9 | 51.2 |
| 2018 | 48.5 | 49.2 | 49.5 | 50.0 | 50.9 | 51.6 | 51.9 | 51.9 | 52.1 | 52.0 | 51.3 | 51.4 | 50.9 |
| 2019 | 50.1 | 50.5 | 51.1 | 52.4 | 52.4 | 53.1 | 53.4 | 53.6 | 53.6 | 54.4 | 53.0 | 51.7 | 52.4 |

## 1. Employment by Industry: Arkansas, 2011–2019—*Continued*

(Numbers in thousands, not seasonally adjusted)

| Industry and year | January | February | March | April | May | June | July | August | September | October | November | December | Annual average |
|---|---|---|---|---|---|---|---|---|---|---|---|---|---|
| **Manufacturing** | | | | | | | | | | | | | |
| 2011 | 159.8 | 159.7 | 160.3 | 160.4 | 160.1 | 158.6 | 159.5 | 158.9 | 158.6 | 157.4 | 157.0 | 156.8 | 158.9 |
| 2012 | 155.8 | 155.4 | 156.1 | 156.0 | 156.4 | 156.2 | 156.6 | 156.0 | 155.1 | 153.8 | 153.5 | 154.2 | 155.4 |
| 2013 | 153.2 | 152.9 | 153.0 | 152.4 | 152.6 | 152.8 | 152.5 | 152.7 | 152.9 | 153.1 | 152.9 | 152.8 | 152.8 |
| 2014 | 152.4 | 152.5 | 152.9 | 153.4 | 154.0 | 154.6 | 155.0 | 155.1 | 155.4 | 155.6 | 154.9 | 155.8 | 154.3 |
| 2015 | 156.1 | 155.8 | 155.4 | 154.9 | 154.5 | 155.2 | 155.3 | 155.1 | 155.3 | 154.7 | 154.6 | 155.3 | 155.2 |
| 2016 | 154.3 | 154.3 | 154.0 | 153.7 | 153.9 | 154.9 | 155.4 | 155.4 | 155.7 | 155.5 | 155.6 | 156.2 | 154.9 |
| 2017 | 155.8 | 156.2 | 156.5 | 156.0 | 156.2 | 157.1 | 157.5 | 157.9 | 158.1 | 158.5 | 159.0 | 159.6 | 157.4 |
| 2018 | 158.9 | 159.8 | 160.1 | 159.4 | 159.8 | 160.5 | 160.8 | 160.9 | 161.3 | 161.7 | 162.4 | 163.1 | 160.7 |
| 2019 | 162.5 | 163.0 | 162.8 | 161.9 | 162.3 | 162.7 | 161.8 | 162.1 | 161.5 | 162.9 | 162.4 | 162.4 | 162.4 |
| **Trade, Transportation, and Utilities** | | | | | | | | | | | | | |
| 2011 | 233.4 | 231.0 | 233.5 | 237.7 | 236.6 | 237.5 | 239.2 | 238.6 | 238.3 | 239.9 | 242.8 | 245.0 | 237.8 |
| 2012 | 237.8 | 236.6 | 239.1 | 240.3 | 241.3 | 241.9 | 241.0 | 241.3 | 241.0 | 240.9 | 244.6 | 246.1 | 241.0 |
| 2013 | 237.8 | 237.7 | 239.3 | 239.6 | 239.5 | 239.9 | 240.8 | 241.4 | 240.8 | 242.1 | 245.6 | 246.2 | 240.9 |
| 2014 | 238.8 | 238.1 | 240.2 | 242.4 | 243.3 | 244.3 | 244.0 | 245.3 | 245.4 | 246.5 | 250.8 | 253.0 | 244.3 |
| 2015 | 244.9 | 244.6 | 245.7 | 248.1 | 250.3 | 251.2 | 250.5 | 251.7 | 250.8 | 252.1 | 255.7 | 257.1 | 250.2 |
| 2016 | 249.1 | 248.3 | 249.7 | 250.1 | 251.0 | 251.4 | 251.6 | 251.7 | 251.5 | 252.1 | 256.0 | 256.4 | 251.6 |
| 2017 | 248.9 | 247.8 | 248.0 | 248.4 | 249.3 | 249.9 | 249.9 | 250.9 | 250.1 | 250.2 | 254.1 | 255.4 | 250.2 |
| 2018 | 249.1 | 248.4 | 249.6 | 250.1 | 251.4 | 250.7 | 251.1 | 251.9 | 251.4 | 252.3 | 257.4 | 257.4 | 251.7 |
| 2019 | 251.4 | 249.7 | 250.2 | 250.7 | 251.4 | 251.4 | 250.8 | 251.0 | 251.1 | 252.5 | 256.7 | 258.4 | 252.1 |
| **Wholesale Trade** | | | | | | | | | | | | | |
| 2011 | 45.1 | 45.0 | 45.4 | 46.4 | 46.1 | 46.2 | 46.8 | 46.5 | 46.3 | 46.6 | 46.4 | 46.6 | 46.1 |
| 2012 | 46.0 | 46.1 | 46.6 | 47.3 | 47.5 | 47.6 | 46.9 | 46.8 | 46.5 | 46.3 | 46.2 | 46.4 | 46.7 |
| 2013 | 46.0 | 46.2 | 46.6 | 46.7 | 46.7 | 46.6 | 46.4 | 46.2 | 45.9 | 46.0 | 45.3 | 45.1 | 46.1 |
| 2014 | 45.0 | 45.3 | 45.6 | 45.9 | 46.1 | 46.3 | 46.1 | 46.2 | 45.9 | 46.0 | 45.9 | 45.9 | 45.9 |
| 2015 | 45.3 | 45.4 | 45.5 | 45.5 | 45.8 | 45.8 | 45.8 | 45.7 | 45.4 | 45.6 | 45.5 | 45.5 | 45.6 |
| 2016 | 45.0 | 45.2 | 45.4 | 45.4 | 45.5 | 45.5 | 45.6 | 45.5 | 45.4 | 45.4 | 45.4 | 45.6 | 45.4 |
| 2017 | 45.2 | 45.5 | 45.8 | 45.7 | 45.9 | 46.0 | 46.2 | 46.3 | 46.1 | 46.2 | 46.4 | 46.6 | 46.0 |
| 2018 | 46.7 | 47.0 | 47.1 | 47.1 | 47.2 | 47.2 | 47.5 | 47.3 | 47.2 | 47.3 | 47.2 | 47.3 | 47.2 |
| 2019 | 47.0 | 47.1 | 47.3 | 47.6 | 47.8 | 47.8 | 47.7 | 47.5 | 47.3 | 48.2 | 48.8 | 48.9 | 47.8 |
| **Retail Trade** | | | | | | | | | | | | | |
| 2011 | 129.5 | 127.5 | 129.1 | 131.4 | 130.5 | 130.9 | 131.7 | 131.3 | 130.4 | 132.0 | 135.1 | 136.2 | 131.3 |
| 2012 | 131.0 | 129.9 | 131.3 | 132.1 | 132.6 | 132.7 | 132.6 | 132.5 | 132.4 | 132.4 | 136.1 | 136.7 | 132.7 |
| 2013 | 130.7 | 130.4 | 131.5 | 131.9 | 131.8 | 131.9 | 133.4 | 133.8 | 133.4 | 134.6 | 138.5 | 139.1 | 133.4 |
| 2014 | 133.3 | 132.3 | 133.6 | 135.4 | 135.7 | 136.4 | 136.1 | 136.8 | 136.4 | 137.6 | 141.5 | 142.6 | 136.5 |
| 2015 | 136.7 | 136.5 | 137.2 | 139.2 | 140.8 | 141.2 | 140.4 | 141.6 | 140.8 | 142.0 | 145.8 | 146.2 | 140.7 |
| 2016 | 140.3 | 139.8 | 140.9 | 142.1 | 142.6 | 142.3 | 142.5 | 142.6 | 141.7 | 142.6 | 146.1 | 145.6 | 142.4 |
| 2017 | 140.8 | 139.6 | 139.5 | 140.2 | 140.7 | 140.5 | 140.2 | 140.7 | 140.0 | 140.3 | 143.5 | 143.5 | 140.8 |
| 2018 | 138.6 | 137.6 | 138.2 | 138.8 | 139.5 | 138.4 | 138.4 | 138.9 | 138.0 | 138.8 | 142.4 | 141.6 | 139.1 |
| 2019 | 136.6 | 135.2 | 135.3 | 135.6 | 136.4 | 136.0 | 135.7 | 135.8 | 135.8 | 136.1 | 138.5 | 138.9 | 136.3 |
| **Transportation and Utilities** | | | | | | | | | | | | | |
| 2011 | 58.8 | 58.5 | 59.0 | 59.9 | 60.0 | 60.4 | 60.7 | 60.8 | 61.6 | 61.3 | 61.3 | 62.2 | 60.4 |
| 2012 | 60.8 | 60.6 | 61.2 | 60.9 | 61.2 | 61.6 | 61.5 | 62.0 | 62.1 | 62.2 | 62.3 | 63.0 | 61.6 |
| 2013 | 61.1 | 61.1 | 61.2 | 61.0 | 61.0 | 61.4 | 61.0 | 61.4 | 61.5 | 61.5 | 61.8 | 62.0 | 61.3 |
| 2014 | 60.5 | 60.5 | 61.0 | 61.1 | 61.5 | 61.6 | 61.8 | 62.3 | 63.1 | 62.9 | 63.4 | 64.5 | 62.0 |
| 2015 | 62.9 | 62.7 | 63.0 | 63.4 | 63.7 | 64.2 | 64.3 | 64.4 | 64.6 | 64.5 | 64.4 | 65.4 | 64.0 |
| 2016 | 63.8 | 63.3 | 63.4 | 62.6 | 62.9 | 63.6 | 63.5 | 63.6 | 64.4 | 64.1 | 64.5 | 65.2 | 63.7 |
| 2017 | 62.9 | 62.7 | 62.7 | 62.5 | 62.7 | 63.4 | 63.5 | 63.9 | 64.0 | 63.7 | 64.2 | 65.3 | 63.5 |
| 2018 | 63.8 | 63.8 | 64.3 | 64.2 | 64.7 | 65.1 | 65.2 | 65.7 | 66.2 | 66.2 | 67.8 | 68.5 | 65.5 |
| 2019 | 67.8 | 67.4 | 67.6 | 67.5 | 67.2 | 67.6 | 67.4 | 67.7 | 68.0 | 68.2 | 69.4 | 70.6 | 68.0 |
| **Information** | | | | | | | | | | | | | |
| 2011 | 15.0 | 15.0 | 14.9 | 14.9 | 14.9 | 14.9 | 14.9 | 14.9 | 14.7 | 14.7 | 14.7 | 14.7 | 14.9 |
| 2012 | 14.6 | 14.6 | 14.4 | 14.4 | 14.5 | 14.5 | 14.3 | 14.3 | 14.2 | 14.2 | 14.2 | 14.2 | 14.4 |
| 2013 | 14.0 | 14.0 | 13.9 | 13.8 | 13.9 | 13.9 | 13.9 | 13.8 | 13.6 | 13.6 | 13.6 | 13.6 | 13.8 |
| 2014 | 13.3 | 13.3 | 13.2 | 13.1 | 13.1 | 13.0 | 13.1 | 12.9 | 12.7 | 12.6 | 12.6 | 12.6 | 13.0 |
| 2015 | 12.4 | 12.4 | 12.3 | 12.3 | 12.5 | 12.6 | 13.0 | 12.7 | 12.8 | 12.6 | 12.7 | 12.8 | 12.6 |
| 2016 | 12.5 | 12.5 | 12.5 | 12.5 | 12.4 | 12.5 | 12.4 | 12.3 | 12.2 | 12.3 | 12.3 | 12.4 | 12.4 |
| 2017 | 12.1 | 12.1 | 12.0 | 12.0 | 11.9 | 11.8 | 11.6 | 11.5 | 11.3 | 11.3 | 11.4 | 11.1 | 11.7 |
| 2018 | 11.4 | 11.3 | 11.2 | 11.1 | 11.3 | 11.3 | 11.2 | 11.2 | 11.2 | 11.3 | 11.4 | 11.4 | 11.3 |
| 2019 | 11.3 | 11.3 | 11.4 | 11.4 | 11.4 | 11.5 | 11.2 | 11.2 | 11.1 | 11.3 | 11.3 | 11.2 | 11.3 |

## 1. Employment by Industry: Arkansas, 2011–2019—*Continued*

(Numbers in thousands, not seasonally adjusted)

| Industry and year | January | February | March | April | May | June | July | August | September | October | November | December | Annual average |
|---|---|---|---|---|---|---|---|---|---|---|---|---|---|
| **Financial Activities** | | | | | | | | | | | | | |
| 2011 | 48.2 | 48.0 | 48.2 | 48.7 | 48.4 | 48.6 | 49.0 | 48.7 | 48.3 | 48.7 | 48.7 | 49.0 | 48.5 |
| 2012 | 48.5 | 48.6 | 48.8 | 49.1 | 49.5 | 49.8 | 49.7 | 50.1 | 49.8 | 50.0 | 50.2 | 50.5 | 49.6 |
| 2013 | 50.1 | 50.3 | 50.5 | 50.8 | 51.2 | 51.5 | 51.5 | 51.9 | 51.6 | 52.0 | 52.1 | 52.2 | 51.3 |
| 2014 | 51.5 | 51.8 | 52.0 | 52.1 | 52.5 | 52.7 | 52.6 | 52.7 | 52.2 | 52.6 | 52.7 | 52.9 | 52.4 |
| 2015 | 52.5 | 52.6 | 52.7 | 53.2 | 53.7 | 54.1 | 54.5 | 55.0 | 54.8 | 55.5 | 55.7 | 56.0 | 54.2 |
| 2016 | 55.7 | 55.9 | 56.0 | 56.5 | 56.6 | 57.0 | 57.3 | 57.6 | 57.6 | 58.1 | 58.5 | 58.5 | 57.1 |
| 2017 | 58.4 | 58.8 | 59.2 | 59.5 | 59.6 | 59.8 | 60.0 | 60.0 | 59.4 | 59.9 | 59.8 | 60.0 | 59.5 |
| 2018 | 59.8 | 59.8 | 59.7 | 60.1 | 60.7 | 61.1 | 61.4 | 61.7 | 61.4 | 62.2 | 62.3 | 62.3 | 61.0 |
| 2019 | 62.0 | 62.2 | 62.2 | 62.6 | 62.7 | 63.0 | 63.1 | 63.3 | 62.6 | 62.9 | 62.1 | 61.7 | 62.5 |
| **Professional and Business Services** | | | | | | | | | | | | | |
| 2011 | 118.9 | 119.8 | 121.7 | 123.9 | 122.5 | 123.0 | 125.0 | 125.5 | 125.0 | 125.9 | 124.8 | 124.7 | 123.4 |
| 2012 | 121.8 | 123.0 | 124.6 | 126.2 | 126.0 | 125.6 | 125.8 | 126.1 | 126.0 | 127.1 | 126.4 | 127.1 | 125.5 |
| 2013 | 125.3 | 127.8 | 128.8 | 130.2 | 130.3 | 128.0 | 127.6 | 127.8 | 130.8 | 133.1 | 133.5 | 131.4 | 129.6 |
| 2014 | 128.8 | 133.2 | 134.5 | 134.6 | 135.2 | 132.8 | 131.5 | 133.1 | 136.4 | 138.7 | 138.9 | 139.2 | 134.7 |
| 2015 | 133.1 | 138.5 | 137.4 | 140.1 | 141.0 | 138.6 | 137.8 | 139.3 | 142.4 | 143.7 | 144.3 | 144.4 | 140.1 |
| 2016 | 138.0 | 142.9 | 144.0 | 145.7 | 144.7 | 142.4 | 141.8 | 143.0 | 145.9 | 147.0 | 146.7 | 146.3 | 144.0 |
| 2017 | 141.0 | 145.4 | 146.6 | 147.5 | 147.7 | 144.9 | 143.5 | 144.5 | 147.5 | 148.6 | 148.3 | 148.0 | 146.1 |
| 2018 | 142.8 | 146.5 | 147.3 | 148.7 | 148.4 | 145.0 | 145.1 | 145.7 | 147.7 | 148.2 | 147.7 | 147.3 | 146.7 |
| 2019 | 143.0 | 146.1 | 146.3 | 146.8 | 146.5 | 143.7 | 142.2 | 143.6 | 145.1 | 147.2 | 147.0 | 147.4 | 145.4 |
| **Education and Health Services** | | | | | | | | | | | | | |
| 2011 | 165.4 | 165.2 | 166.5 | 168.0 | 167.0 | 163.5 | 164.2 | 166.2 | 170.0 | 171.1 | 171.7 | 171.3 | 167.5 |
| 2012 | 169.5 | 170.0 | 170.8 | 170.3 | 170.1 | 167.4 | 165.6 | 169.5 | 172.0 | 173.5 | 173.5 | 173.4 | 170.5 |
| 2013 | 170.4 | 171.6 | 171.5 | 172.4 | 172.5 | 169.2 | 168.2 | 170.3 | 172.8 | 172.9 | 173.6 | 172.9 | 171.5 |
| 2014 | 170.7 | 171.3 | 171.9 | 172.3 | 172.9 | 169.5 | 168.4 | 170.4 | 173.1 | 173.8 | 174.1 | 174.7 | 171.9 |
| 2015 | 172.8 | 173.3 | 173.5 | 174.6 | 175.0 | 172.3 | 171.7 | 174.1 | 177.4 | 178.3 | 178.8 | 179.1 | 175.1 |
| 2016 | 177.9 | 178.7 | 178.8 | 180.3 | 180.5 | 177.8 | 178.4 | 180.5 | 185.7 | 186.7 | 186.9 | 187.2 | 181.6 |
| 2017 | 185.1 | 186.4 | 187.1 | 188.1 | 188.4 | 186.0 | 184.5 | 186.6 | 190.6 | 191.6 | 192.0 | 192.1 | 188.2 |
| 2018 | 189.7 | 190.6 | 191.3 | 191.6 | 192.1 | 189.2 | 187.9 | 190.0 | 193.5 | 194.1 | 194.0 | 194.6 | 191.6 |
| 2019 | 193.1 | 193.8 | 193.9 | 193.9 | 193.5 | 190.1 | 189.5 | 191.5 | 194.5 | 195.5 | 195.9 | 197.6 | 193.6 |
| **Leisure and Hospitality** | | | | | | | | | | | | | |
| 2011 | 93.8 | 94.0 | 97.3 | 101.3 | 102.1 | 103.3 | 103.7 | 103.7 | 102.5 | 101.4 | 100.1 | 99.2 | 100.2 |
| 2012 | 96.6 | 98.3 | 101.7 | 104.0 | 105.3 | 107.2 | 105.4 | 105.9 | 104.3 | 102.2 | 101.3 | 101.4 | 102.8 |
| 2013 | 99.1 | 100.3 | 102.9 | 106.0 | 107.7 | 109.4 | 108.6 | 108.3 | 106.7 | 104.5 | 103.6 | 102.3 | 105.0 |
| 2014 | 101.1 | 102.2 | 105.3 | 108.6 | 110.7 | 112.5 | 110.4 | 111.1 | 109.9 | 107.6 | 106.9 | 106.4 | 107.7 |
| 2015 | 104.4 | 106.1 | 107.9 | 111.6 | 114.7 | 115.7 | 113.8 | 115.0 | 114.7 | 112.7 | 112.1 | 111.8 | 111.7 |
| 2016 | 108.9 | 110.8 | 113.8 | 117.0 | 119.0 | 119.3 | 117.4 | 118.6 | 117.5 | 115.5 | 113.8 | 112.7 | 115.4 |
| 2017 | 110.7 | 112.5 | 115.3 | 118.1 | 119.4 | 120.0 | 118.1 | 119.4 | 118.3 | 117.2 | 116.2 | 114.6 | 116.7 |
| 2018 | 112.6 | 114.4 | 117.1 | 119.6 | 121.3 | 121.0 | 120.1 | 122.0 | 119.7 | 119.2 | 117.4 | 116.2 | 118.4 |
| 2019 | 114.9 | 117.0 | 119.0 | 122.1 | 122.9 | 122.4 | 122.6 | 123.5 | 121.2 | 119.8 | 117.3 | 116.5 | 119.9 |
| **Other Services** | | | | | | | | | | | | | |
| 2011 | 42.8 | 42.6 | 43.2 | 43.8 | 43.5 | 43.8 | 44.3 | 43.6 | 43.4 | 43.6 | 43.5 | 43.6 | 43.5 |
| 2012 | 42.9 | 43.0 | 43.4 | 43.6 | 43.8 | 44.5 | 43.7 | 43.6 | 43.4 | 43.4 | 43.2 | 43.3 | 43.5 |
| 2013 | 42.7 | 42.8 | 43.1 | 43.3 | 43.4 | 43.8 | 43.7 | 43.4 | 43.4 | 43.2 | 43.0 | 43.0 | 43.2 |
| 2014 | 42.8 | 42.9 | 43.2 | 43.7 | 43.9 | 44.6 | 44.5 | 44.5 | 44.1 | 43.7 | 43.6 | 43.5 | 43.8 |
| 2015 | 42.9 | 43.0 | 43.0 | 43.4 | 44.0 | 44.9 | 45.4 | 45.4 | 45.4 | 45.5 | 45.9 | 46.5 | 44.6 |
| 2016 | 46.5 | 46.5 | 46.9 | 47.0 | 47.2 | 48.1 | 48.2 | 48.0 | 48.2 | 47.9 | 47.8 | 48.0 | 47.5 |
| 2017 | 48.0 | 48.2 | 48.5 | 49.1 | 49.7 | 50.9 | 51.2 | 51.4 | 51.8 | 52.0 | 52.4 | 53.1 | 50.5 |
| 2018 | 52.7 | 52.8 | 53.0 | 53.8 | 54.7 | 55.7 | 56.3 | 56.7 | 57.4 | 57.7 | 58.3 | 58.8 | 55.7 |
| 2019 | 59.2 | 59.2 | 59.4 | 59.6 | 59.8 | 60.1 | 59.8 | 59.6 | 59.5 | 60.2 | 60.0 | 60.2 | 59.7 |
| **Government** | | | | | | | | | | | | | |
| 2011 | 216.7 | 218.7 | 220.1 | 220.9 | 220.8 | 213.8 | 199.1 | 206.1 | 216.8 | 220.9 | 221.6 | 220.1 | 216.3 |
| 2012 | 216.0 | 219.3 | 220.0 | 220.3 | 221.5 | 214.2 | 201.4 | 205.3 | 216.4 | 220.2 | 221.8 | 220.9 | 216.4 |
| 2013 | 215.6 | 219.2 | 219.3 | 219.5 | 219.4 | 212.1 | 199.4 | 203.7 | 215.5 | 217.2 | 217.5 | 217.0 | 214.6 |
| 2014 | 212.3 | 215.8 | 216.4 | 216.5 | 217.5 | 210.6 | 198.4 | 202.6 | 214.2 | 215.4 | 217.5 | 217.2 | 212.9 |
| 2015 | 213.2 | 215.4 | 215.8 | 215.8 | 216.8 | 210.1 | 198.2 | 202.6 | 213.7 | 214.6 | 215.7 | 216.2 | 212.3 |
| 2016 | 212.2 | 214.8 | 216.3 | 216.5 | 216.9 | 210.6 | 197.9 | 202.6 | 213.3 | 213.1 | 214.0 | 214.2 | 211.9 |
| 2017 | 209.9 | 212.8 | 213.2 | 215.5 | 214.7 | 209.6 | 197.6 | 201.2 | 213.8 | 215.3 | 216.0 | 215.1 | 211.2 |
| 2018 | 211.5 | 214.4 | 215.5 | 215.9 | 215.1 | 210.2 | 198.1 | 201.6 | 214.4 | 215.8 | 217.0 | 215.8 | 212.1 |
| 2019 | 212.1 | 214.6 | 215.1 | 216.0 | 215.2 | 208.4 | 196.9 | 200.4 | 213.0 | 213.9 | 214.8 | 213.9 | 211.2 |

## 2. Average Weekly Hours by Selected Industry: Arkansas, 2015–2019

(Not seasonally adjusted)

| Industry and year | January | February | March | April | May | June | July | August | September | October | November | December | Annual average |
|---|---|---|---|---|---|---|---|---|---|---|---|---|---|
| **Total Private** | | | | | | | | | | | | | |
| 2015 | 34.6 | 34.7 | 34.5 | 34.6 | 34.3 | 34.3 | 34.4 | 34.9 | 34.2 | 34.5 | 34.8 | 34.3 | 34.5 |
| 2016 | 34.1 | 34.2 | 33.8 | 34.1 | 34.6 | 34.6 | 34.7 | 34.5 | 34.3 | 34.8 | 34.6 | 34.6 | 34.4 |
| 2017 | 34.6 | 34.5 | 34.5 | 34.9 | 34.7 | 35.0 | 35.1 | 34.9 | 35.0 | 35.3 | 34.8 | 35.2 | 34.9 |
| 2018 | 34.4 | 34.7 | 35.1 | 35.3 | 34.8 | 35.4 | 35.3 | 35.2 | 35.9 | 35.3 | 35.0 | 35.4 | 35.1 |
| 2019 | 34.8 | 34.5 | 34.8 | 35.2 | 34.9 | 35.8 | 34.7 | 35.2 | 35.6 | 34.7 | 34.5 | 35.1 | 35.0 |
| **Goods-Producing** | | | | | | | | | | | | | |
| 2015 | 41.0 | 40.5 | 39.9 | 40.5 | 40.0 | 40.4 | 40.1 | 41.2 | 39.6 | 41.1 | 40.7 | 40.1 | 40.4 |
| 2016 | 39.9 | 39.9 | 39.0 | 40.6 | 40.5 | 41.6 | 40.8 | 41.6 | 41.0 | 41.4 | 41.0 | 40.9 | 40.7 |
| 2017 | 40.5 | 40.2 | 40.0 | 39.9 | 40.4 | 41.5 | 40.8 | 41.3 | 41.3 | 42.0 | 41.4 | 41.6 | 40.9 |
| 2018 | 40.3 | 40.7 | 41.4 | 41.7 | 41.5 | 41.7 | 41.2 | 41.8 | 42.2 | 42.0 | 41.0 | 41.0 | 41.4 |
| 2019 | 40.2 | 39.5 | 40.0 | 40.0 | 39.9 | 40.9 | 38.9 | 40.8 | 41.2 | 39.5 | 39.1 | 39.8 | 40.0 |
| **Construction** | | | | | | | | | | | | | |
| 2015 | 38.9 | 36.7 | 35.6 | 37.9 | 37.3 | 39.3 | 37.7 | 38.5 | 35.4 | 37.5 | 37.6 | 37.7 | 37.5 |
| 2016 | 37.5 | 37.4 | 34.1 | 38.4 | 38.3 | 40.3 | 39.1 | 40.3 | 39.9 | 38.4 | 38.0 | 38.5 | 38.4 |
| 2017 | 39.1 | 38.5 | 39.2 | 38.3 | 39.5 | 41.2 | 41.2 | 41.2 | 40.9 | 41.2 | 39.0 | 38.9 | 39.9 |
| 2018 | 36.9 | 37.5 | 39.1 | 39.7 | 40.9 | 40.7 | 40.5 | 39.5 | 39.6 | 39.6 | 37.7 | 38.3 | 39.2 |
| 2019 | 36.6 | 36.0 | 36.8 | 39.1 | 38.7 | 40.4 | 38.4 | 41.5 | 42.4 | 39.7 | 37.7 | 39.9 | 39.0 |
| **Manufacturing** | | | | | | | | | | | | | |
| 2015 | 41.4 | 41.4 | 41.1 | 40.8 | 40.6 | 40.4 | 40.6 | 41.6 | 40.9 | 41.2 | 40.8 | 40.8 | 41.0 |
| 2016 | 40.7 | 40.9 | 41.0 | 41.2 | 40.9 | 41.7 | 40.9 | 41.6 | 40.9 | 41.9 | 41.6 | 41.3 | 41.2 |
| 2017 | 40.6 | 40.5 | 40.0 | 40.3 | 40.5 | 41.5 | 40.4 | 41.2 | 41.3 | 42.0 | 42.2 | 42.5 | 41.1 |
| 2018 | 42.0 | 42.3 | 42.5 | 42.7 | 41.8 | 42.0 | 41.1 | 42.5 | 42.8 | 42.9 | 42.3 | 41.8 | 42.2 |
| 2019 | 41.4 | 40.7 | 41.1 | 40.3 | 40.6 | 41.1 | 39.0 | 40.2 | 40.3 | 39.4 | 39.2 | 39.0 | 40.2 |
| **Trade, Transportation, and Utilities** | | | | | | | | | | | | | |
| 2015 | 35.4 | 35.5 | 35.7 | 35.4 | 35.9 | 35.4 | 35.3 | 36.1 | 35.6 | 35.0 | 35.4 | 35.0 | 35.5 |
| 2016 | 34.5 | 35.0 | 34.6 | 34.4 | 35.1 | 35.1 | 35.0 | 34.7 | 34.3 | 34.7 | 33.9 | 34.4 | 34.6 |
| 2017 | 34.4 | 34.2 | 34.2 | 35.5 | 34.9 | 35.3 | 35.4 | 35.4 | 35.8 | 35.6 | 35.0 | 35.5 | 35.1 |
| 2018 | 35.1 | 35.2 | 36.1 | 36.2 | 35.9 | 36.4 | 36.7 | 36.1 | 36.6 | 35.3 | 35.2 | 35.9 | 35.9 |
| 2019 | 35.1 | 34.5 | 35.0 | 35.5 | 34.9 | 35.6 | 34.8 | 34.8 | 34.9 | 34.5 | 34.2 | 35.1 | 34.9 |
| **Financial Activities** | | | | | | | | | | | | | |
| 2015 | 36.7 | 37.0 | 37.2 | 35.7 | 35.9 | 35.9 | 36.0 | 36.3 | 35.7 | 35.7 | 37.0 | 36.3 | 36.3 |
| 2016 | 36.9 | 36.9 | 36.6 | 36.7 | 37.1 | 36.1 | 36.8 | 36.6 | 36.6 | 37.5 | 36.7 | 37.2 | 36.8 |
| 2017 | 38.2 | 37.3 | 37.3 | 38.5 | 37.7 | 37.1 | 38.3 | 37.5 | 37.1 | 38.5 | 37.3 | 37.6 | 37.7 |
| 2018 | 37.8 | 37.8 | 37.6 | 37.7 | 36.9 | 37.0 | 37.8 | 37.7 | 37.8 | 37.6 | 37.8 | 38.2 | 37.6 |
| 2019 | 38.0 | 37.6 | 37.5 | 37.3 | 36.8 | 37.5 | 36.7 | 36.2 | 37.3 | 36.9 | 37.2 | 37.9 | 37.2 |
| **Professional and Business Services** | | | | | | | | | | | | | |
| 2015 | 34.9 | 35.8 | 35.7 | 36.2 | 35.7 | 35.8 | 36.1 | 36.1 | 36.3 | 36.1 | 36.7 | 35.8 | 35.9 |
| 2016 | 35.1 | 35.2 | 34.6 | 35.0 | 35.7 | 35.2 | 35.6 | 34.8 | 34.2 | 34.6 | 34.6 | 34.7 | 34.9 |
| 2017 | 34.3 | 34.3 | 34.6 | 35.3 | 34.6 | 34.7 | 35.3 | 34.7 | 35.0 | 35.0 | 34.6 | 35.3 | 34.8 |
| 2018 | 34.1 | 34.9 | 35.2 | 35.7 | 35.4 | 35.6 | 35.6 | 34.9 | 35.7 | 34.7 | 35.3 | 35.8 | 35.2 |
| 2019 | 35.5 | 34.9 | 36.0 | 36.7 | 36.6 | 37.0 | 36.3 | 36.8 | 36.8 | 36.1 | 35.7 | 36.7 | 36.3 |
| **Education and Health Services** | | | | | | | | | | | | | |
| 2015 | 33.1 | 33.5 | 33.0 | 33.4 | 33.3 | 33.3 | 33.4 | 33.6 | 33.4 | 33.4 | 34.3 | 33.9 | 33.5 |
| 2016 | 33.8 | 33.5 | 33.1 | 33.2 | 34.0 | 33.9 | 34.2 | 33.7 | 34.2 | 34.4 | 34.9 | 35.0 | 34.0 |
| 2017 | 34.8 | 34.8 | 34.1 | 34.3 | 33.8 | 33.8 | 34.0 | 33.7 | 33.5 | 33.7 | 33.5 | 33.2 | 33.9 |
| 2018 | 32.5 | 32.6 | 32.3 | 32.8 | 32.2 | 33.1 | 32.5 | 32.3 | 32.8 | 32.7 | 32.4 | 32.7 | 32.6 |
| 2019 | 32.1 | 32.3 | 31.9 | 32.7 | 32.8 | 32.8 | 32.0 | 32.7 | 33.1 | 32.9 | 32.9 | 33.5 | 32.6 |
| **Leisure and Hospitality** | | | | | | | | | | | | | |
| 2015 | 25.6 | 25.5 | 25.6 | 25.3 | 25.6 | 25.7 | 26.1 | 26.0 | 25.2 | 25.4 | 25.2 | 25.3 | 25.5 |
| 2016 | 24.6 | 25.3 | 25.3 | 25.0 | 24.9 | 24.9 | 25.2 | 24.8 | 24.7 | 25.3 | 25.1 | 24.6 | 25.0 |
| 2017 | 25.1 | 24.5 | 25.2 | 24.6 | 25.3 | 25.4 | 25.3 | 24.9 | 25.0 | 25.7 | 25.2 | 25.4 | 25.1 |
| 2018 | 24.8 | 25.1 | 25.6 | 25.7 | 25.4 | 26.1 | 26.1 | 25.9 | 26.6 | 25.9 | 25.7 | 26.2 | 25.8 |
| 2019 | 25.6 | 26.3 | 26.6 | 26.4 | 26.2 | 27.4 | 26.7 | 26.4 | 26.8 | 25.7 | 25.9 | 26.5 | 26.4 |

## 3. Average Hourly Earnings by Selected Industry: Arkansas, 2015–2019

(Dollars, not seasonally adjusted)

| Industry and year | January | February | March | April | May | June | July | August | September | October | November | December | Annual average |
|---|---|---|---|---|---|---|---|---|---|---|---|---|---|
| **Total Private** | | | | | | | | | | | | | |
| 2015 | 19.39 | 19.44 | 19.61 | 19.38 | 19.42 | 19.29 | 19.40 | 19.61 | 19.51 | 19.54 | 19.74 | 19.71 | 19.51 |
| 2016 | 20.05 | 19.94 | 19.96 | 20.04 | 20.08 | 19.96 | 20.24 | 20.10 | 20.10 | 20.37 | 20.20 | 20.25 | 20.11 |
| 2017 | 20.38 | 20.45 | 20.42 | 20.63 | 20.42 | 20.39 | 20.62 | 20.59 | 20.81 | 20.72 | 20.74 | 20.86 | 20.59 |
| 2018 | 21.03 | 20.98 | 20.92 | 20.99 | 20.77 | 20.65 | 21.04 | 20.94 | 21.28 | 21.05 | 21.25 | 21.71 | 21.05 |
| 2019 | 21.58 | 21.93 | 21.70 | 21.90 | 22.00 | 21.96 | 22.21 | 22.33 | 22.52 | 22.61 | 22.78 | 22.92 | 22.21 |
| **Goods-Producing** | | | | | | | | | | | | | |
| 2015 | 19.69 | 19.85 | 20.20 | 20.12 | 20.08 | 19.94 | 20.05 | 20.28 | 20.28 | 20.32 | 20.43 | 20.41 | 20.14 |
| 2016 | 20.26 | 20.30 | 20.26 | 20.25 | 20.22 | 19.95 | 20.11 | 19.99 | 20.15 | 20.37 | 20.32 | 20.72 | 20.24 |
| 2017 | 20.62 | 21.00 | 20.82 | 20.87 | 20.75 | 20.72 | 20.75 | 20.80 | 20.79 | 20.55 | 20.91 | 21.03 | 20.80 |
| 2018 | 20.79 | 20.97 | 21.15 | 20.98 | 20.97 | 20.92 | 21.18 | 21.14 | 21.64 | 21.43 | 21.38 | 22.06 | 21.22 |
| 2019 | 21.41 | 21.54 | 21.60 | 22.17 | 22.43 | 22.16 | 23.10 | 22.72 | 23.06 | 23.29 | 23.27 | 23.49 | 22.52 |
| **Construction** | | | | | | | | | | | | | |
| 2015 | 20.33 | 20.58 | 21.12 | 20.94 | 20.96 | 20.70 | 20.76 | 21.12 | 21.20 | 21.88 | 21.40 | 21.28 | 21.03 |
| 2016 | 21.19 | 21.47 | 21.56 | 21.09 | 20.79 | 20.65 | 20.96 | 21.07 | 21.13 | 21.56 | 21.81 | 21.87 | 21.25 |
| 2017 | 21.89 | 22.15 | 22.02 | 21.61 | 21.79 | 21.71 | 21.64 | 22.17 | 22.15 | 21.79 | 22.04 | 22.13 | 21.92 |
| 2018 | 22.29 | 22.33 | 22.56 | 22.20 | 21.98 | 21.93 | 22.14 | 22.18 | 22.71 | 22.75 | 22.20 | 23.64 | 22.41 |
| 2019 | 22.88 | 22.67 | 22.67 | 23.28 | 23.46 | 22.59 | 23.64 | 23.04 | 23.35 | 24.28 | 24.55 | 24.30 | 23.40 |
| **Manufacturing** | | | | | | | | | | | | | |
| 2015 | 19.35 | 19.42 | 19.82 | 19.72 | 19.50 | 19.45 | 19.56 | 19.65 | 19.56 | 19.51 | 19.55 | 19.67 | 19.56 |
| 2016 | 19.54 | 19.43 | 19.47 | 19.59 | 19.67 | 19.38 | 19.38 | 19.12 | 19.37 | 19.52 | 19.34 | 19.97 | 19.48 |
| 2017 | 19.50 | 20.03 | 19.81 | 20.15 | 19.91 | 19.93 | 19.89 | 19.86 | 19.83 | 19.81 | 20.11 | 20.28 | 19.93 |
| 2018 | 19.95 | 20.20 | 20.09 | 20.05 | 20.14 | 20.19 | 20.44 | 20.43 | 20.62 | 20.37 | 20.42 | 20.79 | 20.31 |
| 2019 | 20.49 | 20.76 | 20.83 | 21.37 | 21.66 | 21.81 | 22.77 | 22.54 | 22.81 | 22.57 | 22.56 | 23.00 | 21.92 |
| **Trade, Transportation, and Utilities** | | | | | | | | | | | | | |
| 2015 | 19.54 | 19.77 | 20.12 | 19.55 | 19.50 | 19.44 | 19.54 | 19.73 | 19.51 | 19.59 | 19.76 | 19.47 | 19.63 |
| 2016 | 19.78 | 19.48 | 19.66 | 19.57 | 19.85 | 19.63 | 19.81 | 19.85 | 19.77 | 19.92 | 19.82 | 19.91 | 19.75 |
| 2017 | 19.84 | 19.90 | 19.95 | 19.63 | 19.70 | 19.84 | 19.90 | 19.71 | 20.09 | 20.10 | 20.12 | 20.22 | 19.92 |
| 2018 | 20.96 | 20.61 | 20.81 | 20.91 | 20.95 | 20.74 | 21.11 | 21.10 | 21.71 | 21.39 | 21.55 | 21.87 | 21.15 |
| 2019 | 21.94 | 22.42 | 22.05 | 22.11 | 21.93 | 22.48 | 22.36 | 22.51 | 23.33 | 23.06 | 22.78 | 23.02 | 22.50 |
| **Financial Activities** | | | | | | | | | | | | | |
| 2015 | 23.26 | 23.26 | 22.90 | 23.69 | 23.50 | 22.44 | 22.76 | 22.89 | 22.99 | 22.77 | 23.53 | 23.64 | 23.14 |
| 2016 | 23.38 | 24.03 | 24.03 | 24.41 | 24.76 | 24.88 | 24.80 | 25.34 | 25.92 | 26.68 | 26.16 | 25.32 | 24.99 |
| 2017 | 26.32 | 26.52 | 25.86 | 26.18 | 25.46 | 25.80 | 26.18 | 26.29 | 26.56 | 27.01 | 26.30 | 25.92 | 26.20 |
| 2018 | 26.18 | 26.93 | 26.20 | 26.91 | 26.74 | 26.86 | 27.06 | 27.09 | 27.25 | 26.64 | 26.66 | 27.36 | 26.83 |
| 2019 | 26.32 | 26.69 | 26.32 | 27.31 | 27.09 | 26.19 | 26.35 | 27.05 | 28.43 | 28.56 | 29.36 | 29.37 | 27.42 |
| **Professional and Business Services** | | | | | | | | | | | | | |
| 2015 | 21.60 | 21.06 | 21.30 | 20.82 | 20.93 | 21.15 | 21.06 | 21.32 | 20.83 | 20.99 | 21.18 | 21.02 | 21.10 |
| 2016 | 21.20 | 20.93 | 21.03 | 21.36 | 21.78 | 21.55 | 21.63 | 21.36 | 21.41 | 21.74 | 21.12 | 21.19 | 21.36 |
| 2017 | 21.45 | 21.36 | 21.17 | 21.45 | 21.31 | 21.06 | 21.16 | 21.07 | 21.47 | 21.49 | 21.11 | 21.45 | 21.30 |
| 2018 | 22.02 | 21.79 | 21.46 | 21.59 | 21.22 | 21.05 | 21.76 | 21.53 | 21.48 | 20.95 | 21.31 | 21.51 | 21.47 |
| 2019 | 21.75 | 22.31 | 22.19 | 21.57 | 22.06 | 21.53 | 22.38 | 22.68 | 22.72 | 22.89 | 23.53 | 24.21 | 22.49 |
| **Education and Health Services** | | | | | | | | | | | | | |
| 2015 | 21.09 | 21.12 | 21.09 | 20.66 | 21.01 | 20.85 | 20.91 | 20.91 | 20.78 | 20.81 | 20.75 | 20.72 | 20.89 |
| 2016 | 21.13 | 21.33 | 21.40 | 21.71 | 21.43 | 21.59 | 22.24 | 22.12 | 22.03 | 22.54 | 22.28 | 22.65 | 21.88 |
| 2017 | 22.79 | 22.23 | 22.67 | 23.20 | 22.93 | 22.74 | 23.01 | 22.96 | 23.18 | 22.82 | 22.66 | 22.87 | 22.84 |
| 2018 | 22.71 | 22.39 | 22.51 | 22.42 | 22.01 | 22.13 | 22.29 | 22.16 | 22.34 | 21.84 | 22.15 | 22.55 | 22.29 |
| 2019 | 22.15 | 22.11 | 22.19 | 21.91 | 22.04 | 22.46 | 22.33 | 22.42 | 22.24 | 22.31 | 22.24 | 22.35 | 22.23 |
| **Leisure and Hospitality** | | | | | | | | | | | | | |
| 2015 | 11.14 | 11.23 | 11.40 | 11.22 | 11.27 | 11.12 | 11.11 | 11.38 | 11.50 | 11.42 | 11.62 | 11.71 | 11.34 |
| 2016 | 11.78 | 11.76 | 11.63 | 11.53 | 11.71 | 11.68 | 11.68 | 11.68 | 11.78 | 11.76 | 11.78 | 11.78 | 11.71 |
| 2017 | 11.82 | 12.19 | 12.21 | 12.23 | 12.41 | 12.14 | 12.09 | 12.12 | 12.21 | 12.11 | 12.18 | 12.22 | 12.16 |
| 2018 | 12.19 | 12.31 | 12.21 | 12.29 | 12.32 | 12.22 | 12.22 | 12.24 | 12.38 | 12.52 | 12.74 | 12.88 | 12.38 |
| 2019 | 12.68 | 13.03 | 13.16 | 13.14 | 13.26 | 13.16 | 13.09 | 13.14 | 13.05 | 13.07 | 13.05 | 13.15 | 13.09 |

## 4. Average Weekly Earnings by Selected Industry: Arkansas, 2015–2019

(Dollars, not seasonally adjusted)

| Industry and year | January | February | March | April | May | June | July | August | September | October | November | December | Annual average |
|---|---|---|---|---|---|---|---|---|---|---|---|---|---|
| **Total Private** | | | | | | | | | | | | | |
| 2015 | 671.24 | 674.92 | 676.55 | 670.55 | 666.11 | 661.65 | 667.36 | 684.39 | 667.24 | 674.13 | 686.95 | 676.05 | 673.10 |
| 2016 | 683.71 | 681.95 | 674.65 | 683.36 | 694.77 | 690.62 | 702.33 | 693.45 | 689.43 | 708.88 | 698.92 | 700.65 | 691.78 |
| 2017 | 704.80 | 705.53 | 704.49 | 719.99 | 708.57 | 713.65 | 723.76 | 718.59 | 728.35 | 731.42 | 723.83 | 734.27 | 718.59 |
| 2018 | 723.43 | 728.01 | 734.29 | 740.95 | 722.80 | 731.01 | 742.71 | 737.09 | 763.95 | 743.07 | 743.75 | 768.53 | 738.86 |
| 2019 | 750.98 | 756.59 | 755.16 | 770.88 | 767.80 | 786.17 | 771.03 | 786.02 | 801.71 | 784.57 | 785.91 | 804.49 | 777.35 |
| **Goods-Producing** | | | | | | | | | | | | | |
| 2015 | 807.29 | 803.93 | 805.98 | 814.86 | 803.20 | 805.58 | 804.01 | 835.95 | 803.09 | 835.15 | 831.50 | 818.44 | 813.66 |
| 2016 | 808.37 | 809.97 | 790.14 | 822.15 | 818.91 | 829.92 | 820.49 | 831.58 | 826.15 | 843.32 | 833.12 | 847.45 | 823.77 |
| 2017 | 835.11 | 844.20 | 832.80 | 832.71 | 838.30 | 859.88 | 846.60 | 859.04 | 858.63 | 863.10 | 865.67 | 874.85 | 850.72 |
| 2018 | 837.84 | 853.48 | 875.61 | 874.87 | 870.26 | 872.36 | 872.62 | 883.65 | 913.21 | 900.06 | 876.58 | 904.46 | 878.51 |
| 2019 | 860.68 | 850.83 | 864.00 | 886.80 | 894.96 | 906.34 | 898.59 | 926.98 | 950.07 | 919.96 | 909.86 | 934.90 | 900.80 |
| **Construction** | | | | | | | | | | | | | |
| 2015 | 790.84 | 755.29 | 751.87 | 793.63 | 781.81 | 813.51 | 782.65 | 813.12 | 750.48 | 820.50 | 804.64 | 802.26 | 788.63 |
| 2016 | 794.63 | 802.98 | 735.20 | 809.86 | 796.26 | 832.20 | 819.54 | 849.12 | 843.09 | 827.90 | 828.78 | 842.00 | 816.00 |
| 2017 | 855.90 | 852.78 | 863.18 | 827.66 | 860.71 | 894.45 | 891.57 | 913.40 | 905.94 | 897.75 | 859.56 | 860.86 | 874.61 |
| 2018 | 822.50 | 837.38 | 882.10 | 881.34 | 898.98 | 892.55 | 896.67 | 876.11 | 899.32 | 900.90 | 836.94 | 905.41 | 878.47 |
| 2019 | 837.41 | 816.12 | 834.26 | 910.25 | 907.90 | 912.64 | 907.78 | 956.16 | 990.04 | 963.92 | 925.54 | 969.57 | 912.60 |
| **Manufacturing** | | | | | | | | | | | | | |
| 2015 | 801.09 | 803.99 | 814.60 | 804.58 | 791.70 | 785.78 | 794.14 | 817.44 | 800.00 | 803.81 | 797.64 | 802.54 | 801.96 |
| 2016 | 795.28 | 794.69 | 798.27 | 807.11 | 804.50 | 808.15 | 792.64 | 795.39 | 792.23 | 817.89 | 804.54 | 824.76 | 802.58 |
| 2017 | 791.70 | 811.22 | 792.40 | 812.05 | 806.36 | 827.10 | 803.56 | 818.23 | 818.98 | 832.02 | 848.64 | 861.90 | 819.12 |
| 2018 | 837.90 | 854.46 | 853.83 | 856.14 | 841.85 | 847.98 | 840.08 | 868.28 | 882.54 | 873.87 | 863.77 | 869.02 | 857.08 |
| 2019 | 848.29 | 844.93 | 856.11 | 861.21 | 879.40 | 896.39 | 888.03 | 906.11 | 919.24 | 889.26 | 884.35 | 897.00 | 881.18 |
| **Trade, Transportation, and Utilities** | | | | | | | | | | | | | |
| 2015 | 691.72 | 701.84 | 718.28 | 692.07 | 700.05 | 688.18 | 689.76 | 712.25 | 694.56 | 685.65 | 699.50 | 681.45 | 696.87 |
| 2016 | 682.41 | 681.80 | 680.24 | 673.21 | 696.74 | 689.01 | 693.35 | 688.80 | 678.11 | 691.22 | 671.90 | 684.90 | 683.35 |
| 2017 | 682.50 | 680.58 | 682.29 | 696.87 | 687.53 | 700.35 | 704.46 | 697.73 | 719.22 | 715.56 | 704.20 | 717.81 | 699.19 |
| 2018 | 735.70 | 725.47 | 751.24 | 756.94 | 752.11 | 754.94 | 774.74 | 761.71 | 794.59 | 755.07 | 758.56 | 785.13 | 759.29 |
| 2019 | 770.09 | 773.49 | 771.75 | 784.91 | 765.36 | 800.29 | 778.13 | 783.35 | 814.22 | 795.57 | 779.08 | 808.00 | 785.25 |
| **Financial Activities** | | | | | | | | | | | | | |
| 2015 | 853.64 | 860.62 | 851.88 | 845.73 | 843.65 | 805.60 | 819.36 | 830.91 | 820.74 | 812.89 | 870.61 | 858.13 | 839.98 |
| 2016 | 862.72 | 886.71 | 879.50 | 895.85 | 918.60 | 898.17 | 912.64 | 927.44 | 948.67 | 1,000.50 | 960.07 | 941.90 | 919.63 |
| 2017 | 1,005.42 | 989.20 | 964.58 | 1,007.93 | 959.84 | 957.18 | 1,002.69 | 985.88 | 985.38 | 1,039.89 | 980.99 | 974.59 | 987.74 |
| 2018 | 989.60 | 1,017.95 | 985.12 | 1,014.51 | 986.71 | 993.82 | 1,022.87 | 1,021.29 | 1,030.05 | 1,001.66 | 1,007.75 | 1,045.15 | 1,008.81 |
| 2019 | 1,000.16 | 1,003.54 | 987.00 | 1,018.66 | 996.91 | 982.13 | 967.05 | 979.21 | 1,060.44 | 1,053.86 | 1,092.19 | 1,113.12 | 1,020.02 |
| **Professional and Business Services** | | | | | | | | | | | | | |
| 2015 | 753.84 | 753.95 | 760.41 | 753.68 | 747.20 | 757.17 | 760.27 | 769.65 | 756.13 | 757.74 | 777.31 | 752.52 | 757.49 |
| 2016 | 744.12 | 736.74 | 727.64 | 747.60 | 777.55 | 758.56 | 770.03 | 743.33 | 732.22 | 752.20 | 730.75 | 735.29 | 745.46 |
| 2017 | 735.74 | 732.65 | 732.48 | 757.19 | 737.33 | 730.78 | 746.95 | 731.13 | 751.45 | 752.15 | 730.41 | 757.19 | 741.24 |
| 2018 | 750.88 | 760.47 | 755.39 | 770.76 | 751.19 | 749.38 | 774.66 | 751.40 | 766.84 | 726.97 | 752.24 | 770.06 | 755.74 |
| 2019 | 772.13 | 778.62 | 798.84 | 791.62 | 807.40 | 796.61 | 812.39 | 834.62 | 836.10 | 826.33 | 840.02 | 888.51 | 816.39 |
| **Education and Health Services** | | | | | | | | | | | | | |
| 2015 | 698.08 | 707.52 | 695.97 | 690.04 | 699.63 | 694.31 | 698.39 | 702.58 | 694.05 | 695.05 | 711.73 | 702.41 | 699.82 |
| 2016 | 714.19 | 714.56 | 708.34 | 720.77 | 728.62 | 731.90 | 760.61 | 745.44 | 753.43 | 775.38 | 777.57 | 792.75 | 743.92 |
| 2017 | 793.09 | 773.60 | 773.05 | 795.76 | 775.03 | 768.61 | 782.34 | 773.75 | 776.53 | 769.03 | 759.11 | 759.28 | 774.28 |
| 2018 | 738.08 | 729.91 | 727.07 | 735.38 | 708.72 | 732.50 | 724.43 | 715.77 | 732.75 | 714.17 | 717.66 | 737.39 | 726.65 |
| 2019 | 711.02 | 714.15 | 707.86 | 716.46 | 722.91 | 736.69 | 714.56 | 733.13 | 736.14 | 734.00 | 731.70 | 748.73 | 724.70 |
| **Leisure and Hospitality** | | | | | | | | | | | | | |
| 2015 | 285.18 | 286.37 | 291.84 | 283.87 | 288.51 | 285.78 | 289.97 | 295.88 | 290.05 | 290.32 | 292.82 | 296.26 | 289.17 |
| 2016 | 289.79 | 297.53 | 294.24 | 288.25 | 291.58 | 290.83 | 294.34 | 289.66 | 290.97 | 297.53 | 295.43 | 289.79 | 292.75 |
| 2017 | 296.68 | 298.66 | 307.69 | 300.86 | 313.97 | 308.36 | 305.88 | 301.79 | 305.25 | 311.48 | 306.94 | 310.39 | 305.22 |
| 2018 | 302.31 | 308.98 | 312.58 | 315.85 | 312.93 | 318.94 | 318.94 | 317.02 | 329.31 | 324.27 | 327.42 | 337.46 | 319.40 |
| 2019 | 324.61 | 342.69 | 350.06 | 346.90 | 347.41 | 360.58 | 349.77 | 346.90 | 349.74 | 335.90 | 338.00 | 348.48 | 345.58 |

# CALIFORNIA
*At a Glance*

Population:
  2010 census: 37,253,956
  2019 estimate: 39,512,223

Percent change in population:
  2010–2019: 6.1%

Percent change in total nonfarm employment:
  2011–2019: 20.7%

Industry with the largest growth in employment, 2011–2019 (percent):
  Construction, 57.2%

Industry with the largest decline or smallest growth in employment, 2011–2019 (percent):
  Mining and logging, -15.7%

Civilian labor force:
  2010: 18,336,271
  2019: 19,411,572

Unemployment rate and rank among states (highest to lowest):
  2010: 12.2%, 3rd
  2019: 4.0%, 13th

Over-the-year change in unemployment rates:
  2017–2018: -0.5%
  2018–2019: -0.3%

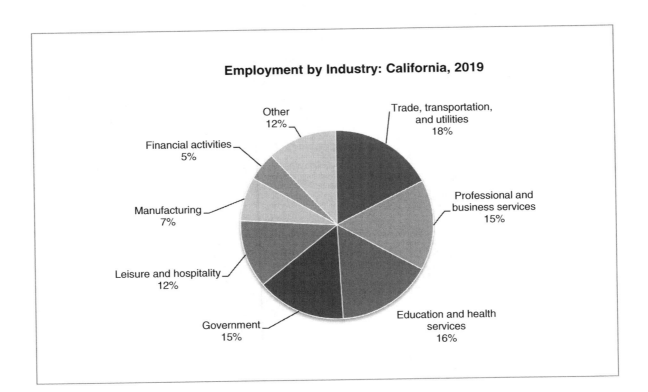

**Employment by Industry: California, 2019**

Other 12%

Financial activities 5%

Manufacturing 7%

Leisure and hospitality 12%

Government 15%

Trade, transportation, and utilities 18%

Professional and business services 15%

Education and health services 16%

## 1. Employment by Industry: California, 2011–2019

(Numbers in thousands, not seasonally adjusted)

| Industry and year | January | February | March | April | May | June | July | August | September | October | November | December | Annual average |
|---|---|---|---|---|---|---|---|---|---|---|---|---|---|
| **Total Nonfarm** | | | | | | | | | | | | | |
| 2011 | 14,197.7 | 14,280.3 | 14,339.6 | 14,405.2 | 14,452.1 | 14,471.0 | 14,324.0 | 14,370.6 | 14,467.3 | 14,574.8 | 14,655.2 | 14,677.7 | 14,434.6 |
| 2012 | 14,435.0 | 14,532.0 | 14,626.3 | 14,664.3 | 14,763.1 | 14,830.1 | 14,657.9 | 14,737.6 | 14,803.1 | 14,945.7 | 15,061.6 | 15,084.0 | 14,761.7 |
| 2013 | 14,796.1 | 14,921.8 | 14,999.8 | 15,065.0 | 15,148.2 | 15,178.7 | 15,032.4 | 15,145.8 | 15,200.6 | 15,344.3 | 15,482.3 | 15,498.1 | 15,151.1 |
| 2014 | 15,229.7 | 15,326.9 | 15,410.8 | 15,477.3 | 15,564.1 | 15,595.2 | 15,435.9 | 15,573.6 | 15,645.4 | 15,800.0 | 15,914.5 | 15,938.7 | 15,576.0 |
| 2015 | 15,661.7 | 15,757.4 | 15,845.8 | 15,919.0 | 16,000.0 | 16,038.6 | 15,980.5 | 16,077.4 | 16,142.5 | 16,330.6 | 16,424.5 | 16,447.9 | 16,052.2 |
| 2016 | 16,150.2 | 16,261.6 | 16,283.8 | 16,431.0 | 16,481.3 | 16,468.7 | 16,394.0 | 16,469.5 | 16,552.6 | 16,694.2 | 16,786.8 | 16,793.0 | 16,480.6 |
| 2017 | 16,462.4 | 16,581.8 | 16,671.5 | 16,728.1 | 16,823.5 | 16,873.4 | 16,721.6 | 16,804.0 | 16,889.3 | 17,042.3 | 17,151.1 | 17,175.7 | 16,827.1 |
| 2018 | 16,867.4 | 16,996.3 | 17,047.5 | 17,087.0 | 17,146.7 | 17,201.9 | 17,040.4 | 17,149.2 | 17,199.3 | 17,371.6 | 17,474.7 | 17,489.3 | 17,172.6 |
| 2019 | 17,143.5 | 17,250.5 | 17,309.2 | 17,352.1 | 17,415.3 | 17,453.9 | 17,310.9 | 17,423.9 | 17,438.7 | 17,593.6 | 17,697.6 | 17,711.8 | 17,425.1 |
| **Total Private** | | | | | | | | | | | | | |
| 2011 | 11,773.4 | 11,834.7 | 11,870.4 | 11,935.6 | 11,982.3 | 12,013.5 | 12,045.7 | 12,098.0 | 12,130.9 | 12,166.9 | 12,229.2 | 12,276.1 | 12,029.7 |
| 2012 | 12,052.6 | 12,123.7 | 12,198.2 | 12,238.6 | 12,329.5 | 12,404.3 | 12,406.2 | 12,480.2 | 12,485.6 | 12,559.9 | 12,654.9 | 12,691.9 | 12,385.5 |
| 2013 | 12,432.8 | 12,530.4 | 12,587.1 | 12,652.7 | 12,725.3 | 12,765.3 | 12,793.5 | 12,874.0 | 12,864.9 | 12,945.1 | 13,058.5 | 13,091.9 | 12,776.8 |
| 2014 | 12,836.8 | 12,911.9 | 12,970.9 | 13,025.8 | 13,101.5 | 13,143.7 | 13,156.7 | 13,264.5 | 13,264.4 | 13,349.2 | 13,440.6 | 13,478.4 | 13,162.0 |
| 2015 | 13,215.5 | 13,291.4 | 13,360.2 | 13,422.8 | 13,497.4 | 13,541.6 | 13,650.0 | 13,716.6 | 13,706.9 | 13,828.3 | 13,903.0 | 13,936.7 | 13,589.2 |
| 2016 | 13,659.4 | 13,748.6 | 13,743.0 | 13,883.7 | 13,921.1 | 13,923.9 | 14,012.3 | 14,056.3 | 14,059.3 | 14,137.1 | 14,209.6 | 14,223.8 | 13,964.8 |
| 2017 | 13,918.9 | 14,016.5 | 14,085.4 | 14,138.7 | 14,220.2 | 14,279.4 | 14,309.5 | 14,369.8 | 14,366.1 | 14,452.3 | 14,541.8 | 14,575.5 | 14,272.8 |
| 2018 | 14,293.4 | 14,401.6 | 14,432.8 | 14,465.5 | 14,516.0 | 14,575.7 | 14,611.1 | 14,683.4 | 14,650.6 | 14,759.8 | 14,840.6 | 14,861.8 | 14,591.0 |
| 2019 | 14,548.9 | 14,635.8 | 14,672.7 | 14,706.6 | 14,761.9 | 14,810.1 | 14,854.6 | 14,923.1 | 14,866.7 | 14,945.6 | 15,026.8 | 15,052.8 | 14,817.1 |
| **Goods Producing** | | | | | | | | | | | | | |
| 2011 | 1,790.7 | 1,797.3 | 1,800.3 | 1,817.5 | 1,833.5 | 1,849.7 | 1,871.9 | 1,886.5 | 1,884.9 | 1,872.4 | 1,855.8 | 1,844.8 | 1,842.1 |
| 2012 | 1,824.0 | 1,827.8 | 1,836.4 | 1,837.4 | 1,864.8 | 1,891.7 | 1,907.9 | 1,923.9 | 1,920.9 | 1,912.5 | 1,900.9 | 1,890.9 | 1,878.3 |
| 2013 | 1,866.1 | 1,880.6 | 1,888.5 | 1,894.6 | 1,910.5 | 1,932.2 | 1,954.0 | 1,973.6 | 1,968.0 | 1,963.6 | 1,956.6 | 1,946.7 | 1,927.9 |
| 2014 | 1,920.5 | 1,935.2 | 1,944.3 | 1,948.5 | 1,967.4 | 1,987.1 | 2,006.9 | 2,030.8 | 2,029.1 | 2,020.6 | 2,011.3 | 1,998.6 | 1,983.4 |
| 2015 | 1,986.8 | 1,998.0 | 2,011.8 | 2,022.7 | 2,042.4 | 2,065.5 | 2,097.2 | 2,115.5 | 2,108.0 | 2,105.5 | 2,092.8 | 2,084.8 | 2,060.9 |
| 2016 | 2,054.5 | 2,069.6 | 2,064.6 | 2,087.5 | 2,097.9 | 2,112.0 | 2,142.7 | 2,150.0 | 2,143.6 | 2,132.6 | 2,119.8 | 2,109.7 | 2,107.0 |
| 2017 | 2,064.5 | 2,081.8 | 2,100.5 | 2,111.6 | 2,132.3 | 2,157.8 | 2,176.8 | 2,190.6 | 2,187.1 | 2,181.8 | 2,171.6 | 2,170.6 | 2,143.9 |
| 2018 | 2,138.7 | 2,168.0 | 2,165.0 | 2,178.1 | 2,192.9 | 2,215.0 | 2,236.4 | 2,248.1 | 2,243.7 | 2,240.9 | 2,225.4 | 2,215.5 | 2,205.6 |
| 2019 | 2,175.1 | 2,187.2 | 2,201.9 | 2,210.4 | 2,225.2 | 2,245.5 | 2,257.9 | 2,270.5 | 2,260.2 | 2,248.0 | 2,232.9 | 2,217.2 | 2,227.7 |
| **Service-Providing** | | | | | | | | | | | | | |
| 2011 | 12,407.0 | 12,483.0 | 12,539.3 | 12,587.7 | 12,618.6 | 12,621.3 | 12,452.1 | 12,484.1 | 12,582.4 | 12,702.4 | 12,799.4 | 12,832.9 | 12,592.5 |
| 2012 | 12,611.0 | 12,704.2 | 12,789.9 | 12,826.9 | 12,898.3 | 12,938.4 | 12,750.0 | 12,813.7 | 12,882.2 | 13,033.2 | 13,160.7 | 13,193.1 | 12,883.5 |
| 2013 | 12,930.0 | 13,041.2 | 13,111.3 | 13,170.4 | 13,237.7 | 13,246.5 | 13,078.4 | 13,172.2 | 13,232.6 | 13,380.7 | 13,525.7 | 13,551.4 | 13,223.2 |
| 2014 | 13,309.2 | 13,391.7 | 13,466.5 | 13,528.8 | 13,596.7 | 13,608.1 | 13,429.0 | 13,542.8 | 13,616.3 | 13,779.4 | 13,903.2 | 13,940.1 | 13,592.7 |
| 2015 | 13,674.9 | 13,759.4 | 13,834.0 | 13,896.3 | 13,957.6 | 13,973.1 | 13,883.3 | 13,961.9 | 14,034.5 | 14,225.1 | 14,331.7 | 14,363.1 | 13,991.2 |
| 2016 | 14,095.7 | 14,192.0 | 14,219.2 | 14,343.5 | 14,383.4 | 14,356.7 | 14,251.3 | 14,319.5 | 14,409.0 | 14,561.6 | 14,667.0 | 14,683.3 | 14,373.5 |
| 2017 | 14,397.9 | 14,500.0 | 14,571.0 | 14,616.5 | 14,691.2 | 14,715.6 | 14,544.8 | 14,613.4 | 14,702.2 | 14,860.5 | 14,979.5 | 15,005.1 | 14,683.1 |
| 2018 | 14,728.7 | 14,828.3 | 14,882.5 | 14,908.9 | 14,953.8 | 14,986.9 | 14,804.0 | 14,901.1 | 14,955.6 | 15,130.7 | 15,249.3 | 15,273.8 | 14,967.0 |
| 2019 | 14,968.4 | 15,063.3 | 15,107.3 | 15,141.7 | 15,190.1 | 15,208.4 | 15,053.0 | 15,153.4 | 15,178.5 | 15,345.6 | 15,464.7 | 15,494.6 | 15,197.4 |
| **Mining and Logging** | | | | | | | | | | | | | |
| 2011 | 24.7 | 24.9 | 24.8 | 25.5 | 26.2 | 26.8 | 27.8 | 28.1 | 28.1 | 28.2 | 28.0 | 27.6 | 26.7 |
| 2012 | 27.3 | 26.9 | 26.9 | 27.0 | 28.1 | 28.9 | 29.6 | 29.8 | 29.3 | 29.2 | 28.9 | 28.2 | 28.3 |
| 2013 | 27.4 | 27.5 | 27.3 | 27.8 | 28.6 | 29.0 | 29.1 | 29.0 | 28.8 | 28.8 | 28.5 | 28.0 | 28.3 |
| 2014 | 27.9 | 27.9 | 27.8 | 28.4 | 29.2 | 29.6 | 30.2 | 30.3 | 30.4 | 30.2 | 30.0 | 29.3 | 29.3 |
| 2015 | 27.8 | 27.1 | 26.8 | 27.0 | 26.8 | 26.9 | 26.9 | 26.6 | 26.2 | 25.7 | 25.0 | 24.3 | 26.4 |
| 2016 | 23.5 | 22.8 | 22.2 | 21.9 | 22.3 | 22.7 | 22.6 | 22.2 | 22.0 | 22.0 | 21.7 | 21.3 | 22.3 |
| 2017 | 20.8 | 20.6 | 20.5 | 21.1 | 21.9 | 22.4 | 22.6 | 22.7 | 22.6 | 22.6 | 22.3 | 22.2 | 21.9 |
| 2018 | 21.7 | 21.7 | 21.6 | 21.7 | 22.3 | 22.6 | 23.0 | 23.1 | 23.1 | 23.1 | 22.8 | 22.4 | 22.4 |
| 2019 | 21.8 | 21.8 | 21.7 | 21.9 | 22.6 | 22.8 | 23.2 | 23.1 | 23.0 | 23.0 | 22.7 | 22.4 | 22.5 |
| **Construction** | | | | | | | | | | | | | |
| 2011 | 532.8 | 535.1 | 534.4 | 545.9 | 554.4 | 562.9 | 578.8 | 584.9 | 584.2 | 580.8 | 575.7 | 567.5 | 561.5 |
| 2012 | 556.4 | 556.3 | 559.3 | 561.1 | 579.1 | 595.4 | 605.9 | 612.3 | 613.4 | 617.1 | 615.7 | 610.0 | 590.2 |
| 2013 | 598.0 | 606.9 | 613.0 | 618.1 | 628.4 | 640.1 | 652.8 | 661.9 | 658.5 | 662.3 | 660.5 | 652.2 | 637.7 |
| 2014 | 638.3 | 645.6 | 651.8 | 656.1 | 667.7 | 676.3 | 686.2 | 697.7 | 697.2 | 697.4 | 696.3 | 682.7 | 674.4 |
| 2015 | 681.6 | 688.0 | 698.6 | 707.4 | 720.1 | 732.3 | 749.8 | 760.2 | 756.1 | 767.5 | 765.7 | 757.8 | 732.1 |
| 2016 | 737.7 | 748.4 | 744.5 | 764.2 | 770.1 | 777.5 | 794.4 | 799.4 | 797.6 | 799.6 | 792.4 | 782.5 | 775.7 |
| 2017 | 746.8 | 761.5 | 780.7 | 793.2 | 806.3 | 821.0 | 830.9 | 837.2 | 837.9 | 839.8 | 835.9 | 832.7 | 810.3 |
| 2018 | 814.7 | 836.7 | 829.7 | 845.3 | 854.6 | 867.4 | 876.3 | 883.8 | 881.6 | 885.6 | 877.2 | 869.0 | 860.2 |
| 2019 | 842.8 | 847.7 | 860.8 | 870.9 | 882.2 | 895.5 | 904.5 | 910.6 | 905.2 | 901.5 | 892.7 | 877.3 | 882.6 |

## 1. Employment by Industry: California, 2011–2019—*Continued*

(Numbers in thousands, not seasonally adjusted)

| Industry and year | January | February | March | April | May | June | July | August | September | October | November | December | Annual average |
|---|---|---|---|---|---|---|---|---|---|---|---|---|---|
| **Manufacturing** | | | | | | | | | | | | | |
| 2011 | 1,233.3 | 1,237.3 | 1,241.1 | 1,246.1 | 1,252.9 | 1,260.1 | 1,265.4 | 1,273.6 | 1,272.6 | 1,263.5 | 1,252.1 | 1,249.7 | 1,254.0 |
| 2012 | 1,240.4 | 1,244.7 | 1,250.2 | 1,249.2 | 1,257.5 | 1,267.4 | 1,272.5 | 1,281.9 | 1,278.1 | 1,266.1 | 1,256.3 | 1,252.8 | 1,259.8 |
| 2013 | 1,240.8 | 1,246.3 | 1,248.2 | 1,248.7 | 1,253.5 | 1,263.2 | 1,272.2 | 1,282.6 | 1,280.7 | 1,272.5 | 1,267.7 | 1,266.6 | 1,261.9 |
| 2014 | 1,254.4 | 1,261.6 | 1,264.6 | 1,264.1 | 1,270.5 | 1,281.2 | 1,290.6 | 1,302.8 | 1,301.6 | 1,292.9 | 1,285.0 | 1,286.6 | 1,279.7 |
| 2015 | 1,277.4 | 1,282.9 | 1,286.3 | 1,288.3 | 1,295.5 | 1,306.4 | 1,320.5 | 1,328.8 | 1,325.6 | 1,312.4 | 1,302.1 | 1,302.7 | 1,302.4 |
| 2016 | 1,293.3 | 1,298.4 | 1,297.9 | 1,301.3 | 1,305.5 | 1,311.9 | 1,325.6 | 1,328.4 | 1,324.0 | 1,311.0 | 1,305.7 | 1,305.8 | 1,309.1 |
| 2017 | 1,296.9 | 1,299.8 | 1,299.3 | 1,297.2 | 1,304.1 | 1,314.4 | 1,323.2 | 1,330.7 | 1,326.5 | 1,319.4 | 1,313.3 | 1,315.6 | 1,311.7 |
| 2018 | 1,302.3 | 1,309.6 | 1,313.8 | 1,311.1 | 1,316.0 | 1,325.0 | 1,337.1 | 1,341.2 | 1,339.0 | 1,332.2 | 1,325.4 | 1,324.1 | 1,323.1 |
| 2019 | 1,310.5 | 1,317.7 | 1,319.4 | 1,317.6 | 1,320.4 | 1,327.2 | 1,330.2 | 1,336.8 | 1,332.0 | 1,323.5 | 1,317.5 | 1,317.5 | 1,322.5 |
| **Trade, Transportation, and Utilities** | | | | | | | | | | | | | |
| 2011 | 2,626.3 | 2,610.2 | 2,609.3 | 2,625.2 | 2,637.3 | 2,643.7 | 2,652.6 | 2,665.4 | 2,666.2 | 2,684.8 | 2,749.5 | 2,777.2 | 2,662.3 |
| 2012 | 2,686.2 | 2,655.3 | 2,658.6 | 2,665.2 | 2,683.8 | 2,696.0 | 2,702.9 | 2,713.2 | 2,715.6 | 2,734.5 | 2,818.5 | 2,838.0 | 2,714.0 |
| 2013 | 2,731.0 | 2,715.3 | 2,712.9 | 2,717.5 | 2,736.5 | 2,748.5 | 2,758.7 | 2,771.2 | 2,764.6 | 2,789.4 | 2,875.4 | 2,906.0 | 2,768.9 |
| 2014 | 2,797.2 | 2,778.5 | 2,777.7 | 2,785.7 | 2,800.7 | 2,812.5 | 2,818.9 | 2,838.8 | 2,837.5 | 2,860.0 | 2,940.5 | 2,974.9 | 2,835.2 |
| 2015 | 2,867.6 | 2,846.4 | 2,851.3 | 2,855.0 | 2,872.8 | 2,878.1 | 2,904.4 | 2,920.0 | 2,917.9 | 2,943.6 | 3,013.1 | 3,034.8 | 2,908.8 |
| 2016 | 2,929.0 | 2,913.6 | 2,911.2 | 2,927.9 | 2,935.6 | 2,929.7 | 2,957.6 | 2,971.9 | 2,965.7 | 2,995.8 | 3,070.7 | 3,094.2 | 2,966.9 |
| 2017 | 2,995.2 | 2,961.1 | 2,963.0 | 2,973.3 | 2,983.8 | 2,988.9 | 3,000.7 | 3,015.9 | 3,012.3 | 3,039.8 | 3,123.8 | 3,145.8 | 3,017.0 |
| 2018 | 3,036.3 | 3,010.3 | 3,008.3 | 3,003.5 | 3,014.9 | 3,019.4 | 3,035.4 | 3,044.6 | 3,039.3 | 3,061.6 | 3,142.5 | 3,158.4 | 3,047.9 |
| 2019 | 3,051.7 | 3,014.5 | 3,007.8 | 3,005.5 | 3,017.7 | 3,021.5 | 3,041.6 | 3,053.1 | 3,039.2 | 3,063.4 | 3,141.1 | 3,165.9 | 3,051.9 |
| **Wholesale Trade** | | | | | | | | | | | | | |
| 2011 | 631.1 | 633.8 | 634.2 | 640.8 | 642.5 | 643.2 | 645.4 | 647.3 | 647.0 | 646.8 | 646.6 | 647.4 | 642.2 |
| 2012 | 641.9 | 644.9 | 647.5 | 650.4 | 655.3 | 657.9 | 659.5 | 662.5 | 661.6 | 664.5 | 665.4 | 665.8 | 656.4 |
| 2013 | 659.3 | 662.4 | 664.3 | 667.1 | 670.8 | 673.3 | 674.5 | 675.7 | 674.4 | 675.1 | 678.2 | 680.5 | 671.3 |
| 2014 | 675.2 | 679.4 | 680.8 | 680.0 | 682.5 | 683.9 | 683.7 | 685.8 | 685.0 | 685.6 | 688.3 | 689.9 | 683.3 |
| 2015 | 681.2 | 684.6 | 684.5 | 686.8 | 689.9 | 690.4 | 694.8 | 696.0 | 694.7 | 695.5 | 696.3 | 697.3 | 691.0 |
| 2016 | 689.1 | 691.7 | 689.5 | 692.6 | 693.3 | 691.7 | 697.4 | 697.5 | 695.1 | 693.8 | 693.2 | 694.6 | 693.3 |
| 2017 | 688.0 | 690.2 | 690.3 | 694.1 | 696.7 | 698.5 | 699.1 | 698.6 | 696.5 | 698.6 | 699.8 | 701.6 | 696.0 |
| 2018 | 693.6 | 696.6 | 695.8 | 696.8 | 700.0 | 699.9 | 701.1 | 701.1 | 697.4 | 701.0 | 701.5 | 702.1 | 698.9 |
| 2019 | 692.0 | 695.0 | 693.8 | 694.0 | 696.5 | 696.0 | 696.7 | 695.5 | 691.3 | 694.4 | 691.5 | 692.6 | 694.1 |
| **Retail Trade** | | | | | | | | | | | | | |
| 2011 | 1,530.9 | 1,512.0 | 1,509.6 | 1,514.0 | 1,520.6 | 1,525.6 | 1,532.2 | 1,539.3 | 1,539.3 | 1,556.7 | 1,620.9 | 1,643.7 | 1,545.4 |
| 2012 | 1,569.8 | 1,537.1 | 1,535.5 | 1,535.9 | 1,545.1 | 1,548.5 | 1,552.5 | 1,557.6 | 1,557.7 | 1,573.9 | 1,655.0 | 1,667.0 | 1,569.6 |
| 2013 | 1,579.2 | 1,558.3 | 1,554.9 | 1,556.3 | 1,567.1 | 1,574.8 | 1,579.9 | 1,587.2 | 1,581.5 | 1,603.2 | 1,680.9 | 1,703.7 | 1,593.9 |
| 2014 | 1,614.4 | 1,590.5 | 1,590.1 | 1,594.8 | 1,599.7 | 1,607.0 | 1,612.1 | 1,623.4 | 1,618.0 | 1,636.0 | 1,708.0 | 1,731.4 | 1,627.1 |
| 2015 | 1,647.4 | 1,626.1 | 1,625.2 | 1,626.4 | 1,636.1 | 1,637.2 | 1,650.1 | 1,657.9 | 1,655.0 | 1,674.8 | 1,735.4 | 1,749.6 | 1,660.1 |
| 2016 | 1,669.6 | 1,652.9 | 1,648.6 | 1,654.8 | 1,657.8 | 1,653.4 | 1,666.5 | 1,674.1 | 1,667.2 | 1,689.7 | 1,750.4 | 1,761.5 | 1,678.9 |
| 2017 | 1,693.0 | 1,664.6 | 1,660.3 | 1,666.5 | 1,667.9 | 1,667.9 | 1,673.7 | 1,680.6 | 1,675.4 | 1,692.2 | 1,757.2 | 1,766.9 | 1,688.9 |
| 2018 | 1,695.0 | 1,670.5 | 1,665.8 | 1,659.8 | 1,664.2 | 1,661.8 | 1,672.4 | 1,676.3 | 1,669.2 | 1,680.8 | 1,743.5 | 1,752.8 | 1,684.3 |
| 2019 | 1,672.5 | 1,645.5 | 1,638.1 | 1,633.7 | 1,636.3 | 1,634.2 | 1,643.7 | 1,648.1 | 1,636.7 | 1,652.8 | 1,717.2 | 1,732.2 | 1,657.6 |
| **Transportation and Utilities** | | | | | | | | | | | | | |
| 2011 | 464.3 | 464.4 | 465.5 | 470.4 | 474.2 | 474.9 | 475.0 | 478.8 | 479.9 | 481.3 | 482.0 | 486.1 | 474.7 |
| 2012 | 474.5 | 473.3 | 475.6 | 478.9 | 483.4 | 489.6 | 490.9 | 493.1 | 496.3 | 496.1 | 498.1 | 505.2 | 487.9 |
| 2013 | 492.5 | 494.6 | 493.7 | 494.1 | 498.6 | 500.4 | 504.3 | 508.3 | 508.7 | 511.1 | 516.3 | 521.8 | 503.7 |
| 2014 | 507.6 | 508.6 | 506.8 | 510.9 | 518.5 | 521.6 | 523.1 | 529.6 | 534.5 | 538.4 | 544.2 | 553.6 | 524.8 |
| 2015 | 539.0 | 535.7 | 541.6 | 541.8 | 546.8 | 550.5 | 559.5 | 566.1 | 568.2 | 573.3 | 581.4 | 587.9 | 557.7 |
| 2016 | 570.3 | 569.0 | 573.1 | 580.5 | 584.5 | 584.6 | 593.7 | 600.3 | 603.4 | 612.3 | 627.1 | 638.1 | 594.7 |
| 2017 | 614.2 | 606.3 | 612.4 | 612.7 | 619.2 | 622.5 | 627.9 | 636.7 | 640.4 | 649.0 | 666.8 | 677.3 | 632.1 |
| 2018 | 647.7 | 643.2 | 646.7 | 646.9 | 650.7 | 657.7 | 661.9 | 667.0 | 672.7 | 679.8 | 697.5 | 703.5 | 664.6 |
| 2019 | 687.2 | 674.0 | 675.9 | 677.8 | 684.9 | 691.3 | 701.2 | 709.5 | 711.2 | 716.2 | 732.4 | 741.1 | 700.2 |
| **Information** | | | | | | | | | | | | | |
| 2011 | 430.9 | 431.2 | 432.7 | 428.2 | 427.8 | 430.0 | 431.6 | 433.5 | 429.8 | 431.6 | 429.6 | 433.8 | 430.9 |
| 2012 | 426.9 | 428.0 | 430.7 | 433.4 | 432.3 | 432.6 | 437.7 | 440.0 | 435.6 | 440.6 | 447.0 | 451.1 | 436.3 |
| 2013 | 440.1 | 442.9 | 444.9 | 445.6 | 445.6 | 450.2 | 448.3 | 451.9 | 451.7 | 455.4 | 462.2 | 461.6 | 450.0 |
| 2014 | 454.7 | 454.6 | 457.7 | 461.4 | 459.0 | 461.2 | 463.0 | 469.1 | 468.0 | 472.1 | 472.1 | 474.3 | 463.9 |
| 2015 | 467.3 | 476.5 | 480.2 | 480.5 | 480.9 | 489.0 | 489.6 | 493.2 | 494.0 | 501.7 | 505.1 | 505.3 | 488.6 |
| 2016 | 510.5 | 519.0 | 517.9 | 527.8 | 532.4 | 528.6 | 528.2 | 531.5 | 528.5 | 525.0 | 534.3 | 533.0 | 526.4 |
| 2017 | 515.8 | 537.5 | 520.8 | 519.5 | 520.1 | 524.2 | 527.5 | 530.4 | 533.7 | 536.7 | 538.8 | 546.9 | 529.3 |
| 2018 | 535.6 | 546.1 | 544.3 | 530.6 | 529.4 | 541.2 | 538.7 | 547.9 | 547.5 | 548.1 | 551.7 | 556.9 | 543.2 |
| 2019 | 553.5 | 569.6 | 563.3 | 546.0 | 546.5 | 555.6 | 554.7 | 564.4 | 569.4 | 569.6 | 582.5 | 575.9 | 562.6 |

## 1. Employment by Industry: California, 2011–2019—*Continued*

(Numbers in thousands, not seasonally adjusted)

| Industry and year | January | February | March | April | May | June | July | August | September | October | November | December | Annual average |
|---|---|---|---|---|---|---|---|---|---|---|---|---|---|
| **Financial Activities** | | | | | | | | | | | | | |
| 2011 | 758.8 | 760.5 | 761.4 | 759.2 | 760.2 | 763.1 | 763.3 | 763.7 | 762.2 | 763.6 | 763.7 | 767.9 | 762.3 |
| 2012 | 761.6 | 765.4 | 769.2 | 767.6 | 770.8 | 774.7 | 777.3 | 778.2 | 775.6 | 779.6 | 780.3 | 784.2 | 773.7 |
| 2013 | 775.3 | 778.6 | 779.3 | 781.5 | 784.2 | 785.7 | 787.8 | 787.3 | 781.8 | 785.1 | 784.6 | 785.1 | 783.0 |
| 2014 | 775.5 | 776.4 | 776.3 | 777.9 | 781.5 | 784.5 | 785.6 | 786.3 | 782.5 | 786.3 | 788.8 | 791.5 | 782.8 |
| 2015 | 784.7 | 787.8 | 788.5 | 794.0 | 798.7 | 801.5 | 810.7 | 811.1 | 806.8 | 814.7 | 815.1 | 817.1 | 802.6 |
| 2016 | 810.5 | 813.1 | 812.7 | 820.3 | 822.0 | 822.1 | 830.5 | 830.5 | 826.3 | 829.0 | 830.2 | 831.9 | 823.3 |
| 2017 | 823.4 | 825.2 | 825.2 | 828.4 | 832.1 | 833.4 | 837.7 | 836.6 | 832.4 | 838.4 | 837.8 | 841.3 | 832.7 |
| 2018 | 833.1 | 836.1 | 834.5 | 836.0 | 837.6 | 839.2 | 842.4 | 841.5 | 833.6 | 840.9 | 839.3 | 840.8 | 837.9 |
| 2019 | 830.0 | 833.5 | 832.2 | 835.0 | 837.5 | 840.6 | 847.1 | 847.7 | 841.0 | 849.5 | 849.6 | 850.5 | 841.2 |
| **Professional and Business Services** | | | | | | | | | | | | | |
| 2011 | 2,077.2 | 2,100.6 | 2,107.4 | 2,115.6 | 2,117.6 | 2,127.3 | 2,147.1 | 2,160.3 | 2,171.8 | 2,187.0 | 2,193.9 | 2,199.8 | 2,142.1 |
| 2012 | 2,165.0 | 2,197.5 | 2,212.6 | 2,218.0 | 2,227.3 | 2,249.4 | 2,250.9 | 2,270.7 | 2,272.4 | 2,302.7 | 2,314.1 | 2,315.7 | 2,249.7 |
| 2013 | 2,266.7 | 2,297.8 | 2,309.4 | 2,323.3 | 2,328.0 | 2,335.3 | 2,353.8 | 2,376.9 | 2,375.2 | 2,393.4 | 2,406.3 | 2,405.3 | 2,347.6 |
| 2014 | 2,358.9 | 2,378.8 | 2,391.2 | 2,399.7 | 2,408.6 | 2,415.2 | 2,419.5 | 2,444.1 | 2,443.0 | 2,477.8 | 2,491.4 | 2,495.7 | 2,427.0 |
| 2015 | 2,425.2 | 2,439.2 | 2,452.9 | 2,456.4 | 2,456.4 | 2,467.1 | 2,498.3 | 2,513.5 | 2,505.3 | 2,547.4 | 2,561.4 | 2,567.0 | 2,490.8 |
| 2016 | 2,496.1 | 2,512.6 | 2,497.4 | 2,518.3 | 2,510.7 | 2,516.7 | 2,538.4 | 2,547.9 | 2,553.0 | 2,562.6 | 2,566.0 | 2,561.1 | 2,531.7 |
| 2017 | 2,507.0 | 2,531.2 | 2,547.8 | 2,546.1 | 2,559.3 | 2,577.5 | 2,597.0 | 2,609.2 | 2,606.4 | 2,625.9 | 2,640.7 | 2,640.1 | 2,582.4 |
| 2018 | 2,593.1 | 2,618.7 | 2,628.0 | 2,640.4 | 2,643.2 | 2,657.0 | 2,675.2 | 2,693.7 | 2,689.2 | 2,722.7 | 2,735.8 | 2,736.3 | 2,669.4 |
| 2019 | 2,663.7 | 2,684.9 | 2,689.1 | 2,702.6 | 2,702.6 | 2,717.2 | 2,731.4 | 2,751.0 | 2,734.7 | 2,754.5 | 2,758.1 | 2,763.4 | 2,721.1 |
| **Education and Health Services** | | | | | | | | | | | | | |
| 2011 | 2,134.9 | 2,160.6 | 2,168.5 | 2,173.9 | 2,171.4 | 2,151.2 | 2,118.8 | 2,124.3 | 2,158.7 | 2,183.6 | 2,196.5 | 2,210.5 | 2,162.7 |
| 2012 | 2,181.0 | 2,218.0 | 2,235.9 | 2,233.5 | 2,238.4 | 2,223.4 | 2,190.7 | 2,206.8 | 2,232.1 | 2,265.2 | 2,276.2 | 2,289.7 | 2,232.6 |
| 2013 | 2,265.2 | 2,297.5 | 2,309.8 | 2,318.8 | 2,320.7 | 2,291.1 | 2,264.1 | 2,279.7 | 2,303.9 | 2,338.7 | 2,354.2 | 2,359.9 | 2,308.6 |
| 2014 | 2,333.1 | 2,363.3 | 2,374.8 | 2,374.2 | 2,377.3 | 2,355.5 | 2,334.5 | 2,356.6 | 2,384.5 | 2,418.2 | 2,429.3 | 2,433.5 | 2,377.9 |
| 2015 | 2,409.8 | 2,439.9 | 2,450.4 | 2,459.2 | 2,463.0 | 2,440.9 | 2,434.3 | 2,445.9 | 2,472.4 | 2,510.9 | 2,521.0 | 2,527.4 | 2,464.6 |
| 2016 | 2,494.3 | 2,526.3 | 2,532.0 | 2,553.5 | 2,556.8 | 2,535.0 | 2,515.2 | 2,524.2 | 2,556.8 | 2,604.6 | 2,615.0 | 2,620.9 | 2,552.9 |
| 2017 | 2,591.7 | 2,627.9 | 2,645.2 | 2,648.2 | 2,655.3 | 2,636.4 | 2,609.1 | 2,627.3 | 2,658.9 | 2,693.4 | 2,703.9 | 2,706.2 | 2,650.3 |
| 2018 | 2,679.7 | 2,710.9 | 2,722.3 | 2,717.3 | 2,717.4 | 2,704.4 | 2,677.9 | 2,704.0 | 2,719.2 | 2,762.7 | 2,773.2 | 2,777.0 | 2,722.2 |
| 2019 | 2,749.9 | 2,788.0 | 2,796.7 | 2,799.3 | 2,803.8 | 2,782.8 | 2,770.9 | 2,792.1 | 2,805.9 | 2,839.7 | 2,852.3 | 2,859.2 | 2,803.4 |
| **Leisure and Hospitality** | | | | | | | | | | | | | |
| 2011 | 1,476.0 | 1,490.3 | 1,505.7 | 1,523.7 | 1,540.1 | 1,553.5 | 1,564.3 | 1,569.0 | 1,560.3 | 1,545.9 | 1,543.6 | 1,545.6 | 1,534.8 |
| 2012 | 1,519.0 | 1,537.0 | 1,556.9 | 1,582.2 | 1,605.2 | 1,625.7 | 1,632.6 | 1,641.5 | 1,626.2 | 1,615.5 | 1,610.8 | 1,616.2 | 1,597.4 |
| 2013 | 1,588.7 | 1,610.9 | 1,633.2 | 1,657.5 | 1,683.3 | 1,703.2 | 1,709.5 | 1,714.7 | 1,701.0 | 1,697.8 | 1,696.2 | 1,705.8 | 1,675.2 |
| 2014 | 1,677.1 | 1,699.0 | 1,719.9 | 1,743.2 | 1,768.2 | 1,787.0 | 1,791.6 | 1,800.6 | 1,781.5 | 1,774.7 | 1,768.8 | 1,773.2 | 1,757.1 |
| 2015 | 1,744.5 | 1,768.6 | 1,787.9 | 1,812.6 | 1,837.2 | 1,852.8 | 1,866.9 | 1,870.4 | 1,855.4 | 1,855.0 | 1,846.3 | 1,854.1 | 1,829.3 |
| 2016 | 1,824.4 | 1,847.3 | 1,860.2 | 1,895.2 | 1,911.2 | 1,925.3 | 1,941.7 | 1,943.1 | 1,926.7 | 1,925.4 | 1,916.1 | 1,918.1 | 1,902.9 |
| 2017 | 1,875.3 | 1,899.0 | 1,925.1 | 1,947.1 | 1,969.2 | 1,990.6 | 1,992.9 | 1,992.0 | 1,966.9 | 1,967.3 | 1,958.6 | 1,959.2 | 1,953.6 |
| 2018 | 1,918.9 | 1,946.5 | 1,964.3 | 1,987.0 | 2,005.5 | 2,022.3 | 2,030.6 | 2,029.8 | 2,006.0 | 2,004.0 | 1,997.6 | 2,005.4 | 1,993.2 |
| 2019 | 1,963.5 | 1,989.8 | 2,011.0 | 2,032.3 | 2,049.6 | 2,066.8 | 2,069.4 | 2,063.3 | 2,038.4 | 2,039.6 | 2,031.7 | 2,042.6 | 2,033.2 |
| **Other Services** | | | | | | | | | | | | | |
| 2011 | 478.6 | 484.0 | 485.1 | 492.3 | 494.4 | 495.0 | 496.1 | 495.3 | 497.0 | 498.0 | 496.6 | 496.5 | 492.4 |
| 2012 | 488.9 | 494.7 | 497.9 | 501.3 | 506.9 | 510.8 | 506.2 | 505.9 | 507.2 | 509.3 | 507.1 | 506.1 | 503.5 |
| 2013 | 499.7 | 506.8 | 509.1 | 513.9 | 516.5 | 519.1 | 517.3 | 518.7 | 518.7 | 521.7 | 523.0 | 521.5 | 515.5 |
| 2014 | 519.8 | 526.1 | 529.0 | 535.2 | 538.8 | 540.7 | 536.7 | 538.2 | 538.3 | 539.5 | 538.4 | 536.7 | 534.8 |
| 2015 | 529.6 | 535.0 | 537.2 | 542.4 | 546.0 | 546.7 | 548.6 | 547.0 | 547.1 | 549.5 | 548.2 | 546.2 | 543.6 |
| 2016 | 540.1 | 547.1 | 547.0 | 553.2 | 554.5 | 554.5 | 558.0 | 557.2 | 558.7 | 562.1 | 557.5 | 554.9 | 553.7 |
| 2017 | 546.0 | 552.8 | 557.8 | 564.5 | 568.1 | 570.6 | 567.8 | 567.8 | 568.4 | 569.0 | 566.6 | 565.4 | 563.7 |
| 2018 | 558.0 | 565.0 | 566.1 | 572.6 | 575.1 | 577.2 | 574.5 | 574.0 | 572.1 | 578.9 | 575.1 | 571.5 | 571.7 |
| 2019 | 561.5 | 568.3 | 570.7 | 575.5 | 579.0 | 580.1 | 581.6 | 581.0 | 577.9 | 581.3 | 578.6 | 578.1 | 576.1 |
| **Government** | | | | | | | | | | | | | |
| 2011 | 2,424.3 | 2,445.6 | 2,469.2 | 2,469.6 | 2,469.8 | 2,457.5 | 2,278.3 | 2,272.6 | 2,336.4 | 2,407.9 | 2,426.0 | 2,401.6 | 2,404.9 |
| 2012 | 2,382.4 | 2,408.3 | 2,428.1 | 2,425.7 | 2,433.6 | 2,425.8 | 2,251.7 | 2,257.4 | 2,317.5 | 2,385.8 | 2,406.7 | 2,392.1 | 2,376.3 |
| 2013 | 2,363.3 | 2,391.4 | 2,412.7 | 2,412.3 | 2,422.9 | 2,413.4 | 2,238.9 | 2,271.8 | 2,335.7 | 2,399.2 | 2,423.8 | 2,406.2 | 2,374.3 |
| 2014 | 2,392.9 | 2,415.0 | 2,439.9 | 2,451.5 | 2,462.6 | 2,451.5 | 2,279.2 | 2,309.1 | 2,381.0 | 2,450.8 | 2,473.9 | 2,460.3 | 2,414.0 |
| 2015 | 2,446.2 | 2,466.0 | 2,485.6 | 2,496.2 | 2,502.6 | 2,497.0 | 2,330.5 | 2,360.8 | 2,435.6 | 2,502.3 | 2,521.5 | 2,511.2 | 2,463.0 |
| 2016 | 2,490.8 | 2,513.0 | 2,540.8 | 2,547.3 | 2,560.2 | 2,544.8 | 2,381.7 | 2,413.2 | 2,493.3 | 2,557.1 | 2,577.2 | 2,569.2 | 2,515.7 |
| 2017 | 2,543.5 | 2,565.3 | 2,586.1 | 2,589.4 | 2,603.3 | 2,594.0 | 2,412.1 | 2,434.2 | 2,523.2 | 2,590.0 | 2,609.3 | 2,600.2 | 2,554.2 |
| 2018 | 2,574.0 | 2,594.7 | 2,614.7 | 2,621.5 | 2,630.7 | 2,626.2 | 2,429.3 | 2,465.8 | 2,548.7 | 2,611.8 | 2,634.1 | 2,627.5 | 2,581.6 |
| 2019 | 2,594.6 | 2,614.7 | 2,636.5 | 2,645.5 | 2,653.4 | 2,643.8 | 2,456.3 | 2,500.8 | 2,572.0 | 2,648.0 | 2,670.8 | 2,659.0 | 2,608.0 |

## 2. Average Weekly Hours by Selected Industry: California, 2015–2019

(Not seasonally adjusted)

| Industry and year | January | February | March | April | May | June | July | August | September | October | November | December | Annual average |
|---|---|---|---|---|---|---|---|---|---|---|---|---|---|
| **Total Private** | | | | | | | | | | | | | |
| 2015 | 34.1 | 34.9 | 35.0 | 34.3 | 34.3 | 34.5 | 34.5 | 35.4 | 34.4 | 34.5 | 35.1 | 34.5 | 34.6 |
| 2016 | 34.2 | 34.3 | 34.2 | 34.4 | 35.0 | 34.4 | 34.5 | 34.5 | 34.3 | 35.0 | 34.2 | 34.2 | 34.4 |
| 2017 | 34.5 | 34.0 | 34.2 | 34.9 | 34.3 | 34.4 | 35.1 | 34.6 | 34.4 | 35.1 | 34.4 | 34.5 | 34.5 |
| 2018 | 34.1 | 34.4 | 34.2 | 35.2 | 34.5 | 34.6 | 35.2 | 34.6 | 35.2 | 34.4 | 34.2 | 35.1 | 34.6 |
| 2019 | 34.0 | 34.0 | 34.2 | 34.2 | 34.2 | 35.1 | 34.3 | 34.5 | 35.0 | 34.3 | 34.2 | 34.9 | 34.4 |
| **Goods Producing** | | | | | | | | | | | | | |
| 2015 | 38.5 | 38.8 | 39.1 | 38.8 | 38.6 | 38.9 | 38.9 | 39.6 | 38.2 | 39.3 | 39.2 | 39.3 | 38.9 |
| 2016 | 38.5 | 38.5 | 38.3 | 38.8 | 38.8 | 38.9 | 38.7 | 38.9 | 38.8 | 39.1 | 38.4 | 38.4 | 38.7 |
| 2017 | 37.5 | 37.6 | 38.5 | 38.4 | 38.8 | 39.1 | 39.0 | 39.2 | 39.0 | 39.2 | 38.8 | 39.2 | 38.7 |
| 2018 | 37.8 | 38.9 | 38.4 | 39.3 | 39.0 | 39.0 | 39.1 | 39.2 | 39.4 | 39.1 | 38.2 | 38.7 | 38.9 |
| 2019 | 37.8 | 37.2 | 38.5 | 38.4 | 38.3 | 38.9 | 38.3 | 38.8 | 38.8 | 38.7 | 38.4 | 38.7 | 38.4 |
| **Construction** | | | | | | | | | | | | | |
| 2015 | 36.6 | 36.7 | 37.2 | 36.9 | 36.5 | 37.2 | 37.1 | 37.7 | 34.9 | 37.7 | 36.8 | 37.2 | 36.9 |
| 2016 | 36.2 | 36.3 | 35.3 | 36.6 | 37.0 | 37.3 | 37.4 | 37.6 | 37.1 | 37.7 | 36.6 | 36.4 | 36.8 |
| 2017 | 34.7 | 35.1 | 37.2 | 36.7 | 37.5 | 37.8 | 37.7 | 38.1 | 37.8 | 37.9 | 37.3 | 37.9 | 37.2 |
| 2018 | 35.1 | 37.3 | 36.0 | 37.6 | 37.5 | 37.4 | 37.5 | 37.6 | 37.7 | 37.6 | 36.1 | 37.2 | 37.1 |
| 2019 | 35.3 | 34.4 | 37.0 | 37.1 | 36.7 | 37.6 | 37.2 | 37.9 | 37.6 | 37.8 | 37.2 | 37.5 | 37.0 |
| **Manufacturing** | | | | | | | | | | | | | |
| 2015 | 40.0 | 40.4 | 40.5 | 40.2 | 40.2 | 40.1 | 40.2 | 40.9 | 40.3 | 40.3 | 40.7 | 40.7 | 40.4 |
| 2016 | 40.0 | 39.9 | 40.2 | 40.3 | 40.3 | 40.3 | 39.9 | 40.1 | 40.2 | 40.3 | 40.0 | 39.8 | 40.1 |
| 2017 | 39.4 | 39.3 | 39.6 | 39.8 | 39.8 | 40.1 | 40.0 | 40.0 | 39.9 | 40.2 | 40.0 | 40.2 | 39.9 |
| 2018 | 39.7 | 40.0 | 40.0 | 40.4 | 39.9 | 40.1 | 40.2 | 40.3 | 40.6 | 40.2 | 39.7 | 40.6 | 40.1 |
| 2019 | 39.5 | 39.2 | 39.7 | 39.5 | 39.5 | 39.8 | 39.1 | 39.4 | 39.7 | 39.4 | 39.4 | 39.7 | 39.5 |
| **Trade, Transportation, and Utilities** | | | | | | | | | | | | | |
| 2015 | 34.4 | 35.4 | 35.6 | 35.2 | 35.2 | 35.4 | 35.5 | 36.2 | 35.9 | 35.3 | 35.7 | 35.1 | 35.4 |
| 2016 | 34.7 | 35.1 | 34.9 | 35.3 | 35.6 | 35.3 | 35.4 | 35.3 | 35.2 | 35.8 | 34.9 | 35.1 | 35.2 |
| 2017 | 35.2 | 35.0 | 35.1 | 36.0 | 35.5 | 35.5 | 36.2 | 35.7 | 35.6 | 35.9 | 35.4 | 35.4 | 35.6 |
| 2018 | 35.1 | 35.2 | 35.2 | 36.1 | 35.5 | 35.6 | 36.1 | 35.5 | 35.7 | 34.9 | 34.7 | 35.1 | 35.4 |
| 2019 | 34.3 | 34.3 | 34.2 | 34.5 | 34.7 | 35.3 | 34.9 | 35.0 | 35.3 | 34.5 | 34.3 | 35.1 | 34.7 |
| **Information** | | | | | | | | | | | | | |
| 2015 | 37.2 | 38.0 | 37.4 | 36.7 | 36.4 | 36.7 | 37.3 | 37.8 | 36.9 | 36.9 | 37.7 | 36.9 | 37.2 |
| 2016 | 37.7 | 37.0 | 36.9 | 36.9 | 37.6 | 37.1 | 37.1 | 37.0 | 37.3 | 37.5 | 37.1 | 37.0 | 37.2 |
| 2017 | 38.2 | 36.8 | 36.8 | 37.6 | 36.7 | 37.1 | 38.0 | 37.0 | 37.3 | 38.1 | 37.3 | 37.2 | 37.3 |
| 2018 | 37.5 | 37.0 | 37.2 | 38.0 | 36.8 | 37.0 | 38.1 | 37.4 | 38.3 | 36.9 | 37.0 | 38.6 | 37.5 |
| 2019 | 36.8 | 36.9 | 37.3 | 36.8 | 36.6 | 38.3 | 36.8 | 36.5 | 37.4 | 36.0 | 35.9 | 37.2 | 36.9 |
| **Financial Activities** | | | | | | | | | | | | | |
| 2015 | 36.8 | 37.8 | 37.8 | 36.9 | 36.9 | 37.0 | 36.8 | 38.0 | 37.0 | 36.8 | 37.8 | 37.0 | 37.2 |
| 2016 | 36.9 | 36.9 | 36.7 | 36.3 | 37.2 | 36.5 | 36.6 | 36.6 | 36.1 | 37.0 | 35.7 | 35.7 | 36.5 |
| 2017 | 36.6 | 35.5 | 35.6 | 36.8 | 35.8 | 36.2 | 37.3 | 36.5 | 36.3 | 37.3 | 36.3 | 36.3 | 36.4 |
| 2018 | 36.6 | 36.4 | 36.4 | 37.7 | 36.6 | 36.7 | 37.6 | 36.6 | 38.0 | 36.5 | 36.1 | 37.0 | 36.8 |
| 2019 | 36.7 | 36.9 | 37.1 | 37.4 | 37.3 | 38.4 | 37.6 | 37.6 | 38.8 | 37.5 | 37.7 | 38.6 | 37.6 |
| **Professional and Business Services** | | | | | | | | | | | | | |
| 2015 | 35.5 | 36.6 | 36.8 | 35.9 | 35.8 | 36.1 | 35.8 | 37.2 | 35.8 | 36.3 | 37.2 | 36.2 | 36.3 |
| 2016 | 35.7 | 35.9 | 35.8 | 36.1 | 36.8 | 35.9 | 35.9 | 36.0 | 35.9 | 37.0 | 36.0 | 35.9 | 36.1 |
| 2017 | 36.6 | 35.9 | 36.1 | 37.1 | 36.0 | 35.9 | 36.9 | 36.1 | 35.9 | 37.1 | 36.2 | 36.2 | 36.3 |
| 2018 | 35.8 | 36.4 | 36.1 | 37.4 | 36.2 | 36.3 | 37.0 | 36.2 | 37.2 | 36.4 | 36.2 | 37.5 | 36.6 |
| 2019 | 36.0 | 36.1 | 36.5 | 36.5 | 36.5 | 37.6 | 36.3 | 36.6 | 37.6 | 36.8 | 36.6 | 37.3 | 36.7 |
| **Education and Health Services** | | | | | | | | | | | | | |
| 2015 | 33.3 | 34.0 | 33.8 | 33.0 | 33.0 | 33.0 | 33.0 | 33.8 | 33.1 | 32.8 | 33.8 | 32.9 | 33.3 |
| 2016 | 33.1 | 33.1 | 33.2 | 33.3 | 34.0 | 33.2 | 33.2 | 33.3 | 33.4 | 34.1 | 33.4 | 33.4 | 33.4 |
| 2017 | 34.2 | 33.5 | 33.5 | 34.0 | 33.4 | 33.5 | 34.3 | 33.5 | 33.5 | 34.2 | 33.7 | 33.3 | 33.7 |
| 2018 | 33.4 | 33.3 | 33.3 | 34.2 | 33.5 | 33.6 | 34.4 | 33.3 | 34.4 | 33.6 | 33.6 | 34.5 | 33.8 |
| 2019 | 33.5 | 33.8 | 33.6 | 33.5 | 33.5 | 34.4 | 33.7 | 33.6 | 34.3 | 33.5 | 33.7 | 34.4 | 33.8 |
| **Leisure and Hospitality** | | | | | | | | | | | | | |
| 2015 | 26.4 | 27.4 | 27.4 | 26.8 | 26.8 | 27.0 | 27.1 | 28.0 | 26.8 | 26.8 | 27.4 | 26.7 | 27.1 |
| 2016 | 26.5 | 26.8 | 26.7 | 26.5 | 27.6 | 26.9 | 27.1 | 26.9 | 26.3 | 27.1 | 26.2 | 26.0 | 26.7 |
| 2017 | 26.6 | 26.0 | 26.1 | 26.9 | 26.1 | 26.2 | 27.1 | 26.4 | 26.1 | 26.8 | 25.9 | 26.1 | 26.4 |
| 2018 | 25.9 | 26.2 | 26.1 | 26.8 | 26.3 | 26.6 | 27.2 | 26.7 | 27.0 | 26.3 | 26.1 | 26.9 | 26.5 |
| 2019 | 26.2 | 26.1 | 26.0 | 26.1 | 26.1 | 27.0 | 26.1 | 26.1 | 26.4 | 25.7 | 25.7 | 26.4 | 26.2 |
| **Other services** | | | | | | | | | | | | | |
| 2015 | 31.0 | 32.2 | 32.4 | 31.4 | 31.4 | 31.5 | 32.0 | 33.1 | 31.8 | 31.9 | 32.1 | 31.6 | 31.9 |
| 2016 | 31.3 | 31.6 | 31.5 | 31.6 | 32.5 | 32.0 | 32.2 | 32.4 | 32.0 | 32.9 | 31.8 | 31.5 | 31.9 |
| 2017 | 31.8 | 31.4 | 32.1 | 32.4 | 31.7 | 32.2 | 32.8 | 31.9 | 31.4 | 32.0 | 31.7 | 31.4 | 31.8 |
| 2018 | 30.3 | 31.1 | 30.4 | 31.9 | 31.4 | 32.2 | 33.0 | 32.0 | 32.8 | 31.7 | 31.5 | 32.5 | 31.7 |
| 2019 | 30.7 | 30.9 | 31.1 | 31.4 | 31.2 | 32.4 | 31.5 | 31.7 | 32.1 | 31.1 | 31.3 | 31.6 | 31.4 |

## 3.  Average Hourly Earnings by Selected Industry: California, 2015–2019

(Dollars, not seasonally adjusted)

| Industry and year | January | February | March | April | May | June | July | August | September | October | November | December | Annual average |
|---|---|---|---|---|---|---|---|---|---|---|---|---|---|
| **Total Private** | | | | | | | | | | | | | |
| 2015 | 28.12 | 28.22 | 28.10 | 27.99 | 28.04 | 27.93 | 27.97 | 28.14 | 27.95 | 28.19 | 28.48 | 28.35 | 28.13 |
| 2016 | 28.59 | 28.64 | 28.55 | 28.71 | 29.06 | 28.68 | 28.81 | 28.93 | 29.19 | 29.58 | 29.31 | 29.49 | 28.97 |
| 2017 | 29.91 | 29.77 | 29.60 | 30.05 | 29.79 | 29.69 | 30.18 | 29.90 | 30.24 | 30.67 | 30.30 | 30.45 | 30.05 |
| 2018 | 30.60 | 30.63 | 30.62 | 30.87 | 30.68 | 30.60 | 31.02 | 30.76 | 31.29 | 31.25 | 31.32 | 31.96 | 30.97 |
| 2019 | 32.05 | 32.11 | 32.06 | 32.24 | 32.10 | 32.40 | 32.35 | 32.37 | 32.86 | 32.69 | 32.84 | 33.18 | 32.44 |
| **Goods Producing** | | | | | | | | | | | | | |
| 2015 | 29.77 | 29.52 | 29.43 | 29.45 | 29.47 | 29.44 | 29.46 | 29.40 | 29.42 | 29.70 | 29.82 | 29.95 | 29.57 |
| 2016 | 30.12 | 29.90 | 29.93 | 30.02 | 30.41 | 30.31 | 30.45 | 30.55 | 30.70 | 31.07 | 30.94 | 31.38 | 30.49 |
| 2017 | 31.64 | 31.83 | 31.71 | 31.92 | 31.71 | 31.80 | 32.33 | 32.01 | 32.30 | 32.49 | 32.41 | 32.85 | 32.09 |
| 2018 | 32.74 | 32.75 | 32.76 | 32.78 | 32.68 | 32.82 | 32.90 | 32.67 | 33.05 | 33.33 | 33.54 | 34.23 | 33.02 |
| 2019 | 34.44 | 34.60 | 34.42 | 34.79 | 34.57 | 34.77 | 35.00 | 34.91 | 35.06 | 35.11 | 35.26 | 35.74 | 34.89 |
| **Construction** | | | | | | | | | | | | | |
| 2015 | 31.33 | 31.03 | 31.16 | 31.24 | 30.91 | 31.14 | 31.41 | 31.44 | 31.51 | 31.49 | 31.69 | 31.79 | 31.35 |
| 2016 | 31.95 | 31.83 | 31.84 | 31.70 | 32.01 | 32.09 | 32.48 | 32.46 | 32.70 | 32.79 | 32.58 | 33.24 | 32.32 |
| 2017 | 33.45 | 33.63 | 33.57 | 33.22 | 33.30 | 33.36 | 33.82 | 33.88 | 34.20 | 34.11 | 34.32 | 35.09 | 33.85 |
| 2018 | 34.39 | 34.46 | 34.92 | 34.76 | 34.78 | 35.14 | 35.41 | 35.58 | 35.75 | 35.86 | 35.78 | 36.60 | 35.30 |
| 2019 | 37.25 | 37.12 | 37.07 | 37.45 | 37.12 | 37.13 | 37.18 | 37.56 | 37.54 | 37.51 | 37.26 | 37.80 | 37.34 |
| **Manufacturing** | | | | | | | | | | | | | |
| 2015 | 28.94 | 28.68 | 28.60 | 28.60 | 28.78 | 28.57 | 28.50 | 28.35 | 28.44 | 28.77 | 28.75 | 28.87 | 28.65 |
| 2016 | 29.01 | 28.75 | 28.86 | 29.09 | 29.43 | 29.25 | 29.24 | 29.39 | 29.47 | 30.00 | 29.90 | 30.19 | 29.38 |
| 2017 | 30.58 | 30.71 | 30.44 | 31.04 | 30.55 | 30.65 | 31.20 | 30.69 | 30.97 | 31.48 | 31.18 | 31.39 | 30.91 |
| 2018 | 31.58 | 31.45 | 31.47 | 31.48 | 31.26 | 31.21 | 31.13 | 30.88 | 31.39 | 31.74 | 32.14 | 32.73 | 31.54 |
| 2019 | 32.84 | 33.17 | 32.81 | 33.12 | 32.94 | 33.21 | 33.33 | 32.81 | 33.09 | 33.16 | 33.63 | 34.01 | 33.18 |
| **Trade, Transportation, and Utilities** | | | | | | | | | | | | | |
| 2015 | 22.76 | 22.67 | 22.31 | 22.41 | 22.62 | 22.46 | 22.47 | 22.74 | 22.52 | 22.77 | 23.03 | 22.94 | 22.64 |
| 2016 | 23.19 | 23.26 | 22.95 | 23.32 | 23.54 | 23.20 | 23.32 | 23.43 | 23.60 | 24.05 | 23.77 | 23.84 | 23.46 |
| 2017 | 24.37 | 23.67 | 23.47 | 23.93 | 23.55 | 23.50 | 23.90 | 23.50 | 23.52 | 23.79 | 23.30 | 23.50 | 23.67 |
| 2018 | 23.52 | 23.36 | 23.39 | 23.79 | 23.71 | 23.55 | 23.86 | 23.60 | 23.93 | 23.86 | 23.84 | 24.16 | 23.72 |
| 2019 | 24.59 | 24.60 | 24.71 | 24.90 | 24.72 | 24.97 | 24.96 | 24.94 | 25.13 | 25.19 | 25.29 | 25.36 | 24.95 |
| **Information** | | | | | | | | | | | | | |
| 2015 | 41.02 | 41.90 | 41.99 | 42.24 | 42.32 | 41.62 | 41.34 | 42.11 | 41.50 | 41.36 | 41.60 | 41.11 | 41.67 |
| 2016 | 40.61 | 40.84 | 40.50 | 40.52 | 41.52 | 40.50 | 40.60 | 40.64 | 41.03 | 41.98 | 41.12 | 41.06 | 40.91 |
| 2017 | 41.84 | 42.02 | 42.20 | 43.36 | 43.15 | 42.78 | 43.01 | 42.72 | 43.88 | 44.97 | 43.63 | 43.47 | 43.10 |
| 2018 | 43.95 | 44.72 | 44.73 | 45.88 | 45.76 | 45.41 | 46.09 | 45.65 | 47.13 | 47.08 | 46.86 | 48.11 | 45.97 |
| 2019 | 48.47 | 49.29 | 49.70 | 49.68 | 50.87 | 51.33 | 50.82 | 51.37 | 52.14 | 51.04 | 51.49 | 52.28 | 50.72 |
| **Financial Activities** | | | | | | | | | | | | | |
| 2015 | 33.90 | 34.09 | 34.28 | 33.52 | 33.44 | 33.28 | 33.09 | 33.31 | 33.17 | 33.40 | 34.15 | 33.68 | 33.61 |
| 2016 | 33.60 | 34.39 | 34.05 | 34.25 | 35.44 | 33.62 | 33.87 | 34.83 | 35.52 | 36.30 | 36.23 | 35.46 | 34.80 |
| 2017 | 35.43 | 35.40 | 34.79 | 36.06 | 35.99 | 35.83 | 36.84 | 36.77 | 37.01 | 38.31 | 37.39 | 37.28 | 36.44 |
| 2018 | 37.61 | 38.14 | 38.07 | 38.21 | 38.23 | 37.01 | 37.90 | 38.21 | 38.58 | 39.33 | 39.00 | 39.32 | 38.30 |
| 2019 | 39.00 | 38.06 | 37.82 | 38.55 | 38.19 | 38.63 | 38.28 | 38.64 | 39.47 | 39.19 | 40.15 | 40.24 | 38.86 |
| **Professional and Business Services** | | | | | | | | | | | | | |
| 2015 | 35.28 | 35.91 | 35.97 | 35.59 | 35.79 | 35.66 | 36.06 | 36.19 | 35.69 | 35.68 | 36.44 | 35.82 | 35.85 |
| 2016 | 36.45 | 36.59 | 36.64 | 36.87 | 37.62 | 37.01 | 37.37 | 37.26 | 37.49 | 38.07 | 37.43 | 37.69 | 37.21 |
| 2017 | 38.69 | 38.34 | 38.09 | 38.77 | 38.13 | 37.86 | 38.62 | 38.08 | 38.58 | 39.32 | 38.59 | 38.75 | 38.49 |
| 2018 | 38.94 | 39.00 | 39.02 | 39.80 | 39.35 | 39.27 | 40.27 | 39.35 | 40.37 | 39.61 | 39.93 | 40.94 | 39.67 |
| 2019 | 40.60 | 40.75 | 40.49 | 40.97 | 40.97 | 41.54 | 41.12 | 40.97 | 42.07 | 41.42 | 41.55 | 42.35 | 41.24 |
| **Education and Health Services** | | | | | | | | | | | | | |
| 2015 | 28.53 | 28.45 | 28.19 | 28.22 | 28.11 | 28.09 | 28.19 | 28.26 | 28.12 | 28.47 | 28.43 | 28.71 | 28.32 |
| 2016 | 28.62 | 28.64 | 28.61 | 28.67 | 28.66 | 28.69 | 28.76 | 28.78 | 29.01 | 29.10 | 28.95 | 29.34 | 28.82 |
| 2017 | 29.20 | 29.33 | 29.36 | 29.70 | 29.71 | 29.65 | 30.00 | 29.75 | 30.18 | 30.30 | 30.48 | 30.59 | 29.86 |
| 2018 | 30.77 | 30.50 | 30.48 | 30.28 | 30.32 | 30.58 | 30.85 | 30.77 | 30.73 | 30.82 | 30.92 | 31.37 | 30.70 |
| 2019 | 31.56 | 31.44 | 31.38 | 31.24 | 31.00 | 31.03 | 31.29 | 31.24 | 31.30 | 31.23 | 31.29 | 31.48 | 31.29 |
| **Leisure and Hospitality** | | | | | | | | | | | | | |
| 2015 | 16.03 | 16.15 | 16.15 | 16.23 | 16.27 | 16.19 | 16.08 | 16.14 | 16.27 | 16.31 | 16.35 | 16.46 | 16.22 |
| 2016 | 16.77 | 16.84 | 16.92 | 17.01 | 17.09 | 17.11 | 17.12 | 17.21 | 17.34 | 17.32 | 17.32 | 17.53 | 17.13 |
| 2017 | 17.61 | 17.72 | 17.60 | 17.63 | 17.75 | 17.61 | 17.66 | 17.72 | 17.87 | 17.89 | 17.96 | 18.12 | 17.76 |
| 2018 | 18.05 | 18.11 | 18.10 | 18.22 | 18.04 | 17.99 | 18.10 | 18.19 | 18.56 | 18.63 | 18.71 | 19.07 | 18.32 |
| 2019 | 19.04 | 19.20 | 19.23 | 19.28 | 19.26 | 19.38 | 19.45 | 19.56 | 19.87 | 20.00 | 20.07 | 20.27 | 19.55 |
| **Other services** | | | | | | | | | | | | | |
| 2015 | 23.27 | 23.36 | 23.42 | 23.06 | 23.39 | 23.26 | 22.89 | 23.26 | 23.44 | 23.30 | 23.42 | 23.15 | 23.27 |
| 2016 | 23.61 | 23.50 | 23.72 | 23.39 | 23.29 | 22.90 | 22.83 | 23.05 | 23.17 | 23.84 | 23.86 | 24.29 | 23.45 |
| 2017 | 25.26 | 25.13 | 24.86 | 25.48 | 25.34 | 25.05 | 25.87 | 25.99 | 26.35 | 26.61 | 26.41 | 26.38 | 25.73 |
| 2018 | 26.69 | 26.61 | 26.75 | 26.44 | 26.14 | 26.08 | 26.12 | 26.17 | 26.73 | 26.68 | 26.98 | 27.72 | 26.59 |
| 2019 | 28.13 | 28.03 | 27.65 | 27.59 | 27.27 | 27.25 | 27.70 | 27.48 | 28.24 | 28.13 | 28.40 | 29.21 | 27.92 |

## 4. Average Weekly Earnings by Selected Industry: California, 2015–2019

(Dollars, not seasonally adjusted)

| Industry and year | January | February | March | April | May | June | July | August | September | October | November | December | Annual average |
|---|---|---|---|---|---|---|---|---|---|---|---|---|---|
| **Total Private** | | | | | | | | | | | | | |
| 2015 | 958.89 | 984.88 | 983.50 | 960.06 | 961.77 | 963.59 | 964.97 | 996.16 | 961.48 | 972.56 | 999.65 | 978.08 | 973.30 |
| 2016 | 977.78 | 982.35 | 976.41 | 987.62 | 1,017.10 | 986.59 | 993.95 | 998.09 | 1,001.22 | 1,035.30 | 1,002.40 | 1,008.56 | 996.57 |
| 2017 | 1,031.90 | 1,012.18 | 1,012.32 | 1,048.75 | 1,021.80 | 1,021.34 | 1,059.32 | 1,034.54 | 1,040.26 | 1,076.52 | 1,042.32 | 1,050.53 | 1,036.73 |
| 2018 | 1,043.46 | 1,053.67 | 1,047.20 | 1,086.62 | 1,058.46 | 1,058.76 | 1,091.90 | 1,064.30 | 1,101.41 | 1,075.00 | 1,071.14 | 1,121.80 | 1,071.56 |
| 2019 | 1,089.70 | 1,091.74 | 1,096.79 | 1,102.61 | 1,097.82 | 1,137.24 | 1,109.61 | 1,116.77 | 1,150.10 | 1,121.27 | 1,123.13 | 1,157.98 | 1,115.94 |
| **Goods Producing** | | | | | | | | | | | | | |
| 2015 | 1,146.15 | 1,144.99 | 1,150.71 | 1,142.66 | 1,137.54 | 1,145.22 | 1,145.99 | 1,164.24 | 1,123.84 | 1,167.21 | 1,168.94 | 1,177.04 | 1,150.27 |
| 2016 | 1,159.62 | 1,151.15 | 1,146.32 | 1,164.78 | 1,179.91 | 1,179.06 | 1,178.42 | 1,188.40 | 1,191.16 | 1,215.23 | 1,188.10 | 1,204.99 | 1,179.96 |
| 2017 | 1,186.50 | 1,196.81 | 1,220.84 | 1,225.73 | 1,230.35 | 1,243.38 | 1,260.87 | 1,254.79 | 1,259.70 | 1,273.61 | 1,257.51 | 1,287.72 | 1,241.88 |
| 2018 | 1,237.95 | 1,273.98 | 1,257.98 | 1,288.25 | 1,274.52 | 1,279.98 | 1,286.39 | 1,280.66 | 1,302.17 | 1,303.20 | 1,281.23 | 1,341.82 | 1,284.48 |
| 2019 | 1,301.83 | 1,287.12 | 1,325.17 | 1,335.94 | 1,324.03 | 1,352.55 | 1,340.50 | 1,354.51 | 1,360.33 | 1,358.76 | 1,353.98 | 1,383.14 | 1,339.78 |
| **Construction** | | | | | | | | | | | | | |
| 2015 | 1,146.68 | 1,138.80 | 1,159.15 | 1,152.76 | 1,128.22 | 1,158.41 | 1,165.31 | 1,185.29 | 1,099.70 | 1,187.17 | 1,166.19 | 1,182.59 | 1,156.82 |
| 2016 | 1,156.59 | 1,155.43 | 1,123.95 | 1,160.22 | 1,184.37 | 1,196.96 | 1,214.75 | 1,220.50 | 1,213.17 | 1,236.18 | 1,192.43 | 1,209.94 | 1,189.38 |
| 2017 | 1,160.72 | 1,180.41 | 1,248.80 | 1,219.54 | 1,248.75 | 1,261.01 | 1,275.01 | 1,291.21 | 1,292.76 | 1,293.15 | 1,280.51 | 1,330.29 | 1,259.22 |
| 2018 | 1,207.44 | 1,285.73 | 1,257.12 | 1,306.98 | 1,304.25 | 1,314.24 | 1,327.88 | 1,337.81 | 1,347.78 | 1,348.34 | 1,291.66 | 1,361.52 | 1,309.63 |
| 2019 | 1,314.93 | 1,276.93 | 1,371.59 | 1,389.40 | 1,362.30 | 1,396.09 | 1,383.10 | 1,423.52 | 1,411.50 | 1,417.88 | 1,386.07 | 1,417.50 | 1,381.58 |
| **Manufacturing** | | | | | | | | | | | | | |
| 2015 | 1,157.60 | 1,158.67 | 1,158.30 | 1,149.72 | 1,156.96 | 1,145.66 | 1,145.70 | 1,159.52 | 1,146.13 | 1,159.43 | 1,170.13 | 1,175.01 | 1,157.46 |
| 2016 | 1,160.40 | 1,147.13 | 1,160.17 | 1,172.33 | 1,186.03 | 1,178.78 | 1,166.68 | 1,178.54 | 1,184.69 | 1,209.00 | 1,196.00 | 1,201.56 | 1,178.14 |
| 2017 | 1,204.85 | 1,206.90 | 1,205.42 | 1,235.39 | 1,215.89 | 1,229.07 | 1,248.00 | 1,227.60 | 1,235.70 | 1,265.50 | 1,247.20 | 1,261.88 | 1,233.31 |
| 2018 | 1,253.73 | 1,258.00 | 1,258.80 | 1,271.79 | 1,247.27 | 1,251.52 | 1,251.43 | 1,244.46 | 1,274.43 | 1,275.95 | 1,275.96 | 1,328.84 | 1,264.75 |
| 2019 | 1,297.18 | 1,300.26 | 1,302.56 | 1,308.24 | 1,301.13 | 1,321.76 | 1,303.20 | 1,292.71 | 1,313.67 | 1,306.50 | 1,325.02 | 1,350.20 | 1,310.61 |
| **Trade, Transportation, and Utilities** | | | | | | | | | | | | | |
| 2015 | 782.94 | 802.52 | 794.24 | 788.83 | 796.22 | 795.08 | 797.69 | 823.19 | 808.47 | 803.78 | 822.17 | 805.19 | 801.46 |
| 2016 | 804.69 | 816.43 | 800.96 | 823.20 | 838.02 | 818.96 | 825.53 | 827.08 | 830.72 | 860.99 | 829.57 | 836.78 | 825.79 |
| 2017 | 857.82 | 828.45 | 823.80 | 861.48 | 836.03 | 834.25 | 865.18 | 838.95 | 837.31 | 854.06 | 824.82 | 838.95 | 842.65 |
| 2018 | 825.55 | 822.27 | 823.33 | 858.82 | 841.71 | 838.38 | 861.35 | 837.80 | 854.30 | 832.71 | 827.25 | 848.02 | 839.69 |
| 2019 | 843.44 | 843.78 | 845.08 | 859.05 | 857.78 | 881.44 | 871.10 | 872.90 | 887.09 | 869.06 | 867.45 | 890.14 | 865.77 |
| **Information** | | | | | | | | | | | | | |
| 2015 | 1,525.94 | 1,592.20 | 1,570.43 | 1,550.21 | 1,540.45 | 1,527.45 | 1,541.98 | 1,591.76 | 1,531.35 | 1,526.18 | 1,568.32 | 1,516.96 | 1,550.12 |
| 2016 | 1,531.00 | 1,511.08 | 1,494.45 | 1,495.19 | 1,561.15 | 1,502.55 | 1,506.26 | 1,503.68 | 1,530.42 | 1,574.25 | 1,525.55 | 1,519.22 | 1,521.85 |
| 2017 | 1,598.29 | 1,546.34 | 1,552.96 | 1,630.34 | 1,583.61 | 1,587.14 | 1,634.38 | 1,580.64 | 1,636.72 | 1,713.36 | 1,627.40 | 1,617.08 | 1,607.63 |
| 2018 | 1,648.13 | 1,654.64 | 1,663.96 | 1,743.44 | 1,683.97 | 1,680.17 | 1,756.03 | 1,707.31 | 1,805.08 | 1,737.25 | 1,733.82 | 1,857.05 | 1,723.88 |
| 2019 | 1,783.70 | 1,818.80 | 1,853.81 | 1,828.22 | 1,861.84 | 1,965.94 | 1,870.18 | 1,875.01 | 1,950.04 | 1,837.44 | 1,848.49 | 1,944.82 | 1,871.57 |
| **Financial Activities** | | | | | | | | | | | | | |
| 2015 | 1,247.52 | 1,288.60 | 1,295.78 | 1,236.89 | 1,233.94 | 1,231.36 | 1,217.71 | 1,265.78 | 1,227.29 | 1,229.12 | 1,290.87 | 1,246.16 | 1,250.29 |
| 2016 | 1,239.84 | 1,268.99 | 1,249.64 | 1,243.28 | 1,318.37 | 1,227.13 | 1,239.64 | 1,274.78 | 1,282.27 | 1,343.10 | 1,293.41 | 1,265.92 | 1,270.20 |
| 2017 | 1,296.74 | 1,256.70 | 1,238.52 | 1,327.01 | 1,288.44 | 1,297.05 | 1,374.13 | 1,342.11 | 1,343.46 | 1,428.96 | 1,357.26 | 1,353.26 | 1,326.42 |
| 2018 | 1,376.53 | 1,388.30 | 1,385.75 | 1,440.52 | 1,399.22 | 1,358.27 | 1,425.04 | 1,398.49 | 1,466.04 | 1,435.55 | 1,407.90 | 1,454.84 | 1,409.44 |
| 2019 | 1,431.30 | 1,404.41 | 1,403.12 | 1,441.77 | 1,424.49 | 1,483.39 | 1,439.33 | 1,452.86 | 1,531.44 | 1,469.63 | 1,513.66 | 1,553.26 | 1,461.14 |
| **Professional and Business Services** | | | | | | | | | | | | | |
| 2015 | 1,252.44 | 1,314.31 | 1,323.70 | 1,277.68 | 1,281.28 | 1,287.33 | 1,290.95 | 1,346.27 | 1,277.70 | 1,295.18 | 1,355.57 | 1,296.68 | 1,301.36 |
| 2016 | 1,301.27 | 1,313.58 | 1,311.71 | 1,331.01 | 1,384.42 | 1,328.66 | 1,341.58 | 1,341.36 | 1,345.89 | 1,408.59 | 1,347.48 | 1,353.07 | 1,343.28 |
| 2017 | 1,416.05 | 1,376.41 | 1,375.05 | 1,438.37 | 1,372.68 | 1,359.17 | 1,425.08 | 1,374.69 | 1,385.02 | 1,458.77 | 1,396.96 | 1,402.75 | 1,397.19 |
| 2018 | 1,394.05 | 1,419.60 | 1,408.62 | 1,488.52 | 1,424.47 | 1,425.50 | 1,489.99 | 1,424.47 | 1,501.76 | 1,441.80 | 1,445.47 | 1,535.25 | 1,451.92 |
| 2019 | 1,461.60 | 1,471.08 | 1,477.89 | 1,495.41 | 1,495.41 | 1,561.90 | 1,492.66 | 1,499.50 | 1,581.83 | 1,524.26 | 1,520.73 | 1,579.66 | 1,513.51 |
| **Education and Health Services** | | | | | | | | | | | | | |
| 2015 | 950.05 | 967.30 | 952.82 | 931.26 | 927.63 | 926.97 | 930.27 | 955.19 | 930.77 | 933.82 | 960.93 | 944.56 | 943.06 |
| 2016 | 947.32 | 947.98 | 949.85 | 954.71 | 974.44 | 952.84 | 954.83 | 958.37 | 968.93 | 992.31 | 966.93 | 979.96 | 962.59 |
| 2017 | 998.64 | 982.56 | 983.56 | 1,009.80 | 992.31 | 993.28 | 1,029.00 | 996.63 | 1,011.03 | 1,036.60 | 1,027.18 | 1,018.65 | 1,006.28 |
| 2018 | 1,027.72 | 1,015.65 | 1,014.98 | 1,035.58 | 1,015.72 | 1,027.49 | 1,061.24 | 1,024.64 | 1,057.11 | 1,035.55 | 1,038.91 | 1,082.27 | 1,037.66 |
| 2019 | 1,057.26 | 1,062.67 | 1,054.37 | 1,046.54 | 1,038.50 | 1,067.43 | 1,054.47 | 1,049.66 | 1,073.59 | 1,046.21 | 1,054.47 | 1,082.91 | 1,057.60 |
| **Leisure and Hospitality** | | | | | | | | | | | | | |
| 2015 | 423.19 | 442.51 | 442.51 | 434.96 | 436.04 | 437.13 | 435.77 | 451.92 | 436.04 | 437.11 | 447.99 | 439.48 | 439.56 |
| 2016 | 444.41 | 451.31 | 451.76 | 450.77 | 471.68 | 460.26 | 464.22 | 462.95 | 456.04 | 469.37 | 453.78 | 455.78 | 457.37 |
| 2017 | 468.43 | 460.72 | 459.36 | 474.25 | 463.28 | 461.38 | 478.59 | 467.81 | 466.67 | 479.72 | 465.16 | 472.93 | 468.86 |
| 2018 | 467.50 | 474.48 | 472.41 | 488.30 | 474.45 | 478.53 | 492.32 | 485.67 | 501.12 | 489.97 | 488.33 | 512.98 | 485.48 |
| 2019 | 498.85 | 501.12 | 499.98 | 503.21 | 502.69 | 523.26 | 507.65 | 510.52 | 524.57 | 514.00 | 515.80 | 535.13 | 512.21 |
| **Other Services** | | | | | | | | | | | | | |
| 2015 | 721.37 | 752.19 | 758.81 | 724.08 | 734.45 | 732.69 | 732.48 | 769.91 | 745.39 | 743.27 | 751.78 | 731.54 | 742.31 |
| 2016 | 738.99 | 742.60 | 747.18 | 739.12 | 756.93 | 732.80 | 735.13 | 746.82 | 741.44 | 784.34 | 758.75 | 765.14 | 748.06 |
| 2017 | 803.27 | 789.08 | 798.01 | 825.55 | 803.28 | 806.61 | 848.54 | 829.08 | 827.39 | 851.52 | 818.71 | 828.33 | 818.21 |
| 2018 | 808.71 | 827.57 | 813.20 | 843.44 | 820.80 | 818.91 | 861.96 | 837.44 | 876.74 | 845.76 | 849.87 | 900.90 | 842.90 |
| 2019 | 863.59 | 866.13 | 859.92 | 866.33 | 850.82 | 882.90 | 872.55 | 871.12 | 906.50 | 874.84 | 888.92 | 923.04 | 876.69 |

# COLORADO
## *At a Glance*

Population:
  2010 census: 5,029,196
  2019 estimate: 5,758,736

Percent change in population:
  2010–2019: 14.5%

Percent change in total nonfarm employment:
  2011–2019: 23.4%

Industry with the largest growth in employment, 2011–2019 (percent):
  Construction, 58.9%

Industry with the largest decline or smallest growth in employment, 2011–2019 (percent):
  Mining and logging, 3.6%

Civilian labor force:
  2010: 2,724,417
  2019: 3,148,766

Unemployment rate and rank among states (highest to lowest):
  2010: 8.7%, 24th
  2019: 2.8%, 43rd

Over-the-year change in unemployment rates:
  2017–2018: 0.4%
  2018–2019: -0.4%

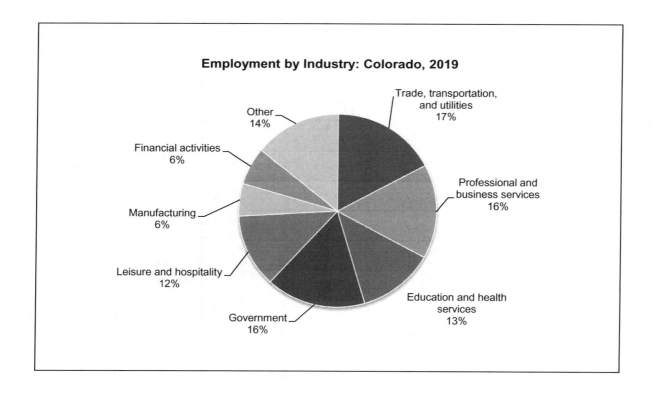

**Employment by Industry: Colorado, 2019**

- Trade, transportation, and utilities 17%
- Professional and business services 16%
- Education and health services 13%
- Government 16%
- Leisure and hospitality 12%
- Manufacturing 6%
- Financial activities 6%
- Other 14%

## 1. Employment by Industry: Colorado, 2011–2019

(Numbers in thousands, not seasonally adjusted)

| Industry and year | January | February | March | April | May | June | July | August | September | October | November | December | Annual average |
|---|---|---|---|---|---|---|---|---|---|---|---|---|---|
| **Total Nonfarm** | | | | | | | | | | | | | |
| 2011 | 2,201.8 | 2,212.1 | 2,227.7 | 2,246.8 | 2,251.4 | 2,273.4 | 2,262.1 | 2,272.9 | 2,278.8 | 2,276.4 | 2,283.4 | 2,300.5 | 2,257.3 |
| 2012 | 2,248.4 | 2,261.9 | 2,281.2 | 2,291.4 | 2,301.8 | 2,329.3 | 2,317.9 | 2,327.7 | 2,329.0 | 2,339.9 | 2,349.7 | 2,362.3 | 2,311.7 |
| 2013 | 2,309.9 | 2,331.0 | 2,348.4 | 2,357.3 | 2,370.1 | 2,395.3 | 2,388.3 | 2,402.2 | 2,402.0 | 2,408.0 | 2,420.1 | 2,433.6 | 2,380.5 |
| 2014 | 2,389.7 | 2,405.1 | 2,421.9 | 2,438.6 | 2,452.6 | 2,478.0 | 2,470.5 | 2,487.1 | 2,488.0 | 2,500.2 | 2,505.2 | 2,527.1 | 2,463.7 |
| 2015 | 2,481.4 | 2,498.3 | 2,508.7 | 2,521.7 | 2,530.6 | 2,555.3 | 2,550.3 | 2,554.8 | 2,557.1 | 2,567.0 | 2,575.5 | 2,591.6 | 2,541.0 |
| 2016 | 2,543.2 | 2,558.4 | 2,570.0 | 2,587.0 | 2,582.2 | 2,614.4 | 2,615.5 | 2,622.0 | 2,627.5 | 2,624.6 | 2,631.1 | 2,645.2 | 2,601.8 |
| 2017 | 2,590.8 | 2,612.5 | 2,630.8 | 2,641.6 | 2,647.2 | 2,678.4 | 2,671.9 | 2,679.2 | 2,680.7 | 2,686.4 | 2,692.7 | 2,711.7 | 2,660.3 |
| 2018 | 2,661.1 | 2,679.8 | 2,696.4 | 2,710.8 | 2,716.7 | 2,749.8 | 2,743.8 | 2,752.7 | 2,736.2 | 2,748.6 | 2,760.2 | 2,771.1 | 2,727.3 |
| 2019 | 2,723.5 | 2,743.6 | 2,749.6 | 2,760.9 | 2,774.3 | 2,798.4 | 2,804.6 | 2,815.1 | 2,798.3 | 2,806.2 | 2,820.1 | 2,832.2 | 2,785.6 |
| **Total Private** | | | | | | | | | | | | | |
| 2011 | 1,818.9 | 1,816.7 | 1,829.8 | 1,846.9 | 1,848.6 | 1,881.6 | 1,891.0 | 1,901.1 | 1,883.9 | 1,875.7 | 1,882.1 | 1,902.3 | 1,864.9 |
| 2012 | 1,865.1 | 1,866.0 | 1,882.1 | 1,891.1 | 1,898.0 | 1,935.9 | 1,945.3 | 1,950.6 | 1,931.3 | 1,937.0 | 1,945.0 | 1,961.1 | 1,917.4 |
| 2013 | 1,918.7 | 1,926.1 | 1,941.0 | 1,949.3 | 1,957.6 | 1,995.2 | 2,008.1 | 2,017.2 | 1,994.4 | 1,993.7 | 2,004.4 | 2,022.7 | 1,977.4 |
| 2014 | 1,991.2 | 1,996.2 | 2,010.2 | 2,025.8 | 2,034.9 | 2,071.8 | 2,086.4 | 2,098.6 | 2,078.0 | 2,080.9 | 2,083.6 | 2,111.1 | 2,055.7 |
| 2015 | 2,075.4 | 2,082.0 | 2,090.1 | 2,100.6 | 2,104.2 | 2,141.2 | 2,157.2 | 2,158.6 | 2,137.8 | 2,138.9 | 2,143.8 | 2,164.6 | 2,124.5 |
| 2016 | 2,126.2 | 2,130.4 | 2,138.6 | 2,152.5 | 2,150.7 | 2,189.9 | 2,210.1 | 2,211.2 | 2,191.1 | 2,187.9 | 2,189.3 | 2,206.2 | 2,173.7 |
| 2017 | 2,168.4 | 2,175.7 | 2,189.2 | 2,199.9 | 2,201.4 | 2,247.3 | 2,256.1 | 2,256.1 | 2,236.9 | 2,238.7 | 2,248.2 | 2,265.6 | 2,223.6 |
| 2018 | 2,229.9 | 2,235.5 | 2,247.8 | 2,261.0 | 2,261.2 | 2,305.4 | 2,317.7 | 2,316.0 | 2,288.3 | 2,294.1 | 2,304.3 | 2,318.9 | 2,281.7 |
| 2019 | 2,283.6 | 2,291.1 | 2,293.6 | 2,302.8 | 2,306.4 | 2,348.0 | 2,368.7 | 2,369.5 | 2,338.8 | 2,340.0 | 2,352.3 | 2,368.2 | 2,330.3 |
| **Goods Producing** | | | | | | | | | | | | | |
| 2011 | 254.9 | 253.6 | 257.5 | 263.9 | 266.3 | 272.6 | 275.5 | 277.4 | 276.0 | 276.8 | 275.2 | 273.1 | 268.6 |
| 2012 | 265.0 | 264.5 | 267.0 | 271.0 | 275.9 | 281.4 | 283.3 | 284.3 | 282.4 | 284.8 | 283.3 | 281.4 | 277.0 |
| 2013 | 273.6 | 275.1 | 278.8 | 281.8 | 288.1 | 295.0 | 297.6 | 300.2 | 298.2 | 300.8 | 301.2 | 299.8 | 290.9 |
| 2014 | 294.9 | 295.5 | 299.2 | 304.9 | 311.1 | 316.9 | 321.1 | 322.4 | 321.5 | 323.1 | 322.1 | 322.0 | 312.9 |
| 2015 | 314.0 | 314.2 | 314.5 | 317.0 | 320.0 | 324.7 | 326.6 | 325.5 | 323.5 | 323.8 | 322.0 | 319.7 | 320.5 |
| 2016 | 312.2 | 312.2 | 314.3 | 317.4 | 319.6 | 324.9 | 327.8 | 327.4 | 326.2 | 327.2 | 325.9 | 324.1 | 321.6 |
| 2017 | 317.6 | 319.9 | 324.1 | 328.1 | 331.3 | 338.9 | 340.6 | 341.2 | 339.7 | 341.9 | 341.6 | 340.6 | 333.8 |
| 2018 | 335.0 | 337.2 | 340.9 | 345.1 | 347.9 | 355.1 | 356.1 | 356.4 | 354.4 | 354.9 | 354.3 | 353.2 | 349.2 |
| 2019 | 347.1 | 349.7 | 351.0 | 354.3 | 357.4 | 363.5 | 365.8 | 365.1 | 361.8 | 360.8 | 359.0 | 358.1 | 357.8 |
| **Service-Providing** | | | | | | | | | | | | | |
| 2011 | 1,946.9 | 1,958.5 | 1,970.2 | 1,982.9 | 1,985.1 | 2,000.8 | 1,986.6 | 1,995.5 | 2,002.8 | 1,999.6 | 2,008.2 | 2,027.4 | 1,988.7 |
| 2012 | 1,983.4 | 1,997.4 | 2,014.2 | 2,020.4 | 2,025.9 | 2,047.9 | 2,034.6 | 2,043.4 | 2,046.6 | 2,055.1 | 2,066.4 | 2,080.9 | 2,034.7 |
| 2013 | 2,036.3 | 2,055.9 | 2,069.6 | 2,075.5 | 2,082.0 | 2,100.3 | 2,090.7 | 2,102.0 | 2,103.8 | 2,107.2 | 2,118.9 | 2,133.8 | 2,089.7 |
| 2014 | 2,094.8 | 2,109.6 | 2,122.7 | 2,133.7 | 2,141.5 | 2,161.1 | 2,149.4 | 2,164.7 | 2,166.5 | 2,177.1 | 2,183.1 | 2,205.1 | 2,150.8 |
| 2015 | 2,167.4 | 2,184.1 | 2,194.2 | 2,204.7 | 2,210.6 | 2,230.6 | 2,223.7 | 2,229.3 | 2,233.6 | 2,243.2 | 2,253.5 | 2,271.9 | 2,220.6 |
| 2016 | 2,231.0 | 2,246.2 | 2,255.7 | 2,269.6 | 2,262.6 | 2,289.5 | 2,287.7 | 2,294.6 | 2,301.3 | 2,297.4 | 2,305.2 | 2,321.1 | 2,280.2 |
| 2017 | 2,273.2 | 2,292.6 | 2,306.7 | 2,313.5 | 2,315.9 | 2,339.5 | 2,331.3 | 2,338.0 | 2,341.0 | 2,344.5 | 2,351.1 | 2,371.1 | 2,326.5 |
| 2018 | 2,326.1 | 2,342.6 | 2,355.5 | 2,365.7 | 2,368.8 | 2,394.7 | 2,387.7 | 2,396.3 | 2,381.8 | 2,393.7 | 2,405.9 | 2,417.9 | 2,378.1 |
| 2019 | 2,376.4 | 2,393.9 | 2,398.6 | 2,406.6 | 2,416.9 | 2,434.9 | 2,438.8 | 2,450.0 | 2,436.5 | 2,445.4 | 2,461.1 | 2,474.1 | 2,427.8 |
| **Mining and Logging** | | | | | | | | | | | | | |
| 2011 | 25.7 | 25.9 | 26.3 | 26.8 | 27.2 | 27.9 | 28.5 | 28.9 | 28.7 | 29.5 | 29.8 | 30.1 | 27.9 |
| 2012 | 30.0 | 30.2 | 30.3 | 30.2 | 30.4 | 30.7 | 30.7 | 30.6 | 30.1 | 30.1 | 29.9 | 29.9 | 30.3 |
| 2013 | 29.5 | 29.6 | 29.6 | 29.6 | 30.0 | 30.5 | 30.8 | 31.2 | 31.1 | 31.4 | 31.6 | 31.8 | 30.6 |
| 2014 | 31.8 | 32.1 | 32.3 | 32.7 | 33.2 | 33.7 | 34.5 | 35.0 | 35.2 | 35.8 | 36.1 | 36.4 | 34.1 |
| 2015 | 35.6 | 34.5 | 33.1 | 31.6 | 31.1 | 30.7 | 30.3 | 29.7 | 28.9 | 28.0 | 27.5 | 27.1 | 30.7 |
| 2016 | 26.0 | 25.4 | 24.6 | 23.7 | 23.3 | 23.1 | 22.8 | 22.9 | 22.9 | 22.9 | 23.0 | 23.4 | 23.7 |
| 2017 | 23.5 | 24.0 | 24.4 | 24.9 | 25.4 | 26.2 | 26.3 | 26.5 | 26.6 | 27.1 | 27.4 | 27.5 | 25.8 |
| 2018 | 27.3 | 27.5 | 28.0 | 28.1 | 28.3 | 28.7 | 28.8 | 29.0 | 28.9 | 29.1 | 29.4 | 29.5 | 28.6 |
| 2019 | 29.1 | 29.2 | 29.3 | 29.3 | 29.2 | 29.3 | 29.3 | 29.2 | 28.5 | 28.5 | 28.3 | 27.7 | 28.9 |
| **Construction** | | | | | | | | | | | | | |
| 2011 | 104.3 | 102.7 | 105.3 | 110.1 | 111.6 | 116.0 | 117.5 | 118.6 | 117.5 | 117.5 | 115.7 | 113.0 | 112.5 |
| 2012 | 106.5 | 105.4 | 107.4 | 111.0 | 115.1 | 119.2 | 120.5 | 121.4 | 120.5 | 122.4 | 121.1 | 119.4 | 115.8 |
| 2013 | 113.4 | 114.4 | 117.5 | 120.3 | 125.8 | 131.1 | 133.2 | 135.1 | 133.7 | 135.8 | 135.7 | 134.0 | 127.5 |
| 2014 | 130.0 | 130.0 | 133.0 | 137.5 | 142.2 | 146.3 | 148.8 | 149.3 | 148.0 | 148.7 | 146.8 | 146.1 | 142.2 |
| 2015 | 139.8 | 140.6 | 141.9 | 145.6 | 148.4 | 151.9 | 154.0 | 153.5 | 152.6 | 154.0 | 152.3 | 150.4 | 148.8 |
| 2016 | 145.0 | 145.2 | 148.0 | 151.9 | 154.2 | 158.8 | 160.9 | 160.8 | 160.3 | 161.1 | 159.7 | 157.1 | 155.3 |
| 2017 | 151.9 | 153.6 | 156.7 | 159.8 | 162.2 | 167.3 | 168.6 | 169.2 | 168.3 | 169.7 | 169.0 | 167.5 | 163.7 |
| 2018 | 162.9 | 164.6 | 166.9 | 170.1 | 172.8 | 177.8 | 178.5 | 178.7 | 177.4 | 177.5 | 176.4 | 174.4 | 173.2 |
| 2019 | 169.6 | 171.2 | 172.0 | 175.6 | 178.6 | 183.3 | 184.9 | 184.9 | 182.9 | 182.2 | 180.7 | 179.7 | 178.8 |

## 1. Employment by Industry: Colorado, 2011–2019—*Continued*

(Numbers in thousands, not seasonally adjusted)

| Industry and year | January | February | March | April | May | June | July | August | September | October | November | December | Annual average |
|---|---|---|---|---|---|---|---|---|---|---|---|---|---|
| **Manufacturing** | | | | | | | | | | | | | |
| 2011 | 124.9 | 125.0 | 125.9 | 127.0 | 127.5 | 128.7 | 129.5 | 129.9 | 129.8 | 129.8 | 129.7 | 130.0 | 128.1 |
| 2012 | 128.5 | 128.9 | 129.3 | 129.8 | 130.4 | 131.5 | 132.1 | 132.3 | 131.8 | 132.3 | 132.3 | 132.1 | 130.9 |
| 2013 | 130.7 | 131.1 | 131.7 | 131.9 | 132.3 | 133.4 | 133.6 | 133.9 | 133.4 | 133.6 | 133.9 | 134.0 | 132.8 |
| 2014 | 133.1 | 133.4 | 133.9 | 134.7 | 135.7 | 136.9 | 137.8 | 138.1 | 138.3 | 138.6 | 139.2 | 139.5 | 136.6 |
| 2015 | 138.6 | 139.1 | 139.5 | 139.8 | 140.5 | 142.1 | 142.3 | 142.3 | 142.0 | 141.8 | 142.2 | 142.2 | 141.0 |
| 2016 | 141.2 | 141.6 | 141.7 | 141.8 | 142.1 | 143.0 | 144.1 | 143.7 | 143.0 | 143.2 | 143.2 | 143.6 | 142.7 |
| 2017 | 142.2 | 142.3 | 143.0 | 143.4 | 143.7 | 145.4 | 145.7 | 145.5 | 144.8 | 145.1 | 145.2 | 145.6 | 144.3 |
| 2018 | 144.8 | 145.1 | 146.0 | 146.9 | 146.8 | 148.6 | 148.8 | 148.7 | 148.1 | 148.3 | 148.5 | 149.3 | 147.5 |
| 2019 | 148.4 | 149.3 | 149.7 | 149.4 | 149.6 | 150.9 | 151.6 | 151.0 | 150.4 | 150.1 | 150.0 | 150.7 | 150.1 |
| **Trade, Transportation, and Utilities** | | | | | | | | | | | | | |
| 2011 | 395.1 | 392.5 | 393.7 | 397.0 | 398.9 | 402.5 | 403.8 | 404.6 | 401.7 | 403.5 | 410.7 | 415.5 | 401.6 |
| 2012 | 402.5 | 399.0 | 401.0 | 402.5 | 405.1 | 409.8 | 411.1 | 411.2 | 409.7 | 413.3 | 422.4 | 426.9 | 409.5 |
| 2013 | 412.6 | 410.6 | 411.7 | 412.9 | 415.5 | 419.9 | 421.4 | 423.3 | 420.6 | 423.0 | 432.1 | 437.8 | 420.1 |
| 2014 | 424.0 | 422.3 | 423.3 | 425.3 | 427.8 | 433.4 | 434.2 | 435.5 | 433.2 | 436.2 | 444.5 | 452.2 | 432.7 |
| 2015 | 438.2 | 436.4 | 437.1 | 438.7 | 440.3 | 445.5 | 448.3 | 448.3 | 445.4 | 448.9 | 457.0 | 463.9 | 445.7 |
| 2016 | 448.1 | 445.8 | 446.1 | 448.0 | 449.5 | 453.1 | 456.2 | 456.4 | 453.7 | 456.4 | 463.9 | 469.9 | 453.9 |
| 2017 | 456.1 | 453.3 | 453.3 | 454.5 | 455.2 | 460.5 | 462.4 | 462.8 | 460.8 | 463.6 | 473.7 | 479.2 | 461.3 |
| 2018 | 465.7 | 461.4 | 462.5 | 463.0 | 464.5 | 469.2 | 471.9 | 472.4 | 469.3 | 472.6 | 484.5 | 488.0 | 470.4 |
| 2019 | 476.2 | 471.9 | 470.5 | 468.7 | 469.8 | 475.6 | 478.6 | 478.5 | 475.1 | 477.5 | 489.8 | 495.6 | 477.3 |
| **Wholesale Trade** | | | | | | | | | | | | | |
| 2011 | 90.4 | 90.5 | 90.9 | 91.4 | 91.8 | 92.2 | 92.5 | 92.6 | 92.4 | 92.2 | 92.3 | 92.5 | 91.8 |
| 2012 | 91.6 | 91.9 | 92.5 | 93.2 | 93.6 | 94.4 | 94.7 | 94.8 | 94.6 | 95.1 | 95.2 | 95.6 | 93.9 |
| 2013 | 94.5 | 94.9 | 95.3 | 95.7 | 96.1 | 96.8 | 96.9 | 97.0 | 96.6 | 97.0 | 97.3 | 97.6 | 96.3 |
| 2014 | 97.0 | 97.6 | 97.9 | 98.6 | 99.2 | 99.8 | 100.3 | 100.8 | 100.5 | 101.0 | 101.5 | 102.2 | 99.7 |
| 2015 | 101.4 | 101.9 | 101.9 | 102.4 | 102.9 | 103.3 | 103.8 | 103.9 | 103.5 | 104.2 | 104.4 | 104.7 | 103.2 |
| 2016 | 103.7 | 103.9 | 103.9 | 104.5 | 104.6 | 104.7 | 105.3 | 105.0 | 104.7 | 105.1 | 105.2 | 105.3 | 104.7 |
| 2017 | 104.8 | 105.1 | 105.5 | 105.8 | 106.1 | 106.8 | 107.0 | 107.1 | 106.8 | 107.0 | 107.0 | 107.1 | 106.3 |
| 2018 | 106.7 | 107.0 | 107.2 | 107.4 | 107.8 | 108.7 | 109.3 | 108.8 | 108.4 | 109.0 | 109.2 | 109.3 | 108.2 |
| 2019 | 108.6 | 109.2 | 109.1 | 108.9 | 109.3 | 110.4 | 111.3 | 111.2 | 110.6 | 109.8 | 111.2 | 111.4 | 110.1 |
| **Retail Trade** | | | | | | | | | | | | | |
| 2011 | 234.5 | 232.4 | 233.1 | 235.9 | 237.3 | 239.9 | 240.5 | 241.3 | 239.0 | 240.5 | 247.0 | 249.8 | 239.3 |
| 2012 | 239.5 | 235.7 | 237.2 | 238.1 | 240.1 | 243.2 | 243.9 | 243.8 | 242.6 | 244.4 | 252.5 | 255.1 | 243.0 |
| 2013 | 243.5 | 241.1 | 242.1 | 243.1 | 245.0 | 248.4 | 249.5 | 250.8 | 248.6 | 249.9 | 257.5 | 260.9 | 248.4 |
| 2014 | 249.6 | 247.4 | 248.4 | 249.7 | 251.0 | 255.2 | 255.5 | 255.8 | 254.1 | 256.3 | 263.2 | 267.4 | 254.5 |
| 2015 | 255.7 | 254.0 | 255.5 | 256.8 | 258.3 | 262.3 | 264.2 | 264.4 | 262.2 | 264.7 | 271.6 | 275.4 | 262.1 |
| 2016 | 263.0 | 261.5 | 262.6 | 263.7 | 265.2 | 268.1 | 270.1 | 270.0 | 267.7 | 269.9 | 276.2 | 278.6 | 268.1 |
| 2017 | 267.7 | 265.0 | 265.6 | 266.8 | 267.5 | 271.0 | 272.3 | 272.2 | 269.6 | 271.3 | 279.0 | 281.3 | 270.8 |
| 2018 | 271.3 | 267.7 | 268.5 | 268.8 | 270.3 | 273.1 | 275.2 | 274.9 | 271.3 | 272.8 | 281.3 | 282.6 | 273.2 |
| 2019 | 273.5 | 270.2 | 269.3 | 268.4 | 268.9 | 272.0 | 272.7 | 272.1 | 269.1 | 271.2 | 279.0 | 279.6 | 272.2 |
| **Transportation and Utilities** | | | | | | | | | | | | | |
| 2011 | 70.2 | 69.6 | 69.7 | 69.7 | 69.8 | 70.4 | 70.8 | 70.7 | 70.3 | 70.8 | 71.4 | 73.2 | 70.6 |
| 2012 | 71.4 | 71.4 | 71.3 | 71.2 | 71.4 | 72.2 | 72.5 | 72.6 | 72.5 | 73.8 | 74.7 | 76.2 | 72.6 |
| 2013 | 74.6 | 74.6 | 74.3 | 74.1 | 74.4 | 74.7 | 75.0 | 75.5 | 75.4 | 76.1 | 77.3 | 79.3 | 75.4 |
| 2014 | 77.4 | 77.3 | 77.0 | 77.0 | 77.6 | 78.4 | 78.4 | 78.9 | 78.6 | 78.9 | 79.8 | 82.6 | 78.5 |
| 2015 | 81.1 | 80.5 | 79.7 | 79.5 | 79.1 | 79.9 | 80.3 | 80.0 | 79.7 | 80.0 | 81.0 | 83.8 | 80.4 |
| 2016 | 81.4 | 80.4 | 79.6 | 79.8 | 79.7 | 80.3 | 80.8 | 81.4 | 81.3 | 81.4 | 82.5 | 86.0 | 81.2 |
| 2017 | 83.6 | 83.2 | 82.2 | 81.9 | 81.6 | 82.7 | 83.1 | 83.5 | 84.4 | 85.3 | 87.7 | 90.8 | 84.2 |
| 2018 | 87.7 | 86.7 | 86.8 | 86.8 | 86.4 | 87.4 | 87.4 | 88.7 | 89.6 | 90.8 | 94.0 | 96.1 | 89.0 |
| 2019 | 94.1 | 92.5 | 92.1 | 91.4 | 91.6 | 93.2 | 94.6 | 95.2 | 95.4 | 96.5 | 99.6 | 104.6 | 95.1 |
| **Information** | | | | | | | | | | | | | |
| 2011 | 72.3 | 72.2 | 71.8 | 71.8 | 71.6 | 71.5 | 71.2 | 71.1 | 70.9 | 70.7 | 70.8 | 70.6 | 71.4 |
| 2012 | 70.2 | 70.2 | 70.3 | 69.7 | 69.8 | 70.0 | 69.6 | 69.5 | 69.2 | 69.4 | 69.7 | 69.9 | 69.8 |
| 2013 | 69.6 | 69.7 | 69.7 | 69.4 | 69.6 | 70.2 | 70.4 | 70.3 | 69.7 | 69.5 | 70.1 | 70.1 | 69.9 |
| 2014 | 70.1 | 70.2 | 70.1 | 69.6 | 69.8 | 70.5 | 71.0 | 71.2 | 70.0 | 70.2 | 70.5 | 70.7 | 70.3 |
| 2015 | 70.3 | 70.6 | 70.4 | 70.0 | 70.3 | 70.9 | 71.3 | 71.3 | 70.6 | 70.6 | 71.1 | 71.3 | 70.7 |
| 2016 | 71.1 | 71.5 | 71.5 | 71.5 | 71.6 | 72.0 | 72.8 | 72.8 | 71.8 | 72.0 | 72.3 | 72.1 | 71.9 |
| 2017 | 71.4 | 71.7 | 71.4 | 71.0 | 70.8 | 71.8 | 71.9 | 72.0 | 71.6 | 72.1 | 73.3 | 73.5 | 71.9 |
| 2018 | 73.8 | 74.5 | 74.3 | 74.7 | 75.0 | 75.9 | 76.0 | 75.6 | 75.1 | 75.6 | 75.9 | 75.9 | 75.2 |
| 2019 | 75.8 | 76.0 | 75.3 | 75.6 | 75.6 | 76.4 | 76.4 | 76.3 | 75.8 | 76.7 | 76.3 | 75.8 | 76.0 |

## 1. Employment by Industry: Colorado, 2011–2019—*Continued*

(Numbers in thousands, not seasonally adjusted)

| Industry and year | January | February | March | April | May | June | July | August | September | October | November | December | Annual average |
|---|---|---|---|---|---|---|---|---|---|---|---|---|---|
| **Financial Activities** | | | | | | | | | | | | | |
| 2011 | 143.6 | 143.4 | 143.5 | 143.3 | 142.8 | 144.0 | 144.1 | 144.4 | 143.7 | 143.3 | 144.3 | 146.3 | 143.9 |
| 2012 | 144.4 | 144.7 | 145.4 | 145.3 | 145.2 | 146.8 | 147.3 | 147.7 | 146.8 | 147.9 | 148.3 | 150.3 | 146.7 |
| 2013 | 148.6 | 149.5 | 150.3 | 150.1 | 149.7 | 151.3 | 152.1 | 152.2 | 151.3 | 151.5 | 151.9 | 153.4 | 151.0 |
| 2014 | 151.5 | 152.0 | 152.2 | 152.5 | 152.4 | 153.7 | 154.7 | 155.1 | 154.1 | 155.0 | 155.7 | 157.8 | 153.9 |
| 2015 | 156.2 | 156.9 | 157.3 | 157.4 | 157.4 | 159.0 | 160.2 | 160.5 | 159.5 | 160.4 | 160.7 | 162.7 | 159.0 |
| 2016 | 161.4 | 161.6 | 161.8 | 162.2 | 162.1 | 163.9 | 165.3 | 165.7 | 164.6 | 165.2 | 165.4 | 167.0 | 163.9 |
| 2017 | 165.5 | 166.1 | 166.6 | 167.0 | 166.9 | 169.0 | 169.4 | 169.2 | 168.3 | 169.1 | 169.3 | 171.1 | 168.1 |
| 2018 | 169.4 | 170.0 | 170.2 | 170.7 | 170.4 | 172.3 | 173.4 | 172.8 | 171.4 | 172.2 | 172.5 | 174.1 | 171.6 |
| 2019 | 172.5 | 173.2 | 173.3 | 172.7 | 172.3 | 173.6 | 174.8 | 174.9 | 173.7 | 175.1 | 174.8 | 175.3 | 173.9 |
| **Professional and Business Services** | | | | | | | | | | | | | |
| 2011 | 328.6 | 330.0 | 330.8 | 338.8 | 341.4 | 344.8 | 346.4 | 348.9 | 346.6 | 346.7 | 347.2 | 347.8 | 341.5 |
| 2012 | 340.3 | 342.3 | 345.0 | 351.8 | 355.8 | 360.9 | 363.0 | 365.2 | 362.7 | 367.5 | 365.1 | 363.7 | 356.9 |
| 2013 | 356.4 | 359.6 | 362.9 | 368.1 | 371.6 | 376.7 | 378.7 | 381.3 | 378.2 | 380.4 | 379.2 | 378.5 | 372.6 |
| 2014 | 370.2 | 372.2 | 374.1 | 381.0 | 384.5 | 390.0 | 391.5 | 396.8 | 393.6 | 397.0 | 393.4 | 394.8 | 386.6 |
| 2015 | 386.8 | 388.7 | 390.0 | 394.9 | 397.5 | 401.4 | 404.3 | 405.5 | 402.3 | 404.9 | 402.8 | 402.0 | 398.4 |
| 2016 | 393.4 | 395.0 | 395.8 | 403.5 | 403.8 | 408.9 | 413.5 | 413.2 | 411.2 | 412.2 | 410.4 | 407.7 | 405.7 |
| 2017 | 398.5 | 400.6 | 403.2 | 409.6 | 412.3 | 417.7 | 419.6 | 419.8 | 417.4 | 419.8 | 418.6 | 415.9 | 412.8 |
| 2018 | 406.9 | 411.2 | 413.1 | 420.2 | 423.0 | 428.2 | 433.6 | 432.8 | 428.0 | 432.1 | 429.9 | 428.2 | 423.9 |
| 2019 | 421.2 | 425.0 | 426.2 | 433.8 | 437.2 | 443.2 | 449.5 | 451.2 | 446.2 | 449.0 | 449.3 | 447.7 | 440.0 |
| **Education and Health Services** | | | | | | | | | | | | | |
| 2011 | 267.2 | 269.2 | 270.6 | 271.7 | 272.3 | 271.6 | 271.1 | 273.4 | 274.8 | 276.4 | 276.9 | 279.4 | 272.9 |
| 2012 | 276.6 | 279.3 | 280.1 | 280.4 | 280.8 | 280.5 | 279.9 | 281.5 | 282.6 | 285.2 | 286.2 | 288.2 | 281.8 |
| 2013 | 280.4 | 282.7 | 283.4 | 284.8 | 285.2 | 283.7 | 283.8 | 286.2 | 286.8 | 289.6 | 291.5 | 292.7 | 285.9 |
| 2014 | 290.3 | 293.1 | 294.4 | 296.6 | 297.5 | 296.3 | 295.9 | 299.0 | 299.8 | 303.3 | 304.6 | 305.6 | 298.0 |
| 2015 | 304.7 | 307.5 | 308.8 | 311.4 | 312.3 | 312.0 | 312.5 | 314.0 | 314.7 | 319.2 | 320.7 | 321.4 | 313.3 |
| 2016 | 318.8 | 321.3 | 322.4 | 325.5 | 325.7 | 324.9 | 325.6 | 326.9 | 327.8 | 329.6 | 330.1 | 330.4 | 325.8 |
| 2017 | 327.9 | 330.7 | 332.2 | 333.9 | 334.4 | 334.0 | 332.8 | 334.2 | 334.9 | 337.1 | 338.0 | 338.8 | 334.1 |
| 2018 | 336.2 | 338.9 | 339.7 | 340.8 | 341.1 | 339.9 | 339.0 | 340.4 | 339.9 | 343.1 | 344.2 | 345.1 | 340.7 |
| 2019 | 342.0 | 345.1 | 345.0 | 346.1 | 346.5 | 345.5 | 345.4 | 347.7 | 346.7 | 350.8 | 354.9 | 355.7 | 347.6 |
| **Leisure and Hospitality** | | | | | | | | | | | | | |
| 2011 | 265.4 | 264.1 | 269.4 | 267.0 | 261.6 | 279.5 | 284.1 | 286.0 | 275.8 | 264.6 | 263.4 | 275.4 | 271.4 |
| 2012 | 272.0 | 271.5 | 278.1 | 275.0 | 269.8 | 289.3 | 293.7 | 294.0 | 281.6 | 272.5 | 274.0 | 284.3 | 279.7 |
| 2013 | 281.2 | 282.6 | 287.4 | 285.3 | 280.3 | 299.6 | 305.1 | 304.7 | 291.7 | 281.4 | 280.7 | 292.4 | 289.4 |
| 2014 | 291.7 | 292.4 | 297.9 | 296.3 | 291.8 | 309.3 | 315.3 | 315.4 | 304.2 | 294.0 | 291.0 | 305.5 | 300.4 |
| 2015 | 303.0 | 305.4 | 309.2 | 307.9 | 303.0 | 322.6 | 328.1 | 327.8 | 317.0 | 306.5 | 305.0 | 318.4 | 312.8 |
| 2016 | 316.1 | 317.4 | 320.8 | 318.3 | 312.0 | 334.0 | 339.8 | 339.5 | 327.3 | 316.9 | 313.5 | 327.6 | 323.6 |
| 2017 | 324.9 | 325.9 | 330.3 | 327.7 | 322.1 | 345.5 | 349.6 | 347.2 | 335.3 | 326.3 | 325.3 | 337.7 | 333.2 |
| 2018 | 334.8 | 333.9 | 338.0 | 336.4 | 328.4 | 351.9 | 354.9 | 353.1 | 338.5 | 331.7 | 331.4 | 343.2 | 339.7 |
| 2019 | 338.3 | 339.1 | 340.8 | 339.5 | 334.7 | 355.7 | 363.0 | 361.0 | 346.0 | 335.3 | 334.6 | 347.1 | 344.6 |
| **Other Services** | | | | | | | | | | | | | |
| 2011 | 91.8 | 91.7 | 92.5 | 93.4 | 93.7 | 95.1 | 94.8 | 95.3 | 94.4 | 93.7 | 93.6 | 94.2 | 93.7 |
| 2012 | 94.1 | 94.5 | 95.2 | 95.4 | 95.6 | 97.2 | 97.4 | 97.2 | 96.3 | 96.4 | 96.0 | 96.4 | 96.0 |
| 2013 | 96.3 | 96.3 | 96.8 | 96.9 | 97.6 | 98.8 | 99.0 | 99.0 | 97.9 | 97.5 | 97.7 | 98.0 | 97.7 |
| 2014 | 98.5 | 98.5 | 99.0 | 99.6 | 100.0 | 101.7 | 102.7 | 103.2 | 101.6 | 102.1 | 101.8 | 102.5 | 100.9 |
| 2015 | 102.2 | 102.3 | 102.8 | 103.3 | 103.4 | 105.1 | 105.9 | 105.7 | 104.8 | 104.6 | 104.5 | 105.2 | 104.2 |
| 2016 | 105.1 | 105.6 | 105.9 | 106.1 | 106.4 | 108.2 | 109.1 | 109.3 | 108.5 | 108.4 | 107.8 | 107.4 | 107.3 |
| 2017 | 106.5 | 107.5 | 108.1 | 108.1 | 108.4 | 109.9 | 109.8 | 109.7 | 108.9 | 108.8 | 108.4 | 108.8 | 108.6 |
| 2018 | 108.1 | 108.4 | 109.1 | 110.1 | 110.9 | 112.9 | 112.8 | 112.5 | 111.7 | 111.9 | 111.6 | 111.2 | 110.9 |
| 2019 | 110.5 | 111.1 | 111.5 | 112.1 | 112.9 | 114.5 | 115.2 | 114.8 | 113.5 | 114.8 | 113.6 | 112.9 | 113.1 |
| **Government** | | | | | | | | | | | | | |
| 2011 | 382.9 | 395.4 | 397.9 | 399.9 | 402.8 | 391.8 | 371.1 | 371.8 | 394.9 | 400.7 | 401.3 | 398.2 | 392.4 |
| 2012 | 383.3 | 395.9 | 399.1 | 400.3 | 403.8 | 393.4 | 372.6 | 377.1 | 397.7 | 402.9 | 404.7 | 401.2 | 394.3 |
| 2013 | 391.2 | 404.9 | 407.4 | 408.0 | 412.5 | 400.1 | 380.2 | 385.0 | 407.6 | 414.3 | 415.7 | 410.9 | 403.2 |
| 2014 | 398.5 | 408.9 | 411.7 | 412.8 | 417.7 | 406.2 | 384.1 | 388.5 | 410.0 | 419.3 | 421.6 | 416.0 | 407.9 |
| 2015 | 406.0 | 416.3 | 418.6 | 421.1 | 426.4 | 414.1 | 393.1 | 396.2 | 419.3 | 428.1 | 431.7 | 427.0 | 416.5 |
| 2016 | 417.0 | 428.0 | 431.4 | 434.5 | 431.5 | 424.5 | 405.4 | 410.8 | 436.4 | 436.7 | 441.8 | 439.0 | 428.1 |
| 2017 | 422.4 | 436.8 | 441.6 | 441.7 | 445.8 | 431.1 | 415.8 | 423.1 | 443.8 | 447.7 | 444.5 | 446.1 | 436.7 |
| 2018 | 431.2 | 444.3 | 448.6 | 449.8 | 455.5 | 444.4 | 426.1 | 436.7 | 447.9 | 454.5 | 455.9 | 452.2 | 445.6 |
| 2019 | 439.9 | 452.5 | 456.0 | 458.1 | 467.9 | 450.4 | 435.9 | 445.6 | 459.5 | 466.2 | 467.8 | 464.0 | 455.3 |

## 2. Average Weekly Hours by Selected Industry: Colorado, 2015–2019

(Not seasonally adjusted)

| Industry and year | January | February | March | April | May | June | July | August | September | October | November | December | Annual average |
|---|---|---|---|---|---|---|---|---|---|---|---|---|---|
| **Total Private** | | | | | | | | | | | | | |
| 2015 | 33.6 | 34.4 | 34.4 | 33.6 | 33.7 | 34.0 | 34.1 | 34.8 | 33.9 | 33.9 | 34.0 | 33.2 | 34.0 |
| 2016 | 33.4 | 33.2 | 33.3 | 33.2 | 33.9 | 33.7 | 33.8 | 33.8 | 33.7 | 34.2 | 33.3 | 33.2 | 33.5 |
| 2017 | 33.1 | 32.9 | 32.9 | 33.7 | 33.8 | 33.8 | 34.4 | 33.8 | 33.5 | 33.9 | 33.4 | 33.3 | 33.5 |
| 2018 | 33.2 | 33.3 | 33.5 | 33.9 | 33.9 | 33.9 | 34.4 | 33.8 | 34.2 | 33.4 | 33.3 | 33.7 | 33.7 |
| 2019 | 32.7 | 33.1 | 32.6 | 32.7 | 33.2 | 34.3 | 33.5 | 33.6 | 34.1 | 33.1 | 33.2 | 33.8 | 33.3 |
| **Goods-Producing** | | | | | | | | | | | | | |
| 2015 | 39.3 | 40.1 | 40.3 | 39.4 | 39.0 | 40.0 | 40.0 | 40.8 | 39.8 | 40.2 | 40.1 | 40.0 | 39.9 |
| 2016 | 39.5 | 39.0 | 39.1 | 39.3 | 39.6 | 39.9 | 39.7 | 39.7 | 39.8 | 39.9 | 39.5 | 38.1 | 39.4 |
| 2017 | 38.7 | 39.0 | 38.8 | 39.7 | 39.6 | 40.7 | 40.3 | 39.9 | 40.2 | 40.1 | 39.9 | 39.4 | 39.7 |
| 2018 | 39.0 | 39.2 | 39.8 | 40.1 | 40.5 | 40.7 | 40.3 | 39.7 | 40.2 | 40.2 | 39.3 | 40.1 | 39.9 |
| 2019 | 38.8 | 39.3 | 38.5 | 40.4 | 40.0 | 41.3 | 40.6 | 40.9 | 40.9 | 40.2 | 41.2 | 41.7 | 40.3 |
| **Construction** | | | | | | | | | | | | | |
| 2015 | 37.8 | 38.7 | 39.0 | 38.7 | 37.6 | 39.4 | 39.8 | 40.9 | 39.0 | 40.3 | 39.5 | 39.9 | 39.2 |
| 2016 | 38.7 | 37.9 | 38.5 | 38.9 | 39.7 | 40.0 | 39.6 | 40.1 | 39.8 | 39.5 | 38.8 | 36.6 | 39.0 |
| 2017 | 36.7 | 38.0 | 37.5 | 38.1 | 38.1 | 39.8 | 39.1 | 38.7 | 38.9 | 38.5 | 38.4 | 37.6 | 38.3 |
| 2018 | 37.1 | 36.9 | 38.2 | 38.2 | 39.4 | 39.6 | 39.2 | 39.0 | 39.1 | 40.1 | 38.5 | 39.3 | 38.7 |
| 2019 | 37.7 | 38.3 | 37.0 | 38.7 | 38.1 | 40.1 | 39.2 | 40.0 | 39.8 | 39.1 | 39.8 | 39.9 | 39.0 |
| **Manufacturing** | | | | | | | | | | | | | |
| 2015 | 39.3 | 40.3 | 40.4 | 39.2 | 39.7 | 40.1 | 39.9 | 40.2 | 40.1 | 39.8 | 40.0 | 39.6 | 39.9 |
| 2016 | 39.8 | 39.5 | 39.4 | 39.6 | 39.3 | 39.3 | 39.5 | 38.9 | 39.5 | 40.0 | 39.7 | 39.6 | 39.5 |
| 2017 | 40.4 | 39.3 | 39.3 | 40.2 | 39.9 | 40.2 | 40.2 | 40.2 | 39.8 | 39.9 | 39.7 | 39.5 | 39.9 |
| 2018 | 39.6 | 39.5 | 39.6 | 39.9 | 39.8 | 40.1 | 39.9 | 39.4 | 39.8 | 39.4 | 39.7 | 39.8 | 39.7 |
| 2019 | 39.4 | 39.3 | 39.2 | 39.8 | 40.1 | 40.5 | 40.7 | 40.0 | 39.9 | 39.5 | 40.6 | 41.1 | 40.0 |
| **Trade, Transportation, and Utilities** | | | | | | | | | | | | | |
| 2015 | 33.7 | 34.6 | 34.5 | 33.4 | 34.0 | 34.2 | 34.5 | 34.7 | 34.5 | 34.2 | 34.3 | 34.0 | 34.2 |
| 2016 | 33.7 | 33.7 | 33.4 | 33.4 | 33.6 | 33.7 | 33.6 | 33.7 | 33.3 | 33.8 | 33.0 | 33.5 | 33.5 |
| 2017 | 33.3 | 33.2 | 32.9 | 33.5 | 32.8 | 33.2 | 33.9 | 33.4 | 33.2 | 33.7 | 33.4 | 33.3 | 33.3 |
| 2018 | 33.2 | 33.3 | 33.0 | 33.6 | 33.9 | 33.8 | 34.5 | 33.6 | 34.2 | 33.1 | 33.2 | 33.6 | 33.6 |
| 2019 | 33.2 | 32.6 | 32.1 | 32.6 | 33.0 | 33.9 | 33.2 | 33.0 | 33.3 | 32.3 | 32.0 | 33.1 | 32.9 |
| **Financial Activities** | | | | | | | | | | | | | |
| 2015 | 36.8 | 37.7 | 37.5 | 36.5 | 36.4 | 36.0 | 36.1 | 37.4 | 36.3 | 36.1 | 37.6 | 36.2 | 36.7 |
| 2016 | 36.8 | 36.5 | 36.3 | 36.8 | 37.4 | 37.1 | 36.9 | 36.9 | 37.0 | 37.9 | 37.1 | 36.5 | 36.9 |
| 2017 | 37.7 | 36.6 | 36.5 | 37.8 | 36.5 | 36.6 | 37.5 | 36.9 | 36.8 | 37.4 | 36.8 | 37.1 | 37.0 |
| 2018 | 36.8 | 36.8 | 36.7 | 37.7 | 36.3 | 36.7 | 37.6 | 36.4 | 37.9 | 36.9 | 36.4 | 37.3 | 37.0 |
| 2019 | 36.2 | 35.9 | 36.0 | 36.3 | 36.6 | 37.9 | 36.8 | 36.9 | 37.7 | 36.5 | 36.8 | 37.7 | 36.8 |
| **Professional and Business Services** | | | | | | | | | | | | | |
| 2015 | 36.2 | 37.0 | 37.2 | 36.5 | 36.6 | 36.6 | 36.6 | 37.2 | 36.2 | 36.2 | 36.2 | 35.1 | 36.5 |
| 2016 | 35.4 | 35.3 | 35.3 | 35.6 | 36.2 | 35.9 | 36.0 | 36.0 | 36.5 | 37.0 | 36.0 | 35.8 | 35.9 |
| 2017 | 35.9 | 35.3 | 35.4 | 36.3 | 35.5 | 36.3 | 36.6 | 35.9 | 35.4 | 35.4 | 35.0 | 35.3 | 35.7 |
| 2018 | 35.4 | 34.8 | 35.4 | 36.1 | 35.7 | 36.4 | 37.0 | 36.8 | 37.1 | 35.9 | 36.1 | 36.8 | 36.1 |
| 2019 | 35.7 | 36.1 | 35.4 | 35.6 | 35.9 | 37.1 | 36.3 | 36.8 | 37.3 | 36.1 | 36.1 | 36.4 | 36.2 |
| **Education and Health Services** | | | | | | | | | | | | | |
| 2015 | 31.3 | 32.0 | 31.9 | 31.1 | 31.1 | 30.9 | 30.6 | 31.4 | 30.7 | 30.6 | 31.4 | 30.5 | 31.1 |
| 2016 | 31.1 | 31.0 | 31.3 | 31.1 | 31.7 | 30.8 | 31.5 | 31.3 | 31.5 | 31.7 | 31.3 | 31.6 | 31.3 |
| 2017 | 32.2 | 31.9 | 31.9 | 32.9 | 32.0 | 32.2 | 32.9 | 32.5 | 31.9 | 32.4 | 32.1 | 31.9 | 32.2 |
| 2018 | 31.7 | 31.7 | 31.8 | 32.1 | 31.7 | 31.4 | 31.6 | 31.1 | 31.4 | 30.7 | 30.9 | 31.7 | 31.5 |
| 2019 | 30.9 | 31.3 | 30.8 | 31.3 | 31.5 | 32.1 | 31.0 | 31.6 | 32.0 | 31.6 | 31.4 | 32.1 | 31.5 |
| **Leisure and Hospitality** | | | | | | | | | | | | | |
| 2015 | 25.9 | 26.7 | 26.9 | 26.0 | 26.1 | 26.6 | 26.8 | 27.6 | 26.1 | 26.2 | 25.2 | 25.0 | 26.3 |
| 2016 | 25.3 | 25.5 | 25.9 | 24.4 | 26.1 | 26.2 | 26.5 | 26.4 | 25.7 | 26.0 | 24.8 | 25.0 | 25.7 |
| 2017 | 24.7 | 24.7 | 25.2 | 24.2 | 24.6 | 26.0 | 26.7 | 26.1 | 25.4 | 25.6 | 24.5 | 24.7 | 25.2 |
| 2018 | 25.5 | 25.5 | 25.6 | 24.8 | 25.5 | 26.0 | 26.5 | 26.2 | 25.8 | 25.0 | 23.8 | 24.6 | 25.4 |
| 2019 | 24.0 | 25.0 | 24.8 | 23.8 | 25.1 | 26.3 | 26.1 | 25.5 | 25.7 | 24.8 | 24.4 | 24.9 | 25.0 |
| **Other Services** | | | | | | | | | | | | | |
| 2015 | 29.8 | 31.0 | 31.1 | 30.1 | 30.4 | 32.2 | 32.3 | 33.6 | 32.5 | 32.7 | 34.2 | 32.8 | 31.9 |
| 2016 | 33.5 | 33.0 | 33.0 | 33.1 | 34.2 | 33.3 | 34.1 | 34.2 | 33.7 | 35.6 | 33.4 | 33.7 | 33.7 |
| 2017 | 33.9 | 33.5 | 33.6 | 35.1 | 33.8 | 34.4 | 36.0 | 35.2 | 35.1 | 36.2 | 35.4 | 35.2 | 34.8 |
| 2018 | 34.7 | 35.0 | 34.3 | 35.6 | 34.6 | 34.1 | 34.0 | 32.9 | 33.8 | 33.0 | 32.6 | 33.0 | 34.0 |
| 2019 | 32.4 | 32.8 | 31.9 | 32.3 | 33.3 | 34.2 | 32.9 | 34.2 | 34.5 | 33.5 | 34.4 | 33.8 | 33.4 |

## 3. Average Hourly Earnings by Selected Industry: Colorado, 2015–2019

(Dollars, not seasonally adjusted)

| Industry and year | January | February | March | April | May | June | July | August | September | October | November | December | Annual average |
|---|---|---|---|---|---|---|---|---|---|---|---|---|---|
| **Total Private** | | | | | | | | | | | | | |
| 2015 | 26.64 | 26.74 | 26.81 | 26.85 | 26.82 | 26.41 | 26.76 | 27.00 | 26.81 | 27.06 | 27.25 | 27.02 | 26.85 |
| 2016 | 27.41 | 27.47 | 27.31 | 27.42 | 27.31 | 26.80 | 26.62 | 26.60 | 26.76 | 27.24 | 26.97 | 26.95 | 27.07 |
| 2017 | 27.42 | 27.44 | 27.26 | 27.74 | 27.16 | 27.25 | 27.65 | 27.46 | 27.77 | 27.95 | 27.94 | 28.12 | 27.60 |
| 2018 | 28.21 | 28.42 | 28.39 | 28.79 | 28.51 | 28.66 | 28.78 | 28.90 | 29.38 | 29.55 | 29.57 | 29.88 | 28.92 |
| 2019 | 30.10 | 29.95 | 30.26 | 30.35 | 30.22 | 30.19 | 30.25 | 30.12 | 30.79 | 30.53 | 30.66 | 31.00 | 30.37 |
| **Goods-Producing** | | | | | | | | | | | | | |
| 2015 | 29.10 | 29.28 | 29.42 | 29.57 | 29.54 | 29.43 | 29.88 | 30.08 | 29.96 | 29.96 | 30.19 | 30.13 | 29.72 |
| 2016 | 30.93 | 31.22 | 31.22 | 31.17 | 31.00 | 30.57 | 30.49 | 30.25 | 30.20 | 30.48 | 30.63 | 30.86 | 30.74 |
| 2017 | 30.90 | 31.01 | 30.58 | 30.71 | 30.13 | 29.71 | 29.80 | 29.83 | 30.12 | 30.13 | 30.31 | 30.87 | 30.33 |
| 2018 | 30.97 | 30.71 | 31.02 | 30.89 | 30.84 | 30.55 | 30.74 | 31.07 | 31.16 | 31.59 | 31.88 | 32.50 | 31.16 |
| 2019 | 32.33 | 32.54 | 32.73 | 32.46 | 32.15 | 31.69 | 32.01 | 32.08 | 32.41 | 32.65 | 32.77 | 33.91 | 32.48 |
| **Construction** | | | | | | | | | | | | | |
| 2015 | 28.06 | 28.64 | 28.22 | 28.44 | 28.21 | 27.83 | 28.04 | 27.75 | 27.61 | 27.78 | 27.73 | 27.41 | 27.96 |
| 2016 | 27.86 | 28.08 | 27.81 | 27.56 | 27.49 | 27.25 | 27.37 | 27.09 | 27.00 | 27.14 | 26.96 | 26.85 | 27.36 |
| 2017 | 26.92 | 26.76 | 26.74 | 27.08 | 26.86 | 26.85 | 26.65 | 26.93 | 27.33 | 27.29 | 27.84 | 28.34 | 27.14 |
| 2018 | 28.31 | 28.56 | 28.61 | 28.49 | 28.65 | 28.52 | 28.71 | 29.07 | 29.26 | 29.90 | 29.93 | 30.39 | 29.05 |
| 2019 | 30.04 | 30.50 | 30.52 | 30.41 | 30.06 | 29.58 | 29.79 | 30.10 | 30.79 | 30.80 | 30.90 | 31.91 | 30.45 |
| **Manufacturing** | | | | | | | | | | | | | |
| 2015 | 28.40 | 28.31 | 29.19 | 29.66 | 29.61 | 29.76 | 30.63 | 30.83 | 30.50 | 30.69 | 31.14 | 31.49 | 30.03 |
| 2016 | 32.05 | 31.89 | 32.14 | 32.41 | 32.22 | 32.00 | 31.85 | 31.93 | 31.91 | 32.47 | 32.89 | 33.16 | 32.24 |
| 2017 | 32.67 | 32.36 | 31.72 | 31.48 | 31.49 | 31.18 | 30.45 | 30.32 | 30.75 | 30.89 | 30.61 | 31.16 | 31.25 |
| 2018 | 31.59 | 30.75 | 31.09 | 31.22 | 31.15 | 30.66 | 30.77 | 31.48 | 31.37 | 31.22 | 31.97 | 32.21 | 31.29 |
| 2019 | 32.77 | 33.00 | 33.38 | 33.58 | 33.26 | 32.75 | 32.63 | 33.01 | 32.42 | 32.20 | 32.26 | 32.54 | 32.81 |
| **Trade, Transportation, and Utilities** | | | | | | | | | | | | | |
| 2015 | 22.87 | 22.93 | 23.08 | 23.07 | 22.97 | 22.65 | 22.98 | 23.21 | 23.02 | 23.06 | 22.88 | 22.65 | 22.95 |
| 2016 | 23.22 | 23.23 | 23.59 | 23.44 | 23.26 | 23.12 | 22.61 | 22.67 | 22.90 | 22.87 | 22.37 | 21.99 | 22.93 |
| 2017 | 22.31 | 22.14 | 22.29 | 22.31 | 21.66 | 21.28 | 21.81 | 21.61 | 22.15 | 21.88 | 21.77 | 21.92 | 21.93 |
| 2018 | 22.48 | 23.08 | 22.80 | 23.55 | 23.03 | 23.34 | 23.49 | 23.40 | 23.67 | 23.35 | 23.30 | 23.94 | 23.29 |
| 2019 | 24.49 | 23.96 | 24.33 | 23.96 | 23.69 | 24.07 | 24.13 | 23.98 | 24.84 | 24.45 | 24.66 | 24.58 | 24.26 |
| **Financial Activities** | | | | | | | | | | | | | |
| 2015 | 30.77 | 30.85 | 31.23 | 31.59 | 31.57 | 30.63 | 31.35 | 31.94 | 31.38 | 31.64 | 31.63 | 30.86 | 31.29 |
| 2016 | 30.82 | 30.69 | 30.76 | 31.12 | 31.53 | 30.38 | 30.43 | 30.55 | 31.07 | 31.84 | 31.64 | 31.18 | 31.00 |
| 2017 | 31.72 | 31.86 | 30.97 | 31.94 | 31.54 | 31.12 | 31.63 | 31.61 | 31.66 | 31.95 | 31.71 | 31.85 | 31.63 |
| 2018 | 32.32 | 32.67 | 33.09 | 34.30 | 34.06 | 33.08 | 34.44 | 34.51 | 35.55 | 35.44 | 35.42 | 35.02 | 34.17 |
| 2019 | 34.76 | 34.27 | 34.21 | 34.82 | 34.11 | 35.29 | 34.77 | 34.43 | 35.15 | 34.90 | 34.52 | 34.94 | 34.69 |
| **Professional and Business Services** | | | | | | | | | | | | | |
| 2015 | 32.56 | 32.48 | 32.30 | 32.13 | 31.86 | 31.45 | 32.05 | 32.43 | 32.18 | 32.44 | 33.32 | 33.26 | 32.37 |
| 2016 | 33.65 | 34.00 | 33.40 | 33.00 | 32.61 | 31.82 | 31.91 | 31.65 | 31.37 | 31.92 | 31.62 | 31.92 | 32.38 |
| 2017 | 31.19 | 31.53 | 31.32 | 32.26 | 31.65 | 31.54 | 32.40 | 31.95 | 32.10 | 32.72 | 33.04 | 33.60 | 32.11 |
| 2018 | 34.10 | 34.53 | 33.95 | 34.39 | 33.93 | 34.37 | 34.45 | 34.81 | 35.50 | 35.62 | 35.92 | 36.80 | 34.88 |
| 2019 | 37.55 | 37.51 | 38.13 | 37.88 | 38.01 | 37.74 | 37.69 | 37.86 | 38.84 | 38.22 | 38.30 | 38.74 | 38.05 |
| **Education and Health Services** | | | | | | | | | | | | | |
| 2015 | 24.87 | 25.31 | 25.30 | 25.24 | 25.46 | 25.81 | 26.09 | 25.83 | 25.99 | 26.19 | 26.49 | 26.43 | 25.75 |
| 2016 | 26.13 | 26.03 | 25.79 | 25.94 | 25.62 | 25.60 | 25.57 | 25.49 | 25.74 | 26.10 | 25.62 | 25.98 | 25.80 |
| 2017 | 25.77 | 25.88 | 25.76 | 26.05 | 25.89 | 25.93 | 25.89 | 25.89 | 25.72 | 25.91 | 25.90 | 26.22 | 25.90 |
| 2018 | 25.61 | 25.90 | 26.25 | 26.38 | 25.81 | 25.95 | 26.40 | 26.57 | 27.36 | 27.35 | 28.18 | 28.08 | 26.65 |
| 2019 | 28.16 | 28.12 | 28.47 | 28.55 | 28.73 | 28.61 | 28.97 | 28.85 | 29.29 | 29.38 | 29.11 | 29.15 | 28.79 |
| **Leisure and Hospitality** | | | | | | | | | | | | | |
| 2015 | 15.82 | 15.70 | 16.04 | 15.89 | 15.80 | 15.36 | 15.43 | 15.64 | 15.20 | 15.65 | 15.43 | 15.92 | 15.65 |
| 2016 | 15.86 | 16.14 | 16.18 | 16.26 | 16.39 | 16.18 | 16.32 | 16.44 | 16.63 | 17.14 | 16.74 | 17.03 | 16.44 |
| 2017 | 17.62 | 17.71 | 17.78 | 17.25 | 17.32 | 17.00 | 17.32 | 17.19 | 17.54 | 18.34 | 17.86 | 18.30 | 17.59 |
| 2018 | 18.17 | 18.40 | 18.71 | 18.66 | 18.52 | 18.08 | 18.05 | 18.20 | 18.31 | 18.61 | 18.95 | 19.04 | 18.46 |
| 2019 | 19.31 | 19.45 | 19.68 | 19.48 | 19.32 | 19.02 | 19.09 | 19.18 | 19.44 | 19.76 | 19.77 | 20.15 | 19.46 |
| **Other Services** | | | | | | | | | | | | | |
| 2015 | 23.03 | 23.24 | 23.44 | 23.27 | 23.32 | 22.68 | 23.03 | 23.63 | 23.66 | 24.30 | 24.23 | 23.52 | 23.46 |
| 2016 | 23.42 | 23.46 | 23.39 | 23.87 | 24.12 | 23.12 | 22.76 | 23.47 | 24.54 | 25.05 | 24.60 | 25.49 | 23.95 |
| 2017 | 25.39 | 26.35 | 25.94 | 26.92 | 26.38 | 26.61 | 26.88 | 26.16 | 26.48 | 26.17 | 26.83 | 25.90 | 26.34 |
| 2018 | 25.94 | 25.77 | 25.24 | 25.39 | 25.30 | 26.02 | 26.06 | 26.37 | 26.18 | 27.10 | 27.31 | 26.78 | 26.11 |
| 2019 | 25.96 | 26.82 | 25.96 | 25.78 | 25.85 | 25.02 | 24.79 | 24.64 | 25.13 | 25.01 | 25.19 | 25.70 | 25.47 |

## 4. Average Weekly Earnings by Selected Industry: Colorado, 2015–2019

(Dollars, not seasonally adjusted)

| Industry and year | January | February | March | April | May | June | July | August | September | October | November | December | Annual average |
|---|---|---|---|---|---|---|---|---|---|---|---|---|---|
| **Total Private** | | | | | | | | | | | | | |
| 2015 | 895.10 | 919.86 | 922.26 | 902.16 | 903.83 | 897.94 | 912.52 | 939.60 | 908.86 | 917.33 | 926.50 | 897.06 | 912.90 |
| 2016 | 915.49 | 912.00 | 909.42 | 910.34 | 925.81 | 903.16 | 899.76 | 899.08 | 901.81 | 931.61 | 898.10 | 894.74 | 906.85 |
| 2017 | 907.60 | 902.78 | 896.85 | 934.84 | 918.01 | 921.05 | 951.16 | 928.15 | 930.30 | 947.51 | 933.20 | 936.40 | 924.60 |
| 2018 | 936.57 | 946.39 | 951.07 | 975.98 | 966.49 | 971.57 | 990.03 | 976.82 | 1,004.80 | 986.97 | 975.81 | 1,006.96 | 974.60 |
| 2019 | 984.27 | 991.35 | 986.48 | 992.45 | 1,003.30 | 1,035.52 | 1,013.38 | 1,012.03 | 1,049.94 | 1,010.54 | 1,017.91 | 1,047.80 | 1,011.32 |
| **Goods-Producing** | | | | | | | | | | | | | |
| 2015 | 1,143.63 | 1,174.13 | 1,185.63 | 1,165.06 | 1,152.06 | 1,177.20 | 1,195.20 | 1,227.26 | 1,192.41 | 1,204.39 | 1,210.62 | 1,205.20 | 1,185.83 |
| 2016 | 1,221.74 | 1,217.58 | 1,220.70 | 1,224.98 | 1,227.60 | 1,219.74 | 1,210.45 | 1,200.93 | 1,201.96 | 1,216.15 | 1,209.89 | 1,175.77 | 1,211.16 |
| 2017 | 1,195.83 | 1,209.39 | 1,186.50 | 1,219.19 | 1,193.15 | 1,209.20 | 1,200.94 | 1,190.22 | 1,210.82 | 1,208.21 | 1,209.37 | 1,216.28 | 1,204.10 |
| 2018 | 1,207.83 | 1,203.83 | 1,234.60 | 1,238.69 | 1,249.02 | 1,243.39 | 1,238.82 | 1,233.48 | 1,252.63 | 1,269.92 | 1,252.88 | 1,303.25 | 1,243.28 |
| 2019 | 1,254.40 | 1,278.82 | 1,260.11 | 1,311.38 | 1,286.00 | 1,308.80 | 1,299.61 | 1,312.07 | 1,325.57 | 1,312.53 | 1,350.12 | 1,414.05 | 1,308.94 |
| **Construction** | | | | | | | | | | | | | |
| 2015 | 1,060.67 | 1,108.37 | 1,100.58 | 1,100.63 | 1,060.70 | 1,096.50 | 1,115.99 | 1,134.98 | 1,076.79 | 1,119.53 | 1,095.34 | 1,093.66 | 1,096.03 |
| 2016 | 1,078.18 | 1,064.23 | 1,070.69 | 1,072.08 | 1,091.35 | 1,090.00 | 1,083.85 | 1,086.31 | 1,074.60 | 1,072.03 | 1,046.05 | 982.71 | 1,067.04 |
| 2017 | 987.96 | 1,016.88 | 1,002.75 | 1,031.75 | 1,023.37 | 1,068.63 | 1,042.02 | 1,042.19 | 1,063.14 | 1,050.67 | 1,069.06 | 1,065.58 | 1,039.46 |
| 2018 | 1,050.30 | 1,053.86 | 1,092.90 | 1,088.32 | 1,128.81 | 1,129.39 | 1,125.43 | 1,133.73 | 1,144.07 | 1,198.99 | 1,152.31 | 1,194.33 | 1,124.24 |
| 2019 | 1,132.51 | 1,168.15 | 1,129.24 | 1,176.87 | 1,145.29 | 1,186.16 | 1,167.77 | 1,204.00 | 1,225.44 | 1,204.28 | 1,229.82 | 1,273.21 | 1,187.55 |
| **Manufacturing** | | | | | | | | | | | | | |
| 2015 | 1,116.12 | 1,140.89 | 1,179.28 | 1,162.67 | 1,175.52 | 1,193.38 | 1,222.14 | 1,239.37 | 1,223.05 | 1,221.46 | 1,245.60 | 1,247.00 | 1,198.20 |
| 2016 | 1,275.59 | 1,259.66 | 1,266.32 | 1,283.44 | 1,266.25 | 1,257.60 | 1,258.08 | 1,242.08 | 1,260.45 | 1,298.80 | 1,305.73 | 1,313.14 | 1,273.48 |
| 2017 | 1,319.87 | 1,271.75 | 1,246.60 | 1,265.50 | 1,256.45 | 1,253.44 | 1,224.09 | 1,218.86 | 1,223.85 | 1,232.51 | 1,215.22 | 1,230.82 | 1,246.88 |
| 2018 | 1,250.96 | 1,214.63 | 1,231.16 | 1,245.68 | 1,239.77 | 1,229.47 | 1,227.72 | 1,240.31 | 1,248.53 | 1,230.07 | 1,269.21 | 1,281.96 | 1,242.21 |
| 2019 | 1,291.14 | 1,296.90 | 1,308.50 | 1,336.48 | 1,333.73 | 1,326.38 | 1,328.04 | 1,320.40 | 1,293.56 | 1,271.90 | 1,309.76 | 1,337.39 | 1,312.40 |
| **Trade, Transportation, and Utilities** | | | | | | | | | | | | | |
| 2015 | 770.72 | 793.38 | 796.26 | 770.54 | 780.98 | 774.63 | 792.81 | 805.39 | 794.19 | 788.65 | 784.78 | 770.10 | 784.89 |
| 2016 | 782.51 | 782.85 | 787.91 | 782.90 | 781.54 | 779.14 | 759.70 | 763.98 | 762.57 | 773.01 | 738.21 | 736.67 | 768.16 |
| 2017 | 742.92 | 735.05 | 733.34 | 747.39 | 710.45 | 706.50 | 739.36 | 721.77 | 735.38 | 737.36 | 727.12 | 729.94 | 730.27 |
| 2018 | 746.34 | 768.56 | 752.40 | 791.28 | 780.72 | 788.89 | 810.41 | 786.24 | 809.51 | 772.89 | 773.56 | 804.38 | 782.54 |
| 2019 | 813.07 | 781.10 | 780.99 | 781.10 | 781.77 | 815.97 | 801.12 | 791.34 | 827.17 | 789.74 | 789.12 | 813.60 | 798.15 |
| **Financial Activities** | | | | | | | | | | | | | |
| 2015 | 1,132.34 | 1,163.05 | 1,171.13 | 1,153.04 | 1,149.15 | 1,102.68 | 1,131.74 | 1,194.56 | 1,139.09 | 1,142.20 | 1,189.29 | 1,117.13 | 1,148.34 |
| 2016 | 1,134.18 | 1,120.19 | 1,116.59 | 1,145.22 | 1,179.22 | 1,127.10 | 1,122.87 | 1,127.30 | 1,149.59 | 1,206.74 | 1,173.84 | 1,138.07 | 1,143.90 |
| 2017 | 1,195.84 | 1,166.08 | 1,130.41 | 1,207.33 | 1,151.21 | 1,138.99 | 1,186.13 | 1,166.41 | 1,165.09 | 1,194.93 | 1,166.93 | 1,181.64 | 1,170.31 |
| 2018 | 1,189.38 | 1,202.26 | 1,214.40 | 1,293.11 | 1,236.38 | 1,214.04 | 1,294.94 | 1,256.16 | 1,347.35 | 1,307.74 | 1,289.29 | 1,306.25 | 1,264.29 |
| 2019 | 1,258.31 | 1,230.29 | 1,231.56 | 1,263.97 | 1,248.43 | 1,337.49 | 1,279.54 | 1,270.47 | 1,325.16 | 1,273.85 | 1,270.34 | 1,317.24 | 1,276.59 |
| **Professional and Business Services** | | | | | | | | | | | | | |
| 2015 | 1,178.67 | 1,201.76 | 1,201.56 | 1,172.75 | 1,166.08 | 1,151.07 | 1,173.03 | 1,206.40 | 1,164.92 | 1,174.33 | 1,206.18 | 1,167.43 | 1,181.51 |
| 2016 | 1,191.21 | 1,200.20 | 1,179.02 | 1,174.80 | 1,180.48 | 1,142.34 | 1,148.76 | 1,139.40 | 1,145.01 | 1,181.04 | 1,138.32 | 1,142.74 | 1,162.44 |
| 2017 | 1,119.72 | 1,113.01 | 1,108.73 | 1,171.04 | 1,123.58 | 1,144.90 | 1,185.84 | 1,147.01 | 1,136.34 | 1,158.29 | 1,156.40 | 1,186.08 | 1,146.33 |
| 2018 | 1,207.14 | 1,201.64 | 1,201.83 | 1,241.48 | 1,211.30 | 1,251.07 | 1,274.65 | 1,281.01 | 1,317.05 | 1,278.76 | 1,296.71 | 1,354.24 | 1,259.17 |
| 2019 | 1,340.54 | 1,354.11 | 1,349.80 | 1,348.53 | 1,364.56 | 1,400.15 | 1,368.15 | 1,393.25 | 1,448.73 | 1,379.74 | 1,382.63 | 1,410.14 | 1,377.41 |
| **Education and Health Services** | | | | | | | | | | | | | |
| 2015 | 778.43 | 809.92 | 807.07 | 784.96 | 791.81 | 797.53 | 798.35 | 811.06 | 797.89 | 801.41 | 831.79 | 806.12 | 800.83 |
| 2016 | 812.64 | 806.93 | 807.23 | 806.73 | 812.15 | 788.48 | 805.46 | 797.84 | 810.81 | 827.37 | 801.91 | 820.97 | 807.54 |
| 2017 | 829.79 | 825.57 | 821.74 | 857.05 | 828.48 | 834.95 | 851.78 | 841.43 | 820.47 | 839.48 | 831.39 | 836.42 | 833.98 |
| 2018 | 811.84 | 821.03 | 834.75 | 846.80 | 818.18 | 814.83 | 834.24 | 826.33 | 859.10 | 839.65 | 870.76 | 890.14 | 839.48 |
| 2019 | 870.14 | 880.16 | 876.88 | 893.62 | 905.00 | 918.38 | 898.07 | 911.66 | 937.28 | 928.41 | 914.05 | 935.72 | 906.89 |
| **Leisure and Hospitality** | | | | | | | | | | | | | |
| 2015 | 409.74 | 419.19 | 431.48 | 413.14 | 412.38 | 408.58 | 413.52 | 431.66 | 396.72 | 410.03 | 388.84 | 398.00 | 411.60 |
| 2016 | 401.26 | 411.57 | 419.06 | 396.74 | 427.78 | 423.92 | 432.48 | 434.02 | 427.39 | 445.64 | 415.15 | 425.75 | 422.51 |
| 2017 | 435.21 | 437.44 | 448.06 | 417.45 | 426.07 | 442.00 | 462.44 | 448.66 | 445.52 | 469.50 | 437.57 | 452.01 | 443.27 |
| 2018 | 463.34 | 469.20 | 478.98 | 462.77 | 472.26 | 470.08 | 478.33 | 476.84 | 472.40 | 465.25 | 451.01 | 468.38 | 468.88 |
| 2019 | 463.44 | 486.25 | 488.06 | 463.62 | 484.93 | 500.23 | 498.25 | 489.09 | 499.61 | 490.05 | 482.39 | 501.74 | 486.50 |
| **Other Services** | | | | | | | | | | | | | |
| 2015 | 686.29 | 720.44 | 728.98 | 700.43 | 708.93 | 730.30 | 743.87 | 793.97 | 768.95 | 794.61 | 828.67 | 771.46 | 748.37 |
| 2016 | 784.57 | 774.18 | 771.87 | 790.10 | 824.90 | 769.90 | 776.12 | 802.67 | 827.00 | 891.78 | 821.64 | 859.01 | 807.12 |
| 2017 | 860.72 | 882.73 | 871.58 | 944.89 | 891.64 | 915.38 | 967.68 | 920.83 | 929.45 | 947.35 | 949.78 | 911.68 | 916.63 |
| 2018 | 900.12 | 901.95 | 865.73 | 903.88 | 875.38 | 887.28 | 886.04 | 867.57 | 884.88 | 894.30 | 890.31 | 883.74 | 887.74 |
| 2019 | 841.10 | 879.70 | 828.12 | 832.69 | 860.81 | 855.68 | 815.59 | 842.69 | 866.99 | 837.84 | 866.54 | 868.66 | 850.70 |

# CONNECTICUT
## *At a Glance*

Population:
  2010 census: 3,574,097
  2019 estimate: 3,565,287

Percent change in population:
  2010–2019: -0.2%

Percent change in total nonfarm employment:
  2011–2019: 3.6%

Industry with the largest growth in employment, 2011–2019 (percent):
  Transportation and utilities, 19.4%

Industry with the largest decline or smallest growth in employment, 2011–2019 (percent):
  Mining and logging, -16.7%

Civilian labor force:
  2010: 1,911,712
  2019: 1,913,530

Unemployment rate and rank among states (highest to lowest):
  2010: 9.1%, 22nd
  2019: 3.7%, 19th

Over-the-year change in unemployment rates:
  2017–2018: -0.6%
  2018–2019: -0.4%

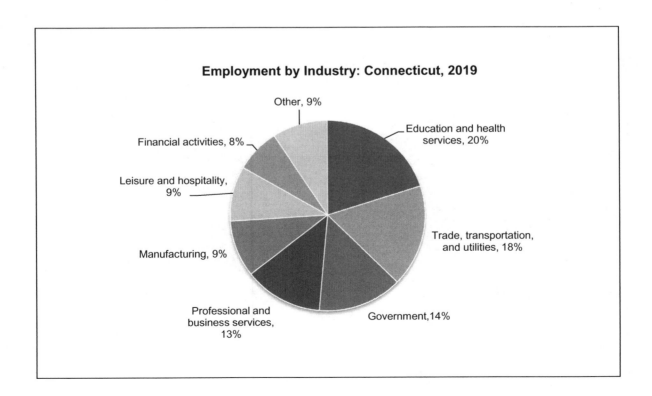

**Employment by Industry: Connecticut, 2019**

- Other, 9%
- Education and health services, 20%
- Financial activities, 8%
- Leisure and hospitality, 9%
- Trade, transportation, and utilities, 18%
- Manufacturing, 9%
- Professional and business services, 13%
- Government, 14%

## 1. Employment by Industry: Connecticut, 2011–2019

(Numbers in thousands, not seasonally adjusted)

| Industry and year | January | February | March | April | May | June | July | August | September | October | November | December | Annual average |
|---|---|---|---|---|---|---|---|---|---|---|---|---|---|
| **Total Nonfarm** | | | | | | | | | | | | | |
| 2011 | 1,591.9 | 1,603.4 | 1,606.0 | 1,633.7 | 1,638.7 | 1,637.7 | 1,622.7 | 1,614.7 | 1,639.6 | 1,643.7 | 1,651.3 | 1,656.5 | 1,628.3 |
| 2012 | 1,607.2 | 1,619.0 | 1,626.5 | 1,638.4 | 1,649.6 | 1,653.4 | 1,632.7 | 1,626.8 | 1,651.1 | 1,659.8 | 1,668.8 | 1,673.3 | 1,642.2 |
| 2013 | 1,618.5 | 1,622.1 | 1,633.0 | 1,655.7 | 1,666.2 | 1,675.4 | 1,654.6 | 1,645.3 | 1,661.6 | 1,668.2 | 1,679.3 | 1,676.8 | 1,654.7 |
| 2014 | 1,631.2 | 1,631.0 | 1,640.3 | 1,666.1 | 1,678.3 | 1,683.2 | 1,660.1 | 1,655.1 | 1,674.2 | 1,683.9 | 1,693.4 | 1,695.7 | 1,666.0 |
| 2015 | 1,649.8 | 1,648.0 | 1,655.2 | 1,676.7 | 1,693.8 | 1,700.6 | 1,670.1 | 1,663.9 | 1,683.0 | 1,697.1 | 1,705.0 | 1,704.3 | 1,679.0 |
| 2016 | 1,655.0 | 1,658.4 | 1,669.0 | 1,682.0 | 1,696.6 | 1,699.9 | 1,678.7 | 1,671.1 | 1,689.7 | 1,696.9 | 1,704.8 | 1,704.7 | 1,683.9 |
| 2017 | 1,661.6 | 1,662.6 | 1,667.9 | 1,683.6 | 1,698.7 | 1,708.0 | 1,680.9 | 1,675.1 | 1,692.7 | 1,698.8 | 1,709.2 | 1,709.1 | 1,687.4 |
| 2018 | 1,659.1 | 1,665.3 | 1,668.0 | 1,681.5 | 1,699.2 | 1,710.5 | 1,684.4 | 1,679.6 | 1,696.3 | 1,705.1 | 1,714.7 | 1,715.9 | 1,690.0 |
| 2019 | 1,660.1 | 1,664.5 | 1,667.5 | 1,684.4 | 1,696.0 | 1,701.1 | 1,680.9 | 1,672.3 | 1,692.0 | 1,700.1 | 1,710.1 | 1,711.0 | 1,686.7 |
| **Total Private** | | | | | | | | | | | | | |
| 2011 | 1,348.1 | 1,350.3 | 1,352.3 | 1,377.4 | 1,386.9 | 1,397.9 | 1,394.6 | 1,389.6 | 1,390.3 | 1,389.8 | 1,396.4 | 1,402.0 | 1,381.3 |
| 2012 | 1,365.9 | 1,366.3 | 1,373.7 | 1,386.0 | 1,400.9 | 1,414.3 | 1,405.9 | 1,401.8 | 1,402.9 | 1,407.8 | 1,414.4 | 1,419.0 | 1,396.6 |
| 2013 | 1,375.2 | 1,372.2 | 1,382.0 | 1,403.8 | 1,416.1 | 1,430.2 | 1,423.1 | 1,420.0 | 1,416.8 | 1,419.6 | 1,428.1 | 1,426.8 | 1,409.5 |
| 2014 | 1,388.1 | 1,383.2 | 1,390.8 | 1,414.6 | 1,428.4 | 1,439.9 | 1,433.4 | 1,428.7 | 1,427.9 | 1,434.0 | 1,441.0 | 1,444.9 | 1,421.2 |
| 2015 | 1,406.1 | 1,400.3 | 1,406.3 | 1,426.5 | 1,444.8 | 1,459.2 | 1,445.2 | 1,439.5 | 1,438.0 | 1,448.0 | 1,453.5 | 1,455.4 | 1,435.2 |
| 2016 | 1,413.5 | 1,412.2 | 1,421.3 | 1,434.4 | 1,447.9 | 1,462.6 | 1,456.9 | 1,450.6 | 1,448.8 | 1,451.9 | 1,457.1 | 1,458.9 | 1,443.0 |
| 2017 | 1,422.0 | 1,418.2 | 1,422.9 | 1,439.4 | 1,454.9 | 1,472.3 | 1,460.4 | 1,454.6 | 1,453.6 | 1,456.5 | 1,465.3 | 1,466.4 | 1,448.9 |
| 2018 | 1,423.3 | 1,423.9 | 1,425.5 | 1,440.8 | 1,458.7 | 1,476.2 | 1,465.1 | 1,460.3 | 1,458.2 | 1,465.1 | 1,471.9 | 1,474.4 | 1,453.6 |
| 2019 | 1,423.4 | 1,422.8 | 1,425.5 | 1,443.7 | 1,455.4 | 1,469.1 | 1,462.6 | 1,454.5 | 1,452.8 | 1,458.8 | 1,466.1 | 1,468.7 | 1,450.3 |
| **Goods Producing** | | | | | | | | | | | | | |
| 2011 | 208.5 | 208.3 | 209.3 | 213.5 | 216.1 | 219.3 | 219.8 | 220.0 | 218.7 | 217.8 | 217.7 | 215.8 | 215.4 |
| 2012 | 209.8 | 209.1 | 209.6 | 212.2 | 214.1 | 216.9 | 217.1 | 217.1 | 215.5 | 215.9 | 214.9 | 214.3 | 213.9 |
| 2013 | 208.9 | 208.0 | 209.0 | 212.9 | 215.7 | 218.1 | 219.0 | 218.3 | 216.8 | 216.0 | 215.0 | 213.1 | 214.2 |
| 2014 | 207.1 | 206.0 | 206.6 | 211.5 | 214.0 | 216.5 | 217.8 | 217.9 | 216.4 | 216.9 | 215.6 | 214.2 | 213.4 |
| 2015 | 208.8 | 207.2 | 208.3 | 213.5 | 216.9 | 220.1 | 219.5 | 219.8 | 218.7 | 218.9 | 217.8 | 216.6 | 215.5 |
| 2016 | 211.0 | 209.5 | 211.2 | 214.8 | 217.1 | 220.0 | 220.9 | 220.7 | 218.5 | 218.2 | 217.6 | 215.9 | 216.3 |
| 2017 | 210.6 | 209.8 | 211.1 | 215.2 | 218.4 | 222.4 | 223.0 | 222.7 | 220.5 | 220.8 | 219.7 | 217.9 | 217.7 |
| 2018 | 211.5 | 211.8 | 212.8 | 216.8 | 220.3 | 224.1 | 225.0 | 224.6 | 223.0 | 224.2 | 223.8 | 222.6 | 220.0 |
| 2019 | 215.8 | 215.4 | 216.8 | 221.3 | 223.5 | 226.3 | 227.7 | 226.1 | 224.3 | 225.0 | 224.0 | 221.4 | 222.3 |
| **Service-Providing** | | | | | | | | | | | | | |
| 2011 | 1,383.4 | 1,395.1 | 1,396.7 | 1,420.2 | 1,422.6 | 1,418.4 | 1,402.9 | 1,394.7 | 1,420.9 | 1,425.9 | 1,433.6 | 1,440.7 | 1,412.9 |
| 2012 | 1,397.4 | 1,409.9 | 1,416.9 | 1,426.2 | 1,435.5 | 1,436.5 | 1,415.6 | 1,409.7 | 1,435.6 | 1,443.9 | 1,453.9 | 1,459.0 | 1,428.3 |
| 2013 | 1,409.6 | 1,414.1 | 1,424.0 | 1,442.8 | 1,450.5 | 1,457.3 | 1,435.6 | 1,427.0 | 1,444.8 | 1,452.2 | 1,464.3 | 1,463.7 | 1,440.5 |
| 2014 | 1,424.1 | 1,425.0 | 1,433.7 | 1,454.6 | 1,464.3 | 1,466.7 | 1,442.3 | 1,437.2 | 1,457.8 | 1,467.0 | 1,477.8 | 1,481.5 | 1,452.7 |
| 2015 | 1,441.0 | 1,440.8 | 1,446.9 | 1,463.2 | 1,476.9 | 1,480.5 | 1,450.6 | 1,444.1 | 1,464.3 | 1,478.2 | 1,487.2 | 1,487.7 | 1,463.5 |
| 2016 | 1,444.0 | 1,448.9 | 1,457.8 | 1,467.2 | 1,479.5 | 1,479.9 | 1,457.8 | 1,450.4 | 1,471.2 | 1,478.7 | 1,487.2 | 1,488.8 | 1,467.6 |
| 2017 | 1,451.0 | 1,452.8 | 1,456.8 | 1,468.4 | 1,480.3 | 1,485.6 | 1,457.9 | 1,452.4 | 1,472.2 | 1,478.0 | 1,489.5 | 1,491.2 | 1,469.7 |
| 2018 | 1,447.6 | 1,453.5 | 1,455.2 | 1,464.7 | 1,478.9 | 1,486.4 | 1,459.4 | 1,455.0 | 1,473.3 | 1,480.9 | 1,490.9 | 1,493.3 | 1,469.9 |
| 2019 | 1,444.3 | 1,449.1 | 1,450.7 | 1,463.1 | 1,472.5 | 1,474.8 | 1,453.2 | 1,446.2 | 1,467.7 | 1,475.1 | 1,486.1 | 1,489.6 | 1,464.4 |
| **Mining and Logging** | | | | | | | | | | | | | |
| 2011 | 0.5 | 0.5 | 0.5 | 0.5 | 0.6 | 0.6 | 0.6 | 0.6 | 0.6 | 0.6 | 0.6 | 0.6 | 0.6 |
| 2012 | 0.5 | 0.5 | 0.5 | 0.6 | 0.6 | 0.6 | 0.6 | 0.6 | 0.6 | 0.6 | 0.6 | 0.5 | 0.6 |
| 2013 | 0.5 | 0.5 | 0.5 | 0.5 | 0.6 | 0.6 | 0.6 | 0.6 | 0.6 | 0.6 | 0.6 | 0.6 | 0.6 |
| 2014 | 0.5 | 0.4 | 0.4 | 0.5 | 0.6 | 0.6 | 0.6 | 0.6 | 0.6 | 0.6 | 0.6 | 0.6 | 0.6 |
| 2015 | 0.5 | 0.5 | 0.5 | 0.5 | 0.6 | 0.6 | 0.6 | 0.6 | 0.6 | 0.6 | 0.6 | 0.6 | 0.6 |
| 2016 | 0.5 | 0.5 | 0.5 | 0.6 | 0.6 | 0.6 | 0.6 | 0.6 | 0.6 | 0.6 | 0.6 | 0.6 | 0.6 |
| 2017 | 0.5 | 0.5 | 0.5 | 0.5 | 0.6 | 0.6 | 0.6 | 0.6 | 0.6 | 0.6 | 0.6 | 0.5 | 0.6 |
| 2018 | 0.5 | 0.5 | 0.5 | 0.5 | 0.5 | 0.5 | 0.6 | 0.6 | 0.6 | 0.6 | 0.6 | 0.5 | 0.5 |
| 2019 | 0.5 | 0.5 | 0.5 | 0.5 | 0.5 | 0.5 | 0.6 | 0.6 | 0.6 | 0.5 | 0.5 | 0.5 | 0.5 |
| **Construction** | | | | | | | | | | | | | |
| 2011 | 45.6 | 45.3 | 45.9 | 50.1 | 52.1 | 53.8 | 54.8 | 55.0 | 54.6 | 54.2 | 54.2 | 52.0 | 51.5 |
| 2012 | 47.1 | 46.2 | 47.1 | 50.0 | 51.4 | 52.8 | 53.9 | 54.2 | 53.8 | 54.3 | 53.5 | 52.4 | 51.4 |
| 2013 | 47.7 | 46.9 | 48.0 | 52.1 | 54.5 | 55.7 | 56.9 | 57.1 | 56.7 | 56.2 | 55.7 | 53.5 | 53.4 |
| 2014 | 48.6 | 48.0 | 48.8 | 53.9 | 56.6 | 58.0 | 59.4 | 59.7 | 59.2 | 59.5 | 58.4 | 56.7 | 55.6 |
| 2015 | 52.1 | 50.8 | 51.5 | 56.5 | 59.4 | 60.8 | 60.9 | 61.4 | 60.8 | 61.7 | 60.7 | 59.3 | 58.0 |
| 2016 | 54.7 | 53.3 | 55.0 | 58.7 | 60.7 | 61.9 | 62.5 | 62.6 | 61.5 | 61.1 | 60.4 | 57.8 | 59.2 |
| 2017 | 53.1 | 52.4 | 53.2 | 57.1 | 59.7 | 61.5 | 61.9 | 61.9 | 61.3 | 61.2 | 59.8 | 57.4 | 58.4 |
| 2018 | 52.1 | 52.2 | 53.2 | 56.8 | 59.7 | 61.5 | 62.0 | 62.1 | 61.9 | 62.5 | 61.7 | 59.9 | 58.8 |
| 2019 | 54.2 | 53.9 | 54.9 | 59.5 | 61.2 | 62.2 | 63.1 | 62.7 | 62.1 | 62.7 | 61.4 | 59.6 | 59.8 |

## 1. Employment by Industry: Connecticut, 2011–2019—*Continued*

(Numbers in thousands, not seasonally adjusted)

| Industry and year | January | February | March | April | May | June | July | August | September | October | November | December | Annual average |
|---|---|---|---|---|---|---|---|---|---|---|---|---|---|
| **Manufacturing** | | | | | | | | | | | | | |
| 2011 | 162.4 | 162.5 | 162.9 | 162.9 | 163.4 | 164.9 | 164.4 | 164.4 | 163.5 | 163.0 | 162.9 | 163.2 | 163.4 |
| 2012 | 162.2 | 162.4 | 162.0 | 161.6 | 162.1 | 163.5 | 162.6 | 162.3 | 161.1 | 161.0 | 160.8 | 161.4 | 161.9 |
| 2013 | 160.7 | 160.6 | 160.5 | 160.3 | 160.6 | 161.8 | 161.5 | 160.6 | 159.5 | 159.2 | 158.7 | 159.0 | 160.3 |
| 2014 | 158.0 | 157.6 | 157.4 | 157.1 | 156.8 | 157.9 | 157.8 | 157.6 | 156.6 | 156.8 | 156.6 | 156.9 | 157.3 |
| 2015 | 156.2 | 155.9 | 156.3 | 156.5 | 156.9 | 158.7 | 158.0 | 157.8 | 157.3 | 156.6 | 156.5 | 156.7 | 157.0 |
| 2016 | 155.8 | 155.7 | 155.7 | 155.5 | 155.8 | 157.5 | 157.8 | 157.5 | 156.4 | 156.5 | 156.6 | 157.5 | 156.5 |
| 2017 | 157.0 | 156.9 | 157.4 | 157.6 | 158.1 | 160.3 | 160.5 | 160.2 | 158.6 | 159.0 | 159.3 | 160.0 | 158.7 |
| 2018 | 158.9 | 159.1 | 159.1 | 159.5 | 160.1 | 162.1 | 162.4 | 161.9 | 160.5 | 161.1 | 161.5 | 162.2 | 160.7 |
| 2019 | 161.1 | 161.0 | 161.4 | 161.3 | 161.8 | 163.6 | 164.0 | 162.8 | 161.6 | 161.8 | 162.1 | 161.3 | 162.0 |
| **Trade, Transportation, and Utilities** | | | | | | | | | | | | | |
| 2011 | 285.8 | 282.3 | 282.4 | 286.4 | 288.2 | 290.8 | 285.2 | 284.6 | 286.8 | 288.4 | 294.5 | 300.7 | 288.0 |
| 2012 | 289.7 | 284.4 | 286.3 | 285.5 | 290.2 | 292.9 | 286.4 | 285.9 | 289.2 | 292.3 | 300.0 | 303.5 | 290.5 |
| 2013 | 290.7 | 284.9 | 287.5 | 289.9 | 292.8 | 296.0 | 289.9 | 290.0 | 292.1 | 295.0 | 302.3 | 306.9 | 293.2 |
| 2014 | 293.6 | 288.8 | 290.1 | 292.1 | 294.8 | 297.2 | 291.2 | 290.2 | 293.3 | 296.5 | 303.5 | 308.1 | 295.0 |
| 2015 | 295.0 | 289.4 | 290.6 | 291.5 | 296.5 | 299.6 | 291.6 | 290.9 | 294.8 | 298.8 | 306.5 | 310.8 | 296.3 |
| 2016 | 297.1 | 292.6 | 293.9 | 293.8 | 297.6 | 298.5 | 293.3 | 292.0 | 295.2 | 298.2 | 305.3 | 309.9 | 297.3 |
| 2017 | 298.3 | 292.0 | 291.8 | 292.4 | 296.7 | 298.7 | 292.0 | 290.9 | 295.5 | 298.3 | 307.5 | 311.1 | 297.1 |
| 2018 | 298.2 | 292.4 | 292.2 | 290.9 | 296.5 | 299.1 | 292.2 | 291.1 | 294.3 | 297.4 | 307.0 | 309.3 | 296.7 |
| 2019 | 294.9 | 288.2 | 287.0 | 286.7 | 289.7 | 291.6 | 286.8 | 286.6 | 290.3 | 292.7 | 300.8 | 305.0 | 291.7 |
| **Wholesale Trade** | | | | | | | | | | | | | |
| 2011 | 61.4 | 61.5 | 61.6 | 62.2 | 62.4 | 62.8 | 62.8 | 62.7 | 62.4 | 62.1 | 62.0 | 62.3 | 62.2 |
| 2012 | 61.7 | 61.7 | 61.9 | 62.2 | 62.3 | 62.7 | 62.4 | 62.2 | 62.0 | 62.4 | 62.3 | 62.4 | 62.2 |
| 2013 | 61.4 | 61.4 | 61.8 | 62.0 | 62.3 | 62.7 | 62.5 | 62.4 | 62.1 | 62.1 | 62.1 | 62.4 | 62.1 |
| 2014 | 61.4 | 61.2 | 61.4 | 61.9 | 62.2 | 62.4 | 62.2 | 61.9 | 61.8 | 61.8 | 61.7 | 61.9 | 61.8 |
| 2015 | 61.3 | 61.2 | 61.4 | 61.7 | 62.0 | 62.3 | 61.8 | 61.6 | 61.5 | 61.3 | 61.1 | 61.4 | 61.6 |
| 2016 | 60.8 | 60.9 | 61.1 | 61.5 | 61.8 | 62.2 | 61.9 | 61.8 | 61.7 | 61.5 | 61.4 | 61.6 | 61.5 |
| 2017 | 61.3 | 61.1 | 61.2 | 61.3 | 61.7 | 62.2 | 61.7 | 61.7 | 61.6 | 61.3 | 61.5 | 61.9 | 61.5 |
| 2018 | 61.2 | 61.1 | 61.4 | 61.3 | 61.5 | 61.9 | 61.6 | 61.3 | 61.0 | 61.0 | 61.1 | 61.2 | 61.3 |
| 2019 | 59.5 | 59.5 | 59.5 | 59.9 | 60.2 | 60.5 | 60.2 | 59.8 | 59.3 | 59.5 | 59.1 | 59.2 | 59.7 |
| **Retail Trade** | | | | | | | | | | | | | |
| 2011 | 179.2 | 175.5 | 175.3 | 178.1 | 179.3 | 181.0 | 179.1 | 179.5 | 177.9 | 179.8 | 185.7 | 190.3 | 180.1 |
| 2012 | 181.9 | 176.7 | 178.1 | 177.9 | 181.0 | 182.9 | 180.6 | 180.6 | 179.2 | 181.8 | 189.1 | 191.4 | 181.8 |
| 2013 | 181.9 | 177.2 | 178.0 | 179.8 | 181.9 | 184.2 | 182.5 | 183.2 | 181.0 | 183.8 | 190.5 | 193.5 | 183.1 |
| 2014 | 183.9 | 179.4 | 180.2 | 181.7 | 183.5 | 185.5 | 183.7 | 183.3 | 181.7 | 184.4 | 190.7 | 193.6 | 184.3 |
| 2015 | 184.3 | 179.5 | 180.2 | 180.6 | 184.3 | 186.7 | 183.3 | 183.7 | 182.2 | 185.6 | 191.9 | 194.5 | 184.7 |
| 2016 | 185.0 | 180.7 | 181.7 | 181.7 | 183.9 | 185.5 | 184.1 | 183.8 | 181.8 | 184.7 | 190.7 | 192.5 | 184.7 |
| 2017 | 185.5 | 179.9 | 179.6 | 180.9 | 182.9 | 184.3 | 182.9 | 182.2 | 180.1 | 182.8 | 189.7 | 191.1 | 183.5 |
| 2018 | 183.0 | 177.9 | 177.4 | 177.9 | 180.2 | 181.7 | 179.7 | 179.5 | 177.3 | 179.5 | 186.7 | 188.0 | 180.7 |
| 2019 | 179.4 | 173.7 | 172.8 | 173.3 | 174.4 | 175.7 | 174.4 | 173.6 | 171.4 | 173.1 | 178.6 | 179.6 | 175.0 |
| **Transportation and Utilities** | | | | | | | | | | | | | |
| 2011 | 45.2 | 45.3 | 45.5 | 46.1 | 46.5 | 47.0 | 43.3 | 42.4 | 46.5 | 46.5 | 46.8 | 48.1 | 45.8 |
| 2012 | 46.1 | 46.0 | 46.3 | 45.4 | 46.9 | 47.3 | 43.4 | 43.1 | 48.0 | 48.1 | 48.6 | 49.7 | 46.6 |
| 2013 | 47.4 | 46.3 | 47.7 | 48.1 | 48.6 | 49.1 | 44.9 | 44.4 | 49.0 | 49.1 | 49.7 | 51.0 | 47.9 |
| 2014 | 48.3 | 48.2 | 48.5 | 48.5 | 49.1 | 49.3 | 45.3 | 45.0 | 49.8 | 50.3 | 51.1 | 52.6 | 48.8 |
| 2015 | 49.4 | 48.7 | 49.0 | 49.2 | 50.2 | 50.6 | 46.5 | 45.6 | 51.1 | 51.9 | 53.5 | 54.9 | 50.1 |
| 2016 | 51.3 | 51.0 | 51.1 | 50.6 | 51.9 | 50.8 | 47.3 | 46.4 | 51.7 | 52.0 | 53.2 | 55.8 | 51.1 |
| 2017 | 51.5 | 51.0 | 51.0 | 50.2 | 52.1 | 52.2 | 47.4 | 47.0 | 53.8 | 54.2 | 56.3 | 58.1 | 52.1 |
| 2018 | 54.0 | 53.4 | 53.4 | 51.7 | 54.8 | 55.5 | 50.9 | 50.3 | 56.0 | 56.9 | 59.2 | 60.1 | 54.7 |
| 2019 | 56.0 | 55.0 | 54.7 | 53.5 | 55.1 | 55.4 | 52.2 | 53.2 | 59.6 | 60.1 | 63.1 | 66.2 | 57.0 |
| **Information** | | | | | | | | | | | | | |
| 2011 | 31.6 | 31.6 | 31.6 | 31.5 | 31.3 | 31.4 | 31.5 | 31.5 | 31.2 | 31.1 | 31.4 | 31.2 | 31.4 |
| 2012 | 31.3 | 31.6 | 31.0 | 31.0 | 31.3 | 31.1 | 31.2 | 31.7 | 31.4 | 31.5 | 32.0 | 31.5 | 31.4 |
| 2013 | 31.6 | 32.4 | 32.1 | 31.7 | 32.2 | 32.3 | 32.5 | 32.5 | 31.9 | 31.9 | 32.2 | 32.2 | 32.1 |
| 2014 | 31.9 | 31.9 | 32.1 | 32.1 | 32.1 | 32.1 | 32.3 | 32.5 | 31.8 | 31.5 | 32.6 | 32.6 | 32.1 |
| 2015 | 32.2 | 32.2 | 32.3 | 32.4 | 32.5 | 32.7 | 32.6 | 32.8 | 32.4 | 32.4 | 32.8 | 32.6 | 32.5 |
| 2016 | 32.3 | 32.5 | 32.2 | 32.2 | 32.3 | 32.4 | 32.7 | 33.1 | 32.3 | 32.4 | 32.5 | 32.1 | 32.4 |
| 2017 | 31.7 | 31.9 | 31.8 | 31.7 | 31.7 | 31.7 | 31.5 | 31.7 | 31.3 | 31.2 | 31.7 | 31.5 | 31.6 |
| 2018 | 31.6 | 32.1 | 31.6 | 31.6 | 31.6 | 31.8 | 31.7 | 31.9 | 31.5 | 31.6 | 31.7 | 31.7 | 31.7 |
| 2019 | 31.2 | 31.5 | 31.4 | 31.2 | 31.3 | 31.6 | 31.8 | 31.9 | 31.4 | 31.7 | 31.1 | 31.5 | 31.5 |

## 1. Employment by Industry: Connecticut, 2011–2019—*Continued*

(Numbers in thousands, not seasonally adjusted)

| Industry and year | January | February | March | April | May | June | July | August | September | October | November | December | Annual average |
|---|---|---|---|---|---|---|---|---|---|---|---|---|---|
| **Financial Activities** | | | | | | | | | | | | | |
| 2011 | 135.4 | 135.2 | 135.2 | 134.8 | 134.9 | 135.5 | 136.6 | 136.3 | 134.3 | 133.8 | 133.9 | 133.9 | 135.0 |
| 2012 | 132.9 | 132.7 | 132.9 | 132.5 | 133.0 | 134.6 | 134.8 | 134.1 | 132.7 | 132.4 | 132.1 | 132.2 | 133.1 |
| 2013 | 131.7 | 131.1 | 130.8 | 130.5 | 130.2 | 132.1 | 132.3 | 131.5 | 129.5 | 129.1 | 129.0 | 129.2 | 130.6 |
| 2014 | 128.1 | 127.7 | 127.5 | 127.4 | 128.3 | 129.7 | 130.3 | 130.0 | 128.7 | 128.9 | 129.0 | 129.3 | 128.7 |
| 2015 | 128.9 | 128.8 | 129.0 | 129.4 | 129.9 | 131.6 | 131.9 | 131.7 | 129.9 | 129.9 | 129.9 | 130.0 | 130.1 |
| 2016 | 129.2 | 128.9 | 129.4 | 129.3 | 129.5 | 131.1 | 131.0 | 130.6 | 129.0 | 128.8 | 128.5 | 128.4 | 129.5 |
| 2017 | 127.9 | 127.4 | 127.3 | 127.4 | 127.7 | 129.6 | 129.7 | 129.1 | 127.4 | 127.2 | 126.7 | 126.8 | 127.9 |
| 2018 | 125.5 | 125.4 | 125.3 | 124.8 | 125.0 | 127.1 | 126.9 | 126.3 | 125.0 | 124.9 | 124.7 | 124.8 | 125.5 |
| 2019 | 123.1 | 123.1 | 122.9 | 122.9 | 123.2 | 124.8 | 125.8 | 125.0 | 123.6 | 123.2 | 123.6 | 124.4 | 123.8 |
| **Professional and Business Services** | | | | | | | | | | | | | |
| 2011 | 193.1 | 194.9 | 194.7 | 201.6 | 201.4 | 203.5 | 203.0 | 202.5 | 203.0 | 203.9 | 205.6 | 205.9 | 201.1 |
| 2012 | 199.3 | 199.9 | 203.4 | 207.8 | 207.9 | 210.0 | 209.4 | 209.3 | 209.2 | 209.1 | 209.6 | 209.0 | 207.0 |
| 2013 | 201.4 | 203.5 | 204.0 | 209.6 | 210.5 | 213.2 | 212.7 | 214.1 | 213.0 | 213.6 | 214.2 | 213.1 | 210.2 |
| 2014 | 206.6 | 207.8 | 208.9 | 215.5 | 217.4 | 218.8 | 217.7 | 217.3 | 216.3 | 217.6 | 218.4 | 218.6 | 215.1 |
| 2015 | 212.6 | 214.0 | 214.6 | 219.6 | 221.1 | 223.4 | 220.9 | 220.3 | 219.4 | 221.5 | 221.8 | 220.7 | 219.2 |
| 2016 | 213.0 | 214.0 | 215.5 | 220.1 | 219.8 | 222.8 | 221.3 | 221.1 | 220.5 | 220.5 | 220.0 | 220.3 | 219.1 |
| 2017 | 213.2 | 213.8 | 215.5 | 219.9 | 219.6 | 222.6 | 222.0 | 221.8 | 220.9 | 221.5 | 222.6 | 221.5 | 219.6 |
| 2018 | 213.9 | 215.6 | 216.5 | 220.1 | 221.5 | 224.0 | 223.6 | 224.4 | 222.8 | 223.8 | 224.2 | 222.1 | 221.0 |
| 2019 | 211.7 | 213.2 | 213.8 | 220.0 | 220.4 | 222.7 | 222.4 | 222.2 | 220.2 | 221.4 | 222.6 | 223.6 | 219.5 |
| **Education and Health Services** | | | | | | | | | | | | | |
| 2011 | 310.1 | 313.0 | 312.5 | 315.8 | 314.7 | 310.9 | 308.8 | 306.8 | 314.0 | 315.8 | 316.9 | 317.2 | 313.0 |
| 2012 | 312.6 | 317.5 | 316.6 | 317.8 | 317.9 | 314.9 | 311.9 | 310.1 | 317.9 | 321.2 | 322.3 | 324.1 | 317.1 |
| 2013 | 315.9 | 318.8 | 319.8 | 323.0 | 321.1 | 318.6 | 315.4 | 314.4 | 321.5 | 324.7 | 327.1 | 324.5 | 320.4 |
| 2014 | 319.7 | 321.1 | 321.5 | 326.2 | 324.9 | 322.2 | 319.5 | 318.5 | 325.8 | 328.9 | 330.6 | 330.7 | 324.1 |
| 2015 | 324.9 | 326.2 | 325.3 | 328.5 | 327.8 | 325.8 | 322.2 | 320.0 | 325.5 | 330.4 | 331.6 | 331.5 | 326.6 |
| 2016 | 325.5 | 328.7 | 329.3 | 330.0 | 329.2 | 327.3 | 326.1 | 324.2 | 331.7 | 334.2 | 336.2 | 335.5 | 329.8 |
| 2017 | 330.3 | 333.9 | 333.1 | 335.6 | 335.9 | 332.7 | 327.3 | 326.1 | 334.0 | 335.7 | 336.9 | 338.1 | 333.3 |
| 2018 | 330.9 | 335.9 | 334.5 | 337.6 | 337.1 | 333.8 | 329.2 | 328.2 | 335.9 | 338.4 | 339.2 | 341.3 | 335.2 |
| 2019 | 334.4 | 339.5 | 338.7 | 341.1 | 339.5 | 336.6 | 332.0 | 330.9 | 339.7 | 344.3 | 346.5 | 346.7 | 339.2 |
| **Leisure and Hospitality** | | | | | | | | | | | | | |
| 2011 | 124.3 | 125.7 | 127.1 | 133.6 | 139.7 | 144.8 | 147.9 | 146.4 | 142.3 | 139.5 | 136.6 | 137.1 | 137.1 |
| 2012 | 130.4 | 131.0 | 133.8 | 138.6 | 145.4 | 151.6 | 152.1 | 150.9 | 145.3 | 143.3 | 141.2 | 142.3 | 142.2 |
| 2013 | 134.3 | 132.7 | 137.4 | 144.5 | 151.4 | 156.8 | 157.9 | 156.2 | 150.2 | 147.8 | 146.6 | 145.8 | 146.8 |
| 2014 | 139.8 | 138.7 | 142.3 | 147.4 | 154.0 | 159.4 | 160.1 | 158.1 | 152.5 | 150.4 | 148.1 | 148.0 | 149.9 |
| 2015 | 141.1 | 140.0 | 143.1 | 148.5 | 156.1 | 161.3 | 161.4 | 158.5 | 153.3 | 152.2 | 149.2 | 149.1 | 151.2 |
| 2016 | 142.1 | 142.6 | 145.8 | 150.0 | 157.7 | 164.2 | 165.1 | 163.1 | 157.0 | 155.1 | 152.7 | 152.0 | 154.0 |
| 2017 | 146.1 | 145.7 | 148.2 | 152.7 | 159.7 | 167.9 | 168.2 | 165.9 | 158.7 | 157.1 | 155.1 | 154.2 | 156.6 |
| 2018 | 147.6 | 146.9 | 148.2 | 153.5 | 160.9 | 168.8 | 169.1 | 167.0 | 160.2 | 159.5 | 155.5 | 156.8 | 157.8 |
| 2019 | 148.1 | 147.8 | 150.2 | 155.3 | 162.2 | 168.8 | 169.3 | 165.7 | 158.7 | 157.0 | 153.2 | 151.8 | 157.3 |
| **Other Services** | | | | | | | | | | | | | |
| 2011 | 59.3 | 59.3 | 59.5 | 60.2 | 60.6 | 61.7 | 61.8 | 61.5 | 60.0 | 59.5 | 59.8 | 60.2 | 60.3 |
| 2012 | 59.9 | 60.1 | 60.1 | 60.6 | 61.1 | 62.3 | 63.0 | 62.7 | 61.7 | 62.1 | 62.3 | 62.1 | 61.5 |
| 2013 | 60.7 | 60.8 | 61.4 | 61.7 | 62.2 | 63.1 | 63.4 | 63.0 | 61.8 | 61.5 | 61.7 | 62.0 | 61.9 |
| 2014 | 61.3 | 61.2 | 61.8 | 62.4 | 62.9 | 64.0 | 64.5 | 64.2 | 63.1 | 63.3 | 63.2 | 63.4 | 62.9 |
| 2015 | 62.6 | 62.5 | 63.1 | 63.1 | 64.0 | 64.7 | 65.1 | 65.5 | 64.0 | 63.9 | 63.9 | 64.1 | 63.9 |
| 2016 | 63.3 | 63.4 | 64.0 | 64.2 | 64.7 | 66.3 | 66.5 | 65.8 | 64.6 | 64.5 | 64.3 | 64.8 | 64.7 |
| 2017 | 63.9 | 63.7 | 64.1 | 64.5 | 65.2 | 66.7 | 66.7 | 66.4 | 65.3 | 64.7 | 65.1 | 65.3 | 65.1 |
| 2018 | 64.1 | 63.8 | 64.4 | 65.5 | 65.8 | 67.5 | 67.4 | 66.8 | 65.5 | 65.3 | 65.8 | 65.8 | 65.6 |
| 2019 | 64.2 | 64.1 | 64.7 | 65.2 | 65.6 | 66.7 | 66.8 | 66.1 | 64.6 | 63.5 | 64.3 | 64.3 | 65.0 |
| **Government** | | | | | | | | | | | | | |
| 2011 | 243.8 | 253.1 | 253.7 | 256.3 | 251.8 | 239.8 | 228.1 | 225.1 | 249.3 | 253.9 | 254.9 | 254.5 | 247.0 |
| 2012 | 241.3 | 252.7 | 252.8 | 252.4 | 248.7 | 239.1 | 226.8 | 225.0 | 248.2 | 252.0 | 254.4 | 254.3 | 245.6 |
| 2013 | 243.3 | 249.9 | 251.0 | 251.9 | 250.1 | 245.2 | 231.5 | 225.3 | 244.8 | 248.6 | 251.2 | 250.0 | 245.2 |
| 2014 | 243.1 | 247.8 | 249.5 | 251.5 | 249.9 | 243.3 | 226.7 | 226.4 | 246.3 | 249.9 | 252.4 | 250.8 | 244.8 |
| 2015 | 243.7 | 247.7 | 248.9 | 250.2 | 249.0 | 241.4 | 224.9 | 224.4 | 245.0 | 249.1 | 251.5 | 248.9 | 243.7 |
| 2016 | 241.5 | 246.2 | 247.7 | 247.6 | 248.7 | 237.3 | 221.8 | 220.5 | 240.9 | 245.0 | 247.7 | 245.8 | 240.9 |
| 2017 | 239.6 | 244.4 | 245.0 | 244.2 | 243.8 | 235.7 | 220.5 | 220.5 | 239.1 | 242.3 | 243.9 | 242.7 | 238.5 |
| 2018 | 235.8 | 241.4 | 242.5 | 240.7 | 240.5 | 234.3 | 219.3 | 219.3 | 238.1 | 240.0 | 242.8 | 241.5 | 236.4 |
| 2019 | 236.7 | 241.7 | 242.0 | 240.7 | 240.6 | 232.0 | 218.3 | 217.8 | 239.2 | 241.3 | 244.0 | 242.3 | 236.4 |

## 2. Average Weekly Hours by Selected Industry: Connecticut, 2015–2019

(Not seasonally adjusted)

| Industry and year | January | February | March | April | May | June | July | August | September | October | November | December | Annual average |
|---|---|---|---|---|---|---|---|---|---|---|---|---|---|
| **Total Private** | | | | | | | | | | | | | |
| 2015 | 33.5 | 33.4 | 33.6 | 33.4 | 33.3 | 33.3 | 33.4 | 34.0 | 33.4 | 33.7 | 33.8 | 33.6 | 33.5 |
| 2016 | 33.2 | 33.1 | 33.2 | 33.4 | 34.0 | 33.6 | 33.6 | 33.6 | 33.9 | 34.2 | 33.7 | 33.7 | 33.6 |
| 2017 | 33.7 | 33.0 | 32.9 | 33.7 | 33.6 | 33.6 | 33.9 | 33.8 | 33.9 | 34.1 | 33.9 | 33.9 | 33.7 |
| 2018 | 33.6 | 33.7 | 33.3 | 34.1 | 33.8 | 33.7 | 34.2 | 33.8 | 34.2 | 33.9 | 33.7 | 34.2 | 33.9 |
| 2019 | 33.4 | 33.2 | 33.6 | 34.0 | 33.8 | 33.9 | 33.9 | 33.9 | 34.3 | 33.9 | 33.8 | 34.1 | 33.8 |
| **Goods-Producing** | | | | | | | | | | | | | |
| 2015 | 39.6 | 38.9 | 39.9 | 39.4 | 39.2 | 39.1 | 39.1 | 39.9 | 39.2 | 39.7 | 40.2 | 40.2 | 39.5 |
| 2016 | 39.8 | 39.2 | 39.7 | 39.7 | 40.9 | 40.6 | 40.3 | 40.1 | 40.6 | 40.3 | 40.2 | 39.4 | 40.1 |
| 2017 | 38.9 | 38.1 | 38.3 | 39.0 | 39.0 | 39.1 | 39.2 | 39.1 | 39.2 | 39.5 | 39.3 | 39.9 | 39.1 |
| 2018 | 39.0 | 39.1 | 38.2 | 40.0 | 39.0 | 39.0 | 40.1 | 39.5 | 39.8 | 39.7 | 39.2 | 40.4 | 39.4 |
| 2019 | 38.3 | 38.1 | 38.9 | 39.3 | 38.8 | 39.4 | 38.8 | 38.8 | 39.5 | 39.2 | 39.5 | 39.8 | 39.0 |
| **Construction** | | | | | | | | | | | | | |
| 2015 | 38.2 | 36.3 | 38.6 | 39.0 | 39.7 | 38.8 | 39.6 | 39.7 | 38.6 | 40.2 | 39.2 | 39.8 | 39.0 |
| 2016 | 38.6 | 37.2 | 38.4 | 38.4 | 40.2 | 39.5 | 39.0 | 38.8 | 39.9 | 38.8 | 38.7 | 37.0 | 38.7 |
| 2017 | 36.8 | 35.8 | 36.1 | 37.5 | 38.5 | 38.9 | 37.7 | 38.3 | 38.3 | 37.5 | 38.3 | 37.4 | 37.6 |
| 2018 | 36.8 | 36.4 | 35.6 | 37.6 | 38.7 | 38.5 | 39.6 | 38.8 | 37.2 | 38.9 | 37.1 | 39.0 | 37.9 |
| 2019 | 36.9 | 35.2 | 38.0 | 38.1 | 39.1 | 38.6 | 38.8 | 38.8 | 38.6 | 37.8 | 38.6 | 37.7 | 38.1 |
| **Manufacturing** | | | | | | | | | | | | | |
| 2015 | 40.1 | 40.0 | 40.6 | 39.8 | 39.1 | 39.3 | 38.9 | 40.0 | 39.6 | 40.2 | 41.3 | 41.0 | 40.0 |
| 2016 | 40.8 | 40.5 | 40.8 | 40.8 | 41.5 | 41.3 | 41.2 | 40.9 | 41.0 | 41.2 | 41.1 | 40.9 | 41.0 |
| 2017 | 40.1 | 39.4 | 39.4 | 39.9 | 39.5 | 39.5 | 40.2 | 39.7 | 39.8 | 40.6 | 39.9 | 40.9 | 39.9 |
| 2018 | 39.8 | 40.0 | 39.2 | 40.9 | 40.0 | 40.0 | 40.9 | 40.3 | 41.5 | 40.7 | 40.8 | 42.2 | 40.5 |
| 2019 | 40.0 | 39.8 | 40.0 | 40.4 | 39.9 | 40.8 | 39.5 | 39.4 | 40.3 | 40.1 | 40.2 | 41.0 | 40.1 |
| **Trade, Transportation, and Utilities** | | | | | | | | | | | | | |
| 2015 | 32.6 | 32.4 | 32.7 | 33.0 | 32.9 | 32.8 | 33.1 | 33.4 | 33.6 | 33.4 | 32.8 | 33.1 | 33.0 |
| 2016 | 32.4 | 32.6 | 32.5 | 32.6 | 33.1 | 33.1 | 32.8 | 32.8 | 33.3 | 33.2 | 32.7 | 33.0 | 32.8 |
| 2017 | 32.4 | 31.9 | 31.3 | 32.2 | 32.2 | 32.3 | 32.7 | 32.4 | 32.9 | 32.5 | 32.9 | 32.9 | 32.4 |
| 2018 | 32.4 | 32.5 | 32.2 | 33.0 | 33.0 | 33.1 | 33.3 | 33.5 | 33.9 | 33.3 | 33.5 | 33.5 | 33.1 |
| 2019 | 32.9 | 32.6 | 33.2 | 33.4 | 33.5 | 33.7 | 33.5 | 33.4 | 34.1 | 33.5 | 33.2 | 34.1 | 33.4 |
| **Financial Activities** | | | | | | | | | | | | | |
| 2015 | 38.2 | 39.1 | 39.0 | 38.2 | 38.1 | 38.1 | 37.9 | 39.0 | 37.9 | 38.1 | 39.4 | 37.5 | 38.4 |
| 2016 | 37.2 | 37.5 | 37.5 | 37.4 | 38.4 | 37.1 | 37.1 | 36.8 | 37.1 | 38.6 | 37.1 | 36.9 | 37.4 |
| 2017 | 38.0 | 36.5 | 36.5 | 38.2 | 36.9 | 36.7 | 38.0 | 37.0 | 37.0 | 38.0 | 37.0 | 36.9 | 37.2 |
| 2018 | 37.3 | 37.1 | 37.1 | 37.9 | 36.9 | 36.8 | 38.0 | 36.8 | 37.4 | 36.5 | 36.3 | 37.4 | 37.1 |
| 2019 | 36.4 | 36.9 | 36.5 | 36.7 | 36.7 | 38.0 | 37.0 | 37.1 | 38.0 | 37.2 | 37.3 | 38.2 | 37.2 |
| **Professional and Business Services** | | | | | | | | | | | | | |
| 2015 | 34.8 | 34.9 | 35.1 | 34.7 | 34.7 | 34.8 | 34.6 | 35.2 | 34.2 | 34.7 | 35.2 | 35.0 | 34.8 |
| 2016 | 34.3 | 34.6 | 34.5 | 34.9 | 35.6 | 35.2 | 35.1 | 34.9 | 34.8 | 35.6 | 34.8 | 34.8 | 34.9 |
| 2017 | 35.4 | 34.6 | 34.6 | 35.5 | 35.7 | 35.8 | 36.1 | 35.7 | 35.5 | 35.5 | 34.9 | 34.6 | 35.3 |
| 2018 | 34.6 | 34.5 | 33.7 | 34.9 | 34.7 | 34.4 | 34.7 | 34.0 | 34.6 | 34.2 | 33.7 | 34.9 | 34.4 |
| 2019 | 33.9 | 33.5 | 33.6 | 34.6 | 34.7 | 35.0 | 34.5 | 34.8 | 35.2 | 34.5 | 34.7 | 34.8 | 34.5 |
| **Education and Health Services** | | | | | | | | | | | | | |
| 2015 | 31.3 | 31.0 | 31.1 | 31.2 | 31.0 | 31.2 | 31.4 | 31.7 | 31.2 | 31.4 | 31.4 | 31.0 | 31.2 |
| 2016 | 31.3 | 30.9 | 31.2 | 31.3 | 31.5 | 31.3 | 31.7 | 31.7 | 31.9 | 31.8 | 32.0 | 31.9 | 31.5 |
| 2017 | 32.1 | 31.8 | 31.8 | 32.1 | 32.1 | 32.3 | 32.5 | 32.4 | 32.4 | 32.3 | 32.6 | 32.3 | 32.2 |
| 2018 | 32.2 | 32.4 | 32.0 | 32.3 | 32.3 | 32.2 | 32.4 | 32.5 | 32.6 | 32.6 | 32.4 | 32.6 | 32.4 |
| 2019 | 32.3 | 32.3 | 32.7 | 32.9 | 32.7 | 32.4 | 32.6 | 32.9 | 33.1 | 33.1 | 32.9 | 32.6 | 32.7 |
| **Leisure and Hospitality** | | | | | | | | | | | | | |
| 2015 | 25.4 | 25.0 | 25.5 | 26.1 | 26.0 | 25.8 | 26.0 | 26.4 | 25.6 | 26.0 | 25.7 | 25.8 | 25.8 |
| 2016 | 24.9 | 25.5 | 25.7 | 26.7 | 26.8 | 26.4 | 26.5 | 26.1 | 25.9 | 26.1 | 25.7 | 25.3 | 26.0 |
| 2017 | 25.0 | 24.1 | 24.3 | 25.3 | 25.6 | 25.6 | 26.3 | 26.0 | 25.8 | 26.1 | 25.9 | 25.9 | 25.5 |
| 2018 | 25.4 | 25.9 | 25.8 | 26.3 | 26.6 | 26.4 | 26.9 | 26.5 | 26.2 | 26.1 | 25.6 | 25.7 | 26.1 |
| 2019 | 24.6 | 24.9 | 25.6 | 25.6 | 25.7 | 25.5 | 26.4 | 25.7 | 25.4 | 25.1 | 25.0 | 25.1 | 25.4 |
| **Other Services** | | | | | | | | | | | | | |
| 2015 | 29.2 | 29.2 | 28.9 | 29.0 | 28.8 | 28.9 | 30.0 | 29.7 | 29.7 | 30.5 | 30.7 | 30.9 | 29.6 |
| 2016 | 30.3 | 30.0 | 30.5 | 31.2 | 31.0 | 30.2 | 30.8 | 31.9 | 32.3 | 32.0 | 31.5 | 31.4 | 31.1 |
| 2017 | 31.5 | 30.4 | 31.4 | 31.4 | 31.8 | 31.6 | 31.4 | 32.0 | 31.6 | 32.1 | 31.6 | 32.0 | 31.6 |
| 2018 | 30.8 | 30.4 | 30.8 | 32.3 | 31.6 | 31.6 | 31.8 | 31.2 | 31.8 | 32.2 | 32.1 | 32.1 | 31.6 |
| 2019 | 31.2 | 30.1 | 31.0 | 30.5 | 30.2 | 31.2 | 32.1 | 32.4 | 32.3 | 30.6 | 31.0 | 30.3 | 31.1 |

## 3. Average Hourly Earnings by Selected Industry: Connecticut, 2015–2019

(Dollars, not seasonally adjusted)

| Industry and year | January | February | March | April | May | June | July | August | September | October | November | December | Annual average |
|---|---|---|---|---|---|---|---|---|---|---|---|---|---|
| **Total Private** | | | | | | | | | | | | | |
| 2015 | 28.54 | 29.13 | 29.04 | 28.73 | 28.68 | 28.75 | 28.79 | 29.35 | 29.49 | 29.49 | 29.89 | 29.80 | 29.14 |
| 2016 | 30.28 | 30.32 | 30.10 | 30.52 | 30.71 | 30.04 | 30.18 | 30.39 | 30.38 | 30.95 | 30.57 | 30.66 | 30.43 |
| 2017 | 31.36 | 31.30 | 31.39 | 31.63 | 31.03 | 30.78 | 31.08 | 30.82 | 31.00 | 31.47 | 30.94 | 31.18 | 31.16 |
| 2018 | 31.73 | 31.58 | 31.83 | 32.06 | 31.40 | 31.41 | 31.86 | 31.78 | 32.65 | 32.31 | 32.30 | 33.58 | 32.05 |
| 2019 | 33.37 | 32.82 | 32.98 | 33.03 | 32.57 | 32.79 | 32.34 | 32.49 | 33.38 | 33.19 | 33.45 | 33.82 | 33.02 |
| **Goods-Producing** | | | | | | | | | | | | | |
| 2015 | 31.01 | 30.88 | 30.84 | 30.74 | 30.52 | 30.27 | 30.61 | 31.00 | 31.25 | 31.39 | 31.55 | 31.67 | 30.98 |
| 2016 | 31.87 | 32.22 | 31.94 | 31.90 | 31.89 | 31.60 | 31.50 | 31.20 | 31.10 | 30.90 | 30.55 | 30.56 | 31.43 |
| 2017 | 31.04 | 31.42 | 31.20 | 30.47 | 31.06 | 31.19 | 31.04 | 31.50 | 31.52 | 31.90 | 31.92 | 31.96 | 31.36 |
| 2018 | 32.77 | 32.71 | 33.53 | 33.59 | 33.48 | 33.48 | 33.95 | 34.00 | 35.03 | 35.01 | 34.30 | 36.59 | 34.06 |
| 2019 | 36.10 | 35.52 | 36.06 | 36.31 | 35.77 | 35.82 | 35.91 | 35.98 | 36.73 | 36.49 | 36.34 | 36.96 | 36.17 |
| **Construction** | | | | | | | | | | | | | |
| 2015 | 31.28 | 30.72 | 31.84 | 31.31 | 31.05 | 30.76 | 31.19 | 30.78 | 30.95 | 31.37 | 31.07 | 30.93 | 31.10 |
| 2016 | 31.29 | 31.18 | 31.20 | 30.86 | 30.51 | 30.44 | 30.57 | 30.69 | 30.83 | 30.85 | 30.62 | 31.17 | 30.83 |
| 2017 | 31.24 | 31.70 | 31.98 | 31.81 | 30.76 | 30.99 | 31.15 | 31.88 | 31.13 | 31.65 | 31.75 | 31.23 | 31.43 |
| 2018 | 32.02 | 31.25 | 31.68 | 30.06 | 30.01 | 30.42 | 31.26 | 32.06 | 32.41 | 33.15 | 32.15 | 33.51 | 31.68 |
| 2019 | 32.39 | 32.96 | 32.97 | 33.60 | 33.48 | 33.30 | 33.80 | 34.19 | 34.74 | 34.76 | 35.16 | 35.46 | 33.94 |
| **Manufacturing** | | | | | | | | | | | | | |
| 2015 | 30.93 | 31.23 | 30.60 | 30.67 | 30.32 | 30.09 | 30.38 | 30.92 | 31.23 | 31.28 | 31.60 | 31.81 | 30.93 |
| 2016 | 31.90 | 32.41 | 32.05 | 32.15 | 32.34 | 31.98 | 31.78 | 31.28 | 31.04 | 30.80 | 30.43 | 30.27 | 31.53 |
| 2017 | 30.81 | 31.17 | 30.80 | 30.17 | 30.96 | 31.06 | 30.75 | 31.13 | 31.47 | 31.81 | 31.81 | 32.01 | 31.17 |
| 2018 | 33.04 | 33.20 | 33.94 | 34.65 | 34.64 | 34.55 | 34.70 | 34.50 | 35.73 | 35.79 | 35.64 | 37.15 | 34.82 |
| 2019 | 36.88 | 35.84 | 36.23 | 37.14 | 36.59 | 36.99 | 36.92 | 37.05 | 38.09 | 37.69 | 37.33 | 38.02 | 37.07 |
| **Trade, Transportation, and Utilities** | | | | | | | | | | | | | |
| 2015 | 24.45 | 25.08 | 24.57 | 24.30 | 24.53 | 24.23 | 24.18 | 24.23 | 24.89 | 25.01 | 25.29 | 25.17 | 24.67 |
| 2016 | 26.08 | 26.40 | 26.42 | 27.09 | 26.97 | 26.21 | 26.67 | 26.43 | 26.68 | 27.34 | 26.20 | 25.77 | 26.52 |
| 2017 | 26.78 | 26.82 | 27.22 | 27.20 | 26.76 | 26.35 | 26.80 | 26.24 | 26.36 | 26.41 | 25.99 | 26.01 | 26.57 |
| 2018 | 25.97 | 26.04 | 25.92 | 26.07 | 25.55 | 25.92 | 26.04 | 25.80 | 26.39 | 26.06 | 25.98 | 26.82 | 26.05 |
| 2019 | 27.12 | 27.09 | 26.85 | 27.32 | 27.31 | 27.94 | 27.64 | 27.75 | 28.32 | 28.05 | 28.25 | 28.20 | 27.66 |
| **Financial Activities** | | | | | | | | | | | | | |
| 2015 | 42.42 | 43.82 | 44.04 | 43.07 | 43.31 | 43.61 | 44.33 | 46.01 | 44.45 | 44.49 | 44.79 | 44.95 | 44.11 |
| 2016 | 44.56 | 43.39 | 42.31 | 45.62 | 45.89 | 43.88 | 44.33 | 46.15 | 44.49 | 47.30 | 45.57 | 44.58 | 44.85 |
| 2017 | 47.54 | 46.31 | 47.21 | 49.68 | 47.12 | 46.06 | 47.10 | 46.75 | 46.33 | 48.17 | 45.94 | 46.04 | 47.03 |
| 2018 | 47.61 | 46.80 | 46.93 | 49.73 | 47.33 | 46.76 | 48.02 | 48.34 | 49.93 | 48.10 | 48.48 | 50.28 | 48.19 |
| 2019 | 48.73 | 48.13 | 47.59 | 47.81 | 47.14 | 48.57 | 47.15 | 48.17 | 50.67 | 48.91 | 50.76 | 51.56 | 48.78 |
| **Professional and Business Services** | | | | | | | | | | | | | |
| 2015 | 32.07 | 32.67 | 33.10 | 33.11 | 32.76 | 33.84 | 33.97 | 34.71 | 34.50 | 33.96 | 34.46 | 33.95 | 33.60 |
| 2016 | 35.43 | 35.27 | 35.10 | 34.73 | 35.35 | 34.95 | 34.87 | 34.89 | 35.23 | 35.11 | 35.00 | 36.09 | 35.17 |
| 2017 | 36.36 | 35.91 | 36.24 | 35.99 | 35.41 | 35.39 | 35.78 | 35.00 | 35.69 | 36.09 | 35.67 | 35.90 | 35.78 |
| 2018 | 36.80 | 36.62 | 36.80 | 36.23 | 35.53 | 35.41 | 36.28 | 36.42 | 36.71 | 36.46 | 36.47 | 37.24 | 36.41 |
| 2019 | 37.93 | 36.97 | 36.99 | 36.42 | 35.89 | 35.92 | 35.73 | 35.49 | 36.04 | 36.02 | 36.55 | 37.00 | 36.40 |
| **Education and Health Services** | | | | | | | | | | | | | |
| 2015 | 25.72 | 26.12 | 25.94 | 26.05 | 26.06 | 26.18 | 26.05 | 26.06 | 26.45 | 26.39 | 26.67 | 27.10 | 26.23 |
| 2016 | 27.20 | 27.31 | 27.41 | 27.48 | 27.58 | 27.57 | 27.80 | 28.19 | 28.33 | 28.24 | 28.83 | 28.81 | 27.91 |
| 2017 | 28.76 | 28.81 | 28.66 | 28.95 | 28.56 | 28.56 | 28.44 | 28.55 | 28.72 | 28.73 | 28.43 | 28.82 | 28.67 |
| 2018 | 29.04 | 28.42 | 28.59 | 28.88 | 28.97 | 29.28 | 29.28 | 29.29 | 29.74 | 29.64 | 29.49 | 29.93 | 29.22 |
| 2019 | 29.60 | 29.36 | 29.48 | 29.69 | 29.32 | 29.43 | 29.16 | 29.23 | 29.42 | 29.64 | 29.42 | 29.58 | 29.45 |
| **Leisure and Hospitality** | | | | | | | | | | | | | |
| 2015 | 16.20 | 16.55 | 16.36 | 16.50 | 16.42 | 16.06 | 15.85 | 15.92 | 15.96 | 16.35 | 16.57 | 16.60 | 16.27 |
| 2016 | 16.72 | 16.91 | 16.63 | 16.46 | 16.66 | 16.21 | 16.23 | 16.34 | 16.61 | 16.97 | 17.10 | 17.33 | 16.67 |
| 2017 | 17.36 | 17.67 | 17.63 | 17.74 | 17.75 | 17.17 | 17.06 | 16.94 | 17.09 | 17.31 | 17.21 | 17.67 | 17.37 |
| 2018 | 17.83 | 17.70 | 17.79 | 17.66 | 17.64 | 17.23 | 17.40 | 17.17 | 17.54 | 17.53 | 17.48 | 17.54 | 17.53 |
| 2019 | 17.53 | 18.17 | 18.06 | 17.99 | 17.79 | 17.39 | 17.04 | 17.36 | 17.76 | 18.06 | 18.14 | 18.38 | 17.79 |
| **Other Services** | | | | | | | | | | | | | |
| 2015 | 22.27 | 22.66 | 22.19 | 21.68 | 22.23 | 21.98 | 20.95 | 21.13 | 21.58 | 22.24 | 22.34 | 22.08 | 21.94 |
| 2016 | 22.30 | 22.42 | 22.70 | 22.66 | 23.28 | 22.80 | 22.56 | 22.74 | 23.02 | 23.53 | 23.95 | 24.18 | 23.02 |
| 2017 | 24.82 | 25.42 | 24.93 | 25.04 | 25.12 | 24.74 | 25.46 | 24.78 | 25.26 | 25.21 | 24.95 | 25.62 | 25.11 |
| 2018 | 24.89 | 25.49 | 25.82 | 25.18 | 25.08 | 24.70 | 24.73 | 24.76 | 25.03 | 24.95 | 25.58 | 25.18 | 25.11 |
| 2019 | 25.22 | 25.64 | 25.21 | 24.67 | 25.46 | 24.59 | 24.36 | 23.96 | 25.27 | 25.29 | 25.35 | 25.97 | 25.07 |

## 4. Average Weekly Earnings by Selected Industry: Connecticut, 2015–2019

(Dollars, not seasonally adjusted)

| Industry and year | January | February | March | April | May | June | July | August | September | October | November | December | Annual average |
|---|---|---|---|---|---|---|---|---|---|---|---|---|---|
| **Total Private** | | | | | | | | | | | | | |
| 2015 | 956.09 | 972.94 | 975.74 | 959.58 | 955.04 | 957.38 | 961.59 | 997.90 | 984.97 | 993.81 | 1,010.28 | 1,001.28 | 976.19 |
| 2016 | 1,005.30 | 1,003.59 | 999.32 | 1,019.37 | 1,044.14 | 1,009.34 | 1,014.05 | 1,021.10 | 1,029.88 | 1,058.49 | 1,030.21 | 1,033.24 | 1,022.45 |
| 2017 | 1,056.83 | 1,032.90 | 1,032.73 | 1,065.93 | 1,042.61 | 1,034.21 | 1,053.61 | 1,041.72 | 1,050.90 | 1,073.13 | 1,048.87 | 1,057.00 | 1,050.09 |
| 2018 | 1,066.13 | 1,064.25 | 1,059.94 | 1,093.25 | 1,061.32 | 1,058.52 | 1,089.61 | 1,074.16 | 1,116.63 | 1,095.31 | 1,088.51 | 1,148.44 | 1,086.50 |
| 2019 | 1,114.56 | 1,089.62 | 1,108.13 | 1,123.02 | 1,100.87 | 1,111.58 | 1,096.33 | 1,101.41 | 1,144.93 | 1,125.14 | 1,130.61 | 1,153.26 | 1,116.08 |
| **Goods-Producing** | | | | | | | | | | | | | |
| 2015 | 1,228.00 | 1,201.23 | 1,230.52 | 1,211.16 | 1,196.38 | 1,183.56 | 1,196.85 | 1,236.90 | 1,225.00 | 1,246.18 | 1,268.31 | 1,273.13 | 1,223.71 |
| 2016 | 1,268.43 | 1,263.02 | 1,268.02 | 1,266.43 | 1,304.30 | 1,282.96 | 1,269.45 | 1,251.12 | 1,262.66 | 1,245.27 | 1,228.11 | 1,204.06 | 1,260.34 |
| 2017 | 1,207.46 | 1,197.10 | 1,194.96 | 1,188.33 | 1,211.34 | 1,219.53 | 1,216.77 | 1,231.65 | 1,235.58 | 1,260.05 | 1,254.46 | 1,275.20 | 1,226.18 |
| 2018 | 1,278.03 | 1,278.96 | 1,280.85 | 1,343.60 | 1,305.72 | 1,305.72 | 1,361.40 | 1,343.00 | 1,394.19 | 1,389.90 | 1,344.56 | 1,478.24 | 1,341.96 |
| 2019 | 1,382.63 | 1,353.31 | 1,402.73 | 1,426.98 | 1,387.88 | 1,411.31 | 1,393.31 | 1,396.02 | 1,450.84 | 1,430.41 | 1,435.43 | 1,471.01 | 1,410.63 |
| **Construction** | | | | | | | | | | | | | |
| 2015 | 1,194.90 | 1,115.14 | 1,229.02 | 1,221.09 | 1,232.69 | 1,193.49 | 1,235.12 | 1,221.97 | 1,194.67 | 1,261.07 | 1,217.94 | 1,231.01 | 1,212.90 |
| 2016 | 1,207.79 | 1,159.90 | 1,198.08 | 1,185.02 | 1,226.50 | 1,202.38 | 1,192.23 | 1,190.77 | 1,230.12 | 1,196.98 | 1,184.99 | 1,153.29 | 1,193.12 |
| 2017 | 1,149.63 | 1,134.86 | 1,154.48 | 1,192.88 | 1,184.26 | 1,205.51 | 1,174.36 | 1,221.00 | 1,192.28 | 1,186.88 | 1,216.03 | 1,168.00 | 1,181.77 |
| 2018 | 1,178.34 | 1,137.50 | 1,127.81 | 1,130.26 | 1,161.39 | 1,171.17 | 1,237.90 | 1,243.93 | 1,205.65 | 1,289.54 | 1,192.77 | 1,306.89 | 1,200.67 |
| 2019 | 1,195.19 | 1,160.19 | 1,252.86 | 1,280.16 | 1,309.07 | 1,285.38 | 1,311.44 | 1,326.57 | 1,340.96 | 1,313.93 | 1,357.18 | 1,336.84 | 1,293.11 |
| **Manufacturing** | | | | | | | | | | | | | |
| 2015 | 1,240.29 | 1,249.20 | 1,242.36 | 1,220.67 | 1,185.51 | 1,182.54 | 1,181.78 | 1,236.80 | 1,236.71 | 1,257.46 | 1,305.08 | 1,304.21 | 1,237.20 |
| 2016 | 1,301.52 | 1,312.61 | 1,307.64 | 1,311.72 | 1,342.11 | 1,320.77 | 1,309.34 | 1,279.35 | 1,272.64 | 1,268.96 | 1,250.67 | 1,238.04 | 1,292.73 |
| 2017 | 1,235.48 | 1,228.10 | 1,213.52 | 1,203.78 | 1,222.92 | 1,226.87 | 1,236.15 | 1,235.86 | 1,252.51 | 1,291.49 | 1,269.22 | 1,309.21 | 1,243.68 |
| 2018 | 1,314.99 | 1,328.00 | 1,330.45 | 1,417.19 | 1,385.60 | 1,382.00 | 1,419.23 | 1,390.35 | 1,482.80 | 1,456.65 | 1,454.11 | 1,567.73 | 1,410.21 |
| 2019 | 1,475.20 | 1,426.43 | 1,449.20 | 1,500.46 | 1,459.94 | 1,509.19 | 1,458.34 | 1,459.77 | 1,535.03 | 1,511.37 | 1,500.67 | 1,558.82 | 1,486.51 |
| **Trade, Transportation, and Utilities** | | | | | | | | | | | | | |
| 2015 | 797.07 | 812.59 | 803.44 | 801.90 | 807.04 | 794.74 | 800.36 | 809.28 | 836.30 | 835.33 | 829.51 | 833.13 | 814.11 |
| 2016 | 844.99 | 860.64 | 858.65 | 883.13 | 892.71 | 867.55 | 874.78 | 866.90 | 888.44 | 907.69 | 856.74 | 850.41 | 869.86 |
| 2017 | 867.67 | 855.56 | 851.99 | 875.84 | 861.67 | 851.11 | 876.36 | 850.18 | 867.24 | 858.33 | 855.07 | 855.73 | 860.87 |
| 2018 | 841.43 | 846.30 | 834.62 | 860.31 | 843.15 | 857.95 | 867.13 | 864.30 | 894.62 | 867.80 | 870.33 | 898.47 | 862.26 |
| 2019 | 892.25 | 883.13 | 891.42 | 912.49 | 914.89 | 941.58 | 925.94 | 926.85 | 965.71 | 939.68 | 937.90 | 961.62 | 923.84 |
| **Financial Activities** | | | | | | | | | | | | | |
| 2015 | 1,620.44 | 1,713.36 | 1,717.56 | 1,645.27 | 1,650.11 | 1,661.54 | 1,680.11 | 1,794.39 | 1,684.66 | 1,695.07 | 1,764.73 | 1,685.63 | 1,693.82 |
| 2016 | 1,657.63 | 1,627.13 | 1,586.63 | 1,706.19 | 1,762.18 | 1,627.95 | 1,644.64 | 1,698.32 | 1,650.58 | 1,825.78 | 1,690.65 | 1,645.00 | 1,677.39 |
| 2017 | 1,806.52 | 1,690.32 | 1,723.17 | 1,897.78 | 1,738.73 | 1,690.40 | 1,789.80 | 1,729.75 | 1,714.21 | 1,830.46 | 1,699.78 | 1,698.88 | 1,749.52 |
| 2018 | 1,775.85 | 1,736.28 | 1,741.10 | 1,884.77 | 1,746.48 | 1,720.77 | 1,824.76 | 1,778.91 | 1,867.38 | 1,755.65 | 1,759.82 | 1,880.47 | 1,787.85 |
| 2019 | 1,773.77 | 1,776.00 | 1,737.04 | 1,754.63 | 1,730.04 | 1,845.66 | 1,744.55 | 1,787.11 | 1,925.46 | 1,819.45 | 1,893.35 | 1,969.59 | 1,814.62 |
| **Professional and Business Services** | | | | | | | | | | | | | |
| 2015 | 1,116.04 | 1,140.18 | 1,161.81 | 1,148.92 | 1,136.77 | 1,177.63 | 1,175.36 | 1,221.79 | 1,179.90 | 1,178.41 | 1,212.99 | 1,188.25 | 1,169.28 |
| 2016 | 1,215.25 | 1,220.34 | 1,210.95 | 1,212.08 | 1,258.46 | 1,230.24 | 1,223.94 | 1,217.66 | 1,226.00 | 1,249.92 | 1,218.00 | 1,255.93 | 1,227.43 |
| 2017 | 1,287.14 | 1,242.49 | 1,253.90 | 1,277.65 | 1,264.14 | 1,266.96 | 1,291.66 | 1,249.50 | 1,267.00 | 1,281.20 | 1,244.88 | 1,242.14 | 1,263.03 |
| 2018 | 1,273.28 | 1,263.39 | 1,240.16 | 1,264.43 | 1,232.89 | 1,218.10 | 1,258.92 | 1,238.28 | 1,270.17 | 1,246.93 | 1,229.04 | 1,299.68 | 1,252.50 |
| 2019 | 1,285.83 | 1,238.50 | 1,242.86 | 1,260.13 | 1,245.38 | 1,257.20 | 1,232.69 | 1,235.05 | 1,268.61 | 1,242.69 | 1,268.29 | 1,287.60 | 1,255.80 |
| **Education and Health Services** | | | | | | | | | | | | | |
| 2015 | 805.04 | 809.72 | 806.73 | 812.76 | 807.86 | 816.82 | 817.97 | 826.10 | 825.24 | 828.65 | 837.44 | 840.10 | 818.38 |
| 2016 | 851.36 | 843.88 | 855.19 | 860.12 | 868.77 | 862.94 | 881.26 | 893.62 | 903.73 | 898.03 | 922.56 | 919.04 | 879.17 |
| 2017 | 923.20 | 916.16 | 911.39 | 929.30 | 916.78 | 922.49 | 924.30 | 925.02 | 930.53 | 927.98 | 926.82 | 930.89 | 923.17 |
| 2018 | 935.09 | 920.81 | 914.88 | 932.82 | 935.73 | 942.82 | 948.67 | 951.93 | 969.52 | 966.26 | 955.48 | 975.72 | 946.73 |
| 2019 | 956.08 | 948.33 | 964.00 | 976.80 | 958.76 | 953.53 | 950.62 | 961.67 | 973.80 | 981.08 | 967.92 | 964.31 | 963.02 |
| **Leisure and Hospitality** | | | | | | | | | | | | | |
| 2015 | 411.48 | 413.75 | 417.18 | 430.65 | 426.92 | 414.35 | 412.10 | 420.29 | 408.58 | 425.10 | 425.85 | 428.28 | 419.77 |
| 2016 | 416.33 | 431.21 | 427.39 | 439.48 | 446.49 | 427.94 | 430.10 | 426.47 | 430.20 | 442.92 | 439.47 | 438.45 | 433.42 |
| 2017 | 434.00 | 425.85 | 428.41 | 448.82 | 454.40 | 439.55 | 448.68 | 440.70 | 440.92 | 451.79 | 445.74 | 457.65 | 442.94 |
| 2018 | 452.88 | 458.43 | 458.98 | 464.46 | 469.22 | 454.87 | 468.06 | 455.01 | 459.55 | 457.53 | 447.49 | 450.78 | 457.53 |
| 2019 | 431.24 | 452.43 | 462.34 | 460.54 | 457.20 | 443.45 | 449.86 | 446.15 | 451.10 | 453.31 | 453.50 | 461.34 | 451.87 |
| **Other Services** | | | | | | | | | | | | | |
| 2015 | 650.28 | 661.67 | 641.29 | 628.72 | 640.22 | 635.22 | 628.50 | 627.56 | 640.93 | 678.32 | 685.84 | 682.27 | 649.42 |
| 2016 | 675.69 | 672.60 | 692.35 | 706.99 | 721.68 | 688.56 | 694.85 | 725.41 | 743.55 | 752.96 | 754.43 | 759.25 | 715.92 |
| 2017 | 781.83 | 772.77 | 782.80 | 786.26 | 798.82 | 781.78 | 799.44 | 792.96 | 798.22 | 809.24 | 788.42 | 819.84 | 793.48 |
| 2018 | 766.61 | 774.90 | 795.26 | 813.31 | 792.53 | 780.52 | 786.41 | 772.51 | 795.95 | 803.39 | 821.12 | 808.28 | 793.48 |
| 2019 | 786.86 | 771.76 | 781.51 | 752.44 | 768.89 | 767.21 | 781.96 | 776.30 | 816.22 | 773.87 | 785.85 | 786.89 | 779.68 |

# DELAWARE
## *At a Glance*

Population:
  2010 census: 897,934
  2019 estimate: 973,764

Percent change in population:
  2010–2019: 8.4%

Percent change in total nonfarm employment:
  2011–2019: 11.7%

Industry with the largest growth in employment, 2011–2019 (percent):
  Transportation and utilities, 43.9%

Industry with the largest decline or smallest growth in employment, 2011–2019 (percent):
  Information, -31.6%

Civilian labor force:
  2010: 434,419
  2019: 487,263

Unemployment rate and rank among states (highest to lowest):
  2010: 8.4%, 29th
  2019: 3.8%, 18th

Over-the-year change in unemployment rates:
  2017–2018: -0.7%
  2018–2019: 0.0%

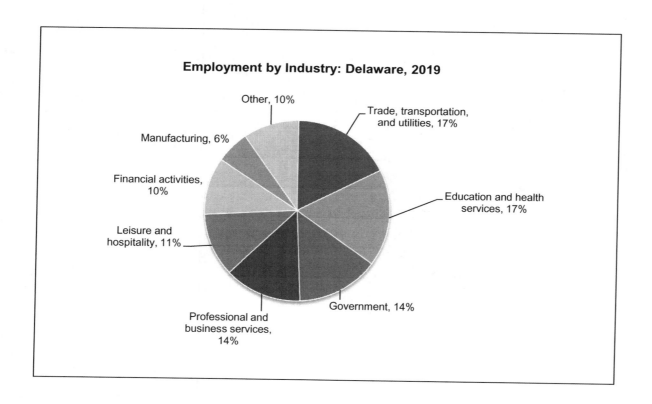

**Employment by Industry: Delaware, 2019**

- Other, 10%
- Trade, transportation, and utilities, 17%
- Manufacturing, 6%
- Financial activities, 10%
- Education and health services, 17%
- Leisure and hospitality, 11%
- Government, 14%
- Professional and business services, 14%

# 1. Employment by Industry: Delaware, 2011–2019

(Numbers in thousands, not seasonally adjusted)

| Industry and year | January | February | March | April | May | June | July | August | September | October | November | December | Annual average |
|---|---|---|---|---|---|---|---|---|---|---|---|---|---|
| **Total Nonfarm** | | | | | | | | | | | | | |
| 2011 | 406.1 | 407.5 | 411.8 | 419.4 | 420.2 | 421.1 | 420.0 | 417.9 | 419.5 | 417.9 | 419.9 | 420.7 | 416.8 |
| 2012 | 406.3 | 407.5 | 412.6 | 416.4 | 422.2 | 422.9 | 422.3 | 421.6 | 421.4 | 423.6 | 427.0 | 427.2 | 419.3 |
| 2013 | 412.6 | 414.6 | 419.7 | 424.7 | 430.1 | 432.1 | 431.7 | 432.1 | 431.9 | 434.4 | 439.0 | 436.5 | 428.3 |
| 2014 | 423.7 | 423.3 | 428.1 | 433.8 | 440.6 | 442.4 | 441.3 | 440.6 | 440.5 | 443.0 | 448.0 | 448.8 | 437.8 |
| 2015 | 433.3 | 433.6 | 438.3 | 443.1 | 451.0 | 453.2 | 453.8 | 450.7 | 451.0 | 452.3 | 457.2 | 456.8 | 447.9 |
| 2016 | 440.5 | 441.0 | 445.7 | 450.7 | 454.3 | 456.9 | 458.3 | 455.4 | 454.8 | 455.3 | 458.3 | 458.4 | 452.5 |
| 2017 | 446.1 | 446.4 | 449.8 | 453.8 | 457.2 | 461.8 | 460.7 | 458.2 | 458.9 | 457.8 | 461.8 | 461.8 | 456.2 |
| 2018 | 448.3 | 450.5 | 454.0 | 459.4 | 465.4 | 467.4 | 466.0 | 463.3 | 462.0 | 464.6 | 466.4 | 466.7 | 461.2 |
| 2019 | 454.5 | 455.9 | 461.0 | 464.9 | 468.3 | 470.3 | 470.9 | 469.2 | 466.6 | 468.5 | 469.7 | 468.0 | 465.7 |
| **Total Private** | | | | | | | | | | | | | |
| 2011 | 343.4 | 343.8 | 346.7 | 353.2 | 355.0 | 358.8 | 359.3 | 357.8 | 356.0 | 352.9 | 354.7 | 355.7 | 353.1 |
| 2012 | 344.1 | 343.5 | 347.4 | 351.4 | 356.7 | 360.4 | 361.4 | 361.8 | 358.1 | 358.7 | 361.8 | 362.1 | 355.6 |
| 2013 | 351.2 | 350.5 | 354.2 | 359.1 | 364.4 | 369.0 | 370.5 | 371.9 | 368.0 | 368.9 | 373.0 | 371.0 | 364.3 |
| 2014 | 359.2 | 357.8 | 361.8 | 367.7 | 374.2 | 379.0 | 379.5 | 380.2 | 375.8 | 377.0 | 381.8 | 382.7 | 373.1 |
| 2015 | 369.2 | 368.8 | 370.7 | 376.6 | 383.8 | 388.4 | 391.1 | 389.5 | 385.8 | 385.9 | 390.7 | 390.2 | 382.6 |
| 2016 | 375.9 | 376.0 | 379.1 | 383.5 | 387.2 | 392.9 | 395.0 | 394.0 | 389.5 | 388.2 | 390.6 | 391.2 | 386.9 |
| 2017 | 380.5 | 380.6 | 382.0 | 386.1 | 389.5 | 396.8 | 397.2 | 396.5 | 392.6 | 390.9 | 394.7 | 394.8 | 390.2 |
| 2018 | 383.5 | 384.5 | 386.8 | 391.9 | 397.6 | 402.6 | 402.1 | 400.9 | 395.5 | 397.1 | 398.6 | 398.8 | 395.0 |
| 2019 | 389.1 | 389.3 | 393.1 | 397.0 | 400.5 | 405.0 | 406.4 | 405.8 | 399.6 | 399.6 | 400.6 | 399.4 | 398.8 |
| **Goods Producing** | | | | | | | | | | | | | |
| 2011 | 44.1 | 44.0 | 44.8 | 45.9 | 46.1 | 46.0 | 45.8 | 45.1 | 45.2 | 45.3 | 44.8 | 44.6 | 45.1 |
| 2012 | 43.1 | 42.8 | 43.1 | 43.8 | 44.4 | 44.6 | 45.3 | 45.2 | 45.0 | 44.9 | 45.0 | 44.8 | 44.3 |
| 2013 | 44.1 | 43.6 | 43.9 | 44.6 | 44.9 | 45.3 | 45.5 | 45.8 | 45.6 | 46.3 | 45.8 | 44.8 | 45.0 |
| 2014 | 43.7 | 43.6 | 44.5 | 45.1 | 45.9 | 46.7 | 46.8 | 46.9 | 46.6 | 46.7 | 46.7 | 46.5 | 45.8 |
| 2015 | 45.0 | 45.0 | 45.0 | 46.1 | 46.8 | 47.1 | 47.5 | 47.7 | 47.9 | 47.2 | 46.7 | 46.7 | 46.6 |
| 2016 | 45.6 | 45.8 | 46.5 | 46.3 | 46.6 | 47.2 | 47.6 | 47.9 | 47.6 | 47.8 | 47.8 | 47.8 | 47.0 |
| 2017 | 46.9 | 47.2 | 47.7 | 47.8 | 47.6 | 48.2 | 48.3 | 48.0 | 48.1 | 48.0 | 48.4 | 48.5 | 47.9 |
| 2018 | 47.4 | 47.9 | 48.3 | 48.9 | 49.2 | 50.0 | 50.0 | 50.1 | 49.9 | 50.1 | 50.0 | 50.6 | 49.4 |
| 2019 | 49.5 | 49.5 | 50.1 | 50.3 | 50.3 | 50.7 | 50.6 | 50.6 | 50.2 | 50.5 | 50.2 | 49.8 | 50.2 |
| **Service-Providing** | | | | | | | | | | | | | |
| 2011 | 362.0 | 363.5 | 367.0 | 373.5 | 374.1 | 375.1 | 374.2 | 372.8 | 374.3 | 372.6 | 375.1 | 376.1 | 371.7 |
| 2012 | 363.2 | 364.7 | 369.5 | 372.6 | 377.8 | 378.3 | 377.0 | 376.4 | 376.4 | 378.7 | 382.0 | 382.4 | 374.9 |
| 2013 | 368.5 | 371.0 | 375.8 | 380.1 | 385.2 | 386.8 | 386.2 | 386.3 | 386.3 | 388.1 | 393.2 | 391.7 | 383.3 |
| 2014 | 380.0 | 379.7 | 383.6 | 388.7 | 394.7 | 395.7 | 394.5 | 393.7 | 393.9 | 396.3 | 401.3 | 402.3 | 392.0 |
| 2015 | 388.3 | 388.6 | 393.3 | 397.0 | 404.2 | 406.1 | 406.3 | 403.0 | 403.1 | 405.1 | 410.5 | 410.1 | 401.3 |
| 2016 | 394.9 | 395.2 | 399.2 | 404.4 | 407.7 | 409.7 | 410.7 | 407.5 | 407.2 | 407.5 | 410.5 | 410.6 | 405.4 |
| 2017 | 399.2 | 399.2 | 402.1 | 406.0 | 409.6 | 413.6 | 412.4 | 410.2 | 410.8 | 409.8 | 413.4 | 413.3 | 408.3 |
| 2018 | 400.9 | 402.6 | 405.7 | 410.5 | 416.2 | 417.4 | 416.0 | 413.2 | 412.1 | 414.5 | 416.4 | 416.1 | 411.8 |
| 2019 | 405.0 | 406.4 | 410.9 | 414.6 | 418.0 | 419.6 | 420.3 | 418.6 | 416.4 | 418.0 | 419.5 | 418.2 | 415.5 |
| **Mining, Logging, and Construction** | | | | | | | | | | | | | |
| 2011 | 18.7 | 18.6 | 19.3 | 20.2 | 20.1 | 19.9 | 19.6 | 19.1 | 19.2 | 19.3 | 18.9 | 18.8 | 19.3 |
| 2012 | 17.7 | 17.3 | 17.5 | 18.1 | 18.5 | 18.7 | 19.1 | 19.2 | 19.0 | 19.1 | 19.3 | 19.2 | 18.6 |
| 2013 | 18.6 | 18.3 | 18.6 | 19.3 | 19.6 | 19.9 | 20.2 | 20.5 | 20.3 | 20.8 | 20.4 | 19.6 | 19.7 |
| 2014 | 18.9 | 18.7 | 19.4 | 20.0 | 20.7 | 21.2 | 21.4 | 21.3 | 21.0 | 21.0 | 21.0 | 20.8 | 20.5 |
| 2015 | 19.4 | 19.4 | 19.5 | 20.4 | 21.1 | 21.1 | 21.6 | 21.7 | 21.9 | 21.5 | 21.0 | 20.8 | 20.8 |
| 2016 | 19.8 | 19.9 | 20.8 | 20.5 | 20.6 | 21.0 | 21.4 | 21.6 | 21.5 | 21.7 | 21.6 | 21.5 | 21.0 |
| 2017 | 20.7 | 20.9 | 21.6 | 21.8 | 21.5 | 21.9 | 22.0 | 21.9 | 22.0 | 21.7 | 21.7 | 21.6 | 21.6 |
| 2018 | 20.6 | 21.0 | 21.4 | 22.0 | 22.3 | 22.7 | 22.9 | 22.9 | 22.8 | 22.9 | 22.9 | 23.2 | 22.3 |
| 2019 | 22.2 | 22.1 | 22.8 | 23.0 | 23.1 | 23.4 | 23.3 | 23.3 | 23.0 | 23.2 | 23.0 | 22.7 | 22.9 |
| **Manufacturing** | | | | | | | | | | | | | |
| 2011 | 25.4 | 25.4 | 25.5 | 25.7 | 26.0 | 26.1 | 26.2 | 26.0 | 26.0 | 26.0 | 25.9 | 25.8 | 25.8 |
| 2012 | 25.4 | 25.5 | 25.6 | 25.7 | 25.9 | 25.9 | 26.2 | 26.0 | 26.0 | 25.8 | 25.7 | 25.6 | 25.8 |
| 2013 | 25.5 | 25.3 | 25.3 | 25.3 | 25.3 | 25.4 | 25.3 | 25.3 | 25.3 | 25.5 | 25.4 | 25.2 | 25.3 |
| 2014 | 24.8 | 24.9 | 25.1 | 25.1 | 25.2 | 25.5 | 25.4 | 25.6 | 25.6 | 25.7 | 25.7 | 25.7 | 25.4 |
| 2015 | 25.6 | 25.6 | 25.5 | 25.7 | 25.7 | 26.0 | 25.9 | 26.0 | 26.0 | 25.7 | 25.7 | 25.9 | 25.8 |
| 2016 | 25.8 | 25.9 | 25.7 | 25.8 | 26.0 | 26.2 | 26.2 | 26.3 | 26.1 | 26.1 | 26.2 | 26.3 | 26.1 |
| 2017 | 26.2 | 26.3 | 26.1 | 26.0 | 26.1 | 26.3 | 26.3 | 26.1 | 26.1 | 26.3 | 26.7 | 26.9 | 26.3 |
| 2018 | 26.8 | 26.9 | 26.9 | 26.9 | 26.9 | 27.3 | 27.1 | 27.2 | 27.1 | 27.2 | 27.1 | 27.4 | 27.1 |
| 2019 | 27.3 | 27.4 | 27.3 | 27.3 | 27.2 | 27.3 | 27.3 | 27.3 | 27.2 | 27.3 | 27.2 | 27.1 | 27.3 |

## 1. Employment by Industry: Delaware, 2011–2019—*Continued*

(Numbers in thousands, not seasonally adjusted)

| Industry and year | January | February | March | April | May | June | July | August | September | October | November | December | Annual average |
|---|---|---|---|---|---|---|---|---|---|---|---|---|---|
| **Trade, Transportation, and Utilities** | | | | | | | | | | | | | |
| 2011 | 73.9 | 73.3 | 73.6 | 75.0 | 75.2 | 75.9 | 75.6 | 75.3 | 75.4 | 75.1 | 77.6 | 78.4 | 75.4 |
| 2012 | 74.3 | 73.4 | 74.3 | 74.4 | 75.7 | 75.9 | 75.7 | 75.6 | 75.2 | 76.1 | 78.9 | 79.2 | 75.7 |
| 2013 | 75.0 | 74.2 | 75.0 | 75.8 | 76.7 | 77.3 | 77.3 | 77.8 | 77.9 | 78.9 | 81.4 | 82.1 | 77.5 |
| 2014 | 77.5 | 76.6 | 77.1 | 77.9 | 78.7 | 79.5 | 79.7 | 80.3 | 79.7 | 80.1 | 82.5 | 83.8 | 79.5 |
| 2015 | 79.0 | 78.5 | 78.8 | 79.7 | 80.4 | 81.1 | 81.5 | 81.7 | 81.2 | 82.5 | 85.2 | 85.8 | 81.3 |
| 2016 | 80.8 | 80.1 | 80.8 | 81.3 | 81.6 | 81.7 | 82.1 | 82.2 | 82.0 | 81.8 | 83.6 | 84.0 | 81.8 |
| 2017 | 80.4 | 79.2 | 79.1 | 79.7 | 80.0 | 80.7 | 80.2 | 81.1 | 81.1 | 81.0 | 83.7 | 84.2 | 80.9 |
| 2018 | 79.7 | 79.1 | 79.3 | 80.0 | 80.8 | 80.9 | 80.5 | 80.5 | 80.1 | 80.5 | 83.1 | 83.9 | 80.7 |
| 2019 | 80.3 | 79.9 | 80.3 | 80.4 | 80.5 | 80.9 | 80.9 | 80.6 | 80.1 | 80.3 | 83.3 | 84.5 | 81.0 |
| **Wholesale Trade** | | | | | | | | | | | | | |
| 2011 | 12.4 | 12.4 | 12.4 | 12.5 | 12.4 | 12.4 | 12.5 | 12.4 | 12.4 | 12.3 | 12.3 | 12.4 | 12.4 |
| 2012 | 12.3 | 12.3 | 12.5 | 12.4 | 12.3 | 12.3 | 12.3 | 12.3 | 12.2 | 12.1 | 12.1 | 12.1 | 12.3 |
| 2013 | 11.9 | 11.9 | 12.0 | 12.0 | 12.1 | 12.1 | 12.0 | 12.0 | 12.0 | 11.8 | 11.9 | 12.0 | 12.0 |
| 2014 | 11.7 | 11.6 | 11.7 | 11.8 | 11.9 | 11.9 | 11.8 | 11.8 | 11.7 | 11.6 | 11.7 | 11.8 | 11.8 |
| 2015 | 11.5 | 11.4 | 11.5 | 11.5 | 11.6 | 11.7 | 11.5 | 11.5 | 11.4 | 11.4 | 11.4 | 11.4 | 11.5 |
| 2016 | 11.2 | 11.2 | 11.2 | 11.2 | 11.3 | 11.2 | 11.1 | 11.0 | 10.9 | 10.7 | 10.7 | 10.7 | 11.0 |
| 2017 | 10.6 | 10.5 | 10.4 | 10.6 | 10.6 | 10.7 | 10.6 | 10.6 | 10.5 | 10.6 | 10.6 | 10.6 | 10.6 |
| 2018 | 10.5 | 10.5 | 10.5 | 10.8 | 10.8 | 10.9 | 10.8 | 10.9 | 10.8 | 10.8 | 10.8 | 10.9 | 10.8 |
| 2019 | 10.8 | 10.9 | 10.9 | 11.0 | 10.9 | 11.1 | 11.2 | 11.2 | 11.0 | 11.1 | 11.0 | 11.1 | 11.0 |
| **Retail Trade** | | | | | | | | | | | | | |
| 2011 | 49.2 | 48.6 | 48.9 | 50.1 | 50.3 | 51.1 | 51.4 | 51.4 | 50.5 | 50.2 | 52.6 | 53.1 | 50.6 |
| 2012 | 49.6 | 48.7 | 49.3 | 49.9 | 50.7 | 51.2 | 51.3 | 51.1 | 50.0 | 50.5 | 53.0 | 53.1 | 50.7 |
| 2013 | 49.5 | 48.9 | 49.5 | 50.2 | 51.0 | 51.7 | 52.1 | 52.5 | 51.5 | 52.2 | 54.4 | 54.8 | 51.5 |
| 2014 | 50.9 | 50.2 | 50.6 | 51.4 | 52.1 | 53.2 | 53.3 | 53.3 | 52.2 | 52.5 | 54.5 | 55.2 | 52.5 |
| 2015 | 51.5 | 50.9 | 51.1 | 51.9 | 52.5 | 53.4 | 53.7 | 53.6 | 52.6 | 53.4 | 55.8 | 55.9 | 53.0 |
| 2016 | 52.3 | 51.8 | 52.4 | 53.0 | 53.4 | 54.2 | 54.7 | 54.8 | 53.7 | 53.7 | 55.3 | 55.6 | 53.7 |
| 2017 | 52.6 | 52.1 | 52.1 | 52.8 | 53.2 | 54.0 | 54.0 | 54.0 | 53.0 | 53.1 | 55.5 | 55.7 | 53.5 |
| 2018 | 52.5 | 52.1 | 52.3 | 52.6 | 53.3 | 53.9 | 53.9 | 53.6 | 52.4 | 52.6 | 54.4 | 54.6 | 53.2 |
| 2019 | 51.8 | 51.5 | 51.7 | 51.7 | 51.9 | 52.5 | 52.5 | 52.3 | 51.3 | 51.7 | 54.2 | 54.8 | 52.3 |
| **Transportation and Utilities** | | | | | | | | | | | | | |
| 2011 | 12.3 | 12.3 | 12.3 | 12.4 | 12.5 | 12.4 | 11.7 | 11.5 | 12.5 | 12.6 | 12.7 | 12.9 | 12.3 |
| 2012 | 12.4 | 12.4 | 12.5 | 12.1 | 12.7 | 12.4 | 12.1 | 12.2 | 13.0 | 13.5 | 13.8 | 14.0 | 12.8 |
| 2013 | 13.6 | 13.4 | 13.5 | 13.6 | 13.6 | 13.5 | 13.2 | 13.3 | 14.4 | 14.9 | 15.1 | 15.3 | 14.0 |
| 2014 | 14.9 | 14.8 | 14.8 | 14.7 | 14.7 | 14.4 | 14.6 | 15.2 | 15.8 | 16.0 | 16.3 | 16.8 | 15.3 |
| 2015 | 16.0 | 16.2 | 16.2 | 16.3 | 16.3 | 16.0 | 16.3 | 16.6 | 17.2 | 17.7 | 18.0 | 18.5 | 16.8 |
| 2016 | 17.3 | 17.1 | 17.2 | 17.1 | 16.9 | 16.3 | 16.3 | 16.4 | 17.4 | 17.4 | 17.6 | 17.7 | 17.1 |
| 2017 | 17.2 | 16.6 | 16.6 | 16.3 | 16.2 | 16.0 | 15.6 | 16.5 | 17.6 | 17.3 | 17.6 | 17.9 | 16.8 |
| 2018 | 16.7 | 16.5 | 16.5 | 16.6 | 16.7 | 16.1 | 15.8 | 16.0 | 16.9 | 17.1 | 17.9 | 18.4 | 16.8 |
| 2019 | 17.7 | 17.5 | 17.7 | 17.7 | 17.7 | 17.3 | 17.2 | 17.1 | 17.8 | 17.5 | 18.1 | 18.6 | 17.7 |
| **Information** | | | | | | | | | | | | | |
| 2011 | 5.8 | 5.8 | 5.8 | 5.8 | 5.6 | 5.8 | 5.7 | 5.2 | 5.7 | 5.5 | 5.6 | 5.7 | 5.7 |
| 2012 | 5.6 | 5.6 | 5.6 | 5.5 | 5.5 | 5.5 | 5.4 | 5.5 | 5.3 | 5.3 | 5.3 | 5.3 | 5.5 |
| 2013 | 5.3 | 5.4 | 5.3 | 5.3 | 5.2 | 5.2 | 5.2 | 5.2 | 5.1 | 5.0 | 5.1 | 5.0 | 5.2 |
| 2014 | 5.1 | 4.9 | 4.9 | 4.9 | 5.0 | 4.9 | 4.9 | 5.0 | 4.8 | 4.9 | 4.9 | 4.8 | 4.9 |
| 2015 | 4.8 | 4.7 | 4.7 | 4.7 | 4.8 | 4.7 | 4.7 | 4.6 | 4.6 | 4.7 | 4.7 | 4.7 | 4.7 |
| 2016 | 4.6 | 4.6 | 4.6 | 4.6 | 4.3 | 4.7 | 4.7 | 4.7 | 4.7 | 4.6 | 4.6 | 4.7 | 4.6 |
| 2017 | 4.6 | 4.6 | 4.6 | 4.5 | 4.5 | 4.6 | 4.5 | 4.5 | 4.4 | 4.3 | 4.4 | 4.3 | 4.5 |
| 2018 | 4.2 | 4.3 | 4.2 | 4.1 | 4.1 | 4.2 | 4.0 | 4.0 | 3.9 | 3.9 | 4.0 | 3.9 | 4.1 |
| 2019 | 3.9 | 3.9 | 3.9 | 3.8 | 3.9 | 3.9 | 3.9 | 3.9 | 3.9 | 3.9 | 4.0 | 3.8 | 3.9 |
| **Financial Activities** | | | | | | | | | | | | | |
| 2011 | 42.3 | 42.4 | 42.3 | 42.4 | 42.2 | 42.8 | 43.1 | 42.8 | 42.3 | 41.4 | 41.3 | 41.7 | 42.3 |
| 2012 | 41.3 | 41.3 | 41.5 | 41.5 | 42.1 | 42.7 | 43.3 | 43.5 | 42.7 | 42.8 | 42.9 | 43.3 | 42.4 |
| 2013 | 42.9 | 43.2 | 43.3 | 43.3 | 43.5 | 44.2 | 44.7 | 44.7 | 44.1 | 44.0 | 44.3 | 44.5 | 43.9 |
| 2014 | 44.1 | 44.2 | 44.1 | 44.3 | 44.7 | 45.3 | 45.5 | 45.7 | 45.3 | 45.4 | 45.6 | 46.2 | 45.0 |
| 2015 | 45.7 | 46.0 | 46.1 | 46.3 | 46.2 | 46.6 | 47.0 | 47.3 | 47.2 | 46.9 | 47.1 | 46.9 | 46.6 |
| 2016 | 46.7 | 46.8 | 46.9 | 46.9 | 46.8 | 47.4 | 47.5 | 47.5 | 46.9 | 47.0 | 47.3 | 47.6 | 47.1 |
| 2017 | 47.3 | 47.4 | 47.5 | 47.5 | 47.7 | 48.6 | 48.6 | 48.6 | 48.1 | 47.9 | 47.9 | 48.0 | 47.9 |
| 2018 | 47.5 | 47.7 | 47.6 | 47.4 | 47.6 | 48.0 | 48.1 | 47.7 | 47.1 | 47.6 | 47.7 | 47.7 | 47.6 |
| 2019 | 47.5 | 47.6 | 47.6 | 47.7 | 47.6 | 47.9 | 48.1 | 47.8 | 47.5 | 47.6 | 47.5 | 47.7 | 47.7 |

# 1. Employment by Industry: Delaware, 2011–2019—*Continued*

(Numbers in thousands, not seasonally adjusted)

| Industry and year | January | February | March | April | May | June | July | August | September | October | November | December | Annual average |
|---|---|---|---|---|---|---|---|---|---|---|---|---|---|
| **Professional and Business Services** | | | | | | | | | | | | | |
| 2011 | 53.9 | 54.3 | 54.3 | 55.9 | 55.4 | 55.7 | 55.8 | 55.9 | 55.8 | 56.1 | 57.1 | 57.6 | 55.7 |
| 2012 | 54.9 | 54.6 | 55.2 | 56.1 | 55.9 | 55.9 | 56.0 | 56.2 | 56.0 | 57.0 | 58.5 | 58.6 | 56.2 |
| 2013 | 55.9 | 55.5 | 56.5 | 57.5 | 57.8 | 58.2 | 58.7 | 59.3 | 58.9 | 59.4 | 62.2 | 60.7 | 58.4 |
| 2014 | 58.1 | 57.1 | 57.8 | 59.0 | 59.7 | 60.0 | 60.0 | 59.8 | 59.6 | 60.7 | 64.2 | 63.6 | 60.0 |
| 2015 | 59.9 | 58.9 | 59.1 | 59.2 | 60.6 | 61.1 | 61.8 | 60.7 | 60.1 | 61.7 | 65.1 | 64.6 | 61.1 |
| 2016 | 60.5 | 59.6 | 59.7 | 60.6 | 61.1 | 62.7 | 62.8 | 62.1 | 61.1 | 61.7 | 63.3 | 64.2 | 61.6 |
| 2017 | 61.1 | 60.5 | 60.2 | 61.5 | 61.7 | 63.1 | 63.0 | 62.5 | 61.8 | 61.8 | 63.7 | 64.7 | 62.1 |
| 2018 | 61.5 | 61.3 | 61.8 | 63.0 | 63.5 | 64.2 | 64.3 | 63.8 | 63.1 | 63.8 | 64.7 | 64.2 | 63.3 |
| 2019 | 61.9 | 61.6 | 62.1 | 63.0 | 63.0 | 63.7 | 64.2 | 64.7 | 63.4 | 64.4 | 64.7 | 63.2 | 63.3 |
| **Education and Health Services** | | | | | | | | | | | | | |
| 2011 | 64.8 | 65.3 | 66.0 | 66.5 | 66.3 | 65.7 | 65.6 | 65.8 | 66.4 | 67.1 | 67.2 | 67.8 | 66.2 |
| 2012 | 66.7 | 67.0 | 67.6 | 67.9 | 68.2 | 68.0 | 67.6 | 67.8 | 68.6 | 69.2 | 69.5 | 69.8 | 68.2 |
| 2013 | 68.7 | 69.2 | 69.6 | 69.5 | 69.8 | 69.3 | 69.2 | 69.7 | 70.1 | 70.7 | 71.4 | 71.7 | 69.9 |
| 2014 | 70.8 | 71.2 | 71.9 | 72.1 | 72.5 | 71.9 | 71.6 | 71.8 | 72.6 | 73.4 | 73.9 | 74.1 | 72.3 |
| 2015 | 73.5 | 74.0 | 74.2 | 75.1 | 75.4 | 75.3 | 75.1 | 74.6 | 75.3 | 76.0 | 76.3 | 76.4 | 75.1 |
| 2016 | 75.5 | 76.1 | 76.4 | 76.5 | 76.8 | 76.2 | 76.2 | 76.1 | 76.8 | 77.4 | 77.5 | 77.6 | 76.6 |
| 2017 | 76.2 | 77.3 | 77.4 | 77.7 | 78.0 | 77.2 | 77.2 | 77.2 | 78.1 | 78.9 | 79.1 | 79.1 | 77.8 |
| 2018 | 78.5 | 78.8 | 79.4 | 79.7 | 80.0 | 79.4 | 78.7 | 78.7 | 79.6 | 80.8 | 81.1 | 81.1 | 79.7 |
| 2019 | 80.2 | 80.8 | 81.4 | 81.4 | 81.4 | 80.7 | 80.4 | 80.6 | 81.0 | 81.4 | 81.5 | 81.8 | 81.1 |
| **Leisure and Hospitality** | | | | | | | | | | | | | |
| 2011 | 40.5 | 40.6 | 41.8 | 43.6 | 46.0 | 48.5 | 49.3 | 49.3 | 47.0 | 44.3 | 43.1 | 41.9 | 44.7 |
| 2012 | 40.3 | 40.8 | 42.0 | 44.0 | 46.6 | 49.3 | 49.6 | 49.4 | 47.0 | 45.0 | 43.3 | 42.7 | 45.0 |
| 2013 | 41.1 | 41.2 | 42.3 | 44.6 | 48.0 | 50.8 | 51.2 | 50.7 | 47.9 | 46.2 | 44.3 | 43.7 | 46.0 |
| 2014 | 41.7 | 41.9 | 43.1 | 45.8 | 49.0 | 51.9 | 52.3 | 51.9 | 48.7 | 47.2 | 45.3 | 45.0 | 47.0 |
| 2015 | 43.0 | 43.3 | 44.5 | 46.9 | 50.8 | 53.5 | 54.7 | 54.1 | 50.9 | 48.3 | 47.0 | 46.5 | 48.6 |
| 2016 | 43.9 | 44.6 | 45.7 | 48.5 | 51.1 | 54.0 | 55.2 | 54.6 | 51.8 | 49.3 | 47.9 | 46.7 | 49.4 |
| 2017 | 45.5 | 45.9 | 46.9 | 48.5 | 51.1 | 55.2 | 56.4 | 55.7 | 52.6 | 50.4 | 48.9 | 47.5 | 50.4 |
| 2018 | 46.4 | 47.1 | 47.9 | 50.3 | 53.8 | 57.0 | 57.7 | 57.4 | 53.4 | 51.9 | 49.6 | 49.0 | 51.8 |
| 2019 | 47.4 | 47.7 | 49.4 | 51.7 | 55.1 | 58.2 | 59.4 | 58.7 | 54.9 | 52.4 | 50.4 | 49.8 | 52.9 |
| **Other Services** | | | | | | | | | | | | | |
| 2011 | 18.1 | 18.1 | 18.1 | 18.1 | 18.2 | 18.4 | 18.4 | 18.4 | 18.2 | 18.1 | 18.0 | 18.0 | 18.2 |
| 2012 | 17.9 | 18.0 | 18.1 | 18.2 | 18.3 | 18.5 | 18.5 | 18.6 | 18.3 | 18.4 | 18.4 | 18.4 | 18.3 |
| 2013 | 18.2 | 18.2 | 18.3 | 18.5 | 18.5 | 18.7 | 18.7 | 18.7 | 18.4 | 18.4 | 18.5 | 18.5 | 18.5 |
| 2014 | 18.2 | 18.3 | 18.4 | 18.6 | 18.7 | 18.8 | 18.7 | 18.8 | 18.5 | 18.6 | 18.7 | 18.7 | 18.6 |
| 2015 | 18.3 | 18.4 | 18.3 | 18.6 | 18.8 | 19.0 | 18.8 | 18.8 | 18.6 | 18.6 | 18.6 | 18.6 | 18.6 |
| 2016 | 18.3 | 18.4 | 18.5 | 18.8 | 18.9 | 19.0 | 18.9 | 18.9 | 18.6 | 18.6 | 18.6 | 18.6 | 18.7 |
| 2017 | 18.5 | 18.5 | 18.6 | 18.9 | 18.9 | 19.2 | 19.0 | 18.9 | 18.4 | 18.6 | 18.6 | 18.5 | 18.7 |
| 2018 | 18.3 | 18.3 | 18.3 | 18.5 | 18.6 | 18.9 | 18.8 | 18.7 | 18.4 | 18.5 | 18.4 | 18.4 | 18.5 |
| 2019 | 18.4 | 18.3 | 18.3 | 18.7 | 18.7 | 19.0 | 18.9 | 18.9 | 18.6 | 19.1 | 19.0 | 18.8 | 18.7 |
| **Government** | | | | | | | | | | | | | |
| 2011 | 62.7 | 63.7 | 65.1 | 66.2 | 65.2 | 62.3 | 60.7 | 60.1 | 63.5 | 65.0 | 65.2 | 65.0 | 63.7 |
| 2012 | 62.2 | 64.0 | 65.2 | 65.0 | 65.5 | 62.5 | 60.9 | 59.8 | 63.3 | 64.9 | 65.2 | 65.1 | 63.6 |
| 2013 | 61.4 | 64.1 | 65.5 | 65.6 | 65.7 | 63.1 | 61.2 | 60.2 | 63.9 | 65.5 | 66.0 | 65.5 | 64.0 |
| 2014 | 64.5 | 65.5 | 66.3 | 66.1 | 66.4 | 63.4 | 61.8 | 60.4 | 64.7 | 66.0 | 66.2 | 66.1 | 64.8 |
| 2015 | 64.1 | 64.8 | 67.6 | 66.5 | 67.2 | 64.8 | 62.7 | 61.2 | 65.2 | 66.4 | 66.5 | 66.6 | 65.3 |
| 2016 | 64.6 | 65.0 | 66.6 | 67.2 | 67.1 | 64.0 | 63.3 | 61.4 | 65.3 | 67.1 | 67.7 | 67.2 | 65.5 |
| 2017 | 65.6 | 65.8 | 67.8 | 67.7 | 67.7 | 65.0 | 63.5 | 61.7 | 66.3 | 66.9 | 67.1 | 67.0 | 66.0 |
| 2018 | 64.8 | 66.0 | 67.2 | 67.5 | 67.8 | 64.8 | 63.9 | 62.4 | 66.5 | 67.5 | 67.8 | 67.9 | 66.2 |
| 2019 | 65.4 | 66.6 | 67.9 | 67.9 | 67.8 | 65.3 | 64.5 | 63.4 | 67.0 | 68.9 | 69.1 | 68.6 | 66.9 |

## 2. Average Weekly Hours by Selected Industry: Delaware, 2015–2019

(Not seasonally adjusted)

| Industry and year | January | February | March | April | May | June | July | August | September | October | November | December | Annual average |
|---|---|---|---|---|---|---|---|---|---|---|---|---|---|
| **Total Private** | | | | | | | | | | | | | |
| 2015 | 33.1 | 33.3 | 33.3 | 33.2 | 33.4 | 33.0 | 33.4 | 33.5 | 33.2 | 32.5 | 32.4 | 33.6 | 33.2 |
| 2016 | 33.3 | 33.2 | 33.3 | 33.2 | 33.3 | 33.4 | 33.7 | 33.2 | 33.0 | 33.3 | 32.6 | 32.8 | 33.2 |
| 2017 | 32.3 | 32.1 | 32.2 | 33.1 | 32.3 | 33.4 | 34.0 | 33.5 | 33.1 | 32.9 | 32.8 | 32.8 | 32.9 |
| 2018 | 32.9 | 32.8 | 32.5 | 33.2 | 32.8 | 33.0 | 33.7 | 33.5 | 33.2 | 32.5 | 32.8 | 33.2 | 33.0 |
| 2019 | 32.4 | 32.6 | 33.1 | 33.2 | 32.8 | 33.1 | 33.3 | 33.5 | 33.6 | 33.0 | 32.8 | 32.8 | 33.0 |
| **Goods-Producing** | | | | | | | | | | | | | |
| 2015 | 39.0 | 38.0 | 37.9 | 39.4 | 39.3 | 39.0 | 38.9 | 39.1 | 38.7 | 38.4 | 36.9 | 38.6 | 38.6 |
| 2016 | 39.2 | 37.7 | 38.7 | 38.3 | 39.0 | 39.4 | 39.8 | 40.0 | 40.5 | 40.3 | 39.1 | 38.9 | 39.3 |
| 2017 | 39.6 | 38.4 | 38.2 | 40.1 | 39.5 | 40.0 | 39.8 | 39.2 | 39.8 | 39.6 | 40.0 | 39.4 | 39.5 |
| 2018 | 40.3 | 39.6 | 39.1 | 40.8 | 40.4 | 40.3 | 40.8 | 40.3 | 39.8 | 39.6 | 40.1 | 40.1 | 40.1 |
| 2019 | 39.4 | 39.3 | 39.7 | 40.7 | 39.8 | 39.0 | 39.5 | 40.4 | 40.9 | 40.4 | 39.7 | 38.9 | 39.8 |
| **Mining, Logging, and Construction** | | | | | | | | | | | | | |
| 2015 | 36.9 | 36.3 | 36.8 | 38.4 | 36.7 | 37.6 | 36.4 | 37.0 | 36.4 | 36.1 | 34.5 | 37.3 | 36.7 |
| 2016 | 36.8 | 36.0 | 38.0 | 37.2 | 37.5 | 38.8 | 39.4 | 39.8 | 40.3 | 41.2 | 39.1 | 37.6 | 38.5 |
| 2017 | 36.8 | 37.2 | 36.3 | 38.3 | 38.0 | 37.8 | 37.8 | 37.3 | 38.6 | 38.6 | 38.4 | 37.7 | 37.8 |
| 2018 | 36.5 | 37.1 | 36.7 | 38.6 | 38.5 | 38.5 | 39.0 | 38.4 | 37.2 | 36.8 | 36.9 | 38.5 | 37.7 |
| 2019 | 37.5 | 36.2 | 37.5 | 39.3 | 37.0 | 36.4 | 37.2 | 38.2 | 39.9 | 39.0 | 38.1 | 36.7 | 37.8 |
| **Manufacturing** | | | | | | | | | | | | | |
| 2015 | 40.6 | 39.3 | 38.7 | 40.2 | 41.4 | 40.0 | 40.9 | 40.9 | 40.8 | 40.4 | 38.9 | 39.5 | 40.1 |
| 2016 | 41.0 | 39.2 | 39.1 | 39.1 | 40.3 | 39.9 | 40.1 | 40.1 | 40.6 | 39.4 | 39.2 | 39.9 | 39.8 |
| 2017 | 41.8 | 39.4 | 39.8 | 41.4 | 40.8 | 41.7 | 41.5 | 40.7 | 40.8 | 40.4 | 41.4 | 40.8 | 40.9 |
| 2018 | 43.2 | 41.5 | 40.9 | 42.5 | 42.1 | 42.0 | 42.1 | 41.8 | 41.9 | 41.9 | 42.8 | 41.4 | 42.0 |
| 2019 | 41.1 | 41.8 | 41.4 | 41.9 | 42.1 | 41.3 | 41.5 | 42.3 | 41.8 | 41.6 | 41.1 | 40.7 | 41.5 |
| **Trade, Transportation, and Utilities** | | | | | | | | | | | | | |
| 2015 | 32.4 | 32.7 | 32.9 | 33.2 | 34.2 | 34.0 | 34.1 | 34.2 | 34.6 | 33.1 | 33.4 | 35.2 | 33.7 |
| 2016 | 34.3 | 34.1 | 33.5 | 33.8 | 33.7 | 33.9 | 33.7 | 33.2 | 33.4 | 33.6 | 33.1 | 33.8 | 33.7 |
| 2017 | 33.1 | 32.6 | 32.8 | 33.3 | 33.1 | 33.0 | 33.1 | 32.8 | 33.4 | 33.2 | 32.4 | 33.1 | 33.0 |
| 2018 | 31.8 | 31.8 | 31.8 | 32.4 | 32.5 | 33.0 | 33.2 | 33.1 | 33.1 | 32.1 | 33.0 | 32.8 | 32.5 |
| 2019 | 31.6 | 31.9 | 32.8 | 32.2 | 31.9 | 32.3 | 32.7 | 32.9 | 33.4 | 32.4 | 32.2 | 33.2 | 32.5 |
| **Financial Activities** | | | | | | | | | | | | | |
| 2015 | 37.5 | 38.5 | 38.3 | 38.2 | 38.2 | 38.4 | 38.6 | 38.8 | 38.4 | 38.3 | 38.8 | 38.5 | 38.4 |
| 2016 | 38.8 | 38.4 | 38.8 | 38.6 | 39.3 | 39.2 | 38.9 | 38.9 | 39.0 | 39.0 | 39.0 | 39.2 | 38.9 |
| 2017 | 40.1 | 38.7 | 38.8 | 39.5 | 37.8 | 38.5 | 39.4 | 38.2 | 38.0 | 38.1 | 37.4 | 37.4 | 38.5 |
| 2018 | 37.5 | 37.4 | 37.9 | 38.7 | 36.9 | 37.4 | 38.5 | 37.2 | 38.5 | 37.2 | 37.2 | 38.3 | 37.7 |
| 2019 | 37.0 | 37.4 | 36.7 | 37.1 | 36.4 | 37.6 | 36.5 | 36.0 | 37.7 | 36.7 | 37.1 | 37.9 | 37.0 |
| **Professional and Business Services** | | | | | | | | | | | | | |
| 2015 | 34.4 | 35.5 | 35.8 | 36.1 | 35.4 | 34.4 | 33.9 | 34.2 | 32.7 | 32.8 | 33.7 | 34.1 | 34.4 |
| 2016 | 33.6 | 34.4 | 34.8 | 34.9 | 35.4 | 34.4 | 34.8 | 34.0 | 33.7 | 35.5 | 33.6 | 33.6 | 34.4 |
| 2017 | 32.8 | 33.7 | 33.8 | 34.8 | 33.8 | 34.0 | 35.3 | 34.8 | 34.5 | 33.3 | 32.9 | 33.1 | 33.9 |
| 2018 | 32.7 | 33.5 | 33.7 | 34.6 | 34.3 | 35.5 | 35.6 | 35.7 | 35.8 | 34.2 | 34.4 | 35.2 | 34.6 |
| 2019 | 33.9 | 34.1 | 35.1 | 35.5 | 35.4 | 35.6 | 35.0 | 35.5 | 36.0 | 35.5 | 34.8 | 35.4 | 35.2 |
| **Education and Health Services** | | | | | | | | | | | | | |
| 2015 | 32.6 | 32.5 | 32.1 | 31.7 | 31.9 | 32.3 | 32.3 | 32.0 | 32.1 | 31.7 | 32.0 | 32.4 | 32.1 |
| 2016 | 32.4 | 32.3 | 32.4 | 32.4 | 32.3 | 32.6 | 33.2 | 32.9 | 32.5 | 32.5 | 32.2 | 32.0 | 32.5 |
| 2017 | 32.8 | 32.6 | 32.4 | 32.9 | 32.4 | 32.7 | 32.9 | 33.0 | 32.6 | 33.0 | 32.8 | 32.5 | 32.7 |
| 2018 | 33.1 | 32.9 | 32.2 | 32.7 | 32.3 | 32.3 | 32.2 | 32.4 | 32.1 | 31.9 | 31.7 | 31.3 | 32.2 |
| 2019 | 31.8 | 31.2 | 31.4 | 31.6 | 30.9 | 31.0 | 31.6 | 31.4 | 30.5 | 30.4 | 30.4 | 29.8 | 31.0 |
| **Leisure and Hospitality** | | | | | | | | | | | | | |
| 2015 | 24.3 | 24.4 | 24.6 | 24.5 | 24.9 | 24.5 | 26.0 | 26.3 | 25.0 | 24.3 | 23.8 | 23.5 | 24.7 |
| 2016 | 23.0 | 23.6 | 23.6 | 23.7 | 23.9 | 25.2 | 25.7 | 25.4 | 24.2 | 23.9 | 23.4 | 23.6 | 24.2 |
| 2017 | 23.1 | 23.3 | 23.9 | 23.9 | 23.3 | 24.6 | 25.8 | 25.6 | 24.3 | 23.7 | 24.1 | 24.0 | 24.2 |
| 2018 | 23.8 | 24.1 | 24.0 | 24.4 | 24.3 | 25.1 | 26.3 | 26.1 | 24.6 | 24.0 | 23.3 | 23.8 | 24.5 |
| 2019 | 22.7 | 23.4 | 23.9 | 24.0 | 24.3 | 25.1 | 26.0 | 26.2 | 24.5 | 24.3 | 24.2 | 23.9 | 24.4 |

## 3. Average Hourly Earnings by Selected Industry: Delaware, 2015–2019

(Dollars, not seasonally adjusted)

| Industry and year | January | February | March | April | May | June | July | August | September | October | November | December | Annual average |
|---|---|---|---|---|---|---|---|---|---|---|---|---|---|
| **Total Private** | | | | | | | | | | | | | |
| 2015 | 22.07 | 22.53 | 22.56 | 22.27 | 22.12 | 22.08 | 22.12 | 22.67 | 22.87 | 23.35 | 23.62 | 23.27 | 22.63 |
| 2016 | 24.00 | 24.13 | 24.25 | 24.42 | 24.38 | 23.76 | 23.85 | 24.09 | 24.43 | 25.33 | 25.16 | 24.97 | 24.40 |
| 2017 | 25.79 | 25.84 | 25.74 | 26.00 | 25.23 | 26.73 | 26.63 | 26.21 | 26.61 | 26.82 | 26.38 | 26.58 | 26.22 |
| 2018 | 25.83 | 26.07 | 26.33 | 26.08 | 25.68 | 25.49 | 25.96 | 25.80 | 26.54 | 26.66 | 26.77 | 27.21 | 26.20 |
| 2019 | 26.41 | 26.57 | 26.88 | 26.81 | 26.68 | 26.77 | 26.65 | 26.46 | 27.48 | 27.20 | 27.42 | 27.97 | 26.94 |
| **Goods-Producing** | | | | | | | | | | | | | |
| 2015 | 24.70 | 25.16 | 25.06 | 24.42 | 24.44 | 24.87 | 25.00 | 25.50 | 25.39 | 25.21 | 25.34 | 25.25 | 25.03 |
| 2016 | 25.10 | 25.28 | 25.50 | 25.34 | 25.17 | 25.24 | 25.68 | 25.92 | 25.58 | 25.97 | 26.20 | 25.66 | 25.56 |
| 2017 | 25.63 | 25.64 | 26.04 | 26.34 | 25.86 | 25.39 | 25.59 | 25.44 | 25.92 | 25.58 | 25.29 | 25.41 | 25.68 |
| 2018 | 24.74 | 25.06 | 25.68 | 25.75 | 25.74 | 25.48 | 26.11 | 25.77 | 25.57 | 26.14 | 26.11 | 27.37 | 25.80 |
| 2019 | 26.47 | 26.88 | 27.35 | 27.78 | 27.86 | 28.10 | 27.90 | 27.75 | 28.32 | 27.93 | 28.51 | 29.19 | 27.84 |
| **Mining, Logging, and Construction** | | | | | | | | | | | | | |
| 2015 | 28.19 | 28.67 | 28.51 | 27.70 | 28.27 | 28.35 | 28.60 | 28.86 | 28.07 | 28.05 | 27.83 | 28.02 | 28.26 |
| 2016 | 28.43 | 29.32 | 28.89 | 28.74 | 28.89 | 28.45 | 28.69 | 29.28 | 29.07 | 29.48 | 29.83 | 29.00 | 29.02 |
| 2017 | 28.86 | 28.64 | 29.04 | 29.03 | 28.78 | 27.73 | 27.62 | 27.19 | 28.10 | 27.44 | 26.58 | 27.39 | 28.02 |
| 2018 | 26.79 | 26.59 | 27.42 | 27.60 | 27.69 | 26.76 | 27.32 | 27.03 | 26.44 | 27.97 | 27.56 | 28.15 | 27.29 |
| 2019 | 27.69 | 28.02 | 28.58 | 29.14 | 30.03 | 30.51 | 29.89 | 30.16 | 30.80 | 30.62 | 31.07 | 31.92 | 29.88 |
| **Manufacturing** | | | | | | | | | | | | | |
| 2015 | 22.30 | 22.70 | 22.56 | 21.93 | 21.66 | 22.21 | 22.33 | 22.96 | 23.37 | 23.09 | 23.54 | 23.14 | 22.65 |
| 2016 | 22.81 | 22.43 | 22.83 | 22.77 | 22.42 | 22.74 | 23.26 | 23.17 | 22.74 | 22.92 | 23.22 | 23.09 | 22.87 |
| 2017 | 23.38 | 23.39 | 23.77 | 24.26 | 23.62 | 23.62 | 24.04 | 24.09 | 24.18 | 24.11 | 24.32 | 23.94 | 23.89 |
| 2018 | 23.41 | 23.99 | 24.44 | 24.37 | 24.26 | 24.51 | 25.16 | 24.80 | 24.92 | 24.78 | 25.06 | 26.75 | 24.70 |
| 2019 | 25.56 | 26.09 | 26.42 | 26.71 | 26.23 | 26.28 | 26.38 | 25.89 | 26.32 | 25.79 | 26.50 | 27.17 | 26.28 |
| **Trade, Transportation, and Utilities** | | | | | | | | | | | | | |
| 2015 | 19.01 | 18.97 | 18.95 | 18.66 | 18.44 | 18.67 | 18.55 | 18.90 | 18.76 | 19.11 | 19.03 | 19.02 | 18.84 |
| 2016 | 19.22 | 19.13 | 19.30 | 19.54 | 19.95 | 19.57 | 19.64 | 20.15 | 20.16 | 20.74 | 20.59 | 20.08 | 19.84 |
| 2017 | 21.00 | 20.82 | 20.94 | 21.60 | 21.06 | 21.64 | 21.47 | 21.10 | 21.50 | 21.89 | 21.23 | 21.51 | 21.32 |
| 2018 | 21.92 | 21.86 | 21.92 | 22.44 | 21.82 | 21.54 | 22.14 | 22.27 | 22.23 | 21.94 | 22.09 | 22.01 | 22.02 |
| 2019 | 22.34 | 22.25 | 22.20 | 22.69 | 22.11 | 21.69 | 21.62 | 21.25 | 21.52 | 21.12 | 21.59 | 21.27 | 21.80 |
| **Financial Activities** | | | | | | | | | | | | | |
| 2015 | 25.22 | 25.64 | 25.81 | 25.87 | 26.09 | 26.09 | 26.79 | 27.10 | 27.98 | 28.42 | 28.91 | 29.02 | 26.93 |
| 2016 | 28.25 | 29.05 | 29.12 | 28.34 | 28.01 | 27.14 | 27.16 | 26.92 | 26.30 | 26.67 | 26.66 | 27.32 | 27.57 |
| 2017 | 26.30 | 26.57 | 26.52 | 26.65 | 25.26 | 24.97 | 26.20 | 26.33 | 27.37 | 28.01 | 28.71 | 27.90 | 26.72 |
| 2018 | 28.16 | 28.05 | 29.40 | 29.16 | 28.84 | 28.35 | 29.33 | 30.03 | 30.98 | 30.83 | 30.65 | 31.96 | 29.65 |
| 2019 | 32.42 | 32.31 | 32.99 | 33.01 | 33.20 | 32.25 | 32.41 | 33.28 | 34.07 | 33.37 | 33.82 | 34.72 | 33.16 |
| **Professional and Business Services** | | | | | | | | | | | | | |
| 2015 | 27.55 | 27.46 | 27.23 | 27.34 | 27.05 | 26.82 | 26.84 | 28.19 | 28.60 | 29.04 | 29.47 | 28.77 | 27.86 |
| 2016 | 30.11 | 30.03 | 29.56 | 29.88 | 30.30 | 30.13 | 30.31 | 30.60 | 31.24 | 32.28 | 31.71 | 31.57 | 30.65 |
| 2017 | 33.34 | 33.17 | 32.82 | 32.09 | 31.25 | 31.30 | 32.53 | 31.50 | 32.07 | 32.14 | 32.10 | 32.71 | 32.24 |
| 2018 | 32.72 | 32.64 | 32.09 | 31.79 | 30.82 | 31.37 | 32.33 | 31.32 | 32.82 | 32.38 | 32.75 | 33.37 | 32.20 |
| 2019 | 31.30 | 33.36 | 33.68 | 31.49 | 31.36 | 33.25 | 33.87 | 33.64 | 34.36 | 33.43 | 33.60 | 34.19 | 33.14 |
| **Education and Health Services** | | | | | | | | | | | | | |
| 2015 | 23.81 | 23.87 | 24.11 | 24.42 | 24.27 | 24.12 | 24.79 | 24.84 | 25.37 | 26.40 | 25.98 | 26.16 | 24.85 |
| 2016 | 26.27 | 26.22 | 26.28 | 27.13 | 27.30 | 27.13 | 27.38 | 27.58 | 28.23 | 29.17 | 29.18 | 29.33 | 27.61 |
| 2017 | 28.44 | 28.49 | 28.05 | 28.27 | 27.75 | 27.45 | 27.13 | 27.32 | 27.35 | 27.77 | 27.15 | 27.75 | 27.74 |
| 2018 | 27.96 | 28.38 | 29.35 | 28.94 | 28.57 | 28.58 | 28.96 | 29.09 | 29.22 | 29.23 | 28.65 | 28.43 | 28.78 |
| 2019 | 27.91 | 27.84 | 27.89 | 28.01 | 27.89 | 28.00 | 28.40 | 27.98 | 29.22 | 29.46 | 29.29 | 29.71 | 28.46 |
| **Leisure and Hospitality** | | | | | | | | | | | | | |
| 2015 | 12.94 | 13.13 | 13.08 | 13.08 | 13.22 | 13.02 | 12.93 | 12.91 | 13.19 | 13.35 | 13.70 | 13.88 | 13.19 |
| 2016 | 13.63 | 13.62 | 13.74 | 13.57 | 13.46 | 12.95 | 13.06 | 13.46 | 13.89 | 14.02 | 14.03 | 14.19 | 13.61 |
| 2017 | 14.38 | 14.76 | 14.66 | 14.77 | 14.86 | 14.25 | 14.24 | 14.41 | 14.40 | 14.69 | 14.41 | 14.77 | 14.54 |
| 2018 | 14.52 | 14.65 | 14.73 | 14.51 | 14.72 | 14.58 | 14.77 | 14.83 | 15.01 | 15.30 | 15.13 | 15.37 | 14.84 |
| 2019 | 15.03 | 15.11 | 15.28 | 15.05 | 15.37 | 15.19 | 15.22 | 14.98 | 15.31 | 15.74 | 15.60 | 16.08 | 15.32 |

## 4. Average Weekly Earnings by Selected Industry: Delaware, 2015–2019

(Dollars, not seasonally adjusted)

| Industry and year | January | February | March | April | May | June | July | August | September | October | November | December | Annual average |
|---|---|---|---|---|---|---|---|---|---|---|---|---|---|
| **Total Private** | | | | | | | | | | | | | |
| 2015 | 730.52 | 750.25 | 751.25 | 739.36 | 738.81 | 728.64 | 738.81 | 759.45 | 759.28 | 758.88 | 765.29 | 781.87 | 751.32 |
| 2016 | 799.20 | 801.12 | 807.53 | 810.74 | 811.85 | 793.58 | 803.75 | 799.79 | 806.19 | 843.49 | 820.22 | 819.02 | 810.08 |
| 2017 | 833.02 | 829.46 | 828.83 | 860.60 | 814.93 | 892.78 | 905.42 | 878.04 | 880.79 | 882.38 | 865.26 | 871.82 | 862.64 |
| 2018 | 849.81 | 855.10 | 855.73 | 865.86 | 842.30 | 841.17 | 874.85 | 864.30 | 881.13 | 866.45 | 878.06 | 903.37 | 864.60 |
| 2019 | 855.68 | 866.18 | 889.73 | 890.09 | 875.10 | 886.09 | 887.45 | 886.41 | 923.33 | 897.60 | 899.38 | 917.42 | 889.02 |
| **Goods-Producing** | | | | | | | | | | | | | |
| 2015 | 963.30 | 956.08 | 949.77 | 962.15 | 960.49 | 969.93 | 972.50 | 997.05 | 982.59 | 968.06 | 935.05 | 974.65 | 966.16 |
| 2016 | 983.92 | 953.06 | 986.85 | 970.52 | 981.63 | 994.46 | 1,022.06 | 1,036.80 | 1,035.99 | 1,046.59 | 1,024.42 | 998.17 | 1,004.51 |
| 2017 | 1,014.95 | 984.58 | 994.73 | 1,056.23 | 1,021.47 | 1,015.60 | 1,018.48 | 997.25 | 1,031.62 | 1,012.97 | 1,011.60 | 1,001.15 | 1,014.36 |
| 2018 | 997.02 | 992.38 | 1,004.09 | 1,050.60 | 1,039.90 | 1,026.84 | 1,065.29 | 1,038.53 | 1,017.69 | 1,035.14 | 1,047.01 | 1,097.54 | 1,034.58 |
| 2019 | 1,042.92 | 1,056.38 | 1,085.80 | 1,130.65 | 1,108.83 | 1,095.90 | 1,102.05 | 1,121.10 | 1,158.29 | 1,128.37 | 1,131.85 | 1,135.49 | 1,108.03 |
| **Mining, Logging, and Construction** | | | | | | | | | | | | | |
| 2015 | 1,040.21 | 1,040.72 | 1,049.17 | 1,063.68 | 1,037.51 | 1,065.96 | 1,041.04 | 1,067.82 | 1,021.75 | 1,012.61 | 960.14 | 1,045.15 | 1,037.14 |
| 2016 | 1,046.22 | 1,055.52 | 1,097.82 | 1,069.13 | 1,083.38 | 1,103.86 | 1,130.39 | 1,165.34 | 1,171.52 | 1,214.58 | 1,166.35 | 1,090.40 | 1,117.27 |
| 2017 | 1,062.05 | 1,065.41 | 1,054.15 | 1,111.85 | 1,093.64 | 1,048.19 | 1,044.04 | 1,014.19 | 1,084.66 | 1,059.18 | 1,020.67 | 1,032.60 | 1,059.16 |
| 2018 | 977.84 | 986.49 | 1,006.31 | 1,065.36 | 1,066.07 | 1,030.26 | 1,065.48 | 1,037.95 | 983.57 | 1,029.30 | 1,016.96 | 1,083.78 | 1,028.83 |
| 2019 | 1,038.38 | 1,014.32 | 1,071.75 | 1,145.20 | 1,111.11 | 1,110.56 | 1,111.91 | 1,152.11 | 1,228.92 | 1,194.18 | 1,183.77 | 1,171.46 | 1,129.46 |
| **Manufacturing** | | | | | | | | | | | | | |
| 2015 | 905.38 | 892.11 | 873.07 | 881.59 | 896.72 | 888.40 | 913.30 | 939.06 | 953.50 | 932.84 | 915.71 | 914.03 | 908.27 |
| 2016 | 935.21 | 879.26 | 892.65 | 890.31 | 903.53 | 907.33 | 932.73 | 929.12 | 923.24 | 903.05 | 910.22 | 921.29 | 910.23 |
| 2017 | 977.28 | 921.57 | 946.05 | 1,004.36 | 963.70 | 984.95 | 997.66 | 980.46 | 986.54 | 974.04 | 1,006.85 | 976.75 | 977.10 |
| 2018 | 1,011.31 | 995.59 | 999.60 | 1,035.73 | 1,021.35 | 1,029.42 | 1,059.24 | 1,036.64 | 1,044.15 | 1,038.28 | 1,072.57 | 1,107.45 | 1,037.40 |
| 2019 | 1,050.52 | 1,090.56 | 1,093.79 | 1,119.15 | 1,104.28 | 1,085.36 | 1,094.77 | 1,095.15 | 1,100.18 | 1,072.86 | 1,089.15 | 1,105.82 | 1,090.62 |
| **Trade, Transportation, and Utilities** | | | | | | | | | | | | | |
| 2015 | 615.92 | 620.32 | 623.46 | 619.51 | 630.65 | 634.78 | 632.56 | 646.38 | 649.10 | 632.54 | 635.60 | 669.50 | 634.91 |
| 2016 | 659.25 | 652.33 | 646.55 | 660.45 | 672.32 | 663.42 | 661.87 | 668.98 | 673.34 | 696.86 | 681.53 | 678.70 | 668.61 |
| 2017 | 695.10 | 678.73 | 686.83 | 719.28 | 697.09 | 714.12 | 710.66 | 692.08 | 718.10 | 726.75 | 687.85 | 711.98 | 703.56 |
| 2018 | 697.06 | 695.15 | 697.06 | 727.06 | 709.15 | 710.82 | 735.05 | 737.14 | 735.81 | 704.27 | 728.97 | 721.93 | 715.65 |
| 2019 | 705.94 | 709.78 | 728.16 | 730.62 | 705.31 | 700.59 | 706.97 | 699.13 | 718.77 | 684.29 | 695.20 | 706.16 | 708.50 |
| **Financial Activities** | | | | | | | | | | | | | |
| 2015 | 945.75 | 987.14 | 988.52 | 988.23 | 996.64 | 1,001.86 | 1,034.09 | 1,051.48 | 1,074.43 | 1,088.49 | 1,121.71 | 1,117.27 | 1,034.11 |
| 2016 | 1,096.10 | 1,115.52 | 1,129.86 | 1,093.92 | 1,100.79 | 1,063.89 | 1,056.52 | 1,047.19 | 1,025.70 | 1,040.13 | 1,039.74 | 1,070.94 | 1,072.47 |
| 2017 | 1,054.63 | 1,028.26 | 1,028.98 | 1,052.68 | 954.83 | 961.35 | 1,032.28 | 1,005.81 | 1,040.06 | 1,067.18 | 1,073.75 | 1,043.46 | 1,028.72 |
| 2018 | 1,056.00 | 1,049.07 | 1,114.26 | 1,128.49 | 1,064.20 | 1,060.29 | 1,129.21 | 1,117.12 | 1,192.73 | 1,146.88 | 1,140.18 | 1,224.07 | 1,117.81 |
| 2019 | 1,199.54 | 1,208.39 | 1,210.73 | 1,224.67 | 1,208.48 | 1,212.60 | 1,182.97 | 1,198.08 | 1,284.44 | 1,224.68 | 1,254.72 | 1,315.89 | 1,226.92 |
| **Professional and Business Services** | | | | | | | | | | | | | |
| 2015 | 947.72 | 974.83 | 974.83 | 986.97 | 957.57 | 922.61 | 909.88 | 964.10 | 935.22 | 952.51 | 993.14 | 981.06 | 958.38 |
| 2016 | 1,011.70 | 1,033.03 | 1,028.69 | 1,042.81 | 1,072.62 | 1,036.47 | 1,054.79 | 1,040.40 | 1,052.79 | 1,145.94 | 1,065.46 | 1,060.75 | 1,054.36 |
| 2017 | 1,093.55 | 1,117.83 | 1,109.32 | 1,116.73 | 1,056.25 | 1,064.20 | 1,148.31 | 1,096.20 | 1,106.42 | 1,070.26 | 1,056.09 | 1,082.70 | 1,092.94 |
| 2018 | 1,069.94 | 1,093.44 | 1,081.43 | 1,099.93 | 1,057.13 | 1,113.64 | 1,150.95 | 1,118.12 | 1,174.96 | 1,107.40 | 1,126.60 | 1,174.62 | 1,114.12 |
| 2019 | 1,061.07 | 1,137.58 | 1,182.17 | 1,117.90 | 1,110.14 | 1,183.70 | 1,185.45 | 1,194.22 | 1,236.96 | 1,186.77 | 1,169.28 | 1,210.33 | 1,166.53 |
| **Education and Health Services** | | | | | | | | | | | | | |
| 2015 | 776.21 | 775.78 | 773.93 | 774.11 | 774.21 | 779.08 | 800.72 | 794.88 | 814.38 | 836.88 | 831.36 | 847.58 | 797.69 |
| 2016 | 851.15 | 846.91 | 851.47 | 879.01 | 881.79 | 884.44 | 909.02 | 907.38 | 917.48 | 948.03 | 939.60 | 938.56 | 897.33 |
| 2017 | 932.83 | 928.77 | 908.82 | 930.08 | 899.10 | 897.62 | 892.58 | 901.56 | 891.61 | 916.41 | 890.52 | 901.88 | 907.10 |
| 2018 | 925.48 | 933.70 | 945.07 | 946.34 | 922.81 | 923.13 | 932.51 | 942.52 | 937.96 | 932.44 | 908.21 | 889.86 | 926.72 |
| 2019 | 887.54 | 868.61 | 875.75 | 885.12 | 861.80 | 868.00 | 897.44 | 878.57 | 891.21 | 895.58 | 890.42 | 885.36 | 882.26 |
| **Leisure and Hospitality** | | | | | | | | | | | | | |
| 2015 | 314.44 | 320.37 | 321.77 | 320.46 | 329.18 | 318.99 | 336.18 | 339.53 | 329.75 | 324.41 | 326.06 | 326.18 | 325.79 |
| 2016 | 313.49 | 321.43 | 324.26 | 321.61 | 321.69 | 326.34 | 335.64 | 341.88 | 336.14 | 335.08 | 328.30 | 334.88 | 329.36 |
| 2017 | 332.18 | 343.91 | 350.37 | 353.00 | 346.24 | 350.55 | 367.39 | 368.90 | 349.92 | 348.15 | 347.28 | 354.48 | 351.87 |
| 2018 | 345.58 | 353.07 | 353.52 | 354.04 | 357.70 | 365.96 | 388.45 | 387.06 | 369.25 | 367.20 | 352.53 | 365.81 | 363.58 |
| 2019 | 341.18 | 353.57 | 365.19 | 361.20 | 373.49 | 381.27 | 395.72 | 392.48 | 375.10 | 382.48 | 377.52 | 384.31 | 373.81 |

# DISTRICT OF COLUMBIA
*At a Glance*

Population:
  2010 census: 601,723
  2019 estimate: 705,749

Percent change in population:
  2010–2019: 17.3%

Percent change in total nonfarm employment:
  2011–2019: 9.9%

Industry with the largest growth in employment, 2011–2019 (percent):
  Leisure and hospitality, 31.1%

Industry with the largest decline or smallest growth in employment, 2011–2019 (percent):
  Government, -3.7%

Civilian labor force:
  2010: 346,065
  2019: 409,969

Unemployment rate and rank among states (highest to lowest):
  2010: 9.4%, 21st
  2019: 5.5%, 2nd

Over-the-year change in unemployment rates:
  2017–2018: -0.4%
  2018–2019: -0.2%

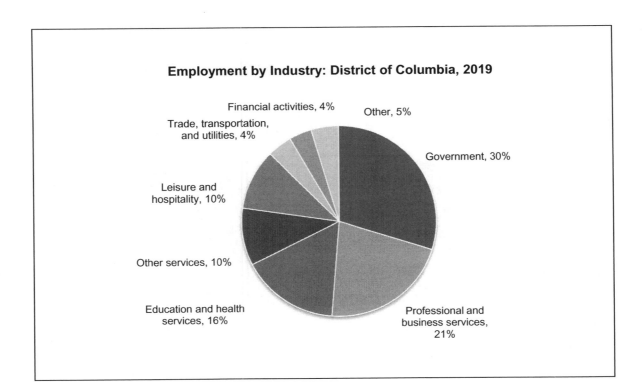

**Employment by Industry: District of Columbia, 2019**

Financial activities, 4%
Other, 5%
Trade, transportation, and utilities, 4%
Government, 30%
Leisure and hospitality, 10%
Other services, 10%
Education and health services, 16%
Professional and business services, 21%

## 1. Employment by Industry: District of Columbia, 2011–2019

(Numbers in thousands, not seasonally adjusted)

| Industry and year | January | February | March | April | May | June | July | August | September | October | November | December | Annual average |
|---|---|---|---|---|---|---|---|---|---|---|---|---|---|
| **Total Nonfarm** | | | | | | | | | | | | | |
| 2011 | 713.8 | 716.9 | 721.5 | 727.7 | 723.8 | 726.3 | 740.8 | 724.7 | 730.2 | 729.5 | 729.2 | 728.5 | 726.1 |
| 2012 | 720.6 | 723.9 | 728.5 | 729.1 | 732.2 | 730.5 | 740.7 | 726.4 | 733.4 | 741.1 | 742.7 | 741.5 | 732.6 |
| 2013 | 729.6 | 734.3 | 737.5 | 744.2 | 744.8 | 739.0 | 752.8 | 738.8 | 747.4 | 748.8 | 752.7 | 750.6 | 743.4 |
| 2014 | 732.8 | 737.5 | 740.9 | 746.2 | 745.4 | 747.0 | 759.0 | 744.4 | 752.0 | 757.1 | 758.6 | 756.9 | 748.2 |
| 2015 | 748.1 | 753.9 | 755.9 | 759.1 | 758.7 | 760.0 | 777.0 | 761.8 | 765.9 | 774.5 | 775.9 | 776.9 | 764.0 |
| 2016 | 762.2 | 770.7 | 773.2 | 779.1 | 774.9 | 774.9 | 787.8 | 773.4 | 778.7 | 783.7 | 784.9 | 781.9 | 777.1 |
| 2017 | 771.3 | 777.9 | 783.1 | 783.0 | 781.9 | 783.8 | 794.0 | 780.3 | 785.2 | 791.4 | 791.8 | 790.2 | 784.5 |
| 2018 | 779.9 | 787.9 | 791.2 | 793.1 | 791.2 | 793.6 | 802.2 | 788.4 | 792.2 | 798.6 | 799.2 | 795.8 | 792.8 |
| 2019 | 784.2 | 793.6 | 796.6 | 797.7 | 793.4 | 798.9 | 808.2 | 793.7 | 797.8 | 804.2 | 807.0 | 804.5 | 798.3 |
| **Total Private** | | | | | | | | | | | | | |
| 2011 | 466.5 | 470.0 | 474.2 | 481.2 | 476.8 | 477.4 | 479.7 | 477.7 | 483.1 | 485.3 | 485.5 | 484.9 | 478.5 |
| 2012 | 477.9 | 482.2 | 486.0 | 487.9 | 490.4 | 486.6 | 485.5 | 483.9 | 491.5 | 497.9 | 499.6 | 499.0 | 489.0 |
| 2013 | 489.1 | 494.3 | 497.1 | 504.4 | 505.0 | 498.7 | 502.3 | 500.7 | 507.7 | 508.8 | 512.8 | 510.5 | 502.6 |
| 2014 | 499.9 | 504.1 | 507.2 | 513.4 | 512.1 | 512.8 | 512.0 | 510.7 | 516.1 | 520.2 | 522.3 | 520.1 | 512.6 |
| 2015 | 512.3 | 517.5 | 519.4 | 522.6 | 521.7 | 522.5 | 526.0 | 525.0 | 528.0 | 537.1 | 538.2 | 537.5 | 525.7 |
| 2016 | 524.3 | 532.2 | 534.5 | 540.7 | 535.5 | 534.5 | 535.0 | 534.0 | 538.0 | 542.8 | 543.5 | 540.0 | 536.3 |
| 2017 | 530.3 | 537.6 | 541.5 | 544.0 | 541.9 | 543.2 | 542.6 | 541.8 | 545.8 | 553.0 | 553.8 | 552.2 | 544.0 |
| 2018 | 541.8 | 550.3 | 553.7 | 555.7 | 553.4 | 555.1 | 553.6 | 550.9 | 555.0 | 561.7 | 562.3 | 559.0 | 554.4 |
| 2019 | 548.2 | 556.4 | 559.5 | 561.1 | 557.3 | 561.6 | 559.1 | 555.7 | 559.5 | 566.5 | 567.7 | 565.1 | 559.8 |
| **Goods Producing** | | | | | | | | | | | | | |
| 2011 | 12.1 | 12.1 | 12.3 | 12.8 | 13.0 | 13.2 | 14.1 | 14.1 | 13.8 | 13.6 | 13.5 | 13.6 | 13.2 |
| 2012 | 13.5 | 13.8 | 14.1 | 14.5 | 14.7 | 14.9 | 15.0 | 15.0 | 14.9 | 15.2 | 14.9 | 14.8 | 14.6 |
| 2013 | 14.5 | 14.6 | 14.7 | 14.5 | 14.9 | 15.1 | 15.7 | 15.8 | 15.3 | 15.1 | 15.1 | 15.0 | 15.0 |
| 2014 | 14.8 | 14.7 | 14.9 | 15.0 | 15.2 | 15.5 | 15.9 | 15.9 | 15.6 | 15.7 | 15.5 | 15.3 | 15.3 |
| 2015 | 14.6 | 14.5 | 14.6 | 14.9 | 15.2 | 15.3 | 16.0 | 16.2 | 15.9 | 16.9 | 16.9 | 17.0 | 15.7 |
| 2016 | 17.0 | 16.7 | 17.1 | 16.9 | 17.0 | 17.2 | 15.9 | 16.0 | 15.9 | 16.5 | 16.3 | 16.4 | 16.6 |
| 2017 | 15.7 | 16.0 | 16.1 | 16.7 | 16.9 | 17.2 | 17.2 | 17.0 | 16.9 | 16.7 | 16.5 | 16.5 | 16.6 |
| 2018 | 16.5 | 16.8 | 17.1 | 17.2 | 17.1 | 17.4 | 17.2 | 17.1 | 16.9 | 17.0 | 16.8 | 16.8 | 17.0 |
| 2019 | 15.9 | 16.0 | 16.1 | 16.2 | 16.4 | 16.6 | 16.4 | 16.4 | 16.2 | 16.3 | 16.1 | 15.9 | 16.2 |
| **Service-Providing** | | | | | | | | | | | | | |
| 2011 | 701.7 | 704.8 | 709.2 | 714.9 | 710.8 | 713.1 | 726.7 | 710.6 | 716.4 | 715.9 | 715.7 | 714.9 | 712.9 |
| 2012 | 707.1 | 710.1 | 714.4 | 714.6 | 717.5 | 715.6 | 725.7 | 711.4 | 718.5 | 725.9 | 727.8 | 726.7 | 717.9 |
| 2013 | 715.1 | 719.7 | 722.8 | 729.7 | 729.9 | 723.9 | 737.1 | 723.0 | 732.1 | 733.7 | 737.6 | 735.6 | 728.4 |
| 2014 | 718.0 | 722.8 | 726.0 | 731.2 | 730.2 | 731.5 | 743.1 | 728.5 | 736.4 | 741.4 | 743.1 | 741.6 | 732.8 |
| 2015 | 733.5 | 739.4 | 741.3 | 744.2 | 743.5 | 744.7 | 761.0 | 745.6 | 750.0 | 757.6 | 759.0 | 759.9 | 748.3 |
| 2016 | 745.2 | 754.0 | 756.1 | 762.2 | 757.9 | 757.7 | 771.9 | 757.4 | 762.8 | 767.2 | 768.6 | 765.5 | 760.5 |
| 2017 | 755.6 | 761.9 | 767.0 | 766.3 | 765.0 | 766.6 | 776.8 | 763.3 | 768.3 | 774.7 | 775.3 | 773.7 | 767.9 |
| 2018 | 763.4 | 771.1 | 774.1 | 775.9 | 774.1 | 776.2 | 785.0 | 771.3 | 775.3 | 781.6 | 782.4 | 779.0 | 775.8 |
| 2019 | 768.3 | 777.6 | 780.5 | 781.5 | 777.0 | 782.3 | 791.8 | 777.3 | 781.6 | 787.9 | 790.9 | 788.6 | 782.1 |
| **Mining, Logging, and Construction** | | | | | | | | | | | | | |
| 2011 | 11.0 | 11.1 | 11.2 | 11.7 | 11.9 | 12.1 | 13.0 | 13.1 | 12.8 | 12.6 | 12.5 | 12.6 | 12.1 |
| 2012 | 12.5 | 12.8 | 13.0 | 13.5 | 13.7 | 13.9 | 14.0 | 14.0 | 13.9 | 14.2 | 13.9 | 13.8 | 13.6 |
| 2013 | 13.5 | 13.6 | 13.7 | 13.5 | 13.9 | 14.1 | 14.7 | 14.8 | 14.3 | 14.1 | 14.1 | 14.0 | 14.0 |
| 2014 | 13.8 | 13.7 | 13.9 | 14.0 | 14.2 | 14.5 | 14.9 | 14.9 | 14.6 | 14.6 | 14.4 | 14.2 | 14.3 |
| 2015 | 13.6 | 13.5 | 13.6 | 13.9 | 14.2 | 14.3 | 14.9 | 15.1 | 14.8 | 15.8 | 15.8 | 15.9 | 14.6 |
| 2016 | 15.8 | 15.5 | 15.9 | 15.7 | 15.8 | 15.9 | 14.7 | 14.8 | 14.7 | 15.3 | 15.1 | 15.2 | 15.4 |
| 2017 | 14.5 | 14.8 | 14.9 | 15.4 | 15.6 | 15.9 | 15.9 | 15.7 | 15.6 | 15.4 | 15.2 | 15.3 | 15.4 |
| 2018 | 15.2 | 15.5 | 15.8 | 15.9 | 15.8 | 16.0 | 15.8 | 15.7 | 15.6 | 15.6 | 15.4 | 15.5 | 15.7 |
| 2019 | 14.6 | 14.7 | 14.8 | 14.8 | 15.0 | 15.2 | 15.1 | 15.1 | 14.8 | 14.9 | 14.7 | 14.5 | 14.9 |
| **Manufacturing** | | | | | | | | | | | | | |
| 2011 | 1.1 | 1.0 | 1.1 | 1.1 | 1.1 | 1.1 | 1.1 | 1.0 | 1.0 | 1.0 | 1.0 | 1.0 | 1.1 |
| 2012 | 1.0 | 1.0 | 1.1 | 1.0 | 1.0 | 1.0 | 1.0 | 1.0 | 1.0 | 1.0 | 1.0 | 1.0 | 1.0 |
| 2013 | 1.0 | 1.0 | 1.0 | 1.0 | 1.0 | 1.0 | 1.0 | 1.0 | 1.0 | 1.0 | 1.0 | 1.0 | 1.0 |
| 2014 | 1.0 | 1.0 | 1.0 | 1.0 | 1.0 | 1.0 | 1.0 | 1.0 | 1.0 | 1.1 | 1.1 | 1.1 | 1.0 |
| 2015 | 1.0 | 1.0 | 1.0 | 1.0 | 1.0 | 1.0 | 1.1 | 1.1 | 1.1 | 1.1 | 1.1 | 1.1 | 1.1 |
| 2016 | 1.2 | 1.2 | 1.2 | 1.2 | 1.2 | 1.3 | 1.2 | 1.2 | 1.2 | 1.2 | 1.2 | 1.2 | 1.2 |
| 2017 | 1.2 | 1.2 | 1.2 | 1.3 | 1.3 | 1.3 | 1.3 | 1.3 | 1.3 | 1.3 | 1.3 | 1.2 | 1.3 |
| 2018 | 1.3 | 1.3 | 1.3 | 1.3 | 1.3 | 1.4 | 1.4 | 1.4 | 1.3 | 1.4 | 1.4 | 1.3 | 1.3 |
| 2019 | 1.3 | 1.3 | 1.3 | 1.4 | 1.4 | 1.4 | 1.3 | 1.3 | 1.4 | 1.4 | 1.4 | 1.4 | 1.4 |

## 1. Employment by Industry: District of Columbia, 2011–2019—*Continued*

(Numbers in thousands, not seasonally adjusted)

| Industry and year | January | February | March | April | May | June | July | August | September | October | November | December | Annual average |
|---|---|---|---|---|---|---|---|---|---|---|---|---|---|
| **Trade, Transportation, and Utilities** | | | | | | | | | | | | | |
| 2011 | 27.2 | 27.0 | 27.1 | 27.4 | 27.2 | 27.2 | 27.1 | 27.1 | 27.3 | 27.9 | 28.1 | 28.3 | 27.4 |
| 2012 | 27.3 | 27.4 | 27.5 | 27.7 | 28.0 | 28.1 | 28.0 | 27.9 | 28.2 | 28.3 | 29.1 | 29.4 | 28.1 |
| 2013 | 28.4 | 28.5 | 28.6 | 28.6 | 28.7 | 28.7 | 28.7 | 28.7 | 29.1 | 29.4 | 30.5 | 30.6 | 29.0 |
| 2014 | 29.4 | 29.5 | 29.8 | 30.5 | 30.5 | 30.7 | 30.3 | 30.5 | 30.7 | 31.2 | 32.1 | 32.1 | 30.6 |
| 2015 | 31.4 | 31.3 | 31.3 | 31.5 | 31.6 | 32.1 | 32.3 | 32.1 | 32.5 | 32.8 | 33.4 | 33.7 | 32.2 |
| 2016 | 32.1 | 32.3 | 32.3 | 32.6 | 32.7 | 33.1 | 32.7 | 32.6 | 32.8 | 33.1 | 33.7 | 33.7 | 32.8 |
| 2017 | 32.7 | 32.9 | 33.1 | 33.0 | 33.1 | 33.4 | 33.2 | 33.2 | 33.5 | 33.5 | 34.3 | 34.4 | 33.4 |
| 2018 | 33.0 | 33.0 | 33.1 | 32.9 | 33.0 | 32.8 | 33.1 | 32.8 | 32.9 | 33.6 | 34.1 | 34.1 | 33.2 |
| 2019 | 32.6 | 32.6 | 32.5 | 32.7 | 33.2 | 33.4 | 33.0 | 33.0 | 33.4 | 33.5 | 34.2 | 34.6 | 33.2 |
| **Wholesale Trade** | | | | | | | | | | | | | |
| 2011 | 4.5 | 4.5 | 4.6 | 4.5 | 4.5 | 4.5 | 4.5 | 4.7 | 4.6 | 4.8 | 4.8 | 4.8 | 4.6 |
| 2012 | 4.7 | 4.9 | 4.8 | 4.9 | 5.0 | 5.0 | 5.0 | 5.0 | 5.1 | 5.0 | 5.0 | 5.0 | 5.0 |
| 2013 | 4.8 | 4.9 | 4.9 | 4.8 | 4.8 | 4.8 | 4.9 | 4.8 | 4.9 | 4.8 | 4.9 | 4.8 | 4.8 |
| 2014 | 4.7 | 4.8 | 4.9 | 4.9 | 4.9 | 4.9 | 4.9 | 4.9 | 4.9 | 5.0 | 5.0 | 5.0 | 4.9 |
| 2015 | 5.0 | 5.0 | 5.0 | 4.7 | 4.7 | 4.7 | 4.8 | 4.7 | 4.8 | 4.8 | 4.9 | 4.9 | 4.8 |
| 2016 | 5.0 | 5.0 | 5.0 | 5.0 | 5.0 | 5.0 | 5.0 | 5.1 | 5.0 | 5.0 | 4.9 | 4.9 | 5.0 |
| 2017 | 5.0 | 5.0 | 5.0 | 4.8 | 4.8 | 4.8 | 4.8 | 4.9 | 4.9 | 4.9 | 4.9 | 4.9 | 4.9 |
| 2018 | 4.8 | 4.9 | 4.8 | 4.7 | 4.7 | 4.8 | 4.9 | 4.9 | 4.9 | 5.1 | 5.1 | 5.2 | 4.9 |
| 2019 | 5.0 | 5.0 | 5.0 | 5.0 | 5.0 | 5.0 | 5.1 | 5.2 | 5.3 | 5.2 | 5.3 | 5.3 | 5.1 |
| **Retail Trade** | | | | | | | | | | | | | |
| 2011 | 18.6 | 18.4 | 18.3 | 18.6 | 18.5 | 18.4 | 18.3 | 18.1 | 18.5 | 18.9 | 19.2 | 19.5 | 18.6 |
| 2012 | 18.6 | 18.5 | 18.6 | 18.6 | 18.8 | 18.8 | 18.8 | 18.7 | 18.9 | 19.1 | 20.0 | 20.3 | 19.0 |
| 2013 | 19.5 | 19.5 | 19.5 | 19.6 | 19.7 | 19.6 | 19.6 | 19.8 | 20.1 | 20.5 | 21.5 | 21.7 | 20.1 |
| 2014 | 20.7 | 20.6 | 20.7 | 21.3 | 21.2 | 21.3 | 21.0 | 21.1 | 21.4 | 21.7 | 22.6 | 22.7 | 21.4 |
| 2015 | 22.0 | 21.8 | 21.8 | 22.1 | 22.1 | 22.3 | 22.4 | 22.4 | 22.7 | 23.1 | 23.7 | 23.9 | 22.5 |
| 2016 | 22.6 | 22.7 | 22.7 | 22.8 | 22.9 | 23.2 | 22.7 | 22.5 | 22.7 | 23.0 | 23.7 | 23.7 | 22.9 |
| 2017 | 22.8 | 23.0 | 23.1 | 23.0 | 23.1 | 23.2 | 23.1 | 23.1 | 23.3 | 23.4 | 24.1 | 24.3 | 23.3 |
| 2018 | 23.0 | 22.9 | 22.9 | 22.8 | 22.8 | 22.6 | 22.7 | 22.5 | 22.7 | 23.2 | 23.8 | 23.8 | 23.0 |
| 2019 | 22.7 | 22.7 | 22.6 | 22.7 | 23.1 | 23.3 | 22.9 | 22.8 | 23.2 | 23.4 | 24.0 | 24.4 | 23.2 |
| **Transportation and Utilities** | | | | | | | | | | | | | |
| 2011 | 4.1 | 4.1 | 4.2 | 4.3 | 4.2 | 4.3 | 4.3 | 4.3 | 4.2 | 4.2 | 4.1 | 4.0 | 4.2 |
| 2012 | 4.0 | 4.0 | 4.1 | 4.2 | 4.2 | 4.3 | 4.2 | 4.2 | 4.2 | 4.2 | 4.1 | 4.1 | 4.2 |
| 2013 | 4.1 | 4.1 | 4.2 | 4.2 | 4.2 | 4.3 | 4.2 | 4.1 | 4.1 | 4.1 | 4.1 | 4.1 | 4.2 |
| 2014 | 4.0 | 4.1 | 4.2 | 4.3 | 4.4 | 4.5 | 4.4 | 4.5 | 4.4 | 4.5 | 4.5 | 4.4 | 4.4 |
| 2015 | 4.4 | 4.5 | 4.5 | 4.7 | 4.8 | 5.1 | 5.1 | 5.0 | 5.0 | 4.9 | 4.8 | 4.9 | 4.8 |
| 2016 | 4.5 | 4.6 | 4.6 | 4.8 | 4.8 | 4.9 | 5.0 | 5.0 | 5.1 | 5.1 | 5.1 | 5.1 | 4.9 |
| 2017 | 4.9 | 4.9 | 5.0 | 5.2 | 5.2 | 5.4 | 5.3 | 5.2 | 5.3 | 5.2 | 5.3 | 5.2 | 5.2 |
| 2018 | 5.2 | 5.2 | 5.4 | 5.4 | 5.5 | 5.4 | 5.5 | 5.4 | 5.3 | 5.3 | 5.2 | 5.1 | 5.3 |
| 2019 | 4.9 | 4.9 | 4.9 | 5.0 | 5.1 | 5.1 | 5.0 | 5.0 | 4.9 | 4.9 | 4.9 | 4.9 | 5.0 |
| **Information** | | | | | | | | | | | | | |
| 2011 | 18.3 | 18.5 | 18.6 | 18.8 | 18.5 | 18.7 | 18.4 | 17.9 | 18.2 | 18.0 | 18.0 | 18.2 | 18.3 |
| 2012 | 17.5 | 17.7 | 17.6 | 17.3 | 17.4 | 17.7 | 17.4 | 17.7 | 17.3 | 17.3 | 17.6 | 17.4 | 17.5 |
| 2013 | 17.1 | 17.2 | 17.2 | 16.9 | 17.1 | 17.1 | 17.3 | 17.4 | 16.9 | 16.6 | 16.9 | 16.7 | 17.0 |
| 2014 | 17.1 | 17.1 | 17.1 | 17.2 | 17.3 | 17.4 | 17.6 | 17.3 | 17.2 | 17.1 | 17.1 | 17.1 | 17.2 |
| 2015 | 16.6 | 16.7 | 16.7 | 17.1 | 17.2 | 17.3 | 17.4 | 17.3 | 17.2 | 17.5 | 17.5 | 17.6 | 17.2 |
| 2016 | 16.9 | 17.1 | 17.0 | 17.0 | 16.8 | 17.1 | 17.2 | 17.2 | 17.1 | 17.3 | 17.4 | 17.3 | 17.1 |
| 2017 | 17.1 | 17.4 | 17.5 | 17.8 | 17.9 | 18.0 | 18.1 | 18.1 | 18.1 | 17.9 | 18.1 | 18.4 | 17.9 |
| 2018 | 18.3 | 18.7 | 18.7 | 18.8 | 18.9 | 19.6 | 19.8 | 19.4 | 19.4 | 19.4 | 19.6 | 19.5 | 19.2 |
| 2019 | 19.5 | 19.8 | 19.7 | 19.6 | 19.6 | 20.3 | 20.2 | 20.1 | 20.2 | 20.5 | 20.7 | 20.4 | 20.1 |
| **Financial Activities** | | | | | | | | | | | | | |
| 2011 | 26.7 | 26.6 | 26.8 | 27.1 | 27.1 | 27.0 | 27.3 | 27.5 | 27.5 | 27.5 | 27.6 | 27.7 | 27.2 |
| 2012 | 27.7 | 27.7 | 27.7 | 27.7 | 27.7 | 27.9 | 27.7 | 27.6 | 27.6 | 27.8 | 27.9 | 27.8 | 27.7 |
| 2013 | 27.6 | 27.8 | 28.0 | 28.2 | 28.1 | 28.5 | 28.5 | 28.6 | 28.3 | 28.9 | 29.0 | 29.2 | 28.4 |
| 2014 | 29.1 | 29.2 | 29.3 | 29.1 | 29.3 | 29.6 | 29.8 | 29.7 | 29.5 | 29.5 | 29.6 | 29.6 | 29.4 |
| 2015 | 29.5 | 29.6 | 29.7 | 29.2 | 29.2 | 29.3 | 29.6 | 29.5 | 29.2 | 29.1 | 29.2 | 29.0 | 29.3 |
| 2016 | 29.1 | 29.1 | 29.2 | 29.4 | 29.3 | 29.4 | 29.7 | 29.7 | 29.6 | 29.5 | 29.4 | 29.5 | 29.4 |
| 2017 | 29.3 | 29.4 | 29.4 | 29.3 | 29.4 | 29.7 | 29.9 | 29.7 | 29.4 | 29.5 | 29.6 | 29.7 | 29.5 |
| 2018 | 29.4 | 29.6 | 29.6 | 29.3 | 29.5 | 29.8 | 30.0 | 29.9 | 29.5 | 29.6 | 29.4 | 29.5 | 29.6 |
| 2019 | 29.4 | 29.7 | 29.6 | 29.7 | 29.6 | 30.1 | 30.2 | 30.1 | 29.7 | 29.9 | 29.6 | 30.0 | 29.8 |

## 1. Employment by Industry: District of Columbia, 2011–2019—*Continued*

(Numbers in thousands, not seasonally adjusted)

| Industry and year | January | February | March | April | May | June | July | August | September | October | November | December | Annual average |
|---|---|---|---|---|---|---|---|---|---|---|---|---|---|
| **Professional and Business Services** | | | | | | | | | | | | | |
| 2011 | 146.7 | 147.4 | 148.4 | 150.4 | 150.5 | 151.8 | 152.7 | 152.1 | 150.3 | 151.8 | 151.5 | 151.0 | 150.4 |
| 2012 | 150.7 | 151.5 | 152.7 | 152.6 | 152.9 | 154.4 | 155.6 | 154.9 | 153.7 | 156.2 | 156.9 | 156.5 | 154.1 |
| 2013 | 153.3 | 154.6 | 154.9 | 155.0 | 154.9 | 156.1 | 157.8 | 157.5 | 156.0 | 156.5 | 157.7 | 156.6 | 155.9 |
| 2014 | 153.7 | 154.6 | 155.2 | 155.9 | 156.3 | 158.4 | 159.1 | 158.1 | 158.2 | 159.1 | 159.3 | 159.4 | 157.3 |
| 2015 | 158.2 | 159.3 | 159.5 | 160.0 | 160.8 | 162.8 | 163.5 | 163.1 | 162.0 | 164.5 | 164.3 | 164.2 | 161.9 |
| 2016 | 162.1 | 163.3 | 163.6 | 165.0 | 164.7 | 165.7 | 166.5 | 165.2 | 164.1 | 165.9 | 166.3 | 165.9 | 164.9 |
| 2017 | 164.7 | 165.0 | 165.1 | 165.7 | 165.6 | 167.9 | 167.6 | 166.2 | 165.0 | 166.7 | 167.3 | 167.5 | 166.2 |
| 2018 | 165.4 | 166.5 | 166.7 | 166.5 | 167.0 | 169.4 | 169.1 | 168.2 | 167.5 | 170.8 | 170.8 | 170.1 | 168.2 |
| 2019 | 166.6 | 168.5 | 168.7 | 169.3 | 169.5 | 172.1 | 172.4 | 171.2 | 171.1 | 174.6 | 174.7 | 174.0 | 171.1 |
| **Education and Health Services** | | | | | | | | | | | | | |
| 2011 | 112.7 | 113.6 | 114.1 | 114.3 | 110.3 | 108.5 | 109.4 | 108.6 | 115.4 | 115.1 | 115.3 | 115.2 | 112.7 |
| 2012 | 113.5 | 114.0 | 114.0 | 114.6 | 114.4 | 107.8 | 105.4 | 106.3 | 115.4 | 118.2 | 119.2 | 119.5 | 113.5 |
| 2013 | 116.9 | 118.5 | 118.8 | 123.0 | 122.2 | 113.3 | 114.9 | 114.5 | 123.2 | 124.9 | 125.7 | 125.4 | 120.1 |
| 2014 | 121.4 | 122.8 | 122.9 | 123.9 | 120.7 | 118.1 | 117.3 | 117.4 | 122.8 | 125.4 | 126.3 | 125.6 | 122.1 |
| 2015 | 121.7 | 125.1 | 125.1 | 125.7 | 122.1 | 119.5 | 121.7 | 121.7 | 126.3 | 131.7 | 132.2 | 130.9 | 125.3 |
| 2016 | 125.8 | 130.2 | 129.9 | 130.5 | 126.1 | 122.5 | 124.4 | 124.9 | 129.0 | 131.2 | 131.8 | 129.9 | 128.0 |
| 2017 | 126.5 | 130.5 | 130.7 | 129.3 | 125.8 | 123.7 | 123.7 | 124.8 | 129.9 | 132.9 | 133.5 | 131.6 | 128.6 |
| 2018 | 128.9 | 132.9 | 133.0 | 133.2 | 129.5 | 126.4 | 125.6 | 126.6 | 131.3 | 133.4 | 134.7 | 132.6 | 130.7 |
| 2019 | 131.0 | 133.7 | 134.2 | 133.0 | 128.5 | 127.3 | 125.7 | 125.7 | 128.9 | 131.5 | 132.7 | 130.7 | 130.2 |
| **Leisure and Hospitality** | | | | | | | | | | | | | |
| 2011 | 57.2 | 58.5 | 60.1 | 63.9 | 63.5 | 63.5 | 62.6 | 63.0 | 63.8 | 64.3 | 64.2 | 63.2 | 62.3 |
| 2012 | 60.7 | 62.5 | 64.4 | 66.3 | 67.7 | 67.4 | 66.7 | 66.0 | 66.3 | 66.6 | 65.4 | 64.7 | 65.4 |
| 2013 | 63.1 | 64.6 | 66.3 | 69.3 | 69.9 | 69.9 | 69.2 | 68.6 | 69.4 | 68.2 | 68.5 | 67.5 | 67.9 |
| 2014 | 65.4 | 66.5 | 68.3 | 71.6 | 72.4 | 71.7 | 70.5 | 70.6 | 71.2 | 71.4 | 71.4 | 70.2 | 70.1 |
| 2015 | 70.1 | 70.4 | 71.8 | 73.8 | 74.9 | 74.6 | 73.8 | 74.0 | 73.9 | 73.5 | 73.5 | 73.7 | 73.2 |
| 2016 | 70.2 | 72.1 | 73.7 | 77.2 | 76.6 | 76.3 | 74.8 | 74.9 | 76.1 | 75.6 | 74.6 | 73.5 | 74.6 |
| 2017 | 71.3 | 72.7 | 75.5 | 78.1 | 79.0 | 78.1 | 77.3 | 77.8 | 78.5 | 80.3 | 78.8 | 78.1 | 77.1 |
| 2018 | 75.0 | 76.9 | 79.4 | 81.1 | 81.6 | 82.0 | 80.9 | 79.8 | 80.9 | 80.8 | 79.9 | 79.3 | 79.8 |
| 2019 | 77.4 | 79.5 | 81.8 | 83.6 | 83.4 | 83.6 | 82.5 | 81.4 | 82.7 | 82.4 | 81.6 | 80.4 | 81.7 |
| **Other Services** | | | | | | | | | | | | | |
| 2011 | 65.6 | 66.3 | 66.8 | 66.5 | 66.7 | 67.5 | 68.1 | 67.4 | 66.8 | 67.1 | 67.3 | 67.7 | 67.0 |
| 2012 | 67.0 | 67.6 | 68.0 | 67.2 | 67.6 | 68.4 | 69.7 | 68.5 | 68.1 | 68.3 | 68.6 | 68.9 | 68.2 |
| 2013 | 68.2 | 68.5 | 68.6 | 68.9 | 69.2 | 70.0 | 70.2 | 69.6 | 69.5 | 69.2 | 69.4 | 69.5 | 69.2 |
| 2014 | 69.0 | 69.7 | 69.7 | 70.2 | 70.4 | 71.4 | 71.5 | 71.2 | 70.9 | 70.8 | 71.0 | 70.8 | 70.6 |
| 2015 | 70.2 | 70.6 | 70.7 | 70.4 | 70.7 | 71.6 | 71.7 | 71.1 | 71.0 | 71.1 | 71.2 | 71.4 | 71.0 |
| 2016 | 71.1 | 71.4 | 71.7 | 72.1 | 72.3 | 73.2 | 73.8 | 73.5 | 73.4 | 73.7 | 74.0 | 73.8 | 72.8 |
| 2017 | 73.0 | 73.7 | 74.1 | 74.1 | 74.2 | 75.2 | 75.6 | 75.0 | 74.5 | 75.5 | 75.7 | 76.0 | 74.7 |
| 2018 | 75.3 | 75.9 | 76.1 | 76.7 | 76.8 | 77.7 | 77.9 | 77.1 | 76.6 | 77.1 | 77.0 | 77.1 | 76.8 |
| 2019 | 75.8 | 76.6 | 76.9 | 77.0 | 77.1 | 78.2 | 78.7 | 77.8 | 77.3 | 77.8 | 78.1 | 79.1 | 77.5 |
| **Government** | | | | | | | | | | | | | |
| 2011 | 247.3 | 246.9 | 247.3 | 246.5 | 247.0 | 248.9 | 261.1 | 247.0 | 247.1 | 244.2 | 243.7 | 243.6 | 247.6 |
| 2012 | 242.7 | 241.7 | 242.5 | 241.2 | 241.8 | 243.9 | 255.2 | 242.5 | 241.9 | 243.2 | 243.1 | 242.5 | 243.5 |
| 2013 | 240.5 | 240.0 | 240.4 | 239.8 | 239.8 | 240.3 | 250.5 | 238.1 | 239.7 | 240.0 | 239.9 | 240.1 | 240.8 |
| 2014 | 232.9 | 233.4 | 233.7 | 232.8 | 233.3 | 234.2 | 247.0 | 233.7 | 235.9 | 236.9 | 236.3 | 236.8 | 235.6 |
| 2015 | 235.8 | 236.4 | 236.5 | 236.5 | 237.0 | 237.5 | 251.0 | 236.8 | 237.9 | 237.4 | 237.7 | 239.4 | 238.3 |
| 2016 | 237.9 | 238.5 | 238.7 | 238.4 | 239.4 | 240.4 | 252.8 | 239.4 | 240.7 | 240.9 | 241.4 | 241.9 | 240.9 |
| 2017 | 241.0 | 240.3 | 241.6 | 239.0 | 240.0 | 240.6 | 251.4 | 238.5 | 239.4 | 238.4 | 238.0 | 238.0 | 240.5 |
| 2018 | 238.1 | 237.6 | 237.5 | 237.4 | 237.8 | 238.5 | 248.6 | 237.5 | 237.2 | 236.9 | 236.9 | 236.8 | 238.4 |
| 2019 | 236.0 | 237.2 | 237.1 | 236.6 | 236.1 | 237.3 | 249.1 | 238.0 | 238.3 | 237.7 | 239.3 | 239.4 | 238.5 |

## 2. Average Weekly Hours by Selected Industry: District of Columbia, 2015–2019

(Not seasonally adjusted)

| Industry and year | January | February | March | April | May | June | July | August | September | October | November | December | Annual average |
|---|---|---|---|---|---|---|---|---|---|---|---|---|---|
| **Total Private** | | | | | | | | | | | | | |
| 2015 | 35.3 | 36.8 | 36.4 | 35.5 | 35.8 | 35.6 | 35.0 | 35.9 | 35.0 | 35.3 | 36.0 | 35.2 | 35.6 |
| 2016 | 35.2 | 35.3 | 35.4 | 35.6 | 36.4 | 35.6 | 35.4 | 35.3 | 35.4 | 36.3 | 35.4 | 35.4 | 35.6 |
| 2017 | 36.1 | 35.5 | 35.3 | 36.4 | 35.1 | 35.0 | 35.9 | 35.0 | 35.1 | 36.0 | 35.0 | 35.1 | 35.5 |
| 2018 | 34.7 | 34.6 | 34.7 | 36.1 | 34.8 | 35.0 | 35.8 | 34.7 | 35.8 | 34.6 | 35.0 | 36.2 | 35.2 |
| 2019 | 34.4 | 35.1 | 35.1 | 35.4 | 35.6 | 36.6 | 35.3 | 35.2 | 36.3 | 35.2 | 35.3 | 36.4 | 35.5 |
| **Goods-Producing** | | | | | | | | | | | | | |
| 2015 | 38.3 | 40.1 | 40.4 | 39.0 | 40.5 | 40.6 | 39.0 | 39.7 | 38.2 | 40.6 | 37.7 | 40.9 | 39.6 |
| 2016 | 41.3 | 39.9 | 42.3 | 40.2 | 38.4 | 40.9 | 39.5 | 40.0 | 40.7 | 38.5 | 37.8 | 34.4 | 39.5 |
| 2017 | 36.9 | 36.9 | 35.7 | 37.1 | 34.7 | 36.7 | 35.8 | 35.3 | 36.1 | 35.7 | 36.6 | 37.1 | 36.1 |
| 2018 | 37.9 | 37.5 | 38.9 | 39.7 | 39.2 | 39.6 | 40.8 | 41.3 | 39.5 | 36.3 | 36.6 | 37.7 | 38.8 |
| 2019 | 35.2 | 35.1 | 36.6 | 38.1 | 38.7 | 39.2 | 38.6 | 39.5 | 38.0 | 38.0 | 36.6 | 36.1 | 37.4 |
| **Trade, Transportation, and Utilities** | | | | | | | | | | | | | |
| 2015 | 34.9 | 36.1 | 35.1 | 34.9 | 35.0 | 34.6 | 34.4 | 34.7 | 35.7 | 34.7 | 35.4 | 35.1 | 35.0 |
| 2016 | 33.9 | 34.2 | 34.4 | 34.4 | 34.4 | 33.9 | 33.9 | 33.4 | 33.9 | 33.4 | 33.7 | 33.5 | 33.9 |
| 2017 | 34.0 | 33.2 | 32.4 | 33.9 | 33.6 | 32.8 | 33.0 | 31.9 | 32.5 | 32.6 | 32.8 | 32.3 | 32.9 |
| 2018 | 31.6 | 31.4 | 31.8 | 32.6 | 32.0 | 32.4 | 32.5 | 31.8 | 32.6 | 32.1 | 31.9 | 31.9 | 32.1 |
| 2019 | 31.3 | 30.8 | 31.3 | 31.2 | 31.3 | 31.4 | 31.0 | 30.7 | 31.5 | 31.1 | 31.0 | 31.6 | 31.2 |
| **Professional and Business Services** | | | | | | | | | | | | | |
| 2015 | 36.0 | 37.8 | 37.5 | 36.2 | 36.3 | 36.3 | 35.4 | 37.4 | 35.7 | 36.1 | 37.1 | 36.1 | 36.5 |
| 2016 | 36.1 | 36.2 | 36.1 | 36.3 | 37.3 | 36.3 | 36.4 | 36.3 | 36.4 | 37.6 | 36.0 | 36.6 | 36.5 |
| 2017 | 37.7 | 37.0 | 36.3 | 38.0 | 36.4 | 36.5 | 37.8 | 36.6 | 36.7 | 38.0 | 36.3 | 36.5 | 37.0 |
| 2018 | 36.2 | 36.2 | 35.8 | 37.8 | 35.8 | 35.6 | 36.8 | 35.4 | 36.7 | 34.9 | 35.5 | 37.4 | 36.2 |
| 2019 | 34.8 | 35.9 | 35.7 | 36.1 | 36.6 | 38.8 | 36.7 | 37.0 | 38.6 | 37.0 | 37.2 | 38.7 | 36.9 |
| **Leisure and Hospitality** | | | | | | | | | | | | | |
| 2015 | 28.2 | 29.1 | 29.9 | 30.2 | 30.7 | 30.0 | 29.0 | 28.7 | 28.2 | 28.8 | 29.0 | 28.5 | 29.2 |
| 2016 | 27.3 | 29.0 | 29.2 | 29.7 | 29.2 | 28.2 | 28.3 | 27.6 | 27.5 | 28.2 | 28.4 | 28.0 | 28.4 |
| 2017 | 27.0 | 27.5 | 29.8 | 28.9 | 28.0 | 26.8 | 26.8 | 27.3 | 26.7 | 27.2 | 27.0 | 27.5 | 27.5 |
| 2018 | 25.9 | 25.6 | 26.9 | 27.8 | 27.5 | 28.3 | 27.6 | 27.3 | 27.7 | 27.7 | 27.5 | 28.6 | 27.4 |
| 2019 | 25.3 | 26.8 | 27.2 | 28.7 | 28.4 | 28.6 | 27.4 | 27.9 | 28.0 | 28.2 | 28.1 | 28.2 | 27.7 |
| **Other Services** | | | | | | | | | | | | | |
| 2015 | 35.7 | 37.2 | 36.1 | 34.9 | 35.4 | 34.8 | 35.1 | 36.2 | 35.5 | 35.6 | 36.8 | 35.2 | 35.7 |
| 2016 | 35.6 | 35.2 | 35.1 | 35.7 | 36.6 | 35.5 | 35.0 | 35.2 | 35.6 | 37.0 | 35.7 | 35.6 | 35.6 |
| 2017 | 36.8 | 35.8 | 35.6 | 37.2 | 35.8 | 36.5 | 37.7 | 36.5 | 36.5 | 37.6 | 36.0 | 35.5 | 36.5 |
| 2018 | 35.0 | 35.4 | 35.1 | 36.9 | 35.3 | 35.6 | 36.9 | 35.5 | 36.9 | 35.8 | 36.4 | 37.5 | 36.0 |
| 2019 | 36.8 | 37.6 | 37.6 | 37.3 | 37.4 | 38.0 | 37.3 | 36.2 | 37.7 | 36.6 | 36.8 | 38.1 | 37.3 |

## 3. Average Hourly Earnings by Selected Industry: District of Columbia, 2015–2019

(Dollars, not seasonally adjusted)

| Industry and year | January | February | March | April | May | June | July | August | September | October | November | December | Annual average |
|---|---|---|---|---|---|---|---|---|---|---|---|---|---|
| **Total Private** | | | | | | | | | | | | | |
| 2015 | 39.63 | 40.55 | 40.56 | 38.99 | 38.24 | 38.36 | 37.71 | 38.04 | 37.44 | 36.12 | 37.42 | 36.94 | 38.33 |
| 2016 | 36.60 | 36.98 | 36.91 | 37.47 | 38.79 | 37.85 | 38.41 | 39.16 | 39.06 | 40.10 | 39.63 | 39.88 | 38.42 |
| 2017 | 41.00 | 39.89 | 40.00 | 39.97 | 39.67 | 39.59 | 41.07 | 40.50 | 40.88 | 42.00 | 41.49 | 41.79 | 40.67 |
| 2018 | 42.03 | 42.69 | 42.54 | 42.79 | 42.17 | 42.22 | 43.21 | 42.86 | 44.14 | 43.46 | 43.73 | 45.13 | 43.10 |
| 2019 | 45.08 | 44.77 | 45.28 | 45.48 | 45.09 | 45.90 | 45.10 | 45.40 | 45.87 | 45.26 | 45.27 | 46.71 | 45.44 |
| **Goods-Producing** | | | | | | | | | | | | | |
| 2015 | 28.72 | 29.95 | 30.38 | 29.77 | 29.68 | 29.88 | 29.53 | 30.58 | 32.00 | 30.74 | 32.38 | 31.96 | 30.50 |
| 2016 | 31.82 | 31.01 | 30.41 | 30.23 | 30.87 | 30.18 | 30.42 | 30.18 | 29.97 | 29.65 | 29.57 | 30.89 | 30.44 |
| 2017 | 30.81 | 31.56 | 31.76 | 31.56 | 31.81 | 32.13 | 32.19 | 33.25 | 32.62 | 33.13 | 34.05 | 34.42 | 32.45 |
| 2018 | 34.49 | 34.35 | 33.40 | 34.28 | 33.23 | 34.30 | 34.52 | 33.56 | 33.65 | 33.82 | 33.30 | 34.59 | 33.96 |
| 2019 | 34.58 | 34.61 | 35.07 | 35.31 | 35.07 | 34.95 | 35.97 | 35.69 | 36.08 | 36.04 | 36.18 | 36.63 | 35.52 |
| **Trade, Transportation, and Utilities** | | | | | | | | | | | | | |
| 2015 | 24.18 | 24.74 | 24.88 | 24.46 | 24.54 | 24.63 | 25.01 | 26.11 | 25.43 | 25.82 | 26.63 | 25.68 | 25.19 |
| 2016 | 26.90 | 26.65 | 27.40 | 27.37 | 27.78 | 27.55 | 27.80 | 28.03 | 27.92 | 26.87 | 26.41 | 26.26 | 27.24 |
| 2017 | 27.29 | 26.29 | 25.57 | 26.27 | 26.31 | 25.65 | 26.74 | 26.62 | 26.25 | 26.69 | 26.30 | 25.78 | 26.31 |
| 2018 | 27.35 | 26.93 | 26.64 | 26.84 | 26.67 | 26.27 | 26.60 | 26.56 | 26.41 | 26.10 | 26.33 | 26.25 | 26.58 |
| 2019 | 26.37 | 26.26 | 26.16 | 26.17 | 25.81 | 26.45 | 27.29 | 27.08 | 26.39 | 26.14 | 26.72 | 26.99 | 26.49 |
| **Professional and Business Services** | | | | | | | | | | | | | |
| 2015 | 48.04 | 48.88 | 48.55 | 47.02 | 47.33 | 47.18 | 46.99 | 47.82 | 47.36 | 46.96 | 48.18 | 47.77 | 47.68 |
| 2016 | 47.70 | 47.46 | 46.87 | 46.93 | 48.57 | 47.49 | 47.49 | 47.81 | 47.42 | 48.77 | 47.68 | 47.64 | 47.66 |
| 2017 | 48.62 | 47.04 | 46.89 | 47.58 | 46.81 | 46.88 | 48.15 | 47.01 | 47.65 | 48.70 | 48.84 | 49.48 | 47.81 |
| 2018 | 49.04 | 49.55 | 50.56 | 50.95 | 50.39 | 51.00 | 51.95 | 51.75 | 53.40 | 52.43 | 52.73 | 54.89 | 51.57 |
| 2019 | 54.26 | 54.03 | 54.62 | 54.82 | 54.79 | 55.99 | 55.06 | 55.16 | 55.92 | 54.51 | 54.55 | 56.28 | 55.02 |
| **Leisure and Hospitality** | | | | | | | | | | | | | |
| 2015 | 18.08 | 17.97 | 18.49 | 18.07 | 17.94 | 17.71 | 17.64 | 17.67 | 17.79 | 17.85 | 17.86 | 17.70 | 17.90 |
| 2016 | 16.88 | 16.81 | 17.44 | 17.42 | 17.64 | 17.74 | 17.95 | 17.66 | 18.22 | 18.24 | 18.89 | 19.49 | 17.87 |
| 2017 | 19.20 | 19.22 | 20.38 | 19.59 | 19.61 | 18.97 | 19.73 | 18.89 | 19.45 | 20.60 | 18.82 | 19.00 | 19.47 |
| 2018 | 19.72 | 21.14 | 19.75 | 20.05 | 19.78 | 19.78 | 19.67 | 20.10 | 20.13 | 20.47 | 21.18 | 21.65 | 20.28 |
| 2019 | 20.94 | 20.74 | 21.75 | 21.74 | 22.22 | 22.01 | 21.71 | 22.07 | 22.67 | 23.14 | 23.57 | 24.72 | 22.30 |
| **Other Services** | | | | | | | | | | | | | |
| 2015 | 45.35 | 46.56 | 46.83 | 45.39 | 45.09 | 45.26 | 44.73 | 46.26 | 45.50 | 44.42 | 45.68 | 45.38 | 45.54 |
| 2016 | 46.12 | 46.80 | 47.07 | 47.43 | 48.33 | 46.96 | 47.59 | 48.02 | 47.48 | 48.22 | 47.60 | 48.23 | 47.50 |
| 2017 | 49.88 | 48.76 | 49.16 | 50.09 | 49.72 | 49.04 | 50.05 | 49.48 | 50.03 | 50.96 | 49.49 | 49.81 | 49.72 |
| 2018 | 51.31 | 52.49 | 52.76 | 53.44 | 53.68 | 53.29 | 53.48 | 53.80 | 55.75 | 55.59 | 54.81 | 56.00 | 53.89 |
| 2019 | 56.65 | 55.90 | 56.77 | 57.56 | 56.91 | 56.91 | 55.31 | 56.71 | 56.44 | 56.48 | 56.33 | 57.64 | 56.64 |

## 4. Average Weekly Earnings by Selected Industry: District of Columbia, 2015–2019

(Dollars, not seasonally adjusted)

| Industry and year | January | February | March | April | May | June | July | August | September | October | November | December | Annual average |
|---|---|---|---|---|---|---|---|---|---|---|---|---|---|
| **Total Private** | | | | | | | | | | | | | |
| 2015 | 1,398.94 | 1,492.24 | 1,476.38 | 1,384.15 | 1,368.99 | 1,365.62 | 1,319.85 | 1,365.64 | 1,310.40 | 1,275.04 | 1,347.12 | 1,300.29 | 1,364.55 |
| 2016 | 1,288.32 | 1,305.39 | 1,306.61 | 1,333.93 | 1,412.32 | 1,347.82 | 1,359.71 | 1,382.35 | 1,383.08 | 1,455.99 | 1,402.90 | 1,411.75 | 1,367.75 |
| 2017 | 1,480.46 | 1,412.46 | 1,412.35 | 1,454.91 | 1,392.77 | 1,389.61 | 1,474.77 | 1,417.85 | 1,435.24 | 1,512.00 | 1,452.15 | 1,466.83 | 1,443.79 |
| 2018 | 1,458.44 | 1,477.07 | 1,476.14 | 1,544.72 | 1,467.52 | 1,477.70 | 1,546.92 | 1,487.24 | 1,580.21 | 1,503.72 | 1,530.90 | 1,629.19 | 1,517.12 |
| 2019 | 1,550.75 | 1,571.43 | 1,589.33 | 1,609.99 | 1,605.20 | 1,679.94 | 1,592.03 | 1,598.08 | 1,665.08 | 1,593.15 | 1,598.03 | 1,700.24 | 1,613.12 |
| **Goods-Producing** | | | | | | | | | | | | | |
| 2015 | 1,099.98 | 1,201.00 | 1,227.35 | 1,161.03 | 1,202.04 | 1,213.13 | 1,151.67 | 1,214.03 | 1,222.40 | 1,248.04 | 1,220.73 | 1,307.16 | 1,207.80 |
| 2016 | 1,314.17 | 1,237.30 | 1,286.34 | 1,215.25 | 1,185.41 | 1,234.36 | 1,201.59 | 1,207.20 | 1,219.78 | 1,141.53 | 1,117.75 | 1,062.62 | 1,202.38 |
| 2017 | 1,136.89 | 1,164.56 | 1,133.83 | 1,170.88 | 1,103.81 | 1,179.17 | 1,152.40 | 1,173.73 | 1,177.58 | 1,182.74 | 1,246.23 | 1,276.98 | 1,171.45 |
| 2018 | 1,307.17 | 1,288.13 | 1,299.26 | 1,360.92 | 1,302.62 | 1,358.28 | 1,408.42 | 1,386.03 | 1,329.18 | 1,227.67 | 1,218.78 | 1,304.04 | 1,317.65 |
| 2019 | 1,217.22 | 1,214.81 | 1,283.56 | 1,345.31 | 1,357.21 | 1,370.04 | 1,388.44 | 1,409.76 | 1,371.04 | 1,369.52 | 1,324.19 | 1,322.34 | 1,328.45 |
| **Trade, Transportation, and Utilities** | | | | | | | | | | | | | |
| 2015 | 843.88 | 893.11 | 873.29 | 853.65 | 858.90 | 852.20 | 860.34 | 906.02 | 907.85 | 895.95 | 942.70 | 901.37 | 881.65 |
| 2016 | 911.91 | 911.43 | 942.56 | 941.53 | 955.63 | 933.95 | 942.42 | 936.20 | 946.49 | 897.46 | 890.02 | 879.71 | 923.44 |
| 2017 | 927.86 | 872.83 | 828.47 | 890.55 | 884.02 | 841.32 | 882.42 | 849.18 | 853.13 | 870.09 | 862.64 | 832.69 | 865.60 |
| 2018 | 864.26 | 845.60 | 847.15 | 874.98 | 853.44 | 851.15 | 864.50 | 844.61 | 860.97 | 837.81 | 839.93 | 837.38 | 853.22 |
| 2019 | 825.38 | 808.81 | 818.81 | 816.50 | 807.85 | 830.53 | 845.99 | 831.36 | 831.29 | 812.95 | 828.32 | 852.88 | 826.49 |
| **Professional and Business Services** | | | | | | | | | | | | | |
| 2015 | 1,729.44 | 1,847.66 | 1,820.63 | 1,702.12 | 1,718.08 | 1,712.63 | 1,663.45 | 1,788.47 | 1,690.75 | 1,695.26 | 1,787.48 | 1,724.50 | 1,740.32 |
| 2016 | 1,721.97 | 1,718.05 | 1,692.01 | 1,703.56 | 1,811.66 | 1,723.89 | 1,728.64 | 1,735.50 | 1,726.09 | 1,833.75 | 1,772.89 | 1,806.02 | 1,768.97 |
| 2017 | 1,832.97 | 1,740.48 | 1,702.11 | 1,808.04 | 1,703.88 | 1,711.12 | 1,820.07 | 1,720.57 | 1,748.76 | 1,850.60 | 1,772.89 | 1,806.02 | 1,768.97 |
| 2018 | 1,775.25 | 1,793.71 | 1,810.05 | 1,925.91 | 1,803.96 | 1,815.60 | 1,911.76 | 1,831.95 | 1,959.78 | 1,829.81 | 1,871.92 | 2,052.89 | 1,866.83 |
| 2019 | 1,888.25 | 1,939.68 | 1,949.93 | 1,979.00 | 2,005.31 | 2,172.41 | 2,020.70 | 2,040.92 | 2,158.51 | 2,016.87 | 2,029.26 | 2,178.04 | 2,030.24 |
| **Leisure and Hospitality** | | | | | | | | | | | | | |
| 2015 | 509.86 | 522.93 | 552.85 | 545.71 | 550.76 | 531.3 | 511.56 | 507.13 | 501.68 | 514.08 | 517.94 | 504.45 | 522.68 |
| 2016 | 460.82 | 487.49 | 509.25 | 517.37 | 515.09 | 500.27 | 507.99 | 487.42 | 501.05 | 514.37 | 536.48 | 545.72 | 507.51 |
| 2017 | 518.4 | 528.55 | 607.32 | 566.15 | 549.08 | 508.4 | 528.76 | 515.7 | 519.32 | 560.32 | 508.14 | 522.5 | 535.43 |
| 2018 | 510.75 | 541.18 | 531.28 | 557.39 | 543.95 | 559.77 | 542.89 | 548.73 | 557.6 | 567.02 | 582.45 | 619.19 | 555.67 |
| 2019 | 529.78 | 555.83 | 591.6 | 623.94 | 631.05 | 629.49 | 594.85 | 615.75 | 634.76 | 652.55 | 662.32 | 697.1 | 617.71 |
| **Other Services** | | | | | | | | | | | | | |
| 2015 | 1,619 | 1,732.03 | 1,690.56 | 1,584.11 | 1,596.19 | 1,575.05 | 1,570.02 | 1,674.61 | 1,615.25 | 1,581.35 | 1,681.02 | 1,597.38 | 1,625.78 |
| 2016 | 1,641.87 | 1,647.36 | 1,652.16 | 1,693.25 | 1,768.88 | 1,667.08 | 1,665.65 | 1,690.30 | 1,690.29 | 1,784.14 | 1,699.32 | 1,716.99 | 1,691 |
| 2017 | 1,835.58 | 1,745.61 | 1,750.10 | 1,863.35 | 1,779.98 | 1,789.96 | 1,886.89 | 1,806.02 | 1,826.10 | 1,916.10 | 1,781.64 | 1,768.26 | 1,814.78 |
| 2018 | 1,795.85 | 1,858.15 | 1,851.88 | 1,971.94 | 1,894.90 | 1,897.12 | 1,973.41 | 1,909.90 | 2,057.18 | 1,990.12 | 1,995.08 | 2,100 | 1,940.04 |
| 2019 | 2,084.72 | 2,101.84 | 2,134.55 | 2,146.99 | 2,128.43 | 2,162.58 | 2,063.06 | 2,052.90 | 2,127.79 | 2,067.17 | 2,072.94 | 2,196.08 | 2,112.67 |

# FLORIDA
## *At a Glance*

Population:
2010 census: 18,801,310
2019 estimate: 21,477,737

Percent change in population:
2010–2019: 14.2%

Percent change in total nonfarm employment:
2011–2019: 23.4%

Industry with the largest growth in employment, 2011–2019 (percent):
Construction, 68.5%

Industry with the largest decline or smallest growth in employment, 2011–2019 (percent):
Information, 2.3%

Civilian labor force:
2010: 9,212,066
2019: 10,336,749

Unemployment rate and rank among states (highest to lowest):
2010: 11.1%, 6th
2019: 3.1%, 37th

Over-the-year change in unemployment rates:
2017–2018: -0.6%
2018–2019: -0.5%

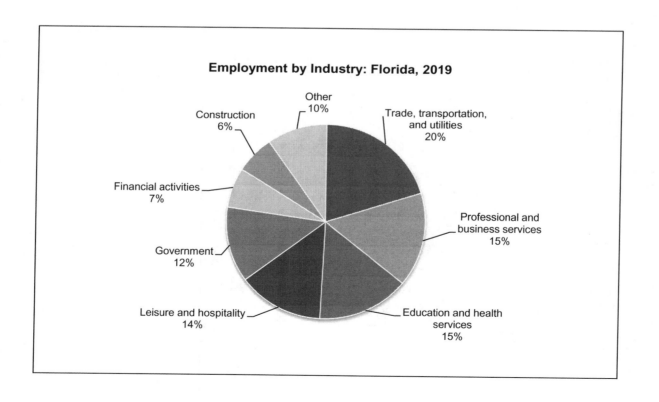

**Employment by Industry: Florida, 2019**

- Other 10%
- Construction 6%
- Trade, transportation, and utilities 20%
- Financial activities 7%
- Professional and business services 15%
- Government 12%
- Leisure and hospitality 14%
- Education and health services 15%

# 1. Employment by Industry: Florida, 2011–2019

(Numbers in thousands, not seasonally adjusted)

| Industry and year | January | February | March | April | May | June | July | August | September | October | November | December | Annual average |
|---|---|---|---|---|---|---|---|---|---|---|---|---|---|
| **Total Nonfarm** | | | | | | | | | | | | | |
| 2011 | 7,175.7 | 7,227.1 | 7,274.0 | 7,311.1 | 7,280.9 | 7,166.9 | 7,129.1 | 7,214.6 | 7,242.2 | 7,283.8 | 7,359.7 | 7,392.9 | 7,254.8 |
| 2012 | 7,285.4 | 7,348.2 | 7,408.3 | 7,427.4 | 7,417.5 | 7,323.2 | 7,268.9 | 7,366.7 | 7,383.1 | 7,455.5 | 7,544.2 | 7,569.1 | 7,399.8 |
| 2013 | 7,446.3 | 7,523.4 | 7,577.1 | 7,587.2 | 7,589.1 | 7,497.9 | 7,461.9 | 7,569.7 | 7,582.8 | 7,650.9 | 7,754.9 | 7,785.1 | 7,585.5 |
| 2014 | 7,665.3 | 7,738.4 | 7,794.6 | 7,824.0 | 7,830.8 | 7,731.6 | 7,702.4 | 7,814.6 | 7,833.3 | 7,921.5 | 8,017.5 | 8,060.7 | 7,827.9 |
| 2015 | 7,943.1 | 8,016.5 | 8,068.0 | 8,094.7 | 8,100.9 | 8,008.2 | 7,987.1 | 8,092.5 | 8,109.3 | 8,224.5 | 8,321.4 | 8,362.8 | 8,110.8 |
| 2016 | 8,238.8 | 8,315.1 | 8,361.0 | 8,397.5 | 8,386.6 | 8,274.0 | 8,275.1 | 8,371.4 | 8,408.6 | 8,467.9 | 8,567.4 | 8,596.0 | 8,388.3 |
| 2017 | 8,488.0 | 8,550.5 | 8,590.9 | 8,593.5 | 8,594.4 | 8,492.9 | 8,455.5 | 8,549.9 | 8,390.6 | 8,637.1 | 8,746.1 | 8,775.1 | 8,572.0 |
| 2018 | 8,656.0 | 8,736.1 | 8,777.2 | 8,780.3 | 8,773.6 | 8,676.4 | 8,646.2 | 8,769.1 | 8,780.0 | 8,860.3 | 8,964.5 | 8,975.3 | 8,782.9 |
| 2019 | 8,863.2 | 8,941.1 | 8,965.4 | 8,964.2 | 8,950.3 | 8,838.6 | 8,821.7 | 8,937.0 | 8,923.1 | 9,010.0 | 9,088.4 | 9,128.3 | 8,952.6 |
| **Total Private** | | | | | | | | | | | | | |
| 2011 | 6,059.0 | 6,099.8 | 6,148.2 | 6,185.0 | 6,167.0 | 6,145.7 | 6,114.4 | 6,128.8 | 6,147.3 | 6,173.4 | 6,249.1 | 6,287.9 | 6,158.8 |
| 2012 | 6,188.6 | 6,238.6 | 6,299.4 | 6,324.2 | 6,324.8 | 6,315.5 | 6,266.9 | 6,289.5 | 6,295.0 | 6,354.8 | 6,440.4 | 6,471.3 | 6,317.4 |
| 2013 | 6,353.8 | 6,420.2 | 6,472.4 | 6,484.9 | 6,496.7 | 6,492.3 | 6,465.5 | 6,496.1 | 6,497.8 | 6,554.2 | 6,652.9 | 6,689.5 | 6,506.4 |
| 2014 | 6,577.9 | 6,641.0 | 6,693.1 | 6,725.9 | 6,740.2 | 6,729.8 | 6,703.4 | 6,742.1 | 6,749.9 | 6,823.9 | 6,916.5 | 6,962.3 | 6,750.5 |
| 2015 | 6,853.9 | 6,914.9 | 6,963.1 | 6,989.5 | 7,003.0 | 6,999.6 | 6,980.4 | 7,010.5 | 7,016.8 | 7,115.0 | 7,210.7 | 7,257.4 | 7,026.2 |
| 2016 | 7,138.7 | 7,203.7 | 7,246.3 | 7,280.8 | 7,276.2 | 7,249.8 | 7,253.6 | 7,276.4 | 7,295.5 | 7,349.3 | 7,443.7 | 7,475.0 | 7,290.8 |
| 2017 | 7,373.5 | 7,422.6 | 7,460.2 | 7,468.4 | 7,474.4 | 7,462.8 | 7,428.8 | 7,452.0 | 7,279.2 | 7,511.0 | 7,615.7 | 7,646.9 | 7,466.3 |
| 2018 | 7,533.0 | 7,603.3 | 7,641.4 | 7,647.2 | 7,648.1 | 7,635.4 | 7,614.9 | 7,657.8 | 7,654.3 | 7,722.8 | 7,820.7 | 7,835.9 | 7,667.9 |
| 2019 | 7,734.9 | 7,800.3 | 7,821.9 | 7,821.8 | 7,816.5 | 7,786.7 | 7,782.6 | 7,817.5 | 7,787.1 | 7,863.4 | 7,937.4 | 7,983.0 | 7,829.4 |
| **Goods Producing** | | | | | | | | | | | | | |
| 2011 | 643.3 | 645.8 | 648.8 | 651.6 | 653.2 | 655.7 | 656.3 | 657.6 | 660.0 | 657.1 | 658.5 | 658.9 | 653.9 |
| 2012 | 649.1 | 652.3 | 658.2 | 657.6 | 662.3 | 667.4 | 665.7 | 670.8 | 672.4 | 674.2 | 677.7 | 677.4 | 665.4 |
| 2013 | 666.4 | 672.6 | 679.0 | 683.2 | 690.3 | 695.6 | 697.4 | 704.3 | 706.5 | 708.5 | 713.4 | 715.5 | 694.4 |
| 2014 | 706.3 | 713.6 | 717.3 | 722.9 | 731.3 | 736.6 | 739.4 | 744.8 | 747.4 | 752.9 | 754.4 | 756.1 | 735.3 |
| 2015 | 748.3 | 755.2 | 761.4 | 766.5 | 774.1 | 782.4 | 785.5 | 789.7 | 793.4 | 805.0 | 808.8 | 811.6 | 781.8 |
| 2016 | 804.5 | 813.5 | 819.4 | 826.6 | 831.5 | 837.7 | 842.6 | 845.2 | 850.6 | 853.0 | 858.6 | 860.7 | 837.0 |
| 2017 | 852.9 | 861.9 | 868.4 | 868.2 | 873.9 | 881.5 | 879.6 | 883.3 | 850.2 | 887.0 | 891.6 | 895.2 | 874.5 |
| 2018 | 888.3 | 902.2 | 909.4 | 911.6 | 914.9 | 924.3 | 924.2 | 929.5 | 931.6 | 937.1 | 940.3 | 942.6 | 921.3 |
| 2019 | 935.7 | 943.9 | 947.8 | 946.6 | 950.9 | 955.7 | 956.1 | 959.9 | 958.9 | 970.8 | 971.5 | 971.5 | 955.8 |
| **Service-Providing** | | | | | | | | | | | | | |
| 2011 | 6,532.4 | 6,581.3 | 6,625.2 | 6,659.5 | 6,627.7 | 6,511.2 | 6,472.8 | 6,557.0 | 6,582.2 | 6,626.7 | 6,701.2 | 6,734.0 | 6,600.9 |
| 2012 | 6,636.3 | 6,695.9 | 6,750.1 | 6,769.8 | 6,755.2 | 6,655.8 | 6,603.2 | 6,695.9 | 6,710.7 | 6,781.3 | 6,866.5 | 6,891.7 | 6,734.4 |
| 2013 | 6,779.9 | 6,850.8 | 6,898.1 | 6,904.0 | 6,898.8 | 6,802.3 | 6,764.5 | 6,865.4 | 6,876.3 | 6,942.4 | 7,041.5 | 7,069.6 | 6,891.1 |
| 2014 | 6,959.0 | 7,024.8 | 7,077.3 | 7,101.1 | 7,099.5 | 6,995.0 | 6,963.0 | 7,069.8 | 7,085.9 | 7,168.6 | 7,263.1 | 7,304.6 | 7,092.6 |
| 2015 | 7,194.8 | 7,261.3 | 7,306.6 | 7,328.2 | 7,326.8 | 7,225.8 | 7,201.6 | 7,302.8 | 7,315.9 | 7,419.5 | 7,512.6 | 7,551.2 | 7,328.9 |
| 2016 | 7,434.3 | 7,501.6 | 7,541.6 | 7,570.9 | 7,555.1 | 7,436.3 | 7,432.5 | 7,526.2 | 7,558.0 | 7,614.9 | 7,708.8 | 7,735.3 | 7,551.3 |
| 2017 | 7,635.1 | 7,688.6 | 7,722.5 | 7,725.3 | 7,720.5 | 7,611.4 | 7,575.9 | 7,666.6 | 7,540.4 | 7,750.1 | 7,854.5 | 7,879.9 | 7,697.6 |
| 2018 | 7,767.7 | 7,833.9 | 7,867.8 | 7,868.7 | 7,858.7 | 7,752.1 | 7,722.0 | 7,839.6 | 7,848.4 | 7,923.2 | 8,024.2 | 8,032.7 | 7,861.6 |
| 2019 | 7,927.5 | 7,997.2 | 8,017.6 | 8,017.6 | 7,999.4 | 7,882.9 | 7,865.6 | 7,977.1 | 7,964.2 | 8,039.2 | 8,116.9 | 8,156.8 | 7,996.8 |
| **Mining and Logging** | | | | | | | | | | | | | |
| 2011 | 334.3 | 336.0 | 338.5 | 340.0 | 340.6 | 342.0 | 343.1 | 343.7 | 346.3 | 343.2 | 343.9 | 343.5 | 341.3 |
| 2012 | 334.4 | 336.7 | 340.9 | 340.7 | 344.3 | 348.8 | 348.3 | 352.6 | 354.9 | 356.1 | 358.5 | 357.8 | 347.8 |
| 2013 | 350.1 | 354.3 | 359.4 | 362.4 | 367.8 | 371.6 | 374.8 | 380.7 | 382.3 | 383.8 | 386.5 | 387.3 | 371.8 |
| 2014 | 379.3 | 385.1 | 388.8 | 393.4 | 399.7 | 404.4 | 407.4 | 411.6 | 413.6 | 417.2 | 417.9 | 418.5 | 403.1 |
| 2015 | 412.9 | 418.2 | 422.5 | 426.8 | 432.4 | 438.2 | 441.1 | 444.4 | 447.4 | 456.4 | 459.1 | 460.6 | 438.3 |
| 2016 | 455.3 | 462.4 | 466.7 | 473.2 | 477.0 | 481.7 | 485.6 | 487.9 | 492.9 | 495.1 | 498.7 | 499.7 | 481.4 |
| 2017 | 494.0 | 500.4 | 505.3 | 505.5 | 510.0 | 515.5 | 515.0 | 518.3 | 492.8 | 523.0 | 525.6 | 527.5 | 511.1 |
| 2018 | 523.5 | 535.0 | 540.4 | 542.4 | 544.2 | 551.1 | 550.8 | 555.0 | 556.7 | 560.5 | 562.2 | 563.1 | 548.7 |
| 2019 | 557.0 | 562.1 | 565.4 | 564.5 | 567.4 | 570.5 | 571.6 | 574.8 | 574.8 | 582.6 | 582.0 | 582.1 | 571.2 |
| **Construction** | | | | | | | | | | | | | |
| 2011 | 328.6 | 330.3 | 332.8 | 334.4 | 335.0 | 336.4 | 337.5 | 338.1 | 340.7 | 337.6 | 338.3 | 337.9 | 335.6 |
| 2012 | 328.8 | 331.1 | 335.3 | 335.1 | 338.7 | 343.2 | 342.7 | 347.0 | 349.3 | 350.6 | 352.9 | 352.1 | 342.2 |
| 2013 | 344.4 | 348.6 | 353.7 | 356.8 | 362.2 | 366.1 | 369.2 | 375.1 | 376.7 | 378.2 | 380.9 | 381.6 | 366.1 |
| 2014 | 373.7 | 379.5 | 383.2 | 387.7 | 394.0 | 398.7 | 401.7 | 405.9 | 408.0 | 411.5 | 412.3 | 412.8 | 397.4 |
| 2015 | 407.2 | 412.5 | 416.8 | 421.0 | 426.6 | 432.4 | 435.3 | 438.6 | 441.6 | 450.6 | 453.4 | 454.9 | 432.6 |
| 2016 | 449.5 | 456.7 | 460.9 | 467.4 | 471.2 | 475.9 | 479.8 | 482.3 | 487.3 | 489.6 | 493.1 | 494.2 | 475.7 |
| 2017 | 488.3 | 494.7 | 499.6 | 499.9 | 504.4 | 509.9 | 509.5 | 512.7 | 487.3 | 517.4 | 520.0 | 521.8 | 505.5 |
| 2018 | 517.8 | 529.3 | 534.7 | 536.7 | 538.5 | 545.3 | 545.0 | 549.2 | 550.9 | 554.8 | 556.4 | 557.4 | 543.0 |
| 2019 | 551.2 | 556.3 | 559.6 | 558.7 | 561.6 | 564.8 | 565.9 | 569.1 | 569.1 | 576.9 | 576.3 | 576.4 | 565.5 |

## 1. Employment by Industry: Florida, 2011–2019—*Continued*

(Numbers in thousands, not seasonally adjusted)

| Industry and year | January | February | March | April | May | June | July | August | September | October | November | December | Annual average |
|---|---|---|---|---|---|---|---|---|---|---|---|---|---|
| **Manufacturing** | | | | | | | | | | | | | |
| 2011 | 309.0 | 309.8 | 310.3 | 311.6 | 312.6 | 313.7 | 313.2 | 313.9 | 313.7 | 313.9 | 314.6 | 315.4 | 312.6 |
| 2012 | 314.7 | 315.6 | 317.3 | 316.9 | 318.0 | 318.6 | 317.4 | 318.2 | 317.5 | 318.1 | 319.2 | 319.6 | 317.6 |
| 2013 | 316.3 | 318.3 | 319.6 | 320.8 | 322.5 | 324.0 | 322.6 | 323.6 | 324.2 | 324.7 | 326.9 | 328.2 | 322.6 |
| 2014 | 327.0 | 328.5 | 328.5 | 329.5 | 331.6 | 332.2 | 332.0 | 333.2 | 333.8 | 335.7 | 336.5 | 337.6 | 332.2 |
| 2015 | 335.4 | 337.0 | 338.9 | 339.7 | 341.7 | 344.2 | 344.4 | 345.3 | 346.0 | 348.6 | 349.7 | 351.0 | 343.5 |
| 2016 | 349.2 | 351.1 | 352.7 | 353.4 | 354.5 | 356.0 | 357.0 | 357.3 | 357.7 | 357.9 | 359.9 | 361.0 | 355.6 |
| 2017 | 358.9 | 361.5 | 363.1 | 362.7 | 363.9 | 366.0 | 364.6 | 365.0 | 357.4 | 364.0 | 366.0 | 367.7 | 363.4 |
| 2018 | 364.8 | 367.2 | 369.0 | 369.2 | 370.7 | 373.2 | 373.4 | 374.5 | 374.9 | 376.6 | 378.1 | 379.5 | 372.6 |
| 2019 | 378.7 | 381.8 | 382.4 | 382.1 | 383.5 | 385.2 | 384.5 | 385.1 | 384.1 | 388.2 | 389.5 | 389.4 | 384.5 |
| **Trade, Transportation, and Utilities** | | | | | | | | | | | | | |
| 2011 | 1,479.1 | 1,477.2 | 1,481.9 | 1,490.3 | 1,488.9 | 1,486.2 | 1,484.4 | 1,488.8 | 1,490.1 | 1,501.7 | 1,541.4 | 1,560.6 | 1,497.6 |
| 2012 | 1,517.1 | 1,514.3 | 1,520.6 | 1,520.7 | 1,524.9 | 1,521.6 | 1,513.5 | 1,516.2 | 1,518.1 | 1,531.3 | 1,575.9 | 1,592.3 | 1,530.5 |
| 2013 | 1,544.3 | 1,544.4 | 1,548.2 | 1,549.4 | 1,553.5 | 1,555.3 | 1,551.1 | 1,556.0 | 1,556.0 | 1,573.6 | 1,622.9 | 1,645.7 | 1,566.7 |
| 2014 | 1,590.8 | 1,593.4 | 1,598.1 | 1,602.5 | 1,604.5 | 1,603.9 | 1,599.2 | 1,607.7 | 1,609.1 | 1,630.1 | 1,682.0 | 1,708.8 | 1,619.2 |
| 2015 | 1,654.8 | 1,654.4 | 1,658.4 | 1,659.8 | 1,662.1 | 1,665.6 | 1,659.3 | 1,667.0 | 1,662.9 | 1,683.7 | 1,732.1 | 1,756.9 | 1,676.4 |
| 2016 | 1,693.1 | 1,693.3 | 1,696.2 | 1,699.9 | 1,701.3 | 1,696.6 | 1,698.4 | 1,702.3 | 1,702.0 | 1,715.8 | 1,766.5 | 1,787.3 | 1,712.7 |
| 2017 | 1,735.7 | 1,727.4 | 1,727.3 | 1,728.3 | 1,728.6 | 1,725.5 | 1,721.4 | 1,725.4 | 1,690.9 | 1,738.7 | 1,803.2 | 1,821.5 | 1,739.5 |
| 2018 | 1,771.8 | 1,767.4 | 1,767.5 | 1,764.5 | 1,766.7 | 1,764.4 | 1,760.7 | 1,764.5 | 1,766.2 | 1,778.7 | 1,837.5 | 1,852.3 | 1,780.2 |
| 2019 | 1,805.4 | 1,794.7 | 1,793.4 | 1,787.0 | 1,786.2 | 1,784.7 | 1,787.5 | 1,789.7 | 1,785.6 | 1,804.1 | 1,846.9 | 1,876.0 | 1,803.4 |
| **Wholesale Trade** | | | | | | | | | | | | | |
| 2011 | 304.4 | 305.7 | 306.5 | 307.7 | 307.2 | 306.4 | 305.5 | 305.5 | 306.0 | 307.0 | 308.2 | 311.1 | 306.8 |
| 2012 | 306.7 | 308.5 | 309.9 | 310.9 | 311.8 | 311.0 | 309.9 | 310.3 | 310.8 | 312.9 | 315.0 | 316.1 | 311.2 |
| 2013 | 311.6 | 313.5 | 314.3 | 314.0 | 314.9 | 313.8 | 312.0 | 312.5 | 312.9 | 314.5 | 317.0 | 318.6 | 314.1 |
| 2014 | 315.5 | 317.8 | 318.1 | 318.9 | 320.5 | 319.5 | 318.8 | 320.5 | 320.7 | 323.4 | 326.3 | 328.2 | 320.7 |
| 2015 | 325.1 | 326.2 | 327.0 | 326.7 | 327.6 | 327.4 | 326.7 | 327.3 | 327.6 | 330.0 | 331.7 | 333.5 | 328.1 |
| 2016 | 329.5 | 331.0 | 331.3 | 332.4 | 332.8 | 331.0 | 330.8 | 331.5 | 331.7 | 332.5 | 335.0 | 337.1 | 332.2 |
| 2017 | 333.9 | 335.2 | 336.1 | 336.7 | 338.2 | 337.5 | 337.0 | 336.9 | 333.9 | 337.7 | 340.0 | 342.4 | 337.1 |
| 2018 | 341.2 | 343.6 | 344.3 | 344.5 | 344.9 | 344.7 | 344.9 | 345.6 | 345.9 | 347.6 | 350.1 | 351.3 | 345.7 |
| 2019 | 349.4 | 352.1 | 351.8 | 351.1 | 352.1 | 352.0 | 353.0 | 353.3 | 352.6 | 353.3 | 356.4 | 359.1 | 353.0 |
| **Retail Trade** | | | | | | | | | | | | | |
| 2011 | 943.9 | 939.8 | 942.3 | 947.9 | 947.2 | 945.3 | 944.1 | 948.5 | 948.8 | 958.6 | 994.1 | 1,004.8 | 955.4 |
| 2012 | 972.6 | 966.8 | 971.0 | 970.6 | 973.6 | 970.6 | 964.5 | 966.9 | 968.1 | 977.6 | 1,016.8 | 1,026.2 | 978.8 |
| 2013 | 989.4 | 986.4 | 988.3 | 989.2 | 992.2 | 995.0 | 994.3 | 997.8 | 996.8 | 1,011.4 | 1,054.7 | 1,069.7 | 1,005.4 |
| 2014 | 1,025.7 | 1,024.7 | 1,027.6 | 1,031.0 | 1,030.9 | 1,031.3 | 1,027.6 | 1,032.9 | 1,032.5 | 1,048.1 | 1,091.1 | 1,106.9 | 1,042.5 |
| 2015 | 1,065.0 | 1,065.4 | 1,068.3 | 1,067.5 | 1,068.3 | 1,070.9 | 1,064.5 | 1,070.2 | 1,064.4 | 1,078.8 | 1,116.8 | 1,129.9 | 1,077.5 |
| 2016 | 1,083.2 | 1,082.3 | 1,083.8 | 1,085.3 | 1,085.7 | 1,082.8 | 1,084.4 | 1,088.2 | 1,085.6 | 1,096.5 | 1,137.5 | 1,147.7 | 1,095.3 |
| 2017 | 1,108.2 | 1,100.8 | 1,098.6 | 1,099.9 | 1,097.9 | 1,094.6 | 1,090.9 | 1,094.0 | 1,064.1 | 1,100.1 | 1,148.5 | 1,156.5 | 1,104.5 |
| 2018 | 1,118.3 | 1,113.4 | 1,112.7 | 1,109.0 | 1,108.6 | 1,104.6 | 1,101.5 | 1,102.6 | 1,101.5 | 1,107.1 | 1,149.9 | 1,152.5 | 1,115.1 |
| 2019 | 1,116.9 | 1,108.7 | 1,107.8 | 1,102.2 | 1,100.0 | 1,096.6 | 1,096.3 | 1,097.6 | 1,092.1 | 1,105.7 | 1,138.3 | 1,147.3 | 1,109.1 |
| **Transportation and Utilities** | | | | | | | | | | | | | |
| 2011 | 230.8 | 231.7 | 233.1 | 234.7 | 234.5 | 234.5 | 234.8 | 234.8 | 235.3 | 236.1 | 239.1 | 244.7 | 235.3 |
| 2012 | 237.8 | 239.0 | 239.7 | 239.2 | 239.5 | 240.0 | 239.1 | 239.0 | 239.2 | 240.8 | 244.1 | 250.0 | 240.6 |
| 2013 | 243.3 | 244.5 | 245.6 | 246.2 | 246.4 | 246.5 | 244.8 | 245.7 | 246.3 | 247.7 | 251.2 | 257.4 | 247.1 |
| 2014 | 249.6 | 250.9 | 252.4 | 252.6 | 253.1 | 253.1 | 252.8 | 254.3 | 255.9 | 258.6 | 264.6 | 273.7 | 256.0 |
| 2015 | 264.7 | 262.8 | 263.1 | 265.6 | 266.2 | 267.3 | 268.1 | 269.5 | 270.9 | 274.9 | 283.6 | 293.5 | 270.9 |
| 2016 | 280.4 | 280.0 | 281.1 | 282.2 | 282.8 | 282.8 | 283.2 | 282.6 | 284.7 | 286.8 | 294.0 | 302.5 | 285.3 |
| 2017 | 293.6 | 291.4 | 292.6 | 291.7 | 292.5 | 293.4 | 293.5 | 294.5 | 292.9 | 300.9 | 314.7 | 322.6 | 297.9 |
| 2018 | 312.3 | 310.4 | 310.5 | 311.0 | 313.2 | 315.1 | 314.3 | 316.3 | 318.8 | 324.0 | 337.5 | 348.5 | 319.3 |
| 2019 | 339.1 | 333.9 | 333.8 | 333.7 | 334.1 | 336.1 | 338.2 | 338.8 | 340.9 | 345.1 | 352.2 | 369.6 | 341.3 |
| **Information** | | | | | | | | | | | | | |
| 2011 | 136.3 | 136.4 | 136.3 | 135.9 | 136.0 | 135.9 | 135.8 | 135.5 | 135.3 | 135.1 | 135.6 | 135.4 | 135.8 |
| 2012 | 134.2 | 134.1 | 133.9 | 133.9 | 133.6 | 133.5 | 133.5 | 133.1 | 132.0 | 134.0 | 134.0 | 134.1 | 133.7 |
| 2013 | 132.9 | 133.2 | 133.7 | 133.6 | 133.6 | 134.4 | 134.6 | 134.6 | 134.0 | 134.7 | 135.4 | 135.9 | 134.2 |
| 2014 | 135.6 | 136.2 | 136.1 | 136.2 | 136.2 | 137.2 | 136.8 | 135.9 | 135.1 | 135.7 | 136.9 | 136.8 | 136.2 |
| 2015 | 135.7 | 135.9 | 135.8 | 135.6 | 136.5 | 136.3 | 136.8 | 136.9 | 136.1 | 137.1 | 138.2 | 139.0 | 136.7 |
| 2016 | 136.4 | 137.3 | 136.8 | 136.9 | 137.6 | 137.4 | 138.1 | 138.4 | 136.5 | 136.9 | 138.7 | 138.5 | 137.5 |
| 2017 | 137.8 | 139.6 | 139.4 | 138.3 | 139.4 | 138.9 | 137.9 | 138.4 | 135.2 | 136.9 | 139.1 | 139.7 | 138.4 |
| 2018 | 138.0 | 140.6 | 139.5 | 138.5 | 139.4 | 139.5 | 138.6 | 139.9 | 137.9 | 138.5 | 140.7 | 140.8 | 139.3 |
| 2019 | 138.2 | 140.2 | 139.2 | 139.3 | 140.1 | 139.4 | 138.5 | 138.4 | 137.0 | 138.6 | 139.1 | 139.0 | 138.9 |

## 1. Employment by Industry: Florida, 2011–2019—*Continued*

(Numbers in thousands, not seasonally adjusted)

| Industry and year | January | February | March | April | May | June | July | August | September | October | November | December | Annual average |
|---|---|---|---|---|---|---|---|---|---|---|---|---|---|
| **Financial Activities** | | | | | | | | | | | | | |
| 2011 | 479.2 | 481.1 | 483.6 | 484.8 | 484.7 | 485.4 | 487.3 | 488.7 | 489.8 | 490.8 | 491.8 | 495.4 | 486.9 |
| 2012 | 489.2 | 492.2 | 494.8 | 496.9 | 498.3 | 500.5 | 500.6 | 501.6 | 500.8 | 505.3 | 507.6 | 510.1 | 499.8 |
| 2013 | 503.7 | 506.4 | 509.1 | 510.5 | 511.6 | 514.3 | 514.7 | 515.7 | 514.6 | 517.4 | 519.7 | 521.9 | 513.3 |
| 2014 | 513.5 | 515.5 | 518.1 | 519.6 | 521.6 | 522.7 | 523.9 | 524.6 | 523.4 | 527.4 | 529.3 | 531.6 | 522.6 |
| 2015 | 526.8 | 528.7 | 531.0 | 532.4 | 533.8 | 535.1 | 536.9 | 537.7 | 535.8 | 541.1 | 543.7 | 545.1 | 535.7 |
| 2016 | 540.1 | 542.3 | 543.4 | 546.0 | 546.8 | 547.6 | 548.8 | 549.7 | 550.2 | 553.9 | 556.0 | 560.2 | 548.8 |
| 2017 | 554.9 | 557.5 | 559.5 | 560.0 | 561.2 | 563.8 | 564.2 | 564.4 | 561.3 | 569.1 | 570.2 | 570.9 | 563.1 |
| 2018 | 565.8 | 569.2 | 571.0 | 572.4 | 573.4 | 575.2 | 576.7 | 577.8 | 576.8 | 581.3 | 584.5 | 585.2 | 575.8 |
| 2019 | 581.3 | 584.6 | 585.1 | 587.8 | 588.4 | 590.8 | 591.9 | 594.2 | 592.0 | 596.9 | 599.6 | 598.5 | 590.9 |
| **Professional and Business Services** | | | | | | | | | | | | | |
| 2011 | 1019.5 | 1033.1 | 1040.4 | 1048.0 | 1040.9 | 1039.0 | 1031.8 | 1034.4 | 1038.0 | 1044.0 | 1054.1 | 1061.4 | 1040.4 |
| 2012 | 1039.7 | 1055.7 | 1066.9 | 1080.4 | 1078.8 | 1078.5 | 1070.9 | 1077.4 | 1078.3 | 1099.4 | 1111.5 | 1114.4 | 1079.3 |
| 2013 | 1087.5 | 1105.6 | 1114.1 | 1115.4 | 1120.1 | 1119.3 | 1116.3 | 1124.0 | 1124.6 | 1139.3 | 1152.0 | 1154.1 | 1122.7 |
| 2014 | 1132.8 | 1145.6 | 1151.5 | 1160.0 | 1166.9 | 1163.3 | 1161.5 | 1173.0 | 1174.4 | 1192.5 | 1204.5 | 1210.0 | 1169.7 |
| 2015 | 1189.1 | 1201.9 | 1206.6 | 1217.7 | 1222.8 | 1220.2 | 1223.2 | 1227.5 | 1228.6 | 1253.0 | 1265.7 | 1270.5 | 1227.2 |
| 2016 | 1254.7 | 1267.2 | 1275.3 | 1283.9 | 1280.8 | 1277.5 | 1285.2 | 1291.3 | 1293.2 | 1311.7 | 1321.0 | 1317.8 | 1288.3 |
| 2017 | 1305.2 | 1312.3 | 1315.9 | 1320.2 | 1321.5 | 1324.9 | 1324.9 | 1327.7 | 1297.2 | 1350.1 | 1360.6 | 1359.8 | 1326.7 |
| 2018 | 1335.4 | 1344.6 | 1349.5 | 1354.6 | 1355.2 | 1358.5 | 1360.1 | 1368.1 | 1364.3 | 1386.5 | 1397.5 | 1390.8 | 1363.8 |
| 2019 | 1367.8 | 1381.5 | 1381.8 | 1388.3 | 1385.9 | 1385.5 | 1391.1 | 1399.4 | 1390.8 | 1405.7 | 1410.9 | 1417.2 | 1392.2 |
| **Education and Health Services** | | | | | | | | | | | | | |
| 2011 | 1,077.4 | 1,085.1 | 1,087.5 | 1,096.2 | 1,094.8 | 1,083.9 | 1,075.1 | 1,082.4 | 1,094.2 | 1,100.2 | 1,107.1 | 1,108.5 | 1,091.0 |
| 2012 | 1,093.8 | 1,101.9 | 1,106.3 | 1,112.0 | 1,113.0 | 1,104.3 | 1,091.8 | 1,103.6 | 1,113.0 | 1,119.9 | 1,125.1 | 1,126.7 | 1,109.3 |
| 2013 | 1,115.0 | 1,125.9 | 1,129.6 | 1,131.7 | 1,131.3 | 1,120.3 | 1,108.0 | 1,121.1 | 1,128.3 | 1,137.7 | 1,145.1 | 1,145.6 | 1,128.3 |
| 2014 | 1,134.4 | 1,145.3 | 1,148.8 | 1,158.4 | 1,159.8 | 1,149.6 | 1,140.9 | 1,157.2 | 1,166.4 | 1,177.9 | 1,184.6 | 1,188.1 | 1,159.3 |
| 2015 | 1,176.4 | 1,186.8 | 1,191.2 | 1,196.0 | 1,199.9 | 1,190.4 | 1,180.9 | 1,193.8 | 1,205.6 | 1,221.7 | 1,229.0 | 1,230.5 | 1,200.2 |
| 2016 | 1,219.8 | 1,229.6 | 1,232.3 | 1,243.1 | 1,243.4 | 1,229.3 | 1,227.7 | 1,239.9 | 1,252.9 | 1,263.1 | 1,268.9 | 1,274.0 | 1,243.7 |
| 2017 | 1,261.0 | 1,272.8 | 1,274.5 | 1,279.0 | 1,280.3 | 1,267.7 | 1,256.4 | 1,272.1 | 1,261.3 | 1,289.5 | 1,294.9 | 1,297.6 | 1,275.6 |
| 2018 | 1,284.9 | 1,297.8 | 1,300.8 | 1,304.2 | 1,302.6 | 1,290.8 | 1,282.0 | 1,303.2 | 1,311.9 | 1,322.5 | 1,329.1 | 1,330.1 | 1,305.0 |
| 2019 | 1,322.0 | 1,335.9 | 1,334.6 | 1,339.3 | 1,340.8 | 1,323.6 | 1,318.5 | 1,337.7 | 1,341.3 | 1,358.4 | 1,362.6 | 1,364.9 | 1,340.0 |
| **Leisure and Hospitality** | | | | | | | | | | | | | |
| 2011 | 931.6 | 946.6 | 973.1 | 979.7 | 970.6 | 963.2 | 948.9 | 947.2 | 945.5 | 949.1 | 964.1 | 970.6 | 957.5 |
| 2012 | 968.0 | 988.7 | 1,017.0 | 1,019.1 | 1,010.8 | 1,006.3 | 990.7 | 987.0 | 980.1 | 988.5 | 1,005.1 | 1,011.7 | 997.8 |
| 2013 | 1,001.8 | 1,027.3 | 1,052.2 | 1,052.4 | 1,047.3 | 1,043.8 | 1,035.6 | 1,031.6 | 1,024.1 | 1,030.9 | 1,049.2 | 1,054.3 | 1,037.5 |
| 2014 | 1,047.5 | 1,070.9 | 1,100.0 | 1,102.7 | 1,096.3 | 1,093.6 | 1,080.4 | 1,076.5 | 1,071.3 | 1,081.9 | 1,097.6 | 1,102.8 | 1,085.1 |
| 2015 | 1,096.7 | 1,123.3 | 1,147.9 | 1,149.0 | 1,140.9 | 1,135.9 | 1,125.4 | 1,124.5 | 1,120.1 | 1,135.9 | 1,152.1 | 1,160.7 | 1,134.4 |
| 2016 | 1,147.8 | 1,174.8 | 1,194.6 | 1,195.4 | 1,186.3 | 1,175.6 | 1,166.2 | 1,163.1 | 1,162.2 | 1,166.4 | 1,183.0 | 1,186.6 | 1,175.2 |
| 2017 | 1,179.9 | 1,202.9 | 1,225.7 | 1,225.3 | 1,220.0 | 1,211.3 | 1,197.0 | 1,193.7 | 1,144.3 | 1,191.6 | 1,205.7 | 1,209.7 | 1,200.6 |
| 2018 | 1,199.6 | 1,229.0 | 1,249.2 | 1,247.0 | 1,241.6 | 1,228.5 | 1,220.3 | 1,222.8 | 1,214.1 | 1,223.3 | 1,237.2 | 1,240.7 | 1,229.4 |
| 2019 | 1,233.3 | 1,265.3 | 1,284.5 | 1,278.4 | 1,269.5 | 1,252.2 | 1,245.7 | 1,246.2 | 1,230.5 | 1,239.7 | 1,253.3 | 1,263.4 | 1,255.2 |
| **Other Services** | | | | | | | | | | | | | |
| 2011 | 292.6 | 294.5 | 296.6 | 298.5 | 297.9 | 296.4 | 294.8 | 294.2 | 294.4 | 295.4 | 296.5 | 297.1 | 295.7 |
| 2012 | 297.5 | 299.4 | 301.7 | 303.6 | 303.1 | 303.4 | 300.2 | 299.8 | 300.3 | 302.2 | 303.5 | 304.6 | 301.6 |
| 2013 | 302.2 | 304.8 | 306.5 | 308.7 | 309.0 | 309.3 | 307.8 | 308.8 | 309.7 | 312.1 | 315.2 | 316.5 | 309.2 |
| 2014 | 317.0 | 320.5 | 323.2 | 323.6 | 323.6 | 322.9 | 321.3 | 322.4 | 322.8 | 325.5 | 327.2 | 328.1 | 323.2 |
| 2015 | 326.1 | 328.7 | 330.8 | 332.5 | 332.9 | 333.7 | 332.4 | 333.4 | 334.3 | 337.5 | 341.1 | 343.1 | 333.9 |
| 2016 | 342.3 | 345.7 | 348.3 | 349.0 | 348.5 | 348.1 | 346.6 | 346.5 | 347.9 | 348.5 | 351.0 | 349.9 | 347.7 |
| 2017 | 346.1 | 348.2 | 349.5 | 349.1 | 349.5 | 349.2 | 347.4 | 347.0 | 338.8 | 348.1 | 350.4 | 352.5 | 348.0 |
| 2018 | 349.2 | 352.5 | 354.5 | 354.4 | 354.3 | 354.2 | 352.3 | 352.0 | 351.5 | 354.9 | 353.9 | 353.4 | 353.1 |
| 2019 | 351.2 | 354.2 | 355.5 | 355.1 | 354.7 | 354.8 | 353.3 | 352.0 | 351.0 | 349.2 | 353.5 | 352.5 | 353.1 |
| **Government** | | | | | | | | | | | | | |
| 2011 | 1,116.7 | 1,127.3 | 1,125.8 | 1,126.1 | 1,113.9 | 1,021.2 | 1,014.7 | 1,085.8 | 1,094.9 | 1,110.4 | 1,110.6 | 1,105.0 | 1,096.0 |
| 2012 | 1,096.8 | 1,109.6 | 1,108.9 | 1,103.2 | 1,092.7 | 1,007.7 | 1,002.0 | 1,077.2 | 1,088.1 | 1,100.7 | 1,103.8 | 1,097.8 | 1,082.4 |
| 2013 | 1,092.5 | 1,103.2 | 1,104.7 | 1,102.3 | 1,094.4 | 1,005.6 | 996.4 | 1,073.6 | 1,085.0 | 1,096.7 | 1,102.0 | 1,095.6 | 1,079.2 |
| 2014 | 1,087.4 | 1,097.4 | 1,101.5 | 1,098.1 | 1,090.6 | 1,001.8 | 999.0 | 1,072.5 | 1,083.4 | 1,097.6 | 1,101.0 | 1,098.4 | 1,077.4 |
| 2015 | 1,089.2 | 1,101.6 | 1,104.9 | 1,105.2 | 1,097.9 | 1,008.6 | 1,006.7 | 1,082.0 | 1,092.5 | 1,109.5 | 1,110.7 | 1,105.4 | 1,084.5 |
| 2016 | 1,100.1 | 1,111.4 | 1,114.7 | 1,116.7 | 1,110.4 | 1,024.2 | 1,021.5 | 1,095.0 | 1,113.1 | 1,118.6 | 1,123.7 | 1,121.0 | 1,097.5 |
| 2017 | 1,114.5 | 1,127.9 | 1,130.7 | 1,125.1 | 1,120.0 | 1,030.1 | 1,026.7 | 1,097.9 | 1,111.4 | 1,126.1 | 1,130.4 | 1,128.2 | 1,105.8 |
| 2018 | 1,123.0 | 1,132.8 | 1,135.8 | 1,133.1 | 1,125.5 | 1,041.0 | 1,031.3 | 1,111.3 | 1,125.7 | 1,137.5 | 1,143.8 | 1,139.4 | 1,115.0 |
| 2019 | 1,128.3 | 1,140.8 | 1,143.5 | 1,142.4 | 1,133.8 | 1,051.9 | 1,039.1 | 1,119.5 | 1,136.0 | 1,146.6 | 1,151.0 | 1,145.3 | 1,123.2 |

## 2. Average Weekly Hours by Selected Industry: Florida, 2015–2019

(Not seasonally adjusted)

| Industry and year | January | February | March | April | May | June | July | August | September | October | November | December | Annual average |
|---|---|---|---|---|---|---|---|---|---|---|---|---|---|
| **Total Private** | | | | | | | | | | | | | |
| 2015 | 34.1 | 34.7 | 34.7 | 34.3 | 34.2 | 34.1 | 34.2 | 34.5 | 33.9 | 34.1 | 34.5 | 34.3 | 34.3 |
| 2016 | 34.2 | 34.2 | 34.2 | 34.2 | 34.3 | 33.9 | 34.1 | 33.8 | 33.7 | 33.9 | 34.0 | 34.2 | 34.0 |
| 2017 | 34.4 | 34.3 | 34.3 | 34.6 | 34.1 | 34.1 | 34.5 | 34.2 | 32.7 | 35.1 | 34.9 | 35.0 | 34.3 |
| 2018 | 34.7 | 35.0 | 35.0 | 35.1 | 34.6 | 34.8 | 34.9 | 34.7 | 34.8 | 34.4 | 34.7 | 34.7 | 34.8 |
| 2019 | 34.4 | 34.5 | 34.5 | 34.5 | 34.2 | 34.5 | 34.0 | 33.9 | 34.1 | 34.0 | 34.0 | 34.4 | 34.3 |
| **Goods-Producing** | | | | | | | | | | | | | |
| 2015 | 39.4 | 39.6 | 40.2 | 39.8 | 39.9 | 40.1 | 39.9 | 40.1 | 38.7 | 40.1 | 40.5 | 40.4 | 39.9 |
| 2016 | 39.4 | 39.3 | 39.3 | 39.5 | 39.3 | 38.5 | 39.0 | 39.1 | 39.4 | 39.3 | 40.0 | 40.2 | 39.4 |
| 2017 | 40.2 | 40.2 | 40.1 | 39.6 | 40.0 | 39.8 | 40.2 | 40.5 | 35.3 | 41.1 | 40.9 | 41.2 | 39.9 |
| 2018 | 40.5 | 40.7 | 40.5 | 40.6 | 40.3 | 40.8 | 40.6 | 40.9 | 40.7 | 40.5 | 40.9 | 40.7 | 40.6 |
| 2019 | 40.3 | 40.0 | 40.4 | 40.2 | 40.2 | 40.4 | 40.0 | 40.0 | 40.2 | 40.0 | 40.0 | 40.3 | 40.2 |
| **Construction** | | | | | | | | | | | | | |
| 2015 | 38.1 | 38.6 | 39.4 | 38.8 | 39.2 | 39.4 | 39.2 | 39.6 | 38.0 | 40.1 | 40.2 | 40.2 | 39.3 |
| 2016 | 38.6 | 38.9 | 38.7 | 38.8 | 38.9 | 38.2 | 38.7 | 39.0 | 39.5 | 39.1 | 40.0 | 39.9 | 39.0 |
| 2017 | 39.8 | 39.8 | 39.8 | 39.0 | 39.5 | 39.0 | 39.8 | 40.0 | 33.9 | 40.0 | 40.1 | 40.1 | 39.0 |
| 2018 | 39.6 | 39.5 | 39.5 | 39.6 | 39.6 | 40.1 | 40.1 | 40.5 | 40.0 | 40.1 | 40.4 | 40.1 | 39.9 |
| 2019 | 39.8 | 38.9 | 39.9 | 39.7 | 39.8 | 40.0 | 39.7 | 39.8 | 40.0 | 40.0 | 40.0 | 40.2 | 39.8 |
| **Manufacturing** | | | | | | | | | | | | | |
| 2015 | 40.7 | 40.5 | 40.9 | 40.7 | 40.4 | 40.7 | 40.5 | 40.6 | 39.6 | 40.2 | 40.9 | 40.8 | 40.5 |
| 2016 | 40.5 | 40.0 | 40.1 | 40.3 | 39.9 | 39.5 | 39.9 | 39.8 | 39.8 | 40.1 | 40.5 | 41.0 | 40.1 |
| 2017 | 40.8 | 40.9 | 40.8 | 40.6 | 40.7 | 40.8 | 40.7 | 41.2 | 37.3 | 42.6 | 42.0 | 43.2 | 41.0 |
| 2018 | 42.1 | 42.6 | 42.1 | 42.1 | 41.4 | 41.7 | 41.3 | 41.5 | 41.7 | 41.1 | 41.4 | 41.3 | 41.7 |
| 2019 | 40.6 | 41.3 | 40.8 | 40.7 | 40.4 | 40.7 | 40.2 | 40.0 | 40.4 | 39.7 | 39.6 | 40.1 | 40.4 |
| **Trade, Transportation, and Utilities** | | | | | | | | | | | | | |
| 2015 | 34.4 | 34.9 | 34.8 | 34.6 | 34.5 | 34.3 | 34.4 | 34.4 | 34.2 | 34.2 | 34.3 | 34.4 | 34.4 |
| 2016 | 34.1 | 34.0 | 33.9 | 34.0 | 33.9 | 33.5 | 33.3 | 33.0 | 33.1 | 33.1 | 33.8 | 34.4 | 33.6 |
| 2017 | 33.3 | 33.3 | 33.4 | 33.6 | 33.1 | 33.1 | 33.7 | 33.4 | 32.4 | 34.0 | 33.9 | 34.0 | 33.4 |
| 2018 | 33.5 | 33.5 | 33.9 | 34.0 | 33.8 | 33.9 | 33.9 | 33.7 | 34.1 | 33.4 | 33.6 | 33.9 | 33.8 |
| 2019 | 33.7 | 33.5 | 33.7 | 33.7 | 33.3 | 33.6 | 33.4 | 33.5 | 33.9 | 33.5 | 33.7 | 34.1 | 33.6 |
| **Financial Activities** | | | | | | | | | | | | | |
| 2015 | 37.7 | 38.7 | 38.4 | 37.7 | 37.6 | 37.6 | 37.8 | 38.3 | 37.6 | 37.7 | 38.4 | 38.0 | 38.0 |
| 2016 | 37.8 | 38.0 | 37.9 | 37.7 | 37.9 | 37.5 | 37.8 | 37.6 | 37.9 | 38.4 | 37.8 | 38.2 | 37.9 |
| 2017 | 38.4 | 37.9 | 37.6 | 38.1 | 37.6 | 37.7 | 38.3 | 37.8 | 37.4 | 38.6 | 38.2 | 38.2 | 38.0 |
| 2018 | 38.2 | 38.2 | 38.1 | 38.8 | 37.5 | 37.8 | 38.6 | 38.1 | 38.8 | 38.0 | 37.9 | 38.0 | 38.2 |
| 2019 | 37.9 | 37.6 | 37.6 | 37.8 | 37.4 | 38.1 | 37.3 | 37.3 | 38.2 | 37.4 | 37.2 | 37.9 | 37.6 |
| **Professional and Business Services** | | | | | | | | | | | | | |
| 2015 | 35.0 | 36.0 | 35.8 | 35.6 | 35.7 | 35.7 | 35.6 | 36.3 | 35.4 | 35.6 | 36.0 | 35.6 | 35.7 |
| 2016 | 35.5 | 35.4 | 35.5 | 35.9 | 36.2 | 35.7 | 35.8 | 35.7 | 36.0 | 36.5 | 36.0 | 35.8 | 35.8 |
| 2017 | 36.5 | 36.2 | 36.0 | 36.8 | 36.0 | 36.1 | 36.7 | 36.1 | 34.7 | 36.9 | 36.6 | 36.4 | 36.3 |
| 2018 | 36.3 | 36.6 | 36.6 | 36.9 | 36.4 | 36.6 | 36.7 | 36.4 | 37.3 | 36.5 | 36.3 | 36.7 | 36.6 |
| 2019 | 36.0 | 36.5 | 36.4 | 36.6 | 36.4 | 37.1 | 36.4 | 36.4 | 36.6 | 36.3 | 36.3 | 36.7 | 36.5 |
| **Education and Health Services** | | | | | | | | | | | | | |
| 2015 | 35.1 | 35.1 | 35.2 | 34.8 | 34.8 | 34.7 | 34.8 | 34.9 | 34.6 | 34.5 | 34.9 | 34.5 | 34.8 |
| 2016 | 35.2 | 35.0 | 34.9 | 35.0 | 35.0 | 34.7 | 34.7 | 34.4 | 34.2 | 34.1 | 34.0 | 34.1 | 34.6 |
| 2017 | 34.3 | 34.2 | 33.7 | 34.1 | 34.0 | 33.8 | 34.3 | 34.0 | 34.0 | 34.3 | 34.3 | 34.5 | 34.1 |
| 2018 | 34.2 | 34.5 | 34.3 | 34.6 | 34.2 | 34.2 | 34.2 | 34.2 | 34.5 | 34.3 | 34.5 | 34.4 | 34.3 |
| 2019 | 34.1 | 34.3 | 34.1 | 33.7 | 33.8 | 34.0 | 33.6 | 33.8 | 34.2 | 34.0 | 33.8 | 34.3 | 34.0 |
| **Leisure and Hospitality** | | | | | | | | | | | | | |
| 2015 | 28.4 | 29.1 | 29.2 | 28.4 | 27.8 | 27.7 | 27.8 | 28.0 | 27.0 | 27.1 | 27.7 | 27.5 | 28.0 |
| 2016 | 27.6 | 28.3 | 28.3 | 28.0 | 27.6 | 27.7 | 27.9 | 27.4 | 26.9 | 26.9 | 27.8 | 27.5 | 27.7 |
| 2017 | 27.9 | 28.2 | 29.0 | 28.9 | 27.9 | 28.0 | 28.1 | 27.9 | 25.0 | 28.1 | 28.1 | 28.3 | 28.0 |
| 2018 | 28.4 | 29.4 | 29.6 | 29.0 | 28.2 | 28.3 | 28.5 | 28.0 | 27.3 | 27.5 | 28.2 | 28.3 | 28.4 |
| 2019 | 28.2 | 28.4 | 28.7 | 28.0 | 27.5 | 27.6 | 27.2 | 26.6 | 26.2 | 26.6 | 27.0 | 27.2 | 27.4 |
| **Other Services** | | | | | | | | | | | | | |
| 2015 | 32.7 | 32.7 | 33.1 | 32.4 | 31.9 | 32.5 | 32.4 | 33.0 | 32.7 | 33.2 | 33.3 | 33.4 | 32.8 |
| 2016 | 33.2 | 33.4 | 33.4 | 33.4 | 34.0 | 33.9 | 33.8 | 33.7 | 33.4 | 33.3 | 33.4 | 33.2 | 33.5 |
| 2017 | 33.4 | 33.3 | 33.0 | 33.0 | 32.8 | 33.1 | 33.2 | 33.3 | 30.0 | 32.5 | 32.0 | 33.1 | 32.7 |
| 2018 | 32.8 | 33.7 | 33.6 | 33.9 | 33.3 | 33.7 | 34.1 | 33.6 | 33.4 | 33.0 | 33.7 | 34.3 | 33.6 |
| 2019 | 33.8 | 34.2 | 33.9 | 34.6 | 34.1 | 34.6 | 34.8 | 34.8 | 33.8 | 34.3 | 34.8 | 34.8 | 34.4 |

## 3. Average Hourly Earnings by Selected Industry: Florida, 2015–2019

(Dollars, not seasonally adjusted)

| Industry and year | January | February | March | April | May | June | July | August | September | October | November | December | Annual average |
|---|---|---|---|---|---|---|---|---|---|---|---|---|---|
| **Total Private** | | | | | | | | | | | | | |
| 2015 | 22.32 | 22.53 | 22.45 | 22.42 | 22.51 | 22.41 | 22.55 | 22.80 | 22.80 | 22.81 | 22.98 | 22.88 | 22.63 |
| 2016 | 22.73 | 22.88 | 23.12 | 23.06 | 23.33 | 23.23 | 23.11 | 23.36 | 23.48 | 23.93 | 23.69 | 23.74 | 23.31 |
| 2017 | 23.90 | 23.84 | 23.78 | 24.12 | 23.92 | 23.67 | 24.05 | 23.96 | 24.80 | 24.11 | 24.06 | 24.29 | 24.04 |
| 2018 | 24.38 | 24.42 | 24.40 | 24.79 | 24.80 | 24.72 | 24.87 | 24.72 | 25.20 | 25.11 | 25.01 | 25.32 | 24.81 |
| 2019 | 25.42 | 25.48 | 25.37 | 25.53 | 25.45 | 25.58 | 25.57 | 25.81 | 25.96 | 25.77 | 25.84 | 26.13 | 25.66 |
| **Goods-Producing** | | | | | | | | | | | | | |
| 2015 | 23.01 | 22.92 | 22.95 | 22.93 | 23.03 | 22.90 | 23.12 | 23.43 | 23.36 | 23.23 | 23.41 | 23.18 | 23.13 |
| 2016 | 23.30 | 23.31 | 23.45 | 23.80 | 23.91 | 24.14 | 24.46 | 24.48 | 24.68 | 24.97 | 24.86 | 25.08 | 24.22 |
| 2017 | 25.06 | 24.95 | 24.99 | 25.36 | 25.40 | 25.20 | 25.46 | 25.18 | 26.10 | 24.72 | 24.83 | 25.07 | 25.18 |
| 2018 | 25.19 | 25.29 | 25.36 | 25.72 | 25.99 | 25.91 | 25.77 | 25.83 | 26.16 | 26.31 | 26.13 | 26.35 | 25.84 |
| 2019 | 26.51 | 26.28 | 26.55 | 26.99 | 26.88 | 27.03 | 27.14 | 27.31 | 27.41 | 27.43 | 27.30 | 27.60 | 27.04 |
| **Construction** | | | | | | | | | | | | | |
| 2015 | 22.44 | 22.41 | 22.48 | 22.68 | 22.66 | 22.64 | 22.75 | 23.07 | 22.93 | 22.89 | 23.31 | 23.33 | 22.81 |
| 2016 | 23.12 | 23.18 | 22.94 | 23.28 | 23.28 | 23.20 | 23.65 | 23.46 | 23.85 | 24.27 | 24.22 | 24.45 | 23.59 |
| 2017 | 24.53 | 24.47 | 24.63 | 24.90 | 25.08 | 24.94 | 25.01 | 24.88 | 25.82 | 24.22 | 24.43 | 24.73 | 24.79 |
| 2018 | 24.99 | 24.74 | 24.84 | 25.25 | 25.54 | 25.43 | 25.11 | 25.30 | 25.66 | 25.84 | 25.37 | 25.49 | 25.30 |
| 2019 | 25.41 | 25.42 | 25.53 | 26.08 | 26.10 | 26.40 | 26.57 | 26.72 | 26.88 | 26.94 | 26.65 | 26.91 | 26.31 |
| **Manufacturing** | | | | | | | | | | | | | |
| 2015 | 23.74 | 23.57 | 23.58 | 23.29 | 23.56 | 23.27 | 23.62 | 23.93 | 23.97 | 23.72 | 23.57 | 24.06 | 23.66 |
| 2016 | 24.39 | 24.24 | 24.70 | 24.96 | 25.13 | 25.62 | 25.76 | 26.07 | 26.00 | 26.11 | 25.91 | 26.06 | 25.42 |
| 2017 | 25.93 | 25.72 | 25.58 | 25.97 | 25.85 | 25.54 | 26.12 | 25.64 | 26.49 | 25.49 | 25.45 | 25.59 | 25.77 |
| 2018 | 25.51 | 26.08 | 26.11 | 26.37 | 26.62 | 26.61 | 26.80 | 26.64 | 26.92 | 27.02 | 27.26 | 27.63 | 26.63 |
| 2019 | 28.15 | 27.56 | 28.09 | 28.37 | 28.05 | 28.00 | 28.01 | 28.22 | 28.18 | 28.11 | 28.26 | 28.32 | 28.11 |
| **Trade, Transportation, and Utilities** | | | | | | | | | | | | | |
| 2015 | 19.58 | 19.82 | 19.55 | 19.68 | 20.12 | 20.02 | 20.28 | 20.44 | 20.58 | 20.05 | 20.08 | 20.45 | 20.06 |
| 2016 | 20.35 | 20.49 | 21.10 | 20.68 | 20.78 | 21.41 | 20.82 | 20.86 | 20.65 | 20.72 | 20.46 | 20.13 | 20.70 |
| 2017 | 20.60 | 20.55 | 20.66 | 21.10 | 20.89 | 20.87 | 21.24 | 20.75 | 21.84 | 21.10 | 21.30 | 21.34 | 21.02 |
| 2018 | 21.52 | 21.68 | 21.81 | 22.45 | 22.25 | 22.20 | 22.37 | 21.81 | 22.32 | 22.35 | 22.24 | 22.58 | 22.13 |
| 2019 | 22.87 | 22.92 | 22.67 | 22.79 | 22.68 | 22.79 | 22.75 | 22.91 | 22.95 | 22.94 | 22.96 | 22.82 | 22.84 |
| **Financial Activities** | | | | | | | | | | | | | |
| 2015 | 26.34 | 27.22 | 28.07 | 27.22 | 27.14 | 27.09 | 27.04 | 27.87 | 27.30 | 27.17 | 28.03 | 27.74 | 27.36 |
| 2016 | 27.17 | 27.72 | 27.78 | 26.86 | 28.09 | 26.83 | 26.87 | 28.48 | 27.75 | 28.76 | 28.82 | 28.37 | 27.80 |
| 2017 | 28.87 | 28.73 | 28.17 | 29.12 | 28.68 | 27.65 | 28.66 | 29.06 | 28.87 | 28.97 | 29.17 | 29.12 | 28.76 |
| 2018 | 29.31 | 29.67 | 29.50 | 30.45 | 30.96 | 30.68 | 31.21 | 31.17 | 31.86 | 31.28 | 32.18 | 32.25 | 30.88 |
| 2019 | 31.91 | 32.32 | 31.43 | 31.75 | 31.96 | 32.23 | 31.79 | 32.81 | 32.68 | 32.15 | 32.67 | 33.55 | 32.27 |
| **Professional and Business Services** | | | | | | | | | | | | | |
| 2015 | 25.90 | 26.05 | 26.03 | 25.94 | 25.74 | 25.63 | 25.84 | 26.12 | 26.22 | 26.30 | 26.69 | 26.39 | 26.08 |
| 2016 | 26.42 | 26.67 | 26.61 | 26.85 | 27.10 | 27.04 | 27.03 | 26.69 | 27.05 | 27.74 | 27.56 | 27.97 | 27.07 |
| 2017 | 28.04 | 28.03 | 28.14 | 28.50 | 28.06 | 27.95 | 28.46 | 28.40 | 29.59 | 28.79 | 28.27 | 28.62 | 28.40 |
| 2018 | 29.00 | 28.90 | 28.66 | 28.81 | 28.82 | 28.92 | 29.30 | 29.28 | 29.94 | 29.66 | 29.29 | 29.75 | 29.20 |
| 2019 | 29.54 | 29.81 | 29.56 | 29.57 | 29.70 | 30.03 | 30.10 | 30.26 | 30.19 | 29.80 | 29.95 | 30.71 | 29.94 |
| **Education and Health Services** | | | | | | | | | | | | | |
| 2015 | 24.01 | 24.27 | 24.31 | 24.38 | 24.19 | 24.11 | 24.18 | 24.23 | 24.44 | 24.70 | 24.61 | 24.38 | 24.32 |
| 2016 | 24.13 | 24.37 | 24.48 | 24.49 | 24.39 | 24.32 | 24.42 | 24.57 | 24.93 | 25.49 | 25.27 | 25.52 | 24.70 |
| 2017 | 25.40 | 25.42 | 25.40 | 25.59 | 25.53 | 25.24 | 25.41 | 25.49 | 26.01 | 25.72 | 25.72 | 26.18 | 25.59 |
| 2018 | 26.26 | 26.11 | 26.19 | 26.15 | 26.16 | 26.16 | 26.09 | 26.31 | 26.35 | 26.33 | 26.23 | 26.48 | 26.24 |
| 2019 | 26.36 | 26.33 | 26.50 | 26.64 | 26.28 | 26.24 | 26.37 | 26.40 | 26.52 | 26.58 | 26.78 | 26.81 | 26.49 |
| **Leisure and Hospitality** | | | | | | | | | | | | | |
| 2015 | 14.51 | 14.57 | 14.33 | 14.34 | 14.39 | 14.09 | 14.24 | 14.17 | 14.25 | 14.57 | 14.62 | 14.68 | 14.40 |
| 2016 | 14.76 | 14.82 | 14.89 | 14.95 | 14.95 | 14.76 | 14.82 | 14.88 | 15.07 | 15.35 | 15.35 | 15.49 | 15.01 |
| 2017 | 15.55 | 15.73 | 15.72 | 15.58 | 15.41 | 15.05 | 15.15 | 15.15 | 15.32 | 15.45 | 15.54 | 15.60 | 15.44 |
| 2018 | 15.88 | 16.14 | 16.18 | 16.20 | 15.96 | 15.82 | 15.89 | 15.82 | 15.94 | 16.09 | 16.23 | 16.43 | 16.05 |
| 2019 | 16.39 | 16.95 | 16.94 | 16.84 | 16.70 | 16.51 | 16.25 | 16.33 | 16.37 | 16.57 | 16.73 | 16.81 | 16.62 |
| **Other Services** | | | | | | | | | | | | | |
| 2015 | 19.54 | 19.76 | 19.74 | 19.69 | 19.97 | 20.22 | 20.46 | 20.55 | 20.26 | 20.35 | 20.79 | 20.57 | 20.17 |
| 2016 | 20.55 | 20.74 | 20.84 | 21.11 | 21.14 | 21.22 | 21.59 | 21.48 | 21.95 | 21.82 | 21.37 | 21.19 | 21.25 |
| 2017 | 20.81 | 20.76 | 20.73 | 20.67 | 20.37 | 19.93 | 19.98 | 19.95 | 20.69 | 19.96 | 20.15 | 20.60 | 20.38 |
| 2018 | 19.96 | 20.38 | 20.41 | 20.77 | 20.62 | 20.44 | 20.63 | 20.14 | 20.45 | 20.57 | 20.12 | 20.65 | 20.43 |
| 2019 | 20.94 | 21.18 | 21.26 | 21.25 | 21.09 | 21.12 | 20.93 | 21.33 | 21.76 | 21.39 | 21.29 | 22.20 | 21.31 |

## 4. Average Weekly Earnings by Selected Industry: Florida, 2015–2019

(Dollars, not seasonally adjusted)

| Industry and year | January | February | March | April | May | June | July | August | September | October | November | December | Annual average |
|---|---|---|---|---|---|---|---|---|---|---|---|---|---|
| **Total Private** | | | | | | | | | | | | | |
| 2015 | 761.11 | 781.79 | 779.02 | 769.01 | 769.84 | 764.18 | 771.21 | 786.60 | 772.92 | 777.82 | 792.81 | 784.78 | 776.21 |
| 2016 | 777.37 | 782.50 | 790.70 | 788.65 | 800.22 | 787.50 | 788.05 | 789.57 | 791.28 | 811.23 | 805.46 | 811.91 | 792.54 |
| 2017 | 822.16 | 817.71 | 815.65 | 834.55 | 815.67 | 807.15 | 829.73 | 819.43 | 810.96 | 846.26 | 839.69 | 850.15 | 824.57 |
| 2018 | 845.99 | 854.70 | 854.00 | 870.13 | 858.08 | 860.26 | 867.96 | 857.78 | 876.96 | 863.78 | 867.85 | 878.60 | 863.39 |
| 2019 | 874.45 | 879.06 | 875.27 | 880.79 | 870.39 | 882.51 | 869.38 | 874.96 | 885.24 | 876.18 | 878.56 | 898.87 | 880.14 |
| **Goods-Producing** | | | | | | | | | | | | | |
| 2015 | 906.59 | 907.63 | 922.59 | 912.61 | 918.90 | 918.29 | 922.49 | 939.54 | 904.03 | 931.52 | 948.11 | 936.47 | 922.89 |
| 2016 | 918.02 | 916.08 | 921.59 | 940.10 | 939.66 | 929.39 | 953.94 | 957.17 | 972.39 | 981.32 | 994.40 | 1,008.22 | 954.27 |
| 2017 | 1,007.41 | 1,002.99 | 1,002.10 | 1,004.26 | 1,016.00 | 1,002.96 | 1,023.49 | 1,019.79 | 921.33 | 1,015.99 | 1,015.55 | 1,032.88 | 1,004.68 |
| 2018 | 1,020.20 | 1,029.30 | 1,027.08 | 1,044.23 | 1,047.40 | 1,057.13 | 1,046.26 | 1,056.45 | 1,064.71 | 1,065.56 | 1,068.72 | 1,072.45 | 1,049.10 |
| 2019 | 1,068.35 | 1,051.20 | 1,072.62 | 1,085.00 | 1,080.58 | 1,092.01 | 1,085.60 | 1,092.40 | 1,101.88 | 1,097.20 | 1,092.00 | 1,112.28 | 1,087.01 |
| **Construction** | | | | | | | | | | | | | |
| 2015 | 854.96 | 865.03 | 885.71 | 879.98 | 888.27 | 892.02 | 891.80 | 913.57 | 871.34 | 917.89 | 937.06 | 937.87 | 896.43 |
| 2016 | 892.43 | 901.70 | 887.78 | 903.26 | 905.59 | 886.24 | 915.26 | 914.94 | 942.08 | 948.96 | 968.80 | 975.56 | 920.01 |
| 2017 | 976.29 | 973.91 | 980.27 | 971.10 | 990.66 | 972.66 | 995.40 | 995.20 | 875.30 | 968.80 | 979.64 | 991.67 | 974.25 |
| 2018 | 989.60 | 977.23 | 981.18 | 999.90 | 1,011.38 | 1,019.74 | 1,006.91 | 1,024.65 | 1,026.40 | 1,036.18 | 1,024.95 | 1,022.15 | 1,009.47 |
| 2019 | 1,011.32 | 988.84 | 1,018.65 | 1,035.38 | 1,038.78 | 1,056.00 | 1,054.83 | 1,063.46 | 1,075.20 | 1,077.60 | 1,066.00 | 1,081.78 | 1,047.14 |
| **Manufacturing** | | | | | | | | | | | | | |
| 2015 | 966.22 | 954.59 | 964.42 | 947.90 | 951.82 | 947.09 | 956.61 | 971.56 | 949.21 | 953.54 | 964.01 | 981.65 | 958.23 |
| 2016 | 987.80 | 969.60 | 990.47 | 1,005.89 | 1,002.69 | 1,011.99 | 1,027.82 | 1,037.59 | 1,034.80 | 1,047.01 | 1,049.36 | 1,068.46 | 1,019.34 |
| 2017 | 1,057.94 | 1,051.95 | 1,043.66 | 1,054.38 | 1,052.10 | 1,042.03 | 1,063.08 | 1,056.37 | 988.08 | 1,085.87 | 1,068.90 | 1,105.49 | 1,056.57 |
| 2018 | 1,073.97 | 1,111.01 | 1,099.23 | 1,110.18 | 1,102.07 | 1,109.64 | 1,106.84 | 1,105.56 | 1,122.56 | 1,110.52 | 1,128.56 | 1,141.12 | 1,110.47 |
| 2019 | 1,142.89 | 1,138.23 | 1,146.07 | 1,154.66 | 1,133.22 | 1,139.60 | 1,126.00 | 1,128.80 | 1,138.47 | 1,115.97 | 1,119.10 | 1,135.63 | 1,135.64 |
| **Trade, Transportation, and Utilities** | | | | | | | | | | | | | |
| 2015 | 673.55 | 691.72 | 680.34 | 680.93 | 694.14 | 686.69 | 697.63 | 703.14 | 703.84 | 685.71 | 688.74 | 703.48 | 690.06 |
| 2016 | 693.94 | 696.66 | 715.29 | 703.12 | 704.44 | 717.24 | 693.31 | 688.38 | 683.52 | 685.83 | 677.23 | 680.39 | 695.52 |
| 2017 | 685.98 | 684.32 | 690.04 | 708.96 | 691.46 | 690.80 | 715.79 | 693.05 | 707.62 | 717.40 | 722.07 | 725.56 | 702.07 |
| 2018 | 720.92 | 726.28 | 739.36 | 763.30 | 752.05 | 752.58 | 758.34 | 735.00 | 761.11 | 746.49 | 747.26 | 765.46 | 747.99 |
| 2019 | 770.72 | 767.82 | 763.98 | 768.02 | 755.24 | 765.74 | 759.85 | 767.49 | 778.01 | 768.49 | 773.75 | 778.16 | 767.42 |
| **Financial Activities** | | | | | | | | | | | | | |
| 2015 | 993.02 | 1,053.41 | 1,077.89 | 1,026.19 | 1,020.46 | 1,018.58 | 1,022.11 | 1,067.42 | 1,026.48 | 1,024.31 | 1,076.35 | 1,054.12 | 1,039.68 |
| 2016 | 1,027.03 | 1,053.36 | 1,052.86 | 1,012.62 | 1,064.61 | 1,006.13 | 1,015.69 | 1,070.85 | 1,051.73 | 1,104.38 | 1,089.40 | 1,083.73 | 1,053.62 |
| 2017 | 1,108.61 | 1,088.87 | 1,059.19 | 1,109.47 | 1,078.37 | 1,042.41 | 1,097.68 | 1,098.47 | 1,079.74 | 1,118.24 | 1,114.29 | 1,112.38 | 1,092.88 |
| 2018 | 1,119.64 | 1,133.39 | 1,123.95 | 1,181.46 | 1,161.00 | 1,159.70 | 1,204.71 | 1,187.58 | 1,236.17 | 1,188.64 | 1,219.62 | 1,225.50 | 1,179.62 |
| 2019 | 1,209.39 | 1,215.23 | 1,181.77 | 1,200.15 | 1,195.30 | 1,227.96 | 1,185.77 | 1,223.81 | 1,248.38 | 1,202.41 | 1,215.32 | 1,271.55 | 1,213.35 |
| **Professional and Business Services** | | | | | | | | | | | | | |
| 2015 | 906.50 | 937.80 | 931.87 | 923.46 | 918.92 | 914.99 | 919.90 | 948.16 | 928.19 | 936.28 | 960.84 | 939.48 | 931.06 |
| 2016 | 937.91 | 944.12 | 944.66 | 963.92 | 981.02 | 965.33 | 967.67 | 952.83 | 973.80 | 1,012.51 | 992.16 | 1,001.33 | 969.11 |
| 2017 | 1,023.46 | 1,014.69 | 1,013.04 | 1,048.80 | 1,010.16 | 1,009.00 | 1,044.48 | 1,025.24 | 1,026.77 | 1,062.35 | 1,034.68 | 1,041.77 | 1,030.92 |
| 2018 | 1,052.70 | 1,057.74 | 1,048.96 | 1,063.09 | 1,049.05 | 1,058.47 | 1,075.31 | 1,065.79 | 1,116.76 | 1,082.59 | 1,063.23 | 1,091.83 | 1,068.72 |
| 2019 | 1,063.44 | 1,088.07 | 1,075.98 | 1,082.26 | 1,081.08 | 1,114.11 | 1,095.64 | 1,101.46 | 1,104.95 | 1,081.74 | 1,087.19 | 1,127.06 | 1,092.81 |
| **Education and Health Services** | | | | | | | | | | | | | |
| 2015 | 842.75 | 851.88 | 855.71 | 848.42 | 841.81 | 836.62 | 841.46 | 845.63 | 845.62 | 852.15 | 858.89 | 841.11 | 846.34 |
| 2016 | 849.38 | 852.95 | 854.35 | 857.15 | 853.65 | 843.90 | 847.37 | 845.21 | 852.61 | 869.21 | 859.18 | 870.23 | 854.62 |
| 2017 | 871.22 | 869.36 | 855.98 | 872.62 | 868.02 | 853.11 | 871.56 | 866.66 | 884.34 | 882.20 | 882.20 | 903.21 | 872.62 |
| 2018 | 898.09 | 900.80 | 898.32 | 904.79 | 894.67 | 894.67 | 892.28 | 899.80 | 909.08 | 903.12 | 904.94 | 910.91 | 900.03 |
| 2019 | 898.88 | 903.12 | 903.65 | 897.77 | 888.26 | 892.16 | 886.03 | 892.32 | 906.98 | 903.72 | 905.16 | 919.58 | 900.66 |
| **Leisure and Hospitality** | | | | | | | | | | | | | |
| 2015 | 412.08 | 423.99 | 418.44 | 407.26 | 400.04 | 390.29 | 395.87 | 396.76 | 384.75 | 394.85 | 404.97 | 403.98 | 403.20 |
| 2016 | 407.38 | 419.41 | 421.39 | 418.60 | 412.62 | 408.85 | 413.48 | 407.71 | 405.38 | 412.92 | 426.73 | 425.98 | 415.78 |
| 2017 | 433.85 | 443.59 | 455.88 | 450.26 | 429.94 | 421.40 | 425.72 | 422.69 | 383.00 | 434.15 | 436.67 | 441.48 | 432.32 |
| 2018 | 450.99 | 474.52 | 478.93 | 469.80 | 450.07 | 447.71 | 452.87 | 442.96 | 435.16 | 442.48 | 457.69 | 464.97 | 455.82 |
| 2019 | 462.20 | 481.38 | 486.18 | 471.52 | 459.25 | 455.68 | 442.00 | 434.38 | 428.89 | 440.76 | 451.71 | 457.23 | 455.39 |
| **Other Services** | | | | | | | | | | | | | |
| 2015 | 638.96 | 646.15 | 653.39 | 637.96 | 637.04 | 657.15 | 662.90 | 678.15 | 662.50 | 675.62 | 692.31 | 687.04 | 661.58 |
| 2016 | 682.26 | 692.72 | 696.06 | 705.07 | 718.76 | 719.36 | 729.74 | 723.88 | 733.13 | 726.61 | 713.76 | 703.51 | 711.88 |
| 2017 | 695.05 | 691.31 | 684.09 | 682.11 | 668.14 | 659.68 | 663.34 | 664.34 | 620.70 | 648.70 | 644.80 | 681.86 | 666.43 |
| 2018 | 654.69 | 686.81 | 685.78 | 704.10 | 686.65 | 688.83 | 703.48 | 676.70 | 683.03 | 678.81 | 678.04 | 708.30 | 686.45 |
| 2019 | 707.77 | 724.36 | 720.71 | 735.25 | 719.17 | 730.75 | 728.36 | 742.28 | 735.49 | 733.68 | 740.89 | 772.56 | 733.06 |

# GEORGIA
*At a Glance*

Population:
  2010 census: 9,687,653
  2019 estimate: 10,617,423

Percent change in population:
  2010–2019: 9.6%

Percent change in total nonfarm employment:
  2011–2019: 18.3%

Industry with the largest growth in employment, 2011–2019 (percent):
  Mining, Logging, and Construction: 36.8%

Industry with the largest decline or smallest growth in employment, 2011–2019 (percent):
  Government, 0.7%

Civilian labor force:
  2010: 4,696,676
  2019: 5,110,318

Unemployment rate and rank among states (highest to lowest):
  2010: 10.5%, 9th
  2019: 3.4%, 28th

Over-the-year change in unemployment rates:
  2017–2018: -0.8%
  2018–2019: -0.5%

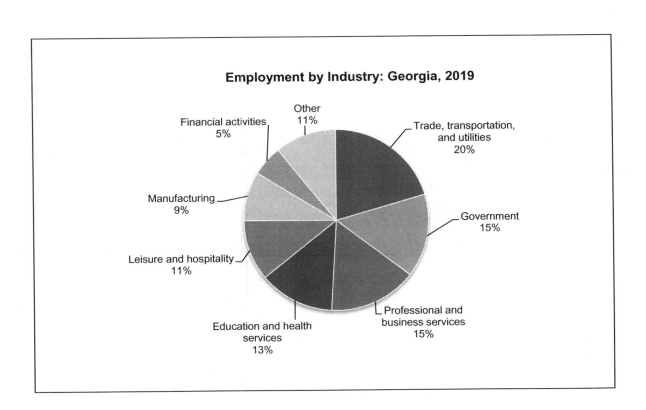

**Employment by Industry: Georgia, 2019**

- Other 11%
- Financial activities 5%
- Trade, transportation, and utilities 20%
- Government 15%
- Manufacturing 9%
- Professional and business services 15%
- Leisure and hospitality 11%
- Education and health services 13%

## 1. Employment by Industry: Georgia, 2011–2019

(Numbers in thousands, not seasonally adjusted)

| Industry and year | January | February | March | April | May | June | July | August | September | October | November | December | Annual average |
|---|---|---|---|---|---|---|---|---|---|---|---|---|---|
| **Total Nonfarm** | | | | | | | | | | | | | |
| 2011 | 3,804.5 | 3,855.6 | 3,876.8 | 3,916.6 | 3,926.3 | 3,904.2 | 3,885.5 | 3,910.3 | 3,909.4 | 3,929.2 | 3,948.5 | 3,935.2 | 3,900.2 |
| 2012 | 3,876.3 | 3,897.9 | 3,921.3 | 3,955.0 | 3,972.0 | 3,957.1 | 3,926.0 | 3,961.1 | 3,955.0 | 3,992.2 | 4,022.7 | 4,009.8 | 3,953.9 |
| 2013 | 3,949.9 | 3,977.8 | 3,992.9 | 4,026.6 | 4,039.6 | 4,023.3 | 4,005.4 | 4,043.6 | 4,043.3 | 4,078.2 | 4,107.1 | 4,101.4 | 4,032.4 |
| 2014 | 4,035.8 | 4,045.3 | 4,087.1 | 4,128.9 | 4,152.7 | 4,138.7 | 4,129.4 | 4,174.0 | 4,171.6 | 4,198.9 | 4,232.7 | 4,241.9 | 4,144.8 |
| 2015 | 4,160.8 | 4,187.1 | 4,207.7 | 4,235.5 | 4,261.3 | 4,261.7 | 4,242.7 | 4,277.3 | 4,281.5 | 4,321.0 | 4,344.1 | 4,356.2 | 4,261.4 |
| 2016 | 4,277.4 | 4,301.8 | 4,314.8 | 4,360.3 | 4,372.9 | 4,368.8 | 4,352.1 | 4,385.8 | 4,397.8 | 4,417.4 | 4,452.1 | 4,455.1 | 4,371.4 |
| 2017 | 4,367.0 | 4,392.9 | 4,419.3 | 4,436.0 | 4,449.8 | 4,456.9 | 4,428.5 | 4,468.4 | 4,455.8 | 4,499.9 | 4,529.9 | 4,527.1 | 4,452.6 |
| 2018 | 4,442.2 | 4,474.7 | 4,501.9 | 4,513.3 | 4,532.1 | 4,535.1 | 4,515.9 | 4,558.5 | 4,556.1 | 4,579.6 | 4,613.4 | 4,608.5 | 4,535.9 |
| 2019 | 4,548.7 | 4,575.5 | 4,592.5 | 4,598.1 | 4,613.5 | 4,609.4 | 4,586.9 | 4,624.3 | 4,619.8 | 4,651.0 | 4,674.7 | 4,671.7 | 4,613.8 |
| **Total Private** | | | | | | | | | | | | | |
| 2010 | 3,117.4 | 3,161.9 | 3,181.0 | 3,224.8 | 3,232.8 | 3,223.2 | 3,224.8 | 3,237.2 | 3,225.5 | 3,240.3 | 3,256.7 | 3,246.3 | 3,214.3 |
| 2011 | 3,194.5 | 3,211.0 | 3,229.2 | 3,262.9 | 3,282.1 | 3,276.1 | 3,271.2 | 3,288.7 | 3,272.3 | 3,303.2 | 3,327.7 | 3,320.5 | 3,270.0 |
| 2012 | 3,266.8 | 3,289.2 | 3,303.2 | 3,336.7 | 3,354.7 | 3,353.0 | 3,356.0 | 3,377.8 | 3,366.1 | 3,394.8 | 3,420.2 | 3,417.6 | 3,353.0 |
| 2013 | 3,364.4 | 3,369.3 | 3,408.0 | 3,447.6 | 3,470.2 | 3,470.0 | 3,480.8 | 3,503.6 | 3,493.2 | 3,516.1 | 3,545.1 | 3,559.3 | 3,469.0 |
| 2014 | 3,486.2 | 3,506.9 | 3,526.7 | 3,554.2 | 3,582.6 | 3,592.8 | 3,593.0 | 3,606.9 | 3,603.7 | 3,636.3 | 3,656.7 | 3,671.8 | 3,584.8 |
| 2015 | 3,601.0 | 3,619.4 | 3,636.2 | 3,676.3 | 3,689.9 | 3,693.2 | 3,701.9 | 3,711.6 | 3,713.7 | 3,729.5 | 3,758.1 | 3,766.8 | 3,691.5 |
| 2016 | 3,688.5 | 3,707.9 | 3,732.2 | 3,747.2 | 3,763.2 | 3,776.8 | 3,771.3 | 3,788.3 | 3,767.5 | 3,807.9 | 3,834.8 | 3,835.5 | 3,768.4 |
| 2017 | 3,755.9 | 3,783.6 | 3,809.5 | 3,821.4 | 3,837.2 | 3,851.3 | 3,852.1 | 3,870.4 | 3,863.1 | 3,882.3 | 3,912.0 | 3,909.8 | 3,845.7 |
| 2018 | 3,861.9 | 3,882.7 | 3,897.8 | 3,903.7 | 3,919.5 | 3,928.7 | 3,922.3 | 3,936.6 | 3,926.7 | 3,953.5 | 3,974.7 | 3,973.7 | 3,923.5 |
| 2019 | | | | | | | | | | | | | |
| **Goods Producing** | | | | | | | | | | | | | |
| 2011 | 490.5 | 499.5 | 502.9 | 507.1 | 508.5 | 509.0 | 509.9 | 510.0 | 507.3 | 506.1 | 505.1 | 502.6 | 504.9 |
| 2012 | 497.8 | 499.3 | 500.8 | 502.8 | 504.3 | 504.7 | 505.7 | 507.0 | 506.4 | 507.8 | 508.9 | 506.3 | 504.3 |
| 2013 | 501.9 | 504.3 | 507.2 | 507.1 | 510.2 | 511.7 | 514.0 | 516.3 | 515.9 | 518.0 | 520.5 | 519.9 | 512.3 |
| 2014 | 517.2 | 519.8 | 524.5 | 527.6 | 531.5 | 534.7 | 538.4 | 541.9 | 542.5 | 544.7 | 545.2 | 547.0 | 534.6 |
| 2015 | 543.4 | 547.3 | 548.1 | 551.5 | 555.2 | 558.3 | 558.9 | 560.1 | 561.3 | 563.9 | 564.1 | 567.4 | 556.6 |
| 2016 | 562.9 | 566.6 | 569.0 | 572.5 | 573.9 | 577.5 | 580.8 | 582.0 | 583.0 | 583.0 | 585.8 | 587.7 | 577.1 |
| 2017 | 582.7 | 586.5 | 588.6 | 587.3 | 590.0 | 594.7 | 594.0 | 594.8 | 594.0 | 596.4 | 597.3 | 600.5 | 592.2 |
| 2018 | 595.1 | 602.2 | 605.0 | 604.5 | 607.9 | 612.7 | 612.1 | 613.9 | 615.3 | 615.2 | 613.7 | 616.7 | 609.5 |
| 2019 | 612.5 | 616.5 | 618.3 | 617.8 | 620.5 | 623.2 | 622.3 | 622.6 | 621.8 | 617.1 | 617.9 | 616.5 | 618.9 |
| **Service-Providing** | | | | | | | | | | | | | |
| 2011 | 3,314.0 | 3,356.1 | 3,373.9 | 3,409.5 | 3,417.8 | 3,395.2 | 3,375.6 | 3,400.3 | 3,402.1 | 3,423.1 | 3,443.4 | 3,432.6 | 3,395.3 |
| 2012 | 3,378.5 | 3,398.6 | 3,420.5 | 3,452.2 | 3,467.7 | 3,452.4 | 3,420.3 | 3,454.1 | 3,448.6 | 3,484.4 | 3,513.8 | 3,503.5 | 3,449.6 |
| 2013 | 3,448.0 | 3,473.5 | 3,485.7 | 3,519.5 | 3,529.4 | 3,511.6 | 3,491.4 | 3,527.3 | 3,527.4 | 3,560.2 | 3,586.6 | 3,581.5 | 3,520.2 |
| 2014 | 3,518.6 | 3,525.5 | 3,562.6 | 3,601.3 | 3,621.2 | 3,604.0 | 3,591.0 | 3,632.1 | 3,629.1 | 3,654.2 | 3,687.5 | 3,694.9 | 3,610.2 |
| 2015 | 3,617.4 | 3,639.8 | 3,659.6 | 3,684.0 | 3,706.1 | 3,703.4 | 3,683.8 | 3,717.2 | 3,720.2 | 3,757.1 | 3,780.0 | 3,788.8 | 3,704.8 |
| 2016 | 3,714.5 | 3,735.2 | 3,745.8 | 3,787.8 | 3,799.0 | 3,791.3 | 3,771.3 | 3,803.8 | 3,814.8 | 3,834.4 | 3,866.3 | 3,867.4 | 3,794.3 |
| 2017 | 3,784.3 | 3,806.4 | 3,830.7 | 3,848.7 | 3,859.8 | 3,862.2 | 3,834.5 | 3,873.6 | 3,861.8 | 3,903.5 | 3,932.6 | 3,926.6 | 3,860.4 |
| 2018 | 3,847.1 | 3,872.5 | 3,896.9 | 3,908.8 | 3,924.2 | 3,922.4 | 3,903.8 | 3,944.6 | 3,940.8 | 3,964.4 | 3,999.7 | 3,991.8 | 3,926.4 |
| 2019 | 3,936.2 | 3,959.0 | 3,974.2 | 3,980.3 | 3,993.0 | 3,986.2 | 3,964.6 | 4,001.7 | 3,998.0 | 4,033.9 | 4,056.8 | 4,055.2 | 3,994.9 |
| **Mining, Logging, and Construction** | | | | | | | | | | | | | |
| 2011 | 147.6 | 153.3 | 156.0 | 157.9 | 157.6 | 157.9 | 158.5 | 158.1 | 157.3 | 156.4 | 154.7 | 152.2 | 155.6 |
| 2012 | 147.9 | 149.1 | 149.7 | 150.6 | 150.6 | 150.8 | 152.4 | 153.3 | 152.3 | 153.3 | 153.4 | 150.9 | 151.2 |
| 2013 | 148.2 | 149.7 | 151.9 | 152.4 | 155.2 | 156.1 | 157.8 | 159.3 | 159.4 | 160.5 | 161.9 | 160.2 | 156.1 |
| 2014 | 158.3 | 159.8 | 162.2 | 164.2 | 166.6 | 168.2 | 170.8 | 172.2 | 172.7 | 174.7 | 174.0 | 174.4 | 168.2 |
| 2015 | 171.4 | 173.6 | 173.5 | 177.1 | 178.2 | 180.2 | 180.7 | 181.2 | 181.4 | 183.4 | 182.6 | 183.9 | 178.9 |
| 2016 | 179.7 | 182.2 | 184.0 | 186.3 | 187.5 | 189.8 | 192.5 | 192.6 | 193.8 | 193.8 | 194.9 | 194.9 | 189.3 |
| 2017 | 191.3 | 193.2 | 194.5 | 193.6 | 195.8 | 198.1 | 197.0 | 197.2 | 197.4 | 198.5 | 198.3 | 199.5 | 196.2 |
| 2018 | 195.5 | 199.8 | 202.1 | 203.0 | 204.9 | 207.3 | 207.6 | 207.9 | 208.5 | 208.7 | 206.5 | 208.1 | 205.0 |
| 2019 | 207.5 | 210.3 | 211.6 | 211.2 | 213.7 | 215.7 | 214.6 | 214.7 | 214.0 | 213.4 | 213.9 | 213.0 | 212.8 |
| **Manufacturing** | | | | | | | | | | | | | |
| 2011 | 342.9 | 346.2 | 346.9 | 349.2 | 350.9 | 351.1 | 351.4 | 351.9 | 350.0 | 349.7 | 350.4 | 350.4 | 349.3 |
| 2012 | 349.9 | 350.2 | 351.1 | 352.2 | 353.7 | 353.9 | 353.3 | 353.7 | 354.1 | 354.5 | 355.5 | 355.4 | 353.1 |
| 2013 | 353.7 | 354.6 | 355.3 | 354.7 | 355.0 | 355.6 | 356.2 | 357.0 | 356.5 | 357.5 | 358.6 | 359.7 | 356.2 |
| 2014 | 358.9 | 360.0 | 362.3 | 363.4 | 364.9 | 366.5 | 367.6 | 369.7 | 369.8 | 370.0 | 371.2 | 372.6 | 366.4 |
| 2015 | 372.0 | 373.7 | 374.6 | 374.4 | 377.0 | 378.1 | 378.2 | 378.9 | 379.9 | 380.5 | 381.5 | 383.5 | 377.7 |
| 2016 | 383.2 | 384.4 | 385.0 | 386.2 | 386.4 | 387.7 | 388.3 | 389.4 | 389.2 | 389.2 | 390.9 | 392.8 | 387.7 |
| 2017 | 391.4 | 393.3 | 394.1 | 393.7 | 394.2 | 396.6 | 397.0 | 397.6 | 396.6 | 397.9 | 399.0 | 401.0 | 396.0 |
| 2018 | 399.6 | 402.4 | 402.9 | 401.5 | 403.0 | 405.4 | 404.5 | 406.0 | 406.8 | 406.5 | 407.2 | 408.6 | 404.5 |
| 2019 | 405.0 | 406.2 | 406.7 | 406.6 | 406.8 | 407.5 | 407.7 | 407.9 | 407.8 | 403.7 | 404.0 | 403.5 | 406.1 |

# 1. Employment by Industry: Georgia, 2011–2019—*Continued*

(Numbers in thousands, not seasonally adjusted)

| Industry and year | January | February | March | April | May | June | July | August | September | October | November | December | Annual average |
|---|---|---|---|---|---|---|---|---|---|---|---|---|---|
| **Trade, Transportation, and Utilities** | | | | | | | | | | | | | |
| 2011 | 790.7 | 795.2 | 797.3 | 804.5 | 807.6 | 805.9 | 806.4 | 807.9 | 804.3 | 814.0 | 827.9 | 830.4 | 807.7 |
| 2012 | 809.1 | 806.0 | 808.1 | 813.5 | 818.6 | 815.4 | 815.8 | 816.8 | 813.3 | 823.7 | 842.2 | 843.4 | 818.8 |
| 2013 | 817.1 | 815.0 | 815.2 | 819.3 | 823.8 | 824.5 | 828.2 | 832.1 | 828.7 | 838.8 | 856.0 | 862.6 | 830.1 |
| 2014 | 836.9 | 832.1 | 838.0 | 845.5 | 850.2 | 850.5 | 852.9 | 855.6 | 854.0 | 866.3 | 887.0 | 897.2 | 855.5 |
| 2015 | 864.4 | 861.3 | 865.9 | 870.8 | 876.6 | 880.0 | 879.8 | 882.1 | 881.9 | 894.8 | 914.0 | 921.6 | 882.8 |
| 2016 | 890.3 | 887.5 | 890.9 | 893.8 | 897.2 | 897.4 | 898.9 | 898.2 | 898.8 | 906.2 | 928.2 | 938.1 | 902.1 |
| 2017 | 905.4 | 903.2 | 906.0 | 905.9 | 907.8 | 909.9 | 910.6 | 912.0 | 909.6 | 919.8 | 943.5 | 948.1 | 915.2 |
| 2018 | 916.7 | 916.0 | 919.5 | 922.0 | 925.7 | 926.1 | 927.8 | 928.6 | 928.6 | 936.3 | 962.2 | 966.6 | 931.3 |
| 2019 | 940.1 | 933.8 | 936.2 | 934.8 | 938.7 | 940.1 | 940.3 | 937.3 | 938.1 | 946.4 | 967.0 | 974.8 | 944.0 |
| **Wholesale Trade** | | | | | | | | | | | | | |
| 2011 | 187.0 | 188.0 | 187.9 | 190.0 | 190.8 | 190.1 | 191.2 | 191.7 | 190.8 | 192.4 | 192.4 | 191.5 | 190.3 |
| 2012 | 190.6 | 191.7 | 191.6 | 193.1 | 194.3 | 193.5 | 194.7 | 195.2 | 194.0 | 196.4 | 196.8 | 196.2 | 194.0 |
| 2013 | 194.2 | 195.1 | 194.5 | 195.8 | 196.1 | 195.8 | 196.2 | 196.4 | 195.3 | 197.8 | 198.4 | 198.0 | 196.1 |
| 2014 | 197.2 | 197.8 | 197.9 | 199.0 | 199.8 | 200.0 | 200.8 | 201.3 | 200.9 | 202.7 | 204.1 | 204.3 | 200.5 |
| 2015 | 202.2 | 203.3 | 203.9 | 204.5 | 205.7 | 206.0 | 206.9 | 207.2 | 206.8 | 209.1 | 209.2 | 208.9 | 206.1 |
| 2016 | 206.6 | 206.4 | 206.9 | 207.8 | 208.0 | 208.2 | 208.1 | 207.7 | 207.7 | 207.7 | 207.8 | 208.5 | 207.6 |
| 2017 | 206.2 | 207.2 | 207.6 | 207.6 | 207.9 | 209.0 | 209.6 | 209.4 | 209.7 | 210.2 | 210.7 | 211.3 | 208.9 |
| 2018 | 210.0 | 211.3 | 212.0 | 212.1 | 212.8 | 214.3 | 215.4 | 214.9 | 214.9 | 216.7 | 217.3 | 217.9 | 214.1 |
| 2019 | 215.3 | 216.3 | 216.3 | 215.4 | 216.5 | 217.3 | 216.2 | 216.6 | 216.0 | 218.9 | 219.2 | 220.0 | 217.0 |
| **Retail Trade** | | | | | | | | | | | | | |
| 2011 | 435.6 | 437.0 | 438.6 | 443.2 | 444.5 | 442.9 | 443.0 | 443.1 | 440.2 | 447.5 | 460.2 | 461.4 | 444.8 |
| 2012 | 444.8 | 440.8 | 442.5 | 445.4 | 448.4 | 446.2 | 446.2 | 446.4 | 444.1 | 451.6 | 468.6 | 468.0 | 449.4 |
| 2013 | 447.0 | 445.6 | 446.4 | 449.5 | 452.4 | 453.2 | 456.6 | 459.5 | 457.6 | 464.0 | 478.7 | 483.1 | 457.8 |
| 2014 | 461.6 | 457.4 | 460.7 | 464.7 | 467.0 | 466.6 | 468.3 | 469.1 | 467.7 | 474.5 | 492.0 | 497.0 | 470.6 |
| 2015 | 470.7 | 469.0 | 472.4 | 477.5 | 479.7 | 481.6 | 479.9 | 481.2 | 481.0 | 487.2 | 503.2 | 506.2 | 482.5 |
| 2016 | 482.9 | 481.5 | 484.2 | 486.7 | 488.2 | 486.9 | 488.5 | 488.1 | 487.6 | 493.1 | 509.8 | 512.6 | 490.8 |
| 2017 | 491.6 | 489.7 | 491.0 | 491.8 | 492.1 | 491.8 | 491.9 | 492.1 | 487.9 | 494.4 | 512.4 | 513.0 | 495.0 |
| 2018 | 492.1 | 489.6 | 491.6 | 492.3 | 494.1 | 491.8 | 492.8 | 491.7 | 490.5 | 492.9 | 510.7 | 510.4 | 495.0 |
| 2019 | 492.9 | 488.1 | 489.7 | 490.4 | 492.5 | 491.4 | 490.4 | 488.9 | 487.5 | 490.8 | 506.3 | 509.5 | 493.2 |
| **Transportation and Utilities** | | | | | | | | | | | | | |
| 2011 | 168.1 | 170.2 | 170.8 | 171.3 | 172.3 | 172.9 | 172.2 | 173.1 | 173.3 | 174.1 | 175.3 | 177.5 | 172.6 |
| 2012 | 173.7 | 173.5 | 174.0 | 175.0 | 175.9 | 175.7 | 174.9 | 175.2 | 175.2 | 175.7 | 176.8 | 179.2 | 175.4 |
| 2013 | 175.9 | 174.3 | 174.3 | 174.0 | 175.3 | 175.5 | 175.4 | 176.2 | 175.8 | 177.0 | 178.9 | 181.5 | 176.2 |
| 2014 | 178.1 | 176.9 | 179.4 | 181.8 | 183.4 | 183.9 | 183.8 | 185.2 | 185.4 | 189.1 | 190.9 | 195.9 | 184.5 |
| 2015 | 191.5 | 189.0 | 189.6 | 188.8 | 191.2 | 192.4 | 193.0 | 193.7 | 194.1 | 198.5 | 201.6 | 206.5 | 194.2 |
| 2016 | 200.8 | 199.6 | 199.8 | 199.3 | 201.0 | 202.3 | 202.3 | 202.4 | 203.5 | 205.4 | 210.6 | 217.0 | 203.7 |
| 2017 | 207.6 | 206.3 | 207.4 | 206.5 | 207.8 | 209.1 | 209.1 | 210.5 | 212.0 | 215.2 | 220.4 | 223.8 | 211.3 |
| 2018 | 214.6 | 215.1 | 215.9 | 217.6 | 218.8 | 220.0 | 219.6 | 222.0 | 223.2 | 226.7 | 234.2 | 238.3 | 222.2 |
| 2019 | 231.9 | 229.4 | 230.2 | 229.0 | 229.7 | 231.4 | 233.7 | 231.8 | 234.6 | 236.7 | 241.5 | 245.3 | 233.8 |
| **Information** | | | | | | | | | | | | | |
| 2011 | 97.0 | 97.8 | 97.7 | 98.4 | 98.3 | 97.7 | 98.5 | 98.7 | 98.3 | 98.7 | 100.2 | 98.4 | 98.3 |
| 2012 | 98.3 | 99.5 | 99.4 | 99.1 | 100.3 | 100.1 | 100.8 | 101.1 | 100.8 | 102.1 | 102.6 | 102.6 | 100.6 |
| 2013 | 100.4 | 101.5 | 101.7 | 102.7 | 103.5 | 102.7 | 103.4 | 103.7 | 103.7 | 105.6 | 105.5 | 105.7 | 103.3 |
| 2014 | 105.5 | 106.4 | 107.0 | 108.0 | 108.7 | 110.1 | 110.1 | 109.4 | 109.0 | 111.0 | 111.7 | 111.8 | 109.1 |
| 2015 | 108.6 | 109.5 | 109.6 | 110.7 | 113.0 | 113.1 | 115.3 | 113.3 | 111.3 | 115.8 | 116.7 | 116.9 | 112.8 |
| 2016 | 110.5 | 112.4 | 110.7 | 113.6 | 113.2 | 113.4 | 114.9 | 112.7 | 113.9 | 115.0 | 115.9 | 114.5 | 113.4 |
| 2017 | 114.6 | 116.3 | 116.3 | 117.3 | 118.1 | 118.0 | 117.4 | 120.0 | 117.4 | 123.6 | 123.2 | 120.2 | 118.5 |
| 2018 | 114.0 | 115.0 | 115.4 | 113.4 | 113.4 | 113.6 | 113.3 | 114.9 | 115.3 | 117.7 | 117.7 | 114.2 | 114.8 |
| 2019 | 114.8 | 118.5 | 118.0 | 115.6 | 115.3 | 117.6 | 117.5 | 120.0 | 116.3 | 116.9 | 118.1 | 115.9 | 117.0 |
| **Financial Activities** | | | | | | | | | | | | | |
| 2011 | 219.3 | 219.9 | 220.0 | 222.8 | 223.4 | 223.7 | 224.2 | 225.1 | 225.0 | 226.2 | 226.5 | 226.6 | 223.6 |
| 2012 | 225.4 | 225.9 | 226.2 | 226.1 | 226.3 | 226.4 | 227.3 | 227.6 | 226.3 | 228.2 | 229.3 | 229.0 | 227.0 |
| 2013 | 226.8 | 227.7 | 228.0 | 228.8 | 229.2 | 229.2 | 229.6 | 230.1 | 228.5 | 230.3 | 231.5 | 230.8 | 229.2 |
| 2014 | 229.1 | 229.3 | 229.6 | 230.3 | 231.1 | 231.1 | 231.6 | 232.2 | 230.4 | 232.3 | 232.5 | 232.6 | 231.0 |
| 2015 | 230.7 | 231.1 | 231.5 | 232.6 | 233.4 | 234.0 | 234.2 | 233.7 | 232.7 | 234.5 | 234.8 | 235.3 | 233.2 |
| 2016 | 233.7 | 233.8 | 234.0 | 235.1 | 236.4 | 237.0 | 238.5 | 238.3 | 237.9 | 239.1 | 239.4 | 239.6 | 236.9 |
| 2017 | 236.6 | 237.6 | 238.5 | 238.6 | 240.1 | 241.8 | 242.2 | 242.2 | 242.0 | 243.8 | 243.7 | 244.7 | 241.0 |
| 2018 | 241.1 | 242.9 | 243.5 | 243.9 | 244.7 | 246.2 | 246.7 | 247.0 | 246.9 | 247.9 | 250.3 | 248.9 | 245.8 |
| 2019 | 245.9 | 247.3 | 247.8 | 248.5 | 249.5 | 250.3 | 251.8 | 253.8 | 251.1 | 251.6 | 252.0 | 252.4 | 250.2 |

## 1. Employment by Industry: Georgia, 2011–2019—*Continued*

(Numbers in thousands, not seasonally adjusted)

| Industry and year | January | February | March | April | May | June | July | August | September | October | November | December | Annual average |
|---|---|---|---|---|---|---|---|---|---|---|---|---|---|
| **Professional and Business Services** | | | | | | | | | | | | | |
| 2011 | 532.9 | 546.2 | 550.6 | 560.7 | 559.0 | 559.6 | 559.5 | 563.8 | 564.5 | 565.5 | 567.7 | 566.3 | 558.0 |
| 2012 | 552.6 | 559.9 | 564.5 | 572.1 | 575.4 | 579.5 | 575.5 | 580.8 | 577.7 | 584.2 | 588.5 | 587.5 | 574.9 |
| 2013 | 577.6 | 587.8 | 591.2 | 597.3 | 599.2 | 601.7 | 601.1 | 606.3 | 606.2 | 612.8 | 616.4 | 613.7 | 600.9 |
| 2014 | 605.3 | 607.5 | 620.1 | 624.5 | 629.4 | 630.5 | 635.0 | 640.6 | 640.2 | 642.7 | 647.5 | 647.0 | 630.9 |
| 2015 | 631.9 | 639.3 | 643.3 | 643.5 | 650.5 | 653.1 | 654.3 | 657.8 | 658.4 | 663.8 | 662.5 | 665.2 | 652.0 |
| 2016 | 652.6 | 658.2 | 660.6 | 667.7 | 668.6 | 669.2 | 676.8 | 681.6 | 683.6 | 687.3 | 688.7 | 689.6 | 673.7 |
| 2017 | 672.8 | 677.3 | 682.6 | 684.2 | 685.5 | 690.3 | 692.3 | 697.9 | 692.9 | 702.2 | 706.8 | 705.3 | 690.8 |
| 2018 | 689.4 | 695.8 | 701.4 | 701.0 | 699.9 | 704.5 | 705.0 | 712.2 | 709.6 | 716.7 | 721.3 | 717.8 | 706.2 |
| 2019 | 707.3 | 711.7 | 712.6 | 712.5 | 714.6 | 719.1 | 716.2 | 716.8 | 716.0 | 723.5 | 720.7 | 721.2 | 716.0 |
| **Education and Health Services** | | | | | | | | | | | | | |
| 2011 | 477.5 | 484.3 | 484.1 | 488.7 | 487.9 | 479.9 | 480.1 | 486.5 | 487.8 | 493.7 | 493.9 | 491.7 | 486.3 |
| 2012 | 488.0 | 492.8 | 493.1 | 497.5 | 498.3 | 490.9 | 489.6 | 499.1 | 500.0 | 505.9 | 507.4 | 505.7 | 497.4 |
| 2013 | 503.4 | 508.2 | 508.3 | 513.2 | 514.1 | 506.7 | 504.0 | 513.0 | 514.6 | 519.8 | 523.2 | 521.1 | 512.5 |
| 2014 | 516.0 | 518.1 | 521.2 | 524.7 | 526.2 | 519.7 | 519.5 | 530.2 | 531.6 | 533.2 | 535.5 | 537.5 | 526.1 |
| 2015 | 532.6 | 536.5 | 537.7 | 538.9 | 541.1 | 536.8 | 536.2 | 544.8 | 548.2 | 555.3 | 557.4 | 557.7 | 543.6 |
| 2016 | 555.1 | 560.4 | 561.1 | 564.1 | 564.7 | 558.4 | 556.9 | 564.9 | 567.7 | 572.5 | 573.7 | 573.2 | 564.4 |
| 2017 | 566.1 | 570.5 | 573.0 | 572.8 | 574.1 | 568.7 | 566.8 | 574.3 | 575.3 | 580.3 | 582.0 | 581.7 | 573.8 |
| 2018 | 577.1 | 582.6 | 583.5 | 584.9 | 586.4 | 581.5 | 582.5 | 591.5 | 593.5 | 597.2 | 599.2 | 598.6 | 588.2 |
| 2019 | 598.6 | 604.2 | 604.6 | 605.2 | 606.2 | 600.1 | 598.1 | 609.6 | 616.1 | 624.8 | 629.0 | 627.6 | 610.3 |
| **Leisure and Hospitality** | | | | | | | | | | | | | |
| 2011 | 358.5 | 365.8 | 375.1 | 387.8 | 392.5 | 391.3 | 390.5 | 390.8 | 385.0 | 382.8 | 382.4 | 378.8 | 381.8 |
| 2012 | 372.6 | 376.0 | 385.5 | 398.5 | 404.9 | 404.2 | 401.3 | 402.2 | 395.1 | 397.1 | 394.9 | 393.7 | 393.8 |
| 2013 | 387.9 | 392.1 | 399.3 | 414.6 | 420.3 | 421.6 | 420.8 | 422.2 | 415.5 | 416.3 | 414.1 | 412.0 | 411.4 |
| 2014 | 403.6 | 404.8 | 416.1 | 433.1 | 438.4 | 437.7 | 437.3 | 438.5 | 431.6 | 432.1 | 431.6 | 432.3 | 428.1 |
| 2015 | 422.0 | 428.1 | 436.5 | 450.9 | 456.5 | 459.8 | 456.0 | 458.1 | 453.8 | 452.5 | 451.8 | 451.7 | 448.1 |
| 2016 | 441.2 | 445.2 | 454.1 | 472.1 | 477.7 | 480.4 | 475.7 | 475.7 | 471.7 | 469.0 | 469.2 | 467.1 | 466.6 |
| 2017 | 454.5 | 459.9 | 469.8 | 482.4 | 487.4 | 491.8 | 487.0 | 487.6 | 478.4 | 484.4 | 481.4 | 478.4 | 478.6 |
| 2018 | 467.2 | 472.5 | 483.5 | 492.9 | 498.3 | 503.5 | 501.4 | 499.9 | 491.9 | 488.9 | 486.4 | 485.7 | 489.3 |
| 2019 | 481.1 | 487.9 | 496.6 | 504.2 | 509.5 | 511.5 | 509.1 | 509.5 | 502.8 | 508.7 | 504.3 | 499.6 | 502.1 |
| **Other Services** | | | | | | | | | | | | | |
| 2011 | 151.0 | 153.2 | 153.3 | 154.8 | 155.6 | 156.1 | 155.7 | 154.4 | 153.3 | 153.3 | 153.0 | 151.5 | 153.8 |
| 2012 | 150.7 | 151.6 | 151.6 | 153.3 | 154.0 | 154.9 | 155.2 | 154.1 | 152.7 | 154.2 | 153.9 | 152.3 | 153.2 |
| 2013 | 151.7 | 152.6 | 152.3 | 153.7 | 154.4 | 154.9 | 154.9 | 154.1 | 153.0 | 153.2 | 153.0 | 151.8 | 153.3 |
| 2014 | 150.8 | 151.3 | 151.5 | 153.9 | 154.7 | 155.7 | 156.0 | 155.2 | 153.9 | 153.8 | 154.1 | 153.9 | 153.7 |
| 2015 | 152.6 | 153.8 | 154.1 | 155.3 | 156.3 | 157.7 | 158.3 | 157.0 | 156.1 | 155.7 | 155.4 | 156.0 | 155.7 |
| 2016 | 154.7 | 155.3 | 155.8 | 157.4 | 158.2 | 159.9 | 159.4 | 158.2 | 157.1 | 157.4 | 157.2 | 157.0 | 157.3 |
| 2017 | 155.8 | 156.6 | 157.4 | 158.7 | 160.2 | 161.6 | 161.0 | 159.5 | 157.9 | 157.4 | 156.9 | 156.6 | 158.3 |
| 2018 | 155.3 | 156.6 | 157.7 | 158.8 | 160.9 | 163.2 | 163.3 | 162.4 | 162.0 | 162.4 | 161.2 | 161.3 | 160.4 |
| 2019 | 161.6 | 162.8 | 163.7 | 165.1 | 165.2 | 166.8 | 167.0 | 167.0 | 164.5 | 164.5 | 165.7 | 165.7 | 165.0 |
| **Government** | | | | | | | | | | | | | |
| 2011 | 687.1 | 693.7 | 695.8 | 691.8 | 693.5 | 681.0 | 660.7 | 673.1 | 683.9 | 688.9 | 691.8 | 688.9 | 685.9 |
| 2012 | 681.8 | 686.9 | 692.1 | 692.1 | 689.9 | 681.0 | 654.8 | 672.4 | 682.7 | 689.0 | 695.0 | 689.3 | 683.9 |
| 2013 | 683.1 | 688.6 | 689.7 | 689.9 | 684.9 | 670.3 | 649.4 | 665.8 | 677.2 | 683.4 | 686.9 | 683.8 | 679.4 |
| 2014 | 671.4 | 676.0 | 679.1 | 681.3 | 682.5 | 668.7 | 648.6 | 670.4 | 678.4 | 682.8 | 687.6 | 682.6 | 675.8 |
| 2015 | 674.6 | 680.2 | 681.0 | 681.3 | 678.7 | 668.9 | 649.7 | 670.4 | 677.8 | 684.7 | 687.4 | 684.4 | 676.6 |
| 2016 | 676.4 | 682.4 | 678.6 | 684.0 | 683.0 | 675.6 | 650.2 | 674.2 | 684.1 | 687.9 | 694.0 | 688.3 | 679.9 |
| 2017 | 678.5 | 685.0 | 687.1 | 688.8 | 686.6 | 680.1 | 657.2 | 680.1 | 688.3 | 692.0 | 695.1 | 691.6 | 684.2 |
| 2018 | 686.3 | 691.1 | 692.4 | 691.9 | 694.9 | 683.8 | 663.8 | 688.1 | 693.0 | 697.3 | 701.4 | 698.7 | 690.2 |
| 2019 | 686.8 | 692.8 | 694.7 | 694.4 | 694.0 | 680.7 | 664.6 | 687.7 | 693.1 | 697.5 | 700.0 | 698.0 | 690.4 |

## 2. Average Weekly Hours by Selected Industry: Georgia, 2015–2019

(Not seasonally adjusted)

| Industry and year | January | February | March | April | May | June | July | August | September | October | November | December | Annual average |
|---|---|---|---|---|---|---|---|---|---|---|---|---|---|
| **Total Private** | | | | | | | | | | | | | |
| 2015 | 34.8 | 35.3 | 35.3 | 34.8 | 35.1 | 35.2 | 35.1 | 35.6 | 34.8 | 34.8 | 35.1 | 34.8 | 35.1 |
| 2016 | 34.4 | 34.7 | 34.7 | 34.8 | 35.2 | 34.9 | 34.8 | 34.6 | 34.6 | 35.2 | 34.8 | 34.9 | 34.8 |
| 2017 | 34.7 | 34.4 | 34.4 | 34.8 | 34.5 | 34.9 | 35.0 | 34.6 | 33.9 | 35.2 | 34.7 | 34.7 | 34.7 |
| 2018 | 34.2 | 34.6 | 34.8 | 35.2 | 34.8 | 35.0 | 35.2 | 34.8 | 35.2 | 34.6 | 34.7 | 35.3 | 34.9 |
| 2019 | 34.5 | 34.6 | 34.8 | 34.5 | 34.6 | 35.3 | 34.8 | 34.9 | 35.1 | 34.7 | 34.8 | 35.2 | 34.8 |
| **Goods-Producing** | | | | | | | | | | | | | |
| 2015 | 40.7 | 40.4 | 40.6 | 40.5 | 41.4 | 41.4 | 41.7 | 42.3 | 40.8 | 41.6 | 41.0 | 41.9 | 41.2 |
| 2016 | 40.3 | 40.4 | 41.0 | 40.7 | 41.4 | 41.5 | 40.6 | 40.7 | 41.0 | 41.3 | 41.4 | 41.0 | 40.9 |
| 2017 | 39.8 | 39.9 | 40.0 | 40.3 | 40.6 | 41.2 | 41.3 | 41.0 | 39.5 | 41.5 | 41.5 | 41.2 | 40.7 |
| 2018 | 39.9 | 41.1 | 41.4 | 41.9 | 41.5 | 41.5 | 41.8 | 42.0 | 41.9 | 41.2 | 41.4 | 42.9 | 41.5 |
| 2019 | 42.1 | 41.7 | 41.9 | 41.6 | 41.8 | 42.2 | 41.5 | 41.9 | 41.6 | 41.4 | 40.9 | 41.1 | 41.6 |
| **Construction** | | | | | | | | | | | | | |
| 2015 | 40.0 | 39.5 | 39.8 | 39.7 | 42.2 | 42.0 | 42.3 | 42.3 | 40.4 | 42.5 | 41.2 | 42.4 | 41.2 |
| 2016 | 40.4 | 40.3 | 41.4 | 40.8 | 41.6 | 41.2 | 41.6 | 40.9 | 41.4 | 40.9 | 41.0 | 39.5 | 40.9 |
| 2017 | 39.2 | 39.4 | 39.0 | 39.8 | 40.5 | 40.5 | 40.8 | 40.1 | 38.6 | 41.1 | 40.4 | 40.1 | 40.0 |
| 2018 | 37.7 | 39.9 | 41.0 | 42.2 | 41.5 | 41.0 | 41.1 | 41.3 | 41.1 | 40.7 | 40.1 | 41.8 | 40.8 |
| 2019 | 42.1 | 41.6 | 42.0 | 41.9 | 41.6 | 41.9 | 41.8 | 42.0 | 41.5 | 41.4 | 39.8 | 39.7 | 41.4 |
| **Manufacturing** | | | | | | | | | | | | | |
| 2015 | 41.3 | 41.0 | 41.1 | 41.0 | 40.8 | 40.9 | 41.2 | 42.2 | 40.9 | 40.9 | 40.7 | 41.4 | 41.1 |
| 2016 | 40.0 | 40.1 | 40.4 | 40.3 | 40.9 | 41.3 | 39.6 | 40.2 | 40.4 | 41.3 | 41.4 | 41.7 | 40.6 |
| 2017 | 40.1 | 40.0 | 40.3 | 40.4 | 40.6 | 41.6 | 41.4 | 41.5 | 40.1 | 41.7 | 42.2 | 41.8 | 41.0 |
| 2018 | 41.3 | 41.8 | 41.7 | 41.8 | 41.5 | 41.8 | 42.3 | 42.4 | 42.5 | 41.5 | 42.6 | 43.9 | 42.1 |
| 2019 | 42.4 | 42.0 | 42.0 | 41.5 | 41.9 | 42.4 | 41.4 | 41.9 | 41.6 | 41.5 | 41.7 | 42.2 | 41.9 |
| **Trade, Transportation, and Utilities** | | | | | | | | | | | | | |
| 2015 | 34.7 | 35.4 | 35.3 | 35.0 | 35.2 | 34.9 | 34.8 | 35.1 | 34.3 | 34.5 | 34.7 | 34.6 | 34.9 |
| 2016 | 34.2 | 34.6 | 34.1 | 34.3 | 34.6 | 34.3 | 34.3 | 34.2 | 34.1 | 34.5 | 34.2 | 34.4 | 34.3 |
| 2017 | 33.9 | 33.8 | 33.9 | 34.5 | 34.0 | 34.3 | 34.9 | 34.4 | 33.9 | 34.6 | 34.6 | 34.8 | 34.3 |
| 2018 | 34.2 | 34.3 | 34.4 | 34.5 | 34.5 | 35.2 | 35.3 | 34.8 | 35.1 | 34.4 | 34.5 | 34.7 | 34.7 |
| 2019 | 33.8 | 33.7 | 33.8 | 33.8 | 33.9 | 34.6 | 34.6 | 34.5 | 34.6 | 34.4 | 34.5 | 34.8 | 34.3 |
| **Financial Activities** | | | | | | | | | | | | | |
| 2015 | 36.6 | 38.1 | 38.1 | 36.9 | 36.9 | 37.3 | 37.1 | 38.6 | 37.4 | 37.1 | 38.9 | 37.6 | 37.5 |
| 2016 | 37.4 | 37.3 | 37.3 | 37.2 | 38.4 | 37.3 | 37.2 | 37.0 | 37.3 | 37.9 | 36.8 | 36.8 | 37.3 |
| 2017 | 38.5 | 37.3 | 36.9 | 38.2 | 36.6 | 36.7 | 38.2 | 36.6 | 36.8 | 38.7 | 37.1 | 36.8 | 37.4 |
| 2018 | 36.8 | 37.1 | 36.7 | 38.0 | 36.7 | 37.0 | 38.0 | 37.1 | 38.4 | 36.8 | 37.5 | 38.3 | 37.4 |
| 2019 | 36.9 | 36.9 | 36.7 | 36.2 | 36.4 | 37.7 | 36.6 | 36.7 | 37.9 | 36.9 | 37.5 | 38.4 | 37.1 |
| **Professional and Business Services** | | | | | | | | | | | | | |
| 2015 | 35.9 | 36.5 | 36.3 | 35.6 | 35.7 | 36.0 | 35.4 | 36.0 | 35.2 | 35.5 | 35.9 | 35.2 | 35.8 |
| 2016 | 34.5 | 34.7 | 35.0 | 35.4 | 35.8 | 35.3 | 35.4 | 35.5 | 35.1 | 36.3 | 35.0 | 35.2 | 35.3 |
| 2017 | 35.3 | 34.9 | 34.8 | 35.6 | 35.1 | 35.7 | 36.0 | 35.4 | 34.6 | 36.3 | 35.3 | 35.5 | 35.4 |
| 2018 | 34.8 | 35.3 | 35.7 | 36.6 | 36.2 | 36.1 | 36.2 | 35.7 | 36.4 | 35.6 | 35.5 | 36.3 | 35.9 |
| 2019 | 35.4 | 35.6 | 35.5 | 35.2 | 35.3 | 36.1 | 35.3 | 35.6 | 36.1 | 35.3 | 35.4 | 36.1 | 35.6 |
| **Education and Health Services** | | | | | | | | | | | | | |
| 2015 | 34.9 | 35.2 | 35.3 | 34.7 | 34.8 | 34.7 | 34.9 | 35.3 | 34.9 | 35.1 | 35.6 | 35.1 | 35.0 |
| 2016 | 35.3 | 35.2 | 35.3 | 35.1 | 35.3 | 34.9 | 35.2 | 34.6 | 34.7 | 35.6 | 35.5 | 35.7 | 35.2 |
| 2017 | 35.8 | 35.3 | 35.3 | 35.4 | 35.3 | 35.3 | 35.4 | 35.4 | 34.8 | 35.4 | 34.9 | 34.8 | 35.3 |
| 2018 | 34.6 | 34.6 | 34.4 | 34.6 | 34.4 | 34.4 | 34.4 | 34.1 | 34.4 | 33.9 | 34.2 | 34.6 | 34.4 |
| 2019 | 34.0 | 34.1 | 34.5 | 33.7 | 34.3 | 34.9 | 34.6 | 34.7 | 35.0 | 34.5 | 34.8 | 34.9 | 34.5 |
| **Leisure and Hospitality** | | | | | | | | | | | | | |
| 2015 | 26.2 | 26.8 | 26.7 | 26.8 | 26.8 | 26.7 | 26.5 | 27.0 | 26.4 | 26.7 | 26.6 | 26.4 | 26.6 |
| 2016 | 25.9 | 26.8 | 26.8 | 27.1 | 27.2 | 27.1 | 26.9 | 26.4 | 26.1 | 26.6 | 26.5 | 26.6 | 26.7 |
| 2017 | 26.0 | 26.5 | 26.6 | 26.7 | 26.6 | 26.6 | 26.5 | 26.0 | 25.5 | 26.7 | 26.5 | 26.2 | 26.4 |
| 2018 | 25.8 | 26.6 | 27.1 | 27.1 | 26.8 | 27.1 | 27.1 | 26.5 | 26.4 | 26.5 | 26.5 | 26.8 | 26.7 |
| 2019 | 26.0 | 26.4 | 26.4 | 27.5 | 27.3 | 27.9 | 27.2 | 27.1 | 26.8 | 26.9 | 26.7 | 26.9 | 26.9 |
| **Other Services** | | | | | | | | | | | | | |
| 2015 | 33.1 | 33.8 | 34.7 | 34.0 | 34.3 | 34.2 | 34.5 | 35.0 | 34.5 | 34.1 | 34.2 | 33.8 | 34.2 |
| 2016 | 33.6 | 34.9 | 34.1 | 33.8 | 34.1 | 33.9 | 33.8 | 33.0 | 33.2 | 33.4 | 33.1 | 32.8 | 33.6 |
| 2017 | 33.0 | 32.6 | 32.3 | 33.0 | 32.9 | 32.4 | 32.8 | 32.0 | 30.2 | 31.8 | 31.9 | 31.4 | 32.2 |
| 2018 | 30.7 | 31.8 | 32.3 | 32.0 | 30.5 | 31.2 | 31.1 | 30.3 | 30.8 | 31.5 | 29.6 | 30.1 | 31.0 |
| 2019 | 30.0 | 30.3 | 30.6 | 30.4 | 30.6 | 31.3 | 29.9 | 31.1 | 31.1 | 30.7 | 30.7 | 30.3 | 30.6 |

## 3. Average Hourly Earnings by Selected Industry: Georgia, 2015–2019

(Dollars, not seasonally adjusted)

| Industry and year | January | February | March | April | May | June | July | August | September | October | November | December | Annual average |
|---|---|---|---|---|---|---|---|---|---|---|---|---|---|
| **Total Private** | | | | | | | | | | | | | |
| 2015 | 23.89 | 24.08 | 23.92 | 23.65 | 23.50 | 23.34 | 23.51 | 23.74 | 23.62 | 23.88 | 24.09 | 23.87 | 23.76 |
| 2016 | 24.16 | 24.01 | 23.97 | 23.98 | 24.27 | 23.91 | 24.10 | 24.19 | 24.24 | 24.82 | 24.39 | 24.50 | 24.22 |
| 2017 | 25.24 | 24.88 | 24.82 | 25.33 | 24.96 | 24.92 | 25.44 | 25.47 | 25.88 | 25.87 | 25.58 | 25.83 | 25.35 |
| 2018 | 26.08 | 26.22 | 26.02 | 26.48 | 26.06 | 25.96 | 26.32 | 26.23 | 26.86 | 26.73 | 26.57 | 26.85 | 26.37 |
| 2019 | 26.89 | 26.75 | 26.56 | 26.50 | 26.37 | 26.55 | 26.28 | 26.47 | 26.67 | 26.80 | 26.56 | 26.98 | 26.62 |
| **Goods-Producing** | | | | | | | | | | | | | |
| 2015 | 23.30 | 23.48 | 23.13 | 23.15 | 23.07 | 22.93 | 23.19 | 23.29 | 23.44 | 23.47 | 23.88 | 23.82 | 23.35 |
| 2016 | 24.13 | 23.93 | 24.24 | 24.14 | 24.19 | 24.00 | 24.10 | 24.04 | 24.07 | 24.12 | 23.75 | 23.95 | 24.05 |
| 2017 | 24.14 | 24.04 | 23.92 | 23.97 | 23.88 | 23.95 | 24.22 | 23.97 | 24.37 | 24.17 | 24.30 | 24.34 | 24.11 |
| 2018 | 24.16 | 24.27 | 24.39 | 24.76 | 24.61 | 24.46 | 24.72 | 24.56 | 25.33 | 25.41 | 25.30 | 25.07 | 24.76 |
| 2019 | 25.21 | 25.47 | 25.36 | 25.48 | 25.35 | 25.41 | 25.36 | 25.34 | 25.82 | 26.08 | 25.82 | 26.22 | 25.57 |
| **Construction** | | | | | | | | | | | | | |
| 2015 | 22.88 | 23.19 | 23.09 | 23.26 | 23.18 | 22.87 | 23.10 | 23.30 | 23.36 | 23.51 | 24.14 | 23.85 | 23.32 |
| 2016 | 24.35 | 24.10 | 24.36 | 24.36 | 24.42 | 24.58 | 24.38 | 24.46 | 24.51 | 25.04 | 24.62 | 25.00 | 24.52 |
| 2017 | 24.57 | 24.84 | 24.84 | 24.73 | 24.35 | 24.95 | 24.99 | 24.87 | 25.40 | 25.07 | 25.58 | 25.39 | 24.97 |
| 2018 | 25.09 | 25.40 | 25.28 | 25.68 | 25.24 | 25.28 | 25.61 | 25.52 | 26.30 | 26.67 | 26.61 | 26.59 | 25.78 |
| 2019 | 26.29 | 26.81 | 26.54 | 26.54 | 26.81 | 26.79 | 26.94 | 26.74 | 27.14 | 27.06 | 27.39 | 27.82 | 26.90 |
| **Manufacturing** | | | | | | | | | | | | | |
| 2015 | 23.38 | 23.46 | 22.97 | 23.03 | 22.91 | 22.90 | 23.19 | 23.23 | 23.45 | 23.37 | 23.67 | 23.75 | 23.28 |
| 2016 | 23.77 | 23.60 | 23.85 | 23.83 | 23.87 | 23.31 | 23.46 | 23.38 | 23.44 | 23.18 | 22.96 | 23.10 | 23.47 |
| 2017 | 23.64 | 23.34 | 23.11 | 23.46 | 23.54 | 23.34 | 23.80 | 23.39 | 23.72 | 23.43 | 23.36 | 23.54 | 23.47 |
| 2018 | 23.46 | 23.48 | 23.77 | 24.12 | 23.76 | 23.54 | 23.91 | 23.66 | 24.28 | 24.20 | 23.97 | 23.55 | 23.81 |
| 2019 | 24.00 | 24.15 | 24.17 | 24.40 | 24.11 | 24.26 | 24.10 | 24.16 | 24.71 | 25.12 | 24.69 | 25.10 | 24.41 |
| **Trade, Transportation, and Utilities** | | | | | | | | | | | | | |
| 2015 | 22.44 | 22.26 | 22.25 | 21.94 | 21.68 | 21.43 | 21.56 | 21.48 | 21.49 | 21.58 | 21.33 | 21.30 | 21.72 |
| 2016 | 21.67 | 21.22 | 21.70 | 21.72 | 21.68 | 21.60 | 21.77 | 21.62 | 21.82 | 22.40 | 21.90 | 22.23 | 21.78 |
| 2017 | 23.29 | 22.65 | 22.52 | 22.85 | 22.52 | 22.91 | 23.08 | 23.13 | 23.29 | 22.90 | 22.89 | 22.92 | 22.91 |
| 2018 | 23.37 | 23.32 | 23.22 | 23.89 | 23.60 | 23.59 | 23.94 | 23.71 | 24.03 | 23.71 | 23.22 | 23.76 | 23.62 |
| 2019 | 23.94 | 23.77 | 23.48 | 23.46 | 23.37 | 23.51 | 23.35 | 23.45 | 23.67 | 23.68 | 23.63 | 23.76 | 23.59 |
| **Financial Activities** | | | | | | | | | | | | | |
| 2015 | 29.47 | 29.98 | 30.16 | 29.33 | 29.46 | 29.03 | 29.06 | 29.32 | 29.13 | 29.09 | 28.95 | 28.45 | 29.28 |
| 2016 | 28.52 | 29.42 | 28.79 | 28.60 | 30.46 | 29.06 | 29.84 | 31.68 | 30.85 | 32.65 | 32.11 | 32.36 | 30.37 |
| 2017 | 32.69 | 32.45 | 32.49 | 33.40 | 32.94 | 32.04 | 33.17 | 32.84 | 33.62 | 34.14 | 33.57 | 33.13 | 33.05 |
| 2018 | 33.95 | 33.90 | 34.12 | 33.91 | 33.12 | 32.84 | 34.19 | 34.21 | 34.85 | 34.58 | 34.69 | 35.82 | 34.19 |
| 2019 | 36.16 | 35.82 | 35.55 | 35.33 | 34.33 | 35.43 | 34.77 | 34.90 | 35.10 | 34.46 | 34.37 | 35.58 | 35.15 |
| **Professional and Business Services** | | | | | | | | | | | | | |
| 2015 | 28.37 | 29.04 | 28.69 | 28.12 | 27.89 | 27.72 | 28.13 | 28.89 | 28.55 | 29.18 | 30.09 | 29.68 | 28.70 |
| 2016 | 30.41 | 30.15 | 29.70 | 29.93 | 30.57 | 29.75 | 29.98 | 29.99 | 30.07 | 30.61 | 30.10 | 29.90 | 30.10 |
| 2017 | 30.92 | 30.30 | 29.76 | 30.67 | 30.14 | 29.84 | 30.97 | 30.74 | 31.13 | 31.44 | 30.74 | 31.42 | 30.68 |
| 2018 | 31.35 | 32.09 | 31.60 | 32.16 | 31.63 | 31.47 | 31.99 | 31.46 | 32.42 | 32.27 | 32.30 | 32.67 | 31.96 |
| 2019 | 32.17 | 32.19 | 32.14 | 32.40 | 32.23 | 32.26 | 31.56 | 32.03 | 32.26 | 32.07 | 32.04 | 33.11 | 32.21 |
| **Education and Health Services** | | | | | | | | | | | | | |
| 2015 | 24.94 | 25.05 | 24.90 | 25.14 | 24.83 | 24.98 | 24.91 | 25.02 | 25.06 | 25.86 | 25.52 | 25.50 | 25.15 |
| 2016 | 25.39 | 25.55 | 25.13 | 25.38 | 25.22 | 25.46 | 25.60 | 25.75 | 25.77 | 26.38 | 26.32 | 26.32 | 25.69 |
| 2017 | 26.59 | 26.88 | 27.20 | 27.80 | 27.58 | 27.62 | 27.90 | 28.69 | 29.05 | 29.44 | 27.90 | 28.31 | 27.91 |
| 2018 | 28.85 | 29.08 | 28.86 | 29.20 | 28.74 | 28.62 | 29.00 | 29.73 | 29.57 | 30.15 | 29.95 | 30.06 | 29.32 |
| 2019 | 30.20 | 29.86 | 30.17 | 30.00 | 29.56 | 29.68 | 29.44 | 29.72 | 29.27 | 30.49 | 29.06 | 29.11 | 29.71 |
| **Leisure and Hospitality** | | | | | | | | | | | | | |
| 2015 | 12.47 | 12.48 | 12.57 | 12.47 | 12.58 | 12.38 | 12.47 | 12.58 | 12.58 | 12.59 | 12.70 | 12.74 | 12.55 |
| 2016 | 12.75 | 12.70 | 12.74 | 12.77 | 12.71 | 12.45 | 12.54 | 12.54 | 12.73 | 12.83 | 12.65 | 12.78 | 12.68 |
| 2017 | 12.87 | 12.92 | 12.92 | 13.03 | 13.14 | 13.07 | 13.03 | 13.06 | 13.08 | 13.13 | 13.06 | 13.39 | 13.06 |
| 2018 | 13.22 | 13.22 | 13.21 | 13.38 | 13.45 | 13.29 | 13.31 | 13.28 | 13.38 | 13.51 | 13.51 | 13.70 | 13.37 |
| 2019 | 13.65 | 13.65 | 13.53 | 13.81 | 13.70 | 13.54 | 13.62 | 13.61 | 13.70 | 13.85 | 13.75 | 13.82 | 13.69 |
| **Other Services** | | | | | | | | | | | | | |
| 2015 | 20.76 | 20.86 | 20.58 | 21.14 | 20.99 | 21.03 | 20.91 | 22.00 | 21.56 | 21.61 | 21.60 | 21.59 | 21.22 |
| 2016 | 21.54 | 21.22 | 21.31 | 20.80 | 20.98 | 20.29 | 20.84 | 21.01 | 20.68 | 20.85 | 20.85 | 20.53 | 20.91 |
| 2017 | 20.54 | 21.16 | 20.99 | 20.83 | 20.66 | 20.98 | 20.83 | 21.40 | 21.46 | 21.36 | 21.47 | 21.95 | 21.13 |
| 2018 | 21.99 | 22.50 | 23.02 | 23.89 | 23.48 | 23.38 | 23.01 | 23.91 | 24.59 | 24.66 | 24.84 | 24.41 | 23.64 |
| 2019 | 25.24 | 24.61 | 24.32 | 24.10 | 23.98 | 24.12 | 24.13 | 23.59 | 23.73 | 23.54 | 23.91 | 24.02 | 24.10 |

## 4. Average Weekly Earnings by Selected Industry: Georgia, 2015–2019

(Dollars, not seasonally adjusted)

| Industry and year | January | February | March | April | May | June | July | August | September | October | November | December | Annual average |
|---|---|---|---|---|---|---|---|---|---|---|---|---|---|
| **Total Private** | | | | | | | | | | | | | |
| 2015 | 831.37 | 850.02 | 844.73 | 823.02 | 824.85 | 819.23 | 825.20 | 845.14 | 821.98 | 831.02 | 845.56 | 830.68 | 833.98 |
| 2016 | 831.10 | 833.15 | 831.76 | 834.50 | 854.30 | 834.46 | 838.68 | 836.97 | 838.70 | 873.66 | 848.77 | 855.05 | 842.86 |
| 2017 | 875.83 | 855.87 | 853.81 | 881.48 | 861.12 | 869.71 | 890.40 | 881.26 | 877.33 | 910.62 | 887.63 | 896.30 | 879.65 |
| 2018 | 891.94 | 907.21 | 905.50 | 932.10 | 906.89 | 908.60 | 926.46 | 912.80 | 945.47 | 924.86 | 921.98 | 947.81 | 920.31 |
| 2019 | 927.71 | 922.88 | 924.29 | 914.25 | 912.40 | 937.22 | 914.54 | 923.80 | 936.12 | 929.96 | 924.29 | 949.70 | 926.38 |
| **Goods-Producing** | | | | | | | | | | | | | |
| 2015 | 948.72 | 948.59 | 939.08 | 937.58 | 955.10 | 949.30 | 967.02 | 985.17 | 956.35 | 976.35 | 979.08 | 998.06 | 962.02 |
| 2016 | 972.44 | 966.77 | 993.84 | 982.50 | 1,001.47 | 996.00 | 978.46 | 978.43 | 986.87 | 996.16 | 983.25 | 981.95 | 983.65 |
| 2017 | 960.77 | 959.20 | 956.80 | 965.99 | 969.53 | 986.74 | 1,000.29 | 982.77 | 962.62 | 1,003.06 | 1,008.45 | 1,002.81 | 981.28 |
| 2018 | 963.98 | 997.50 | 1,009.75 | 1,037.44 | 1,021.32 | 1,015.09 | 1,033.30 | 1,031.52 | 1,061.33 | 1,046.89 | 1,047.42 | 1,075.50 | 1,027.54 |
| 2019 | 1,061.34 | 1,062.10 | 1,062.58 | 1,059.97 | 1,059.63 | 1,072.30 | 1,052.44 | 1,061.75 | 1,074.11 | 1,079.71 | 1,056.04 | 1,077.64 | 1,063.71 |
| **Construction** | | | | | | | | | | | | | |
| 2015 | 915.20 | 916.01 | 918.98 | 923.42 | 978.20 | 960.54 | 977.13 | 985.59 | 943.74 | 999.18 | 994.57 | 1,011.24 | 960.78 |
| 2016 | 983.74 | 971.23 | 1,008.50 | 993.89 | 1,015.87 | 1,012.70 | 1,014.21 | 1,000.41 | 1,014.71 | 1,024.14 | 1,009.42 | 987.50 | 1,002.87 |
| 2017 | 963.14 | 978.70 | 968.76 | 984.25 | 986.18 | 1,010.48 | 1,019.59 | 997.29 | 980.44 | 1,030.38 | 1,033.43 | 1,018.14 | 998.80 |
| 2018 | 945.89 | 1,013.46 | 1,036.48 | 1,083.70 | 1,047.46 | 1,036.48 | 1,052.57 | 1,053.98 | 1,080.93 | 1,085.47 | 1,067.06 | 1,111.46 | 1,051.82 |
| 2019 | 1,106.81 | 1,115.30 | 1,114.68 | 1,112.03 | 1,115.30 | 1,122.50 | 1,126.09 | 1,123.08 | 1,126.31 | 1,120.28 | 1,090.12 | 1,104.45 | 1,113.66 |
| **Manufacturing** | | | | | | | | | | | | | |
| 2015 | 965.59 | 961.86 | 944.07 | 944.23 | 934.73 | 936.61 | 955.43 | 980.31 | 959.11 | 955.83 | 963.37 | 983.25 | 956.81 |
| 2016 | 950.80 | 946.36 | 963.54 | 960.35 | 976.28 | 962.70 | 929.02 | 939.88 | 946.98 | 957.33 | 950.54 | 963.27 | 952.88 |
| 2017 | 947.96 | 933.60 | 931.33 | 947.78 | 955.72 | 970.94 | 985.32 | 970.69 | 951.17 | 977.03 | 985.79 | 983.97 | 962.27 |
| 2018 | 968.90 | 981.46 | 991.21 | 1,008.22 | 986.04 | 983.97 | 1,011.39 | 1,003.18 | 1,031.90 | 1,004.30 | 1,021.12 | 1,033.85 | 1,002.40 |
| 2019 | 1,017.60 | 1,014.30 | 1,015.14 | 1,012.60 | 1,010.21 | 1,028.62 | 997.74 | 1,012.30 | 1,027.94 | 1,042.48 | 1,029.57 | 1,059.22 | 1,022.78 |
| **Trade, Transportation, and Utilities** | | | | | | | | | | | | | |
| 2015 | 778.67 | 788.00 | 785.43 | 767.90 | 763.14 | 747.91 | 750.29 | 753.95 | 737.11 | 744.51 | 740.15 | 736.98 | 758.03 |
| 2016 | 741.11 | 734.21 | 739.97 | 745.00 | 750.13 | 740.88 | 746.71 | 739.40 | 744.06 | 772.80 | 748.98 | 764.71 | 747.05 |
| 2017 | 789.53 | 765.57 | 763.43 | 788.33 | 765.68 | 785.81 | 805.49 | 795.67 | 789.53 | 792.34 | 791.99 | 797.62 | 785.81 |
| 2018 | 799.25 | 799.88 | 798.77 | 824.21 | 814.20 | 830.37 | 845.08 | 825.11 | 843.45 | 815.62 | 801.09 | 824.47 | 819.61 |
| 2019 | 809.17 | 801.05 | 793.62 | 792.95 | 792.24 | 813.45 | 807.91 | 809.03 | 818.98 | 814.59 | 815.24 | 826.85 | 809.14 |
| **Financial Activities** | | | | | | | | | | | | | |
| 2015 | 1,078.60 | 1,142.24 | 1,149.10 | 1,082.28 | 1,087.07 | 1,082.82 | 1,078.13 | 1,131.75 | 1,089.46 | 1,079.24 | 1,126.16 | 1,069.72 | 1,098.00 |
| 2016 | 1,066.65 | 1,097.37 | 1,073.87 | 1,063.92 | 1,169.66 | 1,083.94 | 1,110.05 | 1,172.16 | 1,150.71 | 1,237.44 | 1,181.65 | 1,190.85 | 1,132.80 |
| 2017 | 1,258.57 | 1,210.39 | 1,198.88 | 1,275.88 | 1,205.60 | 1,175.87 | 1,267.09 | 1,201.94 | 1,237.22 | 1,321.22 | 1,245.45 | 1,219.18 | 1,236.07 |
| 2018 | 1,249.36 | 1,257.69 | 1,252.20 | 1,288.58 | 1,215.50 | 1,215.08 | 1,299.22 | 1,269.19 | 1,338.24 | 1,272.54 | 1,300.88 | 1,371.91 | 1,278.71 |
| 2019 | 1,334.30 | 1,321.76 | 1,304.69 | 1,278.95 | 1,249.61 | 1,335.71 | 1,272.58 | 1,280.83 | 1,330.29 | 1,271.57 | 1,288.88 | 1,366.27 | 1,304.07 |
| **Professional and Business Services** | | | | | | | | | | | | | |
| 2015 | 1,018.48 | 1,059.96 | 1,041.45 | 1,001.07 | 995.67 | 997.92 | 995.80 | 1,040.04 | 1,004.96 | 1,035.89 | 1,080.23 | 1,044.74 | 1,027.46 |
| 2016 | 1,049.15 | 1,046.21 | 1,039.50 | 1,059.52 | 1,094.41 | 1,050.18 | 1,061.29 | 1,064.65 | 1,055.46 | 1,111.14 | 1,053.50 | 1,052.48 | 1,062.53 |
| 2017 | 1,091.48 | 1,057.47 | 1,035.65 | 1,091.85 | 1,057.91 | 1,065.29 | 1,114.92 | 1,088.20 | 1,077.10 | 1,141.27 | 1,085.12 | 1,115.41 | 1,086.07 |
| 2018 | 1,090.98 | 1,132.78 | 1,128.12 | 1,177.06 | 1,145.01 | 1,136.07 | 1,158.04 | 1,123.12 | 1,180.09 | 1,148.81 | 1,146.65 | 1,185.92 | 1,147.36 |
| 2019 | 1,138.82 | 1,145.96 | 1,140.97 | 1,140.48 | 1,137.72 | 1,164.59 | 1,114.07 | 1,140.27 | 1,164.59 | 1,132.07 | 1,134.22 | 1,195.27 | 1,146.68 |
| **Education and Health Services** | | | | | | | | | | | | | |
| 2015 | 870.41 | 881.76 | 878.97 | 872.36 | 864.08 | 866.81 | 869.36 | 883.21 | 874.59 | 907.69 | 908.51 | 895.05 | 880.25 |
| 2016 | 896.27 | 899.36 | 887.09 | 890.84 | 890.27 | 888.55 | 901.12 | 890.95 | 894.22 | 939.13 | 934.36 | 939.62 | 904.29 |
| 2017 | 951.92 | 948.86 | 960.16 | 984.12 | 973.57 | 974.99 | 987.66 | 1,015.63 | 1,010.94 | 1,042.18 | 973.71 | 985.19 | 985.22 |
| 2018 | 998.21 | 1,006.17 | 992.78 | 1,010.32 | 988.66 | 984.53 | 997.60 | 1,013.79 | 1,017.21 | 1,022.09 | 1,024.29 | 1,040.08 | 1,008.61 |
| 2019 | 1,026.80 | 1,018.23 | 1,040.87 | 1,011.00 | 1,013.91 | 1,035.83 | 1,018.62 | 1,031.28 | 1,024.45 | 1,051.91 | 1,011.29 | 1,015.94 | 1,025.00 |
| **Leisure and Hospitality** | | | | | | | | | | | | | |
| 2015 | 326.71 | 334.46 | 335.62 | 334.20 | 337.14 | 330.55 | 330.46 | 339.66 | 332.11 | 336.15 | 337.82 | 336.34 | 333.83 |
| 2016 | 330.23 | 340.36 | 341.43 | 346.07 | 345.71 | 337.40 | 337.33 | 331.06 | 332.25 | 341.28 | 335.23 | 339.95 | 338.56 |
| 2017 | 334.62 | 342.38 | 343.67 | 347.90 | 349.52 | 347.66 | 345.30 | 339.56 | 333.54 | 350.57 | 346.09 | 350.82 | 344.78 |
| 2018 | 341.08 | 351.65 | 357.99 | 362.60 | 360.46 | 360.16 | 360.70 | 351.92 | 353.23 | 358.02 | 358.02 | 367.16 | 356.98 |
| 2019 | 354.90 | 360.36 | 357.19 | 379.78 | 374.01 | 377.77 | 370.46 | 368.83 | 367.16 | 372.57 | 367.13 | 371.76 | 368.26 |
| **Other Services** | | | | | | | | | | | | | |
| 2015 | 687.16 | 705.07 | 714.13 | 718.76 | 719.96 | 719.23 | 721.40 | 770.00 | 743.82 | 736.90 | 738.72 | 729.74 | 725.72 |
| 2016 | 723.74 | 740.58 | 726.67 | 703.04 | 715.42 | 687.83 | 704.39 | 693.33 | 686.58 | 696.39 | 690.14 | 673.38 | 702.58 |
| 2017 | 677.82 | 689.82 | 677.98 | 687.39 | 679.71 | 679.75 | 683.22 | 684.80 | 648.09 | 679.25 | 684.89 | 689.23 | 680.39 |
| 2018 | 675.09 | 715.50 | 743.55 | 764.48 | 716.14 | 729.46 | 715.61 | 724.47 | 757.37 | 776.79 | 735.26 | 734.74 | 732.84 |
| 2019 | 757.20 | 745.68 | 744.19 | 732.64 | 733.79 | 754.96 | 721.49 | 733.65 | 738.00 | 722.68 | 734.04 | 727.81 | 737.46 |

# HAWAII
## *At a Glance*

Population:
  2010 census: 1,360,301
  2019 estimate: 1,415,872

Percent change in population:
  2010–2019: 4.1%

Percent change in total nonfarm employment:
  2011–2019: 10.3%

Industry with the largest growth in employment, 2011–2019 (percent):
  Mining, Logging, and Construction, 26.1%

Industry with the largest decline or smallest growth in employment, 2011–2019 (percent):
  Information, 1.2%

Civilian labor force:
  2010: 647,249
  2019: 664,992

Unemployment rate and rank among states (highest to lowest):
  2010: 6.9%, 43rd
  2019: 2.7%, 46th

Over-the-year change in unemployment rates:
  2017–2018: 0.1%
  2018–2019: 0.2%

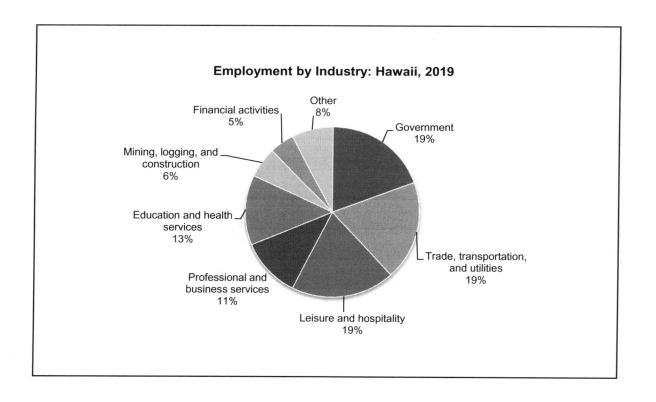

**Employment by Industry: Hawaii, 2019**

- Other 8%
- Financial activities 5%
- Government 19%
- Mining, logging, and construction 6%
- Education and health services 13%
- Trade, transportation, and utilities 19%
- Professional and business services 11%
- Leisure and hospitality 19%

# 1. Employment by Industry: Hawaii, 2011–2019

(Numbers in thousands, not seasonally adjusted)

| Industry and year | January | February | March | April | May | June | July | August | September | October | November | December | Annual average |
|---|---|---|---|---|---|---|---|---|---|---|---|---|---|
| **Total Nonfarm** | | | | | | | | | | | | | |
| 2011 | 582.0 | 593.1 | 596.9 | 593.8 | 595.1 | 592.2 | 589.0 | 586.2 | 595.1 | 598.4 | 604.5 | 609.8 | 594.7 |
| 2012 | 586.1 | 601.7 | 604.2 | 605.7 | 608.8 | 607.4 | 600.9 | 607.1 | 608.8 | 612.9 | 624.1 | 624.3 | 607.7 |
| 2013 | 601.8 | 616.8 | 620.2 | 617.1 | 622.0 | 618.9 | 615.0 | 612.7 | 620.8 | 625.3 | 632.4 | 635.8 | 619.9 |
| 2014 | 620.0 | 624.8 | 628.4 | 626.6 | 630.2 | 626.3 | 620.5 | 623.5 | 628.9 | 632.3 | 640.4 | 639.6 | 628.5 |
| 2015 | 628.6 | 634.3 | 637.9 | 636.7 | 639.1 | 637.2 | 631.6 | 634.9 | 637.9 | 644.0 | 649.6 | 655.7 | 639.0 |
| 2016 | 637.2 | 644.7 | 647.5 | 645.7 | 648.5 | 645.3 | 641.1 | 644.3 | 649.9 | 650.3 | 659.4 | 657.6 | 647.6 |
| 2017 | 646.9 | 653.3 | 657.3 | 655.4 | 657.6 | 655.4 | 647.2 | 646.0 | 655.5 | 656.4 | 661.3 | 667.2 | 655.0 |
| 2018 | 650.7 | 658.0 | 661.1 | 658.0 | 659.8 | 658.7 | 648.1 | 652.4 | 655.4 | 658.9 | 667.5 | 670.4 | 658.3 |
| 2019 | 652.0 | 659.6 | 660.8 | 652.9 | 656.2 | 651.6 | 646.0 | 646.2 | 653.9 | 658.0 | 662.5 | 668.2 | 655.7 |
| **Total Private** | | | | | | | | | | | | | |
| 2010 | 461.8 | 466.2 | 469.2 | 466.7 | 466.9 | 466.7 | 469.4 | 470.7 | 472.6 | 472.5 | 477.1 | 481.7 | 470.1 |
| 2011 | 471.0 | 474.2 | 475.9 | 477.2 | 479.8 | 481.5 | 482.2 | 484.5 | 486.4 | 492.1 | 495.4 | 482.1 |
| 2012 | 486.1 | 488.8 | 491.8 | 491.7 | 492.8 | 493.9 | 496.2 | 496.7 | 497.0 | 498.3 | 504.4 | 507.1 | 495.4 |
| 2013 | 495.3 | 496.5 | 499.8 | 498.7 | 500.7 | 500.1 | 501.2 | 502.7 | 504.1 | 505.2 | 508.9 | 513.4 | 502.2 |
| 2014 | 503.8 | 506.0 | 509.2 | 508.0 | 509.7 | 511.0 | 512.9 | 513.3 | 513.2 | 516.4 | 521.2 | 525.9 | 512.6 |
| 2015 | 514.3 | 516.8 | 518.5 | 519.1 | 519.4 | 519.1 | 522.3 | 524.6 | 524.5 | 522.6 | 527.5 | 530.5 | 521.6 |
| 2016 | 522.2 | 524.1 | 527.9 | 526.4 | 528.1 | 529.4 | 530.1 | 531.4 | 531.2 | 530.1 | 533.7 | 538.6 | 529.4 |
| 2017 | 528.4 | 530.2 | 533.3 | 531.1 | 531.0 | 533.4 | 530.5 | 533.1 | 531.4 | 532.4 | 536.1 | 540.6 | 532.6 |
| 2018 | 528.3 | 530.4 | 531.7 | 525.2 | 526.3 | 525.3 | 527.5 | 529.1 | 528.0 | 529.6 | 532.7 | 538.1 | 529.4 |
| 2019 | | | | | | | | | | | | | |
| **Goods Producing** | | | | | | | | | | | | | |
| 2011 | 41.4 | 42.0 | 42.2 | 42.5 | 42.6 | 43.1 | 43.7 | 43.8 | 44.0 | 43.5 | 43.6 | 43.7 | 43.0 |
| 2012 | 42.8 | 42.7 | 42.8 | 42.7 | 42.9 | 43.5 | 43.8 | 44.2 | 44.5 | 44.7 | 45.0 | 45.1 | 43.7 |
| 2013 | 44.1 | 44.4 | 45.0 | 44.9 | 45.7 | 45.5 | 45.9 | 46.0 | 46.2 | 46.0 | 46.4 | 46.6 | 45.6 |
| 2014 | 45.2 | 45.5 | 45.9 | 45.7 | 46.4 | 46.9 | 47.6 | 48.1 | 48.2 | 48.4 | 48.4 | 48.5 | 47.1 |
| 2015 | 47.1 | 47.4 | 48.1 | 48.5 | 49.2 | 49.9 | 50.9 | 51.1 | 51.1 | 52.4 | 52.8 | 53.4 | 50.2 |
| 2016 | 52.4 | 53.0 | 53.3 | 53.2 | 53.5 | 53.7 | 54.2 | 54.2 | 53.6 | 53.0 | 53.0 | 52.8 | 53.3 |
| 2017 | 51.0 | 51.4 | 51.8 | 51.4 | 51.8 | 52.2 | 52.0 | 52.1 | 52.0 | 51.4 | 51.7 | 51.9 | 51.7 |
| 2018 | 50.6 | 50.8 | 51.3 | 51.6 | 51.5 | 52.0 | 52.3 | 52.2 | 52.1 | 52.3 | 52.1 | 52.1 | 51.7 |
| 2019 | 50.5 | 50.7 | 51.6 | 51.0 | 51.0 | 50.9 | 51.2 | 51.2 | 51.1 | 51.9 | 51.4 | 51.8 | 51.2 |
| **Service-Providing** | | | | | | | | | | | | | |
| 2011 | 540.6 | 551.1 | 554.7 | 551.3 | 552.5 | 549.1 | 545.3 | 542.4 | 551.1 | 554.9 | 560.9 | 566.1 | 551.7 |
| 2012 | 543.3 | 559.0 | 561.4 | 563.0 | 565.9 | 563.9 | 557.1 | 562.9 | 564.3 | 568.2 | 579.1 | 579.2 | 563.9 |
| 2013 | 557.7 | 572.4 | 575.2 | 572.2 | 576.3 | 573.4 | 569.1 | 566.7 | 574.6 | 579.3 | 586.0 | 589.2 | 574.3 |
| 2014 | 574.8 | 579.3 | 582.5 | 580.9 | 583.8 | 579.4 | 572.9 | 575.4 | 580.7 | 583.9 | 592.0 | 591.1 | 581.4 |
| 2015 | 581.5 | 586.9 | 589.8 | 588.2 | 589.9 | 587.3 | 580.7 | 583.8 | 586.8 | 591.6 | 596.8 | 602.3 | 588.8 |
| 2016 | 584.8 | 591.7 | 594.2 | 592.5 | 595.0 | 591.6 | 586.9 | 590.1 | 596.3 | 597.3 | 606.4 | 604.8 | 594.3 |
| 2017 | 595.9 | 601.9 | 605.5 | 604.0 | 605.8 | 603.2 | 595.2 | 593.9 | 603.5 | 605.0 | 609.6 | 615.3 | 603.2 |
| 2018 | 600.1 | 607.2 | 609.8 | 606.4 | 608.3 | 606.7 | 595.8 | 600.2 | 603.3 | 606.6 | 615.4 | 618.3 | 606.5 |
| 2019 | 601.5 | 608.9 | 609.2 | 601.9 | 605.2 | 600.7 | 594.8 | 595.0 | 602.8 | 606.1 | 611.1 | 616.4 | 604.5 |
| **Mining, Logging, and Construction** | | | | | | | | | | | | | |
| 2011 | 28.2 | 28.6 | 28.8 | 29.1 | 29.1 | 29.7 | 30.2 | 30.1 | 30.3 | 29.9 | 29.8 | 30.0 | 29.5 |
| 2012 | 29.2 | 29.1 | 29.3 | 29.3 | 29.6 | 30.1 | 30.3 | 30.6 | 30.9 | 31.1 | 31.2 | 31.3 | 30.2 |
| 2013 | 30.5 | 30.8 | 31.3 | 31.4 | 32.0 | 31.8 | 32.1 | 32.2 | 32.2 | 32.1 | 32.3 | 32.5 | 31.8 |
| 2014 | 31.4 | 31.7 | 31.9 | 31.9 | 32.6 | 32.8 | 33.3 | 33.6 | 33.9 | 34.1 | 34.0 | 34.0 | 32.9 |
| 2015 | 32.8 | 33.1 | 33.8 | 34.3 | 34.9 | 35.6 | 36.5 | 36.6 | 36.8 | 38.0 | 38.3 | 38.8 | 35.8 |
| 2016 | 38.1 | 38.6 | 38.9 | 38.8 | 39.1 | 39.2 | 39.7 | 39.6 | 39.1 | 38.5 | 38.5 | 38.1 | 38.9 |
| 2017 | 36.8 | 37.0 | 37.3 | 36.9 | 37.2 | 37.5 | 37.3 | 37.4 | 37.2 | 36.6 | 36.8 | 36.9 | 37.1 |
| 2018 | 35.8 | 36.1 | 36.6 | 36.9 | 37.0 | 37.6 | 37.9 | 37.9 | 37.8 | 38.0 | 37.7 | 37.7 | 37.3 |
| 2019 | 36.3 | 36.5 | 37.4 | 37.0 | 37.0 | 36.9 | 37.3 | 37.2 | 37.1 | 38.0 | 37.4 | 37.7 | 37.2 |
| **Manufacturing** | | | | | | | | | | | | | |
| 2011 | 13.2 | 13.4 | 13.4 | 13.4 | 13.5 | 13.4 | 13.5 | 13.7 | 13.7 | 13.6 | 13.8 | 13.7 | 13.5 |
| 2012 | 13.6 | 13.6 | 13.5 | 13.4 | 13.3 | 13.4 | 13.5 | 13.6 | 13.6 | 13.6 | 13.8 | 13.8 | 13.6 |
| 2013 | 13.6 | 13.6 | 13.7 | 13.5 | 13.7 | 13.7 | 13.8 | 13.8 | 14.0 | 13.9 | 14.1 | 14.1 | 13.8 |
| 2014 | 13.8 | 13.8 | 14.0 | 13.8 | 13.8 | 14.1 | 14.3 | 14.5 | 14.3 | 14.3 | 14.4 | 14.5 | 14.1 |
| 2015 | 14.3 | 14.3 | 14.3 | 14.2 | 14.3 | 14.3 | 14.4 | 14.5 | 14.3 | 14.4 | 14.5 | 14.6 | 14.4 |
| 2016 | 14.3 | 14.4 | 14.4 | 14.4 | 14.4 | 14.5 | 14.5 | 14.6 | 14.5 | 14.5 | 14.5 | 14.7 | 14.5 |
| 2017 | 14.2 | 14.4 | 14.5 | 14.5 | 14.6 | 14.7 | 14.7 | 14.7 | 14.8 | 14.8 | 14.9 | 15.0 | 14.7 |
| 2018 | 14.8 | 14.7 | 14.7 | 14.7 | 14.5 | 14.4 | 14.4 | 14.3 | 14.3 | 14.3 | 14.4 | 14.4 | 14.5 |
| 2019 | 14.2 | 14.2 | 14.2 | 14.0 | 14.0 | 14.0 | 13.9 | 14.0 | 14.0 | 13.9 | 14.0 | 14.1 | 14.0 |

## 1. Employment by Industry: Hawaii, 2011–2019—*Continued*

(Numbers in thousands, not seasonally adjusted)

| Industry and year | January | February | March | April | May | June | July | August | September | October | November | December | Annual average |
|---|---|---|---|---|---|---|---|---|---|---|---|---|---|
| **Trade, Transportation, and Utilities** | | | | | | | | | | | | | |
| 2011 | 111.6 | 111.1 | 111.3 | 110.8 | 110.9 | 111.1 | 111.9 | 111.9 | 112.1 | 113.1 | 115.3 | 117.0 | 112.3 |
| 2012 | 114.2 | 113.6 | 114.2 | 113.8 | 114.4 | 115.1 | 115.4 | 115.6 | 115.8 | 116.2 | 119.4 | 120.6 | 115.7 |
| 2013 | 116.7 | 116.3 | 116.9 | 116.5 | 116.6 | 117.2 | 117.4 | 117.7 | 117.8 | 117.9 | 120.4 | 122.0 | 117.8 |
| 2014 | 118.0 | 117.1 | 117.4 | 117.2 | 117.6 | 117.9 | 118.4 | 118.0 | 118.1 | 118.9 | 121.4 | 123.6 | 118.6 |
| 2015 | 120.2 | 119.5 | 119.9 | 119.5 | 119.6 | 119.9 | 120.3 | 120.3 | 120.0 | 120.6 | 123.0 | 124.5 | 120.6 |
| 2016 | 120.8 | 120.0 | 119.9 | 119.6 | 119.8 | 119.6 | 120.7 | 121.2 | 121.5 | 121.8 | 124.4 | 126.3 | 121.3 |
| 2017 | 122.7 | 121.5 | 121.8 | 121.4 | 121.8 | 122.2 | 122.6 | 123.1 | 123.0 | 123.4 | 125.7 | 127.3 | 123.0 |
| 2018 | 124.3 | 123.2 | 123.4 | 123.6 | 123.7 | 124.0 | 124.3 | 124.4 | 123.9 | 124.1 | 126.9 | 127.8 | 124.5 |
| 2019 | 124.9 | 123.6 | 123.4 | 122.3 | 122.5 | 123.0 | 123.0 | 123.1 | 122.8 | 122.6 | 124.8 | 126.1 | 123.5 |
| **Wholesale Trade** | | | | | | | | | | | | | |
| 2011 | 17.6 | 17.6 | 17.6 | 17.6 | 17.7 | 17.7 | 17.8 | 17.8 | 17.8 | 17.9 | 17.9 | 18.1 | 17.8 |
| 2012 | 17.8 | 17.8 | 17.9 | 17.8 | 17.8 | 18.0 | 18.0 | 18.0 | 18.1 | 18.1 | 18.1 | 18.2 | 18.0 |
| 2013 | 18.0 | 17.9 | 18.1 | 18.0 | 18.0 | 18.0 | 18.0 | 18.0 | 18.0 | 18.0 | 18.0 | 18.0 | 18.0 |
| 2014 | 17.9 | 17.9 | 18.0 | 17.9 | 18.0 | 18.1 | 18.0 | 18.0 | 18.0 | 18.2 | 18.2 | 18.5 | 18.1 |
| 2015 | 18.2 | 18.2 | 18.3 | 18.2 | 18.3 | 18.3 | 18.4 | 18.4 | 18.3 | 18.3 | 18.3 | 18.4 | 18.3 |
| 2016 | 18.1 | 18.0 | 18.0 | 18.2 | 18.2 | 18.2 | 18.3 | 18.3 | 18.3 | 18.3 | 18.4 | 18.5 | 18.2 |
| 2017 | 18.3 | 18.2 | 18.3 | 18.2 | 18.3 | 18.4 | 18.3 | 18.4 | 18.4 | 18.3 | 18.4 | 18.5 | 18.3 |
| 2018 | 18.3 | 18.3 | 18.3 | 18.3 | 18.3 | 18.4 | 18.3 | 18.3 | 18.3 | 18.3 | 18.3 | 18.5 | 18.3 |
| 2019 | 18.4 | 18.4 | 18.4 | 18.2 | 18.2 | 18.3 | 18.1 | 18.1 | 18.1 | 18.2 | 18.1 | 18.2 | 18.2 |
| **Retail Trade** | | | | | | | | | | | | | |
| 2011 | 67.0 | 66.3 | 66.5 | 66.2 | 66.2 | 66.4 | 66.9 | 66.9 | 67.1 | 67.6 | 69.7 | 70.9 | 67.3 |
| 2012 | 68.6 | 68.1 | 68.2 | 67.9 | 68.4 | 68.7 | 68.8 | 68.8 | 68.8 | 69.2 | 72.0 | 73.0 | 69.2 |
| 2013 | 69.7 | 69.2 | 69.5 | 69.1 | 69.1 | 69.5 | 69.7 | 69.8 | 69.8 | 69.8 | 72.3 | 73.5 | 70.1 |
| 2014 | 70.0 | 69.1 | 69.2 | 69.1 | 69.2 | 69.8 | 70.1 | 69.8 | 70.0 | 70.3 | 72.5 | 74.0 | 70.3 |
| 2015 | 71.1 | 70.4 | 70.7 | 70.4 | 70.3 | 70.5 | 70.7 | 70.8 | 70.7 | 71.2 | 73.5 | 74.4 | 71.2 |
| 2016 | 71.4 | 70.7 | 70.6 | 70.0 | 69.9 | 69.7 | 70.4 | 70.6 | 71.0 | 71.3 | 73.3 | 74.5 | 71.1 |
| 2017 | 71.9 | 70.7 | 70.8 | 70.7 | 70.9 | 71.1 | 71.4 | 71.5 | 71.2 | 71.7 | 74.0 | 74.9 | 71.7 |
| 2018 | 72.7 | 71.6 | 71.6 | 71.6 | 71.7 | 71.8 | 72.3 | 72.3 | 71.9 | 72.1 | 74.5 | 74.9 | 72.4 |
| 2019 | 72.5 | 71.3 | 71.1 | 70.4 | 70.5 | 70.8 | 70.9 | 70.7 | 70.6 | 69.9 | 71.9 | 72.7 | 71.1 |
| **Transportation and Utilities** | | | | | | | | | | | | | |
| 2011 | 27.0 | 27.2 | 27.2 | 27.0 | 27.0 | 27.0 | 27.2 | 27.2 | 27.2 | 27.6 | 27.7 | 28.0 | 27.3 |
| 2012 | 27.8 | 27.7 | 28.1 | 28.1 | 28.2 | 28.4 | 28.6 | 28.8 | 28.9 | 28.9 | 29.3 | 29.4 | 28.5 |
| 2013 | 29.0 | 29.2 | 29.3 | 29.4 | 29.5 | 29.7 | 29.7 | 29.9 | 30.0 | 30.1 | 30.1 | 30.5 | 29.7 |
| 2014 | 30.1 | 30.1 | 30.2 | 30.2 | 30.4 | 30.0 | 30.3 | 30.2 | 30.1 | 30.4 | 30.7 | 31.1 | 30.3 |
| 2015 | 30.9 | 30.9 | 30.9 | 30.9 | 31.0 | 31.1 | 31.2 | 31.1 | 31.0 | 31.1 | 31.2 | 31.7 | 31.1 |
| 2016 | 31.3 | 31.3 | 31.3 | 31.4 | 31.7 | 31.7 | 32.0 | 32.3 | 32.2 | 32.2 | 32.7 | 33.3 | 32.0 |
| 2017 | 32.5 | 32.6 | 32.7 | 32.5 | 32.6 | 32.7 | 32.9 | 33.2 | 33.4 | 33.4 | 33.3 | 33.9 | 33.0 |
| 2018 | 33.3 | 33.3 | 33.5 | 33.7 | 33.7 | 33.8 | 33.7 | 33.8 | 33.7 | 33.7 | 34.1 | 34.4 | 33.7 |
| 2019 | 34.0 | 33.9 | 33.9 | 33.7 | 33.8 | 33.9 | 34.0 | 34.3 | 34.1 | 34.5 | 34.8 | 35.2 | 34.2 |
| **Information** | | | | | | | | | | | | | |
| 2011 | 8.6 | 9.5 | 10.2 | 8.2 | 8.1 | 7.9 | 8.4 | 8.4 | 8.3 | 8.4 | 8.7 | 8.8 | 8.6 |
| 2012 | 8.4 | 8.5 | 8.6 | 8.5 | 8.5 | 7.9 | 8.2 | 8.4 | 8.5 | 8.7 | 9.3 | 9.0 | 8.5 |
| 2013 | 8.4 | 8.5 | 8.6 | 8.5 | 8.1 | 8.0 | 9.7 | 8.5 | 8.9 | 9.5 | 9.7 | 10.0 | 8.9 |
| 2014 | 8.4 | 8.5 | 8.6 | 8.4 | 8.9 | 8.2 | 8.3 | 8.8 | 8.9 | 8.6 | 8.8 | 8.8 | 8.6 |
| 2015 | 8.6 | 8.7 | 8.7 | 8.5 | 8.4 | 8.3 | 8.8 | 8.7 | 8.6 | 8.8 | 9.7 | 9.8 | 8.8 |
| 2016 | 8.3 | 8.7 | 8.5 | 8.6 | 9.1 | 8.6 | 8.8 | 9.8 | 9.2 | 8.8 | 9.8 | 8.8 | 8.9 |
| 2017 | 9.0 | 9.2 | 9.3 | 9.2 | 9.9 | 9.1 | 9.2 | 10.1 | 9.3 | 8.3 | 8.4 | 8.7 | 9.1 |
| 2018 | 8.5 | 9.0 | 9.1 | 9.6 | 9.8 | 9.9 | 8.3 | 10.0 | 9.4 | 8.8 | 9.4 | 9.2 | 9.3 |
| 2019 | 8.9 | 10.0 | 8.7 | 8.0 | 8.9 | 7.8 | 8.1 | 9.2 | 8.7 | 8.5 | 8.9 | 8.8 | 8.7 |
| **Financial Activities** | | | | | | | | | | | | | |
| 2011 | 27.0 | 27.1 | 27.2 | 27.1 | 27.2 | 27.1 | 27.3 | 27.3 | 27.1 | 27.2 | 27.4 | 27.4 | 27.2 |
| 2012 | 27.0 | 27.2 | 27.2 | 27.2 | 27.2 | 27.5 | 27.5 | 27.5 | 27.5 | 27.5 | 27.6 | 27.7 | 27.4 |
| 2013 | 27.4 | 27.4 | 27.7 | 27.8 | 27.9 | 27.9 | 27.9 | 27.8 | 27.9 | 27.9 | 28.0 | 28.2 | 27.8 |
| 2014 | 27.8 | 27.8 | 28.1 | 28.0 | 28.2 | 28.3 | 28.5 | 28.5 | 28.4 | 28.5 | 28.5 | 28.8 | 28.3 |
| 2015 | 28.4 | 28.6 | 28.7 | 28.8 | 28.9 | 29.0 | 29.0 | 28.9 | 28.7 | 28.7 | 28.6 | 28.9 | 28.8 |
| 2016 | 28.9 | 29.0 | 29.0 | 29.0 | 29.1 | 29.2 | 29.5 | 29.6 | 29.4 | 29.3 | 29.4 | 29.5 | 29.2 |
| 2017 | 29.3 | 29.3 | 29.5 | 29.3 | 29.4 | 29.4 | 29.4 | 29.3 | 29.4 | 29.5 | 29.5 | 29.8 | 29.4 |
| 2018 | 29.4 | 29.5 | 29.6 | 29.7 | 29.5 | 29.6 | 29.7 | 29.6 | 29.5 | 29.7 | 29.8 | 30.0 | 29.6 |
| 2019 | 29.5 | 29.7 | 29.8 | 29.9 | 29.9 | 29.9 | 30.0 | 29.8 | 29.8 | 29.9 | 30.1 | 30.1 | 29.9 |

# 1. Employment by Industry: Hawaii, 2011–2019—*Continued*

(Numbers in thousands, not seasonally adjusted)

| Industry and year | January | February | March | April | May | June | July | August | September | October | November | December | Annual average |
|---|---|---|---|---|---|---|---|---|---|---|---|---|---|
| **Professional and Business Services** | | | | | | | | | | | | | |
| 2011 | 67.3 | 68.3 | 68.9 | 69.2 | 68.7 | 68.8 | 68.6 | 69.3 | 69.5 | 69.7 | 70.2 | 71.4 | 69.2 |
| 2012 | 68.7 | 69.4 | 69.7 | 70.3 | 70.7 | 70.8 | 70.5 | 71.3 | 70.7 | 71.4 | 72.2 | 72.5 | 70.7 |
| 2013 | 71.5 | 72.4 | 72.7 | 72.7 | 72.3 | 72.4 | 72.9 | 73.4 | 73.2 | 74.2 | 75.2 | 75.1 | 73.2 |
| 2014 | 74.2 | 74.3 | 75.0 | 75.2 | 74.8 | 74.9 | 74.4 | 74.9 | 75.0 | 75.0 | 75.5 | 76.0 | 74.9 |
| 2015 | 74.6 | 74.9 | 75.4 | 75.0 | 74.8 | 75.0 | 75.1 | 74.6 | 74.5 | 75.2 | 75.2 | 75.4 | 75.0 |
| 2016 | 73.4 | 74.2 | 74.1 | 74.5 | 73.6 | 73.5 | 73.9 | 74.0 | 74.0 | 73.7 | 74.2 | 74.5 | 74.0 |
| 2017 | 73.2 | 73.5 | 74.0 | 73.7 | 73.6 | 74.7 | 74.3 | 74.3 | 73.7 | 73.9 | 74.4 | 74.7 | 74.0 |
| 2018 | 73.2 | 73.5 | 74.2 | 73.9 | 73.7 | 74.2 | 74.1 | 74.5 | 74.2 | 74.9 | 75.4 | 75.8 | 74.3 |
| 2019 | 74.1 | 74.4 | 74.6 | 73.2 | 73.0 | 73.0 | 74.0 | 74.2 | 73.6 | 74.6 | 74.5 | 75.7 | 74.1 |
| **Education and Health Services** | | | | | | | | | | | | | |
| 2011 | 75.5 | 77.2 | 77.3 | 77.2 | 77.5 | 76.5 | 77.1 | 76.7 | 77.7 | 77.7 | 78.6 | 79.0 | 77.3 |
| 2012 | 76.5 | 78.0 | 77.5 | 78.3 | 79.0 | 78.3 | 78.2 | 78.6 | 79.5 | 79.5 | 79.9 | 80.7 | 78.7 |
| 2013 | 79.2 | 80.2 | 80.7 | 80.7 | 80.7 | 80.8 | 80.0 | 80.3 | 80.8 | 80.3 | 81.7 | 81.2 | 80.6 |
| 2014 | 79.4 | 80.2 | 80.7 | 80.6 | 80.6 | 80.0 | 79.9 | 80.2 | 81.1 | 81.5 | 81.9 | 82.7 | 80.7 |
| 2015 | 81.6 | 82.9 | 83.6 | 83.5 | 83.5 | 83.1 | 82.7 | 82.8 | 84.0 | 84.4 | 84.7 | 85.5 | 83.5 |
| 2016 | 83.4 | 83.7 | 84.9 | 85.0 | 84.6 | 84.1 | 84.4 | 84.1 | 85.5 | 84.8 | 85.1 | 85.6 | 84.6 |
| 2017 | 84.7 | 85.3 | 86.1 | 86.3 | 86.1 | 85.2 | 86.2 | 85.6 | 87.7 | 87.3 | 87.5 | 88.5 | 86.4 |
| 2018 | 86.7 | 87.7 | 88.4 | 87.4 | 87.1 | 87.2 | 85.7 | 86.1 | 87.2 | 87.0 | 88.0 | 88.2 | 87.2 |
| 2019 | 85.9 | 87.4 | 88.0 | 86.8 | 86.8 | 85.5 | 85.9 | 86.2 | 87.4 | 88.5 | 88.9 | 89.0 | 87.2 |
| **Leisure and Hospitality** | | | | | | | | | | | | | |
| 2011 | 104.4 | 104.8 | 105.9 | 105.4 | 105.5 | 105.8 | 106.0 | 106.8 | 107.1 | 106.2 | 106.7 | 107.7 | 106.0 |
| 2012 | 107.3 | 108.4 | 109.4 | 109.7 | 110.2 | 111.5 | 111.8 | 112.0 | 111.5 | 111.3 | 111.6 | 112.8 | 110.6 |
| 2013 | 112.0 | 112.7 | 113.2 | 113.5 | 114.4 | 115.0 | 115.3 | 115.8 | 114.8 | 115.2 | 115.8 | 116.6 | 114.5 |
| 2014 | 115.4 | 116.1 | 116.8 | 116.6 | 117.1 | 116.8 | 117.0 | 117.0 | 117.1 | 117.0 | 117.0 | 117.4 | 116.8 |
| 2015 | 116.3 | 116.8 | 117.3 | 116.9 | 117.8 | 118.1 | 118.7 | 119.5 | 118.8 | 118.8 | 119.5 | 120.8 | 118.3 |
| 2016 | 119.6 | 120.6 | 121.1 | 121.3 | 121.8 | 122.4 | 122.8 | 123.7 | 123.1 | 123.2 | 123.4 | 124.8 | 122.3 |
| 2017 | 124.3 | 125.6 | 126.9 | 126.5 | 126.9 | 127.8 | 127.8 | 128.2 | 127.4 | 127.7 | 127.8 | 128.8 | 127.1 |
| 2018 | 127.3 | 127.8 | 128.5 | 126.6 | 127.0 | 127.5 | 127.4 | 127.7 | 126.4 | 127.0 | 125.8 | 128.8 | 127.3 |
| 2019 | 126.1 | 126.1 | 127.0 | 125.7 | 125.9 | 126.7 | 127.0 | 127.2 | 126.4 | 125.5 | 125.7 | 128.3 | 126.5 |
| **Other Services** | | | | | | | | | | | | | |
| 2011 | 26.0 | 26.2 | 26.2 | 26.3 | 26.4 | 26.4 | 26.4 | 26.5 | 26.8 | 26.7 | 26.6 | 26.7 | 26.4 |
| 2012 | 26.1 | 26.4 | 26.5 | 26.7 | 26.9 | 26.9 | 26.8 | 26.9 | 27.1 | 27.1 | 27.1 | 27.0 | 26.8 |
| 2013 | 26.8 | 26.9 | 27.0 | 27.1 | 27.1 | 27.1 | 27.1 | 27.2 | 27.4 | 27.3 | 27.2 | 27.4 | 27.1 |
| 2014 | 26.9 | 27.0 | 27.3 | 27.0 | 27.1 | 27.1 | 27.1 | 27.2 | 27.3 | 27.3 | 27.4 | 27.6 | 27.2 |
| 2015 | 27.0 | 27.2 | 27.5 | 27.3 | 27.5 | 27.7 | 27.4 | 27.4 | 27.5 | 27.5 | 27.7 | 27.6 | 27.4 |
| 2016 | 27.5 | 27.6 | 27.7 | 27.9 | 27.9 | 28.0 | 28.0 | 28.0 | 28.2 | 28.0 | 28.2 | 28.2 | 27.9 |
| 2017 | 28.0 | 28.3 | 28.5 | 28.6 | 28.6 | 28.8 | 28.6 | 28.7 | 28.7 | 28.6 | 28.7 | 28.9 | 28.6 |
| 2018 | 28.4 | 28.7 | 28.8 | 28.7 | 28.7 | 29.0 | 28.7 | 28.6 | 28.7 | 28.1 | 28.7 | 28.7 | 28.7 |
| 2019 | 28.4 | 28.5 | 28.6 | 28.3 | 28.3 | 28.5 | 28.3 | 28.2 | 28.2 | 28.1 | 28.4 | 28.3 | 28.3 |
| **Government** | | | | | | | | | | | | | |
| 2011 | 120.2 | 126.9 | 127.7 | 127.1 | 128.2 | 125.5 | 119.6 | 115.5 | 122.5 | 125.9 | 127.4 | 128.1 | 124.6 |
| 2012 | 115.1 | 127.5 | 128.3 | 128.5 | 129.0 | 125.9 | 118.7 | 122.6 | 123.7 | 126.5 | 132.0 | 128.9 | 125.6 |
| 2013 | 115.7 | 128.0 | 128.4 | 125.4 | 129.2 | 125.0 | 118.8 | 116.0 | 123.8 | 127.0 | 128.0 | 128.7 | 124.5 |
| 2014 | 124.7 | 128.3 | 128.6 | 127.9 | 129.5 | 126.2 | 119.3 | 120.8 | 124.8 | 127.1 | 131.5 | 126.2 | 126.2 |
| 2015 | 124.8 | 128.3 | 128.7 | 128.7 | 129.4 | 126.2 | 118.7 | 121.6 | 124.7 | 127.6 | 128.4 | 129.8 | 126.4 |
| 2016 | 122.9 | 127.9 | 129.0 | 126.6 | 129.1 | 126.2 | 118.8 | 119.7 | 125.4 | 127.7 | 131.9 | 127.1 | 126.0 |
| 2017 | 124.7 | 129.2 | 129.4 | 129.0 | 129.5 | 126.0 | 117.1 | 114.6 | 124.3 | 126.3 | 127.6 | 128.6 | 125.5 |
| 2018 | 122.3 | 127.8 | 127.8 | 126.9 | 128.8 | 125.3 | 117.6 | 119.3 | 124.0 | 126.5 | 131.4 | 129.8 | 125.6 |
| 2019 | 123.7 | 129.2 | 129.1 | 127.7 | 129.9 | 126.3 | 118.5 | 117.1 | 125.9 | 128.4 | 129.8 | 130.1 | 126.3 |

## 2. Average Weekly Hours by Selected Industry: Hawaii, 2015–2019

(Not seasonally adjusted)

| Industry and year | January | February | March | April | May | June | July | August | September | October | November | December | Annual average |
|---|---|---|---|---|---|---|---|---|---|---|---|---|---|
| **Total Private** | | | | | | | | | | | | | |
| 2015 | 33.3 | 34.2 | 34.1 | 33.1 | 33.0 | 32.9 | 33.3 | 34.0 | 32.6 | 32.6 | 33.5 | 33.0 | 33.3 |
| 2016 | 32.8 | 32.7 | 32.6 | 32.7 | 33.6 | 32.5 | 32.9 | 32.7 | 32.3 | 33.6 | 32.1 | 32.5 | 32.7 |
| 2017 | 33.7 | 32.7 | 32.3 | 33.8 | 32.6 | 32.8 | 34.1 | 32.8 | 32.8 | 33.6 | 33.0 | 32.9 | 33.1 |
| 2018 | 33.0 | 32.5 | 32.5 | 33.4 | 32.3 | 32.5 | 33.9 | 32.4 | 33.4 | 32.4 | 32.5 | 33.4 | 32.9 |
| 2019 | 32.3 | 31.8 | 32.1 | 32.3 | 32.5 | 33.4 | 32.6 | 32.5 | 33.7 | 32.6 | 32.6 | 33.7 | 32.7 |
| **Goods-Producing** | | | | | | | | | | | | | |
| 2015 | 36.6 | 36.6 | 36.9 | 37.4 | 37.8 | 35.0 | 36.8 | 36.5 | 34.4 | 36.6 | 35.9 | 38.5 | 36.6 |
| 2016 | 38.5 | 37.5 | 37.7 | 37.1 | 37.5 | 36.4 | 37.2 | 37.3 | 36.2 | 37.7 | 35.2 | 36.6 | 37.1 |
| 2017 | 36.6 | 36.7 | 37.1 | 36.4 | 37.1 | 35.2 | 37.9 | 37.2 | 36.4 | 37.2 | 37.5 | 36.9 | 36.9 |
| 2018 | 37.1 | 35.4 | 36.8 | 37.2 | 36.2 | 34.2 | 37.2 | 36.2 | 36.2 | 37.3 | 36.2 | 38.3 | 36.5 |
| 2019 | 36.7 | 35.6 | 36.8 | 37.2 | 37.3 | 35.1 | 37.2 | 37.2 | 38.7 | 37.2 | 36.9 | 38.9 | 37.1 |
| **Mining, Logging, and Construction** | | | | | | | | | | | | | |
| 2015 | 36.2 | 36.3 | 37.1 | 37.6 | 37.6 | 34.3 | 36.1 | 35.7 | 33.4 | 35.9 | 35.3 | 38.2 | 36.1 |
| 2016 | 38.3 | 37.6 | 37.2 | 37.0 | 37.2 | 36.2 | 36.8 | 37.2 | 35.7 | 37.4 | 34.4 | 36.4 | 36.8 |
| 2017 | 36.7 | 36.4 | 36.9 | 35.5 | 36.9 | 34.7 | 38.1 | 37.2 | 36.3 | 37.3 | 38.7 | 37.7 | 36.8 |
| 2018 | 38.3 | 35.7 | 37.7 | 38.0 | 36.4 | 34.4 | 37.8 | 36.8 | 36.8 | 37.8 | 36.8 | 39.7 | 37.2 |
| 2019 | 37.8 | 36.2 | 37.7 | 37.8 | 37.4 | 34.9 | 37.6 | 37.6 | 39.1 | 37.3 | 36.3 | 39.0 | 37.4 |
| **Manufacturing** | | | | | | | | | | | | | |
| 2015 | 37.6 | 37.2 | 36.6 | 36.8 | 38.3 | 36.6 | 38.5 | 38.7 | 36.6 | 38.5 | 37.5 | 39.2 | 37.7 |
| 2016 | 39.1 | 37.5 | 38.8 | 37.2 | 38.1 | 37.0 | 38.0 | 37.4 | 37.4 | 38.5 | 37.6 | 37.5 | 37.8 |
| 2017 | 36.2 | 37.7 | 37.7 | 38.7 | 37.9 | 36.4 | 37.6 | 37.1 | 36.7 | 37.2 | 34.4 | 35.1 | 36.9 |
| 2018 | 34.1 | 34.4 | 34.6 | 35.1 | 35.6 | 33.9 | 35.8 | 34.4 | 34.8 | 35.9 | 34.9 | 34.9 | 34.9 |
| 2019 | 34.2 | 34.1 | 34.8 | 35.7 | 37.0 | 35.9 | 36.0 | 36.3 | 37.6 | 37.1 | 38.6 | 38.6 | 36.2 |
| **Trade, Transportation, and Utilities** | | | | | | | | | | | | | |
| 2015 | 33.7 | 34.7 | 34.7 | 33.5 | 33.4 | 34.2 | 34.0 | 34.6 | 34.3 | 33.8 | 34.4 | 33.8 | 34.1 |
| 2016 | 33.8 | 33.6 | 33.5 | 33.6 | 34.0 | 33.5 | 34.1 | 33.6 | 33.5 | 34.8 | 33.4 | 33.7 | 33.8 |
| 2017 | 34.7 | 33.6 | 33.0 | 34.8 | 33.1 | 33.8 | 34.8 | 33.0 | 33.4 | 34.5 | 33.8 | 34.1 | 33.9 |
| 2018 | 34.0 | 33.4 | 33.0 | 34.5 | 33.3 | 34.3 | 35.7 | 33.8 | 35.5 | 33.8 | 34.0 | 35.1 | 34.2 |
| 2019 | 33.3 | 33.0 | 33.5 | 33.2 | 33.4 | 35.1 | 33.4 | 33.3 | 35.0 | 33.6 | 33.4 | 35.0 | 33.8 |
| **Professional and Business Services** | | | | | | | | | | | | | |
| 2015 | 34.2 | 34.6 | 34.8 | 34.3 | 33.8 | 33.3 | 33.7 | 34.1 | 33.0 | 33.4 | 35.0 | 34.6 | 34.1 |
| 2016 | 33.2 | 33.2 | 33.4 | 34.1 | 35.0 | 33.3 | 34.2 | 34.9 | 35.1 | 36.0 | 35.1 | 36.0 | 34.5 |
| 2017 | 36.5 | 35.0 | 35.3 | 35.8 | 34.9 | 34.3 | 35.7 | 34.7 | 34.7 | 35.0 | 34.6 | 34.5 | 35.1 |
| 2018 | 34.5 | 34.0 | 34.8 | 35.0 | 33.9 | 34.3 | 34.7 | 33.8 | 34.6 | 33.6 | 33.5 | 34.6 | 34.3 |
| 2019 | 33.4 | 33.4 | 33.6 | 33.8 | 33.7 | 34.8 | 34.2 | 34.1 | 35.1 | 33.8 | 34.3 | 35.2 | 34.1 |
| **Education and Health Services** | | | | | | | | | | | | | |
| 2015 | 31.9 | 32.7 | 31.7 | 31.5 | 31.2 | 31.6 | 31.7 | 32.9 | 31.6 | 31.2 | 32.1 | 31.6 | 31.8 |
| 2016 | 31.7 | 31.9 | 31.6 | 31.7 | 32.9 | 31.7 | 32.1 | 31.4 | 31.1 | 31.6 | 30.7 | 30.7 | 31.6 |
| 2017 | 32.5 | 31.7 | 31.5 | 32.7 | 31.8 | 32.0 | 33.0 | 32.1 | 32.5 | 32.8 | 32.1 | 32.4 | 32.3 |
| 2018 | 32.8 | 32.4 | 32.0 | 33.2 | 32.3 | 32.4 | 33.4 | 32.4 | 33.5 | 32.5 | 32.6 | 32.4 | 32.7 |
| 2019 | 31.9 | 31.7 | 31.7 | 32.3 | 32.3 | 32.7 | 32.3 | 31.9 | 33.1 | 32.3 | 32.3 | 33.2 | 32.3 |
| **Leisure and Hospitality** | | | | | | | | | | | | | |
| 2015 | 29.6 | 31.1 | 31.0 | 29.2 | 29.6 | 29.6 | 30.0 | 31.0 | 28.8 | 28.7 | 30.3 | 28.5 | 29.8 |
| 2016 | 28.8 | 28.8 | 28.3 | 28.8 | 30.5 | 28.9 | 28.9 | 28.8 | 28.3 | 29.9 | 28.4 | 28.4 | 28.9 |
| 2017 | 30.4 | 28.8 | 28.3 | 29.9 | 28.7 | 29.4 | 30.7 | 29.3 | 29.2 | 29.8 | 29.4 | 28.6 | 29.4 |
| 2018 | 29.0 | 28.8 | 28.5 | 28.9 | 27.5 | 27.5 | 29.1 | 27.4 | 27.9 | 27.2 | 27.7 | 28.1 | 28.1 |
| 2019 | 28.2 | 27.8 | 28.0 | 28.1 | 28.5 | 29.5 | 28.1 | 27.8 | 28.4 | 27.8 | 27.6 | 28.4 | 28.2 |

## 3. Average Hourly Earnings by Selected Industry: Hawaii, 2015–2019

(Dollars, not seasonally adjusted)

| Industry and year | January | February | March | April | May | June | July | August | September | October | November | December | Annual average |
|---|---|---|---|---|---|---|---|---|---|---|---|---|---|
| **Total Private** | | | | | | | | | | | | | |
| 2015 | 24.54 | 24.63 | 24.64 | 24.62 | 24.64 | 24.47 | 24.47 | 24.54 | 24.49 | 24.75 | 24.87 | 25.10 | 24.65 |
| 2016 | 25.16 | 25.30 | 25.19 | 25.34 | 25.38 | 25.49 | 25.48 | 25.44 | 25.69 | 25.65 | 25.50 | 25.61 | 25.44 |
| 2017 | 25.80 | 25.69 | 25.71 | 25.92 | 25.96 | 25.88 | 26.23 | 26.38 | 26.47 | 26.70 | 26.58 | 26.93 | 26.19 |
| 2018 | 27.39 | 27.20 | 27.35 | 27.88 | 27.50 | 27.69 | 27.84 | 27.89 | 28.12 | 27.84 | 28.02 | 28.44 | 27.77 |
| 2019 | 28.13 | 28.27 | 28.24 | 28.46 | 28.71 | 28.50 | 28.82 | 28.83 | 29.27 | 29.51 | 29.26 | 29.68 | 28.81 |
| **Goods-Producing** | | | | | | | | | | | | | |
| 2015 | 33.57 | 32.78 | 33.17 | 33.56 | 33.30 | 32.63 | 32.30 | 32.43 | 32.79 | 33.17 | 32.51 | 33.15 | 32.95 |
| 2016 | 32.80 | 32.53 | 32.42 | 33.15 | 32.45 | 33.08 | 32.85 | 33.34 | 33.30 | 33.72 | 33.54 | 33.90 | 33.08 |
| 2017 | 34.51 | 33.51 | 33.63 | 34.14 | 34.36 | 34.00 | 35.07 | 34.26 | 34.54 | 34.39 | 34.36 | 34.48 | 34.28 |
| 2018 | 35.34 | 35.37 | 35.48 | 35.81 | 35.66 | 34.83 | 35.51 | 36.57 | 37.03 | 36.04 | 36.76 | 37.49 | 36.01 |
| 2019 | 38.05 | 37.81 | 38.03 | 37.92 | 37.85 | 37.63 | 37.83 | 38.08 | 38.99 | 39.14 | 38.36 | 39.18 | 38.25 |
| **Mining, Logging and Construction** | | | | | | | | | | | | | |
| 2015 | 40.19 | 38.91 | 38.97 | 39.11 | 38.98 | 38.11 | 37.23 | 37.43 | 38.14 | 38.41 | 37.28 | 37.98 | 38.37 |
| 2016 | 37.75 | 37.17 | 37.18 | 37.75 | 37.07 | 37.77 | 37.60 | 38.00 | 38.29 | 38.81 | 38.94 | 39.25 | 37.95 |
| 2017 | 39.56 | 38.58 | 38.51 | 39.37 | 39.39 | 38.73 | 39.82 | 39.01 | 39.34 | 39.09 | 38.52 | 38.66 | 39.05 |
| 2018 | 39.36 | 39.81 | 39.83 | 40.43 | 40.32 | 39.09 | 39.74 | 41.01 | 41.82 | 40.63 | 41.50 | 42.06 | 40.49 |
| 2019 | 42.88 | 42.68 | 42.58 | 42.69 | 42.87 | 42.91 | 42.69 | 42.86 | 43.87 | 44.09 | 43.58 | 44.20 | 43.17 |
| **Manufacturing** | | | | | | | | | | | | | |
| 2015 | 18.89 | 18.92 | 19.24 | 19.86 | 19.69 | 19.90 | 20.62 | 20.74 | 20.29 | 20.35 | 20.66 | 20.63 | 19.99 |
| 2016 | 19.90 | 20.02 | 20.11 | 20.81 | 20.20 | 20.60 | 20.32 | 20.79 | 20.46 | 20.61 | 20.39 | 20.36 | 20.38 |
| 2017 | 21.29 | 20.90 | 21.36 | 21.91 | 21.89 | 22.53 | 22.84 | 22.22 | 22.59 | 22.74 | 22.77 | 23.41 | 22.20 |
| 2018 | 24.42 | 24.10 | 23.72 | 23.25 | 23.49 | 23.52 | 23.73 | 24.04 | 23.57 | 23.22 | 23.65 | 23.89 | 23.72 |
| 2019 | 24.30 | 24.43 | 25.02 | 24.57 | 24.39 | 24.08 | 24.25 | 24.92 | 25.51 | 25.55 | 25.24 | 25.62 | 24.84 |
| **Trade, Transportation, and Utilities** | | | | | | | | | | | | | |
| 2015 | 23.91 | 24.45 | 24.33 | 24.43 | 24.10 | 23.70 | 23.63 | 24.02 | 23.70 | 23.77 | 24.15 | 24.12 | 24.03 |
| 2016 | 24.26 | 24.40 | 24.24 | 24.46 | 24.67 | 24.84 | 24.76 | 24.95 | 25.23 | 25.04 | 24.62 | 24.51 | 24.67 |
| 2017 | 25.22 | 24.87 | 25.20 | 25.63 | 25.55 | 25.60 | 25.41 | 25.63 | 25.81 | 25.96 | 25.39 | 25.68 | 25.50 |
| 2018 | 26.01 | 26.09 | 26.24 | 27.06 | 26.77 | 26.66 | 26.84 | 26.86 | 27.23 | 26.95 | 26.88 | 27.83 | 26.80 |
| 2019 | 27.04 | 26.93 | 27.14 | 27.89 | 28.23 | 28.25 | 28.42 | 28.58 | 28.51 | 27.99 | 28.11 | 28.86 | 28.00 |
| **Professional and Business Services** | | | | | | | | | | | | | |
| 2015 | 23.34 | 23.46 | 23.40 | 23.14 | 23.46 | 23.49 | 23.35 | 23.30 | 23.20 | 23.85 | 24.23 | 23.65 | 23.49 |
| 2016 | 23.21 | 24.08 | 23.94 | 24.27 | 25.07 | 25.18 | 25.45 | 25.55 | 26.04 | 25.97 | 25.89 | 26.09 | 25.08 |
| 2017 | 25.52 | 26.04 | 25.77 | 25.98 | 25.68 | 25.67 | 26.09 | 25.55 | 25.40 | 26.00 | 25.53 | 25.45 | 25.72 |
| 2018 | 25.96 | 25.60 | 25.88 | 25.94 | 25.76 | 26.08 | 26.36 | 26.28 | 26.25 | 25.66 | 26.27 | 26.54 | 26.05 |
| 2019 | 26.33 | 26.20 | 26.88 | 26.34 | 26.42 | 26.34 | 26.63 | 26.29 | 26.95 | 26.90 | 27.36 | 27.96 | 26.73 |
| **Education and Health Services** | | | | | | | | | | | | | |
| 2015 | 26.98 | 27.18 | 26.52 | 25.97 | 26.32 | 26.69 | 26.84 | 26.64 | 26.87 | 27.52 | 27.26 | 27.72 | 26.88 |
| 2016 | 27.83 | 27.95 | 27.82 | 27.55 | 26.95 | 26.56 | 26.59 | 26.21 | 26.38 | 26.24 | 26.08 | 26.10 | 26.86 |
| 2017 | 26.61 | 27.08 | 27.08 | 27.14 | 27.57 | 28.04 | 28.57 | 29.16 | 29.51 | 29.69 | 30.08 | 30.29 | 28.42 |
| 2018 | 30.71 | 30.81 | 31.15 | 31.93 | 30.96 | 31.72 | 31.59 | 31.75 | 32.32 | 32.72 | 33.21 | 32.15 | 31.75 |
| 2019 | 32.33 | 32.78 | 32.87 | 32.73 | 33.28 | 32.50 | 32.95 | 33.40 | 33.52 | 33.81 | 33.46 | 33.76 | 33.12 |
| **Leisure and Hospitality** | | | | | | | | | | | | | |
| 2015 | 19.25 | 19.15 | 19.17 | 18.93 | 19.20 | 19.44 | 19.73 | 19.45 | 19.38 | 19.13 | 19.63 | 19.51 | 19.33 |
| 2016 | 20.29 | 19.96 | 19.81 | 19.64 | 19.94 | 20.30 | 20.48 | 20.08 | 20.21 | 20.18 | 20.17 | 20.36 | 20.12 |
| 2017 | 21.17 | 20.95 | 20.75 | 20.94 | 20.78 | 21.06 | 21.21 | 21.21 | 20.92 | 20.90 | 20.92 | 21.39 | 21.02 |
| 2018 | 21.50 | 21.74 | 21.48 | 21.47 | 20.84 | 21.33 | 20.96 | 21.11 | 20.53 | 20.38 | 20.50 | 20.57 | 21.04 |
| 2019 | 21.03 | 21.11 | 20.58 | 21.07 | 20.78 | 21.04 | 21.44 | 21.39 | 21.55 | 21.65 | 21.61 | 21.80 | 21.25 |

## 4. Average Weekly Earnings by Selected Industry: Hawaii 2015–2019

(Dollars, not seasonally adjusted)

| Industry and year | January | February | March | April | May | June | July | August | September | October | November | December | Annual average |
|---|---|---|---|---|---|---|---|---|---|---|---|---|---|
| **Total Private** | | | | | | | | | | | | | |
| 2015 | 817.18 | 842.35 | 840.22 | 814.92 | 813.12 | 805.06 | 814.85 | 834.36 | 798.37 | 806.85 | 833.15 | 828.30 | 820.85 |
| 2016 | 825.25 | 827.31 | 821.19 | 828.62 | 852.77 | 828.43 | 838.29 | 831.89 | 829.79 | 861.84 | 818.55 | 832.33 | 831.89 |
| 2017 | 869.46 | 840.06 | 830.43 | 876.10 | 846.30 | 848.86 | 894.44 | 865.26 | 868.22 | 897.12 | 877.14 | 886.00 | 866.89 |
| 2018 | 903.87 | 884.00 | 888.88 | 931.19 | 888.25 | 899.93 | 943.78 | 903.64 | 939.21 | 902.02 | 910.65 | 949.90 | 913.63 |
| 2019 | 908.60 | 898.99 | 906.50 | 919.26 | 933.08 | 951.90 | 939.53 | 936.98 | 986.40 | 962.03 | 953.88 | 1,000.22 | 942.09 |
| **Goods-Producing** | | | | | | | | | | | | | |
| 2015 | 1,228.66 | 1,199.75 | 1,223.97 | 1,255.14 | 1,258.74 | 1,142.05 | 1,188.64 | 1,183.70 | 1,127.98 | 1,214.02 | 1,167.11 | 1,276.28 | 1,205.97 |
| 2016 | 1,262.80 | 1,219.88 | 1,222.23 | 1,229.87 | 1,216.88 | 1,204.11 | 1,222.02 | 1,243.58 | 1,205.46 | 1,271.24 | 1,180.61 | 1,240.74 | 1,227.27 |
| 2017 | 1,263.07 | 1,229.82 | 1,247.67 | 1,242.70 | 1,274.76 | 1,196.80 | 1,329.15 | 1,274.47 | 1,257.26 | 1,279.31 | 1,288.50 | 1,272.31 | 1,264.93 |
| 2018 | 1,311.11 | 1,252.10 | 1,305.66 | 1,332.13 | 1,290.89 | 1,191.19 | 1,320.97 | 1,323.83 | 1,340.49 | 1,344.29 | 1,330.71 | 1,435.87 | 1,314.37 |
| 2019 | 1,396.44 | 1,346.04 | 1,399.50 | 1,410.62 | 1,411.81 | 1,320.81 | 1,407.28 | 1,416.58 | 1,508.91 | 1,456.01 | 1,415.48 | 1,524.10 | 1,419.08 |
| **Mining, Logging, and Construction** | | | | | | | | | | | | | |
| 2015 | 1,454.88 | 1,412.43 | 1,445.79 | 1,470.54 | 1,465.65 | 1,307.17 | 1,344.00 | 1,336.25 | 1,273.88 | 1,378.92 | 1,315.98 | 1,450.84 | 1,385.16 |
| 2016 | 1,445.83 | 1,397.59 | 1,383.10 | 1,396.75 | 1,379.00 | 1,367.27 | 1,383.68 | 1,413.60 | 1,366.95 | 1,451.49 | 1,339.54 | 1,428.70 | 1,396.56 |
| 2017 | 1,451.85 | 1,404.31 | 1,421.02 | 1,397.64 | 1,453.49 | 1,343.93 | 1,517.14 | 1,451.17 | 1,428.04 | 1,458.06 | 1,490.72 | 1,457.48 | 1,437.04 |
| 2018 | 1,507.49 | 1,421.22 | 1,501.59 | 1,536.34 | 1,467.65 | 1,344.70 | 1,502.17 | 1,509.17 | 1,538.98 | 1,535.81 | 1,527.20 | 1,669.78 | 1,506.23 |
| 2019 | 1,620.86 | 1,545.02 | 1,605.27 | 1,613.68 | 1,603.34 | 1,497.56 | 1,605.14 | 1,611.54 | 1,715.32 | 1,644.56 | 1,581.95 | 1,723.80 | 1,614.56 |
| **Manufacturing** | | | | | | | | | | | | | |
| 2015 | 710.26 | 703.82 | 704.18 | 730.85 | 754.13 | 728.34 | 793.87 | 802.64 | 742.61 | 783.48 | 774.75 | 808.70 | 753.62 |
| 2016 | 778.09 | 750.75 | 780.27 | 774.13 | 769.62 | 762.20 | 772.16 | 777.55 | 765.20 | 793.49 | 766.66 | 763.50 | 770.36 |
| 2017 | 770.70 | 787.93 | 805.27 | 847.92 | 829.63 | 820.09 | 858.78 | 824.36 | 829.05 | 845.93 | 783.29 | 821.69 | 819.18 |
| 2018 | 832.72 | 829.04 | 820.71 | 816.08 | 836.24 | 797.33 | 849.53 | 826.98 | 820.24 | 833.60 | 825.39 | 833.76 | 827.83 |
| 2019 | 831.06 | 833.06 | 870.70 | 877.15 | 902.43 | 864.47 | 873.00 | 904.60 | 959.18 | 947.91 | 974.26 | 988.93 | 899.21 |
| **Trade, Transportation, and Utilities** | | | | | | | | | | | | | |
| 2015 | 805.77 | 848.42 | 844.25 | 818.41 | 804.94 | 810.54 | 803.42 | 831.09 | 812.91 | 803.43 | 830.76 | 815.26 | 819.42 |
| 2016 | 819.99 | 819.84 | 812.04 | 821.86 | 838.78 | 832.14 | 844.32 | 838.32 | 845.21 | 871.39 | 822.31 | 825.99 | 833.85 |
| 2017 | 875.13 | 835.63 | 831.60 | 891.92 | 845.71 | 865.28 | 884.27 | 845.79 | 862.05 | 895.62 | 858.18 | 875.69 | 864.45 |
| 2018 | 884.34 | 871.41 | 865.92 | 933.57 | 891.44 | 914.44 | 958.19 | 907.87 | 966.67 | 910.91 | 913.92 | 976.83 | 916.56 |
| 2019 | 900.43 | 888.69 | 909.19 | 925.95 | 942.88 | 991.58 | 949.23 | 951.71 | 997.85 | 940.46 | 938.87 | 1,010.10 | 946.40 |
| **Professional and Business Services** | | | | | | | | | | | | | |
| 2015 | 798.23 | 811.72 | 814.32 | 793.70 | 792.95 | 782.22 | 786.90 | 794.53 | 765.60 | 796.59 | 848.05 | 818.29 | 801.01 |
| 2016 | 770.57 | 799.46 | 799.60 | 827.61 | 877.45 | 838.49 | 870.39 | 891.70 | 914.00 | 934.92 | 908.74 | 939.24 | 865.26 |
| 2017 | 931.48 | 911.40 | 909.68 | 930.08 | 896.23 | 880.48 | 931.41 | 886.59 | 881.38 | 910.00 | 883.34 | 878.03 | 902.77 |
| 2018 | 895.62 | 870.40 | 900.62 | 907.90 | 873.26 | 894.54 | 914.69 | 888.26 | 908.25 | 862.18 | 880.05 | 918.28 | 893.52 |
| 2019 | 879.42 | 875.08 | 903.17 | 890.29 | 890.35 | 916.63 | 910.75 | 896.49 | 945.95 | 909.22 | 938.45 | 984.19 | 911.49 |
| **Education and Health Services** | | | | | | | | | | | | | |
| 2015 | 860.66 | 888.79 | 840.68 | 818.06 | 821.18 | 843.40 | 850.83 | 876.46 | 849.09 | 858.62 | 875.05 | 875.95 | 854.78 |
| 2016 | 882.21 | 891.61 | 879.11 | 873.34 | 886.66 | 841.95 | 853.54 | 822.99 | 820.42 | 829.18 | 800.66 | 801.27 | 848.78 |
| 2017 | 864.83 | 858.44 | 853.02 | 887.48 | 876.73 | 897.28 | 942.81 | 936.04 | 959.08 | 973.83 | 965.57 | 981.40 | 917.97 |
| 2018 | 1,007.29 | 998.24 | 996.80 | 1,060.08 | 1,000.01 | 1,027.73 | 1,055.11 | 1,028.70 | 1,082.72 | 1,063.40 | 1,082.65 | 1,041.66 | 1,038.23 |
| 2019 | 1,031.33 | 1,039.13 | 1,041.98 | 1,057.18 | 1,074.94 | 1,062.75 | 1,064.29 | 1,065.46 | 1,109.51 | 1,092.06 | 1,080.76 | 1,120.83 | 1,069.78 |
| **Leisure and Hospitality** | | | | | | | | | | | | | |
| 2015 | 569.80 | 595.57 | 594.27 | 552.76 | 568.32 | 575.42 | 591.90 | 602.95 | 558.14 | 549.03 | 594.79 | 556.04 | 576.03 |
| 2016 | 584.35 | 574.85 | 560.62 | 565.63 | 608.17 | 586.67 | 591.87 | 578.30 | 571.94 | 603.38 | 572.83 | 578.22 | 581.47 |
| 2017 | 643.57 | 603.36 | 587.23 | 626.11 | 596.39 | 619.16 | 651.15 | 621.45 | 610.86 | 622.82 | 615.05 | 611.75 | 617.99 |
| 2018 | 623.50 | 626.11 | 612.18 | 620.48 | 573.10 | 586.58 | 609.94 | 578.41 | 572.79 | 554.34 | 567.85 | 578.02 | 591.22 |
| 2019 | 593.05 | 586.86 | 576.24 | 592.07 | 592.23 | 620.68 | 602.46 | 594.64 | 612.02 | 601.87 | 596.44 | 619.12 | 599.25 |

# IDAHO
## *At a Glance*

Population:
 2010 census: 1,567,582
 2019 estimate: 1,787,065

Percent change in population:
 2010–2019: 14.0%

Percent change in total nonfarm employment:
 2011–2019: 24.4%

Industry with the largest growth in employment, 2011–2019 (percent):
 Mining, Logging, and Construction, 64.9%

Industry with the largest decline or smallest growth in employment, 2011–2019 (percent):
 Information, -5.3%

Civilian labor force:
 2010: 761,056
 2019: 881,891

Unemployment rate and rank among states (highest to lowest):
 2010: 9.0%, 23rd
 2019: 2.9%, 41st

Over-the-year change in unemployment rates:
 2017–2018: -0.3%
 2018–2019: 0.0%

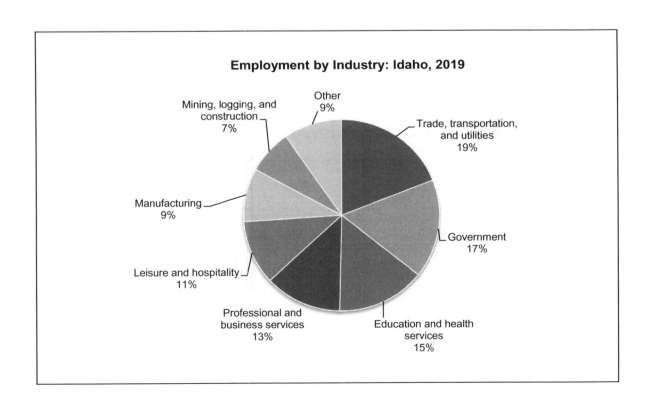

**Employment by Industry: Idaho, 2019**

- Mining, logging, and construction 7%
- Other 9%
- Trade, transportation, and utilities 19%
- Manufacturing 9%
- Government 17%
- Leisure and hospitality 11%
- Professional and business services 13%
- Education and health services 15%

## 1. Employment by Industry: Idaho, 2011–2019

(Numbers in thousands, not seasonally adjusted)

| Industry and year | January | February | March | April | May | June | July | August | September | October | November | December | Annual average |
|---|---|---|---|---|---|---|---|---|---|---|---|---|---|
| **Total Nonfarm** | | | | | | | | | | | | | |
| 2011 | 585.7 | 592.0 | 594.9 | 605.3 | 612.1 | 615.7 | 616.4 | 617.8 | 623.5 | 621.6 | 620.8 | 618.5 | 610.4 |
| 2012 | 596.4 | 602.5 | 607.6 | 613.4 | 623.9 | 627.9 | 626.2 | 628.2 | 634.3 | 634.9 | 634.4 | 630.9 | 621.7 |
| 2013 | 611.7 | 619.4 | 625.6 | 630.7 | 641.0 | 644.5 | 641.7 | 642.6 | 645.8 | 650.5 | 648.7 | 645.6 | 637.3 |
| 2014 | 630.8 | 637.5 | 642.9 | 649.4 | 657.1 | 661.7 | 659.5 | 659.3 | 661.6 | 664.1 | 661.9 | 660.6 | 653.9 |
| 2015 | 646.1 | 652.1 | 659.2 | 664.3 | 673.9 | 678.6 | 679.0 | 676.2 | 682.6 | 683.9 | 682.5 | 681.2 | 671.6 |
| 2016 | 666.7 | 675.4 | 682.4 | 687.8 | 694.5 | 700.8 | 702.8 | 701.1 | 706.7 | 705.8 | 705.2 | 701.6 | 694.2 |
| 2017 | 688.8 | 695.5 | 703.7 | 707.4 | 716.7 | 725.1 | 720.9 | 720.3 | 725.3 | 725.7 | 725.2 | 723.2 | 714.8 |
| 2018 | 710.3 | 719.6 | 724.7 | 731.3 | 740.1 | 748.9 | 747.0 | 746.2 | 746.6 | 750.8 | 749.6 | 747.3 | 738.5 |
| 2019 | 733.8 | 741.4 | 745.4 | 753.4 | 762.7 | 769.2 | 767.5 | 767.6 | 768.8 | 768.1 | 766.7 | 765.9 | 759.2 |
| **Total Private** | | | | | | | | | | | | | |
| 2011 | 472.5 | 473.3 | 475.6 | 485.2 | 491.0 | 498.4 | 505.2 | 506.5 | 505.9 | 502.3 | 502.0 | 499.7 | 493.1 |
| 2012 | 483.1 | 484.7 | 489.4 | 494.3 | 503.1 | 510.9 | 515.9 | 517.4 | 515.9 | 514.0 | 514.1 | 511.1 | 504.5 |
| 2013 | 496.2 | 499.7 | 505.5 | 511.1 | 519.9 | 527.0 | 531.8 | 533.0 | 528.2 | 530.2 | 529.2 | 527.1 | 519.9 |
| 2014 | 515.6 | 518.1 | 522.4 | 529.0 | 536.0 | 543.6 | 547.8 | 547.8 | 543.0 | 542.6 | 541.0 | 541.0 | 535.7 |
| 2015 | 530.1 | 532.2 | 538.4 | 543.2 | 551.0 | 559.4 | 566.2 | 564.7 | 562.3 | 561.2 | 560.4 | 560.0 | 552.4 |
| 2016 | 549.3 | 553.7 | 559.6 | 565.5 | 570.9 | 579.5 | 587.4 | 586.6 | 583.9 | 581.0 | 581.1 | 578.8 | 573.1 |
| 2017 | 568.6 | 572.3 | 579.5 | 582.7 | 590.3 | 601.0 | 604.2 | 604.2 | 601.0 | 598.8 | 599.0 | 597.6 | 591.6 |
| 2018 | 588.8 | 593.8 | 598.2 | 604.4 | 612.3 | 623.3 | 628.1 | 627.5 | 620.6 | 622.0 | 621.7 | 619.9 | 613.4 |
| 2019 | 611.0 | 613.8 | 617.2 | 624.8 | 633.0 | 642.4 | 648.0 | 648.0 | 640.5 | 636.1 | 635.3 | 635.6 | 632.1 |
| **Goods Producing** | | | | | | | | | | | | | |
| 2011 | 82.5 | 82.7 | 83.5 | 86.1 | 88.5 | 91.1 | 92.6 | 93.2 | 93.0 | 93.7 | 92.9 | 90.4 | 89.2 |
| 2012 | 86.6 | 86.4 | 87.1 | 88.9 | 91.9 | 94.8 | 96.2 | 96.8 | 96.1 | 96.5 | 95.7 | 94.1 | 92.6 |
| 2013 | 90.7 | 91.6 | 93.2 | 94.6 | 97.6 | 100.0 | 100.8 | 101.6 | 100.6 | 101.0 | 99.6 | 97.7 | 97.4 |
| 2014 | 95.1 | 94.8 | 95.5 | 97.4 | 99.8 | 102.3 | 103.7 | 104.0 | 103.5 | 103.6 | 102.1 | 101.0 | 100.2 |
| 2015 | 98.1 | 98.6 | 100.3 | 102.0 | 104.3 | 106.7 | 107.5 | 107.9 | 107.1 | 107.8 | 106.9 | 105.3 | 104.4 |
| 2016 | 103.1 | 103.9 | 105.8 | 108.0 | 109.7 | 111.9 | 113.9 | 114.2 | 113.3 | 111.7 | 111.2 | 109.7 | 109.7 |
| 2017 | 107.1 | 108.0 | 110.3 | 111.7 | 114.3 | 117.5 | 118.5 | 119.0 | 118.2 | 118.5 | 117.9 | 116.5 | 114.8 |
| 2018 | 113.8 | 115.2 | 116.4 | 117.8 | 120.9 | 123.9 | 125.1 | 125.3 | 124.2 | 124.2 | 123.9 | 122.2 | 121.1 |
| 2019 | 119.8 | 120.0 | 121.0 | 122.7 | 125.5 | 128.4 | 129.5 | 129.8 | 128.4 | 127.0 | 125.3 | 123.5 | 125.1 |
| **Service-Providing** | | | | | | | | | | | | | |
| 2011 | 503.2 | 509.3 | 511.4 | 519.2 | 523.6 | 524.6 | 523.8 | 524.6 | 530.5 | 527.9 | 527.9 | 528.1 | 521.2 |
| 2012 | 509.8 | 516.1 | 520.5 | 524.5 | 532.0 | 533.1 | 530.0 | 531.4 | 538.2 | 538.4 | 538.7 | 536.8 | 529.1 |
| 2013 | 521.0 | 527.8 | 532.4 | 536.1 | 543.4 | 544.5 | 540.9 | 541.0 | 545.2 | 549.5 | 549.1 | 547.9 | 539.9 |
| 2014 | 535.7 | 542.7 | 547.4 | 552.0 | 557.3 | 559.4 | 555.8 | 555.3 | 558.1 | 560.5 | 559.8 | 559.6 | 553.6 |
| 2015 | 548.0 | 553.5 | 558.9 | 562.3 | 569.6 | 571.9 | 571.5 | 568.3 | 575.5 | 576.1 | 575.6 | 575.9 | 567.3 |
| 2016 | 563.6 | 571.5 | 576.6 | 579.8 | 584.8 | 588.9 | 588.9 | 586.9 | 593.4 | 594.1 | 594.0 | 591.9 | 584.5 |
| 2017 | 581.7 | 587.5 | 593.4 | 595.7 | 602.4 | 607.6 | 602.4 | 601.3 | 607.1 | 607.2 | 607.3 | 606.7 | 600.0 |
| 2018 | 596.5 | 604.4 | 608.3 | 613.5 | 619.2 | 625.0 | 621.9 | 620.9 | 622.4 | 626.6 | 625.7 | 625.1 | 617.5 |
| 2019 | 614.0 | 621.4 | 624.4 | 630.7 | 637.2 | 640.8 | 638.0 | 637.8 | 640.4 | 641.1 | 641.4 | 642.4 | 634.1 |
| **Mining, Logging, and Construction** | | | | | | | | | | | | | |
| 2011 | 29.1 | 29.0 | 29.5 | 31.6 | 33.6 | 36.0 | 37.5 | 37.8 | 37.3 | 37.3 | 37.0 | 34.9 | 34.2 |
| 2012 | 31.4 | 31.1 | 31.4 | 32.7 | 35.0 | 37.1 | 38.4 | 38.7 | 38.3 | 37.9 | 37.0 | 35.8 | 35.4 |
| 2013 | 32.5 | 33.0 | 34.2 | 35.3 | 37.6 | 39.5 | 40.3 | 40.9 | 40.4 | 40.3 | 39.3 | 37.5 | 37.6 |
| 2014 | 35.5 | 35.1 | 35.7 | 37.3 | 39.5 | 41.4 | 42.5 | 43.1 | 42.6 | 42.1 | 41.1 | 40.1 | 39.7 |
| 2015 | 37.6 | 38.0 | 39.4 | 40.6 | 42.4 | 44.0 | 44.7 | 44.8 | 43.8 | 43.9 | 42.9 | 42.0 | 42.0 |
| 2016 | 39.9 | 40.5 | 41.9 | 44.0 | 45.6 | 47.3 | 48.6 | 48.9 | 48.5 | 47.5 | 46.9 | 45.3 | 45.4 |
| 2017 | 42.6 | 43.2 | 45.0 | 46.3 | 48.5 | 50.8 | 51.6 | 51.8 | 51.1 | 51.0 | 50.1 | 49.0 | 48.4 |
| 2018 | 46.7 | 47.8 | 48.7 | 50.1 | 52.8 | 55.2 | 56.0 | 56.3 | 55.4 | 55.2 | 54.5 | 53.0 | 52.6 |
| 2019 | 51.5 | 51.5 | 52.2 | 54.1 | 56.7 | 59.0 | 60.0 | 60.5 | 59.4 | 58.6 | 57.7 | 56.1 | 56.4 |
| **Manufacturing** | | | | | | | | | | | | | |
| 2011 | 53.4 | 53.7 | 54.0 | 54.5 | 54.9 | 55.1 | 55.1 | 55.4 | 55.7 | 56.4 | 55.9 | 55.5 | 55.0 |
| 2012 | 55.2 | 55.3 | 55.7 | 56.2 | 56.9 | 57.7 | 57.8 | 58.1 | 57.8 | 58.6 | 58.7 | 58.3 | 57.2 |
| 2013 | 58.2 | 58.6 | 59.0 | 59.3 | 60.0 | 60.5 | 60.5 | 60.7 | 60.2 | 60.7 | 60.3 | 60.2 | 59.9 |
| 2014 | 59.6 | 59.7 | 59.8 | 60.1 | 60.3 | 60.9 | 61.2 | 60.9 | 60.9 | 61.5 | 61.0 | 60.9 | 60.6 |
| 2015 | 60.5 | 60.6 | 60.9 | 61.4 | 61.9 | 62.7 | 62.8 | 63.1 | 63.3 | 63.9 | 64.0 | 63.3 | 62.4 |
| 2016 | 63.2 | 63.4 | 63.9 | 64.0 | 64.1 | 64.6 | 65.3 | 65.3 | 64.8 | 64.2 | 64.3 | 64.4 | 64.3 |
| 2017 | 64.5 | 64.8 | 65.3 | 65.4 | 65.8 | 66.7 | 66.9 | 67.2 | 67.1 | 67.5 | 67.8 | 67.5 | 66.4 |
| 2018 | 67.1 | 67.4 | 67.7 | 67.7 | 68.1 | 68.7 | 69.1 | 69.0 | 68.8 | 69.0 | 69.4 | 69.2 | 68.4 |
| 2019 | 68.3 | 68.5 | 68.8 | 68.6 | 68.8 | 69.4 | 69.5 | 69.3 | 69.0 | 68.4 | 67.6 | 67.4 | 68.6 |

# 1. Employment by Industry: Idaho, 2011–2019—*Continued*

(Numbers in thousands, not seasonally adjusted)

| Industry and year | January | February | March | April | May | June | July | August | September | October | November | December | Annual average |
|---|---|---|---|---|---|---|---|---|---|---|---|---|---|
| **Trade, Transportation, and Utilities** | | | | | | | | | | | | | |
| 2011 | 117.6 | 117.0 | 117.5 | 119.4 | 120.4 | 120.8 | 122.5 | 123.3 | 123.5 | 123.6 | 125.5 | 125.7 | 121.4 |
| 2012 | 121.4 | 120.5 | 121.5 | 122.0 | 123.8 | 124.7 | 125.9 | 126.2 | 126.2 | 126.7 | 128.7 | 128.5 | 124.7 |
| 2013 | 123.5 | 123.3 | 124.0 | 125.2 | 126.6 | 127.2 | 128.5 | 128.8 | 128.6 | 129.0 | 130.4 | 130.8 | 127.2 |
| 2014 | 126.9 | 126.1 | 127.0 | 128.6 | 129.8 | 130.7 | 131.6 | 131.8 | 131.4 | 132.1 | 134.0 | 134.6 | 130.4 |
| 2015 | 130.5 | 130.3 | 131.6 | 132.5 | 133.8 | 134.6 | 136.1 | 136.1 | 135.9 | 136.7 | 138.7 | 139.1 | 134.7 |
| 2016 | 133.9 | 134.0 | 134.7 | 135.7 | 136.0 | 136.7 | 138.0 | 138.7 | 138.7 | 139.2 | 140.9 | 140.9 | 137.3 |
| 2017 | 136.4 | 135.9 | 136.6 | 137.2 | 138.1 | 139.2 | 140.0 | 140.6 | 140.2 | 140.7 | 142.7 | 143.2 | 139.2 |
| 2018 | 139.5 | 139.0 | 139.5 | 140.3 | 141.7 | 142.4 | 143.3 | 144.5 | 143.6 | 143.6 | 145.6 | 145.6 | 142.4 |
| 2019 | 142.5 | 141.8 | 142.2 | 143.2 | 144.2 | 144.7 | 145.2 | 146.0 | 145.4 | 145.6 | 147.0 | 147.8 | 144.6 |
| **Wholesale Trade** | | | | | | | | | | | | | |
| 2011 | 23.9 | 24.0 | 24.2 | 24.7 | 24.9 | 24.9 | 25.4 | 25.4 | 25.4 | 25.5 | 25.3 | 25.3 | 24.9 |
| 2012 | 24.9 | 25.0 | 25.4 | 25.7 | 26.0 | 26.0 | 26.7 | 26.2 | 26.3 | 26.4 | 26.2 | 26.2 | 25.9 |
| 2013 | 26.0 | 26.3 | 26.4 | 26.7 | 26.8 | 26.9 | 27.6 | 26.9 | 27.1 | 27.1 | 26.8 | 26.8 | 26.8 |
| 2014 | 26.7 | 26.7 | 27.1 | 27.3 | 27.4 | 27.5 | 28.0 | 27.3 | 27.2 | 27.2 | 27.2 | 27.3 | 27.2 |
| 2015 | 26.8 | 27.1 | 27.2 | 27.1 | 27.3 | 27.4 | 28.0 | 27.7 | 27.6 | 27.6 | 27.7 | 27.7 | 27.4 |
| 2016 | 27.4 | 27.7 | 27.9 | 27.9 | 27.9 | 28.0 | 28.4 | 28.4 | 28.2 | 28.1 | 28.2 | 28.1 | 28.0 |
| 2017 | 27.6 | 27.9 | 28.1 | 28.2 | 28.4 | 28.5 | 28.7 | 28.7 | 28.6 | 28.6 | 28.6 | 28.8 | 28.4 |
| 2018 | 28.8 | 29.1 | 29.2 | 29.4 | 29.6 | 29.7 | 30.0 | 30.2 | 29.9 | 30.2 | 30.1 | 30.1 | 29.7 |
| 2019 | 30.0 | 30.3 | 30.5 | 30.7 | 30.9 | 31.1 | 31.3 | 31.5 | 31.3 | 31.0 | 31.0 | 31.0 | 30.9 |
| **Retail Trade** | | | | | | | | | | | | | |
| 2011 | 72.9 | 72.2 | 72.5 | 73.8 | 74.8 | 75.2 | 76.1 | 76.4 | 76.3 | 76.5 | 78.6 | 78.4 | 75.3 |
| 2012 | 75.1 | 74.3 | 74.9 | 75.4 | 76.8 | 77.6 | 78.1 | 78.2 | 77.8 | 78.2 | 80.5 | 80.1 | 77.3 |
| 2013 | 76.0 | 75.5 | 76.1 | 77.5 | 78.7 | 79.3 | 80.0 | 80.4 | 79.8 | 79.9 | 81.6 | 81.6 | 78.9 |
| 2014 | 78.1 | 77.4 | 78.1 | 79.4 | 80.6 | 81.5 | 81.7 | 81.8 | 81.1 | 81.7 | 83.6 | 83.6 | 80.7 |
| 2015 | 80.4 | 80.2 | 81.2 | 82.3 | 83.4 | 84.3 | 85.1 | 85.1 | 84.5 | 85.1 | 87.1 | 87.0 | 83.8 |
| 2016 | 83.0 | 82.8 | 83.3 | 84.4 | 84.8 | 85.7 | 86.6 | 86.7 | 86.4 | 87.0 | 88.5 | 88.1 | 85.6 |
| 2017 | 85.1 | 84.4 | 84.8 | 85.3 | 85.8 | 86.9 | 87.6 | 87.7 | 87.1 | 87.3 | 89.1 | 88.8 | 86.7 |
| 2018 | 85.8 | 84.9 | 85.3 | 85.9 | 87.0 | 87.8 | 88.4 | 88.5 | 87.7 | 87.6 | 89.5 | 89.0 | 87.3 |
| 2019 | 86.5 | 85.9 | 86.1 | 87.0 | 87.7 | 88.1 | 88.3 | 88.2 | 87.5 | 88.1 | 90.0 | 89.8 | 87.8 |
| **Transportation and Utilities** | | | | | | | | | | | | | |
| 2011 | 20.8 | 20.8 | 20.8 | 20.9 | 20.7 | 20.7 | 21.0 | 21.5 | 21.8 | 21.6 | 21.6 | 22.0 | 21.2 |
| 2012 | 21.4 | 21.2 | 21.2 | 20.9 | 21.0 | 21.1 | 21.1 | 21.8 | 22.1 | 22.1 | 22.0 | 22.2 | 21.5 |
| 2013 | 21.5 | 21.5 | 21.5 | 21.0 | 21.1 | 21.0 | 20.9 | 21.5 | 21.7 | 22.0 | 22.0 | 22.4 | 21.5 |
| 2014 | 22.1 | 22.0 | 21.8 | 21.9 | 21.8 | 21.7 | 21.9 | 22.7 | 23.1 | 23.2 | 23.2 | 23.7 | 22.4 |
| 2015 | 23.3 | 23.0 | 23.2 | 23.1 | 23.1 | 22.9 | 23.0 | 23.3 | 23.8 | 24.0 | 23.9 | 24.4 | 23.4 |
| 2016 | 23.5 | 23.5 | 23.5 | 23.4 | 23.3 | 23.0 | 23.0 | 23.6 | 24.1 | 24.1 | 24.2 | 24.7 | 23.7 |
| 2017 | 23.7 | 23.6 | 23.7 | 23.7 | 23.9 | 23.8 | 23.7 | 24.2 | 24.5 | 24.8 | 25.0 | 25.6 | 24.2 |
| 2018 | 24.9 | 25.0 | 25.0 | 25.0 | 25.1 | 24.9 | 24.9 | 25.8 | 26.0 | 25.8 | 26.0 | 26.5 | 25.4 |
| 2019 | 26.0 | 25.6 | 25.6 | 25.5 | 25.6 | 25.5 | 25.6 | 26.3 | 26.6 | 26.5 | 26.0 | 27.0 | 26.0 |
| **Information** | | | | | | | | | | | | | |
| 2011 | 9.4 | 9.3 | 9.3 | 9.5 | 9.6 | 9.6 | 9.6 | 9.6 | 9.4 | 9.4 | 9.4 | 9.5 | 9.5 |
| 2012 | 9.4 | 9.4 | 9.4 | 9.3 | 9.4 | 9.4 | 9.5 | 9.5 | 9.2 | 9.3 | 9.3 | 9.3 | 9.4 |
| 2013 | 9.1 | 9.1 | 9.3 | 9.4 | 9.4 | 9.4 | 9.4 | 9.4 | 9.1 | 9.2 | 9.4 | 9.3 | 9.3 |
| 2014 | 9.1 | 9.2 | 9.2 | 9.3 | 9.4 | 9.4 | 9.4 | 9.5 | 9.1 | 9.3 | 9.5 | 9.5 | 9.3 |
| 2015 | 9.1 | 9.2 | 9.2 | 9.2 | 9.3 | 9.3 | 9.3 | 9.2 | 9.1 | 9.3 | 9.4 | 9.5 | 9.3 |
| 2016 | 8.8 | 8.9 | 8.9 | 9.0 | 9.0 | 9.0 | 9.1 | 9.2 | 9.0 | 9.2 | 9.2 | 9.3 | 9.1 |
| 2017 | 9.0 | 9.0 | 9.0 | 8.9 | 9.0 | 9.0 | 9.0 | 9.0 | 8.9 | 8.9 | 9.0 | 8.9 | 9.0 |
| 2018 | 8.9 | 8.9 | 8.9 | 8.9 | 8.9 | 9.0 | 9.0 | 8.9 | 8.8 | 8.8 | 8.8 | 8.9 | 8.9 |
| 2019 | 8.8 | 8.8 | 8.8 | 8.9 | 9.0 | 9.0 | 9.0 | 9.1 | 9.0 | 9.0 | 9.2 | 9.4 | 9.0 |
| **Financial Activities** | | | | | | | | | | | | | |
| 2011 | 29.2 | 29.2 | 29.2 | 29.5 | 29.7 | 29.9 | 30.4 | 30.3 | 30.3 | 30.2 | 30.2 | 30.3 | 29.9 |
| 2012 | 29.5 | 29.4 | 29.4 | 29.9 | 30.0 | 30.2 | 30.5 | 30.5 | 30.3 | 30.5 | 30.5 | 30.7 | 30.1 |
| 2013 | 30.1 | 30.3 | 30.4 | 30.5 | 30.8 | 30.9 | 31.1 | 31.2 | 30.8 | 31.0 | 31.1 | 31.5 | 30.8 |
| 2014 | 31.4 | 31.8 | 32.0 | 32.0 | 32.2 | 32.4 | 32.9 | 32.7 | 32.4 | 32.2 | 32.3 | 32.3 | 32.2 |
| 2015 | 32.2 | 32.2 | 32.3 | 32.5 | 32.6 | 32.9 | 33.4 | 33.1 | 32.9 | 33.0 | 32.8 | 32.9 | 32.7 |
| 2016 | 32.5 | 32.6 | 32.8 | 32.9 | 33.1 | 33.5 | 34.1 | 33.9 | 33.8 | 33.9 | 34.0 | 34.3 | 33.5 |
| 2017 | 33.9 | 34.0 | 34.2 | 34.3 | 34.5 | 34.8 | 35.2 | 35.2 | 34.9 | 35.0 | 35.1 | 35.4 | 34.7 |
| 2018 | 34.9 | 35.1 | 35.3 | 35.6 | 36.0 | 36.3 | 36.7 | 36.4 | 36.1 | 36.3 | 36.3 | 36.4 | 36.0 |
| 2019 | 36.0 | 36.1 | 36.1 | 36.4 | 36.7 | 37.0 | 37.6 | 37.4 | 37.2 | 36.8 | 36.8 | 37.2 | 36.8 |

## 1. Employment by Industry: Idaho, 2011–2019—*Continued*

(Numbers in thousands, not seasonally adjusted)

| Industry and year | January | February | March | April | May | June | July | August | September | October | November | December | Annual average |
|---|---|---|---|---|---|---|---|---|---|---|---|---|---|
| **Professional and Business Services** | | | | | | | | | | | | | |
| 2011 | 74.0 | 74.0 | 74.4 | 75.9 | 76.7 | 77.6 | 78.7 | 79.6 | 79.3 | 78.4 | 78.0 | 77.0 | 77.0 |
| 2012 | 73.2 | 73.9 | 75.4 | 76.3 | 77.4 | 78.8 | 79.1 | 80.3 | 79.7 | 79.5 | 79.9 | 78.1 | 77.6 |
| 2013 | 74.8 | 75.6 | 77.2 | 77.7 | 79.4 | 81.0 | 81.2 | 82.3 | 81.5 | 82.5 | 82.6 | 82.0 | 79.8 |
| 2014 | 78.6 | 79.9 | 80.9 | 82.1 | 82.3 | 83.1 | 82.7 | 83.4 | 83.1 | 82.9 | 82.7 | 82.3 | 82.0 |
| 2015 | 80.3 | 80.3 | 81.3 | 82.4 | 83.1 | 84.1 | 85.4 | 86.0 | 85.5 | 84.2 | 84.1 | 83.4 | 83.3 |
| 2016 | 83.0 | 83.8 | 85.4 | 87.7 | 88.2 | 89.2 | 90.3 | 90.4 | 89.7 | 89.8 | 90.0 | 88.9 | 88.0 |
| 2017 | 87.6 | 88.3 | 89.8 | 90.7 | 92.0 | 93.2 | 93.2 | 93.6 | 92.9 | 92.1 | 92.3 | 91.6 | 91.4 |
| 2018 | 88.9 | 90.8 | 91.8 | 93.6 | 94.1 | 96.0 | 96.6 | 96.7 | 95.2 | 95.5 | 95.4 | 94.0 | 94.1 |
| 2019 | 91.2 | 92.3 | 93.2 | 95.4 | 96.6 | 98.0 | 99.1 | 99.5 | 98.2 | 98.4 | 98.9 | 97.9 | 96.6 |
| **Education and Health Services** | | | | | | | | | | | | | |
| 2011 | 84.7 | 85.3 | 85.5 | 85.8 | 86.1 | 86.1 | 85.1 | 83.6 | 85.9 | 86.8 | 86.9 | 87.3 | 85.8 |
| 2012 | 85.9 | 86.8 | 87.2 | 87.2 | 87.7 | 87.5 | 86.6 | 85.3 | 87.9 | 88.8 | 88.9 | 89.0 | 87.4 |
| 2013 | 88.0 | 89.3 | 89.6 | 90.2 | 90.2 | 89.4 | 89.6 | 88.3 | 89.0 | 91.7 | 92.0 | 92.0 | 89.9 |
| 2014 | 91.8 | 92.6 | 92.6 | 93.2 | 93.3 | 92.6 | 92.6 | 91.2 | 92.4 | 94.3 | 94.3 | 94.7 | 93.0 |
| 2015 | 93.9 | 95.0 | 95.6 | 96.2 | 96.1 | 96.1 | 96.3 | 94.2 | 96.5 | 97.9 | 98.3 | 98.5 | 96.2 |
| 2016 | 97.5 | 98.7 | 99.1 | 98.5 | 98.9 | 98.7 | 98.7 | 96.9 | 99.8 | 100.3 | 100.9 | 100.3 | 99.0 |
| 2017 | 100.9 | 102.1 | 103.2 | 102.1 | 102.3 | 102.2 | 101.7 | 99.7 | 102.5 | 103.5 | 103.7 | 103.2 | 102.3 |
| 2018 | 104.4 | 105.6 | 105.9 | 105.8 | 106.0 | 105.9 | 105.9 | 104.2 | 104.7 | 108.3 | 108.5 | 108.5 | 106.1 |
| 2019 | 109.4 | 110.4 | 110.7 | 111.0 | 111.1 | 110.7 | 110.7 | 109.2 | 109.7 | 111.3 | 111.9 | 112.4 | 110.7 |
| **Leisure and Hospitality** | | | | | | | | | | | | | |
| 2011 | 54.6 | 55.2 | 55.7 | 58.0 | 58.8 | 61.9 | 64.3 | 65.2 | 63.1 | 59.0 | 57.8 | 58.1 | 59.3 |
| 2012 | 56.1 | 57.2 | 58.2 | 59.4 | 61.4 | 63.7 | 65.8 | 66.7 | 64.8 | 61.0 | 59.7 | 60.0 | 61.2 |
| 2013 | 58.8 | 59.1 | 60.3 | 61.9 | 64.0 | 66.8 | 68.5 | 68.5 | 66.1 | 63.9 | 62.1 | 61.9 | 63.5 |
| 2014 | 61.0 | 61.8 | 63.0 | 64.0 | 66.6 | 70.1 | 71.4 | 71.7 | 68.0 | 65.5 | 63.5 | 64.1 | 65.9 |
| 2015 | 63.3 | 63.8 | 65.1 | 65.3 | 68.3 | 71.8 | 74.1 | 74.3 | 71.7 | 68.7 | 66.7 | 67.7 | 68.4 |
| 2016 | 67.2 | 68.3 | 69.2 | 69.8 | 71.8 | 76.0 | 78.0 | 78.3 | 75.1 | 72.5 | 70.6 | 71.3 | 72.3 |
| 2017 | 69.8 | 70.9 | 72.1 | 73.3 | 75.3 | 79.7 | 81.1 | 81.6 | 78.4 | 75.3 | 73.5 | 74.1 | 75.4 |
| 2018 | 73.7 | 74.4 | 75.5 | 77.4 | 79.3 | 83.8 | 85.3 | 85.1 | 82.3 | 79.5 | 77.3 | 78.5 | 79.3 |
| 2019 | 77.7 | 78.5 | 79.2 | 80.9 | 83.2 | 87.2 | 89.5 | 89.8 | 85.8 | 81.3 | 79.0 | 80.2 | 82.7 |
| **Other Services** | | | | | | | | | | | | | |
| 2011 | 20.5 | 20.6 | 20.5 | 21.0 | 21.2 | 21.4 | 22.0 | 21.7 | 21.4 | 21.2 | 21.3 | 21.4 | 21.2 |
| 2012 | 21.0 | 21.1 | 21.2 | 21.3 | 21.5 | 21.8 | 22.3 | 22.1 | 21.7 | 21.7 | 21.4 | 21.4 | 21.5 |
| 2013 | 21.2 | 21.4 | 21.5 | 21.6 | 21.9 | 22.3 | 22.7 | 22.9 | 22.5 | 21.9 | 22.0 | 21.9 | 22.0 |
| 2014 | 21.7 | 21.9 | 22.2 | 22.4 | 22.6 | 23.0 | 23.5 | 23.5 | 23.1 | 22.7 | 22.6 | 22.5 | 22.6 |
| 2015 | 22.7 | 22.8 | 23.0 | 23.1 | 23.5 | 23.9 | 24.1 | 23.9 | 23.6 | 23.6 | 23.5 | 23.6 | 23.4 |
| 2016 | 23.3 | 23.5 | 23.7 | 23.9 | 24.2 | 24.5 | 25.3 | 25.0 | 24.5 | 24.4 | 24.3 | 24.1 | 24.2 |
| 2017 | 23.9 | 24.1 | 24.3 | 24.5 | 24.8 | 25.4 | 25.5 | 25.5 | 25.0 | 24.8 | 24.8 | 24.7 | 24.8 |
| 2018 | 24.7 | 24.8 | 24.9 | 25.0 | 25.4 | 26.0 | 26.2 | 26.4 | 25.7 | 25.8 | 25.9 | 25.8 | 25.6 |
| 2019 | 25.6 | 25.9 | 26.0 | 26.3 | 26.7 | 27.4 | 27.4 | 27.2 | 26.8 | 26.7 | 27.2 | 27.2 | 26.7 |
| **Government** | | | | | | | | | | | | | |
| 2011 | 113.2 | 118.7 | 119.3 | 120.1 | 121.1 | 117.3 | 111.2 | 111.3 | 117.6 | 119.3 | 118.8 | 118.8 | 117.2 |
| 2012 | 113.3 | 117.8 | 118.2 | 119.1 | 120.8 | 117.0 | 110.3 | 110.8 | 118.4 | 120.9 | 120.3 | 119.8 | 117.2 |
| 2013 | 115.5 | 119.7 | 120.1 | 119.6 | 121.1 | 117.5 | 109.9 | 109.6 | 117.6 | 120.3 | 119.5 | 118.5 | 117.4 |
| 2014 | 115.2 | 119.4 | 120.5 | 120.4 | 121.1 | 118.1 | 111.7 | 111.5 | 118.6 | 121.5 | 120.9 | 119.6 | 118.2 |
| 2015 | 116.0 | 119.9 | 120.8 | 121.1 | 122.9 | 119.2 | 112.8 | 111.5 | 120.3 | 122.7 | 122.1 | 121.2 | 119.2 |
| 2016 | 117.4 | 121.7 | 122.8 | 122.3 | 123.6 | 121.3 | 115.4 | 114.5 | 122.8 | 124.8 | 124.1 | 122.8 | 121.1 |
| 2017 | 120.2 | 123.2 | 124.2 | 124.7 | 126.4 | 124.1 | 116.7 | 116.1 | 124.3 | 126.9 | 126.2 | 125.6 | 123.2 |
| 2018 | 121.5 | 125.8 | 126.5 | 126.9 | 127.8 | 125.6 | 118.9 | 118.7 | 126.0 | 128.8 | 127.9 | 127.4 | 125.2 |
| 2019 | 122.8 | 127.6 | 128.2 | 128.6 | 129.7 | 126.8 | 119.5 | 119.6 | 128.3 | 132.0 | 131.4 | 130.3 | 127.1 |

## 2. Average Weekly Hours by Selected Industry: Idaho, 2015–2019

(Not seasonally adjusted)

| Industry and year | January | February | March | April | May | June | July | August | September | October | November | December | Annual average |
|---|---|---|---|---|---|---|---|---|---|---|---|---|---|
| **Total Private** | | | | | | | | | | | | | |
| 2015 | 32.6 | 33.5 | 33.6 | 33.3 | 33.3 | 33.6 | 33.9 | 34.5 | 33.1 | 33.1 | 33.5 | 32.7 | 33.4 |
| 2016 | 32.5 | 32.4 | 32.4 | 32.7 | 33.6 | 33.0 | 33.4 | 33.2 | 32.9 | 33.6 | 32.9 | 32.4 | 32.9 |
| 2017 | 32.5 | 32.7 | 33.0 | 34.0 | 33.7 | 33.9 | 34.6 | 34.2 | 34.1 | 34.8 | 33.9 | 33.8 | 33.8 |
| 2018 | 33.2 | 33.6 | 33.5 | 34.4 | 34.1 | 34.3 | 34.9 | 34.3 | 34.8 | 33.8 | 33.8 | 34.2 | 34.1 |
| 2019 | 32.9 | 32.7 | 33.2 | 33.6 | 33.8 | 34.7 | 33.7 | 34.2 | 34.6 | 34.0 | 33.6 | 33.9 | 33.7 |
| **Goods-Producing** | | | | | | | | | | | | | |
| 2015 | 38.1 | 38.8 | 39.1 | 39.2 | 39.2 | 39.3 | 39.8 | 40.1 | 38.0 | 38.8 | 38.4 | 37.8 | 38.9 |
| 2016 | 38.2 | 37.4 | 37.6 | 38.3 | 38.9 | 39.1 | 39.0 | 39.1 | 38.9 | 39.3 | 39.1 | 37.4 | 38.6 |
| 2017 | 37.0 | 37.9 | 38.4 | 39.3 | 40.1 | 39.9 | 40.1 | 40.4 | 40.2 | 40.6 | 39.8 | 39.0 | 39.4 |
| 2018 | 37.9 | 39.3 | 38.2 | 39.0 | 39.7 | 40.0 | 39.6 | 39.9 | 40.7 | 39.6 | 39.6 | 39.3 | 39.4 |
| 2019 | 38.4 | 37.4 | 38.9 | 39.8 | 40.3 | 40.7 | 40.2 | 40.8 | 40.4 | 40.0 | 39.7 | 39.8 | 39.7 |
| **Construction** | | | | | | | | | | | | | |
| 2015 | 35.2 | 36.3 | 36.5 | 37.8 | 38.6 | 38.8 | 39.0 | 39.5 | 36.7 | 37.4 | 36.7 | 35.6 | 37.4 |
| 2016 | 36.5 | 35.6 | 36.0 | 37.0 | 37.8 | 38.5 | 38.2 | 38.3 | 38.2 | 38.0 | 37.6 | 35.8 | 37.4 |
| 2017 | 34.1 | 35.6 | 36.8 | 38.6 | 39.9 | 39.5 | 39.2 | 40.2 | 39.2 | 39.8 | 37.8 | 36.9 | 38.3 |
| 2018 | 34.8 | 36.6 | 36.5 | 37.3 | 39.0 | 39.6 | 39.1 | 39.5 | 40.4 | 38.4 | 38.7 | 37.4 | 38.2 |
| 2019 | 36.2 | 33.5 | 37.2 | 38.1 | 39.2 | 39.9 | 39.3 | 40.1 | 39.8 | 39.2 | 38.4 | 38.5 | 38.4 |
| **Manufacturing** | | | | | | | | | | | | | |
| 2015 | 39.0 | 39.4 | 39.7 | 39.2 | 39.0 | 38.9 | 39.7 | 40.0 | 38.3 | 39.2 | 39.2 | 39.2 | 39.2 |
| 2016 | 39.2 | 38.5 | 39.0 | 39.4 | 40.1 | 40.0 | 39.7 | 39.8 | 39.6 | 40.2 | 40.5 | 38.8 | 39.6 |
| 2017 | 39.5 | 39.6 | 39.9 | 40.1 | 40.5 | 40.7 | 41.2 | 41.1 | 41.4 | 41.6 | 41.9 | 40.8 | 40.7 |
| 2018 | 40.4 | 41.3 | 39.6 | 40.6 | 40.2 | 40.2 | 40.0 | 39.8 | 40.7 | 40.7 | 40.5 | 41.2 | 40.4 |
| 2019 | 40.2 | 40.9 | 40.1 | 40.9 | 40.4 | 40.4 | 40.1 | 40.5 | 40.2 | 40.0 | 40.4 | 40.6 | 40.4 |
| **Trade, Transportation, and Utilities** | | | | | | | | | | | | | |
| 2015 | 32.8 | 33.5 | 33.8 | 33.0 | 33.5 | 33.6 | 34.0 | 34.5 | 33.8 | 33.1 | 33.4 | 33.5 | 33.5 |
| 2016 | 32.3 | 32.3 | 32.5 | 32.7 | 33.5 | 33.0 | 33.0 | 32.8 | 32.6 | 33.2 | 32.2 | 32.4 | 32.7 |
| 2017 | 32.1 | 32.4 | 32.6 | 34.0 | 33.6 | 34.0 | 34.6 | 34.0 | 33.7 | 34.8 | 33.8 | 34.0 | 33.6 |
| 2018 | 33.3 | 33.7 | 34.0 | 34.5 | 34.3 | 34.6 | 35.5 | 34.7 | 34.9 | 34.2 | 33.8 | 34.4 | 34.3 |
| 2019 | 32.6 | 32.1 | 32.4 | 32.4 | 32.8 | 33.9 | 32.8 | 33.0 | 33.6 | 32.6 | 32.2 | 32.8 | 32.8 |
| **Financial Activities** | | | | | | | | | | | | | |
| 2015 | 37.7 | 39.0 | 37.6 | 38.0 | 37.8 | 37.6 | 37.4 | 38.4 | 36.6 | 37.1 | 38.5 | 36.4 | 37.7 |
| 2016 | 37.4 | 37.1 | 36.8 | 36.8 | 38.3 | 36.7 | 36.5 | 36.2 | 36.7 | 38.0 | 37.4 | 36.8 | 37.1 |
| 2017 | 38.3 | 37.1 | 37.6 | 39.2 | 37.9 | 38.4 | 40.1 | 38.7 | 39.0 | 40.1 | 38.7 | 38.9 | 38.7 |
| 2018 | 38.0 | 38.1 | 38.5 | 39.8 | 38.1 | 38.2 | 39.6 | 38.6 | 38.9 | 38.4 | 38.7 | 39.5 | 38.7 |
| 2019 | 38.2 | 38.4 | 38.1 | 38.0 | 37.7 | 38.2 | 37.3 | 37.5 | 38.3 | 37.8 | 37.8 | 37.9 | 37.9 |
| **Professional and Business Services** | | | | | | | | | | | | | |
| 2015 | 35.2 | 36.1 | 36.1 | 35.7 | 35.0 | 35.4 | 35.1 | 36.7 | 35.3 | 35.3 | 35.9 | 34.9 | 35.6 |
| 2016 | 34.8 | 35.1 | 35.1 | 35.2 | 35.8 | 35.1 | 35.8 | 35.6 | 35.9 | 36.2 | 35.1 | 34.6 | 35.4 |
| 2017 | 35.2 | 35.1 | 35.1 | 36.8 | 35.9 | 35.7 | 36.4 | 35.8 | 35.8 | 36.6 | 35.6 | 35.6 | 35.8 |
| 2018 | 35.3 | 35.4 | 35.6 | 36.5 | 35.9 | 35.7 | 36.1 | 35.3 | 36.3 | 34.3 | 34.6 | 34.8 | 35.5 |
| 2019 | 34.2 | 34.6 | 34.9 | 35.7 | 35.7 | 36.5 | 35.5 | 36.1 | 36.6 | 36.3 | 35.3 | 35.4 | 35.6 |
| **Education and Health Services** | | | | | | | | | | | | | |
| 2015 | 29.3 | 30.3 | 30.1 | 29.8 | 29.5 | 29.8 | 29.9 | 30.6 | 29.7 | 29.4 | 30.2 | 29.2 | 29.8 |
| 2016 | 28.9 | 28.6 | 28.8 | 28.9 | 29.5 | 29.4 | 29.6 | 29.6 | 29.4 | 30.3 | 29.5 | 29.4 | 29.3 |
| 2017 | 30.0 | 30.0 | 29.7 | 30.3 | 29.5 | 30.1 | 30.7 | 30.2 | 31.0 | 30.9 | 30.9 | 30.4 | 30.3 |
| 2018 | 30.7 | 30.2 | 30.3 | 31.2 | 30.6 | 30.8 | 31.0 | 30.7 | 31.0 | 30.7 | 31.1 | 31.8 | 30.8 |
| 2019 | 30.0 | 30.2 | 30.7 | 31.3 | 31.4 | 32.1 | 30.8 | 31.1 | 31.7 | 31.2 | 30.8 | 31.0 | 31.0 |
| **Leisure and Hospitality** | | | | | | | | | | | | | |
| 2015 | 23.2 | 24.7 | 24.8 | 23.5 | 24.0 | 24.7 | 26.2 | 26.6 | 24.7 | 24.6 | 24.8 | 23.9 | 24.7 |
| 2016 | 23.5 | 24.3 | 23.8 | 24.0 | 25.4 | 24.5 | 25.1 | 25.0 | 23.5 | 24.5 | 23.5 | 23.2 | 24.2 |
| 2017 | 23.6 | 23.9 | 24.3 | 24.6 | 24.5 | 24.8 | 26.0 | 25.4 | 23.9 | 24.5 | 23.4 | 23.3 | 24.4 |
| 2018 | 23.1 | 23.1 | 23.2 | 24.4 | 23.9 | 24.4 | 25.7 | 25.1 | 24.8 | 22.9 | 22.8 | 23.5 | 24.0 |
| 2019 | 22.4 | 22.4 | 22.9 | 22.6 | 23.1 | 25.1 | 24.1 | 24.3 | 23.9 | 22.5 | 22.6 | 23.3 | 23.3 |

## 3. Average Hourly Earnings by Selected Industry: Idaho, 2015–2019

(Dollars, not seasonally adjusted)

| Industry and year | January | February | March | April | May | June | July | August | September | October | November | December | Annual average |
|---|---|---|---|---|---|---|---|---|---|---|---|---|---|
| **Total Private** | | | | | | | | | | | | | |
| 2015 | 21.97 | 22.07 | 21.75 | 21.87 | 21.86 | 21.74 | 21.63 | 21.99 | 21.84 | 22.05 | 22.24 | 22.30 | 21.94 |
| 2016 | 22.54 | 22.48 | 22.45 | 22.70 | 22.48 | 21.99 | 21.91 | 22.01 | 22.12 | 22.32 | 22.24 | 22.23 | 22.28 |
| 2017 | 22.63 | 22.39 | 22.13 | 22.41 | 22.28 | 22.09 | 22.34 | 22.16 | 22.24 | 22.49 | 22.27 | 22.51 | 22.33 |
| 2018 | 22.53 | 22.66 | 22.65 | 22.89 | 22.74 | 22.58 | 22.79 | 22.57 | 22.95 | 22.93 | 22.69 | 22.91 | 22.74 |
| 2019 | 22.84 | 22.68 | 22.68 | 22.83 | 22.78 | 22.94 | 23.26 | 23.36 | 23.67 | 23.74 | 23.82 | 23.70 | 23.20 |
| **Goods-Producing** | | | | | | | | | | | | | |
| 2015 | 23.10 | 23.13 | 23.06 | 23.18 | 22.99 | 23.12 | 22.92 | 22.89 | 22.74 | 22.59 | 22.34 | 23.27 | 22.94 |
| 2016 | 23.05 | 22.55 | 22.38 | 22.72 | 22.36 | 22.22 | 22.00 | 22.03 | 22.20 | 22.44 | 22.50 | 22.57 | 22.41 |
| 2017 | 22.59 | 22.23 | 22.46 | 22.74 | 22.79 | 22.86 | 23.05 | 22.49 | 22.64 | 23.04 | 22.85 | 23.44 | 22.78 |
| 2018 | 23.08 | 23.14 | 23.58 | 23.67 | 23.74 | 23.66 | 24.05 | 23.96 | 23.82 | 23.73 | 23.99 | 24.08 | 23.72 |
| 2019 | 23.23 | 23.01 | 22.91 | 23.29 | 23.59 | 23.79 | 24.16 | 24.18 | 24.36 | 24.39 | 24.76 | 24.90 | 23.90 |
| **Construction** | | | | | | | | | | | | | |
| 2015 | 21.28 | 21.39 | 21.26 | 21.17 | 20.99 | 20.95 | 20.60 | 20.92 | 21.09 | 21.12 | 21.31 | 21.65 | 21.13 |
| 2016 | 21.50 | 20.51 | 20.90 | 21.31 | 20.79 | 20.69 | 20.54 | 20.84 | 21.51 | 21.79 | 21.95 | 22.24 | 21.21 |
| 2017 | 22.40 | 22.29 | 22.67 | 22.76 | 23.03 | 23.21 | 23.28 | 23.00 | 23.21 | 23.63 | 23.16 | 23.90 | 23.08 |
| 2018 | 23.76 | 24.08 | 24.38 | 24.46 | 24.68 | 24.42 | 25.25 | 24.96 | 24.73 | 24.59 | 24.98 | 25.01 | 24.64 |
| 2019 | 24.41 | 24.24 | 23.90 | 24.43 | 24.56 | 25.03 | 25.58 | 25.00 | 25.33 | 25.64 | 25.84 | 26.59 | 25.09 |
| **Manufacturing** | | | | | | | | | | | | | |
| 2015 | 23.82 | 23.68 | 23.55 | 24.14 | 23.83 | 24.07 | 24.07 | 23.74 | 23.50 | 23.23 | 22.68 | 23.73 | 23.67 |
| 2016 | 23.50 | 23.32 | 22.90 | 23.25 | 23.01 | 22.72 | 22.63 | 22.44 | 22.16 | 22.59 | 22.48 | 22.31 | 22.77 |
| 2017 | 22.31 | 21.93 | 22.03 | 22.45 | 22.16 | 22.01 | 22.40 | 21.80 | 21.93 | 22.29 | 22.32 | 23.00 | 22.22 |
| 2018 | 22.50 | 22.20 | 22.63 | 22.71 | 22.70 | 22.79 | 22.71 | 22.87 | 22.84 | 22.94 | 23.07 | 23.23 | 22.77 |
| 2019 | 22.23 | 22.06 | 22.03 | 22.30 | 22.63 | 22.71 | 23.09 | 23.37 | 23.44 | 23.16 | 23.66 | 24.01 | 22.89 |
| **Trade, Transportation, and Utilities** | | | | | | | | | | | | | |
| 2015 | 19.53 | 19.38 | 19.39 | 19.18 | 19.37 | 19.26 | 19.53 | 20.05 | 19.83 | 19.87 | 20.05 | 19.64 | 19.60 |
| 2016 | 19.93 | 19.92 | 19.82 | 19.85 | 19.61 | 19.22 | 19.38 | 19.33 | 19.45 | 19.66 | 19.01 | 18.85 | 19.50 |
| 2017 | 19.60 | 19.02 | 19.15 | 19.53 | 19.46 | 19.08 | 19.64 | 19.64 | 19.62 | 19.54 | 19.42 | 19.40 | 19.43 |
| 2018 | 19.55 | 19.84 | 19.83 | 20.42 | 20.33 | 20.16 | 20.41 | 20.11 | 21.10 | 20.99 | 20.39 | 20.79 | 20.34 |
| 2019 | 20.93 | 20.68 | 20.88 | 21.15 | 21.26 | 21.19 | 21.66 | 21.68 | 22.02 | 21.84 | 21.75 | 21.95 | 21.42 |
| **Financial Activities** | | | | | | | | | | | | | |
| 2015 | 23.59 | 23.79 | 24.17 | 24.32 | 24.43 | 24.72 | 24.91 | 26.13 | 25.63 | 25.21 | 25.09 | 25.52 | 24.79 |
| 2016 | 25.12 | 25.17 | 25.16 | 25.28 | 25.11 | 24.19 | 24.21 | 25.08 | 24.74 | 25.58 | 25.07 | 24.94 | 24.97 |
| 2017 | 26.01 | 26.50 | 25.41 | 25.16 | 24.83 | 24.33 | 24.08 | 24.67 | 24.85 | 24.84 | 24.37 | 24.62 | 24.96 |
| 2018 | 25.04 | 25.11 | 24.89 | 24.99 | 24.49 | 24.81 | 25.19 | 25.20 | 25.23 | 24.69 | 24.14 | 24.77 | 24.88 |
| 2019 | 24.27 | 23.56 | 24.53 | 24.57 | 24.36 | 25.13 | 24.55 | 24.86 | 25.68 | 25.68 | 25.86 | 26.05 | 24.93 |
| **Professional and Business Services** | | | | | | | | | | | | | |
| 2015 | 27.35 | 27.63 | 27.55 | 27.48 | 27.58 | 27.34 | 27.32 | 27.79 | 28.17 | 28.52 | 28.81 | 28.52 | 27.84 |
| 2016 | 29.48 | 30.07 | 29.77 | 30.08 | 30.22 | 29.37 | 29.11 | 29.72 | 29.55 | 29.19 | 28.89 | 28.57 | 29.50 |
| 2017 | 28.68 | 28.42 | 28.53 | 28.88 | 28.18 | 27.51 | 28.15 | 27.34 | 26.89 | 27.60 | 26.72 | 26.57 | 27.78 |
| 2018 | 27.41 | 27.55 | 27.23 | 27.85 | 27.11 | 27.40 | 27.53 | 26.71 | 26.90 | 26.86 | 26.86 | 27.81 | 27.27 |
| 2019 | 28.74 | 28.35 | 28.09 | 28.33 | 27.04 | 27.61 | 27.17 | 27.79 | 27.77 | 27.94 | 28.14 | 28.14 | 27.91 |
| **Education and Health Services** | | | | | | | | | | | | | |
| 2015 | 22.42 | 21.99 | 21.71 | 21.73 | 21.35 | 21.34 | 21.09 | 21.14 | 21.21 | 21.15 | 21.22 | 21.51 | 21.48 |
| 2016 | 21.50 | 21.70 | 21.98 | 22.42 | 22.38 | 22.21 | 22.43 | 22.00 | 22.60 | 22.31 | 22.51 | 23.03 | 22.26 |
| 2017 | 22.99 | 23.33 | 22.46 | 22.87 | 22.81 | 22.60 | 23.02 | 22.25 | 22.02 | 22.30 | 22.72 | 22.99 | 22.69 |
| 2018 | 22.84 | 23.07 | 22.93 | 22.72 | 22.70 | 22.80 | 23.19 | 22.87 | 22.35 | 22.09 | 21.99 | 21.87 | 22.61 |
| 2019 | 21.60 | 21.52 | 21.68 | 21.43 | 21.29 | 21.18 | 21.64 | 21.36 | 21.21 | 21.54 | 22.05 | 21.85 | 21.53 |
| **Leisure and Hospitality** | | | | | | | | | | | | | |
| 2015 | 12.02 | 12.09 | 12.08 | 12.12 | 11.92 | 11.81 | 11.79 | 11.92 | 11.94 | 11.82 | 11.80 | 12.12 | 11.95 |
| 2016 | 12.00 | 12.08 | 12.03 | 12.26 | 12.11 | 12.04 | 12.23 | 12.23 | 12.33 | 12.43 | 12.28 | 12.53 | 12.21 |
| 2017 | 12.72 | 12.62 | 12.60 | 12.67 | 12.63 | 12.43 | 12.75 | 12.72 | 12.86 | 13.01 | 12.87 | 13.13 | 12.75 |
| 2018 | 13.13 | 13.18 | 13.11 | 12.86 | 12.86 | 12.86 | 13.05 | 13.35 | 13.49 | 13.66 | 13.13 | 13.92 | 13.23 |
| 2019 | 13.93 | 14.01 | 14.07 | 13.75 | 13.96 | 13.80 | 13.90 | 14.13 | 14.32 | 14.34 | 14.30 | 14.62 | 14.09 |

## 4. Average Weekly Earnings by Selected Industry: Idaho, 2015–2019

(Dollars, not seasonally adjusted)

| Industry and year | January | February | March | April | May | June | July | August | September | October | November | December | Annual average |
|---|---|---|---|---|---|---|---|---|---|---|---|---|---|
| **Total Private** | | | | | | | | | | | | | |
| 2015 | 716.22 | 739.35 | 730.80 | 728.27 | 727.94 | 730.46 | 733.26 | 758.66 | 722.90 | 729.86 | 745.04 | 729.21 | 732.80 |
| 2016 | 730.30 | 728.35 | 727.38 | 742.29 | 755.33 | 725.67 | 731.79 | 730.73 | 727.75 | 749.95 | 731.70 | 720.25 | 733.01 |
| 2017 | 735.48 | 732.15 | 730.29 | 761.94 | 750.84 | 748.85 | 772.96 | 757.87 | 758.38 | 782.65 | 754.95 | 760.84 | 754.75 |
| 2018 | 748.00 | 761.38 | 758.78 | 787.42 | 775.43 | 774.49 | 795.37 | 774.15 | 798.66 | 775.03 | 766.92 | 783.52 | 775.43 |
| 2019 | 751.44 | 741.64 | 752.98 | 767.09 | 769.96 | 796.02 | 783.86 | 798.91 | 818.98 | 807.16 | 800.35 | 803.43 | 781.84 |
| **Goods-Producing** | | | | | | | | | | | | | |
| 2015 | 880.11 | 897.44 | 901.65 | 908.66 | 901.21 | 908.62 | 912.22 | 917.89 | 864.12 | 876.49 | 857.86 | 879.61 | 892.37 |
| 2016 | 880.51 | 843.37 | 841.49 | 870.18 | 869.80 | 868.80 | 858.00 | 861.37 | 863.58 | 881.89 | 879.75 | 844.12 | 865.03 |
| 2017 | 835.83 | 842.52 | 862.46 | 893.68 | 913.88 | 912.11 | 924.71 | 908.60 | 910.13 | 935.42 | 909.43 | 914.16 | 897.53 |
| 2018 | 874.73 | 909.40 | 900.76 | 923.13 | 942.48 | 946.40 | 952.38 | 956.00 | 969.47 | 939.71 | 950.00 | 946.74 | 934.57 |
| 2019 | 892.42 | 860.57 | 891.20 | 926.94 | 950.68 | 968.25 | 971.23 | 986.54 | 984.14 | 975.60 | 982.97 | 991.02 | 948.83 |
| **Construction** | | | | | | | | | | | | | |
| 2015 | 749.06 | 776.46 | 775.99 | 800.23 | 810.21 | 812.86 | 803.40 | 826.34 | 774.00 | 789.89 | 782.08 | 770.74 | 790.26 |
| 2016 | 784.75 | 730.16 | 752.40 | 788.47 | 785.48 | 796.57 | 784.63 | 798.17 | 821.68 | 828.02 | 825.32 | 796.19 | 793.25 |
| 2017 | 763.84 | 793.52 | 834.26 | 878.54 | 918.90 | 916.80 | 912.58 | 924.60 | 909.83 | 940.47 | 875.45 | 881.91 | 883.96 |
| 2018 | 826.85 | 881.33 | 889.87 | 912.36 | 962.52 | 967.03 | 987.28 | 985.92 | 999.09 | 944.26 | 966.73 | 935.37 | 941.25 |
| 2019 | 883.64 | 812.04 | 889.08 | 930.78 | 962.75 | 998.70 | 1,005.29 | 1,002.50 | 1,008.13 | 1,005.09 | 992.26 | 1,023.72 | 963.46 |
| **Manufacturing** | | | | | | | | | | | | | |
| 2015 | 928.98 | 932.99 | 934.94 | 946.29 | 929.37 | 936.32 | 955.58 | 949.60 | 900.05 | 910.62 | 889.06 | 930.22 | 927.86 |
| 2016 | 921.20 | 897.82 | 893.10 | 916.05 | 922.70 | 908.80 | 898.41 | 893.11 | 877.54 | 908.12 | 910.44 | 865.63 | 901.69 |
| 2017 | 881.25 | 868.43 | 879.00 | 900.25 | 897.48 | 895.81 | 922.88 | 895.98 | 907.90 | 927.26 | 935.21 | 938.40 | 904.35 |
| 2018 | 909.00 | 916.86 | 896.15 | 922.03 | 912.54 | 916.16 | 908.40 | 910.23 | 929.59 | 933.66 | 934.34 | 957.08 | 919.91 |
| 2019 | 893.65 | 902.25 | 883.40 | 912.07 | 914.25 | 917.48 | 925.91 | 946.49 | 942.29 | 926.40 | 955.86 | 974.81 | 924.76 |
| **Trade, Transportation, and Utilities** | | | | | | | | | | | | | |
| 2015 | 640.58 | 649.23 | 655.38 | 632.93 | 648.90 | 647.14 | 664.02 | 691.73 | 670.25 | 658.03 | 670.00 | 657.94 | 656.60 |
| 2016 | 643.74 | 643.42 | 644.15 | 649.10 | 656.94 | 634.26 | 639.54 | 634.02 | 634.07 | 652.71 | 612.12 | 610.74 | 637.65 |
| 2017 | 629.16 | 616.25 | 624.29 | 664.02 | 653.86 | 648.72 | 679.54 | 667.76 | 661.19 | 679.99 | 656.40 | 659.60 | 652.85 |
| 2018 | 651.02 | 668.61 | 674.22 | 704.49 | 697.32 | 697.54 | 724.56 | 697.82 | 736.39 | 717.86 | 689.18 | 715.18 | 697.66 |
| 2019 | 682.32 | 663.83 | 676.51 | 685.26 | 697.33 | 718.34 | 710.45 | 715.44 | 739.87 | 711.98 | 700.35 | 719.96 | 702.58 |
| **Financial Activities** | | | | | | | | | | | | | |
| 2015 | 889.34 | 927.81 | 908.79 | 924.16 | 923.45 | 929.47 | 931.63 | 1,003.39 | 938.06 | 935.29 | 965.97 | 928.93 | 934.58 |
| 2016 | 939.49 | 933.81 | 925.89 | 930.30 | 961.71 | 887.77 | 883.67 | 907.90 | 907.96 | 972.04 | 937.62 | 917.79 | 926.39 |
| 2017 | 996.18 | 983.15 | 955.42 | 986.27 | 941.06 | 934.27 | 965.61 | 954.73 | 969.15 | 996.08 | 943.12 | 957.72 | 965.95 |
| 2018 | 951.52 | 956.69 | 958.27 | 994.60 | 933.07 | 947.74 | 997.52 | 972.72 | 981.45 | 948.10 | 934.22 | 978.42 | 962.86 |
| 2019 | 927.11 | 904.70 | 934.59 | 933.66 | 918.37 | 959.97 | 915.72 | 932.25 | 983.54 | 970.70 | 977.51 | 987.30 | 944.85 |
| **Professional and Business Services** | | | | | | | | | | | | | |
| 2015 | 962.72 | 997.44 | 994.56 | 981.04 | 965.30 | 967.84 | 958.93 | 1,019.89 | 994.40 | 1,006.76 | 1,034.28 | 995.35 | 991.10 |
| 2016 | 1,025.90 | 1,055.46 | 1,044.93 | 1,058.82 | 1,081.88 | 1,030.89 | 1,042.14 | 1,058.03 | 1,060.85 | 1,056.68 | 1,014.04 | 988.52 | 1,044.30 |
| 2017 | 1,009.54 | 997.54 | 1,001.40 | 1,062.78 | 1,011.66 | 982.11 | 1,024.66 | 978.77 | 962.66 | 1,010.16 | 951.23 | 945.89 | 994.52 |
| 2018 | 967.57 | 975.27 | 969.39 | 1,016.53 | 973.25 | 978.18 | 993.83 | 942.86 | 976.47 | 921.30 | 929.36 | 967.79 | 968.09 |
| 2019 | 982.91 | 980.91 | 980.34 | 1,011.38 | 965.33 | 1,007.77 | 964.54 | 1,003.22 | 1,016.38 | 1,014.22 | 993.34 | 996.16 | 993.60 |
| **Education and Health Services** | | | | | | | | | | | | | |
| 2015 | 656.91 | 666.30 | 653.47 | 647.55 | 629.83 | 635.93 | 630.59 | 646.88 | 629.94 | 621.81 | 640.84 | 628.09 | 640.10 |
| 2016 | 621.35 | 620.62 | 633.02 | 647.94 | 660.21 | 652.97 | 663.93 | 651.20 | 664.44 | 675.99 | 664.05 | 677.08 | 652.22 |
| 2017 | 689.70 | 699.90 | 667.06 | 692.96 | 672.90 | 680.26 | 706.71 | 671.95 | 682.62 | 689.07 | 702.05 | 698.90 | 687.51 |
| 2018 | 701.19 | 696.71 | 694.78 | 708.86 | 694.62 | 702.24 | 718.89 | 702.11 | 692.85 | 678.16 | 683.89 | 695.47 | 696.39 |
| 2019 | 648.00 | 649.90 | 665.58 | 670.76 | 668.51 | 679.88 | 666.51 | 664.30 | 672.36 | 672.05 | 679.14 | 677.35 | 667.43 |
| **Leisure and Hospitality** | | | | | | | | | | | | | |
| 2015 | 278.86 | 298.62 | 299.58 | 284.82 | 286.08 | 291.71 | 308.90 | 317.07 | 294.92 | 290.77 | 292.64 | 289.67 | 295.17 |
| 2016 | 282.00 | 293.54 | 286.31 | 294.24 | 307.59 | 294.98 | 306.97 | 305.75 | 289.76 | 304.54 | 288.58 | 290.70 | 295.48 |
| 2017 | 300.19 | 301.62 | 306.18 | 311.68 | 309.44 | 308.26 | 331.50 | 323.09 | 307.35 | 318.75 | 301.16 | 305.93 | 311.10 |
| 2018 | 303.30 | 304.46 | 304.15 | 313.78 | 307.35 | 313.78 | 335.39 | 335.09 | 334.55 | 312.81 | 304.84 | 327.36 | 317.52 |
| 2019 | 312.03 | 314.05 | 322.20 | 310.75 | 322.48 | 346.38 | 334.99 | 343.36 | 342.25 | 322.65 | 323.18 | 340.65 | 328.30 |

# ILLINOIS
## *At a Glance*

Population:
2010 census: 12,830,632
2019 estimate: 12,671,821

Percent change in population:
2010–2019: -1.2%

Percent change in total nonfarm employment:
2011–2019: 7.8%

Industry with the largest growth in employment, 2011–2019 (percent):
Transportation and utilities, 24.9%

Industry with the largest decline or smallest growth in employment, 2011–2019 (percent):
Government, -1.6%

Civilian labor force:
2010: 6,625,321
2019: 6,446,610

Unemployment rate and rank among states (highest to lowest):
2010: 10.4%, 11th
2019: 4.0%, 13th

Over-the-year change in unemployment rates:
2017–2018: -0.6%
2018–2019: -0.3%

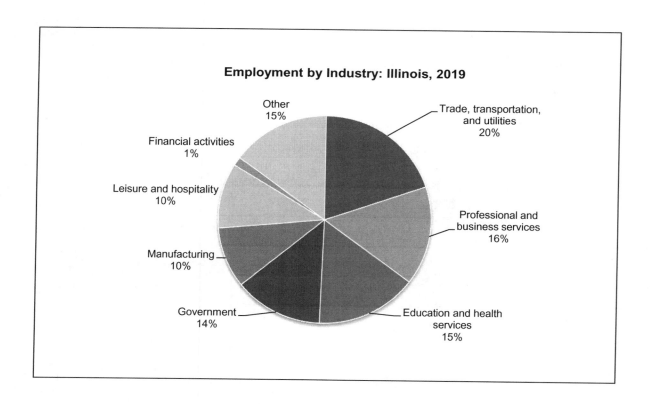

**Employment by Industry: Illinois, 2019**

- Other 15%
- Trade, transportation, and utilities 20%
- Financial activities 1%
- Professional and business services 16%
- Leisure and hospitality 10%
- Manufacturing 10%
- Education and health services 15%
- Government 14%

## 1. Employment by Industry: Illinois, 2011–2019

(Numbers in thousands, not seasonally adjusted)

| Industry and year | January | February | March | April | May | June | July | August | September | October | November | December | Annual average |
|---|---|---|---|---|---|---|---|---|---|---|---|---|---|
| **Total Nonfarm** | | | | | | | | | | | | | |
| 2011 | 5,526.1 | 5,546.3 | 5,590.7 | 5,670.4 | 5,709.2 | 5,720.3 | 5,680.8 | 5,698.5 | 5,736.0 | 5,747.2 | 5,758.3 | 5,746.7 | 5,677.5 |
| 2012 | 5,597.9 | 5,624.0 | 5,678.0 | 5,735.6 | 5,785.4 | 5,799.4 | 5,745.3 | 5,764.8 | 5,806.7 | 5,815.1 | 5,836.5 | 5,822.6 | 5,750.9 |
| 2013 | 5,659.1 | 5,688.1 | 5,723.8 | 5,773.2 | 5,832.8 | 5,848.9 | 5,800.4 | 5,822.4 | 5,854.3 | 5,868.5 | 5,885.2 | 5,882.1 | 5,803.2 |
| 2014 | 5,715.4 | 5,735.9 | 5,781.8 | 5,854.9 | 5,918.6 | 5,932.1 | 5,879.7 | 5,896.3 | 5,926.8 | 5,960.9 | 5,971.9 | 5,969.9 | 5,878.7 |
| 2015 | 5,789.3 | 5,817.6 | 5,854.2 | 5,946.4 | 6,016.1 | 6,031.2 | 5,984.8 | 5,987.7 | 6,015.9 | 6,053.7 | 6,052.4 | 6,048.0 | 5,966.4 |
| 2016 | 5,872.5 | 5,896.4 | 5,929.2 | 6,005.0 | 6,039.3 | 6,057.7 | 6,018.1 | 6,022.6 | 6,056.3 | 6,082.1 | 6,094.8 | 6,076.8 | 6,012.6 |
| 2017 | 5,899.5 | 5,929.8 | 5,974.5 | 6,027.5 | 6,083.9 | 6,116.6 | 6,059.3 | 6,077.4 | 6,099.9 | 6,121.0 | 6,139.7 | 6,131.9 | 6,055.1 |
| 2018 | 5,951.1 | 5,986.5 | 6,041.1 | 6,066.1 | 6,127.7 | 6,161.7 | 6,116.0 | 6,127.5 | 6,143.6 | 6,158.6 | 6,180.4 | 6,159.7 | 6,101.7 |
| 2019 | 5,991.4 | 6,005.9 | 6,048.7 | 6,102.1 | 6,158.2 | 6,183.8 | 6,134.9 | 6,143.2 | 6,149.1 | 6,178.9 | 6,169.3 | 6,150.1 | 6,118.0 |
| **Total Private** | | | | | | | | | | | | | |
| 2010 | 4,696.8 | 4,696.2 | 4,739.6 | 4,811.3 | 4,848.2 | 4,886.9 | 4,882.4 | 4,902.6 | 4,892.5 | 4,897.3 | 4,904.6 | 4,904.5 | 4,838.6 |
| 2011 | 4,776.7 | 4,780.2 | 4,830.3 | 4,884.7 | 4,929.3 | 4,971.3 | 4,960.6 | 4,982.0 | 4,970.7 | 4,969.9 | 4,987.9 | 4,981.0 | 4,918.7 |
| 2012 | 4,837.8 | 4,847.7 | 4,881.2 | 4,927.7 | 4,985.7 | 5,025.0 | 5,016.9 | 5,041.4 | 5,020.6 | 5,030.8 | 5,044.6 | 5,043.9 | 4,975.3 |
| 2013 | 4,901.4 | 4,905.9 | 4,946.9 | 5,014.8 | 5,073.2 | 5,110.6 | 5,096.7 | 5,116.3 | 5,092.9 | 5,119.2 | 5,129.6 | 5,128.4 | 5,053.0 |
| 2014 | 4,976.4 | 4,984.9 | 5,016.7 | 5,104.0 | 5,168.3 | 5,203.6 | 5,198.3 | 5,205.1 | 5,184.0 | 5,212.8 | 5,215.5 | 5,209.3 | 5,139.9 |
| 2015 | 5,064.8 | 5,068.5 | 5,095.8 | 5,170.8 | 5,202.8 | 5,231.2 | 5,234.7 | 5,243.9 | 5,222.9 | 5,251.0 | 5,262.4 | 5,237.7 | 5,190.5 |
| 2016 | 5,098.0 | 5,105.2 | 5,145.6 | 5,197.2 | 5,249.4 | 5,294.9 | 5,280.2 | 5,296.0 | 5,269.5 | 5,288.9 | 5,306.7 | 5,297.8 | 5,235.8 |
| 2017 | 5,151.4 | 5,164.7 | 5,211.2 | 5,237.6 | 5,292.2 | 5,339.9 | 5,336.1 | 5,344.3 | 5,312.0 | 5,325.4 | 5,342.6 | 5,324.8 | 5,281.9 |
| 2018 | 5,186.8 | 5,182.1 | 5,217.0 | 5,270.0 | 5,317.9 | 5,358.6 | 5,350.1 | 5,355.0 | 5,312.6 | 5,336.3 | 5,320.3 | 5,304.4 | 5,292.6 |
| 2019 | | | | | | | | | | | | | |
| **Goods Producing** | | | | | | | | | | | | | |
| 2011 | 744.0 | 743.0 | 755.4 | 773.5 | 784.6 | 797.1 | 799.8 | 802.6 | 796.6 | 793.7 | 788.3 | 777.1 | 779.6 |
| 2012 | 750.0 | 749.4 | 761.8 | 775.9 | 784.5 | 796.9 | 801.2 | 802.1 | 799.6 | 797.9 | 791.0 | 781.8 | 782.7 |
| 2013 | 753.2 | 753.7 | 759.7 | 768.5 | 783.4 | 794.7 | 797.1 | 799.0 | 795.2 | 794.1 | 791.6 | 778.9 | 780.8 |
| 2014 | 753.1 | 753.1 | 765.1 | 780.3 | 794.4 | 806.6 | 809.8 | 812.5 | 809.6 | 812.5 | 808.0 | 800.4 | 792.1 |
| 2015 | 771.5 | 771.7 | 780.8 | 798.3 | 811.7 | 822.2 | 823.6 | 823.8 | 821.0 | 819.5 | 813.2 | 803.2 | 805.0 |
| 2016 | 775.6 | 775.8 | 785.4 | 799.2 | 806.8 | 817.4 | 818.2 | 817.3 | 812.8 | 811.5 | 807.8 | 792.5 | 801.7 |
| 2017 | 766.7 | 768.4 | 778.7 | 793.0 | 806.8 | 821.2 | 822.5 | 823.8 | 820.7 | 820.8 | 817.5 | 808.8 | 804.1 |
| 2018 | 783.6 | 787.5 | 801.7 | 811.1 | 826.1 | 839.4 | 839.6 | 839.4 | 836.1 | 835.7 | 830.9 | 822.5 | 821.1 |
| 2019 | 796.1 | 795.4 | 806.9 | 819.6 | 830.2 | 839.3 | 840.0 | 838.3 | 832.8 | 828.7 | 816.3 | 801.6 | 820.4 |
| **Service-Providing** | | | | | | | | | | | | | |
| 2011 | 4,782.1 | 4,803.3 | 4,835.3 | 4,896.9 | 4,924.6 | 4,923.2 | 4,881.0 | 4,895.9 | 4,939.4 | 4,953.5 | 4,970.0 | 4,969.6 | 4,897.9 |
| 2012 | 4,847.9 | 4,874.6 | 4,916.2 | 4,959.7 | 5,000.9 | 5,002.5 | 4,944.1 | 4,962.7 | 5,007.1 | 5,017.2 | 5,045.4 | 5,040.8 | 4,968.3 |
| 2013 | 4,905.9 | 4,934.4 | 4,964.1 | 5,004.7 | 5,049.4 | 5,054.2 | 5,003.3 | 5,023.4 | 5,059.1 | 5,074.4 | 5,093.6 | 5,103.2 | 5,022.5 |
| 2014 | 4,962.3 | 4,982.8 | 5,016.7 | 5,074.6 | 5,124.2 | 5,125.5 | 5,069.9 | 5,083.8 | 5,117.2 | 5,148.4 | 5,163.9 | 5,169.5 | 5,086.6 |
| 2015 | 5,017.8 | 5,045.9 | 5,073.4 | 5,148.1 | 5,204.4 | 5,209.0 | 5,161.2 | 5,163.9 | 5,194.9 | 5,234.2 | 5,239.2 | 5,244.8 | 5,161.4 |
| 2016 | 5,096.9 | 5,120.6 | 5,143.8 | 5,205.8 | 5,232.5 | 5,240.3 | 5,199.9 | 5,205.3 | 5,243.5 | 5,270.6 | 5,287.0 | 5,284.3 | 5,210.9 |
| 2017 | 5,132.8 | 5,161.4 | 5,195.8 | 5,234.5 | 5,277.1 | 5,295.4 | 5,236.8 | 5,253.6 | 5,279.2 | 5,300.2 | 5,322.2 | 5,323.1 | 5,251.0 |
| 2018 | 5,167.5 | 5,199.0 | 5,239.4 | 5,255.0 | 5,301.6 | 5,322.3 | 5,276.4 | 5,288.1 | 5,307.5 | 5,322.9 | 5,349.5 | 5,337.2 | 5,280.5 |
| 2019 | 5,195.3 | 5,210.5 | 5,241.8 | 5,282.5 | 5,328.0 | 5,344.5 | 5,294.9 | 5,304.9 | 5,316.3 | 5,350.2 | 5,353.0 | 5,348.5 | 5,297.5 |
| **Mining, Logging, and Construction** | | | | | | | | | | | | | |
| 2011 | 177.9 | 176.5 | 186.2 | 201.6 | 211.2 | 219.2 | 222.4 | 224.1 | 220.3 | 216.4 | 210.2 | 198.5 | 205.4 |
| 2012 | 175.7 | 173.5 | 182.9 | 195.3 | 202.1 | 209.6 | 213.1 | 213.7 | 212.1 | 212.3 | 205.0 | 196.2 | 199.3 |
| 2013 | 174.0 | 174.1 | 179.4 | 190.0 | 203.8 | 211.2 | 217.1 | 218.1 | 217.2 | 216.6 | 211.8 | 199.4 | 201.1 |
| 2014 | 178.2 | 177.6 | 186.8 | 202.5 | 214.3 | 222.6 | 227.7 | 229.6 | 229.1 | 230.6 | 225.2 | 215.8 | 211.7 |
| 2015 | 191.9 | 191.2 | 199.4 | 218.3 | 228.8 | 235.1 | 238.1 | 239.7 | 238.6 | 238.8 | 232.9 | 222.6 | 223.0 |
| 2016 | 200.6 | 200.2 | 210.0 | 223.8 | 230.6 | 239.0 | 241.0 | 241.5 | 239.8 | 240.0 | 234.9 | 219.5 | 226.7 |
| 2017 | 199.0 | 202.3 | 210.3 | 222.7 | 233.2 | 240.5 | 242.2 | 243.1 | 241.5 | 241.5 | 236.2 | 225.1 | 228.1 |
| 2018 | 204.7 | 205.6 | 218.1 | 227.2 | 239.8 | 248.8 | 249.2 | 249.2 | 248.1 | 247.1 | 240.0 | 230.0 | 234.0 |
| 2019 | 209.4 | 206.7 | 218.1 | 232.7 | 242.8 | 249.2 | 251.6 | 252.0 | 250.3 | 248.4 | 235.7 | 221.9 | 234.9 |
| **Manufacturing** | | | | | | | | | | | | | |
| 2011 | 566.1 | 566.5 | 569.2 | 571.9 | 573.4 | 577.9 | 577.4 | 578.5 | 576.3 | 577.3 | 578.1 | 578.6 | 574.3 |
| 2012 | 574.3 | 575.9 | 578.9 | 580.6 | 582.4 | 587.3 | 588.1 | 588.4 | 587.5 | 585.6 | 586.1 | 585.6 | 583.4 |
| 2013 | 579.2 | 579.6 | 580.3 | 578.5 | 579.6 | 583.5 | 580.0 | 580.9 | 578.0 | 577.5 | 579.8 | 579.5 | 579.7 |
| 2014 | 574.9 | 575.5 | 578.3 | 577.8 | 580.1 | 584.0 | 582.1 | 582.9 | 580.5 | 581.9 | 582.8 | 584.6 | 580.5 |
| 2015 | 579.6 | 580.5 | 581.4 | 580.0 | 582.9 | 587.1 | 585.5 | 584.1 | 582.4 | 580.7 | 580.3 | 580.6 | 582.1 |
| 2016 | 575.0 | 575.6 | 575.4 | 575.4 | 576.2 | 578.4 | 577.2 | 575.8 | 573.0 | 571.5 | 572.9 | 573.0 | 575.0 |
| 2017 | 567.7 | 566.1 | 568.4 | 570.3 | 573.6 | 580.7 | 580.3 | 580.7 | 579.2 | 579.3 | 581.3 | 583.7 | 575.9 |
| 2018 | 578.9 | 581.9 | 583.6 | 583.9 | 586.3 | 590.6 | 590.4 | 590.2 | 588.0 | 588.6 | 590.9 | 592.5 | 587.2 |
| 2019 | 586.7 | 588.7 | 588.8 | 586.9 | 587.4 | 590.1 | 588.4 | 586.3 | 582.5 | 580.3 | 580.6 | 579.7 | 585.5 |

## 1. Employment by Industry: Illinois, 2011–2019—*Continued*

(Numbers in thousands, not seasonally adjusted)

| Industry and year | January | February | March | April | May | June | July | August | September | October | November | December | Annual average |
|---|---|---|---|---|---|---|---|---|---|---|---|---|---|
| **Trade, Transportation, and Utilities** | | | | | | | | | | | | | |
| 2011 | 1,123.7 | 1,114.5 | 1,120.0 | 1,131.0 | 1,137.9 | 1,143.3 | 1,139.6 | 1,143.7 | 1,143.3 | 1,150.0 | 1,169.1 | 1,183.0 | 1,141.6 |
| 2012 | 1,139.2 | 1,128.2 | 1,136.4 | 1,141.0 | 1,149.9 | 1,153.5 | 1,151.4 | 1,154.5 | 1,153.2 | 1,160.8 | 1,186.3 | 1,192.5 | 1,153.9 |
| 2013 | 1,145.6 | 1,136.5 | 1,140.6 | 1,147.1 | 1,157.4 | 1,164.1 | 1,161.1 | 1,165.9 | 1,162.8 | 1,168.8 | 1,190.4 | 1,203.4 | 1,162.0 |
| 2014 | 1,156.3 | 1,145.2 | 1,152.1 | 1,161.3 | 1,173.7 | 1,181.0 | 1,176.7 | 1,181.6 | 1,179.4 | 1,188.0 | 1,210.3 | 1,222.8 | 1,177.4 |
| | | | | | | | | | | | | | |
| 2015 | 1,175.1 | 1,167.0 | 1,172.6 | 1,184.4 | 1,197.0 | 1,204.8 | 1,200.1 | 1,203.7 | 1,201.7 | 1,210.7 | 1,230.0 | 1,238.8 | 1,198.8 |
| 2016 | 1,190.8 | 1,183.8 | 1,187.3 | 1,200.0 | 1,204.4 | 1,207.0 | 1,206.4 | 1,208.5 | 1,203.8 | 1,219.4 | 1,238.9 | 1,252.0 | 1,208.5 |
| 2017 | 1,202.4 | 1,191.6 | 1,194.0 | 1,197.2 | 1,202.6 | 1,209.6 | 1,206.0 | 1,208.9 | 1,206.7 | 1,214.5 | 1,241.2 | 1,251.5 | 1,210.5 |
| 2018 | 1,206.8 | 1,194.4 | 1,199.9 | 1,199.7 | 1,208.4 | 1,214.5 | 1,212.5 | 1,210.4 | 1,203.2 | 1,210.4 | 1,235.8 | 1,242.5 | 1,211.5 |
| 2019 | 1,203.3 | 1,186.0 | 1,189.3 | 1,193.8 | 1,200.8 | 1,209.3 | 1,205.2 | 1,205.3 | 1,198.8 | 1,206.7 | 1,224.5 | 1,236.3 | 1,204.9 |
| **Wholesale Trade** | | | | | | | | | | | | | |
| 2011 | 281.8 | 281.8 | 283.5 | 286.2 | 287.3 | 289.6 | 289.9 | 289.4 | 288.5 | 289.0 | 288.6 | 289.6 | 287.1 |
| 2012 | 286.6 | 286.9 | 289.8 | 291.1 | 292.6 | 295.0 | 293.8 | 293.4 | 292.7 | 293.3 | 293.6 | 293.8 | 291.9 |
| 2013 | 290.6 | 290.6 | 292.3 | 293.9 | 295.7 | 298.3 | 297.2 | 296.1 | 295.3 | 295.8 | 296.3 | 296.6 | 294.9 |
| 2014 | 292.9 | 292.9 | 294.1 | 294.8 | 296.9 | 298.5 | 297.4 | 296.8 | 295.2 | 297.1 | 297.8 | 297.4 | 296.0 |
| | | | | | | | | | | | | | |
| 2015 | 293.6 | 292.9 | 294.5 | 296.8 | 299.1 | 301.0 | 299.7 | 298.4 | 296.8 | 296.6 | 295.9 | 296.0 | 296.8 |
| 2016 | 291.0 | 290.9 | 291.6 | 294.4 | 294.6 | 296.6 | 296.2 | 295.3 | 295.1 | 295.0 | 295.0 | 295.2 | 294.2 |
| 2017 | 290.6 | 291.1 | 292.1 | 293.9 | 295.3 | 297.9 | 297.3 | 295.8 | 294.4 | 295.5 | 295.4 | 296.4 | 294.6 |
| 2018 | 291.9 | 292.8 | 294.5 | 293.6 | 294.3 | 296.5 | 296.0 | 294.3 | 293.3 | 294.2 | 293.8 | 294.7 | 294.2 |
| 2019 | 291.4 | 291.7 | 293.0 | 295.4 | 296.3 | 299.3 | 298.4 | 296.6 | 294.2 | 293.6 | 292.4 | 291.9 | 294.5 |
| **Retail Trade** | | | | | | | | | | | | | |
| 2011 | 587.2 | 577.7 | 580.4 | 587.0 | 591.4 | 596.0 | 594.8 | 597.3 | 592.5 | 598.3 | 616.5 | 626.0 | 595.4 |
| 2012 | 593.2 | 582.1 | 585.6 | 587.2 | 592.5 | 596.9 | 596.4 | 595.9 | 591.7 | 598.6 | 622.3 | 625.0 | 597.3 |
| 2013 | 592.9 | 583.8 | 585.5 | 587.8 | 594.7 | 602.0 | 600.8 | 601.8 | 597.5 | 602.9 | 621.5 | 630.6 | 600.2 |
| 2014 | 595.6 | 585.1 | 588.6 | 595.8 | 602.7 | 609.7 | 608.2 | 608.5 | 604.5 | 610.8 | 629.5 | 637.1 | 606.3 |
| | | | | | | | | | | | | | |
| 2015 | 603.5 | 596.3 | 599.7 | 605.8 | 613.0 | 619.7 | 618.5 | 619.8 | 616.6 | 623.0 | 639.9 | 644.1 | 616.7 |
| 2016 | 613.0 | 606.6 | 607.8 | 615.4 | 618.4 | 621.9 | 621.9 | 621.7 | 613.1 | 621.1 | 637.5 | 643.5 | 620.2 |
| 2017 | 615.2 | 605.4 | 605.5 | 607.9 | 609.5 | 615.1 | 612.5 | 610.7 | 602.9 | 608.5 | 628.4 | 633.3 | 612.9 |
| 2018 | 603.0 | 591.8 | 594.7 | 596.1 | 601.8 | 605.3 | 604.1 | 600.8 | 592.1 | 595.3 | 614.1 | 616.3 | 601.3 |
| 2019 | 590.9 | 577.4 | 579.0 | 580.9 | 584.7 | 589.1 | 587.4 | 584.8 | 577.2 | 584.3 | 599.0 | 605.7 | 586.7 |
| **Transportation and Utilities** | | | | | | | | | | | | | |
| 2011 | 254.7 | 255.0 | 256.1 | 257.8 | 259.2 | 257.7 | 254.9 | 257.0 | 262.3 | 262.7 | 264.0 | 267.4 | 259.1 |
| 2012 | 259.4 | 259.2 | 261.0 | 262.7 | 264.8 | 261.6 | 261.2 | 265.2 | 268.8 | 268.9 | 270.4 | 273.7 | 264.7 |
| 2013 | 262.1 | 262.1 | 262.8 | 265.4 | 267.0 | 263.8 | 263.1 | 268.0 | 270.0 | 270.1 | 272.6 | 276.2 | 266.9 |
| 2014 | 267.8 | 267.2 | 269.4 | 270.7 | 274.1 | 272.8 | 271.1 | 276.3 | 279.7 | 280.1 | 283.0 | 288.3 | 275.0 |
| | | | | | | | | | | | | | |
| 2015 | 278.0 | 277.8 | 278.4 | 281.8 | 284.9 | 284.1 | 281.9 | 285.5 | 288.3 | 291.1 | 294.2 | 298.7 | 285.4 |
| 2016 | 286.8 | 286.3 | 287.9 | 290.2 | 291.4 | 288.5 | 288.3 | 291.5 | 295.6 | 303.3 | 306.4 | 313.3 | 294.1 |
| 2017 | 296.6 | 295.1 | 296.4 | 295.4 | 297.8 | 296.6 | 296.2 | 302.4 | 309.4 | 310.5 | 317.4 | 321.8 | 303.0 |
| 2018 | 311.9 | 309.8 | 310.7 | 310.0 | 312.3 | 312.7 | 312.4 | 315.3 | 317.8 | 320.9 | 327.9 | 331.5 | 316.1 |
| 2019 | 321.0 | 316.9 | 317.3 | 317.5 | 319.8 | 320.9 | 319.4 | 323.9 | 327.4 | 328.8 | 333.1 | 338.7 | 323.7 |
| **Information** | | | | | | | | | | | | | |
| 2011 | 100.5 | 99.9 | 100.1 | 100.4 | 100.7 | 101.1 | 101.4 | 101.3 | 99.8 | 99.9 | 100.4 | 100.4 | 100.5 |
| 2012 | 100.1 | 99.7 | 100.2 | 100.4 | 101.2 | 100.2 | 100.3 | 100.3 | 99.0 | 99.8 | 100.1 | 100.5 | 100.2 |
| 2013 | 99.2 | 98.8 | 98.8 | 100.0 | 99.9 | 99.9 | 98.8 | 98.3 | 97.3 | 98.0 | 98.5 | 98.9 | 98.9 |
| 2014 | 97.7 | 97.8 | 98.8 | 99.4 | 98.8 | 99.3 | 99.1 | 99.8 | 98.1 | 99.3 | 99.4 | 100.3 | 99.0 |
| | | | | | | | | | | | | | |
| 2015 | 99.6 | 99.6 | 99.6 | 101.0 | 101.6 | 101.3 | 100.2 | 100.5 | 99.1 | 100.4 | 100.8 | 101.1 | 100.4 |
| 2016 | 97.6 | 97.2 | 97.5 | 98.2 | 97.7 | 97.0 | 97.0 | 98.9 | 97.3 | 100.8 | 101.5 | 100.8 | 98.5 |
| 2017 | 99.4 | 99.8 | 100.0 | 98.4 | 98.6 | 98.3 | 97.0 | 97.8 | 95.5 | 94.9 | 94.9 | 94.8 | 97.5 |
| 2018 | 94.6 | 94.4 | 94.7 | 94.3 | 94.0 | 94.3 | 95.3 | 96.1 | 93.9 | 94.8 | 95.3 | 94.9 | 94.7 |
| 2019 | 95.2 | 95.4 | 95.5 | 95.0 | 95.0 | 95.3 | 94.6 | 95.9 | 94.5 | 96.6 | 95.2 | 96.7 | 95.4 |
| **Financial Activities** | | | | | | | | | | | | | |
| 2011 | 369.9 | 369.7 | 369.5 | 370.2 | 370.9 | 373.5 | 375.3 | 375.3 | 372.4 | 374.3 | 373.1 | 373.9 | 372.3 |
| 2012 | 369.9 | 370.5 | 371.3 | 373.0 | 374.7 | 378.3 | 379.3 | 379.9 | 377.5 | 377.1 | 376.8 | 378.6 | 375.6 |
| 2013 | 375.2 | 375.5 | 375.7 | 378.1 | 378.7 | 382.6 | 382.4 | 381.9 | 379.4 | 379.7 | 378.9 | 379.6 | 379.0 |
| 2014 | 375.4 | 374.9 | 375.1 | 375.4 | 377.2 | 380.2 | 381.3 | 382.4 | 378.1 | 379.3 | 378.4 | 379.8 | 378.1 |
| | | | | | | | | | | | | | |
| 2015 | 376.7 | 376.6 | 376.6 | 380.4 | 382.5 | 386.5 | 387.5 | 387.6 | 383.0 | 384.3 | 383.6 | 384.6 | 382.5 |
| 2016 | 380.6 | 381.0 | 381.3 | 384.1 | 384.9 | 388.3 | 391.1 | 391.4 | 387.8 | 389.6 | 389.2 | 390.1 | 386.6 |
| 2017 | 387.8 | 388.1 | 388.9 | 390.8 | 392.1 | 397.6 | 400.7 | 400.7 | 396.9 | 397.7 | 397.7 | 399.8 | 394.9 |
| 2018 | 394.7 | 395.4 | 396.9 | 399.4 | 400.5 | 405.9 | 408.2 | 408.5 | 404.4 | 406.6 | 406.8 | 407.0 | 402.9 |
| 2019 | 403.2 | 405.3 | 406.3 | 409.4 | 409.7 | 414.8 | 416.6 | 417.0 | 411.8 | 412.8 | 412.9 | 413.5 | 411.1 |

## 1. Employment by Industry: Illinois, 2011–2019—*Continued*

(Numbers in thousands, not seasonally adjusted)

| Industry and year | January | February | March | April | May | June | July | August | September | October | November | December | Annual average |
|---|---|---|---|---|---|---|---|---|---|---|---|---|---|
| **Professional and Business Services** | | | | | | | | | | | | | |
| 2011 | 787.7 | 791.2 | 797.1 | 818.5 | 818.8 | 829.8 | 835.4 | 840.7 | 840.8 | 845.0 | 844.3 | 840.0 | 824.1 |
| 2012 | 817.5 | 820.3 | 829.7 | 848.8 | 855.4 | 868.4 | 867.7 | 875.3 | 875.4 | 874.9 | 878.6 | 872.6 | 857.1 |
| 2013 | 839.0 | 846.9 | 853.2 | 868.5 | 879.7 | 891.1 | 893.4 | 902.5 | 898.9 | 908.4 | 909.5 | 906.9 | 883.2 |
| 2014 | 871.3 | 877.3 | 882.3 | 901.8 | 911.4 | 920.8 | 919.5 | 926.1 | 922.3 | 928.9 | 929.5 | 921.5 | 909.4 |
| 2015 | 885.5 | 890.2 | 892.1 | 914.4 | 922.6 | 930.7 | 937.3 | 937.8 | 932.7 | 945.2 | 941.2 | 933.3 | 921.9 |
| 2016 | 905.8 | 908.0 | 909.4 | 924.5 | 924.6 | 933.6 | 940.6 | 944.5 | 944.7 | 950.7 | 950.6 | 939.3 | 931.4 |
| 2017 | 906.2 | 909.4 | 917.2 | 931.1 | 939.6 | 952.8 | 952.1 | 956.8 | 952.7 | 960.6 | 964.2 | 956.4 | 941.6 |
| 2018 | 917.7 | 927.2 | 930.2 | 932.5 | 938.9 | 952.4 | 959.5 | 964.9 | 962.6 | 962.9 | 967.5 | 954.5 | 947.6 |
| 2019 | 919.2 | 925.0 | 924.2 | 936.5 | 945.6 | 958.2 | 959.9 | 965.3 | 956.1 | 959.6 | 952.6 | 935.8 | 944.8 |
| **Education and Health Services** | | | | | | | | | | | | | |
| 2011 | 837.3 | 844.8 | 850.0 | 848.7 | 849.5 | 844.2 | 835.6 | 837.4 | 850.8 | 857.1 | 860.4 | 863.7 | 848.3 |
| 2012 | 852.4 | 861.7 | 865.7 | 864.2 | 863.9 | 861.1 | 850.8 | 854.3 | 866.4 | 869.8 | 873.3 | 874.3 | 863.2 |
| 2013 | 866.4 | 876.2 | 881.1 | 876.1 | 876.5 | 869.0 | 859.0 | 866.1 | 876.2 | 882.4 | 886.5 | 887.8 | 875.3 |
| 2014 | 875.8 | 884.6 | 888.6 | 890.1 | 890.0 | 881.2 | 872.0 | 875.5 | 884.1 | 893.8 | 897.6 | 899.6 | 886.1 |
| 2015 | 885.8 | 892.3 | 896.4 | 902.4 | 905.7 | 897.0 | 891.5 | 892.0 | 901.0 | 911.1 | 914.2 | 914.6 | 900.3 |
| 2016 | 904.1 | 911.5 | 913.3 | 919.2 | 921.0 | 911.8 | 905.8 | 906.8 | 915.7 | 923.3 | 925.8 | 924.1 | 915.2 |
| 2017 | 914.3 | 923.5 | 927.7 | 927.2 | 928.9 | 918.6 | 910.0 | 912.1 | 922.8 | 931.0 | 934.6 | 934.1 | 923.7 |
| 2018 | 922.2 | 933.0 | 938.1 | 936.6 | 936.8 | 928.6 | 918.9 | 920.9 | 931.5 | 937.8 | 941.4 | 940.2 | 932.2 |
| 2019 | 928.7 | 934.9 | 940.3 | 941.9 | 942.0 | 931.1 | 925.0 | 927.7 | 937.2 | 954.1 | 955.8 | 954.4 | 939.4 |
| **Leisure and Hospitality** | | | | | | | | | | | | | |
| 2011 | 488.5 | 487.6 | 500.1 | 519.6 | 534.4 | 544.1 | 542.6 | 549.5 | 538.5 | 527.7 | 520.6 | 516.1 | 522.4 |
| 2012 | 501.1 | 503.1 | 516.0 | 532.8 | 548.8 | 558.8 | 557.7 | 564.4 | 549.9 | 540.8 | 532.8 | 531.4 | 536.5 |
| 2013 | 513.4 | 513.5 | 524.1 | 541.1 | 560.0 | 571.2 | 571.8 | 574.0 | 559.7 | 549.7 | 540.0 | 538.1 | 546.4 |
| 2014 | 524.3 | 524.5 | 534.3 | 554.8 | 573.5 | 584.2 | 581.9 | 584.3 | 570.1 | 565.2 | 555.0 | 552.2 | 558.7 |
| 2015 | 533.9 | 538.0 | 547.3 | 571.5 | 594.1 | 605.4 | 603.6 | 606.1 | 594.2 | 589.8 | 580.8 | 581.5 | 578.9 |
| 2016 | 561.5 | 561.8 | 571.3 | 594.5 | 611.2 | 622.5 | 622.0 | 623.1 | 610.3 | 604.3 | 597.8 | 587.5 | 597.3 |
| 2017 | 572.6 | 575.8 | 588.4 | 606.8 | 627.0 | 640.0 | 636.1 | 640.6 | 622.1 | 616.2 | 604.1 | 598.4 | 610.7 |
| 2018 | 581.5 | 581.7 | 596.7 | 611.3 | 633.1 | 647.3 | 644.9 | 647.9 | 627.1 | 622.1 | 610.1 | 607.6 | 617.6 |
| 2019 | 588.9 | 588.1 | 600.4 | 618.4 | 637.3 | 651.6 | 650.7 | 649.0 | 627.6 | 623.0 | 608.3 | 609.4 | 621.1 |
| **Other Services** | | | | | | | | | | | | | |
| 2011 | 245.2 | 245.5 | 247.4 | 249.4 | 251.4 | 253.8 | 252.7 | 252.1 | 250.3 | 249.6 | 248.4 | 250.3 | 249.7 |
| 2012 | 246.5 | 247.3 | 249.2 | 248.6 | 250.9 | 254.1 | 252.2 | 251.2 | 249.7 | 248.8 | 248.9 | 249.3 | 249.7 |
| 2013 | 245.8 | 246.6 | 248.0 | 248.3 | 250.1 | 252.4 | 253.3 | 253.7 | 251.1 | 249.7 | 249.2 | 250.3 | 249.9 |
| 2014 | 247.5 | 248.5 | 250.6 | 251.7 | 254.2 | 257.3 | 256.4 | 254.1 | 251.2 | 252.2 | 251.4 | 251.8 | 252.2 |
| 2015 | 248.3 | 249.5 | 251.3 | 251.6 | 253.1 | 255.7 | 254.5 | 253.6 | 251.3 | 251.8 | 251.7 | 252.2 | 252.1 |
| 2016 | 248.8 | 249.4 | 250.3 | 251.1 | 252.2 | 253.6 | 253.6 | 253.4 | 250.5 | 251.4 | 250.8 | 251.4 | 251.4 |
| 2017 | 248.6 | 248.6 | 250.7 | 252.7 | 253.8 | 256.8 | 255.8 | 255.3 | 252.1 | 253.2 | 252.5 | 254.0 | 252.8 |
| 2018 | 250.3 | 251.1 | 253.0 | 252.7 | 254.4 | 257.5 | 257.2 | 256.2 | 253.2 | 255.1 | 254.8 | 255.6 | 254.3 |
| 2019 | 252.2 | 252.0 | 254.1 | 255.4 | 257.3 | 259.0 | 258.1 | 256.5 | 253.8 | 254.8 | 254.7 | 256.7 | 255.4 |
| **Government** | | | | | | | | | | | | | |
| 2011 | 829.3 | 850.1 | 851.1 | 859.1 | 861.0 | 833.4 | 798.4 | 795.9 | 843.5 | 849.9 | 853.7 | 842.2 | 839.0 |
| 2012 | 821.2 | 843.8 | 847.7 | 850.9 | 856.1 | 828.1 | 784.7 | 782.8 | 836.0 | 845.2 | 848.6 | 841.6 | 832.2 |
| 2013 | 821.3 | 840.4 | 842.6 | 845.5 | 847.1 | 823.9 | 783.5 | 781.0 | 833.7 | 837.7 | 840.6 | 838.2 | 828.0 |
| 2014 | 814.0 | 830.0 | 834.9 | 840.1 | 845.4 | 821.5 | 783.0 | 780.0 | 833.9 | 841.7 | 842.3 | 841.5 | 825.7 |
| 2015 | 812.9 | 832.7 | 837.5 | 842.4 | 847.8 | 827.6 | 786.5 | 782.6 | 831.9 | 840.9 | 836.9 | 838.7 | 826.5 |
| 2016 | 807.7 | 827.9 | 833.4 | 834.2 | 836.5 | 826.5 | 783.4 | 778.7 | 833.4 | 831.1 | 832.4 | 839.1 | 822.0 |
| 2017 | 801.5 | 824.6 | 828.9 | 830.3 | 834.5 | 821.7 | 779.1 | 781.4 | 830.4 | 832.1 | 833.0 | 834.1 | 819.3 |
| 2018 | 799.7 | 821.8 | 829.9 | 828.5 | 835.5 | 821.8 | 779.9 | 783.2 | 831.6 | 833.2 | 837.8 | 834.9 | 819.8 |
| 2019 | 804.6 | 823.8 | 831.7 | 832.1 | 840.3 | 825.2 | 784.8 | 788.2 | 836.5 | 842.6 | 849.0 | 845.7 | 825.4 |

## 2. Average Weekly Hours by Selected Industry: Illinois, 2015–2019

(Not seasonally adjusted)

| Industry and year | January | February | March | April | May | June | July | August | September | October | November | December | Annual average |
|---|---|---|---|---|---|---|---|---|---|---|---|---|---|
| **Total Private** | | | | | | | | | | | | | |
| 2015 | 34.1 | 34.6 | 34.6 | 34.3 | 34.4 | 34.5 | 34.4 | 34.9 | 34.3 | 34.6 | 34.9 | 34.4 | 34.5 |
| 2016 | 34.0 | 33.9 | 34.0 | 34.0 | 34.4 | 34.2 | 34.2 | 34.1 | 34.2 | 34.7 | 34.2 | 33.9 | 34.1 |
| 2017 | 34.0 | 33.8 | 33.7 | 34.2 | 33.9 | 34.2 | 34.4 | 34.2 | 34.2 | 34.5 | 34.3 | 34.2 | 34.1 |
| 2018 | 33.8 | 33.9 | 34.1 | 34.5 | 34.1 | 34.3 | 34.8 | 34.2 | 34.9 | 34.2 | 34.2 | 34.5 | 34.3 |
| 2019 | 33.6 | 33.8 | 33.7 | 33.8 | 33.9 | 34.5 | 33.9 | 34.0 | 34.5 | 34.1 | 33.9 | 34.4 | 34.0 |
| **Goods-Producing** | | | | | | | | | | | | | |
| 2015 | 39.5 | 39.6 | 39.7 | 39.7 | 39.9 | 39.8 | 39.5 | 40.1 | 39.0 | 39.4 | 39.5 | 39.8 | 39.6 |
| 2016 | 39.3 | 39.0 | 39.3 | 39.4 | 39.7 | 39.9 | 39.6 | 39.5 | 39.6 | 40.0 | 39.9 | 39.1 | 39.5 |
| 2017 | 38.7 | 38.9 | 38.8 | 38.8 | 39.6 | 39.9 | 39.5 | 40.2 | 40.0 | 39.7 | 40.1 | 40.0 | 39.5 |
| 2018 | 39.3 | 39.2 | 40.0 | 40.0 | 39.6 | 40.0 | 40.4 | 40.0 | 40.4 | 39.9 | 39.7 | 40.4 | 39.9 |
| 2019 | 39.5 | 39.6 | 39.5 | 39.6 | 39.8 | 40.2 | 39.9 | 40.0 | 40.0 | 39.8 | 39.1 | 40.0 | 39.8 |
| **Construction** | | | | | | | | | | | | | |
| 2015 | 37.0 | 36.6 | 36.9 | 37.4 | 37.4 | 38.0 | 37.7 | 38.7 | 35.8 | 39.7 | 38.6 | 38.6 | 37.7 |
| 2016 | 36.4 | 36.6 | 37.2 | 38.3 | 38.1 | 39.0 | 38.6 | 38.7 | 38.5 | 39.3 | 38.8 | 37.3 | 38.1 |
| 2017 | 36.4 | 36.9 | 36.6 | 37.1 | 38.1 | 38.8 | 37.3 | 38.7 | 38.3 | 37.3 | 37.5 | 37.1 | 37.6 |
| 2018 | 35.8 | 35.8 | 37.6 | 37.0 | 37.3 | 38.0 | 38.7 | 38.3 | 39.0 | 38.2 | 37.3 | 38.0 | 37.6 |
| 2019 | 37.0 | 37.2 | 37.5 | 37.5 | 37.9 | 38.8 | 39.2 | 39.1 | 38.4 | 38.3 | 36.0 | 37.2 | 37.9 |
| **Manufacturing** | | | | | | | | | | | | | |
| 2015 | 40.6 | 40.8 | 40.8 | 40.7 | 41.0 | 40.6 | 40.2 | 40.6 | 40.2 | 40.5 | 41.0 | 41.4 | 40.7 |
| 2016 | 41.1 | 40.6 | 40.8 | 40.5 | 40.7 | 40.9 | 40.7 | 40.4 | 40.4 | 40.6 | 40.7 | 40.9 | 40.7 |
| 2017 | 40.6 | 40.5 | 40.4 | 40.1 | 40.8 | 41.0 | 41.0 | 41.4 | 41.4 | 41.4 | 41.8 | 41.8 | 41.0 |
| 2018 | 41.3 | 41.1 | 41.5 | 41.7 | 41.1 | 41.4 | 41.5 | 41.1 | 41.3 | 40.8 | 41.0 | 41.6 | 41.3 |
| 2019 | 40.6 | 40.7 | 40.7 | 40.8 | 40.4 | 40.6 | 40.0 | 40.3 | 40.7 | 40.5 | 40.6 | 41.2 | 40.6 |
| **Trade, Transportation, and Utilities** | | | | | | | | | | | | | |
| 2015 | 34.5 | 35.0 | 35.1 | 34.7 | 34.9 | 34.9 | 35.0 | 35.2 | 35.1 | 35.2 | 35.3 | 34.9 | 35.0 |
| 2016 | 34.2 | 34.2 | 34.3 | 34.2 | 34.5 | 34.5 | 34.4 | 34.4 | 34.7 | 34.9 | 34.2 | 34.1 | 34.4 |
| 2017 | 33.8 | 33.9 | 34.0 | 34.8 | 34.2 | 34.7 | 35.0 | 34.6 | 34.7 | 35.3 | 34.8 | 34.9 | 34.6 |
| 2018 | 34.3 | 34.4 | 34.7 | 35.0 | 35.0 | 35.1 | 35.4 | 34.9 | 35.6 | 34.7 | 34.9 | 35.0 | 34.9 |
| 2019 | 33.9 | 34.3 | 34.1 | 34.2 | 34.3 | 34.9 | 34.3 | 34.4 | 34.8 | 34.5 | 34.3 | 34.8 | 34.4 |
| **Information** | | | | | | | | | | | | | |
| 2015 | 36.2 | 36.7 | 36.6 | 36.1 | 35.8 | 36.4 | 36.4 | 36.6 | 35.9 | 35.6 | 36.3 | 35.5 | 36.2 |
| 2016 | 35.7 | 35.2 | 35.3 | 35.2 | 35.5 | 35.0 | 35.2 | 35.1 | 35.3 | 35.6 | 35.2 | 35.3 | 35.3 |
| 2017 | 35.8 | 34.5 | 34.9 | 36.1 | 35.2 | 35.2 | 36.1 | 35.6 | 36.3 | 37.4 | 36.7 | 36.3 | 35.8 |
| 2018 | 36.7 | 36.3 | 36.9 | 37.5 | 37.4 | 36.4 | 38.1 | 37.2 | 38.1 | 37.2 | 37.2 | 37.8 | 37.2 |
| 2019 | 36.5 | 37.0 | 37.0 | 37.2 | 37.0 | 37.7 | 36.6 | 37.0 | 37.9 | 36.5 | 36.4 | 37.0 | 37.0 |
| **Financial Activities** | | | | | | | | | | | | | |
| 2015 | 36.5 | 37.9 | 37.7 | 36.7 | 36.7 | 36.8 | 36.6 | 37.7 | 36.6 | 36.5 | 37.6 | 36.6 | 37.0 |
| 2016 | 36.6 | 36.6 | 36.4 | 36.5 | 37.4 | 36.6 | 36.7 | 36.5 | 36.7 | 37.7 | 36.7 | 36.6 | 36.7 |
| 2017 | 37.5 | 36.5 | 36.4 | 37.5 | 36.0 | 36.4 | 37.5 | 36.4 | 36.1 | 37.2 | 36.4 | 36.1 | 36.7 |
| 2018 | 36.3 | 36.3 | 36.2 | 37.6 | 36.3 | 36.4 | 37.6 | 36.5 | 37.8 | 36.3 | 36.1 | 37.6 | 36.8 |
| 2019 | 36.4 | 36.2 | 36.1 | 36.3 | 36.5 | 37.9 | 36.3 | 36.6 | 37.8 | 36.8 | 36.7 | 37.6 | 36.8 |
| **Professional and Business Services** | | | | | | | | | | | | | |
| 2015 | 35.3 | 36.4 | 35.9 | 35.7 | 35.7 | 36.1 | 35.9 | 36.9 | 35.6 | 36.8 | 37.3 | 36.4 | 36.2 |
| 2016 | 35.8 | 35.6 | 35.9 | 36.1 | 36.6 | 36.2 | 36.2 | 36.0 | 36.1 | 37.0 | 36.0 | 35.7 | 36.1 |
| 2017 | 36.3 | 36.0 | 35.6 | 36.0 | 35.9 | 36.2 | 36.2 | 36.1 | 35.9 | 36.5 | 36.0 | 35.8 | 36.0 |
| 2018 | 35.1 | 35.6 | 35.4 | 36.2 | 35.6 | 35.9 | 36.2 | 35.5 | 36.3 | 35.9 | 35.7 | 35.7 | 35.8 |
| 2019 | 34.7 | 35.1 | 35.0 | 35.2 | 35.1 | 36.1 | 35.1 | 35.3 | 35.9 | 35.0 | 34.9 | 35.7 | 35.3 |
| **Education and Health Services** | | | | | | | | | | | | | |
| 2015 | 32.4 | 32.4 | 32.5 | 32.3 | 32.3 | 32.3 | 32.3 | 32.6 | 32.4 | 32.2 | 32.6 | 32.3 | 32.4 |
| 2016 | 32.2 | 32.2 | 32.1 | 32.0 | 32.2 | 32.1 | 32.1 | 31.9 | 32.1 | 32.2 | 32.1 | 32.1 | 32.1 |
| 2017 | 32.4 | 31.8 | 31.7 | 32.0 | 31.6 | 31.7 | 32.2 | 31.9 | 31.8 | 31.9 | 32.1 | 31.9 | 31.9 |
| 2018 | 32.0 | 31.8 | 31.8 | 32.3 | 31.8 | 32.0 | 32.6 | 32.0 | 32.8 | 31.9 | 32.3 | 32.5 | 32.2 |
| 2019 | 32.0 | 31.9 | 31.8 | 31.9 | 32.0 | 32.3 | 32.0 | 32.1 | 32.6 | 32.4 | 32.5 | 32.6 | 32.2 |
| **Leisure and Hospitality** | | | | | | | | | | | | | |
| 2015 | 24.8 | 25.7 | 26.0 | 25.8 | 26.1 | 26.3 | 26.3 | 26.5 | 26.0 | 26.0 | 25.7 | 25.5 | 25.9 |
| 2016 | 24.6 | 25.0 | 25.1 | 25.3 | 25.7 | 25.5 | 25.5 | 25.5 | 25.3 | 25.6 | 25.5 | 24.9 | 25.3 |
| 2017 | 24.7 | 25.0 | 25.3 | 25.5 | 25.5 | 25.9 | 25.8 | 25.7 | 25.7 | 26.1 | 25.5 | 25.7 | 25.5 |
| 2018 | 24.7 | 24.9 | 25.6 | 25.5 | 25.8 | 25.9 | 26.1 | 25.5 | 25.8 | 25.6 | 25.1 | 25.3 | 25.5 |
| 2019 | 24.4 | 24.8 | 25.2 | 25.0 | 25.1 | 25.6 | 25.2 | 25.2 | 25.3 | 25.2 | 24.9 | 25.3 | 25.1 |
| **Other Services** | | | | | | | | | | | | | |
| 2015 | 32.1 | 32.8 | 33.3 | 32.5 | 32.3 | 32.2 | 32.4 | 33.3 | 32.7 | 32.7 | 33.7 | 32.5 | 32.7 |
| 2016 | 32.6 | 31.8 | 32.1 | 32.0 | 32.4 | 32.3 | 32.7 | 32.3 | 32.6 | 33.5 | 32.9 | 33.1 | 32.5 |
| 2017 | 33.1 | 32.8 | 32.4 | 32.8 | 32.4 | 32.5 | 32.9 | 32.4 | 32.1 | 31.9 | 31.6 | 31.7 | 32.4 |
| 2018 | 31.5 | 31.7 | 31.9 | 32.2 | 31.1 | 31.9 | 32.5 | 31.5 | 32.5 | 31.2 | 31.1 | 31.5 | 31.7 |
| 2019 | 30.5 | 30.9 | 31.4 | 31.5 | 31.2 | 32.7 | 32.2 | 31.8 | 32.6 | 32.1 | 32.4 | 33.1 | 31.9 |

# 3. Average Hourly Earnings by Selected Industry: Illinois, 2015–2019

(Dollars, not seasonally adjusted)

| Industry and year | January | February | March | April | May | June | July | August | September | October | November | December | Annual average |
|---|---|---|---|---|---|---|---|---|---|---|---|---|---|
| **Total Private** | | | | | | | | | | | | | |
| 2015 | 25.83 | 26.21 | 26.03 | 25.82 | 25.80 | 25.69 | 25.79 | 26.05 | 26.00 | 26.14 | 26.50 | 26.29 | 26.01 |
| 2016 | 26.58 | 26.45 | 26.47 | 26.53 | 26.69 | 26.27 | 26.41 | 26.48 | 26.59 | 26.91 | 26.69 | 26.68 | 26.56 |
| 2017 | 26.92 | 26.66 | 26.56 | 26.86 | 26.48 | 26.40 | 26.87 | 26.56 | 26.90 | 27.10 | 27.01 | 27.16 | 26.79 |
| 2018 | 27.20 | 27.26 | 27.16 | 27.64 | 27.19 | 27.14 | 27.75 | 27.62 | 28.26 | 28.16 | 28.14 | 28.59 | 27.68 |
| 2019 | 28.42 | 28.71 | 28.53 | 28.58 | 28.41 | 28.66 | 28.78 | 28.82 | 29.22 | 28.98 | 29.12 | 29.46 | 28.81 |
| **Goods-Producing** | | | | | | | | | | | | | |
| 2015 | 27.67 | 27.94 | 27.93 | 27.86 | 28.06 | 28.23 | 28.70 | 28.86 | 28.57 | 28.95 | 29.11 | 29.02 | 28.42 |
| 2016 | 28.43 | 28.33 | 28.46 | 28.79 | 29.10 | 28.83 | 29.03 | 29.12 | 29.06 | 29.17 | 28.95 | 28.91 | 28.85 |
| 2017 | 28.50 | 28.50 | 28.53 | 28.46 | 28.58 | 28.78 | 29.03 | 29.02 | 29.40 | 29.12 | 29.26 | 29.23 | 28.88 |
| 2018 | 28.90 | 28.78 | 29.12 | 29.39 | 29.66 | 29.54 | 30.13 | 30.42 | 31.02 | 31.01 | 30.73 | 31.03 | 30.00 |
| 2019 | 30.31 | 30.48 | 30.59 | 31.18 | 31.22 | 31.46 | 31.73 | 31.62 | 31.90 | 31.93 | 31.62 | 31.91 | 31.34 |
| **Construction** | | | | | | | | | | | | | |
| 2015 | 35.22 | 36.18 | 36.34 | 36.05 | 36.24 | 36.28 | 36.78 | 36.98 | 36.39 | 36.36 | 36.96 | 37.24 | 36.45 |
| 2016 | 35.95 | 35.90 | 36.27 | 36.20 | 36.52 | 36.27 | 36.66 | 36.72 | 36.88 | 36.86 | 36.78 | 37.10 | 36.53 |
| 2017 | 36.54 | 36.38 | 36.45 | 35.54 | 35.89 | 35.90 | 36.40 | 36.66 | 37.49 | 36.73 | 37.56 | 37.75 | 36.61 |
| 2018 | 37.26 | 36.93 | 37.24 | 37.21 | 37.39 | 37.28 | 38.01 | 38.06 | 38.80 | 38.50 | 38.49 | 38.98 | 37.88 |
| 2019 | 38.26 | 39.13 | 39.04 | 39.72 | 39.20 | 38.95 | 39.52 | 39.26 | 39.18 | 39.65 | 39.58 | 39.58 | 39.27 |
| **Manufacturing** | | | | | | | | | | | | | |
| 2015 | 25.30 | 25.40 | 25.22 | 24.97 | 25.07 | 25.16 | 25.45 | 25.46 | 25.50 | 25.65 | 25.77 | 25.68 | 25.39 |
| 2016 | 25.79 | 25.66 | 25.53 | 25.74 | 25.94 | 25.56 | 25.70 | 25.69 | 25.44 | 25.58 | 25.35 | 25.57 | 25.63 |
| 2017 | 25.41 | 25.34 | 25.27 | 25.47 | 25.26 | 25.41 | 25.62 | 25.35 | 25.61 | 25.69 | 25.58 | 25.75 | 25.48 |
| 2018 | 25.70 | 25.60 | 25.62 | 25.99 | 26.06 | 25.79 | 26.16 | 26.55 | 26.77 | 26.89 | 26.99 | 27.39 | 26.29 |
| 2019 | 26.83 | 26.78 | 26.88 | 27.20 | 27.32 | 27.53 | 27.58 | 27.58 | 28.13 | 27.95 | 27.99 | 28.51 | 27.52 |
| **Trade, Transportation, and Utilities** | | | | | | | | | | | | | |
| 2015 | 23.35 | 23.38 | 23.05 | 23.22 | 23.15 | 23.05 | 23.06 | 23.39 | 23.37 | 23.03 | 23.40 | 23.17 | 23.22 |
| 2016 | 23.62 | 23.30 | 23.35 | 23.58 | 23.76 | 23.45 | 23.54 | 23.44 | 23.60 | 23.87 | 23.71 | 23.64 | 23.57 |
| 2017 | 23.91 | 23.40 | 23.42 | 23.74 | 23.55 | 23.45 | 23.90 | 23.63 | 23.87 | 24.06 | 24.22 | 24.13 | 23.78 |
| 2018 | 24.36 | 24.17 | 23.89 | 24.65 | 24.25 | 24.38 | 24.95 | 24.80 | 25.24 | 25.09 | 24.74 | 25.13 | 24.64 |
| 2019 | 25.33 | 25.60 | 25.24 | 25.27 | 25.10 | 25.42 | 25.23 | 25.08 | 25.39 | 25.26 | 25.45 | 25.76 | 25.35 |
| **Financial Activities** | | | | | | | | | | | | | |
| 2015 | 34.64 | 35.90 | 36.55 | 35.75 | 35.61 | 34.84 | 34.82 | 35.32 | 35.45 | 35.60 | 36.24 | 35.51 | 35.52 |
| 2016 | 36.74 | 36.56 | 36.47 | 36.93 | 37.22 | 35.78 | 36.42 | 36.81 | 36.99 | 37.36 | 36.99 | 36.73 | 36.75 |
| 2017 | 37.68 | 36.92 | 37.40 | 38.40 | 37.39 | 36.80 | 37.38 | 36.50 | 37.05 | 37.45 | 37.08 | 37.21 | 37.27 |
| 2018 | 37.21 | 37.32 | 37.42 | 38.91 | 37.52 | 37.06 | 38.06 | 37.42 | 39.03 | 38.50 | 38.84 | 39.00 | 38.04 |
| 2019 | 38.39 | 38.62 | 38.22 | 38.30 | 38.12 | 38.69 | 38.50 | 38.78 | 39.35 | 38.76 | 39.08 | 39.62 | 38.71 |
| **Professional and Business Services** | | | | | | | | | | | | | |
| 2015 | 28.98 | 29.91 | 29.49 | 28.91 | 28.79 | 28.60 | 28.70 | 28.89 | 28.91 | 28.59 | 29.27 | 28.94 | 28.99 |
| 2016 | 29.82 | 29.59 | 29.70 | 29.69 | 29.83 | 29.33 | 29.32 | 29.47 | 29.60 | 30.15 | 30.00 | 30.11 | 29.72 |
| 2017 | 30.58 | 30.32 | 30.10 | 30.65 | 29.58 | 29.57 | 30.51 | 29.62 | 30.20 | 30.68 | 30.09 | 30.54 | 30.20 |
| 2018 | 31.25 | 31.34 | 31.55 | 31.95 | 31.02 | 30.91 | 31.73 | 31.00 | 31.86 | 31.56 | 31.81 | 32.79 | 31.57 |
| 2019 | 32.88 | 33.58 | 33.79 | 33.31 | 32.73 | 32.85 | 33.31 | 33.21 | 34.18 | 33.68 | 34.00 | 34.73 | 33.52 |
| **Education and Health Services** | | | | | | | | | | | | | |
| 2015 | 24.61 | 24.63 | 24.64 | 24.52 | 24.61 | 24.61 | 24.54 | 24.57 | 24.76 | 25.64 | 25.65 | 25.56 | 24.87 |
| 2016 | 25.43 | 25.58 | 25.54 | 25.01 | 25.04 | 24.91 | 25.06 | 25.12 | 25.09 | 25.21 | 25.11 | 25.08 | 25.18 |
| 2017 | 25.16 | 25.32 | 24.89 | 25.06 | 25.08 | 24.94 | 25.18 | 25.26 | 25.27 | 25.40 | 25.43 | 25.81 | 25.23 |
| 2018 | 24.96 | 25.45 | 24.97 | 24.85 | 24.84 | 24.89 | 25.17 | 25.34 | 25.64 | 25.74 | 25.85 | 25.93 | 25.31 |
| 2019 | 25.52 | 25.68 | 25.30 | 25.18 | 25.27 | 25.44 | 25.73 | 25.80 | 25.70 | 25.72 | 25.94 | 25.63 | 25.58 |
| **Leisure and Hospitality** | | | | | | | | | | | | | |
| 2015 | 14.07 | 14.16 | 13.99 | 14.02 | 14.07 | 14.04 | 14.17 | 14.19 | 14.35 | 14.40 | 14.49 | 14.64 | 14.22 |
| 2016 | 14.55 | 14.57 | 14.66 | 14.69 | 14.78 | 14.70 | 14.67 | 14.72 | 14.87 | 15.05 | 15.05 | 15.40 | 14.81 |
| 2017 | 15.11 | 15.18 | 15.20 | 15.27 | 15.52 | 15.27 | 15.13 | 15.28 | 15.49 | 15.48 | 15.51 | 15.66 | 15.34 |
| 2018 | 15.47 | 15.46 | 15.51 | 15.60 | 15.70 | 15.58 | 15.80 | 15.85 | 15.93 | 16.38 | 16.40 | 16.79 | 15.87 |
| 2019 | 16.58 | 16.74 | 16.74 | 16.80 | 16.80 | 16.69 | 16.64 | 17.02 | 17.23 | 17.23 | 17.42 | 17.81 | 16.97 |
| **Other Services** | | | | | | | | | | | | | |
| 2015 | 25.35 | 25.64 | 25.15 | 25.06 | 25.22 | 25.09 | 25.04 | 25.64 | 25.40 | 25.85 | 25.97 | 26.48 | 25.49 |
| 2016 | 26.43 | 26.55 | 26.26 | 26.94 | 27.26 | 26.48 | 26.17 | 26.37 | 26.69 | 27.06 | 26.39 | 26.23 | 26.57 |
| 2017 | 26.44 | 25.98 | 26.10 | 26.03 | 25.31 | 25.09 | 25.18 | 25.51 | 26.23 | 26.56 | 26.28 | 26.51 | 25.93 |
| 2018 | 26.96 | 27.12 | 27.20 | 27.54 | 26.81 | 26.10 | 26.76 | 26.89 | 27.50 | 27.42 | 27.55 | 28.20 | 27.17 |
| 2019 | 28.48 | 28.62 | 28.53 | 28.92 | 28.71 | 28.73 | 28.62 | 29.23 | 29.72 | 29.28 | 29.55 | 30.41 | 29.08 |

## 4. Average Weekly Earnings by Selected Industry: Illinois, 2015–2019

(Dollars, not seasonally adjusted)

| Industry and year | January | February | March | April | May | June | July | August | September | October | November | December | Annual average |
|---|---|---|---|---|---|---|---|---|---|---|---|---|---|
| **Total Private** | | | | | | | | | | | | | |
| 2015 | 880.80 | 906.87 | 900.64 | 885.63 | 887.52 | 886.31 | 887.18 | 909.15 | 891.80 | 904.44 | 924.85 | 904.38 | 897.35 |
| 2016 | 903.72 | 896.66 | 899.98 | 902.02 | 918.48 | 898.43 | 903.22 | 902.97 | 909.38 | 933.78 | 912.80 | 904.45 | 905.70 |
| 2017 | 915.28 | 901.11 | 895.07 | 918.61 | 897.67 | 902.88 | 924.33 | 908.35 | 919.98 | 934.95 | 926.44 | 928.87 | 913.54 |
| 2018 | 919.36 | 924.11 | 926.16 | 953.58 | 927.18 | 930.90 | 965.70 | 944.60 | 986.27 | 963.07 | 962.39 | 986.36 | 949.42 |
| 2019 | 954.91 | 970.40 | 961.46 | 966.00 | 963.10 | 988.77 | 975.64 | 979.88 | 1,008.09 | 988.22 | 987.17 | 1,013.42 | 979.54 |
| **Goods-Producing** | | | | | | | | | | | | | |
| 2015 | 1,092.97 | 1,106.42 | 1,108.82 | 1,105.65 | 1,119.59 | 1,123.55 | 1,133.65 | 1,157.29 | 1,114.23 | 1,140.63 | 1,149.85 | 1,155.00 | 1,125.43 |
| 2016 | 1,117.30 | 1,104.87 | 1,118.48 | 1,134.33 | 1,155.27 | 1,150.32 | 1,149.59 | 1,150.24 | 1,150.78 | 1,166.80 | 1,155.11 | 1,130.38 | 1,139.58 |
| 2017 | 1,102.95 | 1,108.65 | 1,106.96 | 1,104.25 | 1,131.77 | 1,148.32 | 1,146.69 | 1,166.20 | 1,176.00 | 1,156.06 | 1,173.33 | 1,169.20 | 1,140.76 |
| 2018 | 1,135.77 | 1,128.18 | 1,165.20 | 1,176.00 | 1,174.54 | 1,181.60 | 1,217.25 | 1,216.80 | 1,253.21 | 1,237.30 | 1,219.98 | 1,253.61 | 1,197.00 |
| 2019 | 1,197.25 | 1,207.01 | 1,208.31 | 1,234.73 | 1,242.56 | 1,264.69 | 1,266.03 | 1,264.80 | 1,276.00 | 1,270.81 | 1,236.34 | 1,276.40 | 1,247.33 |
| **Construction** | | | | | | | | | | | | | |
| 2015 | 1,303.14 | 1,324.19 | 1,340.95 | 1,348.27 | 1,355.38 | 1,378.64 | 1,386.61 | 1,431.13 | 1,302.76 | 1,443.49 | 1,426.66 | 1,437.46 | 1,374.17 |
| 2016 | 1,308.58 | 1,313.94 | 1,349.24 | 1,386.46 | 1,391.41 | 1,414.53 | 1,415.08 | 1,421.06 | 1,419.88 | 1,448.60 | 1,427.06 | 1,383.83 | 1,391.79 |
| 2017 | 1,330.06 | 1,342.42 | 1,334.07 | 1,318.53 | 1,367.41 | 1,392.53 | 1,357.35 | 1,418.74 | 1,435.87 | 1,370.03 | 1,408.50 | 1,400.53 | 1,376.54 |
| 2018 | 1,333.91 | 1,322.09 | 1,400.22 | 1,376.77 | 1,394.65 | 1,416.64 | 1,470.99 | 1,457.70 | 1,513.20 | 1,470.70 | 1,435.68 | 1,481.24 | 1,424.29 |
| 2019 | 1,415.62 | 1,455.64 | 1,464.00 | 1,489.50 | 1,485.68 | 1,511.26 | 1,549.18 | 1,535.07 | 1,504.51 | 1,518.60 | 1,424.88 | 1,472.38 | 1,488.33 |
| **Manufacturing** | | | | | | | | | | | | | |
| 2015 | 1,027.18 | 1,036.32 | 1,028.98 | 1,016.28 | 1,027.87 | 1,021.50 | 1,023.09 | 1,033.68 | 1,025.10 | 1,038.83 | 1,056.57 | 1,063.15 | 1,033.37 |
| 2016 | 1,059.97 | 1,041.80 | 1,041.62 | 1,042.47 | 1,055.76 | 1,045.40 | 1,045.99 | 1,037.88 | 1,027.78 | 1,038.55 | 1,031.75 | 1,045.81 | 1,043.14 |
| 2017 | 1,031.65 | 1,026.27 | 1,020.91 | 1,021.35 | 1,030.61 | 1,041.81 | 1,050.42 | 1,049.49 | 1,060.25 | 1,063.57 | 1,069.66 | 1,076.35 | 1,044.68 |
| 2018 | 1,061.41 | 1,052.16 | 1,063.23 | 1,083.78 | 1,071.07 | 1,067.71 | 1,085.64 | 1,091.21 | 1,105.60 | 1,097.11 | 1,106.59 | 1,139.42 | 1,085.78 |
| 2019 | 1,089.30 | 1,089.95 | 1,094.02 | 1,109.76 | 1,103.73 | 1,117.72 | 1,103.20 | 1,111.47 | 1,144.89 | 1,131.98 | 1,136.39 | 1,174.61 | 1,117.31 |
| **Trade, Transportation, and Utilities** | | | | | | | | | | | | | |
| 2015 | 805.58 | 818.30 | 809.06 | 805.73 | 807.94 | 804.45 | 807.10 | 823.33 | 820.29 | 810.66 | 826.02 | 808.63 | 812.70 |
| 2016 | 807.80 | 796.86 | 800.91 | 806.44 | 819.72 | 809.03 | 809.78 | 806.34 | 819.27 | 833.06 | 810.88 | 806.12 | 810.81 |
| 2017 | 808.16 | 793.26 | 796.28 | 826.15 | 805.41 | 813.37 | 836.50 | 817.60 | 828.29 | 849.32 | 842.86 | 842.14 | 822.79 |
| 2018 | 835.55 | 831.45 | 828.98 | 862.75 | 848.75 | 855.74 | 883.23 | 865.52 | 898.54 | 870.62 | 863.43 | 879.55 | 859.94 |
| 2019 | 858.69 | 878.08 | 860.68 | 864.23 | 860.93 | 887.16 | 865.39 | 862.75 | 883.57 | 871.47 | 872.94 | 896.45 | 872.04 |
| **Financial Activities** | | | | | | | | | | | | | |
| 2015 | 1,264.36 | 1,360.61 | 1,377.94 | 1,312.03 | 1,306.89 | 1,282.11 | 1,274.41 | 1,331.56 | 1,297.47 | 1,299.40 | 1,362.62 | 1,299.67 | 1,314.24 |
| 2016 | 1,344.68 | 1,338.10 | 1,327.51 | 1,347.95 | 1,392.03 | 1,309.91 | 1,336.61 | 1,343.57 | 1,357.53 | 1,408.47 | 1,357.53 | 1,344.32 | 1,348.73 |
| 2017 | 1,413.00 | 1,347.58 | 1,361.36 | 1,440.00 | 1,346.04 | 1,339.52 | 1,401.75 | 1,328.60 | 1,337.51 | 1,393.14 | 1,349.71 | 1,343.28 | 1,367.81 |
| 2018 | 1,350.72 | 1,354.72 | 1,354.60 | 1,463.02 | 1,361.98 | 1,348.98 | 1,431.06 | 1,365.83 | 1,475.33 | 1,397.55 | 1,402.12 | 1,466.40 | 1,399.87 |
| 2019 | 1,397.40 | 1,398.04 | 1,379.74 | 1,390.29 | 1,391.38 | 1,466.35 | 1,397.55 | 1,419.35 | 1,487.43 | 1,426.37 | 1,434.24 | 1,489.71 | 1,424.53 |
| **Professional and Business Services** | | | | | | | | | | | | | |
| 2015 | 1,022.99 | 1,088.72 | 1,058.69 | 1,032.09 | 1,027.80 | 1,032.46 | 1,030.33 | 1,066.04 | 1,029.20 | 1,052.11 | 1,091.77 | 1,053.42 | 1,049.44 |
| 2016 | 1,067.56 | 1,053.40 | 1,066.23 | 1,071.81 | 1,091.78 | 1,061.75 | 1,061.38 | 1,060.92 | 1,068.56 | 1,115.55 | 1,080.00 | 1,074.93 | 1,072.89 |
| 2017 | 1,110.05 | 1,091.52 | 1,071.56 | 1,103.40 | 1,061.92 | 1,070.43 | 1,104.46 | 1,069.28 | 1,084.18 | 1,119.82 | 1,083.24 | 1,093.33 | 1,087.20 |
| 2018 | 1,096.88 | 1,115.70 | 1,116.87 | 1,156.59 | 1,104.31 | 1,109.67 | 1,148.63 | 1,100.50 | 1,156.52 | 1,133.00 | 1,135.62 | 1,170.60 | 1,130.21 |
| 2019 | 1,140.94 | 1,178.66 | 1,182.65 | 1,172.51 | 1,148.82 | 1,185.89 | 1,169.18 | 1,172.31 | 1,227.06 | 1,178.80 | 1,186.60 | 1,239.86 | 1,183.26 |
| **Education and Health Services** | | | | | | | | | | | | | |
| 2015 | 797.36 | 798.01 | 800.80 | 792.00 | 794.90 | 794.90 | 792.64 | 800.98 | 802.22 | 825.61 | 836.19 | 825.59 | 805.79 |
| 2016 | 818.85 | 823.68 | 819.83 | 800.32 | 806.29 | 799.61 | 804.43 | 801.33 | 805.39 | 811.76 | 806.03 | 805.07 | 808.28 |
| 2017 | 815.18 | 805.18 | 789.01 | 801.92 | 792.53 | 790.60 | 810.80 | 805.79 | 803.59 | 810.26 | 816.30 | 823.34 | 804.84 |
| 2018 | 798.72 | 809.31 | 794.05 | 802.66 | 789.91 | 796.48 | 820.54 | 810.88 | 840.99 | 821.11 | 834.96 | 842.73 | 814.98 |
| 2019 | 816.64 | 819.19 | 804.54 | 803.24 | 808.64 | 821.71 | 823.36 | 828.18 | 837.82 | 833.33 | 843.05 | 835.54 | 823.68 |
| **Leisure and Hospitality** | | | | | | | | | | | | | |
| 2015 | 348.94 | 363.91 | 363.74 | 361.72 | 367.23 | 369.25 | 372.67 | 376.04 | 373.10 | 374.40 | 372.39 | 373.32 | 368.30 |
| 2016 | 357.93 | 364.25 | 367.97 | 371.66 | 379.85 | 375.11 | 374.09 | 375.36 | 376.21 | 385.28 | 383.78 | 383.46 | 374.69 |
| 2017 | 373.22 | 379.50 | 384.56 | 389.38 | 395.76 | 395.49 | 390.35 | 392.70 | 398.09 | 404.03 | 395.51 | 402.46 | 391.17 |
| 2018 | 382.11 | 384.95 | 397.06 | 397.80 | 405.06 | 403.52 | 412.38 | 404.18 | 410.99 | 419.33 | 411.64 | 424.79 | 404.69 |
| 2019 | 404.55 | 415.15 | 421.85 | 420.00 | 421.68 | 427.26 | 419.33 | 428.90 | 435.92 | 434.20 | 433.76 | 450.59 | 425.95 |
| **Other Services** | | | | | | | | | | | | | |
| 2015 | 813.74 | 840.99 | 837.50 | 814.45 | 814.61 | 807.90 | 811.30 | 853.81 | 830.58 | 845.30 | 875.19 | 860.60 | 833.52 |
| 2016 | 861.62 | 844.29 | 842.95 | 862.08 | 883.22 | 855.30 | 855.76 | 851.75 | 870.09 | 906.51 | 868.23 | 868.21 | 863.53 |
| 2017 | 875.16 | 852.14 | 845.64 | 853.78 | 820.04 | 815.43 | 828.42 | 826.52 | 841.98 | 847.26 | 830.45 | 840.37 | 840.13 |
| 2018 | 849.24 | 859.70 | 867.68 | 886.79 | 833.79 | 832.59 | 869.70 | 847.04 | 893.75 | 855.50 | 856.81 | 888.30 | 861.29 |
| 2019 | 868.64 | 884.36 | 895.84 | 910.98 | 895.75 | 939.47 | 921.56 | 929.51 | 968.87 | 939.89 | 957.42 | 1,006.57 | 927.65 |

# INDIANA
## *At a Glance*

Population:
  2010 census: 6,483,802
  2019 estimate: 6,732,219

Percent change in population:
  2010–2019: 3.8%

Percent change in total nonfarm employment:
  2011–2019: 11.2%

Industry with the largest growth in employment, 2011–2019 (percent):
  Transportation and utilities, 23.2%

Industry with the largest decline or smallest growth in employment, 2011–2019 (percent):
  Information, -17.7%

Civilian labor force:
  2010: 3,175,192
  2019: 3,387,366

Unemployment rate and rank among states (highest to lowest):
  2010: 10.4%, 11th
  2019: 3.3%, 30th

Over-the-year change in unemployment rates:
  2017–2018: -0.1%
  2018–2019: -0.2%

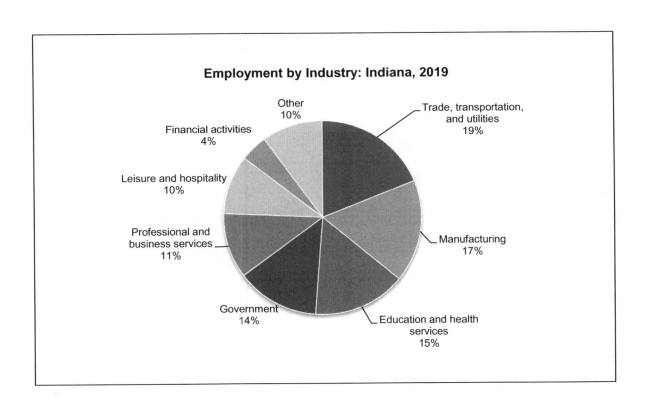

**Employment by Industry: Indiana, 2019**

- Other 10%
- Trade, transportation, and utilities 19%
- Financial activities 4%
- Manufacturing 17%
- Leisure and hospitality 10%
- Professional and business services 11%
- Education and health services 15%
- Government 14%

## 1. Employment by Industry: Indiana, 2011–2019

(Numbers in thousands, not seasonally adjusted)

| Industry and year | January | February | March | April | May | June | July | August | September | October | November | December | Annual average |
|---|---|---|---|---|---|---|---|---|---|---|---|---|---|
| **Total Nonfarm** | | | | | | | | | | | | | |
| 2011 | 2,768.3 | 2,779.6 | 2,811.8 | 2,853.0 | 2,876.7 | 2,841.3 | 2,811.9 | 2,847.8 | 2,893.0 | 2,895.6 | 2,897.0 | 2,899.2 | 2,847.9 |
| 2012 | 2,829.7 | 2,850.0 | 2,878.0 | 2,904.7 | 2,927.9 | 2,906.3 | 2,853.2 | 2,914.2 | 2,946.5 | 2,948.0 | 2,953.4 | 2,948.9 | 2,905.1 |
| 2013 | 2,863.2 | 2,891.2 | 2,910.8 | 2,938.2 | 2,951.1 | 2,935.6 | 2,884.3 | 2,954.2 | 2,974.4 | 2,982.4 | 3,006.1 | 3,001.3 | 2,941.1 |
| 2014 | 2,889.0 | 2,917.0 | 2,945.5 | 2,981.9 | 3,010.3 | 2,992.6 | 2,936.6 | 2,990.7 | 3,012.2 | 3,026.2 | 3,043.1 | 3,046.8 | 2,982.7 |
| 2015 | 2,958.2 | 2,974.8 | 2,997.7 | 3,033.8 | 3,060.3 | 3,047.3 | 2,994.7 | 3,042.5 | 3,069.7 | 3,080.5 | 3,094.6 | 3,097.9 | 3,037.7 |
| 2016 | 3,008.9 | 3,032.1 | 3,052.9 | 3,079.3 | 3,093.8 | 3,072.2 | 3,039.4 | 3,081.5 | 3,116.2 | 3,113.0 | 3,126.4 | 3,118.7 | 3,077.9 |
| 2017 | 3,045.9 | 3,063.1 | 3,084.8 | 3,110.8 | 3,133.9 | 3,125.2 | 3,070.3 | 3,113.5 | 3,142.8 | 3,146.3 | 3,159.3 | 3,160.1 | 3,113.0 |
| 2018 | 3,078.9 | 3,098.4 | 3,120.6 | 3,138.8 | 3,164.8 | 3,158.1 | 3,109.4 | 3,156.4 | 3,173.1 | 3,181.4 | 3,190.8 | 3,187.6 | 3,146.5 |
| 2019 | 3,130.2 | 3,144.8 | 3,156.5 | 3,167.5 | 3,193.1 | 3,169.0 | 3,116.5 | 3,167.2 | 3,184.1 | 3,186.6 | 3,194.7 | 3,184.3 | 3,166.2 |
| **Total Private** | | | | | | | | | | | | | |
| 2010 | 2,338.9 | 2,342.5 | 2,372.8 | 2,410.6 | 2,430.3 | 2,430.4 | 2,428.9 | 2,445.5 | 2,453.1 | 2,453.8 | 2,453.6 | 2,455.7 | 2,418.0 |
| 2011 | 2,396.2 | 2,410.2 | 2,435.9 | 2,465.1 | 2,491.1 | 2,498.7 | 2,486.5 | 2,500.8 | 2,507.8 | 2,506.6 | 2,512.3 | 2,512.8 | 2,477.0 |
| 2012 | 2,438.5 | 2,453.3 | 2,472.3 | 2,499.2 | 2,525.9 | 2,534.2 | 2,522.2 | 2,540.8 | 2,542.0 | 2,544.5 | 2,564.2 | 2,560.9 | 2,516.5 |
| 2013 | 2,472.2 | 2,481.4 | 2,507.7 | 2,544.8 | 2,577.3 | 2,583.2 | 2,565.1 | 2,580.3 | 2,579.9 | 2,588.6 | 2,603.9 | 2,606.2 | 2,557.6 |
| 2014 | 2,530.0 | 2,539.7 | 2,562.3 | 2,597.5 | 2,627.1 | 2,633.9 | 2,622.7 | 2,632.7 | 2,629.4 | 2,642.3 | 2,654.5 | 2,656.3 | 2,610.7 |
| 2015 | 2,580.2 | 2,594.6 | 2,612.9 | 2,643.5 | 2,662.0 | 2,665.8 | 2,666.7 | 2,671.4 | 2,675.8 | 2,676.6 | 2,687.6 | 2,681.3 | 2,651.5 |
| 2016 | 2,616.6 | 2,629.3 | 2,647.7 | 2,674.5 | 2,697.1 | 2,713.0 | 2,696.3 | 2,700.8 | 2,701.7 | 2,706.8 | 2,717.8 | 2,717.0 | 2,684.9 |
| 2017 | 2,648.6 | 2,663.1 | 2,683.5 | 2,701.7 | 2,726.7 | 2,743.0 | 2,732.0 | 2,737.2 | 2,733.5 | 2,739.2 | 2,747.5 | 2,743.8 | 2,716.7 |
| 2018 | 2,697.1 | 2,708.0 | 2,717.1 | 2,733.5 | 2,754.2 | 2,759.2 | 2,740.9 | 2,750.5 | 2,744.3 | 2,746.9 | 2,748.6 | 2,742.1 | 2,736.9 |
| 2019 | | | | | | | | | | | | | |
| **Goods Producing** | | | | | | | | | | | | | |
| 2011 | 561.9 | 561.8 | 572.1 | 583.5 | 590.3 | 598.6 | 599.2 | 604.0 | 604.0 | 605.6 | 599.2 | 598.5 | 589.9 |
| 2012 | 587.7 | 589.2 | 597.9 | 607.3 | 615.2 | 625.4 | 625.6 | 626.8 | 623.1 | 622.4 | 617.8 | 616.4 | 612.9 |
| 2013 | 600.4 | 604.7 | 609.3 | 616.5 | 622.8 | 631.4 | 627.6 | 631.8 | 628.1 | 629.3 | 629.1 | 625.5 | 621.4 |
| 2014 | 609.4 | 611.5 | 620.6 | 629.6 | 637.7 | 648.5 | 645.4 | 649.8 | 646.3 | 647.7 | 647.8 | 646.7 | 636.8 |
| 2015 | 631.7 | 631.8 | 638.2 | 645.7 | 653.9 | 662.0 | 661.6 | 663.6 | 660.0 | 659.7 | 659.5 | 657.6 | 652.1 |
| 2016 | 641.9 | 642.9 | 648.2 | 656.9 | 661.8 | 670.0 | 671.3 | 671.1 | 668.9 | 668.9 | 669.0 | 666.4 | 661.4 |
| 2017 | 655.7 | 657.7 | 663.6 | 670.5 | 677.2 | 686.3 | 685.5 | 684.1 | 683.6 | 683.0 | 683.8 | 683.2 | 676.2 |
| 2018 | 670.0 | 672.8 | 678.8 | 683.7 | 689.8 | 700.4 | 698.6 | 699.0 | 696.4 | 697.4 | 695.2 | 693.4 | 689.6 |
| 2019 | 684.2 | 686.0 | 689.1 | 691.9 | 696.9 | 704.7 | 694.5 | 699.8 | 696.5 | 695.6 | 695.0 | 693.1 | 693.9 |
| **Service-Providing** | | | | | | | | | | | | | |
| 2011 | 2,206.4 | 2,217.8 | 2,239.7 | 2,269.5 | 2,286.4 | 2,242.7 | 2,212.7 | 2,243.8 | 2,289.0 | 2,290.0 | 2,297.8 | 2,300.7 | 2,258.0 |
| 2012 | 2,242.0 | 2,260.8 | 2,280.1 | 2,297.4 | 2,312.7 | 2,280.9 | 2,227.6 | 2,287.4 | 2,323.4 | 2,325.6 | 2,335.6 | 2,332.5 | 2,292.2 |
| 2013 | 2,262.8 | 2,286.5 | 2,301.5 | 2,321.7 | 2,328.3 | 2,304.2 | 2,256.7 | 2,322.4 | 2,346.3 | 2,353.1 | 2,377.0 | 2,375.8 | 2,319.7 |
| 2014 | 2,279.6 | 2,305.5 | 2,324.9 | 2,352.3 | 2,372.6 | 2,344.1 | 2,291.2 | 2,340.9 | 2,365.9 | 2,378.5 | 2,395.3 | 2,400.1 | 2,345.9 |
| 2015 | 2,326.5 | 2,343.0 | 2,359.5 | 2,388.1 | 2,406.4 | 2,385.3 | 2,333.1 | 2,378.9 | 2,409.7 | 2,420.8 | 2,435.1 | 2,440.3 | 2,385.6 |
| 2016 | 2,367.0 | 2,389.2 | 2,404.7 | 2,422.4 | 2,432.0 | 2,402.2 | 2,368.1 | 2,410.4 | 2,447.3 | 2,444.1 | 2,457.4 | 2,452.3 | 2,416.4 |
| 2017 | 2,390.2 | 2,405.4 | 2,421.2 | 2,440.3 | 2,456.7 | 2,438.9 | 2,384.8 | 2,429.4 | 2,459.2 | 2,463.3 | 2,475.5 | 2,476.9 | 2,436.8 |
| 2018 | 2,408.9 | 2,425.6 | 2,441.8 | 2,455.1 | 2,475.0 | 2,457.7 | 2,410.8 | 2,457.4 | 2,476.7 | 2,484.0 | 2,495.6 | 2,494.2 | 2,456.9 |
| 2019 | 2,446.0 | 2,458.8 | 2,467.4 | 2,475.6 | 2,496.2 | 2,464.3 | 2,422.0 | 2,467.4 | 2,487.6 | 2,491.0 | 2,499.7 | 2,491.2 | 2,472.3 |
| **Mining and Logging** | | | | | | | | | | | | | |
| 2011 | 6.3 | 6.4 | 6.6 | 6.7 | 6.8 | 6.9 | 6.9 | 7.0 | 6.9 | 7.0 | 7.0 | 6.9 | 6.8 |
| 2012 | 6.8 | 6.8 | 6.9 | 7.0 | 7.1 | 7.1 | 7.1 | 7.1 | 7.0 | 7.0 | 6.9 | 6.8 | 7.0 |
| 2013 | 6.7 | 6.7 | 6.7 | 6.9 | 7.0 | 7.1 | 7.1 | 7.1 | 7.2 | 7.1 | 7.1 | 7.1 | 7.0 |
| 2014 | 6.7 | 6.6 | 6.9 | 7.2 | 7.3 | 7.5 | 7.4 | 7.4 | 7.3 | 7.1 | 7.2 | 7.2 | 7.2 |
| 2015 | 6.9 | 6.7 | 6.8 | 6.9 | 7.0 | 7.0 | 6.9 | 6.9 | 6.7 | 6.7 | 6.7 | 6.5 | 6.8 |
| 2016 | 6.2 | 6.3 | 6.2 | 6.3 | 6.3 | 6.3 | 6.3 | 6.3 | 6.3 | 6.1 | 5.9 | 5.9 | 6.2 |
| 2017 | 5.7 | 5.7 | 5.8 | 6.0 | 6.0 | 6.1 | 6.1 | 6.1 | 6.2 | 6.2 | 6.4 | 6.1 | 6.0 |
| 2018 | 5.9 | 6.0 | 6.0 | 6.2 | 6.2 | 6.3 | 6.4 | 6.4 | 6.4 | 6.3 | 6.3 | 6.3 | 6.2 |
| 2019 | 5.9 | 5.9 | 6.0 | 6.0 | 6.1 | 6.1 | 6.1 | 6.1 | 6.1 | 6.1 | 5.9 | 5.8 | 6.0 |
| **Construction** | | | | | | | | | | | | | |
| 2011 | 104.3 | 102.3 | 108.0 | 115.9 | 121.3 | 124.5 | 128.5 | 129.2 | 129.2 | 129.3 | 127.5 | 122.1 | 120.2 |
| 2012 | 112.5 | 111.2 | 116.9 | 123.8 | 127.4 | 130.9 | 131.9 | 132.0 | 131.6 | 130.8 | 127.5 | 123.7 | 125.0 |
| 2013 | 111.2 | 112.2 | 116.0 | 122.0 | 126.0 | 129.6 | 130.6 | 129.2 | 127.4 | 128.4 | 126.8 | 121.0 | 123.4 |
| 2014 | 108.3 | 107.5 | 113.4 | 120.3 | 124.8 | 129.8 | 131.7 | 130.4 | 128.9 | 129.6 | 128.2 | 124.1 | 123.1 |
| 2015 | 112.9 | 112.4 | 116.6 | 124.5 | 129.8 | 132.5 | 133.4 | 134.4 | 133.1 | 134.0 | 132.9 | 129.8 | 127.2 |
| 2016 | 117.2 | 116.6 | 121.1 | 129.9 | 133.4 | 136.9 | 138.4 | 138.5 | 139.2 | 139.9 | 138.5 | 132.8 | 131.9 |
| 2017 | 124.3 | 124.7 | 129.7 | 136.6 | 141.3 | 144.3 | 145.3 | 144.5 | 144.6 | 143.5 | 141.8 | 138.1 | 138.2 |
| 2018 | 126.8 | 127.5 | 132.8 | 138.0 | 142.3 | 147.4 | 148.1 | 148.0 | 147.0 | 148.1 | 145.2 | 142.2 | 141.1 |
| 2019 | 135.2 | 135.0 | 138.3 | 144.0 | 148.1 | 152.0 | 151.2 | 151.0 | 150.6 | 153.2 | 148.9 | 146.3 | 146.2 |

## 1. Employment by Industry: Indiana, 2011–2019—*Continued*

(Numbers in thousands, not seasonally adjusted)

| Industry and year | January | February | March | April | May | June | July | August | September | October | November | December | Annual average |
|---|---|---|---|---|---|---|---|---|---|---|---|---|---|
| **Manufacturing** | | | | | | | | | | | | | |
| 2011 | 451.3 | 453.1 | 457.5 | 460.9 | 462.2 | 467.2 | 463.8 | 467.8 | 467.9 | 469.3 | 464.7 | 469.5 | 462.9 |
| 2012 | 468.4 | 471.2 | 474.1 | 476.5 | 480.7 | 487.4 | 486.6 | 487.7 | 484.5 | 484.6 | 483.4 | 485.9 | 480.9 |
| 2013 | 482.5 | 485.8 | 486.6 | 487.6 | 489.8 | 494.7 | 489.9 | 495.5 | 493.5 | 493.8 | 495.2 | 497.4 | 491.0 |
| 2014 | 494.4 | 497.4 | 500.3 | 502.1 | 505.6 | 511.2 | 506.3 | 512.0 | 510.1 | 511.0 | 512.4 | 515.4 | 506.5 |
| 2015 | 511.9 | 512.7 | 514.8 | 514.3 | 517.1 | 522.5 | 521.3 | 522.3 | 520.2 | 519.0 | 519.9 | 521.3 | 518.1 |
| 2016 | 518.5 | 520.0 | 520.9 | 520.7 | 522.1 | 526.8 | 526.6 | 526.3 | 523.4 | 522.9 | 524.6 | 527.7 | 523.4 |
| 2017 | 525.7 | 527.3 | 528.1 | 527.9 | 529.9 | 535.9 | 534.1 | 533.5 | 532.8 | 533.3 | 535.6 | 539.0 | 531.9 |
| 2018 | 537.3 | 539.3 | 540.0 | 539.5 | 541.3 | 546.7 | 544.1 | 544.6 | 543.0 | 543.0 | 543.7 | 544.9 | 542.3 |
| 2019 | 543.1 | 545.1 | 544.8 | 541.9 | 542.7 | 546.6 | 537.2 | 542.7 | 539.8 | 536.3 | 540.2 | 541.0 | 541.8 |
| **Trade, Transportation, and Utilities** | | | | | | | | | | | | | |
| 2011 | 538.1 | 535.1 | 538.4 | 545.2 | 550.6 | 552.5 | 552.4 | 553.2 | 551.1 | 555.6 | 564.8 | 568.0 | 550.4 |
| 2012 | 548.6 | 545.0 | 549.1 | 553.3 | 559.7 | 562.8 | 560.9 | 560.3 | 559.8 | 563.5 | 576.2 | 577.7 | 559.7 |
| 2013 | 552.5 | 551.0 | 553.4 | 558.8 | 566.7 | 570.7 | 567.6 | 569.6 | 568.3 | 571.6 | 584.3 | 587.7 | 566.9 |
| 2014 | 561.3 | 558.5 | 562.2 | 566.6 | 573.2 | 575.7 | 574.0 | 574.8 | 572.7 | 575.7 | 587.1 | 592.0 | 572.8 |
| 2015 | 568.4 | 565.6 | 568.9 | 573.4 | 581.1 | 584.7 | 583.7 | 585.6 | 583.2 | 589.0 | 599.3 | 604.5 | 582.3 |
| 2016 | 584.6 | 583.4 | 585.8 | 588.9 | 592.8 | 593.8 | 595.2 | 594.6 | 594.1 | 595.6 | 606.2 | 609.4 | 593.7 |
| 2017 | 588.8 | 586.1 | 587.3 | 591.2 | 594.5 | 597.9 | 594.7 | 594.9 | 593.7 | 596.5 | 608.7 | 611.1 | 595.5 |
| 2018 | 588.7 | 586.1 | 588.5 | 589.5 | 596.2 | 599.2 | 598.8 | 597.9 | 597.6 | 600.8 | 613.3 | 615.4 | 597.7 |
| 2019 | 598.0 | 593.8 | 594.0 | 595.5 | 600.3 | 601.7 | 598.2 | 597.7 | 595.7 | 596.4 | 607.2 | 611.0 | 599.1 |
| **Wholesale Trade** | | | | | | | | | | | | | |
| 2011 | 111.6 | 111.8 | 112.6 | 113.7 | 114.6 | 115.2 | 115.7 | 115.0 | 114.4 | 114.5 | 114.6 | 114.5 | 114.0 |
| 2012 | 113.4 | 113.6 | 114.4 | 115.1 | 116.0 | 116.9 | 117.0 | 116.0 | 115.6 | 115.5 | 115.3 | 115.3 | 115.3 |
| 2013 | 113.5 | 114.0 | 114.7 | 115.6 | 116.5 | 117.3 | 117.3 | 116.5 | 115.9 | 116.0 | 116.1 | 116.2 | 115.8 |
| 2014 | 114.3 | 114.5 | 115.3 | 116.1 | 117.4 | 118.1 | 118.1 | 117.7 | 116.9 | 116.9 | 117.2 | 117.6 | 116.7 |
| 2015 | 116.3 | 116.6 | 117.3 | 118.0 | 119.0 | 119.3 | 118.7 | 118.3 | 117.4 | 117.5 | 117.4 | 117.4 | 117.8 |
| 2016 | 116.3 | 116.3 | 116.8 | 117.4 | 117.9 | 118.4 | 118.3 | 117.5 | 117.0 | 117.1 | 117.1 | 117.2 | 117.3 |
| 2017 | 116.5 | 116.9 | 117.3 | 117.9 | 118.7 | 120.0 | 119.7 | 119.5 | 118.8 | 118.9 | 119.0 | 119.3 | 118.5 |
| 2018 | 118.2 | 118.7 | 119.3 | 119.6 | 120.7 | 121.6 | 122.0 | 121.5 | 121.2 | 121.9 | 121.7 | 122.0 | 120.7 |
| 2019 | 121.7 | 122.1 | 122.3 | 123.1 | 124.0 | 124.6 | 124.2 | 123.5 | 122.5 | 121.7 | 121.5 | 121.7 | 122.7 |
| **Retail Trade** | | | | | | | | | | | | | |
| 2011 | 301.2 | 297.1 | 299.3 | 303.5 | 306.7 | 307.2 | 306.1 | 306.8 | 304.7 | 308.4 | 316.5 | 318.9 | 306.4 |
| 2012 | 304.5 | 299.8 | 302.1 | 305.0 | 309.2 | 310.4 | 309.1 | 308.3 | 307.8 | 310.5 | 321.3 | 321.3 | 309.1 |
| 2013 | 303.1 | 300.7 | 302.0 | 306.0 | 311.4 | 313.9 | 311.7 | 313.1 | 311.4 | 314.4 | 324.2 | 326.5 | 311.5 |
| 2014 | 306.5 | 303.8 | 305.9 | 309.5 | 313.0 | 314.5 | 313.1 | 313.7 | 311.9 | 314.8 | 324.2 | 326.7 | 313.1 |
| 2015 | 309.6 | 307.1 | 308.9 | 312.5 | 317.1 | 319.1 | 318.0 | 318.7 | 317.0 | 321.1 | 329.5 | 331.4 | 317.5 |
| 2016 | 315.6 | 315.0 | 316.3 | 319.8 | 322.4 | 323.3 | 322.6 | 322.0 | 321.7 | 324.1 | 332.6 | 333.5 | 322.4 |
| 2017 | 321.3 | 318.6 | 318.9 | 322.1 | 324.4 | 325.1 | 322.4 | 321.8 | 320.5 | 323.0 | 332.6 | 332.8 | 323.6 |
| 2018 | 318.3 | 315.7 | 317.6 | 317.3 | 321.6 | 322.8 | 322.0 | 320.2 | 319.2 | 320.7 | 329.9 | 330.2 | 321.3 |
| 2019 | 317.8 | 314.5 | 315.0 | 314.4 | 317.5 | 317.8 | 314.9 | 313.8 | 311.6 | 313.8 | 321.8 | 323.0 | 316.3 |
| **Transportation and Utilities** | | | | | | | | | | | | | |
| 2011 | 125.3 | 126.2 | 126.5 | 128.0 | 129.3 | 130.1 | 130.6 | 131.4 | 132.0 | 132.7 | 133.7 | 134.6 | 130.0 |
| 2012 | 130.7 | 131.6 | 132.6 | 133.2 | 134.5 | 135.5 | 134.8 | 136.0 | 136.4 | 137.5 | 139.6 | 141.1 | 135.3 |
| 2013 | 135.9 | 136.3 | 136.7 | 137.2 | 138.8 | 139.5 | 138.6 | 140.0 | 141.0 | 141.2 | 144.0 | 145.0 | 139.5 |
| 2014 | 140.5 | 140.2 | 141.0 | 141.0 | 142.8 | 143.1 | 142.8 | 143.4 | 143.9 | 144.0 | 145.7 | 147.7 | 143.0 |
| 2015 | 142.5 | 141.9 | 142.7 | 142.9 | 145.0 | 146.3 | 147.0 | 148.6 | 148.8 | 150.4 | 152.4 | 155.7 | 147.0 |
| 2016 | 152.7 | 152.1 | 152.7 | 151.7 | 152.5 | 152.1 | 154.3 | 155.1 | 155.4 | 154.4 | 156.5 | 158.7 | 154.0 |
| 2017 | 151.0 | 150.6 | 151.1 | 151.2 | 151.4 | 152.8 | 152.6 | 153.6 | 154.4 | 154.6 | 157.1 | 159.0 | 153.3 |
| 2018 | 152.2 | 151.7 | 151.6 | 152.6 | 153.9 | 154.8 | 154.8 | 156.2 | 157.2 | 158.2 | 161.7 | 163.2 | 155.7 |
| 2019 | 158.5 | 157.2 | 156.7 | 158.0 | 158.8 | 159.3 | 159.1 | 160.4 | 161.6 | 160.9 | 163.9 | 166.3 | 160.1 |
| **Information** | | | | | | | | | | | | | |
| 2011 | 34.5 | 34.3 | 34.5 | 34.5 | 35.0 | 35.2 | 35.2 | 35.3 | 35.2 | 35.2 | 35.5 | 35.6 | 35.0 |
| 2012 | 35.7 | 35.7 | 35.9 | 35.7 | 36.0 | 36.2 | 36.0 | 35.9 | 35.6 | 35.9 | 36.0 | 36.0 | 35.9 |
| 2013 | 35.9 | 35.8 | 36.0 | 36.0 | 36.0 | 36.3 | 36.5 | 36.1 | 35.7 | 35.7 | 35.8 | 36.0 | 36.0 |
| 2014 | 35.5 | 35.4 | 35.6 | 35.5 | 35.7 | 36.0 | 35.9 | 35.6 | 34.9 | 34.6 | 34.6 | 34.5 | 35.3 |
| 2015 | 34.2 | 34.0 | 33.9 | 33.8 | 34.0 | 34.3 | 34.1 | 33.7 | 33.2 | 33.0 | 33.2 | 33.3 | 33.7 |
| 2016 | 32.9 | 33.0 | 32.9 | 32.9 | 33.1 | 33.2 | 32.9 | 32.7 | 32.4 | 32.7 | 32.4 | 32.5 | 32.8 |
| 2017 | 32.5 | 32.3 | 32.6 | 32.0 | 32.2 | 32.1 | 31.6 | 31.2 | 30.6 | 30.5 | 30.8 | 30.9 | 31.6 |
| 2018 | 30.0 | 29.8 | 29.8 | 29.7 | 29.7 | 29.8 | 29.4 | 29.1 | 28.8 | 28.7 | 28.7 | 28.8 | 29.4 |
| 2019 | 28.8 | 28.8 | 28.7 | 28.7 | 29.1 | 29.3 | 29.0 | 28.6 | 28.3 | 28.4 | 28.4 | 29.0 | 28.8 |

## 1. Employment by Industry: Indiana, 2011–2019—*Continued*

(Numbers in thousands, not seasonally adjusted)

| Industry and year | January | February | March | April | May | June | July | August | September | October | November | December | Annual average |
|---|---|---|---|---|---|---|---|---|---|---|---|---|---|
| **Financial Activities** | | | | | | | | | | | | | |
| 2011 | 130.9 | 130.9 | 131.3 | 131.0 | 131.9 | 132.5 | 132.6 | 132.0 | 130.9 | 130.7 | 130.3 | 130.5 | 131.3 |
| 2012 | 129.0 | 128.9 | 129.2 | 129.5 | 130.2 | 131.0 | 130.8 | 130.3 | 129.4 | 129.2 | 129.0 | 129.4 | 129.7 |
| 2013 | 127.6 | 127.3 | 127.3 | 127.8 | 128.9 | 129.8 | 130.0 | 129.6 | 128.6 | 128.4 | 128.3 | 128.8 | 128.5 |
| 2014 | 126.2 | 126.2 | 126.4 | 126.7 | 127.8 | 129.0 | 129.2 | 129.3 | 128.8 | 129.0 | 129.4 | 129.5 | 128.1 |
| 2015 | 128.3 | 128.6 | 129.0 | 129.2 | 130.5 | 132.0 | 132.1 | 132.5 | 131.7 | 132.5 | 132.4 | 133.2 | 131.0 |
| 2016 | 131.6 | 131.8 | 132.0 | 132.6 | 133.5 | 134.8 | 135.7 | 135.7 | 134.8 | 135.0 | 134.8 | 135.4 | 134.0 |
| 2017 | 133.5 | 134.0 | 134.3 | 135.0 | 135.9 | 137.7 | 137.8 | 138.1 | 137.3 | 137.5 | 137.6 | 138.2 | 136.4 |
| 2018 | 136.5 | 137.1 | 137.5 | 138.1 | 139.0 | 140.9 | 141.5 | 141.1 | 139.9 | 139.9 | 140.0 | 140.2 | 139.3 |
| 2019 | 139.2 | 139.6 | 139.8 | 140.9 | 141.9 | 143.1 | 143.1 | 142.8 | 141.3 | 143.1 | 142.0 | 141.0 | 141.5 |
| **Professional and Business Services** | | | | | | | | | | | | | |
| 2011 | 276.9 | 277.9 | 283.8 | 290.5 | 288.9 | 288.8 | 289.2 | 294.1 | 297.2 | 297.6 | 297.6 | 296.7 | 289.9 |
| 2012 | 284.3 | 290.2 | 294.7 | 299.0 | 301.2 | 304.9 | 302.3 | 306.3 | 307.2 | 307.0 | 306.6 | 304.8 | 300.7 |
| 2013 | 292.4 | 293.8 | 298.7 | 304.7 | 305.8 | 309.0 | 310.7 | 316.0 | 317.1 | 318.0 | 326.5 | 324.3 | 309.8 |
| 2014 | 306.6 | 307.5 | 312.5 | 322.0 | 325.8 | 324.7 | 321.3 | 327.3 | 328.1 | 332.4 | 337.7 | 335.9 | 323.5 |
| 2015 | 319.3 | 318.5 | 322.4 | 332.5 | 334.2 | 335.4 | 334.0 | 335.1 | 333.1 | 337.1 | 341.5 | 340.2 | 331.9 |
| 2016 | 322.4 | 322.2 | 325.4 | 333.8 | 333.2 | 335.1 | 337.7 | 339.7 | 340.4 | 340.1 | 343.1 | 339.9 | 334.4 |
| 2017 | 324.8 | 325.5 | 329.9 | 334.8 | 336.6 | 340.6 | 338.4 | 341.7 | 342.2 | 343.2 | 346.0 | 344.6 | 337.4 |
| 2018 | 333.5 | 334.7 | 338.8 | 341.5 | 341.9 | 344.9 | 343.5 | 347.1 | 344.9 | 346.7 | 350.1 | 345.9 | 342.8 |
| 2019 | 336.2 | 337.3 | 338.9 | 344.9 | 345.7 | 346.9 | 345.2 | 349.2 | 345.5 | 347.7 | 345.4 | 344.7 | 344.0 |
| **Education and Health Services** | | | | | | | | | | | | | |
| 2011 | 419.6 | 423.6 | 424.6 | 428.9 | 427.3 | 412.2 | 411.8 | 416.3 | 430.4 | 430.4 | 431.1 | 432.3 | 424.0 |
| 2012 | 425.6 | 431.9 | 431.3 | 434.5 | 433.1 | 417.9 | 413.7 | 421.6 | 439.8 | 439.9 | 442.0 | 443.0 | 431.2 |
| 2013 | 434.7 | 442.9 | 442.7 | 441.5 | 439.8 | 426.5 | 422.5 | 429.0 | 441.3 | 442.8 | 445.5 | 443.9 | 437.8 |
| 2014 | 433.3 | 439.4 | 440.0 | 442.6 | 443.1 | 430.7 | 423.9 | 427.8 | 440.3 | 443.7 | 445.8 | 446.9 | 438.1 |
| 2015 | 437.9 | 448.3 | 449.5 | 452.8 | 452.3 | 439.9 | 435.4 | 439.6 | 451.8 | 458.2 | 459.8 | 459.2 | 448.7 |
| 2016 | 450.3 | 460.5 | 460.6 | 460.8 | 460.1 | 447.7 | 444.8 | 448.5 | 461.5 | 467.1 | 468.5 | 466.9 | 458.1 |
| 2017 | 459.9 | 468.8 | 468.6 | 470.6 | 471.1 | 464.9 | 458.3 | 460.8 | 471.7 | 475.6 | 475.4 | 474.5 | 468.4 |
| 2018 | 466.7 | 475.0 | 475.7 | 477.2 | 477.3 | 470.9 | 464.6 | 468.1 | 479.1 | 482.0 | 482.5 | 482.3 | 475.1 |
| 2019 | 475.8 | 484.8 | 483.4 | 483.4 | 482.9 | 473.8 | 472.4 | 475.4 | 485.7 | 487.9 | 490.3 | 488.0 | 482.0 |
| **Leisure and Hospitality** | | | | | | | | | | | | | |
| 2011 | 259.7 | 261.1 | 268.7 | 277.3 | 286.2 | 289.3 | 287.5 | 289.7 | 284.1 | 278.9 | 275.5 | 274.3 | 277.7 |
| 2012 | 266.2 | 269.6 | 277.1 | 284.7 | 293.6 | 297.5 | 294.8 | 297.3 | 291.2 | 286.1 | 282.5 | 282.5 | 285.3 |
| 2013 | 272.8 | 274.6 | 280.5 | 289.0 | 299.7 | 302.6 | 299.7 | 301.2 | 296.4 | 291.8 | 287.6 | 286.8 | 290.2 |
| 2014 | 273.8 | 275.7 | 281.9 | 292.9 | 303.8 | 307.2 | 304.5 | 305.7 | 299.7 | 296.6 | 292.7 | 291.7 | 293.9 |
| 2015 | 282.0 | 284.4 | 290.7 | 299.7 | 310.1 | 313.5 | 310.2 | 312.0 | 306.6 | 302.9 | 298.6 | 298.2 | 300.7 |
| 2016 | 288.1 | 291.7 | 298.3 | 307.5 | 316.5 | 319.2 | 317.1 | 317.9 | 312.8 | 306.9 | 303.5 | 300.6 | 306.7 |
| 2017 | 292.5 | 295.8 | 301.1 | 309.8 | 317.7 | 320.3 | 317.6 | 318.8 | 312.3 | 309.5 | 304.7 | 303.5 | 308.6 |
| 2018 | 294.1 | 297.8 | 303.4 | 309.7 | 319.7 | 322.0 | 321.1 | 321.5 | 314.2 | 310.8 | 305.2 | 305.2 | 310.4 |
| 2019 | 301.9 | 304.3 | 309.0 | 314.3 | 322.8 | 324.0 | 323.0 | 322.4 | 317.3 | 313.5 | 305.8 | 301.8 | 313.3 |
| **Other Services** | | | | | | | | | | | | | |
| 2011 | 117.3 | 117.8 | 119.4 | 119.7 | 120.1 | 121.3 | 121.0 | 120.9 | 120.2 | 119.8 | 119.6 | 119.8 | 119.7 |
| 2012 | 119.1 | 119.7 | 120.7 | 121.1 | 122.1 | 123.0 | 122.4 | 122.3 | 121.7 | 122.6 | 122.2 | 123.0 | 121.7 |
| 2013 | 122.2 | 123.2 | 124.4 | 124.9 | 126.2 | 127.9 | 127.6 | 127.5 | 126.5 | 126.9 | 127.1 | 127.9 | 126.0 |
| 2014 | 126.1 | 127.2 | 128.5 | 128.9 | 130.2 | 131.4 | 130.9 | 130.0 | 129.1 | 128.9 | 128.8 | 129.0 | 129.1 |
| 2015 | 128.2 | 128.5 | 129.7 | 130.4 | 131.0 | 132.1 | 131.6 | 130.6 | 129.8 | 129.9 | 130.2 | 130.1 | 130.2 |
| 2016 | 128.4 | 129.1 | 129.7 | 130.1 | 131.0 | 132.0 | 132.0 | 131.2 | 130.9 | 130.3 | 130.1 | 130.2 | 130.4 |
| 2017 | 128.9 | 129.1 | 130.3 | 130.6 | 131.9 | 133.2 | 132.4 | 131.2 | 130.3 | 131.0 | 130.8 | 131.0 | 130.9 |
| 2018 | 129.1 | 129.8 | 131.0 | 132.3 | 133.1 | 134.9 | 134.5 | 133.4 | 132.6 | 132.9 | 132.5 | 132.6 | 132.4 |
| 2019 | 133.0 | 133.4 | 134.2 | 133.9 | 134.6 | 135.7 | 135.5 | 134.6 | 134.0 | 134.3 | 134.5 | 133.5 | 134.3 |
| **Government** | | | | | | | | | | | | | |
| 2011 | 429.4 | 437.1 | 439.0 | 442.4 | 446.4 | 410.9 | 383.0 | 402.3 | 439.9 | 441.8 | 443.4 | 443.5 | 429.9 |
| 2012 | 433.5 | 439.8 | 442.1 | 439.6 | 436.8 | 407.6 | 366.7 | 413.4 | 438.7 | 441.4 | 441.1 | 436.1 | 428.1 |
| 2013 | 424.7 | 437.9 | 438.5 | 439.0 | 425.2 | 401.4 | 361.2 | 413.4 | 432.4 | 437.9 | 441.9 | 440.4 | 424.6 |
| 2014 | 416.8 | 435.6 | 437.8 | 437.1 | 433.0 | 409.4 | 371.5 | 410.4 | 432.3 | 437.6 | 439.2 | 440.6 | 425.1 |
| 2015 | 428.2 | 435.1 | 435.4 | 436.3 | 433.2 | 413.4 | 372.0 | 409.8 | 440.3 | 438.2 | 440.1 | 441.6 | 427.0 |
| 2016 | 428.7 | 437.5 | 440.0 | 435.8 | 431.8 | 406.4 | 372.7 | 410.1 | 440.4 | 436.4 | 438.8 | 437.4 | 426.3 |
| 2017 | 429.3 | 433.8 | 437.1 | 436.3 | 436.8 | 412.2 | 374.0 | 412.7 | 441.1 | 439.5 | 441.5 | 443.1 | 428.1 |
| 2018 | 430.3 | 435.3 | 437.1 | 437.1 | 438.1 | 415.1 | 377.4 | 419.2 | 439.6 | 442.2 | 443.4 | 443.8 | 429.9 |
| 2019 | 433.1 | 436.8 | 439.4 | 434.0 | 438.9 | 409.8 | 375.6 | 416.7 | 439.8 | 439.7 | 446.1 | 442.2 | 429.3 |

## 2. Average Weekly Hours by Selected Industry: Indiana, 2015–2019

(Not seasonally adjusted)

| Industry and year | January | February | March | April | May | June | July | August | September | October | November | December | Annual average |
|---|---|---|---|---|---|---|---|---|---|---|---|---|---|
| **Total Private** | | | | | | | | | | | | | |
| 2015 | 34.7 | 35.0 | 35.0 | 34.8 | 35.0 | 34.9 | 34.8 | 35.3 | 34.5 | 34.9 | 35.0 | 35.1 | 34.9 |
| 2016 | 34.5 | 34.3 | 34.3 | 34.5 | 34.8 | 34.7 | 34.7 | 34.9 | 34.9 | 35.2 | 35.1 | 34.7 | 34.7 |
| 2017 | 34.7 | 34.5 | 34.6 | 34.7 | 34.8 | 35.4 | 35.4 | 35.5 | 35.2 | 35.4 | 35.6 | 35.7 | 35.1 |
| 2018 | 34.8 | 35.1 | 35.2 | 35.1 | 34.9 | 35.1 | 35.4 | 35.1 | 35.3 | 35.1 | 35.0 | 35.5 | 35.1 |
| 2019 | 34.3 | 34.6 | 34.6 | 35.0 | 34.9 | 35.5 | 35.1 | 35.4 | 35.6 | 35.1 | 35.3 | 35.9 | 35.1 |
| **Goods-Producing** | | | | | | | | | | | | | |
| 2015 | 40.5 | 40.6 | 40.6 | 40.1 | 40.6 | 40.3 | 39.7 | 40.9 | 39.5 | 40.9 | 41.2 | 41.0 | 40.5 |
| 2016 | 40.0 | 39.5 | 39.4 | 39.7 | 40.2 | 39.5 | 39.3 | 40.0 | 40.2 | 41.0 | 40.3 | 40.1 | 39.9 |
| 2017 | 39.9 | 40.1 | 39.8 | 39.9 | 40.8 | 41.5 | 40.9 | 41.7 | 41.1 | 41.5 | 41.4 | 41.3 | 40.8 |
| 2018 | 39.7 | 40.0 | 40.7 | 39.7 | 39.6 | 39.8 | 40.0 | 40.0 | 40.4 | 40.7 | 40.2 | 41.3 | 40.2 |
| 2019 | 39.7 | 39.5 | 39.6 | 40.5 | 40.4 | 41.2 | 40.5 | 40.9 | 41.7 | 40.8 | 41.4 | 42.1 | 40.7 |
| **Construction** | | | | | | | | | | | | | |
| 2015 | 37.8 | 37.7 | 37.2 | 38.6 | 39.5 | 40.0 | 38.7 | 39.8 | 36.3 | 39.5 | 38.7 | 38.7 | 38.6 |
| 2016 | 36.5 | 37.0 | 37.4 | 38.7 | 38.8 | 39.6 | 39.3 | 39.0 | 39.3 | 40.2 | 39.8 | 37.3 | 38.6 |
| 2017 | 36.8 | 38.2 | 37.4 | 38.3 | 39.8 | 40.5 | 39.4 | 40.6 | 39.5 | 40.0 | 39.8 | 40.3 | 39.3 |
| 2018 | 38.0 | 38.5 | 38.8 | 39.2 | 40.3 | 39.8 | 41.1 | 40.1 | 39.8 | 41.2 | 40.4 | 40.4 | 39.8 |
| 2019 | 39.3 | 37.9 | 38.4 | 39.3 | 40.4 | 40.3 | 40.8 | 40.6 | 41.1 | 40.7 | 39.7 | 40.1 | 39.9 |
| **Manufacturing** | | | | | | | | | | | | | |
| 2015 | 41.1 | 41.3 | 41.5 | 40.6 | 40.9 | 40.4 | 40.0 | 41.3 | 40.6 | 41.2 | 41.9 | 41.7 | 41.0 |
| 2016 | 41.0 | 40.6 | 40.4 | 40.5 | 41.0 | 39.9 | 39.7 | 40.8 | 41.0 | 41.7 | 41.0 | 41.5 | 40.8 |
| 2017 | 41.3 | 41.0 | 40.8 | 40.5 | 41.3 | 41.7 | 41.4 | 42.0 | 41.5 | 42.0 | 42.0 | 41.6 | 41.4 |
| 2018 | 40.2 | 40.4 | 41.3 | 41.9 | 41.1 | 41.4 | 41.1 | 41.4 | 42.0 | 41.8 | 41.3 | 42.7 | 41.4 |
| 2019 | 40.8 | 40.9 | 40.8 | 41.7 | 41.7 | 42.6 | 41.4 | 41.9 | 42.7 | 41.5 | 42.6 | 43.4 | 41.8 |
| **Trade, Transportation, and Utilities** | | | | | | | | | | | | | |
| 2015 | 33.7 | 34.5 | 34.7 | 34.5 | 34.9 | 34.5 | 34.9 | 34.8 | 34.7 | 34.4 | 34.4 | 35.0 | 34.6 |
| 2016 | 34.3 | 34.2 | 34.0 | 34.0 | 34.4 | 34.4 | 34.3 | 34.4 | 34.4 | 34.4 | 34.8 | 34.2 | 34.3 |
| 2017 | 34.0 | 33.3 | 33.7 | 34.5 | 34.1 | 34.6 | 34.9 | 34.5 | 34.4 | 34.6 | 35.0 | 35.5 | 34.4 |
| 2018 | 34.5 | 34.3 | 34.5 | 35.0 | 34.7 | 34.8 | 34.7 | 34.9 | 34.7 | 33.9 | 34.5 | 34.7 | 34.6 |
| 2019 | 33.7 | 33.5 | 33.7 | 33.9 | 33.9 | 34.4 | 34.3 | 34.7 | 34.7 | 34.2 | 34.3 | 35.1 | 34.2 |
| **Financial Activities** | | | | | | | | | | | | | |
| 2015 | 36.8 | 37.2 | 37.3 | 36.3 | 36.6 | 36.4 | 36.1 | 37.4 | 36.3 | 35.9 | 36.2 | 35.2 | 36.5 |
| 2016 | 36.8 | 35.8 | 35.6 | 36.0 | 36.2 | 35.5 | 36.7 | 36.4 | 36.8 | 37.3 | 36.8 | 37.0 | 36.4 |
| 2017 | 38.6 | 37.4 | 37.5 | 38.0 | 37.7 | 37.6 | 38.7 | 38.0 | 38.0 | 38.5 | 38.2 | 37.8 | 38.0 |
| 2018 | 38.1 | 37.9 | 37.9 | 38.0 | 36.8 | 36.3 | 37.2 | 35.9 | 36.6 | 35.9 | 36.3 | 36.8 | 37.0 |
| 2019 | 36.3 | 36.7 | 36.6 | 37.0 | 36.5 | 37.2 | 36.6 | 36.7 | 36.8 | 36.3 | 36.5 | 37.1 | 36.7 |
| **Professional and Business Services** | | | | | | | | | | | | | |
| 2015 | 36.2 | 36.3 | 36.2 | 36.0 | 36.2 | 36.0 | 35.7 | 36.4 | 34.7 | 35.4 | 35.3 | 35.5 | 35.8 |
| 2016 | 34.4 | 34.6 | 35.0 | 35.4 | 35.7 | 35.6 | 35.5 | 35.4 | 34.9 | 36.3 | 35.7 | 35.3 | 35.3 |
| 2017 | 35.7 | 35.4 | 35.0 | 35.6 | 35.2 | 35.7 | 35.5 | 35.8 | 35.5 | 35.7 | 35.9 | 36.1 | 35.6 |
| 2018 | 34.7 | 35.9 | 35.2 | 35.7 | 36.0 | 35.7 | 36.4 | 35.4 | 35.8 | 35.5 | 34.8 | 35.8 | 35.6 |
| 2019 | 34.0 | 34.5 | 34.2 | 34.4 | 34.5 | 35.0 | 34.4 | 34.9 | 35.0 | 35.1 | 34.7 | 35.5 | 34.7 |
| **Education and Health Services** | | | | | | | | | | | | | |
| 2015 | 33.6 | 33.6 | 33.6 | 33.9 | 33.8 | 33.8 | 33.8 | 34.0 | 33.8 | 33.7 | 33.9 | 34.0 | 33.8 |
| 2016 | 33.9 | 33.8 | 33.9 | 34.0 | 34.2 | 34.4 | 34.4 | 34.3 | 34.5 | 34.3 | 34.4 | 34.2 | 34.2 |
| 2017 | 33.8 | 33.6 | 33.7 | 33.4 | 33.5 | 33.8 | 33.8 | 33.9 | 33.6 | 33.5 | 34.0 | 34.2 | 33.7 |
| 2018 | 34.0 | 34.4 | 34.2 | 34.1 | 34.4 | 34.7 | 34.9 | 34.7 | 35.1 | 35.1 | 34.9 | 35.0 | 34.6 |
| 2019 | 34.2 | 34.8 | 34.7 | 34.8 | 34.5 | 34.5 | 34.5 | 34.7 | 34.9 | 34.6 | 34.9 | 35.2 | 34.7 |
| **Leisure and Hospitality** | | | | | | | | | | | | | |
| 2015 | 24.7 | 25.3 | 25.3 | 25.1 | 25.3 | 25.5 | 25.7 | 25.5 | 24.8 | 25.0 | 24.7 | 25.2 | 25.2 |
| 2016 | 24.2 | 24.6 | 24.7 | 24.7 | 24.3 | 24.8 | 25.1 | 24.9 | 24.8 | 24.5 | 24.3 | 23.8 | 24.6 |
| 2017 | 23.9 | 24.4 | 24.9 | 24.7 | 24.8 | 25.7 | 25.8 | 25.9 | 25.4 | 25.4 | 25.3 | 25.0 | 25.1 |
| 2018 | 24.3 | 25.1 | 25.3 | 25.1 | 25.3 | 26.1 | 26.5 | 25.9 | 25.3 | 25.4 | 25.0 | 24.8 | 25.4 |
| 2019 | 23.7 | 24.3 | 24.3 | 24.7 | 24.7 | 25.8 | 25.5 | 25.5 | 25.2 | 24.9 | 25.3 | 25.5 | 25.0 |
| **Other Services** | | | | | | | | | | | | | |
| 2015 | 29.2 | 29.1 | 29.8 | 29.6 | 29.4 | 30.4 | 29.7 | 29.7 | 29.4 | 28.6 | 28.9 | 29.7 | 29.5 |
| 2016 | 28.9 | 28.5 | 28.7 | 29.3 | 30.2 | 30.8 | 30.7 | 29.1 | 29.7 | 29.4 | 29.6 | 29.3 | 29.5 |
| 2017 | 29.8 | 29.6 | 29.6 | 29.8 | 28.9 | 29.8 | 30.3 | 29.5 | 29.4 | 29.6 | 29.3 | 28.7 | 29.5 |
| 2018 | 28.8 | 29.0 | 29.3 | 29.2 | 29.1 | 29.9 | 30.7 | 29.9 | 29.6 | 29.7 | 30.1 | 30.4 | 29.6 |
| 2019 | 30.2 | 29.6 | 30.3 | 29.9 | 30.2 | 30.7 | 30.0 | 30.6 | 30.5 | 30.1 | 30.2 | 30.3 | 30.2 |

## 3. Average Hourly Earnings by Selected Industry: Indiana, 2015–2019

(Dollars, not seasonally adjusted)

| Industry and year | January | February | March | April | May | June | July | August | September | October | November | December | Annual average |
|---|---|---|---|---|---|---|---|---|---|---|---|---|---|
| **Total Private** | | | | | | | | | | | | | |
| 2015 | 23.00 | 22.86 | 22.78 | 22.71 | 22.65 | 22.65 | 22.75 | 22.97 | 22.93 | 22.89 | 23.07 | 23.00 | 22.85 |
| 2016 | 23.32 | 23.24 | 23.15 | 23.45 | 23.41 | 23.20 | 23.40 | 23.36 | 23.60 | 24.09 | 23.85 | 24.15 | 23.52 |
| 2017 | 24.39 | 24.37 | 24.09 | 24.55 | 24.40 | 24.04 | 24.52 | 24.30 | 24.70 | 24.77 | 24.47 | 24.84 | 24.45 |
| 2018 | 25.02 | 24.98 | 25.12 | 25.28 | 24.73 | 24.36 | 24.63 | 24.78 | 24.93 | 24.94 | 24.92 | 25.25 | 24.91 |
| 2019 | 25.29 | 25.57 | 25.55 | 25.35 | 25.28 | 25.41 | 25.47 | 25.42 | 25.81 | 25.86 | 25.89 | 26.05 | 25.58 |
| **Goods-Producing** | | | | | | | | | | | | | |
| 2015 | 25.30 | 25.29 | 25.36 | 25.13 | 25.03 | 25.17 | 25.23 | 25.50 | 25.42 | 25.26 | 25.65 | 25.40 | 25.31 |
| 2016 | 25.48 | 25.58 | 25.55 | 25.85 | 25.84 | 25.46 | 25.57 | 25.76 | 25.80 | 26.43 | 26.23 | 26.23 | 25.82 |
| 2017 | 26.77 | 26.49 | 26.46 | 27.11 | 26.91 | 26.89 | 27.23 | 26.70 | 26.93 | 27.07 | 26.72 | 27.19 | 26.88 |
| 2018 | 27.14 | 27.27 | 26.78 | 27.64 | 27.10 | 27.15 | 27.44 | 27.22 | 27.84 | 27.93 | 27.84 | 27.95 | 27.45 |
| 2019 | 27.16 | 27.46 | 27.03 | 27.00 | 27.12 | 27.22 | 27.24 | 27.21 | 27.40 | 27.28 | 27.44 | 27.75 | 27.28 |
| **Construction** | | | | | | | | | | | | | |
| 2015 | 26.94 | 26.83 | 27.31 | 27.13 | 26.33 | 26.58 | 26.70 | 27.19 | 27.05 | 27.33 | 27.07 | 26.88 | 26.94 |
| 2016 | 27.20 | 27.15 | 27.31 | 27.73 | 27.71 | 27.17 | 26.95 | 27.29 | 27.82 | 27.92 | 27.86 | 27.83 | 27.51 |
| 2017 | 27.65 | 27.32 | 27.89 | 28.83 | 29.20 | 29.78 | 29.64 | 29.30 | 29.55 | 29.27 | 29.01 | 28.74 | 28.91 |
| 2018 | 28.57 | 28.32 | 28.61 | 28.53 | 28.60 | 28.24 | 28.77 | 28.43 | 29.23 | 29.85 | 29.24 | 29.77 | 28.86 |
| 2019 | 29.01 | 29.39 | 29.08 | 28.87 | 28.90 | 28.60 | 28.89 | 29.08 | 29.17 | 28.95 | 29.17 | 28.83 | 28.99 |
| **Manufacturing** | | | | | | | | | | | | | |
| 2015 | 24.79 | 24.84 | 24.82 | 24.52 | 24.64 | 24.74 | 24.79 | 24.99 | 24.99 | 24.65 | 25.26 | 25.01 | 24.84 |
| 2016 | 25.10 | 25.25 | 25.14 | 25.38 | 25.36 | 24.99 | 25.22 | 25.36 | 25.22 | 26.02 | 25.77 | 25.83 | 25.39 |
| 2017 | 26.57 | 26.29 | 26.01 | 26.52 | 26.06 | 25.69 | 26.25 | 25.61 | 25.82 | 26.16 | 25.76 | 26.54 | 26.10 |
| 2018 | 26.56 | 26.79 | 26.52 | 27.21 | 26.38 | 26.60 | 27.05 | 26.88 | 27.43 | 27.24 | 27.37 | 27.35 | 26.95 |
| 2019 | 26.57 | 26.90 | 26.41 | 26.41 | 26.15 | 26.46 | 26.35 | 26.28 | 26.53 | 26.31 | 26.69 | 27.26 | 26.53 |
| **Trade, Transportation, and Utilities** | | | | | | | | | | | | | |
| 2015 | 20.94 | 20.64 | 20.78 | 20.74 | 20.56 | 20.46 | 20.44 | 20.37 | 20.41 | 20.02 | 20.13 | 20.14 | 20.46 |
| 2016 | 20.29 | 20.04 | 20.01 | 20.45 | 20.48 | 20.52 | 20.94 | 20.64 | 21.27 | 21.54 | 21.12 | 21.35 | 20.73 |
| 2017 | 20.80 | 20.76 | 20.47 | 20.40 | 20.16 | 20.63 | 21.13 | 20.91 | 21.47 | 21.58 | 21.10 | 21.53 | 20.92 |
| 2018 | 22.21 | 21.94 | 21.83 | 21.51 | 21.24 | 21.63 | 21.70 | 21.54 | 22.00 | 22.00 | 21.72 | 22.38 | 21.81 |
| 2019 | 22.57 | 22.19 | 22.61 | 22.41 | 22.10 | 22.37 | 21.97 | 21.96 | 22.35 | 22.46 | 22.37 | 22.42 | 22.31 |
| **Financial Activities** | | | | | | | | | | | | | |
| 2015 | 23.31 | 23.08 | 23.03 | 23.13 | 23.22 | 22.85 | 23.49 | 23.88 | 24.24 | 24.31 | 24.39 | 24.96 | 23.66 |
| 2016 | 25.33 | 25.59 | 26.00 | 26.30 | 26.23 | 25.82 | 25.64 | 25.37 | 25.91 | 26.66 | 26.50 | 27.36 | 26.06 |
| 2017 | 26.24 | 26.42 | 26.48 | 28.02 | 27.05 | 27.36 | 27.14 | 27.17 | 27.87 | 27.74 | 27.97 | 28.62 | 27.35 |
| 2018 | 27.37 | 28.50 | 28.40 | 28.89 | 28.44 | 28.56 | 28.71 | 28.84 | 29.48 | 29.09 | 28.90 | 29.79 | 28.74 |
| 2019 | 28.86 | 28.81 | 28.30 | 28.64 | 28.22 | 28.71 | 29.05 | 29.32 | 29.88 | 29.58 | 30.23 | 30.73 | 29.20 |
| **Professional and Business Services** | | | | | | | | | | | | | |
| 2015 | 25.33 | 25.73 | 25.42 | 24.87 | 24.72 | 24.99 | 25.08 | 25.33 | 25.53 | 25.12 | 25.17 | 25.00 | 25.19 |
| 2016 | 26.07 | 25.68 | 25.66 | 25.92 | 25.92 | 25.45 | 26.22 | 25.60 | 25.99 | 26.14 | 25.51 | 26.04 | 25.85 |
| 2017 | 26.96 | 26.48 | 26.23 | 26.58 | 26.28 | 25.97 | 26.64 | 26.25 | 26.17 | 26.11 | 25.69 | 25.89 | 26.26 |
| 2018 | 26.55 | 26.26 | 26.38 | 26.23 | 26.05 | 25.57 | 25.86 | 25.23 | 25.73 | 25.36 | 25.36 | 25.78 | 25.86 |
| 2019 | 25.94 | 25.74 | 26.04 | 26.07 | 26.29 | 26.68 | 27.02 | 26.96 | 27.39 | 27.06 | 27.01 | 27.20 | 26.63 |
| **Education and Health Services** | | | | | | | | | | | | | |
| 2015 | 24.20 | 24.32 | 24.16 | 24.62 | 24.76 | 24.55 | 24.77 | 24.92 | 24.62 | 25.06 | 24.94 | 24.79 | 24.65 |
| 2016 | 25.19 | 24.97 | 24.78 | 25.21 | 25.30 | 25.10 | 25.24 | 25.53 | 25.45 | 26.06 | 26.00 | 25.92 | 25.40 |
| 2017 | 26.77 | 27.04 | 26.53 | 26.82 | 26.52 | 24.65 | 25.22 | 24.98 | 25.60 | 25.70 | 25.66 | 26.32 | 25.99 |
| 2018 | 26.17 | 26.00 | 26.48 | 26.78 | 26.13 | 25.29 | 26.04 | 26.62 | 26.16 | 26.44 | 26.18 | 26.26 | 26.21 |
| 2019 | 26.93 | 27.05 | 26.89 | 26.38 | 26.54 | 26.72 | 27.50 | 27.32 | 27.77 | 28.40 | 28.28 | 28.34 | 27.35 |
| **Leisure and Hospitality** | | | | | | | | | | | | | |
| 2015 | 12.78 | 12.91 | 12.81 | 12.75 | 12.62 | 12.51 | 12.44 | 12.57 | 12.77 | 13.02 | 13.30 | 13.55 | 12.83 |
| 2016 | 13.34 | 13.50 | 13.27 | 13.25 | 13.29 | 12.94 | 13.01 | 13.28 | 13.51 | 13.63 | 13.79 | 13.88 | 13.38 |
| 2017 | 13.74 | 13.54 | 13.45 | 13.52 | 13.57 | 13.28 | 13.55 | 13.67 | 14.07 | 14.35 | 14.36 | 14.25 | 13.78 |
| 2018 | 14.38 | 14.27 | 14.38 | 14.67 | 14.29 | 13.91 | 13.94 | 14.01 | 13.94 | 13.83 | 14.04 | 14.22 | 14.15 |
| 2019 | 14.36 | 14.33 | 14.22 | 14.26 | 14.11 | 13.66 | 13.64 | 13.83 | 14.04 | 14.35 | 14.33 | 14.50 | 14.13 |
| **Other Services** | | | | | | | | | | | | | |
| 2015 | 17.62 | 17.56 | 17.57 | 17.42 | 17.61 | 17.52 | 17.36 | 18.31 | 18.30 | 18.29 | 18.71 | 18.95 | 17.93 |
| 2016 | 19.28 | 19.59 | 20.19 | 20.50 | 20.26 | 20.07 | 19.75 | 20.47 | 20.06 | 20.60 | 20.33 | 20.86 | 20.16 |
| 2017 | 20.97 | 20.95 | 20.95 | 21.32 | 21.12 | 20.41 | 20.62 | 21.73 | 22.08 | 22.44 | 22.22 | 22.54 | 21.44 |
| 2018 | 22.94 | 22.25 | 22.44 | 22.31 | 22.42 | 21.85 | 21.29 | 22.61 | 22.06 | 21.69 | 21.46 | 21.34 | 22.04 |
| 2019 | 21.63 | 21.67 | 21.55 | 22.01 | 22.19 | 22.17 | 21.63 | 22.25 | 22.69 | 23.08 | 22.90 | 22.97 | 22.23 |

## 4. Average Weekly Earnings by Selected Industry: Indiana, 2015–2019

(Dollars, not seasonally adjusted)

| Industry and year | January | February | March | April | May | June | July | August | September | October | November | December | Annual average |
|---|---|---|---|---|---|---|---|---|---|---|---|---|---|
| **Total Private** | | | | | | | | | | | | | |
| 2015 | 798.10 | 800.10 | 797.30 | 790.31 | 792.75 | 790.49 | 791.70 | 810.84 | 791.09 | 798.86 | 807.45 | 807.30 | 797.47 |
| 2016 | 804.54 | 797.13 | 794.05 | 809.03 | 814.67 | 805.04 | 811.98 | 815.26 | 823.64 | 847.97 | 837.14 | 838.01 | 816.14 |
| 2017 | 846.33 | 840.77 | 833.51 | 851.89 | 849.12 | 851.02 | 868.01 | 862.65 | 869.44 | 876.86 | 871.13 | 886.79 | 858.20 |
| 2018 | 870.70 | 876.80 | 884.22 | 887.33 | 863.08 | 855.04 | 871.90 | 869.78 | 880.03 | 875.39 | 872.20 | 896.38 | 874.34 |
| 2019 | 867.45 | 884.72 | 884.03 | 887.25 | 882.27 | 902.06 | 894.00 | 899.87 | 918.84 | 907.69 | 913.92 | 935.20 | 897.86 |
| **Goods-Producing** | | | | | | | | | | | | | |
| 2015 | 1,024.65 | 1,026.77 | 1,029.62 | 1,007.71 | 1,016.22 | 1,014.35 | 1,001.63 | 1,042.95 | 1,004.09 | 1,033.13 | 1,056.78 | 1,041.40 | 1,025.06 |
| 2016 | 1,019.20 | 1,010.41 | 1,006.67 | 1,026.25 | 1,038.77 | 1,005.67 | 1,004.90 | 1,030.40 | 1,037.16 | 1,083.63 | 1,057.07 | 1,051.82 | 1,030.22 |
| 2017 | 1,068.12 | 1,062.25 | 1,053.11 | 1,081.69 | 1,097.93 | 1,115.94 | 1,113.71 | 1,113.39 | 1,106.82 | 1,123.41 | 1,106.21 | 1,122.95 | 1,096.70 |
| 2018 | 1,077.46 | 1,090.80 | 1,089.95 | 1,097.31 | 1,073.16 | 1,080.57 | 1,097.60 | 1,088.80 | 1,124.74 | 1,136.75 | 1,119.17 | 1,154.34 | 1,103.49 |
| 2019 | 1,078.25 | 1,084.67 | 1,070.39 | 1,093.50 | 1,095.65 | 1,121.46 | 1,103.22 | 1,112.89 | 1,142.58 | 1,113.02 | 1,136.02 | 1,168.28 | 1,110.30 |
| **Construction** | | | | | | | | | | | | | |
| 2015 | 1,018.33 | 1,011.49 | 1,015.93 | 1,047.22 | 1,040.04 | 1,063.20 | 1,033.29 | 1,082.16 | 981.92 | 1,079.54 | 1,047.61 | 1,040.26 | 1,039.88 |
| 2016 | 992.80 | 1,004.55 | 1,021.39 | 1,073.15 | 1,075.15 | 1,075.93 | 1,059.14 | 1,064.31 | 1,093.33 | 1,122.38 | 1,108.83 | 1,038.06 | 1,061.89 |
| 2017 | 1,017.52 | 1,043.62 | 1,043.09 | 1,104.19 | 1,162.16 | 1,206.09 | 1,167.82 | 1,189.58 | 1,167.23 | 1,170.80 | 1,154.60 | 1,158.22 | 1,136.16 |
| 2018 | 1,085.66 | 1,090.32 | 1,110.07 | 1,118.38 | 1,152.58 | 1,123.95 | 1,182.45 | 1,140.04 | 1,163.35 | 1,229.82 | 1,181.30 | 1,202.71 | 1,148.63 |
| 2019 | 1,140.09 | 1,113.88 | 1,116.67 | 1,134.59 | 1,167.56 | 1,152.58 | 1,178.71 | 1,180.65 | 1,198.89 | 1,178.27 | 1,158.05 | 1,156.08 | 1,156.70 |
| **Manufacturing** | | | | | | | | | | | | | |
| 2015 | 1,018.87 | 1,025.89 | 1,030.03 | 995.51 | 1,007.78 | 999.50 | 991.60 | 1,032.09 | 1,014.59 | 1,015.58 | 1,058.39 | 1,042.92 | 1,018.44 |
| 2016 | 1,029.10 | 1,025.15 | 1,015.66 | 1,027.89 | 1,039.76 | 997.10 | 1,001.23 | 1,034.69 | 1,034.02 | 1,085.03 | 1,056.57 | 1,071.95 | 1,035.91 |
| 2017 | 1,097.34 | 1,077.89 | 1,061.21 | 1,074.06 | 1,076.28 | 1,071.27 | 1,086.75 | 1,075.62 | 1,071.53 | 1,098.72 | 1,081.92 | 1,104.06 | 1,080.54 |
| 2018 | 1,067.71 | 1,082.32 | 1,095.28 | 1,140.10 | 1,084.22 | 1,101.24 | 1,111.76 | 1,112.83 | 1,152.06 | 1,138.63 | 1,130.38 | 1,167.85 | 1,115.73 |
| 2019 | 1,084.06 | 1,100.21 | 1,077.53 | 1,101.30 | 1,090.46 | 1,127.20 | 1,090.89 | 1,101.13 | 1,132.83 | 1,091.87 | 1,136.99 | 1,183.08 | 1,108.95 |
| **Trade, Transportation, and Utilities** | | | | | | | | | | | | | |
| 2015 | 705.68 | 712.08 | 721.07 | 715.53 | 717.54 | 705.87 | 713.36 | 708.88 | 708.23 | 688.69 | 692.47 | 704.90 | 707.92 |
| 2016 | 695.95 | 685.37 | 680.34 | 695.30 | 704.51 | 705.89 | 718.24 | 710.02 | 731.69 | 740.98 | 734.98 | 730.17 | 711.04 |
| 2017 | 707.20 | 691.31 | 689.84 | 703.80 | 687.46 | 713.80 | 737.44 | 721.40 | 738.57 | 746.67 | 738.50 | 764.32 | 719.65 |
| 2018 | 766.25 | 752.54 | 753.14 | 752.85 | 737.03 | 752.72 | 752.99 | 751.75 | 763.40 | 745.80 | 749.34 | 776.59 | 754.63 |
| 2019 | 760.61 | 743.37 | 761.96 | 759.70 | 749.19 | 769.53 | 753.57 | 762.01 | 775.55 | 768.13 | 767.29 | 786.94 | 763.00 |
| **Financial Activities** | | | | | | | | | | | | | |
| 2015 | 857.81 | 858.58 | 859.02 | 839.62 | 849.85 | 831.74 | 847.99 | 893.11 | 879.91 | 872.73 | 882.92 | 878.59 | 863.59 |
| 2016 | 932.14 | 916.12 | 925.60 | 946.80 | 949.53 | 916.61 | 940.99 | 923.47 | 953.49 | 994.42 | 975.20 | 1,012.32 | 948.58 |
| 2017 | 1,012.86 | 988.11 | 993.00 | 1,064.76 | 1,019.79 | 1,028.74 | 1,050.32 | 1,032.46 | 1,059.06 | 1,067.99 | 1,068.45 | 1,081.84 | 1,039.30 |
| 2018 | 1,042.80 | 1,080.15 | 1,076.36 | 1,097.82 | 1,046.59 | 1,036.73 | 1,068.01 | 1,035.36 | 1,078.97 | 1,044.33 | 1,049.07 | 1,096.27 | 1,063.38 |
| 2019 | 1,047.62 | 1,057.33 | 1,035.78 | 1,059.68 | 1,030.03 | 1,068.01 | 1,063.23 | 1,076.04 | 1,099.58 | 1,073.75 | 1,103.40 | 1,140.08 | 1,071.64 |
| **Professional and Business Services** | | | | | | | | | | | | | |
| 2015 | 916.95 | 934.00 | 920.20 | 895.32 | 894.86 | 899.64 | 895.36 | 922.01 | 885.89 | 889.25 | 888.50 | 887.50 | 901.80 |
| 2016 | 896.81 | 888.53 | 898.10 | 917.57 | 925.34 | 906.02 | 930.81 | 906.24 | 907.05 | 948.88 | 910.71 | 919.21 | 912.51 |
| 2017 | 962.47 | 937.39 | 918.05 | 946.25 | 925.06 | 927.13 | 945.72 | 939.75 | 929.04 | 932.13 | 922.27 | 934.63 | 934.86 |
| 2018 | 921.29 | 942.73 | 928.58 | 936.41 | 937.80 | 912.85 | 941.30 | 893.14 | 921.13 | 900.28 | 882.53 | 922.92 | 920.62 |
| 2019 | 881.96 | 888.03 | 890.57 | 896.81 | 907.01 | 933.80 | 929.49 | 940.90 | 958.65 | 949.81 | 937.25 | 965.60 | 924.06 |
| **Education and Health Services** | | | | | | | | | | | | | |
| 2015 | 813.12 | 817.15 | 811.78 | 834.62 | 836.89 | 829.79 | 837.23 | 847.28 | 832.16 | 844.52 | 845.47 | 842.86 | 833.17 |
| 2016 | 853.94 | 843.99 | 840.04 | 857.14 | 865.26 | 863.44 | 868.26 | 875.68 | 878.03 | 893.86 | 894.40 | 886.46 | 868.68 |
| 2017 | 904.83 | 908.54 | 894.06 | 895.79 | 888.42 | 833.17 | 852.44 | 846.82 | 860.16 | 860.95 | 872.44 | 900.14 | 875.86 |
| 2018 | 889.78 | 894.40 | 905.62 | 913.20 | 898.87 | 877.56 | 908.80 | 923.71 | 918.22 | 928.04 | 913.68 | 919.10 | 906.87 |
| 2019 | 921.01 | 941.34 | 933.08 | 918.02 | 915.63 | 921.84 | 948.75 | 948.00 | 969.17 | 982.64 | 986.97 | 997.57 | 949.05 |
| **Leisure and Hospitality** | | | | | | | | | | | | | |
| 2015 | 315.67 | 326.62 | 324.09 | 320.03 | 319.29 | 319.01 | 319.71 | 320.54 | 316.70 | 325.50 | 328.51 | 341.46 | 323.32 |
| 2016 | 322.83 | 332.10 | 327.77 | 327.28 | 322.95 | 320.91 | 326.55 | 330.67 | 335.05 | 333.94 | 335.10 | 330.34 | 329.15 |
| 2017 | 328.39 | 330.38 | 334.91 | 333.94 | 336.54 | 341.30 | 349.59 | 354.05 | 357.38 | 364.49 | 363.31 | 356.25 | 345.88 |
| 2018 | 349.43 | 358.18 | 363.81 | 368.22 | 361.54 | 363.05 | 369.41 | 362.86 | 352.68 | 351.28 | 351.00 | 352.66 | 359.41 |
| 2019 | 340.33 | 348.22 | 345.55 | 352.22 | 348.52 | 352.43 | 347.82 | 352.67 | 353.81 | 357.32 | 362.55 | 369.75 | 353.25 |
| **Other Services** | | | | | | | | | | | | | |
| 2015 | 514.50 | 511.00 | 523.59 | 515.63 | 517.73 | 532.61 | 515.59 | 543.81 | 538.02 | 523.09 | 540.72 | 562.82 | 528.94 |
| 2016 | 557.19 | 558.32 | 579.45 | 600.65 | 611.85 | 618.16 | 606.33 | 595.68 | 595.78 | 605.64 | 601.77 | 611.20 | 594.72 |
| 2017 | 624.91 | 620.12 | 620.12 | 635.34 | 610.37 | 608.22 | 624.79 | 641.04 | 649.15 | 664.22 | 651.05 | 646.90 | 632.48 |
| 2018 | 660.67 | 645.25 | 657.49 | 651.45 | 652.42 | 653.32 | 653.60 | 676.04 | 652.98 | 644.19 | 645.95 | 648.74 | 652.38 |
| 2019 | 653.23 | 641.43 | 652.97 | 658.1 | 670.14 | 680.62 | 648.9 | 680.85 | 692.05 | 694.71 | 691.58 | 695.99 | 671.35 |

# IOWA
## *At a Glance*

Population:
2010 census: 3,046,355
2019 estimate: 3,155,070

Percent change in population:
2010–2019: 3.6%

Percent change in total nonfarm employment:
2011–2019: 6.7%

Industry with the largest growth in employment, 2011–2019 (percent):
Construction, 25.2%

Industry with the largest decline or smallest growth in employment, 2011–2019 (percent):
Information, -23.9%

Civilian labor force:
2010: 1,678,281
2019: 1,738,824

Unemployment rate and rank among states (highest to lowest):
2010: 6.0%, 47th
2019: 2.7%, 46th

Over-the-year change in unemployment rates:
2017–2018: -0.5%
2018–2019: 0.1%

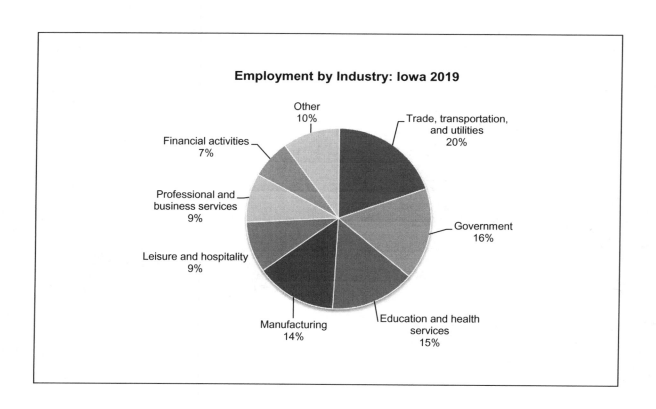

**Employment by Industry: Iowa 2019**

- Other 10%
- Trade, transportation, and utilities 20%
- Financial activities 7%
- Professional and business services 9%
- Government 16%
- Leisure and hospitality 9%
- Manufacturing 14%
- Education and health services 15%

## 1. Employment by Industry: Iowa, 2011–2019

(Numbers in thousands, not seasonally adjusted)

| Industry and year | January | February | March | April | May | June | July | August | September | October | November | December | Annual average |
|---|---|---|---|---|---|---|---|---|---|---|---|---|---|
| **Total Nonfarm** | | | | | | | | | | | | | |
| 2011 | 1,443.9 | 1,449.9 | 1,460.9 | 1,489.2 | 1,500.3 | 1,499.8 | 1,477.8 | 1,480.0 | 1,501.6 | 1,509.5 | 1,513.7 | 1,507.7 | 1,486.2 |
| 2012 | 1,467.4 | 1,474.5 | 1,488.9 | 1,510.7 | 1,524.1 | 1,524.2 | 1,500.5 | 1,505.5 | 1,519.7 | 1,528.8 | 1,533.7 | 1,527.4 | 1,508.8 |
| 2013 | 1,484.0 | 1,493.2 | 1,501.7 | 1,520.7 | 1,542.0 | 1,543.6 | 1,527.6 | 1,532.6 | 1,545.2 | 1,547.9 | 1,554.4 | 1,547.6 | 1,528.4 |
| 2014 | 1,504.0 | 1,512.5 | 1,522.5 | 1,548.1 | 1,564.4 | 1,564.0 | 1,540.5 | 1,545.4 | 1,561.8 | 1,566.1 | 1,569.9 | 1,565.2 | 1,547.0 |
| 2015 | 1,525.8 | 1,532.9 | 1,543.2 | 1,564.8 | 1,577.3 | 1,578.9 | 1,556.7 | 1,555.1 | 1,567.6 | 1,578.3 | 1,580.9 | 1,575.5 | 1,561.4 |
| 2016 | 1,535.0 | 1,543.7 | 1,554.9 | 1,578.9 | 1,585.0 | 1,582.3 | 1,565.9 | 1,567.8 | 1,581.7 | 1,588.0 | 1,588.2 | 1,578.6 | 1,570.8 |
| 2017 | 1,536.4 | 1,547.5 | 1,554.9 | 1,578.1 | 1,585.8 | 1,589.5 | 1,565.8 | 1,568.0 | 1,580.0 | 1,588.5 | 1,591.9 | 1,586.4 | 1,572.7 |
| 2018 | 1,547.9 | 1,558.1 | 1,563.8 | 1,583.1 | 1,600.5 | 1,602.5 | 1,579.2 | 1,578.7 | 1,590.4 | 1,599.5 | 1,604.3 | 1,594.6 | 1,583.6 |
| 2019 | 1,557.8 | 1,561.8 | 1,567.4 | 1,591.5 | 1,602.8 | 1,599.6 | 1,579.2 | 1,580.1 | 1,591.2 | 1,604.1 | 1,604.0 | 1,589.0 | 1,585.7 |
| **Total Private** | | | | | | | | | | | | | |
| 2011 | 1,194.4 | 1,194.4 | 1,204.4 | 1,231.3 | 1,241.1 | 1,244.5 | 1,241.9 | 1,243.6 | 1,247.6 | 1,251.7 | 1,254.9 | 1,249.5 | 1,233.3 |
| 2012 | 1,215.8 | 1,218.4 | 1,232.1 | 1,252.4 | 1,264.2 | 1,269.8 | 1,265.9 | 1,266.1 | 1,265.3 | 1,270.5 | 1,273.9 | 1,268.2 | 1,255.2 |
| 2013 | 1,233.9 | 1,236.7 | 1,244.7 | 1,263.3 | 1,281.2 | 1,287.3 | 1,288.8 | 1,290.8 | 1,288.3 | 1,288.4 | 1,293.5 | 1,287.3 | 1,273.7 |
| 2014 | 1,251.4 | 1,254.9 | 1,264.3 | 1,289.3 | 1,303.8 | 1,309.7 | 1,304.5 | 1,306.4 | 1,303.3 | 1,304.9 | 1,307.3 | 1,303.9 | 1,292.0 |
| 2015 | 1,271.1 | 1,273.4 | 1,283.8 | 1,305.0 | 1,316.1 | 1,323.2 | 1,320.3 | 1,318.1 | 1,312.3 | 1,317.0 | 1,318.0 | 1,312.9 | 1,305.9 |
| 2016 | 1,279.2 | 1,282.8 | 1,294.0 | 1,316.9 | 1,322.0 | 1,323.4 | 1,328.5 | 1,326.8 | 1,322.9 | 1,324.6 | 1,323.1 | 1,314.3 | 1,313.2 |
| 2017 | 1,276.8 | 1,284.4 | 1,291.4 | 1,313.7 | 1,321.4 | 1,328.0 | 1,323.9 | 1,322.1 | 1,319.1 | 1,323.5 | 1,325.8 | 1,321.5 | 1,312.6 |
| 2018 | 1,287.4 | 1,294.2 | 1,300.1 | 1,318.2 | 1,335.1 | 1,340.0 | 1,336.9 | 1,333.1 | 1,330.0 | 1,334.2 | 1,336.9 | 1,328.8 | 1,322.9 |
| 2019 | 1,298.8 | 1,298.6 | 1,302.8 | 1,325.7 | 1,336.0 | 1,340.5 | 1,338.1 | 1,336.2 | 1,329.6 | 1,337.3 | 1,335.7 | 1,323.1 | 1,325.2 |
| **Goods Producing** | | | | | | | | | | | | | |
| 2011 | 254.2 | 253.5 | 257.6 | 267.0 | 272.2 | 277.4 | 279.8 | 279.8 | 278.7 | 277.4 | 276.3 | 271.1 | 270.4 |
| 2012 | 261.7 | 261.0 | 266.4 | 275.1 | 280.5 | 285.3 | 286.5 | 286.2 | 283.7 | 283.7 | 281.7 | 278.3 | 277.5 |
| 2013 | 268.8 | 268.6 | 270.9 | 278.1 | 286.0 | 291.4 | 293.5 | 294.3 | 292.0 | 292.4 | 291.6 | 286.5 | 284.5 |
| 2014 | 276.4 | 276.4 | 280.3 | 290.9 | 297.3 | 302.4 | 303.3 | 303.5 | 300.6 | 299.6 | 298.6 | 294.0 | 293.6 |
| 2015 | 284.9 | 284.1 | 287.4 | 296.1 | 299.4 | 304.0 | 305.0 | 303.5 | 300.8 | 301.1 | 299.4 | 295.0 | 296.7 |
| 2016 | 284.3 | 282.9 | 289.4 | 297.0 | 299.2 | 304.0 | 306.1 | 306.1 | 303.4 | 301.8 | 298.5 | 292.8 | 297.1 |
| 2017 | 281.0 | 280.9 | 284.6 | 292.4 | 296.3 | 301.0 | 301.4 | 300.4 | 299.6 | 300.0 | 299.4 | 296.3 | 294.4 |
| 2018 | 285.2 | 285.9 | 290.2 | 298.0 | 304.7 | 310.8 | 312.0 | 310.9 | 309.3 | 308.9 | 308.7 | 304.0 | 302.4 |
| 2019 | 294.9 | 292.0 | 294.5 | 304.7 | 310.2 | 315.5 | 316.4 | 315.1 | 311.4 | 312.7 | 310.1 | 302.7 | 306.7 |
| **Service-Providing** | | | | | | | | | | | | | |
| 2011 | 1,189.7 | 1,196.4 | 1,203.3 | 1,222.2 | 1,228.1 | 1,222.4 | 1,198.0 | 1,200.2 | 1,222.9 | 1,232.1 | 1,237.4 | 1,236.6 | 1,215.8 |
| 2012 | 1,205.7 | 1,213.5 | 1,222.5 | 1,235.6 | 1,243.6 | 1,238.9 | 1,214.0 | 1,219.3 | 1,236.0 | 1,245.1 | 1,252.0 | 1,249.1 | 1,231.3 |
| 2013 | 1,215.2 | 1,224.6 | 1,230.8 | 1,242.6 | 1,256.0 | 1,252.2 | 1,234.1 | 1,238.3 | 1,253.2 | 1,255.5 | 1,262.8 | 1,261.1 | 1,243.9 |
| 2014 | 1,227.6 | 1,236.1 | 1,242.2 | 1,257.2 | 1,267.1 | 1,261.6 | 1,237.2 | 1,241.9 | 1,261.2 | 1,266.5 | 1,271.3 | 1,271.2 | 1,253.4 |
| 2015 | 1,240.9 | 1,248.8 | 1,255.8 | 1,268.7 | 1,277.9 | 1,274.9 | 1,251.7 | 1,251.6 | 1,266.8 | 1,277.2 | 1,281.5 | 1,280.5 | 1,264.7 |
| 2016 | 1,250.7 | 1,260.8 | 1,265.5 | 1,281.9 | 1,285.8 | 1,278.3 | 1,259.8 | 1,261.7 | 1,278.3 | 1,286.2 | 1,289.7 | 1,285.8 | 1,273.7 |
| 2017 | 1,255.4 | 1,266.6 | 1,270.3 | 1,285.7 | 1,289.5 | 1,288.5 | 1,264.4 | 1,267.6 | 1,280.4 | 1,288.5 | 1,292.5 | 1,290.1 | 1,278.3 |
| 2018 | 1,262.7 | 1,272.2 | 1,273.6 | 1,285.1 | 1,295.8 | 1,291.7 | 1,267.2 | 1,267.8 | 1,281.1 | 1,290.6 | 1,295.6 | 1,290.6 | 1,281.2 |
| 2019 | 1,262.9 | 1,269.8 | 1,272.9 | 1,286.8 | 1,292.6 | 1,284.1 | 1,262.8 | 1,265.0 | 1,279.8 | 1,291.4 | 1,293.9 | 1,286.3 | 1,279.0 |
| **Mining and Logging** | | | | | | | | | | | | | |
| 2011 | 1.7 | 1.8 | 1.8 | 2.2 | 2.3 | 2.4 | 2.4 | 2.4 | 2.4 | 2.4 | 2.3 | 2.2 | 2.2 |
| 2012 | 1.8 | 1.9 | 2.1 | 2.2 | 2.4 | 2.4 | 2.4 | 2.4 | 2.4 | 2.3 | 2.3 | 2.2 | 2.2 |
| 2013 | 1.8 | 1.8 | 2.0 | 2.1 | 2.4 | 2.5 | 2.5 | 2.5 | 2.5 | 2.4 | 2.4 | 2.3 | 2.3 |
| 2014 | 1.8 | 1.8 | 1.9 | 2.2 | 2.4 | 2.5 | 2.4 | 2.4 | 2.4 | 2.3 | 2.3 | 2.2 | 2.2 |
| 2015 | 1.8 | 1.9 | 2.1 | 2.3 | 2.4 | 2.5 | 2.5 | 2.5 | 2.4 | 2.3 | 2.2 | 2.1 | 2.3 |
| 2016 | 1.7 | 1.7 | 1.9 | 2.4 | 2.4 | 2.5 | 2.5 | 2.5 | 2.5 | 2.3 | 2.2 | 2.1 | 2.2 |
| 2017 | 1.9 | 2.0 | 2.2 | 2.4 | 2.5 | 2.5 | 2.5 | 2.5 | 2.5 | 2.5 | 2.5 | 2.4 | 2.4 |
| 2018 | 1.9 | 2.2 | 2.4 | 2.4 | 2.6 | 2.7 | 2.7 | 2.7 | 2.6 | 2.6 | 2.6 | 2.5 | 2.5 |
| 2019 | 2.2 | 2.2 | 2.4 | 2.4 | 2.6 | 2.6 | 2.6 | 2.6 | 2.6 | 2.5 | 2.4 | 2.3 | 2.5 |
| **Construction** | | | | | | | | | | | | | |
| 2011 | 50.6 | 49.6 | 52.1 | 60.8 | 64.5 | 67.4 | 69.0 | 69.3 | 68.6 | 68.3 | 66.8 | 61.4 | 62.4 |
| 2012 | 54.1 | 52.9 | 56.5 | 63.8 | 67.4 | 69.9 | 70.5 | 70.6 | 69.2 | 69.2 | 67.0 | 63.9 | 64.6 |
| 2013 | 56.1 | 55.3 | 56.5 | 63.0 | 69.5 | 72.8 | 74.9 | 75.6 | 74.1 | 74.4 | 73.3 | 67.9 | 67.8 |
| 2014 | 59.9 | 59.5 | 62.4 | 72.0 | 77.0 | 80.3 | 81.3 | 82.2 | 81.2 | 81.1 | 79.7 | 74.9 | 74.3 |
| 2015 | 67.2 | 66.8 | 69.3 | 77.8 | 80.2 | 82.8 | 84.2 | 83.9 | 82.7 | 83.6 | 82.4 | 78.0 | 78.2 |
| 2016 | 68.6 | 67.9 | 73.4 | 81.1 | 82.8 | 85.6 | 88.0 | 88.4 | 87.3 | 86.7 | 83.8 | 77.3 | 80.9 |
| 2017 | 66.9 | 66.9 | 69.5 | 75.7 | 78.7 | 81.2 | 81.1 | 80.9 | 79.9 | 79.6 | 78.3 | 74.1 | 76.1 |
| 2018 | 65.0 | 65.0 | 68.7 | 74.8 | 80.0 | 83.5 | 84.3 | 84.3 | 82.9 | 82.0 | 80.8 | 75.7 | 77.3 |
| 2019 | 68.2 | 65.5 | 67.1 | 76.6 | 81.2 | 84.0 | 85.3 | 85.5 | 83.5 | 84.1 | 81.1 | 75.2 | 78.1 |

## 1. Employment by Industry: Iowa, 2011–2019—*Continued*

(Numbers in thousands, not seasonally adjusted)

| Industry and year | January | February | March | April | May | June | July | August | September | October | November | December | Annual average |
|---|---|---|---|---|---|---|---|---|---|---|---|---|---|
| **Manufacturing** | | | | | | | | | | | | | |
| 2011 | 201.9 | 202.1 | 203.7 | 204.0 | 205.4 | 207.6 | 208.4 | 208.1 | 207.7 | 206.7 | 207.2 | 207.5 | 205.9 |
| 2012 | 205.8 | 206.2 | 207.8 | 209.1 | 210.7 | 213.0 | 213.6 | 213.2 | 212.1 | 212.2 | 212.4 | 212.2 | 210.7 |
| 2013 | 210.9 | 211.5 | 212.4 | 213.0 | 214.1 | 216.1 | 216.1 | 216.2 | 215.4 | 215.6 | 215.9 | 216.3 | 214.5 |
| 2014 | 214.7 | 215.1 | 216.0 | 216.7 | 217.9 | 219.6 | 219.6 | 218.9 | 217.0 | 216.2 | 216.6 | 216.9 | 217.1 |
| 2015 | 215.9 | 215.4 | 216.0 | 216.0 | 216.8 | 218.7 | 218.3 | 217.1 | 215.7 | 215.2 | 214.8 | 214.9 | 216.2 |
| 2016 | 214.0 | 213.3 | 214.1 | 213.5 | 214.0 | 215.9 | 215.6 | 215.2 | 213.6 | 212.8 | 212.5 | 213.4 | 214.0 |
| 2017 | 212.2 | 212.0 | 212.9 | 214.3 | 215.1 | 217.3 | 217.8 | 217.0 | 217.2 | 217.9 | 218.6 | 219.8 | 216.0 |
| 2018 | 218.3 | 218.7 | 219.1 | 220.8 | 222.1 | 224.6 | 225.0 | 223.9 | 223.8 | 224.3 | 225.3 | 225.8 | 222.6 |
| 2019 | 224.5 | 224.3 | 225.0 | 225.7 | 226.4 | 228.9 | 228.5 | 227.0 | 225.3 | 226.1 | 226.6 | 225.2 | 226.1 |
| **Trade, Transportation, and Utilities** | | | | | | | | | | | | | |
| 2011 | 295.4 | 293.8 | 295.8 | 300.4 | 303.6 | 304.9 | 304.0 | 303.7 | 302.3 | 304.9 | 309.8 | 311.9 | 302.5 |
| 2012 | 300.9 | 298.8 | 300.2 | 303.7 | 306.8 | 308.5 | 308.1 | 307.7 | 306.8 | 308.6 | 314.6 | 315.6 | 306.7 |
| 2013 | 304.1 | 302.5 | 304.3 | 307.3 | 310.9 | 312.7 | 312.3 | 311.5 | 309.9 | 311.8 | 317.6 | 318.4 | 310.3 |
| 2014 | 306.8 | 305.0 | 306.1 | 310.1 | 312.1 | 314.1 | 312.4 | 311.9 | 310.2 | 312.8 | 318.3 | 320.9 | 311.7 |
| 2015 | 310.4 | 308.7 | 310.2 | 312.6 | 314.7 | 317.2 | 316.1 | 314.6 | 312.4 | 315.3 | 319.8 | 321.0 | 314.4 |
| 2016 | 311.1 | 309.8 | 310.6 | 314.0 | 315.1 | 315.6 | 317.4 | 316.5 | 313.7 | 315.3 | 319.7 | 322.1 | 315.1 |
| 2017 | 311.1 | 309.7 | 310.1 | 313.6 | 314.9 | 316.3 | 315.2 | 314.2 | 311.8 | 314.0 | 318.9 | 320.8 | 314.2 |
| 2018 | 309.9 | 307.6 | 307.7 | 310.6 | 313.6 | 315.1 | 313.9 | 312.4 | 309.9 | 311.9 | 318.3 | 319.2 | 312.5 |
| 2019 | 310.0 | 305.7 | 306.5 | 309.1 | 310.7 | 311.5 | 311.3 | 309.6 | 307.7 | 310.4 | 315.8 | 315.1 | 310.3 |
| **Wholesale Trade** | | | | | | | | | | | | | |
| 2011 | 64.5 | 64.4 | 65.0 | 66.5 | 67.0 | 67.2 | 67.2 | 66.6 | 66.8 | 67.9 | 68.2 | 67.7 | 66.6 |
| 2012 | 66.3 | 66.4 | 67.5 | 68.6 | 68.9 | 69.1 | 68.9 | 68.3 | 68.3 | 68.6 | 68.8 | 68.0 | 68.1 |
| 2013 | 66.8 | 66.9 | 67.3 | 68.6 | 69.8 | 69.7 | 69.2 | 68.7 | 67.8 | 68.8 | 69.4 | 68.5 | 68.5 |
| 2014 | 67.1 | 67.0 | 67.3 | 69.0 | 69.5 | 69.6 | 69.0 | 68.4 | 67.7 | 68.8 | 69.1 | 68.3 | 68.4 |
| 2015 | 66.7 | 66.4 | 66.8 | 68.1 | 68.0 | 68.2 | 67.7 | 67.1 | 66.5 | 67.4 | 67.4 | 66.5 | 67.2 |
| 2016 | 65.4 | 65.3 | 66.0 | 67.1 | 67.0 | 66.9 | 66.9 | 66.2 | 66.1 | 66.6 | 66.7 | 66.0 | 66.4 |
| 2017 | 64.9 | 65.0 | 65.5 | 66.6 | 66.9 | 67.0 | 66.6 | 66.1 | 65.8 | 66.4 | 66.5 | 66.3 | 66.1 |
| 2018 | 65.0 | 64.9 | 65.5 | 66.2 | 66.9 | 66.9 | 66.6 | 65.9 | 65.7 | 66.4 | 66.6 | 66.3 | 66.1 |
| 2019 | 65.1 | 64.8 | 65.2 | 66.7 | 67.1 | 67.2 | 66.9 | 66.2 | 65.7 | 65.9 | 66.1 | 65.4 | 66.0 |
| **Retail Trade** | | | | | | | | | | | | | |
| 2011 | 170.8 | 169.1 | 170.1 | 172.6 | 174.7 | 175.5 | 175.1 | 175.0 | 173.3 | 174.8 | 179.0 | 180.9 | 174.2 |
| 2012 | 173.5 | 171.3 | 171.2 | 173.1 | 175.3 | 176.1 | 176.1 | 176.0 | 174.8 | 176.3 | 181.8 | 182.6 | 175.7 |
| 2013 | 174.6 | 172.8 | 173.8 | 175.6 | 177.3 | 178.7 | 178.9 | 178.6 | 177.8 | 178.8 | 183.3 | 183.9 | 177.8 |
| 2014 | 176.6 | 175.0 | 175.3 | 176.8 | 178.0 | 179.1 | 178.2 | 177.9 | 176.4 | 177.8 | 182.2 | 183.7 | 178.1 |
| 2015 | 177.1 | 175.9 | 176.8 | 178.9 | 180.9 | 182.3 | 181.6 | 180.9 | 179.1 | 181.3 | 185.1 | 186.0 | 180.5 |
| 2016 | 180.0 | 179.4 | 179.3 | 181.8 | 183.1 | 182.9 | 183.7 | 183.7 | 181.2 | 182.6 | 186.1 | 187.0 | 182.6 |
| 2017 | 180.6 | 179.4 | 178.9 | 181.3 | 182.1 | 182.7 | 182.1 | 181.6 | 179.7 | 180.9 | 184.9 | 185.3 | 181.6 |
| 2018 | 178.7 | 177.0 | 176.1 | 177.9 | 179.5 | 180.1 | 179.3 | 178.3 | 176.1 | 177.0 | 182.0 | 181.7 | 178.6 |
| 2019 | 176.0 | 173.1 | 173.1 | 173.9 | 174.7 | 175.0 | 174.8 | 173.9 | 172.8 | 174.9 | 178.3 | 178.3 | 174.9 |
| **Transportation and Utilities** | | | | | | | | | | | | | |
| 2011 | 60.1 | 60.3 | 60.7 | 61.3 | 61.9 | 62.2 | 61.7 | 62.1 | 62.2 | 62.2 | 62.6 | 63.3 | 61.7 |
| 2012 | 61.1 | 61.1 | 61.5 | 62.0 | 62.6 | 63.3 | 63.1 | 63.4 | 63.7 | 63.7 | 64.0 | 65.0 | 62.9 |
| 2013 | 62.7 | 62.8 | 63.2 | 63.1 | 63.8 | 64.3 | 64.2 | 64.2 | 64.3 | 64.2 | 64.9 | 66.0 | 64.0 |
| 2014 | 63.1 | 63.0 | 63.5 | 64.3 | 64.6 | 65.4 | 65.2 | 65.6 | 66.1 | 66.2 | 67.0 | 68.9 | 65.2 |
| 2015 | 66.6 | 66.4 | 66.6 | 65.6 | 65.8 | 66.7 | 66.8 | 66.6 | 66.8 | 66.6 | 67.3 | 68.5 | 66.7 |
| 2016 | 65.7 | 65.1 | 65.3 | 65.1 | 65.0 | 65.8 | 66.8 | 66.6 | 66.4 | 66.1 | 66.9 | 69.1 | 66.2 |
| 2017 | 65.6 | 65.3 | 65.7 | 65.7 | 65.9 | 66.6 | 66.5 | 66.5 | 66.3 | 66.7 | 67.5 | 69.2 | 66.5 |
| 2018 | 66.2 | 65.7 | 66.1 | 66.5 | 67.2 | 68.1 | 68.0 | 68.2 | 68.1 | 68.5 | 69.7 | 71.2 | 67.8 |
| 2019 | 68.9 | 67.8 | 68.2 | 68.5 | 68.9 | 69.3 | 69.6 | 69.5 | 69.2 | 69.6 | 71.4 | 71.4 | 69.4 |
| **Information** | | | | | | | | | | | | | |
| 2011 | 28.3 | 28.4 | 28.4 | 28.4 | 28.5 | 28.1 | 28.0 | 27.8 | 27.6 | 27.5 | 27.7 | 27.6 | 28.0 |
| 2012 | 27.3 | 27.5 | 27.6 | 27.3 | 27.2 | 27.2 | 26.9 | 26.6 | 26.3 | 26.6 | 26.8 | 26.6 | 27.0 |
| 2013 | 26.1 | 26.5 | 26.6 | 26.5 | 26.6 | 26.4 | 26.2 | 26.1 | 25.8 | 25.6 | 25.7 | 25.8 | 26.2 |
| 2014 | 25.9 | 25.9 | 26.0 | 26.2 | 26.2 | 26.0 | 25.7 | 25.5 | 25.4 | 25.6 | 25.3 | 25.5 | 25.8 |
| 2015 | 25.1 | 25.3 | 25.2 | 25.1 | 25.2 | 25.0 | 24.2 | 23.9 | 23.4 | 23.6 | 23.6 | 23.3 | 24.4 |
| 2016 | 23.1 | 23.1 | 22.8 | 22.8 | 22.8 | 22.8 | 22.9 | 22.7 | 22.4 | 22.3 | 22.2 | 22.2 | 22.7 |
| 2017 | 22.1 | 22.0 | 22.0 | 22.0 | 22.1 | 22.3 | 22.4 | 22.3 | 22.1 | 22.0 | 22.1 | 22.1 | 22.1 |
| 2018 | 22.0 | 22.1 | 22.1 | 22.1 | 22.1 | 22.3 | 22.2 | 22.1 | 22.0 | 21.9 | 21.9 | 21.9 | 22.1 |
| 2019 | 21.7 | 21.7 | 21.6 | 21.5 | 21.4 | 21.5 | 21.3 | 21.2 | 20.8 | 20.9 | 20.9 | 21.1 | 21.3 |

# 1. Employment by Industry: Iowa, 2011–2019—*Continued*

(Numbers in thousands, not seasonally adjusted)

| Industry and year | January | February | March | April | May | June | July | August | September | October | November | December | Annual average |
|---|---|---|---|---|---|---|---|---|---|---|---|---|---|
| **Financial Activities** | | | | | | | | | | | | | |
| 2011 | 101.0 | 100.6 | 100.6 | 100.7 | 100.9 | 101.2 | 101.5 | 101.7 | 100.8 | 100.5 | 100.8 | 101.3 | 101.0 |
| 2012 | 100.5 | 100.3 | 100.8 | 101.4 | 101.9 | 102.8 | 102.8 | 102.6 | 102.0 | 102.4 | 102.6 | 103.3 | 102.0 |
| 2013 | 102.8 | 102.7 | 102.9 | 103.5 | 103.9 | 104.6 | 104.7 | 104.6 | 103.9 | 104.3 | 104.6 | 104.9 | 104.0 |
| 2014 | 103.7 | 103.5 | 103.6 | 103.8 | 103.9 | 105.0 | 104.7 | 105.0 | 104.2 | 104.4 | 104.4 | 105.0 | 104.3 |
| 2015 | 104.2 | 104.2 | 104.8 | 105.1 | 105.6 | 106.7 | 106.8 | 106.8 | 106.2 | 106.4 | 106.8 | 107.8 | 106.0 |
| 2016 | 107.5 | 107.5 | 107.7 | 107.8 | 108.1 | 108.9 | 109.5 | 109.1 | 108.6 | 108.6 | 108.6 | 109.4 | 108.4 |
| 2017 | 108.5 | 108.4 | 108.5 | 108.9 | 109.3 | 110.3 | 110.6 | 110.3 | 109.4 | 109.4 | 109.4 | 110.2 | 109.4 |
| 2018 | 109.7 | 109.4 | 109.1 | 109.1 | 109.9 | 110.6 | 111.1 | 110.8 | 109.8 | 110.0 | 110.1 | 110.4 | 110.0 |
| 2019 | 109.0 | 108.9 | 109.1 | 109.4 | 109.9 | 110.8 | 111.0 | 110.9 | 109.7 | 109.5 | 108.8 | 109.0 | 109.7 |
| **Professional and Business Services** | | | | | | | | | | | | | |
| 2011 | 121.6 | 121.8 | 121.6 | 125.1 | 124.2 | 124.9 | 127.2 | 127.7 | 128.2 | 129.3 | 129.1 | 127.5 | 125.7 |
| 2012 | 124.9 | 125.9 | 127.5 | 129.8 | 129.4 | 131.4 | 132.5 | 132.4 | 132.1 | 132.3 | 131.4 | 129.7 | 129.9 |
| 2013 | 127.0 | 127.7 | 128.5 | 131.2 | 131.4 | 133.4 | 134.0 | 135.0 | 134.2 | 135.2 | 135.6 | 134.8 | 132.3 |
| 2014 | 131.3 | 132.3 | 131.9 | 136.2 | 137.0 | 138.2 | 138.8 | 139.8 | 138.3 | 139.7 | 138.9 | 137.6 | 136.7 |
| 2015 | 134.7 | 135.2 | 135.7 | 139.1 | 139.7 | 141.1 | 140.7 | 141.3 | 138.9 | 139.8 | 139.4 | 137.5 | 138.6 |
| 2016 | 134.2 | 135.1 | 134.9 | 139.3 | 138.3 | 139.0 | 141.2 | 140.9 | 139.9 | 140.9 | 140.1 | 138.2 | 138.5 |
| 2017 | 133.6 | 135.1 | 135.3 | 140.2 | 139.4 | 141.1 | 141.2 | 141.2 | 139.9 | 139.9 | 140.0 | 138.3 | 138.8 |
| 2018 | 135.9 | 137.3 | 136.8 | 139.3 | 140.0 | 141.0 | 142.3 | 141.7 | 140.5 | 141.0 | 140.8 | 138.2 | 139.6 |
| 2019 | 136.4 | 137.2 | 136.2 | 140.3 | 139.8 | 141.0 | 141.6 | 141.4 | 139.5 | 141.1 | 140.2 | 137.0 | 139.3 |
| **Education and Health Services** | | | | | | | | | | | | | |
| 2011 | 215.6 | 218.0 | 219.1 | 221.5 | 218.6 | 211.3 | 205.6 | 206.0 | 216.6 | 224.0 | 225.0 | 225.2 | 217.2 |
| 2012 | 219.6 | 222.8 | 224.2 | 223.8 | 221.6 | 214.2 | 208.4 | 209.6 | 218.5 | 225.5 | 226.8 | 226.1 | 220.1 |
| 2013 | 221.5 | 223.6 | 224.2 | 223.8 | 223.5 | 215.7 | 214.3 | 215.0 | 223.8 | 225.0 | 225.8 | 226.1 | 221.9 |
| 2014 | 220.3 | 223.5 | 225.7 | 226.5 | 225.1 | 218.2 | 214.8 | 215.3 | 223.7 | 226.6 | 227.1 | 227.5 | 222.9 |
| 2015 | 222.4 | 225.1 | 226.8 | 228.6 | 226.8 | 220.5 | 219.3 | 219.8 | 227.5 | 230.7 | 231.0 | 231.5 | 225.8 |
| 2016 | 227.3 | 231.3 | 232.7 | 234.7 | 232.5 | 223.2 | 221.8 | 222.2 | 230.9 | 234.8 | 235.3 | 234.1 | 230.1 |
| 2017 | 229.0 | 235.1 | 235.7 | 236.6 | 234.9 | 227.7 | 224.6 | 225.7 | 233.2 | 237.8 | 238.2 | 237.7 | 233.0 |
| 2018 | 233.3 | 238.4 | 238.7 | 239.0 | 238.3 | 229.8 | 225.4 | 226.4 | 235.5 | 238.7 | 239.0 | 237.7 | 235.0 |
| 2019 | 233.7 | 240.2 | 239.7 | 239.5 | 237.5 | 229.1 | 225.0 | 226.6 | 235.6 | 238.4 | 239.3 | 238.0 | 235.2 |
| **Leisure and Hospitality** | | | | | | | | | | | | | |
| 2011 | 122.1 | 122.2 | 124.9 | 131.7 | 136.4 | 139.6 | 138.7 | 139.8 | 136.5 | 131.1 | 129.4 | 127.9 | 131.7 |
| 2012 | 124.0 | 125.4 | 128.3 | 133.7 | 138.8 | 141.9 | 142.5 | 142.6 | 138.2 | 133.3 | 131.8 | 130.8 | 134.3 |
| 2013 | 126.4 | 127.9 | 130.0 | 135.3 | 140.7 | 144.5 | 144.9 | 145.2 | 140.4 | 135.5 | 134.1 | 132.2 | 136.4 |
| 2014 | 128.8 | 130.1 | 132.1 | 136.8 | 142.7 | 145.8 | 145.0 | 145.7 | 141.8 | 137.1 | 135.5 | 134.5 | 138.0 |
| 2015 | 130.8 | 132.3 | 134.8 | 139.4 | 145.4 | 148.8 | 148.6 | 148.8 | 144.1 | 140.8 | 138.9 | 137.5 | 140.9 |
| 2016 | 133.1 | 134.6 | 137.3 | 142.7 | 147.1 | 150.4 | 150.0 | 150.2 | 145.3 | 142.6 | 140.7 | 137.9 | 142.7 |
| 2017 | 134.5 | 136.1 | 138.0 | 142.7 | 146.8 | 150.8 | 150.3 | 150.3 | 145.9 | 143.3 | 140.7 | 138.7 | 143.2 |
| 2018 | 134.8 | 136.8 | 138.4 | 142.9 | 148.9 | 151.8 | 151.7 | 151.1 | 145.8 | 144.3 | 140.7 | 139.8 | 143.9 |
| 2019 | 136.3 | 136.2 | 138.0 | 143.7 | 148.4 | 151.9 | 152.1 | 152.1 | 146.3 | 145.4 | 141.1 | 141.4 | 144.4 |
| **Other Services** | | | | | | | | | | | | | |
| 2011 | 56.2 | 56.1 | 56.4 | 56.5 | 56.7 | 57.1 | 57.1 | 57.1 | 56.9 | 57.0 | 56.8 | 57.0 | 56.7 |
| 2012 | 56.9 | 56.7 | 57.1 | 57.6 | 58.0 | 58.5 | 58.2 | 58.4 | 57.7 | 58.1 | 58.2 | 57.8 | 57.8 |
| 2013 | 57.2 | 57.2 | 57.3 | 57.6 | 58.2 | 58.6 | 58.9 | 59.1 | 58.3 | 58.6 | 58.5 | 58.6 | 58.2 |
| 2014 | 58.2 | 58.2 | 58.6 | 58.8 | 59.5 | 60.0 | 59.8 | 59.7 | 59.1 | 59.1 | 59.2 | 58.9 | 59.1 |
| 2015 | 58.6 | 58.5 | 58.9 | 59.0 | 59.3 | 59.9 | 59.6 | 59.4 | 59.0 | 59.3 | 59.1 | 59.3 | 59.2 |
| 2016 | 58.6 | 58.5 | 58.6 | 58.6 | 58.9 | 59.5 | 59.6 | 59.1 | 58.7 | 58.3 | 58.0 | 57.6 | 58.7 |
| 2017 | 57.0 | 57.1 | 57.2 | 57.3 | 57.7 | 58.5 | 58.2 | 57.7 | 57.2 | 57.1 | 57.1 | 57.4 | 57.5 |
| 2018 | 56.6 | 56.7 | 57.1 | 57.2 | 57.6 | 58.6 | 58.3 | 57.7 | 57.2 | 57.5 | 57.4 | 57.6 | 57.5 |
| 2019 | 56.8 | 56.7 | 57.2 | 57.5 | 58.1 | 59.2 | 59.4 | 59.3 | 58.6 | 58.9 | 59.5 | 58.8 | 58.3 |
| **Government** | | | | | | | | | | | | | |
| 2011 | 249.5 | 255.5 | 256.5 | 257.9 | 259.2 | 255.3 | 235.9 | 236.4 | 254.0 | 257.8 | 258.8 | 258.2 | 252.9 |
| 2012 | 251.6 | 256.1 | 256.8 | 258.3 | 259.9 | 254.4 | 234.6 | 239.4 | 254.4 | 258.3 | 259.8 | 259.2 | 253.6 |
| 2013 | 250.1 | 256.5 | 257.0 | 257.4 | 260.8 | 256.3 | 238.8 | 241.8 | 256.9 | 259.5 | 260.9 | 260.3 | 254.7 |
| 2014 | 252.6 | 257.6 | 258.2 | 258.8 | 260.6 | 254.3 | 236.0 | 239.0 | 258.5 | 261.2 | 262.6 | 261.3 | 255.1 |
| 2015 | 254.7 | 259.5 | 259.4 | 259.8 | 261.2 | 255.7 | 236.4 | 237.0 | 255.3 | 261.3 | 262.9 | 262.6 | 255.5 |
| 2016 | 255.8 | 260.9 | 260.9 | 262.0 | 263.0 | 258.9 | 237.4 | 241.0 | 258.8 | 263.4 | 265.1 | 264.3 | 257.6 |
| 2017 | 259.6 | 263.1 | 263.5 | 264.4 | 264.4 | 261.5 | 241.9 | 245.9 | 260.9 | 265.0 | 266.1 | 264.9 | 260.1 |
| 2018 | 260.5 | 263.9 | 263.7 | 264.9 | 265.4 | 262.5 | 242.3 | 245.6 | 260.4 | 265.3 | 267.4 | 265.8 | 260.6 |
| 2019 | 259.0 | 263.2 | 264.6 | 265.8 | 266.8 | 259.1 | 241.1 | 243.9 | 261.6 | 266.8 | 268.3 | 265.9 | 260.5 |

## 2. Average Weekly Hours by Selected Industry: Iowa, 2015–2019

(Not seasonally adjusted)

| Industry and year | January | February | March | April | May | June | July | August | September | October | November | December | Annual average |
|---|---|---|---|---|---|---|---|---|---|---|---|---|---|
| **Total Private** | | | | | | | | | | | | | |
| 2015 | 34.2 | 34.8 | 34.7 | 34.7 | 34.6 | 34.8 | 34.9 | 35.3 | 34.5 | 34.8 | 34.7 | 34.3 | 34.7 |
| 2016 | 33.8 | 33.8 | 34.0 | 34.4 | 34.6 | 35.1 | 34.8 | 34.8 | 34.7 | 35.1 | 34.7 | 34.2 | 34.5 |
| 2017 | 34.1 | 34.0 | 33.8 | 34.6 | 34.2 | 34.6 | 34.5 | 34.4 | 34.4 | 34.6 | 34.7 | 34.3 | 34.4 |
| 2018 | 33.6 | 33.7 | 33.9 | 34.2 | 34.4 | 34.7 | 34.9 | 34.5 | 34.8 | 34.7 | 34.6 | 34.7 | 34.4 |
| 2019 | 33.9 | 33.8 | 33.9 | 34.3 | 34.3 | 35.2 | 34.6 | 34.6 | 34.6 | 34.1 | 34.0 | 34.1 | 34.3 |
| **Goods-Producing** | | | | | | | | | | | | | |
| 2015 | 40.3 | 40.5 | 40.6 | 41.1 | 40.9 | 41.1 | 41.1 | 41.8 | 40.0 | 41.7 | 41.3 | 41.3 | 41.0 |
| 2016 | 39.3 | 39.9 | 40.6 | 41.5 | 41.2 | 42.9 | 41.8 | 41.8 | 41.8 | 42.2 | 42.7 | 40.6 | 41.4 |
| 2017 | 39.6 | 40.0 | 40.0 | 40.4 | 40.4 | 40.9 | 40.5 | 40.6 | 40.7 | 40.8 | 41.0 | 40.4 | 40.5 |
| 2018 | 38.9 | 39.2 | 39.4 | 39.8 | 40.3 | 40.7 | 40.9 | 40.3 | 41.2 | 40.2 | 40.0 | 40.3 | 40.1 |
| 2019 | 39.5 | 38.6 | 38.9 | 39.7 | 39.8 | 41.3 | 40.6 | 40.7 | 40.1 | 40.0 | 39.4 | 39.4 | 39.9 |
| **Construction** | | | | | | | | | | | | | |
| 2015 | 38.6 | 38.7 | 39.3 | 40.8 | 40.9 | 41.5 | 42.1 | 43.1 | 39.1 | 42.2 | 41.9 | 40.8 | 40.8 |
| 2016 | 36.8 | 36.2 | 39.4 | 42.0 | 41.0 | 44.0 | 41.4 | 42.1 | 41.7 | 42.3 | 40.8 | 38.5 | 40.7 |
| 2017 | 36.9 | 37.4 | 37.5 | 39.5 | 39.5 | 40.7 | 40.3 | 40.7 | 40.5 | 38.8 | 39.7 | 38.1 | 39.2 |
| 2018 | 34.9 | 35.6 | 37.0 | 38.3 | 40.0 | 40.1 | 40.8 | 40.1 | 42.0 | 38.2 | 39.0 | 39.8 | 39.0 |
| 2019 | 37.6 | 35.0 | 36.2 | 38.9 | 38.8 | 42.6 | 42.6 | 42.5 | 41.0 | 40.7 | 39.7 | 40.6 | 39.9 |
| **Manufacturing** | | | | | | | | | | | | | |
| 2015 | 41.1 | 41.4 | 41.4 | 41.6 | 41.2 | 41.2 | 40.9 | 41.4 | 40.7 | 41.7 | 41.2 | 41.2 | 41.2 |
| 2016 | 40.1 | 40.4 | 40.3 | 40.3 | 40.1 | 40.3 | 40.1 | 40.0 | 39.9 | 40.3 | 41.3 | 40.4 | 40.3 |
| 2017 | 39.5 | 40.0 | 40.1 | 40.1 | 40.2 | 40.4 | 39.8 | 39.8 | 40.2 | 41.2 | 40.8 | 40.6 | 40.2 |
| 2018 | 39.6 | 39.8 | 39.7 | 39.8 | 39.7 | 39.9 | 39.9 | 39.4 | 39.8 | 40.5 | 39.8 | 39.9 | 39.8 |
| 2019 | 39.8 | 39.6 | 39.7 | 39.7 | 39.9 | 40.2 | 39.2 | 39.4 | 39.4 | 39.5 | 39.1 | 38.8 | 39.5 |
| **Trade, Transportation, and Utilities** | | | | | | | | | | | | | |
| 2015 | 31.7 | 32.2 | 31.8 | 31.9 | 32.1 | 32.5 | 32.5 | 32.8 | 33.0 | 32.5 | 32.1 | 31.8 | 32.2 |
| 2016 | 31.8 | 31.8 | 31.7 | 32.0 | 32.2 | 32.5 | 32.3 | 32.2 | 32.3 | 32.4 | 31.9 | 32.1 | 32.1 |
| 2017 | 32.4 | 32.1 | 32.3 | 33.0 | 32.7 | 33.0 | 32.9 | 32.8 | 32.7 | 32.6 | 32.9 | 32.5 | 32.7 |
| 2018 | 31.9 | 32.1 | 33.0 | 32.9 | 33.7 | 33.8 | 33.8 | 33.4 | 33.2 | 32.8 | 32.6 | 32.5 | 33.0 |
| 2019 | 31.7 | 31.8 | 31.9 | 32.4 | 32.5 | 33.0 | 32.7 | 32.8 | 32.9 | 32.2 | 32.2 | 32.3 | 32.4 |
| **Financial Activities** | | | | | | | | | | | | | |
| 2015 | 38.2 | 39.2 | 39.0 | 38.7 | 38.2 | 38.3 | 38.2 | 38.7 | 38.1 | 38.1 | 39.0 | 37.7 | 38.4 |
| 2016 | 37.9 | 38.0 | 37.7 | 38.0 | 38.8 | 37.9 | 38.0 | 37.8 | 37.8 | 39.0 | 37.7 | 37.5 | 38.0 |
| 2017 | 38.2 | 37.1 | 36.8 | 37.6 | 37.2 | 37.6 | 38.0 | 37.6 | 37.5 | 38.4 | 37.8 | 38.0 | 37.6 |
| 2018 | 38.2 | 38.1 | 37.8 | 38.6 | 37.9 | 38.1 | 38.5 | 38.0 | 38.7 | 38.1 | 38.1 | 38.6 | 38.2 |
| 2019 | 38.3 | 38.5 | 38.5 | 38.3 | 38.3 | 39.0 | 38.4 | 38.3 | 38.9 | 38.2 | 38.8 | 39.2 | 38.6 |
| **Professional and Business Services** | | | | | | | | | | | | | |
| 2015 | 34.9 | 36.1 | 36.2 | 35.9 | 35.9 | 35.7 | 36.3 | 36.7 | 35.3 | 36.1 | 36.2 | 35.8 | 35.9 |
| 2016 | 35.1 | 34.9 | 35.1 | 35.9 | 35.9 | 35.8 | 35.6 | 35.7 | 35.4 | 36.1 | 35.0 | 34.7 | 35.4 |
| 2017 | 34.5 | 34.6 | 34.4 | 35.1 | 34.8 | 35.1 | 35.4 | 35.2 | 35.2 | 35.0 | 35.2 | 34.6 | 34.9 |
| 2018 | 33.9 | 34.3 | 34.5 | 35.1 | 35.5 | 35.6 | 35.9 | 35.5 | 36.2 | 35.4 | 35.3 | 34.3 | 35.1 |
| 2019 | 34.4 | 34.6 | 34.8 | 35.1 | 35.0 | 36.1 | 35.2 | 34.5 | 35.1 | 34.6 | 34.5 | 34.5 | 34.9 |
| **Education and Health Services** | | | | | | | | | | | | | |
| 2015 | 31.8 | 31.9 | 31.7 | 31.6 | 31.6 | 31.9 | 32.3 | 32.5 | 32.1 | 31.9 | 32.3 | 31.7 | 31.9 |
| 2016 | 32.0 | 31.4 | 31.3 | 31.8 | 32.0 | 32.2 | 32.0 | 32.0 | 32.2 | 32.3 | 32.5 | 32.3 | 32.0 |
| 2017 | 32.5 | 31.9 | 31.2 | 32.1 | 31.3 | 31.5 | 31.9 | 31.3 | 31.6 | 31.6 | 31.6 | 31.2 | 31.6 |
| 2018 | 31.1 | 30.6 | 30.6 | 31.5 | 30.8 | 31.1 | 31.8 | 31.2 | 31.3 | 30.9 | 30.9 | 31.2 | 31.1 |
| 2019 | 30.5 | 30.5 | 30.4 | 30.8 | 30.9 | 31.7 | 31.4 | 31.7 | 31.6 | 31.3 | 31.4 | 31.6 | 31.1 |
| **Leisure and Hospitality** | | | | | | | | | | | | | |
| 2015 | 23.5 | 24.7 | 24.8 | 24.2 | 24.4 | 24.8 | 25.2 | 25.7 | 24.5 | 24.3 | 24.1 | 23.8 | 24.5 |
| 2016 | 23.4 | 23.7 | 24.0 | 23.7 | 24.1 | 24.7 | 24.7 | 24.7 | 24.2 | 24.4 | 23.9 | 23.8 | 24.1 |
| 2017 | 23.7 | 23.9 | 23.7 | 24.3 | 23.8 | 24.5 | 24.5 | 24.1 | 23.7 | 24.2 | 23.9 | 24.0 | 24.0 |
| 2018 | 23.2 | 23.4 | 23.8 | 23.8 | 24.2 | 24.6 | 24.8 | 24.0 | 23.7 | 23.5 | 23.4 | 23.9 | 23.9 |
| 2019 | 22.7 | 22.7 | 23.0 | 23.5 | 23.2 | 24.0 | 24.0 | 23.7 | 23.6 | 23.1 | 22.9 | 22.6 | 23.3 |
| **Other Services** | | | | | | | | | | | | | |
| 2015 | 30.0 | 30.5 | 29.4 | 28.7 | 28.7 | 29.2 | 29.6 | 29.4 | 28.5 | 28.3 | 26.9 | 26.9 | 28.8 |
| 2016 | 26.8 | 25.9 | 26.5 | 25.8 | 27.1 | 28.5 | 28.2 | 28.7 | 28.7 | 28.6 | 29.3 | 29.4 | 27.8 |
| 2017 | 29.1 | 29.2 | 28.1 | 28.1 | 28.6 | 30.2 | 30.1 | 30.1 | 29.9 | 30.6 | 30.3 | 30.7 | 29.6 |
| 2018 | 30.1 | 30.6 | 30.6 | 30.7 | 30.8 | 31.8 | 31.0 | 31.7 | 31.5 | 31.2 | 31.6 | 31.8 | 31.1 |
| 2019 | 31.2 | 31.0 | 31.3 | 32.8 | 31.7 | 33.4 | 31.7 | 32.5 | 32.1 | 31.0 | 31.1 | 31.3 | 31.8 |

# 3. Average Hourly Earnings by Selected Industry: Iowa, 2015–2019

(Dollars, not seasonally adjusted)

| Industry and year | January | February | March | April | May | June | July | August | September | October | November | December | Annual average |
|---|---|---|---|---|---|---|---|---|---|---|---|---|---|
| **Total Private** | | | | | | | | | | | | | |
| 2015 | 21.91 | 22.12 | 22.21 | 22.32 | 22.43 | 22.18 | 22.27 | 22.90 | 22.90 | 23.33 | 23.00 | 23.04 | 22.55 |
| 2016 | 23.11 | 23.01 | 23.23 | 23.42 | 23.35 | 23.11 | 23.07 | 22.90 | 23.01 | 23.33 | 23.04 | 23.12 | 23.14 |
| 2017 | 23.17 | 23.07 | 23.24 | 23.29 | 22.95 | 22.84 | 23.21 | 23.07 | 23.31 | 23.34 | 23.51 | 23.69 | 23.22 |
| 2018 | 23.69 | 23.50 | 23.61 | 23.70 | 23.63 | 23.68 | 23.89 | 23.92 | 24.42 | 24.24 | 24.26 | 24.46 | 23.92 |
| 2019 | 24.37 | 24.61 | 24.41 | 24.49 | 24.55 | 24.49 | 24.64 | 24.77 | 25.12 | 25.04 | 25.11 | 25.28 | 24.74 |
| **Goods-Producing** | | | | | | | | | | | | | |
| 2015 | 23.17 | 23.55 | 23.55 | 23.56 | 23.64 | 23.54 | 23.92 | 24.19 | 24.10 | 24.89 | 24.72 | 24.54 | 23.96 |
| 2016 | 24.62 | 24.53 | 24.75 | 25.15 | 25.26 | 25.09 | 24.76 | 24.59 | 24.67 | 25.06 | 24.48 | 24.87 | 24.82 |
| 2017 | 24.78 | 24.25 | 24.45 | 24.50 | 23.99 | 24.06 | 24.54 | 24.19 | 24.36 | 24.29 | 24.60 | 24.94 | 24.41 |
| 2018 | 24.40 | 24.37 | 24.54 | 24.86 | 24.96 | 25.28 | 25.85 | 25.59 | 25.82 | 25.62 | 25.89 | 26.21 | 25.31 |
| 2019 | 25.75 | 25.99 | 26.08 | 25.93 | 26.31 | 26.18 | 26.47 | 26.53 | 26.50 | 26.55 | 26.71 | 26.93 | 26.33 |
| **Construction** | | | | | | | | | | | | | |
| 2015 | 26.04 | 25.94 | 26.12 | 25.31 | 25.04 | 25.40 | 25.23 | 25.80 | 26.14 | 26.74 | 26.79 | 27.17 | 25.97 |
| 2016 | 26.95 | 26.88 | 26.34 | 27.16 | 26.53 | 26.24 | 25.62 | 25.16 | 25.23 | 25.48 | 25.25 | 25.50 | 25.97 |
| 2017 | 25.15 | 25.10 | 25.15 | 24.39 | 24.42 | 24.11 | 24.59 | 24.49 | 24.76 | 24.90 | 25.09 | 25.20 | 24.75 |
| 2018 | 25.21 | 25.52 | 25.13 | 26.19 | 26.25 | 27.02 | 27.55 | 27.33 | 27.58 | 27.57 | 28.05 | 28.29 | 26.92 |
| 2019 | 27.63 | 28.11 | 28.16 | 27.35 | 27.76 | 27.36 | 27.65 | 27.51 | 27.05 | 27.65 | 27.76 | 28.19 | 27.65 |
| **Manufacturing** | | | | | | | | | | | | | |
| 2015 | 22.11 | 22.66 | 22.61 | 22.77 | 22.91 | 22.61 | 23.21 | 23.44 | 23.20 | 23.79 | 23.28 | 22.94 | 22.96 |
| 2016 | 23.14 | 23.14 | 23.43 | 23.82 | 23.95 | 23.68 | 23.61 | 23.25 | 23.46 | 23.95 | 23.29 | 23.86 | 23.55 |
| 2017 | 24.08 | 23.48 | 23.83 | 24.51 | 23.72 | 23.97 | 24.37 | 23.88 | 24.01 | 23.99 | 24.19 | 24.78 | 24.07 |
| 2018 | 24.24 | 24.10 | 24.38 | 24.44 | 24.34 | 24.38 | 24.41 | 24.18 | 24.37 | 24.20 | 24.48 | 24.93 | 24.37 |
| 2019 | 24.55 | 24.79 | 24.90 | 25.04 | 25.08 | 25.22 | 25.40 | 25.45 | 25.65 | 25.33 | 25.59 | 25.77 | 25.23 |
| **Trade, Transportation, and Utilities** | | | | | | | | | | | | | |
| 2015 | 19.22 | 19.55 | 19.56 | 20.11 | 20.23 | 19.53 | 19.80 | 20.68 | 20.62 | 21.14 | 20.57 | 20.95 | 20.17 |
| 2016 | 21.28 | 21.00 | 21.19 | 21.48 | 21.03 | 20.80 | 20.89 | 20.78 | 21.19 | 21.33 | 21.13 | 20.93 | 21.08 |
| 2017 | 21.32 | 21.38 | 21.35 | 21.84 | 21.10 | 20.88 | 21.23 | 21.04 | 21.36 | 21.05 | 21.13 | 21.00 | 21.22 |
| 2018 | 21.63 | 21.42 | 21.52 | 21.48 | 21.50 | 21.49 | 21.43 | 21.51 | 22.39 | 22.10 | 21.90 | 22.26 | 21.72 |
| 2019 | 21.96 | 22.02 | 21.79 | 22.20 | 22.06 | 22.00 | 22.06 | 22.28 | 22.49 | 22.31 | 22.14 | 22.10 | 22.12 |
| **Financial Activities** | | | | | | | | | | | | | |
| 2015 | 27.61 | 27.28 | 27.79 | 28.13 | 28.19 | 27.87 | 27.77 | 28.15 | 28.16 | 28.42 | 28.73 | 28.73 | 28.07 |
| 2016 | 28.84 | 28.89 | 29.64 | 29.70 | 29.96 | 29.43 | 29.47 | 29.23 | 29.57 | 30.16 | 30.24 | 30.00 | 29.60 |
| 2017 | 30.12 | 30.15 | 30.80 | 30.72 | 30.54 | 30.13 | 30.62 | 30.52 | 30.73 | 30.85 | 31.13 | 31.47 | 30.65 |
| 2018 | 31.32 | 31.14 | 31.58 | 31.81 | 31.60 | 31.86 | 32.06 | 31.93 | 32.35 | 31.97 | 32.02 | 32.15 | 31.82 |
| 2019 | 31.99 | 32.09 | 32.32 | 32.73 | 32.58 | 32.57 | 32.91 | 33.30 | 33.91 | 33.91 | 33.81 | 34.23 | 33.03 |
| **Professional and Business Services** | | | | | | | | | | | | | |
| 2015 | 23.12 | 23.64 | 23.52 | 23.05 | 23.68 | 23.72 | 23.94 | 24.33 | 24.44 | 24.57 | 24.73 | 24.54 | 23.95 |
| 2016 | 24.73 | 24.73 | 24.77 | 24.70 | 25.11 | 25.06 | 25.27 | 24.87 | 24.93 | 25.46 | 25.44 | 25.85 | 25.08 |
| 2017 | 25.17 | 25.14 | 25.44 | 25.60 | 25.73 | 25.62 | 25.76 | 25.49 | 25.61 | 26.03 | 25.72 | 26.42 | 25.65 |
| 2018 | 26.08 | 25.79 | 25.92 | 25.78 | 25.72 | 25.58 | 25.71 | 25.73 | 25.87 | 25.46 | 25.27 | 25.90 | 25.73 |
| 2019 | 25.84 | 26.18 | 26.05 | 25.84 | 25.98 | 26.25 | 25.97 | 25.81 | 26.76 | 26.46 | 26.54 | 26.20 | 26.16 |
| **Education and Health Services** | | | | | | | | | | | | | |
| 2015 | 20.20 | 20.40 | 20.68 | 20.69 | 20.74 | 20.92 | 20.55 | 20.68 | 20.88 | 21.09 | 20.97 | 21.19 | 20.75 |
| 2016 | 21.01 | 21.06 | 21.23 | 21.10 | 21.00 | 20.98 | 21.13 | 21.00 | 21.20 | 21.39 | 21.13 | 21.14 | 21.12 |
| 2017 | 21.32 | 21.19 | 21.28 | 21.17 | 21.10 | 21.28 | 21.41 | 21.59 | 21.59 | 21.60 | 21.83 | 21.61 | 21.41 |
| 2018 | 21.63 | 21.31 | 21.25 | 21.19 | 21.23 | 21.03 | 20.91 | 21.13 | 21.25 | 21.06 | 21.25 | 21.06 | 21.19 |
| 2019 | 21.36 | 21.42 | 21.07 | 21.19 | 21.12 | 21.35 | 21.64 | 21.52 | 21.92 | 21.94 | 22.35 | 22.68 | 21.64 |
| **Leisure and Hospitality** | | | | | | | | | | | | | |
| 2015 | 12.72 | 12.61 | 12.30 | 12.43 | 12.47 | 12.19 | 12.22 | 12.49 | 12.46 | 12.60 | 12.79 | 12.95 | 12.51 |
| 2016 | 12.82 | 12.84 | 12.74 | 12.94 | 12.80 | 12.49 | 12.63 | 12.51 | 12.84 | 12.87 | 12.85 | 13.06 | 12.78 |
| 2017 | 12.79 | 13.02 | 12.89 | 12.81 | 12.88 | 12.50 | 12.78 | 12.81 | 13.03 | 13.05 | 13.15 | 13.28 | 12.91 |
| 2018 | 13.52 | 13.48 | 13.46 | 13.51 | 13.50 | 13.27 | 13.33 | 13.46 | 13.77 | 13.88 | 13.92 | 14.08 | 13.59 |
| 2019 | 14.20 | 14.32 | 14.10 | 14.21 | 14.20 | 13.76 | 13.85 | 14.00 | 14.10 | 14.22 | 14.23 | 14.43 | 14.13 |
| **Other Services** | | | | | | | | | | | | | |
| 2015 | 20.57 | 21.11 | 21.09 | 21.14 | 21.37 | 20.48 | 20.50 | 20.61 | 20.56 | 20.61 | 20.07 | 19.97 | 20.68 |
| 2016 | 19.82 | 19.38 | 19.45 | 20.05 | 19.82 | 19.27 | 19.40 | 19.49 | 20.26 | 19.80 | 18.91 | 18.62 | 19.52 |
| 2017 | 18.60 | 19.27 | 19.11 | 19.22 | 18.96 | 18.34 | 18.20 | 18.03 | 18.14 | 18.48 | 18.40 | 18.38 | 18.58 |
| 2018 | 18.41 | 18.58 | 18.67 | 18.81 | 18.97 | 19.08 | 19.39 | 19.71 | 19.65 | 19.52 | 20.33 | 20.60 | 19.32 |
| 2019 | 20.63 | 20.82 | 20.53 | 20.77 | 21.39 | 21.43 | 21.33 | 21.25 | 21.25 | 21.27 | 22.04 | 21.86 | 21.22 |

## 4. Average Weekly Earnings by Selected Industry: Iowa, 2015–2019

(Dollars, not seasonally adjusted)

| Industry and year | January | February | March | April | May | June | July | August | September | October | November | December | Annual average |
|---|---|---|---|---|---|---|---|---|---|---|---|---|---|
| **Total Private** | | | | | | | | | | | | | |
| 2015 | 749.32 | 769.78 | 770.69 | 774.50 | 776.08 | 771.86 | 777.22 | 808.37 | 790.05 | 811.88 | 798.10 | 790.27 | 782.49 |
| 2016 | 781.12 | 777.74 | 789.82 | 807.99 | 807.91 | 811.16 | 802.84 | 796.92 | 798.45 | 818.88 | 799.49 | 790.70 | 798.33 |
| 2017 | 790.10 | 784.38 | 785.51 | 805.83 | 784.89 | 790.26 | 803.07 | 793.61 | 801.86 | 807.56 | 815.80 | 812.57 | 798.77 |
| 2018 | 795.98 | 791.95 | 800.38 | 810.54 | 812.87 | 821.70 | 833.76 | 825.24 | 849.82 | 841.13 | 839.40 | 848.76 | 822.85 |
| 2019 | 826.14 | 831.82 | 827.50 | 840.01 | 842.07 | 862.05 | 852.54 | 857.04 | 869.15 | 853.86 | 853.74 | 862.05 | 848.58 |
| **Goods-Producing** | | | | | | | | | | | | | |
| 2015 | 933.75 | 953.78 | 956.13 | 968.32 | 966.88 | 967.49 | 983.11 | 1,011.14 | 964.00 | 1,037.91 | 1,020.94 | 1,013.50 | 982.36 |
| 2016 | 967.57 | 978.75 | 1,004.85 | 1,043.73 | 1,040.71 | 1,076.36 | 1,034.97 | 1,027.86 | 1,031.21 | 1,057.53 | 1,045.30 | 1,009.72 | 1,027.55 |
| 2017 | 981.29 | 970.00 | 978.00 | 989.80 | 969.20 | 984.05 | 993.87 | 982.11 | 991.45 | 991.03 | 1,008.60 | 1,007.58 | 988.61 |
| 2018 | 949.16 | 955.30 | 966.88 | 989.43 | 1,005.89 | 1,028.90 | 1,057.27 | 1,031.28 | 1,063.78 | 1,029.92 | 1,035.60 | 1,056.26 | 1,014.93 |
| 2019 | 1,017.13 | 1,003.21 | 1,014.51 | 1,029.42 | 1,047.14 | 1,081.23 | 1,074.68 | 1,079.77 | 1,062.65 | 1,062.00 | 1,052.37 | 1,061.04 | 1,050.57 |
| **Construction** | | | | | | | | | | | | | |
| 2015 | 1,005.14 | 1,003.88 | 1,026.52 | 1,032.65 | 1,024.14 | 1,054.10 | 1,062.17 | 1,111.98 | 1,022.07 | 1,128.43 | 1,122.50 | 1,108.54 | 1,059.58 |
| 2016 | 991.76 | 973.06 | 1,037.80 | 1,140.72 | 1,087.73 | 1,154.56 | 1,060.67 | 1,059.24 | 1,052.09 | 1,077.80 | 1,030.20 | 981.75 | 1,056.98 |
| 2017 | 928.04 | 938.74 | 943.13 | 963.41 | 964.59 | 981.28 | 990.98 | 996.74 | 1,002.78 | 966.12 | 996.07 | 960.12 | 970.20 |
| 2018 | 879.83 | 908.51 | 929.81 | 1,003.08 | 1,050.00 | 1,083.50 | 1,124.04 | 1,095.93 | 1,158.36 | 1,053.17 | 1,093.95 | 1,125.94 | 1,049.88 |
| 2019 | 1,038.89 | 983.85 | 1,019.39 | 1,063.92 | 1,077.09 | 1,165.54 | 1,177.89 | 1,169.18 | 1,109.05 | 1,125.36 | 1,102.07 | 1,144.51 | 1,103.24 |
| **Manufacturing** | | | | | | | | | | | | | |
| 2015 | 908.72 | 938.12 | 936.05 | 947.23 | 943.89 | 931.53 | 949.29 | 970.42 | 944.24 | 992.04 | 959.14 | 945.13 | 945.95 |
| 2016 | 927.91 | 934.86 | 944.23 | 959.95 | 960.40 | 954.30 | 946.76 | 930.00 | 936.05 | 965.19 | 961.88 | 963.94 | 949.07 |
| 2017 | 951.16 | 939.20 | 955.58 | 982.85 | 953.54 | 968.39 | 969.93 | 950.42 | 965.20 | 988.39 | 986.95 | 1,006.07 | 967.61 |
| 2018 | 959.90 | 959.18 | 967.89 | 972.71 | 966.30 | 972.76 | 973.96 | 952.69 | 969.93 | 980.10 | 974.30 | 994.71 | 969.93 |
| 2019 | 977.09 | 981.68 | 988.53 | 994.09 | 1,000.69 | 1,013.84 | 995.68 | 1,002.73 | 1,010.61 | 1,000.54 | 1,000.57 | 999.88 | 996.59 |
| **Trade, Transportation, and Utilities** | | | | | | | | | | | | | |
| 2015 | 609.27 | 629.51 | 622.01 | 641.51 | 649.38 | 634.73 | 643.50 | 678.30 | 680.46 | 687.05 | 660.30 | 666.21 | 649.47 |
| 2016 | 676.70 | 667.80 | 671.72 | 687.36 | 677.17 | 676.00 | 674.75 | 669.12 | 684.44 | 691.09 | 674.05 | 671.85 | 676.67 |
| 2017 | 690.77 | 686.30 | 689.61 | 720.72 | 689.97 | 689.04 | 698.47 | 690.11 | 698.47 | 686.23 | 695.18 | 682.50 | 693.89 |
| 2018 | 690.00 | 687.58 | 710.16 | 706.69 | 724.55 | 726.36 | 724.33 | 718.43 | 743.35 | 724.88 | 713.94 | 723.45 | 716.76 |
| 2019 | 696.13 | 700.24 | 695.10 | 719.28 | 716.95 | 726.00 | 721.36 | 730.78 | 739.92 | 718.38 | 712.91 | 713.83 | 716.69 |
| **Financial Activities** | | | | | | | | | | | | | |
| 2015 | 1,054.70 | 1,069.38 | 1,083.81 | 1,088.63 | 1,076.86 | 1,067.42 | 1,060.81 | 1,089.41 | 1,072.90 | 1,082.80 | 1,120.47 | 1,083.12 | 1,077.89 |
| 2016 | 1,093.04 | 1,097.82 | 1,117.43 | 1,128.60 | 1,162.45 | 1,115.40 | 1,119.86 | 1,104.89 | 1,117.75 | 1,176.24 | 1,140.05 | 1,125.00 | 1,124.80 |
| 2017 | 1,150.58 | 1,118.57 | 1,133.44 | 1,155.07 | 1,136.09 | 1,132.89 | 1,163.56 | 1,147.55 | 1,152.38 | 1,184.64 | 1,176.71 | 1,195.86 | 1,152.44 |
| 2018 | 1,196.42 | 1,186.43 | 1,193.72 | 1,227.87 | 1,197.64 | 1,213.87 | 1,234.31 | 1,213.34 | 1,251.95 | 1,218.06 | 1,219.96 | 1,240.99 | 1,215.52 |
| 2019 | 1,225.22 | 1,235.47 | 1,244.32 | 1,253.56 | 1,247.81 | 1,270.23 | 1,263.74 | 1,275.39 | 1,319.10 | 1,295.36 | 1,311.83 | 1,341.82 | 1,274.96 |
| **Professional and Business Services** | | | | | | | | | | | | | |
| 2015 | 806.89 | 853.40 | 851.42 | 827.50 | 850.11 | 846.80 | 869.02 | 892.91 | 862.73 | 886.98 | 895.23 | 878.53 | 859.81 |
| 2016 | 868.02 | 863.08 | 869.43 | 886.73 | 901.45 | 897.15 | 899.61 | 887.86 | 882.52 | 919.11 | 890.40 | 897.00 | 887.83 |
| 2017 | 868.37 | 869.84 | 875.48 | 898.56 | 895.75 | 899.26 | 911.90 | 897.60 | 901.47 | 911.05 | 905.34 | 914.13 | 895.19 |
| 2018 | 884.11 | 884.60 | 894.24 | 904.88 | 913.06 | 910.65 | 922.99 | 913.42 | 936.49 | 901.28 | 892.03 | 888.37 | 903.12 |
| 2019 | 888.90 | 905.83 | 906.54 | 906.98 | 909.30 | 947.63 | 914.14 | 890.45 | 939.28 | 915.52 | 915.63 | 903.90 | 912.98 |
| **Education and Health Services** | | | | | | | | | | | | | |
| 2015 | 642.36 | 650.76 | 655.56 | 653.80 | 655.38 | 667.35 | 663.77 | 672.10 | 670.25 | 672.77 | 677.33 | 671.72 | 661.93 |
| 2016 | 672.32 | 661.28 | 664.50 | 670.98 | 672.00 | 675.56 | 676.16 | 672.00 | 682.64 | 690.90 | 686.73 | 682.82 | 675.84 |
| 2017 | 692.90 | 675.96 | 663.94 | 679.56 | 660.43 | 670.32 | 682.98 | 675.77 | 682.24 | 682.56 | 689.83 | 674.23 | 676.56 |
| 2018 | 672.69 | 652.09 | 650.25 | 667.49 | 653.88 | 654.03 | 664.94 | 659.26 | 665.13 | 650.75 | 656.63 | 657.07 | 659.01 |
| 2019 | 651.48 | 653.31 | 640.53 | 652.65 | 652.61 | 676.80 | 679.50 | 682.18 | 692.67 | 686.72 | 701.79 | 716.69 | 673.00 |
| **Leisure and Hospitality** | | | | | | | | | | | | | |
| 2015 | 298.92 | 311.47 | 305.04 | 300.81 | 304.27 | 302.31 | 307.94 | 320.99 | 305.27 | 306.18 | 308.24 | 308.21 | 306.50 |
| 2016 | 299.99 | 304.31 | 305.76 | 306.68 | 308.48 | 308.50 | 311.96 | 309.00 | 310.73 | 314.03 | 307.12 | 310.83 | 308.00 |
| 2017 | 303.12 | 311.18 | 305.49 | 311.28 | 306.54 | 306.25 | 313.11 | 308.72 | 308.81 | 315.81 | 314.29 | 318.72 | 309.84 |
| 2018 | 313.66 | 315.43 | 320.35 | 321.54 | 326.70 | 326.44 | 330.58 | 323.04 | 326.35 | 326.18 | 325.73 | 336.51 | 324.80 |
| 2019 | 322.34 | 325.06 | 324.30 | 333.94 | 329.44 | 330.24 | 332.40 | 331.80 | 332.76 | 328.48 | 325.87 | 326.12 | 329.23 |
| **Other Services** | | | | | | | | | | | | | |
| 2015 | 617.10 | 643.86 | 620.05 | 606.72 | 613.32 | 598.02 | 606.80 | 605.93 | 585.96 | 583.26 | 539.88 | 537.19 | 595.58 |
| 2016 | 531.18 | 501.94 | 515.43 | 517.29 | 537.12 | 549.20 | 547.08 | 559.36 | 581.46 | 566.28 | 554.06 | 547.43 | 542.66 |
| 2017 | 541.26 | 562.68 | 536.99 | 540.08 | 542.26 | 553.87 | 547.82 | 542.70 | 542.39 | 565.49 | 557.52 | 564.27 | 549.97 |
| 2018 | 554.14 | 568.55 | 571.30 | 577.47 | 584.28 | 606.74 | 601.09 | 624.81 | 618.98 | 609.02 | 642.43 | 655.08 | 600.85 |
| 2019 | 643.66 | 645.42 | 642.59 | 681.26 | 678.06 | 715.76 | 676.16 | 690.63 | 682.13 | 659.37 | 685.44 | 684.22 | 674.80 |

# KANSAS
## *At a Glance*

Population:
  2010 census: 2,853,118
  2019 estimate: 2,913,314

Percent change in population:
  2010–2019: 2.1%

Percent change in total nonfarm employment:
  2011–2019: 6.2%

Industry with the largest growth in employment, 2011–2019 (percent):
  Transportation and utilities, 22.5%

Industry with the largest decline or smallest growth in employment, 2011–2019 (percent):
  Mining and Logging, -25.3%

Civilian labor force:
  2010: 1,500,764
  2019: 1,486,620

Unemployment rate and rank among states (highest to lowest):
  2010: 7.1%, 41st
  2019: 3.2%, 35th

Over-the-year change in unemployment rates:
  2017–2018: -0.3%
  2018–2019: -0.1%

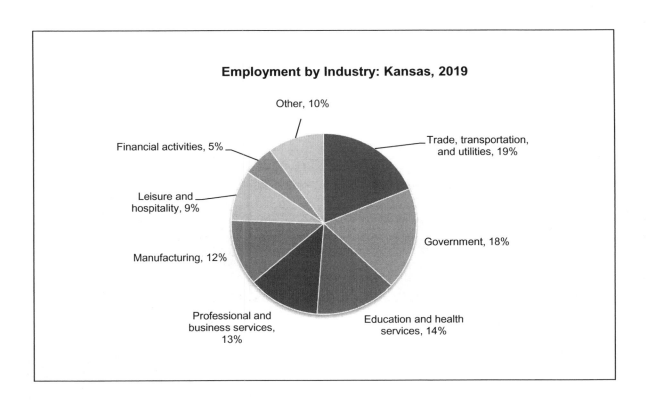

**Employment by Industry: Kansas, 2019**

- Other, 10%
- Trade, transportation, and utilities, 19%
- Financial activities, 5%
- Government, 18%
- Leisure and hospitality, 9%
- Manufacturing, 12%
- Education and health services, 14%
- Professional and business services, 13%

## 1. Employment by Industry: Kansas, 2011–2019

(Numbers in thousands, not seasonally adjusted)

| Industry and year | January | February | March | April | May | June | July | August | September | October | November | December | Annual average |
|---|---|---|---|---|---|---|---|---|---|---|---|---|---|
| **Total Nonfarm** | | | | | | | | | | | | | |
| 2011 | 1,316.2 | 1,317.8 | 1,327.4 | 1,348.3 | 1,354.7 | 1,341.7 | 1,326.0 | 1,329.2 | 1,349.0 | 1,358.3 | 1,360.5 | 1,355.8 | 1,340.4 |
| 2012 | 1,332.5 | 1,340.4 | 1,352.0 | 1,360.7 | 1,371.4 | 1,366.7 | 1,337.8 | 1,344.7 | 1,361.6 | 1,375.4 | 1,378.2 | 1,375.7 | 1,358.1 |
| 2013 | 1,342.2 | 1,353.4 | 1,359.5 | 1,375.9 | 1,381.2 | 1,375.1 | 1,354.7 | 1,360.5 | 1,383.2 | 1,392.2 | 1,398.0 | 1,395.9 | 1,372.7 |
| 2014 | 1,359.7 | 1,370.9 | 1,382.0 | 1,395.4 | 1,404.2 | 1,397.0 | 1,375.7 | 1,380.1 | 1,397.9 | 1,409.4 | 1,412.9 | 1,412.7 | 1,391.5 |
| 2015 | 1,375.1 | 1,387.9 | 1,393.2 | 1,403.0 | 1,411.0 | 1,406.1 | 1,385.2 | 1,387.6 | 1,405.3 | 1,417.5 | 1,419.4 | 1,418.6 | 1,400.8 |
| 2016 | 1,382.3 | 1,393.0 | 1,398.3 | 1,414.0 | 1,413.8 | 1,404.0 | 1,387.6 | 1,389.1 | 1,411.4 | 1,420.4 | 1,422.4 | 1,418.3 | 1,404.6 |
| 2017 | 1,380.2 | 1,395.8 | 1,401.3 | 1,403.8 | 1,407.5 | 1,401.3 | 1,385.9 | 1,389.3 | 1,410.7 | 1,420.8 | 1,427.3 | 1,425.5 | 1,404.1 |
| 2018 | 1,388.6 | 1,403.5 | 1,406.0 | 1,416.8 | 1,421.6 | 1,415.0 | 1,399.2 | 1,409.2 | 1,422.9 | 1,432.3 | 1,438.1 | 1,434.9 | 1,415.7 |
| 2019 | 1,399.3 | 1,410.0 | 1,411.8 | 1,431.3 | 1,433.7 | 1,424.1 | 1,404.6 | 1,418.5 | 1,427.2 | 1,435.8 | 1,439.2 | 1,440.4 | 1,423.0 |
| **Total Private** | | | | | | | | | | | | | |
| 2011 | 1,054.6 | 1,054.4 | 1,062.2 | 1,080.2 | 1,085.7 | 1,085.4 | 1,087.8 | 1,089.2 | 1,086.6 | 1,092.5 | 1,094.7 | 1,093.0 | 1,080.5 |
| 2012 | 1,074.8 | 1,077.5 | 1,087.5 | 1,096.2 | 1,103.7 | 1,111.5 | 1,103.3 | 1,104.8 | 1,102.5 | 1,109.5 | 1,111.9 | 1,111.6 | 1,099.6 |
| 2013 | 1,086.2 | 1,090.1 | 1,095.9 | 1,110.0 | 1,117.2 | 1,124.2 | 1,122.5 | 1,124.7 | 1,122.6 | 1,127.6 | 1,132.6 | 1,132.3 | 1,115.5 |
| 2014 | 1,105.3 | 1,108.7 | 1,118.5 | 1,131.8 | 1,140.6 | 1,144.8 | 1,141.6 | 1,143.7 | 1,138.4 | 1,144.7 | 1,147.9 | 1,149.4 | 1,134.6 |
| 2015 | 1,120.4 | 1,125.3 | 1,129.4 | 1,138.7 | 1,146.8 | 1,153.1 | 1,152.0 | 1,152.1 | 1,146.8 | 1,154.4 | 1,156.1 | 1,156.6 | 1,144.3 |
| 2016 | 1,129.6 | 1,132.1 | 1,135.6 | 1,150.1 | 1,151.5 | 1,152.2 | 1,155.4 | 1,154.2 | 1,152.1 | 1,156.4 | 1,158.5 | 1,154.8 | 1,148.5 |
| 2017 | 1,127.5 | 1,133.9 | 1,138.7 | 1,141.1 | 1,145.2 | 1,150.6 | 1,153.2 | 1,153.4 | 1,151.6 | 1,156.6 | 1,162.2 | 1,161.5 | 1,148.0 |
| 2018 | 1,134.8 | 1,140.5 | 1,142.3 | 1,152.4 | 1,157.7 | 1,163.5 | 1,164.8 | 1,164.3 | 1,160.3 | 1,166.0 | 1,170.7 | 1,168.7 | 1,157.2 |
| 2019 | 1,144.4 | 1,145.1 | 1,147.5 | 1,164.6 | 1,165.6 | 1,169.7 | 1,169.9 | 1,172.8 | 1,163.7 | 1,168.5 | 1,171.0 | 1,173.4 | 1,163.0 |
| **Goods Producing** | | | | | | | | | | | | | |
| 2011 | 210.9 | 210.3 | 214.2 | 218.3 | 219.8 | 222.0 | 223.8 | 223.8 | 223.0 | 224.5 | 223.3 | 222.1 | 219.7 |
| 2012 | 218.6 | 218.4 | 222.5 | 222.6 | 225.1 | 227.3 | 227.8 | 227.4 | 227.0 | 226.9 | 225.6 | 223.2 | 224.4 |
| 2013 | 218.6 | 219.5 | 221.5 | 225.2 | 227.0 | 229.2 | 229.6 | 229.9 | 229.7 | 230.3 | 230.7 | 229.4 | 226.7 |
| 2014 | 224.2 | 226.3 | 228.7 | 231.1 | 232.8 | 235.5 | 234.1 | 234.4 | 232.7 | 233.0 | 231.8 | 231.0 | 231.3 |
| 2015 | 223.1 | 226.3 | 227.9 | 227.6 | 230.9 | 232.7 | 232.3 | 231.2 | 231.1 | 231.1 | 230.5 | 229.6 | 229.5 |
| 2016 | 224.0 | 223.8 | 225.8 | 227.3 | 227.6 | 229.3 | 229.3 | 229.3 | 228.9 | 228.9 | 228.4 | 226.4 | 227.4 |
| 2017 | 222.7 | 224.4 | 225.9 | 224.9 | 226.1 | 229.5 | 229.7 | 228.3 | 228.9 | 229.1 | 228.6 | 228.9 | 227.3 |
| 2018 | 222.8 | 225.8 | 227.3 | 229.3 | 231.1 | 234.7 | 235.7 | 236.0 | 235.7 | 236.4 | 236.3 | 236.0 | 232.3 |
| 2019 | 232.0 | 232.4 | 234.2 | 239.7 | 239.1 | 242.3 | 240.1 | 240.6 | 238.8 | 236.0 | 237.0 | 236.4 | 237.4 |
| **Service-Providing** | | | | | | | | | | | | | |
| 2011 | 1,105.3 | 1,107.5 | 1,113.2 | 1,130.0 | 1,134.9 | 1,119.7 | 1,102.2 | 1,105.4 | 1,126.0 | 1,133.8 | 1,137.2 | 1,133.7 | 1,120.7 |
| 2012 | 1,113.9 | 1,122.0 | 1,129.5 | 1,138.1 | 1,146.3 | 1,139.4 | 1,110.0 | 1,117.3 | 1,134.6 | 1,148.5 | 1,152.6 | 1,152.5 | 1,133.7 |
| 2013 | 1,123.6 | 1,133.9 | 1,138.0 | 1,150.7 | 1,154.2 | 1,145.9 | 1,125.1 | 1,130.6 | 1,153.5 | 1,161.9 | 1,167.3 | 1,166.5 | 1,145.9 |
| 2014 | 1,135.5 | 1,144.6 | 1,153.3 | 1,164.3 | 1,171.4 | 1,161.5 | 1,141.6 | 1,145.7 | 1,165.2 | 1,176.4 | 1,181.1 | 1,181.7 | 1,160.2 |
| 2015 | 1,152.0 | 1,161.6 | 1,165.3 | 1,175.4 | 1,180.1 | 1,173.4 | 1,152.9 | 1,156.4 | 1,174.2 | 1,186.4 | 1,188.9 | 1,189.0 | 1,171.3 |
| 2016 | 1,158.3 | 1,169.2 | 1,172.5 | 1,186.7 | 1,186.2 | 1,174.7 | 1,158.3 | 1,159.8 | 1,182.5 | 1,191.5 | 1,194.0 | 1,191.9 | 1,177.1 |
| 2017 | 1,157.5 | 1,171.4 | 1,175.4 | 1,178.9 | 1,181.4 | 1,171.8 | 1,156.2 | 1,161.0 | 1,181.8 | 1,191.7 | 1,198.7 | 1,196.6 | 1,176.9 |
| 2018 | 1,165.8 | 1,177.7 | 1,178.7 | 1,187.5 | 1,190.5 | 1,180.3 | 1,163.5 | 1,173.2 | 1,187.2 | 1,195.9 | 1,201.8 | 1,198.9 | 1,183.4 |
| 2019 | 1,167.3 | 1,177.6 | 1,177.6 | 1,191.6 | 1,194.6 | 1,181.8 | 1,164.5 | 1,177.9 | 1,188.4 | 1,199.8 | 1,202.2 | 1,204.0 | 1,185.6 |
| **Mining and Logging** | | | | | | | | | | | | | |
| 2011 | 8.4 | 8.3 | 8.5 | 8.8 | 8.8 | 9.0 | 9.5 | 9.5 | 9.4 | 9.5 | 9.5 | 9.6 | 9.1 |
| 2012 | 9.5 | 9.5 | 9.6 | 9.6 | 9.8 | 10.0 | 10.3 | 10.3 | 10.1 | 10.5 | 10.5 | 10.5 | 10.0 |
| 2013 | 10.1 | 10.1 | 10.1 | 10.4 | 10.5 | 10.5 | 10.7 | 10.6 | 10.5 | 10.6 | 10.7 | 10.8 | 10.5 |
| 2014 | 10.4 | 10.3 | 10.4 | 10.6 | 10.7 | 10.6 | 10.6 | 10.6 | 10.5 | 10.5 | 10.4 | 10.3 | 10.5 |
| 2015 | 9.9 | 9.3 | 8.9 | 8.6 | 8.6 | 8.6 | 8.5 | 8.4 | 8.1 | 7.8 | 7.7 | 7.7 | 8.5 |
| 2016 | 7.2 | 6.9 | 6.8 | 6.7 | 6.8 | 6.8 | 6.9 | 6.9 | 6.8 | 6.7 | 6.8 | 6.7 | 6.8 |
| 2017 | 6.6 | 6.6 | 6.7 | 6.7 | 6.7 | 6.8 | 6.8 | 6.8 | 6.8 | 6.8 | 6.7 | 6.7 | 6.7 |
| 2018 | 6.6 | 6.6 | 6.7 | 6.8 | 6.7 | 6.8 | 6.9 | 7.0 | 7.0 | 6.9 | 6.9 | 6.9 | 6.8 |
| 2019 | 6.7 | 6.7 | 6.7 | 6.8 | 6.8 | 6.8 | 6.9 | 6.9 | 6.8 | 6.9 | 6.8 | 6.7 | 6.8 |
| **Construction** | | | | | | | | | | | | | |
| 2011 | 47.1 | 46.8 | 49.9 | 52.6 | 53.9 | 55.2 | 56.0 | 55.8 | 55.6 | 56.3 | 54.7 | 53.1 | 53.1 |
| 2012 | 50.5 | 50.5 | 53.9 | 54.8 | 56.2 | 57.8 | 57.6 | 57.2 | 56.7 | 56.2 | 54.9 | 53.5 | 55.0 |
| 2013 | 50.0 | 50.9 | 52.1 | 55.4 | 56.7 | 59.0 | 59.7 | 60.2 | 59.9 | 60.1 | 59.6 | 57.9 | 56.8 |
| 2014 | 55.3 | 54.6 | 57.4 | 59.8 | 61.6 | 62.6 | 63.2 | 62.3 | 61.1 | 61.4 | 59.7 | 58.7 | 59.8 |
| 2015 | 55.1 | 56.1 | 58.3 | 61.5 | 61.8 | 62.7 | 63.8 | 63.4 | 62.7 | 63.3 | 62.5 | 61.2 | 61.0 |
| 2016 | 57.3 | 57.2 | 59.8 | 61.2 | 61.6 | 63.5 | 64.0 | 63.4 | 63.1 | 63.2 | 62.3 | 60.3 | 61.4 |
| 2017 | 57.5 | 58.4 | 59.9 | 59.3 | 60.1 | 61.8 | 62.4 | 61.8 | 60.8 | 61.0 | 60.2 | 59.8 | 60.3 |
| 2018 | 56.4 | 56.8 | 58.7 | 60.0 | 61.4 | 63.4 | 64.2 | 64.3 | 64.0 | 64.3 | 63.3 | 62.2 | 61.6 |
| 2019 | 59.6 | 59.3 | 61.4 | 65.6 | 64.7 | 66.7 | 65.9 | 65.4 | 64.5 | 63.6 | 62.6 | 62.2 | 63.5 |

## 1. Employment by Industry: Kansas, 2011–2019—*Continued*

(Numbers in thousands, not seasonally adjusted)

| Industry and year | January | February | March | April | May | June | July | August | September | October | November | December | Annual average |
|---|---|---|---|---|---|---|---|---|---|---|---|---|---|
| **Manufacturing** | | | | | | | | | | | | | |
| 2011 | 155.4 | 155.2 | 155.8 | 156.9 | 157.1 | 157.8 | 158.3 | 158.5 | 158.0 | 158.7 | 159.1 | 159.4 | 157.5 |
| 2012 | 158.6 | 158.4 | 159.0 | 158.2 | 159.1 | 159.5 | 159.9 | 159.9 | 160.2 | 160.2 | 160.2 | 159.2 | 159.4 |
| 2013 | 158.5 | 158.5 | 159.3 | 159.4 | 159.8 | 159.7 | 159.2 | 159.1 | 159.3 | 159.6 | 160.4 | 160.7 | 159.5 |
| 2014 | 158.5 | 161.4 | 160.9 | 160.7 | 160.5 | 162.3 | 160.3 | 161.5 | 161.1 | 161.1 | 161.7 | 162.0 | 161.0 |
| 2015 | 158.1 | 160.9 | 160.7 | 157.5 | 160.5 | 161.4 | 160.0 | 159.4 | 160.3 | 160.0 | 160.3 | 160.7 | 160.0 |
| 2016 | 159.5 | 159.7 | 159.2 | 159.4 | 159.2 | 159.0 | 158.4 | 159.0 | 159.0 | 159.0 | 159.3 | 159.4 | 159.2 |
| 2017 | 158.6 | 159.4 | 159.3 | 158.9 | 159.3 | 160.9 | 160.5 | 159.7 | 161.3 | 161.3 | 161.7 | 162.4 | 160.3 |
| 2018 | 159.8 | 162.4 | 161.9 | 162.5 | 163.0 | 164.5 | 164.6 | 164.7 | 164.7 | 165.2 | 166.1 | 166.9 | 163.9 |
| 2019 | 165.7 | 166.4 | 166.1 | 167.3 | 167.6 | 168.8 | 167.3 | 168.3 | 167.5 | 165.5 | 167.6 | 167.5 | 167.1 |
| **Trade, Transportation, and Utilities** | | | | | | | | | | | | | |
| 2011 | 249.5 | 248.3 | 247.6 | 252.4 | 253.9 | 253.4 | 253.2 | 253.3 | 252.4 | 254.6 | 258.6 | 259.6 | 253.1 |
| 2012 | 252.4 | 250.6 | 251.6 | 253.2 | 254.9 | 256.8 | 253.7 | 253.9 | 253.6 | 256.1 | 260.0 | 261.0 | 254.8 |
| 2013 | 252.9 | 251.8 | 252.3 | 253.7 | 255.3 | 256.7 | 256.3 | 257.4 | 256.5 | 258.9 | 263.4 | 265.1 | 256.7 |
| 2014 | 256.2 | 254.2 | 257.0 | 258.8 | 260.5 | 261.3 | 261.2 | 261.9 | 260.4 | 263.2 | 267.4 | 269.8 | 261.0 |
| 2015 | 261.0 | 258.8 | 259.5 | 261.2 | 263.6 | 265.3 | 264.7 | 265.1 | 263.9 | 266.8 | 270.5 | 271.8 | 264.4 |
| 2016 | 263.1 | 262.6 | 262.6 | 265.5 | 266.5 | 266.2 | 267.3 | 266.9 | 265.8 | 268.2 | 272.8 | 274.6 | 266.8 |
| 2017 | 264.9 | 264.0 | 263.6 | 263.1 | 264.4 | 264.3 | 265.5 | 267.9 | 267.8 | 269.6 | 275.8 | 276.6 | 267.3 |
| 2018 | 267.6 | 265.7 | 265.2 | 266.4 | 268.3 | 268.2 | 268.0 | 268.0 | 267.3 | 269.7 | 275.0 | 275.7 | 268.8 |
| 2019 | 267.0 | 264.1 | 263.3 | 265.2 | 265.9 | 265.5 | 266.2 | 267.3 | 265.7 | 268.3 | 271.9 | 274.0 | 267.0 |
| **Wholesale Trade** | | | | | | | | | | | | | |
| 2011 | 55.7 | 55.7 | 56.0 | 56.6 | 56.9 | 57.5 | 57.6 | 57.1 | 56.7 | 56.8 | 56.7 | 56.8 | 56.7 |
| 2012 | 56.2 | 56.2 | 56.4 | 56.3 | 56.7 | 58.0 | 57.0 | 56.7 | 56.2 | 56.4 | 56.2 | 56.3 | 56.6 |
| 2013 | 55.9 | 55.8 | 55.8 | 56.2 | 56.4 | 57.2 | 58.5 | 58.0 | 57.4 | 57.9 | 57.8 | 57.9 | 57.1 |
| 2014 | 57.1 | 56.7 | 57.9 | 57.9 | 58.4 | 59.1 | 59.5 | 58.9 | 58.5 | 58.9 | 58.7 | 58.8 | 58.4 |
| 2015 | 58.5 | 58.4 | 58.5 | 58.4 | 58.9 | 59.8 | 59.8 | 59.2 | 58.6 | 59.2 | 58.9 | 58.7 | 58.9 |
| 2016 | 58.0 | 58.0 | 57.7 | 58.5 | 58.8 | 59.4 | 59.7 | 59.0 | 58.6 | 58.8 | 58.5 | 58.3 | 58.6 |
| 2017 | 57.6 | 57.7 | 57.8 | 57.8 | 58.1 | 59.0 | 59.3 | 58.8 | 58.4 | 58.7 | 58.6 | 58.4 | 58.4 |
| 2018 | 58.2 | 58.1 | 58.3 | 58.6 | 58.7 | 59.4 | 59.2 | 58.6 | 58.2 | 58.3 | 58.4 | 58.2 | 58.5 |
| 2019 | 57.8 | 57.6 | 57.6 | 57.9 | 58.0 | 58.2 | 58.8 | 58.2 | 57.8 | 58.5 | 58.2 | 58.0 | 58.1 |
| **Retail Trade** | | | | | | | | | | | | | |
| 2011 | 139.3 | 138.2 | 139.2 | 141.3 | 142.2 | 142.0 | 141.8 | 141.6 | 140.8 | 142.4 | 146.2 | 146.7 | 141.8 |
| 2012 | 141.5 | 139.8 | 140.7 | 141.7 | 142.7 | 143.1 | 142.6 | 142.2 | 142.1 | 143.6 | 147.5 | 148.1 | 143.0 |
| 2013 | 141.4 | 140.5 | 141.2 | 142.2 | 143.1 | 144.0 | 143.9 | 144.5 | 144.2 | 145.5 | 149.4 | 150.7 | 144.2 |
| 2014 | 144.0 | 142.7 | 143.8 | 145.4 | 146.2 | 146.7 | 146.6 | 146.7 | 145.5 | 147.3 | 151.2 | 152.5 | 146.6 |
| 2015 | 145.9 | 144.6 | 145.3 | 147.1 | 148.8 | 150.1 | 149.6 | 149.4 | 148.4 | 150.7 | 153.9 | 154.2 | 149.0 |
| 2016 | 148.6 | 148.2 | 148.5 | 150.1 | 150.3 | 149.9 | 150.7 | 150.0 | 148.5 | 150.1 | 153.4 | 153.8 | 150.2 |
| 2017 | 148.2 | 147.2 | 146.9 | 146.6 | 147.2 | 146.6 | 147.4 | 147.5 | 145.8 | 147.1 | 150.9 | 151.0 | 147.7 |
| 2018 | 145.6 | 144.4 | 144.3 | 144.9 | 145.9 | 145.5 | 145.3 | 144.8 | 143.6 | 144.8 | 148.4 | 147.9 | 145.5 |
| 2019 | 142.4 | 140.6 | 140.3 | 141.7 | 142.2 | 141.9 | 141.9 | 141.9 | 140.5 | 142.0 | 144.5 | 145.0 | 142.1 |
| **Transportation and Utilities** | | | | | | | | | | | | | |
| 2011 | 54.5 | 54.4 | 52.4 | 54.5 | 54.8 | 53.9 | 53.8 | 54.6 | 54.9 | 55.4 | 55.7 | 56.1 | 54.6 |
| 2012 | 54.7 | 54.6 | 54.5 | 55.2 | 55.5 | 55.7 | 54.1 | 55.0 | 55.3 | 56.1 | 56.3 | 56.6 | 55.3 |
| 2013 | 55.6 | 55.5 | 55.3 | 55.3 | 55.8 | 55.5 | 53.9 | 54.9 | 54.9 | 55.5 | 56.2 | 56.5 | 55.4 |
| 2014 | 55.1 | 54.8 | 55.3 | 55.5 | 55.9 | 55.5 | 55.1 | 56.3 | 56.4 | 57.0 | 57.5 | 58.5 | 56.1 |
| 2015 | 56.6 | 55.8 | 55.7 | 55.7 | 55.9 | 55.4 | 55.3 | 56.5 | 56.9 | 56.9 | 57.7 | 58.9 | 56.4 |
| 2016 | 56.5 | 56.4 | 56.4 | 56.9 | 57.4 | 56.9 | 56.9 | 57.9 | 58.7 | 59.3 | 60.9 | 62.5 | 58.1 |
| 2017 | 59.1 | 59.1 | 58.9 | 58.7 | 59.1 | 58.7 | 58.8 | 61.6 | 63.6 | 63.8 | 66.3 | 67.2 | 61.2 |
| 2018 | 63.8 | 63.2 | 62.6 | 62.9 | 63.7 | 63.3 | 63.5 | 64.6 | 65.5 | 66.6 | 68.2 | 69.6 | 64.8 |
| 2019 | 66.8 | 65.9 | 65.4 | 65.6 | 65.7 | 65.4 | 65.5 | 67.2 | 67.4 | 67.8 | 69.2 | 71.0 | 66.9 |
| **Information** | | | | | | | | | | | | | |
| 2011 | 25.2 | 25.1 | 25.0 | 24.6 | 23.9 | 23.8 | 23.6 | 23.3 | 22.9 | 22.9 | 22.9 | 22.9 | 23.8 |
| 2012 | 23.3 | 23.0 | 23.1 | 23.0 | 23.0 | 23.0 | 22.8 | 22.6 | 22.4 | 22.5 | 22.5 | 22.5 | 22.8 |
| 2013 | 22.1 | 22.1 | 22.0 | 22.1 | 22.1 | 22.2 | 22.5 | 22.5 | 22.2 | 22.2 | 22.3 | 22.5 | 22.2 |
| 2014 | 22.4 | 22.2 | 22.1 | 22.1 | 22.1 | 22.1 | 22.1 | 21.9 | 21.5 | 21.6 | 21.6 | 21.6 | 21.9 |
| 2015 | 21.2 | 21.2 | 21.2 | 21.1 | 21.1 | 21.2 | 21.2 | 21.1 | 20.7 | 20.8 | 20.9 | 21.0 | 21.1 |
| 2016 | 21.0 | 21.0 | 20.8 | 20.8 | 20.7 | 20.7 | 20.7 | 20.5 | 20.1 | 19.8 | 19.9 | 19.9 | 20.5 |
| 2017 | 20.0 | 19.8 | 19.7 | 19.6 | 19.6 | 19.4 | 19.3 | 19.1 | 18.8 | 18.9 | 18.9 | 18.9 | 19.3 |
| 2018 | 18.9 | 18.9 | 18.8 | 19.0 | 18.9 | 18.8 | 18.8 | 18.7 | 18.5 | 18.5 | 18.5 | 18.4 | 18.7 |
| 2019 | 18.2 | 18.2 | 18.1 | 18.2 | 18.1 | 18.0 | 18.1 | 18.1 | 17.9 | 18.0 | 18.2 | 18.5 | 18.1 |

## 1. Employment by Industry: Kansas, 2011–2019—*Continued*

(Numbers in thousands, not seasonally adjusted)

| Industry and year | January | February | March | April | May | June | July | August | September | October | November | December | Annual average |
|---|---|---|---|---|---|---|---|---|---|---|---|---|---|
| **Financial Activities** | | | | | | | | | | | | | |
| 2011 | 71.9 | 71.8 | 72.0 | 72.7 | 73.8 | 74.0 | 74.5 | 74.6 | 74.2 | 74.7 | 74.8 | 75.2 | 73.7 |
| 2012 | 74.7 | 75.3 | 75.7 | 76.1 | 76.2 | 76.9 | 77.0 | 76.9 | 76.2 | 76.6 | 77.0 | 77.3 | 76.3 |
| 2013 | 76.5 | 76.7 | 76.5 | 77.3 | 77.9 | 78.9 | 79.0 | 78.8 | 78.2 | 78.3 | 78.5 | 78.6 | 77.9 |
| 2014 | 77.4 | 77.3 | 77.5 | 77.6 | 77.9 | 78.4 | 78.4 | 78.6 | 78.1 | 78.5 | 78.6 | 78.9 | 78.1 |
| 2015 | 78.1 | 78.2 | 78.4 | 78.5 | 78.6 | 79.1 | 79.5 | 79.3 | 78.3 | 78.7 | 78.8 | 78.9 | 78.7 |
| 2016 | 79.1 | 78.9 | 78.6 | 79.7 | 79.7 | 79.7 | 80.1 | 80.0 | 79.1 | 79.0 | 78.9 | 78.8 | 79.3 |
| 2017 | 78.1 | 78.1 | 77.9 | 77.7 | 77.6 | 78.2 | 78.5 | 78.2 | 77.4 | 77.8 | 77.8 | 77.9 | 77.9 |
| 2018 | 76.7 | 76.7 | 76.5 | 77.0 | 77.2 | 78.0 | 78.0 | 77.8 | 77.0 | 77.4 | 77.3 | 77.5 | 77.3 |
| 2019 | 76.6 | 76.6 | 76.4 | 77.0 | 77.1 | 77.6 | 78.1 | 78.2 | 77.4 | 77.6 | 77.3 | 78.0 | 77.3 |
| **Professional and Business Services** | | | | | | | | | | | | | |
| 2011 | 154.6 | 155.4 | 156.9 | 160.4 | 159.4 | 158.4 | 160.0 | 160.9 | 161.2 | 162.4 | 162.7 | 161.3 | 159.5 |
| 2012 | 159.4 | 160.6 | 162.2 | 165.0 | 165.2 | 167.1 | 165.6 | 166.3 | 166.5 | 169.6 | 169.2 | 169.7 | 165.5 |
| 2013 | 166.3 | 167.8 | 169.5 | 173.3 | 172.8 | 175.1 | 176.1 | 177.0 | 177.2 | 177.6 | 178.5 | 179.1 | 174.2 |
| 2014 | 174.5 | 175.9 | 177.6 | 180.4 | 180.6 | 182.2 | 181.7 | 182.5 | 181.8 | 183.7 | 184.2 | 184.8 | 180.8 |
| 2015 | 177.9 | 178.8 | 179.3 | 181.6 | 181.4 | 182.4 | 183.1 | 183.6 | 182.5 | 184.4 | 183.8 | 184.1 | 181.9 |
| 2016 | 177.1 | 177.1 | 177.3 | 180.6 | 179.3 | 179.4 | 181.5 | 181.3 | 182.2 | 182.9 | 182.6 | 181.7 | 180.3 |
| 2017 | 174.9 | 175.6 | 176.8 | 179.9 | 179.6 | 180.6 | 182.8 | 182.0 | 181.6 | 182.1 | 182.4 | 182.1 | 180.0 |
| 2018 | 176.9 | 178.2 | 178.7 | 181.6 | 180.4 | 181.7 | 182.9 | 182.7 | 181.8 | 181.4 | 181.7 | 180.7 | 180.7 |
| 2019 | 175.6 | 175.9 | 175.8 | 179.7 | 179.1 | 180.4 | 180.8 | 181.3 | 179.5 | 180.3 | 179.6 | 179.5 | 179.0 |
| **Education and Health Services** | | | | | | | | | | | | | |
| 2011 | 183.8 | 184.2 | 184.3 | 185.9 | 186.3 | 184.4 | 183.2 | 183.8 | 185.3 | 186.5 | 187.0 | 186.9 | 185.1 |
| 2012 | 184.5 | 185.2 | 185.5 | 186.2 | 186.9 | 186.2 | 184.3 | 185.2 | 186.7 | 188.2 | 188.9 | 189.5 | 186.4 |
| 2013 | 186.9 | 187.0 | 187.3 | 188.3 | 188.7 | 187.9 | 185.8 | 186.2 | 187.3 | 188.8 | 189.4 | 189.0 | 187.7 |
| 2014 | 187.1 | 187.6 | 187.8 | 189.9 | 191.0 | 190.0 | 188.7 | 189.1 | 190.9 | 192.2 | 193.2 | 193.0 | 190.0 |
| 2015 | 192.0 | 193.2 | 192.9 | 195.1 | 195.2 | 194.0 | 193.5 | 193.4 | 194.1 | 195.9 | 196.4 | 196.4 | 194.3 |
| 2016 | 194.7 | 195.9 | 195.5 | 197.0 | 196.6 | 194.9 | 195.3 | 194.7 | 196.8 | 198.1 | 198.1 | 197.6 | 196.3 |
| 2017 | 195.1 | 196.8 | 196.8 | 197.1 | 196.7 | 196.0 | 195.4 | 195.6 | 196.9 | 198.8 | 199.3 | 198.9 | 197.0 |
| 2018 | 197.2 | 198.6 | 198.0 | 198.5 | 198.6 | 198.5 | 197.6 | 197.7 | 199.1 | 201.2 | 201.9 | 201.6 | 199.0 |
| 2019 | 199.9 | 201.0 | 201.3 | 201.7 | 202.2 | 201.1 | 200.4 | 201.2 | 201.6 | 204.5 | 204.5 | 204.7 | 202.0 |
| **Leisure and Hospitality** | | | | | | | | | | | | | |
| 2011 | 108.3 | 108.5 | 111.4 | 115.1 | 117.9 | 119.2 | 118.9 | 119.1 | 117.0 | 115.9 | 114.8 | 114.4 | 115.0 |
| 2012 | 112.3 | 114.3 | 116.9 | 120.2 | 122.5 | 124.5 | 122.8 | 123.3 | 120.4 | 119.7 | 119.1 | 118.9 | 119.6 |
| 2013 | 114.9 | 116.4 | 118.2 | 121.1 | 124.6 | 125.6 | 124.7 | 124.4 | 122.7 | 122.4 | 120.5 | 119.6 | 121.3 |
| 2014 | 115.6 | 116.7 | 119.0 | 122.7 | 126.8 | 126.8 | 127.0 | 126.9 | 124.6 | 123.6 | 122.4 | 122.1 | 122.9 |
| 2015 | 119.5 | 120.9 | 122.7 | 125.6 | 127.9 | 129.9 | 129.4 | 129.7 | 127.1 | 126.8 | 125.6 | 125.1 | 125.9 |
| 2016 | 121.1 | 122.8 | 124.7 | 128.2 | 130.4 | 131.6 | 130.8 | 131.1 | 128.4 | 128.4 | 126.7 | 125.1 | 127.4 |
| 2017 | 121.8 | 124.4 | 127.2 | 128.1 | 130.7 | 132.5 | 131.9 | 132.0 | 129.7 | 128.8 | 128.0 | 127.0 | 128.5 |
| 2018 | 124.1 | 125.6 | 126.9 | 129.4 | 132.1 | 133.0 | 132.9 | 132.5 | 130.2 | 129.7 | 128.6 | 128.0 | 129.4 |
| 2019 | 124.6 | 125.9 | 127.3 | 130.7 | 132.6 | 133.6 | 134.0 | 133.9 | 130.7 | 132.0 | 130.2 | 130.2 | 130.5 |
| **Other Services** | | | | | | | | | | | | | |
| 2011 | 50.4 | 50.8 | 50.8 | 50.8 | 50.7 | 50.2 | 50.6 | 50.4 | 50.6 | 51.0 | 50.6 | 50.6 | 50.6 |
| 2012 | 49.6 | 50.1 | 50.0 | 49.9 | 49.9 | 49.7 | 49.3 | 49.2 | 49.7 | 49.9 | 49.6 | 49.5 | 49.7 |
| 2013 | 48.0 | 48.8 | 48.6 | 49.0 | 48.8 | 48.6 | 48.5 | 48.5 | 48.8 | 49.1 | 49.3 | 49.0 | 48.8 |
| 2014 | 47.9 | 48.5 | 48.8 | 49.2 | 48.9 | 48.5 | 48.4 | 48.4 | 48.4 | 48.9 | 48.7 | 48.2 | 48.6 |
| 2015 | 47.6 | 47.9 | 47.5 | 48.0 | 48.1 | 48.5 | 48.3 | 48.7 | 49.1 | 49.9 | 49.6 | 49.7 | 48.6 |
| 2016 | 49.5 | 50.0 | 50.3 | 51.0 | 50.7 | 50.4 | 50.4 | 50.4 | 50.8 | 51.1 | 51.1 | 50.7 | 50.5 |
| 2017 | 50.0 | 50.8 | 50.8 | 50.7 | 50.5 | 50.1 | 50.1 | 50.3 | 50.5 | 51.5 | 51.4 | 51.2 | 50.7 |
| 2018 | 50.6 | 51.0 | 50.9 | 51.2 | 51.1 | 50.6 | 50.9 | 50.9 | 50.7 | 51.7 | 51.4 | 50.8 | 51.0 |
| 2019 | 50.5 | 51.0 | 51.1 | 52.4 | 51.5 | 51.2 | 52.2 | 52.2 | 52.1 | 51.8 | 52.3 | 52.1 | 51.7 |
| **Government** | | | | | | | | | | | | | |
| 2011 | 261.6 | 263.4 | 265.2 | 268.1 | 269.0 | 256.3 | 238.2 | 240.0 | 262.4 | 265.8 | 265.8 | 262.8 | 259.9 |
| 2012 | 257.7 | 262.9 | 264.5 | 264.5 | 267.7 | 255.2 | 234.5 | 239.9 | 259.1 | 265.9 | 266.3 | 264.1 | 258.5 |
| 2013 | 256.0 | 263.3 | 263.6 | 265.9 | 264.0 | 250.9 | 232.2 | 235.8 | 260.6 | 264.6 | 265.4 | 263.6 | 257.2 |
| 2014 | 254.4 | 262.2 | 263.5 | 263.6 | 263.6 | 252.2 | 234.1 | 236.4 | 259.5 | 264.7 | 265.0 | 263.3 | 256.9 |
| 2015 | 254.7 | 262.6 | 263.8 | 264.3 | 264.2 | 253.0 | 233.2 | 235.5 | 258.5 | 263.1 | 263.3 | 262.0 | 256.5 |
| 2016 | 252.7 | 260.9 | 262.7 | 263.9 | 262.3 | 251.8 | 232.2 | 234.9 | 259.3 | 264.0 | 263.9 | 263.5 | 256.0 |
| 2017 | 252.7 | 261.9 | 262.6 | 262.7 | 262.3 | 250.7 | 232.7 | 235.9 | 259.1 | 264.2 | 265.1 | 264.0 | 256.2 |
| 2018 | 253.8 | 263.0 | 263.7 | 264.4 | 263.9 | 251.5 | 234.4 | 244.9 | 262.6 | 266.3 | 267.4 | 266.2 | 258.5 |
| 2019 | 254.9 | 264.9 | 264.3 | 266.7 | 268.1 | 254.4 | 234.7 | 245.7 | 263.5 | 267.3 | 268.2 | 267.0 | 260.0 |

## 2. Average Weekly Hours by Selected Industry: Kansas, 2015–2019

(Not seasonally adjusted)

| Industry and year | January | February | March | April | May | June | July | August | September | October | November | December | Annual average |
|---|---|---|---|---|---|---|---|---|---|---|---|---|---|
| **Total Private** | | | | | | | | | | | | | |
| 2015 | 34.0 | 34.5 | 34.5 | 34.0 | 34.1 | 34.5 | 34.4 | 34.9 | 33.8 | 34.0 | 34.2 | 33.7 | 34.2 |
| 2016 | 33.5 | 33.4 | 33.4 | 33.3 | 33.6 | 34.0 | 33.7 | 33.7 | 33.8 | 34.4 | 33.9 | 33.7 | 33.7 |
| 2017 | 33.7 | 33.8 | 33.7 | 34.1 | 33.6 | 34.3 | 34.6 | 34.1 | 34.1 | 34.4 | 34.1 | 34.1 | 34.1 |
| 2018 | 33.5 | 33.6 | 33.8 | 34.4 | 33.9 | 34.5 | 34.8 | 34.3 | 34.7 | 34.2 | 34.1 | 34.6 | 34.2 |
| 2019 | 33.9 | 33.8 | 33.9 | 34.5 | 34.1 | 35.2 | 34.6 | 34.4 | 35.0 | 34.3 | 34.5 | 34.6 | 34.4 |
| **Goods Producing** | | | | | | | | | | | | | |
| 2015 | 40.0 | 39.9 | 40.3 | 40.1 | 39.6 | 40.2 | 40.1 | 40.5 | 39.1 | 40.2 | 40.0 | 40.0 | 40.0 |
| 2016 | 39.1 | 39.1 | 39.6 | 39.2 | 39.1 | 40.2 | 39.2 | 39.9 | 39.7 | 40.5 | 40.2 | 39.7 | 39.6 |
| 2017 | 38.8 | 39.5 | 39.6 | 39.7 | 39.8 | 40.4 | 40.3 | 40.7 | 40.6 | 40.6 | 40.9 | 41.0 | 40.2 |
| 2018 | 39.0 | 39.9 | 40.2 | 40.2 | 40.5 | 40.9 | 40.7 | 40.5 | 40.7 | 40.3 | 40.5 | 40.7 | 40.3 |
| 2019 | 39.3 | 38.8 | 39.1 | 40.4 | 39.4 | 40.6 | 39.8 | 40.4 | 41.0 | 40.4 | 40.6 | 40.6 | 40.0 |
| **Construction** | | | | | | | | | | | | | |
| 2015 | 38.1 | 37.7 | 39.0 | 36.9 | 36.1 | 37.6 | 37.5 | 40.0 | 36.4 | 38.7 | 38.1 | 36.7 | 37.7 |
| 2016 | 35.9 | 36.0 | 37.4 | 37.5 | 37.3 | 39.3 | 37.6 | 38.7 | 37.6 | 39.6 | 38.9 | 37.6 | 37.8 |
| 2017 | 35.5 | 36.4 | 36.8 | 37.1 | 37.0 | 38.6 | 38.6 | 38.7 | 38.3 | 38.4 | 38.4 | 38.1 | 37.7 |
| 2018 | 34.8 | 37.0 | 36.8 | 37.9 | 38.7 | 39.3 | 39.3 | 38.4 | 39.1 | 38.0 | 38.7 | 39.3 | 38.1 |
| 2019 | 38.4 | 37.5 | 37.5 | 40.7 | 38.4 | 41.3 | 40.3 | 40.7 | 40.7 | 39.7 | 39.1 | 39.5 | 39.5 |
| **Manufacturing** | | | | | | | | | | | | | |
| 2015 | 40.7 | 40.9 | 41.0 | 41.2 | 41.0 | 41.0 | 40.9 | 40.7 | 40.9 | 41.1 | 41.5 | 42.4 | 41.1 |
| 2016 | 41.5 | 41.4 | 41.4 | 40.9 | 40.7 | 41.2 | 40.6 | 40.8 | 41.3 | 41.3 | 41.3 | 41.2 | 41.1 |
| 2017 | 40.3 | 41.0 | 41.1 | 40.9 | 41.3 | 41.1 | 41.1 | 42.1 | 42.1 | 42.1 | 42.9 | 43.4 | 41.6 |
| 2018 | 42.3 | 41.9 | 42.3 | 41.8 | 41.7 | 42.1 | 41.8 | 41.9 | 41.9 | 41.9 | 41.8 | 41.8 | 41.9 |
| 2019 | 40.5 | 40.0 | 40.2 | 40.5 | 40.1 | 40.3 | 39.7 | 40.4 | 41.3 | 41.0 | 41.6 | 41.6 | 40.6 |
| **Trade, Transportation, and Utilities** | | | | | | | | | | | | | |
| 2015 | 33.4 | 34.5 | 34.5 | 33.9 | 33.8 | 34.2 | 34.4 | 34.8 | 34.2 | 33.8 | 33.9 | 33.4 | 34.1 |
| 2016 | 32.9 | 32.9 | 32.6 | 32.9 | 32.7 | 33.1 | 33.6 | 33.0 | 32.8 | 33.9 | 33.0 | 33.4 | 33.1 |
| 2017 | 33.4 | 33.1 | 33.4 | 33.9 | 33.4 | 34.1 | 34.4 | 33.6 | 33.6 | 33.6 | 33.5 | 33.6 | 33.6 |
| 2018 | 33.1 | 33.2 | 33.8 | 34.1 | 34.0 | 34.8 | 34.6 | 33.6 | 34.1 | 33.2 | 33.2 | 33.1 | 33.7 |
| 2019 | 32.6 | 32.6 | 32.7 | 33.0 | 32.5 | 33.5 | 33.5 | 32.8 | 33.0 | 32.8 | 32.5 | 32.8 | 32.9 |
| **Financial Activities** | | | | | | | | | | | | | |
| 2015 | 35.5 | 36.6 | 36.4 | 35.9 | 36.1 | 36.1 | 36.3 | 37.4 | 36.2 | 36.2 | 37.4 | 36.6 | 36.4 |
| 2016 | 36.4 | 36.5 | 36.8 | 37.1 | 37.6 | 36.9 | 37.3 | 37.0 | 36.5 | 37.8 | 36.6 | 36.5 | 36.9 |
| 2017 | 37.9 | 37.1 | 36.3 | 37.3 | 36.2 | 36.4 | 37.3 | 36.3 | 36.8 | 37.8 | 36.9 | 36.8 | 36.9 |
| 2018 | 36.9 | 37.0 | 36.1 | 37.5 | 35.9 | 36.3 | 37.5 | 36.7 | 37.7 | 36.7 | 36.5 | 37.7 | 36.9 |
| 2019 | 36.4 | 36.8 | 36.5 | 36.7 | 36.6 | 37.2 | 36.5 | 35.9 | 37.2 | 35.6 | 36.3 | 36.8 | 36.6 |
| **Professional and Business Services** | | | | | | | | | | | | | |
| 2015 | 35.9 | 36.4 | 36.8 | 36.3 | 36.5 | 37.0 | 36.3 | 37.0 | 35.8 | 36.2 | 36.1 | 35.6 | 36.3 |
| 2016 | 35.4 | 35.1 | 34.9 | 34.8 | 35.2 | 35.1 | 34.6 | 34.4 | 34.7 | 35.6 | 34.8 | 33.8 | 34.9 |
| 2017 | 34.5 | 34.6 | 34.5 | 34.9 | 34.6 | 35.8 | 35.8 | 35.5 | 35.5 | 36.3 | 36.1 | 36.0 | 35.4 |
| 2018 | 35.4 | 35.7 | 35.6 | 36.5 | 35.7 | 36.1 | 36.6 | 36.1 | 36.7 | 36.4 | 36.0 | 37.0 | 36.1 |
| 2019 | 36.4 | 36.5 | 36.7 | 37.5 | 37.4 | 38.4 | 37.9 | 37.5 | 38.5 | 37.7 | 37.4 | 37.6 | 37.5 |
| **Education and Health Services** | | | | | | | | | | | | | |
| 2015 | 32.4 | 32.7 | 32.5 | 31.9 | 32.1 | 32.4 | 32.4 | 33.1 | 32.4 | 32.2 | 33.0 | 31.7 | 32.4 |
| 2016 | 32.5 | 32.2 | 32.2 | 32.0 | 32.6 | 32.5 | 32.2 | 32.3 | 32.6 | 32.8 | 32.3 | 32.4 | 32.4 |
| 2017 | 32.8 | 32.2 | 31.9 | 32.8 | 31.7 | 31.9 | 32.6 | 31.8 | 31.9 | 32.3 | 31.6 | 31.7 | 32.1 |
| 2018 | 31.8 | 31.7 | 31.6 | 32.5 | 31.6 | 32.2 | 32.8 | 32.4 | 32.7 | 32.0 | 32.3 | 32.3 | 32.2 |
| 2019 | 31.5 | 31.4 | 31.5 | 31.8 | 31.6 | 32.6 | 31.9 | 32.3 | 32.3 | 31.5 | 32.5 | 32.6 | 32.0 |
| **Leisure and Hospitality** | | | | | | | | | | | | | |
| 2015 | 22.8 | 23.3 | 23.3 | 23.0 | 23.6 | 24.2 | 23.7 | 24.1 | 23.0 | 23.5 | 23.4 | 22.6 | 23.4 |
| 2016 | 22.2 | 22.5 | 23.0 | 22.9 | 22.9 | 23.7 | 23.6 | 23.8 | 23.7 | 23.7 | 23.8 | 23.4 | 23.3 |
| 2017 | 23.0 | 23.9 | 24.0 | 24.2 | 24.0 | 24.7 | 25.1 | 24.6 | 23.9 | 24.4 | 24.0 | 23.7 | 24.1 |
| 2018 | 23.1 | 23.7 | 24.2 | 24.3 | 24.0 | 24.8 | 24.9 | 24.6 | 24.5 | 24.2 | 23.8 | 24.1 | 24.2 |
| 2019 | 23.2 | 23.2 | 23.7 | 23.9 | 23.7 | 25.0 | 24.4 | 24.0 | 24.1 | 23.8 | 23.7 | 23.6 | 23.9 |
| **Other Services** | | | | | | | | | | | | | |
| 2015 | 29.6 | 29.2 | 28.2 | 29.3 | 30.2 | 30.6 | 30.5 | 31.3 | 29.2 | 29.7 | 29.5 | 29.3 | 29.7 |
| 2016 | 30.0 | 30.1 | 29.2 | 29.8 | 30.5 | 31.5 | 30.6 | 30.8 | 29.7 | 30.2 | 29.2 | 29.8 | 30.1 |
| 2017 | 29.7 | 30.9 | 30.1 | 29.8 | 30.0 | 31.6 | 32.1 | 31.0 | 30.0 | 30.8 | 30.5 | 29.7 | 30.5 |
| 2018 | 29.2 | 29.8 | 29.7 | 30.5 | 30.2 | 31.3 | 31.8 | 31.1 | 31.4 | 30.4 | 29.8 | 31.1 | 30.5 |
| 2019 | 31.7 | 31.4 | 31.2 | 32.5 | 32.2 | 33.9 | 33.8 | 32.9 | 32.6 | 33.0 | 32.3 | 32.3 | 32.5 |

## 3. Average Hourly Earnings by Selected Industry: Kansas, 2015–2019

(Dollars, not seasonally adjusted)

| Industry and year | January | February | March | April | May | June | July | August | September | October | November | December | Annual average |
|---|---|---|---|---|---|---|---|---|---|---|---|---|---|
| **Total Private** | | | | | | | | | | | | | |
| 2015 | 22.56 | 22.70 | 22.51 | 22.35 | 22.37 | 22.20 | 22.39 | 22.58 | 22.62 | 22.64 | 22.84 | 22.92 | 22.56 |
| 2016 | 22.81 | 22.75 | 22.57 | 22.87 | 22.70 | 22.36 | 22.60 | 22.72 | 22.85 | 23.09 | 22.95 | 22.99 | 22.77 |
| 2017 | 23.34 | 23.24 | 23.13 | 23.26 | 23.01 | 22.79 | 23.12 | 23.08 | 23.31 | 23.46 | 23.26 | 23.45 | 23.20 |
| 2018 | 23.55 | 23.81 | 23.63 | 23.97 | 23.79 | 23.85 | 24.11 | 24.02 | 24.35 | 24.45 | 24.57 | 24.97 | 24.10 |
| 2019 | 25.13 | 25.27 | 25.20 | 25.21 | 25.28 | 25.36 | 25.32 | 25.41 | 25.76 | 25.55 | 25.67 | 25.97 | 25.43 |
| **Goods Producing** | | | | | | | | | | | | | |
| 2015 | 24.54 | 24.14 | 24.27 | 23.83 | 24.09 | 24.16 | 24.27 | 24.50 | 24.43 | 24.56 | 24.67 | 24.96 | 24.37 |
| 2016 | 24.78 | 24.84 | 24.67 | 24.90 | 24.54 | 24.40 | 24.52 | 24.83 | 24.82 | 25.02 | 24.92 | 25.00 | 24.77 |
| 2017 | 25.17 | 25.02 | 24.71 | 24.51 | 24.19 | 24.24 | 24.27 | 23.89 | 24.10 | 24.14 | 23.93 | 24.42 | 24.37 |
| 2018 | 24.53 | 24.37 | 24.12 | 24.48 | 24.33 | 24.42 | 24.70 | 24.54 | 24.59 | 24.62 | 24.71 | 25.20 | 24.55 |
| 2019 | 25.09 | 25.15 | 24.96 | 25.20 | 25.30 | 25.39 | 25.41 | 25.36 | 25.37 | 25.22 | 25.66 | 26.23 | 25.37 |
| **Construction** | | | | | | | | | | | | | |
| 2015 | 24.50 | 24.37 | 24.23 | 23.71 | 23.89 | 24.09 | 24.30 | 24.81 | 24.98 | 24.90 | 24.85 | 24.78 | 24.46 |
| 2016 | 25.47 | 25.39 | 25.09 | 25.25 | 25.05 | 25.10 | 25.11 | 25.57 | 25.71 | 25.82 | 25.60 | 25.84 | 25.42 |
| 2017 | 25.60 | 25.41 | 25.27 | 25.41 | 25.11 | 24.95 | 24.89 | 24.70 | 25.13 | 25.31 | 25.24 | 25.50 | 25.20 |
| 2018 | 26.15 | 25.75 | 25.54 | 25.58 | 25.75 | 25.77 | 25.86 | 25.51 | 26.08 | 25.64 | 26.14 | 26.15 | 25.83 |
| 2019 | 26.36 | 26.64 | 26.41 | 26.65 | 27.16 | 26.94 | 27.26 | 27.31 | 27.50 | 27.20 | 27.88 | 28.21 | 27.14 |
| **Manufacturing** | | | | | | | | | | | | | |
| 2015 | 24.37 | 24.23 | 24.48 | 23.97 | 24.21 | 24.23 | 24.42 | 24.40 | 24.10 | 24.40 | 24.63 | 26.14 | 24.47 |
| 2016 | 25.55 | 25.56 | 25.16 | 25.29 | 24.84 | 24.44 | 24.56 | 24.80 | 24.67 | 24.78 | 24.71 | 24.59 | 24.91 |
| 2017 | 24.59 | 24.23 | 23.79 | 23.39 | 23.14 | 23.36 | 23.33 | 22.84 | 22.94 | 22.94 | 22.71 | 23.50 | 23.39 |
| 2018 | 23.42 | 23.39 | 23.14 | 23.69 | 23.29 | 23.39 | 23.81 | 23.99 | 23.71 | 24.03 | 23.89 | 24.24 | 23.67 |
| 2019 | 24.21 | 24.29 | 24.13 | 24.18 | 24.14 | 24.42 | 24.26 | 24.16 | 24.28 | 24.26 | 24.61 | 25.33 | 24.36 |
| **Trade, Transportation, and Utilities** | | | | | | | | | | | | | |
| 2015 | 21.62 | 21.82 | 21.78 | 22.14 | 21.92 | 21.66 | 21.47 | 21.64 | 21.49 | 21.73 | 21.78 | 21.70 | 21.73 |
| 2016 | 21.75 | 21.75 | 21.60 | 21.76 | 21.85 | 21.33 | 21.58 | 21.87 | 22.40 | 22.36 | 22.34 | 22.18 | 21.90 |
| 2017 | 22.84 | 22.49 | 21.81 | 22.22 | 22.16 | 21.78 | 22.21 | 22.09 | 22.31 | 22.38 | 21.89 | 21.47 | 22.13 |
| 2018 | 21.88 | 21.96 | 22.10 | 22.27 | 22.18 | 22.19 | 22.35 | 22.21 | 22.80 | 22.35 | 22.63 | 22.55 | 22.29 |
| 2019 | 23.07 | 22.56 | 22.36 | 22.33 | 22.52 | 22.58 | 22.74 | 22.62 | 23.32 | 23.20 | 22.90 | 22.76 | 22.75 |
| **Financial Activities** | | | | | | | | | | | | | |
| 2015 | 28.63 | 29.08 | 28.02 | 27.46 | 27.63 | 27.14 | 27.17 | 28.04 | 27.46 | 27.67 | 27.52 | 27.35 | 27.76 |
| 2016 | 27.41 | 27.12 | 26.97 | 27.95 | 27.80 | 27.38 | 27.86 | 27.66 | 27.92 | 28.56 | 28.28 | 28.34 | 27.77 |
| 2017 | 29.09 | 28.59 | 29.48 | 29.85 | 29.33 | 28.35 | 29.14 | 29.89 | 29.25 | 29.61 | 30.12 | 29.53 | 29.35 |
| 2018 | 29.20 | 30.28 | 29.74 | 31.25 | 30.72 | 31.70 | 32.12 | 31.85 | 31.76 | 31.51 | 31.85 | 32.13 | 31.19 |
| 2019 | 31.93 | 32.43 | 32.40 | 32.44 | 32.44 | 32.44 | 31.65 | 32.37 | 31.83 | 32.12 | 32.58 | 32.51 | 32.26 |
| **Professional and Business Services** | | | | | | | | | | | | | |
| 2015 | 23.99 | 24.87 | 24.98 | 24.49 | 24.57 | 24.32 | 24.82 | 25.24 | 25.52 | 25.13 | 25.61 | 25.36 | 24.91 |
| 2016 | 25.23 | 25.22 | 24.99 | 25.54 | 25.16 | 24.72 | 25.17 | 25.46 | 25.36 | 25.76 | 25.41 | 26.02 | 25.34 |
| 2017 | 26.62 | 26.74 | 26.96 | 27.30 | 26.57 | 26.17 | 26.67 | 26.50 | 26.67 | 27.09 | 26.84 | 27.71 | 26.82 |
| 2018 | 28.28 | 28.44 | 27.95 | 28.31 | 28.36 | 28.43 | 28.94 | 28.85 | 29.39 | 29.98 | 29.87 | 30.65 | 28.96 |
| 2019 | 30.94 | 31.25 | 31.39 | 31.20 | 31.34 | 31.92 | 31.68 | 32.04 | 32.87 | 31.92 | 32.01 | 32.85 | 31.79 |
| **Education and Health Services** | | | | | | | | | | | | | |
| 2015 | 21.79 | 21.59 | 21.40 | 21.16 | 21.03 | 20.89 | 20.76 | 20.86 | 21.11 | 21.05 | 21.25 | 21.69 | 21.21 |
| 2016 | 21.43 | 21.20 | 20.97 | 21.30 | 20.94 | 20.79 | 20.99 | 20.78 | 20.74 | 21.10 | 20.88 | 20.72 | 20.99 |
| 2017 | 20.81 | 21.11 | 21.00 | 21.39 | 21.47 | 21.45 | 21.59 | 21.55 | 22.16 | 22.12 | 22.12 | 22.28 | 21.59 |
| 2018 | 22.00 | 22.27 | 22.01 | 22.05 | 21.89 | 21.87 | 22.04 | 22.14 | 22.28 | 22.30 | 22.28 | 22.58 | 22.14 |
| 2019 | 22.91 | 23.33 | 23.20 | 23.26 | 23.23 | 23.03 | 23.38 | 23.09 | 22.92 | 23.28 | 23.26 | 23.26 | 23.18 |
| **Leisure and Hospitality** | | | | | | | | | | | | | |
| 2015 | 11.80 | 11.93 | 11.84 | 11.79 | 11.77 | 11.72 | 11.82 | 11.82 | 12.11 | 12.07 | 12.13 | 12.18 | 11.91 |
| 2016 | 12.05 | 12.00 | 11.90 | 11.87 | 11.89 | 11.69 | 11.81 | 11.79 | 11.94 | 12.06 | 12.05 | 12.26 | 11.94 |
| 2017 | 12.32 | 12.23 | 12.21 | 12.23 | 12.30 | 12.19 | 12.14 | 12.23 | 12.37 | 12.39 | 12.51 | 12.63 | 12.31 |
| 2018 | 12.64 | 12.64 | 12.68 | 12.70 | 12.64 | 12.50 | 12.53 | 12.47 | 12.71 | 12.88 | 12.81 | 13.04 | 12.68 |
| 2019 | 13.01 | 13.11 | 13.03 | 13.14 | 13.17 | 13.03 | 13.02 | 13.15 | 13.47 | 13.64 | 13.74 | 13.92 | 13.29 |
| **Other Services** | | | | | | | | | | | | | |
| 2015 | 21.73 | 21.20 | 21.28 | 20.66 | 20.58 | 20.78 | 20.68 | 20.47 | 20.50 | 21.25 | 21.62 | 21.52 | 21.02 |
| 2016 | 21.34 | 21.46 | 21.65 | 21.43 | 21.89 | 21.97 | 22.08 | 21.90 | 22.16 | 21.60 | 21.47 | 21.46 | 21.70 |
| 2017 | 21.47 | 20.75 | 20.91 | 20.72 | 21.07 | 21.52 | 21.37 | 21.46 | 21.00 | 21.22 | 20.82 | 20.88 | 21.10 |
| 2018 | 21.59 | 20.81 | 20.77 | 21.21 | 20.71 | 20.59 | 21.34 | 21.32 | 21.54 | 22.02 | 22.34 | 22.26 | 21.38 |
| 2019 | 21.78 | 21.66 | 22.03 | 21.62 | 21.94 | 22.33 | 22.31 | 22.64 | 23.19 | 22.93 | 23.47 | 23.14 | 22.43 |

# 4. Average Weekly Earnings by Selected Industry: Kansas, 2015–2019

(Dollars, not seasonally adjusted)

| Industry and year | January | February | March | April | May | June | July | August | September | October | November | December | Annual average |
|---|---|---|---|---|---|---|---|---|---|---|---|---|---|
| **Total Private** | | | | | | | | | | | | | |
| 2015 | 767.04 | 783.15 | 776.60 | 759.90 | 762.82 | 765.90 | 770.22 | 788.04 | 764.56 | 769.76 | 781.13 | 772.40 | 771.55 |
| 2016 | 764.14 | 759.85 | 753.84 | 761.57 | 762.72 | 760.24 | 761.62 | 765.66 | 772.33 | 794.30 | 778.01 | 774.76 | 767.35 |
| 2017 | 786.56 | 785.51 | 779.48 | 793.17 | 773.14 | 781.70 | 799.95 | 787.03 | 792.54 | 807.02 | 793.17 | 799.65 | 791.12 |
| 2018 | 788.93 | 800.02 | 798.69 | 824.57 | 806.48 | 822.83 | 839.03 | 823.89 | 844.95 | 836.19 | 837.84 | 863.96 | 824.22 |
| 2019 | 851.91 | 854.13 | 854.28 | 869.75 | 862.05 | 892.67 | 876.07 | 874.10 | 901.60 | 876.37 | 885.62 | 898.56 | 874.79 |
| **Goods Producing** | | | | | | | | | | | | | |
| 2015 | 981.60 | 963.19 | 978.08 | 955.58 | 953.96 | 971.23 | 973.23 | 992.25 | 955.21 | 987.31 | 986.80 | 998.40 | 974.80 |
| 2016 | 968.90 | 971.24 | 976.93 | 976.08 | 959.51 | 980.88 | 961.18 | 990.72 | 985.35 | 1,013.31 | 1,001.78 | 992.50 | 980.89 |
| 2017 | 976.60 | 988.29 | 978.52 | 973.05 | 962.76 | 979.30 | 978.08 | 972.32 | 978.46 | 980.08 | 978.74 | 1,001.22 | 979.67 |
| 2018 | 956.67 | 972.36 | 969.62 | 984.10 | 985.37 | 998.78 | 1,005.29 | 993.87 | 1,000.81 | 992.19 | 1,000.76 | 1,025.64 | 989.37 |
| 2019 | 986.04 | 975.82 | 975.94 | 1,018.08 | 996.82 | 1,030.83 | 1,011.32 | 1,024.54 | 1,040.17 | 1,018.89 | 1,041.80 | 1,064.94 | 1,014.80 |
| **Construction** | | | | | | | | | | | | | |
| 2015 | 933.45 | 918.75 | 944.97 | 874.90 | 862.43 | 905.78 | 911.25 | 992.40 | 909.27 | 963.63 | 946.79 | 909.43 | 922.14 |
| 2016 | 914.37 | 914.04 | 938.37 | 946.88 | 934.37 | 986.43 | 944.14 | 989.56 | 966.70 | 1,022.47 | 995.84 | 971.58 | 960.88 |
| 2017 | 908.80 | 924.92 | 929.94 | 942.71 | 929.07 | 963.07 | 960.75 | 955.89 | 962.48 | 971.90 | 969.22 | 971.55 | 950.04 |
| 2018 | 910.02 | 952.75 | 939.87 | 969.48 | 996.53 | 1,012.76 | 1,016.30 | 979.58 | 1,019.73 | 974.32 | 1,011.62 | 1,027.70 | 984.12 |
| 2019 | 1,012.22 | 999.00 | 990.38 | 1,084.66 | 1,042.94 | 1,112.62 | 1,098.58 | 1,111.52 | 1,119.25 | 1,079.84 | 1,090.11 | 1,114.30 | 1,072.03 |
| **Manufacturing** | | | | | | | | | | | | | |
| 2015 | 991.86 | 991.01 | 1,003.68 | 987.56 | 992.61 | 993.43 | 998.78 | 993.08 | 985.69 | 1,002.84 | 1,022.15 | 1,108.34 | 1,005.72 |
| 2016 | 1,060.33 | 1,058.18 | 1,041.62 | 1,034.36 | 1,010.99 | 1,006.93 | 997.14 | 1,011.84 | 1,018.87 | 1,023.41 | 1,020.52 | 1,013.11 | 1,023.80 |
| 2017 | 990.98 | 993.43 | 977.77 | 956.65 | 955.68 | 960.10 | 958.86 | 961.56 | 965.77 | 965.77 | 974.26 | 1,019.90 | 973.02 |
| 2018 | 990.67 | 980.04 | 978.82 | 990.24 | 971.19 | 984.72 | 995.26 | 1,005.18 | 993.45 | 1,006.86 | 998.60 | 1,013.23 | 991.77 |
| 2019 | 980.51 | 971.60 | 970.03 | 979.29 | 968.01 | 984.13 | 963.12 | 976.06 | 1,002.76 | 994.66 | 1,023.78 | 1,053.73 | 989.02 |
| **Trade, Transportation, and Utilities** | | | | | | | | | | | | | |
| 2015 | 722.11 | 752.79 | 751.41 | 750.55 | 740.90 | 740.77 | 738.57 | 753.07 | 734.96 | 734.47 | 738.34 | 724.78 | 740.99 |
| 2016 | 715.58 | 715.58 | 704.16 | 715.90 | 714.50 | 706.02 | 725.09 | 721.71 | 734.72 | 758.00 | 737.22 | 740.81 | 724.89 |
| 2017 | 762.86 | 744.42 | 728.45 | 753.26 | 740.14 | 742.70 | 764.02 | 742.22 | 749.62 | 751.97 | 733.32 | 721.39 | 743.57 |
| 2018 | 724.23 | 729.07 | 746.98 | 759.41 | 754.12 | 772.21 | 773.31 | 746.26 | 777.48 | 742.02 | 751.32 | 746.41 | 751.17 |
| 2019 | 752.08 | 735.46 | 731.17 | 736.89 | 731.90 | 756.43 | 761.79 | 741.94 | 769.56 | 760.96 | 744.25 | 746.53 | 748.48 |
| **Financial Activities** | | | | | | | | | | | | | |
| 2015 | 1,016.37 | 1,064.33 | 1,019.93 | 985.81 | 997.44 | 979.75 | 986.27 | 1,048.70 | 994.05 | 1,001.65 | 1,029.25 | 1,001.01 | 1,010.46 |
| 2016 | 997.72 | 989.88 | 992.50 | 1,036.95 | 1,045.28 | 1,010.32 | 1,039.18 | 1,023.42 | 1,019.08 | 1,079.57 | 1,035.05 | 1,034.41 | 1,024.71 |
| 2017 | 1,102.51 | 1,060.69 | 1,070.12 | 1,113.41 | 1,061.75 | 1,031.94 | 1,086.92 | 1,085.01 | 1,076.40 | 1,119.26 | 1,111.43 | 1,086.70 | 1,083.02 |
| 2018 | 1,077.48 | 1,120.36 | 1,073.61 | 1,171.88 | 1,102.85 | 1,150.71 | 1,204.50 | 1,168.90 | 1,197.35 | 1,156.42 | 1,162.53 | 1,211.30 | 1,150.91 |
| 2019 | 1,162.25 | 1,193.42 | 1,182.60 | 1,190.55 | 1,187.30 | 1,206.77 | 1,155.23 | 1,162.08 | 1,184.08 | 1,143.47 | 1,182.65 | 1,196.37 | 1,180.72 |
| **Professional and Business Services** | | | | | | | | | | | | | |
| 2015 | 861.24 | 905.27 | 919.26 | 888.99 | 896.81 | 899.84 | 900.97 | 933.88 | 913.62 | 909.71 | 924.52 | 902.82 | 904.23 |
| 2016 | 893.14 | 885.22 | 872.15 | 888.79 | 885.63 | 867.67 | 870.88 | 875.82 | 879.99 | 917.06 | 884.27 | 879.48 | 884.37 |
| 2017 | 918.39 | 925.20 | 930.12 | 952.77 | 919.32 | 936.89 | 954.79 | 940.75 | 946.79 | 983.37 | 968.92 | 997.56 | 949.43 |
| 2018 | 1,001.11 | 1,015.31 | 995.02 | 1,033.32 | 1,012.45 | 1,026.32 | 1,059.20 | 1,041.49 | 1,078.61 | 1,091.27 | 1,075.32 | 1,134.05 | 1,045.46 |
| 2019 | 1,126.22 | 1,140.63 | 1,152.01 | 1,170.00 | 1,172.12 | 1,225.73 | 1,200.67 | 1,201.50 | 1,265.50 | 1,203.38 | 1,197.17 | 1,235.16 | 1,192.13 |
| **Education and Health Services** | | | | | | | | | | | | | |
| 2015 | 706.00 | 705.99 | 695.50 | 675.00 | 675.06 | 676.84 | 672.62 | 690.47 | 683.96 | 677.81 | 701.25 | 687.57 | 687.20 |
| 2016 | 696.48 | 682.64 | 675.23 | 681.60 | 682.64 | 675.68 | 675.88 | 671.19 | 676.12 | 692.08 | 674.42 | 671.33 | 680.08 |
| 2017 | 682.57 | 679.74 | 669.90 | 701.59 | 680.60 | 684.26 | 703.83 | 685.29 | 706.90 | 714.48 | 698.99 | 706.28 | 693.04 |
| 2018 | 699.60 | 705.96 | 695.52 | 716.63 | 691.72 | 704.21 | 722.91 | 717.34 | 728.56 | 713.60 | 719.64 | 729.33 | 712.91 |
| 2019 | 721.67 | 732.56 | 730.80 | 739.67 | 734.07 | 750.78 | 745.82 | 745.81 | 740.32 | 733.32 | 755.95 | 758.28 | 741.76 |
| **Leisure and Hospitality** | | | | | | | | | | | | | |
| 2015 | 269.04 | 277.97 | 275.87 | 271.17 | 277.77 | 283.38 | 279.90 | 284.86 | 278.53 | 283.65 | 283.84 | 275.27 | 278.69 |
| 2016 | 267.51 | 270.00 | 273.70 | 271.82 | 272.28 | 277.05 | 278.72 | 280.60 | 282.98 | 285.82 | 286.79 | 286.88 | 278.20 |
| 2017 | 283.36 | 292.30 | 293.04 | 295.97 | 295.20 | 301.09 | 304.71 | 300.86 | 295.64 | 302.32 | 300.24 | 299.33 | 296.67 |
| 2018 | 291.98 | 299.57 | 306.86 | 308.61 | 303.36 | 310.00 | 312.00 | 306.76 | 311.40 | 311.70 | 304.88 | 314.26 | 306.86 |
| 2019 | 301.83 | 304.15 | 308.81 | 314.05 | 312.13 | 325.75 | 317.69 | 315.60 | 324.63 | 324.63 | 325.64 | 328.51 | 317.63 |
| **Other Services** | | | | | | | | | | | | | |
| 2015 | 643.21 | 619.04 | 600.10 | 605.34 | 621.52 | 635.87 | 630.74 | 640.71 | 598.60 | 631.13 | 637.79 | 630.54 | 624.29 |
| 2016 | 640.20 | 645.95 | 632.18 | 638.61 | 667.65 | 692.06 | 675.65 | 674.52 | 658.15 | 652.32 | 626.92 | 639.51 | 653.17 |
| 2017 | 637.66 | 641.18 | 629.39 | 617.46 | 632.10 | 680.03 | 685.98 | 665.26 | 630.00 | 653.58 | 635.01 | 620.14 | 643.55 |
| 2018 | 630.43 | 620.14 | 616.87 | 646.91 | 625.44 | 644.47 | 678.61 | 663.05 | 676.36 | 669.41 | 665.73 | 692.29 | 652.09 |
| 2019 | 690.43 | 680.12 | 687.34 | 702.65 | 706.47 | 756.99 | 754.08 | 744.86 | 755.99 | 756.69 | 758.08 | 747.42 | 728.98 |

# KENTUCKY
## *At a Glance*

Population:
2010 census: 4,339,367
2019 estimate: 4,467,673

Percent change in population:
2010–2019: 3.0%

Percent change in total nonfarm employment:
2011–2019: 8.7%

Industry with the largest growth in employment, 2011–2019 (percent):
Transportation and Utilities, 26.5%

Industry with the largest decline or smallest growth in employment, 2011–2019 (percent):
Mining and Logging, -56.3%

Civilian labor force:
2010: 2,054,375
2019: 2,072,586

Unemployment rate and rank among states (highest to lowest):
2010: 10.2%, 16th
2019: 4.3%, 9th

Over-the-year change in unemployment rates:
2017–2018: -0.6%
2018–2019: 0.0%

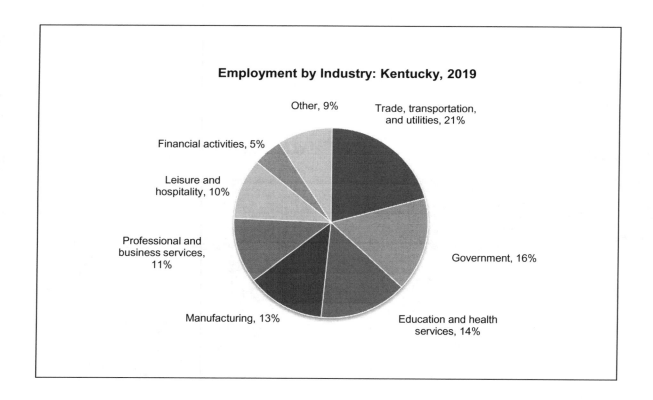

**Employment by Industry: Kentucky, 2019**

Other, 9%
Trade, transportation, and utilities, 21%
Financial activities, 5%
Leisure and hospitality, 10%
Professional and business services, 11%
Government, 16%
Manufacturing, 13%
Education and health services, 14%

## 1. Employment by Industry: Kentucky, 2011–2019

(Numbers in thousands, not seasonally adjusted)

| Industry and year | January | February | March | April | May | June | July | August | September | October | November | December | Annual average |
|---|---|---|---|---|---|---|---|---|---|---|---|---|---|
| **Total Nonfarm** | | | | | | | | | | | | | |
| 2011 | 1,739.1 | 1,744.3 | 1,762.2 | 1,783.4 | 1,786.9 | 1,792.3 | 1,773.7 | 1,792.0 | 1,800.8 | 1,800.9 | 1,814.1 | 1,814.6 | 1,783.7 |
| 2012 | 1,772.0 | 1,776.7 | 1,794.5 | 1,809.5 | 1,822.1 | 1,825.5 | 1,801.7 | 1,813.2 | 1,819.5 | 1,823.5 | 1,837.6 | 1,838.8 | 1,811.2 |
| 2013 | 1,791.2 | 1,794.7 | 1,809.6 | 1,825.6 | 1,837.7 | 1,835.1 | 1,817.3 | 1,837.4 | 1,842.5 | 1,846.4 | 1,863.9 | 1,865.2 | 1,830.6 |
| 2014 | 1,812.4 | 1,810.5 | 1,829.2 | 1,854.1 | 1,866.1 | 1,863.7 | 1,849.2 | 1,867.0 | 1,871.0 | 1,878.8 | 1,892.5 | 1,899.1 | 1,857.8 |
| 2015 | 1,847.7 | 1,844.9 | 1,854.3 | 1,876.0 | 1,893.3 | 1,893.6 | 1,873.6 | 1,888.9 | 1,896.6 | 1,906.5 | 1,924.1 | 1,928.4 | 1,885.7 |
| 2016 | 1,872.9 | 1,875.9 | 1,887.2 | 1,906.4 | 1,917.0 | 1,912.5 | 1,903.1 | 1,913.5 | 1,920.6 | 1,922.2 | 1,933.7 | 1,936.1 | 1,908.4 |
| 2017 | 1,885.7 | 1,892.8 | 1,904.6 | 1,917.9 | 1,926.5 | 1,930.5 | 1,906.2 | 1,914.0 | 1,929.1 | 1,934.9 | 1,952.5 | 1,948.3 | 1,920.3 |
| 2018 | 1,890.8 | 1,902.2 | 1,913.0 | 1,929.5 | 1,939.0 | 1,943.4 | 1,917.1 | 1,928.8 | 1,938.4 | 1,941.7 | 1,961.9 | 1,954.8 | 1,930.1 |
| 2019 | 1,909.9 | 1,913.6 | 1,924.5 | 1,935.9 | 1,948.8 | 1,948.8 | 1,930.2 | 1,941.1 | 1,949.0 | 1,954.3 | 1,959.3 | 1,949.5 | 1,938.7 |
| **Total Private** | | | | | | | | | | | | | |
| 2011 | 1,423.4 | 1,423.7 | 1,439.4 | 1,458.9 | 1,462.4 | 1,471.7 | 1,465.6 | 1,477.8 | 1,478.1 | 1,476.3 | 1,487.8 | 1,488.0 | 1,462.8 |
| 2012 | 1,449.9 | 1,450.1 | 1,465.8 | 1,479.0 | 1,492.6 | 1,501.9 | 1,493.0 | 1,499.4 | 1,496.6 | 1,498.1 | 1,511.0 | 1,512.5 | 1,487.5 |
| 2013 | 1,470.6 | 1,469.1 | 1,482.5 | 1,496.5 | 1,508.4 | 1,511.5 | 1,506.4 | 1,520.4 | 1,516.3 | 1,522.2 | 1,537.8 | 1,539.0 | 1,506.7 |
| 2014 | 1,491.8 | 1,488.3 | 1,505.1 | 1,526.7 | 1,538.7 | 1,541.6 | 1,537.8 | 1,547.8 | 1,546.2 | 1,554.1 | 1,567.2 | 1,575.1 | 1,535.0 |
| 2015 | 1,529.0 | 1,525.0 | 1,533.8 | 1,552.2 | 1,570.0 | 1,575.9 | 1,570.7 | 1,578.6 | 1,578.3 | 1,585.6 | 1,602.1 | 1,606.6 | 1,567.3 |
| 2016 | 1,557.1 | 1,558.7 | 1,567.5 | 1,586.1 | 1,596.2 | 1,598.1 | 1,599.8 | 1,601.1 | 1,602.6 | 1,605.2 | 1,615.3 | 1,618.0 | 1,592.2 |
| 2017 | 1,571.7 | 1,575.7 | 1,586.1 | 1,597.6 | 1,605.4 | 1,614.8 | 1,605.7 | 1,608.4 | 1,610.8 | 1,616.4 | 1,632.3 | 1,628.5 | 1,604.5 |
| 2018 | 1,580.1 | 1,586.5 | 1,595.3 | 1,611.8 | 1,620.0 | 1,629.6 | 1,620.9 | 1,626.1 | 1,622.4 | 1,625.9 | 1,645.9 | 1,640.1 | 1,617.1 |
| 2019 | 1,601.6 | 1,600.2 | 1,609.9 | 1,621.1 | 1,631.8 | 1,637.5 | 1,635.2 | 1,638.9 | 1,633.9 | 1,639.2 | 1,644.3 | 1,635.1 | 1,627.4 |
| **Goods Producing** | | | | | | | | | | | | | |
| 2011 | 292.6 | 293.2 | 296.8 | 301.8 | 303.0 | 307.3 | 302.9 | 308.8 | 309.2 | 308.1 | 309.2 | 307.4 | 303.4 |
| 2012 | 302.4 | 300.8 | 305.5 | 308.2 | 311.2 | 315.3 | 314.9 | 316.1 | 315.8 | 315.4 | 315.4 | 314.0 | 311.3 |
| 2013 | 306.7 | 306.2 | 308.8 | 310.8 | 314.3 | 317.2 | 314.3 | 318.4 | 319.4 | 319.7 | 320.1 | 319.4 | 314.6 |
| 2014 | 311.4 | 311.8 | 316.6 | 320.5 | 324.7 | 327.2 | 327.8 | 330.4 | 330.3 | 330.9 | 332.0 | 330.5 | 324.5 |
| 2015 | 323.2 | 322.4 | 323.5 | 325.8 | 331.8 | 333.8 | 332.1 | 336.2 | 336.6 | 336.3 | 336.0 | 335.7 | 331.1 |
| 2016 | 327.7 | 327.3 | 330.5 | 334.2 | 336.2 | 338.9 | 339.7 | 339.1 | 339.3 | 337.8 | 338.8 | 338.1 | 335.6 |
| 2017 | 331.2 | 332.3 | 335.5 | 336.9 | 338.5 | 340.9 | 340.5 | 340.4 | 340.5 | 340.1 | 340.5 | 339.4 | 338.1 |
| 2018 | 331.8 | 332.9 | 335.6 | 338.0 | 340.3 | 342.8 | 341.6 | 343.2 | 341.9 | 342.5 | 343.1 | 343.0 | 339.7 |
| 2019 | 338.4 | 337.7 | 340.2 | 341.5 | 343.6 | 344.9 | 346.0 | 346.6 | 344.8 | 341.3 | 341.9 | 340.7 | 342.3 |
| **Service-Providing** | | | | | | | | | | | | | |
| 2011 | 1,446.5 | 1,451.1 | 1,465.4 | 1,481.6 | 1,483.9 | 1,485.0 | 1,470.8 | 1,483.2 | 1,491.6 | 1,492.8 | 1,504.9 | 1,507.2 | 1,480.3 |
| 2012 | 1,469.6 | 1,475.9 | 1,489.0 | 1,501.3 | 1,510.9 | 1,510.2 | 1,486.8 | 1,497.1 | 1,503.7 | 1,508.1 | 1,522.2 | 1,524.8 | 1,500.0 |
| 2013 | 1,484.5 | 1,488.5 | 1,500.8 | 1,514.8 | 1,523.4 | 1,517.9 | 1,503.0 | 1,519.0 | 1,523.1 | 1,526.7 | 1,543.8 | 1,545.8 | 1,515.9 |
| 2014 | 1,501.0 | 1,498.7 | 1,512.6 | 1,533.6 | 1,541.4 | 1,536.5 | 1,521.4 | 1,536.6 | 1,540.7 | 1,547.9 | 1,560.5 | 1,568.6 | 1,533.3 |
| 2015 | 1,524.5 | 1,522.5 | 1,530.8 | 1,550.2 | 1,561.5 | 1,559.8 | 1,541.5 | 1,552.7 | 1,560.0 | 1,570.2 | 1,588.1 | 1,592.7 | 1,554.5 |
| 2016 | 1,545.2 | 1,548.6 | 1,556.7 | 1,572.2 | 1,580.8 | 1,573.6 | 1,563.4 | 1,574.4 | 1,581.3 | 1,584.4 | 1,594.9 | 1,598.0 | 1,572.8 |
| 2017 | 1,554.5 | 1,560.5 | 1,569.1 | 1,581.0 | 1,588.0 | 1,589.6 | 1,565.7 | 1,573.6 | 1,588.6 | 1,594.8 | 1,612.0 | 1,608.9 | 1,582.2 |
| 2018 | 1,559.0 | 1,569.3 | 1,577.4 | 1,591.5 | 1,598.7 | 1,600.6 | 1,575.5 | 1,585.6 | 1,596.5 | 1,599.2 | 1,618.8 | 1,611.8 | 1,590.3 |
| 2019 | 1,571.5 | 1,575.9 | 1,584.3 | 1,594.4 | 1,605.2 | 1,603.9 | 1,584.2 | 1,594.5 | 1,604.2 | 1,613.0 | 1,617.4 | 1,608.8 | 1,596.4 |
| **Mining and Logging** | | | | | | | | | | | | | |
| 2011 | 22.0 | 22.1 | 22.3 | 22.7 | 22.9 | 23.2 | 23.4 | 23.5 | 23.4 | 23.2 | 23.2 | 23.3 | 22.9 |
| 2012 | 23.0 | 22.5 | 22.1 | 21.6 | 21.1 | 21.0 | 20.4 | 19.9 | 19.5 | 18.7 | 18.6 | 18.1 | 20.5 |
| 2013 | 17.6 | 17.2 | 17.6 | 17.5 | 17.6 | 17.8 | 17.7 | 17.6 | 17.5 | 17.2 | 17.1 | 16.9 | 17.4 |
| 2014 | 16.2 | 16.1 | 16.3 | 16.4 | 16.7 | 16.8 | 16.7 | 16.8 | 16.7 | 16.7 | 16.6 | 16.5 | 16.5 |
| 2015 | 15.3 | 15.1 | 14.6 | 14.4 | 14.4 | 14.3 | 14.0 | 13.7 | 13.5 | 13.3 | 12.8 | 12.4 | 14.0 |
| 2016 | 11.6 | 11.1 | 11.0 | 10.5 | 10.4 | 10.4 | 10.2 | 10.1 | 10.1 | 10.2 | 10.3 | 10.3 | 10.5 |
| 2017 | 10.1 | 10.2 | 10.4 | 10.4 | 10.4 | 10.4 | 10.3 | 10.3 | 10.2 | 10.2 | 10.0 | 9.8 | 10.2 |
| 2018 | 9.3 | 9.3 | 9.5 | 10.0 | 10.1 | 10.2 | 10.4 | 10.3 | 10.4 | 10.5 | 10.6 | 10.7 | 10.1 |
| 2019 | 10.6 | 10.5 | 10.7 | 10.5 | 10.6 | 9.9 | 10.0 | 9.8 | 9.6 | 9.2 | 9.3 | 9.0 | 10.0 |
| **Construction** | | | | | | | | | | | | | |
| 2011 | 60.4 | 60.7 | 63.7 | 67.5 | 69.0 | 71.3 | 70.9 | 71.3 | 70.6 | 69.5 | 69.4 | 67.3 | 67.6 |
| 2012 | 62.2 | 62.3 | 64.3 | 66.9 | 68.4 | 69.9 | 70.1 | 70.0 | 69.7 | 69.0 | 68.5 | 66.5 | 67.3 |
| 2013 | 61.4 | 61.5 | 63.5 | 65.7 | 68.3 | 70.0 | 71.1 | 71.4 | 71.9 | 71.7 | 71.3 | 69.4 | 68.1 |
| 2014 | 64.1 | 64.1 | 68.4 | 71.3 | 73.8 | 75.3 | 75.9 | 76.1 | 76.7 | 77.2 | 76.8 | 74.4 | 72.8 |
| 2015 | 69.1 | 68.8 | 70.0 | 74.5 | 76.5 | 77.7 | 80.0 | 79.0 | 79.0 | 79.3 | 78.3 | 77.1 | 75.8 |
| 2016 | 71.3 | 70.7 | 73.2 | 76.8 | 78.0 | 79.4 | 79.8 | 78.9 | 79.2 | 78.4 | 78.2 | 76.7 | 76.7 |
| 2017 | 71.5 | 72.0 | 74.9 | 76.1 | 77.8 | 79.6 | 80.0 | 79.9 | 80.4 | 80.2 | 79.0 | 77.2 | 77.4 |
| 2018 | 71.7 | 72.4 | 74.8 | 77.1 | 79.1 | 80.6 | 80.8 | 80.7 | 80.8 | 80.1 | 79.3 | 78.3 | 78.0 |
| 2019 | 75.0 | 74.2 | 77.0 | 79.2 | 81.2 | 82.5 | 83.4 | 84.0 | 83.3 | 82.8 | 81.1 | 79.5 | 80.3 |

## 1. Employment by Industry: Kentucky, 2011–2019—*Continued*

(Numbers in thousands, not seasonally adjusted)

| Industry and year | January | February | March | April | May | June | July | August | September | October | November | December | Annual average |
|---|---|---|---|---|---|---|---|---|---|---|---|---|---|
| **Manufacturing** | | | | | | | | | | | | | |
| 2011 | 210.2 | 210.4 | 210.8 | 211.6 | 211.1 | 212.8 | 208.6 | 214.0 | 215.2 | 215.4 | 216.6 | 216.8 | 212.8 |
| 2012 | 217.2 | 216.0 | 219.1 | 219.7 | 221.7 | 224.4 | 224.4 | 226.2 | 226.6 | 227.7 | 228.3 | 229.4 | 223.4 |
| 2013 | 227.7 | 227.5 | 227.7 | 227.6 | 228.4 | 229.4 | 225.5 | 229.4 | 230.0 | 230.8 | 231.7 | 233.1 | 229.1 |
| 2014 | 231.1 | 231.6 | 231.9 | 232.8 | 234.2 | 235.1 | 235.2 | 237.5 | 236.9 | 237.0 | 238.6 | 239.6 | 235.1 |
| 2015 | 238.8 | 238.5 | 238.9 | 236.9 | 240.9 | 241.8 | 238.1 | 243.5 | 244.1 | 243.7 | 244.9 | 246.2 | 241.4 |
| 2016 | 244.8 | 245.5 | 246.3 | 246.9 | 247.8 | 249.1 | 249.7 | 250.1 | 250.0 | 249.2 | 250.3 | 251.1 | 248.4 |
| 2017 | 249.6 | 250.1 | 250.2 | 250.4 | 250.3 | 250.9 | 250.2 | 250.2 | 249.9 | 249.7 | 251.5 | 252.4 | 250.5 |
| 2018 | 250.8 | 251.2 | 251.3 | 250.9 | 251.1 | 252.0 | 250.4 | 252.2 | 250.7 | 251.9 | 253.2 | 254.0 | 251.6 |
| 2019 | 252.8 | 253.0 | 252.5 | 251.8 | 251.8 | 252.5 | 252.6 | 252.8 | 251.9 | 249.3 | 251.5 | 252.2 | 252.1 |
| **Trade, Transportation, and Utilities** | | | | | | | | | | | | | |
| 2011 | 358.7 | 356.7 | 359.8 | 362.0 | 363.0 | 365.1 | 364.6 | 366.1 | 365.1 | 366.9 | 376.1 | 379.4 | 365.3 |
| 2012 | 363.5 | 361.7 | 364.6 | 366.0 | 368.8 | 370.3 | 368.2 | 368.9 | 368.8 | 368.6 | 376.4 | 379.1 | 368.7 |
| 2013 | 364.0 | 362.2 | 364.5 | 365.5 | 368.2 | 369.6 | 368.5 | 370.6 | 369.7 | 371.2 | 380.1 | 385.1 | 369.9 |
| 2014 | 368.6 | 366.4 | 369.2 | 371.3 | 374.6 | 376.4 | 375.0 | 377.8 | 377.2 | 379.8 | 388.0 | 395.3 | 376.6 |
| 2015 | 379.4 | 376.9 | 378.8 | 381.0 | 384.5 | 386.1 | 384.9 | 387.1 | 386.2 | 388.7 | 396.5 | 400.9 | 385.9 |
| 2016 | 387.9 | 386.7 | 388.9 | 391.1 | 393.3 | 392.7 | 395.3 | 396.0 | 394.7 | 395.8 | 404.3 | 410.0 | 394.7 |
| 2017 | 392.7 | 390.9 | 392.3 | 393.2 | 395.9 | 397.3 | 395.9 | 397.3 | 398.5 | 400.3 | 412.4 | 416.0 | 398.6 |
| 2018 | 399.4 | 397.1 | 398.4 | 398.7 | 400.9 | 403.5 | 402.8 | 402.3 | 400.6 | 402.6 | 416.0 | 419.0 | 403.4 |
| 2019 | 405.3 | 400.1 | 400.2 | 398.9 | 401.3 | 402.9 | 403.6 | 403.1 | 402.0 | 403.3 | 407.5 | 406.0 | 402.9 |
| **Wholesale Trade** | | | | | | | | | | | | | |
| 2011 | 70.1 | 70.4 | 70.7 | 70.5 | 70.5 | 70.9 | 71.3 | 71.5 | 71.4 | 71.2 | 71.3 | 71.7 | 71.0 |
| 2012 | 70.6 | 70.8 | 71.0 | 71.1 | 71.4 | 71.7 | 71.5 | 71.9 | 72.0 | 71.9 | 72.0 | 72.2 | 71.5 |
| 2013 | 71.9 | 72.1 | 72.3 | 72.3 | 72.5 | 72.9 | 72.6 | 72.9 | 72.7 | 72.3 | 72.5 | 72.9 | 72.5 |
| 2014 | 72.2 | 72.3 | 72.6 | 72.6 | 72.9 | 73.0 | 72.6 | 73.0 | 72.7 | 72.4 | 72.5 | 73.2 | 72.7 |
| 2015 | 72.1 | 72.1 | 72.0 | 72.1 | 72.7 | 73.0 | 73.0 | 73.2 | 73.0 | 73.0 | 73.2 | 73.7 | 72.8 |
| 2016 | 73.1 | 72.9 | 73.2 | 73.3 | 73.7 | 73.6 | 73.7 | 73.3 | 73.1 | 72.7 | 73.1 | 73.7 | 73.3 |
| 2017 | 72.9 | 73.2 | 73.4 | 74.1 | 74.5 | 74.8 | 74.4 | 74.2 | 74.1 | 73.9 | 74.2 | 75.0 | 74.1 |
| 2018 | 74.3 | 74.6 | 74.6 | 74.7 | 74.7 | 75.2 | 75.3 | 75.1 | 74.7 | 75.0 | 75.4 | 75.9 | 75.0 |
| 2019 | 75.2 | 75.4 | 75.8 | 75.8 | 76.1 | 76.4 | 76.2 | 76.1 | 75.7 | 74.8 | 75.2 | 74.6 | 75.6 |
| **Retail Trade** | | | | | | | | | | | | | |
| 2011 | 198.3 | 196.2 | 198.3 | 200.7 | 201.3 | 201.5 | 200.6 | 201.2 | 199.3 | 201.2 | 207.0 | 208.7 | 201.2 |
| 2012 | 199.8 | 197.3 | 199.7 | 201.3 | 203.5 | 204.2 | 202.8 | 202.4 | 201.8 | 202.8 | 209.0 | 209.6 | 202.9 |
| 2013 | 199.7 | 198.1 | 199.6 | 200.9 | 202.8 | 203.5 | 203.0 | 203.6 | 202.4 | 203.9 | 210.1 | 212.4 | 203.3 |
| 2014 | 200.9 | 199.4 | 200.9 | 203.3 | 204.9 | 205.8 | 204.7 | 205.7 | 204.2 | 205.8 | 212.0 | 215.3 | 205.2 |
| 2015 | 205.4 | 204.2 | 206.0 | 208.0 | 210.2 | 211.2 | 209.7 | 210.3 | 209.1 | 210.3 | 216.2 | 218.5 | 209.9 |
| 2016 | 209.4 | 209.3 | 210.9 | 213.4 | 214.5 | 213.7 | 214.7 | 214.9 | 213.3 | 215.2 | 220.9 | 222.1 | 214.4 |
| 2017 | 213.2 | 211.1 | 211.7 | 212.8 | 214.2 | 214.2 | 213.1 | 213.3 | 213.3 | 214.2 | 221.5 | 221.4 | 214.5 |
| 2018 | 212.1 | 211.1 | 212.0 | 212.9 | 214.9 | 214.7 | 214.0 | 213.2 | 211.7 | 211.7 | 219.3 | 219.2 | 213.9 |
| 2019 | 211.5 | 208.3 | 208.8 | 208.4 | 210.1 | 209.9 | 209.4 | 208.9 | 207.8 | 209.4 | 210.4 | 209.9 | 209.4 |
| **Transportation and Utilities** | | | | | | | | | | | | | |
| 2011 | 90.3 | 90.1 | 90.8 | 90.8 | 91.2 | 92.7 | 92.7 | 93.4 | 94.4 | 94.5 | 97.8 | 99.0 | 93.1 |
| 2012 | 93.1 | 93.6 | 93.9 | 93.6 | 93.9 | 94.4 | 93.9 | 94.6 | 95.0 | 93.9 | 95.4 | 97.3 | 94.4 |
| 2013 | 92.4 | 92.0 | 92.6 | 92.3 | 92.9 | 93.2 | 92.9 | 94.1 | 94.6 | 95.0 | 97.5 | 99.8 | 94.1 |
| 2014 | 95.5 | 94.7 | 95.7 | 95.4 | 96.8 | 97.6 | 97.7 | 99.1 | 100.3 | 101.6 | 103.5 | 106.8 | 98.7 |
| 2015 | 101.9 | 100.6 | 100.8 | 100.9 | 101.6 | 101.9 | 102.2 | 103.6 | 104.1 | 105.4 | 107.1 | 108.7 | 103.2 |
| 2016 | 105.4 | 104.5 | 104.8 | 104.4 | 105.1 | 105.4 | 106.9 | 107.8 | 108.3 | 107.9 | 110.3 | 114.2 | 107.1 |
| 2017 | 106.6 | 106.6 | 107.2 | 106.3 | 107.2 | 108.3 | 108.4 | 109.8 | 111.1 | 112.2 | 116.7 | 119.6 | 110.0 |
| 2018 | 113.0 | 111.4 | 111.8 | 111.1 | 111.3 | 113.6 | 113.5 | 114.0 | 114.2 | 115.9 | 121.3 | 123.9 | 114.6 |
| 2019 | 118.6 | 116.4 | 115.6 | 114.7 | 115.1 | 116.6 | 118.0 | 118.1 | 118.5 | 119.1 | 121.9 | 121.5 | 117.8 |
| **Information** | | | | | | | | | | | | | |
| 2011 | 25.3 | 25.1 | 25.0 | 24.9 | 24.9 | 24.9 | 24.9 | 24.9 | 24.6 | 24.7 | 25.1 | 25.2 | 25.0 |
| 2012 | 24.9 | 24.8 | 24.5 | 24.5 | 24.6 | 24.5 | 24.5 | 24.4 | 24.1 | 24.1 | 24.4 | 24.4 | 24.5 |
| 2013 | 24.3 | 24.2 | 24.3 | 24.1 | 24.2 | 24.2 | 24.1 | 24.2 | 23.8 | 23.8 | 23.9 | 23.9 | 24.1 |
| 2014 | 24.1 | 23.9 | 23.9 | 23.7 | 23.8 | 23.9 | 23.7 | 23.8 | 23.5 | 23.6 | 23.5 | 23.3 | 23.7 |
| 2015 | 23.1 | 23.0 | 22.9 | 22.6 | 22.7 | 22.8 | 22.8 | 22.7 | 22.4 | 22.4 | 22.7 | 22.6 | 22.7 |
| 2016 | 22.6 | 22.7 | 22.7 | 22.6 | 22.8 | 23.0 | 23.1 | 23.3 | 23.2 | 23.0 | 23.0 | 23.1 | 22.9 |
| 2017 | 22.6 | 22.6 | 22.7 | 22.6 | 22.7 | 22.7 | 22.6 | 22.4 | 22.2 | 22.1 | 21.8 | 21.9 | 22.4 |
| 2018 | 22.0 | 22.1 | 22.0 | 21.9 | 22.1 | 22.2 | 21.8 | 21.8 | 21.9 | 21.8 | 22.0 | 21.8 | 22.0 |
| 2019 | 21.6 | 21.8 | 21.8 | 21.6 | 21.8 | 21.8 | 21.7 | 21.6 | 21.4 | 21.4 | 21.2 | 21.3 | 21.6 |

# 1. Employment by Industry: Kentucky, 2011–2019—*Continued*

(Numbers in thousands, not seasonally adjusted)

| Industry and year | January | February | March | April | May | June | July | August | September | October | November | December | Annual average |
|---|---|---|---|---|---|---|---|---|---|---|---|---|---|
| **Financial Activities** | | | | | | | | | | | | | |
| 2011 | 84.4 | 84.6 | 84.7 | 84.2 | 84.3 | 85.0 | 85.2 | 85.5 | 85.6 | 85.4 | 85.4 | 86.0 | 85.0 |
| 2012 | 85.5 | 85.4 | 85.8 | 85.7 | 86.1 | 87.0 | 87.4 | 87.5 | 87.7 | 87.5 | 87.9 | 88.3 | 86.8 |
| 2013 | 87.8 | 87.7 | 88.1 | 88.1 | 88.5 | 89.0 | 89.5 | 89.9 | 89.5 | 89.1 | 89.3 | 89.7 | 88.9 |
| 2014 | 88.9 | 88.6 | 88.7 | 89.1 | 89.8 | 90.2 | 90.8 | 90.9 | 90.8 | 91.1 | 91.6 | 92.3 | 90.2 |
| 2015 | 91.2 | 91.2 | 91.3 | 91.1 | 91.8 | 92.5 | 92.8 | 92.9 | 92.7 | 92.6 | 93.1 | 93.4 | 92.2 |
| 2016 | 92.7 | 92.9 | 92.8 | 92.9 | 93.5 | 93.9 | 94.2 | 94.0 | 93.9 | 94.2 | 94.1 | 95.1 | 93.7 |
| 2017 | 93.5 | 93.5 | 93.7 | 93.7 | 94.0 | 94.7 | 94.1 | 94.1 | 93.9 | 93.8 | 93.7 | 93.7 | 93.9 |
| 2018 | 92.3 | 92.1 | 92.1 | 92.6 | 93.1 | 93.7 | 93.6 | 93.9 | 93.7 | 93.4 | 93.6 | 94.0 | 93.2 |
| 2019 | 92.7 | 92.7 | 92.7 | 92.7 | 93.4 | 93.8 | 94.1 | 94.2 | 93.8 | 94.2 | 93.3 | 93.5 | 93.4 |
| **Professional and Business Services** | | | | | | | | | | | | | |
| 2011 | 182.1 | 181.4 | 183.6 | 187.2 | 185.8 | 187.7 | 188.7 | 192.2 | 192.8 | 193.5 | 195.2 | 198.1 | 189.0 |
| 2012 | 188.9 | 188.1 | 189.6 | 192.3 | 193.3 | 195.7 | 194.2 | 197.1 | 196.6 | 199.4 | 203.7 | 206.7 | 195.5 |
| 2013 | 196.1 | 194.4 | 196.4 | 199.8 | 201.1 | 201.9 | 201.0 | 207.0 | 205.7 | 210.2 | 217.8 | 218.9 | 204.2 |
| 2014 | 207.5 | 203.3 | 207.0 | 211.1 | 213.0 | 212.0 | 211.6 | 214.8 | 213.9 | 218.4 | 225.7 | 228.2 | 213.9 |
| 2015 | 214.9 | 210.7 | 212.3 | 215.2 | 217.7 | 219.6 | 218.4 | 220.0 | 219.8 | 222.6 | 230.0 | 233.4 | 219.6 |
| 2016 | 218.0 | 215.1 | 213.0 | 216.2 | 217.0 | 216.1 | 214.9 | 215.9 | 217.8 | 220.5 | 224.3 | 223.9 | 217.7 |
| 2017 | 214.7 | 212.0 | 211.5 | 212.7 | 212.6 | 215.3 | 214.1 | 215.6 | 217.6 | 219.9 | 224.0 | 223.1 | 216.1 |
| 2018 | 212.6 | 213.0 | 213.3 | 216.4 | 215.6 | 217.7 | 216.0 | 217.8 | 218.4 | 220.0 | 224.7 | 220.6 | 217.2 |
| 2019 | 211.7 | 209.9 | 211.6 | 212.7 | 213.8 | 215.6 | 215.6 | 216.8 | 217.6 | 223.6 | 224.8 | 223.7 | 216.5 |
| **Education and Health Services** | | | | | | | | | | | | | |
| 2011 | 255.0 | 255.7 | 256.4 | 257.5 | 257.2 | 255.9 | 255.4 | 256.7 | 259.5 | 259.8 | 259.9 | 258.7 | 257.3 |
| 2012 | 257.0 | 258.7 | 259.6 | 259.5 | 259.8 | 259.6 | 257.9 | 259.3 | 260.5 | 261.7 | 262.4 | 262.4 | 259.9 |
| 2013 | 259.1 | 260.5 | 261.5 | 261.8 | 261.0 | 258.5 | 259.0 | 260.6 | 261.6 | 263.2 | 263.0 | 261.9 | 261.0 |
| 2014 | 258.6 | 260.1 | 259.9 | 260.9 | 259.3 | 257.9 | 256.3 | 258.2 | 261.5 | 263.5 | 261.1 | 262.9 | 260.0 |
| 2015 | 259.5 | 261.6 | 262.1 | 263.6 | 263.1 | 261.7 | 260.8 | 261.8 | 265.3 | 269.1 | 268.9 | 269.7 | 263.9 |
| 2016 | 264.1 | 267.5 | 267.2 | 266.6 | 266.5 | 266.0 | 265.9 | 267.5 | 270.7 | 272.7 | 271.7 | 272.8 | 268.3 |
| 2017 | 267.9 | 271.7 | 271.5 | 273.3 | 271.7 | 272.6 | 269.7 | 270.8 | 273.6 | 276.1 | 277.4 | 276.5 | 272.7 |
| 2018 | 272.1 | 275.8 | 275.6 | 278.8 | 277.2 | 277.9 | 274.7 | 276.8 | 279.9 | 280.7 | 283.0 | 282.1 | 277.9 |
| 2019 | 277.9 | 281.7 | 281.3 | 283.3 | 282.3 | 282.4 | 280.1 | 282.8 | 284.6 | 286.5 | 287.8 | 287.7 | 283.2 |
| **Leisure and Hospitality** | | | | | | | | | | | | | |
| 2011 | 157.5 | 159.1 | 164.6 | 173.4 | 176.2 | 177.6 | 175.8 | 175.8 | 173.9 | 170.6 | 170.0 | 166.4 | 170.1 |
| 2012 | 161.3 | 164.2 | 169.2 | 176.1 | 182.3 | 182.9 | 179.8 | 180.5 | 177.8 | 176.3 | 175.8 | 172.7 | 174.9 |
| 2013 | 168.4 | 169.3 | 173.8 | 181.2 | 185.8 | 185.8 | 185.3 | 185.3 | 182.2 | 180.9 | 179.6 | 176.1 | 179.5 |
| 2014 | 169.8 | 171.0 | 176.0 | 185.9 | 188.9 | 189.8 | 188.6 | 188.0 | 185.1 | 183.5 | 181.3 | 179.3 | 182.3 |
| 2015 | 175.0 | 176.3 | 179.4 | 189.4 | 194.1 | 194.7 | 194.7 | 193.4 | 191.3 | 189.9 | 190.0 | 186.5 | 187.9 |
| 2016 | 180.1 | 182.0 | 187.3 | 196.7 | 200.7 | 201.4 | 201.0 | 200.5 | 197.5 | 194.8 | 193.7 | 189.5 | 193.8 |
| 2017 | 184.4 | 187.3 | 192.8 | 199.2 | 203.7 | 204.8 | 203.0 | 202.0 | 198.8 | 198.4 | 197.2 | 192.5 | 197.0 |
| 2018 | 185.6 | 188.6 | 192.8 | 199.2 | 204.5 | 205.4 | 204.7 | 204.3 | 200.6 | 199.3 | 197.7 | 193.9 | 198.1 |
| 2019 | 189.4 | 191.3 | 196.3 | 204.4 | 209.5 | 209.6 | 208.1 | 207.4 | 203.7 | 202.6 | 201.0 | 197.2 | 201.7 |
| **Other Services** | | | | | | | | | | | | | |
| 2011 | 67.8 | 67.9 | 68.5 | 67.9 | 68.0 | 68.2 | 68.1 | 67.8 | 67.4 | 67.3 | 66.9 | 66.8 | 67.7 |
| 2012 | 66.4 | 66.4 | 67.0 | 66.7 | 66.5 | 66.6 | 66.1 | 65.6 | 65.3 | 65.1 | 65.0 | 64.9 | 66.0 |
| 2013 | 64.2 | 64.6 | 65.1 | 65.2 | 65.3 | 65.3 | 64.7 | 64.7 | 64.4 | 64.1 | 64.0 | 64.0 | 64.6 |
| 2014 | 62.9 | 63.2 | 63.8 | 64.2 | 64.6 | 64.2 | 64.0 | 63.9 | 63.9 | 63.3 | 64.0 | 63.3 | 63.8 |
| 2015 | 62.7 | 62.9 | 63.5 | 63.5 | 64.3 | 64.7 | 64.2 | 64.5 | 64.0 | 64.0 | 64.9 | 64.4 | 64.0 |
| 2016 | 64.0 | 64.5 | 65.1 | 65.8 | 66.2 | 66.1 | 65.7 | 65.8 | 65.5 | 66.4 | 65.4 | 65.5 | 65.5 |
| 2017 | 64.7 | 65.4 | 66.1 | 66.0 | 66.3 | 66.5 | 65.8 | 65.8 | 65.7 | 65.7 | 65.3 | 65.4 | 65.7 |
| 2018 | 64.3 | 64.9 | 65.5 | 66.2 | 66.3 | 66.4 | 65.7 | 66.0 | 65.4 | 65.6 | 65.8 | 65.7 | 65.7 |
| 2019 | 64.6 | 65.0 | 65.8 | 66.0 | 66.1 | 66.5 | 66.0 | 66.4 | 66.0 | 66.3 | 66.8 | 65.0 | 65.9 |
| **Government** | | | | | | | | | | | | | |
| 2011 | 315.7 | 320.6 | 322.8 | 324.5 | 324.5 | 320.6 | 308.1 | 314.2 | 322.7 | 324.6 | 326.3 | 326.6 | 320.9 |
| 2012 | 322.1 | 326.6 | 328.7 | 329.5 | 330.5 | 323.6 | 308.7 | 313.8 | 322.9 | 325.4 | 326.6 | 326.3 | 323.7 |
| 2013 | 320.6 | 325.6 | 327.1 | 329.1 | 329.3 | 323.6 | 310.9 | 317.0 | 326.2 | 324.2 | 326.1 | 326.2 | 323.8 |
| 2014 | 320.6 | 322.2 | 324.1 | 327.4 | 327.4 | 322.1 | 311.4 | 319.2 | 324.8 | 324.7 | 325.3 | 324.0 | 322.8 |
| 2015 | 318.7 | 319.9 | 320.5 | 323.8 | 323.3 | 317.7 | 302.9 | 310.3 | 318.3 | 320.9 | 322.0 | 321.8 | 318.3 |
| 2016 | 315.8 | 317.2 | 319.7 | 320.3 | 320.8 | 314.4 | 303.3 | 311.4 | 318.0 | 317.0 | 318.4 | 318.1 | 316.2 |
| 2017 | 314.0 | 317.1 | 318.5 | 320.3 | 321.1 | 315.7 | 300.5 | 305.6 | 318.3 | 318.5 | 320.2 | 319.8 | 315.8 |
| 2018 | 310.7 | 315.7 | 317.7 | 317.7 | 319.0 | 313.8 | 296.2 | 302.7 | 316.0 | 315.8 | 316.0 | 314.7 | 313.0 |
| 2019 | 308.3 | 313.4 | 314.6 | 314.8 | 317.0 | 311.3 | 295.0 | 302.2 | 315.1 | 315.1 | 315.0 | 314.4 | 311.4 |

## 2. Average Weekly Hours by Selected Industry: Kentucky, 2015–2019

(Not seasonally adjusted)

| Industry and year | January | February | March | April | May | June | July | August | September | October | November | December | Annual average |
|---|---|---|---|---|---|---|---|---|---|---|---|---|---|
| **Total Private** | | | | | | | | | | | | | |
| 2015 | 34.9 | 34.4 | 35.0 | 35.1 | 35.2 | 35.5 | 35.4 | 35.7 | 35.3 | 35.5 | 35.7 | 35.8 | 35.3 |
| 2016 | 34.8 | 34.8 | 35.1 | 35.1 | 35.0 | 35.5 | 35.2 | 35.0 | 35.1 | 35.4 | 35.3 | 35.4 | 35.1 |
| 2017 | 35.3 | 34.9 | 34.8 | 34.9 | 34.6 | 35.1 | 35.3 | 35.3 | 35.1 | 35.3 | 35.0 | 35.2 | 35.1 |
| 2018 | 33.8 | 34.7 | 34.8 | 35.0 | 34.8 | 35.2 | 35.3 | 35.1 | 35.5 | 35.5 | 35.2 | 35.5 | 35.0 |
| 2019 | 34.9 | 34.8 | 34.8 | 34.8 | 35.0 | 35.5 | 35.2 | 35.3 | 35.5 | 35.0 | 35.0 | 35.3 | 35.1 |
| **Goods-Producing** | | | | | | | | | | | | | |
| 2015 | 41.1 | 39.8 | 40.5 | 40.9 | 41.4 | 41.6 | 41.0 | 41.8 | 40.8 | 41.2 | 41.2 | 42.0 | 41.1 |
| 2016 | 40.1 | 39.6 | 39.9 | 40.2 | 40.0 | 41.2 | 40.1 | 40.6 | 40.9 | 40.7 | 41.2 | 40.9 | 40.5 |
| 2017 | 40.6 | 40.3 | 40.1 | 40.1 | 40.2 | 40.8 | 41.1 | 41.4 | 40.8 | 41.4 | 40.8 | 41.4 | 40.8 |
| 2018 | 39.1 | 40.4 | 40.3 | 41.1 | 40.8 | 40.6 | 40.8 | 42.0 | 42.1 | 42.0 | 41.3 | 41.9 | 41.0 |
| 2019 | 41.2 | 41.2 | 41.2 | 41.2 | 41.4 | 41.9 | 41.5 | 42.1 | 41.7 | 41.4 | 41.3 | 40.8 | 41.4 |
| **Construction** | | | | | | | | | | | | | |
| 2015 | 38.4 | 36.9 | 37.1 | 38.0 | 39.8 | 39.9 | 39.3 | 40.3 | 38.0 | 40.7 | 39.3 | 40.4 | 39.1 |
| 2016 | 38.3 | 36.4 | 38.1 | 39.3 | 37.9 | 40.4 | 39.1 | 39.2 | 39.3 | 39.4 | 39.3 | 39.1 | 38.9 |
| 2017 | 39.0 | 39.1 | 38.9 | 39.0 | 38.4 | 40.1 | 41.4 | 40.8 | 39.4 | 40.3 | 39.0 | 39.2 | 39.6 |
| 2018 | 35.9 | 37.1 | 37.0 | 38.5 | 39.2 | 38.9 | 40.2 | 39.1 | 39.4 | 39.5 | 38.0 | 38.9 | 38.5 |
| 2019 | 38.5 | 38.8 | 39.4 | 39.3 | 39.3 | 40.6 | 40.8 | 40.9 | 40.9 | 40.0 | 39.1 | 39.0 | 39.7 |
| **Manufacturing** | | | | | | | | | | | | | |
| 2015 | 41.2 | 39.9 | 40.8 | 41.2 | 41.4 | 41.8 | 40.9 | 41.7 | 41.2 | 41.2 | 41.7 | 42.5 | 41.3 |
| 2016 | 40.7 | 41.2 | 41.0 | 40.9 | 41.1 | 41.9 | 40.7 | 41.3 | 41.6 | 41.5 | 42.2 | 41.8 | 41.3 |
| 2017 | 41.2 | 40.8 | 40.6 | 40.6 | 40.9 | 41.0 | 40.9 | 41.5 | 41.2 | 41.4 | 41.1 | 41.9 | 41.1 |
| 2018 | 39.7 | 41.1 | 41.1 | 41.8 | 41.1 | 41.0 | 40.9 | 42.3 | 42.5 | 42.2 | 41.9 | 42.4 | 41.5 |
| 2019 | 41.5 | 41.5 | 41.2 | 41.4 | 41.7 | 41.9 | 41.3 | 42.2 | 41.7 | 41.8 | 41.9 | 41.2 | 41.6 |
| **Trade, Transportation, and Utilities** | | | | | | | | | | | | | |
| 2015 | 34.7 | 34.7 | 35.3 | 35.7 | 35.9 | 36.0 | 35.8 | 36.2 | 36.0 | 35.9 | 36.2 | 36.3 | 35.7 |
| 2016 | 34.6 | 35.2 | 35.0 | 34.8 | 34.7 | 35.2 | 35.4 | 34.5 | 34.2 | 34.6 | 34.0 | 34.5 | 34.7 |
| 2017 | 33.6 | 33.5 | 33.7 | 33.9 | 33.7 | 33.7 | 33.9 | 33.8 | 33.7 | 33.5 | 33.5 | 33.8 | 33.7 |
| 2018 | 31.9 | 32.5 | 33.1 | 33.3 | 33.3 | 33.9 | 33.9 | 33.8 | 34.2 | 34.1 | 34.1 | 34.2 | 33.5 |
| 2019 | 33.6 | 33.4 | 33.6 | 33.6 | 34.1 | 34.7 | 34.6 | 35.0 | 34.5 | 34.2 | 34.3 | 35.2 | 34.2 |
| **Financial Activities** | | | | | | | | | | | | | |
| 2015 | 35.9 | 36.0 | 36.9 | 36.0 | 36.3 | 36.7 | 36.7 | 37.1 | 36.6 | 37.2 | 37.6 | 37.0 | 36.7 |
| 2016 | 36.6 | 35.8 | 35.9 | 36.3 | 36.9 | 36.7 | 36.3 | 36.3 | 36.0 | 36.6 | 35.8 | 35.3 | 36.2 |
| 2017 | 36.3 | 35.6 | 35.8 | 36.9 | 35.8 | 36.4 | 37.1 | 36.7 | 37.1 | 38.2 | 37.4 | 37.6 | 36.7 |
| 2018 | 37.7 | 38.0 | 37.8 | 38.4 | 37.6 | 37.6 | 37.7 | 36.9 | 38.2 | 37.1 | 37.6 | 38.1 | 37.7 |
| 2019 | 37.8 | 37.5 | 37.2 | 37.4 | 37.7 | 38.1 | 37.5 | 37.3 | 38.0 | 37.4 | 37.7 | 38.6 | 37.7 |
| **Professional and Business Services** | | | | | | | | | | | | | |
| 2015 | 34.9 | 34.8 | 35.1 | 35.5 | 35.5 | 35.7 | 36.1 | 36.2 | 35.1 | 35.6 | 35.9 | 36.2 | 35.6 |
| 2016 | 35.3 | 35.5 | 35.9 | 36.1 | 36.3 | 36.9 | 36.4 | 36.8 | 36.8 | 37.4 | 37.0 | 37.3 | 36.5 |
| 2017 | 37.0 | 36.7 | 36.4 | 36.4 | 35.7 | 36.3 | 36.6 | 36.1 | 36.3 | 36.4 | 36.2 | 35.8 | 36.3 |
| 2018 | 34.9 | 35.9 | 35.6 | 36.0 | 35.4 | 36.3 | 35.9 | 35.3 | 35.6 | 35.6 | 35.2 | 35.0 | 35.6 |
| 2019 | 34.6 | 34.3 | 34.8 | 34.8 | 34.8 | 35.4 | 34.4 | 35.2 | 35.0 | 34.1 | 34.5 | 35.1 | 34.7 |
| **Education and Health Services** | | | | | | | | | | | | | |
| 2015 | 34.7 | 34.2 | 34.6 | 34.5 | 34.5 | 34.7 | 35.0 | 35.2 | 35.0 | 34.9 | 35.3 | 34.8 | 34.8 |
| 2016 | 34.5 | 34.6 | 34.8 | 35.0 | 35.0 | 34.6 | 34.4 | 34.1 | 34.4 | 34.7 | 34.7 | 34.6 | 34.6 |
| 2017 | 35.4 | 34.6 | 34.6 | 34.8 | 34.4 | 34.9 | 35.0 | 34.2 | 34.1 | 34.1 | 34.4 | 34.3 | 34.6 |
| 2018 | 33.5 | 34.4 | 34.3 | 34.3 | 34.1 | 34.3 | 34.6 | 34.3 | 34.9 | 35.0 | 34.6 | 34.9 | 34.4 |
| 2019 | 34.4 | 34.1 | 33.9 | 33.8 | 33.8 | 34.2 | 33.9 | 33.3 | 34.1 | 33.4 | 33.7 | 33.7 | 33.9 |
| **Leisure and Hospitality** | | | | | | | | | | | | | |
| 2015 | 24.2 | 23.8 | 24.7 | 24.8 | 24.3 | 24.9 | 24.9 | 24.9 | 24.6 | 25.1 | 24.9 | 25.4 | 24.7 |
| 2016 | 24.1 | 24.3 | 25.0 | 25.2 | 25.0 | 25.5 | 25.7 | 25.5 | 25.6 | 25.8 | 25.8 | 25.9 | 25.3 |
| 2017 | 25.6 | 25.3 | 25.5 | 25.6 | 25.5 | 26.4 | 26.8 | 26.6 | 26.2 | 26.4 | 26.0 | 26.3 | 26.0 |
| 2018 | 24.8 | 26.0 | 26.4 | 26.5 | 26.7 | 26.9 | 27.2 | 26.4 | 26.2 | 26.8 | 26.1 | 26.4 | 26.4 |
| 2019 | 25.2 | 25.5 | 25.8 | 25.5 | 25.9 | 26.6 | 26.7 | 26.0 | 26.0 | 26.1 | 25.6 | 25.9 | 25.9 |

# 3. Average Hourly Earnings by Selected Industry: Kentucky, 2015–2019

(Dollars, not seasonally adjusted)

| Industry and year | January | February | March | April | May | June | July | August | September | October | November | December | Annual average |
|---|---|---|---|---|---|---|---|---|---|---|---|---|---|
| **Total Private** | | | | | | | | | | | | | |
| 2015 | 21.21 | 21.26 | 21.17 | 21.13 | 21.08 | 20.97 | 21.16 | 21.14 | 21.08 | 20.90 | 20.94 | 20.98 | 21.08 |
| 2016 | 21.25 | 21.06 | 21.13 | 21.27 | 21.16 | 21.10 | 21.24 | 21.14 | 21.24 | 21.55 | 21.34 | 21.58 | 21.26 |
| 2017 | 21.92 | 21.74 | 21.76 | 22.01 | 21.87 | 21.67 | 21.94 | 21.74 | 21.86 | 21.82 | 21.73 | 21.80 | 21.82 |
| 2018 | 22.18 | 21.86 | 21.82 | 22.21 | 22.04 | 21.78 | 22.13 | 21.88 | 22.18 | 22.09 | 22.43 | 22.73 | 22.11 |
| 2019 | 22.80 | 22.86 | 22.64 | 22.58 | 22.60 | 22.76 | 22.73 | 22.68 | 23.01 | 22.97 | 23.06 | 23.20 | 22.83 |
| **Goods-Producing** | | | | | | | | | | | | | |
| 2015 | 22.71 | 22.71 | 22.75 | 22.94 | 22.78 | 22.68 | 23.10 | 22.72 | 22.62 | 22.73 | 22.93 | 22.97 | 22.80 |
| 2016 | 22.77 | 22.75 | 22.80 | 22.97 | 23.13 | 23.02 | 23.16 | 22.85 | 22.76 | 23.04 | 22.86 | 23.32 | 22.95 |
| 2017 | 23.42 | 23.24 | 23.14 | 23.37 | 23.41 | 23.47 | 23.36 | 23.25 | 23.20 | 23.18 | 22.99 | 23.03 | 23.25 |
| 2018 | 22.98 | 22.64 | 22.77 | 23.08 | 23.07 | 22.65 | 23.11 | 22.86 | 23.14 | 22.78 | 23.06 | 23.13 | 22.94 |
| 2019 | 23.32 | 23.00 | 23.29 | 22.97 | 23.30 | 23.71 | 23.47 | 23.53 | 23.88 | 24.01 | 24.39 | 24.51 | 23.62 |
| **Construction** | | | | | | | | | | | | | |
| 2015 | 23.11 | 23.46 | 23.61 | 23.73 | 23.50 | 23.72 | 24.63 | 23.99 | 23.45 | 23.42 | 23.90 | 23.92 | 23.72 |
| 2016 | 24.03 | 24.71 | 24.05 | 24.29 | 24.97 | 24.94 | 24.15 | 24.12 | 23.63 | 24.36 | 23.87 | 23.91 | 24.25 |
| 2017 | 23.67 | 24.23 | 24.54 | 24.88 | 24.88 | 25.27 | 25.03 | 25.15 | 25.43 | 25.40 | 25.44 | 25.97 | 25.01 |
| 2018 | 25.37 | 25.43 | 25.63 | 25.75 | 25.86 | 24.97 | 24.84 | 24.42 | 25.09 | 24.85 | 25.23 | 25.28 | 25.21 |
| 2019 | 25.04 | 25.12 | 25.07 | 24.79 | 24.87 | 25.27 | 24.82 | 24.55 | 24.84 | 25.01 | 25.51 | 25.80 | 25.05 |
| **Manufacturing** | | | | | | | | | | | | | |
| 2015 | 22.24 | 22.15 | 22.17 | 22.38 | 22.19 | 21.89 | 22.13 | 21.80 | 21.94 | 21.96 | 22.04 | 22.03 | 22.07 |
| 2016 | 21.66 | 21.50 | 21.74 | 21.93 | 21.96 | 21.74 | 22.32 | 21.91 | 22.04 | 22.14 | 22.11 | 22.78 | 21.99 |
| 2017 | 23.00 | 22.50 | 22.20 | 22.40 | 22.40 | 22.32 | 22.32 | 21.99 | 22.12 | 22.04 | 21.81 | 21.77 | 22.24 |
| 2018 | 21.93 | 21.46 | 21.57 | 21.90 | 21.77 | 21.49 | 22.17 | 22.00 | 22.09 | 21.63 | 21.91 | 21.98 | 21.83 |
| 2019 | 22.26 | 21.85 | 22.30 | 21.74 | 22.21 | 22.74 | 22.54 | 22.76 | 23.17 | 23.23 | 23.59 | 23.61 | 22.67 |
| **Trade, Transportation, and Utilities** | | | | | | | | | | | | | |
| 2015 | 20.04 | 20.00 | 19.89 | 20.10 | 20.01 | 20.18 | 20.09 | 20.25 | 20.17 | 20.08 | 20.03 | 19.89 | 20.06 |
| 2016 | 20.70 | 20.30 | 20.44 | 20.48 | 19.95 | 20.05 | 20.39 | 20.40 | 20.50 | 20.79 | 20.29 | 20.46 | 20.40 |
| 2017 | 20.95 | 20.68 | 20.77 | 21.16 | 21.05 | 21.04 | 21.17 | 21.01 | 21.24 | 20.91 | 20.85 | 20.74 | 20.96 |
| 2018 | 21.20 | 20.93 | 20.83 | 21.36 | 21.01 | 20.99 | 21.48 | 21.19 | 21.22 | 21.54 | 21.70 | 21.90 | 21.29 |
| 2019 | 22.15 | 22.40 | 22.32 | 22.25 | 22.21 | 22.50 | 22.34 | 21.90 | 22.42 | 22.20 | 22.16 | 22.05 | 22.24 |
| **Financial Activities** | | | | | | | | | | | | | |
| 2015 | 22.31 | 22.68 | 22.44 | 22.92 | 22.25 | 22.34 | 22.69 | 23.16 | 22.86 | 23.11 | 23.07 | 23.14 | 22.75 |
| 2016 | 23.44 | 24.08 | 23.95 | 23.71 | 23.58 | 23.25 | 23.64 | 23.34 | 23.86 | 24.66 | 24.39 | 25.02 | 23.91 |
| 2017 | 26.03 | 26.09 | 26.19 | 26.78 | 26.04 | 26.28 | 27.22 | 26.47 | 26.64 | 26.90 | 27.19 | 27.34 | 26.61 |
| 2018 | 28.31 | 27.79 | 27.14 | 27.73 | 27.84 | 27.35 | 27.81 | 26.88 | 26.86 | 26.30 | 26.37 | 26.83 | 27.27 |
| 2019 | 26.15 | 26.59 | 26.17 | 26.58 | 26.92 | 27.20 | 26.68 | 26.89 | 26.67 | 26.78 | 26.53 | 27.26 | 26.70 |
| **Professional and Business Services** | | | | | | | | | | | | | |
| 2015 | 20.84 | 21.33 | 21.54 | 21.09 | 21.24 | 21.28 | 21.88 | 22.29 | 22.16 | 22.19 | 22.33 | 22.21 | 21.71 |
| 2016 | 22.82 | 22.57 | 22.66 | 22.65 | 23.07 | 22.71 | 22.48 | 22.02 | 21.95 | 22.25 | 22.20 | 22.13 | 22.45 |
| 2017 | 22.89 | 23.16 | 23.19 | 23.65 | 23.51 | 23.02 | 23.51 | 23.50 | 23.32 | 23.28 | 23.15 | 23.52 | 23.31 |
| 2018 | 24.10 | 23.77 | 23.79 | 23.78 | 23.56 | 23.19 | 23.31 | 23.17 | 23.67 | 23.30 | 23.37 | 23.38 | 23.53 |
| 2019 | 23.35 | 23.24 | 23.11 | 22.85 | 22.83 | 22.84 | 23.22 | 23.35 | 23.80 | 23.80 | 23.82 | 24.35 | 23.39 |
| **Education and Health Services** | | | | | | | | | | | | | |
| 2015 | 24.34 | 24.18 | 24.02 | 23.65 | 23.87 | 23.48 | 23.47 | 23.12 | 23.26 | 23.29 | 22.89 | 23.22 | 23.56 |
| 2016 | 23.08 | 22.71 | 22.75 | 22.41 | 22.10 | 22.27 | 22.56 | 22.66 | 22.70 | 22.96 | 22.88 | 22.99 | 22.67 |
| 2017 | 22.84 | 22.70 | 22.75 | 22.62 | 22.66 | 22.39 | 22.89 | 22.51 | 22.55 | 22.68 | 22.52 | 22.54 | 22.64 |
| 2018 | 23.30 | 23.00 | 23.00 | 23.64 | 23.17 | 23.07 | 23.57 | 23.43 | 23.64 | 23.77 | 24.18 | 24.40 | 23.52 |
| 2019 | 24.72 | 24.80 | 23.86 | 24.09 | 23.85 | 24.13 | 24.79 | 24.84 | 24.71 | 25.07 | 24.42 | 24.58 | 24.49 |
| **Leisure and Hospitality** | | | | | | | | | | | | | |
| 2015 | 11.37 | 11.55 | 11.36 | 11.41 | 11.33 | 11.19 | 11.31 | 11.44 | 11.34 | 11.47 | 11.51 | 11.58 | 11.40 |
| 2016 | 11.46 | 11.55 | 11.59 | 11.53 | 11.69 | 11.55 | 11.48 | 11.59 | 11.70 | 11.82 | 11.76 | 12.01 | 11.65 |
| 2017 | 11.95 | 12.12 | 12.20 | 12.10 | 12.18 | 11.90 | 12.04 | 12.11 | 12.29 | 12.44 | 12.40 | 12.69 | 12.20 |
| 2018 | 12.57 | 12.69 | 12.61 | 12.55 | 12.57 | 12.50 | 12.52 | 12.54 | 12.83 | 12.80 | 12.82 | 13.04 | 12.67 |
| 2019 | 12.82 | 12.89 | 12.82 | 12.90 | 12.86 | 12.65 | 12.72 | 12.80 | 13.00 | 12.92 | 12.97 | 13.09 | 12.87 |

## 4. Average Weekly Earnings by Selected Industry: Kentucky, 2015–2019

(Dollars, not seasonally adjusted)

| Industry and year | January | February | March | April | May | June | July | August | September | October | November | December | Annual average |
|---|---|---|---|---|---|---|---|---|---|---|---|---|---|
| **Total Private** | | | | | | | | | | | | | |
| 2015 | 740.23 | 731.34 | 740.95 | 741.66 | 742.02 | 744.44 | 749.06 | 754.70 | 744.12 | 741.95 | 747.56 | 751.08 | 744.12 |
| 2016 | 739.50 | 732.89 | 741.66 | 746.58 | 740.60 | 749.05 | 747.65 | 739.90 | 745.52 | 762.87 | 753.30 | 763.93 | 746.23 |
| 2017 | 773.78 | 758.73 | 757.25 | 768.15 | 756.70 | 760.62 | 774.48 | 767.42 | 767.29 | 770.25 | 760.55 | 767.36 | 765.88 |
| 2018 | 749.68 | 758.54 | 759.34 | 777.35 | 766.99 | 766.66 | 781.19 | 767.99 | 787.39 | 784.20 | 789.54 | 806.92 | 773.85 |
| 2019 | 795.72 | 795.53 | 787.87 | 785.78 | 791.00 | 807.98 | 800.10 | 800.60 | 816.86 | 803.95 | 807.10 | 818.96 | 801.33 |
| **Goods-Producing** | | | | | | | | | | | | | |
| 2015 | 933.38 | 903.86 | 921.38 | 938.25 | 943.09 | 943.49 | 947.10 | 949.70 | 922.90 | 936.48 | 944.72 | 964.74 | 937.08 |
| 2016 | 913.08 | 900.90 | 909.72 | 923.39 | 925.20 | 948.42 | 928.72 | 927.71 | 930.88 | 937.73 | 941.83 | 953.79 | 929.48 |
| 2017 | 950.85 | 936.57 | 927.91 | 937.14 | 941.08 | 957.58 | 960.10 | 962.55 | 946.56 | 959.65 | 937.99 | 953.44 | 948.60 |
| 2018 | 898.52 | 914.66 | 917.63 | 948.59 | 941.26 | 919.59 | 942.89 | 960.12 | 974.19 | 956.76 | 952.38 | 969.15 | 940.54 |
| 2019 | 960.78 | 947.60 | 959.55 | 946.36 | 964.62 | 993.45 | 974.01 | 990.61 | 995.80 | 994.01 | 1007.31 | 1000.01 | 977.87 |
| **Construction** | | | | | | | | | | | | | |
| 2015 | 887.42 | 865.67 | 875.93 | 901.74 | 935.30 | 946.43 | 967.96 | 966.80 | 891.10 | 953.19 | 939.27 | 966.37 | 927.45 |
| 2016 | 920.35 | 899.44 | 916.31 | 954.60 | 946.36 | 1007.58 | 944.27 | 945.50 | 928.66 | 959.78 | 938.09 | 934.88 | 943.33 |
| 2017 | 923.13 | 947.39 | 954.61 | 970.32 | 955.39 | 1013.33 | 1036.24 | 1026.12 | 1001.94 | 1023.62 | 992.16 | 1018.02 | 990.40 |
| 2018 | 910.78 | 943.45 | 948.31 | 991.38 | 1013.71 | 971.33 | 998.57 | 954.82 | 988.55 | 981.58 | 958.74 | 983.39 | 970.59 |
| 2019 | 964.04 | 974.66 | 987.76 | 974.25 | 977.39 | 1025.96 | 1012.66 | 1004.10 | 1015.96 | 1000.40 | 997.44 | 1006.20 | 994.49 |
| **Manufacturing** | | | | | | | | | | | | | |
| 2015 | 916.29 | 883.79 | 904.54 | 922.06 | 918.67 | 915.00 | 905.12 | 909.06 | 903.93 | 904.75 | 919.07 | 936.28 | 911.49 |
| 2016 | 881.54 | 885.80 | 891.34 | 896.94 | 902.56 | 910.91 | 908.42 | 904.88 | 916.86 | 918.81 | 933.04 | 952.20 | 908.19 |
| 2017 | 947.60 | 918.00 | 901.32 | 909.44 | 916.16 | 915.17 | 913.30 | 912.59 | 911.34 | 912.46 | 896.39 | 912.16 | 914.06 |
| 2018 | 870.62 | 882.01 | 886.53 | 915.42 | 894.75 | 881.09 | 906.75 | 930.60 | 938.83 | 912.79 | 918.03 | 931.95 | 905.95 |
| 2019 | 923.79 | 906.78 | 918.76 | 900.04 | 926.16 | 952.81 | 930.90 | 960.47 | 966.19 | 971.01 | 988.42 | 972.73 | 943.07 |
| **Trade, Transportation, and Utilities** | | | | | | | | | | | | | |
| 2015 | 695.39 | 694.00 | 702.12 | 717.57 | 718.36 | 726.48 | 719.22 | 733.05 | 726.12 | 720.87 | 725.09 | 722.01 | 716.14 |
| 2016 | 716.22 | 714.56 | 715.40 | 712.70 | 692.27 | 705.76 | 721.81 | 703.80 | 701.10 | 719.33 | 689.86 | 705.87 | 707.88 |
| 2017 | 703.92 | 692.78 | 699.95 | 717.32 | 709.39 | 709.05 | 717.66 | 710.14 | 715.79 | 700.49 | 698.48 | 701.01 | 706.35 |
| 2018 | 676.28 | 680.23 | 689.47 | 711.29 | 699.63 | 711.56 | 728.17 | 716.22 | 725.72 | 734.51 | 739.97 | 748.98 | 713.22 |
| 2019 | 744.24 | 748.16 | 749.95 | 747.60 | 757.36 | 780.75 | 772.96 | 766.50 | 773.49 | 759.24 | 760.09 | 776.16 | 760.61 |
| **Financial Activities** | | | | | | | | | | | | | |
| 2015 | 800.93 | 816.48 | 828.04 | 825.12 | 807.68 | 819.88 | 832.72 | 859.24 | 836.68 | 859.69 | 867.43 | 856.18 | 834.93 |
| 2016 | 857.90 | 862.06 | 859.81 | 860.67 | 870.10 | 853.28 | 858.13 | 847.24 | 858.96 | 902.56 | 873.16 | 883.21 | 865.54 |
| 2017 | 944.89 | 928.80 | 937.60 | 988.18 | 932.23 | 956.59 | 1009.86 | 971.45 | 988.34 | 1027.58 | 1016.91 | 1027.98 | 976.59 |
| 2018 | 1067.29 | 1056.02 | 1025.89 | 1064.83 | 1046.78 | 1028.36 | 1048.44 | 991.87 | 1026.05 | 975.73 | 991.51 | 1022.22 | 1028.08 |
| 2019 | 988.47 | 997.13 | 973.52 | 994.09 | 1014.88 | 1036.32 | 1000.50 | 1003.00 | 1013.46 | 1001.57 | 1000.18 | 1052.24 | 1006.59 |
| **Professional and Business Services** | | | | | | | | | | | | | |
| 2015 | 727.32 | 742.28 | 756.05 | 748.70 | 754.02 | 759.70 | 789.87 | 806.90 | 777.82 | 789.96 | 801.65 | 804.00 | 772.88 |
| 2016 | 805.55 | 801.24 | 813.49 | 817.67 | 837.44 | 838.00 | 818.27 | 810.34 | 807.76 | 832.15 | 821.40 | 825.45 | 819.43 |
| 2017 | 846.93 | 849.97 | 844.12 | 860.86 | 839.31 | 835.63 | 860.47 | 848.35 | 846.52 | 847.39 | 838.03 | 842.02 | 846.15 |
| 2018 | 841.09 | 853.34 | 846.92 | 856.08 | 834.02 | 841.80 | 836.83 | 817.90 | 842.65 | 829.48 | 822.62 | 818.30 | 837.67 |
| 2019 | 807.91 | 797.13 | 804.23 | 795.18 | 794.48 | 808.54 | 798.77 | 821.92 | 833.00 | 811.58 | 821.79 | 854.69 | 811.63 |
| **Education and Health Services** | | | | | | | | | | | | | |
| 2015 | 844.60 | 826.96 | 831.09 | 815.93 | 823.52 | 814.76 | 821.45 | 813.82 | 814.10 | 812.82 | 808.02 | 808.06 | 819.89 |
| 2016 | 796.26 | 785.77 | 791.70 | 784.35 | 773.50 | 770.54 | 776.06 | 772.71 | 780.88 | 796.71 | 793.94 | 795.45 | 784.38 |
| 2017 | 808.54 | 785.42 | 787.15 | 787.18 | 779.50 | 781.41 | 801.15 | 769.84 | 768.96 | 773.39 | 774.69 | 773.12 | 783.34 |
| 2018 | 780.55 | 791.20 | 788.90 | 810.85 | 790.10 | 791.30 | 815.52 | 803.65 | 825.04 | 831.95 | 836.63 | 851.56 | 809.09 |
| 2019 | 850.37 | 845.68 | 808.85 | 814.24 | 806.13 | 825.25 | 840.38 | 827.17 | 842.61 | 837.34 | 822.95 | 828.35 | 830.21 |
| **Leisure and Hospitality** | | | | | | | | | | | | | |
| 2015 | 275.15 | 274.89 | 280.59 | 282.97 | 275.32 | 278.63 | 281.62 | 284.86 | 278.96 | 287.90 | 286.60 | 294.13 | 281.58 |
| 2016 | 276.19 | 280.67 | 289.75 | 290.56 | 292.25 | 294.53 | 295.04 | 295.55 | 299.52 | 304.96 | 303.41 | 311.06 | 294.75 |
| 2017 | 305.92 | 306.64 | 311.10 | 309.76 | 310.59 | 314.16 | 322.67 | 322.13 | 322.00 | 328.42 | 322.40 | 333.75 | 317.20 |
| 2018 | 311.74 | 329.94 | 332.90 | 332.58 | 335.62 | 336.25 | 340.54 | 331.06 | 336.15 | 343.04 | 334.60 | 344.26 | 334.49 |
| 2019 | 323.06 | 328.70 | 330.76 | 328.95 | 333.07 | 336.49 | 339.62 | 332.80 | 338.00 | 337.21 | 332.03 | 339.03 | 333.33 |

# LOUISIANA
*At a Glance*

Population:
  2010 census: 4,533,372
  2019 estimate: 4,648,794

Percent change in population:
  2010–2019: 2.5%

Percent change in total nonfarm employment:
  2011–2019: 4.4%

Industry with the largest growth in employment, 2011–2019(percent):
  Leisure and hospitality, 18.6%

Industry with the largest decline or smallest growth in employment, 2011–2019 (percent):
  Mining and logging, -32.9%

Civilian labor force:
  2010: 2,086,076
  2019: 2,095,452

Unemployment rate and rank among states (highest to lowest):
  2010: 8.0%, 35th
  2019: 4.8%, 6th

Over-the-year change in unemployment rates:
  2017–2018: -0.2%
  2018–2019: -0.1%

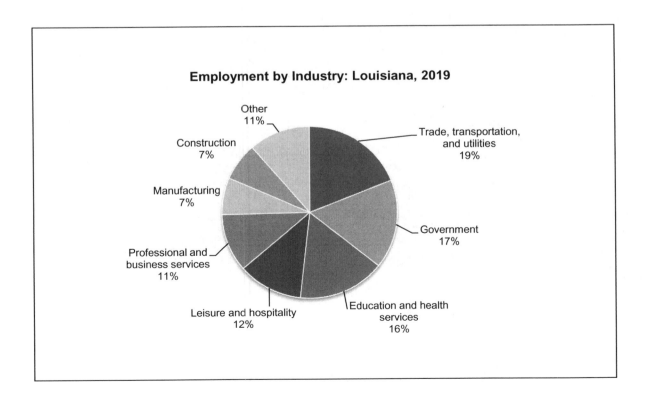

**Employment by Industry: Louisiana, 2019**

Other 11%
Construction 7%
Manufacturing 7%
Professional and business services 11%
Leisure and hospitality 12%
Education and health services 16%
Government 17%
Trade, transportation, and utilities 19%

## 1. Employment by Industry: Louisiana, 2011–2019

(Numbers in thousands, not seasonally adjusted)

| Industry and year | January | February | March | April | May | June | July | August | September | October | November | December | Annual average |
|---|---|---|---|---|---|---|---|---|---|---|---|---|---|
| **Total Nonfarm** | | | | | | | | | | | | | |
| 2011 | 1,875.2 | 1,889.6 | 1,901.2 | 1,910.3 | 1,911.8 | 1,899.9 | 1,890.9 | 1,898.4 | 1,913.0 | 1,920.8 | 1,927.8 | 1,927.4 | 1,905.5 |
| 2012 | 1,897.6 | 1,911.6 | 1,923.3 | 1,937.6 | 1,944.1 | 1,934.2 | 1,910.7 | 1,920.3 | 1,924.3 | 1,942.3 | 1,954.7 | 1,954.1 | 1,929.6 |
| 2013 | 1,920.8 | 1,940.0 | 1,948.9 | 1,956.5 | 1,959.7 | 1,956.1 | 1,938.8 | 1,953.4 | 1,959.7 | 1,977.1 | 1,988.2 | 1,979.6 | 1,956.6 |
| 2014 | 1,950.5 | 1,961.5 | 1,973.5 | 1,980.1 | 1,989.2 | 1,984.4 | 1,972.5 | 1,986.8 | 1,994.2 | 2,012.8 | 2,020.9 | 2,021.6 | 1,987.3 |
| 2015 | 1,985.6 | 1,991.1 | 1,992.7 | 1,998.8 | 2,003.3 | 1,995.8 | 1,984.4 | 1,988.6 | 1,990.9 | 2,009.9 | 2,010.3 | 2,005.1 | 1,996.4 |
| 2016 | 1,968.0 | 1,971.7 | 1,976.3 | 1,984.0 | 1,985.7 | 1,975.1 | 1,961.5 | 1,956.4 | 1,974.1 | 1,981.6 | 1,985.7 | 1,978.0 | 1,974.8 |
| 2017 | 1,952.5 | 1,969.8 | 1,972.7 | 1,976.3 | 1,984.6 | 1,976.8 | 1,956.1 | 1,964.6 | 1,971.8 | 1,984.9 | 1,992.8 | 1,989.1 | 1,974.3 |
| 2018 | 1,957.5 | 1,970.7 | 1,988.2 | 1,994.0 | 1,997.4 | 1,990.6 | 1,969.9 | 1,984.3 | 1,987.0 | 2,009.0 | 2,015.5 | 2,004.6 | 1,989.1 |
| 2019 | 1,976.6 | 1,990.3 | 1,992.1 | 2,000.8 | 2,001.3 | 1,987.6 | 1,960.3 | 1,979.3 | 1,981.1 | 1,994.7 | 2,006.3 | 1,994.9 | 1,988.8 |
| **Total Private** | | | | | | | | | | | | | |
| 2011 | 1,514.8 | 1,525.0 | 1,536.7 | 1,546.0 | 1,549.1 | 1,543.5 | 1,545.0 | 1,550.8 | 1,553.7 | 1,557.2 | 1,563.7 | 1,566.3 | 1,546.0 |
| 2012 | 1,544.9 | 1,554.7 | 1,567.2 | 1,580.5 | 1,588.1 | 1,584.5 | 1,572.3 | 1,580.7 | 1,575.6 | 1,588.4 | 1,600.1 | 1,600.3 | 1,578.1 |
| 2013 | 1,577.4 | 1,591.9 | 1,601.0 | 1,609.0 | 1,613.1 | 1,615.5 | 1,609.2 | 1,624.8 | 1,620.0 | 1,636.1 | 1,644.9 | 1,638.9 | 1,615.2 |
| 2014 | 1,617.8 | 1,624.4 | 1,637.7 | 1,645.1 | 1,654.6 | 1,654.1 | 1,654.4 | 1,665.6 | 1,661.1 | 1,676.9 | 1,683.1 | 1,686.9 | 1,655.1 |
| 2015 | 1,657.1 | 1,658.1 | 1,661.0 | 1,665.9 | 1,671.0 | 1,667.6 | 1,667.3 | 1,668.8 | 1,659.8 | 1,676.9 | 1,675.2 | 1,673.5 | 1,666.9 |
| 2016 | 1,640.8 | 1,640.5 | 1,646.1 | 1,652.8 | 1,652.8 | 1,647.1 | 1,645.8 | 1,639.0 | 1,643.0 | 1,647.1 | 1,649.1 | 1,644.2 | 1,645.7 |
| 2017 | 1,624.2 | 1,636.8 | 1,640.6 | 1,643.1 | 1,650.9 | 1,649.1 | 1,640.2 | 1,646.5 | 1,642.3 | 1,650.5 | 1,657.6 | 1,655.2 | 1,644.8 |
| 2018 | 1,630.0 | 1,638.1 | 1,654.7 | 1,658.7 | 1,664.3 | 1,663.4 | 1,654.4 | 1,663.8 | 1,656.9 | 1,673.8 | 1,679.3 | 1,671.6 | 1,659.1 |
| 2019 | 1,649.5 | 1,657.2 | 1,659.3 | 1,665.0 | 1,667.0 | 1,660.5 | 1,643.5 | 1,656.1 | 1,648.2 | 1,657.5 | 1,667.7 | 1,659.2 | 1,657.6 |
| **Goods Producing** | | | | | | | | | | | | | |
| 2011 | 308.0 | 310.9 | 314.1 | 317.0 | 316.8 | 316.7 | 319.7 | 319.5 | 321.0 | 320.7 | 318.1 | 316.7 | 316.6 |
| 2012 | 316.1 | 319.9 | 322.8 | 323.4 | 326.4 | 328.1 | 323.7 | 326.0 | 326.8 | 328.6 | 328.2 | 325.5 | 324.6 |
| 2013 | 320.8 | 325.5 | 328.9 | 329.1 | 330.8 | 333.7 | 332.9 | 334.6 | 334.8 | 338.9 | 336.5 | 331.9 | 331.5 |
| 2014 | 331.7 | 333.9 | 338.0 | 337.0 | 342.0 | 342.0 | 345.8 | 347.8 | 348.4 | 352.0 | 346.4 | 344.0 | 342.4 |
| 2015 | 338.4 | 336.3 | 334.9 | 331.4 | 330.8 | 331.7 | 333.5 | 333.0 | 331.5 | 335.3 | 329.1 | 324.9 | 332.6 |
| 2016 | 317.5 | 316.5 | 316.9 | 313.9 | 313.5 | 315.8 | 316.8 | 311.9 | 314.5 | 316.0 | 312.6 | 310.5 | 314.7 |
| 2017 | 310.3 | 314.3 | 315.7 | 316.1 | 318.7 | 320.4 | 320.2 | 320.5 | 317.8 | 320.8 | 317.9 | 317.6 | 317.5 |
| 2018 | 312.7 | 316.9 | 323.7 | 322.7 | 325.1 | 328.9 | 327.4 | 327.3 | 325.4 | 330.3 | 327.6 | 324.2 | 324.4 |
| 2019 | 319.0 | 320.4 | 322.5 | 319.2 | 319.4 | 317.7 | 312.8 | 313.8 | 311.9 | 312.6 | 312.1 | 310.5 | 316.0 |
| **Service-Providing** | | | | | | | | | | | | | |
| 2011 | 1,567.2 | 1,578.7 | 1,587.1 | 1,593.3 | 1,595.0 | 1,583.2 | 1,571.2 | 1,578.9 | 1,592.0 | 1,600.1 | 1,609.7 | 1,610.7 | 1,588.9 |
| 2012 | 1,581.5 | 1,591.7 | 1,600.5 | 1,614.2 | 1,617.7 | 1,606.1 | 1,587.0 | 1,594.3 | 1,597.5 | 1,613.7 | 1,626.5 | 1,628.6 | 1,604.9 |
| 2013 | 1,600.0 | 1,614.5 | 1,620.0 | 1,627.4 | 1,628.9 | 1,622.4 | 1,605.9 | 1,618.8 | 1,624.9 | 1,638.2 | 1,651.7 | 1,647.7 | 1,625.0 |
| 2014 | 1,618.8 | 1,627.6 | 1,635.5 | 1,643.1 | 1,647.2 | 1,642.4 | 1,626.7 | 1,639.0 | 1,645.8 | 1,660.8 | 1,674.5 | 1,677.6 | 1,644.9 |
| 2015 | 1,647.2 | 1,654.8 | 1,657.8 | 1,667.4 | 1,672.5 | 1,664.1 | 1,650.9 | 1,655.6 | 1,659.4 | 1,674.6 | 1,681.2 | 1,680.2 | 1,663.8 |
| 2016 | 1,650.5 | 1,655.2 | 1,659.4 | 1,670.1 | 1,672.2 | 1,659.3 | 1,644.7 | 1,644.5 | 1,659.6 | 1,665.6 | 1,673.1 | 1,667.5 | 1,660.1 |
| 2017 | 1,642.2 | 1,655.5 | 1,657.0 | 1,660.2 | 1,665.9 | 1,656.4 | 1,635.9 | 1,644.1 | 1,654.0 | 1,664.1 | 1,674.9 | 1,671.5 | 1,656.8 |
| 2018 | 1,644.8 | 1,653.8 | 1,664.5 | 1,671.3 | 1,672.3 | 1,661.7 | 1,642.5 | 1,657.0 | 1,661.6 | 1,678.7 | 1,687.9 | 1,680.4 | 1,664.7 |
| 2019 | 1,657.6 | 1,669.9 | 1,669.6 | 1,681.6 | 1,681.9 | 1,669.9 | 1,647.5 | 1,665.5 | 1,669.2 | 1,682.1 | 1,694.2 | 1,684.4 | 1,672.8 |
| **Mining and Logging** | | | | | | | | | | | | | |
| 2011 | 52.7 | 53.2 | 53.4 | 54.4 | 54.3 | 55.0 | 55.9 | 56.1 | 56.2 | 56.0 | 56.1 | 56.2 | 55.0 |
| 2012 | 57.3 | 58.0 | 57.7 | 56.4 | 57.0 | 56.9 | 55.2 | 55.5 | 54.9 | 55.1 | 55.1 | 54.7 | 56.2 |
| 2013 | 54.4 | 54.9 | 55.1 | 55.5 | 55.8 | 56.3 | 56.5 | 56.8 | 56.3 | 56.3 | 56.1 | 55.7 | 55.8 |
| 2014 | 55.6 | 55.4 | 55.5 | 55.2 | 55.8 | 55.8 | 56.5 | 56.4 | 56.2 | 56.3 | 56.0 | 55.9 | 55.9 |
| 2015 | 54.7 | 52.5 | 51.1 | 49.0 | 48.7 | 47.5 | 47.3 | 46.9 | 45.9 | 44.9 | 43.5 | 43.1 | 47.9 |
| 2016 | 42.2 | 41.0 | 40.0 | 38.8 | 38.1 | 37.8 | 37.9 | 37.3 | 37.0 | 36.7 | 36.2 | 36.3 | 38.3 |
| 2017 | 35.3 | 35.3 | 35.4 | 35.4 | 35.7 | 36.1 | 36.3 | 36.1 | 35.9 | 36.0 | 36.0 | 36.1 | 35.8 |
| 2018 | 35.8 | 35.9 | 36.1 | 36.5 | 36.7 | 36.9 | 37.2 | 37.2 | 37.1 | 37.2 | 36.9 | 36.7 | 36.7 |
| 2019 | 36.4 | 36.4 | 36.7 | 37.0 | 37.1 | 37.1 | 37.1 | 37.2 | 36.6 | 36.9 | 36.8 | 37.3 | 36.9 |
| **Construction** | | | | | | | | | | | | | |
| 2011 | 118.4 | 120.3 | 122.8 | 124.4 | 123.5 | 122.5 | 123.4 | 122.5 | 123.1 | 122.3 | 120.3 | 118.8 | 121.9 |
| 2012 | 119.2 | 122.1 | 124.4 | 125.2 | 126.5 | 127.6 | 125.2 | 127.0 | 128.8 | 130.6 | 130.1 | 127.8 | 126.2 |
| 2013 | 124.5 | 128.4 | 131.1 | 130.6 | 131.1 | 132.3 | 131.4 | 132.2 | 132.8 | 135.6 | 133.6 | 129.7 | 131.1 |
| 2014 | 129.7 | 132.8 | 136.6 | 135.4 | 138.8 | 138.2 | 141.2 | 142.9 | 144.2 | 146.8 | 141.8 | 139.6 | 139.0 |
| 2015 | 136.6 | 137.5 | 138.9 | 138.0 | 137.9 | 139.8 | 141.8 | 142.1 | 142.6 | 147.6 | 143.8 | 140.7 | 140.6 |
| 2016 | 136.8 | 137.6 | 139.8 | 138.3 | 138.7 | 141.6 | 143.1 | 139.7 | 142.5 | 144.6 | 142.1 | 139.9 | 140.4 |
| 2017 | 141.4 | 144.8 | 146.1 | 146.2 | 148.3 | 148.8 | 149.1 | 149.4 | 147.5 | 149.8 | 146.8 | 142.2 | 147.0 |
| 2018 | 143.0 | 147.1 | 153.0 | 151.6 | 153.3 | 155.7 | 154.5 | 154.0 | 152.5 | 155.9 | 153.3 | 149.8 | 152.0 |
| 2019 | 145.3 | 146.6 | 148.0 | 144.7 | 144.5 | 142.3 | 137.8 | 139.1 | 138.2 | 139.2 | 138.4 | 135.7 | 141.7 |

## 1. Employment by Industry: Louisiana, 2011–2019—*Continued*

(Numbers in thousands, not seasonally adjusted)

| Industry and year | January | February | March | April | May | June | July | August | September | October | November | December | Annual average |
|---|---|---|---|---|---|---|---|---|---|---|---|---|---|
| **Manufacturing** | | | | | | | | | | | | | |
| 2011 | 136.9 | 137.4 | 137.9 | 138.2 | 139.0 | 139.2 | 140.4 | 140.9 | 141.7 | 142.4 | 141.7 | 141.7 | 139.8 |
| 2012 | 139.6 | 139.8 | 140.7 | 141.8 | 142.9 | 143.6 | 143.3 | 143.5 | 143.1 | 143.0 | 143.0 | 143.0 | 142.3 |
| 2013 | 141.9 | 142.2 | 142.7 | 143.0 | 143.9 | 145.1 | 145.0 | 145.6 | 145.7 | 147.0 | 146.8 | 146.5 | 144.6 |
| 2014 | 146.4 | 145.7 | 145.9 | 146.4 | 147.4 | 148.0 | 148.1 | 148.5 | 148.0 | 148.9 | 148.6 | 148.5 | 147.5 |
| 2015 | 147.1 | 146.3 | 144.9 | 144.4 | 144.2 | 144.4 | 144.4 | 144.0 | 143.0 | 142.8 | 141.8 | 141.1 | 144.0 |
| 2016 | 138.5 | 137.9 | 137.1 | 136.8 | 136.7 | 136.4 | 135.8 | 134.9 | 135.0 | 134.7 | 134.3 | 134.3 | 136.0 |
| 2017 | 133.6 | 134.2 | 134.2 | 134.5 | 134.7 | 135.5 | 134.8 | 135.0 | 134.4 | 135.0 | 135.1 | 135.3 | 134.7 |
| 2018 | 133.9 | 133.9 | 134.6 | 134.6 | 135.1 | 136.3 | 135.7 | 136.1 | 135.8 | 137.2 | 137.4 | 137.7 | 135.7 |
| 2019 | 137.3 | 137.4 | 137.8 | 137.5 | 137.8 | 138.3 | 137.9 | 137.5 | 137.1 | 136.5 | 136.9 | 137.5 | 137.5 |
| **Trade, Transportation, and Utilities** | | | | | | | | | | | | | |
| 2011 | 369.7 | 368.8 | 370.6 | 373.0 | 373.9 | 373.0 | 373.8 | 373.8 | 373.1 | 374.5 | 381.2 | 384.1 | 374.1 |
| 2012 | 373.5 | 372.0 | 374.7 | 376.2 | 377.5 | 377.2 | 375.5 | 375.8 | 374.7 | 378.8 | 387.5 | 389.5 | 377.7 |
| 2013 | 377.9 | 376.5 | 379.7 | 380.1 | 380.3 | 381.4 | 380.8 | 382.4 | 383.1 | 384.7 | 391.0 | 395.5 | 382.8 |
| 2014 | 383.1 | 381.6 | 384.2 | 385.5 | 387.2 | 388.5 | 387.9 | 389.6 | 389.4 | 391.8 | 399.4 | 405.2 | 389.5 |
| 2015 | 392.3 | 389.4 | 391.1 | 391.7 | 392.6 | 393.0 | 392.0 | 392.6 | 390.3 | 393.5 | 398.9 | 401.4 | 393.2 |
| 2016 | 388.9 | 386.7 | 387.8 | 387.9 | 387.6 | 386.5 | 386.3 | 385.5 | 384.5 | 386.3 | 392.6 | 394.9 | 388.0 |
| 2017 | 383.3 | 380.9 | 381.9 | 381.8 | 382.2 | 381.6 | 379.5 | 380.5 | 378.6 | 379.5 | 387.2 | 388.7 | 382.1 |
| 2018 | 379.3 | 377.4 | 379.5 | 379.4 | 380.8 | 379.4 | 378.8 | 380.4 | 378.6 | 381.0 | 389.6 | 389.9 | 381.2 |
| 2019 | 380.4 | 377.6 | 377.9 | 378.4 | 379.1 | 377.7 | 376.5 | 377.8 | 375.7 | 377.5 | 384.0 | 383.3 | 378.8 |
| **Wholesale Trade** | | | | | | | | | | | | | |
| 2011 | 71.5 | 71.7 | 72.0 | 71.4 | 71.9 | 71.9 | 72.4 | 72.4 | 72.4 | 72.5 | 72.6 | 72.7 | 72.1 |
| 2012 | 71.8 | 72.0 | 72.3 | 72.6 | 72.6 | 72.7 | 72.4 | 72.4 | 72.0 | 72.3 | 72.5 | 72.5 | 72.3 |
| 2013 | 72.6 | 72.7 | 73.1 | 73.0 | 73.1 | 73.2 | 73.1 | 73.4 | 73.3 | 73.4 | 73.5 | 73.4 | 73.2 |
| 2014 | 72.3 | 72.5 | 72.8 | 72.9 | 73.3 | 73.3 | 73.2 | 73.4 | 73.6 | 73.6 | 73.6 | 73.8 | 73.2 |
| 2015 | 73.0 | 72.7 | 72.9 | 72.5 | 72.5 | 72.4 | 72.2 | 72.2 | 71.7 | 72.0 | 71.6 | 71.7 | 72.3 |
| 2016 | 71.1 | 71.0 | 70.7 | 70.9 | 70.7 | 70.4 | 70.6 | 70.5 | 70.4 | 70.2 | 69.8 | 70.0 | 70.5 |
| 2017 | 68.9 | 69.4 | 69.6 | 69.6 | 69.7 | 69.8 | 69.8 | 69.9 | 69.8 | 69.3 | 69.2 | 69.3 | 69.5 |
| 2018 | 68.9 | 69.3 | 69.6 | 69.5 | 69.7 | 69.7 | 69.8 | 70.1 | 69.5 | 69.8 | 69.5 | 69.5 | 69.6 |
| 2019 | 68.7 | 69.0 | 69.2 | 69.2 | 69.3 | 69.1 | 68.9 | 69.1 | 68.8 | 68.5 | 68.6 | 68.2 | 68.9 |
| **Retail Trade** | | | | | | | | | | | | | |
| 2011 | 218.7 | 217.7 | 219.2 | 221.2 | 221.4 | 220.6 | 220.1 | 219.5 | 218.6 | 219.9 | 226.4 | 228.1 | 221.0 |
| 2012 | 220.4 | 218.8 | 220.4 | 221.2 | 222.0 | 221.7 | 220.9 | 220.3 | 219.5 | 222.9 | 230.6 | 231.8 | 222.5 |
| 2013 | 221.3 | 219.3 | 221.4 | 221.7 | 221.9 | 223.0 | 222.8 | 223.6 | 224.2 | 225.0 | 231.0 | 233.8 | 224.1 |
| 2014 | 223.6 | 222.4 | 223.8 | 224.9 | 225.8 | 227.4 | 226.8 | 227.2 | 226.6 | 228.6 | 235.8 | 239.6 | 227.7 |
| 2015 | 229.3 | 228.5 | 230.4 | 231.1 | 231.9 | 233.0 | 232.4 | 232.8 | 231.3 | 234.5 | 240.6 | 241.9 | 233.1 |
| 2016 | 233.0 | 232.1 | 233.6 | 234.4 | 234.2 | 234.4 | 234.1 | 233.3 | 232.3 | 234.8 | 241.4 | 242.7 | 235.0 |
| 2017 | 233.8 | 231.3 | 231.8 | 231.7 | 231.8 | 231.3 | 229.2 | 229.8 | 228.1 | 229.4 | 236.1 | 236.0 | 231.7 |
| 2018 | 228.3 | 225.8 | 227.3 | 226.7 | 227.4 | 226.6 | 225.6 | 225.6 | 224.5 | 225.9 | 233.0 | 232.0 | 227.4 |
| 2019 | 225.0 | 222.3 | 222.2 | 222.4 | 223.0 | 222.5 | 221.2 | 221.1 | 219.6 | 221.5 | 226.1 | 224.6 | 222.6 |
| **Transportation and Utilities** | | | | | | | | | | | | | |
| 2011 | 79.5 | 79.4 | 79.4 | 80.4 | 80.6 | 80.5 | 81.3 | 81.9 | 82.1 | 82.1 | 82.2 | 83.3 | 81.1 |
| 2012 | 81.3 | 81.2 | 82.0 | 82.4 | 82.9 | 82.8 | 82.2 | 83.1 | 83.2 | 83.6 | 84.4 | 85.2 | 82.9 |
| 2013 | 84.0 | 84.5 | 85.2 | 85.4 | 85.3 | 85.2 | 84.9 | 85.4 | 85.6 | 86.3 | 86.5 | 88.3 | 85.6 |
| 2014 | 87.2 | 86.7 | 87.6 | 87.7 | 88.1 | 87.8 | 87.9 | 89.0 | 89.2 | 89.6 | 90.0 | 91.8 | 88.6 |
| 2015 | 90.0 | 88.2 | 87.8 | 88.1 | 88.2 | 87.6 | 87.4 | 87.6 | 87.3 | 87.0 | 86.7 | 87.8 | 87.8 |
| 2016 | 84.8 | 83.6 | 83.5 | 82.6 | 82.7 | 81.7 | 81.6 | 81.7 | 81.8 | 81.3 | 81.4 | 82.2 | 82.4 |
| 2017 | 80.6 | 80.2 | 80.5 | 80.5 | 80.7 | 80.5 | 80.5 | 80.8 | 80.7 | 80.8 | 81.9 | 83.4 | 80.9 |
| 2018 | 82.1 | 82.3 | 82.6 | 83.2 | 83.7 | 83.1 | 83.4 | 84.7 | 84.6 | 85.3 | 87.1 | 88.4 | 84.2 |
| 2019 | 86.7 | 86.3 | 86.5 | 86.8 | 86.8 | 86.1 | 86.4 | 87.6 | 87.3 | 87.5 | 89.3 | 90.5 | 87.3 |
| **Information** | | | | | | | | | | | | | |
| 2011 | 23.4 | 23.5 | 25.1 | 23.7 | 24.6 | 24.0 | 22.9 | 22.9 | 23.0 | 23.6 | 23.5 | 24.2 | 23.7 |
| 2012 | 23.2 | 23.9 | 23.9 | 27.1 | 28.0 | 25.4 | 24.8 | 24.7 | 24.3 | 23.9 | 25.0 | 25.7 | 25.0 |
| 2013 | 25.4 | 26.9 | 26.3 | 27.0 | 27.7 | 28.0 | 25.5 | 25.5 | 24.4 | 26.3 | 27.6 | 25.7 | 26.4 |
| 2014 | 23.6 | 25.0 | 26.0 | 26.3 | 27.8 | 27.0 | 26.6 | 25.3 | 24.3 | 25.4 | 27.4 | 26.8 | 26.0 |
| 2015 | 24.8 | 26.6 | 25.5 | 27.5 | 29.0 | 28.1 | 27.5 | 26.2 | 24.9 | 25.1 | 25.8 | 26.2 | 26.4 |
| 2016 | 24.8 | 24.6 | 24.5 | 24.1 | 23.9 | 23.4 | 23.9 | 23.9 | 22.3 | 22.6 | 24.1 | 22.5 | 23.7 |
| 2017 | 21.9 | 24.2 | 23.8 | 24.1 | 25.0 | 22.8 | 22.3 | 22.5 | 22.1 | 22.6 | 22.9 | 22.5 | 23.1 |
| 2018 | 22.5 | 23.7 | 24.4 | 24.0 | 24.0 | 22.8 | 21.8 | 21.6 | 21.5 | 22.2 | 23.5 | 22.7 | 22.9 |
| 2019 | 21.5 | 23.5 | 23.0 | 23.7 | 23.3 | 22.1 | 21.7 | 22.1 | 21.0 | 20.8 | 22.4 | 21.1 | 22.2 |

## 1. Employment by Industry: Louisiana, 2011–2019—*Continued*

(Numbers in thousands, not seasonally adjusted)

| Industry and year | January | February | March | April | May | June | July | August | September | October | November | December | Annual average |
|---|---|---|---|---|---|---|---|---|---|---|---|---|---|
| **Financial Activities** | | | | | | | | | | | | | |
| 2011 | 91.9 | 92.3 | 92.3 | 91.8 | 91.9 | 91.6 | 91.6 | 91.3 | 91.7 | 91.9 | 91.7 | 91.7 | 91.8 |
| 2012 | 90.8 | 91.2 | 91.6 | 91.4 | 91.5 | 91.6 | 91.4 | 91.4 | 91.1 | 91.7 | 92.4 | 92.7 | 91.6 |
| 2013 | 91.4 | 91.4 | 91.6 | 91.9 | 92.4 | 92.9 | 92.9 | 93.3 | 93.5 | 93.8 | 93.6 | 93.2 | 92.7 |
| 2014 | 92.2 | 92.1 | 92.0 | 92.3 | 92.8 | 93.1 | 93.6 | 94.2 | 94.0 | 94.4 | 94.6 | 94.6 | 93.3 |
| 2015 | 93.6 | 93.5 | 93.6 | 93.2 | 93.3 | 93.6 | 93.3 | 93.4 | 92.7 | 93.3 | 93.3 | 93.4 | 93.4 |
| 2016 | 92.4 | 92.4 | 92.3 | 92.7 | 93.0 | 92.4 | 93.3 | 92.9 | 93.2 | 93.4 | 93.0 | 92.8 | 92.8 |
| 2017 | 91.7 | 91.9 | 91.8 | 91.9 | 92.2 | 92.2 | 92.5 | 92.4 | 92.2 | 92.4 | 92.6 | 92.8 | 92.2 |
| 2018 | 91.6 | 92.0 | 92.1 | 92.4 | 92.4 | 92.5 | 92.7 | 92.4 | 91.8 | 92.4 | 92.4 | 92.5 | 92.3 |
| 2019 | 91.4 | 91.8 | 91.5 | 91.9 | 92.4 | 92.4 | 92.2 | 92.6 | 92.4 | 92.4 | 92.7 | 92.3 | 92.2 |
| **Professional and Business Services** | | | | | | | | | | | | | |
| 2011 | 190.9 | 193.6 | 193.5 | 195.1 | 195.1 | 194.6 | 194.2 | 196.1 | 196.2 | 197.3 | 197.3 | 197.6 | 195.1 |
| 2012 | 195.6 | 197.8 | 199.6 | 203.7 | 204.2 | 202.8 | 201.7 | 202.0 | 201.3 | 204.0 | 204.2 | 202.9 | 201.7 |
| 2013 | 200.3 | 206.5 | 205.5 | 205.4 | 205.2 | 205.2 | 205.2 | 207.2 | 205.3 | 209.6 | 210.6 | 209.7 | 206.3 |
| 2014 | 207.5 | 208.5 | 210.2 | 211.7 | 209.7 | 210.2 | 209.9 | 210.4 | 210.0 | 213.5 | 214.7 | 216.2 | 211.0 |
| 2015 | 211.5 | 212.2 | 213.1 | 214.8 | 214.4 | 212.9 | 214.0 | 214.3 | 211.8 | 215.3 | 213.9 | 212.4 | 213.4 |
| 2016 | 208.9 | 210.1 | 210.0 | 214.2 | 212.4 | 209.3 | 209.2 | 207.7 | 211.0 | 211.2 | 209.8 | 207.5 | 210.1 |
| 2017 | 205.7 | 209.2 | 208.7 | 207.9 | 208.6 | 207.9 | 208.4 | 208.6 | 208.9 | 212.2 | 213.9 | 211.5 | 209.3 |
| 2018 | 209.2 | 210.2 | 212.1 | 213.5 | 212.5 | 212.8 | 212.7 | 213.7 | 212.8 | 216.9 | 216.5 | 214.4 | 213.1 |
| 2019 | 213.4 | 215.8 | 216.5 | 217.9 | 216.4 | 215.7 | 214.6 | 215.3 | 214.3 | 217.4 | 217.9 | 214.8 | 215.8 |
| **Education and Health Services** | | | | | | | | | | | | | |
| 2011 | 272.5 | 274.7 | 275.7 | 277.1 | 276.6 | 273.1 | 273.5 | 276.1 | 279.0 | 281.2 | 282.7 | 282.2 | 277.0 |
| 2012 | 277.8 | 280.1 | 281.6 | 282.5 | 283.1 | 281.4 | 279.3 | 283.1 | 283.4 | 286.5 | 287.0 | 286.9 | 282.7 |
| 2013 | 286.7 | 288.5 | 288.8 | 289.1 | 288.7 | 284.9 | 284.4 | 292.1 | 293.1 | 295.7 | 297.8 | 296.7 | 290.7 |
| 2014 | 295.3 | 295.9 | 296.1 | 297.2 | 297.5 | 294.3 | 294.1 | 299.7 | 300.9 | 303.2 | 303.0 | 302.4 | 298.3 |
| 2015 | 301.4 | 301.8 | 301.8 | 304.0 | 304.3 | 301.1 | 300.6 | 304.7 | 305.7 | 309.0 | 309.1 | 309.4 | 304.4 |
| 2016 | 306.2 | 306.9 | 307.2 | 309.7 | 310.0 | 307.8 | 307.9 | 310.9 | 312.4 | 313.1 | 313.1 | 313.9 | 309.9 |
| 2017 | 311.6 | 313.3 | 313.2 | 314.0 | 314.2 | 312.9 | 308.9 | 313.3 | 314.9 | 315.4 | 316.2 | 315.7 | 313.6 |
| 2018 | 311.7 | 313.5 | 313.2 | 315.2 | 315.8 | 312.3 | 310.0 | 316.0 | 316.1 | 319.7 | 319.6 | 319.9 | 315.3 |
| 2019 | 317.2 | 318.7 | 317.9 | 320.6 | 320.9 | 318.6 | 315.9 | 321.8 | 322.1 | 323.9 | 323.9 | 322.1 | 320.3 |
| **Leisure and Hospitality** | | | | | | | | | | | | | |
| 2011 | 192.6 | 195.0 | 198.9 | 201.6 | 203.7 | 203.6 | 202.2 | 203.9 | 202.5 | 201.1 | 202.4 | 203.1 | 200.9 |
| 2012 | 201.6 | 203.1 | 205.9 | 208.6 | 209.5 | 209.6 | 208.0 | 209.7 | 206.1 | 206.6 | 207.4 | 208.6 | 207.1 |
| 2013 | 206.6 | 207.6 | 210.7 | 214.8 | 216.1 | 217.1 | 215.4 | 217.6 | 213.7 | 213.3 | 215.7 | 214.3 | 213.6 |
| 2014 | 212.4 | 215.0 | 218.5 | 221.9 | 224.0 | 225.2 | 222.8 | 224.7 | 220.5 | 222.5 | 223.7 | 223.6 | 221.2 |
| 2015 | 221.3 | 224.1 | 226.5 | 228.3 | 231.0 | 231.6 | 230.6 | 229.2 | 227.8 | 230.0 | 230.1 | 230.7 | 228.4 |
| 2016 | 227.1 | 228.4 | 232.1 | 234.8 | 237.1 | 236.5 | 233.3 | 231.5 | 230.6 | 230.4 | 229.9 | 228.6 | 231.7 |
| 2017 | 226.2 | 229.4 | 231.7 | 233.6 | 236.0 | 236.8 | 234.5 | 234.8 | 234.2 | 234.0 | 233.6 | 233.3 | 233.2 |
| 2018 | 230.1 | 231.2 | 236.2 | 237.9 | 239.5 | 240.4 | 237.3 | 238.7 | 237.1 | 237.2 | 236.3 | 234.6 | 236.4 |
| 2019 | 233.2 | 235.5 | 236.1 | 239.3 | 241.1 | 241.7 | 235.9 | 238.4 | 236.9 | 238.4 | 241.0 | 241.6 | 238.3 |
| **Other Services** | | | | | | | | | | | | | |
| 2011 | 65.8 | 66.2 | 66.5 | 66.7 | 66.5 | 66.9 | 67.1 | 67.2 | 67.2 | 66.9 | 66.8 | 66.7 | 66.7 |
| 2012 | 66.3 | 66.7 | 67.1 | 67.6 | 67.9 | 68.4 | 67.9 | 68.0 | 67.9 | 68.3 | 68.4 | 68.5 | 67.8 |
| 2013 | 68.3 | 69.0 | 69.5 | 71.6 | 71.9 | 72.3 | 72.1 | 72.1 | 72.1 | 72.0 | 72.1 | 71.9 | 71.2 |
| 2014 | 72.0 | 72.4 | 72.7 | 73.2 | 73.6 | 73.8 | 73.7 | 73.9 | 73.6 | 74.1 | 73.9 | 74.1 | 73.4 |
| 2015 | 73.8 | 74.2 | 74.5 | 75.0 | 75.6 | 75.6 | 75.8 | 75.4 | 75.1 | 75.4 | 75.0 | 75.1 | 75.0 |
| 2016 | 75.0 | 74.9 | 75.3 | 75.5 | 75.3 | 75.4 | 75.1 | 74.7 | 74.5 | 74.1 | 74.0 | 73.5 | 74.8 |
| 2017 | 73.5 | 73.6 | 73.8 | 73.7 | 74.0 | 74.5 | 73.9 | 73.9 | 73.6 | 73.6 | 73.3 | 73.1 | 73.7 |
| 2018 | 72.9 | 73.2 | 73.5 | 73.6 | 74.2 | 74.3 | 73.7 | 73.7 | 73.6 | 74.1 | 73.8 | 73.4 | 73.7 |
| 2019 | 73.4 | 73.9 | 73.9 | 74.0 | 74.4 | 74.6 | 73.9 | 74.3 | 73.9 | 74.5 | 73.7 | 73.5 | 74.0 |
| **Government** | | | | | | | | | | | | | |
| 2011 | 360.4 | 364.6 | 364.5 | 364.3 | 362.7 | 356.4 | 345.9 | 347.6 | 359.3 | 363.6 | 364.1 | 361.1 | 359.5 |
| 2012 | 352.7 | 356.9 | 356.1 | 357.1 | 356.0 | 349.7 | 338.4 | 339.6 | 348.7 | 353.9 | 354.6 | 353.8 | 351.5 |
| 2013 | 343.4 | 348.1 | 347.9 | 347.5 | 346.6 | 340.6 | 329.6 | 328.6 | 339.7 | 341.0 | 343.3 | 340.7 | 341.4 |
| 2014 | 332.7 | 337.1 | 335.8 | 335.0 | 334.6 | 330.3 | 318.1 | 321.2 | 333.1 | 335.9 | 337.8 | 334.7 | 332.2 |
| 2015 | 328.5 | 333.0 | 331.7 | 332.9 | 332.3 | 328.2 | 317.1 | 319.8 | 331.1 | 333.0 | 335.1 | 331.6 | 329.5 |
| 2016 | 327.2 | 331.2 | 330.2 | 331.2 | 332.9 | 328.0 | 315.7 | 317.4 | 331.1 | 334.5 | 336.6 | 333.8 | 329.2 |
| 2017 | 328.3 | 333.0 | 332.1 | 333.2 | 333.7 | 327.7 | 315.9 | 318.1 | 329.5 | 334.4 | 335.2 | 333.9 | 329.6 |
| 2018 | 327.5 | 332.6 | 333.5 | 335.3 | 333.1 | 327.2 | 315.5 | 320.5 | 330.1 | 335.2 | 336.2 | 333.0 | 330.0 |
| 2019 | 327.1 | 333.1 | 332.8 | 335.8 | 334.3 | 327.1 | 316.8 | 323.2 | 332.9 | 337.2 | 338.6 | 335.7 | 331.2 |

## 2. Average Weekly Hours by Selected Industry: Louisiana, 2015–2019

(Not seasonally adjusted)

| Industry and year | January | February | March | April | May | June | July | August | September | October | November | December | Annual average |
|---|---|---|---|---|---|---|---|---|---|---|---|---|---|
| **Total Private** | | | | | | | | | | | | | |
| 2015 | 35.9 | 36.4 | 35.9 | 35.7 | 35.8 | 35.9 | 35.9 | 36.3 | 35.4 | 35.9 | 35.9 | 35.8 | 35.9 |
| 2016 | 35.3 | 35.1 | 34.6 | 35.0 | 35.5 | 35.2 | 35.1 | 34.2 | 34.9 | 35.6 | 35.1 | 35.2 | 35.1 |
| 2017 | 35.4 | 35.4 | 35.4 | 35.4 | 35.4 | 35.3 | 35.8 | 35.3 | 35.5 | 35.9 | 35.5 | 35.4 | 35.5 |
| 2018 | 34.9 | 35.5 | 36.3 | 36.4 | 36.2 | 36.4 | 36.4 | 36.0 | 36.4 | 36.0 | 36.0 | 36.6 | 36.1 |
| 2019 | 36.2 | 36.3 | 36.2 | 36.1 | 36.0 | 36.5 | 35.4 | 36.2 | 36.8 | 36.1 | 36.0 | 36.5 | 36.2 |
| **Goods Producing** | | | | | | | | | | | | | |
| 2015 | 42.2 | 42.1 | 40.6 | 41.0 | 41.5 | 41.3 | 41.3 | 41.8 | 40.3 | 42.5 | 42.3 | 42.4 | 41.6 |
| 2016 | 41.8 | 40.6 | 39.3 | 40.8 | 41.9 | 41.3 | 41.2 | 39.8 | 41.1 | 42.6 | 41.3 | 41.7 | 41.1 |
| 2017 | 41.7 | 42.4 | 42.4 | 40.7 | 42.5 | 42.0 | 42.6 | 41.7 | 42.8 | 42.3 | 42.0 | 42.1 | 42.1 |
| 2018 | 41.4 | 42.8 | 44.4 | 43.9 | 44.7 | 44.6 | 43.6 | 43.1 | 43.0 | 43.4 | 43.4 | 44.1 | 43.5 |
| 2019 | 43.1 | 43.7 | 43.6 | 42.9 | 42.3 | 43.3 | 41.0 | 43.2 | 43.7 | 43.0 | 43.0 | 43.8 | 43.1 |
| **Construction** | | | | | | | | | | | | | |
| 2015 | 40.3 | 40.6 | 38.6 | 40.0 | 40.9 | 41.5 | 41.4 | 41.5 | 38.6 | 41.8 | 41.5 | 42.3 | 40.8 |
| 2016 | 40.7 | 40.6 | 37.8 | 40.2 | 42.2 | 41.5 | 40.9 | 38.7 | 41.1 | 42.6 | 40.6 | 40.3 | 40.6 |
| 2017 | 41.4 | 42.1 | 41.5 | 38.5 | 41.9 | 41.2 | 41.4 | 40.6 | 41.4 | 41.4 | 40.5 | 40.9 | 41.1 |
| 2018 | 39.7 | 41.0 | 42.9 | 42.0 | 43.4 | 43.1 | 42.7 | 41.9 | 42.0 | 43.8 | 41.7 | 42.9 | 42.3 |
| 2019 | 41.9 | 42.5 | 43.1 | 41.8 | 41.6 | 42.6 | 39.3 | 42.7 | 43.4 | 42.8 | 41.9 | 43.0 | 42.2 |
| **Manufacturing** | | | | | | | | | | | | | |
| 2015 | 43.9 | 43.2 | 42.5 | 42.2 | 41.9 | 40.9 | 41.1 | 41.2 | 40.7 | 42.3 | 42.3 | 42.1 | 42.0 |
| 2016 | 42.0 | 39.9 | 40.1 | 40.9 | 40.6 | 40.4 | 40.2 | 39.4 | 40.2 | 41.3 | 41.0 | 42.1 | 40.7 |
| 2017 | 41.3 | 42.2 | 42.1 | 41.6 | 42.1 | 41.9 | 42.6 | 42.3 | 43.9 | 43.2 | 43.2 | 43.0 | 42.4 |
| 2018 | 42.3 | 43.8 | 44.8 | 45.2 | 45.0 | 44.8 | 43.9 | 43.8 | 43.3 | 42.2 | 44.3 | 44.7 | 44.0 |
| 2019 | 42.7 | 43.3 | 42.8 | 42.5 | 41.5 | 42.8 | 41.2 | 42.2 | 42.7 | 41.9 | 42.3 | 43.2 | 42.4 |
| **Trade, Transportation, and Utilities** | | | | | | | | | | | | | |
| 2015 | 35.8 | 36.0 | 36.2 | 36.6 | 36.6 | 36.4 | 36.6 | 36.8 | 36.0 | 35.5 | 36.0 | 36.1 | 36.2 |
| 2016 | 35.2 | 35.4 | 34.9 | 35.2 | 35.7 | 35.6 | 35.6 | 34.5 | 35.4 | 35.5 | 35.0 | 35.5 | 35.3 |
| 2017 | 35.1 | 35.0 | 35.2 | 35.6 | 35.3 | 35.1 | 35.4 | 35.3 | 35.2 | 35.2 | 35.2 | 35.0 | 35.2 |
| 2018 | 34.7 | 35.0 | 35.5 | 36.0 | 35.3 | 35.7 | 35.7 | 35.2 | 35.6 | 35.1 | 35.3 | 35.7 | 35.4 |
| 2019 | 35.7 | 35.6 | 35.5 | 35.8 | 36.1 | 36.4 | 35.8 | 36.2 | 36.9 | 36.4 | 36.2 | 36.8 | 36.1 |
| **Financial Activities** | | | | | | | | | | | | | |
| 2015 | 37.6 | 38.7 | 38.5 | 37.5 | 37.9 | 38.0 | 37.9 | 38.9 | 37.4 | 37.4 | 38.6 | 37.3 | 38.0 |
| 2016 | 37.5 | 37.5 | 37.6 | 36.7 | 37.3 | 37.3 | 36.7 | 36.0 | 36.4 | 37.6 | 36.2 | 36.3 | 36.9 |
| 2017 | 36.5 | 35.8 | 35.8 | 36.3 | 35.2 | 35.8 | 37.2 | 35.7 | 36.6 | 37.4 | 36.8 | 36.7 | 36.3 |
| 2018 | 37.1 | 37.4 | 37.5 | 38.4 | 37.6 | 38.5 | 38.7 | 39.2 | 39.6 | 37.8 | 38.2 | 39.4 | 38.3 |
| 2019 | 40.1 | 39.4 | 38.4 | 38.0 | 38.1 | 39.3 | 38.9 | 39.4 | 40.2 | 39.5 | 39.5 | 39.6 | 39.2 |
| **Professional and Business Services** | | | | | | | | | | | | | |
| 2015 | 37.8 | 38.4 | 37.8 | 37.3 | 37.1 | 37.2 | 37.3 | 38.3 | 37.1 | 37.7 | 38.3 | 37.4 | 37.6 |
| 2016 | 36.8 | 36.5 | 36.5 | 36.7 | 37.6 | 37.3 | 37.1 | 36.9 | 37.5 | 38.5 | 37.4 | 37.7 | 37.2 |
| 2017 | 38.1 | 37.6 | 36.8 | 37.8 | 37.0 | 37.6 | 38.1 | 37.5 | 37.3 | 38.5 | 37.7 | 37.1 | 37.6 |
| 2018 | 36.7 | 36.5 | 37.1 | 37.9 | 37.3 | 37.6 | 38.6 | 37.7 | 38.4 | 37.6 | 37.7 | 38.3 | 37.6 |
| 2019 | 37.1 | 37.4 | 38.3 | 38.1 | 37.5 | 38.3 | 36.9 | 37.7 | 38.1 | 36.7 | 36.8 | 36.8 | 37.5 |
| **Education and Health Services** | | | | | | | | | | | | | |
| 2015 | 33.9 | 33.9 | 33.7 | 33.5 | 33.3 | 33.7 | 34.1 | 34.1 | 33.9 | 34.0 | 34.2 | 34.0 | 33.9 |
| 2016 | 34.1 | 33.7 | 33.4 | 33.6 | 33.9 | 33.8 | 33.9 | 33.5 | 33.4 | 33.9 | 33.5 | 33.5 | 33.7 |
| 2017 | 34.1 | 33.5 | 33.4 | 33.7 | 33.2 | 33.4 | 34.0 | 33.5 | 33.8 | 34.0 | 33.8 | 34.0 | 33.7 |
| 2018 | 33.5 | 33.9 | 34.1 | 34.1 | 33.6 | 33.8 | 33.9 | 33.8 | 34.7 | 33.4 | 33.5 | 34.1 | 33.9 |
| 2019 | 33.9 | 34.0 | 33.4 | 33.4 | 33.5 | 33.6 | 33.7 | 33.3 | 33.6 | 33.0 | 33.3 | 33.8 | 33.5 |
| **Leisure and Hospitality** | | | | | | | | | | | | | |
| 2015 | 27.3 | 28.6 | 28.3 | 28.1 | 28.3 | 28.5 | 28.2 | 28.0 | 27.4 | 27.8 | 27.9 | 27.4 | 28.0 |
| 2016 | 26.7 | 27.6 | 27.7 | 27.6 | 27.4 | 27.2 | 26.9 | 25.7 | 26.4 | 26.9 | 27.5 | 26.9 | 27.0 |
| 2017 | 27.0 | 27.4 | 27.7 | 27.5 | 27.3 | 26.9 | 27.2 | 26.7 | 26.6 | 27.3 | 27.2 | 27.2 | 27.2 |
| 2018 | 26.1 | 27.2 | 27.7 | 27.5 | 27.2 | 27.3 | 27.5 | 26.8 | 26.6 | 26.7 | 26.3 | 27.0 | 27.0 |
| 2019 | 26.4 | 26.5 | 26.6 | 26.4 | 26.3 | 26.7 | 24.7 | 25.9 | 26.0 | 25.8 | 25.6 | 26.4 | 26.1 |

## 3. Average Hourly Earnings Selected Industry: Louisiana, 2015–2019

(Dollars, not seasonally adjusted)

| Industry and year | January | February | March | April | May | June | July | August | September | October | November | December | Annual average |
|---|---|---|---|---|---|---|---|---|---|---|---|---|---|
| **Total Private** | | | | | | | | | | | | | |
| 2015 | 22.13 | 22.15 | 22.32 | 22.26 | 21.98 | 21.94 | 21.93 | 22.24 | 22.15 | 22.31 | 22.55 | 22.38 | 22.20 |
| 2016 | 22.51 | 22.39 | 22.41 | 22.53 | 22.63 | 22.47 | 22.49 | 22.65 | 22.87 | 23.11 | 22.87 | 22.83 | 22.65 |
| 2017 | 23.09 | 23.03 | 23.00 | 22.85 | 22.81 | 22.76 | 23.07 | 22.90 | 23.02 | 23.15 | 23.09 | 23.09 | 22.99 |
| 2018 | 23.31 | 23.34 | 23.21 | 23.37 | 23.31 | 23.19 | 23.49 | 23.39 | 23.75 | 23.89 | 23.79 | 23.83 | 23.49 |
| 2019 | 23.89 | 23.89 | 24.06 | 24.20 | 23.97 | 24.00 | 24.38 | 24.20 | 24.38 | 24.44 | 24.37 | 24.62 | 24.20 |
| **Goods Producing** | | | | | | | | | | | | | |
| 2015 | 26.39 | 26.30 | 26.74 | 26.41 | 26.12 | 25.93 | 26.18 | 26.38 | 26.39 | 26.27 | 26.51 | 26.58 | 26.35 |
| 2016 | 26.76 | 26.84 | 27.06 | 26.89 | 26.75 | 26.59 | 26.74 | 26.89 | 27.20 | 27.26 | 26.94 | 26.83 | 26.90 |
| 2017 | 26.80 | 27.06 | 27.14 | 26.74 | 26.58 | 26.36 | 26.92 | 26.74 | 26.62 | 26.96 | 26.80 | 27.16 | 26.82 |
| 2018 | 27.10 | 26.97 | 26.66 | 26.78 | 26.56 | 26.52 | 26.84 | 26.53 | 26.95 | 27.13 | 26.89 | 27.46 | 26.86 |
| 2019 | 26.85 | 27.32 | 27.76 | 27.86 | 27.91 | 27.93 | 28.05 | 27.83 | 28.13 | 28.32 | 28.38 | 28.50 | 27.90 |
| **Construction** | | | | | | | | | | | | | |
| 2015 | 25.27 | 25.29 | 25.61 | 25.26 | 24.74 | 24.39 | 24.72 | 24.55 | 24.66 | 25.09 | 25.14 | 25.34 | 25.00 |
| 2016 | 25.22 | 25.23 | 25.55 | 25.72 | 25.39 | 25.27 | 25.44 | 25.54 | 26.44 | 26.72 | 26.31 | 26.60 | 25.80 |
| 2017 | 26.80 | 27.19 | 26.76 | 26.08 | 26.21 | 26.03 | 26.37 | 26.07 | 26.39 | 26.46 | 26.42 | 26.66 | 26.46 |
| 2018 | 26.51 | 26.89 | 26.61 | 26.77 | 26.72 | 26.13 | 26.32 | 25.61 | 26.13 | 26.27 | 26.53 | 27.09 | 26.46 |
| 2019 | 26.07 | 26.79 | 27.01 | 27.12 | 27.22 | 26.97 | 27.16 | 27.37 | 27.99 | 28.31 | 28.62 | 28.90 | 27.45 |
| **Manufacturing** | | | | | | | | | | | | | |
| 2015 | 25.76 | 25.54 | 26.44 | 26.02 | 25.83 | 25.83 | 25.88 | 26.33 | 26.26 | 25.46 | 25.93 | 25.95 | 25.93 |
| 2016 | 26.28 | 26.51 | 26.52 | 26.07 | 25.90 | 25.74 | 26.09 | 26.24 | 25.95 | 26.10 | 25.89 | 25.60 | 26.07 |
| 2017 | 25.45 | 25.71 | 26.04 | 26.16 | 25.84 | 25.54 | 26.27 | 25.84 | 25.86 | 26.29 | 25.93 | 26.33 | 25.94 |
| 2018 | 26.17 | 25.77 | 25.50 | 25.68 | 25.41 | 25.64 | 26.05 | 25.46 | 25.73 | 25.81 | 25.35 | 25.74 | 25.69 |
| 2019 | 25.52 | 25.74 | 26.48 | 26.68 | 26.67 | 26.91 | 26.90 | 27.03 | 27.35 | 27.50 | 27.50 | 27.58 | 26.82 |
| **Trade, Transportation, and Utilities** | | | | | | | | | | | | | |
| 2015 | 20.62 | 20.61 | 20.86 | 20.86 | 20.62 | 20.89 | 20.50 | 20.94 | 20.76 | 20.78 | 20.50 | 20.79 | 20.73 |
| 2016 | 20.72 | 20.37 | 20.13 | 20.37 | 20.40 | 20.30 | 20.04 | 20.30 | 20.39 | 20.24 | 20.02 | 19.82 | 20.26 |
| 2017 | 20.07 | 20.03 | 19.93 | 20.28 | 20.16 | 20.20 | 20.50 | 20.42 | 20.78 | 20.79 | 21.05 | 20.64 | 20.40 |
| 2018 | 20.92 | 20.95 | 21.04 | 21.38 | 21.56 | 21.42 | 21.92 | 21.88 | 22.22 | 22.23 | 22.33 | 21.90 | 21.65 |
| 2019 | 22.07 | 22.09 | 22.67 | 22.69 | 22.57 | 22.53 | 23.29 | 23.08 | 23.07 | 22.98 | 22.77 | 22.95 | 22.73 |
| **Financial Activities** | | | | | | | | | | | | | |
| 2015 | 23.63 | 23.89 | 23.97 | 24.67 | 23.98 | 24.12 | 24.53 | 24.92 | 24.85 | 24.96 | 26.12 | 25.40 | 24.59 |
| 2016 | 25.54 | 25.55 | 25.53 | 26.12 | 25.99 | 24.70 | 25.12 | 26.01 | 26.04 | 26.89 | 26.47 | 26.30 | 25.85 |
| 2017 | 27.74 | 26.94 | 28.09 | 27.43 | 26.63 | 25.79 | 26.22 | 26.38 | 26.41 | 26.53 | 26.66 | 26.74 | 26.79 |
| 2018 | 27.32 | 27.72 | 27.32 | 27.05 | 26.90 | 26.16 | 26.44 | 26.04 | 26.78 | 25.74 | 25.76 | 26.40 | 26.63 |
| 2019 | 26.77 | 26.64 | 26.22 | 28.19 | 27.15 | 27.97 | 27.89 | 28.05 | 28.01 | 27.91 | 28.23 | 29.38 | 27.71 |
| **Professional and Business Services** | | | | | | | | | | | | | |
| 2015 | 25.70 | 26.16 | 26.21 | 25.90 | 25.52 | 25.59 | 25.56 | 26.00 | 25.60 | 25.75 | 26.26 | 25.50 | 25.82 |
| 2016 | 25.55 | 25.48 | 25.72 | 25.24 | 25.59 | 25.43 | 25.48 | 25.14 | 25.40 | 25.93 | 25.68 | 25.98 | 25.55 |
| 2017 | 26.22 | 25.85 | 25.93 | 25.82 | 25.91 | 26.35 | 26.86 | 26.26 | 26.17 | 26.19 | 25.94 | 26.19 | 26.14 |
| 2018 | 26.55 | 26.68 | 26.09 | 26.29 | 25.77 | 25.81 | 26.34 | 26.04 | 26.46 | 26.52 | 27.29 | 26.97 | 26.40 |
| 2019 | 27.37 | 26.55 | 26.66 | 26.73 | 26.88 | 26.54 | 27.20 | 26.88 | 27.48 | 27.40 | 27.70 | 28.58 | 27.16 |
| **Education and Health Services** | | | | | | | | | | | | | |
| 2015 | 18.33 | 18.40 | 18.65 | 19.04 | 18.91 | 18.58 | 18.50 | 18.78 | 19.00 | 19.49 | 19.98 | 19.98 | 18.98 |
| 2016 | 20.04 | 20.29 | 20.66 | 21.33 | 21.67 | 21.77 | 21.83 | 21.92 | 22.30 | 22.59 | 22.83 | 22.77 | 21.67 |
| 2017 | 23.09 | 22.95 | 22.84 | 22.96 | 22.80 | 22.74 | 22.81 | 22.77 | 22.89 | 23.02 | 22.93 | 22.73 | 22.88 |
| 2018 | 22.86 | 22.79 | 22.72 | 23.03 | 22.91 | 22.91 | 23.11 | 23.02 | 23.12 | 23.30 | 23.38 | 23.71 | 23.07 |
| 2019 | 23.45 | 23.41 | 23.25 | 23.06 | 22.44 | 22.63 | 22.21 | 22.45 | 22.54 | 22.53 | 22.69 | 22.57 | 22.77 |
| **Leisure and Hospitality** | | | | | | | | | | | | | |
| 2015 | 13.29 | 13.12 | 13.07 | 13.06 | 12.96 | 12.87 | 12.87 | 12.88 | 12.98 | 13.16 | 13.16 | 13.31 | 13.06 |
| 2016 | 13.32 | 13.35 | 13.60 | 13.53 | 13.35 | 13.21 | 13.16 | 13.34 | 13.35 | 13.53 | 13.48 | 13.51 | 13.39 |
| 2017 | 13.47 | 13.51 | 13.57 | 13.56 | 13.41 | 13.24 | 13.14 | 13.11 | 13.27 | 13.35 | 13.49 | 13.56 | 13.39 |
| 2018 | 13.36 | 13.65 | 13.62 | 13.58 | 13.51 | 13.52 | 13.43 | 13.51 | 13.44 | 13.63 | 13.74 | 13.57 | 13.57 |
| 2019 | 13.65 | 13.76 | 13.83 | 13.76 | 13.82 | 13.55 | 13.63 | 13.57 | 13.59 | 13.76 | 13.83 | 13.90 | 13.72 |

# 4. Average Weekly Earnings Selected Industry: Louisiana, 2015–2019

(Dollars, not seasonally adjusted)

| Industry and year | January | February | March | April | May | June | July | August | September | October | November | December | Annual average |
|---|---|---|---|---|---|---|---|---|---|---|---|---|---|
| **Total Private** | | | | | | | | | | | | | |
| 2015 | 794.47 | 806.26 | 801.29 | 794.68 | 786.88 | 787.65 | 787.29 | 807.31 | 784.11 | 800.93 | 809.55 | 801.20 | 796.98 |
| 2016 | 794.60 | 785.89 | 775.39 | 788.55 | 803.37 | 790.94 | 789.40 | 774.63 | 798.16 | 822.72 | 802.74 | 803.62 | 795.02 |
| 2017 | 817.39 | 815.26 | 814.20 | 808.89 | 807.47 | 803.43 | 825.91 | 808.37 | 817.21 | 831.09 | 819.70 | 817.39 | 816.15 |
| 2018 | 813.52 | 828.57 | 842.52 | 850.67 | 843.82 | 844.12 | 855.04 | 842.04 | 864.50 | 860.04 | 856.44 | 872.18 | 847.99 |
| 2019 | 864.82 | 867.21 | 870.97 | 873.62 | 862.92 | 876.00 | 863.05 | 876.04 | 897.18 | 882.28 | 877.32 | 898.63 | 876.04 |
| **Goods Producing** | | | | | | | | | | | | | |
| 2015 | 1,113.66 | 1,107.23 | 1,085.64 | 1,082.81 | 1,083.98 | 1,070.91 | 1,081.23 | 1,102.68 | 1,063.52 | 1,116.48 | 1,121.37 | 1,126.99 | 1,096.16 |
| 2016 | 1,118.57 | 1,089.70 | 1,063.46 | 1,097.11 | 1,120.83 | 1,098.17 | 1,101.69 | 1,070.22 | 1,117.92 | 1,161.28 | 1,112.62 | 1,118.81 | 1,105.59 |
| 2017 | 1,117.56 | 1,147.34 | 1,150.74 | 1,088.32 | 1,129.65 | 1,107.12 | 1,146.79 | 1,115.06 | 1,139.34 | 1,140.41 | 1,125.60 | 1,143.44 | 1,129.12 |
| 2018 | 1,121.94 | 1,154.32 | 1,183.70 | 1,175.64 | 1,187.23 | 1,182.79 | 1,170.22 | 1,143.44 | 1,158.85 | 1,177.44 | 1,167.03 | 1,210.99 | 1,168.41 |
| 2019 | 1,157.24 | 1,193.88 | 1,210.34 | 1,195.19 | 1,180.59 | 1,209.37 | 1,150.05 | 1,202.26 | 1,229.28 | 1,217.76 | 1,220.34 | 1,248.30 | 1,202.49 |
| **Construction** | | | | | | | | | | | | | |
| 2015 | 1,018.38 | 1,026.37 | 988.55 | 1,010.40 | 1,011.87 | 1,012.19 | 1,023.41 | 1,018.83 | 951.88 | 1,048.76 | 1,043.31 | 1,071.88 | 1,020.00 |
| 2016 | 1,026.45 | 1,024.34 | 965.79 | 1,033.94 | 1,071.46 | 1,048.71 | 1,040.50 | 988.40 | 1,086.68 | 1,138.27 | 1,068.19 | 1,071.98 | 1,047.48 |
| 2017 | 1,109.52 | 1,144.70 | 1,110.54 | 1,004.08 | 1,098.62 | 1,072.85 | 1,091.72 | 1,058.44 | 1,092.55 | 1,095.44 | 1,070.01 | 1,090.39 | 1,087.51 |
| 2018 | 1,052.45 | 1,102.49 | 1,141.57 | 1,124.34 | 1,159.65 | 1,126.20 | 1,123.86 | 1,073.06 | 1,097.46 | 1,150.63 | 1,106.30 | 1,162.16 | 1,119.26 |
| 2019 | 1,092.33 | 1,138.58 | 1,164.13 | 1,133.62 | 1,132.35 | 1,148.92 | 1,067.39 | 1,168.70 | 1,214.77 | 1,211.67 | 1,199.18 | 1,242.70 | 1,158.39 |
| **Manufacturing** | | | | | | | | | | | | | |
| 2015 | 1,130.86 | 1,103.33 | 1,123.70 | 1,098.04 | 1,082.28 | 1,056.45 | 1,063.67 | 1,084.80 | 1,068.78 | 1,076.96 | 1,096.84 | 1,092.50 | 1,089.06 |
| 2016 | 1,103.76 | 1,057.75 | 1,063.45 | 1,066.26 | 1,051.54 | 1,039.90 | 1,048.82 | 1,033.86 | 1,043.19 | 1,077.93 | 1,061.49 | 1,077.76 | 1,061.05 |
| 2017 | 1,051.09 | 1,084.96 | 1,096.28 | 1,088.26 | 1,087.86 | 1,070.13 | 1,119.10 | 1,093.03 | 1,135.25 | 1,135.73 | 1,120.18 | 1,132.19 | 1,099.86 |
| 2018 | 1,106.99 | 1,128.73 | 1,142.40 | 1,160.74 | 1,143.45 | 1,148.67 | 1,143.60 | 1,115.15 | 1,114.11 | 1,089.18 | 1,123.01 | 1,150.58 | 1,130.36 |
| 2019 | 1,089.70 | 1,114.54 | 1,133.34 | 1,133.90 | 1,106.81 | 1,151.75 | 1,108.28 | 1,140.67 | 1,167.85 | 1,152.25 | 1,163.25 | 1,191.46 | 1,137.17 |
| **Trade, Transportation, and Utilities** | | | | | | | | | | | | | |
| 2015 | 738.20 | 741.96 | 755.13 | 763.48 | 754.69 | 760.40 | 750.30 | 770.59 | 747.36 | 737.69 | 738.00 | 750.52 | 750.43 |
| 2016 | 729.34 | 721.10 | 702.54 | 717.02 | 728.28 | 722.68 | 713.42 | 700.35 | 721.81 | 718.52 | 700.70 | 703.61 | 715.18 |
| 2017 | 704.46 | 701.05 | 701.54 | 721.97 | 711.65 | 709.02 | 725.70 | 720.83 | 731.46 | 731.81 | 740.96 | 722.40 | 718.08 |
| 2018 | 725.92 | 733.25 | 746.92 | 769.68 | 761.07 | 764.69 | 782.54 | 770.18 | 791.03 | 780.27 | 788.25 | 781.83 | 766.41 |
| 2019 | 787.90 | 786.40 | 804.79 | 812.30 | 814.78 | 820.09 | 833.78 | 835.50 | 851.28 | 836.47 | 824.27 | 844.56 | 820.55 |
| **Financial Activities** | | | | | | | | | | | | | |
| 2015 | 888.49 | 924.54 | 922.85 | 925.13 | 908.84 | 916.56 | 929.69 | 969.39 | 929.39 | 933.50 | 1,008.23 | 947.42 | 934.42 |
| 2016 | 957.75 | 958.13 | 959.93 | 958.60 | 969.43 | 921.31 | 921.90 | 936.36 | 947.86 | 1,011.06 | 958.21 | 954.69 | 953.87 |
| 2017 | 1,012.51 | 964.45 | 1,005.62 | 995.71 | 937.38 | 923.28 | 975.38 | 941.77 | 966.61 | 992.22 | 981.09 | 981.36 | 972.48 |
| 2018 | 1,013.57 | 1,036.73 | 1,024.50 | 1,038.72 | 1,011.44 | 1,007.16 | 1,023.23 | 1,020.77 | 1,060.49 | 972.97 | 984.03 | 1,040.16 | 1,019.93 |
| 2019 | 1,073.48 | 1,049.62 | 1,006.85 | 1,071.22 | 1,034.42 | 1,099.22 | 1,084.92 | 1,105.17 | 1,126.00 | 1,102.45 | 1,115.09 | 1,163.45 | 1,086.23 |
| **Professional and Business Services** | | | | | | | | | | | | | |
| 2015 | 971.46 | 1,004.54 | 990.74 | 966.07 | 946.79 | 951.95 | 953.39 | 995.80 | 949.76 | 970.78 | 1,005.76 | 953.70 | 970.83 |
| 2016 | 940.24 | 930.02 | 938.78 | 926.31 | 962.18 | 948.54 | 945.31 | 927.67 | 952.50 | 998.31 | 960.43 | 979.45 | 950.46 |
| 2017 | 998.98 | 971.96 | 954.22 | 976.00 | 958.67 | 990.76 | 1,023.37 | 984.75 | 976.14 | 1,008.32 | 977.94 | 971.65 | 982.86 |
| 2018 | 974.39 | 973.82 | 967.94 | 996.39 | 961.22 | 970.46 | 1,016.72 | 981.71 | 1,016.06 | 997.15 | 1,028.83 | 1,032.95 | 992.64 |
| 2019 | 1,015.43 | 992.97 | 1,021.08 | 1,018.41 | 1,008.00 | 1,016.48 | 1,003.68 | 1,013.38 | 1,046.99 | 1,005.58 | 1,019.36 | 1,051.74 | 1,018.50 |
| **Education and Health Services** | | | | | | | | | | | | | |
| 2015 | 621.39 | 623.76 | 628.51 | 637.84 | 629.70 | 626.15 | 630.85 | 640.40 | 644.10 | 662.66 | 683.32 | 679.32 | 643.42 |
| 2016 | 683.36 | 683.77 | 690.04 | 716.69 | 734.61 | 735.83 | 740.04 | 734.32 | 744.82 | 765.80 | 764.81 | 762.80 | 730.28 |
| 2017 | 787.37 | 768.83 | 762.86 | 773.75 | 756.96 | 759.52 | 775.54 | 762.80 | 773.68 | 782.68 | 775.03 | 772.82 | 771.06 |
| 2018 | 765.81 | 772.58 | 774.75 | 785.32 | 769.78 | 774.36 | 783.43 | 778.08 | 802.26 | 778.22 | 783.23 | 808.51 | 782.07 |
| 2019 | 794.96 | 795.94 | 776.55 | 770.20 | 751.74 | 760.37 | 748.48 | 747.59 | 757.34 | 743.49 | 755.58 | 762.87 | 762.80 |
| **Leisure and Hospitality** | | | | | | | | | | | | | |
| 2015 | 362.82 | 375.23 | 369.88 | 366.99 | 366.77 | 366.80 | 362.93 | 360.64 | 355.65 | 365.85 | 367.16 | 364.69 | 365.68 |
| 2016 | 355.64 | 368.46 | 376.72 | 373.43 | 365.79 | 359.31 | 354.00 | 342.84 | 352.44 | 363.96 | 370.70 | 363.42 | 361.53 |
| 2017 | 363.69 | 370.17 | 375.89 | 372.90 | 366.09 | 356.16 | 357.41 | 350.04 | 352.98 | 364.46 | 366.93 | 368.83 | 364.21 |
| 2018 | 348.70 | 371.28 | 377.27 | 373.45 | 367.47 | 369.10 | 369.33 | 362.07 | 357.50 | 363.92 | 361.36 | 372.60 | 366.39 |
| 2019 | 360.36 | 364.64 | 367.88 | 363.26 | 363.47 | 361.79 | 336.66 | 351.46 | 353.34 | 355.01 | 354.05 | 366.96 | 358.09 |

# MAINE
*At a Glance*

Population:
  2010 census: 1,328,361
  2019 estimate: 1,344,212

Percent change in population:
  2010–2019: 1.2%

Percent change in total nonfarm employment:
  2011–2019: 6.8%

Industry with the largest growth in employment, 2011–2019 (percent):
  Professional and business services, 16.8%

Industry with the largest decline or smallest growth in employment, 2011–2019 (percent):
  Information, -13.3%

Civilian labor force:
  2010: 695,182
  2019: 692,739

Unemployment rate and rank among states (highest to lowest):
  2010: 8.1%, 32nd
  2019: 3.0%, 38th

Over-the-year change in unemployment rates:
  2017–2018: -0.2%
  2018–2019: -0.2%

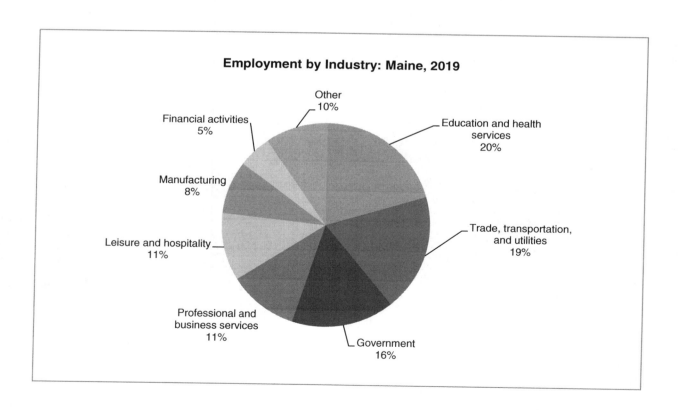

**Employment by Industry: Maine, 2019**

- Other 10%
- Financial activities 5%
- Manufacturing 8%
- Leisure and hospitality 11%
- Professional and business services 11%
- Government 16%
- Trade, transportation, and utilities 19%
- Education and health services 20%

# 1. Employment by Industry: Maine, 2011–2019

(Numbers in thousands, not seasonally adjusted)

| Industry and year | January | February | March | April | May | June | July | August | September | October | November | December | Annual average |
|---|---|---|---|---|---|---|---|---|---|---|---|---|---|
| **Total Nonfarm** | | | | | | | | | | | | | |
| 2011 | 572.3 | 574.2 | 575.4 | 583.0 | 594.5 | 605.8 | 610.6 | 610.2 | 609.0 | 606.4 | 601.4 | 597.5 | 595.0 |
| 2012 | 575.1 | 577.2 | 578.9 | 587.6 | 602.3 | 613.3 | 613.7 | 613.4 | 610.9 | 608.9 | 601.7 | 598.8 | 598.5 |
| 2013 | 577.9 | 578.2 | 579.9 | 588.8 | 604.5 | 616.4 | 619.9 | 618.9 | 616.4 | 615.0 | 605.3 | 603.3 | 602.0 |
| 2014 | 580.3 | 581.7 | 583.6 | 591.7 | 607.6 | 621.2 | 622.9 | 622.8 | 619.1 | 617.1 | 609.4 | 608.4 | 605.5 |
| 2015 | 586.4 | 585.4 | 588.2 | 598.0 | 613.6 | 626.5 | 630.3 | 629.5 | 624.5 | 621.2 | 613.9 | 612.9 | 610.9 |
| 2016 | 593.4 | 595.1 | 597.6 | 606.8 | 619.7 | 634.0 | 638.1 | 636.7 | 631.0 | 627.7 | 622.0 | 619.4 | 618.5 |
| 2017 | 601.6 | 600.7 | 604.6 | 611.3 | 624.2 | 641.2 | 642.4 | 640.9 | 636.8 | 632.3 | 626.4 | 626.4 | 624.1 |
| 2018 | 606.9 | 609.0 | 610.3 | 618.5 | 631.6 | 648.3 | 646.9 | 644.7 | 641.7 | 641.1 | 633.2 | 632.0 | 630.4 |
| 2019 | 615.0 | 615.9 | 617.4 | 623.5 | 636.8 | 650.8 | 651.3 | 652.0 | 648.6 | 645.6 | 635.1 | 633.7 | 635.5 |
| **Total Private** | | | | | | | | | | | | | |
| 2011 | 469.2 | 468.9 | 469.8 | 478.0 | 489.9 | 504.1 | 518.4 | 518.9 | 506.7 | 501.9 | 496.1 | 493.2 | 492.9 |
| 2012 | 474.1 | 473.4 | 474.7 | 483.8 | 497.4 | 512.3 | 521.8 | 521.4 | 509.3 | 504.4 | 497.3 | 494.5 | 497.0 |
| 2013 | 476.3 | 475.2 | 476.3 | 485.4 | 500.8 | 516.6 | 529.2 | 528.8 | 516.1 | 511.6 | 502.3 | 500.2 | 501.6 |
| 2014 | 480.8 | 480.3 | 481.3 | 489.5 | 505.4 | 520.4 | 532.5 | 532.8 | 518.6 | 514.0 | 506.1 | 505.0 | 505.6 |
| 2015 | 486.9 | 484.3 | 486.2 | 496.2 | 512.2 | 526.9 | 539.1 | 538.5 | 524.4 | 519.1 | 511.4 | 510.7 | 511.3 |
| 2016 | 494.8 | 493.9 | 495.5 | 504.6 | 517.7 | 533.4 | 546.5 | 545.0 | 530.0 | 524.9 | 518.2 | 516.8 | 518.4 |
| 2017 | 502.4 | 499.4 | 502.3 | 509.0 | 522.3 | 540.8 | 550.6 | 549.4 | 535.4 | 529.4 | 523.0 | 523.3 | 523.9 |
| 2018 | 507.6 | 507.3 | 508.3 | 515.8 | 529.4 | 546.5 | 556.5 | 554.5 | 540.1 | 537.0 | 529.3 | 528.1 | 530.0 |
| 2019 | 513.7 | 513.2 | 514.4 | 520.2 | 534.0 | 549.0 | 559.7 | 560.5 | 545.7 | 540.6 | 530.6 | 529.2 | 534.2 |
| **Goods Producing** | | | | | | | | | | | | | |
| 2011 | 74.7 | 73.8 | 74.1 | 75.3 | 77.9 | 80.5 | 81.5 | 82.0 | 81.3 | 81.0 | 80.8 | 79.4 | 78.5 |
| 2012 | 75.1 | 74.5 | 74.6 | 76.7 | 79.4 | 81.5 | 82.1 | 82.1 | 81.3 | 80.8 | 79.8 | 77.9 | 78.8 |
| 2013 | 74.1 | 73.5 | 73.6 | 75.2 | 78.3 | 80.7 | 81.9 | 82.2 | 81.3 | 81.2 | 80.4 | 78.4 | 78.4 |
| 2014 | 73.9 | 73.7 | 73.7 | 75.1 | 78.7 | 81.2 | 82.0 | 82.3 | 81.3 | 81.1 | 81.3 | 79.7 | 78.7 |
| 2015 | 75.3 | 74.3 | 74.5 | 76.5 | 79.4 | 81.9 | 83.0 | 83.3 | 82.4 | 82.1 | 82.1 | 80.8 | 79.6 |
| 2016 | 76.9 | 76.3 | 76.5 | 78.0 | 80.5 | 83.0 | 83.6 | 83.6 | 82.3 | 82.1 | 82.2 | 80.9 | 80.5 |
| 2017 | 77.7 | 76.9 | 77.5 | 78.7 | 80.8 | 83.9 | 84.3 | 84.8 | 84.0 | 84.1 | 84.0 | 82.9 | 81.6 |
| 2018 | 79.3 | 79.2 | 79.9 | 81.2 | 83.6 | 85.8 | 86.4 | 86.7 | 85.8 | 85.9 | 85.8 | 84.8 | 83.7 |
| 2019 | 82.0 | 81.2 | 81.6 | 82.4 | 85.2 | 87.3 | 88.0 | 88.4 | 87.4 | 87.7 | 87.2 | 85.2 | 85.3 |
| **Service-Providing** | | | | | | | | | | | | | |
| 2011 | 497.6 | 500.4 | 501.3 | 507.7 | 516.6 | 525.3 | 529.1 | 528.2 | 527.7 | 525.4 | 520.6 | 518.1 | 516.5 |
| 2012 | 500.0 | 502.7 | 504.3 | 510.9 | 522.9 | 531.8 | 531.6 | 531.3 | 529.6 | 528.1 | 521.9 | 520.9 | 519.7 |
| 2013 | 503.8 | 504.7 | 506.3 | 513.6 | 526.2 | 535.7 | 538.0 | 536.7 | 535.1 | 533.8 | 524.9 | 524.9 | 523.6 |
| 2014 | 506.4 | 508.0 | 509.9 | 516.6 | 528.9 | 540.0 | 540.9 | 540.5 | 537.8 | 536.0 | 528.1 | 528.7 | 526.8 |
| 2015 | 511.1 | 511.1 | 513.7 | 521.5 | 534.2 | 544.6 | 547.3 | 546.2 | 542.1 | 539.1 | 531.8 | 532.1 | 531.2 |
| 2016 | 516.5 | 518.8 | 521.1 | 528.8 | 539.2 | 551.0 | 554.5 | 553.1 | 548.7 | 545.6 | 539.8 | 538.5 | 538.0 |
| 2017 | 523.9 | 523.8 | 527.1 | 532.6 | 543.4 | 557.3 | 558.1 | 556.1 | 552.8 | 548.2 | 542.4 | 543.5 | 542.4 |
| 2018 | 527.6 | 529.8 | 530.4 | 537.3 | 548.0 | 562.5 | 560.5 | 558.0 | 555.9 | 555.2 | 547.4 | 547.2 | 546.7 |
| 2019 | 533.0 | 534.7 | 535.8 | 541.1 | 551.6 | 563.5 | 563.3 | 563.6 | 561.2 | 557.9 | 547.9 | 548.5 | 550.2 |
| **Mining and Logging** | | | | | | | | | | | | | |
| 2011 | 2.6 | 2.6 | 2.6 | 1.9 | 1.8 | 2.4 | 2.7 | 2.7 | 2.7 | 2.7 | 2.7 | 2.7 | 2.5 |
| 2012 | 2.6 | 2.6 | 2.5 | 1.8 | 1.9 | 2.4 | 2.6 | 2.7 | 2.7 | 2.7 | 2.6 | 2.6 | 2.5 |
| 2013 | 2.6 | 2.6 | 2.4 | 1.8 | 1.9 | 2.3 | 2.5 | 2.6 | 2.6 | 2.6 | 2.6 | 2.6 | 2.4 |
| 2014 | 2.6 | 2.6 | 2.6 | 2.1 | 1.7 | 2.3 | 2.6 | 2.6 | 2.6 | 2.6 | 2.6 | 2.6 | 2.5 |
| 2015 | 2.5 | 2.5 | 2.6 | 2.0 | 1.8 | 2.3 | 2.6 | 2.6 | 2.6 | 2.5 | 2.5 | 2.5 | 2.4 |
| 2016 | 2.4 | 2.5 | 2.3 | 1.7 | 1.7 | 2.3 | 2.4 | 2.4 | 2.4 | 2.4 | 2.4 | 2.4 | 2.3 |
| 2017 | 2.3 | 2.3 | 2.3 | 1.7 | 1.6 | 2.1 | 2.3 | 2.3 | 2.4 | 2.4 | 2.3 | 2.3 | 2.2 |
| 2018 | 2.3 | 2.3 | 2.3 | 1.9 | 1.7 | 2.1 | 2.3 | 2.3 | 2.4 | 2.3 | 2.3 | 2.3 | 2.2 |
| 2019 | 2.3 | 2.3 | 2.3 | 1.8 | 1.7 | 2.1 | 2.3 | 2.3 | 2.3 | 2.3 | 2.3 | 2.2 | 2.2 |
| **Construction** | | | | | | | | | | | | | |
| 2011 | 22.0 | 21.3 | 21.4 | 23.2 | 25.3 | 27.0 | 27.7 | 27.7 | 27.6 | 27.6 | 26.9 | 25.6 | 25.3 |
| 2012 | 22.9 | 22.2 | 22.3 | 24.5 | 26.6 | 27.4 | 27.7 | 27.8 | 27.4 | 27.1 | 26.1 | 24.7 | 25.6 |
| 2013 | 22.3 | 21.9 | 21.9 | 23.9 | 26.1 | 27.2 | 27.8 | 28.0 | 27.8 | 27.8 | 26.8 | 25.3 | 25.6 |
| 2014 | 22.7 | 22.5 | 22.5 | 23.9 | 26.7 | 27.7 | 28.3 | 28.4 | 28.0 | 27.9 | 27.2 | 25.8 | 26.0 |
| 2015 | 23.3 | 22.7 | 22.7 | 24.5 | 27.2 | 28.4 | 29.0 | 29.0 | 28.4 | 28.5 | 27.9 | 26.9 | 26.5 |
| 2016 | 24.8 | 24.3 | 24.5 | 26.3 | 28.1 | 29.2 | 29.7 | 29.4 | 28.8 | 28.8 | 28.3 | 27.3 | 27.5 |
| 2017 | 25.5 | 24.9 | 25.2 | 26.7 | 28.4 | 29.9 | 30.2 | 30.3 | 30.0 | 30.2 | 29.7 | 28.8 | 28.3 |
| 2018 | 26.6 | 26.4 | 26.8 | 28.1 | 30.3 | 31.0 | 31.2 | 31.1 | 30.8 | 30.9 | 30.2 | 29.1 | 29.4 |
| 2019 | 27.6 | 27.0 | 27.1 | 28.3 | 30.5 | 31.4 | 31.6 | 31.7 | 31.3 | 31.5 | 30.4 | 29.0 | 29.8 |

## 1. Employment by Industry: Maine, 2011–2019—*Continued*

(Numbers in thousands, not seasonally adjusted)

| Industry and year | January | February | March | April | May | June | July | August | September | October | November | December | Annual average |
|---|---|---|---|---|---|---|---|---|---|---|---|---|---|
| **Manufacturing** | | | | | | | | | | | | | |
| 2011 | 50.1 | 49.9 | 50.1 | 50.2 | 50.8 | 51.1 | 51.1 | 51.6 | 51.0 | 50.7 | 51.2 | 51.1 | 50.7 |
| 2012 | 49.6 | 49.7 | 49.8 | 50.4 | 50.9 | 51.7 | 51.8 | 51.6 | 51.2 | 51.0 | 51.1 | 50.6 | 50.8 |
| 2013 | 49.2 | 49.0 | 49.3 | 49.5 | 50.3 | 51.2 | 51.6 | 51.6 | 50.9 | 50.8 | 51.0 | 50.5 | 50.4 |
| 2014 | 48.6 | 48.6 | 48.6 | 49.1 | 50.3 | 51.2 | 51.1 | 51.3 | 50.7 | 50.6 | 51.5 | 51.3 | 50.2 |
| 2015 | 49.5 | 49.1 | 49.2 | 50.0 | 50.4 | 51.2 | 51.4 | 51.7 | 51.4 | 51.1 | 51.7 | 51.4 | 50.7 |
| 2016 | 49.7 | 49.5 | 49.7 | 50.0 | 50.7 | 51.5 | 51.5 | 51.8 | 51.1 | 50.9 | 51.5 | 51.2 | 50.8 |
| 2017 | 49.9 | 49.7 | 50.0 | 50.3 | 50.8 | 51.9 | 51.8 | 52.2 | 51.6 | 51.5 | 52.0 | 51.8 | 51.1 |
| 2018 | 50.4 | 50.5 | 50.8 | 51.2 | 51.6 | 52.7 | 52.9 | 53.3 | 52.6 | 52.7 | 53.3 | 53.4 | 52.1 |
| 2019 | 52.1 | 51.9 | 52.2 | 52.3 | 53.0 | 53.8 | 54.1 | 54.4 | 53.8 | 53.9 | 54.5 | 54.0 | 53.3 |
| **Trade, Transportation, and Utilities** | | | | | | | | | | | | | |
| 2011 | 113.8 | 111.6 | 110.8 | 112.2 | 114.1 | 117.3 | 118.8 | 119.4 | 117.3 | 118.6 | 120.4 | 121.2 | 116.3 |
| 2012 | 114.5 | 112.2 | 111.7 | 112.4 | 115.2 | 118.5 | 119.2 | 119.7 | 117.3 | 118.6 | 121.0 | 121.1 | 116.8 |
| 2013 | 113.8 | 111.4 | 110.9 | 112.1 | 115.1 | 119.0 | 121.1 | 121.5 | 119.2 | 119.9 | 121.7 | 122.6 | 117.4 |
| 2014 | 115.1 | 113.7 | 113.0 | 114.2 | 116.8 | 119.8 | 121.3 | 121.9 | 119.6 | 120.4 | 122.1 | 123.2 | 118.4 |
| 2015 | 115.8 | 113.9 | 113.4 | 115.0 | 117.8 | 121.0 | 122.6 | 122.7 | 120.2 | 120.7 | 121.9 | 123.1 | 119.0 |
| 2016 | 116.6 | 115.0 | 114.9 | 116.1 | 118.5 | 121.7 | 123.2 | 123.2 | 120.8 | 120.5 | 122.0 | 122.9 | 119.6 |
| 2017 | 117.3 | 114.8 | 114.8 | 115.8 | 118.1 | 121.6 | 123.2 | 123.0 | 120.3 | 120.4 | 121.7 | 122.9 | 119.5 |
| 2018 | 117.4 | 115.5 | 115.2 | 116.1 | 118.3 | 121.2 | 122.1 | 121.4 | 119.5 | 119.7 | 121.5 | 122.0 | 119.2 |
| 2019 | 117.3 | 115.7 | 114.7 | 115.6 | 117.4 | 120.1 | 121.6 | 121.9 | 119.3 | 118.6 | 119.3 | 121.0 | 118.5 |
| **Wholesale Trade** | | | | | | | | | | | | | |
| 2011 | 18.5 | 18.4 | 18.3 | 18.6 | 18.7 | 19.2 | 19.5 | 19.5 | 19.3 | 19.2 | 19.1 | 19.2 | 19.0 |
| 2012 | 18.7 | 18.6 | 18.6 | 18.9 | 19.3 | 19.8 | 19.9 | 19.9 | 19.6 | 19.5 | 19.4 | 19.3 | 19.3 |
| 2013 | 18.7 | 18.7 | 18.7 | 18.8 | 19.3 | 19.9 | 20.1 | 20.1 | 19.8 | 19.7 | 19.5 | 19.5 | 19.4 |
| 2014 | 18.9 | 18.8 | 18.9 | 19.1 | 19.6 | 20.0 | 20.2 | 20.2 | 20.0 | 20.0 | 19.8 | 19.7 | 19.6 |
| 2015 | 19.3 | 19.2 | 19.2 | 19.4 | 19.8 | 20.2 | 20.5 | 20.5 | 20.2 | 20.1 | 19.8 | 19.8 | 19.8 |
| 2016 | 19.2 | 19.1 | 19.2 | 19.4 | 19.8 | 20.1 | 20.4 | 20.3 | 20.0 | 19.8 | 19.5 | 19.4 | 19.7 |
| 2017 | 19.0 | 18.8 | 18.9 | 19.1 | 19.5 | 19.9 | 20.0 | 19.9 | 19.7 | 19.6 | 19.4 | 19.4 | 19.4 |
| 2018 | 19.0 | 19.0 | 19.0 | 19.2 | 19.6 | 19.9 | 20.1 | 20.0 | 19.6 | 19.7 | 19.6 | 19.6 | 19.5 |
| 2019 | 19.2 | 19.1 | 19.1 | 19.2 | 19.5 | 19.8 | 20.0 | 20.1 | 19.8 | 19.4 | 19.1 | 19.4 | 19.5 |
| **Retail Trade** | | | | | | | | | | | | | |
| 2011 | 79.4 | 77.6 | 77.0 | 78.0 | 79.7 | 81.9 | 83.1 | 83.6 | 81.4 | 82.6 | 84.2 | 84.6 | 81.1 |
| 2012 | 79.7 | 77.7 | 77.4 | 78.0 | 80.0 | 82.3 | 83.1 | 83.5 | 81.1 | 82.3 | 84.4 | 84.2 | 81.1 |
| 2013 | 79.0 | 76.8 | 76.4 | 77.4 | 79.6 | 82.3 | 84.2 | 84.5 | 82.2 | 82.8 | 84.3 | 84.7 | 81.2 |
| 2014 | 79.6 | 78.4 | 77.8 | 78.7 | 80.4 | 82.5 | 83.9 | 84.3 | 82.0 | 82.5 | 83.9 | 84.6 | 81.6 |
| 2015 | 79.3 | 77.9 | 77.6 | 78.7 | 80.7 | 83.1 | 84.3 | 84.4 | 82.0 | 82.6 | 83.8 | 84.7 | 81.6 |
| 2016 | 80.1 | 78.8 | 78.7 | 79.4 | 81.0 | 83.3 | 84.7 | 84.7 | 82.3 | 82.3 | 83.8 | 84.2 | 81.9 |
| 2017 | 80.2 | 78.2 | 78.2 | 79.0 | 80.3 | 82.7 | 84.2 | 84.1 | 81.4 | 81.4 | 82.7 | 83.3 | 81.3 |
| 2018 | 80.0 | 78.3 | 78.2 | 79.0 | 80.3 | 82.5 | 83.5 | 82.9 | 81.1 | 80.9 | 82.6 | 82.8 | 81.0 |
| 2019 | 79.5 | 78.3 | 77.7 | 78.6 | 79.7 | 81.5 | 82.9 | 83.0 | 80.5 | 80.3 | 80.9 | 81.7 | 80.4 |
| **Transportation and Utilities** | | | | | | | | | | | | | |
| 2011 | 15.9 | 15.6 | 15.5 | 15.6 | 15.7 | 16.2 | 16.2 | 16.3 | 16.6 | 16.8 | 17.1 | 17.4 | 16.2 |
| 2012 | 16.1 | 15.9 | 15.7 | 15.5 | 15.9 | 16.4 | 16.2 | 16.3 | 16.6 | 16.8 | 17.2 | 17.6 | 16.4 |
| 2013 | 16.1 | 15.9 | 15.8 | 15.9 | 16.2 | 16.8 | 16.8 | 16.9 | 17.2 | 17.4 | 17.9 | 18.4 | 16.8 |
| 2014 | 16.6 | 16.5 | 16.3 | 16.4 | 16.8 | 17.3 | 17.2 | 17.4 | 17.6 | 17.9 | 18.4 | 18.9 | 17.3 |
| 2015 | 17.2 | 16.8 | 16.6 | 16.9 | 17.3 | 17.7 | 17.8 | 17.8 | 18.0 | 18.0 | 18.3 | 18.6 | 17.6 |
| 2016 | 17.3 | 17.1 | 17.0 | 17.3 | 17.7 | 18.3 | 18.1 | 18.2 | 18.5 | 18.4 | 18.7 | 19.3 | 18.0 |
| 2017 | 18.1 | 17.8 | 17.7 | 17.7 | 18.3 | 19.0 | 19.0 | 19.0 | 19.2 | 19.4 | 19.6 | 20.2 | 18.8 |
| 2018 | 18.4 | 18.2 | 18.0 | 17.9 | 18.4 | 18.8 | 18.5 | 18.5 | 18.8 | 19.1 | 19.3 | 19.6 | 18.6 |
| 2019 | 18.6 | 18.3 | 17.9 | 17.8 | 18.2 | 18.8 | 18.7 | 18.8 | 19.0 | 18.9 | 19.3 | 19.9 | 18.7 |
| **Information** | | | | | | | | | | | | | |
| 2011 | 8.4 | 8.3 | 8.3 | 8.3 | 8.3 | 8.3 | 8.4 | 8.3 | 8.2 | 8.1 | 8.1 | 8.1 | 8.3 |
| 2012 | 8.0 | 8.0 | 8.0 | 7.9 | 7.9 | 7.9 | 7.9 | 7.9 | 7.8 | 7.8 | 7.8 | 7.8 | 7.9 |
| 2013 | 7.8 | 7.7 | 7.7 | 7.7 | 7.7 | 7.7 | 7.7 | 7.7 | 7.6 | 7.5 | 7.5 | 7.5 | 7.7 |
| 2014 | 7.5 | 7.4 | 7.4 | 7.4 | 7.4 | 7.6 | 7.6 | 7.6 | 7.6 | 7.6 | 7.2 | 7.2 | 7.5 |
| 2015 | 7.3 | 7.3 | 7.5 | 7.6 | 7.7 | 7.9 | 7.9 | 7.8 | 7.6 | 7.7 | 7.8 | 7.7 | 7.7 |
| 2016 | 7.7 | 7.7 | 7.7 | 7.7 | 7.8 | 7.8 | 7.9 | 7.8 | 7.7 | 7.7 | 7.7 | 7.7 | 7.7 |
| 2017 | 7.6 | 7.5 | 7.5 | 7.4 | 7.5 | 7.5 | 7.5 | 7.5 | 7.4 | 7.4 | 7.4 | 7.5 | 7.5 |
| 2018 | 7.5 | 7.4 | 7.4 | 7.5 | 7.5 | 7.6 | 7.5 | 7.6 | 7.3 | 7.3 | 7.2 | 7.3 | 7.4 |
| 2019 | 7.2 | 7.2 | 7.2 | 7.1 | 7.2 | 7.2 | 7.2 | 7.2 | 7.1 | 7.2 | 7.4 | 7.3 | 7.2 |

# 1. Employment by Industry: Maine, 2011–2019—*Continued*

(Numbers in thousands, not seasonally adjusted)

| Industry and year | January | February | March | April | May | June | July | August | September | October | November | December | Annual average |
|---|---|---|---|---|---|---|---|---|---|---|---|---|---|
| **Financial Activities** | | | | | | | | | | | | | |
| 2011 | 30.0 | 30.1 | 30.2 | 30.0 | 30.3 | 30.7 | 31.0 | 31.0 | 30.4 | 30.4 | 30.2 | 30.4 | 30.4 |
| 2012 | 29.9 | 29.8 | 29.8 | 29.9 | 30.2 | 30.6 | 30.9 | 30.8 | 30.2 | 30.0 | 29.8 | 29.9 | 30.2 |
| 2013 | 29.8 | 29.7 | 29.9 | 30.0 | 30.4 | 30.8 | 31.2 | 31.1 | 30.6 | 30.4 | 30.4 | 30.4 | 30.4 |
| 2014 | 29.9 | 29.8 | 29.9 | 30.0 | 30.4 | 30.8 | 31.0 | 31.2 | 30.5 | 30.4 | 30.3 | 30.4 | 30.4 |
| 2015 | 30.1 | 30.0 | 30.0 | 30.2 | 30.6 | 31.0 | 31.3 | 31.4 | 30.8 | 30.7 | 30.6 | 30.8 | 30.6 |
| 2016 | 30.5 | 30.5 | 30.6 | 30.8 | 31.2 | 31.6 | 31.9 | 31.9 | 31.3 | 31.1 | 30.8 | 31.0 | 31.1 |
| 2017 | 30.8 | 30.7 | 30.9 | 30.9 | 31.3 | 31.9 | 32.2 | 32.2 | 31.8 | 31.6 | 31.6 | 31.7 | 31.5 |
| 2018 | 31.2 | 31.3 | 31.3 | 31.6 | 32.1 | 32.5 | 32.8 | 32.8 | 32.4 | 32.5 | 32.5 | 32.5 | 32.1 |
| 2019 | 32.3 | 32.4 | 32.3 | 32.3 | 32.8 | 33.4 | 33.6 | 33.7 | 33.2 | 33.1 | 33.0 | 33.1 | 32.9 |
| **Professional and Business Services** | | | | | | | | | | | | | |
| 2011 | 56.6 | 57.0 | 57.1 | 58.8 | 59.4 | 60.4 | 61.0 | 61.2 | 60.9 | 60.5 | 60.5 | 59.2 | 59.4 |
| 2012 | 58.0 | 57.8 | 58.0 | 59.6 | 60.2 | 61.4 | 61.5 | 61.6 | 61.3 | 61.4 | 60.9 | 60.5 | 60.2 |
| 2013 | 58.9 | 59.6 | 59.3 | 61.0 | 62.3 | 63.7 | 64.2 | 64.4 | 63.8 | 63.6 | 62.8 | 62.7 | 62.2 |
| 2014 | 60.7 | 61.4 | 61.7 | 63.1 | 64.9 | 66.0 | 66.1 | 66.2 | 65.6 | 65.5 | 64.7 | 64.1 | 64.2 |
| 2015 | 62.5 | 63.3 | 63.3 | 64.4 | 66.6 | 67.2 | 67.3 | 67.2 | 66.3 | 66.4 | 65.6 | 65.2 | 65.4 |
| 2016 | 63.8 | 64.0 | 63.8 | 66.0 | 67.0 | 68.3 | 68.7 | 68.5 | 67.6 | 67.4 | 66.7 | 66.6 | 66.5 |
| 2017 | 64.8 | 65.3 | 65.3 | 66.3 | 67.8 | 69.0 | 69.0 | 68.9 | 67.9 | 68.2 | 67.8 | 67.5 | 67.3 |
| 2018 | 66.9 | 67.2 | 67.3 | 68.3 | 69.8 | 71.1 | 71.4 | 71.3 | 70.2 | 70.4 | 69.9 | 69.0 | 69.4 |
| 2019 | 67.4 | 68.0 | 67.9 | 68.8 | 69.7 | 71.0 | 71.2 | 71.3 | 70.0 | 70.3 | 69.2 | 68.2 | 69.4 |
| **Education and Health Services** | | | | | | | | | | | | | |
| 2011 | 117.1 | 119.3 | 119.6 | 120.1 | 119.9 | 118.1 | 118.0 | 118.2 | 120.2 | 122.0 | 122.1 | 122.0 | 119.7 |
| 2012 | 119.5 | 121.6 | 121.6 | 121.9 | 122.2 | 119.9 | 119.6 | 119.0 | 121.5 | 123.1 | 122.9 | 122.7 | 121.3 |
| 2013 | 120.6 | 122.4 | 122.4 | 122.9 | 122.2 | 120.2 | 119.9 | 119.7 | 122.5 | 123.6 | 123.4 | 122.7 | 121.9 |
| 2014 | 121.6 | 122.3 | 122.5 | 122.9 | 121.9 | 120.6 | 119.9 | 119.9 | 122.4 | 123.4 | 123.5 | 122.8 | 122.0 |
| 2015 | 122.3 | 122.7 | 123.3 | 123.9 | 123.2 | 122.1 | 121.9 | 121.7 | 124.0 | 124.2 | 124.4 | 124.3 | 123.2 |
| 2016 | 124.3 | 125.0 | 125.7 | 125.5 | 124.9 | 123.1 | 123.3 | 123.0 | 125.7 | 126.7 | 127.0 | 126.9 | 125.1 |
| 2017 | 126.7 | 127.2 | 128.0 | 128.0 | 127.2 | 126.0 | 125.2 | 124.7 | 127.5 | 127.5 | 127.9 | 128.1 | 127.0 |
| 2018 | 126.9 | 127.7 | 127.6 | 127.7 | 126.9 | 125.3 | 124.7 | 124.5 | 127.1 | 128.2 | 128.7 | 128.7 | 127.0 |
| 2019 | 127.5 | 128.6 | 129.1 | 129.7 | 129.2 | 127.6 | 127.1 | 127.8 | 130.6 | 131.4 | 131.8 | 130.8 | 129.3 |
| **Leisure and Hospitality** | | | | | | | | | | | | | |
| 2011 | 49.3 | 49.5 | 50.3 | 53.6 | 59.9 | 68.5 | 79.1 | 78.4 | 68.4 | 61.3 | 54.2 | 53.1 | 60.5 |
| 2012 | 49.6 | 50.0 | 51.3 | 55.5 | 62.3 | 72.2 | 79.9 | 79.8 | 69.8 | 62.6 | 55.1 | 54.6 | 61.9 |
| 2013 | 51.3 | 50.9 | 52.3 | 56.0 | 63.9 | 73.3 | 81.8 | 81.0 | 70.3 | 64.7 | 55.5 | 55.3 | 63.0 |
| 2014 | 51.7 | 51.7 | 52.7 | 56.2 | 64.3 | 73.0 | 82.8 | 82.0 | 70.4 | 64.3 | 56.0 | 56.6 | 63.5 |
| 2015 | 52.9 | 52.3 | 53.5 | 57.5 | 65.5 | 73.9 | 82.9 | 82.4 | 71.7 | 65.8 | 57.6 | 57.2 | 64.4 |
| 2016 | 53.9 | 54.2 | 55.0 | 59.1 | 66.1 | 75.8 | 85.2 | 84.6 | 72.8 | 67.6 | 60.1 | 59.2 | 66.1 |
| 2017 | 56.1 | 55.9 | 57.1 | 60.4 | 67.8 | 78.6 | 86.6 | 85.9 | 74.7 | 68.4 | 60.9 | 60.8 | 67.8 |
| 2018 | 56.9 | 57.3 | 58.0 | 61.6 | 68.9 | 80.2 | 88.6 | 87.4 | 75.6 | 70.5 | 61.5 | 61.6 | 69.0 |
| 2019 | 58.3 | 58.3 | 59.7 | 62.3 | 70.1 | 79.8 | 88.0 | 87.4 | 75.9 | 69.7 | 60.1 | 60.8 | 69.2 |
| **Other Services** | | | | | | | | | | | | | |
| 2011 | 19.3 | 19.3 | 19.4 | 19.7 | 20.1 | 20.3 | 20.6 | 20.4 | 20.0 | 20.0 | 19.8 | 19.8 | 19.9 |
| 2012 | 19.5 | 19.5 | 19.7 | 19.9 | 20.0 | 20.3 | 20.7 | 20.5 | 20.1 | 20.1 | 20.0 | 20.0 | 20.0 |
| 2013 | 20.0 | 20.0 | 20.2 | 20.5 | 20.9 | 21.2 | 21.4 | 21.2 | 20.8 | 20.7 | 20.6 | 20.6 | 20.7 |
| 2014 | 20.4 | 20.3 | 20.4 | 20.6 | 21.0 | 21.4 | 21.8 | 21.7 | 21.2 | 21.3 | 21.0 | 21.0 | 21.0 |
| 2015 | 20.7 | 20.5 | 20.7 | 21.1 | 21.4 | 21.9 | 22.2 | 22.0 | 21.4 | 21.5 | 21.4 | 21.6 | 21.4 |
| 2016 | 21.1 | 21.2 | 21.3 | 21.4 | 21.7 | 22.1 | 22.7 | 22.4 | 21.8 | 21.8 | 21.7 | 21.6 | 21.7 |
| 2017 | 21.4 | 21.1 | 21.2 | 21.5 | 21.8 | 22.3 | 22.6 | 22.4 | 21.8 | 21.8 | 21.7 | 21.9 | 21.8 |
| 2018 | 21.5 | 21.7 | 21.6 | 21.8 | 22.3 | 22.8 | 23.0 | 22.8 | 22.2 | 22.5 | 22.2 | 22.2 | 22.2 |
| 2019 | 21.7 | 21.8 | 21.9 | 22.0 | 22.4 | 22.6 | 23.0 | 22.8 | 22.2 | 22.6 | 22.6 | 22.8 | 22.4 |
| **Government** | | | | | | | | | | | | | |
| 2011 | 103.1 | 105.3 | 105.6 | 105.0 | 104.6 | 101.7 | 92.2 | 91.3 | 102.3 | 104.5 | 105.3 | 104.3 | 102.1 |
| 2012 | 101.0 | 103.8 | 104.2 | 103.8 | 104.9 | 101.0 | 91.9 | 92.0 | 101.6 | 104.5 | 104.4 | 104.3 | 101.5 |
| 2013 | 101.6 | 103.0 | 103.6 | 103.4 | 103.7 | 99.8 | 90.7 | 90.1 | 100.3 | 103.4 | 103.0 | 103.1 | 100.5 |
| 2014 | 99.5 | 101.4 | 102.3 | 102.2 | 102.2 | 100.8 | 90.4 | 90.0 | 100.5 | 103.1 | 103.3 | 103.4 | 99.9 |
| 2015 | 99.5 | 101.1 | 102.0 | 101.8 | 101.4 | 99.6 | 91.2 | 91.0 | 100.1 | 102.1 | 102.5 | 102.2 | 99.5 |
| 2016 | 98.6 | 101.2 | 102.1 | 102.2 | 102.0 | 100.6 | 91.6 | 91.7 | 101.0 | 102.8 | 103.8 | 102.6 | 100.0 |
| 2017 | 99.2 | 101.3 | 102.3 | 102.3 | 101.9 | 100.4 | 91.8 | 91.5 | 101.4 | 102.9 | 103.4 | 103.1 | 100.1 |
| 2018 | 99.3 | 101.7 | 102.0 | 102.7 | 102.2 | 101.8 | 90.4 | 90.2 | 101.6 | 104.1 | 103.9 | 103.9 | 100.3 |
| 2019 | 101.3 | 102.7 | 103.0 | 103.3 | 102.8 | 101.8 | 91.6 | 91.5 | 102.9 | 105.0 | 104.5 | 104.5 | 101.2 |

## 2. Average Weekly Hours by Selected Industry: Maine, 2015–2019

(Not seasonally adjusted)

| Industry and year | January | February | March | April | May | June | July | August | September | October | November | December | Annual average |
|---|---|---|---|---|---|---|---|---|---|---|---|---|---|
| **Total Private** | | | | | | | | | | | | | |
| 2015 | 33.9 | 34.0 | 34.1 | 33.9 | 34.3 | 34.3 | 34.6 | 34.7 | 34.5 | 34.3 | 34.3 | 34.1 | 34.3 |
| 2016 | 33.5 | 33.6 | 33.8 | 33.8 | 34.0 | 33.9 | 34.1 | 34.2 | 34.0 | 34.4 | 34.0 | 33.7 | 33.9 |
| 2017 | 33.6 | 33.0 | 33.6 | 34.0 | 34.1 | 34.1 | 34.5 | 34.5 | 34.3 | 34.2 | 34.1 | 33.9 | 34.0 |
| 2018 | 33.7 | 33.9 | 33.2 | 34.3 | 34.3 | 34.4 | 34.8 | 34.5 | 34.3 | 34.2 | 33.8 | 34.5 | 34.2 |
| 2019 | 33.7 | 33.1 | 33.4 | 33.4 | 33.7 | 33.9 | 34.1 | 34.3 | 34.4 | 33.9 | 33.9 | 34.3 | 33.8 |
| **Goods-Producing** | | | | | | | | | | | | | |
| 2015 | 40.2 | 39.7 | 40.1 | 40.2 | 41.4 | 41.5 | 41.8 | 41.8 | 40.9 | 41.8 | 41.2 | 41.4 | 41.0 |
| 2016 | 40.5 | 39.9 | 40.7 | 40.6 | 41.3 | 41.4 | 41.6 | 41.6 | 41.2 | 41.6 | 40.9 | 39.9 | 40.9 |
| 2017 | 40.5 | 38.7 | 40.0 | 40.6 | 40.9 | 41.3 | 41.2 | 41.6 | 41.4 | 41.2 | 40.7 | 40.3 | 40.7 |
| 2018 | 40.3 | 39.9 | 38.0 | 40.1 | 40.3 | 40.1 | 40.3 | 40.4 | 40.1 | 39.6 | 38.8 | 40.3 | 39.9 |
| 2019 | 39.3 | 38.4 | 39.3 | 39.3 | 40.4 | 39.9 | 40.2 | 40.4 | 40.3 | 40.2 | 39.5 | 40.4 | 39.8 |
| **Construction** | | | | | | | | | | | | | |
| 2015 | 37.3 | 37.2 | 37.1 | 38.5 | 40.7 | 41.0 | 41.6 | 40.7 | 39.5 | 40.9 | 40.4 | 40.1 | 39.7 |
| 2016 | 39.1 | 37.7 | 39.2 | 39.3 | 41.1 | 41.6 | 42.1 | 41.4 | 41.1 | 41.3 | 40.4 | 39.1 | 40.3 |
| 2017 | 39.6 | 36.7 | 37.9 | 39.4 | 40.2 | 40.8 | 40.3 | 41.6 | 41.6 | 40.8 | 40.4 | 39.4 | 40.0 |
| 2018 | 39.4 | 39.1 | 36.8 | 39.7 | 40.8 | 40.1 | 40.6 | 39.8 | 39.1 | 38.6 | 37.1 | 38.8 | 39.2 |
| 2019 | 37.2 | 36.5 | 38.0 | 38.3 | 40.1 | 39.8 | 40.0 | 40.5 | 39.9 | 40.0 | 38.9 | 39.6 | 39.1 |
| **Manufacturing** | | | | | | | | | | | | | |
| 2015 | 40.3 | 39.6 | 40.5 | 40.1 | 40.9 | 40.9 | 40.8 | 41.4 | 40.8 | 41.6 | 41.1 | 41.6 | 40.8 |
| 2016 | 40.5 | 40.3 | 40.9 | 40.8 | 41.1 | 40.9 | 41.2 | 41.5 | 41.1 | 41.6 | 40.7 | 40.0 | 40.9 |
| 2017 | 40.7 | 38.9 | 40.4 | 40.7 | 40.7 | 41.0 | 41.2 | 41.1 | 41.0 | 41.1 | 40.6 | 40.5 | 40.6 |
| 2018 | 40.4 | 39.8 | 38.4 | 39.6 | 39.2 | 39.5 | 39.3 | 40.3 | 40.5 | 40.0 | 39.7 | 40.9 | 39.8 |
| 2019 | 40.3 | 39.1 | 39.7 | 39.6 | 40.2 | 39.6 | 39.9 | 40.3 | 40.5 | 40.4 | 39.8 | 40.5 | 40.0 |
| **Trade, Transportation, and Utilities** | | | | | | | | | | | | | |
| 2015 | 33.1 | 33.8 | 33.4 | 33.1 | 33.7 | 33.4 | 34.3 | 34.2 | 34.8 | 33.7 | 33.5 | 34.1 | 33.8 |
| 2016 | 33.3 | 33.5 | 33.4 | 33.9 | 33.7 | 33.9 | 34.6 | 34.8 | 34.3 | 34.6 | 34.2 | 34.6 | 34.1 |
| 2017 | 33.6 | 32.9 | 33.8 | 33.9 | 34.4 | 34.5 | 35.1 | 34.9 | 34.3 | 34.0 | 34.1 | 34.5 | 34.2 |
| 2018 | 33.6 | 33.6 | 33.0 | 34.0 | 34.3 | 34.1 | 34.7 | 34.7 | 34.3 | 33.9 | 34.0 | 34.1 | 34.0 |
| 2019 | 33.5 | 32.9 | 33.2 | 33.0 | 33.3 | 33.6 | 34.1 | 34.2 | 33.8 | 33.0 | 33.5 | 34.0 | 33.5 |
| **Professional and Business Services** | | | | | | | | | | | | | |
| 2015 | 33.7 | 34.1 | 34.6 | 33.9 | 34.1 | 34.4 | 34.3 | 34.8 | 34.3 | 34.7 | 35.1 | 34.4 | 34.4 |
| 2016 | 33.2 | 33.6 | 33.9 | 34.4 | 35.0 | 34.3 | 34.2 | 33.7 | 33.5 | 34.8 | 34.2 | 33.9 | 34.1 |
| 2017 | 35.1 | 34.0 | 34.5 | 35.2 | 34.7 | 34.7 | 35.4 | 34.8 | 35.1 | 35.3 | 34.2 | 34.5 | 34.8 |
| 2018 | 34.2 | 34.5 | 33.7 | 35.1 | 35.1 | 35.3 | 35.8 | 35.4 | 35.4 | 35.3 | 35.2 | 35.9 | 35.1 |
| 2019 | 34.8 | 34.7 | 35.0 | 35.0 | 35.5 | 35.9 | 35.4 | 35.3 | 36.0 | 35.3 | 35.0 | 36.2 | 35.4 |
| **Education and Health Services** | | | | | | | | | | | | | |
| 2015 | 34.4 | 34.3 | 34.1 | 34.1 | 34.1 | 34.0 | 34.0 | 33.7 | 33.9 | 33.5 | 33.7 | 33.4 | 33.9 |
| 2016 | 33.1 | 33.3 | 33.1 | 33.0 | 33.0 | 33.1 | 33.1 | 33.5 | 33.6 | 33.3 | 33.3 | 33.1 | 33.2 |
| 2017 | 32.8 | 32.0 | 32.3 | 32.4 | 32.5 | 32.4 | 32.6 | 32.5 | 32.7 | 32.4 | 32.6 | 32.4 | 32.5 |
| 2018 | 32.2 | 32.4 | 32.3 | 32.9 | 32.7 | 33.0 | 33.1 | 32.7 | 33.1 | 32.9 | 32.7 | 33.2 | 32.8 |
| 2019 | 32.7 | 32.3 | 32.5 | 32.6 | 32.7 | 32.8 | 32.4 | 32.6 | 33.1 | 32.8 | 32.8 | 32.9 | 32.7 |
| **Leisure and Hospitality** | | | | | | | | | | | | | |
| 2015 | 24.5 | 24.3 | 25.1 | 25.2 | 25.6 | 26.2 | 27.3 | 27.9 | 26.4 | 25.8 | 25.3 | 24.4 | 25.8 |
| 2016 | 24.3 | 25.0 | 24.9 | 24.7 | 25.1 | 25.5 | 27.0 | 27.4 | 26.0 | 26.0 | 24.9 | 23.3 | 25.5 |
| 2017 | 24.0 | 23.5 | 25.0 | 25.6 | 25.6 | 26.5 | 27.6 | 28.1 | 26.7 | 26.5 | 25.8 | 24.7 | 26.0 |
| 2018 | 24.8 | 25.5 | 24.3 | 25.6 | 26.1 | 26.8 | 28.6 | 28.1 | 27.1 | 27.4 | 25.2 | 25.8 | 26.5 |
| 2019 | 24.8 | 24.9 | 25.0 | 25.4 | 25.8 | 26.9 | 28.4 | 28.6 | 27.6 | 26.9 | 25.9 | 25.3 | 26.5 |

## 3. Average Hourly Earnings by Selected Industry: Maine, 2015–2019

(Dollars, not seasonally adjusted)

| Industry and year | January | February | March | April | May | June | July | August | September | October | November | December | Annual average |
|---|---|---|---|---|---|---|---|---|---|---|---|---|---|
| **Total Private** | | | | | | | | | | | | | |
| 2015 | 21.93 | 22.00 | 22.11 | 21.94 | 21.67 | 21.46 | 21.42 | 21.54 | 21.82 | 22.01 | 22.20 | 22.24 | 21.85 |
| 2016 | 22.36 | 22.29 | 22.22 | 22.28 | 22.20 | 21.88 | 21.77 | 21.87 | 22.38 | 22.55 | 22.66 | 22.66 | 22.25 |
| 2017 | 23.05 | 23.43 | 23.44 | 23.24 | 23.28 | 22.79 | 22.74 | 22.84 | 23.32 | 23.39 | 23.56 | 23.66 | 23.22 |
| 2018 | 23.85 | 23.77 | 23.92 | 23.90 | 23.63 | 23.46 | 23.32 | 23.49 | 24.00 | 24.11 | 24.35 | 24.58 | 23.86 |
| 2019 | 24.67 | 25.08 | 25.17 | 25.26 | 25.18 | 24.84 | 24.53 | 24.53 | 24.99 | 24.96 | 24.84 | 25.06 | 24.92 |
| **Goods-Producing** | | | | | | | | | | | | | |
| 2015 | 23.64 | 23.35 | 23.13 | 23.18 | 22.89 | 22.80 | 22.93 | 23.37 | 22.85 | 23.22 | 23.26 | 23.68 | 23.19 |
| 2016 | 23.38 | 23.43 | 23.65 | 23.62 | 23.79 | 23.44 | 23.40 | 23.25 | 23.51 | 23.81 | 24.11 | 24.01 | 23.62 |
| 2017 | 23.64 | 24.00 | 24.06 | 23.67 | 24.04 | 23.53 | 23.78 | 23.79 | 24.27 | 24.15 | 24.13 | 24.43 | 23.96 |
| 2018 | 24.39 | 24.23 | 24.54 | 24.54 | 24.09 | 24.15 | 23.89 | 23.87 | 24.05 | 24.20 | 24.21 | 24.86 | 24.25 |
| 2019 | 24.74 | 24.93 | 25.40 | 25.49 | 25.24 | 25.60 | 25.49 | 25.30 | 25.62 | 25.23 | 25.11 | 25.53 | 25.31 |
| **Construction** | | | | | | | | | | | | | |
| 2015 | 23.30 | 23.27 | 22.67 | 22.81 | 22.44 | 21.98 | 22.24 | 22.71 | 22.31 | 22.44 | 22.74 | 23.07 | 22.63 |
| 2016 | 23.27 | 23.98 | 23.31 | 23.31 | 23.11 | 23.30 | 23.19 | 22.87 | 23.49 | 23.90 | 23.55 | 23.98 | 23.43 |
| 2017 | 24.01 | 24.24 | 24.55 | 24.16 | 23.82 | 23.54 | 23.64 | 23.58 | 23.97 | 23.68 | 23.92 | 24.47 | 23.94 |
| 2018 | 24.55 | 24.65 | 24.89 | 24.94 | 24.44 | 24.11 | 23.61 | 23.91 | 23.92 | 23.89 | 24.35 | 25.06 | 24.33 |
| 2019 | 25.33 | 25.67 | 25.80 | 25.84 | 25.14 | 25.31 | 25.63 | 25.39 | 25.96 | 25.69 | 25.55 | 25.96 | 25.60 |
| **Manufacturing** | | | | | | | | | | | | | |
| 2015 | 24.29 | 23.86 | 23.79 | 23.70 | 23.41 | 23.57 | 23.71 | 24.16 | 23.52 | 24.00 | 23.71 | 24.21 | 23.83 |
| 2016 | 23.69 | 23.46 | 23.96 | 23.80 | 24.17 | 23.71 | 23.74 | 23.68 | 23.78 | 24.02 | 24.80 | 24.30 | 23.93 |
| 2017 | 23.69 | 24.17 | 23.96 | 23.73 | 24.51 | 23.92 | 24.25 | 24.21 | 24.76 | 24.76 | 24.57 | 24.73 | 24.28 |
| 2018 | 24.61 | 24.24 | 24.57 | 24.46 | 24.25 | 24.53 | 24.50 | 24.20 | 24.49 | 24.69 | 24.43 | 24.97 | 24.50 |
| 2019 | 24.63 | 24.84 | 25.20 | 25.02 | 24.95 | 25.45 | 25.08 | 24.96 | 25.18 | 24.66 | 24.71 | 25.09 | 24.98 |
| **Trade, Transportation, and Utilities** | | | | | | | | | | | | | |
| 2015 | 19.88 | 19.83 | 19.91 | 19.97 | 20.09 | 20.00 | 20.10 | 20.03 | 20.26 | 20.28 | 20.45 | 20.22 | 20.09 |
| 2016 | 20.87 | 20.59 | 20.49 | 20.38 | 20.29 | 19.98 | 19.86 | 19.84 | 20.13 | 20.08 | 20.12 | 20.02 | 20.21 |
| 2017 | 20.68 | 21.04 | 21.08 | 20.53 | 20.90 | 20.42 | 20.11 | 20.25 | 20.40 | 20.23 | 20.25 | 20.31 | 20.51 |
| 2018 | 20.33 | 20.27 | 20.17 | 20.08 | 20.10 | 20.01 | 20.05 | 20.29 | 20.47 | 20.72 | 21.07 | 20.86 | 20.37 |
| 2019 | 20.98 | 21.38 | 21.44 | 21.12 | 21.11 | 20.80 | 20.64 | 20.59 | 20.86 | 20.73 | 20.51 | 20.48 | 20.88 |
| **Professional and Business Services** | | | | | | | | | | | | | |
| 2015 | 24.47 | 24.31 | 24.51 | 24.21 | 23.73 | 23.95 | 24.26 | 24.19 | 24.50 | 24.11 | 24.47 | 24.31 | 24.25 |
| 2016 | 24.73 | 24.89 | 24.49 | 24.66 | 24.40 | 24.07 | 24.60 | 24.74 | 25.19 | 25.18 | 25.06 | 25.15 | 24.76 |
| 2017 | 25.72 | 26.34 | 26.61 | 26.11 | 25.71 | 25.75 | 26.06 | 25.85 | 26.26 | 26.09 | 26.48 | 26.84 | 26.15 |
| 2018 | 26.73 | 26.77 | 27.40 | 27.27 | 26.66 | 26.55 | 26.85 | 27.07 | 27.65 | 27.61 | 27.71 | 28.15 | 27.20 |
| 2019 | 28.60 | 28.50 | 28.60 | 28.77 | 29.04 | 28.39 | 28.45 | 28.62 | 29.34 | 29.16 | 29.45 | 30.20 | 28.93 |
| **Education and Health Services** | | | | | | | | | | | | | |
| 2015 | 21.96 | 21.94 | 22.03 | 21.86 | 21.47 | 21.38 | 21.40 | 21.79 | 21.94 | 22.25 | 22.21 | 22.23 | 21.87 |
| 2016 | 21.93 | 21.96 | 21.98 | 22.08 | 22.08 | 22.02 | 21.99 | 21.99 | 22.14 | 22.36 | 22.32 | 22.40 | 22.11 |
| 2017 | 22.71 | 23.22 | 23.45 | 23.87 | 24.04 | 23.83 | 24.04 | 24.17 | 24.21 | 24.30 | 24.31 | 24.36 | 23.88 |
| 2018 | 24.75 | 24.65 | 24.51 | 24.62 | 24.55 | 24.75 | 24.95 | 24.83 | 24.86 | 24.99 | 24.98 | 24.93 | 24.78 |
| 2019 | 25.02 | 25.17 | 25.19 | 25.57 | 25.62 | 25.74 | 26.11 | 26.28 | 26.18 | 26.48 | 26.24 | 26.66 | 25.86 |
| **Leisure and Hospitality** | | | | | | | | | | | | | |
| 2015 | 13.41 | 13.60 | 13.51 | 13.76 | 13.57 | 13.48 | 13.37 | 13.54 | 13.86 | 14.18 | 14.25 | 14.62 | 13.74 |
| 2016 | 14.36 | 14.15 | 14.12 | 14.36 | 14.26 | 14.05 | 14.03 | 14.27 | 14.72 | 15.06 | 14.85 | 15.22 | 14.43 |
| 2017 | 15.15 | 15.40 | 15.35 | 15.42 | 15.39 | 15.09 | 14.90 | 15.20 | 15.54 | 15.82 | 15.76 | 15.86 | 15.38 |
| 2018 | 15.95 | 16.07 | 16.34 | 16.20 | 16.28 | 16.11 | 15.80 | 16.06 | 16.56 | 16.93 | 17.09 | 17.13 | 16.35 |
| 2019 | 17.10 | 17.38 | 17.49 | 17.32 | 17.01 | 16.73 | 16.23 | 16.44 | 16.96 | 17.35 | 17.24 | 17.42 | 16.98 |

## 4. Average Weekly Earnings by Selected Industry: Maine, 2015–2019

(Dollars, not seasonally adjusted)

| Industry and year | January | February | March | April | May | June | July | August | September | October | November | December | Annual average |
|---|---|---|---|---|---|---|---|---|---|---|---|---|---|
| **Total Private** | | | | | | | | | | | | | |
| 2015 | 743.43 | 748.00 | 753.95 | 743.77 | 743.28 | 736.08 | 741.13 | 747.44 | 752.79 | 754.94 | 761.46 | 758.38 | 749.46 |
| 2016 | 749.06 | 748.94 | 751.04 | 753.06 | 754.80 | 741.73 | 742.36 | 747.95 | 760.92 | 775.72 | 770.44 | 763.64 | 754.28 |
| 2017 | 774.48 | 773.19 | 787.58 | 790.16 | 793.85 | 777.14 | 784.53 | 787.98 | 799.88 | 799.94 | 803.40 | 802.07 | 789.48 |
| 2018 | 803.75 | 805.80 | 794.14 | 819.77 | 810.51 | 807.02 | 811.54 | 810.41 | 823.20 | 824.56 | 823.03 | 848.01 | 816.01 |
| 2019 | 831.38 | 830.15 | 840.68 | 843.68 | 848.57 | 842.08 | 836.47 | 841.38 | 859.66 | 846.14 | 842.08 | 859.56 | 842.30 |
| **Goods-Producing** | | | | | | | | | | | | | |
| 2015 | 950.33 | 927.00 | 927.51 | 931.84 | 947.65 | 946.20 | 958.47 | 976.87 | 934.57 | 970.60 | 958.31 | 980.35 | 950.79 |
| 2016 | 946.89 | 934.86 | 962.56 | 958.97 | 982.53 | 970.42 | 973.44 | 967.20 | 968.61 | 990.50 | 986.10 | 958.00 | 966.06 |
| 2017 | 957.42 | 928.80 | 962.40 | 961.00 | 983.24 | 971.79 | 979.74 | 989.66 | 1,004.78 | 994.98 | 982.09 | 984.53 | 975.17 |
| 2018 | 982.92 | 966.78 | 932.52 | 984.05 | 970.83 | 968.42 | 962.77 | 964.35 | 964.41 | 958.32 | 939.35 | 1,001.86 | 967.58 |
| 2019 | 972.28 | 957.31 | 998.22 | 1,001.76 | 1,019.70 | 1,021.44 | 1,024.70 | 1,022.12 | 1,032.49 | 1,014.25 | 991.85 | 1,031.41 | 1,007.34 |
| **Construction** | | | | | | | | | | | | | |
| 2015 | 869.09 | 865.64 | 841.06 | 878.19 | 913.31 | 901.18 | 925.18 | 924.30 | 881.25 | 917.80 | 918.70 | 925.11 | 898.41 |
| 2016 | 909.86 | 904.05 | 913.75 | 916.08 | 949.82 | 969.28 | 976.30 | 946.82 | 965.44 | 987.07 | 951.42 | 937.62 | 944.23 |
| 2017 | 950.80 | 889.61 | 930.45 | 951.90 | 957.56 | 960.43 | 952.69 | 980.93 | 997.15 | 966.14 | 966.37 | 964.12 | 957.60 |
| 2018 | 967.27 | 963.82 | 915.95 | 990.12 | 997.15 | 966.81 | 958.57 | 951.62 | 935.27 | 922.15 | 903.39 | 972.33 | 953.74 |
| 2019 | 942.28 | 936.96 | 980.40 | 989.67 | 1,008.11 | 1,007.34 | 1,025.20 | 1,028.30 | 1,035.80 | 1,027.60 | 993.90 | 1,028.02 | 1,000.96 |
| **Manufacturing** | | | | | | | | | | | | | |
| 2015 | 978.89 | 944.86 | 963.50 | 950.37 | 957.47 | 964.01 | 967.37 | 1,000.22 | 959.62 | 998.40 | 974.48 | 1,007.14 | 972.26 |
| 2016 | 959.45 | 945.44 | 979.96 | 971.04 | 993.39 | 969.74 | 978.09 | 982.72 | 977.36 | 999.23 | 1,009.36 | 972.00 | 978.74 |
| 2017 | 964.18 | 940.21 | 967.98 | 965.81 | 997.56 | 980.72 | 999.10 | 995.03 | 1,015.16 | 1,017.64 | 997.54 | 1,001.57 | 985.77 |
| 2018 | 994.24 | 964.75 | 943.49 | 968.62 | 950.60 | 968.94 | 962.85 | 975.26 | 991.85 | 987.60 | 969.87 | 1,021.27 | 975.10 |
| 2019 | 992.59 | 971.24 | 1,000.44 | 990.79 | 1,002.99 | 1,007.82 | 1,000.69 | 1,005.89 | 1,019.79 | 996.26 | 983.46 | 1,016.15 | 999.20 |
| **Trade, Transportation, and Utilities** | | | | | | | | | | | | | |
| 2015 | 658.03 | 670.25 | 664.99 | 661.01 | 677.03 | 668.00 | 689.43 | 685.03 | 705.05 | 683.44 | 685.08 | 689.50 | 679.04 |
| 2016 | 694.97 | 689.77 | 684.37 | 690.88 | 683.77 | 677.32 | 687.16 | 690.43 | 690.46 | 694.77 | 688.10 | 692.69 | 689.16 |
| 2017 | 694.85 | 692.22 | 712.50 | 695.97 | 718.96 | 704.49 | 705.86 | 706.73 | 699.72 | 687.82 | 690.53 | 700.70 | 701.44 |
| 2018 | 683.09 | 681.07 | 665.61 | 682.72 | 689.43 | 682.34 | 695.74 | 704.06 | 702.12 | 702.41 | 716.38 | 711.33 | 692.58 |
| 2019 | 702.83 | 703.40 | 711.81 | 696.96 | 702.96 | 698.88 | 703.82 | 704.18 | 705.07 | 684.09 | 687.09 | 696.32 | 699.48 |
| **Professional and Business Services** | | | | | | | | | | | | | |
| 2015 | 824.64 | 828.97 | 848.05 | 820.72 | 809.19 | 823.88 | 832.12 | 841.81 | 840.35 | 836.62 | 858.90 | 836.26 | 834.20 |
| 2016 | 821.04 | 836.30 | 830.21 | 848.30 | 854.00 | 825.60 | 841.32 | 833.74 | 843.87 | 876.26 | 857.05 | 852.59 | 844.32 |
| 2017 | 902.77 | 895.56 | 918.05 | 919.07 | 892.14 | 893.53 | 922.52 | 899.58 | 921.73 | 920.98 | 905.62 | 925.98 | 910.02 |
| 2018 | 914.17 | 923.57 | 923.38 | 957.18 | 935.77 | 937.22 | 961.23 | 958.28 | 978.81 | 974.63 | 975.39 | 1,010.59 | 954.72 |
| 2019 | 995.28 | 988.95 | 1,001.00 | 1,006.95 | 1,030.92 | 1,019.20 | 1,007.13 | 1,010.29 | 1,056.24 | 1,029.35 | 1,030.75 | 1,093.24 | 1,024.12 |
| **Education and Health Services** | | | | | | | | | | | | | |
| 2015 | 755.42 | 752.54 | 751.22 | 745.43 | 732.13 | 726.92 | 727.60 | 734.32 | 743.77 | 745.38 | 748.48 | 742.48 | 741.39 |
| 2016 | 725.88 | 731.27 | 727.54 | 728.64 | 728.64 | 728.86 | 727.87 | 736.67 | 743.90 | 744.59 | 743.26 | 741.44 | 734.05 |
| 2017 | 744.89 | 743.04 | 757.44 | 773.39 | 781.30 | 772.09 | 783.70 | 785.53 | 791.67 | 787.32 | 792.51 | 789.26 | 776.10 |
| 2018 | 796.95 | 798.66 | 791.67 | 810.00 | 802.79 | 816.75 | 825.85 | 811.94 | 822.87 | 822.17 | 816.85 | 827.68 | 812.78 |
| 2019 | 818.15 | 812.99 | 818.68 | 833.58 | 837.77 | 844.27 | 845.96 | 856.73 | 866.56 | 868.54 | 860.67 | 877.11 | 845.62 |
| **Leisure and Hospitality** | | | | | | | | | | | | | |
| 2015 | 328.55 | 330.48 | 339.10 | 346.75 | 347.39 | 353.18 | 365.00 | 377.77 | 365.90 | 365.84 | 360.53 | 356.73 | 354.49 |
| 2016 | 348.95 | 353.75 | 351.59 | 354.69 | 357.93 | 358.28 | 378.81 | 391.00 | 382.72 | 391.56 | 369.77 | 354.63 | 367.97 |
| 2017 | 363.60 | 361.90 | 383.75 | 394.75 | 393.98 | 399.89 | 411.24 | 427.12 | 414.92 | 419.23 | 406.61 | 391.74 | 399.88 |
| 2018 | 395.56 | 409.79 | 397.06 | 414.72 | 424.91 | 431.75 | 451.88 | 451.29 | 448.78 | 463.88 | 430.67 | 441.95 | 433.28 |
| 2019 | 424.08 | 432.76 | 437.25 | 439.93 | 438.86 | 450.04 | 460.93 | 470.18 | 468.10 | 466.72 | 446.52 | 440.73 | 449.97 |

# MARYLAND
*At a Glance*

Population:
  2010 census: 5,773,552
  2019 estimate: 6,045,680

Percent change in population:
  2010–2019: 4.7%

Percent change in total nonfarm employment:
  2011–2019:  8.7%

Industry with the largest growth in employment, 2011–2019 (percent):
  Transportation and utilities, 31.8%

Industry with the largest decline or smallest growth in employment, 2011–2019 (percent):
  Information, -11.5%

Civilian labor force:
  2010: 3,073,826
  2019: 3,260,667

Unemployment rate and rank among states (highest to lowest):
  2010: 7.7%, 38th
  2019: 3.6%, 21st

Over-the-year change in unemployment rates:
  2017–2018: -0.3%
  2018–2019: -0.3%

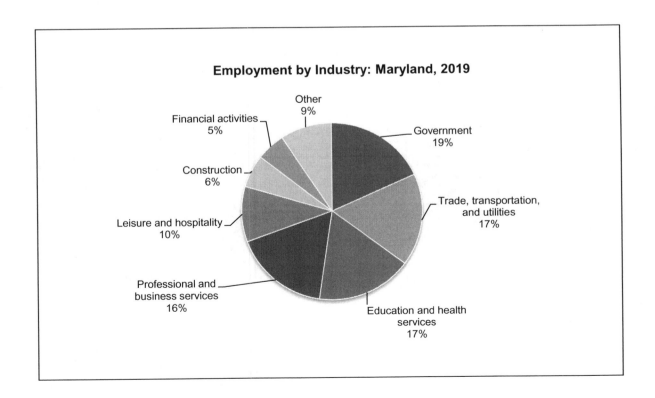

**Employment by Industry: Maryland, 2019**

- Other 9%
- Financial activities 5%
- Construction 6%
- Leisure and hospitality 10%
- Professional and business services 16%
- Education and health services 17%
- Government 19%
- Trade, transportation, and utilities 17%

## 1. Employment by Industry: Maryland, 2011–2019

(Numbers in thousands, not seasonally adjusted)

| Industry and year | January | February | March | April | May | June | July | August | September | October | November | December | Annual average |
|---|---|---|---|---|---|---|---|---|---|---|---|---|---|
| **Total Nonfarm** | | | | | | | | | | | | | |
| 2011 | 2,478.2 | 2,495.1 | 2,522.9 | 2,547.4 | 2,561.9 | 2,569.0 | 2,560.8 | 2,550.1 | 2,560.2 | 2,571.4 | 2,575.7 | 2,580.9 | 2,547.8 |
| 2012 | 2,510.7 | 2,527.1 | 2,556.4 | 2,571.3 | 2,590.3 | 2,601.3 | 2,582.4 | 2,582.2 | 2,593.3 | 2,602.2 | 2,608.2 | 2,614.1 | 2,578.3 |
| 2013 | 2,539.3 | 2,555.8 | 2,579.1 | 2,598.4 | 2,619.6 | 2,630.1 | 2,610.8 | 2,608.8 | 2,613.6 | 2,618.2 | 2,632.3 | 2,627.3 | 2,602.8 |
| 2014 | 2,549.4 | 2,561.3 | 2,584.6 | 2,615.6 | 2,642.7 | 2,654.2 | 2,628.4 | 2,635.7 | 2,642.5 | 2,654.2 | 2,664.5 | 2,665.9 | 2,624.9 |
| 2015 | 2,583.1 | 2,600.1 | 2,617.8 | 2,655.0 | 2,684.3 | 2,693.8 | 2,675.7 | 2,673.8 | 2,678.1 | 2,698.1 | 2,706.2 | 2,709.2 | 2,664.6 |
| 2016 | 2,624.7 | 2,636.0 | 2,661.5 | 2,695.7 | 2,708.8 | 2,715.5 | 2,702.8 | 2,704.1 | 2,715.3 | 2,723.0 | 2,738.4 | 2,740.0 | 2,697.2 |
| 2017 | 2,660.4 | 2,680.0 | 2,696.9 | 2,718.4 | 2,741.1 | 2,754.7 | 2,733.7 | 2,731.1 | 2,735.0 | 2,748.1 | 2,762.2 | 2,754.2 | 2,726.3 |
| 2018 | 2,681.3 | 2,705.2 | 2,723.6 | 2,742.5 | 2,765.4 | 2,779.3 | 2,766.0 | 2,761.9 | 2,759.0 | 2,771.7 | 2,788.0 | 2,780.1 | 2,752.0 |
| 2019 | 2,712.8 | 2,728.1 | 2,746.1 | 2,765.3 | 2,786.6 | 2,799.4 | 2,778.3 | 2,770.6 | 2,768.1 | 2,777.9 | 2,795.6 | 2,797.5 | 2,768.9 |
| **Total Private** | | | | | | | | | | | | | |
| 2011 | 1,985.2 | 1,985.9 | 2,006.9 | 2,033.8 | 2,049.0 | 2,069.0 | 2,074.7 | 2,069.4 | 2,059.3 | 2,056.2 | 2,063.5 | 2,068.3 | 2,043.4 |
| 2012 | 2,018.7 | 2,017.4 | 2,041.2 | 2,057.3 | 2,077.8 | 2,105.2 | 2,104.0 | 2,104.6 | 2,093.4 | 2,089.3 | 2,094.3 | 2,100.9 | 2,075.3 |
| 2013 | 2,046.0 | 2,046.7 | 2,065.6 | 2,084.4 | 2,106.4 | 2,129.1 | 2,130.0 | 2,129.1 | 2,113.4 | 2,108.0 | 2,118.5 | 2,117.2 | 2,099.5 |
| 2014 | 2,059.0 | 2,054.6 | 2,074.8 | 2,105.2 | 2,133.5 | 2,154.0 | 2,153.5 | 2,156.3 | 2,140.0 | 2,142.8 | 2,149.9 | 2,154.8 | 2,123.2 |
| 2015 | 2,092.5 | 2,093.0 | 2,107.1 | 2,142.2 | 2,171.0 | 2,190.0 | 2,197.1 | 2,194.2 | 2,174.1 | 2,187.3 | 2,192.5 | 2,195.2 | 2,161.4 |
| 2016 | 2,132.6 | 2,130.1 | 2,149.4 | 2,183.1 | 2,197.5 | 2,216.9 | 2,226.3 | 2,224.2 | 2,211.4 | 2,211.6 | 2,223.8 | 2,225.2 | 2,194.3 |
| 2017 | 2,165.3 | 2,168.9 | 2,182.0 | 2,204.3 | 2,225.6 | 2,250.9 | 2,256.7 | 2,253.2 | 2,235.1 | 2,236.4 | 2,246.6 | 2,242.3 | 2,222.3 |
| 2018 | 2,187.9 | 2,193.4 | 2,208.2 | 2,227.9 | 2,249.7 | 2,273.6 | 2,282.2 | 2,276.7 | 2,253.2 | 2,258.6 | 2,273.0 | 2,266.1 | 2,245.9 |
| 2019 | 2,214.5 | 2,216.1 | 2,230.0 | 2,249.3 | 2,269.1 | 2,292.2 | 2,295.2 | 2,289.2 | 2,262.2 | 2,265.0 | 2,279.7 | 2,283.7 | 2,262.2 |
| **Goods Producing** | | | | | | | | | | | | | |
| 2011 | 253.6 | 252.3 | 254.8 | 259.5 | 261.2 | 264.4 | 265.8 | 264.9 | 262.1 | 261.2 | 260.4 | 259.7 | 260.0 |
| 2012 | 252.2 | 250.2 | 252.5 | 255.0 | 255.8 | 260.4 | 261.6 | 261.4 | 258.7 | 257.9 | 257.5 | 256.8 | 256.7 |
| 2013 | 249.6 | 248.6 | 250.6 | 254.8 | 256.9 | 259.7 | 260.8 | 261.2 | 259.2 | 257.5 | 258.1 | 254.8 | 256.7 |
| 2014 | 247.7 | 246.0 | 248.9 | 254.8 | 257.8 | 261.2 | 261.6 | 262.6 | 260.9 | 260.9 | 261.3 | 259.7 | 257.0 |
| 2015 | 250.8 | 250.5 | 252.2 | 257.8 | 261.0 | 264.8 | 267.3 | 268.6 | 267.1 | 268.9 | 268.6 | 268.2 | 262.2 |
| 2016 | 260.4 | 258.1 | 262.1 | 266.8 | 268.8 | 271.7 | 273.2 | 273.3 | 272.2 | 272.1 | 271.9 | 272.0 | 268.6 |
| 2017 | 263.5 | 264.8 | 265.7 | 269.2 | 271.1 | 275.3 | 275.8 | 276.2 | 274.3 | 273.9 | 274.3 | 273.4 | 271.5 |
| 2018 | 265.3 | 266.7 | 268.9 | 271.3 | 273.3 | 276.8 | 279.9 | 280.2 | 278.1 | 278.5 | 278.2 | 277.3 | 274.5 |
| 2019 | 272.6 | 272.1 | 274.6 | 277.6 | 279.4 | 283.3 | 284.6 | 285.1 | 282.6 | 285.0 | 283.8 | 283.1 | 280.3 |
| **Service-Providing** | | | | | | | | | | | | | |
| 2011 | 2,224.6 | 2,242.8 | 2,268.1 | 2,287.9 | 2,300.7 | 2,304.6 | 2,295.0 | 2,285.2 | 2,298.1 | 2,310.2 | 2,315.3 | 2,321.2 | 2,287.8 |
| 2012 | 2,258.5 | 2,276.9 | 2,303.9 | 2,316.3 | 2,334.5 | 2,340.9 | 2,320.8 | 2,320.8 | 2,334.6 | 2,344.3 | 2,350.7 | 2,357.3 | 2,321.6 |
| 2013 | 2,289.7 | 2,307.2 | 2,328.5 | 2,343.6 | 2,362.7 | 2,370.4 | 2,350.0 | 2,347.6 | 2,354.4 | 2,360.7 | 2,374.2 | 2,372.5 | 2,346.8 |
| 2014 | 2,301.7 | 2,315.3 | 2,335.7 | 2,360.8 | 2,384.9 | 2,393.0 | 2,366.8 | 2,373.1 | 2,381.6 | 2,393.3 | 2,403.2 | 2,406.2 | 2,368.0 |
| 2015 | 2,332.3 | 2,349.6 | 2,365.6 | 2,397.2 | 2,423.3 | 2,429.0 | 2,408.4 | 2,405.2 | 2,411.0 | 2,429.2 | 2,437.6 | 2,441.0 | 2,402.5 |
| 2016 | 2,364.3 | 2,377.9 | 2,399.4 | 2,428.9 | 2,440.0 | 2,443.8 | 2,429.6 | 2,430.8 | 2,443.1 | 2,450.9 | 2,466.5 | 2,468.0 | 2,428.6 |
| 2017 | 2,396.9 | 2,415.2 | 2,431.2 | 2,449.2 | 2,470.0 | 2,479.4 | 2,457.9 | 2,454.9 | 2,460.7 | 2,474.2 | 2,487.9 | 2,480.8 | 2,454.9 |
| 2018 | 2,416.0 | 2,438.5 | 2,454.7 | 2,471.2 | 2,492.1 | 2,502.5 | 2,486.1 | 2,481.7 | 2,480.9 | 2,493.2 | 2,509.8 | 2,502.8 | 2,477.5 |
| 2019 | 2,440.2 | 2,456.0 | 2,471.5 | 2,487.7 | 2,507.2 | 2,516.1 | 2,493.7 | 2,485.5 | 2,485.5 | 2,492.9 | 2,511.8 | 2,514.4 | 2,488.5 |
| **Mining and Logging** | | | | | | | | | | | | | |
| 2011 | 1.3 | 1.3 | 1.4 | 1.4 | 1.4 | 1.4 | 1.5 | 1.5 | 1.5 | 1.5 | 1.5 | 1.5 | 1.4 |
| 2012 | 1.4 | 1.4 | 1.4 | 1.5 | 1.5 | 1.5 | 1.5 | 1.5 | 1.5 | 1.5 | 1.5 | 1.5 | 1.5 |
| 2013 | 1.3 | 1.3 | 1.4 | 1.4 | 1.4 | 1.4 | 1.4 | 1.5 | 1.5 | 1.4 | 1.4 | 1.4 | 1.4 |
| 2014 | 1.5 | 1.5 | 1.6 | 1.7 | 1.7 | 1.7 | 1.7 | 1.7 | 1.7 | 1.7 | 1.7 | 1.6 | 1.7 |
| 2015 | 1.5 | 1.6 | 1.6 | 1.6 | 1.6 | 1.6 | 1.7 | 1.7 | 1.7 | 1.5 | 1.5 | 1.5 | 1.6 |
| 2016 | 1.4 | 1.4 | 1.4 | 1.5 | 1.5 | 1.5 | 1.4 | 1.4 | 1.4 | 1.4 | 1.4 | 1.4 | 1.4 |
| 2017 | 1.3 | 1.3 | 1.3 | 1.3 | 1.3 | 1.3 | 1.3 | 1.3 | 1.3 | 1.3 | 1.3 | 1.3 | 1.3 |
| 2018 | 1.3 | 1.2 | 1.3 | 1.3 | 1.3 | 1.3 | 1.3 | 1.3 | 1.3 | 1.3 | 1.3 | 1.3 | 1.3 |
| 2019 | 1.3 | 1.3 | 1.3 | 1.3 | 1.3 | 1.3 | 1.3 | 1.3 | 1.3 | 1.3 | 1.3 | 1.3 | 1.3 |
| **Construction** | | | | | | | | | | | | | |
| 2011 | 136.7 | 136.0 | 138.1 | 142.4 | 143.9 | 146.6 | 148.2 | 147.6 | 146.0 | 145.6 | 145.1 | 144.3 | 143.4 |
| 2012 | 138.1 | 137.3 | 139.3 | 141.5 | 142.4 | 145.9 | 147.1 | 147.5 | 146.9 | 146.7 | 146.1 | 145.2 | 143.7 |
| 2013 | 139.4 | 138.7 | 140.5 | 144.8 | 146.8 | 149.1 | 150.3 | 150.8 | 149.9 | 148.6 | 149.0 | 146.0 | 146.2 |
| 2014 | 141.0 | 139.5 | 142.3 | 147.6 | 150.5 | 153.1 | 153.8 | 154.7 | 153.7 | 153.3 | 153.0 | 151.8 | 149.5 |
| 2015 | 144.2 | 143.8 | 145.5 | 150.9 | 153.9 | 156.5 | 158.3 | 159.6 | 158.9 | 160.9 | 160.3 | 159.6 | 154.4 |
| 2016 | 153.9 | 152.0 | 155.8 | 159.8 | 161.1 | 163.5 | 165.1 | 165.0 | 164.4 | 164.3 | 163.5 | 163.3 | 161.0 |
| 2017 | 156.3 | 157.2 | 157.7 | 160.7 | 162.2 | 165.7 | 166.1 | 166.3 | 165.0 | 164.2 | 164.1 | 163.1 | 162.4 |
| 2018 | 156.3 | 157.7 | 159.5 | 161.1 | 162.7 | 165.1 | 167.4 | 167.7 | 166.2 | 166.2 | 165.5 | 164.5 | 163.3 |
| 2019 | 160.8 | 159.9 | 162.1 | 164.0 | 165.6 | 168.4 | 169.1 | 169.6 | 168.0 | 169.4 | 168.4 | 167.9 | 166.1 |

## 1. Employment by Industry: Maryland, 2011–2019—*Continued*

(Numbers in thousands, not seasonally adjusted)

| Industry and year | January | February | March | April | May | June | July | August | September | October | November | December | Annual average |
|---|---|---|---|---|---|---|---|---|---|---|---|---|---|
| **Manufacturing** | | | | | | | | | | | | | |
| 2011 | 115.6 | 115.0 | 115.3 | 115.7 | 115.9 | 116.4 | 116.1 | 115.8 | 114.6 | 114.1 | 113.8 | 113.9 | 115.2 |
| 2012 | 112.7 | 111.5 | 111.8 | 112.0 | 111.9 | 113.0 | 113.0 | 112.4 | 110.3 | 109.7 | 109.9 | 110.1 | 111.5 |
| 2013 | 108.9 | 108.6 | 108.7 | 108.6 | 108.7 | 109.2 | 109.1 | 108.9 | 107.8 | 107.5 | 107.7 | 107.4 | 108.4 |
| 2014 | 105.2 | 105.0 | 105.0 | 105.5 | 105.6 | 106.4 | 106.1 | 106.2 | 105.5 | 105.9 | 106.6 | 106.3 | 105.8 |
| 2015 | 105.1 | 105.1 | 105.1 | 105.3 | 105.5 | 106.7 | 107.3 | 107.3 | 106.5 | 106.5 | 106.8 | 107.1 | 106.2 |
| 2016 | 105.1 | 104.7 | 104.9 | 105.5 | 106.2 | 106.7 | 106.7 | 106.9 | 106.4 | 106.4 | 107.0 | 107.3 | 106.2 |
| 2017 | 105.9 | 106.3 | 106.7 | 107.2 | 107.6 | 108.3 | 108.4 | 108.6 | 108.0 | 108.4 | 108.9 | 109.0 | 107.8 |
| 2018 | 107.7 | 107.8 | 108.1 | 108.9 | 109.3 | 110.4 | 111.2 | 111.2 | 110.6 | 111.1 | 111.5 | 111.6 | 110.0 |
| 2019 | 110.5 | 110.9 | 111.2 | 112.3 | 112.5 | 113.6 | 114.2 | 114.2 | 113.3 | 114.3 | 114.1 | 113.9 | 112.9 |
| **Trade, Transportation, and Utilities** | | | | | | | | | | | | | |
| 2011 | 435.9 | 431.3 | 434.0 | 438.4 | 441.4 | 444.0 | 442.7 | 443.7 | 442.9 | 446.2 | 455.9 | 463.1 | 443.3 |
| 2012 | 443.5 | 438.6 | 443.2 | 444.5 | 448.1 | 450.6 | 447.5 | 447.5 | 448.3 | 450.5 | 461.7 | 467.8 | 449.3 |
| 2013 | 445.5 | 440.0 | 442.3 | 443.9 | 448.3 | 451.3 | 449.8 | 450.3 | 448.9 | 451.6 | 463.0 | 469.9 | 450.4 |
| 2014 | 448.1 | 441.1 | 444.4 | 448.0 | 451.7 | 455.9 | 454.2 | 455.3 | 453.5 | 457.5 | 468.8 | 477.0 | 454.6 |
| 2015 | 453.7 | 447.9 | 449.6 | 455.3 | 460.0 | 464.7 | 462.9 | 462.5 | 461.4 | 467.2 | 476.9 | 483.3 | 462.1 |
| 2016 | 460.1 | 455.3 | 457.8 | 462.0 | 465.2 | 467.0 | 465.9 | 467.1 | 466.3 | 469.8 | 481.5 | 486.5 | 467.0 |
| 2017 | 464.2 | 457.1 | 457.8 | 462.1 | 465.5 | 469.0 | 467.4 | 468.0 | 466.7 | 470.5 | 485.7 | 487.7 | 468.5 |
| 2018 | 466.3 | 461.0 | 461.2 | 463.1 | 466.3 | 469.8 | 469.3 | 468.9 | 467.5 | 473.3 | 489.9 | 492.0 | 470.7 |
| 2019 | 467.6 | 460.4 | 460.7 | 460.9 | 464.6 | 468.2 | 467.6 | 467.8 | 466.7 | 472.9 | 483.0 | 488.8 | 469.1 |
| **Wholesale Trade** | | | | | | | | | | | | | |
| 2011 | 83.9 | 84.0 | 84.4 | 84.9 | 85.5 | 85.6 | 85.9 | 85.8 | 85.3 | 85.2 | 85.0 | 85.1 | 85.1 |
| 2012 | 83.9 | 84.1 | 84.9 | 85.2 | 85.9 | 86.3 | 86.0 | 85.9 | 85.4 | 85.4 | 85.3 | 85.3 | 85.3 |
| 2013 | 84.1 | 84.1 | 84.4 | 84.7 | 84.9 | 85.1 | 84.5 | 84.3 | 83.8 | 83.7 | 83.8 | 83.9 | 84.3 |
| 2014 | 82.6 | 82.5 | 82.6 | 83.0 | 83.6 | 83.9 | 83.8 | 83.8 | 83.3 | 83.4 | 83.4 | 84.1 | 83.3 |
| 2015 | 82.9 | 82.9 | 83.1 | 84.1 | 84.5 | 85.0 | 85.2 | 84.9 | 84.5 | 84.8 | 84.7 | 84.6 | 84.3 |
| 2016 | 83.9 | 83.7 | 83.7 | 84.4 | 84.7 | 84.8 | 84.9 | 85.0 | 84.5 | 84.7 | 84.7 | 84.6 | 84.5 |
| 2017 | 83.8 | 83.6 | 84.0 | 84.5 | 84.9 | 85.5 | 85.4 | 85.3 | 84.8 | 84.8 | 84.8 | 84.8 | 84.7 |
| 2018 | 84.0 | 84.2 | 84.1 | 84.8 | 85.3 | 86.1 | 86.2 | 86.4 | 86.1 | 86.2 | 86.1 | 86.3 | 85.5 |
| 2019 | 85.9 | 85.9 | 86.2 | 86.7 | 86.9 | 87.2 | 86.9 | 86.9 | 86.2 | 88.0 | 87.4 | 88.1 | 86.9 |
| **Retail Trade** | | | | | | | | | | | | | |
| 2011 | 276.4 | 272.2 | 274.1 | 276.8 | 278.6 | 280.8 | 280.1 | 281.1 | 279.2 | 282.6 | 291.2 | 296.5 | 280.8 |
| 2012 | 281.6 | 276.8 | 280.1 | 280.5 | 282.9 | 284.6 | 283.5 | 283.5 | 282.7 | 285.1 | 295.0 | 298.4 | 284.6 |
| 2013 | 281.9 | 277.7 | 279.2 | 280.6 | 283.6 | 285.9 | 286.6 | 287.2 | 284.2 | 286.8 | 296.2 | 300.2 | 285.8 |
| 2014 | 284.6 | 279.4 | 281.5 | 283.9 | 286.0 | 289.4 | 289.9 | 290.4 | 287.0 | 290.3 | 298.5 | 303.1 | 288.7 |
| 2015 | 286.6 | 282.0 | 283.4 | 286.8 | 290.0 | 293.4 | 292.1 | 291.9 | 288.9 | 292.8 | 300.5 | 303.6 | 291.0 |
| 2016 | 288.7 | 284.4 | 286.9 | 288.0 | 290.4 | 291.9 | 292.0 | 292.5 | 289.3 | 292.2 | 300.0 | 302.8 | 291.6 |
| 2017 | 288.2 | 282.8 | 283.4 | 285.7 | 287.5 | 289.7 | 289.0 | 289.2 | 286.0 | 288.7 | 299.3 | 299.7 | 289.1 |
| 2018 | 285.2 | 280.8 | 281.2 | 282.7 | 285.3 | 286.9 | 287.6 | 287.4 | 284.0 | 287.2 | 300.8 | 302.2 | 287.6 |
| 2019 | 280.9 | 275.4 | 276.7 | 275.8 | 277.8 | 279.4 | 279.4 | 279.4 | 275.9 | 280.9 | 289.6 | 291.5 | 280.2 |
| **Transportation and Utilities** | | | | | | | | | | | | | |
| 2011 | 75.6 | 75.1 | 75.5 | 76.7 | 77.3 | 77.6 | 76.7 | 76.8 | 78.4 | 78.4 | 79.7 | 81.5 | 77.4 |
| 2012 | 78.0 | 77.7 | 78.2 | 78.8 | 79.3 | 79.7 | 78.0 | 78.1 | 80.2 | 80.0 | 81.4 | 84.1 | 79.5 |
| 2013 | 79.5 | 78.2 | 78.7 | 78.6 | 79.8 | 80.3 | 78.7 | 78.8 | 80.9 | 81.1 | 83.0 | 85.8 | 80.3 |
| 2014 | 80.9 | 79.2 | 80.3 | 81.1 | 82.1 | 82.6 | 80.5 | 81.1 | 83.2 | 83.8 | 86.9 | 89.8 | 82.6 |
| 2015 | 84.2 | 83.0 | 83.1 | 84.4 | 85.5 | 86.3 | 85.6 | 85.7 | 88.0 | 89.6 | 91.7 | 95.1 | 86.9 |
| 2016 | 87.5 | 87.2 | 87.2 | 89.6 | 90.1 | 90.3 | 89.0 | 89.6 | 92.5 | 92.9 | 96.8 | 99.1 | 91.0 |
| 2017 | 92.2 | 90.7 | 90.4 | 91.9 | 93.1 | 93.8 | 93.0 | 93.5 | 95.9 | 97.0 | 101.6 | 103.2 | 94.7 |
| 2018 | 97.1 | 96.0 | 95.9 | 95.6 | 95.7 | 96.8 | 95.5 | 95.1 | 97.4 | 99.9 | 103.0 | 103.5 | 97.6 |
| 2019 | 100.8 | 99.1 | 97.8 | 98.4 | 99.9 | 101.6 | 101.3 | 101.5 | 104.6 | 104.0 | 106.0 | 109.2 | 102.0 |
| **Information** | | | | | | | | | | | | | |
| 2011 | 41.3 | 41.9 | 42.1 | 41.4 | 41.2 | 41.1 | 41.2 | 38.1 | 40.2 | 40.2 | 40.9 | 40.7 | 40.9 |
| 2012 | 39.8 | 39.9 | 39.9 | 38.8 | 39.1 | 40.5 | 40.4 | 40.5 | 40.1 | 39.5 | 39.8 | 40.7 | 39.9 |
| 2013 | 39.7 | 39.8 | 40.0 | 39.5 | 39.6 | 39.7 | 39.8 | 39.8 | 39.2 | 39.2 | 39.8 | 39.6 | 39.6 |
| 2014 | 40.2 | 38.8 | 38.8 | 38.6 | 39.6 | 38.7 | 38.9 | 39.9 | 38.3 | 39.3 | 38.9 | 39.0 | 39.1 |
| 2015 | 38.8 | 38.3 | 38.4 | 39.0 | 39.2 | 38.3 | 38.8 | 38.4 | 37.8 | 38.9 | 38.7 | 38.6 | 38.6 |
| 2016 | 37.6 | 37.9 | 37.7 | 38.9 | 36.0 | 39.0 | 38.9 | 38.3 | 38.1 | 37.8 | 38.0 | 38.5 | 38.1 |
| 2017 | 37.5 | 38.2 | 38.0 | 37.6 | 37.6 | 38.0 | 37.5 | 37.3 | 37.1 | 37.1 | 37.2 | 37.3 | 37.5 |
| 2018 | 36.2 | 36.7 | 36.5 | 36.5 | 36.6 | 36.9 | 36.3 | 36.2 | 35.3 | 35.7 | 35.9 | 35.6 | 36.2 |
| 2019 | 35.1 | 35.2 | 35.5 | 35.3 | 35.3 | 35.7 | 35.7 | 35.7 | 35.3 | 35.3 | 35.5 | 34.5 | 35.3 |

## 1. Employment by Industry: Maryland, 2011–2019—*Continued*

(Numbers in thousands, not seasonally adjusted)

| Industry and year | January | February | March | April | May | June | July | August | September | October | November | December | Annual average |
|---|---|---|---|---|---|---|---|---|---|---|---|---|---|
| **Financial Activities** | | | | | | | | | | | | | |
| 2011 | 142.3 | 142.6 | 143.0 | 143.3 | 143.3 | 144.1 | 144.2 | 143.5 | 142.6 | 142.7 | 142.3 | 142.7 | 143.1 |
| 2012 | 141.7 | 141.7 | 141.8 | 141.6 | 142.4 | 143.7 | 144.3 | 144.3 | 143.7 | 143.8 | 144.2 | 144.7 | 143.2 |
| 2013 | 143.5 | 143.5 | 143.9 | 144.4 | 145.0 | 146.4 | 147.0 | 146.5 | 145.6 | 145.2 | 145.3 | 145.5 | 145.2 |
| 2014 | 143.4 | 143.3 | 143.1 | 143.8 | 144.5 | 145.7 | 146.1 | 146.1 | 144.9 | 145.4 | 145.5 | 146.0 | 144.8 |
| 2015 | 144.4 | 144.7 | 144.8 | 145.4 | 145.7 | 147.0 | 147.0 | 146.6 | 144.6 | 144.9 | 144.6 | 144.5 | 145.4 |
| 2016 | 142.3 | 142.3 | 141.9 | 143.1 | 143.6 | 144.6 | 145.6 | 145.7 | 145.0 | 145.1 | 144.9 | 145.5 | 144.1 |
| 2017 | 143.9 | 144.4 | 144.7 | 145.2 | 146.1 | 148.0 | 149.6 | 149.7 | 148.3 | 148.3 | 146.8 | 146.8 | 146.8 |
| 2018 | 145.6 | 145.9 | 146.2 | 146.4 | 146.6 | 147.3 | 147.9 | 147.3 | 145.7 | 145.0 | 144.7 | 144.3 | 146.1 |
| 2019 | 143.2 | 143.3 | 143.2 | 143.3 | 143.4 | 144.4 | 145.4 | 144.7 | 143.0 | 144.0 | 143.8 | 143.7 | 143.8 |
| **Professional and Business Services** | | | | | | | | | | | | | |
| 2011 | 385.9 | 387.0 | 391.5 | 398.4 | 398.9 | 404.2 | 407.4 | 408.3 | 407.1 | 407.4 | 408.5 | 408.1 | 401.1 |
| 2012 | 398.4 | 399.1 | 405.2 | 408.2 | 411.0 | 415.7 | 416.1 | 419.3 | 417.6 | 417.9 | 419.0 | 417.5 | 412.1 |
| 2013 | 408.3 | 410.9 | 416.2 | 416.9 | 418.6 | 422.7 | 423.0 | 425.9 | 423.5 | 422.5 | 424.2 | 421.2 | 419.5 |
| 2014 | 411.2 | 413.8 | 417.6 | 424.6 | 428.2 | 431.0 | 431.8 | 432.8 | 429.6 | 431.3 | 431.2 | 429.9 | 426.1 |
| 2015 | 417.9 | 419.5 | 422.8 | 431.6 | 434.7 | 437.4 | 441.1 | 442.2 | 436.5 | 442.4 | 442.4 | 439.6 | 434.0 |
| 2016 | 429.3 | 429.7 | 433.2 | 441.3 | 441.6 | 445.5 | 448.3 | 450.3 | 446.1 | 446.4 | 446.5 | 443.5 | 441.8 |
| 2017 | 434.8 | 435.2 | 438.6 | 442.1 | 444.5 | 449.6 | 450.9 | 451.7 | 448.3 | 448.4 | 448.6 | 446.2 | 444.9 |
| 2018 | 438.7 | 440.9 | 445.2 | 449.9 | 452.2 | 456.7 | 460.7 | 461.4 | 456.7 | 458.6 | 460.4 | 455.3 | 453.1 |
| 2019 | 450.4 | 452.8 | 455.8 | 461.1 | 463.7 | 468.7 | 469.5 | 470.0 | 463.8 | 466.2 | 470.1 | 467.3 | 463.3 |
| **Education and Health Services** | | | | | | | | | | | | | |
| 2011 | 402.2 | 406.4 | 408.0 | 408.8 | 408.4 | 405.3 | 405.9 | 404.7 | 409.1 | 412.8 | 414.2 | 414.1 | 408.3 |
| 2012 | 411.5 | 415.5 | 417.5 | 418.2 | 418.1 | 416.7 | 416.3 | 414.6 | 418.7 | 422.4 | 422.6 | 424.5 | 418.1 |
| 2013 | 418.4 | 422.4 | 424.1 | 425.1 | 424.9 | 422.8 | 421.8 | 420.4 | 424.1 | 427.6 | 428.7 | 428.7 | 424.1 |
| 2014 | 422.0 | 424.9 | 427.6 | 428.4 | 429.1 | 428.1 | 427.0 | 426.9 | 430.7 | 433.5 | 435.6 | 436.5 | 429.2 |
| 2015 | 430.7 | 434.7 | 436.4 | 439.9 | 440.7 | 438.2 | 438.0 | 436.0 | 439.4 | 445.3 | 447.5 | 447.1 | 439.5 |
| 2016 | 440.5 | 443.4 | 445.6 | 448.7 | 448.3 | 443.6 | 447.8 | 444.5 | 449.3 | 454.3 | 456.0 | 456.3 | 448.2 |
| 2017 | 449.0 | 453.9 | 455.7 | 456.8 | 456.9 | 454.8 | 460.0 | 457.5 | 461.3 | 466.3 | 467.4 | 467.4 | 458.9 |
| 2018 | 462.5 | 467.0 | 468.1 | 468.7 | 469.1 | 467.7 | 467.2 | 464.8 | 467.4 | 472.8 | 474.7 | 473.4 | 468.6 |
| 2019 | 469.2 | 474.5 | 475.7 | 475.8 | 475.2 | 472.7 | 472.4 | 469.6 | 471.3 | 472.9 | 475.7 | 476.7 | 473.5 |
| **Leisure and Hospitality** | | | | | | | | | | | | | |
| 2011 | 211.8 | 212.1 | 220.4 | 229.9 | 240.5 | 250.7 | 252.7 | 252.2 | 242.7 | 233.6 | 229.2 | 227.7 | 233.6 |
| 2012 | 220.8 | 221.7 | 229.8 | 239.0 | 251.1 | 264.4 | 264.7 | 264.7 | 254.8 | 246.6 | 239.4 | 238.4 | 244.6 |
| 2013 | 232.3 | 232.7 | 239.4 | 249.0 | 261.9 | 274.5 | 275.5 | 273.5 | 261.6 | 254.1 | 248.9 | 247.2 | 254.2 |
| 2014 | 237.1 | 237.5 | 244.3 | 255.7 | 270.5 | 279.9 | 280.3 | 279.8 | 269.0 | 262.5 | 256.1 | 254.0 | 260.6 |
| 2015 | 244.9 | 245.9 | 250.8 | 262.6 | 278.1 | 287.1 | 288.8 | 287.1 | 275.4 | 267.9 | 261.9 | 261.9 | 267.7 |
| 2016 | 251.1 | 251.9 | 258.9 | 269.4 | 280.7 | 291.6 | 291.7 | 290.7 | 280.7 | 272.7 | 271.6 | 269.7 | 273.4 |
| 2017 | 260.2 | 262.8 | 268.4 | 277.7 | 289.7 | 300.6 | 299.8 | 298.2 | 285.5 | 278.2 | 272.9 | 269.7 | 280.3 |
| 2018 | 260.7 | 262.4 | 268.6 | 278.0 | 291.0 | 302.7 | 304.5 | 302.4 | 288.5 | 280.3 | 274.6 | 273.7 | 282.3 |
| 2019 | 263.0 | 264.1 | 270.2 | 280.3 | 291.9 | 302.9 | 303.6 | 300.3 | 284.8 | 273.8 | 272.7 | 273.3 | 281.7 |
| **Other Services** | | | | | | | | | | | | | |
| 2011 | 112.2 | 112.3 | 113.1 | 114.1 | 114.1 | 115.2 | 114.8 | 114.0 | 112.6 | 112.1 | 112.1 | 112.2 | 113.2 |
| 2012 | 110.8 | 110.7 | 111.3 | 112.0 | 112.2 | 113.2 | 113.1 | 112.3 | 111.5 | 110.7 | 110.1 | 110.5 | 111.5 |
| 2013 | 108.7 | 108.8 | 109.1 | 110.8 | 111.2 | 112.0 | 112.3 | 111.5 | 111.3 | 110.3 | 110.5 | 110.3 | 110.6 |
| 2014 | 109.3 | 109.2 | 110.1 | 111.3 | 112.1 | 113.5 | 113.6 | 112.9 | 113.1 | 112.4 | 112.5 | 112.7 | 111.9 |
| 2015 | 111.3 | 111.5 | 112.1 | 110.6 | 111.6 | 112.5 | 113.2 | 112.8 | 111.9 | 111.8 | 111.9 | 112.0 | 111.9 |
| 2016 | 111.3 | 111.5 | 112.2 | 112.9 | 113.3 | 113.9 | 114.9 | 114.3 | 113.7 | 113.4 | 113.4 | 113.2 | 113.2 |
| 2017 | 112.2 | 112.5 | 113.1 | 113.6 | 114.2 | 115.6 | 115.7 | 114.6 | 113.6 | 113.7 | 113.7 | 113.8 | 113.9 |
| 2018 | 112.6 | 112.8 | 113.5 | 114.0 | 114.6 | 115.7 | 116.4 | 115.5 | 114.0 | 114.4 | 114.6 | 114.5 | 114.4 |
| 2019 | 113.4 | 113.7 | 114.3 | 115.0 | 115.6 | 116.3 | 116.4 | 116.0 | 114.7 | 114.9 | 115.1 | 116.3 | 115.1 |
| **Government** | | | | | | | | | | | | | |
| 2011 | 493.0 | 509.2 | 516.0 | 513.6 | 512.9 | 500.0 | 486.1 | 480.7 | 500.9 | 515.2 | 512.2 | 512.6 | 504.4 |
| 2012 | 492.0 | 509.7 | 515.2 | 514.0 | 512.5 | 496.1 | 478.4 | 477.6 | 499.9 | 512.9 | 513.9 | 513.2 | 503.0 |
| 2013 | 493.3 | 509.1 | 513.5 | 514.0 | 513.2 | 501.0 | 480.8 | 479.7 | 500.2 | 510.2 | 513.8 | 510.1 | 503.2 |
| 2014 | 490.4 | 506.7 | 509.8 | 510.4 | 509.2 | 500.2 | 474.9 | 479.4 | 502.5 | 511.4 | 514.6 | 511.1 | 501.7 |
| 2015 | 490.6 | 507.1 | 510.7 | 512.8 | 513.3 | 503.8 | 478.6 | 479.6 | 504.0 | 510.8 | 513.7 | 514.0 | 503.3 |
| 2016 | 492.1 | 505.9 | 512.1 | 512.6 | 511.3 | 498.6 | 476.5 | 479.9 | 503.9 | 511.4 | 514.6 | 514.8 | 502.8 |
| 2017 | 495.1 | 511.1 | 514.9 | 514.1 | 515.5 | 503.8 | 477.0 | 477.9 | 499.9 | 511.7 | 515.6 | 511.9 | 502.8 |
| 2018 | 493.4 | 511.8 | 515.4 | 514.6 | 515.7 | 505.7 | 483.8 | 485.2 | 505.8 | 513.1 | 515.0 | 514.0 | 504.0 |
| 2019 | 498.3 | 512.0 | 516.1 | 516.0 | 517.5 | 507.2 | 483.1 | 481.4 | 505.9 | 512.9 | 515.9 | 513.8 | 506.7 |

## 2. Average Weekly Hours by Selected Industry: Maryland, 2015–2019

(Not seasonally adjusted)

| Industry and year | January | February | March | April | May | June | July | August | September | October | November | December | Annual average |
|---|---|---|---|---|---|---|---|---|---|---|---|---|---|
| **Total Private** | | | | | | | | | | | | | |
| 2015 | 33.3 | 33.9 | 34.0 | 34.0 | 34.2 | 34.2 | 34.3 | 34.5 | 34.3 | 34.5 | 34.4 | 34.2 | 34.2 |
| 2016 | 33.5 | 33.6 | 34.0 | 34.2 | 34.1 | 34.3 | 34.2 | 34.2 | 34.4 | 34.7 | 34.2 | 34.0 | 34.1 |
| 2017 | 34.1 | 34.0 | 33.7 | 34.7 | 34.1 | 34.4 | 34.6 | 34.1 | 34.4 | 34.6 | 34.3 | 34.4 | 34.3 |
| 2018 | 33.8 | 34.2 | 34.2 | 34.9 | 34.5 | 34.5 | 35.0 | 34.5 | 34.9 | 34.6 | 34.3 | 34.7 | 34.5 |
| 2019 | 34.0 | 33.9 | 34.3 | 34.3 | 34.2 | 34.4 | 34.2 | 34.3 | 34.6 | 34.2 | 34.2 | 34.0 | 34.2 |
| **Goods-Producing** | | | | | | | | | | | | | |
| 2015 | 37.5 | 37.8 | 38.6 | 38.9 | 39.6 | 40.0 | 39.9 | 39.8 | 39.4 | 40.6 | 39.1 | 40.3 | 39.3 |
| 2016 | 38.9 | 38.1 | 39.3 | 39.5 | 38.4 | 39.5 | 39.1 | 39.4 | 39.4 | 39.3 | 38.2 | 37.7 | 38.9 |
| 2017 | 38.0 | 38.3 | 37.3 | 38.3 | 38.4 | 39.1 | 38.9 | 38.7 | 39.2 | 39.4 | 39.5 | 39.8 | 38.7 |
| 2018 | 38.2 | 38.5 | 39.2 | 39.6 | 39.3 | 38.7 | 39.0 | 39.3 | 38.5 | 38.9 | 38.2 | 39.9 | 38.9 |
| 2019 | 38.4 | 37.9 | 39.0 | 39.6 | 38.9 | 38.8 | 38.9 | 39.3 | 39.8 | 39.6 | 39.2 | 38.3 | 39.0 |
| **Mining, Logging, and Construction** | | | | | | | | | | | | | |
| 2015 | 35.9 | 36.7 | 36.9 | 37.8 | 39.2 | 39.5 | 39.4 | 39.0 | 37.6 | 39.9 | 37.7 | 39.9 | 38.3 |
| 2016 | 38.5 | 36.6 | 39.1 | 39.0 | 37.8 | 39.7 | 39.3 | 39.4 | 39.4 | 39.5 | 37.6 | 37.3 | 38.6 |
| 2017 | 37.7 | 37.8 | 36.3 | 38.0 | 37.6 | 38.4 | 38.2 | 37.6 | 37.6 | 37.7 | 38.2 | 38.6 | 37.8 |
| 2018 | 36.7 | 37.1 | 38.2 | 39.1 | 38.4 | 37.9 | 38.2 | 39.1 | 37.7 | 38.9 | 37.6 | 39.6 | 38.2 |
| 2019 | 38.4 | 37.5 | 39.3 | 40.3 | 39.6 | 39.4 | 39.7 | 40.5 | 40.9 | 40.6 | 39.8 | 38.1 | 39.5 |
| **Manufacturing** | | | | | | | | | | | | | |
| 2015 | 39.7 | 39.3 | 41.1 | 40.4 | 40.2 | 40.7 | 40.7 | 41.0 | 42.0 | 41.7 | 41.2 | 41.0 | 40.7 |
| 2016 | 39.4 | 40.3 | 39.7 | 40.4 | 39.3 | 39.3 | 38.8 | 39.3 | 39.3 | 39.0 | 39.0 | 38.3 | 39.3 |
| 2017 | 38.5 | 39.0 | 38.7 | 38.8 | 39.7 | 40.3 | 39.9 | 40.3 | 41.7 | 42.0 | 41.4 | 41.6 | 40.2 |
| 2018 | 40.4 | 40.5 | 40.8 | 40.4 | 40.7 | 39.8 | 40.2 | 39.5 | 39.8 | 38.9 | 39.0 | 40.2 | 40.0 |
| 2019 | 38.3 | 38.4 | 38.5 | 38.6 | 38.0 | 38.0 | 37.7 | 37.4 | 38.1 | 38.0 | 38.3 | 38.7 | 38.2 |
| **Trade, Transportation, and Utilities** | | | | | | | | | | | | | |
| 2015 | 32.8 | 33.2 | 33.4 | 33.4 | 33.7 | 33.5 | 34.0 | 33.8 | 34.2 | 33.4 | 33.6 | 33.6 | 33.6 |
| 2016 | 32.3 | 32.7 | 32.8 | 32.9 | 33.3 | 33.7 | 33.6 | 33.4 | 33.9 | 34.2 | 34.0 | 34.3 | 33.4 |
| 2017 | 34.3 | 33.9 | 33.5 | 34.2 | 33.8 | 34.0 | 34.4 | 33.8 | 34.3 | 35.0 | 34.8 | 34.6 | 34.2 |
| 2018 | 34.2 | 34.2 | 34.3 | 34.5 | 34.3 | 34.4 | 34.4 | 34.2 | 34.6 | 34.0 | 34.2 | 34.3 | 34.3 |
| 2019 | 33.4 | 33.4 | 33.5 | 33.8 | 33.7 | 33.9 | 33.7 | 33.7 | 34.1 | 33.2 | 33.2 | 33.6 | 33.6 |
| **Financial Activities** | | | | | | | | | | | | | |
| 2015 | 37.6 | 38.2 | 38.3 | 37.5 | 37.9 | 37.7 | 37.6 | 38.5 | 38.0 | 38.1 | 38.0 | 37.6 | 37.9 |
| 2016 | 37.7 | 38.1 | 38.3 | 37.8 | 38.6 | 38.5 | 38.6 | 38.3 | 38.0 | 38.6 | 38.0 | 38.3 | 38.2 |
| 2017 | 38.3 | 37.8 | 37.8 | 38.3 | 37.3 | 37.6 | 38.1 | 37.3 | 37.3 | 37.3 | 37.6 | 37.1 | 37.7 |
| 2018 | 37.3 | 37.3 | 37.5 | 38.2 | 36.9 | 37.2 | 38.2 | 37.2 | 38.2 | 37.4 | 38.1 | 38.3 | 37.7 |
| 2019 | 38.1 | 37.6 | 37.5 | 37.5 | 37.4 | 38.2 | 37.7 | 38.1 | 38.3 | 37.5 | 37.7 | 38.0 | 37.8 |
| **Professional and Business Services** | | | | | | | | | | | | | |
| 2015 | 34.3 | 35.4 | 35.4 | 35.5 | 35.4 | 35.4 | 35.2 | 36.0 | 35.4 | 36.1 | 36.4 | 35.7 | 35.5 |
| 2016 | 35.2 | 35.2 | 35.9 | 36.3 | 36.5 | 36.6 | 36.1 | 36.2 | 36.2 | 37.4 | 36.6 | 36.1 | 36.2 |
| 2017 | 36.4 | 36.3 | 36.2 | 37.8 | 36.6 | 37.0 | 37.0 | 36.8 | 37.0 | 37.3 | 36.7 | 36.7 | 36.8 |
| 2018 | 36.1 | 36.7 | 36.5 | 37.6 | 36.8 | 36.2 | 37.2 | 36.1 | 37.1 | 36.8 | 36.2 | 36.6 | 36.7 |
| 2019 | 35.7 | 35.9 | 36.4 | 36.1 | 35.9 | 36.4 | 35.4 | 36.1 | 36.2 | 35.5 | 35.8 | 35.8 | 35.9 |
| **Education and Health Services** | | | | | | | | | | | | | |
| 2015 | 32.6 | 33.0 | 32.8 | 32.6 | 32.7 | 32.8 | 33.0 | 32.9 | 32.9 | 33.2 | 33.5 | 32.8 | 32.9 |
| 2016 | 33.3 | 33.0 | 33.2 | 33.2 | 33.1 | 33.1 | 33.6 | 33.4 | 33.4 | 33.5 | 33.6 | 33.3 | 33.3 |
| 2017 | 33.2 | 33.0 | 33.0 | 33.3 | 33.1 | 33.0 | 33.4 | 33.2 | 33.1 | 32.8 | 32.7 | 33.1 | 33.1 |
| 2018 | 33.3 | 33.3 | 33.0 | 33.5 | 33.2 | 33.5 | 33.4 | 33.2 | 33.9 | 33.2 | 33.4 | 33.2 | 33.3 |
| 2019 | 33.3 | 33.1 | 33.3 | 33.2 | 33.4 | 33.8 | 33.7 | 33.8 | 33.9 | 33.7 | 33.8 | 33.4 | 33.5 |
| **Leisure and Hospitality** | | | | | | | | | | | | | |
| 2015 | 25.2 | 25.3 | 25.8 | 26.1 | 26.8 | 27.3 | 27.6 | 28.0 | 26.9 | 26.7 | 26.7 | 26.5 | 26.6 |
| 2016 | 24.9 | 26.0 | 26.0 | 26.1 | 26.1 | 26.1 | 26.4 | 26.3 | 26.2 | 25.8 | 25.6 | 25.3 | 25.9 |
| 2017 | 25.1 | 25.4 | 25.3 | 26.2 | 26.2 | 25.6 | 26.1 | 25.5 | 25.4 | 25.7 | 25.4 | 25.2 | 25.6 |
| 2018 | 24.3 | 25.1 | 24.8 | 25.7 | 25.8 | 26.7 | 27.5 | 26.8 | 26.2 | 26.3 | 26.1 | 26.0 | 26.0 |
| 2019 | 25.4 | 25.6 | 26.0 | 26.0 | 25.9 | 26.3 | 26.9 | 26.8 | 26.5 | 26.3 | 26.5 | 25.9 | 26.2 |
| **Other Services** | | | | | | | | | | | | | |
| 2015 | 32.1 | 33.3 | 33.5 | 33.6 | 34.0 | 33.6 | 33.7 | 32.9 | 32.6 | 32.3 | 32.5 | 32.3 | 33.0 |
| 2016 | 31.3 | 31.5 | 31.8 | 32.0 | 31.9 | 32.6 | 32.3 | 32.2 | 31.6 | 31.4 | 30.7 | 30.6 | 31.7 |
| 2017 | 31.1 | 31.6 | 30.5 | 31.5 | 31.4 | 31.7 | 32.5 | 32.1 | 32.6 | 32.2 | 31.6 | 31.8 | 31.7 |
| 2018 | 31.8 | 32.0 | 32.5 | 33.4 | 33.9 | 33.1 | 33.3 | 33.6 | 34.3 | 34.0 | 33.7 | 34.6 | 33.3 |
| 2019 | 34.0 | 35.0 | 34.6 | 34.4 | 34.9 | 35.1 | 35.4 | 34.9 | 35.1 | 35.3 | 34.9 | 35.2 | 34.9 |

## 3. Average Hourly Earnings by Selected Industry: Maryland, 2015–2019

(Dollars, not seasonally adjusted)

| Industry and year | January | February | March | April | May | June | July | August | September | October | November | December | Annual average |
|---|---|---|---|---|---|---|---|---|---|---|---|---|---|
| **Total Private** | | | | | | | | | | | | | |
| 2015 | 27.66 | 27.73 | 27.79 | 27.36 | 27.15 | 27.01 | 26.93 | 27.44 | 27.34 | 27.33 | 27.81 | 27.46 | 27.41 |
| 2016 | 27.83 | 27.78 | 27.63 | 27.64 | 27.93 | 27.36 | 27.44 | 27.67 | 27.92 | 28.28 | 28.27 | 28.00 | 27.82 |
| 2017 | 28.79 | 28.29 | 28.31 | 28.42 | 27.95 | 27.83 | 28.40 | 28.31 | 28.61 | 29.23 | 29.15 | 29.38 | 28.56 |
| 2018 | 29.83 | 30.15 | 29.96 | 30.33 | 29.84 | 29.57 | 29.87 | 29.51 | 30.22 | 30.14 | 30.21 | 30.68 | 30.02 |
| 2019 | 30.34 | 30.33 | 30.17 | 30.21 | 30.18 | 30.35 | 30.04 | 29.98 | 30.57 | 30.47 | 30.79 | 31.13 | 30.38 |
| **Goods-Producing** | | | | | | | | | | | | | |
| 2015 | 26.73 | 26.59 | 26.56 | 26.26 | 26.23 | 26.36 | 26.19 | 26.21 | 26.30 | 26.05 | 26.37 | 26.44 | 26.35 |
| 2016 | 26.03 | 26.20 | 26.25 | 26.43 | 26.84 | 26.50 | 26.86 | 27.03 | 27.53 | 27.62 | 28.29 | 28.48 | 27.01 |
| 2017 | 28.79 | 28.84 | 28.95 | 28.87 | 28.74 | 29.02 | 29.58 | 29.03 | 29.62 | 29.50 | 29.77 | 30.02 | 29.24 |
| 2018 | 30.17 | 30.12 | 30.05 | 30.09 | 30.14 | 30.36 | 30.23 | 29.94 | 30.00 | 29.85 | 29.62 | 30.04 | 30.05 |
| 2019 | 29.78 | 29.95 | 29.88 | 29.58 | 29.73 | 29.87 | 29.78 | 29.90 | 29.94 | 30.07 | 30.45 | 31.05 | 30.00 |
| **Mining, Logging, and Construction** | | | | | | | | | | | | | |
| 2015 | 27.62 | 27.31 | 27.17 | 27.07 | 26.87 | 26.91 | 26.85 | 26.51 | 26.49 | 26.34 | 26.26 | 26.66 | 26.82 |
| 2016 | 26.52 | 26.47 | 26.40 | 26.77 | 26.89 | 26.49 | 27.00 | 27.49 | 27.80 | 27.87 | 28.54 | 28.97 | 27.28 |
| 2017 | 29.53 | 29.62 | 29.93 | 29.43 | 29.62 | 30.16 | 30.84 | 30.22 | 30.58 | 30.56 | 30.81 | 31.11 | 30.21 |
| 2018 | 31.56 | 31.67 | 31.63 | 31.52 | 31.58 | 31.97 | 32.20 | 31.55 | 31.54 | 31.13 | 30.99 | 31.55 | 31.57 |
| 2019 | 30.82 | 30.83 | 31.00 | 30.44 | 30.35 | 30.61 | 30.50 | 30.49 | 30.55 | 31.19 | 31.63 | 32.31 | 30.89 |
| **Manufacturing** | | | | | | | | | | | | | |
| 2015 | 25.61 | 25.66 | 25.80 | 25.17 | 25.31 | 25.58 | 25.23 | 25.78 | 26.04 | 25.62 | 26.53 | 26.12 | 25.71 |
| 2016 | 25.33 | 25.84 | 26.02 | 25.94 | 26.76 | 26.52 | 26.64 | 26.31 | 27.10 | 27.22 | 27.92 | 27.75 | 26.61 |
| 2017 | 27.72 | 27.71 | 27.58 | 28.05 | 27.47 | 27.35 | 27.72 | 27.31 | 28.30 | 28.05 | 28.31 | 28.50 | 27.85 |
| 2018 | 28.33 | 28.02 | 27.86 | 28.02 | 28.09 | 28.06 | 27.39 | 27.53 | 27.79 | 27.91 | 27.65 | 27.84 | 27.87 |
| 2019 | 28.24 | 28.70 | 28.19 | 28.25 | 28.76 | 28.73 | 28.66 | 28.95 | 28.96 | 28.29 | 28.62 | 29.21 | 28.63 |
| **Trade, Transportation, and Utilities** | | | | | | | | | | | | | |
| 2015 | 22.65 | 22.69 | 22.27 | 22.40 | 22.04 | 21.99 | 22.02 | 22.30 | 22.11 | 22.68 | 22.66 | 22.29 | 22.34 |
| 2016 | 22.96 | 22.86 | 23.08 | 23.45 | 23.31 | 23.14 | 23.59 | 23.70 | 23.86 | 23.79 | 23.72 | 23.34 | 23.41 |
| 2017 | 23.90 | 23.82 | 23.93 | 24.58 | 24.00 | 24.03 | 24.80 | 24.31 | 24.18 | 24.28 | 23.64 | 24.20 | 24.14 |
| 2018 | 24.41 | 24.56 | 24.38 | 24.21 | 24.17 | 23.76 | 23.88 | 23.93 | 24.17 | 24.13 | 23.77 | 24.00 | 24.11 |
| 2019 | 23.64 | 23.53 | 23.52 | 23.33 | 23.28 | 23.16 | 23.17 | 23.03 | 23.11 | 23.12 | 22.68 | 23.19 | 23.23 |
| **Financial Activities** | | | | | | | | | | | | | |
| 2015 | 33.76 | 34.57 | 34.96 | 35.50 | 35.58 | 35.11 | 35.45 | 36.52 | 36.66 | 36.36 | 37.73 | 36.82 | 35.75 |
| 2016 | 36.33 | 37.14 | 37.52 | 37.84 | 37.86 | 37.37 | 37.18 | 39.41 | 39.66 | 39.94 | 39.75 | 39.28 | 38.28 |
| 2017 | 40.57 | 40.20 | 39.20 | 39.70 | 38.83 | 38.01 | 37.58 | 38.47 | 36.81 | 37.97 | 37.60 | 37.59 | 38.54 |
| 2018 | 38.65 | 39.13 | 37.98 | 38.24 | 38.45 | 37.36 | 37.77 | 38.22 | 37.58 | 37.77 | 38.84 | 38.39 | 38.20 |
| 2019 | 38.70 | 38.31 | 37.98 | 38.31 | 39.06 | 38.08 | 37.79 | 38.63 | 38.81 | 39.12 | 40.08 | 40.50 | 38.78 |
| **Professional and Business Services** | | | | | | | | | | | | | |
| 2015 | 34.97 | 34.94 | 34.95 | 33.84 | 33.67 | 33.44 | 33.49 | 34.44 | 33.97 | 33.52 | 34.62 | 34.24 | 34.17 |
| 2016 | 35.01 | 34.76 | 33.78 | 33.63 | 34.43 | 33.25 | 33.41 | 33.51 | 33.71 | 34.22 | 34.39 | 34.67 | 34.06 |
| 2017 | 35.42 | 34.48 | 34.41 | 34.53 | 33.93 | 33.65 | 35.12 | 34.59 | 35.29 | 36.63 | 35.87 | 36.26 | 35.02 |
| 2018 | 36.94 | 36.70 | 36.50 | 37.94 | 36.98 | 36.64 | 37.92 | 36.91 | 37.99 | 38.01 | 38.12 | 38.84 | 37.47 |
| 2019 | 38.23 | 38.75 | 38.76 | 38.91 | 38.88 | 39.65 | 39.85 | 39.74 | 40.79 | 40.64 | 41.09 | 42.02 | 39.78 |
| **Education and Health Services** | | | | | | | | | | | | | |
| 2015 | 26.34 | 26.08 | 26.11 | 25.96 | 25.66 | 25.58 | 25.68 | 25.52 | 26.01 | 25.45 | 25.38 | 25.38 | 25.76 |
| 2016 | 25.28 | 25.20 | 25.22 | 25.42 | 25.52 | 25.36 | 25.54 | 25.30 | 25.47 | 25.33 | 25.11 | 24.95 | 25.31 |
| 2017 | 25.25 | 25.22 | 25.29 | 25.55 | 25.79 | 25.84 | 25.80 | 25.23 | 25.33 | 25.39 | 25.35 | 25.44 | 25.46 |
| 2018 | 25.74 | 26.16 | 26.47 | 26.87 | 26.73 | 26.75 | 27.24 | 27.27 | 27.77 | 27.85 | 28.12 | 28.09 | 27.09 |
| 2019 | 27.80 | 27.72 | 27.60 | 27.67 | 27.61 | 27.47 | 27.41 | 27.08 | 27.40 | 27.23 | 27.64 | 27.29 | 27.49 |
| **Leisure and Hospitality** | | | | | | | | | | | | | |
| 2015 | 14.75 | 14.80 | 14.97 | 15.24 | 15.28 | 14.95 | 14.61 | 14.85 | 15.01 | 15.27 | 15.40 | 15.44 | 15.05 |
| 2016 | 15.52 | 15.43 | 15.50 | 15.38 | 15.41 | 15.24 | 15.11 | 15.25 | 15.62 | 15.35 | 15.26 | 15.40 | 15.37 |
| 2017 | 15.49 | 15.77 | 15.75 | 15.45 | 15.70 | 15.22 | 14.95 | 15.19 | 15.73 | 15.31 | 15.44 | 15.63 | 15.46 |
| 2018 | 15.79 | 16.06 | 15.70 | 15.55 | 15.51 | 15.15 | 15.14 | 15.25 | 15.88 | 15.64 | 15.97 | 16.70 | 15.67 |
| 2019 | 16.62 | 16.83 | 16.74 | 17.13 | 17.05 | 16.94 | 16.76 | 16.88 | 17.55 | 16.69 | 16.64 | 17.07 | 16.91 |
| **Other Services** | | | | | | | | | | | | | |
| 2015 | 26.11 | 26.02 | 26.29 | 25.40 | 25.36 | 25.82 | 26.05 | 27.68 | 27.09 | 27.66 | 27.60 | 27.10 | 26.51 |
| 2016 | 28.24 | 28.31 | 28.86 | 27.82 | 28.49 | 28.00 | 28.10 | 28.42 | 28.98 | 29.92 | 29.22 | 29.24 | 28.63 |
| 2017 | 29.97 | 29.01 | 29.60 | 29.43 | 28.67 | 28.84 | 29.17 | 30.10 | 30.34 | 30.27 | 30.10 | 30.33 | 29.65 |
| 2018 | 30.66 | 30.64 | 30.47 | 30.49 | 29.98 | 31.10 | 30.79 | 30.02 | 30.55 | 30.68 | 30.73 | 31.45 | 30.63 |
| 2019 | 31.38 | 31.00 | 31.00 | 31.33 | 31.13 | 32.09 | 31.97 | 31.68 | 31.95 | 31.41 | 31.31 | 32.26 | 31.55 |

## 4. Average Weekly Earnings by Selected Industry: Maryland, 2015–2019

(Dollars, not seasonally adjusted)

| Industry and year | January | February | March | April | May | June | July | August | September | October | November | December | Annual average |
|---|---|---|---|---|---|---|---|---|---|---|---|---|---|
| **Total Private** | | | | | | | | | | | | | |
| 2015 | 921.08 | 940.05 | 944.86 | 930.25 | 928.53 | 923.74 | 923.70 | 946.68 | 937.76 | 942.89 | 956.66 | 939.13 | 937.42 |
| 2016 | 932.31 | 933.41 | 939.42 | 945.29 | 952.41 | 938.45 | 938.45 | 946.31 | 960.45 | 981.32 | 966.83 | 952.00 | 948.66 |
| 2017 | 981.74 | 961.86 | 954.05 | 986.17 | 953.10 | 957.35 | 982.64 | 965.37 | 984.18 | 1,011.36 | 999.85 | 1,010.67 | 979.61 |
| 2018 | 1,008.25 | 1,031.13 | 1,024.63 | 1,058.52 | 1,029.48 | 1,020.17 | 1,045.45 | 1,018.10 | 1,054.68 | 1,042.84 | 1,036.20 | 1,064.60 | 1,035.69 |
| 2019 | 1,031.56 | 1,028.19 | 1,034.83 | 1,036.20 | 1,032.16 | 1,044.04 | 1,027.37 | 1,028.31 | 1,057.72 | 1,042.07 | 1,053.02 | 1,058.42 | 1,039.00 |
| **Goods-Producing** | | | | | | | | | | | | | |
| 2015 | 1,002.38 | 1,005.10 | 1,025.22 | 1,021.51 | 1,038.71 | 1,054.40 | 1,044.98 | 1,043.16 | 1,036.22 | 1,057.63 | 1,031.07 | 1,065.53 | 1,035.56 |
| 2016 | 1,012.57 | 998.22 | 1,031.63 | 1,043.99 | 1,030.66 | 1,046.75 | 1,050.23 | 1,064.98 | 1,084.68 | 1,085.47 | 1,080.68 | 1,073.70 | 1,050.69 |
| 2017 | 1,094.02 | 1,104.57 | 1,079.84 | 1,105.72 | 1,103.62 | 1,134.68 | 1,150.66 | 1,123.46 | 1,161.10 | 1,162.30 | 1,175.92 | 1,194.80 | 1,131.59 |
| 2018 | 1,152.49 | 1,159.62 | 1,177.96 | 1,191.56 | 1,184.50 | 1,174.93 | 1,178.97 | 1,176.64 | 1,155.00 | 1,161.17 | 1,131.48 | 1,198.60 | 1,168.95 |
| 2019 | 1,143.55 | 1,135.11 | 1,165.32 | 1,171.37 | 1,156.50 | 1,158.96 | 1,158.44 | 1,175.07 | 1,191.61 | 1,190.77 | 1,193.64 | 1,189.22 | 1,170.00 |
| **Mining, Logging, and Construction** | | | | | | | | | | | | | |
| 2015 | 991.56 | 1,002.28 | 1,002.57 | 1,023.25 | 1,053.30 | 1,062.95 | 1,057.89 | 1,033.89 | 996.02 | 1,050.97 | 990.00 | 1,063.73 | 1,027.21 |
| 2016 | 1,021.02 | 968.80 | 1,032.24 | 1,044.03 | 1,016.44 | 1,051.65 | 1,061.10 | 1,083.11 | 1,095.32 | 1,100.87 | 1,073.10 | 1,080.58 | 1,053.01 |
| 2017 | 1,113.28 | 1,119.64 | 1,086.46 | 1,118.34 | 1,113.71 | 1,158.14 | 1,178.09 | 1,136.27 | 1,149.81 | 1,152.11 | 1,176.94 | 1,200.85 | 1,141.94 |
| 2018 | 1,158.25 | 1,174.96 | 1,208.27 | 1,232.43 | 1,212.67 | 1,211.66 | 1,230.04 | 1,233.61 | 1,189.06 | 1,210.96 | 1,165.22 | 1,249.38 | 1,205.97 |
| 2019 | 1,183.49 | 1,156.13 | 1,218.30 | 1,226.73 | 1,201.86 | 1,206.03 | 1,210.85 | 1,234.85 | 1,249.50 | 1,266.31 | 1,258.87 | 1,231.01 | 1,220.16 |
| **Manufacturing** | | | | | | | | | | | | | |
| 2015 | 1,016.72 | 1,008.44 | 1,060.38 | 1,016.87 | 1,017.46 | 1,041.11 | 1,026.86 | 1,056.98 | 1,093.68 | 1,068.35 | 1,093.04 | 1,070.92 | 1,046.40 |
| 2016 | 998.00 | 1,041.35 | 1,032.99 | 1,047.98 | 1,051.67 | 1,042.24 | 1,033.63 | 1,033.98 | 1,065.03 | 1,061.58 | 1,088.88 | 1,062.83 | 1,045.77 |
| 2017 | 1,067.22 | 1,080.69 | 1,067.35 | 1,088.34 | 1,090.56 | 1,102.21 | 1,106.03 | 1,100.59 | 1,180.11 | 1,178.10 | 1,172.03 | 1,185.60 | 1,119.57 |
| 2018 | 1,144.53 | 1,134.81 | 1,136.69 | 1,132.01 | 1,143.26 | 1,116.79 | 1,101.08 | 1,087.44 | 1,106.04 | 1,085.70 | 1,078.35 | 1,119.17 | 1,114.80 |
| 2019 | 1,081.59 | 1,102.08 | 1,085.32 | 1,090.45 | 1,092.88 | 1,091.74 | 1,080.48 | 1,082.73 | 1,103.38 | 1,075.02 | 1,096.15 | 1,130.43 | 1,093.67 |
| **Trade, Transportation, and Utilities** | | | | | | | | | | | | | |
| 2015 | 742.92 | 753.31 | 743.82 | 748.16 | 742.75 | 736.67 | 748.68 | 753.74 | 756.16 | 757.51 | 761.38 | 748.94 | 750.62 |
| 2016 | 741.61 | 747.52 | 757.02 | 771.51 | 776.22 | 779.82 | 792.62 | 791.58 | 808.85 | 813.62 | 806.48 | 800.56 | 781.89 |
| 2017 | 819.77 | 807.50 | 801.66 | 840.64 | 811.20 | 817.02 | 853.12 | 821.68 | 829.37 | 849.80 | 822.67 | 837.32 | 825.59 |
| 2018 | 834.82 | 839.95 | 836.23 | 835.25 | 829.03 | 817.34 | 821.47 | 818.41 | 836.28 | 820.42 | 812.93 | 823.20 | 826.97 |
| 2019 | 789.58 | 785.90 | 787.92 | 788.55 | 784.54 | 785.12 | 780.83 | 776.11 | 788.05 | 767.58 | 752.98 | 779.18 | 780.53 |
| **Financial Activities** | | | | | | | | | | | | | |
| 2015 | 1,269.38 | 1,320.57 | 1,338.97 | 1,331.25 | 1,348.48 | 1,323.65 | 1,332.92 | 1,406.02 | 1,393.08 | 1,385.32 | 1,433.74 | 1,384.43 | 1,354.93 |
| 2016 | 1,369.64 | 1,415.03 | 1,437.02 | 1,430.35 | 1,461.40 | 1,438.75 | 1,435.15 | 1,509.40 | 1,507.08 | 1,541.68 | 1,510.50 | 1,504.42 | 1,462.30 |
| 2017 | 1,553.83 | 1,519.56 | 1,481.76 | 1,520.51 | 1,448.36 | 1,429.18 | 1,431.80 | 1,434.93 | 1,373.01 | 1,416.28 | 1,413.76 | 1,394.59 | 1,452.96 |
| 2018 | 1,441.65 | 1,459.55 | 1,424.25 | 1,460.77 | 1,418.81 | 1,389.79 | 1,442.81 | 1,421.78 | 1,435.56 | 1,412.60 | 1,479.80 | 1,470.34 | 1,440.14 |
| 2019 | 1,474.47 | 1,440.46 | 1,424.25 | 1,436.63 | 1,460.84 | 1,454.66 | 1,424.68 | 1,471.80 | 1,486.42 | 1,467.00 | 1,511.02 | 1,539.00 | 1,465.88 |
| **Professional and Business Services** | | | | | | | | | | | | | |
| 2015 | 1,199.47 | 1,236.88 | 1,237.23 | 1,201.32 | 1,191.92 | 1,183.78 | 1,178.85 | 1,239.84 | 1,202.54 | 1,210.07 | 1,260.17 | 1,222.37 | 1,213.04 |
| 2016 | 1,232.35 | 1,223.55 | 1,212.70 | 1,220.77 | 1,256.70 | 1,216.95 | 1,206.10 | 1,213.06 | 1,220.30 | 1,279.83 | 1,258.67 | 1,251.59 | 1,232.97 |
| 2017 | 1,289.29 | 1,251.62 | 1,245.64 | 1,305.23 | 1,241.84 | 1,245.05 | 1,299.44 | 1,272.91 | 1,305.73 | 1,366.30 | 1,316.43 | 1,330.74 | 1,288.74 |
| 2018 | 1,333.53 | 1,346.89 | 1,332.25 | 1,426.54 | 1,360.86 | 1,326.37 | 1,410.62 | 1,332.45 | 1,409.43 | 1,398.77 | 1,379.94 | 1,421.54 | 1,375.15 |
| 2019 | 1,364.81 | 1,391.13 | 1,410.86 | 1,404.65 | 1,395.79 | 1,443.26 | 1,410.69 | 1,434.61 | 1,476.60 | 1,442.72 | 1,471.02 | 1,504.32 | 1,428.10 |
| **Education and Health Services** | | | | | | | | | | | | | |
| 2015 | 858.68 | 860.64 | 856.41 | 846.30 | 839.08 | 839.02 | 847.44 | 839.61 | 855.73 | 844.94 | 850.23 | 832.46 | 847.50 |
| 2016 | 841.82 | 831.60 | 837.30 | 843.94 | 844.71 | 839.42 | 858.14 | 845.02 | 850.70 | 848.56 | 843.70 | 830.84 | 842.82 |
| 2017 | 838.30 | 832.26 | 834.57 | 850.82 | 853.65 | 852.72 | 861.72 | 837.64 | 838.42 | 832.79 | 828.95 | 842.06 | 842.73 |
| 2018 | 857.14 | 871.13 | 873.51 | 900.15 | 887.44 | 896.13 | 909.82 | 905.36 | 941.40 | 924.62 | 939.21 | 932.59 | 902.10 |
| 2019 | 925.74 | 917.53 | 919.08 | 918.64 | 922.17 | 928.49 | 923.72 | 915.30 | 928.86 | 917.65 | 934.23 | 911.49 | 920.92 |
| **Leisure and Hospitality** | | | | | | | | | | | | | |
| 2015 | 371.70 | 374.44 | 386.23 | 397.76 | 409.50 | 408.14 | 403.24 | 415.80 | 403.77 | 407.71 | 411.18 | 409.16 | 400.33 |
| 2016 | 386.45 | 401.18 | 403.00 | 401.42 | 402.20 | 397.76 | 398.90 | 401.08 | 409.24 | 396.03 | 390.66 | 389.62 | 398.08 |
| 2017 | 388.80 | 400.56 | 398.48 | 404.79 | 411.34 | 389.63 | 390.20 | 387.35 | 399.54 | 393.47 | 392.18 | 393.88 | 395.78 |
| 2018 | 383.70 | 403.11 | 389.36 | 399.64 | 400.16 | 404.51 | 416.35 | 408.70 | 416.06 | 411.33 | 416.82 | 434.20 | 407.42 |
| 2019 | 422.15 | 430.85 | 435.24 | 445.38 | 441.60 | 445.52 | 450.84 | 452.38 | 465.08 | 438.95 | 440.96 | 442.11 | 443.04 |
| **Other Services** | | | | | | | | | | | | | |
| 2015 | 838.13 | 866.47 | 880.72 | 853.44 | 862.24 | 867.55 | 877.89 | 910.67 | 883.13 | 893.42 | 897.00 | 875.33 | 874.83 |
| 2016 | 883.91 | 891.77 | 917.75 | 890.24 | 908.83 | 912.80 | 907.63 | 915.12 | 915.77 | 939.49 | 897.05 | 894.74 | 907.57 |
| 2017 | 932.07 | 916.72 | 902.80 | 927.05 | 900.24 | 914.23 | 948.03 | 966.21 | 989.08 | 974.69 | 951.16 | 964.49 | 939.91 |
| 2018 | 974.99 | 980.48 | 990.28 | 1,018.37 | 1,016.32 | 1,029.41 | 1,025.31 | 1,008.67 | 1,047.87 | 1,043.12 | 1,035.60 | 1,088.17 | 1,019.98 |
| 2019 | 1,066.92 | 1,085.00 | 1,072.60 | 1,077.75 | 1,086.44 | 1,126.36 | 1,131.74 | 1,105.63 | 1,121.45 | 1,108.77 | 1,092.72 | 1,135.55 | 1,101.10 |

# MASSACHUSETTS
## *At a Glance*

Population:
  2010 census: 6,547,629
  2019 estimate: 6,892,503

Percent change in population
  2010–2019: 5.3%

Percent change in total nonfarm employment:
  2011–2019: 13.2%

Industry with the largest growth in employment, 2011–2019 (percent):
  Construction, 46.3%

Industry with the largest decline or smallest growth in employment, 2011–2019 (percent):
  Mining and logging, -9.1%

Civilian labor force:
  2010: 3,480,083
  2019: 3,817,437

Unemployment rate and rank among states (highest to lowest):
  2010: 8.3%, 30th
  2019: 2.9%, 41st

Over-the-year change in unemployment rates:
  2017–2018: -0.3%
  2018–2019: -0.5%

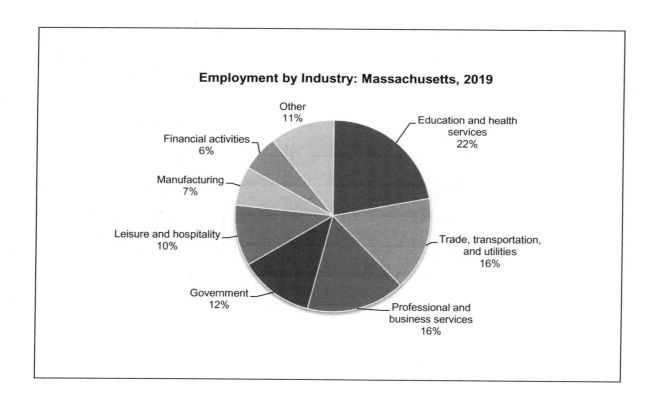

**Employment by Industry: Massachusetts, 2019**

- Other 11%
- Financial activities 6%
- Manufacturing 7%
- Leisure and hospitality 10%
- Government 12%
- Education and health services 22%
- Trade, transportation, and utilities 16%
- Professional and business services 16%

# 1. Employment by Industry: Massachusetts, 2011–2019

(Numbers in thousands, not seasonally adjusted)

| Industry and year | January | February | March | April | May | June | July | August | September | October | November | December | Annual average |
|---|---|---|---|---|---|---|---|---|---|---|---|---|---|
| **Total Nonfarm** | | | | | | | | | | | | | |
| 2011 | 3,166.6 | 3,179.3 | 3,194.1 | 3,250.8 | 3,271.4 | 3,288.8 | 3,283.3 | 3,266.7 | 3,294.5 | 3,307.6 | 3,304.8 | 3,305.0 | 3,259.4 |
| 2012 | 3,216.5 | 3,226.8 | 3,254.1 | 3,291.6 | 3,320.8 | 3,359.5 | 3,328.5 | 3,320.0 | 3,339.5 | 3,354.8 | 3,359.4 | 3,353.1 | 3,310.4 |
| 2013 | 3,258.8 | 3,273.2 | 3,298.5 | 3,353.6 | 3,387.6 | 3,417.1 | 3,383.8 | 3,378.4 | 3,390.0 | 3,413.1 | 3,416.1 | 3,414.7 | 3,365.4 |
| 2014 | 3,313.3 | 3,332.0 | 3,353.3 | 3,413.6 | 3,449.7 | 3,476.8 | 3,457.2 | 3,436.9 | 3,462.7 | 3,491.9 | 3,499.2 | 3,499.9 | 3,432.2 |
| 2015 | 3,384.5 | 3,387.8 | 3,417.6 | 3,478.6 | 3,523.7 | 3,553.0 | 3,537.2 | 3,519.4 | 3,518.4 | 3,553.3 | 3,557.5 | 3,556.8 | 3,499.0 |
| 2016 | 3,450.0 | 3,468.7 | 3,494.6 | 3,551.7 | 3,579.3 | 3,607.6 | 3,608.1 | 3,592.7 | 3,598.1 | 3,607.0 | 3,613.6 | 3,610.1 | 3,565.1 |
| 2017 | 3,506.8 | 3,520.3 | 3,540.2 | 3,595.1 | 3,626.9 | 3,672.8 | 3,647.9 | 3,634.0 | 3,635.5 | 3,652.4 | 3,657.3 | 3,654.6 | 3,612.0 |
| 2018 | 3,546.9 | 3,574.4 | 3,587.0 | 3,637.4 | 3,671.7 | 3,714.3 | 3,682.9 | 3,665.1 | 3,669.6 | 3,695.3 | 3,698.6 | 3,696.7 | 3,653.3 |
| 2019 | 3,592.3 | 3,616.8 | 3,631.1 | 3,674.3 | 3,710.2 | 3,747.2 | 3,726.5 | 3,708.2 | 3,701.9 | 3,728.1 | 3,729.6 | 3,711.3 | 3,689.8 |
| **Total Private** | | | | | | | | | | | | | |
| 2011 | 2,733.8 | 2,734.1 | 2,748.5 | 2,805.4 | 2,823.9 | 2,852.8 | 2,881.4 | 2,873.3 | 2,858.2 | 2,864.5 | 2,861.0 | 2,859.3 | 2,824.7 |
| 2012 | 2,784.8 | 2,782.9 | 2,807.1 | 2,844.9 | 2,872.5 | 2,920.5 | 2,924.8 | 2,922.3 | 2,899.2 | 2,907.9 | 2,907.8 | 2,903.5 | 2,873.2 |
| 2013 | 2,825.0 | 2,822.2 | 2,846.1 | 2,897.0 | 2,931.5 | 2,972.7 | 2,975.1 | 2,976.4 | 2,948.3 | 2,959.2 | 2,958.0 | 2,956.2 | 2,922.3 |
| 2014 | 2,869.3 | 2,873.9 | 2,894.6 | 2,949.0 | 2,986.5 | 3,025.8 | 3,040.1 | 3,027.7 | 3,008.7 | 3,029.1 | 3,029.5 | 3,032.5 | 2,980.6 |
| 2015 | 2,940.2 | 2,928.6 | 2,954.4 | 3,013.1 | 3,062.4 | 3,098.6 | 3,117.9 | 3,111.2 | 3,069.7 | 3,092.9 | 3,093.8 | 3,091.7 | 3,047.9 |
| 2016 | 3,005.2 | 3,009.4 | 3,028.6 | 3,087.9 | 3,115.2 | 3,153.5 | 3,185.8 | 3,178.8 | 3,140.4 | 3,143.9 | 3,143.1 | 3,143.8 | 3,111.3 |
| 2017 | 3,057.8 | 3,059.6 | 3,079.1 | 3,131.7 | 3,163.5 | 3,215.8 | 3,228.4 | 3,222.2 | 3,183.0 | 3,190.4 | 3,191.7 | 3,189.6 | 3,159.4 |
| 2018 | 3,100.3 | 3,112.8 | 3,126.9 | 3,173.7 | 3,206.8 | 3,255.1 | 3,261.5 | 3,253.5 | 3,211.8 | 3,231.2 | 3,227.9 | 3,228.1 | 3,199.1 |
| 2019 | 3,144.7 | 3,153.0 | 3,166.3 | 3,207.3 | 3,239.5 | 3,285.7 | 3,300.4 | 3,291.4 | 3,242.8 | 3,260.8 | 3,257.1 | 3,240.6 | 3,232.5 |
| **Goods Producing** | | | | | | | | | | | | | |
| 2011 | 345.6 | 342.0 | 344.5 | 356.2 | 362.5 | 369.5 | 373.7 | 374.2 | 370.7 | 369.3 | 367.1 | 363.6 | 361.6 |
| 2012 | 352.3 | 348.8 | 352.9 | 360.8 | 365.4 | 373.7 | 374.7 | 375.1 | 372.1 | 372.6 | 371.1 | 367.9 | 365.6 |
| 2013 | 355.8 | 353.1 | 355.7 | 364.3 | 372.6 | 379.3 | 381.3 | 382.2 | 379.0 | 378.0 | 375.9 | 372.4 | 370.8 |
| 2014 | 361.5 | 358.2 | 360.1 | 369.4 | 377.6 | 384.0 | 386.3 | 386.7 | 383.2 | 384.3 | 384.2 | 381.3 | 376.4 |
| 2015 | 369.5 | 364.6 | 367.5 | 380.2 | 389.3 | 395.5 | 397.5 | 397.7 | 392.8 | 394.2 | 393.3 | 391.1 | 386.1 |
| 2016 | 379.0 | 373.4 | 377.5 | 386.6 | 392.7 | 399.0 | 400.4 | 399.9 | 396.0 | 396.0 | 394.4 | 391.9 | 390.6 |
| 2017 | 379.3 | 376.0 | 378.4 | 388.8 | 395.4 | 403.3 | 406.7 | 407.3 | 403.6 | 404.2 | 402.6 | 398.5 | 395.3 |
| 2018 | 385.7 | 385.4 | 388.1 | 397.4 | 404.9 | 412.5 | 412.4 | 411.0 | 407.4 | 408.9 | 406.6 | 404.0 | 402.0 |
| 2019 | 394.6 | 392.6 | 394.8 | 403.7 | 409.6 | 416.0 | 416.4 | 416.1 | 412.1 | 412.6 | 411.0 | 404.6 | 407.0 |
| **Service-Providing** | | | | | | | | | | | | | |
| 2011 | 2,821.0 | 2,837.3 | 2,849.6 | 2,894.6 | 2,908.9 | 2,919.3 | 2,909.6 | 2,892.5 | 2,923.8 | 2,938.3 | 2,937.7 | 2,941.4 | 2,897.8 |
| 2012 | 2,864.2 | 2,878.0 | 2,901.2 | 2,930.8 | 2,955.4 | 2,985.8 | 2,953.8 | 2,944.9 | 2,967.4 | 2,982.2 | 2,988.3 | 2,985.2 | 2,944.8 |
| 2013 | 2,903.0 | 2,920.1 | 2,942.8 | 2,989.3 | 3,015.0 | 3,037.8 | 3,002.5 | 2,996.2 | 3,011.0 | 3,035.1 | 3,040.2 | 3,042.3 | 2,994.6 |
| 2014 | 2,951.8 | 2,973.8 | 2,993.2 | 3,044.2 | 3,072.1 | 3,092.8 | 3,070.9 | 3,050.2 | 3,079.5 | 3,107.6 | 3,115.0 | 3,118.6 | 3,055.8 |
| 2015 | 3,015.0 | 3,023.2 | 3,050.1 | 3,098.4 | 3,134.4 | 3,157.5 | 3,139.7 | 3,121.7 | 3,125.6 | 3,159.1 | 3,164.2 | 3,165.7 | 3,112.9 |
| 2016 | 3,071.0 | 3,095.3 | 3,117.1 | 3,165.1 | 3,186.6 | 3,208.6 | 3,207.7 | 3,192.8 | 3,202.1 | 3,211.0 | 3,219.2 | 3,218.2 | 3,174.6 |
| 2017 | 3,127.5 | 3,144.3 | 3,161.8 | 3,206.3 | 3,231.5 | 3,269.5 | 3,241.2 | 3,226.7 | 3,231.9 | 3,248.2 | 3,254.7 | 3,256.1 | 3,216.6 |
| 2018 | 3,161.2 | 3,189.0 | 3,198.9 | 3,240.0 | 3,266.8 | 3,301.8 | 3,270.5 | 3,254.1 | 3,262.2 | 3,286.4 | 3,292.0 | 3,292.7 | 3,251.3 |
| 2019 | 3,197.7 | 3,224.2 | 3,236.3 | 3,270.6 | 3,300.6 | 3,331.2 | 3,310.1 | 3,292.1 | 3,289.8 | 3,315.5 | 3,318.6 | 3,306.7 | 3,282.8 |
| **Mining and Logging** | | | | | | | | | | | | | |
| 2011 | 0.9 | 0.9 | 0.9 | 1.1 | 1.2 | 1.2 | 1.2 | 1.2 | 1.2 | 1.2 | 1.1 | 1.1 | 1.1 |
| 2012 | 0.9 | 0.8 | 0.9 | 0.9 | 1.0 | 1.0 | 1.0 | 1.0 | 1.0 | 1.0 | 1.0 | 1.0 | 1.0 |
| 2013 | 0.8 | 0.8 | 0.9 | 1.0 | 1.0 | 1.0 | 1.0 | 1.1 | 1.1 | 1.1 | 1.0 | 1.0 | 1.0 |
| 2014 | 0.9 | 0.9 | 0.9 | 1.0 | 1.1 | 1.1 | 1.1 | 1.1 | 1.1 | 1.1 | 1.1 | 1.0 | 1.0 |
| 2015 | 0.9 | 0.9 | 0.9 | 1.1 | 1.1 | 1.1 | 1.2 | 1.1 | 1.2 | 1.1 | 1.1 | 1.1 | 1.1 |
| 2016 | 1.0 | 1.0 | 1.0 | 1.1 | 1.2 | 1.2 | 1.2 | 1.2 | 1.2 | 1.2 | 1.1 | 1.1 | 1.1 |
| 2017 | 1.0 | 1.0 | 1.0 | 1.1 | 1.1 | 1.2 | 1.2 | 1.2 | 1.2 | 1.2 | 1.2 | 1.1 | 1.1 |
| 2018 | 1.0 | 1.0 | 1.0 | 1.1 | 1.1 | 1.1 | 1.1 | 1.1 | 1.1 | 1.1 | 1.1 | 1.0 | 1.1 |
| 2019 | 0.9 | 0.9 | 0.9 | 1.0 | 1.1 | 1.1 | 1.1 | 1.1 | 1.1 | 1.1 | 1.1 | 1.0 | 1.0 |
| **Construction** | | | | | | | | | | | | | |
| 2011 | 96.8 | 94.2 | 95.8 | 105.9 | 111.7 | 116.7 | 120.7 | 121.1 | 119.4 | 118.0 | 116.4 | 112.6 | 110.8 |
| 2012 | 103.4 | 100.4 | 103.9 | 111.5 | 115.6 | 120.5 | 123.5 | 123.9 | 122.1 | 122.5 | 121.3 | 118.0 | 115.6 |
| 2013 | 108.9 | 106.8 | 108.7 | 116.9 | 124.3 | 128.5 | 131.9 | 132.3 | 130.2 | 129.6 | 127.6 | 123.3 | 122.4 |
| 2014 | 114.9 | 112.4 | 113.9 | 122.9 | 130.5 | 135.1 | 138.1 | 138.2 | 136.5 | 137.2 | 136.5 | 133.1 | 129.1 |
| 2015 | 123.8 | 119.0 | 121.4 | 133.3 | 141.8 | 145.9 | 148.9 | 149.4 | 146.6 | 148.2 | 146.9 | 144.4 | 139.1 |
| 2016 | 135.0 | 130.6 | 134.1 | 143.2 | 148.7 | 152.3 | 155.0 | 154.4 | 152.5 | 152.7 | 151.4 | 148.1 | 146.5 |
| 2017 | 137.6 | 134.8 | 137.2 | 147.0 | 153.3 | 158.3 | 161.5 | 161.9 | 160.2 | 160.4 | 158.8 | 153.6 | 152.1 |
| 2018 | 143.4 | 143.7 | 146.0 | 154.9 | 161.7 | 166.5 | 167.1 | 166.6 | 164.7 | 165.8 | 163.3 | 159.4 | 158.6 |
| 2019 | 150.5 | 148.8 | 150.5 | 159.3 | 164.6 | 168.8 | 169.9 | 170.2 | 168.4 | 168.0 | 166.3 | 160.3 | 162.1 |

## 1. Employment by Industry: Massachusetts, 2011–2019—*Continued*

(Numbers in thousands, not seasonally adjusted)

| Industry and year | January | February | March | April | May | June | July | August | September | October | November | December | Annual average |
|---|---|---|---|---|---|---|---|---|---|---|---|---|---|
| **Manufacturing** | | | | | | | | | | | | | |
| 2011 | 247.9 | 246.9 | 247.8 | 249.2 | 249.6 | 251.6 | 251.8 | 251.9 | 250.1 | 250.1 | 249.6 | 249.9 | 249.7 |
| 2012 | 248.0 | 247.6 | 248.1 | 248.4 | 248.8 | 252.2 | 250.2 | 250.2 | 249.0 | 249.1 | 248.8 | 248.9 | 249.1 |
| 2013 | 246.1 | 245.5 | 246.1 | 246.4 | 247.3 | 249.8 | 248.4 | 248.8 | 247.7 | 247.3 | 247.3 | 248.1 | 247.4 |
| 2014 | 245.7 | 244.9 | 245.3 | 245.5 | 246.0 | 247.8 | 247.1 | 247.4 | 245.6 | 246.0 | 246.6 | 247.2 | 246.3 |
| 2015 | 244.8 | 244.7 | 245.2 | 245.8 | 246.4 | 248.5 | 247.4 | 247.2 | 245.0 | 244.9 | 245.3 | 245.6 | 245.9 |
| 2016 | 243.0 | 241.8 | 242.4 | 242.3 | 242.8 | 245.5 | 244.2 | 244.3 | 242.3 | 242.1 | 241.9 | 242.7 | 242.9 |
| 2017 | 240.7 | 240.2 | 240.2 | 240.7 | 241.0 | 243.8 | 244.0 | 244.2 | 242.2 | 242.6 | 242.6 | 243.8 | 242.2 |
| 2018 | 241.3 | 240.7 | 241.1 | 241.4 | 242.1 | 244.9 | 244.2 | 243.3 | 241.6 | 242.0 | 242.2 | 243.6 | 242.4 |
| 2019 | 243.2 | 242.9 | 243.4 | 243.4 | 243.9 | 246.1 | 245.4 | 244.8 | 242.6 | 243.5 | 243.6 | 243.3 | 243.8 |
| **Trade, Transportation, and Utilities** | | | | | | | | | | | | | |
| 2011 | 541.1 | 533.9 | 533.9 | 540.3 | 544.3 | 551.1 | 548.9 | 548.7 | 547.7 | 551.8 | 559.5 | 567.0 | 547.4 |
| 2012 | 545.2 | 535.0 | 537.1 | 539.8 | 547.7 | 557.6 | 552.1 | 551.8 | 549.9 | 554.7 | 565.0 | 570.4 | 550.5 |
| 2013 | 547.8 | 539.0 | 540.7 | 546.2 | 553.8 | 563.2 | 557.3 | 557.9 | 555.7 | 558.3 | 567.4 | 575.4 | 555.2 |
| 2014 | 555.2 | 547.3 | 548.3 | 553.7 | 560.1 | 568.6 | 562.7 | 552.3 | 562.2 | 567.7 | 577.7 | 586.7 | 561.9 |
| 2015 | 563.0 | 550.5 | 552.7 | 559.2 | 567.0 | 576.3 | 572.3 | 571.9 | 568.0 | 572.7 | 581.4 | 588.3 | 568.6 |
| 2016 | 567.4 | 559.4 | 560.6 | 566.4 | 572.3 | 580.9 | 579.1 | 578.5 | 573.4 | 576.7 | 585.6 | 594.3 | 574.6 |
| 2017 | 574.0 | 564.0 | 564.1 | 570.4 | 576.4 | 587.5 | 584.1 | 583.5 | 579.0 | 582.2 | 592.0 | 598.9 | 579.7 |
| 2018 | 579.5 | 570.2 | 568.1 | 571.4 | 578.3 | 588.5 | 582.9 | 581.1 | 575.8 | 577.9 | 589.5 | 596.9 | 580.0 |
| 2019 | 578.0 | 568.8 | 567.2 | 568.9 | 576.4 | 585.1 | 582.4 | 581.0 | 576.0 | 580.2 | 586.9 | 593.5 | 578.7 |
| **Wholesale Trade** | | | | | | | | | | | | | |
| 2011 | 120.4 | 120.2 | 119.9 | 121.3 | 121.3 | 121.6 | 122.5 | 121.8 | 120.4 | 120.4 | 120.0 | 120.1 | 120.8 |
| 2012 | 119.1 | 118.8 | 119.2 | 120.3 | 120.9 | 122.1 | 122.2 | 122.3 | 121.0 | 121.7 | 121.7 | 121.6 | 120.9 |
| 2013 | 120.4 | 120.2 | 120.6 | 121.5 | 121.9 | 123.0 | 123.5 | 123.4 | 122.4 | 122.8 | 122.7 | 122.7 | 122.1 |
| 2014 | 121.4 | 121.1 | 121.3 | 122.4 | 122.8 | 123.8 | 124.0 | 123.7 | 122.6 | 122.8 | 122.9 | 123.0 | 122.7 |
| 2015 | 121.4 | 120.6 | 120.7 | 122.3 | 122.8 | 123.9 | 124.5 | 124.3 | 123.2 | 123.5 | 123.4 | 123.5 | 122.8 |
| 2016 | 122.3 | 122.0 | 122.1 | 123.5 | 123.8 | 124.8 | 126.0 | 125.9 | 124.6 | 124.8 | 124.4 | 124.5 | 124.1 |
| 2017 | 123.2 | 123.1 | 123.3 | 124.5 | 125.0 | 126.3 | 126.5 | 126.2 | 124.6 | 124.7 | 124.6 | 124.7 | 124.7 |
| 2018 | 123.5 | 123.5 | 123.7 | 123.7 | 124.0 | 125.5 | 125.1 | 124.6 | 123.1 | 123.8 | 123.6 | 123.8 | 124.0 |
| 2019 | 122.5 | 122.1 | 122.0 | 122.7 | 123.5 | 124.3 | 125.1 | 124.9 | 123.4 | 124.7 | 124.8 | 125.0 | 123.8 |
| **Retail Trade** | | | | | | | | | | | | | |
| 2011 | 338.8 | 332.0 | 331.9 | 336.1 | 339.0 | 344.0 | 345.0 | 346.5 | 341.7 | 346.2 | 354.4 | 360.4 | 343.0 |
| 2012 | 343.3 | 333.8 | 335.1 | 336.4 | 342.3 | 349.3 | 348.1 | 348.6 | 343.1 | 347.0 | 357.6 | 360.8 | 345.5 |
| 2013 | 343.6 | 334.9 | 336.1 | 339.8 | 345.4 | 351.8 | 349.9 | 351.6 | 345.3 | 347.6 | 356.6 | 362.7 | 347.1 |
| 2014 | 347.2 | 339.6 | 339.9 | 343.2 | 347.1 | 352.7 | 351.3 | 342.1 | 347.5 | 352.8 | 361.8 | 367.3 | 349.4 |
| 2015 | 351.3 | 340.4 | 342.2 | 345.7 | 351.3 | 357.7 | 357.1 | 357.5 | 349.8 | 354.3 | 362.9 | 368.0 | 353.2 |
| 2016 | 352.5 | 345.3 | 346.3 | 349.3 | 353.3 | 359.3 | 360.1 | 360.7 | 351.7 | 353.9 | 362.2 | 367.6 | 355.2 |
| 2017 | 353.5 | 344.3 | 344.2 | 348.5 | 352.0 | 359.3 | 359.9 | 360.3 | 351.9 | 355.0 | 364.2 | 368.0 | 355.1 |
| 2018 | 354.8 | 346.5 | 344.1 | 346.7 | 351.7 | 358.5 | 358.7 | 357.8 | 349.3 | 350.6 | 362.0 | 366.6 | 353.9 |
| 2019 | 353.6 | 344.6 | 343.3 | 343.6 | 348.1 | 354.2 | 355.1 | 354.8 | 346.6 | 349.8 | 356.2 | 359.4 | 350.8 |
| **Transportation and Utilities** | | | | | | | | | | | | | |
| 2011 | 81.9 | 81.7 | 82.1 | 82.9 | 84.0 | 85.5 | 81.4 | 80.4 | 85.6 | 85.2 | 85.1 | 86.5 | 83.5 |
| 2012 | 82.8 | 82.4 | 82.8 | 83.1 | 84.5 | 86.2 | 81.8 | 80.9 | 85.8 | 86.0 | 85.7 | 88.0 | 84.2 |
| 2013 | 83.8 | 83.9 | 84.0 | 84.9 | 86.5 | 88.4 | 83.9 | 82.9 | 88.0 | 87.9 | 88.1 | 90.0 | 86.0 |
| 2014 | 86.6 | 86.6 | 87.1 | 88.1 | 90.2 | 92.1 | 87.4 | 86.5 | 92.1 | 92.1 | 93.0 | 96.4 | 89.9 |
| 2015 | 90.3 | 89.5 | 89.8 | 91.2 | 92.9 | 94.7 | 90.7 | 90.1 | 95.0 | 94.9 | 95.1 | 96.8 | 92.6 |
| 2016 | 92.6 | 92.1 | 92.2 | 93.6 | 95.2 | 96.8 | 93.0 | 91.9 | 97.1 | 98.0 | 99.0 | 102.2 | 95.3 |
| 2017 | 97.3 | 96.6 | 96.6 | 97.4 | 99.4 | 101.9 | 97.7 | 97.0 | 102.5 | 102.5 | 103.2 | 106.2 | 99.9 |
| 2018 | 101.2 | 100.2 | 100.3 | 101.0 | 102.6 | 104.5 | 99.1 | 98.7 | 103.4 | 103.5 | 103.9 | 106.5 | 102.1 |
| 2019 | 101.9 | 102.1 | 101.9 | 102.6 | 104.8 | 106.6 | 102.2 | 101.3 | 106.0 | 105.7 | 105.9 | 109.1 | 104.2 |
| **Information** | | | | | | | | | | | | | |
| 2011 | 83.6 | 83.7 | 84.1 | 84.1 | 84.6 | 85.8 | 87.1 | 83.5 | 85.7 | 85.8 | 85.6 | 86.0 | 85.0 |
| 2012 | 85.7 | 85.4 | 85.7 | 86.0 | 86.6 | 88.5 | 89.6 | 88.9 | 86.4 | 86.5 | 86.0 | 85.9 | 86.8 |
| 2013 | 85.0 | 85.1 | 85.1 | 85.6 | 86.0 | 87.7 | 88.1 | 87.9 | 86.7 | 86.3 | 88.0 | 86.6 | 86.5 |
| 2014 | 85.0 | 85.2 | 85.3 | 86.0 | 86.9 | 88.2 | 88.6 | 88.2 | 87.1 | 87.2 | 87.4 | 87.8 | 86.9 |
| 2015 | 87.5 | 87.2 | 87.5 | 87.9 | 88.1 | 89.4 | 89.9 | 89.6 | 88.3 | 88.9 | 89.1 | 89.2 | 88.6 |
| 2016 | 88.9 | 89.0 | 88.4 | 89.4 | 86.3 | 90.2 | 91.1 | 91.7 | 90.6 | 90.6 | 90.6 | 90.6 | 89.8 |
| 2017 | 89.8 | 91.0 | 90.7 | 91.2 | 92.6 | 92.4 | 93.0 | 93.7 | 92.0 | 91.7 | 92.0 | 92.1 | 91.9 |
| 2018 | 90.7 | 91.4 | 90.4 | 90.4 | 90.1 | 91.6 | 92.1 | 92.9 | 91.1 | 92.5 | 92.3 | 91.8 | 91.4 |
| 2019 | 90.0 | 90.5 | 90.3 | 90.4 | 92.0 | 93.3 | 95.3 | 96.0 | 92.4 | 92.7 | 94.6 | 94.0 | 92.6 |

# 1. Employment by Industry: Massachusetts, 2011–2019—*Continued*

(Numbers in thousands, not seasonally adjusted)

| Industry and year | January | February | March | April | May | June | July | August | September | October | November | December | Annual average |
|---|---|---|---|---|---|---|---|---|---|---|---|---|---|
| **Financial Activities** | | | | | | | | | | | | | |
| 2011 | 212.4 | 212.1 | 212.1 | 213.0 | 213.3 | 215.5 | 217.4 | 217.4 | 214.7 | 213.9 | 213.1 | 213.5 | 214.0 |
| 2012 | 211.4 | 211.5 | 211.5 | 211.8 | 212.8 | 215.9 | 216.5 | 216.7 | 213.4 | 213.0 | 212.7 | 213.3 | 213.4 |
| 2013 | 211.1 | 211.2 | 211.6 | 211.9 | 213.2 | 216.1 | 216.8 | 217.4 | 213.8 | 213.5 | 213.4 | 214.1 | 213.7 |
| 2014 | 211.6 | 211.4 | 211.6 | 212.6 | 214.3 | 217.1 | 218.1 | 218.0 | 214.7 | 215.0 | 215.1 | 215.8 | 214.6 |
| 2015 | 213.5 | 213.0 | 213.1 | 214.1 | 215.6 | 218.7 | 222.0 | 222.2 | 218.0 | 218.6 | 218.9 | 219.1 | 217.2 |
| 2016 | 217.6 | 217.7 | 217.2 | 218.7 | 219.8 | 222.6 | 225.6 | 225.6 | 221.4 | 220.6 | 220.3 | 221.4 | 220.7 |
| 2017 | 218.8 | 219.0 | 218.8 | 219.4 | 220.7 | 225.0 | 225.8 | 225.8 | 222.0 | 221.6 | 221.0 | 222.0 | 221.7 |
| 2018 | 219.5 | 219.8 | 220.0 | 220.8 | 221.5 | 225.4 | 226.2 | 226.0 | 222.5 | 222.6 | 222.5 | 222.7 | 222.5 |
| 2019 | 221.8 | 221.9 | 221.4 | 221.9 | 222.9 | 225.9 | 229.0 | 228.6 | 224.1 | 223.6 | 223.9 | 223.8 | 224.1 |
| **Professional and Business Services** | | | | | | | | | | | | | |
| 2011 | 467.8 | 468.7 | 468.7 | 485.3 | 485.6 | 492.2 | 497.5 | 495.9 | 493.1 | 496.4 | 496.2 | 493.9 | 486.8 |
| 2012 | 480.2 | 480.6 | 486.8 | 497.7 | 500.1 | 509.6 | 510.5 | 510.5 | 506.4 | 508.8 | 509.6 | 505.1 | 500.5 |
| 2013 | 492.7 | 495.9 | 498.5 | 512.3 | 516.1 | 523.8 | 525.2 | 525.9 | 519.7 | 522.6 | 523.7 | 520.4 | 514.7 |
| 2014 | 506.3 | 507.3 | 509.1 | 523.8 | 528.1 | 536.2 | 539.5 | 540.6 | 535.6 | 539.5 | 538.8 | 535.9 | 528.4 |
| 2015 | 521.5 | 521.6 | 524.8 | 540.3 | 547.2 | 555.3 | 559.4 | 559.2 | 550.9 | 557.1 | 557.2 | 552.8 | 545.6 |
| 2016 | 536.8 | 539.1 | 541.3 | 558.4 | 560.7 | 569.6 | 576.9 | 576.5 | 569.0 | 571.7 | 571.7 | 567.8 | 561.6 |
| 2017 | 553.4 | 555.5 | 558.7 | 571.7 | 574.2 | 584.4 | 588.3 | 586.4 | 579.0 | 581.8 | 582.6 | 577.0 | 574.4 |
| 2018 | 563.9 | 566.3 | 570.0 | 583.5 | 587.6 | 599.0 | 603.3 | 603.5 | 594.5 | 599.5 | 602.5 | 598.4 | 589.3 |
| 2019 | 579.2 | 583.7 | 583.8 | 599.3 | 602.4 | 612.4 | 616.2 | 616.0 | 606.5 | 610.3 | 609.1 | 599.7 | 601.6 |
| **Education and Health Services** | | | | | | | | | | | | | |
| 2011 | 682.9 | 694.2 | 698.1 | 700.0 | 693.4 | 677.9 | 682.9 | 680.7 | 695.2 | 704.6 | 709.3 | 709.3 | 694.0 |
| 2012 | 696.5 | 708.2 | 712.4 | 711.7 | 706.9 | 694.5 | 694.6 | 693.2 | 706.4 | 717.3 | 721.8 | 722.0 | 707.1 |
| 2013 | 708.1 | 715.8 | 721.4 | 725.8 | 720.7 | 708.9 | 707.0 | 703.6 | 714.3 | 726.6 | 729.5 | 731.3 | 717.8 |
| 2014 | 711.5 | 726.5 | 731.9 | 740.3 | 735.4 | 724.0 | 727.9 | 725.3 | 734.4 | 749.9 | 755.2 | 755.8 | 734.8 |
| 2015 | 734.9 | 748.3 | 754.9 | 760.6 | 760.3 | 747.0 | 749.0 | 745.3 | 754.0 | 770.1 | 775.4 | 774.3 | 756.2 |
| 2016 | 756.3 | 772.0 | 775.8 | 781.1 | 778.7 | 761.4 | 770.9 | 766.6 | 778.5 | 787.1 | 791.4 | 791.6 | 776.0 |
| 2017 | 773.2 | 787.2 | 792.4 | 796.0 | 792.9 | 781.4 | 782.4 | 779.3 | 790.4 | 797.8 | 802.5 | 804.8 | 790.0 |
| 2018 | 781.4 | 798.7 | 802.6 | 807.4 | 802.8 | 789.9 | 789.5 | 784.4 | 796.5 | 810.8 | 813.5 | 814.8 | 799.4 |
| 2019 | 796.4 | 813.2 | 819.1 | 820.1 | 813.4 | 800.7 | 801.2 | 797.5 | 807.2 | 823.1 | 828.8 | 824.3 | 812.1 |
| **Leisure and Hospitality** | | | | | | | | | | | | | |
| 2011 | 284.9 | 283.6 | 289.5 | 307.0 | 319.9 | 337.2 | 347.4 | 347.1 | 330.9 | 322.9 | 310.4 | 306.0 | 315.6 |
| 2012 | 296.1 | 295.9 | 301.5 | 316.3 | 330.8 | 353.8 | 358.2 | 358.6 | 341.2 | 331.8 | 318.3 | 315.4 | 326.5 |
| 2013 | 303.1 | 300.7 | 309.3 | 325.0 | 341.7 | 361.5 | 365.1 | 365.5 | 350.1 | 345.2 | 331.1 | 326.3 | 335.6 |
| 2014 | 311.0 | 310.3 | 318.1 | 331.2 | 350.3 | 369.1 | 376.4 | 376.8 | 357.8 | 352.1 | 337.9 | 335.8 | 343.9 |
| 2015 | 319.8 | 314.6 | 322.6 | 337.7 | 360.2 | 377.0 | 385.8 | 384.3 | 363.2 | 356.9 | 344.5 | 342.7 | 350.8 |
| 2016 | 327.8 | 327.4 | 334.4 | 351.8 | 368.0 | 388.6 | 398.0 | 397.1 | 375.8 | 365.4 | 353.8 | 350.7 | 361.6 |
| 2017 | 336.3 | 334.3 | 341.4 | 358.5 | 374.3 | 399.5 | 404.3 | 403.1 | 380.5 | 374.9 | 362.8 | 360.0 | 369.2 |
| 2018 | 345.1 | 346.4 | 351.9 | 364.8 | 382.2 | 403.2 | 409.2 | 409.5 | 386.0 | 381.4 | 363.6 | 362.0 | 375.4 |
| 2019 | 349.7 | 347.3 | 353.2 | 365.2 | 383.6 | 408.2 | 413.5 | 411.0 | 387.0 | 379.7 | 365.3 | 363.9 | 377.3 |
| **Other Services** | | | | | | | | | | | | | |
| 2011 | 115.5 | 115.9 | 117.6 | 119.5 | 120.3 | 123.6 | 126.5 | 125.8 | 120.2 | 119.8 | 119.8 | 120.0 | 120.4 |
| 2012 | 117.4 | 117.5 | 119.2 | 120.8 | 122.2 | 126.9 | 128.6 | 127.5 | 123.4 | 123.2 | 123.3 | 123.5 | 122.8 |
| 2013 | 121.4 | 121.4 | 123.8 | 125.9 | 127.4 | 132.2 | 134.3 | 134.0 | 129.0 | 128.7 | 129.0 | 129.7 | 128.1 |
| 2014 | 127.2 | 127.7 | 130.2 | 132.0 | 133.8 | 138.6 | 140.6 | 139.8 | 133.7 | 133.4 | 133.2 | 133.4 | 133.6 |
| 2015 | 130.5 | 128.8 | 131.3 | 133.1 | 134.7 | 139.4 | 142.0 | 141.0 | 134.5 | 134.4 | 134.0 | 134.2 | 134.8 |
| 2016 | 131.4 | 131.4 | 133.4 | 135.5 | 136.7 | 141.2 | 143.8 | 142.9 | 135.7 | 135.8 | 135.3 | 135.5 | 136.6 |
| 2017 | 133.0 | 132.6 | 134.6 | 135.7 | 137.0 | 142.3 | 143.8 | 143.1 | 136.5 | 136.2 | 136.2 | 136.3 | 137.3 |
| 2018 | 134.5 | 134.6 | 135.8 | 138.0 | 139.4 | 145.0 | 145.9 | 145.1 | 138.0 | 137.6 | 137.4 | 137.5 | 139.1 |
| 2019 | 135.0 | 135.0 | 136.5 | 137.8 | 139.2 | 144.1 | 146.4 | 145.2 | 137.5 | 138.6 | 137.5 | 136.8 | 139.1 |
| **Government** | | | | | | | | | | | | | |
| 2011 | 432.8 | 445.2 | 445.6 | 445.4 | 447.5 | 436.0 | 401.9 | 393.4 | 436.3 | 443.1 | 443.8 | 445.7 | 434.7 |
| 2012 | 431.7 | 443.9 | 447.0 | 446.7 | 448.3 | 439.0 | 403.7 | 397.7 | 440.3 | 446.9 | 451.6 | 449.6 | 437.2 |
| 2013 | 433.8 | 451.0 | 452.4 | 456.6 | 456.1 | 444.4 | 408.7 | 402.0 | 441.7 | 453.9 | 458.1 | 458.5 | 443.1 |
| 2014 | 444.0 | 458.1 | 458.7 | 464.6 | 463.2 | 451.0 | 417.1 | 409.2 | 454.0 | 462.8 | 469.7 | 467.4 | 451.7 |
| 2015 | 444.3 | 459.2 | 463.2 | 465.5 | 461.3 | 454.4 | 419.3 | 408.2 | 448.7 | 460.4 | 463.7 | 465.1 | 451.1 |
| 2016 | 444.8 | 459.3 | 466.0 | 463.8 | 464.1 | 454.1 | 422.3 | 413.9 | 457.7 | 463.1 | 470.5 | 466.3 | 453.8 |
| 2017 | 449.0 | 460.7 | 461.1 | 463.4 | 463.4 | 457.0 | 419.5 | 411.8 | 452.5 | 462.0 | 465.6 | 465.0 | 452.6 |
| 2018 | 446.6 | 461.6 | 460.1 | 463.7 | 464.9 | 459.2 | 421.4 | 411.6 | 457.8 | 464.1 | 470.7 | 468.6 | 454.2 |
| 2019 | 447.6 | 463.8 | 464.8 | 467.0 | 470.7 | 461.5 | 426.1 | 416.8 | 459.1 | 467.3 | 472.5 | 470.7 | 457.3 |

## 2. Average Weekly Hours by Selected Industry: Massachusetts, 2015–2019

(Not seasonally adjusted)

| Industry and year | January | February | March | April | May | June | July | August | September | October | November | December | Annual average |
|---|---|---|---|---|---|---|---|---|---|---|---|---|---|
| **Total Private** | | | | | | | | | | | | | |
| 2015 | 33.1 | 33.0 | 33.4 | 33.3 | 33.5 | 33.5 | 33.6 | 33.9 | 33.5 | 33.5 | 33.8 | 33.7 | 33.5 |
| 2016 | 33.2 | 33.0 | 33.2 | 33.3 | 33.7 | 33.5 | 33.6 | 33.5 | 33.5 | 33.8 | 33.4 | 33.5 | 33.5 |
| 2017 | 33.6 | 33.0 | 33.0 | 33.6 | 33.4 | 33.4 | 33.7 | 33.5 | 33.6 | 33.7 | 33.5 | 33.5 | 33.5 |
| 2018 | 33.1 | 33.2 | 32.5 | 33.6 | 33.4 | 33.4 | 33.7 | 33.5 | 33.6 | 33.2 | 33.4 | 33.8 | 33.4 |
| 2019 | 33.0 | 33.0 | 32.9 | 33.1 | 33.1 | 33.4 | 33.3 | 33.3 | 33.5 | 33.1 | 33.2 | 33.4 | 33.2 |
| **Goods-Producing** | | | | | | | | | | | | | |
| 2015 | 39.3 | 38.0 | 39.5 | 39.2 | 39.6 | 39.9 | 39.5 | 39.9 | 38.8 | 39.4 | 39.5 | 40.3 | 39.4 |
| 2016 | 39.6 | 38.9 | 39.6 | 39.4 | 40.0 | 40.1 | 39.9 | 39.8 | 39.9 | 39.6 | 39.5 | 39.6 | 39.7 |
| 2017 | 39.7 | 38.2 | 38.4 | 38.9 | 39.1 | 39.3 | 39.1 | 39.4 | 39.6 | 39.2 | 39.7 | 39.4 | 39.2 |
| 2018 | 38.9 | 39.0 | 37.3 | 39.2 | 39.5 | 39.8 | 39.2 | 39.3 | 38.9 | 38.6 | 38.9 | 40.2 | 39.1 |
| 2019 | 39.4 | 39.3 | 39.2 | 39.0 | 39.3 | 39.0 | 39.1 | 39.4 | 39.4 | 38.8 | 38.8 | 38.8 | 39.1 |
| **Construction** | | | | | | | | | | | | | |
| 2015 | 37.4 | 35.1 | 37.8 | 37.7 | 38.9 | 39.3 | 38.9 | 39.2 | 37.5 | 38.0 | 37.7 | 39.2 | 38.1 |
| 2016 | 38.1 | 36.5 | 38.1 | 37.9 | 39.0 | 39.6 | 39.2 | 38.9 | 39.5 | 38.4 | 38.0 | 37.9 | 38.5 |
| 2017 | 37.8 | 36.5 | 36.3 | 38.0 | 38.1 | 38.5 | 38.0 | 38.6 | 38.7 | 37.9 | 38.7 | 38.5 | 38.0 |
| 2018 | 37.3 | 37.5 | 34.8 | 38.2 | 39.1 | 39.7 | 39.0 | 39.2 | 38.6 | 38.3 | 38.5 | 40.4 | 38.4 |
| 2019 | 39.5 | 39.2 | 39.2 | 39.0 | 39.7 | 39.3 | 40.1 | 40.3 | 39.9 | 38.7 | 38.3 | 38.2 | 39.3 |
| **Manufacturing** | | | | | | | | | | | | | |
| 2015 | 40.5 | 39.7 | 40.5 | 40.1 | 40.1 | 40.3 | 40.0 | 40.5 | 39.8 | 40.1 | 40.5 | 40.7 | 40.2 |
| 2016 | 40.2 | 40.0 | 40.3 | 40.1 | 40.4 | 40.3 | 40.3 | 40.4 | 40.2 | 40.4 | 40.5 | 40.6 | 40.3 |
| 2017 | 40.7 | 39.6 | 39.9 | 40.3 | 40.4 | 40.5 | 40.4 | 40.4 | 40.7 | 40.4 | 40.6 | 40.3 | 40.4 |
| 2018 | 40.2 | 40.1 | 39.1 | 39.9 | 39.7 | 39.7 | 39.2 | 39.3 | 39.2 | 38.9 | 39.2 | 40.1 | 39.6 |
| 2019 | 39.4 | 39.4 | 39.2 | 39.0 | 39.0 | 38.8 | 38.4 | 38.8 | 39.2 | 38.9 | 39.2 | 39.4 | 39.1 |
| **Trade, Transportation, and Utilities** | | | | | | | | | | | | | |
| 2015 | 32.4 | 32.1 | 32.7 | 32.9 | 33.1 | 33.3 | 33.5 | 33.1 | 33.1 | 32.9 | 33.3 | 33.6 | 33.0 |
| 2016 | 32.6 | 32.4 | 32.7 | 33.0 | 33.3 | 33.5 | 33.6 | 33.4 | 33.8 | 33.8 | 33.7 | 34.5 | 33.4 |
| 2017 | 33.3 | 32.8 | 32.9 | 33.5 | 33.4 | 33.3 | 33.6 | 33.3 | 33.4 | 33.3 | 33.4 | 33.9 | 33.3 |
| 2018 | 32.6 | 32.4 | 31.7 | 33.0 | 33.3 | 33.0 | 33.0 | 33.0 | 33.1 | 32.6 | 33.0 | 33.0 | 32.8 |
| 2019 | 32.1 | 31.8 | 31.7 | 32.2 | 32.3 | 32.8 | 32.5 | 32.4 | 32.8 | 32.2 | 32.5 | 33.2 | 32.4 |
| **Financial Activities** | | | | | | | | | | | | | |
| 2015 | 36.5 | 37.1 | 37.1 | 36.7 | 36.6 | 36.5 | 36.7 | 37.4 | 36.7 | 36.7 | 37.3 | 36.6 | 36.8 |
| 2016 | 36.2 | 36.3 | 36.5 | 36.2 | 37.1 | 36.7 | 36.8 | 36.8 | 36.8 | 37.7 | 37.0 | 37.3 | 36.8 |
| 2017 | 37.9 | 37.5 | 37.2 | 38.0 | 37.3 | 37.1 | 38.0 | 37.1 | 37.5 | 38.1 | 37.8 | 37.8 | 37.6 |
| 2018 | 37.7 | 37.7 | 37.5 | 38.1 | 37.2 | 37.6 | 38.1 | 37.5 | 38.3 | 37.6 | 37.8 | 38.3 | 37.8 |
| 2019 | 38.1 | 38.2 | 38.2 | 38.1 | 38.1 | 38.1 | 37.6 | 37.6 | 38.2 | 37.6 | 38.1 | 38.0 | 38.0 |
| **Professional and Business Services** | | | | | | | | | | | | | |
| 2015 | 35.4 | 36.0 | 36.1 | 35.9 | 36.2 | 36.1 | 35.8 | 36.8 | 36.0 | 36.3 | 37.1 | 36.7 | 36.2 |
| 2016 | 36.3 | 35.7 | 36.1 | 36.2 | 37.0 | 36.4 | 36.1 | 36.0 | 35.9 | 36.7 | 35.9 | 35.8 | 36.2 |
| 2017 | 36.1 | 35.4 | 35.2 | 36.4 | 35.7 | 35.9 | 36.2 | 35.7 | 36.0 | 36.4 | 36.0 | 36.1 | 35.9 |
| 2018 | 35.7 | 36.1 | 35.5 | 36.9 | 36.3 | 36.4 | 36.8 | 36.3 | 36.8 | 35.9 | 35.8 | 37.2 | 36.3 |
| 2019 | 35.8 | 35.6 | 35.7 | 35.7 | 35.9 | 36.6 | 35.8 | 36.0 | 36.5 | 35.7 | 36.0 | 36.5 | 36.0 |
| **Education and Health Services** | | | | | | | | | | | | | |
| 2015 | 31.8 | 31.7 | 31.7 | 31.5 | 31.5 | 31.7 | 31.8 | 31.9 | 32.1 | 32.1 | 31.9 | 31.7 | 31.8 |
| 2016 | 31.5 | 31.5 | 31.5 | 31.6 | 31.6 | 31.4 | 31.8 | 31.7 | 31.7 | 31.8 | 31.5 | 31.6 | 31.6 |
| 2017 | 32.0 | 31.7 | 31.6 | 31.7 | 31.7 | 31.6 | 31.8 | 31.9 | 31.9 | 32.0 | 31.7 | 31.5 | 31.8 |
| 2018 | 31.6 | 31.5 | 31.0 | 31.5 | 31.3 | 31.4 | 31.7 | 31.6 | 31.5 | 31.6 | 31.7 | 31.5 | 31.5 |
| 2019 | 31.4 | 31.2 | 31.1 | 31.2 | 31.2 | 31.3 | 31.3 | 31.2 | 31.3 | 31.1 | 31.3 | 31.0 | 31.2 |
| **Leisure and Hospitality** | | | | | | | | | | | | | |
| 2015 | 24.6 | 24.1 | 25.3 | 25.4 | 26.1 | 25.6 | 26.2 | 26.2 | 25.7 | 25.4 | 25.2 | 25.1 | 25.4 |
| 2016 | 24.2 | 24.8 | 24.6 | 25.1 | 25.4 | 25.3 | 25.8 | 25.4 | 25.2 | 25.0 | 25.0 | 24.2 | 25.0 |
| 2017 | 24.0 | 23.9 | 24.5 | 25.3 | 25.4 | 25.5 | 26.0 | 26.2 | 25.7 | 25.4 | 24.8 | 24.5 | 25.1 |
| 2018 | 23.7 | 24.2 | 23.7 | 24.6 | 24.7 | 24.9 | 25.7 | 25.7 | 25.0 | 24.8 | 24.2 | 24.6 | 24.7 |
| 2019 | 23.3 | 23.8 | 24.0 | 24.3 | 24.7 | 24.9 | 25.8 | 25.7 | 25.3 | 25.1 | 24.7 | 24.7 | 24.7 |
| **Other Services** | | | | | | | | | | | | | |
| 2015 | 29.3 | 29.1 | 29.3 | 29.3 | 28.8 | 28.7 | 29.9 | 30.5 | 29.8 | 28.9 | 29.6 | 29.6 | 29.4 |
| 2016 | 29.5 | 28.6 | 28.7 | 28.9 | 29.1 | 29.0 | 30.4 | 30.5 | 29.2 | 29.0 | 28.6 | 28.6 | 29.2 |
| 2017 | 28.7 | 28.3 | 28.7 | 29.1 | 29.1 | 29.0 | 30.5 | 30.1 | 29.6 | 29.6 | 29.8 | 30.1 | 29.4 |
| 2018 | 30.0 | 30.1 | 29.5 | 30.0 | 30.4 | 29.8 | 31.2 | 31.6 | 31.3 | 30.9 | 31.2 | 31.1 | 30.6 |
| 2019 | 30.4 | 30.5 | 30.4 | 30.4 | 30.3 | 30.4 | 31.2 | 31.4 | 30.9 | 30.5 | 30.3 | 30.1 | 30.6 |

## 3. Average Hourly Earnings by Selected Industry: Massachusetts, 2015–2019

(Dollars, not seasonally adjusted)

| Industry and year | January | February | March | April | May | June | July | August | September | October | November | December | Annual average |
|---|---|---|---|---|---|---|---|---|---|---|---|---|---|
| **Total Private** | | | | | | | | | | | | | |
| 2015 | 30.53 | 30.59 | 30.39 | 30.24 | 30.10 | 29.82 | 29.80 | 30.16 | 30.34 | 30.71 | 31.05 | 30.85 | 30.38 |
| 2016 | 31.28 | 31.12 | 30.94 | 30.91 | 30.92 | 30.53 | 30.65 | 30.56 | 31.07 | 31.53 | 31.38 | 31.44 | 31.03 |
| 2017 | 32.04 | 31.95 | 31.88 | 32.03 | 31.47 | 31.35 | 31.58 | 31.21 | 31.70 | 32.07 | 32.15 | 32.05 | 31.79 |
| 2018 | 32.29 | 32.61 | 32.83 | 32.96 | 32.66 | 32.51 | 32.60 | 32.42 | 33.19 | 33.10 | 33.19 | 33.69 | 32.84 |
| 2019 | 33.44 | 33.79 | 33.78 | 33.80 | 33.59 | 33.78 | 33.52 | 33.72 | 34.44 | 34.34 | 34.28 | 34.66 | 33.93 |
| **Goods-Producing** | | | | | | | | | | | | | |
| 2015 | 31.74 | 31.70 | 31.55 | 31.67 | 31.67 | 31.44 | 31.68 | 32.08 | 31.81 | 32.33 | 32.45 | 32.34 | 31.88 |
| 2016 | 31.90 | 31.95 | 32.16 | 31.95 | 31.95 | 31.95 | 32.16 | 32.16 | 32.27 | 32.36 | 32.22 | 32.49 | 32.13 |
| 2017 | 32.82 | 33.20 | 33.53 | 33.82 | 33.53 | 33.71 | 33.57 | 33.57 | 34.09 | 34.12 | 34.34 | 34.69 | 33.76 |
| 2018 | 34.41 | 34.45 | 34.96 | 34.71 | 34.82 | 34.95 | 35.02 | 34.67 | 35.17 | 35.53 | 35.94 | 35.89 | 35.05 |
| 2019 | 35.30 | 35.79 | 35.95 | 35.81 | 35.65 | 35.81 | 36.05 | 35.99 | 36.24 | 35.90 | 36.37 | 36.41 | 35.94 |
| **Construction** | | | | | | | | | | | | | |
| 2015 | 36.38 | 36.43 | 36.57 | 36.70 | 36.11 | 35.59 | 35.98 | 36.19 | 35.82 | 36.68 | 36.64 | 37.17 | 36.34 |
| 2016 | 36.52 | 36.39 | 36.69 | 36.53 | 36.74 | 36.59 | 36.61 | 36.64 | 36.56 | 36.44 | 36.41 | 37.14 | 36.61 |
| 2017 | 37.50 | 37.23 | 37.41 | 37.31 | 36.91 | 37.26 | 36.92 | 36.63 | 36.86 | 36.30 | 36.56 | 37.09 | 36.98 |
| 2018 | 36.62 | 36.75 | 37.43 | 36.65 | 37.03 | 37.06 | 37.59 | 37.02 | 37.54 | 37.90 | 39.00 | 38.03 | 37.40 |
| 2019 | 37.73 | 37.76 | 38.16 | 38.08 | 38.13 | 38.35 | 38.45 | 38.61 | 38.70 | 38.51 | 38.72 | 38.78 | 38.34 |
| **Manufacturing** | | | | | | | | | | | | | |
| 2015 | 29.41 | 29.51 | 29.16 | 29.12 | 29.18 | 29.03 | 29.11 | 29.57 | 29.44 | 29.60 | 29.80 | 29.31 | 29.35 |
| 2016 | 29.16 | 29.46 | 29.49 | 29.19 | 29.00 | 28.89 | 29.24 | 29.26 | 29.50 | 29.78 | 29.35 | 29.49 | 29.32 |
| 2017 | 29.96 | 30.40 | 30.89 | 31.35 | 31.37 | 31.40 | 31.39 | 31.42 | 32.14 | 32.58 | 32.68 | 32.92 | 31.55 |
| 2018 | 32.82 | 32.80 | 33.17 | 33.16 | 32.89 | 33.07 | 32.75 | 32.66 | 32.97 | 33.14 | 33.10 | 33.51 | 33.00 |
| 2019 | 33.26 | 33.83 | 33.88 | 33.98 | 33.55 | 33.63 | 33.75 | 33.54 | 33.97 | 33.83 | 34.18 | 34.22 | 33.80 |
| **Trade, Transportation, and Utilities** | | | | | | | | | | | | | |
| 2015 | 25.20 | 24.72 | 24.82 | 25.08 | 24.78 | 24.47 | 25.02 | 24.61 | 24.73 | 25.45 | 25.32 | 25.18 | 24.95 |
| 2016 | 26.08 | 25.60 | 25.56 | 25.31 | 25.31 | 25.71 | 25.87 | 25.92 | 26.00 | 26.34 | 26.91 | 26.74 | 26.22 | 26.03 |
| 2017 | 26.78 | 26.55 | 26.52 | 26.52 | 26.07 | 26.01 | 26.42 | 25.81 | 26.28 | 26.79 | 26.71 | 26.21 | 26.39 |
| 2018 | 26.63 | 27.01 | 27.24 | 27.08 | 27.03 | 26.89 | 27.42 | 27.14 | 27.81 | 27.91 | 27.56 | 27.12 | 27.24 |
| 2019 | 27.34 | 28.08 | 28.07 | 28.04 | 27.72 | 28.02 | 27.82 | 27.92 | 28.73 | 28.79 | 28.20 | 27.79 | 28.04 |
| **Financial Activities** | | | | | | | | | | | | | |
| 2015 | 37.54 | 37.25 | 37.81 | 37.86 | 37.42 | 37.61 | 37.68 | 38.54 | 38.06 | 38.79 | 39.10 | 38.95 | 38.06 |
| 2016 | 40.10 | 39.78 | 38.90 | 40.22 | 39.90 | 38.42 | 40.26 | 39.47 | 40.03 | 41.05 | 40.92 | 40.25 | 39.95 |
| 2017 | 41.01 | 41.22 | 41.90 | 42.22 | 41.08 | 41.22 | 41.68 | 41.73 | 42.30 | 42.57 | 42.73 | 42.31 | 41.83 |
| 2018 | 41.91 | 42.59 | 42.39 | 43.05 | 43.25 | 42.92 | 42.81 | 42.43 | 42.63 | 42.49 | 43.22 | 44.16 | 42.82 |
| 2019 | 43.42 | 43.62 | 43.40 | 44.33 | 44.19 | 44.80 | 44.77 | 46.03 | 46.28 | 46.72 | 45.52 | 46.29 | 44.95 |
| **Professional and Business Services** | | | | | | | | | | | | | |
| 2015 | 38.89 | 39.18 | 39.15 | 38.28 | 38.32 | 37.77 | 37.93 | 38.70 | 38.70 | 38.71 | 39.33 | 38.65 | 38.63 |
| 2016 | 39.52 | 39.98 | 39.75 | 39.67 | 39.76 | 38.97 | 39.03 | 38.92 | 39.88 | 40.25 | 39.92 | 40.34 | 39.66 |
| 2017 | 41.61 | 41.20 | 41.20 | 41.25 | 40.43 | 40.05 | 40.57 | 40.10 | 40.23 | 40.72 | 40.67 | 40.04 | 40.66 |
| 2018 | 40.96 | 41.51 | 41.66 | 41.89 | 41.21 | 40.74 | 41.15 | 41.11 | 41.94 | 41.35 | 41.63 | 42.70 | 41.49 |
| 2019 | 42.39 | 42.66 | 42.78 | 42.84 | 42.48 | 42.93 | 42.73 | 42.74 | 43.40 | 43.19 | 43.28 | 44.58 | 43.01 |
| **Education and Health Services** | | | | | | | | | | | | | |
| 2015 | 28.99 | 28.77 | 28.34 | 28.36 | 28.49 | 28.16 | 27.81 | 28.11 | 28.71 | 28.66 | 29.09 | 29.11 | 28.55 |
| 2016 | 28.77 | 28.38 | 28.11 | 28.25 | 28.10 | 27.87 | 28.14 | 27.89 | 27.95 | 28.07 | 28.15 | 28.40 | 28.17 |
| 2017 | 28.17 | 28.18 | 27.86 | 28.05 | 27.86 | 27.92 | 28.00 | 27.67 | 28.09 | 28.30 | 28.46 | 28.85 | 28.12 |
| 2018 | 28.66 | 28.75 | 28.75 | 29.31 | 29.12 | 29.20 | 29.09 | 28.97 | 29.46 | 29.26 | 29.12 | 29.91 | 29.14 |
| 2019 | 29.40 | 29.51 | 29.38 | 29.31 | 29.25 | 29.28 | 29.17 | 29.15 | 29.73 | 29.85 | 29.76 | 30.05 | 29.49 |
| **Leisure and Hospitality** | | | | | | | | | | | | | |
| 2015 | 15.58 | 15.76 | 15.66 | 15.60 | 15.68 | 15.57 | 15.75 | 15.87 | 15.94 | 16.06 | 16.07 | 16.36 | 15.83 |
| 2016 | 16.42 | 16.47 | 16.59 | 16.48 | 16.52 | 16.22 | 16.18 | 16.49 | 16.84 | 17.00 | 17.13 | 17.46 | 16.64 |
| 2017 | 17.37 | 17.55 | 17.54 | 17.40 | 17.59 | 17.28 | 17.21 | 17.27 | 17.63 | 17.71 | 17.86 | 17.97 | 17.52 |
| 2018 | 17.91 | 18.10 | 18.25 | 18.05 | 18.15 | 17.59 | 17.52 | 17.72 | 18.36 | 18.64 | 18.73 | 19.15 | 18.16 |
| 2019 | 19.15 | 19.56 | 19.50 | 19.42 | 19.49 | 19.31 | 18.90 | 19.23 | 20.13 | 19.96 | 20.20 | 20.77 | 19.63 |
| **Other Services** | | | | | | | | | | | | | |
| 2015 | 24.14 | 24.88 | 24.64 | 24.58 | 24.70 | 24.61 | 23.56 | 23.98 | 25.47 | 25.74 | 25.89 | 26.12 | 24.85 |
| 2016 | 26.00 | 26.55 | 26.21 | 26.08 | 26.69 | 26.30 | 25.19 | 25.17 | 26.98 | 27.29 | 27.12 | 27.27 | 26.38 |
| 2017 | 27.69 | 28.11 | 27.76 | 27.87 | 27.79 | 26.97 | 26.24 | 26.02 | 27.47 | 27.27 | 27.49 | 27.48 | 27.32 |
| 2018 | 27.91 | 28.06 | 28.57 | 28.29 | 27.98 | 27.62 | 26.82 | 27.12 | 29.25 | 29.54 | 29.08 | 29.05 | 28.26 |
| 2019 | 29.19 | 29.18 | 29.66 | 29.57 | 29.37 | 29.19 | 27.43 | 27.89 | 29.98 | 29.25 | 29.23 | 29.57 | 29.10 |

## 4. Average Weekly Earnings by Selected Industry: Massachusetts, 2015–2019

(Dollars, not seasonally adjusted)

| Industry and year | January | February | March | April | May | June | July | August | September | October | November | December | Annual average |
|---|---|---|---|---|---|---|---|---|---|---|---|---|---|
| **Total Private** | | | | | | | | | | | | | |
| 2015 | 1,010.54 | 1,009.47 | 1,015.03 | 1,006.99 | 1,008.35 | 998.97 | 1,001.28 | 1,022.42 | 1,016.39 | 1,028.79 | 1,049.49 | 1,039.65 | 1,017.73 |
| 2016 | 1,038.50 | 1,026.96 | 1,027.21 | 1,029.30 | 1,042.00 | 1,022.76 | 1,029.84 | 1,023.76 | 1,040.85 | 1,065.71 | 1,048.09 | 1,053.24 | 1,039.51 |
| 2017 | 1,076.54 | 1,054.35 | 1,052.04 | 1,076.21 | 1,051.10 | 1,047.09 | 1,064.25 | 1,045.54 | 1,065.12 | 1,080.76 | 1,077.03 | 1,073.68 | 1,064.97 |
| 2018 | 1,068.80 | 1,082.65 | 1,066.98 | 1,107.46 | 1,090.84 | 1,085.83 | 1,098.62 | 1,086.07 | 1,115.18 | 1,098.92 | 1,108.55 | 1,138.72 | 1,096.86 |
| 2019 | 1,103.52 | 1,115.07 | 1,111.36 | 1,118.78 | 1,111.83 | 1,128.25 | 1,116.22 | 1,122.88 | 1,153.74 | 1,136.65 | 1,138.10 | 1,157.64 | 1,126.48 |
| **Goods-Producing** | | | | | | | | | | | | | |
| 2015 | 1,247.38 | 1,204.60 | 1,246.23 | 1,241.46 | 1,254.13 | 1,254.46 | 1,251.36 | 1,279.99 | 1,234.23 | 1,273.80 | 1,281.78 | 1,303.30 | 1,256.07 |
| 2016 | 1,263.24 | 1,242.86 | 1,273.54 | 1,258.83 | 1,278.00 | 1,281.20 | 1,283.18 | 1,279.97 | 1,287.57 | 1,281.46 | 1,272.69 | 1,286.60 | 1,275.56 |
| 2017 | 1,302.95 | 1,268.24 | 1,287.55 | 1,315.60 | 1,311.02 | 1,324.41 | 1,312.59 | 1,322.66 | 1,349.96 | 1,337.50 | 1,363.30 | 1,366.79 | 1,323.39 |
| 2018 | 1,338.55 | 1,343.55 | 1,304.01 | 1,360.63 | 1,375.39 | 1,391.01 | 1,372.78 | 1,362.53 | 1,368.11 | 1,371.46 | 1,398.07 | 1,442.78 | 1,370.46 |
| 2019 | 1,390.82 | 1,406.55 | 1,409.24 | 1,396.59 | 1,401.05 | 1,396.59 | 1,409.56 | 1,418.01 | 1,427.86 | 1,392.92 | 1,411.16 | 1,412.71 | 1,405.25 |
| **Construction** | | | | | | | | | | | | | |
| 2015 | 1,360.61 | 1,278.69 | 1,382.35 | 1,383.59 | 1,404.68 | 1,398.69 | 1,399.62 | 1,418.65 | 1,343.25 | 1,393.84 | 1,381.33 | 1,457.06 | 1,384.55 |
| 2016 | 1,391.41 | 1,328.24 | 1,397.89 | 1,384.49 | 1,432.86 | 1,448.96 | 1,435.11 | 1,425.30 | 1,444.12 | 1,399.30 | 1,383.58 | 1,407.61 | 1,409.49 |
| 2017 | 1,417.50 | 1,358.90 | 1,357.98 | 1,417.78 | 1,406.27 | 1,434.51 | 1,402.96 | 1,413.92 | 1,426.48 | 1,375.77 | 1,414.87 | 1,427.97 | 1,405.24 |
| 2018 | 1,365.93 | 1,378.13 | 1,302.22 | 1,400.03 | 1,447.87 | 1,471.28 | 1,466.01 | 1,451.18 | 1,449.04 | 1,451.57 | 1,501.50 | 1,536.41 | 1,436.16 |
| 2019 | 1,490.34 | 1,480.19 | 1,495.87 | 1,485.12 | 1,513.76 | 1,507.16 | 1,541.85 | 1,555.98 | 1,544.13 | 1,490.34 | 1,482.98 | 1,481.40 | 1,506.76 |
| **Manufacturing** | | | | | | | | | | | | | |
| 2015 | 1,191.11 | 1,171.55 | 1,180.98 | 1,167.71 | 1,170.12 | 1,169.91 | 1,164.40 | 1,197.59 | 1,171.71 | 1,186.96 | 1,206.90 | 1,192.92 | 1,179.87 |
| 2016 | 1,172.23 | 1,178.40 | 1,188.45 | 1,170.52 | 1,171.60 | 1,164.27 | 1,178.37 | 1,182.10 | 1,185.90 | 1,203.11 | 1,188.68 | 1,197.29 | 1,181.60 |
| 2017 | 1,219.67 | 1,204.14 | 1,233.13 | 1,262.46 | 1,267.66 | 1,271.70 | 1,268.78 | 1,269.68 | 1,307.78 | 1,316.23 | 1,326.81 | 1,326.68 | 1,274.62 |
| 2018 | 1,319.36 | 1,315.28 | 1,296.95 | 1,323.08 | 1,305.73 | 1,312.88 | 1,283.80 | 1,283.54 | 1,292.42 | 1,289.15 | 1,297.52 | 1,343.75 | 1,306.80 |
| 2019 | 1,310.44 | 1,332.90 | 1,328.10 | 1,325.22 | 1,308.45 | 1,304.84 | 1,296.00 | 1,301.35 | 1,331.62 | 1,315.99 | 1,339.86 | 1,348.27 | 1,321.58 |
| **Trade, Transportation, and Utilities** | | | | | | | | | | | | | |
| 2015 | 816.48 | 793.51 | 811.61 | 825.13 | 820.22 | 814.85 | 838.17 | 814.59 | 818.56 | 837.31 | 843.16 | 846.05 | 823.35 |
| 2016 | 850.21 | 829.44 | 835.81 | 835.23 | 856.14 | 866.65 | 870.91 | 868.40 | 890.29 | 909.56 | 901.14 | 904.59 | 869.40 |
| 2017 | 891.77 | 870.84 | 872.51 | 888.42 | 870.74 | 866.13 | 887.71 | 859.47 | 877.75 | 892.11 | 892.11 | 888.52 | 878.79 |
| 2018 | 868.14 | 875.12 | 863.51 | 893.64 | 900.10 | 887.37 | 904.86 | 895.62 | 920.51 | 909.87 | 909.48 | 894.96 | 893.47 |
| 2019 | 877.61 | 892.94 | 889.82 | 902.89 | 895.36 | 919.06 | 904.15 | 904.61 | 942.34 | 927.04 | 916.50 | 922.63 | 908.50 |
| **Financial Activities** | | | | | | | | | | | | | |
| 2015 | 1,370.21 | 1,381.98 | 1,402.75 | 1,389.46 | 1,369.57 | 1,372.77 | 1,382.86 | 1,441.40 | 1,396.80 | 1,423.59 | 1,458.43 | 1,425.57 | 1,400.61 |
| 2016 | 1,451.62 | 1,444.01 | 1,419.85 | 1,455.96 | 1,480.29 | 1,410.01 | 1,481.57 | 1,452.50 | 1,473.10 | 1,547.59 | 1,514.04 | 1,501.33 | 1,470.16 |
| 2017 | 1,554.28 | 1,545.75 | 1,558.68 | 1,604.36 | 1,532.28 | 1,529.26 | 1,583.84 | 1,548.18 | 1,586.25 | 1,621.92 | 1,615.19 | 1,599.32 | 1,572.81 |
| 2018 | 1,580.01 | 1,605.64 | 1,589.63 | 1,640.21 | 1,608.90 | 1,613.79 | 1,631.06 | 1,591.13 | 1,632.73 | 1,597.62 | 1,633.72 | 1,691.33 | 1,618.60 |
| 2019 | 1,654.30 | 1,666.28 | 1,657.88 | 1,688.97 | 1,683.64 | 1,706.88 | 1,683.35 | 1,730.73 | 1,767.90 | 1,756.67 | 1,734.31 | 1,759.02 | 1,708.10 |
| **Professional and Business Services** | | | | | | | | | | | | | |
| 2015 | 1,376.71 | 1,410.48 | 1,413.32 | 1,374.25 | 1,387.18 | 1,363.50 | 1,357.89 | 1,424.16 | 1,393.20 | 1,405.17 | 1,459.14 | 1,418.46 | 1,398.41 |
| 2016 | 1,434.58 | 1,427.29 | 1,434.98 | 1,436.05 | 1,471.12 | 1,418.51 | 1,408.98 | 1,401.12 | 1,431.69 | 1,477.18 | 1,433.13 | 1,444.17 | 1,435.69 |
| 2017 | 1,502.12 | 1,458.48 | 1,450.24 | 1,501.50 | 1,443.35 | 1,437.80 | 1,468.63 | 1,431.57 | 1,448.28 | 1,482.21 | 1,464.12 | 1,445.44 | 1,459.69 |
| 2018 | 1,462.27 | 1,498.51 | 1,478.93 | 1,545.74 | 1,495.92 | 1,482.94 | 1,514.32 | 1,492.29 | 1,543.39 | 1,484.47 | 1,490.35 | 1,588.44 | 1,506.09 |
| 2019 | 1,517.56 | 1,518.70 | 1,527.25 | 1,529.39 | 1,525.03 | 1,571.24 | 1,529.73 | 1,538.64 | 1,584.10 | 1,541.88 | 1,558.08 | 1,627.17 | 1,548.36 |
| **Education and Health Services** | | | | | | | | | | | | | |
| 2015 | 921.88 | 912.01 | 898.38 | 893.34 | 897.44 | 892.67 | 884.36 | 896.71 | 921.59 | 919.99 | 927.97 | 922.79 | 907.89 |
| 2016 | 906.26 | 893.97 | 885.47 | 892.70 | 887.96 | 875.12 | 894.85 | 884.11 | 886.02 | 892.63 | 886.73 | 897.44 | 890.17 |
| 2017 | 901.44 | 893.31 | 880.38 | 889.19 | 883.16 | 882.27 | 890.40 | 882.67 | 896.07 | 905.60 | 902.18 | 908.78 | 894.22 |
| 2018 | 905.66 | 905.63 | 891.25 | 923.27 | 911.46 | 916.88 | 922.15 | 915.45 | 927.99 | 924.62 | 923.10 | 942.17 | 917.91 |
| 2019 | 923.16 | 920.71 | 913.72 | 914.47 | 912.60 | 916.46 | 913.02 | 909.48 | 930.55 | 928.34 | 931.49 | 931.55 | 920.09 |
| **Leisure and Hospitality** | | | | | | | | | | | | | |
| 2015 | 383.27 | 379.82 | 396.20 | 396.24 | 409.25 | 398.59 | 412.65 | 415.79 | 409.66 | 407.92 | 404.96 | 410.64 | 402.08 |
| 2016 | 397.36 | 408.46 | 408.11 | 413.65 | 419.61 | 410.37 | 417.44 | 418.85 | 424.37 | 425.00 | 428.25 | 422.53 | 416.00 |
| 2017 | 416.88 | 419.45 | 429.73 | 440.22 | 446.79 | 440.64 | 447.46 | 452.47 | 453.09 | 449.83 | 442.93 | 440.27 | 439.75 |
| 2018 | 424.47 | 438.02 | 432.53 | 444.03 | 448.31 | 437.99 | 450.26 | 455.40 | 459.00 | 462.27 | 453.27 | 471.09 | 448.55 |
| 2019 | 446.20 | 465.53 | 468.00 | 471.91 | 481.40 | 480.82 | 487.88 | 494.21 | 509.29 | 501.00 | 498.94 | 513.02 | 484.86 |
| **Other Services** | | | | | | | | | | | | | |
| 2015 | 707.30 | 724.01 | 721.95 | 720.19 | 711.36 | 706.31 | 704.44 | 731.39 | 759.01 | 743.89 | 766.34 | 773.15 | 730.59 |
| 2016 | 767.00 | 759.33 | 752.51 | 754.00 | 776.97 | 762.70 | 765.78 | 767.69 | 787.82 | 791.41 | 775.63 | 779.92 | 770.30 |
| 2017 | 794.70 | 795.51 | 796.71 | 811.02 | 808.69 | 782.13 | 800.32 | 783.20 | 813.11 | 807.19 | 819.20 | 827.15 | 803.21 |
| 2018 | 837.30 | 844.61 | 842.82 | 848.70 | 850.59 | 823.08 | 836.78 | 856.99 | 915.53 | 912.79 | 907.30 | 903.46 | 864.76 |
| 2019 | 887.38 | 889.99 | 901.66 | 898.93 | 889.91 | 887.38 | 855.82 | 875.75 | 926.38 | 892.13 | 885.67 | 890.06 | 890.46 |

# MICHIGAN
*At a Glance*

Population:
  2010 census: 9,883,640
  2019 estimate: 9,986,857

Percent change in population:
  2010–2019: 1.0%

Percent change in total nonfarm employment:
  2011–2019: 12.2%

Industry with the largest growth in employment, 2011–2019 (percent):
  Construction, 38.4%

Industry with the largest decline or smallest growth in employment, 2011–2019 (percent):
  Mining and logging, -1.4%

Civilian labor force:
  2010: 4,798,954
  2019: 4,937,266

Unemployment rate and rank among states (highest to lowest):
  2010: 12.6%, 2nd
  2019: 4.1%, 11th

Over-the-year change in unemployment rates:
  2017–2018: -0.5%
  2018–2019: 0.0%

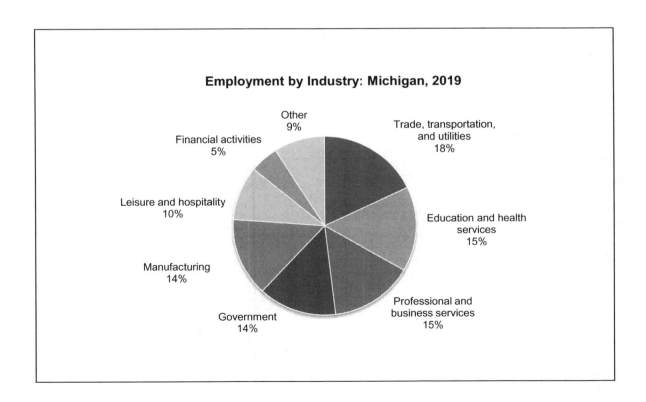

**Employment by Industry: Michigan, 2019**

- Other 9%
- Financial activities 5%
- Leisure and hospitality 10%
- Manufacturing 14%
- Government 14%
- Trade, transportation, and utilities 18%
- Education and health services 15%
- Professional and business services 15%

## 1. Employment by Industry: Michigan, 2011–2019

(Numbers in thousands, not seasonally adjusted)

| Industry and year | January | February | March | April | May | June | July | August | September | October | November | December | Annual average |
|---|---|---|---|---|---|---|---|---|---|---|---|---|---|
| **Total Nonfarm** | | | | | | | | | | | | | |
| 2011 | 3,832.1 | 3,847.0 | 3,874.4 | 3,926.5 | 3,973.0 | 3,986.0 | 3,931.6 | 3,952.6 | 4,012.7 | 4,033.8 | 4,038.6 | 4,017.3 | 3,952.1 |
| 2012 | 3,929.5 | 3,948.4 | 3,976.6 | 4,015.6 | 4,061.2 | 4,068.9 | 4,007.2 | 4,026.5 | 4,076.5 | 4,095.1 | 4,102.9 | 4,093.3 | 4,033.5 |
| 2013 | 4,004.3 | 4,029.4 | 4,051.5 | 4,068.6 | 4,138.5 | 4,149.9 | 4,072.6 | 4,105.9 | 4,156.8 | 4,181.3 | 4,185.7 | 4,169.6 | 4,109.5 |
| 2014 | 4,065.2 | 4,098.6 | 4,114.9 | 4,136.5 | 4,212.1 | 4,242.6 | 4,163.2 | 4,180.2 | 4,215.7 | 4,245.6 | 4,253.9 | 4,251.7 | 4,181.7 |
| 2015 | 4,141.4 | 4,157.7 | 4,173.8 | 4,205.8 | 4,274.3 | 4,289.9 | 4,225.2 | 4,237.3 | 4,275.8 | 4,313.0 | 4,316.0 | 4,307.5 | 4,243.1 |
| 2016 | 4,214.6 | 4,232.9 | 4,249.9 | 4,300.3 | 4,341.7 | 4,364.5 | 4,308.8 | 4,315.3 | 4,364.4 | 4,379.7 | 4,394.4 | 4,370.0 | 4,319.7 |
| 2017 | 4,281.8 | 4,297.2 | 4,317.4 | 4,345.8 | 4,400.2 | 4,427.6 | 4,341.7 | 4,363.8 | 4,400.6 | 4,418.0 | 4,427.0 | 4,408.0 | 4,369.1 |
| 2018 | 4,319.3 | 4,348.6 | 4,375.2 | 4,387.3 | 4,442.8 | 4,478.5 | 4,397.9 | 4,418.0 | 4,439.1 | 4,473.9 | 4,477.4 | 4,454.3 | 4,417.7 |
| 2019 | 4,355.9 | 4,374.8 | 4,394.4 | 4,412.5 | 4,462.8 | 4,485.4 | 4,411.2 | 4,437.9 | 4,454.4 | 4,457.4 | 4,480.1 | 4,464.4 | 4,432.6 |
| **Total Private** | | | | | | | | | | | | | |
| 2011 | 3,207.1 | 3,210.8 | 3,236.0 | 3,288.9 | 3,349.5 | 3,376.6 | 3,366.5 | 3,390.9 | 3,393.0 | 3,401.8 | 3,403.9 | 3,391.4 | 3,334.7 |
| 2012 | 3,313.7 | 3,320.5 | 3,348.3 | 3,388.0 | 3,445.3 | 3,472.8 | 3,451.7 | 3,470.8 | 3,464.2 | 3,472.2 | 3,476.6 | 3,475.8 | 3,425.0 |
| 2013 | 3,401.2 | 3,413.4 | 3,436.5 | 3,453.2 | 3,534.3 | 3,564.1 | 3,525.6 | 3,560.9 | 3,552.1 | 3,564.0 | 3,567.4 | 3,558.9 | 3,511.0 |
| 2014 | 3,468.1 | 3,487.8 | 3,503.7 | 3,525.2 | 3,612.8 | 3,657.8 | 3,617.1 | 3,634.8 | 3,616.4 | 3,630.3 | 3,636.2 | 3,640.9 | 3,585.9 |
| 2015 | 3,546.7 | 3,549.4 | 3,564.2 | 3,596.3 | 3,674.1 | 3,709.4 | 3,679.8 | 3,693.1 | 3,681.1 | 3,697.6 | 3,699.9 | 3,696.3 | 3,649.0 |
| 2016 | 3,619.2 | 3,622.7 | 3,635.9 | 3,686.4 | 3,743.4 | 3,777.7 | 3,756.7 | 3,763.1 | 3,755.2 | 3,760.6 | 3,769.9 | 3,752.8 | 3,720.3 |
| 2017 | 3,680.8 | 3,683.5 | 3,701.3 | 3,729.9 | 3,795.0 | 3,834.2 | 3,784.9 | 3,808.3 | 3,785.4 | 3,793.6 | 3,800.6 | 3,787.1 | 3,765.4 |
| 2018 | 3,716.8 | 3,728.6 | 3,752.9 | 3,766.1 | 3,834.7 | 3,882.2 | 3,837.4 | 3,853.7 | 3,821.9 | 3,844.6 | 3,843.0 | 3,828.1 | 3,809.2 |
| 2019 | 3,749.6 | 3,753.6 | 3,769.1 | 3,787.7 | 3,846.7 | 3,886.0 | 3,845.5 | 3,863.7 | 3,830.4 | 3,823.9 | 3,844.0 | 3,831.8 | 3,819.3 |
| **Goods Producing** | | | | | | | | | | | | | |
| 2011 | 593.3 | 593.7 | 599.0 | 615.3 | 633.3 | 647.6 | 647.7 | 658.6 | 657.9 | 658.5 | 658.1 | 651.9 | 634.6 |
| 2012 | 636.5 | 635.0 | 642.0 | 652.0 | 666.9 | 678.6 | 680.3 | 685.0 | 683.8 | 683.0 | 679.0 | 675.8 | 666.5 |
| 2013 | 659.0 | 659.8 | 664.9 | 668.5 | 690.2 | 702.4 | 696.0 | 710.5 | 710.0 | 712.2 | 710.3 | 698.9 | 690.2 |
| 2014 | 682.4 | 691.3 | 693.7 | 701.5 | 725.7 | 746.9 | 741.5 | 749.1 | 741.1 | 742.1 | 743.0 | 739.2 | 724.8 |
| 2015 | 718.0 | 717.7 | 719.8 | 730.7 | 749.9 | 764.3 | 760.8 | 766.5 | 764.7 | 762.5 | 762.1 | 754.7 | 747.6 |
| 2016 | 742.7 | 739.5 | 741.9 | 759.4 | 770.2 | 784.0 | 779.7 | 781.3 | 781.2 | 780.4 | 783.6 | 771.7 | 768.0 |
| 2017 | 761.5 | 760.8 | 763.5 | 774.5 | 790.6 | 803.5 | 789.8 | 803.7 | 796.1 | 796.8 | 795.9 | 788.1 | 785.4 |
| 2018 | 772.7 | 778.6 | 785.0 | 792.9 | 809.2 | 822.1 | 816.4 | 822.3 | 816.4 | 819.6 | 815.3 | 809.3 | 805.0 |
| 2019 | 787.2 | 792.8 | 794.7 | 799.2 | 811.3 | 825.5 | 817.2 | 824.8 | 818.5 | 802.4 | 814.3 | 807.6 | 808.0 |
| **Service-Providing** | | | | | | | | | | | | | |
| 2011 | 3,238.8 | 3,253.3 | 3,275.4 | 3,311.2 | 3,339.7 | 3,338.4 | 3,283.9 | 3,294.0 | 3,354.8 | 3,375.3 | 3,380.5 | 3,365.4 | 3,317.6 |
| 2012 | 3,293.0 | 3,313.4 | 3,334.6 | 3,363.6 | 3,394.3 | 3,390.3 | 3,326.9 | 3,341.5 | 3,392.7 | 3,412.1 | 3,423.9 | 3,417.5 | 3,367.0 |
| 2013 | 3,345.3 | 3,369.6 | 3,386.6 | 3,400.1 | 3,448.3 | 3,447.5 | 3,376.6 | 3,395.4 | 3,446.8 | 3,469.1 | 3,475.4 | 3,470.7 | 3,419.3 |
| 2014 | 3,382.8 | 3,407.3 | 3,421.2 | 3,435.0 | 3,486.4 | 3,495.7 | 3,421.7 | 3,431.1 | 3,474.6 | 3,503.5 | 3,510.9 | 3,512.5 | 3,456.9 |
| 2015 | 3,423.4 | 3,440.0 | 3,454.0 | 3,475.1 | 3,524.4 | 3,525.6 | 3,464.4 | 3,470.8 | 3,511.1 | 3,550.5 | 3,553.9 | 3,552.8 | 3,495.5 |
| 2016 | 3,471.9 | 3,493.4 | 3,508.0 | 3,540.9 | 3,571.5 | 3,580.5 | 3,529.1 | 3,534.0 | 3,583.2 | 3,599.3 | 3,610.8 | 3,598.3 | 3,551.7 |
| 2017 | 3,520.3 | 3,536.4 | 3,553.9 | 3,571.3 | 3,609.6 | 3,624.1 | 3,551.9 | 3,560.1 | 3,604.5 | 3,621.2 | 3,631.1 | 3,619.9 | 3,583.7 |
| 2018 | 3,546.6 | 3,570.0 | 3,590.2 | 3,594.4 | 3,633.6 | 3,656.4 | 3,581.5 | 3,595.7 | 3,622.7 | 3,654.3 | 3,662.1 | 3,645.0 | 3,612.7 |
| 2019 | 3,568.7 | 3,582.0 | 3,599.7 | 3,613.3 | 3,651.5 | 3,659.9 | 3,594.0 | 3,613.1 | 3,635.9 | 3,655.0 | 3,665.8 | 3,656.8 | 3,624.6 |
| **Mining and Logging** | | | | | | | | | | | | | |
| 2011 | 6.7 | 6.7 | 6.7 | 7.0 | 7.5 | 7.8 | 7.9 | 7.9 | 7.8 | 7.9 | 7.8 | 7.6 | 7.4 |
| 2012 | 7.4 | 7.5 | 7.3 | 7.7 | 8.0 | 8.0 | 8.0 | 8.1 | 8.2 | 8.1 | 7.9 | 7.7 | 7.8 |
| 2013 | 7.5 | 7.5 | 7.5 | 7.5 | 8.1 | 8.3 | 8.4 | 8.5 | 8.4 | 8.4 | 8.3 | 8.0 | 8.0 |
| 2014 | 7.8 | 7.9 | 7.9 | 7.9 | 8.3 | 8.6 | 8.6 | 8.6 | 8.5 | 8.5 | 8.3 | 8.1 | 8.3 |
| 2015 | 7.7 | 7.6 | 7.5 | 7.5 | 7.8 | 8.0 | 7.7 | 7.7 | 7.7 | 7.7 | 7.7 | 7.4 | 7.7 |
| 2016 | 7.1 | 7.0 | 7.0 | 7.1 | 7.2 | 7.4 | 7.4 | 7.4 | 7.2 | 7.4 | 7.0 | 6.9 | 7.2 |
| 2017 | 6.6 | 6.5 | 6.6 | 7.0 | 7.3 | 7.5 | 7.5 | 7.5 | 7.4 | 7.4 | 7.3 | 7.1 | 7.1 |
| 2018 | 6.6 | 6.8 | 6.9 | 7.0 | 7.3 | 7.6 | 7.6 | 7.6 | 7.6 | 7.5 | 7.4 | 7.2 | 7.3 |
| 2019 | 6.9 | 7.0 | 7.1 | 7.1 | 7.4 | 7.6 | 7.7 | 7.7 | 7.6 | 7.6 | 7.4 | 7.0 | 7.3 |
| **Construction** | | | | | | | | | | | | | |
| 2011 | 108.0 | 104.9 | 107.4 | 114.5 | 126.1 | 133.9 | 138.9 | 139.6 | 137.6 | 135.7 | 132.3 | 124.6 | 125.3 |
| 2012 | 113.2 | 110.1 | 114.0 | 122.1 | 129.9 | 135.4 | 137.9 | 138.7 | 138.5 | 137.6 | 133.1 | 127.9 | 128.2 |
| 2013 | 118.3 | 115.4 | 117.2 | 121.1 | 135.7 | 140.4 | 144.5 | 145.7 | 144.7 | 145.2 | 140.7 | 133.0 | 133.5 |
| 2014 | 122.8 | 122.2 | 122.8 | 128.9 | 144.0 | 151.5 | 153.6 | 155.5 | 154.9 | 153.7 | 149.4 | 142.4 | 141.8 |
| 2015 | 130.6 | 128.6 | 131.4 | 140.5 | 152.0 | 158.4 | 159.1 | 159.6 | 158.4 | 158.8 | 154.5 | 147.3 | 148.3 |
| 2016 | 137.2 | 135.4 | 138.9 | 149.4 | 159.6 | 163.5 | 165.4 | 165.9 | 165.4 | 165.8 | 162.6 | 151.9 | 155.1 |
| 2017 | 143.5 | 142.0 | 145.6 | 154.9 | 166.7 | 172.8 | 174.4 | 175.2 | 173.1 | 172.1 | 167.3 | 158.6 | 162.2 |
| 2018 | 149.3 | 149.1 | 153.4 | 160.4 | 173.9 | 180.8 | 182.0 | 182.4 | 178.5 | 180.0 | 173.8 | 166.0 | 169.1 |
| 2019 | 156.6 | 153.6 | 156.7 | 164.0 | 177.1 | 182.5 | 185.4 | 185.6 | 183.7 | 186.7 | 178.7 | 170.4 | 173.4 |

## 1. Employment by Industry: Michigan, 2011–2019—*Continued*

(Numbers in thousands, not seasonally adjusted)

| Industry and year | January | February | March | April | May | June | July | August | September | October | November | December | Annual average |
|---|---|---|---|---|---|---|---|---|---|---|---|---|---|
| **Manufacturing** | | | | | | | | | | | | | |
| 2011 | 478.6 | 482.1 | 484.9 | 493.8 | 499.7 | 505.9 | 500.9 | 511.1 | 512.5 | 514.9 | 518.0 | 519.7 | 501.8 |
| 2012 | 515.9 | 517.4 | 520.7 | 522.2 | 529.0 | 535.2 | 534.4 | 538.2 | 537.1 | 537.3 | 538.0 | 540.2 | 530.5 |
| 2013 | 533.2 | 536.9 | 540.2 | 539.9 | 546.4 | 553.7 | 543.1 | 556.3 | 556.9 | 558.6 | 561.3 | 557.9 | 548.7 |
| 2014 | 551.8 | 561.2 | 563.0 | 564.7 | 573.4 | 586.8 | 579.3 | 585.0 | 577.7 | 579.9 | 585.3 | 588.7 | 574.7 |
| 2015 | 579.7 | 581.5 | 580.9 | 582.7 | 590.1 | 597.9 | 594.0 | 599.2 | 598.6 | 596.0 | 599.9 | 600.0 | 591.7 |
| 2016 | 598.4 | 597.1 | 596.0 | 602.9 | 603.4 | 613.1 | 606.9 | 608.0 | 608.6 | 607.2 | 614.0 | 612.9 | 605.7 |
| 2017 | 611.4 | 612.3 | 611.3 | 612.6 | 616.6 | 623.2 | 607.9 | 621.0 | 615.6 | 617.3 | 621.3 | 622.4 | 616.1 |
| 2018 | 616.8 | 622.7 | 624.7 | 625.5 | 628.0 | 633.7 | 626.8 | 632.3 | 630.3 | 632.1 | 634.1 | 636.1 | 628.6 |
| 2019 | 623.7 | 632.2 | 630.9 | 628.1 | 626.8 | 635.4 | 624.1 | 631.5 | 627.2 | 608.1 | 628.2 | 630.2 | 627.2 |
| **Trade, Transportation, and Utilities** | | | | | | | | | | | | | |
| 2011 | 704.1 | 698.3 | 699.9 | 709.1 | 720.4 | 726.4 | 728.3 | 728.4 | 724.5 | 728.7 | 741.5 | 745.6 | 721.3 |
| 2012 | 714.9 | 707.9 | 712.5 | 717.5 | 729.2 | 734.8 | 734.7 | 734.3 | 730.1 | 734.6 | 751.3 | 753.7 | 729.6 |
| 2013 | 725.7 | 721.1 | 724.4 | 727.9 | 741.5 | 749.7 | 750.4 | 751.4 | 745.3 | 750.5 | 764.1 | 770.7 | 743.6 |
| 2014 | 739.4 | 735.6 | 737.1 | 743.3 | 757.5 | 765.1 | 761.7 | 763.1 | 758.9 | 764.8 | 779.8 | 787.0 | 757.8 |
| 2015 | 755.8 | 749.9 | 752.0 | 758.9 | 771.6 | 778.2 | 772.8 | 773.6 | 769.8 | 775.0 | 789.4 | 795.5 | 770.2 |
| 2016 | 765.1 | 760.3 | 762.1 | 770.3 | 781.2 | 786.6 | 784.2 | 785.8 | 780.8 | 786.1 | 799.4 | 802.9 | 780.4 |
| 2017 | 774.6 | 767.9 | 771.1 | 778.2 | 786.9 | 793.1 | 787.9 | 790.2 | 785.0 | 790.5 | 804.4 | 807.0 | 786.4 |
| 2018 | 778.1 | 772.7 | 775.1 | 777.3 | 790.3 | 797.0 | 793.6 | 795.8 | 789.7 | 796.2 | 811.5 | 813.5 | 790.9 |
| 2019 | 788.4 | 778.5 | 779.9 | 783.2 | 794.7 | 800.5 | 799.1 | 800.4 | 793.6 | 799.1 | 812.4 | 820.8 | 795.9 |
| **Wholesale Trade** | | | | | | | | | | | | | |
| 2011 | 150.2 | 150.6 | 151.4 | 153.1 | 154.9 | 155.9 | 156.1 | 156.5 | 155.7 | 155.8 | 156.2 | 156.2 | 154.4 |
| 2012 | 154.2 | 154.8 | 155.8 | 157.3 | 159.2 | 160.4 | 160.6 | 160.5 | 159.7 | 160.0 | 159.9 | 160.4 | 158.6 |
| 2013 | 159.2 | 159.7 | 160.8 | 161.4 | 163.3 | 164.3 | 164.1 | 164.0 | 163.1 | 163.1 | 163.2 | 164.0 | 162.5 |
| 2014 | 162.5 | 163.1 | 163.4 | 164.7 | 167.2 | 168.4 | 167.4 | 167.6 | 166.1 | 165.8 | 166.2 | 167.0 | 165.8 |
| 2015 | 164.8 | 165.0 | 165.6 | 166.7 | 168.5 | 169.7 | 168.6 | 168.5 | 166.9 | 166.9 | 167.0 | 167.5 | 167.1 |
| 2016 | 165.5 | 165.8 | 166.0 | 167.9 | 169.8 | 170.8 | 170.5 | 170.2 | 168.8 | 168.9 | 169.1 | 169.2 | 168.5 |
| 2017 | 167.4 | 167.8 | 168.8 | 170.6 | 172.2 | 173.4 | 172.5 | 172.4 | 170.9 | 170.4 | 170.4 | 170.8 | 170.6 |
| 2018 | 169.4 | 170.2 | 170.6 | 170.9 | 172.7 | 174.0 | 173.2 | 172.8 | 171.5 | 171.9 | 171.6 | 172.0 | 171.7 |
| 2019 | 170.3 | 170.5 | 170.7 | 171.0 | 172.7 | 173.5 | 173.4 | 173.0 | 171.2 | 171.7 | 170.9 | 171.9 | 171.7 |
| **Retail Trade** | | | | | | | | | | | | | |
| 2011 | 439.4 | 433.7 | 434.1 | 440.6 | 447.8 | 451.0 | 452.8 | 451.8 | 448.2 | 452.3 | 464.3 | 467.0 | 448.6 |
| 2012 | 441.8 | 434.3 | 437.5 | 440.9 | 448.6 | 451.7 | 452.2 | 451.2 | 447.5 | 451.2 | 467.4 | 467.6 | 449.3 |
| 2013 | 444.4 | 439.1 | 441.1 | 443.6 | 453.0 | 458.6 | 460.8 | 460.5 | 455.6 | 459.8 | 472.1 | 476.0 | 455.4 |
| 2014 | 449.2 | 445.2 | 446.2 | 451.5 | 460.4 | 465.3 | 463.6 | 464.2 | 460.7 | 467.0 | 480.5 | 482.9 | 461.4 |
| 2015 | 457.2 | 453.1 | 454.6 | 458.8 | 467.8 | 472.0 | 468.8 | 470.2 | 466.7 | 471.5 | 483.7 | 486.4 | 467.6 |
| 2016 | 463.0 | 459.4 | 460.5 | 466.5 | 473.7 | 476.9 | 475.9 | 477.2 | 471.9 | 476.2 | 487.6 | 489.2 | 473.2 |
| 2017 | 467.5 | 462.2 | 463.6 | 468.2 | 473.4 | 477.0 | 474.7 | 475.2 | 470.5 | 475.1 | 486.3 | 485.6 | 473.3 |
| 2018 | 465.2 | 459.2 | 460.5 | 462.2 | 471.1 | 474.8 | 473.6 | 473.6 | 466.6 | 470.0 | 482.0 | 481.4 | 470.0 |
| 2019 | 462.5 | 454.6 | 455.6 | 458.1 | 465.4 | 467.6 | 466.3 | 466.2 | 460.4 | 464.8 | 473.2 | 476.5 | 464.3 |
| **Transportation and Utilities** | | | | | | | | | | | | | |
| 2011 | 114.5 | 114.0 | 114.4 | 115.4 | 117.7 | 119.5 | 119.4 | 120.1 | 120.6 | 120.6 | 121.0 | 122.4 | 118.3 |
| 2012 | 118.9 | 118.8 | 119.2 | 119.3 | 121.4 | 122.7 | 121.9 | 122.6 | 122.9 | 123.4 | 124.0 | 125.7 | 121.7 |
| 2013 | 122.1 | 122.3 | 122.5 | 122.9 | 125.2 | 126.8 | 125.5 | 126.9 | 126.6 | 127.6 | 128.8 | 130.7 | 125.7 |
| 2014 | 127.7 | 127.3 | 127.5 | 127.1 | 129.9 | 131.4 | 130.7 | 131.3 | 132.1 | 132.0 | 133.1 | 137.1 | 130.6 |
| 2015 | 133.8 | 131.8 | 131.8 | 133.4 | 135.3 | 136.5 | 135.4 | 134.9 | 136.2 | 136.6 | 138.7 | 141.6 | 135.5 |
| 2016 | 136.6 | 135.1 | 135.6 | 135.9 | 137.7 | 138.9 | 137.8 | 138.4 | 140.1 | 141.0 | 142.7 | 144.5 | 138.7 |
| 2017 | 139.7 | 137.9 | 138.7 | 139.4 | 141.3 | 142.7 | 140.7 | 142.6 | 143.6 | 145.0 | 147.7 | 150.6 | 142.5 |
| 2018 | 143.5 | 143.3 | 144.0 | 144.2 | 146.5 | 148.2 | 146.8 | 149.4 | 151.6 | 154.3 | 157.9 | 160.1 | 149.2 |
| 2019 | 155.6 | 153.4 | 153.6 | 154.1 | 156.6 | 159.4 | 159.4 | 161.2 | 162.0 | 162.6 | 168.3 | 172.4 | 159.9 |
| **Information** | | | | | | | | | | | | | |
| 2011 | 53.8 | 53.5 | 53.4 | 52.1 | 52.7 | 52.8 | 53.1 | 53.2 | 52.7 | 53.6 | 53.8 | 53.8 | 53.2 |
| 2012 | 53.4 | 53.2 | 53.1 | 52.9 | 53.2 | 53.2 | 53.6 | 54.2 | 52.9 | 53.2 | 53.5 | 53.6 | 53.3 |
| 2013 | 54.0 | 54.2 | 54.4 | 55.0 | 55.4 | 55.9 | 56.0 | 56.1 | 55.3 | 55.3 | 56.0 | 56.1 | 55.3 |
| 2014 | 56.3 | 56.0 | 56.3 | 57.1 | 57.4 | 58.2 | 59.0 | 58.6 | 57.1 | 57.9 | 58.0 | 57.6 | 57.5 |
| 2015 | 56.5 | 56.3 | 56.3 | 55.9 | 56.6 | 57.2 | 57.7 | 56.8 | 56.4 | 56.0 | 56.4 | 56.5 | 56.6 |
| 2016 | 56.7 | 56.5 | 56.7 | 56.9 | 57.5 | 58.1 | 58.5 | 57.9 | 57.4 | 56.8 | 57.4 | 57.1 | 57.3 |
| 2017 | 56.5 | 56.3 | 56.8 | 56.2 | 56.7 | 56.9 | 56.7 | 56.4 | 56.1 | 56.0 | 56.3 | 56.7 | 56.5 |
| 2018 | 55.9 | 55.5 | 55.4 | 55.9 | 56.5 | 56.9 | 56.6 | 56.4 | 55.3 | 55.8 | 56.0 | 55.5 | 56.0 |
| 2019 | 55.5 | 55.2 | 55.2 | 54.9 | 55.3 | 55.8 | 56.1 | 55.6 | 54.8 | 54.9 | 54.9 | 54.3 | 55.2 |

## 1. Employment by Industry: Michigan, 2011–2019—*Continued*

(Numbers in thousands, not seasonally adjusted)

| Industry and year | January | February | March | April | May | June | July | August | September | October | November | December | Annual average |
|---|---|---|---|---|---|---|---|---|---|---|---|---|---|
| **Financial Activities** | | | | | | | | | | | | | |
| 2011 | 190.7 | 191.1 | 191.8 | 191.3 | 192.5 | 194.4 | 196.0 | 196.8 | 194.4 | 193.7 | 193.9 | 194.7 | 193.4 |
| 2012 | 192.5 | 192.9 | 193.7 | 194.9 | 196.6 | 198.8 | 200.3 | 200.5 | 197.7 | 197.7 | 197.9 | 198.8 | 196.9 |
| 2013 | 198.9 | 199.6 | 199.9 | 201.5 | 203.8 | 206.9 | 207.7 | 207.8 | 204.0 | 203.3 | 203.4 | 203.4 | 203.4 |
| 2014 | 202.8 | 202.5 | 202.4 | 202.7 | 205.5 | 207.9 | 208.1 | 208.1 | 205.0 | 203.9 | 204.1 | 205.0 | 204.8 |
| 2015 | 203.5 | 203.2 | 203.4 | 205.0 | 208.2 | 211.1 | 211.8 | 212.1 | 209.3 | 209.7 | 209.8 | 210.5 | 208.1 |
| 2016 | 209.8 | 209.7 | 209.9 | 211.5 | 214.1 | 216.9 | 218.3 | 218.5 | 215.7 | 215.5 | 215.6 | 216.8 | 214.4 |
| 2017 | 217.1 | 217.0 | 216.8 | 217.7 | 219.5 | 223.1 | 222.9 | 222.3 | 219.0 | 218.1 | 217.9 | 218.1 | 219.1 |
| 2018 | 217.5 | 217.7 | 218.1 | 218.9 | 221.0 | 224.6 | 224.6 | 224.1 | 220.7 | 220.8 | 220.3 | 221.0 | 220.8 |
| 2019 | 220.2 | 220.4 | 220.8 | 221.7 | 223.9 | 227.1 | 227.8 | 227.9 | 225.1 | 225.4 | 226.3 | 227.4 | 224.5 |
| **Professional and Business Services** | | | | | | | | | | | | | |
| 2011 | 537.1 | 542.3 | 548.9 | 560.9 | 569.5 | 564.2 | 552.3 | 561.5 | 575.1 | 585.2 | 584.6 | 574.7 | 563.0 |
| 2012 | 568.6 | 574.2 | 578.6 | 590.5 | 599.1 | 591.8 | 576.4 | 585.7 | 595.3 | 603.9 | 603.2 | 599.4 | 588.9 |
| 2013 | 593.3 | 600.1 | 606.1 | 606.8 | 623.0 | 617.7 | 591.4 | 606.8 | 618.4 | 626.4 | 627.2 | 623.3 | 611.7 |
| 2014 | 606.5 | 613.3 | 616.3 | 617.5 | 633.4 | 633.8 | 612.4 | 619.0 | 627.7 | 639.2 | 638.9 | 637.7 | 624.6 |
| 2015 | 622.8 | 626.2 | 627.3 | 635.9 | 646.5 | 644.6 | 627.1 | 630.8 | 638.6 | 651.2 | 648.8 | 643.8 | 637.0 |
| 2016 | 631.4 | 634.0 | 635.5 | 646.0 | 652.4 | 652.3 | 638.6 | 641.1 | 651.1 | 658.5 | 659.0 | 651.9 | 646.0 |
| 2017 | 640.3 | 642.0 | 646.9 | 648.6 | 659.9 | 660.9 | 638.8 | 643.1 | 650.0 | 656.4 | 659.5 | 652.2 | 649.9 |
| 2018 | 646.4 | 651.8 | 657.4 | 658.1 | 667.1 | 673.8 | 648.5 | 654.4 | 657.9 | 669.2 | 669.6 | 658.6 | 659.4 |
| 2019 | 646.7 | 651.8 | 653.1 | 655.2 | 661.7 | 664.0 | 642.2 | 647.9 | 651.0 | 657.4 | 664.2 | 653.0 | 654.0 |
| **Education and Health Services** | | | | | | | | | | | | | |
| 2011 | 610.6 | 614.9 | 617.7 | 621.8 | 621.9 | 618.3 | 615.7 | 616.8 | 623.5 | 630.1 | 632.8 | 632.8 | 621.4 |
| 2012 | 622.9 | 630.2 | 632.2 | 631.9 | 632.2 | 630.1 | 623.6 | 625.4 | 630.8 | 638.0 | 640.8 | 642.0 | 631.7 |
| 2013 | 629.6 | 636.0 | 638.2 | 639.1 | 639.3 | 637.3 | 631.2 | 632.9 | 638.1 | 643.6 | 647.1 | 645.6 | 638.2 |
| 2014 | 634.6 | 641.4 | 643.2 | 641.2 | 643.3 | 640.7 | 631.4 | 632.8 | 638.1 | 643.9 | 646.6 | 648.0 | 640.4 |
| 2015 | 639.0 | 644.4 | 647.4 | 644.9 | 648.4 | 646.6 | 640.5 | 644.0 | 646.6 | 657.7 | 660.0 | 661.9 | 648.5 |
| 2016 | 651.2 | 657.2 | 658.4 | 661.1 | 663.9 | 660.3 | 656.3 | 656.9 | 662.7 | 667.5 | 669.9 | 670.7 | 661.3 |
| 2017 | 660.0 | 665.8 | 667.3 | 668.7 | 672.1 | 669.8 | 664.7 | 666.3 | 671.5 | 676.8 | 679.6 | 680.4 | 670.3 |
| 2018 | 672.5 | 678.1 | 680.5 | 679.6 | 680.3 | 678.3 | 670.7 | 671.3 | 674.1 | 680.2 | 682.2 | 682.3 | 677.5 |
| 2019 | 674.4 | 679.1 | 681.6 | 683.1 | 684.8 | 681.8 | 674.1 | 677.6 | 679.5 | 685.7 | 689.4 | 687.9 | 681.6 |
| **Leisure and Hospitality** | | | | | | | | | | | | | |
| 2011 | 353.6 | 352.7 | 359.8 | 372.0 | 391.3 | 403.2 | 404.1 | 406.0 | 397.0 | 384.2 | 372.2 | 370.2 | 380.5 |
| 2012 | 360.0 | 361.5 | 369.2 | 380.0 | 398.2 | 413.2 | 411.3 | 413.7 | 402.7 | 391.8 | 381.3 | 382.7 | 388.8 |
| 2013 | 372.3 | 373.7 | 378.3 | 385.0 | 410.4 | 422.0 | 420.4 | 422.8 | 410.5 | 402.5 | 389.5 | 390.9 | 398.2 |
| 2014 | 377.8 | 378.8 | 385.3 | 393.4 | 419.7 | 433.4 | 431.6 | 433.5 | 419.2 | 409.1 | 397.5 | 398.2 | 406.5 |
| 2015 | 386.4 | 386.9 | 392.5 | 399.5 | 425.4 | 438.1 | 439.4 | 439.9 | 427.9 | 417.5 | 405.8 | 405.2 | 413.7 |
| 2016 | 396.6 | 399.2 | 404.7 | 414.7 | 435.7 | 449.3 | 451.4 | 452.1 | 438.1 | 428.2 | 417.7 | 415.0 | 425.2 |
| 2017 | 406.2 | 408.5 | 413.2 | 422.2 | 443.3 | 458.6 | 457.2 | 459.4 | 442.6 | 433.7 | 421.9 | 419.7 | 432.2 |
| 2018 | 410.6 | 410.3 | 416.7 | 419.3 | 444.0 | 460.5 | 459.5 | 461.4 | 442.1 | 435.5 | 421.7 | 422.1 | 433.6 |
| 2019 | 413.3 | 412.0 | 419.1 | 424.9 | 447.1 | 461.2 | 460.2 | 461.1 | 442.0 | 434.9 | 417.3 | 416.9 | 434.2 |
| **Other Services** | | | | | | | | | | | | | |
| 2011 | 163.9 | 164.3 | 165.5 | 166.4 | 167.9 | 169.7 | 169.3 | 169.6 | 167.9 | 167.8 | 167.0 | 167.7 | 167.3 |
| 2012 | 164.9 | 165.6 | 167.0 | 168.3 | 169.9 | 172.3 | 171.5 | 172.0 | 170.9 | 170.0 | 169.6 | 169.8 | 169.3 |
| 2013 | 168.4 | 168.9 | 170.3 | 169.4 | 170.7 | 172.2 | 172.5 | 172.6 | 170.5 | 170.2 | 169.8 | 170.0 | 170.5 |
| 2014 | 168.3 | 168.9 | 169.4 | 168.5 | 170.3 | 171.8 | 171.4 | 170.6 | 169.3 | 169.4 | 168.3 | 168.2 | 169.5 |
| 2015 | 164.7 | 164.8 | 165.5 | 165.5 | 167.5 | 169.3 | 169.7 | 169.4 | 167.8 | 168.0 | 167.6 | 168.2 | 167.3 |
| 2016 | 165.7 | 166.3 | 166.7 | 166.5 | 168.4 | 170.2 | 169.7 | 169.5 | 168.2 | 167.6 | 167.3 | 166.7 | 167.7 |
| 2017 | 164.6 | 165.2 | 165.7 | 163.8 | 166.0 | 168.3 | 166.9 | 166.9 | 165.1 | 165.3 | 165.1 | 164.9 | 165.7 |
| 2018 | 163.1 | 163.9 | 164.7 | 164.1 | 166.3 | 169.0 | 167.5 | 168.0 | 165.7 | 167.3 | 166.4 | 165.8 | 166.0 |
| 2019 | 163.9 | 163.8 | 164.7 | 165.5 | 167.9 | 170.1 | 168.8 | 168.4 | 165.9 | 164.1 | 165.2 | 163.9 | 166.0 |
| **Government** | | | | | | | | | | | | | |
| 2011 | 625.0 | 636.2 | 638.4 | 637.6 | 623.5 | 609.4 | 565.1 | 561.7 | 619.7 | 632.0 | 634.7 | 625.9 | 617.4 |
| 2012 | 615.8 | 627.9 | 628.3 | 627.6 | 615.9 | 596.1 | 555.5 | 555.7 | 612.3 | 622.9 | 626.3 | 617.5 | 608.5 |
| 2013 | 603.1 | 616.0 | 615.0 | 615.4 | 604.2 | 585.8 | 547.0 | 545.0 | 604.7 | 617.3 | 618.3 | 610.7 | 598.5 |
| 2014 | 597.1 | 610.8 | 611.2 | 611.3 | 599.3 | 584.8 | 546.1 | 545.4 | 599.3 | 615.3 | 617.7 | 610.8 | 595.8 |
| 2015 | 594.7 | 608.3 | 609.6 | 609.5 | 600.2 | 580.5 | 545.4 | 544.2 | 594.7 | 615.4 | 616.1 | 611.2 | 594.2 |
| 2016 | 595.4 | 610.2 | 614.0 | 613.9 | 598.3 | 586.8 | 552.1 | 552.2 | 609.2 | 619.1 | 624.5 | 617.2 | 599.4 |
| 2017 | 601.0 | 613.7 | 616.1 | 615.9 | 605.2 | 593.4 | 556.8 | 555.5 | 615.2 | 624.4 | 626.4 | 620.9 | 603.7 |
| 2018 | 602.5 | 620.0 | 622.3 | 621.2 | 608.1 | 596.3 | 560.5 | 564.3 | 617.2 | 629.3 | 634.4 | 626.2 | 608.5 |
| 2019 | 606.3 | 621.2 | 625.3 | 624.8 | 616.1 | 599.4 | 565.7 | 574.2 | 624.0 | 633.5 | 636.1 | 632.6 | 613.3 |

## 2. Average Weekly Hours by Selected Industry: Michigan, 2015–2019

(Not seasonally adjusted)

| Industry and year | January | February | March | April | May | June | July | August | September | October | November | December | Annual average |
|---|---|---|---|---|---|---|---|---|---|---|---|---|---|
| **Total Private** | | | | | | | | | | | | | |
| 2015 | 34.2 | 34.3 | 34.5 | 34.2 | 34.5 | 34.6 | 34.4 | 35.0 | 34.3 | 34.5 | 34.7 | 34.6 | 34.5 |
| 2016 | 34.1 | 34.0 | 34.1 | 34.4 | 34.5 | 34.5 | 34.5 | 34.6 | 34.7 | 34.8 | 34.4 | 34.4 | 34.4 |
| 2017 | 34.3 | 34.3 | 34.3 | 34.5 | 34.7 | 34.7 | 34.6 | 34.6 | 34.6 | 34.7 | 34.5 | 34.5 | 34.5 |
| 2018 | 34.1 | 34.4 | 34.5 | 34.6 | 34.7 | 35.0 | 34.9 | 34.8 | 35.1 | 34.6 | 34.5 | 34.7 | 34.7 |
| 2019 | 34.0 | 34.1 | 34.3 | 34.3 | 34.2 | 34.5 | 34.3 | 34.6 | 34.8 | 34.4 | 34.0 | 34.4 | 34.3 |
| **Goods-Producing** | | | | | | | | | | | | | |
| 2015 | 40.5 | 40.5 | 40.9 | 40.5 | 41.2 | 41.4 | 40.5 | 41.8 | 40.2 | 41.8 | 41.5 | 41.7 | 41.1 |
| 2016 | 40.6 | 40.3 | 40.6 | 41.0 | 40.7 | 41.1 | 40.6 | 40.8 | 41.2 | 41.4 | 40.9 | 40.8 | 40.8 |
| 2017 | 40.6 | 40.5 | 40.5 | 39.9 | 41.1 | 41.2 | 40.7 | 41.4 | 41.5 | 41.4 | 40.9 | 41.1 | 40.9 |
| 2018 | 40.7 | 40.7 | 40.9 | 41.1 | 41.1 | 41.6 | 41.0 | 41.1 | 41.5 | 41.0 | 40.7 | 41.1 | 41.0 |
| 2019 | 39.8 | 39.4 | 39.9 | 39.9 | 40.1 | 40.3 | 39.7 | 40.5 | 40.8 | 40.7 | 39.5 | 40.8 | 40.1 |
| **Construction** | | | | | | | | | | | | | |
| 2015 | 38.1 | 37.6 | 38.4 | 38.5 | 39.6 | 39.9 | 39.4 | 40.1 | 37.6 | 40.5 | 39.0 | 39.5 | 39.1 |
| 2016 | 37.7 | 37.4 | 37.7 | 38.7 | 39.1 | 40.0 | 40.4 | 39.9 | 39.9 | 40.4 | 39.5 | 38.1 | 39.2 |
| 2017 | 37.9 | 38.0 | 37.5 | 38.9 | 40.6 | 40.9 | 40.0 | 41.5 | 41.2 | 39.5 | 38.4 | 37.8 | 39.4 |
| 2018 | 37.6 | 37.5 | 37.7 | 38.3 | 39.5 | 41.1 | 40.8 | 40.1 | 39.7 | 40.3 | 38.5 | 38.9 | 39.2 |
| 2019 | 37.2 | 36.8 | 37.4 | 37.8 | 39.3 | 39.2 | 40.3 | 40.2 | 39.4 | 40.6 | 37.1 | 38.7 | 38.7 |
| **Manufacturing** | | | | | | | | | | | | | |
| 2015 | 41.3 | 41.8 | 42.3 | 41.8 | 42.4 | 42.7 | 41.1 | 42.5 | 40.4 | 41.7 | 41.8 | 41.9 | 41.8 |
| 2016 | 40.9 | 40.6 | 40.9 | 41.4 | 40.9 | 41.3 | 40.4 | 40.9 | 41.5 | 41.9 | 41.1 | 41.6 | 41.1 |
| 2017 | 41.3 | 41.4 | 41.8 | 40.9 | 41.9 | 42.0 | 41.5 | 41.9 | 42.1 | 42.8 | 42.0 | 42.8 | 41.9 |
| 2018 | 42.1 | 42.1 | 42.4 | 42.4 | 42.1 | 42.1 | 41.4 | 41.9 | 42.5 | 41.6 | 41.8 | 42.1 | 42.0 |
| 2019 | 41.2 | 40.8 | 40.9 | 40.8 | 40.6 | 41.0 | 39.9 | 41.0 | 41.6 | 40.8 | 40.6 | 41.7 | 40.9 |
| **Trade, Transportation, and Utilities** | | | | | | | | | | | | | |
| 2015 | 33.3 | 33.3 | 33.5 | 33.4 | 33.6 | 33.4 | 33.6 | 33.9 | 33.6 | 33.2 | 33.5 | 33.6 | 33.5 |
| 2016 | 33.0 | 32.9 | 33.0 | 33.2 | 33.4 | 33.5 | 33.8 | 33.6 | 33.7 | 33.7 | 33.4 | 33.5 | 33.4 |
| 2017 | 33.2 | 33.2 | 33.1 | 33.9 | 34.0 | 34.1 | 34.3 | 33.9 | 34.1 | 34.0 | 33.9 | 34.1 | 33.8 |
| 2018 | 33.4 | 33.5 | 33.6 | 33.6 | 34.1 | 34.1 | 34.4 | 33.9 | 34.1 | 33.2 | 33.7 | 33.7 | 33.8 |
| 2019 | 33.1 | 33.2 | 33.2 | 33.3 | 33.4 | 33.6 | 33.7 | 33.8 | 33.8 | 33.4 | 33.3 | 33.6 | 33.5 |
| **Financial Activities** | | | | | | | | | | | | | |
| 2015 | 36.4 | 37.0 | 37.3 | 36.9 | 37.1 | 37.0 | 36.9 | 36.9 | 36.5 | 36.4 | 36.9 | 36.7 | 36.8 |
| 2016 | 37.0 | 36.8 | 36.8 | 36.7 | 37.3 | 37.0 | 36.8 | 36.8 | 36.6 | 37.1 | 36.7 | 36.9 | 36.9 |
| 2017 | 37.0 | 36.6 | 36.7 | 37.2 | 36.8 | 36.4 | 37.0 | 36.5 | 36.5 | 37.2 | 36.6 | 36.7 | 36.8 |
| 2018 | 36.5 | 36.6 | 36.6 | 37.0 | 36.2 | 36.6 | 36.9 | 36.6 | 37.0 | 36.3 | 36.1 | 37.0 | 36.6 |
| 2019 | 36.5 | 36.2 | 36.3 | 36.5 | 36.1 | 36.7 | 36.2 | 36.4 | 37.2 | 36.5 | 36.6 | 36.9 | 36.5 |
| **Professional and Business Services** | | | | | | | | | | | | | |
| 2015 | 35.7 | 36.1 | 36.2 | 35.7 | 36.0 | 36.1 | 35.7 | 36.4 | 35.4 | 36.0 | 36.2 | 35.7 | 35.9 |
| 2016 | 35.3 | 35.5 | 35.6 | 36.1 | 36.3 | 36.2 | 35.8 | 36.3 | 36.3 | 36.8 | 35.8 | 36.0 | 36.0 |
| 2017 | 36.1 | 36.0 | 36.1 | 36.4 | 36.3 | 36.4 | 35.2 | 35.1 | 35.1 | 35.9 | 35.3 | 35.4 | 35.8 |
| 2018 | 34.8 | 35.4 | 35.6 | 36.1 | 36.0 | 36.3 | 36.1 | 35.9 | 36.6 | 36.2 | 36.0 | 36.3 | 35.9 |
| 2019 | 35.5 | 36.0 | 36.4 | 36.4 | 35.9 | 36.4 | 35.8 | 36.1 | 36.5 | 36.0 | 35.3 | 36.2 | 36.0 |
| **Education and Health Services** | | | | | | | | | | | | | |
| 2015 | 32.7 | 32.8 | 32.9 | 32.8 | 32.9 | 32.8 | 32.8 | 33.1 | 32.9 | 32.6 | 33.1 | 32.9 | 32.9 |
| 2016 | 32.9 | 32.8 | 32.8 | 32.9 | 33.1 | 32.9 | 33.3 | 33.1 | 33.4 | 33.2 | 33.0 | 32.8 | 33.0 |
| 2017 | 33.0 | 32.9 | 33.0 | 33.2 | 32.9 | 32.9 | 33.0 | 33.1 | 33.2 | 33.1 | 33.2 | 33.0 | 33.0 |
| 2018 | 33.0 | 33.2 | 33.2 | 33.3 | 33.4 | 33.5 | 33.4 | 33.5 | 34.0 | 33.6 | 33.5 | 33.4 | 33.4 |
| 2019 | 33.1 | 33.1 | 33.3 | 33.1 | 33.1 | 33.1 | 33.2 | 32.9 | 33.3 | 32.9 | 32.9 | 32.4 | 33.0 |
| **Leisure and Hospitality** | | | | | | | | | | | | | |
| 2015 | 23.2 | 23.6 | 23.6 | 23.5 | 24.0 | 24.3 | 25.0 | 25.3 | 24.5 | 24.1 | 23.8 | 23.8 | 24.1 |
| 2016 | 23.0 | 23.5 | 23.6 | 23.9 | 24.3 | 24.7 | 25.2 | 25.5 | 24.8 | 24.5 | 24.3 | 23.7 | 24.3 |
| 2017 | 23.9 | 23.9 | 24.1 | 24.0 | 24.6 | 24.8 | 25.5 | 25.3 | 24.7 | 24.5 | 24.1 | 24.1 | 24.5 |
| 2018 | 23.7 | 24.1 | 24.2 | 24.2 | 24.8 | 25.4 | 25.8 | 25.5 | 24.8 | 24.4 | 23.7 | 24.1 | 24.6 |
| 2019 | 23.4 | 23.8 | 24.2 | 24.0 | 24.1 | 24.9 | 25.1 | 25.5 | 24.7 | 24.5 | 24.1 | 24.3 | 24.4 |
| **Other Services** | | | | | | | | | | | | | |
| 2015 | 32.4 | 32.1 | 32.4 | 31.9 | 32.2 | 32.7 | 32.4 | 33.2 | 32.8 | 32.5 | 32.4 | 31.8 | 32.4 |
| 2016 | 31.1 | 31.2 | 31.3 | 31.7 | 32.1 | 31.1 | 31.6 | 31.7 | 31.3 | 31.6 | 31.1 | 31.3 | 31.4 |
| 2017 | 30.6 | 31.3 | 31.1 | 31.5 | 31.4 | 31.8 | 31.2 | 31.5 | 31.3 | 31.3 | 31.3 | 31.4 | 31.3 |
| 2018 | 30.8 | 31.6 | 31.2 | 31.2 | 31.1 | 31.2 | 31.2 | 31.4 | 31.3 | 31.3 | 31.4 | 31.2 | 31.2 |
| 2019 | 30.8 | 30.6 | 30.5 | 30.4 | 31.3 | 31.6 | 31.4 | 31.5 | 31.3 | 31.2 | 30.5 | 30.6 | 31.0 |

## 3. Average Hourly Earnings by Selected Industry: Michigan, 2015–2019

(Dollars, not seasonally adjusted)

| Industry and year | January | February | March | April | May | June | July | August | September | October | November | December | Annual average |
|---|---|---|---|---|---|---|---|---|---|---|---|---|---|
| **Total Private** | | | | | | | | | | | | | |
| 2015 | 23.88 | 23.97 | 23.95 | 23.77 | 23.63 | 23.54 | 23.83 | 24.21 | 24.19 | 24.25 | 24.34 | 24.27 | 23.98 |
| 2016 | 24.25 | 24.16 | 24.16 | 23.98 | 23.95 | 23.66 | 23.79 | 23.72 | 23.85 | 24.17 | 24.12 | 24.22 | 24.00 |
| 2017 | 24.65 | 24.44 | 24.34 | 24.69 | 24.27 | 24.13 | 24.36 | 24.14 | 24.54 | 24.79 | 24.79 | 25.11 | 24.52 |
| 2018 | 25.29 | 25.12 | 25.00 | 25.33 | 25.16 | 25.19 | 25.41 | 25.28 | 25.81 | 25.85 | 26.01 | 26.24 | 25.48 |
| 2019 | 26.26 | 26.38 | 26.34 | 26.44 | 26.26 | 26.40 | 26.32 | 26.39 | 26.82 | 26.77 | 26.99 | 27.18 | 26.55 |
| **Goods-Producing** | | | | | | | | | | | | | |
| 2015 | 25.08 | 25.09 | 25.16 | 25.12 | 24.93 | 24.84 | 24.97 | 25.57 | 25.61 | 25.36 | 25.41 | 25.57 | 25.23 |
| 2016 | 25.20 | 25.15 | 25.25 | 24.62 | 24.70 | 24.58 | 24.89 | 24.80 | 24.99 | 25.20 | 25.17 | 25.57 | 25.01 |
| 2017 | 25.93 | 25.56 | 25.63 | 26.04 | 25.70 | 25.76 | 26.01 | 25.70 | 25.90 | 25.89 | 25.69 | 26.06 | 25.82 |
| 2018 | 26.15 | 26.10 | 26.06 | 26.06 | 26.18 | 26.34 | 26.66 | 26.71 | 26.92 | 26.96 | 26.92 | 26.74 | 26.49 |
| 2019 | 26.80 | 26.83 | 26.88 | 27.16 | 27.13 | 27.21 | 27.85 | 27.76 | 27.98 | 28.14 | 27.97 | 28.04 | 27.49 |
| **Construction** | | | | | | | | | | | | | |
| 2015 | 26.19 | 26.28 | 26.65 | 26.71 | 26.25 | 26.27 | 26.51 | 26.71 | 26.64 | 26.95 | 27.06 | 27.31 | 26.64 |
| 2016 | 26.56 | 26.83 | 26.92 | 26.85 | 26.88 | 26.82 | 27.08 | 26.92 | 27.06 | 27.04 | 27.16 | 27.49 | 26.98 |
| 2017 | 27.47 | 27.33 | 27.82 | 27.36 | 27.40 | 27.26 | 27.54 | 27.93 | 27.98 | 27.63 | 27.37 | 28.15 | 27.61 |
| 2018 | 28.02 | 28.00 | 28.32 | 27.63 | 28.19 | 28.22 | 28.51 | 28.51 | 28.93 | 29.09 | 28.87 | 29.57 | 28.51 |
| 2019 | 29.50 | 29.54 | 29.35 | 29.23 | 29.60 | 29.51 | 30.13 | 30.08 | 30.46 | 30.75 | 30.48 | 30.78 | 29.98 |
| **Manufacturing** | | | | | | | | | | | | | |
| 2015 | 24.99 | 25.00 | 24.99 | 24.86 | 24.64 | 24.65 | 24.74 | 25.43 | 25.51 | 25.07 | 24.97 | 25.05 | 24.99 |
| 2016 | 24.85 | 24.76 | 24.85 | 24.03 | 24.14 | 23.98 | 24.28 | 24.21 | 24.42 | 24.68 | 24.60 | 25.05 | 24.49 |
| 2017 | 25.50 | 25.07 | 25.01 | 25.57 | 25.12 | 25.24 | 25.46 | 24.91 | 25.18 | 25.39 | 25.21 | 25.50 | 25.26 |
| 2018 | 25.66 | 25.59 | 25.41 | 25.58 | 25.47 | 25.65 | 25.96 | 25.89 | 26.11 | 26.07 | 26.14 | 25.71 | 25.77 |
| 2019 | 25.94 | 25.98 | 26.11 | 26.46 | 26.23 | 26.36 | 26.95 | 26.86 | 27.06 | 27.06 | 27.11 | 27.13 | 26.60 |
| **Trade, Transportation, and Utilities** | | | | | | | | | | | | | |
| 2015 | 20.62 | 20.64 | 20.46 | 20.46 | 20.43 | 20.47 | 20.71 | 20.96 | 20.96 | 20.81 | 20.91 | 20.53 | 20.66 |
| 2016 | 20.94 | 20.70 | 20.57 | 20.62 | 20.40 | 20.26 | 20.28 | 20.45 | 19.98 | 20.26 | 20.19 | 19.95 | 20.38 |
| 2017 | 20.57 | 20.63 | 20.51 | 20.87 | 20.56 | 20.65 | 21.07 | 21.06 | 21.37 | 21.73 | 21.94 | 22.08 | 21.10 |
| 2018 | 22.34 | 22.30 | 21.61 | 22.11 | 21.98 | 21.95 | 22.05 | 21.93 | 22.46 | 22.50 | 22.43 | 22.60 | 22.19 |
| 2019 | 22.59 | 22.88 | 22.92 | 22.90 | 22.67 | 22.73 | 22.60 | 22.76 | 23.25 | 22.85 | 23.05 | 23.25 | 22.87 |
| **Financial Activities** | | | | | | | | | | | | | |
| 2015 | 26.81 | 27.37 | 27.59 | 27.70 | 27.36 | 26.88 | 27.00 | 27.45 | 27.59 | 27.64 | 28.57 | 27.86 | 27.49 |
| 2016 | 27.49 | 27.67 | 27.39 | 27.76 | 27.91 | 27.14 | 27.17 | 27.52 | 28.28 | 28.52 | 28.84 | 29.08 | 27.90 |
| 2017 | 29.36 | 29.18 | 28.84 | 30.12 | 29.30 | 28.48 | 29.28 | 28.72 | 29.73 | 30.07 | 30.16 | 30.82 | 29.50 |
| 2018 | 30.58 | 31.00 | 30.69 | 31.61 | 31.14 | 30.96 | 31.65 | 31.30 | 31.82 | 31.55 | 31.72 | 32.51 | 31.38 |
| 2019 | 31.97 | 31.68 | 31.76 | 31.95 | 32.36 | 33.23 | 32.19 | 32.36 | 32.77 | 32.63 | 33.63 | 33.49 | 32.51 |
| **Professional and Business Services** | | | | | | | | | | | | | |
| 2015 | 29.79 | 29.88 | 29.95 | 29.14 | 29.07 | 29.06 | 30.31 | 30.78 | 30.28 | 30.19 | 30.22 | 30.49 | 29.93 |
| 2016 | 30.21 | 30.16 | 30.20 | 29.89 | 29.88 | 29.47 | 29.68 | 29.04 | 29.40 | 29.77 | 29.33 | 29.43 | 29.70 |
| 2017 | 30.15 | 29.55 | 29.19 | 29.59 | 28.92 | 28.72 | 28.99 | 28.47 | 28.97 | 29.32 | 29.25 | 30.09 | 29.27 |
| 2018 | 29.91 | 29.09 | 29.19 | 29.83 | 29.57 | 29.79 | 30.27 | 29.80 | 30.56 | 30.07 | 30.57 | 31.01 | 29.98 |
| 2019 | 30.76 | 31.13 | 31.08 | 30.99 | 30.90 | 31.45 | 30.82 | 31.16 | 31.63 | 31.52 | 31.93 | 32.45 | 31.32 |
| **Education and Health Services** | | | | | | | | | | | | | |
| 2015 | 23.69 | 23.72 | 23.57 | 23.58 | 23.49 | 23.49 | 23.90 | 24.02 | 24.13 | 24.67 | 24.38 | 24.39 | 23.92 |
| 2016 | 24.38 | 24.33 | 24.50 | 24.55 | 24.49 | 24.53 | 24.83 | 24.72 | 24.69 | 24.95 | 25.00 | 24.97 | 24.66 |
| 2017 | 25.05 | 24.99 | 24.86 | 25.13 | 24.77 | 24.74 | 24.91 | 24.57 | 24.88 | 24.97 | 24.95 | 24.97 | 24.90 |
| 2018 | 25.68 | 25.38 | 25.53 | 25.64 | 25.68 | 25.87 | 26.19 | 26.05 | 26.42 | 26.67 | 27.16 | 27.68 | 26.17 |
| 2019 | 28.09 | 27.98 | 27.76 | 27.80 | 27.63 | 27.51 | 27.86 | 27.83 | 27.78 | 27.87 | 27.99 | 28.23 | 27.86 |
| **Leisure and Hospitality** | | | | | | | | | | | | | |
| 2015 | 12.58 | 12.55 | 12.59 | 12.54 | 12.43 | 12.28 | 12.26 | 12.43 | 12.47 | 12.55 | 12.54 | 12.69 | 12.49 |
| 2016 | 12.68 | 12.62 | 12.65 | 12.67 | 12.75 | 12.58 | 12.81 | 12.92 | 13.00 | 13.17 | 13.31 | 13.59 | 12.90 |
| 2017 | 13.56 | 13.56 | 13.77 | 13.81 | 13.80 | 13.57 | 13.75 | 13.90 | 14.13 | 14.18 | 14.21 | 14.17 | 13.87 |
| 2018 | 14.14 | 14.20 | 14.30 | 14.41 | 14.34 | 14.04 | 14.00 | 14.01 | 14.16 | 14.42 | 14.33 | 14.50 | 14.23 |
| 2019 | 14.43 | 14.42 | 14.32 | 14.43 | 14.43 | 14.44 | 14.31 | 14.37 | 14.74 | 14.71 | 14.83 | 15.12 | 14.54 |
| **Other Services** | | | | | | | | | | | | | |
| 2015 | 21.03 | 21.27 | 21.02 | 21.10 | 21.52 | 21.27 | 21.25 | 21.44 | 21.51 | 21.12 | 21.49 | 21.00 | 21.25 |
| 2016 | 20.98 | 20.85 | 21.06 | 20.86 | 21.49 | 20.69 | 20.82 | 20.87 | 20.89 | 20.90 | 21.18 | 21.17 | 20.98 |
| 2017 | 21.78 | 21.44 | 21.56 | 21.50 | 21.47 | 21.52 | 21.83 | 21.98 | 22.17 | 22.59 | 22.60 | 22.89 | 21.94 |
| 2018 | 22.99 | 22.69 | 22.64 | 22.99 | 22.72 | 22.39 | 22.37 | 22.37 | 23.16 | 23.25 | 23.22 | 23.64 | 22.87 |
| 2019 | 23.61 | 24.16 | 23.95 | 24.64 | 23.72 | 23.77 | 23.39 | 23.40 | 24.26 | 24.33 | 24.65 | 24.55 | 24.03 |

# 4. Average Weekly Earnings by Selected Industry: Michigan, 2015–2019

(Dollars, not seasonally adjusted)

| Industry and year | January | February | March | April | May | June | July | August | September | October | November | December | Annual average |
|---|---|---|---|---|---|---|---|---|---|---|---|---|---|
| **Total Private** | | | | | | | | | | | | | |
| 2015 | 816.70 | 821.83 | 825.93 | 812.93 | 815.24 | 814.48 | 819.75 | 847.35 | 829.72 | 836.63 | 844.60 | 839.74 | 827.31 |
| 2016 | 826.93 | 821.44 | 823.86 | 824.91 | 826.28 | 816.27 | 820.76 | 820.71 | 827.60 | 841.12 | 829.73 | 833.17 | 825.60 |
| 2017 | 845.50 | 838.29 | 834.86 | 851.81 | 842.17 | 837.31 | 842.86 | 835.24 | 849.08 | 860.21 | 855.26 | 866.30 | 845.94 |
| 2018 | 862.39 | 864.13 | 862.50 | 876.42 | 873.05 | 881.65 | 886.81 | 879.74 | 905.93 | 894.41 | 897.35 | 910.53 | 884.16 |
| 2019 | 892.84 | 899.56 | 903.46 | 906.89 | 898.09 | 910.80 | 902.78 | 913.09 | 933.34 | 920.89 | 917.66 | 934.99 | 910.67 |
| **Goods-Producing** | | | | | | | | | | | | | |
| 2015 | 1,015.74 | 1,016.15 | 1,029.04 | 1,017.36 | 1,027.12 | 1,028.38 | 1,011.29 | 1,068.83 | 1,029.52 | 1,060.05 | 1,054.52 | 1,066.27 | 1,036.95 |
| 2016 | 1,023.12 | 1,013.55 | 1,025.15 | 1,009.42 | 1,005.29 | 1,010.24 | 1,010.53 | 1,011.84 | 1,029.59 | 1,043.28 | 1,029.45 | 1,043.26 | 1,020.41 |
| 2017 | 1,052.76 | 1,035.18 | 1,038.02 | 1,039.00 | 1,056.27 | 1,061.31 | 1,058.61 | 1,063.98 | 1,074.85 | 1,071.85 | 1,050.72 | 1,071.07 | 1,056.04 |
| 2018 | 1,064.31 | 1,062.27 | 1,065.85 | 1,071.07 | 1,076.00 | 1,095.74 | 1,093.06 | 1,097.78 | 1,117.18 | 1,105.36 | 1,095.64 | 1,099.01 | 1,086.09 |
| 2019 | 1,066.64 | 1,057.10 | 1,072.51 | 1,083.68 | 1,087.91 | 1,096.56 | 1,105.65 | 1,124.28 | 1,141.58 | 1,145.30 | 1,104.82 | 1,144.03 | 1,102.35 |
| **Construction** | | | | | | | | | | | | | |
| 2015 | 997.84 | 988.13 | 1,023.36 | 1,028.34 | 1,039.50 | 1,048.17 | 1,044.49 | 1,071.07 | 1,001.66 | 1,091.48 | 1,055.34 | 1,078.75 | 1,041.62 |
| 2016 | 1,001.31 | 1,003.44 | 1,014.88 | 1,039.10 | 1,051.01 | 1,072.80 | 1,094.03 | 1,074.11 | 1,079.69 | 1,092.42 | 1,072.82 | 1,047.37 | 1,057.62 |
| 2017 | 1,041.11 | 1,038.54 | 1,043.25 | 1,064.30 | 1,112.44 | 1,114.93 | 1,101.20 | 1,159.10 | 1,152.78 | 1,091.39 | 1,051.01 | 1,064.07 | 1,087.83 |
| 2018 | 1,053.55 | 1,050.00 | 1,067.66 | 1,058.23 | 1,113.51 | 1,159.84 | 1,163.21 | 1,143.25 | 1,148.52 | 1,172.33 | 1,111.50 | 1,150.27 | 1,117.59 |
| 2019 | 1,097.40 | 1,087.07 | 1,097.69 | 1,104.89 | 1,163.28 | 1,156.79 | 1,214.24 | 1,209.22 | 1,200.12 | 1,248.45 | 1,130.81 | 1,191.19 | 1,160.23 |
| **Manufacturing** | | | | | | | | | | | | | |
| 2015 | 1,032.09 | 1,045.00 | 1,057.08 | 1,039.15 | 1,044.74 | 1,052.56 | 1,016.81 | 1,080.78 | 1,030.60 | 1,045.42 | 1,043.75 | 1,049.60 | 1,044.58 |
| 2016 | 1,016.37 | 1,005.26 | 1,016.37 | 994.84 | 987.33 | 990.37 | 980.91 | 990.19 | 1,013.43 | 1,034.09 | 1,011.06 | 1,042.08 | 1,006.54 |
| 2017 | 1,053.15 | 1,037.90 | 1,045.42 | 1,045.81 | 1,052.53 | 1,060.08 | 1,056.59 | 1,043.73 | 1,060.08 | 1,086.69 | 1,058.82 | 1,091.40 | 1,058.39 |
| 2018 | 1,080.29 | 1,077.34 | 1,077.38 | 1,084.59 | 1,072.29 | 1,079.87 | 1,074.74 | 1,084.79 | 1,109.68 | 1,084.51 | 1,092.65 | 1,082.39 | 1,082.34 |
| 2019 | 1,068.73 | 1,059.98 | 1,067.90 | 1,079.57 | 1,064.94 | 1,080.76 | 1,075.31 | 1,101.26 | 1,125.70 | 1,104.05 | 1,100.67 | 1,131.32 | 1,087.94 |
| **Trade, Transportation, and Utilities** | | | | | | | | | | | | | |
| 2015 | 686.65 | 687.31 | 685.41 | 683.36 | 686.45 | 683.70 | 695.86 | 710.54 | 704.26 | 690.89 | 700.49 | 689.81 | 692.11 |
| 2016 | 691.02 | 681.03 | 678.81 | 684.58 | 681.36 | 678.71 | 685.46 | 687.12 | 673.33 | 682.76 | 674.35 | 668.33 | 680.69 |
| 2017 | 682.92 | 684.92 | 678.88 | 707.49 | 699.04 | 704.17 | 722.70 | 713.93 | 728.72 | 738.82 | 743.77 | 752.93 | 713.18 |
| 2018 | 746.16 | 747.05 | 726.10 | 742.90 | 749.52 | 748.50 | 758.52 | 743.43 | 765.89 | 747.00 | 755.89 | 761.62 | 750.02 |
| 2019 | 747.73 | 759.62 | 760.94 | 762.57 | 757.18 | 763.73 | 761.62 | 769.29 | 785.85 | 763.19 | 767.57 | 781.20 | 766.15 |
| **Financial Activities** | | | | | | | | | | | | | |
| 2015 | 975.88 | 1,012.69 | 1,029.11 | 1,022.13 | 1,015.06 | 994.56 | 996.30 | 1,012.91 | 1,007.04 | 1,006.10 | 1,054.23 | 1,022.46 | 1,011.63 |
| 2016 | 1,017.13 | 1,018.26 | 1,007.95 | 1,018.79 | 1,041.04 | 1,004.18 | 999.86 | 1,012.74 | 1,035.05 | 1,058.09 | 1,058.43 | 1,073.05 | 1,029.51 |
| 2017 | 1,086.32 | 1,067.99 | 1,058.43 | 1,120.46 | 1,078.24 | 1,036.67 | 1,083.36 | 1,048.28 | 1,085.15 | 1,118.60 | 1,103.86 | 1,131.09 | 1,085.60 |
| 2018 | 1,116.17 | 1,134.60 | 1,123.25 | 1,169.57 | 1,127.27 | 1,133.14 | 1,167.89 | 1,145.58 | 1,177.34 | 1,145.27 | 1,145.09 | 1,202.87 | 1,148.51 |
| 2019 | 1,166.91 | 1,146.82 | 1,152.89 | 1,166.18 | 1,168.20 | 1,219.54 | 1,165.28 | 1,177.90 | 1,219.04 | 1,191.00 | 1,230.86 | 1,235.78 | 1,186.62 |
| **Professional and Business Services** | | | | | | | | | | | | | |
| 2015 | 1,063.50 | 1,078.67 | 1,084.19 | 1,040.30 | 1,046.52 | 1,049.07 | 1,082.07 | 1,120.39 | 1,071.91 | 1,086.84 | 1,093.96 | 1,088.49 | 1,074.49 |
| 2016 | 1,066.41 | 1,070.68 | 1,075.12 | 1,079.03 | 1,084.64 | 1,066.81 | 1,062.54 | 1,054.15 | 1,067.22 | 1,095.54 | 1,050.01 | 1,059.48 | 1,069.20 |
| 2017 | 1,088.42 | 1,063.80 | 1,053.76 | 1,077.08 | 1,049.80 | 1,045.41 | 1,020.45 | 999.30 | 1,016.85 | 1,052.59 | 1,032.53 | 1,065.19 | 1,047.87 |
| 2018 | 1,040.87 | 1,029.79 | 1,039.16 | 1,076.86 | 1,064.52 | 1,081.38 | 1,092.75 | 1,069.82 | 1,118.50 | 1,088.53 | 1,100.52 | 1,125.66 | 1,076.28 |
| 2019 | 1,091.98 | 1,120.68 | 1,131.31 | 1,128.04 | 1,109.31 | 1,144.78 | 1,103.36 | 1,124.88 | 1,154.50 | 1,134.72 | 1,127.13 | 1,174.69 | 1,127.52 |
| **Education and Health Services** | | | | | | | | | | | | | |
| 2015 | 774.66 | 778.02 | 775.45 | 773.42 | 772.82 | 770.47 | 783.92 | 795.06 | 793.88 | 804.24 | 806.98 | 802.43 | 786.97 |
| 2016 | 802.10 | 798.02 | 803.60 | 807.70 | 810.62 | 807.04 | 826.84 | 818.23 | 824.65 | 828.34 | 825.00 | 819.02 | 813.78 |
| 2017 | 826.65 | 822.17 | 820.38 | 834.32 | 814.93 | 813.95 | 822.03 | 813.27 | 826.02 | 826.51 | 828.34 | 824.01 | 821.70 |
| 2018 | 847.44 | 842.62 | 847.60 | 853.81 | 857.71 | 866.65 | 874.75 | 872.68 | 898.28 | 896.11 | 909.86 | 924.51 | 874.08 |
| 2019 | 929.78 | 926.14 | 924.41 | 920.18 | 914.55 | 910.58 | 924.95 | 915.61 | 925.07 | 916.92 | 920.87 | 914.65 | 919.38 |
| **Leisure and Hospitality** | | | | | | | | | | | | | |
| 2015 | 292.09 | 296.42 | 297.36 | 294.69 | 298.32 | 298.40 | 306.50 | 314.48 | 305.52 | 302.46 | 298.45 | 302.02 | 301.01 |
| 2016 | 291.64 | 296.57 | 298.54 | 302.81 | 309.83 | 310.73 | 322.81 | 329.46 | 322.40 | 322.67 | 323.43 | 322.08 | 313.47 |
| 2017 | 324.08 | 324.08 | 331.86 | 331.44 | 339.48 | 336.54 | 350.63 | 351.67 | 349.01 | 347.41 | 342.46 | 341.50 | 339.82 |
| 2018 | 335.12 | 342.22 | 346.06 | 348.72 | 355.63 | 356.62 | 361.20 | 357.26 | 351.17 | 351.85 | 339.62 | 349.45 | 350.06 |
| 2019 | 337.66 | 343.20 | 346.54 | 346.32 | 347.76 | 359.56 | 359.18 | 366.44 | 364.08 | 360.40 | 357.40 | 367.42 | 354.78 |
| **Other Services** | | | | | | | | | | | | | |
| 2015 | 681.37 | 682.77 | 681.05 | 673.09 | 692.94 | 695.53 | 688.50 | 711.81 | 705.53 | 686.40 | 696.28 | 667.80 | 688.50 |
| 2016 | 652.48 | 650.52 | 659.18 | 661.26 | 689.83 | 643.46 | 657.91 | 661.58 | 653.86 | 660.44 | 658.70 | 662.62 | 658.77 |
| 2017 | 666.47 | 671.07 | 670.52 | 677.25 | 674.16 | 684.34 | 681.10 | 692.37 | 693.92 | 707.07 | 707.38 | 718.75 | 686.72 |
| 2018 | 708.09 | 717.00 | 706.37 | 717.29 | 706.59 | 698.57 | 697.94 | 702.42 | 724.91 | 727.73 | 729.11 | 737.57 | 713.54 |
| 2019 | 727.19 | 739.30 | 730.48 | 749.06 | 742.44 | 751.13 | 734.45 | 737.10 | 759.34 | 759.10 | 751.83 | 751.23 | 744.93 |

# MINNESOTA
## *At a Glance*

Population:
    2010 census: 5,303,925
    2019 estimate: 5,639,632

Percent change in population:
    2010–2019: 6.3%

Percent change in total nonfarm employment:
    2011–2019:  11.0%

Industry with the largest growth in employment, 2011–2019 (percent):
    Construction, 38.5%

Industry with the largest decline or smallest growth in employment, 2011–2019 (percent):
    Information, -11.2%

Civilian labor force:
    2010: 2,938,795
    2019: 3,109,648

Unemployment rate and rank among states (highest to lowest):
    2010: 7.4%, 39th
    2019: 3.2%, 35th

Over-the-year change in unemployment rates:
    2017–2018: -0.5%
    2018–2019: 0.3%

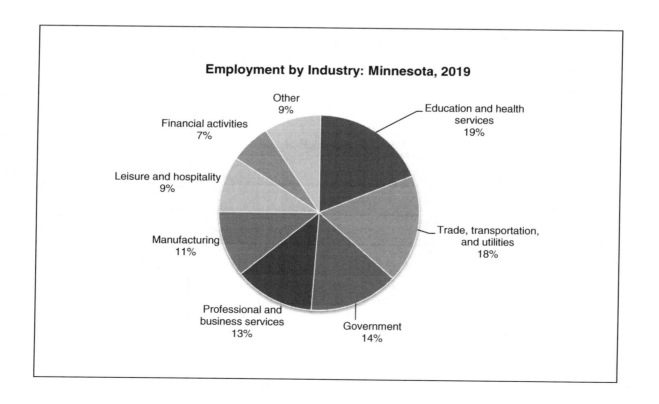

**Employment by Industry: Minnesota, 2019**

Other 9%
Financial activities 7%
Leisure and hospitality 9%
Manufacturing 11%
Professional and business services 13%
Government 14%
Education and health services 19%
Trade, transportation, and utilities 18%

## 1. Employment by Industry: Minnesota, 2011–2019

(Numbers in thousands, not seasonally adjusted)

| Industry and year | January | February | March | April | May | June | July | August | September | October | November | December | Annual average |
|---|---|---|---|---|---|---|---|---|---|---|---|---|---|
| **Total Nonfarm** | | | | | | | | | | | | | |
| 2011 | 2,603.7 | 2,609.9 | 2,619.1 | 2,668.3 | 2,705.5 | 2,723.8 | 2,670.8 | 2,702.2 | 2,723.1 | 2,729.0 | 2,724.2 | 2,715.3 | 2,682.9 |
| 2012 | 2,647.1 | 2,653.7 | 2,668.9 | 2,710.5 | 2,740.8 | 2,762.3 | 2,722.7 | 2,740.1 | 2,757.2 | 2,772.4 | 2,772.5 | 2,760.4 | 2,725.7 |
| 2013 | 2,700.1 | 2,712.6 | 2,720.4 | 2,743.9 | 2,791.7 | 2,813.0 | 2,768.1 | 2,788.3 | 2,805.7 | 2,822.5 | 2,817.6 | 2,805.8 | 2,774.1 |
| 2014 | 2,733.3 | 2,742.5 | 2,745.1 | 2,786.9 | 2,833.0 | 2,857.4 | 2,828.5 | 2,839.1 | 2,839.6 | 2,856.3 | 2,853.7 | 2,844.2 | 2,813.3 |
| 2015 | 2,775.1 | 2,786.7 | 2,793.3 | 2,843.1 | 2,880.9 | 2,900.6 | 2,877.3 | 2,881.4 | 2,879.3 | 2,902.4 | 2,899.5 | 2,887.2 | 2,858.9 |
| 2016 | 2,822.9 | 2,832.9 | 2,836.7 | 2,885.5 | 2,913.7 | 2,924.9 | 2,918.6 | 2,927.6 | 2,928.7 | 2,939.6 | 2,934.3 | 2,918.1 | 2,898.6 |
| 2017 | 2,873.4 | 2,880.7 | 2,888.5 | 2,920.8 | 2,950.5 | 2,980.9 | 2,956.0 | 2,957.7 | 2,959.1 | 2,971.3 | 2,967.3 | 2,953.5 | 2,938.3 |
| 2018 | 2,905.4 | 2,912.4 | 2,907.7 | 2,931.5 | 2,980.5 | 3,005.2 | 2,985.3 | 2,985.8 | 2,981.1 | 2,995.0 | 2,993.4 | 2,976.9 | 2,963.4 |
| 2019 | 2,925.6 | 2,924.7 | 2,922.6 | 2,956.8 | 3,002.7 | 3,022.4 | 3,003.0 | 3,005.1 | 2,992.2 | 3,008.7 | 2,994.6 | 2,972.9 | 2,977.6 |
| **Total Private** | | | | | | | | | | | | | |
| 2011 | 2190.1 | 2188.6 | 2198.1 | 2246.3 | 2284.0 | 2306.0 | 2309.8 | 2324.7 | 2317.7 | 2309.9 | 2303.0 | 2294.2 | 2272.7 |
| 2012 | 2237.1 | 2235.7 | 2250.6 | 2289.8 | 2320.5 | 2345.8 | 2347.0 | 2360.9 | 2349.4 | 2350.3 | 2345.6 | 2336.1 | 2314.1 |
| 2013 | 2286.7 | 2290.1 | 2299.7 | 2322.5 | 2368.6 | 2396.5 | 2395.1 | 2410.7 | 2395.2 | 2397.3 | 2388.4 | 2379.5 | 2360.9 |
| 2014 | 2317.3 | 2317.3 | 2320.4 | 2359.5 | 2405.3 | 2434.4 | 2436.1 | 2449.2 | 2427.0 | 2428.3 | 2422.8 | 2416.2 | 2394.5 |
| 2015 | 2357.1 | 2361.5 | 2370.1 | 2415.8 | 2453.2 | 2478.7 | 2483.6 | 2490.7 | 2467.2 | 2475.0 | 2469.2 | 2458.0 | 2440.0 |
| 2016 | 2401.9 | 2405.8 | 2409.1 | 2461.1 | 2488.4 | 2505.2 | 2524.1 | 2532.9 | 2513.5 | 2512.4 | 2505.0 | 2493.0 | 2479.4 |
| 2017 | 2448.8 | 2451.7 | 2460.5 | 2493.8 | 2525.1 | 2554.5 | 2555.8 | 2559.4 | 2537.3 | 2537.4 | 2531.0 | 2522.2 | 2514.8 |
| 2018 | 2477.6 | 2479.4 | 2476.4 | 2500.9 | 2548.6 | 2573.3 | 2581.8 | 2585.1 | 2560.7 | 2562.6 | 2559.5 | 2545.9 | 2537.7 |
| 2019 | 2498.3 | 2494.7 | 2492.9 | 2526.5 | 2569.1 | 2588.5 | 2598.4 | 2603.2 | 2570.1 | 2574.3 | 2557.9 | 2540.0 | 2551.2 |
| **Goods Producing** | | | | | | | | | | | | | |
| 2011 | 373.0 | 371.3 | 373.7 | 386.1 | 399.5 | 411.3 | 417.2 | 420.5 | 416.2 | 414.6 | 407.2 | 398.0 | 399.1 |
| 2012 | 383.1 | 381.1 | 386.5 | 398.8 | 409.4 | 421.7 | 424.9 | 427.4 | 422.5 | 420.1 | 412.4 | 404.1 | 407.7 |
| 2013 | 390.0 | 388.9 | 392.6 | 399.1 | 416.0 | 428.6 | 431.6 | 435.8 | 431.4 | 429.3 | 423.3 | 413.0 | 415.0 |
| 2014 | 399.7 | 398.7 | 400.8 | 410.9 | 428.3 | 442.1 | 446.7 | 449.8 | 443.8 | 442.4 | 435.0 | 427.9 | 427.2 |
| 2015 | 413.8 | 413.3 | 416.8 | 431.2 | 443.0 | 455.3 | 460.0 | 460.4 | 453.3 | 451.0 | 443.8 | 434.5 | 439.7 |
| 2016 | 417.1 | 415.8 | 418.8 | 433.4 | 444.0 | 453.9 | 458.7 | 459.5 | 453.4 | 451.3 | 444.3 | 432.5 | 440.2 |
| 2017 | 420.8 | 421.0 | 425.1 | 435.0 | 447.7 | 460.1 | 463.0 | 463.1 | 456.3 | 456.7 | 448.2 | 439.5 | 444.7 |
| 2018 | 425.5 | 424.4 | 426.7 | 433.4 | 451.6 | 466.8 | 470.5 | 471.4 | 465.7 | 463.7 | 457.5 | 448.3 | 450.5 |
| 2019 | 434.4 | 432.8 | 435.7 | 445.3 | 462.6 | 474.3 | 477.9 | 478.9 | 472.8 | 473.5 | 456.0 | 444.5 | 457.4 |
| **Service-Providing** | | | | | | | | | | | | | |
| 2011 | 2,230.7 | 2,238.6 | 2,245.4 | 2,282.2 | 2,306.0 | 2,312.5 | 2,253.6 | 2,281.7 | 2,306.9 | 2,314.4 | 2,317.0 | 2,317.3 | 2,283.9 |
| 2012 | 2,264.0 | 2,272.6 | 2,282.4 | 2,311.7 | 2,331.4 | 2,340.6 | 2,297.8 | 2,312.7 | 2,334.7 | 2,352.3 | 2,360.1 | 2,356.3 | 2,318.1 |
| 2013 | 2,310.1 | 2,323.7 | 2,327.8 | 2,344.8 | 2,375.7 | 2,384.4 | 2,336.5 | 2,352.5 | 2,374.3 | 2,393.2 | 2,394.3 | 2,392.8 | 2,359.2 |
| 2014 | 2,333.6 | 2,343.8 | 2,344.3 | 2,376.0 | 2,404.7 | 2,415.3 | 2,381.8 | 2,389.3 | 2,395.8 | 2,413.9 | 2,418.7 | 2,416.3 | 2,386.1 |
| 2015 | 2,361.3 | 2,373.4 | 2,376.5 | 2,411.9 | 2,437.9 | 2,445.3 | 2,417.3 | 2,421.0 | 2,426.0 | 2,451.4 | 2,455.7 | 2,452.7 | 2,419.2 |
| 2016 | 2,405.8 | 2,417.1 | 2,417.9 | 2,452.1 | 2,469.7 | 2,471.0 | 2,459.9 | 2,468.1 | 2,475.3 | 2,488.3 | 2,490.0 | 2,485.6 | 2,458.4 |
| 2017 | 2,452.6 | 2,459.7 | 2,463.4 | 2,485.8 | 2,502.8 | 2,520.8 | 2,493.0 | 2,494.6 | 2,502.8 | 2,514.6 | 2,519.1 | 2,514.0 | 2,493.6 |
| 2018 | 2,479.9 | 2,488.0 | 2,481.0 | 2,498.1 | 2,528.9 | 2,538.4 | 2,514.8 | 2,514.4 | 2,515.4 | 2,531.3 | 2,535.9 | 2,528.6 | 2,512.9 |
| 2019 | 2,491.2 | 2,491.9 | 2,486.9 | 2,511.5 | 2,540.1 | 2,548.1 | 2,525.1 | 2,526.2 | 2,519.4 | 2,535.2 | 2,538.6 | 2,528.4 | 2,520.2 |
| **Mining and Logging** | | | | | | | | | | | | | |
| 2011 | 6.0 | 6.2 | 6.1 | 6.1 | 6.5 | 6.8 | 7.0 | 7.1 | 6.9 | 7.0 | 6.9 | 6.6 | 6.6 |
| 2012 | 6.6 | 6.6 | 6.6 | 6.8 | 7.0 | 7.3 | 7.4 | 7.5 | 7.2 | 7.2 | 7.1 | 6.8 | 7.0 |
| 2013 | 6.6 | 6.6 | 6.7 | 6.6 | 6.9 | 7.2 | 7.2 | 7.4 | 7.2 | 7.2 | 7.1 | 6.9 | 7.0 |
| 2014 | 6.6 | 6.7 | 6.7 | 6.8 | 7.1 | 7.3 | 7.6 | 7.6 | 7.4 | 7.5 | 7.4 | 7.1 | 7.2 |
| 2015 | 6.8 | 6.9 | 7.0 | 7.1 | 7.3 | 7.4 | 7.6 | 7.2 | 6.9 | 6.8 | 6.7 | 6.4 | 7.0 |
| 2016 | 5.5 | 5.4 | 5.7 | 5.7 | 6.4 | 6.4 | 6.6 | 6.7 | 6.7 | 6.8 | 6.5 | 6.2 | 6.2 |
| 2017 | 6.1 | 6.2 | 6.3 | 6.3 | 6.6 | 6.8 | 6.8 | 6.8 | 6.8 | 6.8 | 6.8 | 6.6 | 6.6 |
| 2018 | 6.3 | 6.4 | 6.5 | 6.2 | 6.6 | 6.9 | 7.0 | 7.0 | 6.9 | 6.8 | 6.7 | 6.4 | 6.6 |
| 2019 | 6.1 | 6.2 | 6.4 | 6.3 | 6.7 | 6.8 | 6.9 | 7.0 | 6.8 | 6.8 | 6.6 | 6.1 | 6.6 |
| **Construction** | | | | | | | | | | | | | |
| 2011 | 74.2 | 72.7 | 74.5 | 83.3 | 93.6 | 101.1 | 103.8 | 105.6 | 103.8 | 102.5 | 97.3 | 88.8 | 91.8 |
| 2012 | 77.4 | 75.9 | 79.7 | 90.0 | 98.0 | 104.4 | 106.9 | 108.2 | 105.2 | 104.0 | 98.2 | 91.4 | 94.9 |
| 2013 | 80.5 | 80.0 | 82.4 | 88.9 | 102.7 | 110.3 | 113.4 | 116.2 | 114.2 | 112.8 | 107.7 | 98.1 | 100.6 |
| 2014 | 87.9 | 86.7 | 88.9 | 96.5 | 110.6 | 119.3 | 122.1 | 123.4 | 120.4 | 119.0 | 112.3 | 105.2 | 107.7 |
| 2015 | 94.4 | 93.9 | 96.3 | 109.3 | 119.2 | 127.0 | 130.2 | 130.6 | 126.6 | 125.1 | 118.6 | 110.8 | 115.2 |
| 2016 | 97.3 | 96.4 | 98.6 | 112.2 | 121.1 | 127.1 | 129.8 | 129.6 | 126.8 | 125.3 | 120.1 | 110.0 | 116.2 |
| 2017 | 100.7 | 100.8 | 104.2 | 113.6 | 124.1 | 131.4 | 133.2 | 133.3 | 130.0 | 129.2 | 121.9 | 114.8 | 119.8 |
| 2018 | 103.2 | 102.1 | 103.6 | 109.2 | 124.9 | 134.6 | 136.9 | 137.1 | 134.2 | 132.2 | 126.5 | 118.0 | 121.9 |
| 2019 | 107.2 | 105.6 | 108.0 | 117.5 | 132.5 | 140.4 | 142.1 | 143.1 | 140.9 | 140.3 | 127.9 | 119.4 | 127.1 |

## 1. Employment by Industry: Minnesota, 2011–2019—*Continued*

(Numbers in thousands, not seasonally adjusted)

| Industry and year | January | February | March | April | May | June | July | August | September | October | November | December | Annual average |
|---|---|---|---|---|---|---|---|---|---|---|---|---|---|
| **Manufacturing** | | | | | | | | | | | | | |
| 2011 | 292.8 | 292.4 | 293.1 | 296.7 | 299.4 | 303.4 | 306.4 | 307.8 | 305.5 | 305.1 | 303.0 | 302.6 | 300.7 |
| 2012 | 299.1 | 298.6 | 300.2 | 302.0 | 304.4 | 310.0 | 310.6 | 311.7 | 310.1 | 308.9 | 307.1 | 305.9 | 305.7 |
| 2013 | 302.9 | 302.3 | 303.5 | 303.6 | 306.4 | 311.1 | 311.0 | 312.2 | 310.0 | 309.3 | 308.5 | 308.0 | 307.4 |
| 2014 | 305.2 | 305.3 | 305.2 | 307.6 | 310.6 | 315.5 | 317.0 | 318.8 | 316.0 | 315.9 | 315.3 | 315.6 | 312.3 |
| 2015 | 312.6 | 312.5 | 313.5 | 314.8 | 316.5 | 320.9 | 322.2 | 322.6 | 319.8 | 319.1 | 318.5 | 317.3 | 317.5 |
| 2016 | 314.3 | 314.0 | 314.5 | 315.5 | 316.5 | 320.4 | 322.3 | 323.2 | 319.9 | 319.2 | 317.7 | 316.3 | 317.8 |
| 2017 | 314.0 | 314.0 | 314.6 | 315.1 | 317.0 | 321.9 | 323.0 | 323.0 | 319.5 | 320.7 | 319.5 | 318.1 | 318.4 |
| 2018 | 316.0 | 315.9 | 316.6 | 318.0 | 320.1 | 325.3 | 326.6 | 327.3 | 324.6 | 324.7 | 324.3 | 323.9 | 321.9 |
| 2019 | 321.1 | 321.0 | 321.3 | 321.5 | 323.4 | 327.1 | 328.9 | 328.8 | 325.1 | 326.4 | 321.5 | 319.0 | 323.8 |
| **Trade, Transportation, and Utilities** | | | | | | | | | | | | | |
| 2011 | 480.2 | 476.3 | 477.8 | 487.4 | 494.2 | 496.2 | 494.5 | 495.4 | 495.7 | 497.3 | 504.5 | 507.9 | 492.3 |
| 2012 | 490.4 | 483.8 | 486.5 | 493.5 | 499.8 | 501.9 | 498.5 | 500.1 | 498.5 | 503.0 | 512.1 | 512.4 | 498.4 |
| 2013 | 496.9 | 491.8 | 492.9 | 496.2 | 505.6 | 510.1 | 506.0 | 509.5 | 507.5 | 511.1 | 518.5 | 522.0 | 505.7 |
| 2014 | 501.6 | 496.8 | 497.6 | 505.4 | 512.7 | 516.5 | 513.9 | 515.4 | 510.7 | 515.7 | 522.8 | 528.3 | 511.5 |
| 2015 | 508.8 | 504.4 | 505.7 | 514.5 | 520.9 | 525.3 | 522.3 | 523.5 | 519.1 | 524.5 | 531.5 | 534.6 | 519.6 |
| 2016 | 516.7 | 513.7 | 514.2 | 523.3 | 528.5 | 529.5 | 530.4 | 531.8 | 526.9 | 531.1 | 537.0 | 541.3 | 527.0 |
| 2017 | 527.1 | 522.7 | 522.5 | 528.7 | 534.1 | 537.6 | 535.0 | 535.0 | 530.6 | 534.4 | 542.4 | 546.5 | 533.1 |
| 2018 | 530.9 | 526.5 | 525.8 | 527.7 | 535.9 | 536.6 | 536.0 | 535.2 | 530.3 | 531.9 | 542.3 | 545.6 | 533.7 |
| 2019 | 531.1 | 522.3 | 520.6 | 524.9 | 532.2 | 532.6 | 531.1 | 530.8 | 525.0 | 530.5 | 538.0 | 542.5 | 530.1 |
| **Wholesale Trade** | | | | | | | | | | | | | |
| 2011 | 117.6 | 117.7 | 118.1 | 120.5 | 122.2 | 122.4 | 123.0 | 122.9 | 121.5 | 121.7 | 121.5 | 121.2 | 120.9 |
| 2012 | 120.2 | 120.3 | 121.3 | 123.5 | 124.4 | 125.7 | 126.1 | 125.4 | 123.9 | 124.4 | 124.4 | 124.3 | 123.7 |
| 2013 | 122.5 | 122.5 | 122.9 | 124.1 | 126.2 | 127.1 | 127.0 | 126.7 | 125.1 | 125.7 | 126.1 | 125.4 | 125.1 |
| 2014 | 123.6 | 123.5 | 123.9 | 125.3 | 127.5 | 128.3 | 128.3 | 128.1 | 126.4 | 127.1 | 127.4 | 127.2 | 126.4 |
| 2015 | 125.1 | 124.9 | 125.3 | 127.5 | 127.9 | 129.0 | 129.2 | 128.8 | 126.9 | 127.4 | 127.5 | 126.9 | 127.2 |
| 2016 | 124.9 | 124.9 | 125.1 | 127.5 | 128.2 | 128.0 | 128.7 | 128.4 | 126.4 | 126.4 | 126.3 | 125.8 | 126.7 |
| 2017 | 125.6 | 125.3 | 125.7 | 127.1 | 128.4 | 129.2 | 129.5 | 129.2 | 127.4 | 127.8 | 128.0 | 127.9 | 127.6 |
| 2018 | 126.5 | 126.6 | 126.8 | 127.6 | 129.1 | 130.0 | 129.3 | 128.9 | 126.8 | 127.5 | 127.5 | 127.4 | 127.8 |
| 2019 | 127.2 | 126.9 | 126.7 | 127.8 | 129.4 | 129.9 | 130.1 | 129.4 | 127.2 | 127.1 | 127.4 | 127.2 | 128.0 |
| **Retail Trade** | | | | | | | | | | | | | |
| 2011 | 272.6 | 268.4 | 269.1 | 275.6 | 280.0 | 283.0 | 282.5 | 284.2 | 281.6 | 282.2 | 289.5 | 292.2 | 280.1 |
| 2012 | 279.3 | 272.8 | 274.4 | 277.8 | 282.3 | 284.9 | 283.1 | 284.7 | 281.7 | 284.7 | 293.4 | 293.5 | 282.7 |
| 2013 | 282.0 | 276.5 | 277.5 | 279.6 | 285.5 | 290.4 | 288.8 | 291.2 | 287.5 | 288.5 | 295.1 | 298.6 | 286.8 |
| 2014 | 283.2 | 278.9 | 279.4 | 284.0 | 288.4 | 292.4 | 292.2 | 293.1 | 287.1 | 289.9 | 296.4 | 300.4 | 288.8 |
| 2015 | 286.6 | 282.4 | 283.3 | 287.9 | 293.5 | 298.0 | 296.7 | 298.1 | 292.5 | 295.7 | 302.0 | 304.1 | 293.4 |
| 2016 | 291.9 | 288.9 | 289.4 | 294.7 | 298.4 | 300.7 | 302.9 | 303.3 | 296.3 | 299.2 | 304.2 | 306.3 | 298.0 |
| 2017 | 295.9 | 292.0 | 292.0 | 296.1 | 299.2 | 302.4 | 302.1 | 302.2 | 295.5 | 297.9 | 304.6 | 307.0 | 298.9 |
| 2018 | 296.5 | 292.2 | 291.6 | 292.4 | 298.6 | 301.2 | 301.8 | 301.3 | 294.6 | 295.1 | 304.4 | 306.3 | 298.0 |
| 2019 | 294.5 | 287.4 | 286.4 | 288.9 | 293.2 | 295.0 | 294.7 | 294.1 | 287.3 | 292.1 | 298.5 | 301.9 | 292.8 |
| **Transportation and Utilities** | | | | | | | | | | | | | |
| 2011 | 90.0 | 90.2 | 90.6 | 91.3 | 92.0 | 90.8 | 89.0 | 88.3 | 92.6 | 93.4 | 93.5 | 94.5 | 91.4 |
| 2012 | 90.9 | 90.7 | 90.8 | 92.2 | 93.1 | 91.3 | 89.3 | 90.0 | 92.9 | 93.9 | 94.3 | 94.6 | 92.0 |
| 2013 | 92.4 | 92.8 | 92.5 | 92.5 | 93.9 | 92.6 | 90.2 | 91.6 | 94.9 | 96.9 | 97.3 | 98.0 | 93.8 |
| 2014 | 94.8 | 94.4 | 94.3 | 96.1 | 96.8 | 95.8 | 93.4 | 94.2 | 97.2 | 98.7 | 99.0 | 100.7 | 96.3 |
| 2015 | 97.1 | 97.1 | 97.1 | 99.1 | 99.5 | 98.3 | 96.4 | 96.6 | 99.7 | 101.4 | 102.0 | 103.6 | 99.0 |
| 2016 | 99.9 | 99.9 | 99.7 | 101.1 | 101.9 | 100.8 | 98.8 | 100.1 | 104.2 | 105.5 | 106.5 | 109.2 | 102.3 |
| 2017 | 105.6 | 105.4 | 104.8 | 105.5 | 106.5 | 106.0 | 103.4 | 103.6 | 107.7 | 108.7 | 109.8 | 111.6 | 106.6 |
| 2018 | 107.9 | 107.7 | 107.4 | 107.7 | 108.2 | 105.4 | 104.9 | 105.0 | 108.9 | 109.3 | 110.4 | 111.9 | 107.9 |
| 2019 | 109.4 | 108.0 | 107.5 | 108.2 | 109.6 | 107.7 | 106.3 | 107.3 | 110.5 | 111.3 | 112.1 | 113.4 | 109.3 |
| **Information** | | | | | | | | | | | | | |
| 2011 | 52.6 | 52.2 | 52.0 | 52.7 | 52.7 | 53.0 | 53.2 | 53.6 | 52.9 | 52.7 | 52.6 | 52.7 | 52.7 |
| 2012 | 51.4 | 51.4 | 51.5 | 51.0 | 51.4 | 51.5 | 51.6 | 51.6 | 51.2 | 51.3 | 51.1 | 51.3 | 51.4 |
| 2013 | 50.6 | 50.8 | 50.7 | 50.8 | 51.0 | 51.0 | 51.5 | 51.3 | 50.5 | 50.4 | 50.6 | 50.7 | 50.8 |
| 2014 | 50.3 | 50.2 | 49.9 | 49.9 | 50.1 | 50.5 | 50.8 | 50.8 | 49.9 | 50.0 | 49.8 | 50.2 | 50.2 |
| 2015 | 49.1 | 48.9 | 48.8 | 48.7 | 49.0 | 49.4 | 49.7 | 49.7 | 48.7 | 48.6 | 48.9 | 48.6 | 49.0 |
| 2016 | 47.9 | 48.0 | 47.9 | 48.2 | 48.3 | 48.3 | 48.7 | 49.1 | 49.1 | 48.6 | 48.5 | 48.5 | 48.4 |
| 2017 | 48.2 | 48.1 | 48.2 | 48.2 | 48.2 | 48.5 | 48.3 | 48.7 | 47.7 | 47.5 | 47.8 | 47.9 | 48.1 |
| 2018 | 47.5 | 47.6 | 47.1 | 47.1 | 47.2 | 47.6 | 47.8 | 48.0 | 46.9 | 46.8 | 46.8 | 46.8 | 47.3 |
| 2019 | 46.9 | 46.8 | 46.5 | 46.8 | 46.9 | 47.1 | 47.5 | 47.7 | 46.8 | 46.0 | 46.4 | 46.0 | 46.8 |

# 1. Employment by Industry: Minnesota, 2011–2019—*Continued*

(Numbers in thousands, not seasonally adjusted)

| Industry and year | January | February | March | April | May | June | July | August | September | October | November | December | Annual average |
|---|---|---|---|---|---|---|---|---|---|---|---|---|---|
| **Financial Activities** | | | | | | | | | | | | | |
| 2011 | 163.5 | 163.5 | 163.4 | 163.5 | 164.2 | 164.8 | 165.5 | 165.8 | 164.2 | 164.0 | 163.8 | 164.1 | 164.2 |
| 2012 | 164.2 | 164.7 | 164.8 | 166.6 | 167.9 | 170.0 | 170.9 | 171.4 | 170.5 | 171.3 | 171.8 | 172.6 | 168.9 |
| 2013 | 171.9 | 172.4 | 172.7 | 172.4 | 173.3 | 175.1 | 175.8 | 175.7 | 173.9 | 174.1 | 174.3 | 174.5 | 173.8 |
| 2014 | 172.8 | 172.6 | 172.6 | 173.1 | 174.2 | 176.3 | 176.7 | 176.5 | 174.4 | 174.6 | 174.6 | 175.4 | 174.5 |
| 2015 | 175.4 | 175.5 | 175.7 | 177.0 | 178.3 | 180.2 | 182.0 | 182.0 | 179.6 | 180.3 | 180.5 | 181.1 | 179.0 |
| 2016 | 179.7 | 179.9 | 180.2 | 181.8 | 182.4 | 183.9 | 186.3 | 186.4 | 184.8 | 185.2 | 185.3 | 185.9 | 183.5 |
| 2017 | 185.5 | 185.8 | 186.1 | 186.4 | 187.4 | 189.8 | 191.0 | 190.7 | 188.6 | 188.6 | 188.4 | 189.3 | 188.1 |
| 2018 | 188.1 | 188.2 | 188.3 | 189.3 | 189.9 | 192.0 | 193.5 | 193.3 | 191.2 | 191.9 | 191.9 | 192.3 | 190.8 |
| 2019 | 190.9 | 191.1 | 191.1 | 191.5 | 192.4 | 194.7 | 195.8 | 195.7 | 193.0 | 191.9 | 191.6 | 191.3 | 192.6 |
| **Professional and Business Services** | | | | | | | | | | | | | |
| 2011 | 326.7 | 327.6 | 329.4 | 338.2 | 340.3 | 343.7 | 348.3 | 352.4 | 351.0 | 352.5 | 351.3 | 349.5 | 342.6 |
| 2012 | 338.2 | 338.2 | 339.9 | 347.0 | 348.6 | 352.4 | 355.2 | 358.7 | 355.4 | 358.3 | 356.8 | 356.4 | 350.4 |
| 2013 | 347.4 | 350.6 | 351.8 | 355.4 | 358.2 | 363.7 | 364.7 | 368.6 | 364.8 | 369.7 | 366.8 | 366.6 | 360.7 |
| 2014 | 354.5 | 355.3 | 355.2 | 360.3 | 364.3 | 369.2 | 372.6 | 375.8 | 370.3 | 374.7 | 375.9 | 371.1 | 366.6 |
| 2015 | 360.5 | 361.7 | 361.4 | 370.5 | 373.8 | 375.5 | 378.4 | 379.5 | 372.9 | 380.5 | 380.2 | 376.1 | 372.6 |
| 2016 | 366.6 | 368.6 | 365.7 | 376.0 | 376.9 | 379.1 | 384.5 | 384.7 | 382.9 | 386.7 | 383.6 | 381.4 | 378.1 |
| 2017 | 371.9 | 371.1 | 372.1 | 377.5 | 379.0 | 382.1 | 384.1 | 384.6 | 380.6 | 384.1 | 384.3 | 380.2 | 379.3 |
| 2018 | 375.5 | 376.0 | 371.9 | 378.3 | 382.1 | 384.0 | 387.8 | 388.3 | 384.2 | 389.0 | 387.5 | 382.2 | 382.2 |
| 2019 | 375.2 | 377.3 | 374.8 | 381.8 | 385.0 | 386.3 | 389.5 | 390.3 | 383.8 | 386.1 | 385.0 | 381.4 | 383.0 |
| **Education and Health Services** | | | | | | | | | | | | | |
| 2011 | 460.6 | 464.3 | 464.4 | 469.9 | 470.4 | 464.5 | 459.5 | 461.8 | 468.8 | 472.4 | 473.8 | 474.2 | 467.1 |
| 2012 | 467.9 | 473.8 | 474.1 | 476.8 | 476.6 | 469.8 | 467.4 | 470.8 | 479.0 | 484.2 | 486.3 | 485.4 | 476.0 |
| 2013 | 481.6 | 487.4 | 487.0 | 491.3 | 491.2 | 483.8 | 480.9 | 483.6 | 490.5 | 496.2 | 498.2 | 496.4 | 489.0 |
| 2014 | 490.6 | 496.2 | 496.0 | 499.8 | 499.5 | 492.2 | 488.9 | 491.6 | 499.8 | 503.6 | 505.7 | 504.7 | 497.4 |
| 2015 | 497.4 | 504.7 | 505.2 | 506.9 | 507.3 | 500.2 | 498.6 | 500.7 | 510.0 | 514.4 | 516.7 | 515.2 | 506.4 |
| 2016 | 512.5 | 517.9 | 517.4 | 523.6 | 521.8 | 513.0 | 514.5 | 517.7 | 524.0 | 525.8 | 531.6 | 531.2 | 520.9 |
| 2017 | 526.2 | 533.1 | 532.9 | 537.2 | 535.8 | 530.8 | 528.0 | 529.4 | 538.2 | 541.5 | 543.9 | 543.3 | 535.0 |
| 2018 | 538.4 | 544.9 | 544.9 | 549.0 | 548.3 | 541.2 | 538.8 | 539.6 | 547.1 | 551.6 | 554.2 | 551.8 | 545.8 |
| 2019 | 547.2 | 551.5 | 550.6 | 554.5 | 553.3 | 545.5 | 544.7 | 546.1 | 552.8 | 558.5 | 558.0 | 552.9 | 551.3 |
| **Leisure and Hospitality** | | | | | | | | | | | | | |
| 2011 | 220.8 | 220.4 | 223.8 | 233.7 | 247.5 | 255.9 | 255.1 | 258.3 | 252.7 | 241.1 | 234.6 | 232.3 | 239.7 |
| 2012 | 227.7 | 228.4 | 232.5 | 240.6 | 251.0 | 260.6 | 261.4 | 263.7 | 256.6 | 246.2 | 239.3 | 238.0 | 245.5 |
| 2013 | 233.3 | 232.9 | 235.9 | 241.3 | 256.4 | 266.4 | 266.4 | 269.1 | 261.1 | 252.1 | 243.2 | 243.0 | 250.2 |
| 2014 | 236.7 | 236.9 | 237.5 | 247.7 | 262.6 | 272.6 | 271.7 | 274.5 | 264.7 | 253.7 | 245.9 | 245.6 | 254.2 |
| 2015 | 240.3 | 240.8 | 243.6 | 252.8 | 266.4 | 277.0 | 277.1 | 279.3 | 269.9 | 260.9 | 253.1 | 253.0 | 259.5 |
| 2016 | 248.1 | 248.1 | 250.4 | 259.3 | 270.7 | 280.7 | 283.6 | 286.0 | 275.6 | 267.1 | 258.5 | 256.2 | 265.4 |
| 2017 | 254.0 | 255.0 | 257.9 | 264.8 | 276.4 | 287.9 | 289.4 | 291.0 | 279.9 | 269.5 | 261.6 | 261.0 | 270.7 |
| 2018 | 259.0 | 259.1 | 259.1 | 263.1 | 279.7 | 289.4 | 291.6 | 293.9 | 282.0 | 273.3 | 265.1 | 265.3 | 273.4 |
| 2019 | 260.6 | 260.7 | 261.1 | 267.6 | 282.1 | 291.6 | 295.4 | 297.2 | 281.9 | 274.4 | 268.1 | 266.5 | 275.6 |
| **Other Services** | | | | | | | | | | | | | |
| 2011 | 112.7 | 113.0 | 113.6 | 114.8 | 115.2 | 116.6 | 116.5 | 116.9 | 116.2 | 115.3 | 115.2 | 115.5 | 115.1 |
| 2012 | 114.2 | 114.3 | 114.8 | 115.5 | 115.8 | 117.9 | 117.1 | 117.2 | 115.7 | 115.9 | 115.8 | 115.9 | 115.8 |
| 2013 | 115.0 | 115.3 | 116.1 | 116.0 | 116.9 | 117.8 | 116.8 | 117.1 | 115.5 | 114.4 | 113.5 | 113.3 | 115.6 |
| 2014 | 111.1 | 110.6 | 110.8 | 112.4 | 113.6 | 115.0 | 114.8 | 114.8 | 113.4 | 113.6 | 113.1 | 113.0 | 113.0 |
| 2015 | 111.8 | 112.2 | 112.9 | 114.2 | 114.5 | 115.8 | 115.5 | 115.6 | 113.7 | 114.8 | 114.5 | 114.9 | 114.2 |
| 2016 | 113.3 | 113.8 | 114.5 | 115.5 | 115.8 | 116.8 | 117.4 | 117.7 | 116.8 | 116.6 | 116.2 | 116.0 | 115.9 |
| 2017 | 115.1 | 114.9 | 115.7 | 116.0 | 116.5 | 117.7 | 117.0 | 116.9 | 115.4 | 115.1 | 114.4 | 114.5 | 115.8 |
| 2018 | 112.7 | 112.7 | 112.6 | 113.0 | 113.9 | 115.7 | 115.8 | 115.4 | 113.3 | 114.4 | 114.2 | 113.6 | 113.9 |
| 2019 | 112.0 | 112.2 | 112.5 | 114.1 | 114.6 | 116.4 | 116.5 | 116.5 | 114.0 | 113.4 | 114.8 | 114.9 | 114.3 |
| **Government** | | | | | | | | | | | | | |
| 2011 | 413.6 | 421.3 | 421.0 | 422.0 | 421.5 | 417.8 | 361.0 | 377.5 | 405.4 | 419.1 | 421.2 | 421.1 | 410.2 |
| 2012 | 410.0 | 418.0 | 418.3 | 420.7 | 420.3 | 416.5 | 375.7 | 379.2 | 407.8 | 422.1 | 426.9 | 424.3 | 411.7 |
| 2013 | 413.4 | 422.5 | 420.7 | 421.4 | 423.1 | 416.5 | 373.0 | 377.6 | 410.5 | 425.2 | 429.2 | 426.3 | 413.3 |
| 2014 | 416.0 | 425.2 | 424.7 | 427.4 | 427.7 | 423.0 | 392.4 | 389.9 | 412.6 | 428.0 | 430.9 | 428.0 | 418.8 |
| 2015 | 418.0 | 425.2 | 423.2 | 427.3 | 427.7 | 421.9 | 393.7 | 390.7 | 412.1 | 427.4 | 430.3 | 429.2 | 418.9 |
| 2016 | 421.0 | 427.1 | 427.6 | 424.4 | 425.3 | 419.7 | 394.5 | 394.7 | 415.2 | 427.2 | 429.3 | 425.1 | 419.3 |
| 2017 | 424.6 | 429.0 | 428.0 | 427.0 | 425.4 | 426.4 | 400.2 | 398.3 | 421.8 | 433.9 | 436.3 | 431.3 | 423.5 |
| 2018 | 427.8 | 433.0 | 431.3 | 430.6 | 431.9 | 431.9 | 403.5 | 400.7 | 420.4 | 432.4 | 433.9 | 431.0 | 425.7 |
| 2019 | 427.3 | 430.0 | 429.7 | 430.3 | 433.6 | 433.9 | 404.6 | 401.9 | 422.1 | 434.4 | 436.7 | 432.9 | 426.5 |

## 2. Average Weekly Hours by Selected Industry: Minnesota, 2015–2019

(Not seasonally adjusted)

| Industry and year | January | February | March | April | May | June | July | August | September | October | November | December | Annual average |
|---|---|---|---|---|---|---|---|---|---|---|---|---|---|
| **Total Private** | | | | | | | | | | | | | |
| 2015 | 33.5 | 33.9 | 33.9 | 33.6 | 33.8 | 34.1 | 34.2 | 34.8 | 33.9 | 34.0 | 34.2 | 33.7 | 34.0 |
| 2016 | 33.5 | 33.4 | 33.5 | 33.7 | 34.3 | 34.3 | 34.1 | 34.1 | 34.1 | 34.5 | 34.2 | 33.9 | 34.0 |
| 2017 | 34.0 | 33.8 | 33.8 | 34.2 | 33.9 | 34.1 | 34.4 | 34.2 | 34.1 | 34.4 | 34.1 | 33.9 | 34.1 |
| 2018 | 33.5 | 33.7 | 33.7 | 34.0 | 34.0 | 34.1 | 34.3 | 34.3 | 34.4 | 33.6 | 33.8 | 34.1 | 34.0 |
| 2019 | 33.3 | 33.3 | 33.4 | 33.2 | 33.8 | 34.5 | 33.9 | 34.1 | 34.1 | 33.6 | 33.6 | 33.9 | 33.7 |
| **Goods-Producing** | | | | | | | | | | | | | |
| 2015 | 39.2 | 39.3 | 39.2 | 39.1 | 39.7 | 40.1 | 39.6 | 40.4 | 38.9 | 39.5 | 39.3 | 39.1 | 39.5 |
| 2016 | 38.8 | 38.8 | 38.8 | 39.1 | 39.2 | 39.7 | 39.2 | 39.5 | 39.9 | 39.5 | 39.6 | 38.7 | 39.2 |
| 2017 | 38.6 | 39.1 | 39.5 | 39.0 | 39.6 | 39.8 | 39.9 | 40.3 | 40.4 | 39.9 | 39.5 | 39.6 | 39.6 |
| 2018 | 38.9 | 39.1 | 39.4 | 39.1 | 39.8 | 40.1 | 39.9 | 40.4 | 40.6 | 39.7 | 39.5 | 39.8 | 39.7 |
| 2019 | 39.0 | 38.9 | 39.2 | 38.4 | 39.9 | 40.7 | 39.8 | 40.3 | 39.8 | 39.9 | 39.4 | 39.1 | 39.6 |
| **Construction** | | | | | | | | | | | | | |
| 2015 | 36.3 | 37.0 | 37.0 | 38.2 | 40.2 | 41.6 | 41.2 | 42.1 | 38.6 | 40.3 | 38.8 | 38.1 | 39.3 |
| 2016 | 37.5 | 37.6 | 37.9 | 38.4 | 38.9 | 40.9 | 41.0 | 40.4 | 40.8 | 41.0 | 40.0 | 37.8 | 39.5 |
| 2017 | 37.5 | 38.4 | 38.6 | 38.7 | 40.1 | 40.5 | 40.4 | 41.0 | 40.4 | 40.2 | 38.9 | 38.4 | 39.5 |
| 2018 | 37.2 | 37.4 | 37.9 | 37.2 | 39.2 | 40.8 | 40.4 | 40.6 | 40.3 | 38.5 | 38.9 | 39.3 | 39.1 |
| 2019 | 38.4 | 37.5 | 37.9 | 36.1 | 39.5 | 41.4 | 40.2 | 40.9 | 39.1 | 39.2 | 38.5 | 37.5 | 39.0 |
| **Manufacturing** | | | | | | | | | | | | | |
| 2015 | 39.8 | 39.8 | 39.8 | 39.3 | 39.6 | 39.6 | 39.0 | 39.9 | 39.4 | 39.6 | 40.0 | 39.8 | 39.6 |
| 2016 | 39.4 | 39.3 | 39.5 | 39.6 | 39.6 | 39.5 | 38.6 | 39.3 | 39.6 | 38.8 | 39.4 | 39.0 | 39.3 |
| 2017 | 39.0 | 39.3 | 39.9 | 39.3 | 39.4 | 39.5 | 39.7 | 39.9 | 40.3 | 39.6 | 39.6 | 39.9 | 39.6 |
| 2018 | 39.5 | 39.7 | 39.9 | 39.9 | 40.1 | 39.7 | 39.5 | 40.1 | 40.5 | 39.8 | 39.4 | 39.6 | 39.8 |
| 2019 | 38.8 | 39.1 | 39.5 | 39.3 | 40.0 | 40.3 | 39.6 | 40.0 | 40.3 | 40.3 | 39.9 | 39.9 | 39.8 |
| **Trade, Transportation, and Utilities** | | | | | | | | | | | | | |
| 2015 | 32.7 | 33.2 | 32.8 | 32.6 | 32.7 | 33.0 | 33.3 | 33.8 | 33.3 | 32.9 | 33.0 | 32.9 | 33.0 |
| 2016 | 32.0 | 32.2 | 32.3 | 32.3 | 33.2 | 33.0 | 33.1 | 32.7 | 32.9 | 33.2 | 32.7 | 32.9 | 32.7 |
| 2017 | 32.3 | 31.7 | 31.8 | 32.4 | 31.9 | 32.2 | 32.8 | 32.4 | 32.2 | 32.0 | 32.6 | 32.8 | 32.3 |
| 2018 | 31.7 | 31.9 | 31.7 | 32.1 | 32.5 | 32.4 | 32.8 | 32.6 | 32.8 | 31.7 | 32.3 | 32.2 | 32.2 |
| 2019 | 31.3 | 31.6 | 31.6 | 31.5 | 32.3 | 32.5 | 32.1 | 32.2 | 32.3 | 31.4 | 31.4 | 32.4 | 31.9 |
| **Financial Activities** | | | | | | | | | | | | | |
| 2015 | 37.0 | 37.4 | 37.3 | 36.9 | 36.6 | 36.8 | 36.5 | 37.5 | 36.5 | 36.7 | 37.6 | 36.7 | 37.0 |
| 2016 | 37.3 | 37.2 | 37.0 | 36.9 | 38.0 | 37.4 | 37.2 | 36.8 | 37.2 | 38.1 | 37.2 | 37.3 | 37.3 |
| 2017 | 38.6 | 37.7 | 37.5 | 38.6 | 37.5 | 37.8 | 38.8 | 37.5 | 37.6 | 38.5 | 37.6 | 37.4 | 37.9 |
| 2018 | 38.1 | 37.8 | 37.5 | 38.6 | 37.7 | 38.0 | 37.9 | 37.7 | 38.1 | 38.0 | 37.7 | 38.2 | 37.9 |
| 2019 | 38.1 | 37.6 | 37.5 | 37.3 | 37.4 | 38.1 | 37.4 | 37.8 | 37.9 | 38.1 | 38.3 | 38.5 | 37.8 |
| **Professional and Business Services** | | | | | | | | | | | | | |
| 2015 | 35.2 | 36.3 | 36.4 | 35.5 | 35.7 | 35.9 | 35.8 | 37.1 | 35.2 | 36.4 | 37.0 | 35.6 | 36.0 |
| 2016 | 35.3 | 35.2 | 35.5 | 35.3 | 36.5 | 35.9 | 35.6 | 35.8 | 35.7 | 36.7 | 35.6 | 35.1 | 35.7 |
| 2017 | 35.9 | 35.8 | 35.5 | 36.4 | 36.0 | 36.1 | 36.2 | 36.0 | 35.8 | 36.8 | 36.2 | 35.4 | 36.0 |
| 2018 | 34.8 | 35.7 | 35.6 | 36.2 | 35.8 | 35.9 | 36.2 | 36.1 | 36.7 | 35.5 | 36.0 | 36.9 | 36.0 |
| 2019 | 36.0 | 36.0 | 36.2 | 36.0 | 36.2 | 37.4 | 36.3 | 36.7 | 37.4 | 36.8 | 37.0 | 37.3 | 36.6 |
| **Education and Health Services** | | | | | | | | | | | | | |
| 2015 | 31.4 | 31.7 | 31.8 | 31.8 | 32.0 | 32.2 | 32.5 | 32.4 | 32.5 | 32.3 | 32.6 | 32.5 | 32.1 |
| 2016 | 32.3 | 32.0 | 32.0 | 32.2 | 32.5 | 32.1 | 32.1 | 32.2 | 32.1 | 32.6 | 32.5 | 32.5 | 32.3 |
| 2017 | 32.9 | 32.3 | 32.3 | 32.7 | 32.1 | 32.3 | 32.7 | 32.5 | 32.7 | 33.4 | 33.1 | 32.9 | 32.7 |
| 2018 | 32.9 | 33.0 | 32.7 | 33.0 | 32.9 | 33.0 | 33.0 | 33.0 | 32.8 | 32.2 | 32.2 | 32.6 | 32.8 |
| 2019 | 31.8 | 31.8 | 32.0 | 31.7 | 31.8 | 32.0 | 31.7 | 31.7 | 31.9 | 31.2 | 31.3 | 31.5 | 31.7 |
| **Leisure and Hospitality** | | | | | | | | | | | | | |
| 2015 | 22.4 | 23.1 | 23.4 | 22.7 | 23.0 | 24.0 | 24.1 | 24.7 | 23.6 | 23.5 | 23.4 | 22.6 | 23.4 |
| 2016 | 22.8 | 22.7 | 22.8 | 23.0 | 23.5 | 24.0 | 23.6 | 23.7 | 22.6 | 23.3 | 22.4 | 22.0 | 23.1 |
| 2017 | 22.0 | 22.1 | 22.2 | 22.1 | 22.1 | 23.1 | 23.3 | 22.8 | 22.2 | 22.5 | 21.5 | 21.2 | 22.3 |
| 2018 | 21.1 | 21.4 | 21.5 | 21.4 | 21.6 | 22.2 | 22.9 | 22.5 | 22.3 | 21.4 | 20.8 | 21.5 | 21.7 |
| 2019 | 20.8 | 20.6 | 20.7 | 20.9 | 21.1 | 22.3 | 22.5 | 22.6 | 21.7 | 21.6 | 21.2 | 21.6 | 21.5 |
| **Other Services** | | | | | | | | | | | | | |
| 2015 | 30.4 | 31.3 | 30.5 | 30.1 | 30.6 | 30.1 | 31.0 | 31.2 | 29.8 | 29.6 | 30.2 | 29.0 | 30.3 |
| 2016 | 29.7 | 29.8 | 29.1 | 29.3 | 30.0 | 29.6 | 28.4 | 29.3 | 29.1 | 29.6 | 28.8 | 28.5 | 29.3 |
| 2017 | 28.0 | 28.1 | 28.2 | 28.8 | 28.8 | 28.8 | 29.0 | 28.3 | 27.9 | 28.8 | 28.0 | 28.7 | 28.5 |
| 2018 | 28.4 | 28.8 | 29.0 | 29.1 | 28.8 | 29.1 | 29.1 | 29.0 | 29.0 | 28.7 | 29.1 | 29.8 | 29.0 |
| 2019 | 29.1 | 29.3 | 30.6 | 30.4 | 30.7 | 31.7 | 31.4 | 31.8 | 31.1 | 31.3 | 31.2 | 31.8 | 30.9 |

# 3. Average Hourly Earnings by Selected Industry: Minnesota, 2015–2019

(Dollars, not seasonally adjusted)

| Industry and year | January | February | March | April | May | June | July | August | September | October | November | December | Annual average |
|---|---|---|---|---|---|---|---|---|---|---|---|---|---|
| **Total Private** | | | | | | | | | | | | | |
| 2015 | 26.08 | 26.08 | 26.32 | 25.98 | 25.79 | 25.71 | 25.80 | 25.98 | 26.00 | 26.39 | 26.32 | 26.36 | 26.06 |
| 2016 | 26.71 | 26.54 | 27.05 | 26.90 | 26.99 | 26.64 | 26.95 | 26.88 | 27.32 | 27.63 | 27.78 | 27.85 | 27.11 |
| 2017 | 28.20 | 28.26 | 28.28 | 28.88 | 28.25 | 27.94 | 28.42 | 28.20 | 28.58 | 28.77 | 28.54 | 28.67 | 28.42 |
| 2018 | 28.71 | 28.57 | 28.88 | 29.03 | 28.88 | 28.77 | 29.08 | 28.88 | 29.38 | 29.35 | 29.32 | 29.82 | 29.06 |
| 2019 | 29.92 | 29.95 | 29.85 | 30.07 | 29.81 | 29.99 | 30.27 | 30.27 | 30.69 | 30.76 | 30.85 | 31.19 | 30.31 |
| **Goods-Producing** | | | | | | | | | | | | | |
| 2015 | 26.72 | 26.42 | 26.38 | 26.57 | 26.44 | 26.35 | 26.58 | 26.58 | 26.37 | 26.74 | 26.29 | 26.26 | 26.48 |
| 2016 | 26.61 | 26.62 | 26.53 | 27.11 | 27.21 | 27.37 | 28.11 | 27.80 | 28.31 | 28.55 | 28.26 | 28.43 | 27.60 |
| 2017 | 28.32 | 28.35 | 28.06 | 28.67 | 28.62 | 28.37 | 28.67 | 28.44 | 28.61 | 28.76 | 28.43 | 28.57 | 28.49 |
| 2018 | 28.52 | 28.26 | 28.23 | 28.42 | 28.45 | 28.47 | 28.62 | 28.47 | 28.87 | 28.99 | 28.71 | 29.00 | 28.59 |
| 2019 | 29.42 | 29.24 | 29.27 | 29.30 | 29.64 | 29.68 | 30.13 | 30.22 | 30.48 | 30.47 | 30.40 | 30.63 | 29.92 |
| **Construction** | | | | | | | | | | | | | |
| 2015 | 30.49 | 30.73 | 30.78 | 30.36 | 30.73 | 30.31 | 30.27 | 30.60 | 30.68 | 30.84 | 30.19 | 30.48 | 30.53 |
| 2016 | 30.63 | 30.31 | 30.61 | 30.95 | 31.29 | 31.53 | 31.80 | 31.59 | 32.26 | 32.46 | 32.33 | 32.53 | 31.59 |
| 2017 | 32.06 | 32.03 | 32.20 | 31.70 | 32.18 | 32.30 | 32.34 | 32.53 | 32.37 | 33.03 | 32.15 | 32.27 | 32.29 |
| 2018 | 32.43 | 31.98 | 32.27 | 32.71 | 32.50 | 32.21 | 32.50 | 32.71 | 33.16 | 33.42 | 33.26 | 33.29 | 32.73 |
| 2019 | 33.69 | 33.25 | 32.83 | 32.79 | 33.44 | 32.94 | 33.55 | 34.00 | 34.08 | 34.05 | 33.70 | 33.96 | 33.55 |
| **Manufacturing** | | | | | | | | | | | | | |
| 2015 | 25.42 | 24.98 | 24.91 | 25.12 | 24.71 | 24.58 | 24.90 | 24.75 | 24.55 | 24.97 | 24.73 | 24.70 | 24.86 |
| 2016 | 25.19 | 25.30 | 25.07 | 25.63 | 25.58 | 25.59 | 26.30 | 25.94 | 26.44 | 26.66 | 26.41 | 26.83 | 25.91 |
| 2017 | 26.91 | 26.90 | 26.44 | 27.31 | 26.92 | 26.44 | 26.86 | 26.44 | 26.82 | 26.78 | 26.77 | 27.04 | 26.80 |
| 2018 | 27.00 | 26.82 | 26.70 | 26.76 | 26.69 | 26.72 | 26.82 | 26.47 | 26.88 | 27.07 | 26.73 | 27.20 | 26.82 |
| 2019 | 27.42 | 27.42 | 27.59 | 27.70 | 27.67 | 27.87 | 28.20 | 28.10 | 28.43 | 28.35 | 28.63 | 29.05 | 28.04 |
| **Trade, Transportation, and Utilities** | | | | | | | | | | | | | |
| 2015 | 22.92 | 22.72 | 22.68 | 22.63 | 22.52 | 22.10 | 22.24 | 22.20 | 22.21 | 22.27 | 22.01 | 22.03 | 22.37 |
| 2016 | 21.96 | 21.79 | 21.69 | 21.93 | 22.01 | 21.76 | 21.56 | 21.46 | 21.74 | 21.77 | 21.62 | 21.18 | 21.70 |
| 2017 | 21.93 | 21.68 | 21.39 | 22.30 | 21.84 | 21.77 | 22.25 | 22.05 | 22.59 | 22.57 | 22.47 | 22.16 | 22.09 |
| 2018 | 22.68 | 22.82 | 22.44 | 23.35 | 23.30 | 23.37 | 23.73 | 23.30 | 24.12 | 23.68 | 23.71 | 24.13 | 23.39 |
| 2019 | 24.28 | 24.78 | 24.83 | 24.83 | 24.57 | 24.97 | 24.98 | 25.30 | 25.63 | 25.43 | 25.31 | 25.49 | 25.04 |
| **Financial Activities** | | | | | | | | | | | | | |
| 2015 | 30.88 | 31.59 | 31.64 | 31.79 | 32.24 | 32.39 | 32.43 | 32.27 | 32.20 | 32.59 | 32.98 | 33.45 | 32.21 |
| 2016 | 32.21 | 33.33 | 33.61 | 33.96 | 34.45 | 34.01 | 34.92 | 34.92 | 35.19 | 35.82 | 36.13 | 36.33 | 34.59 |
| 2017 | 35.89 | 37.11 | 35.91 | 36.59 | 36.82 | 36.71 | 37.78 | 36.97 | 37.62 | 38.78 | 37.97 | 38.57 | 37.23 |
| 2018 | 38.13 | 38.29 | 39.01 | 39.38 | 39.07 | 38.95 | 40.17 | 39.91 | 40.50 | 40.31 | 40.62 | 41.24 | 39.64 |
| 2019 | 39.95 | 39.67 | 38.87 | 39.12 | 38.89 | 39.51 | 40.06 | 40.08 | 40.16 | 39.98 | 39.90 | 40.69 | 39.74 |
| **Professional and Business Services** | | | | | | | | | | | | | |
| 2015 | 30.97 | 30.86 | 31.58 | 30.79 | 31.20 | 31.19 | 31.25 | 31.71 | 32.13 | 32.15 | 32.91 | 32.99 | 31.66 |
| 2016 | 33.72 | 33.25 | 34.54 | 33.06 | 33.41 | 32.70 | 33.47 | 33.18 | 33.40 | 33.79 | 33.79 | 34.47 | 33.56 |
| 2017 | 34.83 | 34.43 | 35.11 | 35.39 | 34.26 | 33.79 | 34.84 | 34.46 | 34.51 | 34.58 | 34.49 | 35.25 | 34.66 |
| 2018 | 34.21 | 34.01 | 34.66 | 34.93 | 34.32 | 34.83 | 35.15 | 35.63 | 35.78 | 35.80 | 35.70 | 36.05 | 35.10 |
| 2019 | 36.02 | 35.76 | 36.03 | 36.49 | 36.09 | 36.62 | 36.53 | 36.47 | 37.05 | 36.49 | 36.89 | 37.20 | 36.48 |
| **Education and Health Services** | | | | | | | | | | | | | |
| 2015 | 26.37 | 26.65 | 27.10 | 26.58 | 26.01 | 26.16 | 26.33 | 26.56 | 26.55 | 27.14 | 26.71 | 26.87 | 26.59 |
| 2016 | 27.04 | 27.23 | 27.57 | 27.79 | 27.74 | 27.18 | 27.31 | 27.14 | 27.39 | 27.66 | 27.47 | 27.77 | 27.44 |
| 2017 | 28.07 | 28.45 | 28.95 | 29.60 | 28.60 | 28.76 | 29.13 | 29.06 | 29.37 | 29.46 | 29.38 | 29.68 | 29.05 |
| 2018 | 30.02 | 29.81 | 30.18 | 30.01 | 29.97 | 29.57 | 29.72 | 29.55 | 29.61 | 29.45 | 29.35 | 29.63 | 29.74 |
| 2019 | 30.02 | 29.97 | 29.50 | 29.96 | 29.47 | 29.40 | 29.88 | 29.16 | 29.28 | 29.88 | 29.86 | 30.28 | 29.72 |
| **Leisure and Hospitality** | | | | | | | | | | | | | |
| 2015 | 14.66 | 14.87 | 14.89 | 14.88 | 14.51 | 14.55 | 14.62 | 15.12 | 15.23 | 15.37 | 15.48 | 15.50 | 14.97 |
| 2016 | 15.37 | 15.56 | 15.90 | 15.61 | 15.59 | 15.14 | 15.30 | 15.54 | 16.10 | 16.35 | 16.60 | 16.68 | 15.80 |
| 2017 | 16.75 | 16.82 | 16.95 | 16.88 | 16.56 | 16.04 | 16.05 | 16.22 | 16.64 | 16.82 | 17.28 | 17.30 | 16.67 |
| 2018 | 17.20 | 17.18 | 17.20 | 17.37 | 17.10 | 16.54 | 16.34 | 16.41 | 16.76 | 16.99 | 17.34 | 17.41 | 16.96 |
| 2019 | 17.11 | 17.35 | 17.55 | 17.49 | 17.47 | 17.13 | 16.95 | 17.03 | 17.46 | 17.65 | 17.65 | 17.88 | 17.38 |
| **Other Services** | | | | | | | | | | | | | |
| 2015 | 22.53 | 22.21 | 22.06 | 22.29 | 22.14 | 21.83 | 21.68 | 22.44 | 22.74 | 23.10 | 22.75 | 22.86 | 22.38 |
| 2016 | 22.55 | 22.36 | 22.77 | 22.48 | 22.57 | 22.35 | 22.57 | 21.98 | 22.39 | 22.51 | 23.03 | 23.34 | 22.57 |
| 2017 | 23.03 | 22.52 | 22.61 | 23.55 | 23.62 | 22.77 | 23.05 | 22.90 | 23.22 | 22.76 | 23.03 | 23.29 | 23.03 |
| 2018 | 22.80 | 22.61 | 22.11 | 21.92 | 22.01 | 21.84 | 21.79 | 21.87 | 22.43 | 22.36 | 22.89 | 23.58 | 22.35 |
| 2019 | 24.15 | 24.19 | 24.54 | 24.85 | 24.77 | 24.71 | 24.69 | 25.25 | 25.23 | 24.90 | 25.17 | 25.43 | 24.84 |

## 4. Average Weekly Earnings by Selected Industry: Minnesota, 2015–2019

(Dollars, not seasonally adjusted)

| Industry and year | January | February | March | April | May | June | July | August | September | October | November | December | Annual average |
|---|---|---|---|---|---|---|---|---|---|---|---|---|---|
| **Total Private** | | | | | | | | | | | | | |
| 2015 | 873.68 | 884.11 | 892.25 | 872.93 | 871.70 | 876.71 | 882.36 | 904.10 | 881.40 | 897.26 | 900.14 | 888.33 | 886.04 |
| 2016 | 894.79 | 886.44 | 906.18 | 906.53 | 925.76 | 913.75 | 919.00 | 916.61 | 931.61 | 953.24 | 950.08 | 944.12 | 921.74 |
| 2017 | 958.80 | 955.19 | 955.86 | 987.70 | 957.68 | 952.75 | 977.65 | 964.44 | 974.58 | 989.69 | 973.21 | 971.91 | 969.12 |
| 2018 | 961.79 | 962.81 | 973.26 | 987.02 | 981.92 | 981.06 | 997.44 | 990.58 | 1,010.67 | 986.16 | 991.02 | 1,016.86 | 988.04 |
| 2019 | 996.34 | 997.34 | 996.99 | 998.32 | 1,007.58 | 1,034.66 | 1,026.15 | 1,032.21 | 1,046.53 | 1,033.54 | 1,036.56 | 1,057.34 | 1,021.45 |
| **Goods-Producing** | | | | | | | | | | | | | |
| 2015 | 1,047.42 | 1,038.31 | 1,034.10 | 1,038.89 | 1,049.67 | 1,056.64 | 1,052.57 | 1,073.83 | 1,025.79 | 1,056.23 | 1,033.20 | 1,026.77 | 1,045.96 |
| 2016 | 1,032.47 | 1,032.86 | 1,029.36 | 1,060.00 | 1,066.63 | 1,086.59 | 1,101.91 | 1,098.10 | 1,129.57 | 1,127.73 | 1,119.10 | 1,100.24 | 1,081.92 |
| 2017 | 1,093.15 | 1,108.49 | 1,108.37 | 1,118.13 | 1,133.35 | 1,129.13 | 1,143.93 | 1,146.13 | 1,155.84 | 1,147.52 | 1,122.99 | 1,131.37 | 1,128.20 |
| 2018 | 1,109.43 | 1,104.97 | 1,112.26 | 1,111.22 | 1,132.31 | 1,141.65 | 1,141.94 | 1,150.19 | 1,172.12 | 1,150.90 | 1,134.05 | 1,154.20 | 1,135.02 |
| 2019 | 1,147.38 | 1,137.44 | 1,147.38 | 1,125.12 | 1,182.64 | 1,207.98 | 1,199.17 | 1,217.87 | 1,213.10 | 1,215.75 | 1,197.76 | 1,197.63 | 1,184.83 |
| **Construction** | | | | | | | | | | | | | |
| 2015 | 1,106.79 | 1,137.01 | 1,138.86 | 1,159.75 | 1,235.35 | 1,260.90 | 1,247.12 | 1,288.26 | 1,184.25 | 1,242.85 | 1,171.37 | 1,161.29 | 1,199.83 |
| 2016 | 1,148.63 | 1,139.66 | 1,160.12 | 1,188.48 | 1,217.18 | 1,289.58 | 1,303.80 | 1,276.24 | 1,316.21 | 1,330.86 | 1,293.20 | 1,229.63 | 1,247.81 |
| 2017 | 1,202.25 | 1,229.95 | 1,242.92 | 1,226.79 | 1,290.42 | 1,308.15 | 1,306.54 | 1,333.73 | 1,307.75 | 1,327.81 | 1,250.64 | 1,239.17 | 1,275.46 |
| 2018 | 1,206.40 | 1,196.05 | 1,223.03 | 1,216.81 | 1,274.00 | 1,314.17 | 1,313.00 | 1,328.03 | 1,336.35 | 1,286.67 | 1,293.81 | 1,308.30 | 1,279.74 |
| 2019 | 1,293.70 | 1,246.88 | 1,244.26 | 1,183.72 | 1,320.88 | 1,363.72 | 1,348.71 | 1,390.60 | 1,332.53 | 1,334.76 | 1,297.45 | 1,273.50 | 1,308.45 |
| **Manufacturing** | | | | | | | | | | | | | |
| 2015 | 1,011.72 | 994.20 | 991.42 | 987.22 | 978.52 | 973.37 | 971.10 | 987.53 | 967.27 | 988.81 | 989.20 | 983.06 | 984.46 |
| 2016 | 992.49 | 994.29 | 990.27 | 1,014.95 | 1,012.97 | 1,010.81 | 1,015.18 | 1,019.44 | 1,047.02 | 1,034.41 | 1,040.55 | 1,046.37 | 1,018.26 |
| 2017 | 1,049.49 | 1,057.17 | 1,054.96 | 1,073.28 | 1,060.65 | 1,044.38 | 1,066.34 | 1,054.96 | 1,080.85 | 1,060.49 | 1,060.09 | 1,078.90 | 1,061.28 |
| 2018 | 1,066.50 | 1,064.75 | 1,065.33 | 1,067.72 | 1,070.27 | 1,060.78 | 1,059.39 | 1,061.45 | 1,088.64 | 1,077.39 | 1,053.16 | 1,077.12 | 1,067.44 |
| 2019 | 1,063.90 | 1,072.12 | 1,089.81 | 1,088.61 | 1,106.80 | 1,123.16 | 1,116.72 | 1,124.00 | 1,145.73 | 1,142.51 | 1,142.34 | 1,159.10 | 1,115.99 |
| **Trade, Transportation, and Utilities** | | | | | | | | | | | | | |
| 2015 | 749.48 | 754.30 | 743.90 | 737.74 | 736.40 | 729.30 | 740.59 | 750.36 | 739.59 | 732.68 | 726.33 | 724.79 | 738.21 |
| 2016 | 702.72 | 701.64 | 700.59 | 708.34 | 730.73 | 718.08 | 713.64 | 701.74 | 715.25 | 722.76 | 706.97 | 696.82 | 709.59 |
| 2017 | 708.34 | 687.26 | 680.20 | 722.52 | 696.70 | 700.99 | 729.80 | 714.42 | 727.40 | 722.24 | 732.52 | 726.85 | 713.51 |
| 2018 | 718.96 | 727.96 | 711.35 | 749.54 | 757.25 | 757.19 | 778.34 | 759.58 | 791.14 | 750.66 | 765.83 | 776.99 | 753.16 |
| 2019 | 759.96 | 783.05 | 784.63 | 782.15 | 793.61 | 811.53 | 801.86 | 814.66 | 827.85 | 798.50 | 794.73 | 825.88 | 798.78 |
| **Financial Activities** | | | | | | | | | | | | | |
| 2015 | 1,142.56 | 1,181.47 | 1,180.17 | 1,173.05 | 1,179.98 | 1,191.95 | 1,183.70 | 1,210.13 | 1,175.30 | 1,196.05 | 1,240.05 | 1,227.62 | 1,191.77 |
| 2016 | 1,201.43 | 1,239.88 | 1,243.57 | 1,253.12 | 1,309.10 | 1,271.97 | 1,299.02 | 1,285.06 | 1,309.07 | 1,364.74 | 1,344.04 | 1,355.11 | 1,290.21 |
| 2017 | 1,385.35 | 1,399.05 | 1,346.63 | 1,412.37 | 1,380.75 | 1,387.64 | 1,465.86 | 1,386.38 | 1,414.51 | 1,493.03 | 1,427.67 | 1,442.52 | 1,411.02 |
| 2018 | 1,452.75 | 1,447.36 | 1,462.88 | 1,520.07 | 1,472.94 | 1,480.10 | 1,522.44 | 1,504.61 | 1,543.05 | 1,531.78 | 1,531.37 | 1,575.37 | 1,502.36 |
| 2019 | 1,522.10 | 1,491.59 | 1,457.63 | 1,459.18 | 1,454.49 | 1,505.33 | 1,498.24 | 1,515.02 | 1,522.06 | 1,523.24 | 1,528.17 | 1,566.57 | 1,502.17 |
| **Professional and Business Services** | | | | | | | | | | | | | |
| 2015 | 1,090.14 | 1,120.22 | 1,149.51 | 1,093.05 | 1,113.84 | 1,119.72 | 1,118.75 | 1,176.44 | 1,130.98 | 1,170.26 | 1,217.67 | 1,174.44 | 1,139.76 |
| 2016 | 1,190.32 | 1,170.40 | 1,226.17 | 1,167.02 | 1,219.47 | 1,173.93 | 1,191.53 | 1,187.84 | 1,192.38 | 1,240.09 | 1,202.92 | 1,209.90 | 1,198.09 |
| 2017 | 1,250.40 | 1,232.59 | 1,246.41 | 1,288.20 | 1,233.36 | 1,219.82 | 1,261.21 | 1,240.56 | 1,235.46 | 1,272.54 | 1,248.54 | 1,247.85 | 1,247.76 |
| 2018 | 1,190.51 | 1,214.16 | 1,233.90 | 1,264.47 | 1,228.66 | 1,250.40 | 1,272.43 | 1,286.24 | 1,313.13 | 1,270.90 | 1,285.20 | 1,330.25 | 1,263.60 |
| 2019 | 1,296.72 | 1,287.36 | 1,304.29 | 1,313.64 | 1,306.46 | 1,369.59 | 1,326.04 | 1,338.45 | 1,385.67 | 1,342.83 | 1,364.93 | 1,387.56 | 1,335.17 |
| **Education and Health Services** | | | | | | | | | | | | | |
| 2015 | 828.02 | 844.81 | 861.78 | 845.24 | 832.32 | 842.35 | 855.73 | 860.54 | 862.88 | 876.62 | 870.75 | 873.28 | 853.54 |
| 2016 | 873.39 | 871.36 | 882.24 | 894.84 | 901.55 | 872.48 | 876.65 | 873.91 | 879.22 | 901.72 | 892.78 | 902.53 | 886.31 |
| 2017 | 923.50 | 918.94 | 935.09 | 967.92 | 918.06 | 928.95 | 952.55 | 944.45 | 960.40 | 983.96 | 972.48 | 976.47 | 949.94 |
| 2018 | 987.66 | 983.73 | 986.89 | 990.33 | 986.01 | 975.81 | 980.76 | 975.15 | 971.21 | 948.29 | 945.07 | 965.94 | 975.47 |
| 2019 | 954.64 | 953.05 | 944.00 | 949.73 | 937.15 | 940.80 | 947.20 | 924.37 | 934.03 | 932.26 | 934.62 | 953.82 | 942.12 |
| **Leisure and Hospitality** | | | | | | | | | | | | | |
| 2015 | 328.38 | 343.50 | 348.43 | 337.78 | 333.73 | 349.20 | 352.34 | 373.46 | 359.43 | 361.20 | 362.23 | 350.30 | 350.30 |
| 2016 | 350.44 | 353.21 | 362.52 | 359.03 | 366.37 | 363.36 | 361.08 | 368.30 | 363.86 | 380.96 | 371.84 | 366.96 | 364.98 |
| 2017 | 368.50 | 371.72 | 376.29 | 373.05 | 365.98 | 370.52 | 373.97 | 369.82 | 369.41 | 378.45 | 371.52 | 366.76 | 371.74 |
| 2018 | 362.92 | 367.65 | 369.80 | 371.72 | 369.36 | 367.19 | 374.19 | 369.23 | 373.75 | 363.59 | 360.67 | 374.32 | 368.03 |
| 2019 | 355.89 | 357.41 | 363.29 | 365.54 | 368.62 | 382.00 | 381.38 | 384.88 | 378.88 | 381.24 | 374.18 | 386.21 | 373.67 |
| **Other Services** | | | | | | | | | | | | | |
| 2015 | 684.91 | 695.17 | 672.83 | 670.93 | 677.48 | 657.08 | 672.08 | 700.13 | 677.65 | 683.76 | 687.05 | 662.94 | 678.11 |
| 2016 | 669.74 | 666.33 | 662.61 | 658.66 | 677.10 | 661.56 | 640.99 | 644.01 | 651.55 | 666.30 | 663.26 | 665.19 | 661.30 |
| 2017 | 644.84 | 632.81 | 637.60 | 678.24 | 680.26 | 655.78 | 668.45 | 648.07 | 647.84 | 655.49 | 644.84 | 668.42 | 656.36 |
| 2018 | 647.52 | 651.17 | 641.19 | 637.87 | 633.89 | 635.54 | 634.09 | 634.23 | 650.47 | 641.73 | 666.10 | 702.68 | 648.15 |
| 2019 | 702.77 | 708.77 | 750.92 | 755.44 | 760.44 | 783.31 | 775.27 | 802.95 | 784.65 | 779.37 | 785.30 | 808.67 | 767.56 |

# MISSISSIPPI
*At a Glance*

Population:
  2010 census: 2,967,297
  2019 estimate: 2,976,149

Percent change in population:
  2010–2019: 0.3%

Percent change in total nonfarm employment:
  2011–2019: 6.0%

Industry with the largest growth in employment, 2011–2019 (percent):
  Transportation and utilities, 25.7%

Industry with the largest decline or smallest growth in employment, 2011–2019 (percent):
  Mining and logging, -25.3%

Civilian labor force:
  2010: 1,306,608
  2019: 1,276,118

Unemployment rate and rank among states (highest to lowest):
  2010: 10.4%, 11th
  2019: 5.4%, 3rd

Over-the-year change in unemployment rates:
  2017–2018: -0.3%
  2018–2019: 0.6%

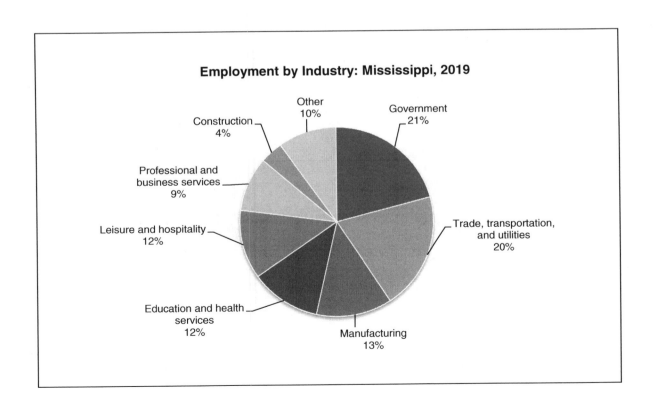

**Employment by Industry: Mississippi, 2019**

- Other 10%
- Government 21%
- Construction 4%
- Professional and business services 9%
- Trade, transportation, and utilities 20%
- Leisure and hospitality 12%
- Education and health services 12%
- Manufacturing 13%

## 1. Employment by Industry: Mississippi, 2011–2019

(Numbers in thousands, not seasonally adjusted)

| Industry and year | January | February | March | April | May | June | July | August | September | October | November | December | Annual average |
|---|---|---|---|---|---|---|---|---|---|---|---|---|---|
| **Total Nonfarm** | | | | | | | | | | | | | |
| 2011 | 1,078.3 | 1,084.0 | 1,094.2 | 1,099.9 | 1,100.1 | 1,093.7 | 1,078.5 | 1,088.8 | 1,099.0 | 1,098.8 | 1,101.5 | 1,097.8 | 1,092.9 |
| 2012 | 1,085.3 | 1,095.5 | 1,103.6 | 1,107.4 | 1,108.1 | 1,100.6 | 1,086.5 | 1,101.9 | 1,107.7 | 1,107.5 | 1,112.8 | 1,110.7 | 1,102.3 |
| 2013 | 1,092.5 | 1,104.6 | 1,110.2 | 1,114.7 | 1,115.1 | 1,110.1 | 1,094.1 | 1,108.8 | 1,118.6 | 1,118.1 | 1,125.3 | 1,123.0 | 1,111.3 |
| 2014 | 1,107.3 | 1,110.7 | 1,116.8 | 1,124.3 | 1,124.3 | 1,118.2 | 1,104.7 | 1,118.4 | 1,125.8 | 1,128.8 | 1,135.1 | 1,135.0 | 1,120.8 |
| 2015 | 1,113.9 | 1,122.9 | 1,124.7 | 1,134.2 | 1,139.2 | 1,129.8 | 1,120.7 | 1,131.0 | 1,140.0 | 1,145.9 | 1,150.1 | 1,152.1 | 1,133.7 |
| 2016 | 1,133.5 | 1,143.3 | 1,146.0 | 1,150.7 | 1,149.4 | 1,138.3 | 1,133.6 | 1,143.3 | 1,152.5 | 1,153.2 | 1,158.1 | 1,153.6 | 1,146.3 |
| 2017 | 1,137.5 | 1,147.2 | 1,150.5 | 1,154.8 | 1,153.8 | 1,147.6 | 1,136.8 | 1,148.3 | 1,156.0 | 1,157.9 | 1,165.8 | 1,161.6 | 1,151.5 |
| 2018 | 1,138.3 | 1,146.0 | 1,151.6 | 1,157.0 | 1,157.4 | 1,150.0 | 1,137.4 | 1,152.6 | 1,158.7 | 1,161.8 | 1,170.4 | 1,164.5 | 1,153.8 |
| 2019 | 1,148.1 | 1,154.8 | 1,156.1 | 1,159.7 | 1,161.5 | 1,155.4 | 1,143.9 | 1,157.2 | 1,160.8 | 1,166.9 | 1,171.2 | 1,164.8 | 1,158.4 |
| **Total Private** | | | | | | | | | | | | | |
| 2011 | 833.1 | 836.5 | 845.9 | 851.1 | 852.0 | 849.5 | 841.9 | 847.0 | 851.5 | 849.8 | 853.0 | 852.8 | 847.0 |
| 2012 | 839.9 | 847.1 | 854.3 | 858.6 | 859.5 | 856.7 | 851.2 | 860.2 | 860.7 | 858.6 | 863.8 | 865.0 | 856.3 |
| 2013 | 847.8 | 856.3 | 861.5 | 865.8 | 866.9 | 866.7 | 859.7 | 868.1 | 871.3 | 870.4 | 877.7 | 879.3 | 866.0 |
| 2014 | 864.1 | 864.2 | 869.6 | 876.6 | 877.5 | 876.0 | 870.3 | 878.3 | 879.2 | 881.0 | 888.3 | 891.7 | 876.4 |
| 2015 | 871.6 | 877.4 | 878.4 | 888.6 | 893.1 | 888.8 | 886.5 | 891.6 | 894.6 | 899.2 | 904.0 | 909.4 | 890.3 |
| 2016 | 890.9 | 896.6 | 898.8 | 902.9 | 902.7 | 896.7 | 899.1 | 903.8 | 906.1 | 906.4 | 911.6 | 911.1 | 902.2 |
| 2017 | 896.0 | 901.9 | 904.0 | 909.7 | 910.1 | 908.4 | 903.5 | 909.6 | 910.7 | 912.4 | 920.6 | 920.1 | 908.9 |
| 2018 | 898.5 | 903.1 | 907.4 | 913.9 | 915.3 | 911.4 | 905.9 | 915.0 | 915.3 | 918.1 | 926.6 | 925.2 | 913.0 |
| 2019 | 908.9 | 911.6 | 911.8 | 916.2 | 917.9 | 916.3 | 911.2 | 918.1 | 915.5 | 921.1 | 925.5 | 923.6 | 916.5 |
| **Goods Producing** | | | | | | | | | | | | | |
| 2011 | 190.0 | 190.3 | 193.4 | 193.7 | 195.3 | 195.4 | 193.4 | 193.1 | 193.9 | 193.4 | 192.6 | 192.5 | 193.1 |
| 2012 | 191.1 | 193.0 | 194.5 | 195.9 | 195.9 | 195.6 | 194.4 | 195.3 | 195.2 | 195.0 | 194.5 | 194.8 | 194.6 |
| 2013 | 191.5 | 194.0 | 194.6 | 195.8 | 197.9 | 198.7 | 197.4 | 198.1 | 199.0 | 199.7 | 199.3 | 198.7 | 197.1 |
| 2014 | 196.9 | 196.7 | 198.7 | 199.3 | 200.1 | 200.4 | 198.0 | 197.7 | 197.1 | 197.4 | 196.5 | 197.0 | 198.0 |
| 2015 | 193.7 | 195.1 | 194.5 | 195.9 | 197.1 | 197.2 | 196.9 | 196.0 | 196.7 | 196.3 | 195.0 | 196.0 | 195.9 |
| 2016 | 194.5 | 195.4 | 196.0 | 194.5 | 193.9 | 193.6 | 194.3 | 194.1 | 194.8 | 194.1 | 194.1 | 194.4 | 194.5 |
| 2017 | 193.0 | 194.1 | 194.2 | 194.0 | 194.1 | 195.4 | 194.1 | 194.9 | 195.1 | 195.3 | 195.8 | 195.5 | 194.6 |
| 2018 | 192.4 | 193.6 | 195.0 | 196.7 | 197.1 | 196.7 | 195.6 | 195.5 | 195.9 | 196.2 | 196.4 | 196.9 | 195.7 |
| 2019 | 195.8 | 197.6 | 198.1 | 197.3 | 198.4 | 199.5 | 197.9 | 198.1 | 197.7 | 199.6 | 199.8 | 199.5 | 198.3 |
| **Service-Providing** | | | | | | | | | | | | | |
| 2011 | 888.3 | 893.7 | 900.8 | 906.2 | 904.8 | 898.3 | 885.1 | 895.7 | 905.1 | 905.4 | 908.9 | 905.3 | 899.8 |
| 2012 | 894.2 | 902.5 | 909.1 | 911.5 | 912.2 | 905.0 | 892.1 | 906.6 | 912.5 | 912.5 | 918.3 | 915.9 | 907.7 |
| 2013 | 901.0 | 910.6 | 915.6 | 918.9 | 917.2 | 911.4 | 896.7 | 910.7 | 919.6 | 918.4 | 926.0 | 924.3 | 914.2 |
| 2014 | 910.4 | 914.0 | 918.1 | 925.0 | 924.2 | 917.8 | 906.7 | 920.7 | 928.7 | 931.4 | 938.6 | 938.0 | 922.8 |
| 2015 | 920.2 | 927.8 | 930.2 | 938.3 | 942.1 | 932.6 | 923.8 | 935.0 | 943.3 | 949.6 | 955.1 | 956.1 | 937.8 |
| 2016 | 939.0 | 947.9 | 950.0 | 956.2 | 955.5 | 944.7 | 939.3 | 949.2 | 957.7 | 959.1 | 964.0 | 959.2 | 951.8 |
| 2017 | 944.5 | 953.1 | 956.3 | 960.8 | 959.7 | 952.2 | 942.7 | 953.4 | 960.9 | 962.6 | 970.0 | 966.1 | 956.9 |
| 2018 | 945.9 | 952.4 | 956.6 | 960.3 | 960.3 | 953.3 | 941.8 | 957.1 | 962.8 | 965.6 | 974.0 | 967.6 | 958.1 |
| 2019 | 952.3 | 957.2 | 958.0 | 962.4 | 963.1 | 955.9 | 946.0 | 959.1 | 963.1 | 967.3 | 971.4 | 965.3 | 960.1 |
| **Mining and Logging** | | | | | | | | | | | | | |
| 2011 | 8.8 | 8.8 | 9.0 | 9.0 | 9.1 | 9.1 | 9.3 | 9.3 | 9.2 | 9.1 | 9.1 | 9.0 | 9.1 |
| 2012 | 9.0 | 9.1 | 9.2 | 9.3 | 9.3 | 9.3 | 9.4 | 9.4 | 9.4 | 9.2 | 9.3 | 9.2 | 9.3 |
| 2013 | 8.9 | 9.0 | 9.0 | 9.1 | 9.2 | 9.2 | 9.3 | 9.3 | 9.2 | 9.1 | 9.1 | 9.1 | 9.1 |
| 2014 | 9.1 | 8.9 | 9.0 | 9.0 | 9.1 | 9.3 | 9.3 | 9.4 | 9.4 | 9.4 | 9.4 | 9.3 | 9.2 |
| 2015 | 8.9 | 8.7 | 8.3 | 8.2 | 8.2 | 8.1 | 7.9 | 7.9 | 7.8 | 7.5 | 7.4 | 7.3 | 8.0 |
| 2016 | 7.2 | 7.1 | 6.9 | 6.7 | 6.8 | 6.8 | 6.8 | 6.9 | 7.0 | 7.0 | 7.0 | 7.0 | 6.9 |
| 2017 | 7.0 | 6.9 | 7.0 | 6.9 | 6.9 | 7.0 | 6.9 | 7.0 | 7.0 | 6.9 | 6.9 | 6.9 | 6.9 |
| 2018 | 6.7 | 6.8 | 6.9 | 6.9 | 6.9 | 6.9 | 6.9 | 6.9 | 6.9 | 6.9 | 6.9 | 6.9 | 6.9 |
| 2019 | 6.9 | 6.9 | 6.9 | 6.9 | 6.9 | 6.8 | 6.8 | 6.7 | 6.7 | 6.9 | 6.9 | 6.7 | 6.8 |
| **Construction** | | | | | | | | | | | | | |
| 2011 | 46.9 | 47.2 | 49.1 | 49.3 | 50.3 | 50.5 | 49.3 | 48.8 | 49.5 | 49.1 | 48.2 | 47.2 | 48.8 |
| 2012 | 46.0 | 47.6 | 48.8 | 50.0 | 49.8 | 48.9 | 47.9 | 48.4 | 48.7 | 48.4 | 47.9 | 47.6 | 48.3 |
| 2013 | 46.2 | 48.6 | 49.3 | 50.3 | 52.2 | 52.9 | 52.6 | 52.5 | 53.0 | 53.2 | 52.0 | 50.5 | 51.1 |
| 2014 | 48.8 | 48.6 | 50.3 | 50.9 | 51.5 | 51.2 | 50.1 | 49.0 | 48.3 | 47.7 | 46.9 | 46.8 | 49.2 |
| 2015 | 44.5 | 45.8 | 45.8 | 46.5 | 46.8 | 46.4 | 47.1 | 46.2 | 46.5 | 46.2 | 45.2 | 45.5 | 46.0 |
| 2016 | 43.8 | 44.8 | 45.7 | 44.7 | 44.3 | 44.1 | 44.7 | 44.1 | 44.5 | 44.2 | 44.0 | 43.3 | 44.4 |
| 2017 | 42.4 | 43.0 | 43.4 | 43.5 | 43.2 | 43.6 | 43.6 | 43.7 | 44.2 | 44.4 | 44.2 | 43.1 | 43.5 |
| 2018 | 41.4 | 42.3 | 43.7 | 45.4 | 45.6 | 44.6 | 44.1 | 43.8 | 44.0 | 44.0 | 43.7 | 43.5 | 43.8 |
| 2019 | 42.7 | 43.5 | 44.3 | 43.9 | 45.0 | 45.8 | 44.9 | 44.8 | 44.7 | 44.9 | 44.5 | 43.5 | 44.4 |

# 1. Employment by Industry: Mississippi, 2011–2019—*Continued*

(Numbers in thousands, not seasonally adjusted)

| Industry and year | January | February | March | April | May | June | July | August | September | October | November | December | Annual average |
|---|---|---|---|---|---|---|---|---|---|---|---|---|---|
| **Manufacturing** | | | | | | | | | | | | | |
| 2011 | 134.3 | 134.3 | 135.3 | 135.4 | 135.9 | 135.8 | 134.8 | 135.0 | 135.2 | 135.2 | 135.3 | 136.3 | 135.2 |
| 2012 | 136.1 | 136.3 | 136.5 | 136.6 | 136.8 | 137.4 | 137.1 | 137.5 | 137.1 | 137.4 | 137.3 | 138.0 | 137.0 |
| 2013 | 136.4 | 136.4 | 136.3 | 136.4 | 136.5 | 136.6 | 135.5 | 136.3 | 136.8 | 137.4 | 138.2 | 139.1 | 136.8 |
| 2014 | 139.0 | 139.2 | 139.4 | 139.4 | 139.5 | 139.9 | 138.6 | 139.3 | 139.4 | 140.3 | 140.2 | 140.9 | 139.6 |
| 2015 | 140.3 | 140.6 | 140.4 | 141.2 | 142.1 | 142.7 | 141.9 | 141.9 | 142.4 | 142.6 | 142.4 | 143.2 | 141.8 |
| 2016 | 143.5 | 143.5 | 143.4 | 143.1 | 142.8 | 142.7 | 142.8 | 143.1 | 143.3 | 142.9 | 143.1 | 144.1 | 143.2 |
| 2017 | 143.6 | 144.2 | 143.8 | 143.6 | 144.0 | 144.8 | 143.6 | 144.2 | 143.9 | 144.0 | 144.7 | 145.5 | 144.2 |
| 2018 | 144.3 | 144.5 | 144.4 | 144.4 | 144.6 | 145.2 | 144.6 | 144.8 | 145.0 | 145.3 | 145.8 | 146.5 | 145.0 |
| 2019 | 146.2 | 147.2 | 146.9 | 146.5 | 146.5 | 146.9 | 146.2 | 146.6 | 146.3 | 147.8 | 148.4 | 149.3 | 147.1 |
| **Trade, Transportation, and Utilities** | | | | | | | | | | | | | |
| 2011 | 212.5 | 212.1 | 214.1 | 215.1 | 215.4 | 214.7 | 214.0 | 214.8 | 214.5 | 214.8 | 218.9 | 221.2 | 215.2 |
| 2012 | 214.3 | 213.8 | 214.6 | 215.2 | 216.2 | 215.9 | 215.5 | 215.8 | 215.4 | 215.1 | 219.6 | 221.2 | 216.1 |
| 2013 | 213.4 | 212.9 | 213.5 | 214.4 | 215.3 | 216.4 | 216.3 | 217.4 | 217.4 | 217.5 | 223.3 | 225.8 | 217.0 |
| 2014 | 217.6 | 217.0 | 217.8 | 218.5 | 218.9 | 219.9 | 219.7 | 220.9 | 220.2 | 221.9 | 227.0 | 229.6 | 220.8 |
| 2015 | 221.3 | 220.9 | 221.1 | 223.7 | 224.5 | 224.8 | 223.6 | 224.5 | 224.5 | 226.5 | 231.8 | 234.5 | 225.1 |
| 2016 | 226.7 | 226.2 | 226.3 | 228.5 | 228.9 | 228.3 | 229.2 | 229.4 | 229.7 | 231.4 | 236.7 | 238.4 | 230.0 |
| 2017 | 230.7 | 229.4 | 229.0 | 229.7 | 229.8 | 230.3 | 230.3 | 231.2 | 230.7 | 232.0 | 237.6 | 238.8 | 231.6 |
| 2018 | 230.2 | 229.1 | 229.6 | 229.7 | 230.9 | 230.7 | 230.2 | 230.2 | 229.9 | 231.0 | 237.6 | 238.4 | 231.5 |
| 2019 | 231.8 | 229.5 | 229.4 | 230.3 | 230.5 | 230.4 | 229.8 | 229.7 | 229.4 | 230.6 | 234.6 | 235.6 | 231.0 |
| **Wholesale Trade** | | | | | | | | | | | | | |
| 2011 | 33.8 | 33.9 | 33.8 | 33.8 | 33.9 | 33.7 | 33.8 | 34.2 | 34.1 | 33.8 | 33.8 | 34.3 | 33.9 |
| 2012 | 34.1 | 34.2 | 33.9 | 33.7 | 33.8 | 33.8 | 33.8 | 34.1 | 33.9 | 33.5 | 33.6 | 33.8 | 33.9 |
| 2013 | 33.9 | 33.9 | 33.6 | 33.5 | 33.7 | 33.7 | 33.5 | 33.9 | 33.8 | 33.4 | 33.4 | 33.9 | 33.7 |
| 2014 | 33.7 | 33.8 | 33.4 | 33.5 | 33.5 | 33.6 | 33.6 | 34.0 | 33.7 | 33.6 | 33.6 | 34.2 | 33.7 |
| 2015 | 34.1 | 34.1 | 33.6 | 33.8 | 33.9 | 33.9 | 33.7 | 34.0 | 33.9 | 33.9 | 33.8 | 34.1 | 33.9 |
| 2016 | 34.0 | 33.9 | 33.5 | 33.5 | 33.7 | 33.7 | 33.8 | 34.2 | 34.2 | 34.1 | 34.0 | 34.4 | 33.9 |
| 2017 | 34.5 | 34.6 | 34.3 | 34.1 | 34.1 | 34.2 | 34.1 | 34.5 | 34.2 | 34.2 | 34.0 | 34.5 | 34.3 |
| 2018 | 34.2 | 34.3 | 33.9 | 33.8 | 34.0 | 34.1 | 34.0 | 34.4 | 34.3 | 34.2 | 34.1 | 34.6 | 34.2 |
| 2019 | 34.7 | 34.7 | 34.6 | 34.4 | 34.4 | 34.4 | 34.4 | 34.6 | 34.4 | 34.7 | 34.5 | 34.5 | 34.5 |
| **Retail Trade** | | | | | | | | | | | | | |
| 2011 | 131.2 | 130.8 | 132.4 | 133.4 | 133.5 | 133.1 | 132.4 | 132.3 | 131.7 | 132.4 | 136.3 | 137.7 | 133.1 |
| 2012 | 132.4 | 131.7 | 132.6 | 133.3 | 133.8 | 133.5 | 133.2 | 132.7 | 132.1 | 132.6 | 136.8 | 137.7 | 133.5 |
| 2013 | 130.8 | 130.2 | 131.1 | 131.8 | 132.3 | 133.3 | 133.6 | 133.7 | 133.6 | 133.7 | 138.8 | 140.4 | 133.6 |
| 2014 | 133.7 | 133.3 | 134.4 | 134.8 | 134.9 | 135.6 | 135.3 | 135.4 | 134.9 | 135.8 | 140.4 | 142.0 | 135.9 |
| 2015 | 135.5 | 135.3 | 135.8 | 137.6 | 138.1 | 138.3 | 137.5 | 137.6 | 137.3 | 138.5 | 143.0 | 144.4 | 138.2 |
| 2016 | 138.5 | 138.7 | 139.0 | 140.7 | 140.5 | 139.8 | 140.3 | 139.8 | 139.9 | 141.1 | 145.2 | 145.5 | 140.8 |
| 2017 | 140.3 | 139.3 | 139.5 | 140.2 | 140.1 | 140.0 | 140.0 | 139.8 | 139.8 | 139.4 | 143.9 | 143.8 | 140.5 |
| 2018 | 138.3 | 137.5 | 138.1 | 138.3 | 138.8 | 138.0 | 137.7 | 137.1 | 136.6 | 136.9 | 141.6 | 141.3 | 138.4 |
| 2019 | 136.8 | 135.2 | 135.5 | 135.9 | 136.2 | 135.7 | 135.0 | 134.3 | 134.1 | 135.1 | 138.4 | 138.2 | 135.9 |
| **Transportation and Utilities** | | | | | | | | | | | | | |
| 2011 | 47.5 | 47.4 | 47.9 | 47.9 | 48.0 | 47.9 | 47.8 | 48.3 | 48.7 | 48.6 | 48.8 | 49.2 | 48.2 |
| 2012 | 47.8 | 47.9 | 48.1 | 48.2 | 48.6 | 48.6 | 48.5 | 49.0 | 49.4 | 49.0 | 49.2 | 49.7 | 48.7 |
| 2013 | 48.7 | 48.8 | 48.8 | 49.1 | 49.3 | 49.4 | 49.2 | 49.8 | 50.0 | 50.4 | 51.1 | 51.5 | 49.7 |
| 2014 | 50.2 | 49.9 | 50.0 | 50.2 | 50.5 | 50.7 | 50.8 | 51.5 | 51.6 | 52.5 | 53.0 | 53.4 | 51.2 |
| 2015 | 51.7 | 51.5 | 51.7 | 52.3 | 52.5 | 52.6 | 52.4 | 52.9 | 53.3 | 54.1 | 55.0 | 56.0 | 53.0 |
| 2016 | 54.2 | 53.6 | 53.8 | 54.3 | 54.7 | 54.8 | 55.1 | 55.4 | 55.6 | 56.2 | 57.5 | 58.5 | 55.3 |
| 2017 | 55.9 | 55.5 | 55.2 | 55.4 | 55.6 | 56.1 | 56.4 | 56.9 | 57.1 | 58.0 | 59.7 | 60.5 | 56.9 |
| 2018 | 57.7 | 57.3 | 57.6 | 57.6 | 58.1 | 58.6 | 58.5 | 58.7 | 59.0 | 59.9 | 61.9 | 62.5 | 59.0 |
| 2019 | 60.3 | 59.6 | 59.3 | 60.0 | 59.9 | 60.3 | 60.4 | 60.8 | 60.9 | 60.8 | 61.7 | 62.9 | 60.6 |
| **Information** | | | | | | | | | | | | | |
| 2011 | 12.0 | 12.0 | 12.0 | 11.9 | 12.0 | 12.1 | 12.1 | 12.1 | 12.1 | 12.1 | 12.2 | 12.4 | 12.1 |
| 2012 | 12.5 | 12.5 | 12.5 | 12.5 | 12.5 | 12.5 | 12.6 | 12.4 | 12.4 | 12.4 | 12.7 | 12.7 | 12.5 |
| 2013 | 12.8 | 12.8 | 12.7 | 12.7 | 12.6 | 12.8 | 12.7 | 12.7 | 12.8 | 12.8 | 12.9 | 13.2 | 12.8 |
| 2014 | 13.8 | 13.0 | 13.0 | 12.8 | 12.7 | 12.8 | 12.8 | 13.0 | 13.0 | 13.1 | 13.4 | 13.3 | 13.1 |
| 2015 | 12.8 | 12.8 | 12.7 | 12.5 | 12.8 | 12.7 | 12.7 | 12.5 | 12.6 | 12.7 | 12.7 | 12.8 | 12.7 |
| 2016 | 12.4 | 12.3 | 12.1 | 12.0 | 12.2 | 12.2 | 12.3 | 12.2 | 12.0 | 12.1 | 12.2 | 12.1 | 12.2 |
| 2017 | 11.7 | 11.8 | 11.8 | 11.7 | 11.8 | 11.7 | 11.6 | 11.5 | 11.3 | 11.4 | 11.4 | 11.3 | 11.6 |
| 2018 | 11.1 | 11.1 | 11.0 | 11.0 | 10.9 | 11.0 | 11.0 | 11.0 | 10.9 | 10.9 | 11.1 | 11.0 | 11.0 |
| 2019 | 10.8 | 10.8 | 10.9 | 10.8 | 10.7 | 10.8 | 10.8 | 10.5 | 10.5 | 10.6 | 10.8 | 10.7 | 10.7 |

## 1. Employment by Industry: Mississippi, 2011–2019—*Continued*

(Numbers in thousands, not seasonally adjusted)

| Industry and year | January | February | March | April | May | June | July | August | September | October | November | December | Annual average |
|---|---|---|---|---|---|---|---|---|---|---|---|---|---|
| **Financial Activities** | | | | | | | | | | | | | |
| 2011 | 43.9 | 44.0 | 44.0 | 44.3 | 44.1 | 44.4 | 44.2 | 44.3 | 44.2 | 44.1 | 44.2 | 44.2 | 44.2 |
| 2012 | 43.9 | 43.9 | 44.0 | 44.1 | 44.3 | 44.3 | 44.3 | 44.4 | 44.2 | 43.9 | 44.0 | 44.0 | 44.1 |
| 2013 | 43.6 | 43.8 | 43.9 | 43.9 | 43.8 | 43.9 | 43.7 | 43.8 | 43.6 | 43.8 | 43.9 | 43.9 | 43.8 |
| 2014 | 43.2 | 43.3 | 43.2 | 43.1 | 43.5 | 43.5 | 43.4 | 43.6 | 43.4 | 43.4 | 43.7 | 43.7 | 43.4 |
| 2015 | 43.3 | 43.3 | 43.3 | 43.4 | 43.7 | 43.7 | 43.8 | 43.8 | 43.6 | 43.9 | 44.1 | 44.4 | 43.7 |
| 2016 | 43.8 | 43.9 | 43.8 | 44.1 | 44.1 | 44.1 | 44.3 | 44.3 | 44.1 | 44.2 | 44.2 | 44.2 | 44.1 |
| 2017 | 43.8 | 43.8 | 43.9 | 43.9 | 44.0 | 44.4 | 44.2 | 44.2 | 44.2 | 44.4 | 44.3 | 44.4 | 44.1 |
| 2018 | 44.2 | 44.2 | 44.3 | 44.3 | 44.5 | 44.6 | 44.6 | 44.6 | 44.4 | 44.5 | 44.6 | 44.7 | 44.5 |
| 2019 | 44.5 | 44.5 | 44.4 | 44.5 | 44.7 | 44.8 | 44.7 | 44.7 | 44.4 | 44.2 | 44.4 | 44.4 | 44.5 |
| **Professional and Business Services** | | | | | | | | | | | | | |
| 2011 | 91.9 | 92.9 | 94.1 | 94.9 | 94.2 | 93.7 | 91.7 | 92.7 | 93.7 | 93.7 | 94.0 | 93.2 | 93.4 |
| 2012 | 91.5 | 93.9 | 95.8 | 96.0 | 96.1 | 95.5 | 93.5 | 96.8 | 97.4 | 97.7 | 98.7 | 98.8 | 96.0 |
| 2013 | 96.6 | 99.6 | 100.5 | 99.8 | 98.9 | 98.1 | 95.3 | 98.7 | 97.9 | 97.8 | 99.1 | 100.6 | 98.6 |
| 2014 | 99.1 | 99.0 | 99.0 | 101.0 | 100.0 | 99.3 | 98.3 | 101.6 | 102.2 | 102.7 | 105.0 | 106.4 | 101.1 |
| 2015 | 102.4 | 103.5 | 103.4 | 104.9 | 105.0 | 103.6 | 103.8 | 106.7 | 106.8 | 108.9 | 110.1 | 112.3 | 106.0 |
| 2016 | 107.8 | 109.6 | 109.3 | 108.4 | 107.1 | 105.8 | 106.2 | 107.3 | 107.8 | 108.6 | 108.8 | 109.0 | 108.0 |
| 2017 | 106.0 | 108.1 | 108.1 | 108.5 | 107.5 | 106.6 | 104.8 | 106.3 | 106.8 | 108.3 | 110.6 | 111.5 | 107.8 |
| 2018 | 106.8 | 107.3 | 108.0 | 108.9 | 107.6 | 106.9 | 105.7 | 108.9 | 110.6 | 112.5 | 115.6 | 114.6 | 109.5 |
| 2019 | 108.7 | 109.1 | 107.9 | 107.9 | 108.2 | 106.9 | 106.4 | 108.6 | 107.9 | 108.0 | 108.7 | 107.8 | 108.0 |
| **Education and Health Services** | | | | | | | | | | | | | |
| 2011 | 131.7 | 132.5 | 132.7 | 133.0 | 131.3 | 128.9 | 127.6 | 130.2 | 134.5 | 134.9 | 134.6 | 133.6 | 132.1 |
| 2012 | 132.7 | 134.1 | 134.4 | 134.2 | 132.2 | 129.7 | 129.0 | 132.0 | 134.5 | 135.4 | 135.3 | 134.5 | 133.2 |
| 2013 | 133.4 | 134.7 | 135.0 | 135.7 | 133.6 | 130.4 | 129.3 | 131.6 | 135.7 | 136.1 | 136.2 | 135.1 | 133.9 |
| 2014 | 133.7 | 134.5 | 134.6 | 135.5 | 134.2 | 131.3 | 131.7 | 135.0 | 137.3 | 137.7 | 138.3 | 137.6 | 135.1 |
| 2015 | 136.7 | 137.9 | 138.0 | 138.6 | 138.7 | 134.8 | 134.4 | 136.4 | 139.4 | 140.7 | 140.8 | 139.9 | 138.0 |
| 2016 | 138.9 | 140.1 | 140.2 | 141.1 | 141.0 | 137.0 | 136.9 | 139.9 | 141.9 | 142.5 | 142.4 | 141.9 | 140.3 |
| 2017 | 141.8 | 143.6 | 143.8 | 145.1 | 144.4 | 141.2 | 140.7 | 143.4 | 146.1 | 146.1 | 146.3 | 145.2 | 144.0 |
| 2018 | 143.6 | 145.4 | 144.5 | 145.7 | 145.3 | 142.0 | 141.6 | 145.5 | 146.5 | 147.4 | 147.1 | 146.2 | 145.1 |
| 2019 | 145.7 | 146.9 | 147.0 | 147.1 | 146.8 | 144.1 | 143.4 | 147.2 | 148.0 | 149.5 | 149.3 | 148.9 | 147.0 |
| **Leisure and Hospitality** | | | | | | | | | | | | | |
| 2011 | 113.8 | 115.4 | 118.1 | 120.6 | 121.8 | 122.2 | 121.1 | 122.2 | 121.0 | 119.1 | 118.9 | 118.2 | 119.4 |
| 2012 | 116.4 | 118.4 | 120.7 | 122.7 | 124.1 | 124.7 | 123.4 | 124.9 | 123.0 | 120.8 | 120.6 | 120.5 | 121.7 |
| 2013 | 118.2 | 119.9 | 122.5 | 124.7 | 125.9 | 127.0 | 126.0 | 126.9 | 126.0 | 123.9 | 124.2 | 123.3 | 124.0 |
| 2014 | 121.3 | 122.1 | 124.5 | 127.6 | 129.1 | 129.3 | 127.2 | 127.2 | 126.9 | 125.8 | 125.1 | 124.7 | 125.9 |
| 2015 | 122.2 | 124.4 | 125.8 | 129.7 | 131.3 | 131.8 | 131.2 | 131.9 | 131.2 | 130.4 | 129.6 | 129.6 | 129.1 |
| 2016 | 126.9 | 129.0 | 130.9 | 134.1 | 135.3 | 135.3 | 135.4 | 136.4 | 135.6 | 133.3 | 133.0 | 130.9 | 133.0 |
| 2017 | 129.1 | 130.9 | 132.8 | 136.3 | 137.9 | 137.9 | 137.1 | 137.5 | 135.7 | 134.2 | 133.8 | 132.6 | 134.7 |
| 2018 | 129.4 | 131.4 | 133.8 | 136.3 | 137.7 | 137.9 | 136.0 | 138.2 | 136.0 | 134.6 | 133.4 | 132.8 | 134.8 |
| 2019 | 131.3 | 132.8 | 133.7 | 137.9 | 138.1 | 139.0 | 137.7 | 138.9 | 137.2 | 137.2 | 136.6 | 135.8 | 136.4 |
| **Other Services** | | | | | | | | | | | | | |
| 2011 | 37.3 | 37.3 | 37.5 | 37.6 | 37.9 | 38.1 | 37.8 | 37.6 | 37.6 | 37.7 | 37.6 | 37.5 | 37.6 |
| 2012 | 37.5 | 37.5 | 37.8 | 38.0 | 38.2 | 38.5 | 38.5 | 38.6 | 38.6 | 38.3 | 38.4 | 38.5 | 38.2 |
| 2013 | 38.3 | 38.6 | 38.8 | 38.8 | 38.9 | 39.4 | 39.0 | 38.9 | 38.9 | 38.8 | 38.8 | 38.7 | 38.8 |
| 2014 | 38.5 | 38.6 | 38.8 | 38.8 | 39.0 | 39.5 | 39.2 | 39.3 | 39.1 | 39.0 | 39.3 | 39.4 | 39.0 |
| 2015 | 39.2 | 39.5 | 39.6 | 39.9 | 40.0 | 40.2 | 40.1 | 39.8 | 39.8 | 39.8 | 39.9 | 39.9 | 39.8 |
| 2016 | 39.9 | 40.1 | 40.2 | 40.2 | 40.2 | 40.4 | 40.5 | 40.2 | 40.2 | 40.2 | 40.2 | 40.2 | 40.2 |
| 2017 | 39.9 | 40.2 | 40.4 | 40.5 | 40.6 | 40.9 | 40.7 | 40.6 | 40.8 | 40.7 | 40.8 | 40.8 | 40.6 |
| 2018 | 40.8 | 41.0 | 41.2 | 41.3 | 41.3 | 41.6 | 41.2 | 41.1 | 41.1 | 41.0 | 40.8 | 40.6 | 41.1 |
| 2019 | 40.3 | 40.4 | 40.4 | 40.4 | 40.5 | 40.8 | 40.5 | 40.4 | 40.4 | 41.4 | 41.3 | 40.9 | 40.6 |
| **Government** | | | | | | | | | | | | | |
| 2011 | 245.2 | 247.5 | 248.3 | 248.8 | 248.1 | 244.2 | 236.6 | 241.8 | 247.5 | 249.0 | 248.5 | 245.0 | 245.9 |
| 2012 | 245.4 | 248.4 | 249.3 | 248.8 | 248.6 | 243.9 | 235.3 | 241.7 | 247.0 | 248.9 | 249.0 | 245.7 | 246.0 |
| 2013 | 244.7 | 248.3 | 248.7 | 248.9 | 248.2 | 243.4 | 234.4 | 240.7 | 247.3 | 247.7 | 247.6 | 243.7 | 245.3 |
| 2014 | 243.2 | 246.5 | 247.2 | 247.7 | 246.8 | 242.2 | 234.4 | 240.1 | 246.6 | 247.8 | 246.8 | 243.3 | 244.4 |
| 2015 | 242.3 | 245.5 | 246.3 | 245.6 | 246.1 | 241.0 | 234.2 | 239.4 | 245.4 | 246.7 | 246.1 | 242.7 | 243.4 |
| 2016 | 242.6 | 246.7 | 247.2 | 247.8 | 246.7 | 241.6 | 234.5 | 239.5 | 246.4 | 246.8 | 246.5 | 242.5 | 244.1 |
| 2017 | 241.5 | 245.3 | 246.5 | 245.1 | 243.7 | 239.2 | 233.3 | 238.7 | 245.3 | 245.5 | 245.2 | 241.5 | 242.6 |
| 2018 | 239.8 | 242.9 | 244.2 | 243.1 | 242.1 | 238.6 | 231.5 | 237.6 | 243.4 | 243.7 | 243.8 | 239.3 | 240.8 |
| 2019 | 239.2 | 243.2 | 244.3 | 243.5 | 243.6 | 239.1 | 232.7 | 239.1 | 245.3 | 245.8 | 245.7 | 241.2 | 241.9 |

## 2. Average Weekly Hours by Selected Industry: Mississippi, 2015–2019

(Not seasonally adjusted)

| Industry and year | January | February | March | April | May | June | July | August | September | October | November | December | Annual average |
|---|---|---|---|---|---|---|---|---|---|---|---|---|---|
| **Total Private** | | | | | | | | | | | | | |
| 2015 | 35.0 | 35.5 | 35.5 | 34.5 | 34.8 | 34.9 | 34.9 | 35.5 | 34.6 | 35.0 | 35.3 | 34.9 | 35.0 |
| 2016 | 34.9 | 34.8 | 34.5 | 34.5 | 35.0 | 34.6 | 35.0 | 34.6 | 34.8 | 35.4 | 34.9 | 35.0 | 34.8 |
| 2017 | 35.0 | 34.8 | 34.7 | 34.7 | 34.8 | 35.0 | 35.3 | 34.9 | 34.9 | 35.1 | 34.8 | 34.9 | 34.9 |
| 2018 | 33.9 | 34.7 | 34.7 | 35.0 | 34.6 | 34.8 | 35.0 | 34.5 | 34.8 | 34.5 | 34.4 | 35.3 | 34.7 |
| 2019 | 34.5 | 34.6 | 34.6 | 34.6 | 34.6 | 35.3 | 34.4 | 34.9 | 35.3 | 34.6 | 34.9 | 35.2 | 34.8 |
| **Goods-Producing** | | | | | | | | | | | | | |
| 2015 | 41.1 | 40.9 | 41.0 | 39.6 | 40.4 | 40.5 | 40.1 | 41.1 | 39.7 | 41.1 | 41.7 | 41.8 | 40.7 |
| 2016 | 41.5 | 41.4 | 41.1 | 41.3 | 42.1 | 41.3 | 42.0 | 41.3 | 41.6 | 42.3 | 41.7 | 42.0 | 41.6 |
| 2017 | 41.2 | 41.4 | 41.0 | 40.0 | 40.9 | 41.5 | 41.7 | 41.0 | 41.5 | 41.4 | 41.6 | 42.0 | 41.3 |
| 2018 | 39.7 | 41.6 | 41.5 | 41.5 | 41.0 | 41.6 | 41.0 | 41.2 | 40.8 | 40.6 | 40.1 | 41.7 | 41.0 |
| 2019 | 40.5 | 40.1 | 39.8 | 40.0 | 40.1 | 41.3 | 40.0 | 41.0 | 41.8 | 40.5 | 41.5 | 41.4 | 40.7 |
| **Construction** | | | | | | | | | | | | | |
| 2015 | 40.2 | 39.9 | 39.9 | 40.7 | 42.9 | 41.6 | 41.7 | 41.7 | 39.7 | 42.9 | 42.7 | 43.3 | 41.4 |
| 2016 | 43.1 | 43.0 | 41.2 | 40.8 | 44.0 | 43.4 | 43.0 | 41.6 | 42.6 | 42.6 | 41.5 | 40.7 | 42.3 |
| 2017 | 41.1 | 41.2 | 40.1 | 40.9 | 41.1 | 41.9 | 41.6 | 40.5 | 41.7 | 41.9 | 42.2 | 41.8 | 41.3 |
| 2018 | 36.7 | 38.8 | 40.5 | 41.5 | 42.1 | 40.2 | 40.1 | 39.4 | 39.2 | 39.9 | 37.0 | 38.9 | 39.5 |
| 2019 | 38.7 | 37.5 | 38.4 | 39.5 | 40.5 | 41.5 | 39.8 | 40.6 | 42.3 | 38.8 | 39.0 | 38.6 | 39.6 |
| **Manufacturing** | | | | | | | | | | | | | |
| 2015 | 41.6 | 41.3 | 41.7 | 41.7 | 41.8 | 42.3 | 41.5 | 42.7 | 41.4 | 42.2 | 42.9 | 42.9 | 42.0 |
| 2016 | 42.3 | 42.3 | 42.3 | 42.7 | 42.5 | 41.6 | 42.6 | 42.2 | 42.0 | 42.9 | 42.5 | 43.2 | 42.4 |
| 2017 | 41.8 | 42.0 | 41.7 | 40.2 | 41.2 | 41.7 | 42.0 | 41.4 | 41.6 | 41.5 | 41.6 | 41.9 | 41.6 |
| 2018 | 40.3 | 41.6 | 41.1 | 40.9 | 40.0 | 41.5 | 40.7 | 41.2 | 41.0 | 40.5 | 40.9 | 42.3 | 41.0 |
| 2019 | 40.3 | 40.3 | 39.6 | 39.8 | 39.4 | 40.5 | 39.0 | 40.3 | 40.7 | 40.5 | 41.5 | 41.6 | 40.3 |
| **Trade, Transportation, and Utilities** | | | | | | | | | | | | | |
| 2015 | 34.3 | 35.1 | 35.2 | 34.5 | 34.9 | 34.7 | 34.6 | 34.7 | 34.2 | 33.9 | 34.1 | 33.7 | 34.5 |
| 2016 | 33.4 | 33.1 | 32.7 | 32.8 | 33.3 | 33.4 | 33.8 | 33.4 | 33.3 | 34.1 | 33.9 | 33.9 | 33.4 |
| 2017 | 33.8 | 33.6 | 34.5 | 34.9 | 34.6 | 34.5 | 34.6 | 34.9 | 34.8 | 35.2 | 34.7 | 35.1 | 34.6 |
| 2018 | 34.3 | 34.4 | 34.7 | 34.6 | 34.6 | 34.5 | 35.1 | 34.3 | 34.6 | 34.2 | 34.3 | 35.0 | 34.6 |
| 2019 | 34.8 | 35.0 | 34.8 | 36.0 | 35.7 | 36.6 | 35.8 | 35.9 | 36.2 | 35.9 | 35.9 | 35.9 | 35.7 |
| **Financial Activities** | | | | | | | | | | | | | |
| 2015 | 37.4 | 38.8 | 39.1 | 36.8 | 36.8 | 37.1 | 37.0 | 39.4 | 37.0 | 37.3 | 39.0 | 36.8 | 37.7 |
| 2016 | 37.2 | 37.1 | 37.0 | 37.5 | 38.7 | 37.0 | 37.1 | 36.5 | 36.5 | 37.6 | 36.1 | 36.1 | 37.0 |
| 2017 | 37.1 | 36.4 | 35.9 | 36.6 | 36.3 | 36.6 | 37.4 | 35.8 | 36.5 | 36.8 | 35.5 | 35.3 | 36.4 |
| 2018 | 35.1 | 35.6 | 35.8 | 36.9 | 35.0 | 35.2 | 36.4 | 35.6 | 37.6 | 36.4 | 36.7 | 38.9 | 36.3 |
| 2019 | 37.3 | 37.6 | 37.0 | 37.4 | 37.7 | 38.8 | 37.6 | 37.5 | 39.5 | 37.3 | 37.6 | 38.7 | 37.9 |
| **Professional and Business Services** | | | | | | | | | | | | | |
| 2015 | 35.0 | 36.1 | 36.1 | 35.2 | 35.3 | 35.5 | 35.5 | 36.6 | 35.0 | 36.0 | 36.0 | 35.7 | 35.7 |
| 2016 | 35.0 | 35.0 | 34.8 | 34.3 | 35.0 | 35.2 | 34.8 | 35.0 | 35.3 | 35.5 | 34.7 | 35.1 | 35.0 |
| 2017 | 35.1 | 34.8 | 34.1 | 33.9 | 34.5 | 34.4 | 34.6 | 34.3 | 34.0 | 35.1 | 34.4 | 34.0 | 34.4 |
| 2018 | 32.7 | 33.6 | 33.5 | 34.5 | 33.9 | 34.9 | 34.8 | 34.6 | 34.7 | 34.6 | 34.7 | 35.5 | 34.3 |
| 2019 | 34.0 | 34.5 | 34.3 | 34.6 | 34.2 | 34.3 | 33.8 | 34.7 | 34.4 | 34.3 | 35.1 | 35.3 | 34.5 |
| **Education and Health Services** | | | | | | | | | | | | | |
| 2015 | 33.4 | 33.7 | 33.3 | 33.4 | 33.1 | 33.0 | 33.3 | 34.0 | 33.5 | 33.7 | 34.2 | 33.6 | 33.5 |
| 2016 | 34.3 | 34.0 | 33.9 | 34.0 | 34.3 | 34.3 | 34.5 | 34.2 | 34.7 | 35.1 | 35.0 | 34.9 | 34.4 |
| 2017 | 35.2 | 34.7 | 34.3 | 34.8 | 34.3 | 34.5 | 35.0 | 34.5 | 34.3 | 34.5 | 34.6 | 34.2 | 34.6 |
| 2018 | 34.1 | 34.2 | 34.1 | 34.6 | 34.0 | 33.9 | 34.2 | 33.6 | 34.1 | 33.3 | 34.1 | 34.0 | 34.0 |
| 2019 | 33.7 | 33.7 | 33.6 | 33.6 | 33.7 | 33.9 | 33.3 | 33.5 | 33.7 | 33.3 | 33.3 | 33.8 | 33.6 |
| **Leisure and Hospitality** | | | | | | | | | | | | | |
| 2015 | 26.8 | 28.3 | 28.0 | 27.7 | 27.5 | 27.8 | 28.1 | 27.4 | 26.9 | 27.2 | 27.3 | 27.0 | 27.5 |
| 2016 | 26.8 | 27.5 | 27.1 | 27.2 | 27.8 | 27.4 | 27.8 | 26.9 | 27.2 | 27.4 | 27.1 | 27.0 | 27.3 |
| 2017 | 27.0 | 27.3 | 27.5 | 28.0 | 27.9 | 27.9 | 27.9 | 27.3 | 27.2 | 27.1 | 27.1 | 27.0 | 27.4 |
| 2018 | 26.1 | 27.3 | 27.5 | 27.3 | 27.7 | 27.3 | 27.6 | 26.9 | 27.0 | 27.2 | 26.4 | 26.8 | 27.1 |
| 2019 | 26.4 | 26.9 | 27.7 | 26.8 | 27.6 | 28.1 | 27.4 | 27.4 | 27.3 | 27.4 | 26.8 | 27.0 | 27.2 |

## 3. Average Hourly Earnings by Selected Industry: Mississippi, 2015–2019

(Dollars, not seasonally adjusted)

| Industry and year | January | February | March | April | May | June | July | August | September | October | November | December | Annual average |
|---|---|---|---|---|---|---|---|---|---|---|---|---|---|
| **Total Private** | | | | | | | | | | | | | |
| 2015 | 19.25 | 19.51 | 19.68 | 19.53 | 19.35 | 19.34 | 19.52 | 19.68 | 19.67 | 19.60 | 19.81 | 19.80 | 19.56 |
| 2016 | 19.82 | 19.88 | 19.83 | 20.10 | 20.19 | 20.06 | 20.20 | 20.07 | 20.15 | 20.37 | 20.29 | 20.30 | 20.11 |
| 2017 | 20.51 | 20.55 | 20.41 | 20.52 | 20.26 | 20.31 | 20.57 | 20.67 | 20.90 | 20.75 | 20.72 | 20.42 | 20.55 |
| 2018 | 20.10 | 19.84 | 19.90 | 20.02 | 20.04 | 20.05 | 20.43 | 20.16 | 20.49 | 20.50 | 20.40 | 21.12 | 20.26 |
| 2019 | 20.87 | 20.70 | 21.16 | 21.23 | 21.45 | 21.71 | 21.75 | 21.62 | 22.13 | 22.00 | 22.10 | 22.12 | 21.57 |
| **Goods-Producing** | | | | | | | | | | | | | |
| 2015 | 20.14 | 20.41 | 20.84 | 20.87 | 20.65 | 20.68 | 20.83 | 20.77 | 20.75 | 20.79 | 21.08 | 21.41 | 20.77 |
| 2016 | 21.29 | 21.37 | 21.35 | 21.90 | 22.46 | 22.82 | 22.82 | 22.62 | 22.93 | 23.03 | 23.12 | 23.31 | 22.42 |
| 2017 | 23.04 | 22.73 | 22.77 | 22.70 | 22.56 | 22.59 | 22.87 | 22.88 | 22.97 | 22.90 | 22.81 | 22.73 | 22.80 |
| 2018 | 22.82 | 22.53 | 22.45 | 22.44 | 22.53 | 22.42 | 22.60 | 22.37 | 22.90 | 22.73 | 22.87 | 23.15 | 22.65 |
| 2019 | 22.79 | 22.90 | 22.88 | 22.88 | 22.91 | 22.91 | 23.11 | 23.14 | 23.46 | 23.38 | 23.60 | 23.89 | 23.16 |
| **Construction** | | | | | | | | | | | | | |
| 2015 | 21.63 | 21.41 | 22.35 | 21.83 | 21.55 | 21.86 | 21.59 | 21.60 | 21.67 | 21.64 | 21.90 | 22.26 | 21.77 |
| 2016 | 21.98 | 22.11 | 22.46 | 22.26 | 22.42 | 22.77 | 22.27 | 22.06 | 22.26 | 22.24 | 22.46 | 22.96 | 22.35 |
| 2017 | 22.44 | 22.71 | 22.70 | 22.48 | 22.36 | 22.52 | 22.33 | 22.64 | 22.27 | 22.40 | 22.63 | 22.79 | 22.52 |
| 2018 | 22.83 | 22.78 | 22.38 | 22.31 | 22.19 | 22.27 | 22.50 | 22.07 | 22.66 | 21.97 | 22.55 | 22.71 | 22.42 |
| 2019 | 22.89 | 23.58 | 23.64 | 23.24 | 23.35 | 23.10 | 23.22 | 22.91 | 23.28 | 23.15 | 23.56 | 23.53 | 23.28 |
| **Manufacturing** | | | | | | | | | | | | | |
| 2015 | 19.48 | 19.91 | 20.14 | 20.23 | 20.16 | 19.90 | 20.23 | 20.17 | 20.22 | 20.34 | 20.70 | 21.04 | 20.21 |
| 2016 | 20.98 | 21.07 | 20.96 | 21.68 | 22.32 | 22.75 | 22.98 | 22.77 | 23.16 | 23.31 | 23.34 | 23.43 | 22.40 |
| 2017 | 23.25 | 22.77 | 22.85 | 22.82 | 22.65 | 22.67 | 23.14 | 23.06 | 23.20 | 23.12 | 22.91 | 22.74 | 22.93 |
| 2018 | 22.86 | 22.51 | 22.47 | 22.48 | 22.51 | 22.29 | 22.52 | 22.35 | 22.84 | 22.82 | 22.64 | 23.00 | 22.61 |
| 2019 | 22.45 | 22.35 | 22.67 | 22.36 | 22.66 | 22.80 | 23.00 | 23.15 | 23.47 | 23.33 | 23.43 | 23.68 | 22.95 |
| **Trade, Transportation, and Utilities** | | | | | | | | | | | | | |
| 2015 | 18.20 | 18.38 | 18.38 | 18.38 | 17.80 | 18.00 | 18.22 | 18.42 | 18.39 | 18.47 | 18.33 | 18.03 | 18.25 |
| 2016 | 18.26 | 18.11 | 18.26 | 18.70 | 18.89 | 18.39 | 18.76 | 18.61 | 19.18 | 19.35 | 18.94 | 18.66 | 18.68 |
| 2017 | 19.41 | 20.01 | 19.62 | 19.86 | 20.06 | 20.05 | 20.20 | 20.69 | 21.05 | 20.79 | 20.58 | 19.77 | 20.18 |
| 2018 | 19.47 | 19.53 | 19.55 | 20.13 | 20.16 | 19.75 | 20.13 | 19.98 | 19.90 | 20.24 | 19.99 | 20.52 | 19.95 |
| 2019 | 20.69 | 20.88 | 20.55 | 20.71 | 20.93 | 20.74 | 21.64 | 21.41 | 22.11 | 21.66 | 21.06 | 20.74 | 21.09 |
| **Financial Activities** | | | | | | | | | | | | | |
| 2015 | 23.14 | 24.14 | 24.13 | 23.75 | 23.72 | 23.75 | 23.85 | 24.15 | 24.02 | 24.03 | 25.23 | 24.88 | 24.07 |
| 2016 | 24.02 | 25.04 | 24.14 | 24.06 | 23.94 | 23.43 | 23.46 | 23.54 | 23.04 | 23.44 | 23.21 | 22.92 | 23.69 |
| 2017 | 23.51 | 23.70 | 23.70 | 23.26 | 22.06 | 21.70 | 21.97 | 21.89 | 22.41 | 22.28 | 21.92 | 22.26 | 22.55 |
| 2018 | 22.44 | 22.13 | 21.83 | 22.74 | 22.86 | 22.39 | 23.54 | 23.06 | 24.25 | 23.29 | 23.40 | 24.18 | 23.03 |
| 2019 | 23.48 | 23.63 | 23.89 | 23.91 | 23.88 | 25.13 | 25.04 | 24.83 | 25.20 | 25.44 | 25.44 | 26.02 | 24.67 |
| **Professional and Business Services** | | | | | | | | | | | | | |
| 2015 | 21.69 | 22.39 | 22.53 | 22.12 | 21.96 | 21.42 | 21.28 | 21.57 | 21.51 | 21.18 | 21.42 | 21.17 | 21.68 |
| 2016 | 21.19 | 21.12 | 20.80 | 20.90 | 20.98 | 20.52 | 20.58 | 20.11 | 20.05 | 20.68 | 20.69 | 21.11 | 20.73 |
| 2017 | 21.10 | 21.08 | 20.99 | 21.34 | 20.95 | 21.26 | 21.36 | 20.94 | 21.30 | 21.00 | 21.04 | 20.46 | 21.07 |
| 2018 | 20.47 | 20.25 | 20.61 | 20.05 | 20.32 | 20.34 | 21.15 | 20.80 | 21.19 | 21.36 | 20.84 | 21.40 | 20.74 |
| 2019 | 21.82 | 21.67 | 22.21 | 22.23 | 22.17 | 22.79 | 22.47 | 22.10 | 23.06 | 22.81 | 23.05 | 23.65 | 22.50 |
| **Education and Health Services** | | | | | | | | | | | | | |
| 2015 | 20.13 | 20.18 | 20.42 | 20.38 | 20.55 | 20.61 | 20.96 | 21.00 | 21.04 | 21.01 | 20.95 | 21.29 | 20.71 |
| 2016 | 21.11 | 21.19 | 21.34 | 21.34 | 21.19 | 21.35 | 21.56 | 21.53 | 21.20 | 21.12 | 21.21 | 21.11 | 21.27 |
| 2017 | 21.24 | 21.17 | 21.16 | 21.17 | 20.98 | 21.24 | 21.53 | 21.58 | 21.40 | 21.41 | 21.51 | 21.51 | 21.33 |
| 2018 | 21.55 | 21.76 | 21.78 | 21.87 | 21.75 | 21.86 | 21.99 | 21.40 | 21.44 | 21.61 | 21.02 | 21.03 | 21.59 |
| 2019 | 20.96 | 20.70 | 21.01 | 20.94 | 20.86 | 21.17 | 21.16 | 20.90 | 21.30 | 21.52 | 21.81 | 21.34 | 21.14 |
| **Leisure and Hospitality** | | | | | | | | | | | | | |
| 2015 | 11.99 | 11.98 | 12.04 | 11.96 | 11.97 | 11.84 | 11.87 | 11.87 | 11.92 | 11.69 | 11.80 | 11.75 | 11.89 |
| 2016 | 11.97 | 12.00 | 11.96 | 12.05 | 12.00 | 11.86 | 11.94 | 11.94 | 12.05 | 12.10 | 11.94 | 12.09 | 11.99 |
| 2017 | 11.98 | 12.14 | 12.17 | 12.27 | 12.28 | 12.20 | 12.22 | 12.20 | 12.20 | 12.41 | 12.25 | 12.05 | 12.20 |
| 2018 | 12.15 | 12.23 | 12.17 | 12.24 | 12.20 | 12.15 | 12.21 | 12.25 | 12.32 | 12.38 | 12.45 | 12.58 | 12.28 |
| 2019 | 12.33 | 12.38 | 12.33 | 12.30 | 12.50 | 12.46 | 12.58 | 12.66 | 12.69 | 12.86 | 12.82 | 12.97 | 12.57 |

## 4. Average Weekly Earnings by Selected Industry: Mississippi, 2015–2019

(Dollars, not seasonally adjusted)

| Industry and year | January | February | March | April | May | June | July | August | September | October | November | December | Annual average |
|---|---|---|---|---|---|---|---|---|---|---|---|---|---|
| **Total Private** | | | | | | | | | | | | | |
| 2015 | 673.75 | 692.61 | 698.64 | 673.79 | 673.38 | 674.97 | 681.25 | 698.64 | 680.58 | 686.00 | 699.29 | 691.02 | 684.60 |
| 2016 | 691.72 | 691.82 | 684.14 | 693.45 | 706.65 | 694.08 | 707.00 | 694.42 | 701.22 | 721.10 | 708.12 | 710.50 | 699.83 |
| 2017 | 717.85 | 715.14 | 708.23 | 712.04 | 705.05 | 710.85 | 726.12 | 721.38 | 729.41 | 728.33 | 721.06 | 712.66 | 717.20 |
| 2018 | 681.39 | 688.45 | 690.53 | 700.70 | 693.38 | 697.74 | 715.05 | 695.52 | 713.05 | 707.25 | 701.76 | 745.54 | 703.02 |
| 2019 | 720.02 | 716.22 | 732.14 | 734.56 | 742.17 | 766.36 | 748.20 | 754.54 | 781.19 | 761.20 | 771.29 | 778.62 | 750.64 |
| **Goods-Producing** | | | | | | | | | | | | | |
| 2015 | 827.75 | 834.77 | 854.44 | 826.45 | 834.26 | 837.54 | 835.28 | 853.65 | 823.78 | 854.47 | 879.04 | 894.94 | 845.34 |
| 2016 | 883.54 | 884.72 | 877.49 | 904.47 | 945.57 | 942.47 | 958.44 | 934.21 | 953.89 | 974.17 | 964.10 | 979.02 | 932.67 |
| 2017 | 949.25 | 941.02 | 933.57 | 908.00 | 922.70 | 937.49 | 953.68 | 938.08 | 953.26 | 948.06 | 948.90 | 954.66 | 941.64 |
| 2018 | 905.95 | 937.25 | 931.68 | 931.26 | 923.73 | 932.67 | 926.60 | 921.64 | 934.32 | 922.84 | 917.09 | 965.36 | 928.65 |
| 2019 | 923.00 | 918.29 | 910.62 | 915.20 | 918.69 | 946.18 | 924.40 | 948.74 | 980.63 | 946.89 | 979.40 | 989.05 | 942.61 |
| **Construction** | | | | | | | | | | | | | |
| 2015 | 869.12 | 854.26 | 891.77 | 888.48 | 924.50 | 909.38 | 900.30 | 900.72 | 860.30 | 928.36 | 935.13 | 963.86 | 901.28 |
| 2016 | 947.34 | 950.73 | 925.35 | 908.21 | 986.48 | 988.22 | 957.61 | 917.70 | 948.28 | 947.42 | 932.09 | 934.47 | 945.41 |
| 2017 | 922.28 | 935.65 | 910.27 | 919.43 | 919.00 | 943.59 | 928.93 | 916.92 | 928.66 | 938.56 | 954.99 | 952.62 | 930.08 |
| 2018 | 837.86 | 883.86 | 906.39 | 925.87 | 934.20 | 895.25 | 902.25 | 869.56 | 888.27 | 876.60 | 834.35 | 883.42 | 885.59 |
| 2019 | 885.84 | 884.25 | 907.78 | 917.98 | 945.68 | 958.65 | 924.16 | 930.15 | 984.74 | 898.22 | 918.84 | 908.26 | 921.89 |
| **Manufacturing** | | | | | | | | | | | | | |
| 2015 | 810.37 | 822.28 | 839.84 | 843.59 | 842.69 | 841.77 | 839.55 | 861.26 | 837.11 | 858.35 | 888.03 | 902.62 | 848.82 |
| 2016 | 887.45 | 891.26 | 886.61 | 925.74 | 948.60 | 946.40 | 978.95 | 960.89 | 972.72 | 1000.00 | 991.95 | 1012.18 | 949.76 |
| 2017 | 971.85 | 956.34 | 952.85 | 917.36 | 933.18 | 945.34 | 971.88 | 954.68 | 965.12 | 959.48 | 953.06 | 952.81 | 953.89 |
| 2018 | 921.26 | 936.42 | 923.52 | 919.43 | 900.40 | 925.04 | 916.56 | 920.82 | 936.44 | 924.21 | 925.98 | 972.90 | 927.01 |
| 2019 | 904.74 | 900.71 | 897.73 | 889.93 | 892.80 | 923.40 | 897.00 | 932.95 | 955.23 | 944.87 | 972.35 | 985.09 | 924.89 |
| **Trade, Transportation, and Utilities** | | | | | | | | | | | | | |
| 2015 | 624.26 | 645.14 | 646.98 | 634.11 | 621.22 | 624.60 | 630.41 | 639.17 | 628.94 | 626.13 | 625.05 | 607.61 | 629.63 |
| 2016 | 609.88 | 599.44 | 597.10 | 613.36 | 629.04 | 614.23 | 634.09 | 621.57 | 638.69 | 659.84 | 642.07 | 632.57 | 623.91 |
| 2017 | 656.06 | 672.34 | 676.89 | 693.11 | 694.08 | 691.73 | 698.92 | 722.08 | 732.54 | 731.81 | 714.13 | 693.93 | 698.23 |
| 2018 | 667.82 | 671.83 | 678.39 | 696.50 | 697.54 | 681.38 | 706.56 | 685.31 | 688.54 | 692.21 | 685.66 | 718.20 | 690.27 |
| 2019 | 720.01 | 730.80 | 715.14 | 745.56 | 747.20 | 759.08 | 774.71 | 768.62 | 800.38 | 777.59 | 756.05 | 744.57 | 752.91 |
| **Financial Activities** | | | | | | | | | | | | | |
| 2015 | 865.44 | 936.63 | 943.48 | 874.00 | 872.90 | 881.13 | 882.45 | 951.51 | 888.74 | 896.32 | 983.97 | 915.58 | 907.44 |
| 2016 | 893.54 | 928.98 | 893.18 | 902.25 | 926.48 | 866.91 | 870.37 | 859.21 | 840.96 | 881.34 | 837.88 | 827.41 | 876.53 |
| 2017 | 872.22 | 862.68 | 850.83 | 851.32 | 800.78 | 794.22 | 821.68 | 783.66 | 817.97 | 819.90 | 778.16 | 785.78 | 820.82 |
| 2018 | 787.64 | 787.83 | 781.51 | 839.11 | 800.10 | 788.13 | 856.86 | 820.94 | 911.80 | 847.76 | 858.78 | 940.60 | 835.99 |
| 2019 | 875.80 | 888.49 | 883.93 | 894.23 | 900.28 | 975.04 | 941.50 | 931.13 | 995.40 | 948.91 | 956.54 | 1006.97 | 934.99 |
| **Professional and Business Services** | | | | | | | | | | | | | |
| 2015 | 759.15 | 808.28 | 813.33 | 778.62 | 775.19 | 760.41 | 755.44 | 789.46 | 752.85 | 762.48 | 771.12 | 755.77 | 773.98 |
| 2016 | 741.65 | 739.20 | 723.84 | 716.87 | 734.30 | 722.30 | 716.18 | 703.85 | 708.12 | 734.14 | 717.94 | 740.96 | 725.55 |
| 2017 | 740.61 | 733.58 | 715.76 | 723.43 | 722.78 | 731.34 | 739.06 | 718.24 | 724.20 | 737.10 | 723.78 | 695.64 | 724.81 |
| 2018 | 669.37 | 680.40 | 690.44 | 691.73 | 688.85 | 709.87 | 736.02 | 719.68 | 735.29 | 739.06 | 723.15 | 759.70 | 711.38 |
| 2019 | 741.88 | 747.62 | 761.80 | 769.16 | 758.21 | 781.70 | 759.49 | 766.87 | 793.26 | 782.38 | 809.06 | 834.85 | 776.25 |
| **Education and Health Services** | | | | | | | | | | | | | |
| 2015 | 672.34 | 680.07 | 679.99 | 680.69 | 680.21 | 680.13 | 697.97 | 714.00 | 704.84 | 708.04 | 716.49 | 715.34 | 693.79 |
| 2016 | 724.07 | 720.46 | 723.43 | 725.56 | 726.82 | 732.31 | 743.82 | 736.33 | 735.64 | 741.31 | 742.35 | 736.74 | 731.69 |
| 2017 | 747.65 | 734.60 | 725.79 | 736.72 | 719.61 | 732.78 | 753.55 | 744.51 | 734.02 | 738.65 | 744.25 | 735.64 | 738.02 |
| 2018 | 734.86 | 744.19 | 742.70 | 756.70 | 739.50 | 741.05 | 752.06 | 719.04 | 731.10 | 719.61 | 716.78 | 715.02 | 734.06 |
| 2019 | 706.35 | 697.59 | 705.94 | 703.58 | 702.98 | 717.66 | 704.63 | 700.15 | 717.81 | 716.62 | 726.27 | 721.29 | 710.30 |
| **Leisure and Hospitality** | | | | | | | | | | | | | |
| 2015 | 321.33 | 339.03 | 337.12 | 331.29 | 329.18 | 329.15 | 333.55 | 325.24 | 320.65 | 317.97 | 322.14 | 317.25 | 326.98 |
| 2016 | 320.80 | 330.00 | 324.12 | 328.03 | 333.88 | 324.96 | 331.93 | 321.19 | 327.76 | 331.54 | 323.57 | 326.43 | 327.33 |
| 2017 | 323.46 | 331.42 | 334.68 | 343.56 | 342.61 | 340.38 | 340.94 | 333.06 | 331.84 | 336.31 | 331.98 | 325.35 | 334.28 |
| 2018 | 317.12 | 333.88 | 334.68 | 334.15 | 337.94 | 331.70 | 337.00 | 329.79 | 332.64 | 336.74 | 328.68 | 337.14 | 332.79 |
| 2019 | 325.51 | 333.02 | 341.54 | 329.64 | 345.00 | 350.13 | 344.69 | 346.88 | 346.44 | 352.36 | 343.58 | 350.19 | 341.90 |

# MISSOURI
## *At a Glance*

Population:
    2010 census: 5,988,927
    2019 estimate: 6,137,428

Percent change in population:
    2010–2019: 2.5%

Percent change in total nonfarm employment:
    2011–2019: 8.6%

Industry with the largest growth in employment, 2011–2019 (percent):
    Construction, 22.4%

Industry with the largest decline or smallest growth in employment, 2011–2019 (percent):
    Information, -19.4%

Civilian labor force:
    2010: 3,056,484
    2019: 3,083,245

Unemployment rate and rank among states (highest to lowest):
    2010: 9.6%, 19th
    2019: 3.3%, 30th

Over-the-year change in unemployment rates:
    2017–2018: -0.5%
    2018–2019: 0.1%

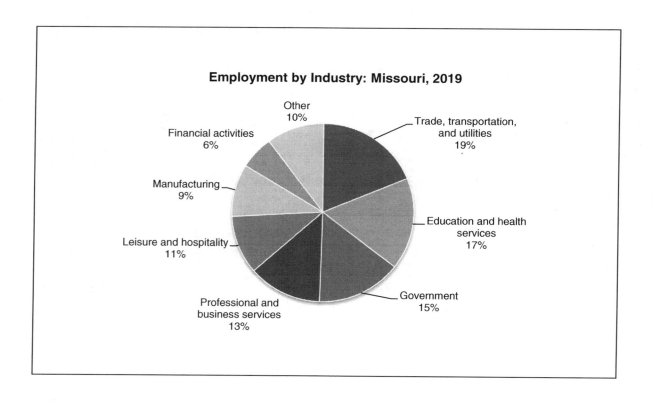

**Employment by Industry: Missouri, 2019**

- Other 10%
- Trade, transportation, and utilities 19%
- Financial activities 6%
- Education and health services 17%
- Manufacturing 9%
- Government 15%
- Leisure and hospitality 11%
- Professional and business services 13%

# 1. Employment by Industry: Missouri, 2011–2019

(Numbers in thousands, not seasonally adjusted)

| Industry and year | January | February | March | April | May | June | July | August | September | October | November | December | Annual average |
|---|---|---|---|---|---|---|---|---|---|---|---|---|---|
| **Total Nonfarm** | | | | | | | | | | | | | |
| 2011 | 2,612.9 | 2,618.3 | 2,652.7 | 2,693.0 | 2,704.4 | 2,695.3 | 2,652.3 | 2,660.4 | 2,691.2 | 2,696.1 | 2,699.1 | 2,697.6 | 2,672.8 |
| 2012 | 2,631.7 | 2,643.1 | 2,673.8 | 2,699.5 | 2,717.3 | 2,713.5 | 2,664.9 | 2,681.7 | 2,705.4 | 2,719.6 | 2,725.4 | 2,723.3 | 2,691.6 |
| 2013 | 2,653.1 | 2,671.4 | 2,692.0 | 2,727.0 | 2,746.7 | 2,740.2 | 2,691.6 | 2,710.2 | 2,734.4 | 2,749.4 | 2,751.4 | 2,745.2 | 2,717.7 |
| 2014 | 2,667.8 | 2,688.0 | 2,710.6 | 2,759.7 | 2,778.1 | 2,767.6 | 2,723.3 | 2,742.8 | 2,760.9 | 2,783.7 | 2,786.4 | 2,785.7 | 2,746.2 |
| 2015 | 2,724.5 | 2,742.5 | 2,761.2 | 2,810.8 | 2,833.1 | 2,829.3 | 2,791.7 | 2,799.4 | 2,821.7 | 2,842.2 | 2,847.5 | 2,846.4 | 2,804.2 |
| 2016 | 2,775.6 | 2,791.8 | 2,815.5 | 2,860.3 | 2,868.0 | 2,870.8 | 2,828.8 | 2,842.6 | 2,868.0 | 2,880.2 | 2,879.1 | 2,871.6 | 2,846.0 |
| 2017 | 2,810.3 | 2,833.9 | 2,850.7 | 2,882.6 | 2,893.9 | 2,901.3 | 2,851.2 | 2,861.2 | 2,885.9 | 2,893.6 | 2,899.2 | 2,896.1 | 2,871.7 |
| 2018 | 2,823.5 | 2,842.1 | 2,862.7 | 2,890.5 | 2,901.5 | 2,915.0 | 2,870.2 | 2,878.5 | 2,895.8 | 2,913.0 | 2,914.4 | 2,908.5 | 2,884.6 |
| 2019 | 2,849.8 | 2,860.7 | 2,877.4 | 2,915.3 | 2,926.5 | 2,925.4 | 2,886.3 | 2,897.5 | 2,914.3 | 2,927.5 | 2,928.1 | 2,910.2 | 2,901.6 |
| **Total Private** | | | | | | | | | | | | | |
| 2011 | 2,170.3 | 2,170.6 | 2,202.6 | 2,239.0 | 2,249.4 | 2,259.2 | 2,258.3 | 2,259.1 | 2,250.5 | 2,248.9 | 2,249.7 | 2,248.7 | 2,233.9 |
| 2012 | 2,194.7 | 2,196.0 | 2,224.4 | 2,247.9 | 2,265.1 | 2,278.5 | 2,272.7 | 2,277.2 | 2,264.2 | 2,271.1 | 2,276.0 | 2,275.0 | 2,253.6 |
| 2013 | 2,216.4 | 2,224.9 | 2,243.2 | 2,276.3 | 2,295.9 | 2,306.9 | 2,303.0 | 2,310.6 | 2,298.3 | 2,305.6 | 2,306.4 | 2,301.5 | 2,282.4 |
| 2014 | 2,237.0 | 2,247.2 | 2,268.3 | 2,313.5 | 2,330.7 | 2,337.1 | 2,336.0 | 2,344.5 | 2,326.0 | 2,341.5 | 2,343.7 | 2,344.6 | 2,314.2 |
| 2015 | 2,292.0 | 2,297.9 | 2,314.4 | 2,364.5 | 2,385.2 | 2,393.6 | 2,399.7 | 2,399.2 | 2,386.1 | 2,401.7 | 2,405.2 | 2,404.1 | 2,370.3 |
| 2016 | 2,344.6 | 2,353.6 | 2,373.9 | 2,418.1 | 2,423.6 | 2,434.6 | 2,435.1 | 2,439.4 | 2,427.8 | 2,434.8 | 2,433.4 | 2,426.2 | 2,412.1 |
| 2017 | 2,376.3 | 2,392.6 | 2,408.3 | 2,438.5 | 2,448.1 | 2,462.3 | 2,455.5 | 2,458.4 | 2,447.3 | 2,449.9 | 2,454.6 | 2,452.2 | 2,437.0 |
| 2018 | 2,389.4 | 2,401.7 | 2,420.2 | 2,447.0 | 2,457.0 | 2,474.0 | 2,473.6 | 2,476.4 | 2,458.6 | 2,468.3 | 2,468.7 | 2,463.8 | 2,449.9 |
| 2019 | 2,416.0 | 2,419.5 | 2,434.0 | 2,469.2 | 2,478.6 | 2,485.5 | 2,488.7 | 2,492.2 | 2,472.1 | 2,480.7 | 2,481.2 | 2,464.0 | 2,465.1 |
| **Goods Producing** | | | | | | | | | | | | | |
| 2011 | 342.5 | 341.3 | 349.3 | 356.2 | 359.6 | 364.6 | 366.6 | 363.8 | 364.4 | 361.9 | 359.3 | 357.7 | 357.3 |
| 2012 | 350.3 | 349.5 | 356.0 | 359.5 | 362.1 | 367.1 | 367.3 | 367.7 | 364.6 | 363.6 | 361.4 | 359.8 | 360.7 |
| 2013 | 351.0 | 352.8 | 355.4 | 361.1 | 366.5 | 371.9 | 370.9 | 372.7 | 371.2 | 370.3 | 368.2 | 364.4 | 364.7 |
| 2014 | 353.3 | 356.3 | 362.9 | 368.4 | 372.8 | 376.8 | 377.7 | 379.0 | 377.2 | 377.7 | 376.5 | 375.9 | 371.2 |
| 2015 | 367.2 | 367.8 | 372.1 | 378.0 | 381.9 | 385.9 | 387.1 | 386.4 | 385.3 | 385.5 | 384.1 | 384.7 | 380.5 |
| 2016 | 375.8 | 376.2 | 381.1 | 387.8 | 388.4 | 394.5 | 394.3 | 394.6 | 393.3 | 394.1 | 393.0 | 391.6 | 388.7 |
| 2017 | 382.8 | 385.7 | 387.3 | 391.0 | 393.8 | 400.2 | 399.9 | 399.8 | 398.5 | 395.2 | 396.6 | 397.0 | 394.0 |
| 2018 | 385.1 | 388.5 | 393.5 | 396.9 | 398.1 | 407.1 | 405.0 | 407.0 | 405.7 | 405.6 | 402.9 | 404.0 | 400.0 |
| 2019 | 398.5 | 397.3 | 401.1 | 407.4 | 409.6 | 414.4 | 412.2 | 414.8 | 411.9 | 409.8 | 409.4 | 407.0 | 407.8 |
| **Service-Providing** | | | | | | | | | | | | | |
| 2011 | 2,270.4 | 2,277.0 | 2,303.4 | 2,336.8 | 2,344.8 | 2,330.7 | 2,285.7 | 2,296.6 | 2,326.8 | 2,334.2 | 2,339.8 | 2,339.9 | 2,315.5 |
| 2012 | 2,281.4 | 2,293.6 | 2,317.8 | 2,340.0 | 2,355.2 | 2,346.4 | 2,297.6 | 2,314.0 | 2,340.8 | 2,356.0 | 2,364.0 | 2,363.5 | 2,330.9 |
| 2013 | 2,302.1 | 2,318.6 | 2,336.6 | 2,365.9 | 2,380.2 | 2,368.3 | 2,320.7 | 2,337.5 | 2,363.2 | 2,379.1 | 2,383.2 | 2,380.8 | 2,353.0 |
| 2014 | 2,314.5 | 2,331.7 | 2,347.7 | 2,391.3 | 2,405.3 | 2,390.8 | 2,345.6 | 2,363.8 | 2,383.7 | 2,406.0 | 2,409.9 | 2,409.8 | 2,375.0 |
| 2015 | 2,357.3 | 2,374.7 | 2,389.1 | 2,432.8 | 2,451.2 | 2,443.4 | 2,404.6 | 2,413.0 | 2,436.4 | 2,456.7 | 2,463.4 | 2,461.7 | 2,423.7 |
| 2016 | 2,399.8 | 2,415.6 | 2,434.4 | 2,472.5 | 2,479.6 | 2,476.3 | 2,434.5 | 2,448.0 | 2,474.7 | 2,486.1 | 2,486.1 | 2,480.0 | 2,457.3 |
| 2017 | 2,427.5 | 2,448.2 | 2,463.4 | 2,491.6 | 2,500.1 | 2,501.1 | 2,451.3 | 2,461.4 | 2,487.4 | 2,498.4 | 2,502.6 | 2,499.1 | 2,477.7 |
| 2018 | 2,438.4 | 2,453.6 | 2,469.2 | 2,493.6 | 2,503.4 | 2,507.9 | 2,465.2 | 2,471.5 | 2,490.1 | 2,507.4 | 2,511.5 | 2,504.5 | 2,484.7 |
| 2019 | 2,451.3 | 2,463.4 | 2,476.3 | 2,507.9 | 2,516.9 | 2,511.0 | 2,474.1 | 2,482.7 | 2,502.4 | 2,517.7 | 2,518.7 | 2,503.2 | 2,493.8 |
| **Mining and Logging** | | | | | | | | | | | | | |
| 2011 | 3.9 | 3.8 | 4.2 | 4.3 | 4.3 | 4.4 | 4.4 | 4.4 | 4.4 | 4.3 | 4.3 | 4.1 | 4.2 |
| 2012 | 3.9 | 3.9 | 4.1 | 4.2 | 4.2 | 4.3 | 4.2 | 4.2 | 4.2 | 4.2 | 4.1 | 4.1 | 4.1 |
| 2013 | 3.8 | 3.9 | 3.9 | 4.1 | 4.2 | 4.2 | 4.3 | 4.3 | 4.2 | 4.1 | 4.1 | 3.9 | 4.1 |
| 2014 | 3.6 | 3.7 | 3.9 | 4.1 | 4.1 | 4.2 | 4.2 | 4.2 | 4.3 | 4.2 | 4.2 | 4.1 | 4.1 |
| 2015 | 4.0 | 4.0 | 4.1 | 4.2 | 4.2 | 4.1 | 4.1 | 4.2 | 4.2 | 4.1 | 4.1 | 4.0 | 4.1 |
| 2016 | 4.0 | 3.9 | 4.0 | 4.1 | 4.1 | 4.2 | 4.2 | 4.1 | 4.1 | 4.1 | 4.1 | 4.1 | 4.1 |
| 2017 | 4.0 | 4.1 | 4.1 | 4.2 | 4.2 | 4.2 | 4.3 | 4.3 | 4.3 | 4.3 | 4.3 | 4.3 | 4.2 |
| 2018 | 4.1 | 4.2 | 4.3 | 4.3 | 4.4 | 4.5 | 4.5 | 4.5 | 4.4 | 4.4 | 4.3 | 4.3 | 4.4 |
| 2019 | 4.2 | 4.2 | 4.3 | 4.4 | 4.4 | 4.5 | 4.5 | 4.5 | 4.5 | 4.5 | 4.4 | 4.2 | 4.4 |
| **Construction** | | | | | | | | | | | | | |
| 2011 | 91.7 | 90.5 | 96.9 | 102.8 | 105.3 | 108.4 | 110.4 | 109.7 | 108.7 | 107.3 | 104.9 | 102.8 | 103.3 |
| 2012 | 96.1 | 94.9 | 99.7 | 102.6 | 105.7 | 108.4 | 109.2 | 109.6 | 108.2 | 107.3 | 105.8 | 104.7 | 104.4 |
| 2013 | 96.8 | 97.5 | 99.5 | 104.1 | 108.6 | 112.5 | 114.6 | 113.8 | 113.2 | 113.0 | 111.0 | 107.2 | 107.7 |
| 2014 | 100.7 | 99.1 | 105.4 | 108.9 | 111.6 | 114.0 | 115.9 | 115.8 | 114.6 | 114.3 | 112.6 | 111.5 | 110.4 |
| 2015 | 104.1 | 104.2 | 107.6 | 112.8 | 115.2 | 117.3 | 119.0 | 119.4 | 118.5 | 119.5 | 118.3 | 117.9 | 114.5 |
| 2016 | 111.1 | 110.2 | 114.5 | 120.5 | 121.1 | 124.8 | 125.3 | 125.4 | 124.8 | 124.9 | 123.7 | 122.0 | 120.7 |
| 2017 | 115.5 | 116.7 | 118.6 | 121.3 | 123.5 | 127.1 | 127.4 | 127.2 | 126.1 | 125.9 | 124.3 | 123.0 | 123.1 |
| 2018 | 113.1 | 114.9 | 119.1 | 121.6 | 124.5 | 127.7 | 127.8 | 127.2 | 126.4 | 125.2 | 122.3 | 122.5 | 122.7 |
| 2019 | 118.4 | 116.2 | 120.4 | 125.7 | 127.5 | 130.5 | 131.9 | 131.7 | 130.3 | 130.5 | 128.2 | 125.8 | 126.4 |

## 1. Employment by Industry: Missouri, 2011–2019—*Continued*

(Numbers in thousands, not seasonally adjusted)

| Industry and year | January | February | March | April | May | June | July | August | September | October | November | December | Annual average |
|---|---|---|---|---|---|---|---|---|---|---|---|---|---|
| **Manufacturing** | | | | | | | | | | | | | |
| 2011 | 246.9 | 247.0 | 248.2 | 249.1 | 250.0 | 251.8 | 251.8 | 249.7 | 251.3 | 250.3 | 250.1 | 250.8 | 249.8 |
| 2012 | 250.3 | 250.7 | 252.2 | 252.7 | 252.2 | 254.4 | 253.9 | 253.9 | 252.2 | 252.1 | 251.5 | 251.0 | 252.3 |
| 2013 | 250.4 | 251.4 | 252.0 | 252.9 | 253.7 | 255.2 | 252.0 | 254.6 | 253.8 | 253.2 | 253.1 | 253.3 | 253.0 |
| 2014 | 249.0 | 253.5 | 253.6 | 255.4 | 257.1 | 258.6 | 257.6 | 259.0 | 258.3 | 259.2 | 259.7 | 260.3 | 256.8 |
| 2015 | 259.1 | 259.6 | 260.4 | 261.0 | 262.5 | 264.5 | 264.0 | 262.8 | 262.6 | 261.9 | 261.7 | 262.8 | 261.9 |
| 2016 | 260.7 | 262.1 | 262.6 | 263.2 | 263.2 | 265.5 | 264.8 | 265.1 | 264.4 | 265.1 | 265.2 | 265.5 | 264.0 |
| 2017 | 263.3 | 264.9 | 264.6 | 265.5 | 266.1 | 268.9 | 268.2 | 268.3 | 268.1 | 265.0 | 268.0 | 269.7 | 266.7 |
| 2018 | 267.9 | 269.4 | 270.1 | 271.0 | 269.2 | 274.9 | 272.7 | 275.3 | 274.9 | 276.0 | 276.3 | 277.2 | 272.9 |
| 2019 | 275.9 | 276.9 | 276.4 | 277.3 | 277.7 | 279.4 | 275.8 | 278.6 | 277.1 | 274.8 | 276.8 | 277.0 | 277.0 |
| **Trade, Transportation, and Utilities** | | | | | | | | | | | | | |
| 2011 | 505.8 | 502.5 | 507.0 | 514.2 | 515.8 | 515.5 | 512.3 | 513.1 | 512.1 | 513.0 | 521.7 | 525.0 | 513.2 |
| 2012 | 506.4 | 501.5 | 505.1 | 507.8 | 512.1 | 512.5 | 509.8 | 511.1 | 510.7 | 513.6 | 524.0 | 526.2 | 511.7 |
| 2013 | 505.8 | 501.7 | 503.9 | 510.2 | 514.1 | 515.6 | 514.1 | 516.4 | 514.9 | 518.8 | 528.9 | 533.2 | 514.8 |
| 2014 | 512.2 | 508.7 | 512.1 | 517.6 | 521.5 | 523.8 | 521.0 | 523.1 | 521.5 | 525.2 | 535.2 | 539.9 | 521.8 |
| 2015 | 521.0 | 517.4 | 520.0 | 533.1 | 537.9 | 539.5 | 538.7 | 539.0 | 537.3 | 542.0 | 550.9 | 554.8 | 536.0 |
| 2016 | 535.4 | 533.5 | 536.1 | 541.4 | 543.7 | 542.9 | 543.4 | 543.6 | 541.2 | 544.6 | 553.4 | 556.8 | 543.0 |
| 2017 | 539.5 | 537.1 | 539.0 | 542.0 | 543.3 | 544.0 | 541.4 | 541.7 | 539.9 | 543.4 | 553.6 | 556.5 | 543.5 |
| 2018 | 538.6 | 535.6 | 537.4 | 541.7 | 544.9 | 545.0 | 544.8 | 545.9 | 543.5 | 546.5 | 557.4 | 558.7 | 545.0 |
| 2019 | 542.0 | 537.2 | 538.3 | 540.4 | 542.7 | 542.1 | 541.9 | 542.6 | 540.3 | 543.9 | 551.3 | 552.0 | 542.9 |
| **Wholesale Trade** | | | | | | | | | | | | | |
| 2011 | 112.9 | 113.1 | 113.8 | 115.1 | 115.1 | 115.8 | 115.7 | 115.2 | 114.9 | 114.9 | 114.9 | 115.6 | 114.8 |
| 2012 | 114.6 | 114.7 | 115.6 | 115.9 | 116.4 | 117.2 | 116.7 | 116.6 | 116.1 | 116.1 | 116.1 | 116.4 | 116.0 |
| 2013 | 114.3 | 114.6 | 115.1 | 116.8 | 117.4 | 117.8 | 117.6 | 117.5 | 117.2 | 117.7 | 117.9 | 118.6 | 116.9 |
| 2014 | 116.9 | 117.3 | 117.7 | 118.3 | 119.0 | 119.6 | 119.4 | 119.2 | 118.3 | 118.3 | 118.3 | 118.6 | 118.4 |
| 2015 | 117.0 | 116.8 | 117.0 | 117.8 | 118.4 | 118.8 | 119.4 | 118.4 | 117.4 | 117.7 | 117.6 | 118.0 | 117.9 |
| 2016 | 116.8 | 116.8 | 117.1 | 118.2 | 118.2 | 118.8 | 119.6 | 118.3 | 117.4 | 117.5 | 117.6 | 118.1 | 117.9 |
| 2017 | 117.3 | 117.7 | 118.1 | 118.8 | 119.1 | 120.2 | 119.9 | 119.3 | 119.3 | 119.4 | 120.0 | 120.8 | 119.2 |
| 2018 | 119.0 | 119.5 | 119.9 | 120.6 | 121.0 | 121.9 | 122.4 | 121.9 | 121.8 | 122.4 | 123.0 | 123.6 | 121.4 |
| 2019 | 122.2 | 122.3 | 122.1 | 122.8 | 123.2 | 124.2 | 124.8 | 124.4 | 123.7 | 124.4 | 123.7 | 123.9 | 123.5 |
| **Retail Trade** | | | | | | | | | | | | | |
| 2011 | 296.1 | 292.5 | 295.7 | 300.3 | 302.2 | 303.0 | 301.5 | 301.8 | 300.4 | 301.8 | 310.5 | 312.5 | 301.5 |
| 2012 | 298.4 | 294.4 | 297.1 | 299.1 | 301.9 | 302.5 | 301.5 | 300.6 | 300.1 | 302.5 | 312.6 | 313.3 | 302.0 |
| 2013 | 297.6 | 293.5 | 294.8 | 298.4 | 301.2 | 303.4 | 302.3 | 302.9 | 301.1 | 304.3 | 313.3 | 316.0 | 302.4 |
| 2014 | 299.7 | 296.3 | 298.9 | 302.9 | 305.4 | 308.0 | 306.4 | 306.5 | 305.1 | 308.2 | 317.5 | 320.4 | 306.3 |
| 2015 | 304.7 | 302.0 | 304.3 | 308.6 | 311.8 | 314.1 | 312.7 | 312.8 | 311.0 | 315.3 | 323.2 | 325.2 | 312.1 |
| 2016 | 310.1 | 308.7 | 310.5 | 314.5 | 316.2 | 316.3 | 316.9 | 316.6 | 314.3 | 316.8 | 324.8 | 326.0 | 316.0 |
| 2017 | 312.0 | 309.4 | 310.6 | 312.5 | 313.3 | 314.3 | 313.8 | 312.9 | 310.4 | 313.2 | 322.0 | 322.8 | 313.9 |
| 2018 | 309.2 | 305.8 | 307.3 | 309.4 | 311.6 | 312.0 | 312.0 | 310.9 | 308.5 | 309.9 | 318.8 | 318.2 | 311.1 |
| 2019 | 305.3 | 301.3 | 301.9 | 303.3 | 304.8 | 304.5 | 303.9 | 301.7 | 300.0 | 304.0 | 310.9 | 310.5 | 304.3 |
| **Transportation and Utilities** | | | | | | | | | | | | | |
| 2011 | 96.8 | 96.9 | 97.5 | 98.8 | 98.5 | 96.7 | 95.1 | 96.1 | 96.8 | 96.3 | 96.3 | 96.9 | 96.9 |
| 2012 | 93.4 | 92.4 | 92.4 | 92.8 | 93.8 | 92.8 | 91.6 | 93.9 | 94.5 | 95.0 | 95.3 | 96.5 | 93.7 |
| 2013 | 93.9 | 93.6 | 94.0 | 95.0 | 95.5 | 94.4 | 94.2 | 96.0 | 96.6 | 96.8 | 97.7 | 98.6 | 95.5 |
| 2014 | 95.6 | 95.1 | 95.5 | 96.4 | 97.1 | 96.2 | 95.2 | 97.4 | 98.1 | 98.7 | 99.4 | 100.9 | 97.1 |
| 2015 | 99.3 | 98.6 | 98.7 | 106.7 | 107.7 | 106.6 | 106.6 | 107.8 | 108.9 | 109.0 | 110.1 | 111.6 | 106.0 |
| 2016 | 108.5 | 108.0 | 108.5 | 108.7 | 109.3 | 107.8 | 106.9 | 108.7 | 109.5 | 110.3 | 111.0 | 112.7 | 109.2 |
| 2017 | 110.2 | 110.0 | 110.3 | 110.7 | 110.9 | 109.5 | 107.7 | 109.5 | 110.2 | 110.8 | 111.6 | 112.9 | 110.4 |
| 2018 | 110.4 | 110.3 | 110.2 | 111.7 | 112.3 | 111.1 | 110.4 | 113.1 | 113.2 | 114.2 | 115.6 | 116.9 | 112.5 |
| 2019 | 114.5 | 113.6 | 114.3 | 114.3 | 114.7 | 113.4 | 113.2 | 116.5 | 116.6 | 115.5 | 116.7 | 117.6 | 115.1 |
| **Information** | | | | | | | | | | | | | |
| 2011 | 58.6 | 58.4 | 58.3 | 59.3 | 59.6 | 59.8 | 60.0 | 59.9 | 59.9 | 59.4 | 59.4 | 59.5 | 59.3 |
| 2012 | 58.8 | 58.5 | 58.4 | 58.5 | 58.8 | 58.8 | 59.1 | 58.8 | 58.5 | 58.2 | 58.1 | 58.1 | 58.6 |
| 2013 | 57.6 | 57.9 | 58.0 | 57.5 | 57.8 | 58.0 | 57.7 | 57.5 | 57.1 | 57.3 | 57.3 | 57.5 | 57.6 |
| 2014 | 56.6 | 56.6 | 56.8 | 56.7 | 56.7 | 56.9 | 56.7 | 56.1 | 55.5 | 55.1 | 55.0 | 54.9 | 56.1 |
| 2015 | 54.6 | 54.4 | 54.3 | 54.4 | 54.7 | 54.8 | 55.0 | 54.4 | 53.6 | 53.5 | 53.6 | 53.9 | 54.3 |
| 2016 | 53.1 | 53.1 | 53.1 | 52.3 | 52.5 | 52.6 | 52.3 | 52.2 | 51.9 | 51.9 | 51.7 | 51.8 | 52.4 |
| 2017 | 51.3 | 51.2 | 51.3 | 51.1 | 51.3 | 51.5 | 51.5 | 51.3 | 51.0 | 50.5 | 50.2 | 50.1 | 51.0 |
| 2018 | 49.6 | 49.4 | 49.2 | 49.2 | 49.4 | 49.6 | 49.4 | 48.8 | 48.6 | 48.6 | 48.8 | 49.0 | 49.1 |
| 2019 | 48.5 | 48.5 | 48.4 | 48.2 | 47.9 | 48.2 | 48.1 | 47.9 | 47.4 | 46.9 | 46.6 | 46.5 | 47.8 |

## 1. Employment by Industry: Missouri, 2011–2019—*Continued*

(Numbers in thousands, not seasonally adjusted)

| Industry and year | January | February | March | April | May | June | July | August | September | October | November | December | Annual average |
|---|---|---|---|---|---|---|---|---|---|---|---|---|---|
| **Financial Activities** | | | | | | | | | | | | | |
| 2011 | 159.2 | 159.4 | 159.7 | 160.2 | 160.4 | 160.8 | 161.6 | 162.0 | 161.0 | 162.0 | 162.3 | 162.4 | 160.9 |
| 2012 | 160.8 | 161.4 | 162.1 | 161.9 | 162.6 | 163.3 | 163.8 | 164.1 | 162.8 | 163.9 | 164.2 | 163.8 | 162.9 |
| 2013 | 161.2 | 161.6 | 161.7 | 163.2 | 163.7 | 164.4 | 165.3 | 164.9 | 163.7 | 163.8 | 163.9 | 163.4 | 163.4 |
| 2014 | 161.4 | 161.7 | 161.5 | 163.3 | 164.2 | 164.7 | 165.5 | 165.4 | 163.9 | 164.4 | 164.4 | 164.7 | 163.8 |
| 2015 | 163.2 | 163.3 | 163.5 | 164.9 | 166.2 | 167.3 | 168.2 | 167.8 | 166.2 | 166.8 | 167.1 | 167.3 | 166.0 |
| 2016 | 165.8 | 166.2 | 166.4 | 167.5 | 168.2 | 169.3 | 170.0 | 169.9 | 169.1 | 169.1 | 169.5 | 170.0 | 168.4 |
| 2017 | 169.3 | 170.0 | 170.7 | 171.1 | 172.3 | 173.9 | 173.6 | 173.3 | 172.0 | 171.9 | 171.5 | 171.7 | 171.8 |
| 2018 | 170.0 | 170.1 | 170.0 | 170.8 | 171.7 | 172.9 | 173.5 | 173.4 | 171.9 | 173.5 | 174.1 | 173.4 | 172.1 |
| 2019 | 172.3 | 172.8 | 173.1 | 174.5 | 175.2 | 176.4 | 177.4 | 177.0 | 175.1 | 175.2 | 174.9 | 174.7 | 174.9 |
| **Professional and Business Services** | | | | | | | | | | | | | |
| 2011 | 318.7 | 320.4 | 325.1 | 331.2 | 329.5 | 331.2 | 329.8 | 330.1 | 330.0 | 331.1 | 331.7 | 332.7 | 328.5 |
| 2012 | 325.9 | 327.1 | 331.9 | 336.1 | 336.2 | 339.1 | 337.5 | 338.2 | 337.3 | 340.3 | 342.1 | 342.3 | 336.2 |
| 2013 | 332.9 | 336.8 | 341.7 | 345.9 | 346.6 | 349.0 | 348.9 | 351.3 | 349.2 | 352.5 | 352.9 | 353.1 | 346.7 |
| 2014 | 341.6 | 344.7 | 347.8 | 356.1 | 356.1 | 357.5 | 356.7 | 360.1 | 358.4 | 362.9 | 363.7 | 364.9 | 355.9 |
| 2015 | 354.8 | 358.1 | 361.9 | 368.8 | 369.4 | 369.5 | 372.4 | 373.6 | 372.7 | 378.1 | 379.2 | 379.1 | 369.8 |
| 2016 | 367.1 | 371.2 | 374.1 | 382.5 | 380.3 | 381.2 | 381.4 | 383.8 | 382.9 | 384.0 | 382.9 | 379.9 | 379.3 |
| 2017 | 370.8 | 375.2 | 379.0 | 385.4 | 382.9 | 385.0 | 383.2 | 384.6 | 385.1 | 386.4 | 387.6 | 384.7 | 382.5 |
| 2018 | 374.5 | 379.2 | 382.7 | 386.4 | 384.7 | 387.1 | 387.8 | 388.3 | 385.9 | 387.0 | 385.4 | 382.9 | 384.3 |
| 2019 | 375.9 | 376.9 | 377.9 | 385.3 | 383.0 | 383.1 | 384.3 | 385.2 | 383.0 | 384.7 | 385.6 | 379.9 | 382.1 |
| **Education and Health Services** | | | | | | | | | | | | | |
| 2011 | 425.9 | 429.5 | 430.9 | 432.2 | 430.4 | 426.5 | 426.4 | 427.0 | 430.9 | 433.0 | 434.4 | 433.8 | 430.1 |
| 2012 | 429.1 | 432.8 | 432.9 | 433.3 | 433.0 | 430.0 | 430.5 | 432.5 | 435.5 | 439.0 | 439.7 | 440.6 | 434.1 |
| 2013 | 434.9 | 440.2 | 438.5 | 443.9 | 441.7 | 436.0 | 436.7 | 437.5 | 439.3 | 444.9 | 445.3 | 442.7 | 440.1 |
| 2014 | 437.2 | 443.1 | 439.9 | 447.9 | 445.6 | 439.5 | 442.0 | 442.8 | 443.9 | 451.5 | 452.5 | 449.7 | 444.6 |
| 2015 | 449.4 | 452.8 | 449.9 | 458.0 | 456.5 | 451.8 | 455.4 | 454.9 | 455.4 | 462.9 | 463.6 | 459.5 | 455.8 |
| 2016 | 456.2 | 460.2 | 459.2 | 466.2 | 463.6 | 458.5 | 462.9 | 463.5 | 466.1 | 472.5 | 472.6 | 469.7 | 464.3 |
| 2017 | 466.7 | 473.2 | 470.7 | 476.9 | 475.7 | 469.8 | 472.1 | 472.7 | 475.0 | 480.5 | 480.8 | 479.2 | 474.4 |
| 2018 | 472.7 | 478.6 | 476.0 | 479.9 | 477.4 | 472.0 | 475.9 | 475.1 | 475.8 | 484.2 | 483.9 | 481.2 | 477.7 |
| 2019 | 477.5 | 483.4 | 481.1 | 486.2 | 484.6 | 478.1 | 483.0 | 484.5 | 485.1 | 492.8 | 492.5 | 485.6 | 484.5 |
| **Leisure and Hospitality** | | | | | | | | | | | | | |
| 2011 | 248.8 | 248.2 | 260.1 | 271.2 | 279.3 | 285.4 | 286.0 | 288.0 | 277.8 | 274.1 | 266.7 | 263.5 | 270.8 |
| 2012 | 251.0 | 252.5 | 264.2 | 276.0 | 284.7 | 291.4 | 288.6 | 289.2 | 280.1 | 277.6 | 271.6 | 269.4 | 274.7 |
| 2013 | 258.7 | 259.0 | 268.7 | 281.3 | 291.8 | 297.3 | 295.1 | 296.0 | 289.7 | 285.1 | 277.3 | 274.8 | 281.2 |
| 2014 | 263.5 | 264.4 | 274.5 | 289.5 | 298.9 | 302.4 | 301.1 | 303.1 | 291.7 | 290.9 | 283.0 | 280.9 | 287.0 |
| 2015 | 269.1 | 270.9 | 278.7 | 292.5 | 303.2 | 308.2 | 306.7 | 307.4 | 300.8 | 297.5 | 291.5 | 289.4 | 293.0 |
| 2016 | 276.8 | 278.5 | 288.5 | 303.5 | 309.7 | 317.1 | 312.6 | 314.2 | 306.6 | 301.8 | 293.8 | 290.5 | 299.5 |
| 2017 | 280.8 | 285.1 | 294.7 | 304.7 | 312.1 | 319.9 | 316.5 | 318.2 | 309.9 | 306.1 | 298.9 | 297.4 | 303.7 |
| 2018 | 284.7 | 286.0 | 296.3 | 305.8 | 314.3 | 322.2 | 319.6 | 321.0 | 311.3 | 306.7 | 300.5 | 299.0 | 305.6 |
| 2019 | 286.7 | 288.7 | 298.5 | 310.3 | 318.2 | 324.5 | 323.4 | 322.5 | 312.9 | 311.0 | 304.2 | 300.5 | 308.5 |
| **Other Services** | | | | | | | | | | | | | |
| 2011 | 110.8 | 110.9 | 112.2 | 114.5 | 114.8 | 115.4 | 115.6 | 115.2 | 114.4 | 114.4 | 114.2 | 114.1 | 113.9 |
| 2012 | 112.4 | 112.7 | 113.8 | 114.8 | 115.6 | 116.3 | 116.1 | 115.6 | 114.7 | 114.9 | 114.9 | 114.8 | 114.7 |
| 2013 | 114.3 | 114.9 | 115.3 | 113.2 | 113.7 | 114.7 | 114.3 | 114.3 | 113.2 | 112.9 | 112.6 | 112.4 | 113.8 |
| 2014 | 111.2 | 111.7 | 112.8 | 114.0 | 114.9 | 115.5 | 115.3 | 114.9 | 113.9 | 113.8 | 113.4 | 113.7 | 113.8 |
| 2015 | 112.7 | 113.2 | 114.0 | 114.8 | 115.4 | 116.6 | 116.2 | 115.7 | 114.8 | 115.4 | 115.2 | 115.4 | 115.0 |
| 2016 | 114.4 | 114.7 | 115.4 | 116.9 | 117.2 | 118.5 | 118.2 | 117.6 | 116.7 | 116.8 | 116.5 | 115.9 | 116.6 |
| 2017 | 115.1 | 115.1 | 115.6 | 116.3 | 116.7 | 118.0 | 117.3 | 116.8 | 115.9 | 115.9 | 115.4 | 115.6 | 116.1 |
| 2018 | 114.2 | 114.3 | 115.1 | 116.3 | 116.5 | 118.1 | 117.6 | 116.9 | 115.9 | 116.2 | 115.7 | 115.6 | 116.0 |
| 2019 | 114.6 | 114.7 | 115.6 | 116.9 | 117.4 | 118.7 | 118.4 | 117.7 | 116.4 | 116.4 | 116.7 | 117.8 | 116.8 |
| **Government** | | | | | | | | | | | | | |
| 2011 | 442.6 | 447.7 | 450.1 | 454.0 | 455.0 | 436.1 | 394.0 | 401.3 | 440.7 | 447.2 | 449.4 | 448.9 | 438.9 |
| 2012 | 437.0 | 447.1 | 449.4 | 451.6 | 452.2 | 435.0 | 392.2 | 404.5 | 441.2 | 448.5 | 449.4 | 448.3 | 438.0 |
| 2013 | 436.7 | 446.5 | 448.8 | 450.7 | 450.8 | 433.3 | 388.6 | 399.6 | 436.1 | 443.8 | 445.0 | 443.7 | 435.3 |
| 2014 | 430.8 | 440.8 | 442.3 | 446.2 | 447.4 | 430.5 | 387.3 | 398.3 | 434.9 | 442.2 | 442.7 | 441.1 | 432.0 |
| 2015 | 432.5 | 444.6 | 446.8 | 446.3 | 447.9 | 435.7 | 392.0 | 400.2 | 435.6 | 440.5 | 442.3 | 442.3 | 433.9 |
| 2016 | 431.0 | 438.2 | 441.6 | 442.2 | 444.4 | 436.2 | 393.7 | 403.2 | 440.2 | 445.4 | 445.7 | 445.4 | 433.9 |
| 2017 | 434.0 | 441.3 | 442.4 | 441.1 | 445.8 | 439.0 | 395.7 | 402.8 | 438.6 | 443.7 | 444.6 | 443.9 | 434.7 |
| 2018 | 434.1 | 440.4 | 442.5 | 443.5 | 444.5 | 441.0 | 396.6 | 402.1 | 437.2 | 444.7 | 445.7 | 444.7 | 434.8 |
| 2019 | 433.8 | 441.2 | 443.4 | 446.1 | 447.9 | 439.9 | 397.6 | 405.3 | 442.2 | 446.8 | 446.9 | 446.2 | 436.4 |

## 2. Average Weekly Hours by Selected Industry: Missouri, 2015–2019

(Not seasonally adjusted)

| Industry and year | January | February | March | April | May | June | July | August | September | October | November | December | Annual average |
|---|---|---|---|---|---|---|---|---|---|---|---|---|---|
| **Total Private** | | | | | | | | | | | | | |
| 2015 | 33.7 | 34.2 | 34.2 | 34.0 | 33.5 | 33.7 | 33.7 | 34.4 | 33.6 | 33.8 | 34.0 | 33.7 | 33.9 |
| 2016 | 33.4 | 33.3 | 33.3 | 33.7 | 33.7 | 33.3 | 33.3 | 33.2 | 33.3 | 33.8 | 33.1 | 33.0 | 33.4 |
| 2017 | 33.1 | 33.1 | 33.3 | 34.0 | 33.6 | 33.7 | 34.1 | 33.7 | 33.6 | 33.8 | 33.2 | 33.1 | 33.5 |
| 2018 | 32.6 | 32.9 | 33.2 | 33.8 | 33.6 | 34.0 | 34.5 | 33.9 | 34.4 | 33.9 | 33.5 | 33.8 | 33.7 |
| 2019 | 33.1 | 33.1 | 33.3 | 33.6 | 33.4 | 34.3 | 33.7 | 33.7 | 34.1 | 33.5 | 33.5 | 33.9 | 33.6 |
| **Goods-Producing** | | | | | | | | | | | | | |
| 2015 | 38.8 | 39.1 | 38.6 | 39.0 | 39.0 | 39.7 | 39.2 | 40.0 | 38.2 | 39.6 | 38.7 | 39.5 | 39.1 |
| 2016 | 38.7 | 39.1 | 39.3 | 39.6 | 39.4 | 39.8 | 39.7 | 39.7 | 39.9 | 40.3 | 39.0 | 39.2 | 39.5 |
| 2017 | 38.4 | 39.5 | 39.4 | 39.2 | 39.7 | 40.0 | 40.3 | 40.5 | 40.5 | 40.4 | 39.6 | 40.0 | 39.8 |
| 2018 | 38.8 | 39.2 | 39.2 | 40.3 | 40.2 | 40.5 | 41.3 | 40.6 | 41.1 | 40.2 | 39.4 | 40.2 | 40.1 |
| 2019 | 39.6 | 39.3 | 39.5 | 40.0 | 39.5 | 39.6 | 39.3 | 39.1 | 39.7 | 38.8 | 38.3 | 38.9 | 39.3 |
| **Construction** | | | | | | | | | | | | | |
| 2015 | 36.4 | 35.6 | 36.1 | 36.3 | 35.9 | 37.6 | 36.7 | 38.0 | 34.9 | 38.2 | 35.5 | 38.2 | 36.6 |
| 2016 | 36.0 | 36.5 | 36.5 | 36.4 | 35.8 | 37.9 | 37.0 | 36.9 | 37.4 | 38.3 | 35.6 | 36.9 | 36.8 |
| 2017 | 34.4 | 36.4 | 35.9 | 36.1 | 36.4 | 36.9 | 37.3 | 36.6 | 37.2 | 37.2 | 35.7 | 35.4 | 36.3 |
| 2018 | 33.4 | 34.7 | 35.6 | 36.6 | 36.9 | 37.0 | 37.6 | 36.4 | 37.0 | 35.6 | 34.2 | 35.9 | 35.9 |
| 2019 | 33.9 | 33.9 | 35.4 | 36.8 | 35.9 | 36.4 | 35.6 | 35.0 | 36.7 | 35.4 | 34.1 | 35.3 | 35.4 |
| **Manufacturing** | | | | | | | | | | | | | |
| 2015 | 39.9 | 40.7 | 39.7 | 40.2 | 40.4 | 40.8 | 40.5 | 41.0 | 39.9 | 40.6 | 40.7 | 40.3 | 40.4 |
| 2016 | 40.2 | 40.5 | 40.8 | 41.3 | 41.3 | 40.8 | 41.1 | 41.1 | 41.2 | 41.4 | 40.8 | 40.5 | 40.9 |
| 2017 | 40.6 | 41.2 | 41.1 | 40.7 | 41.3 | 41.5 | 41.8 | 42.7 | 42.3 | 42.1 | 41.6 | 42.2 | 41.6 |
| 2018 | 41.3 | 41.4 | 40.9 | 42.0 | 41.7 | 42.1 | 43.0 | 42.5 | 43.0 | 41.7 | 41.1 | 41.6 | 41.9 |
| 2019 | 41.6 | 41.2 | 41.0 | 41.2 | 40.9 | 40.9 | 40.8 | 40.8 | 40.8 | 40.2 | 40.1 | 40.5 | 40.8 |
| **Trade, Transportation, and Utilities** | | | | | | | | | | | | | |
| 2015 | 33.1 | 33.5 | 33.5 | 33.6 | 33.4 | 33.9 | 33.9 | 34.2 | 34.1 | 34.1 | 34.1 | 34.1 | 33.8 |
| 2016 | 33.3 | 33.3 | 33.2 | 33.7 | 33.6 | 34.1 | 33.7 | 33.7 | 33.9 | 34.4 | 33.4 | 33.4 | 33.6 |
| 2017 | 33.1 | 33.4 | 33.9 | 34.6 | 33.9 | 33.9 | 33.9 | 33.5 | 33.5 | 33.4 | 33.0 | 33.0 | 33.6 |
| 2018 | 32.4 | 32.6 | 33.1 | 33.4 | 33.6 | 34.0 | 34.3 | 33.7 | 34.1 | 33.7 | 33.5 | 33.6 | 33.5 |
| 2019 | 32.6 | 33.0 | 33.4 | 33.5 | 33.7 | 34.5 | 33.7 | 33.8 | 34.1 | 33.5 | 33.4 | 33.6 | 33.6 |
| **Financial Activities** | | | | | | | | | | | | | |
| 2015 | 36.5 | 37.6 | 37.6 | 36.9 | 36.8 | 36.8 | 37.1 | 37.8 | 36.5 | 36.2 | 37.2 | 36.2 | 36.9 |
| 2016 | 36.0 | 35.3 | 35.7 | 36.3 | 37.0 | 34.4 | 34.8 | 34.7 | 34.4 | 35.3 | 34.6 | 34.7 | 35.3 |
| 2017 | 36.3 | 35.3 | 34.8 | 36.7 | 35.8 | 35.5 | 36.6 | 35.7 | 35.6 | 36.8 | 35.5 | 35.6 | 35.9 |
| 2018 | 35.7 | 35.7 | 35.7 | 37.4 | 36.2 | 36.3 | 37.7 | 36.6 | 37.6 | 37.1 | 36.4 | 37.4 | 36.7 |
| 2019 | 36.9 | 37.2 | 36.7 | 37.0 | 36.8 | 38.0 | 36.8 | 36.9 | 37.6 | 36.6 | 37.0 | 37.4 | 37.1 |
| **Professional and Business Services** | | | | | | | | | | | | | |
| 2015 | 35.8 | 36.7 | 36.5 | 36.1 | 35.6 | 35.7 | 35.5 | 37.1 | 35.8 | 36.3 | 36.4 | 35.6 | 36.1 |
| 2016 | 35.4 | 35.2 | 35.3 | 35.9 | 36.1 | 35.8 | 36.1 | 35.6 | 35.5 | 36.5 | 35.8 | 35.6 | 35.7 |
| 2017 | 36.0 | 35.5 | 35.4 | 36.6 | 35.3 | 36.1 | 36.1 | 36.1 | 35.7 | 35.5 | 35.0 | 34.6 | 35.7 |
| 2018 | 34.1 | 34.7 | 34.7 | 35.0 | 35.0 | 35.6 | 35.3 | 35.2 | 35.7 | 34.8 | 34.2 | 34.5 | 34.9 |
| 2019 | 33.6 | 33.8 | 33.8 | 34.4 | 33.9 | 35.0 | 34.4 | 34.6 | 34.9 | 34.3 | 34.0 | 34.9 | 34.3 |
| **Education and Health Services** | | | | | | | | | | | | | |
| 2015 | 32.8 | 33.1 | 33.1 | 32.8 | 33.0 | 32.3 | 33.0 | 33.5 | 33.2 | 32.3 | 33.9 | 33.0 | 33.0 |
| 2016 | 33.5 | 32.6 | 32.6 | 32.6 | 33.1 | 32.6 | 32.7 | 32.6 | 32.9 | 33.2 | 32.7 | 32.7 | 32.8 |
| 2017 | 33.8 | 33.2 | 32.8 | 33.6 | 32.6 | 32.7 | 33.4 | 32.5 | 32.7 | 33.3 | 32.7 | 32.5 | 33.0 |
| 2018 | 32.3 | 31.9 | 32.3 | 33.3 | 32.2 | 32.3 | 33.7 | 32.5 | 33.5 | 32.7 | 32.5 | 32.9 | 32.7 |
| 2019 | 32.4 | 31.7 | 32.0 | 32.6 | 32.1 | 33.4 | 32.7 | 32.4 | 33.0 | 32.2 | 32.5 | 32.9 | 32.5 |
| **Leisure and Hospitality** | | | | | | | | | | | | | |
| 2015 | 24.9 | 25.9 | 26.6 | 26.1 | 25.3 | 26.0 | 25.8 | 25.7 | 25.7 | 25.8 | 25.4 | 25.0 | 25.7 |
| 2016 | 24.9 | 25.3 | 25.5 | 25.5 | 25.7 | 25.6 | 25.9 | 25.6 | 25.1 | 25.2 | 25.0 | 24.1 | 25.3 |
| 2017 | 23.4 | 24.3 | 24.7 | 24.7 | 25.2 | 25.7 | 26.1 | 25.3 | 25.0 | 25.3 | 24.8 | 24.9 | 25.0 |
| 2018 | 23.7 | 24.5 | 24.8 | 24.9 | 24.8 | 25.5 | 25.6 | 25.2 | 25.2 | 24.7 | 24.7 | 25.1 | 24.9 |
| 2019 | 23.2 | 23.8 | 25.2 | 24.9 | 24.7 | 25.6 | 25.2 | 25.0 | 25.0 | 25.2 | 25.3 | 25.3 | 24.9 |

# 3. Average Hourly Earnings by Selected Industry: Missouri, 2015–2019

(Dollars, not seasonally adjusted)

| Industry and year | January | February | March | April | May | June | July | August | September | October | November | December | Annual average |
|---|---|---|---|---|---|---|---|---|---|---|---|---|---|
| **Total Private** | | | | | | | | | | | | | |
| 2015 | 21.90 | 22.10 | 22.03 | 21.86 | 22.07 | 21.89 | 21.88 | 21.97 | 21.95 | 21.93 | 22.09 | 22.01 | 21.97 |
| 2016 | 22.11 | 22.03 | 22.07 | 22.02 | 22.18 | 22.03 | 22.28 | 22.17 | 22.71 | 22.98 | 23.09 | 23.19 | 22.41 |
| 2017 | 23.89 | 23.44 | 23.51 | 23.84 | 23.45 | 23.41 | 23.93 | 23.69 | 24.08 | 24.26 | 24.27 | 24.18 | 23.83 |
| 2018 | 24.48 | 24.58 | 24.41 | 24.79 | 24.54 | 24.19 | 24.64 | 24.52 | 24.95 | 24.78 | 24.73 | 25.13 | 24.65 |
| 2019 | 25.09 | 25.12 | 25.15 | 25.09 | 25.10 | 25.22 | 25.27 | 25.39 | 25.76 | 25.59 | 25.72 | 26.06 | 25.38 |
| **Goods-Producing** | | | | | | | | | | | | | |
| 2015 | 25.31 | 24.95 | 25.08 | 24.57 | 24.66 | 24.61 | 24.81 | 25.24 | 25.59 | 25.35 | 25.33 | 25.78 | 25.11 |
| 2016 | 25.20 | 25.08 | 25.75 | 25.45 | 25.75 | 25.54 | 25.91 | 25.89 | 26.29 | 26.73 | 26.77 | 26.91 | 25.95 |
| 2017 | 26.72 | 27.00 | 27.02 | 27.43 | 26.92 | 27.10 | 27.64 | 27.59 | 27.66 | 27.86 | 27.57 | 27.53 | 27.34 |
| 2018 | 27.96 | 27.87 | 27.76 | 28.37 | 27.93 | 27.73 | 28.23 | 27.87 | 27.99 | 27.63 | 28.07 | 28.00 | 27.95 |
| 2019 | 27.98 | 28.19 | 28.02 | 28.30 | 28.30 | 28.44 | 28.47 | 28.59 | 28.71 | 28.52 | 28.94 | 29.60 | 28.50 |
| **Construction** | | | | | | | | | | | | | |
| 2015 | 27.78 | 27.81 | 28.23 | 27.88 | 28.04 | 27.74 | 28.17 | 28.19 | 28.27 | 28.41 | 28.20 | 29.09 | 28.16 |
| 2016 | 27.92 | 27.72 | 28.07 | 28.13 | 28.70 | 28.11 | 28.45 | 29.01 | 29.33 | 29.77 | 29.06 | 29.26 | 28.65 |
| 2017 | 28.41 | 29.01 | 29.18 | 29.25 | 28.99 | 29.09 | 29.15 | 29.79 | 29.76 | 29.97 | 29.62 | 29.63 | 29.33 |
| 2018 | 30.35 | 29.93 | 29.72 | 30.40 | 30.24 | 30.39 | 30.22 | 30.00 | 29.97 | 30.42 | 30.33 | 30.38 | 30.20 |
| 2019 | 30.69 | 30.89 | 31.12 | 31.28 | 31.40 | 31.52 | 31.41 | 31.71 | 31.48 | 31.27 | 32.04 | 32.31 | 31.44 |
| **Manufacturing** | | | | | | | | | | | | | |
| 2015 | 23.77 | 23.31 | 23.32 | 22.57 | 22.42 | 22.32 | 22.50 | 23.20 | 23.33 | 22.89 | 23.38 | 23.35 | 23.03 |
| 2016 | 23.38 | 23.44 | 24.28 | 23.78 | 23.93 | 23.84 | 24.29 | 23.98 | 24.10 | 24.76 | 25.18 | 25.30 | 24.19 |
| 2017 | 25.50 | 25.68 | 25.80 | 26.38 | 25.81 | 25.87 | 26.65 | 26.44 | 26.56 | 26.82 | 26.65 | 26.68 | 26.24 |
| 2018 | 27.09 | 26.87 | 26.82 | 27.43 | 26.74 | 26.39 | 27.20 | 26.82 | 27.03 | 26.31 | 27.03 | 26.88 | 26.88 |
| 2019 | 26.33 | 26.62 | 26.35 | 26.22 | 26.26 | 26.45 | 26.82 | 26.88 | 27.16 | 27.06 | 27.26 | 27.79 | 26.76 |
| **Trade, Transportation, and Utilities** | | | | | | | | | | | | | |
| 2015 | 19.72 | 19.88 | 19.85 | 19.83 | 19.87 | 19.46 | 19.56 | 19.60 | 19.61 | 19.61 | 19.58 | 19.29 | 19.65 |
| 2016 | 19.71 | 19.41 | 19.50 | 19.63 | 19.59 | 19.98 | 19.62 | 20.12 | 20.20 | 20.64 | 20.38 | 20.75 | 19.97 |
| 2017 | 22.44 | 21.11 | 21.21 | 21.55 | 21.18 | 21.27 | 21.63 | 21.33 | 21.71 | 21.93 | 21.79 | 21.83 | 21.58 |
| 2018 | 22.04 | 21.64 | 21.42 | 22.05 | 21.91 | 21.92 | 22.07 | 22.16 | 22.89 | 22.89 | 22.43 | 23.11 | 22.22 |
| 2019 | 23.19 | 23.01 | 23.18 | 23.05 | 22.90 | 23.56 | 23.76 | 23.34 | 23.95 | 23.74 | 23.44 | 23.49 | 23.39 |
| **Financial Activities** | | | | | | | | | | | | | |
| 2015 | 25.83 | 26.43 | 26.31 | 26.03 | 25.91 | 25.53 | 25.30 | 25.84 | 25.87 | 25.77 | 26.29 | 26.05 | 25.93 |
| 2016 | 26.78 | 26.52 | 26.32 | 26.72 | 26.31 | 25.49 | 26.76 | 26.31 | 27.66 | 28.34 | 28.31 | 27.78 | 26.94 |
| 2017 | 28.92 | 29.00 | 29.40 | 29.46 | 29.09 | 29.72 | 31.25 | 30.39 | 31.17 | 31.21 | 31.50 | 31.80 | 30.25 |
| 2018 | 31.47 | 31.87 | 32.01 | 31.84 | 31.54 | 30.81 | 31.52 | 31.20 | 31.70 | 30.79 | 31.00 | 31.25 | 31.41 |
| 2019 | 31.76 | 31.43 | 30.93 | 31.36 | 31.50 | 31.42 | 31.09 | 31.69 | 31.82 | 32.14 | 31.99 | 32.38 | 31.63 |
| **Professional and Business Services** | | | | | | | | | | | | | |
| 2015 | 25.80 | 26.52 | 26.55 | 26.28 | 26.35 | 26.24 | 26.34 | 26.86 | 26.95 | 26.80 | 27.33 | 26.96 | 26.59 |
| 2016 | 27.55 | 27.61 | 27.05 | 26.91 | 27.10 | 26.68 | 26.99 | 26.87 | 27.17 | 27.51 | 27.49 | 27.76 | 27.22 |
| 2017 | 28.99 | 29.10 | 29.05 | 29.34 | 28.88 | 28.58 | 29.48 | 28.97 | 29.55 | 29.69 | 28.87 | 29.11 | 29.14 |
| 2018 | 29.41 | 29.91 | 29.65 | 29.50 | 29.41 | 28.99 | 29.88 | 29.89 | 30.31 | 29.62 | 29.88 | 30.27 | 29.73 |
| 2019 | 30.50 | 30.31 | 30.59 | 29.83 | 29.79 | 29.81 | 29.80 | 30.20 | 30.42 | 30.25 | 30.76 | 31.32 | 30.30 |
| **Education and Health Services** | | | | | | | | | | | | | |
| 2015 | 18.52 | 18.72 | 18.75 | 18.82 | 18.64 | 18.98 | 18.99 | 18.36 | 18.09 | 18.12 | 18.18 | 18.32 | 18.54 |
| 2016 | 18.09 | 18.34 | 18.70 | 18.83 | 19.17 | 19.13 | 19.31 | 19.29 | 19.67 | 19.53 | 19.96 | 19.87 | 19.16 |
| 2017 | 19.73 | 19.90 | 20.03 | 20.16 | 20.00 | 19.98 | 19.83 | 19.57 | 19.67 | 19.62 | 19.41 | 19.41 | 19.78 |
| 2018 | 19.34 | 19.80 | 19.42 | 19.50 | 19.74 | 19.50 | 19.66 | 20.10 | 19.99 | 20.14 | 20.34 | 20.71 | 19.86 |
| 2019 | 20.47 | 20.71 | 21.60 | 21.60 | 21.77 | 21.71 | 21.72 | 21.88 | 21.77 | 22.06 | 21.93 | 22.06 | 21.61 |
| **Leisure and Hospitality** | | | | | | | | | | | | | |
| 2015 | 12.95 | 13.04 | 12.96 | 12.96 | 13.28 | 13.09 | 13.07 | 13.09 | 13.11 | 13.34 | 13.23 | 13.42 | 13.13 |
| 2016 | 13.33 | 13.51 | 13.35 | 13.51 | 13.46 | 13.27 | 13.40 | 13.36 | 13.75 | 13.72 | 13.57 | 13.90 | 13.51 |
| 2017 | 13.99 | 13.93 | 14.10 | 13.93 | 13.75 | 13.75 | 13.79 | 13.91 | 14.27 | 14.21 | 14.39 | 14.60 | 14.05 |
| 2018 | 14.82 | 14.80 | 14.71 | 14.85 | 14.73 | 14.42 | 14.38 | 14.53 | 14.77 | 14.71 | 14.68 | 15.06 | 14.70 |
| 2019 | 15.21 | 14.97 | 15.02 | 14.90 | 14.83 | 14.89 | 14.79 | 14.67 | 14.84 | 14.87 | 14.73 | 14.91 | 14.88 |

## 4. Average Weekly Earnings by Selected Industry: Missouri, 2015–2019

(Dollars, not seasonally adjusted)

| Industry and year | January | February | March | April | May | June | July | August | September | October | November | December | Annual average |
|---|---|---|---|---|---|---|---|---|---|---|---|---|---|
| **Total Private** | | | | | | | | | | | | | |
| 2015 | 738.03 | 755.82 | 753.43 | 743.24 | 739.35 | 737.69 | 737.36 | 755.77 | 737.52 | 741.23 | 751.06 | 741.74 | 744.78 |
| 2016 | 738.47 | 733.60 | 734.93 | 742.07 | 747.47 | 733.60 | 741.92 | 736.04 | 756.24 | 776.72 | 764.28 | 765.27 | 748.49 |
| 2017 | 790.76 | 775.86 | 782.88 | 810.56 | 787.92 | 788.92 | 816.01 | 798.35 | 809.09 | 819.99 | 805.76 | 800.36 | 798.31 |
| 2018 | 798.05 | 808.68 | 810.41 | 837.90 | 824.54 | 822.46 | 850.08 | 831.23 | 858.28 | 837.56 | 828.46 | 849.39 | 830.71 |
| 2019 | 830.48 | 831.47 | 837.50 | 843.02 | 838.34 | 865.05 | 851.60 | 855.64 | 878.42 | 857.27 | 861.62 | 883.43 | 852.77 |
| **Goods-Producing** | | | | | | | | | | | | | |
| 2015 | 982.03 | 975.55 | 968.09 | 958.23 | 961.74 | 977.02 | 972.55 | 1,009.60 | 977.54 | 1,003.86 | 980.27 | 1,018.31 | 981.80 |
| 2016 | 975.24 | 980.63 | 1,011.98 | 1,007.82 | 1,014.55 | 1,016.49 | 1,028.63 | 1,027.83 | 1,048.97 | 1,077.22 | 1,044.03 | 1,054.87 | 1,025.03 |
| 2017 | 1,026.05 | 1,066.50 | 1,064.59 | 1,075.26 | 1,068.72 | 1,084.00 | 1,113.89 | 1,117.40 | 1,120.23 | 1,125.54 | 1,091.77 | 1,101.20 | 1,088.13 |
| 2018 | 1,084.85 | 1,092.50 | 1,088.19 | 1,143.31 | 1,122.79 | 1,123.07 | 1,165.90 | 1,131.52 | 1,150.39 | 1,110.73 | 1,105.96 | 1,125.60 | 1,120.80 |
| 2019 | 1,108.01 | 1,107.87 | 1,106.79 | 1,132.00 | 1,117.85 | 1,126.22 | 1,118.87 | 1,117.87 | 1,139.79 | 1,106.58 | 1,108.40 | 1,151.44 | 1,120.05 |
| **Construction** | | | | | | | | | | | | | |
| 2015 | 1,011.19 | 990.04 | 1,019.10 | 1,012.04 | 1,006.64 | 1,043.02 | 1,033.84 | 1,071.22 | 986.62 | 1,085.26 | 1,000.75 | 1,111.24 | 1,030.66 |
| 2016 | 1,005.12 | 1,011.78 | 1,024.56 | 1,023.93 | 1,027.46 | 1,065.37 | 1,052.65 | 1,070.47 | 1,096.94 | 1,140.19 | 1,034.54 | 1,079.69 | 1,054.32 |
| 2017 | 977.30 | 1,055.96 | 1,047.56 | 1,055.93 | 1,055.24 | 1,073.42 | 1,087.30 | 1,090.31 | 1,107.07 | 1,114.88 | 1,057.43 | 1,048.90 | 1,064.68 |
| 2018 | 1,013.69 | 1,038.57 | 1,058.03 | 1,112.64 | 1,115.86 | 1,124.43 | 1,136.27 | 1,092.00 | 1,108.89 | 1,082.95 | 1,037.29 | 1,090.64 | 1,084.18 |
| 2019 | 1,040.39 | 1,047.17 | 1,101.65 | 1,151.10 | 1,127.26 | 1,147.33 | 1,118.20 | 1,109.85 | 1,155.32 | 1,106.96 | 1,092.56 | 1,140.54 | 1,112.98 |
| **Manufacturing** | | | | | | | | | | | | | |
| 2015 | 948.42 | 948.72 | 925.80 | 907.31 | 905.77 | 910.66 | 911.25 | 951.20 | 930.87 | 929.33 | 951.57 | 941.01 | 930.41 |
| 2016 | 939.88 | 949.32 | 990.62 | 982.11 | 988.31 | 972.67 | 998.32 | 985.58 | 992.92 | 1,025.06 | 1,027.34 | 1,024.65 | 989.37 |
| 2017 | 1,035.30 | 1,058.02 | 1,060.38 | 1,073.67 | 1,065.95 | 1,073.61 | 1,113.97 | 1,128.99 | 1,123.49 | 1,129.12 | 1,108.64 | 1,125.90 | 1,091.58 |
| 2018 | 1,118.82 | 1,112.42 | 1,096.94 | 1,152.06 | 1,115.06 | 1,111.02 | 1,169.60 | 1,139.85 | 1,162.29 | 1,097.13 | 1,110.93 | 1,118.21 | 1,126.27 |
| 2019 | 1,095.33 | 1,096.74 | 1,080.35 | 1,080.26 | 1,074.03 | 1,081.81 | 1,094.26 | 1,096.70 | 1,108.13 | 1,087.81 | 1,093.13 | 1,125.50 | 1,091.81 |
| **Trade, Transportation, and Utilities** | | | | | | | | | | | | | |
| 2015 | 652.73 | 665.98 | 664.98 | 666.29 | 663.66 | 659.69 | 663.08 | 670.32 | 668.70 | 668.70 | 667.68 | 657.79 | 664.17 |
| 2016 | 656.34 | 646.35 | 647.40 | 661.53 | 658.22 | 681.32 | 661.19 | 678.04 | 684.78 | 710.02 | 680.69 | 693.05 | 670.99 |
| 2017 | 742.76 | 705.07 | 719.02 | 745.63 | 718.00 | 721.05 | 733.26 | 714.56 | 727.29 | 732.46 | 719.07 | 720.39 | 725.09 |
| 2018 | 714.10 | 705.46 | 709.00 | 736.47 | 736.18 | 745.28 | 757.00 | 746.79 | 780.55 | 771.39 | 751.41 | 776.50 | 744.37 |
| 2019 | 755.99 | 759.33 | 774.21 | 772.18 | 771.73 | 812.82 | 800.71 | 788.89 | 816.70 | 795.29 | 782.90 | 789.26 | 785.90 |
| **Financial Activities** | | | | | | | | | | | | | |
| 2015 | 942.80 | 993.77 | 989.26 | 960.51 | 953.49 | 939.50 | 938.63 | 976.75 | 944.26 | 932.87 | 977.99 | 943.01 | 956.82 |
| 2016 | 964.08 | 936.16 | 939.62 | 969.94 | 973.47 | 876.86 | 931.25 | 912.96 | 951.50 | 1,000.40 | 979.53 | 963.97 | 950.98 |
| 2017 | 1,049.80 | 1,023.70 | 1,023.12 | 1,081.18 | 1,041.42 | 1,055.06 | 1,143.75 | 1,084.92 | 1,109.65 | 1,148.53 | 1,118.25 | 1,132.08 | 1,085.98 |
| 2018 | 1,123.48 | 1,137.76 | 1,142.76 | 1,190.82 | 1,141.75 | 1,118.40 | 1,188.30 | 1,141.92 | 1,191.92 | 1,142.31 | 1,128.40 | 1,168.75 | 1,152.75 |
| 2019 | 1,171.94 | 1,169.20 | 1,135.13 | 1,160.32 | 1,159.20 | 1,193.96 | 1,144.11 | 1,169.36 | 1,196.43 | 1,176.32 | 1,183.63 | 1,211.01 | 1,173.47 |
| **Professional and Business Services** | | | | | | | | | | | | | |
| 2015 | 923.64 | 973.28 | 969.08 | 948.71 | 938.06 | 936.77 | 935.07 | 996.51 | 964.81 | 972.84 | 994.81 | 959.78 | 959.90 |
| 2016 | 975.27 | 971.87 | 954.87 | 966.07 | 978.31 | 955.14 | 974.34 | 956.57 | 964.54 | 1,004.12 | 984.14 | 988.26 | 971.75 |
| 2017 | 1,043.64 | 1,033.05 | 1,028.37 | 1,073.84 | 1,019.46 | 1,031.74 | 1,064.23 | 1,045.82 | 1,054.94 | 1,054.00 | 1,010.45 | 1,007.21 | 1,040.30 |
| 2018 | 1,002.88 | 1,037.88 | 1,028.86 | 1,032.50 | 1,029.35 | 1,032.04 | 1,054.76 | 1,052.13 | 1,082.07 | 1,030.78 | 1,021.90 | 1,044.32 | 1,037.58 |
| 2019 | 1,024.80 | 1,024.48 | 1,033.94 | 1,026.15 | 1,009.88 | 1,043.35 | 1,025.12 | 1,044.92 | 1,061.66 | 1,037.58 | 1,045.84 | 1,093.07 | 1,039.29 |
| **Education and Health Services** | | | | | | | | | | | | | |
| 2015 | 607.46 | 619.63 | 620.63 | 617.30 | 615.12 | 613.05 | 626.67 | 615.06 | 600.59 | 585.28 | 616.30 | 604.56 | 611.82 |
| 2016 | 606.02 | 597.88 | 609.62 | 613.86 | 634.53 | 623.64 | 631.44 | 628.85 | 647.14 | 648.40 | 652.69 | 649.75 | 628.45 |
| 2017 | 666.87 | 660.68 | 656.98 | 677.38 | 652.00 | 653.35 | 662.32 | 636.03 | 643.21 | 653.35 | 634.71 | 630.83 | 652.74 |
| 2018 | 624.68 | 631.62 | 627.27 | 649.35 | 635.63 | 629.85 | 662.54 | 653.25 | 669.67 | 658.58 | 661.05 | 681.36 | 649.42 |
| 2019 | 663.23 | 656.51 | 691.20 | 704.16 | 698.82 | 725.11 | 710.24 | 708.91 | 718.41 | 710.33 | 712.73 | 725.77 | 702.33 |
| **Leisure and Hospitality** | | | | | | | | | | | | | |
| 2015 | 322.46 | 337.74 | 344.74 | 338.26 | 335.98 | 340.34 | 337.21 | 336.41 | 336.93 | 344.17 | 336.04 | 335.50 | 337.44 |
| 2016 | 331.92 | 341.80 | 340.43 | 344.51 | 345.92 | 339.71 | 347.06 | 342.02 | 345.13 | 345.74 | 339.25 | 334.99 | 341.80 |
| 2017 | 327.37 | 338.50 | 348.27 | 344.07 | 346.50 | 353.38 | 359.92 | 351.92 | 356.75 | 359.51 | 356.87 | 363.54 | 351.25 |
| 2018 | 351.23 | 362.60 | 364.81 | 369.77 | 365.30 | 367.71 | 368.13 | 366.16 | 372.20 | 363.34 | 362.60 | 378.01 | 366.03 |
| 2019 | 352.87 | 356.29 | 378.50 | 371.01 | 366.30 | 381.18 | 372.71 | 366.75 | 371.00 | 374.72 | 372.67 | 377.22 | 370.51 |

# MONTANA
## *At a Glance*

Population:
  2010 census: 989,415
  2019 estimate: 1,068,778

Percent change in population:
  2010–2019:  8.0%

Percent change in total nonfarm employment:
  2011–2019: 12.2%

Industry with the largest growth in employment, 2011–2019 (percent):
  Construction, 32.6%

Industry with the largest decline or smallest growth in employment, 2011–2019 (percent):
  Information, -13.9%

Civilian labor force:
  2010: 500,525
  2019: 533,497

Unemployment rate and rank among states (highest to lowest):
  2010: 7.3%, 40th
  2019: 3.5%, 25th

Over-the-year change in unemployment rates:
  2017–2018: -0.3%
  2018–2019: -0.1%

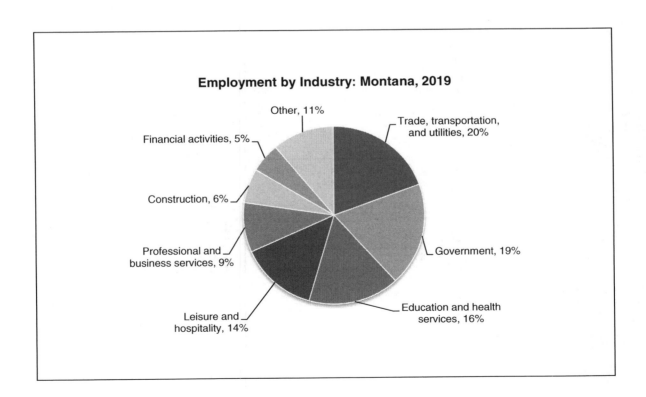

**Employment by Industry: Montana, 2019**

Other, 11%
Financial activities, 5%
Trade, transportation, and utilities, 20%
Construction, 6%
Professional and business services, 9%
Government, 19%
Leisure and hospitality, 14%
Education and health services, 16%

## 1. Employment by Industry: Montana, 2011–2019

(Numbers in thousands, not seasonally adjusted)

| Industry and year | January | February | March | April | May | June | July | August | September | October | November | December | Annual average |
|---|---|---|---|---|---|---|---|---|---|---|---|---|---|
| **Total Nonfarm** | | | | | | | | | | | | | |
| 2011 | 413.7 | 415.8 | 419.8 | 425.7 | 433.4 | 438.5 | 437.3 | 440.4 | 441.2 | 438.2 | 434.6 | 434.6 | 431.1 |
| 2012 | 422.8 | 423.9 | 427.8 | 434.5 | 443.6 | 448.4 | 448.3 | 450.1 | 449.9 | 447.0 | 443.0 | 443.6 | 440.2 |
| 2013 | 432.3 | 435.5 | 438.7 | 444.5 | 452.5 | 456.6 | 454.2 | 457.0 | 455.6 | 454.7 | 450.9 | 450.8 | 448.6 |
| 2014 | 437.8 | 441.1 | 442.7 | 449.1 | 456.2 | 462.0 | 461.4 | 462.5 | 460.3 | 457.4 | 452.7 | 454.7 | 453.2 |
| 2015 | 444.9 | 448.9 | 452.8 | 458.7 | 464.6 | 469.3 | 468.8 | 469.6 | 468.2 | 468.5 | 464.8 | 465.9 | 462.1 |
| 2016 | 452.6 | 455.8 | 459.4 | 465.3 | 471.4 | 476.6 | 474.3 | 475.4 | 474.9 | 471.9 | 469.5 | 468.9 | 468.0 |
| 2017 | 457.9 | 459.9 | 463.7 | 469.9 | 476.8 | 482.7 | 479.5 | 480.5 | 478.6 | 476.8 | 472.9 | 474.0 | 472.8 |
| 2018 | 463.7 | 465.1 | 468.2 | 473.1 | 481.8 | 488.3 | 485.3 | 486.3 | 484.0 | 482.7 | 480.5 | 481.9 | 478.4 |
| 2019 | 470.0 | 470.6 | 471.7 | 478.9 | 487.6 | 492.5 | 492.2 | 493.6 | 489.8 | 488.3 | 485.5 | 484.4 | 483.8 |
| **Total Private** | | | | | | | | | | | | | |
| 2011 | 324.3 | 324.8 | 327.8 | 333.9 | 340.2 | 347.7 | 352.9 | 354.6 | 350.4 | 347.0 | 343.8 | 344.0 | 341.0 |
| 2012 | 334.1 | 334.3 | 337.4 | 344.2 | 351.2 | 359.3 | 362.1 | 364.5 | 359.6 | 356.0 | 352.0 | 353.1 | 350.7 |
| 2013 | 342.0 | 344.0 | 346.8 | 353.1 | 360.4 | 367.4 | 370.4 | 372.2 | 366.2 | 363.0 | 359.7 | 361.0 | 358.9 |
| 2014 | 349.7 | 349.7 | 351.0 | 357.8 | 364.1 | 372.3 | 375.8 | 377.0 | 370.0 | 365.7 | 360.9 | 363.8 | 363.2 |
| 2015 | 356.4 | 357.9 | 360.9 | 366.4 | 371.7 | 379.7 | 383.6 | 384.0 | 377.6 | 375.5 | 372.5 | 373.9 | 371.7 |
| 2016 | 363.8 | 364.9 | 367.3 | 372.9 | 377.6 | 384.9 | 388.6 | 388.9 | 383.4 | 378.9 | 376.5 | 376.5 | 377.0 |
| 2017 | 367.7 | 368.7 | 371.9 | 377.6 | 383.8 | 391.7 | 393.0 | 393.6 | 386.5 | 383.4 | 380.7 | 382.6 | 381.8 |
| 2018 | 374.0 | 374.7 | 377.3 | 381.9 | 389.4 | 398.0 | 399.2 | 400.0 | 393.0 | 390.5 | 388.5 | 390.7 | 388.1 |
| 2019 | 380.8 | 379.9 | 380.7 | 387.5 | 394.2 | 402.3 | 405.0 | 406.1 | 398.1 | 395.4 | 392.9 | 392.6 | 393.0 |
| **Goods Producing** | | | | | | | | | | | | | |
| 2011 | 41.6 | 41.6 | 42.5 | 45.4 | 47.3 | 49.3 | 50.9 | 51.7 | 51.4 | 51.5 | 49.9 | 48.1 | 47.6 |
| 2012 | 44.8 | 44.5 | 45.4 | 48.5 | 50.5 | 52.0 | 52.8 | 53.5 | 53.3 | 53.5 | 51.7 | 50.6 | 50.1 |
| 2013 | 46.3 | 46.8 | 47.7 | 50.4 | 53.7 | 54.3 | 54.5 | 55.1 | 54.3 | 54.6 | 53.5 | 51.7 | 51.9 |
| 2014 | 48.1 | 47.7 | 48.5 | 51.1 | 53.6 | 56.0 | 56.7 | 56.6 | 55.3 | 56.0 | 53.5 | 53.0 | 53.0 |
| 2015 | 49.8 | 50.0 | 50.7 | 52.3 | 54.3 | 56.2 | 57.1 | 56.8 | 55.4 | 56.0 | 54.3 | 53.0 | 53.8 |
| 2016 | 49.4 | 49.5 | 50.2 | 52.5 | 54.2 | 55.8 | 56.2 | 56.4 | 55.3 | 55.3 | 54.8 | 52.8 | 53.5 |
| 2017 | 49.6 | 50.3 | 51.3 | 53.5 | 56.0 | 57.2 | 57.3 | 57.4 | 56.2 | 56.5 | 55.0 | 54.3 | 54.6 |
| 2018 | 51.0 | 51.1 | 52.3 | 54.9 | 57.9 | 59.1 | 59.6 | 60.0 | 59.1 | 60.0 | 59.3 | 58.2 | 56.9 |
| 2019 | 54.6 | 53.1 | 53.3 | 56.4 | 58.8 | 60.9 | 61.5 | 62.0 | 60.6 | 61.4 | 59.8 | 57.7 | 58.3 |
| **Service-Providing** | | | | | | | | | | | | | |
| 2011 | 372.1 | 374.2 | 377.3 | 380.3 | 386.1 | 389.2 | 386.4 | 388.7 | 389.8 | 386.7 | 384.7 | 386.5 | 383.5 |
| 2012 | 378.0 | 379.4 | 382.4 | 386.0 | 393.1 | 396.4 | 395.5 | 396.6 | 396.6 | 393.5 | 391.3 | 393.0 | 390.2 |
| 2013 | 386.0 | 388.7 | 391.0 | 394.1 | 398.8 | 402.3 | 399.7 | 401.9 | 401.3 | 400.1 | 397.4 | 399.1 | 396.7 |
| 2014 | 389.7 | 393.4 | 394.2 | 398.0 | 402.6 | 406.0 | 404.7 | 405.9 | 405.0 | 401.4 | 399.2 | 401.7 | 400.2 |
| 2015 | 395.1 | 398.9 | 402.1 | 406.4 | 410.3 | 413.1 | 411.7 | 412.8 | 412.8 | 412.5 | 410.5 | 412.9 | 408.3 |
| 2016 | 403.2 | 406.3 | 409.2 | 412.8 | 417.2 | 420.8 | 418.1 | 419.0 | 419.6 | 416.6 | 414.7 | 416.1 | 414.5 |
| 2017 | 408.3 | 409.6 | 412.4 | 416.4 | 420.8 | 425.5 | 422.2 | 423.1 | 422.4 | 420.3 | 417.9 | 419.7 | 418.2 |
| 2018 | 412.7 | 414.0 | 415.9 | 418.2 | 423.9 | 429.2 | 425.7 | 426.3 | 424.9 | 422.7 | 421.2 | 423.7 | 421.5 |
| 2019 | 415.4 | 417.5 | 418.4 | 422.5 | 428.8 | 431.6 | 430.7 | 431.6 | 429.2 | 426.9 | 425.7 | 426.7 | 425.4 |
| **Mining and Logging** | | | | | | | | | | | | | |
| 2011 | 7.4 | 7.5 | 7.6 | 7.6 | 7.8 | 8.0 | 8.5 | 8.8 | 8.6 | 8.7 | 8.8 | 8.7 | 8.2 |
| 2012 | 8.7 | 8.8 | 8.7 | 8.8 | 9.0 | 9.4 | 9.7 | 9.9 | 9.7 | 9.8 | 9.7 | 9.8 | 9.3 |
| 2013 | 9.1 | 9.3 | 9.3 | 9.2 | 9.5 | 9.7 | 9.6 | 9.7 | 9.6 | 9.4 | 9.5 | 9.4 | 9.4 |
| 2014 | 8.9 | 8.8 | 8.7 | 8.7 | 9.0 | 9.2 | 9.4 | 9.5 | 9.4 | 9.5 | 9.3 | 9.2 | 9.1 |
| 2015 | 8.8 | 8.6 | 8.4 | 8.1 | 8.2 | 8.4 | 8.4 | 8.3 | 8.0 | 7.9 | 7.7 | 7.5 | 8.2 |
| 2016 | 7.1 | 7.0 | 6.8 | 6.9 | 7.0 | 7.1 | 7.0 | 7.0 | 6.9 | 6.9 | 6.9 | 6.8 | 7.0 |
| 2017 | 6.7 | 6.7 | 6.6 | 6.5 | 6.7 | 6.9 | 7.1 | 7.2 | 7.0 | 7.1 | 6.9 | 6.9 | 6.9 |
| 2018 | 6.8 | 6.9 | 6.9 | 6.8 | 7.1 | 7.4 | 7.5 | 7.5 | 7.4 | 7.5 | 7.4 | 7.3 | 7.2 |
| 2019 | 7.1 | 7.0 | 6.9 | 6.9 | 7.2 | 7.4 | 7.6 | 7.7 | 7.7 | 7.7 | 7.5 | 7.3 | 7.3 |
| **Construction** | | | | | | | | | | | | | |
| 2011 | 17.9 | 17.8 | 18.5 | 21.3 | 22.9 | 24.5 | 25.5 | 25.9 | 25.9 | 25.6 | 24.0 | 22.1 | 22.7 |
| 2012 | 19.3 | 19.0 | 20.0 | 22.5 | 24.0 | 24.9 | 25.2 | 25.6 | 25.7 | 25.4 | 23.7 | 22.4 | 23.1 |
| 2013 | 19.6 | 19.8 | 20.7 | 23.2 | 26.0 | 26.1 | 26.2 | 26.7 | 26.1 | 26.2 | 24.9 | 23.2 | 24.1 |
| 2014 | 20.8 | 20.5 | 21.5 | 23.8 | 25.8 | 27.7 | 28.1 | 27.9 | 26.9 | 27.2 | 25.2 | 24.6 | 25.0 |
| 2015 | 22.4 | 22.7 | 23.7 | 25.4 | 27.2 | 28.6 | 29.3 | 29.1 | 28.1 | 28.5 | 27.1 | 25.9 | 26.5 |
| 2016 | 23.1 | 23.3 | 24.3 | 26.4 | 27.9 | 29.2 | 29.5 | 29.6 | 28.7 | 28.5 | 27.9 | 26.1 | 27.0 |
| 2017 | 23.5 | 24.1 | 25.1 | 27.5 | 29.6 | 30.3 | 30.1 | 30.1 | 29.1 | 29.1 | 27.8 | 27.1 | 27.8 |
| 2018 | 24.3 | 24.2 | 25.3 | 28.1 | 30.5 | 31.0 | 31.4 | 31.5 | 30.9 | 31.4 | 30.7 | 29.7 | 29.1 |
| 2019 | 27.0 | 25.5 | 25.8 | 28.7 | 30.7 | 32.4 | 32.7 | 33.0 | 31.8 | 32.8 | 31.4 | 29.5 | 30.1 |

# 1. Employment by Industry: Montana, 2011–2019—*Continued*

(Numbers in thousands, not seasonally adjusted)

| Industry and year | January | February | March | April | May | June | July | August | September | October | November | December | Annual average |
|---|---|---|---|---|---|---|---|---|---|---|---|---|---|
| **Manufacturing** | | | | | | | | | | | | | |
| 2011 | 16.3 | 16.3 | 16.4 | 16.5 | 16.6 | 16.8 | 16.9 | 17.0 | 16.9 | 17.2 | 17.1 | 17.3 | 16.8 |
| 2012 | 16.8 | 16.7 | 16.7 | 17.2 | 17.5 | 17.7 | 17.9 | 18.0 | 17.9 | 18.3 | 18.3 | 18.4 | 17.6 |
| 2013 | 17.6 | 17.7 | 17.7 | 18.0 | 18.2 | 18.5 | 18.7 | 18.7 | 18.6 | 19.0 | 19.1 | 19.1 | 18.4 |
| 2014 | 18.4 | 18.4 | 18.3 | 18.6 | 18.8 | 19.1 | 19.2 | 19.2 | 19.0 | 19.3 | 19.0 | 19.2 | 18.9 |
| | | | | | | | | | | | | | |
| 2015 | 18.6 | 18.7 | 18.6 | 18.8 | 18.9 | 19.2 | 19.4 | 19.4 | 19.3 | 19.6 | 19.5 | 19.6 | 19.1 |
| 2016 | 19.2 | 19.2 | 19.1 | 19.2 | 19.3 | 19.5 | 19.7 | 19.8 | 19.7 | 19.9 | 20.0 | 19.9 | 19.5 |
| 2017 | 19.4 | 19.5 | 19.6 | 19.5 | 19.7 | 20.0 | 20.1 | 20.1 | 20.1 | 20.3 | 20.3 | 20.3 | 19.9 |
| 2018 | 19.9 | 20.0 | 20.1 | 20.0 | 20.3 | 20.7 | 20.7 | 21.0 | 20.8 | 21.1 | 21.2 | 21.2 | 20.6 |
| 2019 | 20.5 | 20.6 | 20.6 | 20.8 | 20.9 | 21.1 | 21.2 | 21.3 | 21.1 | 20.9 | 20.9 | 20.9 | 20.9 |
| | | | | | | | | | | | | | |
| **Trade, Transportation, and Utilities** | | | | | | | | | | | | | |
| 2011 | 83.9 | 83.5 | 83.6 | 84.8 | 86.0 | 87.0 | 87.3 | 87.7 | 86.9 | 87.1 | 88.1 | 88.7 | 86.2 |
| 2012 | 85.7 | 85.3 | 85.7 | 86.8 | 88.4 | 89.7 | 89.7 | 90.0 | 89.6 | 90.0 | 91.1 | 91.7 | 88.6 |
| 2013 | 88.3 | 88.1 | 88.4 | 89.8 | 91.4 | 92.1 | 92.1 | 92.6 | 91.6 | 92.2 | 93.2 | 94.1 | 91.2 |
| 2014 | 90.7 | 90.1 | 90.1 | 91.1 | 92.6 | 93.5 | 93.4 | 93.7 | 93.0 | 93.0 | 94.2 | 95.1 | 92.5 |
| | | | | | | | | | | | | | |
| 2015 | 92.1 | 91.7 | 92.3 | 93.3 | 94.3 | 95.1 | 95.1 | 95.3 | 94.6 | 95.2 | 96.4 | 97.0 | 94.4 |
| 2016 | 93.7 | 93.1 | 93.5 | 94.2 | 95.4 | 95.8 | 95.4 | 95.7 | 95.0 | 94.5 | 95.0 | 95.4 | 94.7 |
| 2017 | 92.9 | 92.3 | 92.6 | 93.6 | 94.6 | 95.4 | 95.2 | 95.3 | 94.6 | 94.5 | 95.6 | 95.9 | 94.4 |
| 2018 | 93.4 | 92.9 | 93.1 | 93.5 | 94.9 | 95.9 | 95.6 | 95.7 | 94.8 | 94.4 | 95.6 | 96.4 | 94.7 |
| 2019 | 93.4 | 92.7 | 92.9 | 93.5 | 94.7 | 94.9 | 94.8 | 94.8 | 93.9 | 94.7 | 96.0 | 96.7 | 94.4 |
| | | | | | | | | | | | | | |
| **Wholesale Trade** | | | | | | | | | | | | | |
| 2011 | 15.0 | 15.1 | 15.2 | 15.4 | 15.6 | 15.7 | 15.8 | 15.9 | 15.7 | 15.7 | 15.7 | 15.8 | 15.6 |
| 2012 | 15.6 | 15.6 | 15.9 | 16.1 | 16.2 | 16.4 | 16.5 | 16.5 | 16.4 | 16.4 | 16.4 | 16.4 | 16.2 |
| 2013 | 16.4 | 16.5 | 16.7 | 16.9 | 17.1 | 17.1 | 17.1 | 17.1 | 16.8 | 16.8 | 16.8 | 16.8 | 16.8 |
| 2014 | 16.5 | 16.4 | 16.6 | 16.7 | 16.9 | 17.0 | 17.0 | 17.0 | 16.8 | 16.8 | 16.9 | 16.9 | 16.8 |
| | | | | | | | | | | | | | |
| 2015 | 16.9 | 16.9 | 17.1 | 17.3 | 17.4 | 17.5 | 17.5 | 17.5 | 17.2 | 17.3 | 17.4 | 17.4 | 17.3 |
| 2016 | 17.1 | 17.1 | 17.2 | 17.2 | 17.3 | 17.4 | 17.3 | 17.3 | 17.0 | 17.0 | 17.0 | 16.9 | 17.2 |
| 2017 | 16.8 | 16.8 | 16.9 | 17.0 | 17.2 | 17.3 | 17.3 | 17.3 | 17.0 | 17.1 | 17.2 | 17.0 | 17.1 |
| 2018 | 17.0 | 17.0 | 17.1 | 17.2 | 17.4 | 17.5 | 17.4 | 17.3 | 17.1 | 17.1 | 17.2 | 17.2 | 17.2 |
| 2019 | 16.9 | 16.9 | 17.0 | 17.2 | 17.4 | 17.4 | 17.4 | 17.3 | 17.2 | 17.4 | 17.4 | 17.2 | 17.2 |
| | | | | | | | | | | | | | |
| **Retail Trade** | | | | | | | | | | | | | |
| 2011 | 53.2 | 52.7 | 52.8 | 53.7 | 54.5 | 55.3 | 55.7 | 55.8 | 55.1 | 55.2 | 56.1 | 56.3 | 54.7 |
| 2012 | 53.9 | 53.3 | 53.4 | 54.1 | 55.3 | 56.2 | 56.3 | 56.2 | 55.6 | 56.0 | 57.1 | 57.2 | 55.4 |
| 2013 | 54.1 | 53.6 | 53.7 | 55.0 | 56.0 | 56.8 | 57.2 | 57.3 | 56.4 | 57.0 | 57.9 | 58.3 | 56.1 |
| 2014 | 55.6 | 55.2 | 55.1 | 56.2 | 57.3 | 58.1 | 58.4 | 58.5 | 57.6 | 57.8 | 58.8 | 59.1 | 57.3 |
| | | | | | | | | | | | | | |
| 2015 | 56.8 | 56.5 | 56.9 | 57.9 | 58.8 | 59.5 | 59.7 | 59.8 | 59.0 | 59.4 | 60.4 | 60.5 | 58.8 |
| 2016 | 58.3 | 57.8 | 58.1 | 59.0 | 59.8 | 60.4 | 60.3 | 60.4 | 59.7 | 59.3 | 59.9 | 59.9 | 59.4 |
| 2017 | 58.1 | 57.5 | 57.7 | 58.4 | 59.1 | 59.7 | 59.8 | 59.8 | 59.0 | 59.0 | 60.0 | 59.9 | 59.0 |
| 2018 | 58.0 | 57.6 | 57.7 | 58.0 | 59.1 | 60.1 | 60.0 | 59.9 | 58.9 | 58.6 | 59.6 | 59.8 | 58.9 |
| 2019 | 57.6 | 57.1 | 57.2 | 57.7 | 58.5 | 58.8 | 58.8 | 58.6 | 57.8 | 58.4 | 59.4 | 59.6 | 58.3 |
| | | | | | | | | | | | | | |
| **Transportation and Utilities** | | | | | | | | | | | | | |
| 2011 | 15.7 | 15.7 | 15.6 | 15.7 | 15.9 | 16.0 | 15.8 | 16.0 | 16.1 | 16.2 | 16.3 | 16.6 | 16.0 |
| 2012 | 16.2 | 16.4 | 16.4 | 16.6 | 16.9 | 17.1 | 16.9 | 17.3 | 17.6 | 17.6 | 17.6 | 18.1 | 17.1 |
| 2013 | 17.8 | 18.0 | 18.0 | 17.9 | 18.3 | 18.2 | 17.8 | 18.2 | 18.4 | 18.4 | 18.5 | 19.0 | 18.2 |
| 2014 | 18.6 | 18.5 | 18.4 | 18.2 | 18.4 | 18.4 | 18.0 | 18.2 | 18.6 | 18.4 | 18.5 | 19.1 | 18.4 |
| | | | | | | | | | | | | | |
| 2015 | 18.4 | 18.3 | 18.3 | 18.1 | 18.1 | 18.1 | 17.9 | 18.0 | 18.4 | 18.5 | 18.6 | 19.1 | 18.3 |
| 2016 | 18.3 | 18.2 | 18.2 | 18.0 | 18.3 | 18.0 | 17.8 | 18.0 | 18.3 | 18.2 | 18.1 | 18.6 | 18.2 |
| 2017 | 18.0 | 18.0 | 18.0 | 18.2 | 18.3 | 18.4 | 18.1 | 18.2 | 18.6 | 18.4 | 18.4 | 19.0 | 18.3 |
| 2018 | 18.4 | 18.3 | 18.3 | 18.3 | 18.4 | 18.3 | 18.2 | 18.5 | 18.8 | 18.7 | 18.8 | 19.4 | 18.5 |
| 2019 | 18.9 | 18.7 | 18.7 | 18.6 | 18.8 | 18.7 | 18.6 | 18.9 | 18.9 | 18.9 | 19.2 | 19.9 | 18.9 |
| | | | | | | | | | | | | | |
| **Information** | | | | | | | | | | | | | |
| 2011 | 7.1 | 7.2 | 7.2 | 7.2 | 7.2 | 7.3 | 7.3 | 7.3 | 7.2 | 7.2 | 7.2 | 7.1 | 7.2 |
| 2012 | 6.9 | 7.0 | 6.9 | 6.8 | 6.9 | 6.9 | 6.9 | 7.0 | 6.9 | 6.9 | 7.0 | 7.0 | 6.9 |
| 2013 | 6.8 | 7.0 | 6.9 | 6.8 | 6.9 | 6.8 | 6.8 | 6.8 | 6.7 | 6.7 | 6.7 | 6.7 | 6.8 |
| 2014 | 6.5 | 6.5 | 6.4 | 6.4 | 6.4 | 6.4 | 6.4 | 6.4 | 6.4 | 6.3 | 6.3 | 6.3 | 6.4 |
| | | | | | | | | | | | | | |
| 2015 | 6.3 | 6.4 | 6.3 | 6.3 | 6.4 | 6.4 | 6.4 | 6.4 | 6.4 | 6.4 | 6.5 | 6.4 | 6.4 |
| 2016 | 6.3 | 6.4 | 6.3 | 6.3 | 6.3 | 6.3 | 6.3 | 6.3 | 6.3 | 6.4 | 6.5 | 6.4 | 6.3 |
| 2017 | 6.4 | 6.3 | 6.3 | 6.3 | 6.3 | 6.3 | 6.5 | 6.6 | 6.5 | 6.5 | 6.5 | 6.5 | 6.4 |
| 2018 | 6.4 | 6.5 | 6.5 | 6.3 | 6.4 | 6.4 | 6.3 | 6.4 | 6.3 | 6.3 | 6.3 | 6.3 | 6.4 |
| 2019 | 6.2 | 6.2 | 6.2 | 6.2 | 6.3 | 6.2 | 6.2 | 6.2 | 6.2 | 6.3 | 6.3 | 6.2 | 6.2 |

## 1. Employment by Industry: Montana, 2011–2019—*Continued*

(Numbers in thousands, not seasonally adjusted)

| Industry and year | January | February | March | April | May | June | July | August | September | October | November | December | Annual average |
|---|---|---|---|---|---|---|---|---|---|---|---|---|---|
| **Financial Activities** | | | | | | | | | | | | | |
| 2011 | 20.7 | 20.7 | 20.8 | 20.7 | 20.8 | 21.2 | 21.4 | 21.3 | 21.2 | 21.6 | 21.6 | 21.9 | 21.2 |
| 2012 | 20.9 | 20.9 | 20.9 | 21.0 | 21.3 | 21.7 | 21.9 | 22.0 | 21.9 | 21.9 | 21.8 | 22.2 | 21.5 |
| 2013 | 21.6 | 21.7 | 21.8 | 22.2 | 22.3 | 22.6 | 23.0 | 23.2 | 22.9 | 23.2 | 23.1 | 23.4 | 22.6 |
| 2014 | 22.9 | 23.1 | 23.1 | 23.3 | 23.4 | 23.7 | 24.0 | 24.0 | 23.6 | 23.6 | 23.5 | 23.8 | 23.5 |
| 2015 | 23.4 | 23.4 | 23.5 | 23.4 | 23.6 | 23.9 | 24.1 | 24.2 | 23.9 | 24.0 | 23.9 | 24.3 | 23.8 |
| 2016 | 23.8 | 23.8 | 23.8 | 23.8 | 23.9 | 24.3 | 24.5 | 24.5 | 24.2 | 24.3 | 24.2 | 24.4 | 24.1 |
| 2017 | 24.0 | 23.9 | 24.1 | 24.3 | 24.5 | 24.7 | 24.9 | 24.8 | 24.5 | 24.6 | 24.6 | 24.9 | 24.5 |
| 2018 | 24.4 | 24.4 | 24.4 | 24.6 | 24.8 | 25.2 | 25.5 | 25.4 | 25.2 | 25.4 | 25.4 | 25.7 | 25.0 |
| 2019 | 25.2 | 25.3 | 25.4 | 25.5 | 25.7 | 25.9 | 26.2 | 26.2 | 25.9 | 26.4 | 26.3 | 26.3 | 25.9 |
| **Professional and Business Services** | | | | | | | | | | | | | |
| 2011 | 38.8 | 39.0 | 39.4 | 40.6 | 41.0 | 41.5 | 42.0 | 42.1 | 41.1 | 40.6 | 40.2 | 39.5 | 40.5 |
| 2012 | 38.9 | 39.0 | 39.5 | 40.9 | 41.2 | 41.7 | 42.0 | 41.9 | 40.8 | 40.7 | 39.9 | 39.5 | 40.5 |
| 2013 | 38.1 | 38.3 | 38.6 | 39.6 | 40.1 | 40.8 | 41.5 | 40.9 | 40.0 | 39.9 | 39.3 | 39.0 | 39.7 |
| 2014 | 37.6 | 38.1 | 38.3 | 39.3 | 39.9 | 40.6 | 41.1 | 41.4 | 40.4 | 39.7 | 38.7 | 38.6 | 39.5 |
| 2015 | 38.7 | 39.1 | 39.5 | 40.6 | 40.6 | 41.5 | 42.2 | 42.1 | 41.1 | 40.8 | 40.1 | 39.9 | 40.5 |
| 2016 | 39.0 | 39.4 | 39.9 | 40.7 | 41.0 | 41.4 | 42.2 | 42.0 | 41.0 | 40.8 | 40.4 | 40.2 | 40.7 |
| 2017 | 39.3 | 39.7 | 40.1 | 40.9 | 41.7 | 42.3 | 42.5 | 42.5 | 41.4 | 41.7 | 41.1 | 41.1 | 41.2 |
| 2018 | 40.4 | 40.7 | 40.9 | 41.9 | 42.7 | 43.5 | 43.6 | 43.7 | 42.9 | 43.0 | 42.2 | 41.8 | 42.3 |
| 2019 | 40.8 | 41.5 | 41.4 | 42.4 | 43.6 | 44.1 | 44.9 | 45.5 | 44.4 | 44.6 | 43.9 | 43.2 | 43.4 |
| **Education and Health Services** | | | | | | | | | | | | | |
| 2011 | 63.9 | 64.2 | 64.3 | 64.2 | 64.7 | 64.5 | 63.9 | 64.5 | 65.6 | 66.4 | 66.5 | 67.1 | 65.0 |
| 2012 | 66.8 | 67.2 | 67.3 | 67.5 | 67.9 | 67.3 | 66.6 | 67.2 | 67.7 | 68.1 | 68.4 | 68.8 | 67.6 |
| 2013 | 68.3 | 68.6 | 68.8 | 68.9 | 69.1 | 68.8 | 68.0 | 68.6 | 69.5 | 69.9 | 70.1 | 70.3 | 69.1 |
| 2014 | 69.7 | 69.9 | 70.1 | 70.9 | 70.7 | 70.1 | 69.1 | 69.4 | 70.0 | 70.5 | 70.8 | 71.2 | 70.2 |
| 2015 | 70.7 | 71.1 | 71.4 | 72.3 | 72.3 | 71.9 | 71.1 | 71.5 | 72.4 | 73.2 | 73.6 | 73.7 | 72.1 |
| 2016 | 73.8 | 74.3 | 74.6 | 74.6 | 74.5 | 74.3 | 74.2 | 74.4 | 75.6 | 75.8 | 76.1 | 76.3 | 74.9 |
| 2017 | 76.6 | 76.8 | 77.1 | 77.1 | 77.3 | 76.9 | 76.2 | 76.5 | 77.2 | 77.7 | 78.0 | 78.2 | 77.1 |
| 2018 | 78.1 | 78.4 | 78.4 | 78.2 | 78.0 | 77.4 | 76.5 | 76.9 | 77.3 | 78.0 | 78.3 | 78.8 | 77.9 |
| 2019 | 78.5 | 78.9 | 78.9 | 79.3 | 79.0 | 78.5 | 78.0 | 78.4 | 78.7 | 78.9 | 79.5 | 79.7 | 78.9 |
| **Leisure and Hospitality** | | | | | | | | | | | | | |
| 2011 | 51.9 | 52.1 | 53.3 | 54.2 | 56.2 | 59.8 | 62.9 | 63.0 | 60.0 | 55.6 | 53.4 | 54.5 | 56.4 |
| 2012 | 53.4 | 53.5 | 54.7 | 55.4 | 57.5 | 62.3 | 64.6 | 65.2 | 61.7 | 57.1 | 54.6 | 55.9 | 58.0 |
| 2013 | 55.4 | 56.1 | 57.1 | 57.8 | 59.1 | 64.1 | 66.7 | 67.1 | 63.5 | 58.6 | 55.9 | 57.9 | 59.9 |
| 2014 | 56.8 | 56.8 | 57.1 | 58.0 | 59.6 | 64.3 | 67.1 | 67.6 | 63.7 | 58.6 | 56.1 | 58.4 | 60.3 |
| 2015 | 57.7 | 58.4 | 59.3 | 60.2 | 62.1 | 66.5 | 69.4 | 69.6 | 65.8 | 61.7 | 59.5 | 61.4 | 62.6 |
| 2016 | 59.9 | 60.5 | 61.0 | 62.6 | 64.0 | 68.5 | 71.3 | 71.1 | 67.4 | 63.1 | 60.9 | 62.5 | 64.4 |
| 2017 | 60.8 | 61.1 | 62.0 | 63.4 | 64.7 | 70.1 | 71.8 | 71.8 | 67.5 | 63.3 | 61.3 | 63.0 | 65.1 |
| 2018 | 61.9 | 62.3 | 63.0 | 63.7 | 65.7 | 71.3 | 73.0 | 72.8 | 68.4 | 64.3 | 62.3 | 64.4 | 66.1 |
| 2019 | 63.4 | 63.4 | 63.8 | 65.1 | 66.8 | 72.2 | 73.9 | 73.6 | 69.3 | 63.7 | 62.1 | 63.8 | 66.8 |
| **Other Services** | | | | | | | | | | | | | |
| 2011 | 16.4 | 16.5 | 16.7 | 16.8 | 17.0 | 17.1 | 17.2 | 17.0 | 17.0 | 17.0 | 16.9 | 17.1 | 16.9 |
| 2012 | 16.7 | 16.9 | 17.0 | 17.3 | 17.5 | 17.7 | 17.6 | 17.7 | 17.7 | 17.8 | 17.5 | 17.4 | 17.4 |
| 2013 | 17.2 | 17.4 | 17.5 | 17.6 | 17.8 | 17.9 | 17.8 | 17.9 | 17.7 | 17.9 | 17.9 | 17.9 | 17.7 |
| 2014 | 17.4 | 17.5 | 17.4 | 17.7 | 17.9 | 17.7 | 18.0 | 17.9 | 17.6 | 18.0 | 17.8 | 17.4 | 17.7 |
| 2015 | 17.7 | 17.8 | 17.9 | 18.0 | 18.1 | 18.2 | 18.2 | 18.1 | 18.0 | 18.2 | 18.2 | 18.2 | 18.1 |
| 2016 | 17.9 | 17.9 | 18.0 | 18.2 | 18.3 | 18.5 | 18.5 | 18.5 | 18.6 | 18.7 | 18.6 | 18.5 | 18.4 |
| 2017 | 18.1 | 18.3 | 18.4 | 18.5 | 18.7 | 18.8 | 18.6 | 18.7 | 18.6 | 18.6 | 18.6 | 18.7 | 18.6 |
| 2018 | 18.4 | 18.4 | 18.7 | 18.8 | 19.0 | 19.2 | 19.1 | 19.1 | 19.0 | 19.1 | 19.1 | 19.1 | 18.9 |
| 2019 | 18.7 | 18.8 | 18.8 | 19.1 | 19.3 | 19.6 | 19.5 | 19.4 | 19.1 | 19.4 | 19.0 | 19.0 | 19.1 |
| **Government** | | | | | | | | | | | | | |
| 2011 | 89.4 | 91.0 | 92.0 | 91.8 | 93.2 | 90.8 | 84.4 | 85.8 | 90.8 | 91.2 | 90.8 | 90.6 | 90.2 |
| 2012 | 88.7 | 89.6 | 90.4 | 90.3 | 92.4 | 89.1 | 86.2 | 85.6 | 90.3 | 91.0 | 91.0 | 90.5 | 89.6 |
| 2013 | 90.3 | 91.5 | 91.9 | 91.4 | 92.1 | 89.2 | 83.8 | 84.8 | 89.4 | 91.7 | 91.2 | 89.8 | 89.8 |
| 2014 | 88.1 | 91.4 | 91.7 | 91.3 | 92.1 | 89.7 | 85.6 | 85.5 | 90.3 | 91.7 | 91.8 | 90.9 | 90.0 |
| 2015 | 88.5 | 91.0 | 91.9 | 92.3 | 92.9 | 89.6 | 85.2 | 85.6 | 90.6 | 93.0 | 92.3 | 92.0 | 90.4 |
| 2016 | 88.8 | 90.9 | 92.1 | 92.4 | 93.8 | 91.7 | 85.7 | 86.5 | 91.5 | 93.0 | 93.0 | 92.4 | 91.0 |
| 2017 | 90.2 | 91.2 | 91.8 | 92.3 | 93.0 | 91.0 | 86.5 | 86.9 | 92.1 | 93.4 | 92.2 | 91.4 | 91.0 |
| 2018 | 89.7 | 90.4 | 90.9 | 91.2 | 92.4 | 90.3 | 86.1 | 86.3 | 91.0 | 92.2 | 92.0 | 91.2 | 90.3 |
| 2019 | 89.2 | 90.7 | 91.0 | 91.4 | 93.4 | 90.2 | 87.2 | 87.5 | 91.7 | 92.9 | 92.6 | 91.8 | 90.8 |

## 2. Average Weekly Hours by Selected Industry: Montana, 2015–2019

(Not seasonally adjusted)

| Industry and year | January | February | March | April | May | June | July | August | September | October | November | December | Annual average |
|---|---|---|---|---|---|---|---|---|---|---|---|---|---|
| **Total Private** | | | | | | | | | | | | | |
| 2015 | 32.2 | 32.9 | 32.6 | 32.2 | 32.6 | 32.8 | 33.0 | 33.6 | 32.7 | 32.6 | 33.1 | 32.3 | 32.7 |
| 2016 | 32.2 | 32.3 | 32.3 | 32.4 | 33.0 | 33.1 | 33.2 | 33.4 | 33.0 | 33.4 | 32.7 | 32.4 | 32.8 |
| 2017 | 32.7 | 32.2 | 32.3 | 33.1 | 32.8 | 33.4 | 33.8 | 33.6 | 33.1 | 33.5 | 32.7 | 32.6 | 33.0 |
| 2018 | 32.5 | 32.6 | 32.7 | 33.2 | 33.3 | 33.8 | 34.2 | 33.8 | 34.2 | 33.4 | 33.1 | 33.7 | 33.4 |
| 2019 | 32.8 | 33.0 | 33.0 | 33.2 | 33.3 | 34.3 | 33.7 | 33.7 | 33.9 | 33.2 | 33.1 | 33.7 | 33.4 |
| **Goods-Producing** | | | | | | | | | | | | | |
| 2015 | 36.6 | 37.2 | 37.2 | 37.5 | 38.5 | 38.8 | 38.3 | 38.5 | 37.0 | 37.5 | 37.9 | 37.9 | 37.7 |
| 2016 | 36.8 | 37.2 | 37.3 | 37.9 | 38.1 | 39.1 | 39.2 | 39.1 | 38.9 | 38.5 | 37.9 | 36.2 | 38.1 |
| 2017 | 35.8 | 36.2 | 35.9 | 37.4 | 37.7 | 38.5 | 38.1 | 38.1 | 37.5 | 38.3 | 36.6 | 37.0 | 37.3 |
| 2018 | 36.2 | 36.1 | 37.1 | 37.8 | 38.5 | 39.0 | 39.3 | 39.5 | 40.1 | 39.2 | 38.2 | 39.3 | 38.4 |
| 2019 | 37.8 | 37.9 | 37.7 | 37.7 | 38.2 | 39.1 | 37.3 | 37.9 | 37.5 | 37.7 | 37.7 | 37.4 | 37.8 |
| **Construction** | | | | | | | | | | | | | |
| 2015 | 36.5 | 36.9 | 37.3 | 37.8 | 39.4 | 39.1 | 38.3 | 38.6 | 36.9 | 37.6 | 37.4 | 38.0 | 37.8 |
| 2016 | 36.1 | 36.4 | 36.7 | 37.7 | 37.4 | 38.9 | 38.6 | 39.0 | 38.4 | 37.6 | 37.9 | 35.9 | 37.6 |
| 2017 | 34.8 | 36.1 | 36.1 | 37.3 | 38.2 | 40.0 | 39.2 | 38.5 | 37.8 | 38.7 | 35.9 | 36.3 | 37.5 |
| 2018 | 34.8 | 34.3 | 36.1 | 37.3 | 39.3 | 40.0 | 40.8 | 40.6 | 40.2 | 39.2 | 37.8 | 39.2 | 38.5 |
| 2019 | 37.3 | 37.6 | 37.8 | 37.7 | 39.4 | 40.9 | 38.8 | 39.9 | 38.4 | 38.5 | 37.9 | 37.8 | 38.6 |
| **Trade, Transportation, and Utilities** | | | | | | | | | | | | | |
| 2015 | 32.9 | 33.3 | 33.0 | 32.5 | 32.9 | 33.3 | 33.5 | 34.4 | 33.5 | 33.1 | 33.5 | 33.0 | 33.2 |
| 2016 | 32.7 | 32.7 | 32.4 | 32.4 | 33.0 | 32.9 | 33.0 | 33.1 | 32.7 | 33.0 | 32.3 | 32.6 | 32.7 |
| 2017 | 32.2 | 31.5 | 31.9 | 33.0 | 32.6 | 33.3 | 33.8 | 33.7 | 32.9 | 33.4 | 32.9 | 32.9 | 32.8 |
| 2018 | 32.4 | 32.2 | 32.3 | 32.8 | 33.0 | 33.8 | 34.6 | 33.9 | 34.0 | 32.9 | 32.9 | 33.2 | 33.2 |
| 2019 | 32.1 | 32.7 | 32.3 | 32.6 | 32.6 | 33.3 | 33.8 | 34.0 | 33.5 | 32.7 | 32.6 | 33.4 | 33.0 |
| **Financial Activities** | | | | | | | | | | | | | |
| 2015 | 35.4 | 36.2 | 36.2 | 35.0 | 35.4 | 35.1 | 35.6 | 36.4 | 35.7 | 35.6 | 36.9 | 35.3 | 35.7 |
| 2016 | 36.1 | 35.6 | 35.8 | 36.0 | 35.9 | 35.9 | 36.0 | 36.0 | 36.0 | 36.2 | 36.1 | 35.9 | 35.9 |
| 2017 | 36.5 | 36.5 | 36.4 | 37.5 | 36.6 | 36.6 | 36.6 | 36.2 | 36.7 | 36.3 | 36.6 | 36.6 | 36.6 |
| 2018 | 36.5 | 37.3 | 37.0 | 37.1 | 36.9 | 37.3 | 37.3 | 37.5 | 37.8 | 37.3 | 37.4 | 37.5 | 37.2 |
| 2019 | 37.3 | 38.1 | 37.7 | 37.7 | 37.5 | 38.4 | 37.5 | 37.1 | 37.6 | 36.6 | 37.1 | 38.2 | 37.6 |
| **Professional and Business Services** | | | | | | | | | | | | | |
| 2015 | 34.4 | 35.0 | 34.4 | 33.7 | 34.3 | 34.2 | 34.0 | 34.8 | 34.0 | 33.5 | 34.6 | 34.0 | 34.2 |
| 2016 | 34.5 | 34.9 | 35.7 | 35.3 | 36.2 | 35.9 | 35.0 | 35.6 | 34.8 | 35.9 | 35.1 | 34.6 | 35.3 |
| 2017 | 35.2 | 34.3 | 33.7 | 35.5 | 34.6 | 34.5 | 35.6 | 34.9 | 35.1 | 35.3 | 33.8 | 33.9 | 34.7 |
| 2018 | 34.3 | 35.0 | 34.7 | 35.6 | 35.6 | 36.1 | 35.6 | 35.4 | 36.3 | 35.5 | 34.8 | 35.4 | 35.4 |
| 2019 | 35.0 | 35.5 | 35.6 | 35.8 | 35.4 | 37.3 | 36.1 | 35.6 | 35.9 | 34.7 | 34.9 | 35.2 | 35.6 |
| **Education and Health Services** | | | | | | | | | | | | | |
| 2015 | 33.5 | 34.1 | 34.0 | 33.7 | 33.6 | 33.6 | 33.8 | 34.0 | 33.8 | 33.7 | 34.0 | 33.6 | 33.8 |
| 2016 | 33.3 | 33.3 | 33.3 | 33.6 | 33.7 | 33.7 | 33.6 | 34.2 | 34.1 | 34.6 | 34.2 | 34.1 | 33.8 |
| 2017 | 34.8 | 34.4 | 34.6 | 35.0 | 34.3 | 34.4 | 34.9 | 34.3 | 34.2 | 34.7 | 34.4 | 33.9 | 34.5 |
| 2018 | 34.0 | 34.4 | 34.1 | 34.4 | 34.0 | 33.5 | 33.8 | 33.6 | 34.1 | 33.8 | 34.0 | 34.8 | 34.0 |
| 2019 | 33.7 | 33.7 | 34.0 | 34.3 | 34.5 | 35.2 | 34.5 | 34.9 | 35.2 | 35.4 | 35.2 | 35.5 | 34.7 |
| **Leisure and Hospitality** | | | | | | | | | | | | | |
| 2015 | 22.4 | 23.7 | 23.3 | 22.4 | 23.3 | 24.0 | 25.3 | 25.8 | 23.9 | 23.3 | 23.5 | 22.4 | 23.7 |
| 2016 | 22.6 | 22.5 | 22.6 | 22.6 | 24.3 | 24.8 | 25.7 | 25.4 | 24.2 | 24.5 | 22.8 | 22.8 | 23.8 |
| 2017 | 23.7 | 23.3 | 23.6 | 23.2 | 23.1 | 24.2 | 25.7 | 25.3 | 23.8 | 24.2 | 22.8 | 22.9 | 23.8 |
| 2018 | 22.7 | 22.8 | 23.3 | 23.3 | 23.3 | 24.8 | 26.0 | 25.3 | 25.0 | 23.2 | 22.8 | 24.0 | 23.9 |
| 2019 | 23.1 | 23.0 | 23.5 | 23.0 | 23.8 | 25.7 | 25.8 | 25.7 | 25.3 | 23.7 | 23.0 | 23.9 | 24.2 |

## 3. Average Hourly Earnings by Selected Industry: Montana, 2015–2019

(Dollars, not seasonally adjusted)

| Industry and year | January | February | March | April | May | June | July | August | September | October | November | December | Annual average |
|---|---|---|---|---|---|---|---|---|---|---|---|---|---|
| **Total Private** | | | | | | | | | | | | | |
| 2015 | 21.60 | 21.65 | 21.51 | 21.55 | 21.63 | 21.55 | 21.46 | 21.68 | 21.75 | 21.88 | 22.05 | 21.79 | 21.67 |
| 2016 | 21.54 | 21.50 | 21.36 | 21.82 | 21.92 | 21.67 | 21.95 | 21.90 | 22.37 | 22.63 | 22.41 | 22.32 | 21.96 |
| 2017 | 22.69 | 22.42 | 22.35 | 22.77 | 22.71 | 22.49 | 22.82 | 22.61 | 23.10 | 23.31 | 23.31 | 23.33 | 22.83 |
| 2018 | 23.34 | 23.45 | 23.53 | 23.72 | 23.67 | 23.50 | 23.59 | 23.64 | 24.03 | 23.87 | 23.94 | 24.10 | 23.70 |
| 2019 | 24.19 | 23.99 | 23.95 | 24.30 | 24.15 | 24.35 | 24.29 | 24.23 | 24.76 | 24.61 | 24.78 | 24.72 | 24.36 |
| **Goods-Producing** | | | | | | | | | | | | | |
| 2015 | 24.16 | 24.14 | 24.18 | 24.56 | 24.83 | 24.60 | 24.24 | 24.65 | 25.10 | 24.80 | 24.75 | 23.92 | 24.50 |
| 2016 | 23.89 | 23.74 | 23.57 | 24.04 | 24.20 | 24.49 | 24.29 | 24.17 | 24.54 | 24.43 | 24.47 | 24.33 | 24.20 |
| 2017 | 24.43 | 24.34 | 24.36 | 24.37 | 24.42 | 24.59 | 24.93 | 24.88 | 25.25 | 25.61 | 25.88 | 26.05 | 24.94 |
| 2018 | 25.99 | 26.27 | 26.43 | 26.70 | 26.93 | 27.02 | 26.70 | 26.73 | 27.42 | 27.47 | 27.61 | 28.20 | 26.99 |
| 2019 | 28.26 | 28.46 | 28.33 | 28.07 | 27.46 | 27.84 | 27.99 | 27.82 | 28.29 | 28.10 | 28.38 | 28.33 | 28.10 |
| **Construction** | | | | | | | | | | | | | |
| 2015 | 24.81 | 24.78 | 24.64 | 24.97 | 25.27 | 24.99 | 24.44 | 24.52 | 24.75 | 24.79 | 24.71 | 24.76 | 24.79 |
| 2016 | 24.48 | 24.40 | 23.82 | 24.36 | 24.44 | 24.70 | 24.18 | 24.26 | 24.47 | 24.50 | 24.12 | 24.48 | 24.35 |
| 2017 | 24.39 | 24.86 | 24.63 | 24.60 | 24.97 | 25.33 | 25.22 | 24.99 | 25.54 | 26.02 | 25.80 | 25.92 | 25.22 |
| 2018 | 25.67 | 26.06 | 26.53 | 26.70 | 27.07 | 27.18 | 26.49 | 26.57 | 27.28 | 27.41 | 27.61 | 28.77 | 27.01 |
| 2019 | 28.68 | 29.46 | 29.26 | 28.62 | 28.53 | 28.38 | 28.69 | 28.31 | 28.90 | 28.65 | 28.69 | 28.62 | 28.71 |
| **Trade, Transportation, and Utilities** | | | | | | | | | | | | | |
| 2015 | 19.97 | 19.88 | 19.71 | 19.78 | 19.63 | 19.83 | 20.02 | 19.96 | 20.12 | 20.01 | 20.03 | 19.81 | 19.90 |
| 2016 | 20.15 | 20.08 | 19.98 | 20.38 | 20.54 | 20.37 | 20.67 | 20.29 | 20.53 | 20.29 | 19.81 | 19.55 | 20.22 |
| 2017 | 20.13 | 20.24 | 20.05 | 20.57 | 20.56 | 20.39 | 20.71 | 20.49 | 20.91 | 20.88 | 20.60 | 20.56 | 20.51 |
| 2018 | 20.95 | 21.11 | 20.97 | 21.24 | 21.06 | 21.13 | 21.02 | 21.21 | 21.39 | 20.89 | 20.65 | 20.44 | 21.01 |
| 2019 | 20.67 | 20.61 | 20.50 | 20.51 | 20.17 | 20.31 | 20.23 | 20.77 | 21.05 | 20.99 | 20.99 | 20.92 | 20.64 |
| **Financial Activities** | | | | | | | | | | | | | |
| 2015 | 24.40 | 24.46 | 24.90 | 24.41 | 24.53 | 24.56 | 24.51 | 25.28 | 25.07 | 25.20 | 25.54 | 25.29 | 24.85 |
| 2016 | 24.77 | 25.12 | 25.40 | 25.25 | 25.47 | 24.81 | 25.38 | 25.12 | 25.44 | 25.93 | 25.77 | 25.77 | 25.35 |
| 2017 | 26.34 | 24.78 | 24.82 | 25.30 | 24.89 | 24.80 | 24.99 | 24.87 | 25.26 | 25.25 | 25.11 | 25.27 | 25.14 |
| 2018 | 25.32 | 25.27 | 25.44 | 25.28 | 25.03 | 24.48 | 24.92 | 25.11 | 25.35 | 24.98 | 24.98 | 25.40 | 25.13 |
| 2019 | 25.14 | 24.30 | 24.40 | 24.97 | 24.94 | 25.84 | 25.74 | 25.75 | 26.35 | 25.67 | 26.05 | 26.55 | 25.48 |
| **Professional and Business Services** | | | | | | | | | | | | | |
| 2015 | 23.69 | 24.01 | 23.82 | 23.32 | 23.22 | 23.00 | 23.22 | 23.19 | 23.52 | 24.31 | 24.24 | 24.46 | 23.66 |
| 2016 | 24.23 | 23.94 | 24.09 | 24.39 | 24.76 | 23.85 | 24.01 | 24.00 | 24.57 | 25.16 | 25.10 | 25.48 | 24.46 |
| 2017 | 25.59 | 25.34 | 25.58 | 25.88 | 25.74 | 25.69 | 25.83 | 25.48 | 26.21 | 26.20 | 26.93 | 26.99 | 25.95 |
| 2018 | 26.71 | 26.82 | 26.71 | 26.82 | 26.33 | 25.85 | 26.10 | 25.91 | 26.84 | 25.97 | 26.47 | 26.91 | 26.44 |
| 2019 | 27.07 | 26.83 | 27.23 | 27.58 | 27.85 | 28.21 | 27.98 | 27.82 | 28.66 | 27.91 | 28.11 | 28.88 | 27.86 |
| **Education and Health Services** | | | | | | | | | | | | | |
| 2015 | 22.66 | 23.04 | 22.30 | 21.98 | 22.43 | 22.64 | 22.75 | 23.35 | 22.43 | 22.49 | 22.91 | 22.69 | 22.64 |
| 2016 | 22.57 | 23.07 | 22.23 | 22.71 | 22.54 | 22.45 | 23.46 | 23.89 | 24.05 | 24.33 | 24.02 | 24.03 | 23.29 |
| 2017 | 24.14 | 23.73 | 23.64 | 24.52 | 24.70 | 24.53 | 25.63 | 25.05 | 25.24 | 25.50 | 25.46 | 25.63 | 24.81 |
| 2018 | 25.40 | 25.13 | 25.33 | 25.46 | 25.12 | 25.46 | 26.26 | 26.06 | 25.91 | 25.82 | 26.00 | 26.11 | 25.67 |
| 2019 | 26.74 | 26.40 | 26.12 | 26.55 | 26.60 | 26.35 | 26.76 | 26.40 | 26.64 | 26.91 | 27.02 | 26.63 | 26.60 |
| **Leisure and Hospitality** | | | | | | | | | | | | | |
| 2015 | 12.76 | 12.97 | 12.95 | 13.05 | 13.09 | 12.97 | 13.01 | 13.13 | 13.22 | 13.28 | 13.31 | 13.34 | 13.09 |
| 2016 | 13.45 | 13.66 | 13.49 | 13.71 | 13.71 | 13.60 | 13.85 | 13.73 | 13.81 | 13.94 | 13.82 | 13.99 | 13.73 |
| 2017 | 14.10 | 14.07 | 14.02 | 14.17 | 14.07 | 13.76 | 13.96 | 13.94 | 14.11 | 14.43 | 14.13 | 14.37 | 14.09 |
| 2018 | 14.34 | 14.43 | 14.56 | 14.76 | 14.67 | 14.59 | 14.62 | 14.67 | 15.02 | 15.16 | 15.04 | 15.17 | 14.75 |
| 2019 | 15.07 | 14.85 | 15.10 | 15.01 | 14.96 | 14.72 | 14.66 | 14.65 | 15.27 | 15.15 | 15.25 | 15.20 | 14.98 |

# 4. Average Weekly Earnings by Selected Industry: Montana, 2015–2019

(Dollars, not seasonally adjusted)

| Industry and year | January | February | March | April | May | June | July | August | September | October | November | December | Annual average |
|---|---|---|---|---|---|---|---|---|---|---|---|---|---|
| **Total Private** | | | | | | | | | | | | | |
| 2015 | 695.52 | 712.29 | 701.23 | 693.91 | 705.14 | 706.84 | 708.18 | 728.45 | 711.23 | 713.29 | 729.86 | 703.82 | 708.61 |
| 2016 | 693.59 | 694.45 | 689.93 | 706.97 | 723.36 | 717.28 | 728.74 | 731.46 | 738.21 | 755.84 | 732.81 | 723.17 | 720.29 |
| 2017 | 741.96 | 721.92 | 721.91 | 753.69 | 744.89 | 751.17 | 771.32 | 759.70 | 764.61 | 780.89 | 762.24 | 760.56 | 753.39 |
| 2018 | 758.55 | 764.47 | 769.43 | 787.50 | 788.21 | 791.95 | 806.78 | 799.03 | 821.83 | 797.26 | 792.41 | 812.17 | 791.58 |
| 2019 | 793.43 | 791.67 | 790.35 | 806.76 | 804.20 | 835.21 | 818.57 | 816.55 | 839.36 | 817.05 | 820.22 | 833.06 | 813.62 |
| **Goods-Producing** | | | | | | | | | | | | | |
| 2015 | 884.26 | 898.01 | 899.50 | 921.00 | 955.96 | 954.48 | 928.39 | 949.03 | 928.70 | 930.00 | 938.03 | 906.57 | 923.65 |
| 2016 | 879.15 | 883.13 | 879.16 | 911.12 | 922.02 | 957.56 | 952.17 | 945.05 | 954.61 | 940.56 | 927.41 | 880.75 | 922.02 |
| 2017 | 874.59 | 881.11 | 874.52 | 911.44 | 920.63 | 946.72 | 949.83 | 947.93 | 946.88 | 980.86 | 947.21 | 963.85 | 930.26 |
| 2018 | 940.84 | 948.35 | 980.55 | 1,009.26 | 1,036.81 | 1,053.39 | 1,049.31 | 1,055.84 | 1,099.54 | 1,076.82 | 1,054.70 | 1,108.26 | 1,036.42 |
| 2019 | 1,068.23 | 1,078.63 | 1,068.04 | 1,058.24 | 1,048.97 | 1,088.54 | 1,044.03 | 1,054.38 | 1,060.88 | 1,059.37 | 1,069.93 | 1,059.54 | 1,062.18 |
| **Construction** | | | | | | | | | | | | | |
| 2015 | 905.57 | 914.38 | 919.07 | 943.87 | 995.64 | 977.11 | 936.05 | 946.47 | 913.28 | 932.10 | 924.15 | 940.88 | 937.06 |
| 2016 | 883.74 | 888.16 | 874.19 | 918.37 | 914.06 | 960.83 | 933.35 | 946.14 | 939.65 | 921.20 | 914.15 | 878.83 | 915.56 |
| 2017 | 848.77 | 897.45 | 889.14 | 917.58 | 953.85 | 1,013.20 | 988.62 | 962.12 | 965.41 | 1,006.97 | 926.22 | 940.90 | 945.75 |
| 2018 | 893.32 | 893.86 | 957.73 | 995.91 | 1,063.85 | 1,087.20 | 1,080.79 | 1,078.74 | 1,096.66 | 1,074.47 | 1,043.66 | 1,127.78 | 1,039.89 |
| 2019 | 1,069.76 | 1,107.70 | 1,106.03 | 1,078.97 | 1,124.08 | 1,160.74 | 1,113.17 | 1,129.57 | 1,109.76 | 1,103.03 | 1,087.35 | 1,081.84 | 1,108.21 |
| **Trade, Transportation, and Utilities** | | | | | | | | | | | | | |
| 2015 | 657.01 | 662.00 | 650.43 | 642.85 | 645.83 | 660.34 | 670.67 | 686.62 | 674.02 | 662.33 | 671.01 | 653.73 | 660.68 |
| 2016 | 658.91 | 656.62 | 647.35 | 660.31 | 677.82 | 670.17 | 682.11 | 671.60 | 671.33 | 669.57 | 639.86 | 637.33 | 661.19 |
| 2017 | 648.19 | 637.56 | 639.60 | 678.81 | 670.26 | 678.99 | 700.00 | 690.51 | 687.94 | 697.39 | 677.74 | 676.42 | 672.73 |
| 2018 | 678.78 | 679.74 | 677.33 | 696.67 | 694.98 | 714.19 | 727.29 | 719.02 | 727.26 | 687.28 | 679.39 | 678.61 | 697.53 |
| 2019 | 663.51 | 673.95 | 662.15 | 668.63 | 657.54 | 676.32 | 683.77 | 706.18 | 705.18 | 686.37 | 684.27 | 698.73 | 681.12 |
| **Financial Activities** | | | | | | | | | | | | | |
| 2015 | 863.76 | 885.45 | 901.38 | 854.35 | 868.36 | 862.06 | 872.56 | 920.19 | 895.00 | 897.12 | 942.43 | 892.74 | 887.15 |
| 2016 | 894.20 | 894.27 | 909.32 | 909.00 | 914.37 | 890.68 | 913.68 | 904.32 | 915.84 | 938.67 | 930.30 | 925.14 | 910.07 |
| 2017 | 961.41 | 904.47 | 903.45 | 948.75 | 910.97 | 907.68 | 914.63 | 900.29 | 927.04 | 916.58 | 919.03 | 924.88 | 920.12 |
| 2018 | 924.18 | 942.57 | 941.28 | 937.89 | 923.61 | 913.10 | 929.52 | 941.63 | 958.23 | 931.75 | 934.25 | 952.50 | 934.84 |
| 2019 | 937.72 | 925.83 | 919.88 | 941.37 | 935.25 | 992.26 | 965.25 | 955.33 | 990.76 | 939.52 | 966.46 | 1,014.21 | 958.05 |
| **Professional and Business Services** | | | | | | | | | | | | | |
| 2015 | 814.94 | 840.35 | 819.41 | 785.88 | 796.45 | 786.60 | 789.48 | 807.01 | 799.68 | 814.39 | 838.70 | 831.64 | 809.17 |
| 2016 | 835.94 | 835.51 | 860.01 | 860.97 | 896.31 | 856.22 | 840.35 | 854.40 | 855.04 | 903.24 | 881.01 | 881.61 | 863.44 |
| 2017 | 900.77 | 869.16 | 862.05 | 918.74 | 890.60 | 886.31 | 919.55 | 889.25 | 919.97 | 924.86 | 909.90 | 914.96 | 900.47 |
| 2018 | 916.15 | 938.70 | 926.84 | 954.79 | 937.35 | 933.19 | 929.16 | 917.21 | 974.29 | 921.94 | 921.16 | 952.61 | 935.98 |
| 2019 | 947.45 | 952.47 | 969.39 | 987.36 | 985.89 | 1,052.23 | 1,010.08 | 990.39 | 1,028.89 | 968.48 | 981.04 | 1,016.58 | 991.82 |
| **Education and Health Services** | | | | | | | | | | | | | |
| 2015 | 759.11 | 785.66 | 758.20 | 740.73 | 753.65 | 760.70 | 768.95 | 793.90 | 758.13 | 757.91 | 778.94 | 762.38 | 765.23 |
| 2016 | 751.58 | 768.23 | 740.26 | 763.06 | 759.60 | 756.57 | 788.26 | 817.04 | 820.11 | 841.82 | 821.48 | 819.42 | 787.20 |
| 2017 | 840.07 | 816.31 | 817.94 | 858.20 | 847.21 | 843.83 | 894.49 | 859.22 | 863.21 | 884.85 | 875.82 | 868.86 | 855.95 |
| 2018 | 863.60 | 864.47 | 863.75 | 875.82 | 854.08 | 852.91 | 887.59 | 875.62 | 883.53 | 872.72 | 884.00 | 908.63 | 872.78 |
| 2019 | 901.14 | 889.68 | 888.08 | 910.67 | 917.70 | 927.52 | 923.22 | 921.36 | 937.73 | 952.61 | 951.10 | 945.37 | 923.02 |
| **Leisure and Hospitality** | | | | | | | | | | | | | |
| 2015 | 285.82 | 307.39 | 301.74 | 292.32 | 305 | 311.28 | 329.41 | 339.01 | 315.96 | 309.42 | 312.79 | 298.82 | 310.23 |
| 2016 | 303.97 | 307.35 | 304.87 | 309.85 | 333.15 | 337.28 | 355.95 | 348.74 | 334.2 | 341.53 | 315.1 | 318.97 | 326.77 |
| 2017 | 334.17 | 327.83 | 330.87 | 328.74 | 325.02 | 332.99 | 359.03 | 352.68 | 335.82 | 349.21 | 322.16 | 329.07 | 335.34 |
| 2018 | 325.52 | 329 | 339.25 | 343.91 | 341.81 | 361.83 | 380.12 | 371.15 | 375.5 | 351.71 | 342.91 | 364.08 | 352.53 |
| 2019 | 348.12 | 341.55 | 354.85 | 345.23 | 356.05 | 378.3 | 378.23 | 376.51 | 386.33 | 359.06 | 350.75 | 363.28 | 362.52 |

# NEBRASKA
## *At a Glance*

Population:
  2010 census: 1,826,341
  2019 estimate: 1,934,408

Percent change in population:
  2010–2019: 5.9%

Percent change in total nonfarm employment:
  2011–2019: 7.8%

Industry with the largest growth in employment, 2011–2019 (percent):
  Construction, 32.1%

Industry with the largest decline or smallest growth in employment, 2011–2019 (percent):
  Information, -2.3%

Civilian labor force:
  2010: 993,398
  2019: 1,035,240

Unemployment rate and rank among states (highest to lowest):
  2010: 4.6%, 50th
  2019: 3.0%, 38th

Over-the-year change in unemployment rates:
  2017–2018: 0.0%
  2018–2019: 0.1%

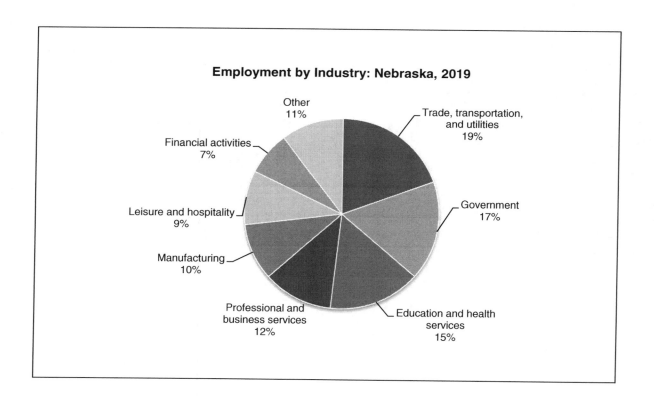

**Employment by Industry: Nebraska, 2019**

- Other 11%
- Trade, transportation, and utilities 19%
- Financial activities 7%
- Government 17%
- Leisure and hospitality 9%
- Manufacturing 10%
- Professional and business services 12%
- Education and health services 15%

# 1. Employment by Industry: Nebraska, 2011–2019

(Numbers in thousands, not seasonally adjusted)

| Industry and year | January | February | March | April | May | June | July | August | September | October | November | December | Annual average |
|---|---|---|---|---|---|---|---|---|---|---|---|---|---|
| **Total Nonfarm** | | | | | | | | | | | | | |
| 2011 | 928.5 | 931.8 | 939.1 | 953.6 | 960.7 | 959.9 | 950.4 | 952.9 | 957.5 | 964.5 | 966.9 | 965.7 | 952.6 |
| 2012 | 945.0 | 947.7 | 957.6 | 967.4 | 977.9 | 976.8 | 967.0 | 969.3 | 973.5 | 979.2 | 981.4 | 981.5 | 968.7 |
| 2013 | 955.6 | 959.6 | 965.7 | 975.8 | 989.2 | 987.5 | 978.2 | 982.6 | 986.4 | 993.1 | 995.6 | 994.7 | 980.3 |
| 2014 | 970.8 | 975.7 | 981.4 | 991.9 | 1,002.7 | 1,000.2 | 989.8 | 992.6 | 996.6 | 1,002.8 | 1,002.9 | 1,005.7 | 992.8 |
| 2015 | 980.6 | 985.9 | 992.9 | 1,005.3 | 1,013.9 | 1,014.2 | 1,006.3 | 1,009.2 | 1,011.9 | 1,018.7 | 1,018.9 | 1,020.4 | 1,006.5 |
| 2016 | 992.5 | 996.1 | 1,006.0 | 1,015.8 | 1,024.4 | 1,023.0 | 1,015.7 | 1,016.0 | 1,022.5 | 1,024.9 | 1,023.8 | 1,020.3 | 1,015.1 |
| 2017 | 998.2 | 1,004.2 | 1,010.7 | 1,019.3 | 1,026.4 | 1,027.9 | 1,016.3 | 1,018.6 | 1,020.5 | 1,026.4 | 1,028.4 | 1,028.6 | 1,018.8 |
| 2018 | 1,002.5 | 1,007.1 | 1,013.8 | 1,021.6 | 1,033.4 | 1,034.2 | 1,025.2 | 1,025.3 | 1,028.0 | 1,030.4 | 1,034.2 | 1,030.4 | 1,023.8 |
| 2019 | 1,009.9 | 1,010.3 | 1,012.5 | 1,024.6 | 1,036.0 | 1,034.9 | 1,026.5 | 1,028.6 | 1,029.8 | 1,036.5 | 1,037.6 | 1,037.5 | 1,027.1 |
| **Total Private** | | | | | | | | | | | | | |
| 2010 | 761.3 | 762.3 | 769.3 | 782.2 | 788.5 | 791.8 | 791.3 | 792.1 | 790.9 | 793.2 | 795.5 | 795.1 | 784.5 |
| 2011 | 777.8 | 778.0 | 787.7 | 796.5 | 804.4 | 809.8 | 807.2 | 807.9 | 805.3 | 808.1 | 809.9 | 810.8 | 800.3 |
| 2012 | 788.5 | 790.2 | 796.1 | 805.1 | 815.1 | 818.8 | 817.7 | 821.0 | 818.0 | 820.7 | 823.1 | 823.3 | 811.5 |
| 2013 | 802.8 | 804.8 | 810.5 | 820.7 | 828.3 | 831.6 | 829.5 | 830.8 | 826.3 | 829.5 | 829.6 | 833.2 | 823.1 |
| 2014 | 812.5 | 814.8 | 821.2 | 831.5 | 838.8 | 843.7 | 843.6 | 844.9 | 841.2 | 843.5 | 844.0 | 846.1 | 835.5 |
| 2015 | 822.3 | 823.5 | 832.0 | 840.7 | 846.9 | 849.3 | 850.7 | 851.7 | 848.1 | 848.3 | 847.1 | 844.8 | 842.1 |
| 2016 | 826.5 | 830.5 | 836.3 | 844.2 | 849.6 | 853.0 | 851.2 | 852.3 | 847.5 | 850.7 | 852.8 | 853.7 | 845.7 |
| 2017 | 830.9 | 833.8 | 839.4 | 846.6 | 855.8 | 859.6 | 859.3 | 859.1 | 854.4 | 854.7 | 858.4 | 855.6 | 850.6 |
| 2018 | 837.4 | 836.8 | 839.0 | 849.5 | 858.2 | 860.4 | 860.7 | 861.6 | 856.2 | 859.8 | 860.2 | 861.6 | 853.5 |
| 2019 | | | | | | | | | | | | | |
| **Goods Producing** | | | | | | | | | | | | | |
| 2011 | 128.7 | 128.4 | 130.7 | 134.1 | 136.0 | 137.8 | 138.1 | 137.4 | 137.0 | 137.1 | 137.3 | 135.9 | 134.9 |
| 2012 | 132.5 | 131.6 | 134.1 | 136.5 | 139.1 | 141.4 | 141.3 | 141.4 | 140.8 | 140.9 | 140.5 | 139.7 | 138.3 |
| 2013 | 134.8 | 135.5 | 136.7 | 139.9 | 143.2 | 145.2 | 145.4 | 145.7 | 145.0 | 144.4 | 143.9 | 141.6 | 141.8 |
| 2014 | 138.1 | 138.1 | 139.6 | 144.3 | 146.1 | 148.2 | 148.6 | 148.6 | 147.3 | 147.6 | 146.1 | 145.7 | 144.9 |
| 2015 | 141.0 | 141.7 | 143.8 | 147.2 | 148.8 | 150.2 | 150.6 | 150.6 | 149.6 | 149.6 | 148.7 | 147.5 | 147.4 |
| 2016 | 143.0 | 142.8 | 145.7 | 148.0 | 149.7 | 151.5 | 151.8 | 151.7 | 150.7 | 150.5 | 149.4 | 147.4 | 148.5 |
| 2017 | 143.8 | 145.0 | 147.0 | 149.6 | 151.3 | 153.1 | 153.1 | 153.1 | 152.0 | 152.6 | 152.4 | 151.9 | 150.4 |
| 2018 | 146.5 | 146.8 | 149.0 | 152.0 | 154.0 | 156.1 | 157.5 | 157.4 | 155.7 | 154.8 | 154.8 | 153.0 | 153.1 |
| 2019 | 149.1 | 148.8 | 149.3 | 153.2 | 155.4 | 157.2 | 157.9 | 157.6 | 156.8 | 157.0 | 155.7 | 153.2 | 154.3 |
| **Service-Providing** | | | | | | | | | | | | | |
| 2011 | 799.8 | 803.4 | 808.4 | 819.5 | 824.7 | 822.1 | 812.3 | 815.5 | 820.5 | 827.4 | 829.6 | 829.8 | 817.8 |
| 2012 | 812.5 | 816.1 | 823.5 | 830.9 | 838.8 | 835.4 | 825.7 | 827.9 | 832.7 | 838.3 | 840.9 | 841.8 | 830.4 |
| 2013 | 820.8 | 824.1 | 829.0 | 835.9 | 846.0 | 842.3 | 832.8 | 836.9 | 841.4 | 848.7 | 851.7 | 853.1 | 838.6 |
| 2014 | 832.7 | 837.6 | 841.8 | 847.6 | 856.6 | 852.0 | 841.2 | 844.0 | 849.3 | 855.2 | 856.8 | 860.0 | 847.9 |
| 2015 | 839.6 | 844.2 | 849.1 | 858.1 | 865.1 | 864.0 | 855.7 | 858.6 | 862.3 | 869.1 | 870.2 | 872.9 | 859.1 |
| 2016 | 849.5 | 853.3 | 860.3 | 867.8 | 874.7 | 871.5 | 863.9 | 864.3 | 871.8 | 874.4 | 874.4 | 872.9 | 866.6 |
| 2017 | 854.4 | 859.2 | 863.7 | 869.7 | 875.1 | 874.8 | 863.2 | 865.5 | 868.5 | 873.8 | 876.0 | 876.7 | 868.4 |
| 2018 | 856.0 | 860.3 | 864.8 | 869.6 | 879.4 | 878.1 | 867.7 | 867.9 | 872.3 | 875.6 | 879.4 | 877.4 | 870.7 |
| 2019 | 860.8 | 861.5 | 863.2 | 871.4 | 880.6 | 877.7 | 868.6 | 871.0 | 873.0 | 879.5 | 881.9 | 884.3 | 872.8 |
| **Mining and Logging** | | | | | | | | | | | | | |
| 2011 | 0.9 | 0.9 | 0.9 | 1.0 | 1.1 | 1.1 | 1.1 | 1.1 | 1.1 | 1.1 | 1.1 | 1.0 | 1.0 |
| 2012 | 1.0 | 1.0 | 1.1 | 1.1 | 1.2 | 1.2 | 1.2 | 1.4 | 1.2 | 1.2 | 1.1 | 1.1 | 1.2 |
| 2013 | 0.9 | 1.0 | 1.0 | 1.1 | 1.1 | 1.1 | 1.1 | 1.1 | 1.1 | 1.1 | 1.1 | 1.0 | 1.1 |
| 2014 | 1.1 | 1.0 | 1.1 | 1.2 | 1.2 | 1.2 | 1.2 | 1.2 | 1.1 | 1.2 | 1.2 | 1.1 | 1.2 |
| 2015 | 1.0 | 1.0 | 1.1 | 1.2 | 1.1 | 1.1 | 1.1 | 1.1 | 1.1 | 1.1 | 1.0 | 1.0 | 1.1 |
| 2016 | 0.9 | 0.9 | 1.0 | 1.0 | 1.0 | 1.0 | 1.0 | 1.0 | 1.0 | 1.0 | 1.0 | 1.0 | 1.0 |
| 2017 | 0.9 | 0.9 | 1.0 | 1.1 | 1.1 | 1.1 | 1.1 | 1.1 | 1.1 | 1.1 | 1.1 | 1.1 | 1.1 |
| 2018 | 1.0 | 1.0 | 1.0 | 1.1 | 1.1 | 1.2 | 1.2 | 1.2 | 1.1 | 1.1 | 1.1 | 1.0 | 1.1 |
| 2019 | 1.0 | 1.0 | 1.0 | 1.1 | 1.1 | 1.1 | 1.1 | 1.1 | 1.1 | 1.0 | 1.0 | 0.9 | 1.0 |
| **Construction** | | | | | | | | | | | | | |
| 2011 | 36.0 | 35.6 | 37.4 | 40.2 | 41.6 | 42.9 | 43.1 | 42.8 | 42.3 | 42.2 | 41.5 | 39.9 | 40.5 |
| 2012 | 37.7 | 36.9 | 38.9 | 41.3 | 43.2 | 44.6 | 44.4 | 44.6 | 44.1 | 44.5 | 43.6 | 42.5 | 42.2 |
| 2013 | 38.8 | 38.9 | 39.9 | 42.8 | 45.6 | 47.1 | 47.7 | 47.7 | 47.0 | 46.3 | 45.4 | 43.3 | 44.2 |
| 2014 | 40.4 | 40.1 | 41.7 | 45.8 | 47.6 | 49.2 | 49.7 | 49.3 | 48.5 | 48.9 | 47.2 | 46.6 | 46.3 |
| 2015 | 42.9 | 43.3 | 45.1 | 48.6 | 50.3 | 51.6 | 52.2 | 51.9 | 51.2 | 51.2 | 50.3 | 49.0 | 49.0 |
| 2016 | 45.4 | 45.3 | 47.7 | 50.4 | 51.9 | 53.6 | 53.7 | 53.5 | 52.8 | 52.5 | 51.3 | 49.0 | 50.6 |
| 2017 | 46.1 | 46.8 | 48.5 | 50.9 | 52.2 | 53.7 | 53.7 | 53.5 | 52.7 | 52.7 | 52.0 | 51.0 | 51.2 |
| 2018 | 47.1 | 46.8 | 48.7 | 51.7 | 53.5 | 55.2 | 55.8 | 55.6 | 54.4 | 54.1 | 53.5 | 51.8 | 52.4 |
| 2019 | 48.8 | 48.1 | 48.4 | 52.8 | 54.8 | 56.3 | 56.8 | 56.6 | 56.1 | 56.3 | 54.9 | 52.5 | 53.5 |

## 1. Employment by Industry: Nebraska, 2011–2019—*Continued*

(Numbers in thousands, not seasonally adjusted)

| Industry and year | January | February | March | April | May | June | July | August | September | October | November | December | Annual average |
|---|---|---|---|---|---|---|---|---|---|---|---|---|---|
| **Manufacturing** | | | | | | | | | | | | | |
| 2011 | 91.8 | 91.9 | 92.4 | 92.9 | 93.3 | 93.8 | 93.9 | 93.5 | 93.6 | 93.8 | 94.7 | 95.0 | 93.4 |
| 2012 | 93.8 | 93.7 | 94.1 | 94.1 | 94.7 | 95.6 | 95.7 | 95.4 | 95.5 | 95.2 | 95.8 | 96.1 | 95.0 |
| 2013 | 95.1 | 95.6 | 95.8 | 96.0 | 96.5 | 97.0 | 96.6 | 96.9 | 96.9 | 97.0 | 97.4 | 97.3 | 96.5 |
| 2014 | 96.6 | 97.0 | 96.8 | 97.3 | 97.3 | 97.8 | 97.7 | 98.1 | 97.7 | 97.5 | 97.7 | 98.0 | 97.5 |
| 2015 | 97.1 | 97.4 | 97.6 | 97.4 | 97.4 | 97.5 | 97.3 | 97.6 | 97.3 | 97.3 | 97.4 | 97.5 | 97.4 |
| 2016 | 96.7 | 96.6 | 97.0 | 96.6 | 96.8 | 96.9 | 97.1 | 97.2 | 96.9 | 97.0 | 97.1 | 97.4 | 96.9 |
| 2017 | 96.8 | 97.3 | 97.5 | 97.6 | 98.0 | 98.3 | 98.3 | 98.5 | 98.2 | 98.8 | 99.3 | 99.8 | 98.2 |
| 2018 | 98.4 | 99.0 | 99.3 | 99.2 | 99.4 | 99.7 | 100.5 | 100.6 | 100.2 | 99.6 | 100.2 | 100.2 | 99.7 |
| 2019 | 99.3 | 99.7 | 99.9 | 99.3 | 99.5 | 99.8 | 100.0 | 99.9 | 99.6 | 99.7 | 99.8 | 99.8 | 99.7 |
| **Trade, Transportation, and Utilities** | | | | | | | | | | | | | |
| 2011 | 193.6 | 192.5 | 193.6 | 196.2 | 197.3 | 197.6 | 197.4 | 198.2 | 197.9 | 199.1 | 203.0 | 204.6 | 197.6 |
| 2012 | 197.0 | 195.0 | 196.2 | 198.2 | 199.8 | 199.9 | 199.1 | 198.6 | 198.6 | 200.4 | 204.5 | 206.5 | 199.5 |
| 2013 | 197.8 | 196.1 | 197.1 | 198.4 | 200.8 | 201.4 | 200.8 | 201.3 | 200.5 | 202.1 | 206.4 | 209.3 | 201.0 |
| 2014 | 200.9 | 199.4 | 200.1 | 202.0 | 204.0 | 204.4 | 203.5 | 204.1 | 203.0 | 204.9 | 208.7 | 212.2 | 203.9 |
| 2015 | 202.9 | 202.2 | 202.8 | 204.9 | 206.6 | 207.8 | 206.5 | 207.0 | 205.4 | 207.2 | 210.5 | 212.7 | 206.4 |
| 2016 | 202.7 | 201.6 | 202.1 | 203.5 | 204.6 | 204.5 | 204.3 | 203.8 | 202.6 | 203.7 | 206.4 | 207.5 | 203.9 |
| 2017 | 200.3 | 199.7 | 200.1 | 201.6 | 203.0 | 202.6 | 201.9 | 202.0 | 200.9 | 202.0 | 206.8 | 208.1 | 202.4 |
| 2018 | 199.9 | 199.2 | 199.8 | 200.0 | 201.9 | 202.2 | 201.5 | 200.9 | 199.0 | 200.0 | 205.5 | 206.3 | 201.4 |
| 2019 | 198.6 | 196.5 | 196.4 | 197.6 | 198.8 | 198.4 | 198.1 | 198.3 | 196.2 | 197.5 | 201.5 | 203.5 | 198.5 |
| **Wholesale Trade** | | | | | | | | | | | | | |
| 2011 | 39.6 | 39.6 | 39.9 | 40.5 | 40.8 | 41.1 | 41.1 | 40.8 | 40.7 | 40.9 | 41.0 | 41.1 | 40.6 |
| 2012 | 40.3 | 40.3 | 40.7 | 41.3 | 41.6 | 41.8 | 41.6 | 41.1 | 40.8 | 41.0 | 41.0 | 41.3 | 41.1 |
| 2013 | 40.6 | 40.6 | 41.0 | 41.5 | 42.2 | 42.5 | 42.3 | 41.8 | 41.5 | 41.8 | 41.9 | 42.3 | 41.7 |
| 2014 | 41.9 | 41.6 | 42.1 | 42.6 | 43.1 | 43.5 | 43.4 | 42.8 | 42.3 | 42.3 | 42.2 | 42.5 | 42.5 |
| 2015 | 41.5 | 41.4 | 41.7 | 42.3 | 42.6 | 42.9 | 42.6 | 42.3 | 41.7 | 41.8 | 41.8 | 41.8 | 42.0 |
| 2016 | 41.3 | 41.0 | 41.3 | 41.7 | 42.0 | 42.2 | 42.2 | 41.6 | 41.1 | 41.0 | 40.8 | 40.7 | 41.4 |
| 2017 | 40.1 | 40.1 | 40.3 | 40.9 | 41.2 | 41.4 | 41.2 | 40.7 | 40.2 | 40.4 | 40.5 | 40.8 | 40.7 |
| 2018 | 39.8 | 39.8 | 40.0 | 40.4 | 40.9 | 41.2 | 40.9 | 40.4 | 39.8 | 39.8 | 40.0 | 40.2 | 40.3 |
| 2019 | 39.5 | 39.4 | 39.7 | 40.2 | 40.6 | 40.7 | 40.8 | 40.4 | 39.8 | 39.5 | 39.8 | 40.0 | 40.0 |
| **Retail Trade** | | | | | | | | | | | | | |
| 2011 | 102.8 | 101.9 | 102.4 | 103.9 | 104.6 | 104.6 | 104.3 | 104.8 | 104.2 | 105.2 | 108.7 | 109.7 | 104.8 |
| 2012 | 104.2 | 102.4 | 103.1 | 104.2 | 105.2 | 105.3 | 104.9 | 104.7 | 104.6 | 106.3 | 109.8 | 110.5 | 105.4 |
| 2013 | 104.3 | 103.3 | 103.9 | 104.6 | 105.7 | 106.1 | 106.0 | 106.3 | 105.8 | 107.1 | 110.8 | 112.2 | 106.3 |
| 2014 | 106.3 | 105.2 | 105.3 | 106.8 | 108.0 | 108.2 | 108.0 | 108.4 | 107.6 | 109.0 | 111.8 | 113.4 | 108.2 |
| 2015 | 107.9 | 107.3 | 107.6 | 108.6 | 109.5 | 110.3 | 109.7 | 109.9 | 108.7 | 110.2 | 113.1 | 114.2 | 109.8 |
| 2016 | 108.8 | 108.4 | 108.5 | 109.9 | 110.6 | 110.5 | 110.6 | 110.4 | 109.4 | 110.5 | 113.0 | 113.4 | 110.3 |
| 2017 | 108.5 | 107.8 | 108.0 | 108.9 | 109.5 | 109.1 | 109.1 | 108.8 | 108.0 | 108.8 | 112.6 | 112.7 | 109.3 |
| 2018 | 107.5 | 106.8 | 106.8 | 107.0 | 108.2 | 108.3 | 108.2 | 107.6 | 106.1 | 107.0 | 110.8 | 110.8 | 107.9 |
| 2019 | 105.9 | 104.6 | 104.2 | 104.8 | 105.4 | 105.0 | 104.7 | 104.9 | 103.6 | 104.9 | 107.7 | 107.8 | 105.3 |
| **Transportation and Utilities** | | | | | | | | | | | | | |
| 2011 | 51.2 | 51.0 | 51.3 | 51.8 | 51.9 | 51.9 | 52.0 | 52.6 | 53.0 | 53.0 | 53.3 | 53.8 | 52.2 |
| 2012 | 52.5 | 52.3 | 52.4 | 52.7 | 53.0 | 52.8 | 52.6 | 52.8 | 53.2 | 53.1 | 53.7 | 54.7 | 53.0 |
| 2013 | 52.9 | 52.2 | 52.2 | 52.3 | 52.9 | 52.8 | 52.5 | 53.2 | 53.2 | 53.2 | 53.7 | 54.8 | 53.0 |
| 2014 | 52.7 | 52.6 | 52.7 | 52.6 | 52.9 | 52.7 | 52.1 | 52.9 | 53.1 | 53.6 | 54.7 | 56.3 | 53.2 |
| 2015 | 53.5 | 53.5 | 53.5 | 54.0 | 54.5 | 54.6 | 54.2 | 54.8 | 55.0 | 55.2 | 55.6 | 56.7 | 54.6 |
| 2016 | 52.6 | 52.2 | 52.3 | 51.9 | 52.0 | 51.8 | 51.5 | 51.8 | 52.1 | 52.2 | 52.6 | 53.4 | 52.2 |
| 2017 | 51.7 | 51.8 | 51.8 | 51.8 | 52.3 | 52.1 | 51.9 | 52.4 | 52.7 | 52.8 | 53.7 | 54.6 | 52.5 |
| 2018 | 52.6 | 52.6 | 53.0 | 52.6 | 52.8 | 52.7 | 52.4 | 52.9 | 53.1 | 53.2 | 54.7 | 55.3 | 53.2 |
| 2019 | 53.2 | 52.5 | 52.5 | 52.6 | 52.8 | 52.7 | 52.6 | 53.0 | 52.8 | 53.1 | 54.0 | 55.7 | 53.1 |
| **Information** | | | | | | | | | | | | | |
| 2011 | 17.4 | 17.5 | 17.4 | 17.3 | 17.3 | 17.5 | 17.8 | 17.7 | 17.7 | 17.7 | 17.8 | 17.8 | 17.6 |
| 2012 | 17.7 | 17.8 | 17.8 | 17.8 | 17.7 | 17.8 | 17.7 | 17.8 | 17.7 | 17.7 | 17.8 | 17.8 | 17.8 |
| 2013 | 17.7 | 17.8 | 17.8 | 17.7 | 17.7 | 17.7 | 17.7 | 17.7 | 17.7 | 17.7 | 17.8 | 17.8 | 17.7 |
| 2014 | 17.8 | 17.7 | 17.6 | 17.6 | 17.6 | 17.7 | 17.7 | 17.8 | 17.8 | 17.8 | 17.8 | 17.8 | 17.8 |
| 2015 | 17.9 | 18.0 | 18.0 | 18.1 | 18.2 | 18.3 | 18.4 | 18.5 | 18.3 | 18.5 | 18.5 | 18.6 | 18.3 |
| 2016 | 18.5 | 18.5 | 18.4 | 18.5 | 18.3 | 18.3 | 18.4 | 18.4 | 18.5 | 18.5 | 18.5 | 18.6 | 18.5 |
| 2017 | 18.4 | 18.4 | 18.3 | 18.3 | 18.2 | 18.2 | 18.2 | 18.1 | 17.9 | 18.0 | 17.9 | 18.0 | 18.2 |
| 2018 | 17.8 | 17.9 | 17.7 | 17.7 | 17.6 | 17.7 | 17.7 | 17.7 | 17.5 | 17.5 | 17.4 | 17.4 | 17.6 |
| 2019 | 17.4 | 17.4 | 17.3 | 17.3 | 17.2 | 17.5 | 17.3 | 17.2 | 17.1 | 16.9 | 16.9 | 16.9 | 17.2 |

# 1. Employment by Industry: Nebraska, 2011–2019—*Continued*

(Numbers in thousands, not seasonally adjusted)

| Industry and year | January | February | March | April | May | June | July | August | September | October | November | December | Annual average |
|---|---|---|---|---|---|---|---|---|---|---|---|---|---|
| **Financial Activities** | | | | | | | | | | | | | |
| 2011 | 68.9 | 68.9 | 69.0 | 69.6 | 69.7 | 70.0 | 70.0 | 70.0 | 69.9 | 69.9 | 70.1 | 70.5 | 69.7 |
| 2012 | 69.8 | 69.7 | 69.9 | 70.1 | 70.4 | 70.8 | 70.8 | 70.7 | 70.4 | 70.6 | 70.7 | 71.1 | 70.4 |
| 2013 | 70.3 | 70.4 | 70.5 | 70.5 | 70.9 | 71.2 | 71.3 | 71.2 | 70.8 | 71.0 | 71.1 | 71.2 | 70.9 |
| 2014 | 71.0 | 71.0 | 71.1 | 70.8 | 70.9 | 71.3 | 71.4 | 71.0 | 70.6 | 70.7 | 70.7 | 70.7 | 70.9 |
| 2015 | 70.0 | 69.8 | 69.8 | 70.1 | 70.4 | 71.0 | 71.2 | 71.1 | 70.8 | 71.3 | 71.4 | 71.8 | 70.7 |
| 2016 | 71.2 | 71.3 | 71.4 | 71.6 | 71.8 | 72.1 | 72.6 | 72.5 | 71.9 | 71.9 | 71.9 | 72.1 | 71.9 |
| 2017 | 71.7 | 71.8 | 71.9 | 72.2 | 72.3 | 73.0 | 73.2 | 73.2 | 72.9 | 73.2 | 73.0 | 73.4 | 72.7 |
| 2018 | 72.7 | 73.2 | 73.2 | 73.8 | 74.2 | 74.5 | 74.6 | 74.4 | 74.1 | 74.5 | 74.8 | 75.0 | 74.1 |
| 2019 | 74.3 | 74.3 | 74.4 | 74.6 | 75.1 | 75.5 | 75.8 | 75.6 | 75.4 | 75.7 | 75.4 | 75.8 | 75.2 |
| **Professional and Business Services** | | | | | | | | | | | | | |
| 2011 | 99.5 | 100.1 | 100.8 | 102.8 | 102.9 | 103.7 | 104.9 | 104.9 | 105.7 | 105.8 | 105.3 | 105.2 | 103.5 |
| 2012 | 103.9 | 104.8 | 105.4 | 106.7 | 107.1 | 109.3 | 109.3 | 108.9 | 108.8 | 109.0 | 108.7 | 108.4 | 107.5 |
| 2013 | 106.4 | 106.9 | 107.5 | 109.1 | 109.8 | 111.1 | 111.6 | 111.7 | 111.8 | 113.5 | 113.2 | 113.7 | 110.5 |
| 2014 | 110.4 | 111.8 | 112.4 | 113.8 | 114.1 | 115.0 | 115.0 | 114.7 | 114.5 | 114.9 | 114.8 | 115.1 | 113.9 |
| 2015 | 113.5 | 114.4 | 115.1 | 117.4 | 117.6 | 119.1 | 119.4 | 118.8 | 118.8 | 118.5 | 118.2 | 118.2 | 117.4 |
| 2016 | 115.7 | 116.4 | 117.5 | 120.0 | 120.2 | 120.9 | 120.7 | 120.9 | 120.4 | 119.9 | 119.3 | 119.5 | 119.3 |
| 2017 | 116.5 | 116.9 | 117.9 | 119.3 | 118.9 | 119.9 | 120.2 | 119.5 | 119.5 | 120.0 | 119.6 | 119.7 | 119.0 |
| 2018 | 116.0 | 116.9 | 117.5 | 118.9 | 119.3 | 120.3 | 120.3 | 119.7 | 119.9 | 119.8 | 119.9 | 118.9 | 119.0 |
| 2019 | 116.7 | 116.6 | 116.6 | 119.3 | 119.7 | 120.7 | 121.1 | 120.9 | 121.0 | 121.4 | 121.7 | 121.5 | 119.8 |
| **Education and Health Services** | | | | | | | | | | | | | |
| 2011 | 141.1 | 141.9 | 142.2 | 143.1 | 143.5 | 142.2 | 141.3 | 142.0 | 143.0 | 144.7 | 145.1 | 145.2 | 142.9 |
| 2012 | 143.2 | 144.5 | 146.1 | 145.9 | 146.0 | 144.8 | 144.2 | 145.5 | 146.6 | 147.8 | 148.0 | 148.2 | 145.9 |
| 2013 | 145.5 | 146.6 | 147.3 | 147.8 | 147.8 | 146.0 | 145.5 | 146.5 | 147.0 | 148.0 | 148.2 | 148.3 | 147.0 |
| 2014 | 145.7 | 147.3 | 148.5 | 148.5 | 148.6 | 146.7 | 146.1 | 147.2 | 148.0 | 149.4 | 149.3 | 149.8 | 147.9 |
| 2015 | 147.7 | 148.4 | 149.0 | 149.1 | 149.3 | 147.6 | 148.5 | 149.5 | 150.7 | 152.2 | 152.4 | 152.8 | 149.8 |
| 2016 | 150.0 | 151.2 | 152.6 | 151.9 | 152.8 | 151.2 | 152.3 | 153.2 | 154.5 | 155.3 | 155.3 | 154.7 | 152.9 |
| 2017 | 153.2 | 154.7 | 155.2 | 154.4 | 155.2 | 153.2 | 152.8 | 153.6 | 154.5 | 156.1 | 156.1 | 155.9 | 154.6 |
| 2018 | 154.3 | 155.4 | 155.9 | 155.7 | 156.3 | 154.6 | 154.4 | 155.5 | 156.5 | 157.1 | 157.2 | 157.4 | 155.9 |
| 2019 | 155.7 | 156.9 | 157.4 | 156.9 | 158.0 | 155.6 | 156.1 | 156.5 | 157.0 | 158.5 | 158.7 | 159.4 | 157.2 |
| **Leisure and Hospitality** | | | | | | | | | | | | | |
| 2011 | 76.1 | 76.8 | 79.0 | 82.4 | 85.0 | 86.1 | 85.1 | 85.5 | 83.4 | 82.6 | 80.7 | 79.6 | 81.9 |
| 2012 | 77.7 | 78.5 | 81.7 | 84.7 | 87.4 | 88.6 | 87.8 | 88.1 | 85.6 | 85.0 | 83.0 | 82.4 | 84.2 |
| 2013 | 79.8 | 80.5 | 82.2 | 84.7 | 87.8 | 88.9 | 88.4 | 89.9 | 88.4 | 87.4 | 86.1 | 84.9 | 85.8 |
| 2014 | 82.7 | 83.2 | 84.8 | 86.8 | 89.9 | 90.8 | 90.1 | 90.6 | 88.4 | 87.3 | 85.1 | 84.8 | 87.0 |
| 2015 | 82.9 | 83.5 | 85.8 | 87.6 | 90.6 | 92.3 | 91.7 | 92.4 | 90.9 | 89.3 | 87.5 | 87.5 | 88.5 |
| 2016 | 84.8 | 85.3 | 87.8 | 90.4 | 92.7 | 93.8 | 93.7 | 94.5 | 92.8 | 91.6 | 89.4 | 88.3 | 90.4 |
| 2017 | 86.3 | 87.6 | 89.3 | 91.8 | 93.9 | 96.0 | 95.1 | 96.2 | 93.2 | 92.3 | 90.4 | 89.9 | 91.8 |
| 2018 | 87.4 | 88.0 | 89.7 | 91.7 | 95.4 | 96.8 | 95.9 | 96.4 | 94.5 | 93.7 | 91.6 | 90.6 | 92.6 |
| 2019 | 88.9 | 89.4 | 90.8 | 93.6 | 96.7 | 98.0 | 96.6 | 97.8 | 95.1 | 95.3 | 93.0 | 94.0 | 94.1 |
| **Other Services** | | | | | | | | | | | | | |
| 2011 | 36.0 | 36.2 | 36.6 | 36.7 | 36.8 | 36.9 | 36.7 | 36.4 | 36.3 | 36.3 | 36.2 | 36.3 | 36.5 |
| 2012 | 36.0 | 36.1 | 36.5 | 36.6 | 36.9 | 37.2 | 37.0 | 36.9 | 36.8 | 36.7 | 36.7 | 36.7 | 36.7 |
| 2013 | 36.2 | 36.4 | 37.0 | 37.0 | 37.1 | 37.3 | 37.0 | 37.0 | 36.8 | 36.5 | 36.4 | 36.5 | 36.8 |
| 2014 | 36.2 | 36.3 | 36.4 | 36.9 | 37.1 | 37.5 | 37.1 | 36.8 | 36.7 | 36.9 | 36.9 | 36.9 | 36.8 |
| 2015 | 36.6 | 36.8 | 36.9 | 37.1 | 37.3 | 37.4 | 37.3 | 37.0 | 36.7 | 36.9 | 36.8 | 37.0 | 37.0 |
| 2016 | 36.4 | 36.4 | 36.5 | 36.8 | 36.8 | 37.0 | 36.9 | 36.7 | 36.7 | 36.9 | 36.9 | 36.7 | 36.7 |
| 2017 | 36.3 | 36.4 | 36.6 | 37.0 | 36.8 | 37.0 | 36.7 | 36.6 | 36.6 | 36.5 | 36.6 | 36.8 | 36.7 |
| 2018 | 36.3 | 36.4 | 36.6 | 36.8 | 37.1 | 37.4 | 37.4 | 37.1 | 37.2 | 37.3 | 37.2 | 37.0 | 37.0 |
| 2019 | 36.7 | 36.9 | 36.8 | 37.0 | 37.3 | 37.5 | 37.8 | 37.7 | 37.6 | 37.5 | 37.3 | 37.3 | 37.3 |
| **Government** | | | | | | | | | | | | | |
| 2011 | 167.2 | 169.5 | 169.8 | 171.4 | 172.2 | 168.1 | 159.1 | 160.8 | 166.6 | 171.3 | 171.4 | 170.6 | 168.2 |
| 2012 | 167.2 | 169.7 | 169.9 | 170.9 | 173.5 | 167.0 | 159.8 | 161.4 | 168.2 | 171.1 | 171.5 | 170.7 | 168.4 |
| 2013 | 167.1 | 169.4 | 169.6 | 170.7 | 174.1 | 168.7 | 160.5 | 161.6 | 168.4 | 172.4 | 172.5 | 171.4 | 168.9 |
| 2014 | 168.0 | 170.9 | 170.9 | 171.2 | 174.4 | 168.6 | 160.3 | 161.8 | 170.3 | 173.3 | 173.3 | 172.5 | 169.6 |
| 2015 | 168.1 | 171.1 | 171.7 | 173.8 | 175.1 | 170.5 | 162.7 | 164.3 | 170.7 | 175.2 | 174.9 | 174.3 | 171.0 |
| 2016 | 170.2 | 172.6 | 174.0 | 175.1 | 177.5 | 173.7 | 165.0 | 164.3 | 174.4 | 176.6 | 176.7 | 175.5 | 173.0 |
| 2017 | 171.7 | 173.7 | 174.4 | 175.1 | 176.8 | 174.9 | 165.1 | 166.3 | 173.0 | 175.7 | 175.6 | 174.9 | 173.1 |
| 2018 | 171.6 | 173.3 | 174.4 | 175.0 | 177.6 | 174.6 | 165.9 | 166.2 | 173.6 | 175.7 | 175.8 | 174.8 | 173.2 |
| 2019 | 172.5 | 173.5 | 173.5 | 175.1 | 177.8 | 174.5 | 165.8 | 167.0 | 173.6 | 176.7 | 177.4 | 175.9 | 173.6 |

## 2. Average Weekly Hours by Selected Industry: Nebraska, 2015–2019

(Not seasonally adjusted)

| Industry and year | January | February | March | April | May | June | July | August | September | October | November | December | Annual average |
|---|---|---|---|---|---|---|---|---|---|---|---|---|---|
| **Total Private** | | | | | | | | | | | | | |
| 2015 | 33.6 | 34.3 | 34.2 | 33.8 | 33.9 | 34.4 | 34.3 | 34.9 | 33.9 | 34.3 | 34.2 | 33.8 | 34.1 |
| 2016 | 33.4 | 33.3 | 33.4 | 34.0 | 34.1 | 34.2 | 34.0 | 34.1 | 33.8 | 34.5 | 33.6 | 33.6 | 33.8 |
| 2017 | 33.9 | 33.6 | 33.8 | 34.3 | 33.8 | 34.3 | 34.6 | 34.2 | 34.3 | 34.6 | 34.2 | 34.2 | 34.2 |
| 2018 | 33.4 | 33.6 | 33.6 | 34.2 | 33.8 | 34.0 | 34.3 | 33.6 | 34.1 | 33.5 | 33.4 | 33.8 | 33.8 |
| 2019 | 33.1 | 33.0 | 32.7 | 33.5 | 33.4 | 34.4 | 34.0 | 33.6 | 34.1 | 33.6 | 33.6 | 33.8 | 33.6 |
| **Goods-Producing** | | | | | | | | | | | | | |
| 2015 | 40.0 | 41.0 | 40.4 | 40.5 | 40.9 | 41.2 | 41.3 | 42.3 | 40.4 | 41.8 | 40.3 | 40.4 | 40.9 |
| 2016 | 40.2 | 39.4 | 40.0 | 42.1 | 40.6 | 41.8 | 41.8 | 42.4 | 40.5 | 41.2 | 39.9 | 39.5 | 40.8 |
| 2017 | 39.8 | 40.3 | 41.0 | 41.1 | 40.5 | 40.8 | 41.0 | 41.3 | 41.7 | 40.8 | 40.8 | 41.1 | 40.9 |
| 2018 | 39.3 | 40.0 | 39.5 | 40.5 | 40.6 | 40.9 | 40.1 | 40.2 | 40.7 | 39.3 | 39.5 | 40.0 | 40.1 |
| 2019 | 39.6 | 38.2 | 38.0 | 40.0 | 40.2 | 40.9 | 40.8 | 40.6 | 41.1 | 40.0 | 39.8 | 40.0 | 39.9 |
| **Mining, Logging, and Construction** | | | | | | | | | | | | | |
| 2015 | 37.6 | 39.7 | 40.2 | 39.3 | 39.2 | 41.1 | 42.0 | 43.0 | 41.6 | 42.5 | 40.6 | 40.4 | 40.7 |
| 2016 | 38.3 | 38.5 | 39.6 | 42.9 | 40.5 | 42.0 | 42.6 | 42.7 | 38.2 | 39.7 | 38.5 | 36.4 | 40.1 |
| 2017 | 35.8 | 36.6 | 37.3 | 39.4 | 38.8 | 40.1 | 40.1 | 41.3 | 41.1 | 39.8 | 40.8 | 40.3 | 39.4 |
| 2018 | 37.3 | 38.5 | 39.2 | 41.1 | 42.2 | 43.6 | 41.7 | 41.5 | 41.7 | 38.3 | 39.3 | 40.2 | 40.5 |
| 2019 | 38.8 | 37.5 | 37.5 | 39.5 | 39.4 | 40.7 | 40.5 | 40.1 | 41.0 | 38.9 | 38.5 | 38.8 | 39.3 |
| **Manufacturing** | | | | | | | | | | | | | |
| 2015 | 41.1 | 41.6 | 40.5 | 41.1 | 41.8 | 41.2 | 40.9 | 41.9 | 39.7 | 41.4 | 40.1 | 40.4 | 41.0 |
| 2016 | 41.1 | 39.8 | 40.2 | 41.7 | 40.7 | 41.8 | 41.4 | 42.3 | 41.8 | 42.1 | 40.6 | 41.1 | 41.2 |
| 2017 | 41.7 | 42.1 | 42.8 | 42.0 | 41.4 | 41.1 | 41.5 | 41.3 | 42.0 | 41.4 | 40.9 | 41.6 | 41.6 |
| 2018 | 40.4 | 40.6 | 39.7 | 40.1 | 39.7 | 39.4 | 39.3 | 39.6 | 40.1 | 39.8 | 39.7 | 39.9 | 39.9 |
| 2019 | 40.0 | 38.6 | 38.3 | 40.2 | 40.7 | 41.0 | 40.9 | 40.8 | 41.2 | 40.7 | 40.6 | 40.7 | 40.3 |
| **Trade, Transportation, and Utilities** | | | | | | | | | | | | | |
| 2015 | 33.1 | 33.7 | 33.8 | 33.7 | 33.5 | 34.3 | 34.0 | 34.2 | 33.4 | 33.9 | 33.5 | 33.6 | 33.7 |
| 2016 | 32.5 | 32.7 | 32.8 | 33.1 | 33.6 | 33.4 | 33.6 | 33.2 | 33.1 | 33.5 | 32.6 | 32.7 | 33.1 |
| 2017 | 32.3 | 32.0 | 32.1 | 32.8 | 32.4 | 32.9 | 32.5 | 32.3 | 32.7 | 32.8 | 32.8 | 32.6 | 32.5 |
| 2018 | 31.3 | 31.9 | 32.1 | 32.9 | 32.9 | 33.0 | 32.4 | 32.0 | 32.0 | 31.8 | 32.1 | 32.1 | 32.2 |
| 2019 | 30.9 | 31.6 | 31.2 | 31.9 | 32.1 | 32.6 | 31.8 | 31.7 | 31.5 | 31.4 | 31.2 | 31.2 | 31.6 |
| **Financial Activities** | | | | | | | | | | | | | |
| 2015 | 38.1 | 39.2 | 38.9 | 38.0 | 37.9 | 38.1 | 38.0 | 39.7 | 38.0 | 38.2 | 39.0 | 38.1 | 38.4 |
| 2016 | 37.9 | 38.1 | 38.0 | 38.4 | 39.2 | 38.5 | 37.9 | 38.4 | 38.0 | 39.0 | 38.0 | 38.4 | 38.3 |
| 2017 | 39.7 | 38.4 | 38.1 | 39.0 | 37.7 | 38.3 | 39.0 | 37.9 | 38.3 | 38.7 | 38.0 | 38.5 | 38.5 |
| 2018 | 38.5 | 38.2 | 38.4 | 39.1 | 38.3 | 38.8 | 39.3 | 38.2 | 39.5 | 38.4 | 38.2 | 39.4 | 38.7 |
| 2019 | 39.5 | 39.4 | 38.9 | 38.6 | 37.9 | 39.6 | 38.4 | 38.1 | 39.8 | 38.5 | 38.7 | 39.7 | 38.9 |
| **Professional and Business Services** | | | | | | | | | | | | | |
| 2015 | 35.7 | 36.4 | 36.2 | 35.7 | 35.5 | 36.0 | 35.4 | 36.3 | 35.5 | 35.9 | 36.4 | 35.1 | 35.8 |
| 2016 | 35.1 | 34.9 | 35.0 | 35.3 | 35.4 | 35.1 | 34.9 | 35.1 | 35.2 | 36.0 | 34.6 | 34.5 | 35.1 |
| 2017 | 34.8 | 34.2 | 34.5 | 35.5 | 35.1 | 35.5 | 36.0 | 35.4 | 35.0 | 36.1 | 36.1 | 35.4 | 35.3 |
| 2018 | 35.0 | 34.4 | 34.3 | 35.0 | 34.7 | 34.6 | 35.2 | 34.2 | 35.0 | 34.5 | 34.6 | 35.5 | 34.8 |
| 2019 | 34.6 | 34.5 | 34.8 | 35.1 | 35.2 | 36.2 | 35.6 | 35.7 | 36.4 | 36.2 | 36.1 | 36.4 | 35.6 |
| **Education and Health Services** | | | | | | | | | | | | | |
| 2015 | 31.2 | 31.8 | 31.9 | 31.4 | 31.6 | 32.3 | 32.4 | 32.3 | 32.2 | 31.8 | 32.3 | 31.1 | 31.9 |
| 2016 | 30.9 | 30.7 | 30.9 | 31.0 | 31.4 | 31.1 | 31.0 | 30.9 | 30.9 | 31.6 | 30.7 | 30.7 | 31.0 |
| 2017 | 31.1 | 30.8 | 31.2 | 31.9 | 31.3 | 31.6 | 32.1 | 31.7 | 31.7 | 32.3 | 31.6 | 31.7 | 31.6 |
| 2018 | 31.5 | 31.5 | 31.7 | 32.4 | 31.8 | 31.8 | 32.5 | 32.2 | 32.5 | 31.7 | 31.8 | 31.8 | 31.9 |
| 2019 | 31.0 | 31.2 | 30.9 | 31.5 | 31.6 | 32.6 | 32.1 | 32.0 | 32.7 | 32.1 | 32.5 | 32.8 | 31.9 |
| **Leisure and Hospitality** | | | | | | | | | | | | | |
| 2015 | 22.2 | 22.8 | 23.0 | 22.0 | 22.8 | 23.9 | 23.2 | 23.4 | 22.5 | 22.8 | 22.8 | 22.9 | 22.9 |
| 2016 | 22.3 | 22.3 | 22.5 | 22.5 | 22.9 | 23.5 | 22.9 | 22.5 | 22.9 | 23.0 | 22.7 | 22.0 | 22.7 |
| 2017 | 22.3 | 22.4 | 22.3 | 22.1 | 22.1 | 23.6 | 23.6 | 23.2 | 22.7 | 23.2 | 22.8 | 22.7 | 22.8 |
| 2018 | 21.9 | 22.6 | 22.7 | 22.3 | 22.5 | 23.3 | 23.7 | 22.8 | 23.2 | 22.7 | 22.1 | 22.9 | 22.7 |
| 2019 | 21.8 | 21.8 | 22.1 | 22.7 | 22.5 | 24.3 | 23.9 | 23.5 | 23.5 | 23.0 | 23.4 | 23.2 | 23.0 |

# 3. Average Hourly Earnings by Selected Industry: Nebraska, 2015–2019

(Dollars, not seasonally adjusted)

| Industry and year | January | February | March | April | May | June | July | August | September | October | November | December | Annual average |
|---|---|---|---|---|---|---|---|---|---|---|---|---|---|
| **Total Private** | | | | | | | | | | | | | |
| 2015 | 22.00 | 22.05 | 22.10 | 21.85 | 21.90 | 21.69 | 21.87 | 22.42 | 22.48 | 22.33 | 22.64 | 22.53 | 22.16 |
| 2016 | 22.79 | 22.85 | 22.82 | 22.86 | 23.05 | 22.84 | 23.03 | 22.97 | 23.22 | 23.37 | 23.06 | 22.94 | 22.99 |
| 2017 | 23.86 | 23.57 | 23.78 | 24.20 | 24.04 | 23.76 | 24.11 | 23.92 | 24.17 | 24.51 | 24.56 | 24.55 | 24.09 |
| 2018 | 24.77 | 24.45 | 24.55 | 24.95 | 24.46 | 24.45 | 24.70 | 24.47 | 25.21 | 24.70 | 24.66 | 25.28 | 24.72 |
| 2019 | 25.33 | 25.58 | 25.46 | 25.39 | 25.25 | 25.56 | 25.49 | 25.79 | 26.05 | 26.04 | 26.14 | 26.40 | 25.71 |
| **Goods-Producing** | | | | | | | | | | | | | |
| 2015 | 21.18 | 21.20 | 21.09 | 21.11 | 21.26 | 21.09 | 21.14 | 21.52 | 21.89 | 21.60 | 21.69 | 21.41 | 21.35 |
| 2016 | 21.51 | 21.71 | 22.03 | 21.74 | 21.77 | 21.90 | 22.02 | 21.79 | 22.00 | 22.05 | 21.91 | 22.24 | 21.89 |
| 2017 | 22.55 | 22.36 | 22.43 | 22.62 | 22.62 | 22.71 | 22.94 | 23.03 | 23.21 | 23.36 | 23.50 | 23.73 | 22.93 |
| 2018 | 24.05 | 23.78 | 23.82 | 24.17 | 23.42 | 23.83 | 23.99 | 23.95 | 23.86 | 23.85 | 23.76 | 24.38 | 23.90 |
| 2019 | 24.13 | 24.20 | 23.97 | 23.97 | 23.91 | 23.95 | 23.93 | 24.22 | 24.30 | 24.43 | 24.84 | 25.44 | 24.28 |
| **Mining, Logging, and Construction** | | | | | | | | | | | | | |
| 2015 | 22.19 | 22.04 | 21.67 | 21.67 | 21.56 | 21.26 | 21.34 | 21.85 | 22.27 | 22.55 | 22.16 | 22.30 | 21.90 |
| 2016 | 22.78 | 23.02 | 23.04 | 22.62 | 22.74 | 23.01 | 22.94 | 22.56 | 23.25 | 23.24 | 23.12 | 23.75 | 22.99 |
| 2017 | 23.99 | 23.76 | 23.74 | 22.92 | 23.12 | 23.09 | 23.06 | 23.67 | 23.89 | 23.96 | 24.13 | 24.53 | 23.65 |
| 2018 | 25.35 | 25.12 | 25.20 | 25.28 | 24.33 | 24.87 | 25.27 | 25.61 | 25.25 | 25.46 | 25.51 | 26.17 | 25.28 |
| 2019 | 25.13 | 25.05 | 24.88 | 25.15 | 24.24 | 24.33 | 24.64 | 24.77 | 24.94 | 25.14 | 25.61 | 26.12 | 24.99 |
| **Manufacturing** | | | | | | | | | | | | | |
| 2015 | 20.76 | 20.83 | 20.82 | 20.84 | 21.11 | 21.00 | 21.03 | 21.33 | 21.68 | 21.07 | 21.44 | 20.95 | 21.07 |
| 2016 | 20.95 | 21.10 | 21.53 | 21.26 | 21.25 | 21.27 | 21.49 | 21.36 | 21.36 | 21.43 | 21.29 | 21.55 | 21.32 |
| 2017 | 21.95 | 21.75 | 21.85 | 22.47 | 22.37 | 22.50 | 22.87 | 22.67 | 22.85 | 23.04 | 23.17 | 23.32 | 22.57 |
| 2018 | 23.46 | 23.16 | 23.14 | 23.57 | 22.89 | 23.18 | 23.22 | 22.97 | 23.06 | 22.99 | 22.82 | 23.43 | 23.16 |
| 2019 | 23.64 | 23.80 | 23.53 | 23.34 | 23.73 | 23.73 | 23.53 | 23.91 | 23.94 | 24.04 | 24.43 | 25.10 | 23.90 |
| **Trade, Transportation, and Utilities** | | | | | | | | | | | | | |
| 2015 | 19.69 | 19.64 | 19.51 | 19.42 | 19.41 | 19.20 | 19.34 | 20.00 | 19.70 | 19.59 | 19.68 | 19.50 | 19.56 |
| 2016 | 20.09 | 20.36 | 20.14 | 20.13 | 20.61 | 20.36 | 20.61 | 20.55 | 20.69 | 20.71 | 20.38 | 19.96 | 20.38 |
| 2017 | 21.21 | 20.90 | 21.03 | 21.48 | 21.52 | 21.31 | 21.69 | 21.41 | 21.66 | 21.87 | 21.99 | 21.91 | 21.50 |
| 2018 | 21.86 | 21.28 | 21.54 | 21.70 | 21.46 | 21.49 | 21.37 | 21.03 | 21.95 | 21.39 | 20.98 | 21.34 | 21.45 |
| 2019 | 21.86 | 22.21 | 22.16 | 21.79 | 22.08 | 21.79 | 21.64 | 22.02 | 22.63 | 23.16 | 22.62 | 22.56 | 22.21 |
| **Financial Activities** | | | | | | | | | | | | | |
| 2015 | 26.78 | 27.58 | 27.75 | 27.93 | 27.73 | 27.32 | 27.24 | 28.34 | 28.05 | 28.11 | 29.02 | 28.39 | 27.86 |
| 2016 | 28.88 | 28.34 | 28.86 | 29.64 | 29.83 | 29.08 | 29.26 | 29.50 | 29.63 | 30.17 | 29.80 | 29.91 | 29.41 |
| 2017 | 30.51 | 29.78 | 30.43 | 31.54 | 30.41 | 29.72 | 30.41 | 29.79 | 29.89 | 30.37 | 30.03 | 30.06 | 30.25 |
| 2018 | 30.04 | 30.00 | 30.17 | 31.34 | 30.26 | 30.06 | 30.27 | 30.31 | 30.80 | 29.19 | 30.09 | 31.05 | 30.30 |
| 2019 | 30.14 | 31.57 | 31.06 | 31.29 | 31.57 | 32.18 | 32.06 | 33.25 | 33.55 | 32.38 | 33.37 | 34.38 | 32.24 |
| **Professional and Business Services** | | | | | | | | | | | | | |
| 2015 | 26.65 | 26.25 | 26.69 | 26.42 | 26.63 | 26.53 | 26.69 | 26.69 | 26.84 | 26.46 | 26.94 | 27.01 | 26.65 |
| 2016 | 26.85 | 26.95 | 26.78 | 27.00 | 27.16 | 27.02 | 27.30 | 27.01 | 27.13 | 27.48 | 26.78 | 26.03 | 26.96 |
| 2017 | 27.49 | 27.07 | 27.79 | 28.34 | 28.29 | 27.82 | 28.26 | 28.26 | 27.95 | 28.26 | 28.77 | 29.09 | 28.80 | 28.17 |
| 2018 | 29.55 | 29.60 | 29.96 | 29.83 | 29.36 | 29.01 | 29.38 | 29.17 | 30.07 | 29.64 | 29.88 | 30.42 | 29.66 |
| 2019 | 30.58 | 30.20 | 30.33 | 30.04 | 29.99 | 30.37 | 30.69 | 30.87 | 31.01 | 30.70 | 30.55 | 30.69 | 30.51 |
| **Education and Health Services** | | | | | | | | | | | | | |
| 2015 | 22.22 | 22.28 | 22.33 | 22.27 | 22.30 | 22.13 | 22.43 | 22.73 | 22.87 | 22.56 | 22.46 | 22.52 | 22.43 |
| 2016 | 22.68 | 22.45 | 22.24 | 22.15 | 22.10 | 22.32 | 22.25 | 22.14 | 22.70 | 22.24 | 22.26 | 22.14 | 22.30 |
| 2017 | 22.91 | 22.86 | 23.07 | 23.34 | 23.43 | 23.41 | 23.69 | 23.74 | 24.31 | 24.58 | 24.96 | 24.92 | 23.78 |
| 2018 | 24.89 | 24.64 | 24.60 | 24.63 | 24.63 | 24.61 | 24.87 | 24.57 | 25.28 | 25.01 | 24.84 | 25.81 | 24.87 |
| 2019 | 25.90 | 26.03 | 25.91 | 26.08 | 25.60 | 25.66 | 25.83 | 25.93 | 25.89 | 26.06 | 25.84 | 25.87 | 25.88 |
| **Leisure and Hospitality** | | | | | | | | | | | | | |
| 2015 | 12.33 | 12.27 | 12.28 | 12.30 | 12.37 | 12.23 | 12.41 | 12.67 | 12.84 | 12.88 | 13.07 | 13.28 | 12.58 |
| 2016 | 13.34 | 13.68 | 13.33 | 13.53 | 13.42 | 13.13 | 13.25 | 13.28 | 13.33 | 13.31 | 13.35 | 13.59 | 13.37 |
| 2017 | 13.78 | 13.73 | 13.53 | 13.53 | 13.48 | 13.35 | 13.36 | 13.41 | 13.40 | 13.45 | 13.51 | 13.54 | 13.50 |
| 2018 | 13.81 | 13.79 | 13.64 | 13.84 | 13.73 | 13.57 | 13.82 | 13.74 | 13.80 | 13.91 | 14.06 | 14.25 | 13.83 |
| 2019 | 14.11 | 14.21 | 14.35 | 14.24 | 14.23 | 14.24 | 14.26 | 14.41 | 14.68 | 14.82 | 14.76 | 15.04 | 14.45 |

## 4. Average Weekly Earnings by Selected Industry: Nebraska, 2015–2019

(Dollars, not seasonally adjusted)

| Industry and year | January | February | March | April | May | June | July | August | September | October | November | December | Annual average |
|---|---|---|---|---|---|---|---|---|---|---|---|---|---|
| **Total Private** | | | | | | | | | | | | | |
| 2015 | 739.20 | 756.32 | 755.82 | 738.87 | 742.41 | 748.31 | 750.14 | 782.46 | 762.07 | 765.92 | 774.29 | 761.51 | 755.66 |
| 2016 | 761.19 | 760.91 | 762.19 | 774.95 | 786.01 | 781.13 | 783.02 | 782.94 | 784.84 | 806.61 | 774.82 | 770.78 | 777.06 |
| 2017 | 808.85 | 791.95 | 803.76 | 832.14 | 812.55 | 814.97 | 834.21 | 818.06 | 829.03 | 848.05 | 839.95 | 839.61 | 823.88 |
| 2018 | 827.32 | 821.52 | 824.88 | 853.29 | 826.75 | 831.30 | 847.21 | 822.19 | 859.66 | 827.45 | 823.64 | 854.46 | 835.54 |
| 2019 | 838.42 | 841.58 | 832.54 | 850.57 | 843.35 | 879.26 | 866.66 | 866.54 | 888.31 | 874.94 | 878.30 | 892.32 | 863.86 |
| **Goods-Producing** | | | | | | | | | | | | | |
| 2015 | 847.20 | 869.20 | 852.04 | 854.96 | 869.53 | 868.91 | 873.08 | 910.30 | 884.36 | 902.88 | 874.11 | 864.96 | 873.22 |
| 2016 | 864.70 | 855.37 | 881.20 | 915.25 | 883.86 | 917.61 | 920.44 | 923.90 | 891.00 | 908.46 | 874.21 | 878.48 | 893.11 |
| 2017 | 897.49 | 900.71 | 917.39 | 929.68 | 916.11 | 924.30 | 940.54 | 951.14 | 967.86 | 953.09 | 961.15 | 977.68 | 937.84 |
| 2018 | 947.57 | 948.82 | 940.89 | 976.47 | 950.85 | 974.65 | 964.40 | 965.19 | 971.10 | 937.31 | 940.90 | 975.20 | 958.39 |
| 2019 | 955.55 | 924.44 | 910.86 | 958.80 | 961.18 | 979.56 | 976.34 | 980.91 | 998.73 | 977.20 | 988.63 | 1,017.60 | 968.77 |
| **Mining, Logging, and Construction** | | | | | | | | | | | | | |
| 2015 | 834.34 | 874.99 | 871.13 | 851.63 | 845.15 | 873.79 | 896.28 | 939.55 | 926.43 | 958.38 | 899.70 | 900.92 | 891.33 |
| 2016 | 872.47 | 886.27 | 912.38 | 970.40 | 920.97 | 966.42 | 977.24 | 963.31 | 888.15 | 922.63 | 890.12 | 864.50 | 921.90 |
| 2017 | 858.84 | 869.62 | 885.50 | 903.05 | 897.06 | 925.91 | 924.71 | 977.57 | 981.88 | 953.61 | 984.50 | 988.56 | 931.81 |
| 2018 | 945.56 | 967.12 | 987.84 | 1,039.01 | 1,026.73 | 1,084.33 | 1,053.76 | 1,062.82 | 1,052.93 | 975.12 | 1,002.54 | 1,052.03 | 1,023.84 |
| 2019 | 975.04 | 939.38 | 933.00 | 993.43 | 955.06 | 990.23 | 997.92 | 993.28 | 1,022.54 | 977.95 | 985.99 | 1,013.46 | 982.11 |
| **Manufacturing** | | | | | | | | | | | | | |
| 2015 | 853.24 | 866.53 | 843.21 | 856.52 | 882.40 | 865.20 | 860.13 | 893.73 | 860.70 | 872.30 | 859.74 | 846.38 | 863.87 |
| 2016 | 861.05 | 839.78 | 865.51 | 886.54 | 864.88 | 889.09 | 889.69 | 903.53 | 892.85 | 902.20 | 864.37 | 885.71 | 878.38 |
| 2017 | 915.32 | 915.68 | 935.18 | 943.74 | 926.12 | 924.75 | 949.11 | 936.27 | 959.70 | 953.86 | 947.65 | 970.11 | 938.91 |
| 2018 | 947.78 | 940.30 | 918.66 | 945.16 | 908.73 | 913.29 | 912.55 | 909.61 | 924.71 | 915.00 | 905.95 | 934.86 | 924.08 |
| 2019 | 945.60 | 918.68 | 901.20 | 938.27 | 965.81 | 972.93 | 962.38 | 975.53 | 986.33 | 978.43 | 991.86 | 1,021.57 | 963.17 |
| **Trade, Transportation, and Utilities** | | | | | | | | | | | | | |
| 2015 | 651.74 | 661.87 | 659.44 | 654.45 | 650.24 | 658.56 | 657.56 | 684.00 | 657.98 | 664.10 | 659.28 | 655.20 | 659.17 |
| 2016 | 652.93 | 665.77 | 660.59 | 666.30 | 692.50 | 680.02 | 692.50 | 682.26 | 684.84 | 693.79 | 664.39 | 652.69 | 674.58 |
| 2017 | 685.08 | 668.80 | 675.06 | 704.54 | 697.25 | 701.10 | 704.93 | 691.54 | 708.28 | 717.34 | 721.27 | 714.27 | 698.75 |
| 2018 | 684.22 | 678.83 | 691.43 | 713.93 | 706.03 | 709.17 | 692.39 | 672.96 | 702.40 | 680.20 | 673.46 | 685.01 | 690.69 |
| 2019 | 675.47 | 701.84 | 691.39 | 695.10 | 708.77 | 710.35 | 688.15 | 698.03 | 712.85 | 727.22 | 705.74 | 703.87 | 701.84 |
| **Financial Activities** | | | | | | | | | | | | | |
| 2015 | 1,020.32 | 1,081.14 | 1,079.48 | 1,061.34 | 1,050.97 | 1,040.89 | 1,035.12 | 1,125.10 | 1,065.90 | 1,073.80 | 1,131.78 | 1,081.66 | 1,069.82 |
| 2016 | 1,094.55 | 1,079.75 | 1,096.68 | 1,138.18 | 1,169.34 | 1,119.58 | 1,108.95 | 1,132.80 | 1,125.94 | 1,176.63 | 1,132.40 | 1,148.54 | 1,126.40 |
| 2017 | 1,211.25 | 1,143.55 | 1,159.38 | 1,230.06 | 1,146.46 | 1,138.28 | 1,185.99 | 1,129.04 | 1,144.79 | 1,175.32 | 1,141.14 | 1,157.31 | 1,164.63 |
| 2018 | 1,156.54 | 1,146.00 | 1,158.53 | 1,225.39 | 1,158.96 | 1,166.33 | 1,189.61 | 1,157.84 | 1,216.60 | 1,120.90 | 1,149.44 | 1,223.37 | 1,172.61 |
| 2019 | 1,190.53 | 1,243.86 | 1,208.23 | 1,207.79 | 1,196.50 | 1,274.33 | 1,231.10 | 1,266.83 | 1,335.29 | 1,246.63 | 1,291.42 | 1,364.89 | 1,254.14 |
| **Professional and Business Services** | | | | | | | | | | | | | |
| 2015 | 951.41 | 955.50 | 966.18 | 943.19 | 945.37 | 955.08 | 944.83 | 968.85 | 952.82 | 949.91 | 980.62 | 948.05 | 954.07 |
| 2016 | 942.44 | 940.56 | 937.30 | 953.10 | 961.46 | 948.40 | 952.77 | 948.05 | 954.98 | 989.28 | 926.59 | 898.04 | 946.30 |
| 2017 | 956.65 | 925.79 | 958.76 | 1,006.07 | 992.98 | 987.61 | 1,017.36 | 989.43 | 989.10 | 1,038.60 | 1,050.15 | 1,019.52 | 994.40 |
| 2018 | 1,034.25 | 1,018.24 | 1,027.63 | 1,044.05 | 1,018.79 | 1,003.75 | 1,034.18 | 997.61 | 1,052.45 | 1,022.58 | 1,033.85 | 1,079.91 | 1,032.17 |
| 2019 | 1,058.07 | 1,041.90 | 1,055.48 | 1,054.40 | 1,055.65 | 1,099.39 | 1,092.56 | 1,102.06 | 1,128.76 | 1,111.34 | 1,102.86 | 1,117.12 | 1,086.16 |
| **Education and Health Services** | | | | | | | | | | | | | |
| 2015 | 693.26 | 708.50 | 712.33 | 699.28 | 704.68 | 714.80 | 726.73 | 734.18 | 736.41 | 717.41 | 725.46 | 700.37 | 715.52 |
| 2016 | 700.81 | 689.22 | 687.22 | 686.65 | 693.94 | 694.15 | 689.75 | 684.13 | 701.43 | 702.78 | 683.38 | 679.70 | 691.30 |
| 2017 | 712.50 | 704.09 | 719.78 | 744.55 | 733.36 | 739.76 | 760.45 | 752.56 | 770.63 | 793.93 | 788.74 | 789.96 | 751.45 |
| 2018 | 784.04 | 776.16 | 779.82 | 798.01 | 783.23 | 782.60 | 808.28 | 791.15 | 821.60 | 792.82 | 789.91 | 820.76 | 793.35 |
| 2019 | 802.90 | 812.14 | 800.62 | 821.52 | 808.96 | 836.52 | 829.14 | 829.76 | 846.60 | 836.53 | 839.80 | 848.54 | 825.57 |
| **Leisure and Hospitality** | | | | | | | | | | | | | |
| 2015 | 273.73 | 279.76 | 282.44 | 270.60 | 282.04 | 292.30 | 287.91 | 296.48 | 288.90 | 293.66 | 298.00 | 304.11 | 288.08 |
| 2016 | 297.48 | 305.06 | 299.93 | 304.43 | 307.32 | 308.56 | 303.43 | 298.80 | 305.26 | 306.13 | 303.05 | 298.98 | 303.50 |
| 2017 | 307.29 | 307.55 | 301.72 | 299.01 | 297.91 | 315.06 | 315.30 | 311.11 | 304.18 | 312.04 | 308.03 | 307.36 | 307.80 |
| 2018 | 302.44 | 311.65 | 309.63 | 308.63 | 308.93 | 316.18 | 327.53 | 313.27 | 320.16 | 315.76 | 310.73 | 326.33 | 313.94 |
| 2019 | 307.60 | 309.78 | 317.14 | 323.25 | 320.18 | 346.03 | 340.81 | 338.64 | 344.98 | 340.86 | 345.38 | 348.93 | 332.35 |

# NEVADA
## *At a Glance*

Population:
  2010 census: 2,700,551
  2019 estimate: 3,080,156

Percent change in population:
  2010–2019: 14.1%

Percent change in total nonfarm employment:
  2011–2019:  25.9%

Industry with the largest growth in employment, 2011–2019 (percent):
  Construction, 84.3%

Industry with the largest decline or smallest growth in employment, 2011–2019 (percent):
  Mining and logging, 5.0%

Civilian labor force:
  2010: 1,358,578
  2019:  1,542,452

Unemployment rate and rank among states (highest to lowest):
  2010: 13.5%, 1st
  2019: 3.9%, 16th

Over-the-year change in unemployment rates:
  2017–2018: -0.6%
  2018–2019: -0.5%

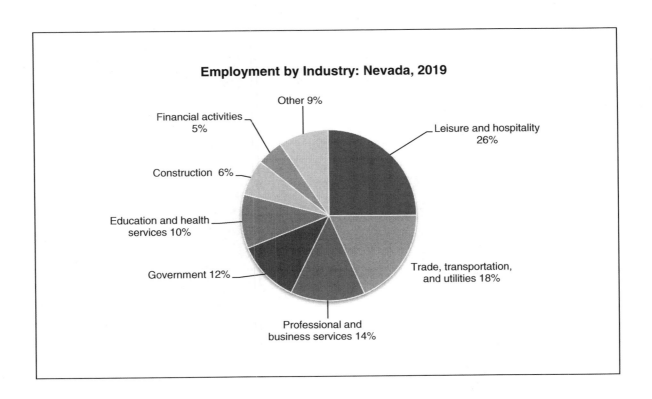

**Employment by Industry: Nevada, 2019**

Other 9%
Financial activities 5%
Leisure and hospitality 26%
Construction  6%
Education and health services 10%
Government 12%
Trade, transportation, and utilities 18%
Professional and business services 14%

## 1. Employment by Industry: Nevada, 2011–2019

(Numbers in thousands, not seasonally adjusted)

| Industry and year | January | February | March | April | May | June | July | August | September | October | November | December | Annual average |
|---|---|---|---|---|---|---|---|---|---|---|---|---|---|
| **Total Nonfarm** | | | | | | | | | | | | | |
| 2011 | 1,106.8 | 1,109.6 | 1,114.8 | 1,126.6 | 1,130.6 | 1,128.7 | 1,122.7 | 1,122.2 | 1,132.4 | 1,137.9 | 1,139.2 | 1,136.9 | 1,125.7 |
| 2012 | 1,120.2 | 1,123.5 | 1,130.9 | 1,139.5 | 1,148.1 | 1,150.0 | 1,139.2 | 1,145.6 | 1,153.8 | 1,160.6 | 1,165.5 | 1,160.6 | 1,144.8 |
| 2013 | 1,145.0 | 1,148.8 | 1,158.4 | 1,168.3 | 1,176.1 | 1,178.9 | 1,171.0 | 1,178.5 | 1,182.9 | 1,189.6 | 1,198.0 | 1,195.3 | 1,174.2 |
| 2014 | 1,179.9 | 1,186.7 | 1,198.1 | 1,208.4 | 1,218.9 | 1,216.2 | 1,209.0 | 1,220.2 | 1,229.6 | 1,239.7 | 1,243.3 | 1,244.1 | 1,216.2 |
| 2015 | 1,227.8 | 1,232.9 | 1,241.5 | 1,252.8 | 1,259.3 | 1,256.5 | 1,249.9 | 1,259.3 | 1,268.8 | 1,281.4 | 1,287.5 | 1,288.8 | 1,258.9 |
| 2016 | 1,263.9 | 1,271.2 | 1,279.8 | 1,292.3 | 1,296.0 | 1,295.3 | 1,298.8 | 1,302.8 | 1,315.9 | 1,319.3 | 1,325.2 | 1,322.9 | 1,298.6 |
| 2017 | 1,306.2 | 1,314.0 | 1,328.6 | 1,328.1 | 1,340.1 | 1,339.1 | 1,336.1 | 1,341.2 | 1,353.5 | 1,361.1 | 1,367.1 | 1,367.7 | 1,340.2 |
| 2018 | 1,344.3 | 1,357.5 | 1,367.1 | 1,371.0 | 1,381.7 | 1,379.7 | 1,378.8 | 1,389.3 | 1,398.5 | 1,409.4 | 1,416.2 | 1,412.2 | 1,383.8 |
| 2019 | 1,390.2 | 1,400.2 | 1,408.0 | 1,413.8 | 1,423.1 | 1,414.5 | 1,412.5 | 1,421.1 | 1,428.2 | 1,431.7 | 1,438.1 | 1,432.3 | 1,417.8 |
| **Total Private** | | | | | | | | | | | | | |
| 2010 | 955.8 | 955.0 | 960.4 | 971.9 | 976.2 | 981.1 | 980.5 | 979.8 | 983.8 | 987.4 | 988.4 | 985.1 | 975.5 |
| 2011 | 973.2 | 973.4 | 979.1 | 987.7 | 995.9 | 1,002.6 | 996.9 | 1,003.4 | 1,003.9 | 1,008.9 | 1,013.0 | 1,007.2 | 995.4 |
| 2012 | 995.4 | 996.9 | 1,005.3 | 1,015.2 | 1,022.6 | 1,029.5 | 1,028.5 | 1,033.1 | 1,031.7 | 1,036.6 | 1,043.7 | 1,039.9 | 1,023.2 |
| 2013 | 1,029.0 | 1,032.9 | 1,042.9 | 1,053.5 | 1,063.3 | 1,067.3 | 1,064.9 | 1,075.0 | 1,075.9 | 1,084.5 | 1,087.6 | 1,087.5 | 1,063.7 |
| 2014 | 1,075.2 | 1,077.4 | 1,084.5 | 1,096.1 | 1,102.2 | 1,104.1 | 1,103.3 | 1,111.7 | 1,112.4 | 1,124.8 | 1,129.2 | 1,129.0 | 1,104.2 |
| 2015 | 1,109.1 | 1,113.0 | 1,119.7 | 1,133.3 | 1,136.4 | 1,143.4 | 1,147.6 | 1,151.1 | 1,156.1 | 1,159.3 | 1,163.7 | 1,160.2 | 1,141.1 |
| 2016 | 1,149.5 | 1,152.2 | 1,165.6 | 1,167.2 | 1,178.0 | 1,182.5 | 1,182.1 | 1,184.9 | 1,188.8 | 1,198.6 | 1,203.3 | 1,202.8 | 1,179.6 |
| 2017 | 1,186.9 | 1,194.2 | 1,203.0 | 1,209.2 | 1,218.7 | 1,221.8 | 1,225.9 | 1,234.3 | 1,233.2 | 1,243.9 | 1,248.5 | 1,244.5 | 1,222.0 |
| 2018 | 1,230.2 | 1,233.4 | 1,240.4 | 1,247.8 | 1,255.5 | 1,255.6 | 1,256.5 | 1,261.7 | 1,259.4 | 1,261.8 | 1,267.9 | 1,261.5 | 1,252.6 |
| 2019 | | | | | | | | | | | | | |
| **Goods-Producing** | | | | | | | | | | | | | |
| 2011 | 102.8 | 102.8 | 101.3 | 102.7 | 103.8 | 105.4 | 106.4 | 106.8 | 106.4 | 106.5 | 105.2 | 104.0 | 104.5 |
| 2012 | 100.8 | 100.6 | 101.8 | 103.4 | 105.5 | 107.7 | 108.6 | 110.5 | 110.3 | 110.5 | 110.2 | 109.5 | 106.6 |
| 2013 | 106.6 | 107.5 | 108.8 | 110.7 | 111.3 | 113.4 | 114.2 | 116.0 | 115.6 | 116.2 | 116.1 | 114.5 | 112.6 |
| 2014 | 113.7 | 113.9 | 114.9 | 116.3 | 118.2 | 119.5 | 121.2 | 122.5 | 122.4 | 123.1 | 122.7 | 122.2 | 119.2 |
| 2015 | 121.0 | 121.6 | 121.8 | 123.3 | 125.3 | 126.4 | 127.1 | 129.2 | 129.2 | 131.5 | 131.2 | 131.5 | 126.6 |
| 2016 | 128.5 | 128.8 | 129.2 | 130.5 | 131.2 | 133.2 | 135.0 | 135.6 | 136.0 | 136.9 | 136.8 | 137.1 | 133.2 |
| 2017 | 135.6 | 137.7 | 141.0 | 142.2 | 144.5 | 147.0 | 147.8 | 148.1 | 149.6 | 150.5 | 149.9 | 150.0 | 145.3 |
| 2018 | 148.5 | 150.7 | 152.2 | 155.7 | 157.7 | 160.6 | 162.0 | 163.8 | 164.5 | 166.0 | 166.2 | 166.7 | 159.6 |
| 2019 | 164.4 | 165.3 | 168.0 | 168.3 | 169.9 | 171.1 | 172.1 | 172.8 | 172.7 | 173.9 | 173.8 | 171.9 | 170.4 |
| **Service-Providing** | | | | | | | | | | | | | |
| 2011 | 1,004.0 | 1,006.8 | 1,013.5 | 1,023.9 | 1,026.8 | 1,023.3 | 1,016.3 | 1,015.4 | 1,026.0 | 1,031.4 | 1,034.0 | 1,032.9 | 1,021.2 |
| 2012 | 1,019.4 | 1,022.9 | 1,029.1 | 1,036.1 | 1,042.6 | 1,042.3 | 1,030.6 | 1,035.1 | 1,043.5 | 1,050.1 | 1,055.3 | 1,051.1 | 1,038.2 |
| 2013 | 1,038.4 | 1,041.3 | 1,049.6 | 1,057.6 | 1,064.8 | 1,065.5 | 1,056.8 | 1,062.5 | 1,067.3 | 1,073.4 | 1,081.9 | 1,080.8 | 1,061.7 |
| 2014 | 1,066.2 | 1,072.8 | 1,083.2 | 1,092.1 | 1,100.7 | 1,096.7 | 1,087.8 | 1,097.7 | 1,107.2 | 1,116.6 | 1,120.6 | 1,121.9 | 1,097.0 |
| 2015 | 1,106.8 | 1,111.3 | 1,119.7 | 1,129.5 | 1,134.0 | 1,130.1 | 1,122.8 | 1,130.1 | 1,139.6 | 1,149.9 | 1,156.3 | 1,157.3 | 1,132.3 |
| 2016 | 1,135.4 | 1,142.4 | 1,150.6 | 1,161.8 | 1,164.8 | 1,162.1 | 1,163.8 | 1,167.2 | 1,179.9 | 1,182.4 | 1,188.4 | 1,185.8 | 1,165.4 |
| 2017 | 1,170.6 | 1,176.3 | 1,187.6 | 1,185.9 | 1,195.6 | 1,192.1 | 1,188.3 | 1,193.1 | 1,203.9 | 1,210.6 | 1,217.2 | 1,217.7 | 1,194.9 |
| 2018 | 1,195.8 | 1,206.8 | 1,214.9 | 1,215.3 | 1,224.0 | 1,219.1 | 1,216.8 | 1,225.5 | 1,234.0 | 1,243.4 | 1,250.0 | 1,245.5 | 1,224.3 |
| 2019 | 1,225.8 | 1,234.9 | 1,240.0 | 1,245.5 | 1,253.2 | 1,243.4 | 1,240.4 | 1,248.3 | 1,255.5 | 1,257.8 | 1,264.3 | 1,260.4 | 1,247.5 |
| **Mining and Logging** | | | | | | | | | | | | | |
| 2011 | 12.8 | 13.0 | 13.2 | 13.4 | 13.7 | 14.3 | 14.6 | 14.6 | 14.5 | 14.5 | 14.6 | 14.7 | 14.0 |
| 2012 | 14.4 | 14.6 | 15.0 | 15.2 | 15.4 | 15.8 | 16.1 | 16.1 | 15.9 | 15.7 | 15.6 | 15.6 | 15.5 |
| 2013 | 15.4 | 15.5 | 15.4 | 15.3 | 15.3 | 15.4 | 15.7 | 15.6 | 15.0 | 14.8 | 14.8 | 14.7 | 15.2 |
| 2014 | 14.4 | 14.1 | 14.2 | 14.2 | 14.3 | 14.5 | 14.6 | 14.6 | 14.4 | 14.6 | 14.7 | 14.7 | 14.4 |
| 2015 | 14.3 | 14.3 | 14.3 | 14.4 | 14.4 | 14.5 | 14.6 | 14.5 | 14.0 | 13.9 | 13.7 | 13.6 | 14.2 |
| 2016 | 13.4 | 13.3 | 13.3 | 13.6 | 13.7 | 13.8 | 14.0 | 14.0 | 13.8 | 13.9 | 14.0 | 14.0 | 13.7 |
| 2017 | 13.9 | 13.9 | 13.9 | 13.9 | 13.9 | 14.2 | 14.5 | 14.5 | 14.4 | 14.4 | 14.4 | 14.4 | 14.2 |
| 2018 | 14.2 | 14.3 | 14.2 | 14.3 | 14.4 | 14.8 | 14.9 | 14.9 | 14.8 | 14.9 | 14.8 | 14.9 | 14.6 |
| 2019 | 14.5 | 14.6 | 14.8 | 14.6 | 14.7 | 14.8 | 14.9 | 14.9 | 14.7 | 14.9 | 14.6 | 14.2 | 14.7 |
| **Construction** | | | | | | | | | | | | | |
| 2011 | 52.4 | 52.1 | 50.2 | 51.3 | 51.9 | 52.6 | 53.3 | 53.5 | 53.1 | 53.1 | 51.9 | 50.6 | 52.2 |
| 2012 | 48.0 | 47.6 | 48.1 | 49.3 | 51.0 | 52.4 | 52.9 | 54.6 | 54.8 | 55.2 | 55.1 | 54.4 | 52.0 |
| 2013 | 51.9 | 52.4 | 53.6 | 55.3 | 55.6 | 57.2 | 57.8 | 59.5 | 59.6 | 60.3 | 60.1 | 58.6 | 56.8 |
| 2014 | 58.1 | 58.6 | 59.5 | 61.0 | 62.5 | 63.4 | 64.9 | 66.3 | 66.4 | 66.9 | 66.3 | 65.8 | 63.3 |
| 2015 | 65.2 | 65.7 | 65.8 | 67.2 | 69.0 | 69.7 | 70.4 | 72.5 | 72.9 | 75.0 | 74.6 | 74.9 | 70.2 |
| 2016 | 72.4 | 72.5 | 72.9 | 73.9 | 74.3 | 75.9 | 77.1 | 77.6 | 78.2 | 78.6 | 78.3 | 78.1 | 75.8 |
| 2017 | 77.1 | 78.8 | 81.5 | 82.0 | 83.9 | 85.4 | 84.6 | 84.4 | 85.3 | 85.9 | 85.0 | 84.6 | 83.2 |
| 2018 | 83.1 | 84.5 | 85.3 | 87.8 | 88.9 | 90.3 | 90.7 | 92.1 | 92.1 | 93.0 | 92.5 | 92.3 | 89.4 |
| 2019 | 90.6 | 91.2 | 93.5 | 94.5 | 95.9 | 96.7 | 97.5 | 98.3 | 98.5 | 99.5 | 100.2 | 98.4 | 96.2 |

# 1. Employment by Industry: Nevada, 2011–2019—*Continued*

(Numbers in thousands, not seasonally adjusted)

| Industry and year | January | February | March | April | May | June | July | August | September | October | November | December | Annual average |
|---|---|---|---|---|---|---|---|---|---|---|---|---|---|
| **Manufacturing** | | | | | | | | | | | | | |
| 2011 | 37.6 | 37.7 | 37.9 | 38.0 | 38.2 | 38.5 | 38.5 | 38.7 | 38.8 | 38.9 | 38.7 | 38.7 | 38.4 |
| 2012 | 38.4 | 38.4 | 38.7 | 38.9 | 39.1 | 39.5 | 39.6 | 39.8 | 39.6 | 39.6 | 39.5 | 39.5 | 39.2 |
| 2013 | 39.3 | 39.6 | 39.8 | 40.1 | 40.4 | 40.8 | 40.7 | 40.9 | 41.0 | 41.1 | 41.2 | 41.2 | 40.5 |
| 2014 | 41.2 | 41.2 | 41.2 | 41.1 | 41.4 | 41.6 | 41.7 | 41.6 | 41.6 | 41.6 | 41.7 | 41.7 | 41.5 |
| 2015 | 41.5 | 41.6 | 41.7 | 41.7 | 41.9 | 42.2 | 42.1 | 42.2 | 42.3 | 42.6 | 42.9 | 43.0 | 42.1 |
| 2016 | 42.7 | 43.0 | 43.0 | 43.0 | 43.2 | 43.5 | 43.9 | 44.0 | 44.0 | 44.4 | 44.5 | 45.0 | 43.7 |
| 2017 | 44.6 | 45.0 | 45.6 | 46.3 | 46.7 | 47.4 | 48.7 | 49.2 | 49.9 | 50.2 | 50.5 | 51.0 | 47.9 |
| 2018 | 51.2 | 51.9 | 52.7 | 53.6 | 54.4 | 55.5 | 56.4 | 56.8 | 57.6 | 58.1 | 58.9 | 59.5 | 55.6 |
| 2019 | 59.3 | 59.5 | 59.7 | 59.2 | 59.3 | 59.6 | 59.7 | 59.6 | 59.5 | 59.5 | 59.0 | 59.3 | 59.4 |
| **Trade, Transportation, and Utilities** | | | | | | | | | | | | | |
| 2011 | 208.6 | 207.1 | 207.7 | 209.1 | 210.1 | 210.8 | 211.7 | 212.4 | 212.8 | 215.0 | 220.7 | 221.7 | 212.3 |
| 2012 | 214.6 | 212.4 | 213.5 | 214.5 | 215.7 | 216.8 | 216.7 | 217.2 | 218.0 | 219.5 | 226.4 | 226.3 | 217.6 |
| 2013 | 217.8 | 215.8 | 215.3 | 216.3 | 219.0 | 220.3 | 221.3 | 221.9 | 222.6 | 224.9 | 231.4 | 233.0 | 221.6 |
| 2014 | 224.4 | 223.2 | 224.6 | 225.8 | 227.2 | 228.1 | 228.4 | 229.8 | 230.7 | 234.0 | 240.1 | 242.2 | 229.9 |
| 2015 | 234.1 | 232.4 | 233.3 | 234.5 | 235.9 | 236.5 | 236.5 | 237.6 | 238.4 | 241.0 | 246.7 | 248.0 | 237.9 |
| 2016 | 236.9 | 236.3 | 236.8 | 238.4 | 239.2 | 239.5 | 240.5 | 242.0 | 242.6 | 244.7 | 251.9 | 252.2 | 241.8 |
| 2017 | 244.8 | 243.0 | 243.0 | 243.6 | 244.9 | 245.9 | 246.5 | 247.7 | 249.0 | 252.1 | 260.4 | 262.4 | 248.6 |
| 2018 | 252.1 | 250.4 | 250.2 | 250.5 | 252.2 | 253.1 | 254.1 | 255.3 | 255.6 | 258.5 | 266.2 | 266.0 | 255.4 |
| 2019 | 258.9 | 256.4 | 256.0 | 256.4 | 259.0 | 260.1 | 260.2 | 261.5 | 261.6 | 264.1 | 270.2 | 270.0 | 261.2 |
| **Wholesale Trade** | | | | | | | | | | | | | |
| 2011 | 32.2 | 32.3 | 32.4 | 32.4 | 32.5 | 32.6 | 32.6 | 32.5 | 32.4 | 32.4 | 32.3 | 32.4 | 32.4 |
| 2012 | 32.0 | 32.0 | 32.2 | 32.2 | 32.3 | 32.4 | 32.5 | 32.4 | 32.3 | 32.4 | 32.4 | 32.5 | 32.3 |
| 2013 | 32.0 | 32.1 | 32.2 | 32.4 | 32.5 | 32.7 | 32.9 | 32.9 | 33.0 | 33.0 | 33.2 | 33.2 | 32.7 |
| 2014 | 32.9 | 33.1 | 33.3 | 33.4 | 33.4 | 33.5 | 33.7 | 33.8 | 33.9 | 33.9 | 33.9 | 34.1 | 33.6 |
| 2015 | 33.7 | 33.8 | 33.9 | 34.0 | 34.0 | 34.1 | 34.1 | 34.1 | 34.2 | 34.3 | 34.3 | 34.4 | 34.1 |
| 2016 | 33.7 | 33.8 | 33.6 | 33.9 | 34.0 | 34.0 | 34.2 | 34.4 | 34.4 | 34.5 | 34.7 | 34.8 | 34.2 |
| 2017 | 34.8 | 34.9 | 35.1 | 35.3 | 35.5 | 35.7 | 35.7 | 35.7 | 35.7 | 35.8 | 35.8 | 36.0 | 35.5 |
| 2018 | 36.1 | 36.3 | 36.3 | 36.7 | 36.9 | 37.2 | 37.4 | 37.5 | 37.5 | 37.9 | 38.0 | 38.1 | 37.2 |
| 2019 | 38.1 | 38.2 | 38.4 | 38.5 | 38.6 | 38.9 | 38.9 | 38.7 | 38.6 | 38.2 | 37.7 | 36.9 | 38.3 |
| **Retail Trade** | | | | | | | | | | | | | |
| 2011 | 126.1 | 124.4 | 124.8 | 125.5 | 126.3 | 126.6 | 127.0 | 127.6 | 127.7 | 129.4 | 134.8 | 135.2 | 128.0 |
| 2012 | 129.8 | 127.8 | 128.6 | 129.2 | 129.9 | 130.6 | 130.3 | 130.7 | 131.2 | 132.4 | 139.0 | 138.5 | 131.5 |
| 2013 | 131.7 | 129.9 | 130.0 | 130.7 | 132.3 | 133.1 | 133.7 | 134.3 | 134.4 | 136.1 | 141.7 | 143.0 | 134.2 |
| 2014 | 135.6 | 134.0 | 134.6 | 135.3 | 136.3 | 136.9 | 137.0 | 138.0 | 138.5 | 141.5 | 146.9 | 148.1 | 138.6 |
| 2015 | 141.0 | 139.5 | 140.5 | 141.3 | 142.1 | 142.4 | 142.3 | 143.1 | 142.8 | 145.0 | 149.7 | 150.0 | 143.3 |
| 2016 | 141.6 | 140.9 | 141.3 | 142.0 | 142.4 | 142.6 | 142.8 | 143.8 | 143.8 | 145.7 | 151.5 | 150.9 | 144.1 |
| 2017 | 144.7 | 143.1 | 142.7 | 143.2 | 144.2 | 144.3 | 144.3 | 144.7 | 145.0 | 147.2 | 153.7 | 154.0 | 145.9 |
| 2018 | 146.3 | 144.9 | 144.5 | 144.5 | 145.7 | 146.1 | 146.8 | 147.8 | 147.8 | 149.1 | 155.3 | 155.0 | 147.8 |
| 2019 | 148.8 | 146.7 | 146.3 | 146.2 | 146.9 | 147.0 | 146.9 | 147.5 | 147.2 | 149.4 | 154.4 | 153.7 | 148.4 |
| **Transportation and Utilities** | | | | | | | | | | | | | |
| 2011 | 50.3 | 50.4 | 50.5 | 51.2 | 51.3 | 51.6 | 52.1 | 52.3 | 52.7 | 53.2 | 53.6 | 54.1 | 51.9 |
| 2012 | 52.8 | 52.6 | 52.7 | 53.1 | 53.5 | 53.8 | 53.9 | 54.1 | 54.5 | 54.7 | 55.0 | 55.3 | 53.8 |
| 2013 | 54.1 | 53.8 | 53.1 | 53.2 | 54.2 | 54.5 | 54.7 | 54.7 | 55.2 | 55.8 | 56.5 | 56.8 | 54.7 |
| 2014 | 55.9 | 56.1 | 56.7 | 57.1 | 57.5 | 57.7 | 57.7 | 58.0 | 58.3 | 58.6 | 59.3 | 60.0 | 57.7 |
| 2015 | 59.4 | 59.1 | 58.9 | 59.2 | 59.8 | 60.0 | 60.1 | 60.4 | 61.4 | 61.7 | 62.7 | 63.6 | 60.5 |
| 2016 | 61.6 | 61.6 | 61.9 | 62.5 | 62.8 | 62.9 | 63.5 | 63.8 | 64.4 | 64.5 | 65.7 | 66.5 | 63.5 |
| 2017 | 65.3 | 65.0 | 65.2 | 65.1 | 65.2 | 65.9 | 66.5 | 67.3 | 68.3 | 69.1 | 70.9 | 72.4 | 67.2 |
| 2018 | 69.7 | 69.2 | 69.4 | 69.3 | 69.6 | 69.8 | 69.9 | 70.0 | 70.3 | 71.5 | 72.9 | 72.9 | 70.4 |
| 2019 | 72.0 | 71.5 | 71.3 | 71.7 | 73.5 | 74.2 | 74.4 | 75.3 | 75.8 | 76.5 | 78.1 | 79.4 | 74.5 |
| **Information** | | | | | | | | | | | | | |
| 2011 | 12.6 | 12.5 | 12.6 | 12.9 | 13.0 | 13.0 | 12.8 | 12.7 | 12.9 | 13.3 | 12.6 | 13.0 | 12.8 |
| 2012 | 12.5 | 12.6 | 12.7 | 12.6 | 12.9 | 12.9 | 12.6 | 13.0 | 12.9 | 13.5 | 14.7 | 13.2 | 13.0 |
| 2013 | 12.3 | 12.6 | 12.8 | 13.0 | 13.3 | 14.2 | 13.4 | 13.2 | 13.2 | 13.3 | 13.6 | 13.4 | 13.2 |
| 2014 | 13.0 | 13.3 | 13.1 | 14.3 | 15.1 | 15.8 | 13.8 | 13.7 | 13.9 | 13.9 | 14.4 | 14.1 | 14.0 |
| 2015 | 13.7 | 14.1 | 13.9 | 14.1 | 14.2 | 14.5 | 14.0 | 14.2 | 13.8 | 14.3 | 15.1 | 14.5 | 14.2 |
| 2016 | 14.5 | 14.7 | 14.1 | 15.2 | 15.0 | 15.2 | 15.1 | 14.4 | 14.5 | 14.6 | 14.4 | 14.3 | 14.7 |
| 2017 | 14.7 | 14.5 | 14.5 | 15.3 | 15.6 | 16.1 | 15.0 | 15.3 | 14.9 | 15.4 | 15.7 | 15.4 | 15.2 |
| 2018 | 15.0 | 15.2 | 15.2 | 16.3 | 16.9 | 16.4 | 15.5 | 15.4 | 15.2 | 15.5 | 16.0 | 15.6 | 15.7 |
| 2019 | 15.2 | 15.8 | 15.6 | 16.4 | 16.6 | 15.8 | 15.6 | 15.6 | 15.5 | 15.7 | 16.0 | 15.8 | 15.8 |

## 1. Employment by Industry: Nevada, 2011–2019—*Continued*

(Numbers in thousands, not seasonally adjusted)

| Industry and year | January | February | March | April | May | June | July | August | September | October | November | December | Annual average |
|---|---|---|---|---|---|---|---|---|---|---|---|---|---|
| **Financial Activities** | | | | | | | | | | | | | |
| 2011 | 52.4 | 52.1 | 52.1 | 52.5 | 52.4 | 52.6 | 52.7 | 52.3 | 52.7 | 52.9 | 52.7 | 53.0 | 52.5 |
| 2012 | 52.6 | 52.7 | 53.0 | 53.9 | 54.2 | 54.6 | 54.5 | 54.8 | 54.9 | 55.7 | 55.7 | 55.8 | 54.4 |
| 2013 | 55.4 | 56.1 | 56.7 | 56.6 | 57.0 | 57.0 | 56.5 | 56.5 | 56.4 | 56.8 | 57.1 | 57.3 | 56.6 |
| 2014 | 56.1 | 56.2 | 56.3 | 56.3 | 57.0 | 56.9 | 56.7 | 57.2 | 57.4 | 58.1 | 58.3 | 58.5 | 57.1 |
| 2015 | 57.9 | 58.4 | 58.5 | 59.4 | 60.0 | 59.9 | 60.3 | 60.4 | 60.5 | 61.7 | 61.7 | 62.4 | 60.1 |
| 2016 | 61.5 | 61.7 | 62.0 | 62.4 | 62.9 | 62.7 | 63.0 | 63.2 | 63.3 | 63.6 | 63.7 | 63.9 | 62.8 |
| 2017 | 63.5 | 64.2 | 64.1 | 64.7 | 65.5 | 65.4 | 66.0 | 66.1 | 66.1 | 66.7 | 66.6 | 66.7 | 65.5 |
| 2018 | 66.4 | 67.3 | 67.6 | 66.9 | 67.5 | 67.4 | 67.8 | 67.9 | 67.6 | 68.0 | 68.0 | 67.5 | 67.5 |
| 2019 | 66.9 | 67.4 | 67.9 | 68.4 | 69.1 | 68.9 | 69.0 | 69.4 | 69.3 | 69.9 | 70.6 | 70.9 | 69.0 |
| **Professional and Business Services** | | | | | | | | | | | | | |
| 2011 | 138.7 | 137.2 | 137.6 | 139.0 | 138.8 | 139.6 | 138.9 | 139.3 | 141.5 | 143.0 | 142.8 | 141.9 | 139.9 |
| 2012 | 144.6 | 143.7 | 142.4 | 143.5 | 144.2 | 145.5 | 141.8 | 145.7 | 146.4 | 148.0 | 147.5 | 145.3 | 144.9 |
| 2013 | 148.9 | 147.2 | 148.9 | 150.4 | 151.3 | 150.3 | 147.8 | 150.8 | 148.9 | 151.6 | 152.8 | 151.7 | 150.1 |
| 2014 | 153.0 | 153.0 | 154.1 | 155.1 | 155.8 | 155.8 | 153.3 | 157.1 | 157.2 | 162.2 | 161.7 | 161.1 | 156.6 |
| 2015 | 163.5 | 161.6 | 162.8 | 166.1 | 165.9 | 164.7 | 163.9 | 167.9 | 167.9 | 172.6 | 173.4 | 173.3 | 167.0 |
| 2016 | 172.1 | 170.5 | 172.4 | 175.4 | 174.3 | 176.5 | 176.0 | 177.1 | 179.9 | 181.2 | 180.9 | 178.1 | 176.2 |
| 2017 | 180.7 | 178.0 | 182.2 | 178.2 | 180.7 | 180.7 | 180.6 | 180.8 | 181.9 | 186.0 | 185.1 | 184.1 | 181.6 |
| 2018 | 184.9 | 184.8 | 185.8 | 187.0 | 188.0 | 187.1 | 189.4 | 193.2 | 192.1 | 197.3 | 195.9 | 193.3 | 189.9 |
| 2019 | 194.2 | 192.0 | 192.0 | 194.4 | 194.4 | 194.3 | 194.3 | 196.5 | 196.5 | 198.5 | 201.2 | 197.8 | 195.5 |
| **Education and Health Services** | | | | | | | | | | | | | |
| 2011 | 103.1 | 104.0 | 104.7 | 105.3 | 105.3 | 105.5 | 104.9 | 105.4 | 105.9 | 106.5 | 107.1 | 107.5 | 105.4 |
| 2012 | 106.9 | 107.8 | 108.1 | 108.6 | 109.1 | 108.6 | 107.4 | 108.7 | 108.5 | 109.1 | 109.2 | 109.6 | 108.5 |
| 2013 | 108.7 | 110.1 | 110.6 | 111.0 | 111.4 | 111.4 | 111.0 | 111.8 | 112.3 | 113.1 | 113.5 | 113.4 | 111.5 |
| 2014 | 112.6 | 113.8 | 114.4 | 114.8 | 115.2 | 115.5 | 115.2 | 116.0 | 116.4 | 117.8 | 118.0 | 118.3 | 115.7 |
| 2015 | 117.0 | 118.1 | 118.8 | 119.6 | 119.8 | 120.3 | 120.5 | 121.5 | 122.3 | 124.2 | 124.2 | 124.7 | 120.9 |
| 2016 | 123.5 | 124.8 | 125.0 | 125.8 | 126.2 | 126.3 | 126.7 | 127.7 | 128.4 | 130.3 | 130.2 | 130.7 | 127.1 |
| 2017 | 129.0 | 130.2 | 130.9 | 132.1 | 132.2 | 132.1 | 130.8 | 133.2 | 134.1 | 135.6 | 136.4 | 136.6 | 132.8 |
| 2018 | 135.9 | 137.5 | 138.3 | 138.3 | 139.0 | 138.9 | 138.3 | 140.4 | 141.1 | 142.3 | 143.0 | 143.2 | 139.7 |
| 2019 | 141.5 | 143.0 | 143.4 | 144.0 | 144.6 | 143.7 | 142.9 | 145.2 | 144.7 | 144.4 | 145.6 | 144.8 | 144.0 |
| **Leisure and Hospitality** | | | | | | | | | | | | | |
| 2011 | 306.0 | 307.5 | 312.4 | 317.9 | 320.1 | 321.3 | 320.1 | 318.0 | 319.0 | 317.9 | 315.1 | 311.7 | 315.6 |
| 2012 | 309.1 | 311.4 | 315.0 | 318.2 | 320.8 | 322.6 | 321.5 | 319.6 | 319.0 | 318.4 | 316.2 | 314.7 | 317.2 |
| 2013 | 313.3 | 315.0 | 319.3 | 323.7 | 325.4 | 328.7 | 330.0 | 328.6 | 328.6 | 326.6 | 325.0 | 322.5 | 323.9 |
| 2014 | 322.1 | 325.2 | 330.8 | 335.4 | 338.8 | 339.6 | 340.1 | 342.6 | 341.9 | 339.0 | 336.6 | 335.6 | 335.6 |
| 2015 | 332.8 | 335.8 | 339.7 | 342.9 | 344.5 | 344.6 | 343.9 | 343.7 | 343.3 | 342.4 | 339.8 | 337.3 | 340.9 |
| 2016 | 334.7 | 338.0 | 341.2 | 346.1 | 347.8 | 350.0 | 350.6 | 350.3 | 350.1 | 346.1 | 344.9 | 343.9 | 345.3 |
| 2017 | 341.5 | 344.8 | 349.7 | 350.4 | 353.5 | 353.9 | 353.7 | 352.2 | 351.8 | 351.0 | 348.0 | 346.6 | 349.8 |
| 2018 | 343.4 | 347.5 | 352.5 | 353.5 | 355.9 | 356.0 | 357.0 | 356.2 | 354.9 | 353.6 | 351.4 | 351.1 | 352.8 |
| 2019 | 348.8 | 352.9 | 356.5 | 358.3 | 359.6 | 359.6 | 360.3 | 358.3 | 357.1 | 353.7 | 349.1 | 349.8 | 355.3 |
| **Other Services** | | | | | | | | | | | | | |
| 2011 | 31.6 | 31.8 | 32.0 | 32.5 | 32.7 | 32.9 | 33.0 | 32.9 | 32.6 | 32.3 | 32.2 | 32.3 | 32.4 |
| 2012 | 32.1 | 32.2 | 32.6 | 33.0 | 33.5 | 33.9 | 33.8 | 33.9 | 33.9 | 34.2 | 33.1 | 32.8 | 33.3 |
| 2013 | 32.4 | 32.6 | 32.9 | 33.5 | 33.9 | 34.2 | 34.3 | 34.3 | 34.1 | 34.1 | 34.2 | 34.1 | 33.7 |
| 2014 | 34.1 | 34.3 | 34.7 | 35.5 | 36.0 | 36.1 | 36.2 | 36.1 | 36.0 | 36.4 | 35.8 | 35.5 | 35.6 |
| 2015 | 35.2 | 35.4 | 35.7 | 36.2 | 36.6 | 37.2 | 37.1 | 37.2 | 37.0 | 37.1 | 37.1 | 37.3 | 36.6 |
| 2016 | 37.4 | 38.2 | 39.0 | 39.5 | 39.8 | 40.0 | 40.7 | 40.8 | 41.3 | 41.9 | 40.9 | 40.0 | 40.0 |
| 2017 | 39.7 | 39.8 | 40.2 | 40.7 | 41.1 | 41.4 | 41.7 | 41.5 | 41.4 | 41.3 | 41.2 | 41.0 | 40.9 |
| 2018 | 40.7 | 40.8 | 41.2 | 41.0 | 41.5 | 42.3 | 41.8 | 42.1 | 42.2 | 42.7 | 41.8 | 41.1 | 41.6 |
| 2019 | 40.3 | 40.6 | 41.0 | 41.6 | 42.3 | 42.1 | 42.1 | 42.4 | 42.0 | 41.6 | 41.4 | 40.5 | 41.5 |
| **Government** | | | | | | | | | | | | | |
| 2011 | 151.0 | 154.6 | 154.4 | 154.7 | 154.4 | 147.6 | 142.2 | 142.4 | 148.6 | 150.5 | 150.8 | 151.8 | 150.3 |
| 2012 | 147.0 | 150.1 | 151.8 | 151.8 | 152.2 | 147.4 | 142.3 | 142.2 | 149.9 | 151.7 | 152.5 | 153.4 | 149.4 |
| 2013 | 149.6 | 151.9 | 153.1 | 153.1 | 153.5 | 149.4 | 142.5 | 145.4 | 151.2 | 153.0 | 154.3 | 155.4 | 151.0 |
| 2014 | 150.9 | 153.8 | 155.2 | 154.9 | 155.6 | 148.9 | 144.1 | 145.2 | 153.7 | 155.2 | 155.7 | 156.6 | 152.5 |
| 2015 | 152.6 | 155.5 | 157.0 | 156.7 | 157.1 | 152.4 | 146.6 | 147.6 | 156.4 | 156.6 | 158.3 | 159.8 | 154.7 |
| 2016 | 154.8 | 158.2 | 160.1 | 159.0 | 159.6 | 151.9 | 151.2 | 151.7 | 159.8 | 160.0 | 161.5 | 162.7 | 157.5 |
| 2017 | 156.7 | 161.8 | 163.0 | 160.9 | 162.1 | 156.6 | 154.0 | 156.3 | 164.7 | 162.5 | 163.8 | 164.9 | 160.6 |
| 2018 | 157.4 | 163.3 | 164.1 | 161.8 | 163.0 | 157.9 | 152.9 | 155.0 | 165.3 | 165.5 | 167.7 | 167.7 | 161.8 |
| 2019 | 160.0 | 166.8 | 167.6 | 166.0 | 167.6 | 158.9 | 156.0 | 159.4 | 168.8 | 169.9 | 170.2 | 170.8 | 165.2 |

## 2. Average Weekly Hours by Selected Industry: Nevada, 2015–2019

(Not seasonally adjusted)

| Industry and year | January | February | March | April | May | June | July | August | September | October | November | December | Annual average |
|---|---|---|---|---|---|---|---|---|---|---|---|---|---|
| **Total Private** | | | | | | | | | | | | | |
| 2015 | 33.2 | 33.5 | 33.6 | 33.4 | 33.5 | 33.6 | 33.7 | 34.1 | 33.7 | 33.6 | 33.9 | 33.4 | 33.6 |
| 2016 | 33.3 | 33.3 | 33.3 | 33.6 | 34.1 | 34.0 | 34.3 | 34.4 | 34.1 | 34.5 | 33.8 | 34.1 | 33.9 |
| 2017 | 34.1 | 33.5 | 33.9 | 34.2 | 34.1 | 34.2 | 34.7 | 34.3 | 34.1 | 34.5 | 34.0 | 33.9 | 34.1 |
| 2018 | 33.6 | 33.6 | 33.9 | 34.0 | 33.8 | 34.1 | 34.5 | 34.4 | 34.6 | 34.0 | 34.3 | 34.5 | 34.1 |
| 2019 | 34.6 | 34.5 | 34.6 | 34.7 | 34.7 | 35.0 | 34.4 | 34.5 | 34.6 | 34.2 | 34.0 | 34.5 | 34.5 |
| **Goods-Producing** | | | | | | | | | | | | | |
| 2015 | 37.7 | 37.7 | 38.7 | 38.7 | 38.4 | 38.8 | 38.1 | 38.3 | 38.0 | 38.5 | 38.1 | 38.2 | 38.3 |
| 2016 | 38.2 | 37.9 | 38.2 | 38.5 | 39.4 | 38.9 | 38.4 | 39.0 | 38.9 | 38.9 | 37.5 | 38.2 | 38.5 |
| 2017 | 37.2 | 37.5 | 37.9 | 37.5 | 38.4 | 38.7 | 39.2 | 39.2 | 38.7 | 39.1 | 38.4 | 39.1 | 38.4 |
| 2018 | 38.0 | 38.7 | 38.9 | 39.1 | 39.6 | 39.5 | 38.9 | 39.8 | 39.6 | 39.1 | 40.0 | 40.4 | 39.3 |
| 2019 | 39.5 | 38.7 | 39.9 | 40.3 | 40.6 | 41.1 | 41.0 | 40.8 | 41.2 | 40.8 | 40.1 | 40.8 | 40.4 |
| **Construction** | | | | | | | | | | | | | |
| 2015 | 36.0 | 36.5 | 37.6 | 37.5 | 37.1 | 37.8 | 37.0 | 37.2 | 37.2 | 38.1 | 36.5 | 36.0 | 37.0 |
| 2016 | 36.3 | 36.6 | 36.7 | 36.9 | 37.6 | 36.5 | 35.7 | 36.5 | 36.4 | 36.6 | 35.0 | 36.1 | 36.4 |
| 2017 | 34.5 | 34.4 | 35.3 | 35.0 | 36.0 | 35.8 | 36.2 | 36.4 | 36.1 | 38.0 | 36.5 | 37.0 | 35.9 |
| 2018 | 35.9 | 37.1 | 37.5 | 37.2 | 37.9 | 37.8 | 37.5 | 38.3 | 37.6 | 38.0 | 38.5 | 39.4 | 37.7 |
| 2019 | 38.8 | 37.6 | 39.2 | 39.7 | 39.4 | 40.1 | 40.5 | 40.4 | 40.5 | 39.9 | 39.1 | 39.8 | 39.6 |
| **Trade, Transportation, and Utilities** | | | | | | | | | | | | | |
| 2015 | 33.9 | 34.5 | 35.5 | 34.6 | 35.2 | 35.4 | 35.6 | 35.9 | 36.3 | 35.7 | 36.6 | 36.0 | 35.4 |
| 2016 | 35.2 | 35.0 | 35.2 | 35.4 | 35.9 | 36.3 | 35.8 | 35.5 | 35.7 | 35.8 | 34.9 | 35.7 | 35.5 |
| 2017 | 35.4 | 35.0 | 35.3 | 36.1 | 35.6 | 35.8 | 36.2 | 35.5 | 35.4 | 35.3 | 35.1 | 35.0 | 35.5 |
| 2018 | 34.9 | 34.6 | 34.7 | 34.9 | 34.6 | 34.7 | 35.3 | 34.4 | 34.9 | 33.8 | 34.1 | 34.2 | 34.6 |
| 2019 | 34.4 | 34.3 | 33.9 | 33.9 | 34.1 | 34.4 | 34.3 | 34.7 | 34.0 | 33.7 | 33.3 | 34.4 | 34.1 |
| **Financial Activities** | | | | | | | | | | | | | |
| 2015 | 37.1 | 37.6 | 37.7 | 37.7 | 37.9 | 37.0 | 37.4 | 37.8 | 38.3 | 37.3 | 37.5 | 36.7 | 37.5 |
| 2016 | 37.0 | 37.1 | 36.5 | 37.6 | 38.1 | 37.7 | 38.3 | 37.6 | 37.3 | 36.6 | 36.7 | 37.5 | 37.3 |
| 2017 | 38.2 | 36.9 | 37.2 | 38.3 | 38.1 | 38.4 | 38.7 | 38.1 | 37.6 | 38.0 | 37.8 | 37.2 | 37.9 |
| 2018 | 37.5 | 37.2 | 37.5 | 38.7 | 37.9 | 37.9 | 38.5 | 38.0 | 38.5 | 37.7 | 35.9 | 37.8 | 37.8 |
| 2019 | 37.2 | 37.1 | 35.6 | 36.2 | 36.1 | 37.8 | 36.4 | 35.5 | 36.2 | 35.6 | 35.2 | 35.4 | 36.2 |
| **Professional and Business Services** | | | | | | | | | | | | | |
| 2015 | 34.9 | 35.2 | 33.9 | 34.3 | 34.1 | 34.3 | 34.6 | 35.8 | 34.0 | 34.1 | 34.2 | 33.9 | 34.4 |
| 2016 | 33.3 | 33.9 | 33.4 | 34.1 | 34.5 | 34.3 | 34.3 | 35.2 | 34.4 | 35.9 | 34.7 | 34.9 | 34.4 |
| 2017 | 35.4 | 34.7 | 34.8 | 35.5 | 35.0 | 35.5 | 35.4 | 35.3 | 34.9 | 35.8 | 34.9 | 34.8 | 35.2 |
| 2018 | 34.0 | 34.3 | 34.8 | 35.0 | 34.4 | 34.8 | 35.3 | 35.9 | 36.2 | 35.3 | 35.2 | 35.9 | 35.1 |
| 2019 | 36.6 | 35.9 | 36.1 | 35.8 | 36.2 | 37.0 | 36.3 | 35.9 | 36.8 | 36.9 | 36.1 | 37.2 | 36.4 |
| **Leisure and Hospitality** | | | | | | | | | | | | | |
| 2015 | 29.8 | 30.1 | 30.2 | 29.9 | 30.1 | 30.2 | 30.5 | 30.4 | 30.0 | 29.7 | 29.9 | 29.4 | 30.0 |
| 2016 | 29.3 | 29.3 | 29.6 | 29.3 | 29.3 | 29.5 | 30.0 | 30.4 | 30.1 | 30.5 | 29.9 | 29.4 | 29.7 |
| 2017 | 29.9 | 29.5 | 30.0 | 30.1 | 30.1 | 29.8 | 30.0 | 29.9 | 29.7 | 29.7 | 29.3 | 28.6 | 29.7 |
| 2018 | 29.3 | 29.0 | 29.5 | 29.4 | 28.8 | 29.2 | 29.6 | 29.7 | 29.7 | 29.6 | 29.6 | 29.0 | 29.4 |
| 2019 | 29.6 | 29.8 | 30.5 | 30.4 | 30.2 | 30.1 | 30.1 | 30.6 | 30.2 | 29.9 | 30.0 | 29.9 | 30.1 |

## 3. Average Hourly Earnings by Selected Industry: Nevada, 2015–2019

(Dollars, not seasonally adjusted)

| Industry and year | January | February | March | April | May | June | July | August | September | October | November | December | Annual average |
|---|---|---|---|---|---|---|---|---|---|---|---|---|---|
| **Total Private** | | | | | | | | | | | | | |
| 2015 | 21.61 | 21.88 | 21.95 | 21.85 | 21.78 | 21.73 | 21.87 | 22.12 | 22.11 | 22.16 | 22.24 | 22.08 | 21.95 |
| 2016 | 22.28 | 22.27 | 22.20 | 22.22 | 22.25 | 22.07 | 21.88 | 22.05 | 22.02 | 22.20 | 22.16 | 22.20 | 22.15 |
| 2017 | 22.70 | 22.51 | 22.48 | 22.48 | 22.34 | 22.33 | 22.42 | 22.50 | 22.51 | 22.67 | 22.64 | 22.70 | 22.52 |
| 2018 | 22.83 | 22.85 | 22.88 | 23.24 | 23.40 | 23.25 | 23.27 | 23.47 | 23.45 | 23.40 | 23.88 | 24.06 | 23.34 |
| 2019 | 24.37 | 23.98 | 23.96 | 24.13 | 24.31 | 24.41 | 24.50 | 24.54 | 24.98 | 24.91 | 24.95 | 25.19 | 24.52 |
| **Goods-Producing** | | | | | | | | | | | | | |
| 2015 | 26.10 | 26.41 | 26.43 | 26.52 | 26.11 | 26.14 | 26.78 | 26.76 | 27.13 | 27.16 | 26.97 | 27.11 | 26.64 |
| 2016 | 27.24 | 27.31 | 27.14 | 27.55 | 27.34 | 27.41 | 27.42 | 27.11 | 27.49 | 27.08 | 27.37 | 27.15 | 27.30 |
| 2017 | 27.94 | 27.65 | 27.44 | 27.23 | 27.42 | 27.55 | 27.73 | 27.91 | 28.18 | 28.45 | 27.95 | 28.27 | 27.82 |
| 2018 | 28.58 | 28.79 | 28.61 | 28.46 | 28.66 | 28.52 | 29.06 | 28.85 | 29.01 | 29.36 | 30.40 | 31.13 | 29.15 |
| 2019 | 31.85 | 31.65 | 32.46 | 33.43 | 32.78 | 32.77 | 33.51 | 33.44 | 34.04 | 33.38 | 33.05 | 33.86 | 33.04 |
| **Construction** | | | | | | | | | | | | | |
| 2015 | 26.21 | 26.40 | 26.64 | 26.71 | 27.16 | 27.06 | 28.25 | 28.26 | 28.40 | 28.36 | 28.00 | 28.08 | 27.50 |
| 2016 | 28.11 | 28.47 | 27.95 | 28.14 | 27.77 | 27.79 | 27.79 | 27.84 | 27.42 | 27.25 | 27.51 | 27.26 | 27.77 |
| 2017 | 28.52 | 28.26 | 27.81 | 27.43 | 27.77 | 27.65 | 27.84 | 28.11 | 28.24 | 28.70 | 28.13 | 28.67 | 28.10 |
| 2018 | 28.77 | 29.13 | 29.02 | 28.30 | 28.80 | 28.76 | 29.36 | 29.33 | 29.43 | 29.91 | 31.08 | 31.77 | 29.51 |
| 2019 | 32.96 | 32.90 | 33.42 | 34.54 | 33.93 | 33.81 | 35.01 | 34.73 | 35.33 | 34.66 | 33.90 | 34.92 | 34.21 |
| **Trade, Transportation, and Utilities** | | | | | | | | | | | | | |
| 2015 | 19.82 | 19.93 | 19.89 | 19.92 | 19.79 | 19.55 | 19.53 | 19.45 | 19.67 | 19.57 | 19.65 | 19.34 | 19.67 |
| 2016 | 20.01 | 19.85 | 20.13 | 20.22 | 20.05 | 19.84 | 20.00 | 20.05 | 20.06 | 20.46 | 20.20 | 20.18 | 20.09 |
| 2017 | 20.64 | 20.76 | 20.46 | 20.50 | 19.97 | 20.06 | 20.06 | 19.90 | 19.70 | 19.80 | 19.41 | 19.67 | 20.07 |
| 2018 | 19.40 | 19.68 | 19.53 | 19.60 | 19.77 | 19.52 | 19.88 | 19.70 | 19.67 | 19.69 | 19.44 | 19.82 | 19.64 |
| 2019 | 20.20 | 20.17 | 20.16 | 20.29 | 20.35 | 20.57 | 20.18 | 20.41 | 20.93 | 20.63 | 20.72 | 20.70 | 20.44 |
| **Financial Activities** | | | | | | | | | | | | | |
| 2015 | 22.19 | 22.69 | 22.96 | 23.49 | 23.85 | 23.89 | 26.20 | 26.57 | 26.11 | 26.33 | 25.98 | 26.49 | 24.76 |
| 2016 | 26.28 | 25.48 | 25.20 | 24.69 | 26.01 | 25.34 | 24.82 | 25.32 | 24.94 | 25.58 | 24.94 | 25.56 | 25.34 |
| 2017 | 24.89 | 25.53 | 25.84 | 25.94 | 25.60 | 25.89 | 26.01 | 26.24 | 26.40 | 26.33 | 26.34 | 26.18 | 25.94 |
| 2018 | 26.65 | 26.84 | 26.90 | 27.05 | 26.96 | 26.76 | 25.82 | 26.13 | 26.57 | 26.05 | 27.26 | 27.33 | 26.69 |
| 2019 | 26.86 | 27.07 | 27.00 | 26.55 | 27.70 | 27.10 | 26.88 | 27.02 | 26.35 | 26.03 | 26.66 | 26.71 | 26.83 |
| **Professional and Business Services** | | | | | | | | | | | | | |
| 2015 | 23.63 | 24.54 | 24.77 | 24.12 | 24.24 | 24.14 | 24.30 | 24.55 | 24.03 | 24.31 | 24.48 | 23.90 | 24.25 |
| 2016 | 24.46 | 24.90 | 24.59 | 24.09 | 24.05 | 23.73 | 23.93 | 23.81 | 23.60 | 24.27 | 24.09 | 24.18 | 24.13 |
| 2017 | 24.74 | 24.40 | 24.44 | 24.52 | 24.76 | 24.05 | 24.55 | 24.74 | 24.53 | 24.65 | 24.84 | 25.24 | 24.62 |
| 2018 | 25.79 | 25.83 | 25.92 | 26.34 | 26.65 | 26.34 | 26.68 | 27.06 | 26.92 | 26.57 | 26.54 | 26.34 | 26.43 |
| 2019 | 26.08 | 25.97 | 25.26 | 25.94 | 25.85 | 26.15 | 26.13 | 26.17 | 26.60 | 26.50 | 25.61 | 25.90 | 26.02 |
| **Leisure and Hospitality** | | | | | | | | | | | | | |
| 2015 | 16.58 | 16.28 | 16.13 | 15.97 | 16.20 | 15.94 | 15.91 | 16.06 | 16.29 | 16.35 | 16.64 | 16.49 | 16.23 |
| 2016 | 16.64 | 16.75 | 16.88 | 16.77 | 16.89 | 17.10 | 16.72 | 16.91 | 17.12 | 16.95 | 17.09 | 16.86 | 16.89 |
| 2017 | 17.45 | 17.31 | 17.35 | 17.42 | 17.17 | 17.30 | 17.09 | 17.17 | 17.42 | 17.20 | 17.28 | 17.14 | 17.27 |
| 2018 | 17.51 | 17.12 | 17.34 | 17.45 | 17.75 | 17.63 | 17.53 | 17.71 | 17.60 | 17.78 | 17.75 | 17.51 | 17.56 |
| 2019 | 17.91 | 17.60 | 17.91 | 17.70 | 17.94 | 17.75 | 17.71 | 17.65 | 17.86 | 17.84 | 17.77 | 18.09 | 17.81 |

# 4. Average Weekly Earnings by Selected Industry: Nevada, 2015–2019

(Dollars, not seasonally adjusted)

| Industry and year | January | February | March | April | May | June | July | August | September | October | November | December | Annual average |
|---|---|---|---|---|---|---|---|---|---|---|---|---|---|
| **Total Private** | | | | | | | | | | | | | |
| 2015 | 717.45 | 732.98 | 737.52 | 729.79 | 729.63 | 730.13 | 737.02 | 754.29 | 745.11 | 744.58 | 753.94 | 737.47 | 737.52 |
| 2016 | 741.92 | 741.59 | 739.26 | 746.59 | 758.73 | 750.38 | 750.48 | 758.52 | 750.88 | 765.90 | 749.01 | 757.02 | 750.89 |
| 2017 | 774.07 | 754.09 | 762.07 | 768.82 | 761.79 | 763.69 | 777.97 | 771.75 | 767.59 | 782.12 | 769.76 | 769.53 | 767.93 |
| 2018 | 767.09 | 767.76 | 775.63 | 790.16 | 790.92 | 792.83 | 802.82 | 807.37 | 811.37 | 795.60 | 819.08 | 830.07 | 795.89 |
| 2019 | 843.20 | 827.31 | 829.02 | 837.31 | 843.56 | 854.35 | 842.80 | 846.63 | 864.31 | 851.92 | 848.30 | 869.06 | 845.94 |
| **Goods-Producing** | | | | | | | | | | | | | |
| 2015 | 983.97 | 995.66 | 1,022.84 | 1,026.32 | 1,002.62 | 1,014.23 | 1,020.32 | 1,024.91 | 1,030.94 | 1,045.66 | 1,027.56 | 1,035.60 | 1,020.31 |
| 2016 | 1,040.57 | 1,035.05 | 1,036.75 | 1,060.68 | 1,077.20 | 1,066.25 | 1,052.93 | 1,057.29 | 1,069.36 | 1,053.41 | 1,026.38 | 1,037.13 | 1,051.05 |
| 2017 | 1,039.37 | 1,036.88 | 1,039.98 | 1,021.13 | 1,052.93 | 1,066.19 | 1,087.02 | 1,094.07 | 1,090.57 | 1,112.40 | 1,073.28 | 1,105.36 | 1,068.29 |
| 2018 | 1,086.04 | 1,114.17 | 1,112.93 | 1,112.79 | 1,134.94 | 1,126.54 | 1,130.43 | 1,148.23 | 1,148.80 | 1,147.98 | 1,216.00 | 1,257.65 | 1,145.60 |
| 2019 | 1,258.08 | 1,224.86 | 1,295.15 | 1,347.23 | 1,330.87 | 1,346.85 | 1,373.91 | 1,364.35 | 1,402.45 | 1,361.90 | 1,325.31 | 1,381.49 | 1,334.82 |
| **Construction** | | | | | | | | | | | | | |
| 2015 | 943.56 | 963.60 | 1,001.66 | 1,001.63 | 1,007.64 | 1,022.87 | 1,045.25 | 1,051.27 | 1,056.48 | 1,080.52 | 1,022.00 | 1,010.88 | 1,017.50 |
| 2016 | 1,020.39 | 1,042.00 | 1,025.77 | 1,038.37 | 1,044.15 | 1,014.34 | 992.10 | 1,016.16 | 998.09 | 997.35 | 962.85 | 984.09 | 1,010.83 |
| 2017 | 983.94 | 972.14 | 981.69 | 960.05 | 999.72 | 989.87 | 1,007.81 | 1,023.20 | 1,019.46 | 1,059.03 | 1,026.75 | 1,060.79 | 1,008.79 |
| 2018 | 1,032.84 | 1,080.72 | 1,088.25 | 1,052.76 | 1,091.52 | 1,087.13 | 1,101.00 | 1,123.34 | 1,106.57 | 1,136.58 | 1,196.58 | 1,251.74 | 1,112.53 |
| 2019 | 1,278.85 | 1,237.04 | 1,310.06 | 1,371.24 | 1,336.84 | 1,355.78 | 1,417.91 | 1,403.09 | 1,430.87 | 1,382.93 | 1,325.49 | 1,389.82 | 1,354.72 |
| **Trade, Transportation, and Utilities** | | | | | | | | | | | | | |
| 2015 | 671.90 | 687.59 | 706.10 | 689.23 | 696.61 | 692.07 | 695.27 | 698.26 | 714.02 | 698.65 | 719.19 | 696.24 | 696.32 |
| 2016 | 704.35 | 694.75 | 708.58 | 715.79 | 719.80 | 720.19 | 716.00 | 711.78 | 716.14 | 732.47 | 704.98 | 720.43 | 713.20 |
| 2017 | 730.66 | 726.60 | 722.24 | 740.05 | 710.93 | 718.15 | 726.17 | 706.45 | 697.38 | 698.94 | 681.29 | 688.45 | 712.49 |
| 2018 | 677.06 | 680.93 | 677.69 | 684.04 | 684.04 | 677.34 | 701.76 | 677.68 | 686.48 | 665.52 | 662.90 | 677.84 | 679.54 |
| 2019 | 694.88 | 691.83 | 683.42 | 687.83 | 693.94 | 707.61 | 692.17 | 708.23 | 711.62 | 695.23 | 689.98 | 712.08 | 697.00 |
| **Financial Activities** | | | | | | | | | | | | | |
| 2015 | 823.25 | 853.14 | 865.59 | 885.57 | 903.92 | 883.93 | 979.88 | 1,004.35 | 1,000.01 | 982.11 | 974.25 | 972.18 | 928.50 |
| 2016 | 972.36 | 945.31 | 919.80 | 928.34 | 990.98 | 955.32 | 950.61 | 952.03 | 930.26 | 936.23 | 915.30 | 958.50 | 945.18 |
| 2017 | 950.80 | 942.06 | 961.25 | 993.50 | 975.36 | 994.18 | 1,006.59 | 999.74 | 992.64 | 1,000.54 | 995.65 | 973.90 | 983.13 |
| 2018 | 999.38 | 998.45 | 1,008.75 | 1,046.84 | 1,021.78 | 1,014.20 | 994.07 | 992.94 | 1,022.95 | 982.09 | 978.63 | 1,033.07 | 1,008.88 |
| 2019 | 999.19 | 1,004.30 | 961.20 | 961.11 | 999.97 | 1,024.38 | 978.43 | 959.21 | 953.87 | 926.67 | 938.43 | 945.53 | 971.25 |
| **Professional and Business Services** | | | | | | | | | | | | | |
| 2015 | 824.69 | 863.81 | 839.70 | 827.32 | 826.58 | 828.00 | 840.78 | 878.89 | 817.02 | 828.97 | 837.22 | 810.21 | 834.20 |
| 2016 | 814.52 | 844.11 | 821.31 | 821.47 | 829.73 | 813.94 | 820.80 | 838.11 | 811.84 | 871.29 | 835.92 | 843.88 | 830.07 |
| 2017 | 875.80 | 846.68 | 850.51 | 870.46 | 866.60 | 853.78 | 869.07 | 873.32 | 856.10 | 882.47 | 866.92 | 878.35 | 866.62 |
| 2018 | 876.86 | 885.97 | 902.02 | 921.90 | 916.76 | 916.63 | 941.80 | 971.45 | 974.50 | 937.92 | 934.21 | 945.61 | 927.69 |
| 2019 | 954.53 | 932.32 | 911.89 | 928.65 | 935.77 | 967.55 | 948.52 | 939.50 | 978.88 | 977.85 | 924.52 | 963.48 | 947.13 |
| **Leisure and Hospitality** | | | | | | | | | | | | | |
| 2015 | 494.08 | 490.03 | 487.13 | 477.50 | 487.62 | 481.39 | 485.26 | 488.22 | 488.70 | 485.60 | 497.54 | 484.81 | 486.90 |
| 2016 | 487.55 | 490.78 | 499.65 | 491.36 | 494.88 | 504.45 | 501.60 | 514.06 | 515.31 | 516.98 | 510.99 | 495.68 | 501.63 |
| 2017 | 521.76 | 510.65 | 520.50 | 524.34 | 516.82 | 515.54 | 512.70 | 513.38 | 517.37 | 510.84 | 506.30 | 490.20 | 512.92 |
| 2018 | 513.04 | 496.48 | 511.53 | 513.03 | 511.20 | 514.80 | 518.89 | 525.99 | 522.72 | 526.29 | 525.40 | 507.79 | 516.26 |
| 2019 | 530.14 | 524.48 | 546.26 | 538.08 | 541.79 | 534.28 | 533.07 | 540.09 | 539.37 | 533.42 | 533.10 | 540.89 | 536.08 |

# NEW HAMPSHIRE
## *At a Glance*

Population:
  2010 census: 1,316,470
  2019 estimate: 1,359,711

Percent change in population:
  2010–2019: 3.3%

Percent change in total nonfarm employment:
  2011–2019: 9.5%

Industry with the largest growth in employment, 2011–2019 (percent):
  Construction, 26.2%

Industry with the largest decline or smallest growth in employment, 2011–2019 (percent):
  Government, -1.7%

Civilian labor force:
  2010: 738,257
  2019: 773,740

Unemployment rate and rank among states (highest to lowest):
  2010: 5.8%, 48th
  2019: 2.5%, 49th

Over-the-year change in unemployment rates:
  2017–2018: -0.1%
  2018–2019: -0.1%

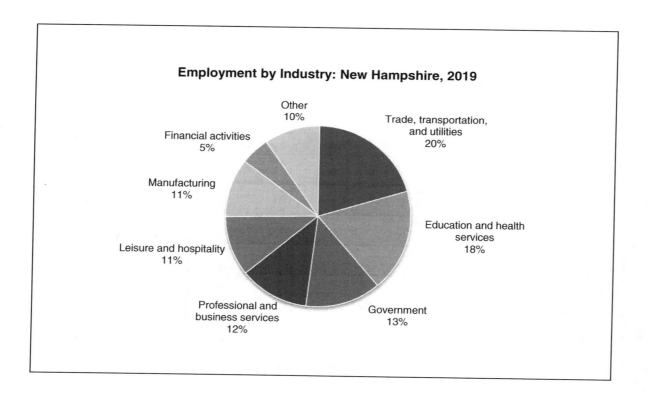

**Employment by Industry: New Hampshire, 2019**

- Other 10%
- Trade, transportation, and utilities 20%
- Financial activities 5%
- Education and health services 18%
- Manufacturing 11%
- Government 13%
- Leisure and hospitality 11%
- Professional and business services 12%

# 1. Employment by Industry: New Hampshire, 2011–2019

(Numbers in thousands, not seasonally adjusted)

| Industry and year | January | February | March | April | May | June | July | August | September | October | November | December | Annual average |
|---|---|---|---|---|---|---|---|---|---|---|---|---|---|
| **Total Nonfarm** | | | | | | | | | | | | | |
| 2011 | 607.1 | 614.9 | 618.0 | 623.8 | 630.0 | 627.6 | 621.4 | 620.3 | 630.9 | 633.4 | 634.3 | 636.4 | 624.8 |
| 2012 | 613.2 | 618.7 | 623.3 | 626.8 | 634.4 | 635.4 | 629.5 | 631.1 | 638.4 | 640.5 | 640.2 | 641.8 | 631.1 |
| 2013 | 618.0 | 625.9 | 627.5 | 632.3 | 642.0 | 640.4 | 633.3 | 635.6 | 639.3 | 645.9 | 646.2 | 649.1 | 636.3 |
| 2014 | 624.7 | 632.8 | 634.5 | 639.9 | 647.2 | 648.7 | 643.0 | 637.0 | 648.7 | 654.2 | 653.3 | 656.5 | 643.4 |
| 2015 | 633.3 | 639.4 | 643.6 | 648.5 | 659.3 | 658.4 | 653.6 | 652.2 | 658.3 | 664.8 | 665.7 | 668.6 | 653.8 |
| 2016 | 646.3 | 656.0 | 656.9 | 663.0 | 669.6 | 668.3 | 665.4 | 665.4 | 673.0 | 675.3 | 675.5 | 677.9 | 666.1 |
| 2017 | 655.1 | 662.0 | 665.0 | 670.1 | 677.4 | 678.7 | 673.4 | 673.2 | 677.2 | 680.9 | 680.1 | 683.9 | 673.1 |
| 2018 | 660.9 | 670.2 | 671.3 | 673.7 | 682.7 | 684.2 | 678.3 | 677.8 | 680.1 | 685.8 | 686.0 | 688.3 | 678.3 |
| 2019 | 669.0 | 677.3 | 678.9 | 681.2 | 689.7 | 689.6 | 684.3 | 685.1 | 686.5 | 690.6 | 687.6 | 690.5 | 684.2 |
| **Total Private** | | | | | | | | | | | | | |
| 2011 | 515.1 | 518.1 | 520.9 | 527.9 | 533.5 | 537.6 | 543.0 | 543.3 | 538.7 | 538.2 | 538.1 | 540.0 | 532.9 |
| 2012 | 521.9 | 524.2 | 527.9 | 532.0 | 539.8 | 547.5 | 549.5 | 551.5 | 545.0 | 545.4 | 544.4 | 545.2 | 539.5 |
| 2013 | 527.8 | 531.4 | 533.6 | 538.4 | 547.9 | 552.4 | 556.2 | 557.1 | 549.3 | 551.4 | 551.6 | 553.7 | 545.9 |
| 2014 | 535.1 | 539.1 | 540.4 | 545.8 | 555.2 | 560.0 | 564.0 | 558.0 | 556.6 | 559.4 | 557.7 | 560.8 | 552.7 |
| 2015 | 543.4 | 546.1 | 549.1 | 554.4 | 565.6 | 570.2 | 575.0 | 574.6 | 567.6 | 571.0 | 570.9 | 573.7 | 563.5 |
| 2016 | 557.1 | 561.3 | 562.6 | 568.7 | 576.6 | 580.7 | 587.1 | 586.3 | 580.6 | 581.4 | 580.5 | 583.0 | 575.5 |
| 2017 | 566.8 | 569.0 | 570.8 | 576.4 | 584.0 | 591.4 | 595.1 | 593.4 | 585.8 | 586.7 | 586.3 | 589.4 | 582.9 |
| 2018 | 571.9 | 577.4 | 577.4 | 580.1 | 589.5 | 596.7 | 599.6 | 598.0 | 588.8 | 592.6 | 592.3 | 594.8 | 588.3 |
| 2019 | 579.9 | 583.9 | 584.3 | 587.7 | 596.2 | 601.6 | 605.5 | 604.3 | 595.4 | 597.1 | 593.8 | 596.1 | 593.8 |
| **Goods Producing** | | | | | | | | | | | | | |
| 2011 | 86.2 | 85.7 | 86.6 | 88.9 | 89.9 | 91.0 | 91.6 | 91.9 | 91.2 | 90.9 | 90.6 | 89.7 | 89.5 |
| 2012 | 86.7 | 86.0 | 86.7 | 88.6 | 89.4 | 90.6 | 90.8 | 91.0 | 90.6 | 90.5 | 89.5 | 88.7 | 89.1 |
| 2013 | 86.5 | 86.0 | 86.4 | 88.1 | 89.8 | 91.2 | 91.2 | 91.5 | 90.7 | 91.0 | 91.1 | 90.4 | 89.5 |
| 2014 | 87.9 | 87.5 | 87.8 | 89.8 | 91.1 | 92.3 | 92.4 | 92.7 | 91.6 | 91.6 | 91.6 | 91.3 | 90.6 |
| 2015 | 89.2 | 88.3 | 88.6 | 90.7 | 92.5 | 94.1 | 94.7 | 94.8 | 94.3 | 94.7 | 94.1 | 93.9 | 92.5 |
| 2016 | 92.1 | 91.4 | 91.6 | 93.6 | 94.8 | 96.2 | 96.8 | 96.6 | 95.7 | 95.8 | 95.8 | 95.5 | 94.7 |
| 2017 | 94.0 | 93.5 | 94.1 | 95.2 | 96.3 | 97.9 | 98.4 | 98.1 | 97.6 | 97.6 | 97.2 | 96.9 | 96.4 |
| 2018 | 95.0 | 95.0 | 95.4 | 97.0 | 98.4 | 100.2 | 100.7 | 100.6 | 99.5 | 100.4 | 100.1 | 99.8 | 98.5 |
| 2019 | 98.4 | 98.2 | 98.5 | 99.1 | 100.5 | 102.0 | 102.3 | 102.1 | 101.3 | 101.3 | 101.0 | 99.7 | 100.4 |
| **Service-Providing** | | | | | | | | | | | | | |
| 2011 | 520.9 | 529.2 | 531.4 | 534.9 | 540.1 | 536.6 | 529.8 | 528.4 | 539.7 | 542.5 | 543.7 | 546.7 | 535.3 |
| 2012 | 526.5 | 532.7 | 536.6 | 538.2 | 545.0 | 544.8 | 538.7 | 540.1 | 547.8 | 550.0 | 550.7 | 553.1 | 542.0 |
| 2013 | 531.5 | 539.9 | 541.1 | 544.2 | 552.2 | 549.2 | 542.1 | 544.1 | 548.6 | 554.9 | 555.1 | 558.7 | 546.8 |
| 2014 | 536.8 | 545.3 | 546.7 | 550.1 | 556.1 | 556.4 | 550.6 | 544.3 | 557.1 | 562.6 | 561.7 | 565.2 | 552.7 |
| 2015 | 544.1 | 551.1 | 555.0 | 557.8 | 566.8 | 564.3 | 558.9 | 557.4 | 564.0 | 570.1 | 571.6 | 574.7 | 561.3 |
| 2016 | 554.2 | 564.6 | 565.3 | 569.4 | 574.8 | 572.1 | 568.6 | 568.8 | 577.3 | 579.5 | 579.7 | 582.4 | 571.4 |
| 2017 | 561.1 | 568.5 | 570.9 | 574.9 | 581.1 | 580.8 | 575.0 | 575.1 | 579.6 | 583.3 | 582.9 | 587.0 | 576.7 |
| 2018 | 565.9 | 575.2 | 575.9 | 576.7 | 584.3 | 584.0 | 577.6 | 577.2 | 580.6 | 585.4 | 585.9 | 588.5 | 579.8 |
| 2019 | 570.6 | 579.1 | 580.4 | 582.1 | 589.2 | 587.6 | 582.0 | 583.0 | 585.2 | 589.3 | 586.6 | 590.8 | 583.8 |
| **Mining and Logging** | | | | | | | | | | | | | |
| 2011 | 0.8 | 0.8 | 0.8 | 0.8 | 0.9 | 0.9 | 1.0 | 1.0 | 1.0 | 1.0 | 1.0 | 0.9 | 0.9 |
| 2012 | 0.8 | 0.8 | 0.8 | 0.9 | 0.9 | 1.0 | 1.0 | 1.0 | 1.0 | 1.0 | 0.9 | 0.9 | 0.9 |
| 2013 | 0.8 | 0.8 | 0.8 | 0.9 | 0.9 | 1.0 | 1.0 | 1.0 | 1.0 | 1.0 | 1.0 | 1.0 | 0.9 |
| 2014 | 0.9 | 0.9 | 0.9 | 0.9 | 1.0 | 1.0 | 1.0 | 1.1 | 1.1 | 1.1 | 1.0 | 1.0 | 1.0 |
| 2015 | 0.9 | 0.9 | 0.9 | 0.9 | 0.9 | 1.0 | 1.0 | 1.0 | 1.0 | 1.0 | 1.0 | 1.0 | 1.0 |
| 2016 | 0.9 | 0.9 | 0.9 | 0.9 | 1.0 | 1.0 | 1.1 | 1.1 | 1.0 | 1.0 | 1.0 | 1.0 | 1.0 |
| 2017 | 0.9 | 0.9 | 0.9 | 0.9 | 0.9 | 1.0 | 1.0 | 1.0 | 1.0 | 1.0 | 0.9 | 1.0 | 1.0 |
| 2018 | 0.9 | 0.9 | 0.9 | 0.9 | 1.0 | 1.0 | 1.0 | 1.1 | 1.0 | 1.0 | 1.0 | 1.0 | 1.0 |
| 2019 | 0.9 | 0.9 | 0.9 | 0.9 | 0.9 | 1.0 | 1.0 | 1.0 | 1.0 | 1.0 | 0.9 | 1.0 | 1.0 |
| **Construction** | | | | | | | | | | | | | |
| 2011 | 19.6 | 19.1 | 19.7 | 21.7 | 22.5 | 23.1 | 23.6 | 23.6 | 23.5 | 23.5 | 23.2 | 22.4 | 22.1 |
| 2012 | 20.0 | 19.5 | 20.1 | 21.8 | 22.6 | 23.2 | 23.5 | 23.7 | 23.7 | 23.6 | 22.8 | 21.9 | 22.2 |
| 2013 | 20.3 | 19.8 | 20.2 | 21.7 | 23.2 | 23.8 | 23.8 | 23.9 | 23.7 | 23.6 | 23.5 | 22.7 | 22.5 |
| 2014 | 20.8 | 20.6 | 20.9 | 22.7 | 23.7 | 24.2 | 24.7 | 24.7 | 24.2 | 24.3 | 24.2 | 23.5 | 23.2 |
| 2015 | 21.8 | 21.1 | 21.2 | 22.9 | 24.5 | 25.2 | 25.7 | 25.8 | 25.9 | 26.2 | 25.5 | 25.1 | 24.2 |
| 2016 | 23.6 | 23.0 | 23.3 | 25.0 | 25.8 | 26.4 | 27.0 | 26.8 | 26.6 | 26.6 | 26.3 | 25.6 | 25.5 |
| 2017 | 24.5 | 24.2 | 24.6 | 25.8 | 26.7 | 27.4 | 27.8 | 27.8 | 27.6 | 27.6 | 27.1 | 26.5 | 26.5 |
| 2018 | 25.0 | 24.8 | 24.9 | 26.2 | 27.3 | 28.1 | 28.4 | 28.3 | 27.8 | 28.2 | 27.6 | 26.9 | 27.0 |
| 2019 | 25.9 | 25.8 | 26.0 | 26.8 | 28.0 | 28.8 | 29.2 | 29.3 | 29.1 | 29.3 | 29.2 | 27.7 | 27.9 |

## 1. Employment by Industry: New Hampshire, 2011–2019—*Continued*

(Numbers in thousands, not seasonally adjusted)

| Industry and year | January | February | March | April | May | June | July | August | September | October | November | December | Annual average |
|---|---|---|---|---|---|---|---|---|---|---|---|---|---|
| **Manufacturing** | | | | | | | | | | | | | |
| 2011 | 65.8 | 65.8 | 66.1 | 66.4 | 66.5 | 67.0 | 67.0 | 67.3 | 66.7 | 66.4 | 66.4 | 66.4 | 66.5 |
| 2012 | 65.9 | 65.7 | 65.8 | 65.9 | 65.9 | 66.4 | 66.3 | 66.3 | 65.9 | 65.9 | 65.8 | 65.9 | 66.0 |
| 2013 | 65.4 | 65.4 | 65.4 | 65.5 | 65.7 | 66.4 | 66.4 | 66.6 | 66.0 | 66.4 | 66.6 | 66.7 | 66.0 |
| 2014 | 66.2 | 66.0 | 66.0 | 66.2 | 66.4 | 67.1 | 66.7 | 66.9 | 66.3 | 66.2 | 66.4 | 66.8 | 66.4 |
| 2015 | 66.5 | 66.3 | 66.5 | 66.9 | 67.1 | 67.9 | 68.0 | 68.0 | 67.4 | 67.5 | 67.6 | 67.8 | 67.3 |
| 2016 | 67.6 | 67.5 | 67.4 | 67.7 | 68.0 | 68.8 | 68.7 | 68.7 | 68.1 | 68.2 | 68.5 | 68.9 | 68.2 |
| 2017 | 68.6 | 68.4 | 68.6 | 68.5 | 68.7 | 69.5 | 69.6 | 69.3 | 69.0 | 69.0 | 69.1 | 69.5 | 69.0 |
| 2018 | 69.1 | 69.3 | 69.6 | 69.9 | 70.1 | 71.1 | 71.3 | 71.2 | 70.7 | 71.2 | 71.5 | 71.9 | 70.6 |
| 2019 | 71.6 | 71.5 | 71.6 | 71.4 | 71.6 | 72.2 | 72.1 | 71.8 | 71.2 | 71.0 | 70.8 | 71.1 | 71.5 |
| **Trade, Transportation, and Utilities** | | | | | | | | | | | | | |
| 2011 | 132.5 | 130.0 | 130.2 | 131.5 | 132.8 | 134.9 | 134.1 | 134.1 | 133.4 | 134.4 | 137.0 | 139.7 | 133.7 |
| 2012 | 134.1 | 131.5 | 132.1 | 132.5 | 134.2 | 137.6 | 136.8 | 137.1 | 135.2 | 135.7 | 139.3 | 140.5 | 135.6 |
| 2013 | 134.6 | 132.2 | 132.6 | 134.0 | 136.0 | 137.9 | 137.3 | 137.3 | 135.5 | 136.0 | 139.1 | 141.4 | 136.2 |
| 2014 | 135.4 | 133.3 | 133.4 | 134.0 | 135.9 | 137.9 | 137.3 | 131.2 | 136.8 | 137.7 | 140.5 | 142.6 | 136.3 |
| 2015 | 136.5 | 133.8 | 133.9 | 134.8 | 137.0 | 138.9 | 138.1 | 138.4 | 136.9 | 138.0 | 141.0 | 143.3 | 137.6 |
| 2016 | 138.0 | 136.3 | 136.3 | 137.3 | 139.2 | 140.7 | 140.4 | 140.5 | 139.3 | 140.0 | 142.8 | 145.1 | 139.7 |
| 2017 | 139.7 | 136.9 | 136.6 | 137.7 | 138.8 | 141.2 | 140.8 | 140.7 | 139.1 | 139.5 | 142.3 | 144.2 | 139.8 |
| 2018 | 138.8 | 137.0 | 136.6 | 137.1 | 138.8 | 140.7 | 139.6 | 139.8 | 138.0 | 139.1 | 142.6 | 144.1 | 139.4 |
| 2019 | 139.9 | 137.0 | 136.7 | 137.5 | 138.6 | 140.5 | 139.8 | 140.3 | 138.2 | 138.6 | 140.5 | 141.8 | 139.1 |
| **Wholesale Trade** | | | | | | | | | | | | | |
| 2011 | 25.6 | 25.6 | 25.7 | 25.9 | 26.0 | 26.1 | 26.1 | 26.0 | 25.9 | 26.0 | 25.9 | 26.1 | 25.9 |
| 2012 | 26.0 | 25.9 | 26.0 | 26.3 | 26.4 | 26.6 | 26.7 | 26.7 | 26.5 | 26.4 | 26.4 | 26.4 | 26.4 |
| 2013 | 26.2 | 26.1 | 26.2 | 26.3 | 26.5 | 26.7 | 26.7 | 26.7 | 26.5 | 26.4 | 26.5 | 26.6 | 26.5 |
| 2014 | 26.4 | 26.4 | 26.5 | 26.6 | 26.8 | 27.0 | 27.1 | 27.2 | 27.0 | 27.0 | 27.1 | 27.1 | 26.9 |
| 2015 | 26.8 | 26.8 | 26.8 | 27.0 | 27.3 | 27.4 | 27.4 | 27.4 | 27.2 | 27.3 | 27.3 | 27.4 | 27.2 |
| 2016 | 27.2 | 27.1 | 27.1 | 27.3 | 27.5 | 27.6 | 27.6 | 27.6 | 27.5 | 27.4 | 27.5 | 27.6 | 27.4 |
| 2017 | 27.4 | 27.3 | 27.3 | 27.6 | 27.7 | 28.1 | 28.0 | 28.0 | 27.7 | 27.7 | 27.8 | 27.9 | 27.7 |
| 2018 | 27.7 | 27.8 | 27.8 | 27.9 | 28.0 | 28.2 | 28.2 | 28.1 | 27.9 | 28.1 | 28.2 | 28.3 | 28.0 |
| 2019 | 28.0 | 27.9 | 27.9 | 28.0 | 28.1 | 28.4 | 28.4 | 28.4 | 28.2 | 28.0 | 27.8 | 28.4 | 28.1 |
| **Retail Trade** | | | | | | | | | | | | | |
| 2011 | 92.3 | 90.0 | 90.0 | 90.9 | 91.8 | 93.6 | 93.7 | 93.9 | 92.4 | 93.4 | 96.2 | 98.2 | 93.0 |
| 2012 | 93.6 | 91.2 | 91.5 | 91.6 | 92.9 | 95.8 | 95.8 | 95.8 | 93.5 | 94.2 | 97.9 | 98.5 | 94.4 |
| 2013 | 93.7 | 91.5 | 91.7 | 92.9 | 94.4 | 95.9 | 96.1 | 96.0 | 93.7 | 94.5 | 97.4 | 99.1 | 94.7 |
| 2014 | 94.3 | 92.2 | 92.1 | 92.7 | 94.0 | 95.5 | 95.7 | 89.4 | 94.3 | 95.2 | 97.8 | 99.4 | 94.4 |
| 2015 | 94.6 | 92.1 | 92.2 | 92.9 | 94.3 | 95.8 | 95.7 | 95.9 | 93.8 | 94.8 | 97.8 | 99.5 | 95.0 |
| 2016 | 95.0 | 93.5 | 93.5 | 94.0 | 95.3 | 96.6 | 97.1 | 97.3 | 95.2 | 96.0 | 98.5 | 99.8 | 96.0 |
| 2017 | 96.1 | 93.4 | 93.2 | 93.8 | 94.7 | 96.4 | 96.6 | 96.6 | 94.5 | 95.1 | 97.8 | 98.8 | 95.6 |
| 2018 | 94.7 | 92.9 | 92.5 | 92.9 | 94.2 | 95.5 | 95.3 | 95.3 | 93.1 | 93.8 | 96.9 | 97.8 | 94.6 |
| 2019 | 94.9 | 92.3 | 92.0 | 92.7 | 93.5 | 94.8 | 94.8 | 95.0 | 92.7 | 93.0 | 94.8 | 94.9 | 93.8 |
| **Transportation and Utilities** | | | | | | | | | | | | | |
| 2011 | 14.6 | 14.4 | 14.5 | 14.7 | 15.0 | 15.2 | 14.3 | 14.2 | 15.1 | 15.0 | 14.9 | 15.4 | 14.8 |
| 2012 | 14.5 | 14.4 | 14.6 | 14.6 | 14.9 | 15.2 | 14.3 | 14.6 | 15.2 | 15.1 | 15.0 | 15.6 | 14.8 |
| 2013 | 14.7 | 14.6 | 14.7 | 14.8 | 15.1 | 15.3 | 14.5 | 14.6 | 15.3 | 15.1 | 15.2 | 15.7 | 15.0 |
| 2014 | 14.7 | 14.7 | 14.8 | 14.7 | 15.1 | 15.4 | 14.5 | 14.6 | 15.5 | 15.5 | 15.6 | 16.1 | 15.1 |
| 2015 | 15.1 | 14.9 | 14.9 | 14.9 | 15.4 | 15.7 | 15.0 | 15.1 | 15.9 | 15.9 | 15.9 | 16.4 | 15.4 |
| 2016 | 15.8 | 15.7 | 15.7 | 16.0 | 16.4 | 16.5 | 15.7 | 15.6 | 16.6 | 16.6 | 16.8 | 17.7 | 16.3 |
| 2017 | 16.2 | 16.2 | 16.1 | 16.3 | 16.4 | 16.7 | 16.2 | 16.1 | 16.9 | 16.7 | 16.7 | 17.5 | 16.5 |
| 2018 | 16.4 | 16.3 | 16.3 | 16.3 | 16.6 | 17.0 | 16.1 | 16.4 | 17.0 | 17.2 | 17.5 | 18.0 | 16.8 |
| 2019 | 17.0 | 16.8 | 16.8 | 16.8 | 17.0 | 17.3 | 16.6 | 16.9 | 17.3 | 17.6 | 17.9 | 18.5 | 17.2 |
| **Information** | | | | | | | | | | | | | |
| 2011 | 11.0 | 11.0 | 11.0 | 11.1 | 11.3 | 11.4 | 11.6 | 11.6 | 11.6 | 11.6 | 11.8 | 11.8 | 11.4 |
| 2012 | 11.8 | 11.9 | 12.0 | 12.0 | 12.1 | 12.2 | 12.3 | 12.3 | 12.0 | 12.0 | 12.0 | 12.1 | 12.1 |
| 2013 | 12.0 | 11.9 | 11.9 | 11.9 | 11.9 | 12.0 | 12.0 | 12.0 | 11.8 | 11.8 | 11.9 | 11.9 | 11.9 |
| 2014 | 12.0 | 12.0 | 12.1 | 12.1 | 12.2 | 12.2 | 12.3 | 12.3 | 12.2 | 12.4 | 12.0 | 11.9 | 12.1 |
| 2015 | 12.1 | 12.1 | 12.5 | 12.6 | 12.7 | 12.8 | 12.8 | 12.7 | 12.5 | 12.5 | 12.6 | 12.6 | 12.5 |
| 2016 | 12.6 | 12.6 | 12.5 | 12.6 | 12.6 | 12.6 | 12.8 | 12.7 | 12.5 | 12.6 | 12.5 | 12.7 | 12.6 |
| 2017 | 12.7 | 12.5 | 12.5 | 12.5 | 12.8 | 13.0 | 13.0 | 12.9 | 12.6 | 12.6 | 12.5 | 12.6 | 12.7 |
| 2018 | 12.5 | 12.5 | 12.4 | 12.4 | 12.5 | 12.8 | 12.8 | 12.8 | 12.4 | 12.3 | 12.4 | 12.4 | 12.5 |
| 2019 | 12.4 | 12.3 | 12.3 | 12.2 | 12.5 | 12.6 | 12.6 | 12.5 | 12.2 | 12.3 | 12.4 | 12.4 | 12.4 |

## 1. Employment by Industry: New Hampshire, 2011–2019—*Continued*

(Numbers in thousands, not seasonally adjusted)

| Industry and year | January | February | March | April | May | June | July | August | September | October | November | December | Annual average |
|---|---|---|---|---|---|---|---|---|---|---|---|---|---|
| **Financial Activities** | | | | | | | | | | | | | |
| 2011 | 33.9 | 33.6 | 33.6 | 33.7 | 33.5 | 33.8 | 33.9 | 33.8 | 33.6 | 33.4 | 33.4 | 33.3 | 33.6 |
| 2012 | 33.1 | 33.1 | 33.2 | 33.3 | 33.6 | 34.3 | 34.3 | 34.5 | 34.0 | 34.1 | 33.9 | 33.9 | 33.8 |
| 2013 | 33.6 | 33.6 | 33.6 | 33.7 | 34.0 | 34.4 | 34.6 | 34.7 | 34.1 | 34.1 | 34.0 | 34.1 | 34.0 |
| 2014 | 33.5 | 33.5 | 33.6 | 33.6 | 33.8 | 34.2 | 34.4 | 34.3 | 33.7 | 33.6 | 33.4 | 33.5 | 33.8 |
| 2015 | 33.2 | 33.2 | 33.2 | 33.3 | 33.6 | 34.1 | 34.7 | 34.8 | 34.4 | 34.3 | 34.4 | 34.4 | 34.0 |
| 2016 | 34.4 | 34.4 | 34.4 | 34.7 | 34.7 | 35.4 | 35.7 | 35.7 | 35.2 | 35.1 | 34.8 | 34.9 | 35.0 |
| 2017 | 34.9 | 34.8 | 34.7 | 34.7 | 35.0 | 35.6 | 35.7 | 35.8 | 35.2 | 35.1 | 35.1 | 35.3 | 35.2 |
| 2018 | 34.9 | 34.9 | 34.8 | 34.9 | 34.9 | 35.4 | 35.4 | 35.3 | 34.7 | 34.7 | 34.7 | 34.8 | 35.0 |
| 2019 | 34.4 | 34.5 | 34.5 | 34.5 | 34.8 | 35.5 | 35.5 | 35.4 | 34.8 | 34.9 | 34.6 | 34.7 | 34.8 |
| **Professional and Business Services** | | | | | | | | | | | | | |
| 2011 | 64.8 | 64.7 | 64.6 | 67.2 | 67.2 | 68.2 | 68.5 | 68.5 | 68.3 | 68.6 | 69.5 | 68.7 | 67.4 |
| 2012 | 67.0 | 66.5 | 67.1 | 69.0 | 69.5 | 70.3 | 70.1 | 70.9 | 70.5 | 70.9 | 71.2 | 70.5 | 69.5 |
| 2013 | 68.8 | 69.6 | 69.2 | 70.6 | 71.9 | 72.7 | 73.3 | 73.5 | 72.7 | 73.5 | 74.3 | 74.1 | 72.0 |
| 2014 | 72.9 | 72.9 | 72.5 | 74.7 | 75.7 | 76.7 | 77.2 | 77.7 | 76.4 | 77.2 | 77.4 | 77.3 | 75.7 |
| 2015 | 75.4 | 76.4 | 76.1 | 77.8 | 78.8 | 79.9 | 80.2 | 80.6 | 80.0 | 80.6 | 80.8 | 80.4 | 78.9 |
| 2016 | 78.3 | 78.2 | 78.0 | 80.2 | 80.6 | 81.4 | 81.8 | 81.9 | 81.3 | 81.7 | 81.5 | 81.2 | 80.5 |
| 2017 | 79.4 | 79.7 | 79.8 | 81.6 | 82.2 | 83.9 | 83.9 | 83.8 | 82.8 | 83.0 | 83.1 | 82.5 | 82.1 |
| 2018 | 81.0 | 81.0 | 81.5 | 81.8 | 82.8 | 84.7 | 84.8 | 84.7 | 83.6 | 83.9 | 83.3 | 82.2 | 82.9 |
| 2019 | 80.9 | 81.6 | 81.4 | 82.7 | 83.4 | 85.0 | 85.4 | 85.5 | 84.6 | 85.3 | 84.5 | 84.4 | 83.7 |
| **Education and Health Services** | | | | | | | | | | | | | |
| 2011 | 106.8 | 113.0 | 114.7 | 114.4 | 114.2 | 107.1 | 106.3 | 105.9 | 111.0 | 114.1 | 114.4 | 114.2 | 111.3 |
| 2012 | 108.1 | 114.0 | 115.2 | 114.8 | 114.7 | 108.2 | 106.8 | 107.0 | 112.1 | 114.8 | 115.7 | 115.8 | 112.3 |
| 2013 | 109.3 | 115.3 | 116.6 | 115.6 | 115.4 | 108.5 | 107.4 | 107.5 | 112.3 | 115.3 | 116.3 | 115.8 | 112.9 |
| 2014 | 108.8 | 115.0 | 116.2 | 116.3 | 115.8 | 109.4 | 108.4 | 108.1 | 113.0 | 116.4 | 117.3 | 117.0 | 113.5 |
| 2015 | 111.0 | 116.6 | 118.3 | 118.3 | 118.4 | 111.3 | 110.4 | 109.7 | 114.6 | 118.6 | 120.2 | 120.1 | 115.6 |
| 2016 | 113.4 | 119.7 | 121.5 | 121.8 | 121.9 | 114.2 | 113.9 | 113.4 | 119.1 | 122.6 | 123.5 | 123.4 | 119.0 |
| 2017 | 116.7 | 122.7 | 123.7 | 124.5 | 124.4 | 117.1 | 116.0 | 115.4 | 120.9 | 124.4 | 125.5 | 125.3 | 121.4 |
| 2018 | 118.2 | 125.2 | 125.2 | 125.7 | 125.8 | 118.5 | 117.3 | 117.1 | 122.6 | 126.4 | 127.5 | 127.3 | 123.1 |
| 2019 | 120.2 | 126.8 | 127.7 | 127.9 | 128.0 | 120.0 | 119.4 | 118.9 | 124.7 | 127.4 | 128.3 | 127.8 | 124.8 |
| **Leisure and Hospitality** | | | | | | | | | | | | | |
| 2011 | 58.0 | 58.1 | 58.0 | 58.9 | 62.1 | 68.2 | 73.7 | 74.1 | 66.8 | 62.6 | 58.8 | 60.0 | 63.3 |
| 2012 | 58.7 | 58.9 | 59.2 | 59.3 | 63.5 | 71.0 | 75.0 | 75.2 | 67.7 | 64.4 | 60.0 | 61.0 | 64.5 |
| 2013 | 60.4 | 60.3 | 60.6 | 61.6 | 65.8 | 72.2 | 76.7 | 76.8 | 68.9 | 66.5 | 61.8 | 62.8 | 66.2 |
| 2014 | 61.5 | 61.8 | 61.7 | 61.9 | 67.0 | 73.2 | 77.7 | 77.5 | 69.2 | 67.0 | 62.1 | 64.0 | 67.1 |
| 2015 | 62.8 | 62.5 | 63.1 | 63.3 | 68.6 | 74.8 | 79.6 | 79.2 | 70.9 | 68.4 | 63.8 | 64.9 | 68.5 |
| 2016 | 64.4 | 64.8 | 64.5 | 64.6 | 68.7 | 75.7 | 80.6 | 80.5 | 73.1 | 69.1 | 65.3 | 66.2 | 69.8 |
| 2017 | 65.6 | 65.1 | 65.5 | 65.7 | 69.9 | 77.4 | 82.0 | 81.6 | 73.1 | 70.1 | 66.3 | 68.2 | 70.9 |
| 2018 | 67.2 | 67.5 | 67.1 | 66.9 | 71.5 | 78.7 | 83.4 | 82.2 | 73.3 | 71.0 | 66.8 | 69.2 | 72.1 |
| 2019 | 69.0 | 68.8 | 68.4 | 68.8 | 73.3 | 79.7 | 83.9 | 83.0 | 74.1 | 71.1 | 66.1 | 68.3 | 72.9 |
| **Other Services** | | | | | | | | | | | | | |
| 2011 | 21.9 | 22.0 | 22.2 | 22.2 | 22.5 | 23.0 | 23.3 | 23.4 | 22.8 | 22.6 | 22.6 | 22.6 | 22.6 |
| 2012 | 22.4 | 22.3 | 22.4 | 22.5 | 22.8 | 23.3 | 23.4 | 23.5 | 22.9 | 23.0 | 22.8 | 22.7 | 22.8 |
| 2013 | 22.6 | 22.5 | 22.7 | 22.9 | 23.1 | 23.5 | 23.7 | 23.8 | 23.3 | 23.2 | 23.1 | 23.2 | 23.1 |
| 2014 | 23.1 | 23.1 | 23.1 | 23.4 | 23.7 | 24.1 | 24.3 | 24.2 | 23.7 | 23.5 | 23.4 | 23.2 | 23.6 |
| 2015 | 23.2 | 23.2 | 23.4 | 23.6 | 24.0 | 24.3 | 24.5 | 24.4 | 24.0 | 23.9 | 24.0 | 24.1 | 23.9 |
| 2016 | 23.9 | 23.9 | 23.8 | 23.9 | 24.1 | 24.5 | 25.1 | 25.0 | 24.4 | 24.5 | 24.3 | 24.0 | 24.3 |
| 2017 | 23.8 | 23.8 | 23.9 | 24.5 | 24.6 | 25.3 | 25.3 | 25.1 | 24.5 | 24.4 | 24.3 | 24.4 | 24.5 |
| 2018 | 24.3 | 24.3 | 24.4 | 24.3 | 24.8 | 25.7 | 25.6 | 25.5 | 24.7 | 24.8 | 24.9 | 25.0 | 24.9 |
| 2019 | 24.7 | 24.7 | 24.8 | 25.0 | 25.1 | 26.3 | 26.6 | 26.6 | 25.5 | 26.2 | 26.4 | 27.0 | 25.7 |
| **Government** | | | | | | | | | | | | | |
| 2011 | 92.0 | 96.8 | 97.1 | 95.9 | 96.5 | 90.0 | 78.4 | 77.0 | 92.2 | 95.2 | 96.2 | 96.4 | 92.0 |
| 2012 | 91.3 | 94.5 | 95.4 | 94.8 | 94.6 | 87.9 | 80.0 | 79.6 | 93.4 | 95.1 | 95.8 | 96.6 | 91.6 |
| 2013 | 90.2 | 94.5 | 93.9 | 93.9 | 94.1 | 88.0 | 77.1 | 78.5 | 90.0 | 94.5 | 94.6 | 95.4 | 90.4 |
| 2014 | 89.6 | 93.7 | 94.1 | 94.1 | 92.0 | 88.7 | 79.0 | 79.0 | 92.1 | 94.8 | 95.6 | 95.7 | 90.7 |
| 2015 | 89.9 | 93.3 | 94.5 | 94.1 | 93.7 | 88.2 | 78.6 | 77.6 | 90.7 | 93.8 | 94.8 | 94.9 | 90.3 |
| 2016 | 89.2 | 94.7 | 94.3 | 94.3 | 93.0 | 87.6 | 78.3 | 79.1 | 92.4 | 93.9 | 95.0 | 94.9 | 90.6 |
| 2017 | 88.3 | 93.0 | 94.2 | 93.7 | 93.4 | 87.3 | 78.3 | 79.8 | 91.4 | 94.2 | 93.8 | 94.5 | 90.2 |
| 2018 | 89.0 | 92.8 | 93.9 | 93.6 | 93.2 | 87.5 | 78.7 | 79.8 | 91.3 | 93.2 | 93.7 | 93.5 | 90.0 |
| 2019 | 89.1 | 93.4 | 94.6 | 93.5 | 93.5 | 88.0 | 78.8 | 80.8 | 91.1 | 93.5 | 93.8 | 94.4 | 90.4 |

## 2. Average Weekly Hours by Selected Industry: New Hampshire, 2015–2019

(Not seasonally adjusted)

| Industry and year | January | February | March | April | May | June | July | August | September | October | November | December | Annual average |
|---|---|---|---|---|---|---|---|---|---|---|---|---|---|
| **Total Private** | | | | | | | | | | | | | |
| 2015 | 32.9 | 32.9 | 33.5 | 33.6 | 33.7 | 33.5 | 33.9 | 34.2 | 33.7 | 33.8 | 33.9 | 33.7 | 33.6 |
| 2016 | 33.3 | 33.2 | 33.1 | 33.6 | 34.0 | 33.7 | 34.0 | 34.0 | 34.2 | 34.5 | 34.1 | 34.0 | 33.8 |
| 2017 | 33.9 | 33.4 | 33.5 | 34.4 | 34.3 | 34.1 | 34.2 | 34.3 | 34.0 | 33.8 | 33.8 | 33.5 | 33.9 |
| 2018 | 33.0 | 33.1 | 32.4 | 33.6 | 33.6 | 33.4 | 33.6 | 33.7 | 33.8 | 33.5 | 33.4 | 33.5 | 33.4 |
| 2019 | 32.8 | 33.0 | 33.1 | 33.2 | 33.4 | 33.5 | 33.6 | 33.8 | 33.6 | 33.4 | 33.6 | 33.5 | 33.4 |
| **Goods-Producing** | | | | | | | | | | | | | |
| 2015 | 38.9 | 38.7 | 39.4 | 39.1 | 39.2 | 39.2 | 39.5 | 39.5 | 38.5 | 38.9 | 39.5 | 39.6 | 39.2 |
| 2016 | 39.5 | 38.8 | 38.8 | 39.2 | 40.0 | 39.8 | 39.7 | 39.7 | 40.0 | 40.0 | 39.4 | 38.4 | 39.4 |
| 2017 | 38.8 | 37.3 | 37.7 | 38.6 | 39.1 | 39.0 | 38.5 | 39.4 | 39.8 | 39.7 | 40.2 | 39.8 | 39.0 |
| 2018 | 39.6 | 39.5 | 38.1 | 39.8 | 40.7 | 40.5 | 39.9 | 40.4 | 40.5 | 40.1 | 39.9 | 40.6 | 40.0 |
| 2019 | 40.7 | 39.3 | 39.2 | 39.4 | 40.1 | 40.2 | 40.2 | 40.4 | 40.4 | 40.1 | 40.3 | 40.2 | 40.0 |
| **Manufacturing** | | | | | | | | | | | | | |
| 2015 | 40.7 | 40.4 | 40.6 | 40.2 | 40.0 | 40.3 | 40.2 | 40.1 | 39.4 | 39.4 | 40.2 | 40.4 | 40.2 |
| 2016 | 40.3 | 39.5 | 39.6 | 39.8 | 40.6 | 40.4 | 40.1 | 39.9 | 40.4 | 40.2 | 40.1 | 39.7 | 40.0 |
| 2017 | 40.2 | 38.6 | 38.8 | 39.2 | 40.0 | 40.3 | 39.7 | 40.8 | 41.2 | 41.3 | 41.3 | 41.4 | 40.2 |
| 2018 | 41.3 | 41.4 | 40.3 | 41.4 | 41.7 | 41.5 | 41.4 | 41.6 | 42.1 | 41.0 | 41.3 | 41.6 | 41.4 |
| 2019 | 42.5 | 41.8 | 41.6 | 41.3 | 41.7 | 41.6 | 41.9 | 41.4 | 41.7 | 41.1 | 41.5 | 41.8 | 41.7 |
| **Trade, Transportation, and Utilities** | | | | | | | | | | | | | |
| 2015 | 31.8 | 32.1 | 32.9 | 33.0 | 33.5 | 33.4 | 33.9 | 34.2 | 34.4 | 33.9 | 33.9 | 34.0 | 33.4 |
| 2016 | 33.0 | 33.0 | 32.8 | 33.3 | 33.7 | 33.5 | 33.8 | 33.6 | 33.7 | 33.8 | 33.6 | 34.5 | 33.5 |
| 2017 | 33.4 | 33.0 | 32.8 | 34.3 | 34.1 | 33.6 | 34.0 | 33.9 | 33.5 | 33.4 | 33.4 | 33.7 | 33.6 |
| 2018 | 32.4 | 32.0 | 32.0 | 33.4 | 33.3 | 33.1 | 33.4 | 33.2 | 33.6 | 33.6 | 33.9 | 33.4 | 33.1 |
| 2019 | 32.3 | 32.6 | 33.1 | 33.5 | 33.7 | 33.4 | 33.4 | 33.6 | 33.3 | 32.8 | 33.2 | 32.9 | 33.1 |
| **Professional and Business Services** | | | | | | | | | | | | | |
| 2015 | 35.0 | 35.2 | 35.6 | 35.4 | 36.3 | 36.1 | 35.7 | 36.0 | 35.4 | 35.7 | 36.3 | 35.8 | 35.7 |
| 2016 | 34.4 | 34.9 | 35.2 | 35.9 | 36.8 | 35.7 | 35.5 | 35.6 | 36.7 | 37.7 | 37.3 | 37.4 | 36.1 |
| 2017 | 37.6 | 36.7 | 36.8 | 38.8 | 38.4 | 37.8 | 37.8 | 37.7 | 37.6 | 36.3 | 36.0 | 35.7 | 37.3 |
| 2018 | 35.3 | 35.6 | 35.2 | 36.0 | 36.3 | 36.2 | 35.8 | 35.9 | 36.7 | 35.9 | 36.3 | 37.0 | 36.0 |
| 2019 | 35.9 | 36.4 | 36.3 | 36.6 | 36.5 | 37.1 | 36.2 | 36.5 | 36.5 | 35.9 | 36.1 | 36.5 | 36.4 |
| **Education and Health Services** | | | | | | | | | | | | | |
| 2015 | 32.6 | 32.3 | 32.7 | 32.8 | 32.4 | 32.7 | 32.7 | 32.7 | 32.0 | 32.2 | 32.0 | 31.7 | 32.4 |
| 2016 | 31.9 | 31.6 | 31.4 | 31.6 | 31.6 | 31.5 | 31.9 | 32.2 | 32.9 | 31.9 | 32.0 | 31.9 | 31.9 |
| 2017 | 31.8 | 31.4 | 31.6 | 31.7 | 31.5 | 31.3 | 31.4 | 31.4 | 31.7 | 31.3 | 31.3 | 31.3 | 31.5 |
| 2018 | 30.9 | 31.5 | 31.0 | 31.5 | 31.3 | 31.2 | 31.6 | 31.5 | 31.5 | 31.3 | 31.5 | 31.6 | 31.4 |
| 2019 | 31.5 | 31.8 | 31.9 | 31.8 | 31.5 | 31.5 | 31.6 | 31.7 | 32.0 | 32.0 | 32.1 | 32.1 | 31.8 |
| **Leisure and Hospitality** | | | | | | | | | | | | | |
| 2015 | 22.9 | 22.9 | 23.7 | 24.3 | 24.3 | 23.9 | 25.8 | 26.2 | 25.4 | 25.2 | 24.7 | 24.3 | 24.5 |
| 2016 | 23.7 | 24.1 | 24.1 | 24.9 | 24.8 | 25.3 | 26.2 | 26.7 | 25.4 | 25.7 | 24.8 | 24.3 | 25.1 |
| 2017 | 24.4 | 23.5 | 24.1 | 24.5 | 25.2 | 26.0 | 26.9 | 27.0 | 25.0 | 24.8 | 24.7 | 23.8 | 25.1 |
| 2018 | 24.0 | 24.1 | 22.7 | 23.8 | 24.6 | 25.3 | 26.3 | 26.6 | 25.5 | 25.0 | 23.4 | 23.6 | 24.7 |
| 2019 | 22.8 | 23.8 | 23.9 | 24.0 | 23.8 | 24.2 | 26.1 | 26.6 | 24.7 | 24.5 | 24.1 | 23.5 | 24.4 |

## 3. Average Hourly Earnings by Selected Industry: New Hampshire, 2015–2019

(Dollars, not seasonally adjusted)

| Industry and year | January | February | March | April | May | June | July | August | September | October | November | December | Annual average |
|---|---|---|---|---|---|---|---|---|---|---|---|---|---|
| **Total Private** | | | | | | | | | | | | | |
| 2015 | 24.61 | 24.92 | 24.82 | 25.09 | 24.93 | 24.64 | 24.52 | 24.52 | 24.87 | 25.21 | 25.45 | 25.28 | 24.91 |
| 2016 | 25.88 | 25.85 | 25.66 | 25.62 | 25.38 | 25.11 | 25.08 | 25.44 | 25.85 | 26.35 | 26.16 | 26.23 | 25.72 |
| 2017 | 26.70 | 26.75 | 26.68 | 26.65 | 25.98 | 25.83 | 25.55 | 25.65 | 26.37 | 26.49 | 26.36 | 26.67 | 26.30 |
| 2018 | 26.68 | 26.89 | 26.84 | 26.79 | 26.35 | 26.17 | 26.19 | 25.93 | 26.82 | 26.86 | 26.66 | 26.91 | 26.59 |
| 2019 | 26.72 | 26.70 | 26.78 | 26.97 | 26.71 | 26.67 | 26.49 | 26.54 | 27.30 | 27.34 | 27.69 | 28.12 | 27.00 |
| **Goods-Producing** | | | | | | | | | | | | | |
| 2015 | 26.19 | 26.60 | 26.51 | 26.66 | 26.64 | 26.26 | 26.39 | 26.28 | 26.86 | 27.12 | 26.61 | 26.98 | 26.59 |
| 2016 | 27.52 | 26.95 | 26.57 | 26.58 | 26.36 | 26.49 | 26.62 | 27.06 | 27.02 | 27.21 | 27.07 | 27.65 | 26.92 |
| 2017 | 26.95 | 27.01 | 27.27 | 27.19 | 26.50 | 26.56 | 26.15 | 26.18 | 26.25 | 26.42 | 26.34 | 26.46 | 26.59 |
| 2018 | 26.10 | 26.19 | 26.71 | 26.74 | 26.35 | 26.39 | 26.49 | 26.19 | 26.50 | 26.45 | 26.42 | 26.83 | 26.45 |
| 2019 | 26.50 | 26.84 | 27.09 | 27.55 | 27.22 | 27.05 | 27.07 | 27.29 | 27.36 | 27.79 | 28.29 | 28.54 | 27.38 |
| **Manufacturing** | | | | | | | | | | | | | |
| 2015 | 25.75 | 26.18 | 26.02 | 26.40 | 26.33 | 25.98 | 26.01 | 25.74 | 26.58 | 26.65 | 26.24 | 26.77 | 26.22 |
| 2016 | 27.28 | 26.70 | 26.54 | 26.71 | 26.46 | 26.84 | 27.07 | 27.42 | 26.86 | 27.36 | 27.02 | 27.48 | 26.98 |
| 2017 | 26.80 | 26.90 | 26.41 | 26.41 | 25.47 | 25.92 | 25.70 | 25.70 | 25.72 | 25.80 | 25.50 | 25.71 | 25.99 |
| 2018 | 25.14 | 25.09 | 25.54 | 25.42 | 25.34 | 25.17 | 25.47 | 25.25 | 25.24 | 25.34 | 25.41 | 25.81 | 25.35 |
| 2019 | 25.60 | 26.02 | 26.21 | 26.67 | 26.52 | 26.30 | 26.41 | 26.72 | 26.77 | 27.30 | 27.51 | 27.89 | 26.65 |
| **Trade, Transportation, and Utilities** | | | | | | | | | | | | | |
| 2015 | 21.72 | 22.14 | 21.53 | 21.81 | 22.02 | 21.65 | 21.80 | 22.16 | 22.46 | 22.79 | 23.01 | 22.24 | 22.12 |
| 2016 | 22.58 | 22.07 | 22.09 | 21.95 | 22.04 | 21.53 | 21.67 | 21.85 | 22.02 | 22.57 | 22.27 | 22.04 | 22.06 |
| 2017 | 22.70 | 22.49 | 22.43 | 22.80 | 22.19 | 22.00 | 22.05 | 22.19 | 22.63 | 22.68 | 22.25 | 22.38 | 22.40 |
| 2018 | 22.86 | 23.09 | 23.29 | 23.45 | 23.23 | 23.09 | 23.28 | 23.07 | 23.76 | 23.80 | 23.33 | 23.75 | 23.34 |
| 2019 | 23.85 | 23.74 | 23.82 | 24.00 | 23.77 | 23.93 | 23.73 | 23.37 | 24.22 | 23.74 | 23.39 | 23.71 | 23.77 |
| **Professional and Business Services** | | | | | | | | | | | | | |
| 2015 | 28.99 | 28.54 | 28.55 | 28.40 | 27.91 | 28.08 | 28.31 | 27.29 | 27.61 | 28.30 | 28.47 | 28.28 | 28.22 |
| 2016 | 29.88 | 30.65 | 30.55 | 29.66 | 28.54 | 28.39 | 29.18 | 29.30 | 29.63 | 30.57 | 30.43 | 30.42 | 29.76 |
| 2017 | 31.75 | 31.89 | 31.69 | 30.43 | 30.21 | 30.94 | 30.39 | 30.04 | 30.72 | 31.13 | 31.00 | 31.48 | 30.95 |
| 2018 | 31.71 | 32.02 | 30.60 | 30.40 | 29.43 | 29.57 | 29.81 | 29.57 | 30.69 | 31.05 | 30.66 | 31.38 | 30.56 |
| 2019 | 30.63 | 31.15 | 31.16 | 30.86 | 31.10 | 31.31 | 31.99 | 32.31 | 32.95 | 32.89 | 33.35 | 33.92 | 31.98 |
| **Education and Health Services** | | | | | | | | | | | | | |
| 2015 | 25.87 | 26.31 | 26.31 | 26.63 | 26.88 | 26.53 | 26.79 | 26.69 | 27.22 | 27.32 | 27.39 | 27.87 | 26.82 |
| 2016 | 28.12 | 28.22 | 28.17 | 28.24 | 27.89 | 27.74 | 28.05 | 28.14 | 28.28 | 28.33 | 28.45 | 28.64 | 28.20 |
| 2017 | 28.72 | 29.29 | 29.16 | 29.42 | 29.32 | 29.58 | 29.84 | 29.5 | 29.33 | 29.48 | 29.66 | 30.05 | 29.45 |
| 2018 | 29.55 | 29.23 | 29.09 | 28.91 | 28.79 | 28.67 | 28.56 | 28.19 | 28.82 | 28.73 | 28.45 | 28.61 | 28.80 |
| 2019 | 28.29 | 28.1 | 27.94 | 27.89 | 28.25 | 28.35 | 28.15 | 28.07 | 28.4 | 28.4 | 28.5 | 28.41 | 28.23 |
| **Leisure and Hospitality** | | | | | | | | | | | | | |
| 2015 | 13.75 | 14.06 | 13.92 | 14.09 | 13.78 | 13.44 | 13.26 | 13.55 | 14.06 | 14.3 | 14.51 | 14.54 | 13.91 |
| 2016 | 14.45 | 14.66 | 14.47 | 14.64 | 14.6 | 14.25 | 13.96 | 14.24 | 14.86 | 14.97 | 14.89 | 14.95 | 14.56 |
| 2017 | 14.7 | 14.91 | 14.93 | 15.05 | 14.94 | 14.51 | 14.17 | 14.27 | 14.75 | 15.02 | 15.11 | 15.05 | 14.75 |
| 2018 | 14.6 | 15.03 | 15.29 | 15.43 | 15.34 | 14.81 | 14.6 | 14.82 | 15.1 | 15.49 | 15.71 | 15.89 | 15.15 |
| 2019 | 15.65 | 15.77 | 15.94 | 16.1 | 16.22 | 16 | 15.61 | 15.6 | 16.36 | 16.9 | 16.79 | 17.09 | 16.14 |

## 4. Average Weekly Earnings by Selected Industry: New Hampshire, 2015–2019

(Dollars, not seasonally adjusted)

| Industry and year | January | February | March | April | May | June | July | August | September | October | November | December | Annual average |
|---|---|---|---|---|---|---|---|---|---|---|---|---|---|
| **Total Private** | | | | | | | | | | | | | |
| 2015 | 809.67 | 819.87 | 831.47 | 843.02 | 840.14 | 825.44 | 831.23 | 838.58 | 838.12 | 852.10 | 862.76 | 851.94 | 836.98 |
| 2016 | 861.80 | 858.22 | 849.35 | 860.83 | 862.92 | 846.21 | 852.72 | 864.96 | 884.07 | 909.08 | 892.06 | 891.82 | 869.34 |
| 2017 | 905.13 | 893.45 | 893.78 | 916.76 | 891.11 | 880.80 | 873.81 | 879.80 | 896.58 | 895.36 | 890.97 | 893.45 | 891.57 |
| 2018 | 880.44 | 890.06 | 869.62 | 900.14 | 885.36 | 874.08 | 879.98 | 873.84 | 906.52 | 899.81 | 890.44 | 901.49 | 888.11 |
| 2019 | 876.42 | 881.10 | 886.42 | 895.40 | 892.11 | 893.45 | 890.06 | 897.05 | 917.28 | 913.16 | 930.38 | 942.02 | 901.80 |
| **Goods-Producing** | | | | | | | | | | | | | |
| 2015 | 1,018.79 | 1,029.42 | 1,044.49 | 1,042.41 | 1,044.29 | 1,029.39 | 1,042.41 | 1,038.06 | 1,034.11 | 1,054.97 | 1,051.10 | 1,068.41 | 1,042.33 |
| 2016 | 1,087.04 | 1,045.66 | 1,030.92 | 1,041.94 | 1,054.40 | 1,054.30 | 1,056.81 | 1,074.28 | 1,080.80 | 1,088.40 | 1,066.56 | 1,061.76 | 1,060.65 |
| 2017 | 1,045.66 | 1,007.47 | 1,028.08 | 1,049.53 | 1,036.15 | 1,035.84 | 1,006.78 | 1,031.49 | 1,044.75 | 1,048.87 | 1,058.87 | 1,053.11 | 1,037.01 |
| 2018 | 1,033.56 | 1,034.51 | 1,017.65 | 1,064.25 | 1,072.45 | 1,068.80 | 1,056.95 | 1,058.08 | 1,073.25 | 1,060.65 | 1,054.16 | 1,089.30 | 1,058.00 |
| 2019 | 1,078.55 | 1,054.81 | 1,061.93 | 1,085.47 | 1,091.52 | 1,087.41 | 1,088.21 | 1,102.52 | 1,105.34 | 1,114.38 | 1,140.09 | 1,147.31 | 1,095.20 |
| **Manufacturing** | | | | | | | | | | | | | |
| 2015 | 1,048.03 | 1,057.67 | 1,056.41 | 1,061.28 | 1,053.20 | 1,046.99 | 1,045.60 | 1,032.17 | 1,047.25 | 1,050.01 | 1,054.85 | 1,081.51 | 1,054.04 |
| 2016 | 1,099.38 | 1,054.65 | 1,050.98 | 1,063.06 | 1,074.28 | 1,084.34 | 1,085.51 | 1,094.06 | 1,085.14 | 1,099.87 | 1,083.50 | 1,090.96 | 1,079.20 |
| 2017 | 1,077.36 | 1,038.34 | 1,024.71 | 1,035.27 | 1,018.80 | 1,044.58 | 1,020.29 | 1,048.56 | 1,059.66 | 1,065.54 | 1,053.15 | 1,064.39 | 1,044.80 |
| 2018 | 1,038.28 | 1,038.73 | 1,029.26 | 1,052.39 | 1,056.68 | 1,044.56 | 1,054.46 | 1,050.40 | 1,062.60 | 1,038.94 | 1,049.43 | 1,073.70 | 1,049.49 |
| 2019 | 1,088.00 | 1,087.64 | 1,090.34 | 1,101.47 | 1,105.88 | 1,094.08 | 1,106.58 | 1,106.21 | 1,116.31 | 1,122.03 | 1,141.67 | 1,165.80 | 1,111.31 |
| **Trade, Transportation, and Utilities** | | | | | | | | | | | | | |
| 2015 | 690.70 | 710.69 | 708.34 | 719.73 | 737.67 | 723.11 | 739.02 | 757.87 | 772.62 | 772.58 | 780.04 | 756.16 | 738.81 |
| 2016 | 745.14 | 728.31 | 724.55 | 730.94 | 742.75 | 721.26 | 732.45 | 734.16 | 742.07 | 762.87 | 748.27 | 760.38 | 739.01 |
| 2017 | 758.18 | 742.17 | 735.70 | 782.04 | 756.68 | 739.20 | 749.70 | 752.24 | 758.11 | 757.51 | 743.15 | 754.21 | 752.64 |
| 2018 | 740.66 | 738.88 | 745.28 | 783.23 | 773.56 | 764.28 | 777.55 | 765.92 | 798.34 | 799.68 | 790.89 | 793.25 | 772.55 |
| 2019 | 770.36 | 773.92 | 788.44 | 804.00 | 801.05 | 799.26 | 792.58 | 785.23 | 806.53 | 778.67 | 776.55 | 780.06 | 786.79 |
| **Professional and Business Services** | | | | | | | | | | | | | |
| 2015 | 1,014.65 | 1,004.61 | 1,016.38 | 1,005.36 | 1,013.13 | 1,013.69 | 1,010.67 | 982.44 | 977.39 | 1,010.31 | 1,033.46 | 1,012.42 | 1,007.45 |
| 2016 | 1,027.87 | 1,069.69 | 1,075.36 | 1,064.79 | 1,050.27 | 1,013.52 | 1,035.89 | 1,043.08 | 1,087.42 | 1,152.49 | 1,135.04 | 1,137.71 | 1,074.34 |
| 2017 | 1,193.80 | 1,170.36 | 1,166.19 | 1,180.68 | 1,160.06 | 1,169.53 | 1,148.74 | 1,132.51 | 1,155.07 | 1,130.02 | 1,116.00 | 1,123.84 | 1,154.44 |
| 2018 | 1,119.36 | 1,139.91 | 1,077.12 | 1,094.40 | 1,068.31 | 1,070.43 | 1,067.20 | 1,061.56 | 1,126.32 | 1,114.70 | 1,112.96 | 1,161.06 | 1,100.16 |
| 2019 | 1,099.62 | 1,133.86 | 1,131.11 | 1,129.48 | 1,135.15 | 1,161.60 | 1,158.04 | 1,179.32 | 1,202.68 | 1,180.75 | 1,203.94 | 1,238.08 | 1,164.07 |
| **Education and Health Services** | | | | | | | | | | | | | |
| 2015 | 843.36 | 849.81 | 860.34 | 873.46 | 870.91 | 867.53 | 876.03 | 872.76 | 871.04 | 879.70 | 876.48 | 883.48 | 868.97 |
| 2016 | 897.03 | 891.75 | 884.54 | 892.38 | 881.32 | 873.81 | 894.80 | 906.11 | 930.74 | 903.73 | 910.40 | 913.62 | 899.58 |
| 2017 | 913.30 | 919.71 | 921.46 | 932.61 | 923.58 | 925.85 | 936.98 | 926.30 | 929.76 | 922.72 | 928.36 | 940.57 | 927.68 |
| 2018 | 913.10 | 920.75 | 901.79 | 910.67 | 901.13 | 894.50 | 902.50 | 887.99 | 907.83 | 899.25 | 896.18 | 904.08 | 904.32 |
| 2019 | 891.14 | 893.58 | 891.29 | 886.90 | 889.88 | 893.03 | 889.54 | 889.82 | 908.80 | 908.80 | 914.85 | 911.96 | 897.71 |
| **Leisure and Hospitality** | | | | | | | | | | | | | |
| 2015 | 314.88 | 321.97 | 329.90 | 342.39 | 334.85 | 321.22 | 342.11 | 355.01 | 357.12 | 360.36 | 358.40 | 353.32 | 340.80 |
| 2016 | 342.47 | 353.31 | 348.73 | 364.54 | 362.08 | 360.53 | 365.75 | 380.21 | 377.44 | 384.73 | 369.27 | 363.29 | 365.46 |
| 2017 | 358.68 | 350.39 | 359.81 | 368.73 | 376.49 | 377.26 | 381.17 | 385.29 | 368.75 | 372.50 | 373.22 | 358.19 | 370.23 |
| 2018 | 350.40 | 362.22 | 347.08 | 367.23 | 377.36 | 374.69 | 383.98 | 394.21 | 385.05 | 387.25 | 367.61 | 375.00 | 374.21 |
| 2019 | 356.82 | 375.33 | 380.97 | 386.40 | 386.04 | 387.20 | 407.42 | 414.96 | 404.09 | 414.05 | 404.64 | 401.62 | 393.82 |

# NEW JERSEY
## At a Glance

Population:
  2010 census: 8,791,894
  2019 estimate: 8,882,190

Percent change in population:
  2010–2019: 1.0%

Percent change in total nonfarm employment:
  2011–2019: 9.2%

Industry with the largest growth in employment, 2011–2019 (percent):
  Construction, 23.0%

Industry with the largest decline or smallest growth in employment, 2011–2019 (percent):
  Information, -10.1%

Civilian labor force:
  2010: 4,555,330
  2019: 4,493,125

Unemployment rate and rank among states (highest to lowest):
  2010: 9.5%, 20th
  2019: 3.6%, 21st

Over-the-year change in unemployment rates:
  2017–2018: -0.5%
  2018–2019: -0.5%

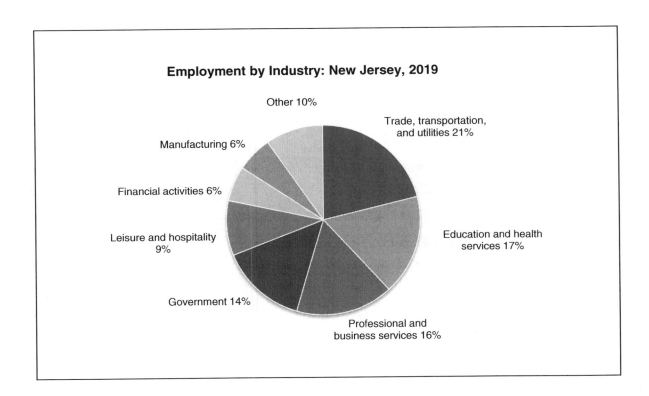

**Employment by Industry: New Jersey, 2019**

Other 10%

Manufacturing 6%

Financial activities 6%

Leisure and hospitality 9%

Government 14%

Trade, transportation, and utilities 21%

Education and health services 17%

Professional and business services 16%

## 1. Employment by Industry: New Jersey, 2011–2019

(Numbers in thousands, not seasonally adjusted)

| Industry and year | January | February | March | April | May | June | July | August | September | October | November | December | Annual average |
|---|---|---|---|---|---|---|---|---|---|---|---|---|---|
| **Total Nonfarm** | | | | | | | | | | | | | |
| 2011 | 3,749.1 | 3,759.1 | 3,788.5 | 3,831.5 | 3,861.1 | 3,911.2 | 3,856.7 | 3,833.6 | 3,857.3 | 3,870.8 | 3,890.0 | 3,897.7 | 3,842.2 |
| 2012 | 3,788.3 | 3,806.1 | 3,843.4 | 3,856.4 | 3,904.2 | 3,965.7 | 3,890.0 | 3,880.8 | 3,902.8 | 3,916.3 | 3,918.8 | 3,943.3 | 3,884.7 |
| 2013 | 3,830.9 | 3,847.7 | 3,881.0 | 3,900.7 | 3,942.0 | 4,001.5 | 3,939.3 | 3,932.8 | 3,946.7 | 3,958.9 | 3,982.9 | 3,982.6 | 3,928.9 |
| 2014 | 3,854.3 | 3,855.6 | 3,887.8 | 3,943.0 | 3,990.4 | 4,038.0 | 3,977.8 | 3,962.4 | 3,979.4 | 3,995.9 | 4,018.0 | 4,029.3 | 3,961.0 |
| 2015 | 3,892.1 | 3,899.7 | 3,932.0 | 3,972.9 | 4,026.0 | 4,074.3 | 4,021.0 | 4,008.0 | 4,022.4 | 4,053.0 | 4,076.0 | 4,082.1 | 4,005.0 |
| 2016 | 3,946.9 | 3,960.5 | 3,997.8 | 4,039.7 | 4,076.0 | 4,134.9 | 4,087.3 | 4,070.7 | 4,092.5 | 4,107.4 | 4,130.7 | 4,140.6 | 4,065.4 |
| 2017 | 4,012.4 | 4,026.9 | 4,049.5 | 4,084.3 | 4,141.0 | 4,210.1 | 4,135.9 | 4,122.0 | 4,138.1 | 4,160.5 | 4,184.3 | 4,193.7 | 4,121.6 |
| 2018 | 4,051.4 | 4,074.3 | 4,090.8 | 4,126.9 | 4,176.0 | 4,242.3 | 4,173.3 | 4,157.1 | 4,165.1 | 4,195.4 | 4,226.0 | 4,225.6 | 4,158.7 |
| 2019 | 4,100.1 | 4,110.2 | 4,134.8 | 4,171.5 | 4,204.4 | 4,270.8 | 4,211.1 | 4,195.6 | 4,201.0 | 4,230.1 | 4,252.3 | 4,256.9 | 4,194.9 |
| **Total Private** | | | | | | | | | | | | | |
| 2011 | 3,135.6 | 3,133.8 | 3,161.1 | 3,201.8 | 3,235.8 | 3,286.8 | 3,271.9 | 3,263.5 | 3,258.0 | 3,247.2 | 3,261.2 | 3,271.6 | 3,227.4 |
| 2012 | 3,179.3 | 3,183.7 | 3,216.6 | 3,233.7 | 3,284.8 | 3,342.3 | 3,309.9 | 3,311.9 | 3,305.2 | 3,294.4 | 3,295.8 | 3,320.4 | 3,273.2 |
| 2013 | 3,218.7 | 3,221.2 | 3,254.1 | 3,284.6 | 3,329.1 | 3,384.5 | 3,362.3 | 3,363.0 | 3,350.5 | 3,337.1 | 3,357.5 | 3,359.5 | 3,318.5 |
| 2014 | 3,246.7 | 3,235.4 | 3,266.6 | 3,314.0 | 3,367.6 | 3,415.7 | 3,396.6 | 3,391.6 | 3,381.3 | 3,377.5 | 3,393.9 | 3,407.4 | 3,349.5 |
| 2015 | 3,290.0 | 3,284.2 | 3,314.9 | 3,353.1 | 3,410.2 | 3,458.8 | 3,446.6 | 3,440.5 | 3,430.7 | 3,440.3 | 3,457.0 | 3,466.5 | 3,399.4 |
| 2016 | 3,347.5 | 3,347.7 | 3,379.9 | 3,423.3 | 3,460.9 | 3,521.5 | 3,513.3 | 3,505.8 | 3,498.6 | 3,495.2 | 3,513.7 | 3,526.8 | 3,461.2 |
| 2017 | 3,411.9 | 3,412.9 | 3,433.3 | 3,469.7 | 3,527.6 | 3,592.2 | 3,558.5 | 3,553.0 | 3,545.5 | 3,548.4 | 3,568.6 | 3,578.5 | 3,516.7 |
| 2018 | 3,454.0 | 3,463.0 | 3,479.7 | 3,514.0 | 3,565.0 | 3,626.5 | 3,597.2 | 3,588.7 | 3,571.9 | 3,583.8 | 3,608.1 | 3,610.9 | 3,555.2 |
| 2019 | 3,501.5 | 3,497.3 | 3,521.6 | 3,556.1 | 3,594.2 | 3,654.0 | 3,628.4 | 3,624.7 | 3,604.5 | 3,614.8 | 3,633.4 | 3,637.1 | 3,589.0 |
| **Goods Producing** | | | | | | | | | | | | | |
| 2011 | 366.1 | 363.8 | 370.2 | 378.1 | 382.0 | 386.6 | 387.2 | 388.4 | 386.1 | 385.1 | 384.3 | 380.9 | 379.9 |
| 2012 | 366.9 | 365.1 | 368.1 | 371.7 | 374.8 | 378.7 | 377.4 | 378.7 | 377.9 | 378.2 | 378.1 | 378.9 | 374.5 |
| 2013 | 365.9 | 364.5 | 369.2 | 376.5 | 380.5 | 384.8 | 384.8 | 387.3 | 386.5 | 387.3 | 387.1 | 381.3 | 379.6 |
| 2014 | 367.6 | 364.1 | 369.7 | 380.7 | 386.9 | 390.2 | 391.7 | 392.7 | 392.6 | 391.7 | 390.7 | 387.9 | 383.9 |
| 2015 | 374.2 | 370.8 | 374.9 | 385.4 | 392.0 | 397.1 | 399.2 | 399.5 | 397.5 | 400.1 | 399.3 | 398.2 | 390.7 |
| 2016 | 385.9 | 383.5 | 389.6 | 395.8 | 400.3 | 405.1 | 406.7 | 406.8 | 404.0 | 405.4 | 404.9 | 402.6 | 399.2 |
| 2017 | 388.6 | 389.6 | 392.0 | 399.8 | 406.3 | 411.7 | 411.6 | 412.2 | 410.2 | 410.6 | 410.6 | 408.9 | 404.3 |
| 2018 | 392.9 | 396.4 | 399.2 | 405.1 | 410.4 | 416.3 | 415.6 | 416.0 | 413.3 | 415.5 | 414.5 | 413.5 | 409.1 |
| 2019 | 401.3 | 399.7 | 403.7 | 410.6 | 414.6 | 418.4 | 419.3 | 419.2 | 417.3 | 417.3 | 417.7 | 412.9 | 412.7 |
| **Service-Providing** | | | | | | | | | | | | | |
| 2011 | 3,383.0 | 3,395.3 | 3,418.3 | 3,453.4 | 3,479.1 | 3,524.6 | 3,469.5 | 3,445.2 | 3,471.2 | 3,485.7 | 3,505.7 | 3,516.8 | 3,462.3 |
| 2012 | 3,421.4 | 3,441.0 | 3,475.3 | 3,484.7 | 3,529.4 | 3,587.0 | 3,512.6 | 3,502.1 | 3,524.9 | 3,538.1 | 3,540.7 | 3,564.4 | 3,510.1 |
| 2013 | 3,465.0 | 3,483.2 | 3,511.8 | 3,524.2 | 3,561.5 | 3,616.7 | 3,554.5 | 3,545.5 | 3,560.2 | 3,571.6 | 3,595.8 | 3,601.3 | 3,549.3 |
| 2014 | 3,486.7 | 3,491.5 | 3,518.1 | 3,562.3 | 3,603.5 | 3,647.8 | 3,586.1 | 3,569.7 | 3,586.8 | 3,604.2 | 3,627.3 | 3,641.4 | 3,577.1 |
| 2015 | 3,517.9 | 3,528.9 | 3,557.1 | 3,587.5 | 3,634.0 | 3,677.2 | 3,621.8 | 3,608.5 | 3,624.9 | 3,652.9 | 3,676.7 | 3,683.9 | 3,614.3 |
| 2016 | 3,561.0 | 3,577.0 | 3,608.2 | 3,643.9 | 3,675.7 | 3,729.8 | 3,680.6 | 3,663.9 | 3,688.5 | 3,702.0 | 3,725.8 | 3,738.0 | 3,666.2 |
| 2017 | 3,623.8 | 3,637.3 | 3,657.5 | 3,684.5 | 3,734.7 | 3,798.4 | 3,724.3 | 3,709.8 | 3,727.9 | 3,749.9 | 3,773.7 | 3,784.8 | 3,717.2 |
| 2018 | 3,658.5 | 3,677.9 | 3,691.6 | 3,721.8 | 3,765.6 | 3,826.0 | 3,757.7 | 3,741.1 | 3,751.8 | 3,779.9 | 3,811.5 | 3,812.1 | 3,749.6 |
| 2019 | 3,698.8 | 3,710.5 | 3,731.1 | 3,760.9 | 3,789.8 | 3,852.4 | 3,791.8 | 3,776.4 | 3,783.7 | 3,812.8 | 3,834.6 | 3,844.0 | 3,782.2 |
| **Mining and Logging** | | | | | | | | | | | | | |
| 2011 | 1.2 | 1.2 | 1.2 | 1.3 | 1.3 | 1.4 | 1.3 | 1.3 | 1.3 | 1.3 | 1.3 | 1.3 | 1.3 |
| 2012 | 1.2 | 1.2 | 1.2 | 1.3 | 1.3 | 1.3 | 1.3 | 1.3 | 1.3 | 1.3 | 1.3 | 1.3 | 1.3 |
| 2013 | 1.2 | 1.1 | 1.2 | 1.3 | 1.3 | 1.4 | 1.4 | 1.4 | 1.4 | 1.4 | 1.4 | 1.4 | 1.3 |
| 2014 | 1.3 | 1.3 | 1.4 | 1.4 | 1.5 | 1.5 | 1.5 | 1.5 | 1.4 | 1.4 | 1.5 | 1.5 | 1.4 |
| 2015 | 1.4 | 1.4 | 1.3 | 1.4 | 1.4 | 1.4 | 1.4 | 1.4 | 1.4 | 1.5 | 1.4 | 1.4 | 1.4 |
| 2016 | 1.3 | 1.3 | 1.3 | 1.3 | 1.4 | 1.4 | 1.4 | 1.3 | 1.3 | 1.3 | 1.3 | 1.3 | 1.3 |
| 2017 | 1.2 | 1.2 | 1.3 | 1.3 | 1.3 | 1.3 | 1.3 | 1.3 | 1.3 | 1.4 | 1.4 | 1.4 | 1.3 |
| 2018 | 1.3 | 1.3 | 1.3 | 1.3 | 1.4 | 1.4 | 1.3 | 1.4 | 1.3 | 1.4 | 1.4 | 1.3 | 1.3 |
| 2019 | 1.3 | 1.3 | 1.3 | 1.3 | 1.4 | 1.4 | 1.4 | 1.5 | 1.5 | 1.5 | 1.5 | 1.5 | 1.4 |
| **Construction** | | | | | | | | | | | | | |
| 2011 | 114.2 | 112.4 | 118.3 | 126.9 | 130.9 | 134.3 | 137.2 | 138.3 | 137.4 | 137.5 | 137.2 | 134.2 | 129.9 |
| 2012 | 123.6 | 122.1 | 123.3 | 127.9 | 129.8 | 132.5 | 133.3 | 134.4 | 133.7 | 134.3 | 134.7 | 135.3 | 130.4 |
| 2013 | 125.8 | 124.6 | 128.0 | 135.8 | 139.2 | 141.6 | 142.6 | 144.4 | 143.6 | 144.1 | 143.5 | 137.6 | 137.6 |
| 2014 | 127.6 | 124.4 | 129.2 | 138.1 | 143.3 | 145.3 | 148.1 | 149.2 | 149.8 | 149.6 | 148.7 | 145.7 | 141.6 |
| 2015 | 134.7 | 132.0 | 135.4 | 145.7 | 150.5 | 153.1 | 155.3 | 155.7 | 153.6 | 156.2 | 155.2 | 152.8 | 148.4 |
| 2016 | 143.0 | 140.3 | 145.3 | 152.0 | 155.3 | 157.8 | 159.7 | 159.8 | 157.8 | 158.7 | 157.7 | 154.8 | 153.5 |
| 2017 | 143.8 | 144.6 | 146.6 | 153.8 | 158.2 | 161.1 | 161.6 | 162.4 | 161.3 | 161.2 | 160.7 | 158.2 | 156.1 |
| 2018 | 145.1 | 148.2 | 150.3 | 156.1 | 160.2 | 163.2 | 163.1 | 163.1 | 161.8 | 163.0 | 161.5 | 159.8 | 158.0 |
| 2019 | 150.5 | 148.7 | 151.5 | 158.4 | 161.6 | 163.2 | 164.6 | 165.8 | 164.8 | 165.6 | 163.9 | 159.1 | 159.8 |

# 1. Employment by Industry: New Jersey, 2011–2019—*Continued*

(Numbers in thousands, not seasonally adjusted)

| Industry and year | January | February | March | April | May | June | July | August | September | October | November | December | Annual average |
|---|---|---|---|---|---|---|---|---|---|---|---|---|---|
| **Manufacturing** | | | | | | | | | | | | | |
| 2011 | 250.7 | 250.2 | 250.7 | 249.9 | 249.8 | 250.9 | 248.7 | 248.8 | 247.4 | 246.3 | 245.8 | 245.4 | 248.7 |
| 2012 | 242.1 | 241.8 | 243.6 | 242.5 | 243.7 | 244.9 | 242.8 | 243.0 | 242.9 | 242.6 | 242.1 | 242.3 | 242.9 |
| 2013 | 238.9 | 238.8 | 240.0 | 239.4 | 240.0 | 241.8 | 240.8 | 241.5 | 241.5 | 241.8 | 242.2 | 242.3 | 240.8 |
| 2014 | 238.7 | 238.4 | 239.1 | 241.2 | 242.1 | 243.4 | 242.1 | 242.0 | 241.4 | 240.7 | 240.5 | 240.7 | 240.9 |
| 2015 | 238.1 | 237.4 | 238.2 | 238.3 | 240.1 | 242.6 | 242.5 | 242.4 | 242.5 | 242.4 | 242.7 | 244.0 | 240.9 |
| 2016 | 241.6 | 241.9 | 243.0 | 242.5 | 243.6 | 245.9 | 245.6 | 245.7 | 244.9 | 245.4 | 245.9 | 246.5 | 244.4 |
| 2017 | 243.6 | 243.8 | 244.1 | 244.7 | 246.8 | 249.3 | 248.7 | 248.5 | 247.6 | 248.0 | 248.5 | 249.3 | 246.9 |
| 2018 | 246.5 | 246.9 | 247.6 | 247.7 | 248.8 | 251.7 | 251.2 | 251.5 | 250.2 | 251.1 | 251.6 | 252.4 | 249.8 |
| 2019 | 249.5 | 249.7 | 250.9 | 250.9 | 251.6 | 253.8 | 253.3 | 251.9 | 251.0 | 250.2 | 252.3 | 252.3 | 251.5 |
| **Trade, Transportation, and Utilities** | | | | | | | | | | | | | |
| 2011 | 803.9 | 796.8 | 799.4 | 803.9 | 809.5 | 819.8 | 812.1 | 811.8 | 813.2 | 817.0 | 833.9 | 846.6 | 814.0 |
| 2012 | 815.0 | 805.6 | 810.2 | 807.0 | 820.3 | 830.9 | 818.7 | 816.4 | 819.4 | 822.4 | 837.8 | 849.8 | 821.1 |
| 2013 | 814.1 | 805.3 | 809.3 | 812.5 | 821.3 | 833.0 | 825.6 | 824.8 | 826.2 | 830.6 | 849.9 | 859.5 | 826.0 |
| 2014 | 823.3 | 813.1 | 818.3 | 823.2 | 833.8 | 844.1 | 836.7 | 836.6 | 837.6 | 842.4 | 861.9 | 875.1 | 837.2 |
| 2015 | 837.4 | 828.3 | 832.3 | 837.6 | 849.5 | 861.4 | 853.6 | 853.2 | 854.0 | 860.1 | 877.8 | 885.3 | 852.5 |
| 2016 | 849.7 | 842.7 | 846.3 | 851.2 | 859.7 | 867.5 | 864.0 | 862.8 | 865.0 | 872.8 | 893.7 | 904.9 | 865.0 |
| 2017 | 869.2 | 859.2 | 859.6 | 863.5 | 872.8 | 885.7 | 878.8 | 878.5 | 880.8 | 883.9 | 908.5 | 917.9 | 879.9 |
| 2018 | 880.7 | 870.7 | 869.7 | 870.3 | 880.1 | 887.9 | 880.6 | 876.3 | 876.3 | 883.9 | 912.3 | 919.5 | 884.0 |
| 2019 | 884.5 | 871.6 | 872.7 | 871.2 | 878.0 | 889.3 | 883.6 | 882.6 | 882.1 | 891.1 | 912.4 | 922.4 | 886.8 |
| **Wholesale Trade** | | | | | | | | | | | | | |
| 2011 | 204.6 | 206.0 | 207.0 | 208.4 | 209.3 | 210.9 | 211.3 | 211.5 | 210.1 | 210.1 | 210.6 | 212.2 | 209.3 |
| 2012 | 209.7 | 210.2 | 211.3 | 210.9 | 212.1 | 214.0 | 213.1 | 212.8 | 212.5 | 211.8 | 212.3 | 212.8 | 212.0 |
| 2013 | 209.2 | 209.1 | 210.1 | 210.5 | 211.5 | 213.2 | 213.0 | 212.9 | 212.4 | 212.1 | 212.4 | 212.5 | 211.6 |
| 2014 | 209.4 | 209.9 | 211.0 | 211.6 | 213.3 | 214.8 | 214.4 | 214.1 | 214.1 | 213.6 | 214.5 | 215.3 | 213.0 |
| 2015 | 211.9 | 211.7 | 212.7 | 213.2 | 214.5 | 215.9 | 215.8 | 215.6 | 214.4 | 214.3 | 214.4 | 215.0 | 214.1 |
| 2016 | 211.5 | 211.7 | 212.6 | 212.9 | 213.9 | 215.0 | 215.5 | 215.3 | 214.5 | 214.4 | 214.9 | 215.5 | 214.0 |
| 2017 | 212.1 | 212.1 | 212.6 | 213.3 | 214.2 | 216.1 | 215.5 | 215.2 | 214.5 | 213.4 | 214.2 | 214.8 | 214.0 |
| 2018 | 212.5 | 212.5 | 212.5 | 213.1 | 214.4 | 215.9 | 216.5 | 215.2 | 214.6 | 215.0 | 215.6 | 216.3 | 214.5 |
| 2019 | 213.5 | 213.6 | 214.1 | 214.2 | 214.7 | 216.2 | 215.5 | 215.1 | 214.6 | 216.2 | 215.4 | 215.0 | 214.8 |
| **Retail Trade** | | | | | | | | | | | | | |
| 2011 | 435.9 | 427.9 | 428.8 | 432.0 | 435.8 | 443.4 | 442.3 | 442.7 | 437.6 | 440.9 | 455.2 | 464.2 | 440.6 |
| 2012 | 441.4 | 431.0 | 433.9 | 433.4 | 441.1 | 448.4 | 444.8 | 444.3 | 439.7 | 443.1 | 457.4 | 465.4 | 443.7 |
| 2013 | 439.9 | 431.5 | 433.7 | 436.0 | 442.8 | 452.2 | 451.6 | 452.2 | 446.8 | 450.6 | 466.6 | 473.6 | 448.1 |
| 2014 | 446.8 | 438.2 | 441.4 | 444.9 | 451.4 | 459.1 | 459.2 | 459.2 | 452.9 | 456.5 | 471.1 | 480.2 | 455.1 |
| 2015 | 452.7 | 444.5 | 446.8 | 450.1 | 458.3 | 466.8 | 464.5 | 465.4 | 460.0 | 463.2 | 477.2 | 481.0 | 460.9 |
| 2016 | 455.5 | 448.1 | 450.2 | 453.3 | 458.8 | 464.9 | 464.9 | 465.5 | 459.2 | 461.9 | 475.8 | 482.9 | 461.8 |
| 2017 | 459.0 | 450.6 | 450.8 | 452.9 | 458.1 | 466.4 | 465.3 | 465.1 | 458.4 | 460.5 | 476.5 | 479.7 | 461.9 |
| 2018 | 457.3 | 449.8 | 449.4 | 449.6 | 456.1 | 461.5 | 459.1 | 457.3 | 451.0 | 451.7 | 467.5 | 471.4 | 456.8 |
| 2019 | 451.8 | 442.1 | 444.2 | 443.9 | 447.6 | 454.5 | 453.4 | 452.4 | 445.4 | 448.1 | 458.8 | 463.3 | 450.5 |
| **Transportation and Utilities** | | | | | | | | | | | | | |
| 2011 | 163.4 | 162.9 | 163.6 | 163.5 | 164.4 | 165.5 | 158.5 | 157.6 | 165.5 | 166.0 | 168.1 | 170.2 | 164.1 |
| 2012 | 163.9 | 164.4 | 165.0 | 162.7 | 167.1 | 168.5 | 160.8 | 159.3 | 167.2 | 167.5 | 168.1 | 171.6 | 165.5 |
| 2013 | 165.0 | 164.7 | 165.5 | 166.0 | 167.0 | 167.6 | 161.0 | 159.7 | 167.0 | 167.9 | 170.9 | 173.4 | 166.3 |
| 2014 | 167.1 | 165.0 | 165.9 | 166.7 | 169.1 | 170.2 | 163.1 | 163.3 | 170.6 | 172.3 | 176.3 | 179.6 | 169.1 |
| 2015 | 172.8 | 172.1 | 172.8 | 174.3 | 176.7 | 178.7 | 173.3 | 172.2 | 179.6 | 182.6 | 186.2 | 189.3 | 177.6 |
| 2016 | 182.7 | 182.9 | 183.5 | 185.0 | 187.0 | 187.6 | 183.6 | 182.0 | 191.3 | 196.5 | 203.0 | 206.5 | 189.3 |
| 2017 | 198.1 | 196.5 | 196.2 | 197.3 | 200.5 | 203.2 | 198.0 | 198.2 | 207.9 | 210.0 | 217.8 | 223.4 | 203.9 |
| 2018 | 210.9 | 208.4 | 207.8 | 207.6 | 209.6 | 210.5 | 205.0 | 203.8 | 210.7 | 217.2 | 229.2 | 231.8 | 212.7 |
| 2019 | 219.2 | 215.9 | 214.4 | 213.1 | 215.7 | 218.6 | 214.7 | 215.1 | 222.1 | 226.8 | 238.2 | 244.1 | 221.5 |
| **Information** | | | | | | | | | | | | | |
| 2011 | 74.1 | 73.9 | 74.0 | 74.9 | 75.1 | 76.2 | 77.5 | 71.5 | 77.2 | 74.9 | 75.1 | 75.1 | 75.0 |
| 2012 | 75.3 | 75.7 | 76.2 | 75.1 | 75.2 | 75.7 | 76.3 | 76.1 | 75.5 | 74.6 | 74.6 | 74.7 | 75.4 |
| 2013 | 73.4 | 73.7 | 73.3 | 73.4 | 73.6 | 74.3 | 74.4 | 74.7 | 73.2 | 73.3 | 73.9 | 73.6 | 73.7 |
| 2014 | 72.8 | 72.7 | 73.0 | 73.8 | 74.1 | 74.4 | 74.3 | 74.3 | 73.6 | 73.0 | 72.4 | 72.9 | 73.4 |
| 2015 | 72.5 | 72.2 | 72.1 | 72.0 | 72.9 | 73.8 | 73.4 | 73.0 | 72.3 | 72.4 | 72.8 | 72.9 | 72.7 |
| 2016 | 71.3 | 71.4 | 71.1 | 71.8 | 67.6 | 72.2 | 73.2 | 72.4 | 71.8 | 71.1 | 71.4 | 72.4 | 71.5 |
| 2017 | 70.9 | 72.0 | 71.4 | 70.7 | 71.0 | 72.2 | 70.6 | 70.7 | 70.4 | 70.1 | 70.5 | 70.8 | 70.9 |
| 2018 | 69.1 | 71.2 | 70.0 | 69.3 | 69.8 | 71.0 | 69.8 | 70.5 | 69.1 | 69.0 | 69.2 | 68.7 | 69.7 |
| 2019 | 66.5 | 66.9 | 66.7 | 66.8 | 67.6 | 68.7 | 67.8 | 69.2 | 67.6 | 67.4 | 67.3 | 66.5 | 67.4 |

## 1. Employment by Industry: New Jersey, 2011–2019—*Continued*

(Numbers in thousands, not seasonally adjusted)

| Industry and year | January | February | March | April | May | June | July | August | September | October | November | December | Annual average |
|---|---|---|---|---|---|---|---|---|---|---|---|---|---|
| **Financial Activities** | | | | | | | | | | | | | |
| 2011 | 245.5 | 245.4 | 245.8 | 245.8 | 246.6 | 249.4 | 248.9 | 249.0 | 246.7 | 244.1 | 244.2 | 244.6 | 246.3 |
| 2012 | 243.0 | 243.0 | 244.1 | 245.2 | 246.9 | 250.2 | 249.5 | 249.6 | 247.4 | 246.7 | 246.7 | 248.5 | 246.7 |
| 2013 | 249.6 | 250.0 | 250.5 | 249.8 | 250.4 | 252.9 | 252.6 | 252.0 | 249.2 | 247.4 | 246.3 | 246.5 | 249.8 |
| 2014 | 241.9 | 241.0 | 241.3 | 241.6 | 242.9 | 245.4 | 245.7 | 245.2 | 242.9 | 242.0 | 242.7 | 243.4 | 243.0 |
| | | | | | | | | | | | | | |
| 2015 | 240.1 | 240.3 | 241.4 | 241.8 | 243.2 | 245.8 | 246.5 | 246.2 | 243.9 | 243.3 | 243.2 | 244.1 | 243.3 |
| 2016 | 240.7 | 240.3 | 240.3 | 241.6 | 242.9 | 246.2 | 248.3 | 248.4 | 246.2 | 246.1 | 245.8 | 246.9 | 244.5 |
| 2017 | 244.9 | 245.5 | 246.9 | 247.2 | 249.1 | 252.7 | 253.1 | 252.7 | 250.4 | 250.3 | 250.7 | 251.9 | 249.6 |
| 2018 | 248.1 | 248.1 | 249.2 | 249.9 | 250.8 | 254.0 | 254.3 | 253.9 | 251.7 | 251.5 | 251.8 | 252.4 | 251.3 |
| 2019 | 250.2 | 249.9 | 250.6 | 251.2 | 252.1 | 255.6 | 255.8 | 255.8 | 252.6 | 250.6 | 251.2 | 251.6 | 252.3 |
| **Professional and Business Services** | | | | | | | | | | | | | |
| 2011 | 586.1 | 587.1 | 593.1 | 603.7 | 606.8 | 615.7 | 614.9 | 617.3 | 617.4 | 619.3 | 620.9 | 618.1 | 608.4 |
| 2012 | 597.0 | 600.8 | 608.9 | 616.3 | 622.5 | 632.4 | 626.6 | 633.5 | 635.2 | 633.3 | 638.5 | 639.5 | 623.7 |
| 2013 | 612.8 | 616.0 | 625.0 | 628.8 | 636.3 | 645.5 | 642.5 | 647.1 | 645.3 | 641.5 | 644.6 | 643.9 | 635.8 |
| 2014 | 618.4 | 619.5 | 621.6 | 633.3 | 639.5 | 646.3 | 643.7 | 645.7 | 647.0 | 651.1 | 655.2 | 655.9 | 639.8 |
| | | | | | | | | | | | | | |
| 2015 | 626.8 | 628.8 | 636.2 | 644.3 | 650.1 | 655.4 | 655.5 | 657.8 | 659.5 | 667.7 | 670.2 | 668.9 | 651.8 |
| 2016 | 637.6 | 639.8 | 647.2 | 660.8 | 664.5 | 674.7 | 672.4 | 673.8 | 676.8 | 674.8 | 679.1 | 681.8 | 665.3 |
| 2017 | 649.3 | 651.0 | 656.0 | 662.6 | 672.8 | 683.7 | 674.0 | 674.5 | 679.3 | 681.8 | 683.7 | 684.0 | 671.1 |
| 2018 | 650.5 | 653.8 | 658.7 | 669.9 | 677.5 | 687.3 | 677.5 | 679.1 | 681.0 | 689.3 | 694.2 | 689.3 | 675.7 |
| 2019 | 660.7 | 663.7 | 668.8 | 682.2 | 683.4 | 694.0 | 685.2 | 688.1 | 690.3 | 696.1 | 698.7 | 695.8 | 683.9 |
| **Education and Health Services** | | | | | | | | | | | | | |
| 2011 | 598.4 | 603.6 | 607.6 | 607.8 | 609.6 | 609.1 | 597.9 | 595.0 | 606.4 | 611.9 | 614.9 | 619.1 | 606.8 |
| 2012 | 611.0 | 619.4 | 624.3 | 620.9 | 626.3 | 625.3 | 611.3 | 609.4 | 621.3 | 628.8 | 626.8 | 632.6 | 621.5 |
| 2013 | 623.6 | 630.1 | 635.6 | 637.3 | 640.6 | 637.0 | 624.0 | 622.1 | 633.8 | 640.7 | 646.3 | 646.3 | 634.8 |
| 2014 | 633.5 | 636.6 | 644.1 | 647.6 | 652.5 | 650.6 | 639.6 | 635.9 | 648.8 | 656.2 | 660.4 | 664.3 | 647.5 |
| | | | | | | | | | | | | | |
| 2015 | 649.9 | 655.0 | 660.8 | 660.5 | 664.3 | 662.8 | 649.7 | 645.6 | 658.5 | 667.6 | 671.6 | 673.7 | 660.0 |
| 2016 | 663.0 | 668.5 | 673.7 | 674.6 | 676.2 | 675.7 | 664.5 | 660.9 | 678.7 | 687.0 | 688.5 | 689.8 | 675.1 |
| 2017 | 682.3 | 687.6 | 692.2 | 695.4 | 700.2 | 698.0 | 681.0 | 677.4 | 696.6 | 706.1 | 708.3 | 710.4 | 694.6 |
| 2018 | 698.4 | 707.1 | 709.3 | 709.0 | 711.7 | 709.0 | 693.1 | 688.0 | 705.4 | 715.0 | 716.8 | 718.1 | 706.7 |
| 2019 | 710.0 | 715.4 | 720.4 | 720.5 | 722.2 | 719.7 | 703.4 | 699.4 | 715.7 | 726.8 | 729.9 | 731.9 | 717.9 |
| **Leisure and Hospitality** | | | | | | | | | | | | | |
| 2011 | 303.7 | 305.2 | 311.7 | 326.9 | 344.2 | 364.1 | 368.7 | 367.1 | 350.5 | 334.2 | 327.4 | 325.8 | 335.8 |
| 2012 | 311.1 | 314.0 | 323.2 | 334.6 | 353.8 | 379.9 | 382.2 | 381.2 | 363.8 | 346.3 | 329.9 | 331.6 | 346.0 |
| 2013 | 317.8 | 319.6 | 328.2 | 341.5 | 360.3 | 386.4 | 388.7 | 386.2 | 370.5 | 350.9 | 343.8 | 342.3 | 353.0 |
| 2014 | 325.7 | 325.0 | 333.4 | 346.9 | 368.8 | 391.9 | 393.2 | 390.7 | 370.8 | 353.6 | 343.1 | 339.8 | 356.9 |
| | | | | | | | | | | | | | |
| 2015 | 324.0 | 324.1 | 331.0 | 345.0 | 369.3 | 389.8 | 397.3 | 395.0 | 377.5 | 360.9 | 353.3 | 354.2 | 360.1 |
| 2016 | 332.6 | 334.6 | 343.6 | 357.2 | 378.0 | 404.5 | 409.9 | 407.2 | 385.9 | 367.3 | 359.5 | 357.2 | 369.8 |
| 2017 | 338.9 | 340.8 | 347.6 | 361.5 | 384.6 | 413.2 | 416.6 | 415.1 | 389.0 | 376.4 | 367.1 | 365.1 | 376.3 |
| 2018 | 347.5 | 348.8 | 356.2 | 370.6 | 392.6 | 424.5 | 431.6 | 431.2 | 404.4 | 387.9 | 377.9 | 377.5 | 387.6 |
| 2019 | 359.2 | 360.7 | 368.3 | 380.6 | 401.8 | 429.9 | 435.8 | 433.7 | 405.7 | 390.5 | 382.3 | 382.2 | 394.2 |
| **Other Services** | | | | | | | | | | | | | |
| 2011 | 157.8 | 158.0 | 159.3 | 160.7 | 162.0 | 165.9 | 164.7 | 163.4 | 160.5 | 160.7 | 160.5 | 161.4 | 161.2 |
| 2012 | 160.0 | 160.1 | 161.6 | 162.9 | 165.0 | 169.2 | 167.9 | 167.0 | 164.7 | 164.1 | 163.4 | 164.8 | 164.2 |
| 2013 | 161.5 | 162.0 | 163.0 | 164.8 | 166.1 | 170.6 | 169.7 | 168.8 | 165.8 | 165.4 | 165.6 | 166.1 | 165.8 |
| 2014 | 163.5 | 163.4 | 165.2 | 166.9 | 169.1 | 172.8 | 171.7 | 170.5 | 168.0 | 167.5 | 167.5 | 168.1 | 167.9 |
| | | | | | | | | | | | | | |
| 2015 | 165.1 | 164.7 | 166.2 | 166.5 | 168.9 | 172.7 | 171.4 | 170.2 | 167.5 | 168.2 | 168.8 | 169.2 | 168.3 |
| 2016 | 166.7 | 166.9 | 168.1 | 170.3 | 171.7 | 175.6 | 174.3 | 173.5 | 170.2 | 170.7 | 170.8 | 171.2 | 170.8 |
| 2017 | 167.8 | 167.2 | 167.6 | 169.0 | 170.8 | 175.0 | 172.8 | 171.9 | 168.8 | 169.2 | 169.2 | 169.5 | 169.9 |
| 2018 | 166.8 | 166.9 | 167.4 | 169.9 | 172.1 | 176.5 | 174.7 | 173.7 | 170.7 | 171.7 | 171.4 | 171.9 | 171.1 |
| 2019 | 169.1 | 169.4 | 170.4 | 173.0 | 174.5 | 178.4 | 177.5 | 176.7 | 173.2 | 175.0 | 173.9 | 173.8 | 173.7 |
| **Government** | | | | | | | | | | | | | |
| 2011 | 613.5 | 625.3 | 627.4 | 629.7 | 625.3 | 624.4 | 584.8 | 570.1 | 599.3 | 623.6 | 628.8 | 626.1 | 614.9 |
| 2012 | 609.0 | 622.4 | 626.8 | 622.7 | 619.4 | 623.4 | 580.1 | 568.9 | 597.6 | 621.9 | 623.0 | 622.9 | 611.5 |
| 2013 | 612.2 | 626.5 | 626.9 | 616.1 | 612.9 | 617.0 | 577.0 | 569.8 | 596.2 | 621.8 | 625.4 | 623.1 | 610.4 |
| 2014 | 607.6 | 620.2 | 621.2 | 629.0 | 622.8 | 622.3 | 581.2 | 570.8 | 598.1 | 618.4 | 624.1 | 621.9 | 611.5 |
| | | | | | | | | | | | | | |
| 2015 | 602.1 | 615.5 | 617.1 | 619.8 | 615.8 | 615.5 | 574.4 | 567.5 | 591.7 | 612.7 | 619.0 | 615.6 | 605.6 |
| 2016 | 599.4 | 612.8 | 617.9 | 616.4 | 615.1 | 613.4 | 574.0 | 564.9 | 593.9 | 612.2 | 617.0 | 613.8 | 604.2 |
| 2017 | 600.5 | 614.0 | 616.2 | 614.6 | 613.4 | 617.9 | 577.4 | 569.0 | 592.6 | 612.1 | 615.7 | 615.2 | 604.9 |
| 2018 | 597.4 | 611.3 | 611.1 | 612.9 | 611.0 | 615.8 | 576.1 | 568.4 | 593.2 | 611.6 | 617.9 | 614.7 | 603.5 |
| 2019 | 598.6 | 612.9 | 613.2 | 615.4 | 610.2 | 616.8 | 582.7 | 570.9 | 596.5 | 615.3 | 618.9 | 619.8 | 605.9 |

## 2. Average Weekly Hours by Selected Industry: New Jersey, 2015–2019

(Not seasonally adjusted)

| Industry and year | January | February | March | April | May | June | July | August | September | October | November | December | Annual average |
|---|---|---|---|---|---|---|---|---|---|---|---|---|---|
| **Total Private** | | | | | | | | | | | | | |
| 2015 | 33.3 | 33.6 | 33.8 | 33.7 | 33.8 | 33.6 | 33.8 | 34.1 | 33.8 | 33.9 | 34.0 | 33.8 | 33.8 |
| 2016 | 33.6 | 33.6 | 33.6 | 33.8 | 34.0 | 33.8 | 34.1 | 34.0 | 34.2 | 34.5 | 34.0 | 34.2 | 34.0 |
| 2017 | 33.9 | 33.3 | 33.3 | 34.3 | 33.9 | 33.9 | 34.2 | 33.9 | 34.0 | 34.3 | 34.1 | 34.1 | 33.9 |
| 2018 | 33.7 | 33.8 | 33.7 | 34.3 | 34.1 | 34.0 | 34.4 | 34.2 | 34.7 | 34.2 | 34.1 | 34.9 | 34.2 |
| 2019 | 34.0 | 33.9 | 34.2 | 34.2 | 34.3 | 34.4 | 34.2 | 34.3 | 34.4 | 33.9 | 33.8 | 34.2 | 34.2 |
| **Goods-Producing** | | | | | | | | | | | | | |
| 2015 | 38.4 | 38.0 | 38.9 | 38.8 | 38.8 | 39.1 | 38.8 | 38.8 | 38.2 | 39.3 | 38.8 | 39.3 | 38.8 |
| 2016 | 38.6 | 38.3 | 38.9 | 39.1 | 39.0 | 39.5 | 39.8 | 39.1 | 39.1 | 39.5 | 38.9 | 39.2 | 39.1 |
| 2017 | 38.0 | 37.5 | 37.4 | 38.6 | 39.7 | 39.7 | 39.4 | 39.7 | 39.7 | 39.6 | 39.6 | 39.6 | 39.1 |
| 2018 | 39.0 | 38.6 | 38.7 | 39.4 | 40.1 | 40.1 | 40.0 | 39.9 | 39.7 | 39.5 | 39.4 | 40.7 | 39.6 |
| 2019 | 39.7 | 38.9 | 39.7 | 39.8 | 39.8 | 39.9 | 39.7 | 40.0 | 40.0 | 40.0 | 39.7 | 39.5 | 39.7 |
| **Construction** | | | | | | | | | | | | | |
| 2015 | 37.2 | 36.9 | 38.0 | 38.1 | 38.8 | 38.6 | 38.1 | 37.9 | 37.3 | 39.3 | 37.4 | 38.3 | 38.0 |
| 2016 | 37.4 | 37.4 | 38.3 | 38.7 | 38.8 | 39.3 | 39.5 | 39.2 | 38.5 | 39.3 | 38.2 | 38.5 | 38.6 |
| 2017 | 37.9 | 37.5 | 37.0 | 38.1 | 39.0 | 39.4 | 39.3 | 39.2 | 38.7 | 38.4 | 38.1 | 38.5 | 38.4 |
| 2018 | 37.9 | 37.2 | 37.3 | 37.6 | 39.4 | 39.2 | 39.7 | 38.8 | 38.1 | 38.7 | 37.4 | 38.4 | 38.3 |
| 2019 | 38.2 | 36.8 | 38.3 | 38.3 | 38.5 | 37.8 | 37.7 | 38.7 | 38.8 | 38.6 | 37.6 | 37.2 | 38.0 |
| **Manufacturing** | | | | | | | | | | | | | |
| 2015 | 38.9 | 38.5 | 39.1 | 39.0 | 38.7 | 39.2 | 39.0 | 39.1 | 38.6 | 38.9 | 39.4 | 39.7 | 39.0 |
| 2016 | 39.1 | 38.8 | 38.8 | 38.9 | 38.4 | 39.0 | 39.0 | 38.9 | 39.4 | 39.4 | 39.3 | 39.6 | 39.0 |
| 2017 | 37.9 | 37.4 | 37.6 | 38.8 | 40.1 | 40.0 | 39.4 | 40.0 | 40.3 | 40.5 | 40.8 | 40.5 | 39.4 |
| 2018 | 40.0 | 39.8 | 39.9 | 40.3 | 40.3 | 40.5 | 39.9 | 40.3 | 40.4 | 39.8 | 40.4 | 41.9 | 40.3 |
| 2019 | 40.5 | 40.0 | 40.5 | 40.5 | 40.5 | 41.1 | 40.8 | 40.6 | 40.5 | 40.7 | 41.0 | 41.0 | 40.6 |
| **Trade, Transportation, and Utilities** | | | | | | | | | | | | | |
| 2015 | 33.4 | 33.6 | 33.8 | 34.0 | 34.2 | 34.0 | 34.3 | 34.5 | 34.7 | 34.0 | 34.3 | 34.2 | 34.1 |
| 2016 | 33.4 | 33.6 | 33.7 | 33.9 | 34.4 | 34.3 | 34.6 | 34.4 | 34.6 | 34.4 | 34.2 | 34.8 | 34.2 |
| 2017 | 34.1 | 33.7 | 33.7 | 34.7 | 34.6 | 34.7 | 34.9 | 34.6 | 35.1 | 34.8 | 35.0 | 35.0 | 34.6 |
| 2018 | 34.2 | 34.0 | 34.2 | 34.7 | 34.6 | 34.6 | 35.0 | 34.8 | 35.2 | 34.6 | 34.8 | 35.1 | 34.7 |
| 2019 | 34.0 | 34.0 | 34.3 | 34.5 | 34.5 | 34.7 | 34.7 | 34.9 | 35.1 | 34.5 | 34.3 | 35.1 | 34.6 |
| **Financial Activities** | | | | | | | | | | | | | |
| 2015 | 36.5 | 37.0 | 37.3 | 36.7 | 36.5 | 36.5 | 36.9 | 37.1 | 36.5 | 36.8 | 37.3 | 36.8 | 36.8 |
| 2016 | 37.0 | 37.1 | 37.1 | 36.8 | 37.7 | 37.0 | 36.8 | 36.9 | 36.8 | 37.5 | 36.6 | 36.5 | 37.0 |
| 2017 | 37.6 | 36.2 | 36.3 | 37.2 | 36.5 | 36.4 | 36.9 | 36.1 | 36.3 | 37.8 | 36.8 | 36.9 | 36.7 |
| 2018 | 36.8 | 37.0 | 36.9 | 37.7 | 36.9 | 37.0 | 37.1 | 36.1 | 37.6 | 36.5 | 36.5 | 37.4 | 37.0 |
| 2019 | 36.8 | 37.2 | 37.5 | 37.5 | 37.5 | 38.5 | 37.4 | 37.5 | 38.5 | 37.2 | 37.3 | 38.3 | 37.6 |
| **Professional and Business Services** | | | | | | | | | | | | | |
| 2015 | 35.3 | 36.0 | 35.8 | 35.5 | 35.6 | 35.5 | 35.5 | 35.9 | 35.2 | 35.8 | 35.8 | 35.7 | 35.6 |
| 2016 | 35.5 | 35.4 | 35.4 | 35.9 | 35.9 | 35.6 | 35.4 | 35.2 | 35.5 | 36.0 | 35.5 | 35.4 | 35.6 |
| 2017 | 35.7 | 34.7 | 34.8 | 35.7 | 35.3 | 35.5 | 35.7 | 35.2 | 35.2 | 35.9 | 35.5 | 35.3 | 35.4 |
| 2018 | 35.0 | 35.2 | 35.1 | 36.0 | 35.5 | 35.6 | 36.0 | 35.6 | 36.2 | 35.7 | 34.9 | 36.1 | 35.6 |
| 2019 | 35.2 | 35.2 | 35.4 | 35.6 | 35.9 | 36.0 | 35.3 | 35.4 | 35.9 | 35.0 | 34.6 | 35.2 | 35.4 |
| **Education and Health Services** | | | | | | | | | | | | | |
| 2015 | 30.8 | 31.0 | 31.2 | 31.1 | 31.3 | 31.3 | 31.5 | 31.7 | 31.5 | 31.6 | 31.8 | 31.6 | 31.4 |
| 2016 | 32.0 | 31.9 | 31.8 | 31.9 | 32.1 | 32.1 | 32.0 | 31.8 | 32.0 | 32.2 | 32.0 | 31.9 | 32.0 |
| 2017 | 32.2 | 31.9 | 31.7 | 32.1 | 31.9 | 32.2 | 32.3 | 32.0 | 32.1 | 32.3 | 32.2 | 32.4 | 32.1 |
| 2018 | 32.2 | 32.2 | 31.9 | 32.3 | 32.1 | 32.2 | 32.2 | 32.3 | 32.6 | 32.5 | 32.6 | 32.9 | 32.3 |
| 2019 | 32.8 | 32.8 | 32.7 | 32.6 | 32.6 | 32.6 | 32.2 | 32.1 | 32.7 | 32.3 | 32.5 | 32.6 | 32.5 |
| **Leisure and Hospitality** | | | | | | | | | | | | | |
| 2015 | 26.0 | 26.1 | 26.2 | 26.9 | 26.7 | 26.6 | 27.4 | 27.7 | 27.1 | 26.8 | 26.8 | 26.5 | 26.8 |
| 2016 | 26.1 | 26.8 | 26.6 | 26.8 | 26.8 | 26.6 | 27.6 | 27.6 | 28.1 | 27.9 | 27.6 | 27.0 | 27.1 |
| 2017 | 26.8 | 26.5 | 26.6 | 27.5 | 27.0 | 26.4 | 27.2 | 26.9 | 26.4 | 26.4 | 26.1 | 25.8 | 26.6 |
| 2018 | 25.2 | 26.1 | 25.4 | 26.0 | 26.0 | 25.9 | 27.2 | 27.1 | 26.9 | 26.9 | 26.1 | 26.5 | 26.3 |
| 2019 | 25.5 | 25.6 | 25.6 | 25.8 | 26.0 | 26.1 | 27.0 | 27.1 | 26.3 | 25.9 | 25.9 | 25.8 | 26.1 |
| **Other Services** | | | | | | | | | | | | | |
| 2015 | 29.1 | 29.1 | 29.2 | 28.8 | 29.2 | 29.3 | 30.0 | 30.9 | 29.8 | 30.1 | 30.3 | 30.1 | 29.7 |
| 2016 | 29.7 | 29.5 | 28.9 | 29.8 | 30.1 | 30.2 | 31.1 | 30.6 | 30.6 | 30.5 | 30.4 | 30.7 | 30.2 |
| 2017 | 31.0 | 30.3 | 29.7 | 30.3 | 29.5 | 29.2 | 30.4 | 29.5 | 29.3 | 29.8 | 30.1 | 30.3 | 29.9 |
| 2018 | 30.5 | 30.1 | 29.9 | 30.7 | 29.8 | 30.0 | 32.0 | 31.3 | 30.4 | 29.8 | 30.1 | 30.7 | 30.4 |
| 2019 | 29.8 | 29.2 | 29.8 | 29.6 | 28.8 | 28.9 | 29.5 | 29.5 | 28.2 | 28.0 | 28.0 | 27.8 | 28.9 |

## 3. Average Hourly Earnings by Selected Industry: New Jersey, 2015–2019

(Dollars, not seasonally adjusted)

| Industry and year | January | February | March | April | May | June | July | August | September | October | November | December | Annual average |
|---|---|---|---|---|---|---|---|---|---|---|---|---|---|
| **Total Private** | | | | | | | | | | | | | |
| 2015 | 27.67 | 28.12 | 28.11 | 27.55 | 27.61 | 27.60 | 27.46 | 27.72 | 27.79 | 27.81 | 28.11 | 27.79 | 27.78 |
| 2016 | 27.92 | 28.07 | 28.05 | 28.11 | 28.15 | 27.76 | 27.75 | 27.86 | 28.15 | 28.66 | 28.32 | 28.47 | 28.11 |
| 2017 | 29.55 | 29.20 | 29.22 | 29.51 | 29.08 | 28.86 | 29.06 | 28.86 | 29.14 | 29.62 | 29.24 | 29.38 | 29.22 |
| 2018 | 29.71 | 29.74 | 29.85 | 30.11 | 29.64 | 29.35 | 29.74 | 29.46 | 30.10 | 30.00 | 30.20 | 30.27 | 29.85 |
| 2019 | 30.47 | 30.53 | 30.58 | 30.40 | 30.05 | 30.15 | 29.87 | 30.09 | 30.77 | 30.42 | 30.35 | 30.67 | 30.36 |
| **Goods-Producing** | | | | | | | | | | | | | |
| 2015 | 29.50 | 29.88 | 29.94 | 29.92 | 30.14 | 29.91 | 30.03 | 29.90 | 29.94 | 30.02 | 30.22 | 30.10 | 29.96 |
| 2016 | 30.38 | 30.27 | 30.29 | 30.57 | 30.80 | 30.53 | 30.24 | 30.55 | 30.57 | 30.94 | 30.65 | 31.15 | 30.58 |
| 2017 | 31.45 | 31.15 | 31.37 | 31.45 | 30.88 | 31.06 | 31.24 | 30.83 | 30.89 | 30.96 | 30.76 | 31.72 | 31.14 |
| 2018 | 31.43 | 31.23 | 31.38 | 32.42 | 31.80 | 32.11 | 32.34 | 32.19 | 32.44 | 32.60 | 32.86 | 32.67 | 32.14 |
| 2019 | 32.42 | 32.55 | 32.90 | 33.08 | 33.37 | 33.21 | 32.98 | 33.24 | 33.45 | 33.56 | 33.82 | 33.80 | 33.20 |
| **Construction** | | | | | | | | | | | | | |
| 2015 | 35.22 | 36.26 | 36.05 | 35.86 | 36.07 | 36.15 | 35.92 | 35.21 | 35.09 | 35.04 | 35.06 | 34.44 | 35.52 |
| 2016 | 34.61 | 34.96 | 35.03 | 34.64 | 34.92 | 34.24 | 34.53 | 34.46 | 35.05 | 35.49 | 35.09 | 35.46 | 34.87 |
| 2017 | 35.42 | 35.74 | 36.15 | 35.94 | 35.08 | 35.54 | 35.43 | 35.02 | 35.19 | 35.21 | 34.75 | 35.90 | 35.43 |
| 2018 | 35.57 | 35.65 | 35.76 | 35.88 | 35.63 | 35.53 | 35.81 | 35.52 | 36.03 | 36.04 | 37.20 | 36.77 | 35.95 |
| 2019 | 36.91 | 37.27 | 37.76 | 37.60 | 37.57 | 37.57 | 36.79 | 37.23 | 37.54 | 37.28 | 38.28 | 37.64 | 37.45 |
| **Manufacturing** | | | | | | | | | | | | | |
| 2015 | 26.74 | 27.12 | 27.19 | 27.01 | 27.18 | 26.86 | 27.10 | 27.18 | 27.28 | 27.39 | 27.77 | 27.87 | 27.23 |
| 2016 | 27.69 | 27.37 | 27.23 | 28.13 | 28.67 | 28.60 | 28.22 | 28.24 | 27.93 | 28.42 | 28.15 | 28.58 | 28.11 |
| 2017 | 29.12 | 28.48 | 28.52 | 28.69 | 28.23 | 28.08 | 28.55 | 28.27 | 28.22 | 28.20 | 28.22 | 28.94 | 28.45 |
| 2018 | 28.55 | 28.13 | 27.71 | 28.21 | 27.62 | 27.98 | 28.38 | 28.54 | 28.91 | 29.23 | 29.14 | 29.26 | 28.48 |
| 2019 | 28.78 | 28.94 | 29.19 | 29.62 | 30.05 | 29.88 | 29.80 | 29.87 | 30.02 | 30.52 | 30.37 | 30.90 | 29.83 |
| **Trade, Transportation, and Utilities** | | | | | | | | | | | | | |
| 2015 | 24.25 | 24.62 | 24.50 | 23.99 | 24.24 | 24.38 | 24.52 | 24.89 | 25.01 | 24.92 | 24.84 | 23.67 | 24.49 |
| 2016 | 23.91 | 24.09 | 24.18 | 24.18 | 24.26 | 24.34 | 24.61 | 24.67 | 25.00 | 25.33 | 25.17 | 25.06 | 24.58 |
| 2017 | 26.16 | 26.08 | 26.21 | 25.95 | 26.18 | 25.84 | 26.41 | 26.06 | 26.29 | 26.44 | 26.18 | 26.10 | 26.16 |
| 2018 | 26.64 | 26.97 | 26.76 | 26.83 | 26.68 | 26.35 | 26.90 | 26.89 | 27.07 | 26.94 | 26.84 | 26.66 | 26.79 |
| 2019 | 27.30 | 27.36 | 27.47 | 27.32 | 27.12 | 27.20 | 27.22 | 27.13 | 27.56 | 27.28 | 27.25 | 27.24 | 27.29 |
| **Financial Activities** | | | | | | | | | | | | | |
| 2015 | 35.22 | 35.95 | 36.25 | 35.45 | 35.81 | 35.75 | 35.33 | 36.06 | 35.92 | 35.64 | 36.43 | 35.82 | 35.80 |
| 2016 | 36.49 | 36.16 | 36.47 | 36.77 | 37.38 | 35.97 | 37.03 | 37.38 | 37.78 | 38.67 | 38.41 | 37.77 | 37.20 |
| 2017 | 39.09 | 38.65 | 38.40 | 39.34 | 38.38 | 38.70 | 39.33 | 39.24 | 38.83 | 39.82 | 39.39 | 39.49 | 39.06 |
| 2018 | 40.84 | 40.62 | 40.49 | 41.54 | 41.39 | 39.85 | 41.28 | 40.73 | 41.15 | 40.63 | 41.84 | 41.77 | 41.01 |
| 2019 | 41.18 | 41.29 | 39.55 | 41.01 | 40.06 | 40.97 | 40.82 | 41.21 | 42.13 | 42.50 | 42.93 | 43.52 | 41.43 |
| **Professional and Business Services** | | | | | | | | | | | | | |
| 2015 | 33.50 | 34.22 | 34.17 | 32.99 | 32.90 | 32.92 | 32.91 | 33.40 | 33.44 | 33.03 | 33.62 | 33.02 | 33.34 |
| 2016 | 33.97 | 34.01 | 34.07 | 34.07 | 34.04 | 33.23 | 33.36 | 33.38 | 33.19 | 34.05 | 33.40 | 33.63 | 33.70 |
| 2017 | 35.33 | 34.99 | 34.97 | 35.93 | 34.97 | 34.46 | 35.34 | 34.83 | 34.95 | 35.84 | 34.92 | 35.36 | 35.16 |
| 2018 | 35.42 | 35.34 | 35.38 | 35.73 | 34.64 | 34.34 | 34.90 | 34.08 | 35.20 | 34.74 | 35.18 | 35.71 | 35.05 |
| 2019 | 36.13 | 35.98 | 35.49 | 34.88 | 34.82 | 35.32 | 35.20 | 35.42 | 36.33 | 35.05 | 35.18 | 36.11 | 35.49 |
| **Education and Health Services** | | | | | | | | | | | | | |
| 2015 | 27.44 | 27.28 | 27.30 | 27.27 | 27.57 | 27.80 | 27.78 | 27.76 | 27.84 | 28.03 | 28.23 | 28.37 | 27.73 |
| 2016 | 27.88 | 28.09 | 27.82 | 27.77 | 27.51 | 27.23 | 27.18 | 27.08 | 27.42 | 27.49 | 27.24 | 27.51 | 27.52 |
| 2017 | 27.40 | 27.39 | 27.21 | 27.24 | 27.13 | 26.94 | 27.06 | 26.97 | 27.05 | 27.13 | 27.04 | 27.16 | 27.14 |
| 2018 | 27.00 | 27.18 | 27.49 | 27.60 | 27.50 | 27.63 | 27.80 | 27.55 | 28.20 | 28.41 | 28.58 | 28.65 | 27.81 |
| 2019 | 27.83 | 27.82 | 28.11 | 27.95 | 27.86 | 28.13 | 28.27 | 28.69 | 28.59 | 28.39 | 28.26 | 28.22 | 28.17 |
| **Leisure and Hospitality** | | | | | | | | | | | | | |
| 2015 | 15.01 | 15.10 | 14.93 | 14.91 | 15.05 | 14.89 | 14.71 | 14.65 | 14.86 | 14.89 | 14.90 | 14.98 | 14.90 |
| 2016 | 14.96 | 14.87 | 14.87 | 14.88 | 14.95 | 14.89 | 14.77 | 14.74 | 15.17 | 15.48 | 15.37 | 15.52 | 15.04 |
| 2017 | 15.71 | 15.64 | 15.62 | 15.96 | 15.89 | 16.78 | 16.44 | 16.47 | 16.78 | 16.76 | 16.71 | 16.93 | 16.32 |
| 2018 | 16.58 | 16.33 | 16.71 | 16.73 | 16.88 | 16.55 | 16.28 | 16.33 | 16.84 | 16.73 | 17.07 | 16.95 | 16.66 |
| 2019 | 17.00 | 17.05 | 17.09 | 17.07 | 16.70 | 16.26 | 16.27 | 16.51 | 16.87 | 16.92 | 16.86 | 17.20 | 16.79 |
| **Other Services** | | | | | | | | | | | | | |
| 2015 | 22.61 | 22.34 | 22.47 | 22.48 | 21.72 | 21.71 | 21.12 | 20.99 | 21.77 | 22.02 | 22.61 | 22.56 | 22.02 |
| 2016 | 22.34 | 23.65 | 23.54 | 23.74 | 23.63 | 23.23 | 22.55 | 22.38 | 23.48 | 24.17 | 23.74 | 24.08 | 23.37 |
| 2017 | 25.91 | 26.00 | 25.74 | 25.85 | 25.72 | 25.55 | 23.94 | 23.75 | 25.45 | 25.16 | 25.19 | 25.55 | 25.31 |
| 2018 | 25.25 | 25.60 | 25.38 | 25.32 | 25.06 | 25.26 | 24.24 | 24.03 | 24.50 | 23.98 | 23.92 | 24.37 | 24.73 |
| 2019 | 24.80 | 24.57 | 25.00 | 24.41 | 24.82 | 24.90 | 23.46 | 24.24 | 25.93 | 25.75 | 25.91 | 26.14 | 24.98 |

## 4. Average Weekly Earnings by Selected Industry: New Jersey, 2015–2019

(Dollars, not seasonally adjusted)

| Industry and year | January | February | March | April | May | June | July | August | September | October | November | December | Annual average |
|---|---|---|---|---|---|---|---|---|---|---|---|---|---|
| **Total Private** | | | | | | | | | | | | | |
| 2015 | 921.41 | 944.83 | 950.12 | 928.44 | 933.22 | 927.36 | 928.15 | 945.25 | 938.96 | 942.76 | 955.74 | 939.30 | 938.96 |
| 2016 | 938.11 | 943.15 | 942.48 | 950.12 | 957.10 | 938.29 | 946.28 | 947.24 | 962.73 | 988.77 | 962.88 | 973.67 | 955.74 |
| 2017 | 1,001.75 | 972.36 | 973.03 | 1,012.19 | 985.81 | 978.35 | 993.85 | 978.35 | 990.76 | 1,015.97 | 997.08 | 1,001.86 | 990.56 |
| 2018 | 1,001.23 | 1,005.21 | 1,005.95 | 1,032.77 | 1,010.72 | 997.90 | 1,023.06 | 1,007.53 | 1,044.47 | 1,026.00 | 1,029.82 | 1,056.42 | 1,020.87 |
| 2019 | 1,035.98 | 1,034.97 | 1,045.84 | 1,039.68 | 1,030.72 | 1,037.16 | 1,021.55 | 1,032.09 | 1,058.49 | 1,031.24 | 1,025.83 | 1,048.91 | 1,038.31 |
| **Goods-Producing** | | | | | | | | | | | | | |
| 2015 | 1,132.80 | 1,135.44 | 1,164.67 | 1,160.90 | 1,169.43 | 1,169.48 | 1,165.16 | 1,160.12 | 1,143.71 | 1,179.79 | 1,172.54 | 1,182.93 | 1,162.45 |
| 2016 | 1,172.67 | 1,159.34 | 1,178.28 | 1,195.29 | 1,201.20 | 1,205.94 | 1,203.55 | 1,194.51 | 1,195.29 | 1,222.13 | 1,192.29 | 1,221.08 | 1,195.68 |
| 2017 | 1,195.10 | 1,168.13 | 1,173.24 | 1,213.97 | 1,225.94 | 1,233.08 | 1,230.86 | 1,223.95 | 1,226.33 | 1,226.02 | 1,218.10 | 1,256.11 | 1,217.57 |
| 2018 | 1,225.77 | 1,205.48 | 1,214.41 | 1,277.35 | 1,275.18 | 1,287.61 | 1,293.60 | 1,284.38 | 1,287.87 | 1,287.70 | 1,294.68 | 1,329.67 | 1,272.74 |
| 2019 | 1,287.07 | 1,266.20 | 1,306.13 | 1,316.58 | 1,328.13 | 1,325.08 | 1,309.31 | 1,329.60 | 1,338.00 | 1,342.40 | 1,342.65 | 1,335.10 | 1,318.04 |
| **Construction** | | | | | | | | | | | | | |
| 2015 | 1,310.18 | 1,337.99 | 1,369.90 | 1,366.27 | 1,399.52 | 1,395.39 | 1,368.55 | 1,334.46 | 1,308.86 | 1,377.07 | 1,311.24 | 1,319.05 | 1,349.76 |
| 2016 | 1,294.41 | 1,307.50 | 1,341.65 | 1,340.57 | 1,354.90 | 1,345.63 | 1,363.94 | 1,350.83 | 1,349.43 | 1,394.76 | 1,340.44 | 1,365.21 | 1,345.98 |
| 2017 | 1,342.42 | 1,340.63 | 1,337.55 | 1,369.31 | 1,368.12 | 1,400.28 | 1,392.40 | 1,372.78 | 1,361.85 | 1,352.06 | 1,323.98 | 1,382.15 | 1,360.51 |
| 2018 | 1,348.10 | 1,326.18 | 1,333.85 | 1,349.09 | 1,403.82 | 1,392.78 | 1,421.66 | 1,378.18 | 1,372.74 | 1,394.75 | 1,391.28 | 1,411.97 | 1,376.89 |
| 2019 | 1,409.96 | 1,371.54 | 1,446.21 | 1,440.08 | 1,446.45 | 1,420.15 | 1,386.98 | 1,440.80 | 1,456.55 | 1,439.01 | 1,439.33 | 1,400.21 | 1,423.10 |
| **Manufacturing** | | | | | | | | | | | | | |
| 2015 | 1,040.19 | 1,044.12 | 1,063.13 | 1,053.39 | 1,051.87 | 1,052.91 | 1,056.90 | 1,062.74 | 1,053.01 | 1,065.47 | 1,094.14 | 1,106.44 | 1,061.97 |
| 2016 | 1,082.68 | 1,061.96 | 1,056.52 | 1,094.26 | 1,100.93 | 1,115.40 | 1,100.58 | 1,098.54 | 1,100.44 | 1,119.75 | 1,106.30 | 1,131.77 | 1,096.29 |
| 2017 | 1,103.65 | 1,065.15 | 1,072.35 | 1,113.17 | 1,132.02 | 1,123.20 | 1,124.87 | 1,130.80 | 1,137.27 | 1,142.10 | 1,151.38 | 1,172.07 | 1,120.93 |
| 2018 | 1,142.00 | 1,119.57 | 1,105.63 | 1,136.86 | 1,113.09 | 1,133.19 | 1,132.36 | 1,150.16 | 1,167.96 | 1,163.35 | 1,177.26 | 1,225.99 | 1,147.74 |
| 2019 | 1,165.59 | 1,157.60 | 1,182.20 | 1,199.61 | 1,217.03 | 1,228.07 | 1,215.84 | 1,212.72 | 1,215.81 | 1,242.16 | 1,245.17 | 1,266.90 | 1,211.10 |
| **Trade, Transportation, and Utilities** | | | | | | | | | | | | | |
| 2015 | 809.95 | 827.23 | 828.10 | 815.66 | 829.01 | 828.92 | 841.04 | 858.71 | 867.85 | 847.28 | 852.01 | 809.51 | 835.11 |
| 2016 | 798.59 | 809.42 | 814.87 | 819.70 | 834.54 | 834.86 | 851.51 | 848.65 | 865.00 | 871.35 | 860.81 | 872.09 | 840.64 |
| 2017 | 892.06 | 878.90 | 883.28 | 900.47 | 905.83 | 896.65 | 921.71 | 901.68 | 922.78 | 920.11 | 916.30 | 913.50 | 905.14 |
| 2018 | 911.09 | 916.98 | 915.19 | 931.00 | 923.13 | 911.71 | 941.50 | 935.77 | 952.86 | 932.12 | 934.03 | 935.77 | 929.61 |
| 2019 | 928.20 | 930.24 | 942.22 | 942.54 | 935.64 | 943.84 | 944.53 | 946.84 | 967.36 | 941.16 | 934.68 | 956.12 | 944.23 |
| **Financial Activities** | | | | | | | | | | | | | |
| 2015 | 1,285.53 | 1,330.15 | 1,352.13 | 1,301.02 | 1,307.07 | 1,304.88 | 1,303.68 | 1,337.83 | 1,311.08 | 1,311.18 | 1,358.84 | 1,318.18 | 1,317.44 |
| 2016 | 1,350.13 | 1,341.54 | 1,353.04 | 1,353.14 | 1,409.23 | 1,330.89 | 1,362.70 | 1,379.32 | 1,390.30 | 1,450.13 | 1,405.81 | 1,378.61 | 1,376.40 |
| 2017 | 1,469.78 | 1,399.13 | 1,393.92 | 1,463.45 | 1,400.87 | 1,408.68 | 1,451.28 | 1,416.56 | 1,409.53 | 1,505.20 | 1,449.55 | 1,457.18 | 1,433.50 |
| 2018 | 1,502.91 | 1,502.94 | 1,494.08 | 1,566.06 | 1,527.29 | 1,474.45 | 1,531.49 | 1,470.35 | 1,547.24 | 1,483.00 | 1,527.16 | 1,562.20 | 1,517.37 |
| 2019 | 1,515.42 | 1,535.99 | 1,483.13 | 1,537.88 | 1,502.25 | 1,577.35 | 1,526.67 | 1,545.38 | 1,622.01 | 1,581.00 | 1,601.29 | 1,666.82 | 1,557.77 |
| **Professional and Business Services** | | | | | | | | | | | | | |
| 2015 | 1,182.55 | 1,231.92 | 1,223.29 | 1,171.15 | 1,171.24 | 1,168.66 | 1,168.31 | 1,199.06 | 1,177.09 | 1,182.47 | 1,203.60 | 1,178.81 | 1,186.90 |
| 2016 | 1,205.94 | 1,203.95 | 1,206.08 | 1,223.11 | 1,222.04 | 1,182.99 | 1,180.94 | 1,174.98 | 1,178.25 | 1,225.80 | 1,185.70 | 1,190.50 | 1,199.72 |
| 2017 | 1,261.28 | 1,214.15 | 1,216.96 | 1,282.70 | 1,234.44 | 1,223.33 | 1,261.64 | 1,226.02 | 1,230.24 | 1,286.66 | 1,239.66 | 1,248.21 | 1,244.66 |
| 2018 | 1,239.70 | 1,243.97 | 1,241.84 | 1,286.64 | 1,230.08 | 1,222.86 | 1,256.76 | 1,213.25 | 1,274.24 | 1,240.22 | 1,227.78 | 1,289.13 | 1,247.78 |
| 2019 | 1,271.78 | 1,266.50 | 1,256.35 | 1,241.73 | 1,250.04 | 1,271.52 | 1,242.56 | 1,253.87 | 1,304.25 | 1,226.75 | 1,217.23 | 1,271.07 | 1,256.35 |
| **Education and Health Services** | | | | | | | | | | | | | |
| 2015 | 845.15 | 845.68 | 851.76 | 848.10 | 862.94 | 870.14 | 875.07 | 879.99 | 876.96 | 885.75 | 897.71 | 896.49 | 870.72 |
| 2016 | 892.16 | 896.07 | 884.68 | 885.86 | 883.07 | 874.08 | 869.76 | 861.14 | 877.44 | 885.18 | 871.68 | 877.57 | 880.64 |
| 2017 | 882.28 | 873.74 | 862.56 | 874.40 | 865.45 | 867.47 | 874.04 | 863.04 | 868.31 | 876.30 | 870.69 | 879.98 | 871.19 |
| 2018 | 869.40 | 875.20 | 876.93 | 891.48 | 882.75 | 889.69 | 895.16 | 889.87 | 919.32 | 923.33 | 931.71 | 942.59 | 898.26 |
| 2019 | 912.82 | 912.50 | 919.20 | 911.17 | 908.24 | 917.04 | 910.29 | 920.95 | 934.89 | 917.00 | 918.45 | 919.97 | 915.53 |
| **Leisure and Hospitality** | | | | | | | | | | | | | |
| 2015 | 390.26 | 394.11 | 391.17 | 401.08 | 401.84 | 396.07 | 403.05 | 405.81 | 402.71 | 399.05 | 399.32 | 396.97 | 399.32 |
| 2016 | 390.46 | 398.52 | 395.54 | 398.78 | 400.66 | 396.07 | 407.65 | 406.82 | 426.28 | 431.89 | 424.21 | 419.04 | 407.58 |
| 2017 | 421.03 | 414.46 | 415.49 | 438.90 | 429.03 | 442.99 | 447.17 | 443.04 | 442.99 | 442.46 | 436.13 | 436.79 | 434.11 |
| 2018 | 417.82 | 426.21 | 424.43 | 434.98 | 438.88 | 428.65 | 442.82 | 442.54 | 453.00 | 450.04 | 445.53 | 449.18 | 438.16 |
| 2019 | 433.50 | 436.48 | 437.50 | 440.41 | 434.20 | 424.39 | 439.29 | 447.42 | 443.68 | 438.23 | 436.67 | 443.76 | 438.22 |
| **Other Services** | | | | | | | | | | | | | |
| 2015 | 657.95 | 650.09 | 656.12 | 647.42 | 634.22 | 636.10 | 633.60 | 648.59 | 648.75 | 662.80 | 685.08 | 679.06 | 653.99 |
| 2016 | 663.50 | 697.68 | 680.31 | 707.45 | 711.26 | 701.55 | 701.31 | 684.83 | 718.49 | 737.19 | 721.70 | 739.26 | 705.77 |
| 2017 | 803.21 | 787.80 | 764.48 | 783.26 | 758.74 | 746.06 | 727.78 | 700.63 | 745.69 | 749.77 | 758.22 | 774.17 | 756.77 |
| 2018 | 770.13 | 770.56 | 758.86 | 777.32 | 746.79 | 757.80 | 775.68 | 752.14 | 744.80 | 714.60 | 719.99 | 748.16 | 751.79 |
| 2019 | 739.04 | 717.44 | 745.00 | 722.54 | 714.82 | 719.61 | 692.07 | 715.08 | 731.23 | 721.00 | 725.48 | 726.69 | 721.92 |

# NEW MEXICO
## *At a Glance*

Population:
    2010 census: 2,059,179
    2019 estimate: 2,096,829

Percent change in population:
    2010–2019: 1.8%

Percent change in total nonfarm employment:
    2011–2019: 6.8%

Industry with the largest growth in employment, 2011–2019 (percent):
    Mining and logging, 21.4%

Industry with the largest decline or smallest growth in employment, 2011–2019 (percent):
    Information, -17.0%

Civilian labor force:
    2010: 936,088
    2019: 954,596

Unemployment rate and rank among states (highest to lowest):
    2010: 8.1%, 32nd
    2019: 4.9%, 4th

Over-the-year change in unemployment rates:
    2017–2018: -1.0%
    2018–2019: 0.0%

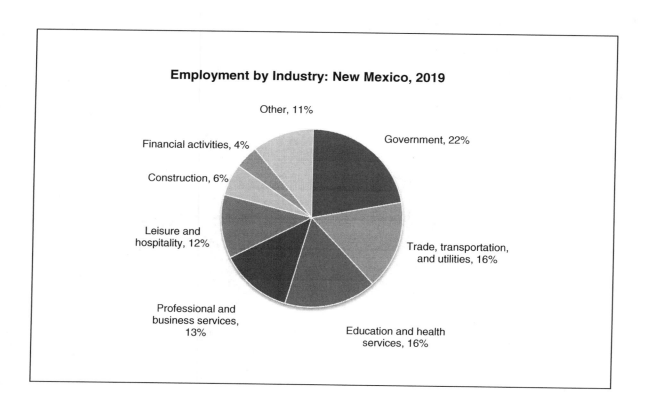

**Employment by Industry: New Mexico, 2019**

- Other, 11%
- Government, 22%
- Financial activities, 4%
- Construction, 6%
- Leisure and hospitality, 12%
- Trade, transportation, and utilities, 16%
- Professional and business services, 13%
- Education and health services, 16%

# 1. Employment by Industry: New Mexico, 2011–2019

(Numbers in thousands, not seasonally adjusted)

| Industry and year | January | February | March | April | May | June | July | August | September | October | November | December | Annual average |
|---|---|---|---|---|---|---|---|---|---|---|---|---|---|
| **Total Nonfarm** | | | | | | | | | | | | | |
| 2011 | 788.0 | 795.9 | 800.1 | 806.5 | 806.9 | 804.2 | 798.6 | 801.4 | 807.6 | 806.5 | 805.7 | 805.9 | 802.3 |
| 2012 | 786.7 | 796.0 | 801.4 | 804.1 | 806.5 | 804.3 | 796.2 | 802.2 | 807.5 | 819.2 | 818.7 | 816.0 | 804.9 |
| 2013 | 799.6 | 806.0 | 807.8 | 815.6 | 819.2 | 806.7 | 803.1 | 811.6 | 813.7 | 820.0 | 820.3 | 820.0 | 812.0 |
| 2014 | 806.0 | 809.9 | 811.6 | 819.2 | 825.6 | 813.4 | 813.4 | 822.4 | 824.2 | 833.3 | 833.2 | 833.3 | 820.5 |
| 2015 | 817.9 | 822.9 | 824.7 | 829.6 | 830.6 | 822.1 | 818.5 | 826.8 | 827.9 | 834.7 | 835.2 | 831.5 | 826.9 |
| 2016 | 818.4 | 826.4 | 825.5 | 832.4 | 832.9 | 822.7 | 819.7 | 827.7 | 832.2 | 832.4 | 832.9 | 833.6 | 828.1 |
| 2017 | 818.4 | 824.6 | 827.8 | 834.3 | 834.4 | 829.8 | 822.7 | 831.4 | 836.1 | 837.9 | 840.0 | 840.3 | 831.5 |
| 2018 | 828.2 | 835.6 | 837.6 | 844.5 | 845.0 | 842.3 | 835.8 | 846.1 | 849.0 | 852.3 | 855.7 | 853.7 | 843.8 |
| 2019 | 841.5 | 849.8 | 851.8 | 856.8 | 858.4 | 851.5 | 850.1 | 861.3 | 862.6 | 865.2 | 868.0 | 865.2 | 856.9 |
| **Total Private** | | | | | | | | | | | | | |
| 2011 | 595.5 | 597.4 | 600.6 | 607.1 | 608.7 | 611.9 | 613.2 | 614.9 | 613.1 | 610.0 | 609.5 | 608.6 | 607.5 |
| 2012 | 598.5 | 601.1 | 605.4 | 608.7 | 610.6 | 614.9 | 613.1 | 616.1 | 614.0 | 622.8 | 622.1 | 620.0 | 612.3 |
| 2013 | 609.7 | 610.9 | 611.6 | 619.2 | 622.1 | 620.9 | 623.0 | 626.6 | 621.6 | 625.7 | 626.4 | 626.2 | 620.3 |
| 2014 | 616.9 | 616.1 | 617.4 | 624.5 | 629.8 | 628.1 | 632.1 | 636.0 | 631.5 | 638.6 | 638.1 | 638.5 | 629.0 |
| 2015 | 628.8 | 629.0 | 629.7 | 636.6 | 638.8 | 637.5 | 640.9 | 642.7 | 637.4 | 642.7 | 641.9 | 639.6 | 637.1 |
| 2016 | 631.3 | 633.6 | 631.7 | 638.4 | 639.9 | 637.8 | 642.6 | 643.9 | 641.5 | 641.3 | 640.6 | 642.4 | 638.8 |
| 2017 | 633.9 | 634.3 | 636.7 | 642.4 | 644.5 | 647.0 | 647.4 | 649.0 | 646.9 | 648.0 | 649.5 | 649.8 | 644.1 |
| 2018 | 643.2 | 645.7 | 647.1 | 653.8 | 657.2 | 658.9 | 659.5 | 663.2 | 659.4 | 662.2 | 664.8 | 664.6 | 656.6 |
| 2019 | 656.1 | 659.4 | 661.2 | 665.9 | 668.9 | 668.3 | 671.9 | 675.3 | 671.1 | 671.7 | 674.7 | 673.5 | 668.2 |
| **Goods Producing** | | | | | | | | | | | | | |
| 2011 | 89.5 | 89.3 | 91.1 | 92.4 | 93.1 | 94.2 | 95.1 | 96.0 | 95.7 | 95.3 | 94.4 | 93.3 | 93.3 |
| 2012 | 91.4 | 91.8 | 92.7 | 93.3 | 94.2 | 95.7 | 95.6 | 96.5 | 96.1 | 98.9 | 97.2 | 96.1 | 95.0 |
| 2013 | 94.1 | 94.7 | 95.0 | 96.3 | 96.8 | 97.6 | 98.2 | 99.6 | 98.9 | 100.3 | 99.2 | 97.5 | 97.4 |
| 2014 | 96.5 | 95.6 | 95.9 | 96.9 | 98.0 | 98.6 | 100.0 | 100.4 | 99.8 | 102.3 | 100.9 | 100.5 | 98.8 |
| 2015 | 98.9 | 97.6 | 96.7 | 97.2 | 96.8 | 97.0 | 97.7 | 97.5 | 96.5 | 97.3 | 95.5 | 94.3 | 96.9 |
| 2016 | 91.9 | 91.4 | 90.3 | 90.4 | 89.7 | 89.7 | 89.6 | 89.5 | 89.6 | 90.1 | 89.1 | 89.1 | 90.0 |
| 2017 | 88.5 | 89.2 | 90.1 | 91.5 | 92.5 | 93.7 | 94.3 | 94.6 | 94.9 | 95.9 | 95.6 | 95.6 | 93.0 |
| 2018 | 95.3 | 96.8 | 97.3 | 98.3 | 98.8 | 99.8 | 99.7 | 100.2 | 100.0 | 101.2 | 101.3 | 101.1 | 99.2 |
| 2019 | 100.3 | 101.1 | 101.8 | 102.6 | 103.8 | 104.0 | 106.7 | 106.8 | 106.0 | 107.6 | 107.0 | 106.2 | 104.5 |
| **Service-Providing** | | | | | | | | | | | | | |
| 2011 | 698.5 | 706.6 | 709.0 | 714.1 | 713.8 | 710.0 | 703.5 | 705.4 | 711.9 | 711.2 | 711.3 | 712.6 | 709.0 |
| 2012 | 695.3 | 704.2 | 708.7 | 710.8 | 712.3 | 708.6 | 700.6 | 705.7 | 711.4 | 720.3 | 721.5 | 719.9 | 709.9 |
| 2013 | 705.5 | 711.3 | 712.8 | 719.3 | 722.4 | 709.1 | 704.9 | 712.0 | 714.8 | 719.7 | 721.1 | 722.5 | 714.6 |
| 2014 | 709.5 | 714.3 | 715.7 | 722.3 | 727.6 | 714.8 | 713.4 | 722.0 | 724.4 | 731.0 | 732.3 | 732.8 | 721.7 |
| 2015 | 719.0 | 725.3 | 728.0 | 732.4 | 733.8 | 725.1 | 720.8 | 729.3 | 731.4 | 737.4 | 739.7 | 737.2 | 730.0 |
| 2016 | 726.5 | 735.0 | 735.2 | 742.0 | 743.2 | 733.0 | 730.1 | 738.2 | 742.6 | 742.3 | 743.8 | 744.5 | 738.0 |
| 2017 | 729.9 | 735.4 | 737.7 | 742.8 | 741.9 | 736.1 | 728.4 | 736.8 | 741.2 | 742.0 | 744.4 | 744.7 | 738.4 |
| 2018 | 732.9 | 738.8 | 740.3 | 746.2 | 746.2 | 742.5 | 736.1 | 745.9 | 749.0 | 751.1 | 754.4 | 752.6 | 744.7 |
| 2019 | 741.2 | 748.7 | 750.0 | 754.2 | 754.6 | 747.5 | 743.4 | 754.5 | 756.6 | 757.6 | 761.0 | 759.0 | 752.4 |
| **Mining and Logging** | | | | | | | | | | | | | |
| 2011 | 19.7 | 20.0 | 20.2 | 20.6 | 21.0 | 21.4 | 21.7 | 22.1 | 22.3 | 22.6 | 22.9 | 23.2 | 21.5 |
| 2012 | 23.2 | 23.4 | 23.3 | 23.5 | 23.8 | 24.2 | 24.4 | 24.5 | 24.6 | 25.1 | 24.9 | 24.9 | 24.2 |
| 2013 | 25.2 | 25.4 | 25.5 | 25.8 | 26.0 | 26.2 | 26.4 | 26.5 | 26.2 | 26.4 | 26.7 | 26.6 | 26.1 |
| 2014 | 26.8 | 26.9 | 27.2 | 27.6 | 27.7 | 28.0 | 28.2 | 28.1 | 28.2 | 28.9 | 29.0 | 29.0 | 28.0 |
| 2015 | 28.9 | 28.1 | 27.0 | 26.3 | 25.7 | 25.4 | 25.4 | 25.3 | 24.7 | 24.1 | 23.4 | 22.9 | 25.6 |
| 2016 | 22.1 | 21.2 | 20.5 | 20.0 | 19.6 | 19.5 | 19.2 | 19.0 | 19.0 | 19.1 | 19.2 | 19.3 | 19.8 |
| 2017 | 19.6 | 20.0 | 20.2 | 20.5 | 20.7 | 21.0 | 21.3 | 21.2 | 21.5 | 22.0 | 22.2 | 22.4 | 21.1 |
| 2018 | 23.0 | 23.8 | 23.8 | 24.1 | 24.3 | 24.8 | 24.9 | 24.9 | 24.9 | 25.4 | 25.6 | 25.9 | 24.6 |
| 2019 | 26.1 | 26.4 | 26.3 | 25.9 | 25.9 | 25.9 | 26.4 | 26.4 | 25.9 | 25.9 | 25.8 | 25.7 | 26.1 |
| **Construction** | | | | | | | | | | | | | |
| 2011 | 40.9 | 40.5 | 41.9 | 42.7 | 43.0 | 43.4 | 43.8 | 43.4 | 42.7 | 42.2 | 41.6 | 40.5 | 42.2 |
| 2012 | 38.9 | 39.2 | 40.2 | 40.5 | 40.9 | 41.8 | 41.5 | 41.6 | 41.1 | 43.2 | 42.5 | 41.8 | 41.1 |
| 2013 | 40.1 | 40.5 | 40.9 | 41.6 | 41.8 | 42.2 | 42.6 | 43.2 | 43.0 | 44.2 | 43.8 | 42.4 | 42.2 |
| 2014 | 41.7 | 40.9 | 40.9 | 41.4 | 42.4 | 42.8 | 43.6 | 43.6 | 43.1 | 45.1 | 44.1 | 43.7 | 42.8 |
| 2015 | 42.3 | 42.1 | 42.2 | 43.5 | 43.5 | 43.7 | 44.3 | 43.9 | 43.7 | 44.8 | 44.4 | 43.7 | 43.5 |
| 2016 | 42.9 | 43.3 | 43.1 | 43.5 | 43.1 | 43.2 | 43.5 | 43.4 | 43.4 | 43.9 | 43.5 | 43.4 | 43.4 |
| 2017 | 42.8 | 43.3 | 44.1 | 45.2 | 45.8 | 46.4 | 46.3 | 46.4 | 46.6 | 46.7 | 46.6 | 46.3 | 45.5 |
| 2018 | 45.8 | 46.5 | 47.0 | 47.5 | 47.5 | 47.8 | 47.4 | 47.4 | 47.2 | 47.8 | 47.8 | 47.3 | 47.3 |
| 2019 | 46.7 | 47.1 | 47.8 | 48.7 | 49.5 | 49.6 | 51.4 | 51.4 | 51.0 | 52.4 | 52.4 | 51.7 | 50.0 |

## 1. Employment by Industry: New Mexico, 2011–2019—*Continued*

(Numbers in thousands, not seasonally adjusted)

| Industry and year | January | February | March | April | May | June | July | August | September | October | November | December | Annual average |
|---|---|---|---|---|---|---|---|---|---|---|---|---|---|
| **Manufacturing** | | | | | | | | | | | | | |
| 2011 | 28.9 | 28.8 | 29.0 | 29.1 | 29.1 | 29.4 | 29.6 | 30.5 | 30.7 | 30.5 | 29.9 | 29.6 | 29.6 |
| 2012 | 29.3 | 29.2 | 29.2 | 29.3 | 29.5 | 29.7 | 29.7 | 30.4 | 30.4 | 30.6 | 29.8 | 29.4 | 29.7 |
| 2013 | 28.8 | 28.8 | 28.6 | 28.9 | 29.0 | 29.2 | 29.2 | 29.9 | 29.7 | 29.7 | 28.7 | 28.5 | 29.1 |
| 2014 | 28.0 | 27.8 | 27.8 | 27.9 | 27.9 | 27.8 | 28.2 | 28.7 | 28.5 | 28.3 | 27.8 | 27.8 | 28.0 |
| 2015 | 27.7 | 27.4 | 27.5 | 27.4 | 27.6 | 27.9 | 28.0 | 28.3 | 28.1 | 28.4 | 27.7 | 27.7 | 27.8 |
| 2016 | 26.9 | 26.9 | 26.7 | 26.9 | 27.0 | 27.0 | 26.9 | 27.1 | 27.2 | 27.1 | 26.4 | 26.4 | 26.9 |
| 2017 | 26.1 | 25.9 | 25.8 | 25.8 | 26.0 | 26.3 | 26.7 | 27.0 | 26.8 | 27.2 | 26.8 | 26.9 | 26.4 |
| 2018 | 26.5 | 26.5 | 26.5 | 26.7 | 27.0 | 27.2 | 27.4 | 27.9 | 27.9 | 28.0 | 27.9 | 27.9 | 27.3 |
| 2019 | 27.5 | 27.6 | 27.7 | 28.0 | 28.4 | 28.5 | 28.9 | 29.0 | 29.1 | 29.3 | 28.8 | 28.8 | 28.5 |
| **Trade, Transportation, and Utilities** | | | | | | | | | | | | | |
| 2011 | 131.9 | 131.0 | 131.3 | 132.7 | 133.4 | 133.4 | 133.0 | 133.6 | 133.6 | 134.8 | 136.9 | 137.6 | 133.6 |
| 2012 | 134.0 | 133.3 | 133.9 | 134.2 | 134.9 | 135.0 | 135.0 | 135.2 | 135.3 | 137.4 | 139.4 | 139.8 | 135.6 |
| 2013 | 135.2 | 134.5 | 134.1 | 135.3 | 136.0 | 136.1 | 137.0 | 137.6 | 136.4 | 138.0 | 140.1 | 141.1 | 136.8 |
| 2014 | 136.5 | 135.9 | 135.9 | 137.1 | 137.6 | 137.3 | 138.3 | 138.6 | 138.3 | 139.8 | 141.4 | 142.5 | 138.3 |
| 2015 | 138.4 | 138.0 | 138.2 | 139.0 | 139.7 | 138.8 | 139.5 | 139.8 | 139.0 | 140.3 | 142.0 | 142.4 | 139.6 |
| 2016 | 138.3 | 137.3 | 137.2 | 138.4 | 138.5 | 137.6 | 138.7 | 139.0 | 138.2 | 139.0 | 140.9 | 140.9 | 138.7 |
| 2017 | 136.8 | 135.5 | 135.3 | 135.7 | 136.0 | 136.0 | 136.2 | 136.6 | 135.8 | 137.0 | 139.5 | 140.0 | 136.7 |
| 2018 | 137.0 | 136.3 | 136.3 | 136.8 | 137.6 | 137.2 | 137.4 | 138.2 | 137.0 | 137.5 | 140.2 | 140.0 | 137.6 |
| 2019 | 136.9 | 135.6 | 135.6 | 135.9 | 136.2 | 135.7 | 136.2 | 136.7 | 135.8 | 137.5 | 140.2 | 140.9 | 136.9 |
| **Wholesale Trade** | | | | | | | | | | | | | |
| 2011 | 20.7 | 20.6 | 20.7 | 20.8 | 21.0 | 21.3 | 21.3 | 21.3 | 21.2 | 21.1 | 20.9 | 21.0 | 21.0 |
| 2012 | 20.8 | 21.0 | 21.2 | 21.2 | 21.4 | 21.7 | 21.8 | 21.6 | 21.5 | 21.7 | 21.6 | 21.6 | 21.4 |
| 2013 | 21.2 | 21.4 | 21.3 | 21.5 | 21.6 | 21.7 | 21.7 | 21.8 | 21.4 | 21.5 | 21.5 | 21.5 | 21.5 |
| 2014 | 21.3 | 21.4 | 21.4 | 21.5 | 21.7 | 21.7 | 21.7 | 21.8 | 21.7 | 21.8 | 21.6 | 21.7 | 21.6 |
| 2015 | 21.3 | 21.3 | 21.4 | 21.5 | 21.6 | 21.6 | 21.7 | 21.6 | 21.4 | 21.6 | 21.5 | 21.5 | 21.5 |
| 2016 | 21.5 | 21.5 | 21.4 | 21.5 | 21.4 | 21.3 | 21.4 | 21.4 | 21.1 | 21.1 | 21.1 | 21.1 | 21.3 |
| 2017 | 20.8 | 20.8 | 20.9 | 20.9 | 21.1 | 21.1 | 21.3 | 21.1 | 20.9 | 20.9 | 20.9 | 21.0 | 21.0 |
| 2018 | 20.9 | 20.9 | 20.8 | 21.0 | 21.1 | 21.3 | 21.5 | 21.5 | 21.3 | 21.2 | 21.2 | 21.3 | 21.2 |
| 2019 | 21.1 | 21.1 | 21.2 | 21.2 | 21.3 | 21.6 | 21.7 | 21.6 | 21.4 | 21.8 | 22.4 | 22.6 | 21.6 |
| **Retail Trade** | | | | | | | | | | | | | |
| 2011 | 89.0 | 88.1 | 88.5 | 89.6 | 90.0 | 89.9 | 89.6 | 89.9 | 89.8 | 90.8 | 93.1 | 93.4 | 90.1 |
| 2012 | 90.2 | 89.2 | 89.5 | 89.9 | 90.2 | 90.3 | 90.3 | 90.3 | 90.4 | 91.9 | 94.0 | 94.2 | 90.9 |
| 2013 | 90.4 | 89.6 | 89.5 | 90.5 | 90.9 | 91.3 | 92.1 | 92.3 | 91.4 | 92.7 | 94.9 | 95.5 | 91.8 |
| 2014 | 91.5 | 90.8 | 91.0 | 91.8 | 91.8 | 92.0 | 92.7 | 92.7 | 92.2 | 93.3 | 95.1 | 95.6 | 92.5 |
| 2015 | 92.5 | 92.0 | 92.1 | 92.8 | 93.4 | 92.9 | 93.4 | 93.6 | 93.1 | 94.0 | 95.8 | 95.9 | 93.5 |
| 2016 | 92.3 | 91.5 | 91.7 | 92.8 | 92.9 | 92.6 | 93.3 | 93.2 | 92.6 | 93.5 | 95.3 | 94.8 | 93.0 |
| 2017 | 91.8 | 90.5 | 90.2 | 90.7 | 90.7 | 91.0 | 90.9 | 91.1 | 90.2 | 91.2 | 93.6 | 93.5 | 91.3 |
| 2018 | 91.1 | 90.4 | 90.5 | 90.6 | 91.2 | 90.9 | 90.8 | 91.0 | 89.9 | 90.4 | 92.8 | 92.3 | 91.0 |
| 2019 | 90.1 | 89.0 | 88.9 | 89.3 | 89.2 | 88.9 | 89.1 | 89.2 | 88.6 | 89.6 | 91.5 | 91.6 | 89.6 |
| **Transportation and Utilities** | | | | | | | | | | | | | |
| 2011 | 22.2 | 22.3 | 22.1 | 22.3 | 22.4 | 22.2 | 22.1 | 22.4 | 22.6 | 22.9 | 22.9 | 23.2 | 22.5 |
| 2012 | 23.0 | 23.1 | 23.2 | 23.1 | 23.3 | 23.0 | 22.9 | 23.3 | 23.4 | 23.8 | 23.8 | 24.0 | 23.3 |
| 2013 | 23.6 | 23.5 | 23.3 | 23.3 | 23.5 | 23.1 | 23.2 | 23.5 | 23.6 | 23.8 | 23.7 | 24.1 | 23.5 |
| 2014 | 23.7 | 23.7 | 23.5 | 23.8 | 24.1 | 23.6 | 23.8 | 24.1 | 24.4 | 24.7 | 24.7 | 25.2 | 24.1 |
| 2015 | 24.6 | 24.7 | 24.7 | 24.7 | 24.7 | 24.3 | 24.4 | 24.6 | 24.5 | 24.7 | 24.7 | 25.0 | 24.6 |
| 2016 | 24.5 | 24.3 | 24.1 | 24.1 | 24.2 | 23.7 | 24.0 | 24.4 | 24.5 | 24.4 | 24.5 | 25.0 | 24.3 |
| 2017 | 24.2 | 24.2 | 24.2 | 24.1 | 24.2 | 23.9 | 24.0 | 24.4 | 24.7 | 24.9 | 25.0 | 25.5 | 24.4 |
| 2018 | 25.0 | 25.0 | 25.0 | 25.2 | 25.3 | 25.0 | 25.1 | 25.7 | 25.8 | 25.9 | 26.2 | 26.4 | 25.5 |
| 2019 | 25.7 | 25.5 | 25.5 | 25.4 | 25.7 | 25.2 | 25.4 | 25.9 | 25.8 | 26.1 | 26.3 | 26.7 | 25.8 |
| **Information** | | | | | | | | | | | | | |
| 2011 | 13.8 | 13.4 | 13.6 | 14.4 | 14.6 | 14.3 | 13.6 | 13.1 | 12.4 | 12.6 | 13.0 | 12.6 | 13.5 |
| 2012 | 13.2 | 13.7 | 14.3 | 13.9 | 13.6 | 13.1 | 13.3 | 14.0 | 13.2 | 13.0 | 14.0 | 13.1 | 13.5 |
| 2013 | 13.1 | 13.6 | 12.9 | 13.6 | 14.2 | 13.6 | 13.2 | 12.8 | 12.3 | 12.4 | 12.6 | 12.3 | 13.1 |
| 2014 | 11.6 | 12.0 | 12.2 | 12.3 | 12.8 | 12.7 | 12.4 | 12.8 | 11.9 | 12.5 | 13.2 | 13.0 | 12.5 |
| 2015 | 11.7 | 12.2 | 12.6 | 13.0 | 13.5 | 13.0 | 13.0 | 13.7 | 12.6 | 12.5 | 12.7 | 11.9 | 12.7 |
| 2016 | 11.5 | 12.8 | 12.3 | 13.4 | 12.9 | 12.7 | 13.3 | 13.2 | 13.2 | 13.3 | 13.8 | 13.6 | 13.0 |
| 2017 | 12.9 | 11.9 | 12.3 | 13.1 | 12.4 | 12.8 | 12.3 | 12.0 | 11.8 | 12.1 | 11.6 | 11.3 | 12.2 |
| 2018 | 11.0 | 11.5 | 11.5 | 11.3 | 11.3 | 11.8 | 11.4 | 11.6 | 11.2 | 11.3 | 11.9 | 11.5 | 11.4 |
| 2019 | 10.4 | 11.1 | 11.2 | 10.7 | 11.3 | 11.4 | 11.8 | 11.2 | 11.3 | 11.3 | 11.6 | 11.1 | 11.2 |

# 1. Employment by Industry: New Mexico, 2011–2019—*Continued*

(Numbers in thousands, not seasonally adjusted)

| Industry and year | January | February | March | April | May | June | July | August | September | October | November | December | Annual average |
|---|---|---|---|---|---|---|---|---|---|---|---|---|---|
| **Financial Activities** | | | | | | | | | | | | | |
| 2011 | 32.5 | 32.4 | 32.4 | 32.6 | 32.5 | 32.5 | 32.7 | 32.6 | 32.5 | 32.5 | 32.5 | 32.7 | 32.5 |
| 2012 | 32.3 | 32.5 | 32.7 | 32.6 | 32.6 | 32.8 | 32.9 | 32.8 | 32.6 | 33.3 | 33.3 | 33.3 | 32.8 |
| 2013 | 33.0 | 32.9 | 32.9 | 33.0 | 33.0 | 33.0 | 33.2 | 33.2 | 33.1 | 33.3 | 33.6 | 33.8 | 33.2 |
| 2014 | 33.1 | 33.1 | 33.2 | 33.2 | 33.2 | 33.2 | 33.4 | 33.3 | 33.0 | 33.3 | 33.3 | 33.4 | 33.2 |
| 2015 | 33.2 | 33.2 | 33.2 | 33.2 | 33.3 | 33.2 | 33.4 | 33.4 | 33.0 | 33.4 | 33.5 | 33.7 | 33.3 |
| 2016 | 33.5 | 33.6 | 33.5 | 33.6 | 33.6 | 33.5 | 33.5 | 33.5 | 33.4 | 33.6 | 33.6 | 33.7 | 33.6 |
| 2017 | 33.6 | 33.6 | 33.6 | 33.9 | 33.9 | 33.9 | 34.1 | 34.1 | 33.9 | 34.2 | 34.2 | 34.3 | 33.9 |
| 2018 | 34.1 | 34.1 | 34.1 | 34.6 | 34.5 | 34.6 | 34.9 | 34.9 | 34.6 | 35.0 | 35.2 | 35.2 | 34.7 |
| 2019 | 35.2 | 35.4 | 35.3 | 35.5 | 35.5 | 35.5 | 35.7 | 35.7 | 35.3 | 35.6 | 35.8 | 36.5 | 35.6 |
| **Professional and Business Services** | | | | | | | | | | | | | |
| 2011 | 98.9 | 101.0 | 99.6 | 100.3 | 100.0 | 100.4 | 101.4 | 101.2 | 101.6 | 99.7 | 99.0 | 98.7 | 100.2 |
| 2012 | 96.6 | 96.7 | 97.2 | 98.5 | 97.8 | 99.1 | 97.9 | 98.2 | 98.2 | 99.3 | 99.2 | 98.3 | 98.1 |
| 2013 | 98.0 | 98.3 | 98.1 | 99.6 | 99.4 | 98.9 | 99.8 | 99.9 | 98.8 | 99.3 | 98.8 | 99.0 | 99.0 |
| 2014 | 98.1 | 98.0 | 97.5 | 99.5 | 99.3 | 98.9 | 100.0 | 100.6 | 98.9 | 99.6 | 99.3 | 99.7 | 99.1 |
| 2015 | 98.4 | 98.5 | 98.4 | 99.4 | 99.2 | 99.5 | 100.8 | 100.9 | 99.8 | 100.7 | 100.4 | 100.4 | 99.7 |
| 2016 | 99.2 | 99.5 | 99.3 | 100.7 | 100.6 | 101.2 | 103.1 | 103.0 | 102.8 | 102.2 | 101.9 | 102.3 | 101.3 |
| 2017 | 102.1 | 102.8 | 102.8 | 104.2 | 103.8 | 104.7 | 105.5 | 105.8 | 105.5 | 104.9 | 105.7 | 105.8 | 104.5 |
| 2018 | 104.5 | 104.8 | 104.7 | 106.2 | 106.3 | 107.2 | 107.9 | 108.8 | 108.8 | 108.9 | 108.9 | 109.3 | 107.2 |
| 2019 | 108.5 | 109.5 | 109.7 | 111.2 | 111.2 | 111.0 | 111.5 | 112.2 | 111.6 | 111.0 | 111.9 | 111.1 | 110.9 |
| **Education and Health Services** | | | | | | | | | | | | | |
| 2011 | 120.5 | 121.0 | 121.6 | 122.2 | 122.2 | 119.4 | 119.3 | 119.9 | 122.9 | 123.0 | 123.1 | 122.6 | 121.5 |
| 2012 | 121.8 | 122.9 | 122.8 | 122.9 | 122.9 | 120.5 | 120.1 | 120.2 | 123.3 | 124.5 | 124.8 | 125.0 | 122.6 |
| 2013 | 123.9 | 124.2 | 124.7 | 125.6 | 125.6 | 121.6 | 120.0 | 121.6 | 125.0 | 125.9 | 126.7 | 126.4 | 124.3 |
| 2014 | 126.1 | 126.7 | 126.7 | 127.5 | 128.1 | 124.0 | 123.4 | 125.5 | 129.4 | 131.1 | 131.4 | 131.3 | 127.6 |
| 2015 | 131.0 | 131.8 | 132.0 | 133.4 | 134.0 | 130.7 | 129.6 | 131.2 | 134.9 | 137.1 | 137.7 | 136.4 | 133.3 |
| 2016 | 137.3 | 138.4 | 138.0 | 139.4 | 139.4 | 135.2 | 134.5 | 136.6 | 139.3 | 140.0 | 139.4 | 140.4 | 138.2 |
| 2017 | 139.3 | 140.1 | 139.9 | 140.2 | 140.1 | 136.5 | 135.1 | 136.6 | 139.4 | 139.8 | 139.9 | 139.5 | 138.9 |
| 2018 | 139.3 | 139.5 | 139.3 | 140.9 | 140.9 | 137.2 | 135.8 | 137.8 | 140.7 | 141.9 | 141.9 | 141.9 | 139.8 |
| 2019 | 140.7 | 141.6 | 141.3 | 141.8 | 141.8 | 138.3 | 137.5 | 140.1 | 142.2 | 143.0 | 143.6 | 143.9 | 141.3 |
| **Leisure and Hospitality** | | | | | | | | | | | | | |
| 2011 | 81.4 | 82.0 | 83.5 | 84.9 | 85.2 | 86.4 | 86.5 | 87.3 | 86.2 | 84.7 | 83.3 | 83.8 | 84.6 |
| 2012 | 82.0 | 82.6 | 84.0 | 85.4 | 86.6 | 88.4 | 88.3 | 89.4 | 87.3 | 87.9 | 86.1 | 86.4 | 86.2 |
| 2013 | 84.9 | 85.1 | 86.2 | 88.1 | 89.1 | 90.0 | 91.4 | 91.9 | 89.3 | 88.8 | 87.8 | 88.6 | 88.4 |
| 2014 | 87.7 | 87.3 | 88.4 | 90.2 | 92.5 | 92.9 | 93.9 | 94.4 | 91.9 | 91.6 | 90.5 | 90.2 | 91.0 |
| 2015 | 89.7 | 89.9 | 90.9 | 93.6 | 94.3 | 94.9 | 96.2 | 95.8 | 93.5 | 93.5 | 92.4 | 93.0 | 93.1 |
| 2016 | 92.3 | 93.0 | 93.5 | 94.6 | 97.0 | 97.5 | 99.1 | 98.8 | 96.8 | 95.1 | 94.0 | 94.8 | 95.5 |
| 2017 | 93.4 | 93.6 | 95.0 | 95.8 | 97.4 | 98.7 | 99.1 | 99.1 | 97.4 | 96.0 | 95.1 | 95.4 | 96.3 |
| 2018 | 94.3 | 94.7 | 95.8 | 97.4 | 99.1 | 100.0 | 101.2 | 101.2 | 98.3 | 97.7 | 96.9 | 97.3 | 97.8 |
| 2019 | 96.0 | 96.7 | 97.9 | 99.7 | 100.2 | 101.2 | 102.2 | 102.7 | 100.1 | 97.3 | 96.1 | 95.7 | 98.8 |
| **Other Services** | | | | | | | | | | | | | |
| 2011 | 27.0 | 27.3 | 27.5 | 27.6 | 27.7 | 31.3 | 31.6 | 31.2 | 28.2 | 27.4 | 27.3 | 27.3 | 28.5 |
| 2012 | 27.2 | 27.6 | 27.8 | 27.9 | 28.0 | 30.3 | 30.0 | 29.8 | 28.0 | 28.5 | 28.1 | 28.0 | 28.4 |
| 2013 | 27.5 | 27.6 | 27.7 | 27.7 | 28.0 | 30.1 | 30.2 | 30.0 | 27.8 | 27.7 | 27.6 | 27.5 | 28.3 |
| 2014 | 27.3 | 27.5 | 27.6 | 27.8 | 28.3 | 30.5 | 30.7 | 30.4 | 28.3 | 28.4 | 28.1 | 27.9 | 28.6 |
| 2015 | 27.5 | 27.8 | 27.7 | 27.8 | 28.0 | 30.4 | 30.7 | 30.4 | 28.1 | 27.9 | 27.7 | 27.5 | 28.5 |
| 2016 | 27.3 | 27.6 | 27.6 | 27.9 | 28.2 | 30.4 | 30.8 | 30.3 | 28.2 | 28.0 | 27.9 | 27.6 | 28.5 |
| 2017 | 27.3 | 27.6 | 27.7 | 28.0 | 28.4 | 30.7 | 30.8 | 30.2 | 28.2 | 28.1 | 27.9 | 27.9 | 28.6 |
| 2018 | 27.7 | 28.0 | 28.1 | 28.3 | 28.7 | 31.1 | 31.2 | 30.5 | 28.8 | 28.7 | 28.5 | 28.3 | 29.0 |
| 2019 | 28.1 | 28.4 | 28.4 | 28.5 | 28.9 | 31.2 | 30.3 | 29.9 | 28.8 | 28.4 | 28.5 | 28.1 | 29.0 |
| **Government** | | | | | | | | | | | | | |
| 2011 | 192.5 | 198.5 | 199.5 | 199.4 | 198.2 | 192.3 | 185.4 | 186.5 | 194.5 | 196.5 | 196.2 | 197.3 | 194.7 |
| 2012 | 188.2 | 194.9 | 196.0 | 195.4 | 195.9 | 189.4 | 183.1 | 186.1 | 193.5 | 196.4 | 196.6 | 196.0 | 192.6 |
| 2013 | 189.9 | 195.1 | 196.2 | 196.4 | 197.1 | 185.8 | 180.1 | 185.0 | 192.1 | 194.3 | 193.9 | 193.8 | 191.6 |
| 2014 | 189.1 | 193.8 | 194.2 | 194.7 | 195.8 | 185.3 | 181.3 | 186.4 | 192.7 | 194.7 | 195.1 | 194.8 | 191.5 |
| 2015 | 189.1 | 193.9 | 195.0 | 193.0 | 191.8 | 184.6 | 177.6 | 184.1 | 190.5 | 192.0 | 193.3 | 191.9 | 189.7 |
| 2016 | 187.1 | 192.8 | 193.8 | 194.0 | 193.0 | 184.9 | 177.1 | 183.8 | 190.7 | 191.1 | 192.3 | 191.2 | 189.3 |
| 2017 | 184.5 | 190.3 | 191.1 | 191.9 | 189.9 | 182.8 | 175.3 | 182.4 | 189.2 | 189.9 | 190.5 | 190.5 | 187.4 |
| 2018 | 185.0 | 189.9 | 190.5 | 190.7 | 187.8 | 183.4 | 176.3 | 182.9 | 189.6 | 190.1 | 190.9 | 189.1 | 187.2 |
| 2019 | 185.4 | 190.4 | 190.6 | 190.9 | 189.5 | 183.2 | 178.2 | 186.0 | 191.5 | 193.5 | 193.3 | 191.7 | 188.7 |

## 2. Average Weekly Hours by Selected Industry: New Mexico, 2015–2019

(Not seasonally adjusted)

| Industry and year | January | February | March | April | May | June | July | August | September | October | November | December | Annual average |
|---|---|---|---|---|---|---|---|---|---|---|---|---|---|
| **Total Private** | | | | | | | | | | | | | |
| 2015 | 33.8 | 34.2 | 34.2 | 33.8 | 33.7 | 34.0 | 34.2 | 34.8 | 33.9 | 34.0 | 34.2 | 33.8 | 34.0 |
| 2016 | 33.2 | 33.3 | 33.2 | 33.4 | 33.7 | 33.3 | 33.4 | 33.5 | 33.3 | 33.8 | 33.2 | 33.0 | 33.4 |
| 2017 | 33.4 | 33.1 | 33.1 | 33.8 | 33.6 | 33.9 | 34.0 | 33.6 | 33.4 | 34.1 | 33.7 | 33.6 | 33.6 |
| 2018 | 33.1 | 33.5 | 33.5 | 34.1 | 33.9 | 33.9 | 34.3 | 33.9 | 34.1 | 33.5 | 33.7 | 34.0 | 33.8 |
| 2019 | 33.3 | 33.4 | 33.4 | 33.7 | 33.6 | 34.6 | 34.0 | 34.5 | 34.4 | 34.3 | 34.1 | 34.5 | 34.0 |
| **Goods-Producing** | | | | | | | | | | | | | |
| 2015 | 38.6 | 39.3 | 38.9 | 39.6 | 39.5 | 39.5 | 39.6 | 40.5 | 38.1 | 39.4 | 40.5 | 40.4 | 39.5 |
| 2016 | 39.2 | 39.4 | 39.2 | 39.8 | 39.5 | 39.7 | 39.7 | 40.3 | 39.9 | 40.5 | 39.9 | 40.1 | 39.8 |
| 2017 | 39.9 | 38.9 | 39.2 | 38.8 | 39.7 | 40.1 | 39.2 | 39.5 | 39.4 | 39.7 | 40.0 | 39.9 | 39.5 |
| 2018 | 38.6 | 38.9 | 39.4 | 39.7 | 40.4 | 40.3 | 40.2 | 40.2 | 39.9 | 39.3 | 40.8 | 41.0 | 39.9 |
| 2019 | 39.9 | 39.0 | 39.1 | 39.8 | 40.2 | 40.5 | 40.4 | 41.0 | 40.5 | 40.7 | 40.3 | 41.5 | 40.3 |
| **Construction** | | | | | | | | | | | | | |
| 2015 | 35.8 | 37.2 | 36.3 | 37.5 | 37.1 | 37.2 | 38.0 | 39.1 | 36.3 | 38.2 | 39.6 | 38.8 | 37.6 |
| 2016 | 38.3 | 39.1 | 38.9 | 39.4 | 38.4 | 39.1 | 39.0 | 39.4 | 39.0 | 40.1 | 39.3 | 39.4 | 39.1 |
| 2017 | 39.5 | 38.0 | 38.3 | 37.8 | 39.3 | 39.6 | 38.9 | 39.4 | 38.5 | 39.2 | 39.6 | 39.7 | 39.0 |
| 2018 | 38.3 | 38.7 | 39.1 | 39.1 | 40.2 | 40.3 | 40.1 | 40.7 | 39.1 | 38.8 | 40.1 | 39.9 | 39.5 |
| 2019 | 39.3 | 38.0 | 37.9 | 38.8 | 39.9 | 40.4 | 39.9 | 40.6 | 39.6 | 40.5 | 39.0 | 40.4 | 39.5 |
| **Trade, Transportation, and Utilities** | | | | | | | | | | | | | |
| 2015 | 33.9 | 34.2 | 34.7 | 34.1 | 34.4 | 34.6 | 34.6 | 35.1 | 34.9 | 34.3 | 33.8 | 34.2 | 34.4 |
| 2016 | 33.1 | 33.2 | 32.3 | 32.9 | 33.5 | 32.9 | 33.6 | 33.8 | 33.9 | 33.9 | 33.1 | 33.1 | 33.3 |
| 2017 | 32.5 | 32.9 | 32.9 | 33.2 | 33.1 | 33.7 | 34.0 | 33.5 | 33.7 | 34.2 | 33.5 | 33.7 | 33.4 |
| 2018 | 32.8 | 33.8 | 33.6 | 34.4 | 34.0 | 34.1 | 34.4 | 34.1 | 34.4 | 33.6 | 33.7 | 34.1 | 33.9 |
| 2019 | 33.6 | 33.6 | 33.3 | 33.2 | 33.6 | 34.4 | 34.4 | 34.7 | 34.4 | 34.5 | 33.9 | 34.8 | 34.0 |
| **Professional and Business Services** | | | | | | | | | | | | | |
| 2015 | 35.4 | 35.5 | 35.6 | 35.1 | 34.7 | 35.0 | 35.0 | 35.8 | 34.7 | 35.2 | 35.7 | 34.6 | 35.2 |
| 2016 | 34.8 | 35.2 | 35.2 | 35.1 | 35.2 | 34.6 | 35.0 | 35.4 | 35.1 | 35.7 | 34.7 | 34.5 | 35.0 |
| 2017 | 35.6 | 35.4 | 35.1 | 36.4 | 35.9 | 35.7 | 35.9 | 35.3 | 35.3 | 35.8 | 35.3 | 35.2 | 35.6 |
| 2018 | 35.2 | 35.6 | 35.2 | 36.4 | 35.7 | 35.5 | 35.9 | 35.2 | 35.7 | 35.0 | 34.9 | 35.8 | 35.5 |
| 2019 | 34.2 | 34.4 | 34.9 | 35.4 | 34.8 | 35.7 | 35.7 | 36.3 | 36.5 | 35.9 | 35.8 | 36.1 | 35.5 |
| **Education and Health Services** | | | | | | | | | | | | | |
| 2015 | 33.5 | 33.8 | 33.6 | 33.3 | 33.4 | 33.6 | 33.6 | 34.0 | 33.9 | 33.6 | 33.8 | 33.4 | 33.6 |
| 2016 | 32.7 | 32.4 | 32.4 | 32.2 | 32.6 | 31.9 | 31.9 | 31.8 | 31.5 | 32.0 | 31.9 | 31.5 | 32.1 |
| 2017 | 32.5 | 31.7 | 31.7 | 32.5 | 32.3 | 32.4 | 32.7 | 32.3 | 32.4 | 32.6 | 32.2 | 32.1 | 32.3 |
| 2018 | 32.0 | 32.2 | 32.4 | 32.7 | 32.5 | 32.3 | 33.3 | 32.7 | 33.1 | 32.6 | 32.5 | 33.1 | 32.6 |
| 2019 | 32.3 | 32.8 | 32.6 | 33.0 | 32.5 | 33.1 | 32.4 | 32.4 | 33.0 | 33.3 | 33.3 | 33.4 | 32.8 |
| **Leisure and Hospitality** | | | | | | | | | | | | | |
| 2015 | 25.3 | 26.2 | 26.2 | 25.2 | 25.5 | 26.1 | 26.6 | 27.0 | 26.1 | 26.1 | 25.8 | 25.7 | 26.0 |
| 2016 | 25.4 | 25.8 | 26.7 | 26.2 | 26.9 | 26.9 | 27.0 | 27.2 | 26.9 | 27.3 | 26.3 | 26.0 | 26.6 |
| 2017 | 26.4 | 26.2 | 27.1 | 27.2 | 26.8 | 26.7 | 27.0 | 26.4 | 25.5 | 26.8 | 25.6 | 25.7 | 26.5 |
| 2018 | 25.3 | 25.6 | 26.2 | 26.4 | 26.1 | 27.1 | 26.9 | 26.4 | 26.2 | 25.9 | 25.4 | 25.8 | 26.1 |
| 2019 | 25.1 | 25.2 | 26.2 | 25.3 | 25.9 | 27.1 | 26.4 | 26.5 | 26.5 | 26.4 | 26.1 | 26.2 | 26.1 |

## 3. Average Hourly Earnings by Selected Industry: New Mexico, 2015–2019

(Dollars, not seasonally adjusted)

| Industry and year | January | February | March | April | May | June | July | August | September | October | November | December | Annual average |
|---|---|---|---|---|---|---|---|---|---|---|---|---|---|
| **Total Private** | | | | | | | | | | | | | |
| 2015 | 20.46 | 20.51 | 20.56 | 20.37 | 20.49 | 20.21 | 20.30 | 20.38 | 20.50 | 20.42 | 20.55 | 20.40 | 20.43 |
| 2016 | 20.59 | 20.64 | 20.48 | 20.36 | 20.36 | 20.32 | 20.44 | 20.48 | 20.71 | 20.93 | 20.82 | 21.03 | 20.60 |
| 2017 | 21.22 | 21.15 | 21.08 | 21.42 | 21.21 | 20.99 | 21.50 | 21.48 | 21.57 | 21.55 | 21.67 | 21.81 | 21.39 |
| 2018 | 21.87 | 21.75 | 21.77 | 22.00 | 21.90 | 21.76 | 22.07 | 22.17 | 22.37 | 22.35 | 22.38 | 22.73 | 22.10 |
| 2019 | 22.73 | 22.67 | 22.84 | 22.98 | 22.84 | 22.88 | 23.07 | 23.13 | 23.33 | 23.09 | 22.89 | 23.19 | 22.97 |
| **Goods-Producing** | | | | | | | | | | | | | |
| 2015 | 23.20 | 23.21 | 23.28 | 22.86 | 23.42 | 23.16 | 23.58 | 23.60 | 23.54 | 23.12 | 23.36 | 23.21 | 23.30 |
| 2016 | 23.36 | 23.14 | 22.91 | 22.44 | 22.34 | 22.69 | 22.66 | 22.57 | 22.76 | 22.67 | 23.07 | 22.64 | 22.77 |
| 2017 | 22.66 | 23.04 | 22.89 | 22.73 | 22.75 | 22.85 | 23.26 | 23.36 | 23.27 | 23.15 | 23.44 | 23.51 | 23.08 |
| 2018 | 23.23 | 23.31 | 23.42 | 23.75 | 23.53 | 23.88 | 24.06 | 24.45 | 24.53 | 24.93 | 25.19 | 25.43 | 24.16 |
| 2019 | 25.97 | 25.62 | 25.83 | 25.75 | 25.87 | 26.11 | 26.20 | 26.14 | 25.97 | 26.14 | 26.09 | 25.98 | 25.98 |
| **Construction** | | | | | | | | | | | | | |
| 2015 | 21.43 | 21.39 | 21.50 | 21.13 | 21.41 | 21.05 | 21.01 | 21.30 | 21.30 | 20.96 | 21.00 | 20.99 | 21.20 |
| 2016 | 21.23 | 20.78 | 21.05 | 20.44 | 20.45 | 21.09 | 21.07 | 21.28 | 21.65 | 21.62 | 22.33 | 21.88 | 21.24 |
| 2017 | 21.86 | 22.30 | 22.09 | 22.06 | 22.34 | 22.51 | 22.76 | 23.00 | 22.85 | 22.65 | 23.02 | 23.28 | 22.57 |
| 2018 | 23.15 | 23.25 | 23.06 | 22.94 | 22.99 | 23.18 | 22.83 | 23.42 | 23.44 | 23.58 | 24.00 | 24.59 | 23.37 |
| 2019 | 25.21 | 24.73 | 24.96 | 24.88 | 25.08 | 25.57 | 25.76 | 25.82 | 25.45 | 25.30 | 25.48 | 25.24 | 25.30 |
| **Trade, Transportation, and Utilities** | | | | | | | | | | | | | |
| 2015 | 17.79 | 17.67 | 17.37 | 17.34 | 17.41 | 17.05 | 16.96 | 17.61 | 17.43 | 17.24 | 17.88 | 17.28 | 17.42 |
| 2016 | 17.37 | 17.24 | 17.38 | 17.13 | 17.25 | 17.32 | 17.32 | 17.66 | 17.87 | 18.04 | 17.97 | 17.92 | 17.54 |
| 2017 | 18.08 | 18.10 | 18.16 | 18.87 | 18.57 | 18.70 | 19.23 | 19.19 | 19.42 | 19.75 | 19.29 | 19.38 | 18.90 |
| 2018 | 19.70 | 19.54 | 19.73 | 20.30 | 20.41 | 20.00 | 20.35 | 20.10 | 20.32 | 19.82 | 19.41 | 19.30 | 19.92 |
| 2019 | 19.32 | 19.43 | 19.51 | 19.63 | 19.55 | 19.88 | 19.87 | 19.87 | 20.22 | 20.37 | 19.88 | 20.52 | 19.85 |
| **Professional and Business Services** | | | | | | | | | | | | | |
| 2015 | 26.28 | 26.49 | 26.40 | 26.30 | 26.58 | 26.42 | 26.27 | 26.39 | 26.35 | 26.24 | 26.11 | 26.40 | 26.35 |
| 2016 | 26.72 | 26.71 | 26.15 | 26.04 | 26.39 | 26.44 | 26.61 | 26.79 | 26.93 | 27.45 | 27.27 | 27.40 | 26.74 |
| 2017 | 27.95 | 28.07 | 28.10 | 28.71 | 28.28 | 27.47 | 28.40 | 28.20 | 27.80 | 27.81 | 28.07 | 28.15 | 28.09 |
| 2018 | 28.51 | 28.30 | 27.87 | 27.84 | 27.31 | 27.51 | 28.10 | 27.80 | 28.49 | 28.54 | 29.12 | 28.55 | 28.16 |
| 2019 | 29.36 | 29.44 | 29.99 | 30.31 | 29.68 | 29.44 | 29.91 | 30.20 | 30.90 | 30.89 | 30.41 | 30.86 | 30.13 |
| **Education and Health Services** | | | | | | | | | | | | | |
| 2015 | 20.68 | 20.79 | 20.66 | 20.13 | 20.05 | 19.87 | 20.22 | 20.32 | 20.55 | 20.51 | 20.50 | 20.51 | 20.40 |
| 2016 | 20.24 | 20.67 | 20.49 | 20.50 | 20.34 | 20.10 | 20.15 | 20.27 | 20.36 | 20.75 | 20.30 | 20.73 | 20.41 |
| 2017 | 20.93 | 20.82 | 20.70 | 20.56 | 20.53 | 20.48 | 20.72 | 20.72 | 20.68 | 20.60 | 20.81 | 21.19 | 20.73 |
| 2018 | 21.52 | 21.13 | 21.13 | 21.17 | 21.04 | 20.93 | 21.03 | 20.79 | 20.77 | 20.54 | 20.88 | 21.29 | 21.02 |
| 2019 | 21.41 | 21.15 | 21.35 | 21.33 | 21.53 | 21.64 | 21.98 | 22.12 | 21.99 | 21.79 | 21.56 | 21.78 | 21.64 |
| **Leisure and Hospitality** | | | | | | | | | | | | | |
| 2015 | 12.34 | 12.66 | 12.67 | 12.44 | 12.75 | 12.51 | 12.56 | 12.51 | 12.65 | 12.72 | 12.71 | 12.89 | 12.62 |
| 2016 | 12.97 | 13.17 | 13.11 | 13.04 | 12.98 | 13.16 | 13.31 | 13.18 | 13.10 | 13.13 | 12.94 | 13.05 | 13.10 |
| 2017 | 12.87 | 12.83 | 12.90 | 12.68 | 12.61 | 12.77 | 12.93 | 13.05 | 13.04 | 12.97 | 12.94 | 13.03 | 12.88 |
| 2018 | 13.20 | 13.40 | 13.48 | 13.44 | 13.67 | 13.47 | 14.11 | 14.18 | 13.93 | 14.13 | 13.90 | 13.92 | 13.74 |
| 2019 | 13.86 | 13.85 | 14.04 | 13.98 | 13.79 | 13.71 | 13.91 | 13.97 | 14.01 | 14.04 | 14.12 | 14.39 | 13.97 |

## 4. Average Weekly Earnings by Selected Industry: New Mexico, 2015–2019

(Dollars, not seasonally adjusted)

| Industry and year | January | February | March | April | May | June | July | August | September | October | November | December | Annual average |
|---|---|---|---|---|---|---|---|---|---|---|---|---|---|
| **Total Private** | | | | | | | | | | | | | |
| 2015 | 691.55 | 701.44 | 703.15 | 688.51 | 690.51 | 687.14 | 694.26 | 709.22 | 694.95 | 694.28 | 702.81 | 689.52 | 694.62 |
| 2016 | 683.59 | 687.31 | 679.94 | 680.02 | 686.13 | 676.66 | 683.03 | 686.42 | 689.64 | 707.43 | 691.22 | 693.99 | 688.04 |
| 2017 | 708.75 | 700.07 | 697.75 | 724.00 | 712.66 | 711.56 | 731.00 | 721.73 | 720.44 | 734.86 | 730.28 | 732.82 | 718.70 |
| 2018 | 723.90 | 728.63 | 729.30 | 750.20 | 742.41 | 737.66 | 757.00 | 751.56 | 762.82 | 748.73 | 754.21 | 772.82 | 746.98 |
| 2019 | 756.91 | 757.18 | 762.86 | 774.43 | 767.42 | 791.65 | 784.38 | 795.67 | 802.55 | 791.99 | 780.55 | 800.06 | 780.98 |
| **Goods-Producing** | | | | | | | | | | | | | |
| 2015 | 895.52 | 912.15 | 905.59 | 905.26 | 925.09 | 914.82 | 933.77 | 955.80 | 896.87 | 910.93 | 946.08 | 937.68 | 920.35 |
| 2016 | 915.71 | 911.72 | 898.07 | 893.11 | 882.43 | 900.79 | 899.60 | 909.57 | 908.12 | 918.14 | 920.49 | 907.86 | 906.25 |
| 2017 | 904.13 | 896.26 | 897.29 | 881.92 | 903.18 | 916.29 | 911.79 | 922.72 | 916.84 | 919.06 | 937.60 | 938.05 | 911.66 |
| 2018 | 896.68 | 906.76 | 922.75 | 942.88 | 950.61 | 962.36 | 967.21 | 982.89 | 978.75 | 979.75 | 1,027.75 | 1,042.63 | 963.98 |
| 2019 | 1,036.20 | 999.18 | 1,009.95 | 1,024.85 | 1,039.97 | 1,057.46 | 1,058.48 | 1,071.74 | 1,051.79 | 1,063.90 | 1,051.43 | 1,078.17 | 1,046.99 |
| **Construction** | | | | | | | | | | | | | |
| 2015 | 767.19 | 795.71 | 780.45 | 792.38 | 794.31 | 783.06 | 798.38 | 832.83 | 773.19 | 800.67 | 831.60 | 814.41 | 797.12 |
| 2016 | 813.11 | 812.50 | 818.85 | 805.34 | 785.28 | 824.62 | 821.73 | 838.43 | 844.35 | 866.96 | 877.57 | 862.07 | 830.48 |
| 2017 | 863.47 | 847.40 | 846.05 | 833.87 | 877.96 | 891.40 | 885.36 | 906.20 | 879.73 | 887.88 | 911.59 | 924.22 | 880.23 |
| 2018 | 886.65 | 899.78 | 901.65 | 896.95 | 924.20 | 934.15 | 915.48 | 953.19 | 916.50 | 914.90 | 962.40 | 981.14 | 923.12 |
| 2019 | 990.75 | 939.74 | 945.98 | 965.34 | 1,000.69 | 1,033.03 | 1,027.82 | 1,048.29 | 1,007.82 | 1,024.65 | 993.72 | 1,019.70 | 999.35 |
| **Trade, Transportation, and Utilities** | | | | | | | | | | | | | |
| 2015 | 603.08 | 604.31 | 602.74 | 591.29 | 598.90 | 589.93 | 586.82 | 618.11 | 608.31 | 591.33 | 604.34 | 590.98 | 599.25 |
| 2016 | 574.95 | 572.37 | 561.37 | 563.58 | 577.88 | 569.83 | 581.95 | 596.91 | 605.79 | 611.56 | 594.81 | 593.15 | 584.08 |
| 2017 | 587.60 | 595.49 | 597.46 | 626.48 | 614.67 | 630.19 | 653.82 | 642.87 | 654.45 | 675.45 | 646.22 | 653.11 | 631.26 |
| 2018 | 646.16 | 660.45 | 662.93 | 698.32 | 693.94 | 682.00 | 700.04 | 685.41 | 699.01 | 665.95 | 654.12 | 658.13 | 675.29 |
| 2019 | 649.49 | 652.85 | 649.68 | 651.72 | 656.88 | 683.87 | 683.53 | 689.49 | 695.57 | 702.77 | 673.93 | 714.10 | 674.90 |
| **Professional and Business Services** | | | | | | | | | | | | | |
| 2015 | 930.31 | 940.40 | 939.84 | 923.13 | 922.67 | 924.70 | 919.45 | 944.76 | 914.35 | 923.65 | 932.13 | 913.44 | 927.52 |
| 2016 | 929.86 | 940.19 | 920.48 | 914.00 | 928.93 | 914.82 | 931.35 | 948.37 | 945.24 | 979.97 | 946.27 | 945.30 | 935.90 |
| 2017 | 995.02 | 993.68 | 986.31 | 1,045.04 | 1,015.25 | 980.68 | 1,019.56 | 995.46 | 981.34 | 995.60 | 990.87 | 990.88 | 1,000.00 |
| 2018 | 1,003.55 | 1,007.48 | 981.02 | 1,013.38 | 974.97 | 976.61 | 1,008.79 | 978.56 | 1,017.09 | 998.90 | 1,016.29 | 1,022.09 | 999.68 |
| 2019 | 1,004.11 | 1,012.74 | 1,046.65 | 1,072.97 | 1,032.86 | 1,051.01 | 1,067.79 | 1,096.26 | 1,127.85 | 1,108.95 | 1,088.68 | 1,114.05 | 1,069.62 |
| **Education and Health Services** | | | | | | | | | | | | | |
| 2015 | 692.78 | 702.70 | 694.18 | 670.33 | 669.67 | 667.63 | 679.39 | 690.88 | 696.65 | 689.14 | 692.90 | 685.03 | 685.44 |
| 2016 | 661.85 | 669.71 | 663.88 | 660.10 | 663.08 | 641.19 | 642.79 | 644.59 | 641.34 | 664.00 | 647.57 | 653.00 | 655.16 |
| 2017 | 680.23 | 659.99 | 656.19 | 668.20 | 663.12 | 663.55 | 677.54 | 669.26 | 670.03 | 671.56 | 670.08 | 680.20 | 669.58 |
| 2018 | 688.64 | 680.39 | 684.61 | 692.26 | 683.80 | 676.04 | 700.30 | 679.83 | 687.49 | 669.60 | 678.60 | 704.70 | 685.25 |
| 2019 | 691.54 | 693.72 | 696.01 | 703.89 | 699.73 | 716.28 | 712.15 | 716.69 | 725.67 | 725.61 | 717.95 | 727.45 | 709.79 |
| **Leisure and Hospitality** | | | | | | | | | | | | | |
| 2015 | 312.20 | 331.69 | 331.95 | 313.49 | 325.13 | 326.51 | 334.10 | 337.77 | 330.17 | 331.99 | 327.92 | 331.27 | 328.12 |
| 2016 | 329.44 | 339.79 | 350.04 | 341.65 | 349.16 | 354.00 | 359.37 | 358.50 | 352.39 | 358.45 | 340.32 | 339.30 | 348.46 |
| 2017 | 339.77 | 336.15 | 349.59 | 344.90 | 337.95 | 340.96 | 349.11 | 344.52 | 332.52 | 347.60 | 331.26 | 339.30 | 341.32 |
| 2018 | 333.96 | 343.04 | 353.18 | 354.82 | 356.79 | 365.04 | 379.56 | 374.35 | 364.97 | 365.97 | 353.06 | 359.14 | 358.61 |
| 2019 | 347.89 | 349.02 | 367.85 | 353.69 | 357.16 | 371.54 | 367.22 | 370.21 | 371.27 | 370.66 | 368.53 | 377.02 | 364.62 |

# NEW YORK
## *At a Glance*

Population:
  2010 census: 19,378,102
  2019 estimate: 19,453,561

Percent change in population:
  2010–2019: 0.4%

Percent change in total nonfarm employment:
  2011–2019: 12.6%

Industry with the largest growth in employment, 2011–2019 (percent):
  Construction, 31.3%

Industry with the largest decline or smallest growth in employment, 2011–2019 (percent):
  Manufacturing, -4.3%

Civilian labor force:
  2010: 9,595,362
  2019:  9,514,378

Unemployment rate and rank among states (highest to lowest):
  2010: 8.6%, 27th
  2019: 4.0%, 13th

Over-the-year change in unemployment rates:
  2017–2018: -0.6%
  2018–2019: -0.1%

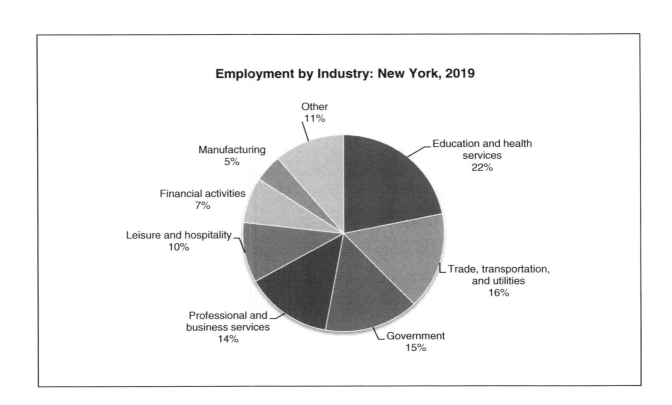

**Employment by Industry: New York, 2019**

- Other 11%
- Manufacturing 5%
- Financial activities 7%
- Leisure and hospitality 10%
- Professional and business services 14%
- Education and health services 22%
- Trade, transportation, and utilities 16%
- Government 15%

## 1. Employment by Industry: New York, 2011–2019

(Numbers in thousands, not seasonally adjusted)

| Industry and year | January | February | March | April | May | June | July | August | September | October | November | December | Annual average |
|---|---|---|---|---|---|---|---|---|---|---|---|---|---|
| **Total Nonfarm** | | | | | | | | | | | | | |
| 2011 | 8,462.4 | 8,525.4 | 8,570.4 | 8,686.4 | 8,718.0 | 8,741.1 | 8,692.8 | 8,660.3 | 8,713.7 | 8,811.4 | 8,850.3 | 8,868.2 | 8,691.7 |
| 2012 | 8,590.8 | 8,672.0 | 8,727.6 | 8,785.9 | 8,866.4 | 8,882.5 | 8,791.2 | 8,780.5 | 8,828.1 | 8,953.7 | 8,954.0 | 9,005.7 | 8,819.9 |
| 2013 | 8,693.8 | 8,770.3 | 8,829.0 | 8,922.8 | 8,978.0 | 9,001.9 | 8,948.7 | 8,925.2 | 8,981.4 | 9,108.3 | 9,155.0 | 9,164.6 | 8,956.6 |
| 2014 | 8,831.1 | 8,919.9 | 8,973.1 | 9,069.5 | 9,153.0 | 9,188.4 | 9,136.1 | 9,121.0 | 9,146.2 | 9,275.0 | 9,320.0 | 9,338.6 | 9,122.7 |
| 2015 | 9,019.1 | 9,090.0 | 9,136.5 | 9,231.1 | 9,325.4 | 9,357.7 | 9,318.9 | 9,288.5 | 9,302.2 | 9,446.2 | 9,489.2 | 9,498.9 | 9,292.0 |
| 2016 | 9,177.1 | 9,257.4 | 9,317.8 | 9,421.7 | 9,447.4 | 9,493.9 | 9,459.3 | 9,429.8 | 9,452.3 | 9,558.6 | 9,600.5 | 9,612.4 | 9,435.7 |
| 2017 | 9,306.9 | 9,396.1 | 9,432.6 | 9,499.9 | 9,584.0 | 9,639.7 | 9,574.2 | 9,551.9 | 9,571.5 | 9,689.0 | 9,737.3 | 9,747.6 | 9,560.9 |
| 2018 | 9,409.8 | 9,521.8 | 9,567.9 | 9,632.9 | 9,709.4 | 9,777.7 | 9,702.4 | 9,673.0 | 9,677.1 | 9,820.1 | 9,864.0 | 9,865.1 | 9,685.1 |
| 2019 | 9,556.2 | 9,645.4 | 9,698.3 | 9,784.5 | 9,829.1 | 9,875.2 | 9,802.8 | 9,767.8 | 9,777.6 | 9,878.7 | 9,918.8 | 9,892.1 | 9,785.5 |
| **Total Private** | | | | | | | | | | | | | |
| 2010 | 6,964.9 | 7,005.8 | 7,047.9 | 7,157.3 | 7,193.8 | 7,228.2 | 7,216.2 | 7,194.8 | 7,240.9 | 7,300.5 | 7,334.4 | 7,354.0 | 7,186.6 |
| 2011 | 7,122.6 | 7,170.6 | 7,223.2 | 7,281.6 | 7,358.1 | 7,386.3 | 7,340.3 | 7,347.2 | 7,376.3 | 7,462.1 | 7,461.6 | 7,507.4 | 7,336.4 |
| 2012 | 7,242.2 | 7,287.4 | 7,343.2 | 7,437.4 | 7,486.6 | 7,521.2 | 7,506.4 | 7,498.6 | 7,544.3 | 7,627.9 | 7,667.7 | 7,678.4 | 7,486.8 |
| 2013 | 7,396.6 | 7,450.0 | 7,498.4 | 7,589.9 | 7,672.2 | 7,714.6 | 7,698.4 | 7,696.5 | 7,707.2 | 7,797.4 | 7,833.8 | 7,853.3 | 7,659.0 |
| 2014 | 7,580.8 | 7,620.6 | 7,661.7 | 7,754.5 | 7,840.8 | 7,879.2 | 7,875.0 | 7,857.1 | 7,853.4 | 7,963.9 | 7,996.0 | 8,004.9 | 7,824.0 |
| 2015 | 7,726.3 | 7,777.9 | 7,830.9 | 7,930.9 | 7,957.3 | 8,008.5 | 8,007.3 | 7,988.8 | 7,992.1 | 8,067.7 | 8,102.6 | 8,110.0 | 7,958.4 |
| 2016 | 7,844.7 | 7,905.8 | 7,938.0 | 8,003.9 | 8,087.4 | 8,148.3 | 8,115.8 | 8,105.7 | 8,107.0 | 8,192.6 | 8,234.8 | 8,243.9 | 8,077.3 |
| 2017 | 7,949.5 | 8,031.2 | 8,073.3 | 8,139.3 | 8,209.5 | 8,275.4 | 8,240.0 | 8,222.2 | 8,205.9 | 8,322.1 | 8,352.5 | 8,356.7 | 8,198.1 |
| 2018 | 8,094.3 | 8,154.9 | 8,202.5 | 8,285.3 | 8,328.3 | 8,371.8 | 8,337.9 | 8,314.0 | 8,304.2 | 8,381.7 | 8,405.7 | 8,383.3 | 8,297.0 |
| 2019 | | | | | | | | | | | | | |
| **Goods Producing** | | | | | | | | | | | | | |
| 2011 | 729.3 | 726.9 | 736.8 | 757.8 | 774.3 | 788.1 | 796.7 | 802.1 | 796.6 | 793.5 | 788.1 | 776.4 | 772.2 |
| 2012 | 746.6 | 743.2 | 752.9 | 767.5 | 780.3 | 794.5 | 798.3 | 801.4 | 796.7 | 796.2 | 787.3 | 783.9 | 779.1 |
| 2013 | 755.2 | 749.7 | 757.8 | 776.3 | 792.2 | 801.4 | 806.9 | 811.9 | 806.3 | 808.9 | 803.3 | 790.0 | 788.3 |
| 2014 | 757.7 | 751.4 | 762.6 | 784.4 | 804.6 | 818.8 | 826.4 | 830.2 | 825.1 | 827.9 | 823.0 | 812.2 | 802.0 |
| 2015 | 777.1 | 770.5 | 782.3 | 806.8 | 826.9 | 839.6 | 847.0 | 849.1 | 841.8 | 847.2 | 842.4 | 832.1 | 821.9 |
| 2016 | 800.1 | 795.2 | 807.3 | 825.3 | 837.9 | 848.5 | 854.9 | 856.7 | 849.9 | 850.5 | 844.4 | 830.3 | 833.4 |
| 2017 | 802.2 | 801.5 | 807.5 | 825.9 | 841.7 | 854.3 | 858.5 | 860.5 | 855.4 | 856.8 | 852.6 | 840.5 | 838.1 |
| 2018 | 806.8 | 812.3 | 819.3 | 834.6 | 853.1 | 866.5 | 871.3 | 871.9 | 865.9 | 870.3 | 862.5 | 853.0 | 849.0 |
| 2019 | 823.7 | 824.0 | 829.5 | 846.4 | 857.1 | 867.0 | 870.0 | 870.4 | 862.9 | 855.0 | 849.8 | 835.2 | 849.3 |
| **Service-Providing** | | | | | | | | | | | | | |
| 2011 | 7,733.1 | 7,798.5 | 7,833.6 | 7,928.6 | 7,943.7 | 7,953.0 | 7,896.1 | 7,858.2 | 7,917.1 | 8,017.9 | 8,062.2 | 8,091.8 | 7,919.5 |
| 2012 | 7,844.2 | 7,928.8 | 7,974.7 | 8,018.4 | 8,086.1 | 8,088.0 | 7,992.9 | 7,979.1 | 8,031.4 | 8,157.5 | 8,166.7 | 8,221.8 | 8,040.8 |
| 2013 | 7,938.6 | 8,020.6 | 8,071.2 | 8,146.5 | 8,185.8 | 8,200.5 | 8,141.8 | 8,113.3 | 8,175.1 | 8,299.4 | 8,351.7 | 8,374.6 | 8,168.3 |
| 2014 | 8,073.4 | 8,168.5 | 8,210.5 | 8,285.1 | 8,348.4 | 8,369.6 | 8,309.7 | 8,290.8 | 8,321.1 | 8,447.1 | 8,497.0 | 8,526.4 | 8,320.6 |
| 2015 | 8,242.0 | 8,319.5 | 8,354.2 | 8,424.3 | 8,498.5 | 8,518.1 | 8,471.9 | 8,439.4 | 8,460.4 | 8,599.0 | 8,646.8 | 8,666.8 | 8,470.1 |
| 2016 | 8,377.0 | 8,462.2 | 8,510.5 | 8,596.4 | 8,609.5 | 8,645.4 | 8,604.4 | 8,573.1 | 8,602.4 | 8,708.1 | 8,756.1 | 8,782.1 | 8,602.3 |
| 2017 | 8,504.7 | 8,594.6 | 8,625.1 | 8,674.0 | 8,742.3 | 8,785.4 | 8,715.7 | 8,691.4 | 8,716.1 | 8,832.2 | 8,884.7 | 8,907.1 | 8,722.8 |
| 2018 | 8,603.0 | 8,709.5 | 8,748.6 | 8,798.3 | 8,856.3 | 8,911.2 | 8,831.1 | 8,801.1 | 8,811.2 | 8,949.8 | 9,001.5 | 9,012.1 | 8,836.1 |
| 2019 | 8,732.5 | 8,821.4 | 8,868.8 | 8,938.1 | 8,972.0 | 9,008.2 | 8,932.8 | 8,897.4 | 8,914.7 | 9,023.7 | 9,069.0 | 9,056.9 | 8,936.3 |
| **Mining and Logging** | | | | | | | | | | | | | |
| 2011 | 4.3 | 4.4 | 4.5 | 5.1 | 5.4 | 5.6 | 5.7 | 5.8 | 5.8 | 5.8 | 5.6 | 5.4 | 5.3 |
| 2012 | 4.5 | 4.6 | 4.9 | 5.3 | 5.5 | 5.6 | 5.7 | 5.6 | 5.6 | 5.6 | 5.3 | 5.0 | 5.3 |
| 2013 | 4.3 | 4.3 | 4.5 | 5.0 | 5.4 | 5.3 | 5.3 | 5.3 | 5.4 | 5.5 | 5.3 | 5.0 | 5.1 |
| 2014 | 4.4 | 4.5 | 4.6 | 5.0 | 5.4 | 5.6 | 5.7 | 5.7 | 5.6 | 5.7 | 5.5 | 5.2 | 5.2 |
| 2015 | 4.6 | 4.6 | 4.7 | 5.1 | 5.5 | 5.7 | 5.8 | 5.7 | 5.7 | 5.6 | 5.5 | 5.3 | 5.3 |
| 2016 | 4.4 | 4.5 | 4.7 | 5.0 | 5.3 | 5.5 | 5.5 | 5.5 | 5.4 | 5.2 | 5.2 | 4.8 | 5.1 |
| 2017 | 4.2 | 4.4 | 4.5 | 4.8 | 5.1 | 5.2 | 5.4 | 5.4 | 5.3 | 5.4 | 5.3 | 5.1 | 5.0 |
| 2018 | 4.6 | 4.7 | 4.8 | 5.2 | 5.5 | 5.7 | 5.8 | 5.8 | 5.8 | 5.7 | 5.6 | 5.2 | 5.4 |
| 2019 | 4.7 | 4.8 | 4.8 | 5.2 | 5.5 | 5.6 | 5.6 | 5.6 | 5.6 | 5.6 | 5.5 | 5.1 | 5.3 |
| **Construction** | | | | | | | | | | | | | |
| 2011 | 273.6 | 270.8 | 279.1 | 296.1 | 310.1 | 319.6 | 329.8 | 333.6 | 328.8 | 325.9 | 321.4 | 310.2 | 308.3 |
| 2012 | 288.1 | 284.0 | 291.7 | 305.5 | 315.0 | 325.0 | 330.6 | 333.3 | 328.8 | 328.9 | 323.4 | 320.0 | 314.5 |
| 2013 | 299.1 | 294.4 | 300.7 | 316.5 | 330.1 | 336.3 | 344.1 | 347.4 | 342.8 | 345.5 | 340.4 | 327.5 | 327.1 |
| 2014 | 304.1 | 298.3 | 308.5 | 328.7 | 346.2 | 355.8 | 365.2 | 367.6 | 364.0 | 366.4 | 361.8 | 351.2 | 343.2 |
| 2015 | 323.7 | 316.7 | 326.2 | 349.3 | 366.9 | 375.2 | 382.2 | 384.7 | 378.9 | 383.6 | 379.7 | 370.2 | 361.4 |
| 2016 | 345.7 | 340.3 | 351.1 | 370.0 | 381.7 | 388.7 | 395.6 | 398.2 | 393.4 | 393.3 | 388.9 | 375.8 | 376.9 |
| 2017 | 355.5 | 353.8 | 358.4 | 377.5 | 391.5 | 400.2 | 405.9 | 408.3 | 404.9 | 405.4 | 401.8 | 390.5 | 387.8 |
| 2018 | 364.2 | 368.3 | 374.3 | 389.2 | 405.6 | 414.8 | 419.5 | 420.2 | 416.6 | 419.9 | 412.6 | 404.1 | 400.8 |
| 2019 | 381.2 | 381.0 | 386.4 | 401.8 | 411.3 | 417.8 | 422.6 | 423.7 | 418.7 | 413.1 | 406.0 | 392.9 | 404.7 |

# 1. Employment by Industry: New York, 2011–2019—*Continued*

(Numbers in thousands, not seasonally adjusted)

| Industry and year | January | February | March | April | May | June | July | August | September | October | November | December | Annual average |
|---|---|---|---|---|---|---|---|---|---|---|---|---|---|
| **Manufacturing** | | | | | | | | | | | | | |
| 2011 | 451.4 | 451.7 | 453.2 | 456.6 | 458.8 | 462.9 | 461.2 | 462.7 | 462.0 | 461.8 | 461.1 | 460.8 | 458.7 |
| 2012 | 454.0 | 454.6 | 456.3 | 456.7 | 459.8 | 463.9 | 462.0 | 462.5 | 462.3 | 461.7 | 458.6 | 458.9 | 459.3 |
| 2013 | 451.8 | 451.0 | 452.6 | 454.8 | 456.7 | 459.8 | 457.5 | 459.2 | 458.1 | 457.9 | 457.6 | 457.5 | 456.2 |
| 2014 | 449.2 | 448.6 | 449.5 | 450.7 | 453.0 | 457.4 | 455.5 | 456.9 | 455.5 | 455.8 | 455.7 | 455.8 | 453.6 |
| 2015 | 448.8 | 449.2 | 451.4 | 452.4 | 454.5 | 458.7 | 459.0 | 458.7 | 457.2 | 458.0 | 457.2 | 456.6 | 455.1 |
| 2016 | 450.0 | 450.4 | 451.5 | 450.3 | 450.9 | 454.3 | 453.8 | 453.0 | 451.1 | 452.0 | 450.3 | 449.7 | 451.4 |
| 2017 | 442.5 | 443.3 | 444.6 | 443.6 | 445.1 | 448.9 | 447.2 | 446.8 | 445.2 | 446.0 | 445.5 | 444.9 | 445.3 |
| 2018 | 438.0 | 439.3 | 440.2 | 440.2 | 442.0 | 446.0 | 446.0 | 445.9 | 443.5 | 444.7 | 444.3 | 443.7 | 442.8 |
| 2019 | 437.8 | 438.2 | 438.3 | 439.4 | 440.3 | 443.6 | 441.8 | 441.1 | 438.6 | 436.3 | 438.3 | 437.2 | 439.2 |
| **Trade, Transportation, and Utilities** | | | | | | | | | | | | | |
| 2011 | 1,464.5 | 1,447.3 | 1,449.5 | 1,461.7 | 1,474.2 | 1,493.9 | 1,474.5 | 1,478.4 | 1,488.3 | 1,500.9 | 1,531.5 | 1,554.5 | 1,484.9 |
| 2012 | 1,494.5 | 1,474.2 | 1,478.9 | 1,481.3 | 1,503.0 | 1,520.2 | 1,492.1 | 1,497.2 | 1,508.5 | 1,523.3 | 1,553.1 | 1,574.4 | 1,508.4 |
| 2013 | 1,501.9 | 1,478.8 | 1,489.2 | 1,500.6 | 1,516.4 | 1,536.9 | 1,522.6 | 1,520.0 | 1,532.8 | 1,547.6 | 1,585.0 | 1,604.1 | 1,528.0 |
| 2014 | 1,531.6 | 1,513.4 | 1,517.9 | 1,529.6 | 1,545.3 | 1,563.6 | 1,547.3 | 1,547.5 | 1,556.3 | 1,574.0 | 1,607.2 | 1,627.5 | 1,555.1 |
| 2015 | 1,555.8 | 1,535.7 | 1,537.0 | 1,544.4 | 1,564.3 | 1,581.3 | 1,562.1 | 1,560.6 | 1,567.6 | 1,580.6 | 1,612.5 | 1,627.7 | 1,569.1 |
| 2016 | 1,557.5 | 1,540.8 | 1,543.2 | 1,553.7 | 1,561.2 | 1,576.3 | 1,558.1 | 1,554.8 | 1,563.7 | 1,579.1 | 1,609.5 | 1,627.3 | 1,568.8 |
| 2017 | 1,562.3 | 1,540.0 | 1,540.5 | 1,544.5 | 1,562.7 | 1,577.2 | 1,558.1 | 1,554.7 | 1,563.3 | 1,576.6 | 1,612.1 | 1,628.9 | 1,568.4 |
| 2018 | 1,559.8 | 1,540.9 | 1,539.5 | 1,544.9 | 1,560.2 | 1,574.1 | 1,553.6 | 1,547.9 | 1,555.0 | 1,570.1 | 1,606.7 | 1,620.0 | 1,564.4 |
| 2019 | 1,555.4 | 1,531.2 | 1,533.0 | 1,538.8 | 1,548.0 | 1,563.2 | 1,543.0 | 1,534.3 | 1,542.2 | 1,554.7 | 1,581.9 | 1,593.7 | 1,551.6 |
| **Wholesale Trade** | | | | | | | | | | | | | |
| 2011 | 322.1 | 321.6 | 323.0 | 325.6 | 327.4 | 330.1 | 330.2 | 330.6 | 329.2 | 330.0 | 330.0 | 331.6 | 327.6 |
| 2012 | 326.7 | 327.4 | 328.6 | 329.6 | 331.1 | 333.6 | 332.7 | 332.3 | 330.4 | 332.5 | 332.1 | 333.8 | 330.9 |
| 2013 | 328.1 | 328.2 | 328.9 | 330.7 | 332.1 | 335.3 | 335.5 | 334.9 | 333.5 | 333.6 | 334.6 | 335.9 | 332.6 |
| 2014 | 330.7 | 330.2 | 330.5 | 332.9 | 334.9 | 337.2 | 337.3 | 337.2 | 335.5 | 336.8 | 338.2 | 339.3 | 335.1 |
| 2015 | 334.1 | 333.6 | 334.4 | 334.9 | 337.0 | 339.5 | 339.9 | 339.3 | 337.2 | 338.2 | 338.5 | 339.8 | 337.2 |
| 2016 | 333.4 | 333.5 | 333.1 | 333.5 | 334.1 | 336.1 | 336.1 | 335.4 | 333.2 | 333.9 | 334.2 | 335.2 | 334.3 |
| 2017 | 329.3 | 329.7 | 330.2 | 332.4 | 334.2 | 336.8 | 336.0 | 335.3 | 334.2 | 333.9 | 334.7 | 335.5 | 333.5 |
| 2018 | 328.6 | 328.7 | 329.4 | 329.0 | 330.4 | 332.8 | 332.9 | 331.5 | 329.6 | 330.3 | 331.1 | 331.8 | 330.5 |
| 2019 | 326.1 | 325.9 | 326.6 | 326.6 | 327.5 | 329.9 | 329.3 | 327.8 | 326.1 | 323.6 | 324.5 | 323.4 | 326.4 |
| **Retail Trade** | | | | | | | | | | | | | |
| 2011 | 877.8 | 863.1 | 863.2 | 873.4 | 881.5 | 895.7 | 892.8 | 897.0 | 892.3 | 904.5 | 932.1 | 949.1 | 893.5 |
| 2012 | 905.6 | 885.4 | 887.6 | 891.1 | 905.0 | 916.7 | 912.0 | 912.7 | 908.9 | 921.3 | 949.8 | 962.0 | 913.2 |
| 2013 | 908.9 | 892.7 | 896.3 | 903.4 | 915.2 | 930.1 | 929.4 | 930.6 | 926.1 | 938.2 | 971.3 | 984.6 | 927.2 |
| 2014 | 927.7 | 912.4 | 914.5 | 921.4 | 931.0 | 945.5 | 942.9 | 945.5 | 939.1 | 953.1 | 980.8 | 993.9 | 942.3 |
| 2015 | 939.9 | 922.9 | 923.1 | 928.1 | 941.1 | 953.0 | 948.1 | 948.1 | 941.6 | 952.0 | 979.4 | 986.4 | 947.0 |
| 2016 | 937.0 | 922.0 | 923.1 | 931.0 | 936.8 | 947.6 | 945.4 | 944.9 | 938.3 | 951.2 | 977.0 | 986.1 | 945.0 |
| 2017 | 940.5 | 919.9 | 918.5 | 924.5 | 934.5 | 943.7 | 940.2 | 938.4 | 930.3 | 942.5 | 970.9 | 979.4 | 940.3 |
| 2018 | 933.6 | 918.1 | 915.6 | 918.7 | 929.1 | 937.4 | 932.4 | 930.0 | 920.7 | 929.3 | 959.2 | 963.8 | 932.3 |
| 2019 | 920.2 | 900.7 | 901.8 | 906.4 | 912.2 | 920.8 | 915.7 | 912.2 | 903.3 | 914.2 | 936.5 | 943.3 | 915.6 |
| **Transportation and Utilities** | | | | | | | | | | | | | |
| 2011 | 264.6 | 262.6 | 263.3 | 262.7 | 265.3 | 268.1 | 251.5 | 250.8 | 266.8 | 266.4 | 269.4 | 273.8 | 263.8 |
| 2012 | 262.2 | 261.4 | 262.7 | 260.6 | 266.9 | 269.9 | 247.4 | 252.2 | 269.2 | 269.5 | 271.2 | 278.6 | 264.3 |
| 2013 | 264.9 | 257.9 | 264.0 | 266.5 | 269.1 | 271.5 | 257.7 | 254.5 | 273.2 | 275.8 | 279.1 | 283.6 | 268.2 |
| 2014 | 273.2 | 270.8 | 272.9 | 275.3 | 279.4 | 280.9 | 267.1 | 264.8 | 281.7 | 284.1 | 288.2 | 294.3 | 277.7 |
| 2015 | 281.8 | 279.2 | 279.5 | 281.4 | 286.2 | 288.8 | 274.1 | 273.2 | 288.8 | 290.4 | 294.6 | 301.5 | 285.0 |
| 2016 | 287.1 | 285.3 | 287.0 | 289.2 | 290.3 | 292.6 | 276.6 | 274.5 | 292.2 | 294.0 | 298.3 | 306.0 | 289.4 |
| 2017 | 292.5 | 290.4 | 291.8 | 287.6 | 294.0 | 296.7 | 281.9 | 281.0 | 298.8 | 300.2 | 306.5 | 314.0 | 294.6 |
| 2018 | 297.6 | 294.1 | 294.5 | 297.2 | 300.7 | 303.9 | 288.3 | 286.4 | 304.7 | 310.5 | 316.4 | 324.4 | 301.6 |
| 2019 | 309.1 | 304.6 | 304.6 | 305.8 | 308.3 | 312.5 | 298.0 | 294.3 | 312.8 | 316.9 | 320.9 | 327.0 | 309.6 |
| **Information** | | | | | | | | | | | | | |
| 2011 | 252.0 | 252.8 | 254.1 | 256.5 | 256.8 | 258.3 | 259.3 | 244.1 | 258.8 | 257.9 | 258.9 | 260.1 | 255.8 |
| 2012 | 255.2 | 256.1 | 256.8 | 258.8 | 261.0 | 262.6 | 260.4 | 260.1 | 258.9 | 260.5 | 261.4 | 261.7 | 259.5 |
| 2013 | 253.8 | 255.3 | 256.8 | 258.8 | 260.6 | 263.1 | 262.8 | 264.2 | 263.5 | 265.6 | 267.3 | 268.0 | 261.7 |
| 2014 | 260.1 | 263.3 | 264.2 | 262.6 | 263.2 | 267.2 | 265.2 | 266.3 | 264.1 | 267.1 | 267.2 | 269.3 | 265.0 |
| 2015 | 261.8 | 263.2 | 263.5 | 262.9 | 263.8 | 265.9 | 268.5 | 267.0 | 266.0 | 270.4 | 271.4 | 272.5 | 266.4 |
| 2016 | 262.3 | 263.4 | 265.0 | 266.9 | 255.4 | 269.0 | 273.9 | 272.9 | 271.0 | 272.7 | 273.6 | 275.0 | 268.4 |
| 2017 | 264.5 | 268.0 | 269.0 | 266.4 | 268.1 | 272.3 | 274.1 | 276.5 | 276.1 | 277.0 | 279.4 | 280.4 | 272.7 |
| 2018 | 265.3 | 272.9 | 275.5 | 270.7 | 272.7 | 279.0 | 277.0 | 278.0 | 275.2 | 279.0 | 281.3 | 278.4 | 275.4 |
| 2019 | 268.8 | 273.2 | 276.0 | 277.0 | 279.1 | 281.1 | 280.2 | 282.7 | 279.5 | 278.6 | 284.1 | 278.7 | 278.3 |

## 1. Employment by Industry: New York, 2011–2019—*Continued*

(Numbers in thousands, not seasonally adjusted)

| Industry and year | January | February | March | April | May | June | July | August | September | October | November | December | Annual average |
|---|---|---|---|---|---|---|---|---|---|---|---|---|---|
| **Financial Activities** | | | | | | | | | | | | | |
| 2011 | 671.4 | 672.1 | 673.5 | 675.4 | 676.9 | 687.5 | 692.3 | 693.5 | 683.9 | 682.8 | 682.9 | 686.0 | 681.5 |
| 2012 | 676.5 | 678.1 | 677.6 | 676.9 | 678.2 | 688.1 | 690.7 | 689.7 | 679.7 | 682.5 | 682.0 | 686.9 | 682.2 |
| 2013 | 671.1 | 673.0 | 672.7 | 674.6 | 675.5 | 685.6 | 690.6 | 689.4 | 680.3 | 682.5 | 684.9 | 689.6 | 680.8 |
| 2014 | 679.1 | 680.9 | 682.6 | 682.5 | 686.4 | 699.1 | 703.9 | 703.6 | 693.9 | 696.0 | 697.5 | 702.8 | 692.4 |
| 2015 | 692.7 | 693.7 | 694.8 | 695.8 | 699.1 | 711.0 | 716.6 | 716.1 | 705.4 | 709.1 | 710.0 | 713.1 | 704.8 |
| 2016 | 705.4 | 706.0 | 706.3 | 705.9 | 708.7 | 719.1 | 723.5 | 723.6 | 710.2 | 711.0 | 712.4 | 716.9 | 712.4 |
| 2017 | 705.6 | 707.2 | 708.1 | 705.7 | 709.0 | 722.7 | 726.5 | 726.7 | 715.1 | 716.6 | 718.2 | 722.2 | 715.3 |
| 2018 | 710.4 | 713.4 | 712.8 | 711.4 | 714.3 | 728.6 | 733.5 | 732.4 | 720.1 | 723.7 | 725.1 | 726.8 | 721.0 |
| 2019 | 719.0 | 721.0 | 720.7 | 721.4 | 723.6 | 735.7 | 741.0 | 740.8 | 727.1 | 729.4 | 728.3 | 728.4 | 728.0 |
| **Professional and Business Services** | | | | | | | | | | | | | |
| 2011 | 1,093.1 | 1,098.8 | 1,107.3 | 1,130.9 | 1,131.4 | 1,149.5 | 1,155.5 | 1,154.2 | 1,149.6 | 1,150.7 | 1,157.3 | 1,157.6 | 1,136.3 |
| 2012 | 1,127.4 | 1,133.4 | 1,144.7 | 1,160.5 | 1,166.5 | 1,184.1 | 1,184.6 | 1,187.4 | 1,180.1 | 1,193.9 | 1,196.8 | 1,199.6 | 1,171.6 |
| 2013 | 1,162.6 | 1,168.9 | 1,177.8 | 1,194.6 | 1,198.6 | 1,214.9 | 1,220.7 | 1,219.5 | 1,209.9 | 1,221.8 | 1,224.8 | 1,225.0 | 1,203.3 |
| 2014 | 1,184.6 | 1,193.2 | 1,198.4 | 1,220.6 | 1,229.4 | 1,243.2 | 1,250.6 | 1,251.5 | 1,240.6 | 1,251.8 | 1,258.4 | 1,259.4 | 1,231.8 |
| 2015 | 1,223.6 | 1,230.4 | 1,234.4 | 1,256.8 | 1,266.5 | 1,284.4 | 1,291.2 | 1,288.6 | 1,275.2 | 1,290.4 | 1,293.2 | 1,290.5 | 1,268.8 |
| 2016 | 1,253.3 | 1,259.1 | 1,268.0 | 1,287.6 | 1,289.9 | 1,307.2 | 1,316.2 | 1,313.9 | 1,306.1 | 1,313.5 | 1,318.1 | 1,314.2 | 1,295.6 |
| 2017 | 1,275.9 | 1,285.2 | 1,290.0 | 1,305.0 | 1,314.4 | 1,335.4 | 1,338.5 | 1,334.5 | 1,326.6 | 1,331.5 | 1,338.4 | 1,338.2 | 1,317.8 |
| 2018 | 1,297.2 | 1,307.3 | 1,315.5 | 1,329.5 | 1,340.0 | 1,364.6 | 1,367.0 | 1,366.0 | 1,351.2 | 1,363.5 | 1,370.3 | 1,367.2 | 1,344.9 |
| 2019 | 1,328.9 | 1,338.3 | 1,346.5 | 1,368.8 | 1,372.0 | 1,392.5 | 1,396.1 | 1,393.8 | 1,378.3 | 1,397.8 | 1,394.7 | 1,390.7 | 1,374.9 |
| **Education and Health Services** | | | | | | | | | | | | | |
| 2011 | 1,689.0 | 1,731.9 | 1,738.8 | 1,752.9 | 1,726.7 | 1,668.4 | 1,644.1 | 1,633.5 | 1,695.8 | 1,755.8 | 1,766.0 | 1,771.1 | 1,714.5 |
| 2012 | 1,718.4 | 1,764.6 | 1,775.9 | 1,778.5 | 1,768.5 | 1,704.7 | 1,675.8 | 1,672.7 | 1,740.8 | 1,799.6 | 1,800.5 | 1,812.8 | 1,751.1 |
| 2013 | 1,758.4 | 1,808.7 | 1,820.1 | 1,832.0 | 1,802.2 | 1,745.6 | 1,718.8 | 1,715.9 | 1,799.6 | 1,849.2 | 1,862.3 | 1,863.7 | 1,798.0 |
| 2014 | 1,797.4 | 1,848.0 | 1,860.5 | 1,868.6 | 1,853.8 | 1,807.8 | 1,781.7 | 1,781.2 | 1,837.2 | 1,892.4 | 1,906.6 | 1,908.5 | 1,845.3 |
| 2015 | 1,847.4 | 1,894.7 | 1,905.0 | 1,913.8 | 1,897.9 | 1,850.9 | 1,828.5 | 1,821.8 | 1,869.2 | 1,943.4 | 1,959.4 | 1,962.9 | 1,891.2 |
| 2016 | 1,898.2 | 1,950.9 | 1,962.5 | 1,977.4 | 1,959.3 | 1,913.5 | 1,889.6 | 1,884.3 | 1,937.2 | 1,997.6 | 2,012.9 | 2,018.0 | 1,950.1 |
| 2017 | 1,954.0 | 2,011.0 | 2,019.7 | 2,023.5 | 2,012.0 | 1,971.1 | 1,937.1 | 1,932.9 | 1,986.6 | 2,054.9 | 2,070.1 | 2,073.0 | 2,003.8 |
| 2018 | 2,008.0 | 2,070.7 | 2,081.6 | 2,095.4 | 2,079.0 | 2,033.9 | 2,006.0 | 2,001.8 | 2,050.4 | 2,129.7 | 2,142.0 | 2,145.5 | 2,070.3 |
| 2019 | 2,087.4 | 2,147.1 | 2,163.3 | 2,172.1 | 2,154.4 | 2,105.9 | 2,074.0 | 2,067.1 | 2,125.7 | 2,185.5 | 2,200.5 | 2,196.7 | 2,140.0 |
| **Leisure and Hospitality** | | | | | | | | | | | | | |
| 2011 | 704.0 | 712.6 | 722.7 | 751.6 | 780.0 | 807.7 | 820.6 | 818.0 | 795.5 | 785.5 | 775.8 | 773.0 | 770.6 |
| 2012 | 734.7 | 750.2 | 762.6 | 782.5 | 820.9 | 849.3 | 858.7 | 861.0 | 833.0 | 824.1 | 800.3 | 805.8 | 806.9 |
| 2013 | 764.1 | 776.0 | 790.1 | 818.2 | 855.8 | 886.2 | 897.1 | 891.2 | 867.3 | 863.3 | 850.2 | 847.4 | 842.2 |
| 2014 | 802.8 | 814.2 | 824.8 | 850.2 | 893.9 | 918.6 | 927.4 | 921.6 | 896.7 | 890.5 | 875.1 | 874.1 | 874.2 |
| 2015 | 829.9 | 838.8 | 849.5 | 876.4 | 920.5 | 941.6 | 957.8 | 951.4 | 927.9 | 917.2 | 901.0 | 898.9 | 900.9 |
| 2016 | 850.6 | 860.9 | 875.6 | 906.1 | 934.2 | 963.5 | 980.1 | 973.5 | 945.7 | 932.0 | 920.1 | 917.4 | 921.6 |
| 2017 | 876.2 | 888.6 | 897.7 | 923.6 | 966.3 | 999.3 | 1,009.2 | 1,008.6 | 973.5 | 964.8 | 949.5 | 945.8 | 950.3 |
| 2018 | 896.3 | 905.7 | 918.8 | 940.2 | 974.6 | 1,010.5 | 1,015.8 | 1,010.2 | 976.7 | 968.4 | 947.6 | 949.3 | 959.5 |
| 2019 | 902.8 | 909.1 | 922.1 | 945.4 | 977.0 | 1,007.8 | 1,016.3 | 1,009.5 | 975.9 | 963.2 | 947.7 | 942.5 | 959.9 |
| **Other Services** | | | | | | | | | | | | | |
| 2011 | 361.6 | 363.4 | 365.2 | 370.5 | 373.5 | 374.8 | 373.2 | 371.0 | 372.4 | 373.4 | 373.9 | 375.3 | 370.7 |
| 2012 | 369.3 | 370.8 | 373.8 | 375.6 | 379.7 | 382.8 | 379.7 | 377.7 | 378.6 | 382.0 | 380.2 | 382.3 | 377.7 |
| 2013 | 375.1 | 377.0 | 378.7 | 382.3 | 385.3 | 387.5 | 386.9 | 386.5 | 384.6 | 389.0 | 389.9 | 390.6 | 384.5 |
| 2014 | 383.3 | 385.6 | 387.4 | 391.4 | 395.6 | 396.3 | 395.9 | 394.6 | 393.3 | 397.7 | 398.8 | 399.5 | 393.3 |
| 2015 | 392.5 | 393.6 | 395.2 | 397.6 | 401.8 | 404.5 | 403.3 | 402.5 | 400.3 | 405.6 | 406.1 | 407.2 | 400.9 |
| 2016 | 398.9 | 401.6 | 403.0 | 408.0 | 410.7 | 411.4 | 411.0 | 409.1 | 408.3 | 411.3 | 411.6 | 410.9 | 408.0 |
| 2017 | 404.0 | 404.3 | 405.5 | 409.3 | 413.2 | 416.0 | 413.8 | 411.3 | 410.4 | 414.4 | 414.5 | 414.9 | 411.0 |
| 2018 | 405.7 | 408.0 | 410.3 | 412.6 | 415.6 | 418.2 | 415.8 | 414.0 | 411.4 | 417.4 | 417.0 | 416.5 | 413.5 |
| 2019 | 408.3 | 411.0 | 411.4 | 415.4 | 417.1 | 418.6 | 417.3 | 415.4 | 412.6 | 417.5 | 418.7 | 417.4 | 415.1 |
| **Government** | | | | | | | | | | | | | |
| 2011 | 1,497.5 | 1,519.6 | 1,522.5 | 1,529.1 | 1,524.2 | 1,512.9 | 1,476.6 | 1,465.5 | 1,472.8 | 1,510.9 | 1,515.9 | 1,514.2 | 1,505.1 |
| 2012 | 1,468.2 | 1,501.4 | 1,504.4 | 1,504.3 | 1,508.3 | 1,496.2 | 1,450.9 | 1,433.3 | 1,451.8 | 1,491.6 | 1,492.4 | 1,498.3 | 1,483.4 |
| 2013 | 1,451.6 | 1,482.9 | 1,485.8 | 1,485.4 | 1,491.4 | 1,480.7 | 1,442.3 | 1,426.6 | 1,437.1 | 1,480.4 | 1,487.3 | 1,486.2 | 1,469.8 |
| 2014 | 1,434.5 | 1,469.9 | 1,474.7 | 1,479.6 | 1,480.8 | 1,473.8 | 1,437.7 | 1,424.5 | 1,439.0 | 1,477.6 | 1,486.2 | 1,485.3 | 1,463.6 |
| 2015 | 1,438.3 | 1,469.4 | 1,474.8 | 1,476.6 | 1,484.6 | 1,478.5 | 1,443.9 | 1,431.4 | 1,448.8 | 1,482.3 | 1,493.2 | 1,494.0 | 1,468.0 |
| 2016 | 1,450.8 | 1,479.5 | 1,486.9 | 1,490.8 | 1,490.1 | 1,485.4 | 1,452.0 | 1,441.0 | 1,460.2 | 1,490.9 | 1,497.9 | 1,502.4 | 1,477.3 |
| 2017 | 1,462.2 | 1,490.3 | 1,494.6 | 1,496.0 | 1,496.6 | 1,491.4 | 1,458.4 | 1,446.2 | 1,464.5 | 1,496.4 | 1,502.5 | 1,503.7 | 1,483.6 |
| 2018 | 1,460.3 | 1,490.6 | 1,494.6 | 1,493.6 | 1,499.9 | 1,502.3 | 1,462.4 | 1,450.8 | 1,471.2 | 1,498.0 | 1,511.5 | 1,508.4 | 1,487.0 |
| 2019 | 1,461.9 | 1,490.5 | 1,495.8 | 1,499.2 | 1,500.8 | 1,503.4 | 1,464.9 | 1,453.8 | 1,473.4 | 1,497.0 | 1,513.1 | 1,508.8 | 1,488.6 |

## 2. Average Weekly Hours by Selected Industry: New York, 2015–2019

(Not seasonally adjusted)

| Industry and year | January | February | March | April | May | June | July | August | September | October | November | December | Annual average |
|---|---|---|---|---|---|---|---|---|---|---|---|---|---|
| **Total Private** | | | | | | | | | | | | | |
| 2015 | 33.5 | 33.7 | 33.8 | 33.5 | 33.7 | 33.7 | 33.8 | 34.2 | 33.7 | 33.7 | 34.0 | 33.7 | 33.8 |
| 2016 | 33.4 | 33.2 | 33.3 | 33.3 | 33.6 | 33.5 | 33.7 | 33.8 | 33.7 | 33.8 | 33.5 | 33.6 | 33.5 |
| 2017 | 33.5 | 33.1 | 32.8 | 33.5 | 33.3 | 33.4 | 33.7 | 33.5 | 33.4 | 33.7 | 33.4 | 33.4 | 33.4 |
| 2018 | 32.9 | 33.0 | 32.9 | 33.4 | 33.2 | 33.3 | 33.6 | 33.4 | 33.6 | 33.2 | 33.0 | 33.6 | 33.3 |
| 2019 | 32.9 | 32.9 | 32.9 | 32.9 | 32.9 | 33.3 | 33.1 | 33.2 | 33.4 | 32.8 | 32.9 | 33.2 | 33.0 |
| **Goods-Producing** | | | | | | | | | | | | | |
| 2015 | 38.7 | 38.0 | 38.8 | 38.9 | 39.3 | 39.1 | 39.1 | 39.0 | 38.2 | 38.9 | 38.8 | 39.0 | 38.8 |
| 2016 | 38.5 | 37.7 | 38.7 | 38.5 | 38.7 | 38.8 | 38.7 | 38.4 | 38.5 | 38.2 | 37.8 | 37.8 | 38.4 |
| 2017 | 37.4 | 36.9 | 36.4 | 37.8 | 38.2 | 38.4 | 38.0 | 38.3 | 38.7 | 38.6 | 38.5 | 38.4 | 38.0 |
| 2018 | 37.7 | 37.9 | 37.7 | 38.4 | 38.6 | 38.8 | 38.7 | 38.5 | 38.2 | 38.6 | 37.9 | 38.9 | 38.3 |
| 2019 | 37.7 | 37.6 | 38.0 | 38.2 | 38.3 | 38.4 | 38.3 | 38.6 | 38.7 | 38.1 | 38.0 | 38.6 | 38.2 |
| **Construction** | | | | | | | | | | | | | |
| 2015 | 36.6 | 35.6 | 37.1 | 37.5 | 38.6 | 38.2 | 38.6 | 38.5 | 37.3 | 38.1 | 37.8 | 38.3 | 37.7 |
| 2016 | 37.5 | 35.9 | 38.0 | 37.6 | 37.9 | 38.1 | 37.9 | 37.7 | 37.9 | 37.0 | 36.4 | 36.7 | 37.4 |
| 2017 | 36.0 | 35.2 | 34.7 | 36.5 | 37.1 | 37.3 | 37.0 | 37.5 | 37.7 | 37.4 | 37.1 | 37.3 | 36.8 |
| 2018 | 36.3 | 36.9 | 36.3 | 37.2 | 37.8 | 38.1 | 38.0 | 37.7 | 37.4 | 38.2 | 36.9 | 38.4 | 37.5 |
| 2019 | 37.6 | 37.5 | 38.1 | 38.1 | 38.2 | 38.0 | 38.0 | 38.1 | 38.2 | 37.4 | 37.1 | 37.3 | 37.8 |
| **Manufacturing** | | | | | | | | | | | | | |
| 2015 | 40.1 | 39.6 | 39.9 | 39.7 | 39.7 | 39.7 | 39.3 | 39.2 | 38.7 | 39.3 | 39.4 | 39.4 | 39.5 |
| 2016 | 39.2 | 38.9 | 39.1 | 39.1 | 39.3 | 39.3 | 39.3 | 38.9 | 38.9 | 39.2 | 39.0 | 38.8 | 39.1 |
| 2017 | 38.6 | 38.3 | 37.9 | 38.4 | 38.7 | 38.8 | 38.3 | 38.5 | 39.1 | 39.3 | 39.4 | 39.2 | 38.7 |
| 2018 | 38.8 | 38.6 | 38.9 | 39.4 | 39.2 | 39.3 | 39.2 | 39.1 | 38.8 | 38.8 | 39.1 | 39.5 | 39.1 |
| 2019 | 38.0 | 38.0 | 38.3 | 38.6 | 38.6 | 39.1 | 38.9 | 39.4 | 39.6 | 39.0 | 39.1 | 40.0 | 38.9 |
| **Trade, Transportation, and Utilities** | | | | | | | | | | | | | |
| 2015 | 34.0 | 34.2 | 34.2 | 34.0 | 34.1 | 33.9 | 34.1 | 34.4 | 34.6 | 34.1 | 34.5 | 34.0 | 34.2 |
| 2016 | 33.3 | 33.3 | 33.1 | 33.3 | 33.6 | 33.5 | 33.8 | 34.0 | 34.1 | 33.9 | 33.7 | 34.3 | 33.7 |
| 2017 | 33.3 | 32.9 | 32.9 | 33.4 | 33.2 | 33.3 | 33.6 | 33.5 | 33.7 | 33.5 | 33.7 | 33.9 | 33.4 |
| 2018 | 32.8 | 32.8 | 32.8 | 33.3 | 33.2 | 33.5 | 33.7 | 33.4 | 33.6 | 33.1 | 33.2 | 33.7 | 33.3 |
| 2019 | 32.6 | 32.5 | 32.3 | 32.6 | 32.5 | 32.8 | 32.7 | 32.8 | 33.2 | 32.5 | 32.4 | 33.0 | 32.7 |
| **Financial Activities** | | | | | | | | | | | | | |
| 2015 | 36.6 | 37.9 | 37.9 | 37.0 | 37.3 | 37.4 | 37.4 | 38.6 | 37.5 | 37.6 | 37.7 | 37.4 | 37.5 |
| 2016 | 37.3 | 37.0 | 36.8 | 36.4 | 37.1 | 36.4 | 36.7 | 36.7 | 35.8 | 37.1 | 36.8 | 36.6 | 36.7 |
| 2017 | 37.2 | 36.8 | 36.6 | 37.8 | 37.2 | 37.8 | 38.6 | 37.9 | 37.5 | 38.6 | 37.7 | 37.4 | 37.6 |
| 2018 | 37.3 | 37.3 | 37.2 | 38.2 | 37.4 | 37.5 | 37.9 | 37.4 | 37.9 | 37.4 | 37.2 | 38.0 | 37.6 |
| 2019 | 37.2 | 37.4 | 37.2 | 37.0 | 37.2 | 37.8 | 37.0 | 37.1 | 37.9 | 37.0 | 37.1 | 38.0 | 37.3 |
| **Professional and Business Services** | | | | | | | | | | | | | |
| 2015 | 34.7 | 35.5 | 35.4 | 34.5 | 34.7 | 34.8 | 34.4 | 35.3 | 34.4 | 34.8 | 35.6 | 34.8 | 34.9 |
| 2016 | 34.6 | 34.5 | 34.6 | 34.7 | 35.3 | 35.1 | 35.3 | 35.5 | 35.2 | 35.7 | 34.9 | 34.9 | 35.0 |
| 2017 | 35.4 | 34.8 | 34.4 | 35.3 | 34.6 | 34.7 | 35.3 | 34.6 | 34.3 | 35.0 | 34.3 | 34.2 | 34.7 |
| 2018 | 33.9 | 34.3 | 34.2 | 35.3 | 34.4 | 34.5 | 35.2 | 34.7 | 35.6 | 34.7 | 34.4 | 35.3 | 34.7 |
| 2019 | 34.2 | 34.6 | 34.6 | 34.7 | 34.4 | 35.3 | 34.6 | 34.9 | 35.6 | 34.5 | 34.6 | 35.2 | 34.8 |
| **Education and Health Services** | | | | | | | | | | | | | |
| 2015 | 31.8 | 31.8 | 31.8 | 31.8 | 31.9 | 32.0 | 32.2 | 32.3 | 32.1 | 31.9 | 32.0 | 31.9 | 32.0 |
| 2016 | 32.1 | 31.9 | 31.7 | 31.7 | 31.8 | 31.8 | 32.0 | 32.1 | 32.2 | 32.1 | 32.0 | 32.1 | 32.0 |
| 2017 | 32.3 | 32.1 | 31.7 | 31.8 | 31.9 | 31.9 | 32.0 | 32.0 | 31.8 | 31.9 | 31.8 | 31.8 | 31.9 |
| 2018 | 31.6 | 31.4 | 31.4 | 31.4 | 31.3 | 31.3 | 31.4 | 31.6 | 31.5 | 31.2 | 31.3 | 31.5 | 31.4 |
| 2019 | 31.7 | 31.5 | 31.4 | 31.3 | 31.2 | 31.4 | 31.4 | 31.6 | 31.4 | 31.3 | 31.4 | 31.4 | 31.4 |
| **Leisure and Hospitality** | | | | | | | | | | | | | |
| 2015 | 27.7 | 27.9 | 27.8 | 28.3 | 28.6 | 28.3 | 28.7 | 29.0 | 28.1 | 28.3 | 28.2 | 28.2 | 28.3 |
| 2016 | 27.2 | 27.7 | 27.8 | 28.1 | 28.3 | 28.4 | 28.7 | 28.9 | 28.5 | 28.4 | 28.2 | 28.1 | 28.2 |
| 2017 | 27.5 | 27.2 | 27.4 | 28.1 | 28.2 | 28.3 | 28.6 | 28.4 | 28.1 | 28.2 | 27.9 | 28.0 | 28.0 |
| 2018 | 27.1 | 27.6 | 27.4 | 27.4 | 28.1 | 28.1 | 28.4 | 28.2 | 28.0 | 28.0 | 27.6 | 28.1 | 27.8 |
| 2019 | 26.9 | 27.1 | 27.2 | 27.3 | 27.4 | 27.4 | 27.9 | 27.8 | 27.2 | 27.0 | 26.8 | 26.6 | 27.2 |
| **Other Services** | | | | | | | | | | | | | |
| 2015 | 31.2 | 31.7 | 31.4 | 31.2 | 31.5 | 30.8 | 31.4 | 32.0 | 31.2 | 31.1 | 31.3 | 30.9 | 31.3 |
| 2016 | 30.9 | 30.8 | 30.8 | 30.8 | 31.3 | 31.1 | 31.4 | 31.5 | 31.1 | 31.0 | 30.8 | 30.9 | 31.0 |
| 2017 | 31.0 | 30.3 | 30.1 | 31.0 | 30.5 | 30.9 | 31.4 | 31.0 | 30.8 | 31.3 | 30.8 | 31.2 | 30.9 |
| 2018 | 30.9 | 30.8 | 30.8 | 31.1 | 30.7 | 30.7 | 31.7 | 31.5 | 31.6 | 31.1 | 30.9 | 31.5 | 31.1 |
| 2019 | 30.8 | 30.7 | 30.9 | 30.7 | 31.0 | 31.6 | 31.9 | 31.8 | 31.3 | 31.0 | 31.3 | 31.4 | 31.2 |

## 3. Average Hourly Earnings by Selected Industry: New York, 2015–2019

(Dollars, not seasonally adjusted)

| Industry and year | January | February | March | April | May | June | July | August | September | October | November | December | Annual average |
|---|---|---|---|---|---|---|---|---|---|---|---|---|---|
| **Total Private** | | | | | | | | | | | | | |
| 2015 | 28.78 | 29.11 | 29.05 | 28.91 | 28.62 | 28.52 | 28.52 | 28.84 | 28.70 | 28.83 | 29.30 | 29.08 | 28.85 |
| 2016 | 29.33 | 29.51 | 29.31 | 29.16 | 29.23 | 28.73 | 29.01 | 29.36 | 29.21 | 29.69 | 29.39 | 29.33 | 29.27 |
| 2017 | 30.16 | 29.98 | 29.99 | 30.30 | 29.75 | 29.60 | 30.09 | 29.72 | 30.04 | 30.45 | 30.15 | 30.42 | 30.06 |
| 2018 | 30.76 | 30.90 | 30.89 | 31.19 | 30.76 | 30.66 | 31.26 | 30.89 | 31.42 | 31.33 | 31.56 | 31.97 | 31.14 |
| 2019 | 31.93 | 32.07 | 31.80 | 31.87 | 31.83 | 32.24 | 31.92 | 32.14 | 32.75 | 32.35 | 32.55 | 33.02 | 32.21 |
| **Goods-Producing** | | | | | | | | | | | | | |
| 2015 | 29.65 | 29.38 | 29.89 | 29.63 | 29.63 | 29.71 | 29.89 | 29.84 | 30.03 | 30.36 | 30.58 | 30.84 | 29.96 |
| 2016 | 30.34 | 30.17 | 30.65 | 30.71 | 30.66 | 30.37 | 30.65 | 30.84 | 30.80 | 30.81 | 30.69 | 30.75 | 30.62 |
| 2017 | 30.85 | 30.63 | 31.04 | 30.93 | 30.95 | 31.01 | 31.46 | 31.55 | 31.58 | 31.57 | 31.82 | 32.20 | 31.31 |
| 2018 | 32.24 | 32.63 | 32.49 | 32.69 | 32.63 | 32.80 | 33.07 | 33.24 | 33.37 | 33.76 | 33.52 | 34.01 | 33.05 |
| 2019 | 33.95 | 33.82 | 33.87 | 34.06 | 34.03 | 33.70 | 33.67 | 33.82 | 34.06 | 33.61 | 33.76 | 33.72 | 33.84 |
| **Construction** | | | | | | | | | | | | | |
| 2015 | 35.76 | 35.19 | 36.15 | 35.58 | 35.12 | 35.79 | 36.04 | 35.92 | 36.09 | 36.73 | 37.16 | 37.89 | 36.14 |
| 2016 | 37.27 | 37.25 | 37.77 | 37.39 | 36.60 | 36.31 | 37.10 | 37.14 | 37.11 | 37.22 | 37.01 | 37.10 | 37.10 |
| 2017 | 37.23 | 37.12 | 37.51 | 36.93 | 36.92 | 36.81 | 37.21 | 37.41 | 37.29 | 37.26 | 37.75 | 38.14 | 37.30 |
| 2018 | 38.16 | 38.59 | 38.65 | 38.62 | 38.28 | 38.01 | 38.27 | 38.66 | 38.58 | 39.22 | 38.85 | 39.38 | 38.61 |
| 2019 | 39.06 | 38.71 | 38.61 | 38.86 | 38.83 | 38.21 | 38.15 | 38.75 | 39.14 | 38.47 | 38.57 | 38.80 | 38.68 |
| **Manufacturing** | | | | | | | | | | | | | |
| 2015 | 26.13 | 26.19 | 26.20 | 25.89 | 25.76 | 25.42 | 25.35 | 25.19 | 25.46 | 25.37 | 25.40 | 25.67 | 25.67 |
| 2016 | 25.63 | 25.62 | 25.63 | 25.76 | 26.18 | 25.76 | 25.55 | 25.80 | 25.57 | 25.65 | 25.66 | 25.83 | 25.72 |
| 2017 | 25.94 | 25.74 | 26.13 | 26.08 | 25.95 | 26.07 | 26.35 | 26.17 | 26.42 | 26.46 | 26.41 | 26.83 | 26.21 |
| 2018 | 27.14 | 27.40 | 27.24 | 27.41 | 27.27 | 27.75 | 27.77 | 27.72 | 28.06 | 27.96 | 28.06 | 28.53 | 27.70 |
| 2019 | 28.70 | 28.80 | 28.89 | 29.02 | 28.94 | 28.92 | 28.85 | 28.65 | 28.84 | 28.70 | 29.05 | 28.95 | 28.86 |
| **Trade, Transportation, and Utilities** | | | | | | | | | | | | | |
| 2015 | 22.83 | 23.18 | 23.19 | 23.41 | 22.92 | 22.89 | 22.87 | 22.94 | 22.97 | 23.27 | 23.46 | 23.89 | 23.15 |
| 2016 | 23.91 | 24.05 | 23.98 | 23.95 | 23.73 | 23.43 | 23.72 | 24.48 | 23.63 | 23.85 | 23.75 | 23.44 | 23.82 |
| 2017 | 24.37 | 24.40 | 24.30 | 24.56 | 24.47 | 24.37 | 24.61 | 24.61 | 24.33 | 24.58 | 24.68 | 24.45 | 24.42 | 24.46 |
| 2018 | 25.15 | 25.21 | 25.68 | 25.66 | 25.61 | 25.15 | 25.39 | 25.53 | 25.80 | 25.80 | 25.73 | 25.90 | 25.55 |
| 2019 | 26.59 | 26.34 | 26.37 | 26.07 | 25.87 | 26.34 | 26.47 | 26.99 | 27.06 | 26.97 | 26.97 | 26.90 | 26.58 |
| **Financial Activities** | | | | | | | | | | | | | |
| 2015 | 43.44 | 44.02 | 43.73 | 43.39 | 43.12 | 42.62 | 42.23 | 43.28 | 42.62 | 42.95 | 43.98 | 42.40 | 43.15 |
| 2016 | 41.99 | 43.81 | 43.18 | 42.29 | 43.65 | 41.74 | 42.00 | 43.74 | 43.17 | 44.62 | 43.38 | 43.61 | 43.10 |
| 2017 | 44.43 | 44.26 | 43.80 | 44.90 | 43.26 | 42.51 | 43.73 | 42.55 | 43.19 | 44.92 | 43.35 | 44.23 | 43.76 |
| 2018 | 44.52 | 44.10 | 43.71 | 44.36 | 43.91 | 43.69 | 44.96 | 43.49 | 45.06 | 44.00 | 44.64 | 45.35 | 44.32 |
| 2019 | 44.51 | 44.89 | 44.00 | 44.34 | 43.79 | 45.86 | 44.57 | 45.10 | 46.66 | 45.59 | 46.26 | 46.73 | 45.20 |
| **Professional and Business Services** | | | | | | | | | | | | | |
| 2015 | 35.89 | 36.45 | 36.19 | 35.79 | 35.64 | 35.31 | 35.31 | 35.89 | 35.38 | 35.48 | 36.30 | 35.73 | 35.78 |
| 2016 | 36.52 | 36.57 | 35.96 | 35.90 | 35.71 | 35.05 | 35.63 | 35.64 | 36.00 | 36.72 | 36.25 | 36.39 | 36.00 |
| 2017 | 38.13 | 37.27 | 37.50 | 37.95 | 36.75 | 36.66 | 37.45 | 36.55 | 37.29 | 38.34 | 37.76 | 38.00 | 37.47 |
| 2018 | 37.62 | 37.84 | 37.84 | 38.47 | 37.84 | 37.92 | 39.14 | 38.15 | 39.20 | 39.08 | 39.55 | 40.11 | 38.58 |
| 2019 | 39.14 | 39.36 | 39.31 | 39.36 | 39.60 | 40.64 | 40.51 | 40.25 | 41.26 | 40.65 | 40.72 | 42.08 | 40.26 |
| **Education and Health Services** | | | | | | | | | | | | | |
| 2015 | 25.02 | 25.02 | 24.83 | 25.04 | 24.80 | 24.74 | 24.94 | 24.82 | 24.88 | 24.65 | 24.99 | 24.95 | 24.89 |
| 2016 | 25.27 | 25.27 | 25.12 | 25.13 | 25.08 | 25.09 | 25.33 | 25.14 | 25.32 | 25.30 | 25.21 | 25.18 | 25.20 |
| 2017 | 25.48 | 25.53 | 25.78 | 25.75 | 25.55 | 25.59 | 25.80 | 25.73 | 25.98 | 25.75 | 25.84 | 26.00 | 25.73 |
| 2018 | 26.50 | 26.53 | 26.38 | 26.48 | 26.25 | 26.33 | 26.78 | 26.38 | 26.57 | 26.59 | 26.85 | 27.03 | 26.56 |
| 2019 | 27.21 | 27.39 | 27.29 | 27.24 | 27.12 | 27.19 | 27.18 | 27.11 | 27.56 | 27.34 | 27.51 | 27.55 | 27.31 |
| **Leisure and Hospitality** | | | | | | | | | | | | | |
| 2015 | 18.16 | 18.28 | 18.18 | 18.24 | 17.84 | 17.38 | 17.25 | 17.32 | 17.89 | 18.17 | 18.64 | 18.60 | 17.98 |
| 2016 | 18.77 | 18.83 | 18.92 | 19.23 | 19.25 | 18.80 | 18.63 | 18.98 | 19.49 | 19.70 | 19.76 | 19.67 | 19.17 |
| 2017 | 19.75 | 19.70 | 19.71 | 19.80 | 19.61 | 19.01 | 18.97 | 19.03 | 19.48 | 19.92 | 19.99 | 20.32 | 19.59 |
| 2018 | 20.40 | 20.82 | 20.63 | 20.77 | 20.30 | 20.01 | 19.79 | 19.92 | 20.23 | 20.64 | 21.06 | 21.62 | 20.50 |
| 2019 | 21.60 | 21.66 | 21.51 | 21.69 | 21.71 | 21.30 | 20.65 | 20.80 | 21.62 | 21.71 | 21.64 | 22.12 | 21.49 |
| **Other Services** | | | | | | | | | | | | | |
| 2015 | 25.42 | 26.15 | 26.44 | 26.21 | 26.36 | 26.71 | 26.25 | 26.56 | 27.29 | 26.98 | 27.23 | 27.20 | 26.57 |
| 2016 | 27.08 | 27.44 | 27.20 | 26.87 | 27.09 | 26.81 | 26.75 | 26.49 | 26.77 | 27.27 | 27.88 | 27.58 | 27.10 |
| 2017 | 27.94 | 28.37 | 28.04 | 28.08 | 27.65 | 27.05 | 26.96 | 26.98 | 27.12 | 27.14 | 27.20 | 27.15 | 27.47 |
| 2018 | 27.40 | 27.47 | 27.58 | 27.91 | 27.21 | 27.24 | 27.14 | 26.94 | 27.79 | 27.70 | 28.38 | 28.85 | 27.64 |
| 2019 | 29.02 | 29.18 | 29.20 | 29.13 | 29.10 | 29.07 | 27.66 | 27.51 | 28.39 | 28.28 | 28.72 | 29.52 | 28.73 |

## 4. Average Weekly Earnings by Selected Industry: New York, 2015–2019

(Dollars, not seasonally adjusted)

| Industry and year | January | February | March | April | May | June | July | August | September | October | November | December | Annual average |
|---|---|---|---|---|---|---|---|---|---|---|---|---|---|
| **Total Private** | | | | | | | | | | | | | |
| 2015 | 964.13 | 981.01 | 981.89 | 968.49 | 964.49 | 961.12 | 963.98 | 986.33 | 967.19 | 971.57 | 996.20 | 980.00 | 975.13 |
| 2016 | 979.62 | 979.73 | 976.02 | 971.03 | 982.13 | 962.46 | 977.64 | 992.37 | 984.38 | 1,003.52 | 984.57 | 985.49 | 980.55 |
| 2017 | 1,010.36 | 992.34 | 983.67 | 1,015.05 | 990.68 | 988.64 | 1,014.03 | 995.62 | 1,003.34 | 1,026.17 | 1,007.01 | 1,016.03 | 1,004.00 |
| 2018 | 1,012.00 | 1,019.70 | 1,016.28 | 1,041.75 | 1,021.23 | 1,020.98 | 1,050.34 | 1,031.73 | 1,055.71 | 1,040.16 | 1,041.48 | 1,074.19 | 1,036.96 |
| 2019 | 1,050.50 | 1,055.10 | 1,046.22 | 1,048.52 | 1,047.21 | 1,073.59 | 1,056.55 | 1,067.05 | 1,093.85 | 1,061.08 | 1,070.90 | 1,096.26 | 1,062.93 |
| **Goods-Producing** | | | | | | | | | | | | | |
| 2015 | 1,147.46 | 1,116.44 | 1,159.73 | 1,152.61 | 1,164.46 | 1,161.66 | 1,168.70 | 1,163.76 | 1,147.15 | 1,181.00 | 1,186.50 | 1,202.76 | 1,162.45 |
| 2016 | 1,168.09 | 1,137.41 | 1,186.16 | 1,182.34 | 1,186.54 | 1,178.36 | 1,186.16 | 1,184.26 | 1,185.80 | 1,176.94 | 1,160.08 | 1,162.35 | 1,175.81 |
| 2017 | 1,153.79 | 1,130.25 | 1,129.86 | 1,169.15 | 1,182.29 | 1,190.78 | 1,195.48 | 1,208.37 | 1,222.15 | 1,218.60 | 1,225.07 | 1,236.48 | 1,189.78 |
| 2018 | 1,215.45 | 1,236.68 | 1,224.87 | 1,255.30 | 1,259.52 | 1,272.64 | 1,279.81 | 1,279.74 | 1,274.73 | 1,303.14 | 1,270.41 | 1,322.99 | 1,265.82 |
| 2019 | 1,279.92 | 1,271.63 | 1,287.06 | 1,301.09 | 1,303.35 | 1,294.08 | 1,289.56 | 1,305.45 | 1,318.12 | 1,280.54 | 1,282.88 | 1,301.59 | 1,292.69 |
| **Construction** | | | | | | | | | | | | | |
| 2015 | 1,308.82 | 1,252.76 | 1,341.17 | 1,334.25 | 1,355.63 | 1,367.18 | 1,391.14 | 1,382.92 | 1,346.16 | 1,399.41 | 1,404.65 | 1,451.19 | 1,362.48 |
| 2016 | 1,397.63 | 1,337.28 | 1,435.26 | 1,405.86 | 1,387.14 | 1,383.41 | 1,406.09 | 1,400.18 | 1,406.47 | 1,377.14 | 1,347.16 | 1,361.57 | 1,387.54 |
| 2017 | 1,340.28 | 1,306.62 | 1,301.60 | 1,347.95 | 1,369.73 | 1,373.01 | 1,376.77 | 1,402.88 | 1,405.83 | 1,393.52 | 1,400.53 | 1,422.62 | 1,372.64 |
| 2018 | 1,385.21 | 1,423.97 | 1,403.00 | 1,436.66 | 1,446.98 | 1,448.18 | 1,454.26 | 1,457.48 | 1,442.89 | 1,498.20 | 1,433.57 | 1,512.19 | 1,447.88 |
| 2019 | 1,468.66 | 1,451.63 | 1,471.04 | 1,480.57 | 1,483.31 | 1,451.98 | 1,449.70 | 1,476.38 | 1,495.15 | 1,438.78 | 1,430.95 | 1,447.24 | 1,462.10 |
| **Manufacturing** | | | | | | | | | | | | | |
| 2015 | 1,047.81 | 1,037.12 | 1,045.38 | 1,027.83 | 1,022.67 | 1,009.17 | 996.26 | 987.45 | 985.30 | 997.04 | 1,000.76 | 1,011.40 | 1,013.97 |
| 2016 | 1,004.70 | 996.62 | 1,002.13 | 1,007.22 | 1,028.87 | 1,012.37 | 1,004.12 | 1,003.62 | 994.67 | 1,005.48 | 1,000.74 | 1,002.20 | 1,005.65 |
| 2017 | 1,001.28 | 985.84 | 990.33 | 1,001.47 | 1,004.27 | 1,011.52 | 1,009.21 | 1,007.55 | 1,033.02 | 1,039.88 | 1,040.55 | 1,051.74 | 1,014.33 |
| 2018 | 1,053.03 | 1,057.64 | 1,059.64 | 1,079.95 | 1,068.98 | 1,090.58 | 1,088.58 | 1,083.85 | 1,088.73 | 1,084.85 | 1,097.15 | 1,126.94 | 1,083.07 |
| 2019 | 1,090.60 | 1,094.40 | 1,106.49 | 1,120.17 | 1,117.08 | 1,130.77 | 1,122.27 | 1,128.81 | 1,142.06 | 1,119.30 | 1,135.86 | 1,158.00 | 1,122.65 |
| **Trade, Transportation, and Utilities** | | | | | | | | | | | | | |
| 2015 | 776.22 | 792.76 | 793.10 | 795.94 | 781.57 | 775.97 | 779.87 | 789.14 | 794.76 | 793.51 | 809.37 | 812.26 | 791.73 |
| 2016 | 796.20 | 800.87 | 793.74 | 797.54 | 797.33 | 784.91 | 801.74 | 832.32 | 805.78 | 808.52 | 800.38 | 803.99 | 802.73 |
| 2017 | 811.52 | 802.76 | 799.47 | 820.30 | 812.40 | 811.52 | 826.90 | 815.06 | 828.35 | 826.78 | 823.97 | 827.84 | 816.96 |
| 2018 | 824.92 | 826.89 | 842.30 | 854.48 | 850.25 | 842.53 | 855.64 | 852.70 | 866.88 | 853.98 | 854.24 | 872.83 | 850.82 |
| 2019 | 866.83 | 856.05 | 851.75 | 849.88 | 840.78 | 863.95 | 865.57 | 885.27 | 898.39 | 876.53 | 873.83 | 887.70 | 869.17 |
| **Financial Activities** | | | | | | | | | | | | | |
| 2015 | 1,589.90 | 1,668.36 | 1,657.37 | 1,605.43 | 1,608.38 | 1,593.99 | 1,579.40 | 1,670.61 | 1,598.25 | 1,614.92 | 1,658.05 | 1,585.76 | 1,618.13 |
| 2016 | 1,566.23 | 1,620.97 | 1,589.02 | 1,539.36 | 1,619.42 | 1,519.34 | 1,541.40 | 1,605.26 | 1,545.49 | 1,655.40 | 1,596.38 | 1,596.13 | 1,581.77 |
| 2017 | 1,652.80 | 1,628.77 | 1,603.08 | 1,697.22 | 1,609.27 | 1,606.88 | 1,687.98 | 1,612.65 | 1,619.63 | 1,733.91 | 1,634.30 | 1,654.20 | 1,645.38 |
| 2018 | 1,660.60 | 1,644.93 | 1,626.01 | 1,694.55 | 1,642.23 | 1,638.38 | 1,703.98 | 1,626.53 | 1,707.77 | 1,645.60 | 1,660.61 | 1,723.30 | 1,666.43 |
| 2019 | 1,655.77 | 1,678.89 | 1,636.80 | 1,640.58 | 1,628.99 | 1,733.51 | 1,649.09 | 1,673.21 | 1,768.41 | 1,686.83 | 1,716.25 | 1,775.74 | 1,685.96 |
| **Professional and Business Services** | | | | | | | | | | | | | |
| 2015 | 1,245.38 | 1,293.98 | 1,281.13 | 1,234.76 | 1,236.71 | 1,228.79 | 1,214.66 | 1,266.92 | 1,217.07 | 1,234.70 | 1,292.28 | 1,243.40 | 1,248.72 |
| 2016 | 1,263.59 | 1,261.67 | 1,244.22 | 1,245.73 | 1,260.56 | 1,230.26 | 1,257.74 | 1,265.22 | 1,267.20 | 1,310.90 | 1,259.54 | 1,265.13 | 1,260.00 |
| 2017 | 1,349.80 | 1,297.00 | 1,290.00 | 1,339.64 | 1,271.55 | 1,272.10 | 1,321.99 | 1,264.63 | 1,279.05 | 1,341.90 | 1,295.17 | 1,299.60 | 1,300.21 |
| 2018 | 1,275.32 | 1,297.91 | 1,294.13 | 1,357.99 | 1,301.70 | 1,308.24 | 1,377.73 | 1,323.81 | 1,395.52 | 1,356.08 | 1,360.52 | 1,415.88 | 1,338.73 |
| 2019 | 1,338.59 | 1,361.86 | 1,360.13 | 1,365.79 | 1,362.24 | 1,434.59 | 1,401.65 | 1,404.73 | 1,468.86 | 1,402.43 | 1,408.91 | 1,481.22 | 1,401.05 |
| **Education and Health Services** | | | | | | | | | | | | | |
| 2015 | 795.64 | 795.64 | 789.59 | 796.27 | 791.12 | 791.68 | 803.07 | 801.69 | 798.65 | 786.34 | 799.68 | 795.91 | 796.48 |
| 2016 | 811.17 | 806.11 | 796.30 | 796.62 | 797.54 | 797.86 | 810.56 | 806.99 | 815.30 | 812.13 | 806.72 | 808.28 | 806.40 |
| 2017 | 823.00 | 819.51 | 817.23 | 818.85 | 815.05 | 816.32 | 825.60 | 823.36 | 826.16 | 821.43 | 821.71 | 826.80 | 820.79 |
| 2018 | 837.40 | 833.04 | 828.33 | 831.47 | 821.63 | 824.13 | 840.89 | 833.61 | 836.96 | 829.61 | 840.41 | 851.45 | 833.98 |
| 2019 | 862.56 | 862.79 | 856.91 | 852.61 | 846.14 | 853.77 | 853.45 | 856.68 | 865.38 | 855.74 | 863.81 | 865.07 | 857.53 |
| **Leisure and Hospitality** | | | | | | | | | | | | | |
| 2015 | 503.03 | 510.01 | 505.40 | 516.19 | 510.22 | 491.85 | 495.08 | 502.28 | 502.71 | 514.21 | 525.65 | 524.52 | 508.83 |
| 2016 | 510.54 | 521.59 | 525.98 | 540.36 | 544.78 | 533.92 | 534.68 | 548.52 | 555.47 | 559.48 | 557.23 | 552.73 | 540.59 |
| 2017 | 543.13 | 535.84 | 540.05 | 556.38 | 553.00 | 537.98 | 542.54 | 540.45 | 547.39 | 561.74 | 557.72 | 568.96 | 548.52 |
| 2018 | 552.84 | 574.63 | 565.26 | 569.10 | 570.43 | 562.28 | 562.04 | 561.74 | 566.44 | 577.92 | 581.26 | 607.52 | 569.90 |
| 2019 | 581.04 | 586.99 | 585.07 | 592.14 | 594.85 | 583.62 | 576.14 | 578.24 | 588.06 | 586.17 | 579.95 | 588.39 | 584.53 |
| **Other Services** | | | | | | | | | | | | | |
| 2015 | 793.10 | 828.96 | 830.22 | 817.75 | 830.34 | 822.67 | 824.25 | 849.92 | 851.45 | 839.08 | 852.30 | 840.48 | 831.64 |
| 2016 | 836.77 | 845.15 | 837.76 | 827.60 | 847.92 | 833.79 | 839.95 | 834.44 | 832.55 | 845.37 | 858.70 | 852.22 | 840.10 |
| 2017 | 866.14 | 859.61 | 844.00 | 870.48 | 843.33 | 835.85 | 846.54 | 836.38 | 835.30 | 849.48 | 837.76 | 847.08 | 848.82 |
| 2018 | 846.66 | 846.08 | 849.46 | 868.00 | 835.35 | 836.27 | 860.34 | 848.61 | 878.16 | 861.47 | 876.94 | 908.78 | 859.60 |
| 2019 | 893.82 | 895.83 | 902.28 | 894.29 | 902.10 | 918.61 | 882.35 | 874.82 | 888.61 | 876.68 | 898.94 | 926.93 | 896.38 |

# NORTH CAROLINA
## *At a Glance*

Population:
  2010 census: 9,535,483
  2019 estimate: 10,488,084

Percent change in population:
  2010–2019: 10.0%

Percent change in total nonfarm employment:
  2011–2019: 17.0%

Industry with the largest growth in employment, 2011–2019 (percent):
  Construction, 33.6%

Industry with the largest decline or smallest growth in employment, 2011–2019 (percent):
  Mining and logging, 1.8%

Civilian labor force:
  2010: 4,616,691
  2019: 5,080,444

Unemployment rate and rank among states (highest to lowest):
  2010: 10.9%, 7th
  2019: 3.9%, 16th

Over-the-year change in unemployment rates:
  2017–2018: -0.5%
  2018–2019: -0.1%

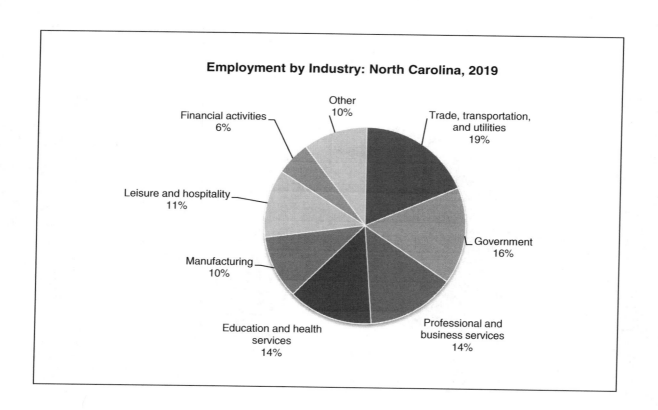

**Employment by Industry: North Carolina, 2019**

- Other 10%
- Trade, transportation, and utilities 19%
- Financial activities 6%
- Leisure and hospitality 11%
- Government 16%
- Manufacturing 10%
- Professional and business services 14%
- Education and health services 14%

## 1. Employment by Industry: North Carolina, 2011–2019

(Numbers in thousands, not seasonally adjusted)

| Industry and year | January | February | March | April | May | June | July | August | September | October | November | December | Annual average |
|---|---|---|---|---|---|---|---|---|---|---|---|---|---|
| **Total Nonfarm** | | | | | | | | | | | | | |
| 2011 | 3,823.5 | 3,858.7 | 3,888.4 | 3,919.5 | 3,940.3 | 3,911.7 | 3,837.7 | 3,905.7 | 3,942.4 | 3,957.1 | 3,972.5 | 3,966.7 | 3,910.4 |
| 2012 | 3,897.0 | 3,921.3 | 3,954.6 | 3,979.8 | 4,012.9 | 3,972.2 | 3,896.7 | 3,974.6 | 4,014.5 | 4,036.3 | 4,055.6 | 4,051.0 | 3,980.5 |
| 2013 | 3,963.1 | 3,992.3 | 4,021.5 | 4,048.6 | 4,076.5 | 4,040.8 | 3,969.7 | 4,045.7 | 4,088.8 | 4,113.4 | 4,130.5 | 4,129.0 | 4,051.7 |
| 2014 | 4,038.6 | 4,039.2 | 4,086.9 | 4,130.0 | 4,166.4 | 4,136.3 | 4,062.7 | 4,133.3 | 4,170.2 | 4,205.8 | 4,222.4 | 4,225.3 | 4,134.8 |
| 2015 | 4,140.3 | 4,163.5 | 4,182.7 | 4,219.7 | 4,260.2 | 4,236.2 | 4,165.4 | 4,228.3 | 4,269.9 | 4,307.9 | 4,323.9 | 4,328.8 | 4,235.6 |
| 2016 | 4,238.7 | 4,263.8 | 4,296.2 | 4,337.2 | 4,361.4 | 4,338.0 | 4,271.2 | 4,328.3 | 4,370.3 | 4,388.2 | 4,415.3 | 4,407.9 | 4,334.7 |
| 2017 | 4,318.8 | 4,354.7 | 4,375.5 | 4,394.0 | 4,426.6 | 4,411.4 | 4,344.9 | 4,404.1 | 4,431.5 | 4,463.3 | 4,480.8 | 4,473.3 | 4,406.6 |
| 2018 | 4,393.9 | 4,431.9 | 4,457.9 | 4,479.4 | 4,517.0 | 4,499.3 | 4,434.9 | 4,497.9 | 4,483.1 | 4,548.6 | 4,568.0 | 4,547.3 | 4,488.3 |
| 2019 | 4,501.7 | 4,528.1 | 4,546.8 | 4,571.1 | 4,601.2 | 4,588.2 | 4,518.2 | 4,579.1 | 4,585.5 | 4,617.8 | 4,633.3 | 4,619.4 | 4,574.2 |
| **Total Private** | | | | | | | | | | | | | |
| 2011 | 3,101.5 | 3,130.2 | 3,155.6 | 3,185.6 | 3,205.6 | 3,226.9 | 3,230.7 | 3,241.6 | 3,231.5 | 3,232.3 | 3,241.2 | 3,241.4 | 3,202.0 |
| 2012 | 3,178.9 | 3,195.3 | 3,225.4 | 3,249.9 | 3,278.9 | 3,298.4 | 3,298.9 | 3,309.0 | 3,298.3 | 3,303.4 | 3,316.3 | 3,318.1 | 3,272.6 |
| 2013 | 3,239.3 | 3,259.6 | 3,285.5 | 3,313.2 | 3,340.3 | 3,364.8 | 3,367.4 | 3,380.7 | 3,370.5 | 3,378.0 | 3,392.5 | 3,394.8 | 3,340.6 |
| 2014 | 3,316.9 | 3,312.5 | 3,356.9 | 3,395.3 | 3,429.1 | 3,452.2 | 3,457.3 | 3,469.4 | 3,455.3 | 3,473.5 | 3,483.7 | 3,493.8 | 3,424.7 |
| 2015 | 3,413.2 | 3,430.7 | 3,447.6 | 3,483.5 | 3,522.4 | 3,546.1 | 3,553.5 | 3,559.9 | 3,549.5 | 3,570.8 | 3,582.0 | 3,588.6 | 3,520.7 |
| 2016 | 3,513.6 | 3,528.5 | 3,553.5 | 3,597.7 | 3,620.4 | 3,638.3 | 3,647.0 | 3,652.9 | 3,639.9 | 3,643.5 | 3,664.1 | 3,663.1 | 3,613.5 |
| 2017 | 3,586.3 | 3,612.9 | 3,630.4 | 3,649.2 | 3,681.6 | 3,711.2 | 3,716.2 | 3,722.1 | 3,694.9 | 3,716.9 | 3,730.0 | 3,726.8 | 3,681.5 |
| 2018 | 3,658.1 | 3,687.4 | 3,709.0 | 3,730.7 | 3,764.0 | 3,790.4 | 3,797.8 | 3,808.3 | 3,750.0 | 3,803.9 | 3,816.6 | 3,800.5 | 3,759.7 |
| 2019 | 3,762.8 | 3,781.3 | 3,796.7 | 3,819.2 | 3,849.2 | 3,878.2 | 3,876.9 | 3,881.3 | 3,843.5 | 3,867.2 | 3,876.5 | 3,867.4 | 3,841.7 |
| **Goods Producing** | | | | | | | | | | | | | |
| 2011 | 597.4 | 603.2 | 608.0 | 610.4 | 614.5 | 617.8 | 618.5 | 619.7 | 619.0 | 615.2 | 614.1 | 613.3 | 612.6 |
| 2012 | 605.5 | 608.4 | 613.6 | 614.7 | 618.5 | 621.2 | 621.6 | 621.7 | 622.3 | 621.0 | 621.4 | 621.5 | 617.6 |
| 2013 | 609.8 | 612.4 | 615.6 | 617.6 | 621.3 | 626.0 | 626.2 | 626.2 | 627.1 | 627.0 | 627.0 | 627.4 | 622.0 |
| 2014 | 616.8 | 617.4 | 624.0 | 625.7 | 631.0 | 636.2 | 638.2 | 639.7 | 641.4 | 645.2 | 645.9 | 647.6 | 634.1 |
| 2015 | 639.5 | 642.5 | 646.0 | 649.7 | 655.4 | 660.0 | 661.6 | 663.0 | 663.1 | 665.6 | 664.9 | 667.0 | 656.5 |
| 2016 | 659.4 | 661.6 | 664.4 | 668.2 | 669.7 | 673.9 | 676.6 | 676.0 | 675.8 | 673.7 | 676.7 | 677.3 | 671.1 |
| 2017 | 667.5 | 673.8 | 675.4 | 676.9 | 680.1 | 686.5 | 687.7 | 687.8 | 687.0 | 687.4 | 688.5 | 690.6 | 682.4 |
| 2018 | 683.0 | 688.2 | 692.3 | 693.4 | 698.1 | 705.1 | 707.6 | 708.5 | 705.1 | 710.0 | 710.1 | 709.9 | 700.9 |
| 2019 | 707.2 | 709.7 | 711.1 | 711.0 | 714.2 | 719.5 | 719.8 | 718.8 | 716.5 | 718.9 | 721.3 | 717.9 | 715.5 |
| **Service-Providing** | | | | | | | | | | | | | |
| 2011 | 3,226.1 | 3,255.5 | 3,280.4 | 3,309.1 | 3,325.8 | 3,293.9 | 3,219.2 | 3,286.0 | 3,323.4 | 3,341.9 | 3,358.4 | 3,353.4 | 3,297.8 |
| 2012 | 3,291.5 | 3,312.9 | 3,341.0 | 3,365.1 | 3,394.4 | 3,351.0 | 3,275.1 | 3,352.9 | 3,392.2 | 3,415.3 | 3,434.2 | 3,429.5 | 3,362.9 |
| 2013 | 3,353.3 | 3,379.9 | 3,405.9 | 3,431.0 | 3,455.2 | 3,414.8 | 3,343.5 | 3,419.5 | 3,461.7 | 3,486.4 | 3,503.5 | 3,501.6 | 3,429.7 |
| 2014 | 3,421.8 | 3,421.8 | 3,462.9 | 3,504.3 | 3,535.4 | 3,500.1 | 3,424.5 | 3,493.6 | 3,528.8 | 3,560.6 | 3,576.5 | 3,577.7 | 3,500.7 |
| 2015 | 3,500.8 | 3,521.0 | 3,536.7 | 3,570.0 | 3,604.8 | 3,576.2 | 3,503.8 | 3,565.3 | 3,606.8 | 3,642.3 | 3,659.0 | 3,661.8 | 3,579.0 |
| 2016 | 3,579.3 | 3,602.2 | 3,631.8 | 3,669.0 | 3,691.7 | 3,664.1 | 3,594.6 | 3,652.3 | 3,694.5 | 3,714.5 | 3,738.6 | 3,730.6 | 3,663.6 |
| 2017 | 3,651.3 | 3,680.9 | 3,700.1 | 3,717.1 | 3,746.5 | 3,724.9 | 3,657.2 | 3,716.3 | 3,744.5 | 3,775.9 | 3,792.3 | 3,782.7 | 3,724.1 |
| 2018 | 3,710.9 | 3,743.7 | 3,765.6 | 3,786.0 | 3,818.9 | 3,794.2 | 3,727.3 | 3,789.4 | 3,778.0 | 3,838.6 | 3,857.9 | 3,837.4 | 3,787.3 |
| 2019 | 3,794.5 | 3,818.4 | 3,835.7 | 3,860.1 | 3,887.0 | 3,868.7 | 3,798.4 | 3,860.3 | 3,869.0 | 3,898.9 | 3,912.0 | 3,901.5 | 3,858.7 |
| **Mining and Logging** | | | | | | | | | | | | | |
| 2011 | 5.5 | 5.6 | 5.6 | 5.5 | 5.5 | 5.6 | 5.7 | 5.7 | 5.7 | 5.6 | 5.6 | 5.6 | 5.6 |
| 2012 | 5.5 | 5.5 | 5.6 | 5.5 | 5.5 | 5.6 | 5.6 | 5.6 | 5.6 | 5.6 | 5.6 | 5.5 | 5.6 |
| 2013 | 5.4 | 5.4 | 5.4 | 5.5 | 5.5 | 5.5 | 5.5 | 5.6 | 5.6 | 5.6 | 5.6 | 5.6 | 5.5 |
| 2014 | 5.4 | 5.4 | 5.5 | 5.5 | 5.5 | 5.6 | 5.6 | 5.6 | 5.6 | 5.5 | 5.5 | 5.5 | 5.5 |
| 2015 | 5.5 | 5.5 | 5.5 | 5.5 | 5.5 | 5.6 | 5.6 | 5.6 | 5.6 | 5.6 | 5.5 | 5.5 | 5.5 |
| 2016 | 5.6 | 5.5 | 5.6 | 5.6 | 5.6 | 5.7 | 5.7 | 5.7 | 5.7 | 5.6 | 5.6 | 5.6 | 5.6 |
| 2017 | 5.6 | 5.6 | 5.7 | 5.5 | 5.6 | 5.6 | 5.8 | 5.8 | 5.8 | 5.8 | 5.9 | 5.9 | 5.7 |
| 2018 | 5.8 | 5.8 | 5.9 | 5.8 | 5.8 | 5.9 | 5.9 | 5.9 | 5.7 | 5.7 | 5.7 | 5.6 | 5.8 |
| 2019 | 5.7 | 5.7 | 5.7 | 5.7 | 5.8 | 5.8 | 5.8 | 5.9 | 5.7 | 5.7 | 5.7 | 5.6 | 5.7 |
| **Construction** | | | | | | | | | | | | | |
| 2011 | 162.5 | 167.2 | 170.7 | 172.9 | 175.2 | 176.8 | 177.7 | 177.7 | 177.1 | 174.8 | 173.7 | 172.8 | 173.3 |
| 2012 | 166.5 | 167.6 | 171.2 | 172.1 | 173.4 | 173.5 | 174.0 | 174.3 | 173.6 | 172.9 | 172.4 | 172.1 | 172.0 |
| 2013 | 165.6 | 166.6 | 169.5 | 172.2 | 174.3 | 175.7 | 176.3 | 176.8 | 176.8 | 176.6 | 176.8 | 175.5 | 173.6 |
| 2014 | 169.7 | 169.3 | 173.9 | 175.6 | 178.7 | 180.9 | 182.7 | 183.5 | 183.4 | 185.2 | 184.5 | 184.3 | 179.3 |
| 2015 | 178.4 | 180.1 | 182.3 | 186.1 | 189.8 | 191.7 | 193.4 | 193.9 | 193.7 | 194.8 | 193.7 | 194.2 | 189.3 |
| 2016 | 190.6 | 191.6 | 195.0 | 199.0 | 200.2 | 202.5 | 204.2 | 204.0 | 204.5 | 204.2 | 205.1 | 204.9 | 200.5 |
| 2017 | 198.8 | 202.5 | 204.3 | 206.1 | 207.9 | 211.0 | 212.1 | 211.9 | 211.8 | 212.4 | 212.7 | 213.4 | 208.7 |
| 2018 | 209.3 | 211.8 | 215.1 | 216.4 | 219.5 | 223.1 | 224.3 | 224.7 | 222.8 | 227.1 | 226.9 | 225.8 | 220.6 |
| 2019 | 225.5 | 226.7 | 228.9 | 229.8 | 231.9 | 234.6 | 234.5 | 234.2 | 233.5 | 233.6 | 233.6 | 231.2 | 231.5 |

## 1. Employment by Industry: North Carolina, 2011–2019—*Continued*

(Numbers in thousands, not seasonally adjusted)

| Industry and year | January | February | March | April | May | June | July | August | September | October | November | December | Annual average |
|---|---|---|---|---|---|---|---|---|---|---|---|---|---|
| **Manufacturing** | | | | | | | | | | | | | |
| 2011 | 429.4 | 430.4 | 431.7 | 432.0 | 433.8 | 435.4 | 435.1 | 436.3 | 436.2 | 434.8 | 434.8 | 434.9 | 433.7 |
| 2012 | 433.5 | 435.3 | 436.8 | 437.1 | 439.6 | 442.1 | 442.0 | 441.8 | 443.1 | 442.5 | 443.4 | 443.9 | 440.1 |
| 2013 | 438.8 | 440.4 | 440.7 | 439.9 | 441.5 | 444.8 | 444.4 | 443.8 | 444.7 | 444.8 | 444.6 | 446.3 | 442.9 |
| 2014 | 441.7 | 442.7 | 444.6 | 444.6 | 446.8 | 449.7 | 449.9 | 450.6 | 452.4 | 454.5 | 455.9 | 457.8 | 449.3 |
| 2015 | 455.6 | 456.9 | 458.2 | 458.1 | 460.1 | 462.7 | 462.6 | 463.5 | 463.8 | 465.2 | 465.7 | 467.3 | 461.6 |
| 2016 | 463.2 | 464.5 | 463.8 | 463.6 | 463.9 | 465.7 | 466.7 | 466.3 | 465.6 | 463.9 | 466.0 | 466.8 | 465.0 |
| 2017 | 463.1 | 465.7 | 465.4 | 465.3 | 466.6 | 469.9 | 469.8 | 470.1 | 469.4 | 469.2 | 469.9 | 471.3 | 468.0 |
| 2018 | 467.9 | 470.6 | 471.3 | 471.2 | 472.8 | 476.1 | 477.4 | 477.9 | 476.6 | 477.2 | 477.5 | 478.4 | 474.6 |
| 2019 | 476.0 | 477.3 | 476.5 | 475.5 | 476.5 | 479.1 | 479.5 | 478.7 | 477.3 | 479.6 | 482.0 | 481.1 | 478.3 |
| **Trade, Transportation, and Utilities** | | | | | | | | | | | | | |
| 2011 | 707.4 | 707.7 | 712.9 | 718.0 | 721.5 | 724.2 | 728.1 | 729.3 | 726.1 | 730.8 | 743.9 | 750.3 | 725.0 |
| 2012 | 726.9 | 722.9 | 729.2 | 732.8 | 739.0 | 742.4 | 743.4 | 742.2 | 741.1 | 744.8 | 761.3 | 765.7 | 741.0 |
| 2013 | 736.8 | 735.0 | 740.0 | 743.0 | 749.0 | 753.5 | 755.7 | 757.3 | 754.8 | 761.3 | 777.7 | 786.1 | 754.2 |
| 2014 | 756.2 | 749.8 | 757.5 | 762.8 | 768.3 | 773.2 | 772.2 | 774.6 | 771.9 | 779.6 | 796.0 | 805.9 | 772.3 |
| 2015 | 773.3 | 771.9 | 776.9 | 783.1 | 789.1 | 794.6 | 795.4 | 796.7 | 793.7 | 801.4 | 816.8 | 824.8 | 793.1 |
| 2016 | 794.6 | 792.5 | 796.9 | 804.1 | 808.4 | 810.7 | 812.3 | 813.8 | 810.5 | 814.5 | 832.1 | 841.4 | 811.0 |
| 2017 | 810.8 | 808.0 | 810.0 | 811.7 | 816.2 | 821.5 | 823.5 | 824.9 | 819.7 | 826.4 | 843.7 | 850.1 | 822.2 |
| 2018 | 820.9 | 821.3 | 823.6 | 823.8 | 829.5 | 833.0 | 834.0 | 834.8 | 824.8 | 836.3 | 857.1 | 859.7 | 833.2 |
| 2019 | 839.1 | 834.4 | 837.0 | 839.1 | 844.9 | 850.2 | 848.8 | 847.4 | 842.1 | 845.9 | 862.2 | 866.8 | 846.5 |
| **Wholesale Trade** | | | | | | | | | | | | | |
| 2011 | 161.0 | 162.0 | 162.8 | 163.7 | 163.9 | 164.4 | 165.3 | 165.3 | 165.2 | 165.0 | 165.5 | 165.7 | 164.2 |
| 2012 | 164.0 | 164.8 | 166.4 | 167.3 | 168.1 | 168.6 | 169.0 | 169.1 | 168.7 | 169.0 | 169.2 | 169.0 | 167.8 |
| 2013 | 166.6 | 167.7 | 168.7 | 168.4 | 169.0 | 169.6 | 169.7 | 170.1 | 169.9 | 170.2 | 170.8 | 171.0 | 169.3 |
| 2014 | 169.3 | 169.7 | 170.7 | 170.7 | 171.3 | 171.9 | 172.0 | 172.6 | 172.0 | 172.7 | 172.8 | 173.2 | 171.6 |
| 2015 | 170.8 | 171.5 | 172.5 | 172.6 | 173.4 | 174.1 | 174.4 | 174.6 | 173.8 | 174.6 | 175.1 | 175.5 | 173.6 |
| 2016 | 173.8 | 174.4 | 175.1 | 176.7 | 177.0 | 177.2 | 177.6 | 177.5 | 176.9 | 177.1 | 177.4 | 177.9 | 176.6 |
| 2017 | 176.0 | 177.0 | 177.2 | 177.5 | 178.4 | 179.7 | 179.9 | 180.2 | 179.5 | 180.3 | 180.3 | 181.1 | 178.9 |
| 2018 | 179.4 | 180.5 | 181.2 | 180.9 | 181.2 | 182.7 | 182.8 | 183.5 | 182.2 | 184.3 | 184.7 | 184.6 | 182.3 |
| 2019 | 185.0 | 185.8 | 186.1 | 186.8 | 187.2 | 188.6 | 187.9 | 188.1 | 187.1 | 187.3 | 189.0 | 188.4 | 187.3 |
| **Retail Trade** | | | | | | | | | | | | | |
| 2011 | 430.4 | 429.2 | 432.6 | 435.9 | 439.1 | 440.5 | 443.1 | 443.8 | 440.0 | 444.7 | 456.8 | 461.2 | 441.4 |
| 2012 | 443.2 | 438.6 | 442.1 | 445.2 | 450.2 | 452.5 | 453.2 | 451.8 | 450.3 | 453.4 | 469.1 | 471.3 | 451.7 |
| 2013 | 447.9 | 446.4 | 449.4 | 452.5 | 457.0 | 460.2 | 462.2 | 462.4 | 459.8 | 465.4 | 479.6 | 485.2 | 460.7 |
| 2014 | 460.6 | 455.7 | 460.9 | 465.8 | 469.4 | 472.5 | 471.8 | 472.8 | 469.7 | 475.9 | 490.4 | 496.0 | 471.8 |
| 2015 | 471.3 | 469.6 | 472.8 | 477.5 | 482.0 | 486.0 | 486.5 | 487.0 | 484.6 | 490.5 | 503.4 | 507.0 | 484.9 |
| 2016 | 483.9 | 482.8 | 485.7 | 491.4 | 495.1 | 496.2 | 497.5 | 498.4 | 495.1 | 498.7 | 512.4 | 515.7 | 496.1 |
| 2017 | 493.2 | 490.8 | 492.3 | 493.2 | 495.6 | 498.4 | 499.5 | 499.3 | 494.5 | 499.6 | 514.5 | 515.6 | 498.9 |
| 2018 | 495.0 | 494.0 | 495.2 | 495.6 | 500.0 | 500.9 | 501.6 | 500.6 | 490.8 | 497.6 | 513.4 | 512.9 | 499.8 |
| 2019 | 496.7 | 493.4 | 494.7 | 496.1 | 500.2 | 502.4 | 501.9 | 499.7 | 495.4 | 498.8 | 509.8 | 510.2 | 499.9 |
| **Transportation and Utilities** | | | | | | | | | | | | | |
| 2011 | 116.0 | 116.5 | 117.5 | 118.4 | 118.5 | 119.3 | 119.7 | 120.2 | 120.9 | 121.1 | 121.6 | 123.4 | 119.4 |
| 2012 | 119.7 | 119.5 | 120.7 | 120.3 | 120.7 | 121.3 | 121.2 | 121.3 | 122.1 | 122.4 | 123.0 | 125.4 | 121.5 |
| 2013 | 122.3 | 120.9 | 121.9 | 122.1 | 123.0 | 123.7 | 123.8 | 124.8 | 125.1 | 125.7 | 127.3 | 129.9 | 124.2 |
| 2014 | 126.3 | 124.4 | 125.9 | 126.3 | 127.6 | 128.8 | 128.4 | 129.2 | 130.2 | 131.0 | 132.8 | 136.7 | 129.0 |
| 2015 | 131.2 | 130.8 | 131.6 | 133.0 | 133.7 | 134.5 | 134.5 | 135.1 | 135.3 | 136.3 | 138.3 | 142.3 | 134.7 |
| 2016 | 136.9 | 135.3 | 136.1 | 136.0 | 136.3 | 137.3 | 137.2 | 137.9 | 138.5 | 138.7 | 142.3 | 147.8 | 138.4 |
| 2017 | 141.6 | 140.2 | 140.5 | 141.0 | 142.2 | 143.4 | 144.1 | 145.4 | 145.7 | 146.5 | 148.9 | 153.4 | 144.4 |
| 2018 | 146.5 | 146.8 | 147.2 | 147.3 | 148.3 | 149.4 | 149.6 | 150.7 | 151.8 | 154.4 | 159.0 | 162.2 | 151.1 |
| 2019 | 157.4 | 155.2 | 156.2 | 156.2 | 157.5 | 159.2 | 159.0 | 159.6 | 159.6 | 159.8 | 163.4 | 168.2 | 159.3 |
| **Information** | | | | | | | | | | | | | |
| 2011 | 65.6 | 65.6 | 65.5 | 66.0 | 66.0 | 66.4 | 66.6 | 66.6 | 65.9 | 66.0 | 66.4 | 66.3 | 66.1 |
| 2012 | 65.9 | 65.9 | 65.7 | 65.8 | 65.7 | 66.2 | 66.2 | 66.0 | 65.3 | 65.4 | 65.8 | 66.0 | 65.8 |
| 2013 | 65.8 | 66.1 | 66.0 | 66.0 | 66.6 | 66.7 | 67.2 | 67.2 | 66.6 | 67.3 | 68.2 | 68.5 | 66.9 |
| 2014 | 67.3 | 67.6 | 67.7 | 67.7 | 68.4 | 69.2 | 69.7 | 70.0 | 69.6 | 70.2 | 70.6 | 71.2 | 69.1 |
| 2015 | 70.4 | 70.8 | 70.8 | 70.9 | 72.4 | 72.7 | 72.9 | 72.8 | 72.3 | 72.8 | 73.5 | 73.8 | 72.2 |
| 2016 | 73.0 | 74.2 | 73.5 | 74.3 | 75.0 | 74.7 | 75.2 | 74.4 | 73.5 | 74.5 | 74.8 | 74.8 | 74.3 |
| 2017 | 73.9 | 74.3 | 74.2 | 74.4 | 74.3 | 74.5 | 74.5 | 74.5 | 73.6 | 73.8 | 74.6 | 74.6 | 74.3 |
| 2018 | 74.4 | 74.9 | 74.7 | 74.8 | 76.5 | 76.0 | 75.7 | 75.1 | 74.5 | 75.1 | 75.5 | 75.4 | 75.2 |
| 2019 | 75.4 | 76.1 | 76.0 | 75.2 | 75.9 | 76.5 | 76.2 | 75.9 | 75.7 | 76.0 | 77.2 | 78.6 | 76.2 |

## 1. Employment by Industry: North Carolina, 2011–2019—Continued

(Numbers in thousands, not seasonally adjusted)

| Industry and year | January | February | March | April | May | June | July | August | September | October | November | December | Annual average |
|---|---|---|---|---|---|---|---|---|---|---|---|---|---|
| **Financial Activities** | | | | | | | | | | | | | |
| 2011 | 200.8 | 201.3 | 201.5 | 202.1 | 203.6 | 205.7 | 206.3 | 206.9 | 204.8 | 204.7 | 204.3 | 204.5 | 203.9 |
| 2012 | 201.8 | 202.6 | 204.0 | 204.6 | 205.6 | 207.7 | 207.9 | 208.2 | 206.7 | 207.6 | 207.3 | 207.5 | 206.0 |
| 2013 | 205.1 | 205.7 | 206.3 | 208.5 | 209.7 | 212.1 | 212.4 | 212.9 | 211.4 | 211.4 | 211.1 | 211.4 | 209.8 |
| 2014 | 210.9 | 211.0 | 211.9 | 212.8 | 214.6 | 217.2 | 218.8 | 219.6 | 218.3 | 218.0 | 218.0 | 218.8 | 215.8 |
| 2015 | 216.4 | 217.6 | 218.0 | 219.3 | 221.4 | 224.2 | 226.1 | 226.0 | 225.3 | 226.2 | 226.0 | 227.1 | 222.8 |
| 2016 | 225.2 | 226.1 | 226.4 | 227.9 | 229.3 | 232.0 | 234.1 | 234.6 | 232.9 | 233.7 | 233.4 | 234.3 | 230.8 |
| 2017 | 231.2 | 232.0 | 233.0 | 234.4 | 235.9 | 239.2 | 241.4 | 241.1 | 239.5 | 240.5 | 239.9 | 240.7 | 237.4 |
| 2018 | 238.6 | 240.0 | 241.1 | 242.2 | 243.5 | 246.8 | 247.5 | 247.6 | 245.3 | 246.7 | 246.6 | 246.7 | 244.4 |
| 2019 | 244.1 | 245.6 | 245.9 | 248.4 | 250.6 | 254.6 | 256.3 | 257.6 | 255.4 | 257.7 | 256.5 | 258.8 | 252.6 |
| **Professional and Business Services** | | | | | | | | | | | | | |
| 2011 | 491.4 | 501.2 | 504.6 | 510.5 | 509.8 | 514.3 | 517.4 | 521.7 | 525.3 | 527.4 | 527.4 | 526.6 | 514.8 |
| 2012 | 515.9 | 523.4 | 527.5 | 531.8 | 533.5 | 537.0 | 534.6 | 541.0 | 540.3 | 543.4 | 543.3 | 543.1 | 534.6 |
| 2013 | 527.3 | 536.4 | 540.2 | 545.1 | 546.5 | 549.8 | 549.8 | 558.0 | 558.8 | 563.2 | 563.2 | 559.9 | 549.9 |
| 2014 | 547.9 | 549.1 | 558.1 | 569.3 | 571.1 | 575.2 | 577.8 | 581.2 | 580.5 | 586.2 | 583.9 | 584.5 | 572.1 |
| 2015 | 570.9 | 576.9 | 577.2 | 586.0 | 589.4 | 592.4 | 595.4 | 600.7 | 601.8 | 608.0 | 608.3 | 605.5 | 592.7 |
| 2016 | 590.5 | 595.0 | 599.6 | 608.0 | 607.5 | 610.8 | 613.2 | 615.1 | 616.6 | 618.3 | 619.4 | 614.1 | 609.0 |
| 2017 | 602.2 | 609.9 | 613.0 | 614.4 | 616.8 | 624.0 | 624.0 | 625.4 | 622.5 | 628.5 | 630.8 | 626.4 | 619.8 |
| 2018 | 614.4 | 621.5 | 624.1 | 630.9 | 631.0 | 636.4 | 639.4 | 645.4 | 638.2 | 651.5 | 647.7 | 641.0 | 635.1 |
| 2019 | 635.9 | 641.5 | 643.5 | 646.7 | 646.9 | 652.7 | 652.6 | 658.0 | 651.2 | 655.7 | 654.0 | 643.9 | 648.6 |
| **Education and Health Services** | | | | | | | | | | | | | |
| 2011 | 532.4 | 538.6 | 538.8 | 541.4 | 540.9 | 536.7 | 533.2 | 536.2 | 540.7 | 544.9 | 546.7 | 546.1 | 539.7 |
| 2012 | 541.4 | 546.2 | 546.5 | 547.0 | 549.1 | 545.8 | 543.2 | 546.4 | 551.1 | 556.0 | 557.4 | 558.2 | 549.0 |
| 2013 | 550.7 | 556.2 | 557.5 | 558.0 | 559.0 | 555.4 | 554.2 | 557.9 | 562.3 | 564.4 | 565.9 | 565.3 | 558.9 |
| 2014 | 557.8 | 560.3 | 565.5 | 568.0 | 569.7 | 564.7 | 565.1 | 569.4 | 571.0 | 576.3 | 577.7 | 576.6 | 568.5 |
| 2015 | 566.6 | 571.8 | 571.0 | 572.2 | 574.3 | 569.5 | 567.8 | 569.3 | 574.3 | 582.1 | 583.6 | 582.8 | 573.8 |
| 2016 | 575.0 | 579.7 | 581.8 | 585.9 | 587.0 | 581.3 | 582.0 | 586.6 | 590.2 | 594.7 | 596.5 | 595.5 | 586.4 |
| 2017 | 590.3 | 597.2 | 596.1 | 598.1 | 600.3 | 594.6 | 594.3 | 598.5 | 600.0 | 608.8 | 608.4 | 606.4 | 599.4 |
| 2018 | 602.5 | 610.3 | 610.2 | 612.5 | 614.5 | 608.7 | 608.3 | 613.3 | 610.2 | 622.1 | 623.6 | 619.7 | 613.0 |
| 2019 | 619.3 | 625.7 | 624.6 | 627.7 | 629.0 | 623.4 | 622.4 | 627.6 | 626.5 | 631.7 | 631.1 | 626.3 | 626.3 |
| **Leisure and Hospitality** | | | | | | | | | | | | | |
| 2011 | 371.1 | 376.4 | 387.3 | 400.3 | 411.7 | 421.4 | 420.2 | 421.7 | 411.9 | 404.9 | 400.4 | 396.2 | 402.0 |
| 2012 | 384.5 | 388.4 | 400.4 | 413.5 | 425.9 | 434.4 | 437.5 | 439.2 | 427.4 | 421.3 | 415.6 | 412.1 | 416.7 |
| 2013 | 400.4 | 403.0 | 413.4 | 428.1 | 440.3 | 451.6 | 453.2 | 453.1 | 442.5 | 437.1 | 432.2 | 430.4 | 432.1 |
| 2014 | 415.7 | 413.3 | 426.2 | 442.1 | 457.8 | 466.2 | 465.2 | 465.2 | 454.7 | 449.9 | 443.9 | 441.7 | 445.2 |
| 2015 | 430.3 | 432.9 | 440.7 | 454.2 | 470.5 | 481.7 | 482.1 | 480.4 | 470.0 | 466.2 | 460.5 | 459.3 | 460.7 |
| 2016 | 448.8 | 452.1 | 462.8 | 479.8 | 492.8 | 502.4 | 500.8 | 499.9 | 488.6 | 483.0 | 479.9 | 475.5 | 480.5 |
| 2017 | 461.5 | 468.1 | 478.4 | 488.5 | 505.9 | 516.2 | 516.6 | 516.6 | 500.6 | 498.4 | 491.4 | 485.3 | 494.0 |
| 2018 | 472.7 | 478.8 | 489.8 | 499.9 | 516.0 | 527.4 | 528.0 | 526.9 | 498.3 | 506.1 | 500.0 | 492.5 | 503.0 |
| 2019 | 485.9 | 491.4 | 500.4 | 512.6 | 527.7 | 539.1 | 538.7 | 535.3 | 516.6 | 520.7 | 513.3 | 513.6 | 516.3 |
| **Other Services** | | | | | | | | | | | | | |
| 2011 | 135.4 | 136.2 | 137.0 | 136.9 | 137.6 | 140.4 | 140.4 | 139.5 | 137.8 | 138.4 | 138.0 | 138.1 | 138.0 |
| 2012 | 137.0 | 137.5 | 138.5 | 139.7 | 141.6 | 143.7 | 144.5 | 144.3 | 144.1 | 143.9 | 144.2 | 144.0 | 141.9 |
| 2013 | 143.4 | 144.8 | 146.5 | 146.9 | 147.9 | 149.7 | 148.7 | 148.1 | 147.0 | 146.3 | 147.2 | 145.8 | 146.9 |
| 2014 | 144.3 | 144.0 | 146.0 | 146.9 | 148.2 | 150.3 | 150.3 | 149.7 | 147.9 | 148.1 | 147.7 | 147.5 | 147.6 |
| 2015 | 145.8 | 146.3 | 147.0 | 148.1 | 149.9 | 151.0 | 152.2 | 151.0 | 149.0 | 148.5 | 148.4 | 148.3 | 148.8 |
| 2016 | 147.1 | 147.3 | 148.1 | 149.5 | 150.7 | 152.5 | 152.8 | 152.5 | 151.8 | 151.1 | 151.3 | 150.2 | 150.4 |
| 2017 | 148.9 | 149.6 | 150.3 | 150.8 | 152.1 | 154.7 | 154.2 | 153.3 | 152.0 | 153.1 | 152.7 | 152.7 | 152.0 |
| 2018 | 151.6 | 152.4 | 153.2 | 153.2 | 154.9 | 157.0 | 157.3 | 156.7 | 153.6 | 156.1 | 156.0 | 155.6 | 154.8 |
| 2019 | 155.9 | 156.9 | 158.2 | 158.5 | 160.0 | 162.2 | 162.1 | 160.7 | 159.5 | 160.6 | 160.9 | 161.5 | 159.8 |
| **Government** | | | | | | | | | | | | | |
| 2011 | 722.0 | 728.5 | 732.8 | 733.9 | 734.7 | 684.8 | 607.0 | 664.1 | 710.9 | 724.8 | 731.3 | 725.3 | 708.3 |
| 2012 | 718.1 | 726.0 | 729.2 | 729.9 | 734.0 | 673.8 | 597.8 | 665.6 | 716.2 | 732.9 | 739.3 | 732.9 | 708.0 |
| 2013 | 723.8 | 732.7 | 736.0 | 735.4 | 736.2 | 676.0 | 602.3 | 665.0 | 718.3 | 735.4 | 738.0 | 734.2 | 711.1 |
| 2014 | 721.7 | 726.7 | 730.0 | 734.7 | 737.3 | 684.1 | 605.4 | 663.9 | 714.9 | 732.3 | 738.7 | 731.5 | 710.1 |
| 2015 | 727.1 | 732.8 | 735.1 | 736.2 | 737.8 | 690.1 | 611.9 | 668.4 | 720.4 | 737.1 | 741.9 | 740.2 | 714.9 |
| 2016 | 725.1 | 735.3 | 742.7 | 739.5 | 741.0 | 699.7 | 624.2 | 675.4 | 730.4 | 744.7 | 751.2 | 744.8 | 721.2 |
| 2017 | 732.5 | 741.8 | 745.1 | 744.8 | 745.0 | 700.2 | 628.7 | 682.0 | 736.6 | 746.4 | 750.8 | 746.5 | 725.0 |
| 2018 | 735.8 | 744.5 | 748.9 | 748.7 | 753.0 | 708.9 | 637.1 | 689.6 | 733.1 | 744.7 | 751.4 | 746.8 | 728.5 |
| 2019 | 738.9 | 746.8 | 750.1 | 751.9 | 752.0 | 710.0 | 641.3 | 697.8 | 742.0 | 750.6 | 756.8 | 752.0 | 732.5 |

## 2. Average Weekly Hours by Selected Industry: North Carolina, 2015–2019

(Not seasonally adjusted)

| Industry and year | January | February | March | April | May | June | July | August | September | October | November | December | Annual average |
|---|---|---|---|---|---|---|---|---|---|---|---|---|---|
| **Total Private** | | | | | | | | | | | | | |
| 2015 | 34.2 | 34.6 | 34.9 | 34.4 | 34.6 | 34.6 | 34.5 | 35.1 | 34.3 | 34.6 | 34.7 | 34.5 | 34.6 |
| 2016 | 33.9 | 34.0 | 34.3 | 34.4 | 34.7 | 34.5 | 34.6 | 34.5 | 34.5 | 34.7 | 34.5 | 34.4 | 34.4 |
| 2017 | 34.0 | 34.4 | 34.3 | 34.7 | 34.5 | 34.7 | 34.9 | 34.4 | 34.5 | 34.9 | 34.5 | 34.4 | 34.5 |
| 2018 | 33.7 | 34.5 | 34.4 | 35.1 | 34.6 | 34.8 | 34.9 | 34.7 | 34.1 | 34.5 | 34.3 | 33.9 | 34.5 |
| 2019 | 34.3 | 34.4 | 34.4 | 34.3 | 34.3 | 34.9 | 34.2 | 34.4 | 34.7 | 34.3 | 34.1 | 34.5 | 34.4 |
| **Goods-Producing** | | | | | | | | | | | | | |
| 2015 | 40.3 | 40.7 | 41.4 | 40.7 | 41.3 | 41.1 | 41.1 | 41.5 | 40.4 | 41.1 | 40.7 | 41.4 | 41.0 |
| 2016 | 39.9 | 39.8 | 40.9 | 40.9 | 40.9 | 41.1 | 40.8 | 40.6 | 41.0 | 40.6 | 41.4 | 40.4 | 40.7 |
| 2017 | 39.3 | 40.4 | 40.4 | 40.1 | 40.8 | 41.1 | 40.6 | 40.3 | 40.4 | 40.8 | 40.8 | 40.6 | 40.5 |
| 2018 | 39.2 | 40.3 | 39.9 | 40.7 | 40.7 | 41.4 | 40.7 | 40.9 | 38.3 | 40.4 | 39.9 | 38.6 | 40.1 |
| 2019 | 40.1 | 39.6 | 40.0 | 40.1 | 40.4 | 40.5 | 39.8 | 40.5 | 40.2 | 40.2 | 39.6 | 39.8 | 40.1 |
| **Construction** | | | | | | | | | | | | | |
| 2015 | 37.2 | 39.0 | 40.3 | 39.3 | 40.9 | 41.1 | 41.1 | 41.4 | 39.6 | 40.6 | 39.4 | 41.2 | 40.1 |
| 2016 | 38.8 | 38.1 | 40.9 | 40.3 | 40.3 | 41.3 | 40.8 | 40.0 | 40.6 | 40.4 | 41.1 | 39.0 | 40.1 |
| 2017 | 36.8 | 39.4 | 39.5 | 39.7 | 40.6 | 41.0 | 40.6 | 39.7 | 39.4 | 39.9 | 40.0 | 40.1 | 39.7 |
| 2018 | 38.1 | 39.3 | 38.5 | 40.5 | 40.7 | 41.0 | 40.0 | 40.1 | 36.3 | 38.8 | 37.7 | 36.3 | 38.9 |
| 2019 | 39.2 | 38.0 | 38.9 | 38.7 | 39.8 | 39.5 | 39.4 | 39.9 | 40.0 | 40.0 | 38.3 | 38.2 | 39.2 |
| **Manufacturing** | | | | | | | | | | | | | |
| 2015 | 41.9 | 41.5 | 42.1 | 41.6 | 41.5 | 41.1 | 41.0 | 41.5 | 40.9 | 41.3 | 41.3 | 41.4 | 41.4 |
| 2016 | 40.4 | 40.6 | 40.7 | 41.2 | 41.2 | 40.9 | 40.6 | 40.9 | 41.1 | 40.7 | 41.6 | 41.3 | 40.9 |
| 2017 | 40.6 | 41.3 | 41.1 | 40.5 | 41.2 | 41.5 | 40.8 | 40.9 | 41.1 | 41.6 | 41.4 | 41.0 | 41.1 |
| 2018 | 40.0 | 40.9 | 40.9 | 40.9 | 40.8 | 41.7 | 41.4 | 41.5 | 39.7 | 41.5 | 41.4 | 40.0 | 40.9 |
| 2019 | 40.5 | 40.4 | 40.5 | 40.7 | 40.7 | 40.9 | 39.8 | 40.6 | 40.1 | 40.2 | 40.4 | 40.7 | 40.5 |
| **Trade, Transportation, and Utilities** | | | | | | | | | | | | | |
| 2015 | 33.8 | 34.2 | 34.4 | 34.3 | 34.5 | 34.4 | 34.6 | 35.1 | 34.7 | 34.6 | 34.4 | 34.3 | 34.4 |
| 2016 | 33.6 | 34.0 | 34.1 | 34.3 | 34.7 | 34.6 | 34.5 | 34.8 | 34.7 | 34.7 | 34.6 | 34.7 | 34.4 |
| 2017 | 34.4 | 34.6 | 34.5 | 35.1 | 34.8 | 34.8 | 35.0 | 34.5 | 34.6 | 34.8 | 34.4 | 34.6 | 34.7 |
| 2018 | 34.0 | 34.5 | 34.5 | 35.1 | 34.7 | 34.8 | 34.9 | 34.6 | 34.1 | 34.2 | 33.8 | 33.4 | 34.4 |
| 2019 | 33.9 | 33.9 | 34.1 | 34.2 | 34.1 | 34.3 | 33.8 | 33.7 | 33.6 | 33.1 | 32.8 | 33.3 | 33.7 |
| **Financial Activities** | | | | | | | | | | | | | |
| 2015 | 37.1 | 38.3 | 38.5 | 37.5 | 37.6 | 37.6 | 37.6 | 38.3 | 37.5 | 37.8 | 38.9 | 38.1 | 37.9 |
| 2016 | 38.2 | 38.2 | 38.4 | 38.5 | 39.2 | 38.6 | 38.7 | 38.3 | 38.3 | 38.9 | 38.0 | 37.9 | 38.4 |
| 2017 | 39.0 | 38.3 | 37.8 | 39.0 | 37.6 | 38.0 | 38.8 | 37.7 | 38.0 | 39.2 | 38.4 | 38.5 | 38.4 |
| 2018 | 37.9 | 38.4 | 37.8 | 38.8 | 37.7 | 37.5 | 38.3 | 37.4 | 38.5 | 37.9 | 37.7 | 38.0 | 38.0 |
| 2019 | 37.5 | 37.9 | 37.6 | 37.5 | 37.2 | 38.3 | 37.1 | 37.4 | 38.7 | 37.7 | 38.3 | 38.6 | 37.8 |
| **Professional and Business Services** | | | | | | | | | | | | | |
| 2015 | 35.7 | 36.3 | 36.7 | 36.0 | 36.0 | 36.2 | 35.8 | 36.7 | 35.4 | 36.2 | 36.7 | 36.1 | 36.2 |
| 2016 | 35.7 | 35.7 | 35.8 | 36.0 | 36.4 | 36.1 | 36.2 | 36.1 | 36.0 | 36.6 | 35.7 | 35.8 | 36.0 |
| 2017 | 35.6 | 35.6 | 35.6 | 36.3 | 35.8 | 36.2 | 36.5 | 35.8 | 36.0 | 36.5 | 35.7 | 35.5 | 35.9 |
| 2018 | 34.7 | 35.6 | 35.6 | 36.6 | 35.4 | 35.9 | 36.4 | 35.8 | 36.0 | 36.0 | 35.3 | 35.4 | 35.7 |
| 2019 | 35.1 | 35.6 | 35.7 | 35.5 | 35.5 | 36.7 | 35.4 | 35.8 | 36.3 | 35.8 | 35.3 | 36.1 | 35.7 |
| **Education and Health Services** | | | | | | | | | | | | | |
| 2015 | 32.6 | 32.4 | 32.7 | 32.1 | 32.2 | 32.2 | 32.0 | 32.5 | 32.1 | 32.2 | 32.4 | 32.2 | 32.3 |
| 2016 | 32.0 | 31.7 | 31.6 | 32.0 | 32.4 | 32.0 | 32.3 | 32.0 | 32.1 | 32.4 | 32.1 | 32.2 | 32.1 |
| 2017 | 32.4 | 32.2 | 32.1 | 32.6 | 32.5 | 32.5 | 32.8 | 32.5 | 32.8 | 33.1 | 32.6 | 32.6 | 32.6 |
| 2018 | 32.3 | 33.0 | 32.7 | 33.2 | 32.9 | 32.9 | 33.1 | 32.9 | 33.0 | 32.9 | 33.1 | 33.2 | 32.9 |
| 2019 | 33.1 | 33.4 | 33.2 | 32.8 | 32.9 | 33.5 | 33.2 | 33.2 | 33.8 | 33.6 | 33.7 | 34.0 | 33.4 |
| **Leisure and Hospitality** | | | | | | | | | | | | | |
| 2015 | 25.3 | 25.7 | 26.0 | 26.0 | 25.9 | 26.1 | 26.1 | 26.5 | 25.6 | 25.6 | 25.6 | 25.6 | 25.8 |
| 2016 | 24.7 | 25.4 | 25.7 | 25.6 | 25.8 | 25.9 | 26.2 | 26.1 | 25.8 | 25.8 | 26.0 | 25.7 | 25.7 |
| 2017 | 24.6 | 25.6 | 25.8 | 26.2 | 26.0 | 26.4 | 26.6 | 26.4 | 25.9 | 26.2 | 25.9 | 25.6 | 25.9 |
| 2018 | 24.8 | 25.8 | 26.1 | 26.4 | 26.4 | 26.7 | 26.5 | 26.5 | 25.1 | 26.6 | 26.2 | 25.5 | 26.1 |
| 2019 | 25.7 | 26.3 | 26.3 | 26.1 | 26.2 | 26.5 | 26.2 | 26.1 | 25.9 | 25.8 | 25.8 | 25.6 | 26.0 |
| **Other Services** | | | | | | | | | | | | | |
| 2015 | 31.1 | 31.3 | 31.9 | 30.7 | 31.2 | 30.8 | 31.2 | 31.4 | 30.8 | 30.6 | 30.5 | 29.5 | 30.9 |
| 2016 | 29.5 | 29.5 | 30.2 | 30.4 | 30.3 | 30.0 | 30.3 | 30.3 | 29.8 | 29.9 | 29.2 | 29.6 | 29.9 |
| 2017 | 28.9 | 29.9 | 29.4 | 30.5 | 29.0 | 29.4 | 30.1 | 29.6 | 28.9 | 29.8 | 29.1 | 29.1 | 29.5 |
| 2018 | 28.7 | 29.5 | 29.8 | 30.8 | 30.5 | 30.7 | 31.6 | 31.1 | 31.0 | 31.5 | 30.4 | 30.0 | 30.5 |
| 2019 | 31.2 | 30.8 | 30.7 | 30.6 | 30.9 | 32.3 | 31.9 | 32.0 | 32.4 | 32.1 | 31.7 | 31.9 | 31.6 |

## 3. Average Hourly Earnings by Selected Industry: North Carolina, 2015–2019

(Dollars, not seasonally adjusted)

| Industry and year | January | February | March | April | May | June | July | August | September | October | November | December | Annual average |
|---|---|---|---|---|---|---|---|---|---|---|---|---|---|
| **Total Private** | | | | | | | | | | | | | |
| 2015 | 22.02 | 22.30 | 21.96 | 22.01 | 22.08 | 21.99 | 22.13 | 22.54 | 22.40 | 22.53 | 22.89 | 22.71 | 22.30 |
| 2016 | 23.03 | 23.25 | 23.24 | 23.31 | 23.51 | 23.34 | 23.31 | 23.46 | 23.53 | 23.85 | 23.68 | 23.58 | 23.43 |
| 2017 | 24.00 | 23.86 | 23.90 | 24.23 | 23.84 | 23.66 | 24.07 | 23.88 | 24.12 | 24.41 | 24.15 | 24.31 | 24.04 |
| 2018 | 24.79 | 24.81 | 24.77 | 25.02 | 24.76 | 24.61 | 24.92 | 24.84 | 25.52 | 25.04 | 25.21 | 25.67 | 25.00 |
| 2019 | 25.45 | 25.35 | 25.25 | 25.26 | 25.22 | 25.31 | 25.21 | 25.41 | 25.55 | 25.49 | 25.91 | 26.01 | 25.45 |
| **Goods-Producing** | | | | | | | | | | | | | |
| 2015 | 21.56 | 21.55 | 21.36 | 21.50 | 21.49 | 21.38 | 21.26 | 21.43 | 21.42 | 21.46 | 21.70 | 21.84 | 21.50 |
| 2016 | 21.70 | 21.91 | 21.88 | 21.98 | 22.08 | 22.14 | 22.02 | 22.06 | 21.85 | 22.32 | 21.97 | 22.31 | 22.02 |
| 2017 | 22.61 | 22.32 | 22.55 | 22.71 | 22.61 | 22.68 | 23.05 | 22.83 | 23.15 | 23.20 | 23.08 | 23.32 | 22.85 |
| 2018 | 23.64 | 23.70 | 23.63 | 23.79 | 23.63 | 23.66 | 23.71 | 23.58 | 23.80 | 23.71 | 23.87 | 24.22 | 23.74 |
| 2019 | 24.01 | 23.97 | 23.99 | 23.82 | 24.08 | 24.09 | 24.26 | 24.06 | 24.37 | 24.14 | 24.25 | 24.58 | 24.14 |
| **Construction** | | | | | | | | | | | | | |
| 2015 | 22.47 | 21.91 | 21.81 | 22.11 | 21.81 | 21.97 | 21.69 | 21.92 | 22.31 | 22.55 | 22.80 | 22.82 | 22.18 |
| 2016 | 22.43 | 22.53 | 22.29 | 22.31 | 22.56 | 22.25 | 22.44 | 22.70 | 22.73 | 22.97 | 22.44 | 22.94 | 22.55 |
| 2017 | 23.41 | 23.10 | 23.01 | 22.90 | 22.86 | 23.10 | 23.41 | 23.16 | 23.71 | 23.61 | 23.60 | 23.73 | 23.30 |
| 2018 | 24.04 | 24.15 | 24.02 | 24.00 | 24.27 | 24.29 | 24.49 | 24.48 | 24.83 | 24.67 | 24.94 | 25.05 | 24.43 |
| 2019 | 24.52 | 24.80 | 25.00 | 24.85 | 25.06 | 25.03 | 25.03 | 24.98 | 25.29 | 25.25 | 25.39 | 25.66 | 25.07 |
| **Manufacturing** | | | | | | | | | | | | | |
| 2015 | 21.25 | 21.44 | 21.19 | 21.27 | 21.35 | 21.09 | 21.01 | 21.15 | 20.97 | 20.89 | 21.14 | 21.31 | 21.17 |
| 2016 | 21.33 | 21.59 | 21.64 | 21.83 | 21.84 | 22.12 | 22.20 | 22.06 | 21.67 | 22.20 | 21.89 | 22.15 | 21.88 |
| 2017 | 22.46 | 22.15 | 22.20 | 22.53 | 22.37 | 22.37 | 22.74 | 22.53 | 22.67 | 22.84 | 22.68 | 23.00 | 22.55 |
| 2018 | 23.32 | 23.36 | 23.32 | 23.58 | 23.19 | 23.17 | 23.27 | 23.04 | 23.30 | 23.23 | 23.28 | 23.74 | 23.32 |
| 2019 | 23.67 | 23.62 | 23.51 | 23.35 | 23.62 | 23.60 | 23.86 | 23.57 | 23.85 | 23.50 | 23.63 | 24.07 | 23.65 |
| **Trade, Transportation, and Utilities** | | | | | | | | | | | | | |
| 2015 | 20.66 | 21.08 | 20.45 | 20.56 | 20.36 | 20.64 | 20.64 | 21.03 | 21.15 | 21.47 | 21.28 | 20.98 | 20.86 |
| 2016 | 21.50 | 21.40 | 21.72 | 21.72 | 21.77 | 21.93 | 22.13 | 21.87 | 21.99 | 22.05 | 22.04 | 21.79 | 21.83 |
| 2017 | 22.15 | 21.79 | 22.38 | 22.72 | 22.34 | 22.17 | 22.52 | 22.13 | 22.52 | 22.64 | 22.28 | 22.13 | 22.31 |
| 2018 | 23.37 | 22.93 | 22.83 | 23.27 | 22.86 | 22.90 | 23.05 | 22.85 | 23.52 | 23.20 | 23.04 | 23.30 | 23.09 |
| 2019 | 23.21 | 23.05 | 22.76 | 22.84 | 22.88 | 22.99 | 22.81 | 22.82 | 23.21 | 23.21 | 23.31 | 22.99 | 23.01 |
| **Financial Activities** | | | | | | | | | | | | | |
| 2015 | 27.12 | 27.12 | 27.98 | 28.01 | 28.68 | 28.25 | 29.04 | 30.33 | 30.50 | 30.69 | 31.56 | 30.85 | 29.21 |
| 2016 | 31.61 | 33.36 | 32.27 | 32.28 | 33.00 | 32.35 | 32.61 | 33.67 | 33.19 | 33.28 | 32.63 | 32.11 | 32.70 |
| 2017 | 32.67 | 33.27 | 32.72 | 33.31 | 32.56 | 32.50 | 33.29 | 33.59 | 33.89 | 33.84 | 32.83 | 32.54 | 33.09 |
| 2018 | 32.65 | 33.07 | 33.43 | 33.66 | 33.83 | 33.30 | 34.58 | 34.67 | 36.00 | 35.92 | 36.48 | 37.13 | 34.57 |
| 2019 | 36.52 | 36.58 | 36.99 | 37.27 | 37.33 | 37.04 | 36.80 | 36.84 | 36.93 | 37.15 | 38.03 | 38.85 | 37.21 |
| **Professional and Business Services** | | | | | | | | | | | | | |
| 2015 | 26.54 | 27.08 | 26.45 | 26.43 | 26.49 | 26.17 | 26.72 | 27.13 | 26.87 | 26.58 | 27.47 | 27.26 | 26.77 |
| 2016 | 27.71 | 28.00 | 28.57 | 28.56 | 28.69 | 28.39 | 28.32 | 28.29 | 28.64 | 28.88 | 28.58 | 28.48 | 28.43 |
| 2017 | 29.09 | 28.86 | 29.03 | 29.31 | 28.40 | 28.09 | 28.70 | 27.78 | 28.19 | 28.98 | 28.44 | 28.87 | 28.64 |
| 2018 | 29.26 | 29.45 | 29.40 | 29.86 | 29.46 | 29.46 | 29.99 | 29.85 | 31.14 | 29.89 | 30.54 | 31.24 | 29.97 |
| 2019 | 30.75 | 30.41 | 30.21 | 30.29 | 30.05 | 30.30 | 30.05 | 29.92 | 30.19 | 30.20 | 31.30 | 31.41 | 30.42 |
| **Education and Health Services** | | | | | | | | | | | | | |
| 2015 | 22.27 | 22.50 | 22.08 | 22.33 | 22.77 | 22.75 | 22.88 | 23.25 | 22.27 | 22.50 | 22.74 | 22.58 | 22.58 |
| 2016 | 22.70 | 22.65 | 22.68 | 22.87 | 23.45 | 23.10 | 22.69 | 23.55 | 23.54 | 23.85 | 24.44 | 23.78 | 23.28 |
| 2017 | 23.64 | 24.33 | 23.71 | 24.18 | 24.48 | 23.83 | 23.98 | 24.80 | 23.93 | 24.21 | 24.29 | 24.35 | 24.15 |
| 2018 | 24.70 | 24.74 | 24.73 | 24.94 | 25.17 | 24.69 | 24.92 | 24.80 | 24.17 | 24.53 | 24.44 | 24.76 | 24.72 |
| 2019 | 24.96 | 24.99 | 25.04 | 25.18 | 25.15 | 25.22 | 25.54 | 26.63 | 25.50 | 25.65 | 26.20 | 25.80 | 25.49 |
| **Leisure and Hospitality** | | | | | | | | | | | | | |
| 2015 | 12.44 | 12.26 | 12.23 | 12.28 | 12.34 | 12.26 | 12.20 | 12.35 | 12.41 | 12.60 | 12.62 | 12.79 | 12.40 |
| 2016 | 12.80 | 12.79 | 12.70 | 12.77 | 12.77 | 12.72 | 12.71 | 12.85 | 12.86 | 12.98 | 12.96 | 13.09 | 12.83 |
| 2017 | 13.07 | 12.88 | 13.00 | 13.04 | 13.11 | 13.14 | 13.19 | 13.23 | 13.37 | 13.44 | 13.68 | 13.81 | 13.25 |
| 2018 | 13.83 | 13.94 | 13.85 | 13.89 | 13.97 | 13.79 | 13.78 | 13.99 | 14.20 | 14.07 | 14.05 | 14.25 | 13.96 |
| 2019 | 14.30 | 14.29 | 14.41 | 14.34 | 14.34 | 14.32 | 14.27 | 14.34 | 14.45 | 14.54 | 14.59 | 14.62 | 14.40 |
| **Other Services** | | | | | | | | | | | | | |
| 2015 | 18.52 | 18.71 | 18.76 | 18.52 | 18.89 | 18.79 | 18.75 | 19.10 | 19.08 | 18.88 | 19.50 | 19.40 | 18.91 |
| 2016 | 19.68 | 19.72 | 19.65 | 19.83 | 20.19 | 20.08 | 19.93 | 19.97 | 20.40 | 20.54 | 20.83 | 20.67 | 20.12 |
| 2017 | 21.49 | 21.32 | 22.03 | 22.34 | 22.08 | 21.82 | 22.03 | 22.48 | 23.13 | 24.00 | 24.24 | 25.14 | 22.68 |
| 2018 | 24.49 | 24.49 | 25.67 | 25.51 | 25.24 | 25.12 | 25.41 | 25.77 | 26.81 | 25.27 | 25.47 | 25.52 | 25.41 |
| 2019 | 25.01 | 24.42 | 24.04 | 23.67 | 23.00 | 22.40 | 21.96 | 22.69 | 22.75 | 22.37 | 22.49 | 22.95 | 23.12 |

## 4. Average Weekly Earnings by Selected Industry: North Carolina, 2015–2019

(Dollars, not seasonally adjusted)

| Industry and year | January | February | March | April | May | June | July | August | September | October | November | December | Annual average |
|---|---|---|---|---|---|---|---|---|---|---|---|---|---|
| **Total Private** | | | | | | | | | | | | | |
| 2015 | 753.08 | 771.58 | 766.40 | 757.14 | 763.97 | 760.85 | 763.14 | 790.80 | 768.32 | 779.54 | 794.28 | 783.50 | 771.58 |
| 2016 | 780.72 | 790.50 | 797.13 | 801.86 | 815.80 | 805.23 | 806.53 | 809.37 | 812.13 | 827.60 | 816.96 | 811.15 | 805.99 |
| 2017 | 816.00 | 820.78 | 819.77 | 840.78 | 822.48 | 821.00 | 840.04 | 821.47 | 832.14 | 851.91 | 833.18 | 836.26 | 829.38 |
| 2018 | 835.42 | 855.95 | 851.74 | 877.85 | 856.70 | 856.43 | 869.71 | 861.95 | 870.23 | 863.88 | 864.70 | 870.21 | 862.50 |
| 2019 | 872.94 | 872.04 | 868.60 | 866.42 | 865.05 | 883.32 | 862.18 | 874.10 | 886.59 | 874.31 | 883.53 | 897.35 | 875.48 |
| **Goods-Producing** | | | | | | | | | | | | | |
| 2015 | 868.87 | 877.09 | 884.30 | 875.05 | 887.54 | 878.72 | 873.79 | 889.35 | 865.37 | 882.01 | 883.19 | 904.18 | 881.50 |
| 2016 | 865.83 | 872.02 | 894.89 | 898.98 | 903.07 | 909.95 | 898.42 | 895.64 | 895.85 | 906.19 | 909.14 | 900.92 | 896.21 |
| 2017 | 888.18 | 901.73 | 911.02 | 910.67 | 922.49 | 932.15 | 935.83 | 920.05 | 935.26 | 946.56 | 941.66 | 946.79 | 925.43 |
| 2018 | 926.69 | 955.11 | 942.84 | 968.25 | 961.74 | 979.52 | 965.00 | 964.42 | 911.54 | 957.88 | 952.41 | 934.89 | 951.97 |
| 2019 | 962.80 | 949.21 | 959.60 | 955.18 | 972.83 | 975.65 | 965.55 | 974.43 | 979.67 | 970.43 | 960.30 | 978.28 | 968.01 |
| **Construction** | | | | | | | | | | | | | |
| 2015 | 835.88 | 854.49 | 878.94 | 868.92 | 892.03 | 902.97 | 891.46 | 907.49 | 883.48 | 915.53 | 898.32 | 940.18 | 889.42 |
| 2016 | 870.28 | 858.39 | 911.66 | 899.09 | 909.17 | 918.93 | 915.55 | 908.00 | 922.84 | 927.99 | 922.28 | 894.66 | 904.26 |
| 2017 | 861.49 | 910.14 | 908.90 | 909.13 | 928.12 | 947.10 | 950.45 | 919.45 | 934.17 | 942.04 | 944.00 | 951.57 | 925.01 |
| 2018 | 915.92 | 949.10 | 924.77 | 972.00 | 987.79 | 995.89 | 979.60 | 981.65 | 901.33 | 957.20 | 940.24 | 909.32 | 950.33 |
| 2019 | 961.18 | 942.40 | 972.50 | 961.70 | 997.39 | 988.69 | 986.18 | 996.70 | 1,011.60 | 1,010.00 | 972.44 | 980.21 | 982.74 |
| **Manufacturing** | | | | | | | | | | | | | |
| 2015 | 890.38 | 889.76 | 892.10 | 884.83 | 886.03 | 866.80 | 861.41 | 877.73 | 857.67 | 862.76 | 873.08 | 882.23 | 876.44 |
| 2016 | 861.73 | 876.55 | 880.75 | 899.40 | 899.81 | 904.71 | 901.32 | 902.25 | 890.64 | 903.54 | 910.62 | 914.80 | 894.89 |
| 2017 | 911.88 | 914.80 | 912.42 | 912.47 | 921.64 | 928.36 | 927.79 | 921.48 | 931.74 | 950.14 | 938.95 | 943.00 | 926.81 |
| 2018 | 932.80 | 955.42 | 953.79 | 964.42 | 946.15 | 966.19 | 963.38 | 956.16 | 925.01 | 964.05 | 963.79 | 950.00 | 953.79 |
| 2019 | 958.64 | 954.25 | 952.16 | 950.35 | 961.33 | 965.24 | 949.63 | 956.94 | 956.39 | 944.70 | 954.65 | 979.65 | 957.83 |
| **Trade, Transportation, and Utilities** | | | | | | | | | | | | | |
| 2015 | 698.31 | 720.94 | 703.48 | 705.21 | 702.42 | 710.02 | 714.14 | 738.15 | 733.91 | 742.86 | 732.03 | 719.61 | 717.58 |
| 2016 | 722.40 | 727.60 | 740.65 | 745.00 | 755.42 | 758.78 | 763.49 | 761.08 | 763.05 | 765.14 | 762.58 | 756.11 | 750.95 |
| 2017 | 761.96 | 753.93 | 772.11 | 797.47 | 777.43 | 771.52 | 788.20 | 763.49 | 779.19 | 787.87 | 766.43 | 765.70 | 774.16 |
| 2018 | 794.58 | 791.09 | 787.64 | 816.78 | 793.24 | 796.92 | 804.45 | 790.61 | 802.03 | 793.44 | 778.75 | 778.22 | 794.30 |
| 2019 | 786.82 | 781.40 | 776.12 | 781.13 | 780.21 | 788.56 | 770.98 | 769.03 | 779.86 | 768.25 | 764.57 | 765.57 | 775.44 |
| **Financial Activities** | | | | | | | | | | | | | |
| 2015 | 1,006.15 | 1,038.70 | 1,077.23 | 1,050.38 | 1,078.37 | 1,062.20 | 1,091.90 | 1,161.64 | 1,143.75 | 1,160.08 | 1,227.68 | 1,175.39 | 1,107.06 |
| 2016 | 1,207.50 | 1,274.35 | 1,239.17 | 1,242.78 | 1,293.60 | 1,248.71 | 1,262.01 | 1,289.56 | 1,271.18 | 1,294.59 | 1,239.94 | 1,216.97 | 1,255.68 |
| 2017 | 1,274.13 | 1,274.24 | 1,236.82 | 1,299.09 | 1,224.26 | 1,235.00 | 1,291.65 | 1,266.34 | 1,287.82 | 1,326.53 | 1,260.67 | 1,252.79 | 1,270.66 |
| 2018 | 1,237.44 | 1,269.89 | 1,263.65 | 1,306.01 | 1,275.39 | 1,248.75 | 1,324.41 | 1,297.03 | 1,386.39 | 1,361.37 | 1,375.30 | 1,410.94 | 1,313.66 |
| 2019 | 1,369.50 | 1,386.38 | 1,390.82 | 1,397.63 | 1,388.68 | 1,418.63 | 1,365.28 | 1,377.82 | 1,429.19 | 1,400.56 | 1,456.55 | 1,499.61 | 1,406.54 |
| **Professional and Business Services** | | | | | | | | | | | | | |
| 2015 | 947.48 | 983.00 | 970.72 | 951.48 | 953.64 | 947.35 | 956.58 | 995.67 | 951.20 | 962.20 | 1,008.15 | 984.09 | 969.07 |
| 2016 | 989.25 | 999.60 | 1,022.81 | 1,028.16 | 1,044.32 | 1,024.88 | 1,025.18 | 1,021.27 | 1,031.04 | 1,057.01 | 1,020.31 | 1,019.58 | 1,023.48 |
| 2017 | 1,035.60 | 1,027.42 | 1,033.47 | 1,063.95 | 1,016.72 | 1,016.86 | 1,047.55 | 994.52 | 1,014.84 | 1,057.77 | 1,015.31 | 1,024.89 | 1,028.18 |
| 2018 | 1,015.32 | 1,048.42 | 1,046.64 | 1,092.88 | 1,042.88 | 1,057.61 | 1,091.64 | 1,068.63 | 1,121.04 | 1,055.12 | 1,081.12 | 1,115.27 | 1,069.93 |
| 2019 | 1,079.33 | 1,082.60 | 1,078.50 | 1,075.30 | 1,066.78 | 1,112.01 | 1,063.77 | 1,071.14 | 1,095.90 | 1,081.16 | 1,104.89 | 1,133.90 | 1,085.99 |
| **Education and Health Services** | | | | | | | | | | | | | |
| 2015 | 726.00 | 729.00 | 722.02 | 716.79 | 733.19 | 732.55 | 732.16 | 755.63 | 714.87 | 724.50 | 736.78 | 727.08 | 729.33 |
| 2016 | 726.40 | 718.01 | 716.69 | 731.84 | 759.78 | 739.20 | 732.89 | 753.60 | 755.63 | 772.74 | 784.52 | 765.72 | 747.29 |
| 2017 | 765.94 | 783.43 | 761.09 | 788.27 | 795.60 | 774.48 | 786.54 | 806.00 | 784.90 | 801.35 | 791.85 | 793.81 | 787.29 |
| 2018 | 797.81 | 816.42 | 808.67 | 828.01 | 828.09 | 812.30 | 824.85 | 815.92 | 797.61 | 807.04 | 808.96 | 822.03 | 813.29 |
| 2019 | 826.18 | 834.67 | 831.33 | 825.90 | 827.44 | 844.87 | 847.93 | 884.12 | 861.90 | 861.84 | 882.94 | 877.20 | 851.37 |
| **Leisure and Hospitality** | | | | | | | | | | | | | |
| 2015 | 314.73 | 315.08 | 317.98 | 319.28 | 319.61 | 319.99 | 318.42 | 327.28 | 317.70 | 322.56 | 323.07 | 327.42 | 319.92 |
| 2016 | 316.16 | 324.87 | 326.39 | 326.91 | 329.21 | 329.19 | 333.00 | 335.39 | 332.05 | 335.14 | 336.96 | 336.41 | 329.73 |
| 2017 | 321.52 | 329.73 | 335.40 | 341.65 | 340.86 | 346.90 | 350.85 | 349.27 | 346.28 | 352.13 | 354.05 | 353.28 | 343.18 |
| 2018 | 342.74 | 359.39 | 361.49 | 366.70 | 368.81 | 368.19 | 365.17 | 370.74 | 356.42 | 374.26 | 368.37 | 363.38 | 364.36 |
| 2019 | 367.51 | 375.83 | 378.98 | 374.27 | 375.71 | 379.48 | 373.87 | 374.27 | 374.26 | 375.13 | 376.42 | 374.27 | 374.40 |
| **Other Services** | | | | | | | | | | | | | |
| 2015 | 575.97 | 585.62 | 598.44 | 568.56 | 589.37 | 578.73 | 585.00 | 599.74 | 587.66 | 577.73 | 594.75 | 572.30 | 584.32 |
| 2016 | 580.56 | 581.74 | 593.43 | 602.83 | 611.76 | 602.40 | 603.88 | 605.09 | 607.92 | 614.15 | 608.24 | 611.83 | 601.59 |
| 2017 | 621.06 | 637.47 | 647.68 | 681.37 | 640.32 | 641.51 | 663.10 | 665.41 | 668.46 | 715.20 | 705.38 | 731.57 | 669.06 |
| 2018 | 702.86 | 722.46 | 764.97 | 785.71 | 769.82 | 771.18 | 802.96 | 801.45 | 831.11 | 796.01 | 774.29 | 765.60 | 775.01 |
| 2019 | 780.31 | 752.14 | 738.03 | 724.30 | 710.70 | 723.52 | 700.52 | 726.08 | 737.10 | 718.08 | 712.93 | 732.11 | 730.59 |

# NORTH DAKOTA
## *At a Glance*

Population:
  2010 census: 672,591
  2019 estimate: 762,062

Percent change in population:
  2010–2019: 13.3%

Percent change in total nonfarm employment:
  2011–2019: 10.6%

Industry with the largest growth in employment, 2011–2019 (percent):
  Mining and logging, 26.0%

Industry with the largest decline or smallest growth in employment, 2011–2019 (percent):
  Information, -14.1%

Civilian labor force:
  2010: 378,342
  2019: 403,599

Unemployment rate and rank among states (highest to lowest):
  2010: 3.8%, 51st
  2019: 2.4%, 50th

Over-the-year change in unemployment rates:
  2017–2018: -0.1%
  2018–2019: -0.2%

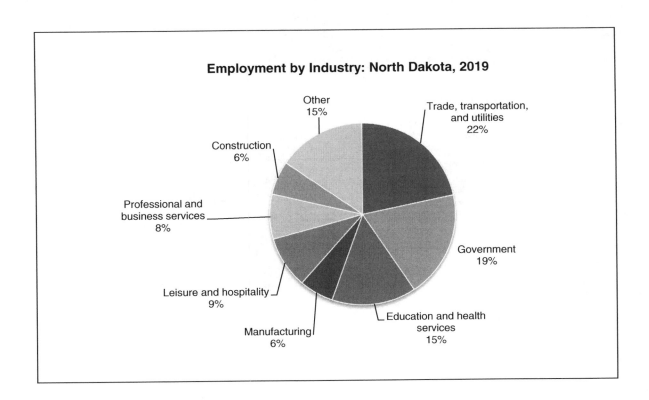

**Employment by Industry: North Dakota, 2019**

Other 15%
Trade, transportation, and utilities 22%
Construction 6%
Professional and business services 8%
Government 19%
Leisure and hospitality 9%
Manufacturing 6%
Education and health services 15%

## 1. Employment by Industry: North Dakota, 2011–2019

(Numbers in thousands, not seasonally adjusted)

| Industry and year | January | February | March | April | May | June | July | August | September | October | November | December | Annual average |
|---|---|---|---|---|---|---|---|---|---|---|---|---|---|
| **Total Nonfarm** | | | | | | | | | | | | | |
| 2011 | 378.1 | 380.1 | 383.4 | 389.7 | 396.7 | 398.4 | 392.5 | 396.2 | 409.0 | 412.8 | 414.2 | 415.7 | 397.2 |
| 2012 | 409.0 | 412.3 | 416.9 | 425.0 | 432.5 | 436.8 | 429.6 | 431.2 | 439.9 | 442.6 | 439.6 | 439.7 | 429.6 |
| 2013 | 428.7 | 432.0 | 434.5 | 436.8 | 447.4 | 450.6 | 442.5 | 444.8 | 454.5 | 457.6 | 457.9 | 453.9 | 445.1 |
| 2014 | 442.0 | 445.8 | 448.3 | 454.6 | 464.1 | 467.5 | 462.9 | 464.3 | 471.4 | 475.9 | 474.9 | 472.8 | 462.0 |
| 2015 | 456.7 | 455.9 | 454.7 | 456.5 | 461.1 | 459.5 | 451.4 | 449.6 | 454.2 | 454.9 | 451.6 | 446.7 | 454.4 |
| 2016 | 429.0 | 429.2 | 428.6 | 434.1 | 439.2 | 438.6 | 435.5 | 434.9 | 440.9 | 440.9 | 438.4 | 433.0 | 435.2 |
| 2017 | 422.3 | 424.0 | 425.2 | 431.1 | 436.4 | 436.8 | 431.0 | 430.5 | 436.3 | 437.5 | 435.6 | 434.2 | 431.7 |
| 2018 | 423.4 | 425.0 | 426.7 | 429.2 | 438.9 | 440.6 | 435.5 | 434.9 | 440.8 | 442.6 | 441.6 | 439.8 | 434.9 |
| 2019 | 429.3 | 430.1 | 431.4 | 436.8 | 444.7 | 445.4 | 439.1 | 439.6 | 443.6 | 445.6 | 443.4 | 440.8 | 439.2 |
| **Total Private** | | | | | | | | | | | | | |
| 2010 | 297.9 | 298.7 | 302.0 | 308.2 | 314.9 | 318.9 | 323.2 | 326.5 | 329.0 | 331.1 | 332.9 | 333.9 | 318.1 |
| 2011 | 329.3 | 331.2 | 335.7 | 343.5 | 351.0 | 357.3 | 359.3 | 361.2 | 359.3 | 360.1 | 357.2 | 357.2 | 350.2 |
| 2012 | 348.2 | 350.3 | 352.6 | 355.2 | 365.0 | 370.1 | 371.5 | 374.2 | 373.7 | 375.3 | 375.5 | 371.2 | 365.2 |
| 2013 | 361.9 | 364.0 | 366.4 | 373.0 | 381.7 | 387.4 | 389.2 | 390.9 | 390.6 | 393.9 | 393.0 | 390.3 | 381.9 |
| 2014 | 376.8 | 374.4 | 372.3 | 373.8 | 377.6 | 378.6 | 376.7 | 375.3 | 372.5 | 370.5 | 366.9 | 362.0 | 373.1 |
| 2015 | 346.4 | 344.6 | 343.7 | 349.2 | 353.1 | 355.2 | 358.5 | 358.2 | 357.2 | 355.8 | 353.2 | 347.8 | 351.9 |
| 2016 | 338.9 | 339.3 | 340.8 | 346.5 | 351.2 | 354.3 | 355.3 | 354.6 | 353.6 | 353.2 | 351.5 | 349.3 | 349.0 |
| 2017 | 340.9 | 341.2 | 342.7 | 345.8 | 354.0 | 358.4 | 359.3 | 358.6 | 357.9 | 358.2 | 357.0 | 354.7 | 352.4 |
| 2018 | 346.4 | 345.8 | 347.2 | 352.6 | 359.2 | 362.8 | 362.8 | 363.2 | 360.2 | 360.4 | 358.0 | 354.9 | 356.1 |
| 2019 | | | | | | | | | | | | | |
| **Goods Producing** | | | | | | | | | | | | | |
| 2011 | 54.9 | 55.0 | 56.5 | 59.9 | 63.4 | 66.0 | 68.7 | 70.4 | 71.6 | 72.8 | 72.8 | 71.4 | 65.3 |
| 2012 | 69.4 | 70.5 | 72.6 | 76.7 | 80.4 | 83.6 | 85.3 | 86.0 | 85.0 | 84.5 | 81.3 | 79.6 | 79.6 |
| 2013 | 76.2 | 76.6 | 77.5 | 79.2 | 84.7 | 87.9 | 88.9 | 90.3 | 89.6 | 89.6 | 88.7 | 84.7 | 84.5 |
| 2014 | 80.5 | 81.1 | 82.1 | 86.1 | 90.7 | 94.5 | 96.0 | 97.3 | 97.1 | 98.2 | 96.9 | 93.6 | 91.2 |
| 2015 | 88.1 | 85.3 | 83.2 | 83.4 | 85.1 | 85.8 | 85.3 | 85.2 | 83.4 | 82.1 | 79.1 | 74.9 | 83.4 |
| 2016 | 67.7 | 66.4 | 65.9 | 69.3 | 71.8 | 74.5 | 76.4 | 76.6 | 75.9 | 74.5 | 71.9 | 67.0 | 71.5 |
| 2017 | 63.1 | 63.3 | 64.1 | 67.3 | 70.5 | 72.7 | 73.7 | 73.4 | 73.3 | 72.9 | 71.0 | 68.7 | 69.5 |
| 2018 | 65.3 | 65.3 | 66.1 | 68.2 | 73.0 | 76.4 | 77.1 | 77.5 | 77.4 | 77.4 | 75.5 | 73.5 | 72.7 |
| 2019 | 70.4 | 70.0 | 70.6 | 73.1 | 76.7 | 79.5 | 80.5 | 80.8 | 79.6 | 79.3 | 75.5 | 73.3 | 75.8 |
| **Service-Providing** | | | | | | | | | | | | | |
| 2011 | 323.2 | 325.1 | 326.9 | 329.8 | 333.3 | 332.4 | 323.8 | 325.8 | 337.4 | 340.0 | 341.4 | 344.3 | 332.0 |
| 2012 | 339.6 | 341.8 | 344.3 | 348.3 | 352.1 | 353.2 | 344.3 | 345.2 | 354.9 | 358.1 | 358.3 | 360.1 | 350.0 |
| 2013 | 352.5 | 355.4 | 357.0 | 357.6 | 362.7 | 362.7 | 353.6 | 354.5 | 364.9 | 368.0 | 369.2 | 369.2 | 360.6 |
| 2014 | 361.5 | 364.7 | 366.2 | 368.5 | 373.4 | 373.0 | 366.9 | 367.0 | 374.3 | 377.7 | 378.0 | 379.2 | 370.9 |
| 2015 | 368.6 | 370.6 | 371.5 | 373.1 | 376.0 | 373.7 | 366.1 | 364.4 | 370.8 | 372.8 | 372.5 | 371.8 | 371.0 |
| 2016 | 361.3 | 362.8 | 362.7 | 364.8 | 367.4 | 364.1 | 359.1 | 358.3 | 365.0 | 366.4 | 366.5 | 366.0 | 363.7 |
| 2017 | 359.2 | 360.7 | 361.1 | 363.8 | 365.9 | 364.1 | 357.3 | 357.1 | 363.0 | 364.6 | 364.6 | 366.0 | 363.7 |
| 2018 | 358.1 | 359.7 | 360.6 | 361.0 | 365.9 | 364.2 | 358.4 | 357.4 | 363.4 | 365.2 | 366.1 | 366.3 | 362.2 |
| 2019 | 358.9 | 360.1 | 360.8 | 363.7 | 368.0 | 365.9 | 358.6 | 358.8 | 364.0 | 366.3 | 367.9 | 367.5 | 363.4 |
| **Mining and Logging** | | | | | | | | | | | | | |
| 2011 | 13.5 | 14.0 | 14.5 | 15.2 | 15.9 | 16.3 | 17.1 | 17.7 | 18.3 | 19.0 | 20.2 | 21.0 | 16.9 |
| 2012 | 21.3 | 22.2 | 23.2 | 23.9 | 24.6 | 25.4 | 26.1 | 26.1 | 25.6 | 25.2 | 24.9 | 24.8 | 24.4 |
| 2013 | 24.6 | 25.1 | 25.5 | 25.5 | 26.0 | 26.4 | 26.3 | 26.6 | 26.6 | 26.9 | 27.6 | 27.4 | 26.2 |
| 2014 | 27.5 | 28.0 | 28.3 | 28.9 | 29.4 | 30.0 | 30.3 | 30.9 | 31.2 | 31.8 | 32.0 | 32.0 | 30.0 |
| 2015 | 30.5 | 28.6 | 26.8 | 24.8 | 23.6 | 23.0 | 22.1 | 21.7 | 20.8 | 19.6 | 19.1 | 18.6 | 23.3 |
| 2016 | 17.2 | 16.6 | 15.5 | 15.0 | 14.6 | 14.5 | 14.6 | 14.7 | 14.9 | 15.1 | 15.4 | 15.5 | 15.3 |
| 2017 | 15.4 | 15.9 | 16.3 | 17.0 | 17.6 | 18.3 | 19.1 | 18.9 | 18.9 | 19.1 | 19.2 | 19.2 | 17.9 |
| 2018 | 19.0 | 19.1 | 19.4 | 20.1 | 20.8 | 21.2 | 21.5 | 21.6 | 21.6 | 21.9 | 21.9 | 21.7 | 20.8 |
| 2019 | 21.4 | 21.4 | 21.3 | 21.3 | 21.5 | 21.9 | 21.9 | 21.8 | 21.4 | 21.0 | 20.5 | 20.4 | 21.3 |
| **Construction** | | | | | | | | | | | | | |
| 2011 | 18.5 | 18.1 | 18.9 | 21.1 | 23.8 | 25.7 | 27.6 | 28.8 | 29.2 | 29.4 | 28.1 | 25.8 | 24.6 |
| 2012 | 23.7 | 23.7 | 24.5 | 27.9 | 30.6 | 32.6 | 33.6 | 34.1 | 33.7 | 33.6 | 31.1 | 29.8 | 29.9 |
| 2013 | 27.1 | 26.9 | 27.3 | 28.8 | 33.1 | 35.6 | 36.7 | 37.8 | 37.2 | 36.6 | 35.3 | 31.7 | 32.8 |
| 2014 | 27.7 | 27.8 | 28.4 | 31.5 | 35.4 | 38.2 | 39.3 | 40.0 | 39.6 | 40.1 | 38.6 | 35.6 | 35.2 |
| 2015 | 32.2 | 31.4 | 31.1 | 33.1 | 35.8 | 37.1 | 37.7 | 37.8 | 37.0 | 36.9 | 34.5 | 31.3 | 34.7 |
| 2016 | 26.0 | 25.4 | 25.9 | 29.7 | 32.7 | 35.3 | 36.9 | 37.1 | 36.3 | 34.7 | 32.0 | 27.5 | 31.6 |
| 2017 | 23.8 | 23.5 | 23.8 | 26.0 | 28.2 | 29.4 | 29.6 | 29.5 | 29.3 | 28.5 | 26.6 | 24.3 | 26.9 |
| 2018 | 21.2 | 21.0 | 21.4 | 22.6 | 26.5 | 29.1 | 29.4 | 29.7 | 29.5 | 28.9 | 27.0 | 25.2 | 26.0 |
| 2019 | 23.0 | 22.6 | 23.2 | 25.6 | 28.8 | 30.9 | 32.1 | 32.3 | 31.5 | 31.3 | 28.5 | 26.8 | 28.1 |

# 1. Employment by Industry: North Dakota, 2011–2019—*Continued*

(Numbers in thousands, not seasonally adjusted)

| Industry and year | January | February | March | April | May | June | July | August | September | October | November | December | Annual average |
|---|---|---|---|---|---|---|---|---|---|---|---|---|---|
| **Manufacturing** | | | | | | | | | | | | | |
| 2011 | 22.9 | 22.9 | 23.1 | 23.6 | 23.7 | 24.0 | 24.0 | 23.9 | 24.1 | 24.4 | 24.5 | 24.6 | 23.8 |
| 2012 | 24.4 | 24.6 | 24.9 | 24.9 | 25.2 | 25.6 | 25.6 | 25.8 | 25.7 | 25.7 | 25.3 | 25.0 | 25.2 |
| 2013 | 24.5 | 24.6 | 24.7 | 24.9 | 25.6 | 25.9 | 25.9 | 25.9 | 25.8 | 26.1 | 25.8 | 25.6 | 25.4 |
| 2014 | 25.3 | 25.3 | 25.4 | 25.7 | 25.9 | 26.3 | 26.4 | 26.4 | 26.3 | 26.3 | 26.3 | 26.0 | 26.0 |
| | | | | | | | | | | | | | |
| 2015 | 25.4 | 25.3 | 25.3 | 25.5 | 25.7 | 25.7 | 25.5 | 25.7 | 25.6 | 25.6 | 25.5 | 25.0 | 25.5 |
| 2016 | 24.5 | 24.4 | 24.5 | 24.6 | 24.5 | 24.7 | 24.9 | 24.8 | 24.7 | 24.7 | 24.5 | 24.0 | 24.6 |
| 2017 | 23.9 | 23.9 | 24.0 | 24.3 | 24.7 | 25.0 | 25.0 | 25.0 | 25.1 | 25.3 | 25.2 | 25.2 | 24.7 |
| 2018 | 25.1 | 25.2 | 25.3 | 25.5 | 25.7 | 26.1 | 26.2 | 26.2 | 26.3 | 26.6 | 26.6 | 26.6 | 26.0 |
| 2019 | 26.0 | 26.0 | 26.1 | 26.2 | 26.4 | 26.7 | 26.5 | 26.7 | 26.7 | 27.0 | 26.5 | 26.1 | 26.4 |
| | | | | | | | | | | | | | |
| **Trade, Transportation, and Utilities** | | | | | | | | | | | | | |
| 2011 | 81.8 | 81.9 | 82.2 | 83.8 | 85.3 | 85.8 | 86.5 | 87.2 | 87.5 | 89.1 | 90.9 | 92.5 | 86.2 |
| 2012 | 91.1 | 91.5 | 92.4 | 94.4 | 96.2 | 97.1 | 97.4 | 97.7 | 97.3 | 98.5 | 99.5 | 100.0 | 96.1 |
| 2013 | 97.7 | 97.9 | 98.3 | 98.9 | 101.1 | 101.4 | 101.7 | 102.3 | 102.3 | 102.9 | 104.3 | 104.8 | 101.1 |
| 2014 | 102.2 | 102.7 | 103.0 | 104.3 | 105.8 | 105.9 | 106.1 | 106.2 | 105.9 | 107.2 | 108.3 | 109.0 | 105.6 |
| | | | | | | | | | | | | | |
| 2015 | 105.4 | 105.1 | 104.7 | 104.9 | 105.0 | 104.5 | 103.8 | 102.4 | 102.0 | 101.9 | 102.1 | 102.0 | 103.7 |
| 2016 | 98.2 | 97.1 | 96.1 | 96.8 | 96.9 | 95.8 | 96.1 | 95.8 | 95.4 | 95.8 | 96.4 | 96.4 | 96.4 |
| 2017 | 94.0 | 93.8 | 93.5 | 94.3 | 95.0 | 94.6 | 94.6 | 94.2 | 94.1 | 94.6 | 95.6 | 95.9 | 94.5 |
| 2018 | 93.4 | 93.2 | 93.1 | 93.4 | 94.8 | 94.3 | 94.3 | 94.0 | 93.6 | 94.2 | 95.4 | 95.3 | 94.1 |
| 2019 | 93.0 | 92.6 | 92.5 | 93.7 | 94.7 | 94.0 | 93.7 | 93.8 | 93.3 | 93.2 | 95.0 | 95.0 | 93.7 |
| | | | | | | | | | | | | | |
| **Wholesale Trade** | | | | | | | | | | | | | |
| 2011 | 21.4 | 21.5 | 21.7 | 22.2 | 22.8 | 23.1 | 22.9 | 22.8 | 22.7 | 23.0 | 23.2 | 23.6 | 22.6 |
| 2012 | 23.5 | 23.7 | 24.1 | 24.9 | 25.4 | 25.6 | 25.6 | 25.6 | 25.4 | 25.5 | 25.6 | 25.7 | 25.1 |
| 2013 | 25.4 | 25.5 | 25.7 | 26.0 | 26.9 | 27.0 | 26.8 | 26.7 | 26.4 | 26.5 | 26.6 | 26.7 | 26.4 |
| 2014 | 26.4 | 26.4 | 26.6 | 27.0 | 27.4 | 27.6 | 27.4 | 27.5 | 27.2 | 27.4 | 27.6 | 27.6 | 27.2 |
| | | | | | | | | | | | | | |
| 2015 | 27.2 | 27.0 | 27.0 | 27.3 | 27.3 | 27.1 | 26.7 | 26.5 | 26.1 | 25.9 | 25.6 | 25.5 | 26.6 |
| 2016 | 24.9 | 24.6 | 24.5 | 24.9 | 24.9 | 24.5 | 24.5 | 24.3 | 23.9 | 23.9 | 23.8 | 23.7 | 24.4 |
| 2017 | 23.5 | 23.6 | 23.7 | 24.1 | 24.4 | 24.3 | 24.1 | 23.9 | 23.6 | 23.7 | 23.8 | 23.7 | 23.9 |
| 2018 | 23.4 | 23.4 | 23.5 | 23.8 | 24.4 | 24.3 | 24.2 | 24.1 | 23.8 | 23.9 | 24.0 | 23.9 | 23.9 |
| 2019 | 23.7 | 23.8 | 23.9 | 24.2 | 24.8 | 24.7 | 24.5 | 24.4 | 24.2 | 24.3 | 24.3 | 24.6 | 24.3 |
| | | | | | | | | | | | | | |
| **Retail Trade** | | | | | | | | | | | | | |
| 2011 | 43.2 | 43.0 | 42.9 | 43.5 | 44.0 | 43.8 | 44.2 | 44.3 | 44.3 | 44.9 | 46.2 | 46.6 | 44.2 |
| 2012 | 45.0 | 44.9 | 44.9 | 45.6 | 46.2 | 46.6 | 46.7 | 46.7 | 46.6 | 47.4 | 48.6 | 49.0 | 46.5 |
| 2013 | 47.4 | 47.3 | 47.3 | 47.3 | 48.1 | 48.2 | 48.5 | 48.9 | 49.0 | 49.4 | 50.5 | 50.9 | 48.6 |
| 2014 | 49.0 | 49.3 | 49.3 | 49.6 | 50.2 | 50.2 | 50.3 | 49.9 | 49.8 | 50.6 | 51.7 | 52.4 | 50.2 |
| | | | | | | | | | | | | | |
| 2015 | 50.0 | 50.0 | 50.0 | 50.1 | 50.5 | 50.5 | 50.5 | 49.9 | 50.0 | 50.4 | 51.2 | 51.4 | 50.4 |
| 2016 | 49.3 | 48.8 | 48.5 | 48.8 | 49.0 | 48.7 | 49.0 | 48.8 | 48.6 | 49.0 | 49.8 | 49.7 | 49.0 |
| 2017 | 48.0 | 47.6 | 47.2 | 47.3 | 47.5 | 47.4 | 47.5 | 47.3 | 47.1 | 47.4 | 48.4 | 48.5 | 47.6 |
| 2018 | 47.0 | 46.9 | 46.7 | 46.6 | 47.2 | 46.8 | 46.8 | 46.4 | 46.0 | 46.6 | 47.6 | 47.4 | 46.8 |
| 2019 | 45.8 | 45.3 | 45.1 | 45.6 | 45.8 | 45.5 | 45.4 | 45.2 | 45.1 | 45.1 | 46.5 | 46.0 | 45.5 |
| | | | | | | | | | | | | | |
| **Transportation and Utilities** | | | | | | | | | | | | | |
| 2011 | 17.2 | 17.4 | 17.6 | 18.1 | 18.5 | 18.9 | 19.4 | 20.1 | 20.5 | 21.2 | 21.5 | 22.3 | 19.4 |
| 2012 | 22.6 | 22.9 | 23.4 | 23.9 | 24.6 | 24.9 | 25.1 | 25.4 | 25.3 | 25.6 | 25.3 | 25.3 | 24.5 |
| 2013 | 24.9 | 25.1 | 25.3 | 25.6 | 26.1 | 26.2 | 26.4 | 26.7 | 26.9 | 27.0 | 27.2 | 27.2 | 26.2 |
| 2014 | 26.8 | 27.0 | 27.1 | 27.7 | 28.2 | 28.1 | 28.4 | 28.8 | 28.9 | 29.2 | 29.0 | 29.0 | 28.2 |
| | | | | | | | | | | | | | |
| 2015 | 28.2 | 28.1 | 27.7 | 27.5 | 27.2 | 26.9 | 26.6 | 26.0 | 25.9 | 25.6 | 25.3 | 25.1 | 26.7 |
| 2016 | 24.0 | 23.7 | 23.1 | 23.1 | 23.0 | 22.6 | 22.6 | 22.7 | 22.9 | 22.9 | 22.8 | 23.0 | 23.0 |
| 2017 | 22.5 | 22.6 | 22.6 | 22.9 | 23.1 | 22.9 | 23.0 | 23.0 | 23.4 | 23.5 | 23.4 | 23.7 | 23.1 |
| 2018 | 23.0 | 22.9 | 22.9 | 23.0 | 23.2 | 23.2 | 23.3 | 23.5 | 23.8 | 23.7 | 23.8 | 24.0 | 23.4 |
| 2019 | 23.5 | 23.5 | 23.5 | 23.9 | 24.1 | 23.8 | 23.8 | 24.2 | 24.0 | 23.8 | 24.2 | 24.4 | 23.9 |
| | | | | | | | | | | | | | |
| **Information** | | | | | | | | | | | | | |
| 2011 | 7.1 | 7.1 | 7.1 | 7.1 | 7.1 | 7.2 | 7.2 | 7.2 | 7.1 | 7.0 | 7.1 | 7.1 | 7.1 |
| 2012 | 7.0 | 6.9 | 6.9 | 6.9 | 6.9 | 7.0 | 7.0 | 7.0 | 6.9 | 6.9 | 6.9 | 6.9 | 6.9 |
| 2013 | 6.9 | 6.8 | 6.7 | 6.7 | 6.8 | 6.9 | 6.9 | 6.9 | 6.8 | 6.8 | 6.8 | 6.8 | 6.8 |
| 2014 | 6.8 | 6.8 | 6.8 | 6.8 | 6.9 | 6.8 | 6.8 | 6.9 | 6.8 | 6.8 | 6.7 | 6.7 | 6.8 |
| | | | | | | | | | | | | | |
| 2015 | 6.6 | 6.6 | 6.6 | 6.6 | 6.6 | 6.6 | 6.6 | 6.6 | 6.6 | 6.6 | 6.7 | 6.7 | 6.6 |
| 2016 | 6.6 | 6.7 | 6.7 | 6.6 | 6.6 | 6.7 | 6.7 | 6.7 | 6.6 | 6.6 | 6.6 | 6.7 | 6.7 |
| 2017 | 6.6 | 6.6 | 6.5 | 6.5 | 6.5 | 6.5 | 6.5 | 6.5 | 6.5 | 6.5 | 6.4 | 6.5 | 6.5 |
| 2018 | 6.5 | 6.3 | 6.3 | 6.2 | 6.2 | 6.2 | 6.2 | 6.2 | 6.2 | 6.1 | 6.1 | 6.2 | 6.2 |
| 2019 | 6.1 | 6.1 | 6.1 | 6.0 | 6.1 | 6.1 | 6.1 | 6.1 | 6.1 | 6.0 | 6.1 | 6.1 | 6.1 |

## 1. Employment by Industry: North Dakota, 2011–2019—*Continued*

(Numbers in thousands, not seasonally adjusted)

| Industry and year | January | February | March | April | May | June | July | August | September | October | November | December | Annual average |
|---|---|---|---|---|---|---|---|---|---|---|---|---|---|
| **Financial Activities** | | | | | | | | | | | | | |
| 2011 | 20.8 | 20.8 | 20.8 | 21.0 | 21.2 | 21.2 | 21.3 | 21.3 | 21.3 | 21.3 | 21.4 | 21.5 | 21.2 |
| 2012 | 21.2 | 21.3 | 21.4 | 21.6 | 21.8 | 22.0 | 22.1 | 22.1 | 22.0 | 22.2 | 22.2 | 22.5 | 21.9 |
| 2013 | 22.2 | 22.3 | 22.5 | 22.6 | 22.8 | 23.0 | 23.1 | 23.2 | 23.1 | 23.4 | 23.5 | 23.6 | 22.9 |
| 2014 | 23.5 | 23.6 | 23.6 | 23.8 | 23.9 | 24.1 | 24.2 | 24.4 | 24.2 | 24.6 | 24.6 | 24.8 | 24.1 |
| 2015 | 24.4 | 24.3 | 24.4 | 24.4 | 24.5 | 24.5 | 24.5 | 24.5 | 24.3 | 24.3 | 24.3 | 24.2 | 24.4 |
| 2016 | 24.0 | 24.0 | 23.9 | 23.7 | 23.8 | 23.8 | 24.1 | 24.1 | 24.0 | 24.2 | 24.4 | 24.4 | 24.0 |
| 2017 | 24.1 | 24.1 | 24.2 | 24.2 | 24.2 | 24.3 | 24.4 | 24.4 | 24.4 | 24.4 | 24.5 | 24.7 | 24.3 |
| 2018 | 24.3 | 24.4 | 24.5 | 24.6 | 24.6 | 24.7 | 24.7 | 24.6 | 24.5 | 24.6 | 24.8 | 24.8 | 24.6 |
| 2019 | 24.6 | 24.5 | 24.7 | 24.7 | 24.7 | 24.8 | 24.7 | 24.8 | 24.6 | 24.6 | 25.1 | 25.2 | 24.8 |
| **Professional and Business Services** | | | | | | | | | | | | | |
| 2011 | 26.9 | 27.1 | 27.7 | 28.0 | 28.1 | 28.6 | 29.7 | 30.1 | 30.2 | 29.9 | 29.7 | 29.7 | 28.8 |
| 2012 | 29.4 | 29.4 | 30.0 | 30.7 | 31.3 | 32.2 | 32.4 | 32.7 | 32.6 | 32.7 | 32.4 | 32.3 | 31.5 |
| 2013 | 31.6 | 32.2 | 32.1 | 32.4 | 32.9 | 33.4 | 33.7 | 33.8 | 33.8 | 34.0 | 33.6 | 33.2 | 33.1 |
| 2014 | 32.7 | 32.9 | 33.5 | 34.2 | 34.8 | 36.0 | 36.5 | 36.2 | 36.5 | 36.6 | 36.1 | 35.6 | 35.1 |
| 2015 | 34.3 | 34.3 | 34.2 | 34.7 | 35.3 | 36.1 | 36.1 | 36.1 | 35.7 | 35.3 | 34.1 | 34.1 | 35.0 |
| 2016 | 32.3 | 32.3 | 32.1 | 33.0 | 33.3 | 33.8 | 34.2 | 34.1 | 33.5 | 33.1 | 32.6 | 32.4 | 33.1 |
| 2017 | 31.7 | 31.8 | 32.0 | 32.7 | 32.9 | 33.7 | 33.7 | 33.7 | 33.1 | 32.6 | 32.1 | 31.9 | 32.7 |
| 2018 | 31.4 | 31.5 | 31.7 | 31.9 | 32.6 | 33.5 | 33.7 | 33.6 | 33.3 | 32.8 | 32.6 | 32.3 | 32.6 |
| 2019 | 31.3 | 31.7 | 31.8 | 32.3 | 33.0 | 33.8 | 33.8 | 34.1 | 33.4 | 33.5 | 33.0 | 32.2 | 32.8 |
| **Education and Health Services** | | | | | | | | | | | | | |
| 2011 | 57.7 | 57.9 | 57.9 | 58.2 | 58.3 | 58.3 | 58.3 | 58.4 | 58.8 | 58.9 | 59.0 | 59.3 | 58.4 |
| 2012 | 59.2 | 59.4 | 59.5 | 59.7 | 59.8 | 60.2 | 59.9 | 60.2 | 60.4 | 60.5 | 60.5 | 61.0 | 60.0 |
| 2013 | 60.4 | 60.8 | 61.0 | 61.1 | 61.1 | 60.9 | 60.8 | 60.9 | 61.3 | 62.0 | 62.0 | 62.1 | 61.2 |
| 2014 | 61.6 | 61.7 | 61.5 | 61.5 | 61.6 | 61.4 | 61.2 | 61.5 | 61.9 | 62.2 | 62.6 | 62.6 | 61.8 |
| 2015 | 62.2 | 62.6 | 62.6 | 62.7 | 62.9 | 62.7 | 62.5 | 62.8 | 63.1 | 63.3 | 64.0 | 63.9 | 62.9 |
| 2016 | 63.4 | 64.0 | 64.2 | 64.6 | 64.6 | 64.2 | 64.8 | 64.8 | 65.3 | 65.7 | 65.9 | 65.9 | 64.8 |
| 2017 | 65.4 | 65.6 | 65.8 | 66.2 | 66.3 | 65.9 | 65.5 | 65.7 | 66.2 | 66.4 | 66.4 | 66.6 | 66.0 |
| 2018 | 66.3 | 66.5 | 66.6 | 66.7 | 66.6 | 66.1 | 65.9 | 65.9 | 66.5 | 66.8 | 67.0 | 67.0 | 66.5 |
| 2019 | 66.7 | 67.0 | 67.0 | 67.6 | 67.5 | 67.1 | 66.6 | 66.6 | 66.9 | 67.5 | 68.0 | 67.7 | 67.2 |
| **Leisure and Hospitality** | | | | | | | | | | | | | |
| 2011 | 33.4 | 33.5 | 34.2 | 34.5 | 35.8 | 36.3 | 36.0 | 36.4 | 36.8 | 36.3 | 36.3 | 36.7 | 35.5 |
| 2012 | 36.1 | 36.3 | 36.9 | 37.4 | 38.5 | 39.1 | 39.0 | 39.4 | 39.1 | 38.7 | 38.2 | 38.7 | 38.1 |
| 2013 | 37.3 | 37.6 | 38.2 | 38.0 | 39.1 | 40.1 | 40.1 | 40.4 | 40.3 | 40.1 | 40.0 | 39.6 | 39.2 |
| 2014 | 38.2 | 38.8 | 39.3 | 39.5 | 41.2 | 41.9 | 41.6 | 41.7 | 41.5 | 41.5 | 41.0 | 41.1 | 40.6 |
| 2015 | 39.3 | 39.6 | 39.9 | 40.6 | 41.6 | 41.9 | 41.6 | 41.6 | 41.4 | 41.0 | 40.7 | 40.3 | 40.8 |
| 2016 | 38.7 | 38.5 | 39.2 | 39.6 | 40.4 | 40.8 | 40.7 | 40.7 | 41.1 | 40.4 | 40.0 | 39.5 | 40.0 |
| 2017 | 38.6 | 38.8 | 39.2 | 39.6 | 40.1 | 41.2 | 41.4 | 41.4 | 40.9 | 40.7 | 40.2 | 39.8 | 40.2 |
| 2018 | 38.6 | 38.9 | 39.2 | 39.5 | 40.8 | 41.7 | 41.9 | 41.4 | 40.9 | 40.9 | 40.1 | 40.2 | 40.3 |
| 2019 | 39.0 | 38.7 | 39.3 | 39.6 | 40.9 | 41.8 | 42.0 | 41.6 | 41.0 | 41.0 | 40.3 | 40.2 | 40.5 |
| **Other Services** | | | | | | | | | | | | | |
| 2011 | 15.3 | 15.4 | 15.6 | 15.7 | 15.7 | 15.5 | 15.5 | 15.5 | 15.7 | 15.8 | 15.7 | 15.7 | 15.6 |
| 2012 | 15.9 | 15.9 | 16.0 | 16.1 | 16.1 | 16.1 | 16.2 | 16.1 | 16.0 | 16.1 | 16.2 | 16.2 | 16.1 |
| 2013 | 15.9 | 16.1 | 16.3 | 16.3 | 16.5 | 16.5 | 16.3 | 16.4 | 16.5 | 16.5 | 16.6 | 16.5 | 16.4 |
| 2014 | 16.4 | 16.4 | 16.6 | 16.8 | 16.8 | 16.8 | 16.8 | 16.7 | 16.7 | 16.8 | 16.8 | 16.9 | 16.7 |
| 2015 | 16.5 | 16.6 | 16.7 | 16.5 | 16.6 | 16.5 | 16.3 | 16.1 | 16.0 | 16.0 | 15.9 | 15.9 | 16.3 |
| 2016 | 15.5 | 15.6 | 15.6 | 15.6 | 15.7 | 15.6 | 15.5 | 15.4 | 15.4 | 15.5 | 15.4 | 15.5 | 15.5 |
| 2017 | 15.4 | 15.3 | 15.5 | 15.7 | 15.7 | 15.4 | 15.5 | 15.3 | 15.1 | 15.1 | 15.3 | 15.2 | 15.4 |
| 2018 | 15.1 | 15.1 | 15.2 | 15.3 | 15.4 | 15.5 | 15.5 | 15.4 | 15.5 | 15.4 | 15.5 | 15.4 | 15.4 |
| 2019 | 15.3 | 15.2 | 15.2 | 15.6 | 15.6 | 15.7 | 15.4 | 15.4 | 15.3 | 15.3 | 15.0 | 15.2 | 15.4 |
| **Government** | | | | | | | | | | | | | |
| 2011 | 80.2 | 81.4 | 81.4 | 81.5 | 81.8 | 79.5 | 69.3 | 69.7 | 80.0 | 81.7 | 81.3 | 81.8 | 79.1 |
| 2012 | 79.7 | 81.1 | 81.2 | 81.5 | 81.5 | 79.5 | 70.3 | 70.0 | 80.6 | 82.5 | 82.4 | 82.5 | 79.4 |
| 2013 | 80.5 | 81.7 | 81.9 | 81.6 | 82.4 | 80.5 | 71.0 | 70.6 | 80.8 | 82.3 | 82.4 | 82.6 | 79.9 |
| 2014 | 80.1 | 81.8 | 81.9 | 81.6 | 82.4 | 80.1 | 73.7 | 73.4 | 80.8 | 82.0 | 81.9 | 82.5 | 80.2 |
| 2015 | 79.9 | 81.5 | 82.4 | 82.7 | 83.5 | 80.9 | 74.7 | 74.3 | 81.7 | 84.4 | 84.7 | 84.7 | 81.3 |
| 2016 | 82.6 | 84.6 | 84.9 | 84.9 | 86.1 | 83.4 | 77.0 | 76.7 | 83.7 | 85.1 | 85.2 | 85.2 | 83.3 |
| 2017 | 83.4 | 84.7 | 84.4 | 84.6 | 85.2 | 82.5 | 75.7 | 75.9 | 82.7 | 84.3 | 84.1 | 84.9 | 82.7 |
| 2018 | 82.5 | 83.8 | 84.0 | 83.4 | 84.9 | 82.2 | 76.2 | 76.3 | 82.9 | 84.4 | 84.6 | 85.1 | 82.5 |
| 2019 | 82.9 | 84.3 | 84.2 | 84.2 | 85.5 | 82.6 | 76.3 | 76.4 | 83.4 | 85.2 | 85.4 | 85.9 | 83.0 |

## 2. Average Weekly Hours by Selected Industry: North Dakota, 2015–2019

(Not seasonally adjusted)

| Industry and year | January | February | March | April | May | June | July | August | September | October | November | December | Annual average |
|---|---|---|---|---|---|---|---|---|---|---|---|---|---|
| **Total Private** | | | | | | | | | | | | | |
| 2015 | 34.5 | 35.0 | 34.9 | 34.6 | 34.7 | 35.3 | 35.4 | 36.0 | 35.2 | 35.4 | 35.3 | 34.7 | 35.1 |
| 2016 | 34.1 | 34.1 | 33.7 | 34.2 | 34.9 | 34.6 | 34.7 | 34.9 | 34.6 | 35.1 | 34.2 | 33.8 | 34.4 |
| 2017 | 34.2 | 33.9 | 33.8 | 35.0 | 35.1 | 35.4 | 35.7 | 35.5 | 35.0 | 35.3 | 34.6 | 34.5 | 34.8 |
| 2018 | 33.6 | 34.3 | 34.4 | 35.2 | 35.5 | 35.9 | 36.3 | 36.0 | 36.2 | 35.1 | 34.8 | 35.5 | 35.2 |
| 2019 | 34.8 | 34.8 | 34.7 | 35.3 | 35.8 | 37.0 | 36.1 | 36.3 | 35.6 | 35.1 | 35.1 | 34.9 | 35.4 |
| **Goods-Producing** | | | | | | | | | | | | | |
| 2015 | 41.5 | 40.6 | 41.8 | 40.8 | 40.6 | 42.3 | 42.3 | 43.3 | 42.2 | 42.5 | 42.0 | 42.2 | 41.8 |
| 2016 | 40.0 | 40.4 | 40.5 | 40.6 | 41.4 | 41.5 | 41.2 | 42.6 | 41.9 | 42.8 | 40.6 | 39.1 | 41.1 |
| 2017 | 39.5 | 39.4 | 39.5 | 40.9 | 42.6 | 42.5 | 43.2 | 43.7 | 42.9 | 44.0 | 41.9 | 41.4 | 41.9 |
| 2018 | 39.7 | 40.9 | 41.7 | 42.1 | 42.8 | 43.2 | 44.6 | 44.5 | 44.3 | 42.9 | 41.8 | 43.1 | 42.7 |
| 2019 | 42.3 | 41.3 | 41.2 | 42.5 | 43.7 | 45.0 | 43.7 | 44.1 | 41.8 | 42.8 | 42.8 | 41.9 | 42.8 |
| **Construction** | | | | | | | | | | | | | |
| 2015 | 41.6 | 39.0 | 41.4 | 41.9 | 40.9 | 44.6 | 44.4 | 45.3 | 43.5 | 44.5 | 42.1 | 41.9 | 42.7 |
| 2016 | 38.6 | 39.9 | 41.0 | 41.9 | 44.1 | 44.2 | 42.9 | 44.1 | 43.9 | 45.0 | 41.5 | 38.6 | 42.4 |
| 2017 | 38.5 | 38.7 | 38.8 | 40.4 | 43.7 | 43.6 | 43.6 | 45.0 | 42.9 | 45.1 | 40.4 | 39.1 | 41.9 |
| 2018 | 35.6 | 37.5 | 38.7 | 38.3 | 41.9 | 42.7 | 44.2 | 44.4 | 44.3 | 42.0 | 40.8 | 41.6 | 41.4 |
| 2019 | 38.6 | 38.2 | 38.2 | 39.7 | 43.0 | 45.4 | 42.7 | 43.9 | 39.9 | 42.2 | 41.8 | 39.7 | 41.3 |
| **Manufacturing** | | | | | | | | | | | | | |
| 2015 | 38.2 | 39.1 | 39.4 | 38.6 | 38.6 | 38.9 | 38.9 | 41.0 | 40.6 | 40.5 | 40.2 | 41.1 | 39.6 |
| 2016 | 39.4 | 39.2 | 39.2 | 39.0 | 39.1 | 39.6 | 39.4 | 40.4 | 39.7 | 40.8 | 39.5 | 39.0 | 39.6 |
| 2017 | 38.5 | 38.2 | 38.8 | 39.4 | 40.2 | 39.3 | 40.1 | 39.6 | 39.8 | 39.1 | 38.8 | 38.6 | 39.2 |
| 2018 | 38.2 | 39.2 | 38.4 | 39.2 | 38.5 | 38.3 | 39.2 | 39.2 | 38.9 | 38.6 | 38.6 | 39.2 | 38.8 |
| 2019 | 39.6 | 39.2 | 38.1 | 38.9 | 39.4 | 39.9 | 39.3 | 39.7 | 39.9 | 39.5 | 39.8 | 38.9 | 39.4 |
| **Trade, Transportation, and Utilities** | | | | | | | | | | | | | |
| 2015 | 35.5 | 36.1 | 35.3 | 35.4 | 35.5 | 35.6 | 35.9 | 36.0 | 35.7 | 35.8 | 35.3 | 34.9 | 35.6 |
| 2016 | 34.2 | 34.0 | 33.8 | 34.7 | 35.4 | 35.4 | 35.4 | 34.9 | 34.9 | 34.9 | 34.5 | 34.3 | 34.7 |
| 2017 | 34.3 | 33.8 | 33.7 | 35.3 | 35.1 | 35.5 | 35.9 | 35.4 | 35.0 | 35.2 | 34.9 | 34.8 | 34.9 |
| 2018 | 34.0 | 34.1 | 34.1 | 34.7 | 36.2 | 35.9 | 36.0 | 35.7 | 36.3 | 35.3 | 35.1 | 35.3 | 35.2 |
| 2019 | 34.8 | 35.1 | 34.8 | 35.4 | 36.4 | 37.0 | 36.4 | 36.9 | 36.2 | 35.4 | 35.3 | 35.1 | 35.7 |
| **Financial Activities** | | | | | | | | | | | | | |
| 2015 | 36.9 | 37.5 | 36.5 | 35.0 | 34.2 | 34.3 | 34.8 | 36.3 | 34.9 | 35.0 | 37.6 | 35.0 | 35.7 |
| 2016 | 35.2 | 34.9 | 34.8 | 35.7 | 37.2 | 35.6 | 36.6 | 35.9 | 37.0 | 38.3 | 36.1 | 36.9 | 36.2 |
| 2017 | 38.3 | 36.6 | 36.9 | 37.3 | 35.2 | 35.9 | 37.1 | 35.8 | 36.2 | 37.1 | 36.5 | 36.6 | 36.7 |
| 2018 | 36.2 | 36.8 | 36.7 | 37.8 | 37.0 | 37.2 | 37.5 | 37.2 | 38.1 | 37.7 | 37.6 | 38.0 | 37.3 |
| 2019 | 37.3 | 37.7 | 37.6 | 38.0 | 36.9 | 38.3 | 37.7 | 37.1 | 37.9 | 37.2 | 36.8 | 37.7 | 37.5 |
| **Professional and Business Services** | | | | | | | | | | | | | |
| 2015 | 36.8 | 38.4 | 38.1 | 38.4 | 38.9 | 39.1 | 38.4 | 39.1 | 38.1 | 38.9 | 37.8 | 36.8 | 38.2 |
| 2016 | 36.0 | 36.8 | 35.9 | 36.0 | 37.7 | 37.0 | 36.3 | 36.9 | 37.3 | 38.3 | 37.2 | 37.5 | 36.9 |
| 2017 | 37.7 | 37.0 | 38.1 | 39.0 | 38.4 | 37.8 | 38.6 | 37.3 | 35.9 | 36.4 | 34.8 | 34.8 | 37.2 |
| 2018 | 33.5 | 34.6 | 35.6 | 37.0 | 36.8 | 36.8 | 37.0 | 36.1 | 37.2 | 35.6 | 35.0 | 35.2 | 35.9 |
| 2019 | 33.8 | 34.8 | 34.7 | 34.5 | 35.5 | 36.9 | 35.1 | 35.4 | 34.9 | 34.4 | 34.7 | 33.8 | 34.9 |
| **Education and Health Services** | | | | | | | | | | | | | |
| 2015 | 31.7 | 32.3 | 32.3 | 32.7 | 32.5 | 32.9 | 32.6 | 32.6 | 32.2 | 32.3 | 32.6 | 32.1 | 32.4 |
| 2016 | 32.1 | 32.3 | 31.7 | 31.7 | 31.8 | 31.8 | 32.0 | 31.6 | 31.4 | 31.5 | 31.9 | 31.8 | 31.8 |
| 2017 | 32.0 | 32.1 | 31.6 | 32.3 | 32.1 | 32.5 | 32.6 | 32.9 | 32.6 | 32.3 | 32.7 | 32.6 | 32.4 |
| 2018 | 32.8 | 33.1 | 32.7 | 33.6 | 33.0 | 34.0 | 34.2 | 33.9 | 34.1 | 33.2 | 33.6 | 34.4 | 33.5 |
| 2019 | 33.7 | 33.5 | 33.6 | 33.9 | 33.8 | 34.8 | 34.1 | 34.2 | 34.2 | 33.7 | 33.8 | 34.3 | 34.0 |
| **Leisure and Hospitality** | | | | | | | | | | | | | |
| 2015 | 22.3 | 23.9 | 23.5 | 22.7 | 23.9 | 24.4 | 24.1 | 25.2 | 23.6 | 23.8 | 24.3 | 24.0 | 23.8 |
| 2016 | 23.9 | 23.5 | 23.1 | 23.4 | 24.1 | 23.5 | 23.4 | 23.7 | 22.0 | 22.8 | 22.6 | 22.1 | 23.2 |
| 2017 | 23.3 | 22.8 | 22.9 | 24.0 | 24.8 | 24.8 | 24.5 | 24.4 | 23.2 | 23.3 | 22.5 | 23.0 | 23.7 |
| 2018 | 22.3 | 22.9 | 23.0 | 23.8 | 23.5 | 24.6 | 24.7 | 24.5 | 24.3 | 22.9 | 23.3 | 23.9 | 23.7 |
| 2019 | 22.7 | 23.1 | 22.8 | 23.3 | 23.4 | 25.0 | 24.6 | 24.2 | 23.8 | 22.5 | 22.7 | 22.7 | 23.4 |
| **Other Services** | | | | | | | | | | | | | |
| 2015 | 24.4 | 25.2 | 25.8 | 25.2 | 26.4 | 26.6 | 26.2 | 27.8 | 26.8 | 26.4 | 27.9 | 27.5 | 26.3 |
| 2016 | 28.2 | 27.5 | 27.1 | 29.2 | 29.3 | 27.6 | 28.9 | 28.7 | 29.2 | 29.7 | 28.9 | 28.9 | 28.6 |
| 2017 | 28.8 | 29.7 | 29.3 | 31.7 | 31.0 | 31.4 | 32.9 | 31.5 | 31.7 | 32.5 | 31.9 | 31.2 | 31.1 |
| 2018 | 30.0 | 32.4 | 31.7 | 32.4 | 31.1 | 31.2 | 31.1 | 31.1 | 30.5 | 30.4 | 31.2 | 32.2 | 31.3 |
| 2019 | 31.4 | 31.1 | 31.6 | 31.6 | 32.0 | 33.1 | 30.8 | 31.4 | 31.1 | 30.8 | 30.0 | 30.1 | 31.3 |

## 3. Average Hourly Earnings by Selected Industry: North Dakota, 2015–2019

(Dollars, not seasonally adjusted)

| Industry and year | January | February | March | April | May | June | July | August | September | October | November | December | Annual average |
|---|---|---|---|---|---|---|---|---|---|---|---|---|---|
| **Total Private** | | | | | | | | | | | | | |
| 2015 | 24.97 | 24.74 | 24.93 | 25.24 | 25.10 | 24.74 | 25.16 | 25.44 | 25.48 | 25.70 | 25.62 | 25.55 | 25.22 |
| 2016 | 25.59 | 25.37 | 25.38 | 25.63 | 25.71 | 25.27 | 25.52 | 25.63 | 25.72 | 25.99 | 25.61 | 25.69 | 25.59 |
| 2017 | 25.88 | 25.72 | 25.76 | 26.19 | 26.10 | 26.10 | 26.31 | 26.21 | 26.38 | 26.51 | 26.56 | 26.47 | 26.19 |
| 2018 | 26.49 | 26.46 | 26.34 | 26.41 | 26.29 | 26.55 | 26.73 | 26.71 | 27.26 | 27.03 | 27.09 | 27.41 | 26.74 |
| 2019 | 27.23 | 27.29 | 27.46 | 27.53 | 27.61 | 27.40 | 27.16 | 27.26 | 27.67 | 27.47 | 27.54 | 27.84 | 27.46 |
| **Goods-Producing** | | | | | | | | | | | | | |
| 2015 | 27.21 | 26.78 | 27.26 | 27.23 | 27.22 | 26.93 | 27.29 | 27.63 | 27.28 | 27.87 | 27.55 | 27.31 | 27.30 |
| 2016 | 27.76 | 27.49 | 27.89 | 28.07 | 27.89 | 27.40 | 27.51 | 27.92 | 27.92 | 28.34 | 27.72 | 28.11 | 27.84 |
| 2017 | 28.43 | 28.01 | 28.09 | 28.69 | 28.65 | 28.35 | 28.57 | 28.68 | 28.60 | 28.92 | 28.46 | 28.59 | 28.52 |
| 2018 | 28.20 | 28.03 | 28.37 | 28.30 | 28.28 | 28.54 | 28.82 | 28.82 | 29.13 | 29.21 | 29.63 | 30.34 | 28.84 |
| 2019 | 30.04 | 29.94 | 30.43 | 31.12 | 31.04 | 30.83 | 29.84 | 29.98 | 30.37 | 30.04 | 30.45 | 31.19 | 30.44 |
| **Construction** | | | | | | | | | | | | | |
| 2015 | 28.59 | 27.62 | 28.24 | 28.06 | 28.04 | 27.84 | 27.71 | 28.39 | 27.54 | 28.41 | 27.58 | 27.97 | 28.00 |
| 2016 | 27.95 | 27.83 | 28.28 | 27.95 | 27.55 | 27.27 | 27.43 | 28.32 | 27.91 | 28.52 | 27.53 | 28.16 | 27.88 |
| 2017 | 28.46 | 28.37 | 28.62 | 28.80 | 28.97 | 28.98 | 29.36 | 28.91 | 28.83 | 29.26 | 28.47 | 28.95 | 28.86 |
| 2018 | 28.86 | 28.71 | 28.78 | 28.94 | 29.24 | 29.22 | 29.08 | 29.05 | 29.47 | 29.87 | 29.88 | 30.49 | 29.34 |
| 2019 | 29.78 | 30.23 | 30.63 | 31.92 | 31.57 | 30.58 | 30.07 | 30.39 | 30.89 | 30.40 | 31.13 | 31.75 | 30.77 |
| **Manufacturing** | | | | | | | | | | | | | |
| 2015 | 21.77 | 21.86 | 22.01 | 22.30 | 22.38 | 22.13 | 22.88 | 22.87 | 23.09 | 23.46 | 23.58 | 23.00 | 22.62 |
| 2016 | 23.85 | 23.75 | 23.96 | 23.94 | 23.81 | 23.69 | 23.59 | 23.75 | 24.03 | 24.28 | 24.19 | 24.24 | 23.92 |
| 2017 | 24.33 | 23.77 | 23.92 | 24.65 | 24.44 | 23.93 | 23.97 | 24.00 | 24.31 | 24.35 | 24.74 | 24.22 | 24.22 |
| 2018 | 24.26 | 23.85 | 24.29 | 24.10 | 23.61 | 23.83 | 23.89 | 23.86 | 24.35 | 24.28 | 25.01 | 24.98 | 24.20 |
| 2019 | 25.63 | 24.96 | 25.57 | 25.64 | 25.44 | 25.65 | 25.74 | 25.85 | 25.75 | 25.60 | 25.51 | 25.79 | 25.60 |
| **Trade, Transportation, and Utilities** | | | | | | | | | | | | | |
| 2015 | 25.36 | 25.01 | 24.99 | 25.47 | 25.09 | 24.98 | 25.16 | 25.34 | 25.42 | 25.32 | 25.07 | 25.01 | 25.19 |
| 2016 | 25.54 | 25.13 | 24.98 | 25.37 | 25.32 | 24.91 | 25.11 | 24.58 | 24.88 | 25.26 | 25.02 | 25.03 | 25.10 |
| 2017 | 25.34 | 25.70 | 25.80 | 26.60 | 26.13 | 26.19 | 26.47 | 25.87 | 25.95 | 25.97 | 25.95 | 25.71 | 25.98 |
| 2018 | 26.06 | 26.14 | 26.42 | 26.53 | 26.46 | 27.28 | 27.70 | 27.33 | 28.00 | 27.37 | 26.95 | 26.64 | 26.92 |
| 2019 | 27.19 | 27.38 | 27.17 | 26.98 | 27.59 | 27.17 | 27.35 | 27.38 | 28.07 | 28.18 | 27.88 | 28.09 | 27.54 |
| **Financial Activities** | | | | | | | | | | | | | |
| 2015 | 24.06 | 24.42 | 25.35 | 25.91 | 26.45 | 26.08 | 27.55 | 27.42 | 25.65 | 26.99 | 27.24 | 26.80 | 26.15 |
| 2016 | 26.68 | 26.37 | 26.13 | 26.74 | 27.07 | 26.43 | 27.01 | 28.03 | 27.61 | 28.54 | 27.70 | 28.30 | 27.24 |
| 2017 | 29.90 | 28.50 | 28.47 | 29.35 | 29.99 | 29.70 | 30.87 | 31.10 | 31.43 | 31.26 | 30.79 | 30.88 | 30.19 |
| 2018 | 32.26 | 32.12 | 31.14 | 31.55 | 31.48 | 32.17 | 31.97 | 32.40 | 32.11 | 31.17 | 31.95 | 32.15 | 31.87 |
| 2019 | 30.29 | 30.59 | 30.36 | 29.93 | 29.95 | 29.63 | 28.90 | 29.78 | 30.32 | 29.61 | 30.10 | 29.88 | 29.94 |
| **Professional and Business Services** | | | | | | | | | | | | | |
| 2015 | 28.00 | 28.06 | 28.12 | 28.68 | 28.83 | 28.00 | 28.82 | 29.30 | 29.43 | 29.17 | 29.50 | 29.24 | 28.76 |
| 2016 | 28.63 | 27.54 | 28.08 | 28.86 | 29.29 | 27.96 | 28.59 | 28.86 | 29.33 | 29.95 | 29.09 | 29.50 | 28.82 |
| 2017 | 26.97 | 27.35 | 27.30 | 27.01 | 27.07 | 27.87 | 27.14 | 27.95 | 28.24 | 28.64 | 28.98 | 29.73 | 27.82 |
| 2018 | 29.02 | 29.18 | 28.16 | 28.33 | 27.82 | 27.51 | 27.92 | 28.10 | 29.22 | 29.59 | 29.45 | 29.51 | 28.63 |
| 2019 | 28.43 | 28.59 | 28.88 | 28.90 | 28.26 | 27.75 | 28.32 | 28.25 | 29.11 | 29.06 | 29.68 | 30.17 | 28.77 |
| **Education and Health Services** | | | | | | | | | | | | | |
| 2015 | 24.27 | 24.41 | 24.17 | 24.44 | 24.46 | 24.21 | 24.45 | 24.90 | 25.42 | 25.43 | 25.59 | 25.70 | 24.79 |
| 2016 | 25.90 | 25.39 | 25.21 | 25.11 | 25.22 | 24.88 | 24.86 | 25.21 | 25.16 | 25.05 | 25.20 | 24.77 | 25.16 |
| 2017 | 24.71 | 24.69 | 24.87 | 24.62 | 24.71 | 24.94 | 25.01 | 24.93 | 25.22 | 25.37 | 25.59 | 25.43 | 25.01 |
| 2018 | 25.60 | 25.92 | 25.48 | 25.30 | 25.20 | 25.11 | 24.93 | 25.15 | 25.65 | 25.69 | 25.87 | 25.90 | 25.48 |
| 2019 | 26.20 | 26.16 | 26.18 | 25.98 | 25.90 | 25.77 | 26.17 | 25.86 | 26.12 | 26.03 | 25.92 | 26.18 | 26.04 |
| **Leisure and Hospitality** | | | | | | | | | | | | | |
| 2015 | 14.16 | 14.06 | 14.15 | 14.28 | 14.14 | 13.99 | 14.06 | 14.13 | 14.35 | 14.40 | 14.43 | 14.50 | 14.22 |
| 2016 | 14.20 | 14.40 | 14.41 | 14.51 | 14.51 | 14.49 | 14.58 | 14.53 | 14.76 | 14.83 | 14.86 | 15.02 | 14.59 |
| 2017 | 15.61 | 15.01 | 15.03 | 15.51 | 15.46 | 15.08 | 15.03 | 15.08 | 15.20 | 15.20 | 15.30 | 15.37 | 15.24 |
| 2018 | 14.92 | 15.10 | 14.89 | 15.12 | 15.03 | 14.80 | 14.83 | 14.86 | 15.03 | 15.11 | 14.87 | 15.43 | 15.00 |
| 2019 | 15.30 | 15.43 | 15.41 | 15.48 | 15.56 | 15.18 | 15.07 | 15.05 | 15.20 | 15.34 | 15.18 | 15.40 | 15.29 |
| **Other Services** | | | | | | | | | | | | | |
| 2015 | 22.88 | 23.10 | 23.43 | 23.04 | 22.85 | 22.91 | 23.37 | 23.22 | 22.78 | 23.03 | 23.54 | 23.48 | 23.14 |
| 2016 | 22.30 | 22.99 | 22.92 | 22.42 | 23.22 | 22.50 | 23.67 | 23.71 | 23.78 | 22.65 | 22.77 | 23.00 | 22.99 |
| 2017 | 21.68 | 21.36 | 21.34 | 22.20 | 22.37 | 22.42 | 22.91 | 22.92 | 23.20 | 23.27 | 22.80 | 22.27 | 22.41 |
| 2018 | 22.52 | 22.31 | 21.77 | 21.96 | 21.34 | 21.57 | 21.30 | 21.38 | 22.15 | 22.31 | 22.82 | 23.16 | 22.05 |
| 2019 | 23.35 | 23.44 | 23.52 | 23.39 | 23.54 | 24.10 | 24.07 | 24.40 | 24.19 | 23.93 | 24.25 | 25.08 | 23.93 |

## 4. Average Weekly Earnings by Selected Industry: North Dakota, 2015–2019

(Dollars, not seasonally adjusted)

| Industry and year | January | February | March | April | May | June | July | August | September | October | November | December | Annual average |
|---|---|---|---|---|---|---|---|---|---|---|---|---|---|
| **Total Private** | | | | | | | | | | | | | |
| 2015 | 861.47 | 865.90 | 870.06 | 873.30 | 870.97 | 873.32 | 888.15 | 915.84 | 896.90 | 909.78 | 904.39 | 886.59 | 885.22 |
| 2016 | 870.06 | 865.12 | 855.31 | 876.55 | 897.28 | 874.34 | 885.54 | 894.49 | 889.91 | 912.25 | 875.86 | 870.89 | 880.30 |
| 2017 | 885.10 | 871.91 | 870.69 | 916.65 | 916.11 | 921.33 | 941.90 | 930.46 | 923.30 | 935.80 | 918.98 | 913.22 | 911.41 |
| 2018 | 890.06 | 907.58 | 906.10 | 929.63 | 933.30 | 953.15 | 970.30 | 961.56 | 986.81 | 948.75 | 945.44 | 973.06 | 941.25 |
| 2019 | 944.88 | 949.69 | 952.86 | 971.81 | 988.44 | 1,013.80 | 980.48 | 987.17 | 985.05 | 964.20 | 966.65 | 971.62 | 972.08 |
| **Goods-Producing** | | | | | | | | | | | | | |
| 2015 | 1,129.22 | 1,087.27 | 1,139.47 | 1,110.98 | 1,105.13 | 1,139.14 | 1,154.37 | 1,196.38 | 1,151.22 | 1,184.48 | 1,157.10 | 1,152.48 | 1,141.14 |
| 2016 | 1,110.40 | 1,110.60 | 1,129.55 | 1,140.05 | 1,155.06 | 1,137.10 | 1,133.41 | 1,189.39 | 1,169.85 | 1,212.95 | 1,125.43 | 1,099.10 | 1,144.22 |
| 2017 | 1,122.99 | 1,103.59 | 1,109.56 | 1,173.42 | 1,220.49 | 1,204.88 | 1,234.22 | 1,253.32 | 1,226.94 | 1,272.48 | 1,192.47 | 1,183.63 | 1,194.99 |
| 2018 | 1,119.54 | 1,146.43 | 1,183.03 | 1,191.43 | 1,210.38 | 1,232.93 | 1,285.37 | 1,282.49 | 1,290.46 | 1,253.11 | 1,238.53 | 1,307.65 | 1,231.47 |
| 2019 | 1,270.69 | 1,236.52 | 1,253.72 | 1,322.60 | 1,356.45 | 1,387.35 | 1,304.01 | 1,322.12 | 1,269.47 | 1,285.71 | 1,303.26 | 1,306.86 | 1,302.83 |
| **Construction** | | | | | | | | | | | | | |
| 2015 | 1,189.34 | 1,077.18 | 1,169.14 | 1,175.71 | 1,146.84 | 1,241.66 | 1,230.32 | 1,286.07 | 1,197.99 | 1,264.25 | 1,161.12 | 1,171.94 | 1,195.60 |
| 2016 | 1,078.87 | 1,110.42 | 1,159.48 | 1,171.11 | 1,214.96 | 1,205.33 | 1,176.75 | 1,248.91 | 1,225.25 | 1,283.40 | 1,142.50 | 1,086.98 | 1,182.11 |
| 2017 | 1,095.71 | 1,097.92 | 1,110.46 | 1,163.52 | 1,265.99 | 1,263.53 | 1,280.10 | 1,300.95 | 1,236.81 | 1,319.63 | 1,150.19 | 1,131.95 | 1,209.23 |
| 2018 | 1,027.42 | 1,076.63 | 1,113.79 | 1,108.40 | 1,225.16 | 1,247.69 | 1,285.34 | 1,289.82 | 1,305.52 | 1,254.54 | 1,219.10 | 1,268.38 | 1,214.68 |
| 2019 | 1,149.51 | 1,154.79 | 1,170.07 | 1,267.22 | 1,357.51 | 1,388.33 | 1,283.99 | 1,334.12 | 1,232.51 | 1,282.88 | 1,301.23 | 1,260.48 | 1,270.80 |
| **Manufacturing** | | | | | | | | | | | | | |
| 2015 | 831.61 | 854.73 | 867.19 | 860.78 | 863.87 | 860.86 | 890.03 | 937.67 | 937.45 | 950.13 | 947.92 | 945.30 | 895.75 |
| 2016 | 939.69 | 931.00 | 939.23 | 933.66 | 930.97 | 938.12 | 929.45 | 959.50 | 953.99 | 990.62 | 955.51 | 945.36 | 947.23 |
| 2017 | 936.71 | 908.01 | 928.10 | 971.21 | 982.49 | 940.45 | 961.20 | 950.40 | 967.54 | 952.09 | 959.91 | 934.89 | 949.42 |
| 2018 | 926.73 | 934.92 | 932.74 | 944.72 | 908.99 | 912.69 | 936.49 | 935.31 | 947.22 | 937.21 | 965.39 | 979.22 | 938.96 |
| 2019 | 1,014.95 | 978.43 | 974.22 | 997.40 | 1,002.34 | 1,023.44 | 1,011.58 | 1,026.64 | 1,027.43 | 1,011.20 | 1,015.30 | 1,003.23 | 1,008.64 |
| **Trade, Transportation, and Utilities** | | | | | | | | | | | | | |
| 2015 | 900.28 | 902.86 | 882.15 | 901.64 | 890.70 | 889.29 | 903.24 | 912.24 | 907.49 | 906.46 | 884.97 | 872.85 | 896.76 |
| 2016 | 873.47 | 854.42 | 844.32 | 880.34 | 896.33 | 881.81 | 888.89 | 857.84 | 868.31 | 881.57 | 863.19 | 858.53 | 870.97 |
| 2017 | 869.16 | 868.66 | 869.46 | 938.98 | 917.16 | 929.75 | 950.27 | 915.80 | 908.25 | 914.14 | 905.66 | 894.71 | 906.70 |
| 2018 | 886.04 | 891.37 | 900.92 | 920.59 | 957.85 | 979.35 | 997.20 | 975.68 | 1,016.40 | 966.16 | 945.95 | 940.39 | 947.58 |
| 2019 | 946.21 | 961.04 | 945.52 | 955.09 | 1,004.28 | 1,005.29 | 995.54 | 1,010.32 | 1,016.13 | 997.57 | 984.16 | 985.96 | 983.18 |
| **Financial Activities** | | | | | | | | | | | | | |
| 2015 | 887.81 | 915.75 | 925.28 | 906.85 | 904.59 | 894.54 | 958.74 | 995.35 | 895.19 | 944.65 | 1,024.22 | 938.00 | 933.56 |
| 2016 | 939.14 | 920.31 | 909.32 | 954.62 | 1,007.00 | 940.91 | 988.57 | 1,006.28 | 1,021.57 | 1,093.08 | 999.97 | 1,044.27 | 986.09 |
| 2017 | 1,145.17 | 1,043.10 | 1,050.54 | 1,094.76 | 1,055.65 | 1,066.23 | 1,145.28 | 1,113.38 | 1,137.77 | 1,159.75 | 1,123.84 | 1,130.21 | 1,107.97 |
| 2018 | 1,167.81 | 1,182.02 | 1,142.84 | 1,192.59 | 1,164.76 | 1,196.72 | 1,198.88 | 1,205.28 | 1,223.39 | 1,175.11 | 1,201.32 | 1,221.70 | 1,188.75 |
| 2019 | 1,129.82 | 1,153.24 | 1,141.54 | 1,137.34 | 1,105.16 | 1,134.83 | 1,089.53 | 1,104.84 | 1,149.13 | 1,101.49 | 1,107.68 | 1,126.48 | 1,122.75 |
| **Professional and Business Services** | | | | | | | | | | | | | |
| 2015 | 1,030.40 | 1,077.50 | 1,071.37 | 1,101.31 | 1,121.49 | 1,094.80 | 1,106.69 | 1,145.63 | 1,121.28 | 1,134.71 | 1,115.10 | 1,076.03 | 1,098.63 |
| 2016 | 1,030.68 | 1,013.47 | 1,008.07 | 1,038.96 | 1,104.23 | 1,034.52 | 1,037.82 | 1,064.93 | 1,094.01 | 1,147.09 | 1,082.15 | 1,106.25 | 1,063.46 |
| 2017 | 1,016.77 | 1,011.95 | 1,040.13 | 1,053.39 | 1,039.49 | 1,053.49 | 1,047.60 | 1,042.54 | 1,013.82 | 1,042.50 | 1,008.50 | 1,034.60 | 1,034.90 |
| 2018 | 972.17 | 1,009.63 | 1,002.50 | 1,048.21 | 1,023.78 | 1,012.37 | 1,033.04 | 1,014.41 | 1,086.98 | 1,053.40 | 1,030.75 | 1,038.75 | 1,027.82 |
| 2019 | 960.93 | 994.93 | 1,002.14 | 997.05 | 1,003.23 | 1,023.98 | 994.03 | 1,000.05 | 1,015.94 | 999.66 | 1,029.90 | 1,019.75 | 1,004.07 |
| **Education and Health Services** | | | | | | | | | | | | | |
| 2015 | 769.36 | 788.44 | 780.69 | 799.19 | 794.95 | 796.51 | 797.07 | 811.74 | 818.52 | 821.39 | 834.23 | 824.97 | 803.20 |
| 2016 | 831.39 | 820.10 | 799.16 | 795.99 | 802.00 | 791.18 | 795.52 | 796.64 | 790.02 | 789.08 | 803.88 | 787.69 | 800.09 |
| 2017 | 790.72 | 792.55 | 785.89 | 795.23 | 793.19 | 810.55 | 815.33 | 820.20 | 822.17 | 819.45 | 836.79 | 829.02 | 810.32 |
| 2018 | 839.68 | 857.95 | 833.20 | 850.08 | 831.60 | 853.74 | 852.61 | 852.59 | 874.67 | 852.91 | 869.23 | 890.96 | 853.58 |
| 2019 | 882.94 | 876.36 | 879.65 | 880.72 | 875.42 | 896.80 | 892.40 | 884.41 | 893.30 | 877.21 | 876.10 | 897.97 | 885.36 |
| **Leisure and Hospitality** | | | | | | | | | | | | | |
| 2015 | 315.77 | 336.03 | 332.53 | 324.16 | 337.95 | 341.36 | 338.85 | 356.08 | 338.66 | 342.72 | 350.65 | 348.00 | 338.44 |
| 2016 | 339.38 | 338.40 | 332.87 | 339.53 | 349.69 | 340.52 | 341.17 | 344.36 | 324.72 | 338.12 | 335.84 | 331.94 | 338.49 |
| 2017 | 363.71 | 342.23 | 344.19 | 372.24 | 383.41 | 373.98 | 368.24 | 367.95 | 352.64 | 354.16 | 344.25 | 353.51 | 361.19 |
| 2018 | 332.72 | 345.79 | 342.47 | 359.86 | 353.21 | 364.08 | 366.30 | 364.07 | 365.23 | 346.02 | 346.47 | 368.78 | 355.50 |
| 2019 | 347.31 | 356.43 | 351.35 | 360.68 | 364.10 | 379.50 | 370.72 | 364.21 | 361.76 | 345.15 | 344.59 | 349.58 | 357.79 |
| **Other Services** | | | | | | | | | | | | | |
| 2015 | 558.27 | 582.12 | 604.49 | 580.61 | 603.24 | 609.41 | 612.29 | 645.52 | 610.50 | 607.99 | 656.77 | 645.70 | 608.58 |
| 2016 | 628.86 | 632.23 | 621.13 | 654.66 | 680.35 | 621.00 | 684.06 | 680.48 | 694.38 | 672.71 | 658.05 | 664.70 | 657.51 |
| 2017 | 624.38 | 634.39 | 625.26 | 703.74 | 693.47 | 703.99 | 753.74 | 721.98 | 735.44 | 756.28 | 727.32 | 694.82 | 696.95 |
| 2018 | 675.60 | 722.84 | 690.11 | 711.50 | 663.67 | 672.98 | 662.43 | 664.92 | 675.58 | 678.22 | 711.98 | 745.75 | 690.17 |
| 2019 | 733.19 | 728.98 | 743.23 | 739.12 | 753.28 | 797.71 | 741.36 | 766.16 | 752.31 | 737.04 | 727.50 | 754.91 | 749.01 |

# OHIO
## *At a Glance*

Population:
2010 census: 11,536,504
2019 estimate: 11,689,100

Percent change in population:
2010–2019: 1.3%

Percent change in total nonfarm employment:
2011–2019: 9.4%

Industry with the largest growth in employment, 2011–2019 (percent):
Construction, 28.3%

Industry with the largest decline or smallest growth in employment, 2011–2019 (percent):
Information, -8.8%

Civilian labor force:
2010: 5,846,886
2019: 5,802,318

Unemployment rate and rank among states (highest to lowest):
2010: 10.3%, 15th
2019: 4.1%, 11th

Over-the-year change in unemployment rates:
2017–2018: -0.5%
2018–2019: -0.4%

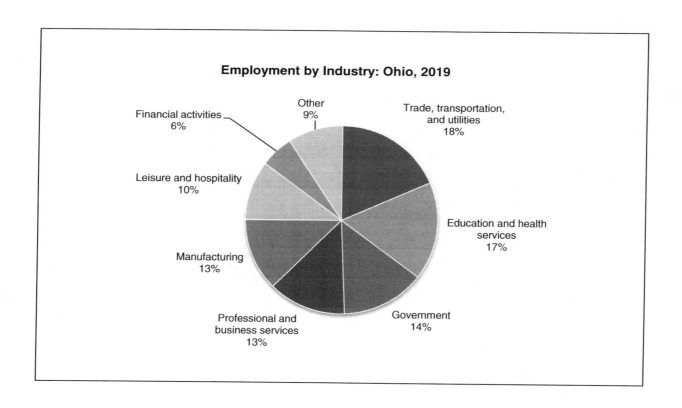

### Employment by Industry: Ohio, 2019

- Other 9%
- Trade, transportation, and utilities 18%
- Education and health services 17%
- Government 14%
- Professional and business services 13%
- Manufacturing 13%
- Leisure and hospitality 10%
- Financial activities 6%

# 1. Employment by Industry: Ohio, 2011–2019

(Numbers in thousands, not seasonally adjusted)

| Industry and year | January | February | March | April | May | June | July | August | September | October | November | December | Annual average |
|---|---|---|---|---|---|---|---|---|---|---|---|---|---|
| **Total Nonfarm** | | | | | | | | | | | | | |
| 2011 | 4,959.4 | 4,981.2 | 5,015.2 | 5,092.4 | 5,132.9 | 5,131.8 | 5,128.2 | 5,145.1 | 5,158.9 | 5,172.9 | 5,192.4 | 5,184.5 | 5,107.9 |
| 2012 | 5,050.8 | 5,082.4 | 5,129.9 | 5,188.9 | 5,247.0 | 5,248.7 | 5,210.2 | 5,223.7 | 5,232.7 | 5,265.5 | 5,275.8 | 5,263.9 | 5,201.6 |
| 2013 | 5,113.4 | 5,142.8 | 5,171.7 | 5,248.9 | 5,317.3 | 5,303.5 | 5,276.0 | 5,297.1 | 5,303.6 | 5,330.8 | 5,355.2 | 5,341.2 | 5,266.8 |
| 2014 | 5,180.3 | 5,203.8 | 5,238.6 | 5,319.4 | 5,391.4 | 5,379.1 | 5,348.3 | 5,378.4 | 5,384.7 | 5,423.6 | 5,442.3 | 5,437.9 | 5,344.0 |
| 2015 | 5,273.5 | 5,295.6 | 5,322.2 | 5,403.3 | 5,473.8 | 5,460.6 | 5,445.8 | 5,456.6 | 5,453.5 | 5,494.1 | 5,505.3 | 5,498.7 | 5,423.6 |
| 2016 | 5,346.9 | 5,369.1 | 5,401.4 | 5,479.4 | 5,522.3 | 5,504.2 | 5,496.6 | 5,501.8 | 5,514.5 | 5,541.2 | 5,560.2 | 5,534.9 | 5,481.0 |
| 2017 | 5,404.8 | 5,427.0 | 5,455.4 | 5,515.1 | 5,562.8 | 5,564.7 | 5,532.4 | 5,546.1 | 5,543.8 | 5,582.6 | 5,596.9 | 5,577.4 | 5,525.8 |
| 2018 | 5,434.3 | 5,469.4 | 5,494.6 | 5,542.4 | 5,593.0 | 5,603.4 | 5,578.6 | 5,591.2 | 5,584.7 | 5,622.1 | 5,633.6 | 5,611.5 | 5,563.2 |
| 2019 | 5,488.3 | 5,504.9 | 5,527.8 | 5,584.8 | 5,629.2 | 5,623.4 | 5,609.0 | 5,616.4 | 5,601.2 | 5,617.7 | 5,624.2 | 5,615.2 | 5,586.8 |
| **Total Private** | | | | | | | | | | | | | |
| 2011 | 4,187.5 | 4,194.6 | 4,226.0 | 4,303.1 | 4,344.3 | 4,365.2 | 4,381.7 | 4,399.7 | 4,385.0 | 4,386.9 | 4,404.2 | 4,403.2 | 4,331.8 |
| 2012 | 4,288.9 | 4,300.1 | 4,343.4 | 4,399.7 | 4,450.9 | 4,484.7 | 4,467.7 | 4,481.9 | 4,460.8 | 4,478.1 | 4,486.8 | 4,480.7 | 4,427.0 |
| 2013 | 4,351.3 | 4,363.9 | 4,393.1 | 4,464.9 | 4,529.2 | 4,555.6 | 4,546.0 | 4,565.1 | 4,537.5 | 4,551.1 | 4,569.6 | 4,564.7 | 4,499.3 |
| 2014 | 4,428.1 | 4,431.5 | 4,465.1 | 4,537.1 | 4,602.5 | 4,626.2 | 4,621.6 | 4,644.1 | 4,608.7 | 4,636.1 | 4,652.4 | 4,653.1 | 4,575.5 |
| 2015 | 4,515.7 | 4,516.3 | 4,543.0 | 4,615.8 | 4,684.6 | 4,703.0 | 4,706.0 | 4,713.6 | 4,679.7 | 4,703.2 | 4,712.7 | 4,711.6 | 4,650.4 |
| 2016 | 4,585.9 | 4,588.3 | 4,620.1 | 4,683.3 | 4,730.7 | 4,746.1 | 4,756.1 | 4,757.6 | 4,731.4 | 4,741.8 | 4,756.8 | 4,743.5 | 4,703.5 |
| 2017 | 4,623.7 | 4,631.8 | 4,659.2 | 4,717.4 | 4,769.3 | 4,803.2 | 4,789.7 | 4,799.4 | 4,761.2 | 4,782.4 | 4,793.1 | 4,782.4 | 4,742.7 |
| 2018 | 4,658.0 | 4,673.3 | 4,697.5 | 4,744.0 | 4,800.6 | 4,837.1 | 4,833.7 | 4,839.0 | 4,797.3 | 4,815.0 | 4,823.6 | 4,809.7 | 4,777.4 |
| 2019 | 4,711.8 | 4,708.8 | 4,726.7 | 4,782.1 | 4,831.7 | 4,856.9 | 4,857.1 | 4,857.9 | 4,813.9 | 4,818.8 | 4,822.4 | 4,821.4 | 4,800.8 |
| **Goods Producing** | | | | | | | | | | | | | |
| 2011 | 786.1 | 784.9 | 794.6 | 811.7 | 822.3 | 834.3 | 844.1 | 852.3 | 849.3 | 849.7 | 849.8 | 843.3 | 826.9 |
| 2012 | 818.8 | 819.3 | 829.1 | 841.8 | 853.4 | 865.6 | 863.4 | 867.9 | 863.7 | 860.8 | 859.3 | 852.4 | 849.6 |
| 2013 | 829.4 | 829.2 | 835.5 | 848.4 | 864.6 | 876.7 | 874.7 | 882.6 | 879.0 | 879.4 | 879.0 | 869.0 | 862.3 |
| 2014 | 845.8 | 845.1 | 855.2 | 871.5 | 889.0 | 901.8 | 901.4 | 909.6 | 905.0 | 907.3 | 906.3 | 898.3 | 886.4 |
| 2015 | 872.5 | 870.7 | 876.5 | 893.4 | 909.5 | 918.1 | 917.2 | 920.9 | 914.9 | 915.2 | 912.4 | 906.1 | 902.3 |
| 2016 | 881.0 | 879.6 | 887.2 | 899.2 | 908.6 | 917.9 | 917.9 | 917.2 | 911.8 | 911.1 | 909.7 | 901.0 | 903.5 |
| 2017 | 881.8 | 882.0 | 891.6 | 906.7 | 921.2 | 935.3 | 930.7 | 935.2 | 926.0 | 928.9 | 927.1 | 920.7 | 915.6 |
| 2018 | 894.5 | 901.8 | 909.6 | 920.5 | 935.4 | 949.5 | 949.6 | 951.1 | 944.9 | 945.4 | 942.3 | 937.1 | 931.8 |
| 2019 | 918.3 | 917.6 | 923.1 | 935.2 | 945.7 | 956.3 | 956.5 | 955.0 | 947.8 | 942.8 | 937.4 | 935.8 | 939.3 |
| **Service-Providing** | | | | | | | | | | | | | |
| 2011 | 4,173.3 | 4,196.3 | 4,220.6 | 4,280.7 | 4,310.6 | 4,297.5 | 4,284.1 | 4,292.8 | 4,309.6 | 4,323.2 | 4,342.6 | 4,341.2 | 4,281.0 |
| 2012 | 4,232.0 | 4,263.1 | 4,300.8 | 4,347.1 | 4,393.6 | 4,383.1 | 4,346.8 | 4,355.8 | 4,369.0 | 4,404.7 | 4,416.5 | 4,411.5 | 4,352.0 |
| 2013 | 4,284.0 | 4,313.6 | 4,336.2 | 4,400.5 | 4,452.7 | 4,426.8 | 4,401.3 | 4,414.5 | 4,424.6 | 4,451.4 | 4,476.2 | 4,472.2 | 4,404.5 |
| 2014 | 4,334.5 | 4,358.7 | 4,383.4 | 4,447.9 | 4,502.4 | 4,477.3 | 4,446.9 | 4,468.8 | 4,479.7 | 4,516.3 | 4,536.0 | 4,539.6 | 4,457.6 |
| 2015 | 4,401.0 | 4,424.9 | 4,445.7 | 4,509.9 | 4,564.3 | 4,542.5 | 4,528.6 | 4,535.7 | 4,538.6 | 4,578.9 | 4,592.9 | 4,592.6 | 4,521.3 |
| 2016 | 4,465.9 | 4,489.5 | 4,514.2 | 4,580.2 | 4,613.7 | 4,586.3 | 4,578.7 | 4,584.6 | 4,602.7 | 4,630.1 | 4,650.5 | 4,633.9 | 4,577.5 |
| 2017 | 4,523.0 | 4,545.0 | 4,563.8 | 4,608.4 | 4,641.6 | 4,629.4 | 4,601.7 | 4,610.9 | 4,617.8 | 4,653.7 | 4,669.8 | 4,656.7 | 4,610.2 |
| 2018 | 4,539.8 | 4,567.6 | 4,585.0 | 4,621.9 | 4,657.6 | 4,653.9 | 4,629.0 | 4,640.1 | 4,639.8 | 4,676.7 | 4,691.3 | 4,674.4 | 4,631.4 |
| 2019 | 4,570.0 | 4,587.3 | 4,604.7 | 4,649.6 | 4,683.5 | 4,667.1 | 4,652.5 | 4,661.4 | 4,653.4 | 4,674.9 | 4,686.8 | 4,679.4 | 4,647.6 |
| **Mining and Logging** | | | | | | | | | | | | | |
| 2011 | 10.7 | 10.7 | 10.9 | 11.2 | 11.3 | 11.4 | 11.6 | 11.7 | 11.7 | 11.7 | 11.6 | 11.4 | 11.3 |
| 2012 | 11.0 | 10.8 | 11.0 | 11.4 | 11.6 | 11.7 | 11.8 | 11.7 | 11.6 | 11.5 | 11.6 | 11.4 | 11.4 |
| 2013 | 11.3 | 11.3 | 11.8 | 12.2 | 12.5 | 12.5 | 12.7 | 12.9 | 12.9 | 13.5 | 13.5 | 13.3 | 12.5 |
| 2014 | 13.1 | 13.3 | 13.7 | 14.2 | 14.6 | 14.9 | 15.4 | 15.8 | 15.7 | 15.8 | 15.9 | 15.8 | 14.9 |
| 2015 | 15.2 | 14.8 | 14.7 | 14.5 | 14.6 | 14.3 | 14.1 | 14.0 | 13.8 | 13.3 | 13.0 | 12.6 | 14.1 |
| 2016 | 11.6 | 11.2 | 11.3 | 11.3 | 11.2 | 11.2 | 11.1 | 11.2 | 11.0 | 11.4 | 11.4 | 11.2 | 11.3 |
| 2017 | 10.4 | 10.6 | 11.0 | 11.2 | 11.3 | 11.4 | 11.7 | 11.9 | 11.9 | 12.0 | 11.9 | 11.7 | 11.4 |
| 2018 | 11.5 | 11.8 | 12.2 | 12.0 | 12.2 | 12.5 | 12.5 | 12.7 | 12.5 | 12.2 | 12.1 | 11.9 | 12.2 |
| 2019 | 11.7 | 11.7 | 12.1 | 12.2 | 12.3 | 12.2 | 12.3 | 12.1 | 11.9 | 11.9 | 11.6 | 11.3 | 11.9 |
| **Construction** | | | | | | | | | | | | | |
| 2011 | 150.2 | 147.9 | 154.2 | 167.0 | 175.1 | 183.0 | 190.7 | 193.6 | 192.6 | 190.8 | 187.7 | 180.8 | 176.1 |
| 2012 | 162.9 | 160.3 | 165.8 | 176.1 | 184.0 | 189.6 | 191.9 | 192.4 | 191.1 | 191.5 | 187.3 | 179.9 | 181.1 |
| 2013 | 163.0 | 161.7 | 166.0 | 176.2 | 188.6 | 195.5 | 198.8 | 201.0 | 199.7 | 200.2 | 196.6 | 185.1 | 186.0 |
| 2014 | 169.1 | 166.6 | 174.9 | 188.0 | 199.9 | 207.3 | 211.0 | 211.9 | 209.5 | 209.4 | 205.1 | 195.6 | 195.7 |
| 2015 | 175.9 | 173.9 | 179.2 | 193.5 | 205.4 | 210.8 | 213.7 | 214.8 | 212.6 | 213.5 | 209.9 | 202.5 | 200.5 |
| 2016 | 185.6 | 184.5 | 192.0 | 203.6 | 211.6 | 217.9 | 218.2 | 217.0 | 214.8 | 214.6 | 212.0 | 201.9 | 206.1 |
| 2017 | 187.6 | 189.6 | 197.3 | 213.4 | 226.2 | 233.3 | 233.0 | 233.0 | 229.8 | 227.3 | 222.1 | 212.9 | 217.1 |
| 2018 | 193.1 | 195.1 | 202.6 | 213.5 | 226.3 | 233.8 | 236.1 | 236.3 | 233.7 | 232.9 | 227.1 | 218.6 | 220.8 |
| 2019 | 204.9 | 202.8 | 209.8 | 222.4 | 231.7 | 238.1 | 239.2 | 239.4 | 237.6 | 236.1 | 227.7 | 221.8 | 226.0 |

## 1. Employment by Industry: Ohio, 2011–2019—*Continued*

(Numbers in thousands, not seasonally adjusted)

| Industry and year | January | February | March | April | May | June | July | August | September | October | November | December | Annual average |
|---|---|---|---|---|---|---|---|---|---|---|---|---|---|
| **Manufacturing** | | | | | | | | | | | | | |
| 2011 | 625.2 | 626.3 | 629.5 | 633.5 | 635.9 | 639.9 | 641.8 | 647.0 | 645.0 | 647.2 | 650.5 | 651.1 | 639.4 |
| 2012 | 644.9 | 648.2 | 652.3 | 654.3 | 657.8 | 664.3 | 659.7 | 663.8 | 661.0 | 657.8 | 660.4 | 661.1 | 657.1 |
| 2013 | 655.1 | 656.2 | 657.7 | 660.0 | 663.5 | 668.7 | 663.2 | 668.7 | 666.4 | 665.7 | 668.9 | 670.6 | 663.7 |
| 2014 | 663.6 | 665.2 | 666.6 | 669.3 | 674.5 | 679.6 | 675.0 | 681.9 | 679.8 | 682.1 | 685.3 | 686.9 | 675.8 |
| 2015 | 681.4 | 682.0 | 682.6 | 685.4 | 689.5 | 693.0 | 689.4 | 692.1 | 688.5 | 688.4 | 689.5 | 691.0 | 687.7 |
| 2016 | 683.8 | 683.9 | 683.9 | 684.3 | 685.8 | 688.8 | 688.6 | 689.0 | 686.0 | 685.1 | 686.3 | 687.9 | 686.1 |
| 2017 | 683.8 | 681.8 | 683.3 | 682.1 | 683.7 | 690.6 | 686.0 | 690.3 | 684.3 | 689.6 | 693.1 | 696.1 | 687.1 |
| 2018 | 689.9 | 694.9 | 694.8 | 695.0 | 696.9 | 703.2 | 701.0 | 702.1 | 698.7 | 700.3 | 703.1 | 706.6 | 698.9 |
| 2019 | 701.7 | 703.1 | 701.2 | 700.6 | 701.7 | 706.0 | 705.0 | 703.5 | 698.3 | 694.8 | 698.1 | 702.7 | 701.4 |
| **Trade, Transportation, and Utilities** | | | | | | | | | | | | | |
| 2011 | 934.0 | 928.4 | 931.6 | 944.5 | 950.5 | 954.9 | 956.7 | 959.6 | 954.8 | 964.0 | 984.6 | 994.9 | 954.9 |
| 2012 | 953.7 | 946.7 | 953.9 | 958.8 | 969.0 | 972.5 | 968.2 | 969.1 | 965.8 | 976.2 | 998.5 | 1,004.5 | 969.7 |
| 2013 | 961.1 | 953.4 | 957.3 | 965.2 | 976.9 | 981.4 | 979.4 | 981.1 | 975.2 | 985.4 | 1,009.7 | 1,019.0 | 978.8 |
| 2014 | 971.6 | 964.7 | 967.9 | 978.2 | 989.2 | 993.4 | 990.8 | 994.9 | 989.1 | 1,002.9 | 1,026.0 | 1,037.8 | 992.2 |
| 2015 | 992.8 | 985.5 | 989.2 | 997.3 | 1,008.1 | 1,010.6 | 1,008.9 | 1,010.7 | 1,004.1 | 1,015.4 | 1,037.6 | 1,047.9 | 1,009.0 |
| 2016 | 1,005.7 | 998.4 | 1,001.2 | 1,006.7 | 1,014.9 | 1,015.5 | 1,015.5 | 1,018.0 | 1,012.0 | 1,022.5 | 1,046.3 | 1,057.4 | 1,017.8 |
| 2017 | 1,012.8 | 1,003.6 | 1,005.0 | 1,010.8 | 1,017.9 | 1,020.6 | 1,019.8 | 1,020.7 | 1,013.5 | 1,025.8 | 1,051.0 | 1,056.0 | 1,021.5 |
| 2018 | 1,016.4 | 1,007.0 | 1,008.4 | 1,012.1 | 1,022.5 | 1,024.4 | 1,024.6 | 1,023.9 | 1,017.0 | 1,027.2 | 1,051.3 | 1,056.0 | 1,024.2 |
| 2019 | 1,022.7 | 1,008.3 | 1,008.4 | 1,011.1 | 1,020.1 | 1,024.0 | 1,027.0 | 1,027.3 | 1,021.5 | 1,029.4 | 1,049.3 | 1,055.1 | 1,025.4 |
| **Wholesale Trade** | | | | | | | | | | | | | |
| 2011 | 209.8 | 210.1 | 210.8 | 213.2 | 214.6 | 215.8 | 217.3 | 217.7 | 216.8 | 217.6 | 217.7 | 218.4 | 215.0 |
| 2012 | 216.8 | 217.6 | 218.6 | 219.3 | 220.9 | 222.5 | 222.3 | 222.2 | 220.8 | 221.8 | 221.8 | 222.2 | 220.6 |
| 2013 | 219.3 | 219.6 | 220.3 | 221.9 | 223.5 | 224.3 | 224.5 | 224.5 | 223.1 | 224.4 | 225.3 | 225.9 | 223.1 |
| 2014 | 223.0 | 224.1 | 225.2 | 226.1 | 228.8 | 229.8 | 230.4 | 230.4 | 229.0 | 229.8 | 230.5 | 231.5 | 228.2 |
| 2015 | 228.0 | 228.7 | 229.8 | 229.9 | 231.5 | 232.1 | 232.1 | 231.6 | 229.3 | 230.1 | 230.5 | 230.6 | 230.4 |
| 2016 | 228.5 | 228.5 | 228.9 | 228.8 | 230.0 | 230.7 | 230.8 | 230.6 | 228.8 | 229.1 | 229.2 | 229.8 | 229.5 |
| 2017 | 227.5 | 228.0 | 228.5 | 229.5 | 230.9 | 232.6 | 232.4 | 232.2 | 230.5 | 231.6 | 232.2 | 233.1 | 230.8 |
| 2018 | 230.4 | 231.1 | 231.9 | 233.2 | 234.9 | 236.6 | 237.3 | 236.6 | 235.1 | 236.3 | 236.9 | 237.2 | 234.8 |
| 2019 | 235.2 | 235.7 | 236.1 | 236.7 | 237.9 | 239.3 | 238.4 | 237.9 | 236.5 | 238.1 | 237.7 | 236.9 | 237.2 |
| **Retail Trade** | | | | | | | | | | | | | |
| 2011 | 544.0 | 538.5 | 540.6 | 549.3 | 552.7 | 555.3 | 555.2 | 556.2 | 550.8 | 558.5 | 576.9 | 583.9 | 555.2 |
| 2012 | 551.1 | 543.5 | 549.1 | 552.8 | 559.2 | 560.1 | 556.6 | 556.5 | 554.0 | 561.8 | 581.6 | 584.2 | 559.2 |
| 2013 | 552.9 | 545.8 | 548.8 | 554.6 | 562.6 | 565.2 | 563.5 | 564.1 | 559.4 | 566.9 | 586.2 | 592.1 | 563.5 |
| 2014 | 555.3 | 549.2 | 550.8 | 559.1 | 564.3 | 566.8 | 563.8 | 566.0 | 560.7 | 571.4 | 589.7 | 594.9 | 566.0 |
| 2015 | 561.0 | 555.4 | 557.8 | 563.8 | 570.5 | 571.8 | 570.1 | 571.0 | 566.1 | 573.8 | 591.7 | 597.4 | 570.9 |
| 2016 | 568.1 | 563.0 | 564.8 | 569.4 | 574.6 | 574.6 | 573.8 | 575.1 | 568.8 | 575.4 | 592.1 | 596.4 | 574.7 |
| 2017 | 567.3 | 560.2 | 560.9 | 565.1 | 568.8 | 569.1 | 568.6 | 568.1 | 561.8 | 570.1 | 589.2 | 590.5 | 570.0 |
| 2018 | 564.7 | 556.5 | 556.7 | 558.1 | 565.3 | 563.5 | 564.0 | 562.5 | 555.9 | 560.6 | 578.3 | 579.2 | 563.8 |
| 2019 | 555.5 | 544.8 | 545.8 | 548.4 | 553.5 | 553.0 | 553.5 | 551.7 | 546.0 | 550.2 | 562.6 | 563.3 | 552.4 |
| **Transportation and Utilities** | | | | | | | | | | | | | |
| 2011 | 180.2 | 179.8 | 180.2 | 182.0 | 183.2 | 183.8 | 184.2 | 185.7 | 187.2 | 187.9 | 190.0 | 192.6 | 184.7 |
| 2012 | 185.8 | 185.6 | 186.2 | 186.7 | 188.9 | 189.9 | 189.3 | 190.4 | 191.0 | 192.6 | 195.1 | 198.1 | 190.0 |
| 2013 | 188.9 | 188.0 | 188.2 | 188.7 | 190.8 | 191.9 | 191.4 | 192.5 | 192.7 | 194.1 | 198.2 | 201.0 | 192.2 |
| 2014 | 193.3 | 191.4 | 191.9 | 193.0 | 196.1 | 196.8 | 196.6 | 198.5 | 199.4 | 201.7 | 205.8 | 211.4 | 198.0 |
| 2015 | 203.8 | 201.4 | 201.6 | 203.6 | 206.1 | 206.7 | 206.7 | 208.1 | 208.7 | 211.5 | 215.4 | 219.9 | 207.8 |
| 2016 | 209.1 | 206.9 | 207.5 | 208.5 | 210.3 | 210.2 | 210.9 | 212.3 | 214.4 | 218.0 | 225.0 | 231.2 | 213.7 |
| 2017 | 218.0 | 215.4 | 215.6 | 216.2 | 218.2 | 218.9 | 218.8 | 220.4 | 221.2 | 224.1 | 229.6 | 232.4 | 220.7 |
| 2018 | 221.3 | 219.4 | 219.8 | 220.8 | 222.3 | 224.3 | 223.3 | 224.8 | 226.0 | 230.3 | 236.1 | 239.6 | 225.7 |
| 2019 | 232.0 | 227.8 | 226.5 | 226.0 | 228.7 | 231.7 | 235.1 | 237.7 | 239.0 | 241.1 | 249.0 | 254.9 | 235.8 |
| **Information** | | | | | | | | | | | | | |
| 2011 | 76.2 | 75.9 | 75.5 | 76.0 | 76.4 | 76.5 | 76.9 | 76.8 | 76.3 | 76.0 | 76.2 | 76.1 | 76.2 |
| 2012 | 75.2 | 75.0 | 74.8 | 74.8 | 75.1 | 75.6 | 75.6 | 75.1 | 74.6 | 74.9 | 75.3 | 75.6 | 75.1 |
| 2013 | 75.0 | 75.5 | 75.6 | 75.6 | 75.6 | 76.0 | 76.1 | 75.8 | 74.9 | 74.6 | 74.5 | 74.9 | 75.3 |
| 2014 | 73.2 | 73.1 | 73.1 | 73.4 | 73.3 | 72.9 | 73.0 | 72.8 | 71.5 | 71.1 | 71.7 | 72.3 | 72.6 |
| 2015 | 70.9 | 71.3 | 71.2 | 71.8 | 71.9 | 72.3 | 72.2 | 72.2 | 71.4 | 71.8 | 72.3 | 72.7 | 71.8 |
| 2016 | 71.6 | 71.7 | 71.8 | 71.7 | 72.1 | 72.5 | 72.8 | 72.7 | 72.2 | 72.0 | 72.5 | 72.4 | 72.2 |
| 2017 | 71.7 | 71.8 | 71.4 | 71.9 | 72.3 | 72.3 | 72.5 | 72.5 | 71.9 | 71.1 | 71.7 | 71.8 | 71.9 |
| 2018 | 71.1 | 71.4 | 70.8 | 71.0 | 71.3 | 71.9 | 71.0 | 70.9 | 70.0 | 70.4 | 70.6 | 70.4 | 70.9 |
| 2019 | 69.6 | 69.9 | 69.6 | 69.2 | 69.6 | 69.9 | 69.9 | 69.2 | 68.5 | 69.6 | 69.5 | 69.8 | 69.5 |

## 1. Employment by Industry: Ohio, 2011–2019—*Continued*

(Numbers in thousands, not seasonally adjusted)

| Industry and year | January | February | March | April | May | June | July | August | September | October | November | December | Annual average |
|---|---|---|---|---|---|---|---|---|---|---|---|---|---|
| **Financial Activities** | | | | | | | | | | | | | |
| 2011 | 277.5 | 277.5 | 277.4 | 277.9 | 278.6 | 278.8 | 278.9 | 278.7 | 277.9 | 277.5 | 277.5 | 277.7 | 278.0 |
| 2012 | 275.7 | 275.7 | 276.4 | 277.9 | 279.6 | 281.5 | 282.5 | 282.4 | 280.4 | 281.8 | 282.7 | 282.8 | 280.0 |
| 2013 | 279.6 | 280.1 | 280.3 | 282.8 | 284.7 | 286.8 | 287.2 | 287.4 | 285.2 | 285.5 | 286.3 | 286.3 | 284.4 |
| 2014 | 283.7 | 284.5 | 284.9 | 285.4 | 288.2 | 290.0 | 290.4 | 291.2 | 288.5 | 289.4 | 290.7 | 290.9 | 288.2 |
| 2015 | 288.6 | 289.0 | 289.0 | 290.7 | 293.4 | 295.6 | 296.4 | 296.9 | 294.1 | 296.0 | 296.2 | 296.2 | 293.5 |
| 2016 | 294.6 | 295.7 | 296.1 | 298.4 | 299.9 | 301.5 | 303.7 | 303.9 | 302.1 | 303.4 | 303.8 | 304.7 | 300.7 |
| 2017 | 302.5 | 302.8 | 303.0 | 304.5 | 306.1 | 308.6 | 308.6 | 308.7 | 306.9 | 307.4 | 306.9 | 308.7 | 306.1 |
| 2018 | 305.7 | 306.7 | 305.8 | 306.8 | 308.9 | 311.2 | 312.4 | 311.6 | 308.3 | 309.3 | 309.0 | 308.7 | 308.7 |
| 2019 | 307.4 | 307.7 | 307.2 | 308.1 | 310.0 | 311.9 | 313.0 | 312.1 | 309.3 | 308.6 | 308.0 | 311.0 | 309.5 |
| **Professional and Business Services** | | | | | | | | | | | | | |
| 2011 | 627.9 | 631.5 | 637.8 | 653.2 | 652.2 | 655.9 | 662.4 | 667.0 | 666.0 | 668.4 | 670.6 | 670.2 | 655.3 |
| 2012 | 652.2 | 656.1 | 662.3 | 674.4 | 676.7 | 681.5 | 681.9 | 687.4 | 684.4 | 692.7 | 691.9 | 687.5 | 677.4 |
| 2013 | 660.9 | 666.1 | 670.9 | 689.2 | 694.9 | 698.9 | 697.6 | 705.2 | 703.2 | 708.9 | 712.0 | 710.8 | 693.2 |
| 2014 | 687.9 | 690.1 | 694.2 | 709.8 | 713.7 | 716.2 | 718.9 | 725.6 | 719.3 | 726.9 | 730.0 | 726.8 | 713.3 |
| 2015 | 700.6 | 698.5 | 701.4 | 715.4 | 722.1 | 725.0 | 729.2 | 731.5 | 723.1 | 735.2 | 733.5 | 728.5 | 720.3 |
| 2016 | 706.8 | 706.8 | 711.3 | 728.3 | 729.5 | 732.1 | 737.5 | 737.5 | 735.0 | 738.1 | 738.5 | 730.3 | 727.6 |
| 2017 | 709.4 | 710.7 | 712.0 | 723.9 | 728.0 | 733.8 | 731.7 | 734.4 | 729.1 | 737.1 | 739.8 | 731.7 | 726.8 |
| 2018 | 711.7 | 715.1 | 717.6 | 726.4 | 729.4 | 736.3 | 738.2 | 740.4 | 734.1 | 741.0 | 744.9 | 736.2 | 730.9 |
| 2019 | 717.6 | 718.6 | 719.0 | 735.8 | 739.2 | 743.0 | 745.1 | 745.5 | 737.7 | 743.0 | 741.7 | 735.1 | 735.1 |
| **Education and Health Services** | | | | | | | | | | | | | |
| 2011 | 839.2 | 847.4 | 848.2 | 853.6 | 855.3 | 841.0 | 837.4 | 838.6 | 852.1 | 859.5 | 861.6 | 862.1 | 849.7 |
| 2012 | 853.0 | 861.1 | 862.6 | 866.1 | 865.9 | 857.5 | 848.9 | 852.5 | 863.1 | 872.3 | 873.9 | 872.3 | 862.4 |
| 2013 | 861.0 | 871.6 | 871.1 | 877.2 | 877.7 | 868.8 | 866.9 | 870.9 | 876.7 | 885.8 | 890.8 | 889.0 | 875.6 |
| 2014 | 874.1 | 881.1 | 883.3 | 888.1 | 888.8 | 877.9 | 876.3 | 880.1 | 886.7 | 897.6 | 901.0 | 900.7 | 886.3 |
| 2015 | 886.5 | 894.1 | 895.5 | 901.5 | 904.2 | 893.9 | 894.6 | 896.9 | 904.0 | 912.2 | 915.8 | 916.3 | 901.3 |
| 2016 | 902.9 | 910.8 | 913.5 | 917.4 | 918.5 | 906.5 | 907.9 | 910.8 | 920.0 | 925.3 | 927.1 | 924.8 | 915.5 |
| 2017 | 913.8 | 922.2 | 924.7 | 927.2 | 928.2 | 920.3 | 916.4 | 919.8 | 926.7 | 933.7 | 935.2 | 933.5 | 925.1 |
| 2018 | 921.7 | 929.7 | 929.7 | 933.1 | 933.1 | 925.2 | 922.4 | 927.4 | 932.0 | 938.2 | 939.0 | 935.5 | 930.6 |
| 2019 | 932.2 | 938.7 | 939.3 | 943.2 | 943.1 | 934.3 | 930.0 | 935.8 | 939.5 | 948.0 | 950.1 | 949.6 | 940.3 |
| **Leisure and Hospitality** | | | | | | | | | | | | | |
| 2011 | 442.6 | 444.6 | 455.6 | 479.5 | 500.9 | 514.4 | 515.0 | 517.1 | 500.8 | 484.0 | 476.1 | 471.2 | 483.5 |
| 2012 | 454.0 | 459.2 | 474.2 | 495.0 | 518.5 | 535.0 | 532.0 | 533.3 | 516.4 | 505.9 | 492.7 | 492.7 | 500.7 |
| 2013 | 474.1 | 477.3 | 490.4 | 513.0 | 540.2 | 551.6 | 550.1 | 548.8 | 532.4 | 521.8 | 508.3 | 507.0 | 517.9 |
| 2014 | 485.9 | 486.9 | 499.5 | 522.1 | 549.1 | 560.8 | 558.3 | 557.8 | 539.0 | 529.6 | 516.3 | 515.1 | 526.7 |
| 2015 | 495.6 | 498.2 | 509.8 | 533.0 | 561.0 | 571.5 | 571.4 | 569.8 | 556.2 | 544.2 | 532.7 | 531.5 | 539.6 |
| 2016 | 513.1 | 514.7 | 527.0 | 547.9 | 571.8 | 583.6 | 584.1 | 581.5 | 564.1 | 554.0 | 543.8 | 539.1 | 552.1 |
| 2017 | 519.3 | 525.4 | 537.0 | 556.9 | 578.6 | 593.1 | 592.0 | 591.3 | 573.6 | 564.4 | 548.6 | 548.5 | 560.7 |
| 2018 | 526.7 | 530.8 | 543.6 | 560.7 | 585.1 | 601.2 | 599.1 | 598.5 | 578.5 | 569.8 | 554.2 | 553.2 | 566.8 |
| 2019 | 534.2 | 537.7 | 548.6 | 566.6 | 589.5 | 600.7 | 599.5 | 597.9 | 577.0 | 566.4 | 552.8 | 552.3 | 568.6 |
| **Other Services** | | | | | | | | | | | | | |
| 2011 | 204.0 | 204.4 | 205.3 | 206.7 | 208.1 | 209.4 | 210.3 | 209.6 | 207.8 | 207.8 | 207.8 | 207.7 | 207.4 |
| 2012 | 206.3 | 207.0 | 210.1 | 210.9 | 212.7 | 215.5 | 215.2 | 214.2 | 212.4 | 213.5 | 212.5 | 212.9 | 211.9 |
| 2013 | 210.2 | 210.7 | 212.0 | 213.5 | 214.6 | 215.4 | 214.0 | 213.3 | 210.9 | 209.7 | 209.0 | 208.7 | 211.8 |
| 2014 | 205.9 | 206.0 | 207.0 | 208.6 | 211.2 | 213.2 | 212.5 | 212.1 | 209.6 | 211.3 | 210.4 | 211.2 | 209.9 |
| 2015 | 208.2 | 209.0 | 210.4 | 212.7 | 214.4 | 216.0 | 216.1 | 214.7 | 211.9 | 213.2 | 212.2 | 212.4 | 212.6 |
| 2016 | 210.2 | 210.6 | 212.0 | 213.7 | 215.4 | 216.5 | 216.7 | 216.0 | 214.2 | 215.4 | 215.1 | 213.8 | 214.1 |
| 2017 | 212.4 | 213.3 | 214.5 | 215.5 | 217.0 | 219.2 | 218.0 | 216.8 | 213.5 | 214.0 | 212.8 | 213.2 | 215.0 |
| 2018 | 210.2 | 210.8 | 212.0 | 213.4 | 214.9 | 217.4 | 216.4 | 215.2 | 212.5 | 213.7 | 212.3 | 212.6 | 213.5 |
| 2019 | 209.8 | 210.3 | 211.5 | 212.9 | 214.5 | 216.8 | 216.1 | 215.1 | 212.6 | 211.0 | 213.6 | 212.7 | 213.1 |
| **Government** | | | | | | | | | | | | | |
| 2011 | 771.9 | 786.6 | 789.2 | 789.3 | 788.6 | 766.6 | 746.5 | 745.4 | 773.9 | 786.0 | 788.2 | 781.3 | 776.1 |
| 2012 | 761.9 | 782.3 | 786.5 | 789.2 | 796.1 | 764.0 | 742.5 | 741.8 | 771.9 | 787.4 | 789.0 | 783.2 | 774.7 |
| 2013 | 762.1 | 778.9 | 778.6 | 784.0 | 788.1 | 747.9 | 730.0 | 732.0 | 766.1 | 779.7 | 785.6 | 776.5 | 767.5 |
| 2014 | 752.2 | 772.3 | 773.5 | 782.3 | 788.9 | 752.9 | 726.7 | 734.3 | 776.0 | 787.5 | 789.9 | 784.8 | 768.4 |
| 2015 | 757.8 | 779.3 | 779.2 | 787.5 | 789.2 | 757.6 | 739.8 | 743.0 | 773.8 | 790.9 | 792.6 | 787.1 | 773.2 |
| 2016 | 761.0 | 780.8 | 781.3 | 796.1 | 791.6 | 758.1 | 740.5 | 744.2 | 783.1 | 799.4 | 803.4 | 791.4 | 777.6 |
| 2017 | 781.1 | 795.2 | 796.2 | 797.7 | 793.5 | 761.5 | 742.7 | 746.7 | 782.6 | 800.2 | 803.8 | 795.0 | 783.0 |
| 2018 | 776.3 | 796.1 | 797.1 | 798.4 | 792.4 | 766.3 | 744.9 | 752.2 | 787.4 | 807.1 | 810.0 | 801.8 | 785.8 |
| 2019 | 776.5 | 796.1 | 801.1 | 802.7 | 797.5 | 766.5 | 751.9 | 758.5 | 787.3 | 798.9 | 801.8 | 793.8 | 786.1 |

## 2. Average Weekly Hours by Selected Industry: Ohio, 2015–2019

(Not seasonally adjusted)

| Industry and year | January | February | March | April | May | June | July | August | September | October | November | December | Annual average |
|---|---|---|---|---|---|---|---|---|---|---|---|---|---|
| **Total Private** | | | | | | | | | | | | | |
| 2015 | 33.7 | 34.1 | 34.3 | 34.1 | 34.2 | 34.2 | 34.2 | 34.6 | 34.1 | 34.4 | 34.7 | 34.5 | 34.3 |
| 2016 | 34.0 | 33.9 | 34.1 | 34.2 | 34.4 | 34.3 | 34.2 | 34.2 | 34.4 | 34.6 | 34.4 | 34.4 | 34.3 |
| 2017 | 34.3 | 34.1 | 34.1 | 34.3 | 34.2 | 34.3 | 34.3 | 34.3 | 34.3 | 34.7 | 34.4 | 34.4 | 34.3 |
| 2018 | 33.6 | 34.1 | 34.2 | 34.5 | 34.2 | 34.4 | 34.4 | 34.3 | 34.5 | 34.2 | 34.2 | 34.6 | 34.3 |
| 2019 | 33.6 | 33.9 | 34.0 | 34.1 | 34.0 | 34.4 | 34.0 | 34.1 | 34.3 | 34.1 | 34.0 | 34.4 | 34.1 |
| **Goods-Producing** | | | | | | | | | | | | | |
| 2015 | 40.2 | 40.2 | 40.5 | 40.3 | 40.5 | 40.6 | 39.9 | 40.6 | 39.6 | 40.8 | 40.3 | 40.4 | 40.3 |
| 2016 | 39.7 | 39.6 | 40.0 | 40.2 | 40.2 | 40.4 | 40.4 | 40.5 | 40.9 | 41.0 | 41.0 | 40.6 | 40.4 |
| 2017 | 40.0 | 40.1 | 39.8 | 40.0 | 40.6 | 41.0 | 40.5 | 41.3 | 40.9 | 41.2 | 41.0 | 40.9 | 40.6 |
| 2018 | 39.5 | 40.6 | 40.6 | 40.9 | 40.4 | 40.7 | 40.3 | 40.7 | 40.8 | 40.9 | 40.5 | 41.1 | 40.6 |
| 2019 | 39.9 | 39.8 | 40.0 | 40.2 | 40.4 | 40.3 | 40.0 | 40.4 | 40.5 | 40.2 | 40.1 | 40.1 | 40.2 |
| **Construction** | | | | | | | | | | | | | |
| 2015 | 36.4 | 37.1 | 37.4 | 38.1 | 39.1 | 38.9 | 39.1 | 40.0 | 37.0 | 40.3 | 38.0 | 38.7 | 38.4 |
| 2016 | 36.8 | 37.1 | 38.2 | 39.0 | 38.2 | 39.8 | 39.8 | 39.3 | 39.7 | 39.8 | 39.5 | 38.0 | 38.8 |
| 2017 | 36.6 | 37.6 | 36.7 | 38.3 | 39.4 | 40.5 | 38.8 | 40.6 | 40.3 | 39.1 | 38.9 | 37.8 | 38.8 |
| 2018 | 36.2 | 37.5 | 38.5 | 39.4 | 39.4 | 39.5 | 40.2 | 40.0 | 39.3 | 39.1 | 38.1 | 39.0 | 38.9 |
| 2019 | 38.3 | 37.8 | 38.2 | 39.0 | 39.4 | 39.0 | 39.7 | 39.5 | 39.5 | 39.4 | 37.8 | 37.6 | 38.8 |
| **Manufacturing** | | | | | | | | | | | | | |
| 2015 | 41.2 | 41.0 | 41.3 | 40.7 | 40.7 | 41.0 | 40.0 | 40.6 | 40.2 | 40.8 | 41.0 | 40.8 | 40.8 |
| 2016 | 40.5 | 40.3 | 40.4 | 40.4 | 40.8 | 40.5 | 40.5 | 40.8 | 41.2 | 41.4 | 41.5 | 41.4 | 40.8 |
| 2017 | 41.1 | 40.9 | 40.9 | 40.6 | 41.1 | 41.2 | 41.1 | 41.5 | 41.2 | 41.9 | 41.6 | 41.9 | 41.3 |
| 2018 | 40.6 | 41.5 | 41.2 | 41.2 | 40.5 | 40.9 | 40.0 | 40.8 | 41.2 | 41.4 | 41.4 | 41.8 | 41.0 |
| 2019 | 40.3 | 40.4 | 40.4 | 40.5 | 40.6 | 40.8 | 40.1 | 40.7 | 41.0 | 40.4 | 41.0 | 41.1 | 40.6 |
| **Trade, Transportation, and Utilities** | | | | | | | | | | | | | |
| 2015 | 33.8 | 34.3 | 34.4 | 34.5 | 34.8 | 34.7 | 34.8 | 35.2 | 35.1 | 34.8 | 35.1 | 35.2 | 34.7 |
| 2016 | 34.2 | 34.4 | 34.2 | 34.7 | 34.9 | 35.0 | 34.9 | 34.8 | 34.8 | 34.8 | 34.6 | 35.3 | 34.7 |
| 2017 | 34.6 | 34.2 | 34.5 | 34.9 | 34.7 | 34.7 | 34.9 | 34.8 | 34.9 | 35.0 | 34.7 | 35.1 | 34.8 |
| 2018 | 33.9 | 34.1 | 34.4 | 34.5 | 34.5 | 34.5 | 34.6 | 34.3 | 34.4 | 34.0 | 34.5 | 34.5 | 34.4 |
| 2019 | 33.6 | 34.0 | 34.0 | 34.3 | 33.9 | 34.1 | 33.6 | 33.9 | 34.1 | 33.7 | 33.6 | 34.3 | 33.9 |
| **Financial Activities** | | | | | | | | | | | | | |
| 2015 | 36.7 | 37.8 | 38.6 | 37.3 | 37.3 | 36.7 | 36.6 | 37.4 | 36.3 | 36.6 | 37.2 | 36.2 | 37.1 |
| 2016 | 36.3 | 35.7 | 35.3 | 35.8 | 36.8 | 35.8 | 36.4 | 35.8 | 35.8 | 37.0 | 36.0 | 35.9 | 36.1 |
| 2017 | 37.2 | 36.1 | 36.3 | 37.0 | 36.2 | 36.5 | 36.6 | 35.8 | 36.2 | 36.9 | 36.2 | 36.1 | 36.4 |
| 2018 | 36.1 | 36.6 | 36.4 | 37.1 | 36.2 | 36.6 | 36.8 | 36.5 | 37.4 | 36.4 | 36.5 | 36.9 | 36.6 |
| 2019 | 36.2 | 36.6 | 36.4 | 36.7 | 36.5 | 37.4 | 36.9 | 36.8 | 37.6 | 36.8 | 36.7 | 37.7 | 36.9 |
| **Professional and Business Services** | | | | | | | | | | | | | |
| 2015 | 34.8 | 35.7 | 35.9 | 35.4 | 35.3 | 35.4 | 35.2 | 35.8 | 35.1 | 35.8 | 36.3 | 35.9 | 35.6 |
| 2016 | 35.4 | 35.4 | 35.6 | 35.6 | 36.0 | 35.2 | 34.7 | 35.1 | 35.4 | 36.0 | 35.3 | 35.3 | 35.4 |
| 2017 | 35.7 | 35.5 | 35.4 | 35.9 | 35.8 | 35.7 | 36.0 | 35.8 | 36.0 | 36.6 | 35.8 | 35.8 | 35.8 |
| 2018 | 35.4 | 35.8 | 35.9 | 36.5 | 35.9 | 36.0 | 36.3 | 35.8 | 36.6 | 36.4 | 36.3 | 37.0 | 36.2 |
| 2019 | 35.8 | 36.0 | 35.7 | 36.2 | 36.2 | 36.7 | 35.7 | 35.8 | 36.3 | 35.9 | 35.6 | 36.2 | 36.0 |
| **Education and Health Services** | | | | | | | | | | | | | |
| 2015 | 31.7 | 31.6 | 31.8 | 31.8 | 32.0 | 32.2 | 32.2 | 32.5 | 32.5 | 32.4 | 32.8 | 32.5 | 32.2 |
| 2016 | 32.7 | 32.2 | 32.4 | 32.4 | 32.5 | 32.4 | 32.4 | 32.5 | 32.5 | 32.7 | 32.8 | 32.5 | 32.5 |
| 2017 | 32.5 | 32.4 | 32.4 | 32.6 | 32.5 | 32.3 | 32.3 | 32.4 | 32.6 | 32.8 | 33.0 | 32.9 | 32.6 |
| 2018 | 32.5 | 32.7 | 32.6 | 32.8 | 32.6 | 32.6 | 32.8 | 32.6 | 32.7 | 32.6 | 32.6 | 32.7 | 32.6 |
| 2019 | 32.2 | 32.1 | 32.2 | 32.1 | 32.2 | 32.6 | 32.5 | 32.3 | 32.7 | 32.4 | 32.7 | 32.9 | 32.4 |
| **Leisure and Hospitality** | | | | | | | | | | | | | |
| 2015 | 23.1 | 23.8 | 24.0 | 23.7 | 24.2 | 24.4 | 24.6 | 24.7 | 23.9 | 24.3 | 24.2 | 24.4 | 24.1 |
| 2016 | 23.5 | 24.1 | 24.2 | 23.9 | 24.2 | 24.6 | 24.6 | 24.4 | 24.0 | 24.3 | 24.2 | 23.7 | 24.2 |
| 2017 | 23.6 | 23.8 | 24.1 | 23.9 | 24.3 | 24.5 | 24.5 | 24.3 | 23.7 | 24.0 | 23.8 | 23.8 | 24.0 |
| 2018 | 22.9 | 23.8 | 24.1 | 24.3 | 24.3 | 24.6 | 24.9 | 24.6 | 24.1 | 24.2 | 24.0 | 24.3 | 24.2 |
| 2019 | 22.8 | 24.0 | 24.3 | 23.9 | 23.7 | 24.4 | 24.1 | 24.1 | 23.6 | 23.4 | 23.3 | 23.4 | 23.8 |
| **Other Services** | | | | | | | | | | | | | |
| 2015 | 30.1 | 30.3 | 31.1 | 30.6 | 30.5 | 31.0 | 30.8 | 31.8 | 30.3 | 30.2 | 30.8 | 31.0 | 30.7 |
| 2016 | 30.8 | 30.9 | 31.9 | 32.3 | 32.1 | 31.7 | 32.2 | 32.4 | 32.7 | 32.7 | 32.2 | 32.6 | 32.0 |
| 2017 | 32.0 | 32.4 | 32.1 | 33.1 | 32.3 | 32.3 | 32.3 | 32.2 | 32.3 | 33.0 | 32.4 | 31.8 | 32.4 |
| 2018 | 31.1 | 31.4 | 31.5 | 32.0 | 31.2 | 31.2 | 31.1 | 30.5 | 30.6 | 30.3 | 29.8 | 30.6 | 30.9 |
| 2019 | 29.4 | 29.9 | 29.6 | 29.6 | 29.1 | 29.9 | 29.0 | 28.9 | 29.8 | 29.7 | 30.1 | 30.3 | 29.6 |

# 3. Average Hourly Earnings by Selected Industry: Ohio, 2015–2019

(Dollars, not seasonally adjusted)

| Industry and year | January | February | March | April | May | June | July | August | September | October | November | December | Annual average |
|---|---|---|---|---|---|---|---|---|---|---|---|---|---|
| **Total Private** | | | | | | | | | | | | | |
| 2015 | 22.65 | 22.76 | 22.78 | 22.68 | 22.58 | 22.44 | 22.57 | 22.84 | 22.93 | 22.79 | 23.00 | 22.95 | 22.75 |
| 2016 | 23.14 | 23.12 | 23.10 | 23.39 | 23.38 | 23.10 | 23.29 | 23.23 | 23.55 | 23.87 | 23.74 | 23.92 | 23.41 |
| 2017 | 24.13 | 23.92 | 23.95 | 24.04 | 23.82 | 23.77 | 24.11 | 23.88 | 24.11 | 24.22 | 24.14 | 24.30 | 24.03 |
| 2018 | 24.64 | 24.54 | 24.55 | 24.74 | 24.43 | 24.35 | 24.78 | 24.75 | 25.23 | 25.14 | 25.09 | 25.44 | 24.81 |
| 2019 | 25.43 | 25.33 | 25.30 | 25.31 | 25.14 | 25.07 | 25.24 | 25.23 | 25.57 | 25.30 | 25.37 | 25.65 | 25.33 |
| **Goods-Producing** | | | | | | | | | | | | | |
| 2015 | 24.60 | 24.54 | 24.68 | 24.72 | 24.71 | 24.59 | 24.90 | 24.94 | 24.95 | 24.71 | 24.74 | 25.05 | 24.76 |
| 2016 | 24.92 | 25.01 | 25.28 | 25.58 | 25.70 | 25.67 | 25.90 | 25.78 | 25.88 | 26.11 | 26.19 | 26.28 | 25.70 |
| 2017 | 26.11 | 26.09 | 26.21 | 26.42 | 26.53 | 26.61 | 26.85 | 26.64 | 27.07 | 27.07 | 27.02 | 27.06 | 26.65 |
| 2018 | 27.07 | 27.07 | 27.21 | 27.28 | 27.24 | 27.03 | 27.39 | 27.46 | 27.69 | 27.86 | 27.77 | 28.38 | 27.47 |
| 2019 | 27.81 | 27.84 | 27.65 | 27.73 | 27.75 | 27.79 | 27.99 | 28.04 | 28.38 | 28.20 | 28.30 | 28.58 | 28.01 |
| **Construction** | | | | | | | | | | | | | |
| 2015 | 25.66 | 25.47 | 25.91 | 25.98 | 26.39 | 26.18 | 26.79 | 26.80 | 26.95 | 26.68 | 26.60 | 26.87 | 26.40 |
| 2016 | 26.76 | 26.81 | 26.89 | 27.52 | 27.57 | 27.31 | 27.15 | 26.99 | 26.96 | 27.23 | 27.15 | 26.86 | 27.09 |
| 2017 | 26.84 | 26.86 | 27.35 | 26.97 | 28.07 | 28.08 | 28.02 | 28.23 | 28.77 | 28.94 | 28.32 | 27.73 | 27.91 |
| 2018 | 27.77 | 28.03 | 28.16 | 28.14 | 28.55 | 28.13 | 28.66 | 29.04 | 29.14 | 29.61 | 29.73 | 29.98 | 28.78 |
| 2019 | 29.51 | 29.74 | 29.11 | 29.24 | 29.50 | 29.59 | 29.85 | 29.82 | 30.15 | 29.71 | 29.67 | 29.88 | 29.66 |
| **Manufacturing** | | | | | | | | | | | | | |
| 2015 | 24.36 | 24.32 | 24.39 | 24.37 | 24.19 | 24.12 | 24.27 | 24.30 | 24.36 | 24.06 | 24.21 | 24.52 | 24.29 |
| 2016 | 24.60 | 24.69 | 25.01 | 25.23 | 25.33 | 25.33 | 25.80 | 25.63 | 25.86 | 26.03 | 26.14 | 26.39 | 25.51 |
| 2017 | 26.13 | 26.06 | 26.02 | 26.41 | 26.05 | 26.14 | 26.49 | 26.04 | 26.46 | 26.45 | 26.65 | 26.93 | 26.32 |
| 2018 | 26.86 | 26.77 | 26.91 | 26.97 | 26.82 | 26.70 | 26.95 | 26.81 | 27.13 | 27.20 | 27.05 | 27.79 | 27.00 |
| 2019 | 27.19 | 27.19 | 27.11 | 27.10 | 27.01 | 27.01 | 27.17 | 27.25 | 27.61 | 27.54 | 27.80 | 28.15 | 27.35 |
| **Trade, Transportation, and Utilities** | | | | | | | | | | | | | |
| 2015 | 21.06 | 21.25 | 21.49 | 21.47 | 21.27 | 21.26 | 21.40 | 21.64 | 21.74 | 21.76 | 21.88 | 21.45 | 21.48 |
| 2016 | 21.97 | 21.85 | 22.02 | 22.40 | 22.12 | 22.00 | 22.19 | 22.09 | 22.39 | 22.66 | 22.29 | 22.24 | 22.19 |
| 2017 | 22.88 | 22.59 | 22.81 | 23.14 | 22.80 | 22.79 | 22.99 | 22.65 | 22.60 | 22.68 | 22.57 | 22.63 | 22.76 |
| 2018 | 23.03 | 22.63 | 22.82 | 23.04 | 22.68 | 22.75 | 23.05 | 23.12 | 23.55 | 23.04 | 22.65 | 22.85 | 22.93 |
| 2019 | 22.86 | 22.76 | 22.98 | 22.87 | 22.77 | 22.59 | 22.80 | 22.96 | 23.27 | 22.93 | 22.73 | 22.91 | 22.87 |
| **Financial Activities** | | | | | | | | | | | | | |
| 2015 | 27.39 | 27.93 | 27.47 | 27.15 | 26.78 | 26.46 | 26.55 | 27.58 | 27.39 | 26.87 | 26.76 | 26.87 | 27.10 |
| 2016 | 26.89 | 27.21 | 27.78 | 27.92 | 28.23 | 28.36 | 28.09 | 28.52 | 29.35 | 30.34 | 30.20 | 30.63 | 28.64 |
| 2017 | 30.80 | 30.81 | 30.84 | 30.78 | 30.18 | 29.92 | 29.90 | 29.76 | 30.15 | 30.06 | 29.56 | 29.87 | 30.22 |
| 2018 | 29.92 | 30.36 | 29.97 | 30.01 | 29.74 | 29.47 | 30.05 | 29.76 | 29.74 | 29.82 | 30.28 | 30.83 | 30.00 |
| 2019 | 30.85 | 31.00 | 30.98 | 30.91 | 31.26 | 31.62 | 31.89 | 32.80 | 32.83 | 32.53 | 33.37 | 34.39 | 32.05 |
| **Professional and Business Services** | | | | | | | | | | | | | |
| 2015 | 25.39 | 25.71 | 25.71 | 25.44 | 25.40 | 25.21 | 25.40 | 25.98 | 25.93 | 25.81 | 26.49 | 26.23 | 25.73 |
| 2016 | 27.03 | 27.07 | 26.71 | 26.93 | 27.06 | 26.66 | 26.93 | 26.87 | 26.82 | 27.07 | 26.86 | 27.11 | 26.93 |
| 2017 | 27.34 | 27.11 | 27.31 | 27.22 | 26.60 | 26.83 | 27.48 | 26.89 | 27.17 | 27.69 | 27.75 | 27.94 | 27.28 |
| 2018 | 28.61 | 28.58 | 28.45 | 28.88 | 28.12 | 27.86 | 28.68 | 28.23 | 28.89 | 28.69 | 28.56 | 28.89 | 28.54 |
| 2019 | 29.17 | 29.25 | 29.16 | 29.12 | 28.78 | 28.73 | 28.78 | 28.54 | 28.99 | 28.58 | 28.87 | 29.13 | 28.92 |
| **Education and Health Services** | | | | | | | | | | | | | |
| 2015 | 23.02 | 22.88 | 22.78 | 22.61 | 22.57 | 22.41 | 22.30 | 22.43 | 22.67 | 22.36 | 22.46 | 22.70 | 22.60 |
| 2016 | 22.48 | 22.25 | 22.20 | 22.51 | 22.83 | 22.26 | 22.22 | 21.94 | 22.41 | 22.55 | 22.31 | 22.61 | 22.38 |
| 2017 | 22.84 | 22.61 | 22.53 | 22.60 | 22.50 | 22.14 | 22.66 | 22.49 | 22.63 | 22.65 | 22.65 | 22.85 | 22.60 |
| 2018 | 23.25 | 22.95 | 22.98 | 23.04 | 22.94 | 23.03 | 23.18 | 23.21 | 23.73 | 23.60 | 23.62 | 23.63 | 23.26 |
| 2019 | 23.58 | 23.34 | 23.25 | 23.27 | 22.65 | 22.55 | 22.77 | 22.64 | 22.72 | 22.63 | 22.59 | 22.64 | 22.88 |
| **Leisure and Hospitality** | | | | | | | | | | | | | |
| 2015 | 12.71 | 12.64 | 12.61 | 12.70 | 12.48 | 12.50 | 12.46 | 12.51 | 12.58 | 12.66 | 12.72 | 12.91 | 12.62 |
| 2016 | 12.88 | 12.88 | 12.93 | 13.11 | 13.14 | 12.86 | 12.98 | 13.05 | 13.25 | 13.46 | 13.48 | 13.67 | 13.14 |
| 2017 | 13.66 | 13.71 | 13.72 | 13.55 | 13.66 | 13.41 | 13.44 | 13.58 | 13.67 | 13.76 | 13.86 | 14.00 | 13.66 |
| 2018 | 13.95 | 13.95 | 13.90 | 13.94 | 13.96 | 13.79 | 13.86 | 13.98 | 14.20 | 14.32 | 14.41 | 14.70 | 14.08 |
| 2019 | 14.74 | 14.79 | 14.69 | 14.87 | 14.86 | 14.57 | 14.91 | 14.75 | 15.01 | 15.03 | 15.13 | 15.32 | 14.89 |
| **Other Services** | | | | | | | | | | | | | |
| 2015 | 20.25 | 20.77 | 20.79 | 20.71 | 21.00 | 20.81 | 21.15 | 21.34 | 21.76 | 21.03 | 21.49 | 21.29 | 21.04 |
| 2016 | 21.08 | 20.81 | 20.44 | 20.75 | 20.82 | 20.85 | 21.24 | 21.04 | 21.17 | 21.20 | 21.41 | 21.51 | 21.03 |
| 2017 | 21.85 | 21.69 | 21.52 | 21.56 | 21.69 | 21.49 | 21.82 | 21.76 | 21.64 | 21.61 | 21.54 | 21.46 | 21.64 |
| 2018 | 21.79 | 22.28 | 22.22 | 22.26 | 22.08 | 22.13 | 22.59 | 22.51 | 22.84 | 22.65 | 23.02 | 23.42 | 22.48 |
| 2019 | 23.57 | 23.27 | 23.35 | 23.27 | 23.22 | 23.22 | 23.07 | 23.34 | 23.47 | 23.44 | 23.09 | 23.31 | 23.30 |

## 4. Average Weekly Earnings by Selected Industry: Ohio, 2015–2019

(Dollars, not seasonally adjusted)

| Industry and year | January | February | March | April | May | June | July | August | September | October | November | December | Annual average |
|---|---|---|---|---|---|---|---|---|---|---|---|---|---|
| **Total Private** | | | | | | | | | | | | | |
| 2015 | 763.31 | 776.12 | 781.35 | 773.39 | 772.24 | 767.45 | 771.89 | 790.26 | 781.91 | 783.98 | 798.10 | 791.78 | 780.33 |
| 2016 | 786.76 | 783.77 | 787.71 | 800.28 | 804.27 | 792.33 | 796.52 | 794.81 | 810.46 | 825.90 | 816.66 | 822.85 | 802.96 |
| 2017 | 827.66 | 815.67 | 816.70 | 824.57 | 814.63 | 815.31 | 826.97 | 819.08 | 826.97 | 840.43 | 830.42 | 835.92 | 824.23 |
| 2018 | 827.90 | 836.81 | 839.61 | 853.53 | 835.51 | 837.64 | 852.43 | 848.93 | 870.44 | 859.79 | 858.08 | 880.22 | 850.98 |
| 2019 | 854.45 | 858.69 | 860.20 | 863.07 | 854.76 | 862.41 | 858.16 | 860.34 | 877.05 | 862.73 | 862.58 | 882.36 | 863.75 |
| **Goods-Producing** | | | | | | | | | | | | | |
| 2015 | 988.92 | 986.51 | 999.54 | 996.22 | 1,000.76 | 998.35 | 993.91 | 1,012.56 | 988.02 | 1,008.17 | 997.02 | 1,012.02 | 997.83 |
| 2016 | 989.32 | 990.40 | 1,011.20 | 1,028.32 | 1,033.14 | 1,037.07 | 1,046.36 | 1,044.09 | 1,058.49 | 1,070.51 | 1,073.79 | 1,066.97 | 1,038.28 |
| 2017 | 1,044.40 | 1,046.21 | 1,043.56 | 1,056.80 | 1,077.12 | 1,091.01 | 1,087.43 | 1,100.23 | 1,107.16 | 1,115.28 | 1,107.82 | 1,106.75 | 1,081.99 |
| 2018 | 1,069.66 | 1,099.45 | 1,105.13 | 1,115.75 | 1,100.90 | 1,100.53 | 1,104.22 | 1,117.62 | 1,130.16 | 1,139.47 | 1,124.69 | 1,166.42 | 1,115.28 |
| 2019 | 1,109.62 | 1,108.03 | 1,106.00 | 1,114.75 | 1,121.10 | 1,119.94 | 1,119.60 | 1,132.82 | 1,149.39 | 1,133.64 | 1,134.83 | 1,146.06 | 1,126.00 |
| **Construction** | | | | | | | | | | | | | |
| 2015 | 934.02 | 944.94 | 969.03 | 989.84 | 1,031.85 | 1,018.40 | 1,047.49 | 1,072.00 | 997.15 | 1,075.20 | 1,010.80 | 1,039.87 | 1,013.76 |
| 2016 | 984.77 | 994.65 | 1,027.20 | 1,073.28 | 1,053.17 | 1,086.94 | 1,074.20 | 1,059.14 | 1,070.31 | 1,083.75 | 1,072.43 | 1,020.68 | 1,051.09 |
| 2017 | 982.34 | 1,009.94 | 1,003.75 | 1,032.95 | 1,105.96 | 1,137.24 | 1,087.18 | 1,146.14 | 1,159.43 | 1,131.55 | 1,101.65 | 1,048.19 | 1,082.91 |
| 2018 | 1,005.27 | 1,051.13 | 1,084.16 | 1,108.72 | 1,124.87 | 1,111.14 | 1,152.13 | 1,161.60 | 1,145.20 | 1,157.75 | 1,132.71 | 1,169.22 | 1,119.54 |
| 2019 | 1,130.23 | 1,124.17 | 1,112.00 | 1,140.36 | 1,162.30 | 1,154.01 | 1,185.05 | 1,177.89 | 1,190.93 | 1,170.57 | 1,121.53 | 1,123.49 | 1,150.81 |
| **Manufacturing** | | | | | | | | | | | | | |
| 2015 | 1,003.63 | 997.12 | 1,007.31 | 992.27 | 984.53 | 988.92 | 970.80 | 986.58 | 979.27 | 981.65 | 992.61 | 1,000.42 | 991.03 |
| 2016 | 996.30 | 995.01 | 1,010.40 | 1,019.29 | 1,033.46 | 1,025.87 | 1,044.90 | 1,045.70 | 1,065.43 | 1,077.64 | 1,084.81 | 1,092.55 | 1,040.81 |
| 2017 | 1,073.94 | 1,065.85 | 1,064.22 | 1,072.25 | 1,070.66 | 1,076.97 | 1,088.74 | 1,080.66 | 1,090.15 | 1,108.26 | 1,108.64 | 1,127.95 | 1,087.02 |
| 2018 | 1,090.52 | 1,110.96 | 1,108.69 | 1,111.16 | 1,086.21 | 1,091.62 | 1,078.00 | 1,093.85 | 1,117.76 | 1,126.08 | 1,119.87 | 1,161.62 | 1,107.00 |
| 2019 | 1,095.76 | 1,098.48 | 1,095.24 | 1,097.55 | 1,096.61 | 1,102.42 | 1,089.52 | 1,109.08 | 1,131.60 | 1,112.62 | 1,139.80 | 1,156.97 | 1,110.41 |
| **Trade, Transportation, and Utilities** | | | | | | | | | | | | | |
| 2015 | 711.83 | 728.88 | 739.26 | 740.72 | 740.20 | 737.72 | 744.72 | 761.73 | 763.07 | 757.25 | 767.99 | 755.04 | 745.36 |
| 2016 | 751.37 | 751.64 | 753.08 | 777.28 | 771.99 | 770.00 | 774.43 | 768.73 | 779.17 | 788.57 | 771.23 | 785.07 | 769.99 |
| 2017 | 791.65 | 772.58 | 786.95 | 807.59 | 791.16 | 790.81 | 802.35 | 788.22 | 788.74 | 793.80 | 783.18 | 794.31 | 792.05 |
| 2018 | 780.72 | 771.68 | 785.01 | 794.88 | 782.46 | 784.88 | 797.53 | 793.02 | 810.12 | 783.36 | 781.43 | 788.33 | 788.79 |
| 2019 | 768.10 | 773.84 | 781.32 | 784.44 | 771.90 | 770.32 | 766.08 | 778.34 | 793.51 | 772.74 | 763.73 | 785.81 | 775.29 |
| **Financial Activities** | | | | | | | | | | | | | |
| 2015 | 1,005.21 | 1,055.75 | 1,060.34 | 1,012.70 | 998.89 | 971.08 | 971.73 | 1,031.49 | 994.26 | 983.44 | 995.47 | 972.69 | 1,005.41 |
| 2016 | 976.11 | 971.40 | 980.63 | 999.54 | 1,038.86 | 1,015.29 | 1,022.48 | 1,021.02 | 1,050.73 | 1,122.58 | 1,087.20 | 1,099.62 | 1,033.90 |
| 2017 | 1,145.76 | 1,112.24 | 1,119.49 | 1,138.86 | 1,092.52 | 1,092.08 | 1,094.34 | 1,065.41 | 1,091.43 | 1,109.21 | 1,070.07 | 1,078.31 | 1,100.01 |
| 2018 | 1,080.11 | 1,111.18 | 1,090.91 | 1,113.37 | 1,076.59 | 1,078.60 | 1,105.84 | 1,086.24 | 1,112.28 | 1,085.45 | 1,105.22 | 1,137.63 | 1,098.00 |
| 2019 | 1,116.77 | 1,134.60 | 1,127.67 | 1,134.40 | 1,140.99 | 1,182.59 | 1,176.74 | 1,207.04 | 1,234.41 | 1,197.10 | 1,224.68 | 1,296.50 | 1,182.65 |
| **Professional and Business Services** | | | | | | | | | | | | | |
| 2015 | 883.57 | 917.85 | 922.99 | 900.58 | 896.62 | 892.43 | 894.08 | 930.08 | 910.14 | 924.00 | 961.59 | 941.66 | 915.99 |
| 2016 | 956.86 | 958.28 | 950.88 | 958.71 | 974.16 | 938.43 | 934.47 | 943.14 | 949.43 | 974.52 | 948.16 | 956.98 | 953.32 |
| 2017 | 976.04 | 962.41 | 966.77 | 977.20 | 952.28 | 957.83 | 989.28 | 962.66 | 978.12 | 1,013.45 | 993.45 | 1,000.25 | 976.62 |
| 2018 | 1,012.79 | 1,023.16 | 1,021.36 | 1,054.12 | 1,009.51 | 1,002.96 | 1,041.08 | 1,010.63 | 1,057.37 | 1,044.32 | 1,036.73 | 1,068.93 | 1,033.15 |
| 2019 | 1,044.29 | 1,053.00 | 1,041.01 | 1,054.14 | 1,041.84 | 1,054.39 | 1,027.45 | 1,021.73 | 1,052.34 | 1,026.02 | 1,027.77 | 1,054.51 | 1,041.12 |
| **Education and Health Services** | | | | | | | | | | | | | |
| 2015 | 729.73 | 723.01 | 724.40 | 719.00 | 722.24 | 721.60 | 718.06 | 728.98 | 736.78 | 724.46 | 736.69 | 737.75 | 727.72 |
| 2016 | 735.10 | 716.45 | 719.28 | 729.32 | 741.98 | 721.22 | 719.93 | 713.05 | 728.33 | 737.39 | 731.77 | 734.83 | 727.35 |
| 2017 | 742.30 | 732.56 | 729.97 | 736.76 | 731.25 | 715.12 | 731.92 | 728.68 | 737.74 | 742.92 | 747.45 | 751.77 | 736.76 |
| 2018 | 755.63 | 750.47 | 749.15 | 755.71 | 747.84 | 750.78 | 760.30 | 756.65 | 775.97 | 769.36 | 770.01 | 772.70 | 758.28 |
| 2019 | 759.28 | 749.21 | 748.65 | 746.97 | 729.33 | 735.13 | 740.03 | 731.27 | 742.94 | 733.21 | 738.69 | 744.86 | 741.31 |
| **Leisure and Hospitality** | | | | | | | | | | | | | |
| 2015 | 293.60 | 301.07 | 302.88 | 300.99 | 302.02 | 305.00 | 306.52 | 309.00 | 300.66 | 307.64 | 307.82 | 315.00 | 304.14 |
| 2016 | 302.68 | 310.41 | 312.91 | 313.33 | 317.99 | 316.36 | 319.31 | 318.42 | 318.00 | 327.08 | 326.22 | 323.98 | 317.99 |
| 2017 | 322.38 | 326.30 | 330.65 | 323.85 | 331.94 | 328.55 | 329.28 | 329.99 | 323.98 | 330.24 | 329.87 | 333.20 | 327.84 |
| 2018 | 319.46 | 332.01 | 334.99 | 338.74 | 339.23 | 339.23 | 345.11 | 343.91 | 342.22 | 346.54 | 345.84 | 357.21 | 340.74 |
| 2019 | 336.07 | 354.96 | 356.97 | 355.39 | 352.18 | 355.51 | 359.33 | 355.48 | 354.24 | 351.70 | 352.53 | 358.49 | 354.38 |
| **Other Services** | | | | | | | | | | | | | |
| 2015 | 609.53 | 629.33 | 646.57 | 633.73 | 640.50 | 645.11 | 651.42 | 678.61 | 659.33 | 635.11 | 661.89 | 659.99 | 645.93 |
| 2016 | 649.26 | 643.03 | 652.04 | 670.23 | 668.32 | 660.95 | 683.93 | 681.70 | 692.26 | 693.24 | 689.40 | 701.23 | 672.96 |
| 2017 | 699.20 | 702.76 | 690.79 | 713.64 | 700.59 | 694.13 | 704.79 | 700.67 | 698.97 | 713.13 | 697.90 | 682.43 | 701.14 |
| 2018 | 677.67 | 699.59 | 699.93 | 712.32 | 688.90 | 690.46 | 702.55 | 686.56 | 698.90 | 686.30 | 686.00 | 716.65 | 694.63 |
| 2019 | 692.96 | 695.77 | 691.16 | 688.79 | 675.70 | 694.28 | 669.03 | 674.53 | 699.41 | 696.17 | 695.01 | 706.29 | 689.68 |

# OKLAHOMA
*At a Glance*

Population:
   2010 census: 3,751,351
   2019 estimate: 3,956,971

Percent change in population:
   2010–2019: 5.5%

Percent change in total nonfarm employment:
   2011–2019: 8.0%

Industry with the largest growth in employment, 2011–2019 (percent):
   Transportation and utilities, 35.0%

Industry with the largest decline or smallest growth in employment, 2011–2019 (percent):
   Information, -14.8%

Civilian labor force:
   2010: 1,768,284
   2019: 1,841,209

Unemployment rate and rank among states (highest to lowest):
   2010: 6.8%, 44th
   2019: 3.3%, 30th

Over-the-year change in unemployment rates:
   2017–2018: -0.8%
   2018–2019: -0.1%

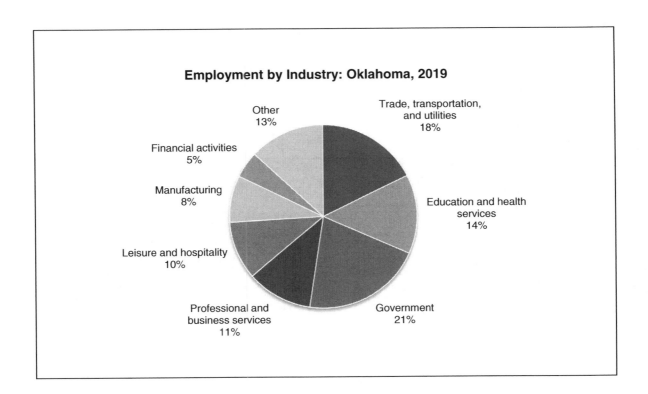

**Employment by Industry: Oklahoma, 2019**

Other
13%

Trade, transportation,
and utilities
18%

Financial activities
5%

Manufacturing
8%

Education and health
services
14%

Leisure and hospitality
10%

Professional and
business services
11%

Government
21%

## 1. Employment by Industry: Oklahoma, 2011–2019

(Numbers in thousands, not seasonally adjusted)

| Industry and year | January | February | March | April | May | June | July | August | September | October | November | December | Annual average |
|---|---|---|---|---|---|---|---|---|---|---|---|---|---|
| **Total Nonfarm** | | | | | | | | | | | | | |
| 2011 | 1,541.6 | 1,541.7 | 1,564.9 | 1,580.7 | 1,584.6 | 1,578.3 | 1,564.9 | 1,573.3 | 1,594.6 | 1,597.8 | 1,602.4 | 1,607.5 | 1,577.7 |
| 2012 | 1,575.0 | 1,589.9 | 1,602.7 | 1,614.9 | 1,622.7 | 1,617.3 | 1,595.8 | 1,608.3 | 1,621.0 | 1,634.4 | 1,642.2 | 1,644.4 | 1,614.1 |
| 2013 | 1,600.9 | 1,614.7 | 1,626.3 | 1,634.2 | 1,645.8 | 1,636.5 | 1,620.9 | 1,633.3 | 1,645.7 | 1,650.6 | 1,660.0 | 1,654.4 | 1,635.3 |
| 2014 | 1,623.1 | 1,633.4 | 1,643.7 | 1,653.0 | 1,662.5 | 1,654.3 | 1,641.9 | 1,654.2 | 1,664.7 | 1,675.5 | 1,683.1 | 1,687.6 | 1,656.4 |
| 2015 | 1,655.0 | 1,662.9 | 1,664.6 | 1,671.8 | 1,675.3 | 1,666.7 | 1,654.6 | 1,659.3 | 1,669.2 | 1,676.4 | 1,680.3 | 1,678.8 | 1,667.9 |
| 2016 | 1,642.4 | 1,652.2 | 1,654.1 | 1,660.7 | 1,658.9 | 1,646.9 | 1,635.2 | 1,644.6 | 1,657.5 | 1,658.8 | 1,664.9 | 1,665.2 | 1,653.5 |
| 2017 | 1,624.6 | 1,639.0 | 1,650.7 | 1,660.5 | 1,666.2 | 1,666.2 | 1,651.4 | 1,660.7 | 1,676.9 | 1,679.4 | 1,685.6 | 1,688.6 | 1,662.5 |
| 2018 | 1,656.1 | 1,668.2 | 1,681.3 | 1,682.1 | 1,692.6 | 1,690.0 | 1,674.6 | 1,686.6 | 1,700.5 | 1,707.6 | 1,714.3 | 1,715.7 | 1,689.1 |
| 2019 | 1,678.5 | 1,692.8 | 1,700.8 | 1,706.3 | 1,710.3 | 1,699.6 | 1,686.5 | 1,693.5 | 1,710.9 | 1,721.2 | 1,722.8 | 1,717.4 | 1,703.4 |
| **Total Private** | | | | | | | | | | | | | |
| 2011 | 1,200.3 | 1,195.5 | 1,216.8 | 1,230.9 | 1,234.6 | 1,240.2 | 1,241.1 | 1,245.9 | 1,248.2 | 1,247.3 | 1,251.0 | 1,254.0 | 1,233.8 |
| 2012 | 1,232.0 | 1,239.4 | 1,250.6 | 1,262.6 | 1,269.8 | 1,277.5 | 1,268.4 | 1,274.3 | 1,272.7 | 1,280.1 | 1,286.2 | 1,289.0 | 1,266.9 |
| 2013 | 1,255.4 | 1,261.3 | 1,271.6 | 1,279.1 | 1,289.2 | 1,294.5 | 1,291.8 | 1,298.8 | 1,297.7 | 1,296.5 | 1,304.1 | 1,300.5 | 1,286.7 |
| 2014 | 1,278.4 | 1,281.4 | 1,290.7 | 1,299.8 | 1,307.2 | 1,312.6 | 1,312.9 | 1,319.0 | 1,316.4 | 1,319.6 | 1,326.5 | 1,332.1 | 1,308.1 |
| 2015 | 1,308.3 | 1,308.6 | 1,310.0 | 1,315.6 | 1,317.5 | 1,322.6 | 1,323.0 | 1,322.0 | 1,317.3 | 1,317.2 | 1,319.8 | 1,318.9 | 1,316.7 |
| 2016 | 1,291.5 | 1,293.9 | 1,294.4 | 1,301.1 | 1,299.9 | 1,301.0 | 1,302.0 | 1,305.5 | 1,304.3 | 1,303.7 | 1,308.5 | 1,308.6 | 1,301.2 |
| 2017 | 1,278.1 | 1,285.2 | 1,295.1 | 1,305.5 | 1,310.7 | 1,322.0 | 1,319.3 | 1,323.4 | 1,326.6 | 1,326.4 | 1,331.8 | 1,335.0 | 1,313.3 |
| 2018 | 1,310.1 | 1,316.1 | 1,328.3 | 1,330.5 | 1,338.9 | 1,348.0 | 1,345.3 | 1,351.2 | 1,352.2 | 1,351.8 | 1,356.6 | 1,358.8 | 1,340.7 |
| 2019 | 1,331.2 | 1,336.3 | 1,343.4 | 1,349.6 | 1,351.5 | 1,355.9 | 1,353.5 | 1,353.8 | 1,354.3 | 1,359.7 | 1,359.7 | 1,355.0 | 1,350.3 |
| **Goods Producing** | | | | | | | | | | | | | |
| 2011 | 244.6 | 244.1 | 249.1 | 253.4 | 254.7 | 258.4 | 260.4 | 261.2 | 262.4 | 263.7 | 264.0 | 265.2 | 256.8 |
| 2012 | 262.2 | 263.7 | 266.5 | 268.4 | 270.6 | 273.9 | 273.3 | 273.8 | 273.2 | 276.5 | 277.2 | 277.5 | 271.4 |
| 2013 | 270.9 | 272.1 | 274.0 | 274.3 | 276.7 | 280.0 | 278.8 | 280.4 | 279.8 | 280.4 | 280.2 | 279.7 | 277.3 |
| 2014 | 275.0 | 275.9 | 277.5 | 277.6 | 279.9 | 282.1 | 284.1 | 286.7 | 286.1 | 287.6 | 288.0 | 289.0 | 282.5 |
| 2015 | 285.4 | 284.0 | 280.6 | 276.2 | 274.0 | 274.9 | 275.1 | 273.4 | 271.5 | 269.4 | 266.7 | 265.0 | 274.7 |
| 2016 | 260.9 | 260.5 | 257.6 | 256.0 | 254.8 | 255.4 | 255.5 | 255.2 | 255.5 | 254.3 | 253.6 | 254.4 | 256.1 |
| 2017 | 250.2 | 252.3 | 253.7 | 254.4 | 256.7 | 261.4 | 262.3 | 263.6 | 264.9 | 264.1 | 263.9 | 265.6 | 259.4 |
| 2018 | 261.9 | 264.4 | 267.2 | 267.7 | 270.1 | 273.7 | 273.6 | 275.9 | 276.8 | 276.9 | 276.7 | 277.3 | 271.9 |
| 2019 | 273.0 | 275.2 | 275.5 | 274.5 | 273.6 | 275.7 | 274.3 | 272.4 | 270.8 | 268.8 | 266.7 | 265.0 | 272.1 |
| **Service-Providing** | | | | | | | | | | | | | |
| 2011 | 1,297.0 | 1,297.6 | 1,315.8 | 1,327.3 | 1,329.9 | 1,319.9 | 1,304.5 | 1,312.1 | 1,332.2 | 1,334.1 | 1,338.4 | 1,342.3 | 1,320.9 |
| 2012 | 1,312.8 | 1,326.2 | 1,336.2 | 1,346.5 | 1,352.1 | 1,343.4 | 1,322.5 | 1,334.5 | 1,347.8 | 1,357.9 | 1,365.0 | 1,366.9 | 1,342.7 |
| 2013 | 1,330.0 | 1,342.6 | 1,352.3 | 1,359.9 | 1,369.1 | 1,356.5 | 1,342.1 | 1,352.9 | 1,365.9 | 1,370.2 | 1,379.8 | 1,374.7 | 1,358.0 |
| 2014 | 1,348.1 | 1,357.5 | 1,366.2 | 1,375.4 | 1,382.6 | 1,372.2 | 1,357.8 | 1,367.5 | 1,378.6 | 1,387.9 | 1,395.1 | 1,398.6 | 1,374.0 |
| 2015 | 1,369.6 | 1,378.9 | 1,384.0 | 1,395.6 | 1,401.3 | 1,391.8 | 1,379.5 | 1,385.9 | 1,397.7 | 1,407.0 | 1,413.6 | 1,413.8 | 1,393.2 |
| 2016 | 1,381.5 | 1,391.7 | 1,396.5 | 1,404.7 | 1,404.1 | 1,391.5 | 1,379.7 | 1,389.4 | 1,402.0 | 1,404.5 | 1,411.3 | 1,410.8 | 1,397.3 |
| 2017 | 1,374.4 | 1,386.7 | 1,397.0 | 1,406.1 | 1,409.5 | 1,404.8 | 1,389.1 | 1,397.1 | 1,412.0 | 1,415.3 | 1,421.7 | 1,423.0 | 1,403.1 |
| 2018 | 1,394.2 | 1,403.8 | 1,414.1 | 1,414.4 | 1,422.5 | 1,416.3 | 1,401.0 | 1,410.7 | 1,423.7 | 1,430.7 | 1,437.6 | 1,438.4 | 1,417.3 |
| 2019 | 1,405.5 | 1,417.6 | 1,425.3 | 1,431.8 | 1,436.7 | 1,423.9 | 1,412.2 | 1,421.1 | 1,440.1 | 1,452.4 | 1,456.1 | 1,452.4 | 1,431.3 |
| **Mining and Logging** | | | | | | | | | | | | | |
| 2011 | 47.5 | 48.0 | 48.8 | 49.5 | 50.3 | 51.6 | 52.9 | 53.4 | 53.9 | 54.8 | 55.3 | 56.1 | 51.8 |
| 2012 | 55.8 | 56.4 | 57.3 | 57.6 | 58.4 | 59.5 | 59.8 | 59.9 | 59.4 | 59.8 | 59.7 | 59.4 | 58.6 |
| 2013 | 59.0 | 59.2 | 59.2 | 59.6 | 60.1 | 60.9 | 60.4 | 60.6 | 60.3 | 60.4 | 60.4 | 60.7 | 60.1 |
| 2014 | 59.7 | 59.6 | 59.9 | 60.1 | 60.8 | 61.9 | 62.7 | 63.7 | 63.8 | 64.3 | 64.8 | 65.0 | 62.2 |
| 2015 | 63.5 | 60.9 | 58.4 | 55.5 | 54.0 | 53.6 | 53.4 | 53.0 | 51.8 | 50.4 | 49.4 | 48.4 | 54.4 |
| 2016 | 47.5 | 46.5 | 45.2 | 44.3 | 43.3 | 43.3 | 43.1 | 42.9 | 42.8 | 43.3 | 43.6 | 44.3 | 44.2 |
| 2017 | 44.1 | 45.1 | 45.7 | 46.5 | 47.2 | 48.6 | 49.1 | 49.6 | 49.9 | 50.1 | 50.4 | 50.9 | 48.1 |
| 2018 | 50.6 | 51.3 | 51.7 | 51.7 | 52.3 | 53.1 | 53.6 | 54.0 | 53.8 | 54.0 | 53.9 | 54.1 | 52.8 |
| 2019 | 52.7 | 52.1 | 51.6 | 51.2 | 50.4 | 50.2 | 48.5 | 47.4 | 46.2 | 45.8 | 44.8 | 43.7 | 48.7 |
| **Construction** | | | | | | | | | | | | | |
| 2011 | 65.1 | 63.9 | 66.8 | 68.6 | 68.7 | 70.0 | 69.5 | 69.7 | 69.8 | 69.7 | 69.0 | 68.8 | 68.3 |
| 2012 | 66.6 | 66.8 | 68.0 | 69.0 | 70.0 | 71.2 | 70.8 | 71.0 | 70.9 | 72.9 | 74.1 | 74.2 | 70.5 |
| 2013 | 69.7 | 70.6 | 72.3 | 72.5 | 74.3 | 76.1 | 75.6 | 77.2 | 77.3 | 77.8 | 77.4 | 76.4 | 74.8 |
| 2014 | 73.6 | 73.7 | 74.7 | 74.1 | 74.8 | 74.9 | 75.7 | 77.3 | 76.6 | 77.1 | 76.5 | 76.5 | 75.5 |
| 2015 | 75.2 | 76.3 | 76.4 | 76.3 | 76.2 | 78.0 | 79.2 | 79.0 | 79.0 | 79.2 | 78.2 | 77.6 | 77.6 |
| 2016 | 75.8 | 76.1 | 76.0 | 76.5 | 76.9 | 78.0 | 78.9 | 79.1 | 79.7 | 78.9 | 77.4 | 77.0 | 77.5 |
| 2017 | 75.1 | 75.0 | 75.9 | 75.4 | 76.5 | 78.4 | 78.7 | 79.2 | 80.2 | 79.2 | 78.4 | 78.5 | 77.5 |
| 2018 | 75.8 | 76.8 | 78.4 | 78.6 | 79.6 | 81.0 | 80.9 | 82.7 | 83.3 | 82.9 | 82.5 | 81.9 | 80.4 |
| 2019 | 79.6 | 81.4 | 82.1 | 81.8 | 81.8 | 83.7 | 84.6 | 84.3 | 84.5 | 83.3 | 82.6 | 82.0 | 82.6 |

# 1. Employment by Industry: Oklahoma, 2011–2019—*Continued*

(Numbers in thousands, not seasonally adjusted)

| Industry and year | January | February | March | April | May | June | July | August | September | October | November | December | Annual average |
|---|---|---|---|---|---|---|---|---|---|---|---|---|---|
| **Manufacturing** | | | | | | | | | | | | | |
| 2011 | 132.0 | 132.2 | 133.5 | 135.3 | 135.7 | 136.8 | 138.0 | 138.1 | 138.7 | 139.2 | 139.7 | 140.3 | 136.6 |
| 2012 | 139.8 | 140.5 | 141.2 | 141.8 | 142.2 | 143.2 | 142.7 | 142.9 | 142.9 | 143.8 | 143.4 | 143.9 | 142.4 |
| 2013 | 142.2 | 142.3 | 142.5 | 142.2 | 142.3 | 143.0 | 142.8 | 142.6 | 142.2 | 142.2 | 142.4 | 142.6 | 142.4 |
| 2014 | 141.7 | 142.6 | 142.9 | 143.4 | 144.3 | 145.3 | 145.7 | 145.7 | 145.7 | 146.2 | 146.7 | 147.5 | 144.8 |
| 2015 | 146.7 | 146.8 | 145.8 | 144.4 | 143.8 | 143.3 | 142.5 | 141.4 | 140.7 | 139.8 | 139.1 | 139.0 | 142.8 |
| 2016 | 137.6 | 137.9 | 136.4 | 135.2 | 134.6 | 134.1 | 133.5 | 133.2 | 133.0 | 132.1 | 132.6 | 133.1 | 134.4 |
| 2017 | 131.0 | 132.2 | 132.1 | 132.5 | 133.0 | 134.4 | 134.5 | 134.8 | 134.8 | 134.8 | 135.1 | 136.2 | 133.8 |
| 2018 | 135.5 | 136.3 | 137.1 | 137.4 | 138.2 | 139.6 | 139.1 | 139.2 | 139.7 | 140.0 | 140.3 | 141.3 | 138.6 |
| 2019 | 140.7 | 141.7 | 141.8 | 141.5 | 141.4 | 141.8 | 141.2 | 140.7 | 140.1 | 139.7 | 139.3 | 139.3 | 140.8 |
| **Trade, Transportation, and Utilities** | | | | | | | | | | | | | |
| 2011 | 268.4 | 266.8 | 271.0 | 273.8 | 274.4 | 275.0 | 274.8 | 276.4 | 275.9 | 277.0 | 282.0 | 284.2 | 275.0 |
| 2012 | 276.5 | 275.3 | 278.2 | 280.0 | 282.0 | 283.3 | 281.9 | 282.0 | 282.1 | 285.2 | 290.9 | 293.3 | 282.6 |
| 2013 | 280.5 | 280.7 | 282.7 | 284.7 | 287.0 | 288.3 | 288.5 | 289.7 | 289.6 | 290.8 | 297.1 | 299.4 | 288.3 |
| 2014 | 290.3 | 289.5 | 291.2 | 291.8 | 293.5 | 295.4 | 294.6 | 295.4 | 295.3 | 297.4 | 303.0 | 307.1 | 295.4 |
| 2015 | 295.7 | 295.3 | 296.5 | 298.2 | 299.5 | 301.2 | 300.5 | 300.3 | 299.6 | 302.2 | 308.0 | 310.7 | 300.6 |
| 2016 | 297.3 | 296.4 | 297.4 | 299.1 | 299.2 | 298.8 | 297.9 | 298.8 | 297.5 | 299.3 | 306.6 | 306.1 | 299.5 |
| 2017 | 294.3 | 292.4 | 292.9 | 294.0 | 294.7 | 295.3 | 295.2 | 295.6 | 295.8 | 298.6 | 305.8 | 306.5 | 296.8 |
| 2018 | 296.2 | 293.9 | 295.5 | 296.1 | 298.0 | 298.6 | 298.7 | 299.5 | 299.9 | 302.1 | 309.5 | 310.1 | 299.8 |
| 2019 | 298.1 | 295.6 | 296.8 | 297.4 | 298.9 | 299.3 | 299.6 | 299.9 | 302.3 | 305.4 | 310.6 | 311.7 | 301.3 |
| **Wholesale Trade** | | | | | | | | | | | | | |
| 2011 | 53.4 | 53.6 | 54.5 | 54.6 | 54.7 | 54.9 | 55.1 | 55.1 | 55.0 | 55.2 | 55.2 | 55.3 | 54.7 |
| 2012 | 55.0 | 55.5 | 56.1 | 56.4 | 56.9 | 57.3 | 56.8 | 56.7 | 56.7 | 57.3 | 57.5 | 57.8 | 56.7 |
| 2013 | 57.0 | 57.2 | 57.4 | 57.5 | 57.9 | 58.3 | 58.0 | 58.0 | 58.0 | 58.1 | 58.4 | 58.4 | 57.9 |
| 2014 | 58.5 | 58.6 | 58.9 | 59.0 | 59.3 | 59.8 | 59.4 | 59.6 | 59.6 | 60.1 | 60.3 | 60.5 | 59.5 |
| 2015 | 59.1 | 59.2 | 59.0 | 58.8 | 58.6 | 59.0 | 58.7 | 58.2 | 57.9 | 58.0 | 57.7 | 57.9 | 58.5 |
| 2016 | 56.8 | 57.0 | 56.8 | 57.0 | 56.9 | 56.8 | 56.6 | 56.4 | 56.1 | 55.9 | 56.1 | 56.1 | 56.5 |
| 2017 | 55.6 | 55.7 | 56.0 | 56.3 | 56.7 | 57.3 | 56.8 | 56.8 | 56.9 | 57.5 | 57.7 | 58.0 | 56.8 |
| 2018 | 56.8 | 56.9 | 57.0 | 57.0 | 57.0 | 57.6 | 57.5 | 57.3 | 57.3 | 58.2 | 58.6 | 58.8 | 57.5 |
| 2019 | 57.6 | 57.6 | 57.7 | 57.7 | 58.0 | 58.3 | 58.5 | 58.3 | 57.9 | 58.3 | 57.8 | 57.5 | 57.9 |
| **Retail Trade** | | | | | | | | | | | | | |
| 2011 | 167.2 | 165.3 | 168.2 | 170.2 | 170.4 | 170.2 | 169.6 | 170.9 | 170.5 | 171.1 | 175.9 | 177.1 | 170.6 |
| 2012 | 170.3 | 168.6 | 170.6 | 171.8 | 172.8 | 173.1 | 172.2 | 172.1 | 172.1 | 174.2 | 179.4 | 180.9 | 173.2 |
| 2013 | 170.0 | 169.4 | 170.9 | 172.4 | 174.0 | 174.5 | 174.7 | 175.8 | 175.8 | 176.9 | 182.4 | 184.3 | 175.1 |
| 2014 | 175.6 | 174.9 | 175.5 | 176.5 | 177.5 | 178.5 | 178.3 | 178.8 | 178.7 | 179.8 | 184.5 | 187.4 | 178.8 |
| 2015 | 178.9 | 179.0 | 180.1 | 181.6 | 182.8 | 183.7 | 183.0 | 183.4 | 183.0 | 184.2 | 188.6 | 190.3 | 183.2 |
| 2016 | 181.4 | 181.3 | 182.7 | 183.9 | 184.1 | 183.9 | 183.0 | 183.7 | 182.4 | 183.2 | 188.3 | 187.6 | 183.8 |
| 2017 | 179.4 | 177.7 | 177.6 | 178.7 | 178.6 | 178.5 | 178.3 | 178.4 | 177.4 | 178.3 | 183.4 | 183.9 | 179.2 |
| 2018 | 177.3 | 175.6 | 176.7 | 177.3 | 178.4 | 177.8 | 177.3 | 177.9 | 177.5 | 177.7 | 182.6 | 182.0 | 178.2 |
| 2019 | 175.1 | 173.4 | 174.4 | 175.0 | 175.9 | 175.4 | 175.4 | 175.7 | 175.9 | 177.5 | 181.0 | 180.6 | 176.3 |
| **Transportation and Utilities** | | | | | | | | | | | | | |
| 2011 | 47.8 | 47.9 | 48.3 | 49.0 | 49.3 | 49.9 | 50.1 | 50.4 | 50.4 | 50.7 | 50.9 | 51.8 | 49.7 |
| 2012 | 51.2 | 51.2 | 51.5 | 51.8 | 52.3 | 52.9 | 52.9 | 53.2 | 53.3 | 53.7 | 54.0 | 54.6 | 52.7 |
| 2013 | 53.5 | 54.1 | 54.4 | 54.8 | 55.1 | 55.5 | 55.8 | 55.9 | 55.8 | 55.8 | 56.3 | 56.7 | 55.3 |
| 2014 | 56.2 | 56.0 | 56.8 | 56.3 | 56.7 | 57.1 | 56.9 | 57.0 | 57.0 | 57.5 | 58.2 | 59.2 | 57.1 |
| 2015 | 57.7 | 57.1 | 57.4 | 57.8 | 58.1 | 58.5 | 58.8 | 58.7 | 58.7 | 60.0 | 61.7 | 62.5 | 58.9 |
| 2016 | 59.1 | 58.1 | 57.9 | 58.2 | 58.2 | 58.1 | 58.3 | 58.7 | 59.0 | 60.2 | 62.2 | 62.4 | 59.2 |
| 2017 | 59.3 | 59.0 | 59.3 | 59.0 | 59.4 | 59.5 | 60.1 | 60.4 | 61.5 | 62.8 | 64.7 | 64.6 | 60.8 |
| 2018 | 62.1 | 61.4 | 61.8 | 61.8 | 62.6 | 63.2 | 63.9 | 64.3 | 65.1 | 66.2 | 68.3 | 69.3 | 64.2 |
| 2019 | 65.4 | 64.6 | 64.7 | 64.7 | 65.0 | 65.6 | 65.7 | 65.9 | 68.5 | 69.6 | 71.8 | 73.6 | 67.1 |
| **Information** | | | | | | | | | | | | | |
| 2011 | 23.3 | 23.1 | 22.9 | 23.0 | 23.1 | 23.1 | 23.2 | 23.1 | 22.8 | 22.9 | 23.0 | 23.0 | 23.0 |
| 2012 | 22.8 | 22.7 | 22.7 | 22.6 | 22.6 | 22.5 | 22.6 | 22.3 | 22.1 | 22.2 | 22.2 | 22.3 | 22.5 |
| 2013 | 21.8 | 21.7 | 21.6 | 21.9 | 22.0 | 22.1 | 22.0 | 21.8 | 21.5 | 21.7 | 21.8 | 21.7 | 21.8 |
| 2014 | 21.4 | 21.3 | 21.3 | 21.3 | 21.3 | 21.3 | 21.5 | 21.2 | 21.1 | 20.8 | 20.9 | 21.2 | 21.2 |
| 2015 | 20.8 | 20.9 | 21.0 | 20.9 | 21.3 | 21.3 | 21.2 | 21.1 | 21.1 | 21.4 | 21.7 | 21.8 | 21.2 |
| 2016 | 21.2 | 21.4 | 21.3 | 21.2 | 21.3 | 21.4 | 21.3 | 21.1 | 20.9 | 20.9 | 21.0 | 21.3 | 21.2 |
| 2017 | 20.9 | 20.9 | 20.9 | 20.8 | 20.8 | 20.7 | 20.5 | 20.3 | 20.1 | 19.9 | 20.0 | 20.2 | 20.5 |
| 2018 | 19.9 | 19.9 | 19.9 | 19.9 | 20.0 | 20.1 | 20.2 | 20.0 | 19.9 | 19.8 | 19.6 | 19.9 | 19.9 |
| 2019 | 19.5 | 19.6 | 19.6 | 19.6 | 19.6 | 19.7 | 19.7 | 19.5 | 19.4 | 19.5 | 19.8 | 19.9 | 19.6 |

## 1. Employment by Industry: Oklahoma, 2011–2019—*Continued*

(Numbers in thousands, not seasonally adjusted)

| Industry and year | January | February | March | April | May | June | July | August | September | October | November | December | Annual average |
|---|---|---|---|---|---|---|---|---|---|---|---|---|---|
| **Financial Activities** | | | | | | | | | | | | | |
| 2011 | 77.0 | 76.8 | 77.3 | 77.6 | 77.5 | 77.9 | 77.9 | 78.1 | 77.7 | 77.8 | 77.8 | 78.2 | 77.6 |
| 2012 | 77.2 | 77.6 | 77.7 | 77.8 | 78.2 | 78.6 | 78.5 | 78.5 | 78.0 | 78.3 | 78.4 | 79.1 | 78.2 |
| 2013 | 78.2 | 78.4 | 78.5 | 78.3 | 78.9 | 79.1 | 79.3 | 79.2 | 79.0 | 79.1 | 79.5 | 79.6 | 78.9 |
| 2014 | 78.7 | 78.8 | 79.0 | 79.2 | 79.4 | 79.8 | 80.0 | 80.1 | 79.4 | 79.5 | 80.0 | 80.5 | 79.5 |
| 2015 | 79.5 | 79.4 | 79.3 | 79.4 | 79.8 | 79.8 | 80.0 | 79.6 | 79.3 | 79.3 | 79.2 | 79.5 | 79.5 |
| 2016 | 78.6 | 78.6 | 78.4 | 78.5 | 78.6 | 78.8 | 79.1 | 79.0 | 78.7 | 78.9 | 78.9 | 79.5 | 78.8 |
| 2017 | 77.9 | 78.1 | 78.4 | 78.7 | 78.9 | 79.4 | 79.0 | 79.1 | 78.9 | 79.0 | 79.1 | 79.7 | 78.9 |
| 2018 | 78.4 | 78.4 | 78.8 | 78.8 | 79.0 | 79.7 | 79.6 | 79.6 | 79.4 | 79.3 | 79.1 | 79.5 | 79.1 |
| 2019 | 78.9 | 79.0 | 79.0 | 79.5 | 79.6 | 79.8 | 79.9 | 79.5 | 79.1 | 79.0 | 79.2 | 80.0 | 79.4 |
| **Professional and Business Services** | | | | | | | | | | | | | |
| 2011 | 171.7 | 171.0 | 174.1 | 176.9 | 176.6 | 176.7 | 177.7 | 178.5 | 178.8 | 179.0 | 177.6 | 177.6 | 176.4 |
| 2012 | 173.4 | 176.8 | 177.5 | 179.1 | 179.5 | 181.9 | 180.5 | 182.7 | 181.6 | 183.3 | 183.1 | 181.2 | 180.1 |
| 2013 | 176.7 | 178.1 | 180.6 | 180.6 | 181.7 | 182.6 | 182.7 | 184.0 | 183.4 | 184.0 | 184.7 | 182.4 | 181.8 |
| 2014 | 179.7 | 180.7 | 182.7 | 184.8 | 185.5 | 186.2 | 186.3 | 187.0 | 185.5 | 187.1 | 187.8 | 186.8 | 185.0 |
| 2015 | 184.9 | 183.9 | 184.3 | 185.4 | 185.0 | 185.2 | 186.1 | 185.8 | 183.7 | 185.0 | 184.1 | 183.7 | 184.8 |
| 2016 | 180.1 | 180.4 | 179.9 | 182.2 | 181.6 | 182.4 | 182.6 | 183.5 | 183.7 | 184.2 | 183.2 | 182.9 | 182.2 |
| 2017 | 179.0 | 181.3 | 183.5 | 185.0 | 185.2 | 188.0 | 188.0 | 188.8 | 189.1 | 189.3 | 188.6 | 188.2 | 186.2 |
| 2018 | 185.2 | 187.6 | 189.3 | 189.1 | 189.4 | 193.2 | 193.4 | 194.1 | 194.0 | 194.4 | 194.1 | 193.3 | 191.4 |
| 2019 | 189.2 | 191.3 | 192.4 | 194.5 | 194.4 | 195.3 | 195.4 | 196.0 | 194.9 | 197.6 | 194.5 | 190.5 | 193.8 |
| **Education and Health Services** | | | | | | | | | | | | | |
| 2011 | 220.5 | 219.6 | 221.6 | 222.5 | 222.9 | 222.7 | 222.0 | 223.3 | 225.2 | 225.3 | 225.8 | 226.1 | 223.1 |
| 2012 | 223.3 | 224.4 | 225.1 | 226.4 | 226.6 | 225.8 | 223.4 | 225.8 | 227.4 | 228.2 | 228.8 | 229.6 | 226.2 |
| 2013 | 226.3 | 227.2 | 227.8 | 227.9 | 228.1 | 226.9 | 225.5 | 227.1 | 228.6 | 229.0 | 229.5 | 228.4 | 227.7 |
| 2014 | 226.2 | 226.8 | 227.3 | 228.5 | 228.3 | 227.5 | 226.4 | 227.6 | 228.7 | 229.4 | 229.9 | 230.4 | 228.1 |
| 2015 | 228.5 | 229.1 | 229.4 | 230.9 | 231.0 | 230.6 | 230.8 | 231.9 | 233.9 | 234.2 | 234.6 | 234.1 | 231.6 |
| 2016 | 232.7 | 233.5 | 233.6 | 234.0 | 233.3 | 231.8 | 232.4 | 233.4 | 235.0 | 235.2 | 235.2 | 235.3 | 233.8 |
| 2017 | 231.3 | 232.7 | 233.2 | 235.5 | 235.9 | 235.4 | 234.5 | 235.3 | 237.4 | 237.6 | 237.4 | 237.7 | 235.3 |
| 2018 | 235.0 | 236.1 | 236.8 | 236.3 | 236.3 | 234.9 | 234.6 | 235.7 | 236.9 | 237.7 | 237.1 | 238.1 | 236.3 |
| 2019 | 236.2 | 237.0 | 237.8 | 238.5 | 238.5 | 238.3 | 237.4 | 238.6 | 240.2 | 241.1 | 240.8 | 241.7 | 238.8 |
| **Leisure and Hospitality** | | | | | | | | | | | | | |
| 2011 | 135.3 | 134.7 | 140.7 | 144.6 | 146.3 | 147.0 | 146.2 | 147.0 | 147.0 | 143.7 | 142.9 | 142.0 | 143.1 |
| 2012 | 139.4 | 141.4 | 145.3 | 148.8 | 150.6 | 151.5 | 148.8 | 150.1 | 149.7 | 147.9 | 147.5 | 148.0 | 147.4 |
| 2013 | 143.7 | 145.6 | 148.7 | 151.9 | 155.0 | 155.1 | 154.7 | 156.5 | 156.1 | 152.4 | 152.2 | 150.4 | 151.9 |
| 2014 | 148.7 | 149.9 | 152.9 | 157.2 | 159.0 | 159.4 | 158.8 | 160.3 | 159.6 | 156.9 | 156.1 | 156.1 | 156.2 |
| 2015 | 152.8 | 154.9 | 157.0 | 162.3 | 164.4 | 166.5 | 165.5 | 166.9 | 165.4 | 163.2 | 163.0 | 161.7 | 162.0 |
| 2016 | 158.3 | 160.4 | 163.5 | 166.9 | 167.4 | 167.8 | 168.2 | 169.5 | 167.8 | 165.7 | 164.5 | 163.3 | 165.3 |
| 2017 | 158.8 | 160.9 | 165.2 | 169.3 | 170.0 | 172.2 | 170.2 | 171.2 | 170.6 | 168.0 | 167.1 | 166.8 | 167.5 |
| 2018 | 163.6 | 165.4 | 169.6 | 172.6 | 175.8 | 176.7 | 174.5 | 175.9 | 174.7 | 171.3 | 170.4 | 170.3 | 171.7 |
| 2019 | 166.6 | 168.5 | 171.9 | 175.2 | 176.3 | 176.3 | 175.8 | 177.2 | 176.9 | 178.2 | 177.2 | 176.0 | 174.7 |
| **Other Services** | | | | | | | | | | | | | |
| 2011 | 59.5 | 59.4 | 60.1 | 59.1 | 59.1 | 59.4 | 58.9 | 58.3 | 58.4 | 57.9 | 57.9 | 57.7 | 58.8 |
| 2012 | 57.2 | 57.5 | 57.6 | 59.5 | 59.7 | 60.0 | 59.4 | 59.1 | 58.6 | 58.5 | 58.1 | 58.0 | 58.6 |
| 2013 | 57.3 | 57.5 | 57.7 | 59.5 | 59.8 | 60.4 | 60.3 | 60.1 | 59.7 | 59.1 | 59.1 | 58.9 | 59.1 |
| 2014 | 58.4 | 58.5 | 58.8 | 59.4 | 60.3 | 60.9 | 61.2 | 60.7 | 60.7 | 60.9 | 60.8 | 61.0 | 60.1 |
| 2015 | 60.7 | 61.1 | 61.9 | 62.3 | 62.5 | 63.1 | 63.8 | 63.0 | 62.8 | 62.5 | 62.5 | 62.4 | 62.4 |
| 2016 | 62.4 | 62.7 | 62.7 | 63.2 | 63.7 | 64.6 | 65.0 | 65.0 | 65.2 | 65.2 | 65.5 | 65.8 | 64.3 |
| 2017 | 65.7 | 66.6 | 67.3 | 67.8 | 68.5 | 69.6 | 69.6 | 69.5 | 69.8 | 69.9 | 69.9 | 70.3 | 68.7 |
| 2018 | 69.9 | 70.4 | 71.2 | 70.0 | 70.3 | 71.1 | 70.7 | 70.5 | 70.6 | 70.3 | 70.1 | 70.3 | 70.5 |
| 2019 | 69.7 | 70.1 | 70.4 | 70.4 | 70.6 | 71.5 | 71.4 | 70.7 | 70.7 | 70.1 | 70.9 | 70.2 | 70.6 |
| **Government** | | | | | | | | | | | | | |
| 2011 | 341.3 | 346.2 | 348.1 | 349.8 | 350.0 | 338.1 | 323.8 | 327.4 | 346.4 | 350.5 | 351.4 | 353.5 | 343.9 |
| 2012 | 343.0 | 350.5 | 352.1 | 352.3 | 352.9 | 339.8 | 327.4 | 334.0 | 348.3 | 354.3 | 356.0 | 355.4 | 347.2 |
| 2013 | 345.5 | 353.4 | 354.7 | 355.1 | 356.6 | 342.0 | 329.1 | 334.5 | 348.0 | 354.1 | 355.9 | 353.9 | 348.6 |
| 2014 | 344.7 | 352.0 | 353.0 | 353.2 | 355.3 | 341.7 | 329.0 | 335.2 | 348.3 | 355.9 | 356.6 | 355.5 | 348.4 |
| 2015 | 346.7 | 354.3 | 354.6 | 356.2 | 357.8 | 344.1 | 331.6 | 337.3 | 351.9 | 359.2 | 360.5 | 359.9 | 351.2 |
| 2016 | 350.9 | 358.3 | 359.7 | 359.6 | 359.0 | 345.9 | 333.2 | 339.1 | 353.2 | 355.1 | 356.4 | 356.6 | 352.3 |
| 2017 | 346.5 | 353.8 | 355.6 | 355.0 | 355.5 | 344.2 | 332.1 | 337.3 | 350.3 | 353.0 | 353.8 | 353.6 | 349.2 |
| 2018 | 346.0 | 352.1 | 353.0 | 351.6 | 353.7 | 342.0 | 329.3 | 335.4 | 348.3 | 355.8 | 357.7 | 356.9 | 348.5 |
| 2019 | 347.3 | 356.5 | 357.4 | 356.7 | 358.8 | 343.7 | 333.0 | 339.7 | 356.6 | 361.5 | 363.1 | 362.4 | 353.1 |

## 2. Average Weekly Hours by Selected Industry: Oklahoma, 2015–2019

(Not seasonally adjusted)

| Industry and year | January | February | March | April | May | June | July | August | September | October | November | December | Annual average |
|---|---|---|---|---|---|---|---|---|---|---|---|---|---|
| **Total Private** | | | | | | | | | | | | | |
| 2015 | 34.7 | 35.1 | 35.1 | 34.4 | 34.2 | 34.8 | 34.5 | 35.3 | 34.3 | 34.7 | 35.1 | 35.1 | 34.8 |
| 2016 | 35.0 | 34.8 | 34.5 | 34.7 | 35.2 | 35.0 | 35.3 | 35.0 | 35.1 | 35.7 | 35.0 | 35.1 | 35.0 |
| 2017 | 35.3 | 35.4 | 35.3 | 35.9 | 35.3 | 35.6 | 36.1 | 35.5 | 35.5 | 36.0 | 35.4 | 35.4 | 35.5 |
| 2018 | 35.0 | 34.9 | 35.3 | 35.6 | 35.3 | 35.6 | 35.8 | 35.5 | 35.9 | 35.7 | 35.7 | 36.3 | 35.6 |
| 2019 | 35.4 | 35.5 | 35.4 | 35.7 | 35.4 | 36.3 | 35.7 | 35.8 | 36.0 | 35.6 | 35.4 | 36.0 | 35.7 |
| **Goods-Producing** | | | | | | | | | | | | | |
| 2015 | 40.7 | 40.4 | 40.2 | 39.9 | 39.3 | 40.7 | 40.0 | 40.9 | 39.5 | 40.9 | 41.3 | 41.2 | 40.4 |
| 2016 | 40.7 | 40.3 | 39.9 | 40.6 | 41.1 | 41.2 | 41.3 | 41.2 | 41.3 | 41.9 | 40.8 | 40.8 | 40.9 |
| 2017 | 40.3 | 40.9 | 41.1 | 41.5 | 41.4 | 41.1 | 41.6 | 41.1 | 41.0 | 41.9 | 41.3 | 41.8 | 41.3 |
| 2018 | 40.9 | 41.4 | 41.9 | 41.3 | 41.6 | 41.7 | 41.3 | 41.3 | 42.2 | 41.3 | 42.0 | 42.7 | 41.6 |
| 2019 | 42.0 | 42.0 | 42.1 | 42.6 | 41.5 | 43.1 | 43.0 | 43.0 | 43.0 | 42.6 | 41.8 | 42.8 | 42.5 |
| **Construction** | | | | | | | | | | | | | |
| 2015 | 40.3 | 40.7 | 40.6 | 41.0 | 39.5 | 41.3 | 41.1 | 41.7 | 39.8 | 41.9 | 42.7 | 42.2 | 41.1 |
| 2016 | 42.3 | 42.3 | 41.2 | 42.8 | 43.1 | 43.3 | 43.5 | 42.4 | 42.5 | 43.1 | 41.1 | 42.0 | 42.5 |
| 2017 | 41.2 | 42.4 | 42.0 | 42.3 | 42.3 | 42.8 | 43.7 | 42.7 | 41.0 | 43.3 | 42.0 | 42.4 | 42.3 |
| 2018 | 40.9 | 41.9 | 42.7 | 41.5 | 41.8 | 41.2 | 41.1 | 41.0 | 41.9 | 39.5 | 40.1 | 41.2 | 41.2 |
| 2019 | 40.6 | 40.6 | 40.9 | 42.1 | 40.2 | 42.6 | 42.5 | 42.6 | 42.6 | 41.6 | 40.5 | 42.8 | 41.7 |
| **Manufacturing** | | | | | | | | | | | | | |
| 2015 | 40.6 | 39.8 | 39.5 | 38.8 | 38.8 | 39.9 | 38.7 | 40.0 | 38.9 | 40.3 | 40.4 | 40.6 | 39.7 |
| 2016 | 39.8 | 39.0 | 39.3 | 39.3 | 39.8 | 39.9 | 40.1 | 40.9 | 40.5 | 40.8 | 40.1 | 39.4 | 39.9 |
| 2017 | 39.0 | 39.1 | 39.8 | 39.6 | 39.9 | 39.2 | 39.2 | 39.3 | 40.4 | 40.2 | 40.5 | 41.0 | 39.8 |
| 2018 | 40.2 | 40.5 | 40.7 | 40.5 | 41.0 | 41.1 | 40.5 | 40.7 | 41.3 | 41.9 | 43.0 | 43.6 | 41.3 |
| 2019 | 42.9 | 42.9 | 42.9 | 43.0 | 42.4 | 42.9 | 43.0 | 42.9 | 42.8 | 43.0 | 44.1 | 43.9 | 43.1 |
| **Trade, Transportation, and Utilities** | | | | | | | | | | | | | |
| 2015 | 34.8 | 35.3 | 35.5 | 34.8 | 35.0 | 35.1 | 35.2 | 36.0 | 35.1 | 34.7 | 34.9 | 35.1 | 35.1 |
| 2016 | 34.7 | 35.3 | 35.0 | 35.2 | 35.3 | 35.5 | 35.2 | 35.0 | 35.2 | 35.4 | 34.4 | 34.9 | 35.1 |
| 2017 | 35.3 | 35.0 | 35.6 | 36.4 | 35.7 | 36.2 | 36.2 | 35.6 | 35.4 | 35.6 | 34.9 | 34.8 | 35.6 |
| 2018 | 34.5 | 34.2 | 34.4 | 34.9 | 34.7 | 35.2 | 35.5 | 35.2 | 35.5 | 34.9 | 34.6 | 35.3 | 34.9 |
| 2019 | 34.6 | 34.5 | 34.6 | 35.1 | 35.3 | 36.2 | 35.7 | 35.6 | 35.7 | 35.2 | 34.8 | 35.6 | 35.2 |
| **Financial Activities** | | | | | | | | | | | | | |
| 2015 | 35.7 | 36.6 | 37.0 | 36.1 | 35.7 | 36.0 | 35.5 | 37.2 | 36.4 | 35.9 | 37.1 | 36.2 | 36.3 |
| 2016 | 35.6 | 35.5 | 35.8 | 36.0 | 37.1 | 35.4 | 35.8 | 35.5 | 36.6 | 36.9 | 35.6 | 35.6 | 35.9 |
| 2017 | 37.3 | 37.9 | 37.0 | 38.1 | 36.1 | 37.1 | 37.9 | 36.2 | 35.9 | 38.0 | 36.0 | 35.9 | 36.9 |
| 2018 | 36.7 | 36.7 | 36.8 | 39.1 | 37.9 | 38.3 | 39.2 | 37.7 | 39.0 | 37.5 | 38.0 | 38.1 | 37.9 |
| 2019 | 36.2 | 37.9 | 37.0 | 36.7 | 35.6 | 38.2 | 36.1 | 36.5 | 37.6 | 36.5 | 37.1 | 37.7 | 36.9 |
| **Professional and Business Services** | | | | | | | | | | | | | |
| 2015 | 35.4 | 36.1 | 35.9 | 35.5 | 34.8 | 35.5 | 34.7 | 35.3 | 33.8 | 35.1 | 35.6 | 35.3 | 35.3 |
| 2016 | 35.9 | 35.4 | 35.6 | 35.9 | 36.4 | 35.9 | 36.6 | 35.8 | 36.4 | 37.0 | 36.6 | 36.6 | 36.2 |
| 2017 | 37.0 | 36.4 | 36.5 | 36.8 | 36.2 | 36.3 | 36.9 | 36.4 | 36.8 | 37.2 | 36.4 | 36.3 | 36.6 |
| 2018 | 35.9 | 35.7 | 36.0 | 36.6 | 36.0 | 36.0 | 35.9 | 35.5 | 35.7 | 35.0 | 35.1 | 35.3 | 35.7 |
| 2019 | 34.6 | 34.8 | 35.5 | 36.4 | 35.8 | 36.6 | 35.8 | 36.0 | 36.7 | 36.4 | 36.2 | 36.8 | 36.0 |
| **Education and Health Services** | | | | | | | | | | | | | |
| 2015 | 33.2 | 33.4 | 33.3 | 32.7 | 33.2 | 33.4 | 33.9 | 34.4 | 33.6 | 33.8 | 34.4 | 33.7 | 33.6 |
| 2016 | 34.0 | 33.3 | 32.9 | 33.1 | 33.6 | 33.7 | 34.3 | 34.2 | 34.3 | 34.8 | 34.4 | 34.4 | 33.9 |
| 2017 | 35.1 | 34.5 | 34.3 | 35.1 | 34.2 | 34.3 | 35.5 | 34.5 | 34.7 | 35.0 | 34.8 | 34.7 | 34.7 |
| 2018 | 35.0 | 34.4 | 34.4 | 35.0 | 34.5 | 34.8 | 35.9 | 35.3 | 35.9 | 34.8 | 35.0 | 35.5 | 35.0 |
| 2019 | 34.8 | 34.7 | 34.2 | 34.3 | 34.5 | 34.9 | 34.2 | 34.2 | 34.3 | 34.2 | 34.6 | 34.8 | 34.5 |
| **Leisure and Hospitality** | | | | | | | | | | | | | |
| 2015 | 25.2 | 26.0 | 26.3 | 25.8 | 25.6 | 26.5 | 25.9 | 26.5 | 26.4 | 26.0 | 26.2 | 26.3 | 26.1 |
| 2016 | 25.3 | 26.5 | 26.2 | 26.0 | 26.8 | 26.5 | 26.7 | 26.8 | 26.0 | 26.7 | 26.5 | 26.2 | 26.4 |
| 2017 | 25.0 | 26.0 | 26.3 | 26.7 | 26.4 | 26.6 | 26.7 | 26.2 | 26.2 | 26.6 | 26.4 | 26.3 | 26.3 |
| 2018 | 25.1 | 25.8 | 26.5 | 26.7 | 26.2 | 26.8 | 25.9 | 26.6 | 26.2 | 25.7 | 25.3 | 25.9 | 26.1 |
| 2019 | 25.2 | 25.8 | 26.1 | 26.0 | 26.0 | 26.7 | 26.1 | 26.7 | 26.1 | 26.2 | 26.0 | 25.9 | 26.1 |

## 3. Average Hourly Earnings by Selected Industry: Oklahoma, 2015–2019

(Dollars, not seasonally adjusted)

| Industry and year | January | February | March | April | May | June | July | August | September | October | November | December | Annual average |
|---|---|---|---|---|---|---|---|---|---|---|---|---|---|
| **Total Private** | | | | | | | | | | | | | |
| 2015 | 21.85 | 21.95 | 21.91 | 21.79 | 21.80 | 21.63 | 21.67 | 21.83 | 21.84 | 21.82 | 21.99 | 21.68 | 21.82 |
| 2016 | 21.68 | 21.84 | 21.88 | 21.91 | 21.99 | 21.80 | 22.09 | 21.94 | 22.23 | 22.37 | 22.31 | 22.35 | 22.03 |
| 2017 | 22.61 | 22.62 | 22.64 | 22.93 | 22.75 | 22.66 | 23.05 | 22.94 | 23.08 | 23.15 | 22.96 | 23.04 | 22.87 |
| 2018 | 23.05 | 23.32 | 23.05 | 23.32 | 23.18 | 23.42 | 23.84 | 23.92 | 24.18 | 24.25 | 24.27 | 24.38 | 23.69 |
| 2019 | 24.43 | 24.59 | 24.31 | 24.30 | 24.31 | 24.43 | 24.34 | 24.41 | 24.67 | 24.40 | 24.49 | 24.63 | 24.44 |
| **Goods-Producing** | | | | | | | | | | | | | |
| 2015 | 23.78 | 23.94 | 24.16 | 23.82 | 24.01 | 23.80 | 23.88 | 24.01 | 24.24 | 24.10 | 24.32 | 24.16 | 24.02 |
| 2016 | 23.63 | 24.04 | 24.02 | 23.76 | 24.26 | 24.14 | 24.20 | 24.33 | 24.36 | 24.58 | 24.59 | 24.66 | 24.21 |
| 2017 | 24.50 | 24.51 | 24.77 | 25.12 | 25.20 | 25.09 | 25.42 | 25.52 | 25.62 | 25.92 | 25.33 | 25.60 | 25.23 |
| 2018 | 25.79 | 26.00 | 26.09 | 26.62 | 26.15 | 26.49 | 26.79 | 26.98 | 27.16 | 26.65 | 26.82 | 27.07 | 26.56 |
| 2019 | 27.30 | 27.29 | 27.27 | 27.07 | 27.43 | 27.61 | 27.39 | 27.64 | 27.88 | 27.82 | 27.83 | 28.05 | 27.55 |
| **Construction** | | | | | | | | | | | | | |
| 2015 | 21.56 | 21.61 | 21.51 | 21.35 | 21.77 | 21.35 | 21.23 | 21.36 | 21.81 | 21.81 | 21.79 | 22.08 | 21.60 |
| 2016 | 21.15 | 21.26 | 21.81 | 21.33 | 21.86 | 21.68 | 22.18 | 21.98 | 22.26 | 22.06 | 22.27 | 22.10 | 21.83 |
| 2017 | 21.82 | 22.05 | 22.02 | 22.12 | 22.79 | 22.64 | 22.55 | 22.92 | 23.08 | 23.38 | 22.79 | 23.00 | 22.61 |
| 2018 | 23.13 | 23.53 | 23.30 | 23.56 | 23.37 | 23.77 | 23.86 | 23.82 | 24.26 | 24.05 | 24.38 | 24.50 | 23.80 |
| 2019 | 24.70 | 24.87 | 24.84 | 24.86 | 24.90 | 25.44 | 25.06 | 25.42 | 25.94 | 26.01 | 25.87 | 25.71 | 25.31 |
| **Manufacturing** | | | | | | | | | | | | | |
| 2015 | 22.51 | 22.69 | 23.00 | 22.89 | 23.08 | 23.16 | 23.53 | 23.74 | 23.95 | 23.76 | 24.15 | 23.82 | 23.35 |
| 2016 | 23.56 | 24.00 | 23.61 | 23.71 | 24.07 | 24.11 | 23.67 | 23.82 | 23.70 | 24.12 | 23.55 | 23.74 | 23.81 |
| 2017 | 23.35 | 23.58 | 23.53 | 23.99 | 23.88 | 23.64 | 24.24 | 24.29 | 24.33 | 24.59 | 24.13 | 24.24 | 23.99 |
| 2018 | 24.52 | 24.75 | 25.03 | 25.32 | 24.79 | 24.71 | 24.96 | 25.52 | 25.27 | 24.97 | 25.21 | 25.49 | 25.05 |
| 2019 | 25.69 | 26.05 | 26.28 | 26.22 | 26.25 | 26.27 | 25.78 | 26.20 | 26.24 | 25.86 | 26.09 | 26.03 | 26.08 |
| **Trade, Transportation, and Utilities** | | | | | | | | | | | | | |
| 2015 | 19.90 | 19.77 | 19.58 | 19.60 | 20.01 | 19.61 | 19.82 | 19.91 | 19.76 | 19.96 | 20.17 | 19.53 | 19.80 |
| 2016 | 19.70 | 19.85 | 20.25 | 20.30 | 20.50 | 20.61 | 21.18 | 20.72 | 20.82 | 20.84 | 21.08 | 20.90 | 20.56 |
| 2017 | 21.23 | 20.78 | 20.98 | 21.36 | 21.40 | 21.19 | 21.90 | 21.65 | 21.96 | 22.05 | 21.72 | 21.83 | 21.51 |
| 2018 | 22.19 | 22.69 | 22.25 | 23.17 | 22.98 | 23.50 | 23.87 | 24.31 | 24.24 | 23.49 | 23.69 | 23.59 | 23.34 |
| 2019 | 23.80 | 24.33 | 24.04 | 24.27 | 24.45 | 24.61 | 24.72 | 24.92 | 25.48 | 25.23 | 24.88 | 24.62 | 24.62 |
| **Financial Activities** | | | | | | | | | | | | | |
| 2015 | 24.18 | 24.62 | 24.34 | 24.74 | 24.73 | 25.02 | 24.91 | 25.62 | 25.14 | 25.70 | 25.84 | 25.86 | 25.06 |
| 2016 | 25.34 | 25.80 | 25.37 | 25.67 | 25.98 | 25.70 | 25.78 | 26.06 | 27.04 | 27.05 | 26.97 | 26.63 | 26.12 |
| 2017 | 27.10 | 27.28 | 26.99 | 27.07 | 26.94 | 26.27 | 27.14 | 26.25 | 25.72 | 25.52 | 25.71 | 25.34 | 26.45 |
| 2018 | 24.80 | 24.65 | 24.36 | 24.18 | 24.51 | 24.14 | 25.03 | 25.36 | 26.01 | 26.04 | 26.00 | 26.57 | 25.14 |
| 2019 | 25.90 | 25.66 | 25.66 | 26.53 | 27.07 | 27.72 | 27.09 | 27.65 | 28.60 | 28.12 | 28.38 | 28.84 | 27.28 |
| **Professional and Business Services** | | | | | | | | | | | | | |
| 2015 | 24.56 | 24.76 | 24.66 | 24.11 | 23.99 | 23.89 | 23.89 | 24.03 | 24.15 | 23.80 | 24.10 | 23.80 | 24.15 |
| 2016 | 23.89 | 23.69 | 23.36 | 23.27 | 23.14 | 22.75 | 22.63 | 22.58 | 22.69 | 23.02 | 22.90 | 23.18 | 23.09 |
| 2017 | 23.40 | 23.22 | 23.14 | 23.01 | 22.36 | 22.26 | 22.43 | 22.40 | 22.61 | 22.99 | 23.15 | 23.44 | 22.86 |
| 2018 | 23.36 | 23.63 | 22.97 | 23.06 | 23.26 | 23.26 | 23.67 | 23.57 | 24.08 | 24.37 | 24.18 | 24.38 | 23.65 |
| 2019 | 24.22 | 24.77 | 24.12 | 24.04 | 24.03 | 24.20 | 24.12 | 24.12 | 24.08 | 23.57 | 24.19 | 24.61 | 24.17 |
| **Education and Health Services** | | | | | | | | | | | | | |
| 2015 | 23.05 | 23.37 | 23.30 | 23.67 | 23.26 | 23.10 | 23.14 | 23.12 | 23.11 | 22.85 | 22.85 | 22.46 | 23.10 |
| 2016 | 22.59 | 23.13 | 23.44 | 23.72 | 23.23 | 22.99 | 23.61 | 23.11 | 23.73 | 23.69 | 23.33 | 23.33 | 23.33 |
| 2017 | 23.33 | 23.37 | 23.61 | 24.26 | 24.09 | 24.31 | 24.45 | 24.45 | 24.54 | 24.33 | 24.28 | 24.13 | 24.10 |
| 2018 | 23.95 | 24.26 | 24.03 | 23.99 | 23.83 | 24.19 | 24.73 | 24.41 | 24.65 | 25.42 | 24.59 | 24.60 | 24.39 |
| 2019 | 24.77 | 24.67 | 24.63 | 24.49 | 24.07 | 23.91 | 24.09 | 23.88 | 24.06 | 24.01 | 24.02 | 24.18 | 24.23 |
| **Leisure and Hospitality** | | | | | | | | | | | | | |
| 2015 | 11.57 | 11.65 | 11.68 | 11.64 | 11.69 | 11.64 | 11.67 | 11.78 | 12.02 | 12.06 | 12.18 | 12.23 | 11.82 |
| 2016 | 12.46 | 12.46 | 12.50 | 12.53 | 12.61 | 12.30 | 12.52 | 12.48 | 12.51 | 12.74 | 12.67 | 12.75 | 12.54 |
| 2017 | 13.07 | 12.91 | 12.83 | 12.82 | 12.84 | 12.72 | 12.58 | 12.63 | 12.74 | 12.64 | 12.66 | 12.72 | 12.76 |
| 2018 | 12.70 | 12.68 | 12.64 | 12.63 | 12.63 | 12.45 | 12.46 | 12.66 | 12.87 | 13.05 | 13.20 | 13.35 | 12.77 |
| 2019 | 13.09 | 13.20 | 12.80 | 12.99 | 13.06 | 12.89 | 12.82 | 12.87 | 12.93 | 13.03 | 13.33 | 13.53 | 13.04 |

## 4. Average Weekly Earnings by Selected Industry: Oklahoma, 2015–2019

(Dollars, not seasonally adjusted)

| Industry and year | January | February | March | April | May | June | July | August | September | October | November | December | Annual average |
|---|---|---|---|---|---|---|---|---|---|---|---|---|---|
| **Total Private** | | | | | | | | | | | | | |
| 2015 | 758.20 | 770.45 | 769.04 | 749.58 | 745.56 | 752.72 | 747.62 | 770.60 | 749.11 | 757.15 | 771.85 | 760.97 | 759.34 |
| 2016 | 758.80 | 760.03 | 754.86 | 760.28 | 774.05 | 763.00 | 779.78 | 767.90 | 780.27 | 798.61 | 780.85 | 784.49 | 771.05 |
| 2017 | 798.13 | 800.75 | 799.19 | 823.19 | 803.08 | 806.70 | 832.11 | 814.37 | 819.34 | 833.40 | 812.78 | 815.62 | 811.89 |
| 2018 | 806.75 | 813.87 | 813.67 | 830.19 | 818.25 | 833.75 | 853.47 | 849.16 | 868.06 | 865.73 | 866.44 | 884.99 | 843.36 |
| 2019 | 864.82 | 872.95 | 860.57 | 867.51 | 860.57 | 886.81 | 868.94 | 873.88 | 888.12 | 868.64 | 866.95 | 886.68 | 872.51 |
| **Goods-Producing** | | | | | | | | | | | | | |
| 2015 | 967.85 | 967.18 | 971.23 | 950.42 | 943.59 | 968.66 | 955.20 | 982.01 | 957.48 | 985.69 | 1004.42 | 995.39 | 970.41 |
| 2016 | 961.74 | 968.81 | 958.40 | 964.66 | 997.09 | 994.57 | 999.46 | 1002.40 | 1006.07 | 1029.90 | 1003.27 | 1006.13 | 990.19 |
| 2017 | 987.35 | 1002.46 | 1018.05 | 1042.48 | 1043.28 | 1031.20 | 1057.47 | 1048.87 | 1050.42 | 1086.05 | 1046.13 | 1070.08 | 1042.00 |
| 2018 | 1054.81 | 1076.40 | 1093.17 | 1099.41 | 1087.84 | 1104.63 | 1106.43 | 1114.27 | 1146.15 | 1100.65 | 1126.44 | 1155.89 | 1104.90 |
| 2019 | 1146.60 | 1146.18 | 1148.07 | 1153.18 | 1138.35 | 1189.99 | 1177.77 | 1188.52 | 1198.84 | 1185.13 | 1163.29 | 1200.54 | 1170.88 |
| **Construction** | | | | | | | | | | | | | |
| 2015 | 868.87 | 879.53 | 873.31 | 875.35 | 859.92 | 881.76 | 872.55 | 890.71 | 868.04 | 913.84 | 930.43 | 931.78 | 887.76 |
| 2016 | 894.65 | 899.30 | 898.57 | 912.92 | 942.17 | 938.74 | 964.83 | 931.95 | 946.05 | 950.79 | 915.30 | 928.20 | 927.78 |
| 2017 | 898.98 | 934.92 | 924.84 | 935.68 | 964.02 | 968.99 | 985.44 | 978.68 | 946.28 | 1012.35 | 957.18 | 975.20 | 956.40 |
| 2018 | 946.02 | 985.91 | 994.91 | 977.74 | 976.87 | 979.32 | 980.65 | 976.62 | 1016.49 | 949.98 | 977.64 | 1009.40 | 980.56 |
| 2019 | 1002.82 | 1009.72 | 1015.96 | 1046.61 | 1000.98 | 1083.74 | 1065.05 | 1082.89 | 1105.04 | 1082.02 | 1047.74 | 1100.39 | 1055.43 |
| **Manufacturing** | | | | | | | | | | | | | |
| 2015 | 913.91 | 903.06 | 908.50 | 888.13 | 895.50 | 924.08 | 910.61 | 949.60 | 931.66 | 957.53 | 975.66 | 967.09 | 927.00 |
| 2016 | 937.69 | 936.00 | 927.87 | 931.80 | 957.99 | 961.99 | 949.17 | 974.24 | 959.85 | 984.10 | 944.36 | 935.36 | 950.02 |
| 2017 | 910.65 | 921.98 | 936.49 | 950.00 | 952.81 | 926.69 | 950.21 | 954.60 | 982.93 | 988.52 | 977.27 | 993.84 | 954.80 |
| 2018 | 985.70 | 1002.38 | 1018.72 | 1025.46 | 1016.39 | 1015.58 | 1010.88 | 1038.66 | 1043.65 | 1046.24 | 1084.03 | 1111.36 | 1034.57 |
| 2019 | 1102.10 | 1117.55 | 1127.41 | 1127.46 | 1113.00 | 1126.98 | 1108.54 | 1123.98 | 1123.07 | 1111.98 | 1150.57 | 1142.72 | 1124.05 |
| **Trade, Transportation, and Utilities** | | | | | | | | | | | | | |
| 2015 | 692.52 | 697.88 | 695.09 | 682.08 | 700.35 | 688.31 | 697.66 | 716.76 | 693.58 | 692.61 | 703.93 | 685.50 | 694.98 |
| 2016 | 683.59 | 700.71 | 708.75 | 714.56 | 723.65 | 731.66 | 745.54 | 725.20 | 732.86 | 737.74 | 725.15 | 729.41 | 721.66 |
| 2017 | 749.42 | 727.30 | 746.89 | 777.50 | 763.98 | 767.08 | 792.78 | 770.74 | 777.38 | 784.98 | 758.03 | 759.68 | 765.76 |
| 2018 | 765.56 | 776.00 | 765.40 | 808.63 | 797.41 | 827.20 | 847.39 | 855.71 | 860.52 | 819.80 | 819.67 | 832.73 | 814.57 |
| 2019 | 823.48 | 839.39 | 831.78 | 851.88 | 863.09 | 890.88 | 882.50 | 887.15 | 909.64 | 888.10 | 865.82 | 876.47 | 866.62 |
| **Financial Activities** | | | | | | | | | | | | | |
| 2015 | 863.23 | 901.09 | 900.58 | 893.11 | 882.86 | 900.72 | 884.31 | 953.06 | 915.10 | 922.63 | 958.66 | 936.13 | 909.68 |
| 2016 | 902.10 | 915.90 | 908.25 | 924.12 | 963.86 | 909.78 | 922.92 | 925.13 | 989.66 | 998.15 | 960.13 | 948.03 | 937.71 |
| 2017 | 1010.83 | 1033.91 | 998.63 | 1031.37 | 972.53 | 974.62 | 1028.61 | 950.25 | 969.76 | 925.56 | 909.71 | 976.01 | |
| 2018 | 910.16 | 904.66 | 896.45 | 945.44 | 928.93 | 924.56 | 981.18 | 956.07 | 1014.39 | 976.50 | 988.00 | 1012.32 | 952.81 |
| 2019 | 937.58 | 972.51 | 949.42 | 973.65 | 963.69 | 1058.90 | 977.95 | 1009.23 | 1075.36 | 1026.38 | 1052.90 | 1087.27 | 1006.63 |
| **Professional and Business Services** | | | | | | | | | | | | | |
| 2015 | 869.42 | 893.84 | 885.29 | 855.91 | 834.85 | 848.10 | 828.98 | 848.26 | 816.27 | 835.38 | 857.96 | 840.14 | 852.50 |
| 2016 | 857.65 | 838.63 | 831.62 | 835.39 | 842.30 | 816.73 | 828.26 | 808.36 | 825.92 | 851.74 | 838.14 | 848.39 | 835.86 |
| 2017 | 865.80 | 845.21 | 844.61 | 846.77 | 809.43 | 808.04 | 827.67 | 815.36 | 832.05 | 855.23 | 842.66 | 850.87 | 836.68 |
| 2018 | 838.62 | 843.59 | 826.92 | 844.00 | 837.36 | 837.36 | 849.75 | 836.74 | 859.66 | 852.95 | 848.72 | 860.61 | 844.31 |
| 2019 | 838.01 | 862.00 | 856.26 | 875.06 | 860.27 | 885.72 | 863.50 | 868.32 | 883.74 | 857.95 | 875.68 | 905.65 | 870.12 |
| **Education and Health Services** | | | | | | | | | | | | | |
| 2015 | 765.26 | 780.56 | 775.89 | 774.01 | 772.23 | 771.54 | 784.45 | 795.33 | 776.50 | 772.33 | 786.04 | 756.90 | 776.16 |
| 2016 | 768.06 | 770.23 | 771.18 | 785.13 | 780.53 | 774.76 | 809.82 | 790.36 | 813.94 | 824.41 | 802.55 | 802.55 | 790.89 |
| 2017 | 818.88 | 806.27 | 809.82 | 851.53 | 823.88 | 833.83 | 867.98 | 843.53 | 851.54 | 851.55 | 844.94 | 837.31 | 836.27 |
| 2018 | 838.25 | 834.54 | 826.63 | 839.65 | 822.14 | 841.81 | 887.81 | 861.67 | 884.94 | 884.62 | 860.65 | 873.30 | 853.65 |
| 2019 | 862.00 | 856.05 | 842.35 | 840.01 | 830.42 | 834.46 | 823.88 | 816.70 | 825.26 | 821.14 | 831.09 | 841.46 | 835.94 |
| **Leisure and Hospitality** | | | | | | | | | | | | | |
| 2015 | 291.56 | 302.90 | 307.18 | 300.31 | 299.26 | 308.46 | 302.25 | 312.17 | 317.33 | 313.56 | 319.12 | 321.65 | 308.50 |
| 2016 | 315.24 | 330.19 | 327.50 | 325.78 | 337.95 | 325.95 | 334.28 | 334.46 | 325.26 | 340.16 | 335.76 | 334.05 | 331.06 |
| 2017 | 326.75 | 335.66 | 337.43 | 342.29 | 338.98 | 338.35 | 335.89 | 330.91 | 333.79 | 336.22 | 334.22 | 334.54 | 335.59 |
| 2018 | 318.77 | 327.14 | 334.96 | 337.22 | 330.91 | 333.66 | 322.71 | 336.76 | 337.19 | 335.39 | 333.96 | 345.77 | 333.30 |
| 2019 | 329.87 | 340.56 | 334.08 | 337.74 | 339.56 | 344.16 | 334.60 | 343.63 | 337.47 | 341.39 | 346.58 | 350.43 | 340.34 |

# OREGON
### *At a Glance*

Population:
  2010 census: 3,831,074
  2019 estimate: 4,217,737

Percent change in population:
  2010–2019: 10.1%

Percent change in total nonfarm employment:
  2011–2019: 19.8%

Industry with the largest growth in employment, 2011–2019 (percent):
  Construction, 58.7%

Industry with the largest decline or smallest growth in employment, 2011–2019 (percent):
  Government, 1.3%

Civilian labor force:
  2010: 1,984,039
  2019: 2,104,069

Unemployment rate and rank among states (highest to lowest):
  2010: 10.6%, 8th
  2019: 3.7%, 19th

Over-the-year change in unemployment rates:
  2017–2018: 0.0%
  2018–2019: -0.4%

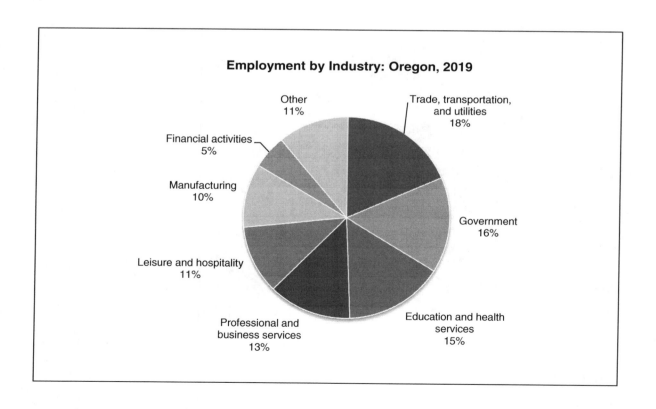

**Employment by Industry: Oregon, 2019**

- Other 11%
- Trade, transportation, and utilities 18%
- Financial activities 5%
- Government 16%
- Manufacturing 10%
- Education and health services 15%
- Leisure and hospitality 11%
- Professional and business services 13%

# 1. Employment by Industry: Oregon, 2011–2019

(Numbers in thousands, not seasonally adjusted)

| Industry and year | January | February | March | April | May | June | July | August | September | October | November | December | Annual average |
|---|---|---|---|---|---|---|---|---|---|---|---|---|---|
| **Total Nonfarm** | | | | | | | | | | | | | |
| 2011 | 1,583.4 | 1,596.2 | 1,603.1 | 1,617.8 | 1,624.7 | 1,634.9 | 1,611.1 | 1,614.8 | 1,628.4 | 1,640.9 | 1,642.3 | 1,638.9 | 1,619.7 |
| 2012 | 1,599.7 | 1,612.8 | 1,620.1 | 1,632.1 | 1,646.0 | 1,654.5 | 1,632.1 | 1,639.4 | 1,649.1 | 1,665.7 | 1,666.1 | 1,661.3 | 1,639.9 |
| 2013 | 1,622.2 | 1,639.2 | 1,647.9 | 1,664.7 | 1,679.7 | 1,686.6 | 1,666.4 | 1,674.6 | 1,689.5 | 1,704.3 | 1,709.4 | 1,705.5 | 1,674.2 |
| 2014 | 1,673.1 | 1,681.3 | 1,693.8 | 1,710.5 | 1,724.8 | 1,734.3 | 1,714.0 | 1,722.9 | 1,738.1 | 1,753.7 | 1,758.3 | 1,759.1 | 1,722.0 |
| | | | | | | | | | | | | | |
| 2015 | 1,725.5 | 1,740.7 | 1,750.2 | 1,772.0 | 1,786.2 | 1,797.6 | 1,776.4 | 1,781.6 | 1,794.3 | 1,813.4 | 1,817.0 | 1,817.3 | 1,781.0 |
| 2016 | 1,782.5 | 1,801.7 | 1,811.5 | 1,827.9 | 1,837.9 | 1,846.9 | 1,825.3 | 1,833.0 | 1,847.0 | 1,861.4 | 1,867.9 | 1,860.5 | 1,833.6 |
| 2017 | 1,815.0 | 1,842.6 | 1,853.8 | 1,871.6 | 1,882.5 | 1,896.9 | 1,871.6 | 1,876.2 | 1,886.8 | 1,899.6 | 1,905.3 | 1,902.1 | 1,875.3 |
| 2018 | 1,871.3 | 1,886.2 | 1,895.1 | 1,905.3 | 1,918.4 | 1,928.7 | 1,900.9 | 1,908.3 | 1,920.6 | 1,936.3 | 1,943.4 | 1,937.9 | 1,912.7 |
| 2019 | 1,908.9 | 1,913.3 | 1,923.0 | 1,935.6 | 1,948.4 | 1,955.6 | 1,931.6 | 1,940.2 | 1,945.3 | 1,960.9 | 1,962.8 | 1,960.8 | 1,940.5 |
| | | | | | | | | | | | | | |
| **Total Private** | | | | | | | | | | | | | |
| 2011 | 1,283.9 | 1,292.7 | 1,299.3 | 1,313.3 | 1,317.8 | 1,327.7 | 1,339.2 | 1,345.3 | 1,349.4 | 1,343.7 | 1,342.4 | 1,341.9 | 1,324.7 |
| 2012 | 1,307.2 | 1,315.1 | 1,321.7 | 1,334.3 | 1,344.5 | 1,353.3 | 1,363.5 | 1,372.1 | 1,371.0 | 1,370.2 | 1,367.9 | 1,366.4 | 1,348.9 |
| 2013 | 1,332.4 | 1,343.7 | 1,352.3 | 1,369.2 | 1,380.9 | 1,388.7 | 1,401.9 | 1,410.7 | 1,412.5 | 1,410.0 | 1,411.6 | 1,409.3 | 1,385.3 |
| 2014 | 1,380.5 | 1,384.4 | 1,396.1 | 1,411.2 | 1,422.2 | 1,431.2 | 1,442.6 | 1,451.8 | 1,454.8 | 1,452.2 | 1,453.7 | 1,455.9 | 1,428.1 |
| | | | | | | | | | | | | | |
| 2015 | 1,425.8 | 1,436.3 | 1,444.4 | 1,462.1 | 1,473.2 | 1,484.0 | 1,499.0 | 1,505.4 | 1,506.3 | 1,506.5 | 1,506.8 | 1,507.8 | 1,479.8 |
| 2016 | 1,477.0 | 1,491.0 | 1,499.1 | 1,514.9 | 1,522.1 | 1,530.1 | 1,541.2 | 1,550.7 | 1,551.0 | 1,547.9 | 1,550.9 | 1,546.6 | 1,526.9 |
| 2017 | 1,508.1 | 1,527.6 | 1,536.4 | 1,554.6 | 1,562.9 | 1,576.2 | 1,583.0 | 1,588.6 | 1,588.0 | 1,585.0 | 1,588.4 | 1,587.2 | 1,565.5 |
| 2018 | 1,577.4 | 1,586.6 | 1,594.4 | 1,604.5 | 1,614.8 | 1,624.1 | 1,630.6 | 1,638.1 | 1,634.1 | 1,635.2 | 1,639.2 | 1,635.9 | 1,617.9 |
| 2019 | 1,610.6 | 1,611.5 | 1,618.9 | 1,631.0 | 1,640.6 | 1,646.9 | 1,656.7 | 1,663.8 | 1,655.4 | 1,654.4 | 1,655.4 | 1,654.8 | 1,641.7 |
| | | | | | | | | | | | | | |
| **Goods Producing** | | | | | | | | | | | | | |
| 2011 | 230.7 | 232.6 | 234.3 | 238.3 | 240.6 | 244.9 | 251.2 | 254.6 | 253.3 | 250.3 | 246.5 | 244.1 | 243.5 |
| 2012 | 238.0 | 239.0 | 239.6 | 242.2 | 246.8 | 251.0 | 257.4 | 260.6 | 257.0 | 255.7 | 249.6 | 246.3 | 248.6 |
| 2013 | 241.7 | 243.8 | 245.7 | 249.8 | 254.0 | 258.2 | 264.5 | 267.0 | 265.6 | 265.1 | 261.5 | 258.9 | 256.3 |
| 2014 | 256.3 | 256.0 | 258.5 | 261.7 | 265.5 | 269.0 | 274.4 | 276.7 | 275.2 | 272.5 | 269.4 | 268.1 | 266.9 |
| | | | | | | | | | | | | | |
| 2015 | 264.9 | 266.2 | 268.1 | 270.9 | 274.4 | 279.1 | 285.3 | 286.3 | 284.9 | 283.3 | 279.8 | 278.2 | 276.8 |
| 2016 | 274.6 | 277.6 | 279.2 | 281.7 | 284.6 | 287.7 | 291.8 | 294.7 | 292.1 | 291.1 | 288.2 | 285.6 | 285.7 |
| 2017 | 278.2 | 282.5 | 285.0 | 289.5 | 293.3 | 298.5 | 303.0 | 304.9 | 302.4 | 302.4 | 299.8 | 299.1 | 294.9 |
| 2018 | 295.4 | 298.1 | 299.7 | 302.1 | 306.1 | 310.4 | 316.1 | 316.8 | 314.1 | 313.8 | 311.5 | 309.9 | 307.8 |
| 2019 | 306.4 | 306.1 | 308.5 | 310.5 | 314.4 | 317.1 | 321.5 | 322.5 | 318.1 | 314.3 | 313.7 | 309.4 | 313.5 |
| | | | | | | | | | | | | | |
| **Service-Providing** | | | | | | | | | | | | | |
| 2011 | 1,352.7 | 1,363.6 | 1,368.8 | 1,379.5 | 1,384.1 | 1,390.0 | 1,359.9 | 1,360.2 | 1,375.1 | 1,390.6 | 1,395.8 | 1,394.8 | 1,376.3 |
| 2012 | 1,361.7 | 1,373.8 | 1,380.5 | 1,389.9 | 1,399.2 | 1,403.5 | 1,374.7 | 1,378.8 | 1,392.1 | 1,410.0 | 1,416.5 | 1,415.0 | 1,391.3 |
| 2013 | 1,380.5 | 1,395.4 | 1,402.2 | 1,414.9 | 1,425.7 | 1,428.4 | 1,401.9 | 1,407.6 | 1,423.9 | 1,439.2 | 1,447.9 | 1,446.6 | 1,417.9 |
| 2014 | 1,416.8 | 1,425.3 | 1,435.3 | 1,448.8 | 1,459.3 | 1,465.3 | 1,439.6 | 1,446.2 | 1,462.9 | 1,481.2 | 1,488.9 | 1,491.0 | 1,455.1 |
| | | | | | | | | | | | | | |
| 2015 | 1,460.6 | 1,474.5 | 1,482.1 | 1,501.1 | 1,511.8 | 1,518.5 | 1,491.1 | 1,495.3 | 1,509.4 | 1,530.1 | 1,537.2 | 1,539.1 | 1,504.2 |
| 2016 | 1,507.9 | 1,524.1 | 1,532.3 | 1,546.2 | 1,553.3 | 1,559.2 | 1,533.5 | 1,538.3 | 1,554.9 | 1,570.3 | 1,579.7 | 1,574.9 | 1,547.9 |
| 2017 | 1,536.8 | 1,560.1 | 1,568.8 | 1,582.1 | 1,589.2 | 1,598.4 | 1,568.6 | 1,571.3 | 1,584.4 | 1,597.2 | 1,605.5 | 1,603.0 | 1,580.5 |
| 2018 | 1,575.9 | 1,588.1 | 1,595.4 | 1,603.2 | 1,612.3 | 1,618.3 | 1,584.8 | 1,591.5 | 1,606.5 | 1,622.5 | 1,631.9 | 1,628.0 | 1,604.9 |
| 2019 | 1,602.5 | 1,607.2 | 1,614.5 | 1,625.1 | 1,634.0 | 1,638.5 | 1,610.1 | 1,617.7 | 1,627.2 | 1,646.6 | 1,649.1 | 1,651.4 | 1,627.0 |
| | | | | | | | | | | | | | |
| **Mining and Logging** | | | | | | | | | | | | | |
| 2011 | 5.9 | 6.1 | 6.1 | 6.2 | 6.4 | 6.6 | 7.0 | 7.1 | 7.2 | 7.1 | 7.0 | 6.9 | 6.6 |
| 2012 | 6.3 | 6.4 | 6.3 | 6.4 | 6.7 | 7.0 | 7.1 | 7.3 | 7.1 | 7.2 | 7.0 | 6.9 | 6.8 |
| 2013 | 6.5 | 6.6 | 6.6 | 6.8 | 7.1 | 7.3 | 7.5 | 7.6 | 7.5 | 7.4 | 7.3 | 7.1 | 7.1 |
| 2014 | 7.0 | 7.0 | 6.9 | 7.0 | 7.1 | 7.3 | 7.5 | 7.6 | 7.4 | 7.3 | 7.3 | 7.1 | 7.2 |
| | | | | | | | | | | | | | |
| 2015 | 7.0 | 7.0 | 7.0 | 7.0 | 7.3 | 7.4 | 7.5 | 7.3 | 7.3 | 7.4 | 7.2 | 7.1 | 7.2 |
| 2016 | 7.0 | 7.0 | 6.9 | 6.9 | 7.2 | 7.2 | 7.3 | 7.4 | 7.3 | 7.2 | 7.1 | 7.0 | 7.1 |
| 2017 | 6.6 | 6.7 | 6.6 | 6.8 | 6.9 | 7.1 | 7.3 | 7.3 | 7.1 | 7.2 | 7.2 | 7.2 | 7.0 |
| 2018 | 7.0 | 7.1 | 7.1 | 7.1 | 7.3 | 7.3 | 7.4 | 7.4 | 7.3 | 7.4 | 7.2 | 7.1 | 7.2 |
| 2019 | 6.9 | 6.8 | 6.7 | 6.8 | 7.0 | 7.0 | 7.1 | 7.1 | 7.0 | 7.0 | 6.9 | 6.6 | 6.9 |
| | | | | | | | | | | | | | |
| **Construction** | | | | | | | | | | | | | |
| 2011 | 62.1 | 62.9 | 63.6 | 66.4 | 67.8 | 70.0 | 72.4 | 73.5 | 73.6 | 72.2 | 70.2 | 68.6 | 68.6 |
| 2012 | 65.0 | 65.4 | 65.4 | 67.1 | 69.6 | 70.9 | 73.9 | 75.7 | 74.0 | 73.1 | 70.0 | 67.9 | 69.8 |
| 2013 | 64.9 | 66.2 | 67.9 | 70.6 | 73.6 | 75.2 | 78.4 | 79.8 | 79.2 | 79.6 | 78.2 | 76.3 | 74.2 |
| 2014 | 74.9 | 74.5 | 76.3 | 78.2 | 80.5 | 81.6 | 83.9 | 84.8 | 84.2 | 82.2 | 80.4 | 79.2 | 80.1 |
| | | | | | | | | | | | | | |
| 2015 | 77.3 | 77.7 | 78.7 | 80.0 | 81.7 | 83.8 | 86.6 | 87.8 | 87.2 | 87.8 | 85.9 | 84.6 | 83.3 |
| 2016 | 82.1 | 84.5 | 85.5 | 88.0 | 89.7 | 91.2 | 93.8 | 95.4 | 95.0 | 94.8 | 93.4 | 91.6 | 90.4 |
| 2017 | 87.2 | 90.2 | 92.1 | 94.9 | 97.2 | 99.7 | 102.2 | 103.6 | 103.1 | 102.8 | 101.1 | 100.5 | 97.9 |
| 2018 | 98.2 | 99.7 | 100.9 | 102.5 | 105.1 | 106.8 | 109.3 | 110.6 | 109.2 | 109.1 | 107.8 | 106.1 | 105.4 |
| 2019 | 103.6 | 103.0 | 105.0 | 106.6 | 109.0 | 110.6 | 113.1 | 114.5 | 112.4 | 110.8 | 110.6 | 107.6 | 108.9 |

## 1. Employment by Industry: Oregon, 2011–2019—*Continued*

(Numbers in thousands, not seasonally adjusted)

| Industry and year | January | February | March | April | May | June | July | August | September | October | November | December | Annual average |
|---|---|---|---|---|---|---|---|---|---|---|---|---|---|
| **Manufacturing** | | | | | | | | | | | | | |
| 2011 | 162.7 | 163.6 | 164.6 | 165.7 | 166.4 | 168.3 | 171.8 | 174.0 | 172.5 | 171.0 | 169.3 | 168.6 | 168.2 |
| 2012 | 166.7 | 167.2 | 167.9 | 168.7 | 170.5 | 173.1 | 176.4 | 177.6 | 175.9 | 175.4 | 172.6 | 171.5 | 172.0 |
| 2013 | 170.3 | 171.0 | 171.2 | 172.4 | 173.3 | 175.7 | 178.6 | 179.6 | 178.9 | 178.1 | 176.0 | 175.5 | 175.1 |
| 2014 | 174.4 | 174.5 | 175.3 | 176.5 | 177.9 | 180.1 | 183.0 | 184.3 | 183.6 | 183.0 | 181.7 | 181.8 | 179.7 |
| 2015 | 180.6 | 181.5 | 182.4 | 183.9 | 185.4 | 187.9 | 191.2 | 191.2 | 190.4 | 188.1 | 186.7 | 186.5 | 186.3 |
| 2016 | 185.5 | 186.1 | 186.8 | 186.8 | 187.7 | 189.3 | 190.7 | 191.9 | 189.8 | 189.1 | 187.7 | 187.0 | 188.2 |
| 2017 | 184.4 | 185.6 | 186.3 | 187.8 | 189.2 | 191.7 | 193.5 | 194.0 | 192.2 | 192.4 | 191.5 | 191.4 | 190.0 |
| 2018 | 190.2 | 191.3 | 191.7 | 192.5 | 193.7 | 196.3 | 199.4 | 198.8 | 197.6 | 197.3 | 196.5 | 196.7 | 195.2 |
| 2019 | 195.9 | 196.3 | 196.8 | 197.1 | 198.4 | 199.5 | 201.3 | 200.9 | 198.7 | 196.5 | 196.2 | 195.2 | 197.7 |
| **Trade, Transportation, and Utilities** | | | | | | | | | | | | | |
| 2011 | 301.4 | 299.3 | 299.7 | 302.0 | 303.7 | 305.5 | 307.1 | 307.8 | 309.0 | 309.8 | 315.4 | 317.4 | 306.5 |
| 2012 | 305.0 | 302.5 | 303.3 | 305.2 | 308.2 | 310.7 | 310.6 | 312.3 | 313.1 | 314.5 | 320.8 | 322.9 | 310.8 |
| 2013 | 310.7 | 309.9 | 310.3 | 313.1 | 316.0 | 317.4 | 319.5 | 322.0 | 323.0 | 323.3 | 329.5 | 331.4 | 318.8 |
| 2014 | 319.7 | 317.1 | 317.5 | 319.9 | 322.9 | 324.6 | 326.6 | 329.2 | 329.9 | 331.6 | 337.7 | 341.4 | 326.5 |
| 2015 | 328.6 | 326.9 | 327.9 | 330.5 | 333.2 | 335.6 | 337.3 | 339.3 | 339.7 | 340.8 | 345.7 | 348.7 | 336.2 |
| 2016 | 335.2 | 334.1 | 334.8 | 336.7 | 338.4 | 340.4 | 342.5 | 345.3 | 344.8 | 345.5 | 352.8 | 354.3 | 342.1 |
| 2017 | 343.8 | 342.4 | 342.7 | 344.3 | 345.9 | 348.0 | 349.2 | 350.7 | 350.9 | 351.4 | 358.6 | 360.2 | 349.0 |
| 2018 | 348.5 | 345.1 | 345.4 | 346.8 | 349.7 | 351.1 | 351.6 | 354.2 | 354.9 | 356.3 | 364.5 | 365.0 | 352.8 |
| 2019 | 354.6 | 349.6 | 349.6 | 351.0 | 353.0 | 354.0 | 356.4 | 357.7 | 358.2 | 360.2 | 363.3 | 367.4 | 356.3 |
| **Wholesale Trade** | | | | | | | | | | | | | |
| 2011 | 65.4 | 65.8 | 66.0 | 66.5 | 66.9 | 66.9 | 67.3 | 67.4 | 67.2 | 67.4 | 67.1 | 66.9 | 66.7 |
| 2012 | 66.0 | 66.5 | 66.7 | 67.5 | 68.1 | 67.9 | 68.4 | 68.7 | 68.6 | 68.7 | 68.5 | 68.4 | 67.8 |
| 2013 | 68.9 | 69.5 | 69.3 | 70.0 | 70.3 | 70.2 | 71.1 | 71.3 | 71.3 | 71.1 | 71.3 | 71.2 | 70.5 |
| 2014 | 70.6 | 70.8 | 70.7 | 70.9 | 70.9 | 71.2 | 71.7 | 71.9 | 72.0 | 72.1 | 72.0 | 72.1 | 71.4 |
| 2015 | 71.4 | 71.8 | 71.6 | 72.0 | 72.3 | 72.4 | 73.2 | 73.6 | 73.6 | 73.5 | 73.8 | 73.9 | 72.8 |
| 2016 | 72.7 | 73.2 | 73.2 | 73.7 | 73.6 | 73.8 | 74.3 | 74.8 | 74.4 | 74.3 | 74.5 | 74.5 | 73.9 |
| 2017 | 74.0 | 74.6 | 74.5 | 74.9 | 75.2 | 75.3 | 75.3 | 75.2 | 75.2 | 75.1 | 75.2 | 75.3 | 75.0 |
| 2018 | 74.4 | 74.8 | 74.7 | 75.0 | 75.5 | 75.7 | 76.0 | 76.4 | 76.2 | 76.0 | 76.3 | 76.6 | 75.6 |
| 2019 | 75.7 | 76.1 | 76.0 | 76.5 | 76.7 | 76.6 | 77.0 | 76.8 | 76.4 | 76.9 | 76.2 | 76.7 | 76.5 |
| **Retail Trade** | | | | | | | | | | | | | |
| 2011 | 183.2 | 180.8 | 180.9 | 182.4 | 183.4 | 184.9 | 186.6 | 187.0 | 187.1 | 187.8 | 193.4 | 194.7 | 186.0 |
| 2012 | 185.2 | 182.1 | 182.5 | 183.8 | 185.9 | 188.1 | 188.9 | 189.7 | 189.3 | 190.8 | 196.9 | 198.1 | 188.4 |
| 2013 | 187.7 | 185.9 | 186.2 | 188.1 | 190.6 | 191.8 | 194.1 | 195.7 | 195.6 | 196.0 | 201.7 | 202.7 | 193.0 |
| 2014 | 192.6 | 189.8 | 190.6 | 192.5 | 195.1 | 196.3 | 198.7 | 200.2 | 200.1 | 201.2 | 206.9 | 208.7 | 197.7 |
| 2015 | 198.2 | 196.4 | 197.4 | 199.9 | 202.0 | 203.3 | 205.7 | 206.9 | 206.4 | 207.1 | 211.0 | 212.2 | 203.9 |
| 2016 | 202.3 | 201.3 | 201.8 | 202.8 | 204.3 | 205.9 | 208.2 | 209.8 | 208.8 | 209.7 | 214.6 | 214.5 | 207.0 |
| 2017 | 207.2 | 205.8 | 206.1 | 207.6 | 208.5 | 210.0 | 211.8 | 212.6 | 212.2 | 212.5 | 218.1 | 217.9 | 210.9 |
| 2018 | 209.8 | 207.0 | 207.2 | 208.1 | 210.0 | 210.8 | 212.1 | 213.3 | 212.4 | 212.7 | 217.4 | 216.3 | 211.4 |
| 2019 | 208.9 | 205.6 | 205.7 | 207.0 | 208.1 | 208.9 | 210.8 | 211.2 | 210.5 | 210.8 | 214.0 | 215.5 | 209.8 |
| **Transportation and Utilities** | | | | | | | | | | | | | |
| 2011 | 52.8 | 52.7 | 52.8 | 53.1 | 53.4 | 53.7 | 53.2 | 53.4 | 54.7 | 54.6 | 54.9 | 55.8 | 53.8 |
| 2012 | 53.8 | 53.9 | 54.1 | 53.9 | 54.2 | 54.7 | 53.3 | 53.9 | 55.2 | 55.0 | 55.4 | 56.4 | 54.5 |
| 2013 | 54.1 | 54.5 | 54.8 | 55.0 | 55.1 | 55.4 | 54.3 | 55.0 | 56.1 | 56.2 | 56.5 | 57.5 | 55.4 |
| 2014 | 56.5 | 56.5 | 56.2 | 56.5 | 56.9 | 57.1 | 56.2 | 57.1 | 57.8 | 58.3 | 58.8 | 60.6 | 57.4 |
| 2015 | 59.0 | 58.7 | 58.9 | 58.6 | 58.9 | 59.9 | 58.4 | 58.8 | 59.7 | 60.2 | 60.9 | 62.6 | 59.6 |
| 2016 | 60.2 | 59.6 | 59.8 | 60.2 | 60.5 | 60.7 | 60.0 | 60.7 | 61.6 | 61.5 | 63.7 | 65.3 | 61.2 |
| 2017 | 62.6 | 62.0 | 62.1 | 61.8 | 62.2 | 62.7 | 62.1 | 62.9 | 63.5 | 63.8 | 65.3 | 67.0 | 63.2 |
| 2018 | 64.3 | 63.3 | 63.5 | 63.7 | 64.2 | 64.6 | 63.5 | 64.5 | 66.3 | 67.6 | 70.8 | 72.1 | 65.7 |
| 2019 | 70.0 | 67.9 | 67.9 | 67.5 | 68.2 | 68.5 | 68.6 | 69.7 | 71.3 | 72.5 | 73.1 | 75.2 | 70.0 |
| **Information** | | | | | | | | | | | | | |
| 2011 | 31.5 | 31.6 | 32.0 | 31.8 | 31.6 | 31.6 | 31.8 | 31.9 | 31.7 | 31.5 | 31.7 | 31.6 | 31.7 |
| 2012 | 31.2 | 31.4 | 31.9 | 32.3 | 32.1 | 32.5 | 32.7 | 32.5 | 32.1 | 32.4 | 32.5 | 32.3 | 32.2 |
| 2013 | 32.0 | 32.1 | 32.2 | 32.2 | 32.0 | 31.9 | 32.0 | 32.3 | 32.5 | 32.6 | 32.7 | 32.7 | 32.3 |
| 2014 | 31.7 | 31.9 | 32.2 | 32.3 | 31.6 | 31.8 | 32.2 | 32.4 | 32.5 | 32.5 | 32.7 | 32.7 | 32.2 |
| 2015 | 32.1 | 32.4 | 32.5 | 32.7 | 32.5 | 32.7 | 33.5 | 33.9 | 33.4 | 32.9 | 33.2 | 33.4 | 32.9 |
| 2016 | 32.7 | 33.2 | 33.3 | 33.2 | 33.6 | 33.5 | 33.3 | 33.7 | 34.6 | 34.1 | 34.1 | 33.8 | 33.6 |
| 2017 | 33.6 | 34.1 | 33.8 | 35.0 | 34.5 | 34.5 | 34.2 | 34.5 | 34.6 | 34.1 | 34.2 | 33.7 | 34.2 |
| 2018 | 33.7 | 34.1 | 34.4 | 34.3 | 34.0 | 34.1 | 34.5 | 34.4 | 34.0 | 34.6 | 35.1 | 34.8 | 34.3 |
| 2019 | 34.4 | 34.3 | 34.1 | 34.6 | 35.4 | 35.1 | 35.1 | 35.4 | 34.9 | 35.5 | 36.3 | 35.8 | 35.1 |

# 1. Employment by Industry: Oregon, 2011–2019—*Continued*

(Numbers in thousands, not seasonally adjusted)

| Industry and year | January | February | March | April | May | June | July | August | September | October | November | December | Annual average |
|---|---|---|---|---|---|---|---|---|---|---|---|---|---|
| **Financial Activities** | | | | | | | | | | | | | |
| 2011 | 91.5 | 91.9 | 91.6 | 91.9 | 92.0 | 92.6 | 92.8 | 92.6 | 91.8 | 91.6 | 91.0 | 91.5 | 91.9 |
| 2012 | 89.7 | 89.8 | 89.5 | 90.1 | 90.1 | 90.5 | 91.8 | 91.9 | 91.2 | 91.4 | 91.1 | 91.3 | 90.7 |
| 2013 | 89.9 | 90.1 | 90.2 | 91.3 | 91.6 | 91.8 | 93.3 | 93.1 | 92.7 | 92.7 | 92.4 | 92.5 | 91.8 |
| 2014 | 90.7 | 90.6 | 90.5 | 91.6 | 92.3 | 93.0 | 93.8 | 94.2 | 93.8 | 93.8 | 93.6 | 94.2 | 92.7 |
| 2015 | 93.0 | 93.0 | 92.9 | 94.2 | 94.8 | 95.1 | 96.3 | 96.7 | 95.8 | 96.5 | 95.9 | 96.5 | 95.1 |
| 2016 | 94.7 | 94.6 | 94.6 | 95.9 | 96.5 | 97.2 | 98.5 | 99.1 | 98.5 | 98.4 | 98.6 | 99.0 | 97.1 |
| 2017 | 97.5 | 97.7 | 98.2 | 98.8 | 99.6 | 100.3 | 101.7 | 101.6 | 100.9 | 101.4 | 101.4 | 101.4 | 100.0 |
| 2018 | 100.4 | 100.7 | 100.9 | 101.6 | 102.2 | 102.5 | 103.8 | 103.9 | 102.8 | 102.9 | 102.5 | 102.5 | 102.2 |
| 2019 | 101.3 | 101.8 | 102.0 | 102.5 | 103.1 | 103.3 | 104.8 | 105.0 | 103.6 | 104.2 | 104.0 | 104.5 | 103.3 |
| **Professional and Business Services** | | | | | | | | | | | | | |
| 2011 | 187.0 | 189.3 | 190.7 | 194.0 | 193.5 | 195.2 | 199.5 | 200.2 | 200.5 | 199.8 | 199.3 | 199.5 | 195.7 |
| 2012 | 195.4 | 197.4 | 198.4 | 200.9 | 201.1 | 203.0 | 205.5 | 206.9 | 205.4 | 205.8 | 205.8 | 206.3 | 202.7 |
| 2013 | 199.5 | 201.6 | 204.0 | 207.3 | 208.2 | 210.5 | 214.4 | 215.9 | 214.9 | 214.7 | 214.4 | 215.0 | 210.0 |
| 2014 | 210.2 | 212.1 | 214.6 | 217.7 | 218.6 | 221.1 | 223.9 | 226.3 | 226.0 | 225.3 | 224.7 | 224.7 | 220.4 |
| 2015 | 219.5 | 221.5 | 223.2 | 227.4 | 228.4 | 230.1 | 233.5 | 234.8 | 234.3 | 235.7 | 235.1 | 235.4 | 229.9 |
| 2016 | 231.2 | 233.7 | 235.4 | 239.0 | 238.8 | 240.3 | 242.9 | 244.1 | 242.4 | 242.4 | 241.7 | 240.5 | 239.4 |
| 2017 | 235.1 | 239.2 | 240.7 | 244.3 | 244.2 | 247.5 | 248.0 | 248.6 | 247.8 | 247.5 | 246.6 | 246.0 | 244.6 |
| 2018 | 243.5 | 246.1 | 247.5 | 248.7 | 248.7 | 250.1 | 251.5 | 253.0 | 252.0 | 252.5 | 251.6 | 251.1 | 249.7 |
| 2019 | 248.2 | 249.0 | 249.9 | 252.9 | 253.3 | 254.4 | 256.3 | 257.3 | 255.0 | 256.1 | 255.5 | 254.8 | 253.6 |
| **Education and Health Services** | | | | | | | | | | | | | |
| 2011 | 229.8 | 233.4 | 234.6 | 235.1 | 233.8 | 230.1 | 225.8 | 226.4 | 233.4 | 237.5 | 238.7 | 238.1 | 233.1 |
| 2012 | 232.6 | 237.7 | 238.8 | 239.6 | 237.8 | 232.8 | 228.9 | 230.0 | 236.9 | 240.7 | 242.0 | 241.8 | 236.6 |
| 2013 | 236.9 | 242.3 | 242.8 | 244.2 | 243.0 | 237.8 | 233.4 | 234.7 | 241.6 | 246.2 | 247.3 | 246.5 | 241.4 |
| 2014 | 242.6 | 246.4 | 248.3 | 249.0 | 247.3 | 243.5 | 239.7 | 240.2 | 248.2 | 252.6 | 254.2 | 254.3 | 247.2 |
| 2015 | 249.9 | 255.6 | 256.0 | 258.1 | 256.5 | 253.0 | 249.7 | 250.6 | 258.0 | 262.3 | 264.3 | 263.5 | 256.5 |
| 2016 | 259.6 | 265.1 | 265.7 | 266.8 | 264.5 | 260.1 | 257.5 | 259.8 | 267.4 | 271.4 | 272.9 | 272.0 | 265.2 |
| 2017 | 265.7 | 273.3 | 274.4 | 275.2 | 273.9 | 269.2 | 265.3 | 266.9 | 274.3 | 277.5 | 279.3 | 278.7 | 272.8 |
| 2018 | 292.5 | 297.1 | 297.8 | 297.5 | 295.8 | 292.0 | 286.7 | 289.0 | 295.5 | 299.4 | 300.9 | 299.4 | 295.3 |
| 2019 | 297.4 | 302.3 | 303.3 | 303.4 | 300.9 | 296.8 | 293.3 | 296.6 | 302.2 | 304.1 | 306.2 | 304.9 | 301.0 |
| **Leisure and Hospitality** | | | | | | | | | | | | | |
| 2011 | 156.2 | 158.3 | 159.9 | 163.4 | 165.6 | 170.6 | 173.8 | 174.6 | 172.3 | 166.2 | 163.0 | 162.9 | 165.6 |
| 2012 | 159.1 | 160.7 | 163.4 | 166.7 | 170.4 | 174.9 | 178.7 | 180.1 | 177.7 | 171.9 | 168.9 | 168.5 | 170.1 |
| 2013 | 164.9 | 166.6 | 169.5 | 173.5 | 177.6 | 182.7 | 186.2 | 187.0 | 183.8 | 177.4 | 175.6 | 174.5 | 176.6 |
| 2014 | 171.6 | 172.5 | 176.2 | 180.3 | 184.5 | 188.3 | 192.2 | 193.1 | 189.4 | 184.1 | 181.7 | 181.1 | 182.9 |
| 2015 | 178.9 | 181.2 | 184.1 | 187.9 | 192.5 | 197.4 | 201.7 | 202.1 | 198.8 | 193.2 | 190.8 | 190.0 | 191.6 |
| 2016 | 187.4 | 190.2 | 193.2 | 197.7 | 201.4 | 206.3 | 210.4 | 209.4 | 206.5 | 200.2 | 198.0 | 197.6 | 199.9 |
| 2017 | 193.0 | 196.0 | 198.9 | 204.1 | 207.6 | 214.0 | 217.2 | 217.0 | 213.1 | 206.8 | 204.8 | 204.3 | 206.4 |
| 2018 | 200.3 | 201.8 | 204.8 | 209.1 | 213.3 | 218.6 | 221.2 | 221.8 | 216.5 | 211.1 | 208.7 | 209.2 | 211.4 |
| 2019 | 204.5 | 204.5 | 207.3 | 211.3 | 215.3 | 221.3 | 224.1 | 224.1 | 218.7 | 214.2 | 210.3 | 212.1 | 214.0 |
| **Other Services** | | | | | | | | | | | | | |
| 2011 | 55.8 | 56.3 | 56.5 | 56.8 | 57.0 | 57.2 | 57.2 | 57.2 | 57.4 | 57.0 | 56.8 | 56.8 | 56.8 |
| 2012 | 56.2 | 56.6 | 56.8 | 57.3 | 58.0 | 57.9 | 57.9 | 57.8 | 57.6 | 57.8 | 57.2 | 57.0 | 57.3 |
| 2013 | 56.8 | 57.3 | 57.6 | 57.8 | 58.5 | 58.4 | 58.6 | 58.7 | 58.4 | 58.0 | 58.2 | 57.8 | 58.0 |
| 2014 | 57.7 | 57.8 | 58.3 | 58.7 | 59.5 | 59.9 | 59.8 | 59.7 | 59.8 | 59.8 | 59.7 | 59.4 | 59.2 |
| 2015 | 58.9 | 59.5 | 59.7 | 60.4 | 60.9 | 61.0 | 61.7 | 61.7 | 61.4 | 61.8 | 62.0 | 62.1 | 60.9 |
| 2016 | 61.6 | 62.5 | 62.9 | 63.9 | 64.3 | 64.6 | 64.3 | 64.6 | 64.7 | 64.8 | 64.6 | 63.8 | 63.9 |
| 2017 | 61.2 | 62.4 | 62.7 | 63.4 | 63.9 | 64.2 | 64.4 | 64.4 | 64.0 | 63.9 | 63.7 | 63.8 | 63.5 |
| 2018 | 63.1 | 63.6 | 63.9 | 64.4 | 65.0 | 65.3 | 65.2 | 65.0 | 64.3 | 64.6 | 64.4 | 64.0 | 64.4 |
| 2019 | 63.8 | 63.9 | 64.2 | 64.8 | 65.2 | 64.9 | 65.2 | 65.2 | 64.7 | 65.8 | 66.1 | 65.9 | 65.0 |
| **Government** | | | | | | | | | | | | | |
| 2011 | 299.5 | 303.5 | 303.8 | 304.5 | 306.9 | 307.2 | 271.9 | 269.5 | 279.0 | 297.2 | 299.9 | 297.0 | 295.0 |
| 2012 | 292.5 | 297.7 | 298.4 | 297.8 | 301.5 | 301.2 | 268.6 | 267.3 | 278.1 | 295.5 | 298.2 | 294.9 | 291.0 |
| 2013 | 289.8 | 295.5 | 295.6 | 295.5 | 298.8 | 297.9 | 264.5 | 263.9 | 277.0 | 294.3 | 297.8 | 296.2 | 288.9 |
| 2014 | 292.6 | 296.9 | 297.7 | 299.3 | 302.6 | 303.1 | 271.4 | 271.1 | 283.3 | 301.5 | 304.6 | 303.2 | 293.9 |
| 2015 | 299.7 | 304.4 | 305.8 | 309.9 | 313.0 | 313.6 | 277.4 | 276.2 | 288.0 | 306.9 | 310.2 | 309.5 | 301.2 |
| 2016 | 305.5 | 310.7 | 312.4 | 313.0 | 315.8 | 316.8 | 284.1 | 282.3 | 296.0 | 313.5 | 317.0 | 313.9 | 306.8 |
| 2017 | 306.9 | 315.0 | 317.4 | 317.0 | 319.6 | 320.7 | 288.6 | 287.6 | 298.8 | 314.6 | 316.9 | 314.9 | 309.8 |
| 2018 | 293.9 | 299.6 | 300.7 | 300.8 | 303.6 | 304.6 | 270.3 | 270.2 | 286.5 | 301.1 | 304.2 | 302.0 | 294.8 |
| 2019 | 298.3 | 301.8 | 304.1 | 304.6 | 307.8 | 308.7 | 274.9 | 276.4 | 289.9 | 306.5 | 307.4 | 306.0 | 298.9 |

## 2. Average Weekly Hours by Selected Industry: Oregon, 2015–2019

(Not seasonally adjusted)

| Industry and year | January | February | March | April | May | June | July | August | September | October | November | December | Annual average |
|---|---|---|---|---|---|---|---|---|---|---|---|---|---|
| **Total Private** | | | | | | | | | | | | | |
| 2015 | 33.3 | 34.6 | 34.4 | 33.6 | 33.7 | 34.0 | 34.0 | 35.0 | 33.8 | 33.7 | 34.5 | 33.5 | 34.0 |
| 2016 | 33.4 | 33.7 | 33.5 | 33.9 | 34.7 | 34.2 | 34.4 | 34.4 | 34.3 | 35.1 | 34.0 | 33.3 | 34.1 |
| 2017 | 33.5 | 33.9 | 33.7 | 34.9 | 33.7 | 34.0 | 34.7 | 34.2 | 34.2 | 34.9 | 33.8 | 33.8 | 34.1 |
| 2018 | 33.3 | 33.9 | 33.6 | 34.7 | 33.9 | 34.0 | 34.7 | 34.2 | 35.0 | 33.9 | 33.8 | 34.4 | 34.1 |
| 2019 | 33.2 | 33.4 | 33.5 | 33.8 | 33.8 | 34.9 | 34.0 | 34.3 | 34.9 | 33.9 | 33.9 | 34.6 | 34.0 |
| **Goods-Producing** | | | | | | | | | | | | | |
| 2015 | 38.9 | 39.7 | 39.4 | 38.8 | 38.6 | 39.2 | 39.2 | 39.6 | 38.1 | 38.7 | 38.9 | 38.5 | 39.0 |
| 2016 | 38.0 | 38.0 | 38.1 | 38.4 | 39.2 | 38.9 | 38.7 | 38.9 | 39.3 | 39.4 | 38.6 | 37.3 | 38.6 |
| 2017 | 36.8 | 38.6 | 38.6 | 39.3 | 38.7 | 39.3 | 39.5 | 39.4 | 39.5 | 39.9 | 38.8 | 38.5 | 38.9 |
| 2018 | 37.6 | 38.1 | 38.1 | 38.8 | 38.6 | 38.6 | 38.7 | 39.0 | 39.4 | 38.7 | 38.3 | 38.9 | 38.6 |
| 2019 | 37.9 | 37.4 | 37.8 | 38.0 | 38.4 | 38.8 | 38.1 | 39.0 | 38.9 | 38.8 | 38.6 | 38.8 | 38.4 |
| **Construction** | | | | | | | | | | | | | |
| 2015 | 36.4 | 36.9 | 36.3 | 36.3 | 35.7 | 37.2 | 37.2 | 37.5 | 35.2 | 36.4 | 35.7 | 35.4 | 36.3 |
| 2016 | 35.6 | 35.6 | 35.6 | 36.9 | 36.8 | 37.5 | 37.2 | 37.6 | 37.6 | 37.2 | 36.3 | 35.0 | 36.6 |
| 2017 | 33.8 | 37.0 | 37.4 | 37.9 | 37.5 | 38.8 | 39.1 | 38.9 | 38.9 | 39.0 | 37.1 | 37.3 | 37.8 |
| 2018 | 36.1 | 36.2 | 36.5 | 37.5 | 38.0 | 38.0 | 38.1 | 39.0 | 38.5 | 38.0 | 36.7 | 37.5 | 37.5 |
| 2019 | 36.9 | 35.7 | 36.8 | 37.2 | 38.2 | 38.7 | 38.4 | 39.6 | 38.3 | 38.9 | 37.9 | 37.3 | 37.9 |
| **Manufacturing** | | | | | | | | | | | | | |
| 2015 | 40.0 | 40.5 | 40.4 | 39.5 | 39.5 | 39.8 | 39.7 | 40.3 | 39.2 | 39.3 | 40.1 | 39.8 | 39.8 |
| 2016 | 39.0 | 38.9 | 39.1 | 39.0 | 40.2 | 39.4 | 39.2 | 39.3 | 39.9 | 40.4 | 39.7 | 39.2 | 39.4 |
| 2017 | 39.1 | 39.8 | 39.7 | 40.4 | 39.7 | 39.8 | 40.1 | 39.9 | 40.1 | 40.5 | 39.8 | 39.3 | 39.9 |
| 2018 | 38.7 | 39.4 | 39.4 | 39.8 | 39.2 | 39.4 | 39.5 | 39.4 | 40.3 | 39.4 | 39.5 | 40.0 | 39.5 |
| 2019 | 38.8 | 38.5 | 38.6 | 38.6 | 38.7 | 39.0 | 37.8 | 38.5 | 39.2 | 38.6 | 38.8 | 39.5 | 38.7 |
| **Trade, Transportation, and Utilities** | | | | | | | | | | | | | |
| 2015 | 33.5 | 35.1 | 35.1 | 34.4 | 34.9 | 34.9 | 35.0 | 35.8 | 35.4 | 34.7 | 35.5 | 34.5 | 34.9 |
| 2016 | 34.2 | 34.5 | 34.7 | 35.4 | 35.9 | 35.3 | 35.6 | 35.5 | 35.4 | 36.1 | 34.9 | 34.8 | 35.2 |
| 2017 | 34.3 | 34.6 | 34.5 | 36.0 | 34.9 | 34.9 | 35.7 | 35.1 | 35.1 | 35.9 | 34.5 | 34.7 | 35.0 |
| 2018 | 34.2 | 35.3 | 34.8 | 35.6 | 35.3 | 35.2 | 35.7 | 35.1 | 35.6 | 34.8 | 34.7 | 35.4 | 35.1 |
| 2019 | 34.4 | 34.8 | 34.9 | 35.2 | 35.3 | 36.4 | 35.6 | 35.6 | 35.9 | 35.0 | 34.7 | 35.6 | 35.3 |
| **Financial Activities** | | | | | | | | | | | | | |
| 2015 | 35.7 | 37.1 | 36.5 | 35.6 | 35.3 | 35.4 | 35.4 | 36.9 | 36.2 | 36.2 | 37.0 | 36.4 | 36.1 |
| 2016 | 37.0 | 36.6 | 36.7 | 36.6 | 38.2 | 37.0 | 37.5 | 37.2 | 38.5 | 39.8 | 38.3 | 37.9 | 37.6 |
| 2017 | 38.4 | 37.7 | 38.7 | 38.0 | 37.1 | 37.4 | 38.1 | 37.4 | 38.3 | 37.7 | 36.7 | 36.8 | 37.7 |
| 2018 | 36.4 | 37.6 | 37.3 | 39.2 | 37.4 | 37.5 | 37.5 | 37.0 | 38.3 | 36.8 | 37.0 | 37.6 | 37.5 |
| 2019 | 36.3 | 36.3 | 36.3 | 36.3 | 36.8 | 37.0 | 36.6 | 37.1 | 38.1 | 36.9 | 36.9 | 36.9 | 36.8 |
| **Professional and Business Services** | | | | | | | | | | | | | |
| 2015 | 34.2 | 35.5 | 35.3 | 34.6 | 34.4 | 35.2 | 35.0 | 36.0 | 34.4 | 34.7 | 35.8 | 34.4 | 35.0 |
| 2016 | 34.5 | 35.0 | 34.5 | 35.0 | 35.9 | 35.0 | 35.0 | 35.0 | 34.7 | 36.3 | 35.2 | 34.1 | 35.0 |
| 2017 | 35.0 | 35.5 | 35.2 | 36.9 | 35.5 | 35.9 | 36.7 | 35.7 | 35.9 | 37.1 | 36.2 | 36.2 | 36.0 |
| 2018 | 35.6 | 36.1 | 35.9 | 37.2 | 35.7 | 35.9 | 36.3 | 35.3 | 37.0 | 35.6 | 35.5 | 36.3 | 36.0 |
| 2019 | 34.7 | 35.0 | 35.1 | 35.4 | 35.2 | 36.9 | 35.0 | 35.6 | 36.9 | 35.6 | 35.7 | 36.7 | 35.7 |
| **Education and Health Services** | | | | | | | | | | | | | |
| 2015 | 32.1 | 33.5 | 33.1 | 32.4 | 32.6 | 32.6 | 32.4 | 33.7 | 32.9 | 32.9 | 34.0 | 33.2 | 33.0 |
| 2016 | 33.3 | 33.2 | 32.8 | 33.2 | 33.8 | 34.1 | 34.2 | 34.1 | 33.1 | 34.2 | 33.3 | 32.7 | 33.5 |
| 2017 | 33.4 | 33.3 | 32.7 | 33.9 | 32.5 | 32.5 | 33.3 | 33.0 | 32.7 | 33.3 | 32.5 | 32.9 | 33.0 |
| 2018 | 32.6 | 32.8 | 32.4 | 33.5 | 32.7 | 32.9 | 33.7 | 33.2 | 34.1 | 32.5 | 32.9 | 33.6 | 33.1 |
| 2019 | 32.5 | 32.5 | 32.4 | 32.7 | 32.7 | 33.6 | 33.2 | 33.0 | 33.8 | 33.0 | 33.2 | 33.9 | 33.0 |
| **Leisure and Hospitality** | | | | | | | | | | | | | |
| 2015 | 24.1 | 25.8 | 25.8 | 24.8 | 25.1 | 25.6 | 26.1 | 27.4 | 25.5 | 25.0 | 25.5 | 24.3 | 25.4 |
| 2016 | 24.0 | 25.0 | 24.3 | 24.8 | 25.7 | 25.1 | 25.9 | 26.6 | 25.8 | 26.3 | 24.7 | 24.2 | 25.2 |
| 2017 | 24.5 | 24.8 | 24.7 | 26.1 | 24.9 | 25.4 | 26.6 | 26.0 | 25.3 | 25.9 | 24.6 | 24.6 | 25.3 |
| 2018 | 24.5 | 24.7 | 24.9 | 25.8 | 24.9 | 25.1 | 26.5 | 25.8 | 25.9 | 24.8 | 24.3 | 24.4 | 25.1 |
| 2019 | 23.2 | 23.5 | 23.7 | 23.9 | 23.8 | 25.4 | 24.5 | 25.1 | 25.7 | 24.3 | 24.2 | 25.0 | 24.4 |
| **Other Services** | | | | | | | | | | | | | |
| 2015 | 28.4 | 30.1 | 28.9 | 28.5 | 28.6 | 29.1 | 29.0 | 29.8 | 28.2 | 28.3 | 28.8 | 26.7 | 28.7 |
| 2016 | 27.0 | 27.7 | 27.4 | 27.8 | 29.4 | 28.0 | 28.8 | 28.7 | 28.1 | 29.8 | 28.4 | 27.7 | 28.2 |
| 2017 | 28.4 | 29.0 | 28.3 | 30.0 | 28.9 | 29.0 | 30.5 | 28.9 | 29.3 | 30.1 | 28.7 | 28.8 | 29.2 |
| 2018 | 28.2 | 29.3 | 29.0 | 30.7 | 29.7 | 30.0 | 31.1 | 29.9 | 31.2 | 29.0 | 29.6 | 30.5 | 29.8 |
| 2019 | 29.2 | 30.5 | 30.1 | 30.4 | 30.0 | 31.1 | 29.7 | 30.4 | 30.0 | 29.0 | 28.7 | 29.3 | 29.9 |

## 3. Average Hourly Earnings by Selected Industry: Oregon, 2015–2019

(Dollars, not seasonally adjusted)

| Industry and year | January | February | March | April | May | June | July | August | September | October | November | December | Annual average |
|---|---|---|---|---|---|---|---|---|---|---|---|---|---|
| **Total Private** | | | | | | | | | | | | | |
| 2015 | 23.36 | 23.34 | 23.38 | 23.32 | 23.36 | 23.28 | 23.32 | 23.43 | 23.57 | 23.78 | 24.01 | 24.12 | 23.53 |
| 2016 | 24.29 | 24.35 | 24.23 | 24.62 | 24.66 | 24.39 | 24.56 | 24.53 | 25.00 | 25.24 | 25.20 | 25.54 | 24.72 |
| 2017 | 26.01 | 25.56 | 25.50 | 25.64 | 25.21 | 25.30 | 25.55 | 25.49 | 25.79 | 25.93 | 25.83 | 26.06 | 25.66 |
| 2018 | 25.95 | 25.83 | 25.83 | 26.04 | 25.90 | 26.01 | 26.27 | 26.21 | 26.53 | 26.50 | 26.56 | 26.98 | 26.22 |
| 2019 | 27.06 | 26.80 | 27.03 | 26.95 | 26.97 | 26.98 | 27.02 | 27.19 | 27.41 | 27.50 | 27.38 | 27.72 | 27.17 |
| **Goods-Producing** | | | | | | | | | | | | | |
| 2015 | 24.32 | 24.17 | 24.25 | 24.36 | 24.21 | 24.39 | 24.49 | 24.49 | 24.41 | 24.71 | 24.78 | 25.12 | 24.48 |
| 2016 | 25.20 | 25.16 | 25.13 | 25.36 | 25.45 | 25.29 | 25.43 | 25.45 | 25.74 | 25.76 | 25.82 | 26.19 | 25.50 |
| 2017 | 26.19 | 25.94 | 25.93 | 26.06 | 26.36 | 26.23 | 26.29 | 26.03 | 26.45 | 26.56 | 26.28 | 26.61 | 26.25 |
| 2018 | 26.62 | 26.31 | 26.68 | 26.92 | 26.84 | 26.80 | 27.22 | 27.29 | 27.42 | 27.69 | 27.65 | 28.39 | 27.16 |
| 2019 | 28.49 | 28.22 | 28.57 | 28.25 | 28.17 | 27.96 | 28.18 | 28.10 | 28.12 | 28.45 | 28.36 | 28.68 | 28.29 |
| **Construction** | | | | | | | | | | | | | |
| 2015 | 28.29 | 28.00 | 28.29 | 28.23 | 28.15 | 28.33 | 28.67 | 28.75 | 28.61 | 28.78 | 28.80 | 29.84 | 28.57 |
| 2016 | 29.57 | 29.23 | 29.35 | 29.51 | 29.68 | 29.39 | 29.61 | 29.88 | 29.85 | 29.91 | 30.19 | 30.08 | 29.70 |
| 2017 | 30.65 | 30.21 | 29.98 | 30.21 | 30.58 | 30.05 | 30.40 | 30.22 | 30.71 | 30.51 | 30.38 | 30.81 | 30.39 |
| 2018 | 30.51 | 30.35 | 30.32 | 30.29 | 29.85 | 29.83 | 30.82 | 30.68 | 30.27 | 30.78 | 30.45 | 31.34 | 30.46 |
| 2019 | 31.59 | 31.62 | 32.48 | 31.69 | 31.78 | 30.98 | 31.26 | 31.16 | 30.95 | 31.20 | 31.47 | 31.90 | 31.49 |
| **Manufacturing** | | | | | | | | | | | | | |
| 2015 | 22.86 | 22.81 | 22.78 | 22.97 | 22.77 | 22.81 | 22.75 | 22.65 | 22.68 | 22.94 | 23.07 | 23.10 | 22.85 |
| 2016 | 23.29 | 23.38 | 23.28 | 23.42 | 23.54 | 23.34 | 23.46 | 23.26 | 23.77 | 23.78 | 23.69 | 24.40 | 23.55 |
| 2017 | 24.19 | 23.88 | 23.92 | 24.03 | 24.25 | 24.27 | 24.16 | 23.86 | 24.16 | 24.51 | 24.25 | 24.41 | 24.16 |
| 2018 | 24.76 | 24.32 | 24.57 | 24.96 | 25.02 | 24.94 | 25.05 | 25.16 | 25.70 | 25.85 | 26.07 | 26.73 | 25.27 |
| 2019 | 26.75 | 26.39 | 26.47 | 26.42 | 26.10 | 26.19 | 26.37 | 26.22 | 26.50 | 26.85 | 26.65 | 27.07 | 26.50 |
| **Trade, Transportation, and Utilities** | | | | | | | | | | | | | |
| 2015 | 19.93 | 19.73 | 19.82 | 19.67 | 19.74 | 19.71 | 19.91 | 19.73 | 19.69 | 19.82 | 19.88 | 19.78 | 19.78 |
| 2016 | 20.31 | 20.29 | 20.36 | 21.25 | 21.65 | 21.23 | 21.84 | 21.74 | 21.98 | 22.32 | 22.21 | 22.21 | 21.47 |
| 2017 | 23.05 | 22.34 | 22.51 | 22.52 | 22.17 | 22.72 | 22.85 | 22.49 | 22.43 | 22.90 | 22.22 | 22.32 | 22.54 |
| 2018 | 21.94 | 22.17 | 22.09 | 22.39 | 22.30 | 22.34 | 22.61 | 22.32 | 22.72 | 22.53 | 22.27 | 22.44 | 22.35 |
| 2019 | 22.28 | 21.93 | 22.23 | 22.53 | 22.62 | 22.84 | 22.65 | 22.89 | 23.44 | 23.36 | 23.19 | 23.58 | 22.80 |
| **Financial Activities** | | | | | | | | | | | | | |
| 2015 | 27.39 | 27.90 | 27.92 | 27.74 | 27.87 | 27.95 | 27.48 | 27.98 | 27.59 | 27.81 | 28.00 | 28.45 | 27.84 |
| 2016 | 27.41 | 28.20 | 28.29 | 29.73 | 28.25 | 27.64 | 28.00 | 27.92 | 28.63 | 29.02 | 28.66 | 28.45 | 28.36 |
| 2017 | 29.35 | 28.64 | 28.52 | 30.17 | 28.70 | 29.81 | 30.58 | 31.71 | 31.24 | 31.35 | 31.43 | 31.70 | 30.27 |
| 2018 | 31.73 | 31.55 | 31.49 | 33.03 | 33.40 | 33.02 | 33.18 | 32.60 | 32.62 | 31.94 | 32.46 | 32.95 | 32.51 |
| 2019 | 32.20 | 31.50 | 31.95 | 33.07 | 33.41 | 34.16 | 33.85 | 34.75 | 34.67 | 34.47 | 33.46 | 35.08 | 33.57 |
| **Professional and Business Services** | | | | | | | | | | | | | |
| 2015 | 26.22 | 26.18 | 26.38 | 26.41 | 26.64 | 26.16 | 26.26 | 26.37 | 26.72 | 26.91 | 27.56 | 27.41 | 26.61 |
| 2016 | 27.57 | 27.85 | 27.73 | 27.80 | 27.97 | 27.71 | 27.33 | 27.49 | 28.20 | 28.54 | 28.12 | 29.03 | 27.95 |
| 2017 | 29.62 | 29.18 | 29.01 | 29.26 | 28.66 | 28.57 | 29.31 | 29.06 | 30.03 | 30.24 | 30.35 | 30.48 | 29.49 |
| 2018 | 30.87 | 30.35 | 30.31 | 30.64 | 30.43 | 30.74 | 31.05 | 31.16 | 31.64 | 31.40 | 31.77 | 32.26 | 31.06 |
| 2019 | 32.63 | 32.44 | 32.99 | 32.94 | 32.92 | 32.73 | 32.54 | 32.70 | 33.02 | 32.80 | 32.76 | 33.13 | 32.80 |
| **Education and Health Services** | | | | | | | | | | | | | |
| 2015 | 26.26 | 26.22 | 26.19 | 26.49 | 26.70 | 26.76 | 27.30 | 27.45 | 27.66 | 27.60 | 27.81 | 27.76 | 27.03 |
| 2016 | 27.92 | 27.99 | 27.97 | 28.20 | 28.04 | 28.09 | 28.60 | 28.41 | 29.11 | 29.15 | 29.05 | 29.44 | 28.50 |
| 2017 | 29.58 | 29.27 | 29.10 | 29.14 | 29.05 | 29.16 | 29.21 | 29.54 | 29.36 | 29.31 | 29.26 | 29.69 | 29.31 |
| 2018 | 29.28 | 29.08 | 28.99 | 28.87 | 28.81 | 28.85 | 29.07 | 28.96 | 28.87 | 28.98 | 28.99 | 29.28 | 29.00 |
| 2019 | 29.53 | 29.50 | 29.44 | 29.26 | 29.30 | 29.31 | 29.63 | 29.74 | 29.67 | 29.70 | 29.72 | 29.89 | 29.56 |
| **Leisure and Hospitality** | | | | | | | | | | | | | |
| 2015 | 14.03 | 14.10 | 14.01 | 14.27 | 14.20 | 13.97 | 13.93 | 14.02 | 14.40 | 14.58 | 14.63 | 14.70 | 14.23 |
| 2016 | 14.62 | 14.69 | 14.76 | 14.76 | 14.89 | 14.91 | 15.06 | 15.03 | 15.10 | 15.23 | 15.19 | 15.38 | 14.97 |
| 2017 | 15.36 | 15.31 | 15.44 | 15.54 | 15.53 | 15.38 | 15.70 | 15.62 | 15.79 | 15.91 | 16.08 | 16.23 | 15.66 |
| 2018 | 16.25 | 16.26 | 16.18 | 16.20 | 16.16 | 16.31 | 16.54 | 16.51 | 16.85 | 16.77 | 16.73 | 17.13 | 16.49 |
| 2019 | 16.93 | 16.89 | 17.02 | 16.92 | 16.91 | 16.88 | 17.08 | 17.11 | 17.20 | 17.47 | 17.42 | 17.77 | 17.14 |
| **Other Services** | | | | | | | | | | | | | |
| 2015 | 21.44 | 21.27 | 21.49 | 21.67 | 21.61 | 21.81 | 21.51 | 21.98 | 22.04 | 22.10 | 22.20 | 22.40 | 21.79 |
| 2016 | 22.47 | 21.96 | 22.13 | 22.23 | 21.98 | 22.27 | 22.15 | 22.34 | 22.75 | 22.53 | 22.35 | 22.73 | 22.32 |
| 2017 | 22.83 | 22.53 | 22.24 | 22.10 | 21.81 | 22.11 | 21.91 | 21.69 | 21.90 | 21.98 | 22.14 | 22.82 | 22.16 |
| 2018 | 22.74 | 22.78 | 22.83 | 22.68 | 21.83 | 22.64 | 23.04 | 23.11 | 23.10 | 23.38 | 23.38 | 23.08 | 22.88 |
| 2019 | 23.06 | 23.11 | 22.85 | 22.98 | 22.94 | 22.25 | 22.26 | 22.31 | 22.41 | 22.20 | 22.07 | 22.19 | 22.55 |

## 4. Average Weekly Earnings by Selected Industry: Oregon, 2015–2019

(Dollars, not seasonally adjusted)

| Industry and year | January | February | March | April | May | June | July | August | September | October | November | December | Annual average |
|---|---|---|---|---|---|---|---|---|---|---|---|---|---|
| **Total Private** | | | | | | | | | | | | | |
| 2015 | 777.89 | 807.56 | 804.27 | 783.55 | 787.23 | 791.52 | 792.88 | 820.05 | 796.67 | 801.39 | 828.35 | 808.02 | 800.02 |
| 2016 | 811.29 | 820.60 | 811.71 | 834.62 | 855.70 | 834.14 | 844.86 | 843.83 | 857.50 | 885.92 | 856.80 | 850.48 | 842.95 |
| 2017 | 871.34 | 866.48 | 859.35 | 894.84 | 849.58 | 860.20 | 886.59 | 871.76 | 882.02 | 904.96 | 873.05 | 880.83 | 875.01 |
| 2018 | 864.14 | 875.64 | 867.89 | 903.59 | 878.01 | 884.34 | 911.57 | 896.38 | 928.55 | 898.35 | 897.73 | 928.11 | 894.10 |
| 2019 | 898.39 | 895.12 | 905.51 | 910.91 | 911.59 | 941.60 | 918.68 | 932.62 | 956.61 | 932.25 | 928.18 | 959.11 | 923.78 |
| **Goods-Producing** | | | | | | | | | | | | | |
| 2015 | 946.05 | 959.55 | 955.45 | 945.17 | 934.51 | 956.09 | 960.01 | 969.80 | 930.02 | 956.28 | 963.94 | 967.12 | 954.72 |
| 2016 | 957.60 | 956.08 | 957.45 | 973.82 | 997.64 | 983.78 | 984.14 | 990.01 | 1,011.58 | 1,014.94 | 996.65 | 976.89 | 984.30 |
| 2017 | 963.79 | 1,001.28 | 1,000.90 | 1,024.16 | 1,020.13 | 1,030.84 | 1,038.46 | 1,025.58 | 1,044.78 | 1,059.74 | 1,019.66 | 1,024.49 | 1,021.13 |
| 2018 | 1,000.91 | 1,002.41 | 1,016.51 | 1,044.50 | 1,036.02 | 1,034.48 | 1,053.41 | 1,064.31 | 1,080.35 | 1,071.60 | 1,059.00 | 1,104.37 | 1,048.38 |
| 2019 | 1,079.77 | 1,055.43 | 1,079.95 | 1,073.50 | 1,081.73 | 1,084.85 | 1,073.66 | 1,095.90 | 1,093.87 | 1,103.86 | 1,094.70 | 1,112.78 | 1,086.34 |
| **Construction** | | | | | | | | | | | | | |
| 2015 | 1,029.76 | 1,033.20 | 1,026.93 | 1,024.75 | 1,004.96 | 1,053.88 | 1,066.52 | 1,078.13 | 1,007.07 | 1,047.59 | 1,028.16 | 1,056.34 | 1,037.09 |
| 2016 | 1,052.69 | 1,040.59 | 1,044.86 | 1,088.92 | 1,092.22 | 1,102.13 | 1,101.49 | 1,123.49 | 1,122.36 | 1,112.65 | 1,095.90 | 1,052.80 | 1,087.02 |
| 2017 | 1,035.97 | 1,117.77 | 1,121.25 | 1,144.96 | 1,146.75 | 1,165.94 | 1,188.64 | 1,175.56 | 1,194.62 | 1,189.89 | 1,127.10 | 1,149.21 | 1,148.74 |
| 2018 | 1,101.41 | 1,098.67 | 1,106.68 | 1,135.88 | 1,134.30 | 1,133.54 | 1,174.24 | 1,196.52 | 1,165.40 | 1,169.64 | 1,117.52 | 1,175.25 | 1,142.25 |
| 2019 | 1,165.67 | 1,128.83 | 1,195.26 | 1,178.87 | 1,214.00 | 1,198.93 | 1,200.38 | 1,233.94 | 1,185.39 | 1,213.68 | 1,192.71 | 1,189.87 | 1,193.47 |
| **Manufacturing** | | | | | | | | | | | | | |
| 2015 | 914.40 | 923.81 | 920.31 | 907.32 | 899.42 | 907.84 | 903.18 | 912.80 | 889.06 | 901.54 | 925.11 | 919.38 | 909.43 |
| 2016 | 908.31 | 909.48 | 910.25 | 913.38 | 946.31 | 919.60 | 919.63 | 914.12 | 948.42 | 960.71 | 940.49 | 956.48 | 927.87 |
| 2017 | 945.83 | 950.42 | 949.62 | 970.81 | 962.73 | 965.95 | 968.82 | 952.01 | 968.82 | 992.66 | 965.15 | 959.31 | 963.98 |
| 2018 | 958.21 | 958.21 | 968.06 | 993.41 | 980.78 | 982.64 | 989.48 | 991.30 | 1,035.71 | 1,018.49 | 1,029.77 | 1,069.20 | 998.17 |
| 2019 | 1,037.90 | 1,016.02 | 1,021.74 | 1,019.81 | 1,010.07 | 1,021.41 | 996.79 | 1,009.47 | 1,038.80 | 1,036.41 | 1,034.02 | 1,069.27 | 1,025.55 |
| **Trade, Transportation, and Utilities** | | | | | | | | | | | | | |
| 2015 | 667.66 | 692.52 | 695.68 | 676.65 | 688.93 | 687.88 | 696.85 | 706.33 | 697.03 | 687.75 | 705.74 | 682.41 | 690.32 |
| 2016 | 694.60 | 700.01 | 706.49 | 752.25 | 777.24 | 749.42 | 777.50 | 771.77 | 778.09 | 805.75 | 775.13 | 772.91 | 755.74 |
| 2017 | 790.62 | 772.96 | 776.60 | 810.72 | 773.73 | 792.93 | 815.75 | 789.40 | 787.29 | 822.11 | 766.59 | 774.50 | 788.90 |
| 2018 | 750.35 | 782.60 | 768.73 | 797.08 | 787.19 | 786.37 | 807.18 | 783.43 | 808.83 | 784.04 | 772.77 | 794.38 | 784.49 |
| 2019 | 766.43 | 763.16 | 775.83 | 793.06 | 798.49 | 831.38 | 806.34 | 814.88 | 841.50 | 817.60 | 804.69 | 839.45 | 804.84 |
| **Financial Activities** | | | | | | | | | | | | | |
| 2015 | 977.82 | 1,035.09 | 1,019.08 | 987.54 | 983.81 | 989.43 | 972.79 | 1,032.46 | 998.76 | 1,006.72 | 1,036.00 | 1,035.58 | 1,005.02 |
| 2016 | 1,014.17 | 1,032.12 | 1,038.24 | 1,088.12 | 1,079.15 | 1,022.68 | 1,050.00 | 1,038.62 | 1,102.26 | 1,155.00 | 1,097.68 | 1,078.26 | 1,066.34 |
| 2017 | 1,127.04 | 1,079.73 | 1,103.72 | 1,146.46 | 1,064.77 | 1,114.89 | 1,165.10 | 1,185.95 | 1,196.49 | 1,181.90 | 1,153.48 | 1,166.56 | 1,141.18 |
| 2018 | 1,154.97 | 1,186.28 | 1,174.58 | 1,294.78 | 1,249.16 | 1,238.25 | 1,244.25 | 1,206.20 | 1,249.35 | 1,175.39 | 1,201.02 | 1,238.92 | 1,219.13 |
| 2019 | 1,168.86 | 1,143.45 | 1,159.79 | 1,200.44 | 1,229.49 | 1,263.92 | 1,238.91 | 1,289.23 | 1,320.93 | 1,271.94 | 1,234.67 | 1,294.45 | 1,235.38 |
| **Professional and Business Services** | | | | | | | | | | | | | |
| 2015 | 896.72 | 929.39 | 931.21 | 913.79 | 916.42 | 920.83 | 919.10 | 949.32 | 919.17 | 933.78 | 986.65 | 942.90 | 931.35 |
| 2016 | 951.17 | 974.75 | 956.69 | 973.00 | 1,004.12 | 969.85 | 956.55 | 962.15 | 978.54 | 1,036.00 | 989.82 | 989.92 | 978.25 |
| 2017 | 1,036.70 | 1,035.89 | 1,021.15 | 1,079.69 | 1,017.43 | 1,025.66 | 1,075.68 | 1,037.44 | 1,078.08 | 1,121.90 | 1,098.67 | 1,103.38 | 1,061.64 |
| 2018 | 1,098.97 | 1,095.64 | 1,088.13 | 1,139.81 | 1,086.35 | 1,103.57 | 1,127.12 | 1,099.95 | 1,170.68 | 1,117.84 | 1,127.84 | 1,171.04 | 1,118.16 |
| 2019 | 1,132.26 | 1,135.40 | 1,157.95 | 1,166.08 | 1,158.78 | 1,207.74 | 1,138.90 | 1,164.12 | 1,218.44 | 1,167.68 | 1,169.53 | 1,215.87 | 1,170.96 |
| **Education and Health Services** | | | | | | | | | | | | | |
| 2015 | 842.95 | 878.37 | 866.89 | 858.28 | 870.42 | 872.38 | 884.52 | 925.07 | 910.01 | 908.04 | 945.54 | 921.63 | 891.99 |
| 2016 | 929.74 | 929.27 | 917.42 | 936.24 | 947.75 | 957.87 | 978.12 | 968.78 | 963.54 | 996.93 | 967.37 | 962.69 | 954.75 |
| 2017 | 987.97 | 974.69 | 951.57 | 987.85 | 944.13 | 947.70 | 972.69 | 974.82 | 960.07 | 976.02 | 950.95 | 976.80 | 967.23 |
| 2018 | 954.53 | 953.82 | 939.28 | 967.15 | 942.09 | 949.17 | 979.66 | 961.47 | 984.47 | 941.85 | 953.77 | 983.81 | 959.90 |
| 2019 | 959.73 | 958.75 | 953.86 | 956.80 | 958.11 | 984.82 | 983.72 | 981.42 | 1,002.85 | 980.10 | 986.70 | 1,013.27 | 975.48 |
| **Leisure and Hospitality** | | | | | | | | | | | | | |
| 2015 | 338.12 | 363.78 | 361.46 | 353.90 | 356.42 | 357.63 | 363.57 | 384.15 | 367.20 | 364.50 | 373.07 | 357.21 | 361.44 |
| 2016 | 350.88 | 367.25 | 358.67 | 366.05 | 382.67 | 374.24 | 390.05 | 399.80 | 389.58 | 400.55 | 375.19 | 372.20 | 377.24 |
| 2017 | 376.32 | 379.69 | 381.37 | 405.59 | 386.70 | 390.65 | 417.62 | 406.12 | 399.49 | 412.07 | 395.57 | 399.26 | 396.20 |
| 2018 | 398.13 | 401.62 | 402.88 | 417.96 | 402.38 | 409.38 | 438.31 | 425.96 | 436.42 | 415.90 | 406.54 | 417.97 | 413.90 |
| 2019 | 392.78 | 396.92 | 403.37 | 404.39 | 402.46 | 428.75 | 418.46 | 429.46 | 442.04 | 424.52 | 421.56 | 444.25 | 418.22 |
| **Other Services** | | | | | | | | | | | | | |
| 2015 | 608.90 | 640.23 | 621.06 | 617.60 | 618.05 | 634.67 | 623.79 | 655.00 | 621.53 | 625.43 | 639.36 | 598.08 | 625.37 |
| 2016 | 606.69 | 608.29 | 606.36 | 617.99 | 646.21 | 623.56 | 637.92 | 641.16 | 639.28 | 671.39 | 634.74 | 629.62 | 629.42 |
| 2017 | 648.37 | 653.37 | 629.39 | 663.00 | 630.31 | 641.19 | 668.26 | 626.84 | 641.67 | 661.60 | 635.42 | 657.22 | 647.07 |
| 2018 | 641.27 | 667.45 | 662.07 | 696.28 | 648.35 | 679.20 | 716.54 | 690.99 | 720.72 | 678.02 | 692.05 | 703.94 | 681.82 |
| 2019 | 673.35 | 704.86 | 687.79 | 698.59 | 688.20 | 691.98 | 661.12 | 678.22 | 672.30 | 643.80 | 633.41 | 650.17 | 674.25 |

# PENNSYLVANIA
*At a Glance*

Population:
2010 census: 12,702,379
2019 estimate: 12,801,989

Percent change in population:
2010–2019: 0.8%

Percent change in total nonfarm employment:
2011–2019: 6.6%

Industry with the largest growth in employment, 2011–2019 (percent):
Construction, 17.6%

Industry with the largest decline or smallest growth in employment, 2011–2019 (percent):
Mining and logging, -13.9%

Civilian labor force:
2010: 6,380,949
2019: 6,491,640

Unemployment rate and rank among states (highest to lowest):
2010: 8.5%, 28th
2019: 4.4%, 8th

Over-the-year change in unemployment rates:
2017–2018: -0.7%
2018–2019: 0.2%

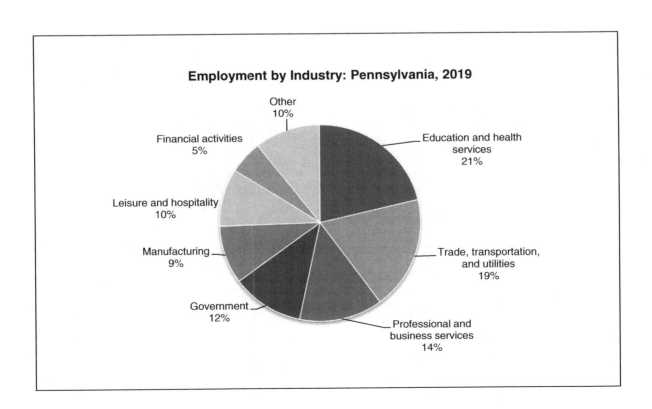

**Employment by Industry: Pennsylvania, 2019**

- Other 10%
- Financial activities 5%
- Leisure and hospitality 10%
- Manufacturing 9%
- Government 12%
- Education and health services 21%
- Trade, transportation, and utilities 19%
- Professional and business services 14%

## 1. Employment by Industry: Pennsylvania, 2011–2019

(Numbers in thousands, not seasonally adjusted)

| Industry and year | January | February | March | April | May | June | July | August | September | October | November | December | Annual average |
|---|---|---|---|---|---|---|---|---|---|---|---|---|---|
| **Total Nonfarm** | | | | | | | | | | | | | |
| 2011 | 5,555.3 | 5,587.4 | 5,631.2 | 5,700.4 | 5,730.7 | 5,729.7 | 5,654.8 | 5,648.0 | 5,713.1 | 5,748.4 | 5,772.6 | 5,759.4 | 5,685.9 |
| 2012 | 5,600.9 | 5,647.6 | 5,702.1 | 5,742.0 | 5,774.9 | 5,760.3 | 5,687.4 | 5,688.4 | 5,748.9 | 5,780.8 | 5,797.9 | 5,781.8 | 5,726.1 |
| 2013 | 5,620.0 | 5,664.1 | 5,702.7 | 5,745.5 | 5,784.7 | 5,771.1 | 5,705.7 | 5,710.5 | 5,766.2 | 5,797.3 | 5,818.9 | 5,800.9 | 5,740.6 |
| 2014 | 5,648.6 | 5,669.3 | 5,717.2 | 5,787.9 | 5,830.4 | 5,825.4 | 5,757.8 | 5,765.7 | 5,824.0 | 5,869.5 | 5,888.3 | 5,879.2 | 5,788.6 |
| 2015 | 5,708.7 | 5,736.3 | 5,760.6 | 5,835.4 | 5,878.0 | 5,869.6 | 5,811.1 | 5,811.4 | 5,865.8 | 5,908.9 | 5,924.9 | 5,913.8 | 5,835.4 |
| 2016 | 5,754.5 | 5,785.4 | 5,828.1 | 5,894.2 | 5,913.0 | 5,892.1 | 5,861.0 | 5,854.5 | 5,927.5 | 5,955.8 | 5,972.2 | 5,956.3 | 5,882.9 |
| 2017 | 5,810.4 | 5,849.0 | 5,871.1 | 5,938.4 | 5,975.8 | 5,958.0 | 5,913.9 | 5,914.8 | 5,985.4 | 6,014.5 | 6,037.8 | 6,026.4 | 5,941.3 |
| 2018 | 5,873.3 | 5,918.6 | 5,946.6 | 6,009.7 | 6,040.5 | 6,029.5 | 5,984.4 | 5,985.7 | 6,046.6 | 6,089.6 | 6,105.8 | 6,086.3 | 6,009.7 |
| 2019 | 5,949.6 | 5,977.9 | 6,010.1 | 6,071.8 | 6,093.0 | 6,073.8 | 6,040.8 | 6,049.2 | 6,092.0 | 6,132.1 | 6,152.2 | 6,121.7 | 6,063.7 |
| **Total Private** | | | | | | | | | | | | | |
| 2011 | 4,793.1 | 4,808.1 | 4,850.2 | 4,919.1 | 4,960.1 | 4,977.6 | 4,966.1 | 4,964.2 | 4,972.8 | 4,992.6 | 5,009.8 | 5,001.0 | 4,934.6 |
| 2012 | 4,870.5 | 4,893.5 | 4,946.6 | 4,986.9 | 5,022.4 | 5,036.7 | 5,014.4 | 5,014.0 | 5,018.9 | 5,036.2 | 5,049.0 | 5,036.9 | 4,993.8 |
| 2013 | 4,897.7 | 4,922.6 | 4,961.3 | 5,003.1 | 5,041.1 | 5,060.9 | 5,044.6 | 5,045.2 | 5,048.5 | 5,065.9 | 5,080.8 | 5,067.3 | 5,019.9 |
| 2014 | 4,935.9 | 4,941.1 | 4,988.6 | 5,056.8 | 5,105.7 | 5,118.7 | 5,101.6 | 5,107.6 | 5,112.2 | 5,144.1 | 5,159.0 | 5,155.0 | 5,077.2 |
| 2015 | 5,008.5 | 5,016.6 | 5,040.3 | 5,110.1 | 5,159.3 | 5,170.9 | 5,157.9 | 5,154.8 | 5,158.3 | 5,191.9 | 5,202.4 | 5,197.1 | 5,130.7 |
| 2016 | 5,057.9 | 5,069.8 | 5,109.6 | 5,175.2 | 5,200.7 | 5,199.1 | 5,205.8 | 5,199.3 | 5,216.4 | 5,236.7 | 5,248.2 | 5,236.9 | 5,179.6 |
| 2017 | 5,113.8 | 5,132.3 | 5,152.9 | 5,218.9 | 5,258.6 | 5,265.4 | 5,258.5 | 5,258.0 | 5,275.0 | 5,297.4 | 5,316.0 | 5,309.8 | 5,238.1 |
| 2018 | 5,176.6 | 5,203.6 | 5,229.6 | 5,292.3 | 5,326.7 | 5,337.1 | 5,329.2 | 5,326.7 | 5,335.1 | 5,371.7 | 5,382.5 | 5,368.9 | 5,306.7 |
| 2019 | 5,249.9 | 5,262.3 | 5,291.4 | 5,352.9 | 5,379.5 | 5,379.7 | 5,379.0 | 5,381.5 | 5,376.3 | 5,409.6 | 5,424.2 | 5,399.5 | 5,357.2 |
| **Goods Producing** | | | | | | | | | | | | | |
| 2011 | 781.1 | 778.6 | 793.4 | 811.4 | 823.6 | 835.5 | 842.0 | 843.7 | 840.0 | 840.6 | 837.4 | 827.8 | 821.3 |
| 2012 | 805.9 | 805.4 | 816.1 | 826.3 | 833.4 | 845.4 | 845.9 | 845.2 | 842.0 | 838.8 | 830.1 | 820.0 | 829.5 |
| 2013 | 798.2 | 797.0 | 806.6 | 819.1 | 830.2 | 840.6 | 842.4 | 843.5 | 840.5 | 838.2 | 831.5 | 817.1 | 825.4 |
| 2014 | 799.2 | 795.7 | 808.0 | 827.1 | 840.7 | 851.4 | 855.6 | 856.2 | 851.2 | 852.4 | 848.0 | 837.7 | 835.3 |
| 2015 | 814.9 | 809.7 | 815.8 | 834.6 | 846.9 | 856.2 | 858.3 | 857.1 | 850.7 | 847.1 | 839.4 | 828.6 | 838.3 |
| 2016 | 805.2 | 797.5 | 808.4 | 821.6 | 829.1 | 838.3 | 841.3 | 839.5 | 833.8 | 833.7 | 829.2 | 820.1 | 824.8 |
| 2017 | 802.7 | 803.3 | 811.1 | 829.8 | 843.7 | 856.0 | 858.7 | 858.0 | 853.4 | 853.2 | 849.7 | 843.1 | 838.6 |
| 2018 | 820.6 | 822.5 | 832.5 | 847.5 | 857.8 | 870.6 | 874.2 | 872.7 | 867.8 | 871.6 | 865.9 | 859.6 | 855.3 |
| 2019 | 841.8 | 839.8 | 848.3 | 864.8 | 872.7 | 880.1 | 882.7 | 880.4 | 872.8 | 873.6 | 867.7 | 856.8 | 865.1 |
| **Service-Providing** | | | | | | | | | | | | | |
| 2011 | 4,774.2 | 4,808.8 | 4,837.8 | 4,889.0 | 4,907.1 | 4,894.2 | 4,812.8 | 4,804.3 | 4,873.1 | 4,907.8 | 4,935.2 | 4,931.6 | 4,864.7 |
| 2012 | 4,795.0 | 4,842.2 | 4,886.0 | 4,915.7 | 4,941.5 | 4,914.9 | 4,841.5 | 4,843.2 | 4,906.9 | 4,942.0 | 4,967.8 | 4,961.8 | 4,896.5 |
| 2013 | 4,821.8 | 4,867.1 | 4,896.1 | 4,926.4 | 4,954.5 | 4,930.5 | 4,863.3 | 4,867.0 | 4,925.7 | 4,959.1 | 4,987.4 | 4,983.8 | 4,915.2 |
| 2014 | 4,849.4 | 4,873.6 | 4,909.2 | 4,960.8 | 4,989.7 | 4,974.0 | 4,902.2 | 4,909.5 | 4,972.8 | 5,017.1 | 5,040.3 | 5,041.5 | 4,953.3 |
| 2015 | 4,893.8 | 4,926.6 | 4,944.8 | 5,000.8 | 5,031.1 | 5,013.4 | 4,952.8 | 4,954.3 | 5,015.1 | 5,061.8 | 5,085.5 | 5,085.2 | 4,997.1 |
| 2016 | 4,949.3 | 4,987.9 | 5,019.7 | 5,072.6 | 5,083.9 | 5,053.8 | 5,019.7 | 5,015.0 | 5,093.7 | 5,122.1 | 5,143.0 | 5,136.2 | 5,058.1 |
| 2017 | 5,007.7 | 5,045.7 | 5,060.0 | 5,108.6 | 5,132.1 | 5,102.0 | 5,055.2 | 5,056.8 | 5,132.0 | 5,161.3 | 5,188.1 | 5,183.3 | 5,102.7 |
| 2018 | 5,052.7 | 5,096.1 | 5,114.1 | 5,162.2 | 5,182.7 | 5,158.9 | 5,110.2 | 5,113.0 | 5,178.8 | 5,218.0 | 5,239.9 | 5,226.7 | 5,154.4 |
| 2019 | 5,107.8 | 5,138.1 | 5,161.8 | 5,207.0 | 5,220.3 | 5,193.7 | 5,158.1 | 5,168.8 | 5,219.2 | 5,258.5 | 5,284.5 | 5,264.9 | 5,198.6 |
| **Mining and Logging** | | | | | | | | | | | | | |
| 2011 | 29.5 | 30.2 | 30.9 | 32.0 | 33.0 | 34.1 | 34.7 | 35.1 | 35.6 | 36.3 | 37.1 | 37.4 | 33.8 |
| 2012 | 37.0 | 37.7 | 38.0 | 37.8 | 37.8 | 38.0 | 37.5 | 37.1 | 36.7 | 36.3 | 36.0 | 35.4 | 37.1 |
| 2013 | 34.7 | 34.9 | 35.5 | 35.9 | 36.4 | 36.7 | 36.7 | 36.4 | 36.3 | 36.5 | 36.3 | 36.1 | 36.0 |
| 2014 | 35.4 | 35.6 | 36.0 | 37.0 | 37.6 | 38.0 | 38.6 | 38.9 | 38.9 | 39.0 | 39.1 | 39.0 | 37.8 |
| 2015 | 38.3 | 36.9 | 36.4 | 35.5 | 35.2 | 35.1 | 34.3 | 33.2 | 32.1 | 31.1 | 30.2 | 29.5 | 34.0 |
| 2016 | 27.4 | 26.3 | 25.9 | 25.1 | 24.9 | 24.6 | 24.3 | 24.2 | 24.2 | 24.3 | 24.4 | 24.4 | 25.0 |
| 2017 | 24.2 | 24.8 | 25.2 | 25.8 | 26.6 | 27.2 | 27.5 | 27.6 | 27.8 | 27.9 | 28.1 | 27.9 | 26.7 |
| 2018 | 27.2 | 27.3 | 27.6 | 28.1 | 28.5 | 28.9 | 29.2 | 29.3 | 29.2 | 29.8 | 29.7 | 29.6 | 28.7 |
| 2019 | 29.0 | 29.1 | 29.5 | 29.6 | 29.7 | 29.6 | 29.6 | 29.2 | 28.3 | 28.7 | 28.8 | 28.3 | 29.1 |
| **Construction** | | | | | | | | | | | | | |
| 2011 | 193.6 | 191.3 | 202.4 | 216.4 | 224.8 | 231.5 | 236.2 | 237.2 | 235.5 | 236.1 | 232.3 | 221.4 | 221.6 |
| 2012 | 204.8 | 204.3 | 212.5 | 221.7 | 226.7 | 233.6 | 235.1 | 235.6 | 236.2 | 235.2 | 227.8 | 218.5 | 224.3 |
| 2013 | 202.0 | 201.2 | 209.2 | 220.3 | 228.8 | 233.9 | 236.8 | 238.9 | 237.8 | 235.3 | 228.4 | 213.8 | 223.9 |
| 2014 | 201.5 | 198.3 | 207.6 | 225.0 | 234.9 | 240.5 | 244.2 | 244.5 | 243.2 | 243.8 | 237.9 | 226.2 | 229.0 |
| 2015 | 209.3 | 205.9 | 211.5 | 230.1 | 240.4 | 246.7 | 249.5 | 251.5 | 250.0 | 250.4 | 244.8 | 234.8 | 235.4 |
| 2016 | 218.3 | 213.3 | 223.4 | 237.4 | 243.4 | 248.5 | 252.4 | 252.0 | 250.4 | 249.9 | 245.3 | 234.6 | 239.1 |
| 2017 | 221.2 | 221.1 | 226.3 | 243.0 | 254.7 | 261.6 | 264.4 | 264.4 | 262.6 | 262.4 | 257.7 | 248.9 | 249.0 |
| 2018 | 230.9 | 232.0 | 239.7 | 252.7 | 260.0 | 267.0 | 269.2 | 268.5 | 268.5 | 266.4 | 261.0 | 253.0 | 255.7 |
| 2019 | 240.1 | 237.4 | 243.5 | 259.6 | 266.2 | 270.8 | 274.1 | 274.9 | 272.2 | 271.7 | 263.7 | 253.1 | 260.6 |

## 1. Employment by Industry: Pennsylvania, 2011–2019—*Continued*

(Numbers in thousands, not seasonally adjusted)

| Industry and year | January | February | March | April | May | June | July | August | September | October | November | December | Annual average |
|---|---|---|---|---|---|---|---|---|---|---|---|---|---|
| **Manufacturing** | | | | | | | | | | | | | |
| 2011 | 558.0 | 557.1 | 560.1 | 563.0 | 565.8 | 569.9 | 571.1 | 571.4 | 568.9 | 568.2 | 568.0 | 569.0 | 565.9 |
| 2012 | 564.1 | 563.4 | 565.6 | 566.8 | 568.9 | 573.8 | 573.3 | 572.5 | 569.1 | 567.3 | 566.3 | 566.1 | 568.1 |
| 2013 | 561.5 | 560.9 | 561.9 | 562.9 | 565.0 | 570.0 | 568.9 | 568.2 | 566.4 | 566.4 | 566.8 | 567.2 | 565.5 |
| 2014 | 562.3 | 561.8 | 564.4 | 565.1 | 568.2 | 572.9 | 572.8 | 572.8 | 569.1 | 569.6 | 571.0 | 572.5 | 568.5 |
| 2015 | 567.3 | 566.9 | 567.9 | 569.0 | 571.3 | 574.4 | 574.5 | 572.4 | 568.6 | 565.6 | 564.4 | 564.3 | 568.9 |
| 2016 | 559.5 | 557.9 | 559.1 | 559.1 | 560.8 | 565.2 | 564.6 | 563.3 | 559.2 | 559.5 | 559.5 | 561.1 | 560.7 |
| 2017 | 557.3 | 557.4 | 559.6 | 561.0 | 562.4 | 567.2 | 566.8 | 566.0 | 563.0 | 562.9 | 563.9 | 566.3 | 562.8 |
| 2018 | 562.5 | 563.2 | 565.2 | 566.7 | 569.3 | 574.7 | 575.8 | 574.9 | 572.2 | 573.3 | 575.2 | 577.0 | 570.8 |
| 2019 | 572.7 | 573.3 | 575.3 | 575.6 | 576.8 | 579.7 | 579.0 | 576.3 | 572.3 | 573.2 | 575.2 | 575.4 | 575.4 |
| **Trade, Transportation, and Utilities** | | | | | | | | | | | | | |
| 2011 | 1,076.5 | 1,065.5 | 1,068.9 | 1,077.8 | 1,085.4 | 1,085.2 | 1,074.2 | 1,074.7 | 1,081.4 | 1,090.8 | 1,112.9 | 1,125.8 | 1,084.9 |
| 2012 | 1,083.6 | 1,072.3 | 1,080.9 | 1,083.8 | 1,093.5 | 1,093.0 | 1,082.4 | 1,083.4 | 1,089.1 | 1,098.8 | 1,125.1 | 1,133.8 | 1,093.3 |
| 2013 | 1,088.2 | 1,077.6 | 1,082.2 | 1,084.9 | 1,093.8 | 1,095.7 | 1,082.6 | 1,085.9 | 1,090.2 | 1,099.5 | 1,122.9 | 1,135.1 | 1,094.9 |
| 2014 | 1,091.0 | 1,077.7 | 1,085.2 | 1,092.0 | 1,103.6 | 1,108.3 | 1,093.6 | 1,097.3 | 1,103.7 | 1,115.4 | 1,138.5 | 1,153.3 | 1,105.0 |
| 2015 | 1,107.1 | 1,093.3 | 1,097.4 | 1,104.2 | 1,116.8 | 1,120.9 | 1,108.0 | 1,108.9 | 1,113.5 | 1,123.1 | 1,145.5 | 1,160.1 | 1,116.6 |
| 2016 | 1,114.1 | 1,102.6 | 1,106.9 | 1,112.1 | 1,120.9 | 1,119.1 | 1,111.5 | 1,111.2 | 1,117.2 | 1,125.9 | 1,148.8 | 1,163.8 | 1,121.2 |
| 2017 | 1,120.0 | 1,105.7 | 1,103.6 | 1,110.7 | 1,116.9 | 1,116.1 | 1,107.5 | 1,109.0 | 1,117.6 | 1,125.6 | 1,152.2 | 1,162.7 | 1,120.6 |
| 2018 | 1,121.2 | 1,110.3 | 1,112.5 | 1,117.1 | 1,126.0 | 1,126.2 | 1,116.4 | 1,115.9 | 1,121.5 | 1,130.5 | 1,156.6 | 1,165.8 | 1,126.7 |
| 2019 | 1,128.3 | 1,110.6 | 1,111.2 | 1,115.3 | 1,121.7 | 1,121.3 | 1,114.6 | 1,116.3 | 1,120.1 | 1,130.2 | 1,151.8 | 1,159.7 | 1,125.1 |
| **Wholesale Trade** | | | | | | | | | | | | | |
| 2011 | 216.9 | 216.7 | 217.7 | 219.0 | 219.8 | 220.3 | 220.2 | 219.8 | 218.5 | 218.8 | 218.6 | 218.7 | 218.8 |
| 2012 | 215.9 | 216.1 | 217.3 | 217.9 | 218.8 | 220.3 | 219.5 | 219.1 | 217.8 | 217.6 | 217.3 | 218.0 | 218.0 |
| 2013 | 215.0 | 215.1 | 216.3 | 216.7 | 217.7 | 218.7 | 218.2 | 218.0 | 217.4 | 216.7 | 216.8 | 217.4 | 217.0 |
| 2014 | 214.8 | 214.5 | 215.3 | 216.0 | 217.7 | 219.4 | 219.9 | 220.0 | 218.6 | 219.3 | 219.8 | 220.2 | 218.0 |
| 2015 | 217.4 | 217.1 | 217.5 | 218.0 | 219.2 | 219.6 | 219.8 | 219.2 | 217.0 | 216.9 | 216.3 | 216.0 | 217.8 |
| 2016 | 213.2 | 212.5 | 212.5 | 213.3 | 214.0 | 214.3 | 214.7 | 214.0 | 212.5 | 212.4 | 212.2 | 212.4 | 213.2 |
| 2017 | 210.6 | 210.5 | 210.6 | 211.5 | 212.8 | 214.5 | 215.2 | 215.1 | 214.2 | 214.5 | 214.9 | 215.6 | 213.3 |
| 2018 | 213.8 | 214.2 | 215.0 | 215.8 | 216.9 | 218.3 | 218.5 | 218.3 | 216.5 | 217.2 | 217.4 | 217.6 | 216.6 |
| 2019 | 215.6 | 215.6 | 215.7 | 216.7 | 217.3 | 218.7 | 219.4 | 219.2 | 217.6 | 218.0 | 215.8 | 215.9 | 217.1 |
| **Retail Trade** | | | | | | | | | | | | | |
| 2011 | 621.4 | 610.4 | 611.8 | 618.0 | 623.4 | 625.0 | 623.7 | 625.4 | 618.7 | 626.9 | 646.8 | 655.9 | 625.6 |
| 2012 | 625.6 | 613.4 | 619.0 | 621.1 | 628.3 | 630.8 | 629.4 | 630.8 | 623.8 | 632.2 | 656.8 | 660.8 | 631.0 |
| 2013 | 626.7 | 616.3 | 618.5 | 620.7 | 627.1 | 631.5 | 629.4 | 630.8 | 623.1 | 631.6 | 651.8 | 660.2 | 630.6 |
| 2014 | 626.2 | 614.1 | 618.7 | 623.3 | 630.6 | 635.3 | 631.7 | 633.5 | 626.1 | 634.1 | 653.5 | 662.4 | 632.5 |
| 2015 | 628.6 | 616.6 | 619.0 | 623.3 | 632.2 | 637.3 | 634.6 | 634.6 | 626.5 | 634.0 | 653.0 | 660.0 | 633.3 |
| 2016 | 628.8 | 619.5 | 622.4 | 626.5 | 632.6 | 635.2 | 635.6 | 635.4 | 625.7 | 632.1 | 649.5 | 656.5 | 633.3 |
| 2017 | 628.8 | 616.8 | 615.1 | 620.1 | 622.3 | 625.4 | 624.2 | 623.6 | 616.2 | 622.6 | 642.3 | 646.5 | 625.3 |
| 2018 | 619.6 | 610.2 | 611.5 | 614.0 | 619.1 | 621.8 | 620.7 | 618.3 | 609.9 | 615.3 | 634.5 | 637.7 | 619.4 |
| 2019 | 612.6 | 599.5 | 600.9 | 603.4 | 607.3 | 608.9 | 608.4 | 607.4 | 599.3 | 605.3 | 623.2 | 623.8 | 608.3 |
| **Transportation and Utilities** | | | | | | | | | | | | | |
| 2011 | 1,076.5 | 1,065.5 | 1,068.9 | 1,077.8 | 1,085.4 | 1,085.2 | 1,074.2 | 1,074.7 | 1,081.4 | 1,090.8 | 1,112.9 | 1,125.8 | 1,084.9 |
| 2012 | 1,083.6 | 1,072.3 | 1,080.9 | 1,083.8 | 1,093.5 | 1,093.0 | 1,082.4 | 1,083.4 | 1,089.1 | 1,098.8 | 1,125.1 | 1,133.8 | 1,093.3 |
| 2013 | 1,088.2 | 1,077.6 | 1,082.2 | 1,084.9 | 1,093.8 | 1,095.7 | 1,082.6 | 1,085.9 | 1,090.2 | 1,099.5 | 1,122.9 | 1,135.1 | 1,094.9 |
| 2014 | 1,091.0 | 1,077.7 | 1,085.2 | 1,092.0 | 1,103.6 | 1,108.3 | 1,093.6 | 1,097.3 | 1,103.7 | 1,115.4 | 1,138.5 | 1,153.3 | 1,105.0 |
| 2015 | 1,107.1 | 1,093.3 | 1,097.4 | 1,104.2 | 1,116.8 | 1,120.9 | 1,108.0 | 1,108.9 | 1,113.5 | 1,123.1 | 1,145.5 | 1,160.1 | 1,116.6 |
| 2016 | 1,114.1 | 1,102.6 | 1,106.9 | 1,112.1 | 1,120.9 | 1,119.1 | 1,111.5 | 1,111.2 | 1,117.2 | 1,125.9 | 1,148.8 | 1,163.8 | 1,121.2 |
| 2017 | 1,120.0 | 1,105.7 | 1,103.6 | 1,110.7 | 1,116.9 | 1,116.1 | 1,107.5 | 1,109.0 | 1,117.6 | 1,125.6 | 1,152.2 | 1,162.7 | 1,120.6 |
| 2018 | 1,121.2 | 1,110.3 | 1,112.5 | 1,117.1 | 1,126.0 | 1,126.2 | 1,116.4 | 1,115.9 | 1,121.5 | 1,130.5 | 1,156.6 | 1,165.8 | 1,126.7 |
| 2019 | 1,128.3 | 1,110.6 | 1,111.2 | 1,115.3 | 1,121.7 | 1,121.3 | 1,114.6 | 1,116.3 | 1,120.1 | 1,130.2 | 1,151.8 | 1,159.7 | 1,125.1 |
| **Information** | | | | | | | | | | | | | |
| 2011 | 90.8 | 90.8 | 90.9 | 91.6 | 92.2 | 92.7 | 92.4 | 87.8 | 91.4 | 91.9 | 92.8 | 90.8 | 91.3 |
| 2012 | 90.1 | 89.6 | 90.7 | 90.1 | 91.4 | 91.1 | 91.0 | 91.5 | 90.5 | 90.0 | 90.9 | 90.1 | 90.6 |
| 2013 | 89.0 | 88.6 | 88.5 | 88.1 | 88.2 | 88.2 | 88.3 | 87.9 | 86.8 | 87.9 | 87.2 | 87.3 | 88.0 |
| 2014 | 85.2 | 85.0 | 85.2 | 86.2 | 85.8 | 86.2 | 86.5 | 86.0 | 85.3 | 85.1 | 85.3 | 85.8 | 85.6 |
| 2015 | 83.8 | 84.1 | 84.6 | 84.6 | 85.2 | 86.1 | 86.1 | 86.5 | 85.4 | 85.1 | 84.9 | 85.4 | 85.2 |
| 2016 | 83.8 | 83.8 | 84.0 | 84.8 | 81.4 | 86.3 | 86.5 | 86.3 | 84.8 | 85.0 | 84.7 | 84.3 | 84.6 |
| 2017 | 83.3 | 83.8 | 83.1 | 83.8 | 84.7 | 86.0 | 85.3 | 85.7 | 84.0 | 84.3 | 84.6 | 84.8 | 84.5 |
| 2018 | 84.0 | 85.2 | 85.3 | 86.5 | 86.3 | 87.0 | 86.6 | 86.5 | 86.4 | 87.1 | 87.3 | 86.9 | 86.3 |
| 2019 | 85.2 | 85.6 | 86.0 | 85.8 | 86.3 | 88.1 | 88.3 | 88.2 | 87.0 | 87.0 | 87.6 | 87.4 | 86.9 |

## 1. Employment by Industry: Pennsylvania, 2011–2019—*Continued*

(Numbers in thousands, not seasonally adjusted)

| Industry and year | January | February | March | April | May | June | July | August | September | October | November | December | Annual average |
|---|---|---|---|---|---|---|---|---|---|---|---|---|---|
| **Financial Activities** | | | | | | | | | | | | | |
| 2011 | 308.2 | 307.1 | 307.2 | 307.5 | 308.4 | 310.6 | 311.1 | 311.2 | 308.3 | 308.1 | 308.2 | 308.9 | 308.7 |
| 2012 | 306.8 | 306.8 | 307.4 | 307.3 | 309.0 | 312.2 | 312.6 | 312.4 | 309.6 | 309.5 | 310.1 | 310.6 | 309.5 |
| 2013 | 308.9 | 309.5 | 310.0 | 311.2 | 312.5 | 315.9 | 316.6 | 317.0 | 313.7 | 314.0 | 314.6 | 315.1 | 313.3 |
| 2014 | 312.6 | 313.0 | 313.3 | 313.4 | 315.3 | 318.2 | 318.9 | 318.8 | 315.0 | 314.9 | 315.1 | 316.2 | 315.4 |
| 2015 | 312.8 | 313.5 | 313.6 | 314.0 | 316.1 | 319.3 | 320.2 | 320.1 | 316.2 | 316.2 | 316.4 | 316.8 | 316.3 |
| 2016 | 314.5 | 314.3 | 314.4 | 315.0 | 316.4 | 319.4 | 320.5 | 320.6 | 317.8 | 317.5 | 318.0 | 318.9 | 317.3 |
| 2017 | 316.6 | 317.7 | 318.4 | 318.3 | 320.3 | 324.0 | 325.1 | 324.8 | 322.0 | 321.6 | 321.9 | 322.6 | 321.1 |
| 2018 | 320.5 | 321.4 | 321.5 | 322.6 | 324.7 | 328.8 | 329.9 | 329.8 | 326.7 | 326.9 | 327.7 | 327.7 | 325.7 |
| 2019 | 326.1 | 326.4 | 326.5 | 327.1 | 329.1 | 332.4 | 333.4 | 332.9 | 329.1 | 330.7 | 330.7 | 332.0 | 329.7 |
| **Professional and Business Services** | | | | | | | | | | | | | |
| 2011 | 693.5 | 695.3 | 701.8 | 717.1 | 720.2 | 725.4 | 724.6 | 727.6 | 728.4 | 733.0 | 735.4 | 732.2 | 719.5 |
| 2012 | 712.5 | 715.3 | 724.3 | 734.8 | 737.8 | 742.7 | 740.5 | 742.0 | 741.4 | 747.5 | 749.1 | 745.5 | 736.1 |
| 2013 | 726.1 | 732.3 | 739.4 | 749.3 | 752.4 | 758.5 | 758.8 | 760.7 | 755.0 | 760.1 | 763.2 | 756.7 | 751.0 |
| 2014 | 737.5 | 739.8 | 746.0 | 761.4 | 766.8 | 770.2 | 768.9 | 772.5 | 769.8 | 777.3 | 784.1 | 780.7 | 764.6 |
| 2015 | 758.4 | 760.2 | 762.3 | 777.3 | 782.4 | 785.4 | 786.2 | 786.4 | 785.3 | 800.1 | 804.7 | 802.2 | 782.6 |
| 2016 | 776.1 | 776.6 | 782.0 | 797.8 | 797.9 | 798.0 | 801.0 | 799.0 | 803.9 | 809.9 | 811.0 | 806.4 | 796.6 |
| 2017 | 786.3 | 784.7 | 787.9 | 801.0 | 805.0 | 805.5 | 804.3 | 804.3 | 807.8 | 812.5 | 814.3 | 808.1 | 801.8 |
| 2018 | 787.5 | 789.2 | 791.9 | 806.0 | 809.2 | 810.5 | 809.6 | 808.9 | 810.0 | 817.7 | 819.6 | 812.3 | 806.0 |
| 2019 | 794.0 | 798.0 | 798.7 | 815.2 | 817.8 | 816.9 | 820.5 | 822.0 | 820.4 | 828.2 | 831.5 | 816.9 | 815.0 |
| **Education and Health Services** | | | | | | | | | | | | | |
| 2011 | 1,123.4 | 1,150.7 | 1,153.0 | 1,154.1 | 1,146.1 | 1,125.9 | 1,118.9 | 1,115.8 | 1,145.5 | 1,163.4 | 1,168.7 | 1,163.7 | 1,144.1 |
| 2012 | 1,138.3 | 1,167.4 | 1,173.0 | 1,172.2 | 1,160.2 | 1,134.2 | 1,126.1 | 1,121.0 | 1,157.0 | 1,175.7 | 1,179.2 | 1,172.3 | 1,156.4 |
| 2013 | 1,146.0 | 1,175.4 | 1,177.4 | 1,176.0 | 1,160.7 | 1,138.8 | 1,131.9 | 1,127.1 | 1,166.1 | 1,183.2 | 1,191.4 | 1,182.3 | 1,163.0 |
| 2014 | 1,159.8 | 1,182.1 | 1,187.4 | 1,195.9 | 1,181.7 | 1,157.1 | 1,151.6 | 1,146.8 | 1,186.4 | 1,205.4 | 1,211.1 | 1,201.7 | 1,180.6 |
| 2015 | 1,175.2 | 1,198.9 | 1,198.6 | 1,206.9 | 1,192.4 | 1,166.3 | 1,162.5 | 1,156.7 | 1,194.8 | 1,216.8 | 1,221.4 | 1,214.3 | 1,192.1 |
| 2016 | 1,194.1 | 1,221.3 | 1,224.0 | 1,233.8 | 1,219.9 | 1,187.5 | 1,188.8 | 1,185.5 | 1,229.8 | 1,245.5 | 1,250.6 | 1,242.6 | 1,218.6 |
| 2017 | 1,220.8 | 1,250.8 | 1,252.2 | 1,256.8 | 1,244.9 | 1,213.8 | 1,213.0 | 1,210.0 | 1,256.0 | 1,273.0 | 1,279.4 | 1,275.1 | 1,245.5 |
| 2018 | 1,248.1 | 1,280.9 | 1,281.5 | 1,288.0 | 1,273.5 | 1,245.3 | 1,240.1 | 1,241.9 | 1,283.9 | 1,304.5 | 1,307.4 | 1,298.6 | 1,274.5 |
| 2019 | 1,275.3 | 1,302.7 | 1,306.9 | 1,311.3 | 1,295.2 | 1,264.6 | 1,257.9 | 1,262.4 | 1,301.0 | 1,322.5 | 1,329.4 | 1,323.4 | 1,296.1 |
| **Leisure and Hospitality** | | | | | | | | | | | | | |
| 2011 | 471.4 | 471.2 | 484.4 | 506.7 | 529.9 | 544.4 | 544.8 | 546.4 | 524.5 | 511.6 | 501.4 | 498.3 | 511.3 |
| 2012 | 482.6 | 485.4 | 500.5 | 518.1 | 541.3 | 558.7 | 557.3 | 561.3 | 535.9 | 523.1 | 512.8 | 512.9 | 524.2 |
| 2013 | 492.7 | 493.6 | 507.3 | 523.5 | 549.8 | 565.9 | 568.3 | 567.8 | 544.1 | 531.7 | 518.8 | 522.6 | 532.2 |
| 2014 | 501.8 | 499.2 | 511.9 | 529.6 | 557.7 | 569.7 | 568.9 | 573.0 | 547.9 | 540.7 | 524.3 | 526.7 | 537.6 |
| 2015 | 506.2 | 506.3 | 515.5 | 535.9 | 564.3 | 577.9 | 578.0 | 581.4 | 558.9 | 549.4 | 535.9 | 534.4 | 545.3 |
| 2016 | 516.9 | 519.6 | 533.3 | 552.1 | 575.3 | 587.5 | 592.4 | 594.2 | 569.8 | 558.6 | 546.4 | 542.7 | 557.4 |
| 2017 | 527.9 | 530.2 | 539.4 | 560.8 | 582.7 | 600.2 | 600.9 | 603.3 | 576.2 | 568.6 | 555.4 | 554.6 | 566.7 |
| 2018 | 538.8 | 537.9 | 547.0 | 565.6 | 588.0 | 603.7 | 606.9 | 606.8 | 578.8 | 572.5 | 557.9 | 558.2 | 571.8 |
| 2019 | 541.5 | 541.8 | 554.7 | 573.0 | 593.7 | 610.0 | 614.2 | 613.7 | 584.2 | 575.3 | 563.0 | 563.8 | 577.4 |
| **Other Services** | | | | | | | | | | | | | |
| 2011 | 248.2 | 248.9 | 250.6 | 252.9 | 254.3 | 257.9 | 258.1 | 257.0 | 253.3 | 253.2 | 253.0 | 253.5 | 253.4 |
| 2012 | 250.7 | 251.3 | 253.7 | 254.3 | 255.8 | 259.4 | 258.6 | 257.2 | 253.4 | 252.8 | 251.7 | 251.7 | 254.2 |
| 2013 | 248.6 | 248.6 | 249.9 | 251.0 | 253.5 | 257.3 | 255.7 | 255.3 | 252.1 | 251.3 | 251.2 | 251.1 | 252.1 |
| 2014 | 248.8 | 248.6 | 251.6 | 251.2 | 254.1 | 257.6 | 257.6 | 257.0 | 252.9 | 252.9 | 252.6 | 252.9 | 253.2 |
| 2015 | 250.1 | 250.6 | 252.5 | 252.6 | 255.2 | 258.8 | 258.6 | 257.7 | 253.5 | 254.1 | 254.2 | 255.3 | 254.4 |
| 2016 | 253.2 | 254.1 | 256.6 | 258.0 | 259.8 | 263.0 | 263.8 | 263.0 | 259.3 | 260.6 | 259.5 | 258.1 | 259.1 |
| 2017 | 256.2 | 256.1 | 257.2 | 257.7 | 260.4 | 263.8 | 263.7 | 262.9 | 258.0 | 258.6 | 258.5 | 258.8 | 259.3 |
| 2018 | 255.9 | 256.2 | 257.4 | 259.0 | 261.2 | 265.0 | 265.5 | 264.2 | 260.0 | 260.9 | 260.1 | 259.8 | 260.4 |
| 2019 | 257.7 | 257.4 | 259.1 | 260.4 | 263.0 | 266.3 | 267.4 | 265.6 | 261.7 | 262.1 | 262.5 | 259.5 | 261.9 |
| **Government** | | | | | | | | | | | | | |
| 2011 | 762.2 | 779.3 | 781.0 | 781.3 | 770.6 | 752.1 | 688.7 | 683.8 | 740.3 | 755.8 | 762.8 | 758.4 | 751.4 |
| 2012 | 730.4 | 754.1 | 755.5 | 755.1 | 752.5 | 723.6 | 673.0 | 674.4 | 730.0 | 744.6 | 748.9 | 744.9 | 732.3 |
| 2013 | 722.3 | 741.5 | 741.4 | 742.4 | 743.6 | 710.2 | 661.1 | 665.3 | 717.7 | 731.4 | 738.1 | 733.6 | 720.7 |
| 2014 | 712.7 | 728.2 | 728.6 | 731.1 | 724.7 | 706.7 | 656.2 | 658.1 | 711.8 | 725.4 | 729.3 | 724.2 | 711.4 |
| 2015 | 700.2 | 719.7 | 720.3 | 725.3 | 718.7 | 698.7 | 653.2 | 656.6 | 707.5 | 717.0 | 722.5 | 716.7 | 704.7 |
| 2016 | 696.6 | 715.6 | 718.5 | 719.0 | 712.3 | 693.0 | 655.2 | 655.2 | 711.1 | 719.1 | 724.0 | 719.4 | 703.3 |
| 2017 | 696.6 | 716.7 | 718.2 | 719.5 | 717.2 | 692.6 | 655.4 | 656.8 | 710.4 | 717.1 | 721.8 | 716.6 | 703.2 |
| 2018 | 696.7 | 715.0 | 717.0 | 717.4 | 713.8 | 692.4 | 655.2 | 659.0 | 711.5 | 717.9 | 723.3 | 717.4 | 703.1 |
| 2019 | 699.7 | 715.6 | 718.7 | 718.9 | 713.5 | 694.1 | 661.8 | 667.7 | 715.7 | 722.5 | 728.0 | 722.2 | 706.5 |

## 2. Average Weekly Hours by Selected Industry: Pennsylvania, 2015–2019

(Not seasonally adjusted)

| Industry and year | January | February | March | April | May | June | July | August | September | October | November | December | Annual average |
|---|---|---|---|---|---|---|---|---|---|---|---|---|---|
| **Total Private** | | | | | | | | | | | | | |
| 2015 | 33.5 | 33.7 | 33.8 | 33.8 | 34.0 | 34.1 | 34.0 | 34.3 | 33.8 | 34.1 | 34.3 | 34.2 | 34.0 |
| 2016 | 33.7 | 33.6 | 33.6 | 33.7 | 33.9 | 33.8 | 33.8 | 33.8 | 33.8 | 34.1 | 33.8 | 33.8 | 33.8 |
| 2017 | 33.7 | 33.5 | 33.1 | 33.9 | 33.8 | 33.9 | 34.0 | 33.9 | 34.1 | 34.1 | 34.1 | 33.9 | 33.8 |
| 2018 | 33.4 | 33.8 | 33.7 | 34.3 | 34.1 | 34.2 | 34.5 | 34.4 | 34.6 | 34.3 | 34.1 | 34.7 | 34.2 |
| 2019 | 34.0 | 33.8 | 34.1 | 34.4 | 34.2 | 34.4 | 34.0 | 34.2 | 34.4 | 34.1 | 34.2 | 34.2 | 34.2 |
| **Goods-Producing** | | | | | | | | | | | | | |
| 2015 | 38.8 | 39.3 | 39.6 | 39.9 | 40.2 | 40.7 | 40.3 | 40.3 | 39.6 | 40.5 | 40.1 | 40.3 | 40.0 |
| 2016 | 39.6 | 39.0 | 39.5 | 39.7 | 39.9 | 40.1 | 39.8 | 40.2 | 40.0 | 40.3 | 40.3 | 40.0 | 39.9 |
| 2017 | 40.1 | 39.5 | 38.5 | 39.6 | 40.3 | 40.4 | 40.0 | 39.9 | 40.4 | 40.1 | 40.6 | 40.1 | 40.0 |
| 2018 | 39.8 | 40.0 | 40.0 | 40.7 | 40.6 | 40.7 | 40.4 | 40.4 | 40.0 | 40.3 | 39.5 | 40.9 | 40.3 |
| 2019 | 40.4 | 39.5 | 40.8 | 41.2 | 40.7 | 40.5 | 40.0 | 40.4 | 40.3 | 39.9 | 39.8 | 39.4 | 40.2 |
| **Construction** | | | | | | | | | | | | | |
| 2015 | 37.3 | 38.3 | 39.4 | 40.6 | 41.7 | 42.5 | 42.2 | 42.0 | 39.6 | 41.0 | 39.4 | 39.5 | 40.4 |
| 2016 | 38.5 | 37.5 | 39.4 | 39.5 | 40.0 | 40.2 | 40.2 | 39.9 | 40.1 | 40.7 | 40.0 | 38.7 | 39.6 |
| 2017 | 38.4 | 37.5 | 36.5 | 38.5 | 39.3 | 40.1 | 39.3 | 39.0 | 39.4 | 38.4 | 38.9 | 37.9 | 38.6 |
| 2018 | 37.4 | 38.0 | 38.0 | 39.3 | 39.9 | 40.0 | 40.4 | 39.7 | 38.2 | 39.3 | 37.3 | 38.3 | 38.9 |
| 2019 | 37.7 | 36.4 | 39.0 | 39.7 | 39.4 | 39.1 | 38.4 | 39.2 | 39.4 | 38.3 | 37.8 | 36.4 | 38.4 |
| **Manufacturing** | | | | | | | | | | | | | |
| 2015 | 39.7 | 39.9 | 39.9 | 39.8 | 39.7 | 40.0 | 39.6 | 39.7 | 39.7 | 40.0 | 40.2 | 40.4 | 39.9 |
| 2016 | 39.8 | 39.4 | 39.5 | 39.8 | 39.9 | 40.0 | 39.5 | 40.3 | 40.0 | 40.2 | 40.6 | 40.8 | 40.0 |
| 2017 | 41.0 | 40.7 | 39.6 | 40.3 | 40.9 | 40.7 | 40.3 | 40.4 | 41.0 | 40.9 | 41.3 | 41.1 | 40.7 |
| 2018 | 40.9 | 40.9 | 40.9 | 41.3 | 40.8 | 40.9 | 40.3 | 40.7 | 41.0 | 40.9 | 40.5 | 41.6 | 40.9 |
| 2019 | 41.0 | 40.3 | 40.9 | 41.3 | 40.5 | 40.5 | 40.1 | 40.5 | 40.2 | 40.1 | 40.3 | 40.4 | 40.5 |
| **Trade, Transportation, and Utilities** | | | | | | | | | | | | | |
| 2015 | 33.5 | 33.7 | 33.8 | 33.8 | 34.3 | 34.3 | 34.2 | 34.5 | 34.4 | 34.2 | 34.5 | 34.8 | 34.2 |
| 2016 | 33.9 | 34.0 | 33.9 | 33.9 | 34.1 | 34.1 | 34.1 | 34.2 | 34.5 | 34.4 | 34.1 | 34.7 | 34.2 |
| 2017 | 34.0 | 33.7 | 33.4 | 34.5 | 34.4 | 34.5 | 34.9 | 34.8 | 35.0 | 34.7 | 35.0 | 35.0 | 34.5 |
| 2018 | 33.9 | 34.0 | 34.2 | 34.5 | 34.7 | 34.5 | 35.0 | 34.9 | 35.2 | 34.7 | 35.0 | 35.2 | 34.7 |
| 2019 | 33.9 | 33.9 | 34.4 | 34.8 | 34.4 | 34.6 | 34.4 | 34.5 | 34.6 | 34.2 | 34.2 | 34.7 | 34.4 |
| **Financial Activities** | | | | | | | | | | | | | |
| 2015 | 37.1 | 37.5 | 37.7 | 37.3 | 37.3 | 37.2 | 36.8 | 37.5 | 36.9 | 36.9 | 37.6 | 36.9 | 37.2 |
| 2016 | 37.0 | 37.0 | 37.0 | 37.2 | 37.4 | 36.9 | 37.3 | 37.3 | 37.2 | 37.5 | 37.5 | 37.3 | 37.2 |
| 2017 | 37.9 | 37.5 | 37.2 | 38.0 | 37.6 | 37.2 | 37.6 | 37.1 | 37.0 | 37.7 | 37.1 | 36.9 | 37.4 |
| 2018 | 37.0 | 37.0 | 36.9 | 37.6 | 36.9 | 37.0 | 37.1 | 36.8 | 37.3 | 36.7 | 36.6 | 37.3 | 37.0 |
| 2019 | 36.8 | 36.7 | 36.5 | 36.7 | 36.6 | 36.8 | 36.6 | 37.1 | 37.3 | 37.0 | 37.0 | 37.0 | 36.8 |
| **Professional and Business Services** | | | | | | | | | | | | | |
| 2015 | 34.9 | 35.5 | 35.7 | 35.5 | 35.8 | 35.8 | 35.8 | 36.4 | 35.2 | 35.9 | 36.5 | 36.0 | 35.8 |
| 2016 | 35.7 | 35.4 | 35.6 | 35.6 | 36.3 | 35.8 | 35.8 | 35.7 | 35.5 | 36.6 | 35.8 | 35.6 | 35.8 |
| 2017 | 35.4 | 35.3 | 34.8 | 36.0 | 35.6 | 35.5 | 36.0 | 35.6 | 35.8 | 36.1 | 35.5 | 35.4 | 35.6 |
| 2018 | 34.7 | 35.2 | 35.3 | 36.3 | 35.8 | 35.8 | 36.3 | 35.8 | 36.4 | 35.9 | 35.4 | 36.5 | 35.8 |
| 2019 | 35.4 | 35.3 | 35.5 | 36.1 | 36.1 | 36.6 | 35.7 | 36.0 | 36.4 | 35.9 | 35.9 | 36.0 | 35.9 |
| **Education and Health Services** | | | | | | | | | | | | | |
| 2015 | 32.7 | 32.5 | 32.6 | 32.5 | 32.6 | 32.5 | 32.7 | 32.7 | 32.6 | 32.6 | 33.0 | 32.9 | 32.7 |
| 2016 | 32.9 | 32.6 | 32.6 | 32.6 | 32.7 | 32.7 | 32.7 | 32.5 | 32.7 | 32.6 | 32.4 | 32.5 | 32.6 |
| 2017 | 32.5 | 32.2 | 32.1 | 32.4 | 32.5 | 32.5 | 32.4 | 32.4 | 32.6 | 32.5 | 32.4 | 32.4 | 32.4 |
| 2018 | 32.4 | 32.7 | 32.5 | 32.9 | 32.8 | 33.1 | 33.6 | 33.4 | 33.7 | 33.5 | 33.6 | 33.6 | 33.2 |
| 2019 | 33.5 | 33.4 | 33.3 | 33.3 | 33.3 | 33.5 | 33.2 | 33.3 | 33.7 | 33.5 | 33.7 | 33.6 | 33.4 |
| **Leisure and Hospitality** | | | | | | | | | | | | | |
| 2015 | 24.2 | 24.6 | 24.6 | 24.9 | 25.1 | 25.1 | 25.0 | 25.6 | 24.7 | 25.1 | 24.8 | 24.6 | 24.9 |
| 2016 | 23.3 | 24.3 | 24.2 | 24.3 | 24.6 | 24.6 | 24.7 | 24.7 | 24.4 | 24.6 | 24.3 | 23.9 | 24.3 |
| 2017 | 24.1 | 24.3 | 24.0 | 24.8 | 24.6 | 24.9 | 24.9 | 24.9 | 24.7 | 25.1 | 25.0 | 25.0 | 24.7 |
| 2018 | 23.9 | 25.0 | 24.8 | 25.4 | 25.3 | 25.3 | 25.4 | 25.4 | 25.3 | 25.3 | 24.3 | 25.0 | 25.0 |
| 2019 | 23.9 | 24.5 | 24.7 | 24.8 | 25.0 | 25.4 | 25.4 | 25.2 | 24.9 | 25.0 | 24.8 | 24.8 | 24.9 |
| **Other Services** | | | | | | | | | | | | | |
| 2015 | 29.4 | 29.3 | 29.4 | 29.1 | 29.2 | 29.1 | 29.9 | 30.3 | 30.0 | 30.0 | 30.1 | 29.6 | 29.6 |
| 2016 | 29.4 | 29.3 | 29.1 | 28.7 | 29.4 | 29.1 | 28.8 | 29.4 | 28.7 | 28.8 | 28.5 | 28.3 | 29.0 |
| 2017 | 28.6 | 28.4 | 28.1 | 29.4 | 28.5 | 28.7 | 29.6 | 29.0 | 29.0 | 28.8 | 29.0 | 28.9 | 28.8 |
| 2018 | 29.0 | 29.2 | 28.5 | 28.9 | 29.2 | 29.0 | 29.9 | 30.5 | 31.0 | 29.8 | 29.7 | 30.3 | 29.6 |
| 2019 | 29.6 | 29.8 | 29.8 | 29.6 | 29.2 | 29.6 | 28.6 | 28.5 | 29.0 | 29.6 | 30.0 | 30.0 | 29.4 |

## 3. Average Hourly Earnings by Selected Industry: Pennsylvania, 2015–2019

(Dollars, not seasonally adjusted)

| Industry and year | January | February | March | April | May | June | July | August | September | October | November | December | Annual average |
|---|---|---|---|---|---|---|---|---|---|---|---|---|---|
| **Total Private** | | | | | | | | | | | | | |
| 2015 | 23.95 | 24.10 | 24.23 | 24.11 | 24.05 | 24.08 | 24.13 | 24.27 | 24.36 | 24.35 | 24.59 | 24.42 | 24.22 |
| 2016 | 24.68 | 24.58 | 24.49 | 24.51 | 24.51 | 24.41 | 24.61 | 24.54 | 24.78 | 25.04 | 24.95 | 25.02 | 24.68 |
| 2017 | 25.20 | 25.03 | 25.07 | 25.21 | 24.86 | 24.86 | 24.98 | 24.90 | 25.16 | 25.35 | 25.15 | 25.45 | 25.10 |
| 2018 | 25.57 | 25.54 | 25.53 | 25.70 | 25.58 | 25.53 | 25.71 | 25.48 | 25.96 | 25.89 | 26.05 | 26.39 | 25.75 |
| 2019 | 26.33 | 26.16 | 25.95 | 25.99 | 25.92 | 25.93 | 25.96 | 25.95 | 26.34 | 26.25 | 26.38 | 26.73 | 26.16 |
| **Goods-Producing** | | | | | | | | | | | | | |
| 2015 | 25.26 | 25.21 | 25.41 | 25.38 | 25.67 | 25.72 | 25.89 | 25.99 | 25.92 | 25.95 | 25.86 | 25.56 | 25.66 |
| 2016 | 25.60 | 25.60 | 25.61 | 25.64 | 25.79 | 26.07 | 26.57 | 26.39 | 26.52 | 26.71 | 26.47 | 26.67 | 26.14 |
| 2017 | 26.70 | 26.61 | 26.78 | 27.09 | 26.70 | 26.93 | 26.92 | 26.95 | 27.08 | 27.00 | 26.78 | 27.22 | 26.90 |
| 2018 | 26.96 | 27.05 | 26.92 | 27.18 | 27.09 | 26.99 | 27.38 | 27.20 | 27.48 | 27.45 | 27.45 | 27.55 | 27.23 |
| 2019 | 27.23 | 27.63 | 27.35 | 27.60 | 27.60 | 27.89 | 28.06 | 28.09 | 28.21 | 28.24 | 28.09 | 28.71 | 27.89 |
| **Construction** | | | | | | | | | | | | | |
| 2015 | 28.83 | 29.09 | 29.14 | 28.76 | 29.32 | 28.91 | 29.20 | 29.31 | 29.33 | 29.52 | 29.52 | 29.72 | 29.23 |
| 2016 | 29.73 | 30.11 | 29.80 | 29.56 | 29.79 | 29.99 | 30.68 | 30.27 | 29.88 | 30.20 | 29.48 | 30.03 | 29.97 |
| 2017 | 29.99 | 30.18 | 30.44 | 30.01 | 30.04 | 30.72 | 30.01 | 29.89 | 30.07 | 29.89 | 29.60 | 30.15 | 30.08 |
| 2018 | 29.93 | 30.35 | 30.14 | 30.40 | 30.30 | 30.27 | 30.43 | 30.44 | 30.68 | 30.86 | 30.76 | 31.09 | 30.48 |
| 2019 | 30.33 | 31.06 | 30.57 | 30.86 | 31.14 | 31.55 | 31.50 | 31.88 | 31.48 | 31.61 | 31.38 | 32.05 | 31.30 |
| **Manufacturing** | | | | | | | | | | | | | |
| 2015 | 23.92 | 23.76 | 23.91 | 23.89 | 23.96 | 24.03 | 24.12 | 24.19 | 24.23 | 24.13 | 24.12 | 24.03 | 24.02 |
| 2016 | 24.21 | 24.09 | 24.03 | 24.08 | 24.14 | 24.38 | 24.65 | 24.47 | 24.86 | 24.98 | 25.02 | 25.17 | 24.51 |
| 2017 | 25.27 | 25.14 | 25.25 | 25.72 | 25.25 | 25.24 | 25.57 | 25.63 | 25.76 | 25.76 | 25.60 | 26.01 | 25.52 |
| 2018 | 25.83 | 25.76 | 25.62 | 25.71 | 25.55 | 25.34 | 25.84 | 25.59 | 26.00 | 25.80 | 25.93 | 25.90 | 25.74 |
| 2019 | 25.83 | 26.12 | 25.90 | 26.00 | 25.81 | 26.03 | 26.30 | 26.17 | 26.54 | 26.52 | 26.46 | 27.14 | 26.23 |
| **Trade, Transportation, and Utilities** | | | | | | | | | | | | | |
| 2015 | 20.88 | 20.78 | 21.36 | 21.41 | 21.21 | 21.09 | 21.04 | 21.13 | 21.11 | 21.05 | 21.04 | 20.75 | 21.07 |
| 2016 | 21.43 | 21.43 | 21.07 | 21.08 | 20.99 | 20.97 | 21.09 | 20.94 | 21.09 | 21.33 | 21.20 | 20.81 | 21.12 |
| 2017 | 21.31 | 21.25 | 21.35 | 21.49 | 21.09 | 21.40 | 21.35 | 21.21 | 21.45 | 21.62 | 21.41 | 21.74 | 21.39 |
| 2018 | 22.08 | 22.00 | 22.23 | 22.63 | 22.86 | 22.67 | 22.84 | 22.70 | 23.09 | 22.88 | 22.72 | 23.01 | 22.65 |
| 2019 | 23.33 | 23.24 | 23.14 | 23.44 | 23.50 | 23.67 | 23.49 | 23.38 | 23.51 | 23.42 | 23.38 | 23.48 | 23.42 |
| **Financial Activities** | | | | | | | | | | | | | |
| 2015 | 31.38 | 31.86 | 31.62 | 31.74 | 31.50 | 31.44 | 31.35 | 32.25 | 31.99 | 32.06 | 32.79 | 33.51 | 31.96 |
| 2016 | 33.04 | 33.13 | 33.53 | 33.42 | 34.03 | 33.43 | 33.68 | 34.40 | 34.84 | 35.31 | 34.91 | 35.19 | 34.08 |
| 2017 | 34.95 | 34.54 | 34.42 | 34.16 | 33.36 | 33.00 | 33.43 | 33.03 | 33.25 | 33.86 | 33.41 | 34.23 | 33.80 |
| 2018 | 34.22 | 34.20 | 34.51 | 34.90 | 35.11 | 34.62 | 35.23 | 35.42 | 36.19 | 35.84 | 36.25 | 37.88 | 35.37 |
| 2019 | 37.10 | 36.85 | 36.76 | 36.50 | 36.27 | 34.41 | 34.40 | 34.57 | 35.61 | 35.33 | 36.07 | 37.17 | 35.91 |
| **Professional and Business Services** | | | | | | | | | | | | | |
| 2015 | 30.72 | 31.16 | 31.11 | 30.50 | 30.53 | 30.81 | 30.92 | 31.13 | 31.31 | 31.25 | 31.92 | 31.49 | 31.08 |
| 2016 | 32.11 | 31.98 | 31.91 | 31.84 | 31.88 | 31.73 | 31.79 | 31.76 | 31.94 | 32.30 | 32.17 | 32.65 | 32.01 |
| 2017 | 33.00 | 32.45 | 32.56 | 32.47 | 31.91 | 31.79 | 32.14 | 31.93 | 32.25 | 32.46 | 32.18 | 32.54 | 32.30 |
| 2018 | 32.49 | 32.62 | 32.37 | 32.51 | 31.83 | 31.89 | 32.32 | 31.83 | 32.48 | 32.19 | 32.74 | 33.58 | 32.41 |
| 2019 | 32.98 | 32.34 | 31.50 | 31.17 | 31.10 | 31.83 | 31.99 | 32.22 | 32.89 | 32.67 | 32.94 | 33.71 | 32.28 |
| **Education and Health Services** | | | | | | | | | | | | | |
| 2015 | 22.40 | 22.58 | 22.48 | 22.48 | 22.46 | 22.57 | 22.73 | 22.81 | 23.15 | 22.84 | 23.10 | 23.10 | 22.73 |
| 2016 | 23.03 | 22.90 | 22.77 | 22.93 | 22.83 | 22.69 | 22.88 | 22.74 | 22.98 | 23.02 | 23.10 | 23.14 | 22.92 |
| 2017 | 23.11 | 23.13 | 23.00 | 23.28 | 23.16 | 23.19 | 23.45 | 23.39 | 23.61 | 23.78 | 23.72 | 23.84 | 23.39 |
| 2018 | 23.87 | 23.72 | 23.62 | 23.50 | 23.42 | 23.74 | 23.60 | 23.35 | 23.84 | 23.88 | 24.16 | 24.13 | 23.74 |
| 2019 | 24.05 | 23.98 | 23.94 | 23.87 | 23.69 | 23.38 | 23.51 | 23.40 | 23.59 | 23.49 | 23.54 | 23.68 | 23.68 |
| **Leisure and Hospitality** | | | | | | | | | | | | | |
| 2015 | 13.92 | 13.92 | 13.82 | 13.91 | 13.75 | 13.66 | 13.47 | 13.44 | 13.71 | 13.79 | 13.87 | 13.91 | 13.76 |
| 2016 | 13.81 | 13.82 | 13.84 | 13.83 | 13.85 | 13.72 | 13.71 | 13.81 | 14.08 | 14.24 | 14.34 | 14.60 | 13.97 |
| 2017 | 14.51 | 14.62 | 14.69 | 14.74 | 14.92 | 14.56 | 14.41 | 14.51 | 14.87 | 15.07 | 15.08 | 15.21 | 14.76 |
| 2018 | 15.45 | 15.30 | 15.42 | 15.22 | 15.40 | 15.02 | 14.95 | 14.88 | 15.13 | 15.13 | 15.35 | 15.41 | 15.21 |
| 2019 | 16.06 | 15.37 | 15.20 | 15.35 | 15.33 | 15.05 | 14.92 | 14.46 | 14.89 | 15.08 | 15.35 | 15.54 | 15.20 |
| **Other Services** | | | | | | | | | | | | | |
| 2015 | 20.82 | 20.73 | 21.19 | 21.00 | 20.80 | 20.56 | 20.34 | 20.28 | 20.65 | 20.83 | 20.74 | 21.11 | 20.75 |
| 2016 | 21.00 | 20.93 | 20.87 | 20.58 | 20.40 | 19.81 | 19.82 | 19.56 | 20.19 | 20.17 | 20.40 | 20.79 | 20.37 |
| 2017 | 20.73 | 20.46 | 20.88 | 21.00 | 21.05 | 20.81 | 20.45 | 20.95 | 21.06 | 21.54 | 21.41 | 21.81 | 21.01 |
| 2018 | 22.18 | 22.25 | 22.26 | 22.79 | 22.85 | 22.76 | 22.81 | 22.71 | 22.94 | 23.77 | 23.84 | 24.02 | 22.94 |
| 2019 | 24.09 | 23.92 | 24.84 | 24.62 | 24.91 | 24.57 | 25.00 | 25.30 | 26.36 | 26.03 | 26.40 | 26.77 | 25.24 |

## 4. Average Weekly Earnings by Selected Industry: Pennsylvania, 2015–2019

(Dollars, not seasonally adjusted)

| Industry and year | January | February | March | April | May | June | July | August | September | October | November | December | Annual average |
|---|---|---|---|---|---|---|---|---|---|---|---|---|---|
| **Total Private** | | | | | | | | | | | | | |
| 2015 | 802.33 | 812.17 | 818.97 | 814.92 | 817.70 | 821.13 | 820.42 | 832.46 | 823.37 | 830.34 | 843.44 | 835.16 | 823.48 |
| 2016 | 831.72 | 825.89 | 822.86 | 825.99 | 830.89 | 825.06 | 831.82 | 829.45 | 837.56 | 853.86 | 843.31 | 845.68 | 834.18 |
| 2017 | 849.24 | 838.51 | 829.82 | 854.62 | 840.27 | 842.75 | 849.32 | 844.11 | 857.96 | 864.44 | 857.62 | 862.76 | 848.38 |
| 2018 | 854.04 | 863.25 | 860.36 | 881.51 | 872.28 | 873.13 | 887.00 | 876.51 | 898.22 | 888.03 | 888.31 | 915.73 | 880.65 |
| 2019 | 895.22 | 884.21 | 884.90 | 894.06 | 886.46 | 891.99 | 882.64 | 887.49 | 906.10 | 895.13 | 902.20 | 914.17 | 894.67 |
| **Goods-Producing** | | | | | | | | | | | | | |
| 2015 | 980.09 | 990.75 | 1,006.24 | 1,012.66 | 1,031.93 | 1,046.80 | 1,043.37 | 1,047.40 | 1,026.43 | 1,050.98 | 1,036.99 | 1,030.07 | 1,026.40 |
| 2016 | 1,013.76 | 998.40 | 1,011.60 | 1,017.91 | 1,029.02 | 1,045.41 | 1,057.49 | 1,060.88 | 1,060.80 | 1,076.41 | 1,066.74 | 1,066.80 | 1,042.99 |
| 2017 | 1,070.67 | 1,051.10 | 1,031.03 | 1,072.76 | 1,076.01 | 1,087.97 | 1,076.80 | 1,075.31 | 1,094.03 | 1,082.70 | 1,087.27 | 1,091.52 | 1,076.00 |
| 2018 | 1,073.01 | 1,082.00 | 1,076.80 | 1,106.23 | 1,099.85 | 1,098.49 | 1,106.15 | 1,098.88 | 1,099.20 | 1,106.24 | 1,084.28 | 1,126.80 | 1,097.37 |
| 2019 | 1,100.09 | 1,091.39 | 1,115.88 | 1,137.12 | 1,123.32 | 1,129.55 | 1,122.40 | 1,134.84 | 1,136.86 | 1,126.78 | 1,117.98 | 1,131.17 | 1,121.18 |
| **Construction** | | | | | | | | | | | | | |
| 2015 | 1,075.36 | 1,114.15 | 1,148.12 | 1,167.66 | 1,222.64 | 1,228.68 | 1,232.24 | 1,231.02 | 1,161.47 | 1,210.32 | 1,163.09 | 1,173.94 | 1,180.89 |
| 2016 | 1,144.61 | 1,129.13 | 1,174.12 | 1,167.62 | 1,191.60 | 1,205.60 | 1,233.34 | 1,207.77 | 1,198.19 | 1,229.14 | 1,179.20 | 1,162.16 | 1,186.81 |
| 2017 | 1,151.62 | 1,131.75 | 1,111.06 | 1,155.39 | 1,180.57 | 1,231.87 | 1,179.39 | 1,165.71 | 1,184.76 | 1,147.78 | 1,151.44 | 1,142.69 | 1,161.09 |
| 2018 | 1,119.38 | 1,153.30 | 1,145.32 | 1,194.72 | 1,208.97 | 1,210.80 | 1,229.37 | 1,208.47 | 1,171.98 | 1,212.80 | 1,147.35 | 1,190.75 | 1,185.67 |
| 2019 | 1,143.44 | 1,130.58 | 1,192.23 | 1,225.14 | 1,226.92 | 1,233.61 | 1,209.60 | 1,249.70 | 1,240.31 | 1,210.66 | 1,186.16 | 1,166.62 | 1,201.92 |
| **Manufacturing** | | | | | | | | | | | | | |
| 2015 | 949.62 | 948.02 | 954.01 | 950.82 | 951.21 | 961.20 | 955.15 | 960.34 | 961.93 | 965.20 | 969.62 | 970.81 | 958.40 |
| 2016 | 963.56 | 949.15 | 949.19 | 958.38 | 963.19 | 975.20 | 973.68 | 986.14 | 994.40 | 1,004.20 | 1,015.81 | 1,026.94 | 980.40 |
| 2017 | 1,036.07 | 1,023.20 | 999.90 | 1,036.52 | 1,032.73 | 1,027.27 | 1,030.47 | 1,035.45 | 1,056.16 | 1,053.58 | 1,057.28 | 1,069.01 | 1,038.66 |
| 2018 | 1,056.45 | 1,053.58 | 1,047.86 | 1,061.82 | 1,042.44 | 1,036.41 | 1,041.35 | 1,041.51 | 1,066.00 | 1,055.22 | 1,050.17 | 1,077.44 | 1,052.77 |
| 2019 | 1,059.03 | 1,052.64 | 1,059.31 | 1,073.80 | 1,045.31 | 1,054.22 | 1,054.63 | 1,059.89 | 1,066.91 | 1,063.45 | 1,066.34 | 1,096.46 | 1,062.32 |
| **Trade, Transportation, and Utilities** | | | | | | | | | | | | | |
| 2015 | 699.48 | 700.29 | 721.97 | 723.66 | 727.50 | 723.39 | 719.57 | 728.99 | 726.18 | 719.91 | 725.88 | 722.10 | 720.59 |
| 2016 | 726.48 | 728.62 | 714.27 | 714.61 | 715.76 | 715.08 | 719.17 | 716.15 | 727.61 | 733.75 | 722.92 | 722.11 | 722.30 |
| 2017 | 724.54 | 716.13 | 713.09 | 741.41 | 725.50 | 738.30 | 745.12 | 738.11 | 750.75 | 750.21 | 749.35 | 760.90 | 737.96 |
| 2018 | 748.51 | 748.00 | 760.27 | 780.74 | 793.24 | 782.12 | 799.40 | 792.23 | 812.77 | 793.94 | 795.20 | 809.95 | 785.96 |
| 2019 | 790.89 | 787.84 | 796.02 | 815.71 | 808.40 | 818.98 | 808.06 | 806.61 | 813.45 | 800.96 | 799.60 | 814.76 | 805.65 |
| **Financial Activities** | | | | | | | | | | | | | |
| 2015 | 1,164.20 | 1,194.75 | 1,192.07 | 1,183.90 | 1,174.95 | 1,169.57 | 1,153.68 | 1,209.38 | 1,180.43 | 1,183.01 | 1,232.90 | 1,236.52 | 1,188.91 |
| 2016 | 1,222.48 | 1,225.81 | 1,240.61 | 1,243.22 | 1,272.72 | 1,233.57 | 1,256.26 | 1,283.12 | 1,296.05 | 1,324.13 | 1,309.13 | 1,312.59 | 1,267.78 |
| 2017 | 1,324.61 | 1,295.25 | 1,280.42 | 1,298.08 | 1,254.34 | 1,227.60 | 1,256.97 | 1,225.41 | 1,230.25 | 1,276.52 | 1,239.51 | 1,263.09 | 1,264.12 |
| 2018 | 1,266.14 | 1,265.40 | 1,273.42 | 1,312.24 | 1,295.56 | 1,280.94 | 1,307.03 | 1,303.46 | 1,349.89 | 1,315.33 | 1,326.75 | 1,412.92 | 1,308.69 |
| 2019 | 1,365.28 | 1,352.40 | 1,341.74 | 1,339.55 | 1,327.48 | 1,266.29 | 1,259.04 | 1,282.55 | 1,328.25 | 1,307.21 | 1,334.59 | 1,375.29 | 1,321.49 |
| **Professional and Business Services** | | | | | | | | | | | | | |
| 2015 | 1,072.13 | 1,106.18 | 1,110.63 | 1,082.75 | 1,092.97 | 1,103.00 | 1,106.94 | 1,133.13 | 1,102.11 | 1,121.88 | 1,165.08 | 1,133.64 | 1,112.66 |
| 2016 | 1,146.33 | 1,132.09 | 1,136.00 | 1,133.50 | 1,157.24 | 1,135.93 | 1,138.08 | 1,133.83 | 1,133.87 | 1,182.18 | 1,151.69 | 1,162.34 | 1,145.96 |
| 2017 | 1,168.20 | 1,145.49 | 1,133.09 | 1,168.92 | 1,136.00 | 1,128.55 | 1,157.04 | 1,136.71 | 1,154.55 | 1,171.81 | 1,142.39 | 1,151.92 | 1,149.88 |
| 2018 | 1,127.40 | 1,148.22 | 1,142.66 | 1,180.11 | 1,139.51 | 1,141.66 | 1,173.22 | 1,139.51 | 1,182.27 | 1,155.62 | 1,159.00 | 1,225.67 | 1,160.28 |
| 2019 | 1,167.49 | 1,141.60 | 1,118.25 | 1,125.24 | 1,122.71 | 1,164.98 | 1,142.04 | 1,159.92 | 1,197.20 | 1,172.85 | 1,182.55 | 1,213.56 | 1,158.85 |
| **Education and Health Services** | | | | | | | | | | | | | |
| 2015 | 732.48 | 733.85 | 732.85 | 730.60 | 732.20 | 733.53 | 743.27 | 745.89 | 754.69 | 744.58 | 762.30 | 759.99 | 743.27 |
| 2016 | 757.69 | 746.54 | 742.30 | 747.52 | 746.54 | 741.96 | 748.18 | 739.05 | 751.45 | 750.45 | 748.44 | 752.05 | 747.19 |
| 2017 | 751.08 | 744.79 | 738.30 | 754.27 | 752.70 | 753.68 | 759.78 | 757.84 | 769.69 | 772.85 | 768.53 | 772.42 | 757.84 |
| 2018 | 773.39 | 775.64 | 767.65 | 773.15 | 768.18 | 785.79 | 792.96 | 779.89 | 803.41 | 799.98 | 811.78 | 810.77 | 788.17 |
| 2019 | 805.68 | 800.93 | 797.20 | 794.87 | 788.88 | 783.23 | 780.53 | 779.22 | 794.98 | 786.92 | 793.30 | 795.65 | 790.91 |
| **Leisure and Hospitality** | | | | | | | | | | | | | |
| 2015 | 336.86 | 342.43 | 339.97 | 346.36 | 345.13 | 342.87 | 336.75 | 344.06 | 338.64 | 346.13 | 343.98 | 342.19 | 342.62 |
| 2016 | 321.77 | 335.83 | 334.93 | 336.07 | 340.71 | 337.51 | 338.64 | 341.11 | 343.55 | 350.30 | 348.46 | 348.94 | 339.47 |
| 2017 | 349.69 | 355.27 | 352.56 | 365.55 | 367.03 | 362.54 | 358.81 | 361.30 | 367.29 | 378.26 | 377.00 | 380.25 | 364.57 |
| 2018 | 369.26 | 382.50 | 382.42 | 386.59 | 389.62 | 380.01 | 379.73 | 377.95 | 382.79 | 382.79 | 373.01 | 385.25 | 380.25 |
| 2019 | 383.83 | 376.57 | 375.44 | 380.68 | 383.25 | 382.27 | 378.97 | 364.39 | 370.76 | 377.00 | 380.68 | 385.39 | 378.48 |
| **Other Services** | | | | | | | | | | | | | |
| 2015 | 612.11 | 607.39 | 622.99 | 611.10 | 607.36 | 598.30 | 608.17 | 614.48 | 619.50 | 624.90 | 624.27 | 624.86 | 614.20 |
| 2016 | 617.40 | 613.25 | 607.32 | 590.65 | 599.76 | 576.47 | 570.82 | 575.06 | 579.45 | 580.90 | 581.40 | 588.36 | 590.73 |
| 2017 | 592.88 | 581.06 | 586.73 | 617.40 | 599.93 | 597.25 | 605.32 | 607.55 | 610.74 | 620.35 | 620.89 | 630.31 | 605.09 |
| 2018 | 643.22 | 649.70 | 634.41 | 658.63 | 667.22 | 660.04 | 682.02 | 692.66 | 711.14 | 708.35 | 708.05 | 727.81 | 679.02 |
| 2019 | 713.06 | 712.82 | 740.23 | 728.75 | 727.37 | 727.27 | 715.00 | 721.05 | 764.44 | 770.49 | 792.00 | 803.10 | 742.06 |

# RHODE ISLAND
## *At a Glance*

Population:
  2010 census: 1,052,567
  2019 estimate: 1,059,361

Percent change in population:
  2010–2019: 0.6%

Percent change in total nonfarm employment:
  2011–2019: 8.5%

Industry with the largest growth in employment, 2011–2019 (percent):
  Construction, 26.8%

Industry with the largest decline or smallest growth in employment, 2011–2019 (percent):
  Information, -29.8%

Civilian labor force:
  2010: 566,704
  2019: 555,554

Unemployment rate and rank among states (highest to lowest):
  2010: 11.2%, 4th
  2019: 3.6%, 21st

Over-the-year change in unemployment rates:
  2017–2018: -0.4%
  2018–2019: -0.4%

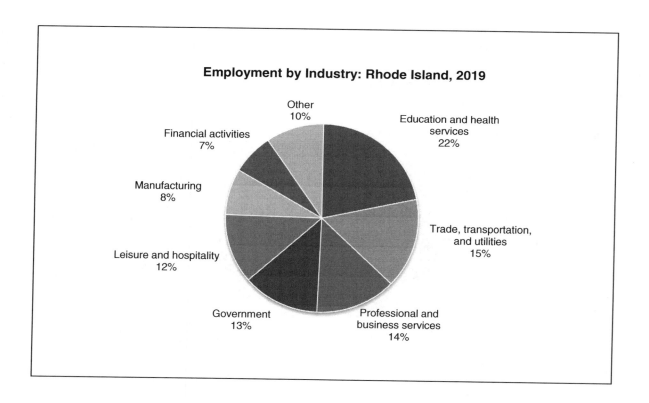

**Employment by Industry: Rhode Island, 2019**

- Other 10%
- Education and health services 22%
- Financial activities 7%
- Manufacturing 8%
- Leisure and hospitality 12%
- Government 13%
- Professional and business services 14%
- Trade, transportation, and utilities 15%

## 1. Employment by Industry: Rhode Island, 2011–2019

(Numbers in thousands, not seasonally adjusted)

| Industry and year | January | February | March | April | May | June | July | August | September | October | November | December | Annual average |
|---|---|---|---|---|---|---|---|---|---|---|---|---|---|
| **Total Nonfarm** | | | | | | | | | | | | | |
| 2011 | 448.3 | 451.6 | 454.6 | 463.8 | 469.6 | 469.8 | 464.3 | 463.8 | 470.8 | 471.1 | 470.9 | 468.9 | 464.0 |
| 2012 | 453.1 | 458.0 | 461.0 | 467.1 | 474.1 | 474.1 | 467.1 | 469.3 | 477.9 | 476.2 | 475.1 | 475.8 | 469.1 |
| 2013 | 459.0 | 461.3 | 465.3 | 471.8 | 479.1 | 480.8 | 475.4 | 476.3 | 483.2 | 484.5 | 483.2 | 481.0 | 475.1 |
| 2014 | 464.8 | 468.2 | 470.3 | 480.3 | 488.1 | 487.5 | 482.9 | 483.1 | 491.1 | 491.0 | 491.0 | 490.8 | 482.4 |
| 2015 | 473.8 | 472.4 | 476.4 | 487.3 | 495.6 | 494.3 | 490.8 | 489.2 | 496.7 | 497.9 | 498.1 | 497.2 | 489.1 |
| 2016 | 479.1 | 482.0 | 485.8 | 493.1 | 497.9 | 498.6 | 494.9 | 493.8 | 499.6 | 500.5 | 499.9 | 497.7 | 493.6 |
| 2017 | 481.5 | 485.1 | 486.9 | 495.7 | 502.0 | 503.5 | 498.9 | 499.3 | 503.3 | 503.3 | 503.8 | 503.0 | 497.2 |
| 2018 | 483.1 | 489.3 | 490.9 | 498.5 | 506.4 | 506.0 | 502.5 | 502.2 | 507.2 | 507.4 | 507.1 | 506.0 | 500.6 |
| 2019 | 490.1 | 494.0 | 494.7 | 502.2 | 507.8 | 508.3 | 503.7 | 503.9 | 508.8 | 511.3 | 510.3 | 507.6 | 503.6 |
| **Total Private** | | | | | | | | | | | | | |
| 2011 | 383.1 | 386.5 | 389.1 | 398.3 | 403.8 | 406.2 | 405.0 | 404.3 | 406.2 | 406.4 | 406.0 | 404.0 | 399.9 |
| 2012 | 388.5 | 393.1 | 396.1 | 402.1 | 408.4 | 411.6 | 408.1 | 409.9 | 413.2 | 411.5 | 410.1 | 410.8 | 405.3 |
| 2013 | 394.5 | 396.9 | 400.3 | 407.0 | 413.4 | 418.1 | 415.5 | 416.7 | 418.4 | 419.4 | 418.1 | 415.7 | 411.2 |
| 2014 | 400.2 | 403.7 | 405.5 | 415.4 | 422.1 | 424.3 | 423.0 | 423.6 | 425.7 | 425.9 | 425.4 | 425.6 | 418.4 |
| 2015 | 408.9 | 407.5 | 411.5 | 422.2 | 429.8 | 431.5 | 431.2 | 430.0 | 432.0 | 433.0 | 433.0 | 431.9 | 425.2 |
| 2016 | 414.3 | 417.0 | 420.5 | 428.0 | 432.4 | 435.6 | 434.6 | 433.9 | 434.4 | 435.0 | 434.2 | 432.1 | 429.3 |
| 2017 | 416.5 | 420.0 | 421.6 | 430.4 | 436.0 | 439.8 | 438.2 | 439.0 | 437.6 | 437.5 | 438.2 | 437.0 | 432.7 |
| 2018 | 417.8 | 423.9 | 425.5 | 433.0 | 439.5 | 442.0 | 441.6 | 441.7 | 440.6 | 441.4 | 441.1 | 439.7 | 435.7 |
| 2019 | 424.4 | 428.2 | 428.4 | 435.9 | 441.2 | 444.2 | 442.8 | 443.0 | 442.4 | 444.7 | 443.7 | 440.8 | 438.3 |
| **Goods Producing** | | | | | | | | | | | | | |
| 2011 | 54.0 | 53.4 | 53.9 | 55.6 | 56.5 | 57.4 | 56.9 | 57.4 | 57.0 | 56.9 | 56.8 | 56.2 | 56.0 |
| 2012 | 53.6 | 53.3 | 54.0 | 55.3 | 55.9 | 57.1 | 56.2 | 57.2 | 56.9 | 57.2 | 56.9 | 56.6 | 55.9 |
| 2013 | 53.9 | 53.2 | 54.2 | 55.5 | 56.6 | 57.4 | 56.5 | 57.9 | 57.8 | 57.8 | 57.9 | 57.2 | 56.3 |
| 2014 | 54.9 | 54.6 | 54.8 | 57.0 | 58.4 | 59.1 | 58.5 | 59.1 | 58.9 | 59.0 | 58.9 | 58.5 | 57.6 |
| 2015 | 56.1 | 55.0 | 55.5 | 57.6 | 58.8 | 59.5 | 59.4 | 59.8 | 59.6 | 59.8 | 60.0 | 59.6 | 58.4 |
| 2016 | 56.7 | 56.2 | 56.9 | 58.3 | 59.2 | 60.0 | 59.7 | 60.1 | 59.6 | 59.9 | 59.6 | 59.0 | 58.8 |
| 2017 | 56.7 | 56.5 | 56.7 | 58.5 | 59.3 | 60.3 | 59.8 | 60.4 | 60.0 | 60.1 | 60.2 | 60.0 | 59.0 |
| 2018 | 57.2 | 58.1 | 58.5 | 59.5 | 60.4 | 60.9 | 60.4 | 61.1 | 60.9 | 60.6 | 60.4 | 60.1 | 59.8 |
| 2019 | 58.3 | 57.8 | 58.2 | 59.8 | 60.4 | 61.2 | 60.6 | 61.2 | 60.9 | 60.7 | 60.2 | 59.5 | 59.9 |
| **Service-Providing** | | | | | | | | | | | | | |
| 2011 | 394.3 | 398.2 | 400.7 | 408.2 | 413.1 | 412.4 | 407.4 | 406.4 | 413.8 | 414.2 | 414.1 | 412.7 | 408.0 |
| 2012 | 399.5 | 404.7 | 407.0 | 411.8 | 418.2 | 417.0 | 410.9 | 412.1 | 421.0 | 419.0 | 418.2 | 419.2 | 413.2 |
| 2013 | 405.1 | 408.1 | 411.1 | 416.3 | 422.5 | 423.4 | 418.9 | 418.4 | 425.4 | 426.7 | 425.3 | 423.8 | 418.8 |
| 2014 | 409.9 | 413.6 | 415.5 | 423.3 | 429.7 | 428.4 | 424.4 | 424.0 | 432.2 | 432.0 | 432.1 | 432.3 | 424.8 |
| 2015 | 417.7 | 417.4 | 420.9 | 429.7 | 436.8 | 434.8 | 431.4 | 429.4 | 437.1 | 438.1 | 438.1 | 437.6 | 430.8 |
| 2016 | 422.4 | 425.8 | 428.9 | 434.8 | 438.7 | 438.6 | 435.2 | 433.7 | 440.0 | 440.6 | 440.3 | 438.7 | 434.8 |
| 2017 | 424.8 | 428.6 | 430.2 | 437.2 | 442.7 | 443.2 | 439.1 | 438.9 | 443.3 | 443.2 | 443.6 | 443.0 | 438.2 |
| 2018 | 425.9 | 431.2 | 432.4 | 439.0 | 446.0 | 445.1 | 442.1 | 441.1 | 446.3 | 446.8 | 446.7 | 445.9 | 440.7 |
| 2019 | 431.8 | 436.2 | 436.5 | 442.4 | 447.4 | 447.1 | 443.1 | 442.7 | 447.9 | 450.6 | 450.1 | 448.1 | 443.7 |
| **Mining and Logging** | | | | | | | | | | | | | |
| 2011 | 0.1 | 0.1 | 0.1 | 0.2 | 0.2 | 0.2 | 0.2 | 0.2 | 0.2 | 0.2 | 0.2 | 0.2 | 0.2 |
| 2012 | 0.2 | 0.2 | 0.2 | 0.2 | 0.2 | 0.2 | 0.2 | 0.2 | 0.2 | 0.3 | 0.2 | 0.2 | 0.2 |
| 2013 | 0.2 | 0.1 | 0.2 | 0.2 | 0.2 | 0.2 | 0.2 | 0.3 | 0.2 | 0.2 | 0.2 | 0.2 | 0.2 |
| 2014 | 0.2 | 0.2 | 0.2 | 0.3 | 0.3 | 0.3 | 0.3 | 0.3 | 0.3 | 0.3 | 0.3 | 0.3 | 0.3 |
| 2015 | 0.2 | 0.2 | 0.2 | 0.3 | 0.3 | 0.3 | 0.3 | 0.3 | 0.3 | 0.3 | 0.3 | 0.3 | 0.3 |
| 2016 | 0.2 | 0.2 | 0.2 | 0.2 | 0.2 | 0.3 | 0.3 | 0.3 | 0.3 | 0.3 | 0.3 | 0.2 | 0.3 |
| 2017 | 0.2 | 0.2 | 0.2 | 0.2 | 0.2 | 0.3 | 0.3 | 0.3 | 0.3 | 0.3 | 0.3 | 0.3 | 0.3 |
| 2018 | 0.2 | 0.2 | 0.2 | 0.2 | 0.2 | 0.2 | 0.3 | 0.3 | 0.3 | 0.2 | 0.2 | 0.2 | 0.2 |
| 2019 | 0.2 | 0.2 | 0.2 | 0.2 | 0.2 | 0.3 | 0.3 | 0.3 | 0.3 | 0.3 | 0.3 | 0.2 | 0.3 |
| **Construction** | | | | | | | | | | | | | |
| 2011 | 13.6 | 13.0 | 13.4 | 15.0 | 15.9 | 16.6 | 17.2 | 17.1 | 16.8 | 16.8 | 16.8 | 16.2 | 15.7 |
| 2012 | 14.3 | 13.8 | 14.5 | 15.7 | 16.1 | 16.9 | 17.2 | 17.1 | 16.8 | 16.8 | 16.7 | 16.3 | 16.0 |
| 2013 | 14.1 | 13.7 | 14.3 | 15.5 | 16.5 | 16.9 | 17.3 | 17.4 | 17.3 | 17.2 | 17.0 | 16.2 | 16.1 |
| 2014 | 14.4 | 14.0 | 14.3 | 16.0 | 17.1 | 17.5 | 17.8 | 17.7 | 17.5 | 17.5 | 17.3 | 16.8 | 16.5 |
| 2015 | 14.8 | 14.0 | 14.4 | 16.2 | 17.3 | 17.8 | 18.3 | 18.3 | 18.2 | 18.3 | 18.3 | 17.9 | 17.0 |
| 2016 | 16.0 | 15.5 | 16.1 | 17.6 | 18.5 | 18.9 | 19.3 | 19.4 | 19.2 | 19.3 | 18.9 | 18.2 | 18.1 |
| 2017 | 16.4 | 16.2 | 16.3 | 17.9 | 18.7 | 19.3 | 19.5 | 19.6 | 19.3 | 19.3 | 19.2 | 18.7 | 18.4 |
| 2018 | 16.5 | 17.2 | 17.4 | 18.7 | 19.6 | 20.1 | 20.3 | 20.4 | 20.3 | 20.3 | 20.1 | 19.7 | 19.2 |
| 2019 | 18.2 | 17.8 | 18.2 | 19.8 | 20.5 | 20.8 | 21.0 | 21.0 | 20.9 | 21.0 | 20.2 | 19.6 | 19.9 |

## 1. Employment by Industry: Rhode Island, 2011–2019—*Continued*

(Numbers in thousands, not seasonally adjusted)

| Industry and year | January | February | March | April | May | June | July | August | September | October | November | December | Annual average |
|---|---|---|---|---|---|---|---|---|---|---|---|---|---|
| **Manufacturing** | | | | | | | | | | | | | |
| 2011 | 40.3 | 40.3 | 40.4 | 40.4 | 40.4 | 40.6 | 39.5 | 40.1 | 40.0 | 39.9 | 39.8 | 39.8 | 40.1 |
| 2012 | 39.1 | 39.3 | 39.3 | 39.4 | 39.6 | 40.0 | 38.8 | 39.9 | 39.9 | 40.1 | 40.0 | 40.1 | 39.6 |
| 2013 | 39.6 | 39.4 | 39.7 | 39.8 | 39.9 | 40.3 | 39.0 | 40.2 | 40.3 | 40.4 | 40.7 | 40.8 | 40.0 |
| 2014 | 40.3 | 40.4 | 40.3 | 40.7 | 41.0 | 41.3 | 40.4 | 41.1 | 41.1 | 41.2 | 41.3 | 41.4 | 40.9 |
| 2015 | 41.1 | 40.8 | 40.9 | 41.1 | 41.2 | 41.4 | 40.8 | 41.2 | 41.1 | 41.2 | 41.4 | 41.4 | 41.1 |
| 2016 | 40.5 | 40.5 | 40.6 | 40.5 | 40.5 | 40.8 | 40.1 | 40.4 | 40.1 | 40.3 | 40.4 | 40.6 | 40.4 |
| 2017 | 40.1 | 40.1 | 40.2 | 40.4 | 40.4 | 40.7 | 40.0 | 40.5 | 40.4 | 40.5 | 40.7 | 41.0 | 40.4 |
| 2018 | 40.5 | 40.7 | 40.9 | 40.6 | 40.6 | 40.6 | 39.8 | 40.4 | 40.3 | 40.1 | 40.1 | 40.2 | 40.4 |
| 2019 | 39.9 | 39.8 | 39.8 | 39.8 | 39.7 | 40.1 | 39.3 | 39.9 | 39.7 | 39.4 | 39.7 | 39.7 | 39.7 |
| **Trade, Transportation, and Utilities** | | | | | | | | | | | | | |
| 2011 | 72.1 | 71.7 | 71.9 | 72.7 | 73.7 | 74.3 | 73.5 | 73.6 | 74.4 | 74.9 | 76.1 | 77.1 | 73.8 |
| 2012 | 73.8 | 73.0 | 73.2 | 73.6 | 74.6 | 75.5 | 74.1 | 74.1 | 74.9 | 75.2 | 76.4 | 76.8 | 74.6 |
| 2013 | 72.6 | 72.2 | 72.0 | 72.6 | 73.7 | 74.6 | 73.9 | 74.0 | 74.4 | 75.1 | 76.2 | 77.1 | 74.0 |
| 2014 | 73.5 | 73.1 | 73.0 | 73.8 | 74.7 | 75.6 | 74.6 | 75.1 | 75.5 | 76.1 | 77.4 | 78.8 | 75.1 |
| 2015 | 75.0 | 74.1 | 74.1 | 75.2 | 76.1 | 77.1 | 76.2 | 76.2 | 76.9 | 77.0 | 78.5 | 79.6 | 76.3 |
| 2016 | 75.6 | 75.0 | 75.0 | 75.4 | 76.2 | 76.8 | 75.9 | 76.0 | 76.5 | 76.8 | 78.3 | 79.0 | 76.4 |
| 2017 | 75.5 | 75.0 | 74.7 | 75.8 | 76.7 | 77.3 | 76.4 | 76.3 | 77.0 | 77.6 | 79.1 | 80.0 | 76.8 |
| 2018 | 76.2 | 76.0 | 75.7 | 76.0 | 77.2 | 77.8 | 76.9 | 76.8 | 77.2 | 77.8 | 79.5 | 80.3 | 77.3 |
| 2019 | 76.7 | 76.0 | 75.5 | 76.0 | 76.5 | 77.6 | 76.3 | 76.4 | 77.1 | 77.6 | 80.1 | 81.2 | 77.3 |
| **Wholesale Trade** | | | | | | | | | | | | | |
| 2011 | 15.7 | 15.8 | 15.9 | 16.0 | 16.3 | 16.4 | 16.5 | 16.5 | 16.6 | 16.7 | 16.7 | 16.9 | 16.3 |
| 2012 | 16.7 | 16.7 | 16.8 | 16.8 | 17.0 | 17.0 | 17.0 | 16.9 | 16.9 | 16.9 | 16.9 | 16.8 | 16.9 |
| 2013 | 16.4 | 16.4 | 16.5 | 16.4 | 16.6 | 16.7 | 16.7 | 16.8 | 16.7 | 16.8 | 16.8 | 16.8 | 16.6 |
| 2014 | 16.6 | 16.7 | 16.7 | 16.6 | 16.8 | 16.8 | 16.8 | 17.0 | 16.9 | 17.0 | 17.0 | 17.1 | 16.8 |
| 2015 | 16.8 | 16.8 | 16.8 | 16.9 | 17.0 | 17.0 | 17.0 | 17.0 | 16.9 | 16.7 | 16.9 | 16.9 | 16.9 |
| 2016 | 16.5 | 16.5 | 16.4 | 16.7 | 16.7 | 16.7 | 16.6 | 16.6 | 16.6 | 16.5 | 16.6 | 16.6 | 16.6 |
| 2017 | 16.4 | 16.4 | 16.4 | 16.4 | 16.5 | 16.5 | 16.5 | 16.4 | 16.3 | 16.5 | 16.6 | 16.6 | 16.5 |
| 2018 | 16.4 | 16.5 | 16.5 | 16.5 | 16.5 | 16.6 | 16.5 | 16.5 | 16.4 | 16.5 | 16.6 | 16.6 | 16.5 |
| 2019 | 16.4 | 16.5 | 16.5 | 16.4 | 16.4 | 16.6 | 16.5 | 16.6 | 16.6 | 16.7 | 17.0 | 17.2 | 16.6 |
| **Retail Trade** | | | | | | | | | | | | | |
| 2011 | 46.0 | 45.5 | 45.6 | 46.1 | 46.6 | 46.9 | 46.8 | 47.1 | 46.7 | 47.2 | 48.4 | 48.8 | 46.8 |
| 2012 | 46.4 | 45.7 | 45.8 | 46.1 | 46.7 | 47.3 | 46.9 | 46.9 | 46.8 | 47.2 | 48.3 | 48.5 | 46.9 |
| 2013 | 45.8 | 45.3 | 45.0 | 45.5 | 46.2 | 46.8 | 46.9 | 46.8 | 46.5 | 47.1 | 48.1 | 48.6 | 46.6 |
| 2014 | 46.2 | 45.8 | 45.6 | 46.4 | 47.0 | 47.5 | 47.4 | 47.5 | 47.2 | 47.7 | 48.8 | 49.6 | 47.2 |
| 2015 | 47.0 | 46.4 | 46.4 | 47.1 | 47.6 | 48.5 | 48.4 | 48.4 | 48.2 | 48.5 | 49.7 | 50.3 | 48.0 |
| 2016 | 47.8 | 47.3 | 47.4 | 47.4 | 47.9 | 48.3 | 48.4 | 48.5 | 48.1 | 48.5 | 49.7 | 49.9 | 48.3 |
| 2017 | 47.7 | 47.2 | 47.0 | 48.0 | 48.6 | 48.9 | 48.8 | 48.9 | 48.6 | 48.8 | 50.1 | 50.3 | 48.6 |
| 2018 | 47.8 | 47.7 | 47.2 | 47.6 | 48.5 | 48.8 | 48.9 | 48.9 | 48.4 | 48.9 | 50.3 | 50.5 | 48.6 |
| 2019 | 48.1 | 47.3 | 47.1 | 47.3 | 47.6 | 48.2 | 48.1 | 47.9 | 47.8 | 48.1 | 49.8 | 49.9 | 48.1 |
| **Transportation and Utilities** | | | | | | | | | | | | | |
| 2011 | 10.4 | 10.4 | 10.4 | 10.6 | 10.8 | 11.0 | 10.2 | 10.0 | 11.1 | 11.0 | 11.0 | 11.4 | 10.7 |
| 2012 | 10.7 | 10.6 | 10.6 | 10.7 | 10.9 | 11.2 | 10.2 | 10.3 | 11.2 | 11.1 | 11.2 | 11.5 | 10.9 |
| 2013 | 10.4 | 10.5 | 10.5 | 10.7 | 10.9 | 11.1 | 10.3 | 10.4 | 11.2 | 11.2 | 11.3 | 11.7 | 10.9 |
| 2014 | 10.7 | 10.6 | 10.7 | 10.8 | 10.9 | 11.3 | 10.4 | 10.6 | 11.4 | 11.4 | 11.6 | 12.1 | 11.0 |
| 2015 | 11.2 | 10.9 | 10.9 | 11.2 | 11.5 | 11.6 | 10.8 | 10.8 | 11.8 | 11.8 | 11.9 | 12.4 | 11.4 |
| 2016 | 11.3 | 11.2 | 11.2 | 11.3 | 11.6 | 11.8 | 10.9 | 10.9 | 11.8 | 11.8 | 12.0 | 12.5 | 11.5 |
| 2017 | 11.4 | 11.4 | 11.3 | 11.4 | 11.6 | 11.9 | 11.1 | 11.0 | 12.1 | 12.3 | 12.4 | 13.1 | 11.8 |
| 2018 | 12.0 | 11.8 | 12.0 | 11.9 | 12.2 | 12.4 | 11.5 | 11.4 | 12.4 | 12.4 | 12.6 | 13.2 | 12.2 |
| 2019 | 12.2 | 12.2 | 11.9 | 12.3 | 12.5 | 12.8 | 11.7 | 11.9 | 12.7 | 12.8 | 13.3 | 14.1 | 12.5 |
| **Information** | | | | | | | | | | | | | |
| 2011 | 8.2 | 8.2 | 8.3 | 8.8 | 8.9 | 8.8 | 8.6 | 7.8 | 8.4 | 8.2 | 8.3 | 8.5 | 8.4 |
| 2012 | 8.1 | 8.2 | 8.2 | 8.0 | 7.8 | 8.0 | 7.7 | 7.8 | 7.6 | 7.6 | 7.5 | 7.6 | 7.8 |
| 2013 | 7.5 | 7.6 | 7.4 | 7.2 | 7.4 | 7.4 | 7.2 | 7.3 | 7.1 | 7.1 | 7.2 | 7.2 | 7.3 |
| 2014 | 7.3 | 7.1 | 7.0 | 7.1 | 7.2 | 7.1 | 7.1 | 7.3 | 7.1 | 7.0 | 7.0 | 7.1 | 7.1 |
| 2015 | 6.8 | 6.7 | 6.8 | 6.9 | 6.9 | 6.7 | 6.8 | 6.7 | 6.8 | 6.9 | 6.2 | 6.1 | 6.7 |
| 2016 | 6.0 | 6.1 | 6.0 | 6.2 | 5.4 | 6.2 | 6.3 | 6.1 | 6.2 | 6.1 | 6.1 | 6.2 | 6.1 |
| 2017 | 6.2 | 6.3 | 6.2 | 6.2 | 6.2 | 6.3 | 6.1 | 6.1 | 6.2 | 6.0 | 6.1 | 6.0 | 6.2 |
| 2018 | 5.8 | 6.0 | 5.9 | 5.8 | 5.8 | 5.8 | 5.7 | 5.9 | 6.0 | 6.1 | 6.0 | 6.0 | 5.9 |
| 2019 | 5.9 | 6.1 | 5.9 | 5.7 | 5.8 | 5.8 | 5.9 | 6.1 | 5.8 | 6.1 | 6.0 | 5.9 | 5.9 |

# 1. Employment by Industry: Rhode Island, 2011–2019—*Continued*

(Numbers in thousands, not seasonally adjusted)

| Industry and year | January | February | March | April | May | June | July | August | September | October | November | December | Annual average |
|---|---|---|---|---|---|---|---|---|---|---|---|---|---|
| **Financial Activities** | | | | | | | | | | | | | |
| 2011 | 32.1 | 32.2 | 32.3 | 32.4 | 32.4 | 32.9 | 32.5 | 32.6 | 32.6 | 32.6 | 32.9 | 32.8 | 32.5 |
| 2012 | 32.6 | 32.8 | 33.0 | 33.0 | 33.4 | 33.6 | 33.5 | 33.5 | 33.6 | 33.6 | 33.6 | 33.7 | 33.3 |
| 2013 | 33.4 | 33.6 | 33.9 | 33.9 | 34.0 | 34.2 | 34.3 | 34.1 | 34.0 | 34.0 | 33.9 | 34.2 | 34.0 |
| 2014 | 33.8 | 33.8 | 33.8 | 34.1 | 34.2 | 34.4 | 34.5 | 34.3 | 34.3 | 34.2 | 34.2 | 34.3 | 34.2 |
| 2015 | 34.0 | 34.1 | 34.4 | 34.6 | 34.9 | 35.1 | 34.9 | 34.8 | 35.1 | 35.7 | 36.1 | 36.2 | 35.0 |
| 2016 | 35.3 | 35.5 | 35.6 | 35.5 | 35.5 | 35.8 | 35.8 | 35.7 | 35.6 | 35.7 | 35.8 | 35.8 | 35.6 |
| 2017 | 35.5 | 35.6 | 35.6 | 35.6 | 35.8 | 36.1 | 36.0 | 36.1 | 36.0 | 35.7 | 35.9 | 35.8 | 35.8 |
| 2018 | 35.3 | 35.4 | 35.3 | 35.4 | 35.3 | 35.5 | 35.5 | 35.4 | 35.2 | 35.4 | 35.3 | 35.2 | 35.4 |
| 2019 | 34.9 | 35.2 | 35.0 | 35.1 | 35.2 | 35.5 | 35.9 | 35.5 | 35.4 | 35.5 | 35.3 | 35.2 | 35.3 |
| **Professional and Business Services** | | | | | | | | | | | | | |
| 2011 | 51.5 | 51.9 | 52.3 | 54.2 | 54.6 | 55.2 | 54.9 | 55.3 | 55.8 | 55.9 | 55.7 | 54.6 | 54.3 |
| 2012 | 52.7 | 53.0 | 54.1 | 56.1 | 56.6 | 57.5 | 56.9 | 57.3 | 57.2 | 57.1 | 57.2 | 57.1 | 56.1 |
| 2013 | 55.0 | 55.6 | 56.1 | 58.4 | 59.0 | 60.3 | 59.6 | 60.2 | 60.2 | 60.6 | 60.4 | 59.7 | 58.8 |
| 2014 | 56.9 | 57.6 | 58.0 | 60.4 | 61.1 | 61.8 | 61.7 | 62.3 | 62.3 | 63.0 | 63.0 | 62.9 | 60.9 |
| 2015 | 60.0 | 60.0 | 60.7 | 63.6 | 64.6 | 64.9 | 65.0 | 64.9 | 64.6 | 65.1 | 65.5 | 65.1 | 63.7 |
| 2016 | 62.9 | 63.0 | 63.6 | 65.6 | 66.0 | 66.5 | 66.5 | 66.8 | 66.9 | 67.2 | 67.1 | 66.6 | 65.7 |
| 2017 | 64.1 | 64.7 | 64.8 | 67.1 | 67.3 | 68.4 | 68.8 | 68.9 | 68.5 | 68.6 | 68.7 | 68.4 | 67.4 |
| 2018 | 65.3 | 65.7 | 66.3 | 68.2 | 68.9 | 69.3 | 69.5 | 69.7 | 69.1 | 69.3 | 69.5 | 68.9 | 68.3 |
| 2019 | 66.2 | 66.5 | 66.2 | 68.0 | 68.5 | 69.0 | 69.2 | 69.4 | 68.8 | 70.0 | 68.9 | 68.2 | 68.2 |
| **Education and Health Services** | | | | | | | | | | | | | |
| 2011 | 99.7 | 102.8 | 103.7 | 104.4 | 104.3 | 99.7 | 98.8 | 98.3 | 101.7 | 104.7 | 104.9 | 104.2 | 102.3 |
| 2012 | 100.7 | 104.7 | 104.9 | 104.1 | 104.6 | 100.0 | 98.7 | 99.0 | 104.7 | 105.8 | 105.6 | 106.4 | 103.3 |
| 2013 | 103.3 | 105.5 | 106.3 | 105.7 | 105.5 | 102.2 | 100.9 | 100.5 | 105.0 | 107.2 | 107.5 | 105.8 | 104.6 |
| 2014 | 103.4 | 105.9 | 106.5 | 107.2 | 106.7 | 102.4 | 101.7 | 101.1 | 106.0 | 107.6 | 108.1 | 107.9 | 105.4 |
| 2015 | 104.4 | 105.8 | 106.9 | 107.7 | 106.9 | 103.3 | 102.6 | 101.7 | 106.1 | 108.2 | 108.5 | 107.9 | 105.8 |
| 2016 | 104.2 | 107.1 | 108.0 | 108.4 | 108.2 | 103.1 | 102.3 | 101.8 | 105.7 | 108.0 | 108.1 | 107.5 | 106.0 |
| 2017 | 104.2 | 106.8 | 108.2 | 108.8 | 108.4 | 103.5 | 102.7 | 102.7 | 105.8 | 107.6 | 108.3 | 107.8 | 106.2 |
| 2018 | 103.3 | 106.8 | 107.4 | 108.8 | 108.6 | 104.2 | 103.6 | 103.1 | 107.0 | 109.5 | 110.1 | 109.4 | 106.8 |
| 2019 | 105.9 | 109.4 | 110.4 | 110.9 | 110.3 | 105.6 | 104.3 | 104.5 | 108.6 | 111.5 | 112.6 | 111.6 | 108.8 |
| **Leisure and Hospitality** | | | | | | | | | | | | | |
| 2011 | 44.0 | 44.6 | 45.0 | 48.1 | 51.1 | 55.0 | 56.1 | 55.8 | 53.8 | 50.9 | 48.9 | 48.2 | 50.1 |
| 2012 | 45.2 | 46.2 | 46.8 | 49.8 | 53.1 | 56.9 | 57.6 | 57.6 | 55.4 | 52.5 | 50.4 | 49.9 | 51.8 |
| 2013 | 46.8 | 47.2 | 48.2 | 51.3 | 54.6 | 58.9 | 59.6 | 59.5 | 57.3 | 55.1 | 52.5 | 51.9 | 53.6 |
| 2014 | 48.4 | 49.4 | 50.1 | 53.3 | 56.9 | 60.4 | 61.0 | 60.6 | 58.6 | 56.3 | 54.0 | 53.2 | 55.2 |
| 2015 | 50.2 | 49.6 | 50.6 | 54.0 | 58.5 | 61.4 | 62.2 | 62.0 | 59.9 | 57.4 | 55.2 | 54.5 | 56.3 |
| 2016 | 51.1 | 51.6 | 52.7 | 55.7 | 58.8 | 63.4 | 63.9 | 63.4 | 60.9 | 58.4 | 56.2 | 55.0 | 57.6 |
| 2017 | 51.9 | 52.6 | 53.0 | 55.6 | 59.3 | 64.2 | 64.5 | 64.7 | 61.2 | 59.0 | 56.8 | 56.0 | 58.2 |
| 2018 | 52.5 | 53.5 | 53.9 | 56.8 | 60.6 | 65.0 | 66.0 | 65.8 | 62.2 | 59.8 | 57.3 | 56.8 | 59.2 |
| 2019 | 53.8 | 54.5 | 54.4 | 57.5 | 61.4 | 65.7 | 66.8 | 66.1 | 62.9 | 61.0 | 58.3 | 57.1 | 60.0 |
| **Other Services** | | | | | | | | | | | | | |
| 2011 | 21.5 | 21.7 | 21.7 | 22.1 | 22.3 | 22.9 | 23.7 | 23.5 | 22.5 | 22.3 | 22.4 | 22.4 | 22.4 |
| 2012 | 21.8 | 21.9 | 21.9 | 22.2 | 22.4 | 23.0 | 23.4 | 23.4 | 22.9 | 22.5 | 22.5 | 22.7 | 22.6 |
| 2013 | 22.0 | 22.0 | 22.2 | 22.4 | 22.6 | 23.1 | 23.5 | 23.2 | 22.6 | 22.5 | 22.5 | 22.6 | 22.6 |
| 2014 | 22.0 | 22.2 | 22.3 | 22.5 | 22.9 | 23.5 | 23.9 | 23.8 | 23.0 | 22.7 | 22.8 | 22.9 | 22.9 |
| 2015 | 22.4 | 22.2 | 22.5 | 22.6 | 23.1 | 23.5 | 24.1 | 23.9 | 23.0 | 22.9 | 23.0 | 22.9 | 23.0 |
| 2016 | 22.5 | 22.5 | 22.7 | 22.9 | 23.1 | 23.8 | 24.2 | 24.0 | 23.0 | 22.9 | 23.0 | 23.0 | 23.1 |
| 2017 | 22.4 | 22.5 | 22.4 | 22.8 | 23.0 | 23.7 | 23.9 | 23.8 | 22.9 | 22.9 | 23.1 | 23.0 | 23.0 |
| 2018 | 22.2 | 22.4 | 22.5 | 22.5 | 22.7 | 23.5 | 24.0 | 23.9 | 23.0 | 22.9 | 22.8 | 23.0 | 23.0 |
| 2019 | 22.7 | 22.7 | 22.8 | 22.9 | 23.1 | 23.8 | 23.8 | 23.8 | 22.9 | 22.6 | 22.3 | 22.1 | 23.0 |
| **Government** | | | | | | | | | | | | | |
| 2011 | 65.2 | 65.1 | 65.5 | 65.5 | 65.8 | 63.6 | 59.3 | 59.5 | 64.6 | 64.7 | 64.9 | 64.9 | 64.1 |
| 2012 | 64.6 | 64.9 | 64.9 | 65.0 | 65.7 | 62.5 | 59.0 | 59.4 | 64.7 | 64.7 | 65.0 | 65.0 | 63.8 |
| 2013 | 64.5 | 64.4 | 65.0 | 64.8 | 65.7 | 62.7 | 59.9 | 59.6 | 64.8 | 65.1 | 65.1 | 65.3 | 63.9 |
| 2014 | 64.6 | 64.5 | 64.8 | 64.9 | 66.0 | 63.2 | 59.9 | 59.5 | 65.4 | 65.1 | 65.6 | 65.2 | 64.1 |
| 2015 | 64.9 | 64.9 | 64.9 | 65.1 | 65.8 | 62.8 | 59.6 | 59.2 | 64.7 | 64.9 | 65.1 | 65.3 | 63.9 |
| 2016 | 64.8 | 65.0 | 65.3 | 65.1 | 65.5 | 63.0 | 60.3 | 59.9 | 65.2 | 65.5 | 65.7 | 65.6 | 64.2 |
| 2017 | 65.0 | 65.1 | 65.3 | 65.3 | 66.0 | 63.7 | 60.7 | 60.3 | 65.7 | 65.8 | 65.6 | 66.0 | 64.5 |
| 2018 | 65.3 | 65.4 | 65.4 | 65.5 | 66.9 | 64.0 | 60.9 | 60.5 | 66.6 | 66.0 | 66.0 | 66.3 | 64.9 |
| 2019 | 65.7 | 65.8 | 66.3 | 66.3 | 66.6 | 64.1 | 60.9 | 60.9 | 66.4 | 66.6 | 66.6 | 66.8 | 65.3 |

## 2. Average Weekly Hours by Selected Industry: Rhode Island, 2015–2019

(Not seasonally adjusted)

| Industry and year | January | February | March | April | May | June | July | August | September | October | November | December | Annual average |
|---|---|---|---|---|---|---|---|---|---|---|---|---|---|
| **Total Private** | | | | | | | | | | | | | |
| 2015 | 32.8 | 32.5 | 32.9 | 32.9 | 33.1 | 33.6 | 33.6 | 33.5 | 33.3 | 32.9 | 33.1 | 32.9 | 33.1 |
| 2016 | 32.5 | 32.4 | 32.5 | 32.5 | 32.9 | 33.0 | 33.0 | 33.0 | 32.8 | 32.4 | 32.3 | 32.7 | 32.7 |
| 2017 | 32.6 | 31.8 | 32.0 | 33.0 | 32.9 | 32.9 | 33.2 | 33.2 | 33.1 | 33.2 | 33.3 | 33.4 | 32.9 |
| 2018 | 33.0 | 33.4 | 32.5 | 33.6 | 33.6 | 33.4 | 33.6 | 33.4 | 33.3 | 33.1 | 33.2 | 33.6 | 33.3 |
| 2019 | 33.2 | 33.0 | 33.1 | 33.0 | 33.2 | 33.2 | 32.7 | 32.9 | 33.2 | 32.7 | 33.1 | 33.0 | 33.0 |
| **Goods-Producing** | | | | | | | | | | | | | |
| 2015 | 38.2 | 37.7 | 38.7 | 38.1 | 37.4 | 38.0 | 37.7 | 37.1 | 37.7 | 37.0 | 37.4 | 38.9 | 37.8 |
| 2016 | 37.9 | 37.6 | 38.4 | 38.0 | 38.4 | 38.8 | 38.4 | 38.2 | 38.2 | 38.1 | 38.2 | 38.8 | 38.3 |
| 2017 | 38.1 | 37.3 | 37.1 | 38.0 | 37.6 | 37.4 | 37.2 | 37.9 | 37.7 | 37.2 | 37.6 | 38.3 | 37.6 |
| 2018 | 36.6 | 37.8 | 35.8 | 38.5 | 38.2 | 37.8 | 37.7 | 37.6 | 37.2 | 37.0 | 37.3 | 38.2 | 37.5 |
| 2019 | 36.9 | 37.1 | 36.8 | 37.4 | 37.5 | 37.3 | 36.7 | 36.9 | 37.4 | 36.5 | 37.3 | 36.7 | 37.0 |
| **Construction** | | | | | | | | | | | | | |
| 2015 | 36.7 | 35.6 | 37.5 | 36.6 | 35.5 | 36.0 | 35.6 | 34.6 | 34.6 | 33.7 | 35.6 | 36.9 | 35.7 |
| 2016 | 35.8 | 33.8 | 36.2 | 35.1 | 36.9 | 37.5 | 37.9 | 37.1 | 36.5 | 36.9 | 36.9 | 36.5 | 36.5 |
| 2017 | 36.3 | 35.7 | 34.5 | 37.1 | 36.8 | 35.9 | 34.5 | 35.8 | 35.8 | 35.5 | 35.2 | 34.6 | 35.7 |
| 2018 | 32.3 | 33.9 | 32.7 | 34.4 | 35.5 | 34.5 | 34.6 | 34.7 | 34.1 | 34.1 | 33.9 | 35.6 | 34.2 |
| 2019 | 35.0 | 34.7 | 34.7 | 35.0 | 35.6 | 34.8 | 34.5 | 35.5 | 35.2 | 34.1 | 35.8 | 35.9 | 35.1 |
| **Manufacturing** | | | | | | | | | | | | | |
| 2015 | 38.9 | 38.5 | 39.2 | 38.8 | 38.3 | 38.9 | 38.6 | 38.1 | 39.0 | 38.4 | 38.2 | 39.9 | 38.7 |
| 2016 | 38.7 | 39.1 | 39.3 | 39.2 | 39.1 | 39.4 | 39.0 | 39.1 | 39.4 | 39.1 | 39.2 | 40.2 | 39.2 |
| 2017 | 39.2 | 38.3 | 38.4 | 38.7 | 38.3 | 38.4 | 38.9 | 39.2 | 39.4 | 39.7 | 40.0 | 41.2 | 39.1 |
| 2018 | 40.1 | 40.8 | 39.1 | 41.3 | 40.9 | 40.6 | 40.4 | 40.2 | 39.8 | 39.3 | 39.9 | 40.2 | 40.2 |
| 2019 | 38.3 | 38.8 | 38.3 | 39.0 | 38.8 | 38.9 | 38.2 | 38.0 | 38.7 | 38.1 | 38.9 | 38.4 | 38.5 |
| **Trade, Transportation, and Utilities** | | | | | | | | | | | | | |
| 2015 | 32.4 | 31.8 | 32.6 | 32.4 | 32.6 | 32.8 | 32.9 | 32.9 | 33.1 | 32.7 | 32.6 | 32.3 | 32.6 |
| 2016 | 31.2 | 31.2 | 31.0 | 31.5 | 31.8 | 32.1 | 32.6 | 32.3 | 32.3 | 32.3 | 32.2 | 32.7 | 31.9 |
| 2017 | 32.2 | 31.4 | 32.3 | 33.5 | 33.4 | 33.4 | 34.0 | 33.6 | 33.7 | 33.5 | 33.8 | 34.1 | 33.3 |
| 2018 | 33.2 | 33.5 | 32.2 | 32.9 | 33.5 | 33.6 | 33.5 | 32.7 | 33.3 | 33.0 | 33.1 | 33.1 | 33.1 |
| 2019 | 33.0 | 32.2 | 32.6 | 32.9 | 32.9 | 33.3 | 33.0 | 33.3 | 33.5 | 33.3 | 32.9 | 33.2 | 33.0 |
| **Financial Activities** | | | | | | | | | | | | | |
| 2015 | 34.0 | 34.1 | 34.4 | 34.6 | 34.9 | 35.1 | 34.9 | 34.8 | 35.1 | 35.7 | 36.1 | 36.2 | 35.0 |
| 2016 | 35.3 | 35.5 | 35.6 | 35.5 | 35.5 | 35.8 | 35.8 | 35.7 | 35.6 | 35.7 | 35.8 | 35.8 | 35.6 |
| 2017 | 35.5 | 35.6 | 35.6 | 35.6 | 35.8 | 36.1 | 36.0 | 36.1 | 36.0 | 35.7 | 35.9 | 35.8 | 35.8 |
| 2018 | 35.3 | 35.4 | 35.3 | 35.4 | 35.3 | 35.5 | 35.5 | 35.4 | 35.2 | 35.4 | 35.3 | 35.2 | 35.4 |
| 2019 | 34.9 | 35.2 | 35.0 | 35.1 | 35.2 | 35.5 | 35.9 | 35.5 | 35.4 | 35.5 | 35.3 | 35.2 | 35.3 |
| **Professional and Business Services** | | | | | | | | | | | | | |
| 2015 | 34.8 | 34.7 | 35.3 | 35.3 | 36.4 | 36.1 | 36.1 | 35.8 | 35.1 | 35.3 | 35.7 | 34.8 | 35.5 |
| 2016 | 35.4 | 34.8 | 35.3 | 35.7 | 35.9 | 36.1 | 35.3 | 35.8 | 35.5 | 34.8 | 34.6 | 35.1 | 35.4 |
| 2017 | 35.1 | 34.6 | 34.6 | 35.2 | 35.8 | 35.8 | 35.2 | 35.5 | 35.8 | 35.3 | 35.5 | 35.2 | 35.3 |
| 2018 | 34.9 | 35.5 | 34.3 | 35.6 | 36.0 | 35.9 | 36.1 | 35.8 | 36.3 | 35.7 | 36.2 | 36.2 | 35.7 |
| 2019 | 36.0 | 35.9 | 36.4 | 36.1 | 37.4 | 37.2 | 36.5 | 36.1 | 36.4 | 36.3 | 36.9 | 36.7 | 36.5 |
| **Education and Health Services** | | | | | | | | | | | | | |
| 2015 | 32.2 | 32.0 | 32.2 | 32.1 | 32.1 | 32.0 | 32.0 | 32.5 | 32.2 | 31.8 | 32.1 | 31.3 | 32.0 |
| 2016 | 31.5 | 31.1 | 31.2 | 30.9 | 31.5 | 31.1 | 31.5 | 31.7 | 31.9 | 32.1 | 31.9 | 32.0 | 31.5 |
| 2017 | 32.5 | 32.2 | 32.2 | 32.8 | 32.8 | 33.0 | 32.7 | 32.1 | 32.6 | 33.0 | 33.1 | 33.2 | 32.7 |
| 2018 | 33.3 | 33.4 | 33.2 | 33.8 | 33.7 | 34.0 | 33.8 | 34.1 | 33.8 | 34.0 | 33.7 | 34.0 | 33.7 |
| 2019 | 33.7 | 33.2 | 33.0 | 32.7 | 32.6 | 32.5 | 32.1 | 32.7 | 33.0 | 32.6 | 32.9 | 32.5 | 32.8 |
| **Leisure and Hospitality** | | | | | | | | | | | | | |
| 2015 | 23.9 | 23.3 | 24.0 | 25.0 | 25.6 | 27.1 | 28.0 | 27.7 | 26.7 | 25.4 | 25.2 | 24.6 | 25.6 |
| 2016 | 23.4 | 24.0 | 23.8 | 23.8 | 24.6 | 25.0 | 25.3 | 25.4 | 24.3 | 23.9 | 24.0 | 23.7 | 24.3 |
| 2017 | 23.2 | 21.9 | 22.8 | 24.3 | 24.1 | 24.1 | 25.0 | 25.3 | 24.2 | 24.2 | 24.1 | 24.1 | 24.0 |
| 2018 | 23.5 | 24.5 | 23.5 | 24.9 | 25.2 | 25.4 | 26.4 | 26.4 | 25.1 | 25.1 | 24.6 | 24.9 | 25.0 |
| 2019 | 24.4 | 25.5 | 25.6 | 24.9 | 25.2 | 25.1 | 26.2 | 26.2 | 25.6 | 24.7 | 24.8 | 24.4 | 25.2 |

## 3. Average Hourly Earnings by Selected Industry: Rhode Island, 2015–2019

(Dollars, not seasonally adjusted)

| Industry and year | January | February | March | April | May | June | July | August | September | October | November | December | Annual average |
|---|---|---|---|---|---|---|---|---|---|---|---|---|---|
| **Total Private** | | | | | | | | | | | | | |
| 2015 | 25.24 | 25.59 | 25.49 | 25.15 | 25.02 | 24.13 | 24.26 | 24.31 | 24.68 | 25.14 | 25.36 | 25.09 | 24.94 |
| 2016 | 25.91 | 26.04 | 25.66 | 26.14 | 25.99 | 25.70 | 25.54 | 25.88 | 25.90 | 26.34 | 26.51 | 26.24 | 25.99 |
| 2017 | 26.88 | 27.01 | 26.81 | 26.91 | 26.72 | 26.48 | 26.63 | 26.67 | 27.08 | 27.32 | 27.43 | 27.65 | 26.97 |
| 2018 | 27.86 | 27.93 | 28.04 | 27.89 | 27.65 | 27.31 | 27.45 | 27.35 | 27.47 | 27.40 | 27.83 | 27.99 | 27.68 |
| 2019 | 28.04 | 28.45 | 28.15 | 28.07 | 27.90 | 27.89 | 27.39 | 27.66 | 27.80 | 28.05 | 28.03 | 28.30 | 27.97 |
| **Goods-Producing** | | | | | | | | | | | | | |
| 2015 | 27.27 | 27.32 | 26.89 | 26.39 | 26.12 | 25.33 | 25.58 | 25.38 | 25.33 | 25.44 | 25.90 | 25.39 | 26.01 |
| 2016 | 25.30 | 24.83 | 24.99 | 25.05 | 25.04 | 25.11 | 25.01 | 25.12 | 25.15 | 25.17 | 25.19 | 24.98 | 25.08 |
| 2017 | 25.30 | 25.10 | 25.25 | 25.08 | 25.19 | 25.37 | 25.44 | 25.08 | 25.46 | 25.05 | 25.28 | 25.68 | 25.27 |
| 2018 | 25.70 | 25.66 | 26.25 | 25.76 | 25.94 | 26.18 | 26.51 | 26.07 | 26.18 | 26.32 | 26.71 | 26.90 | 26.19 |
| 2019 | 27.09 | 26.86 | 26.96 | 27.29 | 27.65 | 27.64 | 28.18 | 28.63 | 28.50 | 29.09 | 29.49 | 30.08 | 28.13 |
| **Construction** | | | | | | | | | | | | | |
| 2015 | 29.25 | 29.70 | 29.25 | 28.52 | 29.11 | 27.78 | 27.57 | 27.72 | 28.82 | 28.60 | 28.89 | 28.83 | 28.63 |
| 2016 | 28.20 | 28.38 | 28.81 | 29.17 | 29.33 | 28.92 | 28.96 | 29.31 | 29.41 | 28.90 | 28.54 | 28.63 | 28.90 |
| 2017 | 29.19 | 28.68 | 28.91 | 28.19 | 28.90 | 28.66 | 28.67 | 28.72 | 29.86 | 29.82 | 30.31 | 31.26 | 29.27 |
| 2018 | 31.27 | 32.03 | 33.43 | 31.71 | 31.77 | 32.04 | 31.56 | 31.01 | 31.55 | 31.88 | 32.03 | 31.78 | 31.82 |
| 2019 | 32.54 | 32.15 | 31.99 | 32.33 | 32.49 | 32.69 | 32.93 | 33.66 | 33.99 | 34.60 | 35.03 | 36.12 | 33.41 |
| **Manufacturing** | | | | | | | | | | | | | |
| 2015 | 24.32 | 24.56 | 24.05 | 23.69 | 23.30 | 22.87 | 23.40 | 23.44 | 23.19 | 23.52 | 24.03 | 23.37 | 23.64 |
| 2016 | 23.60 | 23.25 | 23.25 | 23.15 | 23.05 | 23.34 | 23.26 | 23.25 | 23.28 | 23.50 | 23.68 | 23.43 | 23.34 |
| 2017 | 23.66 | 23.67 | 23.79 | 23.55 | 23.44 | 23.80 | 23.93 | 23.16 | 23.62 | 23.36 | 23.36 | 23.31 | 23.55 |
| 2018 | 23.63 | 23.38 | 24.16 | 23.87 | 23.60 | 23.80 | 24.43 | 24.15 | 23.93 | 23.70 | 24.13 | 24.34 | 23.92 |
| 2019 | 24.09 | 23.97 | 24.08 | 23.72 | 24.13 | 24.05 | 24.47 | 24.51 | 24.16 | 24.51 | 24.95 | 25.25 | 24.32 |
| **Trade, Transportation, and Utilities** | | | | | | | | | | | | | |
| 2015 | 20.48 | 20.31 | 20.09 | 19.66 | 20.01 | 19.88 | 20.02 | 20.01 | 20.23 | 20.66 | 20.55 | 19.70 | 20.13 |
| 2016 | 20.46 | 20.71 | 20.56 | 20.78 | 20.76 | 21.00 | 20.73 | 21.35 | 21.26 | 21.89 | 22.52 | 21.68 | 21.16 |
| 2017 | 22.21 | 22.49 | 23.36 | 23.24 | 23.43 | 23.67 | 23.60 | 23.84 | 24.29 | 24.65 | 24.81 | 24.70 | 23.72 |
| 2018 | 25.49 | 25.55 | 26.40 | 25.88 | 25.79 | 26.27 | 26.74 | 26.59 | 26.94 | 26.88 | 27.21 | 26.88 | 26.39 |
| 2019 | 27.54 | 27.74 | 27.44 | 27.55 | 27.25 | 27.74 | 27.75 | 27.72 | 27.75 | 27.30 | 27.17 | 26.94 | 27.49 |
| **Financial Activities** | | | | | | | | | | | | | |
| 2015 | 34.00 | 34.10 | 34.40 | 34.60 | 34.90 | 35.10 | 34.90 | 34.80 | 35.10 | 35.70 | 36.10 | 36.20 | 35.00 |
| 2016 | 35.30 | 35.50 | 35.60 | 35.50 | 35.50 | 35.80 | 35.80 | 35.70 | 35.60 | 35.70 | 35.80 | 35.80 | 35.60 |
| 2017 | 35.50 | 35.60 | 35.60 | 35.60 | 35.80 | 36.10 | 36.00 | 36.10 | 36.00 | 35.70 | 35.90 | 35.80 | 35.80 |
| 2018 | 35.30 | 35.40 | 35.30 | 35.40 | 35.30 | 35.50 | 35.50 | 35.40 | 35.20 | 35.40 | 35.30 | 35.20 | 35.40 |
| 2019 | 34.90 | 35.20 | 35.00 | 35.10 | 35.20 | 35.50 | 35.90 | 35.50 | 35.40 | 35.50 | 35.30 | 35.20 | 35.30 |
| **Professional and Business Services** | | | | | | | | | | | | | |
| 2015 | 30.40 | 31.09 | 30.94 | 29.84 | 29.73 | 29.29 | 29.50 | 29.88 | 29.78 | 29.91 | 29.83 | 29.22 | 29.93 |
| 2016 | 30.03 | 30.15 | 29.79 | 30.14 | 30.11 | 30.05 | 30.12 | 30.32 | 30.95 | 31.26 | 31.47 | 31.33 | 30.48 |
| 2017 | 32.01 | 31.85 | 31.77 | 31.88 | 31.25 | 31.15 | 31.69 | 31.55 | 31.76 | 31.92 | 31.64 | 32.33 | 31.73 |
| 2018 | 32.85 | 33.08 | 33.17 | 32.99 | 32.08 | 31.88 | 32.03 | 32.16 | 32.28 | 32.63 | 32.39 | 32.34 | 32.48 |
| 2019 | 32.50 | 33.22 | 33.28 | 32.91 | 32.32 | 32.31 | 32.32 | 32.73 | 32.47 | 32.09 | 31.99 | 32.09 | 32.51 |
| **Education and Health Services** | | | | | | | | | | | | | |
| 2015 | 21.99 | 22.68 | 23.17 | 23.66 | 24.12 | 24.18 | 24.63 | 24.77 | 25.50 | 26.15 | 26.66 | 26.98 | 24.55 |
| 2016 | 26.85 | 27.24 | 26.92 | 27.17 | 26.98 | 27.18 | 27.44 | 27.16 | 27.30 | 27.98 | 27.85 | 28.11 | 27.35 |
| 2017 | 28.65 | 28.52 | 28.47 | 29.11 | 29.72 | 29.68 | 29.70 | 30.12 | 30.25 | 30.13 | 29.93 | 29.76 | 29.50 |
| 2018 | 29.57 | 28.99 | 29.14 | 29.31 | 29.01 | 28.86 | 28.45 | 28.02 | 27.95 | 27.52 | 27.60 | 28.14 | 28.54 |
| 2019 | 27.93 | 28.46 | 28.39 | 28.08 | 27.78 | 28.11 | 28.62 | 28.24 | 28.64 | 29.02 | 28.60 | 29.52 | 28.45 |
| **Leisure and Hospitality** | | | | | | | | | | | | | |
| 2015 | 14.40 | 14.58 | 14.66 | 14.49 | 14.39 | 13.99 | 14.27 | 14.50 | 14.84 | 15.25 | 15.02 | 15.42 | 14.63 |
| 2016 | 15.60 | 15.83 | 15.75 | 15.83 | 15.82 | 15.50 | 15.57 | 15.66 | 15.82 | 15.89 | 15.90 | 16.13 | 15.77 |
| 2017 | 16.16 | 16.53 | 16.34 | 16.23 | 16.02 | 16.12 | 16.17 | 15.95 | 16.22 | 16.20 | 16.18 | 16.28 | 16.19 |
| 2018 | 16.40 | 16.50 | 16.58 | 16.51 | 16.67 | 16.51 | 16.65 | 16.58 | 16.81 | 16.64 | 16.87 | 16.96 | 16.64 |
| 2019 | 16.54 | 16.57 | 16.87 | 17.07 | 17.01 | 17.04 | 17.12 | 17.13 | 17.24 | 17.06 | 17.03 | 17.18 | 17.00 |

## 4. Average Weekly Earnings by Selected Industry: Rhode Island, 2015–2019

(Dollars, not seasonally adjusted)

| Industry and year | January | February | March | April | May | June | July | August | September | October | November | December | Annual average |
|---|---|---|---|---|---|---|---|---|---|---|---|---|---|
| **Total Private** | | | | | | | | | | | | | |
| 2015 | 827.87 | 831.68 | 838.62 | 827.44 | 828.16 | 810.77 | 815.14 | 814.39 | 821.84 | 827.11 | 839.42 | 825.46 | 825.51 |
| 2016 | 842.08 | 843.70 | 833.95 | 849.55 | 855.07 | 848.10 | 842.82 | 854.04 | 849.52 | 853.42 | 856.27 | 858.05 | 849.87 |
| 2017 | 876.29 | 858.92 | 857.92 | 888.03 | 879.09 | 871.19 | 884.12 | 885.44 | 896.35 | 907.02 | 913.42 | 923.51 | 887.31 |
| 2018 | 919.38 | 932.86 | 911.30 | 937.10 | 929.04 | 912.15 | 922.32 | 913.49 | 914.75 | 906.94 | 923.96 | 940.46 | 921.74 |
| 2019 | 930.93 | 938.85 | 931.77 | 926.31 | 926.28 | 925.95 | 895.65 | 910.01 | 922.96 | 917.24 | 927.79 | 933.90 | 923.01 |
| **Goods-Producing** | | | | | | | | | | | | | |
| 2015 | 1,041.71 | 1,029.96 | 1,040.64 | 1,005.46 | 976.89 | 962.54 | 964.37 | 941.60 | 954.94 | 941.28 | 968.66 | 987.67 | 983.18 |
| 2016 | 958.87 | 933.61 | 959.62 | 951.90 | 961.54 | 974.27 | 960.38 | 959.58 | 960.73 | 958.98 | 962.26 | 969.22 | 960.56 |
| 2017 | 963.93 | 936.23 | 936.78 | 953.04 | 947.14 | 948.84 | 946.37 | 950.53 | 959.84 | 931.86 | 950.53 | 983.54 | 950.15 |
| 2018 | 940.62 | 969.95 | 939.75 | 991.76 | 990.91 | 989.60 | 999.43 | 980.23 | 973.90 | 973.84 | 996.28 | 1,027.58 | 982.13 |
| 2019 | 999.62 | 996.51 | 992.13 | 1,020.65 | 1,036.88 | 1,030.97 | 1,034.21 | 1,056.45 | 1,065.90 | 1,061.79 | 1,099.98 | 1,103.94 | 1,040.81 |
| **Construction** | | | | | | | | | | | | | |
| 2015 | 1,073.48 | 1,057.32 | 1,096.88 | 1,043.83 | 1,033.41 | 1,000.08 | 981.49 | 959.11 | 997.17 | 963.82 | 1,028.48 | 1,063.83 | 1,022.09 |
| 2016 | 1,009.56 | 959.24 | 1,042.92 | 1,023.87 | 1,082.28 | 1,084.50 | 1,097.58 | 1,087.40 | 1,073.47 | 1,066.41 | 1,053.13 | 1,045.00 | 1,054.85 |
| 2017 | 1,059.60 | 1,023.88 | 997.40 | 1,045.85 | 1,063.52 | 1,028.89 | 989.12 | 1,028.18 | 1,068.99 | 1,058.61 | 1,066.91 | 1,081.60 | 1,044.94 |
| 2018 | 1,010.02 | 1,085.82 | 1,093.16 | 1,090.82 | 1,127.84 | 1,105.38 | 1,091.98 | 1,076.05 | 1,075.86 | 1,087.11 | 1,085.82 | 1,131.37 | 1,088.24 |
| 2019 | 1,138.90 | 1,115.61 | 1,110.05 | 1,131.55 | 1,156.64 | 1,137.61 | 1,136.09 | 1,194.93 | 1,196.45 | 1,179.86 | 1,254.07 | 1,296.71 | 1,172.69 |
| **Manufacturing** | | | | | | | | | | | | | |
| 2015 | 946.05 | 945.56 | 942.76 | 919.17 | 892.39 | 889.64 | 903.24 | 893.06 | 904.41 | 903.17 | 917.95 | 932.46 | 914.87 |
| 2016 | 913.32 | 909.08 | 913.73 | 907.48 | 901.26 | 919.60 | 907.14 | 909.08 | 917.23 | 918.85 | 928.26 | 941.89 | 914.93 |
| 2017 | 927.47 | 906.56 | 913.54 | 911.39 | 897.75 | 913.92 | 930.88 | 907.87 | 930.63 | 927.00 | 934.40 | 960.37 | 920.81 |
| 2018 | 947.56 | 953.50 | 944.66 | 985.83 | 965.24 | 966.69 | 986.97 | 970.83 | 952.41 | 931.41 | 962.79 | 978.47 | 961.58 |
| 2019 | 922.65 | 930.04 | 922.26 | 925.08 | 936.24 | 935.55 | 934.75 | 931.38 | 934.99 | 933.83 | 970.56 | 969.60 | 936.32 |
| **Trade, Transportation, and Utilities** | | | | | | | | | | | | | |
| 2015 | 663.55 | 645.86 | 654.93 | 636.98 | 652.33 | 652.06 | 658.66 | 658.33 | 669.61 | 675.58 | 669.93 | 636.31 | 656.24 |
| 2016 | 638.35 | 646.15 | 637.36 | 654.57 | 660.17 | 674.10 | 675.80 | 689.61 | 686.70 | 707.05 | 725.14 | 708.94 | 675.00 |
| 2017 | 715.16 | 706.19 | 754.53 | 778.54 | 782.56 | 790.58 | 802.40 | 801.02 | 818.57 | 825.78 | 838.58 | 842.27 | 789.88 |
| 2018 | 846.27 | 855.93 | 850.08 | 851.45 | 863.97 | 882.67 | 895.79 | 869.49 | 897.10 | 887.04 | 900.65 | 889.73 | 873.51 |
| 2019 | 908.82 | 893.23 | 894.54 | 906.40 | 896.53 | 923.74 | 915.75 | 923.08 | 929.63 | 909.09 | 893.89 | 894.41 | 907.17 |
| **Professional and Business Services** | | | | | | | | | | | | | |
| 2015 | 1,057.92 | 1,078.82 | 1,092.18 | 1,053.35 | 1,082.17 | 1,057.37 | 1,064.95 | 1,069.70 | 1,045.28 | 1,055.82 | 1,064.93 | 1,016.86 | 1,062.52 |
| 2016 | 1,063.06 | 1,049.22 | 1,051.59 | 1,076.00 | 1,080.95 | 1,084.81 | 1,063.24 | 1,085.46 | 1,098.73 | 1,087.85 | 1,088.86 | 1,099.68 | 1,078.99 |
| 2017 | 1,123.55 | 1,102.01 | 1,099.24 | 1,122.18 | 1,118.75 | 1,115.17 | 1,115.49 | 1,120.03 | 1,137.01 | 1,126.78 | 1,123.22 | 1,138.02 | 1,120.07 |
| 2018 | 1,146.47 | 1,174.34 | 1,137.73 | 1,174.44 | 1,154.88 | 1,144.49 | 1,156.28 | 1,151.33 | 1,171.76 | 1,164.89 | 1,172.52 | 1,170.71 | 1,159.54 |
| 2019 | 1,170.00 | 1,192.60 | 1,211.39 | 1,188.05 | 1,208.77 | 1,201.93 | 1,179.68 | 1,181.55 | 1,181.91 | 1,164.87 | 1,180.43 | 1,177.70 | 1,186.62 |
| **Education and Health Services** | | | | | | | | | | | | | |
| 2015 | 708.08 | 725.76 | 746.07 | 759.49 | 774.25 | 773.76 | 788.16 | 805.03 | 821.10 | 831.57 | 855.79 | 844.47 | 785.60 |
| 2016 | 845.78 | 847.16 | 839.90 | 839.55 | 849.87 | 845.30 | 864.36 | 860.97 | 870.87 | 898.16 | 888.42 | 899.52 | 861.53 |
| 2017 | 931.13 | 918.34 | 916.73 | 954.81 | 974.82 | 979.44 | 971.19 | 966.85 | 986.15 | 994.29 | 990.68 | 988.03 | 964.65 |
| 2018 | 984.68 | 968.27 | 967.45 | 990.68 | 977.64 | 981.24 | 961.61 | 955.48 | 944.71 | 935.68 | 930.12 | 956.76 | 961.80 |
| 2019 | 941.24 | 944.87 | 936.87 | 918.22 | 905.63 | 913.58 | 918.70 | 923.45 | 945.12 | 946.05 | 940.94 | 959.40 | 933.16 |
| **Leisure and Hospitality** | | | | | | | | | | | | | |
| 2015 | 344.16 | 339.71 | 351.84 | 362.25 | 368.38 | 379.13 | 399.56 | 401.65 | 396.23 | 387.35 | 378.50 | 379.33 | 374.53 |
| 2016 | 365.04 | 379.92 | 374.85 | 376.75 | 389.17 | 387.50 | 393.92 | 397.76 | 384.43 | 379.77 | 381.60 | 382.28 | 383.21 |
| 2017 | 374.91 | 362.01 | 372.55 | 394.39 | 386.08 | 388.49 | 404.25 | 403.54 | 392.52 | 392.04 | 389.94 | 392.35 | 388.56 |
| 2018 | 385.40 | 404.25 | 389.63 | 411.10 | 420.08 | 419.35 | 439.56 | 437.71 | 421.93 | 417.66 | 415.00 | 422.30 | 416.00 |
| 2019 | 403.58 | 422.54 | 431.87 | 425.04 | 428.65 | 427.70 | 448.54 | 448.81 | 441.34 | 421.38 | 422.34 | 419.19 | 428.40 |

# SOUTH CAROLINA
## *At a Glance*

Population:
  2010 census: 4,625,364
  2019 estimate: 5,148,714

Percent change in population:
  2010–2019: 11.3%

Percent change in total nonfarm employment:
  2011–2019: 19.5%

Industry with the largest growth in employment, 2011–2019 (percent):
  Construction, 38.3%

Industry with the largest decline or smallest growth in employment, 2011–2019 (percent):
  Information, 5.0%

Civilian labor force:
  2010: 2,155,668
  2019: 2,376,069

Unemployment rate and rank among states (highest to lowest):
  2010: 11.2%, 4th
  2019: 2.8%, 43rd

Over-the-year change in unemployment rates:
  2017–2018: -0.8%
  2018–2019: -0.7%

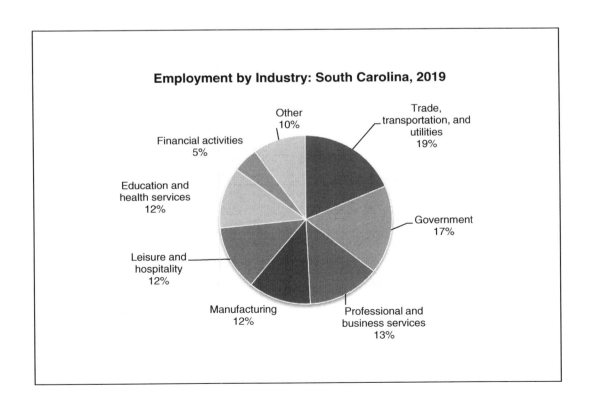

**Employment by Industry: South Carolina, 2019**

- Trade, transportation, and utilities 19%
- Government 17%
- Professional and business services 13%
- Manufacturing 12%
- Leisure and hospitality 12%
- Education and health services 12%
- Financial activities 5%
- Other 10%

## 1. Employment by Industry: South Carolina, 2011–2019

(Numbers in thousands, not seasonally adjusted)

| Industry and year | January | February | March | April | May | June | July | August | September | October | November | December | Annual average |
|---|---|---|---|---|---|---|---|---|---|---|---|---|---|
| **Total Nonfarm** | | | | | | | | | | | | | |
| 2011 | 1,779.2 | 1,798.9 | 1,819.5 | 1,842.5 | 1,851.3 | 1,850.8 | 1,833.8 | 1,839.5 | 1,841.0 | 1,840.4 | 1,847.4 | 1,846.1 | 1,832.5 |
| 2012 | 1,813.6 | 1,830.0 | 1,851.6 | 1,866.0 | 1,877.6 | 1,881.9 | 1,859.9 | 1,866.9 | 1,870.4 | 1,874.8 | 1,891.0 | 1,887.4 | 1,864.3 |
| 2013 | 1,844.4 | 1,860.5 | 1,878.2 | 1,897.0 | 1,911.5 | 1,917.2 | 1,899.7 | 1,906.2 | 1,912.8 | 1,919.0 | 1,932.7 | 1,933.0 | 1,901.0 |
| 2014 | 1,891.7 | 1,898.9 | 1,928.9 | 1,951.2 | 1,966.5 | 1,968.0 | 1,945.9 | 1,953.3 | 1,960.9 | 1,972.6 | 1,987.9 | 1,990.0 | 1,951.3 |
| 2015 | 1,944.8 | 1,960.1 | 1,979.2 | 1,998.3 | 2,016.7 | 2,021.1 | 2,008.6 | 2,014.7 | 2,016.7 | 2,031.0 | 2,042.7 | 2,046.4 | 2,006.7 |
| 2016 | 1,997.4 | 2,015.0 | 2,033.4 | 2,057.0 | 2,068.2 | 2,068.8 | 2,058.8 | 2,063.3 | 2,068.3 | 2,063.0 | 2,084.5 | 2,085.5 | 2,055.3 |
| 2017 | 2,046.4 | 2,064.0 | 2,080.5 | 2,093.8 | 2,107.4 | 2,114.2 | 2,098.6 | 2,098.4 | 2,093.3 | 2,107.8 | 2,125.0 | 2,124.5 | 2,096.2 |
| 2018 | 2,105.5 | 2,123.8 | 2,135.8 | 2,158.4 | 2,170.2 | 2,176.7 | 2,155.1 | 2,160.2 | 2,147.8 | 2,164.7 | 2,181.9 | 2,179.0 | 2,154.9 |
| 2019 | 2,142.9 | 2,155.1 | 2,168.3 | 2,187.1 | 2,199.6 | 2,202.9 | 2,189.8 | 2,196.8 | 2,191.6 | 2,204.1 | 2,217.4 | 2,217.4 | 2,189.4 |
| **Total Private** | | | | | | | | | | | | | |
| 2011 | 1,430.1 | 1,446.6 | 1,465.9 | 1,488.7 | 1,498.7 | 1,503.5 | 1,501.3 | 1,503.8 | 1,492.8 | 1,489.1 | 1,494.9 | 1,494.2 | 1,484.1 |
| 2012 | 1,466.0 | 1,477.0 | 1,497.3 | 1,511.8 | 1,523.1 | 1,531.0 | 1,523.7 | 1,529.0 | 1,518.2 | 1,517.9 | 1,530.0 | 1,528.7 | 1,512.8 |
| 2013 | 1,492.4 | 1,504.0 | 1,520.1 | 1,538.1 | 1,553.5 | 1,565.1 | 1,562.2 | 1,567.2 | 1,560.0 | 1,561.6 | 1,573.7 | 1,575.0 | 1,547.7 |
| 2014 | 1,538.5 | 1,541.7 | 1,570.2 | 1,591.5 | 1,606.5 | 1,613.9 | 1,606.5 | 1,610.3 | 1,603.4 | 1,610.5 | 1,624.9 | 1,626.8 | 1,595.4 |
| 2015 | 1,587.3 | 1,598.0 | 1,616.2 | 1,634.2 | 1,652.6 | 1,663.1 | 1,664.2 | 1,666.6 | 1,655.0 | 1,665.7 | 1,676.0 | 1,678.7 | 1,646.5 |
| 2016 | 1,636.4 | 1,650.1 | 1,666.6 | 1,689.5 | 1,701.4 | 1,707.0 | 1,709.0 | 1,710.8 | 1,703.6 | 1,696.3 | 1,716.3 | 1,716.0 | 1,691.9 |
| 2017 | 1,683.1 | 1,697.1 | 1,711.5 | 1,724.7 | 1,738.5 | 1,749.8 | 1,745.2 | 1,742.4 | 1,725.6 | 1,737.1 | 1,752.0 | 1,751.9 | 1,729.9 |
| 2018 | 1,737.1 | 1,753.0 | 1,763.9 | 1,786.6 | 1,798.4 | 1,810.3 | 1,801.7 | 1,803.4 | 1,778.7 | 1,794.6 | 1,809.3 | 1,806.6 | 1,787.0 |
| 2019 | 1,773.9 | 1,782.7 | 1,794.6 | 1,812.7 | 1,825.1 | 1,832.9 | 1,832.3 | 1,833.5 | 1,817.4 | 1,826.7 | 1,838.0 | 1,837.8 | 1,817.3 |
| **Goods Producing** | | | | | | | | | | | | | |
| 2011 | 287.3 | 291.0 | 294.2 | 295.9 | 297.0 | 298.5 | 298.1 | 298.5 | 298.2 | 298.0 | 298.8 | 299.8 | 296.3 |
| 2012 | 296.6 | 298.7 | 301.0 | 300.6 | 302.2 | 302.8 | 301.2 | 302.4 | 302.1 | 302.7 | 303.5 | 304.3 | 301.5 |
| 2013 | 302.0 | 303.5 | 306.1 | 306.4 | 308.1 | 309.2 | 308.2 | 309.3 | 310.0 | 310.2 | 311.5 | 312.5 | 308.1 |
| 2014 | 309.9 | 310.2 | 313.1 | 314.6 | 317.0 | 318.6 | 317.6 | 317.3 | 318.1 | 319.9 | 321.2 | 322.9 | 316.7 |
| 2015 | 320.5 | 322.3 | 323.6 | 324.2 | 326.3 | 329.0 | 327.8 | 328.1 | 329.2 | 329.5 | 331.1 | 332.0 | 327.0 |
| 2016 | 330.8 | 332.3 | 333.9 | 334.7 | 336.3 | 338.3 | 339.6 | 339.4 | 340.8 | 339.1 | 342.0 | 343.8 | 337.6 |
| 2017 | 341.9 | 343.9 | 345.1 | 344.9 | 347.4 | 350.4 | 350.1 | 345.9 | 345.6 | 345.5 | 347.4 | 349.4 | 346.5 |
| 2018 | 350.9 | 354.3 | 355.2 | 358.0 | 360.2 | 363.3 | 362.1 | 361.7 | 361.3 | 362.7 | 364.3 | 366.1 | 360.0 |
| 2019 | 364.7 | 366.1 | 367.3 | 369.0 | 369.6 | 371.7 | 372.7 | 372.0 | 370.7 | 370.6 | 372.5 | 372.0 | 369.9 |
| **Service-Providing** | | | | | | | | | | | | | |
| 2011 | 1,491.9 | 1,507.9 | 1,525.3 | 1,546.6 | 1,554.3 | 1,552.3 | 1,535.7 | 1,541.0 | 1,542.8 | 1,542.4 | 1,548.6 | 1,546.3 | 1,536.3 |
| 2012 | 1,517.0 | 1,531.3 | 1,550.6 | 1,565.4 | 1,575.4 | 1,579.1 | 1,558.7 | 1,564.5 | 1,568.3 | 1,572.1 | 1,587.5 | 1,583.1 | 1,562.8 |
| 2013 | 1,542.4 | 1,557.0 | 1,572.1 | 1,590.6 | 1,603.4 | 1,608.0 | 1,591.5 | 1,596.9 | 1,602.8 | 1,608.8 | 1,621.2 | 1,620.5 | 1,592.9 |
| 2014 | 1,581.8 | 1,588.7 | 1,615.8 | 1,636.6 | 1,649.5 | 1,649.4 | 1,628.3 | 1,636.0 | 1,642.8 | 1,652.7 | 1,666.7 | 1,667.1 | 1,634.6 |
| 2015 | 1,624.3 | 1,637.8 | 1,655.6 | 1,674.1 | 1,690.4 | 1,692.1 | 1,680.8 | 1,686.6 | 1,687.5 | 1,701.5 | 1,711.6 | 1,714.4 | 1,679.7 |
| 2016 | 1,666.6 | 1,682.7 | 1,699.5 | 1,722.3 | 1,731.9 | 1,730.5 | 1,719.2 | 1,723.9 | 1,727.5 | 1,723.9 | 1,742.5 | 1,741.7 | 1,717.7 |
| 2017 | 1,704.5 | 1,720.1 | 1,735.4 | 1,748.9 | 1,760.0 | 1,763.8 | 1,748.5 | 1,752.5 | 1,747.7 | 1,762.3 | 1,777.6 | 1,775.1 | 1,749.7 |
| 2018 | 1,754.6 | 1,769.5 | 1,780.6 | 1,800.4 | 1,810.0 | 1,813.4 | 1,793.0 | 1,798.5 | 1,786.5 | 1,802.0 | 1,817.6 | 1,812.9 | 1,794.9 |
| 2019 | 1,778.2 | 1,789.0 | 1,801.0 | 1,818.1 | 1,830.0 | 1,831.2 | 1,817.1 | 1,824.8 | 1,820.9 | 1,833.5 | 1,844.9 | 1,845.4 | 1,819.5 |
| **Mining and Logging** | | | | | | | | | | | | | |
| 2011 | 3.9 | 3.9 | 4.0 | 4.0 | 4.0 | 4.0 | 3.9 | 3.9 | 3.9 | 3.9 | 3.9 | 3.9 | 3.9 |
| 2012 | 3.9 | 3.9 | 3.9 | 3.9 | 3.9 | 3.9 | 3.8 | 3.8 | 3.8 | 3.8 | 3.8 | 3.8 | 3.9 |
| 2013 | 3.8 | 3.8 | 3.8 | 3.8 | 3.8 | 3.8 | 3.8 | 3.8 | 3.8 | 3.8 | 3.8 | 3.9 | 3.8 |
| 2014 | 3.8 | 3.7 | 3.8 | 3.8 | 3.9 | 3.9 | 3.9 | 3.9 | 3.9 | 3.9 | 3.9 | 3.9 | 3.9 |
| 2015 | 3.9 | 3.9 | 3.9 | 3.9 | 3.9 | 4.0 | 4.0 | 4.1 | 4.1 | 4.0 | 4.0 | 4.0 | 4.0 |
| 2016 | 4.0 | 4.1 | 4.1 | 4.1 | 4.2 | 4.2 | 4.2 | 4.2 | 4.3 | 4.2 | 4.2 | 4.3 | 4.2 |
| 2017 | 4.2 | 4.2 | 4.3 | 4.2 | 4.3 | 4.3 | 4.3 | 4.3 | 4.2 | 4.2 | 4.2 | 4.2 | 4.2 |
| 2018 | 4.4 | 4.4 | 4.4 | 4.4 | 4.5 | 4.5 | 4.4 | 4.4 | 4.4 | 4.4 | 4.4 | 4.4 | 4.4 |
| 2019 | 4.3 | 4.4 | 4.4 | 4.4 | 4.5 | 4.5 | 4.5 | 4.5 | 4.5 | 4.5 | 4.4 | 4.4 | 4.4 |
| **Construction** | | | | | | | | | | | | | |
| 2011 | 74.5 | 76.1 | 77.3 | 77.9 | 78.6 | 78.8 | 78.5 | 78.3 | 78.0 | 78.0 | 78.0 | 77.6 | 77.6 |
| 2012 | 75.8 | 77.0 | 78.3 | 77.5 | 78.6 | 79.3 | 79.0 | 79.5 | 79.3 | 79.2 | 79.1 | 79.2 | 78.5 |
| 2013 | 78.0 | 77.8 | 79.6 | 80.1 | 81.0 | 81.6 | 82.0 | 82.2 | 82.3 | 82.0 | 82.7 | 83.1 | 81.0 |
| 2014 | 81.5 | 81.6 | 82.9 | 83.5 | 84.7 | 85.4 | 85.2 | 85.7 | 85.4 | 86.0 | 86.4 | 87.0 | 84.6 |
| 2015 | 85.5 | 86.1 | 87.3 | 87.7 | 89.1 | 90.5 | 90.2 | 90.2 | 90.6 | 91.9 | 92.3 | 92.9 | 89.5 |
| 2016 | 92.4 | 93.4 | 95.0 | 95.7 | 96.7 | 98.4 | 99.2 | 99.8 | 99.8 | 99.7 | 100.8 | 101.1 | 97.7 |
| 2017 | 99.6 | 100.3 | 100.8 | 101.8 | 103.3 | 104.6 | 104.1 | 100.4 | 99.2 | 100.1 | 100.2 | 100.8 | 101.3 |
| 2018 | 102.7 | 104.1 | 104.8 | 105.9 | 106.8 | 107.5 | 106.6 | 106.7 | 105.8 | 105.8 | 105.7 | 105.9 | 105.7 |
| 2019 | 104.9 | 105.2 | 105.6 | 106.4 | 106.9 | 107.8 | 107.8 | 107.9 | 107.5 | 108.9 | 109.0 | 109.4 | 107.3 |

## 1. Employment by Industry: South Carolina, 2011–2019—Continued

(Numbers in thousands, not seasonally adjusted)

| Industry and year | January | February | March | April | May | June | July | August | September | October | November | December | Annual average |
|---|---|---|---|---|---|---|---|---|---|---|---|---|---|
| **Manufacturing** | | | | | | | | | | | | | |
| 2011 | 208.9 | 211.0 | 212.9 | 214.0 | 214.4 | 215.7 | 215.7 | 216.3 | 216.3 | 216.1 | 216.9 | 218.3 | 214.7 |
| 2012 | 216.9 | 217.8 | 218.8 | 219.2 | 219.7 | 219.6 | 218.4 | 219.1 | 219.0 | 219.7 | 220.6 | 221.3 | 219.2 |
| 2013 | 220.2 | 221.9 | 222.7 | 222.5 | 223.3 | 223.8 | 222.4 | 223.3 | 223.9 | 224.4 | 225.0 | 225.5 | 223.2 |
| 2014 | 224.6 | 224.9 | 226.4 | 227.3 | 228.4 | 229.3 | 228.5 | 227.7 | 228.8 | 230.0 | 230.9 | 232.0 | 228.2 |
| 2015 | 231.1 | 232.3 | 232.4 | 232.6 | 233.3 | 234.5 | 233.6 | 233.8 | 234.5 | 233.6 | 234.8 | 235.1 | 233.5 |
| 2016 | 234.4 | 234.8 | 234.8 | 234.9 | 235.4 | 235.7 | 236.2 | 235.4 | 236.7 | 235.2 | 237.0 | 238.4 | 235.7 |
| 2017 | 238.1 | 239.4 | 240.0 | 238.9 | 239.8 | 241.5 | 241.7 | 241.2 | 242.2 | 241.2 | 243.0 | 244.4 | 241.0 |
| 2018 | 243.8 | 245.8 | 246.0 | 247.7 | 248.9 | 251.3 | 251.1 | 250.6 | 251.1 | 252.5 | 254.2 | 255.8 | 249.9 |
| 2019 | 255.5 | 256.5 | 257.3 | 258.2 | 258.2 | 259.4 | 260.4 | 259.6 | 258.7 | 257.2 | 259.1 | 258.2 | 258.2 |
| **Trade, Transportation, and Utilities** | | | | | | | | | | | | | |
| 2011 | 341.6 | 342.4 | 344.9 | 348.3 | 349.8 | 351.8 | 351.6 | 351.4 | 348.8 | 350.3 | 355.9 | 358.3 | 349.6 |
| 2012 | 347.4 | 346.3 | 349.4 | 351.1 | 353.7 | 355.9 | 355.3 | 355.2 | 354.1 | 356.4 | 364.5 | 365.6 | 354.6 |
| 2013 | 351.4 | 351.2 | 354.7 | 356.8 | 359.9 | 363.6 | 364.6 | 365.6 | 363.4 | 366.5 | 373.2 | 376.9 | 362.3 |
| 2014 | 363.4 | 361.7 | 366.1 | 368.9 | 372.3 | 376.0 | 374.3 | 374.8 | 373.2 | 376.5 | 384.4 | 388.5 | 373.3 |
| 2015 | 373.5 | 373.2 | 376.6 | 380.5 | 384.1 | 387.6 | 388.6 | 388.9 | 385.0 | 388.4 | 395.5 | 398.4 | 385.0 |
| 2016 | 385.2 | 386.0 | 387.4 | 390.6 | 393.4 | 394.8 | 396.1 | 395.9 | 393.8 | 393.6 | 402.3 | 405.2 | 393.7 |
| 2017 | 392.5 | 391.9 | 393.4 | 393.6 | 395.4 | 397.8 | 397.6 | 397.0 | 392.8 | 397.1 | 405.5 | 409.1 | 397.0 |
| 2018 | 398.7 | 399.2 | 401.1 | 402.0 | 404.3 | 406.7 | 405.2 | 404.3 | 399.5 | 403.9 | 413.9 | 415.6 | 404.5 |
| 2019 | 402.9 | 401.4 | 403.2 | 404.0 | 406.9 | 409.3 | 409.6 | 408.2 | 405.6 | 409.6 | 416.8 | 420.5 | 408.2 |
| **Wholesale Trade** | | | | | | | | | | | | | |
| 2011 | 63.3 | 64.0 | 64.1 | 64.4 | 64.5 | 64.6 | 64.6 | 64.6 | 64.3 | 64.2 | 64.3 | 64.6 | 64.3 |
| 2012 | 64.8 | 65.2 | 65.5 | 65.5 | 65.7 | 66.2 | 65.8 | 65.8 | 65.5 | 65.6 | 65.6 | 65.7 | 65.6 |
| 2013 | 65.4 | 65.7 | 66.1 | 66.3 | 66.6 | 66.9 | 66.5 | 66.8 | 66.5 | 66.5 | 66.8 | 66.9 | 66.4 |
| 2014 | 67.0 | 67.2 | 67.5 | 67.4 | 67.9 | 68.4 | 68.0 | 68.2 | 68.2 | 69.0 | 69.2 | 69.2 | 68.1 |
| 2015 | 69.4 | 69.7 | 70.2 | 70.4 | 70.7 | 70.7 | 70.5 | 70.6 | 70.4 | 70.8 | 70.9 | 71.3 | 70.5 |
| 2016 | 70.9 | 71.2 | 71.3 | 71.6 | 71.7 | 71.8 | 71.9 | 71.8 | 71.7 | 71.4 | 71.8 | 72.1 | 71.6 |
| 2017 | 71.5 | 71.9 | 72.2 | 71.8 | 72.1 | 72.6 | 72.6 | 72.6 | 72.1 | 71.8 | 72.1 | 72.4 | 72.1 |
| 2018 | 71.7 | 72.1 | 72.2 | 72.2 | 72.3 | 72.5 | 72.2 | 72.1 | 71.6 | 72.0 | 72.3 | 72.5 | 72.1 |
| 2019 | 71.9 | 72.3 | 72.6 | 72.9 | 73.4 | 73.7 | 73.6 | 73.4 | 73.1 | 73.1 | 73.6 | 74.1 | 73.1 |
| **Retail Trade** | | | | | | | | | | | | | |
| 2011 | 219.1 | 219.2 | 221.2 | 224.4 | 225.2 | 226.3 | 226.3 | 225.7 | 223.4 | 224.3 | 229.1 | 230.5 | 224.6 |
| 2012 | 221.2 | 219.7 | 222.3 | 223.7 | 225.7 | 226.8 | 226.9 | 226.5 | 225.4 | 227.0 | 234.5 | 234.5 | 226.2 |
| 2013 | 222.7 | 222.1 | 224.8 | 227.0 | 229.3 | 231.9 | 233.0 | 233.4 | 231.5 | 234.3 | 240.0 | 242.2 | 231.0 |
| 2014 | 230.3 | 228.9 | 232.3 | 233.9 | 235.8 | 238.2 | 237.3 | 237.1 | 235.4 | 237.2 | 243.7 | 246.1 | 236.4 |
| 2015 | 233.3 | 232.8 | 235.3 | 238.4 | 241.0 | 244.2 | 244.7 | 244.7 | 241.5 | 244.4 | 251.0 | 252.1 | 242.0 |
| 2016 | 241.0 | 241.6 | 242.8 | 245.2 | 247.1 | 247.5 | 248.1 | 247.7 | 245.6 | 245.1 | 252.4 | 253.3 | 246.5 |
| 2017 | 244.2 | 243.3 | 244.2 | 245.3 | 246.5 | 247.7 | 247.2 | 246.9 | 242.9 | 246.7 | 254.0 | 254.7 | 247.0 |
| 2018 | 247.8 | 247.9 | 249.4 | 250.5 | 252.3 | 253.5 | 252.6 | 251.7 | 247.8 | 251.1 | 258.8 | 258.2 | 251.8 |
| 2019 | 249.0 | 247.7 | 248.9 | 249.1 | 251.3 | 252.8 | 252.8 | 251.5 | 249.3 | 252.7 | 258.6 | 258.2 | 251.8 |
| **Transportation and Utilities** | | | | | | | | | | | | | |
| 2011 | 59.2 | 59.2 | 59.6 | 59.5 | 60.1 | 60.9 | 60.7 | 61.1 | 61.1 | 61.8 | 62.5 | 63.2 | 60.7 |
| 2012 | 61.4 | 61.4 | 61.6 | 61.9 | 62.3 | 62.9 | 62.6 | 62.9 | 63.2 | 63.8 | 64.4 | 65.4 | 62.8 |
| 2013 | 63.3 | 63.4 | 63.8 | 63.5 | 64.0 | 64.8 | 65.1 | 65.4 | 65.4 | 65.7 | 66.4 | 67.8 | 64.9 |
| 2014 | 66.1 | 65.6 | 66.3 | 67.6 | 68.6 | 69.4 | 69.0 | 69.5 | 69.6 | 70.3 | 71.5 | 73.2 | 68.9 |
| 2015 | 70.8 | 70.7 | 71.1 | 71.7 | 72.4 | 72.7 | 73.4 | 73.6 | 73.1 | 73.2 | 73.6 | 75.0 | 72.6 |
| 2016 | 73.3 | 73.2 | 73.3 | 73.8 | 74.6 | 75.5 | 76.1 | 76.4 | 76.5 | 77.1 | 78.1 | 79.8 | 75.6 |
| 2017 | 76.8 | 76.7 | 77.0 | 76.5 | 76.8 | 77.5 | 77.8 | 77.5 | 77.8 | 78.6 | 79.4 | 82.0 | 77.9 |
| 2018 | 79.2 | 79.2 | 79.5 | 79.3 | 79.7 | 80.7 | 80.4 | 80.5 | 80.1 | 80.8 | 82.8 | 84.9 | 80.6 |
| 2019 | 82.0 | 81.4 | 81.7 | 82.0 | 82.2 | 82.8 | 83.2 | 83.3 | 83.2 | 83.8 | 84.6 | 88.2 | 83.2 |
| **Information** | | | | | | | | | | | | | |
| 2011 | 26.0 | 25.7 | 25.9 | 25.7 | 25.7 | 25.8 | 25.8 | 25.7 | 25.3 | 26.0 | 26.1 | 26.1 | 25.8 |
| 2012 | 25.5 | 25.8 | 25.6 | 25.7 | 26.0 | 26.1 | 25.8 | 25.6 | 25.4 | 25.6 | 25.9 | 26.3 | 25.8 |
| 2013 | 26.1 | 26.4 | 26.4 | 26.7 | 26.7 | 26.5 | 26.6 | 26.3 | 26.2 | 26.2 | 26.4 | 26.4 | 26.4 |
| 2014 | 26.0 | 26.0 | 26.1 | 26.4 | 26.5 | 26.5 | 26.5 | 26.3 | 26.1 | 26.4 | 27.0 | 27.0 | 26.4 |
| 2015 | 26.6 | 26.6 | 26.6 | 26.6 | 26.9 | 26.8 | 27.0 | 26.9 | 26.7 | 26.8 | 27.8 | 27.3 | 26.9 |
| 2016 | 26.9 | 26.9 | 27.0 | 27.7 | 27.3 | 27.2 | 27.1 | 27.0 | 26.9 | 27.2 | 27.4 | 27.8 | 27.2 |
| 2017 | 27.3 | 27.5 | 27.7 | 27.4 | 27.8 | 27.9 | 27.4 | 27.5 | 27.5 | 27.4 | 27.5 | 27.7 | 27.6 |
| 2018 | 27.6 | 28.1 | 28.2 | 28.0 | 28.0 | 28.4 | 28.2 | 27.6 | 27.1 | 27.1 | 27.1 | 27.1 | 27.7 |
| 2019 | 26.7 | 26.9 | 27.1 | 27.7 | 27.7 | 27.9 | 27.2 | 27.0 | 26.3 | 26.5 | 26.6 | 27.0 | 27.1 |

## 1. Employment by Industry: South Carolina, 2011–2019—*Continued*

(Numbers in thousands, not seasonally adjusted)

| Industry and year | January | February | March | April | May | June | July | August | September | October | November | December | Annual average |
|---|---|---|---|---|---|---|---|---|---|---|---|---|---|
| **Financial Activities** | | | | | | | | | | | | | |
| 2011 | 89.9 | 89.8 | 90.1 | 90.9 | 91.7 | 92.2 | 92.6 | 92.6 | 91.7 | 91.7 | 92.0 | 92.0 | 91.4 |
| 2012 | 91.3 | 91.7 | 92.2 | 93.4 | 93.8 | 94.9 | 94.8 | 95.1 | 94.3 | 94.1 | 94.4 | 94.9 | 93.7 |
| 2013 | 93.4 | 94.0 | 94.8 | 95.6 | 96.4 | 97.3 | 97.5 | 97.7 | 96.6 | 96.4 | 96.4 | 96.5 | 96.1 |
| 2014 | 95.0 | 95.1 | 95.6 | 96.7 | 97.1 | 97.9 | 97.7 | 97.8 | 96.6 | 96.3 | 96.4 | 96.6 | 96.6 |
| 2015 | 95.5 | 95.7 | 96.1 | 97.0 | 97.7 | 98.7 | 98.8 | 99.0 | 98.1 | 98.7 | 98.9 | 99.3 | 97.8 |
| 2016 | 98.2 | 98.7 | 99.5 | 100.5 | 101.1 | 101.6 | 101.9 | 102.0 | 100.9 | 101.4 | 101.7 | 101.4 | 100.7 |
| 2017 | 100.2 | 100.5 | 101.2 | 101.5 | 102.2 | 102.3 | 103.5 | 103.6 | 102.4 | 102.6 | 102.5 | 102.8 | 102.2 |
| 2018 | 102.5 | 103.0 | 103.3 | 103.6 | 104.3 | 105.1 | 104.9 | 105.0 | 103.6 | 104.4 | 104.5 | 104.3 | 104.0 |
| 2019 | 102.7 | 103.2 | 102.9 | 104.0 | 104.7 | 105.7 | 106.3 | 106.5 | 105.3 | 105.6 | 104.7 | 103.9 | 104.6 |
| **Professional and Business Services** | | | | | | | | | | | | | |
| 2011 | 217.8 | 222.0 | 225.2 | 230.2 | 230.5 | 230.8 | 231.1 | 233.1 | 231.8 | 230.6 | 231.4 | 231.5 | 228.8 |
| 2012 | 227.4 | 230.3 | 234.0 | 237.3 | 238.5 | 239.6 | 236.7 | 239.1 | 236.1 | 235.6 | 239.8 | 240.0 | 236.2 |
| 2013 | 232.9 | 234.9 | 236.3 | 238.5 | 241.2 | 243.4 | 242.1 | 243.8 | 244.1 | 245.7 | 251.3 | 251.7 | 242.2 |
| 2014 | 242.9 | 244.0 | 250.8 | 253.0 | 255.3 | 254.5 | 253.1 | 255.0 | 255.5 | 257.2 | 264.0 | 263.2 | 254.0 |
| 2015 | 251.6 | 253.4 | 255.7 | 258.0 | 262.2 | 262.8 | 263.9 | 265.2 | 265.1 | 270.2 | 272.0 | 274.5 | 262.9 |
| 2016 | 259.2 | 262.9 | 263.8 | 270.2 | 270.4 | 269.8 | 269.3 | 270.8 | 271.6 | 272.7 | 278.3 | 277.0 | 269.7 |
| 2017 | 270.2 | 273.6 | 274.8 | 279.0 | 281.0 | 281.8 | 280.2 | 281.1 | 281.4 | 286.3 | 292.9 | 291.4 | 281.1 |
| 2018 | 287.5 | 290.7 | 292.6 | 293.8 | 294.6 | 295.5 | 293.2 | 295.0 | 293.4 | 299.8 | 303.4 | 301.4 | 295.1 |
| 2019 | 293.4 | 294.6 | 295.4 | 297.4 | 299.2 | 298.4 | 295.5 | 298.0 | 298.0 | 300.3 | 306.1 | 304.5 | 298.4 |
| **Education and Health Services** | | | | | | | | | | | | | |
| 2011 | 209.8 | 212.8 | 213.3 | 214.1 | 214.0 | 211.9 | 210.9 | 211.9 | 213.9 | 214.7 | 215.3 | 214.8 | 213.1 |
| 2012 | 212.7 | 214.9 | 215.3 | 214.6 | 215.0 | 212.6 | 211.9 | 213.4 | 216.3 | 217.8 | 218.4 | 218.1 | 215.1 |
| 2013 | 214.6 | 217.5 | 217.6 | 218.1 | 218.9 | 217.0 | 216.2 | 218.3 | 220.1 | 222.2 | 223.4 | 223.3 | 218.9 |
| 2014 | 221.4 | 222.9 | 224.5 | 227.4 | 227.3 | 225.2 | 224.7 | 227.0 | 228.8 | 231.5 | 232.5 | 232.5 | 227.1 |
| 2015 | 229.3 | 231.9 | 232.7 | 233.6 | 234.6 | 232.9 | 232.3 | 234.8 | 236.0 | 238.2 | 239.4 | 239.1 | 234.6 |
| 2016 | 235.8 | 238.4 | 239.6 | 240.4 | 241.0 | 238.8 | 239.1 | 241.3 | 243.8 | 243.4 | 244.7 | 244.6 | 240.9 |
| 2017 | 241.7 | 245.0 | 245.7 | 245.6 | 245.9 | 244.3 | 243.5 | 245.7 | 246.4 | 249.1 | 249.2 | 249.4 | 246.0 |
| 2018 | 248.0 | 250.8 | 251.5 | 253.7 | 254.1 | 252.9 | 252.3 | 255.0 | 255.3 | 257.2 | 257.7 | 257.3 | 253.8 |
| 2019 | 254.1 | 256.9 | 257.7 | 257.7 | 258.2 | 257.2 | 255.7 | 258.7 | 259.0 | 261.1 | 261.3 | 260.3 | 258.2 |
| **Leisure and Hospitality** | | | | | | | | | | | | | |
| 2011 | 190.2 | 195.0 | 203.7 | 214.7 | 221.0 | 223.5 | 222.1 | 222.1 | 214.8 | 209.9 | 207.6 | 204.1 | 210.7 |
| 2012 | 197.4 | 201.4 | 210.8 | 220.1 | 224.4 | 229.2 | 228.1 | 228.5 | 220.5 | 216.1 | 213.7 | 209.8 | 216.7 |
| 2013 | 202.6 | 206.8 | 213.5 | 225.1 | 231.1 | 236.3 | 235.6 | 234.6 | 227.7 | 222.8 | 220.7 | 216.7 | 222.8 |
| 2014 | 209.7 | 211.4 | 222.1 | 232.6 | 238.5 | 242.4 | 240.2 | 239.6 | 232.8 | 230.2 | 226.8 | 223.7 | 229.2 |
| 2015 | 218.3 | 222.5 | 231.3 | 240.7 | 246.6 | 250.9 | 251.6 | 249.7 | 241.3 | 239.9 | 237.3 | 234.0 | 238.7 |
| 2016 | 227.0 | 231.3 | 241.1 | 250.8 | 257.1 | 261.5 | 260.8 | 259.4 | 250.7 | 244.2 | 244.8 | 241.0 | 247.5 |
| 2017 | 234.8 | 240.1 | 248.2 | 257.3 | 263.0 | 268.4 | 267.1 | 265.9 | 254.1 | 253.7 | 251.6 | 246.6 | 254.2 |
| 2018 | 245.9 | 250.2 | 255.0 | 269.3 | 274.4 | 279.4 | 277.4 | 276.6 | 261.1 | 261.6 | 260.3 | 256.9 | 264.0 |
| 2019 | 251.8 | 255.5 | 262.4 | 273.6 | 279.0 | 282.8 | 284.9 | 282.7 | 272.5 | 272.9 | 270.2 | 269.8 | 271.5 |
| **Other Services** | | | | | | | | | | | | | |
| 2011 | 67.5 | 67.9 | 68.6 | 68.9 | 69.0 | 69.0 | 69.1 | 68.5 | 68.3 | 67.9 | 67.8 | 67.6 | 68.3 |
| 2012 | 67.7 | 67.9 | 69.0 | 69.0 | 69.5 | 69.9 | 69.9 | 69.7 | 69.4 | 69.6 | 69.8 | 69.7 | 69.3 |
| 2013 | 69.4 | 69.7 | 70.7 | 70.9 | 71.2 | 71.8 | 71.4 | 71.6 | 71.9 | 71.6 | 70.8 | 71.0 | 71.0 |
| 2014 | 70.2 | 70.4 | 71.9 | 71.9 | 72.5 | 72.8 | 72.4 | 72.5 | 72.3 | 72.5 | 72.6 | 72.4 | 72.0 |
| 2015 | 72.0 | 72.4 | 73.6 | 73.6 | 74.2 | 74.4 | 74.2 | 74.0 | 73.6 | 74.0 | 74.0 | 74.1 | 73.7 |
| 2016 | 73.3 | 73.6 | 74.3 | 74.6 | 74.8 | 75.0 | 75.1 | 75.0 | 75.1 | 74.7 | 75.1 | 75.2 | 74.7 |
| 2017 | 74.5 | 74.6 | 75.4 | 75.4 | 75.8 | 76.0 | 75.8 | 75.7 | 75.4 | 75.4 | 75.4 | 75.5 | 75.4 |
| 2018 | 76.0 | 76.7 | 77.0 | 78.2 | 78.5 | 79.0 | 78.4 | 78.2 | 77.4 | 77.9 | 78.1 | 77.9 | 77.8 |
| 2019 | 77.6 | 78.1 | 78.6 | 79.3 | 79.8 | 79.9 | 80.4 | 80.4 | 80.0 | 80.1 | 79.8 | 79.8 | 79.5 |
| **Government** | | | | | | | | | | | | | |
| 2011 | 349.1 | 352.3 | 353.6 | 353.8 | 352.6 | 347.3 | 332.5 | 335.7 | 348.2 | 351.3 | 352.5 | 351.9 | 348.4 |
| 2012 | 347.6 | 353.0 | 354.3 | 354.2 | 354.5 | 350.9 | 336.2 | 337.9 | 352.2 | 356.9 | 361.0 | 358.7 | 351.5 |
| 2013 | 352.0 | 356.5 | 358.1 | 358.9 | 358.0 | 352.1 | 337.5 | 339.0 | 352.8 | 357.4 | 359.0 | 358.0 | 353.3 |
| 2014 | 353.2 | 357.2 | 358.7 | 359.7 | 360.0 | 354.1 | 339.4 | 343.0 | 357.5 | 362.1 | 363.0 | 363.2 | 355.9 |
| 2015 | 357.5 | 362.1 | 363.0 | 364.1 | 364.1 | 358.0 | 344.4 | 348.1 | 361.7 | 365.3 | 366.7 | 367.7 | 360.2 |
| 2016 | 361.0 | 364.9 | 366.8 | 367.5 | 366.8 | 361.8 | 349.8 | 352.5 | 364.7 | 366.7 | 368.2 | 369.5 | 363.4 |
| 2017 | 363.3 | 366.9 | 369.0 | 369.1 | 368.9 | 364.4 | 353.4 | 356.0 | 367.7 | 370.7 | 373.0 | 372.6 | 366.3 |
| 2018 | 368.4 | 370.8 | 371.9 | 371.8 | 371.8 | 366.4 | 353.4 | 356.8 | 369.1 | 370.1 | 372.6 | 372.4 | 368.0 |
| 2019 | 369.0 | 372.4 | 373.7 | 374.4 | 374.5 | 370.0 | 357.5 | 363.3 | 374.2 | 377.4 | 379.4 | 379.6 | 372.1 |

## 2. Average Weekly Hours by Selected Industry: South Carolina, 2015–2019

(Not seasonally adjusted)

| Industry and year | January | February | March | April | May | June | July | August | September | October | November | December | Annual average |
|---|---|---|---|---|---|---|---|---|---|---|---|---|---|
| **Total Private** | | | | | | | | | | | | | |
| 2015 | 34.3 | 34.6 | 34.7 | 34.6 | 34.7 | 34.8 | 34.7 | 35.2 | 34.3 | 34.6 | 34.8 | 34.6 | 34.7 |
| 2016 | 34.4 | 34.4 | 34.6 | 34.6 | 34.8 | 34.6 | 34.4 | 34.4 | 34.4 | 34.2 | 34.5 | 34.5 | 34.5 |
| 2017 | 34.4 | 34.4 | 34.5 | 34.7 | 34.6 | 34.9 | 34.8 | 34.8 | 34.0 | 34.8 | 34.7 | 34.7 | 34.6 |
| 2018 | 34.0 | 34.6 | 34.7 | 35.0 | 34.6 | 34.8 | 34.9 | 34.7 | 33.5 | 34.5 | 34.8 | 34.8 | 34.6 |
| 2019 | 34.7 | 34.8 | 34.8 | 34.7 | 34.6 | 34.7 | 34.4 | 34.4 | 34.3 | 34.0 | 34.0 | 34.1 | 34.5 |
| **Goods-Producing** | | | | | | | | | | | | | |
| 2015 | 40.0 | 40.1 | 40.4 | 40.8 | 41.2 | 41.1 | 41.2 | 41.1 | 40.7 | 41.3 | 41.0 | 41.3 | 40.9 |
| 2016 | 40.7 | 40.8 | 42.0 | 41.4 | 41.7 | 41.7 | 40.3 | 40.5 | 41.0 | 40.7 | 41.1 | 41.1 | 41.1 |
| 2017 | 40.1 | 41.1 | 41.1 | 40.8 | 41.4 | 42.0 | 41.0 | 41.3 | 41.2 | 42.1 | 42.3 | 42.6 | 41.4 |
| 2018 | 41.7 | 41.9 | 42.3 | 42.2 | 41.8 | 42.2 | 41.8 | 41.7 | 40.3 | 41.3 | 41.8 | 42.0 | 41.7 |
| 2019 | 42.1 | 41.5 | 42.0 | 41.1 | 41.1 | 41.2 | 41.0 | 40.8 | 40.8 | 40.8 | 40.1 | 40.5 | 41.1 |
| **Construction** | | | | | | | | | | | | | |
| 2015 | 38.1 | 38.5 | 39.4 | 38.9 | 39.7 | 39.7 | 39.5 | 39.7 | 38.8 | 40.5 | 39.7 | 39.9 | 39.4 |
| 2016 | 38.8 | 39.1 | 40.6 | 39.3 | 40.5 | 40.7 | 40.0 | 39.9 | 39.6 | 39.7 | 40.2 | 39.6 | 39.8 |
| 2017 | 39.0 | 39.2 | 39.6 | 38.9 | 40.0 | 40.4 | 40.3 | 40.0 | 38.4 | 40.3 | 41.0 | 40.4 | 39.8 |
| 2018 | 39.6 | 39.7 | 40.1 | 40.1 | 39.8 | 39.9 | 39.9 | 39.4 | 37.2 | 39.1 | 38.7 | 39.5 | 39.4 |
| 2019 | 39.8 | 39.2 | 39.4 | 39.4 | 39.5 | 38.8 | 39.7 | 40.0 | 40.5 | 40.0 | 38.3 | 38.0 | 39.4 |
| **Manufacturing** | | | | | | | | | | | | | |
| 2015 | 41.2 | 41.1 | 41.1 | 41.9 | 42.0 | 41.9 | 42.1 | 41.8 | 41.7 | 41.6 | 41.7 | 42.0 | 41.7 |
| 2016 | 41.6 | 41.5 | 42.5 | 42.3 | 42.2 | 42.1 | 40.3 | 40.7 | 41.7 | 41.3 | 41.6 | 41.9 | 41.6 |
| 2017 | 40.6 | 41.7 | 41.6 | 41.6 | 41.9 | 42.6 | 41.2 | 41.8 | 42.5 | 43.0 | 43.0 | 43.8 | 42.1 |
| 2018 | 42.8 | 43.1 | 43.4 | 43.1 | 42.6 | 43.2 | 42.5 | 42.8 | 41.8 | 42.4 | 43.3 | 43.1 | 42.8 |
| 2019 | 43.0 | 42.5 | 43.2 | 41.9 | 41.8 | 42.4 | 41.6 | 41.2 | 40.9 | 41.1 | 40.8 | 41.7 | 41.8 |
| **Trade, Transportation, and Utilities** | | | | | | | | | | | | | |
| 2015 | 34.4 | 34.7 | 35.3 | 35.0 | 35.2 | 35.2 | 34.9 | 35.5 | 34.5 | 34.6 | 34.8 | 34.5 | 34.9 |
| 2016 | 34.4 | 34.3 | 34.0 | 34.3 | 34.3 | 34.1 | 34.3 | 34.4 | 34.5 | 33.7 | 33.7 | 34.0 | 34.2 |
| 2017 | 33.9 | 33.6 | 33.8 | 34.3 | 34.3 | 34.4 | 34.4 | 34.4 | 33.5 | 34.0 | 34.0 | 34.2 | 34.1 |
| 2018 | 33.2 | 33.6 | 34.0 | 34.4 | 34.2 | 34.1 | 34.5 | 34.3 | 33.2 | 34.2 | 34.1 | 33.9 | 34.0 |
| 2019 | 33.9 | 34.0 | 34.1 | 34.4 | 34.2 | 34.4 | 33.9 | 33.9 | 33.8 | 33.5 | 33.4 | 33.7 | 33.9 |
| **Financial Activities** | | | | | | | | | | | | | |
| 2015 | 36.7 | 37.7 | 37.4 | 36.8 | 36.7 | 37.0 | 37.2 | 38.0 | 36.9 | 37.1 | 38.2 | 37.0 | 37.2 |
| 2016 | 37.1 | 37.3 | 37.2 | 36.9 | 37.8 | 36.9 | 36.9 | 36.4 | 36.3 | 37.4 | 36.6 | 36.8 | 37.0 |
| 2017 | 37.7 | 36.7 | 36.6 | 37.6 | 36.6 | 36.8 | 37.6 | 36.7 | 36.7 | 37.9 | 37.2 | 37.4 | 37.1 |
| 2018 | 37.5 | 37.5 | 37.4 | 37.8 | 36.7 | 36.8 | 37.8 | 37.0 | 37.1 | 37.2 | 37.2 | 38.2 | 37.3 |
| 2019 | 37.4 | 37.9 | 37.7 | 37.6 | 37.3 | 38.3 | 37.3 | 37.1 | 37.7 | 37.2 | 37.4 | 38.3 | 37.6 |
| **Professional and Business Services** | | | | | | | | | | | | | |
| 2015 | 36.7 | 37.1 | 36.6 | 36.4 | 36.5 | 36.5 | 36.1 | 36.9 | 35.8 | 36.2 | 37.3 | 36.9 | 36.6 |
| 2016 | 36.1 | 36.5 | 36.1 | 36.4 | 36.8 | 36.2 | 35.8 | 36.1 | 36.0 | 36.3 | 36.6 | 36.6 | 36.3 |
| 2017 | 36.5 | 36.0 | 36.2 | 36.6 | 36.4 | 36.4 | 36.3 | 36.7 | 35.1 | 36.4 | 36.3 | 36.1 | 36.2 |
| 2018 | 35.3 | 36.3 | 36.5 | 37.3 | 36.9 | 36.9 | 37.4 | 37.2 | 35.6 | 36.1 | 36.7 | 37.0 | 36.6 |
| 2019 | 36.8 | 36.8 | 36.9 | 36.4 | 36.4 | 36.0 | 35.4 | 36.2 | 35.8 | 35.5 | 35.5 | 35.7 | 36.1 |
| **Education and Health Services** | | | | | | | | | | | | | |
| 2015 | 33.2 | 33.4 | 33.3 | 32.8 | 32.8 | 32.6 | 32.7 | 33.6 | 32.8 | 33.0 | 33.3 | 33.0 | 33.0 |
| 2016 | 32.9 | 32.5 | 32.8 | 32.8 | 33.0 | 32.6 | 32.7 | 32.6 | 32.6 | 32.6 | 32.8 | 32.7 | 32.7 |
| 2017 | 32.6 | 32.8 | 32.6 | 32.7 | 32.9 | 32.5 | 32.8 | 32.8 | 32.6 | 32.5 | 32.4 | 32.6 | 32.6 |
| 2018 | 31.9 | 32.1 | 31.9 | 32.0 | 32.1 | 32.1 | 31.7 | 31.9 | 31.8 | 32.0 | 32.2 | 31.9 | 32.0 |
| 2019 | 31.6 | 31.8 | 31.7 | 31.9 | 32.0 | 32.3 | 31.6 | 31.8 | 32.1 | 32.0 | 32.2 | 32.4 | 32.0 |
| **Leisure and Hospitality** | | | | | | | | | | | | | |
| 2015 | 24.6 | 25.1 | 25.7 | 26.0 | 25.8 | 26.4 | 26.7 | 26.6 | 25.2 | 25.0 | 25.0 | 24.7 | 25.6 |
| 2016 | 24.6 | 24.8 | 25.4 | 25.8 | 25.9 | 26.7 | 26.9 | 26.3 | 25.6 | 24.8 | 25.2 | 24.8 | 25.6 |
| 2017 | 24.5 | 24.9 | 25.5 | 26.1 | 25.4 | 26.4 | 26.9 | 26.4 | 24.8 | 25.9 | 25.6 | 25.1 | 25.7 |
| 2018 | 24.7 | 25.7 | 26.0 | 26.0 | 25.6 | 26.3 | 26.6 | 26.5 | 23.4 | 25.6 | 25.4 | 25.0 | 25.6 |
| 2019 | 24.9 | 25.7 | 25.8 | 26.0 | 25.7 | 26.3 | 26.5 | 26.1 | 25.0 | 25.3 | 25.1 | 24.6 | 25.6 |
| **Other Services** | | | | | | | | | | | | | |
| 2015 | 29.9 | 30.0 | 31.3 | 31.5 | 31.9 | 31.5 | 31.7 | 31.1 | 31.1 | 31.3 | 31.1 | 32.4 | 31.2 |
| 2016 | 32.7 | 33.1 | 33.1 | 34.4 | 33.2 | 33.6 | 34.4 | 33.9 | 34.7 | 34.5 | 33.8 | 33.8 | 33.8 |
| 2017 | 34.3 | 34.7 | 34.3 | 34.9 | 33.8 | 33.5 | 33.9 | 32.8 | 33.2 | 34.7 | 33.8 | 33.0 | 33.9 |
| 2018 | 33.5 | 33.6 | 33.3 | 34.4 | 33.5 | 33.9 | 34.5 | 33.8 | 32.0 | 32.9 | 34.0 | 33.6 | 33.6 |
| 2019 | 34.5 | 35.2 | 34.8 | 34.9 | 34.9 | 34.8 | 34.8 | 33.5 | 33.5 | 32.8 | 33.9 | 33.6 | 34.3 |

## 3. Average Hourly Earnings by Selected Industry: South Carolina, 2015–2019

(Dollars, not seasonally adjusted)

| Industry and year | January | February | March | April | May | June | July | August | September | October | November | December | Annual average |
|---|---|---|---|---|---|---|---|---|---|---|---|---|---|
| **Total Private** | | | | | | | | | | | | | |
| 2015 | 21.70 | 21.36 | 21.75 | 21.22 | 21.03 | 20.99 | 21.26 | 21.29 | 21.50 | 21.53 | 21.80 | 21.67 | 21.42 |
| 2016 | 21.87 | 21.79 | 22.17 | 21.93 | 21.87 | 22.07 | 21.93 | 21.95 | 22.24 | 22.53 | 22.49 | 22.46 | 22.11 |
| 2017 | 23.09 | 22.74 | 23.13 | 22.80 | 22.44 | 22.44 | 22.87 | 22.68 | 23.12 | 23.16 | 23.08 | 23.21 | 22.89 |
| 2018 | 23.89 | 23.85 | 23.86 | 23.99 | 23.61 | 23.46 | 23.72 | 23.55 | 24.64 | 24.15 | 24.38 | 24.52 | 23.97 |
| 2019 | 24.30 | 24.50 | 24.30 | 24.43 | 24.23 | 24.56 | 24.53 | 24.71 | 25.36 | 25.08 | 25.34 | 25.37 | 24.72 |
| **Goods-Producing** | | | | | | | | | | | | | |
| 2015 | 22.67 | 22.68 | 22.69 | 22.52 | 22.29 | 22.42 | 22.69 | 22.84 | 22.96 | 23.13 | 23.36 | 23.37 | 22.80 |
| 2016 | 23.39 | 23.33 | 23.55 | 23.47 | 23.47 | 23.59 | 24.20 | 24.04 | 24.33 | 24.02 | 24.08 | 24.27 | 23.81 |
| 2017 | 24.55 | 24.06 | 24.09 | 24.02 | 23.54 | 23.65 | 24.08 | 24.02 | 24.06 | 24.21 | 24.44 | 24.64 | 24.11 |
| 2018 | 24.96 | 24.90 | 24.87 | 25.32 | 25.33 | 25.37 | 25.75 | 25.75 | 26.10 | 26.43 | 26.29 | 26.78 | 25.66 |
| 2019 | 26.18 | 26.42 | 25.96 | 26.40 | 26.15 | 26.50 | 26.51 | 26.53 | 26.81 | 26.66 | 26.94 | 27.28 | 26.53 |
| **Construction** | | | | | | | | | | | | | |
| 2015 | 20.54 | 20.58 | 20.81 | 20.62 | 20.41 | 20.55 | 20.74 | 20.92 | 21.05 | 21.28 | 21.39 | 21.65 | 20.89 |
| 2016 | 21.68 | 21.72 | 22.15 | 21.79 | 21.76 | 21.98 | 22.60 | 22.57 | 23.08 | 23.16 | 22.98 | 22.76 | 22.37 |
| 2017 | 22.97 | 22.65 | 23.15 | 22.75 | 22.34 | 22.60 | 22.97 | 23.14 | 23.34 | 23.09 | 23.08 | 23.94 | 23.00 |
| 2018 | 23.87 | 24.31 | 24.65 | 24.32 | 24.62 | 24.41 | 24.45 | 24.79 | 25.13 | 25.59 | 25.35 | 25.54 | 24.75 |
| 2019 | 25.39 | 25.70 | 25.77 | 25.78 | 25.41 | 25.99 | 25.93 | 25.91 | 26.00 | 25.95 | 26.17 | 26.86 | 25.90 |
| **Manufacturing** | | | | | | | | | | | | | |
| 2015 | 23.56 | 23.57 | 23.50 | 23.35 | 23.11 | 23.26 | 23.59 | 23.75 | 23.86 | 24.03 | 24.34 | 24.25 | 23.68 |
| 2016 | 24.25 | 24.13 | 24.22 | 24.30 | 24.32 | 24.41 | 25.02 | 24.75 | 24.90 | 24.40 | 24.62 | 24.99 | 24.52 |
| 2017 | 25.33 | 24.87 | 24.60 | 24.72 | 24.22 | 24.25 | 24.70 | 24.50 | 24.43 | 24.79 | 25.15 | 24.91 | 24.71 |
| 2018 | 25.43 | 25.10 | 24.85 | 25.48 | 25.39 | 25.57 | 26.18 | 26.00 | 26.36 | 26.66 | 26.56 | 27.25 | 25.91 |
| 2019 | 26.69 | 26.87 | 26.18 | 26.83 | 26.64 | 26.75 | 26.78 | 26.80 | 27.18 | 26.91 | 27.20 | 27.49 | 26.86 |
| **Trade, Transportation, and Utilities** | | | | | | | | | | | | | |
| 2015 | 20.07 | 19.59 | 20.46 | 19.68 | 19.66 | 19.75 | 19.93 | 20.04 | 20.04 | 20.29 | 20.60 | 20.31 | 20.04 |
| 2016 | 20.53 | 20.27 | 21.07 | 20.38 | 20.40 | 20.11 | 20.37 | 20.13 | 20.33 | 20.69 | 20.69 | 20.57 | 20.46 |
| 2017 | 21.02 | 20.97 | 21.57 | 21.73 | 21.33 | 21.36 | 21.57 | 21.56 | 21.77 | 21.92 | 21.06 | 21.05 | 21.41 |
| 2018 | 21.35 | 21.48 | 22.15 | 22.15 | 21.54 | 21.87 | 21.75 | 21.71 | 22.87 | 22.25 | 22.67 | 22.23 | 22.00 |
| 2019 | 22.47 | 22.75 | 22.28 | 22.33 | 22.04 | 22.38 | 22.32 | 22.53 | 23.04 | 22.91 | 22.83 | 22.79 | 22.56 |
| **Financial Activities** | | | | | | | | | | | | | |
| 2015 | 24.95 | 25.20 | 25.10 | 25.01 | 24.56 | 24.31 | 24.84 | 24.58 | 24.54 | 24.31 | 25.17 | 25.07 | 24.80 |
| 2016 | 25.59 | 24.88 | 25.02 | 25.77 | 25.16 | 24.60 | 24.82 | 25.39 | 25.88 | 26.64 | 26.32 | 26.04 | 25.51 |
| 2017 | 26.73 | 25.75 | 24.99 | 26.09 | 25.73 | 25.75 | 26.19 | 26.26 | 26.93 | 27.19 | 27.22 | 27.04 | 26.33 |
| 2018 | 29.77 | 29.25 | 28.03 | 28.60 | 28.50 | 27.57 | 28.49 | 27.79 | 29.00 | 28.13 | 28.88 | 29.06 | 28.59 |
| 2019 | 28.41 | 28.31 | 28.90 | 29.22 | 28.69 | 29.73 | 29.20 | 29.75 | 30.21 | 29.23 | 30.42 | 30.82 | 29.41 |
| **Professional and Business Services** | | | | | | | | | | | | | |
| 2015 | 23.75 | 23.84 | 23.91 | 23.66 | 23.40 | 23.38 | 23.92 | 23.13 | 23.18 | 22.86 | 22.87 | 22.35 | 23.34 |
| 2016 | 22.78 | 22.97 | 22.88 | 23.50 | 23.60 | 23.36 | 23.79 | 23.74 | 24.22 | 24.50 | 24.28 | 24.05 | 23.65 |
| 2017 | 24.67 | 25.19 | 25.09 | 25.76 | 25.02 | 25.01 | 25.93 | 24.77 | 25.51 | 25.26 | 25.37 | 25.88 | 25.29 |
| 2018 | 26.23 | 25.85 | 26.04 | 26.29 | 25.82 | 25.63 | 26.58 | 25.78 | 27.20 | 26.08 | 26.45 | 26.68 | 26.22 |
| 2019 | 26.71 | 27.21 | 27.62 | 27.66 | 27.64 | 27.98 | 28.02 | 27.89 | 28.92 | 28.30 | 28.64 | 28.73 | 27.94 |
| **Education and Health Services** | | | | | | | | | | | | | |
| 2015 | 25.97 | 26.01 | 25.60 | 25.88 | 25.54 | 25.49 | 25.79 | 26.10 | 26.71 | 26.14 | 26.48 | 26.32 | 26.01 |
| 2016 | 26.23 | 26.42 | 25.94 | 26.18 | 25.77 | 25.88 | 26.05 | 25.91 | 25.75 | 26.10 | 26.36 | 26.00 | 26.05 |
| 2017 | 25.78 | 25.82 | 25.95 | 25.83 | 25.82 | 26.25 | 26.87 | 26.74 | 26.94 | 26.70 | 26.58 | 26.65 | 26.33 |
| 2018 | 27.09 | 27.02 | 26.53 | 26.20 | 25.56 | 25.75 | 25.56 | 25.09 | 25.98 | 26.22 | 26.08 | 26.14 | 26.10 |
| 2019 | 26.06 | 26.30 | 25.82 | 26.24 | 26.26 | 26.67 | 26.79 | 27.01 | 27.77 | 27.49 | 27.66 | 27.24 | 26.78 |
| **Leisure and Hospitality** | | | | | | | | | | | | | |
| 2015 | 11.90 | 12.02 | 12.09 | 12.07 | 12.02 | 11.89 | 11.88 | 12.02 | 12.05 | 12.28 | 12.22 | 12.40 | 12.07 |
| 2016 | 12.25 | 12.31 | 12.36 | 12.35 | 12.53 | 12.37 | 12.34 | 12.49 | 12.51 | 12.51 | 12.53 | 12.64 | 12.43 |
| 2017 | 12.58 | 12.48 | 12.47 | 12.78 | 12.83 | 12.55 | 12.48 | 12.53 | 12.57 | 12.72 | 12.73 | 12.82 | 12.63 |
| 2018 | 12.70 | 12.80 | 12.85 | 13.00 | 12.96 | 12.73 | 12.83 | 12.94 | 13.22 | 13.24 | 13.30 | 13.63 | 13.01 |
| 2019 | 13.39 | 13.70 | 13.65 | 13.63 | 13.70 | 13.66 | 13.71 | 13.73 | 13.84 | 13.98 | 13.97 | 14.11 | 13.76 |
| **Other Services** | | | | | | | | | | | | | |
| 2015 | 16.09 | 16.22 | 16.11 | 16.22 | 16.06 | 16.11 | 16.23 | 16.35 | 16.20 | 16.37 | 16.67 | 16.70 | 16.28 |
| 2016 | 17.18 | 17.36 | 17.14 | 17.53 | 18.00 | 17.97 | 18.14 | 17.81 | 17.78 | 18.26 | 19.29 | 19.69 | 18.02 |
| 2017 | 20.35 | 20.54 | 20.70 | 21.09 | 21.13 | 21.28 | 21.65 | 21.80 | 22.47 | 22.36 | 22.73 | 22.35 | 21.53 |
| 2018 | 23.50 | 23.31 | 23.33 | 22.72 | 23.24 | 22.30 | 23.29 | 23.35 | 23.85 | 23.49 | 23.94 | 24.90 | 23.43 |
| 2019 | 24.21 | 24.15 | 24.10 | 23.84 | 23.26 | 22.94 | 22.99 | 23.98 | 24.74 | 24.46 | 24.30 | 24.32 | 23.93 |

# 4. Average Weekly Earnings by Selected Industry: South Carolina, 2015–2019

(Dollars, not seasonally adjusted)

| Industry and year | January | February | March | April | May | June | July | August | September | October | November | December | Annual average |
|---|---|---|---|---|---|---|---|---|---|---|---|---|---|
| **Total Private** | | | | | | | | | | | | | |
| 2015 | 744.31 | 739.06 | 754.73 | 734.21 | 729.74 | 730.45 | 737.72 | 749.41 | 737.45 | 744.94 | 758.64 | 749.78 | 743.27 |
| 2016 | 752.33 | 749.58 | 767.08 | 758.78 | 761.08 | 763.62 | 754.39 | 755.08 | 765.06 | 770.53 | 775.91 | 774.87 | 762.80 |
| 2017 | 794.30 | 782.26 | 797.99 | 791.16 | 776.42 | 783.16 | 795.88 | 789.26 | 786.08 | 805.97 | 800.88 | 805.39 | 791.99 |
| 2018 | 812.26 | 825.21 | 827.94 | 839.65 | 816.91 | 816.41 | 827.83 | 817.19 | 825.44 | 833.18 | 848.42 | 853.30 | 829.36 |
| 2019 | 843.21 | 852.60 | 845.64 | 847.72 | 838.36 | 852.23 | 843.83 | 850.02 | 869.85 | 852.72 | 861.56 | 865.12 | 852.84 |
| **Goods-Producing** | | | | | | | | | | | | | |
| 2015 | 906.80 | 909.47 | 916.68 | 918.82 | 918.35 | 921.46 | 934.83 | 938.72 | 934.47 | 955.27 | 957.76 | 965.18 | 932.52 |
| 2016 | 951.97 | 951.86 | 989.10 | 971.66 | 978.70 | 983.70 | 975.26 | 973.62 | 997.53 | 977.61 | 989.69 | 997.50 | 978.59 |
| 2017 | 984.46 | 988.87 | 990.10 | 980.02 | 974.56 | 993.30 | 987.28 | 992.03 | 991.27 | 1,019.24 | 1,033.81 | 1,049.66 | 998.15 |
| 2018 | 1,040.83 | 1,043.31 | 1,052.00 | 1,068.50 | 1,058.79 | 1,070.61 | 1,076.35 | 1,073.78 | 1,051.83 | 1,091.56 | 1,098.92 | 1,124.76 | 1,070.02 |
| 2019 | 1,102.18 | 1,096.43 | 1,090.32 | 1,085.04 | 1,074.77 | 1,091.80 | 1,086.91 | 1,082.42 | 1,093.85 | 1,087.73 | 1,080.29 | 1,104.84 | 1,090.38 |
| **Construction** | | | | | | | | | | | | | |
| 2015 | 782.57 | 792.33 | 819.91 | 802.12 | 810.28 | 815.84 | 819.23 | 830.52 | 816.74 | 861.84 | 849.18 | 863.84 | 823.07 |
| 2016 | 841.18 | 849.25 | 899.29 | 856.35 | 881.28 | 894.59 | 904.00 | 900.54 | 913.97 | 919.45 | 923.80 | 901.30 | 890.33 |
| 2017 | 895.83 | 887.88 | 916.74 | 884.98 | 893.60 | 913.04 | 925.69 | 925.60 | 896.26 | 930.53 | 946.28 | 967.18 | 915.40 |
| 2018 | 945.25 | 965.11 | 988.47 | 975.23 | 979.88 | 973.96 | 975.56 | 976.73 | 934.84 | 1,000.57 | 981.05 | 1,008.83 | 975.15 |
| 2019 | 1,010.52 | 1,007.44 | 1,015.34 | 1,015.73 | 1,003.70 | 1,008.41 | 1,029.42 | 1,036.40 | 1,053.00 | 1,038.00 | 1,002.31 | 1,020.68 | 1,020.46 |
| **Manufacturing** | | | | | | | | | | | | | |
| 2015 | 970.67 | 968.73 | 965.85 | 978.37 | 970.62 | 974.59 | 993.14 | 992.75 | 994.96 | 999.65 | 1,014.98 | 1,018.50 | 987.46 |
| 2016 | 1,008.80 | 1,001.40 | 1,029.35 | 1,027.89 | 1,026.30 | 1,027.66 | 1,008.31 | 1,007.33 | 1,038.33 | 1,007.72 | 1,024.19 | 1,047.08 | 1,020.03 |
| 2017 | 1,028.40 | 1,037.08 | 1,023.36 | 1,028.35 | 1,014.82 | 1,033.05 | 1,017.64 | 1,024.10 | 1,038.28 | 1,065.97 | 1,081.45 | 1,091.06 | 1,040.29 |
| 2018 | 1,088.40 | 1,081.81 | 1,078.49 | 1,098.19 | 1,081.61 | 1,104.62 | 1,112.65 | 1,112.80 | 1,101.85 | 1,130.38 | 1,150.05 | 1,174.48 | 1,108.95 |
| 2019 | 1,147.67 | 1,141.98 | 1,130.98 | 1,124.18 | 1,113.55 | 1,134.20 | 1,114.05 | 1,104.16 | 1,111.66 | 1,106.00 | 1,109.76 | 1,146.33 | 1,122.75 |
| **Trade, Transportation, and Utilities** | | | | | | | | | | | | | |
| 2015 | 690.41 | 679.77 | 722.24 | 688.80 | 692.03 | 695.20 | 695.56 | 711.42 | 691.38 | 702.03 | 716.88 | 700.70 | 699.40 |
| 2016 | 706.23 | 695.26 | 716.38 | 699.03 | 699.72 | 685.75 | 698.69 | 692.47 | 701.39 | 697.25 | 697.25 | 699.38 | 699.73 |
| 2017 | 712.58 | 704.59 | 729.07 | 745.34 | 731.62 | 734.78 | 742.01 | 741.66 | 729.30 | 745.28 | 716.04 | 719.91 | 730.08 |
| 2018 | 708.82 | 721.73 | 753.10 | 761.96 | 736.67 | 745.77 | 750.38 | 744.65 | 759.28 | 760.95 | 773.05 | 753.60 | 748.00 |
| 2019 | 761.73 | 773.50 | 759.75 | 768.15 | 753.77 | 769.87 | 756.65 | 763.77 | 778.75 | 767.49 | 762.52 | 768.02 | 764.78 |
| **Financial Activities** | | | | | | | | | | | | | |
| 2015 | 915.67 | 950.04 | 938.74 | 920.37 | 901.35 | 899.47 | 924.05 | 934.04 | 905.53 | 901.90 | 961.49 | 927.59 | 922.56 |
| 2016 | 949.39 | 928.02 | 930.74 | 950.91 | 951.05 | 907.74 | 915.86 | 924.20 | 939.44 | 996.34 | 963.31 | 958.27 | 943.87 |
| 2017 | 1,007.72 | 945.03 | 914.63 | 980.98 | 941.72 | 947.60 | 984.74 | 963.74 | 988.33 | 1,030.50 | 1,012.58 | 1,011.30 | 976.84 |
| 2018 | 1,116.38 | 1,096.88 | 1,048.32 | 1,081.08 | 1,045.95 | 1,014.58 | 1,076.92 | 1,028.23 | 1,075.90 | 1,046.44 | 1,074.34 | 1,110.09 | 1,066.41 |
| 2019 | 1,062.53 | 1,072.95 | 1,089.53 | 1,098.67 | 1,070.14 | 1,138.66 | 1,089.16 | 1,103.73 | 1,138.92 | 1,087.36 | 1,137.71 | 1,180.41 | 1,105.82 |
| **Professional and Business Services** | | | | | | | | | | | | | |
| 2015 | 871.63 | 884.46 | 875.11 | 861.22 | 854.10 | 853.37 | 863.51 | 853.50 | 829.84 | 827.53 | 853.05 | 824.72 | 854.24 |
| 2016 | 822.36 | 838.41 | 825.97 | 855.40 | 868.48 | 845.63 | 851.68 | 857.01 | 871.92 | 889.35 | 888.65 | 880.23 | 858.50 |
| 2017 | 900.46 | 906.84 | 908.26 | 942.82 | 910.73 | 910.36 | 941.26 | 909.06 | 895.40 | 919.46 | 920.93 | 934.27 | 915.50 |
| 2018 | 925.92 | 938.36 | 950.46 | 980.62 | 952.76 | 945.75 | 994.09 | 959.02 | 968.32 | 941.49 | 970.72 | 987.16 | 959.65 |
| 2019 | 982.93 | 1,001.33 | 1,019.18 | 1,006.82 | 1,006.10 | 1,007.28 | 991.91 | 1,009.62 | 1,035.34 | 1,004.65 | 1,016.72 | 1,025.66 | 1,008.63 |
| **Education and Health Services** | | | | | | | | | | | | | |
| 2015 | 862.20 | 868.73 | 852.48 | 848.86 | 837.71 | 830.97 | 843.33 | 876.96 | 876.09 | 862.62 | 881.78 | 868.56 | 858.33 |
| 2016 | 862.97 | 858.65 | 850.83 | 858.70 | 850.41 | 843.69 | 851.84 | 844.67 | 839.45 | 850.86 | 864.61 | 850.20 | 851.84 |
| 2017 | 840.43 | 846.90 | 845.97 | 844.64 | 849.48 | 853.13 | 881.34 | 877.07 | 878.24 | 867.75 | 861.19 | 868.79 | 858.36 |
| 2018 | 864.17 | 867.34 | 846.31 | 838.40 | 820.48 | 826.58 | 810.25 | 800.37 | 826.16 | 839.04 | 839.78 | 833.87 | 835.20 |
| 2019 | 823.50 | 836.34 | 818.49 | 837.06 | 840.32 | 861.44 | 846.56 | 858.92 | 891.42 | 879.68 | 890.65 | 882.58 | 856.96 |
| **Leisure and Hospitality** | | | | | | | | | | | | | |
| 2015 | 292.74 | 301.70 | 310.71 | 313.82 | 310.12 | 313.90 | 317.20 | 319.73 | 303.66 | 307.00 | 305.50 | 306.28 | 308.99 |
| 2016 | 301.35 | 305.29 | 313.94 | 318.63 | 324.53 | 330.28 | 331.95 | 328.49 | 320.26 | 310.25 | 315.76 | 313.47 | 318.21 |
| 2017 | 308.21 | 310.75 | 317.99 | 333.56 | 325.88 | 331.32 | 335.71 | 330.79 | 311.74 | 329.45 | 325.89 | 321.78 | 324.59 |
| 2018 | 313.69 | 328.96 | 334.10 | 338.00 | 331.78 | 334.80 | 341.28 | 342.91 | 309.35 | 338.94 | 337.82 | 340.75 | 333.06 |
| 2019 | 333.41 | 352.09 | 352.17 | 354.38 | 352.09 | 359.26 | 363.32 | 358.35 | 346.00 | 353.69 | 350.65 | 347.11 | 352.26 |
| **Other Services** | | | | | | | | | | | | | |
| 2015 | 481.09 | 486.60 | 504.24 | 510.93 | 512.31 | 507.47 | 514.49 | 508.49 | 503.82 | 512.38 | 518.44 | 541.08 | 507.94 |
| 2016 | 561.79 | 574.62 | 567.33 | 603.03 | 597.60 | 603.79 | 624.02 | 603.76 | 616.97 | 629.97 | 652.00 | 665.52 | 609.08 |
| 2017 | 698.01 | 712.74 | 710.01 | 736.04 | 714.19 | 712.88 | 733.94 | 715.04 | 746.00 | 775.89 | 768.27 | 737.55 | 729.87 |
| 2018 | 787.25 | 783.22 | 776.89 | 781.57 | 778.54 | 755.97 | 803.51 | 789.23 | 763.20 | 772.82 | 813.96 | 836.64 | 787.25 |
| 2019 | 835.25 | 850.08 | 838.68 | 832.02 | 811.77 | 798.31 | 800.05 | 803.33 | 828.79 | 802.29 | 823.77 | 817.15 | 820.80 |

# SOUTH DAKOTA
## *At a Glance*

Population:
  2010 census: 814,180
  2019 estimate: 884,659

Percent change in population:
  2010–2019: 8.7%

Percent change in total nonfarm employment:
  2011–2019: 8.1%

Industry with the largest growth in employment, 2011–2019 (percent):
  Construction, 17.4%

Industry with the largest decline or smallest growth in employment, 2011–2019 (percent):
  Information, -14.1%

Civilian labor force:
  2010: 441,339
  2019: 463,997

Unemployment rate and rank among states (highest to lowest):
  2010: 5.0%, 49th
  2019: 3.3%, 30th

Over-the-year change in unemployment rates:
  2017–2018: -0.1%
  2018–2019: 0.2%

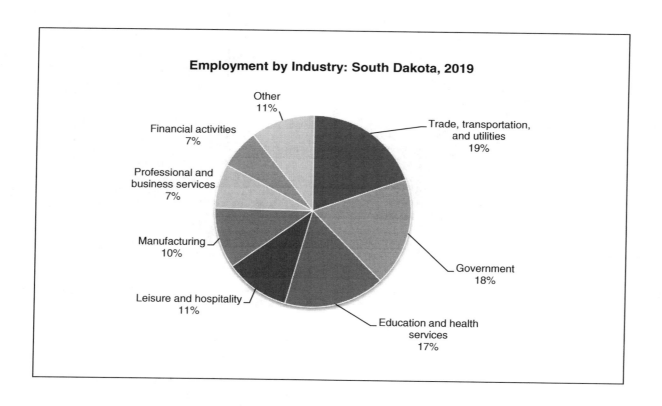

**Employment by Industry: South Dakota, 2019**

- Other 11%
- Financial activities 7%
- Professional and business services 7%
- Manufacturing 10%
- Leisure and hospitality 11%
- Trade, transportation, and utilities 19%
- Government 18%
- Education and health services 17%

# 1. Employment by Industry: South Dakota, 2011–2019

(Numbers in thousands, not seasonally adjusted)

| Industry and year | January | February | March | April | May | June | July | August | September | October | November | December | Annual average |
|---|---|---|---|---|---|---|---|---|---|---|---|---|---|
| **Total Nonfarm** | | | | | | | | | | | | | |
| 2011 | 393.0 | 394.3 | 396.8 | 403.4 | 411.4 | 417.3 | 412.9 | 414.8 | 412.6 | 413.0 | 411.3 | 411.3 | 407.7 |
| 2012 | 399.9 | 400.6 | 404.8 | 411.3 | 418.9 | 424.6 | 419.1 | 420.8 | 418.7 | 418.1 | 417.2 | 415.6 | 414.1 |
| 2013 | 404.7 | 406.0 | 408.9 | 411.6 | 423.5 | 427.5 | 422.3 | 424.6 | 422.4 | 422.3 | 421.9 | 420.1 | 418.0 |
| 2014 | 410.4 | 411.8 | 414.1 | 419.5 | 429.2 | 434.0 | 429.5 | 431.4 | 429.1 | 428.1 | 426.0 | 425.8 | 424.1 |
| 2015 | 414.6 | 416.5 | 419.9 | 425.6 | 433.8 | 438.9 | 434.1 | 434.9 | 432.4 | 432.3 | 430.9 | 430.5 | 428.7 |
| 2016 | 418.5 | 420.4 | 423.3 | 429.5 | 437.1 | 442.2 | 438.6 | 439.5 | 436.9 | 435.7 | 434.6 | 432.5 | 432.4 |
| 2017 | 421.4 | 422.8 | 425.7 | 431.8 | 439.3 | 444.2 | 437.8 | 440.1 | 437.9 | 437.9 | 436.1 | 435.5 | 434.2 |
| 2018 | 424.9 | 426.8 | 429.3 | 431.4 | 443.3 | 448.2 | 442.5 | 445.0 | 442.9 | 441.8 | 440.6 | 440.0 | 438.1 |
| 2019 | 429.3 | 429.7 | 431.2 | 435.3 | 445.7 | 450.4 | 445.4 | 446.6 | 444.8 | 444.8 | 442.9 | 441.2 | 440.6 |
| **Total Private** | | | | | | | | | | | | | |
| 2010 | 315.4 | 315.4 | 317.7 | 324.0 | 331.5 | 337.3 | 338.6 | 341.4 | 335.3 | 334.3 | 332.5 | 332.3 | 329.6 |
| 2011 | 323.0 | 322.9 | 326.4 | 332.6 | 340.0 | 346.0 | 345.7 | 347.8 | 341.4 | 339.0 | 338.1 | 336.9 | 336.7 |
| 2012 | 327.8 | 327.7 | 330.5 | 333.6 | 344.7 | 350.1 | 349.7 | 351.3 | 344.5 | 343.6 | 343.0 | 341.7 | 340.7 |
| 2013 | 333.3 | 333.7 | 335.6 | 340.8 | 349.8 | 355.5 | 355.8 | 357.2 | 350.7 | 349.0 | 346.8 | 347.1 | 346.3 |
| 2014 | 337.9 | 338.6 | 341.5 | 346.9 | 354.1 | 359.9 | 360.0 | 361.3 | 354.3 | 353.4 | 351.7 | 351.4 | 350.9 |
| 2015 | 341.4 | 341.9 | 344.4 | 350.1 | 356.9 | 362.7 | 364.6 | 365.3 | 357.6 | 355.8 | 354.6 | 352.4 | 354.0 |
| 2016 | 343.2 | 343.4 | 346.0 | 352.0 | 358.2 | 363.9 | 363.2 | 365.0 | 358.1 | 357.5 | 355.7 | 355.3 | 355.1 |
| 2017 | 346.6 | 347.2 | 349.1 | 351.4 | 361.7 | 367.3 | 367.4 | 369.5 | 362.7 | 360.8 | 359.7 | 359.2 | 358.6 |
| 2018 | 350.3 | 349.6 | 350.8 | 354.6 | 364.0 | 369.5 | 370.0 | 370.8 | 363.9 | 363.2 | 361.5 | 359.9 | 360.7 |
| 2019 | | | | | | | | | | | | | |
| **Goods Producing** | | | | | | | | | | | | | |
| 2011 | 54.8 | 54.6 | 55.3 | 58.2 | 60.9 | 62.8 | 63.5 | 63.5 | 63.0 | 63.2 | 62.2 | 60.7 | 60.2 |
| 2012 | 58.4 | 58.2 | 59.2 | 61.5 | 63.3 | 65.0 | 65.1 | 64.9 | 64.0 | 63.6 | 62.9 | 61.4 | 62.3 |
| 2013 | 59.0 | 58.5 | 59.3 | 60.7 | 64.1 | 66.0 | 66.0 | 65.9 | 64.8 | 64.6 | 63.8 | 62.2 | 62.9 |
| 2014 | 59.8 | 59.8 | 60.5 | 62.5 | 65.2 | 67.2 | 67.6 | 67.5 | 66.7 | 66.7 | 65.6 | 64.7 | 64.5 |
| 2015 | 62.3 | 62.0 | 63.1 | 65.0 | 66.9 | 68.4 | 68.4 | 68.0 | 67.1 | 66.8 | 65.9 | 64.8 | 65.7 |
| 2016 | 61.8 | 61.6 | 62.7 | 64.6 | 66.6 | 69.4 | 70.0 | 68.9 | 67.6 | 67.1 | 66.2 | 64.6 | 65.9 |
| 2017 | 61.9 | 62.1 | 62.7 | 65.2 | 66.9 | 69.1 | 69.3 | 69.3 | 68.3 | 68.1 | 67.5 | 66.8 | 66.4 |
| 2018 | 64.0 | 64.1 | 64.8 | 66.3 | 69.1 | 71.0 | 71.2 | 71.1 | 70.6 | 70.1 | 69.6 | 68.5 | 68.4 |
| 2019 | 66.3 | 65.8 | 66.3 | 67.8 | 70.5 | 72.1 | 72.7 | 72.3 | 71.4 | 70.2 | 69.4 | 68.1 | 69.4 |
| **Service-Providing** | | | | | | | | | | | | | |
| 2011 | 338.2 | 339.7 | 341.5 | 345.2 | 350.5 | 354.5 | 349.4 | 351.3 | 349.6 | 349.8 | 349.1 | 350.6 | 347.5 |
| 2012 | 341.5 | 342.4 | 345.6 | 349.8 | 355.6 | 359.6 | 354.0 | 355.9 | 354.7 | 354.5 | 354.3 | 354.2 | 351.8 |
| 2013 | 345.7 | 347.5 | 349.6 | 350.9 | 359.4 | 361.5 | 356.3 | 358.7 | 357.6 | 357.7 | 358.1 | 357.9 | 355.1 |
| 2014 | 350.6 | 352.0 | 353.6 | 357.0 | 364.0 | 366.8 | 361.9 | 363.9 | 362.4 | 361.4 | 360.4 | 361.1 | 359.6 |
| 2015 | 352.3 | 354.5 | 356.8 | 360.6 | 366.9 | 370.5 | 365.7 | 366.9 | 365.3 | 365.5 | 365.0 | 365.7 | 363.0 |
| 2016 | 356.7 | 358.8 | 360.6 | 364.9 | 370.5 | 372.8 | 368.6 | 370.6 | 369.3 | 368.6 | 368.4 | 367.9 | 366.5 |
| 2017 | 359.5 | 360.7 | 363.0 | 366.6 | 372.4 | 375.1 | 368.5 | 370.8 | 369.6 | 369.8 | 368.6 | 368.7 | 367.8 |
| 2018 | 360.9 | 362.7 | 364.5 | 365.1 | 374.2 | 377.2 | 371.3 | 373.9 | 372.3 | 371.7 | 371.0 | 371.5 | 369.7 |
| 2019 | 363.0 | 363.9 | 364.9 | 367.5 | 375.2 | 378.3 | 372.7 | 374.3 | 373.4 | 374.6 | 373.5 | 373.1 | 371.2 |
| **Mining and Logging** | | | | | | | | | | | | | |
| 2011 | 0.8 | 0.8 | 0.8 | 0.9 | 1.0 | 1.1 | 1.1 | 1.1 | 1.1 | 1.0 | 1.0 | 0.9 | 1.0 |
| 2012 | 0.9 | 0.8 | 0.9 | 0.9 | 1.0 | 1.0 | 1.0 | 1.1 | 1.0 | 1.0 | 1.0 | 0.9 | 1.0 |
| 2013 | 0.8 | 0.8 | 0.8 | 0.9 | 1.0 | 1.0 | 1.0 | 1.0 | 1.0 | 0.9 | 0.9 | 0.9 | 0.9 |
| 2014 | 0.7 | 0.7 | 0.8 | 0.9 | 1.0 | 1.0 | 1.0 | 1.0 | 1.0 | 0.9 | 0.9 | 0.9 | 0.9 |
| 2015 | 0.8 | 0.8 | 0.8 | 0.9 | 1.0 | 1.0 | 1.0 | 1.0 | 1.0 | 1.0 | 1.0 | 0.9 | 0.9 |
| 2016 | 0.8 | 0.8 | 0.8 | 0.9 | 1.0 | 1.0 | 1.0 | 1.0 | 1.0 | 1.0 | 1.0 | 0.9 | 0.9 |
| 2017 | 0.8 | 0.8 | 0.9 | 1.0 | 1.0 | 1.1 | 1.1 | 1.1 | 1.0 | 1.0 | 1.0 | 0.9 | 1.0 |
| 2018 | 0.8 | 0.8 | 0.9 | 0.9 | 1.0 | 1.1 | 1.1 | 1.1 | 1.1 | 1.0 | 1.0 | 0.9 | 1.0 |
| 2019 | 0.8 | 0.8 | 0.9 | 0.9 | 1.0 | 1.1 | 1.1 | 1.1 | 1.1 | 1.1 | 1.0 | 1.0 | 1.0 |
| **Construction** | | | | | | | | | | | | | |
| 2011 | 16.6 | 16.2 | 16.5 | 18.8 | 20.7 | 22.2 | 22.7 | 22.6 | 22.1 | 22.1 | 20.9 | 19.6 | 20.1 |
| 2012 | 17.6 | 17.1 | 17.9 | 19.7 | 21.0 | 22.2 | 22.2 | 22.1 | 21.3 | 20.8 | 20.1 | 19.1 | 20.1 |
| 2013 | 17.0 | 16.6 | 17.2 | 18.5 | 21.4 | 22.8 | 23.1 | 23.2 | 22.4 | 22.1 | 21.5 | 20.0 | 20.5 |
| 2014 | 18.1 | 17.7 | 18.1 | 19.8 | 22.0 | 23.7 | 23.9 | 23.7 | 23.1 | 22.8 | 21.8 | 20.8 | 21.3 |
| 2015 | 18.7 | 18.6 | 19.7 | 21.6 | 23.2 | 24.5 | 24.8 | 24.4 | 23.5 | 23.2 | 22.4 | 21.4 | 22.2 |
| 2016 | 18.9 | 18.8 | 19.8 | 21.6 | 23.3 | 25.8 | 26.6 | 25.7 | 24.7 | 23.9 | 23.1 | 21.5 | 22.8 |
| 2017 | 19.2 | 19.1 | 19.6 | 21.8 | 23.1 | 24.5 | 24.6 | 24.5 | 23.8 | 23.5 | 22.8 | 22.0 | 22.4 |
| 2018 | 20.0 | 19.7 | 20.2 | 21.5 | 23.9 | 25.1 | 25.2 | 25.3 | 24.7 | 24.3 | 23.6 | 22.5 | 23.0 |
| 2019 | 20.7 | 20.1 | 20.3 | 22.0 | 24.2 | 25.5 | 26.2 | 26.1 | 25.5 | 24.7 | 24.4 | 23.2 | 23.6 |

## 1. Employment by Industry: South Dakota, 2011–2019—*Continued*

(Numbers in thousands, not seasonally adjusted)

| Industry and year | January | February | March | April | May | June | July | August | September | October | November | December | Annual average |
|---|---|---|---|---|---|---|---|---|---|---|---|---|---|
| **Manufacturing** | | | | | | | | | | | | | |
| 2011 | 37.4 | 37.6 | 38.0 | 38.5 | 39.2 | 39.5 | 39.7 | 39.8 | 39.8 | 40.1 | 40.3 | 40.2 | 39.2 |
| 2012 | 39.9 | 40.3 | 40.4 | 40.9 | 41.3 | 41.8 | 41.9 | 41.7 | 41.7 | 41.8 | 41.8 | 41.4 | 41.2 |
| 2013 | 41.2 | 41.1 | 41.3 | 41.3 | 41.7 | 42.2 | 41.9 | 41.7 | 41.4 | 41.6 | 41.4 | 41.3 | 41.5 |
| 2014 | 41.0 | 41.4 | 41.6 | 41.8 | 42.2 | 42.5 | 42.7 | 42.8 | 42.6 | 43.0 | 42.9 | 43.0 | 42.3 |
| 2015 | 42.8 | 42.6 | 42.6 | 42.5 | 42.7 | 42.9 | 42.6 | 42.6 | 42.6 | 42.6 | 42.5 | 42.5 | 42.6 |
| 2016 | 42.1 | 42.0 | 42.1 | 42.1 | 42.3 | 42.6 | 42.4 | 42.2 | 41.9 | 42.2 | 42.1 | 42.2 | 42.2 |
| 2017 | 41.9 | 42.2 | 42.2 | 42.4 | 42.8 | 43.5 | 43.6 | 43.7 | 43.5 | 43.6 | 43.7 | 43.9 | 43.1 |
| 2018 | 43.2 | 43.6 | 43.7 | 43.9 | 44.2 | 44.8 | 44.9 | 44.7 | 44.8 | 44.8 | 45.0 | 45.1 | 44.4 |
| 2019 | 44.8 | 44.9 | 45.1 | 44.9 | 45.3 | 45.5 | 45.4 | 45.1 | 44.8 | 44.4 | 44.0 | 43.9 | 44.8 |
| **Trade, Transportation, and Utilities** | | | | | | | | | | | | | |
| 2011 | 79.5 | 79.1 | 79.4 | 80.7 | 82.0 | 82.5 | 82.5 | 83.0 | 81.6 | 82.0 | 83.0 | 83.6 | 81.6 |
| 2012 | 81.0 | 80.2 | 80.9 | 81.8 | 83.3 | 84.0 | 83.6 | 84.1 | 82.9 | 83.0 | 84.2 | 84.4 | 82.8 |
| 2013 | 81.5 | 81.0 | 81.4 | 82.0 | 84.0 | 84.7 | 84.6 | 84.7 | 83.5 | 84.0 | 85.0 | 85.6 | 83.5 |
| 2014 | 83.4 | 83.1 | 83.4 | 84.3 | 85.7 | 86.8 | 87.1 | 87.4 | 85.9 | 86.1 | 86.9 | 87.6 | 85.6 |
| 2015 | 85.3 | 85.0 | 85.2 | 86.4 | 87.7 | 88.5 | 88.5 | 88.7 | 87.2 | 87.6 | 88.4 | 89.0 | 87.3 |
| 2016 | 86.6 | 86.3 | 86.5 | 87.5 | 88.7 | 89.2 | 89.3 | 89.3 | 87.3 | 87.6 | 88.6 | 88.6 | 88.0 |
| 2017 | 86.1 | 85.5 | 85.7 | 86.5 | 87.6 | 88.0 | 87.9 | 87.8 | 86.3 | 86.8 | 87.8 | 88.2 | 87.0 |
| 2018 | 85.4 | 84.9 | 85.1 | 85.2 | 87.2 | 87.5 | 87.5 | 87.6 | 86.3 | 86.3 | 87.6 | 87.8 | 86.5 |
| 2019 | 85.4 | 84.4 | 84.4 | 85.1 | 86.7 | 87.1 | 87.2 | 87.1 | 85.2 | 86.0 | 86.7 | 87.2 | 86.0 |
| **Wholesale Trade** | | | | | | | | | | | | | |
| 2011 | 18.3 | 18.3 | 18.5 | 18.7 | 19.1 | 19.1 | 19.1 | 19.0 | 18.8 | 19.0 | 19.0 | 19.1 | 18.8 |
| 2012 | 19.0 | 18.9 | 19.2 | 19.4 | 19.6 | 19.7 | 19.5 | 19.4 | 19.1 | 19.3 | 19.3 | 19.3 | 19.3 |
| 2013 | 19.2 | 19.2 | 19.4 | 19.6 | 20.2 | 20.2 | 20.1 | 19.9 | 19.6 | 19.8 | 20.0 | 20.0 | 19.8 |
| 2014 | 20.0 | 20.0 | 20.2 | 20.5 | 20.9 | 21.0 | 21.0 | 20.9 | 20.6 | 20.8 | 20.8 | 20.8 | 20.6 |
| 2015 | 20.6 | 20.6 | 20.8 | 21.0 | 21.3 | 21.3 | 21.2 | 21.1 | 20.8 | 21.0 | 21.0 | 21.0 | 21.0 |
| 2016 | 20.8 | 20.7 | 20.9 | 21.1 | 21.3 | 21.3 | 21.3 | 21.1 | 20.7 | 20.8 | 20.9 | 20.8 | 21.0 |
| 2017 | 20.5 | 20.4 | 20.7 | 20.9 | 21.1 | 21.1 | 21.0 | 20.9 | 20.5 | 20.7 | 20.7 | 20.8 | 20.8 |
| 2018 | 20.4 | 20.4 | 20.5 | 20.6 | 21.2 | 21.2 | 21.1 | 20.9 | 20.7 | 20.7 | 20.8 | 20.9 | 20.8 |
| 2019 | 20.8 | 20.8 | 20.9 | 21.0 | 21.5 | 21.6 | 21.5 | 21.3 | 20.9 | 21.2 | 21.0 | 21.4 | 21.2 |
| **Retail Trade** | | | | | | | | | | | | | |
| 2011 | 48.9 | 48.5 | 48.6 | 49.4 | 50.2 | 50.7 | 50.9 | 51.3 | 50.1 | 50.4 | 51.4 | 51.8 | 50.2 |
| 2012 | 49.8 | 49.1 | 49.4 | 50.2 | 51.2 | 51.7 | 51.6 | 52.2 | 51.0 | 51.0 | 52.2 | 52.4 | 51.0 |
| 2013 | 50.0 | 49.5 | 49.7 | 50.1 | 51.1 | 51.8 | 51.9 | 52.2 | 51.2 | 51.4 | 52.2 | 52.6 | 51.1 |
| 2014 | 50.7 | 50.3 | 50.4 | 50.9 | 51.6 | 52.6 | 53.0 | 53.2 | 52.0 | 51.9 | 52.8 | 53.3 | 51.9 |
| 2015 | 51.6 | 51.3 | 51.3 | 52.1 | 52.9 | 53.7 | 53.8 | 54.0 | 52.9 | 53.0 | 53.8 | 54.2 | 52.9 |
| 2016 | 52.5 | 52.4 | 52.4 | 53.2 | 54.0 | 54.6 | 54.8 | 54.9 | 53.3 | 53.5 | 54.4 | 54.4 | 53.7 |
| 2017 | 52.6 | 52.1 | 52.0 | 52.5 | 53.1 | 53.6 | 53.7 | 53.6 | 52.4 | 52.8 | 53.7 | 53.8 | 53.0 |
| 2018 | 51.8 | 51.5 | 51.6 | 51.4 | 52.5 | 52.8 | 53.0 | 53.1 | 51.9 | 51.8 | 53.0 | 52.9 | 52.3 |
| 2019 | 51.1 | 50.4 | 50.2 | 50.7 | 51.5 | 51.8 | 52.1 | 52.0 | 50.6 | 51.0 | 51.6 | 51.2 | 51.2 |
| **Transportation and Utilities** | | | | | | | | | | | | | |
| 2011 | 12.3 | 12.3 | 12.3 | 12.6 | 12.7 | 12.7 | 12.5 | 12.7 | 12.7 | 12.6 | 12.6 | 12.7 | 12.6 |
| 2012 | 12.2 | 12.2 | 12.3 | 12.2 | 12.5 | 12.6 | 12.5 | 12.5 | 12.8 | 12.7 | 12.7 | 12.7 | 12.5 |
| 2013 | 12.3 | 12.3 | 12.3 | 12.3 | 12.7 | 12.7 | 12.6 | 12.6 | 12.7 | 12.8 | 12.8 | 12.7 | 12.6 |
| 2014 | 12.7 | 12.8 | 12.8 | 12.9 | 13.2 | 13.2 | 13.1 | 13.3 | 13.3 | 13.4 | 13.3 | 13.5 | 13.1 |
| 2015 | 13.1 | 13.1 | 13.1 | 13.3 | 13.5 | 13.5 | 13.5 | 13.6 | 13.5 | 13.6 | 13.6 | 13.8 | 13.4 |
| 2016 | 13.3 | 13.2 | 13.2 | 13.2 | 13.4 | 13.3 | 13.2 | 13.3 | 13.3 | 13.3 | 13.3 | 13.4 | 13.3 |
| 2017 | 13.0 | 13.0 | 13.0 | 13.1 | 13.4 | 13.3 | 13.2 | 13.3 | 13.4 | 13.3 | 13.4 | 13.6 | 13.3 |
| 2018 | 13.2 | 13.0 | 13.0 | 13.2 | 13.5 | 13.5 | 13.4 | 13.6 | 13.7 | 13.7 | 13.7 | 14.0 | 13.5 |
| 2019 | 13.5 | 13.2 | 13.3 | 13.4 | 13.7 | 13.7 | 13.6 | 13.8 | 13.7 | 13.8 | 14.1 | 14.6 | 13.7 |
| **Information** | | | | | | | | | | | | | |
| 2011 | 6.4 | 6.4 | 6.4 | 6.3 | 6.4 | 6.5 | 6.5 | 6.5 | 6.4 | 6.4 | 6.3 | 6.3 | 6.4 |
| 2012 | 6.2 | 6.3 | 6.2 | 6.2 | 6.3 | 6.3 | 6.3 | 6.3 | 6.1 | 6.1 | 6.1 | 6.1 | 6.2 |
| 2013 | 6.0 | 6.0 | 6.0 | 6.0 | 6.1 | 6.1 | 6.1 | 6.2 | 6.0 | 5.9 | 6.0 | 6.0 | 6.0 |
| 2014 | 6.0 | 6.0 | 6.0 | 6.0 | 6.1 | 6.2 | 6.2 | 6.1 | 6.0 | 5.9 | 5.9 | 5.9 | 6.0 |
| 2015 | 5.8 | 5.8 | 5.8 | 5.9 | 5.9 | 5.9 | 5.9 | 6.0 | 5.8 | 5.8 | 5.8 | 5.9 | 5.9 |
| 2016 | 5.8 | 5.8 | 5.8 | 5.8 | 5.8 | 5.9 | 5.8 | 5.8 | 5.7 | 5.7 | 5.7 | 5.7 | 5.8 |
| 2017 | 5.8 | 5.7 | 5.7 | 5.6 | 5.8 | 5.8 | 5.8 | 5.8 | 5.7 | 5.7 | 5.7 | 5.7 | 5.7 |
| 2018 | 5.6 | 5.7 | 5.6 | 5.5 | 5.6 | 5.6 | 5.6 | 5.7 | 5.7 | 5.7 | 5.7 | 5.7 | 5.7 |
| 2019 | 5.4 | 5.5 | 5.5 | 5.4 | 5.5 | 5.6 | 5.5 | 5.5 | 5.5 | 5.4 | 5.5 | 5.6 | 5.5 |

# 1. Employment by Industry: South Dakota, 2011–2019—*Continued*

(Numbers in thousands, not seasonally adjusted)

| Industry and year | January | February | March | April | May | June | July | August | September | October | November | December | Annual average |
|---|---|---|---|---|---|---|---|---|---|---|---|---|---|
| **Financial Activities** | | | | | | | | | | | | | |
| 2011 | 28.3 | 28.3 | 28.3 | 28.1 | 28.1 | 28.3 | 28.1 | 28.1 | 27.9 | 27.9 | 27.9 | 28.2 | 28.1 |
| 2012 | 27.9 | 27.9 | 28.1 | 28.3 | 28.6 | 29.0 | 29.0 | 29.0 | 28.8 | 28.8 | 29.0 | 29.2 | 28.6 |
| 2013 | 29.1 | 29.3 | 29.4 | 29.4 | 29.7 | 30.1 | 30.0 | 30.0 | 29.8 | 29.8 | 30.0 | 30.1 | 29.7 |
| 2014 | 29.6 | 29.6 | 29.6 | 29.7 | 29.9 | 30.0 | 30.0 | 29.9 | 29.6 | 29.6 | 29.6 | 29.7 | 29.7 |
| 2015 | 29.4 | 29.3 | 29.4 | 29.4 | 29.6 | 29.9 | 30.1 | 29.9 | 29.7 | 29.7 | 29.7 | 29.8 | 29.7 |
| 2016 | 29.1 | 29.0 | 29.0 | 29.1 | 29.4 | 29.4 | 29.6 | 29.6 | 29.4 | 29.3 | 29.3 | 29.5 | 29.3 |
| 2017 | 29.0 | 28.9 | 29.0 | 29.1 | 29.3 | 29.5 | 29.5 | 29.5 | 29.3 | 29.3 | 29.3 | 29.4 | 29.3 |
| 2018 | 29.1 | 29.1 | 29.1 | 29.2 | 29.3 | 29.4 | 29.4 | 29.3 | 29.2 | 29.2 | 29.2 | 29.4 | 29.2 |
| 2019 | 28.9 | 28.8 | 28.8 | 28.9 | 29.0 | 29.2 | 29.1 | 29.2 | 28.9 | 28.9 | 29.2 | 29.2 | 29.0 |
| **Professional and Business Services** | | | | | | | | | | | | | |
| 2011 | 27.6 | 27.8 | 28.0 | 28.8 | 29.0 | 29.3 | 29.6 | 29.4 | 29.2 | 29.2 | 29.2 | 29.5 | 28.9 |
| 2012 | 28.4 | 28.5 | 28.8 | 29.3 | 29.4 | 29.8 | 30.0 | 30.1 | 29.7 | 29.4 | 29.3 | 29.3 | 29.3 |
| 2013 | 28.7 | 28.8 | 29.0 | 29.3 | 29.9 | 30.1 | 30.1 | 30.1 | 29.6 | 30.3 | 30.3 | 30.3 | 29.7 |
| 2014 | 29.6 | 29.6 | 29.6 | 30.5 | 31.0 | 31.3 | 31.4 | 31.1 | 30.5 | 30.5 | 30.5 | 30.5 | 30.5 |
| 2015 | 29.8 | 29.9 | 30.2 | 30.7 | 30.9 | 31.3 | 31.6 | 31.4 | 30.8 | 31.1 | 31.1 | 31.1 | 30.8 |
| 2016 | 30.4 | 30.6 | 30.6 | 31.4 | 31.7 | 32.1 | 32.2 | 32.0 | 31.4 | 31.5 | 31.6 | 31.7 | 31.4 |
| 2017 | 30.8 | 30.8 | 31.2 | 31.4 | 31.6 | 32.0 | 31.9 | 32.0 | 31.5 | 31.6 | 31.5 | 31.7 | 31.5 |
| 2018 | 31.1 | 31.5 | 31.7 | 31.8 | 32.3 | 32.8 | 33.1 | 33.1 | 32.5 | 32.5 | 32.5 | 32.4 | 32.3 |
| 2019 | 31.9 | 32.2 | 32.2 | 32.9 | 33.4 | 33.7 | 33.9 | 33.8 | 33.3 | 33.8 | 33.6 | 33.4 | 33.2 |
| **Education and Health Services** | | | | | | | | | | | | | |
| 2011 | 64.5 | 64.7 | 65.0 | 64.9 | 65.5 | 65.4 | 64.9 | 65.2 | 65.3 | 65.9 | 66.2 | 66.5 | 65.3 |
| 2012 | 65.6 | 65.9 | 66.3 | 67.1 | 67.5 | 67.6 | 66.9 | 66.9 | 67.3 | 67.6 | 68.0 | 68.1 | 67.1 |
| 2013 | 67.2 | 67.7 | 68.0 | 68.0 | 68.7 | 68.1 | 67.6 | 67.6 | 67.8 | 68.1 | 68.4 | 68.6 | 68.0 |
| 2014 | 67.7 | 68.1 | 68.3 | 68.4 | 68.9 | 68.6 | 68.0 | 67.9 | 68.1 | 68.4 | 68.5 | 69.0 | 68.3 |
| 2015 | 67.9 | 68.5 | 69.0 | 69.2 | 69.6 | 69.4 | 68.5 | 68.5 | 69.1 | 69.7 | 69.8 | 70.1 | 69.1 |
| 2016 | 69.1 | 69.6 | 70.0 | 70.1 | 70.5 | 69.9 | 69.8 | 70.0 | 70.6 | 70.8 | 71.2 | 71.5 | 70.3 |
| 2017 | 70.4 | 70.8 | 71.4 | 71.9 | 72.0 | 71.7 | 70.8 | 71.0 | 71.6 | 72.0 | 72.1 | 72.4 | 71.5 |
| 2018 | 72.1 | 72.2 | 72.4 | 72.1 | 72.7 | 72.5 | 71.7 | 72.3 | 72.6 | 72.9 | 73.2 | 73.7 | 72.5 |
| 2019 | 72.6 | 73.1 | 73.5 | 72.8 | 73.5 | 73.3 | 72.4 | 73.2 | 73.5 | 74.2 | 74.8 | 74.5 | 73.5 |
| **Leisure and Hospitality** | | | | | | | | | | | | | |
| 2011 | 38.9 | 39.2 | 39.8 | 41.4 | 43.9 | 46.5 | 47.5 | 49.6 | 46.2 | 43.9 | 42.0 | 41.7 | 43.4 |
| 2012 | 39.8 | 40.2 | 41.1 | 42.5 | 45.5 | 48.0 | 48.4 | 50.2 | 46.6 | 44.5 | 42.6 | 42.4 | 44.3 |
| 2013 | 40.4 | 40.5 | 41.4 | 42.1 | 45.8 | 48.5 | 48.8 | 50.5 | 46.9 | 44.9 | 43.4 | 42.9 | 44.7 |
| 2014 | 41.3 | 41.6 | 42.3 | 43.3 | 46.7 | 48.9 | 49.0 | 50.9 | 47.8 | 45.8 | 43.8 | 43.6 | 45.4 |
| 2015 | 41.5 | 42.1 | 42.8 | 44.1 | 47.2 | 49.8 | 50.2 | 52.1 | 48.4 | 46.4 | 44.8 | 44.4 | 46.2 |
| 2016 | 42.5 | 42.8 | 43.5 | 45.1 | 47.6 | 49.8 | 50.8 | 52.7 | 49.0 | 47.2 | 45.5 | 44.4 | 46.7 |
| 2017 | 42.9 | 43.3 | 43.9 | 45.7 | 48.2 | 50.5 | 50.8 | 52.6 | 48.7 | 47.4 | 45.3 | 44.6 | 47.0 |
| 2018 | 43.0 | 43.4 | 44.1 | 44.9 | 48.8 | 51.3 | 51.7 | 53.4 | 49.3 | 47.4 | 45.4 | 45.1 | 47.3 |
| 2019 | 43.4 | 43.4 | 43.6 | 45.1 | 48.6 | 51.2 | 51.9 | 52.6 | 49.2 | 47.4 | 45.3 | 45.3 | 47.3 |
| **Other Services** | | | | | | | | | | | | | |
| 2011 | 15.4 | 15.3 | 15.5 | 15.6 | 15.7 | 16.0 | 16.0 | 16.1 | 15.7 | 15.8 | 15.7 | 15.8 | 15.7 |
| 2012 | 15.7 | 15.7 | 15.8 | 15.9 | 16.1 | 16.3 | 16.4 | 16.3 | 16.0 | 16.0 | 16.0 | 16.0 | 16.0 |
| 2013 | 15.9 | 15.9 | 16.0 | 16.1 | 16.4 | 16.5 | 16.5 | 16.3 | 16.1 | 16.0 | 16.1 | 16.0 | 16.2 |
| 2014 | 15.9 | 15.9 | 15.9 | 16.1 | 16.3 | 16.5 | 16.5 | 16.4 | 16.1 | 16.0 | 16.0 | 16.1 | 16.1 |
| 2015 | 15.9 | 16.0 | 16.0 | 16.2 | 16.3 | 16.7 | 16.8 | 16.7 | 16.2 | 16.3 | 16.2 | 16.3 | 16.3 |
| 2016 | 16.1 | 16.2 | 16.3 | 16.5 | 16.6 | 17.0 | 17.1 | 17.0 | 16.6 | 16.6 | 16.5 | 16.4 | 16.6 |
| 2017 | 16.3 | 16.3 | 16.4 | 16.6 | 16.8 | 17.3 | 17.2 | 17.0 | 16.7 | 16.6 | 16.5 | 16.5 | 16.7 |
| 2018 | 16.3 | 16.3 | 16.3 | 16.4 | 16.7 | 17.2 | 17.2 | 17.0 | 16.7 | 16.8 | 16.7 | 16.7 | 16.7 |
| 2019 | 16.4 | 16.4 | 16.5 | 16.6 | 16.8 | 17.3 | 17.3 | 17.1 | 16.9 | 17.3 | 17.1 | 16.8 | 16.9 |
| **Government** | | | | | | | | | | | | | |
| 2011 | 77.6 | 78.9 | 79.1 | 79.4 | 79.9 | 80.0 | 74.3 | 73.4 | 77.3 | 78.7 | 78.8 | 79.0 | 78.0 |
| 2012 | 76.9 | 77.7 | 78.4 | 78.7 | 78.9 | 78.6 | 73.4 | 73.0 | 77.3 | 79.1 | 79.1 | 78.7 | 77.5 |
| 2013 | 76.9 | 78.3 | 78.4 | 78.0 | 78.8 | 77.4 | 72.6 | 73.3 | 77.9 | 78.7 | 78.9 | 78.4 | 77.3 |
| 2014 | 77.1 | 78.1 | 78.5 | 78.7 | 79.4 | 78.5 | 73.7 | 74.2 | 78.4 | 79.1 | 79.2 | 78.7 | 77.8 |
| 2015 | 76.7 | 77.9 | 78.4 | 78.7 | 79.7 | 79.0 | 74.1 | 73.6 | 78.1 | 78.9 | 79.2 | 79.1 | 77.8 |
| 2016 | 77.1 | 78.5 | 78.9 | 79.4 | 80.2 | 79.5 | 74.0 | 74.2 | 79.3 | 79.9 | 80.0 | 80.1 | 78.4 |
| 2017 | 78.2 | 79.4 | 79.7 | 79.8 | 81.1 | 80.3 | 74.6 | 75.1 | 79.8 | 80.4 | 80.4 | 80.2 | 79.1 |
| 2018 | 78.3 | 79.6 | 80.2 | 80.0 | 81.6 | 80.9 | 75.1 | 75.5 | 80.2 | 81.0 | 80.9 | 80.8 | 79.5 |
| 2019 | 79.0 | 80.1 | 80.4 | 80.7 | 81.7 | 80.9 | 75.4 | 75.8 | 80.9 | 81.6 | 81.4 | 81.3 | 79.9 |

## 2. Average Weekly Hours by Selected Industry: South Dakota, 2015–2019

(Not seasonally adjusted)

| Industry and year | January | February | March | April | May | June | July | August | September | October | November | December | Annual average |
|---|---|---|---|---|---|---|---|---|---|---|---|---|---|
| **Total Private** | | | | | | | | | | | | | |
| 2015 | 33.5 | 34.2 | 34.0 | 33.8 | 33.7 | 34.2 | 34.3 | 34.7 | 33.9 | 34.1 | 34.4 | 33.5 | 34.0 |
| 2016 | 33.6 | 33.4 | 33.6 | 33.9 | 34.5 | 34.6 | 34.4 | 34.1 | 34.1 | 34.5 | 34.0 | 33.1 | 34.0 |
| 2017 | 33.7 | 33.2 | 33.2 | 33.9 | 34.0 | 34.0 | 34.3 | 33.8 | 33.6 | 34.0 | 33.5 | 33.1 | 33.7 |
| 2018 | 33.2 | 33.1 | 33.0 | 33.4 | 33.7 | 34.2 | 34.4 | 33.8 | 34.4 | 33.4 | 33.6 | 34.1 | 33.7 |
| 2019 | 33.7 | 33.7 | 33.1 | 33.0 | 34.0 | 34.5 | 33.7 | 34.4 | 34.4 | 33.7 | 34.1 | 34.4 | 33.9 |
| **Goods-Producing** | | | | | | | | | | | | | |
| 2015 | 38.6 | 39.5 | 39.5 | 39.6 | 39.9 | 40.2 | 41.1 | 41.2 | 40.2 | 40.7 | 40.8 | 39.7 | 40.1 |
| 2016 | 39.9 | 39.5 | 39.7 | 40.8 | 41.3 | 41.2 | 41.5 | 41.6 | 41.2 | 42.0 | 41.7 | 39.5 | 40.8 |
| 2017 | 40.7 | 39.5 | 39.8 | 40.5 | 42.0 | 42.1 | 41.6 | 41.3 | 40.7 | 41.4 | 40.9 | 40.6 | 40.9 |
| 2018 | 40.5 | 39.9 | 39.5 | 39.6 | 39.9 | 41.4 | 41.5 | 40.8 | 41.7 | 40.1 | 41.0 | 41.1 | 40.6 |
| 2019 | 40.0 | 39.5 | 38.0 | 37.1 | 40.0 | 40.5 | 40.0 | 40.1 | 39.2 | 39.3 | 39.9 | 40.2 | 39.5 |
| **Construction** | | | | | | | | | | | | | |
| 2015 | 18.7 | 18.6 | 19.7 | 21.6 | 23.2 | 24.5 | 24.8 | 24.4 | 23.5 | 23.2 | 22.4 | 21.4 | 22.2 |
| 2016 | 18.9 | 18.8 | 19.8 | 21.6 | 23.3 | 25.8 | 26.6 | 25.7 | 24.7 | 23.9 | 23.1 | 21.5 | 22.8 |
| 2017 | 19.2 | 19.1 | 19.6 | 21.8 | 23.1 | 24.5 | 24.6 | 24.5 | 23.8 | 23.5 | 22.8 | 22.0 | 22.4 |
| 2018 | 20.0 | 19.7 | 20.2 | 21.5 | 23.9 | 25.1 | 25.2 | 25.3 | 24.7 | 24.3 | 23.6 | 22.5 | 23.0 |
| 2019 | 20.7 | 20.1 | 20.3 | 22.0 | 24.2 | 25.5 | 26.2 | 26.1 | 25.5 | 24.7 | 24.4 | 23.2 | 23.6 |
| **Manufacturing** | | | | | | | | | | | | | |
| 2015 | 39.6 | 40.5 | 40.2 | 40.3 | 40.9 | 40.2 | 40.9 | 41.1 | 40.1 | 40.5 | 41.4 | 40.6 | 40.5 |
| 2016 | 40.9 | 40.2 | 40.3 | 41.3 | 42.1 | 41.6 | 41.6 | 41.6 | 41.1 | 41.6 | 42.0 | 40.6 | 41.2 |
| 2017 | 42.1 | 40.0 | 40.7 | 41.4 | 41.9 | 42.0 | 41.1 | 41.2 | 40.4 | 40.9 | 41.1 | 41.0 | 41.1 |
| 2018 | 41.8 | 40.6 | 40.1 | 40.1 | 39.0 | 40.1 | 40.0 | 39.6 | 40.6 | 40.4 | 40.8 | 41.4 | 40.4 |
| 2019 | 40.7 | 40.6 | 39.0 | 38.4 | 39.8 | 39.6 | 38.8 | 38.4 | 37.9 | 38.6 | 39.0 | 40.4 | 39.3 |
| **Trade, Transportation, and Utilities** | | | | | | | | | | | | | |
| 2015 | 33.6 | 34.3 | 34.2 | 33.9 | 34.1 | 34.5 | 34.3 | 34.7 | 34.0 | 33.8 | 34.2 | 33.1 | 34.1 |
| 2016 | 32.9 | 32.8 | 33.0 | 33.1 | 34.0 | 34.1 | 33.8 | 33.3 | 33.6 | 33.7 | 33.2 | 32.5 | 33.3 |
| 2017 | 32.8 | 32.5 | 32.5 | 33.4 | 33.8 | 34.0 | 34.4 | 33.7 | 33.7 | 33.7 | 33.1 | 32.9 | 33.4 |
| 2018 | 32.7 | 32.7 | 32.7 | 33.0 | 34.6 | 34.8 | 34.9 | 34.4 | 35.0 | 34.1 | 33.9 | 34.1 | 33.9 |
| 2019 | 33.0 | 33.3 | 32.6 | 32.2 | 33.5 | 34.2 | 33.6 | 34.3 | 34.2 | 33.6 | 33.8 | 34.0 | 33.5 |
| **Financial Activities** | | | | | | | | | | | | | |
| 2015 | 29.4 | 29.3 | 29.4 | 29.4 | 29.6 | 29.9 | 30.1 | 29.9 | 29.7 | 29.7 | 29.7 | 29.8 | 29.7 |
| 2016 | 29.1 | 29.0 | 29.0 | 29.1 | 29.4 | 29.4 | 29.6 | 29.6 | 29.4 | 29.3 | 29.3 | 29.5 | 29.3 |
| 2017 | 29.0 | 28.9 | 29.0 | 29.1 | 29.3 | 29.5 | 29.5 | 29.5 | 29.3 | 29.3 | 29.3 | 29.4 | 29.3 |
| 2018 | 29.1 | 29.1 | 29.1 | 29.2 | 29.3 | 29.4 | 29.4 | 29.3 | 29.2 | 29.2 | 29.2 | 29.4 | 29.2 |
| 2019 | 28.9 | 28.8 | 28.8 | 28.9 | 29.0 | 29.2 | 29.1 | 29.2 | 28.9 | 28.9 | 29.2 | 29.2 | 29.0 |
| **Professional and Business Services** | | | | | | | | | | | | | |
| 2015 | 35.8 | 37.3 | 36.9 | 36.9 | 36.2 | 37.0 | 36.3 | 37.0 | 36.3 | 36.3 | 36.6 | 35.5 | 36.5 |
| 2016 | 35.9 | 36.1 | 36.2 | 36.7 | 38.0 | 37.4 | 36.6 | 36.8 | 36.9 | 37.6 | 36.8 | 35.8 | 36.7 |
| 2017 | 36.5 | 36.8 | 36.3 | 36.3 | 35.6 | 35.4 | 35.5 | 35.1 | 35.7 | 35.9 | 35.2 | 35.0 | 35.8 |
| 2018 | 34.3 | 35.3 | 35.8 | 36.1 | 36.1 | 36.0 | 35.6 | 35.1 | 36.3 | 36.0 | 35.8 | 35.9 | 35.7 |
| 2019 | 35.7 | 35.8 | 36.0 | 36.2 | 36.3 | 35.8 | 34.9 | 35.8 | 36.3 | 35.8 | 35.7 | 35.9 | 35.8 |
| **Education and Health Services** | | | | | | | | | | | | | |
| 2015 | 32.3 | 32.7 | 32.4 | 32.2 | 31.7 | 32.0 | 31.8 | 32.7 | 32.3 | 32.4 | 33.1 | 32.6 | 32.3 |
| 2016 | 32.7 | 32.2 | 32.1 | 32.1 | 32.0 | 32.1 | 32.3 | 31.9 | 32.1 | 32.5 | 31.7 | 31.8 | 32.1 |
| 2017 | 31.9 | 31.4 | 31.3 | 31.9 | 31.2 | 31.4 | 32.3 | 30.9 | 31.3 | 32.0 | 31.1 | 31.1 | 31.5 |
| 2018 | 31.5 | 31.4 | 30.7 | 31.3 | 31.0 | 31.3 | 31.7 | 31.6 | 31.6 | 30.5 | 30.7 | 31.5 | 31.2 |
| 2019 | 31.4 | 30.7 | 30.2 | 31.1 | 31.9 | 31.7 | 31.3 | 32.9 | 32.8 | 32.2 | 32.0 | 32.4 | 31.7 |
| **Leisure and Hospitality** | | | | | | | | | | | | | |
| 2015 | 22.6 | 24.0 | 23.9 | 23.1 | 23.4 | 25.0 | 25.5 | 26.1 | 24.5 | 24.1 | 24.2 | 23.5 | 24.2 |
| 2016 | 23.6 | 23.7 | 24.1 | 24.1 | 25.0 | 25.4 | 25.5 | 26.1 | 24.7 | 24.8 | 23.3 | 23.1 | 24.5 |
| 2017 | 23.9 | 23.7 | 23.9 | 24.3 | 24.0 | 25.6 | 26.1 | 25.9 | 24.5 | 23.9 | 22.9 | 22.7 | 24.3 |
| 2018 | 23.0 | 22.8 | 23.6 | 23.3 | 24.3 | 25.5 | 26.0 | 25.4 | 24.6 | 23.4 | 22.3 | 22.6 | 24.0 |
| 2019 | 22.1 | 22.3 | 22.3 | 22.0 | 22.5 | 24.1 | 24.1 | 24.1 | 23.2 | 22.4 | 22.5 | 22.4 | 22.9 |

## 3. Average Hourly Earnings by Selected Industry: South Dakota, 2015–2019

(Dollars, not seasonally adjusted)

| Industry and year | January | February | March | April | May | June | July | August | September | October | November | December | Annual average |
|---|---|---|---|---|---|---|---|---|---|---|---|---|---|
| **Total Private** | | | | | | | | | | | | | |
| 2015 | 20.94 | 20.93 | 20.88 | 20.91 | 20.99 | 20.72 | 20.68 | 20.79 | 21.04 | 21.32 | 21.23 | 21.39 | 20.98 |
| 2016 | 21.34 | 21.18 | 21.18 | 21.41 | 21.28 | 20.80 | 21.15 | 21.13 | 21.60 | 21.74 | 21.72 | 21.95 | 21.37 |
| 2017 | 22.13 | 22.21 | 22.04 | 22.10 | 21.83 | 21.56 | 21.67 | 21.66 | 22.02 | 22.12 | 21.97 | 22.20 | 21.95 |
| 2018 | 22.11 | 22.26 | 22.18 | 22.57 | 22.37 | 22.23 | 22.77 | 22.58 | 23.00 | 22.90 | 22.92 | 23.44 | 22.62 |
| 2019 | 22.95 | 22.88 | 22.82 | 23.13 | 22.90 | 22.87 | 22.92 | 23.08 | 23.78 | 23.77 | 23.77 | 24.01 | 23.24 |
| **Goods-Producing** | | | | | | | | | | | | | |
| 2015 | 21.85 | 21.77 | 21.60 | 21.63 | 21.49 | 21.55 | 21.31 | 21.58 | 21.54 | 21.96 | 21.78 | 22.05 | 21.67 |
| 2016 | 21.52 | 21.20 | 21.52 | 21.57 | 21.56 | 21.59 | 22.06 | 21.66 | 22.11 | 22.13 | 21.94 | 22.51 | 21.79 |
| 2017 | 22.84 | 22.61 | 22.67 | 22.49 | 22.65 | 22.36 | 22.29 | 22.29 | 22.30 | 22.31 | 22.02 | 22.41 | 22.43 |
| 2018 | 22.27 | 22.57 | 22.56 | 22.69 | 22.74 | 22.82 | 23.05 | 22.92 | 22.87 | 22.71 | 22.85 | 22.97 | 22.76 |
| 2019 | 22.90 | 22.97 | 23.23 | 23.44 | 23.51 | 23.46 | 23.85 | 24.11 | 24.52 | 24.59 | 24.41 | 24.73 | 23.83 |
| **Mining, Logging, and Construction** | | | | | | | | | | | | | |
| 2015 | 22.56 | 22.54 | 22.65 | 22.71 | 22.25 | 22.55 | 22.18 | 22.49 | 22.40 | 22.77 | 22.68 | 23.18 | 22.57 |
| 2016 | 22.83 | 22.89 | 22.82 | 22.74 | 22.96 | 22.82 | 23.02 | 22.89 | 23.13 | 23.59 | 23.31 | 24.30 | 23.11 |
| 2017 | 24.64 | 24.47 | 24.46 | 24.26 | 24.27 | 23.80 | 24.08 | 23.82 | 23.68 | 23.83 | 23.63 | 24.34 | 24.07 |
| 2018 | 25.12 | 25.17 | 24.90 | 25.25 | 24.70 | 24.87 | 24.93 | 25.22 | 25.23 | 25.23 | 25.31 | 25.92 | 25.15 |
| 2019 | 25.92 | 26.06 | 25.96 | 26.33 | 25.61 | 25.11 | 25.78 | 25.80 | 25.99 | 26.26 | 25.77 | 26.82 | 25.93 |
| **Manufacturing** | | | | | | | | | | | | | |
| 2015 | 21.55 | 21.45 | 21.12 | 21.09 | 21.09 | 20.96 | 20.78 | 21.04 | 21.04 | 21.49 | 21.31 | 21.50 | 21.20 |
| 2016 | 20.95 | 20.46 | 20.92 | 20.96 | 20.79 | 20.84 | 21.44 | 20.88 | 21.48 | 21.24 | 21.17 | 21.63 | 21.06 |
| 2017 | 22.07 | 21.76 | 21.86 | 21.60 | 21.74 | 21.51 | 21.20 | 21.39 | 21.49 | 21.42 | 21.15 | 21.43 | 21.55 |
| 2018 | 21.03 | 21.42 | 21.48 | 21.44 | 21.57 | 21.53 | 21.84 | 21.46 | 21.41 | 21.32 | 21.49 | 21.48 | 21.46 |
| 2019 | 21.52 | 21.67 | 22.04 | 22.12 | 22.33 | 22.44 | 22.60 | 22.98 | 23.57 | 23.57 | 23.57 | 23.60 | 22.65 |
| **Trade, Transportation, and Utilities** | | | | | | | | | | | | | |
| 2015 | 19.77 | 19.56 | 19.50 | 19.40 | 19.91 | 19.75 | 19.87 | 19.91 | 20.17 | 20.19 | 20.04 | 20.09 | 19.85 |
| 2016 | 20.14 | 19.96 | 19.82 | 20.38 | 20.47 | 19.70 | 20.15 | 20.24 | 20.42 | 20.53 | 20.62 | 20.69 | 20.26 |
| 2017 | 20.86 | 21.08 | 20.66 | 20.88 | 20.48 | 20.35 | 20.68 | 21.10 | 21.14 | 21.44 | 21.51 | 21.54 | 20.97 |
| 2018 | 21.60 | 21.52 | 21.23 | 21.57 | 21.28 | 21.27 | 21.96 | 21.86 | 22.29 | 21.97 | 22.09 | 22.52 | 21.77 |
| 2019 | 22.63 | 22.96 | 22.26 | 22.70 | 22.59 | 22.69 | 22.54 | 22.97 | 23.37 | 23.01 | 23.52 | 23.39 | 22.89 |
| **Professional and Business Services** | | | | | | | | | | | | | |
| 2015 | 24.42 | 24.43 | 24.69 | 24.68 | 24.23 | 24.05 | 24.57 | 24.73 | 24.80 | 24.96 | 24.98 | 24.64 | 24.60 |
| 2016 | 24.28 | 23.89 | 24.19 | 24.49 | 24.11 | 24.44 | 24.97 | 25.02 | 25.66 | 26.00 | 25.88 | 26.34 | 24.95 |
| 2017 | 26.09 | 26.48 | 26.85 | 27.00 | 27.18 | 27.18 | 27.32 | 26.87 | 27.27 | 26.88 | 26.99 | 27.05 | 26.93 |
| 2018 | 26.55 | 27.24 | 27.08 | 27.42 | 27.34 | 27.71 | 27.94 | 27.74 | 28.26 | 28.02 | 27.33 | 27.48 | 27.52 |
| 2019 | 26.17 | 25.44 | 25.94 | 26.22 | 26.19 | 25.98 | 25.79 | 26.12 | 26.85 | 26.70 | 27.26 | 27.23 | 26.33 |
| **Education and Health Services** | | | | | | | | | | | | | |
| 2015 | 21.81 | 22.31 | 22.08 | 22.12 | 22.42 | 22.04 | 22.08 | 22.42 | 22.73 | 22.99 | 22.76 | 22.81 | 22.38 |
| 2016 | 23.80 | 23.73 | 23.04 | 23.03 | 22.96 | 22.82 | 23.25 | 23.21 | 23.66 | 23.79 | 23.56 | 23.41 | 23.36 |
| 2017 | 23.68 | 23.44 | 23.14 | 22.90 | 22.47 | 22.32 | 22.18 | 22.12 | 22.36 | 22.17 | 22.11 | 22.24 | 22.59 |
| 2018 | 22.19 | 21.78 | 21.61 | 21.75 | 21.78 | 21.55 | 21.86 | 21.45 | 21.44 | 21.62 | 21.66 | 21.84 | 21.71 |
| 2019 | 21.75 | 22.02 | 21.58 | 21.42 | 21.37 | 21.48 | 21.94 | 20.84 | 21.68 | 21.96 | 21.25 | 21.61 | 21.57 |
| **Leisure and Hospitality** | | | | | | | | | | | | | |
| 2015 | 13.10 | 13.01 | 13.10 | 13.15 | 12.88 | 12.33 | 12.52 | 12.63 | 12.88 | 12.99 | 13.14 | 13.04 | 12.87 |
| 2016 | 13.27 | 13.16 | 13.27 | 13.25 | 13.18 | 12.91 | 13.04 | 13.05 | 13.52 | 13.40 | 13.51 | 13.52 | 13.25 |
| 2017 | 13.63 | 13.65 | 13.65 | 13.66 | 13.69 | 13.33 | 13.47 | 13.49 | 13.82 | 14.10 | 14.02 | 14.28 | 13.72 |
| 2018 | 14.19 | 14.35 | 14.42 | 14.33 | 14.07 | 13.79 | 13.83 | 13.94 | 14.01 | 14.04 | 14.18 | 14.62 | 14.12 |
| 2019 | 14.69 | 14.80 | 14.76 | 14.87 | 14.66 | 14.21 | 13.96 | 13.99 | 14.56 | 14.68 | 14.90 | 14.92 | 14.55 |

## 4. Average Weekly Earnings by Selected Industry: South Dakota, 2015–2019

(Dollars, not seasonally adjusted)

| Industry and year | January | February | March | April | May | June | July | August | September | October | November | December | Annual average |
|---|---|---|---|---|---|---|---|---|---|---|---|---|---|
| **Total Private** | | | | | | | | | | | | | |
| 2015 | 701.49 | 715.81 | 709.92 | 706.76 | 707.36 | 708.62 | 709.32 | 721.41 | 713.26 | 727.01 | 730.31 | 716.57 | 713.32 |
| 2016 | 717.02 | 707.41 | 711.65 | 725.80 | 734.16 | 719.68 | 727.56 | 720.53 | 736.56 | 750.03 | 738.48 | 726.55 | 726.58 |
| 2017 | 745.78 | 737.37 | 731.73 | 749.19 | 742.22 | 733.04 | 743.28 | 732.11 | 739.87 | 752.08 | 736.00 | 734.82 | 739.72 |
| 2018 | 734.05 | 736.81 | 731.94 | 753.84 | 753.87 | 760.27 | 783.29 | 763.20 | 791.20 | 764.86 | 770.11 | 799.30 | 762.29 |
| 2019 | 773.42 | 771.06 | 755.34 | 763.29 | 778.60 | 789.02 | 772.40 | 793.95 | 818.03 | 801.05 | 810.56 | 825.94 | 787.84 |
| **Goods-Producing** | | | | | | | | | | | | | |
| 2015 | 843.41 | 859.92 | 853.20 | 856.55 | 857.45 | 866.31 | 875.84 | 889.10 | 865.91 | 893.77 | 888.62 | 875.39 | 868.97 |
| 2016 | 858.65 | 837.40 | 854.34 | 880.06 | 890.43 | 889.51 | 915.49 | 901.06 | 910.93 | 929.46 | 914.90 | 889.15 | 889.03 |
| 2017 | 929.59 | 893.10 | 902.27 | 910.85 | 951.30 | 941.36 | 927.26 | 920.58 | 907.61 | 923.63 | 900.62 | 909.85 | 917.39 |
| 2018 | 901.94 | 900.54 | 891.12 | 898.52 | 907.33 | 944.75 | 956.58 | 935.14 | 953.68 | 910.67 | 936.85 | 944.07 | 924.06 |
| 2019 | 916.00 | 907.32 | 882.74 | 869.62 | 940.40 | 950.13 | 954.00 | 966.81 | 961.18 | 966.39 | 973.96 | 994.15 | 941.29 |
| **Mining, Logging, and Construction** | | | | | | | | | | | | | |
| 2015 | 823.44 | 831.73 | 856.17 | 865.25 | 852.18 | 902.00 | 918.25 | 928.84 | 904.96 | 938.12 | 898.13 | 878.52 | 887.00 |
| 2016 | 858.41 | 865.24 | 876.29 | 905.05 | 918.40 | 924.21 | 946.12 | 949.94 | 952.96 | 1,007.29 | 960.37 | 918.54 | 926.71 |
| 2017 | 931.39 | 942.10 | 924.59 | 943.71 | 1,021.77 | 1,006.74 | 1,018.58 | 990.91 | 977.98 | 1,008.01 | 961.74 | 971.17 | 977.24 |
| 2018 | 949.54 | 964.01 | 956.16 | 969.60 | 1,022.58 | 1,081.85 | 1,099.41 | 1,081.94 | 1,100.03 | 1,001.63 | 1,045.30 | 1,044.58 | 1,031.15 |
| 2019 | 1,003.10 | 961.61 | 939.75 | 908.39 | 1,032.08 | 1,049.60 | 1,082.76 | 1,104.24 | 1,078.59 | 1,060.90 | 1,064.30 | 1,067.44 | 1,034.61 |
| **Manufacturing** | | | | | | | | | | | | | |
| 2015 | 853.38 | 868.73 | 849.02 | 849.93 | 862.58 | 842.59 | 849.90 | 864.74 | 843.70 | 870.35 | 882.23 | 872.90 | 858.60 |
| 2016 | 856.86 | 822.49 | 843.08 | 865.65 | 875.26 | 866.94 | 891.90 | 868.61 | 882.83 | 883.58 | 889.14 | 878.18 | 867.67 |
| 2017 | 929.15 | 870.40 | 889.70 | 894.24 | 910.91 | 903.42 | 871.32 | 881.27 | 868.20 | 876.08 | 869.27 | 878.63 | 885.71 |
| 2018 | 879.05 | 869.65 | 861.35 | 859.74 | 841.23 | 863.35 | 873.60 | 849.82 | 869.25 | 861.33 | 876.79 | 889.27 | 866.98 |
| 2019 | 875.86 | 879.80 | 859.56 | 849.41 | 888.73 | 888.62 | 876.88 | 882.43 | 893.30 | 909.80 | 919.23 | 953.44 | 890.15 |
| **Trade, Transportation, and Utilities** | | | | | | | | | | | | | |
| 2015 | 664.27 | 670.91 | 666.90 | 657.66 | 678.93 | 681.38 | 681.54 | 690.88 | 685.78 | 682.42 | 685.37 | 664.98 | 676.89 |
| 2016 | 662.61 | 654.69 | 654.06 | 674.58 | 695.98 | 681.77 | 681.07 | 673.99 | 686.11 | 691.86 | 684.58 | 672.43 | 674.66 |
| 2017 | 684.21 | 685.10 | 671.45 | 697.39 | 692.22 | 691.90 | 711.39 | 711.07 | 712.42 | 722.53 | 711.98 | 708.67 | 700.40 |
| 2018 | 706.32 | 703.70 | 694.22 | 711.81 | 736.29 | 740.20 | 766.40 | 751.98 | 780.15 | 749.18 | 748.85 | 767.93 | 738.00 |
| 2019 | 746.79 | 764.57 | 725.68 | 730.94 | 756.77 | 776.00 | 757.34 | 787.87 | 799.25 | 773.14 | 794.98 | 795.26 | 766.82 |
| **Professional and Business Services** | | | | | | | | | | | | | |
| 2015 | 874.24 | 911.24 | 911.06 | 910.69 | 877.13 | 889.85 | 891.89 | 915.01 | 900.24 | 906.05 | 914.27 | 874.72 | 897.90 |
| 2016 | 871.65 | 862.43 | 875.68 | 898.78 | 916.18 | 914.06 | 913.90 | 920.74 | 946.85 | 977.60 | 952.38 | 942.97 | 915.67 |
| 2017 | 952.29 | 974.46 | 974.66 | 980.10 | 967.61 | 962.17 | 969.86 | 943.14 | 973.54 | 964.99 | 950.05 | 946.75 | 964.09 |
| 2018 | 910.67 | 961.57 | 969.46 | 989.86 | 986.97 | 997.56 | 994.66 | 973.67 | 1,025.84 | 1,008.72 | 978.41 | 986.53 | 982.46 |
| 2019 | 934.27 | 910.75 | 933.84 | 949.16 | 950.70 | 930.08 | 900.07 | 935.10 | 974.66 | 955.86 | 973.18 | 977.56 | 942.61 |
| **Education and Health Services** | | | | | | | | | | | | | |
| 2015 | 704.46 | 729.54 | 715.39 | 712.26 | 710.71 | 705.28 | 702.14 | 733.13 | 734.18 | 744.88 | 753.36 | 743.61 | 722.87 |
| 2016 | 778.26 | 764.11 | 739.58 | 739.26 | 734.72 | 732.52 | 750.98 | 740.40 | 759.49 | 773.18 | 746.85 | 744.44 | 749.86 |
| 2017 | 755.39 | 736.02 | 724.28 | 730.51 | 701.06 | 700.85 | 716.41 | 683.51 | 699.87 | 709.44 | 687.62 | 691.66 | 711.59 |
| 2018 | 698.99 | 683.89 | 663.43 | 680.78 | 675.18 | 674.52 | 692.96 | 677.82 | 677.50 | 659.41 | 664.96 | 687.96 | 677.35 |
| 2019 | 682.95 | 676.01 | 651.72 | 666.16 | 681.70 | 680.92 | 686.72 | 685.64 | 711.10 | 707.11 | 680.00 | 700.16 | 683.77 |
| **Leisure and Hospitality** | | | | | | | | | | | | | |
| 2015 | 296.06 | 312.24 | 313.09 | 303.77 | 301.39 | 308.25 | 319.26 | 329.64 | 315.56 | 313.06 | 317.99 | 306.44 | 311.45 |
| 2016 | 313.17 | 311.89 | 319.81 | 319.33 | 329.50 | 327.91 | 332.52 | 340.61 | 333.94 | 332.32 | 314.78 | 312.31 | 324.63 |
| 2017 | 325.76 | 323.51 | 326.24 | 331.94 | 328.56 | 341.25 | 351.57 | 349.39 | 338.59 | 336.99 | 321.06 | 324.16 | 333.40 |
| 2018 | 326.37 | 327.18 | 340.31 | 333.89 | 341.90 | 351.65 | 359.58 | 354.08 | 344.65 | 328.54 | 316.21 | 330.41 | 338.88 |
| 2019 | 324.65 | 330.04 | 329.15 | 327.14 | 329.85 | 342.46 | 336.44 | 337.16 | 337.79 | 328.83 | 335.25 | 334.21 | 333.20 |

# TENNESSEE
## *At a Glance*

Population:
  2010 census: 6,346,105
  2019 estimate: 6,829,174

Percent change in population:
  2010–2019:  7.6%

Percent change in total nonfarm employment:
  2011–2019: 17.3%

Industry with the largest growth in employment, 2011–2019 (percent):
  Transportation and utilities, 33.4%

Industry with the largest decline or smallest growth in employment, 2011–2019 (percent):
  Mining and logging, 2.3%

Civilian labor force:
  2010: 3,090,795
  2019: 3,344,849

Unemployment rate and rank among states (highest to lowest):
  2010: 9.7%, 18th
  2019: 3.4%, 28th

Over-the-year change in unemployment rates:
  2017–2018: -0.3%
  2018–2019: -0.1%

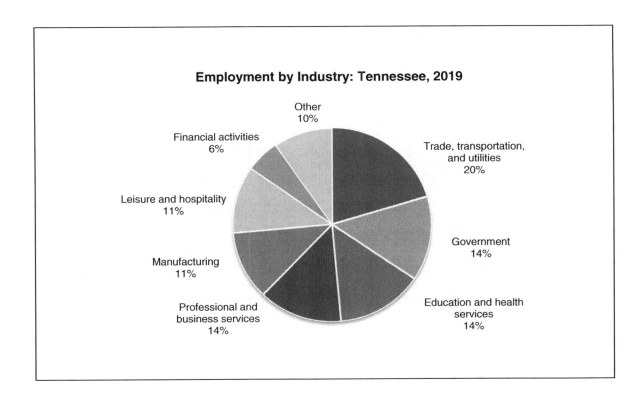

**Employment by Industry: Tennessee, 2019**

Other
10%

Financial activities
6%

Trade, transportation,
and utilities
20%

Leisure and hospitality
11%

Government
14%

Manufacturing
11%

Professional and
business services
14%

Education and health
services
14%

## 1. Employment by Industry: Tennessee, 2011–2019

(Numbers in thousands, not seasonally adjusted)

| Industry and year | January | February | March | April | May | June | July | August | September | October | November | December | Annual average |
|---|---|---|---|---|---|---|---|---|---|---|---|---|---|
| **Total Nonfarm** | | | | | | | | | | | | | |
| 2011 | 2,587.7 | 2,609.2 | 2,632.1 | 2,660.7 | 2,669.2 | 2,646.3 | 2,642.5 | 2,670.2 | 2,688.0 | 2,697.1 | 2,716.3 | 2,715.4 | 2,661.2 |
| 2012 | 2,649.0 | 2,667.3 | 2,698.8 | 2,715.3 | 2,724.8 | 2,705.8 | 2,687.6 | 2,714.7 | 2,734.0 | 2,745.3 | 2,766.3 | 2,768.8 | 2,714.8 |
| 2013 | 2,691.1 | 2,711.2 | 2,733.1 | 2,757.2 | 2,766.6 | 2,744.7 | 2,729.1 | 2,758.1 | 2,778.6 | 2,795.7 | 2,825.5 | 2,827.7 | 2,759.9 |
| 2014 | 2,752.4 | 2,764.4 | 2,791.5 | 2,815.3 | 2,824.8 | 2,800.3 | 2,792.3 | 2,825.2 | 2,847.6 | 2,863.5 | 2,890.6 | 2,897.3 | 2,822.1 |
| 2015 | 2,821.0 | 2,831.5 | 2,845.4 | 2,880.8 | 2,894.8 | 2,875.4 | 2,871.9 | 2,895.3 | 2,922.1 | 2,945.1 | 2,967.0 | 2,973.9 | 2,893.7 |
| 2016 | 2,897.9 | 2,914.4 | 2,938.1 | 2,963.0 | 2,962.9 | 2,944.5 | 2,940.3 | 2,967.8 | 2,997.8 | 3,003.2 | 3,025.1 | 3,028.4 | 2,965.3 |
| 2017 | 2,947.1 | 2,973.5 | 2,987.5 | 3,009.1 | 3,011.5 | 2,995.5 | 2,985.2 | 3,009.7 | 3,037.1 | 3,046.2 | 3,073.8 | 3,072.3 | 3,012.4 |
| 2018 | 2,990.7 | 3,018.1 | 3,037.5 | 3,053.9 | 3,063.6 | 3,047.6 | 3,033.2 | 3,067.2 | 3,090.4 | 3,100.1 | 3,131.5 | 3,125.2 | 3,063.3 |
| 2019 | 3,060.3 | 3,082.6 | 3,096.5 | 3,115.5 | 3,122.4 | 3,104.5 | 3,092.7 | 3,125.6 | 3,145.0 | 3,159.3 | 3,184.7 | 3,175.9 | 3,122.1 |
| **Total Private** | | | | | | | | | | | | | |
| 2011 | 2,158.6 | 2,174.9 | 2,196.6 | 2,225.8 | 2,236.2 | 2,246.3 | 2,246.4 | 2,255.8 | 2,258.5 | 2,263.6 | 2,281.9 | 2,283.7 | 2,235.7 |
| 2012 | 2,226.7 | 2,237.0 | 2,265.4 | 2,282.5 | 2,297.9 | 2,310.3 | 2,295.2 | 2,309.9 | 2,308.8 | 2,314.0 | 2,333.1 | 2,336.6 | 2,293.1 |
| 2013 | 2,273.0 | 2,284.1 | 2,304.4 | 2,320.2 | 2,334.9 | 2,346.7 | 2,335.3 | 2,351.6 | 2,351.5 | 2,361.1 | 2,390.7 | 2,393.4 | 2,337.2 |
| 2014 | 2,329.3 | 2,333.1 | 2,358.5 | 2,381.2 | 2,395.0 | 2,404.2 | 2,398.2 | 2,417.6 | 2,417.9 | 2,428.1 | 2,451.6 | 2,460.0 | 2,397.9 |
| 2015 | 2,395.6 | 2,398.7 | 2,412.9 | 2,447.1 | 2,465.3 | 2,478.2 | 2,477.2 | 2,486.5 | 2,489.9 | 2,506.9 | 2,528.5 | 2,536.8 | 2,468.6 |
| 2016 | 2,472.4 | 2,479.9 | 2,499.1 | 2,527.1 | 2,532.9 | 2,545.9 | 2,544.6 | 2,554.2 | 2,560.3 | 2,562.3 | 2,580.8 | 2,587.6 | 2,537.3 |
| 2017 | 2,520.3 | 2,535.7 | 2,548.9 | 2,569.6 | 2,577.2 | 2,593.0 | 2,585.4 | 2,595.2 | 2,597.3 | 2,603.2 | 2,628.7 | 2,629.5 | 2,582.0 |
| 2018 | 2,559.1 | 2,576.6 | 2,594.4 | 2,609.8 | 2,623.3 | 2,639.2 | 2,629.6 | 2,646.1 | 2,647.0 | 2,651.0 | 2,677.9 | 2,675.7 | 2,627.5 |
| 2019 | 2,624.7 | 2,636.8 | 2,649.7 | 2,669.0 | 2,680.4 | 2,694.8 | 2,688.5 | 2,703.9 | 2,700.4 | 2,709.6 | 2,732.4 | 2,727.9 | 2,684.8 |
| **Goods Producing** | | | | | | | | | | | | | |
| 2011 | 395.3 | 398.4 | 402.9 | 407.6 | 410.1 | 415.0 | 415.7 | 416.5 | 417.9 | 418.9 | 419.2 | 415.7 | 411.1 |
| 2012 | 407.9 | 409.9 | 415.3 | 417.6 | 420.5 | 424.9 | 422.8 | 426.3 | 425.3 | 424.0 | 424.1 | 423.0 | 420.1 |
| 2013 | 415.0 | 417.0 | 419.8 | 420.7 | 423.6 | 426.1 | 424.7 | 427.6 | 428.0 | 429.2 | 429.6 | 428.4 | 424.1 |
| 2014 | 422.4 | 424.0 | 427.6 | 429.7 | 432.8 | 434.2 | 434.2 | 438.3 | 438.3 | 439.2 | 441.2 | 442.3 | 433.7 |
| 2015 | 436.2 | 437.5 | 437.9 | 443.5 | 447.6 | 450.5 | 450.2 | 452.2 | 454.0 | 455.3 | 455.3 | 455.8 | 448.0 |
| 2016 | 450.3 | 451.0 | 455.4 | 457.7 | 459.5 | 463.4 | 464.1 | 464.9 | 465.8 | 464.9 | 465.5 | 467.3 | 460.8 |
| 2017 | 461.4 | 465.2 | 467.2 | 469.9 | 471.0 | 474.1 | 473.0 | 474.0 | 473.1 | 471.9 | 473.2 | 473.4 | 470.6 |
| 2018 | 467.3 | 469.4 | 472.9 | 475.5 | 477.4 | 482.1 | 482.2 | 484.8 | 486.0 | 484.5 | 485.9 | 485.0 | 479.4 |
| 2019 | 481.7 | 484.0 | 486.3 | 488.9 | 491.6 | 494.7 | 494.1 | 493.5 | 492.5 | 486.4 | 489.4 | 489.2 | 489.4 |
| **Service-Providing** | | | | | | | | | | | | | |
| 2011 | 2,192.4 | 2,210.8 | 2,229.2 | 2,253.1 | 2,259.1 | 2,231.3 | 2,226.8 | 2,253.7 | 2,270.1 | 2,278.2 | 2,297.1 | 2,299.7 | 2,250.1 |
| 2012 | 2,241.1 | 2,257.4 | 2,283.5 | 2,297.7 | 2,304.3 | 2,280.9 | 2,264.8 | 2,288.4 | 2,308.7 | 2,321.3 | 2,342.2 | 2,345.8 | 2,294.7 |
| 2013 | 2,276.1 | 2,294.2 | 2,313.3 | 2,336.5 | 2,343.0 | 2,318.6 | 2,304.4 | 2,330.5 | 2,350.6 | 2,366.5 | 2,395.9 | 2,399.3 | 2,335.7 |
| 2014 | 2,330.0 | 2,340.4 | 2,363.9 | 2,385.6 | 2,392.0 | 2,366.1 | 2,358.1 | 2,386.9 | 2,409.3 | 2,424.3 | 2,449.4 | 2,455.0 | 2,388.4 |
| 2015 | 2,384.8 | 2,394.0 | 2,407.5 | 2,437.3 | 2,447.2 | 2,424.9 | 2,421.7 | 2,443.1 | 2,468.1 | 2,489.8 | 2,511.7 | 2,518.1 | 2,445.7 |
| 2016 | 2,447.6 | 2,463.4 | 2,482.7 | 2,505.3 | 2,503.4 | 2,481.1 | 2,476.2 | 2,502.9 | 2,532.0 | 2,538.3 | 2,559.6 | 2,561.1 | 2,504.5 |
| 2017 | 2,485.7 | 2,508.3 | 2,520.3 | 2,539.2 | 2,540.5 | 2,521.4 | 2,512.2 | 2,535.7 | 2,564.0 | 2,574.3 | 2,600.6 | 2,598.9 | 2,541.8 |
| 2018 | 2,523.4 | 2,548.7 | 2,564.6 | 2,578.4 | 2,586.2 | 2,565.5 | 2,551.0 | 2,582.4 | 2,604.4 | 2,615.6 | 2,645.6 | 2,640.2 | 2,583.8 |
| 2019 | 2,578.6 | 2,598.6 | 2,610.2 | 2,626.6 | 2,630.8 | 2,609.8 | 2,598.6 | 2,632.1 | 2,652.5 | 2,672.9 | 2,695.3 | 2,686.7 | 2,632.7 |
| **Mining and Logging** | | | | | | | | | | | | | |
| 2011 | 4.1 | 4.2 | 4.4 | 4.4 | 4.4 | 4.7 | 4.5 | 4.6 | 4.6 | 4.5 | 4.4 | 4.4 | 4.4 |
| 2012 | 4.2 | 4.3 | 4.3 | 4.3 | 4.3 | 4.3 | 4.2 | 4.3 | 4.3 | 4.3 | 4.3 | 4.3 | 4.3 |
| 2013 | 4.2 | 4.3 | 4.4 | 4.4 | 4.4 | 4.4 | 4.3 | 4.4 | 4.3 | 4.3 | 4.2 | 4.2 | 4.3 |
| 2014 | 4.2 | 4.2 | 4.3 | 4.4 | 4.4 | 4.4 | 4.5 | 4.5 | 4.5 | 4.5 | 4.4 | 4.4 | 4.4 |
| 2015 | 4.3 | 4.5 | 4.4 | 4.6 | 4.6 | 4.6 | 4.5 | 4.5 | 4.5 | 4.5 | 4.5 | 4.5 | 4.5 |
| 2016 | 4.3 | 4.3 | 4.0 | 4.0 | 4.0 | 4.0 | 4.0 | 4.0 | 4.1 | 4.0 | 4.0 | 4.0 | 4.1 |
| 2017 | 4.0 | 4.1 | 4.0 | 4.1 | 4.2 | 4.3 | 4.2 | 4.2 | 4.3 | 4.2 | 4.3 | 4.3 | 4.2 |
| 2018 | 4.2 | 4.3 | 4.3 | 4.4 | 4.4 | 4.4 | 4.4 | 4.4 | 4.4 | 4.4 | 4.4 | 4.4 | 4.4 |
| 2019 | 4.3 | 4.4 | 4.4 | 4.4 | 4.5 | 4.5 | 4.6 | 4.5 | 4.6 | 4.5 | 4.5 | 4.4 | 4.5 |
| **Construction** | | | | | | | | | | | | | |
| 2011 | 93.8 | 95.6 | 98.8 | 102.6 | 103.9 | 106.7 | 107.6 | 108.5 | 109.8 | 109.5 | 108.4 | 106.3 | 104.3 |
| 2012 | 100.1 | 100.6 | 103.5 | 103.5 | 105.0 | 106.7 | 106.3 | 107.4 | 107.6 | 106.1 | 105.2 | 103.6 | 104.6 |
| 2013 | 98.0 | 99.3 | 100.8 | 102.3 | 104.3 | 105.5 | 105.5 | 105.9 | 106.1 | 106.4 | 105.6 | 103.8 | 103.6 |
| 2014 | 99.5 | 100.0 | 102.8 | 105.2 | 107.4 | 107.3 | 108.0 | 108.9 | 108.9 | 109.7 | 110.7 | 110.3 | 106.6 |
| 2015 | 105.8 | 106.4 | 106.9 | 110.6 | 113.1 | 114.4 | 115.4 | 115.3 | 116.2 | 117.4 | 116.2 | 114.9 | 112.7 |
| 2016 | 110.1 | 109.6 | 112.2 | 113.6 | 114.2 | 116.3 | 117.2 | 117.2 | 118.2 | 117.7 | 117.5 | 117.2 | 115.1 |
| 2017 | 113.7 | 115.6 | 117.4 | 119.4 | 120.7 | 122.1 | 122.2 | 122.8 | 122.5 | 122.0 | 122.2 | 121.5 | 120.2 |
| 2018 | 117.0 | 118.0 | 120.9 | 122.5 | 124.1 | 127.0 | 126.9 | 127.8 | 128.6 | 127.5 | 127.7 | 126.6 | 124.6 |
| 2019 | 124.2 | 124.8 | 126.8 | 129.3 | 131.4 | 133.1 | 132.6 | 132.5 | 131.9 | 131.8 | 130.0 | 129.2 | 129.8 |

# 1. Employment by Industry: Tennessee, 2011–2019—*Continued*

(Numbers in thousands, not seasonally adjusted)

| Industry and year | January | February | March | April | May | June | July | August | September | October | November | December | Annual average |
|---|---|---|---|---|---|---|---|---|---|---|---|---|---|
| **Manufacturing** | | | | | | | | | | | | | |
| 2011 | 297.4 | 298.6 | 299.7 | 300.6 | 301.8 | 303.6 | 303.6 | 303.4 | 303.5 | 304.9 | 306.4 | 305.0 | 302.4 |
| 2012 | 303.6 | 305.0 | 307.5 | 309.8 | 311.2 | 313.9 | 312.3 | 314.6 | 313.4 | 313.6 | 314.6 | 315.1 | 311.2 |
| 2013 | 312.8 | 313.4 | 314.6 | 314.0 | 314.9 | 316.2 | 314.9 | 317.3 | 317.6 | 318.5 | 319.8 | 320.4 | 316.2 |
| 2014 | 318.7 | 319.8 | 320.5 | 320.1 | 321.0 | 322.5 | 321.7 | 324.9 | 324.9 | 325.0 | 326.1 | 327.6 | 322.7 |
| | | | | | | | | | | | | | |
| 2015 | 326.1 | 326.6 | 326.6 | 328.3 | 329.9 | 331.5 | 330.3 | 332.4 | 333.3 | 333.4 | 334.6 | 336.4 | 330.8 |
| 2016 | 335.9 | 337.1 | 339.2 | 340.1 | 341.3 | 343.1 | 342.9 | 343.7 | 343.5 | 343.2 | 344.0 | 346.1 | 341.7 |
| 2017 | 343.7 | 345.5 | 345.8 | 346.4 | 346.1 | 347.7 | 346.6 | 347.0 | 346.3 | 345.7 | 346.7 | 347.6 | 346.3 |
| 2018 | 346.1 | 347.1 | 347.7 | 348.6 | 348.9 | 350.7 | 350.9 | 352.6 | 353.0 | 352.6 | 353.8 | 354.0 | 350.5 |
| 2019 | 353.2 | 354.8 | 355.1 | 355.2 | 355.7 | 357.1 | 356.9 | 356.5 | 356.0 | 350.1 | 354.9 | 355.6 | 355.1 |
| | | | | | | | | | | | | | |
| **Trade, Transportation, and Utilities** | | | | | | | | | | | | | |
| 2011 | 548.5 | 548.2 | 552.1 | 558.1 | 559.7 | 561.6 | 560.9 | 562.3 | 561.8 | 566.3 | 577.6 | 581.8 | 561.6 |
| 2012 | 563.0 | 559.7 | 566.0 | 568.5 | 571.3 | 572.2 | 570.7 | 572.4 | 574.0 | 576.7 | 589.8 | 593.5 | 573.2 |
| 2013 | 570.8 | 569.3 | 570.7 | 573.3 | 575.6 | 577.8 | 577.4 | 578.6 | 577.2 | 581.3 | 595.4 | 601.2 | 579.1 |
| 2014 | 575.4 | 573.6 | 578.0 | 582.0 | 583.4 | 585.9 | 586.3 | 588.9 | 588.6 | 593.8 | 606.7 | 611.2 | 587.8 |
| | | | | | | | | | | | | | |
| 2015 | 587.2 | 583.6 | 585.9 | 592.2 | 595.7 | 598.3 | 600.8 | 602.2 | 601.1 | 608.1 | 620.1 | 626.2 | 600.1 |
| 2016 | 605.0 | 603.8 | 606.1 | 611.0 | 611.7 | 613.0 | 615.2 | 615.9 | 615.2 | 619.0 | 632.3 | 635.2 | 615.3 |
| 2017 | 612.6 | 610.6 | 611.0 | 613.6 | 614.8 | 616.8 | 617.2 | 619.6 | 619.3 | 622.7 | 637.3 | 641.1 | 619.7 |
| 2018 | 618.0 | 616.3 | 618.9 | 618.9 | 622.6 | 624.0 | 624.1 | 625.7 | 624.6 | 629.1 | 646.3 | 650.0 | 626.5 |
| 2019 | 630.3 | 629.3 | 629.6 | 630.4 | 633.3 | 635.4 | 634.6 | 637.1 | 637.0 | 643.3 | 660.5 | 663.6 | 638.7 |
| | | | | | | | | | | | | | |
| **Wholesale Trade** | | | | | | | | | | | | | |
| 2011 | 113.2 | 113.7 | 114.3 | 115.3 | 115.8 | 116.2 | 116.0 | 116.1 | 116.2 | 116.2 | 116.8 | 116.9 | 115.6 |
| 2012 | 116.0 | 116.8 | 117.4 | 118.0 | 118.6 | 119.1 | 118.7 | 119.1 | 118.8 | 119.0 | 119.0 | 119.1 | 118.3 |
| 2013 | 117.4 | 117.7 | 118.2 | 118.5 | 118.7 | 119.0 | 118.8 | 118.8 | 118.8 | 118.4 | 118.8 | 118.8 | 118.5 |
| 2014 | 117.2 | 117.2 | 117.8 | 117.9 | 118.4 | 118.4 | 118.1 | 118.1 | 118.3 | 117.7 | 118.0 | 118.4 | 118.0 |
| | | | | | | | | | | | | | |
| 2015 | 117.0 | 117.1 | 117.1 | 117.3 | 117.7 | 117.9 | 117.7 | 117.6 | 117.5 | 117.2 | 117.5 | 117.5 | 117.4 |
| 2016 | 116.0 | 116.1 | 116.2 | 116.1 | 116.3 | 116.6 | 116.9 | 117.2 | 117.3 | 117.1 | 117.5 | 117.8 | 116.8 |
| 2017 | 116.8 | 117.5 | 117.7 | 117.7 | 118.2 | 118.4 | 118.2 | 118.3 | 118.3 | 118.4 | 118.9 | 119.0 | 118.1 |
| 2018 | 117.8 | 118.3 | 118.6 | 118.5 | 119.2 | 119.7 | 119.5 | 119.6 | 119.5 | 119.7 | 120.3 | 120.9 | 119.3 |
| 2019 | 119.7 | 120.3 | 120.4 | 120.6 | 121.0 | 121.3 | 121.2 | 121.5 | 121.1 | 121.4 | 121.8 | 121.9 | 121.0 |
| | | | | | | | | | | | | | |
| **Retail Trade** | | | | | | | | | | | | | |
| 2011 | 303.4 | 302.2 | 304.7 | 307.7 | 308.2 | 309.2 | 308.8 | 309.1 | 307.7 | 309.8 | 319.2 | 322.0 | 309.3 |
| 2012 | 308.3 | 304.7 | 309.3 | 310.8 | 312.2 | 312.7 | 311.9 | 311.3 | 310.6 | 313.6 | 324.7 | 325.6 | 313.0 |
| 2013 | 309.9 | 307.6 | 309.0 | 310.3 | 312.5 | 313.9 | 314.2 | 314.5 | 313.5 | 317.1 | 327.5 | 331.0 | 315.1 |
| 2014 | 314.4 | 312.6 | 315.0 | 317.5 | 318.6 | 320.5 | 320.7 | 321.2 | 319.9 | 322.6 | 332.7 | 335.6 | 320.9 |
| | | | | | | | | | | | | | |
| 2015 | 318.0 | 315.5 | 317.5 | 322.0 | 323.9 | 325.4 | 325.3 | 326.2 | 324.5 | 329.4 | 338.6 | 341.3 | 325.6 |
| 2016 | 327.3 | 326.9 | 329.0 | 332.3 | 332.7 | 332.9 | 333.8 | 333.8 | 332.8 | 335.3 | 344.9 | 346.4 | 334.0 |
| 2017 | 333.4 | 331.3 | 331.8 | 333.8 | 334.1 | 334.8 | 334.6 | 334.9 | 333.4 | 335.7 | 346.7 | 347.8 | 336.0 |
| 2018 | 333.3 | 332.2 | 333.8 | 334.5 | 336.2 | 336.2 | 334.6 | 334.3 | 332.1 | 333.6 | 344.1 | 344.4 | 335.8 |
| 2019 | 333.7 | 331.6 | 331.6 | 331.4 | 332.6 | 333.5 | 332.1 | 332.7 | 331.7 | 336.4 | 347.6 | 348.4 | 335.3 |
| | | | | | | | | | | | | | |
| **Transportation and Utilities** | | | | | | | | | | | | | |
| 2011 | 131.9 | 132.3 | 133.1 | 135.1 | 135.7 | 136.2 | 136.1 | 137.1 | 137.9 | 140.3 | 141.6 | 142.9 | 136.7 |
| 2012 | 138.7 | 138.2 | 139.3 | 139.7 | 140.5 | 140.4 | 140.1 | 142.0 | 144.6 | 144.1 | 146.1 | 148.8 | 141.9 |
| 2013 | 143.5 | 144.0 | 143.5 | 144.5 | 144.4 | 144.9 | 144.4 | 145.3 | 144.9 | 145.8 | 149.1 | 151.4 | 145.5 |
| 2014 | 143.8 | 143.8 | 145.2 | 146.6 | 146.4 | 147.0 | 147.5 | 149.6 | 150.4 | 153.5 | 156.0 | 157.2 | 148.9 |
| | | | | | | | | | | | | | |
| 2015 | 152.2 | 151.0 | 151.3 | 152.9 | 154.1 | 155.0 | 157.8 | 158.4 | 159.1 | 161.5 | 164.3 | 167.4 | 157.1 |
| 2016 | 161.7 | 160.8 | 160.9 | 162.6 | 162.7 | 163.5 | 164.5 | 164.9 | 165.1 | 166.6 | 169.9 | 171.0 | 164.5 |
| 2017 | 162.4 | 161.8 | 161.5 | 162.1 | 162.5 | 163.6 | 164.4 | 166.4 | 167.6 | 168.6 | 171.7 | 174.3 | 165.6 |
| 2018 | 166.9 | 165.8 | 166.5 | 165.9 | 167.2 | 168.1 | 170.0 | 171.8 | 173.0 | 175.8 | 181.9 | 184.7 | 171.5 |
| 2019 | 176.9 | 177.4 | 177.6 | 178.4 | 179.7 | 180.6 | 181.3 | 182.9 | 184.2 | 185.5 | 191.1 | 193.3 | 182.4 |
| | | | | | | | | | | | | | |
| **Information** | | | | | | | | | | | | | |
| 2011 | 44.6 | 44.4 | 44.3 | 44.4 | 44.4 | 44.2 | 43.9 | 44.1 | 43.5 | 43.2 | 43.6 | 43.4 | 44.0 |
| 2012 | 43.0 | 43.3 | 43.1 | 43.4 | 44.2 | 44.2 | 42.9 | 43.1 | 42.6 | 43.4 | 43.7 | 44.3 | 43.4 |
| 2013 | 43.7 | 44.1 | 44.3 | 44.0 | 44.5 | 45.1 | 44.5 | 44.4 | 43.9 | 44.0 | 44.7 | 44.6 | 44.3 |
| 2014 | 43.9 | 43.9 | 44.0 | 44.2 | 44.2 | 44.2 | 44.1 | 44.1 | 43.8 | 43.7 | 44.2 | 44.1 | 44.0 |
| | | | | | | | | | | | | | |
| 2015 | 43.6 | 43.7 | 43.8 | 44.1 | 44.4 | 44.9 | 44.8 | 45.0 | 44.7 | 44.8 | 45.8 | 45.8 | 44.6 |
| 2016 | 45.2 | 45.6 | 44.8 | 45.6 | 45.3 | 46.7 | 45.0 | 45.1 | 45.7 | 45.5 | 46.5 | 45.6 | 45.6 |
| 2017 | 45.2 | 45.9 | 45.5 | 45.4 | 45.9 | 47.5 | 45.8 | 45.9 | 45.6 | 46.5 | 47.7 | 46.0 | 46.1 |
| 2018 | 45.3 | 45.4 | 45.3 | 45.7 | 45.4 | 47.2 | 44.3 | 44.6 | 44.8 | 44.5 | 45.0 | 44.3 | 45.2 |
| 2019 | 43.9 | 44.3 | 44.2 | 45.1 | 45.1 | 46.4 | 46.0 | 45.5 | 45.5 | 46.5 | 47.2 | 46.0 | 45.5 |

## 1. Employment by Industry: Tennessee, 2011–2019—*Continued*

(Numbers in thousands, not seasonally adjusted)

| Industry and year | January | February | March | April | May | June | July | August | September | October | November | December | Annual average |
|---|---|---|---|---|---|---|---|---|---|---|---|---|---|
| **Financial Activities** | | | | | | | | | | | | | |
| 2011 | 137.5 | 137.4 | 137.3 | 138.8 | 139.5 | 139.4 | 139.9 | 140.3 | 139.7 | 139.8 | 140.3 | 140.3 | 139.2 |
| 2012 | 139.0 | 139.6 | 139.6 | 139.7 | 140.2 | 140.2 | 140.1 | 140.0 | 139.2 | 139.4 | 139.7 | 140.1 | 139.7 |
| 2013 | 138.6 | 138.5 | 138.8 | 140.0 | 140.7 | 141.4 | 142.6 | 142.8 | 142.6 | 143.2 | 144.1 | 144.5 | 141.5 |
| 2014 | 143.6 | 144.3 | 144.9 | 145.9 | 146.7 | 147.1 | 147.8 | 147.9 | 147.8 | 148.3 | 148.6 | 149.1 | 146.8 |
| 2015 | 148.2 | 148.6 | 148.6 | 149.3 | 150.0 | 151.0 | 151.6 | 152.0 | 151.5 | 152.5 | 153.1 | 154.0 | 150.9 |
| 2016 | 152.2 | 152.7 | 153.1 | 154.5 | 155.5 | 156.4 | 157.2 | 157.9 | 158.1 | 157.8 | 158.3 | 159.0 | 156.1 |
| 2017 | 157.7 | 158.9 | 159.8 | 160.6 | 161.8 | 163.5 | 163.7 | 164.5 | 164.3 | 165.8 | 165.4 | 165.9 | 162.7 |
| 2018 | 164.5 | 165.9 | 166.9 | 167.3 | 168.0 | 169.3 | 169.6 | 169.9 | 170.0 | 169.2 | 169.8 | 169.9 | 168.4 |
| 2019 | 169.3 | 170.0 | 170.0 | 171.0 | 171.8 | 173.1 | 173.8 | 174.1 | 173.9 | 173.7 | 172.8 | 172.9 | 172.2 |
| **Professional and Business Services** | | | | | | | | | | | | | |
| 2011 | 306.3 | 313.0 | 317.4 | 320.9 | 320.7 | 321.8 | 322.2 | 327.2 | 329.4 | 332.8 | 337.8 | 340.2 | 324.1 |
| 2012 | 324.8 | 328.9 | 332.9 | 336.2 | 339.4 | 341.9 | 336.2 | 342.3 | 343.9 | 347.3 | 352.7 | 353.3 | 340.0 |
| 2013 | 339.2 | 342.7 | 346.3 | 348.3 | 351.1 | 353.4 | 347.6 | 357.4 | 360.1 | 365.1 | 378.3 | 378.9 | 355.7 |
| 2014 | 362.6 | 361.4 | 365.1 | 371.7 | 375.2 | 376.2 | 371.5 | 381.0 | 381.8 | 386.6 | 394.6 | 398.6 | 377.2 |
| 2015 | 379.6 | 379.5 | 382.9 | 388.3 | 391.2 | 394.3 | 392.0 | 396.6 | 398.2 | 405.3 | 412.2 | 413.4 | 394.5 |
| 2016 | 394.9 | 395.3 | 397.7 | 403.3 | 402.8 | 404.5 | 402.0 | 407.2 | 409.4 | 411.9 | 414.0 | 418.2 | 405.1 |
| 2017 | 397.8 | 400.0 | 400.8 | 404.8 | 404.9 | 408.6 | 407.5 | 409.2 | 412.1 | 413.7 | 421.3 | 422.1 | 408.6 |
| 2018 | 402.7 | 407.9 | 407.9 | 411.8 | 413.8 | 416.4 | 411.9 | 418.1 | 420.2 | 422.8 | 430.6 | 429.0 | 416.1 |
| 2019 | 416.9 | 418.3 | 419.1 | 423.5 | 422.4 | 426.4 | 424.6 | 430.7 | 429.9 | 434.1 | 436.6 | 436.8 | 426.6 |
| **Education and Health Services** | | | | | | | | | | | | | |
| 2011 | 377.7 | 381.6 | 382.4 | 386.3 | 385.8 | 382.4 | 383.5 | 385.2 | 390.1 | 391.8 | 392.9 | 392.6 | 386.0 |
| 2012 | 389.0 | 392.9 | 395.0 | 395.2 | 393.9 | 392.1 | 391.3 | 394.4 | 399.5 | 400.8 | 401.6 | 401.6 | 395.6 |
| 2013 | 396.5 | 400.5 | 402.1 | 402.2 | 400.9 | 397.5 | 394.9 | 397.7 | 403.1 | 405.0 | 406.3 | 406.0 | 401.1 |
| 2014 | 401.2 | 404.0 | 406.1 | 405.3 | 403.3 | 400.4 | 400.0 | 403.3 | 409.5 | 411.8 | 412.1 | 412.4 | 405.8 |
| 2015 | 408.3 | 410.9 | 412.8 | 414.3 | 412.7 | 409.3 | 409.9 | 412.1 | 418.8 | 420.8 | 422.4 | 423.0 | 414.6 |
| 2016 | 416.5 | 420.8 | 422.4 | 423.5 | 422.1 | 417.9 | 419.0 | 422.5 | 428.5 | 430.6 | 431.7 | 431.2 | 423.9 |
| 2017 | 424.5 | 430.7 | 431.6 | 432.0 | 429.5 | 425.3 | 424.3 | 427.6 | 433.7 | 436.8 | 437.7 | 436.6 | 430.9 |
| 2018 | 429.9 | 436.0 | 437.2 | 436.0 | 434.0 | 430.6 | 429.7 | 433.6 | 439.0 | 441.3 | 442.3 | 440.6 | 435.9 |
| 2019 | 435.4 | 441.5 | 442.5 | 440.1 | 441.1 | 437.6 | 435.6 | 440.5 | 445.8 | 449.0 | 449.9 | 447.7 | 442.2 |
| **Leisure and Hospitality** | | | | | | | | | | | | | |
| 2011 | 249.0 | 251.5 | 259.0 | 268.2 | 273.7 | 278.0 | 276.8 | 277.0 | 273.8 | 268.8 | 268.2 | 267.4 | 267.6 |
| 2012 | 258.2 | 260.1 | 269.6 | 277.8 | 283.4 | 288.5 | 285.3 | 286.6 | 279.9 | 278.2 | 277.4 | 277.0 | 276.8 |
| 2013 | 266.2 | 268.3 | 277.8 | 285.8 | 292.0 | 297.6 | 296.4 | 296.7 | 290.7 | 287.8 | 286.7 | 284.9 | 285.9 |
| 2014 | 276.0 | 277.2 | 286.8 | 296.3 | 302.4 | 308.5 | 307.0 | 307.9 | 302.2 | 298.8 | 298.1 | 296.4 | 296.5 |
| 2015 | 287.4 | 289.2 | 294.8 | 307.9 | 315.0 | 320.1 | 318.5 | 317.9 | 313.1 | 311.4 | 310.8 | 309.8 | 308.0 |
| 2016 | 300.4 | 301.9 | 309.8 | 320.7 | 324.7 | 331.6 | 329.8 | 329.2 | 325.9 | 321.2 | 320.6 | 319.2 | 319.6 |
| 2017 | 310.1 | 312.5 | 320.1 | 329.4 | 334.6 | 340.9 | 338.0 | 338.9 | 333.6 | 330.4 | 330.2 | 328.4 | 328.9 |
| 2018 | 317.0 | 319.9 | 328.4 | 337.0 | 343.7 | 349.5 | 348.0 | 349.8 | 342.6 | 340.0 | 338.6 | 337.4 | 337.7 |
| 2019 | 328.9 | 330.2 | 337.7 | 348.8 | 353.0 | 358.1 | 357.3 | 360.4 | 353.8 | 355.3 | 353.8 | 351.3 | 349.1 |
| **Other Services** | | | | | | | | | | | | | |
| 2011 | 99.7 | 100.4 | 101.2 | 101.5 | 102.3 | 103.9 | 103.5 | 103.2 | 102.3 | 102.0 | 102.3 | 102.3 | 102.1 |
| 2012 | 101.8 | 102.6 | 103.9 | 104.1 | 105.0 | 106.3 | 105.9 | 104.8 | 104.4 | 104.2 | 104.1 | 103.8 | 104.2 |
| 2013 | 103.0 | 103.7 | 104.6 | 105.9 | 106.5 | 107.8 | 107.2 | 106.4 | 105.9 | 105.5 | 105.6 | 104.9 | 105.6 |
| 2014 | 104.2 | 104.7 | 106.0 | 106.1 | 107.0 | 107.7 | 107.3 | 106.2 | 105.9 | 105.9 | 106.1 | 105.9 | 106.1 |
| 2015 | 105.1 | 105.7 | 106.2 | 107.5 | 108.7 | 109.8 | 109.4 | 108.5 | 108.5 | 108.7 | 108.8 | 108.8 | 108.0 |
| 2016 | 107.9 | 108.8 | 109.8 | 110.8 | 111.3 | 112.4 | 112.3 | 111.5 | 111.7 | 111.4 | 111.9 | 111.9 | 111.0 |
| 2017 | 111.0 | 111.9 | 112.9 | 113.9 | 114.7 | 116.3 | 115.9 | 115.5 | 115.6 | 115.4 | 115.9 | 116.0 | 114.6 |
| 2018 | 114.4 | 115.8 | 116.9 | 117.6 | 118.4 | 120.1 | 119.8 | 119.6 | 119.8 | 119.6 | 119.4 | 119.5 | 118.4 |
| 2019 | 118.3 | 119.2 | 120.3 | 121.2 | 122.1 | 123.1 | 122.5 | 122.1 | 122.0 | 121.3 | 122.2 | 120.4 | 121.2 |
| **Government** | | | | | | | | | | | | | |
| 2011 | 429.1 | 434.3 | 435.5 | 434.9 | 433.0 | 400.0 | 396.1 | 414.4 | 429.5 | 433.5 | 434.4 | 431.7 | 425.5 |
| 2012 | 422.3 | 430.3 | 433.4 | 432.8 | 426.9 | 395.5 | 392.4 | 404.8 | 425.2 | 431.3 | 433.2 | 432.2 | 421.7 |
| 2013 | 418.1 | 427.1 | 428.7 | 437.0 | 431.7 | 398.0 | 393.8 | 406.5 | 427.1 | 434.6 | 434.8 | 434.3 | 422.6 |
| 2014 | 423.1 | 431.3 | 433.0 | 434.1 | 429.8 | 396.1 | 394.1 | 407.6 | 429.7 | 435.4 | 439.0 | 437.3 | 424.2 |
| 2015 | 425.4 | 432.8 | 432.5 | 433.7 | 429.5 | 397.2 | 394.7 | 408.8 | 432.2 | 438.2 | 438.5 | 437.1 | 425.1 |
| 2016 | 425.5 | 434.5 | 439.0 | 435.9 | 430.0 | 398.6 | 395.7 | 413.6 | 437.5 | 440.9 | 444.3 | 440.8 | 428.0 |
| 2017 | 426.8 | 437.8 | 438.6 | 439.5 | 434.3 | 402.5 | 399.8 | 414.5 | 439.8 | 443.0 | 445.1 | 442.8 | 430.4 |
| 2018 | 431.6 | 441.5 | 443.1 | 444.1 | 440.3 | 408.4 | 403.6 | 421.1 | 443.4 | 449.1 | 453.6 | 449.5 | 435.8 |
| 2019 | 435.6 | 445.8 | 446.8 | 446.5 | 442.0 | 409.7 | 404.2 | 421.7 | 444.6 | 449.7 | 452.3 | 448.0 | 437.2 |

## 2. Average Weekly Hours by Selected Industry: Tennessee, 2015–2019

(Not seasonally adjusted)

| Industry and year | January | February | March | April | May | June | July | August | September | October | November | December | Annual average |
|---|---|---|---|---|---|---|---|---|---|---|---|---|---|
| **Total Private** | | | | | | | | | | | | | |
| 2015 | 34.7 | 34.7 | 35.2 | 35.0 | 35.1 | 35.3 | 35.2 | 35.8 | 35.0 | 35.2 | 35.5 | 35.6 | 35.2 |
| 2016 | 35.1 | 35.0 | 35.3 | 35.4 | 35.8 | 35.6 | 35.5 | 35.5 | 35.4 | 35.8 | 35.5 | 35.6 | 35.5 |
| 2017 | 35.6 | 35.4 | 35.3 | 35.5 | 35.4 | 35.6 | 35.6 | 35.2 | 35.3 | 35.4 | 35.3 | 35.5 | 35.4 |
| 2018 | 34.0 | 35.0 | 35.2 | 35.8 | 35.4 | 35.7 | 35.8 | 35.4 | 36.0 | 35.5 | 35.3 | 35.6 | 35.4 |
| 2019 | 34.8 | 35.1 | 35.1 | 35.2 | 35.2 | 35.8 | 35.1 | 35.3 | 35.6 | 35.0 | 35.1 | 35.6 | 35.2 |
| **Goods-Producing** | | | | | | | | | | | | | |
| 2015 | 40.8 | 40.1 | 41.3 | 41.1 | 41.2 | 41.4 | 41.0 | 41.6 | 40.7 | 41.4 | 41.8 | 42.3 | 41.2 |
| 2016 | 41.5 | 40.9 | 41.6 | 42.0 | 42.5 | 42.4 | 42.3 | 42.8 | 42.9 | 42.4 | 43.2 | 43.2 | 42.3 |
| 2017 | 42.3 | 42.1 | 42.2 | 41.6 | 42.3 | 42.5 | 41.7 | 41.6 | 41.6 | 41.3 | 42.0 | 42.5 | 42.0 |
| 2018 | 39.7 | 41.6 | 42.4 | 42.6 | 42.0 | 42.6 | 41.7 | 41.6 | 41.6 | 41.6 | 41.4 | 41.3 | 41.7 |
| 2019 | 40.7 | 41.2 | 41.7 | 41.4 | 41.8 | 42.3 | 41.1 | 41.8 | 41.6 | 40.8 | 41.1 | 41.0 | 41.4 |
| **Mining, Logging, and Construction** | | | | | | | | | | | | | |
| 2015 | 37.7 | 37.5 | 37.5 | 38.4 | 40.2 | 40.2 | 40.3 | 39.8 | 38.4 | 40.2 | 39.7 | 40.5 | 39.2 |
| 2016 | 39.6 | 37.0 | 38.6 | 39.5 | 40.5 | 40.6 | 40.2 | 40.7 | 40.3 | 40.6 | 40.3 | 40.1 | 39.9 |
| 2017 | 38.9 | 39.5 | 39.5 | 40.4 | 40.8 | 41.3 | 42.0 | 41.1 | 40.8 | 41.5 | 42.0 | 41.8 | 40.8 |
| 2018 | 37.8 | 39.5 | 41.3 | 42.4 | 42.1 | 42.2 | 41.6 | 41.6 | 41.5 | 41.7 | 40.0 | 40.6 | 41.0 |
| 2019 | 40.8 | 40.0 | 41.1 | 40.4 | 41.5 | 42.5 | 42.5 | 42.6 | 42.0 | 41.4 | 40.8 | 40.5 | 41.3 |
| **Manufacturing** | | | | | | | | | | | | | |
| 2015 | 41.8 | 40.9 | 42.6 | 42.0 | 41.5 | 41.8 | 41.2 | 42.3 | 41.6 | 41.8 | 42.6 | 43.0 | 41.9 |
| 2016 | 42.1 | 42.2 | 42.7 | 42.8 | 43.2 | 43.1 | 43.0 | 43.5 | 43.8 | 43.1 | 44.2 | 44.3 | 43.2 |
| 2017 | 43.5 | 43.0 | 43.1 | 42.0 | 42.9 | 42.9 | 41.6 | 41.8 | 41.9 | 41.2 | 42.0 | 42.7 | 42.4 |
| 2018 | 40.3 | 42.4 | 42.8 | 42.7 | 42.0 | 42.8 | 41.7 | 41.6 | 41.7 | 41.5 | 42.0 | 41.6 | 41.9 |
| 2019 | 40.6 | 41.7 | 41.9 | 41.8 | 41.9 | 42.2 | 40.6 | 41.5 | 41.4 | 40.6 | 41.2 | 41.2 | 41.4 |
| **Trade, Transportation, and Utilities** | | | | | | | | | | | | | |
| 2015 | 34.0 | 33.9 | 34.8 | 34.6 | 34.6 | 34.8 | 34.7 | 34.9 | 34.7 | 34.3 | 34.6 | 35.0 | 34.6 |
| 2016 | 34.4 | 34.3 | 34.4 | 34.6 | 34.8 | 34.9 | 34.7 | 34.5 | 34.6 | 34.9 | 34.4 | 34.8 | 34.6 |
| 2017 | 34.6 | 34.2 | 34.1 | 34.4 | 34.3 | 34.4 | 34.4 | 34.3 | 34.4 | 34.4 | 34.3 | 34.8 | 34.4 |
| 2018 | 33.1 | 33.8 | 34.1 | 34.4 | 34.4 | 34.4 | 34.4 | 34.2 | 34.6 | 34.1 | 33.9 | 34.0 | 34.1 |
| 2019 | 33.4 | 33.4 | 33.6 | 34.1 | 33.7 | 34.3 | 33.9 | 34.5 | 34.9 | 34.3 | 34.1 | 34.7 | 34.1 |
| **Financial Activities** | | | | | | | | | | | | | |
| 2015 | 37.4 | 38.4 | 38.7 | 37.8 | 37.6 | 37.6 | 37.6 | 38.1 | 37.1 | 37.0 | 37.5 | 37.0 | 37.6 |
| 2016 | 37.1 | 37.0 | 36.7 | 36.7 | 37.3 | 36.9 | 37.0 | 37.0 | 36.3 | 37.5 | 36.9 | 37.1 | 37.0 |
| 2017 | 37.9 | 37.4 | 37.2 | 38.1 | 37.2 | 37.5 | 38.7 | 37.5 | 37.7 | 38.7 | 38.0 | 38.1 | 37.8 |
| 2018 | 37.5 | 37.9 | 37.6 | 38.8 | 37.7 | 38.0 | 39.6 | 37.9 | 39.5 | 38.7 | 38.7 | 39.7 | 38.5 |
| 2019 | 38.3 | 38.1 | 37.9 | 38.0 | 37.8 | 38.9 | 38.0 | 38.0 | 39.1 | 38.1 | 38.2 | 39.2 | 38.3 |
| **Professional and Business Services** | | | | | | | | | | | | | |
| 2015 | 35.0 | 35.7 | 35.0 | 35.1 | 35.6 | 36.0 | 35.8 | 37.3 | 35.7 | 36.3 | 36.9 | 37.0 | 36.0 |
| 2016 | 36.5 | 36.3 | 36.5 | 36.7 | 37.3 | 36.9 | 36.7 | 36.6 | 36.4 | 37.4 | 36.5 | 36.5 | 36.7 |
| 2017 | 36.3 | 36.2 | 36.0 | 36.1 | 36.4 | 37.0 | 37.0 | 36.4 | 36.4 | 37.2 | 36.7 | 36.3 | 36.5 |
| 2018 | 35.0 | 35.9 | 36.2 | 37.0 | 36.5 | 37.4 | 37.9 | 37.5 | 38.1 | 37.6 | 37.2 | 37.4 | 37.0 |
| 2019 | 36.5 | 36.8 | 36.9 | 36.8 | 36.8 | 37.2 | 36.5 | 36.8 | 36.6 | 36.3 | 36.7 | 37.0 | 36.7 |
| **Education and Health Services** | | | | | | | | | | | | | |
| 2015 | 34.6 | 34.5 | 34.5 | 34.4 | 34.5 | 34.5 | 34.7 | 35.2 | 34.9 | 34.7 | 35.2 | 34.8 | 34.7 |
| 2016 | 34.9 | 34.9 | 34.9 | 34.7 | 35.1 | 34.8 | 34.9 | 34.8 | 35.0 | 34.9 | 34.8 | 34.8 | 34.9 |
| 2017 | 35.7 | 35.1 | 35.1 | 35.2 | 34.8 | 35.0 | 35.3 | 34.6 | 34.6 | 34.3 | 34.2 | 34.4 | 34.9 |
| 2018 | 33.6 | 34.3 | 34.0 | 35.1 | 34.6 | 34.5 | 35.4 | 34.4 | 35.5 | 34.5 | 34.5 | 35.4 | 34.7 |
| 2019 | 34.6 | 34.5 | 34.0 | 34.2 | 34.5 | 34.9 | 34.6 | 34.0 | 34.6 | 34.0 | 34.4 | 35.1 | 34.4 |
| **Leisure and Hospitality** | | | | | | | | | | | | | |
| 2015 | 25.9 | 25.9 | 26.6 | 27.0 | 26.7 | 27.3 | 27.2 | 27.1 | 26.5 | 26.9 | 26.7 | 26.6 | 26.7 |
| 2016 | 26.0 | 26.5 | 26.8 | 26.8 | 27.0 | 27.2 | 27.0 | 26.9 | 26.4 | 27.1 | 26.8 | 26.2 | 26.7 |
| 2017 | 26.3 | 26.7 | 26.7 | 27.4 | 26.8 | 27.4 | 27.3 | 26.7 | 26.5 | 27.1 | 26.7 | 26.5 | 26.8 |
| 2018 | 25.3 | 26.8 | 26.9 | 27.4 | 27.1 | 27.6 | 27.6 | 26.8 | 27.1 | 27.0 | 26.9 | 27.2 | 27.0 |
| 2019 | 26.0 | 27.0 | 27.2 | 27.1 | 27.1 | 28.1 | 27.7 | 27.4 | 27.6 | 27.6 | 27.2 | 27.4 | 27.3 |
| **Other Services** | | | | | | | | | | | | | |
| 2015 | 32.2 | 32.8 | 32.7 | 32.6 | 33.0 | 33.0 | 33.0 | 33.8 | 32.3 | 32.8 | 32.7 | 32.8 | 32.8 |
| 2016 | 31.7 | 31.9 | 32.2 | 32.7 | 33.0 | 32.2 | 32.4 | 32.1 | 31.8 | 32.2 | 32.1 | 32.7 | 32.2 |
| 2017 | 33.0 | 32.8 | 32.8 | 32.9 | 32.3 | 31.6 | 32.5 | 32.4 | 32.8 | 33.4 | 33.3 | 33.9 | 32.8 |
| 2018 | 30.9 | 31.9 | 32.3 | 33.3 | 32.9 | 32.6 | 32.1 | 32.4 | 33.2 | 32.8 | 32.4 | 31.8 | 32.4 |
| 2019 | 31.8 | 32.4 | 31.8 | 31.5 | 31.6 | 32.1 | 31.1 | 31.5 | 32.1 | 31.9 | 32.0 | 33.0 | 31.9 |

## 3. Average Hourly Earnings by Selected Industry: Tennessee, 2015–2019

(Dollars, not seasonally adjusted)

| Industry and year | January | February | March | April | May | June | July | August | September | October | November | December | Annual average |
|---|---|---|---|---|---|---|---|---|---|---|---|---|---|
| **Total Private** | | | | | | | | | | | | | |
| 2015 | 20.75 | 20.98 | 20.81 | 20.71 | 20.63 | 20.65 | 20.81 | 20.88 | 20.94 | 21.02 | 21.16 | 21.07 | 20.87 |
| 2016 | 21.37 | 21.25 | 21.28 | 21.28 | 21.52 | 21.37 | 21.61 | 21.55 | 21.85 | 22.07 | 21.94 | 22.41 | 21.63 |
| 2017 | 22.60 | 22.41 | 22.21 | 22.54 | 22.29 | 22.23 | 22.57 | 22.45 | 22.74 | 22.65 | 22.76 | 22.89 | 22.53 |
| 2018 | 23.09 | 23.00 | 22.91 | 23.14 | 22.99 | 23.13 | 23.33 | 23.42 | 23.81 | 23.52 | 23.76 | 24.12 | 23.36 |
| 2019 | 23.95 | 24.16 | 23.98 | 23.91 | 23.96 | 24.18 | 24.11 | 24.20 | 24.48 | 24.31 | 24.37 | 24.61 | 24.19 |
| **Goods-Producing** | | | | | | | | | | | | | |
| 2015 | 21.29 | 21.25 | 21.37 | 21.35 | 21.42 | 21.42 | 21.67 | 21.29 | 21.67 | 21.58 | 21.66 | 22.02 | 21.50 |
| 2016 | 22.10 | 22.10 | 22.11 | 22.04 | 22.26 | 22.21 | 22.55 | 22.51 | 22.75 | 22.66 | 22.78 | 23.42 | 22.47 |
| 2017 | 23.15 | 22.96 | 22.92 | 23.08 | 23.16 | 23.21 | 23.54 | 23.36 | 23.80 | 23.57 | 23.72 | 24.09 | 23.38 |
| 2018 | 24.07 | 23.86 | 23.82 | 24.11 | 23.95 | 23.86 | 24.37 | 24.44 | 24.62 | 24.51 | 24.66 | 25.06 | 24.28 |
| 2019 | 24.62 | 24.82 | 24.80 | 25.02 | 24.82 | 25.19 | 25.19 | 25.00 | 25.45 | 25.27 | 25.27 | 25.63 | 25.09 |
| **Mining, Logging, and Construction** | | | | | | | | | | | | | |
| 2015 | 21.92 | 22.10 | 22.48 | 22.08 | 22.01 | 22.45 | 22.44 | 22.19 | 22.49 | 22.67 | 23.16 | 23.49 | 22.47 |
| 2016 | 23.27 | 22.96 | 23.35 | 22.99 | 23.22 | 22.90 | 23.17 | 23.07 | 22.98 | 23.38 | 23.38 | 24.26 | 23.25 |
| 2017 | 24.07 | 23.88 | 23.94 | 24.20 | 24.09 | 23.98 | 24.26 | 24.04 | 24.38 | 24.10 | 24.75 | 24.69 | 24.21 |
| 2018 | 24.83 | 24.91 | 24.67 | 25.01 | 24.58 | 24.36 | 25.00 | 24.82 | 25.43 | 25.81 | 25.88 | 25.72 | 25.09 |
| 2019 | 26.07 | 25.53 | 25.50 | 25.89 | 25.51 | 25.61 | 25.72 | 25.65 | 26.13 | 26.14 | 25.95 | 25.94 | 25.80 |
| **Manufacturing** | | | | | | | | | | | | | |
| 2015 | 21.10 | 20.98 | 21.04 | 21.13 | 21.22 | 21.07 | 21.40 | 20.98 | 21.40 | 21.19 | 21.15 | 21.53 | 21.18 |
| 2016 | 21.72 | 21.85 | 21.72 | 21.74 | 21.95 | 21.98 | 22.34 | 22.33 | 22.68 | 22.42 | 22.59 | 23.16 | 22.22 |
| 2017 | 22.87 | 22.67 | 22.59 | 22.69 | 22.84 | 22.94 | 23.28 | 23.11 | 23.59 | 23.38 | 23.35 | 23.88 | 23.10 |
| 2018 | 23.82 | 23.52 | 23.52 | 23.78 | 23.72 | 23.67 | 24.13 | 24.30 | 24.32 | 24.02 | 24.23 | 24.82 | 23.99 |
| 2019 | 24.09 | 24.57 | 24.55 | 24.71 | 24.56 | 25.03 | 24.97 | 24.74 | 25.19 | 24.92 | 25.02 | 25.51 | 24.82 |
| **Trade, Transportation, and Utilities** | | | | | | | | | | | | | |
| 2015 | 19.37 | 19.37 | 19.12 | 19.41 | 19.07 | 19.20 | 19.25 | 19.05 | 19.10 | 19.11 | 19.13 | 18.90 | 19.17 |
| 2016 | 19.20 | 18.96 | 19.11 | 19.29 | 19.87 | 19.52 | 19.83 | 19.87 | 20.07 | 20.32 | 19.86 | 20.28 | 19.69 |
| 2017 | 20.57 | 20.43 | 20.35 | 20.66 | 20.43 | 20.30 | 20.62 | 20.47 | 20.58 | 20.47 | 20.33 | 20.44 | 20.47 |
| 2018 | 20.38 | 20.53 | 20.33 | 20.38 | 20.32 | 20.66 | 20.66 | 21.01 | 21.40 | 21.12 | 21.30 | 21.46 | 20.80 |
| 2019 | 21.49 | 21.57 | 21.31 | 21.44 | 21.80 | 22.07 | 21.97 | 22.20 | 22.57 | 22.59 | 22.56 | 22.68 | 22.03 |
| **Financial Activities** | | | | | | | | | | | | | |
| 2015 | 25.06 | 25.85 | 25.30 | 25.39 | 25.69 | 25.63 | 25.94 | 27.07 | 25.84 | 26.12 | 26.47 | 26.29 | 25.89 |
| 2016 | 26.49 | 26.50 | 25.99 | 26.42 | 27.04 | 26.54 | 26.60 | 25.94 | 26.36 | 26.75 | 26.68 | 26.43 | 26.48 |
| 2017 | 27.06 | 27.55 | 26.61 | 27.82 | 27.18 | 27.18 | 27.72 | 27.82 | 27.97 | 28.57 | 28.64 | 28.30 | 27.71 |
| 2018 | 28.70 | 28.64 | 28.95 | 29.18 | 29.46 | 30.11 | 31.33 | 31.51 | 30.88 | 30.13 | 31.95 | 32.10 | 30.27 |
| 2019 | 32.66 | 33.38 | 33.74 | 32.53 | 33.62 | 33.71 | 33.50 | 34.25 | 33.77 | 33.21 | 34.12 | 34.27 | 33.57 |
| **Professional and Business Services** | | | | | | | | | | | | | |
| 2015 | 23.68 | 24.34 | 24.55 | 23.83 | 23.77 | 23.69 | 23.89 | 24.31 | 24.53 | 24.45 | 24.77 | 24.28 | 24.18 |
| 2016 | 24.91 | 24.90 | 25.35 | 24.79 | 24.94 | 25.17 | 25.29 | 25.10 | 25.83 | 26.23 | 26.02 | 26.91 | 25.46 |
| 2017 | 27.42 | 27.23 | 26.99 | 27.83 | 27.04 | 26.83 | 27.43 | 27.07 | 27.45 | 27.31 | 27.41 | 27.52 | 27.29 |
| 2018 | 27.76 | 27.48 | 27.52 | 28.00 | 27.31 | 27.72 | 27.69 | 27.52 | 28.04 | 27.36 | 27.78 | 28.62 | 27.74 |
| 2019 | 28.09 | 28.22 | 27.75 | 27.82 | 27.61 | 27.68 | 28.02 | 27.94 | 28.39 | 27.93 | 27.80 | 28.05 | 27.94 |
| **Education and Health Services** | | | | | | | | | | | | | |
| 2015 | 21.70 | 21.94 | 21.61 | 21.64 | 21.62 | 21.75 | 21.87 | 21.91 | 21.83 | 22.25 | 22.21 | 22.07 | 21.87 |
| 2016 | 22.53 | 22.23 | 22.22 | 22.49 | 22.36 | 22.36 | 22.59 | 22.45 | 22.45 | 22.69 | 22.67 | 23.12 | 22.51 |
| 2017 | 23.29 | 22.76 | 22.60 | 22.77 | 22.48 | 22.60 | 22.55 | 22.67 | 22.75 | 22.28 | 22.69 | 22.83 | 22.69 |
| 2018 | 23.36 | 23.22 | 23.14 | 23.52 | 23.65 | 23.56 | 23.21 | 23.16 | 23.78 | 23.64 | 23.69 | 23.84 | 23.48 |
| 2019 | 23.58 | 24.04 | 23.86 | 23.66 | 23.40 | 23.80 | 23.61 | 23.56 | 23.75 | 23.77 | 23.67 | 23.90 | 23.72 |
| **Leisure and Hospitality** | | | | | | | | | | | | | |
| 2015 | 11.77 | 11.94 | 11.87 | 11.87 | 11.89 | 12.02 | 12.15 | 12.13 | 12.35 | 12.33 | 12.36 | 12.38 | 12.09 |
| 2016 | 12.19 | 12.36 | 12.24 | 12.18 | 12.20 | 12.22 | 12.41 | 12.57 | 12.74 | 12.83 | 13.06 | 12.99 | 12.50 |
| 2017 | 12.88 | 13.08 | 12.97 | 12.90 | 13.06 | 12.87 | 13.00 | 13.31 | 13.67 | 13.72 | 13.92 | 14.13 | 13.29 |
| 2018 | 14.30 | 14.41 | 14.31 | 14.38 | 14.41 | 14.19 | 14.38 | 14.60 | 15.07 | 15.25 | 14.54 | 14.77 | 14.55 |
| 2019 | 14.74 | 15.13 | 15.06 | 14.85 | 15.01 | 14.82 | 14.67 | 14.75 | 14.80 | 14.94 | 15.03 | 15.14 | 14.91 |
| **Other Services** | | | | | | | | | | | | | |
| 2015 | 20.23 | 20.35 | 20.11 | 19.83 | 19.46 | 19.28 | 19.31 | 19.13 | 19.37 | 19.20 | 19.43 | 19.64 | 19.60 |
| 2016 | 19.52 | 19.56 | 19.51 | 19.57 | 19.85 | 19.34 | 19.18 | 19.55 | 19.64 | 19.98 | 19.61 | 19.83 | 19.60 |
| 2017 | 20.41 | 19.77 | 19.89 | 20.10 | 19.86 | 19.91 | 20.49 | 19.88 | 20.28 | 20.66 | 20.47 | 20.67 | 20.20 |
| 2018 | 21.13 | 20.70 | 20.54 | 20.51 | 20.49 | 20.59 | 20.82 | 20.79 | 21.36 | 21.10 | 21.54 | 22.55 | 21.01 |
| 2019 | 22.47 | 22.34 | 22.11 | 22.36 | 22.35 | 22.82 | 22.31 | 22.81 | 23.08 | 22.78 | 23.16 | 23.63 | 22.69 |

# 4. Average Weekly Earnings by Selected Industry: Tennessee, 2015–2019

(Dollars, not seasonally adjusted)

| Industry and year | January | February | March | April | May | June | July | August | September | October | November | December | Annual average |
|---|---|---|---|---|---|---|---|---|---|---|---|---|---|
| **Total Private** | | | | | | | | | | | | | |
| 2015 | 720.03 | 728.01 | 732.51 | 724.85 | 724.11 | 728.95 | 732.51 | 747.50 | 732.90 | 739.90 | 751.18 | 750.09 | 734.62 |
| 2016 | 750.09 | 745.88 | 751.18 | 753.31 | 770.42 | 760.77 | 767.16 | 765.03 | 773.49 | 790.11 | 778.87 | 797.80 | 767.87 |
| 2017 | 804.56 | 793.31 | 784.01 | 800.17 | 789.07 | 791.39 | 803.49 | 790.24 | 800.45 | 801.81 | 803.43 | 812.60 | 797.56 |
| 2018 | 785.06 | 805.00 | 806.43 | 828.41 | 813.85 | 825.74 | 835.21 | 829.07 | 857.16 | 834.96 | 838.73 | 858.67 | 826.94 |
| 2019 | 833.46 | 848.02 | 841.70 | 841.63 | 843.39 | 865.64 | 846.26 | 854.26 | 871.49 | 850.85 | 855.39 | 876.12 | 851.49 |
| **Goods-Producing** | | | | | | | | | | | | | |
| 2015 | 868.63 | 850.00 | 882.58 | 877.90 | 882.50 | 886.79 | 888.47 | 885.66 | 881.97 | 893.41 | 905.39 | 931.45 | 885.80 |
| 2016 | 917.15 | 903.89 | 921.99 | 925.68 | 946.05 | 943.93 | 953.87 | 963.43 | 975.98 | 960.78 | 984.10 | 1,011.74 | 950.48 |
| 2017 | 979.25 | 966.62 | 967.22 | 960.13 | 979.67 | 986.43 | 981.62 | 971.78 | 990.08 | 973.44 | 996.24 | 1,023.83 | 981.96 |
| 2018 | 955.58 | 992.58 | 1,009.97 | 1,027.09 | 1,005.90 | 1,016.44 | 1,016.23 | 1,016.70 | 1,024.19 | 1,019.62 | 1,023.39 | 1,034.98 | 1,012.48 |
| 2019 | 1,002.03 | 1,022.58 | 1,034.16 | 1,035.83 | 1,037.48 | 1,065.54 | 1,035.31 | 1,045.00 | 1,058.72 | 1,031.02 | 1,038.60 | 1,050.83 | 1,038.73 |
| **Mining, Logging, and Construction** | | | | | | | | | | | | | |
| 2015 | 826.38 | 828.75 | 843.00 | 847.87 | 884.80 | 902.49 | 904.33 | 883.16 | 863.62 | 911.33 | 919.45 | 951.35 | 880.82 |
| 2016 | 921.49 | 849.52 | 901.31 | 908.11 | 940.41 | 929.74 | 931.43 | 938.95 | 926.09 | 949.23 | 942.21 | 972.83 | 927.68 |
| 2017 | 936.32 | 943.26 | 945.63 | 977.68 | 982.87 | 990.37 | 1,018.92 | 988.04 | 994.70 | 1,000.15 | 1,039.50 | 1,032.04 | 987.77 |
| 2018 | 938.57 | 983.95 | 1,018.87 | 1,060.42 | 1,034.82 | 1,027.99 | 1,040.00 | 1,032.51 | 1,055.35 | 1,076.28 | 1,035.20 | 1,044.23 | 1,028.69 |
| 2019 | 1,063.66 | 1,021.20 | 1,048.05 | 1,045.96 | 1,058.67 | 1,088.43 | 1,093.10 | 1,092.69 | 1,097.46 | 1,082.20 | 1,058.76 | 1,050.57 | 1,065.54 |
| **Manufacturing** | | | | | | | | | | | | | |
| 2015 | 881.98 | 858.08 | 896.30 | 887.46 | 880.63 | 880.73 | 881.68 | 887.45 | 890.24 | 885.74 | 900.99 | 925.79 | 887.44 |
| 2016 | 914.41 | 922.07 | 927.44 | 930.47 | 948.24 | 947.34 | 960.62 | 971.36 | 993.38 | 966.30 | 998.48 | 1,025.99 | 959.90 |
| 2017 | 994.85 | 974.81 | 973.63 | 952.98 | 979.84 | 984.13 | 968.45 | 966.00 | 988.42 | 963.26 | 980.70 | 1,019.68 | 979.44 |
| 2018 | 959.95 | 997.25 | 1,006.66 | 1,015.41 | 996.24 | 1,013.08 | 1,006.22 | 1,010.88 | 1,014.14 | 996.83 | 1,017.66 | 1,032.51 | 1,005.18 |
| 2019 | 978.05 | 1,024.57 | 1,028.65 | 1,032.88 | 1,029.06 | 1,056.27 | 1,013.78 | 1,026.71 | 1,042.87 | 1,011.75 | 1,030.82 | 1,051.01 | 1,027.55 |
| **Trade, Transportation, and Utilities** | | | | | | | | | | | | | |
| 2015 | 658.58 | 656.64 | 665.38 | 671.59 | 659.82 | 668.16 | 667.98 | 664.85 | 662.77 | 655.47 | 661.90 | 661.50 | 663.28 |
| 2016 | 660.48 | 650.33 | 657.38 | 667.43 | 691.48 | 681.25 | 688.10 | 685.52 | 694.42 | 709.17 | 683.18 | 705.74 | 681.27 |
| 2017 | 711.72 | 698.71 | 693.94 | 710.70 | 700.75 | 698.32 | 709.33 | 702.12 | 707.95 | 704.17 | 697.32 | 711.31 | 704.17 |
| 2018 | 674.58 | 693.91 | 693.25 | 701.07 | 699.01 | 710.70 | 710.70 | 718.54 | 740.44 | 720.19 | 722.07 | 729.64 | 709.28 |
| 2019 | 717.77 | 720.44 | 716.02 | 731.10 | 734.66 | 757.00 | 744.78 | 765.90 | 787.69 | 774.84 | 769.30 | 787.00 | 751.22 |
| **Financial Activities** | | | | | | | | | | | | | |
| 2015 | 937.24 | 992.64 | 979.11 | 959.74 | 965.94 | 963.69 | 975.34 | 1,031.37 | 958.66 | 966.44 | 992.63 | 972.73 | 973.46 |
| 2016 | 982.78 | 980.50 | 953.83 | 969.61 | 1,008.59 | 979.33 | 984.20 | 959.78 | 956.87 | 1,003.13 | 984.49 | 980.55 | 979.76 |
| 2017 | 1,025.57 | 1,030.37 | 989.89 | 1,059.94 | 1,011.10 | 1,019.25 | 1,072.76 | 1,043.25 | 1,054.47 | 1,105.66 | 1,088.32 | 1,078.23 | 1,047.44 |
| 2018 | 1,076.25 | 1,085.46 | 1,088.52 | 1,132.18 | 1,110.64 | 1,144.18 | 1,240.67 | 1,194.23 | 1,219.76 | 1,166.03 | 1,236.47 | 1,274.37 | 1,165.40 |
| 2019 | 1,250.88 | 1,271.78 | 1,278.75 | 1,236.14 | 1,270.84 | 1,311.32 | 1,273.00 | 1,301.50 | 1,320.41 | 1,265.30 | 1,303.38 | 1,343.38 | 1,285.73 |
| **Professional and Business Services** | | | | | | | | | | | | | |
| 2015 | 828.80 | 868.94 | 859.25 | 836.43 | 846.21 | 852.84 | 855.26 | 906.76 | 875.72 | 887.54 | 914.01 | 898.36 | 870.48 |
| 2016 | 909.22 | 903.87 | 925.28 | 909.79 | 930.26 | 928.77 | 928.14 | 918.66 | 940.21 | 981.00 | 949.73 | 982.22 | 934.38 |
| 2017 | 995.35 | 985.73 | 971.64 | 1,004.66 | 984.26 | 992.71 | 1,014.91 | 985.35 | 999.18 | 1,015.93 | 1,005.95 | 998.98 | 996.09 |
| 2018 | 971.60 | 986.53 | 996.22 | 1,036.00 | 996.82 | 1,036.73 | 1,049.45 | 1,032.00 | 1,068.32 | 1,028.74 | 1,033.42 | 1,070.39 | 1,026.38 |
| 2019 | 1,025.29 | 1,038.50 | 1,023.98 | 1,023.78 | 1,016.05 | 1,029.70 | 1,022.73 | 1,028.19 | 1,039.07 | 1,013.86 | 1,020.26 | 1,037.85 | 1,025.40 |
| **Education and Health Services** | | | | | | | | | | | | | |
| 2015 | 750.82 | 756.93 | 745.55 | 744.42 | 745.89 | 750.38 | 758.89 | 771.23 | 761.87 | 772.08 | 781.79 | 768.04 | 758.89 |
| 2016 | 786.30 | 775.83 | 775.48 | 780.40 | 784.84 | 778.13 | 788.39 | 781.26 | 785.75 | 791.88 | 788.92 | 804.58 | 785.60 |
| 2017 | 831.45 | 798.88 | 793.26 | 801.50 | 782.30 | 791.00 | 796.02 | 784.38 | 787.15 | 764.20 | 776.00 | 785.35 | 791.88 |
| 2018 | 784.90 | 796.45 | 786.76 | 825.55 | 818.29 | 812.82 | 821.63 | 796.70 | 844.19 | 815.58 | 817.31 | 843.94 | 814.76 |
| 2019 | 815.87 | 829.38 | 811.24 | 809.17 | 807.30 | 830.62 | 816.91 | 801.04 | 821.75 | 808.18 | 814.25 | 838.89 | 815.97 |
| **Leisure and Hospitality** | | | | | | | | | | | | | |
| 2015 | 304.84 | 309.25 | 315.74 | 320.49 | 317.46 | 328.15 | 330.48 | 328.72 | 327.28 | 331.68 | 330.01 | 329.31 | 322.80 |
| 2016 | 316.94 | 327.54 | 328.03 | 326.42 | 332.38 | 335.07 | 338.13 | 336.34 | 347.69 | 350.01 | 340.34 | 333.75 |
| 2017 | 338.74 | 349.24 | 346.30 | 353.46 | 350.01 | 352.64 | 354.90 | 355.38 | 362.26 | 371.81 | 371.66 | 374.45 | 356.17 |
| 2018 | 361.79 | 386.19 | 384.94 | 394.01 | 390.51 | 391.64 | 396.89 | 391.28 | 408.40 | 411.75 | 391.13 | 401.74 | 392.85 |
| 2019 | 383.24 | 408.51 | 409.63 | 402.44 | 406.77 | 416.44 | 406.36 | 404.15 | 408.48 | 412.34 | 408.82 | 414.84 | 407.04 |
| **Other Services** | | | | | | | | | | | | | |
| 2015 | 651.41 | 667.48 | 657.60 | 646.46 | 642.18 | 636.24 | 637.23 | 646.59 | 625.65 | 629.76 | 635.36 | 644.19 | 642.88 |
| 2016 | 618.78 | 623.96 | 628.22 | 639.94 | 655.05 | 622.75 | 621.43 | 627.56 | 624.55 | 643.36 | 629.48 | 648.44 | 631.12 |
| 2017 | 673.53 | 648.46 | 652.39 | 661.29 | 641.48 | 629.16 | 665.93 | 644.11 | 665.18 | 690.04 | 681.65 | 700.71 | 662.56 |
| 2018 | 652.92 | 660.33 | 663.44 | 682.98 | 674.12 | 671.23 | 668.32 | 673.60 | 709.15 | 692.08 | 697.90 | 717.09 | 680.72 |
| 2019 | 714.55 | 723.82 | 703.10 | 704.34 | 706.26 | 732.52 | 693.84 | 718.52 | 740.87 | 726.68 | 741.12 | 779.79 | 723.81 |

# TEXAS
## *At a Glance*

Population:
  2010 census: 25,145,561
  2019 estimate: 28,995,881

Percent change in population:
  2010–2019: 15.3%

Percent change in total nonfarm employment:
  2011–2019:  20.7%

Industry with the largest growth in employment, 2011–2019 (percent):
  Construction, 37.6%

Industry with the largest decline or smallest growth in employment, 2011–2019 (percent):
  Mining and logging, 5.3%

Civilian labor force:
  2010: 12,241,970
  2019: 14,045,312

Unemployment rate and rank among states (highest to lowest):
  2010: 8.1%, 32nd
  2019: 3.5%, 25th

Over-the-year change in unemployment rates:
  2017–2018: -0.5%
  2018–2019: -0.3%

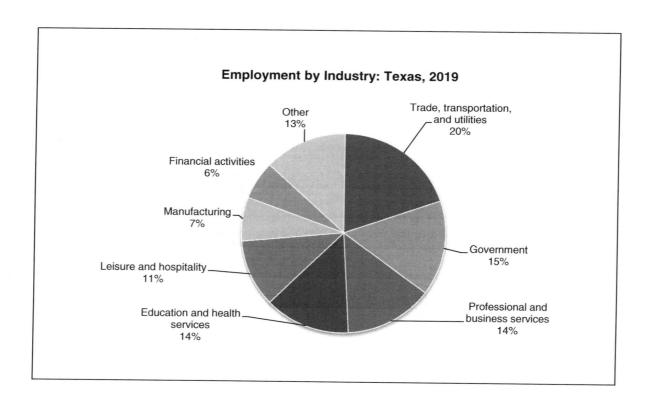

Employment by Industry: Texas, 2019

Other 13%
Trade, transportation, and utilities 20%
Financial activities 6%
Manufacturing 7%
Leisure and hospitality 11%
Education and health services 14%
Government 15%
Professional and business services 14%

# 1. Employment by Industry: Texas, 2011–2019

(Numbers in thousands, not seasonally adjusted)

| Industry and year | January | February | March | April | May | June | July | August | September | October | November | December | Annual average |
|---|---|---|---|---|---|---|---|---|---|---|---|---|---|
| **Total Nonfarm** | | | | | | | | | | | | | |
| 2011 | 10,362.3 | 10,421.5 | 10,518.7 | 10,589.5 | 10,624.0 | 10,660.3 | 10,577.4 | 10,613.1 | 10,667.8 | 10,694.5 | 10,753.2 | 10,784.2 | 10,605.5 |
| 2012 | 10,621.4 | 10,713.9 | 10,800.8 | 10,852.3 | 10,918.1 | 10,964.8 | 10,866.8 | 10,931.4 | 10,975.6 | 11,046.1 | 11,130.5 | 11,157.6 | 10,914.9 |
| 2013 | 10,942.6 | 11,072.0 | 11,142.1 | 11,186.6 | 11,240.4 | 11,284.2 | 11,205.8 | 11,252.7 | 11,297.7 | 11,361.4 | 11,450.4 | 11,458.4 | 11,241.2 |
| 2014 | 11,273.4 | 11,368.4 | 11,441.5 | 11,521.0 | 11,592.9 | 11,635.9 | 11,558.6 | 11,606.1 | 11,651.2 | 11,760.0 | 11,836.5 | 11,879.2 | 11,593.7 |
| | | | | | | | | | | | | | |
| 2015 | 11,672.4 | 11,749.4 | 11,771.2 | 11,820.7 | 11,871.4 | 11,910.8 | 11,841.9 | 11,860.0 | 11,885.8 | 11,967.3 | 12,010.4 | 12,031.0 | 11,866.0 |
| 2016 | 11,830.9 | 11,908.6 | 11,923.4 | 11,987.2 | 12,019.0 | 12,028.3 | 11,974.5 | 11,996.0 | 12,044.7 | 12,100.3 | 12,168.0 | 12,181.1 | 12,013.5 |
| 2017 | 11,994.6 | 12,087.9 | 12,148.5 | 12,183.2 | 12,240.9 | 12,287.5 | 12,172.9 | 12,199.8 | 12,226.7 | 12,335.1 | 12,421.1 | 12,435.1 | 12,227.8 |
| 2018 | 12,222.7 | 12,342.6 | 12,400.9 | 12,436.1 | 12,508.6 | 12,564.8 | 12,489.8 | 12,540.9 | 12,553.7 | 12,660.4 | 12,750.5 | 12,757.2 | 12,519.0 |
| 2019 | 12,548.7 | 12,662.4 | 12,688.7 | 12,728.7 | 12,788.1 | 12,821.5 | 12,765.8 | 12,807.5 | 12,818.3 | 12,938.7 | 13,017.7 | 13,029.8 | 12,801.3 |
| | | | | | | | | | | | | | |
| **Total Private** | | | | | | | | | | | | | |
| 2010 | 8,477.5 | 8,519.3 | 8,614.8 | 8,691.2 | 8,722.5 | 8,794.0 | 8,804.9 | 8,851.9 | 8,849.9 | 8,847.4 | 8,901.6 | 8,942.1 | 8,751.4 |
| 2011 | 8,798.4 | 8,861.6 | 8,943.6 | 9,001.4 | 9,061.0 | 9,144.9 | 9,120.4 | 9,189.5 | 9,167.8 | 9,195.6 | 9,271.9 | 9,298.4 | 9,087.9 |
| 2012 | 9,113.6 | 9,210.0 | 9,273.8 | 9,323.6 | 9,372.3 | 9,448.8 | 9,439.9 | 9,495.6 | 9,469.3 | 9,491.6 | 9,569.4 | 9,583.7 | 9,399.3 |
| 2013 | 9,419.2 | 9,489.3 | 9,555.9 | 9,641.9 | 9,706.9 | 9,779.4 | 9,775.9 | 9,833.6 | 9,809.2 | 9,870.1 | 9,934.8 | 9,979.3 | 9,733.0 |
| 2014 | 9,799.7 | 9,850.0 | 9,868.2 | 9,922.4 | 9,965.8 | 10,028.9 | 10,033.4 | 10,056.3 | 10,013.7 | 10,052.0 | 10,083.0 | 10,102.6 | 9,981.3 |
| | | | | | | | | | | | | | |
| 2015 | 9,925.2 | 9,978.0 | 9,986.6 | 10,051.0 | 10,073.3 | 10,107.0 | 10,125.6 | 10,153.5 | 10,132.1 | 10,153.9 | 10,207.7 | 10,218.4 | 10,092.7 |
| 2016 | 10,063.5 | 10,124.8 | 10,177.7 | 10,215.7 | 10,269.5 | 10,345.2 | 10,312.8 | 10,349.3 | 10,312.0 | 10,376.0 | 10,448.4 | 10,463.9 | 10,288.2 |
| 2017 | 10,286.5 | 10,371.7 | 10,419.6 | 10,466.9 | 10,529.0 | 10,611.3 | 10,609.6 | 10,666.8 | 10,617.8 | 10,691.4 | 10,764.2 | 10,773.4 | 10,567.4 |
| 2018 | 10,599.6 | 10,678.5 | 10,696.6 | 10,746.3 | 10,794.6 | 10,851.4 | 10,865.9 | 10,906.8 | 10,855.5 | 10,937.1 | 11,002.4 | 11,019.1 | 10,829.5 |
| 2019 | | | | | | | | | | | | | |
| | | | | | | | | | | | | | |
| **Goods Producing** | | | | | | | | | | | | | |
| 2011 | 1,583.6 | 1,595.6 | 1,611.0 | 1,619.5 | 1,625.6 | 1,645.6 | 1,659.6 | 1,669.4 | 1,674.6 | 1,674.9 | 1,676.8 | 1,680.3 | 1,643.0 |
| 2012 | 1,668.7 | 1,684.2 | 1,699.4 | 1,708.7 | 1,718.4 | 1,734.8 | 1,737.2 | 1,748.4 | 1,747.2 | 1,754.3 | 1,753.8 | 1,752.1 | 1,725.6 |
| 2013 | 1,732.7 | 1,754.8 | 1,764.2 | 1,767.3 | 1,771.9 | 1,786.7 | 1,787.7 | 1,796.3 | 1,792.2 | 1,793.9 | 1,796.9 | 1,794.7 | 1,778.3 |
| 2014 | 1,781.9 | 1,801.6 | 1,810.0 | 1,828.6 | 1,842.9 | 1,855.9 | 1,863.7 | 1,875.3 | 1,875.1 | 1,887.2 | 1,890.5 | 1,895.9 | 1,850.7 |
| | | | | | | | | | | | | | |
| 2015 | 1,872.2 | 1,870.4 | 1,855.7 | 1,840.8 | 1,837.5 | 1,843.6 | 1,838.4 | 1,834.2 | 1,820.0 | 1,816.5 | 1,803.0 | 1,797.0 | 1,835.8 |
| 2016 | 1,774.9 | 1,777.7 | 1,765.9 | 1,765.0 | 1,759.0 | 1,761.3 | 1,762.0 | 1,758.4 | 1,756.2 | 1,756.3 | 1,748.5 | 1,746.9 | 1,761.0 |
| 2017 | 1,735.1 | 1,754.9 | 1,765.9 | 1,768.0 | 1,781.8 | 1,800.1 | 1,796.1 | 1,799.2 | 1,798.2 | 1,810.1 | 1,815.9 | 1,820.2 | 1,787.1 |
| 2018 | 1,800.4 | 1,826.2 | 1,837.6 | 1,844.9 | 1,858.0 | 1,878.4 | 1,881.3 | 1,891.6 | 1,888.6 | 1,901.2 | 1,906.2 | 1,909.9 | 1,868.7 |
| 2019 | 1,895.1 | 1,916.6 | 1,919.2 | 1,924.7 | 1,931.0 | 1,941.7 | 1,942.2 | 1,945.2 | 1,938.3 | 1,942.2 | 1,952.2 | 1,944.8 | 1,932.8 |
| | | | | | | | | | | | | | |
| **Service-Providing** | | | | | | | | | | | | | |
| 2011 | 8,778.7 | 8,825.9 | 8,907.7 | 8,970.0 | 8,998.4 | 9,014.7 | 8,917.8 | 8,943.7 | 8,993.2 | 9,019.6 | 9,076.4 | 9,103.9 | 8,962.5 |
| 2012 | 8,952.7 | 9,029.7 | 9,101.4 | 9,143.6 | 9,199.7 | 9,230.0 | 9,129.6 | 9,183.0 | 9,228.4 | 9,291.8 | 9,376.7 | 9,405.5 | 9,189.3 |
| 2013 | 9,209.9 | 9,317.2 | 9,377.9 | 9,419.3 | 9,468.5 | 9,497.5 | 9,418.1 | 9,456.4 | 9,505.5 | 9,567.5 | 9,653.5 | 9,663.7 | 9,462.9 |
| 2014 | 9,491.5 | 9,566.8 | 9,631.5 | 9,692.4 | 9,750.0 | 9,780.0 | 9,694.9 | 9,730.8 | 9,776.1 | 9,872.8 | 9,946.0 | 9,983.3 | 9,743.0 |
| | | | | | | | | | | | | | |
| 2015 | 9,800.2 | 9,879.0 | 9,915.5 | 9,979.9 | 10,033.9 | 10,067.2 | 10,003.5 | 10,025.8 | 10,065.8 | 10,150.8 | 10,207.4 | 10,234.0 | 10,030.3 |
| 2016 | 10,056.0 | 10,130.9 | 10,157.5 | 10,222.2 | 10,260.0 | 10,267.0 | 10,212.5 | 10,237.6 | 10,288.5 | 10,344.0 | 10,419.5 | 10,434.2 | 10,252.5 |
| 2017 | 10,259.5 | 10,333.0 | 10,382.6 | 10,415.2 | 10,459.1 | 10,487.4 | 10,376.8 | 10,400.6 | 10,428.5 | 10,525.0 | 10,605.2 | 10,614.9 | 10,440.7 |
| 2018 | 10,422.3 | 10,516.4 | 10,563.3 | 10,591.2 | 10,650.6 | 10,686.4 | 10,608.5 | 10,649.3 | 10,665.1 | 10,759.2 | 10,844.3 | 10,847.3 | 10,650.3 |
| 2019 | 10,653.6 | 10,745.8 | 10,769.5 | 10,804.0 | 10,857.1 | 10,879.8 | 10,823.6 | 10,862.3 | 10,880.0 | 10,996.5 | 11,065.5 | 11,085.0 | 10,868.6 |
| | | | | | | | | | | | | | |
| **Mining and Logging** | | | | | | | | | | | | | |
| 2011 | 218.3 | 220.9 | 223.9 | 227.7 | 229.9 | 235.7 | 240.7 | 244.6 | 246.6 | 250.9 | 253.1 | 256.6 | 237.4 |
| 2012 | 257.0 | 260.3 | 263.5 | 265.8 | 268.0 | 271.9 | 275.0 | 276.1 | 275.4 | 277.9 | 278.8 | 280.4 | 270.8 |
| 2013 | 279.0 | 281.4 | 282.9 | 285.0 | 286.6 | 290.1 | 292.2 | 293.9 | 293.2 | 293.7 | 294.7 | 295.7 | 289.0 |
| 2014 | 296.7 | 299.5 | 301.0 | 304.1 | 306.9 | 311.0 | 315.0 | 317.9 | 317.8 | 320.2 | 321.7 | 322.1 | 311.2 |
| | | | | | | | | | | | | | |
| 2015 | 314.6 | 302.4 | 292.5 | 280.4 | 273.9 | 271.8 | 266.7 | 263.7 | 257.6 | 252.5 | 247.5 | 245.5 | 272.4 |
| 2016 | 235.1 | 229.4 | 223.0 | 215.8 | 211.4 | 209.4 | 207.5 | 206.5 | 204.8 | 205.7 | 204.9 | 206.3 | 213.3 |
| 2017 | 208.8 | 212.6 | 214.2 | 216.7 | 220.0 | 222.9 | 224.9 | 226.3 | 227.1 | 228.5 | 230.0 | 232.3 | 222.0 |
| 2018 | 231.7 | 236.0 | 238.9 | 240.7 | 243.7 | 247.1 | 249.2 | 251.7 | 252.8 | 254.9 | 256.1 | 256.8 | 246.6 |
| 2019 | 255.1 | 255.8 | 254.5 | 254.7 | 254.3 | 253.4 | 250.7 | 249.5 | 245.8 | 244.8 | 242.8 | 236.8 | 249.9 |
| | | | | | | | | | | | | | |
| **Construction** | | | | | | | | | | | | | |
| 2011 | 543.6 | 549.6 | 557.8 | 559.2 | 560.4 | 567.5 | 571.9 | 575.0 | 576.8 | 572.3 | 569.2 | 565.8 | 564.1 |
| 2012 | 557.2 | 564.6 | 573.4 | 576.7 | 584.2 | 589.8 | 586.0 | 594.7 | 595.0 | 600.8 | 598.1 | 593.5 | 584.5 |
| 2013 | 583.2 | 599.2 | 606.8 | 607.7 | 611.6 | 618.3 | 617.8 | 624.0 | 622.5 | 624.2 | 623.9 | 619.9 | 613.3 |
| 2014 | 614.8 | 625.5 | 632.2 | 642.7 | 651.0 | 654.5 | 657.8 | 664.3 | 665.7 | 671.8 | 670.5 | 670.7 | 651.8 |
| | | | | | | | | | | | | | |
| 2015 | 662.3 | 673.6 | 673.4 | 675.4 | 681.2 | 688.1 | 691.7 | 694.2 | 691.4 | 697.6 | 691.0 | 688.7 | 684.1 |
| 2016 | 684.0 | 692.1 | 691.2 | 701.7 | 701.7 | 704.4 | 707.5 | 706.5 | 708.6 | 710.6 | 702.4 | 697.0 | 700.6 |
| 2017 | 688.5 | 699.7 | 707.3 | 706.1 | 714.4 | 721.1 | 714.2 | 714.1 | 713.8 | 722.7 | 723.5 | 720.6 | 712.2 |
| 2018 | 708.5 | 723.1 | 729.3 | 733.2 | 739.2 | 747.0 | 744.7 | 750.2 | 746.3 | 753.1 | 752.1 | 752.4 | 739.9 |
| 2019 | 744.4 | 759.5 | 763.0 | 767.6 | 772.5 | 777.0 | 779.6 | 783.9 | 783.5 | 792.3 | 797.3 | 794.7 | 776.3 |

## 1. Employment by Industry: Texas, 2011–2019—*Continued*

(Numbers in thousands, not seasonally adjusted)

| Industry and year | January | February | March | April | May | June | July | August | September | October | November | December | Annual average |
|---|---|---|---|---|---|---|---|---|---|---|---|---|---|
| **Manufacturing** | | | | | | | | | | | | | |
| 2011 | 821.7 | 825.1 | 829.3 | 832.6 | 835.3 | 842.4 | 847.0 | 849.8 | 851.2 | 851.7 | 854.5 | 857.9 | 841.5 |
| 2012 | 854.5 | 859.3 | 862.5 | 866.2 | 866.2 | 873.1 | 876.2 | 877.6 | 876.8 | 875.6 | 876.9 | 878.2 | 870.3 |
| 2013 | 870.5 | 874.2 | 874.5 | 874.6 | 873.7 | 878.3 | 877.7 | 878.4 | 876.5 | 876.0 | 878.3 | 879.1 | 876.0 |
| 2014 | 870.4 | 876.6 | 876.8 | 881.8 | 885.0 | 890.4 | 890.9 | 893.1 | 891.6 | 895.2 | 898.3 | 903.1 | 887.8 |
| | | | | | | | | | | | | | |
| 2015 | 895.3 | 894.4 | 889.8 | 885.0 | 882.4 | 883.7 | 880.0 | 876.3 | 871.0 | 866.4 | 864.5 | 862.8 | 879.3 |
| 2016 | 855.8 | 856.2 | 851.7 | 847.5 | 845.9 | 847.5 | 847.0 | 845.4 | 842.8 | 840.0 | 841.2 | 843.6 | 847.1 |
| 2017 | 837.8 | 842.6 | 844.4 | 845.2 | 847.4 | 856.1 | 857.0 | 858.8 | 857.3 | 858.9 | 862.4 | 867.3 | 852.9 |
| 2018 | 860.2 | 867.1 | 869.4 | 871.0 | 875.1 | 884.3 | 887.4 | 889.7 | 889.5 | 893.2 | 898.0 | 900.7 | 882.1 |
| 2019 | 895.6 | 901.3 | 901.7 | 902.4 | 904.2 | 911.3 | 911.9 | 911.8 | 909.0 | 905.1 | 912.1 | 913.3 | 906.6 |
| **Trade, Transportation, and Utilities** | | | | | | | | | | | | | |
| 2011 | 2,048.1 | 2,039.5 | 2,055.9 | 2,072.3 | 2,077.6 | 2,087.3 | 2,092.8 | 2,108.5 | 2,101.1 | 2,112.7 | 2,152.2 | 2,180.8 | 2,094.1 |
| 2012 | 2,118.0 | 2,110.1 | 2,121.0 | 2,130.2 | 2,141.9 | 2,155.9 | 2,158.1 | 2,173.0 | 2,164.2 | 2,178.7 | 2,232.3 | 2,251.3 | 2,161.2 |
| 2013 | 2,180.1 | 2,178.0 | 2,183.5 | 2,195.3 | 2,205.3 | 2,218.8 | 2,222.2 | 2,239.7 | 2,233.7 | 2,248.5 | 2,298.9 | 2,323.2 | 2,227.3 |
| 2014 | 2,253.8 | 2,247.3 | 2,253.4 | 2,264.1 | 2,274.6 | 2,291.2 | 2,295.1 | 2,312.3 | 2,307.5 | 2,329.0 | 2,379.2 | 2,413.5 | 2,301.8 |
| | | | | | | | | | | | | | |
| 2015 | 2,340.2 | 2,334.4 | 2,339.3 | 2,350.8 | 2,363.1 | 2,375.3 | 2,377.5 | 2,388.8 | 2,382.5 | 2,398.4 | 2,438.6 | 2,463.6 | 2,379.4 |
| 2016 | 2,388.8 | 2,381.5 | 2,381.8 | 2,390.4 | 2,392.3 | 2,400.7 | 2,407.9 | 2,418.2 | 2,408.3 | 2,427.0 | 2,479.6 | 2,499.7 | 2,414.7 |
| 2017 | 2,427.4 | 2,410.8 | 2,409.8 | 2,416.2 | 2,423.3 | 2,436.2 | 2,434.4 | 2,449.1 | 2,433.8 | 2,460.1 | 2,518.7 | 2,534.8 | 2,446.2 |
| 2018 | 2,459.2 | 2,448.4 | 2,448.7 | 2,455.5 | 2,466.5 | 2,474.6 | 2,476.5 | 2,488.8 | 2,482.5 | 2,497.3 | 2,559.3 | 2,568.6 | 2,485.5 |
| 2019 | 2,499.6 | 2,482.7 | 2,477.2 | 2,479.2 | 2,485.1 | 2,496.4 | 2,503.0 | 2,512.1 | 2,504.3 | 2,534.0 | 2,587.7 | 2,608.6 | 2,514.2 |
| **Wholesale Trade** | | | | | | | | | | | | | |
| 2011 | 485.2 | 488.4 | 491.4 | 495.5 | 498.7 | 501.9 | 503.3 | 505.4 | 507.5 | 509.0 | 510.1 | 513.5 | 500.8 |
| 2012 | 510.9 | 514.6 | 518.1 | 519.6 | 523.2 | 527.4 | 527.0 | 529.2 | 528.7 | 529.9 | 532.0 | 534.6 | 524.6 |
| 2013 | 531.2 | 535.1 | 537.5 | 537.5 | 539.4 | 542.5 | 543.3 | 544.9 | 544.7 | 546.9 | 549.3 | 550.5 | 541.9 |
| 2014 | 546.7 | 550.4 | 551.9 | 553.3 | 556.7 | 561.0 | 562.5 | 566.2 | 566.7 | 570.0 | 572.1 | 574.9 | 561.0 |
| | | | | | | | | | | | | | |
| 2015 | 571.8 | 573.8 | 573.8 | 573.3 | 574.0 | 575.3 | 575.1 | 575.5 | 573.3 | 570.8 | 569.6 | 569.1 | 573.0 |
| 2016 | 569.8 | 570.5 | 568.7 | 569.1 | 568.6 | 569.3 | 570.1 | 570.2 | 569.4 | 567.2 | 567.8 | 569.2 | 569.2 |
| 2017 | 566.0 | 568.0 | 569.7 | 572.4 | 575.5 | 580.4 | 580.0 | 582.0 | 581.0 | 581.9 | 583.3 | 585.9 | 577.2 |
| 2018 | 582.5 | 586.0 | 588.1 | 590.9 | 593.0 | 598.1 | 598.4 | 600.4 | 599.9 | 602.0 | 603.0 | 604.8 | 595.6 |
| 2019 | 601.9 | 605.3 | 605.0 | 606.1 | 607.9 | 611.0 | 612.1 | 612.5 | 610.1 | 614.5 | 617.9 | 620.1 | 610.4 |
| **Retail Trade** | | | | | | | | | | | | | |
| 2011 | 1,139.5 | 1,126.8 | 1,137.2 | 1,147.4 | 1,148.6 | 1,154.0 | 1,155.0 | 1,166.1 | 1,154.1 | 1,165.6 | 1,201.6 | 1,218.4 | 1,159.5 |
| 2012 | 1,168.2 | 1,154.2 | 1,158.3 | 1,165.2 | 1,171.1 | 1,177.4 | 1,180.2 | 1,189.4 | 1,180.9 | 1,194.5 | 1,241.9 | 1,252.0 | 1,186.1 |
| 2013 | 1,192.9 | 1,187.1 | 1,188.2 | 1,198.1 | 1,204.1 | 1,212.2 | 1,216.4 | 1,229.4 | 1,222.2 | 1,233.8 | 1,277.1 | 1,293.4 | 1,221.2 |
| 2014 | 1,237.2 | 1,230.4 | 1,232.5 | 1,238.1 | 1,240.7 | 1,250.4 | 1,252.4 | 1,261.0 | 1,253.1 | 1,265.5 | 1,307.1 | 1,325.2 | 1,257.8 |
| | | | | | | | | | | | | | |
| 2015 | 1,267.3 | 1,263.9 | 1,268.0 | 1,278.2 | 1,287.0 | 1,296.1 | 1,298.1 | 1,305.6 | 1,300.4 | 1,314.2 | 1,347.4 | 1,360.2 | 1,298.9 |
| 2016 | 1,304.8 | 1,299.6 | 1,301.9 | 1,309.4 | 1,310.8 | 1,315.4 | 1,320.1 | 1,328.6 | 1,314.5 | 1,331.9 | 1,372.8 | 1,381.1 | 1,324.2 |
| 2017 | 1,328.0 | 1,313.5 | 1,311.6 | 1,315.8 | 1,316.8 | 1,320.8 | 1,317.9 | 1,324.3 | 1,307.8 | 1,328.4 | 1,372.3 | 1,378.4 | 1,328.0 |
| 2018 | 1,327.4 | 1,313.8 | 1,311.4 | 1,314.5 | 1,320.3 | 1,320.6 | 1,322.6 | 1,329.0 | 1,320.3 | 1,326.7 | 1,372.2 | 1,374.5 | 1,329.4 |
| 2019 | 1,323.8 | 1,308.9 | 1,304.9 | 1,305.3 | 1,306.7 | 1,309.4 | 1,311.7 | 1,316.7 | 1,308.9 | 1,323.2 | 1,362.4 | 1,373.6 | 1,321.3 |
| **Transportation and Utilities** | | | | | | | | | | | | | |
| 2011 | 423.4 | 424.3 | 427.3 | 429.4 | 430.3 | 431.4 | 434.5 | 437.0 | 439.5 | 438.1 | 440.5 | 448.9 | 433.7 |
| 2012 | 438.9 | 441.3 | 444.6 | 445.4 | 447.6 | 451.1 | 450.9 | 454.4 | 454.6 | 454.3 | 458.4 | 464.7 | 450.5 |
| 2013 | 456.0 | 455.8 | 457.8 | 459.7 | 461.8 | 464.1 | 462.5 | 465.4 | 466.8 | 467.8 | 472.5 | 479.3 | 464.1 |
| 2014 | 469.9 | 466.5 | 469.0 | 472.7 | 477.2 | 479.8 | 480.2 | 485.1 | 487.7 | 493.5 | 500.0 | 513.4 | 482.9 |
| | | | | | | | | | | | | | |
| 2015 | 501.1 | 496.7 | 497.5 | 499.3 | 502.1 | 503.9 | 504.3 | 507.7 | 508.8 | 513.4 | 521.6 | 534.3 | 507.6 |
| 2016 | 514.2 | 511.4 | 511.2 | 511.9 | 512.9 | 516.0 | 517.7 | 519.4 | 524.4 | 527.9 | 539.0 | 549.4 | 521.3 |
| 2017 | 533.4 | 529.3 | 528.5 | 528.0 | 531.0 | 535.0 | 536.5 | 542.8 | 545.0 | 549.8 | 563.1 | 570.5 | 541.1 |
| 2018 | 549.3 | 548.6 | 549.2 | 550.1 | 553.2 | 555.9 | 555.5 | 559.4 | 562.3 | 568.6 | 584.1 | 589.3 | 560.5 |
| 2019 | 573.9 | 568.5 | 567.3 | 567.8 | 570.5 | 576.0 | 579.2 | 582.9 | 585.3 | 596.3 | 607.4 | 614.9 | 582.5 |
| **Information** | | | | | | | | | | | | | |
| 2011 | 194.1 | 193.7 | 194.1 | 194.4 | 195.3 | 196.0 | 197.1 | 196.1 | 194.8 | 194.7 | 195.9 | 196.5 | 195.2 |
| 2012 | 195.9 | 195.6 | 196.1 | 196.2 | 196.7 | 197.9 | 197.6 | 197.0 | 195.7 | 196.1 | 198.3 | 198.6 | 196.8 |
| 2013 | 196.4 | 196.9 | 197.7 | 199.0 | 200.4 | 201.9 | 202.3 | 202.4 | 200.2 | 201.3 | 203.7 | 204.6 | 200.6 |
| 2014 | 201.3 | 201.1 | 201.1 | 202.0 | 201.9 | 203.1 | 203.2 | 202.1 | 199.8 | 199.5 | 201.0 | 202.2 | 201.5 |
| | | | | | | | | | | | | | |
| 2015 | 198.2 | 197.7 | 197.8 | 199.8 | 201.0 | 201.8 | 202.4 | 201.9 | 199.3 | 199.6 | 201.6 | 203.1 | 200.4 |
| 2016 | 200.2 | 200.3 | 199.6 | 202.6 | 203.2 | 204.3 | 204.8 | 203.7 | 201.9 | 201.1 | 202.2 | 203.5 | 202.3 |
| 2017 | 201.6 | 202.0 | 203.5 | 203.3 | 203.0 | 204.2 | 204.2 | 203.2 | 201.0 | 202.6 | 203.8 | 205.2 | 203.1 |
| 2018 | 202.7 | 203.2 | 203.0 | 204.0 | 205.6 | 207.3 | 206.7 | 205.2 | 203.8 | 204.5 | 206.1 | 206.8 | 204.9 |
| 2019 | 205.0 | 206.3 | 207.3 | 208.8 | 209.6 | 211.1 | 209.5 | 209.6 | 207.5 | 209.1 | 209.2 | 210.6 | 208.6 |

# 1. Employment by Industry: Texas, 2011–2019—*Continued*

(Numbers in thousands, not seasonally adjusted)

| Industry and year | January | February | March | April | May | June | July | August | September | October | November | December | Annual average |
|---|---|---|---|---|---|---|---|---|---|---|---|---|---|
| **Financial Activities** | | | | | | | | | | | | | |
| 2011 | 629.1 | 631.4 | 634.5 | 636.2 | 637.5 | 641.3 | 644.0 | 645.0 | 645.7 | 647.2 | 648.0 | 651.4 | 640.9 |
| 2012 | 647.0 | 650.1 | 652.8 | 654.4 | 657.8 | 663.1 | 664.4 | 666.6 | 665.9 | 670.5 | 672.7 | 675.7 | 661.8 |
| 2013 | 668.5 | 673.0 | 675.8 | 677.0 | 680.1 | 685.3 | 689.2 | 690.7 | 689.1 | 691.6 | 693.7 | 694.3 | 684.0 |
| 2014 | 686.9 | 689.6 | 691.0 | 693.0 | 696.1 | 700.6 | 703.5 | 706.2 | 704.5 | 709.7 | 711.1 | 713.8 | 700.5 |
| 2015 | 707.5 | 709.8 | 710.9 | 712.8 | 715.6 | 720.6 | 723.1 | 724.0 | 722.5 | 725.4 | 726.3 | 727.7 | 718.9 |
| 2016 | 723.4 | 725.3 | 724.8 | 728.6 | 731.8 | 735.0 | 740.3 | 742.1 | 741.1 | 744.7 | 747.4 | 750.7 | 736.3 |
| 2017 | 745.5 | 748.6 | 750.4 | 753.0 | 756.4 | 762.6 | 765.1 | 766.2 | 767.4 | 771.2 | 770.7 | 772.9 | 760.8 |
| 2018 | 764.9 | 768.9 | 769.4 | 769.7 | 773.0 | 780.2 | 782.6 | 785.6 | 783.1 | 787.9 | 789.4 | 790.8 | 778.8 |
| 2019 | 784.2 | 788.9 | 789.9 | 792.7 | 796.1 | 802.9 | 807.3 | 810.4 | 808.5 | 808.8 | 808.0 | 814.4 | 801.0 |
| **Professional and Business Services** | | | | | | | | | | | | | |
| 2011 | 1,299.9 | 1,313.7 | 1,330.0 | 1,346.0 | 1,342.8 | 1,354.2 | 1,357.3 | 1,369.9 | 1,375.5 | 1,374.2 | 1,380.5 | 1,385.7 | 1,352.5 |
| 2012 | 1,366.0 | 1,382.6 | 1,397.9 | 1,408.9 | 1,415.7 | 1,426.9 | 1,424.2 | 1,445.2 | 1,443.2 | 1,450.3 | 1,461.8 | 1,458.9 | 1,423.5 |
| 2013 | 1,428.2 | 1,449.5 | 1,461.7 | 1,466.1 | 1,469.3 | 1,482.5 | 1,483.9 | 1,500.2 | 1,502.7 | 1,511.7 | 1,522.7 | 1,519.7 | 1,483.2 |
| 2014 | 1,491.1 | 1,507.6 | 1,522.0 | 1,540.6 | 1,547.2 | 1,556.1 | 1,560.3 | 1,577.0 | 1,575.6 | 1,593.6 | 1,599.1 | 1,599.0 | 1,555.8 |
| 2015 | 1,573.8 | 1,584.3 | 1,585.1 | 1,595.0 | 1,593.5 | 1,601.8 | 1,612.9 | 1,620.5 | 1,617.0 | 1,636.9 | 1,639.0 | 1,638.0 | 1,608.2 |
| 2016 | 1,608.2 | 1,619.4 | 1,618.1 | 1,634.1 | 1,627.4 | 1,631.1 | 1,645.4 | 1,653.2 | 1,655.5 | 1,663.4 | 1,667.3 | 1,656.9 | 1,640.0 |
| 2017 | 1,636.8 | 1,651.7 | 1,659.2 | 1,661.9 | 1,663.8 | 1,676.8 | 1,678.4 | 1,686.1 | 1,694.5 | 1,709.5 | 1,714.8 | 1,704.4 | 1,678.2 |
| 2018 | 1,683.6 | 1,705.4 | 1,710.7 | 1,716.3 | 1,720.6 | 1,737.6 | 1,745.6 | 1,759.8 | 1,750.6 | 1,774.6 | 1,781.4 | 1,774.4 | 1,738.4 |
| 2019 | 1,746.8 | 1,766.6 | 1,762.3 | 1,775.1 | 1,777.1 | 1,786.8 | 1,801.6 | 1,814.0 | 1,803.4 | 1,821.3 | 1,824.0 | 1,825.5 | 1,792.0 |
| **Education and Health Services** | | | | | | | | | | | | | |
| 2011 | 1,384.7 | 1,390.6 | 1,398.6 | 1,408.3 | 1,411.7 | 1,409.3 | 1,409.3 | 1,418.9 | 1,430.5 | 1,430.8 | 1,434.7 | 1,438.1 | 1,413.8 |
| 2012 | 1,417.8 | 1,430.4 | 1,436.6 | 1,436.2 | 1,441.9 | 1,440.9 | 1,433.4 | 1,450.5 | 1,460.0 | 1,466.3 | 1,471.7 | 1,476.2 | 1,446.8 |
| 2013 | 1,452.8 | 1,471.1 | 1,477.0 | 1,481.4 | 1,485.1 | 1,479.6 | 1,475.2 | 1,490.8 | 1,497.4 | 1,504.8 | 1,510.1 | 1,508.9 | 1,486.2 |
| 2014 | 1,489.3 | 1,502.2 | 1,506.1 | 1,514.1 | 1,520.7 | 1,514.0 | 1,509.3 | 1,524.8 | 1,531.5 | 1,543.6 | 1,550.0 | 1,552.5 | 1,521.5 |
| 2015 | 1,537.4 | 1,552.5 | 1,555.8 | 1,569.7 | 1,576.2 | 1,570.0 | 1,571.4 | 1,584.6 | 1,590.3 | 1,600.7 | 1,606.6 | 1,608.5 | 1,577.0 |
| 2016 | 1,589.8 | 1,605.1 | 1,606.6 | 1,615.0 | 1,620.6 | 1,610.3 | 1,616.8 | 1,634.4 | 1,643.7 | 1,649.3 | 1,654.3 | 1,657.2 | 1,625.3 |
| 2017 | 1,643.1 | 1,658.6 | 1,661.5 | 1,665.6 | 1,671.4 | 1,667.0 | 1,651.7 | 1,667.5 | 1,669.6 | 1,676.4 | 1,680.6 | 1,684.1 | 1,666.4 |
| 2018 | 1,665.4 | 1,682.5 | 1,684.1 | 1,689.5 | 1,694.5 | 1,692.0 | 1,688.6 | 1,706.3 | 1,709.3 | 1,720.3 | 1,726.0 | 1,727.6 | 1,698.8 |
| 2019 | 1,706.2 | 1,724.0 | 1,724.4 | 1,731.7 | 1,738.8 | 1,729.5 | 1,729.0 | 1,748.0 | 1,748.0 | 1,766.4 | 1,775.8 | 1,772.3 | 1,741.2 |
| **Leisure and Hospitality** | | | | | | | | | | | | | |
| 2011 | 983.4 | 996.8 | 1,028.7 | 1,045.8 | 1,061.4 | 1,074.3 | 1,061.4 | 1,064.2 | 1,055.5 | 1,043.0 | 1,042.9 | 1,039.9 | 1,041.4 |
| 2012 | 1,017.9 | 1,038.1 | 1,065.8 | 1,084.6 | 1,103.4 | 1,123.1 | 1,106.3 | 1,112.3 | 1,104.3 | 1,091.8 | 1,093.1 | 1,097.8 | 1,086.5 |
| 2013 | 1,072.2 | 1,098.0 | 1,122.3 | 1,141.0 | 1,160.5 | 1,177.2 | 1,165.2 | 1,165.2 | 1,153.3 | 1,140.6 | 1,142.1 | 1,139.3 | 1,139.7 |
| 2014 | 1,119.0 | 1,138.8 | 1,168.5 | 1,188.9 | 1,208.6 | 1,228.3 | 1,214.6 | 1,213.2 | 1,203.8 | 1,194.0 | 1,190.3 | 1,190.8 | 1,188.2 |
| 2015 | 1,165.7 | 1,191.6 | 1,212.2 | 1,237.8 | 1,259.4 | 1,279.4 | 1,272.4 | 1,271.6 | 1,262.8 | 1,253.8 | 1,249.4 | 1,248.1 | 1,242.0 |
| 2016 | 1,228.0 | 1,252.1 | 1,272.6 | 1,294.4 | 1,311.7 | 1,327.4 | 1,316.1 | 1,315.0 | 1,302.2 | 1,288.5 | 1,285.8 | 1,282.4 | 1,289.7 |
| 2017 | 1,260.7 | 1,278.9 | 1,304.8 | 1,320.6 | 1,341.0 | 1,358.9 | 1,350.6 | 1,348.1 | 1,321.5 | 1,317.9 | 1,315.0 | 1,316.3 | 1,319.5 |
| 2018 | 1,292.2 | 1,314.5 | 1,339.9 | 1,354.8 | 1,373.2 | 1,393.0 | 1,386.2 | 1,388.3 | 1,362.7 | 1,362.1 | 1,354.2 | 1,358.6 | 1,356.6 |
| 2019 | 1,332.4 | 1,357.3 | 1,378.1 | 1,391.4 | 1,408.7 | 1,427.1 | 1,422.6 | 1,417.6 | 1,399.0 | 1,407.3 | 1,394.4 | 1,393.2 | 1,394.1 |
| **Other Services** | | | | | | | | | | | | | |
| 2011 | 354.6 | 358.0 | 362.0 | 368.7 | 370.6 | 386.0 | 383.4 | 379.9 | 372.2 | 369.9 | 370.6 | 369.4 | 370.4 |
| 2012 | 367.1 | 370.5 | 374.0 | 382.2 | 385.2 | 402.3 | 399.2 | 396.5 | 387.3 | 387.6 | 388.2 | 387.8 | 385.7 |
| 2013 | 382.7 | 388.7 | 391.6 | 396.5 | 399.7 | 416.8 | 414.2 | 410.3 | 400.7 | 399.2 | 401.3 | 399.0 | 400.1 |
| 2014 | 395.9 | 401.1 | 403.8 | 410.6 | 414.9 | 430.2 | 426.2 | 422.7 | 411.4 | 413.5 | 413.6 | 411.6 | 413.0 |
| 2015 | 404.7 | 409.3 | 411.4 | 415.7 | 419.5 | 436.4 | 435.3 | 430.7 | 419.3 | 420.7 | 418.5 | 416.6 | 419.8 |
| 2016 | 411.9 | 416.6 | 417.2 | 420.9 | 427.3 | 436.9 | 432.3 | 428.5 | 423.2 | 423.6 | 422.6 | 421.1 | 423.5 |
| 2017 | 413.3 | 419.3 | 422.6 | 427.1 | 428.8 | 439.4 | 432.3 | 429.9 | 426.0 | 428.2 | 428.9 | 426.0 | 426.8 |
| 2018 | 418.1 | 422.6 | 426.2 | 432.2 | 437.6 | 448.2 | 442.1 | 441.2 | 437.2 | 443.5 | 441.6 | 436.7 | 435.6 |
| 2019 | 430.3 | 436.1 | 438.2 | 442.7 | 448.2 | 455.9 | 450.7 | 449.9 | 446.5 | 448.0 | 451.1 | 449.7 | 445.6 |
| **Government** | | | | | | | | | | | | | |
| 2011 | 1,884.8 | 1,902.2 | 1,903.9 | 1,898.3 | 1,901.5 | 1,866.3 | 1,772.5 | 1,761.2 | 1,817.9 | 1,847.1 | 1,851.6 | 1,842.1 | 1,854.1 |
| 2012 | 1,823.0 | 1,852.3 | 1,857.2 | 1,850.9 | 1,857.1 | 1,819.9 | 1,746.4 | 1,741.9 | 1,807.8 | 1,850.5 | 1,858.6 | 1,859.2 | 1,827.1 |
| 2013 | 1,829.0 | 1,862.0 | 1,868.3 | 1,863.0 | 1,868.1 | 1,835.4 | 1,765.9 | 1,757.1 | 1,828.4 | 1,869.8 | 1,881.0 | 1,874.7 | 1,841.9 |
| 2014 | 1,854.2 | 1,879.1 | 1,885.6 | 1,879.1 | 1,886.0 | 1,856.5 | 1,782.7 | 1,772.5 | 1,842.0 | 1,889.9 | 1,901.7 | 1,899.9 | 1,860.8 |
| 2015 | 1,872.7 | 1,899.4 | 1,903.0 | 1,898.3 | 1,905.6 | 1,881.9 | 1,808.5 | 1,803.7 | 1,872.1 | 1,915.3 | 1,927.4 | 1,928.4 | 1,884.7 |
| 2016 | 1,905.7 | 1,930.6 | 1,936.8 | 1,936.2 | 1,945.7 | 1,921.3 | 1,848.9 | 1,842.5 | 1,912.6 | 1,946.4 | 1,960.3 | 1,962.7 | 1,920.8 |
| 2017 | 1,931.1 | 1,963.1 | 1,970.8 | 1,967.5 | 1,971.4 | 1,942.3 | 1,860.1 | 1,850.5 | 1,914.7 | 1,959.1 | 1,972.7 | 1,971.2 | 1,939.5 |
| 2018 | 1,936.2 | 1,970.9 | 1,981.3 | 1,969.2 | 1,979.6 | 1,953.5 | 1,880.2 | 1,874.1 | 1,935.9 | 1,969.0 | 1,986.3 | 1,983.8 | 1,951.7 |
| 2019 | 1,949.1 | 1,983.9 | 1,992.1 | 1,982.4 | 1,993.5 | 1,970.1 | 1,899.9 | 1,900.7 | 1,962.8 | 2,001.6 | 2,015.3 | 2,010.7 | 1,971.8 |

## 2. Average Weekly Hours by Selected Industry: Texas, 2015–2019

(Not seasonally adjusted)

| Industry and year | January | February | March | April | May | June | July | August | September | October | November | December | Annual average |
|---|---|---|---|---|---|---|---|---|---|---|---|---|---|
| **Total Private** | | | | | | | | | | | | | |
| 2015 | 36.1 | 36.8 | 36.4 | 36.0 | 35.8 | 36.1 | 36.1 | 36.7 | 35.5 | 35.8 | 36.5 | 36.0 | 36.1 |
| 2016 | 35.8 | 35.8 | 35.3 | 35.6 | 36.2 | 36.0 | 35.9 | 35.8 | 35.8 | 36.4 | 35.6 | 35.8 | 35.8 |
| 2017 | 36.0 | 35.4 | 35.6 | 35.8 | 35.7 | 35.9 | 36.4 | 35.9 | 36.1 | 36.5 | 36.0 | 35.9 | 35.9 |
| 2018 | 35.4 | 35.9 | 36.0 | 36.6 | 36.0 | 36.2 | 36.7 | 36.2 | 36.4 | 36.2 | 36.3 | 36.8 | 36.2 |
| 2019 | 35.8 | 36.1 | 36.0 | 36.2 | 35.8 | 36.7 | 36.0 | 36.1 | 36.4 | 35.9 | 35.7 | 36.3 | 36.1 |
| **Goods-Producing** | | | | | | | | | | | | | |
| 2015 | 42.7 | 42.7 | 41.5 | 41.9 | 41.4 | 42.8 | 42.7 | 42.8 | 40.7 | 42.3 | 42.4 | 42.5 | 42.2 |
| 2016 | 41.9 | 41.9 | 40.1 | 41.9 | 42.6 | 42.5 | 42.3 | 42.3 | 42.5 | 43.0 | 41.8 | 42.3 | 42.1 |
| 2017 | 41.9 | 41.8 | 42.0 | 41.3 | 42.9 | 42.9 | 43.2 | 42.3 | 43.8 | 43.8 | 43.0 | 42.9 | 42.7 |
| 2018 | 42.0 | 42.9 | 43.1 | 43.6 | 43.2 | 43.5 | 43.4 | 43.4 | 42.4 | 43.8 | 44.1 | 44.3 | 43.3 |
| 2019 | 43.0 | 43.3 | 43.3 | 43.8 | 43.0 | 44.0 | 43.7 | 44.2 | 44.3 | 43.8 | 43.1 | 43.6 | 43.6 |
| **Construction** | | | | | | | | | | | | | |
| 2015 | 43.1 | 43.4 | 40.9 | 42.2 | 41.0 | 43.3 | 42.9 | 43.0 | 39.7 | 42.1 | 42.2 | 42.4 | 42.2 |
| 2016 | 42.0 | 41.8 | 39.1 | 41.9 | 43.0 | 43.3 | 43.1 | 43.2 | 43.4 | 43.9 | 42.4 | 42.6 | 42.5 |
| 2017 | 42.2 | 42.1 | 42.0 | 40.2 | 42.8 | 42.8 | 43.0 | 42.2 | 43.8 | 43.8 | 43.1 | 42.7 | 42.6 |
| 2018 | 41.6 | 42.5 | 43.6 | 43.7 | 43.2 | 43.4 | 43.1 | 42.4 | 40.5 | 43.3 | 43.9 | 43.6 | 42.9 |
| 2019 | 42.9 | 42.9 | 42.5 | 43.1 | 41.9 | 43.5 | 43.5 | 43.9 | 44.1 | 43.4 | 42.5 | 43.2 | 43.1 |
| **Manufacturing** | | | | | | | | | | | | | |
| 2015 | 41.6 | 41.5 | 41.4 | 41.3 | 41.3 | 41.4 | 41.5 | 41.3 | 40.6 | 41.5 | 41.3 | 41.6 | 41.4 |
| 2016 | 41.0 | 41.5 | 40.9 | 41.5 | 41.7 | 41.6 | 41.2 | 41.1 | 41.5 | 41.6 | 40.7 | 41.7 | 41.3 |
| 2017 | 40.7 | 40.7 | 41.1 | 41.2 | 41.9 | 42.2 | 42.2 | 41.2 | 42.6 | 42.3 | 42.0 | 41.8 | 41.7 |
| 2018 | 41.0 | 41.9 | 41.5 | 42.3 | 42.1 | 42.5 | 42.3 | 43.4 | 43.1 | 43.3 | 43.3 | 44.0 | 42.6 |
| 2019 | 42.4 | 42.8 | 43.3 | 43.6 | 43.2 | 43.6 | 42.9 | 43.6 | 43.4 | 43.1 | 42.7 | 43.0 | 43.1 |
| **Trade, Transportation, and Utilities** | | | | | | | | | | | | | |
| 2015 | 35.8 | 36.7 | 36.6 | 35.9 | 36.0 | 36.0 | 36.3 | 36.6 | 35.9 | 35.9 | 36.4 | 36.2 | 36.2 |
| 2016 | 35.6 | 35.7 | 35.4 | 35.5 | 35.8 | 35.9 | 35.8 | 35.6 | 35.9 | 35.9 | 35.5 | 35.9 | 35.7 |
| 2017 | 35.4 | 35.4 | 35.3 | 36.0 | 35.7 | 35.9 | 36.3 | 35.9 | 36.0 | 36.3 | 36.0 | 36.0 | 35.9 |
| 2018 | 35.1 | 35.5 | 35.8 | 36.1 | 35.8 | 36.1 | 36.5 | 36.0 | 36.2 | 35.4 | 35.1 | 35.3 | 35.7 |
| 2019 | 34.2 | 34.6 | 34.7 | 34.7 | 34.6 | 35.2 | 35.3 | 35.1 | 35.3 | 34.9 | 34.7 | 35.7 | 34.9 |
| **Financial Activities** | | | | | | | | | | | | | |
| 2015 | 38.2 | 39.7 | 39.6 | 38.4 | 38.3 | 38.4 | 38.7 | 39.9 | 38.2 | 38.4 | 39.8 | 38.4 | 38.8 |
| 2016 | 38.8 | 38.7 | 38.5 | 38.7 | 40.0 | 38.4 | 38.5 | 38.5 | 38.4 | 40.0 | 38.5 | 38.4 | 38.8 |
| 2017 | 39.9 | 38.3 | 38.3 | 39.3 | 37.9 | 38.1 | 39.4 | 38.2 | 38.2 | 39.3 | 38.3 | 38.3 | 38.6 |
| 2018 | 38.2 | 38.3 | 37.8 | 39.1 | 37.7 | 37.9 | 39.2 | 38.1 | 39.2 | 38.1 | 38.4 | 39.3 | 38.4 |
| 2019 | 38.3 | 38.5 | 38.5 | 38.0 | 37.9 | 39.1 | 38.0 | 38.1 | 39.0 | 38.0 | 38.0 | 38.8 | 38.4 |
| **Professional and Business Services** | | | | | | | | | | | | | |
| 2015 | 36.9 | 37.9 | 37.9 | 37.3 | 37.2 | 37.5 | 37.4 | 37.6 | 36.3 | 36.8 | 37.6 | 36.9 | 37.3 |
| 2016 | 36.6 | 36.6 | 36.4 | 36.6 | 37.7 | 37.1 | 36.9 | 37.0 | 36.7 | 37.8 | 36.6 | 36.8 | 36.9 |
| 2017 | 37.5 | 36.8 | 36.7 | 37.6 | 37.2 | 37.3 | 37.9 | 37.2 | 37.1 | 37.7 | 36.8 | 36.5 | 37.2 |
| 2018 | 36.3 | 36.6 | 36.9 | 37.7 | 36.6 | 36.5 | 37.1 | 36.6 | 37.1 | 36.9 | 36.8 | 37.5 | 36.9 |
| 2019 | 36.1 | 36.7 | 36.4 | 36.9 | 36.6 | 37.7 | 36.6 | 37.3 | 37.7 | 37.1 | 37.0 | 37.3 | 37.0 |
| **Education and Health Services** | | | | | | | | | | | | | |
| 2015 | 32.9 | 33.4 | 33.0 | 32.8 | 32.6 | 32.6 | 32.6 | 33.3 | 32.3 | 32.2 | 33.2 | 32.4 | 32.8 |
| 2016 | 32.4 | 32.0 | 31.9 | 32.2 | 32.8 | 32.5 | 32.4 | 32.5 | 32.7 | 33.0 | 32.7 | 32.8 | 32.5 |
| 2017 | 33.6 | 32.9 | 32.7 | 33.4 | 32.9 | 32.9 | 33.5 | 33.0 | 33.2 | 33.7 | 33.4 | 33.2 | 33.2 |
| 2018 | 33.1 | 33.4 | 32.9 | 33.8 | 33.1 | 33.0 | 33.8 | 32.8 | 33.8 | 32.9 | 33.0 | 34.3 | 33.3 |
| 2019 | 33.5 | 33.4 | 32.9 | 33.1 | 33.0 | 33.7 | 32.8 | 32.9 | 33.3 | 32.6 | 32.7 | 33.3 | 33.1 |
| **Leisure and Hospitality** | | | | | | | | | | | | | |
| 2015 | 27.6 | 28.7 | 29.0 | 28.2 | 28.1 | 28.4 | 28.4 | 28.7 | 27.6 | 27.8 | 28.3 | 28.1 | 28.2 |
| 2016 | 27.8 | 28.4 | 28.4 | 28.0 | 28.7 | 28.6 | 28.6 | 28.6 | 28.1 | 28.8 | 28.5 | 28.1 | 28.4 |
| 2017 | 28.0 | 27.8 | 28.4 | 28.4 | 27.9 | 28.2 | 28.3 | 28.0 | 27.9 | 28.3 | 27.9 | 28.0 | 28.1 |
| 2018 | 27.2 | 27.8 | 28.3 | 28.2 | 28.1 | 28.2 | 28.3 | 28.2 | 28.1 | 27.8 | 27.9 | 28.3 | 28.0 |
| 2019 | 27.6 | 28.0 | 28.3 | 28.1 | 27.9 | 28.7 | 27.8 | 27.7 | 27.8 | 27.9 | 27.7 | 28.1 | 28.0 |
| **Other Services** | | | | | | | | | | | | | |
| 2015 | 32.8 | 34.1 | 33.3 | 32.6 | 32.7 | 32.2 | 32.3 | 33.6 | 32.5 | 32.6 | 34.0 | 33.8 | 33.0 |
| 2016 | 33.3 | 34.0 | 34.0 | 34.0 | 34.7 | 34.0 | 34.1 | 33.7 | 33.3 | 33.9 | 33.4 | 33.7 | 33.8 |
| 2017 | 33.9 | 33.3 | 33.6 | 32.8 | 33.2 | 32.9 | 32.9 | 33.3 | 33.0 | 34.0 | 33.3 | 33.2 | 33.3 |
| 2018 | 32.8 | 33.8 | 34.8 | 35.2 | 34.2 | 34.3 | 35.0 | 34.4 | 34.6 | 34.9 | 34.7 | 35.5 | 34.5 |
| 2019 | 35.2 | 35.6 | 35.5 | 35.3 | 34.5 | 35.9 | 35.1 | 35.3 | 34.8 | 34.0 | 33.7 | 34.5 | 34.9 |

# 3. Average Hourly Earnings by Selected Industry: Texas, 2015–2019

(Dollars, not seasonally adjusted)

| Industry and year | January | February | March | April | May | June | July | August | September | October | November | December | Annual average |
|---|---|---|---|---|---|---|---|---|---|---|---|---|---|
| **Total Private** | | | | | | | | | | | | | |
| 2015 | 24.36 | 24.56 | 24.46 | 24.30 | 24.28 | 24.16 | 24.13 | 24.52 | 24.36 | 24.50 | 24.62 | 24.35 | 24.39 |
| 2016 | 24.62 | 24.46 | 24.53 | 24.43 | 24.67 | 24.31 | 24.39 | 24.42 | 24.58 | 25.04 | 24.79 | 24.85 | 24.59 |
| 2017 | 25.37 | 25.18 | 25.14 | 25.62 | 25.26 | 25.04 | 25.57 | 25.24 | 25.48 | 25.82 | 25.60 | 25.68 | 25.42 |
| 2018 | 25.74 | 25.70 | 25.62 | 25.86 | 25.56 | 25.58 | 26.01 | 25.85 | 26.22 | 26.03 | 26.17 | 26.56 | 25.91 |
| 2019 | 26.33 | 26.29 | 26.09 | 26.07 | 26.08 | 26.07 | 25.92 | 25.96 | 26.31 | 26.22 | 26.45 | 26.83 | 26.22 |
| **Goods-Producing** | | | | | | | | | | | | | |
| 2015 | 26.44 | 26.74 | 26.86 | 26.64 | 26.71 | 26.42 | 26.28 | 26.64 | 26.60 | 26.67 | 26.91 | 26.89 | 26.65 |
| 2016 | 27.13 | 26.96 | 27.46 | 27.21 | 27.74 | 27.41 | 27.41 | 27.25 | 27.45 | 27.72 | 27.77 | 27.72 | 27.44 |
| 2017 | 28.06 | 27.69 | 27.73 | 27.94 | 27.71 | 27.61 | 28.17 | 27.96 | 28.11 | 28.46 | 28.42 | 28.86 | 28.07 |
| 2018 | 28.89 | 28.83 | 29.13 | 29.16 | 28.74 | 28.82 | 29.08 | 28.71 | 29.16 | 29.05 | 28.64 | 28.83 | 28.92 |
| 2019 | 28.76 | 28.68 | 28.81 | 28.91 | 28.87 | 28.81 | 28.78 | 28.74 | 29.19 | 29.57 | 29.45 | 30.01 | 29.05 |
| **Construction** | | | | | | | | | | | | | |
| 2015 | 24.84 | 25.10 | 25.27 | 25.06 | 25.29 | 24.99 | 24.47 | 24.86 | 24.69 | 24.97 | 24.99 | 25.05 | 24.96 |
| 2016 | 25.48 | 25.24 | 25.94 | 25.55 | 25.72 | 25.60 | 25.25 | 25.39 | 25.38 | 25.26 | 25.48 | 25.29 | 25.46 |
| 2017 | 25.59 | 25.33 | 25.39 | 25.38 | 25.61 | 25.84 | 26.29 | 26.20 | 26.44 | 26.83 | 26.70 | 27.27 | 26.09 |
| 2018 | 27.48 | 27.75 | 27.96 | 28.16 | 27.58 | 27.68 | 27.90 | 27.67 | 28.11 | 28.21 | 27.97 | 28.15 | 27.89 |
| 2019 | 28.11 | 28.21 | 28.39 | 28.23 | 28.24 | 27.80 | 27.65 | 27.87 | 28.22 | 28.44 | 28.30 | 28.66 | 28.18 |
| **Manufacturing** | | | | | | | | | | | | | |
| 2015 | 26.33 | 26.67 | 26.55 | 26.59 | 26.30 | 26.21 | 26.35 | 26.77 | 26.96 | 26.88 | 27.06 | 27.08 | 26.64 |
| 2016 | 27.24 | 27.11 | 27.37 | 27.48 | 27.84 | 27.63 | 28.09 | 27.61 | 27.86 | 28.35 | 28.25 | 28.07 | 27.74 |
| 2017 | 27.91 | 27.57 | 27.72 | 27.74 | 27.52 | 26.89 | 27.49 | 27.23 | 27.40 | 27.51 | 27.64 | 28.07 | 27.56 |
| 2018 | 28.13 | 27.63 | 27.82 | 28.05 | 27.89 | 27.96 | 28.32 | 27.87 | 28.20 | 28.17 | 28.09 | 27.93 | 28.01 |
| 2019 | 27.80 | 27.73 | 27.83 | 28.30 | 28.31 | 28.46 | 28.48 | 28.16 | 28.51 | 29.00 | 28.91 | 29.56 | 28.42 |
| **Trade, Transportation, and Utilities** | | | | | | | | | | | | | |
| 2015 | 22.11 | 22.41 | 22.34 | 22.47 | 22.29 | 22.29 | 22.34 | 22.70 | 22.62 | 22.54 | 22.35 | 22.26 | 22.39 |
| 2016 | 22.68 | 22.58 | 22.98 | 22.72 | 22.71 | 22.42 | 22.30 | 22.20 | 22.24 | 22.70 | 22.23 | 22.26 | 22.50 |
| 2017 | 22.91 | 22.47 | 22.27 | 22.76 | 22.27 | 22.04 | 22.48 | 22.05 | 22.41 | 22.68 | 22.46 | 22.33 | 22.43 |
| 2018 | 22.51 | 22.42 | 22.46 | 22.96 | 22.74 | 22.78 | 23.11 | 22.86 | 23.57 | 23.43 | 23.63 | 23.87 | 23.03 |
| 2019 | 23.48 | 23.56 | 23.53 | 23.51 | 23.27 | 23.13 | 23.14 | 23.17 | 23.42 | 23.17 | 23.20 | 23.61 | 23.35 |
| **Financial Activities** | | | | | | | | | | | | | |
| 2015 | 27.59 | 28.17 | 28.53 | 28.37 | 28.27 | 28.14 | 28.17 | 28.87 | 28.27 | 28.37 | 28.96 | 28.62 | 28.37 |
| 2016 | 29.00 | 28.80 | 28.97 | 28.77 | 29.34 | 28.57 | 29.06 | 29.04 | 29.11 | 30.18 | 29.76 | 29.80 | 29.21 |
| 2017 | 30.24 | 29.91 | 30.17 | 30.65 | 29.58 | 29.14 | 29.76 | 29.85 | 29.84 | 30.51 | 29.94 | 30.07 | 29.97 |
| 2018 | 30.35 | 30.68 | 30.69 | 30.19 | 29.96 | 29.81 | 30.74 | 30.78 | 31.18 | 30.46 | 30.70 | 31.31 | 30.58 |
| 2019 | 31.30 | 30.94 | 30.64 | 30.91 | 31.22 | 31.32 | 30.69 | 30.85 | 30.95 | 30.61 | 31.39 | 31.96 | 31.07 |
| **Professional and Business Services** | | | | | | | | | | | | | |
| 2015 | 28.70 | 29.01 | 28.94 | 28.57 | 28.55 | 28.44 | 28.74 | 29.17 | 28.71 | 28.78 | 29.18 | 28.74 | 28.80 |
| 2016 | 29.29 | 29.29 | 29.17 | 29.14 | 29.45 | 28.98 | 29.18 | 28.83 | 29.13 | 29.90 | 29.47 | 29.32 | 29.26 |
| 2017 | 30.11 | 29.80 | 29.54 | 30.20 | 29.50 | 29.24 | 30.21 | 29.24 | 29.63 | 30.15 | 29.76 | 29.82 | 29.77 |
| 2018 | 29.77 | 29.53 | 29.37 | 29.84 | 29.40 | 29.45 | 30.09 | 29.57 | 30.34 | 29.68 | 30.06 | 30.81 | 29.83 |
| 2019 | 30.56 | 30.23 | 30.18 | 29.89 | 30.21 | 30.69 | 30.43 | 30.28 | 31.49 | 31.11 | 31.31 | 31.53 | 30.67 |
| **Education and Health Services** | | | | | | | | | | | | | |
| 2015 | 24.13 | 24.26 | 24.36 | 24.10 | 24.40 | 24.35 | 24.40 | 24.45 | 24.44 | 24.71 | 24.57 | 24.58 | 24.40 |
| 2016 | 24.56 | 24.64 | 24.55 | 24.53 | 24.36 | 24.37 | 24.38 | 24.30 | 24.39 | 24.59 | 24.62 | 24.72 | 24.50 |
| 2017 | 24.66 | 24.92 | 24.97 | 25.05 | 25.46 | 25.36 | 25.47 | 25.49 | 25.57 | 25.59 | 25.59 | 25.34 | 25.29 |
| 2018 | 24.98 | 24.87 | 24.81 | 24.74 | 24.67 | 24.70 | 25.02 | 25.14 | 24.77 | 24.98 | 25.18 | 25.02 | 24.91 |
| 2019 | 24.93 | 25.00 | 24.84 | 24.64 | 24.54 | 24.46 | 24.47 | 24.40 | 24.11 | 24.31 | 24.24 | 24.57 | 24.54 |
| **Leisure and Hospitality** | | | | | | | | | | | | | |
| 2015 | 12.65 | 12.81 | 12.61 | 12.71 | 12.78 | 12.61 | 12.47 | 12.58 | 12.69 | 12.79 | 12.83 | 12.92 | 12.70 |
| 2016 | 12.88 | 12.92 | 12.86 | 12.88 | 12.89 | 12.73 | 12.76 | 12.76 | 12.89 | 12.97 | 12.97 | 13.21 | 12.89 |
| 2017 | 13.01 | 13.07 | 12.90 | 12.94 | 13.00 | 12.83 | 12.82 | 12.93 | 13.07 | 13.11 | 13.08 | 13.45 | 13.02 |
| 2018 | 13.30 | 13.31 | 13.23 | 13.48 | 13.44 | 13.38 | 13.49 | 13.58 | 13.77 | 13.93 | 14.04 | 14.40 | 13.61 |
| 2019 | 14.09 | 14.26 | 14.07 | 14.21 | 14.25 | 14.00 | 13.93 | 14.09 | 14.24 | 14.25 | 14.32 | 14.47 | 14.18 |
| **Other Services** | | | | | | | | | | | | | |
| 2015 | 21.21 | 20.86 | 20.98 | 20.55 | 20.40 | 20.09 | 19.61 | 19.62 | 19.49 | 19.47 | 19.40 | 19.31 | 20.07 |
| 2016 | 19.62 | 19.53 | 19.45 | 19.41 | 19.26 | 19.17 | 18.89 | 19.39 | 19.59 | 19.98 | 19.62 | 19.98 | 19.49 |
| 2017 | 20.42 | 20.48 | 20.49 | 21.19 | 20.61 | 20.91 | 21.25 | 21.04 | 21.33 | 21.91 | 21.49 | 21.83 | 21.08 |
| 2018 | 22.12 | 22.03 | 21.71 | 22.38 | 22.19 | 21.76 | 21.96 | 22.13 | 23.11 | 23.03 | 23.07 | 23.47 | 22.42 |
| 2019 | 23.00 | 23.24 | 23.30 | 22.96 | 22.74 | 22.61 | 22.78 | 23.19 | 23.69 | 23.50 | 23.40 | 23.82 | 23.18 |

## 4. Average Weekly Earnings by Selected Industry: Texas, 2015–2019

(Dollars, not seasonally adjusted)

| Industry and year | January | February | March | April | May | June | July | August | September | October | November | December | Annual average |
|---|---|---|---|---|---|---|---|---|---|---|---|---|---|
| **Total Private** | | | | | | | | | | | | | |
| 2015 | 879.40 | 903.81 | 890.34 | 874.80 | 869.22 | 872.18 | 871.09 | 899.88 | 864.78 | 877.10 | 898.63 | 876.60 | 880.48 |
| 2016 | 881.40 | 875.67 | 865.91 | 869.71 | 893.05 | 875.52 | 875.96 | 874.24 | 879.96 | 911.46 | 882.52 | 889.63 | 880.32 |
| 2017 | 913.32 | 891.37 | 894.98 | 917.20 | 901.78 | 898.94 | 930.75 | 906.12 | 919.83 | 942.43 | 921.60 | 921.91 | 912.58 |
| 2018 | 911.20 | 922.63 | 922.68 | 946.48 | 920.52 | 926.00 | 954.57 | 935.77 | 954.41 | 942.29 | 949.97 | 977.41 | 937.94 |
| 2019 | 942.61 | 949.07 | 939.24 | 943.73 | 933.66 | 956.77 | 933.12 | 937.16 | 957.68 | 941.30 | 944.27 | 973.93 | 946.54 |
| **Goods-Producing** | | | | | | | | | | | | | |
| 2015 | 1,128.99 | 1,141.80 | 1,114.69 | 1,116.22 | 1,105.79 | 1,130.78 | 1,122.16 | 1,140.19 | 1,082.62 | 1,128.14 | 1,140.98 | 1,142.83 | 1,124.63 |
| 2016 | 1,136.75 | 1,129.62 | 1,101.15 | 1,140.52 | 1,181.72 | 1,164.93 | 1,159.44 | 1,152.68 | 1,166.63 | 1,191.96 | 1,160.79 | 1,172.13 | 1,155.22 |
| 2017 | 1,175.71 | 1,157.44 | 1,164.66 | 1,153.92 | 1,188.76 | 1,184.47 | 1,216.94 | 1,182.71 | 1,231.22 | 1,246.55 | 1,222.06 | 1,238.09 | 1,198.59 |
| 2018 | 1,213.38 | 1,236.81 | 1,255.50 | 1,271.38 | 1,241.57 | 1,254.11 | 1,262.51 | 1,246.45 | 1,236.38 | 1,272.39 | 1,263.02 | 1,277.17 | 1,252.24 |
| 2019 | 1,236.68 | 1,241.84 | 1,247.47 | 1,266.26 | 1,241.41 | 1,267.64 | 1,257.69 | 1,270.31 | 1,293.12 | 1,295.17 | 1,269.30 | 1,308.44 | 1,266.58 |
| **Construction** | | | | | | | | | | | | | |
| 2015 | 1,070.60 | 1,089.34 | 1,033.54 | 1,057.53 | 1,036.89 | 1,082.07 | 1,049.76 | 1,068.98 | 980.19 | 1,051.24 | 1,055.00 | 1,062.54 | 1,053.31 |
| 2016 | 1,070.16 | 1,055.45 | 1,014.65 | 1,070.96 | 1,105.96 | 1,108.48 | 1,088.28 | 1,096.85 | 1,101.06 | 1,108.91 | 1,080.35 | 1,077.35 | 1,082.05 |
| 2017 | 1,079.90 | 1,066.39 | 1,066.38 | 1,020.28 | 1,096.11 | 1,105.95 | 1,130.47 | 1,105.64 | 1,158.07 | 1,175.15 | 1,150.77 | 1,164.43 | 1,111.43 |
| 2018 | 1,143.17 | 1,179.38 | 1,219.06 | 1,230.59 | 1,191.46 | 1,201.31 | 1,202.49 | 1,173.21 | 1,138.46 | 1,221.49 | 1,227.88 | 1,227.34 | 1,196.48 |
| 2019 | 1,205.92 | 1,210.21 | 1,206.58 | 1,216.71 | 1,183.26 | 1,209.30 | 1,202.78 | 1,223.49 | 1,244.50 | 1,234.30 | 1,202.75 | 1,238.11 | 1,214.56 |
| **Manufacturing** | | | | | | | | | | | | | |
| 2015 | 1,095.33 | 1,106.81 | 1,099.17 | 1,098.17 | 1,086.19 | 1,085.09 | 1,093.53 | 1,105.60 | 1,094.58 | 1,115.52 | 1,117.58 | 1,126.53 | 1,102.90 |
| 2016 | 1,116.84 | 1,125.07 | 1,119.43 | 1,140.42 | 1,160.93 | 1,149.41 | 1,157.31 | 1,134.77 | 1,156.19 | 1,179.36 | 1,149.78 | 1,170.52 | 1,145.66 |
| 2017 | 1,135.94 | 1,122.10 | 1,139.29 | 1,142.89 | 1,153.09 | 1,134.76 | 1,160.08 | 1,121.88 | 1,167.24 | 1,163.67 | 1,160.88 | 1,173.33 | 1,149.25 |
| 2018 | 1,153.33 | 1,157.70 | 1,154.53 | 1,186.52 | 1,174.17 | 1,188.30 | 1,197.94 | 1,209.56 | 1,215.42 | 1,219.76 | 1,216.30 | 1,228.92 | 1,193.23 |
| 2019 | 1,178.72 | 1,186.84 | 1,205.04 | 1,233.88 | 1,222.99 | 1,240.86 | 1,221.79 | 1,227.78 | 1,237.33 | 1,249.90 | 1,234.46 | 1,271.08 | 1,224.90 |
| **Trade, Transportation, and Utilities** | | | | | | | | | | | | | |
| 2015 | 791.54 | 822.45 | 817.64 | 806.67 | 802.44 | 802.44 | 810.94 | 830.82 | 812.06 | 809.19 | 813.54 | 805.81 | 810.52 |
| 2016 | 807.41 | 806.11 | 813.49 | 806.56 | 813.02 | 804.88 | 798.34 | 790.32 | 798.42 | 814.93 | 789.17 | 799.13 | 803.25 |
| 2017 | 811.01 | 795.44 | 786.13 | 819.36 | 795.04 | 791.24 | 816.02 | 791.60 | 806.76 | 823.28 | 808.56 | 803.88 | 805.24 |
| 2018 | 790.10 | 795.91 | 804.07 | 828.86 | 814.09 | 822.36 | 843.52 | 822.96 | 853.23 | 829.42 | 829.41 | 842.61 | 822.17 |
| 2019 | 803.02 | 815.18 | 816.49 | 815.80 | 805.14 | 814.18 | 816.84 | 813.27 | 826.73 | 808.63 | 805.04 | 842.88 | 814.92 |
| **Financial Activities** | | | | | | | | | | | | | |
| 2015 | 1,053.94 | 1,118.35 | 1,129.79 | 1,089.41 | 1,082.74 | 1,080.58 | 1,090.18 | 1,151.91 | 1,079.91 | 1,089.41 | 1,152.61 | 1,099.01 | 1,100.76 |
| 2016 | 1,125.20 | 1,114.56 | 1,115.35 | 1,113.40 | 1,173.60 | 1,097.09 | 1,118.81 | 1,118.04 | 1,117.82 | 1,207.20 | 1,145.76 | 1,144.32 | 1,133.35 |
| 2017 | 1,206.58 | 1,145.55 | 1,155.51 | 1,204.55 | 1,121.08 | 1,110.23 | 1,172.54 | 1,140.27 | 1,139.89 | 1,199.04 | 1,146.70 | 1,151.68 | 1,156.84 |
| 2018 | 1,159.37 | 1,175.04 | 1,160.08 | 1,180.43 | 1,129.49 | 1,129.80 | 1,205.01 | 1,172.72 | 1,222.26 | 1,160.53 | 1,178.88 | 1,230.64 | 1,174.27 |
| 2019 | 1,198.79 | 1,191.19 | 1,179.64 | 1,174.58 | 1,183.24 | 1,224.61 | 1,166.22 | 1,175.39 | 1,207.05 | 1,163.18 | 1,192.82 | 1,240.05 | 1,193.09 |
| **Professional and Business Services** | | | | | | | | | | | | | |
| 2015 | 1,059.03 | 1,099.48 | 1,096.83 | 1,065.66 | 1,062.06 | 1,066.50 | 1,074.88 | 1,096.79 | 1,042.17 | 1,059.10 | 1,097.17 | 1,060.51 | 1,074.24 |
| 2016 | 1,072.01 | 1,072.01 | 1,061.79 | 1,066.52 | 1,110.27 | 1,075.16 | 1,076.74 | 1,066.71 | 1,069.07 | 1,130.22 | 1,078.60 | 1,078.98 | 1,079.69 |
| 2017 | 1,129.13 | 1,096.64 | 1,084.12 | 1,135.52 | 1,097.40 | 1,090.65 | 1,144.96 | 1,087.73 | 1,099.27 | 1,136.66 | 1,095.17 | 1,088.43 | 1,107.44 |
| 2018 | 1,080.65 | 1,080.80 | 1,083.75 | 1,124.97 | 1,076.04 | 1,074.93 | 1,116.34 | 1,082.26 | 1,125.61 | 1,095.19 | 1,106.21 | 1,155.38 | 1,100.73 |
| 2019 | 1,103.22 | 1,109.44 | 1,098.55 | 1,102.94 | 1,105.69 | 1,157.01 | 1,113.74 | 1,129.44 | 1,187.17 | 1,154.18 | 1,158.47 | 1,176.07 | 1,134.79 |
| **Education and Health Services** | | | | | | | | | | | | | |
| 2015 | 793.88 | 810.28 | 803.88 | 790.48 | 795.44 | 793.81 | 795.44 | 814.19 | 789.41 | 795.66 | 815.72 | 796.72 | 800.32 |
| 2016 | 795.74 | 788.48 | 783.15 | 789.87 | 799.01 | 792.03 | 789.91 | 789.75 | 797.55 | 811.47 | 805.07 | 810.82 | 796.25 |
| 2017 | 828.58 | 819.87 | 816.52 | 836.67 | 837.63 | 834.34 | 853.25 | 841.17 | 848.92 | 862.38 | 854.71 | 841.29 | 839.63 |
| 2018 | 826.84 | 830.66 | 816.25 | 836.21 | 816.58 | 815.10 | 845.68 | 824.59 | 837.23 | 821.84 | 830.94 | 858.19 | 829.50 |
| 2019 | 835.16 | 835.00 | 817.24 | 815.58 | 809.82 | 824.30 | 802.62 | 802.76 | 802.86 | 792.51 | 792.65 | 818.18 | 812.27 |
| **Leisure and Hospitality** | | | | | | | | | | | | | |
| 2015 | 349.14 | 367.65 | 365.69 | 358.42 | 359.12 | 358.12 | 354.15 | 361.05 | 350.24 | 355.56 | 362.81 | 363.05 | 358.14 |
| 2016 | 358.06 | 366.64 | 364.94 | 360.64 | 370.23 | 364.36 | 364.94 | 364.65 | 361.93 | 373.25 | 369.65 | 371.20 | 366.08 |
| 2017 | 364.28 | 363.35 | 366.36 | 367.50 | 362.70 | 361.81 | 362.81 | 362.04 | 364.65 | 371.01 | 364.93 | 376.60 | 365.86 |
| 2018 | 361.76 | 370.02 | 374.41 | 380.14 | 377.38 | 377.32 | 381.77 | 382.96 | 386.94 | 387.25 | 391.72 | 407.52 | 381.08 |
| 2019 | 388.88 | 399.28 | 398.18 | 399.30 | 397.58 | 401.80 | 387.25 | 390.29 | 395.87 | 397.58 | 396.66 | 406.61 | 397.04 |
| **Other Services** | | | | | | | | | | | | | |
| 2015 | 695.69 | 711.33 | 698.63 | 669.93 | 667.08 | 646.90 | 633.40 | 659.23 | 633.43 | 634.72 | 659.60 | 652.68 | 662.31 |
| 2016 | 653.35 | 664.02 | 661.30 | 659.94 | 668.32 | 651.78 | 644.15 | 653.44 | 652.35 | 677.32 | 655.31 | 673.33 | 658.76 |
| 2017 | 692.24 | 681.98 | 688.46 | 695.03 | 684.25 | 687.94 | 699.13 | 700.63 | 703.89 | 744.94 | 715.62 | 724.76 | 701.96 |
| 2018 | 725.54 | 744.61 | 755.51 | 787.78 | 758.90 | 746.37 | 768.60 | 761.27 | 799.61 | 803.75 | 800.53 | 833.19 | 773.49 |
| 2019 | 809.60 | 827.34 | 827.15 | 810.49 | 784.53 | 811.70 | 799.58 | 818.61 | 824.41 | 799.00 | 788.58 | 821.79 | 808.98 |

# UTAH
## *At a Glance*

Population:
  2010 census: 2,763,885
  2019 estimate: 3,205,958

Percent change in population:
  2010–2019: 16.0%

Percent change in total nonfarm employment:
  2011–2019:  29.3%

Industry with the largest growth in employment, 2011–2019 (percent):
  Construction, 68.5%

Industry with the largest decline or smallest growth in employment, 2011–2019 (percent):
  Mining and logging, -19.7%

Civilian labor force:
  2010: 1,356,097
  2019: 1,607,688

Unemployment rate and rank among states (highest to lowest):
  2010: 7.8%, 37th
  2019: 2.6%, 48th

Over-the-year change in unemployment rates:
  2017–2018: -0.3%
  2018–2019: -0.4%

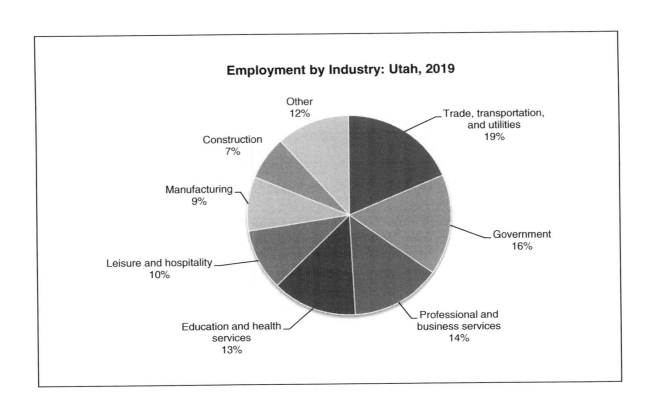

**Employment by Industry: Utah, 2019**

- Other 12%
- Construction 7%
- Manufacturing 9%
- Leisure and hospitality 10%
- Education and health services 13%
- Professional and business services 14%
- Government 16%
- Trade, transportation, and utilities 19%

## 1. Employment by Industry: Utah, 2011–2019

(Numbers in thousands, not seasonally adjusted)

| Industry and year | January | February | March | April | May | June | July | August | September | October | November | December | Annual average |
|---|---|---|---|---|---|---|---|---|---|---|---|---|---|
| **Total Nonfarm** | | | | | | | | | | | | | |
| 2011 | 1,177.1 | 1,182.0 | 1,190.6 | 1,204.7 | 1,203.0 | 1,209.5 | 1,196.9 | 1,207.7 | 1,224.1 | 1,227.6 | 1,231.3 | 1,237.0 | 1,207.6 |
| 2012 | 1,212.0 | 1,218.6 | 1,229.2 | 1,246.4 | 1,251.3 | 1,257.5 | 1,237.2 | 1,249.2 | 1,264.9 | 1,272.2 | 1,281.8 | 1,283.7 | 1,250.3 |
| 2013 | 1,257.5 | 1,265.2 | 1,274.4 | 1,286.5 | 1,287.9 | 1,291.3 | 1,278.8 | 1,287.3 | 1,300.9 | 1,311.5 | 1,319.5 | 1,322.9 | 1,290.3 |
| 2014 | 1,293.1 | 1,300.7 | 1,308.8 | 1,320.1 | 1,322.9 | 1,327.4 | 1,311.5 | 1,324.5 | 1,341.7 | 1,352.1 | 1,358.1 | 1,363.7 | 1,327.1 |
| 2015 | 1,340.2 | 1,350.1 | 1,360.3 | 1,367.4 | 1,371.5 | 1,377.5 | 1,366.0 | 1,375.4 | 1,393.6 | 1,405.4 | 1,410.1 | 1,415.3 | 1,377.7 |
| 2016 | 1,387.3 | 1,399.0 | 1,409.1 | 1,419.4 | 1,420.1 | 1,425.6 | 1,417.3 | 1,425.3 | 1,445.7 | 1,451.4 | 1,454.2 | 1,454.9 | 1,425.8 |
| 2017 | 1,431.2 | 1,441.3 | 1,453.1 | 1,459.0 | 1,461.4 | 1,467.5 | 1,453.2 | 1,464.0 | 1,484.1 | 1,494.3 | 1,502.1 | 1,506.1 | 1,468.1 |
| 2018 | 1,478.0 | 1,493.0 | 1,500.3 | 1,505.7 | 1,509.6 | 1,514.6 | 1,500.6 | 1,514.2 | 1,532.5 | 1,542.4 | 1,549.8 | 1,551.4 | 1,516.0 |
| 2019 | 1,523.7 | 1,535.4 | 1,542.7 | 1,556.8 | 1,561.2 | 1,558.3 | 1,544.3 | 1,559.3 | 1,574.4 | 1,587.1 | 1,593.0 | 1,596.1 | 1,561.0 |
| **Total Private** | | | | | | | | | | | | | |
| 2010 | 958.2 | 960.8 | 967.9 | 980.5 | 978.4 | 986.8 | 992.3 | 999.1 | 1,001.8 | 1,003.3 | 1,007.3 | 1,013.5 | 987.5 |
| 2011 | 989.5 | 994.2 | 1,004.2 | 1,017.9 | 1,023.3 | 1,031.3 | 1,029.5 | 1,039.3 | 1,040.1 | 1,043.9 | 1,053.7 | 1,057.4 | 1,027.0 |
| 2012 | 1,032.9 | 1,038.8 | 1,047.8 | 1,057.9 | 1,057.4 | 1,063.7 | 1,068.8 | 1,075.9 | 1,073.6 | 1,080.4 | 1,088.8 | 1,092.9 | 1,064.9 |
| 2013 | 1,065.6 | 1,070.5 | 1,078.1 | 1,084.8 | 1,085.5 | 1,093.6 | 1,096.8 | 1,108.1 | 1,109.5 | 1,117.1 | 1,123.4 | 1,129.8 | 1,096.9 |
| 2014 | 1,108.2 | 1,115.1 | 1,124.2 | 1,129.5 | 1,131.8 | 1,142.1 | 1,148.1 | 1,156.3 | 1,157.5 | 1,165.9 | 1,171.4 | 1,176.8 | 1,143.9 |
| 2015 | 1,152.1 | 1,160.2 | 1,168.9 | 1,176.5 | 1,175.3 | 1,184.8 | 1,193.6 | 1,200.8 | 1,202.4 | 1,205.0 | 1,207.6 | 1,209.2 | 1,186.4 |
| 2016 | 1,188.6 | 1,195.1 | 1,206.2 | 1,210.4 | 1,210.4 | 1,223.8 | 1,227.9 | 1,235.5 | 1,236.9 | 1,243.8 | 1,251.5 | 1,255.4 | 1,223.8 |
| 2017 | 1,232.4 | 1,243.7 | 1,250.5 | 1,253.7 | 1,255.7 | 1,267.3 | 1,271.1 | 1,281.1 | 1,280.7 | 1,287.8 | 1,295.7 | 1,297.8 | 1,268.1 |
| 2018 | 1,273.6 | 1,281.7 | 1,288.4 | 1,297.2 | 1,298.0 | 1,306.6 | 1,309.5 | 1,319.4 | 1,317.0 | 1,328.3 | 1,333.5 | 1,334.9 | 1,307.3 |
| 2019 | | | | | | | | | | | | | |
| **Goods Producing** | | | | | | | | | | | | | |
| 2011 | 181.7 | 181.3 | 183.1 | 186.6 | 188.5 | 192.0 | 196.1 | 197.8 | 196.9 | 196.3 | 195.4 | 193.7 | 190.8 |
| 2012 | 188.9 | 189.6 | 192.0 | 195.2 | 199.8 | 202.3 | 202.9 | 204.6 | 203.4 | 203.2 | 202.6 | 201.4 | 198.8 |
| 2013 | 195.7 | 196.1 | 198.8 | 202.0 | 205.0 | 207.2 | 209.2 | 210.4 | 209.0 | 208.8 | 208.3 | 206.4 | 204.7 |
| 2014 | 202.1 | 202.9 | 205.5 | 208.2 | 212.1 | 214.2 | 215.1 | 216.3 | 215.8 | 216.8 | 216.3 | 215.1 | 211.7 |
| 2015 | 210.5 | 211.1 | 213.2 | 215.5 | 218.2 | 221.2 | 222.9 | 223.6 | 222.8 | 224.7 | 223.9 | 223.2 | 219.2 |
| 2016 | 217.7 | 219.2 | 221.8 | 224.5 | 226.3 | 228.1 | 230.5 | 230.8 | 230.1 | 230.3 | 229.8 | 228.0 | 226.4 |
| 2017 | 223.9 | 225.9 | 230.0 | 231.1 | 234.3 | 238.6 | 239.7 | 240.4 | 239.6 | 241.1 | 241.5 | 240.9 | 235.6 |
| 2018 | 237.4 | 239.8 | 241.9 | 243.2 | 245.9 | 249.7 | 250.6 | 251.2 | 249.9 | 250.8 | 251.4 | 250.3 | 246.8 |
| 2019 | 245.6 | 246.9 | 249.8 | 252.0 | 256.0 | 258.9 | 260.1 | 261.1 | 259.8 | 261.6 | 261.8 | 259.0 | 256.1 |
| **Service-Providing** | | | | | | | | | | | | | |
| 2011 | 995.4 | 1,000.7 | 1,007.5 | 1,018.1 | 1,014.5 | 1,017.5 | 1,000.8 | 1,009.9 | 1,027.2 | 1,031.3 | 1,035.9 | 1,043.3 | 1,016.8 |
| 2012 | 1,023.1 | 1,029.0 | 1,037.2 | 1,051.2 | 1,051.5 | 1,055.2 | 1,034.3 | 1,044.6 | 1,061.5 | 1,069.0 | 1,079.2 | 1,082.3 | 1,051.5 |
| 2013 | 1,061.8 | 1,069.1 | 1,075.6 | 1,084.5 | 1,082.9 | 1,084.1 | 1,069.6 | 1,076.9 | 1,091.9 | 1,102.7 | 1,111.2 | 1,116.5 | 1,085.6 |
| 2014 | 1,091.0 | 1,097.8 | 1,103.3 | 1,111.9 | 1,110.8 | 1,113.2 | 1,096.4 | 1,108.2 | 1,125.9 | 1,135.3 | 1,141.8 | 1,148.6 | 1,115.4 |
| 2015 | 1,129.7 | 1,139.0 | 1,147.1 | 1,151.9 | 1,153.3 | 1,156.3 | 1,143.1 | 1,151.8 | 1,170.8 | 1,180.7 | 1,186.2 | 1,192.1 | 1,158.5 |
| 2016 | 1,169.6 | 1,179.8 | 1,187.3 | 1,194.9 | 1,193.8 | 1,197.5 | 1,186.8 | 1,194.5 | 1,215.6 | 1,221.1 | 1,224.4 | 1,226.9 | 1,199.4 |
| 2017 | 1,207.3 | 1,215.4 | 1,223.1 | 1,227.9 | 1,227.1 | 1,228.9 | 1,213.5 | 1,223.6 | 1,244.5 | 1,253.2 | 1,260.6 | 1,265.2 | 1,232.5 |
| 2018 | 1,240.6 | 1,253.2 | 1,258.4 | 1,262.5 | 1,263.7 | 1,264.9 | 1,250.0 | 1,263.0 | 1,282.6 | 1,291.6 | 1,298.4 | 1,301.1 | 1,269.2 |
| 2019 | 1,278.1 | 1,288.5 | 1,292.9 | 1,304.8 | 1,305.2 | 1,299.4 | 1,284.2 | 1,298.2 | 1,314.6 | 1,325.5 | 1,331.2 | 1,337.1 | 1,305.0 |
| **Mining and Logging** | | | | | | | | | | | | | |
| 2011 | 10.8 | 10.9 | 11.1 | 11.3 | 11.4 | 11.7 | 12.0 | 12.1 | 12.3 | 12.3 | 12.2 | 12.2 | 11.7 |
| 2012 | 12.1 | 12.3 | 12.5 | 12.6 | 12.8 | 12.8 | 12.8 | 12.9 | 12.8 | 12.7 | 12.6 | 12.4 | 12.6 |
| 2013 | 12.1 | 12.0 | 12.1 | 12.2 | 12.3 | 12.4 | 12.4 | 12.4 | 12.4 | 12.2 | 12.2 | 12.1 | 12.2 |
| 2014 | 11.9 | 11.9 | 12.0 | 12.1 | 12.3 | 12.4 | 12.4 | 12.5 | 12.4 | 12.5 | 12.3 | 12.1 | 12.2 |
| 2015 | 11.7 | 11.1 | 10.9 | 10.6 | 10.6 | 10.5 | 10.4 | 10.3 | 10.1 | 10.0 | 9.8 | 9.5 | 10.5 |
| 2016 | 9.1 | 8.8 | 8.8 | 8.7 | 8.6 | 8.5 | 8.6 | 8.6 | 8.4 | 8.3 | 8.2 | 8.1 | 8.6 |
| 2017 | 8.1 | 8.2 | 8.4 | 8.5 | 8.6 | 8.9 | 8.9 | 8.9 | 8.8 | 9.0 | 9.1 | 8.9 | 8.7 |
| 2018 | 9.1 | 9.1 | 9.2 | 9.3 | 9.4 | 9.6 | 9.6 | 9.6 | 9.6 | 9.8 | 9.8 | 9.6 | 9.5 |
| 2019 | 9.3 | 9.3 | 9.4 | 9.3 | 9.4 | 9.6 | 9.6 | 9.6 | 9.5 | 9.5 | 9.5 | 9.2 | 9.4 |
| **Construction** | | | | | | | | | | | | | |
| 2011 | 59.5 | 58.8 | 60.0 | 62.5 | 64.0 | 66.5 | 69.4 | 70.6 | 69.8 | 68.9 | 68.0 | 66.1 | 65.3 |
| 2012 | 62.2 | 62.6 | 64.2 | 66.8 | 70.2 | 71.9 | 72.3 | 73.6 | 72.6 | 72.3 | 71.7 | 70.5 | 69.2 |
| 2013 | 66.2 | 66.6 | 68.8 | 71.3 | 74.0 | 75.6 | 77.3 | 78.1 | 77.1 | 77.0 | 76.3 | 74.1 | 73.5 |
| 2014 | 71.0 | 71.4 | 73.7 | 76.1 | 78.9 | 80.5 | 81.5 | 82.4 | 82.0 | 82.9 | 82.2 | 80.8 | 78.6 |
| 2015 | 76.8 | 77.8 | 79.8 | 82.0 | 84.0 | 86.4 | 87.9 | 88.6 | 88.2 | 89.3 | 88.6 | 88.2 | 84.8 |
| 2016 | 84.2 | 85.5 | 88.0 | 90.8 | 92.5 | 93.8 | 95.0 | 95.4 | 94.5 | 94.5 | 94.0 | 91.7 | 91.7 |
| 2017 | 88.5 | 89.7 | 93.0 | 94.3 | 96.9 | 100.2 | 101.1 | 101.8 | 101.3 | 102.1 | 101.6 | 100.7 | 97.6 |
| 2018 | 97.8 | 99.3 | 101.1 | 102.5 | 104.5 | 107.1 | 107.4 | 107.7 | 106.6 | 106.6 | 106.4 | 104.7 | 104.3 |
| 2019 | 101.3 | 102.0 | 104.4 | 106.6 | 109.6 | 111.6 | 112.9 | 113.7 | 112.8 | 115.6 | 116.3 | 113.1 | 110.0 |

# 1. Employment by Industry: Utah, 2011–2019—*Continued*

(Numbers in thousands, not seasonally adjusted)

| Industry and year | January | February | March | April | May | June | July | August | September | October | November | December | Annual average |
|---|---|---|---|---|---|---|---|---|---|---|---|---|---|
| **Manufacturing** | | | | | | | | | | | | | |
| 2011 | 111.4 | 111.6 | 112.0 | 112.8 | 113.1 | 113.8 | 114.7 | 115.1 | 114.8 | 115.1 | 115.2 | 115.4 | 113.8 |
| 2012 | 114.6 | 114.7 | 115.3 | 115.8 | 116.8 | 117.6 | 117.8 | 118.1 | 118.0 | 118.2 | 118.3 | 118.5 | 117.0 |
| 2013 | 117.4 | 117.5 | 117.9 | 118.5 | 118.7 | 119.2 | 119.5 | 119.9 | 119.5 | 119.6 | 119.8 | 120.2 | 119.0 |
| 2014 | 119.2 | 119.6 | 119.8 | 120.0 | 120.9 | 121.3 | 121.2 | 121.4 | 121.4 | 121.4 | 121.8 | 122.2 | 120.9 |
| 2015 | 122.0 | 122.2 | 122.5 | 122.9 | 123.6 | 124.3 | 124.6 | 124.7 | 124.5 | 125.4 | 125.5 | 125.5 | 124.0 |
| 2016 | 124.4 | 124.9 | 125.0 | 125.0 | 125.2 | 125.8 | 126.9 | 126.8 | 127.2 | 127.5 | 127.6 | 128.2 | 126.2 |
| 2017 | 127.3 | 128.0 | 128.6 | 128.3 | 128.8 | 129.5 | 129.7 | 129.7 | 129.5 | 130.0 | 130.8 | 131.3 | 129.3 |
| 2018 | 130.5 | 131.4 | 131.6 | 131.4 | 132.0 | 133.0 | 133.6 | 133.9 | 133.7 | 134.4 | 135.2 | 136.0 | 133.1 |
| 2019 | 135.0 | 135.6 | 136.0 | 136.1 | 137.0 | 137.7 | 137.6 | 137.8 | 137.5 | 136.5 | 136.0 | 136.7 | 136.6 |
| **Trade, Transportation, and Utilities** | | | | | | | | | | | | | |
| 2011 | 226.7 | 225.7 | 227.0 | 230.0 | 230.9 | 231.8 | 232.7 | 233.9 | 233.7 | 235.0 | 240.4 | 242.5 | 232.5 |
| 2012 | 234.1 | 233.2 | 234.9 | 237.1 | 239.0 | 240.4 | 240.1 | 240.9 | 241.2 | 242.8 | 249.8 | 250.5 | 240.3 |
| 2013 | 241.4 | 240.5 | 240.9 | 242.3 | 244.1 | 244.8 | 246.0 | 247.1 | 245.6 | 248.0 | 253.5 | 255.6 | 245.8 |
| 2014 | 245.2 | 244.7 | 245.5 | 247.1 | 248.9 | 250.2 | 250.2 | 252.3 | 252.4 | 255.2 | 261.3 | 263.9 | 251.4 |
| 2015 | 255.3 | 255.6 | 256.7 | 257.4 | 258.9 | 259.4 | 261.3 | 263.2 | 262.6 | 264.8 | 270.2 | 272.7 | 261.5 |
| 2016 | 263.3 | 263.6 | 265.6 | 265.9 | 267.4 | 268.4 | 269.4 | 270.9 | 270.8 | 271.7 | 277.6 | 280.0 | 269.6 |
| 2017 | 270.9 | 270.0 | 271.4 | 272.2 | 272.6 | 274.4 | 275.9 | 276.9 | 276.3 | 279.7 | 286.8 | 289.0 | 276.3 |
| 2018 | 277.7 | 277.5 | 279.0 | 279.1 | 281.3 | 282.8 | 284.8 | 286.4 | 287.0 | 290.0 | 297.9 | 299.3 | 285.2 |
| 2019 | 288.4 | 286.6 | 286.6 | 288.0 | 288.5 | 289.2 | 289.3 | 291.1 | 290.4 | 292.8 | 298.3 | 301.2 | 290.9 |
| **Wholesale Trade** | | | | | | | | | | | | | |
| 2011 | 44.0 | 44.3 | 44.6 | 44.9 | 45.2 | 45.4 | 45.5 | 45.7 | 45.6 | 45.7 | 45.8 | 46.0 | 45.2 |
| 2012 | 45.6 | 45.8 | 46.2 | 46.3 | 46.7 | 46.7 | 46.6 | 46.8 | 46.7 | 46.8 | 46.8 | 46.9 | 46.5 |
| 2013 | 46.9 | 47.0 | 47.0 | 47.3 | 47.5 | 47.4 | 47.5 | 47.6 | 47.3 | 47.3 | 47.4 | 47.5 | 47.3 |
| 2014 | 46.9 | 47.1 | 47.1 | 47.5 | 47.7 | 47.8 | 48.0 | 48.2 | 48.0 | 48.6 | 48.7 | 49.0 | 47.9 |
| 2015 | 48.2 | 48.5 | 48.6 | 49.0 | 49.3 | 49.3 | 49.5 | 49.5 | 49.1 | 49.0 | 49.0 | 49.0 | 49.0 |
| 2016 | 48.5 | 48.8 | 48.7 | 48.8 | 48.9 | 48.9 | 49.1 | 49.2 | 49.0 | 49.0 | 49.1 | 49.2 | 48.9 |
| 2017 | 48.8 | 49.0 | 49.2 | 49.3 | 49.6 | 49.9 | 50.1 | 50.1 | 49.9 | 50.3 | 50.4 | 50.6 | 49.8 |
| 2018 | 49.5 | 50.1 | 50.2 | 50.5 | 50.9 | 51.1 | 51.4 | 51.6 | 51.4 | 51.7 | 51.7 | 51.8 | 51.0 |
| 2019 | 51.2 | 51.6 | 51.6 | 51.8 | 51.9 | 51.9 | 52.5 | 52.8 | 52.3 | 51.8 | 51.9 | 52.2 | 52.0 |
| **Retail Trade** | | | | | | | | | | | | | |
| 2011 | 134.8 | 133.6 | 134.4 | 136.8 | 137.4 | 137.7 | 138.5 | 139.3 | 139.0 | 140.4 | 145.2 | 146.2 | 138.6 |
| 2012 | 139.1 | 138.1 | 139.1 | 140.5 | 141.7 | 142.9 | 143.4 | 143.7 | 143.6 | 145.1 | 151.7 | 151.5 | 143.4 |
| 2013 | 143.5 | 142.6 | 143.2 | 145.1 | 146.4 | 147.1 | 147.8 | 148.7 | 147.6 | 149.4 | 154.2 | 155.3 | 147.6 |
| 2014 | 147.3 | 146.8 | 147.5 | 148.6 | 149.9 | 150.7 | 151.3 | 152.7 | 152.5 | 154.1 | 159.0 | 160.5 | 151.7 |
| 2015 | 153.0 | 152.9 | 153.6 | 155.2 | 156.3 | 156.7 | 157.6 | 159.1 | 158.7 | 160.5 | 165.7 | 166.9 | 158.0 |
| 2016 | 159.7 | 159.8 | 161.6 | 161.7 | 162.7 | 163.9 | 164.3 | 165.4 | 165.1 | 166.1 | 171.0 | 171.8 | 164.4 |
| 2017 | 164.2 | 163.5 | 164.2 | 165.1 | 165.2 | 166.2 | 167.3 | 168.3 | 167.2 | 169.6 | 175.4 | 176.1 | 167.7 |
| 2018 | 168.4 | 167.4 | 168.6 | 168.7 | 170.4 | 171.1 | 172.8 | 173.8 | 172.9 | 174.7 | 179.6 | 180.1 | 172.4 |
| 2019 | 172.5 | 171.4 | 171.8 | 172.2 | 172.3 | 172.6 | 172.2 | 172.5 | 172.2 | 174.6 | 178.3 | 179.9 | 173.5 |
| **Transportation and Utilities** | | | | | | | | | | | | | |
| 2011 | 47.9 | 47.8 | 48.0 | 48.3 | 48.3 | 48.7 | 48.7 | 48.9 | 49.1 | 48.9 | 49.4 | 50.3 | 48.7 |
| 2012 | 49.4 | 49.3 | 49.6 | 50.3 | 50.6 | 50.8 | 50.1 | 50.4 | 50.9 | 50.9 | 51.3 | 52.1 | 50.5 |
| 2013 | 51.0 | 50.9 | 50.7 | 49.9 | 50.2 | 50.3 | 50.7 | 50.8 | 50.7 | 51.3 | 51.9 | 52.8 | 50.9 |
| 2014 | 51.0 | 50.8 | 50.9 | 51.0 | 51.3 | 51.7 | 50.9 | 51.4 | 51.9 | 52.5 | 53.6 | 54.4 | 51.8 |
| 2015 | 54.1 | 54.2 | 54.5 | 53.2 | 53.3 | 53.4 | 54.2 | 54.6 | 54.8 | 55.3 | 55.5 | 56.8 | 54.5 |
| 2016 | 55.1 | 55.0 | 55.3 | 55.4 | 55.8 | 55.6 | 56.0 | 56.3 | 56.7 | 56.6 | 57.5 | 59.0 | 56.2 |
| 2017 | 57.9 | 57.5 | 58.0 | 57.8 | 57.8 | 58.3 | 58.5 | 58.5 | 59.2 | 59.8 | 61.0 | 62.3 | 58.9 |
| 2018 | 59.8 | 60.0 | 60.2 | 59.9 | 60.0 | 60.6 | 60.6 | 61.0 | 62.7 | 63.6 | 66.6 | 67.4 | 61.9 |
| 2019 | 64.7 | 63.6 | 63.2 | 64.0 | 64.3 | 64.7 | 64.6 | 65.8 | 65.9 | 66.4 | 68.1 | 69.1 | 65.4 |
| **Information** | | | | | | | | | | | | | |
| 2011 | 28.9 | 29.2 | 29.2 | 29.2 | 29.5 | 29.6 | 29.6 | 29.8 | 29.6 | 29.9 | 30.7 | 30.9 | 29.7 |
| 2012 | 30.2 | 30.5 | 30.7 | 32.0 | 32.7 | 32.8 | 31.4 | 31.6 | 31.1 | 31.3 | 32.4 | 32.5 | 31.6 |
| 2013 | 33.2 | 33.3 | 33.4 | 32.0 | 32.4 | 32.5 | 32.5 | 32.8 | 32.2 | 32.3 | 33.2 | 33.4 | 32.8 |
| 2014 | 32.7 | 33.0 | 33.1 | 32.8 | 32.9 | 33.1 | 33.2 | 33.8 | 33.1 | 33.2 | 33.5 | 33.8 | 33.2 |
| 2015 | 33.0 | 33.4 | 33.5 | 33.6 | 34.2 | 34.5 | 34.9 | 35.4 | 35.0 | 35.5 | 36.3 | 36.3 | 34.6 |
| 2016 | 35.8 | 36.7 | 36.3 | 36.3 | 36.6 | 37.0 | 37.7 | 38.5 | 37.6 | 37.8 | 38.0 | 38.0 | 37.2 |
| 2017 | 38.1 | 38.8 | 38.4 | 38.1 | 38.4 | 38.8 | 38.2 | 38.8 | 38.5 | 39.0 | 39.0 | 38.5 | 38.6 |
| 2018 | 37.5 | 38.2 | 37.5 | 37.6 | 38.4 | 38.6 | 39.0 | 39.8 | 39.0 | 39.2 | 39.3 | 38.7 | 38.6 |
| 2019 | 38.2 | 39.0 | 38.7 | 39.1 | 40.1 | 39.7 | 40.3 | 40.6 | 40.2 | 40.6 | 40.6 | 41.3 | 39.9 |

## 1. Employment by Industry: Utah, 2011–2019—*Continued*

(Numbers in thousands, not seasonally adjusted)

| Industry and year | January | February | March | April | May | June | July | August | September | October | November | December | Annual average |
|---|---|---|---|---|---|---|---|---|---|---|---|---|---|
| **Financial Activities** | | | | | | | | | | | | | |
| 2011 | 67.4 | 67.6 | 67.7 | 68.0 | 67.8 | 68.2 | 68.2 | 68.4 | 68.0 | 68.4 | 68.5 | 69.3 | 68.1 |
| 2012 | 67.9 | 68.2 | 68.2 | 68.6 | 68.6 | 69.2 | 69.5 | 70.3 | 70.1 | 70.6 | 71.0 | 71.9 | 69.5 |
| 2013 | 70.6 | 71.1 | 71.3 | 71.8 | 71.8 | 72.8 | 73.6 | 74.1 | 73.6 | 73.7 | 74.1 | 74.8 | 72.8 |
| 2014 | 73.2 | 73.7 | 73.3 | 73.4 | 73.5 | 74.2 | 75.6 | 76.4 | 75.8 | 76.4 | 76.9 | 77.5 | 75.0 |
| 2015 | 77.1 | 77.6 | 77.9 | 78.0 | 78.2 | 78.7 | 79.4 | 79.6 | 79.4 | 80.0 | 80.2 | 80.9 | 78.9 |
| 2016 | 80.1 | 80.7 | 80.6 | 80.7 | 81.1 | 81.6 | 82.5 | 83.0 | 82.5 | 83.1 | 83.1 | 83.6 | 81.9 |
| 2017 | 82.7 | 83.0 | 82.9 | 82.9 | 83.3 | 84.3 | 84.5 | 85.0 | 84.5 | 85.4 | 85.6 | 86.2 | 84.2 |
| 2018 | 86.1 | 86.7 | 86.6 | 86.4 | 87.1 | 87.9 | 88.3 | 88.8 | 87.8 | 87.7 | 88.0 | 88.7 | 87.5 |
| 2019 | 87.2 | 87.7 | 87.9 | 88.8 | 89.3 | 90.1 | 91.1 | 91.8 | 90.7 | 91.1 | 91.5 | 91.1 | 89.9 |
| **Professional and Business Services** | | | | | | | | | | | | | |
| 2011 | 152.4 | 153.7 | 155.5 | 158.2 | 159.0 | 159.7 | 160.9 | 162.1 | 162.7 | 165.4 | 165.5 | 165.4 | 160.0 |
| 2012 | 159.3 | 161.2 | 163.2 | 165.9 | 167.9 | 169.0 | 169.4 | 172.0 | 171.6 | 174.3 | 174.7 | 174.2 | 168.6 |
| 2013 | 168.4 | 170.7 | 172.7 | 176.0 | 176.5 | 176.6 | 178.5 | 179.9 | 180.3 | 184.3 | 185.9 | 185.5 | 177.9 |
| 2014 | 179.3 | 179.2 | 180.3 | 182.1 | 183.4 | 184.6 | 185.4 | 188.3 | 188.8 | 191.6 | 191.8 | 192.9 | 185.6 |
| 2015 | 186.3 | 187.1 | 189.2 | 191.8 | 193.6 | 195.5 | 196.9 | 198.2 | 197.8 | 200.2 | 201.4 | 201.4 | 195.0 |
| 2016 | 195.6 | 196.0 | 197.7 | 200.1 | 201.2 | 202.5 | 205.4 | 206.8 | 205.5 | 207.2 | 206.1 | 205.0 | 202.4 |
| 2017 | 200.2 | 200.0 | 201.7 | 203.9 | 205.1 | 206.9 | 210.2 | 211.5 | 211.7 | 213.0 | 213.2 | 212.8 | 207.5 |
| 2018 | 207.3 | 209.7 | 211.5 | 214.1 | 215.7 | 217.5 | 219.0 | 220.3 | 219.5 | 221.9 | 222.3 | 220.6 | 216.6 |
| 2019 | 216.6 | 217.9 | 218.6 | 222.5 | 223.5 | 225.7 | 226.2 | 227.9 | 226.9 | 228.7 | 226.6 | 224.5 | 223.8 |
| **Education and Health Services** | | | | | | | | | | | | | |
| 2011 | 157.6 | 158.8 | 159.0 | 159.7 | 155.9 | 155.1 | 153.5 | 155.1 | 160.9 | 162.5 | 163.2 | 163.4 | 158.7 |
| 2012 | 162.2 | 163.2 | 164.0 | 165.7 | 161.6 | 161.0 | 158.9 | 161.4 | 166.8 | 168.9 | 170.3 | 170.4 | 164.5 |
| 2013 | 169.4 | 170.9 | 171.5 | 172.9 | 168.1 | 166.5 | 164.6 | 166.8 | 172.0 | 174.8 | 176.0 | 175.5 | 170.8 |
| 2014 | 173.2 | 175.1 | 176.0 | 174.4 | 170.8 | 169.1 | 168.0 | 170.2 | 175.9 | 178.4 | 180.3 | 179.7 | 174.3 |
| 2015 | 179.9 | 181.8 | 182.4 | 181.5 | 178.6 | 177.6 | 175.8 | 178.5 | 185.6 | 188.5 | 189.7 | 188.9 | 182.4 |
| 2016 | 188.2 | 190.1 | 190.4 | 191.3 | 187.1 | 186.1 | 184.5 | 187.1 | 195.3 | 196.7 | 197.9 | 196.3 | 190.9 |
| 2017 | 195.8 | 197.8 | 198.7 | 199.8 | 195.0 | 192.9 | 190.9 | 193.9 | 200.7 | 203.0 | 204.9 | 203.9 | 198.1 |
| 2018 | 203.7 | 205.8 | 206.0 | 206.1 | 199.3 | 197.4 | 194.5 | 197.9 | 205.2 | 208.6 | 209.6 | 208.7 | 203.6 |
| 2019 | 208.1 | 211.5 | 211.8 | 212.1 | 206.2 | 203.4 | 201.6 | 205.0 | 211.6 | 215.8 | 218.0 | 215.9 | 210.1 |
| **Leisure and Hospitality** | | | | | | | | | | | | | |
| 2011 | 110.5 | 111.2 | 113.0 | 115.1 | 112.7 | 116.0 | 116.4 | 116.9 | 115.4 | 111.5 | 109.4 | 114.1 | 113.5 |
| 2012 | 113.1 | 114.3 | 116.8 | 118.8 | 118.7 | 121.3 | 121.5 | 122.6 | 120.5 | 117.4 | 117.5 | 120.9 | 118.6 |
| 2013 | 119.0 | 120.5 | 123.1 | 124.2 | 122.3 | 126.6 | 127.2 | 127.6 | 124.5 | 122.1 | 121.3 | 125.2 | 123.6 |
| 2014 | 123.6 | 125.2 | 127.3 | 129.5 | 126.5 | 130.2 | 130.8 | 132.3 | 129.9 | 127.8 | 125.6 | 129.2 | 128.2 |
| 2015 | 128.1 | 130.1 | 132.6 | 133.3 | 131.7 | 136.1 | 137.4 | 138.3 | 135.6 | 133.5 | 130.9 | 134.6 | 133.5 |
| 2016 | 132.9 | 135.2 | 137.5 | 138.7 | 136.5 | 141.3 | 143.2 | 143.3 | 140.9 | 138.7 | 135.8 | 139.0 | 138.6 |
| 2017 | 137.8 | 140.2 | 143.3 | 142.4 | 141.4 | 146.8 | 147.0 | 147.9 | 145.4 | 142.5 | 140.4 | 143.9 | 143.3 |
| 2018 | 142.9 | 145.9 | 147.6 | 146.6 | 146.9 | 151.4 | 152.6 | 154.5 | 151.0 | 148.1 | 145.8 | 150.1 | 148.6 |
| 2019 | 148.5 | 150.9 | 153.4 | 153.0 | 152.3 | 156.7 | 157.6 | 158.3 | 155.0 | 154.4 | 153.1 | 159.8 | 154.4 |
| **Other Services** | | | | | | | | | | | | | |
| 2011 | 33.0 | 33.3 | 33.4 | 33.7 | 34.1 | 34.4 | 34.9 | 35.1 | 34.6 | 34.3 | 34.2 | 34.2 | 34.1 |
| 2012 | 33.8 | 34.0 | 34.4 | 34.6 | 35.0 | 35.3 | 35.8 | 35.9 | 35.4 | 35.4 | 35.4 | 35.6 | 35.1 |
| 2013 | 35.2 | 35.7 | 36.1 | 36.7 | 37.2 | 36.7 | 37.2 | 37.2 | 36.4 | 36.4 | 36.5 | 36.5 | 36.5 |
| 2014 | 36.3 | 36.7 | 37.1 | 37.3 | 37.4 | 38.0 | 38.5 | 38.5 | 37.8 | 37.7 | 37.7 | 37.7 | 37.6 |
| 2015 | 38.0 | 38.4 | 38.7 | 38.4 | 38.4 | 39.1 | 39.5 | 39.5 | 38.7 | 38.7 | 38.8 | 38.8 | 38.8 |
| 2016 | 38.5 | 38.7 | 39.0 | 39.0 | 39.1 | 39.8 | 40.4 | 40.4 | 39.7 | 39.5 | 39.3 | 39.3 | 39.4 |
| 2017 | 39.2 | 39.4 | 39.8 | 40.0 | 40.3 | 41.1 | 41.5 | 41.1 | 40.2 | 40.1 | 40.1 | 40.2 | 40.3 |
| 2018 | 39.8 | 40.1 | 40.4 | 40.6 | 41.1 | 42.0 | 42.3 | 42.2 | 41.3 | 41.5 | 41.4 | 41.4 | 41.2 |
| 2019 | 41.0 | 41.2 | 41.6 | 41.7 | 42.1 | 42.9 | 43.3 | 43.6 | 42.4 | 43.3 | 43.6 | 42.1 | 42.4 |
| **Government** | | | | | | | | | | | | | |
| 2011 | 218.9 | 221.2 | 222.7 | 224.2 | 224.6 | 222.7 | 204.6 | 208.6 | 222.3 | 224.3 | 224.0 | 223.5 | 220.1 |
| 2012 | 222.5 | 224.4 | 225.0 | 228.5 | 228.0 | 226.2 | 207.7 | 209.9 | 224.8 | 228.3 | 228.1 | 226.3 | 223.3 |
| 2013 | 224.6 | 226.4 | 226.6 | 228.6 | 230.5 | 227.6 | 210.0 | 211.4 | 227.3 | 231.1 | 230.7 | 230.0 | 225.4 |
| 2014 | 227.5 | 230.2 | 230.7 | 235.3 | 237.4 | 233.8 | 214.7 | 216.4 | 232.2 | 235.0 | 234.7 | 233.9 | 230.2 |
| 2015 | 232.0 | 235.0 | 236.1 | 237.9 | 239.7 | 235.4 | 217.9 | 219.1 | 236.1 | 239.5 | 238.7 | 238.5 | 233.8 |
| 2016 | 235.2 | 238.8 | 240.2 | 242.9 | 244.8 | 240.8 | 223.7 | 224.5 | 243.3 | 246.4 | 246.6 | 245.7 | 239.4 |
| 2017 | 242.6 | 246.2 | 246.9 | 248.6 | 251.0 | 243.7 | 225.3 | 228.5 | 247.2 | 250.5 | 250.6 | 250.7 | 244.3 |
| 2018 | 245.6 | 249.3 | 249.8 | 252.0 | 253.9 | 247.3 | 229.5 | 233.1 | 251.8 | 254.6 | 254.1 | 253.6 | 247.9 |
| 2019 | 250.1 | 253.7 | 254.3 | 259.6 | 263.2 | 251.7 | 234.8 | 239.9 | 257.4 | 258.8 | 259.5 | 261.2 | 253.7 |

## 2. Average Weekly Hours by Selected Industry: Utah, 2015–2019

(Not seasonally adjusted)

| Industry and year | January | February | March | April | May | June | July | August | September | October | November | December | Annual average |
|---|---|---|---|---|---|---|---|---|---|---|---|---|---|
| **Total Private** | | | | | | | | | | | | | |
| 2015 | 34.4 | 35.3 | 35.1 | 34.2 | 34.7 | 34.9 | 34.8 | 35.4 | 34.4 | 34.8 | 34.9 | 34.3 | 34.8 |
| 2016 | 34.0 | 34.2 | 34.3 | 34.4 | 35.3 | 34.8 | 34.8 | 34.9 | 34.5 | 35.4 | 34.8 | 34.8 | 34.7 |
| 2017 | 35.1 | 34.8 | 34.6 | 35.4 | 35.2 | 35.2 | 35.8 | 35.5 | 35.0 | 35.6 | 34.7 | 34.7 | 35.1 |
| 2018 | 34.4 | 34.7 | 34.7 | 35.5 | 35.0 | 35.2 | 35.6 | 34.9 | 35.4 | 34.3 | 34.3 | 34.9 | 34.9 |
| 2019 | 33.7 | 34.1 | 34.0 | 34.3 | 34.8 | 35.7 | 34.9 | 35.0 | 35.4 | 34.8 | 34.7 | 34.7 | 34.7 |
| **Goods-Producing** | | | | | | | | | | | | | |
| 2015 | 37.6 | 38.4 | 38.5 | 38.1 | 38.5 | 38.3 | 37.9 | 38.4 | 36.8 | 38.1 | 37.7 | 37.5 | 38.0 |
| 2016 | 36.3 | 37.0 | 37.7 | 38.0 | 38.0 | 38.1 | 37.6 | 38.0 | 37.8 | 38.6 | 38.1 | 38.1 | 37.8 |
| 2017 | 37.1 | 37.8 | 37.5 | 38.6 | 39.1 | 39.1 | 38.5 | 39.6 | 39.1 | 39.6 | 39.2 | 38.6 | 38.7 |
| 2018 | 37.9 | 38.3 | 38.2 | 38.4 | 38.9 | 39.4 | 39.2 | 39.7 | 39.5 | 39.0 | 39.1 | 39.2 | 38.9 |
| 2019 | 38.1 | 37.9 | 38.1 | 38.8 | 39.3 | 40.1 | 39.7 | 40.2 | 39.6 | 39.9 | 40.2 | 38.4 | 39.2 |
| **Construction** | | | | | | | | | | | | | |
| 2015 | 36.6 | 37.3 | 37.4 | 36.8 | 37.8 | 38.2 | 38.3 | 38.3 | 36.0 | 38.9 | 38.8 | 37.6 | 37.7 |
| 2016 | 35.1 | 35.9 | 37.2 | 38.1 | 37.7 | 37.9 | 37.9 | 38.4 | 38.2 | 38.8 | 37.8 | 36.7 | 37.5 |
| 2017 | 36.2 | 36.9 | 36.9 | 38.7 | 39.6 | 39.8 | 39.7 | 40.2 | 39.3 | 40.3 | 39.2 | 38.2 | 38.8 |
| 2018 | 37.5 | 37.8 | 37.9 | 37.8 | 38.7 | 39.6 | 39.9 | 40.5 | 40.1 | 39.4 | 39.3 | 39.0 | 39.0 |
| 2019 | 37.7 | 37.2 | 37.2 | 38.2 | 40.0 | 41.7 | 40.6 | 41.6 | 40.4 | 40.7 | 40.7 | 37.6 | 39.5 |
| **Manufacturing** | | | | | | | | | | | | | |
| 2015 | 38.6 | 39.3 | 39.4 | 39.2 | 39.3 | 38.6 | 38.3 | 39.1 | 37.9 | 38.1 | 37.3 | 37.6 | 38.6 |
| 2016 | 37.3 | 37.8 | 38.1 | 38.2 | 38.4 | 38.4 | 37.5 | 37.8 | 37.6 | 38.6 | 38.3 | 39.0 | 38.1 |
| 2017 | 37.6 | 38.5 | 37.9 | 38.6 | 38.7 | 38.7 | 37.6 | 39.2 | 38.8 | 39.1 | 39.1 | 38.6 | 38.5 |
| 2018 | 37.9 | 38.4 | 38.1 | 38.8 | 39.1 | 39.4 | 38.6 | 39.1 | 38.9 | 38.9 | 39.0 | 39.5 | 38.8 |
| 2019 | 38.7 | 38.4 | 38.7 | 39.0 | 39.2 | 39.2 | 39.2 | 39.3 | 39.3 | 39.5 | 40.1 | 39.4 | 39.2 |
| **Trade, Transportation, and Utilities** | | | | | | | | | | | | | |
| 2015 | 33.4 | 34.1 | 33.8 | 33.8 | 34.0 | 34.0 | 34.1 | 34.3 | 33.0 | 33.0 | 33.1 | 33.1 | 33.6 |
| 2016 | 32.2 | 32.8 | 32.5 | 33.0 | 33.8 | 33.3 | 33.4 | 33.6 | 32.8 | 33.9 | 32.8 | 33.7 | 33.2 |
| 2017 | 34.2 | 33.6 | 33.9 | 34.9 | 34.0 | 34.4 | 35.2 | 34.4 | 34.2 | 34.3 | 33.6 | 34.1 | 34.2 |
| 2018 | 33.0 | 32.9 | 32.8 | 33.6 | 32.9 | 33.2 | 33.5 | 32.7 | 33.3 | 32.1 | 31.7 | 33.1 | 32.9 |
| 2019 | 31.3 | 31.4 | 31.5 | 31.9 | 32.1 | 33.3 | 32.4 | 32.4 | 33.0 | 32.3 | 32.3 | 33.1 | 32.3 |
| **Financial Activities** | | | | | | | | | | | | | |
| 2015 | 36.6 | 37.1 | 37.4 | 36.4 | 36.4 | 36.5 | 37.0 | 37.5 | 36.6 | 37.3 | 38.4 | 37.2 | 37.0 |
| 2016 | 37.6 | 37.2 | 37.2 | 37.3 | 38.0 | 37.5 | 37.1 | 37.4 | 37.3 | 38.2 | 37.6 | 37.8 | 37.5 |
| 2017 | 38.7 | 37.8 | 37.7 | 38.8 | 38.0 | 38.1 | 38.7 | 38.1 | 38.2 | 38.7 | 37.9 | 37.6 | 38.2 |
| 2018 | 37.3 | 36.6 | 36.4 | 37.3 | 36.2 | 36.6 | 37.3 | 37.0 | 37.7 | 37.2 | 37.4 | 37.7 | 37.1 |
| 2019 | 36.5 | 37.0 | 37.0 | 37.1 | 37.0 | 37.8 | 36.7 | 37.1 | 37.7 | 37.2 | 36.8 | 37.9 | 37.2 |
| **Professional and Business Services** | | | | | | | | | | | | | |
| 2015 | 34.0 | 35.2 | 35.4 | 34.7 | 35.0 | 35.6 | 35.0 | 36.1 | 35.1 | 35.0 | 35.4 | 34.8 | 35.1 |
| 2016 | 34.0 | 34.1 | 34.0 | 34.3 | 35.6 | 34.8 | 35.0 | 34.9 | 34.6 | 35.7 | 34.3 | 33.0 | 34.5 |
| 2017 | 34.0 | 33.3 | 33.2 | 34.3 | 34.1 | 34.6 | 35.6 | 34.5 | 34.1 | 35.5 | 34.8 | 34.6 | 34.4 |
| 2018 | 34.3 | 35.0 | 34.5 | 35.9 | 35.3 | 35.6 | 35.9 | 34.9 | 36.0 | 34.7 | 35.2 | 36.1 | 35.3 |
| 2019 | 34.4 | 35.0 | 34.7 | 35.2 | 35.7 | 37.3 | 35.9 | 36.2 | 37.1 | 35.8 | 36.0 | 36.0 | 35.8 |
| **Education and Health Services** | | | | | | | | | | | | | |
| 2015 | 37.7 | 38.1 | 37.1 | 35.9 | 36.1 | 36.8 | 37.1 | 37.3 | 37.4 | 37.7 | 38.2 | 37.7 | 37.3 |
| 2016 | 38.2 | 37.9 | 38.2 | 38.2 | 39.3 | 38.3 | 38.6 | 38.9 | 38.3 | 39.0 | 39.2 | 39.4 | 38.6 |
| 2017 | 39.4 | 39.7 | 39.1 | 38.6 | 38.9 | 38.7 | 39.0 | 38.8 | 38.1 | 38.5 | 38.5 | 38.6 | 38.8 |
| 2018 | 38.8 | 39.4 | 39.0 | 38.9 | 37.9 | 37.9 | 38.1 | 37.3 | 36.3 | 35.4 | 36.0 | 37.2 | 37.7 |
| 2019 | 37.1 | 37.7 | 37.4 | 37.4 | 38.0 | 38.1 | 37.4 | 37.4 | 38.0 | 37.3 | 37.4 | 37.8 | 37.6 |
| **Leisure and Hospitality** | | | | | | | | | | | | | |
| 2015 | 25.4 | 26.7 | 26.6 | 24.4 | 25.6 | 26.3 | 26.3 | 27.2 | 25.9 | 25.9 | 24.8 | 24.5 | 25.8 |
| 2016 | 25.2 | 25.7 | 25.3 | 24.2 | 25.5 | 25.8 | 25.3 | 25.1 | 24.3 | 25.4 | 23.9 | 24.3 | 25.0 |
| 2017 | 25.1 | 24.4 | 24.3 | 24.5 | 23.7 | 24.8 | 26.0 | 24.8 | 23.8 | 24.2 | 22.5 | 23.0 | 24.3 |
| 2018 | 23.7 | 24.2 | 23.9 | 23.3 | 23.6 | 24.4 | 25.2 | 24.5 | 24.9 | 23.6 | 22.7 | 23.3 | 24.0 |
| 2019 | 22.3 | 23.0 | 22.6 | 22.6 | 23.0 | 24.5 | 23.9 | 23.7 | 23.9 | 23.2 | 22.8 | 23.8 | 23.3 |

## 3. Average Hourly Earnings by Selected Industry: Utah, 2015–2019

(Dollars, not seasonally adjusted)

| Industry and year | January | February | March | April | May | June | July | August | September | October | November | December | Annual average |
|---|---|---|---|---|---|---|---|---|---|---|---|---|---|
| **Total Private** | | | | | | | | | | | | | |
| 2015 | 24.15 | 24.20 | 24.24 | 24.24 | 23.99 | 23.84 | 24.09 | 24.39 | 24.54 | 24.65 | 25.07 | 24.61 | 24.34 |
| 2016 | 24.84 | 24.53 | 24.35 | 24.65 | 24.60 | 24.25 | 24.35 | 24.24 | 24.89 | 24.79 | 24.91 | 24.50 | 24.57 |
| 2017 | 24.93 | 24.61 | 24.78 | 25.46 | 25.04 | 25.16 | 25.50 | 25.02 | 25.44 | 25.56 | 25.39 | 25.21 | 25.18 |
| 2018 | 25.28 | 25.26 | 25.15 | 25.79 | 25.44 | 25.35 | 25.91 | 25.45 | 26.09 | 25.75 | 25.86 | 26.11 | 25.62 |
| 2019 | 26.06 | 26.22 | 26.18 | 26.53 | 26.60 | 27.01 | 26.89 | 27.12 | 27.55 | 27.51 | 27.60 | 28.19 | 26.97 |
| **Goods-Producing** | | | | | | | | | | | | | |
| 2015 | 24.54 | 24.40 | 24.87 | 24.86 | 24.67 | 24.83 | 25.13 | 25.28 | 25.82 | 26.05 | 26.54 | 26.29 | 25.28 |
| 2016 | 26.38 | 26.15 | 26.08 | 26.12 | 26.53 | 26.20 | 26.08 | 26.11 | 26.28 | 26.33 | 26.44 | 26.42 | 26.26 |
| 2017 | 26.34 | 26.16 | 26.67 | 26.69 | 26.59 | 26.71 | 27.46 | 26.66 | 26.91 | 27.28 | 26.98 | 27.35 | 26.83 |
| 2018 | 27.22 | 27.04 | 26.91 | 26.98 | 26.47 | 26.46 | 26.83 | 26.62 | 26.47 | 26.44 | 26.92 | 26.96 | 26.77 |
| 2019 | 26.11 | 27.30 | 27.64 | 27.31 | 27.64 | 27.95 | 27.81 | 27.57 | 27.53 | 27.67 | 27.75 | 28.15 | 27.55 |
| **Construction** | | | | | | | | | | | | | |
| 2015 | 24.38 | 24.38 | 24.70 | 24.68 | 24.54 | 24.52 | 24.24 | 24.50 | 24.91 | 24.91 | 24.74 | 24.88 | 24.62 |
| 2016 | 25.46 | 24.94 | 24.74 | 24.67 | 25.52 | 25.14 | 25.26 | 25.24 | 25.35 | 25.38 | 25.07 | 25.35 | 25.18 |
| 2017 | 25.46 | 25.32 | 25.60 | 25.38 | 25.18 | 25.41 | 25.72 | 25.52 | 26.14 | 26.34 | 26.22 | 26.94 | 25.79 |
| 2018 | 26.63 | 27.00 | 26.61 | 26.75 | 26.22 | 26.51 | 26.99 | 27.14 | 26.87 | 27.04 | 27.72 | 28.09 | 26.97 |
| 2019 | 26.99 | 27.82 | 28.49 | 27.41 | 27.91 | 28.22 | 28.06 | 27.83 | 27.87 | 28.20 | 28.09 | 29.18 | 28.02 |
| **Manufacturing** | | | | | | | | | | | | | |
| 2015 | 23.69 | 23.69 | 24.27 | 24.34 | 24.16 | 24.37 | 24.83 | 24.83 | 25.48 | 25.59 | 26.10 | 25.54 | 24.74 |
| 2016 | 25.59 | 25.60 | 25.82 | 25.97 | 26.20 | 25.94 | 25.76 | 25.82 | 26.07 | 26.23 | 26.61 | 26.31 | 26.00 |
| 2017 | 26.44 | 26.50 | 27.00 | 27.23 | 27.00 | 26.94 | 27.71 | 26.97 | 26.97 | 27.35 | 27.18 | 27.47 | 27.07 |
| 2018 | 27.37 | 26.58 | 26.78 | 26.47 | 26.13 | 25.75 | 26.06 | 25.55 | 25.53 | 25.35 | 25.65 | 25.60 | 26.06 |
| 2019 | 25.71 | 25.57 | 25.76 | 25.98 | 26.11 | 26.46 | 26.11 | 25.84 | 25.76 | 25.79 | 26.16 | 26.12 | 25.95 |
| **Trade, Transportation, and Utilities** | | | | | | | | | | | | | |
| 2015 | 22.54 | 22.95 | 22.85 | 22.88 | 22.18 | 21.97 | 22.37 | 22.48 | 22.74 | 22.73 | 22.21 | 21.67 | 22.46 |
| 2016 | 22.27 | 22.06 | 21.19 | 21.61 | 21.54 | 21.41 | 21.93 | 21.44 | 22.12 | 22.39 | 21.95 | 21.70 | 21.80 |
| 2017 | 22.19 | 22.13 | 21.84 | 22.15 | 21.72 | 22.21 | 22.84 | 22.82 | 23.07 | 23.30 | 22.73 | 22.74 | 22.49 |
| 2018 | 23.18 | 23.16 | 22.61 | 23.16 | 22.94 | 22.91 | 23.78 | 23.41 | 24.24 | 23.66 | 23.22 | 23.85 | 23.35 |
| 2019 | 24.71 | 24.93 | 25.23 | 25.03 | 24.97 | 25.11 | 25.17 | 25.32 | 25.68 | 25.41 | 25.01 | 25.52 | 25.18 |
| **Financial Activities** | | | | | | | | | | | | | |
| 2015 | 27.73 | 28.20 | 28.01 | 28.01 | 27.83 | 27.14 | 27.24 | 28.11 | 28.16 | 27.91 | 28.85 | 28.36 | 27.97 |
| 2016 | 28.21 | 28.97 | 29.05 | 28.69 | 28.48 | 28.25 | 28.19 | 28.03 | 28.26 | 28.73 | 28.93 | 27.99 | 28.48 |
| 2017 | 28.85 | 28.96 | 28.48 | 28.96 | 28.27 | 27.56 | 28.54 | 27.86 | 27.76 | 28.54 | 27.63 | 27.56 | 28.25 |
| 2018 | 27.97 | 28.43 | 28.53 | 29.01 | 28.85 | 28.28 | 28.75 | 28.47 | 28.59 | 27.33 | 27.51 | 27.88 | 28.30 |
| 2019 | 27.81 | 26.87 | 27.44 | 28.93 | 28.95 | 29.81 | 29.87 | 30.04 | 30.24 | 30.29 | 31.40 | 32.31 | 29.53 |
| **Professional and Business Services** | | | | | | | | | | | | | |
| 2015 | 29.32 | 29.65 | 29.40 | 28.51 | 28.48 | 28.05 | 28.13 | 28.94 | 28.82 | 29.16 | 30.14 | 30.13 | 29.06 |
| 2016 | 30.93 | 30.83 | 30.66 | 30.43 | 30.25 | 30.15 | 29.85 | 30.12 | 30.42 | 30.30 | 30.54 | 30.46 | 30.40 |
| 2017 | 31.08 | 30.35 | 30.75 | 32.04 | 31.10 | 31.29 | 31.82 | 31.19 | 32.23 | 31.72 | 31.58 | 31.81 | 31.43 |
| 2018 | 31.46 | 31.80 | 32.07 | 32.61 | 31.62 | 31.13 | 31.71 | 30.85 | 31.08 | 31.02 | 31.57 | 32.49 | 31.62 |
| 2019 | 31.89 | 33.27 | 32.81 | 32.52 | 32.49 | 33.15 | 32.23 | 33.34 | 33.95 | 33.69 | 34.08 | 34.31 | 33.16 |
| **Education and Health Services** | | | | | | | | | | | | | |
| 2015 | 22.33 | 22.28 | 22.27 | 22.48 | 22.62 | 22.84 | 23.31 | 22.91 | 22.99 | 22.89 | 25.22 | 23.28 | 22.97 |
| 2016 | 23.39 | 23.13 | 22.85 | 23.23 | 22.90 | 23.18 | 23.15 | 23.07 | 24.26 | 23.68 | 25.39 | 23.63 | 23.50 |
| 2017 | 24.20 | 23.31 | 23.67 | 24.07 | 23.42 | 24.16 | 24.34 | 23.87 | 25.39 | 24.07 | 26.08 | 24.59 | 24.27 |
| 2018 | 24.15 | 23.84 | 24.31 | 24.92 | 24.77 | 24.81 | 25.45 | 24.72 | 25.85 | 24.91 | 25.09 | 25.10 | 24.81 |
| 2019 | 25.04 | 24.74 | 24.40 | 25.35 | 25.17 | 25.81 | 25.72 | 25.50 | 26.50 | 26.59 | 27.30 | 26.81 | 25.75 |
| **Leisure and Hospitality** | | | | | | | | | | | | | |
| 2015 | 13.47 | 13.67 | 13.64 | 13.39 | 13.37 | 13.23 | 13.39 | 13.59 | 13.57 | 13.64 | 13.63 | 13.86 | 13.54 |
| 2016 | 13.98 | 14.06 | 14.02 | 13.76 | 13.60 | 13.25 | 13.60 | 13.65 | 13.81 | 13.78 | 13.86 | 14.23 | 13.79 |
| 2017 | 14.30 | 14.31 | 14.54 | 14.23 | 14.26 | 14.02 | 14.13 | 14.30 | 14.50 | 14.70 | 14.72 | 14.90 | 14.40 |
| 2018 | 15.06 | 15.04 | 15.13 | 14.96 | 14.93 | 14.59 | 14.75 | 14.72 | 14.97 | 15.05 | 15.37 | 15.55 | 15.00 |
| 2019 | 15.68 | 15.74 | 15.82 | 15.26 | 15.25 | 15.00 | 15.15 | 15.20 | 15.50 | 15.61 | 15.68 | 16.21 | 15.50 |

# 4. Average Weekly Earnings by Selected Industry: Utah, 2015–2019

(Dollars, not seasonally adjusted)

| Industry and year | January | February | March | April | May | June | July | August | September | October | November | December | Annual average |
|---|---|---|---|---|---|---|---|---|---|---|---|---|---|
| **Total Private** | | | | | | | | | | | | | |
| 2015 | 830.76 | 854.26 | 850.82 | 829.01 | 832.45 | 832.02 | 838.33 | 863.41 | 844.18 | 857.82 | 874.94 | 844.12 | 847.03 |
| 2016 | 844.56 | 838.93 | 835.21 | 847.96 | 868.38 | 843.90 | 847.38 | 845.98 | 858.71 | 877.57 | 866.87 | 852.60 | 852.58 |
| 2017 | 877.54 | 856.43 | 857.39 | 901.28 | 878.90 | 885.63 | 912.90 | 888.21 | 890.40 | 909.94 | 881.03 | 874.79 | 883.82 |
| 2018 | 869.63 | 876.52 | 872.71 | 915.55 | 890.40 | 892.32 | 922.40 | 890.75 | 923.59 | 883.23 | 887.00 | 911.24 | 894.14 |
| 2019 | 878.22 | 894.10 | 890.12 | 909.98 | 925.68 | 964.26 | 938.46 | 949.20 | 972.52 | 957.35 | 957.72 | 978.19 | 935.86 |
| **Goods-Producing** | | | | | | | | | | | | | |
| 2015 | 922.70 | 936.96 | 957.50 | 947.17 | 949.80 | 950.99 | 952.43 | 970.75 | 950.18 | 992.51 | 1,000.56 | 985.88 | 960.64 |
| 2016 | 957.59 | 967.55 | 983.22 | 992.56 | 1,008.14 | 998.22 | 980.61 | 992.18 | 993.38 | 1,016.34 | 1,007.36 | 1,006.98 | 992.63 |
| 2017 | 977.21 | 988.85 | 1,000.13 | 1,030.23 | 1,039.67 | 1,044.75 | 1,057.21 | 1,055.74 | 1,052.18 | 1,080.29 | 1,057.62 | 1,055.71 | 1,038.32 |
| 2018 | 1,031.64 | 1,035.63 | 1,027.96 | 1,036.03 | 1,029.68 | 1,042.52 | 1,051.74 | 1,056.81 | 1,045.57 | 1,031.16 | 1,052.57 | 1,056.83 | 1,041.35 |
| 2019 | 994.79 | 1,034.67 | 1,053.08 | 1,059.63 | 1,086.25 | 1,120.80 | 1,104.06 | 1,108.31 | 1,090.19 | 1,104.03 | 1,115.55 | 1,080.96 | 1,079.96 |
| **Construction** | | | | | | | | | | | | | |
| 2015 | 892.31 | 909.37 | 923.78 | 908.22 | 927.61 | 936.66 | 928.39 | 938.35 | 896.76 | 969.00 | 959.91 | 935.49 | 928.17 |
| 2016 | 893.65 | 895.35 | 920.33 | 939.93 | 962.10 | 952.81 | 957.35 | 969.22 | 968.37 | 984.74 | 947.65 | 930.35 | 944.25 |
| 2017 | 921.65 | 934.31 | 944.64 | 982.21 | 997.13 | 1,011.32 | 1,021.08 | 1,025.90 | 1,027.30 | 1,061.50 | 1,027.82 | 1,029.11 | 1,000.65 |
| 2018 | 998.63 | 1,020.60 | 1,008.52 | 1,011.15 | 1,014.71 | 1,049.80 | 1,076.90 | 1,099.17 | 1,077.49 | 1,065.38 | 1,089.40 | 1,095.51 | 1,051.83 |
| 2019 | 1,017.52 | 1,034.90 | 1,059.83 | 1,047.06 | 1,116.40 | 1,176.77 | 1,139.24 | 1,157.73 | 1,125.95 | 1,147.74 | 1,143.26 | 1,097.17 | 1,106.79 |
| **Manufacturing** | | | | | | | | | | | | | |
| 2015 | 914.43 | 931.02 | 956.24 | 954.13 | 949.49 | 940.68 | 950.99 | 970.85 | 965.69 | 974.98 | 973.53 | 960.30 | 954.96 |
| 2016 | 954.51 | 967.68 | 983.74 | 992.05 | 1,006.08 | 996.10 | 966.00 | 976.00 | 980.23 | 1,012.48 | 1,019.16 | 1,026.09 | 990.60 |
| 2017 | 994.14 | 1,020.25 | 1,023.30 | 1,051.08 | 1,044.90 | 1,042.58 | 1,041.90 | 1,057.22 | 1,046.44 | 1,069.39 | 1,062.74 | 1,060.34 | 1,042.20 |
| 2018 | 1,037.32 | 1,020.67 | 1,020.32 | 1,027.04 | 1,021.68 | 1,014.55 | 1,005.92 | 999.01 | 993.12 | 986.12 | 1,000.35 | 1,011.20 | 1,011.13 |
| 2019 | 994.98 | 981.89 | 996.91 | 1,013.22 | 1,023.51 | 1,037.23 | 1,023.51 | 1,015.51 | 1,012.37 | 1,018.71 | 1,049.02 | 1,029.13 | 1,017.24 |
| **Trade, Transportation, and Utilities** | | | | | | | | | | | | | |
| 2015 | 752.84 | 782.60 | 772.33 | 773.34 | 754.12 | 746.98 | 762.82 | 771.06 | 750.42 | 750.09 | 735.15 | 717.28 | 754.66 |
| 2016 | 717.09 | 723.57 | 688.68 | 713.13 | 728.05 | 712.95 | 732.46 | 720.38 | 725.54 | 759.02 | 719.96 | 731.29 | 723.76 |
| 2017 | 758.90 | 743.57 | 740.38 | 773.04 | 738.48 | 764.02 | 803.97 | 785.01 | 788.99 | 799.19 | 763.73 | 775.43 | 769.16 |
| 2018 | 764.94 | 761.96 | 741.61 | 778.18 | 754.73 | 760.61 | 796.63 | 765.51 | 807.19 | 759.49 | 736.07 | 789.44 | 768.22 |
| 2019 | 773.42 | 782.80 | 794.75 | 798.46 | 801.54 | 836.16 | 815.51 | 820.37 | 847.44 | 820.74 | 807.82 | 844.71 | 813.31 |
| **Financial Activities** | | | | | | | | | | | | | |
| 2015 | 1,014.92 | 1,046.22 | 1,047.57 | 1,019.56 | 1,013.01 | 990.61 | 1,007.88 | 1,054.13 | 1,030.66 | 1,041.04 | 1,107.84 | 1,054.99 | 1,034.89 |
| 2016 | 1,060.70 | 1,077.68 | 1,080.66 | 1,070.14 | 1,082.24 | 1,059.38 | 1,045.85 | 1,048.32 | 1,054.10 | 1,097.49 | 1,087.77 | 1,058.02 | 1,068.00 |
| 2017 | 1,116.50 | 1,094.69 | 1,073.70 | 1,123.65 | 1,074.26 | 1,050.04 | 1,104.50 | 1,061.47 | 1,060.43 | 1,104.50 | 1,047.18 | 1,036.26 | 1,079.15 |
| 2018 | 1,043.28 | 1,040.54 | 1,038.49 | 1,082.07 | 1,044.37 | 1,035.05 | 1,072.38 | 1,053.39 | 1,077.84 | 1,016.68 | 1,028.87 | 1,051.08 | 1,049.93 |
| 2019 | 1,015.07 | 994.19 | 1,015.28 | 1,073.30 | 1,071.15 | 1,126.82 | 1,096.23 | 1,114.48 | 1,140.05 | 1,126.79 | 1,155.52 | 1,224.55 | 1,098.52 |
| **Professional and Business Services** | | | | | | | | | | | | | |
| 2015 | 996.88 | 1,043.68 | 1,040.76 | 989.30 | 996.80 | 998.58 | 984.55 | 1,044.73 | 1,011.58 | 1,020.60 | 1,066.96 | 1,048.52 | 1,020.01 |
| 2016 | 1,051.62 | 1,051.30 | 1,042.44 | 1,043.75 | 1,076.90 | 1,049.22 | 1,044.75 | 1,051.19 | 1,052.53 | 1,081.71 | 1,047.52 | 1,005.18 | 1,048.80 |
| 2017 | 1,056.72 | 1,010.66 | 1,020.90 | 1,098.97 | 1,060.51 | 1,082.63 | 1,132.79 | 1,076.06 | 1,099.04 | 1,126.06 | 1,098.98 | 1,100.63 | 1,081.19 |
| 2018 | 1,079.08 | 1,113.00 | 1,106.42 | 1,170.70 | 1,116.19 | 1,108.23 | 1,138.39 | 1,076.67 | 1,118.88 | 1,076.39 | 1,111.26 | 1,172.89 | 1,116.19 |
| 2019 | 1,097.02 | 1,164.45 | 1,138.51 | 1,144.70 | 1,159.89 | 1,236.50 | 1,157.06 | 1,206.91 | 1,259.55 | 1,206.10 | 1,226.88 | 1,235.16 | 1,187.13 |
| **Education and Health Services** | | | | | | | | | | | | | |
| 2015 | 841.84 | 848.87 | 826.22 | 807.03 | 816.58 | 840.51 | 864.80 | 854.54 | 859.83 | 862.95 | 963.40 | 877.66 | 856.78 |
| 2016 | 893.50 | 876.63 | 872.87 | 887.39 | 899.97 | 887.79 | 893.59 | 897.42 | 929.16 | 923.52 | 995.29 | 931.02 | 907.10 |
| 2017 | 953.48 | 925.41 | 925.50 | 929.10 | 911.04 | 934.99 | 949.26 | 926.16 | 967.36 | 926.70 | 1,004.08 | 949.17 | 941.68 |
| 2018 | 937.02 | 939.30 | 948.09 | 969.39 | 938.78 | 940.30 | 969.65 | 922.06 | 938.36 | 881.81 | 903.24 | 933.72 | 935.34 |
| 2019 | 928.98 | 932.70 | 912.56 | 948.09 | 956.46 | 983.36 | 961.93 | 953.70 | 1,007.00 | 991.81 | 1,021.02 | 1,013.42 | 968.20 |
| **Leisure and Hospitality** | | | | | | | | | | | | | |
| 2015 | 342.14 | 364.99 | 362.82 | 326.72 | 342.27 | 347.95 | 352.16 | 369.65 | 351.46 | 353.28 | 338.02 | 339.57 | 349.33 |
| 2016 | 352.30 | 361.34 | 354.71 | 332.99 | 346.80 | 341.85 | 344.08 | 342.62 | 335.58 | 350.01 | 331.25 | 345.79 | 344.75 |
| 2017 | 358.93 | 349.16 | 353.32 | 348.64 | 337.96 | 347.70 | 367.38 | 354.64 | 345.10 | 355.74 | 331.20 | 342.70 | 349.92 |
| 2018 | 356.92 | 363.97 | 361.61 | 348.57 | 352.35 | 356.00 | 371.70 | 360.64 | 372.75 | 355.18 | 348.90 | 362.32 | 360.00 |
| 2019 | 349.66 | 362.02 | 357.53 | 344.88 | 350.75 | 367.50 | 362.09 | 360.24 | 370.45 | 362.15 | 357.50 | 385.80 | 361.15 |

# VERMONT
## *At a Glance*

Population:
2010 census: 625,741
2019 estimate: 623,989

Percent change in population:
2010–2019: -0.3%

Percent change in total nonfarm employment:
2011–2019: 5.1%

Industry with the largest growth in employment, 2011–2019 (percent):
Professional and business services, 18.1%

Industry with the largest decline or smallest growth in employment, 2011–2019 (percent):
Information, -14.0%

Civilian labor force:
2010: 359,402
2019: 342,226

Unemployment rate and rank among states (highest to lowest):
2010: 6.1%, 46th
2019: 2.4%, 50th

Over-the-year change in unemployment rates:
2017–2018: -0.4%
2018–2019: -0.1%

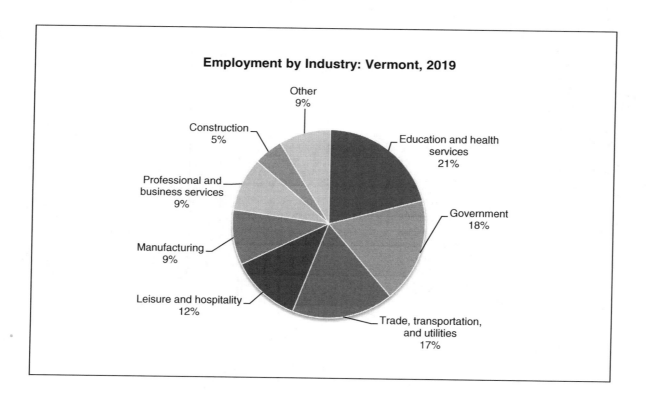

**Employment by Industry: Vermont, 2019**

- Other 9%
- Construction 5%
- Professional and business services 9%
- Manufacturing 9%
- Leisure and hospitality 12%
- Education and health services 21%
- Government 18%
- Trade, transportation, and utilities 17%

# 1. Employment by Industry: Vermont, 2011–2019

(Numbers in thousands, not seasonally adjusted)

| Industry and year | January | February | March | April | May | June | July | August | September | October | November | December | Annual average |
|---|---|---|---|---|---|---|---|---|---|---|---|---|---|
| **Total Nonfarm** | | | | | | | | | | | | | |
| 2011 | 297.0 | 300.2 | 300.1 | 297.1 | 299.4 | 299.2 | 293.0 | 296.9 | 303.3 | 307.5 | 305.4 | 311.1 | 300.9 |
| 2012 | 300.8 | 303.4 | 305.2 | 300.4 | 304.3 | 303.3 | 298.2 | 301.3 | 307.6 | 309.1 | 308.9 | 313.3 | 304.7 |
| 2013 | 303.4 | 305.3 | 307.2 | 304.7 | 305.2 | 305.4 | 298.1 | 303.3 | 308.1 | 312.3 | 311.9 | 315.8 | 306.7 |
| 2014 | 306.6 | 308.9 | 309.4 | 305.6 | 308.5 | 308.9 | 303.0 | 307.5 | 311.8 | 314.8 | 314.2 | 318.1 | 309.8 |
| 2015 | 310.4 | 311.7 | 312.3 | 310.0 | 311.6 | 312.0 | 306.4 | 307.9 | 314.0 | 316.9 | 315.5 | 319.3 | 312.3 |
| 2016 | 310.2 | 312.9 | 312.6 | 310.3 | 311.9 | 312.4 | 308.9 | 310.0 | 315.8 | 318.0 | 316.6 | 320.5 | 313.3 |
| 2017 | 312.0 | 312.4 | 314.4 | 312.2 | 312.9 | 316.4 | 310.1 | 313.0 | 316.7 | 319.3 | 318.8 | 323.1 | 315.1 |
| 2018 | 310.4 | 315.5 | 315.6 | 313.0 | 313.3 | 315.3 | 313.1 | 315.0 | 317.1 | 320.7 | 319.7 | 323.0 | 316.0 |
| 2019 | 313.0 | 316.7 | 318.7 | 314.3 | 314.0 | 315.4 | 312.1 | 313.7 | 316.6 | 319.7 | 317.8 | 321.3 | 316.1 |
| **Total Private** | | | | | | | | | | | | | |
| 2011 | 241.8 | 243.2 | 243.1 | 240.0 | 241.8 | 245.0 | 248.5 | 249.9 | 248.1 | 249.8 | 247.6 | 253.0 | 246.0 |
| 2012 | 245.4 | 246.0 | 247.7 | 242.7 | 246.3 | 249.8 | 253.0 | 254.0 | 251.4 | 251.4 | 250.8 | 255.3 | 249.5 |
| 2013 | 247.2 | 248.0 | 249.6 | 246.8 | 248.2 | 251.7 | 253.0 | 255.0 | 252.1 | 254.0 | 253.5 | 257.6 | 251.4 |
| 2014 | 250.1 | 251.0 | 251.6 | 247.3 | 251.1 | 254.3 | 256.5 | 258.5 | 254.8 | 256.1 | 255.4 | 259.9 | 253.9 |
| 2015 | 253.3 | 253.5 | 254.2 | 251.7 | 254.3 | 257.2 | 259.6 | 259.6 | 257.3 | 258.6 | 257.2 | 261.4 | 256.5 |
| 2016 | 254.0 | 255.0 | 254.6 | 252.3 | 254.7 | 257.6 | 261.3 | 261.3 | 258.8 | 259.3 | 257.7 | 262.4 | 257.4 |
| 2017 | 255.8 | 254.5 | 256.4 | 254.0 | 255.8 | 260.9 | 261.6 | 262.5 | 259.5 | 260.5 | 260.0 | 264.4 | 258.8 |
| 2018 | 256.1 | 257.6 | 258.1 | 255.0 | 255.8 | 259.7 | 263.1 | 263.4 | 260.5 | 261.8 | 261.4 | 264.5 | 259.8 |
| 2019 | 257.7 | 258.5 | 260.7 | 256.1 | 256.2 | 259.9 | 261.8 | 261.8 | 259.0 | 260.3 | 258.8 | 262.2 | 259.4 |
| **Goods Producing** | | | | | | | | | | | | | |
| 2011 | 42.4 | 42.5 | 42.0 | 43.4 | 45.4 | 47.1 | 48.1 | 48.4 | 48.1 | 48.7 | 47.8 | 47.2 | 45.9 |
| 2012 | 44.3 | 44.0 | 44.4 | 45.8 | 47.4 | 48.4 | 48.9 | 48.7 | 48.3 | 48.0 | 47.3 | 46.7 | 46.9 |
| 2013 | 44.2 | 44.2 | 44.4 | 45.1 | 46.9 | 48.0 | 48.3 | 48.2 | 47.8 | 47.8 | 47.5 | 46.9 | 46.6 |
| 2014 | 44.3 | 44.3 | 44.1 | 44.6 | 46.9 | 48.2 | 48.9 | 48.9 | 48.0 | 48.0 | 47.6 | 47.3 | 46.8 |
| 2015 | 44.4 | 44.4 | 44.2 | 45.4 | 47.4 | 48.3 | 48.8 | 48.7 | 48.2 | 47.9 | 47.4 | 46.8 | 46.8 |
| 2016 | 44.2 | 43.8 | 43.6 | 45.2 | 46.6 | 47.7 | 48.0 | 47.8 | 47.1 | 47.1 | 46.4 | 45.7 | 46.1 |
| 2017 | 43.5 | 42.8 | 43.1 | 44.1 | 45.9 | 47.1 | 47.1 | 47.1 | 46.6 | 46.7 | 46.2 | 45.9 | 45.5 |
| 2018 | 43.3 | 43.3 | 43.5 | 44.5 | 46.1 | 47.2 | 47.7 | 47.7 | 47.0 | 47.2 | 46.7 | 46.1 | 45.9 |
| 2019 | 44.0 | 43.7 | 44.0 | 44.7 | 46.3 | 47.4 | 48.1 | 47.9 | 47.4 | 47.5 | 46.5 | 45.4 | 46.1 |
| **Service-Providing** | | | | | | | | | | | | | |
| 2011 | 254.6 | 257.7 | 258.1 | 253.7 | 254.0 | 252.1 | 244.9 | 248.5 | 255.2 | 258.8 | 257.6 | 263.9 | 254.9 |
| 2012 | 256.5 | 259.4 | 260.8 | 254.6 | 256.9 | 254.9 | 249.3 | 252.6 | 259.3 | 261.1 | 261.6 | 266.6 | 257.8 |
| 2013 | 259.2 | 261.1 | 262.8 | 259.6 | 258.3 | 257.4 | 249.8 | 255.1 | 260.3 | 264.5 | 264.4 | 268.9 | 260.1 |
| 2014 | 262.3 | 264.6 | 265.3 | 261.0 | 261.6 | 260.7 | 254.1 | 258.6 | 263.8 | 266.8 | 266.6 | 270.8 | 263.0 |
| 2015 | 266.0 | 267.3 | 268.1 | 264.6 | 264.2 | 263.7 | 257.6 | 259.2 | 265.8 | 269.0 | 268.1 | 272.5 | 265.5 |
| 2016 | 266.0 | 269.1 | 269.0 | 265.1 | 265.3 | 264.7 | 260.9 | 262.2 | 268.7 | 270.9 | 270.2 | 274.8 | 267.2 |
| 2017 | 268.5 | 269.6 | 271.3 | 268.1 | 267.0 | 269.3 | 263.0 | 265.9 | 270.1 | 272.6 | 272.6 | 277.2 | 269.6 |
| 2018 | 267.1 | 272.2 | 272.1 | 268.5 | 267.2 | 268.1 | 265.4 | 267.3 | 270.1 | 273.5 | 273.0 | 276.9 | 270.1 |
| 2019 | 269.0 | 273.0 | 274.7 | 269.6 | 267.7 | 268.0 | 264.0 | 265.8 | 269.2 | 272.2 | 271.3 | 275.9 | 270.0 |
| **Mining and Logging** | | | | | | | | | | | | | |
| 2011 | 0.7 | 0.7 | 0.7 | 0.7 | 0.8 | 0.8 | 0.8 | 0.8 | 0.8 | 0.8 | 0.8 | 0.8 | 0.8 |
| 2012 | 0.7 | 0.7 | 0.7 | 0.8 | 0.8 | 0.8 | 0.9 | 0.9 | 0.9 | 0.9 | 0.8 | 0.8 | 0.8 |
| 2013 | 0.7 | 0.7 | 0.7 | 0.7 | 0.8 | 0.8 | 0.8 | 0.8 | 0.8 | 0.8 | 0.8 | 0.8 | 0.8 |
| 2014 | 0.7 | 0.7 | 0.7 | 0.7 | 0.8 | 0.8 | 0.9 | 0.9 | 0.8 | 0.8 | 0.8 | 0.8 | 0.8 |
| 2015 | 0.7 | 0.8 | 0.8 | 0.8 | 0.8 | 0.9 | 0.9 | 0.9 | 0.9 | 0.9 | 0.8 | 0.8 | 0.8 |
| 2016 | 0.8 | 0.7 | 0.7 | 0.8 | 0.8 | 0.9 | 0.9 | 0.9 | 0.8 | 0.9 | 0.8 | 0.8 | 0.8 |
| 2017 | 0.7 | 0.7 | 0.7 | 0.7 | 0.8 | 0.8 | 0.8 | 0.8 | 0.8 | 0.8 | 0.8 | 0.8 | 0.8 |
| 2018 | 0.7 | 0.7 | 0.7 | 0.8 | 0.8 | 0.9 | 0.9 | 0.8 | 0.8 | 0.8 | 0.8 | 0.8 | 0.8 |
| 2019 | 0.7 | 0.7 | 0.8 | 0.8 | 0.8 | 0.8 | 0.9 | 0.9 | 0.9 | 0.9 | 0.8 | 0.8 | 0.8 |
| **Construction** | | | | | | | | | | | | | |
| 2011 | 11.5 | 11.1 | 11.0 | 12.2 | 13.8 | 15.0 | 15.9 | 16.0 | 16.0 | 16.4 | 15.5 | 14.5 | 14.1 |
| 2012 | 12.5 | 11.9 | 12.1 | 13.4 | 14.6 | 15.4 | 15.9 | 15.8 | 15.4 | 15.2 | 14.6 | 13.6 | 14.2 |
| 2013 | 12.1 | 11.7 | 12.0 | 12.7 | 14.3 | 15.0 | 15.4 | 15.6 | 15.5 | 15.5 | 15.1 | 14.2 | 14.1 |
| 2014 | 12.7 | 12.3 | 12.4 | 13.0 | 14.9 | 15.9 | 16.5 | 16.5 | 16.2 | 16.2 | 15.7 | 15.0 | 14.8 |
| 2015 | 13.2 | 12.8 | 12.8 | 13.9 | 15.7 | 16.3 | 16.8 | 16.7 | 16.4 | 16.2 | 15.8 | 15.1 | 15.1 |
| 2016 | 13.4 | 13.0 | 13.2 | 14.6 | 15.9 | 16.6 | 17.0 | 16.8 | 16.5 | 16.2 | 15.7 | 14.8 | 15.3 |
| 2017 | 13.5 | 13.0 | 13.1 | 14.1 | 15.6 | 16.4 | 16.6 | 16.6 | 16.3 | 16.3 | 15.7 | 15.0 | 15.2 |
| 2018 | 13.5 | 13.3 | 13.4 | 14.2 | 15.6 | 16.3 | 16.6 | 16.7 | 16.3 | 16.4 | 15.8 | 15.0 | 15.3 |
| 2019 | 13.7 | 13.4 | 13.6 | 14.3 | 15.7 | 16.3 | 16.6 | 16.6 | 16.3 | 16.6 | 15.8 | 14.5 | 15.3 |

## 1. Employment by Industry: Vermont, 2011–2019—*Continued*

(Numbers in thousands, not seasonally adjusted)

| Industry and year | January | February | March | April | May | June | July | August | September | October | November | December | Annual average |
|---|---|---|---|---|---|---|---|---|---|---|---|---|---|
| **Manufacturing** | | | | | | | | | | | | | |
| 2011 | 30.2 | 30.7 | 30.3 | 30.5 | 30.8 | 31.3 | 31.4 | 31.6 | 31.3 | 31.5 | 31.5 | 31.9 | 31.1 |
| 2012 | 31.1 | 31.4 | 31.6 | 31.6 | 32.0 | 32.2 | 32.1 | 32.0 | 32.0 | 31.9 | 31.9 | 32.3 | 31.8 |
| 2013 | 31.4 | 31.8 | 31.7 | 31.7 | 31.8 | 32.2 | 32.1 | 31.8 | 31.5 | 31.5 | 31.6 | 31.9 | 31.8 |
| 2014 | 30.9 | 31.3 | 31.0 | 30.9 | 31.2 | 31.5 | 31.5 | 31.5 | 31.0 | 31.0 | 31.1 | 31.5 | 31.2 |
| 2015 | 30.5 | 30.8 | 30.6 | 30.7 | 30.9 | 31.1 | 31.1 | 31.1 | 30.9 | 30.8 | 30.8 | 30.9 | 30.9 |
| 2016 | 30.0 | 30.1 | 29.7 | 29.8 | 29.9 | 30.2 | 30.1 | 30.1 | 29.8 | 30.0 | 29.9 | 30.1 | 30.0 |
| 2017 | 29.3 | 29.1 | 29.3 | 29.3 | 29.5 | 29.9 | 29.7 | 29.7 | 29.5 | 29.6 | 29.7 | 30.1 | 29.6 |
| 2018 | 29.1 | 29.3 | 29.4 | 29.5 | 29.7 | 30.0 | 30.2 | 30.2 | 29.9 | 30.0 | 30.1 | 30.3 | 29.8 |
| 2019 | 29.6 | 29.6 | 29.6 | 29.6 | 29.8 | 30.3 | 30.6 | 30.4 | 30.2 | 30.0 | 29.9 | 30.1 | 30.0 |
| **Trade, Transportation, and Utilities** | | | | | | | | | | | | | |
| 2011 | 55.6 | 55.2 | 54.9 | 54.8 | 55.3 | 56.0 | 55.8 | 55.9 | 55.5 | 56.3 | 57.0 | 57.9 | 55.9 |
| 2012 | 54.7 | 54.3 | 54.1 | 54.4 | 55.1 | 56.0 | 55.8 | 55.8 | 55.6 | 55.8 | 56.7 | 57.6 | 55.5 |
| 2013 | 54.8 | 54.2 | 54.3 | 54.3 | 55.0 | 56.0 | 55.4 | 55.7 | 55.3 | 56.0 | 56.8 | 57.7 | 55.5 |
| 2014 | 54.9 | 54.4 | 54.4 | 54.4 | 55.5 | 56.1 | 55.8 | 55.9 | 55.5 | 56.2 | 57.2 | 58.0 | 55.7 |
| 2015 | 55.3 | 54.7 | 54.6 | 54.5 | 55.2 | 56.0 | 55.6 | 55.4 | 55.0 | 55.7 | 56.4 | 57.4 | 55.5 |
| 2016 | 55.1 | 54.6 | 54.6 | 54.9 | 55.5 | 55.8 | 55.7 | 55.7 | 55.4 | 55.6 | 56.4 | 57.3 | 55.6 |
| 2017 | 55.2 | 54.1 | 54.1 | 54.6 | 55.0 | 55.8 | 55.1 | 55.3 | 54.7 | 55.3 | 56.0 | 56.7 | 55.2 |
| 2018 | 54.3 | 53.8 | 53.6 | 53.9 | 54.5 | 55.0 | 54.7 | 54.8 | 54.3 | 54.8 | 55.6 | 56.1 | 54.6 |
| 2019 | 54.3 | 53.6 | 53.6 | 53.6 | 53.5 | 54.6 | 54.0 | 53.8 | 53.3 | 53.8 | 54.1 | 54.8 | 53.9 |
| **Wholesale Trade** | | | | | | | | | | | | | |
| 2011 | 9.4 | 9.3 | 9.4 | 9.4 | 9.4 | 9.4 | 9.6 | 9.6 | 9.5 | 9.5 | 9.5 | 9.3 | 9.4 |
| 2012 | 9.1 | 9.0 | 9.1 | 9.2 | 9.2 | 9.3 | 9.3 | 9.3 | 9.2 | 9.2 | 9.3 | 9.2 | 9.2 |
| 2013 | 9.0 | 8.9 | 9.0 | 9.0 | 9.1 | 9.3 | 9.2 | 9.3 | 9.1 | 9.2 | 9.2 | 9.3 | 9.1 |
| 2014 | 9.1 | 9.0 | 9.1 | 9.1 | 9.3 | 9.3 | 9.3 | 9.4 | 9.3 | 9.3 | 9.3 | 9.3 | 9.2 |
| 2015 | 9.2 | 9.2 | 9.2 | 9.2 | 9.3 | 9.3 | 9.4 | 9.4 | 9.3 | 9.3 | 9.3 | 9.3 | 9.3 |
| 2016 | 9.3 | 9.3 | 9.3 | 9.5 | 9.6 | 9.5 | 9.5 | 9.5 | 9.4 | 9.3 | 9.3 | 9.3 | 9.4 |
| 2017 | 9.3 | 9.1 | 9.1 | 9.2 | 9.3 | 9.4 | 9.4 | 9.4 | 9.3 | 9.3 | 9.2 | 9.2 | 9.3 |
| 2018 | 8.9 | 8.9 | 9.0 | 9.0 | 9.1 | 9.1 | 9.1 | 9.2 | 9.1 | 9.1 | 9.1 | 9.1 | 9.1 |
| 2019 | 9.1 | 9.0 | 9.1 | 9.1 | 9.0 | 9.2 | 9.1 | 9.1 | 9.0 | 9.2 | 9.2 | 9.3 | 9.1 |
| **Retail Trade** | | | | | | | | | | | | | |
| 2011 | 37.5 | 37.3 | 36.9 | 37.0 | 37.4 | 37.9 | 38.0 | 38.2 | 37.2 | 37.8 | 38.4 | 39.3 | 37.7 |
| 2012 | 37.1 | 36.9 | 36.6 | 36.7 | 37.3 | 38.0 | 38.3 | 38.2 | 37.6 | 37.7 | 38.5 | 39.1 | 37.7 |
| 2013 | 37.1 | 36.8 | 36.6 | 36.9 | 37.4 | 38.1 | 38.1 | 38.2 | 37.5 | 37.9 | 38.5 | 39.2 | 37.7 |
| 2014 | 37.3 | 37.0 | 36.9 | 37.0 | 37.6 | 38.2 | 38.4 | 38.4 | 37.6 | 38.2 | 39.0 | 39.5 | 37.9 |
| 2015 | 37.7 | 37.3 | 37.2 | 37.2 | 37.7 | 38.3 | 38.4 | 38.2 | 37.4 | 38.0 | 38.6 | 39.2 | 37.9 |
| 2016 | 37.7 | 37.4 | 37.3 | 37.5 | 37.8 | 38.4 | 38.7 | 38.6 | 37.9 | 38.1 | 38.8 | 39.3 | 38.1 |
| 2017 | 37.9 | 37.1 | 37.1 | 37.5 | 37.7 | 38.3 | 38.1 | 38.2 | 37.4 | 38.0 | 38.6 | 38.9 | 37.9 |
| 2018 | 37.4 | 37.0 | 36.7 | 37.0 | 37.3 | 37.8 | 37.9 | 37.8 | 37.0 | 37.4 | 38.1 | 38.4 | 37.5 |
| 2019 | 37.0 | 36.6 | 36.4 | 36.4 | 36.4 | 37.0 | 36.9 | 36.8 | 36.0 | 36.2 | 36.6 | 36.9 | 36.6 |
| **Transportation and Utilities** | | | | | | | | | | | | | |
| 2011 | 8.7 | 8.6 | 8.6 | 8.4 | 8.5 | 8.7 | 8.2 | 8.1 | 8.8 | 9.0 | 9.1 | 9.3 | 8.7 |
| 2012 | 8.5 | 8.4 | 8.4 | 8.5 | 8.6 | 8.7 | 8.2 | 8.3 | 8.8 | 8.9 | 8.9 | 9.3 | 8.6 |
| 2013 | 8.7 | 8.5 | 8.7 | 8.4 | 8.5 | 8.6 | 8.1 | 8.2 | 8.7 | 8.9 | 9.1 | 9.2 | 8.6 |
| 2014 | 8.5 | 8.4 | 8.4 | 8.3 | 8.6 | 8.6 | 8.1 | 8.1 | 8.6 | 8.7 | 8.9 | 9.2 | 8.5 |
| 2015 | 8.4 | 8.2 | 8.2 | 8.1 | 8.2 | 8.4 | 7.8 | 7.8 | 8.3 | 8.4 | 8.5 | 8.9 | 8.3 |
| 2016 | 8.1 | 7.9 | 8.0 | 7.9 | 8.1 | 7.9 | 7.5 | 7.6 | 8.1 | 8.2 | 8.3 | 8.7 | 8.0 |
| 2017 | 8.0 | 7.9 | 7.9 | 7.9 | 8.0 | 8.1 | 7.6 | 7.7 | 8.0 | 8.0 | 8.2 | 8.6 | 8.0 |
| 2018 | 8.0 | 7.9 | 7.9 | 7.9 | 8.1 | 8.1 | 7.7 | 7.8 | 8.2 | 8.3 | 8.4 | 8.6 | 8.1 |
| 2019 | 8.2 | 8.0 | 8.1 | 8.1 | 8.1 | 8.4 | 8.0 | 7.9 | 8.3 | 8.4 | 8.3 | 8.6 | 8.2 |
| **Information** | | | | | | | | | | | | | |
| 2011 | 5.2 | 5.3 | 5.2 | 5.0 | 4.9 | 5.0 | 4.9 | 4.9 | 4.8 | 4.8 | 4.8 | 4.8 | 5.0 |
| 2012 | 4.7 | 4.7 | 4.7 | 4.6 | 4.7 | 4.7 | 4.7 | 4.7 | 4.7 | 4.7 | 4.7 | 4.8 | 4.7 |
| 2013 | 4.7 | 4.7 | 4.7 | 4.7 | 4.7 | 4.8 | 4.7 | 4.8 | 4.7 | 4.7 | 4.8 | 4.8 | 4.7 |
| 2014 | 4.8 | 4.8 | 4.9 | 4.8 | 4.8 | 4.9 | 4.8 | 4.8 | 4.8 | 4.8 | 4.4 | 4.4 | 4.8 |
| 2015 | 4.5 | 4.5 | 4.7 | 4.7 | 4.7 | 4.7 | 4.7 | 4.7 | 4.6 | 4.7 | 4.7 | 4.7 | 4.7 |
| 2016 | 4.6 | 4.6 | 4.7 | 4.6 | 4.7 | 4.6 | 4.6 | 4.6 | 4.7 | 4.6 | 4.6 | 4.6 | 4.6 |
| 2017 | 4.6 | 4.6 | 4.6 | 4.5 | 4.5 | 4.5 | 4.4 | 4.4 | 4.4 | 4.4 | 4.4 | 4.4 | 4.5 |
| 2018 | 4.3 | 4.3 | 4.4 | 4.3 | 4.4 | 4.4 | 4.3 | 4.3 | 4.2 | 4.3 | 4.3 | 4.3 | 4.3 |
| 2019 | 4.3 | 4.3 | 4.3 | 4.2 | 4.3 | 4.3 | 4.3 | 4.3 | 4.2 | 4.3 | 4.3 | 4.3 | 4.3 |

## 1. Employment by Industry: Vermont, 2011–2019—*Continued*

(Numbers in thousands, not seasonally adjusted)

| Industry and year | January | February | March | April | May | June | July | August | September | October | November | December | Annual average |
|---|---|---|---|---|---|---|---|---|---|---|---|---|---|
| **Financial Activities** | | | | | | | | | | | | | |
| 2011 | 12.1 | 12.0 | 12.0 | 11.9 | 12.0 | 12.3 | 12.3 | 12.3 | 12.1 | 12.1 | 12.0 | 12.1 | 12.1 |
| 2012 | 12.0 | 11.9 | 12.0 | 11.8 | 12.1 | 12.2 | 12.3 | 12.2 | 12.0 | 11.9 | 11.9 | 12.0 | 12.0 |
| 2013 | 11.8 | 11.8 | 11.8 | 11.8 | 12.1 | 12.3 | 12.3 | 12.3 | 12.1 | 12.1 | 12.0 | 12.1 | 12.0 |
| 2014 | 12.0 | 11.9 | 11.8 | 11.9 | 12.1 | 12.3 | 12.4 | 12.4 | 12.2 | 12.2 | 12.1 | 12.1 | 12.1 |
| 2015 | 12.0 | 12.0 | 11.8 | 11.9 | 12.1 | 12.2 | 12.3 | 12.3 | 12.0 | 12.1 | 11.9 | 11.9 | 12.0 |
| 2016 | 11.9 | 11.9 | 11.8 | 11.9 | 12.0 | 12.2 | 12.2 | 12.2 | 12.0 | 12.0 | 11.9 | 12.1 | 12.0 |
| 2017 | 11.9 | 11.9 | 11.9 | 11.9 | 12.0 | 12.2 | 12.3 | 12.3 | 12.1 | 12.1 | 12.0 | 12.1 | 12.1 |
| 2018 | 11.9 | 11.9 | 11.9 | 11.9 | 12.0 | 12.3 | 12.6 | 12.4 | 12.3 | 12.2 | 12.2 | 12.1 | 12.1 |
| 2019 | 12.2 | 12.1 | 12.1 | 12.1 | 12.3 | 12.4 | 12.6 | 12.5 | 12.3 | 12.1 | 11.9 | 11.9 | 12.2 |
| **Professional and Business Services** | | | | | | | | | | | | | |
| 2011 | 23.0 | 23.2 | 23.4 | 24.1 | 25.0 | 25.5 | 25.7 | 25.9 | 26.0 | 25.9 | 25.7 | 25.5 | 24.9 |
| 2012 | 24.7 | 24.9 | 25.2 | 26.1 | 26.2 | 26.9 | 26.9 | 27.0 | 26.5 | 26.4 | 26.2 | 26.0 | 26.1 |
| 2013 | 25.0 | 25.1 | 25.5 | 26.2 | 26.9 | 27.3 | 27.1 | 27.2 | 26.8 | 26.7 | 26.5 | 26.3 | 26.4 |
| 2014 | 25.2 | 25.4 | 25.6 | 26.0 | 26.9 | 27.6 | 27.5 | 27.4 | 27.1 | 27.2 | 26.9 | 26.7 | 26.6 |
| 2015 | 25.8 | 25.9 | 25.9 | 27.1 | 27.9 | 28.6 | 28.3 | 28.5 | 28.0 | 28.2 | 27.8 | 27.4 | 27.5 |
| 2016 | 26.3 | 26.5 | 26.6 | 27.5 | 28.0 | 28.6 | 29.0 | 29.1 | 28.5 | 28.5 | 28.0 | 27.8 | 27.9 |
| 2017 | 26.9 | 26.9 | 27.2 | 28.3 | 29.0 | 29.7 | 29.5 | 29.5 | 28.9 | 29.2 | 28.7 | 28.4 | 28.5 |
| 2018 | 27.6 | 27.7 | 27.8 | 28.4 | 29.1 | 29.8 | 30.5 | 30.1 | 29.3 | 29.4 | 29.1 | 28.7 | 29.0 |
| 2019 | 28.0 | 28.3 | 28.1 | 28.6 | 29.1 | 30.0 | 30.4 | 30.6 | 30.0 | 30.1 | 29.8 | 29.6 | 29.4 |
| **Education and Health Services** | | | | | | | | | | | | | |
| 2011 | 58.5 | 60.1 | 61.4 | 61.1 | 59.7 | 57.0 | 57.8 | 58.2 | 59.8 | 60.4 | 60.6 | 60.8 | 59.6 |
| 2012 | 59.4 | 60.6 | 62.4 | 61.6 | 60.5 | 58.1 | 59.3 | 60.1 | 60.7 | 62.3 | 62.3 | 62.6 | 60.8 |
| 2013 | 60.6 | 61.8 | 63.5 | 62.8 | 61.5 | 59.2 | 60.1 | 60.8 | 61.5 | 63.1 | 63.4 | 63.2 | 61.8 |
| 2014 | 61.8 | 62.4 | 63.9 | 63.3 | 62.3 | 60.3 | 60.9 | 61.6 | 62.3 | 63.7 | 63.9 | 64.1 | 62.5 |
| 2015 | 62.8 | 63.3 | 64.9 | 64.4 | 63.8 | 61.4 | 62.4 | 62.1 | 63.2 | 64.6 | 64.9 | 65.4 | 63.6 |
| 2016 | 63.6 | 64.6 | 65.9 | 66.0 | 64.6 | 61.9 | 63.2 | 63.2 | 64.4 | 65.7 | 66.0 | 66.3 | 64.6 |
| 2017 | 64.4 | 65.0 | 67.2 | 66.5 | 65.6 | 63.8 | 64.2 | 64.4 | 65.7 | 66.7 | 66.8 | 67.3 | 65.6 |
| 2018 | 65.1 | 66.5 | 68.0 | 68.0 | 66.1 | 63.8 | 64.3 | 64.5 | 66.2 | 67.6 | 68.3 | 68.1 | 66.4 |
| 2019 | 65.6 | 66.8 | 69.4 | 67.8 | 66.3 | 63.0 | 63.2 | 63.6 | 64.9 | 66.5 | 66.9 | 66.6 | 65.9 |
| **Leisure and Hospitality** | | | | | | | | | | | | | |
| 2011 | 35.3 | 35.2 | 34.5 | 29.8 | 29.5 | 32.0 | 33.7 | 34.2 | 31.7 | 31.5 | 29.7 | 34.6 | 32.6 |
| 2012 | 35.6 | 35.6 | 34.8 | 28.5 | 30.3 | 33.4 | 34.9 | 35.3 | 33.5 | 32.2 | 31.7 | 35.6 | 33.5 |
| 2013 | 36.3 | 36.4 | 35.6 | 31.9 | 31.1 | 33.8 | 34.8 | 35.7 | 33.7 | 33.5 | 32.5 | 36.5 | 34.3 |
| 2014 | 37.2 | 37.8 | 36.9 | 32.3 | 32.4 | 34.5 | 35.7 | 37.0 | 34.6 | 33.8 | 33.1 | 37.0 | 35.2 |
| 2015 | 38.4 | 38.7 | 37.9 | 33.5 | 33.0 | 35.5 | 36.9 | 37.4 | 35.9 | 35.0 | 33.8 | 37.4 | 36.1 |
| 2016 | 38.1 | 38.7 | 37.1 | 31.8 | 32.8 | 36.2 | 38.0 | 38.1 | 36.3 | 35.4 | 34.2 | 38.4 | 36.3 |
| 2017 | 39.4 | 39.3 | 38.3 | 34.1 | 33.7 | 37.5 | 38.7 | 39.2 | 36.9 | 35.9 | 35.8 | 39.5 | 37.4 |
| 2018 | 39.7 | 40.0 | 38.8 | 33.8 | 33.4 | 36.8 | 38.4 | 39.1 | 36.8 | 35.9 | 34.9 | 38.8 | 37.2 |
| 2019 | 39.3 | 39.5 | 39.0 | 34.9 | 34.1 | 37.7 | 38.7 | 38.6 | 36.6 | 35.7 | 35.2 | 39.5 | 37.4 |
| **Other Services** | | | | | | | | | | | | | |
| 2011 | 9.7 | 9.7 | 9.7 | 9.9 | 10.0 | 10.1 | 10.2 | 10.1 | 10.1 | 10.1 | 10.0 | 10.1 | 10.0 |
| 2012 | 10.0 | 10.0 | 10.1 | 9.9 | 10.0 | 10.1 | 10.2 | 10.2 | 10.1 | 10.1 | 10.0 | 10.0 | 10.1 |
| 2013 | 9.8 | 9.8 | 9.8 | 10.0 | 10.0 | 10.3 | 10.3 | 10.3 | 10.2 | 10.1 | 10.0 | 10.1 | 10.1 |
| 2014 | 9.9 | 10.0 | 10.0 | 10.0 | 10.2 | 10.4 | 10.5 | 10.5 | 10.3 | 10.2 | 10.2 | 10.3 | 10.2 |
| 2015 | 10.1 | 10.0 | 10.2 | 10.2 | 10.2 | 10.5 | 10.6 | 10.5 | 10.4 | 10.4 | 10.3 | 10.4 | 10.3 |
| 2016 | 10.2 | 10.3 | 10.3 | 10.4 | 10.5 | 10.6 | 10.6 | 10.6 | 10.4 | 10.4 | 10.2 | 10.2 | 10.4 |
| 2017 | 9.9 | 9.9 | 10.0 | 10.0 | 10.1 | 10.3 | 10.3 | 10.3 | 10.2 | 10.2 | 10.1 | 10.1 | 10.1 |
| 2018 | 9.9 | 10.1 | 10.1 | 10.2 | 10.2 | 10.4 | 10.6 | 10.5 | 10.4 | 10.4 | 10.3 | 10.3 | 10.3 |
| 2019 | 10.0 | 10.2 | 10.2 | 10.2 | 10.3 | 10.5 | 10.5 | 10.5 | 10.3 | 10.3 | 10.1 | 10.1 | 10.3 |
| **Government** | | | | | | | | | | | | | |
| 2011 | 55.2 | 57.0 | 57.0 | 57.1 | 57.6 | 54.2 | 44.5 | 47.0 | 55.2 | 57.7 | 57.8 | 58.1 | 54.9 |
| 2012 | 55.4 | 57.4 | 57.5 | 57.7 | 58.0 | 53.5 | 45.2 | 47.3 | 56.2 | 57.7 | 58.1 | 58.0 | 55.2 |
| 2013 | 56.2 | 57.3 | 57.6 | 57.9 | 57.0 | 53.7 | 45.1 | 48.3 | 56.0 | 58.3 | 58.4 | 58.2 | 55.3 |
| 2014 | 56.5 | 57.9 | 57.8 | 58.3 | 57.4 | 54.6 | 46.5 | 49.0 | 57.0 | 58.7 | 58.8 | 58.2 | 55.9 |
| 2015 | 57.1 | 58.2 | 58.1 | 58.3 | 57.3 | 54.8 | 46.8 | 48.3 | 56.7 | 58.3 | 58.3 | 57.9 | 55.8 |
| 2016 | 56.2 | 57.9 | 58.0 | 58.0 | 57.2 | 54.8 | 47.6 | 48.7 | 57.0 | 58.7 | 58.9 | 58.1 | 55.9 |
| 2017 | 56.2 | 57.9 | 58.0 | 58.2 | 57.1 | 55.5 | 48.5 | 50.5 | 57.2 | 58.8 | 58.8 | 58.7 | 56.3 |
| 2018 | 54.3 | 57.9 | 57.5 | 58.0 | 57.5 | 55.6 | 50.0 | 51.6 | 56.6 | 58.9 | 58.3 | 58.5 | 56.2 |
| 2019 | 55.3 | 58.2 | 58.0 | 58.2 | 57.8 | 55.5 | 50.3 | 51.9 | 57.6 | 59.4 | 59.0 | 59.1 | 56.7 |

## 2. Average Weekly Hours by Selected Industry: Vermont, 2015–2019

(Not seasonally adjusted)

| Industry and year | January | February | March | April | May | June | July | August | September | October | November | December | Annual average |
|---|---|---|---|---|---|---|---|---|---|---|---|---|---|
| **Total Private** | | | | | | | | | | | | | |
| 2015 | 32.9 | 33.0 | 33.0 | 33.1 | 33.5 | 33.6 | 33.8 | 33.8 | 33.5 | 33.6 | 33.3 | 32.9 | 33.3 |
| 2016 | 33.0 | 32.9 | 32.9 | 33.3 | 33.8 | 33.7 | 34.0 | 33.8 | 33.8 | 33.7 | 33.3 | 32.6 | 33.4 |
| 2017 | 33.4 | 32.9 | 32.6 | 33.3 | 33.6 | 33.7 | 34.2 | 33.9 | 33.7 | 33.8 | 33.3 | 32.9 | 33.5 |
| 2018 | 32.9 | 33.2 | 32.8 | 33.5 | 33.5 | 33.7 | 33.9 | 33.7 | 33.6 | 33.5 | 33.3 | 33.5 | 33.4 |
| 2019 | 33.2 | 33.2 | 33.2 | 33.3 | 33.6 | 33.9 | 33.8 | 34.0 | 34.1 | 33.8 | 33.4 | 33.4 | 33.6 |
| **Goods-Producing** | | | | | | | | | | | | | |
| 2015 | 37.3 | 37.0 | 37.4 | 37.5 | 37.9 | 37.8 | 37.9 | 37.9 | 37.0 | 37.8 | 38.0 | 38.2 | 37.6 |
| 2016 | 37.9 | 37.2 | 37.4 | 38.0 | 38.0 | 38.2 | 38.1 | 37.9 | 38.0 | 38.0 | 37.8 | 37.8 | 37.9 |
| 2017 | 38.5 | 37.9 | 37.4 | 38.2 | 38.4 | 38.5 | 38.7 | 38.2 | 38.5 | 38.8 | 38.3 | 37.2 | 38.2 |
| 2018 | 37.7 | 38.2 | 37.4 | 37.9 | 38.7 | 38.9 | 38.6 | 39.0 | 38.8 | 38.7 | 38.4 | 39.0 | 38.5 |
| 2019 | 37.8 | 38.1 | 38.6 | 38.6 | 38.4 | 39.2 | 38.5 | 39.8 | 40.0 | 38.9 | 38.5 | 39.0 | 38.8 |
| **Construction** | | | | | | | | | | | | | |
| 2015 | 35.9 | 35.4 | 36.4 | 36.5 | 37.1 | 37.1 | 37.9 | 37.6 | 36.7 | 37.7 | 37.4 | 38.2 | 37.1 |
| 2016 | 37.4 | 36.4 | 36.3 | 37.5 | 38.3 | 38.1 | 38.2 | 37.8 | 38.6 | 38.6 | 37.9 | 37.1 | 37.7 |
| 2017 | 37.5 | 36.4 | 35.7 | 37.0 | 38.5 | 38.9 | 39.1 | 38.5 | 38.8 | 38.5 | 37.6 | 36.8 | 37.9 |
| 2018 | 36.8 | 37.0 | 36.0 | 36.5 | 38.7 | 39.6 | 39.2 | 38.9 | 37.9 | 38.2 | 37.2 | 38.3 | 38.0 |
| 2019 | 36.8 | 37.1 | 37.4 | 37.1 | 38.6 | 39.5 | 38.8 | 40.0 | 40.0 | 38.3 | 37.7 | 38.4 | 38.4 |
| **Manufacturing** | | | | | | | | | | | | | |
| 2015 | 38.1 | 37.9 | 37.9 | 38.0 | 38.3 | 38.1 | 37.8 | 38.0 | 37.1 | 37.8 | 38.3 | 38.1 | 37.9 |
| 2016 | 38.1 | 37.6 | 38.0 | 38.1 | 37.6 | 38.1 | 37.8 | 37.8 | 37.4 | 37.4 | 37.5 | 38.0 | 37.8 |
| 2017 | 38.9 | 38.6 | 38.2 | 38.7 | 38.3 | 38.2 | 38.4 | 38.0 | 38.3 | 38.9 | 38.7 | 37.5 | 38.4 |
| 2018 | 38.2 | 38.9 | 38.2 | 38.7 | 38.7 | 38.5 | 38.2 | 39.0 | 39.3 | 38.9 | 38.9 | 39.2 | 38.7 |
| 2019 | 38.7 | 38.6 | 38.9 | 39.1 | 38.5 | 39.4 | 38.4 | 39.2 | 39.7 | 39.3 | 39.3 | 39.4 | 39.0 |
| **Trade, Transportation, and Utilities** | | | | | | | | | | | | | |
| 2015 | 33.4 | 33.2 | 33.6 | 33.2 | 33.6 | 33.6 | 34.0 | 33.9 | 33.9 | 34.0 | 34.0 | 33.6 | 33.7 |
| 2016 | 33.8 | 33.1 | 33.2 | 33.5 | 33.8 | 33.5 | 33.7 | 33.6 | 33.6 | 33.3 | 33.0 | 32.9 | 33.4 |
| 2017 | 33.0 | 32.5 | 32.3 | 33.1 | 33.2 | 33.2 | 33.6 | 33.2 | 33.1 | 32.9 | 33.2 | 33.0 | 33.0 |
| 2018 | 32.7 | 32.6 | 32.3 | 32.9 | 32.7 | 32.9 | 33.6 | 33.6 | 33.1 | 33.2 | 33.5 | 33.3 | 33.0 |
| 2019 | 33.1 | 32.7 | 32.9 | 33.0 | 33.5 | 33.3 | 33.5 | 33.8 | 33.8 | 33.7 | 33.7 | 33.9 | 33.4 |
| **Professional and Business Services** | | | | | | | | | | | | | |
| 2015 | 34.3 | 35.5 | 35.2 | 34.6 | 34.5 | 35.4 | 35.2 | 35.4 | 34.9 | 35.0 | 35.0 | 34.5 | 35.0 |
| 2016 | 34.5 | 34.8 | 35.0 | 35.4 | 36.0 | 35.7 | 35.2 | 35.0 | 35.1 | 35.6 | 35.0 | 34.4 | 35.1 |
| 2017 | 35.3 | 33.5 | 33.3 | 34.5 | 33.5 | 33.7 | 33.9 | 34.8 | 33.8 | 33.6 | 33.3 | 32.7 | 33.8 |
| 2018 | 32.9 | 32.6 | 32.4 | 33.6 | 33.4 | 33.2 | 33.7 | 32.8 | 33.0 | 32.7 | 31.8 | 32.8 | 32.9 |
| 2019 | 32.6 | 32.0 | 32.7 | 32.6 | 33.1 | 33.9 | 34.0 | 33.3 | 33.7 | 33.4 | 33.2 | 33.0 | 33.1 |
| **Education and Health Services** | | | | | | | | | | | | | |
| 2015 | 33.2 | 33.5 | 33.4 | 33.1 | 33.2 | 33.3 | 33.5 | 33.6 | 33.6 | 33.4 | 33.7 | 33.5 | 33.4 |
| 2016 | 33.7 | 33.6 | 33.6 | 33.5 | 33.7 | 33.6 | 33.9 | 33.8 | 34.2 | 33.6 | 33.7 | 33.2 | 33.7 |
| 2017 | 34.1 | 33.5 | 33.4 | 33.5 | 33.4 | 34.3 | 34.4 | 34.2 | 33.9 | 34.0 | 34.3 | 34.3 | 33.9 |
| 2018 | 34.0 | 33.9 | 34.0 | 34.3 | 34.0 | 34.2 | 34.1 | 34.2 | 34.0 | 33.4 | 33.7 | 33.4 | 33.9 |
| 2019 | 33.3 | 33.4 | 33.4 | 33.1 | 33.2 | 33.5 | 33.5 | 33.6 | 33.6 | 33.3 | 33.5 | 33.2 | 33.4 |
| **Leisure and Hospitality** | | | | | | | | | | | | | |
| 2015 | 24.6 | 25.4 | 24.4 | 24.9 | 25.7 | 25.9 | 26.4 | 26.5 | 25.8 | 25.9 | 23.3 | 23.4 | 25.2 |
| 2016 | 24.3 | 25.1 | 23.7 | 23.5 | 24.5 | 25.4 | 26.6 | 26.5 | 25.5 | 25.9 | 24.2 | 23.4 | 24.9 |
| 2017 | 24.9 | 25.5 | 24.1 | 24.3 | 25.7 | 26.3 | 27.1 | 27.1 | 25.9 | 26.4 | 23.6 | 23.9 | 25.4 |
| 2018 | 24.2 | 25.9 | 24.1 | 23.7 | 24.5 | 25.1 | 26.3 | 26.1 | 25.5 | 25.6 | 23.1 | 23.6 | 24.8 |
| 2019 | 24.6 | 25.2 | 24.4 | 23.8 | 24.3 | 25.2 | 26.8 | 26.7 | 25.7 | 25.9 | 23.7 | 24.5 | 25.1 |

## 3. Average Hourly Earnings by Selected Industry: Vermont, 2015–2019

(Dollars, not seasonally adjusted)

| Industry and year | January | February | March | April | May | June | July | August | September | October | November | December | Annual average |
|---|---|---|---|---|---|---|---|---|---|---|---|---|---|
| **Total Private** | | | | | | | | | | | | | |
| 2015 | 23.57 | 23.67 | 23.88 | 24.14 | 24.13 | 23.96 | 23.93 | 23.99 | 24.12 | 24.12 | 24.57 | 24.67 | 24.06 |
| 2016 | 24.64 | 24.40 | 24.31 | 24.46 | 24.40 | 24.06 | 23.95 | 23.85 | 24.33 | 24.58 | 24.67 | 24.54 | 24.34 |
| 2017 | 24.42 | 24.25 | 24.23 | 24.60 | 24.41 | 24.04 | 24.13 | 24.24 | 24.54 | 24.70 | 24.76 | 24.82 | 24.43 |
| 2018 | 25.05 | 24.97 | 25.08 | 25.40 | 25.21 | 25.13 | 25.21 | 25.07 | 25.61 | 25.84 | 26.12 | 26.00 | 25.39 |
| 2019 | 25.87 | 25.68 | 25.65 | 25.77 | 25.87 | 25.73 | 25.36 | 25.61 | 26.20 | 26.16 | 26.59 | 26.57 | 25.92 |
| **Goods-Producing** | | | | | | | | | | | | | |
| 2015 | 22.83 | 23.02 | 23.36 | 23.53 | 23.42 | 23.35 | 23.49 | 23.43 | 23.75 | 23.56 | 23.80 | 24.22 | 23.49 |
| 2016 | 24.19 | 24.25 | 24.25 | 24.03 | 24.13 | 24.08 | 23.97 | 23.99 | 24.16 | 24.18 | 24.48 | 24.64 | 24.19 |
| 2017 | 24.24 | 24.15 | 24.15 | 24.23 | 24.08 | 24.13 | 23.92 | 24.29 | 24.57 | 24.50 | 24.67 | 25.43 | 24.36 |
| 2018 | 25.11 | 25.20 | 25.42 | 24.89 | 24.96 | 24.96 | 24.94 | 24.89 | 25.00 | 25.31 | 25.25 | 25.49 | 25.12 |
| 2019 | 26.01 | 26.02 | 25.83 | 25.32 | 25.29 | 25.49 | 25.13 | 25.46 | 25.48 | 25.18 | 25.05 | 25.13 | 25.44 |
| **Construction** | | | | | | | | | | | | | |
| 2015 | 23.01 | 23.56 | 23.59 | 23.75 | 23.08 | 22.93 | 23.01 | 22.72 | 22.80 | 22.76 | 22.90 | 23.02 | 23.06 |
| 2016 | 22.99 | 23.61 | 23.41 | 23.25 | 23.12 | 22.97 | 22.94 | 22.54 | 23.08 | 23.30 | 23.75 | 23.75 | 23.21 |
| 2017 | 23.52 | 23.57 | 23.83 | 23.69 | 22.87 | 22.90 | 22.79 | 23.55 | 23.90 | 24.06 | 24.74 | 25.38 | 23.72 |
| 2018 | 25.16 | 25.19 | 25.63 | 25.13 | 24.91 | 24.53 | 24.39 | 24.44 | 24.78 | 25.16 | 25.78 | 26.46 | 25.10 |
| 2019 | 27.23 | 27.05 | 27.26 | 26.79 | 26.45 | 25.88 | 26.00 | 26.36 | 26.07 | 25.96 | 25.95 | 26.13 | 26.38 |
| **Manufacturing** | | | | | | | | | | | | | |
| 2015 | 22.78 | 22.78 | 23.30 | 23.34 | 23.56 | 23.59 | 23.81 | 23.88 | 24.41 | 24.13 | 24.44 | 25.10 | 23.76 |
| 2016 | 25.06 | 24.71 | 24.81 | 24.55 | 24.89 | 24.91 | 25.05 | 25.28 | 25.17 | 25.03 | 25.20 | 25.38 | 25.00 |
| 2017 | 24.89 | 24.71 | 24.58 | 24.73 | 24.90 | 24.98 | 24.80 | 24.89 | 25.13 | 24.91 | 24.73 | 25.57 | 24.90 |
| 2018 | 25.24 | 25.35 | 25.46 | 25.05 | 24.95 | 25.18 | 25.24 | 25.13 | 25.13 | 25.39 | 25.02 | 25.05 | 25.18 |
| 2019 | 25.48 | 25.58 | 25.24 | 24.91 | 24.93 | 25.48 | 24.94 | 25.21 | 25.46 | 25.25 | 25.00 | 25.03 | 25.21 |
| **Trade, Transportation, and Utilities** | | | | | | | | | | | | | |
| 2015 | 19.80 | 19.62 | 19.68 | 19.91 | 20.04 | 20.11 | 20.12 | 20.12 | 20.45 | 20.16 | 20.38 | 21.14 | 20.13 |
| 2016 | 21.01 | 20.54 | 20.54 | 20.63 | 20.66 | 20.45 | 20.55 | 20.63 | 20.64 | 20.70 | 20.79 | 20.79 | 20.66 |
| 2017 | 21.32 | 21.17 | 20.94 | 21.06 | 21.00 | 20.78 | 20.96 | 21.15 | 21.24 | 21.20 | 21.33 | 21.22 | 21.11 |
| 2018 | 21.60 | 21.52 | 21.45 | 21.47 | 21.67 | 21.81 | 21.69 | 21.70 | 22.12 | 22.19 | 22.28 | 22.06 | 21.80 |
| 2019 | 21.79 | 22.08 | 21.99 | 21.86 | 21.84 | 22.14 | 21.85 | 21.85 | 22.45 | 22.09 | 22.66 | 22.66 | 22.11 |
| **Professional and Business Services** | | | | | | | | | | | | | |
| 2015 | 30.95 | 31.45 | 31.60 | 31.37 | 30.93 | 30.08 | 31.02 | 31.02 | 30.69 | 30.51 | 31.02 | 31.04 | 30.96 |
| 2016 | 31.34 | 30.69 | 30.12 | 30.06 | 29.89 | 29.48 | 29.91 | 29.05 | 30.02 | 30.19 | 29.91 | 30.11 | 30.05 |
| 2017 | 30.06 | 31.16 | 30.89 | 31.41 | 30.40 | 30.04 | 30.56 | 30.04 | 29.96 | 29.92 | 29.76 | 30.71 | 30.40 |
| 2018 | 30.94 | 30.55 | 30.92 | 31.23 | 29.96 | 29.59 | 30.30 | 29.98 | 30.17 | 30.42 | 31.30 | 31.22 | 30.53 |
| 2019 | 29.63 | 29.85 | 30.26 | 30.11 | 30.42 | 30.38 | 29.71 | 30.20 | 30.94 | 31.00 | 31.81 | 32.14 | 30.55 |
| **Education and Health Services** | | | | | | | | | | | | | |
| 2015 | 27.01 | 27.25 | 27.50 | 27.52 | 27.33 | 27.19 | 26.92 | 26.89 | 27.03 | 27.64 | 28.29 | 28.76 | 27.45 |
| 2016 | 28.78 | 28.28 | 27.93 | 27.90 | 27.74 | 27.38 | 27.05 | 26.83 | 27.63 | 28.03 | 28.24 | 28.35 | 27.85 |
| 2017 | 27.39 | 27.09 | 27.09 | 27.00 | 27.25 | 26.39 | 26.43 | 26.42 | 26.90 | 27.11 | 27.14 | 26.98 | 26.93 |
| 2018 | 27.24 | 27.16 | 27.20 | 27.36 | 27.27 | 27.43 | 27.67 | 27.64 | 27.94 | 28.71 | 28.57 | 28.65 | 27.74 |
| 2019 | 29.08 | 29.00 | 28.73 | 28.83 | 28.55 | 28.31 | 28.51 | 28.29 | 28.42 | 28.56 | 28.91 | 29.00 | 28.69 |
| **Leisure and Hospitality** | | | | | | | | | | | | | |
| 2015 | 15.25 | 15.32 | 15.35 | 15.94 | 15.83 | 15.99 | 15.78 | 16.13 | 16.34 | 16.40 | 16.38 | 16.03 | 15.88 |
| 2016 | 15.92 | 16.04 | 16.20 | 16.38 | 16.42 | 16.08 | 16.03 | 16.15 | 16.75 | 17.09 | 17.02 | 16.45 | 16.37 |
| 2017 | 16.35 | 16.55 | 16.71 | 16.99 | 16.98 | 16.77 | 16.64 | 16.78 | 17.31 | 17.79 | 17.38 | 16.84 | 16.91 |
| 2018 | 16.88 | 17.14 | 17.19 | 17.84 | 18.01 | 17.77 | 17.83 | 18.06 | 18.51 | 19.10 | 18.43 | 17.64 | 17.85 |
| 2019 | 17.48 | 17.87 | 17.74 | 18.26 | 18.37 | 17.75 | 17.34 | 17.76 | 18.37 | 19.14 | 18.95 | 18.86 | 18.13 |

## 4. Average Weekly Earnings by Selected Industry: Vermont, 2015–2019

(Dollars, not seasonally adjusted)

| Industry and year | January | February | March | April | May | June | July | August | September | October | November | December | Annual average |
|---|---|---|---|---|---|---|---|---|---|---|---|---|---|
| **Total Private** | | | | | | | | | | | | | |
| 2015 | 775.45 | 781.11 | 788.04 | 799.03 | 808.36 | 805.06 | 808.83 | 810.86 | 808.02 | 810.43 | 818.18 | 811.64 | 801.20 |
| 2016 | 813.12 | 802.76 | 799.80 | 814.52 | 824.72 | 810.82 | 814.30 | 806.13 | 822.35 | 828.35 | 821.51 | 800.00 | 812.96 |
| 2017 | 815.63 | 797.83 | 789.90 | 819.18 | 820.18 | 810.15 | 825.25 | 821.74 | 827.00 | 834.86 | 824.51 | 816.58 | 818.41 |
| 2018 | 824.15 | 829.00 | 822.62 | 850.90 | 844.54 | 846.88 | 854.62 | 844.86 | 860.50 | 865.64 | 869.80 | 871.00 | 848.03 |
| 2019 | 858.88 | 852.58 | 851.58 | 858.14 | 869.23 | 872.25 | 857.17 | 870.74 | 893.42 | 884.21 | 888.11 | 887.44 | 870.91 |
| **Goods-Producing** | | | | | | | | | | | | | |
| 2015 | 851.56 | 851.74 | 873.66 | 882.38 | 887.62 | 882.63 | 890.27 | 888.00 | 878.75 | 890.57 | 904.40 | 925.20 | 883.22 |
| 2016 | 916.80 | 902.10 | 906.95 | 913.14 | 916.94 | 919.86 | 913.26 | 909.22 | 918.08 | 918.84 | 925.34 | 931.39 | 916.80 |
| 2017 | 933.24 | 915.29 | 903.21 | 925.59 | 924.67 | 929.01 | 925.70 | 927.88 | 945.95 | 950.60 | 944.86 | 946.00 | 930.55 |
| 2018 | 946.65 | 962.64 | 950.71 | 943.33 | 965.95 | 970.94 | 962.68 | 970.71 | 970.00 | 979.50 | 969.60 | 994.11 | 967.12 |
| 2019 | 983.18 | 991.36 | 997.04 | 977.35 | 971.14 | 999.21 | 967.51 | 1,013.31 | 1,019.20 | 979.50 | 964.43 | 980.07 | 987.07 |
| **Construction** | | | | | | | | | | | | | |
| 2015 | 826.06 | 834.02 | 858.68 | 866.88 | 856.27 | 850.70 | 872.08 | 854.27 | 836.76 | 858.05 | 856.46 | 879.36 | 855.53 |
| 2016 | 859.83 | 859.40 | 849.78 | 871.88 | 885.50 | 875.16 | 876.31 | 852.01 | 890.89 | 899.38 | 900.13 | 881.13 | 875.02 |
| 2017 | 882.00 | 857.95 | 850.73 | 876.53 | 880.50 | 890.81 | 891.09 | 906.68 | 927.32 | 926.31 | 930.22 | 933.98 | 898.99 |
| 2018 | 925.89 | 932.03 | 922.68 | 917.25 | 964.02 | 971.39 | 956.09 | 950.72 | 939.16 | 961.11 | 959.02 | 1,013.42 | 953.80 |
| 2019 | 1,002.06 | 1,003.56 | 1,019.52 | 993.91 | 1,020.97 | 1,022.26 | 1,008.80 | 1,054.40 | 1,042.80 | 994.27 | 978.32 | 1,003.39 | 1,012.99 |
| **Manufacturing** | | | | | | | | | | | | | |
| 2015 | 867.92 | 863.36 | 883.07 | 886.92 | 902.35 | 898.78 | 900.02 | 907.44 | 905.61 | 912.11 | 936.05 | 956.31 | 900.50 |
| 2016 | 954.79 | 929.10 | 942.78 | 935.36 | 935.86 | 949.07 | 946.89 | 955.58 | 941.36 | 936.12 | 945.00 | 964.44 | 945.00 |
| 2017 | 968.22 | 953.81 | 938.96 | 957.05 | 953.67 | 954.24 | 952.32 | 945.82 | 962.48 | 969.00 | 957.05 | 958.88 | 956.16 |
| 2018 | 964.17 | 986.12 | 972.57 | 969.44 | 965.57 | 969.43 | 964.17 | 980.07 | 987.61 | 987.67 | 973.28 | 981.96 | 974.47 |
| 2019 | 986.08 | 987.39 | 981.84 | 973.98 | 959.81 | 1,003.91 | 957.70 | 988.23 | 1,010.76 | 992.33 | 982.50 | 986.18 | 983.19 |
| **Trade, Transportation, and Utilities** | | | | | | | | | | | | | |
| 2015 | 661.32 | 651.38 | 661.25 | 661.01 | 673.34 | 675.70 | 684.08 | 682.07 | 693.26 | 685.44 | 692.92 | 710.30 | 678.38 |
| 2016 | 710.14 | 679.87 | 681.93 | 691.11 | 698.31 | 685.08 | 692.54 | 693.17 | 693.50 | 689.31 | 686.07 | 683.99 | 690.04 |
| 2017 | 703.56 | 688.03 | 676.36 | 697.09 | 697.20 | 689.90 | 704.26 | 702.18 | 703.04 | 697.48 | 708.16 | 700.26 | 696.63 |
| 2018 | 706.32 | 701.55 | 692.84 | 706.36 | 708.61 | 717.55 | 728.78 | 729.12 | 732.17 | 736.71 | 746.38 | 734.60 | 719.40 |
| 2019 | 721.25 | 722.02 | 723.47 | 721.38 | 731.64 | 737.26 | 731.98 | 738.53 | 758.81 | 744.43 | 763.64 | 768.17 | 738.47 |
| **Professional and Business Services** | | | | | | | | | | | | | |
| 2015 | 1,061.59 | 1,116.48 | 1,112.32 | 1,085.40 | 1,067.09 | 1,064.83 | 1,091.90 | 1,098.11 | 1,071.08 | 1,067.85 | 1,085.70 | 1,070.88 | 1,083.60 |
| 2016 | 1,081.23 | 1,068.01 | 1,054.20 | 1,064.12 | 1,076.04 | 1,052.44 | 1,052.83 | 1,016.75 | 1,053.70 | 1,074.76 | 1,046.85 | 1,035.78 | 1,054.76 |
| 2017 | 1,061.12 | 1,043.86 | 1,028.64 | 1,083.65 | 1,018.40 | 1,012.35 | 1,035.98 | 1,045.39 | 1,012.65 | 1,005.31 | 991.01 | 1,004.22 | 1,027.52 |
| 2018 | 1,017.93 | 995.93 | 1,001.81 | 1,049.33 | 1,000.66 | 982.39 | 1,021.11 | 983.34 | 995.61 | 994.73 | 995.34 | 1,024.02 | 1,004.44 |
| 2019 | 965.94 | 955.20 | 989.50 | 981.59 | 1,006.90 | 1,029.88 | 1,010.14 | 1,005.66 | 1,042.68 | 1,035.40 | 1,056.09 | 1,060.62 | 1,011.21 |
| **Education and Health Services** | | | | | | | | | | | | | |
| 2015 | 896.73 | 912.88 | 918.50 | 910.91 | 907.36 | 905.43 | 901.82 | 903.50 | 908.21 | 923.18 | 953.37 | 963.46 | 916.83 |
| 2016 | 969.89 | 950.21 | 938.45 | 934.65 | 934.84 | 919.97 | 917.00 | 906.85 | 944.95 | 941.81 | 951.69 | 941.22 | 938.55 |
| 2017 | 934.00 | 907.52 | 904.81 | 904.50 | 910.15 | 905.18 | 909.19 | 903.56 | 911.91 | 919.03 | 922.76 | 925.41 | 912.93 |
| 2018 | 926.16 | 920.72 | 924.80 | 938.45 | 927.18 | 938.11 | 943.55 | 945.29 | 949.96 | 958.91 | 962.81 | 956.91 | 940.39 |
| 2019 | 968.36 | 968.60 | 959.58 | 954.27 | 947.86 | 948.39 | 955.09 | 950.54 | 954.91 | 951.05 | 968.49 | 962.80 | 958.25 |
| **Leisure and Hospitality** | | | | | | | | | | | | | |
| 2015 | 375.15 | 389.13 | 374.54 | 396.91 | 406.83 | 414.14 | 416.59 | 427.45 | 421.57 | 424.76 | 381.65 | 375.10 | 400.18 |
| 2016 | 386.86 | 402.60 | 383.94 | 384.93 | 402.29 | 408.43 | 426.40 | 427.98 | 427.13 | 442.63 | 411.88 | 384.93 | 407.61 |
| 2017 | 407.12 | 422.03 | 402.71 | 412.86 | 436.39 | 441.05 | 450.94 | 454.74 | 448.33 | 469.66 | 410.17 | 402.48 | 429.51 |
| 2018 | 408.50 | 443.93 | 414.28 | 422.81 | 441.25 | 446.03 | 468.93 | 471.37 | 472.01 | 488.96 | 425.73 | 416.30 | 442.68 |
| 2019 | 430.01 | 450.32 | 432.86 | 434.59 | 446.39 | 447.30 | 464.71 | 474.19 | 472.11 | 495.73 | 449.12 | 462.07 | 455.06 |

# VIRGINIA
## *At a Glance*

Population:
  2010 census: 8,001,024
  2019 estimate: 8,535,519

Percent change in population:
  2010–2019: 6.7%

Percent change in total nonfarm employment:
  2011–2019: 9.9%

Industry with the largest growth in employment, 2011–2019 (percent):
  Transportation and utilities, 23.4%

Industry with the largest decline or smallest growth in employment, 2011–2019 (percent):
  Mining and logging, -27.5%

Civilian labor force:
  2010: 4,157,658
  2019: 4,412,246

Unemployment rate and rank among states (highest to lowest):
  2010: 7.1%, 41st
  2019: 2.8%, 43rd

Over-the-year change in unemployment rates:
  2017–2018: -0.7%
  2018–2019: -0.2%

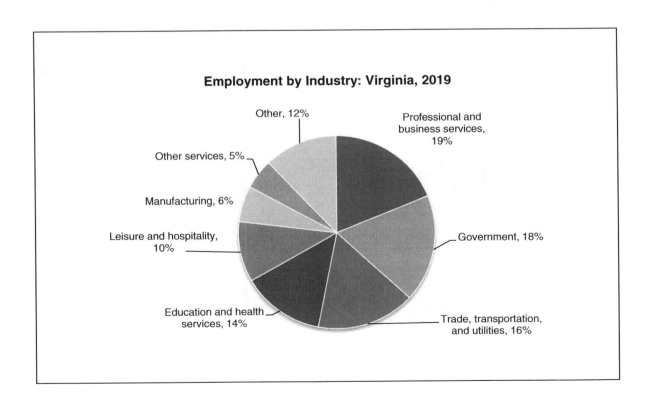

**Employment by Industry: Virginia, 2019**

Other, 12%
Professional and business services, 19%
Other services, 5%
Manufacturing, 6%
Leisure and hospitality, 10%
Government, 18%
Education and health services, 14%
Trade, transportation, and utilities, 16%

## 1. Employment by Industry: Virginia, 2011–2019

(Numbers in thousands, not seasonally adjusted)

| Industry and year | January | February | March | April | May | June | July | August | September | October | November | December | Annual average |
|---|---|---|---|---|---|---|---|---|---|---|---|---|---|
| **Total Nonfarm** | | | | | | | | | | | | | |
| 2011 | 3,611.5 | 3,629.6 | 3,656.3 | 3,692.4 | 3,697.5 | 3,717.2 | 3,701.1 | 3,694.0 | 3,715.7 | 3,723.5 | 3,740.6 | 3,734.5 | 3,692.8 |
| 2012 | 3,659.3 | 3,676.5 | 3,703.9 | 3,728.1 | 3,738.6 | 3,759.1 | 3,724.7 | 3,737.7 | 3,750.8 | 3,772.9 | 3,790.2 | 3,788.3 | 3,735.8 |
| 2013 | 3,700.8 | 3,719.8 | 3,741.0 | 3,764.0 | 3,770.2 | 3,785.1 | 3,761.7 | 3,765.5 | 3,770.7 | 3,776.9 | 3,801.8 | 3,790.0 | 3,762.3 |
| 2014 | 3,710.4 | 3,710.5 | 3,736.7 | 3,783.7 | 3,801.5 | 3,814.7 | 3,787.6 | 3,792.4 | 3,798.7 | 3,811.1 | 3,828.7 | 3,824.9 | 3,783.4 |
| 2015 | 3,758.1 | 3,766.6 | 3,780.1 | 3,841.4 | 3,861.0 | 3,878.0 | 3,877.6 | 3,877.3 | 3,888.3 | 3,915.3 | 3,934.2 | 3,930.3 | 3,859.0 |
| 2016 | 3,836.1 | 3,851.1 | 3,876.8 | 3,918.1 | 3,918.9 | 3,940.3 | 3,916.9 | 3,920.9 | 3,932.0 | 3,947.1 | 3,967.5 | 3,958.0 | 3,915.3 |
| 2017 | 3,877.3 | 3,904.5 | 3,921.8 | 3,952.6 | 3,964.1 | 3,991.5 | 3,964.7 | 3,961.2 | 3,969.8 | 3,989.1 | 4,006.6 | 4,001.7 | 3,958.7 |
| 2018 | 3,929.3 | 3,955.8 | 3,975.6 | 4,004.6 | 4,017.6 | 4,044.3 | 4,020.6 | 4,016.9 | 4,013.0 | 4,040.2 | 4,064.9 | 4,047.3 | 4,010.8 |
| 2019 | 3,981.6 | 4,004.1 | 4,023.6 | 4,052.4 | 4,059.2 | 4,087.6 | 4,066.6 | 4,064.6 | 4,060.7 | 4,082.0 | 4,115.6 | 4,104.3 | 4,058.5 |
| **Total Private** | | | | | | | | | | | | | |
| 2011 | 2,905.1 | 2,911.0 | 2,934.3 | 2,969.3 | 2,979.8 | 3,002.3 | 3,018.1 | 3,014.9 | 3,002.4 | 2,999.7 | 3,011.4 | 3,006.4 | 2,979.6 |
| 2012 | 2,947.9 | 2,953.6 | 2,979.4 | 3,004.3 | 3,019.6 | 3,043.1 | 3,047.2 | 3,057.4 | 3,040.2 | 3,050.7 | 3,062.6 | 3,061.4 | 3,022.3 |
| 2013 | 2,990.9 | 2,997.7 | 3,017.7 | 3,038.6 | 3,049.1 | 3,070.2 | 3,077.2 | 3,084.6 | 3,061.4 | 3,060.5 | 3,079.9 | 3,069.7 | 3,049.8 |
| 2014 | 3,004.0 | 2,995.7 | 3,019.4 | 3,062.7 | 3,084.0 | 3,103.3 | 3,103.2 | 3,109.7 | 3,087.3 | 3,094.6 | 3,107.1 | 3,103.5 | 3,072.9 |
| 2015 | 3,051.7 | 3,047.9 | 3,062.7 | 3,119.7 | 3,143.7 | 3,165.5 | 3,193.3 | 3,196.3 | 3,178.7 | 3,195.5 | 3,209.9 | 3,206.8 | 3,147.6 |
| 2016 | 3,129.7 | 3,131.8 | 3,153.8 | 3,192.7 | 3,199.3 | 3,225.6 | 3,228.4 | 3,235.4 | 3,216.6 | 3,225.3 | 3,240.5 | 3,231.9 | 3,200.9 |
| 2017 | 3,167.5 | 3,181.9 | 3,198.6 | 3,225.4 | 3,241.8 | 3,272.1 | 3,274.3 | 3,273.8 | 3,251.2 | 3,266.0 | 3,277.5 | 3,274.9 | 3,242.1 |
| 2018 | 3,214.4 | 3,228.6 | 3,246.1 | 3,273.8 | 3,289.6 | 3,319.5 | 3,323.2 | 3,322.4 | 3,288.1 | 3,309.9 | 3,328.2 | 3,313.5 | 3,288.1 |
| 2019 | 3,261.4 | 3,269.6 | 3,288.3 | 3,313.7 | 3,325.0 | 3,357.5 | 3,360.5 | 3,358.0 | 3,327.3 | 3,342.6 | 3,365.1 | 3,363.8 | 3,327.7 |
| **Goods Producing** | | | | | | | | | | | | | |
| 2011 | 409.8 | 410.5 | 414.3 | 419.1 | 421.1 | 424.6 | 428.6 | 427.9 | 424.9 | 422.9 | 421.8 | 420.4 | 420.5 |
| 2012 | 411.6 | 410.9 | 414.7 | 416.6 | 418.6 | 422.1 | 425.1 | 424.7 | 423.0 | 421.8 | 420.6 | 419.7 | 419.1 |
| 2013 | 409.8 | 410.4 | 413.2 | 416.0 | 418.1 | 422.4 | 423.5 | 423.8 | 421.6 | 419.7 | 420.0 | 418.0 | 418.0 |
| 2014 | 409.1 | 407.9 | 412.0 | 418.5 | 422.0 | 425.6 | 425.4 | 425.8 | 424.7 | 424.5 | 424.1 | 422.1 | 420.1 |
| 2015 | 414.0 | 413.3 | 416.0 | 425.9 | 429.6 | 432.5 | 435.9 | 435.6 | 433.6 | 434.1 | 432.8 | 431.8 | 427.9 |
| 2016 | 421.0 | 419.2 | 422.6 | 426.4 | 428.4 | 432.2 | 433.4 | 432.9 | 432.9 | 435.1 | 434.5 | 432.6 | 429.3 |
| 2017 | 423.8 | 425.8 | 429.2 | 434.1 | 436.4 | 441.0 | 441.7 | 441.7 | 440.4 | 441.6 | 440.7 | 440.9 | 436.4 |
| 2018 | 431.6 | 435.1 | 438.5 | 442.5 | 446.1 | 451.7 | 453.6 | 453.4 | 450.8 | 452.7 | 452.9 | 451.8 | 446.7 |
| 2019 | 445.5 | 446.5 | 450.2 | 453.3 | 456.1 | 459.4 | 459.6 | 459.4 | 456.3 | 453.2 | 456.3 | 453.1 | 454.1 |
| **Service-Providing** | | | | | | | | | | | | | |
| 2011 | 3,201.7 | 3,219.1 | 3,242.0 | 3,273.3 | 3,276.4 | 3,292.6 | 3,272.5 | 3,266.1 | 3,290.8 | 3,300.6 | 3,318.8 | 3,314.1 | 3,272.3 |
| 2012 | 3,247.7 | 3,265.6 | 3,289.2 | 3,311.5 | 3,320.0 | 3,337.0 | 3,299.6 | 3,313.0 | 3,327.8 | 3,351.1 | 3,369.6 | 3,368.6 | 3,316.7 |
| 2013 | 3,291.0 | 3,309.4 | 3,327.8 | 3,348.0 | 3,352.1 | 3,362.7 | 3,338.2 | 3,341.7 | 3,349.1 | 3,357.2 | 3,381.8 | 3,372.0 | 3,344.3 |
| 2014 | 3,301.3 | 3,302.6 | 3,324.7 | 3,365.2 | 3,379.5 | 3,389.1 | 3,362.2 | 3,366.6 | 3,374.0 | 3,386.6 | 3,404.6 | 3,402.8 | 3,363.3 |
| 2015 | 3,344.1 | 3,353.3 | 3,364.1 | 3,415.5 | 3,431.4 | 3,445.5 | 3,441.7 | 3,441.7 | 3,454.7 | 3,481.2 | 3,501.4 | 3,498.5 | 3,431.1 |
| 2016 | 3,415.1 | 3,431.9 | 3,454.2 | 3,491.7 | 3,490.5 | 3,508.1 | 3,483.5 | 3,488.0 | 3,499.1 | 3,512.0 | 3,533.0 | 3,525.4 | 3,486.0 |
| 2017 | 3,453.7 | 3,478.7 | 3,492.6 | 3,518.5 | 3,527.7 | 3,550.5 | 3,523.5 | 3,519.5 | 3,529.4 | 3,547.5 | 3,565.9 | 3,560.8 | 3,522.4 |
| 2018 | 3,497.7 | 3,520.7 | 3,537.1 | 3,562.1 | 3,571.5 | 3,592.6 | 3,567.0 | 3,563.5 | 3,562.2 | 3,587.5 | 3,612.0 | 3,595.5 | 3,564.1 |
| 2019 | 3,536.1 | 3,557.6 | 3,573.4 | 3,599.1 | 3,603.1 | 3,628.2 | 3,607.0 | 3,605.2 | 3,604.4 | 3,628.8 | 3,659.3 | 3,651.2 | 3,604.5 |
| **Mining and Logging** | | | | | | | | | | | | | |
| 2011 | 10.7 | 10.6 | 10.7 | 10.7 | 10.8 | 10.9 | 11.0 | 11.1 | 11.2 | 11.1 | 11.2 | 11.2 | 10.9 |
| 2012 | 11.1 | 11.1 | 11.1 | 11.0 | 11.0 | 11.1 | 11.0 | 11.0 | 10.8 | 10.3 | 10.5 | 10.4 | 10.9 |
| 2013 | 10.2 | 10.1 | 10.1 | 10.1 | 10.1 | 10.2 | 9.8 | 9.8 | 9.7 | 9.9 | 9.8 | 9.9 | 10.0 |
| 2014 | 9.7 | 9.7 | 9.8 | 9.7 | 9.6 | 9.7 | 9.5 | 9.4 | 9.4 | 9.3 | 9.3 | 9.3 | 9.5 |
| 2015 | 9.4 | 9.3 | 9.2 | 9.2 | 9.1 | 9.0 | 9.1 | 9.1 | 8.8 | 8.6 | 8.5 | 8.5 | 9.0 |
| 2016 | 8.0 | 8.0 | 8.0 | 7.7 | 7.7 | 7.7 | 7.8 | 7.7 | 7.8 | 7.9 | 7.9 | 8.0 | 7.9 |
| 2017 | 7.9 | 8.0 | 8.0 | 7.9 | 7.9 | 8.0 | 8.0 | 8.1 | 8.1 | 7.9 | 7.9 | 7.9 | 8.0 |
| 2018 | 7.8 | 7.9 | 8.0 | 7.9 | 7.9 | 8.0 | 7.9 | 7.8 | 7.9 | 7.9 | 7.9 | 7.9 | 7.9 |
| 2019 | 7.8 | 7.9 | 8.0 | 8.0 | 8.0 | 8.1 | 7.7 | 7.8 | 7.8 | 7.8 | 7.8 | 7.8 | 7.9 |
| **Construction** | | | | | | | | | | | | | |
| 2011 | 171.7 | 172.0 | 174.5 | 178.2 | 179.5 | 181.5 | 184.3 | 183.7 | 180.9 | 179.7 | 178.5 | 177.3 | 178.5 |
| 2012 | 169.7 | 169.0 | 172.3 | 174.8 | 177.2 | 180.5 | 181.4 | 181.0 | 179.3 | 179.3 | 177.9 | 176.9 | 176.6 |
| 2013 | 169.7 | 170.3 | 172.8 | 175.6 | 177.4 | 180.5 | 181.7 | 182.1 | 180.6 | 178.3 | 178.4 | 175.6 | 176.9 |
| 2014 | 169.4 | 168.5 | 171.7 | 177.3 | 179.8 | 182.1 | 182.6 | 183.1 | 182.1 | 182.3 | 181.8 | 179.4 | 178.3 |
| 2015 | 173.3 | 173.0 | 175.2 | 183.6 | 186.8 | 188.5 | 191.0 | 190.8 | 189.1 | 190.0 | 188.7 | 187.7 | 184.8 |
| 2016 | 180.1 | 179.1 | 182.4 | 187.1 | 188.6 | 191.2 | 191.7 | 191.2 | 191.2 | 193.3 | 192.6 | 190.6 | 188.3 |
| 2017 | 183.9 | 185.1 | 187.8 | 191.7 | 194.2 | 197.5 | 197.4 | 197.8 | 196.9 | 197.5 | 196.2 | 195.9 | 193.5 |
| 2018 | 189.2 | 190.8 | 193.3 | 196.5 | 198.6 | 201.9 | 203.1 | 203.2 | 200.0 | 201.8 | 201.5 | 200.2 | 198.3 |
| 2019 | 195.9 | 196.2 | 198.9 | 201.5 | 204.0 | 206.1 | 207.6 | 207.9 | 205.9 | 205.7 | 203.6 | 200.8 | 202.8 |

# 1. Employment by Industry: Virginia, 2011–2019—*Continued*

(Numbers in thousands, not seasonally adjusted)

| Industry and year | January | February | March | April | May | June | July | August | September | October | November | December | Annual average |
|---|---|---|---|---|---|---|---|---|---|---|---|---|---|
| **Manufacturing** | | | | | | | | | | | | | |
| 2011 | 227.4 | 227.9 | 229.1 | 230.2 | 230.8 | 232.2 | 233.3 | 233.1 | 232.8 | 232.1 | 232.1 | 231.9 | 231.1 |
| 2012 | 230.8 | 230.8 | 231.3 | 230.8 | 230.4 | 230.5 | 232.7 | 232.7 | 232.9 | 232.2 | 232.2 | 232.4 | 231.6 |
| 2013 | 229.9 | 230.0 | 230.3 | 230.3 | 230.6 | 231.7 | 232.0 | 231.9 | 231.3 | 231.5 | 231.8 | 232.5 | 231.2 |
| 2014 | 230.0 | 229.7 | 230.5 | 231.5 | 232.6 | 233.8 | 233.3 | 233.3 | 233.2 | 232.9 | 233.0 | 233.4 | 232.3 |
| 2015 | 231.3 | 231.0 | 231.6 | 233.1 | 233.7 | 235.0 | 235.8 | 235.7 | 235.7 | 235.5 | 235.6 | 235.6 | 234.1 |
| 2016 | 232.9 | 232.1 | 232.2 | 231.6 | 232.1 | 233.3 | 233.9 | 234.0 | 233.9 | 233.9 | 234.0 | 234.0 | 233.2 |
| 2017 | 231.8 | 232.7 | 233.4 | 234.5 | 234.3 | 235.5 | 235.8 | 235.8 | 235.4 | 236.2 | 236.6 | 237.1 | 234.9 |
| 2018 | 234.6 | 236.4 | 237.2 | 238.1 | 239.6 | 241.8 | 242.6 | 242.4 | 242.9 | 243.0 | 243.5 | 243.7 | 240.5 |
| 2019 | 241.8 | 242.4 | 243.3 | 243.8 | 244.1 | 245.2 | 244.3 | 243.7 | 242.6 | 239.7 | 244.9 | 244.5 | 243.4 |
| **Trade, Transportation, and Utilities** | | | | | | | | | | | | | |
| 2011 | 619.2 | 614.0 | 616.5 | 622.7 | 625.9 | 628.7 | 629.0 | 630.1 | 626.2 | 629.7 | 644.2 | 652.7 | 628.2 |
| 2012 | 626.5 | 619.5 | 623.6 | 625.3 | 631.0 | 632.7 | 630.6 | 630.7 | 628.7 | 635.8 | 651.9 | 660.3 | 633.1 |
| 2013 | 626.3 | 620.4 | 622.6 | 626.0 | 630.7 | 634.5 | 635.2 | 636.0 | 632.7 | 637.7 | 653.1 | 660.7 | 634.7 |
| 2014 | 631.9 | 624.7 | 628.5 | 633.5 | 638.0 | 641.8 | 641.3 | 642.2 | 638.8 | 643.9 | 658.7 | 667.2 | 640.9 |
| 2015 | 639.2 | 632.8 | 634.2 | 641.2 | 647.4 | 651.8 | 657.5 | 658.5 | 655.5 | 660.2 | 674.7 | 680.8 | 652.8 |
| 2016 | 652.3 | 647.0 | 649.8 | 654.8 | 659.2 | 662.7 | 660.5 | 661.4 | 657.4 | 661.9 | 678.0 | 683.1 | 660.7 |
| 2017 | 656.3 | 649.8 | 650.7 | 654.4 | 658.9 | 663.5 | 662.0 | 662.1 | 658.5 | 661.9 | 677.7 | 681.9 | 661.5 |
| 2018 | 655.3 | 650.7 | 651.7 | 653.5 | 659.5 | 662.0 | 661.3 | 661.2 | 656.9 | 660.7 | 677.9 | 682.1 | 661.1 |
| 2019 | 656.5 | 648.2 | 650.5 | 652.8 | 655.6 | 660.1 | 658.5 | 657.9 | 653.9 | 659.1 | 672.9 | 679.6 | 658.8 |
| **Wholesale Trade** | | | | | | | | | | | | | |
| 2011 | 110.2 | 110.2 | 110.7 | 111.3 | 111.4 | 111.7 | 111.9 | 111.7 | 110.8 | 110.4 | 110.6 | 110.8 | 111.0 |
| 2012 | 109.6 | 109.9 | 110.5 | 110.7 | 111.2 | 111.6 | 111.6 | 111.7 | 111.3 | 111.2 | 111.3 | 111.3 | 111.0 |
| 2013 | 110.1 | 110.3 | 110.7 | 110.4 | 110.5 | 110.6 | 110.5 | 110.4 | 109.9 | 109.9 | 109.9 | 110.0 | 110.3 |
| 2014 | 109.0 | 109.0 | 109.5 | 109.9 | 110.5 | 110.6 | 110.6 | 110.6 | 109.9 | 109.7 | 109.9 | 110.1 | 109.9 |
| 2015 | 108.6 | 108.5 | 108.7 | 109.1 | 109.6 | 110.0 | 111.0 | 110.8 | 110.4 | 110.6 | 110.7 | 110.9 | 109.9 |
| 2016 | 109.3 | 109.1 | 109.4 | 110.2 | 110.5 | 110.6 | 110.5 | 110.4 | 110.2 | 110.4 | 110.5 | 110.8 | 110.2 |
| 2017 | 109.2 | 109.6 | 109.8 | 110.2 | 110.8 | 111.5 | 111.1 | 111.3 | 110.7 | 110.8 | 110.8 | 111.2 | 110.6 |
| 2018 | 109.5 | 109.7 | 109.8 | 110.1 | 110.1 | 110.9 | 110.6 | 110.6 | 109.9 | 110.0 | 110.1 | 110.2 | 110.1 |
| 2019 | 109.0 | 109.5 | 109.7 | 110.2 | 110.6 | 110.9 | 111.0 | 111.1 | 110.2 | 109.9 | 110.1 | 110.4 | 110.2 |
| **Retail Trade** | | | | | | | | | | | | | |
| 2011 | 396.1 | 391.4 | 393.0 | 397.8 | 400.3 | 402.0 | 401.2 | 402.2 | 399.8 | 403.8 | 417.4 | 423.9 | 402.4 |
| 2012 | 403.5 | 395.9 | 399.4 | 400.0 | 403.9 | 404.5 | 402.4 | 402.3 | 400.9 | 407.6 | 423.2 | 429.0 | 406.1 |
| 2013 | 401.2 | 396.3 | 397.6 | 400.8 | 404.6 | 407.4 | 407.5 | 408.1 | 405.5 | 410.2 | 423.9 | 428.8 | 407.7 |
| 2014 | 405.6 | 400.1 | 402.6 | 406.5 | 409.0 | 411.5 | 410.5 | 410.7 | 407.4 | 412.2 | 424.4 | 429.5 | 410.8 |
| 2015 | 407.6 | 402.4 | 403.8 | 408.6 | 413.0 | 415.8 | 417.7 | 418.5 | 416.1 | 420.1 | 432.0 | 434.6 | 415.9 |
| 2016 | 413.6 | 409.6 | 411.9 | 415.0 | 418.3 | 420.5 | 419.1 | 420.1 | 416.1 | 420.2 | 432.8 | 434.8 | 419.3 |
| 2017 | 415.9 | 409.9 | 410.9 | 413.4 | 416.0 | 419.2 | 418.3 | 417.5 | 413.5 | 416.9 | 430.4 | 431.5 | 417.8 |
| 2018 | 413.7 | 408.8 | 409.6 | 410.4 | 415.0 | 415.0 | 413.7 | 412.7 | 408.8 | 410.1 | 423.7 | 423.3 | 413.7 |
| 2019 | 407.8 | 401.0 | 402.6 | 403.9 | 405.1 | 407.6 | 405.9 | 404.7 | 401.8 | 406.1 | 415.9 | 418.7 | 406.8 |
| **Transportation and Utilities** | | | | | | | | | | | | | |
| 2011 | 112.9 | 112.4 | 112.8 | 113.6 | 114.2 | 115.0 | 115.9 | 116.2 | 115.6 | 115.5 | 116.2 | 118.0 | 114.9 |
| 2012 | 113.4 | 113.7 | 113.7 | 114.6 | 115.9 | 116.6 | 116.6 | 116.7 | 116.5 | 117.0 | 117.4 | 120.0 | 116.0 |
| 2013 | 115.0 | 113.8 | 114.3 | 114.8 | 115.6 | 116.5 | 117.2 | 117.5 | 117.3 | 117.6 | 119.3 | 121.9 | 116.7 |
| 2014 | 117.3 | 115.6 | 116.4 | 117.1 | 118.5 | 119.7 | 120.2 | 120.9 | 121.5 | 122.0 | 124.4 | 127.6 | 120.1 |
| 2015 | 123.0 | 121.9 | 121.7 | 123.5 | 124.8 | 126.0 | 128.8 | 129.2 | 129.0 | 129.5 | 132.0 | 135.3 | 127.1 |
| 2016 | 129.4 | 128.3 | 128.5 | 129.6 | 130.4 | 131.6 | 130.9 | 130.9 | 131.1 | 131.3 | 134.7 | 137.5 | 131.2 |
| 2017 | 131.2 | 130.3 | 130.0 | 130.8 | 132.1 | 132.8 | 132.6 | 133.3 | 134.3 | 134.2 | 136.5 | 139.2 | 133.1 |
| 2018 | 132.1 | 132.2 | 132.3 | 133.0 | 134.4 | 136.1 | 137.0 | 137.9 | 138.2 | 140.6 | 144.1 | 148.6 | 137.2 |
| 2019 | 139.7 | 137.7 | 138.2 | 138.7 | 139.9 | 141.6 | 141.6 | 142.1 | 141.9 | 143.1 | 146.9 | 150.5 | 141.8 |
| **Information** | | | | | | | | | | | | | |
| 2011 | 74.7 | 74.6 | 74.7 | 74.1 | 74.3 | 74.5 | 74.8 | 70.2 | 73.5 | 72.7 | 73.3 | 74.2 | 73.8 |
| 2012 | 71.4 | 72.1 | 72.6 | 71.2 | 71.9 | 72.9 | 71.7 | 72.9 | 70.3 | 70.5 | 72.2 | 71.0 | 71.7 |
| 2013 | 70.4 | 72.1 | 72.0 | 71.1 | 71.2 | 71.5 | 71.7 | 72.9 | 70.7 | 71.1 | 72.6 | 71.5 | 71.6 |
| 2014 | 72.3 | 70.9 | 71.0 | 70.9 | 72.4 | 71.4 | 71.5 | 72.4 | 70.4 | 70.9 | 70.1 | 70.1 | 71.2 |
| 2015 | 70.0 | 69.5 | 69.2 | 69.4 | 70.1 | 69.8 | 70.6 | 69.9 | 68.9 | 69.4 | 69.3 | 69.2 | 69.6 |
| 2016 | 68.6 | 68.8 | 68.0 | 68.6 | 66.2 | 69.1 | 69.2 | 68.9 | 68.5 | 67.6 | 67.6 | 68.3 | 68.3 |
| 2017 | 67.9 | 68.4 | 68.3 | 68.0 | 68.3 | 68.7 | 68.4 | 67.9 | 67.7 | 67.5 | 68.4 | 68.2 | 68.1 |
| 2018 | 67.4 | 68.1 | 67.5 | 67.8 | 68.4 | 68.7 | 68.5 | 68.0 | 66.7 | 67.2 | 67.5 | 67.1 | 67.7 |
| 2019 | 66.8 | 67.4 | 67.5 | 67.5 | 68.4 | 68.6 | 68.9 | 69.1 | 68.0 | 68.7 | 69.2 | 69.1 | 68.3 |

## 1. Employment by Industry: Virginia, 2011–2019—*Continued*

(Numbers in thousands, not seasonally adjusted)

| Industry and year | January | February | March | April | May | June | July | August | September | October | November | December | Annual average |
|---|---|---|---|---|---|---|---|---|---|---|---|---|---|
| **Financial Activities** | | | | | | | | | | | | | |
| 2011 | 178.4 | 178.6 | 179.0 | 180.9 | 182.0 | 183.7 | 185.4 | 185.4 | 184.2 | 183.8 | 184.2 | 185.3 | 182.6 |
| 2012 | 183.2 | 184.0 | 184.8 | 186.8 | 187.3 | 189.6 | 190.7 | 190.8 | 189.9 | 190.3 | 190.7 | 191.4 | 188.3 |
| 2013 | 189.2 | 189.7 | 190.4 | 191.4 | 192.1 | 193.9 | 194.8 | 194.6 | 193.0 | 193.4 | 193.6 | 193.9 | 192.5 |
| 2014 | 190.8 | 191.1 | 191.7 | 192.5 | 193.5 | 195.6 | 196.3 | 196.0 | 194.5 | 194.7 | 195.1 | 195.7 | 194.0 |
| 2015 | 194.1 | 194.8 | 195.2 | 195.9 | 197.3 | 198.9 | 200.2 | 200.0 | 198.5 | 199.1 | 199.1 | 199.6 | 197.7 |
| 2016 | 197.5 | 197.5 | 198.1 | 199.5 | 200.7 | 202.2 | 202.9 | 203.3 | 201.5 | 202.3 | 202.8 | 203.6 | 201.0 |
| 2017 | 201.2 | 202.0 | 202.3 | 202.7 | 204.3 | 206.7 | 207.7 | 207.3 | 205.7 | 206.6 | 206.8 | 207.4 | 205.1 |
| 2018 | 204.6 | 205.7 | 205.8 | 206.8 | 208.0 | 210.1 | 210.7 | 210.5 | 208.5 | 209.1 | 209.5 | 209.9 | 208.3 |
| 2019 | 208.3 | 209.1 | 209.1 | 210.4 | 211.7 | 214.1 | 214.6 | 214.2 | 212.5 | 212.0 | 213.9 | 214.6 | 212.0 |
| **Professional and Business Services** | | | | | | | | | | | | | |
| 2011 | 652.9 | 655.6 | 659.6 | 665.7 | 664.1 | 666.5 | 672.9 | 674.9 | 673.9 | 675.5 | 677.4 | 673.3 | 667.7 |
| 2012 | 664.5 | 667.1 | 671.1 | 675.9 | 675.9 | 679.3 | 682.0 | 685.6 | 682.1 | 687.8 | 686.7 | 685.2 | 678.6 |
| 2013 | 675.4 | 677.7 | 680.0 | 682.6 | 681.1 | 683.6 | 683.9 | 686.1 | 679.8 | 680.7 | 685.9 | 680.3 | 681.4 |
| 2014 | 668.9 | 668.5 | 670.9 | 681.2 | 683.4 | 685.3 | 687.2 | 688.2 | 682.5 | 688.0 | 693.1 | 690.4 | 682.3 |
| 2015 | 681.2 | 680.5 | 681.9 | 697.0 | 700.5 | 703.7 | 709.7 | 710.0 | 706.0 | 717.2 | 721.8 | 720.1 | 702.5 |
| 2016 | 700.4 | 702.9 | 705.1 | 712.3 | 711.2 | 715.9 | 719.5 | 722.1 | 719.5 | 724.0 | 726.4 | 725.8 | 715.4 |
| 2017 | 710.4 | 716.3 | 717.4 | 724.3 | 726.7 | 734.9 | 736.9 | 738.0 | 733.6 | 738.4 | 743.3 | 741.1 | 730.1 |
| 2018 | 730.6 | 736.8 | 739.2 | 746.5 | 748.1 | 753.9 | 756.3 | 757.4 | 747.8 | 757.9 | 762.0 | 755.2 | 749.3 |
| 2019 | 749.4 | 752.8 | 753.7 | 762.4 | 765.2 | 772.5 | 774.5 | 775.2 | 766.6 | 772.7 | 777.7 | 775.5 | 766.5 |
| **Education and Health Services** | | | | | | | | | | | | | |
| 2011 | 467.2 | 470.2 | 472.0 | 472.0 | 464.9 | 462.1 | 464.0 | 465.6 | 473.7 | 476.6 | 478.0 | 469.4 | 469.6 |
| 2012 | 473.7 | 477.0 | 478.8 | 480.8 | 473.3 | 472.1 | 472.3 | 478.1 | 486.2 | 491.5 | 493.1 | 487.5 | 480.4 |
| 2013 | 488.5 | 492.9 | 495.3 | 494.8 | 485.9 | 482.0 | 482.7 | 488.0 | 495.6 | 498.4 | 500.6 | 492.5 | 491.4 |
| 2014 | 494.1 | 495.2 | 497.0 | 502.3 | 494.2 | 491.0 | 490.7 | 495.0 | 501.8 | 505.6 | 506.2 | 499.5 | 497.7 |
| 2015 | 504.6 | 506.6 | 507.7 | 515.1 | 507.3 | 504.6 | 508.9 | 513.2 | 520.6 | 526.5 | 528.5 | 522.4 | 513.8 |
| 2016 | 523.8 | 526.2 | 528.0 | 531.9 | 522.5 | 519.2 | 516.9 | 523.7 | 529.0 | 534.0 | 535.9 | 526.7 | 526.5 |
| 2017 | 532.0 | 536.5 | 538.0 | 538.0 | 531.2 | 527.3 | 528.3 | 530.7 | 537.3 | 544.6 | 543.1 | 539.8 | 535.6 |
| 2018 | 543.2 | 546.8 | 548.0 | 550.6 | 539.5 | 538.6 | 538.8 | 540.8 | 549.3 | 555.3 | 556.0 | 547.8 | 546.2 |
| 2019 | 549.0 | 555.6 | 556.9 | 557.2 | 546.2 | 546.1 | 546.7 | 550.0 | 559.0 | 564.5 | 566.2 | 565.3 | 555.2 |
| **Leisure and Hospitality** | | | | | | | | | | | | | |
| 2011 | 319.9 | 323.5 | 333.0 | 346.9 | 359.2 | 371.8 | 372.0 | 370.7 | 357.4 | 350.0 | 344.0 | 342.4 | 349.2 |
| 2012 | 330.2 | 335.2 | 344.8 | 355.2 | 368.3 | 379.5 | 379.3 | 380.4 | 367.2 | 359.4 | 354.2 | 353.3 | 358.9 |
| 2013 | 340.4 | 342.9 | 351.7 | 363.2 | 375.4 | 386.1 | 387.9 | 387.0 | 373.6 | 365.3 | 360.0 | 358.9 | 366.0 |
| 2014 | 345.1 | 345.4 | 354.7 | 368.9 | 384.2 | 394.1 | 392.7 | 392.1 | 378.5 | 371.6 | 364.8 | 363.8 | 371.3 |
| 2015 | 354.7 | 356.4 | 363.0 | 380.0 | 394.6 | 405.5 | 410.3 | 409.4 | 397.8 | 390.9 | 385.4 | 384.9 | 386.1 |
| 2016 | 370.6 | 374.3 | 384.8 | 398.5 | 409.8 | 421.0 | 421.8 | 420.1 | 406.5 | 398.5 | 393.6 | 390.9 | 399.2 |
| 2017 | 376.9 | 383.4 | 391.8 | 404.1 | 415.6 | 427.0 | 426.3 | 424.2 | 407.7 | 404.5 | 397.3 | 395.5 | 404.5 |
| 2018 | 383.4 | 386.7 | 395.7 | 406.8 | 419.6 | 431.8 | 431.2 | 429.3 | 409.1 | 407.1 | 402.3 | 399.8 | 408.6 |
| 2019 | 387.6 | 390.6 | 400.0 | 409.0 | 419.3 | 432.0 | 431.8 | 427.6 | 409.2 | 410.3 | 406.3 | 405.1 | 410.7 |
| **Other Services** | | | | | | | | | | | | | |
| 2011 | 183.0 | 184.0 | 185.2 | 187.9 | 188.3 | 190.4 | 191.4 | 190.1 | 188.6 | 188.5 | 188.5 | 188.7 | 187.9 |
| 2012 | 186.8 | 187.8 | 189.0 | 192.5 | 193.3 | 194.9 | 195.5 | 194.2 | 192.8 | 193.6 | 193.2 | 193.0 | 192.2 |
| 2013 | 190.9 | 191.6 | 192.5 | 193.5 | 194.6 | 196.2 | 197.5 | 196.2 | 194.4 | 194.2 | 194.1 | 193.9 | 194.1 |
| 2014 | 191.8 | 192.0 | 193.6 | 194.9 | 196.3 | 198.5 | 198.1 | 198.0 | 196.1 | 195.4 | 195.0 | 194.7 | 195.4 |
| 2015 | 193.9 | 194.0 | 195.5 | 195.2 | 196.9 | 198.7 | 200.2 | 199.7 | 197.8 | 198.1 | 198.3 | 198.0 | 197.2 |
| 2016 | 195.5 | 195.9 | 197.4 | 200.7 | 201.3 | 203.3 | 204.2 | 203.0 | 201.3 | 201.9 | 201.7 | 200.9 | 200.6 |
| 2017 | 199.2 | 199.7 | 200.9 | 199.8 | 200.4 | 203.0 | 203.5 | 201.9 | 200.3 | 200.9 | 200.2 | 200.1 | 200.8 |
| 2018 | 198.3 | 198.7 | 199.7 | 199.3 | 200.4 | 202.7 | 202.8 | 201.8 | 199.0 | 199.9 | 200.1 | 199.8 | 200.2 |
| 2019 | 198.3 | 199.4 | 200.4 | 201.1 | 202.5 | 204.7 | 205.9 | 204.6 | 201.8 | 202.1 | 202.6 | 201.5 | 202.1 |
| **Government** | | | | | | | | | | | | | |
| 2011 | 706.4 | 718.6 | 722.0 | 723.1 | 717.7 | 714.9 | 683.0 | 679.1 | 713.3 | 723.8 | 729.2 | 728.1 | 713.3 |
| 2012 | 711.4 | 722.9 | 724.5 | 723.8 | 719.0 | 716.0 | 677.5 | 680.3 | 710.6 | 722.2 | 727.6 | 726.9 | 713.6 |
| 2013 | 709.9 | 722.1 | 723.3 | 725.4 | 721.1 | 714.9 | 684.5 | 680.9 | 709.3 | 716.4 | 721.9 | 720.3 | 712.5 |
| 2014 | 706.4 | 714.8 | 717.3 | 721.0 | 717.5 | 711.4 | 684.4 | 682.7 | 711.4 | 716.5 | 721.6 | 721.4 | 710.5 |
| 2015 | 706.4 | 718.7 | 717.4 | 721.7 | 717.3 | 712.5 | 684.3 | 681.0 | 709.6 | 719.8 | 724.3 | 723.5 | 711.4 |
| 2016 | 706.4 | 719.3 | 723.0 | 725.4 | 719.6 | 714.7 | 688.5 | 685.5 | 715.4 | 721.8 | 727.0 | 726.1 | 714.4 |
| 2017 | 709.8 | 722.6 | 723.2 | 727.2 | 722.3 | 719.4 | 690.4 | 687.4 | 718.6 | 723.1 | 729.1 | 726.8 | 716.7 |
| 2018 | 714.9 | 727.2 | 729.5 | 730.8 | 728.0 | 724.8 | 697.4 | 694.5 | 724.9 | 730.3 | 736.7 | 733.8 | 722.7 |
| 2019 | 720.2 | 734.5 | 735.3 | 738.7 | 734.2 | 730.1 | 706.1 | 706.6 | 733.4 | 739.4 | 750.5 | 740.5 | 730.8 |

## 2. Average Weekly Hours by Selected Industry: Virginia, 2015–2019

(Not seasonally adjusted)

| Industry and year | January | February | March | April | May | June | July | August | September | October | November | December | Annual average |
|---|---|---|---|---|---|---|---|---|---|---|---|---|---|
| **Total Private** | | | | | | | | | | | | | |
| 2015 | 34.6 | 35.1 | 35.3 | 35.3 | 35.3 | 35.1 | 35.1 | 35.6 | 35.0 | 34.9 | 35.4 | 35.0 | 35.1 |
| 2016 | 34.7 | 34.7 | 34.8 | 34.9 | 35.1 | 34.9 | 34.9 | 35.1 | 35.1 | 35.3 | 34.9 | 34.8 | 34.9 |
| 2017 | 34.7 | 34.8 | 34.5 | 35.0 | 34.4 | 34.7 | 35.1 | 34.5 | 34.8 | 35.0 | 34.8 | 34.9 | 34.8 |
| 2018 | 34.3 | 34.7 | 34.5 | 35.3 | 34.6 | 34.7 | 35.1 | 34.7 | 34.7 | 34.5 | 34.3 | 34.5 | 34.7 |
| 2019 | 33.9 | 33.9 | 34.3 | 34.5 | 34.5 | 34.9 | 34.1 | 34.5 | 34.8 | 34.3 | 34.2 | 34.3 | 34.3 |
| **Goods-Producing** | | | | | | | | | | | | | |
| 2015 | 38.8 | 38.9 | 39.3 | 40.0 | 40.6 | 40.6 | 39.9 | 40.5 | 39.8 | 40.2 | 40.1 | 40.5 | 39.9 |
| 2016 | 39.9 | 38.3 | 39.1 | 39.5 | 38.8 | 39.5 | 39.7 | 39.8 | 39.4 | 39.4 | 39.2 | 39.0 | 39.3 |
| 2017 | 38.7 | 39.7 | 39.1 | 39.5 | 39.1 | 40.1 | 40.1 | 39.1 | 39.7 | 39.8 | 40.1 | 40.3 | 39.6 |
| 2018 | 38.9 | 39.4 | 39.3 | 40.7 | 40.7 | 39.9 | 40.0 | 40.3 | 38.5 | 40.5 | 40.0 | 39.6 | 39.8 |
| 2019 | 40.5 | 39.7 | 40.9 | 41.0 | 41.1 | 40.9 | 40.2 | 41.3 | 41.2 | 41.0 | 40.3 | 39.6 | 40.6 |
| **Construction** | | | | | | | | | | | | | |
| 2015 | 35.5 | 36.6 | 37.5 | 38.4 | 39.7 | 39.8 | 38.8 | 39.1 | 37.3 | 38.7 | 37.8 | 38.0 | 38.1 |
| 2016 | 37.4 | 35.6 | 37.3 | 38.1 | 37.2 | 38.7 | 39.1 | 39.1 | 39.0 | 39.2 | 38.4 | 37.5 | 38.1 |
| 2017 | 36.5 | 38.0 | 36.4 | 38.5 | 37.4 | 39.0 | 39.1 | 37.9 | 38.8 | 38.6 | 39.0 | 39.6 | 38.3 |
| 2018 | 37.4 | 38.1 | 38.4 | 40.0 | 40.5 | 39.6 | 40.1 | 40.0 | 37.1 | 40.0 | 38.4 | 38.5 | 39.0 |
| 2019 | 39.1 | 38.1 | 40.5 | 41.0 | 40.6 | 40.8 | 40.5 | 41.0 | 41.1 | 40.9 | 39.8 | 38.6 | 40.2 |
| **Manufacturing** | | | | | | | | | | | | | |
| 2015 | 41.7 | 41.0 | 41.0 | 41.6 | 41.5 | 41.4 | 41.1 | 41.9 | 42.5 | 41.7 | 42.3 | 42.8 | 41.7 |
| 2016 | 42.1 | 40.6 | 40.7 | 40.7 | 39.9 | 39.9 | 40.0 | 40.1 | 39.7 | 39.4 | 39.7 | 40.3 | 40.3 |
| 2017 | 40.6 | 41.3 | 40.9 | 39.8 | 40.1 | 40.5 | 40.5 | 40.0 | 40.3 | 40.7 | 41.0 | 40.7 | 40.5 |
| 2018 | 40.1 | 40.4 | 39.7 | 40.9 | 40.3 | 39.8 | 39.4 | 40.2 | 40.0 | 40.4 | 41.4 | 40.4 | 40.2 |
| 2019 | 40.6 | 40.5 | 40.5 | 40.3 | 40.6 | 39.7 | 38.6 | 39.7 | 39.4 | 39.7 | 39.4 | 39.4 | 39.9 |
| **Trade, Transportation, and Utilities** | | | | | | | | | | | | | |
| 2015 | 33.7 | 33.7 | 33.8 | 33.9 | 34.4 | 34.0 | 34.3 | 34.3 | 34.3 | 34.0 | 34.0 | 34.2 | 34.1 |
| 2016 | 33.2 | 33.4 | 33.2 | 33.3 | 33.4 | 33.5 | 33.7 | 33.9 | 34.0 | 33.6 | 33.1 | 33.8 | 33.5 |
| 2017 | 32.9 | 33.1 | 33.3 | 33.7 | 33.4 | 33.1 | 33.5 | 33.3 | 33.6 | 33.2 | 33.3 | 33.5 | 33.3 |
| 2018 | 32.8 | 32.7 | 32.7 | 33.5 | 33.2 | 33.3 | 33.7 | 33.2 | 33.4 | 32.9 | 33.1 | 33.3 | 33.2 |
| 2019 | 32.0 | 32.3 | 32.7 | 32.7 | 32.7 | 33.0 | 32.9 | 32.7 | 33.2 | 33.0 | 32.8 | 33.3 | 32.8 |
| **Professional and Business Services** | | | | | | | | | | | | | |
| 2015 | 36.4 | 37.4 | 37.7 | 37.2 | 37.2 | 36.9 | 36.8 | 37.9 | 36.6 | 36.6 | 37.9 | 37.3 | 37.2 |
| 2016 | 36.9 | 37.0 | 37.2 | 37.7 | 38.2 | 37.5 | 37.2 | 37.4 | 37.5 | 38.2 | 37.4 | 37.2 | 37.5 |
| 2017 | 37.7 | 37.5 | 37.1 | 38.0 | 36.8 | 37.8 | 38.0 | 37.4 | 37.9 | 38.4 | 37.7 | 37.5 | 37.7 |
| 2018 | 37.3 | 37.8 | 37.4 | 38.3 | 37.2 | 37.6 | 37.8 | 37.0 | 37.7 | 36.9 | 36.4 | 37.3 | 37.4 |
| 2019 | 36.4 | 36.6 | 36.8 | 37.9 | 38.0 | 38.4 | 37.1 | 37.5 | 38.2 | 37.5 | 37.3 | 37.8 | 37.5 |
| **Education and Health Services** | | | | | | | | | | | | | |
| 2015 | 34.2 | 34.6 | 34.3 | 34.2 | 34.2 | 34.2 | 34.1 | 34.5 | 34.2 | 34.3 | 34.7 | 33.7 | 34.3 |
| 2016 | 34.6 | 34.5 | 34.6 | 34.7 | 35.1 | 34.8 | 34.6 | 34.7 | 34.7 | 34.8 | 34.4 | 34.4 | 34.7 |
| 2017 | 34.6 | 34.0 | 33.8 | 34.1 | 33.9 | 33.7 | 34.0 | 33.4 | 33.9 | 34.1 | 33.6 | 34.0 | 33.9 |
| 2018 | 33.7 | 34.0 | 33.4 | 33.6 | 33.3 | 33.3 | 34.0 | 33.9 | 33.8 | 33.0 | 32.8 | 32.5 | 33.4 |
| 2019 | 32.6 | 32.3 | 32.4 | 32.6 | 32.4 | 32.8 | 32.2 | 32.6 | 32.8 | 32.2 | 32.6 | 31.9 | 32.4 |
| **Leisure and Hospitality** | | | | | | | | | | | | | |
| 2015 | 25.3 | 25.4 | 26.2 | 26.6 | 26.6 | 26.5 | 26.8 | 27.1 | 26.1 | 26.1 | 26.2 | 25.8 | 26.2 |
| 2016 | 24.7 | 25.6 | 25.9 | 26.3 | 26.4 | 26.4 | 26.7 | 26.5 | 26.4 | 26.8 | 26.7 | 26.2 | 26.2 |
| 2017 | 25.6 | 26.2 | 26.3 | 26.2 | 25.7 | 26.2 | 27.0 | 26.5 | 25.9 | 26.2 | 25.9 | 25.9 | 26.1 |
| 2018 | 25.1 | 25.9 | 25.9 | 26.3 | 26.0 | 26.4 | 26.6 | 26.6 | 25.7 | 26.3 | 25.6 | 25.5 | 26.0 |
| 2019 | 24.7 | 25.0 | 25.4 | 25.8 | 25.6 | 26.4 | 26.0 | 26.4 | 25.8 | 25.9 | 25.6 | 25.3 | 25.7 |
| **Other Services** | | | | | | | | | | | | | |
| 2014 | 32.4 | 32.4 | 32.5 | 32.5 | 31.9 | 32.7 | 32.7 | 32.4 | 31.8 | 32.1 | 32.8 | 32.4 | 32.4 |
| 2015 | 32.5 | 32.5 | 32.7 | 32.2 | 32.9 | 32.4 | 32.2 | 32.3 | 32.2 | 33.0 | 32.0 | 32.4 | 32.4 |
| 2016 | 32.6 | 32.2 | 32.1 | 33.1 | 32.0 | 32.0 | 32.6 | 31.7 | 31.4 | 32.6 | 31.8 | 32.5 | 32.2 |
| 2017 | 31.4 | 31.5 | 31.4 | 32.0 | 31.2 | 31.5 | 32.3 | 31.9 | 32.6 | 32.5 | 32.4 | 32.6 | 31.9 |
| 2018 | 30.4 | 31.5 | 31.9 | 31.5 | 31.5 | 32.0 | 31.3 | 31.6 | 32.5 | 31.4 | 31.6 | 32.4 | 31.6 |

## 3. Average Hourly Earnings by Selected Industry: Virginia, 2015–2019

(Dollars, not seasonally adjusted)

| Industry and year | January | February | March | April | May | June | July | August | September | October | November | December | Annual average |
|---|---|---|---|---|---|---|---|---|---|---|---|---|---|
| **Total Private** | | | | | | | | | | | | | |
| 2015 | 25.79 | 26.30 | 26.23 | 26.04 | 25.94 | 25.79 | 25.81 | 26.34 | 26.26 | 26.36 | 26.55 | 26.26 | 26.14 |
| 2016 | 26.64 | 26.63 | 26.71 | 26.89 | 27.20 | 26.76 | 27.03 | 26.64 | 27.08 | 27.55 | 27.13 | 27.29 | 26.96 |
| 2017 | 27.97 | 27.73 | 27.55 | 28.08 | 27.45 | 27.01 | 27.52 | 27.22 | 27.48 | 27.73 | 27.39 | 27.75 | 27.56 |
| 2018 | 28.09 | 27.87 | 27.97 | 28.26 | 27.97 | 28.05 | 28.46 | 28.28 | 29.07 | 28.53 | 28.65 | 29.46 | 28.39 |
| 2019 | 28.89 | 28.97 | 29.11 | 29.68 | 29.55 | 29.50 | 29.28 | 29.01 | 29.73 | 29.19 | 29.22 | 29.45 | 29.30 |
| **Goods-Producing** | | | | | | | | | | | | | |
| 2015 | 23.52 | 23.61 | 23.55 | 23.50 | 23.39 | 23.29 | 23.46 | 23.36 | 23.73 | 23.72 | 23.75 | 23.66 | 23.54 |
| 2016 | 23.96 | 24.19 | 24.06 | 24.35 | 24.42 | 24.60 | 24.98 | 24.82 | 24.98 | 25.08 | 24.77 | 24.78 | 24.59 |
| 2017 | 25.12 | 24.66 | 24.88 | 25.02 | 24.89 | 24.88 | 24.98 | 25.00 | 25.14 | 24.92 | 24.74 | 25.22 | 24.95 |
| 2018 | 25.19 | 25.01 | 25.08 | 24.98 | 25.01 | 24.84 | 24.75 | 25.24 | 25.29 | 25.70 | 25.47 | 26.31 | 25.24 |
| 2019 | 25.81 | 25.75 | 26.09 | 26.59 | 26.29 | 26.64 | 26.86 | 26.43 | 26.68 | 26.99 | 27.05 | 27.39 | 26.55 |
| **Construction** | | | | | | | | | | | | | |
| 2015 | 24.11 | 24.50 | 24.28 | 23.86 | 23.99 | 23.81 | 24.07 | 23.96 | 24.13 | 24.52 | 24.76 | 24.68 | 24.22 |
| 2016 | 25.19 | 25.51 | 25.47 | 25.66 | 25.50 | 25.51 | 25.49 | 25.62 | 25.67 | 25.65 | 25.61 | 25.59 | 25.54 |
| 2017 | 25.75 | 25.18 | 25.83 | 25.54 | 25.87 | 25.78 | 25.67 | 25.77 | 25.93 | 25.75 | 25.65 | 26.23 | 25.75 |
| 2018 | 26.11 | 26.10 | 26.00 | 25.82 | 26.04 | 25.61 | 25.80 | 26.35 | 26.15 | 26.50 | 25.96 | 26.92 | 26.11 |
| 2019 | 26.07 | 26.07 | 26.23 | 26.28 | 26.39 | 26.76 | 26.93 | 26.54 | 26.97 | 27.55 | 27.66 | 28.17 | 26.81 |
| **Manufacturing** | | | | | | | | | | | | | |
| 2015 | 22.79 | 23.19 | 23.14 | 23.05 | 22.70 | 22.66 | 22.76 | 22.68 | 23.40 | 22.92 | 22.76 | 22.64 | 22.89 |
| 2016 | 22.95 | 23.18 | 22.72 | 23.04 | 22.98 | 23.26 | 23.81 | 23.45 | 23.78 | 23.92 | 23.74 | 23.82 | 23.38 |
| 2017 | 24.06 | 23.73 | 23.77 | 24.36 | 23.84 | 23.89 | 23.98 | 23.96 | 23.97 | 23.97 | 23.71 | 24.04 | 23.94 |
| 2018 | 23.93 | 23.61 | 23.83 | 23.84 | 24.29 | 24.23 | 23.99 | 24.82 | 24.99 | 24.79 | 25.02 | 25.34 | 24.40 |
| 2019 | 25.29 | 25.47 | 25.72 | 25.68 | 25.27 | 25.69 | 26.02 | 25.72 | 25.92 | 25.66 | 25.59 | 25.86 | 25.66 |
| **Trade, Transportation, and Utilities** | | | | | | | | | | | | | |
| 2015 | 19.76 | 20.46 | 20.21 | 20.56 | 20.20 | 20.36 | 20.36 | 20.83 | 20.29 | 20.87 | 20.31 | 20.00 | 20.35 |
| 2016 | 20.71 | 20.04 | 20.35 | 21.24 | 20.87 | 20.95 | 21.47 | 20.98 | 21.34 | 21.77 | 21.30 | 21.37 | 21.04 |
| 2017 | 21.88 | 21.13 | 20.74 | 21.28 | 20.66 | 20.75 | 21.14 | 20.74 | 21.01 | 21.26 | 21.15 | 21.26 | 21.08 |
| 2018 | 21.51 | 21.60 | 21.62 | 21.98 | 21.60 | 21.94 | 22.63 | 22.61 | 23.54 | 23.10 | 22.87 | 23.89 | 22.42 |
| 2019 | 23.73 | 24.19 | 24.51 | 25.32 | 25.56 | 25.17 | 24.85 | 24.59 | 24.50 | 24.00 | 23.93 | 23.37 | 24.47 |
| **Professional and Business Services** | | | | | | | | | | | | | |
| 2015 | 35.19 | 35.87 | 35.49 | 34.82 | 34.81 | 34.56 | 34.87 | 35.55 | 35.50 | 36.06 | 36.36 | 35.50 | 35.39 |
| 2016 | 35.73 | 35.99 | 36.12 | 36.07 | 37.03 | 36.08 | 36.44 | 36.25 | 36.31 | 37.10 | 36.56 | 37.49 | 36.44 |
| 2017 | 38.45 | 37.70 | 37.72 | 38.20 | 37.68 | 36.74 | 37.55 | 37.36 | 37.57 | 37.54 | 36.93 | 37.69 | 37.59 |
| 2018 | 37.89 | 37.17 | 37.37 | 37.50 | 37.46 | 37.78 | 38.33 | 38.04 | 39.11 | 38.05 | 38.99 | 39.49 | 38.10 |
| 2019 | 38.26 | 37.85 | 38.30 | 38.33 | 38.31 | 38.69 | 38.22 | 38.20 | 38.90 | 38.30 | 38.79 | 39.83 | 38.51 |
| **Education and Health Services** | | | | | | | | | | | | | |
| 2015 | 24.77 | 25.02 | 25.40 | 25.50 | 25.72 | 25.85 | 25.45 | 25.98 | 26.22 | 26.04 | 26.00 | 26.94 | 25.75 |
| 2016 | 25.70 | 25.96 | 26.14 | 25.62 | 26.02 | 25.97 | 26.31 | 26.17 | 26.51 | 26.90 | 27.06 | 27.04 | 26.28 |
| 2017 | 27.56 | 27.73 | 27.61 | 27.72 | 27.50 | 27.28 | 27.80 | 27.38 | 27.44 | 27.76 | 27.66 | 27.73 | 27.60 |
| 2018 | 27.91 | 27.51 | 27.80 | 27.99 | 27.66 | 27.47 | 27.32 | 26.74 | 26.90 | 26.74 | 26.84 | 26.61 | 27.29 |
| 2019 | 26.38 | 26.59 | 26.56 | 25.88 | 25.70 | 25.50 | 26.05 | 25.57 | 25.59 | 25.91 | 25.53 | 25.26 | 25.88 |
| **Leisure and Hospitality** | | | | | | | | | | | | | |
| 2015 | 13.32 | 13.44 | 13.39 | 13.34 | 13.27 | 13.06 | 12.93 | 12.83 | 13.12 | 13.27 | 13.34 | 13.40 | 13.22 |
| 2016 | 13.48 | 13.37 | 13.29 | 13.38 | 13.60 | 13.21 | 13.18 | 13.12 | 13.31 | 13.57 | 13.57 | 13.94 | 13.41 |
| 2017 | 13.93 | 13.80 | 14.01 | 14.21 | 14.25 | 13.76 | 13.80 | 13.77 | 13.87 | 14.00 | 14.13 | 14.27 | 13.98 |
| 2018 | 14.33 | 14.42 | 14.37 | 14.41 | 14.47 | 14.15 | 14.22 | 14.36 | 14.46 | 14.59 | 14.83 | 15.03 | 14.46 |
| 2019 | 14.88 | 15.04 | 14.79 | 14.76 | 14.88 | 14.52 | 14.43 | 14.44 | 14.90 | 15.02 | 14.97 | 15.32 | 14.82 |
| **Other Services** | | | | | | | | | | | | | |
| 2014 | 26.23 | 25.79 | 26.22 | 25.80 | 26.37 | 25.91 | 25.82 | 26.21 | 26.64 | 26.62 | 27.15 | 27.37 | 26.34 |
| 2015 | 27.75 | 27.29 | 27.49 | 27.52 | 27.64 | 27.66 | 26.75 | 26.71 | 27.47 | 27.70 | 27.35 | 27.35 | 27.39 |
| 2016 | 27.95 | 27.58 | 27.52 | 27.95 | 27.79 | 27.50 | 27.82 | 27.79 | 27.69 | 28.19 | 27.68 | 27.47 | 27.75 |
| 2017 | 27.84 | 27.69 | 28.16 | 28.58 | 27.82 | 27.89 | 28.39 | 28.47 | 29.24 | 29.26 | 29.32 | 30.93 | 28.64 |
| 2018 | 31.69 | 31.92 | 31.92 | 32.43 | 32.53 | 32.88 | 32.51 | 32.03 | 32.73 | 32.25 | 32.79 | 32.59 | 32.36 |

# 4. Average Weekly Earnings by Selected Industry: Virginia, 2015–2019

(Dollars, not seasonally adjusted)

| Industry and year | January | February | March | April | May | June | July | August | September | October | November | December | Annual average |
|---|---|---|---|---|---|---|---|---|---|---|---|---|---|
| **Total Private** | | | | | | | | | | | | | |
| 2015 | 892.33 | 923.13 | 925.92 | 919.21 | 915.68 | 905.23 | 905.93 | 937.70 | 919.10 | 919.96 | 939.87 | 919.10 | 917.51 |
| 2016 | 924.41 | 924.06 | 929.51 | 938.46 | 954.72 | 933.58 | 943.35 | 935.06 | 950.51 | 972.52 | 946.84 | 949.69 | 940.90 |
| 2017 | 970.56 | 963.96 | 949.79 | 982.10 | 943.59 | 936.55 | 965.25 | 938.75 | 955.61 | 970.20 | 953.17 | 968.48 | 959.09 |
| 2018 | 963.14 | 966.74 | 964.62 | 997.23 | 967.42 | 973.34 | 998.60 | 981.32 | 1,008.73 | 984.29 | 982.70 | 1,016.37 | 985.13 |
| 2019 | 979.03 | 981.74 | 998.13 | 1,023.62 | 1,019.13 | 1,029.20 | 998.45 | 1,000.85 | 1,034.60 | 1,001.22 | 999.32 | 1,010.14 | 1,004.99 |
| **Goods-Producing** | | | | | | | | | | | | | |
| 2015 | 912.58 | 918.43 | 925.52 | 940.00 | 949.63 | 945.57 | 936.05 | 946.08 | 944.45 | 953.54 | 952.38 | 958.23 | 939.25 |
| 2016 | 956.00 | 926.48 | 940.75 | 961.83 | 947.50 | 971.70 | 991.71 | 987.84 | 984.21 | 988.15 | 970.98 | 966.42 | 966.39 |
| 2017 | 972.14 | 979.00 | 972.81 | 988.29 | 973.20 | 997.69 | 1,001.70 | 977.50 | 998.06 | 991.82 | 992.07 | 1,016.37 | 988.02 |
| 2018 | 979.89 | 985.39 | 985.64 | 1,016.69 | 1,017.91 | 991.12 | 990.00 | 1,017.17 | 973.67 | 1,040.85 | 1,018.80 | 1,041.88 | 1,004.55 |
| 2019 | 1,045.31 | 1,022.28 | 1,067.08 | 1,090.19 | 1,080.52 | 1,089.58 | 1,079.77 | 1,091.56 | 1,099.22 | 1,106.59 | 1,090.12 | 1,084.64 | 1,077.93 |
| **Construction** | | | | | | | | | | | | | |
| 2015 | 855.91 | 896.70 | 910.50 | 916.22 | 952.40 | 947.64 | 933.92 | 936.84 | 900.05 | 948.92 | 935.93 | 937.84 | 922.78 |
| 2016 | 942.11 | 908.16 | 950.03 | 977.65 | 948.60 | 987.24 | 996.66 | 1,001.74 | 1,001.13 | 1,005.48 | 983.42 | 959.63 | 973.07 |
| 2017 | 939.88 | 956.84 | 940.21 | 983.29 | 967.54 | 1,005.42 | 1,003.70 | 976.68 | 1,006.08 | 993.95 | 1,000.35 | 1,038.71 | 986.23 |
| 2018 | 976.51 | 994.41 | 998.40 | 1,032.80 | 1,054.62 | 1,014.16 | 1,034.58 | 1,054.00 | 970.17 | 1,060.00 | 996.86 | 1,036.42 | 1,018.29 |
| 2019 | 1,019.34 | 993.27 | 1,062.32 | 1,077.48 | 1,071.43 | 1,091.81 | 1,090.67 | 1,088.14 | 1,108.47 | 1,126.80 | 1,100.87 | 1,087.36 | 1,077.76 |
| **Manufacturing** | | | | | | | | | | | | | |
| 2015 | 950.34 | 950.79 | 948.74 | 958.88 | 942.05 | 938.12 | 935.44 | 950.29 | 994.50 | 955.76 | 962.75 | 968.99 | 954.51 |
| 2016 | 966.20 | 941.11 | 924.70 | 937.73 | 916.90 | 928.07 | 952.40 | 940.35 | 944.07 | 942.45 | 942.48 | 959.95 | 942.21 |
| 2017 | 976.84 | 980.05 | 972.19 | 969.53 | 955.98 | 967.55 | 971.19 | 958.40 | 965.99 | 975.58 | 972.11 | 978.43 | 969.57 |
| 2018 | 959.59 | 953.84 | 946.05 | 975.06 | 978.89 | 964.35 | 945.21 | 997.76 | 999.60 | 1,001.52 | 1,035.83 | 1,023.74 | 980.88 |
| 2019 | 1,026.77 | 1,031.54 | 1,041.66 | 1,034.90 | 1,025.96 | 1,019.89 | 1,004.37 | 1,021.08 | 1,021.25 | 1,018.70 | 1,008.25 | 1,018.88 | 1,023.83 |
| **Trade, Transportation, and Utilities** | | | | | | | | | | | | | |
| 2015 | 665.91 | 689.50 | 683.10 | 696.98 | 694.88 | 692.24 | 698.35 | 714.47 | 695.95 | 709.58 | 690.54 | 684.00 | 693.94 |
| 2016 | 687.57 | 669.34 | 675.62 | 707.29 | 697.06 | 701.83 | 723.54 | 711.22 | 725.56 | 731.47 | 705.03 | 712.21 | 704.84 |
| 2017 | 719.85 | 699.40 | 690.64 | 717.14 | 690.04 | 686.83 | 708.19 | 690.64 | 705.94 | 705.83 | 704.30 | 712.21 | 701.96 |
| 2018 | 705.53 | 706.32 | 706.97 | 736.33 | 717.12 | 730.60 | 762.63 | 750.65 | 786.24 | 759.99 | 757.00 | 795.54 | 744.34 |
| 2019 | 759.36 | 781.34 | 801.48 | 827.96 | 835.81 | 830.61 | 817.57 | 804.09 | 813.40 | 792.00 | 784.90 | 778.22 | 802.62 |
| **Professional and Business Services** | | | | | | | | | | | | | |
| 2015 | 1,280.92 | 1,341.54 | 1,337.97 | 1,295.30 | 1,294.93 | 1,275.26 | 1,283.22 | 1,347.35 | 1,299.30 | 1,319.80 | 1,378.04 | 1,324.15 | 1,316.51 |
| 2016 | 1,318.44 | 1,331.63 | 1,343.66 | 1,359.84 | 1,414.55 | 1,353.00 | 1,355.57 | 1,355.75 | 1,361.63 | 1,417.22 | 1,367.34 | 1,394.63 | 1,366.50 |
| 2017 | 1,449.57 | 1,413.75 | 1,399.41 | 1,451.60 | 1,386.62 | 1,388.77 | 1,426.90 | 1,397.26 | 1,423.90 | 1,441.54 | 1,392.26 | 1,413.38 | 1,417.14 |
| 2018 | 1,413.30 | 1,405.03 | 1,397.64 | 1,436.25 | 1,393.51 | 1,420.53 | 1,448.87 | 1,407.48 | 1,474.45 | 1,404.05 | 1,419.24 | 1,472.98 | 1,424.94 |
| 2019 | 1,392.66 | 1,385.31 | 1,409.44 | 1,452.71 | 1,455.78 | 1,485.70 | 1,417.96 | 1,432.50 | 1,485.98 | 1,436.25 | 1,446.87 | 1,505.57 | 1,444.13 |
| **Education and Health Services** | | | | | | | | | | | | | |
| 2015 | 847.13 | 865.69 | 871.22 | 872.10 | 879.62 | 884.07 | 867.85 | 896.31 | 896.72 | 893.17 | 902.20 | 907.88 | 883.23 |
| 2016 | 889.22 | 895.62 | 904.44 | 889.01 | 913.30 | 903.76 | 910.33 | 908.10 | 919.90 | 936.12 | 930.86 | 930.18 | 911.92 |
| 2017 | 953.58 | 942.82 | 933.22 | 945.25 | 932.25 | 919.34 | 945.20 | 914.49 | 930.22 | 946.62 | 929.38 | 942.82 | 935.64 |
| 2018 | 940.57 | 935.34 | 928.52 | 940.46 | 921.08 | 914.75 | 928.88 | 906.49 | 909.22 | 882.42 | 880.35 | 864.83 | 911.49 |
| 2019 | 859.99 | 858.86 | 860.54 | 843.69 | 832.68 | 836.40 | 838.81 | 833.58 | 839.35 | 834.30 | 832.28 | 805.79 | 838.51 |
| **Leisure and Hospitality** | | | | | | | | | | | | | |
| 2015 | 337.00 | 341.38 | 350.82 | 354.84 | 352.98 | 346.09 | 346.52 | 347.69 | 342.43 | 346.35 | 349.51 | 345.72 | 346.36 |
| 2016 | 332.96 | 342.27 | 344.21 | 351.89 | 359.04 | 348.74 | 351.91 | 347.68 | 351.38 | 363.68 | 362.32 | 365.23 | 351.34 |
| 2017 | 356.61 | 361.56 | 368.46 | 372.30 | 366.23 | 360.51 | 372.60 | 364.91 | 359.23 | 366.80 | 365.97 | 369.59 | 364.88 |
| 2018 | 359.68 | 373.48 | 372.18 | 378.98 | 376.22 | 373.56 | 378.25 | 381.98 | 371.62 | 383.72 | 379.65 | 383.27 | 375.96 |
| 2019 | 367.54 | 376.00 | 375.67 | 380.81 | 380.93 | 383.33 | 375.18 | 381.22 | 384.42 | 389.02 | 383.23 | 387.60 | 380.87 |
| **Other Services** | | | | | | | | | | | | | |
| 2015 | 849.85 | 835.60 | 852.15 | 838.50 | 841.20 | 847.26 | 844.31 | 849.20 | 847.15 | 854.50 | 890.52 | 886.79 | 853.42 |
| 2016 | 901.88 | 886.93 | 898.92 | 886.14 | 909.36 | 896.18 | 861.35 | 862.73 | 884.53 | 914.10 | 875.20 | 886.14 | 887.44 |
| 2017 | 911.17 | 888.08 | 883.39 | 925.15 | 889.28 | 880.00 | 906.93 | 880.94 | 869.47 | 918.99 | 880.22 | 892.78 | 893.55 |
| 2018 | 874.18 | 872.24 | 884.22 | 914.56 | 867.98 | 878.54 | 917.00 | 908.19 | 953.22 | 950.95 | 949.97 | 1,008.32 | 913.62 |
| 2019 | 963.38 | 1,005.48 | 1,018.25 | 1,021.55 | 1,024.70 | 1,052.16 | 1,017.56 | 1,012.15 | 1,063.73 | 1,012.65 | 1,036.16 | 1,055.92 | 1,022.58 |

# WASHINGTON
## *At a Glance*

Population:
  2010 census: 6,724,540
  2019 estimate: 7,614,893

Percent change in population:
  2010–2019: 13.2%

Percent change in total nonfarm employment:
  2011–2019: 20.8%

Industry with the largest growth in employment, 2011–2019 (percent):
  Information, 38.6%

Industry with the largest decline or smallest growth in employment, 2011–2019 (percent):
  Mining and logging, -1.7%

Civilian labor force:
  2010: 3,511,326
  2019: 3,914,154

Unemployment rate and rank among states (highest to lowest):
  2010: 10.0%, 17th
  2019: 4.3%, 9th

Over-the-year change in unemployment rates:
  2017–2018: -0.2%
  2018–2019: -0.2%

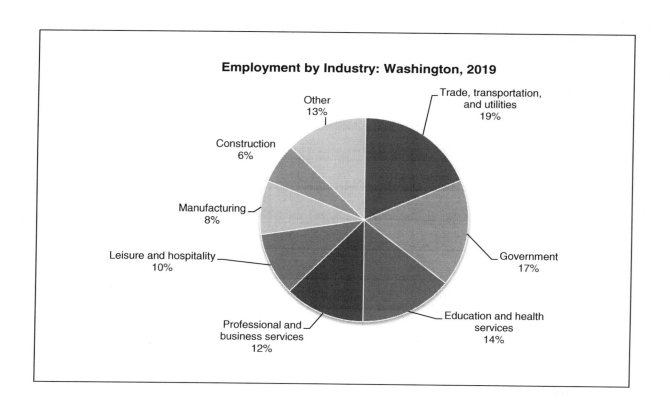

**Employment by Industry: Washington, 2019**

Other 13%

Trade, transportation, and utilities 19%

Construction 6%

Manufacturing 8%

Leisure and hospitality 10%

Government 17%

Professional and business services 12%

Education and health services 14%

# 1. Employment by Industry: Washington, 2011–2019

(Numbers in thousands, not seasonally adjusted)

| Industry and year | January | February | March | April | May | June | July | August | September | October | November | December | Annual average |
|---|---|---|---|---|---|---|---|---|---|---|---|---|---|
| **Total Nonfarm** | | | | | | | | | | | | | |
| 2011 | 2,807.6 | 2,820.2 | 2,832.3 | 2,862.7 | 2,880.6 | 2,893.8 | 2,889.0 | 2,878.0 | 2,895.8 | 2,905.8 | 2,908.6 | 2,895.7 | 2,872.5 |
| 2012 | 2,840.3 | 2,854.8 | 2,876.8 | 2,898.1 | 2,926.6 | 2,945.9 | 2,932.1 | 2,928.1 | 2,943.7 | 2,964.8 | 2,969.3 | 2,955.0 | 2,919.6 |
| 2013 | 2,906.7 | 2,924.6 | 2,939.0 | 2,960.6 | 2,990.3 | 3,001.8 | 2,993.0 | 2,994.6 | 3,012.1 | 3,027.4 | 3,033.6 | 3,024.1 | 2,984.0 |
| 2014 | 2,985.8 | 2,993.0 | 3,011.0 | 3,027.1 | 3,052.1 | 3,070.1 | 3,072.3 | 3,073.8 | 3,091.0 | 3,097.7 | 3,105.8 | 3,107.1 | 3,057.2 |
| | | | | | | | | | | | | | |
| 2015 | 3,061.9 | 3,074.2 | 3,096.1 | 3,121.3 | 3,148.1 | 3,171.5 | 3,163.4 | 3,158.0 | 3,177.9 | 3,183.9 | 3,191.4 | 3,189.2 | 3,144.7 |
| 2016 | 3,153.7 | 3,172.6 | 3,190.8 | 3,223.9 | 3,249.6 | 3,265.8 | 3,261.1 | 3,255.8 | 3,281.9 | 3,279.7 | 3,291.0 | 3,287.3 | 3,242.8 |
| 2017 | 3,234.6 | 3,251.5 | 3,277.0 | 3,300.0 | 3,330.8 | 3,355.7 | 3,341.3 | 3,331.6 | 3,351.2 | 3,354.1 | 3,363.8 | 3,362.1 | 3,321.1 |
| 2018 | 3,325.5 | 3,340.6 | 3,364.8 | 3,377.6 | 3,408.6 | 3,428.4 | 3,414.4 | 3,416.0 | 3,425.6 | 3,435.5 | 3,442.9 | 3,434.4 | 3,401.2 |
| 2019 | 3,396.1 | 3,381.6 | 3,422.1 | 3,449.7 | 3,479.0 | 3,498.3 | 3,493.7 | 3,492.9 | 3,494.4 | 3,501.8 | 3,510.9 | 3,509.6 | 3,469.2 |
| | | | | | | | | | | | | | |
| **Total Private** | | | | | | | | | | | | | |
| 2010 | 2,258.0 | 2,267.1 | 2,278.8 | 2,307.1 | 2,323.5 | 2,344.4 | 2,360.0 | 2,367.3 | 2,372.4 | 2,357.7 | 2,357.6 | 2,354.4 | 2,329.0 |
| 2011 | 2,297.9 | 2,309.0 | 2,328.2 | 2,347.0 | 2,374.1 | 2,399.3 | 2,406.1 | 2,419.3 | 2,418.4 | 2,415.1 | 2,415.7 | 2,411.2 | 2,378.4 |
| 2012 | 2,360.8 | 2,374.5 | 2,388.2 | 2,407.4 | 2,435.8 | 2,453.9 | 2,467.7 | 2,483.1 | 2,483.3 | 2,477.0 | 2,479.2 | 2,477.7 | 2,440.7 |
| 2013 | 2,436.4 | 2,440.3 | 2,455.8 | 2,468.7 | 2,492.1 | 2,516.0 | 2,537.4 | 2,552.1 | 2,550.3 | 2,536.6 | 2,542.8 | 2,550.7 | 2,506.6 |
| 2014 | 2,502.1 | 2,510.8 | 2,529.5 | 2,550.9 | 2,576.0 | 2,604.9 | 2,616.9 | 2,624.9 | 2,623.6 | 2,613.4 | 2,617.5 | 2,622.5 | 2,582.8 |
| | | | | | | | | | | | | | |
| 2015 | 2,581.6 | 2,596.1 | 2,612.6 | 2,642.1 | 2,663.3 | 2,688.2 | 2,701.1 | 2,709.8 | 2,713.6 | 2,693.2 | 2,700.4 | 2,703.6 | 2,667.1 |
| 2016 | 2,652.4 | 2,664.5 | 2,686.8 | 2,706.2 | 2,732.8 | 2,764.6 | 2,766.5 | 2,776.2 | 2,776.1 | 2,758.6 | 2,766.0 | 2,772.2 | 2,735.2 |
| 2017 | 2,734.9 | 2,747.4 | 2,769.7 | 2,779.6 | 2,807.9 | 2,835.7 | 2,841.6 | 2,858.1 | 2,850.2 | 2,842.0 | 2,850.2 | 2,849.4 | 2,813.9 |
| 2018 | 2,808.7 | 2,793.1 | 2,831.2 | 2,855.3 | 2,880.4 | 2,902.6 | 2,918.9 | 2,930.9 | 2,918.1 | 2,907.9 | 2,914.2 | 2,919.1 | 2,881.7 |
| 2019 | | | | | | | | | | | | | |
| | | | | | | | | | | | | | |
| **Goods Producing** | | | | | | | | | | | | | |
| 2011 | 391.0 | 393.6 | 396.4 | 402.0 | 407.2 | 414.2 | 422.1 | 426.7 | 428.9 | 424.9 | 418.3 | 412.4 | 411.5 |
| 2012 | 402.5 | 404.2 | 409.6 | 413.9 | 420.5 | 429.6 | 436.3 | 442.2 | 442.0 | 441.2 | 436.0 | 430.7 | 425.7 |
| 2013 | 422.8 | 426.3 | 429.6 | 432.3 | 439.0 | 445.9 | 452.4 | 457.3 | 457.3 | 453.5 | 447.8 | 442.0 | 442.2 |
| 2014 | 436.8 | 436.9 | 441.5 | 443.3 | 449.2 | 456.9 | 466.0 | 470.2 | 469.9 | 466.6 | 462.3 | 461.5 | 455.1 |
| | | | | | | | | | | | | | |
| 2015 | 456.3 | 457.4 | 461.7 | 465.0 | 469.7 | 477.3 | 483.7 | 484.3 | 482.7 | 479.1 | 473.7 | 471.6 | 471.9 |
| 2016 | 467.1 | 470.7 | 473.1 | 478.7 | 482.9 | 487.8 | 494.3 | 495.1 | 494.4 | 488.5 | 484.5 | 481.5 | 483.2 |
| 2017 | 473.6 | 476.6 | 481.3 | 485.1 | 489.6 | 498.2 | 498.8 | 500.2 | 500.4 | 495.5 | 492.0 | 490.7 | 490.2 |
| 2018 | 484.7 | 489.3 | 495.0 | 498.2 | 505.2 | 511.8 | 516.5 | 519.6 | 518.6 | 517.6 | 515.8 | 513.4 | 507.1 |
| 2019 | 505.2 | 498.7 | 510.2 | 513.9 | 520.9 | 526.0 | 530.0 | 531.6 | 529.4 | 526.7 | 522.2 | 520.8 | 519.6 |
| | | | | | | | | | | | | | |
| **Service-Providing** | | | | | | | | | | | | | |
| 2011 | 2,416.6 | 2,426.6 | 2,435.9 | 2,460.7 | 2,473.4 | 2,479.6 | 2,466.9 | 2,451.3 | 2,466.9 | 2,480.9 | 2,490.3 | 2,483.3 | 2,461.0 |
| 2012 | 2,437.8 | 2,450.6 | 2,467.2 | 2,484.2 | 2,506.1 | 2,516.3 | 2,495.8 | 2,485.9 | 2,501.7 | 2,523.6 | 2,533.3 | 2,524.3 | 2,493.9 |
| 2013 | 2,483.9 | 2,498.3 | 2,509.4 | 2,528.3 | 2,551.3 | 2,555.9 | 2,540.6 | 2,537.3 | 2,554.8 | 2,573.9 | 2,585.8 | 2,582.1 | 2,541.8 |
| 2014 | 2,549.0 | 2,556.1 | 2,569.5 | 2,583.8 | 2,602.9 | 2,613.2 | 2,606.3 | 2,603.6 | 2,621.1 | 2,631.1 | 2,643.5 | 2,645.6 | 2,602.1 |
| | | | | | | | | | | | | | |
| 2015 | 2,605.6 | 2,616.8 | 2,634.4 | 2,656.3 | 2,678.4 | 2,694.2 | 2,679.7 | 2,673.7 | 2,695.2 | 2,704.8 | 2,717.7 | 2,717.6 | 2,672.9 |
| 2016 | 2,686.6 | 2,701.9 | 2,717.7 | 2,745.2 | 2,766.7 | 2,778.0 | 2,766.8 | 2,760.7 | 2,787.5 | 2,791.2 | 2,806.5 | 2,805.8 | 2,759.6 |
| 2017 | 2,761.0 | 2,774.9 | 2,795.7 | 2,814.9 | 2,841.2 | 2,857.5 | 2,842.5 | 2,831.4 | 2,850.8 | 2,858.6 | 2,871.8 | 2,871.4 | 2,831.0 |
| 2018 | 2,840.8 | 2,851.3 | 2,869.8 | 2,879.4 | 2,903.4 | 2,916.6 | 2,897.9 | 2,896.4 | 2,907.0 | 2,917.9 | 2,927.1 | 2,921.0 | 2,894.1 |
| 2019 | 2,890.9 | 2,882.9 | 2,911.9 | 2,935.8 | 2,958.1 | 2,972.3 | 2,963.7 | 2,961.3 | 2,965.0 | 2,975.1 | 2,988.7 | 2,988.8 | 2,949.5 |
| | | | | | | | | | | | | | |
| **Mining and Logging** | | | | | | | | | | | | | |
| 2011 | 5.6 | 5.7 | 5.7 | 5.7 | 5.8 | 6.1 | 6.2 | 6.3 | 6.2 | 6.3 | 6.1 | 6.0 | 6.0 |
| 2012 | 5.7 | 5.6 | 5.6 | 5.6 | 5.7 | 6.0 | 6.1 | 6.2 | 6.2 | 6.2 | 6.0 | 5.9 | 5.9 |
| 2013 | 5.7 | 5.8 | 5.8 | 5.8 | 6.0 | 6.2 | 6.3 | 6.4 | 6.4 | 6.4 | 6.3 | 6.2 | 6.1 |
| 2014 | 6.0 | 6.1 | 6.1 | 5.9 | 6.1 | 6.2 | 6.4 | 6.5 | 6.4 | 6.4 | 6.3 | 6.3 | 6.2 |
| | | | | | | | | | | | | | |
| 2015 | 6.3 | 6.3 | 6.2 | 6.2 | 6.3 | 6.4 | 6.5 | 6.4 | 6.3 | 6.5 | 6.3 | 6.3 | 6.3 |
| 2016 | 6.1 | 6.2 | 6.0 | 6.1 | 6.3 | 6.4 | 6.5 | 6.5 | 6.5 | 6.4 | 6.2 | 6.1 | 6.3 |
| 2017 | 5.9 | 6.0 | 5.9 | 6.0 | 6.2 | 6.4 | 6.4 | 6.4 | 6.4 | 6.3 | 6.2 | 6.3 | 6.2 |
| 2018 | 6.1 | 6.1 | 6.1 | 6.2 | 6.3 | 6.5 | 6.5 | 6.5 | 6.4 | 6.3 | 6.2 | 6.2 | 6.3 |
| 2019 | 6.0 | 5.9 | 5.8 | 5.9 | 6.0 | 6.0 | 6.1 | 5.9 | 5.9 | 5.8 | 5.6 | 5.5 | 5.9 |
| | | | | | | | | | | | | | |
| **Construction** | | | | | | | | | | | | | |
| 2011 | 127.3 | 127.8 | 129.3 | 132.8 | 136.3 | 139.4 | 142.5 | 144.5 | 144.5 | 142.0 | 137.2 | 133.4 | 136.4 |
| 2012 | 125.6 | 126.9 | 130.2 | 133.7 | 137.6 | 141.6 | 144.7 | 148.1 | 147.4 | 147.6 | 144.2 | 141.6 | 139.1 |
| 2013 | 135.2 | 137.4 | 139.9 | 143.0 | 147.7 | 150.8 | 155.2 | 159.0 | 158.7 | 157.1 | 154.1 | 149.9 | 149.0 |
| 2014 | 146.8 | 146.3 | 150.4 | 151.6 | 155.8 | 160.0 | 165.5 | 169.2 | 169.5 | 168.3 | 166.4 | 165.8 | 159.6 |
| | | | | | | | | | | | | | |
| 2015 | 162.3 | 163.3 | 166.2 | 169.9 | 173.5 | 176.4 | 179.8 | 180.3 | 179.1 | 178.2 | 175.3 | 174.3 | 173.2 |
| 2016 | 171.8 | 174.7 | 177.6 | 182.3 | 185.4 | 188.5 | 193.0 | 195.1 | 195.4 | 193.1 | 191.9 | 190.4 | 186.6 |
| 2017 | 184.8 | 187.7 | 192.2 | 195.1 | 199.4 | 204.3 | 205.3 | 207.5 | 208.1 | 206.0 | 204.1 | 202.7 | 199.8 |
| 2018 | 198.8 | 201.6 | 205.7 | 208.6 | 212.9 | 216.5 | 218.1 | 221.6 | 220.0 | 219.6 | 218.1 | 216.0 | 213.1 |
| 2019 | 209.5 | 203.2 | 212.8 | 216.7 | 221.2 | 223.6 | 225.8 | 228.2 | 226.6 | 227.9 | 224.9 | 222.3 | 220.2 |

## 1. Employment by Industry: Washington, 2011–2019—*Continued*

(Numbers in thousands, not seasonally adjusted)

| Industry and year | January | February | March | April | May | June | July | August | September | October | November | December | Annual average |
|---|---|---|---|---|---|---|---|---|---|---|---|---|---|
| **Manufacturing** | | | | | | | | | | | | | |
| 2011 | 258.1 | 260.1 | 261.4 | 263.5 | 265.1 | 268.7 | 273.4 | 275.9 | 278.2 | 276.6 | 275.0 | 273.0 | 269.1 |
| 2012 | 271.2 | 271.7 | 273.8 | 274.6 | 277.2 | 282.0 | 285.5 | 287.9 | 288.4 | 287.4 | 285.8 | 283.2 | 280.7 |
| 2013 | 281.9 | 283.1 | 283.9 | 283.5 | 285.3 | 288.9 | 290.9 | 291.9 | 292.2 | 290.0 | 287.4 | 285.9 | 287.1 |
| 2014 | 284.0 | 284.5 | 285.0 | 285.8 | 287.3 | 290.7 | 294.1 | 294.5 | 294.0 | 291.9 | 289.6 | 289.4 | 289.2 |
| 2015 | 287.7 | 287.8 | 289.3 | 288.9 | 289.9 | 294.5 | 297.4 | 297.6 | 297.3 | 294.4 | 292.1 | 291.0 | 292.3 |
| 2016 | 289.2 | 289.8 | 289.5 | 290.3 | 291.2 | 292.9 | 294.8 | 293.5 | 292.5 | 289.0 | 286.4 | 285.0 | 290.3 |
| 2017 | 282.9 | 282.9 | 283.2 | 284.0 | 284.0 | 287.5 | 287.1 | 286.3 | 285.9 | 283.2 | 281.7 | 281.7 | 284.2 |
| 2018 | 279.8 | 281.6 | 283.2 | 283.4 | 286.0 | 288.8 | 291.9 | 291.5 | 292.2 | 291.7 | 291.5 | 291.2 | 287.7 |
| 2019 | 289.7 | 289.6 | 291.6 | 291.3 | 293.7 | 296.4 | 298.1 | 297.5 | 296.9 | 293.0 | 291.7 | 293.0 | 293.5 |
| **Trade, Transportation, and Utilities** | | | | | | | | | | | | | |
| 2011 | 511.5 | 508.8 | 511.1 | 514.8 | 519.3 | 523.9 | 529.1 | 530.2 | 529.3 | 530.1 | 538.8 | 541.5 | 524.0 |
| 2012 | 521.0 | 517.8 | 520.7 | 523.0 | 530.0 | 536.6 | 539.5 | 541.2 | 540.2 | 542.7 | 552.1 | 553.9 | 534.9 |
| 2013 | 534.4 | 532.6 | 533.3 | 536.5 | 544.4 | 548.8 | 553.5 | 556.7 | 555.5 | 559.7 | 570.0 | 573.5 | 549.9 |
| 2014 | 554.3 | 550.7 | 551.9 | 554.8 | 561.0 | 567.4 | 573.1 | 576.9 | 576.5 | 577.5 | 588.1 | 593.0 | 568.8 |
| 2015 | 572.1 | 569.8 | 573.5 | 576.4 | 582.5 | 589.5 | 591.3 | 594.3 | 593.5 | 593.4 | 603.6 | 607.3 | 587.3 |
| 2016 | 586.8 | 585.1 | 588.7 | 594.3 | 600.3 | 608.7 | 612.1 | 614.1 | 612.3 | 613.8 | 624.6 | 628.4 | 605.8 |
| 2017 | 609.3 | 605.6 | 609.4 | 613.0 | 619.8 | 626.6 | 630.8 | 632.6 | 631.4 | 630.5 | 641.7 | 644.7 | 624.6 |
| 2018 | 629.7 | 623.8 | 626.2 | 625.4 | 631.4 | 637.5 | 639.6 | 642.5 | 639.5 | 638.8 | 648.4 | 649.0 | 636.0 |
| 2019 | 635.3 | 626.3 | 630.1 | 633.0 | 638.9 | 643.2 | 648.5 | 650.2 | 647.1 | 648.5 | 658.1 | 664.5 | 643.6 |
| **Wholesale Trade** | | | | | | | | | | | | | |
| 2011 | 118.3 | 118.7 | 119.4 | 120.1 | 121.2 | 121.7 | 122.3 | 122.1 | 121.9 | 122.6 | 122.4 | 121.5 | 121.0 |
| 2012 | 120.3 | 120.7 | 121.4 | 122.2 | 123.1 | 124.2 | 124.3 | 124.8 | 124.3 | 125.1 | 124.8 | 124.1 | 123.3 |
| 2013 | 122.7 | 123.8 | 124.2 | 124.8 | 125.6 | 126.4 | 127.5 | 127.5 | 127.4 | 128.3 | 128.1 | 127.2 | 126.1 |
| 2014 | 126.3 | 126.7 | 127.0 | 127.2 | 128.1 | 129.2 | 131.1 | 131.0 | 131.2 | 131.0 | 130.9 | 130.4 | 129.2 |
| 2015 | 128.8 | 129.4 | 129.8 | 130.4 | 131.0 | 132.4 | 132.4 | 132.5 | 132.3 | 132.0 | 132.0 | 131.9 | 131.2 |
| 2016 | 129.8 | 130.3 | 130.7 | 131.7 | 132.0 | 132.8 | 133.1 | 133.3 | 133.1 | 132.8 | 132.8 | 132.6 | 132.1 |
| 2017 | 131.1 | 131.6 | 132.0 | 132.5 | 133.3 | 134.1 | 134.3 | 133.8 | 134.1 | 134.2 | 134.2 | 134.2 | 133.3 |
| 2018 | 133.3 | 133.9 | 134.7 | 134.8 | 135.6 | 136.7 | 136.8 | 136.8 | 136.3 | 136.4 | 136.4 | 136.0 | 135.6 |
| 2019 | 134.1 | 134.2 | 134.8 | 136.0 | 136.8 | 136.9 | 137.6 | 137.7 | 137.1 | 138.3 | 138.7 | 138.6 | 136.7 |
| **Retail Trade** | | | | | | | | | | | | | |
| 2011 | 306.3 | 303.3 | 303.8 | 306.0 | 309.0 | 312.2 | 314.1 | 315.7 | 314.1 | 316.3 | 325.1 | 327.3 | 312.8 |
| 2012 | 311.2 | 307.5 | 309.1 | 310.4 | 315.0 | 319.1 | 321.7 | 322.5 | 321.7 | 324.2 | 333.9 | 335.3 | 319.3 |
| 2013 | 320.1 | 317.0 | 317.8 | 320.4 | 326.1 | 329.3 | 332.1 | 334.4 | 332.8 | 336.0 | 345.9 | 349.2 | 330.1 |
| 2014 | 332.9 | 329.4 | 330.5 | 332.2 | 336.2 | 340.4 | 343.3 | 346.0 | 344.8 | 346.4 | 356.8 | 359.8 | 341.6 |
| 2015 | 343.5 | 341.0 | 343.9 | 346.7 | 350.9 | 354.6 | 355.9 | 358.6 | 357.7 | 357.6 | 366.5 | 367.9 | 353.7 |
| 2016 | 353.7 | 352.1 | 354.3 | 357.2 | 361.5 | 366.8 | 369.0 | 370.3 | 368.1 | 370.2 | 378.8 | 380.4 | 365.2 |
| 2017 | 367.7 | 364.4 | 367.4 | 370.5 | 375.5 | 380.1 | 384.1 | 385.1 | 383.4 | 382.5 | 391.8 | 392.5 | 378.8 |
| 2018 | 382.2 | 377.3 | 378.5 | 378.4 | 382.8 | 385.9 | 388.4 | 390.3 | 387.8 | 387.0 | 395.7 | 395.2 | 385.8 |
| 2019 | 386.8 | 379.5 | 381.5 | 383.4 | 387.7 | 390.1 | 393.9 | 394.7 | 392.1 | 393.3 | 400.0 | 403.6 | 390.6 |
| **Transportation and Utilities** | | | | | | | | | | | | | |
| 2011 | 86.9 | 86.8 | 87.9 | 88.7 | 89.1 | 90.0 | 92.7 | 92.4 | 93.3 | 91.2 | 91.3 | 92.7 | 90.3 |
| 2012 | 89.5 | 89.6 | 90.2 | 90.4 | 91.9 | 93.3 | 93.5 | 93.9 | 94.2 | 93.4 | 93.4 | 94.5 | 92.3 |
| 2013 | 91.6 | 91.8 | 91.3 | 91.3 | 92.7 | 93.1 | 93.9 | 94.8 | 95.3 | 95.4 | 96.0 | 97.1 | 93.7 |
| 2014 | 95.1 | 94.6 | 94.4 | 95.4 | 96.7 | 97.8 | 98.7 | 99.9 | 100.5 | 100.1 | 100.4 | 102.8 | 98.0 |
| 2015 | 99.8 | 99.4 | 99.8 | 99.3 | 100.6 | 102.5 | 103.0 | 103.2 | 103.5 | 103.8 | 105.1 | 107.5 | 102.3 |
| 2016 | 103.3 | 102.7 | 103.7 | 105.4 | 106.8 | 109.1 | 110.0 | 110.5 | 111.1 | 110.8 | 113.0 | 115.4 | 108.5 |
| 2017 | 110.5 | 109.6 | 110.0 | 110.0 | 111.0 | 112.4 | 112.4 | 113.7 | 113.9 | 113.8 | 115.7 | 118.0 | 112.6 |
| 2018 | 114.2 | 112.6 | 113.0 | 112.2 | 113.0 | 114.9 | 114.4 | 115.4 | 115.4 | 115.4 | 116.3 | 117.8 | 114.6 |
| 2019 | 114.4 | 112.6 | 113.8 | 113.6 | 114.4 | 116.2 | 117.0 | 117.8 | 117.9 | 116.9 | 119.4 | 122.3 | 116.4 |
| **Information** | | | | | | | | | | | | | |
| 2011 | 102.9 | 103.4 | 103.1 | 103.3 | 103.6 | 104.8 | 105.7 | 106.0 | 104.9 | 104.0 | 104.5 | 104.3 | 104.2 |
| 2012 | 104.0 | 104.4 | 104.0 | 103.8 | 104.6 | 105.9 | 106.0 | 106.0 | 104.5 | 103.9 | 104.4 | 104.9 | 104.7 |
| 2013 | 104.0 | 104.7 | 104.4 | 104.7 | 105.6 | 106.5 | 107.7 | 108.2 | 107.1 | 106.3 | 107.2 | 107.3 | 106.1 |
| 2014 | 106.9 | 107.1 | 107.2 | 107.6 | 108.7 | 110.6 | 112.3 | 113.1 | 112.1 | 110.2 | 110.7 | 110.5 | 109.8 |
| 2015 | 110.0 | 110.9 | 111.1 | 111.3 | 112.5 | 114.3 | 116.4 | 117.5 | 116.8 | 116.1 | 117.1 | 117.4 | 114.3 |
| 2016 | 116.8 | 117.8 | 118.3 | 119.0 | 119.8 | 122.5 | 123.8 | 124.6 | 124.0 | 122.7 | 123.5 | 123.6 | 121.4 |
| 2017 | 123.0 | 123.5 | 124.0 | 123.7 | 124.9 | 127.3 | 128.3 | 129.2 | 128.6 | 127.4 | 127.6 | 128.1 | 126.3 |
| 2018 | 127.6 | 128.7 | 129.4 | 130.4 | 131.5 | 135.6 | 137.4 | 138.6 | 138.1 | 137.2 | 138.0 | 138.2 | 134.2 |
| 2019 | 138.4 | 139.4 | 140.7 | 140.3 | 141.8 | 145.8 | 148.2 | 149.5 | 148.0 | 146.4 | 147.0 | 146.8 | 144.4 |

# 1. Employment by Industry: Washington, 2011–2019—*Continued*

(Numbers in thousands, not seasonally adjusted)

| Industry and year | January | February | March | April | May | June | July | August | September | October | November | December | Annual average |
|---|---|---|---|---|---|---|---|---|---|---|---|---|---|
| **Financial Activities** | | | | | | | | | | | | | |
| 2011 | 136.8 | 136.9 | 137.0 | 137.7 | 137.7 | 138.7 | 139.2 | 139.4 | 139.2 | 138.1 | 138.5 | 138.6 | 138.2 |
| 2012 | 137.0 | 137.7 | 138.3 | 139.0 | 140.2 | 140.9 | 142.2 | 142.1 | 141.1 | 140.9 | 141.0 | 141.3 | 140.1 |
| 2013 | 140.8 | 141.2 | 142.0 | 142.4 | 143.5 | 144.4 | 145.7 | 145.8 | 145.0 | 144.6 | 144.5 | 145.0 | 143.7 |
| 2014 | 143.5 | 143.7 | 144.2 | 144.6 | 144.4 | 145.4 | 146.7 | 147.2 | 146.3 | 145.8 | 145.7 | 146.3 | 145.3 |
| 2015 | 145.4 | 145.8 | 145.9 | 146.8 | 147.7 | 148.6 | 149.7 | 150.0 | 149.2 | 148.1 | 148.1 | 148.3 | 147.8 |
| 2016 | 147.8 | 148.0 | 148.5 | 149.4 | 150.4 | 151.5 | 153.4 | 153.7 | 153.0 | 151.9 | 151.8 | 152.3 | 151.0 |
| 2017 | 150.9 | 151.8 | 152.4 | 152.1 | 153.8 | 155.1 | 155.7 | 156.4 | 155.9 | 154.3 | 154.7 | 154.9 | 154.0 |
| 2018 | 155.0 | 155.6 | 156.4 | 156.4 | 157.9 | 159.2 | 159.7 | 160.0 | 158.9 | 157.8 | 158.5 | 157.4 | 157.7 |
| 2019 | 157.1 | 157.5 | 158.1 | 158.8 | 160.3 | 161.5 | 163.0 | 163.2 | 162.3 | 162.8 | 162.2 | 161.1 | 160.7 |
| **Professional and Business Services** | | | | | | | | | | | | | |
| 2011 | 326.9 | 330.0 | 332.5 | 339.7 | 339.5 | 342.0 | 346.2 | 345.9 | 347.7 | 345.5 | 345.1 | 344.2 | 340.4 |
| 2012 | 336.2 | 339.4 | 342.2 | 347.5 | 350.2 | 354.3 | 353.9 | 357.6 | 358.1 | 359.5 | 358.6 | 356.4 | 351.2 |
| 2013 | 350.0 | 353.2 | 355.6 | 360.5 | 362.0 | 364.6 | 365.6 | 370.0 | 371.1 | 370.7 | 368.3 | 367.3 | 363.2 |
| 2014 | 360.9 | 362.3 | 365.4 | 367.5 | 368.8 | 372.6 | 376.7 | 379.4 | 379.7 | 379.5 | 380.8 | 381.4 | 372.9 |
| 2015 | 372.9 | 374.7 | 378.7 | 383.6 | 386.1 | 389.8 | 392.7 | 394.5 | 396.0 | 394.8 | 395.6 | 396.4 | 388.0 |
| 2016 | 388.9 | 391.1 | 394.2 | 398.5 | 400.4 | 403.5 | 405.7 | 407.0 | 409.9 | 406.0 | 407.0 | 405.6 | 401.5 |
| 2017 | 399.3 | 401.7 | 405.9 | 409.8 | 413.0 | 417.6 | 419.0 | 421.1 | 421.1 | 417.7 | 417.3 | 417.0 | 413.4 |
| 2018 | 411.5 | 414.9 | 419.7 | 419.8 | 422.2 | 427.2 | 427.6 | 431.9 | 430.6 | 428.9 | 429.3 | 428.2 | 424.3 |
| 2019 | 420.3 | 419.4 | 425.3 | 430.9 | 432.1 | 436.4 | 441.2 | 444.7 | 443.4 | 442.5 | 442.4 | 439.8 | 434.9 |
| **Education and Health Services** | | | | | | | | | | | | | |
| 2011 | 427.7 | 431.4 | 432.9 | 433.1 | 433.2 | 430.3 | 425.3 | 424.5 | 430.3 | 435.2 | 436.7 | 436.2 | 431.4 |
| 2012 | 429.3 | 434.2 | 436.5 | 436.1 | 437.3 | 433.5 | 426.7 | 426.6 | 431.8 | 437.0 | 438.6 | 437.5 | 433.8 |
| 2013 | 431.8 | 437.5 | 438.4 | 438.6 | 439.2 | 433.6 | 429.4 | 428.8 | 435.5 | 442.3 | 444.0 | 443.8 | 436.9 |
| 2014 | 440.7 | 446.1 | 445.8 | 445.6 | 446.6 | 441.7 | 438.3 | 437.3 | 442.9 | 446.4 | 447.8 | 448.7 | 444.0 |
| 2015 | 442.9 | 447.5 | 448.2 | 449.9 | 449.7 | 447.6 | 441.5 | 440.7 | 447.0 | 454.1 | 455.9 | 456.6 | 448.5 |
| 2016 | 455.6 | 461.3 | 462.7 | 465.3 | 465.7 | 462.4 | 455.6 | 457.2 | 464.7 | 468.6 | 471.0 | 472.0 | 463.5 |
| 2017 | 465.8 | 472.1 | 474.1 | 474.5 | 475.8 | 473.4 | 467.5 | 470.0 | 477.4 | 483.3 | 486.3 | 486.6 | 475.6 |
| 2018 | 483.0 | 489.6 | 491.6 | 490.5 | 491.3 | 486.9 | 481.7 | 483.7 | 489.6 | 497.1 | 499.3 | 498.8 | 490.3 |
| 2019 | 494.9 | 497.7 | 502.6 | 504.2 | 504.8 | 499.7 | 496.1 | 498.1 | 502.6 | 506.0 | 510.2 | 509.9 | 502.2 |
| **Leisure and Hospitality** | | | | | | | | | | | | | |
| 2011 | 256.2 | 257.1 | 259.6 | 268.8 | 274.3 | 280.4 | 281.7 | 284.1 | 282.8 | 270.9 | 267.3 | 268.4 | 271.0 |
| 2012 | 260.5 | 263.0 | 267.4 | 273.3 | 280.1 | 286.3 | 288.5 | 290.9 | 289.0 | 278.6 | 274.2 | 276.1 | 277.3 |
| 2013 | 269.0 | 270.4 | 275.4 | 282.2 | 290.7 | 298.0 | 300.0 | 302.9 | 299.7 | 288.1 | 285.4 | 287.3 | 287.4 |
| 2014 | 282.4 | 282.3 | 287.4 | 292.8 | 299.8 | 306.5 | 308.1 | 311.8 | 308.3 | 296.7 | 293.6 | 295.1 | 297.1 |
| 2015 | 290.2 | 292.0 | 296.5 | 303.3 | 312.2 | 321.3 | 324.3 | 326.5 | 322.9 | 313.0 | 308.9 | 310.3 | 310.1 |
| 2016 | 304.4 | 307.3 | 311.4 | 319.6 | 325.4 | 332.3 | 336.7 | 338.3 | 336.9 | 324.1 | 320.3 | 322.3 | 323.3 |
| 2017 | 314.1 | 315.9 | 321.3 | 328.9 | 335.5 | 344.2 | 344.6 | 345.1 | 341.2 | 330.0 | 327.0 | 330.4 | 331.5 |
| 2018 | 324.9 | 326.3 | 331.3 | 338.3 | 346.0 | 353.4 | 354.1 | 356.4 | 351.0 | 341.6 | 338.0 | 341.1 | 341.9 |
| 2019 | 332.4 | 329.5 | 337.2 | 346.1 | 352.3 | 359.6 | 361.5 | 363.4 | 357.5 | 348.3 | 344.8 | 347.9 | 348.4 |
| **Other Services** | | | | | | | | | | | | | |
| 2011 | 105.0 | 105.9 | 106.2 | 107.7 | 108.7 | 110.1 | 110.7 | 110.5 | 109.3 | 109.0 | 108.4 | 108.8 | 108.4 |
| 2012 | 107.4 | 108.3 | 109.5 | 110.4 | 111.2 | 112.2 | 113.0 | 112.7 | 111.7 | 111.3 | 110.8 | 110.4 | 110.7 |
| 2013 | 108.0 | 108.6 | 109.5 | 110.2 | 111.4 | 112.1 | 113.4 | 113.4 | 112.1 | 111.8 | 112.0 | 111.5 | 111.2 |
| 2014 | 110.9 | 111.2 | 112.4 | 112.5 | 113.6 | 114.9 | 116.2 | 116.2 | 114.6 | 113.9 | 113.8 | 114.2 | 113.7 |
| 2015 | 112.3 | 112.7 | 113.9 | 114.6 | 115.6 | 116.5 | 117.3 | 117.1 | 115.5 | 114.8 | 114.6 | 114.6 | 115.0 |
| 2016 | 114.2 | 114.8 | 115.7 | 117.3 | 118.4 | 119.5 | 119.5 | 119.8 | 118.4 | 117.6 | 117.7 | 117.9 | 117.6 |
| 2017 | 116.4 | 117.3 | 118.4 | 119.1 | 120.4 | 122.2 | 121.8 | 121.6 | 120.1 | 119.9 | 119.4 | 119.8 | 119.7 |
| 2018 | 118.5 | 119.2 | 120.1 | 120.6 | 122.4 | 124.1 | 125.0 | 125.4 | 123.9 | 123.0 | 122.9 | 123.3 | 122.4 |
| 2019 | 125.1 | 124.6 | 127.0 | 128.1 | 129.3 | 130.4 | 130.4 | 130.2 | 127.8 | 126.7 | 127.3 | 128.3 | 127.9 |
| **Government** | | | | | | | | | | | | | |
| 2011 | 549.6 | 553.1 | 553.5 | 555.6 | 557.1 | 549.4 | 529.0 | 510.7 | 523.4 | 548.1 | 551.0 | 541.3 | 543.5 |
| 2012 | 542.4 | 545.8 | 548.6 | 551.1 | 552.5 | 546.6 | 526.0 | 508.8 | 525.3 | 549.7 | 553.6 | 543.8 | 541.2 |
| 2013 | 545.9 | 550.1 | 550.8 | 553.2 | 554.5 | 547.9 | 525.3 | 511.5 | 528.8 | 550.4 | 554.4 | 546.4 | 543.3 |
| 2014 | 549.4 | 552.7 | 555.2 | 558.4 | 560.0 | 554.1 | 534.9 | 521.7 | 540.7 | 561.1 | 563.0 | 556.4 | 550.6 |
| 2015 | 559.8 | 563.4 | 566.6 | 570.4 | 572.1 | 566.6 | 546.5 | 533.1 | 554.3 | 570.5 | 573.9 | 566.7 | 562.0 |
| 2016 | 572.1 | 576.5 | 578.2 | 581.8 | 586.3 | 577.6 | 560.0 | 546.0 | 568.3 | 586.5 | 590.6 | 583.7 | 575.6 |
| 2017 | 582.2 | 587.0 | 590.2 | 593.8 | 598.0 | 591.1 | 574.8 | 555.4 | 575.1 | 595.5 | 597.8 | 589.9 | 585.9 |
| 2018 | 590.6 | 593.2 | 595.1 | 598.0 | 600.7 | 592.7 | 572.8 | 557.9 | 575.4 | 593.5 | 592.7 | 585.0 | 587.3 |
| 2019 | 587.4 | 588.5 | 590.9 | 594.4 | 598.6 | 595.7 | 574.8 | 562.0 | 576.3 | 593.9 | 596.7 | 590.5 | 587.5 |

## 2. Average Weekly Hours by Selected Industry: Washington, 2015–2019

(Not seasonally adjusted)

| Industry and year | January | February | March | April | May | June | July | August | September | October | November | December | Annual average |
|---|---|---|---|---|---|---|---|---|---|---|---|---|---|
| **Total Private** | | | | | | | | | | | | | |
| 2015 | 33.6 | 34.7 | 34.7 | 34.0 | 34.0 | 34.2 | 34.3 | 35.3 | 34.3 | 34.3 | 35.1 | 34.0 | 34.4 |
| 2016 | 34.0 | 34.2 | 34.1 | 34.4 | 35.2 | 34.5 | 34.6 | 34.9 | 34.6 | 35.4 | 34.5 | 34.4 | 34.6 |
| 2017 | 34.9 | 34.2 | 34.3 | 35.4 | 34.5 | 34.6 | 35.5 | 34.8 | 34.6 | 35.5 | 34.5 | 34.6 | 34.8 |
| 2018 | 34.4 | 34.7 | 34.5 | 35.6 | 34.7 | 34.8 | 35.3 | 34.6 | 35.4 | 34.4 | 34.3 | 35.3 | 34.8 |
| 2019 | 34.1 | 33.2 | 34.1 | 34.1 | 34.4 | 35.2 | 34.5 | 34.7 | 35.3 | 34.5 | 34.5 | 35.0 | 34.5 |
| **Goods-Producing** | | | | | | | | | | | | | |
| 2015 | 39.5 | 39.8 | 39.8 | 39.6 | 39.8 | 40.1 | 39.9 | 40.3 | 39.2 | 40.1 | 39.9 | 39.5 | 39.8 |
| 2016 | 39.2 | 39.2 | 39.4 | 39.5 | 39.9 | 39.5 | 39.5 | 39.6 | 39.5 | 39.8 | 39.5 | 39.2 | 39.5 |
| 2017 | 38.7 | 38.5 | 39.1 | 39.5 | 39.5 | 39.7 | 39.6 | 39.9 | 39.7 | 40.4 | 39.6 | 39.8 | 39.5 |
| 2018 | 39.2 | 39.6 | 39.4 | 40.3 | 39.9 | 40.0 | 39.6 | 39.9 | 40.0 | 40.1 | 40.2 | 40.6 | 39.9 |
| 2019 | 39.7 | 38.1 | 40.0 | 39.7 | 39.9 | 40.3 | 39.8 | 40.2 | 40.0 | 40.4 | 40.1 | 40.0 | 39.9 |
| **Construction** | | | | | | | | | | | | | |
| 2015 | 37.8 | 38.1 | 37.9 | 37.9 | 38.1 | 38.5 | 38.3 | 38.8 | 36.3 | 37.9 | 37.5 | 36.7 | 37.8 |
| 2016 | 36.6 | 36.9 | 37.2 | 37.5 | 38.2 | 37.6 | 37.6 | 38.1 | 37.7 | 37.4 | 37.4 | 36.9 | 37.4 |
| 2017 | 36.0 | 35.7 | 36.8 | 37.4 | 37.8 | 38.3 | 38.4 | 38.5 | 38.0 | 38.8 | 37.5 | 37.5 | 37.6 |
| 2018 | 36.7 | 36.9 | 37.0 | 38.2 | 38.3 | 38.3 | 38.2 | 38.5 | 38.1 | 38.4 | 38.0 | 38.4 | 37.9 |
| 2019 | 37.3 | 34.4 | 37.7 | 37.8 | 38.8 | 38.7 | 38.5 | 38.8 | 38.3 | 38.7 | 38.1 | 37.3 | 37.9 |
| **Manufacturing** | | | | | | | | | | | | | |
| 2015 | 40.4 | 40.7 | 40.8 | 40.6 | 40.7 | 41.0 | 40.8 | 41.1 | 40.7 | 41.2 | 41.1 | 40.9 | 40.8 |
| 2016 | 40.5 | 40.3 | 40.4 | 40.4 | 40.6 | 40.3 | 40.3 | 40.2 | 40.3 | 41.0 | 40.6 | 40.4 | 40.4 |
| 2017 | 40.1 | 39.9 | 40.2 | 40.5 | 40.4 | 40.4 | 40.3 | 40.7 | 40.7 | 41.3 | 40.8 | 41.1 | 40.5 |
| 2018 | 40.5 | 41.0 | 40.7 | 41.5 | 40.9 | 41.1 | 40.5 | 40.8 | 41.1 | 41.1 | 41.3 | 41.7 | 41.0 |
| 2019 | 40.9 | 39.7 | 41.1 | 40.7 | 40.5 | 41 | 40.5 | 40.9 | 40.9 | 41.1 | 40.9 | 41.2 | 40.8 |
| **Trade, Transportation, and Utilities** | | | | | | | | | | | | | |
| 2015 | 34.2 | 35.3 | 35.3 | 34.7 | 35.2 | 35.2 | 35.2 | 36.4 | 35.9 | 35.1 | 36.0 | 35.0 | 35.3 |
| 2016 | 34.9 | 35.4 | 35.2 | 35.9 | 36.6 | 35.6 | 35.8 | 35.9 | 35.7 | 36.3 | 35.3 | 35.9 | 35.7 |
| 2017 | 35.5 | 35.2 | 35.0 | 36.0 | 35.5 | 35.6 | 36.3 | 35.6 | 35.6 | 36.0 | 35.2 | 35.3 | 35.6 |
| 2018 | 34.9 | 35.1 | 35.0 | 35.9 | 35.3 | 35.3 | 36.0 | 35.3 | 35.7 | 34.5 | 34.5 | 35.2 | 35.2 |
| 2019 | 34.2 | 33.1 | 34.1 | 34.3 | 34.6 | 35.2 | 35.1 | 34.7 | 35.2 | 34.4 | 34.2 | 34.7 | 34.5 |
| **Information** | | | | | | | | | | | | | |
| 2015 | 38.1 | 41.3 | 41.3 | 38.3 | 38.2 | 38.2 | 38.2 | 41.0 | 37.9 | 37.9 | 41.2 | 37.7 | 39.1 |
| 2016 | 38.1 | 38.0 | 38.0 | 38.2 | 41.0 | 38.0 | 38.6 | 37.9 | 37.8 | 41.0 | 38.2 | 37.3 | 38.5 |
| 2017 | 41.2 | 37.7 | 37.7 | 40.8 | 37.9 | 38.1 | 41.4 | 37.9 | 37.9 | 41.4 | 37.8 | 38.6 | 39.0 |
| 2018 | 37.6 | 37.8 | 38.3 | 41.2 | 37.9 | 38.4 | 41.6 | 38.1 | 41.5 | 38.2 | 38.3 | 41.3 | 39.2 |
| 2019 | 37.8 | 38.0 | 38.2 | 38.1 | 37.9 | 39.9 | 36.7 | 36.9 | 38.3 | 36.6 | 36.8 | 38.6 | 37.8 |
| **Financial Activities** | | | | | | | | | | | | | |
| 2015 | 35.0 | 36.6 | 36.6 | 35.3 | 35.1 | 35.2 | 35.0 | 36.7 | 35.1 | 35.4 | 37.1 | 35.7 | 35.7 |
| 2016 | 35.7 | 35.9 | 35.7 | 36.0 | 37.1 | 36.0 | 35.4 | 35.8 | 35.7 | 37.0 | 35.7 | 35.3 | 35.9 |
| 2017 | 36.8 | 35.7 | 35.4 | 37.1 | 35.4 | 35.8 | 36.6 | 35.3 | 35.7 | 36.7 | 35.4 | 35.3 | 35.9 |
| 2018 | 35.2 | 35.8 | 35.6 | 37.2 | 36.2 | 36.2 | 37.6 | 36.2 | 37.9 | 36.4 | 36.6 | 37.8 | 36.6 |
| 2019 | 36.8 | 36.3 | 36.5 | 36.5 | 36.4 | 38.3 | 36.9 | 37.4 | 39.4 | 37.5 | 37.6 | 39.1 | 37.4 |
| **Professional and Business Services** | | | | | | | | | | | | | |
| 2015 | 35.0 | 36.4 | 36.4 | 35.5 | 35.3 | 35.5 | 35.2 | 36.5 | 35.6 | 35.7 | 36.5 | 35.2 | 35.7 |
| 2016 | 35.4 | 35.8 | 35.7 | 36.0 | 36.9 | 35.9 | 35.8 | 36.0 | 35.7 | 36.6 | 35.7 | 35.6 | 35.9 |
| 2017 | 36.3 | 35.6 | 35.8 | 36.9 | 35.6 | 35.7 | 36.8 | 35.8 | 35.8 | 36.9 | 36.0 | 35.7 | 36.1 |
| 2018 | 35.9 | 36.2 | 36.2 | 37.1 | 36.1 | 36.4 | 37.3 | 36.4 | 37.8 | 36.7 | 36.2 | 37.4 | 36.6 |
| 2019 | 36.0 | 35.1 | 35.7 | 35.5 | 35.7 | 37.0 | 35.8 | 36.3 | 37.3 | 36.0 | 35.9 | 36.9 | 36.1 |
| **Education and Health Services** | | | | | | | | | | | | | |
| 2015 | 32.5 | 33.4 | 33.1 | 32.4 | 32.3 | 32.5 | 32.9 | 33.7 | 33.1 | 32.9 | 33.8 | 32.5 | 32.9 |
| 2016 | 33.1 | 32.6 | 32.5 | 32.6 | 33.4 | 33.8 | 34.1 | 34.6 | 34.3 | 34.7 | 34.0 | 33.9 | 33.6 |
| 2017 | 34.9 | 34.0 | 33.9 | 34.7 | 33.9 | 34.0 | 34.9 | 34.6 | 34.2 | 35.1 | 34.2 | 34.3 | 34.4 |
| 2018 | 34.9 | 34.5 | 34.3 | 35.2 | 34.2 | 34.1 | 33.0 | 32.5 | 33.7 | 32.3 | 32.7 | 33.5 | 33.7 |
| 2019 | 32.5 | 32.0 | 32.8 | 32.9 | 33.3 | 34.0 | 33.2 | 33.3 | 34.2 | 33.4 | 33.7 | 34.4 | 33.3 |
| **Leisure and Hospitality** | | | | | | | | | | | | | |
| 2015 | 22.8 | 24.2 | 24.3 | 24.0 | 24.0 | 24.5 | 25.0 | 26.3 | 24.8 | 24.6 | 25.1 | 24.1 | 24.5 |
| 2016 | 23.8 | 24.3 | 24.2 | 24.5 | 25.5 | 24.7 | 25.1 | 25.6 | 25.1 | 25.6 | 24.6 | 24.2 | 24.8 |
| 2017 | 25.0 | 24.6 | 24.7 | 26.2 | 25.1 | 25.2 | 26.5 | 25.8 | 25.1 | 25.6 | 24.8 | 24.7 | 25.3 |
| 2018 | 24.4 | 25.2 | 24.6 | 26.0 | 25.4 | 25.7 | 27.0 | 26.2 | 26.6 | 25.7 | 24.6 | 25.9 | 25.6 |
| 2019 | 24.3 | 23.6 | 24.6 | 24.9 | 25.1 | 26.3 | 25.6 | 26.1 | 26.0 | 24.9 | 25.1 | 25.5 | 25.2 |
| **Other Services** | | | | | | | | | | | | | |
| 2015 | 28.1 | 29.8 | 29.4 | 28.5 | 28.6 | 28.8 | 29.0 | 29.7 | 27.7 | 27.5 | 28.8 | 27.7 | 28.6 |
| 2016 | 27.9 | 28.7 | 28.6 | 28.8 | 29.6 | 28.3 | 28.7 | 29.6 | 28.2 | 29.2 | 28.2 | 28.2 | 28.7 |
| 2017 | 28.8 | 28.5 | 28.4 | 29.9 | 28.4 | 28.4 | 29.9 | 29.6 | 28.6 | 29.2 | 28.2 | 28.8 | 28.9 |
| 2018 | 28.0 | 28.4 | 28.6 | 29.4 | 28.2 | 28.2 | 29.6 | 29.0 | 29.1 | 28.7 | 28.0 | 29.7 | 28.7 |
| 2019 | 28.7 | 28.5 | 28.9 | 28.9 | 29.2 | 29.6 | 29.5 | 29.4 | 30.0 | 29.9 | 29.5 | 29.6 | 29.3 |

## 3. Average Hourly Earnings by Selected Industry: Washington, 2015–2019

(Dollars, not seasonally adjusted)

| Industry and year | January | February | March | April | May | June | July | August | September | October | November | December | Annual average |
|---|---|---|---|---|---|---|---|---|---|---|---|---|---|
| **Total Private** | | | | | | | | | | | | | |
| 2015 | 29.46 | 29.50 | 29.49 | 29.35 | 29.36 | 29.12 | 29.10 | 29.41 | 29.76 | 29.97 | 30.36 | 30.25 | 29.60 |
| 2016 | 30.36 | 30.30 | 30.28 | 30.22 | 30.34 | 29.95 | 30.02 | 29.79 | 30.43 | 30.83 | 30.57 | 30.64 | 30.31 |
| 2017 | 31.38 | 31.12 | 31.05 | 31.46 | 31.02 | 30.95 | 31.35 | 31.05 | 31.58 | 31.82 | 31.67 | 31.88 | 31.36 |
| 2018 | 31.96 | 32.23 | 32.24 | 32.60 | 32.21 | 32.37 | 32.61 | 32.42 | 33.41 | 33.10 | 33.51 | 34.00 | 32.73 |
| 2019 | 33.99 | 34.48 | 34.12 | 34.07 | 33.89 | 33.93 | 33.82 | 33.67 | 33.97 | 33.87 | 33.95 | 34.19 | 33.99 |
| **Goods-Producing** | | | | | | | | | | | | | |
| 2015 | 32.48 | 32.61 | 32.90 | 32.82 | 32.80 | 32.73 | 32.46 | 32.58 | 32.80 | 32.71 | 32.80 | 33.37 | 32.75 |
| 2016 | 33.06 | 33.24 | 33.62 | 33.58 | 33.48 | 33.40 | 33.36 | 33.55 | 33.78 | 33.69 | 33.95 | 34.21 | 33.58 |
| 2017 | 34.42 | 34.51 | 34.75 | 34.62 | 34.47 | 34.62 | 34.71 | 34.72 | 35.18 | 35.22 | 35.64 | 35.80 | 34.89 |
| 2018 | 35.74 | 35.63 | 35.85 | 36.01 | 35.97 | 36.17 | 36.28 | 36.34 | 36.61 | 36.55 | 36.89 | 37.10 | 36.27 |
| 2019 | 37.17 | 37.56 | 37.51 | 37.39 | 37.57 | 37.78 | 38.01 | 37.65 | 37.77 | 37.53 | 37.78 | 37.91 | 37.64 |
| **Construction** | | | | | | | | | | | | | |
| 2015 | 31.32 | 31.52 | 31.27 | 31.41 | 31.50 | 31.91 | 31.60 | 31.75 | 31.79 | 31.55 | 31.62 | 32.16 | 31.62 |
| 2016 | 31.46 | 31.64 | 31.99 | 31.71 | 31.61 | 31.74 | 31.98 | 32.31 | 32.56 | 32.66 | 32.85 | 32.79 | 32.12 |
| 2017 | 32.97 | 33.17 | 33.23 | 32.74 | 32.70 | 32.81 | 32.67 | 33.06 | 33.35 | 33.75 | 33.89 | 33.83 | 33.19 |
| 2018 | 33.94 | 34.03 | 34.37 | 34.83 | 35.00 | 34.87 | 35.14 | 35.44 | 35.20 | 34.90 | 35.57 | 35.50 | 34.92 |
| 2019 | 35.91 | 36.15 | 35.92 | 36.58 | 37.15 | 37.49 | 37.85 | 37.63 | 37.64 | 37.45 | 37.51 | 37.82 | 37.13 |
| **Manufacturing** | | | | | | | | | | | | | |
| 2015 | 33.07 | 33.18 | 33.71 | 33.54 | 33.48 | 33.17 | 32.94 | 33.06 | 33.30 | 33.32 | 33.40 | 33.83 | 33.33 |
| 2016 | 33.68 | 33.93 | 34.32 | 34.46 | 34.39 | 34.23 | 34.02 | 34.17 | 34.42 | 34.24 | 34.52 | 34.93 | 34.27 |
| 2017 | 35.15 | 35.20 | 35.56 | 35.63 | 35.43 | 35.67 | 35.88 | 35.69 | 36.22 | 36.09 | 36.62 | 36.87 | 35.84 |
| 2018 | 36.77 | 36.53 | 37.03 | 37.02 | 36.86 | 37.14 | 37.16 | 37.07 | 37.50 | 37.53 | 37.62 | 37.93 | 37.19 |
| 2019 | 37.84 | 38.23 | 38.30 | 37.84 | 37.73 | 37.59 | 37.74 | 37.37 | 37.58 | 37.23 | 37.71 | 37.83 | 37.75 |
| **Trade, Transportation, and Utilities** | | | | | | | | | | | | | |
| 2015 | 24.56 | 24.55 | 24.50 | 24.75 | 24.71 | 24.69 | 24.83 | 25.43 | 26.31 | 26.59 | 26.81 | 26.36 | 25.36 |
| 2016 | 26.61 | 26.28 | 26.16 | 26.17 | 26.08 | 25.60 | 25.56 | 25.16 | 25.30 | 25.70 | 25.17 | 24.86 | 25.71 |
| 2017 | 25.91 | 25.36 | 25.21 | 26.02 | 25.47 | 25.54 | 25.99 | 25.38 | 25.44 | 25.63 | 25.31 | 25.35 | 25.55 |
| 2018 | 25.18 | 25.25 | 25.24 | 25.65 | 25.24 | 25.38 | 25.50 | 25.43 | 26.06 | 25.78 | 25.78 | 26.03 | 25.55 |
| 2019 | 26.23 | 26.44 | 26.01 | 26.18 | 25.62 | 25.86 | 25.28 | 25.41 | 25.38 | 25.47 | 25.59 | 25.51 | 25.74 |
| **Information** | | | | | | | | | | | | | |
| 2015 | 56.22 | 55.92 | 56.27 | 55.88 | 56.36 | 55.97 | 55.96 | 57.74 | 59.72 | 58.88 | 60.42 | 58.73 | 57.37 |
| 2016 | 59.11 | 59.24 | 58.79 | 58.37 | 59.88 | 58.56 | 58.15 | 58.81 | 61.33 | 61.91 | 61.09 | 60.85 | 59.70 |
| 2017 | 60.62 | 60.80 | 61.14 | 62.89 | 61.31 | 60.42 | 60.14 | 59.94 | 63.81 | 61.84 | 61.89 | 61.49 | 61.36 |
| 2018 | 62.49 | 62.63 | 62.58 | 63.72 | 61.88 | 62.42 | 61.33 | 61.12 | 66.08 | 64.85 | 65.09 | 65.87 | 63.38 |
| 2019 | 66.48 | 65.68 | 65.90 | 65.63 | 63.56 | 62.09 | 62.01 | 60.59 | 60.65 | 59.35 | 57.76 | 58.12 | 62.27 |
| **Financial Activities** | | | | | | | | | | | | | |
| 2015 | 29.21 | 29.15 | 29.33 | 29.40 | 29.82 | 28.67 | 29.83 | 29.37 | 28.81 | 29.39 | 28.97 | 28.65 | 29.22 |
| 2016 | 29.62 | 29.36 | 29.47 | 30.18 | 30.54 | 30.61 | 31.12 | 31.33 | 32.05 | 32.68 | 32.25 | 32.86 | 31.02 |
| 2017 | 33.88 | 32.51 | 32.40 | 33.13 | 32.57 | 32.63 | 33.52 | 32.92 | 33.18 | 33.98 | 34.02 | 34.14 | 33.24 |
| 2018 | 34.31 | 35.34 | 34.88 | 35.34 | 35.37 | 35.41 | 35.81 | 36.27 | 36.14 | 35.77 | 37.03 | 37.34 | 35.77 |
| 2019 | 36.61 | 37.43 | 35.99 | 36.65 | 37.44 | 37.08 | 36.45 | 37.49 | 37.15 | 36.86 | 37.85 | 38.82 | 37.16 |
| **Professional and Business Services** | | | | | | | | | | | | | |
| 2015 | 33.71 | 33.92 | 33.65 | 33.27 | 33.38 | 33.06 | 32.95 | 32.83 | 32.74 | 33.13 | 33.69 | 33.78 | 33.34 |
| 2016 | 33.84 | 33.99 | 33.93 | 33.50 | 33.80 | 33.53 | 33.61 | 33.20 | 33.76 | 34.54 | 34.04 | 34.33 | 33.84 |
| 2017 | 35.45 | 35.10 | 34.80 | 35.37 | 34.87 | 34.80 | 35.53 | 34.91 | 35.24 | 36.01 | 35.61 | 36.05 | 35.32 |
| 2018 | 36.35· | 36.57 | 36.63 | 37.02 | 36.50 | 36.71 | 37.35 | 36.74 | 37.86 | 37.33 | 37.84 | 38.78 | 37.15 |
| 2019 | 38.55 | 39.25 | 39.05 | 39.13 | 38.96 | 39.48 | 38.92 | 38.51 | 39.33 | 38.99 | 39.22 | 39.93 | 39.11 |
| **Education and Health Services** | | | | | | | | | | | | | |
| 2015 | 28.46 | 28.32 | 28.13 | 28.11 | 28.11 | 27.81 | 27.60 | 27.99 | 28.26 | 28.39 | 28.71 | 28.72 | 28.22 |
| 2016 | 28.42 | 28.46 | 28.09 | 28.25 | 28.06 | 27.52 | 27.84 | 27.44 | 28.76 | 28.79 | 28.79 | 29.03 | 28.29 |
| 2017 | 29.03 | 29.58 | 29.20 | 29.18 | 29.17 | 28.90 | 29.29 | 29.80 | 29.93 | 29.81 | 29.88 | 30.08 | 29.49 |
| 2018 | 30.02 | 30.87 | 30.56 | 30.56 | 30.61 | 30.53 | 30.90 | 30.81 | 31.71 | 31.38 | 31.74 | 32.16 | 30.98 |
| 2019 | 32.42 | 33.11 | 32.53 | 32.57 | 32.73 | 32.38 | 33.95 | 33.53 | 33.59 | 33.95 | 33.96 | 33.70 | 33.21 |
| **Leisure and Hospitality** | | | | | | | | | | | | | |
| 2015 | 15.95 | 16.04 | 16.15 | 15.98 | 15.97 | 15.91 | 15.80 | 15.85 | 16.01 | 16.12 | 16.16 | 16.48 | 16.03 |
| 2016 | 16.68 | 16.76 | 16.74 | 16.76 | 16.81 | 16.84 | 16.78 | 16.77 | 17.00 | 17.11 | 17.32 | 17.63 | 16.93 |
| 2017 | 17.88 | 18.10 | 18.30 | 18.46 | 18.50 | 18.43 | 18.27 | 18.32 | 18.75 | 18.88 | 19.01 | 19.63 | 18.54 |
| 2018 | 19.57 | 19.75 | 19.74 | 19.95 | 19.95 | 19.87 | 19.73 | 19.85 | 19.84 | 19.93 | 20.68 | 21.12 | 20.00 |
| 2019 | 20.76 | 20.74 | 20.91 | 20.46 | 20.52 | 20.49 | 20.19 | 20.13 | 20.19 | 20.43 | 20.55 | 20.91 | 20.51 |
| **Other Services** | | | | | | | | | | | | | |
| 2015 | 22.70 | 22.45 | 22.11 | 22.26 | 22.13 | 22.22 | 22.37 | 22.59 | 23.02 | 23.28 | 24.58 | 25.06 | 22.88 |
| 2016 | 25.14 | 24.77 | 25.09 | 25.36 | 25.67 | 25.47 | 25.68 | 25.03 | 25.50 | 26.06 | 25.75 | 26.22 | 25.48 |
| 2017 | 27.12 | 26.35 | 26.06 | 26.29 | 25.76 | 25.19 | 25.67 | 25.05 | 26.42 | 26.33 | 26.14 | 26.42 | 26.06 |
| 2018 | 27.25 | 26.89 | 26.76 | 27.67 | 27.38 | 27.20 | 27.14 | 26.37 | 27.76 | 29.00 | 28.70 | 29.24 | 27.62 |
| 2019 | 29.31 | 30.08 | 29.84 | 29.87 | 30.00 | 29.27 | 28.59 | 29.04 | 30.88 | 30.74 | 30.65 | 31.83 | 30.01 |

## 4. Average Weekly Earnings by Selected Industry: Washington, 2015–2019

(Dollars, not seasonally adjusted)

| Industry and year | January | February | March | April | May | June | July | August | September | October | November | December | Annual average |
|---|---|---|---|---|---|---|---|---|---|---|---|---|---|
| **Total Private** | | | | | | | | | | | | | |
| 2015 | 989.86 | 1,023.65 | 1,023.30 | 994.97 | 998.24 | 995.90 | 998.13 | 1,038.17 | 1,020.77 | 1,027.97 | 1,065.64 | 1,028.50 | 1,018.24 |
| 2016 | 1,032.24 | 1,036.26 | 1,032.55 | 1,039.57 | 1,067.97 | 1,033.28 | 1,038.35 | 1,039.67 | 1,052.53 | 1,091.38 | 1,054.67 | 1,054.02 | 1,048.73 |
| 2017 | 1,095.16 | 1,064.30 | 1,065.02 | 1,113.68 | 1,070.19 | 1,070.87 | 1,112.93 | 1,080.54 | 1,092.67 | 1,129.61 | 1,092.62 | 1,103.05 | 1,091.33 |
| 2018 | 1,099.42 | 1,118.38 | 1,112.28 | 1,160.56 | 1,117.69 | 1,126.48 | 1,151.13 | 1,121.73 | 1,186.06 | 1,138.98 | 1,149.39 | 1,199.85 | 1,139.00 |
| 2019 | 1,159.06 | 1,144.74 | 1,163.49 | 1,161.79 | 1,165.82 | 1,194.34 | 1,166.79 | 1,168.35 | 1,198.79 | 1,168.52 | 1,171.28 | 1,196.65 | 1,172.66 |
| **Goods-Producing** | | | | | | | | | | | | | |
| 2015 | 1,282.96 | 1,297.88 | 1,309.42 | 1,299.67 | 1,305.44 | 1,312.47 | 1,295.15 | 1,312.97 | 1,285.76 | 1,311.67 | 1,308.72 | 1,318.12 | 1,303.45 |
| 2016 | 1,295.95 | 1,303.01 | 1,324.63 | 1,326.41 | 1,335.85 | 1,319.30 | 1,317.72 | 1,328.58 | 1,334.31 | 1,340.86 | 1,341.03 | 1,341.03 | 1,326.41 |
| 2017 | 1,332.05 | 1,328.64 | 1,358.73 | 1,367.49 | 1,361.57 | 1,374.41 | 1,374.52 | 1,385.33 | 1,396.65 | 1,422.89 | 1,411.34 | 1,424.84 | 1,378.16 |
| 2018 | 1,401.01 | 1,410.95 | 1,412.49 | 1,451.20 | 1,435.20 | 1,446.80 | 1,436.69 | 1,449.97 | 1,464.40 | 1,465.66 | 1,482.98 | 1,506.26 | 1,447.17 |
| 2019 | 1,475.65 | 1,431.04 | 1,500.40 | 1,484.38 | 1,499.04 | 1,522.53 | 1,512.80 | 1,513.53 | 1,510.80 | 1,516.21 | 1,514.98 | 1,516.40 | 1,501.84 |
| **Construction** | | | | | | | | | | | | | |
| 2015 | 1,183.90 | 1,200.91 | 1,185.13 | 1,190.44 | 1,200.15 | 1,228.54 | 1,210.28 | 1,231.90 | 1,153.98 | 1,195.75 | 1,185.75 | 1,180.27 | 1,195.24 |
| 2016 | 1,151.44 | 1,167.52 | 1,190.03 | 1,189.13 | 1,207.50 | 1,193.42 | 1,202.45 | 1,231.01 | 1,227.51 | 1,221.48 | 1,228.59 | 1,209.95 | 1,201.29 |
| 2017 | 1,186.92 | 1,184.17 | 1,222.86 | 1,224.48 | 1,236.06 | 1,256.62 | 1,254.53 | 1,272.81 | 1,267.30 | 1,309.50 | 1,270.88 | 1,268.63 | 1,247.94 |
| 2018 | 1,245.60 | 1,255.71 | 1,271.69 | 1,330.51 | 1,340.50 | 1,335.52 | 1,342.35 | 1,364.44 | 1,341.12 | 1,340.16 | 1,351.66 | 1,363.20 | 1,323.47 |
| 2019 | 1,339.44 | 1,243.56 | 1,354.18 | 1,382.72 | 1,441.42 | 1,450.86 | 1,457.23 | 1,460.04 | 1,441.61 | 1,449.32 | 1,429.13 | 1,410.69 | 1,407.23 |
| **Manufacturing** | | | | | | | | | | | | | |
| 2015 | 1,336.03 | 1,350.43 | 1,375.37 | 1,361.72 | 1,362.64 | 1,359.97 | 1,343.95 | 1,358.77 | 1,355.31 | 1,372.78 | 1,372.74 | 1,383.65 | 1,359.86 |
| 2016 | 1,364.04 | 1,367.38 | 1,386.53 | 1,392.18 | 1,396.23 | 1,379.47 | 1,371.01 | 1,373.63 | 1,387.13 | 1,403.84 | 1,401.51 | 1,411.17 | 1,384.51 |
| 2017 | 1,409.52 | 1,404.48 | 1,429.51 | 1,443.02 | 1,431.37 | 1,441.07 | 1,445.96 | 1,452.58 | 1,474.15 | 1,490.52 | 1,494.10 | 1,515.36 | 1,451.52 |
| 2018 | 1,489.19 | 1,497.73 | 1,507.12 | 1,536.33 | 1,507.57 | 1,526.45 | 1,504.98 | 1,512.46 | 1,541.25 | 1,542.48 | 1,553.71 | 1,581.68 | 1,524.79 |
| 2019 | 1,547.66 | 1,517.73 | 1,574.13 | 1,540.09 | 1,528.07 | 1,541.19 | 1,528.47 | 1,528.43 | 1,537.02 | 1,530.15 | 1,542.34 | 1,558.60 | 1,540.20 |
| **Trade, Transportation, and Utilities** | | | | | | | | | | | | | |
| 2015 | 839.95 | 866.62 | 864.85 | 858.83 | 869.79 | 869.09 | 874.02 | 925.65 | 944.53 | 933.31 | 965.16 | 922.60 | 895.21 |
| 2016 | 928.69 | 930.31 | 920.83 | 939.50 | 954.53 | 911.36 | 915.05 | 903.24 | 903.21 | 932.91 | 888.50 | 892.47 | 917.85 |
| 2017 | 919.81 | 892.67 | 882.35 | 936.72 | 904.19 | 909.22 | 943.44 | 903.53 | 905.66 | 922.68 | 890.91 | 894.86 | 909.58 |
| 2018 | 878.78 | 886.28 | 883.40 | 920.84 | 890.97 | 895.91 | 918.00 | 897.68 | 930.34 | 889.41 | 889.41 | 916.26 | 899.36 |
| 2019 | 897.07 | 875.16 | 886.94 | 897.97 | 886.45 | 910.27 | 887.33 | 881.73 | 893.38 | 876.17 | 875.18 | 885.20 | 888.03 |
| **Information** | | | | | | | | | | | | | |
| 2015 | 2,141.98 | 2,309.50 | 2,323.95 | 2,140.20 | 2,152.95 | 2,138.05 | 2,137.67 | 2,367.34 | 2,263.39 | 2,231.55 | 2,489.30 | 2,214.12 | 2,243.17 |
| 2016 | 2,252.09 | 2,251.12 | 2,234.02 | 2,229.73 | 2,455.08 | 2,225.28 | 2,244.59 | 2,228.90 | 2,318.27 | 2,538.31 | 2,333.64 | 2,269.71 | 2,298.45 |
| 2017 | 2,497.54 | 2,292.16 | 2,304.98 | 2,565.91 | 2,323.65 | 2,302.00 | 2,489.80 | 2,271.73 | 2,418.40 | 2,560.18 | 2,339.44 | 2,373.51 | 2,393.04 |
| 2018 | 2,349.62 | 2,367.41 | 2,396.81 | 2,625.26 | 2,345.25 | 2,396.93 | 2,551.33 | 2,328.67 | 2,742.32 | 2,477.27 | 2,492.95 | 2,720.43 | 2,484.50 |
| 2019 | 2,512.94 | 2,495.84 | 2,517.38 | 2,500.50 | 2,408.92 | 2,477.39 | 2,275.77 | 2,235.77 | 2,322.90 | 2,172.21 | 2,125.57 | 2,243.43 | 2,353.81 |
| **Financial Activities** | | | | | | | | | | | | | |
| 2015 | 1,022.35 | 1,066.89 | 1,073.48 | 1,037.82 | 1,046.68 | 1,009.18 | 1,044.05 | 1,077.88 | 1,011.23 | 1,040.41 | 1,074.79 | 1,022.81 | 1,043.15 |
| 2016 | 1,057.43 | 1,054.02 | 1,052.08 | 1,086.48 | 1,133.03 | 1,101.96 | 1,101.65 | 1,121.61 | 1,144.19 | 1,209.16 | 1,151.33 | 1,159.96 | 1,113.62 |
| 2017 | 1,246.78 | 1,160.61 | 1,146.96 | 1,229.12 | 1,152.98 | 1,168.15 | 1,226.83 | 1,162.08 | 1,184.53 | 1,247.07 | 1,204.31 | 1,205.14 | 1,193.32 |
| 2018 | 1,207.71 | 1,265.17 | 1,241.73 | 1,314.65 | 1,280.39 | 1,281.84 | 1,346.46 | 1,312.97 | 1,369.71 | 1,302.03 | 1,355.30 | 1,411.45 | 1,309.18 |
| 2019 | 1,347.25 | 1,358.71 | 1,313.64 | 1,337.73 | 1,362.82 | 1,420.16 | 1,345.01 | 1,402.13 | 1,463.71 | 1,382.25 | 1,423.16 | 1,517.86 | 1,389.78 |
| **Professional and Business Services** | | | | | | | | | | | | | |
| 2015 | 1179.85 | 1234.69 | 1224.86 | 1181.09 | 1178.31 | 1173.63 | 1159.84 | 1198.30 | 1165.54 | 1182.74 | 1229.69 | 1189.06 | 1190.24 |
| 2016 | 1197.94 | 1216.84 | 1211.30 | 1206.00 | 1247.22 | 1203.73 | 1203.24 | 1195.20 | 1205.23 | 1264.16 | 1215.23 | 1222.15 | 1214.86 |
| 2017 | 1286.84 | 1249.56 | 1245.84 | 1305.15 | 1241.37 | 1242.36 | 1307.50 | 1249.78 | 1261.59 | 1328.77 | 1281.96 | 1286.99 | 1275.05 |
| 2018 | 1304.97 | 1323.83 | 1326.01 | 1373.44 | 1317.65 | 1336.24 | 1393.16 | 1337.34 | 1431.11 | 1370.01 | 1369.81 | 1450.37 | 1359.69 |
| 2019 | 1387.80 | 1377.68 | 1394.09 | 1389.12 | 1390.87 | 1460.76 | 1393.34 | 1397.91 | 1467.01 | 1403.64 | 1408.00 | 1473.42 | 1411.87 |
| **Education and Health Services** | | | | | | | | | | | | | |
| 2015 | 924.95 | 945.89 | 931.10 | 910.76 | 907.95 | 903.83 | 908.04 | 943.26 | 935.41 | 934.03 | 970.40 | 933.40 | 928.44 |
| 2016 | 940.70 | 927.80 | 912.93 | 920.95 | 937.20 | 930.18 | 949.34 | 949.42 | 986.47 | 999.01 | 978.86 | 984.12 | 950.54 |
| 2017 | 1,013.15 | 1,005.72 | 989.88 | 1,012.55 | 988.86 | 982.60 | 1,022.22 | 1,031.08 | 1,023.61 | 1,046.33 | 1,021.90 | 1,031.74 | 1,014.46 |
| 2018 | 1,047.70 | 1,065.02 | 1,048.21 | 1,075.71 | 1,046.86 | 1,041.07 | 1,019.70 | 1,001.33 | 1,068.63 | 1,013.57 | 1,037.90 | 1,077.36 | 1,044.03 |
| 2019 | 1,053.65 | 1,059.52 | 1,066.98 | 1,071.55 | 1,089.91 | 1,100.92 | 1,127.14 | 1,116.55 | 1,148.78 | 1,133.93 | 1,144.45 | 1,159.28 | 1,105.89 |
| **Leisure and Hospitality** | | | | | | | | | | | | | |
| 2015 | 363.66 | 388.17 | 392.45 | 383.52 | 383.28 | 389.80 | 395.00 | 416.86 | 397.05 | 396.55 | 405.62 | 397.17 | 392.74 |
| 2016 | 396.98 | 407.27 | 405.11 | 410.62 | 428.66 | 415.95 | 421.18 | 429.31 | 426.70 | 438.02 | 426.07 | 426.65 | 419.86 |
| 2017 | 447.00 | 445.26 | 452.01 | 483.65 | 464.35 | 464.44 | 484.16 | 472.66 | 470.63 | 483.33 | 471.45 | 484.86 | 469.06 |
| 2018 | 477.51 | 497.70 | 485.60 | 518.70 | 506.73 | 510.66 | 532.71 | 520.07 | 527.74 | 512.20 | 508.73 | 547.01 | 512.00 |
| 2019 | 504.47 | 489.46 | 514.39 | 509.45 | 515.05 | 538.89 | 516.86 | 525.39 | 524.94 | 508.71 | 515.81 | 533.21 | 516.85 |
| **Other Services** | | | | | | | | | | | | | |
| 2015 | 637.87 | 669.01 | 650.03 | 634.41 | 632.92 | 639.94 | 648.73 | 670.92 | 637.65 | 640.20 | 707.90 | 694.16 | 654.37 |
| 2016 | 701.41 | 710.90 | 717.57 | 730.37 | 759.83 | 720.80 | 737.02 | 740.89 | 719.10 | 760.95 | 726.15 | 739.40 | 731.28 |
| 2017 | 781.06 | 750.98 | 740.10 | 786.07 | 731.58 | 715.40 | 767.53 | 741.48 | 755.61 | 768.84 | 737.15 | 760.90 | 753.13 |
| 2018 | 763.00 | 763.68 | 765.34 | 813.50 | 772.12 | 767.04 | 803.34 | 764.73 | 807.82 | 832.30 | 803.60 | 868.43 | 792.69 |
| 2019 | 841.20 | 857.28 | 862.38 | 863.24 | 876.00 | 866.39 | 843.41 | 853.78 | 926.40 | 919.13 | 904.18 | 942.17 | 879.29 |

# WEST VIRGINIA
## *At a Glance*

Population:
2010 census: 1,852,994
2019 estimate: 1,792,147

Percent change in population:
2010–2019: -3.3%

Percent change in total nonfarm employment:
2011–2019: -0.7%

Industry with the largest growth in employment, 2011–2019 (percent):
Construction, 9.1%

Industry with the largest decline or smallest growth in employment, 2011–2019 (percent):
Mining and logging, -33.5%

Civilian labor force:
2010: 811,125
2019: 796,966

Unemployment rate and rank among states (highest to lowest):
2010: 8.7%, 24th
2019: 4.9%, 4th

Over-the-year change in unemployment rates:
2017–2018: 0.0%
2018–2019: -0.3%

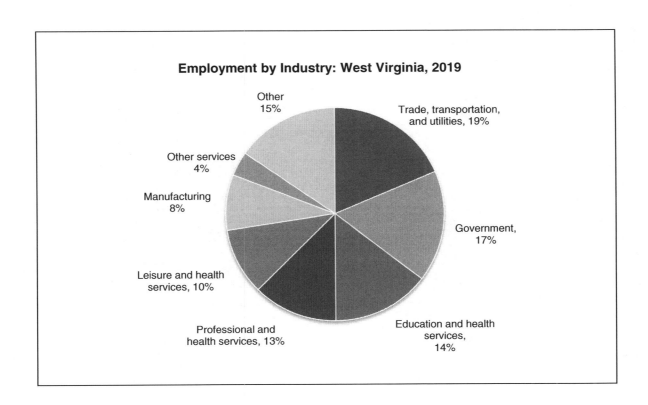

**Employment by Industry: West Virginia, 2019**

Other 15%

Trade, transportation, and utilities, 19%

Other services 4%

Manufacturing 8%

Government, 17%

Leisure and health services, 10%

Education and health services, 14%

Professional and health services, 13%

## 1. Employment by Industry: West Virginia, 2011–2019

(Numbers in thousands, not seasonally adjusted)

| Industry and year | January | February | March | April | May | June | July | August | September | October | November | December | Annual average |
|---|---|---|---|---|---|---|---|---|---|---|---|---|---|
| **Total Nonfarm** | | | | | | | | | | | | | |
| 2011 | 702.7 | 707.1 | 715.3 | 724.7 | 728.7 | 722.2 | 718.1 | 722.9 | 734.6 | 737.1 | 740.7 | 739.9 | 724.5 |
| 2012 | 720.3 | 723.4 | 731.6 | 736.8 | 750.7 | 731.4 | 724.4 | 727.6 | 738.9 | 740.6 | 741.4 | 740.8 | 734.0 |
| 2013 | 719.4 | 721.5 | 728.0 | 733.5 | 739.8 | 732.9 | 725.7 | 729.1 | 734.9 | 737.7 | 741.4 | 738.3 | 731.9 |
| 2014 | 714.3 | 713.6 | 722.7 | 731.0 | 747.1 | 721.7 | 717.8 | 723.9 | 735.4 | 741.3 | 742.3 | 740.3 | 729.3 |
| 2015 | 718.4 | 716.4 | 720.7 | 728.1 | 733.6 | 726.0 | 718.1 | 720.0 | 729.0 | 734.0 | 735.2 | 733.8 | 726.1 |
| 2016 | 708.3 | 706.0 | 714.5 | 719.7 | 729.4 | 712.7 | 706.6 | 709.1 | 719.8 | 722.0 | 733.6 | 721.3 | 716.9 |
| 2017 | 702.6 | 704.2 | 710.6 | 713.5 | 718.4 | 715.8 | 709.7 | 712.5 | 721.9 | 726.4 | 727.2 | 723.3 | 715.5 |
| 2018 | 705.7 | 707.4 | 713.6 | 721.1 | 735.3 | 728.5 | 724.1 | 728.8 | 734.4 | 739.5 | 738.0 | 731.9 | 725.7 |
| 2019 | 711.3 | 711.0 | 715.7 | 722.4 | 724.8 | 723.7 | 715.1 | 720.5 | 721.8 | 726.9 | 723.8 | 717.0 | 719.5 |
| **Total Private** | | | | | | | | | | | | | |
| 2011 | 552.6 | 555.0 | 560.9 | 569.4 | 573.3 | 575.5 | 577.0 | 580.0 | 580.7 | 581.3 | 584.4 | 584.0 | 572.8 |
| 2012 | 566.9 | 568.7 | 574.5 | 580.6 | 583.7 | 584.6 | 582.5 | 584.5 | 585.5 | 584.4 | 583.7 | 583.4 | 580.3 |
| 2013 | 565.5 | 566.7 | 571.4 | 577.2 | 582.2 | 581.2 | 580.8 | 582.6 | 582.3 | 581.3 | 584.4 | 582.0 | 578.1 |
| 2014 | 561.5 | 560.2 | 566.9 | 574.8 | 580.1 | 580.8 | 578.6 | 581.1 | 582.4 | 584.5 | 585.3 | 584.0 | 576.7 |
| 2015 | 565.8 | 562.7 | 565.9 | 572.6 | 577.7 | 576.1 | 573.8 | 574.2 | 575.0 | 576.4 | 577.0 | 575.6 | 572.7 |
| 2016 | 553.6 | 550.7 | 556.7 | 561.8 | 561.9 | 560.0 | 560.3 | 561.2 | 564.9 | 564.5 | 566.5 | 564.3 | 560.5 |
| 2017 | 548.0 | 548.3 | 552.5 | 556.8 | 561.7 | 565.4 | 564.7 | 566.4 | 568.3 | 570.5 | 571.9 | 568.6 | 561.9 |
| 2018 | 554.1 | 554.2 | 559.5 | 565.8 | 572.2 | 577.8 | 579.5 | 582.5 | 583.0 | 585.0 | 584.1 | 579.1 | 573.1 |
| 2019 | 560.7 | 558.5 | 562.2 | 567.7 | 571.1 | 573.3 | 571.8 | 572.2 | 569.1 | 572.2 | 569.4 | 563.7 | 567.7 |
| **Goods Producing** | | | | | | | | | | | | | |
| 2011 | 107.7 | 108.5 | 110.7 | 114.1 | 115.8 | 117.9 | 118.9 | 119.7 | 120.0 | 120.3 | 120.5 | 119.6 | 116.1 |
| 2012 | 115.8 | 115.8 | 117.4 | 119.0 | 119.6 | 121.1 | 119.8 | 119.4 | 119.3 | 119.1 | 116.9 | 115.5 | 118.2 |
| 2013 | 110.7 | 110.5 | 111.8 | 114.5 | 116.4 | 116.2 | 117.1 | 117.3 | 116.7 | 115.9 | 115.0 | 112.0 | 114.5 |
| 2014 | 106.9 | 105.9 | 108.5 | 111.7 | 113.6 | 114.2 | 114.0 | 114.4 | 114.8 | 114.8 | 112.5 | 110.1 | 111.8 |
| 2015 | 105.4 | 104.0 | 105.2 | 107.4 | 109.4 | 108.5 | 107.5 | 107.4 | 106.7 | 106.2 | 104.0 | 101.9 | 106.1 |
| 2016 | 95.8 | 94.2 | 96.7 | 98.4 | 97.2 | 97.8 | 98.2 | 98.1 | 98.5 | 98.3 | 97.5 | 96.4 | 97.3 |
| 2017 | 93.0 | 93.6 | 95.5 | 98.1 | 99.6 | 101.9 | 102.3 | 102.5 | 104.0 | 104.3 | 103.4 | 102.1 | 100.0 |
| 2018 | 97.6 | 97.9 | 101.0 | 104.6 | 108.3 | 112.7 | 115.5 | 117.1 | 118.1 | 118.0 | 114.7 | 110.7 | 109.7 |
| 2019 | 104.2 | 102.3 | 103.4 | 105.6 | 107.7 | 109.0 | 108.5 | 107.7 | 106.3 | 105.9 | 104.4 | 99.9 | 105.4 |
| **Service-Providing** | | | | | | | | | | | | | |
| 2011 | 595.0 | 598.6 | 604.6 | 610.6 | 612.9 | 604.3 | 599.2 | 603.2 | 614.6 | 616.8 | 620.2 | 620.3 | 608.4 |
| 2012 | 604.5 | 607.6 | 614.2 | 617.8 | 631.1 | 610.3 | 604.6 | 608.2 | 619.6 | 621.5 | 624.5 | 625.3 | 615.8 |
| 2013 | 608.7 | 611.0 | 616.2 | 619.0 | 623.4 | 616.7 | 608.6 | 611.8 | 618.2 | 621.8 | 626.4 | 626.3 | 617.3 |
| 2014 | 607.4 | 607.7 | 614.2 | 619.3 | 633.5 | 607.5 | 603.8 | 609.5 | 620.6 | 626.5 | 629.8 | 630.2 | 617.5 |
| 2015 | 613.0 | 612.4 | 615.5 | 620.7 | 624.2 | 617.5 | 610.6 | 612.6 | 622.3 | 627.8 | 631.2 | 631.9 | 620.0 |
| 2016 | 612.5 | 611.8 | 617.8 | 621.3 | 632.2 | 614.9 | 608.4 | 611.0 | 621.3 | 623.7 | 636.1 | 624.9 | 619.7 |
| 2017 | 609.6 | 610.6 | 615.1 | 615.4 | 618.8 | 613.9 | 607.4 | 610.0 | 617.9 | 622.1 | 623.8 | 621.2 | 615.5 |
| 2018 | 608.1 | 609.5 | 612.6 | 616.5 | 627.0 | 615.8 | 608.6 | 611.7 | 616.3 | 621.5 | 623.3 | 621.2 | 616.0 |
| 2019 | 607.1 | 608.7 | 612.3 | 616.8 | 617.1 | 614.7 | 606.6 | 612.8 | 615.5 | 621.0 | 619.4 | 617.1 | 614.1 |
| **Mining and Logging** | | | | | | | | | | | | | |
| 2011 | 31.6 | 32.0 | 32.2 | 32.6 | 32.9 | 33.7 | 33.8 | 34.4 | 34.8 | 35.0 | 35.3 | 35.7 | 33.7 |
| 2012 | 35.2 | 34.9 | 34.7 | 34.0 | 33.7 | 33.7 | 33.1 | 33.0 | 32.8 | 32.6 | 32.5 | 32.2 | 33.5 |
| 2013 | 31.6 | 31.6 | 31.7 | 31.9 | 32.1 | 32.3 | 31.9 | 32.0 | 31.6 | 31.6 | 31.4 | 31.1 | 31.7 |
| 2014 | 30.1 | 30.2 | 30.5 | 30.6 | 30.5 | 30.6 | 30.1 | 30.2 | 30.1 | 30.0 | 29.8 | 29.0 | 30.1 |
| 2015 | 28.5 | 27.8 | 27.6 | 27.3 | 27.0 | 26.0 | 25.5 | 24.9 | 24.9 | 24.7 | 24.0 | 23.3 | 26.0 |
| 2016 | 21.7 | 21.4 | 21.2 | 20.8 | 19.9 | 19.8 | 19.5 | 19.6 | 19.6 | 20.0 | 20.2 | 20.5 | 20.4 |
| 2017 | 20.5 | 20.9 | 21.2 | 21.4 | 21.6 | 22.0 | 22.2 | 22.1 | 22.2 | 22.6 | 22.6 | 22.5 | 21.8 |
| 2018 | 21.9 | 21.9 | 22.1 | 22.5 | 22.7 | 22.8 | 23.1 | 22.9 | 22.9 | 22.8 | 22.7 | 22.9 | 22.6 |
| 2019 | 23.0 | 23.0 | 23.0 | 22.9 | 22.8 | 22.7 | 22.6 | 22.4 | 22.1 | 22.2 | 21.4 | 21.0 | 22.4 |
| **Construction** | | | | | | | | | | | | | |
| 2011 | 27.4 | 27.7 | 29.2 | 32.2 | 33.4 | 34.2 | 35.1 | 35.5 | 35.6 | 35.8 | 35.6 | 34.3 | 33.0 |
| 2012 | 31.3 | 31.6 | 33.3 | 35.6 | 36.4 | 37.6 | 37.3 | 37.9 | 38.2 | 37.7 | 35.9 | 34.3 | 35.6 |
| 2013 | 31.0 | 30.9 | 32.0 | 34.5 | 35.9 | 35.2 | 36.3 | 36.6 | 36.4 | 35.9 | 35.1 | 32.5 | 34.4 |
| 2014 | 29.1 | 28.4 | 30.3 | 33.4 | 35.1 | 35.4 | 35.6 | 36.1 | 36.8 | 36.9 | 35.0 | 33.2 | 33.8 |
| 2015 | 29.3 | 28.6 | 29.8 | 32.6 | 34.6 | 34.4 | 34.2 | 34.7 | 34.2 | 33.9 | 32.4 | 31.0 | 32.5 |
| 2016 | 27.1 | 26.2 | 28.7 | 30.7 | 30.4 | 30.9 | 31.5 | 31.7 | 32.0 | 31.7 | 30.7 | 29.0 | 30.1 |
| 2017 | 26.2 | 26.2 | 27.7 | 29.9 | 31.2 | 32.8 | 33.2 | 33.7 | 35.1 | 35.1 | 34.2 | 32.8 | 31.5 |
| 2018 | 29.4 | 29.6 | 32.1 | 35.2 | 38.5 | 42.8 | 45.4 | 46.9 | 48.0 | 48.0 | 44.8 | 40.5 | 40.1 |
| 2019 | 34.0 | 32.1 | 33.2 | 35.5 | 37.7 | 38.8 | 38.8 | 38.4 | 37.5 | 37.1 | 36.4 | 32.5 | 36.0 |

## 1. Employment by Industry: West Virginia, 2011–2019—*Continued*

(Numbers in thousands, not seasonally adjusted)

| Industry and year | January | February | March | April | May | June | July | August | September | October | November | December | Annual average |
|---|---|---|---|---|---|---|---|---|---|---|---|---|---|
| **Manufacturing** | | | | | | | | | | | | | |
| 2011 | 48.7 | 48.8 | 49.3 | 49.3 | 49.5 | 50.0 | 50.0 | 49.8 | 49.6 | 49.5 | 49.6 | 49.6 | 49.5 |
| 2012 | 49.3 | 49.3 | 49.4 | 49.4 | 49.5 | 49.8 | 49.4 | 48.5 | 48.3 | 48.8 | 48.5 | 49.0 | 49.1 |
| 2013 | 48.1 | 48.0 | 48.1 | 48.1 | 48.4 | 48.7 | 48.9 | 48.7 | 48.7 | 48.4 | 48.5 | 48.4 | 48.4 |
| 2014 | 47.7 | 47.3 | 47.7 | 47.7 | 48.0 | 48.2 | 48.3 | 48.1 | 47.9 | 47.9 | 47.7 | 47.9 | 47.9 |
| 2015 | 47.6 | 47.6 | 47.8 | 47.5 | 47.8 | 48.1 | 47.8 | 47.8 | 47.6 | 47.6 | 47.6 | 47.6 | 47.7 |
| 2016 | 47.0 | 46.6 | 46.8 | 46.9 | 46.9 | 47.1 | 47.2 | 46.8 | 46.9 | 46.6 | 46.6 | 46.9 | 46.9 |
| 2017 | 46.3 | 46.5 | 46.6 | 46.8 | 46.8 | 47.1 | 46.9 | 46.7 | 46.7 | 46.6 | 46.6 | 46.8 | 46.7 |
| 2018 | 46.3 | 46.4 | 46.8 | 46.9 | 47.1 | 47.1 | 47.0 | 47.3 | 47.2 | 47.2 | 47.2 | 47.3 | 47.0 |
| 2019 | 47.2 | 47.2 | 47.2 | 47.2 | 47.2 | 47.5 | 47.1 | 46.9 | 46.7 | 46.6 | 46.6 | 46.4 | 47.0 |
| **Trade, Transportation, and Utilities** | | | | | | | | | | | | | |
| 2011 | 133.4 | 132.5 | 133.1 | 134.4 | 134.8 | 135.1 | 135.2 | 135.7 | 135.5 | 136.1 | 139.1 | 139.6 | 135.4 |
| 2012 | 134.4 | 132.9 | 133.7 | 134.0 | 134.7 | 135.0 | 134.9 | 135.4 | 135.5 | 136.3 | 139.7 | 140.2 | 135.6 |
| 2013 | 134.2 | 133.2 | 133.4 | 134.0 | 134.7 | 135.4 | 135.1 | 135.1 | 135.1 | 136.4 | 140.8 | 141.1 | 135.7 |
| 2014 | 133.8 | 132.5 | 132.6 | 133.8 | 134.5 | 135.0 | 134.1 | 134.8 | 134.5 | 136.8 | 140.8 | 141.2 | 135.4 |
| 2015 | 133.7 | 132.4 | 132.8 | 134.0 | 135.0 | 135.2 | 134.9 | 134.5 | 134.8 | 136.4 | 140.1 | 140.7 | 135.4 |
| 2016 | 132.7 | 131.4 | 132.1 | 133.1 | 133.1 | 132.7 | 132.6 | 132.8 | 133.4 | 134.0 | 137.9 | 138.4 | 133.7 |
| 2017 | 130.9 | 129.0 | 129.1 | 129.2 | 129.9 | 130.4 | 130.0 | 130.2 | 131.0 | 133.1 | 136.7 | 135.6 | 131.3 |
| 2018 | 130.2 | 128.2 | 128.5 | 128.2 | 129.4 | 129.4 | 129.0 | 129.0 | 129.4 | 131.2 | 135.4 | 135.4 | 130.3 |
| 2019 | 128.1 | 126.0 | 126.2 | 126.3 | 126.5 | 126.0 | 126.2 | 125.9 | 126.1 | 128.6 | 131.4 | 131.7 | 127.4 |
| **Wholesale Trade** | | | | | | | | | | | | | |
| 2011 | 22.7 | 22.6 | 22.8 | 23.1 | 23.2 | 23.1 | 23.1 | 23.2 | 23.3 | 23.4 | 23.6 | 23.6 | 23.1 |
| 2012 | 23.1 | 22.9 | 23.1 | 23.1 | 23.1 | 23.1 | 23.0 | 23.0 | 23.1 | 23.3 | 23.7 | 23.5 | 23.2 |
| 2013 | 22.7 | 22.7 | 22.6 | 22.7 | 22.7 | 22.8 | 22.8 | 22.9 | 22.9 | 22.8 | 22.8 | 22.9 | 22.8 |
| 2014 | 22.4 | 22.4 | 22.4 | 22.5 | 22.6 | 22.6 | 22.6 | 22.7 | 22.7 | 22.8 | 22.9 | 22.9 | 22.6 |
| 2015 | 22.4 | 22.3 | 22.3 | 22.4 | 22.3 | 22.3 | 22.2 | 22.1 | 22.0 | 22.1 | 22.1 | 22.0 | 22.2 |
| 2016 | 21.3 | 21.1 | 21.0 | 21.2 | 21.1 | 21.0 | 21.2 | 21.1 | 21.1 | 21.1 | 21.1 | 21.1 | 21.1 |
| 2017 | 20.5 | 20.4 | 20.5 | 20.6 | 20.6 | 20.9 | 20.7 | 20.7 | 20.6 | 20.6 | 20.7 | 20.7 | 20.6 |
| 2018 | 20.3 | 20.2 | 20.3 | 20.2 | 20.3 | 20.4 | 20.4 | 20.4 | 20.4 | 20.6 | 20.7 | 20.6 | 20.4 |
| 2019 | 20.2 | 20.2 | 20.2 | 20.2 | 20.3 | 20.3 | 20.3 | 20.2 | 20.1 | 20.6 | 20.6 | 20.5 | 20.3 |
| **Retail Trade** | | | | | | | | | | | | | |
| 2011 | 85.7 | 84.8 | 85.3 | 86.5 | 86.8 | 87.1 | 87.1 | 87.5 | 87.1 | 87.6 | 90.4 | 90.7 | 87.2 |
| 2012 | 86.7 | 85.4 | 86.1 | 86.4 | 87.1 | 87.3 | 87.4 | 87.8 | 87.6 | 88.2 | 91.1 | 91.4 | 87.7 |
| 2013 | 86.9 | 85.9 | 86.2 | 86.7 | 87.3 | 87.8 | 87.5 | 87.2 | 87.1 | 87.9 | 90.5 | 91.0 | 87.7 |
| 2014 | 86.2 | 85.2 | 85.4 | 86.4 | 86.9 | 87.2 | 86.4 | 86.9 | 86.3 | 86.5 | 89.3 | 89.7 | 86.9 |
| 2015 | 85.4 | 84.6 | 85.0 | 86.0 | 86.8 | 86.8 | 87.0 | 86.9 | 86.9 | 87.6 | 89.8 | 90.1 | 86.9 |
| 2016 | 85.9 | 85.5 | 86.1 | 86.8 | 87.1 | 86.8 | 86.6 | 86.8 | 86.8 | 86.7 | 89.0 | 89.0 | 86.9 |
| 2017 | 85.2 | 83.7 | 83.8 | 84.1 | 84.6 | 84.5 | 84.3 | 84.3 | 84.3 | 85.2 | 87.6 | 87.2 | 84.9 |
| 2018 | 83.3 | 82.5 | 82.7 | 82.8 | 83.6 | 83.1 | 82.8 | 82.4 | 81.9 | 82.2 | 84.5 | 84.3 | 83.0 |
| 2019 | 81.1 | 79.7 | 79.9 | 80.2 | 80.3 | 79.9 | 80.1 | 80.0 | 79.8 | 80.4 | 81.1 | 81.1 | 80.3 |
| **Transportation and Utilities** | | | | | | | | | | | | | |
| 2011 | 25.0 | 25.1 | 25.0 | 24.8 | 24.8 | 24.9 | 25.0 | 25.0 | 25.1 | 25.1 | 25.1 | 25.3 | 25.0 |
| 2012 | 24.6 | 24.6 | 24.5 | 24.5 | 24.5 | 24.6 | 24.5 | 24.6 | 24.8 | 24.8 | 24.9 | 25.3 | 24.7 |
| 2013 | 24.6 | 24.6 | 24.6 | 24.6 | 24.7 | 24.8 | 24.8 | 25.0 | 25.1 | 25.7 | 27.5 | 27.2 | 25.3 |
| 2014 | 25.2 | 24.9 | 24.8 | 24.9 | 25.0 | 25.2 | 25.1 | 25.2 | 25.5 | 27.5 | 28.6 | 28.6 | 25.9 |
| 2015 | 25.9 | 25.5 | 25.5 | 25.6 | 25.9 | 26.1 | 25.7 | 25.5 | 25.9 | 26.7 | 28.2 | 28.6 | 26.3 |
| 2016 | 25.5 | 24.8 | 25.0 | 25.1 | 24.9 | 24.9 | 24.8 | 24.9 | 25.5 | 26.2 | 27.8 | 28.3 | 25.6 |
| 2017 | 25.2 | 24.9 | 24.8 | 24.5 | 24.7 | 25.0 | 25.0 | 25.2 | 26.1 | 27.3 | 28.4 | 27.7 | 25.7 |
| 2018 | 26.6 | 25.5 | 25.5 | 25.2 | 25.5 | 25.9 | 25.8 | 26.2 | 27.1 | 28.4 | 30.2 | 30.5 | 26.9 |
| 2019 | 26.8 | 26.1 | 26.1 | 25.9 | 25.9 | 25.8 | 25.8 | 25.7 | 26.2 | 27.6 | 29.7 | 30.1 | 26.8 |
| **Information** | | | | | | | | | | | | | |
| 2011 | 10.4 | 10.4 | 10.4 | 10.3 | 10.2 | 10.2 | 10.2 | 10.2 | 10.0 | 10.0 | 9.9 | 9.9 | 10.2 |
| 2012 | 9.5 | 9.5 | 9.5 | 9.6 | 9.6 | 9.7 | 9.6 | 9.6 | 9.6 | 9.6 | 9.6 | 9.5 | 9.6 |
| 2013 | 9.3 | 9.4 | 9.5 | 9.5 | 9.6 | 9.6 | 9.7 | 9.7 | 9.7 | 9.7 | 9.8 | 9.8 | 9.6 |
| 2014 | 9.6 | 9.6 | 9.7 | 9.6 | 9.6 | 9.6 | 9.6 | 9.6 | 9.6 | 9.5 | 9.6 | 9.7 | 9.6 |
| 2015 | 9.6 | 9.6 | 9.7 | 9.7 | 9.8 | 9.7 | 9.7 | 9.7 | 9.6 | 9.7 | 9.7 | 9.7 | 9.7 |
| 2016 | 9.6 | 9.6 | 9.6 | 9.5 | 9.5 | 9.5 | 9.5 | 9.5 | 9.5 | 9.5 | 9.6 | 9.5 | 9.5 |
| 2017 | 9.2 | 8.9 | 8.9 | 8.7 | 8.7 | 8.7 | 8.6 | 8.5 | 8.5 | 8.4 | 8.4 | 8.4 | 8.7 |
| 2018 | 8.4 | 8.3 | 7.4 | 8.3 | 8.4 | 8.4 | 8.2 | 8.2 | 8.2 | 8.3 | 8.3 | 8.3 | 8.2 |
| 2019 | 8.2 | 8.1 | 8.1 | 8.0 | 8.1 | 8.0 | 8.0 | 8.0 | 8.0 | 8.1 | 8.0 | 8.0 | 8.1 |

## 1. Employment by Industry: West Virginia, 2011–2019—*Continued*

(Numbers in thousands, not seasonally adjusted)

| Industry and year | January | February | March | April | May | June | July | August | September | October | November | December | Annual average |
|---|---|---|---|---|---|---|---|---|---|---|---|---|---|
| **Financial Activities** | | | | | | | | | | | | | |
| 2011 | 29.7 | 29.4 | 29.3 | 29.4 | 29.5 | 29.6 | 29.8 | 29.7 | 29.6 | 29.8 | 29.7 | 29.8 | 29.6 |
| 2012 | 29.4 | 29.6 | 29.7 | 29.9 | 30.0 | 30.1 | 30.1 | 30.3 | 30.2 | 30.0 | 30.0 | 30.3 | 30.0 |
| 2013 | 29.9 | 30.0 | 30.3 | 30.4 | 30.4 | 30.3 | 30.4 | 30.3 | 30.3 | 30.4 | 30.4 | 30.6 | 30.3 |
| 2014 | 30.1 | 30.0 | 30.2 | 29.9 | 30.0 | 29.9 | 29.9 | 29.8 | 29.6 | 29.5 | 29.5 | 29.5 | 29.8 |
| 2015 | 29.1 | 29.0 | 29.1 | 29.5 | 29.6 | 29.6 | 29.6 | 29.5 | 29.4 | 29.5 | 29.4 | 29.4 | 29.4 |
| 2016 | 29.2 | 29.2 | 29.3 | 29.1 | 29.2 | 29.1 | 29.1 | 29.0 | 29.0 | 28.9 | 28.9 | 29.0 | 29.1 |
| 2017 | 28.6 | 28.7 | 28.9 | 28.8 | 29.0 | 29.0 | 28.8 | 28.8 | 28.8 | 28.8 | 28.7 | 28.8 | 28.8 |
| 2018 | 28.8 | 29.0 | 29.1 | 29.1 | 29.2 | 29.4 | 29.3 | 29.3 | 29.2 | 29.4 | 29.3 | 29.3 | 29.2 |
| 2019 | 28.9 | 28.9 | 29.0 | 29.1 | 29.3 | 29.4 | 29.3 | 29.4 | 29.3 | 29.0 | 29.3 | 29.0 | 29.2 |
| **Professional and Business Services** | | | | | | | | | | | | | |
| 2011 | 61.3 | 61.9 | 62.5 | 63.5 | 62.8 | 63.2 | 63.7 | 64.2 | 64.4 | 64.6 | 65.2 | 65.2 | 63.5 |
| 2012 | 63.4 | 63.7 | 63.9 | 65.2 | 65.0 | 65.1 | 64.7 | 65.2 | 64.9 | 65.1 | 64.7 | 64.7 | 64.6 |
| 2013 | 63.4 | 63.9 | 64.5 | 65.0 | 65.2 | 65.3 | 65.3 | 65.9 | 65.2 | 64.6 | 65.0 | 64.5 | 64.8 |
| 2014 | 63.6 | 63.9 | 64.6 | 66.1 | 66.6 | 67.3 | 67.7 | 68.2 | 67.9 | 68.8 | 68.9 | 69.3 | 66.9 |
| 2015 | 67.0 | 66.5 | 66.5 | 67.0 | 66.7 | 67.3 | 67.4 | 67.9 | 67.0 | 67.4 | 67.2 | 66.9 | 67.1 |
| 2016 | 64.4 | 64.7 | 65.2 | 65.9 | 65.2 | 65.5 | 66.8 | 66.5 | 66.0 | 66.6 | 66.4 | 65.6 | 65.7 |
| 2017 | 64.8 | 65.4 | 65.9 | 66.2 | 66.6 | 67.2 | 67.3 | 67.5 | 67.5 | 67.6 | 67.9 | 67.5 | 66.8 |
| 2018 | 66.4 | 67.2 | 68.1 | 68.8 | 69.0 | 69.6 | 69.7 | 70.1 | 69.8 | 69.6 | 69.6 | 68.7 | 68.9 |
| 2019 | 67.4 | 68.0 | 68.4 | 69.3 | 69.2 | 69.9 | 70.1 | 70.3 | 69.7 | 70.7 | 69.0 | 68.9 | 69.2 |
| **Education and Health Services** | | | | | | | | | | | | | |
| 2011 | 116.9 | 118.7 | 119.5 | 120.4 | 120.8 | 118.9 | 118.4 | 119.1 | 121.3 | 122.1 | 122.7 | 122.8 | 120.1 |
| 2012 | 119.6 | 121.5 | 122.4 | 123.4 | 123.6 | 121.4 | 120.9 | 121.7 | 124.6 | 124.4 | 124.5 | 124.8 | 122.7 |
| 2013 | 121.3 | 123.2 | 123.6 | 123.7 | 124.0 | 121.4 | 120.4 | 121.4 | 124.2 | 124.4 | 124.8 | 125.1 | 123.1 |
| 2014 | 122.0 | 122.5 | 123.7 | 124.3 | 124.6 | 122.2 | 121.0 | 121.9 | 125.0 | 125.1 | 125.5 | 125.7 | 123.6 |
| 2015 | 124.8 | 125.3 | 125.5 | 126.0 | 126.5 | 123.6 | 122.2 | 123.0 | 126.6 | 127.5 | 128.0 | 128.2 | 125.6 |
| 2016 | 125.7 | 125.6 | 126.2 | 127.2 | 127.4 | 123.8 | 122.8 | 123.9 | 128.2 | 128.0 | 128.5 | 128.5 | 126.3 |
| 2017 | 126.9 | 127.4 | 127.5 | 127.6 | 127.6 | 126.0 | 125.8 | 126.9 | 128.2 | 128.8 | 128.9 | 128.8 | 127.5 |
| 2018 | 127.4 | 128.0 | 128.4 | 128.2 | 128.1 | 127.1 | 126.5 | 127.8 | 128.7 | 129.2 | 129.2 | 129.2 | 128.2 |
| 2019 | 128.1 | 128.8 | 129.3 | 129.4 | 129.2 | 128.4 | 127.7 | 128.8 | 129.5 | 130.4 | 130.3 | 129.9 | 129.2 |
| **Leisure and Hospitality** | | | | | | | | | | | | | |
| 2011 | 68.6 | 68.9 | 70.5 | 72.4 | 74.3 | 75.5 | 75.6 | 76.3 | 74.8 | 73.2 | 72.1 | 72.0 | 72.9 |
| 2012 | 69.9 | 70.7 | 72.7 | 74.0 | 75.7 | 76.7 | 77.1 | 77.6 | 76.2 | 74.6 | 73.0 | 73.2 | 74.3 |
| 2013 | 71.7 | 71.5 | 72.9 | 74.3 | 76.3 | 77.4 | 77.2 | 77.4 | 75.6 | 74.5 | 73.2 | 73.6 | 74.6 |
| 2014 | 70.5 | 70.8 | 72.4 | 73.9 | 75.8 | 77.1 | 76.9 | 77.1 | 75.7 | 74.7 | 73.3 | 73.4 | 74.3 |
| 2015 | 71.3 | 71.0 | 72.1 | 74.1 | 75.8 | 77.1 | 77.4 | 77.2 | 76.0 | 74.9 | 73.9 | 74.1 | 74.6 |
| 2016 | 71.8 | 71.6 | 72.9 | 74.0 | 75.7 | 76.9 | 76.7 | 76.8 | 75.8 | 74.7 | 73.3 | 72.5 | 74.4 |
| 2017 | 70.3 | 71.0 | 72.3 | 73.7 | 75.6 | 77.2 | 77.1 | 77.2 | 75.6 | 74.9 | 73.5 | 73.1 | 74.3 |
| 2018 | 71.5 | 71.7 | 72.5 | 73.8 | 75.3 | 76.6 | 76.6 | 76.4 | 75.2 | 74.8 | 73.2 | 73.3 | 74.2 |
| 2019 | 71.9 | 72.4 | 73.4 | 75.2 | 76.4 | 77.6 | 77.7 | 77.7 | 76.0 | 75.4 | 73.0 | 72.5 | 74.9 |
| **Other Services** | | | | | | | | | | | | | |
| 2011 | 24.6 | 24.7 | 24.9 | 24.9 | 25.1 | 25.1 | 25.2 | 25.1 | 25.1 | 25.2 | 25.2 | 25.1 | 25.0 |
| 2012 | 24.9 | 25.0 | 25.2 | 25.5 | 25.5 | 25.5 | 25.4 | 25.3 | 25.2 | 25.3 | 25.3 | 25.2 | 25.3 |
| 2013 | 25.0 | 25.0 | 25.4 | 25.8 | 25.6 | 25.6 | 25.6 | 25.5 | 25.5 | 25.4 | 25.4 | 25.3 | 25.4 |
| 2014 | 25.0 | 25.0 | 25.2 | 25.5 | 25.4 | 25.5 | 25.4 | 25.3 | 25.3 | 25.3 | 25.2 | 25.1 | 25.3 |
| 2015 | 24.9 | 24.9 | 25.0 | 24.9 | 24.9 | 25.1 | 25.1 | 25.0 | 24.9 | 24.8 | 24.7 | 24.7 | 24.9 |
| 2016 | 24.4 | 24.4 | 24.7 | 24.6 | 24.6 | 24.7 | 24.6 | 24.6 | 24.5 | 24.5 | 24.4 | 24.4 | 24.5 |
| 2017 | 24.3 | 24.3 | 24.4 | 24.5 | 24.7 | 25.0 | 24.8 | 24.8 | 24.7 | 24.6 | 24.4 | 24.3 | 24.6 |
| 2018 | 23.8 | 23.9 | 24.5 | 24.8 | 24.5 | 24.6 | 24.7 | 24.6 | 24.4 | 24.5 | 24.4 | 24.2 | 24.4 |
| 2019 | 23.9 | 24.0 | 24.4 | 24.8 | 24.7 | 25.0 | 24.3 | 24.4 | 24.2 | 24.1 | 24.0 | 23.8 | 24.3 |
| **Government** | | | | | | | | | | | | | |
| 2011 | 150.1 | 152.1 | 154.4 | 155.3 | 155.4 | 146.7 | 141.1 | 142.9 | 153.9 | 155.8 | 156.3 | 155.9 | 151.7 |
| 2012 | 153.4 | 154.7 | 157.1 | 156.2 | 167.0 | 146.8 | 141.9 | 143.1 | 153.4 | 156.2 | 157.7 | 157.4 | 153.7 |
| 2013 | 153.9 | 154.8 | 156.6 | 156.3 | 157.6 | 151.7 | 144.9 | 146.5 | 152.6 | 156.4 | 157.0 | 156.3 | 153.7 |
| 2014 | 152.8 | 153.4 | 155.8 | 156.2 | 167.0 | 140.9 | 139.2 | 142.8 | 153.0 | 156.8 | 157.0 | 156.3 | 152.6 |
| 2015 | 152.6 | 153.7 | 154.8 | 155.5 | 155.9 | 149.9 | 144.3 | 145.8 | 154.0 | 157.6 | 158.2 | 158.2 | 153.4 |
| 2016 | 154.7 | 155.3 | 157.8 | 157.9 | 167.5 | 152.7 | 146.3 | 147.9 | 154.9 | 157.5 | 167.1 | 157.0 | 156.4 |
| 2017 | 154.6 | 155.9 | 158.1 | 156.7 | 156.7 | 150.4 | 145.0 | 146.1 | 153.6 | 155.9 | 155.3 | 154.7 | 153.6 |
| 2018 | 151.6 | 153.2 | 154.1 | 155.3 | 163.1 | 150.7 | 144.6 | 146.3 | 151.4 | 154.5 | 153.9 | 152.8 | 152.6 |
| 2019 | 150.6 | 152.5 | 153.5 | 154.7 | 153.7 | 150.4 | 143.3 | 148.3 | 152.7 | 154.7 | 154.4 | 153.3 | 151.8 |

## 2. Average Weekly Hours by Selected Industry: West Virginia, 2015–2019

(Not seasonally adjusted)

| Industry and year | January | February | March | April | May | June | July | August | September | October | November | December | Annual average |
|---|---|---|---|---|---|---|---|---|---|---|---|---|---|
| **Total Private** | | | | | | | | | | | | | |
| 2015 | 34.4 | 34.2 | 34.6 | 34.7 | 35.0 | 34.9 | 35.0 | 35.2 | 34.7 | 35.0 | 35.0 | 34.6 | 34.8 |
| 2016 | 34.3 | 34.4 | 34.9 | 35.1 | 34.9 | 35.3 | 35.3 | 35.2 | 35.2 | 35.5 | 35.3 | 35.3 | 35.1 |
| 2017 | 35.3 | 35.2 | 35.1 | 35.4 | 35.4 | 35.8 | 36.1 | 35.8 | 35.8 | 35.7 | 35.5 | 35.5 | 35.5 |
| 2018 | 34.9 | 35.1 | 35.2 | 35.6 | 35.4 | 35.8 | 35.9 | 35.7 | 35.8 | 35.4 | 35.2 | 35.6 | 35.5 |
| 2019 | 34.9 | 35.1 | 35.4 | 35.5 | 35.7 | 36.2 | 35.6 | 35.6 | 35.9 | 35.5 | 35.6 | 35.5 | 35.6 |
| **Goods-Producing** | | | | | | | | | | | | | |
| 2015 | 39.4 | 38.9 | 39.6 | 39.9 | 41.3 | 40.5 | 40.0 | 41.0 | 39.2 | 41.1 | 39.8 | 40.0 | 40.1 |
| 2016 | 39.3 | 39.1 | 40.2 | 40.5 | 39.4 | 40.4 | 39.8 | 40.6 | 40.6 | 41.3 | 41.3 | 40.5 | 40.2 |
| 2017 | 40.4 | 40.9 | 40.4 | 41.2 | 41.0 | 41.6 | 41.3 | 41.6 | 41.6 | 41.7 | 41.2 | 41.3 | 41.2 |
| 2018 | 40.3 | 40.8 | 40.8 | 41.5 | 41.7 | 42.0 | 41.6 | 42.1 | 41.8 | 42.1 | 41.6 | 42.1 | 41.6 |
| 2019 | 41.1 | 40.9 | 41.3 | 41.4 | 41.3 | 41.3 | 40.7 | 41.6 | 42.1 | 41.2 | 40.9 | 40.8 | 41.2 |
| **Mining and Logging** | | | | | | | | | | | | | |
| 2015 | 47.6 | 44.6 | 46.3 | 46.2 | 45.8 | 45.3 | 45.8 | 46.0 | 43.2 | 46.3 | 46.9 | 46.0 | 45.8 |
| 2016 | 45.8 | 44.4 | 46.0 | 46.5 | 45.5 | 43.9 | 44.1 | 46.1 | 46.4 | 48.4 | 46.6 | 44.8 | 45.7 |
| 2017 | 44.5 | 43.8 | 42.2 | 42.3 | 43.0 | 42.4 | 42.8 | 43.3 | 43.3 | 43.3 | 43.5 | 43.9 | 43.2 |
| 2018 | 43.7 | 44.1 | 43.2 | 43.0 | 42.6 | 42.5 | 41.6 | 43.3 | 43.8 | 42.8 | 43.7 | 44.8 | 43.3 |
| 2019 | 43.6 | 43.9 | 42.9 | 43.7 | 44.6 | 42.7 | 42.0 | 44.5 | 45.0 | 45.8 | 44.6 | 45.4 | 44.0 |
| **Construction** | | | | | | | | | | | | | |
| 2015 | 36.2 | 35.7 | 36.8 | 37.3 | 39.2 | 39.1 | 38.5 | 40.1 | 38.1 | 40.7 | 37.4 | 38.9 | 38.2 |
| 2016 | 37.3 | 36.6 | 38.6 | 38.9 | 38.3 | 41.0 | 40.2 | 40.5 | 40.6 | 40.7 | 40.3 | 38.9 | 39.4 |
| 2017 | 37.7 | 39.1 | 38.2 | 41.3 | 40.7 | 42.7 | 41.9 | 41.7 | 42.1 | 41.8 | 41.6 | 41.3 | 41.0 |
| 2018 | 39.7 | 39.3 | 39.9 | 41.9 | 42.5 | 42.7 | 42.6 | 42.1 | 41.1 | 42.0 | 40.8 | 41.5 | 41.5 |
| 2019 | 40.0 | 39.2 | 40.3 | 40.2 | 40.2 | 40.7 | 39.9 | 40.6 | 41.5 | 39.4 | 38.7 | 38.1 | 39.9 |
| **Manufacturing** | | | | | | | | | | | | | |
| 2015 | 36.5 | 37.5 | 37.5 | 38.1 | 40.2 | 39.0 | 37.9 | 39.1 | 37.9 | 38.8 | 37.9 | 37.8 | 38.2 |
| 2016 | 37.4 | 37.9 | 38.5 | 39.0 | 37.5 | 38.5 | 37.7 | 38.4 | 38.2 | 38.6 | 39.5 | 39.7 | 38.4 |
| 2017 | 40.1 | 40.7 | 40.8 | 40.7 | 40.3 | 40.5 | 40.1 | 40.6 | 40.4 | 40.7 | 39.7 | 40.2 | 40.4 |
| 2018 | 39.1 | 40.2 | 40.2 | 40.4 | 40.5 | 41.2 | 40.5 | 41.4 | 41.6 | 41.9 | 41.4 | 41.4 | 40.8 |
| 2019 | 40.8 | 40.7 | 41.2 | 41.2 | 40.7 | 41.0 | 40.8 | 41.0 | 41.3 | 40.5 | 40.9 | 40.7 | 40.9 |
| **Trade, Transportation, and Utilities** | | | | | | | | | | | | | |
| 2015 | 34.2 | 34.7 | 35.3 | 35.5 | 36.0 | 35.9 | 35.7 | 36.0 | 35.7 | 35.8 | 35.7 | 35.1 | 35.5 |
| 2016 | 34.4 | 34.8 | 34.9 | 35.2 | 35.1 | 35.1 | 35.4 | 35.4 | 35.5 | 35.6 | 35.6 | 35.9 | 35.2 |
| 2017 | 35.4 | 35.2 | 35.3 | 35.1 | 35.5 | 36.0 | 36.0 | 36.0 | 35.7 | 35.1 | 35.2 | 34.9 | 35.4 |
| 2018 | 33.7 | 33.7 | 33.9 | 34.2 | 34.1 | 34.9 | 34.6 | 34.6 | 34.4 | 34.1 | 34.1 | 33.6 | 34.2 |
| 2019 | 32.9 | 33.5 | 34.0 | 34.6 | 34.9 | 35.7 | 35.2 | 35.1 | 35.0 | 34.7 | 35.1 | 34.7 | 34.6 |
| **Financial Activities** | | | | | | | | | | | | | |
| 2015 | 35.5 | 35.9 | 35.8 | 36.1 | 36.1 | 36.6 | 36.0 | 37.0 | 35.6 | 36.2 | 36.6 | 36.1 | 36.1 |
| 2016 | 35.7 | 35.9 | 35.0 | 35.5 | 35.7 | 36.3 | 35.9 | 35.3 | 34.6 | 36.2 | 35.9 | 36.0 | 35.7 |
| 2017 | 36.5 | 35.9 | 35.8 | 36.1 | 35.7 | 35.6 | 36.2 | 35.7 | 35.5 | 36.2 | 35.5 | 35.9 | 35.9 |
| 2018 | 35.1 | 35.2 | 36.1 | 36.1 | 35.6 | 35.5 | 35.6 | 34.8 | 35.4 | 35.0 | 34.5 | 36.0 | 35.4 |
| 2019 | 34.7 | 34.2 | 34.2 | 34.0 | 33.9 | 36.2 | 34.8 | 35.3 | 36.5 | 35.0 | 35.3 | 36.9 | 35.1 |
| **Professional and Business Services** | | | | | | | | | | | | | |
| 2015 | 35.0 | 34.2 | 35.2 | 34.2 | 34.9 | 34.6 | 35.4 | 35.3 | 35.4 | 35.7 | 36.5 | 36.5 | 35.2 |
| 2016 | 35.5 | 35.5 | 36.1 | 36.4 | 36.6 | 36.7 | 36.6 | 36.5 | 36.5 | 38.0 | 37.2 | 37.4 | 36.6 |
| 2017 | 37.1 | 37.2 | 37.1 | 37.5 | 36.6 | 36.9 | 37.8 | 36.8 | 37.1 | 36.6 | 36.3 | 36.2 | 36.9 |
| 2018 | 35.9 | 36.5 | 36.4 | 37.1 | 36.5 | 37.2 | 37.7 | 37.6 | 38.2 | 37.6 | 37.0 | 37.4 | 37.1 |
| 2019 | 36.9 | 36.7 | 37.5 | 37.3 | 37.4 | 39.0 | 38.6 | 38.3 | 39.4 | 38.3 | 37.8 | 38.2 | 38.0 |
| **Education and Health Services** | | | | | | | | | | | | | |
| 2015 | 34.9 | 34.4 | 34.4 | 34.5 | 34.6 | 34.5 | 34.9 | 34.8 | 34.6 | 34.3 | 34.6 | 34.5 | 34.6 |
| 2016 | 34.5 | 34.5 | 34.8 | 34.9 | 35.0 | 35.2 | 35.4 | 34.9 | 35.0 | 35.0 | 34.6 | 34.8 | 34.9 |
| 2017 | 35.2 | 34.7 | 34.8 | 35.0 | 35.1 | 35.3 | 35.7 | 35.3 | 35.4 | 35.4 | 35.1 | 35.1 | 35.2 |
| 2018 | 35.3 | 35.3 | 35.3 | 35.5 | 35.3 | 35.6 | 35.8 | 35.2 | 35.3 | 34.9 | 35.3 | 35.2 | 35.3 |
| 2019 | 35.1 | 35.3 | 35.1 | 35.4 | 35.7 | 35.8 | 35.4 | 35.2 | 35.2 | 35.2 | 35.7 | 35.8 | 35.4 |
| **Leisure and Hospitality** | | | | | | | | | | | | | |
| 2015 | 25.0 | 25.2 | 25.8 | 26.0 | 26.3 | 26.7 | 27.0 | 26.8 | 26.4 | 26.4 | 26.5 | 25.9 | 26.2 |
| 2016 | 25.4 | 26.1 | 27.1 | 26.8 | 26.8 | 27.3 | 27.3 | 27.0 | 26.5 | 26.1 | 26.0 | 25.5 | 26.5 |
| 2017 | 25.0 | 25.7 | 25.6 | 25.5 | 25.9 | 26.6 | 26.9 | 27.0 | 26.8 | 26.4 | 26.3 | 26.3 | 26.2 |
| 2018 | 25.4 | 26.2 | 26.8 | 26.9 | 27.1 | 27.3 | 27.8 | 27.6 | 27.4 | 27.0 | 26.6 | 26.8 | 26.9 |
| 2019 | 26.2 | 26.6 | 26.4 | 26.6 | 27.1 | 27.2 | 27.0 | 26.9 | 26.8 | 26.8 | 27.0 | 26.7 | 26.8 |
| **Other Services** | | | | | | | | | | | | | |
| 2015 | 32.1 | 32.1 | 32.1 | 32.5 | 31.7 | 32.1 | 32.2 | 32.4 | 32.0 | 32.3 | 32.9 | 32.4 | 32.2 |
| 2016 | 31.6 | 32.4 | 31.9 | 32.5 | 32.7 | 33.3 | 32.1 | 32.2 | 32.9 | 33.8 | 33.6 | 33.2 | 32.7 |
| 2017 | 33.0 | 32.8 | 33.4 | 32.9 | 33.5 | 33.7 | 33.4 | 33.4 | 33.6 | 33.7 | 33.3 | 33.6 | 33.3 |
| 2018 | 33.5 | 33.2 | 33.6 | 33.5 | 33.1 | 33.3 | 34.1 | 34.1 | 34.1 | 32.9 | 33.6 | 33.4 | 33.6 |
| 2019 | 33.0 | 33.7 | 32.7 | 32.6 | 32.7 | 33.5 | 33.2 | 32.2 | 32.8 | 33.4 | 32.4 | 30.9 | 32.8 |

## 3. Average Hourly Earnings by Selected Industry: West Virginia, 2015–2019

(Dollars, not seasonally adjusted)

| Industry and year | January | February | March | April | May | June | July | August | September | October | November | December | Annual average |
|---|---|---|---|---|---|---|---|---|---|---|---|---|---|
| **Total Private** | | | | | | | | | | | | | |
| 2015 | 20.91 | 20.88 | 20.80 | 20.67 | 20.65 | 20.60 | 20.70 | 20.84 | 20.89 | 20.86 | 21.03 | 20.83 | 20.80 |
| 2016 | 21.13 | 21.16 | 20.97 | 20.92 | 20.71 | 20.62 | 20.89 | 20.86 | 21.05 | 21.24 | 21.15 | 21.09 | 20.98 |
| 2017 | 21.41 | 21.44 | 21.56 | 21.53 | 21.42 | 21.50 | 21.74 | 21.76 | 22.00 | 22.18 | 22.27 | 22.26 | 21.76 |
| 2018 | 22.69 | 22.67 | 22.47 | 22.93 | 22.74 | 22.70 | 23.03 | 23.01 | 23.26 | 23.44 | 23.40 | 23.64 | 23.00 |
| 2019 | 23.35 | 23.43 | 23.41 | 23.82 | 23.67 | 23.61 | 23.56 | 23.60 | 23.96 | 23.80 | 24.00 | 24.08 | 23.69 |
| **Goods-Producing** | | | | | | | | | | | | | |
| 2015 | 24.96 | 24.71 | 24.84 | 24.90 | 24.65 | 24.73 | 24.56 | 24.82 | 25.26 | 24.99 | 25.28 | 25.09 | 24.89 |
| 2016 | 25.16 | 24.99 | 25.11 | 25.15 | 25.00 | 25.21 | 25.32 | 25.30 | 25.28 | 25.69 | 25.19 | 25.24 | 25.22 |
| 2017 | 25.15 | 25.45 | 25.02 | 25.44 | 25.45 | 25.53 | 25.75 | 25.90 | 26.06 | 26.16 | 25.94 | 25.98 | 25.67 |
| 2018 | 25.38 | 25.10 | 25.03 | 25.33 | 25.23 | 25.70 | 26.06 | 25.87 | 26.15 | 26.31 | 26.59 | 26.87 | 25.83 |
| 2019 | 26.29 | 26.54 | 26.17 | 26.37 | 26.60 | 26.70 | 26.65 | 26.94 | 27.12 | 27.03 | 27.28 | 27.11 | 26.73 |
| **Mining and Logging** | | | | | | | | | | | | | |
| 2015 | 29.89 | 29.86 | 30.10 | 29.68 | 29.78 | 29.71 | 29.48 | 29.31 | 30.16 | 29.38 | 29.47 | 28.87 | 29.65 |
| 2016 | 29.72 | 29.23 | 29.26 | 28.49 | 28.40 | 28.52 | 27.79 | 28.35 | 28.33 | 28.75 | 27.84 | 28.47 | 28.61 |
| 2017 | 28.35 | 29.20 | 29.07 | 28.85 | 28.99 | 28.03 | 28.37 | 28.80 | 28.84 | 28.95 | 29.04 | 28.52 | 28.75 |
| 2018 | 27.74 | 27.22 | 27.32 | 27.65 | 27.70 | 28.29 | 28.72 | 28.81 | 28.84 | 29.45 | 29.39 | 29.84 | 28.43 |
| 2019 | 29.35 | 29.98 | 29.91 | 29.52 | 29.79 | 30.00 | 30.30 | 30.48 | 30.90 | 30.64 | 31.64 | 31.10 | 30.29 |
| **Construction** | | | | | | | | | | | | | |
| 2015 | 24.26 | 23.80 | 24.18 | 24.90 | 24.47 | 25.16 | 24.30 | 24.97 | 25.00 | 25.36 | 25.12 | 25.43 | 24.78 |
| 2016 | 24.60 | 24.95 | 25.67 | 26.36 | 25.96 | 26.03 | 26.51 | 25.82 | 25.98 | 26.12 | 25.60 | 25.08 | 25.76 |
| 2017 | 24.77 | 25.71 | 25.15 | 25.75 | 25.82 | 26.61 | 26.62 | 26.98 | 26.90 | 27.04 | 27.00 | 27.03 | 26.38 |
| 2018 | 26.29 | 26.58 | 26.16 | 26.33 | 26.51 | 26.78 | 27.07 | 27.12 | 27.10 | 27.42 | 28.00 | 28.48 | 27.06 |
| 2019 | 27.90 | 28.01 | 27.46 | 27.93 | 28.18 | 27.86 | 27.49 | 28.26 | 27.96 | 27.95 | 28.38 | 28.17 | 27.96 |
| **Manufacturing** | | | | | | | | | | | | | |
| 2015 | 21.54 | 21.65 | 21.50 | 21.58 | 21.48 | 21.29 | 21.57 | 21.94 | 22.52 | 21.99 | 22.77 | 22.62 | 21.87 |
| 2016 | 22.92 | 22.74 | 22.52 | 22.59 | 22.60 | 23.06 | 23.28 | 23.40 | 23.22 | 23.74 | 23.55 | 23.74 | 23.12 |
| 2017 | 23.77 | 23.50 | 23.04 | 23.61 | 23.46 | 23.51 | 23.79 | 23.63 | 23.97 | 24.03 | 23.48 | 23.89 | 23.64 |
| 2018 | 23.55 | 23.09 | 23.09 | 23.36 | 22.89 | 23.38 | 23.69 | 23.11 | 23.82 | 23.62 | 23.85 | 23.92 | 23.45 |
| 2019 | 23.56 | 23.77 | 23.39 | 23.60 | 23.67 | 24.11 | 24.16 | 24.03 | 24.50 | 24.38 | 24.29 | 24.41 | 23.99 |
| **Trade, Transportation, and Utilities** | | | | | | | | | | | | | |
| 2015 | 18.44 | 18.64 | 18.39 | 18.54 | 18.27 | 18.53 | 18.66 | 18.73 | 18.88 | 19.04 | 18.94 | 18.72 | 18.65 |
| 2016 | 19.23 | 18.85 | 19.42 | 19.78 | 19.40 | 19.42 | 19.77 | 19.49 | 19.80 | 20.07 | 19.78 | 19.45 | 19.54 |
| 2017 | 19.64 | 20.00 | 20.12 | 20.16 | 19.94 | 19.64 | 19.62 | 19.55 | 19.90 | 20.07 | 19.85 | 19.85 | 19.86 |
| 2018 | 20.29 | 20.35 | 20.09 | 20.43 | 20.37 | 20.00 | 20.05 | 20.10 | 20.23 | 20.17 | 19.72 | 19.78 | 20.13 |
| 2019 | 19.92 | 20.56 | 20.57 | 20.76 | 20.91 | 21.06 | 20.90 | 20.74 | 21.04 | 20.84 | 20.91 | 20.88 | 20.76 |
| **Financial Activities** | | | | | | | | | | | | | |
| 2015 | 20.37 | 20.39 | 20.20 | 20.95 | 20.60 | 19.83 | 21.86 | 22.73 | 21.84 | 21.28 | 22.27 | 21.35 | 21.15 |
| 2016 | 21.24 | 21.74 | 21.64 | 21.27 | 21.23 | 20.41 | 20.45 | 20.60 | 21.49 | 21.97 | 22.19 | 22.03 | 21.35 |
| 2017 | 22.26 | 21.90 | 22.22 | 22.74 | 22.00 | 21.55 | 22.10 | 22.01 | 22.22 | 22.38 | 23.04 | 22.55 | 22.25 |
| 2018 | 23.09 | 23.41 | 23.18 | 23.77 | 23.55 | 23.31 | 24.05 | 24.19 | 24.87 | 24.83 | 24.62 | 24.98 | 23.99 |
| 2019 | 24.70 | 24.74 | 24.42 | 24.97 | 24.51 | 24.94 | 25.29 | 25.62 | 25.93 | 26.32 | 26.55 | 26.27 | 25.37 |
| **Professional and Business Services** | | | | | | | | | | | | | |
| 2015 | 20.17 | 20.18 | 20.10 | 20.18 | 19.94 | 19.96 | 20.00 | 20.28 | 20.47 | 20.33 | 20.85 | 19.98 | 20.21 |
| 2016 | 20.23 | 20.31 | 20.08 | 20.41 | 20.48 | 20.46 | 20.82 | 20.89 | 20.87 | 21.16 | 21.12 | 21.56 | 20.71 |
| 2017 | 21.51 | 21.43 | 21.90 | 21.76 | 22.15 | 22.11 | 22.02 | 22.23 | 22.42 | 22.98 | 22.92 | 23.05 | 22.21 |
| 2018 | 23.70 | 24.00 | 23.96 | 24.26 | 24.32 | 24.27 | 24.59 | 24.52 | 24.83 | 24.73 | 24.59 | 24.97 | 24.40 |
| 2019 | 25.21 | 25.00 | 24.98 | 25.46 | 25.54 | 25.76 | 25.65 | 25.10 | 25.51 | 25.76 | 26.26 | 26.38 | 25.56 |
| **Education and Health Services** | | | | | | | | | | | | | |
| 2015 | 22.45 | 22.54 | 22.49 | 22.22 | 22.38 | 22.23 | 22.48 | 22.33 | 22.20 | 22.18 | 22.33 | 22.34 | 22.35 |
| 2016 | 22.83 | 23.10 | 22.16 | 21.70 | 21.58 | 21.36 | 22.05 | 22.05 | 22.18 | 22.06 | 22.21 | 22.12 | 22.11 |
| 2017 | 22.72 | 22.50 | 22.93 | 22.85 | 22.59 | 22.61 | 23.09 | 23.01 | 23.13 | 23.01 | 23.12 | 23.04 | 22.88 |
| 2018 | 23.74 | 23.66 | 23.58 | 24.43 | 24.26 | 24.14 | 24.46 | 24.63 | 24.74 | 24.83 | 25.12 | 25.29 | 24.41 |
| 2019 | 25.09 | 24.96 | 24.91 | 25.27 | 24.49 | 24.35 | 24.26 | 24.43 | 24.93 | 24.72 | 25.00 | 25.35 | 24.81 |
| **Leisure and Hospitality** | | | | | | | | | | | | | |
| 2015 | 11.24 | 11.27 | 11.30 | 11.17 | 11.09 | 11.10 | 11.07 | 11.14 | 11.28 | 11.36 | 11.29 | 11.42 | 11.22 |
| 2016 | 11.55 | 11.67 | 11.65 | 11.64 | 11.75 | 11.55 | 11.60 | 11.69 | 11.83 | 11.96 | 11.93 | 11.92 | 11.73 |
| 2017 | 11.92 | 11.99 | 11.94 | 11.86 | 12.11 | 11.92 | 12.09 | 12.03 | 12.28 | 12.31 | 12.45 | 12.53 | 12.12 |
| 2018 | 12.66 | 12.54 | 12.54 | 12.58 | 12.46 | 12.48 | 12.56 | 12.51 | 12.39 | 12.56 | 12.62 | 12.53 | 12.53 |
| 2019 | 12.49 | 12.45 | 12.37 | 12.41 | 12.36 | 12.12 | 12.12 | 12.23 | 12.37 | 12.26 | 12.26 | 12.50 | 12.32 |
| **Other Services** | | | | | | | | | | | | | |
| 2015 | 21.47 | 20.91 | 21.12 | 20.92 | 20.60 | 20.58 | 20.87 | 20.89 | 20.67 | 20.50 | 20.31 | 20.32 | 20.76 |
| 2016 | 20.41 | 20.63 | 20.67 | 20.57 | 20.19 | 20.09 | 20.60 | 20.81 | 20.69 | 20.29 | 20.62 | 20.33 | 20.49 |
| 2017 | 20.50 | 20.49 | 20.49 | 20.60 | 20.36 | 19.92 | 20.21 | 20.62 | 20.47 | 20.45 | 20.47 | 20.36 | 20.41 |
| 2018 | 20.62 | 20.55 | 20.22 | 20.15 | 20.43 | 19.85 | 19.99 | 19.87 | 19.77 | 20.03 | 20.48 | 20.84 | 20.23 |
| 2019 | 20.74 | 20.89 | 21.24 | 21.12 | 21.19 | 20.46 | 20.47 | 21.05 | 21.73 | 21.04 | 20.93 | 21.43 | 21.02 |

# 4. Average Weekly Earnings by Selected Industry: West Virginia, 2015–2019

(Dollars, not seasonally adjusted)

| Industry and year | January | February | March | April | May | June | July | August | September | October | November | December | Annual average |
|---|---|---|---|---|---|---|---|---|---|---|---|---|---|
| **Total Private** | | | | | | | | | | | | | |
| 2015 | 719.30 | 714.10 | 719.68 | 717.25 | 722.75 | 718.94 | 724.50 | 733.57 | 724.88 | 730.10 | 736.05 | 720.72 | 723.84 |
| 2016 | 724.76 | 727.90 | 731.85 | 734.29 | 722.78 | 727.89 | 737.42 | 734.27 | 740.96 | 754.02 | 746.60 | 744.48 | 736.40 |
| 2017 | 755.77 | 754.69 | 756.76 | 762.16 | 758.27 | 769.70 | 784.81 | 779.01 | 787.60 | 791.83 | 790.59 | 790.23 | 772.48 |
| 2018 | 791.88 | 795.72 | 790.94 | 816.31 | 805.00 | 812.66 | 826.78 | 821.46 | 832.71 | 829.78 | 823.68 | 841.58 | 816.50 |
| 2019 | 814.92 | 822.39 | 828.71 | 845.61 | 845.02 | 854.68 | 838.74 | 840.16 | 860.16 | 844.90 | 854.40 | 854.84 | 843.36 |
| **Goods-Producing** | | | | | | | | | | | | | |
| 2015 | 983.42 | 961.22 | 983.66 | 993.51 | 1,018.05 | 1,001.57 | 982.40 | 1,017.62 | 990.19 | 1,027.09 | 1,006.14 | 1,003.60 | 998.09 |
| 2016 | 988.79 | 977.11 | 1,009.42 | 1,018.58 | 985.00 | 1,018.48 | 1,007.74 | 1,027.18 | 1,026.37 | 1,061.00 | 1,040.35 | 1,022.22 | 1,013.84 |
| 2017 | 1,016.06 | 1,040.91 | 1,010.81 | 1,048.13 | 1,043.45 | 1,062.05 | 1,063.48 | 1,077.44 | 1,084.10 | 1,090.87 | 1,068.73 | 1,072.97 | 1,057.60 |
| 2018 | 1,022.81 | 1,024.08 | 1,021.22 | 1,051.20 | 1,052.09 | 1,079.40 | 1,084.10 | 1,089.13 | 1,093.07 | 1,107.65 | 1,106.14 | 1,131.23 | 1,074.53 |
| 2019 | 1,080.52 | 1,085.49 | 1,080.82 | 1,091.72 | 1,098.58 | 1,102.71 | 1,084.66 | 1,120.70 | 1,141.75 | 1,113.64 | 1,115.75 | 1,106.09 | 1,101.28 |
| **Mining and Logging** | | | | | | | | | | | | | |
| 2015 | 1,422.76 | 1,331.76 | 1,393.63 | 1,371.22 | 1,363.92 | 1,345.86 | 1,350.18 | 1,348.26 | 1,302.91 | 1,360.29 | 1,382.14 | 1,328.02 | 1,357.97 |
| 2016 | 1,361.18 | 1,297.81 | 1,345.96 | 1,324.79 | 1,292.20 | 1,252.03 | 1,225.54 | 1,306.94 | 1,314.51 | 1,391.50 | 1,297.34 | 1,275.46 | 1,307.48 |
| 2017 | 1,261.58 | 1,278.96 | 1,226.75 | 1,220.36 | 1,246.57 | 1,188.47 | 1,214.24 | 1,247.04 | 1,248.77 | 1,253.54 | 1,263.24 | 1,252.03 | 1,242.00 |
| 2018 | 1,212.24 | 1,200.40 | 1,180.22 | 1,188.95 | 1,180.02 | 1,202.33 | 1,194.75 | 1,247.47 | 1,263.19 | 1,260.46 | 1,284.34 | 1,336.83 | 1,231.02 |
| 2019 | 1,279.66 | 1,316.12 | 1,283.14 | 1,290.02 | 1,328.63 | 1,281.00 | 1,272.60 | 1,356.36 | 1,390.50 | 1,403.31 | 1,411.14 | 1,411.94 | 1,332.76 |
| **Construction** | | | | | | | | | | | | | |
| 2015 | 878.21 | 849.66 | 889.82 | 928.77 | 959.22 | 983.76 | 935.55 | 1,001.30 | 952.50 | 1,032.15 | 939.49 | 989.23 | 946.60 |
| 2016 | 917.58 | 913.17 | 990.86 | 1,025.40 | 994.27 | 1,067.23 | 1,065.70 | 1,045.71 | 1,054.79 | 1,063.08 | 1,031.68 | 975.61 | 1,014.94 |
| 2017 | 933.83 | 1,005.26 | 960.73 | 1,063.48 | 1,050.87 | 1,136.25 | 1,115.38 | 1,125.07 | 1,132.49 | 1,130.27 | 1,123.20 | 1,116.34 | 1,081.58 |
| 2018 | 1,043.71 | 1,044.59 | 1,043.78 | 1,103.23 | 1,126.68 | 1,143.51 | 1,153.18 | 1,141.75 | 1,113.81 | 1,151.64 | 1,142.40 | 1,181.92 | 1,122.99 |
| 2019 | 1,116.00 | 1,097.99 | 1,106.64 | 1,122.79 | 1,132.84 | 1,133.90 | 1,096.85 | 1,147.36 | 1,160.34 | 1,101.23 | 1,098.31 | 1,073.28 | 1,115.60 |
| **Manufacturing** | | | | | | | | | | | | | |
| 2015 | 786.21 | 811.88 | 806.25 | 822.20 | 863.50 | 830.31 | 817.50 | 857.85 | 853.51 | 853.21 | 862.98 | 855.04 | 835.43 |
| 2016 | 857.21 | 861.85 | 867.02 | 881.01 | 847.50 | 887.81 | 877.66 | 898.56 | 887.00 | 916.36 | 930.23 | 942.48 | 887.81 |
| 2017 | 953.18 | 956.45 | 940.03 | 960.93 | 945.44 | 952.16 | 953.98 | 959.38 | 968.39 | 978.02 | 932.16 | 960.38 | 955.06 |
| 2018 | 920.81 | 928.22 | 928.22 | 943.74 | 927.05 | 963.26 | 959.45 | 956.75 | 990.91 | 989.68 | 987.39 | 990.29 | 956.76 |
| 2019 | 961.25 | 967.44 | 963.67 | 972.32 | 963.37 | 988.51 | 985.73 | 985.23 | 1,011.85 | 987.39 | 993.46 | 993.49 | 981.19 |
| **Trade, Transportation, and Utilities** | | | | | | | | | | | | | |
| 2015 | 630.65 | 646.81 | 649.17 | 658.17 | 657.72 | 665.23 | 666.16 | 674.28 | 674.02 | 681.63 | 676.16 | 657.07 | 662.08 |
| 2016 | 661.51 | 655.98 | 677.76 | 696.26 | 680.94 | 681.64 | 699.86 | 689.95 | 702.90 | 714.49 | 704.17 | 698.26 | 687.81 |
| 2017 | 695.26 | 704.00 | 710.24 | 707.62 | 707.87 | 707.04 | 706.32 | 703.80 | 710.43 | 704.46 | 698.72 | 692.77 | 703.04 |
| 2018 | 683.77 | 685.80 | 681.05 | 698.71 | 694.62 | 698.00 | 693.73 | 695.46 | 695.91 | 687.80 | 672.45 | 664.61 | 688.45 |
| 2019 | 655.37 | 688.76 | 699.38 | 718.30 | 729.76 | 751.84 | 735.68 | 727.97 | 736.40 | 723.15 | 733.94 | 724.54 | 718.30 |
| **Financial Activities** | | | | | | | | | | | | | |
| 2015 | 723.14 | 732.00 | 723.16 | 756.30 | 743.66 | 725.78 | 786.96 | 841.01 | 777.50 | 770.34 | 815.08 | 770.74 | 763.52 |
| 2016 | 758.27 | 780.47 | 757.40 | 755.09 | 757.91 | 740.88 | 734.16 | 727.18 | 743.55 | 795.31 | 796.62 | 793.08 | 762.20 |
| 2017 | 812.49 | 786.21 | 795.48 | 820.91 | 785.40 | 767.18 | 800.02 | 785.76 | 788.81 | 810.16 | 817.92 | 809.55 | 798.78 |
| 2018 | 810.46 | 824.03 | 836.80 | 858.10 | 838.38 | 827.51 | 856.18 | 841.81 | 880.40 | 869.05 | 849.39 | 899.28 | 849.25 |
| 2019 | 857.09 | 846.11 | 835.16 | 848.98 | 830.89 | 902.83 | 880.09 | 904.39 | 946.45 | 921.20 | 937.22 | 969.36 | 890.49 |
| **Professional and Business Services** | | | | | | | | | | | | | |
| 2015 | 705.95 | 690.16 | 707.52 | 690.16 | 695.91 | 690.62 | 708.00 | 715.88 | 724.64 | 725.78 | 761.03 | 729.27 | 711.39 |
| 2016 | 718.17 | 721.01 | 724.89 | 742.92 | 749.57 | 750.88 | 762.01 | 762.49 | 761.76 | 804.08 | 785.66 | 806.34 | 757.99 |
| 2017 | 798.02 | 797.20 | 812.49 | 816.00 | 810.69 | 815.86 | 832.36 | 818.06 | 831.78 | 841.07 | 832.00 | 834.41 | 819.55 |
| 2018 | 850.83 | 876.00 | 872.14 | 900.05 | 887.68 | 902.84 | 927.04 | 921.95 | 948.51 | 929.85 | 909.83 | 933.88 | 905.24 |
| 2019 | 930.25 | 917.50 | 936.75 | 949.66 | 955.20 | 1,004.64 | 990.09 | 961.33 | 1,005.09 | 986.61 | 992.63 | 1,007.72 | 971.28 |
| **Education and Health Services** | | | | | | | | | | | | | |
| 2015 | 783.51 | 775.38 | 773.66 | 766.59 | 774.35 | 766.94 | 784.55 | 777.08 | 768.12 | 760.77 | 772.62 | 770.73 | 773.31 |
| 2016 | 787.64 | 796.95 | 771.17 | 757.33 | 755.30 | 751.87 | 780.57 | 769.55 | 776.30 | 772.10 | 768.47 | 769.78 | 771.64 |
| 2017 | 799.74 | 780.75 | 797.96 | 799.75 | 792.91 | 798.13 | 824.31 | 812.25 | 818.80 | 814.55 | 811.51 | 808.70 | 805.38 |
| 2018 | 838.02 | 835.20 | 832.37 | 867.27 | 856.38 | 859.74 | 875.67 | 866.98 | 873.32 | 866.57 | 886.74 | 890.21 | 861.67 |
| 2019 | 880.66 | 881.09 | 874.34 | 894.56 | 874.29 | 871.73 | 858.80 | 859.94 | 877.54 | 870.14 | 892.50 | 907.53 | 878.27 |
| **Leisure and Hospitality** | | | | | | | | | | | | | |
| 2015 | 281.00 | 284.00 | 291.54 | 290.42 | 291.67 | 296.37 | 298.89 | 298.55 | 297.79 | 299.90 | 299.19 | 295.78 | 293.96 |
| 2016 | 293.37 | 304.59 | 315.72 | 311.95 | 314.90 | 315.32 | 316.68 | 315.63 | 313.50 | 312.16 | 310.18 | 303.96 | 310.85 |
| 2017 | 298.00 | 308.14 | 305.66 | 302.43 | 313.65 | 317.07 | 325.22 | 324.81 | 329.10 | 324.98 | 327.44 | 329.54 | 317.54 |
| 2018 | 321.56 | 328.55 | 336.07 | 338.40 | 337.67 | 340.70 | 349.17 | 345.28 | 339.49 | 339.12 | 335.69 | 335.80 | 337.06 |
| 2019 | 327.24 | 331.17 | 326.57 | 330.11 | 334.96 | 329.66 | 327.24 | 328.99 | 331.52 | 328.57 | 331.02 | 333.75 | 330.18 |
| **Other Services** | | | | | | | | | | | | | |
| 2015 | 689.19 | 671.21 | 677.95 | 679.90 | 653.02 | 660.62 | 672.01 | 676.84 | 661.44 | 662.15 | 668.20 | 658.37 | 668.47 |
| 2016 | 644.96 | 668.41 | 659.37 | 668.53 | 660.21 | 669.00 | 661.26 | 670.08 | 680.70 | 685.80 | 692.83 | 674.96 | 670.02 |
| 2017 | 676.50 | 672.07 | 684.37 | 677.74 | 682.06 | 671.30 | 675.01 | 688.71 | 687.79 | 689.17 | 681.65 | 684.10 | 679.65 |
| 2018 | 690.77 | 682.26 | 679.39 | 675.03 | 676.23 | 661.01 | 681.66 | 677.57 | 674.16 | 658.99 | 688.13 | 696.06 | 679.73 |
| 2019 | 684.42 | 703.99 | 694.55 | 688.51 | 692.91 | 685.41 | 679.60 | 677.81 | 712.74 | 702.74 | 678.13 | 662.19 | 689.4F |

# WISCONSIN
## *At a Glance*

Population:
  2010 census: 5,686,986
  2019 estimate: 5,822,434

Percent change in population:
  2010–2019: 2.4%

Percent change in total nonfarm employment:
  2011–2019: 8.3%

Industry with the largest growth in employment, 2011–2019 (percent):
  Mining and logging, 40.0%

Industry with the largest decline or smallest growth in employment, 2011–2019 (percent):
  Government, -2.1%

Civilian labor force:
  2010: 3,081,512
  2019: 3,105,142

Unemployment rate and rank among states (highest to lowest):
  2010: 8.7%, 24th
  2019: 3.3%, 30th

Over-the-year change in unemployment rates:
  2017–2018: -0.3%
  2018–2019: 0.3%

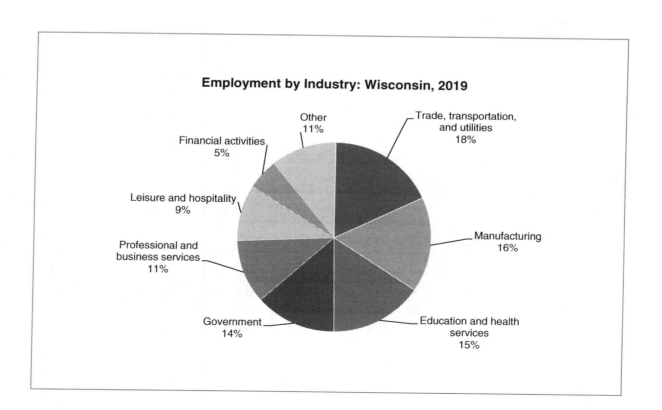

**Employment by Industry: Wisconsin, 2019**

- Other 11%
- Financial activities 5%
- Leisure and hospitality 9%
- Professional and business services 11%
- Government 14%
- Trade, transportation, and utilities 18%
- Manufacturing 16%
- Education and health services 15%

# 1. Employment by Industry: Wisconsin, 2011–2019

(Numbers in thousands, not seasonally adjusted)

| Industry and year | January | February | March | April | May | June | July | August | September | October | November | December | Annual average |
|---|---|---|---|---|---|---|---|---|---|---|---|---|---|
| **Total Nonfarm** | | | | | | | | | | | | | |
| 2011 | 2,676.7 | 2,683.6 | 2,699.6 | 2,737.0 | 2,766.6 | 2,784.4 | 2,770.8 | 2,771.2 | 2,782.4 | 2,786.0 | 2,785.9 | 2,777.5 | 2,751.8 |
| 2012 | 2,690.0 | 2,704.2 | 2,732.6 | 2,768.0 | 2,802.1 | 2,822.0 | 2,790.1 | 2,796.5 | 2,805.2 | 2,818.0 | 2,826.5 | 2,814.1 | 2,780.8 |
| 2013 | 2,719.8 | 2,745.0 | 2,759.2 | 2,778.7 | 2,821.9 | 2,846.6 | 2,823.4 | 2,832.2 | 2,840.6 | 2,848.9 | 2,852.5 | 2,846.5 | 2,809.6 |
| 2014 | 2,764.7 | 2,777.4 | 2,791.2 | 2,826.8 | 2,862.8 | 2,890.1 | 2,869.4 | 2,882.2 | 2,881.6 | 2,891.8 | 2,902.3 | 2,890.4 | 2,852.6 |
| 2015 | 2,807.7 | 2,823.0 | 2,837.2 | 2,876.5 | 2,905.1 | 2,928.9 | 2,913.2 | 2,915.0 | 2,915.5 | 2,928.7 | 2,927.8 | 2,928.5 | 2,892.3 |
| 2016 | 2,850.7 | 2,867.5 | 2,877.4 | 2,921.0 | 2,936.6 | 2,957.4 | 2,949.0 | 2,954.3 | 2,945.5 | 2,953.1 | 2,963.3 | 2,944.9 | 2,926.7 |
| 2017 | 2,873.1 | 2,889.3 | 2,902.1 | 2,935.7 | 2,962.4 | 2,989.1 | 2,971.2 | 2,967.3 | 2,964.3 | 2,973.8 | 2,977.4 | 2,972.9 | 2,948.2 |
| 2018 | 2,903.4 | 2,924.4 | 2,934.9 | 2,955.6 | 2,988.1 | 3,018.3 | 2,997.1 | 3,000.2 | 2,986.9 | 2,996.0 | 3,004.0 | 2,996.1 | 2,975.4 |
| 2019 | 2,923.9 | 2,931.0 | 2,944.1 | 2,973.3 | 2,996.9 | 3,031.2 | 3,004.9 | 2,997.5 | 2,978.6 | 2,999.9 | 2,999.7 | 2,996.3 | 2,981.4 |
| **Total Private** | | | | | | | | | | | | | |
| 2010 | 2,264.5 | 2,257.0 | 2,271.4 | 2,306.2 | 2,338.0 | 2,372.9 | 2,384.0 | 2,390.5 | 2,373.7 | 2,366.9 | 2,363.9 | 2,355.3 | 2,337.0 |
| 2011 | 2,294.2 | 2,292.8 | 2,312.8 | 2,340.7 | 2,373.3 | 2,413.3 | 2,411.8 | 2,417.9 | 2,398.5 | 2,395.8 | 2,396.8 | 2,391.1 | 2,369.9 |
| 2012 | 2,324.9 | 2,324.7 | 2,339.6 | 2,356.0 | 2,405.0 | 2,442.4 | 2,445.2 | 2,456.5 | 2,431.7 | 2,426.6 | 2,429.0 | 2,424.3 | 2,400.5 |
| 2013 | 2,359.5 | 2,359.3 | 2,372.4 | 2,402.2 | 2,444.9 | 2,484.4 | 2,488.6 | 2,497.8 | 2,471.2 | 2,469.3 | 2,471.3 | 2,467.6 | 2,440.7 |
| 2014 | 2,404.7 | 2,403.0 | 2,418.3 | 2,449.8 | 2,487.7 | 2,524.9 | 2,532.9 | 2,537.8 | 2,509.6 | 2,510.2 | 2,508.5 | 2,507.8 | 2,482.9 |
| 2015 | 2,447.6 | 2,448.4 | 2,459.2 | 2,494.0 | 2,521.4 | 2,553.7 | 2,565.7 | 2,567.2 | 2,537.4 | 2,532.4 | 2,530.1 | 2,521.6 | 2,514.9 |
| 2016 | 2,472.2 | 2,472.3 | 2,488.5 | 2,512.4 | 2,545.7 | 2,589.6 | 2,589.9 | 2,590.8 | 2,559.4 | 2,555.5 | 2,557.1 | 2,556.5 | 2,540.8 |
| 2017 | 2,505.8 | 2,507.0 | 2,520.2 | 2,533.7 | 2,571.3 | 2,616.5 | 2,615.3 | 2,618.7 | 2,582.3 | 2,578.4 | 2,578.8 | 2,576.8 | 2,567.1 |
| 2018 | 2,527.9 | 2,519.6 | 2,529.8 | 2,552.7 | 2,586.3 | 2,627.9 | 2,621.7 | 2,621.4 | 2,578.7 | 2,582.5 | 2,579.0 | 2,578.3 | 2,575.5 |
| 2019 | | | | | | | | | | | | | |
| **Goods Producing** | | | | | | | | | | | | | |
| 2011 | 517.5 | 514.9 | 519.8 | 531.6 | 542.4 | 557.0 | 563.5 | 564.6 | 557.7 | 554.1 | 551.6 | 543.9 | 543.2 |
| 2012 | 531.9 | 529.6 | 535.5 | 546.8 | 554.1 | 569.4 | 574.1 | 574.1 | 566.4 | 564.7 | 560.6 | 555.5 | 555.2 |
| 2013 | 542.1 | 540.1 | 543.5 | 547.8 | 561.9 | 575.7 | 580.3 | 582.0 | 573.5 | 571.6 | 568.9 | 560.6 | 562.3 |
| 2014 | 548.8 | 547.2 | 552.0 | 561.6 | 574.3 | 588.6 | 596.1 | 596.9 | 588.5 | 586.0 | 582.7 | 577.0 | 575.0 |
| 2015 | 564.5 | 562.9 | 566.2 | 576.1 | 584.9 | 598.0 | 603.0 | 601.4 | 592.1 | 588.7 | 585.2 | 580.0 | 583.6 |
| 2016 | 566.6 | 564.4 | 568.4 | 577.5 | 584.3 | 597.3 | 601.8 | 600.9 | 591.8 | 589.1 | 586.2 | 579.5 | 584.0 |
| 2017 | 569.6 | 569.2 | 574.1 | 583.4 | 591.7 | 607.1 | 611.0 | 610.0 | 601.1 | 599.3 | 596.7 | 593.2 | 592.2 |
| 2018 | 584.2 | 584.2 | 588.9 | 595.2 | 605.6 | 622.2 | 625.3 | 625.8 | 616.4 | 613.5 | 611.1 | 607.8 | 606.7 |
| 2019 | 598.6 | 595.1 | 597.6 | 605.6 | 614.4 | 627.9 | 630.9 | 628.9 | 618.1 | 615.1 | 612.2 | 606.1 | 612.5 |
| **Service-Providing** | | | | | | | | | | | | | |
| 2011 | 2,159.2 | 2,168.7 | 2,179.8 | 2,205.4 | 2,224.2 | 2,227.4 | 2,207.3 | 2,206.6 | 2,224.7 | 2,231.9 | 2,234.3 | 2,233.6 | 2,208.6 |
| 2012 | 2,158.1 | 2,174.6 | 2,197.1 | 2,221.2 | 2,248.0 | 2,252.6 | 2,216.0 | 2,222.4 | 2,238.8 | 2,253.3 | 2,265.9 | 2,258.6 | 2,225.6 |
| 2013 | 2,177.7 | 2,204.9 | 2,215.7 | 2,230.9 | 2,260.0 | 2,270.9 | 2,243.1 | 2,250.2 | 2,267.1 | 2,277.3 | 2,283.6 | 2,285.9 | 2,247.3 |
| 2014 | 2,215.9 | 2,230.2 | 2,239.2 | 2,265.2 | 2,288.5 | 2,301.5 | 2,273.3 | 2,285.3 | 2,293.1 | 2,305.8 | 2,319.6 | 2,313.4 | 2,277.6 |
| 2015 | 2,243.2 | 2,260.1 | 2,271.0 | 2,300.4 | 2,320.2 | 2,330.9 | 2,310.2 | 2,313.6 | 2,323.4 | 2,340.0 | 2,342.6 | 2,348.5 | 2,308.7 |
| 2016 | 2,284.1 | 2,303.1 | 2,309.0 | 2,343.5 | 2,352.3 | 2,360.1 | 2,347.2 | 2,353.4 | 2,353.7 | 2,364.0 | 2,377.1 | 2,365.4 | 2,342.7 |
| 2017 | 2,303.5 | 2,320.1 | 2,328.0 | 2,352.3 | 2,370.7 | 2,382.0 | 2,360.2 | 2,357.3 | 2,363.2 | 2,374.5 | 2,380.7 | 2,379.7 | 2,356.0 |
| 2018 | 2,319.2 | 2,340.2 | 2,346.0 | 2,360.4 | 2,382.5 | 2,396.1 | 2,371.8 | 2,374.4 | 2,370.5 | 2,382.5 | 2,392.9 | 2,388.3 | 2,368.7 |
| 2019 | 2,325.3 | 2,335.9 | 2,346.5 | 2,367.7 | 2,382.5 | 2,403.3 | 2,374.0 | 2,368.6 | 2,360.5 | 2,384.8 | 2,387.5 | 2,390.2 | 2,368.9 |
| **Mining and Logging** | | | | | | | | | | | | | |
| 2011 | 2.5 | 2.5 | 2.6 | 2.7 | 3.0 | 3.3 | 3.3 | 3.3 | 3.4 | 3.4 | 3.4 | 3.1 | 3.0 |
| 2012 | 2.9 | 2.9 | 3.1 | 3.4 | 3.6 | 3.7 | 3.8 | 3.8 | 3.8 | 3.7 | 3.6 | 3.4 | 3.5 |
| 2013 | 3.2 | 3.2 | 3.2 | 3.4 | 3.8 | 4.0 | 4.0 | 4.1 | 4.0 | 4.0 | 3.9 | 3.6 | 3.7 |
| 2014 | 3.4 | 3.5 | 3.5 | 3.8 | 4.1 | 4.3 | 4.4 | 4.5 | 4.4 | 4.5 | 4.4 | 4.2 | 4.1 |
| 2015 | 3.9 | 4.0 | 4.0 | 4.2 | 4.4 | 4.5 | 4.4 | 4.3 | 4.2 | 4.2 | 4.1 | 3.9 | 4.2 |
| 2016 | 3.5 | 3.5 | 3.6 | 3.7 | 3.9 | 3.9 | 3.9 | 3.9 | 3.8 | 3.9 | 3.8 | 3.6 | 3.8 |
| 2017 | 3.5 | 3.6 | 3.9 | 4.2 | 4.4 | 4.6 | 4.7 | 4.8 | 4.7 | 4.7 | 4.6 | 4.4 | 4.3 |
| 2018 | 4.3 | 4.4 | 4.6 | 4.6 | 4.9 | 5.1 | 5.1 | 5.1 | 4.9 | 4.8 | 4.5 | 4.3 | 4.7 |
| 2019 | 4.2 | 4.0 | 4.1 | 4.1 | 4.3 | 4.4 | 4.5 | 4.4 | 4.3 | 4.2 | 4.1 | 3.9 | 4.2 |
| **Construction** | | | | | | | | | | | | | |
| 2011 | 79.2 | 76.8 | 79.5 | 87.7 | 95.1 | 100.5 | 102.8 | 103.0 | 101.0 | 100.3 | 97.3 | 89.6 | 92.7 |
| 2012 | 79.7 | 78.0 | 81.5 | 90.4 | 95.3 | 100.6 | 101.9 | 102.3 | 100.5 | 101.2 | 98.3 | 93.1 | 93.6 |
| 2013 | 83.6 | 82.9 | 85.2 | 89.4 | 101.0 | 106.3 | 108.8 | 110.2 | 107.6 | 107.2 | 104.4 | 96.1 | 98.6 |
| 2014 | 87.1 | 86.2 | 89.1 | 96.2 | 105.2 | 111.7 | 114.1 | 115.1 | 113.0 | 112.5 | 109.4 | 103.1 | 103.6 |
| 2015 | 94.4 | 93.2 | 95.5 | 105.7 | 112.7 | 117.7 | 120.1 | 119.4 | 116.6 | 116.2 | 113.3 | 108.0 | 109.4 |
| 2016 | 98.3 | 98.1 | 101.0 | 109.5 | 114.8 | 119.8 | 122.2 | 122.3 | 119.7 | 119.0 | 116.8 | 109.4 | 112.6 |
| 2017 | 102.0 | 102.3 | 104.6 | 113.1 | 120.0 | 125.5 | 127.8 | 127.3 | 124.7 | 123.9 | 121.3 | 116.2 | 117.4 |
| 2018 | 108.2 | 108.0 | 111.5 | 117.1 | 125.1 | 131.8 | 132.3 | 132.4 | 129.5 | 127.5 | 124.8 | 119.9 | 122.3 |
| 2019 | 111.9 | 110.2 | 112.3 | 120.2 | 127.3 | 133.1 | 134.2 | 133.9 | 130.9 | 129.6 | 125.6 | 118.7 | 124.0 |

## 1. Employment by Industry: Wisconsin, 2011–2019—*Continued*

(Numbers in thousands, not seasonally adjusted)

| Industry and year | January | February | March | April | May | June | July | August | September | October | November | December | Annual average |
|---|---|---|---|---|---|---|---|---|---|---|---|---|---|
| **Manufacturing** | | | | | | | | | | | | | |
| 2011 | 435.8 | 435.6 | 437.7 | 441.2 | 444.3 | 453.2 | 457.4 | 458.3 | 453.3 | 450.4 | 450.9 | 451.2 | 447.4 |
| 2012 | 449.3 | 448.7 | 450.9 | 453.0 | 455.2 | 465.1 | 468.4 | 468.0 | 462.1 | 459.8 | 458.7 | 459.0 | 458.2 |
| 2013 | 455.3 | 454.0 | 455.1 | 455.0 | 457.1 | 465.4 | 467.5 | 467.7 | 461.9 | 460.4 | 460.6 | 460.9 | 460.1 |
| 2014 | 458.3 | 457.5 | 459.4 | 461.6 | 465.0 | 472.6 | 477.6 | 477.3 | 471.1 | 469.0 | 468.9 | 469.7 | 467.3 |
| 2015 | 466.2 | 465.7 | 466.7 | 466.2 | 467.8 | 475.8 | 478.5 | 477.7 | 471.3 | 468.3 | 467.8 | 468.1 | 470.0 |
| 2016 | 464.8 | 462.8 | 463.8 | 464.3 | 465.6 | 473.6 | 475.7 | 474.7 | 468.3 | 466.2 | 465.6 | 466.5 | 467.7 |
| 2017 | 464.1 | 463.3 | 465.6 | 466.1 | 467.3 | 477.0 | 478.5 | 477.9 | 471.7 | 470.7 | 470.8 | 472.6 | 470.5 |
| 2018 | 471.7 | 471.8 | 472.8 | 473.5 | 475.6 | 485.3 | 487.9 | 488.3 | 482.0 | 481.2 | 481.8 | 483.6 | 479.6 |
| 2019 | 482.5 | 480.9 | 481.2 | 481.3 | 482.8 | 490.4 | 492.2 | 490.6 | 482.9 | 481.3 | 482.5 | 483.5 | 484.3 |
| **Trade, Transportation, and Utilities** | | | | | | | | | | | | | |
| 2011 | 499.5 | 492.9 | 495.0 | 501.2 | 506.0 | 509.3 | 508.7 | 509.9 | 509.5 | 514.1 | 522.8 | 525.2 | 507.8 |
| 2012 | 502.7 | 495.8 | 497.9 | 500.7 | 508.5 | 511.9 | 508.7 | 510.4 | 509.0 | 514.4 | 526.2 | 527.7 | 509.5 |
| 2013 | 504.6 | 499.7 | 501.6 | 505.8 | 514.1 | 519.4 | 515.8 | 517.9 | 515.0 | 519.8 | 530.2 | 534.0 | 514.8 |
| 2014 | 510.5 | 506.4 | 509.0 | 514.3 | 521.3 | 526.1 | 523.5 | 524.5 | 521.4 | 525.5 | 536.4 | 539.8 | 521.6 |
| 2015 | 516.4 | 511.2 | 514.4 | 518.0 | 526.1 | 531.3 | 530.5 | 532.8 | 531.6 | 536.1 | 544.8 | 547.2 | 528.4 |
| 2016 | 526.9 | 523.4 | 525.1 | 531.2 | 536.5 | 538.8 | 539.4 | 539.3 | 535.7 | 539.6 | 548.7 | 551.9 | 536.4 |
| 2017 | 533.2 | 528.3 | 529.5 | 532.2 | 538.6 | 541.3 | 539.8 | 540.9 | 536.8 | 540.8 | 552.1 | 556.0 | 539.1 |
| 2018 | 535.7 | 530.8 | 533.0 | 534.0 | 540.3 | 542.9 | 541.8 | 542.9 | 536.8 | 538.9 | 550.1 | 553.2 | 540.0 |
| 2019 | 534.6 | 526.5 | 527.0 | 529.9 | 534.5 | 538.6 | 534.8 | 536.3 | 529.8 | 533.2 | 541.4 | 542.9 | 534.1 |
| **Wholesale Trade** | | | | | | | | | | | | | |
| 2011 | 109.9 | 109.7 | 110.2 | 111.8 | 112.9 | 114.2 | 115.3 | 114.8 | 113.6 | 113.9 | 113.9 | 114.1 | 112.9 |
| 2012 | 112.5 | 112.3 | 113.0 | 114.4 | 115.1 | 116.5 | 116.4 | 115.8 | 114.3 | 114.6 | 114.8 | 115.0 | 114.6 |
| 2013 | 114.5 | 114.4 | 114.7 | 115.9 | 117.2 | 118.5 | 118.4 | 118.0 | 116.4 | 116.5 | 116.5 | 116.7 | 116.5 |
| 2014 | 114.8 | 114.8 | 115.6 | 116.8 | 118.1 | 119.4 | 119.7 | 119.4 | 117.6 | 117.6 | 117.6 | 117.9 | 117.4 |
| 2015 | 116.8 | 116.5 | 117.1 | 118.4 | 119.7 | 121.2 | 121.6 | 121.3 | 119.5 | 120.2 | 120.4 | 120.5 | 119.4 |
| 2016 | 118.9 | 118.9 | 119.4 | 120.8 | 121.6 | 122.6 | 123.2 | 122.7 | 121.0 | 120.7 | 120.7 | 121.3 | 121.0 |
| 2017 | 119.6 | 119.5 | 119.9 | 120.8 | 122.2 | 123.8 | 123.9 | 123.8 | 122.1 | 122.7 | 122.9 | 123.5 | 122.1 |
| 2018 | 122.0 | 121.9 | 122.4 | 123.0 | 123.9 | 125.8 | 125.5 | 125.1 | 123.2 | 123.4 | 123.5 | 123.9 | 123.6 |
| 2019 | 122.3 | 121.7 | 121.9 | 122.9 | 123.7 | 125.2 | 125.3 | 124.8 | 123.0 | 123.3 | 123.2 | 124.3 | 123.5 |
| **Retail Trade** | | | | | | | | | | | | | |
| 2011 | 289.8 | 283.8 | 285.1 | 288.7 | 291.4 | 294.2 | 294.7 | 296.3 | 293.4 | 297.4 | 306.3 | 308.3 | 294.1 |
| 2012 | 291.3 | 284.7 | 286.0 | 287.5 | 292.0 | 294.8 | 293.9 | 295.8 | 292.6 | 297.4 | 308.9 | 309.6 | 294.5 |
| 2013 | 291.3 | 286.4 | 287.6 | 290.5 | 295.8 | 300.2 | 299.8 | 301.2 | 297.2 | 301.3 | 311.3 | 314.4 | 298.1 |
| 2014 | 296.4 | 292.2 | 293.7 | 297.1 | 301.1 | 304.7 | 304.8 | 305.3 | 300.8 | 304.4 | 314.2 | 316.1 | 302.6 |
| 2015 | 298.3 | 293.7 | 295.6 | 297.3 | 302.4 | 305.8 | 306.2 | 307.5 | 304.3 | 307.7 | 315.9 | 316.6 | 304.3 |
| 2016 | 302.9 | 299.4 | 300.6 | 304.2 | 307.5 | 309.8 | 311.5 | 311.3 | 306.1 | 309.7 | 317.7 | 318.9 | 308.3 |
| 2017 | 306.4 | 302.3 | 303.0 | 304.6 | 307.5 | 310.1 | 310.0 | 310.0 | 304.5 | 307.0 | 317.0 | 318.9 | 308.4 |
| 2018 | 304.3 | 299.9 | 301.3 | 301.5 | 305.6 | 307.6 | 308.3 | 308.3 | 301.3 | 302.7 | 311.8 | 313.5 | 305.5 |
| 2019 | 301.0 | 294.4 | 294.5 | 295.6 | 297.9 | 300.0 | 299.0 | 299.3 | 292.2 | 295.7 | 303.8 | 305.2 | 298.2 |
| **Transportation and Utilities** | | | | | | | | | | | | | |
| 2011 | 99.8 | 99.4 | 99.7 | 100.7 | 101.7 | 100.9 | 98.7 | 98.8 | 102.5 | 102.8 | 102.6 | 102.8 | 100.9 |
| 2012 | 98.9 | 98.8 | 98.9 | 98.8 | 101.4 | 100.6 | 98.4 | 98.8 | 102.1 | 102.4 | 102.5 | 103.1 | 100.4 |
| 2013 | 98.8 | 98.9 | 99.3 | 99.4 | 101.1 | 100.7 | 97.6 | 98.7 | 101.4 | 102.0 | 102.4 | 102.9 | 100.3 |
| 2014 | 99.3 | 99.4 | 99.7 | 100.4 | 102.1 | 102.0 | 99.0 | 99.8 | 103.0 | 103.5 | 104.6 | 105.8 | 101.6 |
| 2015 | 101.3 | 101.0 | 101.7 | 102.3 | 104.0 | 104.3 | 102.7 | 104.0 | 107.8 | 108.2 | 108.5 | 110.1 | 104.7 |
| 2016 | 105.1 | 105.1 | 105.1 | 106.2 | 107.4 | 106.4 | 104.7 | 105.3 | 108.6 | 109.2 | 110.3 | 111.7 | 107.1 |
| 2017 | 107.2 | 106.5 | 106.6 | 106.8 | 108.9 | 107.4 | 105.9 | 107.1 | 110.2 | 111.1 | 112.2 | 113.6 | 108.6 |
| 2018 | 109.4 | 109.0 | 109.3 | 109.5 | 110.8 | 109.5 | 108.0 | 109.5 | 112.3 | 112.8 | 114.8 | 115.8 | 110.9 |
| 2019 | 111.3 | 110.4 | 110.6 | 111.4 | 112.9 | 113.4 | 110.5 | 112.2 | 114.6 | 114.2 | 114.4 | 113.4 | 112.4 |
| **Information** | | | | | | | | | | | | | |
| 2011 | 46.9 | 46.6 | 46.5 | 46.6 | 46.5 | 46.4 | 47.2 | 47.2 | 46.8 | 46.7 | 47.3 | 47.1 | 46.8 |
| 2012 | 46.4 | 46.0 | 45.8 | 45.9 | 45.9 | 46.5 | 46.8 | 47.1 | 46.5 | 46.6 | 47.2 | 47.0 | 46.5 |
| 2013 | 46.9 | 46.7 | 46.5 | 46.7 | 47.2 | 47.2 | 47.7 | 48.0 | 47.1 | 47.4 | 47.8 | 47.9 | 47.3 |
| 2014 | 47.5 | 47.4 | 47.1 | 47.2 | 47.6 | 47.7 | 48.4 | 48.8 | 47.8 | 48.5 | 48.8 | 48.8 | 48.0 |
| 2015 | 48.5 | 48.2 | 47.9 | 48.0 | 48.3 | 48.4 | 49.7 | 50.0 | 49.1 | 49.6 | 49.8 | 49.7 | 48.9 |
| 2016 | 49.2 | 49.1 | 48.9 | 49.0 | 49.0 | 49.0 | 49.5 | 49.8 | 48.7 | 48.8 | 49.0 | 49.0 | 49.1 |
| 2017 | 48.7 | 48.4 | 48.1 | 47.7 | 47.8 | 47.9 | 48.2 | 48.0 | 47.5 | 47.1 | 47.5 | 47.5 | 47.9 |
| 2018 | 47.4 | 47.0 | 46.8 | 46.8 | 46.8 | 46.9 | 47.6 | 47.5 | 47.0 | 47.5 | 47.5 | 47.5 | 47.2 |
| 2019 | 47.2 | 46.8 | 46.7 | 46.3 | 46.5 | 47.2 | 47.6 | 47.3 | 46.7 | 46.8 | 47.0 | 47.3 | 47.0 |

## 1. Employment by Industry: Wisconsin, 2011–2019—*Continued*

(Numbers in thousands, not seasonally adjusted)

| Industry and year | January | February | March | April | May | June | July | August | September | October | November | December | Annual average |
|---|---|---|---|---|---|---|---|---|---|---|---|---|---|
| **Financial Activities** | | | | | | | | | | | | | |
| 2011 | 150.2 | 149.8 | 149.9 | 150.3 | 150.7 | 151.8 | 152.3 | 152.1 | 151.0 | 150.6 | 150.3 | 150.8 | 150.8 |
| 2012 | 150.1 | 149.8 | 150.0 | 150.1 | 150.8 | 152.2 | 152.5 | 152.5 | 150.8 | 150.7 | 150.4 | 150.9 | 150.9 |
| 2013 | 149.4 | 149.2 | 149.5 | 149.4 | 150.3 | 151.9 | 152.6 | 152.4 | 150.6 | 150.3 | 150.0 | 150.5 | 150.5 |
| 2014 | 147.9 | 147.8 | 148.2 | 148.9 | 149.7 | 151.5 | 152.0 | 152.3 | 150.8 | 150.0 | 150.0 | 150.9 | 150.0 |
| 2015 | 149.6 | 149.5 | 149.7 | 150.0 | 151.1 | 152.8 | 153.5 | 153.1 | 151.2 | 151.1 | 151.0 | 151.6 | 151.2 |
| 2016 | 150.0 | 149.8 | 150.0 | 150.7 | 151.3 | 153.1 | 154.4 | 154.3 | 152.5 | 152.2 | 152.1 | 152.5 | 151.9 |
| 2017 | 151.7 | 151.7 | 152.2 | 152.1 | 152.6 | 154.6 | 155.0 | 154.8 | 152.9 | 152.4 | 152.4 | 152.9 | 152.9 |
| 2018 | 151.3 | 151.1 | 151.2 | 151.6 | 152.2 | 154.7 | 155.2 | 155.2 | 153.4 | 153.2 | 153.0 | 153.6 | 153.0 |
| 2019 | 152.7 | 152.6 | 153.0 | 153.2 | 154.0 | 156.1 | 156.6 | 156.3 | 154.4 | 154.1 | 155.3 | 155.2 | 154.5 |
| **Professional and Business Services** | | | | | | | | | | | | | |
| 2011 | 277.4 | 277.8 | 280.7 | 284.0 | 284.9 | 290.9 | 291.5 | 294.1 | 294.2 | 294.2 | 293.9 | 291.3 | 287.9 |
| 2012 | 282.9 | 284.4 | 288.3 | 291.9 | 293.1 | 298.4 | 297.4 | 299.0 | 299.1 | 300.6 | 301.7 | 297.8 | 294.6 |
| 2013 | 287.8 | 291.5 | 295.0 | 294.9 | 299.8 | 304.8 | 306.9 | 309.3 | 307.7 | 307.8 | 309.2 | 308.0 | 301.9 |
| 2014 | 298.2 | 299.4 | 299.3 | 302.5 | 306.4 | 310.0 | 311.5 | 314.3 | 312.3 | 315.5 | 315.5 | 311.8 | 308.1 |
| 2015 | 302.8 | 303.6 | 304.4 | 310.9 | 313.4 | 316.8 | 321.1 | 324.0 | 320.2 | 323.0 | 322.1 | 322.3 | 315.4 |
| 2016 | 314.9 | 316.2 | 315.9 | 321.8 | 321.5 | 324.6 | 327.2 | 328.4 | 326.1 | 326.3 | 325.7 | 322.9 | 322.6 |
| 2017 | 314.6 | 315.3 | 318.5 | 322.7 | 324.9 | 329.1 | 331.6 | 332.3 | 329.5 | 330.8 | 330.6 | 330.0 | 325.8 |
| 2018 | 321.0 | 323.8 | 324.1 | 326.8 | 328.9 | 332.8 | 332.5 | 333.4 | 328.5 | 330.6 | 329.8 | 325.8 | 328.2 |
| 2019 | 319.0 | 321.4 | 321.7 | 325.7 | 326.4 | 330.5 | 329.4 | 330.5 | 325.2 | 329.2 | 329.2 | 327.7 | 326.3 |
| **Education and Health Services** | | | | | | | | | | | | | |
| 2011 | 405.2 | 407.5 | 408.4 | 410.4 | 411.6 | 408.2 | 406.9 | 407.4 | 412.8 | 415.9 | 416.7 | 418.1 | 410.8 |
| 2012 | 410.1 | 415.6 | 418.2 | 417.6 | 419.0 | 418.0 | 412.9 | 415.4 | 420.0 | 424.2 | 425.2 | 426.5 | 418.6 |
| 2013 | 419.7 | 422.2 | 423.8 | 424.1 | 425.2 | 423.9 | 418.4 | 421.4 | 425.2 | 428.7 | 430.0 | 430.5 | 424.4 |
| 2014 | 425.7 | 428.1 | 429.7 | 430.5 | 431.2 | 431.1 | 425.5 | 427.8 | 431.6 | 434.2 | 436.3 | 437.6 | 430.8 |
| 2015 | 430.5 | 433.5 | 435.7 | 436.1 | 437.3 | 436.5 | 431.7 | 432.7 | 436.4 | 440.5 | 442.3 | 444.3 | 436.5 |
| 2016 | 438.8 | 442.2 | 443.7 | 445.7 | 445.9 | 444.6 | 441.5 | 442.4 | 447.0 | 449.1 | 450.3 | 450.5 | 445.1 |
| 2017 | 445.9 | 449.1 | 450.6 | 451.4 | 451.6 | 452.5 | 446.0 | 447.2 | 452.1 | 454.6 | 456.6 | 457.7 | 451.3 |
| 2018 | 452.5 | 455.1 | 456.5 | 457.0 | 457.6 | 459.1 | 452.3 | 454.0 | 457.9 | 460.7 | 462.9 | 463.5 | 457.4 |
| 2019 | 459.0 | 460.5 | 462.2 | 463.0 | 465.0 | 465.4 | 458.9 | 461.0 | 463.5 | 469.5 | 471.3 | 472.6 | 464.3 |
| **Leisure and Hospitality** | | | | | | | | | | | | | |
| 2011 | 232.7 | 232.4 | 235.0 | 245.1 | 258.4 | 270.3 | 275.1 | 276.7 | 264.3 | 253.8 | 244.3 | 241.0 | 252.4 |
| 2012 | 234.4 | 235.4 | 240.4 | 250.2 | 263.9 | 276.5 | 280.2 | 280.6 | 269.0 | 256.6 | 247.8 | 247.6 | 256.9 |
| 2013 | 238.8 | 239.6 | 243.2 | 250.4 | 268.6 | 279.8 | 284.5 | 286.6 | 273.8 | 262.5 | 253.6 | 252.6 | 261.2 |
| 2014 | 242.5 | 243.8 | 246.8 | 255.8 | 271.8 | 284.5 | 286.3 | 287.5 | 273.8 | 264.4 | 256.3 | 255.2 | 264.1 |
| 2015 | 247.3 | 248.5 | 253.1 | 262.8 | 277.9 | 290.9 | 293.5 | 294.4 | 280.7 | 272.8 | 265.3 | 263.4 | 270.9 |
| 2016 | 254.3 | 256.4 | 259.2 | 268.6 | 283.1 | 295.1 | 300.1 | 300.5 | 284.8 | 276.7 | 267.6 | 264.5 | 275.9 |
| 2017 | 259.8 | 261.1 | 265.2 | 271.8 | 286.6 | 303.3 | 305.4 | 305.0 | 287.8 | 279.1 | 270.7 | 268.0 | 280.3 |
| 2018 | 263.6 | 264.8 | 268.6 | 271.0 | 287.4 | 303.5 | 307.1 | 306.4 | 290.0 | 281.4 | 272.4 | 272.8 | 282.4 |
| 2019 | 266.0 | 266.2 | 270.0 | 276.8 | 292.5 | 307.1 | 309.3 | 307.1 | 288.8 | 283.1 | 272.4 | 274.3 | 284.5 |
| **Other Services** | | | | | | | | | | | | | |
| 2011 | 135.1 | 135.1 | 136.1 | 137.0 | 137.5 | 139.0 | 138.8 | 138.5 | 137.4 | 137.5 | 137.0 | 137.9 | 137.2 |
| 2012 | 135.7 | 136.2 | 136.7 | 137.5 | 138.0 | 140.4 | 139.2 | 138.8 | 137.7 | 138.0 | 137.7 | 138.1 | 137.8 |
| 2013 | 135.6 | 135.7 | 136.5 | 136.9 | 137.9 | 139.7 | 139.0 | 138.9 | 138.8 | 138.5 | 139.3 | 140.2 | 138.1 |
| 2014 | 138.4 | 139.2 | 140.3 | 141.4 | 142.6 | 144.9 | 145.3 | 145.7 | 145.0 | 145.2 | 145.3 | 146.5 | 143.3 |
| 2015 | 145.1 | 145.6 | 146.9 | 147.9 | 148.7 | 150.2 | 149.9 | 149.4 | 148.3 | 148.4 | 148.0 | 149.3 | 148.1 |
| 2016 | 146.9 | 146.9 | 148.0 | 149.5 | 149.8 | 151.2 | 151.8 | 151.6 | 150.8 | 150.6 | 150.5 | 150.8 | 149.9 |
| 2017 | 148.7 | 149.2 | 150.3 | 151.1 | 151.9 | 153.8 | 152.9 | 152.6 | 151.7 | 151.4 | 150.9 | 151.7 | 151.4 |
| 2018 | 150.1 | 150.2 | 151.1 | 151.3 | 152.5 | 154.4 | 153.5 | 153.5 | 152.3 | 152.6 | 152.0 | 152.6 | 152.2 |
| 2019 | 150.8 | 150.5 | 151.6 | 152.2 | 153.0 | 155.1 | 154.2 | 154.0 | 152.2 | 151.5 | 150.2 | 152.2 | 152.3 |
| **Government** | | | | | | | | | | | | | |
| 2011 | 412.2 | 426.6 | 428.2 | 430.8 | 428.6 | 411.5 | 386.8 | 380.7 | 408.7 | 419.1 | 422.0 | 422.2 | 414.8 |
| 2012 | 395.8 | 411.4 | 419.8 | 427.3 | 428.8 | 408.7 | 378.3 | 378.6 | 406.7 | 422.2 | 429.7 | 423.0 | 410.9 |
| 2013 | 394.9 | 420.3 | 419.6 | 422.7 | 416.9 | 404.2 | 378.2 | 375.7 | 408.9 | 422.3 | 423.5 | 422.2 | 409.1 |
| 2014 | 405.2 | 418.1 | 418.8 | 424.6 | 417.9 | 405.7 | 380.8 | 384.4 | 410.4 | 422.5 | 431.0 | 422.8 | 411.9 |
| 2015 | 403.0 | 420.0 | 418.9 | 426.7 | 417.4 | 404.0 | 380.3 | 377.2 | 405.9 | 418.5 | 419.3 | 420.7 | 409.3 |
| 2016 | 403.1 | 419.1 | 418.2 | 427.0 | 415.2 | 403.7 | 383.3 | 387.1 | 408.1 | 420.7 | 433.2 | 423.3 | 411.8 |
| 2017 | 400.9 | 417.0 | 413.6 | 423.3 | 416.7 | 399.5 | 381.3 | 376.5 | 404.9 | 418.3 | 420.3 | 416.4 | 407.4 |
| 2018 | 397.6 | 417.4 | 414.7 | 421.9 | 416.8 | 401.8 | 381.8 | 381.5 | 404.6 | 417.6 | 425.2 | 419.3 | 408.4 |
| 2019 | 396.0 | 411.4 | 414.3 | 420.6 | 410.6 | 403.3 | 383.2 | 376.1 | 399.9 | 417.4 | 420.7 | 418.0 | 406.0 |

## 2. Average Weekly Hours by Selected Industry: Wisconsin, 2015–2019

(Not seasonally adjusted)

| Industry and year | January | February | March | April | May | June | July | August | September | October | November | December | Annual average |
|---|---|---|---|---|---|---|---|---|---|---|---|---|---|
| **Total Private** | | | | | | | | | | | | | |
| 2015 | 33.4 | 33.7 | 33.8 | 33.4 | 33.6 | 33.8 | 33.8 | 34.1 | 33.6 | 33.7 | 34.0 | 33.6 | 33.7 |
| 2016 | 33.1 | 33.1 | 33.3 | 33.4 | 33.6 | 33.6 | 33.8 | 33.8 | 33.6 | 34.0 | 33.7 | 33.5 | 33.5 |
| 2017 | 33.6 | 33.3 | 33.3 | 33.8 | 33.5 | 33.8 | 34.2 | 33.9 | 33.8 | 34.1 | 33.9 | 33.8 | 33.8 |
| 2018 | 33.4 | 33.6 | 33.4 | 33.5 | 33.5 | 33.8 | 34.1 | 33.8 | 33.9 | 33.3 | 33.0 | 33.5 | 33.6 |
| 2019 | 33.0 | 32.7 | 32.9 | 33.0 | 33.1 | 33.6 | 33.1 | 33.3 | 33.3 | 33.0 | 33.0 | 33.1 | 33.1 |
| **Goods-Producing** | | | | | | | | | | | | | |
| 2015 | 40.3 | 39.8 | 40.0 | 40.3 | 40.9 | 40.7 | 40.7 | 41.0 | 40.6 | 41.3 | 41.1 | 40.6 | 40.6 |
| 2016 | 39.7 | 39.3 | 39.9 | 40.0 | 40.1 | 40.2 | 40.6 | 40.2 | 40.6 | 40.8 | 41.1 | 40.6 | 40.2 |
| 2017 | 39.8 | 39.7 | 40.1 | 40.0 | 40.4 | 40.2 | 40.5 | 40.8 | 40.8 | 40.8 | 41.1 | 40.0 | 40.3 |
| 2018 | 39.9 | 39.7 | 39.6 | 39.7 | 40.2 | 40.3 | 40.3 | 40.3 | 40.3 | 39.5 | 39.0 | 39.8 | 39.9 |
| 2019 | 39.1 | 38.6 | 39.2 | 38.9 | 39.1 | 39.6 | 39.2 | 39.5 | 39.4 | 39.5 | 39.3 | 39.7 | 39.3 |
| **Construction** | | | | | | | | | | | | | |
| 2015 | 37.9 | 36.0 | 37.8 | 38.6 | 39.7 | 38.6 | 39.0 | 39.7 | 38.4 | 40.7 | 39.0 | 38.6 | 38.7 |
| 2016 | 37.0 | 37.4 | 38.2 | 39.4 | 39.0 | 40.2 | 40.1 | 40.4 | 40.2 | 40.3 | 40.1 | 37.5 | 39.2 |
| 2017 | 37.7 | 37.9 | 38.1 | 39.3 | 40.2 | 39.6 | 39.0 | 40.0 | 40.0 | 40.2 | 40.1 | 37.5 | 39.2 |
| 2018 | 37.7 | 38.0 | 37.7 | 38.3 | 39.2 | 40.2 | 40.5 | 40.3 | 40.3 | 40.2 | 39.4 | 38.2 | 39.2 |
| 2019 | 38.2 | 36.2 | 37.5 | 37.2 | 38.5 | 39.7 | 39.7 | 39.3 | 38.8 | 38.8 | 37.8 | 37.7 | 38.3 |
| **Manufacturing** | | | | | | | | | | | | | |
| 2015 | 40.7 | 40.5 | 40.3 | 40.6 | 41.0 | 41.1 | 41.0 | 41.3 | 40.5 | 40.7 | 41.0 | 40.5 | 40.8 |
| 2016 | 39.8 | 39.3 | 39.9 | 39.8 | 40.1 | 39.9 | 40.3 | 39.7 | 40.3 | 40.5 | 41.0 | 40.4 | 40.1 |
| 2017 | 40.1 | 40.0 | 40.4 | 40.0 | 40.2 | 40.2 | 40.7 | 40.8 | 40.9 | 40.9 | 41.0 | 40.4 | 40.5 |
| 2018 | 40.4 | 40.1 | 40.0 | 40.0 | 40.5 | 40.4 | 40.2 | 40.4 | 40.3 | 39.8 | 39.3 | 39.9 | 40.1 |
| 2019 | 39.2 | 39.3 | 39.7 | 39.4 | 39.3 | 39.6 | 38.9 | 39.6 | 39.7 | 39.8 | 39.9 | 40.4 | 39.6 |
| **Trade, Transportation, and Utilities** | | | | | | | | | | | | | |
| 2015 | 33.2 | 33.8 | 33.9 | 33.4 | 33.9 | 33.8 | 34.0 | 34.0 | 33.5 | 33.4 | 33.7 | 33.6 | 33.7 |
| 2016 | 32.3 | 32.3 | 32.3 | 32.9 | 32.9 | 33.2 | 33.3 | 33.2 | 32.9 | 32.9 | 32.4 | 32.6 | 32.8 |
| 2017 | 32.1 | 31.9 | 32.0 | 32.6 | 32.4 | 32.9 | 33.3 | 33.0 | 33.0 | 33.1 | 33.5 | 33.5 | 32.8 |
| 2018 | 32.8 | 32.7 | 32.8 | 32.7 | 32.9 | 33.0 | 33.2 | 32.5 | 32.6 | 32.0 | 32.3 | 32.5 | 32.7 |
| 2019 | 31.8 | 31.5 | 31.7 | 31.8 | 32.2 | 32.7 | 32.1 | 32.2 | 32.3 | 32.0 | 32.0 | 32.4 | 32.1 |
| **Financial Activities** | | | | | | | | | | | | | |
| 2015 | 36.7 | 37.6 | 37.9 | 36.5 | 36.5 | 36.3 | 36.0 | 37.8 | 37.1 | 36.8 | 37.9 | 37.2 | 37.0 |
| 2016 | 37.4 | 37.3 | 37.9 | 37.4 | 38.3 | 36.8 | 36.5 | 37.3 | 36.8 | 38.1 | 37.5 | 37.4 | 37.4 |
| 2017 | 37.9 | 36.2 | 36.3 | 37.8 | 36.4 | 37.2 | 37.5 | 37.4 | 36.7 | 37.9 | 37.2 | 37.5 | 37.2 |
| 2018 | 37.3 | 37.9 | 37.3 | 38.1 | 37.2 | 37.8 | 38.1 | 37.9 | 38.4 | 37.8 | 37.6 | 38.1 | 37.8 |
| 2019 | 38.0 | 37.5 | 37.6 | 37.4 | 37.1 | 37.1 | 36.8 | 36.9 | 36.7 | 36.7 | 36.9 | 36.9 | 37.1 |
| **Professional and Business Services** | | | | | | | | | | | | | |
| 2015 | 34.1 | 34.6 | 34.8 | 34.1 | 34.5 | 34.6 | 34.4 | 34.8 | 34.0 | 34.4 | 35.1 | 34.3 | 34.5 |
| 2016 | 34.2 | 34.9 | 35.0 | 34.6 | 35.1 | 35.2 | 34.9 | 35.1 | 34.9 | 35.6 | 34.8 | 34.6 | 34.9 |
| 2017 | 35.1 | 35.0 | 34.9 | 35.7 | 35.3 | 36.1 | 36.2 | 35.4 | 35.3 | 35.7 | 35.4 | 35.1 | 35.4 |
| 2018 | 34.7 | 35.2 | 35.1 | 35.4 | 34.6 | 35.3 | 35.7 | 35.3 | 35.1 | 35.4 | 35.1 | 35.0 | 35.4 |
| 2019 | 34.2 | 34.2 | 33.9 | 33.9 | 34.2 | 35.4 | 34.4 | 34.8 | 35.0 | 34.4 | 34.5 | 34.5 | 35.1 |
| **Education and Health Services** | | | | | | | | | | | | | |
| 2015 | 31.2 | 31.4 | 31.2 | 30.9 | 30.9 | 30.8 | 30.9 | 31.1 | 31.0 | 30.8 | 31.0 | 30.9 | 31.0 |
| 2016 | 30.9 | 30.8 | 30.8 | 31.1 | 31.6 | 31.2 | 31.5 | 31.3 | 31.2 | 31.5 | 31.3 | 31.4 | 31.2 |
| 2017 | 32.1 | 31.6 | 31.6 | 32.0 | 31.5 | 31.6 | 32.2 | 31.5 | 31.6 | 31.6 | 31.3 | 31.7 | 31.7 |
| 2018 | 31.4 | 31.3 | 31.2 | 31.3 | 31.3 | 31.5 | 31.7 | 31.7 | 31.8 | 31.1 | 31.1 | 31.5 | 31.4 |
| 2019 | 30.9 | 30.8 | 31.2 | 31.4 | 31.2 | 31.5 | 31.1 | 31.3 | 31.8 | 31.1 | 31.2 | 31.6 | 31.3 |
| **Other Services** | | | | | | | | | | | | | |
| 2015 | 27.6 | 27.6 | 28.1 | 27.1 | 27.2 | 29.0 | 29.2 | 29.5 | 27.8 | 27.7 | 28.0 | 27.8 | 28.1 |
| 2016 | 28.3 | 27.7 | 27.4 | 27.7 | 28.0 | 28.5 | 28.7 | 28.6 | 27.8 | 28.5 | 28.4 | 28.3 | 28.2 |
| 2017 | 28.2 | 27.9 | 27.2 | 27.8 | 27.2 | 27.8 | 27.6 | 27.7 | 26.6 | 26.9 | 27.0 | 27.0 | 27.4 |
| 2018 | 26.4 | 26.9 | 26.5 | 27.3 | 27.2 | 27.7 | 28.8 | 28.8 | 29.0 | 29.0 | 27.0 | 27.0 | 27.8 |
| 2019 | 28.5 | 28.0 | 28.0 | 27.9 | 28.6 | 29.2 | 28.9 | 29.4 | 28.7 | 28.3 | 28.0 | 27.5 | 28.4 |

## 3. Average Hourly Earnings by Selected Industry: Wisconsin, 2015–2019

(Dollars, not seasonally adjusted)

| Industry and year | January | February | March | April | May | June | July | August | September | October | November | December | Annual average |
|---|---|---|---|---|---|---|---|---|---|---|---|---|---|
| **Total Private** | | | | | | | | | | | | | |
| 2015 | 23.57 | 23.60 | 23.54 | 23.53 | 23.41 | 23.09 | 23.11 | 23.25 | 23.38 | 23.61 | 23.69 | 23.81 | 23.46 |
| 2016 | 23.98 | 23.92 | 23.86 | 23.99 | 24.09 | 23.76 | 23.96 | 23.91 | 23.85 | 24.28 | 24.31 | 24.43 | 24.03 |
| 2017 | 24.68 | 24.40 | 24.50 | 24.95 | 24.40 | 24.15 | 24.53 | 24.39 | 24.87 | 25.21 | 25.15 | 25.57 | 24.74 |
| 2018 | 25.96 | 25.85 | 25.87 | 26.42 | 25.94 | 25.61 | 25.76 | 25.62 | 26.06 | 25.95 | 25.97 | 26.19 | 25.93 |
| 2019 | 26.09 | 26.21 | 26.25 | 26.25 | 26.08 | 26.12 | 26.22 | 26.23 | 26.78 | 26.90 | 26.87 | 27.08 | 26.42 |
| **Goods-Producing** | | | | | | | | | | | | | |
| 2015 | 24.44 | 24.53 | 24.61 | 24.73 | 24.62 | 24.38 | 24.48 | 24.55 | 24.48 | 24.66 | 24.63 | 25.08 | 24.60 |
| 2016 | 24.74 | 24.73 | 24.53 | 24.76 | 24.78 | 24.96 | 25.20 | 25.23 | 25.44 | 25.74 | 25.54 | 25.78 | 25.13 |
| 2017 | 25.73 | 25.49 | 25.46 | 25.87 | 25.70 | 25.55 | 25.95 | 25.80 | 26.08 | 26.12 | 26.31 | 26.75 | 25.91 |
| 2018 | 26.83 | 26.73 | 26.56 | 27.19 | 26.80 | 26.76 | 27.02 | 26.91 | 27.18 | 27.33 | 27.27 | 27.72 | 27.03 |
| 2019 | 27.33 | 27.15 | 27.41 | 27.63 | 27.53 | 27.64 | 28.13 | 28.15 | 28.26 | 28.69 | 28.51 | 28.67 | 27.93 |
| **Construction** | | | | | | | | | | | | | |
| 2015 | 27.37 | 27.26 | 27.77 | 27.99 | 27.91 | 27.67 | 27.64 | 27.82 | 27.36 | 27.65 | 27.72 | 27.91 | 27.68 |
| 2016 | 28.19 | 27.76 | 27.69 | 27.77 | 27.52 | 28.10 | 28.56 | 27.89 | 28.20 | 28.07 | 27.88 | 28.55 | 28.02 |
| 2017 | 27.99 | 27.92 | 28.28 | 27.69 | 28.13 | 28.01 | 28.54 | 28.97 | 28.67 | 28.71 | 28.17 | 29.04 | 28.36 |
| 2018 | 29.14 | 29.29 | 29.25 | 29.93 | 29.66 | 29.62 | 29.65 | 30.15 | 30.74 | 31.07 | 30.22 | 31.38 | 30.04 |
| 2019 | 30.75 | 30.62 | 30.85 | 30.69 | 30.12 | 30.50 | 30.53 | 30.59 | 30.70 | 31.80 | 31.44 | 31.80 | 30.86 |
| **Manufacturing** | | | | | | | | | | | | | |
| 2015 | 23.79 | 23.96 | 23.92 | 23.94 | 23.79 | 23.54 | 23.64 | 23.62 | 23.71 | 23.81 | 23.80 | 24.37 | 23.82 |
| 2016 | 23.96 | 24.00 | 23.76 | 23.90 | 24.02 | 23.98 | 24.15 | 24.37 | 24.58 | 25.02 | 24.83 | 25.06 | 24.31 |
| 2017 | 25.15 | 24.87 | 24.75 | 25.36 | 25.16 | 24.98 | 25.34 | 24.96 | 25.38 | 25.43 | 25.86 | 26.21 | 25.29 |
| 2018 | 26.31 | 26.15 | 25.95 | 26.53 | 26.09 | 25.94 | 26.26 | 25.93 | 26.10 | 26.23 | 26.42 | 26.69 | 26.22 |
| 2019 | 26.39 | 26.25 | 26.48 | 26.80 | 26.74 | 26.67 | 27.25 | 27.31 | 27.38 | 27.53 | 27.43 | 27.56 | 26.99 |
| **Trade, Transportation, and Utilities** | | | | | | | | | | | | | |
| 2015 | 20.68 | 20.84 | 20.65 | 20.96 | 20.64 | 20.38 | 20.57 | 20.63 | 20.71 | 20.57 | 20.41 | 20.44 | 20.62 |
| 2016 | 20.93 | 20.87 | 20.92 | 21.16 | 21.23 | 21.08 | 21.15 | 20.82 | 21.32 | 21.48 | 21.55 | 21.53 | 21.17 |
| 2017 | 21.68 | 21.43 | 21.53 | 21.93 | 22.12 | 22.07 | 22.23 | 22.23 | 22.79 | 22.84 | 22.35 | 22.63 | 22.16 |
| 2018 | 23.33 | 23.33 | 23.12 | 23.59 | 23.07 | 23.23 | 22.98 | 23.09 | 23.44 | 23.20 | 22.92 | 23.09 | 23.20 |
| 2019 | 23.20 | 23.61 | 23.57 | 23.52 | 23.22 | 23.42 | 23.35 | 23.37 | 24.09 | 23.92 | 23.80 | 23.83 | 23.58 |
| **Financial Activities** | | | | | | | | | | | | | |
| 2015 | 29.60 | 29.91 | 29.75 | 29.33 | 29.98 | 29.31 | 29.79 | 29.54 | 29.21 | 29.91 | 29.49 | 29.38 | 29.60 |
| 2016 | 30.43 | 30.25 | 29.98 | 30.22 | 30.22 | 29.31 | 29.82 | 29.81 | 30.36 | 30.24 | 30.24 | 30.33 | 30.10 |
| 2017 | 31.41 | 31.23 | 31.61 | 32.32 | 31.50 | 30.58 | 31.50 | 31.04 | 31.53 | 32.43 | 32.14 | 33.29 | 31.72 |
| 2018 | 34.35 | 34.06 | 34.42 | 34.71 | 34.05 | 32.86 | 33.48 | 33.04 | 33.18 | 32.48 | 33.41 | 33.47 | 33.62 |
| 2019 | 32.94 | 33.27 | 33.28 | 33.01 | 32.75 | 32.75 | 32.25 | 32.29 | 33.27 | 32.81 | 32.96 | 32.96 | 32.88 |
| **Professional and Business Services** | | | | | | | | | | | | | |
| 2015 | 26.05 | 25.84 | 25.88 | 25.28 | 25.16 | 25.08 | 24.86 | 25.23 | 25.54 | 25.49 | 26.07 | 26.18 | 25.55 |
| 2016 | 26.36 | 26.49 | 26.35 | 26.77 | 27.32 | 27.01 | 26.83 | 26.92 | 27.09 | 27.81 | 27.96 | 28.36 | 27.11 |
| 2017 | 28.15 | 27.54 | 28.00 | 28.93 | 28.21 | 28.33 | 28.77 | 28.29 | 28.20 | 28.72 | 28.51 | 28.35 | 28.34 |
| 2018 | 28.85 | 28.84 | 28.88 | 29.45 | 29.47 | 29.04 | 29.40 | 29.01 | 29.12 | 28.55 | 28.27 | 28.62 | 28.96 |
| 2019 | 28.62 | 28.77 | 28.70 | 28.88 | 29.13 | 29.93 | 30.22 | 29.84 | 30.26 | 30.22 | 30.27 | 31.21 | 29.68 |
| **Education and Health Services** | | | | | | | | | | | | | |
| 2015 | 24.93 | 24.67 | 24.52 | 24.57 | 24.59 | 24.39 | 24.29 | 24.56 | 24.73 | 24.86 | 25.06 | 25.15 | 24.69 |
| 2016 | 25.06 | 24.93 | 25.00 | 24.66 | 24.90 | 24.71 | 25.26 | 25.33 | 25.36 | 25.71 | 26.01 | 25.75 | 25.23 |
| 2017 | 26.00 | 26.21 | 26.03 | 26.17 | 26.11 | 25.90 | 26.12 | 25.83 | 26.11 | 26.42 | 26.53 | 26.67 | 26.18 |
| 2018 | 27.03 | 26.88 | 26.96 | 27.24 | 26.66 | 26.37 | 26.37 | 25.95 | 26.50 | 26.59 | 26.76 | 26.56 | 26.65 |
| 2019 | 26.87 | 26.77 | 26.89 | 26.88 | 26.75 | 26.86 | 26.99 | 26.87 | 27.11 | 27.20 | 27.37 | 27.27 | 26.99 |
| **Leisure and Hospitality** | | | | | | | | | | | | | |
| 2015 | 12.73 | 13.03 | 12.95 | 13.13 | 13.01 | 12.72 | 12.70 | 12.69 | 13.02 | 13.43 | 13.52 | 13.49 | 13.02 |
| 2016 | 13.43 | 13.59 | 13.58 | 13.68 | 13.49 | 13.02 | 13.08 | 12.99 | 13.50 | 13.84 | 13.73 | 14.00 | 13.47 |
| 2017 | 13.97 | 14.02 | 14.14 | 14.21 | 14.07 | 13.47 | 13.25 | 13.39 | 13.75 | 14.04 | 14.06 | 14.44 | 13.88 |
| 2018 | 14.13 | 14.27 | 14.49 | 14.76 | 14.50 | 14.32 | 14.18 | 14.38 | 14.73 | 14.96 | 14.97 | 15.06 | 14.55 |
| 2019 | 14.80 | 15.03 | 14.89 | 14.88 | 14.84 | 14.45 | 14.63 | 14.68 | 15.03 | 15.44 | 15.37 | 15.79 | 14.97 |
| **Other Services** | | | | | | | | | | | | | |
| 2015 | 19.39 | 19.56 | 19.47 | 19.61 | 19.65 | 19.20 | 19.01 | 19.19 | 19.48 | 18.75 | 19.17 | 19.27 | 19.31 |
| 2016 | 19.09 | 18.93 | 19.09 | 18.95 | 19.10 | 18.62 | 19.06 | 18.91 | 19.35 | 19.81 | 19.88 | 20.37 | 19.27 |
| 2017 | 20.52 | 20.77 | 20.39 | 20.35 | 20.08 | 19.36 | 19.80 | 19.84 | 20.37 | 20.71 | 20.14 | 21.02 | 20.27 |
| 2018 | 21.39 | 20.93 | 21.01 | 21.77 | 21.72 | 21.74 | 21.49 | 21.25 | 21.81 | 21.74 | 21.32 | 21.81 | 21.50 |
| 2019 | 21.46 | 21.17 | 21.17 | 21.22 | 21.02 | 20.42 | 20.28 | 20.54 | 22.32 | 22.23 | 22.53 | 23.19 | 21.45 |

## 4. Average Weekly Earnings by Selected Industry: Wisconsin, 2015–2019

(Dollars, not seasonally adjusted)

| Industry and year | January | February | March | April | May | June | July | August | September | October | November | December | Annual average |
|---|---|---|---|---|---|---|---|---|---|---|---|---|---|
| **Total Private** | | | | | | | | | | | | | |
| 2015 | 787.24 | 795.32 | 795.65 | 785.90 | 786.58 | 780.44 | 781.12 | 792.83 | 785.57 | 795.66 | 805.46 | 800.02 | 790.60 |
| 2016 | 793.74 | 791.75 | 794.54 | 801.27 | 809.42 | 798.34 | 809.85 | 808.16 | 801.36 | 825.52 | 819.25 | 818.41 | 805.01 |
| 2017 | 829.25 | 812.52 | 815.85 | 843.31 | 817.40 | 816.27 | 838.93 | 826.82 | 840.61 | 859.66 | 852.59 | 864.27 | 836.21 |
| 2018 | 867.06 | 868.56 | 864.06 | 885.07 | 868.99 | 865.62 | 878.42 | 865.96 | 883.43 | 864.14 | 857.01 | 877.37 | 871.25 |
| 2019 | 860.97 | 857.07 | 863.63 | 866.25 | 863.25 | 877.63 | 867.88 | 873.46 | 891.77 | 887.70 | 886.71 | 896.35 | 874.50 |
| **Goods-Producing** | | | | | | | | | | | | | |
| 2015 | 984.93 | 976.29 | 984.40 | 996.62 | 1,006.96 | 992.27 | 996.34 | 1,006.55 | 993.89 | 1,018.46 | 1,012.29 | 1,018.25 | 998.76 |
| 2016 | 982.18 | 971.89 | 978.75 | 990.40 | 993.68 | 1,003.39 | 1,023.12 | 1,014.25 | 1,032.86 | 1,050.19 | 1,049.69 | 1,031.20 | 1,010.23 |
| 2017 | 1,024.05 | 1,011.95 | 1,020.95 | 1,034.80 | 1,038.28 | 1,027.11 | 1,050.98 | 1,052.64 | 1,064.06 | 1,065.70 | 1,068.19 | 1,078.03 | 1,044.17 |
| 2018 | 1,070.52 | 1,061.18 | 1,051.78 | 1,079.44 | 1,077.36 | 1,078.43 | 1,088.91 | 1,084.47 | 1,095.35 | 1,079.54 | 1,063.53 | 1,103.26 | 1,078.50 |
| 2019 | 1,068.60 | 1,047.99 | 1,074.47 | 1,074.81 | 1,076.42 | 1,094.54 | 1,102.70 | 1,111.93 | 1,113.44 | 1,133.26 | 1,120.44 | 1,138.20 | 1,097.65 |
| **Construction** | | | | | | | | | | | | | |
| 2015 | 1,037.32 | 981.36 | 1,049.71 | 1,080.41 | 1,108.03 | 1,068.06 | 1,077.96 | 1,104.45 | 1,050.62 | 1,125.36 | 1,081.08 | 1,077.33 | 1,071.22 |
| 2016 | 1,043.03 | 1,038.22 | 1,057.76 | 1,094.14 | 1,073.28 | 1,129.62 | 1,145.26 | 1,126.76 | 1,133.64 | 1,131.22 | 1,117.99 | 1,070.63 | 1,098.38 |
| 2017 | 1,055.22 | 1,058.17 | 1,077.47 | 1,088.22 | 1,130.83 | 1,109.20 | 1,113.06 | 1,158.80 | 1,146.80 | 1,154.14 | 1,109.90 | 1,109.33 | 1,111.71 |
| 2018 | 1,098.58 | 1,113.02 | 1,102.73 | 1,146.32 | 1,162.67 | 1,190.72 | 1,200.83 | 1,215.05 | 1,238.82 | 1,202.41 | 1,160.45 | 1,230.10 | 1,174.56 |
| 2019 | 1,174.65 | 1,108.44 | 1,156.88 | 1,141.67 | 1,159.62 | 1,210.85 | 1,212.04 | 1,202.19 | 1,191.16 | 1,233.84 | 1,188.43 | 1,198.86 | 1,181.94 |
| **Manufacturing** | | | | | | | | | | | | | |
| 2015 | 968.25 | 970.38 | 963.98 | 971.96 | 975.39 | 967.49 | 969.24 | 975.51 | 960.26 | 969.07 | 975.80 | 986.99 | 971.86 |
| 2016 | 953.61 | 943.20 | 948.02 | 951.22 | 963.20 | 956.80 | 973.25 | 967.49 | 990.57 | 1,013.31 | 1,018.03 | 1,012.42 | 974.83 |
| 2017 | 1,008.52 | 994.80 | 999.90 | 1,014.40 | 1,011.43 | 1,004.20 | 1,031.34 | 1,018.37 | 1,038.04 | 1,040.09 | 1,057.67 | 1,069.37 | 1,024.25 |
| 2018 | 1,062.92 | 1,048.62 | 1,038.00 | 1,061.20 | 1,056.65 | 1,047.98 | 1,055.65 | 1,047.57 | 1,051.83 | 1,043.95 | 1,038.31 | 1,064.93 | 1,051.42 |
| 2019 | 1,034.49 | 1,031.63 | 1,051.26 | 1,055.92 | 1,050.88 | 1,056.13 | 1,060.03 | 1,081.48 | 1,086.99 | 1,095.69 | 1,094.46 | 1,113.42 | 1,068.80 |
| **Trade, Transportation, and Utilities** | | | | | | | | | | | | | |
| 2015 | 686.58 | 704.39 | 700.04 | 700.06 | 699.70 | 688.84 | 699.38 | 701.42 | 693.79 | 687.04 | 687.82 | 686.78 | 694.89 |
| 2016 | 676.04 | 674.10 | 675.72 | 696.16 | 698.47 | 699.86 | 704.30 | 691.22 | 701.43 | 706.69 | 698.22 | 701.88 | 694.38 |
| 2017 | 695.93 | 683.62 | 688.96 | 714.92 | 716.69 | 726.10 | 740.26 | 733.59 | 752.07 | 756.00 | 748.73 | 758.11 | 726.85 |
| 2018 | 765.22 | 762.89 | 758.34 | 771.39 | 759.00 | 766.59 | 762.94 | 750.43 | 764.14 | 742.40 | 740.32 | 750.43 | 758.64 |
| 2019 | 737.76 | 743.72 | 747.17 | 747.94 | 747.68 | 765.83 | 749.54 | 752.51 | 778.11 | 765.44 | 761.60 | 772.09 | 756.92 |
| **Financial Activities** | | | | | | | | | | | | | |
| 2014 | 1,086.32 | 1,124.62 | 1,127.53 | 1,070.55 | 1,094.27 | 1,063.95 | 1,072.44 | 1,116.61 | 1,083.69 | 1,100.69 | 1,117.67 | 1,092.94 | 1,095.20 |
| 2015 | 1,138.08 | 1,128.33 | 1,136.24 | 1,130.23 | 1,157.43 | 1,078.61 | 1,088.43 | 1,111.91 | 1,117.25 | 1,152.14 | 1,134.00 | 1,134.34 | 1,125.74 |
| 2016 | 1,190.44 | 1,130.53 | 1,147.44 | 1,221.70 | 1,146.60 | 1,137.58 | 1,181.25 | 1,160.90 | 1,157.15 | 1,229.10 | 1,195.61 | 1,248.38 | 1,179.98 |
| 2017 | 1,281.26 | 1,290.87 | 1,283.87 | 1,322.45 | 1,266.66 | 1,242.11 | 1,275.59 | 1,252.22 | 1,274.11 | 1,227.74 | 1,256.22 | 1,275.21 | 1,270.84 |
| 2018 | 1,251.72 | 1,247.63 | 1,251.33 | 1,234.57 | 1,215.03 | 1,215.03 | 1,186.80 | 1,191.50 | 1,221.01 | 1,204.13 | 1,216.22 | 1,216.22 | 1,219.85 |
| 2019 | | | | | | | | | | | | | |
| **Professional and Business Services** | | | | | | | | | | | | | |
| 2015 | 888.31 | 894.06 | 900.62 | 862.05 | 868.02 | 867.77 | 855.18 | 878.00 | 868.36 | 876.86 | 915.06 | 897.97 | 881.48 |
| 2016 | 901.51 | 924.50 | 922.25 | 926.24 | 958.93 | 950.75 | 936.37 | 944.89 | 945.44 | 990.04 | 973.01 | 981.26 | 946.14 |
| 2017 | 988.07 | 963.90 | 977.20 | 1,032.80 | 995.81 | 1,022.71 | 1,041.47 | 1,001.47 | 995.46 | 1,025.30 | 1,009.25 | 995.09 | 1,003.24 |
| 2018 | 1,001.10 | 1,015.17 | 1,013.69 | 1,042.53 | 1,019.66 | 1,025.11 | 1,049.58 | 1,024.05 | 1,022.11 | 993.54 | 978.14 | 1,001.70 | 1,016.50 |
| 2019 | 978.80 | 983.93 | 972.93 | 979.03 | 996.25 | 1,059.52 | 1,039.57 | 1,038.43 | 1,059.10 | 1,039.57 | 1,044.32 | 1,076.75 | 1,023.96 |
| **Education and Health Services** | | | | | | | | | | | | | |
| 2015 | 777.82 | 774.64 | 765.02 | 759.21 | 759.83 | 751.21 | 750.56 | 763.82 | 766.63 | 765.69 | 776.86 | 777.14 | 765.39 |
| 2016 | 774.35 | 767.84 | 770.00 | 766.93 | 786.84 | 770.95 | 795.69 | 792.83 | 791.23 | 809.87 | 814.11 | 808.55 | 787.18 |
| 2017 | 834.60 | 828.24 | 822.55 | 837.44 | 822.47 | 818.44 | 841.06 | 813.65 | 825.08 | 834.87 | 830.39 | 845.44 | 829.91 |
| 2018 | 848.74 | 841.34 | 841.15 | 852.61 | 834.46 | 830.66 | 835.93 | 822.62 | 842.70 | 826.95 | 832.24 | 836.64 | 836.81 |
| 2019 | 830.28 | 824.52 | 838.97 | 844.03 | 834.60 | 846.09 | 839.39 | 841.03 | 862.10 | 845.92 | 853.94 | 861.73 | 844.79 |
| **Leisure and Hospitality** | | | | | | | | | | | | | |
| 2015 | 277.51 | 293.18 | 290.08 | 290.17 | 286.22 | 288.74 | 290.83 | 294.41 | 287.74 | 295.46 | 294.74 | 294.08 | 290.35 |
| 2016 | 284.72 | 298.98 | 294.69 | 298.22 | 302.18 | 295.55 | 303.46 | 302.67 | 302.40 | 308.63 | 300.69 | 296.80 | 299.03 |
| 2017 | 303.15 | 308.44 | 311.08 | 309.78 | 308.13 | 308.46 | 308.73 | 305.29 | 306.63 | 314.50 | 305.10 | 309.02 | 308.14 |
| 2018 | 302.38 | 315.37 | 315.88 | 314.39 | 319.00 | 325.06 | 331.81 | 327.86 | 325.53 | 327.62 | 309.88 | 320.78 | 320.10 |
| 2019 | 313.76 | 315.63 | 315.67 | 313.97 | 316.09 | 320.79 | 329.18 | 333.24 | 326.15 | 325.78 | 318.16 | 325.27 | 321.86 |
| **Other Services** | | | | | | | | | | | | | |
| 2015 | 535.16 | 539.86 | 547.11 | 531.43 | 534.48 | 556.80 | 555.09 | 566.11 | 541.54 | 519.38 | 536.76 | 535.71 | 542.61 |
| 2016 | 540.25 | 524.36 | 523.07 | 524.92 | 534.80 | 530.67 | 547.02 | 540.83 | 537.93 | 564.59 | 564.59 | 576.47 | 543.41 |
| 2017 | 578.66 | 579.48 | 554.61 | 565.73 | 546.18 | 538.21 | 546.48 | 549.57 | 541.84 | 557.10 | 543.78 | 567.54 | 555.40 |
| 2018 | 564.70 | 563.02 | 556.77 | 594.32 | 590.78 | 602.20 | 618.91 | 612.00 | 632.49 | 630.46 | 596.96 | 612.86 | 597.70 |
| 2019 | 611.61 | 592.76 | 592.76 | 592.04 | 601.17 | 596.26 | 586.09 | 603.88 | 640.58 | 629.11 | 630.84 | 637.73 | 609.18 |

# WYOMING
*At a Glance*

Population:
  2010 census: 563,626
  2019 estimate: 578,759

Percent change in population:
  2010–2019: 2.7%

Percent change in total nonfarm employment:
  2011–2019: .07%

Industry with the largest growth in employment, 2011–2019 (percent):
  Manufacturing, 11.0%

Industry with the largest decline or smallest growth in employment, 2011–2019 (percent):
  Information, -10.5%

Civilian labor force:
  2010: 303,297
  2019: 292,258

Unemployment rate and rank among states (highest to lowest):
  2010: 6.4%, 45th
  2019: 3.6%, 21st

Over-the-year change in unemployment rates:
  2017–2018: -0.3%
  2018–2019: -0.3%

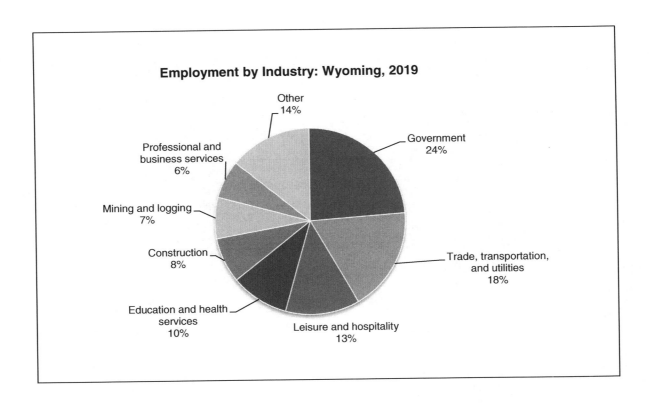

**Employment by Industry: Wyoming, 2019**

Other — 14%
Professional and business services — 6%
Mining and logging — 7%
Construction — 8%
Education and health services — 10%
Leisure and hospitality — 13%
Leisure and hospitality — 13%
Trade, transportation, and utilities — 18%
Government — 24%

## 1. Employment by Industry: Wyoming, 2011–2019

(Numbers in thousands, not seasonally adjusted)

| Industry and year | January | February | March | April | May | June | July | August | September | October | November | December | Annual average |
|---|---|---|---|---|---|---|---|---|---|---|---|---|---|
| **Total Nonfarm** | | | | | | | | | | | | | |
| 2011 | 276.2 | 277.8 | 280.1 | 281.3 | 288.8 | 296.9 | 296.9 | 297.5 | 299.2 | 295.5 | 290.3 | 291.7 | 289.4 |
| 2012 | 283.2 | 284.6 | 286.7 | 287.8 | 294.2 | 300.8 | 299.2 | 299.2 | 299.1 | 296.1 | 291.0 | 291.9 | 292.8 |
| 2013 | 283.9 | 284.5 | 287.0 | 287.6 | 295.2 | 303.2 | 301.5 | 301.0 | 300.1 | 298.2 | 292.4 | 293.2 | 294.0 |
| 2014 | 286.7 | 287.6 | 289.6 | 291.4 | 300.0 | 307.4 | 306.9 | 305.8 | 305.5 | 304.2 | 296.4 | 298.8 | 298.4 |
| 2015 | 291.6 | 291.8 | 292.8 | 293.2 | 298.7 | 303.9 | 303.5 | 302.7 | 302.1 | 299.6 | 291.2 | 291.5 | 296.9 |
| 2016 | 283.1 | 282.4 | 283.2 | 282.7 | 288.1 | 293.6 | 291.6 | 290.6 | 289.1 | 285.8 | 279.7 | 280.4 | 285.9 |
| 2017 | 274.1 | 275.1 | 277.0 | 277.8 | 285.5 | 292.1 | 290.5 | 291.1 | 290.6 | 286.4 | 280.7 | 282.0 | 283.6 |
| 2018 | 276.1 | 276.4 | 278.2 | 279.6 | 287.2 | 293.7 | 292.7 | 292.9 | 291.6 | 290.0 | 285.4 | 286.5 | 285.9 |
| 2019 | 280.9 | 282.6 | 283.7 | 284.3 | 292.3 | 298.5 | 297.2 | 297.9 | 295.5 | 290.6 | 285.3 | 285.8 | 289.6 |
| **Total Private** | | | | | | | | | | | | | |
| 2011 | 205.6 | 205.6 | 207.3 | 208.6 | 214.8 | 223.6 | 227.8 | 229.0 | 226.7 | 222.3 | 217.5 | 218.7 | 217.3 |
| 2012 | 211.9 | 211.6 | 213.3 | 215.2 | 219.9 | 227.7 | 229.7 | 230.9 | 226.5 | 222.6 | 217.9 | 218.6 | 220.5 |
| 2013 | 212.3 | 211.8 | 213.8 | 214.8 | 221.3 | 230.2 | 233.3 | 233.0 | 228.2 | 225.5 | 220.2 | 220.8 | 222.1 |
| 2014 | 216.1 | 215.8 | 217.0 | 219.5 | 227.0 | 235.8 | 238.5 | 238.6 | 234.2 | 232.0 | 224.8 | 226.9 | 227.2 |
| 2015 | 221.8 | 220.8 | 220.8 | 221.6 | 225.7 | 232.2 | 235.8 | 234.8 | 230.1 | 226.6 | 218.7 | 218.9 | 225.7 |
| 2016 | 212.5 | 210.5 | 210.6 | 210.7 | 214.8 | 221.3 | 223.9 | 222.8 | 217.9 | 214.2 | 208.4 | 208.9 | 214.7 |
| 2017 | 204.7 | 204.2 | 205.5 | 206.8 | 213.3 | 221.3 | 224.0 | 224.3 | 220.6 | 216.0 | 210.8 | 212.1 | 213.6 |
| 2018 | 208.4 | 207.3 | 208.6 | 210.0 | 216.9 | 224.4 | 227.1 | 227.0 | 222.3 | 220.2 | 216.0 | 217.2 | 217.1 |
| 2019 | 213.5 | 213.7 | 214.2 | 214.9 | 221.4 | 228.7 | 231.4 | 231.3 | 226.2 | 220.9 | 215.8 | 216.3 | 220.7 |
| **Goods Producing** | | | | | | | | | | | | | |
| 2011 | 52.9 | 52.7 | 53.2 | 54.5 | 56.5 | 58.5 | 59.9 | 60.7 | 61.3 | 61.6 | 60.7 | 59.4 | 57.7 |
| 2012 | 56.1 | 55.7 | 56.4 | 58.3 | 59.2 | 59.8 | 59.9 | 60.6 | 60.4 | 60.1 | 58.8 | 57.4 | 58.6 |
| 2013 | 55.1 | 54.6 | 55.2 | 56.0 | 58.1 | 59.6 | 60.3 | 60.5 | 59.5 | 60.0 | 59.1 | 58.5 | 58.0 |
| 2014 | 56.7 | 56.6 | 57.1 | 58.6 | 61.4 | 63.3 | 63.8 | 63.7 | 63.5 | 63.5 | 61.7 | 60.8 | 60.9 |
| 2015 | 58.3 | 57.4 | 56.7 | 57.1 | 57.3 | 57.3 | 58.2 | 58.2 | 57.5 | 57.4 | 54.9 | 53.1 | 57.0 |
| 2016 | 50.2 | 49.0 | 48.7 | 49.5 | 49.6 | 49.5 | 50.1 | 50.0 | 49.3 | 49.1 | 48.4 | 47.3 | 49.2 |
| 2017 | 45.2 | 45.2 | 45.8 | 47.5 | 48.9 | 49.8 | 50.3 | 50.6 | 50.7 | 50.4 | 49.9 | 49.1 | 48.6 |
| 2018 | 47.6 | 47.2 | 47.7 | 48.6 | 50.1 | 51.3 | 52.1 | 53.1 | 52.5 | 53.3 | 53.3 | 52.6 | 50.8 |
| 2019 | 51.4 | 51.1 | 51.5 | 52.6 | 54.2 | 55.1 | 55.6 | 56.2 | 55.0 | 54.7 | 54.0 | 52.2 | 53.6 |
| **Service-Providing** | | | | | | | | | | | | | |
| 2011 | 223.3 | 225.1 | 226.9 | 226.8 | 232.3 | 238.4 | 237.0 | 236.8 | 237.9 | 233.9 | 229.6 | 232.3 | 231.7 |
| 2012 | 227.1 | 228.9 | 230.3 | 229.5 | 235.0 | 241.0 | 239.3 | 238.6 | 238.7 | 236.0 | 232.2 | 234.5 | 234.3 |
| 2013 | 228.8 | 229.9 | 231.8 | 231.6 | 237.1 | 243.6 | 241.2 | 240.5 | 240.6 | 238.2 | 233.3 | 234.7 | 235.9 |
| 2014 | 230.0 | 231.0 | 232.5 | 232.8 | 238.6 | 244.1 | 243.1 | 242.1 | 242.0 | 240.7 | 234.7 | 238.0 | 237.5 |
| 2015 | 233.3 | 234.4 | 236.1 | 236.1 | 241.4 | 246.6 | 245.3 | 244.5 | 244.6 | 242.2 | 236.3 | 238.4 | 239.9 |
| 2016 | 232.9 | 233.4 | 234.5 | 233.2 | 238.5 | 244.1 | 241.5 | 240.6 | 239.8 | 236.7 | 231.3 | 233.1 | 236.6 |
| 2017 | 228.9 | 229.9 | 231.2 | 230.3 | 236.6 | 242.3 | 240.2 | 240.5 | 239.9 | 236.0 | 230.8 | 232.9 | 235.0 |
| 2018 | 228.5 | 229.2 | 230.5 | 231.0 | 237.1 | 242.4 | 240.6 | 239.8 | 239.1 | 236.7 | 232.1 | 233.9 | 235.1 |
| 2019 | 229.5 | 231.5 | 232.2 | 231.7 | 238.1 | 243.4 | 241.6 | 241.7 | 240.5 | 235.9 | 231.3 | 233.6 | 235.9 |
| **Mining and Logging** | | | | | | | | | | | | | |
| 2011 | 26.2 | 26.2 | 26.3 | 26.4 | 26.7 | 27.3 | 27.8 | 28.1 | 28.2 | 28.5 | 28.6 | 28.8 | 27.4 |
| 2012 | 28.3 | 28.3 | 28.1 | 27.8 | 27.8 | 28.1 | 27.8 | 27.7 | 27.3 | 27.3 | 27.4 | 27.3 | 27.8 |
| 2013 | 26.6 | 26.5 | 26.5 | 26.4 | 26.3 | 26.6 | 26.8 | 26.9 | 26.7 | 26.8 | 26.8 | 27.0 | 26.7 |
| 2014 | 26.9 | 26.8 | 26.9 | 26.9 | 27.0 | 27.4 | 27.6 | 27.8 | 27.7 | 27.8 | 27.9 | 27.9 | 27.4 |
| 2015 | 27.4 | 26.6 | 25.7 | 24.5 | 23.8 | 23.4 | 23.4 | 23.2 | 22.8 | 22.8 | 22.0 | 21.7 | 23.9 |
| 2016 | 21.2 | 20.5 | 19.8 | 19.0 | 18.3 | 18.1 | 18.1 | 18.0 | 18.0 | 18.3 | 18.4 | 18.6 | 18.9 |
| 2017 | 18.5 | 18.7 | 18.9 | 19.1 | 19.4 | 19.7 | 19.8 | 20.0 | 20.1 | 20.4 | 20.6 | 20.7 | 19.7 |
| 2018 | 20.6 | 20.5 | 20.6 | 20.3 | 20.3 | 20.6 | 20.8 | 21.0 | 20.9 | 21.2 | 21.1 | 21.0 | 20.7 |
| 2019 | 21.1 | 21.0 | 21.0 | 20.7 | 20.8 | 21.1 | 20.7 | 20.7 | 20.6 | 20.5 | 21.0 | 20.9 | 20.8 |
| **Construction** | | | | | | | | | | | | | |
| 2011 | 17.9 | 17.8 | 18.3 | 19.3 | 20.9 | 22.1 | 23.0 | 23.3 | 23.8 | 23.5 | 22.5 | 21.0 | 21.1 |
| 2012 | 18.6 | 18.2 | 19.2 | 21.5 | 22.3 | 22.4 | 22.7 | 23.6 | 23.7 | 23.1 | 21.8 | 20.6 | 21.5 |
| 2013 | 19.1 | 18.8 | 19.6 | 20.5 | 22.6 | 23.5 | 23.9 | 24.0 | 23.1 | 23.2 | 22.4 | 21.6 | 21.9 |
| 2014 | 20.2 | 20.3 | 20.6 | 22.3 | 24.8 | 26.1 | 26.3 | 26.0 | 25.9 | 25.6 | 23.7 | 22.8 | 23.7 |
| 2015 | 21.0 | 21.0 | 21.5 | 23.1 | 23.8 | 24.2 | 25.0 | 25.2 | 24.9 | 24.7 | 23.1 | 21.7 | 23.3 |
| 2016 | 19.6 | 19.3 | 19.8 | 21.5 | 22.3 | 22.2 | 22.7 | 22.7 | 22.1 | 21.5 | 20.6 | 19.4 | 21.1 |
| 2017 | 17.5 | 17.4 | 17.7 | 19.4 | 20.4 | 20.8 | 21.0 | 21.0 | 21.0 | 20.3 | 19.5 | 18.7 | 19.6 |
| 2018 | 17.4 | 17.2 | 17.7 | 19.0 | 20.3 | 21.0 | 21.5 | 22.2 | 21.6 | 21.9 | 22.1 | 21.5 | 20.3 |
| 2019 | 20.2 | 20.1 | 20.6 | 22.0 | 23.5 | 23.9 | 24.8 | 25.3 | 24.2 | 23.9 | 22.7 | 21.1 | 22.7 |

# 1. Employment by Industry: Wyoming, 2011–2019—*Continued*

(Numbers in thousands, not seasonally adjusted)

| Industry and year | January | February | March | April | May | June | July | August | September | October | November | December | Annual average |
|---|---|---|---|---|---|---|---|---|---|---|---|---|---|
| **Manufacturing** | | | | | | | | | | | | | |
| 2011 | 8.8 | 8.7 | 8.6 | 8.8 | 8.9 | 9.1 | 9.1 | 9.3 | 9.3 | 9.6 | 9.6 | 9.6 | 9.1 |
| 2012 | 9.2 | 9.2 | 9.1 | 9.0 | 9.1 | 9.3 | 9.4 | 9.3 | 9.4 | 9.7 | 9.6 | 9.5 | 9.3 |
| 2013 | 9.4 | 9.3 | 9.1 | 9.1 | 9.2 | 9.5 | 9.6 | 9.6 | 9.7 | 10.0 | 9.9 | 9.9 | 9.5 |
| 2014 | 9.6 | 9.5 | 9.6 | 9.4 | 9.6 | 9.8 | 9.9 | 9.9 | 9.9 | 10.1 | 10.1 | 10.1 | 9.8 |
| | | | | | | | | | | | | | |
| 2015 | 9.9 | 9.8 | 9.5 | 9.5 | 9.7 | 9.7 | 9.8 | 9.8 | 9.8 | 9.9 | 9.8 | 9.7 | 9.7 |
| 2016 | 9.4 | 9.2 | 9.1 | 9.0 | 9.0 | 9.2 | 9.3 | 9.3 | 9.2 | 9.3 | 9.4 | 9.3 | 9.2 |
| 2017 | 9.2 | 9.1 | 9.2 | 9.0 | 9.1 | 9.3 | 9.5 | 9.6 | 9.6 | 9.7 | 9.8 | 9.7 | 9.4 |
| 2018 | 9.6 | 9.5 | 9.4 | 9.3 | 9.5 | 9.7 | 9.8 | 9.9 | 10.0 | 10.2 | 10.1 | 10.1 | 9.8 |
| 2019 | 10.1 | 10.0 | 9.9 | 9.9 | 9.9 | 10.1 | 10.1 | 10.2 | 10.2 | 10.3 | 10.3 | 10.2 | 10.1 |
| | | | | | | | | | | | | | |
| **Trade, Transportation, and Utilities** | | | | | | | | | | | | | |
| 2011 | 50.7 | 50.6 | 50.8 | 51.3 | 52.2 | 53.4 | 54.0 | 54.0 | 53.5 | 52.8 | 53.1 | 53.5 | 52.5 |
| 2012 | 52.0 | 51.7 | 52.0 | 52.4 | 53.3 | 54.3 | 54.6 | 54.6 | 53.7 | 53.4 | 53.7 | 54.3 | 53.3 |
| 2013 | 52.2 | 52.1 | 52.4 | 52.5 | 53.9 | 55.1 | 55.6 | 55.5 | 54.4 | 54.3 | 54.5 | 54.9 | 54.0 |
| 2014 | 53.3 | 53.0 | 53.2 | 53.5 | 54.6 | 55.8 | 56.2 | 56.4 | 55.4 | 55.5 | 55.6 | 56.4 | 54.9 |
| | | | | | | | | | | | | | |
| 2015 | 55.0 | 54.7 | 55.1 | 55.1 | 55.7 | 56.9 | 57.2 | 56.9 | 55.8 | 55.5 | 55.5 | 55.9 | 55.8 |
| 2016 | 54.3 | 53.6 | 53.4 | 52.9 | 53.4 | 54.4 | 54.7 | 54.3 | 53.2 | 52.9 | 52.8 | 52.8 | 53.6 |
| 2017 | 51.3 | 50.8 | 50.8 | 50.8 | 51.7 | 53.0 | 53.6 | 53.5 | 52.6 | 51.8 | 51.9 | 52.2 | 52.0 |
| 2018 | 51.0 | 50.5 | 50.6 | 51.0 | 51.9 | 53.1 | 53.4 | 53.2 | 52.5 | 51.9 | 52.3 | 52.6 | 52.0 |
| 2019 | 51.2 | 51.0 | 51.1 | 51.2 | 51.9 | 53.1 | 53.2 | 53.0 | 52.2 | 51.8 | 51.8 | 51.9 | 52.0 |
| | | | | | | | | | | | | | |
| **Wholesale Trade** | | | | | | | | | | | | | |
| 2011 | 8.4 | 8.5 | 8.5 | 8.6 | 8.7 | 8.8 | 8.8 | 8.8 | 8.8 | 8.8 | 8.9 | 8.9 | 8.7 |
| 2012 | 8.9 | 8.9 | 9.0 | 9.2 | 9.2 | 9.2 | 9.1 | 9.1 | 9.0 | 9.0 | 9.0 | 9.1 | 9.1 |
| 2013 | 8.9 | 8.9 | 9.0 | 9.0 | 9.1 | 9.1 | 9.1 | 9.1 | 9.1 | 9.2 | 9.2 | 9.2 | 9.1 |
| 2014 | 9.2 | 9.2 | 9.2 | 9.3 | 9.4 | 9.5 | 9.5 | 9.5 | 9.4 | 9.5 | 9.5 | 9.6 | 9.4 |
| | | | | | | | | | | | | | |
| 2015 | 9.5 | 9.5 | 9.6 | 9.5 | 9.5 | 9.5 | 9.4 | 9.3 | 9.2 | 9.2 | 9.1 | 9.1 | 9.4 |
| 2016 | 9.0 | 8.9 | 8.8 | 8.6 | 8.5 | 8.3 | 8.3 | 8.2 | 8.1 | 8.1 | 8.0 | 8.0 | 8.4 |
| 2017 | 7.9 | 7.9 | 8.0 | 8.0 | 8.0 | 8.1 | 8.1 | 8.1 | 8.1 | 8.0 | 8.0 | 8.0 | 8.0 |
| 2018 | 8.0 | 8.0 | 8.1 | 8.1 | 8.2 | 8.3 | 8.3 | 8.3 | 8.2 | 8.3 | 8.3 | 8.4 | 8.2 |
| 2019 | 8.3 | 8.3 | 8.4 | 8.4 | 8.4 | 8.5 | 8.5 | 8.4 | 8.4 | 8.3 | 8.3 | 8.4 | 8.4 |
| | | | | | | | | | | | | | |
| **Retail Trade** | | | | | | | | | | | | | |
| 2011 | 28.2 | 27.9 | 28.1 | 28.4 | 29.0 | 29.9 | 30.4 | 30.3 | 29.8 | 29.3 | 29.5 | 29.7 | 29.2 |
| 2012 | 28.5 | 28.2 | 28.3 | 28.5 | 29.3 | 30.3 | 30.6 | 30.5 | 29.8 | 29.6 | 29.9 | 30.1 | 29.5 |
| 2013 | 28.5 | 28.3 | 28.5 | 28.6 | 29.7 | 30.7 | 31.1 | 30.9 | 30.0 | 29.8 | 30.0 | 30.2 | 29.7 |
| 2014 | 28.7 | 28.5 | 28.7 | 28.9 | 29.7 | 30.6 | 30.9 | 30.9 | 30.1 | 30.1 | 30.1 | 30.5 | 29.8 |
| | | | | | | | | | | | | | |
| 2015 | 29.3 | 29.3 | 29.6 | 30.0 | 30.7 | 31.6 | 32.1 | 31.9 | 31.2 | 31.1 | 31.2 | 31.4 | 30.8 |
| 2016 | 30.2 | 30.0 | 30.0 | 30.0 | 30.6 | 31.6 | 31.8 | 31.6 | 30.8 | 30.6 | 30.5 | 30.4 | 30.7 |
| 2017 | 29.3 | 28.8 | 28.7 | 28.8 | 29.6 | 30.7 | 31.1 | 31.0 | 30.1 | 29.4 | 29.6 | 29.5 | 29.7 |
| 2018 | 28.5 | 28.2 | 28.2 | 28.6 | 29.4 | 30.2 | 30.5 | 30.3 | 29.7 | 29.1 | 29.4 | 29.3 | 29.3 |
| 2019 | 28.4 | 28.2 | 28.2 | 28.3 | 28.9 | 29.7 | 29.8 | 29.7 | 29.1 | 28.8 | 28.7 | 28.6 | 28.9 |
| | | | | | | | | | | | | | |
| **Transportation and Utilities** | | | | | | | | | | | | | |
| 2011 | 14.1 | 14.2 | 14.2 | 14.3 | 14.5 | 14.7 | 14.8 | 14.9 | 14.9 | 14.7 | 14.7 | 14.9 | 14.6 |
| 2012 | 14.6 | 14.6 | 14.7 | 14.7 | 14.8 | 14.8 | 14.9 | 15.0 | 14.9 | 14.8 | 14.8 | 15.1 | 14.8 |
| 2013 | 14.8 | 14.9 | 14.9 | 14.9 | 15.1 | 15.3 | 15.4 | 15.5 | 15.3 | 15.3 | 15.3 | 15.5 | 15.2 |
| 2014 | 15.4 | 15.3 | 15.3 | 15.3 | 15.5 | 15.7 | 15.8 | 16.0 | 15.9 | 15.9 | 16.0 | 16.3 | 15.7 |
| | | | | | | | | | | | | | |
| 2015 | 16.2 | 15.9 | 15.9 | 15.6 | 15.5 | 15.8 | 15.7 | 15.7 | 15.4 | 15.2 | 15.2 | 15.4 | 15.6 |
| 2016 | 15.1 | 14.7 | 14.6 | 14.3 | 14.3 | 14.5 | 14.6 | 14.5 | 14.3 | 14.2 | 14.3 | 14.4 | 14.5 |
| 2017 | 14.1 | 14.1 | 14.1 | 14.0 | 14.1 | 14.2 | 14.4 | 14.4 | 14.4 | 14.4 | 14.3 | 14.7 | 14.3 |
| 2018 | 14.5 | 14.3 | 14.3 | 14.3 | 14.3 | 14.6 | 14.6 | 14.6 | 14.6 | 14.5 | 14.6 | 14.9 | 14.5 |
| 2019 | 14.5 | 14.5 | 14.5 | 14.5 | 14.6 | 14.9 | 14.9 | 14.9 | 14.7 | 14.7 | 14.8 | 14.9 | 14.7 |
| | | | | | | | | | | | | | |
| **Information** | | | | | | | | | | | | | |
| 2011 | 3.8 | 3.8 | 3.8 | 3.8 | 3.9 | 3.9 | 3.9 | 3.9 | 3.8 | 3.8 | 3.8 | 3.9 | 3.8 |
| 2012 | 3.9 | 3.9 | 3.9 | 3.9 | 3.9 | 4.0 | 4.0 | 4.0 | 3.9 | 3.8 | 3.9 | 3.9 | 3.9 |
| 2013 | 3.8 | 3.8 | 3.8 | 3.7 | 3.8 | 3.8 | 3.8 | 3.8 | 3.8 | 3.8 | 3.8 | 3.8 | 3.8 |
| 2014 | 3.8 | 3.7 | 3.7 | 3.7 | 3.8 | 3.8 | 3.8 | 3.8 | 3.8 | 3.8 | 3.8 | 3.8 | 3.8 |
| | | | | | | | | | | | | | |
| 2015 | 3.8 | 3.8 | 3.8 | 3.8 | 3.8 | 3.8 | 3.8 | 3.8 | 3.8 | 3.8 | 3.7 | 3.8 | 3.8 |
| 2016 | 3.8 | 3.8 | 3.7 | 3.7 | 3.7 | 3.8 | 3.8 | 3.8 | 3.7 | 3.7 | 3.7 | 3.7 | 3.7 |
| 2017 | 3.7 | 3.7 | 3.7 | 3.7 | 3.7 | 3.7 | 3.7 | 3.7 | 3.7 | 3.6 | 3.6 | 3.7 | 3.7 |
| 2018 | 3.6 | 3.6 | 3.6 | 3.6 | 3.6 | 3.6 | 3.6 | 3.5 | 3.5 | 3.5 | 3.4 | 3.5 | 3.6 |
| 2019 | 3.4 | 3.4 | 3.4 | 3.4 | 3.4 | 3.4 | 3.4 | 3.4 | 3.4 | 3.4 | 3.4 | 3.4 | 3.4 |

## 1. Employment by Industry: Wyoming, 2011–2019—*Continued*

(Numbers in thousands, not seasonally adjusted)

| Industry and year | January | February | March | April | May | June | July | August | September | October | November | December | Annual average |
|---|---|---|---|---|---|---|---|---|---|---|---|---|---|
| **Financial Activities** | | | | | | | | | | | | | |
| 2011 | 10.7 | 10.6 | 10.6 | 10.7 | 10.7 | 10.8 | 10.8 | 10.9 | 10.8 | 10.7 | 10.7 | 10.7 | 10.7 |
| 2012 | 10.6 | 10.6 | 10.7 | 10.6 | 10.7 | 10.9 | 10.9 | 11.0 | 10.8 | 10.9 | 10.8 | 10.8 | 10.8 |
| 2013 | 10.9 | 10.9 | 10.9 | 11.0 | 11.1 | 11.3 | 11.4 | 11.4 | 11.3 | 11.2 | 11.2 | 11.2 | 11.2 |
| 2014 | 11.0 | 11.0 | 11.0 | 11.0 | 11.2 | 11.4 | 11.4 | 11.5 | 11.4 | 11.4 | 11.3 | 11.4 | 11.3 |
| 2015 | 11.2 | 11.2 | 11.1 | 11.1 | 11.0 | 11.1 | 11.3 | 11.2 | 11.1 | 11.0 | 11.0 | 11.0 | 11.1 |
| 2016 | 10.9 | 10.9 | 10.8 | 10.8 | 10.8 | 11.0 | 11.0 | 10.9 | 10.8 | 10.7 | 10.7 | 10.8 | 10.8 |
| 2017 | 10.7 | 10.7 | 10.7 | 10.7 | 10.8 | 11.1 | 11.0 | 11.0 | 11.0 | 11.0 | 10.9 | 11.1 | 10.9 |
| 2018 | 10.9 | 10.9 | 10.9 | 11.0 | 11.1 | 11.2 | 11.3 | 11.3 | 11.1 | 11.1 | 11.1 | 11.2 | 11.1 |
| 2019 | 11.0 | 11.1 | 11.1 | 11.1 | 11.1 | 11.2 | 11.3 | 11.3 | 11.2 | 11.4 | 11.2 | 11.2 | 11.2 |
| **Professional and Business Services** | | | | | | | | | | | | | |
| 2011 | 16.5 | 16.5 | 16.7 | 17.2 | 17.9 | 18.6 | 18.9 | 19.3 | 18.6 | 18.3 | 18.0 | 17.8 | 17.9 |
| 2012 | 17.2 | 17.3 | 17.4 | 17.8 | 18.1 | 19.0 | 18.8 | 19.1 | 18.5 | 18.3 | 17.8 | 17.7 | 18.1 |
| 2013 | 17.0 | 17.1 | 17.3 | 17.9 | 18.4 | 19.1 | 19.2 | 19.1 | 18.6 | 18.6 | 18.4 | 17.8 | 18.2 |
| 2014 | 17.2 | 17.5 | 17.6 | 18.2 | 18.8 | 19.3 | 19.6 | 19.5 | 19.0 | 19.0 | 18.4 | 18.3 | 18.5 |
| 2015 | 17.6 | 17.7 | 17.7 | 18.3 | 18.8 | 19.2 | 19.7 | 19.7 | 19.1 | 18.8 | 18.3 | 18.0 | 18.6 |
| 2016 | 17.1 | 17.0 | 17.0 | 17.6 | 18.0 | 18.5 | 18.8 | 18.8 | 18.3 | 18.1 | 17.5 | 17.6 | 17.9 |
| 2017 | 17.2 | 17.2 | 17.3 | 17.7 | 18.2 | 18.7 | 19.1 | 19.2 | 18.8 | 18.5 | 18.0 | 17.9 | 18.2 |
| 2018 | 17.4 | 17.2 | 17.5 | 18.1 | 18.8 | 19.4 | 19.8 | 19.8 | 19.4 | 19.4 | 19.1 | 18.8 | 18.7 |
| 2019 | 18.0 | 18.3 | 18.3 | 18.7 | 19.3 | 20.0 | 20.3 | 20.2 | 19.7 | 19.7 | 19.0 | 18.3 | 19.2 |
| **Education and Health Services** | | | | | | | | | | | | | |
| 2011 | 26.9 | 27.2 | 27.4 | 27.0 | 27.1 | 26.1 | 25.8 | 26.1 | 26.9 | 26.9 | 26.6 | 26.9 | 26.7 |
| 2012 | 26.5 | 26.7 | 26.7 | 26.6 | 26.7 | 26.0 | 25.8 | 26.2 | 26.9 | 26.9 | 27.0 | 27.1 | 26.6 |
| 2013 | 26.8 | 26.8 | 27.2 | 27.1 | 27.1 | 26.5 | 26.2 | 26.5 | 27.1 | 27.1 | 27.1 | 27.1 | 26.9 |
| 2014 | 27.0 | 27.0 | 27.1 | 27.2 | 27.3 | 26.5 | 26.2 | 26.4 | 27.0 | 27.5 | 26.9 | 26.9 | 26.9 |
| 2015 | 26.9 | 26.9 | 27.0 | 27.3 | 27.4 | 26.6 | 26.5 | 26.6 | 27.4 | 28.0 | 27.4 | 27.7 | 27.1 |
| 2016 | 27.4 | 27.7 | 28.0 | 28.1 | 28.0 | 27.2 | 27.1 | 27.0 | 27.8 | 28.0 | 27.8 | 27.7 | 27.7 |
| 2017 | 27.7 | 27.8 | 27.9 | 27.8 | 28.0 | 27.4 | 26.9 | 27.1 | 28.0 | 28.0 | 27.9 | 28.2 | 27.7 |
| 2018 | 28.3 | 28.4 | 28.6 | 28.5 | 28.6 | 27.9 | 27.5 | 27.6 | 28.3 | 28.5 | 28.4 | 28.5 | 28.3 |
| 2019 | 28.5 | 28.8 | 28.8 | 28.6 | 28.8 | 28.1 | 27.8 | 28.1 | 28.7 | 28.5 | 28.8 | 29.1 | 28.6 |
| **Leisure and Hospitality** | | | | | | | | | | | | | |
| 2011 | 29.8 | 29.8 | 30.2 | 29.3 | 31.7 | 37.1 | 39.1 | 38.9 | 36.7 | 33.1 | 29.6 | 31.5 | 33.1 |
| 2012 | 30.6 | 30.7 | 31.1 | 30.4 | 32.7 | 38.1 | 40.1 | 39.8 | 36.8 | 33.9 | 30.7 | 32.1 | 33.9 |
| 2013 | 31.3 | 31.3 | 31.7 | 31.1 | 33.4 | 39.0 | 40.9 | 40.5 | 38.0 | 34.8 | 31.0 | 32.5 | 34.6 |
| 2014 | 32.1 | 32.1 | 32.3 | 31.9 | 34.3 | 39.9 | 41.6 | 41.5 | 38.4 | 35.5 | 31.4 | 33.5 | 35.4 |
| 2015 | 33.2 | 33.2 | 33.4 | 32.9 | 35.5 | 40.8 | 42.5 | 42.0 | 39.2 | 36.0 | 31.8 | 33.3 | 36.2 |
| 2016 | 32.8 | 32.6 | 32.9 | 32.0 | 35.1 | 40.8 | 42.3 | 42.0 | 38.8 | 35.8 | 31.7 | 33.2 | 35.8 |
| 2017 | 33.1 | 33.0 | 33.4 | 32.5 | 35.7 | 41.0 | 42.7 | 42.6 | 39.4 | 36.3 | 32.4 | 33.7 | 36.3 |
| 2018 | 33.5 | 33.4 | 33.5 | 32.9 | 36.4 | 41.3 | 42.8 | 42.0 | 38.8 | 36.4 | 32.3 | 33.9 | 36.4 |
| 2019 | 34.0 | 34.0 | 34.0 | 33.3 | 36.6 | 41.4 | 43.3 | 42.7 | 39.7 | 35.2 | 31.3 | 33.9 | 36.6 |
| **Other Services** | | | | | | | | | | | | | |
| 2011 | 14.3 | 14.4 | 14.6 | 14.8 | 14.8 | 15.2 | 15.4 | 15.2 | 15.1 | 15.1 | 15.0 | 15.0 | 14.9 |
| 2012 | 15.0 | 15.0 | 15.1 | 15.2 | 15.3 | 15.6 | 15.6 | 15.6 | 15.5 | 15.3 | 15.2 | 15.3 | 15.3 |
| 2013 | 15.2 | 15.2 | 15.3 | 15.5 | 15.5 | 15.8 | 15.9 | 15.7 | 15.5 | 15.7 | 15.1 | 15.0 | 15.5 |
| 2014 | 15.0 | 14.9 | 15.0 | 15.4 | 15.6 | 15.8 | 15.9 | 15.8 | 15.7 | 15.8 | 15.7 | 15.8 | 15.5 |
| 2015 | 15.8 | 15.9 | 16.0 | 16.0 | 16.2 | 16.5 | 16.6 | 16.4 | 16.2 | 16.2 | 16.1 | 16.1 | 16.2 |
| 2016 | 16.0 | 15.9 | 16.1 | 16.1 | 16.2 | 16.1 | 16.1 | 16.0 | 16.0 | 15.9 | 15.8 | 15.8 | 16.0 |
| 2017 | 15.8 | 15.8 | 15.9 | 16.1 | 16.3 | 16.6 | 16.7 | 16.6 | 16.4 | 16.4 | 16.2 | 16.2 | 16.3 |
| 2018 | 16.1 | 16.1 | 16.2 | 16.3 | 16.4 | 16.6 | 16.6 | 16.5 | 16.2 | 16.1 | 16.1 | 16.1 | 16.3 |
| 2019 | 16.0 | 16.0 | 16.0 | 16.0 | 16.1 | 16.4 | 16.5 | 16.4 | 16.3 | 16.2 | 16.3 | 16.3 | 16.2 |
| **Government** | | | | | | | | | | | | | |
| 2011 | 70.6 | 72.2 | 72.8 | 72.7 | 74.0 | 73.3 | 69.1 | 68.5 | 72.5 | 73.2 | 72.8 | 73.0 | 72.1 |
| 2012 | 71.3 | 73.0 | 73.4 | 72.6 | 74.3 | 73.1 | 69.5 | 68.3 | 72.6 | 73.5 | 73.1 | 73.3 | 72.3 |
| 2013 | 71.6 | 72.7 | 73.2 | 72.8 | 73.9 | 73.0 | 68.2 | 68.0 | 71.9 | 72.7 | 72.2 | 72.4 | 71.9 |
| 2014 | 70.6 | 71.8 | 72.6 | 71.9 | 73.0 | 71.6 | 68.4 | 67.2 | 71.3 | 72.2 | 71.6 | 71.9 | 71.2 |
| 2015 | 69.8 | 71.0 | 72.0 | 71.6 | 73.0 | 71.7 | 67.7 | 67.9 | 72.0 | 73.0 | 72.5 | 72.6 | 71.2 |
| 2016 | 70.6 | 71.9 | 72.6 | 72.0 | 73.3 | 72.3 | 67.7 | 67.8 | 71.2 | 71.6 | 71.3 | 71.5 | 71.2 |
| 2017 | 69.4 | 70.9 | 71.5 | 71.0 | 72.2 | 70.8 | 66.5 | 66.8 | 70.0 | 70.4 | 69.9 | 69.9 | 69.9 |
| 2018 | 67.7 | 69.1 | 69.6 | 69.6 | 70.3 | 69.3 | 65.6 | 65.9 | 69.3 | 69.8 | 69.4 | 69.3 | 68.7 |
| 2019 | 67.4 | 68.9 | 69.5 | 69.4 | 70.9 | 69.8 | 65.8 | 66.6 | 69.3 | 69.7 | 69.5 | 69.5 | 68.9 |

## 2. Average Weekly Hours by Selected Industry: Wyoming, 2015–2019

(Not seasonally adjusted)

| Industry and year | January | February | March | April | May | June | July | August | September | October | November | December | Annual average |
|---|---|---|---|---|---|---|---|---|---|---|---|---|---|
| **Total Private** | | | | | | | | | | | | | |
| 2015 | 34.7 | 35.9 | 35.4 | 34.9 | 35.3 | 35.8 | 35.6 | 36.3 | 34.5 | 34.4 | 34.8 | 33.4 | 35.1 |
| 2016 | 33.5 | 33.4 | 33.3 | 32.1 | 33.1 | 32.9 | 33.2 | 33.7 | 33.3 | 34.0 | 33.2 | 32.5 | 33.2 |
| 2017 | 33.5 | 33.0 | 33.0 | 34.4 | 34.0 | 34.6 | 35.3 | 34.8 | 34.3 | 35.2 | 34.6 | 33.7 | 34.2 |
| 2018 | 33.8 | 33.8 | 34.2 | 34.7 | 34.2 | 34.9 | 35.3 | 35.4 | 36.0 | 34.9 | 35.5 | 36.0 | 34.9 |
| 2019 | 34.9 | 35.2 | 34.3 | 35.0 | 35.4 | 36.7 | 35.9 | 36.4 | 36.6 | 35.6 | 35.4 | 35.6 | 35.6 |
| **Goods-Producing** | | | | | | | | | | | | | |
| 2015 | 40.2 | 40.6 | 40.0 | 40.0 | 41.4 | 41.5 | 41.5 | 41.9 | 39.7 | 41.6 | 41.3 | 39.8 | 40.8 |
| 2016 | 39.2 | 38.4 | 39.4 | 40.0 | 40.4 | 39.8 | 40.0 | 41.4 | 40.8 | 41.5 | 41.2 | 38.7 | 40.1 |
| 2017 | 38.7 | 39.2 | 39.3 | 41.0 | 41.5 | 41.8 | 41.2 | 41.1 | 40.2 | 41.4 | 41.4 | 39.4 | 40.6 |
| 2018 | 40.2 | 39.7 | 40.4 | 41.2 | 41.7 | 42.4 | 42.2 | 42.7 | 42.7 | 41.9 | 43.4 | 44.0 | 41.9 |
| 2019 | 42.5 | 42.7 | 41.0 | 42.3 | 43.3 | 44.1 | 43.4 | 44.4 | 44.1 | 43.4 | 42.9 | 43.0 | 43.1 |
| **Mining and Logging** | | | | | | | | | | | | | |
| 2015 | 43.8 | 44.5 | 44.0 | 42.9 | 44.0 | 42.5 | 42.8 | 43.0 | 41.7 | 42.6 | 43.1 | 42.5 | 43.2 |
| 2016 | 41.7 | 41.5 | 41.4 | 41.5 | 40.0 | 40.5 | 41.7 | 42.9 | 42.6 | 43.7 | 43.1 | 41.6 | 41.9 |
| 2017 | 42.0 | 41.0 | 41.8 | 42.2 | 44.1 | 45.1 | 44.3 | 43.6 | 42.5 | 43.8 | 45.9 | 44.2 | 43.4 |
| 2018 | 44.0 | 43.2 | 43.9 | 44.9 | 43.8 | 45.0 | 45.9 | 45.7 | 46.9 | 44.5 | 46.7 | 49.4 | 45.3 |
| 2019 | 45.1 | 47.0 | 46.4 | 45.6 | 44.4 | 46.7 | 46.8 | 46.7 | 48.2 | 46.5 | 46.5 | 47.7 | 46.5 |
| **Construction** | | | | | | | | | | | | | |
| 2015 | 39.0 | 39.3 | 38.8 | 39.3 | 40.7 | 41.6 | 41.3 | 41.8 | 39.9 | 42.0 | 41.0 | 39.2 | 40.4 |
| 2016 | 37.7 | 36.7 | 38.6 | 39.1 | 40.5 | 39.3 | 39.3 | 41.2 | 40.3 | 40.5 | 40.4 | 38.3 | 39.3 |
| 2017 | 37.7 | 39.9 | 39.3 | 42.1 | 41.6 | 41.1 | 40.4 | 40.4 | 39.3 | 40.8 | 39.4 | 39.0 | 40.1 |
| 2018 | 38.0 | 37.6 | 38.5 | 39.4 | 41.5 | 43.1 | 42.5 | 43.6 | 42.6 | 42.7 | 44.3 | 43.3 | 41.6 |
| 2019 | 41.3 | 40.6 | 38.3 | 41.0 | 43.2 | 43.0 | 41.5 | 43.3 | 41.9 | 41.4 | 40.9 | 40.0 | 41.4 |
| **Trade, Transportation, and Utilities** | | | | | | | | | | | | | |
| 2015 | 34.9 | 36.1 | 35.7 | 35.0 | 35.0 | 36.0 | 35.6 | 35.8 | 35.2 | 34.6 | 34.6 | 33.8 | 35.2 |
| 2016 | 33.4 | 33.7 | 33.3 | 34.1 | 34.4 | 34.4 | 34.5 | 34.7 | 34.5 | 34.9 | 34.0 | 34.7 | 34.2 |
| 2017 | 35.1 | 33.8 | 34.0 | 35.1 | 34.3 | 34.7 | 35.9 | 34.9 | 34.6 | 35.7 | 35.2 | 35.0 | 34.8 |
| 2018 | 33.9 | 34.1 | 34.4 | 35.5 | 35.8 | 35.8 | 36.4 | 36.1 | 36.6 | 35.8 | 35.9 | 36.6 | 35.6 |
| 2019 | 35.7 | 35.4 | 34.7 | 35.1 | 35.8 | 36.9 | 35.8 | 36.0 | 36.5 | 35.8 | 35.5 | 36.2 | 35.8 |
| **Professional and Business Services** | | | | | | | | | | | | | |
| 2015 | 34.0 | 35.1 | 34.9 | 35.4 | 35.1 | 35.4 | 35.4 | 36.8 | 34.9 | 34.2 | 34.8 | 33.4 | 35.0 |
| 2016 | 33.5 | 34.4 | 33.9 | 34.6 | 35.2 | 34.8 | 34.4 | 35.4 | 34.5 | 34.6 | 33.9 | 33.3 | 34.4 |
| 2017 | 35.0 | 33.8 | 32.9 | 35.2 | 34.9 | 35.2 | 35.8 | 34.9 | 35.3 | 35.8 | 34.6 | 33.9 | 34.7 |
| 2018 | 32.9 | 33.3 | 33.3 | 34.0 | 33.4 | 34.3 | 34.0 | 34.3 | 33.6 | 32.7 | 33.2 | 32.2 | 33.4 |
| 2019 | 31.5 | 32.5 | 32.2 | 34.0 | 33.7 | 35.0 | 34.7 | 36.2 | 36.5 | 35.4 | 34.4 | 35.2 | 34.3 |
| **Education and Health Services** | | | | | | | | | | | | | |
| 2015 | 33.4 | 35.1 | 34.6 | 33.8 | 33.8 | 34.2 | 33.3 | 34.6 | 33.6 | 33.6 | 34.9 | 33.1 | 34.0 |
| 2016 | 33.9 | 34.2 | 34.2 | 34.3 | 35.4 | 35.4 | 35.3 | 35.0 | 35.2 | 36.2 | 35.2 | 34.7 | 34.9 |
| 2017 | 35.7 | 35.3 | 34.4 | 35.5 | 33.7 | 33.9 | 34.7 | 33.6 | 34.5 | 34.7 | 34.3 | 33.6 | 34.5 |
| 2018 | 33.6 | 34.1 | 34.1 | 34.9 | 33.1 | 33.3 | 33.8 | 33.3 | 34.7 | 33.4 | 33.0 | 34.1 | 33.8 |
| 2019 | 33.3 | 34.2 | 33.6 | 34.0 | 33.8 | 34.8 | 33.3 | 34.1 | 34.4 | 34.0 | 34.0 | 34.1 | 33.9 |
| **Leisure and Hospitality** | | | | | | | | | | | | | |
| 2015 | 26.1 | 27.4 | 27.2 | 25.9 | 26.7 | 28.6 | 29.5 | 30.2 | 28.3 | 25.2 | 25.0 | 24.5 | 27.2 |
| 2016 | 25.2 | 25.3 | 25.2 | 24.9 | 26.9 | 27.3 | 27.9 | 28.0 | 26.2 | 24.6 | 23.5 | 23.0 | 25.8 |
| 2017 | 24.5 | 24.5 | 24.7 | 23.5 | 24.5 | 27.4 | 28.7 | 28.7 | 26.9 | 25.6 | 24.1 | 24.4 | 25.8 |
| 2018 | 25.4 | 25.5 | 25.8 | 24.1 | 23.9 | 27.0 | 28.0 | 26.8 | 26.4 | 23.5 | 22.8 | 23.6 | 25.3 |
| 2019 | 23.3 | 23.8 | 23.5 | 22.1 | 23.7 | 27.0 | 27.6 | 27.5 | 27.2 | 25.1 | 24.5 | 24.6 | 25.2 |
| **Other Services** | | | | | | | | | | | | | |
| 2015 | 31.4 | 32.9 | 31.8 | 31.3 | 30.0 | 30.3 | 29.8 | 30.5 | 29.3 | 28.4 | 28.8 | 26.7 | 30.1 |
| 2016 | 26.2 | 27.0 | 26.4 | 26.4 | 27.2 | 27.2 | 27.7 | 26.8 | 27.1 | 29.0 | 27.1 | 26.7 | 27.1 |
| 2017 | 27.9 | 27.9 | 27.8 | 29.1 | 27.4 | 28.3 | 29.6 | 28.8 | 29.1 | 29.8 | 28.8 | 28.4 | 28.6 |
| 2018 | 28.0 | 29.0 | 28.2 | 29.3 | 29.1 | 30.3 | 31.9 | 32.2 | 31.8 | 31.3 | 29.4 | 30.4 | 30.1 |
| 2019 | 29.9 | 29.5 | 28.0 | 28.2 | 29.0 | 28.9 | 27.2 | 28.1 | 29.0 | 29.0 | 28.4 | 29.1 | 28.7 |

## 3. Average Hourly Earnings by Selected Industry: Wyoming, 2015–2019

(Dollars, not seasonally adjusted)

| Industry and year | January | February | March | April | May | June | July | August | September | October | November | December | Annual average |
|---|---|---|---|---|---|---|---|---|---|---|---|---|---|
| **Total Private** | | | | | | | | | | | | | |
| 2015 | 23.26 | 23.24 | 23.29 | 23.22 | 23.04 | 22.60 | 22.69 | 22.97 | 23.21 | 23.33 | 23.38 | 23.22 | 23.11 |
| 2016 | 23.01 | 23.16 | 23.21 | 23.49 | 23.27 | 22.65 | 22.72 | 22.83 | 23.25 | 23.76 | 23.77 | 23.65 | 23.22 |
| 2017 | 23.60 | 23.66 | 23.62 | 24.21 | 24.08 | 23.37 | 23.55 | 23.30 | 24.09 | 24.27 | 24.08 | 24.53 | 23.86 |
| 2018 | 24.71 | 24.73 | 24.78 | 25.22 | 25.23 | 24.98 | 25.06 | 25.15 | 25.79 | 25.98 | 26.49 | 26.37 | 25.39 |
| 2019 | 26.42 | 26.50 | 26.54 | 26.64 | 26.58 | 25.76 | 25.55 | 25.78 | 26.23 | 26.34 | 26.52 | 26.71 | 26.28 |
| **Goods-Producing** | | | | | | | | | | | | | |
| 2015 | 27.85 | 27.58 | 27.58 | 27.69 | 27.54 | 27.39 | 27.56 | 27.77 | 27.91 | 27.77 | 28.03 | 28.49 | 27.76 |
| 2016 | 28.55 | 28.63 | 28.65 | 28.47 | 28.64 | 27.99 | 27.95 | 28.09 | 28.47 | 28.77 | 28.39 | 28.57 | 28.43 |
| 2017 | 28.72 | 28.43 | 28.42 | 28.76 | 28.82 | 28.01 | 28.10 | 28.22 | 28.94 | 28.96 | 28.39 | 29.32 | 28.59 |
| 2018 | 29.68 | 29.29 | 29.37 | 29.64 | 29.71 | 29.21 | 29.13 | 29.37 | 29.97 | 29.98 | 30.22 | 30.06 | 29.65 |
| 2019 | 30.87 | 30.40 | 31.16 | 30.99 | 31.03 | 29.97 | 30.01 | 30.28 | 30.66 | 30.71 | 30.88 | 31.32 | 30.68 |
| **Mining and Logging** | | | | | | | | | | | | | |
| 2015 | 34.85 | 34.16 | 34.36 | 34.47 | 34.40 | 35.04 | 35.31 | 36.07 | 36.34 | 35.24 | 35.00 | 35.69 | 35.04 |
| 2016 | 36.30 | 35.79 | 35.89 | 35.35 | 35.77 | 35.87 | 34.82 | 34.14 | 35.14 | 35.54 | 34.95 | 35.10 | 35.40 |
| 2017 | 36.04 | 35.93 | 35.65 | 35.86 | 34.87 | 34.38 | 34.52 | 34.43 | 35.32 | 35.36 | 33.94 | 35.39 | 35.11 |
| 2018 | 35.05 | 34.16 | 34.06 | 34.38 | 34.68 | 33.92 | 33.62 | 33.79 | 34.36 | 34.99 | 34.74 | 33.60 | 34.27 |
| 2019 | 34.31 | 33.45 | 34.53 | 35.38 | 36.25 | 35.97 | 36.69 | 37.69 | 37.72 | 37.97 | 38.53 | 38.94 | 36.46 |
| **Construction** | | | | | | | | | | | | | |
| 2015 | 25.21 | 25.14 | 25.15 | 25.68 | 25.50 | 24.96 | 25.20 | 25.28 | 25.13 | 25.69 | 25.92 | 25.97 | 25.40 |
| 2016 | 25.31 | 25.48 | 25.70 | 25.78 | 26.48 | 25.05 | 25.32 | 26.23 | 25.89 | 26.17 | 25.84 | 26.06 | 25.79 |
| 2017 | 25.64 | 25.07 | 25.24 | 25.59 | 26.14 | 25.43 | 25.35 | 25.72 | 26.40 | 26.27 | 26.65 | 27.22 | 25.90 |
| 2018 | 27.59 | 27.36 | 27.57 | 27.95 | 28.06 | 27.16 | 26.99 | 27.36 | 28.03 | 28.13 | 28.20 | 28.24 | 27.73 |
| 2019 | 28.27 | 28.23 | 28.60 | 28.51 | 28.74 | 27.63 | 27.41 | 27.56 | 27.76 | 28.10 | 27.70 | 27.94 | 28.01 |
| **Trade, Transportation, and Utilities** | | | | | | | | | | | | | |
| 2015 | 21.33 | 21.51 | 21.95 | 21.71 | 21.30 | 21.10 | 21.31 | 21.60 | 20.91 | 20.65 | 20.75 | 20.39 | 21.21 |
| 2016 | 20.62 | 20.63 | 21.05 | 21.15 | 21.31 | 20.77 | 20.98 | 21.17 | 21.56 | 21.69 | 21.81 | 21.59 | 21.19 |
| 2017 | 21.96 | 22.04 | 22.03 | 22.68 | 22.21 | 22.07 | 22.41 | 22.01 | 22.18 | 22.20 | 22.08 | 22.19 | 22.17 |
| 2018 | 22.36 | 22.32 | 22.54 | 23.11 | 22.51 | 22.46 | 22.43 | 22.32 | 23.19 | 22.93 | 23.25 | 23.28 | 22.73 |
| 2019 | 23.33 | 23.54 | 23.69 | 23.70 | 24.40 | 23.52 | 23.13 | 23.60 | 24.52 | 24.42 | 24.46 | 24.90 | 23.93 |
| **Professional and Business Services** | | | | | | | | | | | | | |
| 2015 | 27.52 | 27.27 | 27.23 | 27.03 | 26.63 | 26.10 | 26.03 | 26.12 | 27.55 | 27.16 | 26.39 | 26.38 | 26.77 |
| 2016 | 25.83 | 25.77 | 25.86 | 26.10 | 25.93 | 25.90 | 25.90 | 26.15 | 26.53 | 27.40 | 27.17 | 27.71 | 26.35 |
| 2017 | 27.42 | 27.36 | 26.87 | 27.02 | 26.74 | 26.59 | 26.71 | 26.38 | 26.57 | 26.71 | 26.78 | 27.47 | 26.87 |
| 2018 | 27.93 | 28.05 | 27.16 | 28.09 | 28.07 | 27.79 | 27.72 | 27.51 | 28.90 | 29.14 | 29.77 | 30.08 | 28.35 |
| 2019 | 29.85 | 30.28 | 29.63 | 29.86 | 29.53 | 29.54 | 29.43 | 29.57 | 30.54 | 29.91 | 30.38 | 30.55 | 29.92 |
| **Education and Health Services** | | | | | | | | | | | | | |
| 2015 | 22.37 | 22.87 | 22.83 | 22.65 | 22.68 | 22.65 | 22.85 | 22.94 | 22.82 | 22.60 | 22.71 | 22.42 | 22.70 |
| 2016 | 22.05 | 22.16 | 21.96 | 21.97 | 22.18 | 21.91 | 22.19 | 22.11 | 22.03 | 22.30 | 21.99 | 22.14 | 22.08 |
| 2017 | 22.41 | 22.64 | 22.47 | 22.72 | 23.24 | 23.52 | 23.91 | 23.76 | 23.80 | 24.36 | 23.53 | 24.28 | 23.38 |
| 2018 | 24.06 | 23.61 | 23.62 | 23.41 | 24.00 | 24.35 | 25.11 | 24.79 | 24.50 | 25.15 | 25.33 | 24.90 | 24.39 |
| 2019 | 24.58 | 24.09 | 23.93 | 23.65 | 23.55 | 23.54 | 23.58 | 23.22 | 22.60 | 22.72 | 22.40 | 22.51 | 23.36 |
| **Leisure and Hospitality** | | | | | | | | | | | | | |
| 2015 | 14.06 | 14.30 | 14.14 | 13.91 | 13.56 | 13.44 | 13.36 | 13.46 | 13.70 | 13.68 | 13.63 | 13.74 | 13.72 |
| 2016 | 13.98 | 14.15 | 14.17 | 14.07 | 13.52 | 13.68 | 13.89 | 13.90 | 14.26 | 14.21 | 14.21 | 14.44 | 14.02 |
| 2017 | 14.98 | 15.10 | 14.89 | 14.69 | 14.33 | 14.22 | 14.33 | 14.43 | 14.86 | 14.73 | 14.76 | 15.10 | 14.67 |
| 2018 | 16.03 | 16.08 | 16.15 | 15.59 | 15.60 | 15.34 | 15.43 | 15.66 | 15.63 | 15.44 | 15.42 | 15.95 | 15.68 |
| 2019 | 16.03 | 15.90 | 15.73 | 15.04 | 14.85 | 14.96 | 15.09 | 15.11 | 15.39 | 15.33 | 15.56 | 15.54 | 15.34 |
| **Other Services** | | | | | | | | | | | | | |
| 2015 | 19.93 | 20.89 | 20.72 | 20.07 | 21.27 | 19.96 | 20.84 | 21.65 | 20.65 | 20.01 | 20.53 | 20.68 | 20.60 |
| 2016 | 20.71 | 20.76 | 20.72 | 20.22 | 21.07 | 20.27 | 20.75 | 21.60 | 21.97 | 22.76 | 22.11 | 22.54 | 21.30 |
| 2017 | 21.96 | 21.76 | 21.90 | 22.32 | 22.65 | 21.51 | 21.45 | 21.57 | 21.61 | 21.88 | 21.02 | 21.77 | 21.78 |
| 2018 | 21.40 | 21.19 | 21.73 | 22.00 | 22.37 | 22.67 | 22.11 | 22.51 | 22.13 | 21.69 | 21.25 | 21.73 | 21.91 |
| 2019 | 21.09 | 21.05 | 22.03 | 22.32 | 22.41 | 23.37 | 23.40 | 22.89 | 23.80 | 24.17 | 24.37 | 25.03 | 23.00 |

## 4. Average Weekly Earnings by Selected Industry: Wyoming, 2015–2019

(Dollars, not seasonally adjusted)

| Industry and year | January | February | March | April | May | June | July | August | September | October | November | December | Annual average |
|---|---|---|---|---|---|---|---|---|---|---|---|---|---|
| **Total Private** | | | | | | | | | | | | | |
| 2015 | 807.12 | 834.32 | 824.47 | 810.38 | 813.31 | 809.08 | 807.76 | 833.81 | 800.75 | 802.55 | 813.62 | 775.55 | 811.16 |
| 2016 | 770.84 | 773.54 | 772.89 | 754.03 | 770.24 | 745.19 | 754.30 | 769.37 | 774.23 | 807.84 | 789.16 | 768.63 | 770.90 |
| 2017 | 790.60 | 780.78 | 779.46 | 832.82 | 818.72 | 808.60 | 831.32 | 810.84 | 826.29 | 854.30 | 833.17 | 826.66 | 816.01 |
| 2018 | 835.20 | 835.87 | 847.48 | 875.13 | 862.87 | 871.80 | 884.62 | 890.31 | 928.44 | 906.70 | 940.40 | 949.32 | 886.11 |
| 2019 | 922.06 | 932.80 | 910.32 | 932.40 | 940.93 | 945.39 | 917.25 | 938.39 | 960.02 | 937.70 | 938.81 | 950.88 | 935.57 |
| **Goods-Producing** | | | | | | | | | | | | | |
| 2015 | 1,119.57 | 1,119.75 | 1,103.20 | 1,107.60 | 1,140.16 | 1,136.69 | 1,143.74 | 1,163.56 | 1,108.03 | 1,155.23 | 1,157.64 | 1,133.90 | 1,132.61 |
| 2016 | 1,119.16 | 1,099.39 | 1,128.81 | 1,138.80 | 1,157.06 | 1,114.00 | 1,118.00 | 1,162.93 | 1,161.58 | 1,193.96 | 1,169.67 | 1,105.66 | 1,140.04 |
| 2017 | 1,111.46 | 1,114.46 | 1,116.91 | 1,179.16 | 1,196.03 | 1,170.82 | 1,157.72 | 1,159.84 | 1,163.39 | 1,198.94 | 1,175.35 | 1,155.21 | 1,160.75 |
| 2018 | 1,193.14 | 1,162.81 | 1,186.55 | 1,221.17 | 1,238.91 | 1,238.50 | 1,229.29 | 1,254.10 | 1,279.72 | 1,256.16 | 1,311.55 | 1,322.64 | 1,242.34 |
| 2019 | 1,311.98 | 1,298.08 | 1,277.56 | 1,310.88 | 1,343.60 | 1,321.68 | 1,302.43 | 1,344.43 | 1,352.11 | 1,332.81 | 1,324.75 | 1,346.76 | 1,322.31 |
| **Mining and Logging** | | | | | | | | | | | | | |
| 2015 | 1,526.43 | 1,520.12 | 1,511.84 | 1,478.76 | 1,513.60 | 1,489.20 | 1,511.27 | 1,551.01 | 1,515.38 | 1,501.22 | 1,508.50 | 1,516.83 | 1,513.73 |
| 2016 | 1,513.71 | 1,485.29 | 1,485.85 | 1,467.03 | 1,430.80 | 1,452.74 | 1,451.99 | 1,464.61 | 1,496.96 | 1,553.10 | 1,506.35 | 1,460.16 | 1,483.26 |
| 2017 | 1,513.68 | 1,473.13 | 1,490.17 | 1,513.29 | 1,537.77 | 1,550.54 | 1,529.24 | 1,501.15 | 1,501.10 | 1,548.77 | 1,557.85 | 1,564.24 | 1,523.77 |
| 2018 | 1,542.20 | 1,475.71 | 1,495.23 | 1,543.66 | 1,518.98 | 1,526.40 | 1,543.16 | 1,544.20 | 1,611.48 | 1,557.06 | 1,622.36 | 1,659.84 | 1,552.43 |
| 2019 | 1,547.38 | 1,572.15 | 1,602.19 | 1,613.33 | 1,609.50 | 1,679.80 | 1,717.09 | 1,760.12 | 1,818.10 | 1,765.61 | 1,791.65 | 1,857.44 | 1,695.39 |
| **Construction** | | | | | | | | | | | | | |
| 2015 | 983.19 | 988.00 | 975.82 | 1,009.22 | 1,037.85 | 1,038.34 | 1,040.76 | 1,056.70 | 1,002.69 | 1,078.98 | 1,062.72 | 1,018.02 | 1,026.16 |
| 2016 | 954.19 | 935.12 | 992.02 | 1,008.00 | 1,072.44 | 984.47 | 995.08 | 1,080.68 | 1,043.37 | 1,059.89 | 1,043.94 | 998.10 | 1,013.55 |
| 2017 | 966.63 | 1,000.29 | 991.93 | 1,077.34 | 1,087.42 | 1,045.17 | 1,024.14 | 1,039.09 | 1,037.52 | 1,071.82 | 1,050.01 | 1,061.58 | 1,038.59 |
| 2018 | 1,048.42 | 1,028.74 | 1,061.45 | 1,101.23 | 1,164.49 | 1,170.60 | 1,147.08 | 1,192.90 | 1,194.08 | 1,201.15 | 1,249.26 | 1,222.79 | 1,153.57 |
| 2019 | 1,167.55 | 1,146.14 | 1,095.38 | 1,168.91 | 1,241.57 | 1,188.09 | 1,137.52 | 1,193.35 | 1,163.14 | 1,163.34 | 1,132.93 | 1,117.60 | 1,159.61 |
| **Trade, Transportation, and Utilities** | | | | | | | | | | | | | |
| 2015 | 744.42 | 776.51 | 783.62 | 759.85 | 745.50 | 759.60 | 758.64 | 773.28 | 736.03 | 714.49 | 717.95 | 689.18 | 746.59 |
| 2016 | 688.71 | 695.23 | 700.97 | 721.22 | 733.06 | 714.49 | 723.81 | 734.60 | 743.82 | 756.98 | 741.54 | 749.17 | 724.70 |
| 2017 | 770.80 | 744.95 | 749.02 | 796.07 | 761.80 | 765.83 | 804.52 | 768.15 | 767.43 | 792.54 | 777.22 | 776.65 | 771.52 |
| 2018 | 758.00 | 761.11 | 775.38 | 820.41 | 805.86 | 804.07 | 816.45 | 805.75 | 848.75 | 820.89 | 834.68 | 852.05 | 809.19 |
| 2019 | 832.88 | 833.32 | 822.04 | 831.87 | 873.52 | 867.89 | 828.05 | 849.60 | 894.98 | 874.24 | 868.33 | 901.38 | 856.69 |
| **Professional and Business Services** | | | | | | | | | | | | | |
| 2015 | 935.68 | 957.18 | 950.33 | 956.86 | 934.71 | 923.94 | 921.46 | 961.22 | 961.50 | 928.87 | 918.37 | 881.09 | 936.95 |
| 2016 | 865.31 | 886.49 | 876.65 | 903.06 | 912.74 | 901.32 | 890.96 | 925.71 | 915.29 | 948.04 | 921.06 | 922.74 | 906.44 |
| 2017 | 959.70 | 924.77 | 884.02 | 951.10 | 933.23 | 935.97 | 956.22 | 920.66 | 937.92 | 956.59 | 926.59 | 931.23 | 932.39 |
| 2018 | 918.90 | 934.07 | 904.43 | 955.06 | 937.54 | 953.20 | 942.48 | 943.59 | 971.04 | 952.88 | 988.36 | 968.58 | 946.89 |
| 2019 | 940.28 | 984.10 | 954.09 | 1,015.24 | 995.16 | 1,033.90 | 1,021.22 | 1,070.43 | 1,114.71 | 1,058.81 | 1,045.07 | 1,075.36 | 1,026.26 |
| **Education and Health Services** | | | | | | | | | | | | | |
| 2015 | 747.16 | 802.74 | 789.92 | 765.57 | 766.58 | 774.63 | 760.91 | 793.72 | 766.75 | 759.36 | 792.58 | 742.10 | 771.80 |
| 2016 | 747.50 | 757.87 | 751.03 | 753.57 | 785.17 | 775.61 | 783.31 | 773.85 | 775.46 | 807.26 | 774.05 | 768.26 | 770.59 |
| 2017 | 800.04 | 799.19 | 772.97 | 806.56 | 783.19 | 797.33 | 829.68 | 798.34 | 821.10 | 845.29 | 807.08 | 815.81 | 806.61 |
| 2018 | 808.42 | 805.10 | 805.44 | 817.01 | 794.40 | 810.86 | 848.72 | 825.51 | 850.15 | 840.01 | 835.89 | 849.09 | 824.38 |
| 2019 | 818.51 | 823.88 | 804.05 | 804.10 | 795.99 | 819.19 | 785.21 | 791.80 | 777.44 | 772.48 | 761.60 | 767.59 | 791.90 |
| **Leisure and Hospitality** | | | | | | | | | | | | | |
| 2015 | 366.97 | 391.82 | 384.61 | 360.27 | 362.05 | 384.38 | 394.12 | 406.49 | 387.71 | 344.74 | 340.75 | 336.63 | 373.18 |
| 2016 | 352.30 | 358.00 | 357.08 | 350.34 | 363.69 | 373.46 | 387.53 | 389.20 | 373.61 | 349.57 | 333.94 | 332.12 | 361.72 |
| 2017 | 367.01 | 369.95 | 367.78 | 345.22 | 351.09 | 389.63 | 411.27 | 414.14 | 399.73 | 377.09 | 355.72 | 368.44 | 378.49 |
| 2018 | 407.16 | 410.04 | 416.67 | 375.72 | 372.84 | 414.18 | 432.04 | 419.69 | 412.63 | 362.84 | 351.58 | 376.42 | 396.70 |
| 2019 | 373.50 | 378.42 | 369.66 | 332.38 | 351.95 | 403.92 | 416.48 | 415.53 | 418.61 | 384.78 | 381.22 | 382.28 | 386.57 |
| **Other Services** | | | | | | | | | | | | | |
| 2015 | 625.80 | 687.28 | 658.90 | 628.19 | 638.10 | 604.79 | 621.03 | 660.33 | 605.05 | 568.28 | 591.26 | 552.16 | 620.06 |
| 2016 | 542.60 | 560.52 | 547.01 | 533.81 | 573.10 | 551.34 | 574.78 | 578.88 | 595.39 | 660.04 | 599.18 | 601.82 | 577.23 |
| 2017 | 612.68 | 607.10 | 608.82 | 649.51 | 620.61 | 608.73 | 634.92 | 621.22 | 628.85 | 652.02 | 605.38 | 618.27 | 622.91 |
| 2018 | 599.20 | 614.51 | 612.79 | 644.60 | 650.97 | 686.90 | 705.31 | 724.82 | 703.73 | 678.90 | 624.75 | 660.59 | 659.49 |
| 2019 | 630.59 | 620.98 | 616.84 | 629.42 | 649.89 | 675.39 | 636.48 | 643.21 | 690.20 | 700.93 | 692.11 | 728.37 | 660.10 |

# PART B

# METROPOLITAN STATISTICAL AREA (MSA) DATA

# METROPOLITAN STATISTICAL AREA (MSA) NOTES

Part B provides employment data for the 75 largest metropolitan statistical areas (MSAs) and New England city and town areas (NECTAs) in the United States from 2011 through 2019. As mentioned in the technical notes, all employment data are for MSAs unless otherwise noted. NECTAs are similar to MSAs but are defined by cities and towns rather than counties in the New England region.

According to the 2019 estimates from the Census Bureau, New York-Newark-Jersey City, NY-NJ-PA metro area, was the largest MSA in the United States—with a population of 19,216,182 Los Angeles-Long Beach-Anaheim, CA followed with a population of 13,214,799. Although the New York area was the most populated MSA, it was not among the fastest growing 75 largest MSAs. The fastest growing MSAs between 2018 and 2019 was Austin-Round Rock-Georgetown, TX Metro Area with a growth rate of 2.8 percent followed by Raleigh-Cary, NC Metro Area with a growth rate of 2.1 percent and North Port-Sarasota-Bradenton, FL and Phoenix-Mesa-Chandler, AZ Metro Area with growth rates of 2.0 percent. MSAs in the South and West typically had higher growth rates. Fifteen MSAs among the 75 largest experienced a decline in growth.

Austin-Round Rock-Georgetown, TX was also the fastest growing MSA in terms of total nonfarm employment. Total nonfarm employment grew 37.5 percent there from 2011 to 2019 while it grew 33.5 percent in Riverside-San Bernardino-Ontario, CA. Two of the top five fastest growing MSAs in terms of employment were in were in Florida. Total nonfarm employment grew 32.0 percent in Orlando-Kissimmee-Sanford and 30.7 percent in North Port-Sarasota-Bradenton, FL. Total nonfarm employment increased in all of the 75 largest MSAs from 2011 to 2019.

Among the 75 largest MSAs, the unemployment rate increased in six MSAs, remained stable in nine other MSAs, and declined in sixty MSAs between 2018 and 2019. Jacksonville, FL experienced the greatest increase in unemployment growing from 3.5 percent to 4.6 percent in just one year. Greenville-Anderson, SC experienced the greatest decline in unemployment from 2018 to 2019 declining 1.7 percent followed by Columbia, SC which experienced a 0.9 percent decline in employment. Salt Lake City, UT had the lowest unemployment rate at 2.5 percent in places with a population of 1,000,000 or more while Jacksonville, FL had the highest unemployment rate at 4.6 percent followed by New Orleans-Metairie, LA at 4.5 percent and Buffalo-Cheektowaga, NY and Tucson, AZ at 4.4 percent.

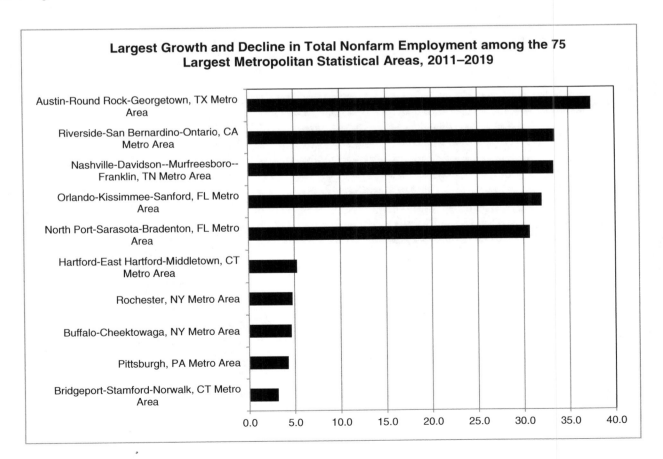

**Largest Growth and Decline in Total Nonfarm Employment among the 75 Largest Metropolitan Statistical Areas, 2011–2019**

## Metropolitan Statistical Areas: Employment and Unemployment Rates

(Seventy-five largest MSAs; ranked by population)

| Rank | Metropolitan statistical area | 2019 Population estimates | Total nonfarm employment | | Percent change in total nonfarm employment, 2011–2019 | Unemployment rates | |
|---|---|---|---|---|---|---|---|
| | | | 2011 | 2019 | | 2018 | 2019 |
| 1 | New York-Newark-Jersey City, NY-NJ-PA Metro Area | 19,216,182 | 8,719.9 | 9,966.9 | 14.3 | 4.0 | 3.7 |
| 2 | Los Angeles-Long Beach-Anaheim, CA Metro Area | 13,214,799 | 5,337.4 | 6,239.5 | 16.9 | 4.2 | 4.0 |
| 3 | Chicago-Naperville-Elgin, IL-IN-WI Metro Area | 9,458,539 | 4,304.6 | 4,760.6 | 10.6 | 4.1 | 3.8 |
| 4 | Dallas-Fort Worth-Arlington, TX Metro Area | 7,573,136 | 3,003.1 | 3,782.7 | 26.0 | 3.5 | 3.3 |
| 5 | Houston-The Woodlands-Sugar Land, TX Metro Area | 7,066,141 | 2,634.5 | 3,156.2 | 19.8 | 4.3 | 3.8 |
| 6 | Washington-Arlington-Alexandria, DC-VA-MD-WV Metro Area | 6,280,487 | 3,023.8 | 3,352.4 | 10.9 | 3.4 | 3.1 |
| 7 | Miami-Fort Lauderdale-Pompano Beach, FL Metro Area | 6,166,488 | 2,234.1 | 2,718.1 | 21.7 | 3.5 | 2.8 |
| 8 | Philadelphia-Camden-Wilmington, PA-NJ-DE-MD Metro Area | 6,102,434 | 2,705.9 | 2,974.3 | 9.9 | 4.2 | 4.1 |
| 9 | Atlanta-Sandy Springs-Alpharetta, GA Metro Area | 6,020,364 | 2,312.1 | 2,849.4 | 23.2 | 3.8 | 3.2 |
| 10 | Phoenix-Mesa-Chandler, AZ Metro Area | 4,948,203 | 1,717.4 | 2,177.3 | 26.8 | 4.1 | 4.1 |
| 11 | Boston-Cambridge-Newton, MA-NH Metro Area | 4,873,019 | 1,642.4 | 1,904.6 | 16.0 | 3.0 | 2.6 |
| 12 | San Francisco-Oakland-Berkeley, CA Metro Area | 4,731,803 | 1,956.8 | 2,480.2 | 26.7 | 2.8 | 2.6 |
| 13 | Riverside-San Bernardino-Ontario, CA Metro Area | 4,650,631 | 1,155.3 | 1,541.8 | 33.5 | 4.3 | 4.0 |
| 14 | Detroit-Warren-Dearborn, MI Metro Area | 4,319,629 | 1,784.8 | 2,038.8 | 14.2 | 4.3 | 4.3 |
| 15 | Seattle-Tacoma-Bellevue, WA Metro Area | 3,979,845 | 1,694.6 | 2,091.2 | 23.4 | 3.7 | 3.3 |
| 16 | Minneapolis-St Paul-Bloomington, MN-WI Metro Area | 3,640,043 | 1,790.0 | 2,031.5 | 13.5 | 2.7 | 3.0 |
| 17 | San Diego-Carlsbad, CA Metro Area | 3,338,330 | 1,250.3 | 1,503.9 | 21.2 | 3.4 | 3.2 |
| 18 | Tampa-St Petersburg-Clearwater, FL Metro Area | 3,194,831 | 1,123.4 | 1384.7 | 23.3 | 3.6 | 3.2 |
| 19 | Denver-Aurora-Lakewood, CO Metro Area | 2,967,239 | 1,214.3 | 1,536.0 | 26.5 | 3.0 | 2.7 |
| 20 | St Louis, MO-IL Metro Area | 2,803,228 | 1,297.7 | 1,393.5 | 7.4 | 3.4 | 3.3 |
| 21 | Baltimore-Columbia-Towson, MD Metro Area | 2,800,053 | 1,293.9 | 1,426.3 | 10.2 | 4.0 | 3.6 |
| 22 | Charlotte-Concord-Gastonia, NC-SC Metro Area | 2,636,883 | 976.2 | 1,235.5 | 26.6 | 3.7 | 3.5 |
| 23 | Orlando-Kissimmee-Sanford, FL Metro Area | 2,608,147 | 1,005.5 | 1,327.1 | 32.0 | 3.4 | 3.0 |
| 24 | San Antonio-New Braunfels, TX Metro Area | 2,550,960 | 871.2 | 1,078.7 | 23.8 | 3.3 | 3.1 |
| 25 | Portland-Vancouver-Hillsboro, OR-WA Metro Area | 2,492,412 | 999.1 | 1,221.2 | 22.2 | 3.8 | 3.5 |
| 26 | Sacramento-Roseville-Folsom, CA Metro Area | 2,363,730 | 829.3 | 1,018.5 | 22.8 | 3.8 | 3.6 |
| 27 | Pittsburgh, PA Metro Area | 2,317,600 | 1,145.2 | 1,194.0 | 4.3 | 4.2 | 4.3 |
| 28 | Las Vegas-Henderson-Paradise, NV Metro Area | 2,266,715 | 808.3 | 1,034.1 | 27.9 | 4.7 | 4.0 |
| 29 | Austin-Round Rock-Georgetown, TX Metro Area | 2,227,083 | 811.9 | 1,116.0 | 37.5 | 2.9 | 2.7 |
| 30 | Cincinnati, OH-KY-IN Metro Area | 2,221,208 | 992.3 | 1,115.1 | 12.4 | 4.0 | 3.7 |
| 31 | Kansas City, MO-KS Metro Area | 2,157,990 | 975.1 | 1,096.1 | 12.4 | 3.3 | 3.3 |
| 32 | Columbus, OH Metro Area | 2,122,271 | 941.4 | 1,111.3 | 18.0 | 3.9 | 3.6 |
| 33 | Indianapolis-Carmel-Anderson, IN Metro Area | 2,074,537 | 929.6 | 1,088.2 | 17.1 | 3.3 | 3.0 |
| 34 | Cleveland-Elyria, OH Metro Area | 2,048,449 | 1,001.1 | 1,079.2 | 7.8 | 4.6 | 4.0 |
| 35 | San Jose-Sunnyvale-Santa Clara, CA Metro Area | 1,990,660 | 895.4 | 1,146.8 | 28.1 | 2.7 | 2.6 |
| 36 | Nashville-Davidson--Murfreesboro--Franklin, TN Metro Area | 1,934,317 | 786.1 | 1,047.9 | 33.3 | 2.8 | 2.6 |
| 37 | Virginia Beach-Norfolk-Newport News, VA-NC Metro Area | 1,768,901 | 740.2 | 795.3 | 7.4 | 3.3 | 3.1 |
| 38 | Providence-Warwick, RI-MA Metro Area | 1,624,578 | 548.0 | 599.3 | 9.4 | 4.0 | 3.6 |
| 39 | Milwaukee-Waukesha, WI Metro Area | 1,575,179 | 814.0 | 874.4 | 7.4 | 3.2 | 3.5 |
| 40 | Jacksonville, FL Metro Area | 1,559,514 | 586.1 | 724.4 | 23.6 | 3.5 | 3.1 |
| 41 | Oklahoma City, OK Metro Area | 1,408,950 | 580.1 | 659.1 | 13.6 | 3.2 | 3.0 |
| 42 | Raleigh, NC Metro Area | 1,390,785 | 509.1 | 650.1 | 27.7 | 3.5 | 3.4 |
| 43 | Memphis, TN-MS-AR Metro Area | 1,346,045 | 595.5 | 654.7 | 9.9 | 4.2 | 4.2 |
| 44 | Richmond, VA Metro Area | 1,291,900 | 600.1 | 686.7 | 14.4 | 3.2 | 2.9 |
| 45 | New Orleans-Metairie, LA Metro Area | 1,270,530 | 539.5 | 583.4 | 8.1 | 4.6 | 4.5 |
| 46 | Louisville/Jefferson County, KY-IN Metro Area | 1,265,108 | 586.4 | 675.2 | 15.1 | 3.9 | 3.8 |
| 47 | Salt Lake City, UT Metro Area | 1,232,696 | 597.8 | 754.3 | 26.2 | 3.0 | 2.5 |
| 48 | Hartford-East Hartford-Middletown, CT Metro Area | 1,204,877 | 554.2 | 583.4 | 5.3 | 4.2 | 3.8 |
| 49 | Buffalo-Cheektowaga, NY Metro Area | 1,127,983 | 540.1 | 565.1 | 4.6 | 4.6 | 4.4 |
| 50 | Birmingham-Hoover, AL Metro Area | 1,090,435 | 498.5 | 546.0 | 9.5 | 3.5 | 2.7 |
| 51 | Grand Rapids-Kentwood, MI Metro Area | 1,077,370 | 468.4 | 567.0 | 21.1 | 3.0 | 2.9 |
| 52 | Rochester, NY Metro Area | 1,069,644 | 515.3 | 539.8 | 4.8 | 4.2 | 4.1 |
| 53 | Tucson, AZ Metro Area | 1,047,279 | 353.8 | 389.6 | 10.1 | 4.4 | 4.4 |
| 54 | Fresno, CA Metro Area | 999,101 | 291.3 | 361.4 | 24.1 | 7.6 | 7.2 |
| 55 | Tulsa, OK Metro Area | 998,626 | 415.5 | 461.4 | 11.0 | 3.5 | 3.3 |

## Metropolitan Statistical Areas: Employment and Unemployment Rates—*Continued*

(Seventy-five largest MSAs; ranked by population)

| Rank | Metropolitan statistical area | 2019 Population estimates | Total nonfarm employment | | Percent change in total nonfarm employment, 2011–2019 | Unemployment rates | |
|---|---|---|---|---|---|---|---|
| | | | 2011 | 2019 | | 2018 | 2019 |
| 56 | Urban Honolulu, HI Metro Area | 974,563 | 437.5 | 471.8 | 7.8 | 2.4 | 2.6 |
| 57 | Omaha-Council Bluffs, NE-IA Metro Area | 949,442 | 464.3 | 507.2 | 9.2 | 3.0 | 3.1 |
| 58 | Worcester, MA-CT Metro Area | 947,404 | 264.1 | 290.2 | 9.9 | 3.6 | 3.2 |
| 59 | Bridgeport-Stamford-Norwalk, CT Metro Area | 943,332 | 393.5 | 405.8 | 3.1 | 4.1 | 3.7 |
| 60 | Greenville-Anderson, SC Metro Area | 920,477 | 362.4 | 433.3 | 19.6 | 3.1 | 2.6 |
| 61 | Albuquerque, NM Metro Area | 918,018 | 372.4 | 398.9 | 7.1 | 4.6 | 4.6 |
| 62 | Bakersfield, CA Metro Area | 900,202 | 237.1 | 273.7 | 15.4 | 8.1 | 7.7 |
| 63 | Albany-Schenectady-Troy, NY Metro Area | 880,381 | 434.2 | 472.3 | 8.8 | 3.8 | 3.7 |
| 64 | Knoxville, TN Metro Area | 869,046 | 364.2 | 405.0 | 11.2 | 3.3 | 3.2 |
| 65 | McAllen-Edinburg-Mission, TX Metro Area | 868,707 | 226.3 | 270.9 | 19.7 | 6.5 | 6.2 |
| 66 | Baton Rouge, LA Metro Area | 854,884 | 370.2 | 412.4 | 11.4 | 4.4 | 4.4 |
| 67 | New Haven, CT Metro Area | 854,757 | 268.6 | 288.7 | 7.5 | 4.1 | 3.6 |
| 68 | Oxnard-Thousand Oaks-Ventura, CA Metro Area | 846,006 | 278.0 | 311.8 | 12.2 | 3.8 | 3.6 |
| 69 | El Paso, TX Metro Area | 844,124 | 283.4 | 324.1 | 14.4 | 4.2 | 3.8 |
| 70 | Allentown-Bethlehem-Easton, PA-NJ Metro Area | 844,052 | 339.8 | 380.9 | 12.1 | 4.4 | 4.4 |
| 71 | Columbia, SC Metro Area | 838,433 | 348.2 | 403.5 | 15.9 | 3.3 | 2.7 |
| 72 | North Port-Sarasota-Bradenton, FL Metro Area | 836,995 | 240.0 | 313.6 | 30.7 | 3.5 | 3.1 |
| 73 | Dayton-Kettering, OH Metro Area | 807,611 | 365.4 | 391.9 | 7.3 | 4.3 | 4.0 |
| 74 | Charleston-North Charleston, SC Metro Area | 802,122 | 295.8 | 375.8 | 27.0 | 2.9 | 2.4 |
| 75 | Greensboro-High Point, NC Metro Area | 771,851 | 338.7 | 364.4 | 7.6 | 4.2 | 4.1 |

## Employment by Industry: New York-Newark-Jersey City, NY-NJ-PA, 2011–2019

(Numbers in thousands, not seasonally adjusted)

| Industry and year | January | February | March | April | May | June | July | August | September | October | November | December | Annual average |
|---|---|---|---|---|---|---|---|---|---|---|---|---|---|
| **Total Nonfarm** | | | | | | | | | | | | | |
| 2011 | 8,493.6 | 8,537.0 | 8,599.7 | 8,703.8 | 8,745.4 | 8,800.2 | 8,741.7 | 8,691.7 | 8,735.4 | 8,813.8 | 8,873.4 | 8,903.0 | 8,719.9 |
| 2012 | 8,632.4 | 8,697.2 | 8,772.5 | 8,813.6 | 8,894.1 | 8,951.7 | 8,842.1 | 8,816.1 | 8,865.5 | 8,960.0 | 8,966.0 | 9,043.2 | 8,854.5 |
| 2013 | 8,745.2 | 8,801.0 | 8,877.6 | 8,967.1 | 9,025.8 | 9,080.1 | 9,020.5 | 8,978.5 | 9,014.7 | 9,138.8 | 9,211.8 | 9,227.9 | 9,007.4 |
| 2014 | 8,909.4 | 8,960.9 | 9,035.2 | 9,138.7 | 9,221.0 | 9,273.4 | 9,219.1 | 9,182.1 | 9,208.5 | 9,330.2 | 9,403.1 | 9,435.6 | 9,193.1 |
| 2015 | 9,121.5 | 9,169.6 | 9,237.1 | 9,327.8 | 9,413.3 | 9,466.4 | 9,420.1 | 9,375.5 | 9,392.2 | 9,528.3 | 9,591.5 | 9,613.5 | 9,388.1 |
| 2016 | 9,298.4 | 9,355.0 | 9,433.5 | 9,524.5 | 9,555.7 | 9,628.9 | 9,583.6 | 9,537.8 | 9,569.5 | 9,662.3 | 9,729.0 | 9,759.9 | 9,553.2 |
| 2017 | 9,462.7 | 9,527.6 | 9,578.2 | 9,635.9 | 9,732.9 | 9,816.3 | 9,734.3 | 9,685.5 | 9,714.5 | 9,824.4 | 9,896.7 | 9,923.6 | 9,711.1 |
| 2018 | 9,585.0 | 9,674.4 | 9,726.2 | 9,787.7 | 9,864.0 | 9,952.6 | 9,848.0 | 9,794.6 | 9,821.8 | 9,962.3 | 10,040.7 | 10,051.0 | 9,842.4 |
| 2019 | 9,745.2 | 9,810.3 | 9,873.0 | 9,954.6 | 9,998.4 | 10,079.0 | 9,980.6 | 9,928.7 | 9,955.1 | 10,052.5 | 10,115.7 | 10,109.3 | 9,966.9 |
| **Total Private** | | | | | | | | | | | | | |
| 2011 | 7,167.1 | 7,193.5 | 7,252.0 | 7,348.8 | 7,397.5 | 7,451.4 | 7,416.5 | 7,389.8 | 7,435.6 | 7,475.5 | 7,527.5 | 7,562.2 | 7,384.8 |
| 2012 | 7,330.3 | 7,369.7 | 7,436.0 | 7,479.0 | 7,560.8 | 7,617.0 | 7,543.8 | 7,546.7 | 7,579.2 | 7,631.9 | 7,638.1 | 7,710.4 | 7,536.9 |
| 2013 | 7,446.9 | 7,476.2 | 7,547.7 | 7,635.0 | 7,694.7 | 7,753.2 | 7,723.5 | 7,712.4 | 7,733.7 | 7,809.9 | 7,875.6 | 7,895.3 | 7,692.0 |
| 2014 | 7,617.9 | 7,644.7 | 7,711.0 | 7,805.0 | 7,890.6 | 7,947.2 | 7,919.4 | 7,908.6 | 7,917.7 | 8,002.0 | 8,063.2 | 8,098.8 | 7,877.2 |
| 2015 | 7,827.5 | 7,850.1 | 7,910.3 | 7,993.8 | 8,079.1 | 8,135.1 | 8,111.4 | 8,090.8 | 8,093.6 | 8,197.4 | 8,247.4 | 8,271.8 | 8,067.4 |
| 2016 | 7,994.9 | 8,027.0 | 8,095.3 | 8,183.6 | 8,215.1 | 8,290.5 | 8,271.8 | 8,251.6 | 8,262.9 | 8,325.0 | 8,383.4 | 8,416.0 | 8,226.4 |
| 2017 | 8,151.8 | 8,192.5 | 8,236.9 | 8,295.5 | 8,392.8 | 8,473.6 | 8,415.8 | 8,398.6 | 8,409.5 | 8,486.5 | 8,552.6 | 8,580.6 | 8,382.2 |
| 2018 | 8,281.7 | 8,344.8 | 8,392.2 | 8,451.1 | 8,523.8 | 8,605.5 | 8,547.4 | 8,518.7 | 8,509.9 | 8,624.8 | 8,687.7 | 8,705.1 | 8,516.1 |
| 2019 | 8,439.7 | 8,480.7 | 8,539.1 | 8,616.0 | 8,660.5 | 8,729.7 | 8,679.4 | 8,647.2 | 8,640.7 | 8,703.2 | 8,756.2 | 8,754.4 | 8,637.2 |
| **Goods Producing** | | | | | | | | | | | | | |
| 2011 | 650.6 | 649.7 | 660.9 | 676.1 | 686.1 | 693.4 | 698.1 | 701.8 | 699.7 | 698.9 | 698.5 | 692.8 | 683.9 |
| 2012 | 665.6 | 664.4 | 672.9 | 681.4 | 687.9 | 695.1 | 696.6 | 700.0 | 698.5 | 700.4 | 697.3 | 700.6 | 688.4 |
| 2013 | 675.6 | 673.7 | 683.1 | 699.1 | 706.0 | 712.3 | 715.6 | 721.0 | 719.3 | 723.1 | 722.4 | 712.5 | 705.3 |
| 2014 | 682.7 | 677.6 | 690.3 | 709.4 | 720.9 | 729.1 | 735.6 | 737.9 | 737.0 | 739.9 | 740.2 | 733.2 | 719.5 |
| 2015 | 702.4 | 696.3 | 707.6 | 728.7 | 741.0 | 749.5 | 754.7 | 757.2 | 753.1 | 760.1 | 759.3 | 753.8 | 738.6 |
| 2016 | 727.8 | 723.7 | 736.6 | 750.5 | 757.1 | 764.3 | 768.5 | 771.1 | 766.5 | 768.3 | 767.2 | 761.4 | 755.3 |
| 2017 | 734.7 | 736.4 | 741.7 | 756.7 | 768.5 | 776.8 | 777.9 | 779.1 | 776.2 | 778.8 | 779.4 | 773.0 | 764.9 |
| 2018 | 740.4 | 748.7 | 754.2 | 765.9 | 775.9 | 785.4 | 786.1 | 786.9 | 784.0 | 789.8 | 787.8 | 783.7 | 774.1 |
| 2019 | 757.3 | 759.3 | 765.5 | 777.8 | 782.8 | 789.6 | 790.0 | 789.5 | 785.4 | 780.7 | 777.5 | 764.2 | 776.6 |
| **Service-Providing** | | | | | | | | | | | | | |
| 2011 | 7,843.0 | 7,887.3 | 7,938.8 | 8,027.7 | 8,059.3 | 8,106.8 | 8,043.6 | 7,989.9 | 8,035.7 | 8,114.9 | 8,174.9 | 8,210.2 | 8,036.0 |
| 2012 | 7,966.8 | 8,032.8 | 8,099.6 | 8,132.2 | 8,206.2 | 8,256.6 | 8,145.5 | 8,116.1 | 8,167.0 | 8,259.6 | 8,268.7 | 8,342.6 | 8,166.1 |
| 2013 | 8,069.6 | 8,127.3 | 8,194.5 | 8,268.0 | 8,319.8 | 8,367.8 | 8,304.9 | 8,257.5 | 8,295.4 | 8,415.7 | 8,489.4 | 8,515.4 | 8,302.1 |
| 2014 | 8,226.7 | 8,283.3 | 8,344.9 | 8,429.3 | 8,500.1 | 8,544.3 | 8,483.5 | 8,444.2 | 8,471.5 | 8,590.3 | 8,662.9 | 8,702.4 | 8,473.6 |
| 2015 | 8,419.1 | 8,473.3 | 8,529.5 | 8,599.1 | 8,672.3 | 8,716.9 | 8,665.4 | 8,618.3 | 8,639.1 | 8,768.2 | 8,832.2 | 8,859.7 | 8,649.4 |
| 2016 | 8,570.6 | 8,631.3 | 8,696.9 | 8,774.0 | 8,798.6 | 8,864.6 | 8,815.1 | 8,766.7 | 8,803.0 | 8,894.0 | 8,961.8 | 8,998.5 | 8,797.9 |
| 2017 | 8,728.0 | 8,791.2 | 8,836.5 | 8,879.2 | 8,964.4 | 9,039.5 | 8,956.4 | 8,906.4 | 8,938.3 | 9,045.6 | 9,117.3 | 9,150.6 | 8,946.1 |
| 2018 | 8,844.6 | 8,925.7 | 8,972.0 | 9,021.8 | 9,088.1 | 9,167.2 | 9,061.9 | 9,007.7 | 9,037.8 | 9,172.5 | 9,252.9 | 9,267.3 | 9,068.3 |
| 2019 | 8,987.9 | 9,051.0 | 9,107.5 | 9,176.8 | 9,215.6 | 9,289.4 | 9,190.6 | 9,139.2 | 9,169.7 | 9,271.8 | 9,338.2 | 9,345.1 | 9,190.2 |
| **Mining, Logging, and Construction** | | | | | | | | | | | | | |
| 2011 | 276.4 | 275.4 | 285.7 | 300.4 | 309.4 | 314.7 | 321.7 | 324.2 | 321.4 | 321.0 | 320.4 | 314.9 | 307.1 |
| 2012 | 293.8 | 291.8 | 298.4 | 308.1 | 312.5 | 317.5 | 321.8 | 324.5 | 321.8 | 323.5 | 322.2 | 324.9 | 313.4 |
| 2013 | 307.6 | 304.5 | 311.7 | 326.7 | 332.4 | 336.8 | 342.6 | 346.9 | 344.7 | 348.3 | 347.4 | 337.4 | 332.3 |
| 2014 | 315.2 | 309.9 | 321.9 | 341.0 | 351.1 | 357.4 | 366.1 | 368.2 | 367.6 | 370.7 | 370.5 | 363.8 | 350.3 |
| 2015 | 338.3 | 332.0 | 342.0 | 363.2 | 373.9 | 379.7 | 385.7 | 388.2 | 383.9 | 390.3 | 389.5 | 383.4 | 370.8 |
| 2016 | 362.7 | 357.3 | 369.3 | 384.6 | 390.5 | 395.2 | 400.7 | 403.4 | 400.1 | 400.5 | 399.3 | 392.9 | 388.0 |
| 2017 | 372.2 | 373.3 | 377.7 | 393.5 | 403.1 | 408.8 | 412.3 | 414.4 | 412.4 | 414.7 | 414.5 | 407.9 | 400.4 |
| 2018 | 380.7 | 387.7 | 392.9 | 405.3 | 414.5 | 420.4 | 423.5 | 424.0 | 422.4 | 427.0 | 424.3 | 419.4 | 411.8 |
| 2019 | 398.6 | 399.8 | 405.0 | 417.1 | 421.5 | 425.5 | 428.6 | 429.6 | 426.7 | 422.8 | 417.4 | 404.5 | 416.4 |
| **Manufacturing** | | | | | | | | | | | | | |
| 2011 | 374.2 | 374.3 | 375.2 | 375.7 | 376.7 | 378.7 | 376.4 | 377.6 | 378.3 | 377.9 | 378.1 | 377.9 | 376.8 |
| 2012 | 371.8 | 372.6 | 374.5 | 373.3 | 375.4 | 377.6 | 374.8 | 375.5 | 376.7 | 376.9 | 375.1 | 375.7 | 375.0 |
| 2013 | 368.0 | 369.2 | 371.4 | 372.4 | 373.6 | 375.5 | 373.0 | 374.1 | 374.6 | 374.8 | 375.0 | 375.1 | 373.1 |
| 2014 | 367.5 | 367.7 | 368.4 | 368.4 | 369.8 | 371.7 | 369.5 | 369.7 | 369.4 | 369.2 | 369.7 | 369.4 | 369.2 |
| 2015 | 364.1 | 364.3 | 365.6 | 365.5 | 367.1 | 369.8 | 369.0 | 369.0 | 369.2 | 369.8 | 369.8 | 370.4 | 367.8 |
| 2016 | 365.1 | 366.4 | 367.3 | 365.9 | 366.6 | 369.1 | 367.8 | 367.7 | 366.4 | 367.8 | 367.9 | 368.5 | 367.2 |
| 2017 | 362.5 | 363.1 | 364.0 | 363.2 | 365.4 | 368.0 | 365.6 | 364.7 | 363.8 | 364.1 | 364.9 | 365.1 | 364.5 |
| 2018 | 359.7 | 361.0 | 361.3 | 360.6 | 361.4 | 365.0 | 362.6 | 362.9 | 361.6 | 362.8 | 363.5 | 364.3 | 362.2 |
| 2019 | 358.7 | 359.5 | 360.5 | 360.7 | 361.3 | 364.1 | 361.4 | 359.9 | 358.7 | 357.9 | 360.1 | 359.7 | 360.2 |

## Employment by Industry: New York-Newark-Jersey City, NY-NJ-PA, 2011–2019—*Continued*

(Numbers in thousands, not seasonally adjusted)

| Industry and year | January | February | March | April | May | June | July | August | September | October | November | December | Annual average |
|---|---|---|---|---|---|---|---|---|---|---|---|---|---|
| **Trade, Transportation, and Utilities** | | | | | | | | | | | | | |
| 2011 | 1,593.9 | 1,576.4 | 1,580.9 | 1,593.6 | 1,603.5 | 1,622.7 | 1,600.3 | 1,600.3 | 1,616.1 | 1,627.8 | 1,663.3 | 1,691.5 | 1,614.2 |
| 2012 | 1,628.9 | 1,609.6 | 1,616.5 | 1,613.5 | 1,634.6 | 1,652.7 | 1,617.6 | 1,620.7 | 1,637.8 | 1,650.7 | 1,682.8 | 1,711.9 | 1,639.8 |
| 2013 | 1,634.3 | 1,611.6 | 1,624.5 | 1,635.5 | 1,649.3 | 1,670.5 | 1,654.1 | 1,651.3 | 1,667.3 | 1,681.7 | 1,725.6 | 1,747.5 | 1,662.8 |
| 2014 | 1,671.8 | 1,650.9 | 1,658.6 | 1,666.7 | 1,682.5 | 1,700.6 | 1,684.1 | 1,683.4 | 1,696.4 | 1,713.4 | 1,753.6 | 1,780.5 | 1,695.2 |
| 2015 | 1,702.8 | 1,682.6 | 1,686.3 | 1,691.6 | 1,709.6 | 1,728.4 | 1,706.2 | 1,703.9 | 1,714.1 | 1,728.1 | 1,765.3 | 1,781.2 | 1,716.7 |
| 2016 | 1,708.9 | 1,692.2 | 1,695.8 | 1,705.4 | 1,712.7 | 1,727.5 | 1,709.3 | 1,705.1 | 1,717.1 | 1,735.5 | 1,774.0 | 1,799.8 | 1,723.6 |
| 2017 | 1,729.6 | 1,706.9 | 1,707.8 | 1,710.9 | 1,729.3 | 1,746.7 | 1,727.0 | 1,724.0 | 1,735.6 | 1,747.3 | 1,793.6 | 1,816.7 | 1,739.6 |
| 2018 | 1,742.1 | 1,720.2 | 1,719.6 | 1,719.3 | 1,733.8 | 1,749.0 | 1,726.2 | 1,717.6 | 1,728.1 | 1,745.0 | 1,794.7 | 1,813.2 | 1,742.4 |
| 2019 | 1,740.7 | 1,714.0 | 1,716.3 | 1,716.8 | 1,724.8 | 1,743.6 | 1,722.4 | 1,712.9 | 1,722.8 | 1,733.6 | 1,770.2 | 1,790.5 | 1,734.1 |
| **Wholesale Trade** | | | | | | | | | | | | | |
| 2011 | 402.5 | 401.4 | 403.4 | 405.1 | 406.2 | 409.1 | 408.4 | 408.7 | 407.5 | 407.9 | 408.2 | 411.1 | 406.6 |
| 2012 | 407.0 | 408.4 | 409.9 | 409.6 | 411.1 | 414.2 | 411.6 | 411.2 | 410.3 | 411.4 | 411.4 | 413.8 | 410.8 |
| 2013 | 406.1 | 406.5 | 407.6 | 410.0 | 411.5 | 415.1 | 415.2 | 414.8 | 413.7 | 414.3 | 415.6 | 417.0 | 412.3 |
| 2014 | 410.0 | 410.2 | 411.6 | 413.3 | 415.0 | 417.4 | 417.9 | 417.1 | 416.4 | 417.3 | 419.2 | 420.7 | 415.5 |
| 2015 | 414.1 | 414.2 | 415.6 | 416.2 | 418.0 | 421.0 | 421.1 | 420.5 | 418.6 | 419.6 | 420.1 | 421.1 | 418.3 |
| 2016 | 414.3 | 414.8 | 414.9 | 414.6 | 414.6 | 416.6 | 416.4 | 415.8 | 413.9 | 414.1 | 414.6 | 416.3 | 415.1 |
| 2017 | 409.3 | 409.7 | 410.3 | 411.6 | 413.8 | 417.1 | 416.1 | 415.4 | 414.1 | 413.0 | 414.7 | 416.6 | 413.5 |
| 2018 | 409.7 | 410.1 | 410.9 | 409.9 | 411.4 | 414.4 | 414.6 | 412.5 | 411.3 | 412.0 | 413.5 | 415.0 | 412.1 |
| 2019 | 407.9 | 407.9 | 408.7 | 407.9 | 408.7 | 411.8 | 410.3 | 408.9 | 407.8 | 404.6 | 404.8 | 404.1 | 407.8 |
| **Retail Trade** | | | | | | | | | | | | | |
| 2011 | 877.7 | 863.0 | 864.2 | 873.0 | 879.8 | 893.1 | 889.5 | 890.9 | 889.3 | 900.3 | 930.8 | 951.7 | 891.9 |
| 2012 | 905.3 | 885.0 | 888.6 | 890.5 | 902.5 | 914.5 | 906.9 | 906.8 | 905.9 | 917.7 | 947.7 | 966.0 | 911.5 |
| 2013 | 911.2 | 895.7 | 900.7 | 906.7 | 917.1 | 932.7 | 931.4 | 932.8 | 930.1 | 941.7 | 979.4 | 995.1 | 931.2 |
| 2014 | 936.8 | 920.1 | 924.2 | 930.4 | 939.8 | 953.3 | 951.3 | 953.3 | 949.0 | 961.7 | 993.6 | 1,012.0 | 952.1 |
| 2015 | 952.3 | 934.7 | 936.2 | 939.0 | 951.0 | 963.6 | 957.2 | 956.8 | 951.7 | 961.2 | 991.8 | 998.9 | 957.9 |
| 2016 | 948.2 | 932.3 | 934.0 | 940.3 | 946.5 | 957.8 | 955.4 | 954.4 | 948.2 | 960.5 | 991.4 | 1,006.6 | 956.3 |
| 2017 | 957.4 | 937.2 | 936.5 | 940.8 | 950.3 | 960.4 | 956.5 | 954.5 | 947.2 | 957.1 | 990.4 | 1,001.5 | 957.5 |
| 2018 | 953.8 | 936.7 | 935.2 | 935.3 | 944.3 | 953.6 | 947.3 | 943.4 | 935.3 | 943.0 | 976.8 | 986.8 | 949.3 |
| 2019 | 942.4 | 921.6 | 924.1 | 925.8 | 930.1 | 940.3 | 936.0 | 931.4 | 922.8 | 931.4 | 956.9 | 968.4 | 935.9 |
| **Transportation and Utilities** | | | | | | | | | | | | | |
| 2011 | 313.7 | 312.0 | 313.3 | 315.5 | 317.5 | 320.5 | 302.4 | 300.7 | 319.3 | 319.6 | 324.3 | 328.7 | 315.6 |
| 2012 | 316.6 | 316.2 | 318.0 | 313.4 | 321.0 | 324.0 | 299.1 | 302.7 | 321.6 | 321.6 | 323.7 | 332.1 | 317.5 |
| 2013 | 317.0 | 309.4 | 316.2 | 318.8 | 320.7 | 322.7 | 307.5 | 303.7 | 323.5 | 325.7 | 330.6 | 335.4 | 319.3 |
| 2014 | 325.0 | 320.6 | 322.8 | 323.0 | 327.7 | 329.9 | 314.9 | 313.0 | 331.0 | 334.4 | 340.8 | 347.8 | 327.6 |
| 2015 | 336.4 | 333.7 | 334.5 | 336.4 | 340.6 | 343.8 | 327.9 | 326.6 | 343.8 | 347.3 | 353.4 | 361.2 | 340.5 |
| 2016 | 346.4 | 345.1 | 346.9 | 350.5 | 351.6 | 353.1 | 337.5 | 334.9 | 355.0 | 360.9 | 368.0 | 376.9 | 352.2 |
| 2017 | 362.9 | 360.0 | 361.0 | 358.5 | 365.2 | 369.2 | 354.4 | 354.1 | 374.3 | 377.2 | 388.5 | 398.6 | 368.7 |
| 2018 | 378.6 | 373.4 | 373.5 | 374.1 | 378.1 | 381.0 | 364.3 | 361.7 | 381.5 | 390.0 | 404.4 | 411.4 | 381.0 |
| 2019 | 390.4 | 384.5 | 383.5 | 383.1 | 386.0 | 391.5 | 376.1 | 372.6 | 392.2 | 397.6 | 408.5 | 418.0 | 390.3 |
| **Information** | | | | | | | | | | | | | |
| 2011 | 269.7 | 270.8 | 272.5 | 275.1 | 275.6 | 277.2 | 279.1 | 262.1 | 278.5 | 276.2 | 277.6 | 279.6 | 274.5 |
| 2012 | 274.8 | 276.1 | 277.6 | 277.8 | 279.7 | 281.7 | 279.0 | 278.8 | 277.1 | 278.8 | 279.7 | 280.2 | 278.4 |
| 2013 | 272.4 | 274.1 | 275.5 | 277.2 | 279.3 | 282.1 | 281.8 | 284.4 | 282.3 | 283.8 | 287.2 | 286.4 | 280.5 |
| 2014 | 278.5 | 281.3 | 282.3 | 281.0 | 281.9 | 285.4 | 283.9 | 285.1 | 282.5 | 284.8 | 284.6 | 286.9 | 283.2 |
| 2015 | 280.1 | 281.6 | 282.1 | 280.8 | 282.0 | 284.9 | 286.8 | 285.2 | 284.2 | 288.3 | 289.8 | 290.8 | 284.7 |
| 2016 | 280.0 | 281.1 | 282.6 | 284.6 | 271.5 | 286.6 | 292.3 | 291.1 | 288.9 | 290.5 | 291.5 | 293.2 | 286.2 |
| 2017 | 282.5 | 286.6 | 287.5 | 284.3 | 286.2 | 290.8 | 291.9 | 294.0 | 293.9 | 294.6 | 297.4 | 298.2 | 290.7 |
| 2018 | 282.7 | 291.0 | 292.8 | 287.3 | 289.7 | 296.4 | 294.6 | 295.6 | 292.6 | 296.5 | 298.9 | 296.2 | 292.9 |
| 2019 | 284.5 | 289.4 | 292.6 | 293.9 | 296.0 | 299.0 | 297.9 | 301.4 | 297.8 | 296.7 | 301.5 | 296.2 | 295.6 |
| **Financial Activities** | | | | | | | | | | | | | |
| 2011 | 732.6 | 733.7 | 734.8 | 736.2 | 738.3 | 749.1 | 752.4 | 753.4 | 744.9 | 742.1 | 742.3 | 745.2 | 742.1 |
| 2012 | 735.6 | 737.6 | 738.4 | 736.7 | 738.4 | 748.0 | 748.9 | 747.2 | 738.7 | 740.3 | 739.6 | 745.3 | 741.2 |
| 2013 | 731.5 | 733.6 | 733.3 | 733.5 | 734.7 | 745.2 | 748.8 | 748.4 | 740.0 | 741.5 | 743.7 | 748.0 | 740.2 |
| 2014 | 736.5 | 738.4 | 740.3 | 739.7 | 743.3 | 755.7 | 759.3 | 758.3 | 749.1 | 750.1 | 751.8 | 756.9 | 748.3 |
| 2015 | 745.2 | 746.6 | 747.6 | 747.8 | 751.1 | 763.4 | 769.5 | 769.1 | 759.4 | 762.4 | 763.3 | 767.2 | 757.7 |
| 2016 | 758.1 | 758.5 | 758.8 | 758.3 | 761.5 | 772.3 | 777.4 | 777.3 | 764.7 | 765.4 | 766.9 | 771.7 | 765.9 |
| 2017 | 761.1 | 763.8 | 765.9 | 763.4 | 767.3 | 781.4 | 784.4 | 784.6 | 774.3 | 776.2 | 777.8 | 782.6 | 773.6 |
| 2018 | 768.8 | 772.0 | 772.6 | 772.2 | 774.5 | 789.5 | 794.2 | 792.9 | 781.3 | 784.7 | 786.0 | 788.6 | 781.4 |
| 2019 | 780.2 | 781.9 | 782.6 | 782.9 | 784.8 | 797.5 | 802.2 | 802.4 | 788.7 | 789.6 | 789.3 | 790.4 | 789.4 |

## Employment by Industry: New York-Newark-Jersey City, NY-NJ-PA, 2011–2019—*Continued*

(Numbers in thousands, not seasonally adjusted)

| Industry and year | January | February | March | April | May | June | July | August | September | October | November | December | Annual average |
|---|---|---|---|---|---|---|---|---|---|---|---|---|---|
| **Professional and Business Services** | | | | | | | | | | | | | |
| 2011 | 1,277.0 | 1,282.4 | 1,294.9 | 1,317.3 | 1,321.0 | 1,339.9 | 1,343.5 | 1,345.2 | 1,342.8 | 1,347.4 | 1,356.7 | 1,356.3 | 1,327.0 |
| 2012 | 1,312.3 | 1,320.9 | 1,336.8 | 1,352.4 | 1,362.6 | 1,381.0 | 1,377.2 | 1,386.6 | 1,384.5 | 1,393.3 | 1,400.8 | 1,408.3 | 1,368.1 |
| 2013 | 1,355.4 | 1,361.5 | 1,375.6 | 1,389.5 | 1,397.5 | 1,415.9 | 1,421.1 | 1,424.6 | 1,416.3 | 1,424.2 | 1,430.1 | 1,431.6 | 1,403.6 |
| 2014 | 1,380.7 | 1,389.1 | 1,395.5 | 1,422.7 | 1,433.2 | 1,448.2 | 1,455.8 | 1,457.5 | 1,447.6 | 1,460.5 | 1,468.9 | 1,471.4 | 1,435.9 |
| 2015 | 1,426.9 | 1,434.7 | 1,445.7 | 1,468.6 | 1,477.6 | 1,495.2 | 1,500.2 | 1,500.7 | 1,492.2 | 1,510.2 | 1,514.4 | 1,513.3 | 1,481.6 |
| 2016 | 1,464.4 | 1,472.1 | 1,486.2 | 1,506.8 | 1,511.4 | 1,531.6 | 1,536.6 | 1,539.0 | 1,535.2 | 1,539.2 | 1,547.0 | 1,547.7 | 1,518.1 |
| 2017 | 1,497.7 | 1,506.9 | 1,514.4 | 1,528.4 | 1,543.3 | 1,566.2 | 1,562.7 | 1,559.3 | 1,556.8 | 1,564.5 | 1,573.7 | 1,574.5 | 1,545.7 |
| 2018 | 1,519.4 | 1,530.5 | 1,540.0 | 1,558.5 | 1,571.3 | 1,595.5 | 1,589.1 | 1,589.8 | 1,581.8 | 1,602.7 | 1,613.2 | 1,609.2 | 1,575.1 |
| 2019 | 1,558.3 | 1,569.2 | 1,580.2 | 1,606.5 | 1,607.9 | 1,631.0 | 1,630.4 | 1,626.5 | 1,615.8 | 1,632.3 | 1,633.9 | 1,630.8 | 1,610.2 |
| **Education and Health Services** | | | | | | | | | | | | | |
| 2011 | 1,601.5 | 1,632.4 | 1,644.0 | 1,649.8 | 1,645.7 | 1,611.1 | 1,580.8 | 1,572.3 | 1,616.5 | 1,652.1 | 1,662.5 | 1,670.1 | 1,628.2 |
| 2012 | 1,626.7 | 1,662.8 | 1,676.5 | 1,676.4 | 1,680.9 | 1,648.2 | 1,613.8 | 1,605.7 | 1,655.8 | 1,689.6 | 1,685.4 | 1,700.0 | 1,660.2 |
| 2013 | 1,656.8 | 1,692.6 | 1,706.1 | 1,719.6 | 1,715.3 | 1,676.7 | 1,648.4 | 1,638.8 | 1,684.1 | 1,736.5 | 1,751.2 | 1,754.0 | 1,698.3 |
| 2014 | 1,700.1 | 1,732.4 | 1,750.5 | 1,760.9 | 1,761.6 | 1,730.2 | 1,704.4 | 1,699.1 | 1,739.3 | 1,791.4 | 1,808.4 | 1,814.4 | 1,749.4 |
| 2015 | 1,762.2 | 1,796.8 | 1,812.0 | 1,820.8 | 1,817.8 | 1,783.7 | 1,755.6 | 1,744.9 | 1,782.7 | 1,845.9 | 1,862.5 | 1,869.0 | 1,804.5 |
| 2016 | 1,816.4 | 1,853.3 | 1,867.4 | 1,878.0 | 1,872.1 | 1,841.9 | 1,814.2 | 1,805.4 | 1,853.7 | 1,901.9 | 1,916.8 | 1,923.7 | 1,862.1 |
| 2017 | 1,875.9 | 1,916.6 | 1,929.4 | 1,930.7 | 1,932.6 | 1,905.4 | 1,866.9 | 1,858.3 | 1,907.9 | 1,964.8 | 1,979.3 | 1,985.4 | 1,921.1 |
| 2018 | 1,932.7 | 1,981.4 | 1,993.2 | 2,001.5 | 1,998.3 | 1,966.5 | 1,936.1 | 1,925.3 | 1,968.3 | 2,035.8 | 2,047.8 | 2,053.2 | 1,986.7 |
| 2019 | 2,010.5 | 2,055.0 | 2,073.0 | 2,081.5 | 2,075.1 | 2,040.2 | 2,003.6 | 1,992.8 | 2,045.5 | 2,095.3 | 2,116.7 | 2,115.1 | 2,058.7 |
| **Leisure and Hospitality** | | | | | | | | | | | | | |
| 2011 | 676.2 | 680.9 | 694.7 | 725.9 | 749.2 | 775.4 | 781.6 | 777.0 | 759.8 | 751.9 | 747.1 | 745.2 | 738.7 |
| 2012 | 709.4 | 720.2 | 736.0 | 756.5 | 787.8 | 815.7 | 819.6 | 818.7 | 797.9 | 787.7 | 763.5 | 771.5 | 773.7 |
| 2013 | 736.5 | 742.8 | 761.4 | 789.8 | 819.4 | 851.8 | 856.8 | 848.3 | 831.3 | 823.6 | 818.5 | 817.7 | 808.2 |
| 2014 | 776.6 | 782.1 | 798.0 | 824.3 | 862.0 | 888.8 | 889.6 | 882.2 | 862.4 | 855.4 | 847.5 | 846.0 | 842.9 |
| 2015 | 805.8 | 808.8 | 824.3 | 849.1 | 888.3 | 913.2 | 923.8 | 916.4 | 896.5 | 887.5 | 876.7 | 879.1 | 872.5 |
| 2016 | 829.5 | 834.0 | 853.9 | 880.8 | 906.9 | 940.6 | 950.0 | 941.5 | 917.4 | 902.4 | 897.9 | 896.4 | 895.9 |
| 2017 | 856.2 | 861.5 | 875.2 | 902.4 | 942.7 | 978.0 | 980.8 | 977.8 | 945.0 | 937.3 | 927.8 | 925.6 | 925.9 |
| 2018 | 879.8 | 883.3 | 900.3 | 923.3 | 953.7 | 991.4 | 994.1 | 985.9 | 952.3 | 943.2 | 932.2 | 933.8 | 939.4 |
| 2019 | 888.9 | 890.0 | 906.2 | 929.7 | 960.3 | 995.5 | 1,002.4 | 992.8 | 959.7 | 943.9 | 937.7 | 937.5 | 945.4 |
| **Other Services** | | | | | | | | | | | | | |
| 2011 | 365.6 | 367.2 | 369.3 | 374.8 | 378.1 | 382.6 | 380.7 | 377.7 | 377.3 | 379.1 | 379.5 | 381.5 | 376.1 |
| 2012 | 377.0 | 378.1 | 381.3 | 384.3 | 388.9 | 394.6 | 391.1 | 389.0 | 388.9 | 391.1 | 389.0 | 392.6 | 387.2 |
| 2013 | 384.4 | 386.3 | 388.2 | 390.8 | 393.2 | 398.7 | 396.9 | 395.6 | 393.1 | 395.5 | 396.9 | 397.6 | 393.1 |
| 2014 | 391.0 | 392.9 | 395.5 | 400.3 | 405.2 | 409.2 | 406.7 | 405.1 | 403.4 | 406.5 | 408.2 | 409.5 | 402.8 |
| 2015 | 402.1 | 402.7 | 404.7 | 406.4 | 411.7 | 416.8 | 414.6 | 413.4 | 411.4 | 414.9 | 416.1 | 417.4 | 411.0 |
| 2016 | 409.8 | 412.1 | 414.0 | 419.2 | 421.9 | 425.7 | 423.5 | 421.1 | 419.4 | 421.8 | 422.1 | 422.1 | 419.4 |
| 2017 | 414.1 | 413.8 | 415.0 | 418.7 | 422.9 | 428.3 | 424.2 | 421.5 | 419.8 | 423.0 | 423.6 | 424.6 | 420.8 |
| 2018 | 415.8 | 417.7 | 419.5 | 423.1 | 426.6 | 431.8 | 427.0 | 424.7 | 421.5 | 427.1 | 427.1 | 427.2 | 424.1 |
| 2019 | 419.3 | 421.9 | 422.7 | 426.9 | 428.8 | 433.3 | 430.5 | 428.9 | 425.0 | 431.1 | 429.4 | 429.7 | 427.3 |
| **Government** | | | | | | | | | | | | | |
| 2011 | 1,326.5 | 1,343.5 | 1,347.7 | 1,355.0 | 1,347.9 | 1,348.8 | 1,325.2 | 1,301.9 | 1,299.8 | 1,338.3 | 1,345.9 | 1,340.8 | 1,335.1 |
| 2012 | 1,302.1 | 1,327.5 | 1,336.5 | 1,334.6 | 1,333.3 | 1,334.7 | 1,298.3 | 1,269.4 | 1,286.3 | 1,328.1 | 1,327.9 | 1,332.8 | 1,317.6 |
| 2013 | 1,298.3 | 1,324.8 | 1,329.9 | 1,332.1 | 1,331.1 | 1,326.9 | 1,297.0 | 1,266.1 | 1,281.0 | 1,328.9 | 1,336.2 | 1,332.6 | 1,315.4 |
| 2014 | 1,291.5 | 1,316.2 | 1,324.2 | 1,333.7 | 1,330.4 | 1,326.2 | 1,299.7 | 1,273.5 | 1,290.8 | 1,328.2 | 1,339.9 | 1,336.8 | 1,315.9 |
| 2015 | 1,294.0 | 1,319.5 | 1,326.8 | 1,334.0 | 1,334.2 | 1,331.3 | 1,308.7 | 1,284.7 | 1,298.6 | 1,330.9 | 1,344.1 | 1,341.7 | 1,320.7 |
| 2016 | 1,303.5 | 1,328.0 | 1,338.2 | 1,340.9 | 1,340.6 | 1,338.4 | 1,311.8 | 1,286.2 | 1,306.6 | 1,337.3 | 1,345.6 | 1,343.9 | 1,326.8 |
| 2017 | 1,310.9 | 1,335.1 | 1,341.3 | 1,340.4 | 1,340.1 | 1,342.7 | 1,318.5 | 1,286.9 | 1,305.0 | 1,337.9 | 1,344.1 | 1,343.0 | 1,328.8 |
| 2018 | 1,303.3 | 1,329.6 | 1,334.0 | 1,336.6 | 1,340.2 | 1,347.1 | 1,300.6 | 1,275.9 | 1,311.9 | 1,337.5 | 1,353.0 | 1,345.9 | 1,326.3 |
| 2019 | 1,305.5 | 1,329.6 | 1,333.9 | 1,338.6 | 1,337.9 | 1,349.3 | 1,301.2 | 1,281.5 | 1,314.4 | 1,349.3 | 1,359.5 | 1,354.9 | 1,329.6 |

## Employment by Industry: Los Angeles-Long Beach-Anaheim, CA, 2011–2019

(Numbers in thousands, not seasonally adjusted)

| Industry and year | January | February | March | April | May | June | July | August | September | October | November | December | Annual average |
|---|---|---|---|---|---|---|---|---|---|---|---|---|---|
| **Total Nonfarm** | | | | | | | | | | | | | |
| 2011 | 5,279.9 | 5,305.5 | 5,325.3 | 5,329.5 | 5,339.1 | 5,340.6 | 5,291.8 | 5,287.8 | 5,332.3 | 5,373.8 | 5,410.2 | 5,432.7 | 5,337.4 |
| 2012 | 5,337.0 | 5,375.4 | 5,410.3 | 5,449.2 | 5,476.2 | 5,485.6 | 5,425.9 | 5,437.9 | 5,473.7 | 5,524.3 | 5,580.1 | 5,600.7 | 5,464.7 |
| 2013 | 5,468.3 | 5,512.7 | 5,533.4 | 5,560.8 | 5,581.0 | 5,585.4 | 5,532.8 | 5,560.5 | 5,587.5 | 5,644.5 | 5,701.5 | 5,716.9 | 5,582.1 |
| 2014 | 5,606.3 | 5,633.1 | 5,657.4 | 5,667.0 | 5,691.0 | 5,683.7 | 5,621.1 | 5,668.8 | 5,703.7 | 5,759.3 | 5,803.4 | 5,821.2 | 5,693.0 |
| 2015 | 5,709.5 | 5,752.6 | 5,776.7 | 5,795.8 | 5,810.2 | 5,815.7 | 5,792.1 | 5,812.7 | 5,853.1 | 5,937.3 | 5,971.4 | 5,985.0 | 5,834.3 |
| 2016 | 5,887.4 | 5,929.6 | 5,929.7 | 5,980.8 | 5,992.4 | 5,959.9 | 5,934.3 | 5,950.4 | 5,990.9 | 6,052.2 | 6,091.3 | 6,103.0 | 5,983.5 |
| 2017 | 5,962.0 | 6,007.0 | 6,024.7 | 6,037.3 | 6,061.6 | 6,062.3 | 6,013.6 | 6,037.4 | 6,086.0 | 6,152.1 | 6,186.3 | 6,206.2 | 6,069.7 |
| 2018 | 6,090.8 | 6,132.2 | 6,144.9 | 6,144.9 | 6,149.6 | 6,159.2 | 6,102.4 | 6,137.5 | 6,167.7 | 6,237.9 | 6,273.4 | 6,291.8 | 6,169.4 |
| 2019 | 6,157.1 | 6,207.1 | 6,216.9 | 6,214.2 | 6,229.7 | 6,235.8 | 6,186.0 | 6,211.8 | 6,239.4 | 6,293.1 | 6,332.7 | 6,349.7 | 6,239.5 |
| **Total Private** | | | | | | | | | | | | | |
| 2011 | 4,555.1 | 4,577.7 | 4,590.9 | 4,596.3 | 4,604.9 | 4,606.0 | 4,613.7 | 4,625.3 | 4,644.6 | 4,658.0 | 4,686.0 | 4,713.1 | 4,622.6 |
| 2012 | 4,627.5 | 4,656.9 | 4,686.0 | 4,727.3 | 4,751.7 | 4,762.4 | 4,757.8 | 4,778.1 | 4,789.2 | 4,820.8 | 4,870.2 | 4,892.4 | 4,760.0 |
| 2013 | 4,770.1 | 4,805.4 | 4,819.5 | 4,849.7 | 4,867.6 | 4,872.3 | 4,871.1 | 4,895.4 | 4,902.3 | 4,939.3 | 4,988.8 | 5,004.9 | 4,882.2 |
| 2014 | 4,904.0 | 4,925.8 | 4,940.2 | 4,948.7 | 4,967.6 | 4,965.1 | 4,955.5 | 4,994.6 | 5,003.5 | 5,039.8 | 5,076.4 | 5,094.1 | 4,984.6 |
| 2015 | 4,990.5 | 5,025.9 | 5,044.2 | 5,059.4 | 5,076.5 | 5,079.8 | 5,105.4 | 5,126.0 | 5,136.7 | 5,198.6 | 5,228.7 | 5,241.6 | 5,109.4 |
| 2016 | 5,154.8 | 5,188.8 | 5,183.3 | 5,233.4 | 5,241.9 | 5,219.3 | 5,238.7 | 5,253.9 | 5,262.4 | 5,303.6 | 5,338.1 | 5,348.6 | 5,247.2 |
| 2017 | 5,217.2 | 5,255.5 | 5,266.7 | 5,279.4 | 5,299.3 | 5,301.8 | 5,310.9 | 5,333.7 | 5,351.2 | 5,396.5 | 5,423.9 | 5,444.9 | 5,323.4 |
| 2018 | 5,340.6 | 5,374.1 | 5,383.4 | 5,381.7 | 5,384.5 | 5,394.9 | 5,393.8 | 5,425.2 | 5,424.5 | 5,477.7 | 5,506.6 | 5,523.0 | 5,417.5 |
| 2019 | 5,402.5 | 5,444.8 | 5,450.2 | 5,445.8 | 5,459.7 | 5,466.1 | 5,470.7 | 5,495.5 | 5,493.3 | 5,525.6 | 5,557.3 | 5,576.0 | 5,482.3 |
| **Goods Producing** | | | | | | | | | | | | | |
| 2011 | 694.8 | 696.5 | 700.0 | 702.7 | 706.4 | 709.1 | 713.2 | 714.1 | 712.8 | 709.4 | 709.5 | 708.3 | 706.4 |
| 2012 | 704.1 | 706.0 | 709.7 | 712.3 | 715.9 | 721.4 | 724.0 | 724.6 | 724.1 | 723.7 | 725.1 | 724.3 | 717.9 |
| 2013 | 717.7 | 723.5 | 724.7 | 725.3 | 728.1 | 733.2 | 735.5 | 738.1 | 736.4 | 738.2 | 739.7 | 738.1 | 731.5 |
| 2014 | 726.6 | 732.4 | 733.6 | 729.9 | 733.4 | 735.5 | 735.7 | 739.6 | 738.6 | 738.2 | 738.6 | 736.9 | 734.9 |
| 2015 | 734.3 | 735.9 | 738.6 | 739.6 | 742.9 | 746.7 | 753.1 | 755.7 | 752.7 | 755.6 | 755.6 | 755.2 | 747.2 |
| 2016 | 746.6 | 751.3 | 749.2 | 753.1 | 753.5 | 752.5 | 756.3 | 756.6 | 755.6 | 754.7 | 754.3 | 753.9 | 753.1 |
| 2017 | 740.5 | 744.8 | 748.8 | 749.3 | 751.2 | 755.3 | 756.8 | 758.6 | 756.3 | 757.1 | 756.6 | 757.7 | 752.8 |
| 2018 | 746.9 | 754.0 | 753.3 | 753.3 | 754.6 | 757.4 | 759.4 | 762.2 | 760.2 | 761.5 | 759.8 | 759.2 | 756.8 |
| 2019 | 748.4 | 751.9 | 754.9 | 755.3 | 756.9 | 760.8 | 762.7 | 763.2 | 759.2 | 760.3 | 754.6 | 757.6 | 757.2 |
| **Service-Providing** | | | | | | | | | | | | | |
| 2011 | 4,585.1 | 4,609.0 | 4,625.3 | 4,626.8 | 4,632.7 | 4,631.5 | 4,578.6 | 4,573.7 | 4,619.5 | 4,664.4 | 4,700.7 | 4,724.4 | 4,631.0 |
| 2012 | 4,632.9 | 4,669.4 | 4,700.6 | 4,736.9 | 4,760.3 | 4,764.2 | 4,701.9 | 4,713.3 | 4,749.6 | 4,800.6 | 4,855.0 | 4,876.4 | 4,746.8 |
| 2013 | 4,750.6 | 4,789.2 | 4,808.7 | 4,835.5 | 4,852.9 | 4,852.2 | 4,797.3 | 4,822.4 | 4,851.1 | 4,906.3 | 4,961.8 | 4,978.8 | 4,850.6 |
| 2014 | 4,879.7 | 4,900.7 | 4,923.8 | 4,937.1 | 4,957.6 | 4,948.2 | 4,885.4 | 4,929.2 | 4,965.1 | 5,021.1 | 5,064.8 | 5,084.3 | 4,958.1 |
| 2015 | 4,975.2 | 5,016.7 | 5,038.1 | 5,056.2 | 5,067.3 | 5,069.0 | 5,039.0 | 5,057.0 | 5,100.4 | 5,181.7 | 5,215.8 | 5,229.8 | 5,087.2 |
| 2016 | 5,140.8 | 5,178.3 | 5,180.5 | 5,227.7 | 5,238.9 | 5,207.4 | 5,178.0 | 5,193.8 | 5,235.3 | 5,297.5 | 5,337.0 | 5,349.1 | 5,230.4 |
| 2017 | 5,221.5 | 5,262.2 | 5,275.9 | 5,288.0 | 5,310.4 | 5,307.0 | 5,256.8 | 5,278.8 | 5,329.7 | 5,395.0 | 5,429.7 | 5,448.5 | 5,317.0 |
| 2018 | 5,343.9 | 5,378.2 | 5,391.6 | 5,391.6 | 5,395.0 | 5,401.8 | 5,343.0 | 5,375.3 | 5,407.5 | 5,476.4 | 5,513.6 | 5,532.6 | 5,412.5 |
| 2019 | 5,408.7 | 5,455.2 | 5,462.0 | 5,458.9 | 5,472.8 | 5,475.0 | 5,423.3 | 5,448.6 | 5,480.2 | 5,532.8 | 5,578.1 | 5,592.1 | 5,482.3 |
| **Mining, Logging, and Construction** | | | | | | | | | | | | | |
| 2011 | 170.4 | 171.0 | 172.6 | 174.4 | 176.8 | 178.5 | 181.4 | 183.1 | 182.6 | 180.7 | 180.8 | 179.2 | 177.6 |
| 2012 | 177.3 | 177.3 | 178.6 | 178.5 | 181.0 | 184.5 | 187.3 | 188.3 | 188.4 | 188.6 | 189.7 | 189.2 | 184.1 |
| 2013 | 187.5 | 189.7 | 191.1 | 192.0 | 194.3 | 197.7 | 199.7 | 201.9 | 200.8 | 202.9 | 202.9 | 201.1 | 196.8 |
| 2014 | 197.1 | 199.9 | 201.6 | 200.9 | 203.9 | 205.1 | 205.8 | 209.4 | 209.2 | 210.4 | 211.2 | 208.5 | 205.3 |
| 2015 | 209.2 | 209.8 | 213.0 | 214.4 | 216.8 | 219.8 | 224.7 | 227.8 | 226.4 | 230.6 | 230.9 | 229.8 | 221.1 |
| 2016 | 226.5 | 229.1 | 228.6 | 232.3 | 233 | 233.1 | 237.2 | 238.5 | 238 | 239.2 | 237.7 | 236.6 | 234.2 |
| 2017 | 227.2 | 232.3 | 236.7 | 239.7 | 241.5 | 244.3 | 247.1 | 249.1 | 248.7 | 250.3 | 249.5 | 249.8 | 243.0 |
| 2018 | 245.5 | 250.7 | 249.7 | 252.6 | 253.7 | 255.2 | 256.7 | 260.2 | 259.2 | 260.7 | 258.6 | 257.2 | 255.0 |
| 2019 | 250.5 | 251.7 | 254.3 | 256.2 | 257.8 | 259.6 | 262.4 | 263.2 | 261.3 | 262.7 | 258.1 | 259.3 | 258.1 |
| **Manufacturing** | | | | | | | | | | | | | |
| 2011 | 524.4 | 525.5 | 527.4 | 528.3 | 529.6 | 530.6 | 531.8 | 531.0 | 530.2 | 528.7 | 528.7 | 529.1 | 528.8 |
| 2012 | 526.8 | 528.7 | 531.1 | 533.8 | 534.9 | 536.9 | 536.7 | 536.3 | 535.7 | 535.1 | 535.4 | 535.1 | 533.9 |
| 2013 | 530.2 | 533.8 | 533.6 | 533.3 | 533.8 | 535.5 | 535.8 | 536.2 | 535.6 | 535.3 | 536.8 | 537.0 | 534.7 |
| 2014 | 529.5 | 532.5 | 532.0 | 529.0 | 529.5 | 530.4 | 529.9 | 530.2 | 529.4 | 527.8 | 527.4 | 528.4 | 529.7 |
| 2015 | 525.1 | 526.1 | 525.6 | 525.2 | 526.1 | 526.9 | 528.4 | 527.9 | 526.3 | 525.0 | 524.7 | 525.4 | 526.1 |
| 2016 | 520.1 | 522.2 | 520.6 | 520.8 | 520.5 | 519.4 | 519.1 | 518.1 | 517.6 | 515.5 | 516.6 | 517.3 | 519 |
| 2017 | 513.3 | 512.5 | 512.1 | 509.6 | 509.7 | 511.0 | 509.7 | 509.5 | 507.6 | 506.8 | 507.1 | 507.9 | 509.7 |
| 2018 | 501.4 | 503.3 | 503.6 | 500.7 | 500.9 | 502.2 | 502.7 | 502.0 | 501.0 | 500.8 | 501.2 | 502.0 | 501.8 |
| 2019 | 497.9 | 500.2 | 500.6 | 499.1 | 499.1 | 501.2 | 500.3 | 500.0 | 497.9 | 497.6 | 496.5 | 498.3 | 499.1 |

## Employment by Industry: Los Angeles-Long Beach-Anaheim, CA, 2011–2019—*Continued*

(Numbers in thousands, not seasonally adjusted)

| Industry and year | January | February | March | April | May | June | July | August | September | October | November | December | Annual average |
|---|---|---|---|---|---|---|---|---|---|---|---|---|---|
| **Trade, Transportation, and Utilities** | | | | | | | | | | | | | |
| 2011 | 992.4 | 988.9 | 986.4 | 990.4 | 992.9 | 994.1 | 996.7 | 1,000.3 | 999.5 | 1,003.9 | 1,026.9 | 1,040.0 | 1,001.0 |
| 2012 | 1,009.0 | 998.8 | 999.8 | 1,006.6 | 1,011.2 | 1,015.1 | 1,014.9 | 1,017.2 | 1,018.3 | 1,024.5 | 1,055.4 | 1,064.6 | 1,019.6 |
| 2013 | 1,028.9 | 1,023.1 | 1,019.6 | 1,021.6 | 1,027.0 | 1,030.6 | 1,032.6 | 1,036.1 | 1,033.7 | 1,042.4 | 1,073.9 | 1,085.1 | 1,037.9 |
| 2014 | 1,049.6 | 1,041.3 | 1,039.0 | 1,041.2 | 1,046.2 | 1,050.0 | 1,051.3 | 1,057.1 | 1,057.4 | 1,066.9 | 1,096.2 | 1,108.9 | 1,058.8 |
| 2015 | 1,071.8 | 1,063.4 | 1,066.0 | 1,062.8 | 1,067.5 | 1,068.7 | 1,075.0 | 1,079.4 | 1,078.7 | 1,088.1 | 1,113.1 | 1,121.4 | 1,079.7 |
| 2016 | 1087.5 | 1078.6 | 1077.8 | 1083 | 1084.8 | 1082 | 1091.9 | 1095.6 | 1093 | 1098.4 | 1122.4 | 1133.5 | 1094 |
| 2017 | 1,102.5 | 1,087.3 | 1,091.8 | 1,093.9 | 1,095.8 | 1,096.8 | 1,099.9 | 1,102.6 | 1,103.3 | 1,112.7 | 1,139.4 | 1,149.2 | 1,106.3 |
| 2018 | 1,113.4 | 1,101.6 | 1,102.6 | 1,100.7 | 1,102.1 | 1,101.7 | 1,107.3 | 1,110.3 | 1,108.5 | 1,116.4 | 1,143.8 | 1,150.6 | 1,113.3 |
| 2019 | 1,114.1 | 1,100.2 | 1,099.6 | 1,098.5 | 1,100.9 | 1,101.2 | 1,105.9 | 1,109.3 | 1,103.0 | 1,111.2 | 1,138.9 | 1,147.5 | 1,110.9 |
| **Wholesale Trade** | | | | | | | | | | | | | |
| 2011 | 277.2 | 278.2 | 278.1 | 279.5 | 279.7 | 279.3 | 279.2 | 279.4 | 279.9 | 279.7 | 279.6 | 280.7 | 279.2 |
| 2012 | 277.9 | 278.7 | 279.4 | 283.9 | 285.1 | 286.0 | 285.6 | 286.7 | 286.5 | 288.0 | 289.0 | 290.8 | 284.8 |
| 2013 | 288.5 | 290.1 | 291.5 | 292.5 | 293.1 | 294.4 | 293.9 | 294.3 | 293.8 | 295.1 | 296.5 | 298.1 | 293.5 |
| 2014 | 295.5 | 297.0 | 297.3 | 296.4 | 297.4 | 297.7 | 298.0 | 299.6 | 299.8 | 300.7 | 301.9 | 302.7 | 298.7 |
| 2015 | 298.8 | 300.3 | 300.3 | 300.2 | 300.7 | 300.8 | 302.0 | 302.2 | 301.4 | 302.5 | 303.0 | 303.2 | 301.3 |
| 2016 | 299.8 | 300.6 | 299.1 | 300.6 | 300.6 | 299.4 | 302.3 | 302.3 | 301.3 | 300.6 | 300.7 | 301.4 | 300.7 |
| 2017 | 297.8 | 298.7 | 299.8 | 299.9 | 300.7 | 301.1 | 300.6 | 300.5 | 300.3 | 301.4 | 302.2 | 303.3 | 300.5 |
| 2018 | 300.7 | 302.1 | 302.2 | 302.4 | 303.3 | 303.5 | 303.6 | 303.3 | 302.3 | 303.9 | 304.4 | 304.7 | 303.0 |
| 2019 | 299.7 | 301.0 | 300.7 | 300.6 | 301.1 | 300.9 | 300.4 | 300.2 | 298.3 | 298.7 | 298.1 | 297.9 | 299.8 |
| **Retail Trade** | | | | | | | | | | | | | |
| 2011 | 533.9 | 527.5 | 526.3 | 527.0 | 529.0 | 530.8 | 533.6 | 535.8 | 535.5 | 539.6 | 561.9 | 571.8 | 537.7 |
| 2012 | 547.1 | 536.3 | 535.7 | 535.6 | 538.5 | 540.0 | 540.8 | 542.7 | 543.2 | 548.0 | 577.1 | 581.9 | 547.2 |
| 2013 | 551.0 | 543.2 | 541.2 | 542.1 | 544.5 | 547.1 | 547.7 | 549.8 | 548.6 | 555.3 | 583.1 | 591.2 | 553.7 |
| 2014 | 560.9 | 551.2 | 550.4 | 552.8 | 554.5 | 557.6 | 558.4 | 562.0 | 560.8 | 567.3 | 593.7 | 602.2 | 564.3 |
| 2015 | 573.4 | 565.3 | 563.8 | 562.1 | 564.8 | 565.4 | 568.8 | 571.6 | 570.5 | 577.4 | 598.7 | 604.4 | 573.9 |
| 2016 | 577.5 | 569.6 | 567.8 | 569.4 | 570.1 | 568.3 | 571.8 | 574.1 | 572.3 | 579.5 | 600.1 | 605.6 | 577.2 |
| 2017 | 583.0 | 571.4 | 569.6 | 571.2 | 571.2 | 571.4 | 573.4 | 575.1 | 574.9 | 581 | 604.3 | 608.4 | 579.6 |
| 2018 | 584.2 | 574.1 | 572.3 | 569.4 | 569.9 | 568.4 | 572.0 | 573.2 | 571.1 | 575.4 | 598.0 | 601.3 | 577.4 |
| 2019 | 574.8 | 564.2 | 561.5 | 558.9 | 558.9 | 559.1 | 561.9 | 563.6 | 559.4 | 566.6 | 589.5 | 594.6 | 567.8 |
| **Transportation and Utilities** | | | | | | | | | | | | | |
| 2011 | 181.3 | 183.2 | 182.0 | 183.9 | 184.2 | 184.0 | 183.9 | 185.1 | 184.1 | 184.6 | 185.4 | 187.5 | 184.1 |
| 2012 | 184.0 | 183.8 | 184.7 | 187.1 | 187.6 | 189.1 | 188.5 | 187.8 | 188.6 | 188.5 | 189.3 | 191.9 | 187.6 |
| 2013 | 189.4 | 189.8 | 186.9 | 187.0 | 189.4 | 189.1 | 191.0 | 192.0 | 191.3 | 192.0 | 194.3 | 195.8 | 190.7 |
| 2014 | 193.2 | 193.1 | 191.3 | 192.0 | 194.3 | 194.7 | 194.9 | 195.5 | 196.8 | 198.9 | 200.6 | 204.0 | 195.8 |
| 2015 | 199.6 | 197.8 | 201.9 | 200.5 | 202.0 | 202.5 | 204.2 | 205.6 | 206.8 | 208.2 | 211.4 | 213.8 | 204.5 |
| 2016 | 210.2 | 208.4 | 210.9 | 213.0 | 214.1 | 214.3 | 217.8 | 219.2 | 219.4 | 218.3 | 221.6 | 226.5 | 216.1 |
| 2017 | 221.7 | 217.2 | 222.4 | 222.8 | 223.9 | 224.3 | 225.9 | 227 | 228.1 | 230.3 | 232.9 | 237.5 | 226.2 |
| 2018 | 228.5 | 225.4 | 228.1 | 228.9 | 228.9 | 229.8 | 231.7 | 233.8 | 235.1 | 237.1 | 241.4 | 244.6 | 232.8 |
| 2019 | 239.6 | 235.0 | 237.4 | 239.0 | 240.9 | 241.2 | 243.6 | 245.5 | 245.3 | 245.9 | 251.3 | 255.0 | 243.3 |
| **Information** | | | | | | | | | | | | | |
| 2011 | 216.5 | 215.7 | 216.9 | 212.9 | 211.7 | 211.6 | 211.2 | 213.6 | 211.8 | 213.1 | 210.5 | 213.8 | 213.3 |
| 2012 | 207.9 | 208.4 | 210.6 | 215.6 | 212.5 | 210.0 | 213.9 | 216.3 | 213.2 | 217.3 | 221.6 | 224.8 | 214.3 |
| 2013 | 216.0 | 217.7 | 219.4 | 219.2 | 218.0 | 219.6 | 215.6 | 219.3 | 221.5 | 224.0 | 227.6 | 226.5 | 220.4 |
| 2014 | 221.9 | 219.8 | 221.6 | 224.0 | 219.8 | 218.7 | 217.2 | 223.1 | 224.2 | 226.8 | 225.5 | 225.8 | 222.4 |
| 2015 | 219.1 | 227.6 | 230.4 | 229.2 | 227.6 | 231.3 | 228.1 | 232.5 | 235.3 | 242.1 | 244.4 | 242.6 | 232.5 |
| 2016 | 249.3 | 256.1 | 254.8 | 263.1 | 265.8 | 256.9 | 251.5 | 254.8 | 252.6 | 249.9 | 255.3 | 253.6 | 255.3 |
| 2017 | 237.6 | 258.4 | 239.5 | 237.1 | 236.8 | 234.2 | 231.9 | 236.2 | 242.9 | 246.4 | 246.8 | 252.6 | 241.7 |
| 2018 | 245.9 | 255.2 | 252.3 | 237.8 | 233.6 | 238.4 | 232.3 | 240.9 | 243.4 | 243.6 | 245.2 | 248.7 | 243.1 |
| 2019 | 246.3 | 259.6 | 251.7 | 233.0 | 231.9 | 234.9 | 229.4 | 238.2 | 246.3 | 245.2 | 253.7 | 250.9 | 243.4 |
| **Financial Activities** | | | | | | | | | | | | | |
| 2011 | 314.6 | 314.8 | 315.5 | 313.3 | 313.5 | 314.8 | 315.2 | 315.7 | 314.7 | 315.8 | 315.7 | 317.9 | 315.1 |
| 2012 | 313.6 | 314.9 | 316.4 | 318.5 | 319.7 | 321.5 | 322.9 | 323.2 | 322.9 | 324.7 | 325.7 | 327.9 | 321.0 |
| 2013 | 324.2 | 325.3 | 325.7 | 326.3 | 326.8 | 327.4 | 328.0 | 327.1 | 324.6 | 326.9 | 327.0 | 327.3 | 326.4 |
| 2014 | 322.0 | 322.5 | 322.1 | 322.9 | 324.8 | 326.0 | 325.3 | 326.0 | 324.3 | 326.5 | 328.6 | 330.4 | 325.1 |
| 2015 | 325.3 | 326.9 | 327.3 | 328.6 | 330.3 | 331.4 | 334.2 | 334.8 | 333.4 | 336.6 | 336.6 | 338.1 | 332.0 |
| 2016 | 333.3 | 334.6 | 334.0 | 336.7 | 337.3 | 336.9 | 339.9 | 339.6 | 337.8 | 340.1 | 341.0 | 342.4 | 337.8 |
| 2017 | 337.8 | 338.2 | 338 | 339.5 | 341 | 341.3 | 342.6 | 341.9 | 340.7 | 343.5 | 343.4 | 345.5 | 341.1 |
| 2018 | 340.8 | 341.9 | 341.4 | 341.1 | 341.9 | 342.5 | 343.6 | 342.7 | 339.4 | 342.4 | 341.7 | 342.4 | 341.8 |
| 2019 | 338.1 | 339.0 | 338.4 | 339.1 | 340.1 | 341.0 | 343.1 | 343.3 | 340.8 | 343.5 | 344.3 | 345.2 | 341.3 |

## Employment by Industry: Los Angeles-Long Beach-Anaheim, CA, 2011–2019—*Continued*

(Numbers in thousands, not seasonally adjusted)

| Industry and year | January | February | March | April | May | June | July | August | September | October | November | December | Annual average |
|---|---|---|---|---|---|---|---|---|---|---|---|---|---|
| **Professional and Business Services** | | | | | | | | | | | | | |
| 2011 | 769.7 | 777.7 | 779.4 | 776.9 | 777.2 | 781.4 | 787.0 | 789.6 | 795.5 | 801.2 | 803.7 | 807.8 | 787.3 |
| 2012 | 789.5 | 803.2 | 811.4 | 816.6 | 820.9 | 827.2 | 825.3 | 830.6 | 834.0 | 844.6 | 852.9 | 855.6 | 826.0 |
| 2013 | 827.9 | 839.0 | 842.2 | 846.7 | 849.0 | 850.2 | 854.6 | 863.6 | 864.2 | 872.8 | 881.9 | 881.9 | 856.2 |
| 2014 | 862.4 | 866.6 | 869.4 | 866.2 | 866.9 | 865.6 | 865.2 | 872.8 | 871.3 | 878.8 | 883.8 | 886.0 | 871.3 |
| 2015 | 862.7 | 870.2 | 871.5 | 876.1 | 874.4 | 876.0 | 883.6 | 885.9 | 885.3 | 902.4 | 904.0 | 903.6 | 883.0 |
| 2016 | 887.3 | 894.7 | 887.8 | 895.9 | 892.8 | 893.4 | 901.9 | 904.7 | 907.9 | 917.1 | 923.6 | 920.7 | 902.3 |
| 2017 | 892.2 | 899.9 | 902.7 | 901 | 903.9 | 909.2 | 920.9 | 926 | 928.3 | 935.2 | 939 | 939.2 | 916.5 |
| 2018 | 919.1 | 925.6 | 929.7 | 936.0 | 933.5 | 941.6 | 947.9 | 954.3 | 953.8 | 971.3 | 977.3 | 977.6 | 947.3 |
| 2019 | 950.6 | 961.7 | 963.6 | 964.4 | 964.9 | 968.9 | 973.0 | 978.8 | 974.7 | 982.0 | 982.6 | 987.4 | 971.1 |
| **Education and Health Services** | | | | | | | | | | | | | |
| 2011 | 844.0 | 855.7 | 859.2 | 857.1 | 854.1 | 842.1 | 830.9 | 832.8 | 849.2 | 859.6 | 864.6 | 869.7 | 851.6 |
| 2012 | 857.5 | 873.6 | 877.9 | 882.7 | 884.5 | 874.1 | 863.5 | 871.4 | 882.8 | 892.8 | 896.7 | 900.7 | 879.9 |
| 2013 | 873.9 | 885.8 | 889.8 | 900.8 | 898.1 | 882.9 | 874.1 | 881.1 | 892.3 | 903.5 | 907.8 | 913.1 | 891.9 |
| 2014 | 899.1 | 911.5 | 915.2 | 916.6 | 916.5 | 903.9 | 894.6 | 906.3 | 920.2 | 932.8 | 936.4 | 937.5 | 915.9 |
| 2015 | 922.4 | 937.0 | 939.4 | 941.9 | 943.0 | 929.8 | 928.0 | 934.9 | 950.2 | 965.6 | 971.1 | 974.1 | 944.8 |
| 2016 | 958.5 | 971.3 | 973.7 | 980.5 | 980.5 | 968.1 | 959.9 | 963.9 | 978.2 | 999.9 | 1,004.3 | 1,007.6 | 978.9 |
| 2017 | 994.1 | 1006.6 | 1012.7 | 1013.9 | 1017 | 1004.9 | 998.5 | 1005.4 | 1022.4 | 1038.3 | 1041.8 | 1042.1 | 1016.5 |
| 2018 | 1,033.9 | 1,045.4 | 1,047.8 | 1,045.6 | 1,044.6 | 1,035.1 | 1,024.7 | 1,036.1 | 1,046.3 | 1,060.9 | 1,063.7 | 1,067.5 | 1,046.0 |
| 2019 | 1,052.8 | 1,068.8 | 1,070.6 | 1,073.7 | 1,074.0 | 1,062.1 | 1,061.9 | 1,070.9 | 1,082.3 | 1,091.6 | 1,096.6 | 1,099.3 | 1,075.4 |
| **Leisure and Hospitality** | | | | | | | | | | | | | |
| 2011 | 546.7 | 550.4 | 554.8 | 563.5 | 568.9 | 572.3 | 578.3 | 579.0 | 578.9 | 573.0 | 573.5 | 573.4 | 567.7 |
| 2012 | 565.5 | 569.6 | 576.5 | 589.3 | 599.5 | 605.0 | 606.4 | 608.3 | 605.9 | 603.8 | 604.0 | 606.3 | 595.0 |
| 2013 | 595.5 | 602.6 | 608.6 | 618.6 | 628.8 | 636.0 | 639.3 | 638.6 | 636.9 | 638.4 | 637.4 | 639.6 | 626.7 |
| 2014 | 630.1 | 636.9 | 643.4 | 650.3 | 661.4 | 665.6 | 668.5 | 671.5 | 668.2 | 670.0 | 667.8 | 669.2 | 658.6 |
| 2015 | 659.0 | 667.1 | 672.4 | 682.0 | 690.1 | 695.5 | 702.8 | 703.2 | 700.2 | 706.0 | 701.7 | 705.4 | 690.5 |
| 2016 | 693.7 | 700.6 | 705.0 | 717.6 | 723.2 | 726.5 | 732.9 | 734.7 | 731.8 | 735.9 | 730.8 | 731.4 | 722.0 |
| 2017 | 712.3 | 717.9 | 728.8 | 738.7 | 746.7 | 752.8 | 754.1 | 756.6 | 749.9 | 754.9 | 749.2 | 750.2 | 742.7 |
| 2018 | 734.6 | 742.3 | 747.9 | 756.5 | 762.5 | 766.3 | 768.6 | 769.0 | 762.7 | 768.5 | 763.5 | 766.9 | 759.1 |
| 2019 | 746.9 | 755.9 | 763.3 | 771.8 | 780.0 | 786.0 | 783.2 | 780.0 | 775.7 | 778.7 | 775.0 | 775.6 | 772.7 |
| **Other Services** | | | | | | | | | | | | | |
| 2011 | 176.4 | 178.0 | 178.7 | 179.5 | 180.2 | 180.6 | 181.2 | 180.2 | 182.2 | 182.0 | 181.6 | 182.2 | 180.2 |
| 2012 | 180.4 | 182.4 | 183.7 | 185.7 | 187.5 | 188.1 | 186.9 | 186.5 | 188.0 | 189.4 | 188.8 | 188.2 | 186.3 |
| 2013 | 186.0 | 188.4 | 189.5 | 191.2 | 191.8 | 192.4 | 191.4 | 191.5 | 192.7 | 193.1 | 193.5 | 193.3 | 191.2 |
| 2014 | 192.3 | 194.8 | 195.9 | 197.6 | 198.6 | 199.8 | 197.7 | 198.2 | 199.3 | 199.8 | 199.5 | 199.4 | 197.7 |
| 2015 | 195.9 | 197.8 | 198.6 | 199.2 | 200.7 | 200.4 | 200.6 | 199.6 | 200.9 | 202.2 | 202.2 | 201.2 | 199.9 |
| 2016 | 198.6 | 201.6 | 201.0 | 203.5 | 204.0 | 203.0 | 204.4 | 204.0 | 205.5 | 207.6 | 206.4 | 205.5 | 203.8 |
| 2017 | 200.2 | 202.4 | 204.4 | 206 | 206.9 | 207.3 | 206.2 | 206.4 | 207.4 | 208.4 | 207.7 | 208.4 | 206.0 |
| 2018 | 206.0 | 208.1 | 208.4 | 210.7 | 211.7 | 211.9 | 210.0 | 209.7 | 210.2 | 213.1 | 211.6 | 210.1 | 210.1 |
| 2019 | 205.3 | 207.7 | 208.1 | 210.0 | 211.0 | 211.2 | 211.5 | 211.8 | 211.3 | 213.1 | 211.6 | 212.5 | 210.4 |
| **Government** | | | | | | | | | | | | | |
| 2011 | 724.8 | 727.8 | 734.4 | 733.2 | 734.2 | 734.6 | 678.1 | 662.5 | 687.7 | 715.8 | 724.2 | 719.6 | 714.7 |
| 2012 | 709.5 | 718.5 | 724.3 | 721.9 | 724.5 | 723.2 | 668.1 | 659.8 | 684.5 | 703.5 | 709.9 | 708.3 | 704.7 |
| 2013 | 698.2 | 707.3 | 713.9 | 711.1 | 713.4 | 713.1 | 661.7 | 665.1 | 685.2 | 705.2 | 712.7 | 712.0 | 699.9 |
| 2014 | 702.3 | 707.3 | 717.2 | 718.3 | 723.4 | 718.6 | 665.6 | 674.2 | 700.2 | 719.5 | 727.0 | 727.1 | 708.4 |
| 2015 | 719.0 | 726.7 | 732.5 | 736.4 | 733.7 | 735.9 | 686.7 | 686.7 | 716.4 | 738.7 | 742.7 | 743.4 | 724.9 |
| 2016 | 732.6 | 740.8 | 746.4 | 747.4 | 750.5 | 740.6 | 695.6 | 696.5 | 728.5 | 748.6 | 753.2 | 754.4 | 736.3 |
| 2017 | 744.8 | 751.5 | 758.0 | 757.9 | 762.3 | 760.5 | 702.7 | 703.7 | 734.8 | 755.6 | 762.4 | 761.3 | 746.3 |
| 2018 | 750.2 | 758.1 | 761.5 | 763.2 | 765.1 | 764.3 | 708.6 | 712.3 | 743.2 | 760.2 | 766.8 | 768.8 | 751.9 |
| 2019 | 754.6 | 762.3 | 766.7 | 768.4 | 770.0 | 769.7 | 715.3 | 716.3 | 746.1 | 767.5 | 775.4 | 773.7 | 757.2 |

## Employment by Industry: Chicago-Naperville-Elgin, IL-IN-WI, 2011–2019

(Numbers in thousands, not seasonally adjusted)

| Industry and year | January | February | March | April | May | June | July | August | September | October | November | December | Annual average |
|---|---|---|---|---|---|---|---|---|---|---|---|---|---|
| **Total Nonfarm** | | | | | | | | | | | | | |
| 2011 | 4,183.3 | 4,193.2 | 4,224.4 | 4,283.9 | 4,317.5 | 4,340.4 | 4,325.7 | 4,335.6 | 4,350.2 | 4,361.2 | 4,375.2 | 4,365.0 | 4,304.6 |
| 2012 | 4,253.2 | 4,266.4 | 4,301.0 | 4,348.1 | 4,390.2 | 4,419.9 | 4,393.0 | 4,406.0 | 4,420.9 | 4,430.1 | 4,450.0 | 4,443.9 | 4,376.9 |
| 2013 | 4,317.2 | 4,340.7 | 4,369.4 | 4,405.5 | 4,461.7 | 4,492.0 | 4,465.3 | 4,479.8 | 4,485.8 | 4,498.1 | 4,515.0 | 4,517.2 | 4,445.6 |
| 2014 | 4,378.3 | 4,394.8 | 4,427.0 | 4,480.6 | 4,536.4 | 4,563.9 | 4,537.6 | 4,546.0 | 4,545.1 | 4,572.9 | 4,585.5 | 4,588.6 | 4,513.1 |
| 2015 | 4,454.6 | 4,470.7 | 4,499.1 | 4,565.3 | 4,624.2 | 4,652.1 | 4,633.5 | 4,632.3 | 4,634.8 | 4,665.3 | 4,670.9 | 4,676.8 | 4,598.3 |
| 2016 | 4,544.4 | 4,555.3 | 4,580.7 | 4,638.6 | 4,671.8 | 4,703.2 | 4,695.4 | 4,693.9 | 4,695.0 | 4,714.4 | 4,726.9 | 4,718.1 | 4,661.5 |
| 2017 | 4,586.7 | 4,602.0 | 4,636.3 | 4,667.0 | 4,716.7 | 4,755.9 | 4,725.7 | 4,728.5 | 4,727.7 | 4,745.1 | 4,761.9 | 4,755.6 | 4,700.8 |
| 2018 | 4,619.3 | 4,637.7 | 4,678.3 | 4,694.0 | 4,746.3 | 4,789.7 | 4,772.8 | 4,774.4 | 4,766.4 | 4,778.1 | 4,800.6 | 4,787.1 | 4,737.1 |
| 2019 | 4,658.3 | 4,663.8 | 4,694.5 | 4,729.9 | 4,781.2 | 4,819.8 | 4,796.4 | 4,797.0 | 4,784.0 | 4,808.4 | 4,802.6 | 4,791.0 | 4,760.6 |
| **Total Private** | | | | | | | | | | | | | |
| 2011 | 3,635.9 | 3,637.9 | 3,666.9 | 3,723.1 | 3,753.4 | 3,786.2 | 3,784.7 | 3,799.8 | 3,797.9 | 3,805.6 | 3,816.8 | 3,812.5 | 3,751.7 |
| 2012 | 3,711.0 | 3,713.3 | 3,745.0 | 3,791.5 | 3,830.4 | 3,866.5 | 3,857.3 | 3,872.7 | 3,870.9 | 3,876.1 | 3,894.2 | 3,892.1 | 3,826.8 |
| 2013 | 3,776.3 | 3,788.7 | 3,814.8 | 3,850.9 | 3,902.7 | 3,938.0 | 3,929.8 | 3,944.4 | 3,935.1 | 3,948.3 | 3,962.8 | 3,965.6 | 3,896.5 |
| 2014 | 3,842.7 | 3,849.1 | 3,877.8 | 3,929.9 | 3,979.6 | 4,013.7 | 4,001.7 | 4,012.9 | 3,995.5 | 4,020.5 | 4,033.4 | 4,035.7 | 3,966.0 |
| 2015 | 3,914.7 | 3,921.2 | 3,947.4 | 4,010.9 | 4,064.5 | 4,098.2 | 4,096.7 | 4,098.9 | 4,084.3 | 4,111.0 | 4,119.4 | 4,123.1 | 4,049.2 |
| 2016 | 4,006.3 | 4,008.8 | 4,029.4 | 4,088.3 | 4,117.9 | 4,147.0 | 4,155.3 | 4,158.0 | 4,139.9 | 4,165.3 | 4,176.7 | 4,160.5 | 4,112.8 |
| 2017 | 4,049.4 | 4,055.5 | 4,086.4 | 4,118.7 | 4,163.9 | 4,200.4 | 4,188.3 | 4,196.2 | 4,174.8 | 4,197.2 | 4,213.0 | 4,205.0 | 4,154.1 |
| 2018 | 4,084.1 | 4,093.5 | 4,127.9 | 4,147.1 | 4,192.4 | 4,235.8 | 4,235.3 | 4,239.2 | 4,212.9 | 4,228.5 | 4,247.4 | 4,234.8 | 4,189.9 |
| 2019 | 4,121.3 | 4,119.6 | 4,144.7 | 4,181.6 | 4,224.5 | 4,263.7 | 4,257.8 | 4,260.0 | 4,228.6 | 4,254.8 | 4,245.9 | 4,236.0 | 4,211.5 |
| **Goods Producing** | | | | | | | | | | | | | |
| 2011 | 533.5 | 532.0 | 540.7 | 554.6 | 563.4 | 570.2 | 572.8 | 574.5 | 570.8 | 569.9 | 566.9 | 557.9 | 558.9 |
| 2012 | 538.6 | 537.1 | 545.5 | 556.1 | 563.1 | 571.5 | 574.1 | 575.3 | 574.2 | 571.8 | 567.7 | 562.4 | 561.5 |
| 2013 | 540.2 | 541.4 | 547.0 | 553.3 | 564.0 | 572.0 | 572.8 | 573.9 | 571.3 | 571.9 | 570.3 | 561.1 | 561.6 |
| 2014 | 539.1 | 540.8 | 548.2 | 559.4 | 569.6 | 578.6 | 580.5 | 581.1 | 579.3 | 583.5 | 582.3 | 576.4 | 568.2 |
| 2015 | 555.1 | 554.5 | 563.0 | 574.6 | 584.1 | 593.2 | 594.1 | 594.0 | 592.7 | 592.9 | 591.5 | 584.2 | 581.2 |
| 2016 | 563.1 | 564.4 | 572.6 | 586.4 | 591.5 | 598.0 | 598.9 | 598.4 | 595.7 | 597.1 | 595.2 | 582.8 | 587.0 |
| 2017 | 564.7 | 566.6 | 574.1 | 583.9 | 593.8 | 602.1 | 603.3 | 603.6 | 602.3 | 601.6 | 599.6 | 592.3 | 590.7 |
| 2018 | 573.2 | 575.5 | 586.3 | 594.2 | 604.7 | 614.5 | 613.3 | 613.5 | 610.9 | 612.0 | 608.1 | 600.8 | 600.6 |
| 2019 | 581.0 | 581.2 | 589.5 | 598.9 | 608.0 | 615.5 | 614.4 | 613.6 | 609.9 | 608.6 | 602.3 | 592.2 | 601.3 |
| **Service-Providing** | | | | | | | | | | | | | |
| 2011 | 3,649.8 | 3,661.2 | 3,683.7 | 3,729.3 | 3,754.1 | 3,770.2 | 3,752.9 | 3,761.1 | 3,779.4 | 3,791.3 | 3,808.3 | 3,807.1 | 3,745.7 |
| 2012 | 3,714.6 | 3,729.3 | 3,755.5 | 3,792.0 | 3,827.1 | 3,848.4 | 3,818.9 | 3,830.7 | 3,846.7 | 3,858.3 | 3,882.3 | 3,881.5 | 3,815.4 |
| 2013 | 3,777.0 | 3,799.3 | 3,822.4 | 3,852.2 | 3,897.7 | 3,920.0 | 3,892.5 | 3,905.9 | 3,914.5 | 3,926.2 | 3,944.7 | 3,956.1 | 3,884.0 |
| 2014 | 3,839.2 | 3,854.0 | 3,878.8 | 3,921.2 | 3,966.8 | 3,985.3 | 3,957.1 | 3,964.9 | 3,965.8 | 3,989.4 | 4,003.2 | 4,012.2 | 3,944.8 |
| 2015 | 3,899.5 | 3,916.2 | 3,936.1 | 3,990.7 | 4,040.1 | 4,058.9 | 4,039.4 | 4,038.3 | 4,042.1 | 4,072.4 | 4,079.4 | 4,092.6 | 4,017.1 |
| 2016 | 3,981.3 | 3,990.9 | 4,008.1 | 4,052.2 | 4,080.3 | 4,105.2 | 4,096.5 | 4,095.5 | 4,099.3 | 4,117.3 | 4,131.7 | 4,135.3 | 4,074.5 |
| 2017 | 4,022.0 | 4,035.4 | 4,062.2 | 4,083.1 | 4,122.9 | 4,153.8 | 4,122.4 | 4,124.9 | 4,125.4 | 4,143.5 | 4,162.3 | 4,163.3 | 4,110.1 |
| 2018 | 4,046.1 | 4,062.2 | 4,092.0 | 4,099.8 | 4,141.6 | 4,175.2 | 4,159.5 | 4,160.9 | 4,155.5 | 4,166.1 | 4,192.5 | 4,186.3 | 4,136.5 |
| 2019 | 4,077.3 | 4,082.6 | 4,105.0 | 4,131.0 | 4,173.2 | 4,204.3 | 4,182.0 | 4,183.4 | 4,174.1 | 4,199.8 | 4,200.3 | 4,198.8 | 4,159.3 |
| **Mining and Logging** | | | | | | | | | | | | | |
| 2011 | 1.2 | 1.2 | 1.3 | 1.5 | 1.5 | 1.5 | 1.6 | 1.5 | 1.5 | 1.5 | 1.5 | 1.3 | 1.4 |
| 2012 | 1.2 | 1.2 | 1.2 | 1.3 | 1.4 | 1.5 | 1.5 | 1.5 | 1.5 | 1.5 | 1.5 | 1.3 | 1.4 |
| 2013 | 1.2 | 1.2 | 1.2 | 1.3 | 1.6 | 1.6 | 1.5 | 1.5 | 1.5 | 1.5 | 1.6 | 1.3 | 1.4 |
| 2014 | 1.2 | 1.2 | 1.2 | 1.4 | 1.5 | 1.6 | 1.6 | 1.6 | 1.6 | 1.6 | 1.6 | 1.3 | 1.5 |
| 2015 | 1.3 | 1.3 | 1.5 | 1.6 | 1.6 | 1.5 | 1.5 | 1.6 | 1.6 | 1.6 | 1.7 | 1.7 | 1.5 |
| 2016 | 1.4 | 1.5 | 1.6 | 1.6 | 1.6 | 1.6 | 1.6 | 1.6 | 1.6 | 1.6 | 1.6 | 1.5 | 1.6 |
| 2017 | 1.3 | 1.3 | 1.4 | 1.6 | 1.6 | 1.7 | 1.6 | 1.7 | 1.6 | 1.6 | 1.6 | 1.6 | 1.6 |
| 2018 | 1.4 | 1.4 | 1.5 | 1.6 | 1.7 | 1.7 | 1.7 | 1.7 | 1.6 | 1.7 | 1.8 | 1.7 | 1.6 |
| 2019 | 1.6 | 1.6 | 1.7 | 1.9 | 1.9 | 1.9 | 1.9 | 1.9 | 1.9 | 1.9 | 1.9 | 1.8 | 1.8 |
| **Construction** | | | | | | | | | | | | | |
| 2011 | 125.8 | 124.2 | 130.5 | 142.2 | 150.1 | 154.3 | 157.7 | 159.5 | 157.3 | 155.8 | 153.2 | 144.3 | 146.2 |
| 2012 | 128.6 | 126.7 | 133.3 | 142.7 | 148.4 | 154.0 | 157.3 | 158.4 | 158.4 | 158.0 | 153.5 | 146.9 | 147.2 |
| 2013 | 129.9 | 130.5 | 135.5 | 143.1 | 152.7 | 157.3 | 160.2 | 160.5 | 160.0 | 160.6 | 157.8 | 148.7 | 149.7 |
| 2014 | 130.6 | 132.1 | 137.7 | 148.8 | 157.6 | 163.7 | 167.0 | 167.5 | 167.0 | 169.6 | 166.9 | 160.0 | 155.7 |
| 2015 | 141.8 | 141.5 | 148.5 | 161.0 | 168.4 | 173.1 | 174.8 | 175.2 | 174.7 | 176.7 | 174.7 | 166.4 | 164.7 |
| 2016 | 149.0 | 149.3 | 156.5 | 168.6 | 172.9 | 177.5 | 179.9 | 180.6 | 180.4 | 182.3 | 179.2 | 166.4 | 170.2 |
| 2017 | 151.8 | 152.8 | 159.0 | 169.2 | 177.8 | 181.8 | 183.4 | 184.0 | 184.3 | 184.4 | 181.1 | 172.3 | 173.5 |
| 2018 | 156.7 | 157.1 | 166.6 | 174.3 | 182.8 | 189.6 | 189.3 | 190.1 | 189.4 | 190.2 | 184.3 | 176.2 | 178.9 |
| 2019 | 159.8 | 159.0 | 167.1 | 177.7 | 185.4 | 190.1 | 190.4 | 191.1 | 190.2 | 190.3 | 184.0 | 173.9 | 179.9 |

## Employment by Industry: Chicago-Naperville-Elgin, IL-IN-WI, 2011–2019—*Continued*

(Numbers in thousands, not seasonally adjusted)

| Industry and year | January | February | March | April | May | June | July | August | September | October | November | December | Annual average |
|---|---|---|---|---|---|---|---|---|---|---|---|---|---|
| **Manufacturing** | | | | | | | | | | | | | |
| 2011 | 406.5 | 406.6 | 408.9 | 410.9 | 411.8 | 414.4 | 413.5 | 413.5 | 412.0 | 412.6 | 412.2 | 412.3 | 411.3 |
| 2012 | 408.8 | 409.2 | 411.0 | 412.1 | 413.3 | 416.0 | 415.3 | 415.4 | 414.3 | 412.3 | 412.7 | 414.2 | 412.9 |
| 2013 | 409.1 | 409.7 | 410.3 | 408.9 | 409.7 | 413.1 | 411.1 | 411.9 | 409.8 | 409.8 | 410.9 | 411.1 | 410.5 |
| 2014 | 407.3 | 407.5 | 409.3 | 409.2 | 410.5 | 413.3 | 411.9 | 412.0 | 410.7 | 412.3 | 413.8 | 414.8 | 411.1 |
| 2015 | 412.0 | 411.7 | 413.0 | 412.0 | 414.1 | 418.6 | 417.8 | 417.2 | 416.4 | 414.6 | 415.1 | 416.1 | 414.9 |
| 2016 | 412.7 | 413.6 | 414.5 | 416.2 | 417.0 | 418.9 | 417.4 | 416.2 | 413.7 | 413.2 | 414.4 | 414.9 | 415.2 |
| 2017 | 411.6 | 412.5 | 413.7 | 413.1 | 414.4 | 418.6 | 418.3 | 417.9 | 416.4 | 415.6 | 416.9 | 418.4 | 415.6 |
| 2018 | 415.1 | 417.0 | 418.2 | 418.3 | 420.2 | 423.2 | 422.3 | 421.7 | 419.9 | 420.1 | 422.0 | 422.9 | 420.1 |
| 2019 | 419.6 | 420.6 | 420.7 | 419.3 | 420.7 | 423.5 | 422.1 | 420.6 | 417.8 | 416.4 | 416.4 | 416.5 | 419.5 |
| **Trade, Transportation, and Utilities** | | | | | | | | | | | | | |
| 2011 | 855.0 | 846.9 | 849.7 | 858.0 | 863.9 | 869.9 | 867.2 | 871.2 | 871.3 | 877.4 | 893.8 | 904.7 | 869.1 |
| 2012 | 871.9 | 861.9 | 866.9 | 869.4 | 877.1 | 882.2 | 881.1 | 883.5 | 882.4 | 889.8 | 911.3 | 917.4 | 882.9 |
| 2013 | 881.7 | 873.8 | 877.1 | 881.6 | 891.2 | 898.6 | 895.8 | 899.0 | 895.9 | 901.5 | 919.7 | 932.2 | 895.7 |
| 2014 | 892.5 | 883.5 | 888.8 | 893.8 | 903.7 | 911.4 | 907.9 | 910.5 | 908.5 | 915.4 | 934.6 | 946.2 | 908.1 |
| 2015 | 908.3 | 901.9 | 906.4 | 913.6 | 924.4 | 933.1 | 931.5 | 933.0 | 932.5 | 939.3 | 956.3 | 965.8 | 928.8 |
| 2016 | 927.4 | 921.0 | 923.8 | 932.0 | 936.7 | 941.4 | 941.9 | 942.9 | 938.1 | 950.8 | 967.3 | 980.8 | 942.0 |
| 2017 | 941.7 | 932.5 | 934.6 | 935.1 | 940.2 | 947.7 | 942.5 | 943.4 | 941.1 | 950.3 | 972.1 | 981.7 | 946.9 |
| 2018 | 945.0 | 934.6 | 938.1 | 937.3 | 943.9 | 950.3 | 950.3 | 948.0 | 942.4 | 948.8 | 971.3 | 979.2 | 949.1 |
| 2019 | 946.9 | 932.7 | 934.7 | 937.3 | 943.1 | 952.0 | 949.5 | 949.4 | 943.8 | 951.6 | 965.1 | 975.1 | 948.4 |
| **Wholesale Trade** | | | | | | | | | | | | | |
| 2011 | 226.6 | 226.6 | 227.4 | 228.9 | 229.8 | 231.7 | 231.8 | 231.9 | 230.9 | 230.9 | 231.3 | 232.6 | 230.0 |
| 2012 | 231.3 | 231.2 | 232.5 | 233.4 | 234.6 | 236.7 | 236.1 | 236.1 | 235.3 | 235.9 | 236.4 | 237.1 | 234.7 |
| 2013 | 234.4 | 234.7 | 236.0 | 236.9 | 238.2 | 240.6 | 240.1 | 239.5 | 239.0 | 238.6 | 239.2 | 240.6 | 238.2 |
| 2014 | 236.3 | 237.1 | 237.8 | 237.7 | 239.1 | 240.3 | 239.4 | 239.1 | 237.5 | 238.6 | 239.3 | 240.2 | 238.5 |
| 2015 | 237.6 | 237.4 | 238.7 | 240.1 | 242.2 | 243.7 | 243.4 | 242.5 | 241.1 | 240.5 | 240.7 | 241.6 | 240.8 |
| 2016 | 236.6 | 236.7 | 237.1 | 238.7 | 239.1 | 241.0 | 240.9 | 240.5 | 238.9 | 239.9 | 240.5 | 241.4 | 239.3 |
| 2017 | 238.0 | 238.6 | 239.4 | 240.4 | 241.9 | 244.1 | 243.4 | 242.6 | 241.6 | 242.8 | 242.7 | 244.2 | 241.6 |
| 2018 | 241.4 | 242.2 | 243.3 | 241.8 | 242.2 | 244.1 | 244.5 | 243.4 | 242.2 | 243.0 | 243.1 | 244.7 | 243.0 |
| 2019 | 241.8 | 242.5 | 243.0 | 244.4 | 244.9 | 247.4 | 247.0 | 245.8 | 244.0 | 244.0 | 243.6 | 242.8 | 244.3 |
| **Retail Trade** | | | | | | | | | | | | | |
| 2011 | 437.1 | 428.9 | 430.3 | 435.2 | 438.8 | 443.4 | 442.5 | 444.8 | 442.1 | 447.9 | 463.1 | 470.6 | 443.7 |
| 2012 | 444.6 | 435.0 | 437.4 | 437.2 | 441.8 | 446.3 | 445.9 | 446.0 | 442.9 | 449.1 | 468.8 | 471.5 | 447.2 |
| 2013 | 446.4 | 438.0 | 439.4 | 440.6 | 447.6 | 454.1 | 452.5 | 453.2 | 449.6 | 455.4 | 471.1 | 479.7 | 452.3 |
| 2014 | 451.0 | 441.7 | 444.6 | 448.4 | 454.0 | 460.6 | 459.7 | 459.4 | 456.5 | 462.3 | 477.7 | 484.0 | 458.3 |
| 2015 | 456.9 | 450.6 | 453.3 | 456.6 | 462.4 | 469.0 | 468.1 | 467.8 | 465.8 | 470.9 | 485.1 | 489.1 | 466.3 |
| 2016 | 464.9 | 458.5 | 460.1 | 464.5 | 467.3 | 471.9 | 472.0 | 471.2 | 464.9 | 471.4 | 484.4 | 490.4 | 470.1 |
| 2017 | 467.9 | 459.8 | 459.7 | 461.1 | 462.5 | 467.8 | 465.1 | 463.0 | 456.9 | 462.7 | 479.2 | 483.8 | 465.8 |
| 2018 | 459.2 | 449.5 | 451.8 | 451.9 | 456.6 | 460.2 | 459.2 | 456.3 | 449.9 | 453.0 | 469.0 | 471.8 | 457.4 |
| 2019 | 451.7 | 439.7 | 441.2 | 441.9 | 444.6 | 449.0 | 447.2 | 445.5 | 438.6 | 444.7 | 456.4 | 463.6 | 447.0 |
| **Transportation and Utilities** | | | | | | | | | | | | | |
| 2011 | 191.3 | 191.4 | 192.0 | 193.9 | 195.3 | 194.8 | 192.9 | 194.5 | 198.3 | 198.6 | 199.4 | 201.5 | 195.3 |
| 2012 | 196.0 | 195.7 | 197.0 | 198.8 | 200.7 | 199.2 | 199.1 | 201.4 | 204.2 | 204.8 | 206.1 | 208.8 | 201.0 |
| 2013 | 200.9 | 201.1 | 201.7 | 204.1 | 205.4 | 203.9 | 203.2 | 206.3 | 207.3 | 207.5 | 209.4 | 211.9 | 205.2 |
| 2014 | 205.2 | 204.7 | 206.4 | 207.7 | 210.6 | 210.5 | 208.8 | 212.0 | 214.5 | 214.5 | 217.6 | 222.0 | 211.2 |
| 2015 | 213.8 | 213.9 | 214.4 | 216.9 | 219.8 | 220.4 | 220.0 | 222.7 | 225.6 | 227.9 | 230.5 | 235.1 | 221.8 |
| 2016 | 225.9 | 225.8 | 226.6 | 228.8 | 230.3 | 228.5 | 229.0 | 231.2 | 234.3 | 239.5 | 242.4 | 249.0 | 232.6 |
| 2017 | 235.8 | 234.1 | 235.5 | 233.6 | 235.8 | 235.8 | 234.0 | 237.8 | 242.6 | 244.8 | 250.2 | 253.7 | 239.5 |
| 2018 | 244.4 | 242.9 | 243.0 | 243.6 | 245.1 | 246.0 | 246.6 | 248.3 | 250.3 | 252.8 | 259.2 | 262.7 | 248.7 |
| 2019 | 253.4 | 250.5 | 250.5 | 251.0 | 253.6 | 255.6 | 255.3 | 258.1 | 261.2 | 262.9 | 265.1 | 268.7 | 257.2 |
| **Information** | | | | | | | | | | | | | |
| 2011 | 79.4 | 79.2 | 79.0 | 79.3 | 79.5 | 80.3 | 80.8 | 80.5 | 79.8 | 80.2 | 80.7 | 80.5 | 79.9 |
| 2012 | 80.5 | 80.3 | 80.1 | 80.5 | 81.0 | 80.8 | 80.8 | 80.5 | 79.9 | 80.5 | 81.1 | 81.0 | 80.6 |
| 2013 | 79.9 | 79.9 | 79.5 | 80.0 | 80.3 | 80.6 | 80.2 | 79.7 | 79.1 | 79.3 | 79.7 | 79.8 | 79.8 |
| 2014 | 78.6 | 78.8 | 79.4 | 79.8 | 79.6 | 80.2 | 80.2 | 80.2 | 78.9 | 79.9 | 79.9 | 80.1 | 79.6 |
| 2015 | 79.4 | 79.2 | 78.6 | 80.1 | 80.7 | 80.3 | 79.8 | 79.7 | 78.6 | 79.3 | 79.5 | 79.6 | 79.6 |
| 2016 | 78.2 | 77.7 | 77.8 | 77.9 | 78.1 | 78.2 | 78.2 | 79.3 | 78.4 | 81.8 | 82.1 | 81.2 | 79.1 |
| 2017 | 80.5 | 80.5 | 80.6 | 79.2 | 79.9 | 79.9 | 79.0 | 79.5 | 77.9 | 77.7 | 77.8 | 77.6 | 79.2 |
| 2018 | 77.4 | 76.9 | 77.1 | 77.1 | 77.4 | 77.9 | 78.7 | 78.6 | 76.8 | 77.9 | 78.5 | 78.1 | 77.7 |
| 2019 | 78.4 | 78.6 | 78.8 | 78.5 | 78.2 | 78.8 | 78.5 | 79.5 | 78.5 | 79.5 | 78.3 | 80.4 | 78.8 |

## Employment by Industry: Chicago-Naperville-Elgin, IL-IN-WI, 2011–2019—*Continued*

(Numbers in thousands, not seasonally adjusted)

| Industry and year | January | February | March | April | May | June | July | August | September | October | November | December | Annual average |
|---|---|---|---|---|---|---|---|---|---|---|---|---|---|
| **Financial Activities** | | | | | | | | | | | | | |
| 2011 | 285.2 | 284.7 | 284.7 | 285.0 | 285.4 | 288.0 | 289.5 | 289.5 | 287.6 | 288.4 | 288.2 | 288.3 | 287.0 |
| 2012 | 285.3 | 285.7 | 286.0 | 286.9 | 288.2 | 291.2 | 292.1 | 292.5 | 290.5 | 290.2 | 289.8 | 290.8 | 289.1 |
| 2013 | 288.2 | 288.6 | 288.3 | 289.1 | 289.9 | 293.6 | 293.6 | 293.0 | 291.4 | 292.0 | 291.3 | 292.1 | 290.9 |
| 2014 | 288.8 | 288.1 | 288.1 | 288.7 | 290.7 | 293.6 | 294.4 | 295.4 | 292.2 | 293.0 | 292.5 | 293.7 | 291.6 |
| 2015 | 291.3 | 291.4 | 291.3 | 293.1 | 295.4 | 299.2 | 300.3 | 300.7 | 297.1 | 298.8 | 298.3 | 299.4 | 296.4 |
| 2016 | 296.3 | 296.9 | 297.2 | 298.8 | 300.0 | 303.0 | 305.7 | 306.1 | 303.0 | 304.3 | 304.0 | 304.8 | 301.7 |
| 2017 | 302.3 | 302.5 | 303.3 | 304.4 | 305.8 | 310.0 | 312.8 | 312.6 | 309.2 | 310.0 | 309.6 | 310.7 | 307.8 |
| 2018 | 305.9 | 306.1 | 306.7 | 306.8 | 308.5 | 313.3 | 315.5 | 315.7 | 312.3 | 314.0 | 313.7 | 314.5 | 311.1 |
| 2019 | 311.6 | 313.6 | 314.2 | 315.8 | 316.5 | 321.6 | 322.9 | 323.1 | 318.6 | 320.4 | 320.6 | 320.9 | 318.3 |
| **Professional and Business Services** | | | | | | | | | | | | | |
| 2011 | 679.3 | 683.4 | 687.7 | 706.3 | 706.9 | 717.0 | 721.5 | 726.8 | 726.9 | 730.5 | 730.9 | 724.8 | 711.8 |
| 2012 | 704.9 | 706.6 | 714.0 | 732.3 | 739.7 | 750.9 | 750.0 | 757.8 | 759.5 | 760.9 | 764.3 | 760.0 | 741.7 |
| 2013 | 733.1 | 739.6 | 745.4 | 758.9 | 771.3 | 781.4 | 784.4 | 792.2 | 791.0 | 800.1 | 802.0 | 799.9 | 774.9 |
| 2014 | 765.4 | 770.6 | 775.1 | 790.8 | 800.4 | 809.1 | 807.3 | 812.8 | 809.1 | 817.1 | 817.3 | 810.9 | 798.8 |
| 2015 | 780.5 | 783.7 | 785.4 | 803.9 | 812.1 | 819.4 | 827.3 | 826.2 | 822.2 | 832.7 | 830.0 | 827.3 | 812.6 |
| 2016 | 801.4 | 801.6 | 801.5 | 813.9 | 814.8 | 823.8 | 831.9 | 834.6 | 833.4 | 837.4 | 838.2 | 828.8 | 821.8 |
| 2017 | 799.0 | 800.9 | 807.2 | 815.3 | 824.2 | 835.3 | 836.3 | 840.6 | 837.1 | 845.0 | 848.0 | 841.2 | 827.5 |
| 2018 | 807.1 | 815.0 | 816.6 | 818.2 | 824.8 | 837.5 | 844.5 | 850.1 | 847.4 | 849.0 | 854.4 | 843.4 | 834.0 |
| 2019 | 810.7 | 816.2 | 815.0 | 824.2 | 833.9 | 846.0 | 848.0 | 852.8 | 845.1 | 851.7 | 847.2 | 833.7 | 835.4 |
| **Education and Health Services** | | | | | | | | | | | | | |
| 2011 | 640.1 | 648.2 | 651.1 | 650.7 | 650.6 | 644.8 | 638.1 | 637.5 | 652.5 | 659.3 | 662.2 | 664.5 | 650.0 |
| 2012 | 652.5 | 662.7 | 663.4 | 665.4 | 665.0 | 659.9 | 651.6 | 651.3 | 666.1 | 671.1 | 674.4 | 674.8 | 663.2 |
| 2013 | 664.0 | 675.9 | 677.9 | 676.1 | 676.7 | 668.9 | 658.9 | 662.0 | 674.6 | 680.8 | 684.7 | 685.1 | 673.8 |
| 2014 | 676.2 | 684.7 | 686.5 | 690.3 | 691.3 | 682.7 | 675.3 | 677.9 | 686.1 | 693.7 | 697.1 | 699.3 | 686.8 |
| 2015 | 688.3 | 695.9 | 699.7 | 704.2 | 707.0 | 698.4 | 692.7 | 692.3 | 700.8 | 710.7 | 712.8 | 712.8 | 701.3 |
| 2016 | 704.6 | 712.1 | 713.6 | 718.0 | 719.4 | 711.5 | 707.1 | 706.3 | 714.9 | 722.2 | 723.8 | 722.6 | 714.7 |
| 2017 | 714.3 | 723.7 | 726.8 | 727.0 | 728.1 | 718.4 | 710.9 | 711.7 | 720.8 | 730.2 | 733.2 | 731.7 | 723.1 |
| 2018 | 721.3 | 731.6 | 735.2 | 734.3 | 734.7 | 727.4 | 719.9 | 720.1 | 730.2 | 736.1 | 739.1 | 737.2 | 730.6 |
| 2019 | 728.4 | 734.5 | 738.6 | 739.9 | 740.1 | 729.4 | 725.1 | 725.9 | 736.0 | 750.2 | 752.2 | 751.9 | 737.7 |
| **Leisure and Hospitality** | | | | | | | | | | | | | |
| 2011 | 375.7 | 375.1 | 384.0 | 398.6 | 411.2 | 421.6 | 421.1 | 426.5 | 417.1 | 408.8 | 403.5 | 400.1 | 403.6 |
| 2012 | 388.3 | 389.4 | 398.2 | 410.7 | 424.4 | 435.2 | 434.3 | 439.5 | 427.0 | 421.2 | 414.7 | 414.6 | 416.5 |
| 2013 | 400.4 | 400.0 | 409.0 | 420.6 | 436.7 | 448.3 | 448.0 | 448.2 | 437.5 | 429.6 | 422.4 | 421.7 | 426.9 |
| 2014 | 410.2 | 409.8 | 417.4 | 432.2 | 447.3 | 458.5 | 456.7 | 457.9 | 446.4 | 442.5 | 434.4 | 433.4 | 437.2 |
| 2015 | 418.8 | 420.8 | 427.9 | 446.3 | 464.5 | 475.8 | 473.2 | 475.7 | 465.1 | 461.4 | 454.9 | 457.4 | 453.5 |
| 2016 | 441.0 | 440.4 | 447.4 | 465.1 | 480.4 | 492.5 | 493.1 | 492.2 | 480.3 | 475.4 | 470.0 | 462.8 | 470.1 |
| 2017 | 452.1 | 453.7 | 463.0 | 476.5 | 493.7 | 506.8 | 504.0 | 505.9 | 489.9 | 484.9 | 475.3 | 471.2 | 481.4 |
| 2018 | 458.8 | 457.7 | 470.1 | 481.4 | 499.1 | 513.3 | 511.7 | 513.0 | 495.0 | 490.8 | 482.6 | 481.4 | 487.9 |
| 2019 | 466.7 | 465.4 | 474.9 | 487.2 | 503.6 | 518.4 | 517.8 | 515.0 | 498.2 | 494.5 | 481.2 | 482.0 | 492.1 |
| **Other Services** | | | | | | | | | | | | | |
| 2011 | 187.7 | 188.4 | 190.0 | 190.6 | 192.5 | 194.4 | 193.7 | 193.3 | 191.9 | 191.1 | 190.6 | 191.7 | 191.3 |
| 2012 | 189.0 | 189.6 | 190.9 | 190.2 | 191.9 | 194.8 | 193.3 | 192.3 | 191.3 | 190.6 | 190.9 | 191.1 | 191.3 |
| 2013 | 188.8 | 189.5 | 190.6 | 191.3 | 192.6 | 194.6 | 196.1 | 196.4 | 194.3 | 193.1 | 192.7 | 193.7 | 192.8 |
| 2014 | 191.9 | 192.8 | 194.3 | 194.9 | 197.0 | 199.6 | 199.4 | 197.1 | 195.0 | 195.4 | 195.3 | 195.7 | 195.7 |
| 2015 | 193.0 | 193.8 | 195.1 | 195.1 | 196.3 | 198.8 | 197.8 | 197.3 | 195.3 | 195.9 | 196.1 | 196.6 | 195.9 |
| 2016 | 194.3 | 194.7 | 195.5 | 196.2 | 197.0 | 198.6 | 198.5 | 198.2 | 196.1 | 196.3 | 196.1 | 196.7 | 196.5 |
| 2017 | 194.8 | 195.1 | 196.8 | 197.3 | 198.2 | 200.2 | 199.5 | 198.9 | 196.5 | 197.5 | 197.4 | 198.6 | 197.6 |
| 2018 | 195.4 | 196.1 | 197.8 | 198.1 | 199.3 | 201.6 | 201.4 | 200.2 | 197.9 | 199.9 | 199.7 | 200.2 | 199.0 |
| 2019 | 197.6 | 197.4 | 199.0 | 199.8 | 201.1 | 202.0 | 201.6 | 200.7 | 198.5 | 198.3 | 199.0 | 199.8 | 199.6 |
| **Government** | | | | | | | | | | | | | |
| 2011 | 547.4 | 555.3 | 557.5 | 560.8 | 564.1 | 554.2 | 541.0 | 535.8 | 552.3 | 555.6 | 558.4 | 552.5 | 552.9 |
| 2012 | 542.2 | 553.1 | 556.0 | 556.6 | 559.8 | 553.4 | 535.7 | 533.3 | 550.0 | 554.0 | 555.8 | 551.8 | 550.1 |
| 2013 | 540.9 | 552.0 | 554.6 | 554.6 | 559.0 | 554.0 | 535.5 | 535.4 | 550.7 | 549.8 | 552.2 | 551.6 | 549.2 |
| 2014 | 535.6 | 545.7 | 549.2 | 550.7 | 556.8 | 550.2 | 535.9 | 533.1 | 549.6 | 552.4 | 552.1 | 552.9 | 547.0 |
| 2015 | 539.9 | 549.5 | 551.7 | 554.4 | 559.7 | 553.9 | 536.8 | 533.4 | 550.5 | 554.3 | 551.5 | 553.7 | 549.1 |
| 2016 | 538.1 | 546.5 | 551.3 | 550.3 | 553.9 | 556.2 | 540.1 | 535.9 | 555.1 | 549.1 | 550.2 | 557.6 | 548.7 |
| 2017 | 537.3 | 546.5 | 549.9 | 548.3 | 552.8 | 555.5 | 537.4 | 532.3 | 552.9 | 547.9 | 548.9 | 550.6 | 546.7 |
| 2018 | 535.2 | 544.2 | 550.4 | 546.9 | 553.9 | 553.9 | 537.5 | 535.2 | 553.5 | 549.6 | 553.2 | 552.3 | 547.2 |
| 2019 | 537.0 | 544.2 | 549.8 | 548.3 | 556.7 | 556.1 | 538.6 | 537.0 | 555.4 | 553.6 | 556.7 | 555.0 | 549.0 |

# Employment by Industry: Dallas-Fort Worth-Arlington, TX, 2011–2019

(Numbers in thousands, not seasonally adjusted)

| Industry and year | January | February | March | April | May | June | July | August | September | October | November | December | Annual average |
|---|---|---|---|---|---|---|---|---|---|---|---|---|---|
| **Total Nonfarm** | | | | | | | | | | | | | |
| 2011 | 2,927.2 | 2,941.2 | 2,968.8 | 2,992.2 | 3,004.3 | 3,019.6 | 3,004.4 | 3,015.5 | 3,026.9 | 3,034.7 | 3,047.6 | 3,055.0 | 3,003.1 |
| 2012 | 3,003.5 | 3,026.6 | 3,049.9 | 3,064.9 | 3,082.3 | 3,098.9 | 3,070.5 | 3,090.5 | 3,098.7 | 3,115.9 | 3,139.4 | 3,147.0 | 3,082.3 |
| 2013 | 3,078.2 | 3,107.5 | 3,127.5 | 3,144.1 | 3,165.7 | 3,186.1 | 3,169.8 | 3,189.5 | 3,199.2 | 3,213.9 | 3,240.6 | 3,242.5 | 3,172.1 |
| 2014 | 3,184.8 | 3,209.9 | 3,231.7 | 3,255.4 | 3,278.4 | 3,298.4 | 3,279.8 | 3,298.0 | 3,306.5 | 3,335.4 | 3,358.8 | 3,374.5 | 3,284.3 |
| 2015 | 3,319.1 | 3,341.7 | 3,347.2 | 3,373.3 | 3,394.7 | 3,413.8 | 3,403.4 | 3,414.8 | 3,418.3 | 3,445.2 | 3,459.4 | 3,471.8 | 3,400.2 |
| 2016 | 3,421.6 | 3,446.6 | 3,453.6 | 3,482.2 | 3,497.6 | 3,507.6 | 3,498.6 | 3,513.0 | 3,527.9 | 3,544.7 | 3,570.4 | 3,579.1 | 3,503.6 |
| 2017 | 3,523.5 | 3,544.9 | 3,557.3 | 3,572.0 | 3,588.2 | 3,609.3 | 3,583.3 | 3,598.4 | 3,608.5 | 3,637.0 | 3,666.6 | 3,666.7 | 3,596.3 |
| 2018 | 3,603.5 | 3,628.2 | 3,639.7 | 3,649.9 | 3,674.3 | 3,697.7 | 3,678.7 | 3,695.6 | 3,698.2 | 3,727.1 | 3,755.3 | 3,760.4 | 3,684.1 |
| 2019 | 3,697.4 | 3,721.5 | 3,730.1 | 3,745.1 | 3,767.8 | 3,788.2 | 3,780.6 | 3,797.8 | 3,801.6 | 3,825.0 | 3,861.3 | 3,875.6 | 3,782.7 |
| **Total Private** | | | | | | | | | | | | | |
| 2011 | 2,522.9 | 2,532.7 | 2,559.7 | 2,581.3 | 2,592.0 | 2,613.9 | 2,617.5 | 2,630.7 | 2,629.9 | 2,631.6 | 2,644.4 | 2,653.6 | 2,600.9 |
| 2012 | 2,607.8 | 2,625.8 | 2,648.5 | 2,663.6 | 2,678.7 | 2,704.2 | 2,692.7 | 2,712.2 | 2,704.2 | 2,712.6 | 2,735.8 | 2,742.2 | 2,685.7 |
| 2013 | 2,680.5 | 2,703.6 | 2,722.1 | 2,738.0 | 2,758.7 | 2,785.3 | 2,784.0 | 2,803.1 | 2,799.8 | 2,805.3 | 2,829.8 | 2,831.7 | 2,770.2 |
| 2014 | 2,781.2 | 2,799.3 | 2,818.9 | 2,842.4 | 2,863.4 | 2,890.8 | 2,889.7 | 2,906.1 | 2,900.8 | 2,919.3 | 2,940.7 | 2,955.7 | 2,875.7 |
| 2015 | 2,907.1 | 2,922.9 | 2,928.2 | 2,954.3 | 2,973.9 | 2,998.1 | 3,006.0 | 3,016.5 | 3,004.9 | 3,022.6 | 3,034.1 | 3,044.9 | 2,984.5 |
| 2016 | 3,000.7 | 3,020.2 | 3,026.0 | 3,054.1 | 3,067.2 | 3,084.0 | 3,092.4 | 3,104.5 | 3,103.2 | 3,114.4 | 3,137.4 | 3,144.3 | 3,079.0 |
| 2017 | 3,095.5 | 3,109.5 | 3,119.9 | 3,133.4 | 3,148.2 | 3,177.7 | 3,171.2 | 3,185.2 | 3,180.1 | 3,197.8 | 3,223.6 | 3,225.3 | 3,164.0 |
| 2018 | 3,170.2 | 3,186.1 | 3,195.3 | 3,207.8 | 3,229.7 | 3,260.6 | 3,260.2 | 3,276.2 | 3,262.9 | 3,284.2 | 3,308.8 | 3,314.8 | 3,246.4 |
| 2019 | 3,259.9 | 3,277.0 | 3,282.9 | 3,298.7 | 3,318.2 | 3,344.8 | 3,355.5 | 3,369.6 | 3,357.5 | 3,372.9 | 3,406.1 | 3,421.2 | 3,338.7 |
| **Goods Producing** | | | | | | | | | | | | | |
| 2011 | 409.2 | 411.4 | 415.4 | 417.6 | 419.1 | 424.5 | 427.3 | 428.7 | 427.8 | 425.9 | 426.5 | 426.9 | 421.7 |
| 2012 | 423.1 | 426.7 | 429.6 | 431.0 | 431.2 | 436.5 | 439.1 | 440.6 | 439.4 | 438.2 | 439.2 | 439.6 | 434.5 |
| 2013 | 433.3 | 436.2 | 439.6 | 439.7 | 442.2 | 446.7 | 448.0 | 449.5 | 448.4 | 445.5 | 446.2 | 444.3 | 443.3 |
| 2014 | 440.4 | 445.3 | 447.4 | 451.8 | 455.5 | 458.9 | 460.8 | 461.8 | 461.0 | 461.9 | 463.2 | 465.1 | 456.1 |
| 2015 | 460.9 | 462.2 | 460.0 | 462.2 | 463.0 | 466.7 | 468.2 | 467.5 | 464.5 | 464.2 | 463.1 | 462.4 | 463.7 |
| 2016 | 460.8 | 464.1 | 463.5 | 467.4 | 467.1 | 470.7 | 473.2 | 473.4 | 472.6 | 472.2 | 472.2 | 473.4 | 469.2 |
| 2017 | 471.0 | 475.7 | 478.3 | 479.5 | 481.4 | 488.6 | 488.7 | 488.2 | 487.2 | 488.1 | 488.6 | 489.7 | 483.8 |
| 2018 | 484.5 | 488.7 | 491.1 | 492.4 | 495.4 | 503.0 | 503.8 | 504.6 | 503.2 | 502.6 | 504.8 | 506.1 | 498.4 |
| 2019 | 504.4 | 508.5 | 510.0 | 511.2 | 513.3 | 520.3 | 520.8 | 520.8 | 519.3 | 518.7 | 524.2 | 525.1 | 516.4 |
| **Service-Providing** | | | | | | | | | | | | | |
| 2011 | 2,518.0 | 2,529.8 | 2,553.4 | 2,574.6 | 2,585.2 | 2,595.1 | 2,577.1 | 2,586.8 | 2,599.1 | 2,608.8 | 2,621.1 | 2,628.1 | 2,581.4 |
| 2012 | 2,580.4 | 2,599.9 | 2,620.3 | 2,633.9 | 2,651.1 | 2,662.4 | 2,631.4 | 2,649.9 | 2,659.3 | 2,677.7 | 2,700.2 | 2,707.4 | 2,647.8 |
| 2013 | 2,644.9 | 2,671.3 | 2,687.9 | 2,704.4 | 2,723.5 | 2,739.4 | 2,721.8 | 2,740.0 | 2,750.8 | 2,768.4 | 2,794.4 | 2,798.2 | 2,728.8 |
| 2014 | 2,744.4 | 2,764.6 | 2,784.3 | 2,803.6 | 2,822.9 | 2,839.5 | 2,819.0 | 2,836.2 | 2,845.5 | 2,873.5 | 2,895.6 | 2,909.4 | 2,828.2 |
| 2015 | 2,858.2 | 2,879.5 | 2,887.2 | 2,911.1 | 2,931.7 | 2,947.1 | 2,935.2 | 2,947.3 | 2,953.8 | 2,981.0 | 2,996.3 | 3,009.4 | 2,936.5 |
| 2016 | 2,960.8 | 2,982.5 | 2,990.1 | 3,014.8 | 3,030.5 | 3,036.9 | 3,025.4 | 3,039.6 | 3,055.3 | 3,072.5 | 3,098.2 | 3,105.7 | 3,034.4 |
| 2017 | 3,052.5 | 3,069.2 | 3,079.0 | 3,092.5 | 3,106.8 | 3,120.7 | 3,094.6 | 3,110.2 | 3,121.3 | 3,148.9 | 3,178.0 | 3,177.0 | 3,112.6 |
| 2018 | 3,119.0 | 3,139.5 | 3,148.6 | 3,157.5 | 3,178.9 | 3,194.7 | 3,174.9 | 3,191.0 | 3,195.0 | 3,224.5 | 3,250.5 | 3,254.3 | 3,185.7 |
| 2019 | 3,193.0 | 3,213.0 | 3,220.1 | 3,233.9 | 3,254.5 | 3,267.9 | 3,259.8 | 3,277.0 | 3,282.3 | 3,306.3 | 3,337.1 | 3,350.5 | 3,266.3 |
| **Mining, Logging, and Construction** | | | | | | | | | | | | | |
| 2011 | 156.1 | 157.3 | 160.0 | 161.2 | 162.1 | 165.1 | 167.1 | 168.1 | 167.0 | 165.3 | 165.5 | 165.9 | 163.4 |
| 2012 | 163.7 | 166.0 | 168.3 | 169.5 | 172.4 | 175.6 | 175.6 | 176.9 | 176.1 | 175.7 | 176.6 | 176.3 | 172.7 |
| 2013 | 172.6 | 174.9 | 177.6 | 178.2 | 180.4 | 183.3 | 185.4 | 187.1 | 186.7 | 184.7 | 185.2 | 183.5 | 181.6 |
| 2014 | 183.6 | 184.9 | 187.2 | 190.3 | 193.1 | 195.6 | 197.2 | 197.9 | 197.9 | 198.7 | 199.1 | 199.4 | 193.7 |
| 2015 | 197.0 | 197.7 | 196.1 | 197.9 | 198.3 | 200.9 | 201.9 | 201.5 | 199.8 | 200.6 | 199.5 | 198.9 | 199.2 |
| 2016 | 197.9 | 200.0 | 199.6 | 203.7 | 203.1 | 205.3 | 206.5 | 207.0 | 207.1 | 206.5 | 205.9 | 206.0 | 204.1 |
| 2017 | 205.1 | 208.0 | 210.1 | 211.0 | 212.5 | 216.3 | 216.0 | 215.5 | 215.1 | 215.5 | 215.5 | 215.2 | 213.0 |
| 2018 | 211.6 | 213.9 | 215.6 | 217.0 | 218.8 | 222.7 | 222.8 | 223.3 | 221.9 | 220.8 | 221.7 | 221.9 | 219.3 |
| 2019 | 220.2 | 221.9 | 223.0 | 224.0 | 225.4 | 229.1 | 230.0 | 229.9 | 228.7 | 232.9 | 233.9 | 234.6 | 227.8 |
| **Manufacturing** | | | | | | | | | | | | | |
| 2011 | 253.1 | 254.1 | 255.4 | 256.4 | 257.0 | 259.4 | 260.2 | 260.6 | 260.8 | 260.6 | 261.0 | 261.0 | 258.3 |
| 2012 | 259.4 | 260.7 | 261.3 | 261.5 | 258.8 | 260.9 | 263.5 | 263.7 | 263.3 | 262.5 | 262.6 | 263.3 | 261.8 |
| 2013 | 260.7 | 261.3 | 262.0 | 261.5 | 261.8 | 263.4 | 262.6 | 262.4 | 261.7 | 260.8 | 261.0 | 260.8 | 261.7 |
| 2014 | 256.8 | 260.4 | 260.2 | 261.5 | 262.4 | 263.3 | 263.6 | 263.9 | 263.1 | 263.2 | 264.1 | 265.7 | 262.4 |
| 2015 | 263.9 | 264.5 | 263.9 | 264.3 | 264.7 | 265.8 | 266.3 | 266.0 | 264.7 | 263.6 | 263.6 | 263.5 | 264.6 |
| 2016 | 262.9 | 264.1 | 263.9 | 263.7 | 264.0 | 265.4 | 266.7 | 266.4 | 265.5 | 265.7 | 266.3 | 267.4 | 265.2 |
| 2017 | 265.9 | 267.7 | 268.2 | 268.5 | 268.9 | 272.3 | 272.7 | 272.7 | 272.1 | 272.6 | 273.1 | 274.5 | 270.8 |
| 2018 | 272.9 | 274.8 | 275.5 | 275.4 | 276.6 | 280.3 | 281.0 | 281.3 | 281.3 | 281.8 | 283.1 | 284.2 | 279.0 |
| 2019 | 284.2 | 286.6 | 287.0 | 287.2 | 287.9 | 291.2 | 290.8 | 290.9 | 290.6 | 285.8 | 290.3 | 290.5 | 288.6 |

## Employment by Industry: Dallas-Fort Worth-Arlington, TX, 2011–2019—*Continued*

(Numbers in thousands, not seasonally adjusted)

| Industry and year | January | February | March | April | May | June | July | August | September | October | November | December | Annual average |
|---|---|---|---|---|---|---|---|---|---|---|---|---|---|
| **Trade, Transportation, and Utilities** | | | | | | | | | | | | | |
| 2011 | 608.4 | 606.1 | 610.8 | 615.8 | 617.2 | 619.5 | 621.1 | 625.8 | 624.7 | 627.7 | 638.5 | 645.8 | 621.8 |
| 2012 | 626.7 | 625.1 | 628.7 | 629.7 | 633.7 | 637.8 | 638.0 | 642.5 | 640.2 | 643.7 | 659.5 | 664.9 | 639.2 |
| 2013 | 642.0 | 641.1 | 642.9 | 645.9 | 649.6 | 654.7 | 655.4 | 661.5 | 660.0 | 665.7 | 682.1 | 688.6 | 657.5 |
| 2014 | 665.6 | 663.1 | 666.5 | 668.6 | 673.5 | 680.2 | 681.7 | 687.3 | 687.3 | 695.0 | 711.1 | 723.2 | 683.6 |
| 2015 | 703.1 | 701.7 | 703.4 | 708.6 | 713.9 | 719.8 | 722.2 | 727.5 | 726.3 | 732.9 | 745.5 | 755.1 | 721.7 |
| 2016 | 732.6 | 731.2 | 731.6 | 735.5 | 737.4 | 741.7 | 745.2 | 749.5 | 748.0 | 756.4 | 775.0 | 784.0 | 747.3 |
| 2017 | 759.6 | 752.6 | 751.6 | 752.5 | 754.7 | 762.1 | 762.8 | 770.3 | 768.0 | 776.4 | 798.3 | 803.1 | 767.7 |
| 2018 | 775.2 | 769.2 | 768.5 | 770.2 | 774.6 | 778.4 | 779.4 | 783.7 | 782.5 | 788.5 | 810.1 | 813.4 | 782.8 |
| 2019 | 787.8 | 780.6 | 779.0 | 779.6 | 782.5 | 788.5 | 792.5 | 795.5 | 794.4 | 804.9 | 826.4 | 832.5 | 795.4 |
| **Wholesale Trade** | | | | | | | | | | | | | |
| 2011 | 165.1 | 166.4 | 166.9 | 167.7 | 168.7 | 169.2 | 169.3 | 169.8 | 170.1 | 170.5 | 170.8 | 171.8 | 168.9 |
| 2012 | 170.2 | 171.5 | 172.4 | 173.1 | 174.4 | 175.4 | 175.4 | 176.1 | 176.0 | 175.5 | 176.4 | 177.2 | 174.5 |
| 2013 | 175.6 | 176.5 | 177.2 | 177.5 | 178.1 | 179.1 | 179.2 | 179.7 | 179.3 | 180.5 | 181.7 | 182.2 | 178.9 |
| 2014 | 179.8 | 180.7 | 181.5 | 181.6 | 182.4 | 183.8 | 184.7 | 185.6 | 185.5 | 186.5 | 186.8 | 187.6 | 183.9 |
| 2015 | 187.7 | 188.8 | 189.1 | 189.4 | 190.4 | 191.3 | 191.9 | 192.6 | 192.0 | 190.7 | 190.3 | 190.2 | 190.4 |
| 2016 | 192.7 | 193.5 | 193.1 | 193.5 | 193.6 | 194.1 | 194.9 | 195.1 | 194.4 | 193.8 | 193.9 | 194.4 | 193.9 |
| 2017 | 192.8 | 192.9 | 192.7 | 192.8 | 193.9 | 195.7 | 195.7 | 196.6 | 196.3 | 196.7 | 196.8 | 197.8 | 195.1 |
| 2018 | 197.1 | 198.0 | 198.1 | 199.0 | 199.9 | 201.5 | 201.2 | 201.7 | 201.3 | 202.2 | 202.3 | 202.8 | 200.4 |
| 2019 | 202.0 | 203.2 | 203.0 | 204.1 | 204.8 | 205.8 | 207.0 | 206.8 | 205.9 | 206.6 | 207.5 | 207.9 | 205.4 |
| **Retail Trade** | | | | | | | | | | | | | |
| 2011 | 306.3 | 302.2 | 305.4 | 309.1 | 309.5 | 311.1 | 312.5 | 316.1 | 313.5 | 317.0 | 326.7 | 331.6 | 313.4 |
| 2012 | 316.6 | 312.7 | 314.4 | 314.7 | 316.5 | 318.5 | 318.4 | 321.1 | 318.2 | 322.4 | 335.9 | 338.1 | 320.6 |
| 2013 | 321.6 | 319.6 | 319.9 | 322.0 | 324.0 | 326.9 | 327.3 | 331.9 | 330.2 | 334.1 | 347.5 | 351.3 | 329.7 |
| 2014 | 334.0 | 331.3 | 332.8 | 333.9 | 335.5 | 339.2 | 339.3 | 342.4 | 340.1 | 344.7 | 357.8 | 363.8 | 341.2 |
| 2015 | 347.6 | 346.0 | 346.5 | 350.1 | 352.5 | 355.8 | 357.3 | 359.4 | 357.6 | 363.1 | 373.0 | 378.0 | 357.2 |
| 2016 | 359.9 | 358.0 | 358.5 | 361.4 | 362.0 | 363.8 | 366.3 | 368.9 | 364.5 | 370.9 | 383.0 | 387.4 | 367.1 |
| 2017 | 371.2 | 366.4 | 366.3 | 367.8 | 368.0 | 371.4 | 371.0 | 373.9 | 369.8 | 375.7 | 390.9 | 393.0 | 373.8 |
| 2018 | 375.1 | 370.0 | 369.6 | 370.2 | 372.1 | 373.0 | 374.4 | 376.4 | 373.5 | 376.2 | 389.4 | 391.8 | 376.0 |
| 2019 | 373.9 | 368.5 | 368.2 | 366.8 | 366.9 | 369.1 | 370.4 | 371.8 | 369.5 | 374.0 | 388.5 | 391.4 | 373.3 |
| **Transportation and Utilities** | | | | | | | | | | | | | |
| 2011 | 137.0 | 137.5 | 138.5 | 139.0 | 139.0 | 139.2 | 139.3 | 139.9 | 141.1 | 140.2 | 141.0 | 142.4 | 139.5 |
| 2012 | 139.9 | 140.9 | 141.9 | 141.9 | 142.8 | 143.9 | 144.2 | 145.3 | 146.0 | 145.8 | 147.2 | 149.6 | 144.1 |
| 2013 | 144.8 | 145.0 | 145.8 | 146.4 | 147.5 | 148.7 | 148.9 | 149.9 | 150.5 | 151.1 | 152.9 | 155.1 | 148.9 |
| 2014 | 151.8 | 151.1 | 152.2 | 153.1 | 155.6 | 157.2 | 157.7 | 159.3 | 161.7 | 163.8 | 166.5 | 171.8 | 158.5 |
| 2015 | 167.8 | 166.9 | 167.8 | 169.1 | 171.0 | 172.7 | 173.0 | 175.5 | 176.7 | 179.1 | 182.2 | 186.9 | 174.1 |
| 2016 | 180.0 | 179.7 | 180.0 | 180.6 | 181.8 | 183.8 | 184.0 | 185.5 | 189.1 | 191.7 | 198.1 | 202.2 | 186.4 |
| 2017 | 195.6 | 193.3 | 192.6 | 191.9 | 192.8 | 195.0 | 196.1 | 199.8 | 201.9 | 204.0 | 210.6 | 212.3 | 198.8 |
| 2018 | 203.0 | 201.2 | 200.8 | 201.0 | 202.6 | 203.9 | 203.8 | 205.6 | 207.7 | 210.1 | 218.4 | 218.8 | 206.4 |
| 2019 | 211.9 | 208.9 | 207.8 | 208.7 | 210.8 | 213.6 | 215.1 | 216.9 | 219.0 | 224.3 | 230.4 | 233.2 | 216.7 |
| **Information** | | | | | | | | | | | | | |
| 2011 | 80.5 | 80.3 | 80.3 | 80.1 | 80.4 | 80.7 | 80.9 | 80.5 | 80.0 | 80.3 | 80.6 | 80.8 | 80.5 |
| 2012 | 79.6 | 79.5 | 79.5 | 79.6 | 79.6 | 80.0 | 79.4 | 79.2 | 78.8 | 79.2 | 80.2 | 80.1 | 79.6 |
| 2013 | 79.8 | 80.1 | 79.9 | 80.4 | 81.1 | 81.3 | 81.7 | 81.8 | 80.9 | 81.5 | 82.1 | 82.5 | 81.1 |
| 2014 | 82.1 | 81.9 | 81.5 | 81.7 | 82.2 | 82.7 | 82.5 | 82.1 | 81.1 | 80.4 | 80.8 | 81.0 | 81.7 |
| 2015 | 79.8 | 79.6 | 79.8 | 80.3 | 80.5 | 80.6 | 81.6 | 81.7 | 80.8 | 80.9 | 81.5 | 82.4 | 80.8 |
| 2016 | 81.5 | 81.6 | 81.6 | 83.0 | 82.9 | 83.5 | 84.0 | 84.1 | 83.6 | 82.8 | 83.4 | 83.8 | 83.0 |
| 2017 | 83.5 | 83.7 | 84.6 | 84.1 | 83.9 | 84.4 | 84.4 | 84.1 | 83.0 | 82.7 | 83.3 | 83.7 | 83.8 |
| 2018 | 83.1 | 83.9 | 83.6 | 83.0 | 83.5 | 84.4 | 83.6 | 82.8 | 81.7 | 81.8 | 82.2 | 82.3 | 83.0 |
| 2019 | 81.2 | 81.5 | 81.3 | 81.6 | 81.7 | 82.3 | 82.1 | 82.1 | 81.2 | 82.3 | 83.1 | 83.3 | 82.0 |
| **Financial Activities** | | | | | | | | | | | | | |
| 2011 | 237.0 | 237.9 | 239.0 | 238.9 | 238.9 | 240.8 | 241.8 | 242.5 | 242.6 | 243.4 | 244.0 | 245.7 | 241.0 |
| 2012 | 243.8 | 245.3 | 246.5 | 247.2 | 248.4 | 250.6 | 250.5 | 250.7 | 250.8 | 252.5 | 253.7 | 255.2 | 249.6 |
| 2013 | 253.1 | 255.0 | 256.8 | 256.9 | 258.6 | 261.0 | 262.8 | 263.3 | 262.7 | 263.0 | 263.8 | 264.3 | 260.1 |
| 2014 | 261.6 | 262.5 | 263.1 | 264.1 | 264.1 | 265.9 | 267.8 | 268.4 | 267.5 | 269.6 | 270.0 | 270.7 | 266.3 |
| 2015 | 268.9 | 269.9 | 270.3 | 271.2 | 272.1 | 273.9 | 275.3 | 275.7 | 275.8 | 276.1 | 276.8 | 277.4 | 273.6 |
| 2016 | 277.4 | 278.4 | 278.6 | 280.5 | 282.0 | 283.2 | 285.0 | 285.7 | 286.4 | 288.0 | 289.1 | 290.3 | 283.7 |
| 2017 | 288.3 | 289.9 | 291.0 | 293.1 | 294.2 | 296.5 | 297.5 | 297.9 | 299.9 | 300.1 | 299.3 | 299.9 | 295.6 |
| 2018 | 298.0 | 299.3 | 299.3 | 298.7 | 300.3 | 303.2 | 304.1 | 305.5 | 305.5 | 308.0 | 309.3 | 310.7 | 303.5 |
| 2019 | 309.8 | 312.5 | 313.7 | 314.5 | 315.9 | 319.7 | 320.8 | 322.4 | 321.9 | 321.5 | 321.5 | 324.3 | 318.2 |

## Employment by Industry: Dallas-Fort Worth-Arlington, TX, 2011–2019—*Continued*

(Numbers in thousands, not seasonally adjusted)

| Industry and year | January | February | March | April | May | June | July | August | September | October | November | December | Annual average |
|---|---|---|---|---|---|---|---|---|---|---|---|---|---|
| **Professional and Business Services** | | | | | | | | | | | | | |
| 2011 | 448.9 | 452.8 | 457.7 | 463.5 | 463.5 | 467.2 | 468.6 | 473.3 | 475.8 | 476.2 | 478.6 | 477.8 | 467.0 |
| 2012 | 469.5 | 474.9 | 480.2 | 484.6 | 488.3 | 491.4 | 486.4 | 495.3 | 494.3 | 499.2 | 504.0 | 499.6 | 489.0 |
| 2013 | 487.2 | 493.4 | 496.7 | 498.6 | 502.0 | 507.3 | 507.7 | 515.3 | 518.3 | 522.0 | 526.3 | 523.7 | 508.2 |
| 2014 | 514.1 | 519.7 | 524.1 | 530.8 | 534.0 | 537.6 | 539.2 | 545.0 | 545.4 | 550.8 | 554.2 | 553.4 | 537.4 |
| 2015 | 546.5 | 550.0 | 550.2 | 555.0 | 556.7 | 558.6 | 563.3 | 566.1 | 564.1 | 572.7 | 573.1 | 572.7 | 560.8 |
| 2016 | 565.7 | 570.5 | 569.2 | 576.2 | 577.0 | 579.4 | 584.7 | 589.2 | 590.5 | 593.0 | 596.6 | 591.7 | 582.0 |
| 2017 | 583.6 | 588.3 | 587.0 | 588.9 | 591.3 | 593.7 | 594.7 | 598.3 | 599.5 | 607.1 | 610.5 | 602.9 | 595.5 |
| 2018 | 598.1 | 604.0 | 604.6 | 609.5 | 613.4 | 617.7 | 622.2 | 627.2 | 623.4 | 632.5 | 634.9 | 630.9 | 618.2 |
| 2019 | 621.5 | 626.5 | 624.4 | 632.3 | 634.6 | 637.2 | 645.6 | 651.9 | 648.5 | 647.0 | 650.9 | 651.4 | 639.3 |
| **Education and Health Services** | | | | | | | | | | | | | |
| 2011 | 360.8 | 361.8 | 365.7 | 368.2 | 369.8 | 369.8 | 369.6 | 371.7 | 375.3 | 375.4 | 376.1 | 378.1 | 370.2 |
| 2012 | 372.4 | 376.0 | 378.2 | 378.2 | 378.5 | 377.6 | 376.1 | 379.3 | 381.0 | 381.9 | 382.7 | 384.0 | 378.8 |
| 2013 | 376.9 | 381.5 | 383.0 | 385.7 | 387.1 | 385.7 | 384.2 | 388.7 | 391.0 | 392.7 | 394.7 | 395.0 | 387.2 |
| 2014 | 390.1 | 394.0 | 395.7 | 396.3 | 398.3 | 397.6 | 395.7 | 400.8 | 403.0 | 405.8 | 408.1 | 409.7 | 399.6 |
| 2015 | 403.5 | 407.7 | 408.6 | 412.6 | 415.9 | 414.9 | 414.7 | 418.4 | 419.2 | 422.2 | 424.1 | 425.6 | 415.6 |
| 2016 | 420.8 | 424.8 | 425.6 | 426.8 | 428.9 | 426.0 | 426.3 | 430.2 | 433.0 | 434.4 | 435.8 | 436.6 | 429.1 |
| 2017 | 434.4 | 439.0 | 440.3 | 441.6 | 442.7 | 442.4 | 438.3 | 442.4 | 444.6 | 446.1 | 447.5 | 448.8 | 442.3 |
| 2018 | 443.7 | 447.5 | 448.2 | 448.5 | 450.1 | 449.7 | 449.0 | 453.2 | 454.4 | 456.6 | 457.7 | 459.7 | 451.5 |
| 2019 | 453.6 | 458.6 | 459.1 | 460.8 | 463.0 | 460.5 | 459.9 | 464.3 | 464.3 | 469.5 | 471.1 | 475.2 | 463.3 |
| **Leisure and Hospitality** | | | | | | | | | | | | | |
| 2011 | 276.1 | 279.3 | 286.7 | 292.5 | 297.1 | 300.7 | 297.3 | 298.6 | 295.7 | 295.6 | 293.3 | 292.1 | 292.1 |
| 2012 | 285.8 | 290.5 | 297.2 | 304.5 | 308.7 | 314.9 | 308.5 | 311.1 | 309.2 | 306.7 | 305.5 | 308.1 | 304.2 |
| 2013 | 298.3 | 304.7 | 311.1 | 318.4 | 324.0 | 329.6 | 325.6 | 325.4 | 323.1 | 320.9 | 320.4 | 319.8 | 318.4 |
| 2014 | 313.0 | 317.7 | 324.7 | 332.5 | 337.5 | 344.3 | 339.1 | 339.1 | 337.5 | 337.2 | 334.8 | 334.7 | 332.7 |
| 2015 | 327.5 | 333.5 | 337.1 | 347.8 | 353.5 | 360.1 | 357.9 | 358.1 | 356.3 | 355.2 | 351.7 | 351.6 | 349.2 |
| 2016 | 345.3 | 351.6 | 357.4 | 365.1 | 370.5 | 374.7 | 370.5 | 370.3 | 368.6 | 367.5 | 364.8 | 364.1 | 364.2 |
| 2017 | 357.5 | 361.4 | 366.9 | 372.7 | 378.4 | 384.2 | 381.0 | 381.0 | 376.0 | 375.3 | 374.2 | 375.7 | 373.7 |
| 2018 | 368.5 | 373.5 | 378.7 | 382.5 | 388.4 | 396.0 | 391.4 | 393.1 | 387.3 | 388.6 | 384.4 | 387.1 | 385.0 |
| 2019 | 378.8 | 384.3 | 389.5 | 392.0 | 398.6 | 405.1 | 403.6 | 402.8 | 398.4 | 399.4 | 399.4 | 401.9 | 396.2 |
| **Other Services** | | | | | | | | | | | | | |
| 2011 | 102.0 | 103.1 | 104.1 | 104.7 | 106.0 | 110.7 | 110.9 | 109.6 | 108.0 | 107.1 | 106.8 | 106.4 | 106.6 |
| 2012 | 106.9 | 107.8 | 108.6 | 108.8 | 110.3 | 115.4 | 114.7 | 113.5 | 110.5 | 111.2 | 111.0 | 110.7 | 110.8 |
| 2013 | 109.9 | 111.6 | 112.1 | 112.4 | 114.1 | 119.0 | 118.6 | 117.6 | 115.4 | 114.0 | 114.2 | 113.5 | 114.4 |
| 2014 | 114.3 | 115.1 | 115.9 | 116.6 | 118.3 | 123.6 | 122.9 | 121.6 | 118.0 | 118.6 | 118.5 | 117.9 | 118.4 |
| 2015 | 116.9 | 118.3 | 118.8 | 116.6 | 118.3 | 123.5 | 122.8 | 121.5 | 117.9 | 118.4 | 118.3 | 117.7 | 119.1 |
| 2016 | 116.6 | 118.0 | 118.5 | 119.6 | 121.4 | 124.8 | 123.5 | 122.1 | 120.5 | 120.1 | 120.5 | 120.4 | 120.5 |
| 2017 | 117.6 | 118.9 | 120.2 | 121.0 | 121.6 | 125.8 | 123.8 | 123.0 | 121.9 | 122.0 | 121.9 | 121.5 | 121.6 |
| 2018 | 119.1 | 120.0 | 121.3 | 123.0 | 124.0 | 128.2 | 126.7 | 126.1 | 124.9 | 125.6 | 125.4 | 124.6 | 124.1 |
| 2019 | 122.8 | 124.5 | 125.9 | 126.7 | 128.6 | 131.2 | 130.2 | 129.8 | 129.5 | 129.6 | 129.5 | 127.5 | 128.0 |
| **Government** | | | | | | | | | | | | | |
| 2011 | 404.3 | 408.5 | 409.1 | 410.9 | 412.3 | 405.7 | 386.9 | 384.8 | 397.0 | 403.1 | 403.2 | 401.4 | 402.3 |
| 2012 | 395.7 | 400.8 | 401.4 | 401.3 | 403.6 | 394.7 | 377.8 | 378.3 | 394.5 | 403.3 | 403.6 | 404.8 | 396.7 |
| 2013 | 397.7 | 403.9 | 405.4 | 406.1 | 407.0 | 400.8 | 385.8 | 386.4 | 399.4 | 408.6 | 410.8 | 410.8 | 401.9 |
| 2014 | 403.6 | 410.6 | 412.8 | 413.0 | 415.0 | 407.6 | 390.1 | 391.9 | 405.7 | 416.1 | 418.1 | 418.8 | 408.6 |
| 2015 | 412.0 | 418.8 | 419.0 | 419.0 | 420.8 | 415.7 | 397.4 | 398.3 | 413.4 | 422.6 | 425.3 | 426.9 | 415.8 |
| 2016 | 420.9 | 426.4 | 427.6 | 428.1 | 430.4 | 423.6 | 406.2 | 408.5 | 424.7 | 430.3 | 433.0 | 434.8 | 424.5 |
| 2017 | 428.0 | 435.4 | 437.4 | 438.6 | 440.0 | 431.6 | 412.1 | 413.2 | 428.4 | 439.2 | 443.0 | 441.4 | 432.4 |
| 2018 | 433.3 | 442.1 | 444.4 | 442.1 | 444.6 | 437.1 | 418.5 | 419.4 | 435.3 | 442.9 | 446.5 | 445.6 | 437.7 |
| 2019 | 437.5 | 444.5 | 447.2 | 446.4 | 449.6 | 443.4 | 425.1 | 428.2 | 444.1 | 452.1 | 455.2 | 454.4 | 444.0 |

## Employment by Industry: Houston-The Woodlands-Sugar Land, TX, 2011–2019

(Numbers in thousands, not seasonally adjusted)

| Industry and year | January | February | March | April | May | June | July | August | September | October | November | December | Annual average |
|---|---|---|---|---|---|---|---|---|---|---|---|---|---|
| **Total Nonfarm** | | | | | | | | | | | | | |
| 2011 | 2,566.4 | 2,582.3 | 2,604.5 | 2,625.4 | 2,631.5 | 2,647.8 | 2,634.2 | 2,641.2 | 2,655.2 | 2,659.6 | 2,675.1 | 2,690.9 | 2,634.5 |
| 2012 | 2,650.4 | 2,675.2 | 2,700.1 | 2,713.1 | 2,733.0 | 2,751.4 | 2,735.6 | 2,751.2 | 2,763.3 | 2,778.1 | 2,797.7 | 2,808.4 | 2,738.1 |
| 2013 | 2,759.4 | 2,796.3 | 2,812.9 | 2,824.0 | 2,837.4 | 2,851.6 | 2,839.6 | 2,845.1 | 2,854.5 | 2,872.3 | 2,889.7 | 2,898.4 | 2,840.1 |
| 2014 | 2,851.9 | 2,881.1 | 2,898.3 | 2,916.0 | 2,935.5 | 2,947.5 | 2,936.9 | 2,946.6 | 2,957.7 | 2,984.4 | 3,000.4 | 3,015.1 | 2,939.3 |
| 2015 | 2,964.7 | 2,984.7 | 2,988.8 | 2,989.8 | 2,997.3 | 3,003.3 | 2,986.9 | 2,984.6 | 2,988.1 | 3,006.5 | 3,006.8 | 3,012.6 | 2,992.8 |
| 2016 | 2,971.9 | 2,987.3 | 2,987.6 | 2,996.5 | 2,999.1 | 2,998.5 | 2,983.2 | 2,978.7 | 2,986.9 | 2,998.7 | 3,007.0 | 3,010.2 | 2,992.1 |
| 2017 | 2,965.0 | 2,991.3 | 3,009.8 | 3,014.6 | 3,030.0 | 3,040.8 | 3,007.4 | 3,010.0 | 3,006.5 | 3,038.9 | 3,059.2 | 3,064.6 | 3,019.8 |
| 2018 | 3,009.7 | 3,048.0 | 3,064.5 | 3,066.5 | 3,084.5 | 3,099.9 | 3,080.9 | 3,089.3 | 3,093.5 | 3,122.7 | 3,141.3 | 3,147.3 | 3,087.3 |
| 2019 | 3,099.1 | 3,132.9 | 3,136.7 | 3,139.5 | 3,155.6 | 3,162.8 | 3,146.6 | 3,150.3 | 3,156.3 | 3,181.9 | 3,203.5 | 3,209.5 | 3,156.2 |
| **Total Private** | | | | | | | | | | | | | |
| 2011 | 2,180.1 | 2,192.6 | 2,214.2 | 2,234.6 | 2,243.2 | 2,267.6 | 2,270.4 | 2,283.7 | 2,283.3 | 2,282.6 | 2,298.0 | 2,314.8 | 2,255.4 |
| 2012 | 2,281.2 | 2,299.1 | 2,323.2 | 2,335.9 | 2,355.2 | 2,382.7 | 2,379.8 | 2,397.9 | 2,393.6 | 2,401.2 | 2,418.9 | 2,429.1 | 2,366.5 |
| 2013 | 2,389.5 | 2,417.0 | 2,432.8 | 2,442.8 | 2,455.4 | 2,477.6 | 2,479.4 | 2,491.2 | 2,478.1 | 2,487.8 | 2,503.0 | 2,512.0 | 2,463.9 |
| 2014 | 2,474.3 | 2,494.2 | 2,510.6 | 2,528.4 | 2,547.1 | 2,563.9 | 2,569.4 | 2,584.6 | 2,575.9 | 2,593.8 | 2,607.0 | 2,622.4 | 2,556.0 |
| 2015 | 2,580.3 | 2,591.8 | 2,594.6 | 2,596.6 | 2,603.3 | 2,614.7 | 2,614.0 | 2,616.1 | 2,600.2 | 2,608.8 | 2,606.6 | 2,612.3 | 2,603.3 |
| 2016 | 2,578.3 | 2,585.7 | 2,584.6 | 2,591.7 | 2,592.6 | 2,596.6 | 2,597.5 | 2,598.4 | 2,587.8 | 2,591.7 | 2,596.5 | 2,597.8 | 2,591.6 |
| 2017 | 2,564.5 | 2,580.4 | 2,596.0 | 2,601.8 | 2,616.1 | 2,632.2 | 2,618.2 | 2,625.9 | 2,603.7 | 2,627.6 | 2,643.8 | 2,648.3 | 2,613.2 |
| 2018 | 2,605.3 | 2,632.2 | 2,647.1 | 2,651.8 | 2,667.5 | 2,688.4 | 2,687.7 | 2,701.3 | 2,687.1 | 2,709.7 | 2,723.2 | 2,728.3 | 2,677.5 |
| 2019 | 2,690.6 | 2,714.0 | 2,716.6 | 2,722.0 | 2,735.7 | 2,747.3 | 2,747.5 | 2,754.9 | 2,741.5 | 2,760.1 | 2,777.1 | 2,782.7 | 2,740.8 |
| **Goods Producing** | | | | | | | | | | | | | |
| 2011 | 470.0 | 476.1 | 479.2 | 481.8 | 482.6 | 490.6 | 494.9 | 498.8 | 502.3 | 504.5 | 504.9 | 507.0 | 491.1 |
| 2012 | 502.0 | 508.4 | 514.5 | 516.4 | 520.4 | 526.1 | 526.2 | 530.5 | 532.6 | 538.7 | 537.7 | 538.2 | 524.3 |
| 2013 | 533.4 | 543.0 | 545.0 | 546.6 | 547.5 | 552.7 | 551.9 | 553.8 | 551.9 | 554.8 | 554.2 | 555.1 | 549.2 |
| 2014 | 551.8 | 559.3 | 560.8 | 564.5 | 568.6 | 571.0 | 573.3 | 577.5 | 578.8 | 583.3 | 584.8 | 587.3 | 571.8 |
| 2015 | 579.6 | 579.3 | 575.3 | 567.8 | 565.5 | 565.3 | 562.1 | 558.7 | 554.4 | 554.5 | 546.3 | 542.4 | 562.6 |
| 2016 | 537.6 | 537.8 | 533.4 | 530.7 | 527.1 | 523.9 | 520.4 | 515.8 | 514.8 | 515.9 | 509.8 | 506.7 | 522.8 |
| 2017 | 503.3 | 509.1 | 512.1 | 510.9 | 514.8 | 515.8 | 510.0 | 511.7 | 510.5 | 516.6 | 516.7 | 516.0 | 512.3 |
| 2018 | 508.9 | 518.2 | 522.1 | 523.3 | 526.8 | 531.2 | 531.3 | 535.7 | 537.3 | 544.7 | 544.0 | 545.5 | 530.8 |
| 2019 | 541.2 | 550.4 | 550.9 | 551.7 | 553.6 | 553.5 | 554.2 | 556.2 | 555.9 | 553.3 | 557.0 | 555.0 | 552.7 |
| **Service-Providing** | | | | | | | | | | | | | |
| 2011 | 2,096.4 | 2,106.2 | 2,125.3 | 2,143.6 | 2,148.9 | 2,157.2 | 2,139.3 | 2,142.4 | 2,152.9 | 2,155.1 | 2,170.2 | 2,183.9 | 2,143.5 |
| 2012 | 2,148.4 | 2,166.8 | 2,185.6 | 2,196.7 | 2,212.6 | 2,225.3 | 2,209.4 | 2,220.7 | 2,230.7 | 2,239.4 | 2,260.0 | 2,270.2 | 2,213.8 |
| 2013 | 2,226.0 | 2,253.3 | 2,267.9 | 2,277.4 | 2,289.9 | 2,298.9 | 2,287.7 | 2,291.3 | 2,302.6 | 2,317.5 | 2,335.5 | 2,343.3 | 2,290.9 |
| 2014 | 2,300.1 | 2,321.8 | 2,337.5 | 2,351.5 | 2,366.9 | 2,376.5 | 2,363.6 | 2,369.1 | 2,378.9 | 2,401.1 | 2,415.6 | 2,427.8 | 2,367.5 |
| 2015 | 2,385.1 | 2,405.4 | 2,413.5 | 2,422.0 | 2,431.8 | 2,438.0 | 2,424.8 | 2,425.9 | 2,433.7 | 2,452.0 | 2,460.5 | 2,470.2 | 2,430.2 |
| 2016 | 2,434.3 | 2,449.5 | 2,454.2 | 2,465.8 | 2,472.0 | 2,474.6 | 2,462.8 | 2,462.9 | 2,472.1 | 2,482.8 | 2,497.2 | 2,503.5 | 2,469.3 |
| 2017 | 2,461.7 | 2,482.2 | 2,497.7 | 2,503.7 | 2,515.2 | 2,525.0 | 2,497.4 | 2,498.3 | 2,496.0 | 2,522.3 | 2,542.5 | 2,548.6 | 2,507.6 |
| 2018 | 2,500.8 | 2,529.8 | 2,542.4 | 2,543.2 | 2,557.7 | 2,568.7 | 2,549.6 | 2,553.6 | 2,556.2 | 2,578.0 | 2,597.3 | 2,601.8 | 2,556.6 |
| 2019 | 2,557.9 | 2,582.5 | 2,585.8 | 2,587.8 | 2,602.0 | 2,609.3 | 2,592.4 | 2,594.1 | 2,600.4 | 2,628.6 | 2,646.5 | 2,654.5 | 2,603.5 |
| **Mining and Logging** | | | | | | | | | | | | | |
| 2011 | 85.4 | 86.4 | 86.9 | 87.9 | 88.2 | 91.0 | 92.7 | 94.1 | 94.3 | 95.7 | 96.3 | 97.6 | 91.4 |
| 2012 | 96.4 | 97.2 | 98.3 | 98.9 | 98.9 | 100.3 | 102.1 | 102.1 | 102.1 | 102.9 | 103.2 | 104.1 | 100.5 |
| 2013 | 103.9 | 104.5 | 105.0 | 106.1 | 106.6 | 108.1 | 109.5 | 109.9 | 109.2 | 110.2 | 110.5 | 110.7 | 107.9 |
| 2014 | 109.7 | 110.5 | 110.1 | 110.2 | 110.8 | 111.5 | 112.6 | 112.7 | 112.3 | 111.9 | 112.8 | 113.0 | 111.5 |
| 2015 | 111.3 | 107.5 | 105.0 | 102.5 | 100.6 | 99.9 | 99.1 | 97.5 | 95.6 | 94.9 | 92.4 | 91.2 | 99.8 |
| 2016 | 89.5 | 88.0 | 86.1 | 83.5 | 81.7 | 81.1 | 79.3 | 78.6 | 77.3 | 77.4 | 76.0 | 75.7 | 81.2 |
| 2017 | 76.1 | 77.0 | 76.7 | 76.9 | 77.8 | 77.7 | 77.7 | 77.8 | 77.3 | 77.9 | 77.7 | 77.9 | 77.4 |
| 2018 | 77.1 | 77.9 | 78.4 | 77.4 | 78.0 | 78.3 | 78.3 | 78.9 | 79.7 | 80.7 | 80.2 | 80.4 | 78.8 |
| 2019 | 80.7 | 81.2 | 80.5 | 80.8 | 80.8 | 80.6 | 79.9 | 79.8 | 79.4 | 79.7 | 78.9 | 78.5 | 80.1 |
| **Construction** | | | | | | | | | | | | | |
| 2011 | 165.9 | 169.6 | 170.8 | 170.9 | 170.7 | 173.3 | 174.5 | 175.9 | 178.0 | 177.7 | 176.1 | 174.5 | 173.2 |
| 2012 | 171.7 | 175.3 | 178.2 | 178.0 | 180.6 | 181.8 | 179.5 | 183.8 | 184.9 | 190.2 | 188.1 | 186.7 | 181.6 |
| 2013 | 183.6 | 190.8 | 191.6 | 192.0 | 192.3 | 193.9 | 192.0 | 193.4 | 192.5 | 194.2 | 192.5 | 192.1 | 191.7 |
| 2014 | 191.5 | 196.9 | 198.3 | 202.2 | 204.4 | 203.7 | 204.0 | 207.5 | 209.4 | 212.4 | 211.1 | 211.8 | 204.4 |
| 2015 | 208.8 | 214.4 | 214.9 | 214.4 | 216.2 | 217.8 | 218.2 | 219.1 | 219.0 | 222.6 | 218.9 | 217.4 | 216.8 |
| 2016 | 216.5 | 219.5 | 219.5 | 222.1 | 222.0 | 220.0 | 219.3 | 216.9 | 218.5 | 220.9 | 216.6 | 213.3 | 218.8 |
| 2017 | 210.1 | 214.2 | 216.4 | 215.6 | 217.8 | 216.9 | 211.0 | 211.6 | 211.6 | 216.9 | 216.0 | 213.9 | 214.3 |
| 2018 | 209.9 | 216.6 | 218.9 | 220.2 | 221.9 | 223.0 | 222.1 | 224.9 | 225.5 | 230.5 | 229.2 | 229.4 | 222.7 |
| 2019 | 226.2 | 233.5 | 234.2 | 235.0 | 236.5 | 235.2 | 236.4 | 239.1 | 240.2 | 240.0 | 242.5 | 241.6 | 236.7 |

## Employment by Industry: Houston-The Woodlands-Sugar Land, TX, 2011–2019—Continued

(Numbers in thousands, not seasonally adjusted)

| Industry and year | January | February | March | April | May | June | July | August | September | October | November | December | Annual average |
|---|---|---|---|---|---|---|---|---|---|---|---|---|---|
| **Manufacturing** | | | | | | | | | | | | | |
| 2011 | 218.7 | 220.1 | 221.5 | 223.0 | 223.7 | 226.3 | 227.7 | 228.8 | 230.0 | 231.1 | 232.5 | 234.9 | 226.5 |
| 2012 | 233.9 | 235.9 | 238.0 | 239.5 | 240.9 | 244.0 | 244.6 | 244.6 | 245.6 | 245.6 | 246.4 | 247.4 | 242.2 |
| 2013 | 245.9 | 247.7 | 248.4 | 248.5 | 248.6 | 250.7 | 250.4 | 250.5 | 250.2 | 250.4 | 251.2 | 252.3 | 249.6 |
| 2014 | 250.6 | 251.9 | 252.4 | 252.1 | 253.4 | 255.8 | 256.7 | 257.3 | 257.1 | 259.0 | 260.9 | 262.5 | 255.8 |
| 2015 | 259.5 | 257.4 | 255.4 | 250.9 | 248.7 | 247.6 | 244.8 | 242.1 | 239.8 | 237.0 | 235.0 | 233.8 | 246.0 |
| 2016 | 231.6 | 230.3 | 227.8 | 225.1 | 223.4 | 222.8 | 221.8 | 220.3 | 219.0 | 217.6 | 217.2 | 217.7 | 222.9 |
| 2017 | 217.1 | 217.9 | 219.0 | 218.4 | 219.2 | 221.2 | 221.3 | 222.3 | 221.6 | 221.8 | 223.0 | 224.2 | 220.6 |
| 2018 | 221.9 | 223.7 | 224.8 | 225.7 | 226.9 | 229.9 | 230.9 | 231.9 | 232.1 | 233.5 | 234.6 | 235.7 | 229.3 |
| 2019 | 234.3 | 235.7 | 236.2 | 235.9 | 236.3 | 237.7 | 237.9 | 237.3 | 236.3 | 233.6 | 235.6 | 234.9 | 236.0 |
| **Trade, Transportation, and Utilities** | | | | | | | | | | | | | |
| 2011 | 527.8 | 525.5 | 529.7 | 533.7 | 534.7 | 538.6 | 538.9 | 543.1 | 540.3 | 543.5 | 554.7 | 564.8 | 539.6 |
| 2012 | 546.5 | 544.3 | 547.5 | 549.4 | 552.5 | 556.4 | 556.8 | 561.1 | 558.1 | 561.9 | 575.8 | 581.4 | 557.6 |
| 2013 | 564.2 | 563.5 | 565.4 | 568.0 | 570.1 | 573.9 | 575.3 | 580.0 | 576.5 | 578.8 | 591.2 | 599.0 | 575.5 |
| 2014 | 584.3 | 582.3 | 583.5 | 585.0 | 587.6 | 591.4 | 593.0 | 598.0 | 594.9 | 599.5 | 611.8 | 621.4 | 594.4 |
| 2015 | 603.4 | 601.8 | 602.1 | 603.8 | 606.7 | 608.2 | 608.5 | 611.0 | 607.9 | 610.8 | 619.9 | 625.9 | 609.2 |
| 2016 | 608.6 | 606.2 | 605.5 | 605.5 | 604.9 | 607.1 | 608.0 | 609.2 | 604.9 | 609.9 | 621.4 | 627.8 | 609.9 |
| 2017 | 611.1 | 607.7 | 607.8 | 608.9 | 611.3 | 614.0 | 612.4 | 614.9 | 607.6 | 617.1 | 630.9 | 636.2 | 615.0 |
| 2018 | 619.2 | 617.4 | 618.1 | 618.4 | 621.0 | 622.9 | 622.9 | 624.7 | 622.2 | 627.5 | 642.8 | 646.9 | 625.3 |
| 2019 | 631.1 | 625.9 | 623.6 | 620.7 | 621.8 | 624.9 | 626.0 | 627.4 | 623.9 | 630.5 | 645.8 | 652.9 | 629.5 |
| **Wholesale Trade** | | | | | | | | | | | | | |
| 2011 | 136.6 | 137.4 | 138.3 | 139.4 | 140.2 | 141.2 | 141.9 | 142.7 | 143.5 | 143.9 | 144.7 | 145.9 | 141.3 |
| 2012 | 145.2 | 146.3 | 147.3 | 147.5 | 148.7 | 150.2 | 150.2 | 151.1 | 151.2 | 151.7 | 152.4 | 153.0 | 149.6 |
| 2013 | 151.9 | 153.5 | 154.3 | 154.4 | 155.3 | 156.5 | 157.1 | 158.1 | 158.5 | 158.7 | 159.7 | 160.1 | 156.5 |
| 2014 | 159.2 | 160.7 | 161.4 | 161.4 | 162.8 | 164.3 | 164.5 | 166.2 | 166.8 | 167.6 | 168.4 | 169.6 | 164.4 |
| 2015 | 168.4 | 169.4 | 169.4 | 168.7 | 168.3 | 168.1 | 167.4 | 167.7 | 166.8 | 166.8 | 166.3 | 166.1 | 167.8 |
| 2016 | 165.4 | 165.5 | 164.4 | 162.9 | 162.4 | 162.1 | 162.0 | 161.8 | 161.4 | 160.2 | 160.5 | 160.9 | 162.5 |
| 2017 | 159.7 | 160.5 | 161.2 | 162.6 | 163.8 | 165.4 | 164.4 | 165.0 | 164.1 | 164.5 | 165.1 | 165.8 | 163.5 |
| 2018 | 164.6 | 165.9 | 166.8 | 167.3 | 167.8 | 168.9 | 169.0 | 169.5 | 169.3 | 170.4 | 170.8 | 171.3 | 168.5 |
| 2019 | 171.0 | 171.8 | 171.6 | 170.8 | 171.1 | 171.8 | 172.0 | 172.2 | 171.7 | 173.5 | 176.1 | 177.4 | 172.6 |
| **Retail Trade** | | | | | | | | | | | | | |
| 2011 | 266.7 | 263.6 | 266.3 | 268.8 | 269.1 | 271.5 | 270.2 | 273.3 | 269.4 | 272.7 | 282.3 | 287.0 | 271.7 |
| 2012 | 274.2 | 270.6 | 271.6 | 272.8 | 274.6 | 276.4 | 276.8 | 279.6 | 276.9 | 280.4 | 292.0 | 295.4 | 278.4 |
| 2013 | 280.4 | 278.5 | 279.1 | 281.4 | 282.6 | 284.7 | 285.8 | 288.4 | 284.9 | 287.0 | 297.5 | 302.6 | 286.1 |
| 2014 | 290.4 | 288.2 | 288.2 | 288.9 | 289.3 | 291.2 | 292.1 | 294.1 | 290.8 | 292.9 | 302.7 | 307.3 | 293.0 |
| 2015 | 293.6 | 292.1 | 292.8 | 294.5 | 297.5 | 299.8 | 300.6 | 302.6 | 300.6 | 303.4 | 311.9 | 315.3 | 300.4 |
| 2016 | 302.9 | 301.4 | 302.2 | 303.2 | 303.6 | 305.5 | 306.0 | 308.0 | 303.6 | 309.1 | 318.8 | 321.6 | 307.2 |
| 2017 | 310.6 | 306.9 | 306.0 | 305.9 | 306.2 | 307.0 | 305.8 | 306.8 | 300.6 | 308.1 | 318.5 | 320.4 | 308.6 |
| 2018 | 310.0 | 306.6 | 305.9 | 305.0 | 306.4 | 306.7 | 306.5 | 307.3 | 304.4 | 306.4 | 317.8 | 318.9 | 308.5 |
| 2019 | 307.4 | 302.9 | 301.2 | 299.6 | 300.2 | 301.3 | 301.4 | 302.2 | 299.4 | 302.6 | 311.5 | 313.9 | 303.6 |
| **Transportation and Utilities** | | | | | | | | | | | | | |
| 2011 | 124.5 | 124.5 | 125.1 | 125.5 | 125.4 | 125.9 | 126.8 | 127.1 | 127.4 | 126.9 | 127.7 | 131.9 | 126.6 |
| 2012 | 127.1 | 127.4 | 128.6 | 129.1 | 129.2 | 129.8 | 129.8 | 130.4 | 130.0 | 129.8 | 131.4 | 133.0 | 129.6 |
| 2013 | 131.9 | 131.5 | 132.0 | 132.2 | 132.2 | 132.7 | 132.4 | 133.5 | 133.1 | 133.1 | 134.0 | 136.3 | 132.9 |
| 2014 | 134.7 | 133.4 | 133.9 | 134.7 | 135.5 | 135.9 | 136.4 | 137.7 | 137.3 | 139.0 | 140.7 | 144.5 | 137.0 |
| 2015 | 141.4 | 140.3 | 139.9 | 140.6 | 140.9 | 140.3 | 140.5 | 140.7 | 140.5 | 140.6 | 141.7 | 144.5 | 141.0 |
| 2016 | 140.3 | 139.3 | 138.9 | 139.4 | 138.9 | 139.5 | 140.0 | 139.4 | 139.9 | 140.6 | 142.1 | 145.3 | 140.3 |
| 2017 | 140.8 | 140.3 | 140.6 | 140.4 | 141.3 | 141.6 | 142.2 | 143.1 | 142.9 | 144.5 | 147.3 | 150.0 | 142.9 |
| 2018 | 144.6 | 144.9 | 145.4 | 146.1 | 146.8 | 147.3 | 147.4 | 147.9 | 148.5 | 150.7 | 154.2 | 156.7 | 148.4 |
| 2019 | 152.7 | 151.2 | 150.8 | 150.3 | 150.5 | 151.8 | 152.6 | 153.0 | 152.8 | 154.4 | 158.2 | 161.6 | 153.3 |
| **Information** | | | | | | | | | | | | | |
| 2011 | 32.5 | 32.4 | 32.2 | 32.2 | 32.4 | 32.5 | 32.3 | 32.2 | 32.0 | 31.8 | 31.8 | 31.9 | 32.2 |
| 2012 | 31.7 | 31.7 | 31.7 | 31.7 | 31.9 | 32.4 | 32.7 | 32.9 | 32.8 | 32.3 | 32.6 | 32.7 | 32.3 |
| 2013 | 32.2 | 32.4 | 32.7 | 32.7 | 32.9 | 33.4 | 33.4 | 33.4 | 33.0 | 33.5 | 33.6 | 33.7 | 33.1 |
| 2014 | 33.0 | 32.9 | 32.9 | 32.9 | 32.8 | 33.0 | 32.8 | 32.5 | 31.9 | 31.9 | 32.0 | 32.2 | 32.6 |
| 2015 | 32.0 | 32.0 | 32.0 | 32.3 | 32.3 | 32.5 | 32.6 | 32.4 | 31.8 | 31.5 | 31.7 | 32.1 | 32.1 |
| 2016 | 32.2 | 32.2 | 32.1 | 32.5 | 32.7 | 33.1 | 33.1 | 32.8 | 32.3 | 32.2 | 32.3 | 32.7 | 32.5 |
| 2017 | 32.3 | 32.2 | 32.5 | 32.5 | 32.5 | 32.6 | 32.6 | 32.2 | 31.3 | 31.2 | 31.5 | 32.0 | 32.1 |
| 2018 | 31.7 | 31.7 | 31.7 | 31.5 | 31.7 | 32.0 | 32.1 | 31.7 | 31.5 | 31.5 | 31.9 | 32.7 | 31.8 |
| 2019 | 31.8 | 32.0 | 32.2 | 32.5 | 32.6 | 33.1 | 32.9 | 32.8 | 32.3 | 32.4 | 32.5 | 32.7 | 32.5 |

## Employment by Industry: Houston-The Woodlands-Sugar Land, TX, 2011–2019—*Continued*

(Numbers in thousands, not seasonally adjusted)

| Industry and year | January | February | March | April | May | June | July | August | September | October | November | December | Annual average |
|---|---|---|---|---|---|---|---|---|---|---|---|---|---|
| **Financial Activities** | | | | | | | | | | | | | |
| 2011 | 138.0 | 138.2 | 138.7 | 138.6 | 138.9 | 139.4 | 140.0 | 140.1 | 140.7 | 141.0 | 140.8 | 140.8 | 139.6 |
| 2012 | 139.5 | 140.2 | 140.7 | 141.2 | 142.0 | 143.1 | 143.1 | 143.3 | 142.6 | 143.9 | 144.0 | 144.5 | 142.3 |
| 2013 | 142.3 | 143.5 | 143.2 | 143.7 | 144.3 | 145.6 | 146.4 | 146.6 | 146.3 | 147.0 | 146.8 | 146.9 | 145.2 |
| 2014 | 145.2 | 146.0 | 145.9 | 146.7 | 147.7 | 148.4 | 149.0 | 149.6 | 149.1 | 150.3 | 150.2 | 150.7 | 148.2 |
| 2015 | 149.2 | 149.8 | 150.1 | 150.5 | 151.1 | 151.5 | 152.1 | 152.3 | 151.8 | 153.1 | 153.1 | 153.4 | 151.5 |
| 2016 | 153.6 | 154.0 | 153.9 | 154.6 | 154.9 | 155.6 | 157.2 | 157.4 | 157.0 | 157.4 | 157.9 | 158.3 | 156.0 |
| 2017 | 157.5 | 158.1 | 158.4 | 158.6 | 159.3 | 160.7 | 161.3 | 161.5 | 160.8 | 162.8 | 162.7 | 163.0 | 160.4 |
| 2018 | 161.7 | 162.7 | 162.7 | 163.2 | 163.6 | 164.9 | 164.7 | 165.3 | 164.1 | 165.2 | 164.8 | 164.8 | 164.0 |
| 2019 | 163.5 | 164.4 | 164.3 | 165.1 | 165.7 | 166.7 | 167.6 | 167.8 | 167.5 | 167.8 | 168.0 | 168.8 | 166.4 |
| **Professional and Business Services** | | | | | | | | | | | | | |
| 2011 | 379.7 | 384.1 | 389.0 | 395.4 | 395.9 | 401.2 | 403.6 | 406.7 | 407.1 | 405.5 | 406.9 | 410.3 | 398.8 |
| 2012 | 407.5 | 412.4 | 417.8 | 421.0 | 424.0 | 430.5 | 432.0 | 436.4 | 435.7 | 434.7 | 437.7 | 439.4 | 427.4 |
| 2013 | 432.5 | 438.5 | 443.8 | 443.9 | 444.8 | 449.8 | 450.8 | 453.1 | 451.3 | 454.2 | 455.1 | 455.2 | 447.8 |
| 2014 | 446.5 | 450.6 | 455.7 | 459.8 | 463.1 | 466.6 | 468.7 | 473.4 | 472.0 | 475.9 | 475.5 | 476.5 | 465.4 |
| 2015 | 469.4 | 472.0 | 471.6 | 472.9 | 472.1 | 475.2 | 476.9 | 477.7 | 474.4 | 477.7 | 475.8 | 476.5 | 474.4 |
| 2016 | 470.6 | 471.2 | 470.3 | 473.7 | 471.2 | 471.4 | 475.2 | 475.8 | 475.2 | 476.0 | 474.5 | 471.8 | 473.1 |
| 2017 | 468.6 | 473.1 | 477.3 | 477.9 | 478.3 | 484.1 | 484.6 | 485.7 | 486.5 | 488.2 | 487.7 | 486.2 | 481.5 |
| 2018 | 480.6 | 487.0 | 489.5 | 487.3 | 488.7 | 496.2 | 498.3 | 501.2 | 496.6 | 500.8 | 500.7 | 499.1 | 493.8 |
| 2019 | 494.3 | 500.4 | 499.7 | 501.9 | 502.9 | 507.7 | 509.4 | 510.6 | 506.2 | 515.3 | 514.8 | 512.7 | 506.3 |
| **Education and Health Services** | | | | | | | | | | | | | |
| 2011 | 309.8 | 311.0 | 312.3 | 314.1 | 315.1 | 314.7 | 314.4 | 316.3 | 318.4 | 318.6 | 320.6 | 321.5 | 315.6 |
| 2012 | 318.0 | 320.9 | 322.7 | 323.6 | 325.6 | 326.0 | 325.1 | 328.8 | 330.9 | 332.7 | 333.6 | 334.6 | 326.9 |
| 2013 | 330.4 | 334.3 | 335.2 | 336.4 | 338.0 | 337.2 | 337.0 | 341.3 | 342.1 | 345.2 | 346.7 | 345.9 | 339.1 |
| 2014 | 341.8 | 344.5 | 345.2 | 347.8 | 349.2 | 347.3 | 348.9 | 352.7 | 354.0 | 358.5 | 359.7 | 360.3 | 350.8 |
| 2015 | 358.0 | 361.6 | 362.8 | 363.9 | 364.9 | 362.8 | 364.5 | 367.5 | 368.9 | 371.5 | 372.4 | 372.6 | 366.0 |
| 2016 | 369.4 | 372.5 | 372.6 | 374.3 | 375.5 | 374.0 | 375.7 | 380.1 | 381.4 | 382.4 | 383.4 | 384.1 | 377.1 |
| 2017 | 379.3 | 382.9 | 383.4 | 385.2 | 387.0 | 386.0 | 383.5 | 386.5 | 384.7 | 387.4 | 388.8 | 389.7 | 385.4 |
| 2018 | 384.7 | 389.5 | 390.6 | 391.5 | 393.0 | 392.6 | 392.1 | 396.5 | 397.2 | 399.1 | 400.7 | 401.4 | 394.1 |
| 2019 | 396.0 | 400.4 | 400.5 | 402.8 | 404.8 | 402.0 | 401.1 | 406.0 | 406.2 | 409.6 | 411.8 | 411.1 | 404.4 |
| **Leisure and Hospitality** | | | | | | | | | | | | | |
| 2011 | 230.5 | 232.8 | 240.5 | 243.9 | 247.7 | 250.6 | 246.5 | 247.9 | 246.4 | 242.6 | 244.0 | 244.0 | 243.1 |
| 2012 | 241.4 | 245.7 | 253.1 | 254.8 | 259.9 | 265.1 | 260.7 | 262.3 | 260.7 | 257.5 | 259.1 | 259.7 | 256.7 |
| 2013 | 255.8 | 262.1 | 267.7 | 270.1 | 275.4 | 278.1 | 277.3 | 277.5 | 273.6 | 271.2 | 272.7 | 273.9 | 271.3 |
| 2014 | 269.1 | 274.4 | 282.2 | 285.0 | 290.6 | 294.8 | 292.3 | 290.9 | 287.9 | 286.2 | 286.0 | 287.3 | 285.6 |
| 2015 | 282.8 | 288.3 | 294.0 | 298.7 | 303.1 | 307.6 | 305.7 | 306.3 | 303.4 | 301.2 | 300.1 | 302.3 | 299.5 |
| 2016 | 300.0 | 304.4 | 309.6 | 312.6 | 317.6 | 320.7 | 317.8 | 318.0 | 313.5 | 308.4 | 308.8 | 309.0 | 311.7 |
| 2017 | 306.4 | 309.1 | 315.5 | 316.4 | 322.1 | 326.5 | 323.7 | 323.5 | 312.9 | 313.4 | 314.5 | 315.2 | 316.6 |
| 2018 | 310.7 | 316.1 | 322.1 | 324.2 | 329.4 | 333.0 | 333.3 | 332.8 | 325.2 | 325.3 | 323.6 | 325.0 | 325.1 |
| 2019 | 320.0 | 326.0 | 330.9 | 331.7 | 337.1 | 341.5 | 340.1 | 338.1 | 334.2 | 335.5 | 330.7 | 332.2 | 333.2 |
| **Other Services** | | | | | | | | | | | | | |
| 2011 | 91.8 | 92.5 | 92.6 | 94.9 | 95.9 | 100.0 | 99.8 | 98.6 | 96.1 | 95.1 | 94.3 | 94.5 | 95.5 |
| 2012 | 94.6 | 95.5 | 95.2 | 97.8 | 98.9 | 103.1 | 103.2 | 102.6 | 100.2 | 99.5 | 98.4 | 98.6 | 99.0 |
| 2013 | 98.7 | 99.7 | 99.8 | 101.4 | 102.4 | 106.9 | 107.3 | 105.5 | 103.4 | 103.1 | 102.7 | 102.3 | 102.8 |
| 2014 | 102.6 | 104.2 | 104.4 | 106.7 | 107.5 | 111.4 | 111.4 | 110.0 | 107.3 | 108.2 | 107.0 | 106.7 | 107.3 |
| 2015 | 105.9 | 107.0 | 106.7 | 106.7 | 107.6 | 111.6 | 111.6 | 110.2 | 107.6 | 108.5 | 107.3 | 107.1 | 108.2 |
| 2016 | 106.3 | 107.4 | 107.2 | 107.8 | 108.7 | 110.8 | 110.1 | 109.3 | 108.7 | 109.5 | 108.4 | 107.4 | 108.5 |
| 2017 | 106.0 | 108.2 | 109.0 | 111.4 | 110.8 | 112.5 | 110.1 | 109.9 | 109.4 | 110.9 | 111.0 | 110.0 | 109.9 |
| 2018 | 107.8 | 109.6 | 110.3 | 112.4 | 113.3 | 115.6 | 113.0 | 113.4 | 113.0 | 115.6 | 114.7 | 113.6 | 112.7 |
| 2019 | 112.7 | 114.5 | 114.5 | 115.6 | 117.2 | 117.9 | 116.2 | 116.0 | 115.3 | 115.7 | 116.5 | 117.3 | 115.8 |
| **Government** | | | | | | | | | | | | | |
| 2011 | 386.3 | 389.7 | 390.3 | 390.8 | 388.3 | 380.2 | 363.8 | 357.5 | 371.9 | 377.0 | 377.1 | 376.1 | 379.1 |
| 2012 | 369.2 | 376.1 | 376.9 | 377.2 | 377.8 | 368.7 | 355.8 | 353.3 | 369.7 | 376.9 | 378.8 | 379.3 | 371.6 |
| 2013 | 369.9 | 379.3 | 380.1 | 381.2 | 382.0 | 374.0 | 360.2 | 353.9 | 376.4 | 384.5 | 386.7 | 386.4 | 376.2 |
| 2014 | 377.6 | 386.9 | 387.7 | 387.6 | 388.4 | 383.6 | 367.5 | 362.0 | 381.8 | 390.6 | 393.4 | 392.7 | 383.3 |
| 2015 | 384.4 | 392.9 | 394.2 | 393.2 | 394.0 | 388.6 | 372.9 | 368.5 | 387.9 | 397.7 | 400.2 | 400.3 | 389.6 |
| 2016 | 393.6 | 401.6 | 403.0 | 404.8 | 406.5 | 401.9 | 385.7 | 380.3 | 399.1 | 407.0 | 410.5 | 412.4 | 400.5 |
| 2017 | 400.5 | 410.9 | 413.8 | 412.8 | 413.9 | 408.6 | 389.2 | 384.1 | 402.8 | 411.3 | 415.4 | 416.3 | 406.6 |
| 2018 | 404.4 | 415.8 | 417.4 | 414.7 | 417.0 | 411.5 | 393.2 | 388.0 | 406.4 | 413.0 | 418.1 | 419.0 | 409.9 |
| 2019 | 408.5 | 418.9 | 420.1 | 417.5 | 419.9 | 415.5 | 399.1 | 395.4 | 414.8 | 421.8 | 426.4 | 426.8 | 415.4 |

# Employment by Industry: Washington-Arlington-Alexandria, DC-VA-MD-WV, 2011–2019

(Numbers in thousands, not seasonally adjusted)

| Industry and year | January | February | March | April | May | June | July | August | September | October | November | December | Annual average |
|---|---|---|---|---|---|---|---|---|---|---|---|---|---|
| **Total Nonfarm** | | | | | | | | | | | | | |
| 2011 | 2,964.4 | 2,973.5 | 2,995.8 | 3,022.2 | 3,023.3 | 3,041.2 | 3,048.3 | 3,022.1 | 3,038.7 | 3,043.7 | 3,053.8 | 3,058.1 | 3,023.8 |
| 2012 | 2,995.4 | 3,009.0 | 3,036.2 | 3,050.4 | 3,064.4 | 3,081.4 | 3,070.9 | 3,058.9 | 3,069.9 | 3,089.9 | 3,102.8 | 3,101.7 | 3,060.9 |
| 2013 | 3,041.2 | 3,053.8 | 3,069.7 | 3,084.9 | 3,097.2 | 3,102.3 | 3,097.4 | 3,081.9 | 3,090.3 | 3,093.4 | 3,113.8 | 3,106.1 | 3,086.0 |
| 2014 | 3,041.9 | 3,048.5 | 3,065.8 | 3,093.2 | 3,113.5 | 3,131.4 | 3,116.0 | 3,103.7 | 3,112.8 | 3,128.2 | 3,140.7 | 3,138.3 | 3,102.8 |
| 2015 | 3,088.2 | 3,100.9 | 3,108.5 | 3,139.0 | 3,159.0 | 3,178.9 | 3,180.2 | 3,161.6 | 3,169.7 | 3,196.1 | 3,209.6 | 3,212.1 | 3,158.7 |
| 2016 | 3,144.5 | 3,155.9 | 3,175.3 | 3,213.1 | 3,218.1 | 3,235.1 | 3,234.0 | 3,222.8 | 3,231.8 | 3,247.9 | 3,266.6 | 3,265.1 | 3,217.5 |
| 2017 | 3,207.0 | 3,227.8 | 3,244.8 | 3,260.4 | 3,275.2 | 3,297.6 | 3,280.1 | 3,263.9 | 3,267.2 | 3,289.3 | 3,303.4 | 3,294.1 | 3,267.6 |
| 2018 | 3,245.3 | 3,269.9 | 3,279.8 | 3,298.5 | 3,312.7 | 3,334.3 | 3,326.8 | 3,310.3 | 3,308.5 | 3,329.1 | 3,342.6 | 3,335.4 | 3,307.8 |
| 2019 | 3,286.4 | 3,305.7 | 3,322.6 | 3,341.9 | 3,353.8 | 3,378.0 | 3,371.8 | 3,345.9 | 3,350.4 | 3,377.2 | 3,398.5 | 3,396.3 | 3,352.4 |
| **Total Private** | | | | | | | | | | | | | |
| 2011 | 2,277.4 | 2,279.1 | 2,297.6 | 2,326.4 | 2,326.1 | 2,346.0 | 2,359.7 | 2,351.2 | 2,344.7 | 2,347.8 | 2,358.1 | 2,361.9 | 2,331.3 |
| 2012 | 2,311.0 | 2,316.4 | 2,338.4 | 2,355.3 | 2,368.5 | 2,387.8 | 2,388.6 | 2,390.5 | 2,379.7 | 2,390.6 | 2,402.1 | 2,401.7 | 2,369.2 |
| 2013 | 2,353.7 | 2,358.6 | 2,372.4 | 2,387.3 | 2,397.9 | 2,407.5 | 2,417.3 | 2,415.7 | 2,402.3 | 2,399.5 | 2,416.2 | 2,411.1 | 2,395.0 |
| 2014 | 2,364.7 | 2,362.8 | 2,378.9 | 2,406.0 | 2,422.2 | 2,441.1 | 2,441.9 | 2,440.5 | 2,424.0 | 2,434.0 | 2,443.8 | 2,443.7 | 2,417.0 |
| 2015 | 2,406.2 | 2,407.7 | 2,414.8 | 2,447.3 | 2,464.5 | 2,483.6 | 2,500.8 | 2,496.0 | 2,478.6 | 2,504.4 | 2,514.5 | 2,516.0 | 2,469.5 |
| 2016 | 2,459.1 | 2,464.5 | 2,480.2 | 2,513.2 | 2,517.3 | 2,536.4 | 2,549.0 | 2,546.5 | 2,532.1 | 2,543.8 | 2,558.4 | 2,557.4 | 2,521.5 |
| 2017 | 2,511.6 | 2,522.1 | 2,536.2 | 2,554.6 | 2,566.2 | 2,591.4 | 2,593.7 | 2,587.3 | 2,567.9 | 2,585.4 | 2,596.0 | 2,590.9 | 2,566.9 |
| 2018 | 2,551.8 | 2,564.2 | 2,573.6 | 2,591.0 | 2,603.3 | 2,627.5 | 2,634.1 | 2,626.1 | 2,604.4 | 2,620.5 | 2,632.0 | 2,626.5 | 2,604.6 |
| 2019 | 2,589.6 | 2,597.9 | 2,612.3 | 2,631.0 | 2,641.5 | 2,671.2 | 2,671.9 | 2,663.3 | 2,640.0 | 2,659.1 | 2,675.1 | 2,676.2 | 2,644.1 |
| **Goods Producing** | | | | | | | | | | | | | |
| 2011 | 188.5 | 187.8 | 189.6 | 194.1 | 195.7 | 198.3 | 201.6 | 201.0 | 198.1 | 196.6 | 196.2 | 196.3 | 195.3 |
| 2012 | 189.9 | 189.4 | 192.1 | 194.5 | 195.5 | 199.4 | 201.2 | 200.6 | 199.3 | 199.4 | 198.5 | 197.5 | 196.4 |
| 2013 | 191.6 | 191.0 | 192.7 | 195.2 | 197.8 | 200.3 | 201.6 | 202.4 | 200.2 | 198.8 | 199.8 | 197.1 | 197.4 |
| 2014 | 192.1 | 190.8 | 193.5 | 198.7 | 201.1 | 203.9 | 203.3 | 204.4 | 202.7 | 203.3 | 203.2 | 201.3 | 199.9 |
| 2015 | 194.1 | 193.9 | 195.0 | 200.7 | 203.5 | 205.8 | 208.5 | 209.2 | 208.1 | 211.2 | 211.8 | 211.2 | 204.4 |
| 2016 | 204.0 | 202.9 | 206.5 | 210.0 | 212.0 | 213.9 | 213.6 | 213.5 | 213.1 | 215.2 | 214.9 | 214.9 | 211.2 |
| 2017 | 207.7 | 208.9 | 210.6 | 214.1 | 215.4 | 218.1 | 218.2 | 217.9 | 216.7 | 216.6 | 215.7 | 214.7 | 214.6 |
| 2018 | 209.1 | 210.5 | 211.9 | 213.6 | 214.9 | 217.9 | 220.4 | 220.3 | 218.5 | 219.7 | 220.1 | 219.7 | 216.4 |
| 2019 | 215.0 | 215.3 | 217.7 | 220.3 | 222.3 | 225.4 | 225.3 | 225.9 | 223.7 | 224.0 | 224.0 | 221.7 | 221.7 |
| **Service-Providing** | | | | | | | | | | | | | |
| 2011 | 2,775.9 | 2,785.7 | 2,806.2 | 2,828.1 | 2,827.6 | 2,842.9 | 2,846.7 | 2,821.1 | 2,840.6 | 2,847.1 | 2,857.6 | 2,861.8 | 2,828.4 |
| 2012 | 2,805.5 | 2,819.6 | 2,844.1 | 2,855.9 | 2,868.9 | 2,882.0 | 2,869.7 | 2,858.3 | 2,870.6 | 2,890.6 | 2,904.3 | 2,904.2 | 2,864.5 |
| 2013 | 2,849.6 | 2,862.8 | 2,877.0 | 2,889.7 | 2,899.4 | 2,902.0 | 2,895.8 | 2,879.5 | 2,890.1 | 2,894.6 | 2,914.0 | 2,909.0 | 2,888.6 |
| 2014 | 2,849.8 | 2,857.7 | 2,872.3 | 2,894.5 | 2,912.4 | 2,927.5 | 2,912.7 | 2,899.3 | 2,910.1 | 2,924.9 | 2,937.5 | 2,937.0 | 2,903.0 |
| 2015 | 2,894.1 | 2,907.0 | 2,913.5 | 2,938.3 | 2,955.5 | 2,973.1 | 2,971.7 | 2,952.4 | 2,961.6 | 2,984.9 | 2,997.8 | 3,000.9 | 2,954.2 |
| 2016 | 2,940.5 | 2,953.0 | 2,968.8 | 3,003.1 | 3,006.1 | 3,021.2 | 3,020.4 | 3,009.3 | 3,018.7 | 3,032.7 | 3,051.7 | 3,050.2 | 3,006.3 |
| 2017 | 2,999.3 | 3,018.9 | 3,034.2 | 3,046.3 | 3,059.8 | 3,079.5 | 3,061.9 | 3,046.0 | 3,050.5 | 3,072.7 | 3,087.7 | 3,079.4 | 3,053.0 |
| 2018 | 3,036.2 | 3,059.4 | 3,067.9 | 3,084.9 | 3,097.8 | 3,116.4 | 3,106.4 | 3,090.0 | 3,090.0 | 3,109.4 | 3,122.5 | 3,115.7 | 3,091.4 |
| 2019 | 3,071.4 | 3,090.4 | 3,104.9 | 3,121.6 | 3,131.5 | 3,152.6 | 3,146.5 | 3,120.0 | 3,126.7 | 3,153.2 | 3,174.5 | 3,174.6 | 3,130.7 |
| **Mining, Logging, and Construction** | | | | | | | | | | | | | |
| 2011 | 135.4 | 135.2 | 137.0 | 141.5 | 143.0 | 145.4 | 148.9 | 148.5 | 146.2 | 144.7 | 144.2 | 143.8 | 142.8 |
| 2012 | 138.1 | 138.6 | 141.0 | 143.3 | 144.4 | 147.8 | 149.5 | 149.1 | 148.1 | 148.5 | 147.2 | 146.4 | 145.2 |
| 2013 | 141.1 | 141.0 | 142.6 | 145.0 | 147.4 | 149.7 | 151.0 | 151.8 | 150.2 | 148.3 | 148.8 | 145.9 | 146.9 |
| 2014 | 141.9 | 140.7 | 143.1 | 146.8 | 149.1 | 151.5 | 151.1 | 152.0 | 150.6 | 150.8 | 150.1 | 148.1 | 148.0 |
| 2015 | 142.0 | 141.7 | 142.6 | 147.7 | 150.3 | 152.2 | 154.5 | 155.0 | 154.1 | 157.1 | 157.2 | 156.7 | 150.9 |
| 2016 | 151.1 | 149.9 | 153.3 | 156.2 | 157.7 | 159.5 | 158.9 | 158.9 | 158.8 | 160.7 | 159.9 | 159.7 | 157.1 |
| 2017 | 153.5 | 154.6 | 156.0 | 159.5 | 160.6 | 163.0 | 163.0 | 162.7 | 161.9 | 161.6 | 160.6 | 159.5 | 159.7 |
| 2018 | 154.8 | 156.1 | 157.3 | 158.8 | 159.9 | 162.2 | 164.1 | 164.2 | 162.9 | 163.8 | 163.6 | 163.2 | 160.9 |
| 2019 | 159.3 | 159.4 | 161.5 | 163.7 | 165.4 | 167.9 | 167.9 | 168.7 | 166.9 | 166.6 | 166.0 | 163.5 | 164.7 |
| **Manufacturing** | | | | | | | | | | | | | |
| 2011 | 53.1 | 52.6 | 52.6 | 52.6 | 52.7 | 52.9 | 52.7 | 52.5 | 51.9 | 51.9 | 52.0 | 52.5 | 52.5 |
| 2012 | 51.8 | 50.8 | 51.1 | 51.2 | 51.1 | 51.6 | 51.7 | 51.5 | 51.2 | 50.9 | 51.3 | 51.1 | 51.3 |
| 2013 | 50.5 | 50.0 | 50.1 | 50.2 | 50.4 | 50.6 | 50.6 | 50.6 | 50.0 | 50.5 | 51.0 | 51.2 | 50.5 |
| 2014 | 50.2 | 50.1 | 50.4 | 51.9 | 52.0 | 52.4 | 52.2 | 52.4 | 52.1 | 52.5 | 53.1 | 53.2 | 51.9 |
| 2015 | 52.1 | 52.2 | 52.4 | 53.0 | 53.2 | 53.6 | 54.0 | 54.2 | 54.0 | 54.1 | 54.6 | 54.5 | 53.5 |
| 2016 | 52.9 | 53.0 | 53.2 | 53.8 | 54.3 | 54.4 | 54.7 | 54.6 | 54.3 | 54.5 | 55.0 | 55.2 | 54.2 |
| 2017 | 54.2 | 54.3 | 54.6 | 54.6 | 54.8 | 55.1 | 55.2 | 55.2 | 54.8 | 55.0 | 55.1 | 55.2 | 54.8 |
| 2018 | 54.3 | 54.4 | 54.6 | 54.8 | 55.0 | 55.7 | 56.3 | 56.1 | 55.6 | 55.9 | 56.5 | 56.5 | 55.5 |
| 2019 | 55.7 | 55.9 | 56.2 | 56.6 | 56.9 | 57.5 | 57.4 | 57.2 | 56.8 | 57.4 | 58.0 | 58.2 | 57.0 |

## Employment by Industry: Washington-Arlington-Alexandria, DC-VA-MD-WV, 2011–2019—*Continued*

(Numbers in thousands, not seasonally adjusted)

| Industry and year | January | February | March | April | May | June | July | August | September | October | November | December | Annual average |
|---|---|---|---|---|---|---|---|---|---|---|---|---|---|
| **Trade, Transportation, and Utilities** | | | | | | | | | | | | | |
| 2011 | 382.3 | 377.4 | 379.0 | 382.7 | 384.1 | 386.8 | 387.3 | 387.3 | 385.1 | 389.3 | 398.1 | 405.2 | 387.1 |
| 2012 | 387.3 | 382.8 | 385.1 | 384.6 | 388.4 | 391.0 | 389.2 | 389.0 | 387.5 | 391.0 | 402.1 | 407.4 | 390.5 |
| 2013 | 388.3 | 383.0 | 384.9 | 385.9 | 388.8 | 391.7 | 392.0 | 392.2 | 390.0 | 393.6 | 404.3 | 411.1 | 392.2 |
| 2014 | 392.1 | 386.5 | 389.0 | 391.3 | 394.8 | 398.1 | 397.8 | 397.7 | 395.4 | 399.2 | 409.0 | 416.5 | 397.3 |
| 2015 | 398.3 | 392.1 | 392.8 | 394.7 | 399.4 | 402.6 | 403.7 | 403.3 | 401.4 | 405.6 | 415.1 | 421.3 | 402.5 |
| 2016 | 400.2 | 395.5 | 397.3 | 400.4 | 403.7 | 405.6 | 406.1 | 405.4 | 402.8 | 406.7 | 417.3 | 423.3 | 405.4 |
| 2017 | 405.0 | 399.4 | 400.6 | 403.0 | 405.5 | 408.9 | 407.6 | 407.5 | 403.9 | 407.4 | 418.8 | 423.0 | 407.6 |
| 2018 | 406.3 | 401.6 | 401.5 | 402.6 | 405.7 | 408.1 | 408.5 | 407.6 | 406.4 | 409.0 | 420.0 | 423.9 | 408.4 |
| 2019 | 407.3 | 400.2 | 401.8 | 401.7 | 405.0 | 409.1 | 408.0 | 408.0 | 405.1 | 408.9 | 417.9 | 426.4 | 408.3 |
| **Wholesale Trade** | | | | | | | | | | | | | |
| 2011 | 62.6 | 62.6 | 62.8 | 62.8 | 62.7 | 62.6 | 62.8 | 62.8 | 62.2 | 62.6 | 62.3 | 62.5 | 62.6 |
| 2012 | 62.1 | 62.4 | 62.7 | 61.8 | 62.5 | 62.8 | 62.8 | 63.1 | 62.8 | 63.0 | 63.1 | 63.0 | 62.7 |
| 2013 | 62.8 | 62.9 | 63.0 | 62.7 | 62.7 | 62.8 | 62.6 | 62.4 | 62.0 | 62.4 | 62.5 | 62.6 | 62.6 |
| 2014 | 61.8 | 61.8 | 62.1 | 61.8 | 62.2 | 62.2 | 62.2 | 62.2 | 61.7 | 61.4 | 61.4 | 61.4 | 61.9 |
| 2015 | 60.9 | 60.7 | 60.7 | 60.4 | 60.7 | 60.8 | 61.5 | 61.2 | 60.9 | 61.1 | 61.1 | 61.3 | 60.9 |
| 2016 | 61.0 | 60.7 | 60.6 | 61.2 | 61.5 | 61.6 | 62.3 | 62.4 | 62.1 | 62.5 | 62.4 | 62.3 | 61.7 |
| 2017 | 62.2 | 62.4 | 62.2 | 62.3 | 62.6 | 62.8 | 62.7 | 62.7 | 62.2 | 62.4 | 62.5 | 62.4 | 62.5 |
| 2018 | 62.4 | 62.6 | 62.4 | 62.3 | 62.5 | 63.2 | 63.2 | 63.3 | 63.2 | 63.5 | 63.6 | 63.3 | 63.0 |
| 2019 | 62.3 | 62.4 | 62.6 | 62.7 | 62.9 | 63.0 | 62.9 | 63.5 | 63.0 | 63.0 | 62.7 | 63.1 | 62.8 |
| **Retail Trade** | | | | | | | | | | | | | |
| 2011 | 258.4 | 254.2 | 255.2 | 258.5 | 259.8 | 261.9 | 261.5 | 261.7 | 260.7 | 264.2 | 272.8 | 277.7 | 262.2 |
| 2012 | 263.6 | 258.7 | 260.8 | 260.5 | 263.0 | 264.7 | 263.4 | 262.9 | 262.1 | 265.2 | 275.4 | 278.2 | 264.9 |
| 2013 | 263.7 | 259.6 | 260.8 | 262.3 | 264.7 | 266.8 | 267.4 | 267.5 | 266.2 | 269.7 | 278.8 | 282.8 | 267.5 |
| 2014 | 268.3 | 264.0 | 265.7 | 267.9 | 270.2 | 272.8 | 272.8 | 272.5 | 270.7 | 274.6 | 282.8 | 287.4 | 272.5 |
| 2015 | 273.8 | 269.5 | 270.3 | 272.1 | 275.5 | 278.1 | 278.3 | 277.9 | 276.7 | 280.9 | 288.8 | 291.5 | 277.8 |
| 2016 | 275.9 | 271.8 | 273.6 | 275.1 | 277.5 | 278.6 | 278.5 | 278.3 | 275.6 | 279.4 | 287.9 | 290.7 | 278.6 |
| 2017 | 277.3 | 272.2 | 273.3 | 274.9 | 276.4 | 278.8 | 277.6 | 277.6 | 274.3 | 277.9 | 287.6 | 288.8 | 278.1 |
| 2018 | 276.6 | 272.2 | 272.2 | 272.7 | 274.9 | 275.3 | 275.0 | 274.1 | 272.4 | 274.1 | 283.2 | 284.4 | 275.6 |
| 2019 | 271.9 | 265.9 | 266.8 | 266.4 | 268.3 | 270.7 | 269.9 | 269.1 | 267.1 | 270.4 | 278.5 | 284.3 | 270.8 |
| **Transportation and Utilities** | | | | | | | | | | | | | |
| 2011 | 61.3 | 60.6 | 61.0 | 61.4 | 61.6 | 62.3 | 63.0 | 62.8 | 62.2 | 62.5 | 63.0 | 65.0 | 62.2 |
| 2012 | 61.6 | 61.7 | 61.6 | 62.3 | 62.9 | 63.5 | 63.0 | 63.0 | 62.6 | 62.8 | 63.6 | 66.2 | 62.9 |
| 2013 | 61.8 | 60.5 | 61.1 | 60.9 | 61.4 | 62.1 | 62.0 | 62.3 | 61.8 | 61.5 | 63.0 | 65.7 | 62.0 |
| 2014 | 62.0 | 60.7 | 61.2 | 61.6 | 62.4 | 63.1 | 62.8 | 63.0 | 63.0 | 63.2 | 64.8 | 67.7 | 63.0 |
| 2015 | 63.6 | 61.9 | 61.8 | 62.2 | 63.2 | 63.7 | 63.9 | 64.2 | 63.8 | 63.6 | 65.2 | 68.5 | 63.8 |
| 2016 | 63.3 | 63.0 | 63.1 | 64.1 | 64.7 | 65.4 | 65.3 | 64.7 | 65.1 | 64.8 | 67.0 | 70.3 | 65.1 |
| 2017 | 65.5 | 64.8 | 65.1 | 65.8 | 66.5 | 67.3 | 67.3 | 67.2 | 67.4 | 67.1 | 68.7 | 71.8 | 67.0 |
| 2018 | 67.3 | 66.8 | 66.9 | 67.6 | 68.3 | 69.6 | 70.3 | 70.2 | 70.8 | 71.4 | 73.2 | 76.2 | 69.9 |
| 2019 | 73.1 | 71.9 | 72.4 | 72.6 | 73.8 | 75.4 | 75.2 | 75.4 | 75.0 | 75.5 | 76.7 | 79.0 | 74.7 |
| **Information** | | | | | | | | | | | | | |
| 2011 | 80.1 | 80.7 | 81.0 | 82.0 | 80.0 | 81.8 | 81.6 | 76.2 | 80.2 | 77.3 | 78.5 | 79.8 | 79.9 |
| 2012 | 76.1 | 77.3 | 78.1 | 76.3 | 77.1 | 78.8 | 77.9 | 79.1 | 77.0 | 76.8 | 78.4 | 77.3 | 77.5 |
| 2013 | 76.5 | 78.0 | 77.9 | 76.5 | 77.2 | 77.2 | 77.6 | 78.7 | 76.6 | 76.7 | 78.5 | 77.3 | 77.4 |
| 2014 | 79.1 | 77.8 | 77.8 | 77.9 | 79.3 | 78.5 | 78.5 | 79.3 | 77.3 | 78.1 | 77.4 | 77.4 | 78.2 |
| 2015 | 77.7 | 77.0 | 76.6 | 77.0 | 77.2 | 76.5 | 76.9 | 76.1 | 75.1 | 76.3 | 76.1 | 76.1 | 76.6 |
| 2016 | 75.0 | 75.4 | 74.4 | 74.7 | 71.8 | 74.7 | 74.9 | 74.5 | 74.2 | 73.7 | 73.8 | 74.2 | 74.3 |
| 2017 | 73.6 | 74.4 | 74.1 | 74.0 | 74.0 | 74.6 | 74.4 | 74.1 | 73.9 | 73.6 | 74.3 | 74.5 | 74.1 |
| 2018 | 73.8 | 74.7 | 74.1 | 74.6 | 74.9 | 76.0 | 75.8 | 75.3 | 74.4 | 75.0 | 75.4 | 75.3 | 74.9 |
| 2019 | 75.1 | 75.9 | 75.9 | 75.9 | 76.2 | 77.4 | 77.7 | 77.5 | 76.8 | 77.6 | 77.8 | 77.0 | 76.7 |
| **Financial Activities** | | | | | | | | | | | | | |
| 2011 | 144.0 | 144.0 | 144.3 | 145.5 | 145.7 | 146.4 | 146.7 | 146.2 | 145.5 | 145.9 | 145.6 | 146.2 | 145.5 |
| 2012 | 144.7 | 145.0 | 145.5 | 146.2 | 146.5 | 147.8 | 148.0 | 147.6 | 147.2 | 147.8 | 147.9 | 148.5 | 146.9 |
| 2013 | 147.3 | 147.6 | 148.3 | 148.6 | 148.9 | 150.3 | 150.8 | 150.5 | 149.2 | 149.9 | 150.1 | 150.6 | 149.3 |
| 2014 | 148.5 | 148.2 | 148.6 | 148.7 | 149.3 | 150.7 | 151.2 | 150.7 | 149.7 | 150.1 | 150.2 | 150.6 | 149.7 |
| 2015 | 150.0 | 150.2 | 150.5 | 149.9 | 150.7 | 152.1 | 153.0 | 152.5 | 151.1 | 152.0 | 151.8 | 152.1 | 151.3 |
| 2016 | 150.8 | 150.9 | 151.1 | 152.3 | 152.8 | 153.9 | 155.0 | 155.0 | 154.0 | 154.6 | 154.7 | 155.5 | 153.4 |
| 2017 | 154.2 | 154.9 | 155.2 | 155.3 | 156.5 | 158.1 | 158.9 | 158.3 | 157.1 | 157.8 | 158.0 | 158.3 | 156.9 |
| 2018 | 157.3 | 157.9 | 158.0 | 157.9 | 158.9 | 160.5 | 161.0 | 160.4 | 159.1 | 159.4 | 159.3 | 159.4 | 159.1 |
| 2019 | 158.4 | 158.9 | 159.1 | 159.9 | 160.4 | 162.0 | 162.5 | 162.3 | 160.7 | 162.2 | 161.4 | 163.0 | 160.9 |

## Employment by Industry: Washington-Arlington-Alexandria, DC-VA-MD-WV, 2011–2019—*Continued*

(Numbers in thousands, not seasonally adjusted)

| Industry and year | January | February | March | April | May | June | July | August | September | October | November | December | Annual average |
|---|---|---|---|---|---|---|---|---|---|---|---|---|---|
| **Professional and Business Services** | | | | | | | | | | | | | |
| 2011 | 683.4 | 685.9 | 691.0 | 694.4 | 693.1 | 698.3 | 705.6 | 705.1 | 699.5 | 703.4 | 703.7 | 702.1 | 697.1 |
| 2012 | 691.8 | 694.7 | 701.0 | 708.3 | 708.6 | 715.1 | 717.4 | 718.7 | 710.6 | 716.4 | 717.1 | 714.0 | 709.5 |
| 2013 | 704.4 | 708.1 | 710.3 | 710.3 | 708.4 | 711.3 | 715.3 | 714.7 | 706.4 | 705.3 | 706.8 | 702.7 | 708.7 |
| 2014 | 693.5 | 696.2 | 697.9 | 704.5 | 707.1 | 711.5 | 715.4 | 713.8 | 707.2 | 711.5 | 712.1 | 710.4 | 706.8 |
| 2015 | 707.1 | 709.0 | 709.9 | 719.1 | 721.5 | 726.3 | 732.5 | 730.8 | 722.8 | 732.0 | 732.4 | 730.4 | 722.8 |
| 2016 | 722.0 | 724.5 | 727.4 | 736.2 | 735.2 | 740.7 | 746.8 | 746.3 | 738.6 | 742.8 | 743.2 | 740.6 | 737.0 |
| 2017 | 734.8 | 736.7 | 738.8 | 742.8 | 743.7 | 753.0 | 756.6 | 754.8 | 746.4 | 752.6 | 754.2 | 750.6 | 747.1 |
| 2018 | 747.6 | 752.5 | 754.5 | 757.3 | 759.0 | 766.4 | 770.6 | 768.7 | 758.4 | 766.5 | 766.6 | 762.4 | 760.9 |
| 2019 | 760.4 | 765.4 | 766.8 | 774.4 | 777.3 | 785.7 | 789.8 | 787.2 | 779.3 | 787.4 | 792.2 | 787.3 | 779.4 |
| **Education and Health Services** | | | | | | | | | | | | | |
| 2011 | 370.1 | 372.0 | 373.9 | 377.3 | 371.4 | 368.3 | 370.3 | 369.1 | 379.1 | 380.8 | 382.2 | 379.8 | 374.5 |
| 2012 | 378.2 | 380.7 | 382.2 | 384.1 | 381.8 | 374.9 | 372.9 | 374.6 | 386.4 | 391.0 | 392.0 | 390.8 | 382.5 |
| 2013 | 387.6 | 391.2 | 392.9 | 396.2 | 393.0 | 382.8 | 385.3 | 384.9 | 396.6 | 398.4 | 400.1 | 397.3 | 392.2 |
| 2014 | 394.1 | 397.1 | 398.8 | 401.2 | 396.7 | 393.8 | 392.7 | 394.0 | 401.2 | 405.3 | 407.3 | 405.2 | 399.0 |
| 2015 | 402.4 | 407.9 | 407.5 | 412.9 | 408.0 | 404.8 | 408.2 | 408.4 | 415.5 | 425.3 | 427.5 | 424.3 | 412.7 |
| 2016 | 418.5 | 424.5 | 425.3 | 429.2 | 422.5 | 416.6 | 419.3 | 419.9 | 425.7 | 430.3 | 432.0 | 427.6 | 424.3 |
| 2017 | 425.2 | 431.0 | 431.9 | 432.4 | 427.7 | 425.5 | 425.4 | 425.5 | 433.1 | 440.1 | 441.2 | 437.7 | 431.4 |
| 2018 | 436.0 | 442.7 | 442.6 | 445.8 | 440.3 | 436.9 | 436.0 | 436.5 | 443.6 | 450.2 | 452.3 | 447.5 | 442.5 |
| 2019 | 446.3 | 451.2 | 452.7 | 452.9 | 446.1 | 445.4 | 442.7 | 442.3 | 447.9 | 452.0 | 455.1 | 453.4 | 449.0 |
| **Leisure and Hospitality** | | | | | | | | | | | | | |
| 2011 | 251.5 | 252.7 | 259.4 | 268.8 | 274.3 | 282.8 | 282.2 | 283.2 | 275.5 | 272.8 | 271.4 | 269.8 | 270.4 |
| 2012 | 262.0 | 264.3 | 271.3 | 278.6 | 287.0 | 295.9 | 295.1 | 295.2 | 287.1 | 283.7 | 281.4 | 280.7 | 281.9 |
| 2013 | 274.6 | 275.8 | 281.3 | 289.4 | 297.7 | 306.5 | 306.4 | 304.7 | 296.5 | 290.6 | 289.8 | 288.4 | 291.8 |
| 2014 | 280.1 | 280.6 | 286.6 | 296.3 | 305.6 | 314.1 | 312.6 | 311.1 | 302.4 | 299.0 | 297.1 | 295.1 | 298.4 |
| 2015 | 290.4 | 291.2 | 295.6 | 305.4 | 315.3 | 324.9 | 326.2 | 325.0 | 315.4 | 312.2 | 309.9 | 310.7 | 310.2 |
| 2016 | 300.3 | 302.0 | 308.6 | 318.7 | 325.9 | 334.7 | 334.2 | 332.6 | 324.5 | 319.7 | 320.3 | 318.4 | 320.0 |
| 2017 | 308.9 | 312.5 | 319.0 | 327.0 | 336.7 | 344.3 | 343.1 | 341.3 | 331.2 | 330.0 | 326.7 | 324.8 | 328.8 |
| 2018 | 315.4 | 317.6 | 323.8 | 331.4 | 340.9 | 350.8 | 350.2 | 347.1 | 335.9 | 331.8 | 329.1 | 329.1 | 333.6 |
| 2019 | 320.1 | 322.7 | 329.4 | 336.2 | 343.8 | 353.4 | 352.1 | 347.6 | 336.3 | 335.5 | 335.4 | 334.6 | 337.3 |
| **Other Services** | | | | | | | | | | | | | |
| 2011 | 177.5 | 178.6 | 179.4 | 181.6 | 181.8 | 183.3 | 184.4 | 183.1 | 181.7 | 181.7 | 182.4 | 182.7 | 181.5 |
| 2012 | 181.0 | 182.2 | 183.1 | 182.7 | 183.6 | 184.9 | 186.9 | 185.7 | 184.6 | 184.5 | 184.7 | 185.5 | 184.1 |
| 2013 | 183.4 | 183.9 | 184.1 | 185.2 | 186.1 | 187.4 | 188.3 | 187.6 | 186.8 | 186.2 | 186.8 | 186.6 | 186.0 |
| 2014 | 185.2 | 185.6 | 186.7 | 187.4 | 188.3 | 190.5 | 190.4 | 189.5 | 188.1 | 187.5 | 187.5 | 187.2 | 187.8 |
| 2015 | 186.2 | 186.4 | 186.9 | 187.6 | 188.9 | 190.6 | 191.8 | 190.7 | 189.2 | 189.8 | 189.9 | 189.9 | 189.0 |
| 2016 | 188.3 | 188.8 | 189.6 | 191.7 | 193.4 | 196.3 | 199.1 | 199.3 | 199.2 | 200.8 | 202.2 | 202.9 | 196.0 |
| 2017 | 202.2 | 204.3 | 206.0 | 206.0 | 206.7 | 208.9 | 209.5 | 207.9 | 205.6 | 207.3 | 207.1 | 207.3 | 206.6 |
| 2018 | 206.3 | 206.7 | 207.2 | 207.8 | 208.7 | 210.9 | 211.6 | 210.2 | 208.1 | 208.9 | 209.2 | 209.2 | 208.7 |
| 2019 | 207.0 | 208.3 | 208.9 | 209.7 | 210.4 | 212.8 | 213.8 | 212.5 | 210.2 | 211.5 | 211.3 | 212.8 | 210.8 |
| **Government** | | | | | | | | | | | | | |
| 2011 | 687.0 | 694.4 | 698.2 | 695.8 | 697.2 | 695.2 | 688.6 | 670.9 | 694.0 | 695.9 | 695.7 | 696.2 | 692.4 |
| 2012 | 684.4 | 692.6 | 697.8 | 695.1 | 695.9 | 693.6 | 682.3 | 668.4 | 690.2 | 699.3 | 700.7 | 700.0 | 691.7 |
| 2013 | 687.5 | 695.2 | 697.3 | 697.6 | 699.3 | 694.8 | 680.1 | 666.2 | 688.0 | 693.9 | 697.6 | 695.0 | 691.0 |
| 2014 | 677.2 | 685.7 | 686.9 | 687.2 | 691.3 | 690.3 | 674.1 | 663.2 | 688.8 | 694.2 | 696.9 | 694.6 | 685.9 |
| 2015 | 682.0 | 693.2 | 693.7 | 691.7 | 694.5 | 695.3 | 679.4 | 665.6 | 691.1 | 691.7 | 695.1 | 696.1 | 689.1 |
| 2016 | 685.4 | 691.4 | 695.1 | 699.9 | 700.8 | 698.7 | 685.0 | 676.3 | 699.7 | 704.1 | 708.2 | 707.7 | 696.0 |
| 2017 | 695.4 | 705.7 | 708.6 | 705.8 | 709.0 | 706.2 | 686.4 | 676.6 | 699.3 | 703.9 | 707.4 | 703.2 | 700.6 |
| 2018 | 693.5 | 705.7 | 706.2 | 707.5 | 709.4 | 706.8 | 692.7 | 684.2 | 704.1 | 708.6 | 710.6 | 708.9 | 703.2 |
| 2019 | 696.8 | 707.8 | 710.3 | 710.9 | 712.3 | 706.8 | 699.9 | 682.6 | 710.4 | 718.1 | 723.4 | 720.1 | 708.3 |

## Employment by Industry: Miami-Fort Lauderdale-West Palm Beach, FL, 2011–2019

(Numbers in thousands, not seasonally adjusted)

| Industry and year | January | February | March | April | May | June | July | August | September | October | November | December | Annual average |
|---|---|---|---|---|---|---|---|---|---|---|---|---|---|
| **Total Nonfarm** | | | | | | | | | | | | | |
| 2011 | 2,211.9 | 2,224.4 | 2,230.5 | 2,242.8 | 2,237.1 | 2,202.7 | 2,186.7 | 2,217.6 | 2,231.2 | 2,249.3 | 2,277.7 | 2,297.3 | 2,234.1 |
| 2012 | 2,261.3 | 2,274.3 | 2,286.8 | 2,289.0 | 2,290.4 | 2,259.4 | 2,237.8 | 2,267.8 | 2,279.9 | 2,306.7 | 2,338.4 | 2,350.8 | 2,286.9 |
| 2013 | 2,313.8 | 2,333.5 | 2,344.7 | 2,345.5 | 2,348.0 | 2,320.0 | 2,303.4 | 2,336.2 | 2,346.3 | 2,367.8 | 2,407.6 | 2,423.0 | 2,349.2 |
| 2014 | 2,383.5 | 2,401.8 | 2,413.2 | 2,421.1 | 2,425.3 | 2,395.9 | 2,380.5 | 2,416.7 | 2,429.6 | 2,460.0 | 2,498.1 | 2,514.0 | 2,428.3 |
| 2015 | 2,472.7 | 2,487.7 | 2,498.9 | 2,501.6 | 2,505.7 | 2,475.5 | 2,465.3 | 2,499.3 | 2,506.1 | 2,544.7 | 2,577.3 | 2,593.7 | 2,510.7 |
| 2016 | 2,552.4 | 2,570.5 | 2,577.6 | 2,590.1 | 2,585.9 | 2,549.1 | 2,543.9 | 2,572.3 | 2,584.9 | 2,603.8 | 2,638.3 | 2,651.7 | 2,585.0 |
| 2017 | 2,614.8 | 2,631.1 | 2,640.7 | 2,638.2 | 2,644.4 | 2,611.6 | 2,595.2 | 2,621.9 | 2,565.9 | 2,643.2 | 2,677.9 | 2,692.8 | 2,631.5 |
| 2018 | 2,653.1 | 2,673.8 | 2,682.1 | 2,679.0 | 2,679.6 | 2,645.3 | 2,637.4 | 2,673.7 | 2,675.8 | 2,704.8 | 2,734.8 | 2,739.6 | 2,681.6 |
| 2019 | 2,702.4 | 2,721.7 | 2,725.1 | 2,724.1 | 2,719.7 | 2,684.0 | 2,678.9 | 2,714.4 | 2,707.1 | 2,729.5 | 2,749.9 | 2,760.7 | 2,718.1 |
| **Total Private** | | | | | | | | | | | | | |
| 2011 | 1,899.8 | 1,910.8 | 1,918.4 | 1,930.8 | 1,927.0 | 1,919.1 | 1,906.2 | 1,914.1 | 1,924.7 | 1,939.6 | 1,969.5 | 1,988.6 | 1,929.1 |
| 2012 | 1,956.0 | 1,967.7 | 1,981.2 | 1,983.4 | 1,985.7 | 1,980.0 | 1,961.1 | 1,969.6 | 1,977.5 | 2,001.2 | 2,032.8 | 2,045.4 | 1,986.8 |
| 2013 | 2,010.5 | 2,027.3 | 2,038.2 | 2,039.3 | 2,041.9 | 2,039.7 | 2,025.5 | 2,037.6 | 2,042.9 | 2,062.7 | 2,100.3 | 2,117.5 | 2,048.6 |
| 2014 | 2,079.5 | 2,095.9 | 2,106.5 | 2,114.4 | 2,119.3 | 2,115.5 | 2,102.9 | 2,118.5 | 2,127.7 | 2,155.0 | 2,191.4 | 2,209.1 | 2,128.0 |
| 2015 | 2,169.6 | 2,182.7 | 2,192.6 | 2,194.5 | 2,198.8 | 2,194.0 | 2,185.7 | 2,199.6 | 2,202.1 | 2,237.0 | 2,269.5 | 2,287.2 | 2,209.4 |
| 2016 | 2,246.9 | 2,262.7 | 2,269.4 | 2,279.6 | 2,276.3 | 2,263.6 | 2,259.2 | 2,268.6 | 2,274.7 | 2,292.8 | 2,325.6 | 2,340.8 | 2,280.0 |
| 2017 | 2,303.9 | 2,318.0 | 2,326.3 | 2,325.0 | 2,330.0 | 2,322.0 | 2,307.1 | 2,314.5 | 2,254.3 | 2,328.8 | 2,362.8 | 2,378.1 | 2,322.6 |
| 2018 | 2,337.6 | 2,356.8 | 2,363.7 | 2,361.6 | 2,361.9 | 2,351.0 | 2,345.5 | 2,358.7 | 2,359.3 | 2,386.3 | 2,415.2 | 2,421.7 | 2,368.3 |
| 2019 | 2,384.3 | 2,401.8 | 2,403.8 | 2,403.3 | 2,399.1 | 2,387.1 | 2,384.4 | 2,396.9 | 2,388.1 | 2,407.6 | 2,426.8 | 2,439.1 | 2,401.9 |
| **Goods Producing** | | | | | | | | | | | | | |
| 2011 | 160.2 | 160.9 | 160.9 | 161.3 | 161.5 | 162.3 | 161.4 | 162.3 | 163.1 | 163.3 | 163.9 | 163.9 | 162.1 |
| 2012 | 161.1 | 161.5 | 162.5 | 161.6 | 162.9 | 164.2 | 163.3 | 165.6 | 166.3 | 166.7 | 167.8 | 167.8 | 164.3 |
| 2013 | 163.8 | 165.9 | 167.1 | 167.0 | 169.5 | 171.1 | 171.9 | 174.5 | 175.1 | 175.9 | 177.2 | 177.6 | 171.4 |
| 2014 | 175.0 | 177.4 | 178.8 | 179.8 | 182.2 | 184.0 | 184.8 | 187.0 | 188.0 | 189.8 | 190.4 | 190.9 | 184.0 |
| 2015 | 188.9 | 191.3 | 193.0 | 193.9 | 196.3 | 198.3 | 198.6 | 200.6 | 201.6 | 205.5 | 206.5 | 207.2 | 198.5 |
| 2016 | 204.1 | 206.4 | 207.4 | 209.2 | 210.1 | 210.7 | 212.1 | 213.6 | 214.6 | 215.2 | 217.0 | 217.0 | 211.5 |
| 2017 | 213.9 | 216.5 | 218.1 | 218.1 | 219.6 | 220.9 | 219.6 | 220.9 | 212.1 | 221.6 | 222.4 | 223.0 | 218.9 |
| 2018 | 220.0 | 223.0 | 224.4 | 225.8 | 227.0 | 229.0 | 228.8 | 230.0 | 232.1 | 233.9 | 233.7 | 233.5 | 228.8 |
| 2019 | 230.8 | 233.1 | 233.7 | 232.3 | 233.3 | 234.5 | 234.9 | 235.9 | 235.6 | 235.4 | 235.4 | 234.4 | 234.1 |
| **Service-Providing** | | | | | | | | | | | | | |
| 2011 | 2,051.7 | 2,063.5 | 2,069.6 | 2,081.5 | 2,075.6 | 2,040.4 | 2,025.3 | 2,055.3 | 2,068.1 | 2,086.0 | 2,113.8 | 2,133.4 | 2,072.0 |
| 2012 | 2,100.2 | 2,112.8 | 2,124.3 | 2,127.4 | 2,127.5 | 2,095.2 | 2,074.5 | 2,102.2 | 2,113.6 | 2,140.0 | 2,170.6 | 2,183.0 | 2,122.6 |
| 2013 | 2,150.0 | 2,167.6 | 2,177.6 | 2,178.5 | 2,178.5 | 2,148.9 | 2,131.5 | 2,161.7 | 2,171.2 | 2,191.9 | 2,230.4 | 2,245.4 | 2,177.8 |
| 2014 | 2,208.5 | 2,224.4 | 2,234.4 | 2,241.3 | 2,243.1 | 2,211.9 | 2,195.7 | 2,229.7 | 2,241.6 | 2,270.2 | 2,307.7 | 2,323.1 | 2,244.3 |
| 2015 | 2,283.8 | 2,296.4 | 2,305.9 | 2,307.7 | 2,309.4 | 2,277.2 | 2,266.7 | 2,298.7 | 2,304.5 | 2,339.2 | 2,370.8 | 2,386.5 | 2,312.2 |
| 2016 | 2,348.3 | 2,364.1 | 2,370.2 | 2,380.9 | 2,375.8 | 2,338.4 | 2,331.8 | 2,358.7 | 2,370.3 | 2,388.6 | 2,421.3 | 2,434.7 | 2,373.6 |
| 2017 | 2,400.9 | 2,414.6 | 2,422.6 | 2,420.1 | 2,424.8 | 2,390.7 | 2,375.6 | 2,401.0 | 2,353.8 | 2,421.6 | 2,455.5 | 2,469.8 | 2,412.6 |
| 2018 | 2,433.1 | 2,450.8 | 2,457.7 | 2,453.2 | 2,452.6 | 2,416.3 | 2,408.6 | 2,443.7 | 2,443.7 | 2,470.9 | 2,501.1 | 2,506.1 | 2,453.2 |
| 2019 | 2,471.6 | 2,488.6 | 2,491.4 | 2,491.8 | 2,486.4 | 2,449.5 | 2,444.0 | 2,478.5 | 2,471.5 | 2,494.1 | 2,514.5 | 2,526.3 | 2,484.0 |
| **Mining and Logging** | | | | | | | | | | | | | |
| 2011 | 0.6 | 0.6 | 0.7 | 0.7 | 0.7 | 0.7 | 0.6 | 0.6 | 0.5 | 0.6 | 0.6 | 0.6 | 0.6 |
| 2012 | 0.6 | 0.6 | 0.6 | 0.6 | 0.7 | 0.7 | 0.6 | 0.6 | 0.6 | 0.6 | 0.6 | 0.6 | 0.6 |
| 2013 | 0.6 | 0.6 | 0.6 | 0.6 | 0.6 | 0.5 | 0.6 | 0.6 | 0.6 | 0.6 | 0.6 | 0.6 | 0.6 |
| 2014 | 0.6 | 0.6 | 0.6 | 0.6 | 0.6 | 0.6 | 0.6 | 0.6 | 0.6 | 0.6 | 0.6 | 0.6 | 0.6 |
| 2015 | 0.6 | 0.6 | 0.6 | 0.6 | 0.6 | 0.6 | 0.6 | 0.6 | 0.6 | 0.6 | 0.6 | 0.6 | 0.6 |
| 2016 | 0.7 | 0.7 | 0.7 | 0.7 | 0.7 | 0.7 | 0.7 | 0.7 | 0.7 | 0.7 | 0.7 | 0.7 | 0.7 |
| 2017 | 0.7 | 0.7 | 0.7 | 0.7 | 0.7 | 0.7 | 0.7 | 0.7 | 0.7 | 0.7 | 0.7 | 0.7 | 0.7 |
| 2018 | 0.7 | 0.7 | 0.7 | 0.7 | 0.7 | 0.7 | 0.7 | 0.7 | 0.7 | 0.7 | 0.7 | 0.7 | 0.7 |
| 2019 | 0.7 | 0.7 | 0.7 | 0.8 | 0.7 | 0.8 | 0.7 | 0.7 | 0.8 | 0.7 | 0.8 | 0.8 | 0.7 |
| **Construction** | | | | | | | | | | | | | |
| 2011 | 84.2 | 84.6 | 84.7 | 84.7 | 84.4 | 84.8 | 84.8 | 85.2 | 86.1 | 85.8 | 86.1 | 85.8 | 85.1 |
| 2012 | 83.6 | 83.6 | 84.3 | 84.3 | 85.2 | 86.5 | 86.4 | 88.1 | 88.8 | 88.9 | 89.5 | 89.5 | 86.6 |
| 2013 | 87.4 | 88.6 | 89.4 | 89.7 | 91.6 | 92.6 | 93.5 | 95.6 | 96.2 | 96.4 | 96.9 | 97.1 | 92.9 |
| 2014 | 94.8 | 96.6 | 98.0 | 99.1 | 100.8 | 102.3 | 103.0 | 104.6 | 105.2 | 106.4 | 106.5 | 106.8 | 102.0 |
| 2015 | 105.3 | 107.1 | 108.2 | 109.2 | 110.7 | 112.3 | 112.9 | 114.3 | 115.3 | 118.1 | 118.8 | 119.1 | 112.6 |
| 2016 | 116.3 | 118.0 | 119.0 | 120.8 | 121.8 | 122.5 | 124.0 | 124.9 | 125.7 | 126.1 | 127.2 | 127.2 | 122.8 |
| 2017 | 125.4 | 127.3 | 128.4 | 128.5 | 129.6 | 130.8 | 130.8 | 131.7 | 124.8 | 132.5 | 132.7 | 133.1 | 129.6 |
| 2018 | 131.3 | 133.5 | 134.6 | 136.0 | 137.1 | 138.7 | 138.5 | 139.3 | 140.9 | 142.5 | 141.8 | 141.6 | 138.0 |
| 2019 | 139.5 | 140.9 | 141.6 | 140.3 | 141.2 | 141.9 | 142.8 | 143.2 | 143.2 | 143.5 | 143.7 | 142.2 | 142.0 |

## Employment by Industry: Miami-Fort Lauderdale-West Palm Beach, FL, 2011–2019—*Continued*

(Numbers in thousands, not seasonally adjusted)

| Industry and year | January | February | March | April | May | June | July | August | September | October | November | December | Annual average |
|---|---|---|---|---|---|---|---|---|---|---|---|---|---|
| **Manufacturing** | | | | | | | | | | | | | |
| 2011 | 75.4 | 75.7 | 75.5 | 75.9 | 76.4 | 76.8 | 76.0 | 76.5 | 76.5 | 76.9 | 77.2 | 77.5 | 76.4 |
| 2012 | 76.9 | 77.3 | 77.6 | 76.7 | 77.0 | 77.0 | 76.3 | 76.9 | 76.9 | 77.2 | 77.7 | 77.7 | 77.1 |
| 2013 | 75.8 | 76.7 | 77.1 | 76.7 | 77.3 | 78.0 | 77.8 | 78.3 | 78.3 | 78.9 | 79.7 | 79.9 | 77.9 |
| 2014 | 79.6 | 80.2 | 80.2 | 80.1 | 80.8 | 81.1 | 81.2 | 81.8 | 82.2 | 82.8 | 83.3 | 83.5 | 81.4 |
| | | | | | | | | | | | | | |
| 2015 | 83.0 | 83.6 | 84.2 | 84.1 | 85.0 | 85.4 | 85.1 | 85.7 | 85.7 | 86.8 | 87.1 | 87.5 | 85.3 |
| 2016 | 87.1 | 87.7 | 87.7 | 87.7 | 87.6 | 87.5 | 87.4 | 88.0 | 88.2 | 88.4 | 89.1 | 89.1 | 88.0 |
| 2017 | 87.8 | 88.5 | 89.0 | 88.9 | 89.3 | 89.4 | 88.1 | 88.5 | 86.6 | 88.4 | 89.0 | 89.2 | 88.6 |
| 2018 | 88.0 | 88.8 | 89.1 | 89.1 | 89.2 | 89.6 | 89.6 | 90.0 | 90.5 | 90.7 | 91.2 | 91.2 | 89.8 |
| 2019 | 90.6 | 91.5 | 91.4 | 91.2 | 91.4 | 91.8 | 91.4 | 92.0 | 91.6 | 91.2 | 90.9 | 91.4 | 91.4 |
| **Trade, Transportation, and Utilities** | | | | | | | | | | | | | |
| 2011 | 511.4 | 510.6 | 511.7 | 515.0 | 514.9 | 515.1 | 514.9 | 517.1 | 519.0 | 525.1 | 538.3 | 546.3 | 520.0 |
| 2012 | 532.3 | 531.1 | 532.4 | 533.2 | 534.8 | 533.4 | 530.0 | 530.7 | 532.6 | 537.9 | 552.9 | 558.1 | 536.6 |
| 2013 | 543.5 | 542.4 | 543.2 | 543.7 | 545.3 | 546.4 | 543.0 | 545.2 | 546.3 | 552.5 | 570.0 | 578.9 | 550.0 |
| 2014 | 558.0 | 557.9 | 558.3 | 559.5 | 560.7 | 561.0 | 559.1 | 563.1 | 563.9 | 571.8 | 589.8 | 598.8 | 566.8 |
| | | | | | | | | | | | | | |
| 2015 | 580.6 | 578.5 | 579.7 | 579.1 | 579.5 | 580.7 | 577.6 | 580.2 | 578.1 | 586.1 | 601.7 | 609.5 | 584.3 |
| 2016 | 588.7 | 587.4 | 587.7 | 589.4 | 589.8 | 587.8 | 587.9 | 588.6 | 588.3 | 591.6 | 608.9 | 616.8 | 592.7 |
| 2017 | 598.3 | 595.2 | 596.0 | 594.5 | 595.1 | 594.2 | 592.8 | 593.6 | 580.0 | 596.1 | 615.7 | 623.1 | 597.9 |
| 2018 | 606.6 | 604.8 | 603.7 | 603.1 | 603.8 | 604.4 | 602.4 | 603.7 | 604.9 | 608.5 | 627.2 | 633.3 | 608.9 |
| 2019 | 615.5 | 612.0 | 611.7 | 609.5 | 608.2 | 608.5 | 609.4 | 610.7 | 609.3 | 617.9 | 628.8 | 636.9 | 614.9 |
| **Wholesale Trade** | | | | | | | | | | | | | |
| 2011 | 131.8 | 132.8 | 133.0 | 134.0 | 133.6 | 133.4 | 133.0 | 133.3 | 133.8 | 135.2 | 136.1 | 137.8 | 134.0 |
| 2012 | 136.5 | 137.5 | 138.4 | 139.0 | 139.3 | 138.6 | 137.8 | 137.8 | 138.2 | 139.0 | 139.9 | 141.0 | 138.6 |
| 2013 | 139.1 | 140.2 | 140.2 | 139.9 | 140.5 | 140.1 | 139.0 | 139.4 | 139.8 | 140.3 | 141.4 | 142.3 | 140.2 |
| 2014 | 140.9 | 141.9 | 141.7 | 141.8 | 142.3 | 141.6 | 140.9 | 141.7 | 142.1 | 143.3 | 144.9 | 145.7 | 142.4 |
| | | | | | | | | | | | | | |
| 2015 | 144.3 | 144.8 | 144.8 | 144.4 | 144.6 | 144.1 | 143.2 | 143.4 | 143.2 | 144.9 | 145.6 | 146.2 | 144.5 |
| 2016 | 144.7 | 145.4 | 145.5 | 145.9 | 146.1 | 145.0 | 144.4 | 144.3 | 144.5 | 144.5 | 146.1 | 147.1 | 145.3 |
| 2017 | 145.4 | 145.8 | 146.3 | 145.8 | 146.5 | 145.8 | 145.0 | 144.9 | 143.4 | 144.9 | 145.7 | 146.6 | 145.5 |
| 2018 | 146.4 | 147.3 | 147.5 | 148.0 | 147.9 | 147.7 | 147.5 | 147.5 | 147.7 | 148.4 | 149.2 | 149.8 | 147.9 |
| 2019 | 147.8 | 149.0 | 148.6 | 148.5 | 148.3 | 148.3 | 148.4 | 148.1 | 148.2 | 148.1 | 148.0 | 149.2 | 148.4 |
| **Retail Trade** | | | | | | | | | | | | | |
| 2011 | 290.2 | 287.7 | 288.3 | 290.3 | 290.8 | 291.0 | 291.3 | 293.1 | 294.4 | 298.6 | 309.5 | 314.1 | 294.9 |
| 2012 | 303.0 | 299.9 | 300.1 | 300.3 | 301.7 | 301.0 | 298.8 | 299.5 | 300.7 | 304.0 | 316.9 | 319.2 | 303.8 |
| 2013 | 308.8 | 306.2 | 306.7 | 307.4 | 308.6 | 309.7 | 308.4 | 310.1 | 310.4 | 315.1 | 330.2 | 336.2 | 313.2 |
| 2014 | 319.2 | 317.6 | 317.9 | 318.9 | 319.6 | 320.5 | 319.5 | 322.3 | 322.2 | 328.2 | 342.2 | 348.2 | 324.7 |
| | | | | | | | | | | | | | |
| 2015 | 333.6 | 331.4 | 332.1 | 331.4 | 331.9 | 333.1 | 330.6 | 332.7 | 330.2 | 335.0 | 347.0 | 351.2 | 335.0 |
| 2016 | 334.9 | 332.6 | 332.4 | 333.5 | 334.2 | 333.3 | 334.0 | 335.4 | 334.0 | 337.0 | 350.3 | 354.5 | 337.2 |
| 2017 | 339.6 | 336.3 | 336.0 | 335.2 | 335.1 | 334.4 | 333.9 | 334.6 | 323.7 | 335.0 | 350.1 | 353.4 | 337.3 |
| 2018 | 340.9 | 337.9 | 336.6 | 335.6 | 335.9 | 335.8 | 333.7 | 334.3 | 334.1 | 335.5 | 348.9 | 350.5 | 338.3 |
| 2019 | 338.2 | 334.1 | 333.6 | 331.9 | 331.5 | 331.0 | 331.2 | 332.6 | 330.7 | 336.7 | 347.0 | 350.3 | 335.7 |
| **Transportation and Utilities** | | | | | | | | | | | | | |
| 2011 | 89.4 | 90.1 | 90.4 | 90.7 | 90.5 | 90.7 | 90.6 | 90.7 | 90.8 | 91.3 | 92.7 | 94.4 | 91.0 |
| 2012 | 92.8 | 93.7 | 93.9 | 93.9 | 93.8 | 93.8 | 93.4 | 93.4 | 93.7 | 94.9 | 96.1 | 97.9 | 94.3 |
| 2013 | 95.6 | 96.0 | 96.3 | 96.4 | 96.2 | 96.6 | 95.6 | 95.7 | 96.1 | 97.1 | 98.4 | 100.4 | 96.7 |
| 2014 | 97.9 | 98.4 | 98.7 | 98.8 | 98.8 | 98.9 | 98.7 | 99.1 | 99.6 | 100.3 | 102.7 | 104.9 | 99.7 |
| | | | | | | | | | | | | | |
| 2015 | 102.7 | 102.3 | 102.8 | 103.3 | 103.0 | 103.5 | 103.8 | 104.1 | 104.7 | 106.2 | 109.1 | 112.1 | 104.8 |
| 2016 | 109.1 | 109.4 | 109.8 | 110.0 | 109.5 | 109.5 | 109.5 | 108.9 | 109.8 | 110.1 | 112.5 | 115.2 | 110.3 |
| 2017 | 113.3 | 113.1 | 113.7 | 113.5 | 113.5 | 114.0 | 113.9 | 114.1 | 112.9 | 116.2 | 119.9 | 123.1 | 115.1 |
| 2018 | 119.3 | 119.6 | 119.6 | 119.5 | 120.0 | 120.9 | 121.2 | 121.9 | 123.1 | 124.6 | 129.1 | 133.0 | 122.7 |
| 2019 | 129.5 | 128.9 | 129.5 | 129.1 | 128.4 | 129.2 | 129.8 | 130.0 | 130.4 | 133.1 | 133.8 | 137.4 | 130.8 |
| **Information** | | | | | | | | | | | | | |
| 2011 | 43.8 | 43.9 | 44.0 | 43.9 | 43.8 | 43.8 | 43.8 | 44.1 | 44.1 | 44.2 | 44.5 | 44.7 | 44.1 |
| 2012 | 44.6 | 44.6 | 45.0 | 45.1 | 45.1 | 44.8 | 45.0 | 45.0 | 44.8 | 45.9 | 45.9 | 46.0 | 45.2 |
| 2013 | 45.5 | 45.5 | 46.1 | 45.8 | 46.0 | 46.2 | 46.4 | 46.5 | 46.5 | 47.1 | 47.2 | 47.5 | 46.4 |
| 2014 | 47.2 | 47.4 | 47.1 | 47.5 | 47.4 | 48.2 | 48.1 | 47.7 | 47.5 | 47.8 | 48.4 | 48.4 | 47.7 |
| | | | | | | | | | | | | | |
| 2015 | 47.6 | 47.5 | 47.8 | 47.6 | 48.2 | 48.1 | 48.0 | 48.6 | 48.2 | 48.4 | 48.4 | 48.8 | 48.1 |
| 2016 | 48.5 | 49.1 | 49.0 | 49.2 | 49.7 | 49.8 | 49.8 | 50.4 | 49.2 | 49.8 | 50.4 | 50.5 | 49.6 |
| 2017 | 50.7 | 52.1 | 51.9 | 51.2 | 51.9 | 51.5 | 50.6 | 51.2 | 49.5 | 50.0 | 51.1 | 51.2 | 51.1 |
| 2018 | 50.2 | 51.5 | 51.5 | 50.4 | 50.8 | 50.8 | 50.5 | 51.9 | 50.5 | 50.6 | 51.7 | 52.0 | 51.0 |
| 2019 | 50.0 | 51.4 | 50.9 | 51.0 | 51.5 | 51.0 | 50.5 | 51.0 | 50.4 | 50.7 | 51.1 | 51.1 | 50.9 |

## Employment by Industry: Miami-Fort Lauderdale-West Palm Beach, FL, 2011–2019—*Continued*

(Numbers in thousands, not seasonally adjusted)

| Industry and year | January | February | March | April | May | June | July | August | September | October | November | December | Annual average |
|---|---|---|---|---|---|---|---|---|---|---|---|---|---|
| **Financial Activities** | | | | | | | | | | | | | |
| 2011 | 153.6 | 154.0 | 154.5 | 155.8 | 156.2 | 156.0 | 156.4 | 157.0 | 157.3 | 158.5 | 159.2 | 160.6 | 156.6 |
| 2012 | 158.7 | 159.4 | 160.0 | 161.0 | 161.5 | 161.8 | 161.7 | 162.0 | 161.4 | 163.3 | 164.1 | 165.1 | 161.7 |
| 2013 | 162.6 | 163.0 | 163.6 | 164.0 | 164.2 | 165.0 | 164.9 | 165.0 | 165.0 | 166.5 | 167.3 | 168.6 | 165.0 |
| 2014 | 166.3 | 167.1 | 167.5 | 168.5 | 169.5 | 169.7 | 169.8 | 169.9 | 170.1 | 172.6 | 173.7 | 174.7 | 170.0 |
| 2015 | 172.9 | 173.8 | 174.0 | 174.4 | 174.8 | 175.3 | 176.1 | 176.4 | 175.7 | 177.7 | 178.5 | 179.3 | 175.7 |
| 2016 | 176.0 | 176.9 | 177.0 | 177.4 | 177.8 | 177.4 | 177.6 | 177.6 | 177.7 | 178.9 | 179.7 | 181.5 | 178.0 |
| 2017 | 180.0 | 180.6 | 180.9 | 180.4 | 180.8 | 181.0 | 181.0 | 181.0 | 179.9 | 182.8 | 182.6 | 184.0 | 181.3 |
| 2018 | 181.1 | 182.2 | 182.6 | 183.5 | 184.0 | 184.1 | 185.0 | 185.0 | 184.9 | 187.0 | 188.1 | 188.5 | 184.7 |
| 2019 | 187.0 | 188.1 | 188.0 | 188.4 | 188.2 | 188.6 | 189.1 | 189.8 | 189.1 | 190.3 | 191.3 | 192.3 | 189.2 |
| **Professional and Business Services** | | | | | | | | | | | | | |
| 2011 | 331.5 | 336.3 | 337.7 | 340.6 | 338.6 | 337.4 | 336.1 | 336.9 | 338.7 | 342.7 | 346.6 | 350.1 | 339.4 |
| 2012 | 341.3 | 345.8 | 349.0 | 350.6 | 350.4 | 351.3 | 349.5 | 350.8 | 352.7 | 361.2 | 366.1 | 368.3 | 353.1 |
| 2013 | 360.8 | 366.5 | 368.6 | 368.9 | 369.0 | 368.3 | 368.2 | 370.4 | 370.5 | 375.9 | 381.6 | 383.3 | 371.0 |
| 2014 | 376.6 | 380.3 | 381.9 | 385.5 | 387.1 | 385.8 | 385.6 | 388.8 | 390.5 | 397.5 | 402.5 | 406.0 | 389.0 |
| 2015 | 394.1 | 398.4 | 398.7 | 400.3 | 402.1 | 400.3 | 402.2 | 404.8 | 405.2 | 415.0 | 419.2 | 421.3 | 405.1 |
| 2016 | 414.1 | 417.8 | 417.7 | 421.4 | 419.8 | 417.8 | 419.5 | 422.8 | 422.4 | 430.8 | 434.8 | 433.8 | 422.7 |
| 2017 | 428.6 | 431.6 | 431.6 | 433.7 | 434.7 | 434.4 | 434.6 | 435.4 | 423.4 | 440.5 | 444.7 | 445.1 | 434.9 |
| 2018 | 436.5 | 440.0 | 441.5 | 442.8 | 442.3 | 440.7 | 442.7 | 444.8 | 442.8 | 452.3 | 454.1 | 451.1 | 444.3 |
| 2019 | 443.2 | 448.2 | 446.7 | 450.1 | 448.4 | 448.4 | 451.7 | 455.7 | 452.4 | 452.6 | 450.7 | 451.6 | 450.0 |
| **Education and Health Services** | | | | | | | | | | | | | |
| 2011 | 338.6 | 341.4 | 341.7 | 344.3 | 343.7 | 340.6 | 334.7 | 336.4 | 340.6 | 342.1 | 343.7 | 343.8 | 341.0 |
| 2012 | 339.2 | 342.3 | 343.8 | 343.2 | 343.1 | 340.4 | 334.6 | 338.6 | 342.0 | 343.7 | 345.3 | 344.8 | 341.8 |
| 2013 | 341.9 | 345.5 | 346.5 | 347.9 | 348.1 | 345.8 | 339.8 | 344.1 | 346.9 | 348.7 | 351.2 | 352.1 | 346.5 |
| 2014 | 349.0 | 352.4 | 353.0 | 355.2 | 355.7 | 353.6 | 349.4 | 354.9 | 358.9 | 361.2 | 362.9 | 364.1 | 355.9 |
| 2015 | 360.6 | 363.7 | 364.9 | 366.3 | 368.4 | 365.8 | 361.6 | 364.7 | 369.4 | 373.9 | 376.4 | 376.8 | 367.7 |
| 2016 | 374.3 | 377.0 | 377.7 | 381.4 | 381.7 | 378.2 | 376.0 | 379.2 | 384.3 | 386.9 | 388.7 | 390.7 | 381.3 |
| 2017 | 387.0 | 391.0 | 392.2 | 393.7 | 395.7 | 391.6 | 386.6 | 390.6 | 387.8 | 397.2 | 399.1 | 400.0 | 392.7 |
| 2018 | 394.9 | 399.1 | 399.9 | 400.3 | 400.3 | 395.9 | 392.8 | 398.9 | 402.0 | 406.5 | 408.6 | 408.4 | 400.6 |
| 2019 | 405.6 | 409.9 | 409.8 | 412.2 | 411.7 | 405.1 | 402.0 | 407.1 | 408.6 | 413.5 | 414.4 | 413.2 | 409.4 |
| **Leisure and Hospitality** | | | | | | | | | | | | | |
| 2011 | 259.2 | 261.7 | 265.3 | 266.4 | 264.5 | 261.0 | 255.6 | 256.6 | 257.6 | 258.5 | 266.8 | 272.1 | 262.1 |
| 2012 | 272.0 | 275.3 | 280.0 | 279.5 | 278.7 | 275.0 | 269.0 | 269.4 | 269.8 | 273.6 | 281.1 | 285.3 | 275.7 |
| 2013 | 283.0 | 287.9 | 291.8 | 290.3 | 288.3 | 285.3 | 280.2 | 280.8 | 280.9 | 283.3 | 291.9 | 294.8 | 286.5 |
| 2014 | 292.8 | 297.4 | 303.0 | 301.5 | 299.7 | 296.6 | 289.7 | 290.5 | 291.8 | 296.0 | 304.0 | 306.1 | 297.4 |
| 2015 | 305.4 | 309.0 | 313.4 | 311.4 | 308.4 | 304.3 | 301.1 | 303.7 | 302.9 | 308.8 | 315.7 | 320.6 | 308.7 |
| 2016 | 318.4 | 324.1 | 328.2 | 326.8 | 323.0 | 317.7 | 312.7 | 313.4 | 315.1 | 316.2 | 322.1 | 326.7 | 320.4 |
| 2017 | 322.9 | 327.5 | 331.8 | 329.9 | 328.6 | 325.3 | 319.3 | 319.7 | 302.9 | 318.3 | 324.2 | 328.0 | 323.2 |
| 2018 | 326.3 | 333.1 | 336.4 | 332.3 | 330.5 | 323.5 | 321.2 | 323.0 | 320.9 | 325.2 | 330.3 | 333.1 | 328.0 |
| 2019 | 331.9 | 337.9 | 341.8 | 338.4 | 337.1 | 330.0 | 326.3 | 327.3 | 323.5 | 327.4 | 333.9 | 338.9 | 332.9 |
| **Other Services** | | | | | | | | | | | | | |
| 2011 | 101.5 | 102.0 | 102.6 | 103.5 | 103.8 | 102.9 | 103.3 | 103.7 | 104.3 | 105.2 | 106.5 | 107.1 | 103.9 |
| 2012 | 106.8 | 107.7 | 108.5 | 109.2 | 109.2 | 109.1 | 108.0 | 107.5 | 107.9 | 108.9 | 109.6 | 110.0 | 108.5 |
| 2013 | 109.4 | 110.6 | 111.3 | 111.7 | 111.5 | 111.6 | 111.1 | 111.1 | 111.7 | 112.8 | 113.9 | 114.7 | 111.8 |
| 2014 | 114.6 | 116.0 | 116.9 | 116.9 | 117.0 | 116.6 | 116.4 | 116.6 | 117.0 | 118.3 | 119.7 | 120.1 | 117.2 |
| 2015 | 119.5 | 120.5 | 121.1 | 121.5 | 121.1 | 121.2 | 120.5 | 120.6 | 121.0 | 121.6 | 123.1 | 123.7 | 121.3 |
| 2016 | 122.8 | 124.0 | 124.7 | 124.8 | 124.4 | 124.2 | 123.6 | 123.0 | 123.1 | 123.4 | 124.0 | 123.8 | 123.8 |
| 2017 | 122.5 | 123.5 | 123.8 | 123.5 | 123.6 | 123.1 | 122.6 | 122.1 | 118.7 | 122.3 | 123.0 | 123.7 | 122.7 |
| 2018 | 122.0 | 123.1 | 123.7 | 123.4 | 123.2 | 122.6 | 122.1 | 121.4 | 121.2 | 122.3 | 121.5 | 121.8 | 122.4 |
| 2019 | 120.3 | 121.2 | 121.2 | 121.4 | 120.7 | 121.0 | 120.5 | 119.4 | 119.2 | 119.8 | 121.2 | 120.7 | 120.6 |
| **Government** | | | | | | | | | | | | | |
| 2011 | 312.1 | 313.6 | 312.1 | 312.0 | 310.1 | 283.6 | 280.5 | 303.5 | 306.5 | 309.7 | 308.2 | 308.7 | 305.1 |
| 2012 | 305.3 | 306.6 | 305.6 | 305.6 | 304.7 | 279.4 | 276.7 | 298.2 | 302.4 | 305.5 | 305.6 | 305.4 | 300.1 |
| 2013 | 303.3 | 306.2 | 306.5 | 306.2 | 306.1 | 280.3 | 277.9 | 298.6 | 303.4 | 305.1 | 307.3 | 305.5 | 300.5 |
| 2014 | 304.0 | 305.9 | 306.7 | 306.7 | 306.0 | 280.4 | 277.6 | 298.2 | 301.9 | 305.0 | 306.7 | 304.9 | 300.3 |
| 2015 | 303.1 | 305.0 | 306.3 | 307.1 | 306.9 | 281.5 | 279.6 | 299.7 | 304.0 | 307.7 | 307.8 | 306.5 | 301.3 |
| 2016 | 305.5 | 307.8 | 308.2 | 310.5 | 309.6 | 285.5 | 284.7 | 303.7 | 310.2 | 311.0 | 312.7 | 310.9 | 305.0 |
| 2017 | 310.9 | 313.1 | 314.4 | 313.2 | 314.4 | 289.6 | 288.1 | 307.4 | 311.6 | 314.4 | 315.1 | 314.7 | 308.9 |
| 2018 | 315.5 | 317.0 | 318.4 | 317.4 | 317.7 | 294.3 | 291.9 | 315.0 | 316.5 | 318.5 | 319.6 | 317.9 | 313.3 |
| 2019 | 318.1 | 319.9 | 321.3 | 320.8 | 320.6 | 296.9 | 294.5 | 317.5 | 319.0 | 321.9 | 323.1 | 321.6 | 316.3 |

# Employment by Industry: Philadelphia-Camden-Wilmington, PA-NJ-DE-MD, 2011–2019

(Numbers in thousands, not seasonally adjusted)

| Industry and year | January | February | March | April | May | June | July | August | September | October | November | December | Annual average |
|---|---|---|---|---|---|---|---|---|---|---|---|---|---|
| **Total Nonfarm** | | | | | | | | | | | | | |
| 2011 | 2,661.6 | 2,673.3 | 2,694.3 | 2,724.3 | 2,725.3 | 2,723.7 | 2,684.9 | 2,674.6 | 2,704.3 | 2,725.1 | 2,739.1 | 2,740.2 | 2,705.9 |
| 2012 | 2,667.9 | 2,684.0 | 2,709.9 | 2,723.6 | 2,735.0 | 2,736.7 | 2,697.9 | 2,695.9 | 2,723.8 | 2,750.4 | 2,766.9 | 2,767.2 | 2,721.6 |
| 2013 | 2,689.2 | 2,708.1 | 2,728.4 | 2,749.9 | 2,758.5 | 2,761.4 | 2,719.2 | 2,717.0 | 2,746.4 | 2,770.3 | 2,791.1 | 2,783.6 | 2,743.6 |
| 2014 | 2,711.9 | 2,717.0 | 2,741.2 | 2,775.1 | 2,789.4 | 2,794.0 | 2,753.6 | 2,752.1 | 2,787.2 | 2,816.2 | 2,835.0 | 2,835.5 | 2,775.7 |
| 2015 | 2,752.5 | 2,765.7 | 2,780.6 | 2,816.8 | 2,835.7 | 2,838.8 | 2,800.4 | 2,795.2 | 2,825.9 | 2,858.7 | 2,875.1 | 2,877.1 | 2,818.5 |
| 2016 | 2,794.6 | 2,808.9 | 2,833.0 | 2,866.5 | 2,873.2 | 2,875.7 | 2,853.6 | 2,847.8 | 2,885.1 | 2,905.0 | 2,918.9 | 2,922.2 | 2,865.4 |
| 2017 | 2,851.1 | 2,863.7 | 2,877.0 | 2,902.9 | 2,919.7 | 2,919.2 | 2,886.8 | 2,884.8 | 2,916.7 | 2,941.2 | 2,959.6 | 2,959.0 | 2,906.8 |
| 2018 | 2,879.6 | 2,899.7 | 2,909.7 | 2,935.9 | 2,947.6 | 2,954.1 | 2,920.2 | 2,916.9 | 2,948.4 | 2,977.5 | 2,993.1 | 2,987.9 | 2,939.2 |
| 2019 | 2,921.5 | 2,932.7 | 2,951.4 | 2,978.8 | 2,985.7 | 2,986.0 | 2,961.9 | 2,961.9 | 2,987.3 | 3,005.2 | 3,013.1 | 3,006.4 | 2,974.3 |
| **Total Private** | | | | | | | | | | | | | |
| 2011 | 2,310.2 | 2,317.3 | 2,336.4 | 2,365.3 | 2,371.0 | 2,373.4 | 2,364.2 | 2,357.7 | 2,366.3 | 2,377.7 | 2,389.7 | 2,390.8 | 2,360.0 |
| 2012 | 2,328.7 | 2,337.7 | 2,362.3 | 2,376.1 | 2,390.1 | 2,396.7 | 2,384.1 | 2,383.7 | 2,390.7 | 2,406.6 | 2,421.3 | 2,421.6 | 2,383.3 |
| 2013 | 2,352.8 | 2,364.5 | 2,383.0 | 2,405.2 | 2,414.2 | 2,422.6 | 2,408.4 | 2,408.8 | 2,415.7 | 2,429.7 | 2,448.2 | 2,442.3 | 2,408.0 |
| 2014 | 2,378.7 | 2,377.0 | 2,399.9 | 2,432.7 | 2,448.6 | 2,456.5 | 2,443.4 | 2,444.5 | 2,456.1 | 2,476.7 | 2,493.8 | 2,496.0 | 2,442.0 |
| 2015 | 2,420.7 | 2,428.1 | 2,440.4 | 2,475.8 | 2,495.6 | 2,502.6 | 2,491.8 | 2,487.3 | 2,494.6 | 2,522.1 | 2,536.0 | 2,538.7 | 2,486.1 |
| 2016 | 2,464.9 | 2,473.1 | 2,494.5 | 2,528.5 | 2,536.4 | 2,543.6 | 2,543.3 | 2,538.5 | 2,552.5 | 2,566.8 | 2,578.5 | 2,582.3 | 2,533.6 |
| 2017 | 2,519.1 | 2,525.6 | 2,537.0 | 2,563.9 | 2,581.4 | 2,585.7 | 2,574.9 | 2,571.7 | 2,582.8 | 2,602.2 | 2,618.6 | 2,618.2 | 2,573.4 |
| 2018 | 2,547.0 | 2,560.6 | 2,569.4 | 2,595.5 | 2,609.2 | 2,618.6 | 2,606.7 | 2,602.3 | 2,611.6 | 2,636.1 | 2,649.3 | 2,645.1 | 2,604.3 |
| 2019 | 2,588.4 | 2,591.7 | 2,608.6 | 2,636.5 | 2,645.6 | 2,651.2 | 2,644.6 | 2,642.3 | 2,647.5 | 2,660.0 | 2,665.8 | 2,659.7 | 2,636.8 |
| **Goods Producing** | | | | | | | | | | | | | |
| 2011 | 276.7 | 275.5 | 281.4 | 287.4 | 288.3 | 290.7 | 291.8 | 292.0 | 290.1 | 290.2 | 288.7 | 285.2 | 286.5 |
| 2012 | 276.8 | 276.6 | 279.5 | 281.4 | 282.2 | 285.7 | 286.0 | 286.4 | 285.6 | 284.9 | 282.9 | 281.6 | 282.5 |
| 2013 | 274.3 | 274.0 | 277.9 | 281.8 | 283.0 | 286.2 | 286.6 | 288.5 | 286.9 | 287.1 | 286.1 | 280.8 | 282.8 |
| 2014 | 274.8 | 273.4 | 279.1 | 283.6 | 286.7 | 289.4 | 290.7 | 290.8 | 289.4 | 289.7 | 289.5 | 287.1 | 285.4 |
| 2015 | 279.0 | 279.3 | 281.6 | 289.0 | 292.5 | 295.2 | 296.8 | 297.3 | 296.0 | 295.5 | 294.3 | 292.8 | 290.8 |
| 2016 | 284.7 | 284.0 | 288.5 | 292.0 | 294.3 | 297.7 | 299.3 | 299.4 | 298.2 | 299.2 | 297.7 | 296.5 | 294.3 |
| 2017 | 289.9 | 290.7 | 291.8 | 296.6 | 299.9 | 302.1 | 302.3 | 301.7 | 299.7 | 299.7 | 299.6 | 297.6 | 297.6 |
| 2018 | 289.2 | 290.5 | 292.9 | 298.3 | 300.3 | 304.4 | 304.7 | 305.0 | 303.8 | 306.4 | 304.2 | 303.3 | 300.3 |
| 2019 | 296.7 | 296.2 | 298.5 | 303.8 | 305.3 | 308.1 | 309.2 | 308.9 | 306.8 | 307.1 | 304.4 | 301.0 | 303.8 |
| **Service-Providing** | | | | | | | | | | | | | |
| 2011 | 2,384.9 | 2,397.8 | 2,412.9 | 2,436.9 | 2,437.0 | 2,433.0 | 2,393.1 | 2,382.6 | 2,414.2 | 2,434.9 | 2,450.4 | 2,455.0 | 2,419.4 |
| 2012 | 2,391.1 | 2,407.4 | 2,430.4 | 2,442.2 | 2,452.8 | 2,451.0 | 2,411.9 | 2,409.5 | 2,438.2 | 2,465.5 | 2,484.0 | 2,485.6 | 2,439.1 |
| 2013 | 2,414.9 | 2,434.1 | 2,450.5 | 2,468.1 | 2,475.5 | 2,475.2 | 2,432.6 | 2,428.5 | 2,459.5 | 2,483.2 | 2,505.0 | 2,502.8 | 2,460.8 |
| 2014 | 2,437.1 | 2,443.6 | 2,462.1 | 2,491.5 | 2,502.7 | 2,504.6 | 2,462.9 | 2,461.3 | 2,497.8 | 2,526.5 | 2,545.5 | 2,548.4 | 2,490.3 |
| 2015 | 2,473.5 | 2,486.4 | 2,499.0 | 2,527.8 | 2,543.2 | 2,543.6 | 2,503.6 | 2,497.9 | 2,529.9 | 2,563.2 | 2,580.8 | 2,584.3 | 2,527.8 |
| 2016 | 2,509.9 | 2,524.9 | 2,544.5 | 2,574.5 | 2,578.9 | 2,578.0 | 2,554.3 | 2,548.4 | 2,586.9 | 2,605.8 | 2,621.2 | 2,625.7 | 2,571.1 |
| 2017 | 2,561.2 | 2,573.0 | 2,585.2 | 2,606.3 | 2,619.8 | 2,617.1 | 2,584.5 | 2,583.1 | 2,617.0 | 2,641.5 | 2,660.0 | 2,661.4 | 2,609.2 |
| 2018 | 2,590.4 | 2,609.2 | 2,616.8 | 2,637.6 | 2,647.3 | 2,649.7 | 2,615.5 | 2,611.9 | 2,644.6 | 2,671.1 | 2,688.9 | 2,684.6 | 2,639.0 |
| 2019 | 2,624.8 | 2,636.5 | 2,652.9 | 2,675.0 | 2,680.4 | 2,677.9 | 2,652.7 | 2,653.0 | 2,680.5 | 2,698.1 | 2,708.7 | 2,705.4 | 2,670.5 |
| **Mining, Logging, and Construction** | | | | | | | | | | | | | |
| 2011 | 90.6 | 90.0 | 95.2 | 100.9 | 101.6 | 103.2 | 104.9 | 105.2 | 104.4 | 104.6 | 103.3 | 100.0 | 100.3 |
| 2012 | 93.4 | 93.5 | 96.0 | 98.2 | 98.9 | 101.4 | 102.3 | 102.9 | 103.0 | 102.6 | 101.3 | 99.9 | 99.5 |
| 2013 | 94.3 | 94.1 | 98.2 | 101.5 | 102.4 | 104.4 | 105.4 | 107.0 | 105.8 | 106.0 | 104.7 | 99.3 | 101.9 |
| 2014 | 95.3 | 94.0 | 99.1 | 104.2 | 106.0 | 107.9 | 109.5 | 109.4 | 108.8 | 109.1 | 108.5 | 105.5 | 104.8 |
| 2015 | 99.1 | 99.3 | 101.4 | 108.8 | 111.4 | 113.4 | 115.0 | 115.7 | 115.2 | 115.4 | 114.0 | 112.1 | 110.1 |
| 2016 | 106.0 | 104.9 | 109.6 | 112.7 | 114.3 | 116.3 | 118.0 | 118.3 | 117.8 | 118.7 | 117.1 | 115.0 | 114.1 |
| 2017 | 110.3 | 111.1 | 112.0 | 116.1 | 118.9 | 119.6 | 119.9 | 119.6 | 118.7 | 118.7 | 117.8 | 115.5 | 116.5 |
| 2018 | 108.8 | 110.3 | 112.9 | 117.8 | 118.7 | 121.0 | 121.3 | 121.8 | 121.0 | 123.0 | 120.9 | 119.1 | 118.1 |
| 2019 | 114.0 | 113.2 | 115.1 | 120.5 | 121.6 | 122.9 | 123.9 | 124.5 | 123.8 | 124.3 | 121.2 | 117.3 | 120.2 |
| **Manufacturing** | | | | | | | | | | | | | |
| 2011 | 186.1 | 185.5 | 186.2 | 186.5 | 186.7 | 187.5 | 186.9 | 186.8 | 185.7 | 185.6 | 185.4 | 185.2 | 186.2 |
| 2012 | 183.4 | 183.1 | 183.5 | 183.2 | 183.3 | 184.3 | 183.7 | 183.5 | 182.6 | 182.3 | 181.6 | 181.7 | 183.0 |
| 2013 | 180.0 | 179.9 | 179.7 | 180.3 | 180.6 | 181.8 | 181.2 | 181.5 | 181.1 | 181.1 | 181.4 | 181.5 | 180.8 |
| 2014 | 179.5 | 179.4 | 180.0 | 179.4 | 180.7 | 181.5 | 181.2 | 181.4 | 180.6 | 180.6 | 181.0 | 181.6 | 180.6 |
| 2015 | 179.9 | 180.0 | 180.2 | 180.2 | 181.1 | 181.8 | 181.8 | 181.6 | 180.8 | 180.1 | 180.3 | 180.7 | 180.7 |
| 2016 | 178.7 | 179.1 | 178.9 | 179.3 | 180.0 | 181.4 | 181.3 | 181.1 | 180.4 | 180.5 | 180.6 | 181.5 | 180.2 |
| 2017 | 179.6 | 179.6 | 179.8 | 180.5 | 181.0 | 182.5 | 182.4 | 182.1 | 181.0 | 181.0 | 181.8 | 182.1 | 181.1 |
| 2018 | 180.4 | 180.2 | 180.0 | 180.5 | 181.6 | 183.4 | 183.4 | 183.2 | 182.8 | 183.4 | 183.3 | 184.2 | 182.2 |
| 2019 | 182.7 | 183.0 | 183.4 | 183.3 | 183.7 | 185.2 | 185.3 | 184.4 | 183.0 | 182.8 | 183.2 | 183.7 | 183.6 |

## Employment by Industry: Philadelphia-Camden-Wilmington, PA-NJ-DE-MD, 2011–2019—*Continued*

(Numbers in thousands, not seasonally adjusted)

| Industry and year | January | February | March | April | May | June | July | August | September | October | November | December | Annual average |
|---|---|---|---|---|---|---|---|---|---|---|---|---|---|
| **Trade, Transportation, and Utilities** | | | | | | | | | | | | | |
| 2011 | 496.5 | 491.3 | 492.2 | 496.1 | 497.9 | 499.1 | 493.8 | 493.1 | 495.4 | 499.2 | 510.8 | 518.4 | 498.7 |
| 2012 | 498.0 | 492.8 | 496.4 | 495.9 | 501.7 | 502.3 | 497.8 | 497.8 | 499.2 | 504.4 | 518.3 | 523.0 | 502.3 |
| 2013 | 501.4 | 496.2 | 498.1 | 499.8 | 503.4 | 506.0 | 501.3 | 502.0 | 503.4 | 508.3 | 521.5 | 528.3 | 505.8 |
| 2014 | 505.6 | 499.8 | 503.4 | 505.6 | 509.7 | 513.0 | 506.6 | 507.1 | 508.0 | 513.5 | 527.0 | 534.0 | 511.1 |
| 2015 | 508.1 | 502.6 | 504.4 | 508.3 | 513.1 | 516.9 | 510.8 | 511.1 | 511.8 | 517.5 | 530.5 | 536.9 | 514.3 |
| 2016 | 512.3 | 507.3 | 509.2 | 511.7 | 515.5 | 516.7 | 514.6 | 514.5 | 515.7 | 520.5 | 533.3 | 540.4 | 517.6 |
| 2017 | 518.6 | 510.9 | 510.7 | 513.0 | 516.5 | 518.3 | 514.3 | 516.0 | 517.9 | 523.2 | 536.9 | 542.7 | 519.9 |
| 2018 | 520.6 | 515.2 | 515.8 | 518.1 | 522.3 | 524.8 | 521.2 | 519.1 | 520.7 | 526.4 | 541.9 | 546.3 | 524.4 |
| 2019 | 529.0 | 520.1 | 521.4 | 521.7 | 524.5 | 527.4 | 525.4 | 525.2 | 525.8 | 530.6 | 540.0 | 544.9 | 528.0 |
| **Wholesale Trade** | | | | | | | | | | | | | |
| 2011 | 117.2 | 117.2 | 117.8 | 118.7 | 118.9 | 119.4 | 119.7 | 119.6 | 119.1 | 119.2 | 119.2 | 119.6 | 118.8 |
| 2012 | 117.6 | 117.8 | 118.7 | 118.7 | 119.0 | 119.7 | 119.3 | 119.1 | 118.3 | 118.4 | 118.2 | 118.7 | 118.6 |
| 2013 | 117.1 | 117.1 | 117.7 | 118.1 | 118.6 | 119.1 | 118.5 | 118.2 | 118.0 | 117.5 | 117.9 | 118.0 | 118.0 |
| 2014 | 116.5 | 116.6 | 117.2 | 117.2 | 117.7 | 118.6 | 117.7 | 117.3 | 116.3 | 116.1 | 116.5 | 116.7 | 117.0 |
| 2015 | 114.0 | 113.9 | 113.9 | 114.5 | 115.2 | 115.8 | 115.4 | 115.5 | 114.6 | 114.6 | 114.5 | 114.6 | 114.7 |
| 2016 | 113.4 | 113.3 | 113.2 | 113.3 | 113.8 | 113.9 | 114.4 | 114.2 | 113.6 | 113.6 | 113.6 | 113.6 | 113.7 |
| 2017 | 113.4 | 112.9 | 113.2 | 113.9 | 114.4 | 115.3 | 115.2 | 115.5 | 115.1 | 115.4 | 115.8 | 116.2 | 114.7 |
| 2018 | 116.0 | 116.2 | 116.5 | 117.0 | 117.4 | 117.9 | 117.9 | 117.9 | 116.9 | 117.3 | 117.2 | 117.2 | 117.1 |
| 2019 | 116.3 | 116.3 | 116.6 | 117.1 | 117.2 | 118.2 | 118.3 | 118.3 | 117.3 | 116.9 | 115.7 | 115.2 | 117.0 |
| **Retail Trade** | | | | | | | | | | | | | |
| 2011 | 288.5 | 283.4 | 283.4 | 286.0 | 287.0 | 287.8 | 285.8 | 286.2 | 284.3 | 288.1 | 298.8 | 304.2 | 288.6 |
| 2012 | 289.8 | 284.0 | 286.4 | 287.0 | 291.0 | 291.6 | 290.6 | 291.3 | 288.9 | 292.9 | 305.9 | 308.4 | 292.3 |
| 2013 | 292.0 | 286.9 | 287.8 | 288.6 | 291.1 | 293.3 | 292.5 | 293.5 | 291.0 | 295.3 | 306.6 | 311.4 | 294.2 |
| 2014 | 294.0 | 288.8 | 291.1 | 292.6 | 295.4 | 297.7 | 296.5 | 297.3 | 294.5 | 298.9 | 310.1 | 314.5 | 297.6 |
| 2015 | 296.4 | 291.1 | 292.6 | 295.0 | 298.7 | 301.7 | 298.8 | 299.0 | 296.0 | 300.3 | 311.0 | 314.1 | 299.6 |
| 2016 | 297.3 | 292.9 | 294.7 | 296.5 | 299.3 | 300.9 | 301.1 | 301.1 | 296.8 | 300.3 | 309.2 | 312.9 | 300.3 |
| 2017 | 298.3 | 293.1 | 292.6 | 294.9 | 296.5 | 297.7 | 296.9 | 296.7 | 293.4 | 296.9 | 307.4 | 310.2 | 297.9 |
| 2018 | 295.6 | 291.1 | 291.4 | 292.7 | 295.8 | 297.4 | 296.2 | 294.7 | 293.4 | 296.9 | 307.4 | 310.2 | 297.9 |
| 2019 | 294.4 | 288.0 | 288.8 | 288.5 | 289.8 | 291.3 | 289.8 | 289.4 | 285.7 | 289.0 | 297.9 | 299.5 | 291.0 |
| **Transportation and Utilities** | | | | | | | | | | | | | |
| 2011 | 90.8 | 90.7 | 91.0 | 91.4 | 92.0 | 91.9 | 88.3 | 87.3 | 92.0 | 91.9 | 92.8 | 94.6 | 91.2 |
| 2012 | 90.6 | 91.0 | 91.3 | 90.2 | 91.7 | 91.0 | 87.9 | 87.4 | 92.0 | 93.1 | 94.2 | 95.9 | 91.4 |
| 2013 | 92.3 | 92.2 | 92.6 | 93.1 | 93.7 | 93.6 | 90.3 | 90.3 | 94.4 | 95.5 | 97.0 | 98.9 | 93.7 |
| 2014 | 95.1 | 94.4 | 95.1 | 95.8 | 96.6 | 96.7 | 92.4 | 92.5 | 97.2 | 98.5 | 100.4 | 102.8 | 96.5 |
| 2015 | 97.7 | 97.6 | 97.9 | 98.8 | 99.2 | 99.4 | 96.6 | 96.6 | 101.2 | 102.6 | 105.0 | 108.2 | 100.1 |
| 2016 | 101.6 | 101.1 | 101.3 | 101.9 | 102.4 | 101.9 | 99.1 | 99.2 | 105.3 | 106.6 | 110.5 | 113.9 | 103.7 |
| 2017 | 106.9 | 104.9 | 104.9 | 104.2 | 105.6 | 105.3 | 102.2 | 103.8 | 109.4 | 110.9 | 113.7 | 116.3 | 107.3 |
| 2018 | 109.0 | 107.9 | 107.9 | 108.4 | 109.1 | 109.5 | 107.1 | 106.5 | 111.9 | 114.0 | 118.8 | 120.9 | 110.9 |
| 2019 | 118.3 | 115.8 | 116.0 | 116.1 | 117.5 | 117.9 | 117.3 | 117.5 | 122.8 | 124.7 | 126.4 | 130.2 | 120.0 |
| **Information** | | | | | | | | | | | | | |
| 2011 | 50.3 | 50.3 | 50.1 | 50.7 | 50.5 | 50.9 | 50.8 | 47.8 | 51.0 | 50.4 | 50.8 | 50.2 | 50.3 |
| 2012 | 49.7 | 49.5 | 49.9 | 49.5 | 49.5 | 49.8 | 49.9 | 50.4 | 49.6 | 49.2 | 50.1 | 49.5 | 49.7 |
| 2013 | 49.2 | 49.3 | 49.1 | 48.4 | 48.2 | 48.0 | 48.0 | 48.1 | 47.2 | 47.3 | 47.2 | 47.4 | 48.1 |
| 2014 | 46.6 | 46.5 | 46.2 | 46.4 | 46.3 | 46.7 | 46.6 | 46.6 | 46.3 | 46.4 | 46.4 | 46.8 | 46.5 |
| 2015 | 45.8 | 46.2 | 46.4 | 46.2 | 46.1 | 46.6 | 46.8 | 46.9 | 46.6 | 46.4 | 46.6 | 47.1 | 46.5 |
| 2016 | 46.2 | 46.2 | 46.2 | 46.6 | 44.4 | 47.0 | 47.2 | 47.1 | 46.3 | 46.3 | 46.5 | 46.6 | 46.4 |
| 2017 | 46.5 | 46.8 | 46.5 | 46.7 | 47.3 | 47.7 | 47.3 | 47.2 | 46.5 | 47.0 | 47.3 | 47.7 | 47.0 |
| 2018 | 47.4 | 48.0 | 47.9 | 48.5 | 48.5 | 49.1 | 48.9 | 48.7 | 48.4 | 48.9 | 49.2 | 49.0 | 48.5 |
| 2019 | 48.4 | 48.5 | 48.5 | 48.7 | 48.9 | 49.8 | 50.2 | 50.4 | 49.5 | 49.6 | 49.6 | 50.1 | 49.4 |
| **Financial Activities** | | | | | | | | | | | | | |
| 2011 | 199.6 | 198.9 | 198.9 | 198.9 | 198.8 | 199.7 | 200.6 | 200.1 | 199.2 | 198.7 | 198.4 | 199.3 | 199.3 |
| 2012 | 198.1 | 198.0 | 198.5 | 198.6 | 199.5 | 201.1 | 202.0 | 202.1 | 200.8 | 200.9 | 201.5 | 202.4 | 200.3 |
| 2013 | 201.7 | 202.5 | 202.5 | 202.9 | 203.0 | 204.7 | 205.1 | 204.8 | 202.9 | 202.5 | 202.8 | 203.3 | 203.2 |
| 2014 | 201.7 | 201.5 | 201.6 | 202.2 | 203.2 | 205.4 | 205.9 | 206.0 | 204.6 | 205.1 | 205.7 | 207.0 | 204.2 |
| 2015 | 205.3 | 205.9 | 206.3 | 207.0 | 208.0 | 210.0 | 210.9 | 210.3 | 209.0 | 209.0 | 209.5 | 210.2 | 208.5 |
| 2016 | 209.2 | 209.5 | 209.8 | 210.2 | 210.7 | 213.0 | 213.5 | 213.8 | 212.2 | 212.4 | 213.1 | 213.7 | 211.8 |
| 2017 | 212.1 | 212.5 | 212.8 | 212.6 | 213.6 | 216.2 | 216.7 | 216.8 | 215.1 | 214.7 | 215.0 | 215.1 | 214.4 |
| 2018 | 214.5 | 215.2 | 215.2 | 215.2 | 215.6 | 217.3 | 217.9 | 217.4 | 215.5 | 216.2 | 216.2 | 216.2 | 216.0 |
| 2019 | 216.1 | 216.2 | 216.3 | 216.7 | 217.3 | 218.8 | 219.5 | 218.9 | 217.1 | 218.5 | 218.9 | 219.0 | 217.8 |

## Employment by Industry: Philadelphia-Camden-Wilmington, PA-NJ-DE-MD, 2011–2019—*Continued*

(Numbers in thousands, not seasonally adjusted)

| Industry and year | January | February | March | April | May | June | July | August | September | October | November | December | Annual average |
|---|---|---|---|---|---|---|---|---|---|---|---|---|---|
| **Professional and Business Services** | | | | | | | | | | | | | |
| 2011 | 408.5 | 408.4 | 412.3 | 420.8 | 419.9 | 422.6 | 420.2 | 420.3 | 421.4 | 424.1 | 425.3 | 424.2 | 419.0 |
| 2012 | 412.1 | 413.5 | 418.5 | 423.4 | 424.7 | 428.1 | 426.3 | 427.5 | 429.5 | 433.9 | 435.6 | 433.1 | 425.5 |
| 2013 | 419.5 | 421.8 | 426.8 | 432.7 | 434.5 | 438.0 | 433.6 | 434.6 | 434.6 | 439.3 | 443.3 | 439.3 | 433.2 |
| 2014 | 427.2 | 425.9 | 429.8 | 440.4 | 443.1 | 445.4 | 440.3 | 441.6 | 445.9 | 451.0 | 455.0 | 454.1 | 441.6 |
| 2015 | 438.4 | 438.2 | 440.4 | 449.3 | 453.7 | 454.9 | 453.0 | 452.0 | 453.4 | 464.1 | 467.6 | 464.8 | 452.5 |
| 2016 | 449.3 | 449.4 | 454.2 | 462.5 | 463.8 | 465.9 | 466.1 | 463.3 | 467.2 | 469.0 | 470.8 | 471.7 | 462.8 |
| 2017 | 456.6 | 455.3 | 458.6 | 465.2 | 469.3 | 471.8 | 467.4 | 466.4 | 470.6 | 475.1 | 477.8 | 476.4 | 467.5 |
| 2018 | 459.9 | 460.8 | 462.0 | 465.1 | 467.5 | 470.2 | 466.8 | 465.9 | 467.5 | 471.8 | 474.9 | 471.3 | 467.0 |
| 2019 | 458.7 | 459.8 | 462.5 | 471.8 | 472.4 | 474.6 | 473.7 | 473.2 | 475.3 | 475.2 | 477.7 | 472.3 | 470.6 |
| **Education and Health Services** | | | | | | | | | | | | | |
| 2011 | 546.9 | 560.7 | 561.2 | 561.7 | 558.2 | 547.3 | 545.5 | 543.5 | 556.5 | 565.0 | 567.9 | 567.7 | 556.8 |
| 2012 | 556.6 | 569.3 | 571.9 | 572.8 | 568.6 | 557.1 | 552.6 | 549.9 | 565.9 | 576.5 | 578.0 | 576.0 | 566.3 |
| 2013 | 564.6 | 577.5 | 579.2 | 579.4 | 573.7 | 563.7 | 560.4 | 558.5 | 576.8 | 585.9 | 590.7 | 586.5 | 574.7 |
| 2014 | 577.0 | 587.0 | 588.8 | 594.5 | 589.1 | 578.7 | 576.9 | 575.8 | 593.6 | 603.5 | 607.4 | 603.7 | 589.7 |
| 2015 | 593.7 | 605.4 | 604.3 | 609.9 | 605.1 | 594.4 | 591.5 | 588.2 | 605.0 | 616.5 | 619.3 | 616.9 | 604.2 |
| 2016 | 606.5 | 618.8 | 619.8 | 628.4 | 622.8 | 610.8 | 610.6 | 609.0 | 629.2 | 637.2 | 639.2 | 637.5 | 622.5 |
| 2017 | 629.0 | 642.1 | 642.2 | 645.7 | 640.8 | 627.3 | 625.3 | 623.1 | 643.0 | 653.2 | 656.4 | 655.1 | 640.3 |
| 2018 | 641.9 | 656.6 | 655.3 | 659.4 | 654.7 | 643.3 | 639.1 | 638.7 | 658.7 | 670.3 | 671.4 | 667.8 | 654.8 |
| 2019 | 658.7 | 670.2 | 672.4 | 675.2 | 669.1 | 656.0 | 650.4 | 651.2 | 669.6 | 678.2 | 680.1 | 677.8 | 667.4 |
| **Leisure and Hospitality** | | | | | | | | | | | | | |
| 2011 | 213.9 | 214.2 | 221.5 | 230.0 | 237.2 | 241.4 | 240.9 | 240.9 | 233.7 | 231.2 | 229.0 | 226.9 | 230.1 |
| 2012 | 219.0 | 219.7 | 228.6 | 234.8 | 243.1 | 250.1 | 248.3 | 248.6 | 240.3 | 237.2 | 235.4 | 236.1 | 236.8 |
| 2013 | 223.6 | 224.5 | 230.2 | 240.2 | 247.8 | 253.8 | 254.0 | 253.4 | 246.7 | 242.2 | 239.9 | 240.5 | 241.4 |
| 2014 | 231.2 | 229.1 | 236.1 | 244.1 | 253.0 | 258.6 | 258.2 | 259.0 | 252.0 | 250.6 | 245.9 | 246.7 | 247.0 |
| 2015 | 235.1 | 235.0 | 240.8 | 249.5 | 259.2 | 265.2 | 263.7 | 263.7 | 256.3 | 256.0 | 250.8 | 252.2 | 252.3 |
| 2016 | 240.3 | 240.9 | 248.5 | 258.0 | 265.0 | 271.0 | 271.1 | 271.0 | 264.9 | 262.2 | 258.3 | 257.0 | 259.0 |
| 2017 | 248.2 | 249.4 | 255.8 | 264.7 | 273.3 | 280.1 | 280.4 | 279.7 | 271.0 | 269.8 | 265.9 | 264.0 | 266.9 |
| 2018 | 254.9 | 255.6 | 260.9 | 270.2 | 278.5 | 286.0 | 285.3 | 285.1 | 275.7 | 274.5 | 269.8 | 269.5 | 272.2 |
| 2019 | 260.0 | 260.1 | 267.8 | 276.6 | 284.6 | 291.5 | 291.6 | 290.9 | 280.4 | 278.0 | 272.8 | 272.5 | 277.2 |
| **Other Services** | | | | | | | | | | | | | |
| 2011 | 117.8 | 118.0 | 118.8 | 119.7 | 120.2 | 121.7 | 120.6 | 120.0 | 119.0 | 118.9 | 118.8 | 118.9 | 119.4 |
| 2012 | 118.4 | 118.3 | 119.0 | 119.7 | 120.8 | 122.5 | 121.2 | 121.0 | 119.8 | 119.6 | 119.5 | 119.9 | 120.0 |
| 2013 | 118.5 | 118.7 | 119.2 | 120.0 | 120.6 | 122.2 | 119.4 | 118.9 | 117.2 | 117.1 | 116.7 | 116.2 | 118.7 |
| 2014 | 114.6 | 113.8 | 114.9 | 115.9 | 117.5 | 119.3 | 118.2 | 117.6 | 116.3 | 116.9 | 116.9 | 116.6 | 116.5 |
| 2015 | 115.3 | 115.5 | 116.2 | 116.6 | 117.9 | 119.4 | 118.3 | 117.8 | 116.5 | 117.1 | 117.4 | 117.8 | 117.2 |
| 2016 | 116.4 | 117.0 | 118.3 | 119.1 | 119.9 | 121.5 | 120.9 | 120.4 | 118.8 | 120.0 | 119.6 | 118.9 | 119.2 |
| 2017 | 118.2 | 117.9 | 118.6 | 119.4 | 120.7 | 122.2 | 121.2 | 120.8 | 119.0 | 119.5 | 119.7 | 119.6 | 119.7 |
| 2018 | 118.6 | 118.7 | 119.4 | 120.7 | 121.8 | 123.5 | 122.8 | 122.4 | 121.3 | 121.6 | 121.7 | 121.7 | 121.2 |
| 2019 | 120.8 | 120.6 | 121.2 | 122.0 | 123.5 | 125.0 | 124.6 | 123.6 | 123.0 | 122.8 | 122.3 | 122.1 | 122.6 |
| **Government** | | | | | | | | | | | | | |
| 2011 | 351.4 | 356.0 | 357.9 | 359.0 | 354.3 | 350.3 | 320.7 | 316.9 | 338.0 | 347.4 | 349.4 | 349.4 | 345.9 |
| 2012 | 339.2 | 346.3 | 347.6 | 347.5 | 344.9 | 340.0 | 313.8 | 312.2 | 333.1 | 343.8 | 345.6 | 345.6 | 338.3 |
| 2013 | 336.4 | 343.6 | 345.4 | 344.7 | 344.3 | 338.8 | 310.8 | 308.2 | 330.7 | 340.6 | 342.9 | 341.3 | 335.6 |
| 2014 | 333.2 | 340.0 | 341.3 | 342.4 | 340.8 | 337.5 | 310.2 | 307.6 | 331.1 | 339.5 | 341.2 | 339.5 | 333.7 |
| 2015 | 331.8 | 337.6 | 340.2 | 341.0 | 340.1 | 336.2 | 308.6 | 307.9 | 331.3 | 336.6 | 339.1 | 338.4 | 332.4 |
| 2016 | 329.7 | 335.8 | 338.5 | 338.0 | 336.8 | 332.1 | 310.3 | 309.3 | 332.6 | 338.2 | 340.4 | 339.9 | 331.8 |
| 2017 | 332.0 | 338.1 | 340.0 | 339.0 | 338.3 | 333.5 | 311.9 | 313.1 | 333.9 | 339.0 | 341.0 | 340.8 | 333.4 |
| 2018 | 332.6 | 339.1 | 340.3 | 340.4 | 338.4 | 335.5 | 313.5 | 314.6 | 336.8 | 341.4 | 343.8 | 342.8 | 334.9 |
| 2019 | 333.1 | 341.0 | 342.8 | 342.3 | 340.1 | 334.8 | 317.3 | 319.6 | 339.8 | 345.2 | 347.3 | 346.7 | 337.5 |

## Employment by Industry: Atlanta-Sandy Springs-Roswell, GA, 2011–2019

(Numbers in thousands, not seasonally adjusted)

| Industry and year | January | February | March | April | May | June | July | August | September | October | November | December | Annual average |
|---|---|---|---|---|---|---|---|---|---|---|---|---|---|
| **Total Nonfarm** | | | | | | | | | | | | | |
| 2011 | 2,248.5 | 2,283.8 | 2,299.9 | 2,314.7 | 2,323.3 | 2,311.9 | 2,306.3 | 2,319.0 | 2,318.6 | 2,331.6 | 2,344.4 | 2,343.7 | 2,312.1 |
| 2012 | 2,305.4 | 2,317.7 | 2,332.5 | 2,350.6 | 2,363.3 | 2,361.1 | 2,343.8 | 2,362.0 | 2,354.3 | 2,376.8 | 2,397.9 | 2,393.4 | 2,354.9 |
| 2013 | 2,357.9 | 2,373.7 | 2,382.9 | 2,402.0 | 2,411.9 | 2,410.1 | 2,402.8 | 2,425.2 | 2,425.0 | 2,448.9 | 2,469.5 | 2,471.0 | 2,415.1 |
| 2014 | 2,428.9 | 2,432.1 | 2,463.3 | 2,484.1 | 2,503.6 | 2,502.1 | 2,500.2 | 2,526.4 | 2,520.6 | 2,543.4 | 2,567.0 | 2,575.3 | 2,503.9 |
| 2015 | 2,520.7 | 2,535.5 | 2,546.9 | 2,559.6 | 2,580.4 | 2,584.8 | 2,576.8 | 2,593.3 | 2,591.5 | 2,621.1 | 2,635.8 | 2,646.1 | 2,582.7 |
| 2016 | 2,603.0 | 2,616.5 | 2,623.9 | 2,650.4 | 2,662.9 | 2,663.6 | 2,660.0 | 2,677.5 | 2,683.0 | 2,696.7 | 2,719.7 | 2,725.9 | 2,665.3 |
| 2017 | 2,667.6 | 2,684.2 | 2,701.0 | 2,708.8 | 2,721.8 | 2,729.7 | 2,717.7 | 2,740.9 | 2,735.4 | 2,761.2 | 2,782.4 | 2,782.7 | 2,727.8 |
| 2018 | 2,725.2 | 2,742.8 | 2,758.9 | 2,764.1 | 2,779.8 | 2,785.1 | 2,780.2 | 2,803.7 | 2,797.2 | 2,817.4 | 2,837.8 | 2,834.9 | 2,785.6 |
| 2019 | 2,804.3 | 2,819.3 | 2,828.3 | 2,828.8 | 2,843.4 | 2,845.4 | 2,838.2 | 2,852.7 | 2,856.0 | 2,878.5 | 2,894.2 | 2,904.0 | 2,849.4 |
| **Total Private** | | | | | | | | | | | | | |
| 2011 | 1,924.7 | 1,956.5 | 1,971.0 | 1,987.8 | 1,996.2 | 1,991.6 | 1,995.8 | 2,003.0 | 1,997.7 | 2,009.0 | 2,018.9 | 2,019.9 | 1,989.3 |
| 2012 | 1,984.3 | 1,994.3 | 2,005.6 | 2,025.0 | 2,039.1 | 2,040.8 | 2,037.4 | 2,047.6 | 2,036.0 | 2,056.1 | 2,072.5 | 2,072.2 | 2,034.2 |
| 2013 | 2,038.5 | 2,052.2 | 2,061.2 | 2,078.4 | 2,090.8 | 2,095.7 | 2,099.7 | 2,113.7 | 2,108.2 | 2,128.4 | 2,145.6 | 2,148.6 | 2,096.8 |
| 2014 | 2,112.8 | 2,113.8 | 2,142.3 | 2,162.3 | 2,181.0 | 2,186.3 | 2,194.5 | 2,209.4 | 2,200.4 | 2,221.1 | 2,240.4 | 2,252.1 | 2,184.7 |
| 2015 | 2,199.8 | 2,211.9 | 2,223.0 | 2,235.8 | 2,257.8 | 2,266.9 | 2,268.9 | 2,275.0 | 2,269.6 | 2,295.6 | 2,307.6 | 2,319.7 | 2,261.0 |
| 2016 | 2,278.9 | 2,290.1 | 2,297.8 | 2,323.2 | 2,335.6 | 2,339.3 | 2,349.9 | 2,354.3 | 2,355.5 | 2,367.2 | 2,386.4 | 2,395.1 | 2,339.4 |
| 2017 | 2,340.6 | 2,353.6 | 2,369.8 | 2,377.8 | 2,392.0 | 2,402.6 | 2,402.2 | 2,414.5 | 2,403.3 | 2,427.8 | 2,446.8 | 2,448.9 | 2,398.3 |
| 2018 | 2,393.2 | 2,408.3 | 2,423.7 | 2,429.1 | 2,443.2 | 2,454.2 | 2,459.2 | 2,470.9 | 2,462.1 | 2,480.8 | 2,499.0 | 2,496.9 | 2,451.7 |
| 2019 | 2,471.8 | 2,484.0 | 2,491.8 | 2,492.3 | 2,506.8 | 2,514.9 | 2,516.6 | 2,519.1 | 2,519.3 | 2,540.4 | 2,555.2 | 2,564.9 | 2,514.8 |
| **Goods Producing** | | | | | | | | | | | | | |
| 2011 | 226.1 | 232.4 | 234.2 | 236.5 | 237.4 | 237.9 | 238.9 | 238.3 | 236.7 | 237.2 | 236.3 | 234.7 | 235.6 |
| 2012 | 231.0 | 232.1 | 232.3 | 233.6 | 234.4 | 234.8 | 235.6 | 235.9 | 235.5 | 236.8 | 237.4 | 236.3 | 234.6 |
| 2013 | 233.8 | 234.9 | 236.6 | 236.5 | 238.8 | 240.2 | 242.4 | 243.1 | 243.7 | 244.6 | 246.0 | 245.3 | 240.5 |
| 2014 | 243.2 | 244.3 | 246.7 | 248.8 | 251.0 | 253.0 | 254.7 | 256.1 | 256.5 | 258.8 | 258.5 | 259.2 | 252.6 |
| 2015 | 256.8 | 259.0 | 259.2 | 261.4 | 263.1 | 265.4 | 266.3 | 267.0 | 268.0 | 270.0 | 269.6 | 271.3 | 264.8 |
| 2016 | 268.6 | 270.7 | 272.5 | 274.4 | 275.7 | 277.6 | 280.2 | 281.0 | 281.8 | 282.3 | 283.3 | 284.1 | 277.7 |
| 2017 | 281.6 | 283.6 | 284.5 | 283.7 | 285.3 | 287.5 | 287.4 | 287.7 | 288.0 | 289.1 | 289.4 | 290.9 | 286.6 |
| 2018 | 287.2 | 290.3 | 292.5 | 292.3 | 294.1 | 296.5 | 297.1 | 298.1 | 298.7 | 300.3 | 299.1 | 300.8 | 295.6 |
| 2019 | 297.9 | 299.8 | 301.2 | 302.4 | 304.2 | 304.8 | 305.3 | 305.0 | 305.6 | 305.0 | 304.8 | 304.3 | 303.4 |
| **Service-Providing** | | | | | | | | | | | | | |
| 2011 | 2,022.4 | 2,051.4 | 2,065.7 | 2,078.2 | 2,085.9 | 2,074.0 | 2,067.4 | 2,080.7 | 2,081.9 | 2,094.4 | 2,108.1 | 2,109.0 | 2,076.6 |
| 2012 | 2,074.4 | 2,085.6 | 2,100.2 | 2,117.0 | 2,128.9 | 2,126.3 | 2,108.2 | 2,126.1 | 2,118.8 | 2,140.0 | 2,160.5 | 2,157.1 | 2,120.3 |
| 2013 | 2,124.1 | 2,138.8 | 2,146.3 | 2,165.5 | 2,173.1 | 2,169.9 | 2,160.4 | 2,182.1 | 2,181.3 | 2,204.3 | 2,223.5 | 2,225.7 | 2,174.6 |
| 2014 | 2,185.7 | 2,187.8 | 2,216.6 | 2,235.3 | 2,252.6 | 2,249.1 | 2,245.5 | 2,270.3 | 2,264.1 | 2,284.6 | 2,308.5 | 2,316.1 | 2,251.4 |
| 2015 | 2,263.9 | 2,276.5 | 2,287.7 | 2,298.2 | 2,317.3 | 2,319.4 | 2,310.5 | 2,326.3 | 2,323.5 | 2,351.1 | 2,366.2 | 2,374.8 | 2,318.0 |
| 2016 | 2,334.4 | 2,345.8 | 2,351.4 | 2,376.0 | 2,387.2 | 2,386.0 | 2,379.8 | 2,396.5 | 2,401.2 | 2,414.4 | 2,436.4 | 2,441.8 | 2,387.6 |
| 2017 | 2,386.0 | 2,400.6 | 2,416.5 | 2,425.1 | 2,436.5 | 2,442.2 | 2,430.3 | 2,453.2 | 2,447.4 | 2,472.1 | 2,493.0 | 2,491.8 | 2,441.2 |
| 2018 | 2,438.0 | 2,452.5 | 2,466.4 | 2,471.8 | 2,485.7 | 2,488.6 | 2,483.1 | 2,505.6 | 2,498.5 | 2,517.1 | 2,538.7 | 2,534.1 | 2,490.0 |
| 2019 | 2,506.4 | 2,519.5 | 2,527.1 | 2,526.4 | 2,539.2 | 2,540.6 | 2,532.9 | 2,547.7 | 2,550.4 | 2,573.5 | 2,589.4 | 2,599.7 | 2,546.1 |
| **Mining, Logging, and Construction** | | | | | | | | | | | | | |
| 2011 | 85.4 | 89.5 | 91.2 | 92.8 | 92.8 | 93.1 | 93.5 | 93.2 | 92.5 | 92.6 | 91.3 | 89.8 | 91.5 |
| 2012 | 86.6 | 87.5 | 87.6 | 88.3 | 88.2 | 88.4 | 89.0 | 89.3 | 88.9 | 89.9 | 90.4 | 89.1 | 88.6 |
| 2013 | 86.9 | 88.0 | 89.7 | 89.8 | 91.6 | 92.8 | 94.6 | 95.5 | 96.0 | 96.8 | 97.9 | 96.9 | 93.0 |
| 2014 | 95.8 | 96.9 | 98.7 | 99.9 | 101.2 | 102.6 | 104.1 | 105.0 | 105.4 | 107.0 | 106.3 | 106.2 | 102.4 |
| 2015 | 104.1 | 105.6 | 105.5 | 107.9 | 108.6 | 109.9 | 110.1 | 110.6 | 110.9 | 112.4 | 111.4 | 112.2 | 109.1 |
| 2016 | 110.2 | 111.9 | 112.9 | 114.0 | 115.1 | 116.6 | 118.7 | 119.1 | 119.9 | 120.0 | 120.3 | 120.3 | 116.6 |
| 2017 | 117.7 | 119.3 | 119.5 | 120.2 | 121.7 | 123.1 | 122.5 | 122.5 | 123.0 | 123.3 | 122.9 | 123.6 | 121.6 |
| 2018 | 120.8 | 122.9 | 124.7 | 125.4 | 126.6 | 128.1 | 128.5 | 129.0 | 129.4 | 129.9 | 128.4 | 129.3 | 126.9 |
| 2019 | 128.3 | 129.5 | 130.5 | 130.7 | 132.3 | 133.0 | 132.5 | 132.0 | 132.1 | 132.2 | 132.1 | 132.2 | 131.5 |
| **Manufacturing** | | | | | | | | | | | | | |
| 2011 | 140.7 | 142.9 | 143.0 | 143.7 | 144.6 | 144.8 | 145.4 | 145.1 | 144.2 | 144.6 | 145.0 | 144.9 | 144.1 |
| 2012 | 144.4 | 144.6 | 144.7 | 145.3 | 146.2 | 146.4 | 146.6 | 146.6 | 146.6 | 146.9 | 147.0 | 147.2 | 146.0 |
| 2013 | 146.9 | 146.9 | 146.9 | 146.7 | 147.2 | 147.4 | 147.8 | 147.6 | 147.7 | 147.8 | 148.1 | 148.4 | 147.5 |
| 2014 | 147.4 | 147.4 | 148.0 | 148.9 | 149.8 | 150.4 | 150.6 | 151.1 | 151.1 | 151.8 | 152.2 | 153.0 | 150.1 |
| 2015 | 152.7 | 153.4 | 153.7 | 153.5 | 154.5 | 155.5 | 156.2 | 156.4 | 157.1 | 157.6 | 158.2 | 159.1 | 155.7 |
| 2016 | 158.4 | 158.8 | 159.6 | 160.4 | 160.6 | 161.0 | 161.5 | 161.9 | 161.9 | 162.3 | 163.0 | 163.8 | 161.1 |
| 2017 | 163.9 | 164.3 | 165.0 | 163.5 | 163.6 | 164.4 | 164.9 | 165.2 | 165.0 | 165.8 | 166.5 | 167.3 | 165.0 |
| 2018 | 166.4 | 167.4 | 167.8 | 166.9 | 167.5 | 168.4 | 168.6 | 169.1 | 169.3 | 170.4 | 170.7 | 171.5 | 168.7 |
| 2019 | 169.6 | 170.3 | 170.7 | 171.7 | 171.9 | 171.8 | 172.8 | 173.0 | 173.5 | 172.8 | 172.7 | 172.1 | 171.9 |

## Employment by Industry: Atlanta-Sandy Springs-Roswell, GA, 2011–2019—*Continued*

(Numbers in thousands, not seasonally adjusted)

| Industry and year | January | February | March | April | May | June | July | August | September | October | November | December | Annual average |
|---|---|---|---|---|---|---|---|---|---|---|---|---|---|
| **Trade, Transportation, and Utilities** | | | | | | | | | | | | | |
| 2011 | 499.2 | 502.7 | 504.7 | 508.3 | 510.1 | 509.8 | 510.6 | 511.4 | 509.0 | 514.6 | 523.5 | 526.6 | 510.9 |
| 2012 | 511.4 | 509.2 | 511.0 | 513.9 | 516.6 | 516.2 | 516.5 | 516.6 | 514.2 | 519.1 | 531.7 | 533.2 | 517.5 |
| 2013 | 516.4 | 514.9 | 514.8 | 515.8 | 519.0 | 520.3 | 522.6 | 525.0 | 523.5 | 528.7 | 540.5 | 545.9 | 524.0 |
| 2014 | 528.0 | 524.5 | 529.0 | 532.6 | 535.6 | 536.6 | 538.9 | 540.0 | 538.4 | 546.9 | 561.0 | 568.1 | 540.0 |
| | | | | | | | | | | | | | |
| 2015 | 548.6 | 546.1 | 548.0 | 549.2 | 553.0 | 554.9 | 555.0 | 555.9 | 554.5 | 562.6 | 575.2 | 580.6 | 557.0 |
| 2016 | 562.3 | 559.4 | 561.2 | 561.9 | 564.5 | 565.4 | 567.1 | 566.6 | 566.5 | 572.2 | 587.4 | 595.4 | 569.2 |
| 2017 | 573.1 | 571.0 | 573.3 | 573.3 | 574.5 | 576.5 | 577.4 | 578.2 | 577.3 | 582.8 | 599.9 | 603.3 | 580.1 |
| 2018 | 581.9 | 581.4 | 583.4 | 585.0 | 587.3 | 588.8 | 590.1 | 589.9 | 589.4 | 595.1 | 612.4 | 616.3 | 591.8 |
| 2019 | 598.7 | 594.8 | 596.9 | 595.9 | 598.2 | 600.2 | 599.7 | 598.0 | 599.9 | 604.6 | 617.7 | 623.6 | 602.4 |
| | | | | | | | | | | | | | |
| **Wholesale Trade** | | | | | | | | | | | | | |
| 2011 | 137.9 | 138.9 | 139.1 | 139.9 | 140.3 | 139.9 | 140.8 | 141.1 | 140.2 | 141.2 | 141.4 | 141.0 | 140.1 |
| 2012 | 140.1 | 140.9 | 140.9 | 141.6 | 142.1 | 141.8 | 142.7 | 142.7 | 141.2 | 142.2 | 142.5 | 142.4 | 141.8 |
| 2013 | 140.7 | 141.4 | 141.0 | 141.5 | 141.8 | 141.8 | 142.1 | 142.3 | 141.5 | 143.1 | 143.8 | 144.1 | 142.1 |
| 2014 | 144.0 | 144.5 | 144.6 | 144.8 | 145.3 | 145.3 | 146.1 | 146.5 | 146.2 | 147.1 | 148.1 | 148.6 | 145.9 |
| | | | | | | | | | | | | | |
| 2015 | 147.7 | 148.2 | 148.5 | 148.7 | 149.3 | 149.2 | 148.8 | 148.9 | 148.3 | 149.8 | 149.8 | 149.7 | 148.9 |
| 2016 | 148.1 | 148.0 | 148.3 | 148.8 | 149.0 | 148.9 | 149.2 | 148.8 | 148.5 | 148.4 | 148.7 | 149.3 | 148.7 |
| 2017 | 148.5 | 149.1 | 149.5 | 148.9 | 148.9 | 149.4 | 149.7 | 149.2 | 149.3 | 149.3 | 150.1 | 150.7 | 149.4 |
| 2018 | 149.8 | 150.7 | 150.8 | 151.0 | 151.5 | 152.5 | 153.2 | 152.5 | 152.5 | 153.7 | 154.4 | 154.9 | 152.3 |
| 2019 | 153.5 | 154.3 | 154.3 | 154.1 | 154.7 | 155.5 | 154.9 | 155.2 | 154.8 | 156.5 | 156.6 | 157.1 | 155.1 |
| | | | | | | | | | | | | | |
| **Retail Trade** | | | | | | | | | | | | | |
| 2011 | 248.8 | 250.0 | 251.2 | 253.7 | 254.3 | 254.2 | 254.3 | 254.6 | 253.1 | 257.4 | 265.3 | 267.4 | 255.4 |
| 2012 | 256.3 | 253.9 | 255.3 | 256.5 | 258.2 | 258.0 | 257.6 | 257.5 | 256.8 | 260.3 | 271.7 | 271.7 | 259.5 |
| 2013 | 259.3 | 258.2 | 258.7 | 259.9 | 261.9 | 262.9 | 264.6 | 266.4 | 265.8 | 269.3 | 278.9 | 282.6 | 265.7 |
| 2014 | 268.3 | 264.7 | 266.8 | 268.3 | 269.6 | 270.4 | 271.3 | 271.5 | 270.4 | 275.4 | 287.4 | 290.9 | 272.9 |
| | | | | | | | | | | | | | |
| 2015 | 274.7 | 273.4 | 275.2 | 277.3 | 278.8 | 280.0 | 279.6 | 280.0 | 279.2 | 283.6 | 294.2 | 296.4 | 281.0 |
| 2016 | 282.1 | 280.2 | 281.8 | 283.3 | 284.4 | 284.1 | 285.4 | 284.7 | 284.1 | 289.0 | 299.9 | 302.2 | 286.8 |
| 2017 | 288.1 | 286.1 | 287.1 | 287.7 | 288.0 | 288.7 | 289.2 | 289.3 | 286.9 | 291.2 | 303.4 | 304.2 | 290.8 |
| 2018 | 289.8 | 287.9 | 288.9 | 289.0 | 290.1 | 289.3 | 290.3 | 289.1 | 288.2 | 290.2 | 301.6 | 302.2 | 291.4 |
| 2019 | 290.4 | 286.6 | 287.6 | 287.9 | 289.3 | 289.1 | 288.1 | 287.1 | 286.9 | 288.6 | 299.8 | 303.2 | 290.4 |
| | | | | | | | | | | | | | |
| **Transportation and Utilities** | | | | | | | | | | | | | |
| 2011 | 112.5 | 113.8 | 114.4 | 114.7 | 115.5 | 115.7 | 115.5 | 115.7 | 115.7 | 116.0 | 116.8 | 118.2 | 115.4 |
| 2012 | 115.0 | 114.4 | 114.8 | 115.8 | 116.3 | 116.4 | 116.2 | 116.4 | 116.2 | 116.6 | 117.5 | 119.1 | 116.2 |
| 2013 | 116.4 | 115.3 | 115.1 | 114.4 | 115.3 | 115.6 | 115.9 | 116.3 | 116.2 | 116.3 | 117.8 | 119.2 | 116.2 |
| 2014 | 115.7 | 115.3 | 117.6 | 119.5 | 120.7 | 120.9 | 121.5 | 122.0 | 121.8 | 124.4 | 125.5 | 128.6 | 121.1 |
| | | | | | | | | | | | | | |
| 2015 | 126.2 | 124.5 | 124.3 | 123.2 | 124.9 | 125.7 | 126.6 | 127.0 | 127.0 | 129.2 | 131.2 | 134.5 | 127.0 |
| 2016 | 132.1 | 131.2 | 131.1 | 129.8 | 131.1 | 132.4 | 132.5 | 133.1 | 133.9 | 134.8 | 138.8 | 143.9 | 133.7 |
| 2017 | 136.5 | 135.8 | 136.7 | 136.7 | 137.6 | 138.4 | 138.5 | 139.7 | 141.1 | 142.3 | 146.4 | 148.4 | 139.8 |
| 2018 | 142.3 | 142.8 | 143.7 | 145.0 | 145.7 | 147.0 | 146.6 | 148.3 | 148.7 | 151.2 | 156.4 | 159.2 | 148.1 |
| 2019 | 154.8 | 153.9 | 155.0 | 153.9 | 154.2 | 155.6 | 156.7 | 155.7 | 158.2 | 159.5 | 161.3 | 163.3 | 156.8 |
| | | | | | | | | | | | | | |
| **Information** | | | | | | | | | | | | | |
| 2011 | 78.3 | 78.4 | 78.9 | 79.1 | 78.9 | 78.3 | 79.0 | 79.3 | 79.0 | 79.5 | 81.0 | 79.2 | 79.1 |
| 2012 | 78.9 | 80.1 | 79.9 | 79.6 | 80.5 | 80.3 | 80.9 | 81.3 | 81.1 | 82.5 | 82.9 | 82.9 | 80.9 |
| 2013 | 81.4 | 82.4 | 82.5 | 83.1 | 83.6 | 82.8 | 84.0 | 84.4 | 84.4 | 86.6 | 86.4 | 86.2 | 84.0 |
| 2014 | 86.6 | 86.9 | 87.8 | 88.4 | 88.7 | 89.4 | 89.6 | 89.6 | 89.1 | 91.3 | 91.9 | 92.0 | 89.3 |
| | | | | | | | | | | | | | |
| 2015 | 89.2 | 90.0 | 90.7 | 91.6 | 93.6 | 93.9 | 96.1 | 93.9 | 92.4 | 96.9 | 97.8 | 98.1 | 93.7 |
| 2016 | 93.9 | 96.1 | 95.2 | 98.0 | 97.3 | 97.7 | 99.7 | 97.6 | 98.8 | 98.9 | 101.1 | 99.3 | 97.8 |
| 2017 | 99.5 | 101.5 | 101.5 | 100.3 | 101.2 | 100.8 | 99.8 | 102.6 | 100.3 | 104.5 | 103.8 | 103.1 | 101.6 |
| 2018 | 98.8 | 99.7 | 97.6 | 98.0 | 97.8 | 97.9 | 97.8 | 99.6 | 99.8 | 102.2 | 102.3 | 98.6 | 99.2 |
| 2019 | 99.0 | 101.9 | 101.8 | 100.0 | 99.6 | 101.5 | 101.2 | 101.0 | 100.0 | 101.6 | 103.6 | 102.0 | 101.1 |
| | | | | | | | | | | | | | |
| **Financial Activities** | | | | | | | | | | | | | |
| 2011 | 149.5 | 150.1 | 150.4 | 150.8 | 151.0 | 151.1 | 151.3 | 151.8 | 151.8 | 152.5 | 152.7 | 152.9 | 151.3 |
| 2012 | 152.8 | 153.3 | 153.7 | 153.7 | 153.5 | 153.8 | 154.0 | 154.1 | 153.2 | 154.6 | 155.6 | 155.7 | 154.0 |
| 2013 | 153.7 | 154.3 | 154.8 | 155.6 | 156.1 | 156.5 | 156.7 | 157.1 | 156.1 | 157.4 | 158.5 | 158.3 | 156.3 |
| 2014 | 156.4 | 156.7 | 157.2 | 157.6 | 158.2 | 158.7 | 159.0 | 159.6 | 158.5 | 160.2 | 160.3 | 160.5 | 158.6 |
| | | | | | | | | | | | | | |
| 2015 | 159.4 | 159.8 | 160.2 | 160.8 | 161.3 | 161.7 | 162.1 | 161.6 | 160.9 | 162.5 | 162.6 | 162.7 | 161.3 |
| 2016 | 162.7 | 162.7 | 162.7 | 163.7 | 164.9 | 165.4 | 166.8 | 167.0 | 166.7 | 167.7 | 167.9 | 168.1 | 165.5 |
| 2017 | 166.0 | 166.7 | 167.5 | 167.8 | 169.0 | 170.2 | 170.5 | 170.5 | 170.4 | 172.1 | 171.9 | 172.2 | 169.6 |
| 2018 | 169.7 | 171.2 | 171.4 | 171.8 | 172.2 | 173.3 | 173.9 | 173.8 | 173.5 | 174.6 | 176.7 | 175.0 | 173.1 |
| 2019 | 173.9 | 174.8 | 175.3 | 175.7 | 176.7 | 177.3 | 179.1 | 179.8 | 179.1 | 179.0 | 178.7 | 179.2 | 177.4 |

## Employment by Industry: Atlanta-Sandy Springs-Roswell, GA, 2011–2019—*Continued*

(Numbers in thousands, not seasonally adjusted)

| Industry and year | January | February | March | April | May | June | July | August | September | October | November | December | Annual average |
|---|---|---|---|---|---|---|---|---|---|---|---|---|---|
| **Professional and Business Services** | | | | | | | | | | | | | |
| 2011 | 404.0 | 414.7 | 418.3 | 417.9 | 417.5 | 417.9 | 419.2 | 422.2 | 422.9 | 425.4 | 426.3 | 428.0 | 419.5 |
| 2012 | 417.9 | 422.1 | 424.9 | 429.7 | 433.0 | 437.5 | 434.1 | 437.5 | 434.6 | 441.2 | 444.6 | 444.5 | 433.5 |
| 2013 | 437.5 | 444.8 | 446.8 | 450.7 | 451.3 | 454.8 | 454.1 | 457.9 | 457.9 | 464.4 | 467.7 | 466.6 | 454.5 |
| 2014 | 461.3 | 462.9 | 473.1 | 474.2 | 478.3 | 480.9 | 485.3 | 489.4 | 488.0 | 492.5 | 495.5 | 496.1 | 481.5 |
| 2015 | 483.4 | 487.9 | 490.5 | 490.2 | 496.5 | 498.7 | 499.7 | 501.1 | 500.5 | 505.9 | 504.3 | 506.4 | 497.1 |
| 2016 | 499.2 | 503.0 | 503.1 | 509.1 | 509.2 | 509.0 | 514.6 | 517.0 | 518.7 | 520.5 | 521.2 | 523.0 | 512.3 |
| 2017 | 510.0 | 513.6 | 517.5 | 519.8 | 520.4 | 524.5 | 528.3 | 531.5 | 528.9 | 535.9 | 540.1 | 539.0 | 525.8 |
| 2018 | 524.9 | 528.6 | 533.0 | 532.4 | 532.6 | 535.6 | 537.4 | 542.4 | 540.1 | 545.6 | 548.1 | 545.5 | 537.2 |
| 2019 | 542.1 | 544.9 | 543.9 | 543.5 | 545.5 | 549.4 | 548.9 | 548.1 | 549.3 | 555.6 | 557.6 | 562.6 | 549.3 |
| **Education and Health Services** | | | | | | | | | | | | | |
| 2011 | 264.8 | 268.9 | 269.8 | 274.8 | 274.6 | 270.0 | 270.6 | 274.7 | 276.4 | 280.2 | 280.4 | 281.2 | 273.9 |
| 2012 | 279.5 | 282.5 | 283.7 | 285.9 | 286.6 | 282.6 | 281.6 | 287.3 | 288.4 | 291.5 | 291.8 | 292.1 | 286.1 |
| 2013 | 291.5 | 294.3 | 294.9 | 297.3 | 298.0 | 294.2 | 292.7 | 298.4 | 299.8 | 302.8 | 305.2 | 305.4 | 297.9 |
| 2014 | 302.3 | 303.2 | 305.9 | 307.7 | 309.3 | 305.6 | 304.9 | 311.8 | 312.7 | 314.1 | 315.7 | 317.1 | 309.2 |
| 2015 | 315.4 | 317.3 | 317.8 | 318.8 | 320.6 | 317.8 | 316.8 | 322.2 | 323.9 | 329.5 | 331.1 | 331.9 | 321.9 |
| 2016 | 330.1 | 333.3 | 333.6 | 335.7 | 336.6 | 332.4 | 332.6 | 337.8 | 339.5 | 342.9 | 343.6 | 343.4 | 336.8 |
| 2017 | 338.8 | 341.7 | 343.6 | 343.7 | 344.8 | 341.3 | 340.4 | 345.5 | 346.8 | 349.4 | 350.7 | 350.8 | 344.8 |
| 2018 | 349.5 | 352.2 | 353.6 | 353.8 | 355.2 | 351.7 | 353.1 | 359.6 | 359.5 | 362.7 | 363.8 | 363.6 | 356.5 |
| 2019 | 365.6 | 368.9 | 369.1 | 367.9 | 368.9 | 364.7 | 365.2 | 370.7 | 374.4 | 379.3 | 381.6 | 384.1 | 371.7 |
| **Leisure and Hospitality** | | | | | | | | | | | | | |
| 2011 | 211.2 | 216.1 | 221.4 | 227.8 | 233.4 | 233.4 | 232.9 | 232.4 | 229.4 | 227.2 | 226.3 | 225.7 | 226.4 |
| 2012 | 221.8 | 223.5 | 228.5 | 235.7 | 241.1 | 241.8 | 240.6 | 241.2 | 236.1 | 236.6 | 234.7 | 234.7 | 234.7 |
| 2013 | 231.8 | 233.7 | 238.2 | 245.6 | 249.9 | 252.5 | 253.0 | 253.8 | 249.4 | 250.4 | 247.9 | 248.1 | 246.2 |
| 2014 | 243.0 | 243.0 | 249.9 | 258.7 | 265.1 | 266.7 | 266.6 | 267.3 | 262.5 | 262.9 | 262.8 | 264.4 | 259.4 |
| 2015 | 253.3 | 257.2 | 261.7 | 267.8 | 273.2 | 277.3 | 275.1 | 276.2 | 273.1 | 272.4 | 271.4 | 272.5 | 269.3 |
| 2016 | 266.7 | 268.9 | 273.4 | 282.8 | 289.2 | 292.4 | 289.5 | 288.6 | 285.7 | 284.6 | 283.9 | 284.0 | 282.5 |
| 2017 | 274.6 | 277.8 | 283.6 | 289.9 | 296.2 | 300.4 | 297.6 | 298.3 | 292.3 | 295.4 | 292.8 | 291.7 | 290.9 |
| 2018 | 284.0 | 286.9 | 293.5 | 296.1 | 302.9 | 307.8 | 306.8 | 305.0 | 299.1 | 297.8 | 295.5 | 296.2 | 297.6 |
| 2019 | 292.9 | 296.5 | 300.7 | 302.8 | 309.9 | 312.2 | 311.9 | 311.1 | 306.3 | 310.8 | 306.4 | 303.5 | 305.4 |
| **Other Services** | | | | | | | | | | | | | |
| 2011 | 91.6 | 93.2 | 93.3 | 92.6 | 93.3 | 93.2 | 93.3 | 92.9 | 92.5 | 92.4 | 92.4 | 91.6 | 92.7 |
| 2012 | 91.0 | 91.5 | 91.6 | 92.9 | 93.4 | 93.8 | 94.1 | 93.7 | 92.9 | 93.8 | 93.8 | 92.8 | 92.9 |
| 2013 | 92.4 | 92.9 | 92.6 | 93.8 | 94.1 | 94.4 | 94.2 | 94.0 | 93.4 | 93.5 | 93.4 | 92.8 | 93.5 |
| 2014 | 92.0 | 92.3 | 92.7 | 94.3 | 94.8 | 95.4 | 95.5 | 95.6 | 94.7 | 94.4 | 94.7 | 94.7 | 94.3 |
| 2015 | 93.7 | 94.6 | 94.9 | 96.0 | 96.5 | 97.2 | 97.8 | 97.1 | 96.3 | 95.8 | 95.6 | 96.2 | 96.0 |
| 2016 | 95.4 | 96.0 | 96.1 | 97.6 | 98.2 | 99.4 | 99.4 | 98.7 | 97.8 | 98.1 | 98.0 | 97.8 | 97.7 |
| 2017 | 97.0 | 97.7 | 98.3 | 99.3 | 100.6 | 101.4 | 100.8 | 100.2 | 99.3 | 98.6 | 98.2 | 97.9 | 99.1 |
| 2018 | 97.2 | 98.0 | 98.7 | 99.7 | 101.1 | 102.6 | 103.0 | 102.5 | 102.0 | 102.5 | 101.1 | 100.9 | 100.8 |
| 2019 | 101.7 | 102.4 | 102.9 | 104.1 | 103.8 | 104.8 | 105.3 | 105.4 | 104.7 | 104.5 | 104.8 | 105.6 | 104.2 |
| **Government** | | | | | | | | | | | | | |
| 2011 | 323.8 | 327.3 | 328.9 | 326.9 | 327.1 | 320.3 | 310.5 | 316.0 | 320.9 | 322.6 | 325.5 | 323.8 | 322.8 |
| 2012 | 321.1 | 323.4 | 326.9 | 325.6 | 324.2 | 320.3 | 306.4 | 314.4 | 318.3 | 320.7 | 325.4 | 321.2 | 320.7 |
| 2013 | 319.4 | 321.5 | 321.7 | 323.6 | 321.1 | 314.4 | 303.1 | 311.5 | 316.8 | 320.5 | 323.9 | 322.4 | 318.3 |
| 2014 | 316.1 | 318.3 | 321.0 | 321.8 | 322.6 | 315.8 | 305.7 | 317.0 | 320.2 | 322.3 | 326.6 | 323.2 | 319.2 |
| 2015 | 320.9 | 323.6 | 323.9 | 323.8 | 322.6 | 317.9 | 307.9 | 318.3 | 321.9 | 325.5 | 328.2 | 326.4 | 321.7 |
| 2016 | 324.1 | 326.4 | 326.1 | 327.2 | 327.3 | 324.3 | 310.1 | 323.2 | 327.5 | 329.5 | 333.3 | 330.8 | 325.8 |
| 2017 | 327.0 | 330.6 | 331.2 | 331.0 | 329.8 | 327.1 | 315.5 | 326.4 | 332.1 | 333.4 | 335.6 | 333.8 | 329.5 |
| 2018 | 332.0 | 334.5 | 335.2 | 335.0 | 336.6 | 330.9 | 321.0 | 332.8 | 335.1 | 336.6 | 338.8 | 338.0 | 333.9 |
| 2019 | 332.5 | 335.3 | 336.5 | 336.5 | 336.6 | 330.5 | 321.6 | 333.6 | 336.7 | 338.1 | 339.0 | 339.1 | 334.7 |

# Employment by Industry: Phoenix-Mesa-Scottsdale, AZ, 2011–2019

(Numbers in thousands, not seasonally adjusted)

| Industry and year | January | February | March | April | May | June | July | August | September | October | November | December | Annual average |
|---|---|---|---|---|---|---|---|---|---|---|---|---|---|
| **Total Nonfarm** | | | | | | | | | | | | | |
| 2011 | 1,693.6 | 1,708.5 | 1,718.9 | 1,727.6 | 1,724.7 | 1,680.7 | 1,666.0 | 1,702.8 | 1,725.5 | 1,739.2 | 1,759.0 | 1,762.5 | 1,717.4 |
| 2012 | 1,732.3 | 1,746.8 | 1,759.6 | 1,760.8 | 1,758.3 | 1,727.7 | 1,707.7 | 1,747.6 | 1,769.3 | 1,786.6 | 1,810.3 | 1,818.1 | 1,760.4 |
| 2013 | 1,779.7 | 1,798.0 | 1,807.7 | 1,813.3 | 1,811.4 | 1,777.4 | 1,762.0 | 1,798.9 | 1,817.5 | 1,838.9 | 1,865.4 | 1,870.4 | 1,811.7 |
| 2014 | 1,828.3 | 1,843.0 | 1,850.1 | 1,855.4 | 1,843.7 | 1,813.5 | 1,797.0 | 1,838.0 | 1,856.0 | 1,884.1 | 1,908.6 | 1,919.4 | 1,853.1 |
| 2015 | 1,879.3 | 1,897.7 | 1,903.0 | 1,911.4 | 1,905.0 | 1,871.5 | 1,865.7 | 1,900.8 | 1,923.3 | 1,957.1 | 1,982.4 | 1,985.4 | 1,915.2 |
| 2016 | 1,945.7 | 1,966.6 | 1,973.5 | 1,982.7 | 1,972.0 | 1,932.8 | 1,932.6 | 1,969.4 | 1,995.6 | 2,014.2 | 2,034.2 | 2,037.7 | 1,979.8 |
| 2017 | 2,000.4 | 2,020.3 | 2,028.6 | 2,040.8 | 2,029.4 | 2,004.4 | 1,989.4 | 2,029.1 | 2,052.4 | 2,077.0 | 2,102.4 | 2,105.8 | 2,040.0 |
| 2018 | 2,070.3 | 2,094.0 | 2,102.1 | 2,102.1 | 2,094.9 | 2,062.2 | 2,056.4 | 2,102.2 | 2,120.7 | 2,146.5 | 2,175.3 | 2,175.8 | 2,108.5 |
| 2019 | 2,145.8 | 2,162.1 | 2,166.8 | 2,166.4 | 2,158.4 | 2,124.2 | 2,123.5 | 2,179.3 | 2,190.0 | 2,216.9 | 2,244.9 | 2,249.5 | 2,177.3 |
| **Total Private** | | | | | | | | | | | | | |
| 2011 | 1,461.1 | 1,470.2 | 1,480.7 | 1,488.9 | 1,486.3 | 1,477.8 | 1,473.6 | 1,483.8 | 1,491.3 | 1,501.9 | 1,520.8 | 1,528.6 | 1,488.8 |
| 2012 | 1,501.2 | 1,509.2 | 1,521.7 | 1,522.3 | 1,524.8 | 1,521.1 | 1,511.2 | 1,526.4 | 1,531.8 | 1,547.6 | 1,569.9 | 1,578.6 | 1,530.5 |
| 2013 | 1,545.0 | 1,558.1 | 1,568.5 | 1,573.4 | 1,574.7 | 1,570.2 | 1,564.1 | 1,578.0 | 1,579.7 | 1,598.0 | 1,624.4 | 1,631.7 | 1,580.5 |
| 2014 | 1,593.1 | 1,602.7 | 1,610.3 | 1,614.7 | 1,612.6 | 1,606.0 | 1,598.8 | 1,614.1 | 1,615.3 | 1,638.9 | 1,663.2 | 1,675.7 | 1,620.5 |
| 2015 | 1,644.0 | 1,654.2 | 1,660.1 | 1,668.9 | 1,669.2 | 1,663.9 | 1,665.5 | 1,678.7 | 1,683.4 | 1,712.0 | 1,735.9 | 1,743.3 | 1,681.6 |
| 2016 | 1,711.5 | 1,723.2 | 1,730.2 | 1,738.7 | 1,735.0 | 1,722.6 | 1,729.0 | 1,742.4 | 1,751.3 | 1,768.2 | 1,786.8 | 1,792.8 | 1,744.3 |
| 2017 | 1,763.0 | 1,774.3 | 1,782.8 | 1,794.1 | 1,791.8 | 1,787.4 | 1,781.8 | 1,797.7 | 1,807.4 | 1,829.2 | 1,853.8 | 1,861.1 | 1,802.0 |
| 2018 | 1,831.9 | 1,847.6 | 1,855.8 | 1,856.2 | 1,853.8 | 1,846.7 | 1,847.6 | 1,866.1 | 1,873.6 | 1,896.4 | 1,924.9 | 1,928.7 | 1,869.1 |
| 2019 | 1,900.4 | 1,912.1 | 1,916.9 | 1,917.3 | 1,913.9 | 1,906.1 | 1,911.7 | 1,935.4 | 1,938.9 | 1,962.9 | 1,990.4 | 1,994.4 | 1,933.4 |
| **Goods Producing** | | | | | | | | | | | | | |
| 2011 | 194.1 | 193.8 | 195.1 | 197.1 | 198.8 | 200.5 | 202.5 | 202.9 | 203.0 | 202.8 | 202.7 | 203.0 | 199.7 |
| 2012 | 201.4 | 202.3 | 204.7 | 205.8 | 207.3 | 210.3 | 211.1 | 212.9 | 213.1 | 213.5 | 213.1 | 212.2 | 209.0 |
| 2013 | 208.7 | 210.4 | 211.8 | 212.5 | 214.4 | 217.2 | 217.4 | 217.8 | 216.8 | 217.6 | 217.3 | 216.6 | 214.9 |
| 2014 | 215.3 | 216.7 | 216.7 | 218.2 | 218.7 | 219.1 | 218.7 | 218.6 | 217.2 | 218.6 | 219.1 | 219.4 | 218.0 |
| 2015 | 216.8 | 218.5 | 219.0 | 221.0 | 222.1 | 223.5 | 224.4 | 224.8 | 224.3 | 226.1 | 226.2 | 227.1 | 222.8 |
| 2016 | 224.8 | 227.1 | 227.5 | 228.0 | 228.6 | 230.9 | 232.1 | 232.4 | 231.7 | 230.9 | 230.8 | 232.2 | 229.8 |
| 2017 | 230.9 | 232.6 | 233.7 | 235.7 | 238.0 | 242.3 | 243.4 | 244.4 | 245.4 | 247.0 | 248.4 | 249.4 | 240.9 |
| 2018 | 247.3 | 250.3 | 252.0 | 252.3 | 253.0 | 257.0 | 258.6 | 259.5 | 259.9 | 260.8 | 262.6 | 263.9 | 256.4 |
| 2019 | 262.7 | 265.4 | 266.5 | 268.2 | 269.5 | 272.3 | 273.8 | 274.5 | 274.5 | 274.6 | 272.8 | 274.3 | 270.8 |
| **Service-Providing** | | | | | | | | | | | | | |
| 2011 | 1,499.5 | 1,514.7 | 1,523.8 | 1,530.5 | 1,525.9 | 1,480.2 | 1,463.5 | 1,499.9 | 1,522.5 | 1,536.4 | 1,556.3 | 1,559.5 | 1,517.7 |
| 2012 | 1,530.9 | 1,544.5 | 1,554.9 | 1,555.0 | 1,551.0 | 1,517.4 | 1,496.6 | 1,534.7 | 1,556.2 | 1,573.1 | 1,597.2 | 1,605.9 | 1,551.5 |
| 2013 | 1,571.0 | 1,587.6 | 1,595.9 | 1,600.8 | 1,597.0 | 1,560.2 | 1,544.6 | 1,581.1 | 1,600.7 | 1,621.3 | 1,648.1 | 1,653.8 | 1,596.8 |
| 2014 | 1,613.0 | 1,626.3 | 1,633.4 | 1,637.2 | 1,625.0 | 1,594.4 | 1,578.3 | 1,619.4 | 1,638.8 | 1,665.5 | 1,689.5 | 1,700.0 | 1,635.1 |
| 2015 | 1,662.5 | 1,679.2 | 1,684.0 | 1,690.4 | 1,682.9 | 1,648.0 | 1,641.3 | 1,676.0 | 1,699.0 | 1,731.0 | 1,756.2 | 1,758.3 | 1,692.4 |
| 2016 | 1,720.9 | 1,739.5 | 1,746.0 | 1,754.7 | 1,743.4 | 1,701.9 | 1,700.5 | 1,737.0 | 1,763.9 | 1,783.3 | 1,803.4 | 1,805.5 | 1,750.0 |
| 2017 | 1,769.5 | 1,787.7 | 1,794.9 | 1,805.1 | 1,791.4 | 1,762.1 | 1,746.0 | 1,784.7 | 1,807.0 | 1,830.0 | 1,854.0 | 1,856.4 | 1,799.1 |
| 2018 | 1,823.0 | 1,843.7 | 1,850.1 | 1,849.8 | 1,841.9 | 1,805.2 | 1,797.8 | 1,842.7 | 1,860.8 | 1,885.7 | 1,912.7 | 1,911.9 | 1,852.1 |
| 2019 | 1,883.1 | 1,896.7 | 1,900.3 | 1,898.2 | 1,888.9 | 1,851.9 | 1,849.7 | 1,904.8 | 1,915.5 | 1,942.3 | 1,972.1 | 1,975.2 | 1,906.6 |
| **Mining and Logging** | | | | | | | | | | | | | |
| 2011 | 3.2 | 3.2 | 3.2 | 3.1 | 3.2 | 3.2 | 3.2 | 3.2 | 3.2 | 3.4 | 3.4 | 3.4 | 3.2 |
| 2012 | 3.4 | 3.4 | 3.4 | 3.4 | 3.4 | 3.5 | 3.6 | 3.6 | 3.7 | 3.6 | 3.6 | 3.6 | 3.5 |
| 2013 | 3.6 | 3.6 | 3.6 | 3.6 | 3.6 | 3.8 | 3.8 | 3.7 | 3.6 | 3.5 | 3.5 | 3.5 | 3.6 |
| 2014 | 3.4 | 3.4 | 3.4 | 3.4 | 3.4 | 3.4 | 3.4 | 3.4 | 3.4 | 3.4 | 3.4 | 3.4 | 3.4 |
| 2015 | 3.4 | 3.4 | 3.4 | 3.3 | 3.4 | 3.4 | 3.5 | 3.4 | 3.3 | 3.2 | 3.2 | 3.2 | 3.3 |
| 2016 | 3.2 | 3.2 | 3.2 | 3.2 | 3.2 | 3.3 | 3.3 | 3.3 | 3.2 | 3.2 | 3.2 | 3.2 | 3.2 |
| 2017 | 3.1 | 3.1 | 3.1 | 3.2 | 3.2 | 3.3 | 3.3 | 3.4 | 3.3 | 3.4 | 3.4 | 3.4 | 3.3 |
| 2018 | 3.4 | 3.5 | 3.5 | 3.5 | 3.5 | 3.5 | 3.6 | 3.6 | 3.6 | 3.6 | 3.6 | 3.6 | 3.5 |
| 2019 | 3.5 | 3.5 | 3.5 | 3.5 | 3.5 | 3.6 | 3.6 | 3.6 | 3.6 | 3.6 | 3.6 | 3.6 | 3.6 |
| **Construction** | | | | | | | | | | | | | |
| 2011 | 79.2 | 78.9 | 80.0 | 81.5 | 82.4 | 83.9 | 85.3 | 85.6 | 85.8 | 85.2 | 84.5 | 83.9 | 83.0 |
| 2012 | 82.5 | 83.0 | 84.8 | 85.5 | 86.5 | 88.5 | 89.4 | 90.9 | 91.3 | 91.9 | 91.5 | 90.2 | 88.0 |
| 2013 | 87.8 | 89.1 | 90.6 | 91.4 | 92.9 | 95.1 | 95.3 | 96.2 | 95.6 | 96.2 | 95.8 | 94.9 | 93.4 |
| 2014 | 93.8 | 94.4 | 94.4 | 95.7 | 96.0 | 96.1 | 95.9 | 95.6 | 94.7 | 95.9 | 96.0 | 95.8 | 95.4 |
| 2015 | 94.8 | 96.0 | 96.7 | 97.9 | 98.6 | 99.2 | 99.6 | 100.0 | 100.0 | 101.6 | 101.5 | 101.7 | 99.0 |
| 2016 | 100.4 | 102.3 | 103.2 | 103.9 | 104.3 | 105.9 | 107.6 | 107.9 | 107.3 | 107.4 | 106.8 | 107.1 | 105.3 |
| 2017 | 106.8 | 108.1 | 109.6 | 110.8 | 112.3 | 114.9 | 115.5 | 116.1 | 116.7 | 117.9 | 118.4 | 119.0 | 113.8 |
| 2018 | 117.8 | 119.8 | 121.1 | 121.8 | 122.5 | 124.6 | 125.7 | 126.4 | 126.7 | 127.5 | 128.7 | 129.4 | 124.3 |
| 2019 | 128.6 | 130.5 | 131.5 | 133.0 | 133.8 | 135.3 | 136.2 | 136.3 | 136.4 | 136.5 | 134.7 | 135.7 | 134.0 |

## Employment by Industry: Phoenix-Mesa-Scottsdale, AZ, 2011–2019—*Continued*

(Numbers in thousands, not seasonally adjusted)

| Industry and year | January | February | March | April | May | June | July | August | September | October | November | December | Annual average |
|---|---|---|---|---|---|---|---|---|---|---|---|---|---|
| **Manufacturing** | | | | | | | | | | | | | |
| 2011 | 111.7 | 111.7 | 111.9 | 112.5 | 113.2 | 113.4 | 114.0 | 114.1 | 114.0 | 114.2 | 114.8 | 115.7 | 113.4 |
| 2012 | 115.5 | 115.9 | 116.5 | 116.9 | 117.4 | 118.3 | 118.1 | 118.4 | 118.1 | 118.0 | 118.0 | 118.4 | 117.5 |
| 2013 | 117.3 | 117.7 | 117.6 | 117.5 | 117.9 | 118.3 | 118.3 | 117.9 | 117.6 | 117.9 | 118.0 | 118.2 | 117.9 |
| 2014 | 118.1 | 118.9 | 118.9 | 119.1 | 119.3 | 119.6 | 119.4 | 119.6 | 119.1 | 119.3 | 119.7 | 120.2 | 119.3 |
| 2015 | 118.6 | 119.1 | 118.9 | 119.8 | 120.1 | 120.9 | 121.3 | 121.4 | 121.0 | 121.3 | 121.5 | 122.2 | 120.5 |
| 2016 | 121.2 | 121.6 | 121.1 | 120.9 | 121.1 | 121.7 | 121.2 | 121.2 | 121.2 | 120.3 | 120.8 | 121.9 | 121.2 |
| 2017 | 121.0 | 121.4 | 121.0 | 121.7 | 122.5 | 124.1 | 124.6 | 124.9 | 125.4 | 125.7 | 126.6 | 127.0 | 123.8 |
| 2018 | 126.1 | 127.0 | 127.4 | 127.0 | 127.0 | 128.9 | 129.3 | 129.5 | 129.6 | 129.7 | 130.3 | 130.9 | 128.6 |
| 2019 | 130.6 | 131.4 | 131.5 | 131.7 | 132.2 | 133.4 | 134.0 | 134.6 | 134.5 | 134.5 | 134.5 | 135.0 | 133.2 |
| **Trade, Transportation, and Utilities** | | | | | | | | | | | | | |
| 2011 | 343.4 | 343.3 | 344.0 | 346.0 | 345.6 | 344.7 | 344.2 | 344.8 | 344.9 | 349.5 | 358.9 | 360.9 | 347.5 |
| 2012 | 349.5 | 347.3 | 348.5 | 348.5 | 349.4 | 348.2 | 347.2 | 347.0 | 347.8 | 352.1 | 363.2 | 365.9 | 351.2 |
| 2013 | 349.8 | 348.8 | 348.5 | 349.3 | 350.3 | 349.9 | 350.2 | 351.7 | 352.7 | 357.2 | 368.1 | 373.4 | 354.2 |
| 2014 | 359.3 | 358.3 | 358.4 | 358.7 | 358.5 | 358.7 | 358.6 | 360.5 | 360.5 | 365.7 | 376.4 | 382.1 | 363.0 |
| 2015 | 368.3 | 367.9 | 368.7 | 369.1 | 369.6 | 370.6 | 371.3 | 373.6 | 375.2 | 381.6 | 392.5 | 394.3 | 375.2 |
| 2016 | 379.0 | 378.9 | 379.6 | 380.7 | 380.6 | 379.3 | 381.5 | 382.4 | 382.6 | 390.2 | 401.1 | 404.7 | 385.1 |
| 2017 | 389.7 | 388.0 | 387.2 | 387.5 | 387.5 | 387.6 | 388.6 | 389.9 | 390.1 | 396.3 | 409.8 | 411.1 | 392.8 |
| 2018 | 399.2 | 396.4 | 396.7 | 396.3 | 397.3 | 396.9 | 398.9 | 399.9 | 401.8 | 407.4 | 421.5 | 423.0 | 402.9 |
| 2019 | 409.0 | 405.1 | 404.3 | 402.9 | 401.8 | 402.3 | 403.4 | 405.5 | 406.6 | 413.0 | 426.8 | 430.8 | 409.3 |
| **Wholesale Trade** | | | | | | | | | | | | | |
| 2011 | 77.1 | 77.7 | 77.7 | 78.1 | 78.0 | 78.0 | 77.7 | 77.5 | 77.3 | 77.4 | 77.4 | 77.3 | 77.6 |
| 2012 | 76.9 | 77.2 | 77.6 | 77.4 | 77.4 | 77.6 | 77.7 | 77.6 | 77.6 | 77.8 | 77.8 | 77.8 | 77.5 |
| 2013 | 76.7 | 77.4 | 77.2 | 77.4 | 77.3 | 77.4 | 77.3 | 77.4 | 77.1 | 77.6 | 77.7 | 78.0 | 77.4 |
| 2014 | 76.6 | 76.9 | 77.1 | 76.8 | 77.0 | 76.8 | 76.9 | 77.1 | 76.9 | 76.8 | 76.7 | 77.3 | 76.9 |
| 2015 | 76.0 | 76.1 | 76.2 | 76.5 | 76.6 | 76.7 | 76.7 | 76.9 | 77.0 | 77.3 | 77.4 | 77.4 | 76.7 |
| 2016 | 76.9 | 77.2 | 76.9 | 77.4 | 77.4 | 77.3 | 78.1 | 77.8 | 77.7 | 78.8 | 78.7 | 79.0 | 77.8 |
| 2017 | 78.1 | 78.5 | 78.5 | 78.3 | 78.4 | 78.4 | 78.4 | 78.6 | 78.6 | 79.1 | 79.2 | 79.3 | 78.6 |
| 2018 | 79.1 | 79.3 | 79.6 | 80.0 | 80.5 | 80.3 | 81.6 | 81.8 | 82.1 | 82.3 | 82.7 | 82.8 | 81.0 |
| 2019 | 81.8 | 82.3 | 82.2 | 82.4 | 82.4 | 82.6 | 82.7 | 82.7 | 82.7 | 83.4 | 84.6 | 85.5 | 82.9 |
| **Retail Trade** | | | | | | | | | | | | | |
| 2011 | 204.1 | 203.3 | 203.9 | 204.9 | 204.4 | 203.1 | 203.1 | 203.6 | 203.4 | 206.9 | 215.6 | 216.6 | 206.1 |
| 2012 | 207.1 | 204.5 | 204.9 | 205.7 | 206.2 | 204.8 | 203.5 | 203.3 | 204.0 | 207.7 | 218.4 | 219.8 | 207.5 |
| 2013 | 206.0 | 204.5 | 204.8 | 205.8 | 206.3 | 205.9 | 206.6 | 207.7 | 208.5 | 211.6 | 221.8 | 225.3 | 209.6 |
| 2014 | 214.0 | 212.9 | 212.6 | 213.7 | 213.1 | 213.3 | 213.4 | 214.3 | 214.5 | 218.7 | 228.5 | 231.8 | 216.7 |
| 2015 | 220.5 | 219.3 | 219.6 | 220.6 | 220.7 | 221.6 | 220.9 | 221.8 | 222.7 | 227.7 | 236.6 | 237.3 | 224.1 |
| 2016 | 225.1 | 224.4 | 224.4 | 224.5 | 224.5 | 223.8 | 224.4 | 225.3 | 225.7 | 231.0 | 240.1 | 241.6 | 227.9 |
| 2017 | 230.4 | 228.9 | 228.9 | 229.3 | 229.2 | 229.3 | 230.0 | 230.5 | 230.1 | 233.8 | 244.4 | 243.6 | 232.4 |
| 2018 | 234.4 | 231.9 | 231.9 | 230.6 | 231.0 | 230.5 | 231.1 | 231.9 | 232.9 | 236.9 | 247.6 | 247.6 | 234.9 |
| 2019 | 235.9 | 232.8 | 232.1 | 231.4 | 230.2 | 230.1 | 230.5 | 231.5 | 232.3 | 236.2 | 245.5 | 246.6 | 234.6 |
| **Transportation and Utilities** | | | | | | | | | | | | | |
| 2011 | 62.2 | 62.3 | 62.4 | 63.0 | 63.2 | 63.6 | 63.4 | 63.7 | 64.2 | 65.2 | 65.9 | 67.0 | 63.8 |
| 2012 | 65.5 | 65.6 | 66.0 | 65.4 | 65.8 | 65.8 | 66.0 | 66.1 | 66.2 | 66.6 | 67.0 | 68.3 | 66.2 |
| 2013 | 67.1 | 66.9 | 66.5 | 66.1 | 66.7 | 66.6 | 66.3 | 66.6 | 67.1 | 68.0 | 68.6 | 70.1 | 67.2 |
| 2014 | 68.7 | 68.5 | 68.7 | 68.2 | 68.4 | 68.6 | 68.3 | 69.1 | 69.1 | 70.2 | 71.2 | 73.0 | 69.3 |
| 2015 | 71.8 | 72.5 | 72.9 | 72.0 | 72.3 | 72.3 | 73.7 | 74.9 | 75.5 | 76.6 | 78.5 | 79.6 | 74.4 |
| 2016 | 77.0 | 77.3 | 78.3 | 78.8 | 78.7 | 78.2 | 79.0 | 79.3 | 79.2 | 80.4 | 82.3 | 84.1 | 79.4 |
| 2017 | 81.2 | 80.6 | 79.8 | 79.9 | 79.9 | 79.9 | 80.2 | 80.8 | 81.4 | 83.4 | 86.2 | 88.2 | 81.8 |
| 2018 | 85.7 | 85.2 | 85.2 | 85.7 | 85.8 | 86.1 | 86.2 | 86.2 | 86.8 | 88.2 | 91.2 | 92.6 | 87.1 |
| 2019 | 91.3 | 90.0 | 90.0 | 89.1 | 89.2 | 89.6 | 90.2 | 91.3 | 91.6 | 93.4 | 96.7 | 98.7 | 91.8 |
| **Information** | | | | | | | | | | | | | |
| 2011 | 28.7 | 28.6 | 28.9 | 29.2 | 29.2 | 29.4 | 29.7 | 29.7 | 29.6 | 30.0 | 30.8 | 30.9 | 29.6 |
| 2012 | 30.9 | 31.2 | 31.5 | 31.8 | 32.3 | 32.3 | 32.4 | 32.7 | 32.3 | 32.4 | 33.4 | 33.6 | 32.2 |
| 2013 | 33.3 | 33.8 | 34.2 | 34.2 | 34.8 | 34.5 | 34.7 | 34.8 | 34.3 | 34.6 | 35.2 | 35.1 | 34.5 |
| 2014 | 35.0 | 35.0 | 35.4 | 35.8 | 36.2 | 36.6 | 37.0 | 36.8 | 36.0 | 36.4 | 36.6 | 36.9 | 36.1 |
| 2015 | 36.7 | 37.8 | 37.0 | 37.5 | 37.9 | 37.7 | 37.5 | 36.9 | 36.2 | 36.3 | 36.8 | 36.8 | 37.1 |
| 2016 | 37.2 | 37.7 | 37.2 | 37.6 | 37.9 | 37.8 | 37.6 | 36.9 | 36.4 | 36.7 | 36.7 | 36.8 | 37.2 |
| 2017 | 36.4 | 37.0 | 37.1 | 37.9 | 38.1 | 38.1 | 38.0 | 37.9 | 37.4 | 37.8 | 37.9 | 38.4 | 37.7 |
| 2018 | 38.6 | 39.1 | 38.7 | 38.9 | 39.1 | 39.0 | 39.0 | 38.8 | 38.3 | 39.0 | 39.9 | 40.0 | 39.0 |
| 2019 | 39.6 | 40.0 | 40.0 | 39.7 | 39.9 | 40.0 | 40.6 | 40.8 | 40.3 | 40.9 | 40.8 | 40.9 | 40.3 |

## Employment by Industry: Phoenix-Mesa-Scottsdale, AZ, 2011–2019—*Continued*

(Numbers in thousands, not seasonally adjusted)

| Industry and year | January | February | March | April | May | June | July | August | September | October | November | December | Annual average |
|---|---|---|---|---|---|---|---|---|---|---|---|---|---|
| **Financial Activities** | | | | | | | | | | | | | |
| 2011 | 142.1 | 142.9 | 143.7 | 144.4 | 144.3 | 144.8 | 145.3 | 145.8 | 146.0 | 146.4 | 147.2 | 148.8 | 145.1 |
| 2012 | 147.2 | 149.0 | 149.3 | 149.0 | 149.1 | 149.1 | 149.3 | 150.2 | 150.5 | 152.3 | 153.6 | 154.5 | 150.3 |
| 2013 | 153.3 | 155.9 | 156.0 | 156.9 | 157.5 | 158.0 | 158.1 | 158.6 | 158.6 | 160.9 | 162.1 | 162.5 | 158.2 |
| 2014 | 160.7 | 161.6 | 161.1 | 160.5 | 160.7 | 160.7 | 160.5 | 161.1 | 161.1 | 162.8 | 163.9 | 164.2 | 161.6 |
| 2015 | 163.1 | 164.5 | 164.9 | 165.2 | 165.8 | 166.4 | 167.4 | 168.4 | 168.6 | 171.0 | 172.5 | 173.7 | 167.6 |
| 2016 | 172.6 | 174.0 | 174.6 | 175.9 | 175.9 | 176.2 | 177.8 | 178.8 | 179.6 | 181.3 | 182.9 | 183.7 | 177.8 |
| 2017 | 182.8 | 183.3 | 184.2 | 184.6 | 184.9 | 185.9 | 187.1 | 187.9 | 188.7 | 189.9 | 191.0 | 191.4 | 186.8 |
| 2018 | 190.5 | 191.6 | 191.4 | 192.2 | 192.4 | 193.1 | 193.7 | 194.7 | 195.2 | 196.9 | 198.4 | 198.8 | 194.1 |
| 2019 | 197.8 | 199.1 | 199.9 | 200.8 | 201.1 | 201.7 | 202.9 | 204.3 | 204.2 | 206.4 | 206.3 | 205.7 | 202.5 |
| **Professional and Business Services** | | | | | | | | | | | | | |
| 2011 | 270.6 | 273.6 | 275.1 | 276.7 | 273.7 | 272.9 | 273.0 | 274.7 | 275.3 | 278.4 | 281.2 | 285.3 | 275.9 |
| 2012 | 276.6 | 277.8 | 279.7 | 280.8 | 281.1 | 283.2 | 282.5 | 285.6 | 285.4 | 289.7 | 295.0 | 298.5 | 284.7 |
| 2013 | 293.1 | 292.3 | 295.1 | 297.0 | 297.3 | 299.9 | 298.9 | 300.4 | 299.1 | 305.0 | 313.0 | 314.7 | 300.5 |
| 2014 | 299.8 | 299.5 | 301.5 | 304.2 | 304.5 | 305.3 | 305.1 | 307.9 | 307.9 | 315.1 | 321.8 | 325.7 | 308.2 |
| 2015 | 314.7 | 314.1 | 314.0 | 317.7 | 317.6 | 318.6 | 320.6 | 322.0 | 322.8 | 330.8 | 337.4 | 340.5 | 322.6 |
| 2016 | 330.8 | 331.3 | 332.0 | 335.8 | 333.8 | 330.7 | 336.1 | 337.7 | 340.1 | 342.8 | 345.0 | 345.6 | 336.8 |
| 2017 | 338.7 | 338.9 | 338.8 | 341.2 | 339.8 | 338.6 | 337.0 | 340.0 | 342.6 | 348.0 | 352.5 | 355.2 | 342.6 |
| 2018 | 347.0 | 349.6 | 350.5 | 350.5 | 349.2 | 350.9 | 351.8 | 355.5 | 356.2 | 363.3 | 368.0 | 369.6 | 355.2 |
| 2019 | 360.7 | 362.7 | 362.9 | 363.3 | 362.2 | 363.7 | 368.2 | 371.2 | 370.5 | 375.7 | 385.2 | 380.1 | 368.9 |
| **Education and Health Services** | | | | | | | | | | | | | |
| 2011 | 244.8 | 246.5 | 247.4 | 248.3 | 249.3 | 244.8 | 244.1 | 249.4 | 252.6 | 254.2 | 255.9 | 256.8 | 249.5 |
| 2012 | 253.9 | 256.3 | 256.9 | 257.1 | 257.2 | 253.8 | 251.0 | 257.2 | 259.3 | 261.2 | 262.8 | 264.2 | 257.6 |
| 2013 | 259.3 | 261.9 | 263.8 | 263.9 | 263.0 | 258.6 | 256.8 | 262.9 | 264.9 | 265.4 | 267.8 | 267.9 | 263.0 |
| 2014 | 265.8 | 267.8 | 268.3 | 269.2 | 269.0 | 265.8 | 265.0 | 271.6 | 273.4 | 276.6 | 278.7 | 280.2 | 271.0 |
| 2015 | 276.8 | 280.1 | 280.6 | 282.2 | 282.2 | 278.8 | 279.6 | 285.7 | 287.3 | 291.9 | 293.8 | 294.2 | 284.4 |
| 2016 | 290.8 | 292.7 | 293.6 | 295.3 | 293.9 | 289.5 | 290.3 | 297.0 | 301.0 | 302.9 | 305.4 | 306.6 | 296.6 |
| 2017 | 303.6 | 307.2 | 308.3 | 310.2 | 309.3 | 305.9 | 304.3 | 311.0 | 314.5 | 317.8 | 319.9 | 321.1 | 311.1 |
| 2018 | 318.1 | 322.1 | 323.1 | 323.7 | 322.0 | 314.2 | 315.3 | 324.6 | 328.0 | 331.4 | 334.3 | 334.6 | 324.3 |
| 2019 | 331.3 | 335.7 | 334.9 | 336.1 | 335.2 | 327.1 | 327.5 | 339.3 | 342.5 | 345.8 | 350.0 | 352.2 | 338.1 |
| **Leisure and Hospitality** | | | | | | | | | | | | | |
| 2011 | 173.7 | 176.9 | 181.7 | 182.4 | 180.4 | 175.9 | 171.1 | 173.3 | 176.8 | 177.8 | 181.4 | 180.7 | 177.7 |
| 2012 | 180.1 | 183.5 | 188.9 | 187.2 | 185.7 | 181.2 | 175.7 | 179.2 | 181.4 | 184.1 | 185.9 | 186.7 | 183.3 |
| 2013 | 185.1 | 190.7 | 195.2 | 195.6 | 193.2 | 188.1 | 184.6 | 188.7 | 190.1 | 193.4 | 196.7 | 197.3 | 191.6 |
| 2014 | 194.2 | 200.0 | 204.7 | 204.1 | 201.1 | 196.1 | 191.0 | 195.1 | 196.4 | 200.1 | 203.1 | 203.8 | 199.1 |
| 2015 | 204.8 | 207.7 | 212.2 | 212.9 | 210.4 | 204.7 | 201.4 | 204.3 | 205.6 | 210.3 | 212.2 | 212.2 | 208.2 |
| 2016 | 211.7 | 216.0 | 219.9 | 219.7 | 217.8 | 212.2 | 208.5 | 212.3 | 214.5 | 217.6 | 218.7 | 217.7 | 215.6 |
| 2017 | 216.2 | 221.7 | 227.7 | 229.8 | 226.6 | 221.6 | 216.7 | 220.2 | 222.0 | 225.2 | 226.4 | 226.8 | 223.4 |
| 2018 | 224.1 | 230.3 | 235.0 | 233.0 | 231.2 | 225.9 | 221.2 | 224.2 | 224.8 | 227.7 | 229.9 | 229.7 | 228.1 |
| 2019 | 229.7 | 233.8 | 238.1 | 236.1 | 233.3 | 228.4 | 224.8 | 229.2 | 229.5 | 234.7 | 235.8 | 238.0 | 232.6 |
| **Other Services** | | | | | | | | | | | | | |
| 2011 | 63.7 | 64.6 | 64.8 | 64.8 | 65.0 | 64.8 | 63.7 | 63.2 | 63.1 | 62.8 | 62.7 | 62.2 | 63.8 |
| 2012 | 61.6 | 61.8 | 62.2 | 62.1 | 62.7 | 63.0 | 62.0 | 61.6 | 62.0 | 62.3 | 62.9 | 63.0 | 62.3 |
| 2013 | 62.4 | 64.3 | 63.9 | 64.0 | 64.2 | 64.0 | 63.4 | 63.1 | 63.2 | 63.9 | 64.2 | 64.2 | 63.7 |
| 2014 | 63.0 | 63.8 | 64.2 | 64.0 | 63.9 | 63.7 | 62.9 | 62.5 | 62.8 | 63.6 | 63.6 | 63.4 | 63.5 |
| 2015 | 62.8 | 63.6 | 63.7 | 63.3 | 63.6 | 63.6 | 63.3 | 63.0 | 63.4 | 64.0 | 64.5 | 64.5 | 63.6 |
| 2016 | 64.6 | 65.5 | 65.8 | 65.7 | 66.5 | 66.0 | 65.1 | 64.9 | 65.4 | 65.8 | 66.2 | 65.5 | 65.6 |
| 2017 | 64.7 | 65.6 | 65.8 | 67.2 | 67.6 | 67.4 | 66.7 | 66.4 | 66.7 | 67.2 | 67.9 | 67.7 | 66.7 |
| 2018 | 67.1 | 68.2 | 68.4 | 69.3 | 69.6 | 69.7 | 69.1 | 68.9 | 69.4 | 69.9 | 70.3 | 69.1 | 69.1 |
| 2019 | 69.6 | 70.3 | 70.3 | 70.2 | 70.9 | 70.6 | 70.5 | 70.6 | 70.8 | 71.8 | 72.7 | 72.4 | 70.9 |
| **Government** | | | | | | | | | | | | | |
| 2011 | 232.5 | 238.3 | 238.2 | 238.7 | 238.4 | 202.9 | 192.4 | 219.0 | 234.2 | 237.3 | 238.2 | 233.9 | 228.7 |
| 2012 | 231.1 | 237.6 | 237.9 | 238.5 | 233.5 | 206.6 | 196.5 | 221.2 | 237.5 | 239.0 | 240.4 | 239.5 | 229.9 |
| 2013 | 234.7 | 239.9 | 239.2 | 239.9 | 236.7 | 207.2 | 197.9 | 220.9 | 237.8 | 240.9 | 241.0 | 238.7 | 231.2 |
| 2014 | 235.2 | 240.3 | 239.8 | 240.7 | 231.1 | 207.5 | 198.2 | 223.9 | 240.7 | 245.2 | 245.4 | 243.7 | 232.6 |
| 2015 | 235.3 | 243.5 | 242.9 | 242.5 | 235.8 | 207.6 | 200.2 | 222.1 | 239.9 | 245.1 | 246.5 | 242.1 | 233.6 |
| 2016 | 234.2 | 243.4 | 243.3 | 244.0 | 237.0 | 210.2 | 203.6 | 227.0 | 244.3 | 246.0 | 247.4 | 244.9 | 235.4 |
| 2017 | 237.4 | 246.0 | 245.8 | 246.7 | 237.6 | 217.0 | 207.6 | 231.4 | 245.0 | 247.8 | 248.6 | 244.7 | 238.0 |
| 2018 | 238.4 | 246.4 | 246.3 | 245.9 | 241.1 | 215.5 | 208.8 | 236.1 | 247.1 | 250.1 | 250.4 | 247.1 | 239.4 |
| 2019 | 245.4 | 250.0 | 249.9 | 249.1 | 244.5 | 218.1 | 211.8 | 243.9 | 251.1 | 254.0 | 254.5 | 255.1 | 244.0 |

## Employment by Industry: Boston-Cambridge-Newton, MA-NH, 2011–2019

(Numbers in thousands, not seasonally adjusted)

| Industry and year | January | February | March | April | May | June | July | August | September | October | November | December | Annual average |
|---|---|---|---|---|---|---|---|---|---|---|---|---|---|
| **Total Nonfarm** | | | | | | | | | | | | | |
| 2011 | 1,601.5 | 1,607.0 | 1,615.1 | 1,639.0 | 1,642.2 | 1,646.1 | 1,649.0 | 1,642.9 | 1,655.2 | 1,666.7 | 1,671.1 | 1,672.4 | 1,642.4 |
| 2012 | 1,631.4 | 1,636.7 | 1,647.3 | 1,661.8 | 1,669.7 | 1,683.3 | 1,677.0 | 1,673.5 | 1,682.0 | 1,695.8 | 1,703.1 | 1,700.8 | 1,671.9 |
| 2013 | 1,660.0 | 1,664.4 | 1,676.8 | 1,701.2 | 1,710.5 | 1,721.4 | 1,707.4 | 1,705.8 | 1,711.5 | 1,729.3 | 1,737.1 | 1,734.0 | 1,705.0 |
| 2014 | 1,687.3 | 1,697.6 | 1,706.9 | 1,731.8 | 1,742.3 | 1,751.8 | 1,746.5 | 1,738.7 | 1,747.7 | 1,767.8 | 1,776.2 | 1,777.4 | 1,739.3 |
| 2015 | 1,727.2 | 1,728.4 | 1,743.7 | 1,771.5 | 1,785.7 | 1,795.4 | 1,793.0 | 1,784.5 | 1,781.6 | 1,806.1 | 1,812.4 | 1,812.7 | 1,778.5 |
| 2016 | 1,764.0 | 1,774.7 | 1,785.8 | 1,811.6 | 1,819.7 | 1,829.2 | 1,835.8 | 1,829.1 | 1,829.8 | 1,838.5 | 1,845.1 | 1,846.8 | 1,817.5 |
| 2017 | 1,799.8 | 1,807.9 | 1,817.0 | 1,840.8 | 1,849.9 | 1,867.9 | 1,856.8 | 1,850.2 | 1,851.2 | 1,864.6 | 1,872.0 | 1,871.2 | 1,845.8 |
| 2018 | 1,825.4 | 1,842.6 | 1,849.1 | 1,870.6 | 1,881.7 | 1,899.2 | 1,887.0 | 1,878.3 | 1,879.2 | 1,896.1 | 1,901.5 | 1,902.9 | 1,876.1 |
| 2019 | 1,858.5 | 1,872.3 | 1,879.0 | 1,897.5 | 1,908.5 | 1,927.4 | 1,918.4 | 1,912.1 | 1,907.0 | 1,927.5 | 1,930.1 | 1,917.1 | 1,904.6 |
| **Total Private** | | | | | | | | | | | | | |
| 2011 | 1,408.1 | 1,411.7 | 1,419.8 | 1,444.2 | 1,447.0 | 1,451.6 | 1,465.0 | 1,461.4 | 1,462.7 | 1,473.3 | 1,477.4 | 1,477.5 | 1,450.0 |
| 2012 | 1,438.9 | 1,442.3 | 1,452.1 | 1,468.1 | 1,475.8 | 1,489.5 | 1,492.9 | 1,491.2 | 1,489.9 | 1,502.7 | 1,507.9 | 1,506.6 | 1,479.8 |
| 2013 | 1,469.5 | 1,470.8 | 1,483.0 | 1,506.1 | 1,514.9 | 1,526.4 | 1,524.3 | 1,524.6 | 1,518.9 | 1,532.8 | 1,538.9 | 1,536.4 | 1,512.2 |
| 2014 | 1,492.9 | 1,500.0 | 1,509.0 | 1,531.8 | 1,542.6 | 1,552.9 | 1,559.3 | 1,553.6 | 1,551.5 | 1,569.0 | 1,574.8 | 1,577.3 | 1,542.9 |
| 2015 | 1,531.6 | 1,530.9 | 1,544.5 | 1,571.7 | 1,586.4 | 1,596.4 | 1,605.5 | 1,601.1 | 1,587.0 | 1,608.6 | 1,613.6 | 1,613.5 | 1,582.6 |
| 2016 | 1,568.3 | 1,576.5 | 1,585.0 | 1,612.3 | 1,619.5 | 1,629.5 | 1,645.7 | 1,642.1 | 1,631.2 | 1,639.3 | 1,643.7 | 1,646.4 | 1,620.0 |
| 2017 | 1,603.2 | 1,609.5 | 1,618.6 | 1,641.7 | 1,650.1 | 1,668.5 | 1,670.8 | 1,666.6 | 1,655.4 | 1,667.0 | 1,673.0 | 1,672.3 | 1,649.7 |
| 2018 | 1,630.0 | 1,644.3 | 1,651.4 | 1,672.2 | 1,682.1 | 1,699.0 | 1,700.5 | 1,694.4 | 1,682.5 | 1,697.8 | 1,701.4 | 1,702.8 | 1,679.9 |
| 2019 | 1,662.9 | 1,673.5 | 1,680.0 | 1,697.9 | 1,707.4 | 1,726.2 | 1,730.4 | 1,726.8 | 1,709.3 | 1,728.0 | 1,728.7 | 1,716.0 | 1,707.3 |
| **Goods Producing** | | | | | | | | | | | | | |
| 2011 | 123.4 | 122.4 | 123.3 | 126.8 | 128.5 | 130.6 | 132.5 | 132.5 | 130.2 | 129.5 | 128.7 | 127.6 | 128.0 |
| 2012 | 124.1 | 122.8 | 123.8 | 127.4 | 129.1 | 132.2 | 134.2 | 134.2 | 133.0 | 133.6 | 133.3 | 132.6 | 130.0 |
| 2013 | 128.1 | 126.9 | 128.2 | 131.2 | 134.7 | 136.9 | 137.8 | 138.0 | 136.8 | 136.2 | 135.5 | 134.5 | 133.7 |
| 2014 | 130.1 | 129.1 | 129.7 | 132.3 | 135.5 | 137.9 | 139.9 | 139.8 | 138.4 | 138.3 | 138.7 | 138.5 | 135.7 |
| 2015 | 134.5 | 133.1 | 134.2 | 138.2 | 141.4 | 144.1 | 144.8 | 144.9 | 142.6 | 143.4 | 143.5 | 142.7 | 140.6 |
| 2016 | 139.4 | 137.1 | 138.2 | 141.3 | 143.4 | 145.9 | 147.4 | 147.1 | 145.6 | 145.5 | 144.9 | 144.4 | 143.4 |
| 2017 | 139.4 | 138.0 | 138.5 | 141.9 | 144.1 | 147.2 | 149.0 | 149.6 | 148.1 | 148.3 | 148.3 | 147.3 | 145.0 |
| 2018 | 143.5 | 143.4 | 144.4 | 147.8 | 150.4 | 153.8 | 154.3 | 153.4 | 152.4 | 152.4 | 151.6 | 151.4 | 149.9 |
| 2019 | 148.7 | 148.0 | 148.9 | 151.9 | 153.9 | 156.5 | 156.9 | 157.1 | 155.3 | 157.3 | 157.1 | 152.5 | 153.7 |
| **Service-Providing** | | | | | | | | | | | | | |
| 2011 | 1,478.1 | 1,484.6 | 1,491.8 | 1,512.2 | 1,513.7 | 1,515.5 | 1,516.5 | 1,510.4 | 1,525.0 | 1,537.2 | 1,542.4 | 1,544.8 | 1,514.4 |
| 2012 | 1,507.3 | 1,513.9 | 1,523.5 | 1,534.4 | 1,540.6 | 1,551.1 | 1,542.8 | 1,539.3 | 1,549.0 | 1,562.2 | 1,569.8 | 1,568.2 | 1,541.8 |
| 2013 | 1,531.9 | 1,537.5 | 1,548.6 | 1,570.0 | 1,575.8 | 1,584.5 | 1,569.6 | 1,567.8 | 1,574.7 | 1,593.1 | 1,601.6 | 1,599.5 | 1,571.2 |
| 2014 | 1,557.2 | 1,568.5 | 1,577.2 | 1,599.5 | 1,606.8 | 1,613.9 | 1,606.6 | 1,598.9 | 1,609.3 | 1,629.5 | 1,637.5 | 1,638.9 | 1,603.7 |
| 2015 | 1,592.7 | 1,595.3 | 1,609.5 | 1,633.3 | 1,644.3 | 1,651.3 | 1,648.2 | 1,639.6 | 1,639.0 | 1,662.7 | 1,668.9 | 1,670.0 | 1,637.9 |
| 2016 | 1,624.6 | 1,637.6 | 1,647.6 | 1,670.3 | 1,676.3 | 1,683.3 | 1,688.4 | 1,682.0 | 1,684.2 | 1,693.0 | 1,700.2 | 1,702.4 | 1,674.2 |
| 2017 | 1,660.4 | 1,669.9 | 1,678.5 | 1,698.9 | 1,705.8 | 1,720.7 | 1,707.8 | 1,700.6 | 1,703.1 | 1,716.3 | 1,723.7 | 1,723.9 | 1,700.8 |
| 2018 | 1,681.9 | 1,699.2 | 1,704.7 | 1,722.8 | 1,731.3 | 1,745.4 | 1,732.7 | 1,724.9 | 1,726.8 | 1,743.7 | 1,749.9 | 1,751.5 | 1,726.2 |
| 2019 | 1,709.8 | 1,724.3 | 1,730.1 | 1,745.6 | 1,754.6 | 1,770.9 | 1,761.5 | 1,755.0 | 1,751.7 | 1,770.2 | 1,773.0 | 1,764.6 | 1,750.9 |
| **Mining, Logging, and Construction** | | | | | | | | | | | | | |
| 2011 | 43.5 | 42.6 | 43.4 | 46.7 | 48.8 | 50.5 | 52.2 | 52.4 | 51.1 | 50.4 | 49.7 | 48.7 | 48.3 |
| 2012 | 45.2 | 44.1 | 45.1 | 47.9 | 49.5 | 51.7 | 53.9 | 54.1 | 53.4 | 53.8 | 53.5 | 52.4 | 50.4 |
| 2013 | 49.1 | 48.3 | 49.3 | 52.2 | 55.1 | 56.8 | 58.3 | 58.5 | 57.6 | 57.1 | 56.4 | 55.2 | 54.5 |
| 2014 | 52.0 | 51.2 | 51.7 | 54.6 | 57.7 | 59.6 | 61.5 | 61.6 | 60.7 | 60.9 | 61.0 | 60.5 | 57.8 |
| 2015 | 57.3 | 55.6 | 56.7 | 60.9 | 63.8 | 65.6 | 66.6 | 66.8 | 65.5 | 66.1 | 65.9 | 65.2 | 63.0 |
| 2016 | 62.6 | 60.9 | 62.0 | 65.1 | 67.0 | 68.7 | 70.0 | 69.5 | 68.5 | 68.2 | 67.7 | 66.9 | 66.4 |
| 2017 | 62.3 | 61.0 | 61.9 | 64.9 | 66.9 | 69.0 | 70.6 | 71.1 | 70.3 | 70.4 | 70.3 | 68.9 | 67.3 |
| 2018 | 65.7 | 66.0 | 66.8 | 70.1 | 72.5 | 74.7 | 75.3 | 74.7 | 74.3 | 74.2 | 73.3 | 72.6 | 71.7 |
| 2019 | 70.1 | 69.4 | 69.9 | 73.1 | 74.8 | 76.4 | 77.1 | 77.4 | 76.6 | 77.8 | 77.6 | 73.6 | 74.5 |
| **Manufacturing** | | | | | | | | | | | | | |
| 2011 | 79.9 | 79.8 | 79.9 | 80.1 | 79.7 | 80.1 | 80.3 | 80.1 | 79.1 | 79.1 | 79.0 | 78.9 | 79.7 |
| 2012 | 78.9 | 78.7 | 78.7 | 79.5 | 79.6 | 80.5 | 80.3 | 80.1 | 79.6 | 79.8 | 79.8 | 80.2 | 79.6 |
| 2013 | 79.0 | 78.6 | 78.9 | 79.0 | 79.6 | 80.1 | 79.5 | 79.5 | 79.2 | 79.1 | 79.1 | 79.3 | 79.2 |
| 2014 | 78.1 | 77.9 | 78.0 | 77.7 | 77.8 | 78.3 | 78.4 | 78.2 | 77.7 | 77.4 | 77.7 | 78.0 | 77.9 |
| 2015 | 77.2 | 77.5 | 77.5 | 77.3 | 77.6 | 78.5 | 78.2 | 78.1 | 77.1 | 77.3 | 77.6 | 77.5 | 77.6 |
| 2016 | 76.8 | 76.2 | 76.2 | 76.2 | 76.4 | 77.2 | 77.4 | 77.6 | 77.1 | 77.3 | 77.2 | 77.5 | 76.9 |
| 2017 | 77.1 | 77.0 | 76.6 | 77.0 | 77.2 | 78.2 | 78.4 | 78.5 | 77.8 | 77.9 | 78.0 | 78.4 | 77.7 |
| 2018 | 77.8 | 77.4 | 77.6 | 77.7 | 77.9 | 79.1 | 79.0 | 78.7 | 78.1 | 78.2 | 78.3 | 78.8 | 78.2 |
| 2019 | 78.6 | 78.6 | 79.0 | 78.8 | 79.1 | 80.1 | 79.8 | 79.7 | 78.7 | 79.5 | 79.5 | 78.9 | 79.2 |

## Employment by Industry: Boston-Cambridge-Newton, MA-NH, 2011–2019—*Continued*

(Numbers in thousands, not seasonally adjusted)

| Industry and year | January | February | March | April | May | June | July | August | September | October | November | December | Annual average |
|---|---|---|---|---|---|---|---|---|---|---|---|---|---|
| **Trade, Transportation, and Utilities** | | | | | | | | | | | | | |
| 2011 | 227.9 | 225.0 | 225.2 | 228.3 | 229.3 | 231.9 | 231.2 | 231.0 | 231.3 | 233.4 | 236.5 | 239.6 | 230.9 |
| 2012 | 230.8 | 226.5 | 227.1 | 227.5 | 230.3 | 233.6 | 231.2 | 230.7 | 230.8 | 234.2 | 238.9 | 240.9 | 231.9 |
| 2013 | 233.3 | 229.5 | 230.3 | 232.1 | 234.4 | 238.2 | 236.2 | 236.4 | 236.5 | 238.4 | 242.2 | 245.9 | 236.1 |
| 2014 | 238.5 | 235.2 | 235.6 | 237.0 | 239.5 | 242.7 | 239.8 | 236.9 | 240.4 | 243.9 | 248.2 | 251.8 | 240.8 |
| 2015 | 243.4 | 237.8 | 239.5 | 242.2 | 245.0 | 248.9 | 247.5 | 247.1 | 245.9 | 249.0 | 252.1 | 255.1 | 246.1 |
| 2016 | 246.9 | 243.4 | 243.9 | 246.4 | 248.7 | 252.6 | 251.4 | 250.8 | 249.7 | 250.3 | 253.4 | 257.3 | 249.6 |
| 2017 | 249.7 | 245.3 | 245.8 | 248.4 | 250.7 | 254.8 | 252.3 | 251.4 | 250.7 | 252.3 | 256.5 | 259.7 | 251.5 |
| 2018 | 251.5 | 247.9 | 247.0 | 248.1 | 250.7 | 255.3 | 252.5 | 251.4 | 250.2 | 252.1 | 256.7 | 259.8 | 251.9 |
| 2019 | 252.4 | 248.6 | 248.4 | 248.5 | 251.2 | 254.9 | 252.9 | 252.4 | 250.5 | 253.3 | 255.3 | 257.5 | 252.2 |
| **Wholesale Trade** | | | | | | | | | | | | | |
| 2011 | 52.8 | 52.7 | 52.9 | 53.5 | 53.4 | 53.5 | 54.0 | 53.9 | 53.3 | 53.5 | 53.3 | 53.3 | 53.3 |
| 2012 | 52.8 | 52.6 | 52.7 | 53.0 | 53.2 | 53.7 | 54.0 | 54.0 | 53.4 | 54.2 | 54.9 | 54.9 | 53.6 |
| 2013 | 54.6 | 54.5 | 54.7 | 55.0 | 55.0 | 55.5 | 56.1 | 56.1 | 55.7 | 56.0 | 56.0 | 56.0 | 55.4 |
| 2014 | 55.7 | 55.6 | 55.6 | 56.0 | 56.2 | 56.7 | 56.8 | 56.6 | 56.2 | 56.5 | 56.7 | 56.7 | 56.3 |
| 2015 | 56.2 | 55.9 | 55.9 | 56.6 | 56.9 | 57.6 | 58.5 | 58.3 | 57.8 | 58.2 | 58.4 | 58.5 | 57.4 |
| 2016 | 57.8 | 57.8 | 57.7 | 58.2 | 58.3 | 58.8 | 59.9 | 59.8 | 59.1 | 59.3 | 59.3 | 59.3 | 58.8 |
| 2017 | 58.9 | 58.8 | 58.9 | 59.0 | 59.3 | 59.9 | 60.0 | 59.8 | 59.0 | 59.0 | 59.0 | 59.1 | 59.2 |
| 2018 | 58.1 | 58.3 | 58.5 | 58.2 | 58.3 | 59.0 | 58.9 | 58.6 | 57.9 | 58.2 | 58.1 | 58.2 | 58.4 |
| 2019 | 57.6 | 57.5 | 57.5 | 57.2 | 57.5 | 57.9 | 58.4 | 58.4 | 57.5 | 57.6 | 57.7 | 58.1 | 57.7 |
| **Retail Trade** | | | | | | | | | | | | | |
| 2011 | 137.4 | 134.6 | 134.4 | 135.8 | 136.4 | 138.1 | 138.2 | 138.8 | 137.7 | 140.1 | 143.6 | 146.4 | 138.5 |
| 2012 | 139.2 | 135.1 | 135.5 | 135.5 | 137.5 | 139.6 | 138.4 | 138.6 | 137.2 | 140.0 | 144.6 | 145.9 | 138.9 |
| 2013 | 140.0 | 136.3 | 136.7 | 137.7 | 139.2 | 141.4 | 140.5 | 141.3 | 139.8 | 141.4 | 145.5 | 148.6 | 140.7 |
| 2014 | 142.4 | 139.3 | 139.3 | 140.3 | 141.8 | 143.9 | 142.6 | 140.7 | 142.1 | 145.5 | 149.6 | 152.2 | 143.3 |
| 2015 | 146.0 | 141.2 | 142.3 | 143.5 | 145.2 | 147.5 | 146.6 | 146.8 | 144.1 | 146.9 | 150.3 | 152.5 | 146.1 |
| 2016 | 146.5 | 143.4 | 143.6 | 144.9 | 146.3 | 148.9 | 148.3 | 148.7 | 145.9 | 147.0 | 150.2 | 153.3 | 147.3 |
| 2017 | 147.5 | 143.6 | 143.9 | 145.5 | 146.6 | 149.0 | 148.6 | 148.5 | 145.9 | 147.8 | 152.0 | 154.1 | 147.8 |
| 2018 | 148.8 | 145.3 | 144.2 | 144.9 | 146.7 | 149.6 | 149.3 | 148.8 | 146.2 | 147.7 | 152.5 | 154.6 | 148.2 |
| 2019 | 149.8 | 145.7 | 145.2 | 144.9 | 146.5 | 148.8 | 148.5 | 148.6 | 145.6 | 148.5 | 150.9 | 152.2 | 147.9 |
| **Transportation and Utilities** | | | | | | | | | | | | | |
| 2011 | 37.7 | 37.7 | 37.9 | 39.0 | 39.5 | 40.3 | 39.0 | 38.3 | 40.3 | 39.8 | 39.6 | 39.9 | 39.1 |
| 2012 | 38.8 | 38.8 | 38.9 | 39.0 | 39.6 | 40.3 | 38.8 | 38.1 | 40.2 | 40.0 | 39.4 | 40.1 | 39.3 |
| 2013 | 38.7 | 38.7 | 38.9 | 39.4 | 40.2 | 41.3 | 39.6 | 39.0 | 41.0 | 41.0 | 40.7 | 41.3 | 40.0 |
| 2014 | 40.4 | 40.3 | 40.7 | 40.7 | 41.5 | 42.1 | 40.4 | 39.6 | 42.1 | 41.9 | 41.9 | 42.9 | 41.2 |
| 2015 | 41.2 | 40.7 | 41.3 | 42.1 | 42.9 | 43.8 | 42.4 | 42.0 | 44.0 | 43.9 | 43.4 | 44.1 | 42.7 |
| 2016 | 42.6 | 42.2 | 42.6 | 43.3 | 44.1 | 44.9 | 43.2 | 42.3 | 44.7 | 44.0 | 43.9 | 44.7 | 43.5 |
| 2017 | 43.3 | 42.9 | 43.0 | 43.9 | 44.8 | 45.9 | 43.7 | 43.1 | 45.8 | 45.5 | 45.5 | 46.5 | 44.5 |
| 2018 | 44.6 | 44.3 | 44.3 | 45.0 | 45.7 | 46.7 | 44.3 | 44.0 | 46.1 | 46.2 | 46.1 | 47.0 | 45.4 |
| 2019 | 45.0 | 45.4 | 45.7 | 46.4 | 47.2 | 48.2 | 46.0 | 45.4 | 47.4 | 47.2 | 46.7 | 47.2 | 46.5 |
| **Information** | | | | | | | | | | | | | |
| 2011 | 53.0 | 53.1 | 53.3 | 53.4 | 53.9 | 54.6 | 55.8 | 54.2 | 55.4 | 55.7 | 55.8 | 56.1 | 54.5 |
| 2012 | 54.0 | 54.0 | 54.0 | 54.4 | 54.5 | 55.9 | 56.7 | 56.0 | 54.3 | 54.5 | 54.4 | 54.2 | 54.7 |
| 2013 | 53.9 | 53.8 | 53.7 | 54.5 | 54.7 | 55.8 | 56.1 | 55.9 | 55.3 | 55.1 | 56.4 | 55.3 | 55.0 |
| 2014 | 54.5 | 54.7 | 54.7 | 55.1 | 55.3 | 56.3 | 56.4 | 56.3 | 55.8 | 56.0 | 56.0 | 56.3 | 55.6 |
| 2015 | 56.2 | 56.0 | 56.4 | 56.5 | 56.6 | 57.5 | 58.0 | 57.8 | 57.2 | 57.6 | 57.5 | 57.7 | 57.1 |
| 2016 | 57.6 | 57.4 | 57.5 | 58.1 | 57.1 | 58.7 | 59.4 | 59.7 | 59.0 | 59.3 | 59.3 | 59.6 | 58.6 |
| 2017 | 59.0 | 59.2 | 59.4 | 59.5 | 59.6 | 60.3 | 60.6 | 60.4 | 59.9 | 60.1 | 60.2 | 60.3 | 59.9 |
| 2018 | 59.8 | 60.2 | 60.0 | 59.9 | 59.5 | 60.6 | 60.9 | 61.0 | 60.0 | 60.5 | 60.5 | 60.5 | 60.3 |
| 2019 | 60.2 | 60.2 | 60.3 | 60.2 | 60.9 | 62.1 | 63.9 | 64.1 | 62.3 | 62.5 | 63.1 | 63.1 | 61.9 |
| **Financial Activities** | | | | | | | | | | | | | |
| 2011 | 143.4 | 142.8 | 142.6 | 143.0 | 143.5 | 144.6 | 146.1 | 146.3 | 144.7 | 144.0 | 143.8 | 144.2 | 144.1 |
| 2012 | 143.0 | 143.2 | 143.1 | 143.1 | 143.8 | 145.7 | 146.1 | 146.3 | 144.2 | 144.2 | 144.1 | 144.6 | 144.3 |
| 2013 | 143.0 | 143.5 | 143.8 | 143.6 | 144.0 | 145.6 | 146.3 | 146.8 | 144.5 | 144.4 | 144.6 | 145.0 | 144.6 |
| 2014 | 143.4 | 143.5 | 143.5 | 143.9 | 144.7 | 146.7 | 147.3 | 147.4 | 145.7 | 146.5 | 146.8 | 147.5 | 145.6 |
| 2015 | 146.2 | 146.2 | 146.1 | 146.4 | 147.2 | 148.9 | 151.9 | 152.4 | 149.5 | 151.0 | 151.4 | 151.8 | 149.1 |
| 2016 | 150.5 | 150.9 | 150.7 | 151.3 | 152.0 | 153.8 | 156.3 | 156.3 | 153.4 | 153.2 | 153.2 | 154.2 | 153.0 |
| 2017 | 152.2 | 152.7 | 152.4 | 152.3 | 153.0 | 155.6 | 155.8 | 156.0 | 153.4 | 153.7 | 153.5 | 154.3 | 153.7 |
| 2018 | 152.4 | 153.0 | 152.9 | 153.6 | 153.7 | 156.2 | 156.6 | 156.5 | 154.3 | 154.3 | 154.6 | 154.9 | 154.4 |
| 2019 | 154.2 | 154.6 | 154.3 | 154.4 | 154.5 | 156.5 | 158.9 | 158.5 | 155.2 | 154.8 | 155.6 | 155.2 | 155.6 |

## Employment by Industry: Boston-Cambridge-Newton, MA-NH, 2011–2019—*Continued*

(Numbers in thousands, not seasonally adjusted)

| Industry and year | January | February | March | April | May | June | July | August | September | October | November | December | Annual average |
|---|---|---|---|---|---|---|---|---|---|---|---|---|---|
| **Professional and Business Services** | | | | | | | | | | | | | |
| 2011 | 296.5 | 296.6 | 297.5 | 305.1 | 305.3 | 308.4 | 312.1 | 310.6 | 309.0 | 311.6 | 312.3 | 313.1 | 306.5 |
| 2012 | 305.4 | 305.9 | 308.5 | 314.0 | 315.4 | 321.0 | 322.7 | 322.7 | 320.9 | 323.8 | 324.9 | 324.7 | 317.5 |
| 2013 | 317.9 | 319.7 | 321.5 | 328.4 | 330.0 | 334.6 | 336.2 | 336.1 | 332.9 | 336.0 | 337.6 | 337.0 | 330.7 |
| 2014 | 329.4 | 329.4 | 330.2 | 336.5 | 338.5 | 343.1 | 345.5 | 345.4 | 342.3 | 344.8 | 345.3 | 345.3 | 339.6 |
| 2015 | 338.6 | 338.1 | 340.2 | 348.2 | 350.9 | 355.8 | 358.3 | 357.8 | 352.9 | 357.0 | 357.6 | 357.1 | 351.0 |
| 2016 | 347.7 | 349.7 | 351.2 | 359.2 | 360.1 | 365.4 | 370.4 | 369.8 | 365.4 | 368.0 | 368.9 | 368.7 | 362.0 |
| 2017 | 360.7 | 361.9 | 364.1 | 369.8 | 370.6 | 377.3 | 379.2 | 378.1 | 373.4 | 375.5 | 377.6 | 376.2 | 372.0 |
| 2018 | 369.6 | 372.1 | 374.0 | 379.6 | 381.7 | 388.7 | 392.3 | 392.3 | 386.6 | 389.3 | 392.7 | 393.1 | 384.3 |
| 2019 | 383.3 | 386.4 | 386.9 | 393.2 | 393.9 | 400.9 | 403.3 | 403.3 | 397.3 | 401.6 | 400.8 | 397.7 | 395.7 |
| **Education and Health Services** | | | | | | | | | | | | | |
| 2011 | 359.9 | 369.0 | 370.9 | 370.7 | 364.9 | 353.1 | 356.3 | 355.3 | 366.2 | 374.7 | 378.1 | 377.4 | 366.4 |
| 2012 | 368.2 | 377.2 | 378.8 | 377.2 | 371.8 | 361.5 | 362.6 | 361.5 | 372.2 | 380.7 | 383.7 | 382.9 | 373.2 |
| 2013 | 373.8 | 380.1 | 382.5 | 385.5 | 380.0 | 370.4 | 368.8 | 366.3 | 374.3 | 383.3 | 386.1 | 385.3 | 378.0 |
| 2014 | 372.9 | 384.8 | 386.6 | 391.8 | 386.6 | 376.1 | 379.5 | 377.0 | 384.8 | 395.2 | 398.9 | 397.8 | 386.0 |
| 2015 | 382.2 | 393.4 | 396.4 | 401.3 | 397.9 | 386.6 | 388.3 | 385.7 | 392.4 | 403.1 | 406.1 | 404.3 | 394.8 |
| 2016 | 391.0 | 403.6 | 404.6 | 407.8 | 404.3 | 391.7 | 397.1 | 394.7 | 403.2 | 409.7 | 413.1 | 412.0 | 402.7 |
| 2017 | 400.2 | 412.1 | 413.6 | 416.9 | 413.4 | 404.3 | 405.2 | 402.9 | 410.7 | 417.2 | 419.9 | 419.3 | 411.3 |
| 2018 | 406.3 | 419.1 | 421.0 | 425.3 | 421.5 | 411.4 | 411.3 | 408.2 | 416.7 | 426.3 | 428.6 | 427.8 | 418.6 |
| 2019 | 415.6 | 428.7 | 430.0 | 432.3 | 427.5 | 417.3 | 417.6 | 415.8 | 423.9 | 434.7 | 438.7 | 433.1 | 426.3 |
| **Leisure and Hospitality** | | | | | | | | | | | | | |
| 2011 | 142.5 | 140.7 | 144.1 | 152.8 | 157.0 | 162.1 | 163.9 | 164.7 | 161.4 | 159.8 | 157.3 | 154.8 | 155.1 |
| 2012 | 150.0 | 149.0 | 152.0 | 159.1 | 164.7 | 171.2 | 171.0 | 171.9 | 168.1 | 165.4 | 162.4 | 160.8 | 162.1 |
| 2013 | 154.8 | 152.6 | 157.1 | 164.4 | 170.4 | 176.9 | 174.7 | 177.1 | 172.7 | 173.5 | 170.5 | 167.7 | 167.7 |
| 2014 | 159.7 | 158.8 | 163.3 | 169.0 | 175.5 | 181.1 | 181.6 | 181.9 | 177.3 | 177.3 | 174.0 | 173.2 | 172.7 |
| 2015 | 165.3 | 161.9 | 165.8 | 172.7 | 180.5 | 185.7 | 187.3 | 186.5 | 179.9 | 180.8 | 178.8 | 178.3 | 177.0 |
| 2016 | 170.2 | 169.4 | 172.9 | 181.4 | 186.7 | 192.6 | 193.9 | 194.4 | 187.9 | 186.1 | 183.7 | 183.2 | 183.5 |
| 2017 | 176.2 | 174.4 | 178.1 | 186.1 | 191.2 | 199.2 | 198.6 | 198.3 | 191.8 | 192.5 | 189.4 | 187.8 | 188.6 |
| 2018 | 180.0 | 181.5 | 184.6 | 189.4 | 195.5 | 201.6 | 201.5 | 200.6 | 194.1 | 194.6 | 188.5 | 187.2 | 191.6 |
| 2019 | 181.5 | 179.7 | 183.2 | 188.7 | 196.3 | 206.7 | 205.1 | 204.2 | 196.1 | 194.6 | 189.8 | 188.7 | 192.9 |
| **Other Services** | | | | | | | | | | | | | |
| 2011 | 61.5 | 62.1 | 62.9 | 64.1 | 64.6 | 66.3 | 67.1 | 66.8 | 64.5 | 64.6 | 64.9 | 64.7 | 64.5 |
| 2012 | 63.4 | 63.7 | 64.8 | 65.4 | 66.2 | 68.4 | 68.4 | 67.9 | 66.4 | 66.3 | 66.2 | 65.9 | 66.1 |
| 2013 | 64.7 | 64.7 | 65.9 | 66.4 | 66.7 | 68.0 | 68.2 | 68.0 | 65.9 | 65.9 | 66.0 | 65.7 | 66.3 |
| 2014 | 64.4 | 64.5 | 65.4 | 66.2 | 67.0 | 69.0 | 69.3 | 68.9 | 66.8 | 67.0 | 66.9 | 66.9 | 66.9 |
| 2015 | 65.2 | 64.4 | 65.9 | 66.2 | 66.9 | 68.9 | 69.4 | 68.9 | 66.6 | 66.7 | 66.6 | 66.5 | 66.9 |
| 2016 | 65.0 | 65.0 | 66.0 | 66.8 | 67.2 | 68.8 | 69.8 | 69.3 | 67.0 | 67.2 | 67.2 | 67.0 | 67.2 |
| 2017 | 65.8 | 65.9 | 66.7 | 66.8 | 67.5 | 69.8 | 70.1 | 69.9 | 67.4 | 67.4 | 67.6 | 67.4 | 67.7 |
| 2018 | 66.9 | 67.1 | 67.5 | 68.5 | 69.1 | 71.4 | 71.1 | 71.0 | 68.2 | 68.3 | 68.2 | 68.1 | 68.8 |
| 2019 | 67.0 | 67.3 | 68.0 | 68.7 | 69.2 | 71.3 | 71.8 | 71.4 | 68.7 | 69.2 | 68.3 | 68.2 | 69.1 |
| **Government** | | | | | | | | | | | | | |
| 2011 | 193.4 | 195.3 | 195.3 | 194.8 | 195.2 | 194.5 | 184.0 | 181.5 | 192.5 | 193.4 | 193.7 | 194.9 | 192.4 |
| 2012 | 192.5 | 194.4 | 195.2 | 193.7 | 193.9 | 193.8 | 184.1 | 182.3 | 192.1 | 193.1 | 195.2 | 194.2 | 192.0 |
| 2013 | 190.5 | 193.6 | 193.8 | 195.1 | 195.6 | 195.0 | 183.1 | 181.2 | 192.6 | 196.5 | 198.2 | 197.6 | 192.7 |
| 2014 | 194.4 | 197.6 | 197.9 | 200.0 | 199.7 | 198.9 | 187.2 | 185.1 | 196.2 | 198.8 | 201.4 | 200.1 | 196.4 |
| 2015 | 195.6 | 197.5 | 199.2 | 199.8 | 199.3 | 199.0 | 187.5 | 183.4 | 194.6 | 197.5 | 198.8 | 199.2 | 196.0 |
| 2016 | 195.7 | 198.2 | 200.8 | 199.3 | 200.2 | 199.7 | 190.1 | 187.0 | 198.6 | 199.2 | 201.4 | 200.4 | 197.6 |
| 2017 | 196.6 | 198.4 | 198.4 | 199.1 | 199.8 | 199.4 | 186.0 | 183.6 | 195.8 | 197.6 | 199.0 | 198.9 | 196.1 |
| 2018 | 195.4 | 198.3 | 197.7 | 198.4 | 199.6 | 200.2 | 186.5 | 183.9 | 196.7 | 198.3 | 200.1 | 200.1 | 196.3 |
| 2019 | 195.6 | 198.8 | 199.0 | 199.6 | 201.1 | 201.2 | 188.0 | 185.3 | 197.7 | 199.5 | 201.4 | 201.1 | 197.4 |

## Employment by Industry: San Francisco-Oakland-Hayward, CA, 2011–2019

(Numbers in thousands, not seasonally adjusted)

| Industry and year | January | February | March | April | May | June | July | August | September | October | November | December | Annual average |
|---|---|---|---|---|---|---|---|---|---|---|---|---|---|
| **Total Nonfarm** | | | | | | | | | | | | | |
| 2011 | 1,914.8 | 1,922.7 | 1,928.0 | 1,946.7 | 1,954.8 | 1,957.1 | 1,955.6 | 1,959.5 | 1,970.2 | 1,983.3 | 1,991.8 | 1,997.6 | 1,956.8 |
| 2012 | 1,963.8 | 1,977.4 | 1,989.3 | 2,013.5 | 2,028.7 | 2,040.0 | 2,033.4 | 2,040.4 | 2,045.1 | 2,061.8 | 2,076.0 | 2,083.7 | 2,029.4 |
| 2013 | 2,040.8 | 2,058.4 | 2,070.0 | 2,082.7 | 2,093.6 | 2,095.0 | 2,090.4 | 2,100.7 | 2,102.4 | 2,122.4 | 2,140.8 | 2,143.9 | 2,095.1 |
| 2014 | 2,105.5 | 2,122.2 | 2,132.2 | 2,146.8 | 2,160.3 | 2,166.2 | 2,161.1 | 2,170.9 | 2,174.6 | 2,192.3 | 2,208.8 | 2,216.5 | 2,163.1 |
| 2015 | 2,184.2 | 2,197.3 | 2,212.7 | 2,226.1 | 2,237.8 | 2,246.1 | 2,253.0 | 2,262.8 | 2,264.2 | 2,286.7 | 2,297.5 | 2,304.6 | 2,247.8 |
| 2016 | 2,270.7 | 2,289.3 | 2,294.3 | 2,316.9 | 2,322.5 | 2,327.4 | 2,331.6 | 2,337.2 | 2,341.9 | 2,359.5 | 2,369.9 | 2,371.6 | 2,327.7 |
| 2017 | 2,330.7 | 2,347.1 | 2,362.2 | 2,365.1 | 2,376.4 | 2,388.7 | 2,377.9 | 2,380.8 | 2,384.8 | 2,402.7 | 2,415.1 | 2,420.8 | 2,379.4 |
| 2018 | 2,378.5 | 2,399.8 | 2,410.3 | 2,418.0 | 2,427.7 | 2,442.5 | 2,430.9 | 2,441.2 | 2,438.6 | 2,457.8 | 2,470.9 | 2,476.4 | 2,432.7 |
| 2019 | 2,429.8 | 2,447.8 | 2,459.2 | 2,465.3 | 2,476.9 | 2,489.4 | 2,484.3 | 2,494.7 | 2,485.1 | 2,502.2 | 2,512.8 | 2,514.6 | 2,480.2 |
| **Total Private** | | | | | | | | | | | | | |
| 2011 | 1,613.8 | 1,619.0 | 1,621.9 | 1,640.0 | 1,647.9 | 1,651.9 | 1,665.2 | 1,669.2 | 1,677.2 | 1,683.6 | 1,691.0 | 1,698.9 | 1,656.6 |
| 2012 | 1,667.6 | 1,678.3 | 1,687.5 | 1,711.5 | 1,726.4 | 1,738.9 | 1,742.7 | 1,751.6 | 1,752.7 | 1,765.0 | 1,774.5 | 1,783.7 | 1,731.7 |
| 2013 | 1,745.1 | 1,760.6 | 1,768.3 | 1,780.1 | 1,791.0 | 1,797.0 | 1,802.9 | 1,812.1 | 1,808.4 | 1,822.4 | 1,837.9 | 1,845.2 | 1,797.6 |
| 2014 | 1,806.6 | 1,821.1 | 1,829.9 | 1,841.2 | 1,853.5 | 1,861.5 | 1,866.0 | 1,877.2 | 1,875.5 | 1,886.6 | 1,899.3 | 1,907.9 | 1,860.5 |
| 2015 | 1,878.4 | 1,890.3 | 1,902.3 | 1,913.6 | 1,924.8 | 1,935.4 | 1,953.1 | 1,960.3 | 1,957.0 | 1,974.3 | 1,982.5 | 1,991.0 | 1,938.6 |
| 2016 | 1,958.4 | 1,974.7 | 1,976.6 | 1,997.9 | 2,001.7 | 2,010.1 | 2,026.7 | 2,029.2 | 2,026.3 | 2,037.7 | 2,045.8 | 2,048.6 | 2,011.1 |
| 2017 | 2,011.7 | 2,026.2 | 2,038.7 | 2,041.5 | 2,050.8 | 2,066.9 | 2,070.0 | 2,072.0 | 2,067.4 | 2,078.9 | 2,089.3 | 2,096.2 | 2,059.1 |
| 2018 | 2,057.7 | 2,076.6 | 2,084.9 | 2,091.5 | 2,100.5 | 2,116.2 | 2,123.6 | 2,129.2 | 2,119.8 | 2,133.5 | 2,144.1 | 2,150.0 | 2,110.6 |
| 2019 | 2,109.9 | 2,124.0 | 2,133.9 | 2,139.4 | 2,149.5 | 2,161.8 | 2,173.4 | 2,179.3 | 2,164.5 | 2,177.3 | 2,184.5 | 2,188.2 | 2,157.1 |
| **Goods Producing** | | | | | | | | | | | | | |
| 2011 | 192.6 | 192.3 | 190.4 | 193.0 | 195.0 | 196.9 | 202.0 | 202.8 | 201.8 | 201.9 | 200.8 | 199.9 | 197.5 |
| 2012 | 196.1 | 196.4 | 196.4 | 198.0 | 202.1 | 205.2 | 208.3 | 208.8 | 209.3 | 209.3 | 208.4 | 207.4 | 203.8 |
| 2013 | 203.7 | 205.6 | 206.4 | 207.2 | 208.8 | 211.3 | 214.2 | 216.2 | 215.7 | 216.7 | 216.8 | 214.6 | 211.4 |
| 2014 | 211.4 | 213.2 | 213.9 | 215.5 | 217.7 | 220.5 | 223.6 | 225.6 | 225.9 | 225.9 | 226.7 | 224.5 | 220.4 |
| 2015 | 225.3 | 226.5 | 228.8 | 227.4 | 229.9 | 232.9 | 237.4 | 239.2 | 239.6 | 241.2 | 241.3 | 240.2 | 234.1 |
| 2016 | 238.3 | 240.5 | 239.3 | 242.9 | 243.9 | 246.8 | 251.7 | 252.9 | 253.4 | 254.1 | 253.2 | 251.3 | 247.4 |
| 2017 | 247.8 | 249.9 | 252.6 | 252.5 | 255.8 | 258.9 | 263.0 | 263.5 | 263.2 | 264.2 | 264.3 | 263.7 | 258.3 |
| 2018 | 260.9 | 265.7 | 265.1 | 267.4 | 268.7 | 270.7 | 274.0 | 273.7 | 273.2 | 273.8 | 273.2 | 272.0 | 269.9 |
| 2019 | 265.8 | 267.0 | 269.3 | 269.3 | 271.2 | 273.7 | 275.0 | 275.1 | 274.0 | 273.7 | 272.3 | 270.3 | 271.4 |
| **Service-Providing** | | | | | | | | | | | | | |
| 2011 | 1,722.2 | 1,730.4 | 1,737.6 | 1,753.7 | 1,759.8 | 1,760.2 | 1,753.6 | 1,756.7 | 1,768.4 | 1,781.4 | 1,791.0 | 1,797.7 | 1,759.4 |
| 2012 | 1,767.7 | 1,781.0 | 1,792.9 | 1,815.5 | 1,826.6 | 1,834.8 | 1,825.1 | 1,831.6 | 1,835.8 | 1,852.5 | 1,867.6 | 1,876.3 | 1,825.6 |
| 2013 | 1,837.1 | 1,852.8 | 1,863.6 | 1,875.5 | 1,884.8 | 1,883.7 | 1,876.2 | 1,884.5 | 1,886.7 | 1,905.7 | 1,924.0 | 1,929.3 | 1,883.7 |
| 2014 | 1,894.1 | 1,909.0 | 1,918.3 | 1,931.3 | 1,942.6 | 1,945.7 | 1,937.5 | 1,945.3 | 1,948.7 | 1,966.4 | 1,982.1 | 1,992.0 | 1,942.8 |
| 2015 | 1,958.9 | 1,970.8 | 1,983.9 | 1,998.7 | 2,007.9 | 2,013.2 | 2,015.6 | 2,023.6 | 2,024.6 | 2,045.5 | 2,056.2 | 2,064.4 | 2,013.6 |
| 2016 | 2,032.4 | 2,048.8 | 2,055.0 | 2,074.0 | 2,078.6 | 2,080.6 | 2,079.9 | 2,084.3 | 2,088.5 | 2,105.4 | 2,116.7 | 2,120.3 | 2,080.4 |
| 2017 | 2,082.9 | 2,097.2 | 2,109.6 | 2,112.6 | 2,120.6 | 2,129.8 | 2,114.9 | 2,117.3 | 2,121.6 | 2,138.5 | 2,150.8 | 2,157.1 | 2,121.1 |
| 2018 | 2,117.6 | 2,134.1 | 2,145.2 | 2,150.6 | 2,159.0 | 2,171.8 | 2,156.9 | 2,167.5 | 2,165.4 | 2,184.0 | 2,197.7 | 2,204.4 | 2,162.9 |
| 2019 | 2,164.0 | 2,180.8 | 2,189.9 | 2,196.0 | 2,205.7 | 2,215.7 | 2,209.3 | 2,219.6 | 2,211.1 | 2,228.5 | 2,240.5 | 2,244.3 | 2,208.8 |
| **Mining and Logging** | | | | | | | | | | | | | |
| 2011 | 0.8 | 0.8 | 0.8 | 0.8 | 0.8 | 0.8 | 0.7 | 0.7 | 0.6 | 0.7 | 0.6 | 0.6 | 0.7 |
| 2012 | 0.6 | 0.6 | 0.6 | 0.6 | 0.6 | 0.6 | 0.6 | 0.7 | 0.6 | 0.6 | 0.6 | 0.6 | 0.6 |
| 2013 | 0.5 | 0.5 | 0.5 | 0.6 | 0.5 | 0.5 | 0.5 | 0.5 | 0.5 | 0.5 | 0.4 | 0.4 | 0.5 |
| 2014 | 0.5 | 0.5 | 0.5 | 0.4 | 0.4 | 0.4 | 0.5 | 0.5 | 0.5 | 0.5 | 0.5 | 0.4 | 0.5 |
| 2015 | 0.5 | 0.4 | 0.4 | 0.4 | 0.4 | 0.4 | 0.4 | 0.4 | 0.4 | 0.4 | 0.4 | 0.4 | 0.4 |
| 2016 | 0.4 | 0.4 | 0.4 | 0.4 | 0.4 | 0.4 | 0.4 | 0.4 | 0.4 | 0.4 | 0.4 | 0.3 | 0.4 |
| 2017 | 0.3 | 0.3 | 0.3 | 0.3 | 0.3 | 0.3 | 0.3 | 0.3 | 0.3 | 0.3 | 0.3 | 0.3 | 0.3 |
| 2018 | 0.3 | 0.3 | 0.3 | 0.3 | 0.3 | 0.3 | 0.3 | 0.3 | 0.3 | 0.3 | 0.3 | 0.3 | 0.3 |
| 2019 | 0.3 | 0.3 | 0.3 | 0.3 | 0.3 | 0.3 | 0.3 | 0.3 | 0.3 | 0.3 | 0.3 | 0.3 | 0.3 |
| **Construction** | | | | | | | | | | | | | |
| 2011 | 75.5 | 75.2 | 73.1 | 75.4 | 77.2 | 78.8 | 83.1 | 84.3 | 84.7 | 84.8 | 83.9 | 83.0 | 79.9 |
| 2012 | 80.3 | 80.5 | 79.9 | 80.9 | 84.4 | 87.1 | 89.7 | 90.2 | 90.7 | 91.2 | 90.6 | 89.6 | 86.3 |
| 2013 | 87.2 | 88.6 | 88.9 | 89.5 | 90.7 | 92.6 | 94.9 | 96.0 | 95.5 | 96.7 | 96.3 | 94.1 | 92.6 |
| 2014 | 91.7 | 93.1 | 93.4 | 94.4 | 96.0 | 98.0 | 100.0 | 101.3 | 101.1 | 100.4 | 100.4 | 97.8 | 97.3 |
| 2015 | 99.7 | 100.7 | 102.4 | 100.8 | 102.6 | 104.2 | 107.0 | 108.5 | 108.5 | 109.8 | 110.1 | 108.7 | 105.3 |
| 2016 | 106.9 | 108.9 | 107.4 | 110.6 | 111.3 | 112.8 | 116.1 | 116.8 | 117.3 | 118.5 | 117.3 | 114.9 | 113.2 |
| 2017 | 111.6 | 112.9 | 114.4 | 115.1 | 117.1 | 118.9 | 121.3 | 121.3 | 121.3 | 121.9 | 122.2 | 121.0 | 118.3 |
| 2018 | 118.5 | 122.5 | 121.6 | 123.6 | 124.7 | 125.9 | 127.4 | 127.1 | 127.6 | 128.4 | 127.6 | 125.8 | 125.1 |
| 2019 | 120.5 | 121.5 | 123.7 | 124.7 | 126.9 | 129.3 | 130.6 | 130.9 | 130.7 | 130.1 | 128.3 | 125.7 | 126.9 |

## Employment by Industry: San Francisco-Oakland-Hayward, CA, 2011–2019—*Continued*

(Numbers in thousands, not seasonally adjusted)

| Industry and year | January | February | March | April | May | June | July | August | September | October | November | December | Annual average |
|---|---|---|---|---|---|---|---|---|---|---|---|---|---|
| **Manufacturing** | | | | | | | | | | | | | |
| 2011 | 116.3 | 116.3 | 116.5 | 116.8 | 117.0 | 117.3 | 118.2 | 117.8 | 116.5 | 116.4 | 116.3 | 116.3 | 116.8 |
| 2012 | 115.2 | 115.3 | 115.9 | 116.5 | 117.1 | 117.5 | 118.0 | 117.9 | 118.0 | 117.5 | 117.2 | 117.2 | 116.9 |
| 2013 | 116.0 | 116.5 | 117.0 | 117.1 | 117.6 | 118.2 | 118.8 | 119.7 | 119.7 | 119.5 | 120.1 | 120.1 | 118.4 |
| 2014 | 119.2 | 119.6 | 120.0 | 120.7 | 121.3 | 122.1 | 123.1 | 123.8 | 124.3 | 125.0 | 125.8 | 126.3 | 122.6 |
| 2015 | 125.1 | 125.4 | 126.0 | 126.2 | 126.9 | 128.3 | 130.0 | 130.3 | 130.7 | 131.0 | 130.8 | 131.1 | 128.5 |
| 2016 | 131.0 | 131.2 | 131.5 | 131.9 | 132.2 | 133.6 | 135.2 | 135.7 | 135.7 | 135.2 | 135.5 | 136.1 | 133.7 |
| 2017 | 135.9 | 136.7 | 137.9 | 137.1 | 138.4 | 139.7 | 141.4 | 141.9 | 141.6 | 142.0 | 141.8 | 142.4 | 139.7 |
| 2018 | 142.1 | 142.9 | 143.2 | 143.5 | 143.7 | 144.5 | 146.3 | 146.3 | 145.3 | 145.1 | 145.3 | 145.9 | 144.5 |
| 2019 | 145.0 | 145.2 | 145.3 | 144.3 | 144.0 | 144.1 | 144.1 | 143.9 | 143.0 | 143.3 | 143.7 | 144.3 | 144.2 |
| **Trade, Transportation, and Utilities** | | | | | | | | | | | | | |
| 2011 | 313.4 | 310.9 | 310.3 | 312.8 | 313.9 | 314.7 | 316.7 | 317.6 | 317.1 | 318.7 | 327.1 | 332.1 | 317.1 |
| 2012 | 321.3 | 317.0 | 317.4 | 321.1 | 323.3 | 324.6 | 326.2 | 327.5 | 327.0 | 329.9 | 340.5 | 345.4 | 326.8 |
| 2013 | 333.0 | 330.2 | 329.5 | 329.5 | 331.4 | 333.5 | 335.0 | 336.3 | 335.8 | 339.7 | 349.3 | 355.7 | 336.6 |
| 2014 | 342.3 | 339.1 | 339.4 | 339.7 | 341.5 | 343.3 | 344.9 | 347.1 | 345.1 | 347.9 | 357.3 | 363.7 | 345.9 |
| 2015 | 352.8 | 349.5 | 349.7 | 350.4 | 352.3 | 354.0 | 357.4 | 358.6 | 357.4 | 360.1 | 368.1 | 373.5 | 357.0 |
| 2016 | 362.4 | 360.7 | 359.5 | 361.4 | 361.3 | 362.1 | 366.6 | 367.9 | 366.0 | 368.8 | 377.0 | 383.2 | 366.4 |
| 2017 | 372.7 | 368.6 | 367.9 | 368.5 | 368.4 | 370.5 | 371.6 | 373.1 | 370.9 | 374.3 | 383.5 | 389.5 | 373.3 |
| 2018 | 377.1 | 373.8 | 373.8 | 371.3 | 372.2 | 373.7 | 376.1 | 377.2 | 374.7 | 375.3 | 384.0 | 389.0 | 376.5 |
| 2019 | 375.5 | 370.6 | 370.3 | 367.8 | 369.3 | 370.0 | 372.5 | 373.8 | 370.8 | 373.3 | 382.2 | 385.7 | 373.5 |
| **Wholesale Trade** | | | | | | | | | | | | | |
| 2011 | 64.1 | 64.2 | 64.4 | 65.0 | 65.4 | 65.5 | 66.1 | 66.2 | 66.3 | 66.5 | 66.8 | 67.0 | 65.6 |
| 2012 | 66.1 | 66.3 | 66.5 | 67.6 | 68.2 | 68.4 | 69.1 | 69.2 | 68.9 | 69.4 | 69.6 | 69.9 | 68.3 |
| 2013 | 69.7 | 69.7 | 69.6 | 69.9 | 70.2 | 70.7 | 71.2 | 71.3 | 71.3 | 71.5 | 71.8 | 72.5 | 70.8 |
| 2014 | 71.5 | 71.7 | 71.7 | 71.6 | 72.0 | 72.2 | 72.7 | 72.9 | 72.7 | 73.2 | 73.5 | 73.8 | 72.5 |
| 2015 | 73.8 | 74.1 | 74.1 | 74.4 | 74.7 | 74.9 | 75.7 | 75.8 | 75.5 | 75.9 | 75.9 | 76.3 | 75.1 |
| 2016 | 75.6 | 75.8 | 75.6 | 76.0 | 76.0 | 76.1 | 77.4 | 77.5 | 77.0 | 77.1 | 77.0 | 77.3 | 76.5 |
| 2017 | 76.7 | 77.0 | 76.8 | 77.0 | 77.4 | 77.7 | 78.0 | 77.9 | 77.1 | 77.5 | 77.5 | 77.8 | 77.4 |
| 2018 | 77.0 | 77.0 | 76.7 | 76.6 | 76.6 | 76.5 | 76.4 | 76.4 | 75.7 | 76.1 | 76.1 | 76.0 | 76.4 |
| 2019 | 74.2 | 74.1 | 74.0 | 73.7 | 74.0 | 73.9 | 74.2 | 74.1 | 73.7 | 74.2 | 74.1 | 74.3 | 74.0 |
| **Retail Trade** | | | | | | | | | | | | | |
| 2011 | 187.7 | 185.1 | 184.6 | 185.5 | 186.0 | 186.6 | 187.7 | 188.4 | 187.7 | 189.2 | 196.8 | 200.1 | 188.8 |
| 2012 | 192.3 | 188.1 | 187.7 | 189.3 | 190.7 | 191.3 | 192.5 | 193.2 | 192.8 | 195.1 | 204.5 | 207.9 | 193.8 |
| 2013 | 197.4 | 194.6 | 194.3 | 193.5 | 194.8 | 196.3 | 197.0 | 198.0 | 197.1 | 199.8 | 208.4 | 212.2 | 198.6 |
| 2014 | 202.5 | 198.7 | 199.0 | 199.2 | 199.9 | 201.2 | 202.1 | 203.4 | 201.4 | 203.6 | 211.8 | 215.4 | 203.2 |
| 2015 | 206.5 | 203.2 | 203.2 | 203.1 | 204.0 | 204.6 | 206.5 | 207.0 | 206.1 | 207.1 | 214.0 | 217.0 | 206.9 |
| 2016 | 208.9 | 206.7 | 205.9 | 206.3 | 206.2 | 206.4 | 208.2 | 208.7 | 207.1 | 208.8 | 215.2 | 218.2 | 208.9 |
| 2017 | 211.1 | 207.5 | 207.0 | 207.7 | 207.5 | 208.3 | 208.8 | 209.6 | 208.0 | 209.7 | 217.2 | 219.8 | 210.2 |
| 2018 | 211.8 | 209.3 | 208.9 | 207.1 | 207.3 | 207.5 | 209.3 | 209.5 | 207.7 | 207.9 | 213.4 | 215.7 | 209.6 |
| 2019 | 207.1 | 203.7 | 202.7 | 201.7 | 202.2 | 202.2 | 204.0 | 204.3 | 202.0 | 204.0 | 211.5 | 213.2 | 204.9 |
| **Transportation and Utilities** | | | | | | | | | | | | | |
| 2011 | 61.6 | 61.6 | 61.3 | 62.3 | 62.5 | 62.6 | 62.9 | 63.0 | 63.1 | 63.0 | 63.5 | 65.0 | 62.7 |
| 2012 | 62.9 | 62.6 | 63.2 | 64.2 | 64.4 | 64.9 | 64.6 | 65.1 | 65.3 | 65.4 | 66.4 | 67.6 | 64.7 |
| 2013 | 65.9 | 65.9 | 65.6 | 66.1 | 66.4 | 66.5 | 66.8 | 67.0 | 67.4 | 68.4 | 69.1 | 71.0 | 67.2 |
| 2014 | 68.3 | 68.7 | 68.7 | 68.9 | 69.6 | 69.9 | 70.1 | 70.8 | 71.0 | 71.1 | 72.0 | 74.5 | 70.3 |
| 2015 | 72.5 | 72.2 | 72.4 | 72.9 | 73.6 | 74.5 | 75.2 | 75.8 | 75.8 | 77.1 | 78.2 | 80.2 | 75.0 |
| 2016 | 77.9 | 78.2 | 78.0 | 79.1 | 79.1 | 79.6 | 81.0 | 81.7 | 81.9 | 82.9 | 84.8 | 87.7 | 81.0 |
| 2017 | 84.9 | 84.1 | 84.1 | 83.8 | 83.5 | 84.5 | 84.8 | 85.6 | 85.8 | 87.1 | 88.8 | 91.9 | 85.7 |
| 2018 | 88.3 | 87.5 | 88.2 | 87.6 | 88.3 | 89.7 | 90.4 | 91.3 | 91.3 | 91.3 | 94.5 | 97.3 | 90.5 |
| 2019 | 94.2 | 92.8 | 93.6 | 92.4 | 93.1 | 93.9 | 94.3 | 95.4 | 95.1 | 95.1 | 96.6 | 98.2 | 94.6 |
| **Information** | | | | | | | | | | | | | |
| 2011 | 64.2 | 64.6 | 65.2 | 65.5 | 66.0 | 66.8 | 67.6 | 68.1 | 67.9 | 68.5 | 69.1 | 69.4 | 66.9 |
| 2012 | 69.8 | 70.4 | 70.6 | 71.5 | 72.0 | 73.1 | 73.5 | 73.8 | 73.6 | 73.7 | 74.4 | 74.9 | 72.6 |
| 2013 | 73.2 | 73.8 | 73.6 | 74.3 | 74.8 | 75.9 | 76.7 | 76.8 | 76.0 | 76.5 | 78.1 | 77.8 | 75.6 |
| 2014 | 77.2 | 77.8 | 78.6 | 78.9 | 79.8 | 80.8 | 82.2 | 83.1 | 82.7 | 83.7 | 84.5 | 85.8 | 81.3 |
| 2015 | 85.8 | 86.8 | 87.6 | 88.8 | 89.9 | 91.9 | 93.5 | 94.1 | 93.5 | 94.1 | 94.7 | 95.3 | 91.3 |
| 2016 | 95.7 | 96.7 | 97.7 | 98.1 | 98.7 | 100.7 | 101.8 | 102.3 | 102.1 | 100.4 | 102.2 | 101.6 | 99.8 |
| 2017 | 102.3 | 102.7 | 103.8 | 103.4 | 103.8 | 107.2 | 109.0 | 109.1 | 108.3 | 108.7 | 109.0 | 110.4 | 106.5 |
| 2018 | 109.8 | 111.0 | 111.8 | 111.8 | 113.0 | 116.8 | 118.4 | 119.1 | 118.4 | 119.1 | 120.2 | 121.1 | 115.9 |
| 2019 | 121.8 | 123.1 | 124.2 | 124.6 | 125.3 | 128.3 | 130.5 | 131.3 | 129.6 | 130.4 | 130.9 | 131.2 | 127.6 |

## Employment by Industry: San Francisco-Oakland-Hayward, CA, 2011–2019—*Continued*

(Numbers in thousands, not seasonally adjusted)

| Industry and year | January | February | March | April | May | June | July | August | September | October | November | December | Annual average |
|---|---|---|---|---|---|---|---|---|---|---|---|---|---|
| **Financial Activities** | | | | | | | | | | | | | |
| 2011 | 122.2 | 122.6 | 122.6 | 122.7 | 122.9 | 123.4 | 124.0 | 124.4 | 124.6 | 124.5 | 124.4 | 125.1 | 123.6 |
| 2012 | 124.4 | 125.2 | 125.5 | 126.3 | 126.9 | 127.9 | 128.1 | 128.5 | 127.9 | 128.7 | 128.4 | 129.4 | 127.3 |
| 2013 | 129.0 | 129.9 | 129.9 | 130.6 | 131.1 | 131.6 | 132.3 | 132.6 | 132.0 | 132.4 | 132.5 | 133.1 | 131.4 |
| 2014 | 131.6 | 132.2 | 132.2 | 132.1 | 132.8 | 133.5 | 134.4 | 134.7 | 134.3 | 134.7 | 135.0 | 135.5 | 133.6 |
| 2015 | 134.7 | 135.5 | 135.8 | 135.4 | 136.4 | 137.7 | 139.4 | 139.6 | 138.6 | 140.0 | 140.2 | 140.9 | 137.9 |
| 2016 | 140.0 | 140.6 | 140.6 | 141.6 | 142.1 | 142.6 | 144.0 | 143.7 | 142.8 | 142.9 | 143.1 | 143.3 | 142.3 |
| 2017 | 141.3 | 142.0 | 142.1 | 142.3 | 142.7 | 143.5 | 143.7 | 143.4 | 142.6 | 143.0 | 143.2 | 143.6 | 142.8 |
| 2018 | 141.8 | 142.4 | 142.1 | 142.7 | 143.1 | 144.2 | 144.9 | 145.2 | 143.9 | 145.2 | 145.1 | 145.6 | 143.9 |
| 2019 | 144.3 | 145.1 | 145.1 | 145.4 | 145.7 | 147.1 | 148.6 | 149.0 | 146.9 | 148.0 | 148.3 | 148.3 | 146.8 |
| **Professional and Business Services** | | | | | | | | | | | | | |
| 2011 | 353.7 | 355.7 | 357.6 | 361.7 | 362.8 | 365.2 | 370.6 | 372.6 | 374.9 | 376.9 | 378.5 | 379.9 | 367.5 |
| 2012 | 376.6 | 379.5 | 382.5 | 389.4 | 391.0 | 396.0 | 397.2 | 400.5 | 400.2 | 405.0 | 405.4 | 406.0 | 394.1 |
| 2013 | 400.8 | 403.4 | 405.5 | 408.6 | 408.5 | 410.3 | 413.9 | 416.9 | 414.1 | 417.8 | 419.9 | 421.5 | 411.8 |
| 2014 | 417.5 | 420.6 | 423.0 | 424.8 | 427.9 | 429.1 | 430.7 | 434.7 | 432.9 | 435.8 | 437.0 | 439.0 | 429.4 |
| 2015 | 433.1 | 435.8 | 438.9 | 443.1 | 442.5 | 445.0 | 451.2 | 454.1 | 451.3 | 456.4 | 456.5 | 457.7 | 447.1 |
| 2016 | 451.7 | 455.1 | 455.0 | 459.6 | 458.2 | 461.3 | 465.8 | 466.1 | 463.5 | 465.5 | 466.0 | 464.1 | 461.0 |
| 2017 | 459.0 | 462.0 | 464.1 | 464.4 | 465.3 | 470.4 | 472.9 | 473.9 | 471.5 | 474.5 | 475.1 | 476.0 | 469.1 |
| 2018 | 469.6 | 473.5 | 475.8 | 479.4 | 481.0 | 485.4 | 488.6 | 491.5 | 488.8 | 493.9 | 495.2 | 496.1 | 484.9 |
| 2019 | 487.6 | 491.0 | 492.1 | 496.0 | 496.4 | 501.6 | 507.6 | 510.2 | 505.4 | 509.5 | 509.1 | 509.4 | 501.3 |
| **Education and Health Services** | | | | | | | | | | | | | |
| 2011 | 291.2 | 294.1 | 294.7 | 295.9 | 295.4 | 290.5 | 288.2 | 287.2 | 293.3 | 296.5 | 297.3 | 298.3 | 293.6 |
| 2012 | 292.9 | 300.0 | 302.6 | 304.2 | 305.0 | 302.3 | 300.5 | 300.6 | 304.2 | 307.0 | 308.7 | 310.5 | 303.2 |
| 2013 | 303.7 | 311.5 | 314.0 | 314.9 | 316.5 | 312.9 | 309.6 | 309.9 | 312.2 | 316.6 | 318.7 | 319.1 | 313.3 |
| 2014 | 311.0 | 318.1 | 319.4 | 320.9 | 320.9 | 317.7 | 314.3 | 314.1 | 317.6 | 322.2 | 324.4 | 324.3 | 318.7 |
| 2015 | 320.0 | 325.2 | 326.4 | 328.1 | 328.7 | 326.9 | 326.6 | 325.8 | 329.0 | 334.5 | 335.8 | 336.6 | 328.6 |
| 2016 | 329.7 | 335.5 | 337.7 | 339.9 | 340.3 | 337.5 | 337.2 | 335.6 | 340.8 | 347.1 | 347.9 | 348.9 | 339.8 |
| 2017 | 341.9 | 348.6 | 351.4 | 349.5 | 350.3 | 347.9 | 342.9 | 342.9 | 347.8 | 351.7 | 353.1 | 353.5 | 348.5 |
| 2018 | 347.8 | 354.0 | 356.6 | 354.7 | 354.7 | 353.9 | 349.0 | 350.3 | 351.9 | 358.0 | 359.9 | 359.1 | 354.2 |
| 2019 | 355.9 | 362.1 | 364.5 | 366.0 | 367.1 | 363.0 | 360.8 | 361.4 | 363.1 | 367.6 | 368.6 | 369.3 | 364.1 |
| **Leisure and Hospitality** | | | | | | | | | | | | | |
| 2011 | 204.3 | 206.3 | 208.3 | 213.8 | 217.4 | 219.6 | 220.5 | 221.4 | 222.2 | 220.8 | 218.1 | 218.5 | 215.9 |
| 2012 | 212.6 | 215.0 | 217.0 | 224.5 | 228.3 | 231.4 | 231.1 | 234.2 | 232.6 | 233.1 | 230.5 | 231.5 | 226.8 |
| 2013 | 224.9 | 228.1 | 230.9 | 235.3 | 240.0 | 241.1 | 240.9 | 243.0 | 242.2 | 242.0 | 241.8 | 242.5 | 237.7 |
| 2014 | 235.6 | 239.1 | 241.9 | 246.4 | 249.8 | 253.4 | 253.1 | 255.1 | 254.3 | 253.5 | 251.7 | 252.6 | 248.9 |
| 2015 | 245.1 | 248.6 | 252.3 | 257.2 | 261.1 | 262.9 | 263.7 | 265.4 | 264.3 | 263.8 | 262.0 | 262.9 | 259.1 |
| 2016 | 257.1 | 261.7 | 262.8 | 269.0 | 271.6 | 272.9 | 273.4 | 274.7 | 272.2 | 272.8 | 270.7 | 270.4 | 269.1 |
| 2017 | 261.7 | 266.8 | 270.5 | 273.6 | 277.0 | 280.4 | 279.0 | 278.4 | 275.9 | 275.2 | 273.9 | 272.4 | 273.7 |
| 2018 | 265.0 | 269.4 | 272.5 | 276.1 | 279.2 | 282.5 | 283.3 | 283.6 | 281.2 | 279.2 | 278.3 | 279.2 | 277.5 |
| 2019 | 272.2 | 277.7 | 280.7 | 281.9 | 285.6 | 288.0 | 287.9 | 289.4 | 286.7 | 286.5 | 284.3 | 285.8 | 283.9 |
| **Other Services** | | | | | | | | | | | | | |
| 2011 | 72.2 | 72.5 | 72.8 | 74.6 | 74.5 | 74.8 | 75.6 | 75.1 | 75.4 | 75.8 | 75.7 | 75.7 | 74.6 |
| 2012 | 73.9 | 74.8 | 75.5 | 76.5 | 77.8 | 78.4 | 77.8 | 77.7 | 77.9 | 78.3 | 78.2 | 78.6 | 77.1 |
| 2013 | 76.8 | 78.1 | 78.5 | 79.7 | 79.9 | 80.4 | 80.3 | 80.4 | 80.4 | 80.7 | 80.8 | 80.9 | 79.7 |
| 2014 | 80.0 | 81.0 | 81.5 | 82.9 | 83.1 | 83.2 | 82.8 | 82.8 | 82.7 | 82.9 | 82.7 | 82.5 | 82.3 |
| 2015 | 81.6 | 82.4 | 82.8 | 83.2 | 84.0 | 84.1 | 83.9 | 83.5 | 83.3 | 84.2 | 83.9 | 83.9 | 83.4 |
| 2016 | 83.5 | 83.9 | 84.0 | 85.4 | 85.6 | 86.2 | 86.2 | 86.0 | 85.5 | 86.1 | 85.7 | 85.8 | 85.3 |
| 2017 | 85.0 | 85.6 | 86.3 | 87.3 | 87.5 | 88.1 | 87.9 | 87.7 | 87.2 | 87.3 | 87.2 | 87.1 | 87.0 |
| 2018 | 85.7 | 86.8 | 87.2 | 88.1 | 88.6 | 89.0 | 89.3 | 88.6 | 87.7 | 89.0 | 88.2 | 87.9 | 88.0 |
| 2019 | 86.8 | 87.4 | 87.7 | 88.4 | 88.9 | 90.1 | 90.5 | 89.1 | 88.0 | 88.3 | 88.8 | 88.2 | 88.5 |
| **Government** | | | | | | | | | | | | | |
| 2011 | 301.0 | 303.7 | 306.1 | 306.7 | 306.9 | 305.2 | 290.4 | 290.3 | 293.0 | 299.7 | 300.8 | 298.7 | 300.2 |
| 2012 | 296.2 | 299.1 | 301.8 | 302.0 | 302.3 | 301.1 | 290.7 | 288.8 | 292.4 | 296.8 | 301.5 | 300.0 | 297.7 |
| 2013 | 295.7 | 297.8 | 301.7 | 302.6 | 302.6 | 298.0 | 287.5 | 288.6 | 294.0 | 300.0 | 302.9 | 298.7 | 297.5 |
| 2014 | 298.9 | 301.1 | 302.3 | 305.6 | 306.8 | 304.7 | 295.1 | 293.7 | 299.1 | 305.7 | 309.5 | 308.6 | 302.6 |
| 2015 | 305.8 | 307.0 | 310.4 | 312.5 | 313.0 | 310.7 | 299.9 | 302.5 | 307.2 | 312.4 | 315.0 | 313.6 | 309.2 |
| 2016 | 312.3 | 314.6 | 317.7 | 319.0 | 320.8 | 317.3 | 304.9 | 308.0 | 315.6 | 321.8 | 324.1 | 323.0 | 316.6 |
| 2017 | 319.0 | 320.9 | 323.5 | 323.6 | 325.6 | 321.8 | 307.9 | 308.8 | 317.4 | 323.8 | 325.8 | 324.6 | 320.2 |
| 2018 | 320.8 | 323.2 | 325.4 | 326.5 | 327.2 | 326.3 | 307.3 | 312.0 | 318.8 | 324.3 | 326.8 | 326.4 | 322.1 |
| 2019 | 319.9 | 323.8 | 325.3 | 325.9 | 327.4 | 327.6 | 310.9 | 315.4 | 320.6 | 324.9 | 328.3 | 326.4 | 323.0 |

## Employment by Industry: Riverside-San Bernardino-Ontario, CA, 2011–2019

(Numbers in thousands, not seasonally adjusted)

| Industry and year | January | February | March | April | May | June | July | August | September | October | November | December | Annual average |
|---|---|---|---|---|---|---|---|---|---|---|---|---|---|
| **Total Nonfarm** | | | | | | | | | | | | | |
| 2011 | 1,145.3 | 1,149.9 | 1,154.4 | 1,158.3 | 1,157.9 | 1,152.0 | 1,135.8 | 1,143.9 | 1,150.2 | 1,161.6 | 1,177.0 | 1,177.2 | 1,155.3 |
| 2012 | 1,165.9 | 1,168.1 | 1,173.9 | 1,183.8 | 1,187.3 | 1,186.3 | 1,167.3 | 1,177.7 | 1,182.7 | 1,201.9 | 1,219.8 | 1,217.2 | 1,186.0 |
| 2013 | 1,208.6 | 1,215.4 | 1,221.8 | 1,227.2 | 1,231.0 | 1,230.3 | 1,211.1 | 1,226.2 | 1,235.0 | 1,253.3 | 1,274.4 | 1,275.9 | 1,234.2 |
| 2014 | 1,258.3 | 1,264.6 | 1,272.1 | 1,280.8 | 1,283.2 | 1,282.2 | 1,266.6 | 1,282.5 | 1,293.3 | 1,313.7 | 1,341.5 | 1,345.7 | 1,290.4 |
| 2015 | 1,324.1 | 1,326.2 | 1,333.4 | 1,340.0 | 1,344.7 | 1,343.3 | 1,335.2 | 1,348.0 | 1,353.5 | 1,382.0 | 1,407.1 | 1,414.7 | 1,354.4 |
| 2016 | 1,383.1 | 1,382.1 | 1,386.2 | 1,397.6 | 1,397.8 | 1,391.9 | 1,385.2 | 1,395.1 | 1,403.2 | 1,426.1 | 1,444.0 | 1,446.8 | 1,403.3 |
| 2017 | 1,424.4 | 1,426.4 | 1,439.0 | 1,440.9 | 1,448.9 | 1,448.9 | 1,434.7 | 1,447.2 | 1,458.6 | 1,480.4 | 1,505.3 | 1,504.1 | 1,454.9 |
| 2018 | 1,482.7 | 1,488.6 | 1,494.3 | 1,498.9 | 1,502.3 | 1,503.6 | 1,488.2 | 1,495.0 | 1,504.3 | 1,526.6 | 1,547.3 | 1,548.8 | 1,506.7 |
| 2019 | 1,524.0 | 1,523.8 | 1,530.8 | 1,537.7 | 1,537.3 | 1,538.6 | 1,530.1 | 1,539.4 | 1,540.4 | 1,554.3 | 1,574.1 | 1,571.1 | 1,541.8 |
| **Total Private** | | | | | | | | | | | | | |
| 2011 | 914.0 | 918.3 | 921.0 | 924.9 | 924.3 | 921.2 | 921.8 | 926.1 | 930.2 | 933.7 | 947.9 | 950.4 | 927.8 |
| 2012 | 937.8 | 940.0 | 944.3 | 954.0 | 957.2 | 960.2 | 958.1 | 962.7 | 966.0 | 975.4 | 990.8 | 990.2 | 961.4 |
| 2013 | 981.7 | 988.2 | 993.2 | 998.7 | 1,001.4 | 1,002.5 | 1,000.1 | 1,009.6 | 1,014.0 | 1,025.7 | 1,044.8 | 1,048.4 | 1,009.0 |
| 2014 | 1,029.9 | 1,036.0 | 1,040.5 | 1,048.0 | 1,050.5 | 1,050.8 | 1,051.5 | 1,062.2 | 1,068.5 | 1,081.5 | 1,107.4 | 1,112.7 | 1,061.6 |
| 2015 | 1,091.7 | 1,092.9 | 1,097.3 | 1,103.6 | 1,107.5 | 1,108.9 | 1,115.8 | 1,122.5 | 1,123.9 | 1,144.7 | 1,167.5 | 1,176.4 | 1,121.1 |
| 2016 | 1,143.3 | 1,142.9 | 1,143.0 | 1,153.1 | 1,152.9 | 1,147.7 | 1,153.8 | 1,159.3 | 1,163.2 | 1,179.7 | 1,194.9 | 1,197.6 | 1,161.0 |
| 2017 | 1,175.2 | 1,177.1 | 1,186.8 | 1,189.6 | 1,195.0 | 1,195.6 | 1,195.3 | 1,205.0 | 1,209.0 | 1,224.6 | 1,246.9 | 1,246.6 | 1,203.9 |
| 2018 | 1,225.0 | 1,231.0 | 1,233.9 | 1,238.4 | 1,241.0 | 1,241.8 | 1,243.5 | 1,248.8 | 1,252.5 | 1,267.5 | 1,285.5 | 1,285.6 | 1,249.5 |
| 2019 | 1,262.0 | 1,262.3 | 1,266.3 | 1,273.3 | 1,272.1 | 1,274.1 | 1,281.2 | 1,287.8 | 1,285.0 | 1,292.0 | 1,310.0 | 1,309.2 | 1,281.3 |
| **Goods Producing** | | | | | | | | | | | | | |
| 2011 | 140.5 | 142.0 | 142.9 | 144.6 | 145.6 | 146.3 | 147.6 | 148.0 | 148.0 | 146.8 | 146.4 | 145.1 | 145.3 |
| 2012 | 144.1 | 144.8 | 146.1 | 147.2 | 149.7 | 152.2 | 153.1 | 154.5 | 154.3 | 154.7 | 153.9 | 153.2 | 150.7 |
| 2013 | 151.9 | 154.0 | 155.3 | 155.4 | 156.6 | 157.6 | 159.7 | 161.5 | 161.8 | 163.4 | 163.7 | 163.2 | 158.7 |
| 2014 | 163.3 | 164.7 | 165.8 | 166.5 | 168.4 | 169.8 | 172.1 | 174.7 | 174.9 | 174.5 | 175.0 | 173.8 | 170.3 |
| 2015 | 173.9 | 176.1 | 177.8 | 178.6 | 180.6 | 182.8 | 186.4 | 188.6 | 187.3 | 189.0 | 188.7 | 187.7 | 183.1 |
| 2016 | 185.8 | 187.2 | 188.3 | 190.6 | 191.3 | 192.0 | 194.3 | 195.3 | 194.4 | 194.2 | 192.7 | 192.7 | 191.6 |
| 2017 | 186.1 | 189.3 | 192.6 | 195.7 | 197.6 | 200.0 | 200.3 | 201.7 | 201.8 | 202.3 | 202.1 | 201.7 | 197.6 |
| 2018 | 199.4 | 203.3 | 203.8 | 205.6 | 207.3 | 209.6 | 210.3 | 211.2 | 210.5 | 210.9 | 209.2 | 208.3 | 207.5 |
| 2019 | 203.9 | 203.9 | 206.0 | 208.2 | 208.9 | 211.0 | 211.5 | 213.1 | 211.5 | 208.3 | 207.1 | 206.1 | 208.3 |
| **Service-Providing** | | | | | | | | | | | | | |
| 2011 | 1,004.8 | 1,007.9 | 1,011.5 | 1,013.7 | 1,012.3 | 1,005.7 | 988.2 | 995.9 | 1,002.2 | 1,014.8 | 1,030.6 | 1,032.1 | 1,010.0 |
| 2012 | 1,021.8 | 1,023.3 | 1,027.8 | 1,036.6 | 1,037.6 | 1,034.1 | 1,014.2 | 1,023.2 | 1,028.4 | 1,047.2 | 1,065.9 | 1,064.0 | 1,035.3 |
| 2013 | 1,056.7 | 1,061.4 | 1,066.5 | 1,071.8 | 1,074.4 | 1,072.7 | 1,051.4 | 1,064.7 | 1,073.2 | 1,089.9 | 1,110.7 | 1,112.7 | 1,075.5 |
| 2014 | 1,095.0 | 1,099.9 | 1,106.3 | 1,114.3 | 1,114.8 | 1,112.4 | 1,094.5 | 1,107.8 | 1,118.4 | 1,139.2 | 1,166.5 | 1,171.9 | 1,120.1 |
| 2015 | 1,150.2 | 1,150.1 | 1,155.6 | 1,161.4 | 1,164.1 | 1,160.5 | 1,148.8 | 1,159.4 | 1,166.2 | 1,193.0 | 1,218.4 | 1,227.0 | 1,171.2 |
| 2016 | 1,197.3 | 1,194.9 | 1,197.9 | 1,207.0 | 1,206.5 | 1,199.9 | 1,190.9 | 1,199.8 | 1,208.8 | 1,231.9 | 1,251.3 | 1,254.1 | 1,211.7 |
| 2017 | 1,238.3 | 1,237.1 | 1,246.4 | 1,245.2 | 1,251.3 | 1,248.9 | 1,234.4 | 1,245.5 | 1,256.8 | 1,278.1 | 1,303.2 | 1,302.4 | 1,257.3 |
| 2018 | 1,283.3 | 1,285.3 | 1,290.5 | 1,293.3 | 1,295.0 | 1,294.0 | 1,277.9 | 1,283.8 | 1,293.8 | 1,315.7 | 1,338.1 | 1,340.5 | 1,299.3 |
| 2019 | 1,320.1 | 1,319.9 | 1,324.8 | 1,329.5 | 1,328.4 | 1,327.6 | 1,318.6 | 1,326.3 | 1,328.9 | 1,346.0 | 1,367.0 | 1,365.0 | 1,333.5 |
| **Mining and Logging** | | | | | | | | | | | | | |
| 2011 | 1.0 | 1.0 | 1.0 | 1.0 | 1.0 | 1.0 | 1.0 | 1.1 | 1.1 | 1.1 | 1.1 | 1.1 | 1.0 |
| 2012 | 1.1 | 1.2 | 1.2 | 1.2 | 1.2 | 1.2 | 1.2 | 1.2 | 1.2 | 1.2 | 1.2 | 1.2 | 1.2 |
| 2013 | 1.2 | 1.2 | 1.2 | 1.2 | 1.2 | 1.2 | 1.2 | 1.2 | 1.2 | 1.2 | 1.2 | 1.2 | 1.2 |
| 2014 | 1.2 | 1.3 | 1.3 | 1.3 | 1.3 | 1.3 | 1.3 | 1.3 | 1.3 | 1.3 | 1.3 | 1.3 | 1.3 |
| 2015 | 1.3 | 1.3 | 1.4 | 1.4 | 1.4 | 1.4 | 1.4 | 1.3 | 1.3 | 1.1 | 1.1 | 1.0 | 1.3 |
| 2016 | 0.9 | 0.9 | 0.9 | 0.9 | 0.9 | 0.9 | 0.9 | 0.9 | 0.9 | 1.0 | 1.0 | 1.0 | 0.9 |
| 2017 | 1.0 | 1.0 | 0.9 | 0.9 | 0.9 | 0.9 | 0.9 | 0.9 | 1.0 | 1.0 | 1.1 | 1.1 | 1.0 |
| 2018 | 1.1 | 1.1 | 1.1 | 1.1 | 1.2 | 1.2 | 1.2 | 1.2 | 1.2 | 1.2 | 1.2 | 1.2 | 1.2 |
| 2019 | 1.2 | 1.2 | 1.2 | 1.2 | 1.2 | 1.2 | 1.2 | 1.2 | 1.2 | 1.2 | 1.2 | 1.2 | 1.2 |
| **Construction** | | | | | | | | | | | | | |
| 2011 | 55.6 | 56.9 | 57.3 | 58.6 | 59.1 | 59.4 | 60.8 | 61.0 | 61.0 | 60.5 | 60.0 | 58.7 | 59.1 |
| 2012 | 58.0 | 58.0 | 58.8 | 59.3 | 61.1 | 63.5 | 64.4 | 65.7 | 65.8 | 66.1 | 65.7 | 65.2 | 62.6 |
| 2013 | 64.7 | 66.4 | 67.1 | 67.5 | 68.1 | 68.9 | 70.9 | 72.4 | 72.7 | 74.0 | 74.1 | 73.5 | 70.0 |
| 2014 | 72.9 | 73.6 | 74.5 | 75.1 | 76.3 | 77.2 | 79.3 | 81.4 | 81.2 | 80.4 | 80.3 | 78.8 | 77.6 |
| 2015 | 78.7 | 80.3 | 81.4 | 82.0 | 83.4 | 85.1 | 88.2 | 90.2 | 89.1 | 90.5 | 90.1 | 88.9 | 85.7 |
| 2016 | 87.7 | 88.7 | 89.4 | 91.1 | 91.5 | 92.1 | 93.8 | 94.9 | 94.3 | 94.3 | 92.8 | 92.8 | 92.0 |
| 2017 | 86.7 | 89.7 | 92.6 | 95.7 | 97.4 | 99.3 | 100.0 | 101.4 | 101.7 | 102.0 | 101.5 | 100.8 | 97.4 |
| 2018 | 98.8 | 101.7 | 101.7 | 103.7 | 105.1 | 106.9 | 107.6 | 108.4 | 107.9 | 108.1 | 106.7 | 105.7 | 105.2 |
| 2019 | 102.0 | 101.1 | 103.1 | 105.1 | 105.9 | 107.7 | 108.7 | 110.5 | 109.6 | 107.1 | 105.3 | 104.4 | 105.9 |

## Employment by Industry: Riverside-San Bernardino-Ontario, CA, 2011–2019—*Continued*

(Numbers in thousands, not seasonally adjusted)

| Industry and year | January | February | March | April | May | June | July | August | September | October | November | December | Annual average |
|---|---|---|---|---|---|---|---|---|---|---|---|---|---|
| **Manufacturing** | | | | | | | | | | | | | |
| 2011 | 83.9 | 84.1 | 84.6 | 85.0 | 85.5 | 85.9 | 85.8 | 85.9 | 85.9 | 85.2 | 85.3 | 85.3 | 85.2 |
| 2012 | 85.0 | 85.6 | 86.1 | 86.7 | 87.4 | 87.5 | 87.5 | 87.6 | 87.3 | 87.4 | 87.0 | 86.8 | 86.8 |
| 2013 | 86.0 | 86.4 | 87.0 | 86.7 | 87.3 | 87.5 | 87.6 | 87.9 | 87.9 | 88.2 | 88.4 | 88.5 | 87.5 |
| 2014 | 89.2 | 89.8 | 90.0 | 90.1 | 90.8 | 91.3 | 91.5 | 92.0 | 92.4 | 92.8 | 93.4 | 93.7 | 91.4 |
| 2015 | 93.9 | 94.5 | 95.0 | 95.2 | 95.8 | 96.3 | 96.8 | 97.1 | 96.9 | 97.4 | 97.5 | 97.8 | 96.2 |
| 2016 | 97.2 | 97.6 | 98.0 | 98.6 | 98.9 | 99.0 | 99.6 | 99.5 | 99.2 | 98.9 | 98.9 | 98.9 | 98.7 |
| 2017 | 98.4 | 98.6 | 99.1 | 99.1 | 99.3 | 99.8 | 99.4 | 99.4 | 99.1 | 99.3 | 99.5 | 99.8 | 99.2 |
| 2018 | 99.5 | 100.5 | 101.0 | 100.8 | 101.0 | 101.5 | 101.5 | 101.6 | 101.4 | 101.6 | 101.3 | 101.4 | 101.1 |
| 2019 | 100.7 | 101.6 | 101.7 | 101.9 | 101.8 | 102.1 | 101.6 | 101.4 | 100.7 | 100.0 | 100.6 | 100.5 | 101.2 |
| **Trade, Transportation, and Utilities** | | | | | | | | | | | | | |
| 2011 | 272.6 | 270.6 | 270.2 | 271.3 | 272.2 | 272.1 | 272.7 | 273.9 | 275.0 | 277.2 | 287.5 | 289.9 | 275.4 |
| 2012 | 281.7 | 278.2 | 278.8 | 282.1 | 283.7 | 284.4 | 284.7 | 286.4 | 287.9 | 291.5 | 304.4 | 305.1 | 287.4 |
| 2013 | 293.2 | 291.8 | 292.0 | 292.7 | 294.6 | 295.4 | 295.4 | 298.0 | 298.4 | 303.9 | 317.6 | 320.9 | 299.5 |
| 2014 | 306.7 | 304.9 | 304.8 | 306.9 | 308.8 | 309.7 | 309.6 | 313.9 | 316.3 | 321.5 | 335.3 | 338.9 | 314.8 |
| 2015 | 324.9 | 322.5 | 323.2 | 323.7 | 326.5 | 326.8 | 331.0 | 334.3 | 335.3 | 341.0 | 352.6 | 355.1 | 333.1 |
| 2016 | 340.3 | 338.6 | 338.9 | 341.1 | 341.2 | 338.7 | 343.2 | 345.6 | 346.5 | 356.5 | 371.2 | 373.3 | 347.9 |
| 2017 | 359.9 | 354.7 | 355.2 | 355.3 | 357.4 | 357.8 | 361.4 | 365.7 | 366.6 | 371.9 | 390.1 | 390.1 | 365.5 |
| 2018 | 374.3 | 370.4 | 369.5 | 371.2 | 373.8 | 374.5 | 375.8 | 377.2 | 379.5 | 385.4 | 401.1 | 402.3 | 379.6 |
| 2019 | 388.4 | 382.3 | 379.6 | 380.1 | 382.4 | 384.2 | 389.8 | 391.4 | 391.6 | 397.2 | 409.4 | 412.3 | 390.7 |
| **Wholesale Trade** | | | | | | | | | | | | | |
| 2011 | 48.0 | 48.3 | 48.4 | 48.5 | 48.6 | 48.6 | 48.7 | 48.8 | 48.9 | 49.0 | 49.0 | 49.0 | 48.7 |
| 2012 | 48.9 | 49.1 | 49.5 | 51.2 | 51.6 | 52.0 | 52.2 | 52.7 | 53.0 | 53.4 | 53.4 | 53.5 | 51.7 |
| 2013 | 54.0 | 54.4 | 55.0 | 55.0 | 55.3 | 55.6 | 55.9 | 56.4 | 56.4 | 56.5 | 57.0 | 57.3 | 55.7 |
| 2014 | 56.8 | 57.1 | 57.4 | 57.9 | 58.3 | 58.2 | 58.3 | 58.1 | 58.3 | 58.8 | 59.1 | 59.2 | 58.1 |
| 2015 | 58.7 | 59.0 | 59.1 | 60.2 | 60.6 | 60.4 | 60.9 | 61.1 | 61.3 | 61.8 | 61.6 | 61.7 | 60.5 |
| 2016 | 61.3 | 61.4 | 61.4 | 61.5 | 61.7 | 61.6 | 62.0 | 62.3 | 62.2 | 61.8 | 61.2 | 61.3 | 61.6 |
| 2017 | 61.1 | 61.3 | 61.7 | 62.2 | 62.4 | 62.4 | 62.5 | 63.0 | 63.1 | 63.7 | 63.7 | 63.8 | 62.6 |
| 2018 | 63.5 | 63.9 | 64.2 | 65.0 | 65.8 | 65.7 | 65.7 | 65.9 | 65.9 | 66.5 | 66.6 | 66.9 | 65.5 |
| 2019 | 66.0 | 66.5 | 66.4 | 66.5 | 66.7 | 66.5 | 67.4 | 66.7 | 66.4 | 66.8 | 66.9 | 67.0 | 66.7 |
| **Retail Trade** | | | | | | | | | | | | | |
| 2011 | 157.4 | 155.1 | 154.6 | 155.6 | 155.9 | 155.7 | 156.4 | 157.2 | 157.2 | 159.1 | 168.5 | 170.3 | 158.6 |
| 2012 | 162.7 | 158.9 | 158.5 | 159.8 | 160.1 | 159.4 | 159.7 | 160.1 | 160.2 | 162.5 | 173.9 | 173.4 | 162.4 |
| 2013 | 163.4 | 161.3 | 160.7 | 161.1 | 162.2 | 162.5 | 162.4 | 163.0 | 162.4 | 165.5 | 176.2 | 178.5 | 164.9 |
| 2014 | 167.8 | 165.6 | 165.6 | 166.5 | 166.5 | 166.7 | 166.9 | 168.1 | 167.8 | 170.3 | 180.4 | 182.6 | 169.6 |
| 2015 | 172.4 | 170.0 | 169.9 | 170.2 | 171.6 | 171.4 | 172.6 | 173.4 | 173.0 | 176.4 | 185.6 | 186.8 | 174.4 |
| 2016 | 177.4 | 175.2 | 175.1 | 175.7 | 175.8 | 174.6 | 176.2 | 176.9 | 176.2 | 179.1 | 188.1 | 188.9 | 178.3 |
| 2017 | 182.8 | 179.0 | 178.6 | 179.0 | 178.7 | 178.1 | 178.6 | 178.9 | 178.0 | 180.0 | 189.4 | 189.5 | 180.9 |
| 2018 | 181.2 | 178.3 | 177.7 | 178.0 | 178.7 | 178.3 | 178.6 | 179.2 | 179.1 | 181.3 | 191.7 | 192.5 | 181.2 |
| 2019 | 182.9 | 179.8 | 178.5 | 178.4 | 179.0 | 178.2 | 179.4 | 179.7 | 178.9 | 181.3 | 188.8 | 191.0 | 181.3 |
| **Transportation and Utilities** | | | | | | | | | | | | | |
| 2011 | 67.2 | 67.2 | 67.2 | 67.2 | 67.7 | 67.8 | 67.6 | 67.9 | 68.9 | 69.1 | 70.0 | 70.6 | 68.2 |
| 2012 | 70.1 | 70.2 | 70.8 | 71.1 | 72.0 | 73.0 | 72.8 | 73.6 | 74.7 | 75.6 | 77.1 | 78.2 | 73.3 |
| 2013 | 75.8 | 76.1 | 76.3 | 76.6 | 77.1 | 77.3 | 77.1 | 78.6 | 79.6 | 81.9 | 84.4 | 85.1 | 78.8 |
| 2014 | 82.1 | 82.2 | 81.8 | 82.5 | 84.0 | 84.8 | 84.4 | 87.7 | 90.2 | 92.4 | 95.8 | 97.1 | 87.1 |
| 2015 | 93.8 | 93.5 | 94.2 | 93.3 | 94.3 | 95.0 | 97.5 | 99.8 | 101.0 | 102.8 | 105.4 | 106.6 | 98.1 |
| 2016 | 101.6 | 102.0 | 102.4 | 103.9 | 103.7 | 102.5 | 105.0 | 106.4 | 108.1 | 115.6 | 121.9 | 123.1 | 108.0 |
| 2017 | 116.0 | 114.4 | 114.9 | 114.1 | 116.3 | 117.3 | 120.3 | 123.8 | 125.5 | 128.2 | 137.0 | 136.8 | 122.1 |
| 2018 | 129.6 | 128.2 | 127.6 | 128.2 | 129.3 | 130.5 | 131.5 | 132.1 | 134.5 | 137.6 | 142.8 | 142.9 | 132.9 |
| 2019 | 139.5 | 136.0 | 134.7 | 135.2 | 136.7 | 139.5 | 143.0 | 145.0 | 146.3 | 149.1 | 153.7 | 154.3 | 142.8 |
| **Information** | | | | | | | | | | | | | |
| 2011 | 13.1 | 13.0 | 12.8 | 12.7 | 12.6 | 12.6 | 12.6 | 12.5 | 12.1 | 12.0 | 11.9 | 11.9 | 12.5 |
| 2012 | 12.2 | 12.1 | 12.1 | 12.0 | 12.0 | 12.1 | 12.1 | 11.9 | 11.8 | 11.8 | 11.9 | 12.0 | 12.0 |
| 2013 | 11.9 | 11.9 | 11.8 | 11.8 | 11.9 | 12.0 | 11.9 | 11.8 | 11.7 | 11.8 | 11.8 | 11.8 | 11.8 |
| 2014 | 11.8 | 11.7 | 11.6 | 11.6 | 11.6 | 11.7 | 11.5 | 11.4 | 11.3 | 11.4 | 11.5 | 11.6 | 11.6 |
| 2015 | 11.6 | 11.6 | 11.6 | 11.8 | 11.8 | 11.5 | 11.7 | 11.7 | 11.5 | 11.8 | 11.9 | 12.0 | 11.7 |
| 2016 | 11.8 | 11.7 | 11.7 | 11.9 | 12.0 | 12.0 | 12.1 | 11.9 | 11.7 | 11.5 | 11.6 | 11.6 | 11.8 |
| 2017 | 11.6 | 11.5 | 11.6 | 11.6 | 11.6 | 11.5 | 11.9 | 11.7 | 11.5 | 11.6 | 11.4 | 11.6 | 11.6 |
| 2018 | 11.4 | 11.3 | 11.4 | 11.5 | 11.5 | 11.5 | 11.6 | 11.5 | 11.3 | 11.3 | 11.4 | 11.5 | 11.4 |
| 2019 | 11.6 | 11.6 | 11.4 | 11.7 | 11.6 | 11.6 | 11.7 | 11.5 | 11.3 | 11.3 | 11.5 | 11.4 | 11.5 |

## Employment by Industry: Riverside-San Bernardino-Ontario, CA, 2011–2019—*Continued*

(Numbers in thousands, not seasonally adjusted)

| Industry and year | January | February | March | April | May | June | July | August | September | October | November | December | Annual average |
|---|---|---|---|---|---|---|---|---|---|---|---|---|---|
| **Financial Activities** | | | | | | | | | | | | | |
| 2011 | 39.8 | 40.1 | 39.9 | 39.9 | 39.6 | 39.6 | 39.3 | 39.4 | 39.3 | 39.4 | 39.5 | 39.5 | 39.6 |
| 2012 | 39.2 | 39.4 | 39.7 | 40.3 | 40.4 | 40.3 | 40.4 | 40.6 | 40.7 | 41.0 | 41.2 | 41.3 | 40.4 |
| 2013 | 40.9 | 41.1 | 41.1 | 41.4 | 41.7 | 41.7 | 41.6 | 41.7 | 41.6 | 41.8 | 41.9 | 41.9 | 41.5 |
| 2014 | 41.7 | 41.7 | 41.7 | 42.8 | 42.9 | 42.8 | 42.7 | 42.7 | 42.6 | 42.9 | 43.1 | 43.2 | 42.6 |
| 2015 | 43.0 | 43.2 | 43.3 | 43.6 | 43.7 | 43.6 | 43.7 | 43.7 | 43.4 | 44.2 | 44.1 | 44.3 | 43.7 |
| 2016 | 44.3 | 44.1 | 43.8 | 44.2 | 44.2 | 44.2 | 44.5 | 44.5 | 44.3 | 44.5 | 44.5 | 44.4 | 44.3 |
| 2017 | 44.0 | 43.9 | 43.8 | 44.3 | 44.2 | 43.8 | 43.8 | 43.8 | 43.6 | 44.0 | 43.9 | 43.9 | 43.9 |
| 2018 | 43.8 | 43.9 | 43.7 | 43.9 | 44.0 | 43.9 | 43.7 | 43.7 | 43.5 | 44.0 | 43.9 | 44.0 | 43.8 |
| 2019 | 43.6 | 43.8 | 43.8 | 44.0 | 44.1 | 43.9 | 44.4 | 44.4 | 44.2 | 44.7 | 44.6 | 44.5 | 44.2 |
| **Professional and Business Services** | | | | | | | | | | | | | |
| 2011 | 122.7 | 124.9 | 125.3 | 125.4 | 124.0 | 123.2 | 124.5 | 127.2 | 127.8 | 128.0 | 127.8 | 126.6 | 125.6 |
| 2012 | 124.6 | 126.5 | 125.7 | 128.0 | 126.7 | 128.0 | 127.1 | 127.5 | 127.0 | 129.7 | 128.3 | 125.8 | 127.1 |
| 2013 | 126.4 | 129.5 | 128.8 | 131.5 | 130.3 | 130.9 | 131.9 | 134.3 | 135.2 | 135.7 | 135.3 | 133.7 | 132.0 |
| 2014 | 130.7 | 133.1 | 133.9 | 136.2 | 134.3 | 134.9 | 136.2 | 137.8 | 139.7 | 141.1 | 151.3 | 152.6 | 138.7 |
| 2015 | 145.2 | 142.7 | 141.8 | 144.0 | 143.2 | 144.2 | 144.1 | 144.0 | 144.3 | 152.1 | 159.9 | 163.8 | 147.4 |
| 2016 | 149.4 | 145.8 | 142.4 | 143.1 | 142.0 | 142.3 | 143.2 | 144.0 | 146.5 | 147.3 | 146.0 | 146.8 | 144.9 |
| 2017 | 145.5 | 145.7 | 147.2 | 144.1 | 143.9 | 145.0 | 144.6 | 146.2 | 147.9 | 150.1 | 151.4 | 150.9 | 146.9 |
| 2018 | 147.7 | 149.3 | 149.6 | 150.3 | 149.1 | 149.4 | 150.6 | 152.1 | 153.0 | 155.3 | 155.3 | 154.9 | 151.4 |
| 2019 | 150.2 | 151.2 | 152.7 | 156.0 | 153.6 | 153.9 | 156.3 | 158.1 | 157.4 | 158.1 | 159.2 | 159.1 | 155.5 |
| **Education and Health Services** | | | | | | | | | | | | | |
| 2011 | 162.9 | 165.2 | 165.5 | 166.7 | 165.9 | 164.4 | 163.8 | 164.3 | 167.1 | 168.6 | 169.8 | 170.5 | 166.2 |
| 2012 | 170.4 | 172.2 | 173.3 | 173.5 | 173.6 | 173.2 | 171.7 | 172.7 | 175.2 | 178.2 | 179.2 | 180.0 | 174.4 |
| 2013 | 184.4 | 185.9 | 187.4 | 187.8 | 188.2 | 188.1 | 185.3 | 187.2 | 189.5 | 191.7 | 193.4 | 193.5 | 188.5 |
| 2014 | 191.4 | 193.4 | 194.3 | 195.5 | 195.1 | 194.2 | 193.3 | 195.5 | 197.1 | 199.5 | 200.4 | 200.9 | 195.9 |
| 2015 | 201.6 | 203.4 | 203.7 | 204.8 | 204.6 | 204.1 | 204.8 | 206.3 | 208.3 | 210.6 | 211.5 | 212.4 | 206.3 |
| 2016 | 210.6 | 212.4 | 212.7 | 216.0 | 215.5 | 213.8 | 212.8 | 214.8 | 216.6 | 221.2 | 221.7 | 220.3 | 215.7 |
| 2017 | 220.3 | 222.0 | 222.9 | 225.0 | 225.5 | 224.5 | 223.3 | 226.1 | 227.9 | 233.6 | 234.5 | 234.3 | 226.7 |
| 2018 | 234.8 | 237.0 | 238.0 | 237.5 | 237.5 | 236.9 | 237.4 | 239.2 | 240.8 | 244.4 | 245.1 | 244.9 | 239.5 |
| 2019 | 244.6 | 247.3 | 247.7 | 247.4 | 247.3 | 247.2 | 248.2 | 250.7 | 251.4 | 254.4 | 257.8 | 256.7 | 250.1 |
| **Leisure and Hospitality** | | | | | | | | | | | | | |
| 2011 | 124.4 | 124.0 | 125.8 | 125.2 | 125.0 | 123.6 | 122.2 | 121.4 | 121.5 | 122.2 | 125.6 | 127.5 | 124.0 |
| 2012 | 126.8 | 127.6 | 129.1 | 130.6 | 130.5 | 129.2 | 128.5 | 128.4 | 128.3 | 128.6 | 131.9 | 133.1 | 129.4 |
| 2013 | 133.2 | 133.8 | 135.7 | 137.0 | 137.0 | 135.5 | 133.4 | 133.7 | 134.3 | 135.7 | 139.2 | 141.7 | 135.9 |
| 2014 | 142.2 | 143.9 | 145.3 | 144.8 | 145.8 | 144.3 | 143.2 | 143.0 | 143.4 | 144.9 | 147.8 | 148.8 | 144.8 |
| 2015 | 148.8 | 150.1 | 152.2 | 152.6 | 152.8 | 151.6 | 149.7 | 149.9 | 149.8 | 151.6 | 154.5 | 156.9 | 151.7 |
| 2016 | 157.1 | 158.7 | 160.5 | 161.3 | 161.8 | 159.9 | 159.3 | 158.7 | 158.4 | 159.6 | 162.5 | 164.0 | 160.2 |
| 2017 | 163.5 | 165.4 | 168.5 | 167.8 | 168.8 | 167.0 | 164.3 | 164.0 | 164.2 | 165.4 | 168.0 | 169.0 | 166.3 |
| 2018 | 168.4 | 170.1 | 172.1 | 172.2 | 171.7 | 169.8 | 168.5 | 168.2 | 168.5 | 170.1 | 173.6 | 174.4 | 170.6 |
| 2019 | 174.2 | 176.5 | 179.2 | 179.5 | 177.6 | 175.8 | 173.2 | 172.4 | 171.9 | 172.6 | 175.2 | 174.6 | 175.2 |
| **Other Services** | | | | | | | | | | | | | |
| 2011 | 38.0 | 38.5 | 38.6 | 39.1 | 39.4 | 39.4 | 39.1 | 39.4 | 39.4 | 39.5 | 39.4 | 39.4 | 39.1 |
| 2012 | 38.8 | 39.2 | 39.5 | 40.3 | 40.6 | 40.8 | 40.5 | 40.7 | 40.8 | 39.9 | 40.0 | 39.7 | 40.1 |
| 2013 | 39.8 | 40.2 | 41.1 | 41.1 | 41.1 | 41.3 | 40.9 | 41.4 | 41.5 | 41.7 | 41.9 | 41.7 | 41.1 |
| 2014 | 42.1 | 42.6 | 43.1 | 43.7 | 43.6 | 43.4 | 42.9 | 43.2 | 43.2 | 42.7 | 43.0 | 42.9 | 43.0 |
| 2015 | 42.7 | 43.3 | 43.7 | 44.5 | 44.3 | 44.3 | 44.4 | 44.0 | 44.0 | 44.4 | 44.3 | 44.2 | 44.0 |
| 2016 | 44.0 | 44.4 | 44.7 | 44.9 | 44.9 | 44.8 | 44.4 | 44.5 | 44.8 | 44.9 | 44.7 | 44.5 | 44.6 |
| 2017 | 44.3 | 44.6 | 45.0 | 45.8 | 46.0 | 46.0 | 45.7 | 45.8 | 45.5 | 45.7 | 45.5 | 45.1 | 45.4 |
| 2018 | 45.2 | 45.7 | 45.8 | 46.2 | 46.1 | 46.2 | 45.6 | 45.7 | 45.4 | 46.1 | 45.9 | 45.3 | 45.8 |
| 2019 | 45.5 | 45.7 | 45.9 | 46.4 | 46.6 | 46.5 | 46.1 | 46.2 | 45.7 | 45.4 | 45.2 | 44.5 | 45.8 |
| **Government** | | | | | | | | | | | | | |
| 2011 | 231.3 | 231.6 | 233.4 | 233.4 | 233.6 | 230.8 | 214.0 | 217.8 | 220.0 | 227.9 | 229.1 | 226.8 | 227.5 |
| 2012 | 228.1 | 228.1 | 229.6 | 229.8 | 230.1 | 226.1 | 209.2 | 215.0 | 216.7 | 226.5 | 229.0 | 227.0 | 224.6 |
| 2013 | 226.9 | 227.2 | 228.6 | 228.5 | 229.6 | 227.8 | 211.0 | 216.6 | 221.0 | 227.6 | 229.6 | 227.5 | 225.2 |
| 2014 | 228.4 | 228.6 | 231.6 | 232.8 | 232.7 | 231.4 | 215.1 | 220.3 | 224.8 | 232.2 | 234.1 | 233.0 | 228.8 |
| 2015 | 232.4 | 233.3 | 236.1 | 236.4 | 237.2 | 234.4 | 219.4 | 225.5 | 229.6 | 237.3 | 239.6 | 238.3 | 233.3 |
| 2016 | 239.8 | 239.2 | 243.2 | 244.5 | 244.9 | 244.2 | 231.4 | 235.8 | 240.0 | 246.4 | 249.1 | 249.2 | 242.3 |
| 2017 | 249.2 | 249.3 | 252.2 | 251.3 | 253.9 | 253.3 | 239.4 | 242.2 | 249.6 | 255.8 | 258.4 | 257.5 | 251.0 |
| 2018 | 257.7 | 257.6 | 260.4 | 260.5 | 261.3 | 261.8 | 244.7 | 246.2 | 251.8 | 259.1 | 261.8 | 263.2 | 257.2 |
| 2019 | 262.0 | 261.5 | 264.5 | 264.4 | 265.2 | 264.5 | 248.9 | 251.6 | 255.4 | 262.3 | 264.1 | 261.9 | 260.5 |

# Employment by Industry: Detroit-Warren-Dearborn, MI, 2011–2019

(Numbers in thousands, not seasonally adjusted)

| Industry and year | January | February | March | April | May | June | July | August | September | October | November | December | Annual average |
|---|---|---|---|---|---|---|---|---|---|---|---|---|---|
| **Total Nonfarm** | | | | | | | | | | | | | |
| 2011 | 1,730.8 | 1,739.1 | 1,750.9 | 1,775.0 | 1,792.9 | 1,800.0 | 1,769.9 | 1,785.4 | 1,805.4 | 1,820.0 | 1,826.9 | 1,821.6 | 1,784.8 |
| 2012 | 1,790.6 | 1,797.4 | 1,811.9 | 1,817.4 | 1,840.0 | 1,849.1 | 1,821.4 | 1,834.4 | 1,842.5 | 1,855.6 | 1,863.6 | 1,862.6 | 1,832.2 |
| 2013 | 1,825.5 | 1,834.2 | 1,844.9 | 1,851.0 | 1,879.3 | 1,889.1 | 1,844.7 | 1,866.3 | 1,877.5 | 1,893.3 | 1,898.1 | 1,891.6 | 1,866.3 |
| 2014 | 1,847.2 | 1,862.2 | 1,870.8 | 1,872.8 | 1,904.6 | 1,924.2 | 1,892.4 | 1,901.7 | 1,903.9 | 1,921.2 | 1,932.3 | 1,934.1 | 1,897.3 |
| 2015 | 1,893.1 | 1,896.3 | 1,904.0 | 1,918.3 | 1,949.9 | 1,960.9 | 1,930.3 | 1,938.8 | 1,945.6 | 1,960.4 | 1,968.5 | 1,966.0 | 1,936.0 |
| 2016 | 1,931.2 | 1,932.6 | 1,938.7 | 1,962.9 | 1,983.3 | 1,996.5 | 1,973.6 | 1,976.2 | 1,988.5 | 1,996.6 | 2,012.7 | 2,002.9 | 1,974.6 |
| 2017 | 1,968.3 | 1,971.4 | 1,978.7 | 1,992.7 | 2,018.2 | 2,034.5 | 1,995.5 | 2,009.9 | 2,013.7 | 2,021.3 | 2,034.7 | 2,026.8 | 2,005.5 |
| 2018 | 1,989.6 | 1,997.6 | 2,010.5 | 2,017.2 | 2,040.9 | 2,057.0 | 2,023.7 | 2,035.3 | 2,031.8 | 2,051.2 | 2,060.2 | 2,052.1 | 2,030.6 |
| 2019 | 2,009.9 | 2,014.8 | 2,021.6 | 2,027.1 | 2,049.8 | 2,063.7 | 2,029.9 | 2,043.7 | 2,041.6 | 2,047.5 | 2,057.3 | 2,058.7 | 2,038.8 |
| **Total Private** | | | | | | | | | | | | | |
| 2011 | 1,531.6 | 1,535.6 | 1,547.3 | 1,571.4 | 1,591.9 | 1,600.4 | 1,586.6 | 1,603.2 | 1,607.9 | 1,619.4 | 1,625.3 | 1,622.2 | 1,586.9 |
| 2012 | 1,596.2 | 1,599.2 | 1,613.4 | 1,619.4 | 1,643.8 | 1,653.3 | 1,642.7 | 1,655.9 | 1,649.3 | 1,661.1 | 1,668.0 | 1,668.8 | 1,639.3 |
| 2013 | 1,636.9 | 1,642.1 | 1,652.9 | 1,659.5 | 1,690.1 | 1,700.1 | 1,671.9 | 1,695.0 | 1,691.1 | 1,703.9 | 1,708.4 | 1,703.7 | 1,679.6 |
| 2014 | 1,663.5 | 1,674.4 | 1,682.5 | 1,683.8 | 1,717.8 | 1,737.8 | 1,721.5 | 1,732.1 | 1,720.7 | 1,733.2 | 1,742.7 | 1,747.5 | 1,713.1 |
| 2015 | 1,711.1 | 1,710.5 | 1,717.3 | 1,730.8 | 1,763.1 | 1,775.6 | 1,760.8 | 1,770.9 | 1,763.0 | 1,773.7 | 1,780.6 | 1,779.6 | 1,753.1 |
| 2016 | 1,749.0 | 1,746.6 | 1,750.5 | 1,775.2 | 1,798.1 | 1,811.0 | 1,801.4 | 1,804.7 | 1,802.9 | 1,808.8 | 1,822.3 | 1,814.8 | 1,790.4 |
| 2017 | 1,784.2 | 1,784.7 | 1,790.7 | 1,804.4 | 1,829.9 | 1,846.3 | 1,822.0 | 1,837.9 | 1,826.5 | 1,831.4 | 1,844.0 | 1,837.5 | 1,820.0 |
| 2018 | 1,804.5 | 1,809.1 | 1,819.6 | 1,826.5 | 1,850.3 | 1,866.6 | 1,848.8 | 1,861.2 | 1,844.1 | 1,858.9 | 1,865.7 | 1,860.5 | 1,843.0 |
| 2019 | 1,822.1 | 1,825.0 | 1,830.2 | 1,835.2 | 1,857.8 | 1,870.9 | 1,852.2 | 1,866.4 | 1,850.5 | 1,853.0 | 1,862.5 | 1,865.4 | 1,849.3 |
| **Goods Producing** | | | | | | | | | | | | | |
| 2011 | 232.4 | 233.9 | 236.2 | 244.6 | 251.3 | 257.2 | 254.1 | 260.6 | 262.0 | 262.8 | 263.7 | 262.1 | 251.7 |
| 2012 | 256.9 | 256.0 | 259.1 | 260.0 | 267.4 | 271.4 | 271.2 | 274.1 | 274.2 | 275.1 | 274.4 | 272.5 | 267.7 |
| 2013 | 267.6 | 267.9 | 269.8 | 272.0 | 280.5 | 284.4 | 277.0 | 286.1 | 286.9 | 288.5 | 287.9 | 280.8 | 279.1 |
| 2014 | 274.9 | 280.5 | 282.0 | 278.6 | 290.1 | 301.7 | 297.9 | 302.9 | 299.1 | 301.7 | 304.0 | 303.8 | 293.1 |
| 2015 | 294.8 | 294.3 | 295.4 | 300.0 | 308.9 | 314.3 | 310.6 | 314.6 | 314.4 | 312.4 | 313.7 | 310.2 | 307.0 |
| 2016 | 306.0 | 302.6 | 303.0 | 313.4 | 318.7 | 323.0 | 317.6 | 318.8 | 321.5 | 321.3 | 325.2 | 318.6 | 315.8 |
| 2017 | 316.1 | 316.5 | 315.8 | 321.6 | 329.0 | 333.8 | 323.1 | 333.4 | 329.4 | 330.9 | 332.1 | 327.2 | 325.7 |
| 2018 | 320.6 | 324.5 | 327.5 | 330.0 | 335.2 | 339.5 | 335.1 | 340.1 | 337.5 | 339.9 | 339.1 | 336.8 | 333.8 |
| 2019 | 323.1 | 328.5 | 329.0 | 330.3 | 337.3 | 340.2 | 332.7 | 339.4 | 338.3 | 334.4 | 335.8 | 333.2 | 333.5 |
| **Service-Providing** | | | | | | | | | | | | | |
| 2011 | 1,498.4 | 1,505.2 | 1,514.7 | 1,530.4 | 1,541.6 | 1,542.8 | 1,515.8 | 1,524.8 | 1,543.4 | 1,557.2 | 1,563.2 | 1,559.5 | 1,533.1 |
| 2012 | 1,533.7 | 1,541.4 | 1,552.8 | 1,557.4 | 1,572.6 | 1,577.7 | 1,550.2 | 1,560.3 | 1,568.3 | 1,580.5 | 1,589.2 | 1,590.1 | 1,564.5 |
| 2013 | 1,557.9 | 1,566.3 | 1,575.1 | 1,579.0 | 1,598.8 | 1,604.7 | 1,567.7 | 1,580.2 | 1,590.6 | 1,604.8 | 1,610.2 | 1,610.8 | 1,587.2 |
| 2014 | 1,572.3 | 1,581.7 | 1,588.8 | 1,594.2 | 1,614.5 | 1,622.5 | 1,594.5 | 1,598.8 | 1,604.8 | 1,619.5 | 1,628.3 | 1,630.3 | 1,604.2 |
| 2015 | 1,598.3 | 1,602.0 | 1,608.6 | 1,618.3 | 1,641.0 | 1,646.6 | 1,619.7 | 1,624.2 | 1,631.2 | 1,648.0 | 1,654.8 | 1,655.8 | 1,629.0 |
| 2016 | 1,625.2 | 1,630.0 | 1,635.7 | 1,649.5 | 1,664.6 | 1,673.5 | 1,656.0 | 1,657.4 | 1,667.0 | 1,675.3 | 1,687.5 | 1,684.3 | 1,658.8 |
| 2017 | 1,652.2 | 1,654.9 | 1,662.9 | 1,671.1 | 1,689.2 | 1,700.7 | 1,672.4 | 1,676.5 | 1,684.3 | 1,690.4 | 1,702.6 | 1,699.6 | 1,679.7 |
| 2018 | 1,669.0 | 1,673.1 | 1,683.0 | 1,687.2 | 1,705.7 | 1,717.5 | 1,688.6 | 1,695.2 | 1,694.3 | 1,711.3 | 1,721.1 | 1,715.3 | 1,696.8 |
| 2019 | 1,686.8 | 1,686.3 | 1,692.6 | 1,696.8 | 1,712.5 | 1,723.5 | 1,697.2 | 1,704.3 | 1,703.3 | 1,713.1 | 1,721.5 | 1,725.5 | 1,705.3 |
| **Mining, Logging, and Construction** | | | | | | | | | | | | | |
| 2011 | 47.4 | 46.2 | 47.3 | 50.3 | 54.7 | 58.6 | 60.4 | 60.6 | 59.7 | 59.0 | 57.8 | 55.2 | 54.8 |
| 2012 | 51.0 | 49.1 | 50.3 | 52.9 | 56.4 | 59.1 | 59.9 | 60.0 | 60.0 | 59.7 | 58.4 | 55.8 | 56.1 |
| 2013 | 52.2 | 50.7 | 51.8 | 53.3 | 59.6 | 61.1 | 62.7 | 62.6 | 61.6 | 61.9 | 60.7 | 57.9 | 58.0 |
| 2014 | 53.1 | 52.6 | 52.9 | 55.3 | 62.2 | 65.5 | 66.3 | 67.9 | 68.0 | 67.7 | 66.1 | 63.4 | 61.8 |
| 2015 | 58.0 | 56.9 | 58.3 | 62.1 | 67.3 | 70.2 | 70.3 | 70.5 | 69.6 | 70.2 | 68.8 | 65.9 | 65.7 |
| 2016 | 61.1 | 60.0 | 61.3 | 65.7 | 70.4 | 71.8 | 72.9 | 73.0 | 72.8 | 72.9 | 71.7 | 66.8 | 68.4 |
| 2017 | 64.0 | 63.2 | 64.4 | 68.5 | 74.2 | 76.7 | 77.5 | 77.9 | 77.1 | 76.7 | 75.0 | 70.4 | 72.1 |
| 2018 | 66.3 | 66.0 | 67.5 | 70.4 | 76.6 | 79.3 | 79.6 | 79.9 | 77.8 | 78.8 | 76.5 | 73.2 | 74.3 |
| 2019 | 68.5 | 67.4 | 68.3 | 71.4 | 77.7 | 79.6 | 80.9 | 81.2 | 80.7 | 81.9 | 77.0 | 73.3 | 75.7 |
| **Manufacturing** | | | | | | | | | | | | | |
| 2011 | 185.0 | 187.7 | 188.9 | 194.3 | 196.6 | 198.6 | 193.7 | 200.0 | 202.3 | 203.8 | 205.9 | 206.9 | 197.0 |
| 2012 | 205.9 | 206.9 | 208.8 | 207.1 | 211.0 | 212.3 | 211.3 | 214.1 | 214.2 | 215.4 | 216.0 | 216.7 | 211.6 |
| 2013 | 215.4 | 217.2 | 218.0 | 218.7 | 220.9 | 223.3 | 214.3 | 223.5 | 225.3 | 226.6 | 227.2 | 222.9 | 221.1 |
| 2014 | 221.8 | 227.9 | 229.1 | 223.3 | 227.9 | 236.2 | 231.6 | 235.0 | 231.1 | 234.0 | 237.9 | 240.4 | 231.4 |
| 2015 | 236.8 | 237.4 | 237.1 | 237.9 | 241.6 | 244.1 | 240.3 | 244.1 | 244.8 | 242.2 | 244.9 | 244.3 | 241.3 |
| 2016 | 244.9 | 242.6 | 241.7 | 247.7 | 248.3 | 251.2 | 244.7 | 245.8 | 248.7 | 248.4 | 253.5 | 251.8 | 247.4 |
| 2017 | 252.1 | 253.3 | 251.4 | 253.1 | 254.8 | 257.1 | 245.6 | 255.5 | 252.3 | 254.2 | 257.1 | 256.8 | 253.6 |
| 2018 | 254.3 | 258.5 | 260.0 | 259.6 | 258.6 | 260.2 | 255.5 | 260.2 | 259.7 | 261.1 | 262.6 | 263.6 | 259.5 |
| 2019 | 254.6 | 261.1 | 260.7 | 258.9 | 259.6 | 260.6 | 251.8 | 258.2 | 257.6 | 252.5 | 258.8 | 259.9 | 257.9 |

## Employment by Industry: Detroit-Warren-Dearborn, MI, 2011–2019—*Continued*

(Numbers in thousands, not seasonally adjusted)

| Industry and year | January | February | March | April | May | June | July | August | September | October | November | December | Annual average |
|---|---|---|---|---|---|---|---|---|---|---|---|---|---|
| **Trade, Transportation, and Utilities** | | | | | | | | | | | | | |
| 2011 | 328.0 | 325.0 | 326.0 | 329.0 | 332.7 | 334.4 | 333.4 | 334.7 | 334.4 | 337.7 | 345.5 | 348.6 | 334.1 |
| 2012 | 337.6 | 334.3 | 335.8 | 334.7 | 339.5 | 341.3 | 338.9 | 340.2 | 339.1 | 343.2 | 352.9 | 354.3 | 341.0 |
| 2013 | 340.8 | 338.3 | 339.0 | 339.1 | 344.4 | 347.5 | 345.6 | 347.5 | 345.9 | 349.1 | 356.9 | 361.4 | 346.3 |
| 2014 | 348.0 | 346.3 | 346.9 | 349.1 | 353.8 | 355.8 | 353.6 | 354.6 | 352.7 | 357.1 | 365.3 | 369.8 | 354.4 |
| 2015 | 355.2 | 352.4 | 352.8 | 354.4 | 359.3 | 361.1 | 358.6 | 359.6 | 357.2 | 360.6 | 369.4 | 373.4 | 359.5 |
| 2016 | 360.1 | 357.5 | 357.7 | 359.6 | 363.8 | 365.2 | 364.3 | 365.4 | 363.8 | 366.8 | 375.3 | 378.3 | 364.8 |
| 2017 | 366.1 | 362.7 | 363.4 | 364.6 | 367.7 | 370.1 | 367.7 | 368.9 | 367.5 | 371.9 | 381.1 | 383.7 | 369.6 |
| 2018 | 370.1 | 366.9 | 367.5 | 367.8 | 372.7 | 374.8 | 373.8 | 375.4 | 373.3 | 378.8 | 388.9 | 390.7 | 375.1 |
| 2019 | 378.8 | 374.2 | 373.9 | 373.6 | 378.0 | 380.7 | 380.9 | 382.2 | 379.1 | 385.0 | 392.2 | 396.7 | 381.3 |
| **Wholesale Trade** | | | | | | | | | | | | | |
| 2011 | 78.9 | 78.9 | 79.3 | 80.3 | 80.6 | 80.8 | 81.1 | 81.3 | 80.9 | 81.1 | 81.6 | 81.6 | 80.5 |
| 2012 | 81.4 | 81.7 | 81.9 | 81.9 | 82.8 | 83.2 | 83.1 | 83.3 | 82.9 | 83.4 | 83.4 | 83.6 | 82.7 |
| 2013 | 83.1 | 83.2 | 83.5 | 83.3 | 83.9 | 84.4 | 84.0 | 84.0 | 83.6 | 83.3 | 83.3 | 83.7 | 83.6 |
| 2014 | 83.1 | 83.2 | 83.2 | 83.2 | 84.3 | 84.7 | 84.1 | 84.3 | 83.8 | 83.7 | 84.0 | 84.4 | 83.8 |
| 2015 | 83.3 | 83.6 | 83.6 | 83.9 | 84.6 | 84.9 | 84.7 | 84.8 | 84.0 | 84.0 | 84.1 | 84.3 | 84.2 |
| 2016 | 83.3 | 83.7 | 83.4 | 84.1 | 84.8 | 85.2 | 84.9 | 85.2 | 84.7 | 84.9 | 85.2 | 85.5 | 84.6 |
| 2017 | 85.0 | 85.3 | 85.5 | 85.3 | 85.9 | 86.4 | 85.8 | 86.0 | 85.5 | 85.5 | 85.4 | 85.9 | 85.6 |
| 2018 | 85.9 | 86.1 | 86.2 | 86.0 | 86.5 | 86.9 | 86.9 | 86.7 | 86.2 | 86.7 | 86.4 | 86.7 | 86.4 |
| 2019 | 85.8 | 85.9 | 85.8 | 84.9 | 85.4 | 85.6 | 85.7 | 85.5 | 84.9 | 85.4 | 84.9 | 85.9 | 85.5 |
| **Retail Trade** | | | | | | | | | | | | | |
| 2011 | 192.9 | 190.1 | 190.6 | 192.6 | 194.9 | 195.5 | 195.1 | 195.8 | 195.3 | 198.4 | 205.2 | 207.5 | 196.2 |
| 2012 | 197.2 | 193.5 | 194.6 | 194.1 | 197.2 | 198.0 | 196.7 | 197.3 | 196.0 | 199.0 | 208.3 | 208.8 | 198.4 |
| 2013 | 197.3 | 194.4 | 194.9 | 195.4 | 199.2 | 201.3 | 200.9 | 201.9 | 200.4 | 203.0 | 210.0 | 212.7 | 201.0 |
| 2014 | 201.0 | 199.1 | 199.7 | 201.7 | 204.8 | 206.2 | 204.9 | 205.5 | 204.0 | 208.3 | 215.7 | 217.6 | 205.7 |
| 2015 | 205.0 | 203.0 | 203.8 | 204.3 | 207.8 | 208.9 | 207.2 | 208.3 | 206.3 | 209.3 | 216.5 | 218.5 | 208.2 |
| 2016 | 208.0 | 205.9 | 206.5 | 207.7 | 210.8 | 211.6 | 211.1 | 211.9 | 209.7 | 212.3 | 219.0 | 220.9 | 211.3 |
| 2017 | 211.2 | 208.5 | 208.9 | 210.0 | 211.9 | 213.1 | 212.0 | 212.3 | 210.6 | 213.5 | 220.5 | 220.6 | 212.8 |
| 2018 | 210.9 | 207.8 | 208.0 | 207.7 | 211.3 | 212.0 | 211.8 | 212.1 | 208.8 | 211.2 | 218.6 | 219.1 | 211.6 |
| 2019 | 210.5 | 207.0 | 207.2 | 207.8 | 210.4 | 210.8 | 210.1 | 210.5 | 207.6 | 210.6 | 215.6 | 217.9 | 210.5 |
| **Transportation and Utilities** | | | | | | | | | | | | | |
| 2011 | 56.2 | 56.0 | 56.1 | 56.1 | 57.2 | 58.1 | 57.2 | 57.6 | 58.2 | 58.2 | 58.7 | 59.5 | 57.4 |
| 2012 | 59.0 | 59.1 | 59.3 | 58.7 | 59.5 | 60.1 | 59.1 | 59.6 | 60.2 | 60.8 | 61.2 | 61.9 | 59.9 |
| 2013 | 60.4 | 60.7 | 60.6 | 60.4 | 61.3 | 61.8 | 60.7 | 61.6 | 61.9 | 62.8 | 63.6 | 65.0 | 61.7 |
| 2014 | 63.9 | 64.0 | 64.0 | 64.2 | 64.7 | 64.9 | 64.6 | 64.8 | 64.9 | 65.1 | 65.6 | 67.8 | 64.9 |
| 2015 | 66.9 | 65.8 | 65.4 | 66.2 | 66.9 | 67.3 | 66.7 | 66.5 | 66.9 | 67.3 | 68.8 | 70.6 | 67.1 |
| 2016 | 68.8 | 67.9 | 67.8 | 67.8 | 68.2 | 68.4 | 68.3 | 68.3 | 69.4 | 69.6 | 71.1 | 71.9 | 69.0 |
| 2017 | 69.9 | 68.9 | 69.0 | 69.3 | 69.9 | 70.6 | 69.9 | 70.6 | 71.4 | 72.9 | 75.2 | 77.2 | 71.2 |
| 2018 | 73.3 | 73.0 | 73.3 | 74.1 | 74.9 | 75.9 | 75.1 | 76.6 | 78.3 | 80.9 | 83.9 | 84.9 | 77.0 |
| 2019 | 82.5 | 81.3 | 80.9 | 80.9 | 82.2 | 84.3 | 85.1 | 86.2 | 86.6 | 89.0 | 91.7 | 92.9 | 85.3 |
| **Information** | | | | | | | | | | | | | |
| 2011 | 26.4 | 26.1 | 26.1 | 25.8 | 26.0 | 26.0 | 26.1 | 26.2 | 26.0 | 26.7 | 26.7 | 26.6 | 26.2 |
| 2012 | 26.8 | 26.6 | 26.7 | 26.3 | 26.5 | 26.3 | 26.6 | 27.0 | 26.2 | 26.4 | 26.6 | 26.6 | 26.6 |
| 2013 | 26.7 | 26.7 | 26.8 | 27.4 | 27.6 | 27.9 | 27.6 | 27.6 | 27.1 | 27.0 | 27.2 | 27.2 | 27.2 |
| 2014 | 27.5 | 27.2 | 27.4 | 27.8 | 27.8 | 28.3 | 28.8 | 28.6 | 27.6 | 28.2 | 28.2 | 27.9 | 27.9 |
| 2015 | 27.2 | 27.0 | 27.0 | 26.8 | 27.3 | 27.7 | 28.3 | 27.7 | 27.6 | 27.3 | 27.5 | 27.1 | 27.4 |
| 2016 | 27.5 | 27.4 | 27.6 | 27.9 | 28.2 | 28.6 | 29.1 | 28.6 | 28.4 | 27.7 | 28.2 | 27.9 | 28.1 |
| 2017 | 27.2 | 27.2 | 27.6 | 27.3 | 27.5 | 27.7 | 27.8 | 27.6 | 27.6 | 27.4 | 27.6 | 27.9 | 27.5 |
| 2018 | 27.1 | 26.7 | 26.7 | 27.2 | 27.6 | 27.8 | 27.5 | 27.5 | 27.0 | 27.0 | 27.2 | 27.0 | 27.2 |
| 2019 | 27.0 | 26.8 | 27.0 | 26.7 | 26.9 | 27.1 | 27.1 | 26.8 | 26.4 | 26.3 | 26.5 | 26.3 | 26.7 |
| **Financial Activities** | | | | | | | | | | | | | |
| 2011 | 96.8 | 97.0 | 97.5 | 98.2 | 98.3 | 99.1 | 99.5 | 99.8 | 98.4 | 97.9 | 97.9 | 98.2 | 98.2 |
| 2012 | 97.7 | 98.0 | 98.5 | 98.5 | 99.3 | 100.7 | 101.8 | 102.3 | 100.5 | 100.9 | 101.2 | 102.2 | 100.1 |
| 2013 | 102.1 | 102.4 | 103.0 | 103.1 | 104.1 | 106.1 | 106.9 | 107.0 | 104.7 | 104.6 | 104.7 | 104.9 | 104.5 |
| 2014 | 104.0 | 104.0 | 103.8 | 103.7 | 105.2 | 106.8 | 106.7 | 107.0 | 105.2 | 105.2 | 105.4 | 105.8 | 105.2 |
| 2015 | 105.3 | 105.4 | 105.7 | 106.6 | 108.1 | 110.1 | 110.2 | 110.5 | 109.2 | 109.6 | 110.0 | 110.3 | 108.4 |
| 2016 | 110.5 | 110.7 | 110.9 | 111.8 | 113.1 | 115.3 | 115.9 | 115.8 | 114.7 | 114.8 | 115.0 | 115.6 | 113.7 |
| 2017 | 115.8 | 115.8 | 115.8 | 116.5 | 117.2 | 119.0 | 119.2 | 118.9 | 117.1 | 116.2 | 116.6 | 116.6 | 117.1 |
| 2018 | 116.4 | 116.5 | 116.6 | 117.0 | 117.8 | 119.5 | 119.9 | 119.6 | 117.9 | 117.9 | 118.1 | 118.7 | 118.0 |
| 2019 | 118.3 | 118.5 | 118.9 | 119.4 | 120.4 | 122.2 | 122.8 | 122.9 | 121.8 | 121.1 | 120.5 | 121.2 | 120.7 |

## Employment by Industry: Detroit-Warren-Dearborn, MI, 2011–2019—*Continued*

(Numbers in thousands, not seasonally adjusted)

| Industry and year | January | February | March | April | May | June | July | August | September | October | November | December | Annual average |
|---|---|---|---|---|---|---|---|---|---|---|---|---|---|
| **Professional and Business Services** | | | | | | | | | | | | | |
| 2011 | 323.1 | 325.4 | 329.3 | 335.3 | 338.8 | 336.9 | 330.3 | 337.3 | 343.1 | 349.5 | 349.8 | 344.4 | 336.9 |
| 2012 | 342.8 | 346.4 | 349.4 | 353.9 | 358.9 | 356.6 | 352.0 | 357.5 | 358.7 | 364.0 | 363.4 | 361.8 | 355.5 |
| 2013 | 357.6 | 360.8 | 364.5 | 365.5 | 373.0 | 372.7 | 358.4 | 368.2 | 371.4 | 376.3 | 375.6 | 373.4 | 368.1 |
| 2014 | 364.2 | 367.6 | 369.1 | 367.7 | 375.3 | 376.4 | 369.7 | 372.9 | 374.1 | 377.3 | 377.2 | 376.5 | 372.3 |
| 2015 | 375.5 | 377.1 | 377.8 | 382.4 | 388.0 | 387.7 | 379.9 | 382.6 | 385.2 | 388.9 | 387.5 | 384.9 | 383.1 |
| 2016 | 379.9 | 380.5 | 380.0 | 386.4 | 390.6 | 392.4 | 388.8 | 390.0 | 391.9 | 395.5 | 396.5 | 392.5 | 388.8 |
| 2017 | 386.5 | 387.1 | 389.3 | 392.6 | 397.9 | 400.2 | 392.5 | 395.4 | 395.2 | 396.2 | 397.6 | 393.2 | 393.6 |
| 2018 | 391.1 | 393.3 | 395.6 | 396.9 | 401.5 | 404.4 | 396.7 | 400.8 | 398.5 | 402.0 | 401.7 | 395.9 | 398.2 |
| 2019 | 391.0 | 392.5 | 391.9 | 392.5 | 394.7 | 396.4 | 389.9 | 393.1 | 391.7 | 391.2 | 394.0 | 391.5 | 392.5 |
| **Education and Health Services** | | | | | | | | | | | | | |
| 2011 | 285.5 | 287.6 | 288.6 | 291.1 | 291.6 | 290.0 | 289.2 | 289.6 | 291.5 | 294.4 | 295.4 | 296.1 | 290.9 |
| 2012 | 291.9 | 295.1 | 296.4 | 294.9 | 295.6 | 295.1 | 293.4 | 293.9 | 294.2 | 297.5 | 298.4 | 299.4 | 295.5 |
| 2013 | 295.0 | 297.8 | 298.4 | 297.8 | 298.3 | 297.4 | 294.7 | 295.5 | 297.2 | 299.8 | 300.7 | 300.6 | 297.8 |
| 2014 | 295.6 | 299.3 | 300.1 | 298.7 | 299.4 | 298.3 | 296.0 | 296.5 | 297.6 | 301.1 | 302.6 | 303.4 | 299.1 |
| 2015 | 298.4 | 300.6 | 301.7 | 300.4 | 302.1 | 301.7 | 300.5 | 303.0 | 301.3 | 308.0 | 308.2 | 309.0 | 302.9 |
| 2016 | 304.7 | 307.1 | 307.5 | 308.3 | 309.5 | 308.1 | 308.0 | 307.5 | 309.0 | 311.2 | 312.3 | 312.7 | 308.8 |
| 2017 | 308.0 | 310.4 | 310.9 | 310.7 | 312.5 | 312.4 | 310.6 | 311.0 | 312.1 | 314.4 | 315.7 | 315.8 | 312.0 |
| 2018 | 313.0 | 315.1 | 316.1 | 316.1 | 316.3 | 316.2 | 314.0 | 314.1 | 313.4 | 316.6 | 316.9 | 316.8 | 315.4 |
| 2019 | 314.8 | 316.4 | 317.4 | 318.7 | 319.5 | 318.7 | 316.3 | 317.3 | 316.9 | 320.1 | 323.0 | 324.3 | 318.6 |
| **Leisure and Hospitality** | | | | | | | | | | | | | |
| 2011 | 165.5 | 166.9 | 169.7 | 173.4 | 178.6 | 181.5 | 179.2 | 180.0 | 177.9 | 175.7 | 172.0 | 171.5 | 174.3 |
| 2012 | 168.6 | 168.7 | 172.5 | 175.3 | 180.2 | 184.3 | 181.7 | 183.1 | 179.1 | 177.1 | 174.6 | 175.6 | 176.7 |
| 2013 | 171.1 | 171.7 | 174.2 | 177.8 | 184.8 | 186.1 | 184.2 | 185.3 | 180.7 | 181.5 | 178.3 | 178.3 | 179.5 |
| 2014 | 172.9 | 173.0 | 176.5 | 181.5 | 188.9 | 192.7 | 190.8 | 191.7 | 187.1 | 185.2 | 183.1 | 183.5 | 183.9 |
| 2015 | 179.7 | 178.6 | 181.7 | 185.2 | 193.5 | 196.2 | 195.6 | 195.6 | 191.4 | 190.2 | 187.9 | 188.0 | 188.6 |
| 2016 | 185.0 | 185.5 | 188.2 | 192.4 | 198.0 | 201.7 | 201.3 | 202.0 | 197.1 | 195.4 | 193.6 | 193.3 | 194.5 |
| 2017 | 189.9 | 190.3 | 192.9 | 196.9 | 202.9 | 207.0 | 205.6 | 207.1 | 202.2 | 199.1 | 197.8 | 197.8 | 199.1 |
| 2018 | 192.1 | 191.7 | 194.8 | 197.2 | 203.9 | 208.4 | 206.7 | 208.0 | 201.4 | 200.7 | 198.2 | 199.4 | 200.2 |
| 2019 | 194.7 | 193.6 | 197.1 | 198.9 | 205.1 | 209.1 | 206.8 | 208.9 | 201.4 | 199.9 | 195.7 | 197.6 | 200.7 |
| **Other Services** | | | | | | | | | | | | | |
| 2011 | 73.9 | 73.7 | 73.9 | 74.0 | 74.6 | 75.3 | 74.8 | 75.0 | 74.6 | 74.7 | 74.3 | 74.7 | 74.5 |
| 2012 | 73.9 | 74.1 | 75.0 | 75.8 | 76.4 | 77.6 | 77.1 | 77.8 | 77.3 | 76.9 | 76.5 | 76.4 | 76.2 |
| 2013 | 76.0 | 76.5 | 77.2 | 76.8 | 77.4 | 78.0 | 77.5 | 77.8 | 77.2 | 77.1 | 77.1 | 77.1 | 77.1 |
| 2014 | 76.4 | 76.5 | 76.7 | 76.7 | 77.3 | 77.8 | 78.0 | 77.9 | 77.3 | 77.4 | 76.9 | 76.8 | 77.1 |
| 2015 | 75.0 | 75.1 | 75.2 | 75.0 | 75.9 | 76.8 | 77.1 | 77.3 | 76.7 | 76.7 | 76.4 | 76.7 | 76.2 |
| 2016 | 75.3 | 75.3 | 75.6 | 75.4 | 76.2 | 76.7 | 76.4 | 76.6 | 76.5 | 76.1 | 76.2 | 75.9 | 76.0 |
| 2017 | 74.6 | 74.7 | 75.0 | 74.2 | 75.2 | 76.1 | 75.5 | 75.6 | 75.4 | 75.3 | 75.5 | 75.3 | 75.2 |
| 2018 | 74.1 | 74.4 | 74.8 | 74.3 | 75.3 | 76.0 | 75.1 | 75.7 | 75.1 | 76.0 | 75.6 | 75.2 | 75.1 |
| 2019 | 74.4 | 74.5 | 75.0 | 75.1 | 75.9 | 76.5 | 75.7 | 75.8 | 74.9 | 75.0 | 74.8 | 74.6 | 75.2 |
| **Government** | | | | | | | | | | | | | |
| 2011 | 199.2 | 203.5 | 203.6 | 203.6 | 201.0 | 199.6 | 183.3 | 182.2 | 197.5 | 200.6 | 201.6 | 199.4 | 197.9 |
| 2012 | 194.4 | 198.2 | 198.5 | 198.0 | 196.2 | 195.8 | 178.7 | 178.5 | 193.2 | 194.5 | 195.6 | 193.8 | 193.0 |
| 2013 | 188.6 | 192.1 | 192.0 | 191.5 | 189.2 | 189.0 | 172.8 | 171.3 | 186.4 | 189.4 | 189.7 | 187.9 | 186.7 |
| 2014 | 183.7 | 187.8 | 188.3 | 189.0 | 186.8 | 186.4 | 170.9 | 169.6 | 183.2 | 188.0 | 189.6 | 186.6 | 184.2 |
| 2015 | 182.0 | 185.8 | 186.7 | 187.5 | 186.8 | 185.3 | 169.5 | 167.9 | 182.6 | 186.7 | 187.9 | 186.4 | 182.9 |
| 2016 | 182.2 | 186.0 | 188.2 | 187.7 | 185.2 | 185.5 | 172.2 | 171.5 | 185.6 | 187.8 | 190.4 | 188.1 | 184.2 |
| 2017 | 184.1 | 186.7 | 188.0 | 188.3 | 188.3 | 188.2 | 173.5 | 172.0 | 187.2 | 189.9 | 190.7 | 189.3 | 185.5 |
| 2018 | 185.1 | 188.5 | 190.9 | 190.7 | 190.6 | 190.4 | 174.9 | 174.1 | 187.7 | 192.3 | 194.5 | 191.6 | 187.6 |
| 2019 | 187.8 | 189.8 | 191.4 | 191.9 | 192.0 | 192.8 | 177.7 | 177.3 | 191.1 | 194.5 | 194.8 | 193.3 | 189.5 |

## Employment by Industry: Seattle-Tacoma-Bellevue, WA, 2011–2019

(Numbers in thousands, not seasonally adjusted)

| Industry and year | January | February | March | April | May | June | July | August | September | October | November | December | Annual average |
|---|---|---|---|---|---|---|---|---|---|---|---|---|---|
| **Total Nonfarm** | | | | | | | | | | | | | |
| 2011 | 1,656.8 | 1,664.7 | 1,669.5 | 1,684.4 | 1,693.4 | 1,704.0 | 1,705.6 | 1,698.6 | 1,706.9 | 1,712.0 | 1,719.7 | 1,719.1 | 1,694.6 |
| 2012 | 1,689.0 | 1,697.5 | 1,708.0 | 1,718.1 | 1,734.3 | 1,746.8 | 1,743.0 | 1,739.5 | 1,747.3 | 1,756.3 | 1,766.3 | 1,764.1 | 1,734.2 |
| 2013 | 1,738.2 | 1,747.9 | 1,754.2 | 1,764.7 | 1,780.6 | 1,790.5 | 1,790.4 | 1,790.3 | 1,797.1 | 1,803.2 | 1,813.7 | 1,814.6 | 1,782.1 |
| 2014 | 1,792.6 | 1,795.8 | 1,803.6 | 1,810.0 | 1,824.6 | 1,836.4 | 1,844.6 | 1,845.8 | 1,850.9 | 1,853.4 | 1,862.2 | 1,867.8 | 1,832.3 |
| 2015 | 1,842.6 | 1,847.8 | 1,859.1 | 1,868.5 | 1,882.5 | 1,901.3 | 1,902.8 | 1,901.7 | 1,910.2 | 1,910.7 | 1,919.2 | 1,923.1 | 1,889.1 |
| 2016 | 1,898.3 | 1,910.6 | 1,919.1 | 1,935.2 | 1,950.1 | 1,963.4 | 1,964.5 | 1,963.1 | 1,971.9 | 1,968.5 | 1,978.9 | 1,983.6 | 1,950.6 |
| 2017 | 1,954.5 | 1,962.2 | 1,974.9 | 1,982.8 | 1,999.1 | 2,015.8 | 2,011.7 | 2,007.9 | 2,011.1 | 2,012.0 | 2,021.9 | 2,027.5 | 1,998.5 |
| 2018 | 2,006.7 | 2,011.2 | 2,021.8 | 2,027.7 | 2,043.5 | 2,056.6 | 2,055.4 | 2,055.7 | 2,055.4 | 2,061.3 | 2,070.7 | 2,070.0 | 2,044.7 |
| 2019 | 2,051.6 | 2,039.7 | 2,064.4 | 2,074.0 | 2,089.6 | 2,106.0 | 2,111.5 | 2,110.6 | 2,106.0 | 2,106.5 | 2,115.4 | 2,119.6 | 2,091.2 |
| **Total Private** | | | | | | | | | | | | | |
| 2011 | 1,393.9 | 1,400.3 | 1,405.2 | 1,419.9 | 1,427.7 | 1,441.1 | 1,449.5 | 1,453.7 | 1,456.5 | 1,450.2 | 1,456.7 | 1,460.2 | 1,434.6 |
| 2012 | 1,428.6 | 1,436.0 | 1,444.9 | 1,454.5 | 1,470.1 | 1,485.1 | 1,487.2 | 1,495.1 | 1,494.6 | 1,493.5 | 1,501.5 | 1,504.0 | 1,474.6 |
| 2013 | 1,476.5 | 1,484.2 | 1,490.3 | 1,500.2 | 1,515.4 | 1,527.4 | 1,535.0 | 1,543.9 | 1,542.3 | 1,539.1 | 1,547.9 | 1,552.3 | 1,521.2 |
| 2014 | 1,528.4 | 1,530.6 | 1,537.2 | 1,542.4 | 1,556.2 | 1,569.7 | 1,584.0 | 1,594.1 | 1,590.6 | 1,585.0 | 1,592.4 | 1,601.1 | 1,567.6 |
| 2015 | 1,573.9 | 1,577.5 | 1,587.2 | 1,595.1 | 1,609.0 | 1,627.8 | 1,637.4 | 1,643.7 | 1,642.6 | 1,637.0 | 1,643.3 | 1,651.1 | 1,618.8 |
| 2016 | 1,626.3 | 1,634.7 | 1,643.0 | 1,657.1 | 1,670.2 | 1,686.0 | 1,693.8 | 1,700.6 | 1,700.2 | 1,689.1 | 1,697.0 | 1,704.4 | 1,675.2 |
| 2017 | 1,675.6 | 1,681.3 | 1,692.3 | 1,699.4 | 1,714.2 | 1,732.8 | 1,734.7 | 1,740.5 | 1,738.2 | 1,728.4 | 1,737.9 | 1,747.3 | 1,718.6 |
| 2018 | 1,725.6 | 1,730.0 | 1,740.5 | 1,744.4 | 1,759.9 | 1,777.9 | 1,782.0 | 1,792.3 | 1,785.0 | 1,780.5 | 1,791.7 | 1,795.4 | 1,767.1 |
| 2019 | 1,776.1 | 1,764.4 | 1,788.3 | 1,796.6 | 1,810.2 | 1,826.6 | 1,838.6 | 1,846.0 | 1,836.0 | 1,828.4 | 1,835.8 | 1,843.2 | 1,815.9 |
| **Goods Producing** | | | | | | | | | | | | | |
| 2011 | 245.1 | 246.2 | 247.2 | 249.6 | 251.8 | 255.9 | 260.5 | 262.3 | 263.8 | 262.4 | 260.7 | 260.2 | 255.5 |
| 2012 | 255.9 | 257.1 | 258.9 | 260.8 | 264.1 | 269.2 | 272.3 | 275.5 | 275.9 | 275.2 | 274.2 | 272.8 | 267.7 |
| 2013 | 270.3 | 271.9 | 273.2 | 273.9 | 276.4 | 280.1 | 283.0 | 285.8 | 285.1 | 282.9 | 281.3 | 280.2 | 278.7 |
| 2014 | 277.0 | 277.5 | 278.9 | 279.2 | 282.0 | 285.4 | 290.1 | 292.1 | 291.7 | 291.1 | 290.3 | 290.6 | 285.5 |
| 2015 | 288.5 | 289.2 | 291.4 | 291.6 | 293.7 | 297.6 | 301.5 | 301.7 | 301.3 | 299.1 | 297.3 | 297.5 | 295.9 |
| 2016 | 295.1 | 297.0 | 297.7 | 299.8 | 301.6 | 303.6 | 306.3 | 305.9 | 305.4 | 301.8 | 300.5 | 299.6 | 301.2 |
| 2017 | 295.9 | 296.4 | 297.8 | 298.8 | 299.6 | 303.1 | 302.8 | 302.7 | 300.0 | 299.6 | 299.9 | 300.0 |
| 2018 | 297.1 | 298.7 | 301.2 | 301.8 | 304.9 | 308.1 | 310.5 | 311.7 | 311.7 | 311.5 | 312.5 | 312.3 | 306.8 |
| 2019 | 308.4 | 304.7 | 311.6 | 312.0 | 314.8 | 317.8 | 319.3 | 320.2 | 319.0 | 317.2 | 316.8 | 317.3 | 314.9 |
| **Service-Providing** | | | | | | | | | | | | | |
| 2011 | 1,411.7 | 1,418.5 | 1,422.3 | 1,434.8 | 1,441.6 | 1,448.1 | 1,445.1 | 1,436.3 | 1,443.1 | 1,449.6 | 1,459.0 | 1,458.9 | 1,439.1 |
| 2012 | 1,433.1 | 1,440.4 | 1,449.1 | 1,457.3 | 1,470.2 | 1,477.6 | 1,470.7 | 1,464.0 | 1,471.4 | 1,481.1 | 1,492.1 | 1,491.3 | 1,466.5 |
| 2013 | 1,467.9 | 1,476.0 | 1,481.0 | 1,490.8 | 1,504.2 | 1,510.4 | 1,507.4 | 1,504.5 | 1,512.0 | 1,520.3 | 1,532.4 | 1,534.4 | 1,503.4 |
| 2014 | 1,515.6 | 1,518.3 | 1,524.7 | 1,530.8 | 1,542.6 | 1,551.0 | 1,554.5 | 1,553.7 | 1,559.2 | 1,562.3 | 1,571.9 | 1,577.2 | 1,546.8 |
| 2015 | 1,554.1 | 1,558.6 | 1,567.7 | 1,576.9 | 1,588.8 | 1,603.7 | 1,601.3 | 1,600.0 | 1,608.9 | 1,611.6 | 1,621.9 | 1,625.6 | 1,593.3 |
| 2016 | 1,603.2 | 1,613.6 | 1,621.4 | 1,635.4 | 1,648.5 | 1,659.8 | 1,658.2 | 1,657.2 | 1,666.5 | 1,666.7 | 1,678.4 | 1,684.0 | 1,649.4 |
| 2017 | 1,658.6 | 1,665.8 | 1,677.1 | 1,684.0 | 1,699.5 | 1,712.7 | 1,708.9 | 1,705.1 | 1,708.4 | 1,712.0 | 1,722.3 | 1,727.6 | 1,698.5 |
| 2018 | 1,709.6 | 1,712.5 | 1,720.6 | 1,725.9 | 1,738.6 | 1,748.5 | 1,744.9 | 1,744.0 | 1,743.7 | 1,749.8 | 1,758.2 | 1,757.7 | 1,737.8 |
| 2019 | 1,743.2 | 1,735.0 | 1,752.8 | 1,762.0 | 1,774.8 | 1,788.2 | 1,792.2 | 1,790.4 | 1,787.0 | 1,789.3 | 1,798.6 | 1,802.3 | 1,776.3 |
| **Mining and Logging** | | | | | | | | | | | | | |
| 2011 | 1.0 | 1.0 | 1.0 | 1.0 | 1.0 | 1.0 | 1.0 | 1.0 | 1.0 | 1.1 | 1.1 | 1.1 | 1.0 |
| 2012 | 1.0 | 1.0 | 1.0 | 1.0 | 1.0 | 1.0 | 1.0 | 1.1 | 1.0 | 1.1 | 1.0 | 1.1 | 1.0 |
| 2013 | 1.0 | 1.0 | 1.0 | 1.0 | 1.0 | 1.1 | 1.0 | 1.1 | 1.1 | 1.0 | 1.0 | 1.0 | 1.0 |
| 2014 | 1.0 | 1.0 | 1.0 | 1.0 | 1.0 | 1.0 | 1.0 | 1.0 | 1.0 | 1.1 | 1.1 | 1.1 | 1.0 |
| 2015 | 1.1 | 1.1 | 1.0 | 1.1 | 1.1 | 1.1 | 1.1 | 1.1 | 1.1 | 1.2 | 1.1 | 1.1 | 1.1 |
| 2016 | 1.0 | 1.0 | 1.0 | 1.1 | 1.1 | 1.1 | 1.1 | 1.1 | 1.1 | 1.1 | 1.1 | 1.1 | 1.1 |
| 2017 | 1.1 | 1.1 | 1.0 | 1.1 | 1.1 | 1.1 | 1.1 | 1.1 | 1.1 | 1.1 | 1.1 | 1.1 | 1.1 |
| 2018 | 1.1 | 1.1 | 1.1 | 1.1 | 1.1 | 1.1 | 1.1 | 1.1 | 1.1 | 1.1 | 1.1 | 1.1 | 1.1 |
| 2019 | 1.1 | 1.1 | 1.1 | 1.1 | 1.1 | 1.1 | 1.1 | 1.1 | 1.1 | 1.1 | 1.1 | 1.1 | 1.1 |
| **Construction** | | | | | | | | | | | | | |
| 2011 | 75.5 | 75.3 | 75.5 | 76.6 | 78.2 | 80.1 | 82.2 | 83.2 | 83.4 | 82.2 | 79.9 | 79.0 | 79.3 |
| 2012 | 75.0 | 76.1 | 76.8 | 78.4 | 80.6 | 83.2 | 85.1 | 87.2 | 87.4 | 87.3 | 85.9 | 85.1 | 82.3 |
| 2013 | 82.5 | 83.9 | 84.6 | 85.7 | 88.0 | 89.9 | 92.6 | 95.0 | 94.6 | 93.7 | 92.6 | 91.1 | 89.5 |
| 2014 | 89.4 | 89.6 | 91.2 | 91.4 | 93.8 | 96.1 | 99.1 | 101.3 | 101.7 | 102.0 | 101.5 | 101.6 | 96.6 |
| 2015 | 99.8 | 100.5 | 102.0 | 103.4 | 105.1 | 107.3 | 109.5 | 109.9 | 109.5 | 109.4 | 108.0 | 108.1 | 106.0 |
| 2016 | 106.5 | 108.5 | 109.4 | 111.4 | 113.0 | 115.0 | 117.0 | 118.3 | 118.3 | 117.2 | 116.8 | 116.4 | 114.0 |
| 2017 | 113.8 | 114.9 | 116.5 | 117.1 | 119.0 | 121.8 | 122.2 | 123.2 | 123.7 | 122.6 | 121.7 | 121.8 | 119.9 |
| 2018 | 120.0 | 121.3 | 123.0 | 123.7 | 125.8 | 127.8 | 128.8 | 130.7 | 129.7 | 129.6 | 129.3 | 128.4 | 126.5 |
| 2019 | 124.8 | 121.0 | 126.4 | 127.0 | 128.8 | 130.7 | 131.8 | 132.9 | 131.9 | 132.3 | 131.2 | 130.7 | 129.1 |

# Employment by Industry: Seattle-Tacoma-Bellevue, WA, 2011–2019—*Continued*

(Numbers in thousands, not seasonally adjusted)

| Industry and year | January | February | March | April | May | June | July | August | September | October | November | December | Annual average |
|---|---|---|---|---|---|---|---|---|---|---|---|---|---|
| **Manufacturing** | | | | | | | | | | | | | |
| 2011 | 168.6 | 169.9 | 170.7 | 172.0 | 172.6 | 174.8 | 177.3 | 178.1 | 179.4 | 179.1 | 179.7 | 180.1 | 175.2 |
| 2012 | 179.9 | 180.0 | 181.1 | 181.4 | 182.5 | 185.0 | 186.2 | 187.2 | 187.5 | 186.8 | 187.3 | 186.7 | 184.3 |
| 2013 | 186.8 | 187.0 | 187.6 | 187.2 | 187.4 | 189.1 | 189.4 | 189.7 | 189.4 | 188.2 | 187.7 | 188.1 | 188.1 |
| 2014 | 186.6 | 186.9 | 186.7 | 186.8 | 187.2 | 188.3 | 190.0 | 189.8 | 189.0 | 188.0 | 187.7 | 187.9 | 187.9 |
| 2015 | 187.6 | 187.6 | 188.4 | 187.1 | 187.5 | 189.2 | 190.9 | 190.7 | 190.7 | 188.5 | 188.2 | 188.3 | 188.7 |
| 2016 | 187.6 | 187.5 | 187.3 | 187.3 | 187.5 | 187.5 | 188.2 | 186.5 | 186.0 | 183.5 | 182.6 | 182.1 | 186.1 |
| 2017 | 181.0 | 180.4 | 180.3 | 180.6 | 179.5 | 180.2 | 179.5 | 178.5 | 177.9 | 176.3 | 176.8 | 177.0 | 179.0 |
| 2018 | 176.0 | 176.3 | 177.1 | 177.0 | 178.0 | 179.2 | 180.6 | 179.9 | 180.9 | 180.8 | 182.1 | 182.8 | 179.2 |
| 2019 | 182.5 | 182.6 | 184.1 | 183.9 | 184.9 | 186.0 | 186.4 | 186.2 | 186.0 | 183.8 | 184.5 | 185.5 | 184.7 |
| **Trade, Transportation, and Utilities** | | | | | | | | | | | | | |
| 2011 | 301.7 | 300.6 | 301.4 | 302.8 | 305.2 | 308.1 | 310.5 | 311.6 | 310.3 | 310.3 | 316.2 | 319.6 | 308.2 |
| 2012 | 308.6 | 306.6 | 307.8 | 308.8 | 312.8 | 316.9 | 319.5 | 320.3 | 319.0 | 320.0 | 326.8 | 329.2 | 316.4 |
| 2013 | 319.3 | 317.4 | 317.9 | 319.0 | 323.5 | 326.7 | 329.7 | 331.6 | 330.4 | 332.0 | 339.6 | 343.1 | 327.5 |
| 2014 | 333.6 | 331.4 | 331.4 | 332.2 | 336.3 | 340.4 | 344.0 | 346.3 | 345.4 | 345.9 | 352.8 | 357.3 | 341.4 |
| 2015 | 346.9 | 344.9 | 346.3 | 346.7 | 350.4 | 354.9 | 356.4 | 358.4 | 357.7 | 357.3 | 364.0 | 368.4 | 354.4 |
| 2016 | 356.1 | 354.6 | 356.5 | 359.4 | 363.4 | 368.7 | 371.9 | 373.6 | 371.9 | 372.6 | 380.2 | 384.6 | 367.8 |
| 2017 | 374.6 | 372.2 | 374.1 | 375.0 | 380.1 | 384.9 | 388.1 | 390.0 | 388.5 | 387.5 | 395.1 | 398.8 | 384.1 |
| 2018 | 389.6 | 385.6 | 385.9 | 384.6 | 387.8 | 391.6 | 393.0 | 394.3 | 392.0 | 391.3 | 397.5 | 399.3 | 391.0 |
| 2019 | 393.7 | 388.2 | 390.3 | 390.5 | 394.0 | 397.7 | 401.7 | 402.9 | 400.4 | 399.4 | 405.7 | 410.5 | 397.9 |
| **Wholesale Trade** | | | | | | | | | | | | | |
| 2011 | 76.4 | 76.7 | 76.9 | 77.3 | 77.6 | 77.8 | 78.0 | 78.0 | 77.8 | 77.5 | 77.5 | 77.7 | 77.4 |
| 2012 | 77.1 | 77.3 | 77.5 | 78.0 | 78.3 | 78.7 | 79.2 | 79.7 | 79.2 | 79.0 | 79.1 | 79.4 | 78.5 |
| 2013 | 78.9 | 79.5 | 79.8 | 79.7 | 79.9 | 80.6 | 81.0 | 81.2 | 81.1 | 80.6 | 81.0 | 81.1 | 80.4 |
| 2014 | 80.8 | 81.0 | 80.9 | 80.6 | 81.1 | 81.6 | 82.5 | 82.6 | 82.7 | 82.1 | 82.3 | 82.7 | 81.7 |
| 2015 | 81.9 | 82.1 | 82.5 | 82.3 | 82.8 | 83.4 | 83.5 | 83.8 | 83.6 | 83.1 | 83.3 | 83.7 | 83.0 |
| 2016 | 82.4 | 82.5 | 82.8 | 83.0 | 83.3 | 83.7 | 84.0 | 84.2 | 84.0 | 83.6 | 84.0 | 84.3 | 83.5 |
| 2017 | 83.8 | 84.1 | 84.4 | 84.4 | 84.9 | 85.5 | 85.5 | 85.6 | 85.6 | 85.4 | 85.7 | 86.1 | 85.1 |
| 2018 | 85.4 | 85.8 | 86.2 | 86.3 | 86.4 | 86.9 | 86.9 | 87.0 | 86.5 | 86.1 | 86.5 | 86.7 | 86.4 |
| 2019 | 85.6 | 85.6 | 86.0 | 86.2 | 86.1 | 86.4 | 86.8 | 86.8 | 86.4 | 85.9 | 86.9 | 86.4 | 86.3 |
| **Retail Trade** | | | | | | | | | | | | | |
| 2011 | 168.3 | 166.7 | 166.5 | 167.1 | 169.0 | 171.1 | 172.3 | 173.4 | 172.1 | 173.3 | 178.8 | 181.1 | 171.6 |
| 2012 | 172.6 | 170.2 | 170.9 | 171.2 | 173.9 | 176.7 | 178.7 | 178.9 | 178.4 | 180.2 | 186.5 | 188.0 | 177.2 |
| 2013 | 180.3 | 178.2 | 178.3 | 179.3 | 182.7 | 184.9 | 187.2 | 188.6 | 187.4 | 189.7 | 196.1 | 198.8 | 186.0 |
| 2014 | 190.2 | 188.1 | 188.2 | 188.4 | 191.0 | 193.9 | 195.9 | 197.4 | 196.3 | 197.5 | 203.8 | 206.4 | 194.8 |
| 2015 | 198.7 | 196.8 | 197.8 | 198.5 | 200.9 | 203.8 | 204.6 | 206.2 | 205.7 | 205.2 | 210.8 | 212.8 | 203.5 |
| 2016 | 204.3 | 203.2 | 204.3 | 205.2 | 207.8 | 211.3 | 213.5 | 214.4 | 212.6 | 214.0 | 219.4 | 221.7 | 211.0 |
| 2017 | 215.3 | 213.4 | 214.8 | 216.2 | 219.9 | 223.3 | 226.4 | 227.2 | 225.5 | 224.6 | 230.3 | 231.8 | 222.2 |
| 2018 | 226.4 | 223.2 | 223.0 | 222.0 | 224.6 | 226.8 | 228.5 | 229.5 | 228.0 | 227.7 | 233.0 | 233.4 | 227.2 |
| 2019 | 231.1 | 226.5 | 227.3 | 227.7 | 230.9 | 233.2 | 236.2 | 236.9 | 234.8 | 235.5 | 239.6 | 242.8 | 233.5 |
| **Transportation and Utilities** | | | | | | | | | | | | | |
| 2011 | 57.0 | 57.2 | 58.0 | 58.4 | 58.6 | 59.2 | 60.2 | 60.2 | 60.4 | 59.5 | 59.9 | 60.8 | 59.1 |
| 2012 | 58.9 | 59.1 | 59.4 | 59.6 | 60.6 | 61.5 | 61.6 | 61.7 | 61.4 | 60.8 | 61.2 | 61.8 | 60.6 |
| 2013 | 60.1 | 59.7 | 59.8 | 60.0 | 60.9 | 61.2 | 61.5 | 61.8 | 61.9 | 61.7 | 62.5 | 63.2 | 61.2 |
| 2014 | 62.6 | 62.3 | 62.3 | 63.2 | 64.2 | 64.9 | 65.6 | 66.3 | 66.4 | 66.3 | 66.7 | 68.2 | 64.9 |
| 2015 | 66.3 | 66.0 | 66.0 | 65.9 | 66.7 | 67.7 | 68.3 | 68.4 | 68.4 | 69.0 | 69.9 | 71.9 | 67.9 |
| 2016 | 69.4 | 68.9 | 69.4 | 71.2 | 72.3 | 73.7 | 74.4 | 75.0 | 75.3 | 75.0 | 76.8 | 78.6 | 73.3 |
| 2017 | 75.5 | 74.7 | 74.9 | 74.4 | 75.3 | 76.1 | 76.2 | 77.2 | 77.4 | 77.5 | 79.1 | 80.9 | 76.6 |
| 2018 | 77.8 | 76.6 | 76.7 | 76.3 | 76.8 | 77.9 | 77.6 | 77.8 | 77.5 | 77.5 | 78.0 | 79.2 | 77.5 |
| 2019 | 77.0 | 76.1 | 77.0 | 76.6 | 77.0 | 78.1 | 78.7 | 79.2 | 79.2 | 78.0 | 79.2 | 81.3 | 78.1 |
| **Information** | | | | | | | | | | | | | |
| 2011 | 87.3 | 88.0 | 87.7 | 87.8 | 88.0 | 89.2 | 90.0 | 90.4 | 89.6 | 88.9 | 89.2 | 88.9 | 88.8 |
| 2012 | 88.8 | 89.3 | 88.9 | 88.8 | 89.6 | 90.6 | 90.7 | 90.9 | 89.6 | 89.1 | 89.6 | 89.4 | 89.6 |
| 2013 | 88.9 | 89.7 | 89.2 | 89.6 | 90.2 | 91.0 | 92.4 | 93.0 | 92.1 | 91.5 | 92.3 | 92.3 | 91.0 |
| 2014 | 92.0 | 92.2 | 92.4 | 92.8 | 93.3 | 94.9 | 96.6 | 97.6 | 96.8 | 95.0 | 95.4 | 95.1 | 94.5 |
| 2015 | 93.6 | 94.5 | 94.7 | 94.6 | 95.5 | 97.2 | 99.4 | 100.4 | 99.6 | 99.4 | 100.2 | 100.3 | 97.5 |
| 2016 | 99.9 | 100.9 | 101.4 | 101.9 | 102.8 | 105.5 | 107.2 | 108.2 | 107.6 | 107.1 | 107.9 | 108.1 | 104.9 |
| 2017 | 107.8 | 108.3 | 108.8 | 108.8 | 109.5 | 111.8 | 112.9 | 113.9 | 113.3 | 112.5 | 112.7 | 113.1 | 111.1 |
| 2018 | 112.2 | 113.2 | 113.8 | 114.9 | 115.9 | 119.8 | 121.5 | 122.8 | 122.2 | 121.4 | 122.2 | 122.2 | 118.5 |
| 2019 | 122.5 | 123.4 | 124.6 | 124.1 | 125.6 | 129.4 | 131.8 | 133.1 | 131.5 | 130.1 | 130.7 | 130.3 | 128.1 |

## Employment by Industry: Seattle-Tacoma-Bellevue, WA, 2011–2019—*Continued*

(Numbers in thousands, not seasonally adjusted)

| Industry and year | January | February | March | April | May | June | July | August | September | October | November | December | Annual average |
|---|---|---|---|---|---|---|---|---|---|---|---|---|---|
| **Financial Activities** | | | | | | | | | | | | | |
| 2011 | 90.7 | 90.9 | 90.7 | 91.1 | 90.7 | 91.0 | 91.1 | 90.9 | 90.6 | 90.2 | 90.4 | 90.2 | 90.7 |
| 2012 | 89.1 | 89.3 | 89.5 | 89.7 | 90.3 | 90.8 | 91.5 | 91.3 | 90.9 | 91.0 | 91.3 | 91.5 | 90.5 |
| 2013 | 91.3 | 91.7 | 92.2 | 92.7 | 93.3 | 93.5 | 94.3 | 94.4 | 93.8 | 93.7 | 93.8 | 94.2 | 93.2 |
| 2014 | 93.2 | 93.3 | 93.6 | 93.8 | 94.1 | 94.6 | 95.4 | 95.7 | 95.1 | 95.0 | 95.1 | 95.4 | 94.5 |
| 2015 | 94.7 | 94.9 | 94.9 | 95.3 | 95.7 | 96.2 | 97.0 | 97.0 | 96.5 | 96.0 | 96.2 | 96.3 | 95.9 |
| 2016 | 95.8 | 96.1 | 96.2 | 96.5 | 97.0 | 97.3 | 98.6 | 98.8 | 98.2 | 97.5 | 97.7 | 98.0 | 97.3 |
| 2017 | 96.9 | 97.5 | 97.9 | 97.9 | 98.9 | 99.7 | 100.0 | 100.4 | 100.0 | 99.2 | 99.7 | 100.0 | 99.0 |
| 2018 | 99.9 | 100.2 | 100.8 | 100.8 | 101.7 | 102.2 | 102.2 | 102.5 | 101.8 | 101.2 | 102.2 | 101.3 | 101.4 |
| 2019 | 101.0 | 101.6 | 101.9 | 102.1 | 102.9 | 103.6 | 104.5 | 104.6 | 104.1 | 104.1 | 103.1 | 103.3 | 103.1 |
| **Professional and Business Services** | | | | | | | | | | | | | |
| 2011 | 220.4 | 222.6 | 224.0 | 228.1 | 228.0 | 229.5 | 232.6 | 233.2 | 234.0 | 234.4 | 234.8 | 234.7 | 229.7 |
| 2012 | 229.0 | 231.4 | 232.7 | 236.6 | 238.7 | 240.9 | 239.9 | 242.7 | 242.8 | 244.3 | 245.0 | 244.8 | 239.1 |
| 2013 | 240.5 | 242.6 | 243.0 | 245.3 | 247.2 | 249.3 | 249.6 | 252.1 | 252.4 | 253.0 | 253.8 | 253.5 | 248.5 |
| 2014 | 249.0 | 249.6 | 251.3 | 252.1 | 253.1 | 255.1 | 258.7 | 261.3 | 261.0 | 262.1 | 262.9 | 264.2 | 256.7 |
| 2015 | 258.7 | 259.4 | 261.8 | 264.3 | 265.9 | 268.8 | 271.2 | 273.5 | 274.1 | 273.9 | 274.9 | 276.5 | 268.6 |
| 2016 | 270.9 | 272.4 | 274.6 | 276.8 | 277.8 | 280.1 | 281.1 | 282.9 | 284.2 | 282.4 | 283.2 | 283.5 | 279.2 |
| 2017 | 278.7 | 279.9 | 282.0 | 283.9 | 285.8 | 288.2 | 289.0 | 290.3 | 289.9 | 289.3 | 290.1 | 290.7 | 286.5 |
| 2018 | 287.1 | 288.7 | 291.3 | 290.4 | 291.8 | 295.1 | 296.1 | 299.3 | 297.4 | 298.0 | 299.5 | 299.5 | 294.5 |
| 2019 | 294.0 | 292.6 | 295.9 | 298.8 | 299.5 | 302.0 | 305.8 | 308.2 | 306.9 | 305.3 | 306.5 | 305.3 | 301.7 |
| **Education and Health Services** | | | | | | | | | | | | | |
| 2011 | 235.0 | 237.5 | 238.2 | 238.6 | 238.6 | 237.4 | 234.2 | 233.6 | 236.8 | 240.0 | 242.0 | 240.9 | 237.7 |
| 2012 | 238.2 | 240.9 | 242.5 | 241.8 | 242.8 | 240.9 | 236.2 | 235.9 | 238.8 | 242.4 | 244.0 | 243.8 | 240.7 |
| 2013 | 239.7 | 243.5 | 244.1 | 244.8 | 244.7 | 242.0 | 239.2 | 239.1 | 242.7 | 246.5 | 248.1 | 248.1 | 243.5 |
| 2014 | 246.2 | 249.4 | 249.2 | 249.0 | 249.6 | 247.0 | 245.3 | 244.9 | 247.4 | 249.5 | 250.4 | 251.1 | 248.3 |
| 2015 | 248.1 | 250.2 | 250.6 | 251.8 | 251.9 | 251.0 | 247.5 | 247.1 | 250.4 | 254.3 | 255.9 | 256.2 | 251.3 |
| 2016 | 255.9 | 259.2 | 260.1 | 261.2 | 261.5 | 259.9 | 256.0 | 257.4 | 260.8 | 263.2 | 264.5 | 264.9 | 260.4 |
| 2017 | 261.9 | 265.4 | 266.5 | 265.6 | 266.4 | 265.5 | 262.2 | 263.2 | 266.7 | 270.6 | 272.4 | 272.5 | 266.6 |
| 2018 | 271.8 | 275.0 | 275.8 | 276.3 | 276.8 | 274.8 | 272.1 | 273.4 | 275.8 | 279.9 | 281.3 | 281.2 | 276.2 |
| 2019 | 279.5 | 280.2 | 283.6 | 283.8 | 284.5 | 281.9 | 280.1 | 281.2 | 282.9 | 284.3 | 286.4 | 285.8 | 282.9 |
| **Leisure and Hospitality** | | | | | | | | | | | | | |
| 2011 | 150.7 | 151.2 | 152.4 | 157.5 | 160.3 | 164.0 | 163.9 | 165.2 | 165.6 | 158.7 | 158.1 | 160.1 | 159.0 |
| 2012 | 154.4 | 156.1 | 158.7 | 161.8 | 165.2 | 168.4 | 169.0 | 170.7 | 170.2 | 164.5 | 163.5 | 165.6 | 164.0 |
| 2013 | 161.2 | 161.6 | 164.5 | 168.3 | 172.8 | 177.0 | 178.1 | 179.5 | 178.1 | 171.7 | 171.1 | 173.2 | 171.4 |
| 2014 | 170.1 | 169.7 | 172.3 | 175.2 | 178.8 | 182.5 | 183.3 | 185.5 | 183.6 | 177.1 | 175.9 | 177.5 | 177.6 |
| 2015 | 174.8 | 175.5 | 177.8 | 181.2 | 185.7 | 191.0 | 192.9 | 194.1 | 192.5 | 186.6 | 184.6 | 185.4 | 185.2 |
| 2016 | 182.7 | 184.1 | 185.7 | 189.8 | 193.1 | 197.4 | 199.5 | 200.3 | 199.7 | 192.3 | 190.6 | 193.2 | 192.4 |
| 2017 | 188.7 | 190.1 | 193.1 | 197.1 | 200.7 | 205.2 | 205.5 | 205.8 | 204.1 | 196.6 | 195.6 | 199.0 | 198.5 |
| 2018 | 195.9 | 196.3 | 198.9 | 202.8 | 207.2 | 211.2 | 210.9 | 212.4 | 209.1 | 203.1 | 202.3 | 205.1 | 204.6 |
| 2019 | 200.3 | 197.7 | 202.9 | 207.3 | 210.4 | 214.6 | 215.6 | 216.3 | 213.1 | 210.0 | 208.7 | 212.2 | 209.1 |
| **Other Services** | | | | | | | | | | | | | |
| 2011 | 63.0 | 63.3 | 63.6 | 64.4 | 65.1 | 66.0 | 66.7 | 66.5 | 65.8 | 65.3 | 65.3 | 65.6 | 65.1 |
| 2012 | 64.6 | 65.3 | 65.9 | 66.2 | 66.6 | 67.4 | 68.1 | 67.8 | 67.4 | 67.0 | 67.1 | 66.9 | 66.7 |
| 2013 | 65.3 | 65.8 | 66.2 | 66.6 | 67.3 | 67.8 | 68.7 | 68.4 | 67.7 | 67.8 | 67.9 | 67.7 | 67.3 |
| 2014 | 67.3 | 67.5 | 68.1 | 68.1 | 69.0 | 69.8 | 70.6 | 70.7 | 69.6 | 69.3 | 69.6 | 69.9 | 69.1 |
| 2015 | 68.6 | 68.9 | 69.7 | 69.6 | 70.2 | 71.1 | 71.5 | 71.5 | 70.5 | 70.4 | 70.2 | 70.5 | 70.2 |
| 2016 | 69.9 | 70.4 | 70.8 | 71.7 | 73.0 | 73.5 | 73.2 | 73.5 | 72.4 | 72.2 | 72.4 | 72.5 | 72.1 |
| 2017 | 71.1 | 71.5 | 72.1 | 72.3 | 73.2 | 74.4 | 74.2 | 74.1 | 73.0 | 72.7 | 72.7 | 73.3 | 72.9 |
| 2018 | 72.0 | 72.3 | 72.8 | 72.8 | 73.8 | 75.1 | 75.7 | 75.9 | 75.0 | 74.1 | 74.2 | 74.5 | 74.0 |
| 2019 | 76.7 | 76.0 | 77.5 | 78.0 | 78.5 | 79.6 | 79.8 | 79.5 | 78.1 | 78.0 | 77.9 | 78.5 | 78.2 |
| **Government** | | | | | | | | | | | | | |
| 2011 | 262.9 | 264.4 | 264.3 | 264.5 | 265.7 | 262.9 | 256.1 | 244.9 | 250.4 | 261.8 | 263.0 | 258.9 | 260.0 |
| 2012 | 260.4 | 261.5 | 263.1 | 263.6 | 264.2 | 261.7 | 255.8 | 244.4 | 252.7 | 262.8 | 264.8 | 260.1 | 259.6 |
| 2013 | 261.7 | 263.7 | 263.9 | 264.5 | 265.2 | 263.1 | 255.4 | 246.4 | 254.8 | 264.1 | 265.8 | 262.3 | 260.9 |
| 2014 | 264.2 | 265.2 | 266.4 | 267.6 | 268.4 | 266.7 | 260.6 | 251.7 | 260.3 | 268.4 | 269.8 | 266.7 | 264.7 |
| 2015 | 268.7 | 270.3 | 271.9 | 273.4 | 273.5 | 273.5 | 265.4 | 258.0 | 267.6 | 273.7 | 275.9 | 272.0 | 270.3 |
| 2016 | 272.0 | 275.9 | 276.1 | 278.1 | 279.9 | 277.4 | 270.7 | 262.5 | 271.7 | 279.4 | 281.9 | 279.2 | 275.4 |
| 2017 | 278.9 | 280.9 | 282.6 | 283.4 | 284.9 | 283.0 | 277.0 | 267.4 | 272.9 | 283.6 | 284.0 | 280.2 | 279.9 |
| 2018 | 281.1 | 281.2 | 281.3 | 283.3 | 283.6 | 278.7 | 273.4 | 263.4 | 270.4 | 280.8 | 279.0 | 274.6 | 277.6 |
| 2019 | 275.5 | 275.3 | 276.1 | 277.4 | 279.4 | 279.4 | 272.9 | 264.6 | 270.0 | 278.1 | 279.6 | 276.4 | 275.4 |

# Employment by Industry: Minneapolis-St. Paul-Bloomington, MN-WI, 2011–2019

(Numbers in thousands, not seasonally adjusted)

| Industry and year | January | February | March | April | May | June | July | August | September | October | November | December | Annual average |
|---|---|---|---|---|---|---|---|---|---|---|---|---|---|
| **Total Nonfarm** | | | | | | | | | | | | | |
| 2011 | 1,738.7 | 1,742.9 | 1,749.4 | 1,782.2 | 1,802.2 | 1,807.8 | 1,779.7 | 1,798.2 | 1,814.7 | 1,821.1 | 1,822.6 | 1,819.9 | 1,790.0 |
| 2012 | 1,776.4 | 1,780.9 | 1,789.6 | 1,812.1 | 1,829.8 | 1,840.4 | 1,814.0 | 1,823.0 | 1,839.2 | 1,849.9 | 1,853.4 | 1,846.2 | 1,821.2 |
| 2013 | 1,813.0 | 1,821.2 | 1,824.5 | 1,841.8 | 1,868.5 | 1,879.5 | 1,851.5 | 1,864.1 | 1,880.4 | 1,892.3 | 1,893.7 | 1,888.6 | 1,859.9 |
| 2014 | 1,843.4 | 1,848.3 | 1,850.3 | 1,875.3 | 1,903.2 | 1,917.2 | 1,900.2 | 1,906.5 | 1,908.4 | 1,920.6 | 1,924.4 | 1,920.9 | 1,893.2 |
| 2015 | 1,877.3 | 1,883.8 | 1,888.1 | 1,918.8 | 1,943.5 | 1,956.0 | 1,940.3 | 1,942.8 | 1,941.0 | 1,957.2 | 1,958.7 | 1,954.1 | 1,930.1 |
| 2016 | 1,912.2 | 1,918.6 | 1,919.3 | 1,954.2 | 1,970.1 | 1,976.5 | 1,976.8 | 1,982.4 | 1,983.4 | 1,989.9 | 1,991.4 | 1,983.8 | 1,963.2 |
| 2017 | 1,955.3 | 1,959.0 | 1,964.3 | 1,983.9 | 2,001.5 | 2,018.4 | 2,004.9 | 2,007.8 | 2,008.5 | 2,017.5 | 2,019.6 | 2,011.9 | 1,996.1 |
| 2018 | 1,985.8 | 1,989.2 | 1,982.2 | 1,998.4 | 2,027.7 | 2,041.3 | 2,031.5 | 2,032.9 | 2,029.0 | 2,040.0 | 2,043.2 | 2,034.6 | 2,019.7 |
| 2019 | 1,999.6 | 1,998.5 | 1,995.5 | 2,017.9 | 2,043.9 | 2,057.0 | 2,048.3 | 2,049.9 | 2,038.7 | 2,050.9 | 2,044.6 | 2,033.5 | 2,031.5 |
| **Total Private** | | | | | | | | | | | | | |
| 2011 | 1,496.9 | 1,495.3 | 1,503.0 | 1,535.6 | 1,554.4 | 1,565.5 | 1,571.4 | 1,579.7 | 1,579.2 | 1,578.5 | 1,579.6 | 1,577.5 | 1,551.4 |
| 2012 | 1,539.2 | 1,539.2 | 1,547.6 | 1,568.1 | 1,585.4 | 1,599.3 | 1,598.1 | 1,604.8 | 1,600.0 | 1,605.2 | 1,606.7 | 1,601.1 | 1,582.9 |
| 2013 | 1,572.9 | 1,575.5 | 1,579.8 | 1,594.3 | 1,621.1 | 1,637.1 | 1,636.7 | 1,646.7 | 1,638.1 | 1,643.3 | 1,642.9 | 1,640.3 | 1,619.1 |
| 2014 | 1,600.1 | 1,599.6 | 1,602.4 | 1,626.0 | 1,653.6 | 1,671.2 | 1,672.6 | 1,680.4 | 1,666.4 | 1,670.8 | 1,673.1 | 1,672.0 | 1,649.0 |
| 2015 | 1,633.0 | 1,635.1 | 1,641.1 | 1,670.0 | 1,694.7 | 1,710.1 | 1,712.0 | 1,716.5 | 1,699.3 | 1,708.3 | 1,709.1 | 1,705.4 | 1,686.2 |
| 2016 | 1,667.5 | 1,670.6 | 1,671.9 | 1,707.2 | 1,723.5 | 1,733.4 | 1,748.0 | 1,753.1 | 1,738.8 | 1,739.9 | 1,740.7 | 1,736.9 | 1,719.3 |
| 2017 | 1,707.1 | 1,707.9 | 1,714.6 | 1,735.0 | 1,753.3 | 1,771.2 | 1,772.4 | 1,776.2 | 1,759.9 | 1,762.5 | 1,764.2 | 1,760.7 | 1,748.8 |
| 2018 | 1,733.8 | 1,733.9 | 1,729.7 | 1,745.8 | 1,774.2 | 1,789.1 | 1,795.1 | 1,798.3 | 1,781.8 | 1,785.6 | 1,789.1 | 1,781.9 | 1,769.9 |
| 2019 | 1,748.3 | 1,745.9 | 1,743.7 | 1,765.5 | 1,790.0 | 1,803.3 | 1,811.4 | 1,814.5 | 1,790.6 | 1,794.2 | 1,787.6 | 1,779.0 | 1,781.2 |
| **Goods Producing** | | | | | | | | | | | | | |
| 2011 | 225.7 | 224.6 | 226.2 | 232.7 | 239.7 | 245.7 | 248.8 | 250.7 | 248.4 | 248.1 | 244.9 | 240.1 | 239.6 |
| 2012 | 231.7 | 231.0 | 234.2 | 240.5 | 245.8 | 252.1 | 254.4 | 255.6 | 252.7 | 252.3 | 248.8 | 244.3 | 245.3 |
| 2013 | 238.1 | 237.8 | 239.6 | 243.7 | 252.6 | 258.5 | 260.7 | 263.2 | 261.0 | 260.5 | 258.1 | 252.9 | 252.2 |
| 2014 | 245.7 | 245.0 | 247.0 | 252.3 | 261.6 | 268.7 | 271.1 | 272.8 | 269.3 | 269.7 | 266.4 | 263.4 | 261.1 |
| 2015 | 255.6 | 255.7 | 257.8 | 266.8 | 273.2 | 279.5 | 282.4 | 282.8 | 278.3 | 278.9 | 275.1 | 269.8 | 271.3 |
| 2016 | 260.9 | 260.3 | 262.3 | 271.1 | 276.3 | 281.1 | 284.8 | 284.7 | 281.1 | 280.2 | 276.4 | 269.5 | 274.1 |
| 2017 | 263.1 | 263.4 | 265.9 | 271.4 | 277.8 | 284.1 | 286.4 | 286.7 | 283.2 | 283.2 | 279.2 | 274.0 | 276.5 |
| 2018 | 267.8 | 266.8 | 268.1 | 271.9 | 281.8 | 290.1 | 292.4 | 293.0 | 289.7 | 288.9 | 285.7 | 280.6 | 281.4 |
| 2019 | 273.8 | 272.6 | 274.7 | 280.0 | 289.4 | 296.1 | 299.4 | 299.6 | 296.1 | 295.5 | 286.0 | 280.3 | 287.0 |
| **Service-Providing** | | | | | | | | | | | | | |
| 2011 | 1,513.0 | 1,518.3 | 1,523.2 | 1,549.5 | 1,562.5 | 1,562.1 | 1,530.9 | 1,547.5 | 1,566.3 | 1,573.0 | 1,577.7 | 1,579.8 | 1,550.3 |
| 2012 | 1,544.7 | 1,549.9 | 1,555.4 | 1,571.6 | 1,584.0 | 1,588.3 | 1,559.6 | 1,567.4 | 1,586.5 | 1,597.6 | 1,604.6 | 1,601.9 | 1,576.0 |
| 2013 | 1,574.9 | 1,583.4 | 1,584.9 | 1,598.1 | 1,615.9 | 1,621.0 | 1,590.8 | 1,600.9 | 1,619.4 | 1,631.8 | 1,635.6 | 1,635.7 | 1,607.7 |
| 2014 | 1,597.7 | 1,603.3 | 1,603.3 | 1,623.0 | 1,641.6 | 1,648.5 | 1,629.1 | 1,633.7 | 1,639.1 | 1,650.9 | 1,658.0 | 1,657.5 | 1,632.1 |
| 2015 | 1,621.7 | 1,628.1 | 1,630.3 | 1,652.0 | 1,670.3 | 1,676.5 | 1,657.9 | 1,660.0 | 1,662.7 | 1,678.3 | 1,683.6 | 1,684.3 | 1,658.8 |
| 2016 | 1,651.3 | 1,658.3 | 1,657.0 | 1,683.1 | 1,693.8 | 1,695.4 | 1,692.0 | 1,697.7 | 1,702.3 | 1,709.7 | 1,715.0 | 1,714.3 | 1,689.2 |
| 2017 | 1,692.2 | 1,695.6 | 1,698.4 | 1,712.5 | 1,723.7 | 1,734.3 | 1,718.5 | 1,721.1 | 1,726.2 | 1,734.3 | 1,740.4 | 1,737.9 | 1,719.6 |
| 2018 | 1,718.0 | 1,722.4 | 1,714.1 | 1,726.5 | 1,745.9 | 1,751.2 | 1,739.1 | 1,739.9 | 1,739.3 | 1,751.1 | 1,757.5 | 1,754.0 | 1,738.3 |
| 2019 | 1,725.8 | 1,725.9 | 1,720.8 | 1,737.9 | 1,754.5 | 1,760.9 | 1,748.9 | 1,750.3 | 1,742.6 | 1,755.4 | 1,758.6 | 1,753.2 | 1,744.6 |
| **Mining, Logging, and Construction** | | | | | | | | | | | | | |
| 2011 | 48.5 | 47.8 | 49.1 | 53.8 | 59.1 | 62.8 | 64.4 | 65.7 | 64.7 | 64.0 | 61.2 | 56.7 | 58.2 |
| 2012 | 50.4 | 50.0 | 52.3 | 57.7 | 61.7 | 65.4 | 67.1 | 68.0 | 66.6 | 66.0 | 62.8 | 58.7 | 60.6 |
| 2013 | 53.7 | 53.9 | 55.3 | 59.1 | 66.8 | 70.4 | 72.7 | 74.8 | 74.0 | 73.2 | 70.4 | 65.1 | 65.8 |
| 2014 | 59.3 | 58.7 | 60.1 | 64.7 | 72.4 | 76.6 | 78.4 | 79.4 | 77.7 | 77.2 | 73.6 | 70.0 | 70.7 |
| 2015 | 64.1 | 64.2 | 65.7 | 73.5 | 79.0 | 82.8 | 84.9 | 85.4 | 82.8 | 82.5 | 78.8 | 73.8 | 76.5 |
| 2016 | 66.5 | 66.2 | 67.7 | 75.8 | 80.5 | 83.4 | 85.1 | 85.1 | 83.8 | 83.0 | 80.0 | 74.0 | 77.6 |
| 2017 | 69.0 | 69.3 | 71.3 | 76.7 | 82.7 | 86.6 | 87.9 | 88.2 | 86.2 | 86.0 | 82.3 | 78.0 | 80.4 |
| 2018 | 72.0 | 71.4 | 72.3 | 75.4 | 84.3 | 89.3 | 90.7 | 91.1 | 89.6 | 88.9 | 85.7 | 80.6 | 82.6 |
| 2019 | 74.8 | 73.6 | 75.2 | 80.7 | 89.2 | 93.6 | 95.1 | 96.1 | 95.0 | 94.2 | 86.3 | 80.9 | 86.2 |
| **Manufacturing** | | | | | | | | | | | | | |
| 2011 | 177.2 | 176.8 | 177.1 | 178.9 | 180.6 | 182.9 | 184.4 | 185.0 | 183.7 | 184.1 | 183.7 | 183.4 | 181.5 |
| 2012 | 181.3 | 181.0 | 181.9 | 182.8 | 184.1 | 186.7 | 187.3 | 187.6 | 186.1 | 186.3 | 186.0 | 185.6 | 184.7 |
| 2013 | 184.4 | 183.9 | 184.3 | 184.6 | 185.8 | 188.1 | 188.0 | 188.4 | 187.0 | 187.3 | 187.7 | 187.8 | 186.4 |
| 2014 | 186.4 | 186.3 | 186.9 | 187.6 | 189.2 | 192.1 | 192.7 | 193.4 | 191.6 | 192.5 | 192.8 | 193.4 | 190.4 |
| 2015 | 191.5 | 191.5 | 192.1 | 193.3 | 194.2 | 196.7 | 197.5 | 197.4 | 195.5 | 196.4 | 196.3 | 196.0 | 194.9 |
| 2016 | 194.4 | 194.1 | 194.6 | 195.3 | 195.8 | 197.7 | 199.7 | 199.6 | 197.3 | 197.2 | 196.4 | 195.5 | 196.5 |
| 2017 | 194.1 | 194.1 | 194.6 | 194.7 | 195.1 | 197.5 | 198.5 | 198.5 | 196.1 | 197.2 | 196.9 | 196.0 | 196.1 |
| 2018 | 195.8 | 195.4 | 195.8 | 196.5 | 197.5 | 200.8 | 201.7 | 201.9 | 200.1 | 200.0 | 200.0 | 200.0 | 198.8 |
| 2019 | 199.0 | 199.0 | 199.5 | 199.3 | 200.2 | 202.5 | 204.3 | 203.5 | 201.1 | 201.3 | 199.7 | 199.4 | 200.7 |

## Employment by Industry: Minneapolis-St. Paul-Bloomington, MN-WI, 2011–2019—*Continued*

(Numbers in thousands, not seasonally adjusted)

| Industry and year | January | February | March | April | May | June | July | August | September | October | November | December | Annual average |
|---|---|---|---|---|---|---|---|---|---|---|---|---|---|
| **Trade, Transportation, and Utilities** | | | | | | | | | | | | | |
| 2011 | 316.7 | 313.4 | 314.6 | 321.0 | 323.8 | 324.9 | 325.3 | 325.4 | 325.7 | 327.0 | 332.7 | 336.0 | 323.9 |
| 2012 | 324.7 | 319.9 | 321.3 | 325.1 | 329.0 | 330.7 | 327.9 | 328.4 | 326.9 | 330.0 | 337.6 | 338.3 | 328.3 |
| 2013 | 328.2 | 324.5 | 324.6 | 326.9 | 331.8 | 335.0 | 332.8 | 335.2 | 333.2 | 335.6 | 341.7 | 345.2 | 332.9 |
| 2014 | 332.7 | 329.2 | 329.5 | 334.0 | 338.0 | 340.9 | 339.8 | 340.8 | 336.7 | 340.2 | 346.5 | 351.3 | 338.3 |
| 2015 | 337.9 | 334.7 | 335.5 | 340.4 | 344.9 | 348.6 | 346.4 | 347.3 | 343.5 | 347.0 | 353.3 | 356.4 | 344.7 |
| 2016 | 344.1 | 342.1 | 342.3 | 347.4 | 351.0 | 352.1 | 353.8 | 354.6 | 350.3 | 352.9 | 358.5 | 363.3 | 351.0 |
| 2017 | 353.5 | 350.2 | 349.8 | 352.9 | 356.1 | 358.9 | 358.1 | 358.1 | 354.3 | 356.8 | 364.0 | 368.3 | 356.8 |
| 2018 | 357.1 | 354.0 | 353.3 | 353.7 | 358.2 | 359.3 | 359.7 | 358.8 | 355.1 | 355.6 | 364.8 | 368.1 | 358.1 |
| 2019 | 358.5 | 351.6 | 350.2 | 352.7 | 356.8 | 358.0 | 357.4 | 357.3 | 352.3 | 355.6 | 361.1 | 365.7 | 356.4 |
| **Wholesale Trade** | | | | | | | | | | | | | |
| 2011 | 85.5 | 85.4 | 85.7 | 87.1 | 87.5 | 87.8 | 88.8 | 88.8 | 87.9 | 87.7 | 87.6 | 87.8 | 87.3 |
| 2012 | 87.4 | 87.4 | 87.8 | 89.0 | 89.7 | 90.7 | 90.7 | 90.3 | 89.2 | 89.2 | 89.3 | 89.4 | 89.2 |
| 2013 | 88.6 | 88.7 | 88.8 | 89.2 | 89.9 | 90.7 | 90.9 | 90.8 | 89.9 | 89.9 | 90.0 | 90.1 | 89.8 |
| 2014 | 89.5 | 89.4 | 89.6 | 90.1 | 91.1 | 92.0 | 92.2 | 92.1 | 90.9 | 91.2 | 91.4 | 91.7 | 90.9 |
| 2015 | 90.4 | 90.4 | 90.6 | 91.5 | 91.9 | 92.8 | 93.3 | 93.0 | 91.6 | 91.8 | 92.0 | 91.9 | 91.8 |
| 2016 | 90.6 | 90.8 | 90.7 | 91.9 | 92.4 | 92.3 | 93.3 | 93.1 | 91.9 | 91.4 | 91.4 | 91.7 | 91.8 |
| 2017 | 91.5 | 91.3 | 91.4 | 91.3 | 91.9 | 92.7 | 93.2 | 92.9 | 91.7 | 92.0 | 92.1 | 92.5 | 92.0 |
| 2018 | 91.5 | 91.6 | 91.8 | 92.2 | 92.7 | 93.6 | 92.9 | 92.7 | 91.3 | 91.7 | 91.8 | 92.0 | 92.2 |
| 2019 | 92.2 | 92.0 | 91.6 | 92.3 | 92.7 | 93.5 | 93.9 | 93.7 | 92.1 | 91.3 | 91.5 | 91.6 | 92.4 |
| **Retail Trade** | | | | | | | | | | | | | |
| 2011 | 169.2 | 166.0 | 166.4 | 170.6 | 172.8 | 174.3 | 174.5 | 175.3 | 173.6 | 174.8 | 180.5 | 182.7 | 173.4 |
| 2012 | 174.0 | 169.5 | 170.3 | 172.6 | 175.2 | 176.9 | 175.6 | 176.2 | 174.0 | 176.6 | 183.6 | 183.9 | 175.7 |
| 2013 | 176.3 | 172.4 | 172.6 | 174.4 | 177.6 | 180.7 | 179.8 | 181.2 | 178.3 | 179.5 | 185.0 | 187.7 | 178.8 |
| 2014 | 178.2 | 175.2 | 175.3 | 178.2 | 180.8 | 183.4 | 183.4 | 184.0 | 179.6 | 182.0 | 187.7 | 190.7 | 181.5 |
| 2015 | 181.4 | 178.2 | 178.6 | 181.4 | 185.2 | 188.7 | 187.5 | 188.6 | 184.4 | 186.4 | 192.0 | 193.6 | 185.5 |
| 2016 | 185.2 | 183.2 | 183.5 | 186.4 | 188.8 | 190.5 | 192.4 | 192.4 | 186.6 | 189.0 | 193.5 | 195.5 | 188.9 |
| 2017 | 188.2 | 185.4 | 185.3 | 188.2 | 190.1 | 192.1 | 192.2 | 192.4 | 187.2 | 189.0 | 194.8 | 197.0 | 190.2 |
| 2018 | 190.1 | 187.1 | 186.3 | 186.2 | 190.3 | 192.2 | 193.0 | 192.6 | 187.9 | 188.0 | 195.8 | 197.6 | 190.6 |
| 2019 | 189.6 | 184.1 | 183.4 | 184.6 | 187.4 | 188.8 | 188.7 | 188.2 | 182.8 | 185.7 | 190.9 | 194.1 | 187.4 |
| **Transportation and Utilities** | | | | | | | | | | | | | |
| 2011 | 62.0 | 62.0 | 62.5 | 63.3 | 63.5 | 62.8 | 62.0 | 61.3 | 64.2 | 64.5 | 64.6 | 65.5 | 63.2 |
| 2012 | 63.3 | 63.0 | 63.2 | 63.5 | 64.1 | 63.1 | 61.6 | 61.9 | 63.7 | 64.2 | 64.7 | 65.0 | 63.4 |
| 2013 | 63.3 | 63.4 | 63.2 | 63.3 | 64.3 | 63.6 | 62.1 | 63.2 | 65.0 | 66.2 | 66.7 | 67.4 | 64.3 |
| 2014 | 65.0 | 64.6 | 64.6 | 65.7 | 66.1 | 65.5 | 64.2 | 64.7 | 66.2 | 67.0 | 67.4 | 68.9 | 65.8 |
| 2015 | 66.1 | 66.1 | 66.3 | 67.5 | 67.8 | 67.1 | 65.6 | 65.7 | 67.5 | 68.8 | 69.3 | 70.9 | 67.4 |
| 2016 | 68.3 | 68.1 | 68.1 | 69.1 | 69.8 | 69.3 | 68.1 | 69.1 | 71.8 | 72.5 | 73.6 | 76.1 | 70.3 |
| 2017 | 73.8 | 73.5 | 73.1 | 73.4 | 74.1 | 74.1 | 72.7 | 72.8 | 75.4 | 75.8 | 77.1 | 78.8 | 74.6 |
| 2018 | 75.5 | 75.3 | 75.2 | 75.3 | 75.2 | 73.5 | 73.8 | 73.5 | 75.9 | 75.9 | 77.2 | 78.5 | 75.4 |
| 2019 | 76.7 | 75.5 | 75.2 | 75.8 | 76.7 | 75.7 | 74.8 | 75.4 | 77.4 | 78.6 | 78.7 | 80.0 | 76.7 |
| **Information** | | | | | | | | | | | | | |
| 2011 | 39.5 | 39.1 | 39.0 | 39.6 | 39.6 | 39.7 | 40.3 | 40.5 | 40.1 | 40.0 | 39.9 | 40.0 | 39.8 |
| 2012 | 38.4 | 38.5 | 38.6 | 38.1 | 38.4 | 38.4 | 38.5 | 38.5 | 38.2 | 38.5 | 38.3 | 38.4 | 38.4 |
| 2013 | 37.7 | 37.8 | 37.9 | 38.0 | 37.9 | 38.0 | 38.5 | 38.2 | 37.7 | 37.6 | 37.7 | 37.9 | 37.9 |
| 2014 | 37.3 | 37.3 | 37.1 | 37.1 | 37.2 | 37.5 | 37.7 | 37.7 | 37.0 | 37.1 | 37.0 | 37.3 | 37.3 |
| 2015 | 36.4 | 36.2 | 36.2 | 36.1 | 36.2 | 36.5 | 36.7 | 36.6 | 35.9 | 35.7 | 35.9 | 35.7 | 36.2 |
| 2016 | 35.3 | 35.4 | 35.4 | 35.4 | 35.5 | 35.6 | 36.0 | 36.3 | 36.4 | 36.0 | 36.0 | 36.0 | 35.8 |
| 2017 | 35.9 | 35.8 | 36.0 | 35.9 | 35.9 | 36.1 | 36.1 | 36.5 | 35.8 | 35.7 | 36.0 | 36.1 | 36.0 |
| 2018 | 35.8 | 35.9 | 35.5 | 35.5 | 35.6 | 35.9 | 36.2 | 36.4 | 35.4 | 35.4 | 35.5 | 35.5 | 35.7 |
| 2019 | 35.5 | 35.5 | 35.3 | 35.5 | 35.6 | 35.9 | 36.2 | 36.5 | 35.8 | 35.6 | 35.6 | 35.5 | 35.7 |
| **Financial Activities** | | | | | | | | | | | | | |
| 2011 | 133.7 | 133.7 | 133.8 | 133.2 | 133.4 | 133.8 | 134.6 | 134.7 | 133.7 | 133.4 | 133.4 | 133.6 | 133.8 |
| 2012 | 134.6 | 135.0 | 135.1 | 136.6 | 137.3 | 138.6 | 138.6 | 138.7 | 137.8 | 138.8 | 139.0 | 139.3 | 137.5 |
| 2013 | 138.9 | 139.1 | 139.2 | 139.2 | 139.8 | 141.3 | 141.8 | 141.8 | 140.5 | 140.8 | 141.0 | 141.2 | 140.4 |
| 2014 | 140.1 | 140.0 | 140.0 | 139.4 | 140.0 | 141.7 | 142.0 | 141.8 | 140.2 | 140.8 | 141.1 | 141.5 | 140.7 |
| 2015 | 142.3 | 142.5 | 142.5 | 143.7 | 144.6 | 146.2 | 147.3 | 147.5 | 145.6 | 146.2 | 146.4 | 146.8 | 145.1 |
| 2016 | 145.7 | 146.1 | 146.0 | 147.4 | 147.6 | 148.9 | 150.9 | 151.1 | 149.8 | 150.4 | 150.6 | 151.0 | 148.8 |
| 2017 | 150.5 | 150.6 | 151.0 | 151.4 | 151.9 | 153.8 | 154.6 | 154.6 | 153.1 | 153.3 | 153.4 | 153.9 | 152.7 |
| 2018 | 153.1 | 153.7 | 153.8 | 154.8 | 155.0 | 157.1 | 158.2 | 158.4 | 156.8 | 157.3 | 157.5 | 158.0 | 156.1 |
| 2019 | 156.5 | 156.8 | 157.0 | 157.3 | 157.8 | 159.9 | 160.9 | 160.6 | 158.8 | 158.6 | 158.3 | 157.9 | 158.4 |

# Employment by Industry: Minneapolis-St. Paul-Bloomington, MN-WI, 2011–2019—*Continued*

(Numbers in thousands, not seasonally adjusted)

| Industry and year | January | February | March | April | May | June | July | August | September | October | November | December | Annual average |
|---|---|---|---|---|---|---|---|---|---|---|---|---|---|
| **Professional and Business Services** | | | | | | | | | | | | | |
| 2011 | 278.7 | 279.4 | 281.1 | 288.9 | 290.1 | 293.0 | 298.3 | 300.7 | 300.8 | 302.5 | 302.8 | 302.8 | 293.3 |
| 2012 | 293.7 | 294.0 | 294.6 | 296.8 | 298.4 | 301.1 | 302.9 | 304.9 | 303.5 | 306.1 | 305.6 | 305.2 | 300.6 |
| 2013 | 298.4 | 301.0 | 301.0 | 302.6 | 304.5 | 308.3 | 309.5 | 311.4 | 309.6 | 313.8 | 312.4 | 312.0 | 307.0 |
| 2014 | 303.3 | 304.0 | 303.5 | 307.2 | 310.7 | 314.0 | 316.7 | 318.0 | 315.7 | 318.8 | 321.0 | 317.5 | 312.5 |
| 2015 | 309.8 | 310.7 | 310.1 | 317.3 | 320.0 | 320.9 | 322.7 | 322.9 | 318.7 | 324.1 | 324.3 | 322.5 | 318.7 |
| 2016 | 314.6 | 316.6 | 313.8 | 321.8 | 322.4 | 323.9 | 328.0 | 328.5 | 327.5 | 330.8 | 328.9 | 328.1 | 323.7 |
| 2017 | 321.2 | 320.3 | 320.8 | 324.5 | 325.7 | 327.3 | 328.7 | 329.6 | 327.0 | 330.6 | 331.3 | 328.3 | 326.3 |
| 2018 | 324.4 | 324.5 | 320.1 | 325.2 | 328.0 | 329.0 | 332.9 | 333.9 | 331.0 | 336.2 | 335.5 | 331.6 | 329.4 |
| 2019 | 323.3 | 325.5 | 323.3 | 329.0 | 331.2 | 331.3 | 334.5 | 335.2 | 329.9 | 332.7 | 332.0 | 329.0 | 329.7 |
| **Education and Health Services** | | | | | | | | | | | | | |
| 2011 | 276.3 | 278.9 | 279.3 | 284.2 | 283.5 | 279.3 | 276.1 | 277.3 | 282.0 | 285.4 | 286.6 | 287.2 | 281.3 |
| 2012 | 283.7 | 287.6 | 287.9 | 289.2 | 289.2 | 284.8 | 282.7 | 283.8 | 290.1 | 293.9 | 295.1 | 294.5 | 288.5 |
| 2013 | 294.1 | 297.8 | 297.6 | 299.9 | 301.2 | 296.7 | 294.5 | 296.3 | 300.1 | 303.7 | 305.4 | 304.9 | 299.4 |
| 2014 | 300.6 | 303.8 | 304.0 | 306.7 | 307.4 | 303.5 | 301.6 | 303.5 | 307.7 | 310.6 | 311.7 | 312.0 | 306.1 |
| 2015 | 306.7 | 310.8 | 311.8 | 312.7 | 314.2 | 310.5 | 308.9 | 310.3 | 315.0 | 317.7 | 319.4 | 319.2 | 313.1 |
| 2016 | 316.9 | 320.0 | 319.9 | 324.5 | 324.6 | 320.0 | 320.0 | 322.4 | 323.9 | 324.7 | 329.9 | 330.1 | 323.1 |
| 2017 | 326.6 | 330.8 | 331.1 | 334.1 | 334.1 | 332.3 | 329.8 | 330.9 | 334.9 | 337.0 | 338.7 | 338.7 | 333.3 |
| 2018 | 335.0 | 338.5 | 339.0 | 341.8 | 341.8 | 338.2 | 335.8 | 336.5 | 340.5 | 343.3 | 345.2 | 343.8 | 340.0 |
| 2019 | 340.6 | 343.2 | 342.3 | 345.2 | 345.0 | 341.3 | 340.2 | 341.0 | 344.7 | 348.4 | 347.7 | 345.5 | 343.8 |
| **Leisure and Hospitality** | | | | | | | | | | | | | |
| 2011 | 150.5 | 150.1 | 152.5 | 158.7 | 166.7 | 170.6 | 168.8 | 170.8 | 169.7 | 163.9 | 161.0 | 159.6 | 161.9 |
| 2012 | 155.2 | 155.8 | 158.3 | 163.7 | 168.9 | 173.6 | 173.6 | 175.3 | 172.5 | 167.1 | 164.0 | 162.9 | 165.9 |
| 2013 | 160.0 | 159.8 | 161.7 | 165.9 | 174.1 | 179.2 | 179.2 | 180.5 | 176.7 | 172.9 | 168.4 | 168.0 | 170.5 |
| 2014 | 163.1 | 163.1 | 163.8 | 170.6 | 179.2 | 184.2 | 183.0 | 185.0 | 180.2 | 174.0 | 170.0 | 170.1 | 173.9 |
| 2015 | 167.1 | 167.1 | 169.2 | 174.2 | 182.5 | 187.7 | 187.6 | 188.9 | 183.8 | 179.4 | 175.5 | 175.7 | 178.2 |
| 2016 | 172.6 | 172.2 | 173.9 | 180.1 | 186.5 | 191.5 | 193.4 | 194.3 | 189.0 | 184.7 | 180.3 | 179.1 | 183.1 |
| 2017 | 177.2 | 177.7 | 180.2 | 184.8 | 191.5 | 197.2 | 197.7 | 198.7 | 192.7 | 186.7 | 182.9 | 182.9 | 187.5 |
| 2018 | 182.5 | 182.4 | 182.1 | 184.7 | 195.1 | 199.3 | 199.6 | 201.2 | 195.0 | 190.0 | 186.1 | 186.2 | 190.4 |
| 2019 | 182.8 | 183.4 | 183.4 | 187.2 | 195.4 | 200.4 | 202.0 | 203.8 | 194.5 | 190.2 | 187.9 | 185.0 | 191.3 |
| **Other Services** | | | | | | | | | | | | | |
| 2011 | 75.8 | 76.1 | 76.5 | 77.3 | 77.6 | 78.5 | 79.2 | 79.6 | 78.8 | 78.2 | 78.3 | 78.2 | 77.8 |
| 2012 | 77.2 | 77.4 | 77.6 | 78.1 | 78.4 | 80.0 | 79.5 | 79.6 | 78.3 | 78.5 | 78.3 | 78.2 | 78.4 |
| 2013 | 77.5 | 77.7 | 78.2 | 78.1 | 79.2 | 80.1 | 79.7 | 80.1 | 79.3 | 78.4 | 78.2 | 78.2 | 78.7 |
| 2014 | 77.3 | 77.2 | 77.5 | 78.7 | 79.5 | 80.7 | 80.7 | 80.8 | 79.6 | 79.6 | 79.4 | 78.9 | 79.2 |
| 2015 | 77.2 | 77.4 | 78.0 | 78.8 | 79.1 | 80.2 | 80.0 | 80.2 | 78.5 | 79.3 | 79.2 | 79.3 | 78.9 |
| 2016 | 77.4 | 77.9 | 78.3 | 79.5 | 79.6 | 80.3 | 81.1 | 81.2 | 80.8 | 80.2 | 80.1 | 79.8 | 79.7 |
| 2017 | 79.1 | 79.1 | 79.8 | 80.0 | 80.3 | 81.5 | 81.0 | 81.1 | 79.8 | 79.2 | 78.7 | 78.5 | 79.8 |
| 2018 | 78.1 | 78.1 | 77.8 | 78.2 | 78.7 | 80.2 | 80.3 | 80.1 | 78.3 | 78.9 | 78.8 | 78.1 | 78.8 |
| 2019 | 77.3 | 77.3 | 77.5 | 78.6 | 78.8 | 80.4 | 80.8 | 80.5 | 78.5 | 77.6 | 79.0 | 80.1 | 78.9 |
| **Government** | | | | | | | | | | | | | |
| 2011 | 241.8 | 247.6 | 246.4 | 246.6 | 247.8 | 242.3 | 208.3 | 218.5 | 235.5 | 242.6 | 243.0 | 242.4 | 238.6 |
| 2012 | 237.2 | 241.7 | 242.0 | 244.0 | 244.4 | 241.1 | 215.9 | 218.2 | 239.2 | 244.7 | 246.7 | 245.1 | 238.4 |
| 2013 | 240.1 | 245.7 | 244.7 | 247.5 | 247.4 | 242.4 | 214.8 | 217.4 | 242.3 | 249.0 | 250.8 | 248.3 | 240.9 |
| 2014 | 243.3 | 248.7 | 247.9 | 249.3 | 249.6 | 246.0 | 227.6 | 226.1 | 242.0 | 249.8 | 251.3 | 248.9 | 244.2 |
| 2015 | 244.3 | 248.7 | 247.0 | 248.8 | 248.8 | 245.9 | 228.3 | 226.3 | 241.7 | 248.9 | 249.6 | 248.7 | 243.9 |
| 2016 | 244.7 | 248.0 | 247.4 | 247.0 | 246.6 | 243.1 | 228.8 | 229.3 | 244.6 | 250.0 | 250.7 | 246.9 | 243.9 |
| 2017 | 248.2 | 251.1 | 249.7 | 248.9 | 248.2 | 247.2 | 232.5 | 231.6 | 248.6 | 255.0 | 255.4 | 251.2 | 247.3 |
| 2018 | 252.0 | 255.3 | 252.5 | 252.6 | 253.5 | 252.2 | 236.4 | 234.6 | 247.2 | 254.4 | 254.1 | 252.7 | 249.8 |
| 2019 | 251.3 | 252.6 | 251.8 | 252.4 | 253.9 | 253.7 | 236.9 | 235.4 | 248.1 | 256.7 | 257.0 | 254.5 | 250.4 |

## Employment by Industry: San Diego-Carlsbad, CA, 2011–2019

(Numbers in thousands, not seasonally adjusted)

| Industry and year | January | February | March | April | May | June | July | August | September | October | November | December | Annual average |
|---|---|---|---|---|---|---|---|---|---|---|---|---|---|
| **Total Nonfarm** | | | | | | | | | | | | | |
| 2011 | 1,233.4 | 1,241.0 | 1,244.6 | 1,247.5 | 1,250.1 | 1,254.0 | 1,243.8 | 1,246.6 | 1,251.0 | 1,256.3 | 1,265.9 | 1,268.9 | 1,250.3 |
| 2012 | 1,244.6 | 1,253.6 | 1,260.7 | 1,278.3 | 1,287.7 | 1,295.7 | 1,280.5 | 1,286.5 | 1,286.6 | 1,297.6 | 1,309.2 | 1,312.3 | 1,282.8 |
| 2013 | 1,288.2 | 1,296.5 | 1,303.9 | 1,309.4 | 1,314.5 | 1,320.6 | 1,309.6 | 1,314.8 | 1,315.4 | 1,331.0 | 1,342.8 | 1,345.1 | 1,316.0 |
| 2014 | 1,315.0 | 1,324.6 | 1,331.5 | 1,335.3 | 1,342.1 | 1,349.7 | 1,338.0 | 1,346.6 | 1,346.7 | 1,359.1 | 1,372.5 | 1,375.2 | 1,344.7 |
| 2015 | 1,352.2 | 1,358.5 | 1,365.3 | 1,371.3 | 1,381.8 | 1,385.8 | 1,386.0 | 1,389.2 | 1,389.4 | 1,405.9 | 1,415.9 | 1,416.3 | 1,384.8 |
| 2016 | 1,391.3 | 1,401.9 | 1,402.1 | 1,416.6 | 1,421.7 | 1,422.7 | 1,420.3 | 1,425.1 | 1,428.2 | 1,439.7 | 1,450.2 | 1,451.0 | 1,422.6 |
| 2017 | 1,424.7 | 1,433.3 | 1,437.1 | 1,445.5 | 1,451.1 | 1,459.4 | 1,445.4 | 1,449.6 | 1,453.7 | 1,468.2 | 1,478.2 | 1,480.2 | 1,452.2 |
| 2018 | 1,459.5 | 1,469.6 | 1,473.6 | 1,477.9 | 1,481.7 | 1,488.7 | 1,475.4 | 1,480.3 | 1,479.1 | 1,492.9 | 1,502.6 | 1,504.6 | 1,482.2 |
| 2019 | 1,482.0 | 1,488.0 | 1,491.4 | 1,498.2 | 1,504.8 | 1,509.3 | 1,499.4 | 1,507.1 | 1,502.3 | 1,514.6 | 1,524.0 | 1,525.2 | 1,503.9 |
| **Total Private** | | | | | | | | | | | | | |
| 2011 | 1,003.3 | 1,008.1 | 1,010.8 | 1,013.7 | 1,017.4 | 1,020.4 | 1,024.1 | 1,029.4 | 1,027.8 | 1,026.7 | 1,034.8 | 1,039.1 | 1,021.3 |
| 2012 | 1,017.9 | 1,024.2 | 1,029.8 | 1,047.5 | 1,056.4 | 1,063.6 | 1,062.4 | 1,067.5 | 1,063.6 | 1,068.2 | 1,077.1 | 1,081.1 | 1,054.9 |
| 2013 | 1,060.6 | 1,066.5 | 1,071.5 | 1,077.5 | 1,082.2 | 1,086.6 | 1,089.1 | 1,093.9 | 1,089.5 | 1,099.7 | 1,108.9 | 1,112.0 | 1,086.5 |
| 2014 | 1,085.7 | 1,092.2 | 1,097.1 | 1,100.6 | 1,106.9 | 1,112.0 | 1,115.7 | 1,123.3 | 1,119.6 | 1,125.2 | 1,135.9 | 1,139.1 | 1,112.8 |
| 2015 | 1,117.7 | 1,122.7 | 1,127.7 | 1,133.1 | 1,142.2 | 1,147.0 | 1,158.6 | 1,162.3 | 1,157.8 | 1,166.6 | 1,173.6 | 1,174.5 | 1,148.7 |
| 2016 | 1,152.9 | 1,160.8 | 1,159.2 | 1,172.9 | 1,176.8 | 1,177.3 | 1,189.1 | 1,190.8 | 1,188.5 | 1,192.9 | 1,201.1 | 1,201.6 | 1,180.3 |
| 2017 | 1,178.1 | 1,183.8 | 1,187.3 | 1,194.9 | 1,200.0 | 1,207.5 | 1,212.2 | 1,215.9 | 1,212.0 | 1,220.5 | 1,228.4 | 1,230.4 | 1,205.9 |
| 2018 | 1,212.2 | 1,220.4 | 1,223.2 | 1,225.9 | 1,229.2 | 1,234.8 | 1,241.1 | 1,244.3 | 1,234.8 | 1,241.9 | 1,249.3 | 1,251.7 | 1,234.1 |
| 2019 | 1,231.0 | 1,236.7 | 1,238.6 | 1,244.9 | 1,250.9 | 1,255.0 | 1,263.3 | 1,267.4 | 1,257.0 | 1,262.4 | 1,270.0 | 1,273.6 | 1,254.2 |
| **Goods Producing** | | | | | | | | | | | | | |
| 2011 | 150.1 | 150.5 | 150.9 | 151.1 | 151.7 | 152.7 | 152.8 | 153.7 | 153.2 | 153.2 | 152.8 | 152.9 | 152.1 |
| 2012 | 150.7 | 151.0 | 152.1 | 153.8 | 155.3 | 156.7 | 157.3 | 158.1 | 157.6 | 158.0 | 159.0 | 158.8 | 155.7 |
| 2013 | 157.2 | 158.1 | 158.7 | 159.5 | 159.6 | 160.8 | 161.8 | 162.6 | 162.1 | 162.7 | 163.6 | 163.8 | 160.9 |
| 2014 | 162.1 | 162.6 | 162.9 | 164.0 | 165.2 | 165.9 | 167.7 | 168.9 | 169.0 | 170.3 | 171.0 | 171.1 | 166.7 |
| 2015 | 169.9 | 170.7 | 172.3 | 173.1 | 175.0 | 176.4 | 179.3 | 180.9 | 180.4 | 180.8 | 181.0 | 181.6 | 176.8 |
| 2016 | 180.5 | 181.8 | 181.7 | 183.0 | 183.7 | 184.6 | 187.1 | 187.2 | 186.5 | 187.5 | 187.9 | 188.2 | 185.0 |
| 2017 | 183.3 | 185.1 | 186.2 | 186.7 | 187.2 | 189.2 | 190.7 | 191.6 | 192.3 | 193.0 | 192.3 | 193.3 | 189.2 |
| 2018 | 192.8 | 194.9 | 194.6 | 194.6 | 195.7 | 197.4 | 198.4 | 198.6 | 197.5 | 197.2 | 197.4 | 197.1 | 196.4 |
| 2019 | 194.8 | 195.6 | 196.8 | 197.5 | 198.7 | 200.3 | 202.1 | 202.8 | 201.6 | 200.1 | 200.7 | 202.5 | 199.5 |
| **Service-Providing** | | | | | | | | | | | | | |
| 2011 | 1,083.3 | 1,090.5 | 1,093.7 | 1,096.4 | 1,098.4 | 1,101.3 | 1,091.0 | 1,092.9 | 1,097.8 | 1,103.1 | 1,113.1 | 1,116.0 | 1,098.1 |
| 2012 | 1,093.9 | 1,102.6 | 1,108.6 | 1,124.5 | 1,132.4 | 1,139.0 | 1,123.2 | 1,128.4 | 1,129.0 | 1,139.6 | 1,150.2 | 1,153.5 | 1,127.1 |
| 2013 | 1,131.0 | 1,138.4 | 1,145.2 | 1,149.9 | 1,154.9 | 1,159.8 | 1,147.8 | 1,152.2 | 1,153.3 | 1,168.3 | 1,179.2 | 1,181.3 | 1,155.1 |
| 2014 | 1,152.9 | 1,162.0 | 1,168.6 | 1,171.3 | 1,176.9 | 1,183.8 | 1,170.3 | 1,177.7 | 1,177.7 | 1,188.8 | 1,201.5 | 1,204.1 | 1,178.0 |
| 2015 | 1,182.3 | 1,187.8 | 1,193.0 | 1,198.2 | 1,206.8 | 1,209.4 | 1,206.7 | 1,208.3 | 1,209.0 | 1,225.1 | 1,234.9 | 1,234.7 | 1,208.0 |
| 2016 | 1,210.8 | 1,220.1 | 1,220.4 | 1,233.6 | 1,238.0 | 1,238.1 | 1,233.2 | 1,237.9 | 1,241.7 | 1,252.2 | 1,262.3 | 1,262.8 | 1,237.6 |
| 2017 | 1,241.4 | 1,248.2 | 1,250.9 | 1,258.8 | 1,263.9 | 1,270.2 | 1,254.7 | 1,258.0 | 1,261.4 | 1,275.2 | 1,285.9 | 1,286.9 | 1,263.0 |
| 2018 | 1,266.7 | 1,274.7 | 1,279.0 | 1,283.3 | 1,286.0 | 1,291.3 | 1,277.0 | 1,281.7 | 1,281.6 | 1,295.7 | 1,305.2 | 1,307.5 | 1,285.8 |
| 2019 | 1,287.2 | 1,292.4 | 1,294.6 | 1,300.7 | 1,306.1 | 1,309.0 | 1,297.3 | 1,304.3 | 1,300.7 | 1,314.5 | 1,323.3 | 1,322.7 | 1,304.4 |
| **Mining and Logging** | | | | | | | | | | | | | |
| 2011 | 0.4 | 0.4 | 0.4 | 0.4 | 0.4 | 0.4 | 0.4 | 0.4 | 0.4 | 0.3 | 0.3 | 0.3 | 0.4 |
| 2012 | 0.3 | 0.3 | 0.3 | 0.4 | 0.4 | 0.4 | 0.3 | 0.4 | 0.3 | 0.3 | 0.3 | 0.3 | 0.4 |
| 2013 | 0.3 | 0.3 | 0.3 | 0.3 | 0.3 | 0.3 | 0.3 | 0.3 | 0.3 | 0.3 | 0.3 | 0.4 | 0.4 |
| 2014 | 0.4 | 0.4 | 0.3 | 0.4 | 0.4 | 0.4 | 0.4 | 0.4 | 0.4 | 0.4 | 0.4 | 0.4 | 0.4 |
| 2015 | 0.4 | 0.3 | 0.3 | 0.3 | 0.3 | 0.3 | 0.3 | 0.3 | 0.3 | 0.3 | 0.3 | 0.3 | 0.3 |
| 2016 | 0.3 | 0.3 | 0.3 | 0.3 | 0.3 | 0.3 | 0.3 | 0.3 | 0.3 | 0.3 | 0.3 | 0.3 | 0.3 |
| 2017 | 0.3 | 0.3 | 0.3 | 0.3 | 0.3 | 0.3 | 0.3 | 0.3 | 0.3 | 0.3 | 0.3 | 0.3 | 0.3 |
| 2018 | 0.3 | 0.3 | 0.3 | 0.3 | 0.4 | 0.4 | 0.4 | 0.4 | 0.4 | 0.4 | 0.4 | 0.4 | 0.4 |
| 2019 | 0.3 | 0.3 | 0.3 | 0.3 | 0.4 | 0.4 | 0.4 | 0.4 | 0.4 | 0.4 | 0.4 | 0.4 | 0.4 |
| **Manufacturing** | | | | | | | | | | | | | |
| 2011 | 96.0 | 95.9 | 96.1 | 96.0 | 96.2 | 96.8 | 96.6 | 96.7 | 96.8 | 96.8 | 96.9 | 97.4 | 96.5 |
| 2012 | 96.2 | 96.5 | 96.6 | 97.4 | 97.9 | 98.2 | 99.2 | 99.5 | 99.3 | 99.4 | 99.7 | 100.0 | 98.3 |
| 2013 | 98.9 | 99.2 | 99.4 | 99.3 | 99.1 | 99.0 | 99.5 | 99.5 | 99.6 | 100.0 | 100.4 | 100.8 | 99.6 |
| 2014 | 100.3 | 100.5 | 100.7 | 101.4 | 101.7 | 102.2 | 102.8 | 103.1 | 103.2 | 103.8 | 104.3 | 104.9 | 102.4 |
| 2015 | 104.4 | 104.8 | 105.5 | 105.4 | 105.9 | 106.5 | 107.5 | 107.9 | 107.6 | 107.6 | 107.7 | 107.9 | 106.6 |
| 2016 | 107.5 | 107.6 | 107.6 | 107.9 | 108.0 | 108.4 | 109.1 | 108.6 | 108.3 | 109.2 | 109.2 | 109.3 | 108.4 |
| 2017 | 108.0 | 108.2 | 108.2 | 108.4 | 108.5 | 109.3 | 110.6 | 110.5 | 110.0 | 110.2 | 110.0 | 110.9 | 109.4 |
| 2018 | 110.7 | 111.0 | 111.3 | 111.2 | 111.8 | 112.8 | 113.4 | 113.2 | 112.6 | 113.0 | 113.3 | 113.7 | 112.3 |
| 2019 | 112.8 | 113.5 | 113.7 | 113.9 | 114.4 | 115.4 | 116.1 | 116.0 | 115.4 | 116.0 | 116.3 | 117.3 | 115.1 |

# Employment by Industry: San Diego-Carlsbad, CA, 2011–2019—Continued

(Numbers in thousands, not seasonally adjusted)

| Industry and year | January | February | March | April | May | June | July | August | September | October | November | December | Annual average |
|---|---|---|---|---|---|---|---|---|---|---|---|---|---|
| **Trade, Transportation, and Utilities** | | | | | | | | | | | | | |
| 2011 | 200.2 | 198.1 | 197.7 | 199.0 | 199.7 | 200.6 | 202.2 | 203.1 | 203.4 | 204.5 | 211.0 | 214.0 | 202.8 |
| 2012 | 206.4 | 204.1 | 203.8 | 206.2 | 207.8 | 208.7 | 208.9 | 209.3 | 209.6 | 211.5 | 220.5 | 222.3 | 209.9 |
| 2013 | 212.3 | 210.6 | 210.5 | 210.7 | 212.0 | 212.4 | 212.8 | 213.4 | 212.3 | 215.1 | 223.0 | 225.6 | 214.2 |
| 2014 | 215.2 | 213.8 | 212.5 | 212.3 | 213.2 | 214.4 | 214.7 | 215.4 | 214.9 | 216.5 | 224.2 | 226.8 | 216.2 |
| 2015 | 217.2 | 215.9 | 214.9 | 215.4 | 216.8 | 217.0 | 219.3 | 219.0 | 218.6 | 221.2 | 227.2 | 228.6 | 219.3 |
| 2016 | 219.0 | 218.3 | 216.7 | 218.4 | 218.4 | 217.7 | 219.6 | 220.6 | 219.1 | 222.6 | 229.4 | 230.9 | 220.9 |
| 2017 | 223.9 | 221.7 | 220.4 | 221.8 | 222.3 | 222.3 | 223.7 | 224.0 | 223.4 | 225.8 | 232.7 | 234.8 | 224.7 |
| 2018 | 225.7 | 223.6 | 222.6 | 222.3 | 223.3 | 222.8 | 223.3 | 224.0 | 223.0 | 224.6 | 232.3 | 234.1 | 225.1 |
| 2019 | 225.4 | 222.8 | 221.0 | 221.0 | 221.9 | 221.6 | 222.9 | 223.7 | 222.1 | 223.2 | 229.9 | 232.9 | 224.0 |
| **Wholesale Trade** | | | | | | | | | | | | | |
| 2011 | 42.5 | 42.9 | 42.8 | 43.1 | 43.2 | 43.2 | 43.3 | 43.4 | 43.4 | 43.7 | 43.9 | 43.9 | 43.3 |
| 2012 | 43.7 | 44.3 | 44.2 | 45.1 | 45.6 | 45.4 | 45.7 | 45.9 | 45.7 | 46.2 | 46.5 | 46.3 | 45.4 |
| 2013 | 45.9 | 46.5 | 46.3 | 45.7 | 46.1 | 45.5 | 45.2 | 45.2 | 45.0 | 45.9 | 46.0 | 45.9 | 45.8 |
| 2014 | 44.9 | 45.6 | 45.2 | 45.0 | 45.0 | 45.1 | 44.7 | 44.8 | 44.6 | 44.3 | 44.5 | 44.6 | 44.9 |
| 2015 | 43.4 | 44.3 | 43.8 | 44.0 | 44.1 | 43.7 | 44.2 | 44.0 | 43.9 | 44.5 | 44.5 | 44.3 | 44.1 |
| 2016 | 43.7 | 44.2 | 43.4 | 43.9 | 43.6 | 43.2 | 43.6 | 43.5 | 43.2 | 44.0 | 44.1 | 44.1 | 43.7 |
| 2017 | 43.4 | 44.0 | 42.7 | 44.0 | 44.0 | 43.8 | 44.1 | 43.9 | 43.7 | 44.1 | 44.1 | 44.2 | 43.8 |
| 2018 | 43.4 | 43.8 | 43.4 | 43.6 | 44.2 | 43.7 | 43.8 | 43.8 | 43.6 | 43.9 | 44.0 | 44.1 | 43.8 |
| 2019 | 43.6 | 44.4 | 43.8 | 44.1 | 44.7 | 44.3 | 44.2 | 44.3 | 43.9 | 44.1 | 44.8 | 44.3 | 44.2 |
| **Retail Trade** | | | | | | | | | | | | | |
| 2011 | 131.6 | 129.5 | 129.1 | 130.1 | 130.7 | 131.4 | 132.8 | 133.4 | 133.6 | 134.8 | 141.0 | 143.3 | 133.4 |
| 2012 | 136.4 | 133.4 | 133.0 | 134.2 | 135.0 | 135.6 | 135.5 | 135.8 | 136.2 | 137.9 | 146.3 | 147.5 | 137.2 |
| 2013 | 139.2 | 137.0 | 137.0 | 137.5 | 138.4 | 139.4 | 140.1 | 140.9 | 140.4 | 142.6 | 150.1 | 152.5 | 141.3 |
| 2014 | 143.6 | 141.5 | 140.9 | 140.9 | 141.4 | 142.2 | 142.8 | 143.7 | 143.2 | 145.0 | 152.3 | 154.1 | 144.3 |
| 2015 | 146.2 | 144.1 | 143.6 | 143.9 | 145.0 | 145.1 | 146.3 | 146.2 | 145.8 | 147.9 | 153.5 | 154.4 | 146.8 |
| 2016 | 146.4 | 145.3 | 144.5 | 145.6 | 145.7 | 145.1 | 146.0 | 146.9 | 145.7 | 148.3 | 154.6 | 155.6 | 147.5 |
| 2017 | 149.6 | 146.8 | 146.3 | 146.7 | 146.7 | 146.6 | 147.5 | 148.0 | 147.5 | 149.3 | 155.7 | 156.7 | 149.0 |
| 2018 | 149.5 | 147.2 | 146.5 | 145.7 | 146.1 | 145.7 | 146.6 | 147.0 | 145.9 | 147.1 | 154.0 | 154.9 | 148.0 |
| 2019 | 147.5 | 145.0 | 143.9 | 143.2 | 143.4 | 143.1 | 144.3 | 144.7 | 143.6 | 144.1 | 149.6 | 152.4 | 145.4 |
| **Transportation and Utilities** | | | | | | | | | | | | | |
| 2011 | 26.1 | 25.7 | 25.8 | 25.8 | 25.8 | 26.0 | 26.1 | 26.3 | 26.4 | 26.0 | 26.1 | 26.8 | 26.1 |
| 2012 | 26.3 | 26.4 | 26.6 | 26.9 | 27.2 | 27.7 | 27.7 | 27.6 | 27.7 | 27.4 | 27.7 | 28.5 | 27.3 |
| 2013 | 27.2 | 27.1 | 27.2 | 27.5 | 27.5 | 27.5 | 27.5 | 27.3 | 26.9 | 26.6 | 26.9 | 27.2 | 27.2 |
| 2014 | 26.7 | 26.7 | 26.4 | 26.4 | 26.8 | 27.1 | 27.2 | 26.9 | 27.1 | 27.2 | 27.4 | 28.1 | 27.0 |
| 2015 | 27.6 | 27.5 | 27.5 | 27.5 | 27.7 | 28.2 | 28.8 | 28.8 | 28.9 | 28.8 | 29.2 | 29.9 | 28.4 |
| 2016 | 28.9 | 28.8 | 28.8 | 28.9 | 29.1 | 29.4 | 30.0 | 30.2 | 30.2 | 30.3 | 30.7 | 31.2 | 29.7 |
| 2017 | 30.9 | 30.9 | 31.4 | 31.1 | 31.6 | 31.9 | 32.1 | 32.1 | 32.2 | 32.4 | 32.9 | 33.9 | 32.0 |
| 2018 | 32.8 | 32.6 | 32.7 | 33.0 | 33.0 | 33.4 | 32.9 | 33.2 | 33.5 | 33.6 | 34.3 | 35.1 | 33.3 |
| 2019 | 34.3 | 33.4 | 33.3 | 33.7 | 33.8 | 34.2 | 34.4 | 34.7 | 34.6 | 35.0 | 35.5 | 36.2 | 34.4 |
| **Information** | | | | | | | | | | | | | |
| 2011 | 24.4 | 24.3 | 24.2 | 24.1 | 24.1 | 24.0 | 24.2 | 24.1 | 24.2 | 24.1 | 24.1 | 24.2 | 24.2 |
| 2012 | 24.4 | 24.3 | 24.3 | 24.5 | 24.5 | 24.6 | 24.5 | 24.4 | 24.2 | 24.3 | 24.3 | 24.4 | 24.4 |
| 2013 | 24.1 | 23.9 | 23.9 | 23.9 | 24.1 | 24.1 | 24.1 | 24.2 | 24.1 | 24.2 | 24.4 | 24.5 | 24.1 |
| 2014 | 24.2 | 24.4 | 24.2 | 24.2 | 24.2 | 24.1 | 24.2 | 24.2 | 24.1 | 24.1 | 23.9 | 23.9 | 24.1 |
| 2015 | 23.4 | 23.4 | 23.3 | 23.4 | 23.5 | 23.4 | 23.7 | 23.6 | 23.3 | 23.4 | 23.3 | 23.4 | 23.4 |
| 2016 | 23.4 | 23.2 | 23.0 | 23.1 | 22.9 | 23.1 | 23.5 | 23.5 | 23.3 | 23.1 | 23.3 | 23.4 | 23.2 |
| 2017 | 23.2 | 23.3 | 23.2 | 23.2 | 23.4 | 23.5 | 23.8 | 23.6 | 23.4 | 23.4 | 23.5 | 23.6 | 23.4 |
| 2018 | 23.5 | 23.5 | 23.5 | 23.7 | 23.7 | 23.6 | 24.0 | 23.8 | 23.5 | 23.5 | 23.5 | 23.7 | 23.6 |
| 2019 | 23.4 | 23.6 | 23.4 | 23.5 | 23.5 | 23.3 | 23.7 | 23.6 | 23.3 | 23.4 | 23.7 | 23.5 | 23.5 |
| **Financial Activities** | | | | | | | | | | | | | |
| 2011 | 66.8 | 67.1 | 66.7 | 67.0 | 66.9 | 67.2 | 67.7 | 67.4 | 67.6 | 68.0 | 67.9 | 68.7 | 67.4 |
| 2012 | 68.0 | 68.3 | 68.6 | 69.5 | 69.6 | 70.0 | 70.7 | 70.6 | 70.1 | 70.6 | 71.0 | 71.2 | 69.9 |
| 2013 | 70.6 | 70.9 | 71.0 | 71.1 | 71.3 | 71.2 | 71.5 | 71.3 | 70.7 | 70.9 | 70.5 | 70.5 | 71.0 |
| 2014 | 69.3 | 69.5 | 69.5 | 69.1 | 69.4 | 69.5 | 70.3 | 70.2 | 69.5 | 69.7 | 69.8 | 69.9 | 69.6 |
| 2015 | 70.1 | 70.1 | 70.2 | 70.8 | 71.2 | 71.2 | 72.4 | 72.0 | 71.3 | 72.5 | 72.4 | 72.4 | 71.4 |
| 2016 | 71.5 | 71.7 | 71.6 | 72.7 | 72.9 | 72.9 | 73.9 | 73.8 | 73.4 | 74.0 | 73.8 | 73.7 | 73.0 |
| 2017 | 73.4 | 73.3 | 73.3 | 73.8 | 74.2 | 74.5 | 75.6 | 75.2 | 74.9 | 75.7 | 75.8 | 76.0 | 74.6 |
| 2018 | 75.4 | 75.7 | 75.4 | 76.0 | 76.2 | 76.1 | 76.7 | 76.4 | 75.4 | 76.6 | 76.2 | 76.2 | 76.0 |
| 2019 | 75.0 | 75.3 | 74.9 | 76.0 | 76.2 | 76.2 | 77.0 | 77.3 | 76.7 | 77.7 | 77.2 | 77.5 | 76.4 |

## Employment by Industry: San Diego-Carlsbad, CA, 2011–2019—*Continued*

(Numbers in thousands, not seasonally adjusted)

| Industry and year | January | February | March | April | May | June | July | August | September | October | November | December | Annual average |
|---|---|---|---|---|---|---|---|---|---|---|---|---|---|
| **Professional and Business Services** | | | | | | | | | | | | | |
| 2011 | 203.3 | 204.7 | 205.2 | 204.4 | 203.3 | 203.5 | 204.9 | 206.5 | 205.0 | 205.3 | 206.0 | 206.8 | 204.9 |
| 2012 | 202.4 | 205.5 | 206.2 | 211.3 | 211.8 | 213.3 | 211.8 | 213.1 | 211.7 | 214.4 | 214.0 | 215.7 | 210.9 |
| 2013 | 213.2 | 215.6 | 216.0 | 215.6 | 216.3 | 217.0 | 218.4 | 219.3 | 219.4 | 224.1 | 224.6 | 224.8 | 218.7 |
| 2014 | 218.3 | 221.2 | 222.0 | 219.4 | 220.1 | 221.0 | 221.6 | 223.5 | 223.0 | 226.0 | 227.0 | 227.5 | 222.6 |
| 2015 | 223.8 | 225.5 | 225.6 | 226.2 | 226.7 | 228.3 | 230.8 | 231.8 | 230.1 | 234.5 | 235.5 | 234.9 | 229.5 |
| 2016 | 231.8 | 233.5 | 231.8 | 234.2 | 233.9 | 233.3 | 236.9 | 236.5 | 236.4 | 235.7 | 235.9 | 236.3 | 234.7 |
| 2017 | 233.2 | 235.2 | 235.5 | 236.1 | 236.1 | 237.6 | 239.4 | 240.7 | 240.0 | 243.5 | 245.5 | 245.2 | 239.0 |
| 2018 | 243.7 | 247.2 | 248.0 | 247.8 | 246.6 | 246.9 | 250.6 | 251.0 | 249.4 | 251.6 | 251.9 | 252.5 | 248.9 |
| 2019 | 250.5 | 253.1 | 252.4 | 254.6 | 254.8 | 255.8 | 258.5 | 259.5 | 257.5 | 259.9 | 261.0 | 261.3 | 256.6 |
| **Education and Health Services** | | | | | | | | | | | | | |
| 2011 | 165.9 | 167.8 | 168.5 | 167.7 | 168.2 | 167.4 | 165.3 | 165.7 | 168.0 | 168.8 | 170.8 | 171.0 | 167.9 |
| 2012 | 168.8 | 170.8 | 172.3 | 174.6 | 176.0 | 175.2 | 173.0 | 173.6 | 175.7 | 177.8 | 178.3 | 178.9 | 174.6 |
| 2013 | 179.2 | 180.6 | 182.0 | 182.7 | 182.2 | 180.3 | 177.2 | 178.3 | 180.1 | 183.3 | 183.7 | 183.4 | 181.1 |
| 2014 | 181.7 | 183.1 | 184.7 | 187.3 | 186.7 | 185.4 | 182.6 | 183.9 | 186.9 | 189.2 | 190.6 | 190.9 | 186.1 |
| 2015 | 189.2 | 189.8 | 191.5 | 192.2 | 192.6 | 191.5 | 190.5 | 191.6 | 193.8 | 195.9 | 196.3 | 197.4 | 192.7 |
| 2016 | 195.2 | 197.4 | 197.0 | 199.6 | 199.8 | 198.1 | 195.9 | 196.5 | 198.9 | 201.0 | 202.4 | 203.0 | 198.7 |
| 2017 | 200.8 | 202.9 | 203.7 | 204.3 | 204.4 | 203.9 | 200.4 | 203.0 | 204.4 | 207.2 | 208.1 | 208.3 | 204.3 |
| 2018 | 206.4 | 207.7 | 208.6 | 209.0 | 208.6 | 207.4 | 205.0 | 207.5 | 208.3 | 211.9 | 212.7 | 213.1 | 208.9 |
| 2019 | 212.0 | 214.2 | 215.7 | 215.6 | 215.7 | 214.7 | 213.2 | 215.7 | 216.1 | 218.6 | 219.6 | 220.8 | 216.0 |
| **Leisure and Hospitality** | | | | | | | | | | | | | |
| 2011 | 146.9 | 148.8 | 150.7 | 152.6 | 155.0 | 156.7 | 158.9 | 160.9 | 158.2 | 154.5 | 154.4 | 154.1 | 154.3 |
| 2012 | 150.0 | 151.9 | 153.8 | 158.3 | 161.5 | 164.7 | 166.6 | 169.1 | 165.3 | 161.8 | 160.9 | 160.9 | 160.4 |
| 2013 | 156.3 | 158.5 | 161.2 | 165.3 | 167.6 | 170.9 | 173.3 | 174.8 | 170.9 | 169.5 | 169.0 | 169.5 | 167.2 |
| 2014 | 164.9 | 166.9 | 170.3 | 172.9 | 176.0 | 179.5 | 181.9 | 184.5 | 179.2 | 176.5 | 176.8 | 176.6 | 175.5 |
| 2015 | 172.7 | 175.2 | 177.7 | 179.3 | 183.2 | 185.7 | 188.4 | 189.1 | 186.2 | 184.4 | 184.2 | 182.7 | 182.4 |
| 2016 | 178.4 | 180.9 | 183.9 | 187.6 | 190.6 | 192.9 | 197.0 | 197.5 | 195.8 | 194.0 | 194.0 | 191.9 | 190.4 |
| 2017 | 187.1 | 188.4 | 190.9 | 194.2 | 197.0 | 200.3 | 202.2 | 202.1 | 197.8 | 196.8 | 195.5 | 194.7 | 195.6 |
| 2018 | 190.5 | 193.2 | 195.8 | 197.3 | 199.7 | 204.4 | 206.9 | 206.9 | 202.1 | 200.3 | 199.3 | 199.3 | 199.6 |
| 2019 | 195.2 | 196.9 | 198.9 | 201.1 | 203.9 | 206.6 | 208.9 | 208.1 | 203.4 | 203.3 | 202.4 | 200.6 | 202.4 |
| **Other Services** | | | | | | | | | | | | | |
| 2011 | 45.7 | 46.8 | 46.9 | 47.8 | 48.5 | 48.3 | 48.1 | 48.0 | 48.2 | 48.3 | 47.8 | 47.4 | 47.7 |
| 2012 | 47.2 | 48.3 | 48.7 | 49.3 | 49.9 | 50.4 | 49.6 | 49.3 | 49.4 | 49.8 | 49.1 | 48.9 | 49.2 |
| 2013 | 47.7 | 48.3 | 48.2 | 48.7 | 49.1 | 49.9 | 50.0 | 50.0 | 49.9 | 49.9 | 50.1 | 49.9 | 49.3 |
| 2014 | 50.0 | 50.7 | 51.0 | 51.4 | 52.1 | 52.2 | 52.7 | 52.7 | 53.0 | 52.9 | 52.6 | 52.4 | 52.0 |
| 2015 | 51.4 | 52.1 | 52.2 | 52.7 | 53.2 | 53.5 | 54.2 | 54.3 | 54.1 | 53.9 | 53.7 | 53.5 | 53.2 |
| 2016 | 53.1 | 54.0 | 53.5 | 54.3 | 54.6 | 54.7 | 55.2 | 55.2 | 55.1 | 55.0 | 54.4 | 54.2 | 54.4 |
| 2017 | 53.2 | 53.9 | 54.1 | 54.8 | 55.4 | 56.2 | 56.4 | 55.7 | 55.8 | 55.1 | 55.0 | 54.5 | 55.0 |
| 2018 | 54.2 | 54.6 | 54.7 | 55.2 | 55.4 | 56.2 | 56.2 | 56.1 | 55.6 | 56.2 | 56.0 | 55.7 | 55.5 |
| 2019 | 54.7 | 55.2 | 55.5 | 55.6 | 56.2 | 56.5 | 57.0 | 56.7 | 56.3 | 56.2 | 55.5 | 54.5 | 55.8 |
| **Government** | | | | | | | | | | | | | |
| 2011 | 230.1 | 232.9 | 233.8 | 233.8 | 232.7 | 233.6 | 219.7 | 217.2 | 223.2 | 229.6 | 231.1 | 229.8 | 229.0 |
| 2012 | 226.7 | 229.4 | 230.9 | 230.8 | 231.3 | 232.1 | 218.1 | 219.0 | 223.0 | 229.4 | 232.1 | 231.2 | 227.8 |
| 2013 | 227.6 | 230.0 | 232.4 | 231.9 | 232.3 | 234.0 | 220.5 | 220.9 | 225.9 | 231.3 | 233.9 | 233.1 | 229.5 |
| 2014 | 229.3 | 232.4 | 234.4 | 234.7 | 235.2 | 237.7 | 222.3 | 223.3 | 227.1 | 233.9 | 236.6 | 236.1 | 231.9 |
| 2015 | 234.5 | 235.8 | 237.6 | 238.2 | 239.6 | 238.8 | 227.4 | 226.9 | 231.6 | 239.3 | 242.3 | 241.8 | 236.2 |
| 2016 | 238.4 | 241.1 | 242.9 | 243.7 | 244.9 | 245.4 | 231.2 | 234.3 | 239.7 | 246.8 | 249.1 | 249.4 | 242.2 |
| 2017 | 246.6 | 249.5 | 249.8 | 250.6 | 251.1 | 251.9 | 233.2 | 233.7 | 241.7 | 247.7 | 249.8 | 249.8 | 246.3 |
| 2018 | 247.3 | 249.2 | 250.4 | 252.0 | 252.5 | 253.9 | 234.3 | 236.0 | 244.3 | 251.0 | 253.3 | 252.9 | 248.1 |
| 2019 | 251.0 | 251.3 | 252.8 | 253.3 | 253.9 | 254.3 | 236.1 | 239.7 | 245.3 | 252.2 | 254.0 | 251.6 | 249.6 |

## Employment by Industry: Tampa-St. Petersburg-Clearwater, FL, 2011–2019

(Numbers in thousands, not seasonally adjusted)

| Industry and year | January | February | March | April | May | June | July | August | September | October | November | December | Annual average |
|---|---|---|---|---|---|---|---|---|---|---|---|---|---|
| **Total Nonfarm** | | | | | | | | | | | | | |
| 2011 | 1,106.5 | 1,115.2 | 1,123.3 | 1,127.0 | 1,123.2 | 1,110.5 | 1,107.5 | 1,121.5 | 1,128.5 | 1,132.2 | 1,139.8 | 1,145.2 | 1,123.4 |
| 2012 | 1,132.1 | 1,140.7 | 1,148.3 | 1,153.0 | 1,152.0 | 1,139.9 | 1,132.2 | 1,146.6 | 1,147.0 | 1,155.1 | 1,165.8 | 1,172.1 | 1,148.7 |
| 2013 | 1,154.9 | 1,165.4 | 1,173.9 | 1,177.3 | 1,178.6 | 1,166.5 | 1,162.7 | 1,176.8 | 1,177.0 | 1,185.6 | 1,198.5 | 1,200.7 | 1,176.5 |
| 2014 | 1,181.7 | 1,190.3 | 1,200.4 | 1,207.9 | 1,210.9 | 1,198.8 | 1,195.2 | 1,209.7 | 1,211.6 | 1,221.7 | 1,234.3 | 1,239.3 | 1,208.5 |
| 2015 | 1,222.1 | 1,234.1 | 1,241.6 | 1,246.6 | 1,248.6 | 1,238.5 | 1,235.8 | 1,248.8 | 1,251.3 | 1,269.8 | 1,285.4 | 1,288.1 | 1,250.9 |
| 2016 | 1,270.3 | 1,281.3 | 1,287.3 | 1,297.8 | 1,295.4 | 1,280.6 | 1,281.0 | 1,292.1 | 1,298.1 | 1,310.0 | 1,320.8 | 1,324.6 | 1,294.9 |
| 2017 | 1,307.8 | 1,315.5 | 1,320.2 | 1,322.2 | 1,320.3 | 1,311.8 | 1,305.7 | 1,319.5 | 1,302.3 | 1,333.9 | 1,349.3 | 1,349.9 | 1,321.5 |
| 2018 | 1,331.1 | 1,343.5 | 1,348.6 | 1,350.5 | 1,348.4 | 1,338.8 | 1,333.7 | 1,352.4 | 1,354.2 | 1,364.9 | 1,378.4 | 1,380.1 | 1,352.1 |
| 2019 | 1,366.3 | 1,378.3 | 1,380.5 | 1,381.7 | 1,382.4 | 1,369.9 | 1,368.7 | 1,383.0 | 1,385.2 | 1,399.2 | 1,409.0 | 1,412.4 | 1,384.7 |
| **Total Private** | | | | | | | | | | | | | |
| 2011 | 951.6 | 957.8 | 966.2 | 970.7 | 968.7 | 966.2 | 964.9 | 969.7 | 973.3 | 976.8 | 984.8 | 990.1 | 970.1 |
| 2012 | 977.5 | 985.6 | 993.5 | 997.3 | 997.3 | 995.8 | 989.4 | 995.7 | 994.2 | 1,001.9 | 1,011.6 | 1,018.3 | 996.5 |
| 2013 | 1,000.6 | 1,009.9 | 1,018.5 | 1,021.9 | 1,025.1 | 1,023.4 | 1,020.8 | 1,025.9 | 1,024.3 | 1,030.9 | 1,043.5 | 1,046.3 | 1,024.3 |
| 2014 | 1,028.8 | 1,036.9 | 1,044.7 | 1,051.9 | 1,055.4 | 1,054.2 | 1,051.9 | 1,058.6 | 1,058.0 | 1,066.3 | 1,079.1 | 1,084.0 | 1,055.8 |
| 2015 | 1,068.3 | 1,078.5 | 1,086.3 | 1,090.6 | 1,093.5 | 1,094.1 | 1,092.1 | 1,096.8 | 1,097.7 | 1,112.6 | 1,127.6 | 1,132.1 | 1,097.5 |
| 2016 | 1,114.1 | 1,123.2 | 1,129.8 | 1,139.5 | 1,138.3 | 1,134.3 | 1,135.5 | 1,138.7 | 1,141.4 | 1,150.9 | 1,161.4 | 1,165.5 | 1,139.4 |
| 2017 | 1,150.0 | 1,155.2 | 1,160.5 | 1,162.8 | 1,162.9 | 1,163.3 | 1,160.5 | 1,166.1 | 1,145.7 | 1,174.9 | 1,190.3 | 1,191.0 | 1,165.3 |
| 2018 | 1,174.0 | 1,184.2 | 1,189.6 | 1,191.5 | 1,191.9 | 1,190.8 | 1,187.9 | 1,198.9 | 1,196.9 | 1,205.6 | 1,218.2 | 1,220.8 | 1,195.9 |
| 2019 | 1,208.3 | 1,218.2 | 1,220.5 | 1,222.1 | 1,224.5 | 1,220.7 | 1,221.5 | 1,228.6 | 1,227.5 | 1,239.6 | 1,247.8 | 1,251.6 | 1,227.6 |
| **Goods Producing** | | | | | | | | | | | | | |
| 2011 | 108.4 | 109.0 | 110.2 | 111.0 | 111.6 | 111.9 | 112.4 | 112.3 | 113.1 | 112.6 | 112.5 | 112.6 | 111.5 |
| 2012 | 110.7 | 111.8 | 112.6 | 112.9 | 113.8 | 114.8 | 114.3 | 115.1 | 114.3 | 114.7 | 115.1 | 115.2 | 113.8 |
| 2013 | 112.7 | 113.5 | 114.7 | 116.2 | 116.7 | 117.6 | 117.6 | 118.4 | 118.5 | 119.2 | 120.2 | 119.9 | 117.1 |
| 2014 | 117.7 | 118.9 | 120.0 | 121.1 | 122.6 | 123.4 | 123.3 | 123.9 | 123.8 | 124.1 | 123.8 | 123.9 | 122.2 |
| 2015 | 122.4 | 123.2 | 124.4 | 125.1 | 126.1 | 127.5 | 128.0 | 128.8 | 129.3 | 130.7 | 131.5 | 131.2 | 127.4 |
| 2016 | 130.0 | 131.4 | 132.8 | 134.3 | 135.2 | 135.8 | 136.3 | 136.5 | 137.3 | 138.4 | 138.2 | 138.6 | 135.4 |
| 2017 | 136.9 | 138.2 | 139.2 | 139.3 | 139.7 | 141.5 | 141.1 | 142.1 | 138.4 | 142.3 | 142.5 | 142.7 | 140.3 |
| 2018 | 141.4 | 143.3 | 144.3 | 144.8 | 144.6 | 145.9 | 146.0 | 146.6 | 146.7 | 147.3 | 147.9 | 148.3 | 145.6 |
| 2019 | 147.4 | 148.5 | 149.1 | 148.8 | 149.7 | 150.1 | 150.4 | 150.8 | 151.4 | 153.3 | 153.4 | 153.6 | 150.5 |
| **Service-Providing** | | | | | | | | | | | | | |
| 2011 | 998.1 | 1,006.2 | 1,013.1 | 1,016.0 | 1,011.6 | 998.6 | 995.1 | 1,009.2 | 1,015.4 | 1,019.6 | 1,027.3 | 1,032.6 | 1,011.9 |
| 2012 | 1,021.4 | 1,028.9 | 1,035.7 | 1,040.1 | 1,038.2 | 1,025.1 | 1,017.9 | 1,031.5 | 1,032.7 | 1,040.4 | 1,050.7 | 1,056.9 | 1,035.0 |
| 2013 | 1,042.2 | 1,051.9 | 1,059.2 | 1,061.1 | 1,061.9 | 1,048.9 | 1,045.1 | 1,058.4 | 1,058.5 | 1,066.4 | 1,078.3 | 1,080.8 | 1,059.4 |
| 2014 | 1,064.0 | 1,071.4 | 1,080.4 | 1,086.8 | 1,088.3 | 1,075.4 | 1,071.9 | 1,085.8 | 1,087.8 | 1,097.6 | 1,110.5 | 1,115.4 | 1,086.3 |
| 2015 | 1,099.7 | 1,110.9 | 1,117.2 | 1,121.5 | 1,122.5 | 1,111.0 | 1,107.8 | 1,120.0 | 1,122.0 | 1,139.1 | 1,153.9 | 1,156.9 | 1,123.5 |
| 2016 | 1,140.3 | 1,149.9 | 1,154.5 | 1,163.5 | 1,160.2 | 1,144.8 | 1,144.7 | 1,155.6 | 1,160.8 | 1,171.6 | 1,182.6 | 1,186.0 | 1,159.5 |
| 2017 | 1,170.9 | 1,177.3 | 1,181.0 | 1,182.9 | 1,180.6 | 1,170.3 | 1,164.6 | 1,177.4 | 1,163.9 | 1,191.6 | 1,206.8 | 1,207.2 | 1,181.2 |
| 2018 | 1,189.7 | 1,200.2 | 1,204.3 | 1,205.7 | 1,203.8 | 1,192.9 | 1,187.7 | 1,205.8 | 1,207.5 | 1,217.6 | 1,230.5 | 1,231.8 | 1,206.5 |
| 2019 | 1,218.9 | 1,229.8 | 1,231.4 | 1,232.9 | 1,232.7 | 1,219.8 | 1,218.3 | 1,232.2 | 1,233.8 | 1,245.9 | 1,255.6 | 1,258.8 | 1,234.2 |
| **Mining and Logging** | | | | | | | | | | | | | |
| 2011 | 0.4 | 0.4 | 0.4 | 0.4 | 0.4 | 0.4 | 0.4 | 0.4 | 0.4 | 0.4 | 0.5 | 0.5 | 0.4 |
| 2012 | 0.5 | 0.5 | 0.5 | 0.5 | 0.5 | 0.5 | 0.5 | 0.5 | 0.4 | 0.5 | 0.5 | 0.5 | 0.5 |
| 2013 | 0.4 | 0.4 | 0.5 | 0.5 | 0.4 | 0.4 | 0.5 | 0.4 | 0.4 | 0.4 | 0.4 | 0.4 | 0.4 |
| 2014 | 0.4 | 0.4 | 0.4 | 0.4 | 0.4 | 0.4 | 0.4 | 0.4 | 0.4 | 0.4 | 0.4 | 0.4 | 0.4 |
| 2015 | 0.3 | 0.3 | 0.4 | 0.4 | 0.4 | 0.4 | 0.4 | 0.4 | 0.3 | 0.3 | 0.3 | 0.3 | 0.4 |
| 2016 | 0.3 | 0.3 | 0.3 | 0.3 | 0.3 | 0.3 | 0.3 | 0.3 | 0.3 | 0.3 | 0.2 | 0.3 | 0.3 |
| 2017 | 0.3 | 0.3 | 0.3 | 0.3 | 0.3 | 0.3 | 0.3 | 0.3 | 0.3 | 0.3 | 0.3 | 0.3 | 0.3 |
| 2018 | 0.3 | 0.3 | 0.3 | 0.3 | 0.3 | 0.3 | 0.3 | 0.3 | 0.3 | 0.3 | 0.3 | 0.3 | 0.3 |
| 2019 | 0.3 | 0.3 | 0.3 | 0.3 | 0.3 | 0.3 | 0.3 | 0.3 | 0.3 | 0.3 | 0.3 | 0.3 | 0.3 |
| **Construction** | | | | | | | | | | | | | |
| 2011 | 50.1 | 50.5 | 51.3 | 52.0 | 52.5 | 52.5 | 52.8 | 52.6 | 53.3 | 53.2 | 52.9 | 52.9 | 52.2 |
| 2012 | 51.3 | 52.0 | 52.6 | 52.8 | 53.6 | 54.4 | 54.0 | 54.5 | 54.5 | 54.7 | 55.0 | 55.1 | 53.7 |
| 2013 | 53.4 | 54.0 | 54.8 | 55.5 | 56.2 | 56.8 | 56.8 | 57.4 | 57.6 | 58.0 | 58.8 | 58.5 | 56.5 |
| 2014 | 56.8 | 57.8 | 58.5 | 59.6 | 60.5 | 61.4 | 61.5 | 61.9 | 61.8 | 61.9 | 61.7 | 61.8 | 60.4 |
| 2015 | 60.9 | 61.6 | 62.4 | 63.2 | 63.9 | 64.8 | 64.9 | 65.5 | 66.0 | 67.1 | 67.6 | 67.4 | 64.6 |
| 2016 | 66.5 | 67.6 | 68.3 | 69.4 | 70.1 | 70.5 | 70.7 | 70.9 | 71.7 | 72.7 | 72.4 | 72.5 | 70.3 |
| 2017 | 70.9 | 71.9 | 72.5 | 72.9 | 73.2 | 74.5 | 74.3 | 75.0 | 72.2 | 75.3 | 75.3 | 75.3 | 73.6 |
| 2018 | 74.7 | 76.3 | 77.1 | 77.7 | 77.4 | 78.4 | 78.4 | 78.8 | 79.1 | 79.3 | 79.5 | 79.7 | 78.0 |
| 2019 | 79.2 | 79.8 | 80.2 | 80.1 | 80.7 | 80.9 | 80.8 | 81.1 | 81.9 | 83.3 | 83.3 | 83.1 | 81.2 |

## Employment by Industry: Tampa-St. Petersburg-Clearwater, FL, 2011–2019—*Continued*

(Numbers in thousands, not seasonally adjusted)

| Industry and year | January | February | March | April | May | June | July | August | September | October | November | December | Annual average |
|---|---|---|---|---|---|---|---|---|---|---|---|---|---|
| **Manufacturing** | | | | | | | | | | | | | |
| 2011 | 57.9 | 58.1 | 58.5 | 58.6 | 58.7 | 59.0 | 59.2 | 59.3 | 59.4 | 59.0 | 59.1 | 59.2 | 58.8 |
| 2012 | 58.9 | 59.3 | 59.5 | 59.6 | 59.7 | 59.9 | 59.8 | 60.1 | 59.4 | 59.5 | 59.6 | 59.6 | 59.6 |
| 2013 | 58.9 | 59.1 | 59.4 | 60.2 | 60.1 | 60.4 | 60.3 | 60.6 | 60.5 | 60.8 | 61.0 | 61.0 | 60.2 |
| 2014 | 60.5 | 60.7 | 61.1 | 61.1 | 61.7 | 61.6 | 61.4 | 61.6 | 61.6 | 61.8 | 61.7 | 61.7 | 61.4 |
| 2015 | 61.2 | 61.3 | 61.6 | 61.5 | 61.8 | 62.3 | 62.7 | 62.9 | 63.0 | 63.3 | 63.6 | 63.5 | 62.4 |
| 2016 | 63.2 | 63.5 | 64.2 | 64.6 | 64.8 | 65.0 | 65.3 | 65.3 | 65.3 | 65.4 | 65.6 | 65.8 | 64.8 |
| 2017 | 65.7 | 66.0 | 66.4 | 66.1 | 66.2 | 66.7 | 66.5 | 66.8 | 65.9 | 66.7 | 66.9 | 67.1 | 66.4 |
| 2018 | 66.4 | 66.7 | 66.9 | 66.8 | 66.9 | 67.2 | 67.3 | 67.5 | 67.3 | 67.7 | 68.1 | 68.3 | 67.3 |
| 2019 | 67.9 | 68.4 | 68.6 | 68.4 | 68.7 | 68.9 | 69.3 | 69.4 | 69.2 | 69.7 | 69.8 | 70.2 | 69.0 |
| **Trade, Transportation, and Utilities** | | | | | | | | | | | | | |
| 2011 | 210.3 | 209.8 | 210.9 | 211.3 | 211.7 | 210.7 | 211.1 | 212.2 | 212.5 | 213.6 | 218.8 | 222.1 | 212.9 |
| 2012 | 217.1 | 216.7 | 216.1 | 216.7 | 217.5 | 216.5 | 216.0 | 216.6 | 216.7 | 218.2 | 224.4 | 226.8 | 218.3 |
| 2013 | 220.1 | 219.9 | 219.7 | 219.6 | 220.6 | 220.5 | 219.8 | 220.6 | 220.6 | 222.9 | 229.7 | 232.5 | 222.2 |
| 2014 | 226.0 | 226.8 | 227.3 | 228.6 | 229.4 | 229.3 | 228.7 | 229.7 | 230.5 | 232.9 | 241.1 | 245.2 | 231.3 |
| 2015 | 236.4 | 236.0 | 236.7 | 236.2 | 237.1 | 237.7 | 236.6 | 237.5 | 237.2 | 241.5 | 248.1 | 251.6 | 239.4 |
| 2016 | 244.2 | 244.7 | 244.7 | 245.8 | 245.8 | 244.1 | 244.3 | 244.5 | 244.4 | 246.9 | 254.5 | 256.8 | 246.7 |
| 2017 | 248.3 | 246.7 | 245.5 | 245.1 | 245.3 | 244.8 | 244.4 | 245.5 | 240.5 | 246.5 | 256.5 | 258.1 | 247.3 |
| 2018 | 249.6 | 248.7 | 248.1 | 247.8 | 247.8 | 246.8 | 246.7 | 247.0 | 245.9 | 248.3 | 256.5 | 258.2 | 249.3 |
| 2019 | 252.3 | 250.8 | 250.3 | 250.0 | 250.0 | 250.2 | 250.8 | 251.4 | 251.2 | 252.8 | 258.2 | 260.4 | 252.4 |
| **Wholesale Trade** | | | | | | | | | | | | | |
| 2011 | 44.9 | 44.9 | 45.2 | 45.2 | 45.6 | 45.3 | 45.5 | 45.8 | 46.1 | 46.2 | 46.6 | 47.2 | 45.7 |
| 2012 | 47.5 | 47.8 | 47.6 | 47.6 | 47.9 | 47.6 | 47.1 | 47.4 | 47.5 | 47.6 | 48.4 | 48.2 | 47.7 |
| 2013 | 48.1 | 48.2 | 48.3 | 47.9 | 48.2 | 47.8 | 47.6 | 47.9 | 47.8 | 48.1 | 48.7 | 48.8 | 48.1 |
| 2014 | 48.6 | 49.0 | 49.2 | 49.4 | 49.7 | 49.5 | 49.5 | 49.7 | 49.7 | 49.9 | 50.4 | 50.9 | 49.6 |
| 2015 | 50.1 | 50.1 | 50.4 | 50.2 | 50.4 | 50.1 | 50.2 | 50.3 | 50.3 | 50.8 | 51.1 | 51.3 | 50.4 |
| 2016 | 50.7 | 50.8 | 50.8 | 51.2 | 51.2 | 50.8 | 51.2 | 51.4 | 51.5 | 51.8 | 52.2 | 52.6 | 51.4 |
| 2017 | 51.8 | 52.2 | 52.2 | 51.8 | 52.0 | 51.9 | 51.9 | 52.0 | 51.5 | 52.2 | 52.5 | 52.8 | 52.1 |
| 2018 | 52.8 | 52.9 | 53.1 | 52.8 | 53.0 | 52.9 | 53.1 | 53.2 | 53.1 | 53.2 | 53.4 | 53.6 | 53.1 |
| 2019 | 53.4 | 53.8 | 53.9 | 53.7 | 54.0 | 53.9 | 54.1 | 54.2 | 54.1 | 54.6 | 54.9 | 54.8 | 54.1 |
| **Retail Trade** | | | | | | | | | | | | | |
| 2011 | 140.0 | 139.6 | 140.2 | 140.7 | 140.5 | 139.8 | 139.8 | 140.6 | 140.5 | 141.5 | 146.0 | 147.6 | 141.4 |
| 2012 | 143.3 | 142.5 | 142.1 | 142.6 | 143.0 | 142.3 | 142.3 | 142.9 | 142.8 | 144.2 | 149.3 | 151.0 | 144.0 |
| 2013 | 145.2 | 144.6 | 144.3 | 144.5 | 145.2 | 145.3 | 145.1 | 145.6 | 145.7 | 147.6 | 153.2 | 155.1 | 146.8 |
| 2014 | 149.5 | 149.7 | 149.8 | 150.8 | 151.1 | 151.1 | 150.5 | 151.2 | 151.4 | 153.1 | 159.6 | 161.6 | 152.5 |
| 2015 | 155.5 | 155.8 | 156.6 | 155.4 | 156.0 | 156.7 | 155.3 | 156.0 | 155.5 | 158.6 | 162.9 | 164.4 | 157.4 |
| 2016 | 160.4 | 161.2 | 161.3 | 161.7 | 161.4 | 160.2 | 159.6 | 159.8 | 159.2 | 161.1 | 166.8 | 168.0 | 161.7 |
| 2017 | 161.1 | 159.7 | 159.0 | 159.5 | 159.2 | 158.6 | 157.9 | 158.8 | 154.8 | 159.2 | 165.8 | 166.9 | 160.0 |
| 2018 | 160.3 | 160.0 | 159.4 | 160.5 | 160.2 | 159.2 | 159.0 | 159.1 | 157.9 | 159.1 | 165.0 | 164.7 | 160.4 |
| 2019 | 159.8 | 158.8 | 158.3 | 158.2 | 157.6 | 156.8 | 157.0 | 157.2 | 156.4 | 157.5 | 161.4 | 162.0 | 158.4 |
| **Transportation and Utilities** | | | | | | | | | | | | | |
| 2011 | 25.4 | 25.3 | 25.5 | 25.4 | 25.6 | 25.6 | 25.8 | 25.8 | 25.9 | 25.9 | 26.2 | 27.3 | 25.8 |
| 2012 | 26.3 | 26.4 | 26.4 | 26.5 | 26.6 | 26.6 | 26.6 | 26.3 | 26.4 | 26.4 | 26.7 | 27.6 | 26.6 |
| 2013 | 26.8 | 27.1 | 27.1 | 27.2 | 27.2 | 27.4 | 27.1 | 27.1 | 27.1 | 27.2 | 27.8 | 28.6 | 27.3 |
| 2014 | 27.9 | 28.1 | 28.3 | 28.4 | 28.6 | 28.7 | 28.7 | 28.8 | 29.4 | 29.9 | 31.1 | 32.7 | 29.2 |
| 2015 | 30.8 | 30.1 | 29.7 | 30.6 | 30.7 | 30.9 | 31.1 | 31.2 | 31.4 | 32.1 | 34.1 | 35.9 | 31.6 |
| 2016 | 33.1 | 32.7 | 32.6 | 32.9 | 33.2 | 33.1 | 33.5 | 33.3 | 33.7 | 34.0 | 35.5 | 36.2 | 33.7 |
| 2017 | 35.4 | 34.8 | 34.3 | 33.8 | 34.1 | 34.3 | 34.6 | 34.7 | 34.2 | 35.1 | 38.2 | 38.4 | 35.2 |
| 2018 | 36.5 | 35.8 | 35.6 | 34.5 | 34.6 | 34.7 | 34.6 | 34.7 | 34.9 | 36.0 | 38.1 | 39.9 | 35.8 |
| 2019 | 39.1 | 38.2 | 38.1 | 38.1 | 38.4 | 39.5 | 39.7 | 40.0 | 40.7 | 40.7 | 41.9 | 43.6 | 39.8 |
| **Information** | | | | | | | | | | | | | |
| 2011 | 25.8 | 25.9 | 25.7 | 25.6 | 25.7 | 25.8 | 26.0 | 25.9 | 25.9 | 26.0 | 26.1 | 26.2 | 25.9 |
| 2012 | 25.8 | 25.7 | 25.7 | 25.7 | 25.6 | 25.8 | 25.7 | 25.6 | 25.6 | 25.9 | 25.9 | 25.9 | 25.7 |
| 2013 | 26.1 | 26.1 | 26.2 | 26.2 | 26.3 | 26.4 | 26.1 | 26.1 | 25.9 | 25.9 | 26.0 | 26.0 | 26.1 |
| 2014 | 25.5 | 25.6 | 25.4 | 25.5 | 25.5 | 25.6 | 25.6 | 25.5 | 25.4 | 25.7 | 25.7 | 25.6 | 25.6 |
| 2015 | 25.5 | 25.6 | 25.4 | 25.5 | 25.6 | 25.7 | 26.0 | 25.8 | 25.9 | 26.0 | 26.2 | 26.4 | 25.8 |
| 2016 | 25.6 | 25.6 | 25.5 | 25.3 | 25.4 | 25.5 | 25.9 | 25.7 | 25.5 | 25.3 | 25.6 | 25.6 | 25.5 |
| 2017 | 25.4 | 25.2 | 25.4 | 25.0 | 25.1 | 25.1 | 25.1 | 25.1 | 24.6 | 24.8 | 25.3 | 25.3 | 25.1 |
| 2018 | 25.1 | 25.5 | 25.1 | 25.4 | 25.6 | 25.7 | 25.6 | 25.6 | 25.6 | 25.7 | 25.9 | 26.1 | 25.6 |
| 2019 | 25.6 | 25.9 | 25.7 | 25.7 | 25.8 | 25.8 | 25.5 | 25.6 | 25.3 | 25.4 | 25.6 | 25.6 | 25.6 |

## Employment by Industry: Tampa-St. Petersburg-Clearwater, FL, 2011–2019—*Continued*

(Numbers in thousands, not seasonally adjusted)

| Industry and year | January | February | March | April | May | June | July | August | September | October | November | December | Annual average |
|---|---|---|---|---|---|---|---|---|---|---|---|---|---|
| **Financial Activities** | | | | | | | | | | | | | |
| 2011 | 89.8 | 90.1 | 90.4 | 90.6 | 90.6 | 91.1 | 91.4 | 92.3 | 93.1 | 93.6 | 93.6 | 94.3 | 91.7 |
| 2012 | 93.5 | 94.0 | 94.6 | 94.7 | 95.0 | 95.6 | 95.7 | 96.1 | 96.3 | 97.0 | 97.7 | 98.3 | 95.7 |
| 2013 | 97.8 | 98.6 | 99.2 | 99.0 | 99.4 | 100.0 | 100.3 | 100.6 | 100.3 | 100.5 | 101.1 | 101.5 | 99.9 |
| 2014 | 100.4 | 100.7 | 101.2 | 101.2 | 101.5 | 101.8 | 102.4 | 102.6 | 102.7 | 102.5 | 103.0 | 103.2 | 101.9 |
| 2015 | 102.4 | 102.6 | 102.8 | 103.0 | 103.4 | 103.6 | 104.5 | 104.8 | 104.5 | 105.2 | 106.2 | 106.3 | 104.1 |
| 2016 | 105.4 | 105.5 | 105.8 | 106.4 | 106.5 | 107.0 | 108.3 | 108.7 | 108.8 | 109.4 | 109.7 | 110.8 | 107.7 |
| 2017 | 110.1 | 110.6 | 110.8 | 111.5 | 111.5 | 112.3 | 113.4 | 113.4 | 113.1 | 114.4 | 114.9 | 115.3 | 112.6 |
| 2018 | 114.4 | 115.2 | 115.5 | 115.4 | 115.9 | 116.4 | 116.7 | 117.5 | 117.6 | 118.6 | 119.2 | 120.0 | 116.9 |
| 2019 | 119.4 | 120.1 | 120.1 | 120.5 | 120.8 | 121.4 | 121.6 | 122.1 | 122.0 | 121.8 | 123.0 | 123.5 | 121.4 |
| **Professional and Business Services** | | | | | | | | | | | | | |
| 2011 | 177.9 | 180.1 | 181.0 | 182.4 | 181.0 | 181.8 | 182.7 | 184.2 | 184.0 | 184.5 | 186.5 | 188.3 | 182.9 |
| 2012 | 186.2 | 188.8 | 190.7 | 191.3 | 190.7 | 190.4 | 190.1 | 192.0 | 190.6 | 193.3 | 195.0 | 196.7 | 191.3 |
| 2013 | 192.5 | 196.0 | 197.3 | 197.9 | 199.4 | 198.4 | 199.2 | 200.3 | 199.1 | 200.1 | 201.7 | 201.6 | 198.6 |
| 2014 | 198.4 | 200.4 | 200.7 | 201.9 | 203.2 | 203.1 | 204.1 | 206.9 | 205.3 | 209.1 | 211.4 | 211.8 | 204.7 |
| 2015 | 210.5 | 213.8 | 214.3 | 215.6 | 216.5 | 216.8 | 218.6 | 220.0 | 218.8 | 222.2 | 225.2 | 226.2 | 218.2 |
| 2016 | 224.0 | 226.3 | 227.2 | 230.3 | 229.8 | 229.0 | 230.5 | 230.7 | 230.6 | 233.1 | 234.1 | 233.9 | 230.0 |
| 2017 | 233.0 | 232.8 | 233.2 | 234.5 | 234.6 | 234.8 | 235.5 | 236.2 | 232.2 | 239.7 | 242.7 | 240.5 | 235.8 |
| 2018 | 237.2 | 238.5 | 238.7 | 239.7 | 239.8 | 240.6 | 241.2 | 243.7 | 242.5 | 245.4 | 247.5 | 246.4 | 241.8 |
| 2019 | 245.4 | 247.3 | 246.5 | 247.8 | 247.0 | 246.1 | 246.6 | 248.5 | 247.6 | 252.8 | 253.0 | 252.8 | 248.5 |
| **Education and Health Services** | | | | | | | | | | | | | |
| 2011 | 179.0 | 180.1 | 181.1 | 182.5 | 181.6 | 179.7 | 178.6 | 179.8 | 181.0 | 182.0 | 182.9 | 182.8 | 180.9 |
| 2012 | 180.7 | 182.0 | 182.9 | 183.5 | 183.1 | 182.0 | 179.2 | 181.1 | 182.1 | 183.1 | 183.7 | 184.2 | 182.3 |
| 2013 | 182.2 | 183.6 | 185.0 | 185.4 | 185.2 | 183.4 | 181.7 | 183.6 | 184.5 | 186.5 | 187.6 | 187.1 | 184.7 |
| 2014 | 185.1 | 186.3 | 187.6 | 188.4 | 188.5 | 186.8 | 185.5 | 188.0 | 188.8 | 191.0 | 192.1 | 192.4 | 188.4 |
| 2015 | 190.2 | 192.4 | 192.8 | 194.4 | 194.5 | 193.6 | 191.6 | 193.3 | 195.1 | 198.6 | 199.7 | 199.8 | 194.7 |
| 2016 | 196.7 | 197.9 | 198.3 | 200.3 | 199.7 | 197.2 | 196.8 | 198.9 | 200.5 | 203.0 | 203.5 | 204.2 | 199.8 |
| 2017 | 202.6 | 204.4 | 205.3 | 205.9 | 205.5 | 204.0 | 202.3 | 204.9 | 203.4 | 207.7 | 208.1 | 208.7 | 205.2 |
| 2018 | 207.7 | 209.4 | 209.8 | 210.7 | 210.0 | 208.7 | 207.0 | 211.5 | 212.5 | 213.8 | 215.3 | 215.3 | 211.0 |
| 2019 | 213.6 | 215.7 | 215.8 | 216.3 | 218.9 | 217.6 | 216.2 | 218.7 | 220.1 | 223.2 | 224.0 | 225.1 | 218.8 |
| **Leisure and Hospitality** | | | | | | | | | | | | | |
| 2011 | 119.1 | 121.2 | 124.8 | 125.2 | 124.5 | 123.7 | 121.5 | 122.1 | 123.0 | 123.8 | 123.8 | 123.2 | 123.0 |
| 2012 | 123.1 | 125.9 | 129.8 | 131.3 | 130.4 | 129.5 | 127.5 | 128.3 | 127.5 | 128.5 | 128.4 | 129.7 | 128.3 |
| 2013 | 128.1 | 130.8 | 134.7 | 135.3 | 135.0 | 134.3 | 133.6 | 133.6 | 132.7 | 133.0 | 134.0 | 134.4 | 133.3 |
| 2014 | 132.7 | 134.7 | 138.7 | 141.6 | 141.2 | 140.6 | 138.9 | 138.7 | 138.3 | 137.8 | 138.9 | 138.7 | 138.4 |
| 2015 | 138.2 | 142.0 | 146.7 | 147.5 | 146.9 | 145.6 | 143.8 | 143.3 | 143.5 | 144.7 | 146.7 | 146.4 | 144.6 |
| 2016 | 144.0 | 147.4 | 151.0 | 152.3 | 151.0 | 150.5 | 148.5 | 148.5 | 148.7 | 149.0 | 150.0 | 149.8 | 149.2 |
| 2017 | 148.7 | 151.9 | 155.7 | 155.8 | 155.3 | 154.7 | 153.0 | 153.2 | 148.7 | 153.6 | 154.1 | 154.0 | 153.2 |
| 2018 | 152.6 | 157.0 | 161.2 | 160.8 | 161.1 | 159.5 | 157.9 | 160.1 | 159.5 | 159.4 | 158.9 | 159.5 | 159.0 |
| 2019 | 157.8 | 162.6 | 165.6 | 165.6 | 164.8 | 161.9 | 162.9 | 164.2 | 162.7 | 163.2 | 163.2 | 163.6 | 163.2 |
| **Other Services** | | | | | | | | | | | | | |
| 2011 | 41.3 | 41.6 | 42.1 | 42.1 | 42.0 | 41.5 | 41.2 | 40.9 | 40.7 | 40.7 | 40.6 | 40.6 | 41.3 |
| 2012 | 40.4 | 40.7 | 41.1 | 41.2 | 41.2 | 41.2 | 40.9 | 40.9 | 41.1 | 41.2 | 41.4 | 41.5 | 41.1 |
| 2013 | 41.1 | 41.4 | 41.7 | 42.3 | 42.5 | 42.8 | 42.5 | 42.7 | 42.7 | 42.8 | 43.2 | 43.3 | 42.4 |
| 2014 | 43.0 | 43.5 | 43.8 | 43.6 | 43.5 | 43.6 | 43.4 | 43.3 | 43.2 | 43.2 | 43.1 | 43.2 | 43.4 |
| 2015 | 42.7 | 42.9 | 43.2 | 43.3 | 43.4 | 43.6 | 43.0 | 43.3 | 43.4 | 43.7 | 44.0 | 44.2 | 43.4 |
| 2016 | 44.2 | 44.4 | 44.5 | 44.8 | 44.9 | 45.2 | 44.9 | 45.2 | 45.6 | 45.8 | 45.8 | 45.8 | 45.1 |
| 2017 | 45.0 | 45.4 | 45.4 | 45.7 | 45.9 | 46.1 | 45.7 | 45.7 | 44.8 | 45.9 | 46.2 | 46.4 | 45.7 |
| 2018 | 46.0 | 46.6 | 46.9 | 46.9 | 47.1 | 47.2 | 46.8 | 46.9 | 46.6 | 47.1 | 47.0 | 47.0 | 46.8 |
| 2019 | 46.8 | 47.3 | 47.4 | 47.4 | 47.5 | 47.6 | 47.5 | 47.3 | 47.2 | 47.1 | 47.4 | 47.0 | 47.3 |
| **Government** | | | | | | | | | | | | | |
| 2011 | 154.9 | 157.4 | 157.1 | 156.3 | 154.5 | 144.3 | 142.6 | 151.8 | 155.2 | 155.4 | 155.0 | 155.1 | 153.3 |
| 2012 | 154.6 | 155.1 | 154.8 | 155.7 | 154.7 | 144.1 | 142.8 | 150.9 | 152.8 | 153.2 | 154.2 | 153.8 | 152.2 |
| 2013 | 154.3 | 155.5 | 155.4 | 155.4 | 153.5 | 143.1 | 141.9 | 150.9 | 152.7 | 154.7 | 155.0 | 154.4 | 152.2 |
| 2014 | 152.9 | 153.4 | 155.7 | 156.0 | 155.5 | 144.6 | 143.3 | 151.1 | 153.6 | 155.4 | 155.2 | 155.3 | 152.7 |
| 2015 | 153.8 | 155.6 | 155.3 | 156.0 | 155.1 | 144.4 | 143.7 | 152.0 | 153.6 | 157.2 | 157.8 | 156.0 | 153.4 |
| 2016 | 156.2 | 158.1 | 157.5 | 158.3 | 157.1 | 146.3 | 145.5 | 153.4 | 156.7 | 159.1 | 159.4 | 159.1 | 155.6 |
| 2017 | 157.8 | 160.3 | 159.7 | 159.4 | 157.4 | 148.5 | 145.2 | 153.4 | 156.6 | 159.0 | 159.0 | 158.9 | 156.3 |
| 2018 | 157.1 | 159.3 | 159.0 | 159.0 | 156.5 | 148.0 | 145.8 | 153.5 | 157.3 | 159.3 | 160.2 | 159.3 | 156.2 |
| 2019 | 158.0 | 160.1 | 160.0 | 159.6 | 157.9 | 149.2 | 147.2 | 154.4 | 157.7 | 159.6 | 161.2 | 160.8 | 157.1 |

## Employment by Industry: Denver-Aurora-Lakewood, CO, 2011–2019

(Numbers in thousands, not seasonally adjusted)

| Industry and year | January | February | March | April | May | June | July | August | September | October | November | December | Annual average |
|---|---|---|---|---|---|---|---|---|---|---|---|---|---|
| **Total Nonfarm** | | | | | | | | | | | | | |
| 2011 | 1,180.9 | 1,184.4 | 1,192.1 | 1,208.4 | 1,218.0 | 1,227.0 | 1,219.5 | 1,224.4 | 1,225.2 | 1,226.5 | 1,231.4 | 1,233.2 | 1,214.3 |
| 2012 | 1,208.0 | 1,213.3 | 1,225.0 | 1,236.8 | 1,249.0 | 1,263.0 | 1,256.6 | 1,258.8 | 1,260.1 | 1,270.0 | 1,276.4 | 1,277.0 | 1,249.5 |
| 2013 | 1,251.1 | 1,260.0 | 1,270.2 | 1,282.1 | 1,294.7 | 1,307.1 | 1,302.9 | 1,310.6 | 1,309.4 | 1,318.5 | 1,324.0 | 1,323.9 | 1,296.2 |
| 2014 | 1,299.6 | 1,305.5 | 1,314.3 | 1,330.7 | 1,344.5 | 1,355.3 | 1,351.5 | 1,363.4 | 1,362.9 | 1,373.9 | 1,374.9 | 1,380.1 | 1,346.4 |
| 2015 | 1,357.0 | 1,365.1 | 1,370.6 | 1,384.9 | 1,396.2 | 1,408.9 | 1,405.4 | 1,411.1 | 1,410.5 | 1,416.4 | 1,421.4 | 1,424.3 | 1,397.7 |
| 2016 | 1,399.0 | 1,405.4 | 1,411.8 | 1,425.9 | 1,431.8 | 1,445.3 | 1,444.4 | 1,447.5 | 1,445.9 | 1,448.7 | 1,451.6 | 1,451.4 | 1,434.1 |
| 2017 | 1,425.0 | 1,432.1 | 1,441.1 | 1,452.0 | 1,463.0 | 1,478.8 | 1,474.4 | 1,477.6 | 1,474.5 | 1,480.5 | 1,487.5 | 1,490.7 | 1,464.8 |
| 2018 | 1,464.3 | 1,471.0 | 1,480.4 | 1,493.4 | 1,503.3 | 1,519.7 | 1,515.9 | 1,518.9 | 1,509.7 | 1,515.7 | 1,520.8 | 1,520.7 | 1,502.8 |
| 2019 | 1,496.2 | 1,504.5 | 1,505.7 | 1,521.0 | 1,533.8 | 1,548.6 | 1,551.2 | 1,555.0 | 1,546.8 | 1,553.3 | 1,555.4 | 1,560.9 | 1,536.0 |
| **Total Private** | | | | | | | | | | | | | |
| 2011 | 1,007.0 | 1,005.1 | 1,012.1 | 1,027.0 | 1,035.1 | 1,046.5 | 1,047.9 | 1,053.0 | 1,046.6 | 1,046.3 | 1,050.9 | 1,053.7 | 1,035.9 |
| 2012 | 1,034.1 | 1,034.1 | 1,044.1 | 1,055.0 | 1,065.6 | 1,080.5 | 1,083.2 | 1,086.4 | 1,080.2 | 1,088.5 | 1,093.2 | 1,095.4 | 1,070.0 |
| 2013 | 1,074.9 | 1,078.0 | 1,087.0 | 1,097.5 | 1,109.1 | 1,123.0 | 1,127.1 | 1,133.5 | 1,123.9 | 1,129.8 | 1,135.6 | 1,137.5 | 1,113.1 |
| 2014 | 1,118.4 | 1,120.5 | 1,128.2 | 1,143.8 | 1,156.3 | 1,168.7 | 1,176.0 | 1,183.5 | 1,175.3 | 1,182.4 | 1,182.5 | 1,190.2 | 1,160.5 |
| 2015 | 1,171.5 | 1,175.4 | 1,180.1 | 1,192.7 | 1,202.2 | 1,216.8 | 1,223.0 | 1,225.2 | 1,216.2 | 1,221.5 | 1,225.4 | 1,229.4 | 1,206.6 |
| 2016 | 1,208.4 | 1,210.4 | 1,215.8 | 1,228.6 | 1,234.3 | 1,248.2 | 1,256.9 | 1,256.3 | 1,248.6 | 1,250.8 | 1,251.8 | 1,253.2 | 1,238.6 |
| 2017 | 1,230.2 | 1,233.0 | 1,240.6 | 1,252.7 | 1,261.7 | 1,279.3 | 1,282.0 | 1,283.0 | 1,274.2 | 1,279.9 | 1,286.5 | 1,290.1 | 1,266.1 |
| 2018 | 1,267.5 | 1,270.2 | 1,278.0 | 1,289.6 | 1,297.6 | 1,314.4 | 1,317.5 | 1,317.6 | 1,305.8 | 1,311.8 | 1,316.5 | 1,318.2 | 1,300.4 |
| 2019 | 1,296.5 | 1,299.8 | 1,300.4 | 1,314.0 | 1,322.8 | 1,340.5 | 1,350.2 | 1,350.9 | 1,337.7 | 1,344.2 | 1,345.9 | 1,352.3 | 1,329.6 |
| **Goods Producing** | | | | | | | | | | | | | |
| 2011 | 126.1 | 125.4 | 127.5 | 130.6 | 131.0 | 133.9 | 134.9 | 135.5 | 134.8 | 134.7 | 134.1 | 132.8 | 131.8 |
| 2012 | 130.0 | 130.0 | 131.7 | 133.5 | 135.5 | 138.6 | 139.4 | 139.9 | 139.5 | 140.7 | 140.2 | 139.3 | 136.5 |
| 2013 | 136.6 | 137.3 | 139.2 | 140.3 | 143.4 | 146.4 | 147.4 | 148.7 | 147.7 | 149.0 | 149.2 | 148.5 | 144.5 |
| 2014 | 146.6 | 147.3 | 149.3 | 152.3 | 154.9 | 157.6 | 159.4 | 160.3 | 160.0 | 160.6 | 160.1 | 160.5 | 155.7 |
| 2015 | 157.8 | 158.6 | 159.5 | 160.8 | 162.3 | 164.8 | 165.6 | 165.4 | 164.8 | 165.3 | 164.8 | 164.3 | 162.8 |
| 2016 | 161.5 | 162.1 | 163.8 | 165.0 | 165.5 | 168.1 | 169.0 | 168.6 | 168.2 | 168.7 | 168.0 | 167.6 | 166.3 |
| 2017 | 164.2 | 165.4 | 167.2 | 168.3 | 169.5 | 173.0 | 173.8 | 174.4 | 173.8 | 174.8 | 174.6 | 174.2 | 171.1 |
| 2018 | 171.7 | 173.3 | 175.7 | 177.1 | 177.7 | 181.1 | 180.9 | 181.0 | 180.1 | 180.3 | 179.7 | 179.4 | 178.2 |
| 2019 | 176.8 | 178.0 | 178.7 | 180.6 | 181.4 | 184.8 | 185.8 | 185.9 | 184.4 | 184.1 | 184.1 | 185.3 | 182.5 |
| **Service-Providing** | | | | | | | | | | | | | |
| 2011 | 1,054.8 | 1,059.0 | 1,064.6 | 1,077.8 | 1,087.0 | 1,093.1 | 1,084.6 | 1,088.9 | 1,090.4 | 1,091.8 | 1,097.3 | 1,100.4 | 1,082.5 |
| 2012 | 1,078.0 | 1,083.3 | 1,093.3 | 1,103.3 | 1,113.5 | 1,124.4 | 1,117.2 | 1,118.9 | 1,120.6 | 1,129.3 | 1,136.2 | 1,137.7 | 1,113.0 |
| 2013 | 1,114.5 | 1,122.7 | 1,131.0 | 1,141.8 | 1,151.3 | 1,160.7 | 1,155.5 | 1,161.9 | 1,161.7 | 1,169.5 | 1,174.8 | 1,175.4 | 1,151.7 |
| 2014 | 1,153.0 | 1,158.2 | 1,165.0 | 1,178.4 | 1,189.6 | 1,197.7 | 1,192.1 | 1,203.1 | 1,202.9 | 1,213.3 | 1,214.8 | 1,219.6 | 1,190.6 |
| 2015 | 1,199.2 | 1,206.5 | 1,211.1 | 1,224.1 | 1,233.9 | 1,244.1 | 1,239.8 | 1,245.7 | 1,245.7 | 1,251.1 | 1,256.6 | 1,260.0 | 1,234.8 |
| 2016 | 1,237.5 | 1,243.3 | 1,248.0 | 1,260.9 | 1,266.3 | 1,277.2 | 1,275.4 | 1,278.9 | 1,277.7 | 1,280.0 | 1,283.6 | 1,283.8 | 1,267.7 |
| 2017 | 1,260.8 | 1,266.7 | 1,273.9 | 1,283.7 | 1,293.5 | 1,305.8 | 1,300.6 | 1,303.2 | 1,300.7 | 1,305.7 | 1,312.9 | 1,316.5 | 1,293.7 |
| 2018 | 1,292.6 | 1,297.7 | 1,304.7 | 1,316.3 | 1,325.6 | 1,338.6 | 1,335.0 | 1,337.9 | 1,329.6 | 1,335.4 | 1,341.1 | 1,341.3 | 1,324.7 |
| 2019 | 1,319.4 | 1,326.5 | 1,327.0 | 1,340.4 | 1,352.4 | 1,363.8 | 1,365.4 | 1,369.1 | 1,362.4 | 1,369.2 | 1,371.3 | 1,375.6 | 1,353.5 |
| **Mining, Logging, and Construction** | | | | | | | | | | | | | |
| 2011 | 64.9 | 64.3 | 66.0 | 68.8 | 68.9 | 71.4 | 72.3 | 72.7 | 72.0 | 72.3 | 71.6 | 70.4 | 69.6 |
| 2012 | 68.1 | 67.9 | 69.2 | 70.8 | 72.5 | 75.0 | 75.5 | 76.1 | 75.7 | 76.8 | 76.3 | 75.5 | 73.3 |
| 2013 | 73.3 | 73.9 | 75.4 | 76.7 | 79.6 | 82.1 | 83.2 | 84.4 | 83.6 | 85.0 | 85.1 | 84.3 | 80.6 |
| 2014 | 83.0 | 83.5 | 85.3 | 87.7 | 89.9 | 92.1 | 93.5 | 94.2 | 93.9 | 94.2 | 93.4 | 93.5 | 90.4 |
| 2015 | 91.2 | 91.8 | 92.4 | 93.5 | 94.6 | 96.3 | 96.9 | 96.7 | 96.2 | 96.8 | 95.9 | 95.4 | 94.8 |
| 2016 | 92.8 | 93.4 | 95.1 | 96.3 | 96.7 | 98.8 | 99.4 | 99.3 | 99.1 | 99.5 | 99.0 | 98.2 | 97.3 |
| 2017 | 95.8 | 96.9 | 98.5 | 99.6 | 100.5 | 103.2 | 104.1 | 104.9 | 104.6 | 105.8 | 105.6 | 104.9 | 102.0 |
| 2018 | 102.9 | 104.4 | 106.2 | 107.5 | 108.1 | 110.7 | 110.7 | 111.0 | 110.3 | 110.3 | 109.8 | 109.0 | 108.4 |
| 2019 | 106.9 | 107.6 | 108.2 | 110.2 | 111.1 | 114.0 | 114.7 | 114.8 | 113.6 | 113.2 | 112.9 | 113.4 | 111.7 |
| **Manufacturing** | | | | | | | | | | | | | |
| 2011 | 61.2 | 61.1 | 61.5 | 61.8 | 62.1 | 62.5 | 62.6 | 62.8 | 62.8 | 62.4 | 62.5 | 62.4 | 62.1 |
| 2012 | 61.9 | 62.1 | 62.5 | 62.7 | 63.0 | 63.6 | 63.9 | 63.8 | 63.8 | 63.9 | 63.9 | 63.8 | 63.2 |
| 2013 | 63.3 | 63.4 | 63.8 | 63.6 | 63.8 | 64.3 | 64.2 | 64.3 | 64.1 | 64.0 | 64.1 | 64.2 | 63.9 |
| 2014 | 63.6 | 63.8 | 64.0 | 64.6 | 65.0 | 65.5 | 65.9 | 66.1 | 66.1 | 66.4 | 66.7 | 67.0 | 65.4 |
| 2015 | 66.6 | 66.8 | 67.1 | 67.3 | 67.7 | 68.5 | 68.7 | 68.7 | 68.6 | 68.5 | 68.9 | 68.9 | 68.0 |
| 2016 | 68.7 | 68.7 | 68.7 | 68.7 | 68.8 | 69.3 | 69.6 | 69.3 | 69.1 | 69.2 | 69.0 | 69.4 | 69.0 |
| 2017 | 68.4 | 68.5 | 68.7 | 68.7 | 69.0 | 69.8 | 69.7 | 69.5 | 69.2 | 69.0 | 69.0 | 69.3 | 69.1 |
| 2018 | 68.8 | 68.9 | 69.5 | 69.6 | 69.6 | 70.4 | 70.2 | 70.0 | 69.8 | 70.0 | 69.9 | 70.4 | 69.8 |
| 2019 | 69.9 | 70.4 | 70.5 | 70.4 | 70.3 | 70.8 | 71.1 | 71.1 | 70.8 | 70.9 | 71.2 | 71.9 | 70.8 |

# Employment by Industry: Denver-Aurora-Lakewood, CO, 2011–2019—*Continued*

(Numbers in thousands, not seasonally adjusted)

| Industry and year | January | February | March | April | May | June | July | August | September | October | November | December | Annual average |
|---|---|---|---|---|---|---|---|---|---|---|---|---|---|
| **Trade, Transportation, and Utilities** | | | | | | | | | | | | | |
| 2011 | 226.3 | 224.5 | 225.3 | 227.4 | 228.8 | 230.0 | 230.8 | 231.2 | 229.9 | 231.6 | 236.0 | 238.0 | 230.0 |
| 2012 | 230.9 | 228.9 | 229.8 | 231.0 | 232.7 | 234.9 | 235.6 | 235.6 | 235.5 | 238.3 | 243.9 | 246.4 | 235.3 |
| 2013 | 238.1 | 236.7 | 237.6 | 238.4 | 240.4 | 242.0 | 242.9 | 244.4 | 243.3 | 244.9 | 250.2 | 253.1 | 242.7 |
| 2014 | 245.2 | 244.3 | 244.7 | 246.3 | 248.1 | 250.6 | 250.8 | 251.7 | 250.2 | 252.5 | 257.5 | 261.3 | 250.3 |
| 2015 | 253.4 | 252.2 | 252.5 | 253.7 | 254.6 | 257.1 | 258.4 | 258.7 | 257.0 | 259.8 | 264.5 | 268.2 | 257.5 |
| 2016 | 259.5 | 258.0 | 258.1 | 259.1 | 260.1 | 261.5 | 263.1 | 262.9 | 261.6 | 263.3 | 268.2 | 272.2 | 262.3 |
| 2017 | 264.3 | 262.5 | 262.4 | 263.2 | 264.1 | 266.4 | 267.0 | 267.3 | 266.4 | 268.9 | 275.9 | 279.5 | 267.3 |
| 2018 | 271.5 | 268.4 | 268.8 | 269.1 | 270.4 | 272.4 | 273.6 | 274.2 | 272.7 | 274.8 | 283.0 | 284.7 | 273.6 |
| 2019 | 277.5 | 274.4 | 273.1 | 273.3 | 274.2 | 277.9 | 279.8 | 279.6 | 278.1 | 281.6 | 287.7 | 293.1 | 279.2 |
| **Wholesale Trade** | | | | | | | | | | | | | |
| 2011 | 61.2 | 61.3 | 61.6 | 61.9 | 62.1 | 62.3 | 62.5 | 62.6 | 62.4 | 62.3 | 62.3 | 62.3 | 62.1 |
| 2012 | 61.9 | 62.1 | 62.5 | 62.9 | 63.1 | 63.6 | 63.9 | 64.0 | 63.9 | 64.2 | 64.2 | 64.6 | 63.4 |
| 2013 | 63.8 | 64.2 | 64.5 | 64.6 | 64.9 | 65.4 | 65.4 | 65.6 | 65.4 | 65.6 | 65.8 | 65.9 | 65.1 |
| 2014 | 65.6 | 66.1 | 66.3 | 66.8 | 67.1 | 67.5 | 68.0 | 68.4 | 68.1 | 68.6 | 68.9 | 69.3 | 67.6 |
| 2015 | 68.7 | 69.1 | 69.2 | 69.2 | 69.5 | 69.8 | 70.1 | 70.4 | 70.1 | 70.7 | 70.8 | 70.9 | 69.9 |
| 2016 | 70.5 | 70.6 | 70.7 | 71.0 | 70.9 | 70.9 | 71.4 | 71.2 | 71.2 | 71.2 | 71.3 | 71.4 | 71.0 |
| 2017 | 71.2 | 71.4 | 71.7 | 71.7 | 71.8 | 72.3 | 72.5 | 72.6 | 72.5 | 72.6 | 72.5 | 72.6 | 72.1 |
| 2018 | 72.4 | 72.6 | 72.7 | 72.8 | 73.0 | 73.4 | 73.8 | 73.6 | 73.3 | 73.5 | 73.5 | 73.6 | 73.2 |
| 2019 | 73.0 | 73.5 | 73.3 | 73.5 | 73.7 | 74.4 | 75.1 | 75.1 | 74.8 | 75.9 | 77.1 | 77.9 | 74.8 |
| **Retail Trade** | | | | | | | | | | | | | |
| 2011 | 119.4 | 117.9 | 118.4 | 119.9 | 121.0 | 121.9 | 122.2 | 122.7 | 121.9 | 123.2 | 127.1 | 128.4 | 122.0 |
| 2012 | 122.7 | 120.4 | 121.1 | 121.8 | 123.3 | 124.6 | 124.7 | 124.6 | 124.5 | 125.7 | 130.6 | 131.9 | 124.7 |
| 2013 | 125.3 | 123.6 | 124.0 | 124.7 | 126.3 | 127.5 | 128.3 | 129.2 | 128.3 | 129.3 | 133.6 | 135.4 | 128.0 |
| 2014 | 128.8 | 127.4 | 127.9 | 128.7 | 129.8 | 131.6 | 131.5 | 131.8 | 130.7 | 132.3 | 136.2 | 138.4 | 131.3 |
| 2015 | 131.8 | 130.6 | 131.4 | 132.2 | 133.2 | 135.1 | 135.6 | 135.9 | 134.5 | 136.5 | 140.3 | 142.2 | 134.9 |
| 2016 | 135.3 | 134.2 | 134.7 | 135.0 | 136.0 | 137.3 | 137.7 | 137.4 | 136.0 | 137.6 | 141.5 | 143.3 | 137.2 |
| 2017 | 137.0 | 135.3 | 135.6 | 136.5 | 137.0 | 138.3 | 138.5 | 138.4 | 136.7 | 138.3 | 143.4 | 145.0 | 138.3 |
| 2018 | 139.5 | 137.1 | 137.3 | 137.5 | 138.5 | 139.4 | 140.2 | 139.9 | 137.9 | 138.7 | 144.3 | 145.0 | 139.6 |
| 2019 | 139.8 | 137.3 | 136.6 | 136.8 | 137.1 | 138.8 | 138.8 | 138.4 | 136.7 | 138.0 | 141.1 | 142.9 | 138.5 |
| **Transportation and Utilities** | | | | | | | | | | | | | |
| 2011 | 45.7 | 45.3 | 45.3 | 45.6 | 45.7 | 45.8 | 46.1 | 45.9 | 45.6 | 46.1 | 46.6 | 47.3 | 45.9 |
| 2012 | 46.3 | 46.4 | 46.2 | 46.3 | 46.3 | 46.7 | 47.0 | 47.0 | 47.1 | 48.4 | 49.1 | 49.9 | 47.2 |
| 2013 | 49.0 | 48.9 | 49.1 | 49.1 | 49.2 | 49.1 | 49.2 | 49.6 | 49.6 | 50.0 | 50.8 | 51.8 | 49.6 |
| 2014 | 50.8 | 50.8 | 50.5 | 50.8 | 51.2 | 51.5 | 51.3 | 51.5 | 51.4 | 51.6 | 52.4 | 53.6 | 51.5 |
| 2015 | 52.9 | 52.5 | 51.9 | 52.3 | 51.9 | 52.2 | 52.7 | 52.4 | 52.4 | 52.6 | 53.4 | 55.1 | 52.7 |
| 2016 | 53.7 | 53.2 | 52.7 | 53.1 | 53.2 | 53.3 | 54.0 | 54.3 | 54.4 | 54.5 | 55.4 | 57.5 | 54.1 |
| 2017 | 56.1 | 55.8 | 55.1 | 55.0 | 55.3 | 55.8 | 56.0 | 56.3 | 57.2 | 58.0 | 60.0 | 61.9 | 56.9 |
| 2018 | 59.6 | 58.7 | 58.8 | 58.8 | 58.9 | 59.6 | 59.6 | 60.7 | 61.5 | 62.6 | 65.2 | 66.1 | 60.8 |
| 2019 | 64.7 | 63.6 | 63.2 | 63.0 | 63.4 | 64.7 | 65.9 | 66.1 | 66.6 | 67.7 | 69.5 | 72.3 | 65.9 |
| **Information** | | | | | | | | | | | | | |
| 2011 | 44.0 | 44.0 | 43.6 | 43.9 | 43.8 | 43.8 | 43.6 | 43.6 | 43.5 | 43.4 | 43.5 | 43.4 | 43.7 |
| 2012 | 43.3 | 43.4 | 43.4 | 43.2 | 43.3 | 43.5 | 43.3 | 43.3 | 43.3 | 43.4 | 43.6 | 43.7 | 43.4 |
| 2013 | 43.8 | 44.2 | 44.2 | 44.2 | 44.4 | 44.9 | 45.0 | 44.9 | 44.5 | 44.4 | 44.7 | 44.7 | 44.5 |
| 2014 | 44.8 | 45.0 | 44.9 | 44.9 | 45.0 | 45.7 | 46.3 | 46.2 | 45.2 | 45.3 | 45.2 | 45.6 | 45.3 |
| 2015 | 45.6 | 45.9 | 46.0 | 45.8 | 46.0 | 46.4 | 46.7 | 46.6 | 46.1 | 45.8 | 46.1 | 46.3 | 46.1 |
| 2016 | 45.9 | 46.3 | 46.3 | 46.5 | 46.6 | 47.1 | 47.5 | 47.4 | 46.6 | 46.7 | 46.9 | 46.9 | 46.7 |
| 2017 | 46.5 | 46.4 | 46.5 | 46.4 | 46.7 | 47.5 | 47.6 | 47.7 | 47.5 | 48.0 | 48.7 | 48.9 | 47.4 |
| 2018 | 49.3 | 49.5 | 49.6 | 50.1 | 50.2 | 50.9 | 50.9 | 50.5 | 50.2 | 50.4 | 50.5 | 50.5 | 50.2 |
| 2019 | 50.5 | 50.3 | 49.9 | 50.4 | 50.4 | 51.1 | 51.3 | 51.0 | 50.7 | 51.6 | 51.2 | 50.9 | 50.8 |
| **Financial Activities** | | | | | | | | | | | | | |
| 2011 | 90.2 | 90.1 | 90.1 | 90.2 | 90.3 | 90.9 | 90.9 | 91.1 | 90.9 | 90.7 | 91.1 | 91.7 | 90.7 |
| 2012 | 90.7 | 90.8 | 91.3 | 91.5 | 92.0 | 92.8 | 93.0 | 93.4 | 93.2 | 94.1 | 94.1 | 94.9 | 92.7 |
| 2013 | 93.9 | 94.5 | 94.9 | 95.3 | 95.6 | 96.5 | 96.7 | 96.9 | 96.6 | 96.8 | 96.9 | 97.1 | 96.0 |
| 2014 | 95.7 | 96.0 | 96.2 | 96.8 | 97.5 | 97.9 | 98.6 | 99.0 | 98.7 | 99.5 | 99.9 | 100.7 | 98.0 |
| 2015 | 99.7 | 100.2 | 100.6 | 101.0 | 101.8 | 102.7 | 103.5 | 103.8 | 103.4 | 104.0 | 104.3 | 104.7 | 102.5 |
| 2016 | 104.2 | 104.3 | 104.5 | 105.0 | 105.4 | 106.3 | 107.0 | 107.0 | 106.7 | 107.2 | 107.4 | 107.7 | 106.1 |
| 2017 | 106.9 | 107.4 | 107.6 | 108.2 | 108.7 | 109.5 | 109.5 | 109.6 | 109.1 | 109.9 | 109.9 | 110.5 | 108.9 |
| 2018 | 109.4 | 109.8 | 110.1 | 110.8 | 111.3 | 112.1 | 112.3 | 112.1 | 111.7 | 112.1 | 112.1 | 112.5 | 111.4 |
| 2019 | 111.4 | 111.6 | 111.8 | 112.0 | 112.2 | 112.6 | 113.4 | 113.4 | 113.0 | 114.2 | 113.6 | 112.5 | 112.6 |

## Employment by Industry: Denver-Aurora-Lakewood, CO, 2011–2019—*Continued*

(Numbers in thousands, not seasonally adjusted)

| Industry and year | January | February | March | April | May | June | July | August | September | October | November | December | Annual average |
|---|---|---|---|---|---|---|---|---|---|---|---|---|---|
| **Professional and Business Services** | | | | | | | | | | | | | |
| 2011 | 204.2 | 204.4 | 205.2 | 210.6 | 212.5 | 213.8 | 214.3 | 215.9 | 214.8 | 215.1 | 216.7 | 217.0 | 212.0 |
| 2012 | 212.5 | 213.4 | 216.2 | 220.1 | 222.1 | 225.4 | 226.3 | 227.9 | 226.6 | 229.3 | 229.2 | 228.3 | 223.1 |
| 2013 | 223.9 | 225.5 | 227.6 | 230.9 | 232.5 | 235.3 | 236.0 | 237.9 | 235.6 | 237.7 | 237.5 | 237.2 | 233.1 |
| 2014 | 232.3 | 233.0 | 234.6 | 238.8 | 240.5 | 243.3 | 245.1 | 248.6 | 247.0 | 249.5 | 246.9 | 247.8 | 242.3 |
| 2015 | 243.5 | 244.8 | 245.7 | 249.2 | 250.9 | 253.1 | 254.6 | 255.8 | 253.8 | 255.5 | 254.5 | 254.4 | 251.3 |
| 2016 | 249.7 | 250.6 | 251.6 | 256.0 | 256.1 | 259.0 | 262.0 | 261.7 | 260.5 | 261.5 | 261.0 | 259.7 | 257.5 |
| 2017 | 254.1 | 255.6 | 257.7 | 261.4 | 262.6 | 266.0 | 267.5 | 267.9 | 266.5 | 268.1 | 268.2 | 266.9 | 263.5 |
| 2018 | 261.3 | 263.5 | 264.9 | 269.2 | 270.5 | 273.4 | 276.9 | 276.6 | 274.0 | 276.2 | 274.7 | 273.9 | 271.3 |
| 2019 | 269.7 | 272.3 | 272.3 | 278.2 | 279.7 | 283.3 | 287.3 | 288.3 | 285.0 | 286.6 | 284.2 | 283.9 | 280.9 |
| **Education and Health Services** | | | | | | | | | | | | | |
| 2011 | 144.8 | 145.9 | 146.4 | 147.0 | 147.5 | 147.4 | 146.9 | 148.4 | 148.8 | 150.0 | 150.5 | 151.9 | 148.0 |
| 2012 | 150.6 | 152.0 | 152.5 | 152.8 | 153.0 | 152.8 | 152.7 | 153.2 | 153.7 | 155.3 | 156.0 | 156.9 | 153.5 |
| 2013 | 155.8 | 157.2 | 157.7 | 159.1 | 159.1 | 158.8 | 159.2 | 160.4 | 161.1 | 162.8 | 164.1 | 164.6 | 160.0 |
| 2014 | 163.1 | 164.7 | 165.4 | 167.4 | 167.9 | 167.0 | 167.1 | 168.5 | 169.2 | 171.4 | 172.1 | 172.7 | 168.0 |
| 2015 | 172.6 | 174.3 | 174.7 | 176.7 | 176.9 | 176.4 | 176.8 | 177.5 | 177.8 | 180.3 | 181.2 | 181.3 | 177.2 |
| 2016 | 180.0 | 181.2 | 181.6 | 183.6 | 183.3 | 182.6 | 183.0 | 183.2 | 183.5 | 183.5 | 183.2 | 183.0 | 182.6 |
| 2017 | 181.3 | 182.2 | 182.9 | 185.7 | 186.2 | 186.0 | 185.6 | 186.1 | 185.2 | 186.3 | 186.8 | 187.2 | 185.1 |
| 2018 | 185.4 | 187.3 | 187.7 | 188.6 | 189.0 | 188.8 | 188.1 | 188.9 | 188.5 | 190.1 | 190.6 | 191.1 | 188.7 |
| 2019 | 188.7 | 190.5 | 190.5 | 191.4 | 192.0 | 191.5 | 191.8 | 192.7 | 192.2 | 193.9 | 196.3 | 196.3 | 192.3 |
| **Leisure and Hospitality** | | | | | | | | | | | | | |
| 2011 | 124.0 | 123.5 | 126.4 | 129.2 | 132.7 | 137.7 | 137.6 | 138.1 | 135.2 | 132.4 | 130.6 | 130.3 | 131.5 |
| 2012 | 127.5 | 127.0 | 130.2 | 133.7 | 137.6 | 142.3 | 142.7 | 142.8 | 138.4 | 137.2 | 136.2 | 136.0 | 136.0 |
| 2013 | 132.7 | 132.9 | 135.7 | 139.0 | 142.7 | 147.9 | 148.6 | 149.0 | 144.3 | 143.4 | 142.1 | 141.5 | 141.7 |
| 2014 | 139.2 | 139.0 | 141.8 | 145.4 | 150.1 | 153.7 | 155.1 | 155.4 | 152.0 | 149.9 | 147.5 | 148.5 | 148.1 |
| 2015 | 145.6 | 146.3 | 147.7 | 152.0 | 156.0 | 161.9 | 162.6 | 162.6 | 158.9 | 156.4 | 155.8 | 155.8 | 155.1 |
| 2016 | 153.1 | 153.2 | 155.0 | 158.3 | 161.8 | 167.2 | 168.6 | 168.6 | 164.8 | 163.0 | 160.6 | 160.1 | 161.2 |
| 2017 | 157.5 | 157.5 | 160.1 | 163.3 | 167.3 | 173.6 | 173.9 | 172.8 | 168.9 | 167.1 | 165.5 | 165.9 | 166.1 |
| 2018 | 162.6 | 161.8 | 164.1 | 167.5 | 170.6 | 177.2 | 176.5 | 176.0 | 170.4 | 169.6 | 167.6 | 168.2 | 169.3 |
| 2019 | 164.7 | 165.1 | 166.3 | 169.6 | 174.0 | 179.8 | 181.0 | 180.3 | 175.2 | 173.1 | 170.3 | 172.6 | 172.7 |
| **Other Services** | | | | | | | | | | | | | |
| 2011 | 47.4 | 47.3 | 47.6 | 48.1 | 48.5 | 49.0 | 48.9 | 49.2 | 48.7 | 48.4 | 48.4 | 48.6 | 48.3 |
| 2012 | 48.6 | 48.6 | 49.0 | 49.2 | 49.4 | 50.2 | 50.2 | 50.3 | 50.0 | 50.2 | 50.0 | 49.9 | 49.6 |
| 2013 | 50.1 | 49.7 | 50.1 | 50.3 | 51.0 | 51.2 | 51.3 | 51.3 | 50.8 | 50.8 | 50.9 | 50.8 | 50.7 |
| 2014 | 51.5 | 51.2 | 51.3 | 51.9 | 52.3 | 52.9 | 53.6 | 53.8 | 53.0 | 53.7 | 53.3 | 53.1 | 52.6 |
| 2015 | 53.3 | 53.1 | 53.4 | 53.5 | 53.7 | 54.4 | 54.8 | 54.8 | 54.4 | 54.4 | 54.2 | 54.4 | 54.0 |
| 2016 | 54.5 | 54.7 | 54.9 | 55.1 | 55.5 | 56.4 | 56.7 | 56.9 | 56.7 | 56.9 | 56.5 | 56.0 | 55.9 |
| 2017 | 55.4 | 56.0 | 56.2 | 56.2 | 56.6 | 57.3 | 57.1 | 57.2 | 56.8 | 56.8 | 56.9 | 57.0 | 56.6 |
| 2018 | 56.3 | 56.6 | 57.1 | 57.2 | 57.9 | 58.5 | 58.3 | 58.3 | 58.2 | 58.3 | 58.3 | 57.9 | 57.7 |
| 2019 | 57.2 | 57.6 | 57.8 | 58.5 | 58.9 | 59.5 | 59.8 | 59.7 | 59.1 | 59.1 | 58.5 | 57.7 | 58.6 |
| **Government** | | | | | | | | | | | | | |
| 2011 | 173.9 | 179.3 | 180.0 | 181.4 | 182.9 | 180.5 | 171.6 | 171.4 | 178.6 | 180.2 | 180.5 | 179.5 | 178.3 |
| 2012 | 173.9 | 179.2 | 180.9 | 181.8 | 183.4 | 182.5 | 173.4 | 172.4 | 179.9 | 181.5 | 183.2 | 181.6 | 179.5 |
| 2013 | 176.2 | 182.0 | 183.2 | 184.6 | 185.6 | 184.1 | 175.8 | 177.1 | 185.5 | 188.7 | 188.4 | 186.4 | 183.1 |
| 2014 | 181.2 | 185.0 | 186.1 | 186.9 | 188.2 | 186.6 | 175.5 | 179.9 | 187.6 | 191.5 | 192.4 | 189.9 | 185.9 |
| 2015 | 185.5 | 189.7 | 190.5 | 192.2 | 194.0 | 192.1 | 182.4 | 185.9 | 194.3 | 194.9 | 196.0 | 194.9 | 191.0 |
| 2016 | 190.6 | 195.0 | 196.0 | 197.3 | 197.5 | 197.1 | 187.5 | 191.2 | 197.3 | 197.9 | 199.8 | 198.2 | 195.5 |
| 2017 | 194.8 | 199.1 | 200.5 | 199.3 | 201.3 | 199.5 | 192.4 | 194.6 | 200.3 | 200.6 | 201.0 | 200.6 | 198.7 |
| 2018 | 196.8 | 200.8 | 202.4 | 203.8 | 205.7 | 205.3 | 198.4 | 201.3 | 203.9 | 203.9 | 204.3 | 202.5 | 202.4 |
| 2019 | 199.7 | 204.7 | 205.3 | 207.0 | 211.0 | 208.1 | 201.0 | 204.1 | 209.1 | 209.1 | 209.5 | 208.6 | 206.4 |

## Employment by Industry: St. Louis, MO, 2011–2019

(Numbers in thousands, not seasonally adjusted)

| Industry and year | January | February | March | April | May | June | July | August | September | October | November | December | Annual average |
|---|---|---|---|---|---|---|---|---|---|---|---|---|---|
| **Total Nonfarm** | | | | | | | | | | | | | |
| 2011 | 1,270.8 | 1,273.5 | 1,286.5 | 1,307.6 | 1,312.8 | 1,308.8 | 1,289.4 | 1,297.9 | 1,306.1 | 1,307.2 | 1,305.8 | 1,306.2 | 1,297.7 |
| 2012 | 1,274.4 | 1,279.9 | 1,292.1 | 1,304.5 | 1,312.5 | 1,309.1 | 1,285.1 | 1,294.2 | 1,302.0 | 1,308.8 | 1,309.2 | 1,311.2 | 1,298.6 |
| 2013 | 1,280.4 | 1,287.3 | 1,294.3 | 1,311.5 | 1,321.8 | 1,317.8 | 1,297.3 | 1,306.7 | 1,315.3 | 1,321.4 | 1,322.1 | 1,323.7 | 1,308.3 |
| 2014 | 1,286.3 | 1,296.6 | 1,305.7 | 1,330.3 | 1,338.1 | 1,333.5 | 1,313.4 | 1,323.9 | 1,330.3 | 1,345.0 | 1,343.8 | 1,344.9 | 1,324.3 |
| 2015 | 1,313.8 | 1,319.5 | 1,325.8 | 1,348.3 | 1,360.6 | 1,359.6 | 1,342.5 | 1,350.5 | 1,359.3 | 1,370.8 | 1,372.1 | 1,373.1 | 1,349.7 |
| 2016 | 1,335.3 | 1,343.9 | 1,351.7 | 1,373.6 | 1,379.3 | 1,379.1 | 1,358.2 | 1,367.8 | 1,377.8 | 1,384.5 | 1,383.7 | 1,380.2 | 1,367.9 |
| 2017 | 1,351.0 | 1,363.2 | 1,368.2 | 1,385.1 | 1,392.2 | 1,397.1 | 1,374.8 | 1,381.1 | 1,388.1 | 1,391.9 | 1,394.9 | 1,393.1 | 1,381.7 |
| 2018 | 1,358.9 | 1,368.4 | 1,374.6 | 1,385.5 | 1,393.1 | 1,396.1 | 1,377.6 | 1,384.8 | 1,390.2 | 1,397.2 | 1,399.4 | 1,397.2 | 1,385.3 |
| 2019 | 1,366.8 | 1,373.6 | 1,379.3 | 1,397.4 | 1,402.1 | 1,401.8 | 1,388.9 | 1,395.8 | 1,401.9 | 1,407.4 | 1,407.1 | 1,400.3 | 1,393.5 |
| **Total Private** | | | | | | | | | | | | | |
| 2011 | 1,104.4 | 1,105.4 | 1,117.7 | 1,137.6 | 1,142.1 | 1,146.8 | 1,147.5 | 1,147.5 | 1,139.1 | 1,139.9 | 1,138.5 | 1,138.8 | 1,133.8 |
| 2012 | 1,111.5 | 1,114.2 | 1,125.5 | 1,136.9 | 1,144.0 | 1,149.1 | 1,145.6 | 1,146.2 | 1,138.5 | 1,144.2 | 1,144.7 | 1,146.4 | 1,137.2 |
| 2013 | 1,120.0 | 1,123.9 | 1,130.2 | 1,142.8 | 1,152.5 | 1,157.0 | 1,157.7 | 1,158.6 | 1,151.4 | 1,156.4 | 1,156.6 | 1,158.0 | 1,147.1 |
| 2014 | 1,125.2 | 1,132.2 | 1,140.7 | 1,166.3 | 1,173.4 | 1,177.2 | 1,177.7 | 1,179.9 | 1,171.0 | 1,182.2 | 1,181.8 | 1,182.6 | 1,165.9 |
| 2015 | 1,156.5 | 1,158.6 | 1,164.7 | 1,186.9 | 1,198.2 | 1,202.1 | 1,205.9 | 1,205.5 | 1,198.7 | 1,207.1 | 1,208.7 | 1,209.5 | 1,191.9 |
| 2016 | 1,177.4 | 1,182.5 | 1,190.1 | 1,211.6 | 1,215.9 | 1,220.6 | 1,221.1 | 1,222.0 | 1,216.2 | 1,222.0 | 1,221.1 | 1,217.3 | 1,209.8 |
| 2017 | 1,193.8 | 1,202.8 | 1,207.9 | 1,225.1 | 1,231.8 | 1,239.6 | 1,238.6 | 1,240.8 | 1,232.4 | 1,235.2 | 1,238.9 | 1,237.6 | 1,227.0 |
| 2018 | 1,208.6 | 1,215.0 | 1,221.3 | 1,232.1 | 1,239.6 | 1,245.2 | 1,246.9 | 1,245.7 | 1,235.8 | 1,241.5 | 1,242.8 | 1,241.1 | 1,234.6 |
| 2019 | 1,215.6 | 1,219.4 | 1,224.5 | 1,242.4 | 1,246.3 | 1,248.3 | 1,256.3 | 1,254.2 | 1,244.4 | 1,248.3 | 1,248.5 | 1,242.1 | 1,240.9 |
| **Goods Producing** | | | | | | | | | | | | | |
| 2011 | 165.3 | 165.4 | 169.3 | 172.6 | 173.9 | 176.2 | 177.1 | 176.2 | 174.0 | 171.7 | 169.3 | 168.2 | 171.6 |
| 2012 | 162.2 | 161.8 | 164.4 | 166.6 | 168.6 | 170.8 | 171.4 | 171.3 | 169.4 | 169.2 | 167.5 | 167.0 | 167.5 |
| 2013 | 162.3 | 162.9 | 163.8 | 166.5 | 169.4 | 173.0 | 173.4 | 173.0 | 171.8 | 171.5 | 169.9 | 168.0 | 168.8 |
| 2014 | 161.5 | 163.4 | 166.7 | 170.1 | 172.6 | 175.4 | 176.6 | 176.5 | 176.1 | 176.0 | 174.1 | 173.4 | 171.9 |
| 2015 | 168.4 | 168.3 | 170.5 | 174.3 | 177.2 | 179.4 | 180.7 | 180.7 | 180.2 | 180.5 | 178.6 | 179.3 | 176.5 |
| 2016 | 173.9 | 173.4 | 175.9 | 178.9 | 179.9 | 183.2 | 183.1 | 182.8 | 182.4 | 183.3 | 182.6 | 181.7 | 180.1 |
| 2017 | 176.2 | 177.9 | 178.6 | 180.1 | 181.6 | 184.8 | 184.2 | 184.5 | 183.3 | 182.9 | 182.0 | 182.4 | 181.5 |
| 2018 | 176.1 | 178.3 | 180.4 | 181.6 | 183.9 | 186.8 | 186.7 | 186.6 | 186.5 | 186.6 | 184.6 | 185.7 | 183.7 |
| 2019 | 181.9 | 182.1 | 184.5 | 187.4 | 188.8 | 191.2 | 192.3 | 191.8 | 190.2 | 186.8 | 187.8 | 186.2 | 187.6 |
| **Service-Providing** | | | | | | | | | | | | | |
| 2011 | 1,105.5 | 1,108.1 | 1,117.2 | 1,135.0 | 1,138.9 | 1,132.6 | 1,112.3 | 1,121.7 | 1,132.1 | 1,135.5 | 1,136.5 | 1,138.0 | 1,126.1 |
| 2012 | 1,112.2 | 1,118.1 | 1,127.7 | 1,137.9 | 1,143.9 | 1,138.3 | 1,113.7 | 1,122.9 | 1,132.6 | 1,139.6 | 1,141.7 | 1,144.2 | 1,131.1 |
| 2013 | 1,118.1 | 1,124.4 | 1,130.5 | 1,145.0 | 1,152.4 | 1,144.8 | 1,123.9 | 1,133.7 | 1,143.5 | 1,149.9 | 1,152.2 | 1,155.7 | 1,139.5 |
| 2014 | 1,124.8 | 1,133.2 | 1,139.0 | 1,160.2 | 1,165.5 | 1,158.1 | 1,136.8 | 1,147.4 | 1,154.2 | 1,169.0 | 1,169.7 | 1,171.5 | 1,152.5 |
| 2015 | 1,145.4 | 1,151.2 | 1,155.3 | 1,174.0 | 1,183.4 | 1,180.2 | 1,161.8 | 1,169.8 | 1,179.1 | 1,190.3 | 1,193.5 | 1,193.8 | 1,173.2 |
| 2016 | 1,161.4 | 1,170.5 | 1,175.8 | 1,194.7 | 1,199.4 | 1,195.9 | 1,175.1 | 1,185.0 | 1,195.4 | 1,201.2 | 1,201.1 | 1,198.5 | 1,187.8 |
| 2017 | 1,174.8 | 1,185.3 | 1,189.6 | 1,205.0 | 1,210.6 | 1,212.3 | 1,190.6 | 1,196.6 | 1,204.8 | 1,209.0 | 1,212.9 | 1,210.7 | 1,200.2 |
| 2018 | 1,182.8 | 1,190.1 | 1,194.2 | 1,203.9 | 1,209.2 | 1,209.3 | 1,190.9 | 1,198.2 | 1,203.7 | 1,210.6 | 1,214.8 | 1,211.5 | 1,201.6 |
| 2019 | 1,184.9 | 1,191.5 | 1,194.8 | 1,210.0 | 1,213.3 | 1,210.6 | 1,196.6 | 1,204.0 | 1,211.7 | 1,220.6 | 1,219.3 | 1,214.1 | 1,206.0 |
| **Mining, Logging, and Construction** | | | | | | | | | | | | | |
| 2011 | 56.5 | 56.5 | 59.8 | 62.9 | 63.9 | 65.2 | 65.4 | 64.7 | 62.7 | 60.5 | 58.6 | 57.0 | 61.1 |
| 2012 | 51.9 | 51.4 | 53.5 | 55.7 | 57.3 | 58.8 | 59.6 | 60.0 | 59.5 | 58.9 | 57.5 | 56.9 | 56.8 |
| 2013 | 52.3 | 52.4 | 53.6 | 56.4 | 59.0 | 61.7 | 62.9 | 62.2 | 61.3 | 60.6 | 59.1 | 57.1 | 58.2 |
| 2014 | 52.9 | 52.1 | 55.8 | 58.3 | 59.8 | 61.4 | 62.5 | 62.5 | 62.4 | 62.2 | 60.5 | 59.6 | 59.2 |
| 2015 | 55.5 | 55.3 | 57.4 | 60.8 | 63.0 | 64.0 | 64.8 | 65.6 | 65.4 | 66.1 | 64.4 | 64.7 | 62.3 |
| 2016 | 60.9 | 59.4 | 62.1 | 65.1 | 66.0 | 68.3 | 68.1 | 68.1 | 68.0 | 68.4 | 67.9 | 66.9 | 65.8 |
| 2017 | 62.8 | 63.6 | 64.6 | 65.8 | 67.0 | 68.8 | 68.8 | 68.9 | 68.2 | 68.0 | 67.1 | 66.7 | 66.7 |
| 2018 | 61.1 | 62.3 | 64.7 | 65.7 | 67.6 | 69.3 | 69.5 | 69.4 | 69.3 | 68.6 | 66.6 | 67.2 | 66.8 |
| 2019 | 64.0 | 63.0 | 65.7 | 68.7 | 69.4 | 70.6 | 71.5 | 71.2 | 70.6 | 70.4 | 68.2 | 67.3 | 68.4 |
| **Manufacturing** | | | | | | | | | | | | | |
| 2011 | 108.8 | 108.9 | 109.5 | 109.7 | 110.0 | 111.0 | 111.7 | 111.5 | 111.3 | 111.2 | 110.7 | 111.2 | 110.5 |
| 2012 | 110.3 | 110.4 | 110.9 | 110.9 | 111.3 | 112.0 | 111.8 | 111.3 | 109.9 | 110.3 | 110.0 | 110.1 | 110.8 |
| 2013 | 110.0 | 110.5 | 110.2 | 110.1 | 110.4 | 111.3 | 110.5 | 110.8 | 110.5 | 110.9 | 110.8 | 110.9 | 110.6 |
| 2014 | 108.6 | 111.3 | 110.9 | 111.8 | 112.8 | 114.0 | 114.1 | 114.0 | 113.7 | 113.8 | 113.6 | 113.8 | 112.7 |
| 2015 | 112.9 | 113.0 | 113.1 | 113.5 | 114.2 | 115.4 | 115.9 | 115.1 | 114.8 | 114.4 | 114.2 | 114.6 | 114.3 |
| 2016 | 113.0 | 114.0 | 113.8 | 113.8 | 113.9 | 114.9 | 115.0 | 114.7 | 114.4 | 114.9 | 114.7 | 114.8 | 114.3 |
| 2017 | 113.4 | 114.3 | 114.0 | 114.3 | 114.6 | 116.0 | 115.4 | 115.6 | 115.1 | 114.9 | 114.9 | 115.7 | 114.9 |
| 2018 | 115.0 | 116.0 | 115.7 | 115.9 | 116.3 | 117.5 | 117.2 | 117.2 | 117.2 | 118.0 | 118.0 | 118.5 | 116.9 |
| 2019 | 117.9 | 119.1 | 118.8 | 118.7 | 119.4 | 120.6 | 120.8 | 120.6 | 119.6 | 116.4 | 119.6 | 118.9 | 119.2 |

## Employment by Industry: St. Louis, MO, 2011–2019—*Continued*

(Numbers in thousands, not seasonally adjusted)

| Industry and year | January | February | March | April | May | June | July | August | September | October | November | December | Annual average |
|---|---|---|---|---|---|---|---|---|---|---|---|---|---|
| **Trade, Transportation, and Utilities** | | | | | | | | | | | | | |
| 2011 | 239.5 | 237.7 | 239.0 | 241.8 | 242.8 | 242.7 | 241.8 | 242.7 | 241.6 | 242.0 | 246.6 | 248.8 | 242.3 |
| 2012 | 240.6 | 238.5 | 240.0 | 242.0 | 243.5 | 243.4 | 242.5 | 243.7 | 243.4 | 245.3 | 250.6 | 252.4 | 243.8 |
| 2013 | 242.5 | 239.8 | 240.2 | 242.5 | 244.2 | 244.5 | 243.8 | 245.4 | 244.6 | 246.8 | 252.0 | 255.3 | 245.1 |
| 2014 | 244.7 | 242.7 | 244.1 | 246.6 | 248.3 | 249.6 | 248.1 | 249.4 | 248.5 | 251.1 | 256.6 | 259.7 | 249.1 |
| 2015 | 249.1 | 246.7 | 248.0 | 249.8 | 251.9 | 252.5 | 252.3 | 253.3 | 252.5 | 254.6 | 259.6 | 262.5 | 252.7 |
| 2016 | 252.5 | 250.9 | 251.7 | 253.9 | 255.0 | 254.4 | 255.2 | 254.4 | 253.7 | 254.6 | 259.4 | 262.1 | 254.8 |
| 2017 | 253.3 | 251.7 | 252.5 | 255.3 | 256.2 | 256.8 | 258.1 | 259.2 | 259.8 | 260.5 | 266.9 | 269.5 | 258.3 |
| 2018 | 259.8 | 257.6 | 258.1 | 258.4 | 260.1 | 259.8 | 259.6 | 259.6 | 258.7 | 260.2 | 266.1 | 267.3 | 260.4 |
| 2019 | 258.1 | 255.0 | 255.1 | 254.9 | 255.7 | 256.1 | 257.1 | 257.9 | 257.4 | 259.6 | 266.5 | 268.6 | 258.5 |
| **Wholesale Trade** | | | | | | | | | | | | | |
| 2011 | 58.6 | 58.6 | 58.7 | 59.0 | 59.1 | 59.5 | 59.8 | 59.7 | 59.4 | 59.4 | 59.5 | 59.5 | 59.2 |
| 2012 | 59.1 | 59.2 | 59.5 | 60.1 | 60.4 | 60.8 | 60.6 | 60.9 | 60.4 | 60.5 | 60.4 | 60.6 | 60.2 |
| 2013 | 59.5 | 59.4 | 59.5 | 59.8 | 60.3 | 60.6 | 60.6 | 60.7 | 60.5 | 60.9 | 61.1 | 61.3 | 60.4 |
| 2014 | 60.5 | 60.6 | 60.8 | 61.2 | 61.5 | 61.9 | 62.1 | 62.1 | 61.5 | 61.6 | 61.8 | 61.9 | 61.5 |
| 2015 | 60.8 | 60.6 | 60.8 | 60.4 | 60.9 | 61.1 | 62.0 | 61.3 | 60.9 | 61.0 | 61.1 | 61.2 | 61.0 |
| 2016 | 60.6 | 60.5 | 60.3 | 60.9 | 61.0 | 61.3 | 62.1 | 61.2 | 61.6 | 60.6 | 60.7 | 60.8 | 61.0 |
| 2017 | 60.5 | 60.7 | 60.7 | 60.8 | 61.2 | 61.7 | 62.1 | 61.6 | 62.0 | 62.2 | 62.6 | 63.2 | 61.6 |
| 2018 | 62.3 | 62.3 | 62.4 | 62.8 | 63.1 | 63.4 | 63.8 | 63.3 | 63.3 | 63.7 | 64.2 | 64.4 | 63.3 |
| 2019 | 63.6 | 63.6 | 63.4 | 63.6 | 63.9 | 64.5 | 65.3 | 65.1 | 65.0 | 64.8 | 64.6 | 64.7 | 64.3 |
| **Retail Trade** | | | | | | | | | | | | | |
| 2011 | 136.7 | 134.8 | 135.7 | 137.7 | 138.3 | 138.9 | 138.6 | 138.4 | 137.0 | 137.5 | 141.9 | 143.4 | 138.2 |
| 2012 | 137.2 | 134.9 | 136.0 | 136.9 | 137.6 | 138.3 | 137.9 | 137.2 | 136.9 | 138.7 | 143.7 | 144.5 | 138.3 |
| 2013 | 137.7 | 135.3 | 135.4 | 137.0 | 138.1 | 139.3 | 138.7 | 138.8 | 137.8 | 139.7 | 144.2 | 146.4 | 139.0 |
| 2014 | 138.2 | 136.2 | 137.3 | 138.9 | 139.9 | 141.6 | 140.7 | 140.6 | 139.4 | 141.4 | 146.2 | 147.9 | 140.7 |
| 2015 | 140.2 | 138.3 | 139.3 | 141.0 | 142.2 | 143.7 | 142.9 | 143.4 | 142.2 | 144.3 | 148.4 | 150.0 | 143.0 |
| 2016 | 142.6 | 141.4 | 142.1 | 143.3 | 144.1 | 144.5 | 144.6 | 143.7 | 141.9 | 143.6 | 147.7 | 148.9 | 144.0 |
| 2017 | 142.6 | 140.9 | 141.8 | 142.7 | 142.9 | 143.7 | 143.6 | 143.1 | 141.3 | 142.7 | 147.2 | 148.1 | 143.4 |
| 2018 | 141.8 | 140.0 | 140.5 | 141.0 | 142.2 | 142.3 | 142.3 | 141.7 | 140.2 | 140.6 | 144.5 | 144.5 | 141.8 |
| 2019 | 138.2 | 136.0 | 136.1 | 136.0 | 136.4 | 136.7 | 136.5 | 134.9 | 133.6 | 136.0 | 142.0 | 141.8 | 137.0 |
| **Transportation and Utilities** | | | | | | | | | | | | | |
| 2011 | 44.2 | 44.3 | 44.6 | 45.1 | 45.4 | 44.3 | 43.4 | 44.6 | 45.2 | 45.1 | 45.2 | 45.9 | 44.8 |
| 2012 | 44.3 | 44.4 | 44.5 | 45.0 | 45.5 | 44.3 | 44.0 | 45.6 | 46.1 | 46.1 | 46.5 | 47.3 | 45.3 |
| 2013 | 45.3 | 45.1 | 45.3 | 45.7 | 45.8 | 44.6 | 44.5 | 45.9 | 46.3 | 46.2 | 46.7 | 47.6 | 45.8 |
| 2014 | 46.0 | 45.9 | 46.0 | 46.5 | 46.9 | 46.1 | 45.3 | 46.7 | 47.6 | 48.1 | 48.6 | 49.9 | 47.0 |
| 2015 | 48.1 | 47.8 | 47.9 | 48.4 | 48.8 | 47.7 | 47.4 | 48.6 | 49.4 | 49.3 | 50.1 | 51.3 | 48.7 |
| 2016 | 49.3 | 49.0 | 49.3 | 49.7 | 49.9 | 48.6 | 48.5 | 49.5 | 50.2 | 50.4 | 51.0 | 52.4 | 49.8 |
| 2017 | 50.2 | 50.1 | 50.0 | 51.8 | 52.1 | 51.4 | 52.4 | 54.5 | 56.5 | 55.6 | 57.1 | 58.2 | 53.3 |
| 2018 | 55.7 | 55.3 | 55.2 | 54.6 | 54.8 | 54.1 | 53.5 | 54.6 | 55.2 | 55.9 | 57.4 | 58.4 | 55.4 |
| 2019 | 56.3 | 55.4 | 55.6 | 55.3 | 55.4 | 54.9 | 55.3 | 57.9 | 58.8 | 58.8 | 59.9 | 62.1 | 57.1 |
| **Information** | | | | | | | | | | | | | |
| 2011 | 30.4 | 30.3 | 30.1 | 30.9 | 31.1 | 31.3 | 31.6 | 31.5 | 31.3 | 30.9 | 30.9 | 30.8 | 30.9 |
| 2012 | 30.6 | 30.5 | 30.4 | 30.0 | 30.2 | 30.2 | 30.3 | 30.1 | 29.7 | 29.3 | 29.2 | 29.2 | 30.0 |
| 2013 | 29.1 | 29.2 | 29.2 | 29.1 | 29.4 | 29.4 | 29.3 | 29.2 | 28.9 | 28.8 | 28.7 | 28.9 | 29.1 |
| 2014 | 28.2 | 28.1 | 28.3 | 28.6 | 28.9 | 29.2 | 29.3 | 29.2 | 28.9 | 28.6 | 28.7 | 28.7 | 28.7 |
| 2015 | 28.6 | 28.6 | 28.6 | 28.7 | 28.8 | 29.0 | 29.0 | 28.9 | 28.5 | 28.4 | 28.4 | 28.6 | 28.7 |
| 2016 | 28.5 | 28.4 | 28.5 | 28.6 | 28.8 | 28.9 | 28.8 | 28.8 | 28.6 | 28.3 | 28.2 | 28.2 | 28.6 |
| 2017 | 28.1 | 27.9 | 27.9 | 27.9 | 28.2 | 28.3 | 28.4 | 28.4 | 28.0 | 27.7 | 27.5 | 27.6 | 28.0 |
| 2018 | 27.4 | 27.4 | 27.3 | 27.3 | 27.6 | 27.7 | 27.7 | 27.4 | 27.2 | 27.2 | 27.3 | 27.3 | 27.4 |
| 2019 | 27.2 | 27.3 | 27.2 | 27.2 | 27.2 | 27.4 | 27.4 | 27.2 | 26.8 | 27.0 | 26.8 | 26.4 | 27.1 |
| **Financial Activities** | | | | | | | | | | | | | |
| 2011 | 82.6 | 82.6 | 82.7 | 84.0 | 84.3 | 84.2 | 85.1 | 85.2 | 84.8 | 85.4 | 85.6 | 85.6 | 84.3 |
| 2012 | 85.0 | 85.4 | 86.0 | 86.5 | 86.8 | 87.2 | 87.4 | 87.5 | 87.2 | 88.1 | 88.5 | 88.3 | 87.0 |
| 2013 | 86.3 | 86.6 | 86.8 | 87.0 | 87.8 | 88.3 | 88.4 | 88.3 | 87.8 | 88.2 | 88.3 | 88.0 | 87.7 |
| 2014 | 87.0 | 87.2 | 87.1 | 87.5 | 87.9 | 88.0 | 88.4 | 88.3 | 87.6 | 88.0 | 88.3 | 88.3 | 87.8 |
| 2015 | 87.3 | 87.2 | 87.4 | 87.9 | 88.4 | 88.9 | 89.4 | 89.2 | 88.3 | 88.8 | 89.1 | 89.2 | 88.4 |
| 2016 | 87.8 | 87.9 | 87.9 | 88.2 | 88.5 | 88.9 | 89.2 | 89.1 | 88.8 | 89.3 | 89.3 | 89.5 | 88.7 |
| 2017 | 89.2 | 89.4 | 89.8 | 90.1 | 90.6 | 91.3 | 91.5 | 91.4 | 90.8 | 90.8 | 90.5 | 90.7 | 90.5 |
| 2018 | 90.8 | 90.9 | 90.7 | 90.6 | 90.9 | 91.5 | 91.6 | 91.4 | 91.0 | 91.8 | 92.2 | 92.1 | 91.3 |
| 2019 | 91.8 | 92.0 | 92.4 | 92.9 | 93.0 | 93.6 | 94.0 | 93.8 | 92.6 | 93.2 | 93.3 | 92.9 | 93.0 |

## Employment by Industry: St. Louis, MO, 2011–2019—*Continued*

(Numbers in thousands, not seasonally adjusted)

| Industry and year | January | February | March | April | May | June | July | August | September | October | November | December | Annual average |
|---|---|---|---|---|---|---|---|---|---|---|---|---|---|
| **Professional and Business Services** | | | | | | | | | | | | | |
| 2011 | 187.1 | 187.9 | 190.0 | 194.2 | 192.6 | 192.9 | 192.6 | 192.2 | 191.4 | 191.7 | 191.5 | 190.8 | 191.2 |
| 2012 | 186.4 | 187.2 | 189.1 | 193.3 | 192.8 | 193.9 | 191.6 | 191.5 | 190.7 | 192.3 | 192.9 | 193.0 | 191.2 |
| 2013 | 189.5 | 191.3 | 194.1 | 197.8 | 198.3 | 199.0 | 200.0 | 201.1 | 200.4 | 201.7 | 202.0 | 202.7 | 198.2 |
| 2014 | 197.0 | 198.9 | 201.0 | 206.1 | 204.9 | 205.6 | 203.3 | 204.5 | 204.3 | 206.2 | 205.7 | 206.0 | 203.6 |
| 2015 | 200.7 | 202.1 | 203.5 | 207.0 | 208.0 | 207.5 | 208.9 | 209.6 | 209.1 | 210.1 | 210.8 | 210.7 | 207.3 |
| 2016 | 205.3 | 207.3 | 208.4 | 213.6 | 212.8 | 213.2 | 212.1 | 213.1 | 212.2 | 213.5 | 212.6 | 210.7 | 211.2 |
| 2017 | 207.0 | 209.0 | 210.9 | 213.6 | 212.9 | 214.7 | 213.8 | 214.7 | 213.4 | 214.1 | 215.2 | 212.3 | 212.6 |
| 2018 | 208.9 | 210.3 | 212.1 | 214.1 | 213.4 | 215.4 | 215.8 | 216.4 | 214.3 | 214.3 | 213.7 | 211.4 | 213.3 |
| 2019 | 207.7 | 208.7 | 209.7 | 213.5 | 212.4 | 213.0 | 214.4 | 215.0 | 213.9 | 216.0 | 212.6 | 210.2 | 212.3 |
| **Education and Health Services** | | | | | | | | | | | | | |
| 2011 | 227.4 | 229.9 | 230.3 | 231.7 | 231.3 | 229.7 | 229.6 | 229.7 | 232.9 | 235.1 | 236.6 | 236.6 | 231.7 |
| 2012 | 234.3 | 237.4 | 237.7 | 234.1 | 233.0 | 230.8 | 230.7 | 230.4 | 233.6 | 235.6 | 235.6 | 236.1 | 234.1 |
| 2013 | 233.1 | 236.8 | 236.0 | 232.9 | 230.9 | 227.6 | 228.0 | 227.7 | 229.9 | 232.4 | 233.0 | 232.1 | 231.7 |
| 2014 | 229.3 | 233.9 | 231.6 | 236.6 | 234.2 | 230.6 | 232.9 | 232.7 | 234.6 | 239.6 | 240.3 | 238.2 | 234.5 |
| 2015 | 238.1 | 240.5 | 238.5 | 244.7 | 243.1 | 240.5 | 242.6 | 241.5 | 243.0 | 248.1 | 248.4 | 246.2 | 242.9 |
| 2016 | 242.9 | 247.3 | 246.3 | 249.7 | 247.7 | 244.1 | 246.6 | 247.3 | 249.0 | 252.8 | 252.8 | 250.5 | 248.1 |
| 2017 | 248.7 | 253.1 | 250.9 | 256.0 | 255.0 | 250.9 | 251.8 | 251.9 | 253.4 | 257.3 | 257.7 | 256.4 | 253.6 |
| 2018 | 251.5 | 256.2 | 253.7 | 257.3 | 255.3 | 250.7 | 253.5 | 252.7 | 253.8 | 259.3 | 259.2 | 257.3 | 255.0 |
| 2019 | 254.8 | 259.2 | 256.8 | 260.9 | 259.3 | 254.6 | 257.8 | 257.7 | 259.3 | 264.1 | 262.4 | 260.3 | 258.9 |
| **Leisure and Hospitality** | | | | | | | | | | | | | |
| 2011 | 127.7 | 127.2 | 131.3 | 136.4 | 140.0 | 143.0 | 142.9 | 143.5 | 137.0 | 137.3 | 132.3 | 132.2 | 135.9 |
| 2012 | 127.4 | 128.3 | 132.4 | 139.0 | 143.2 | 146.5 | 145.5 | 145.7 | 139.2 | 139.1 | 135.2 | 135.3 | 138.1 |
| 2013 | 131.8 | 131.9 | 134.5 | 141.5 | 146.4 | 148.4 | 148.3 | 147.3 | 142.3 | 140.9 | 136.6 | 136.8 | 140.6 |
| 2014 | 131.7 | 131.9 | 135.2 | 143.5 | 148.9 | 150.4 | 150.6 | 151.2 | 143.9 | 145.6 | 141.4 | 141.4 | 143.0 |
| 2015 | 137.7 | 138.3 | 140.8 | 146.9 | 153.0 | 155.6 | 154.6 | 154.4 | 150.0 | 149.1 | 146.4 | 145.4 | 147.7 |
| 2016 | 139.5 | 140.2 | 144.1 | 150.8 | 154.8 | 158.0 | 156.0 | 156.3 | 152.0 | 150.3 | 146.0 | 144.2 | 149.4 |
| 2017 | 141.0 | 143.1 | 145.9 | 150.5 | 155.6 | 160.0 | 158.1 | 158.3 | 152.4 | 150.7 | 148.2 | 147.5 | 150.9 |
| 2018 | 143.6 | 143.9 | 148.0 | 151.9 | 157.3 | 161.1 | 159.9 | 159.8 | 153.6 | 151.2 | 149.0 | 149.1 | 152.4 |
| 2019 | 143.8 | 144.8 | 148.1 | 154.4 | 158.5 | 160.0 | 160.9 | 158.9 | 153.3 | 150.8 | 148.1 | 145.8 | 152.3 |
| **Other Services** | | | | | | | | | | | | | |
| 2011 | 44.4 | 44.4 | 45.0 | 46.0 | 46.1 | 46.8 | 46.8 | 46.5 | 46.1 | 45.8 | 45.7 | 45.8 | 45.8 |
| 2012 | 45.0 | 45.1 | 45.5 | 45.4 | 45.9 | 46.3 | 46.2 | 46.0 | 45.3 | 45.3 | 45.2 | 45.1 | 45.5 |
| 2013 | 45.4 | 45.4 | 45.6 | 45.5 | 46.1 | 46.8 | 46.5 | 46.6 | 45.7 | 46.1 | 46.1 | 46.2 | 46.0 |
| 2014 | 45.8 | 46.1 | 46.7 | 47.3 | 47.7 | 48.4 | 48.5 | 48.1 | 47.1 | 47.1 | 46.7 | 46.9 | 47.2 |
| 2015 | 46.6 | 46.9 | 47.4 | 47.6 | 47.8 | 48.7 | 48.4 | 47.9 | 47.1 | 47.5 | 47.4 | 47.6 | 47.6 |
| 2016 | 47.0 | 47.1 | 47.3 | 47.9 | 48.4 | 49.9 | 50.1 | 50.2 | 49.5 | 49.9 | 50.2 | 50.4 | 49.0 |
| 2017 | 50.3 | 50.7 | 51.4 | 51.6 | 51.7 | 52.8 | 52.7 | 52.4 | 51.3 | 51.2 | 50.9 | 51.2 | 51.5 |
| 2018 | 50.5 | 50.4 | 51.0 | 50.9 | 51.1 | 52.2 | 52.1 | 51.8 | 50.7 | 50.9 | 50.7 | 50.9 | 51.1 |
| 2019 | 50.3 | 50.3 | 50.7 | 51.2 | 51.4 | 52.4 | 52.4 | 51.9 | 50.9 | 50.8 | 51.0 | 51.7 | 51.3 |
| **Government** | | | | | | | | | | | | | |
| 2011 | 166.4 | 168.1 | 168.8 | 170.0 | 170.7 | 162.0 | 141.9 | 150.4 | 167.0 | 167.3 | 167.3 | 167.4 | 163.9 |
| 2012 | 162.9 | 165.7 | 166.6 | 167.6 | 168.5 | 160.0 | 139.5 | 148.0 | 163.5 | 164.6 | 164.5 | 164.8 | 161.4 |
| 2013 | 160.4 | 163.4 | 164.1 | 168.7 | 169.3 | 160.8 | 139.6 | 148.1 | 163.9 | 165.0 | 165.5 | 165.7 | 161.2 |
| 2014 | 161.1 | 164.4 | 165.0 | 164.0 | 164.7 | 156.3 | 135.7 | 144.0 | 159.3 | 162.8 | 162.0 | 162.3 | 158.5 |
| 2015 | 157.3 | 160.9 | 161.1 | 161.4 | 162.4 | 157.5 | 136.6 | 145.0 | 160.6 | 163.7 | 163.4 | 163.6 | 157.8 |
| 2016 | 157.9 | 161.4 | 161.6 | 162.0 | 163.4 | 158.5 | 137.1 | 145.8 | 161.6 | 162.5 | 162.6 | 162.9 | 158.1 |
| 2017 | 157.2 | 160.4 | 160.3 | 160.0 | 160.4 | 157.5 | 136.2 | 140.3 | 155.7 | 156.7 | 156.0 | 155.5 | 154.7 |
| 2018 | 150.3 | 153.4 | 153.3 | 153.4 | 153.5 | 150.9 | 130.7 | 139.1 | 154.4 | 155.7 | 156.6 | 156.1 | 150.6 |
| 2019 | 151.2 | 154.2 | 154.8 | 155.0 | 155.8 | 153.5 | 132.6 | 141.6 | 157.5 | 159.1 | 158.6 | 158.2 | 152.7 |

## Employment by Industry: Baltimore-Columbia-Towson, MD, 2011–2019

(Numbers in thousands, not seasonally adjusted)

| Industry and year | January | February | March | April | May | June | July | August | September | October | November | December | Annual average |
|---|---|---|---|---|---|---|---|---|---|---|---|---|---|
| **Total Nonfarm** | | | | | | | | | | | | | |
| 2011 | 1,255.6 | 1,263.9 | 1,277.8 | 1,295.0 | 1,300.5 | 1,302.3 | 1,295.7 | 1,294.8 | 1,301.2 | 1,308.8 | 1,314.0 | 1,316.8 | 1,293.9 |
| 2012 | 1,284.2 | 1,290.3 | 1,302.9 | 1,311.6 | 1,320.1 | 1,323.0 | 1,312.2 | 1,313.3 | 1,321.3 | 1,328.2 | 1,333.8 | 1,336.6 | 1,314.8 |
| 2013 | 1,303.7 | 1,310.8 | 1,323.1 | 1,331.2 | 1,340.7 | 1,344.6 | 1,333.3 | 1,332.6 | 1,337.5 | 1,341.8 | 1,349.4 | 1,345.6 | 1,332.9 |
| 2014 | 1,305.6 | 1,309.8 | 1,322.0 | 1,342.0 | 1,351.8 | 1,354.1 | 1,342.1 | 1,346.1 | 1,351.5 | 1,359.0 | 1,364.9 | 1,365.4 | 1,342.9 |
| 2015 | 1,325.5 | 1,331.8 | 1,340.0 | 1,360.9 | 1,373.8 | 1,374.2 | 1,371.9 | 1,370.9 | 1,371.3 | 1,386.9 | 1,392.1 | 1,394.5 | 1,366.2 |
| 2016 | 1,352.3 | 1,355.8 | 1,367.4 | 1,385.7 | 1,393.0 | 1,393.6 | 1,386.8 | 1,387.3 | 1,393.1 | 1,399.9 | 1,407.9 | 1,407.8 | 1,385.9 |
| 2017 | 1,366.6 | 1,373.8 | 1,381.9 | 1,394.9 | 1,405.3 | 1,410.0 | 1,405.0 | 1,403.8 | 1,407.1 | 1,415.7 | 1,423.4 | 1,421.0 | 1,400.7 |
| 2018 | 1,385.5 | 1,394.5 | 1,403.6 | 1,413.4 | 1,423.6 | 1,428.9 | 1,420.3 | 1,420.2 | 1,423.0 | 1,428.2 | 1,436.0 | 1,430.7 | 1,417.3 |
| 2019 | 1,401.8 | 1,408.2 | 1,415.6 | 1,424.6 | 1,433.3 | 1,437.5 | 1,426.1 | 1,425.6 | 1,421.6 | 1,432.2 | 1,443.2 | 1,446.3 | 1,426.3 |
| **Total Private** | | | | | | | | | | | | | |
| 2011 | 1,026.0 | 1,028.2 | 1,038.6 | 1,054.8 | 1,062.2 | 1,068.8 | 1,071.7 | 1,070.1 | 1,069.1 | 1,068.9 | 1,075.3 | 1,077.7 | 1,059.3 |
| 2012 | 1,055.6 | 1,055.1 | 1,064.9 | 1,074.4 | 1,084.4 | 1,094.5 | 1,091.5 | 1,093.6 | 1,092.7 | 1,091.9 | 1,097.5 | 1,100.8 | 1,083.1 |
| 2013 | 1,075.7 | 1,077.2 | 1,087.2 | 1,095.7 | 1,105.7 | 1,115.1 | 1,113.6 | 1,113.8 | 1,110.3 | 1,109.8 | 1,115.4 | 1,113.1 | 1,102.7 |
| 2014 | 1,081.4 | 1,079.1 | 1,089.6 | 1,107.5 | 1,120.0 | 1,126.9 | 1,125.6 | 1,128.4 | 1,124.9 | 1,126.5 | 1,130.9 | 1,133.1 | 1,114.5 |
| 2015 | 1,101.8 | 1,102.6 | 1,108.5 | 1,129.2 | 1,142.5 | 1,148.7 | 1,154.8 | 1,153.8 | 1,147.2 | 1,156.4 | 1,160.5 | 1,162.9 | 1,139.1 |
| 2016 | 1,129.9 | 1,128.5 | 1,137.5 | 1,154.6 | 1,162.0 | 1,168.3 | 1,170.4 | 1,171.3 | 1,169.0 | 1,170.7 | 1,177.8 | 1,176.9 | 1,159.7 |
| 2017 | 1,143.6 | 1,145.9 | 1,152.8 | 1,164.9 | 1,175.2 | 1,184.6 | 1,189.7 | 1,189.2 | 1,184.5 | 1,187.2 | 1,193.5 | 1,191.7 | 1,175.2 |
| 2018 | 1,163.2 | 1,166.2 | 1,173.9 | 1,183.2 | 1,193.0 | 1,201.8 | 1,203.7 | 1,202.1 | 1,195.5 | 1,197.8 | 1,204.4 | 1,199.2 | 1,190.3 |
| 2019 | 1,178.8 | 1,180.2 | 1,186.5 | 1,195.4 | 1,203.8 | 1,213.1 | 1,213.5 | 1,212.2 | 1,200.0 | 1,205.9 | 1,215.4 | 1,220.1 | 1,202.1 |
| **Goods Producing** | | | | | | | | | | | | | |
| 2011 | 128.7 | 128.2 | 129.5 | 132.1 | 132.8 | 134.2 | 134.9 | 134.6 | 133.0 | 132.5 | 132.0 | 131.6 | 132.0 |
| 2012 | 128.5 | 127.3 | 128.3 | 129.2 | 129.5 | 131.3 | 131.8 | 131.8 | 130.0 | 129.5 | 129.7 | 129.3 | 129.7 |
| 2013 | 125.9 | 125.1 | 126.0 | 127.9 | 128.6 | 130.2 | 130.9 | 131.1 | 130.1 | 129.4 | 129.1 | 127.4 | 128.5 |
| 2014 | 124.0 | 122.9 | 124.7 | 127.6 | 129.2 | 130.7 | 131.0 | 131.3 | 130.5 | 130.0 | 129.7 | 129.1 | 128.4 |
| 2015 | 125.3 | 124.6 | 125.6 | 128.2 | 129.9 | 131.7 | 133.3 | 133.7 | 133.0 | 133.4 | 132.7 | 132.6 | 130.3 |
| 2016 | 129.4 | 127.9 | 130.1 | 133.0 | 133.7 | 135.3 | 136.0 | 136.0 | 135.0 | 134.4 | 134.2 | 133.7 | 133.2 |
| 2017 | 130.3 | 130.7 | 131.5 | 133.0 | 134.3 | 136.6 | 137.0 | 137.5 | 136.6 | 136.7 | 137.0 | 137.0 | 134.9 |
| 2018 | 133.4 | 134.0 | 135.3 | 137.1 | 137.9 | 139.7 | 141.0 | 141.4 | 140.2 | 140.4 | 139.7 | 139.4 | 138.3 |
| 2019 | 137.3 | 136.9 | 138.3 | 139.3 | 140.3 | 142.1 | 143.3 | 143.6 | 142.1 | 142.6 | 142.1 | 142.3 | 140.9 |
| **Service-Providing** | | | | | | | | | | | | | |
| 2011 | 1,126.9 | 1,135.7 | 1,148.3 | 1,162.9 | 1,167.7 | 1,168.1 | 1,160.8 | 1,160.2 | 1,168.2 | 1,176.3 | 1,182.0 | 1,185.2 | 1,161.9 |
| 2012 | 1,155.7 | 1,163.0 | 1,174.6 | 1,182.4 | 1,190.6 | 1,191.7 | 1,180.4 | 1,181.5 | 1,191.3 | 1,198.7 | 1,204.1 | 1,207.3 | 1,185.1 |
| 2013 | 1,177.8 | 1,185.7 | 1,197.1 | 1,203.3 | 1,212.1 | 1,214.4 | 1,202.4 | 1,201.5 | 1,207.4 | 1,212.4 | 1,220.3 | 1,218.2 | 1,204.4 |
| 2014 | 1,181.6 | 1,186.9 | 1,197.3 | 1,214.4 | 1,222.6 | 1,223.4 | 1,211.1 | 1,214.8 | 1,221.0 | 1,229.0 | 1,235.2 | 1,236.3 | 1,214.5 |
| 2015 | 1,200.2 | 1,207.2 | 1,214.4 | 1,232.7 | 1,243.9 | 1,242.5 | 1,238.6 | 1,237.2 | 1,238.3 | 1,253.5 | 1,259.4 | 1,261.9 | 1,235.8 |
| 2016 | 1,222.9 | 1,227.9 | 1,237.3 | 1,252.7 | 1,259.3 | 1,258.3 | 1,250.8 | 1,251.3 | 1,258.1 | 1,265.5 | 1,273.7 | 1,274.1 | 1,252.7 |
| 2017 | 1,236.3 | 1,243.1 | 1,250.4 | 1,261.9 | 1,271.0 | 1,273.4 | 1,268.0 | 1,266.3 | 1,270.5 | 1,279.0 | 1,286.4 | 1,284.0 | 1,265.9 |
| 2018 | 1,252.1 | 1,260.5 | 1,268.3 | 1,276.3 | 1,285.7 | 1,289.2 | 1,279.3 | 1,278.8 | 1,282.8 | 1,287.8 | 1,296.3 | 1,291.3 | 1,279.0 |
| 2019 | 1,264.5 | 1,271.3 | 1,277.3 | 1,285.3 | 1,293.0 | 1,295.4 | 1,282.8 | 1,282.0 | 1,279.5 | 1,289.6 | 1,301.1 | 1,304.0 | 1,285.5 |
| **Mining, Logging, and Construction** | | | | | | | | | | | | | |
| 2011 | 64.8 | 64.3 | 65.5 | 67.7 | 68.5 | 69.8 | 70.7 | 70.6 | 69.9 | 69.9 | 69.6 | 69.2 | 68.4 |
| 2012 | 66.4 | 65.6 | 66.7 | 67.8 | 68.2 | 69.4 | 69.9 | 70.1 | 69.9 | 69.7 | 69.9 | 69.5 | 68.6 |
| 2013 | 66.9 | 66.2 | 67.2 | 69.4 | 70.2 | 71.5 | 72.3 | 72.6 | 72.2 | 71.9 | 72.0 | 70.4 | 70.2 |
| 2014 | 68.0 | 67.1 | 68.8 | 71.4 | 73.0 | 74.2 | 74.7 | 75.0 | 74.5 | 74.0 | 73.7 | 73.2 | 72.3 |
| 2015 | 69.8 | 69.2 | 70.4 | 73.3 | 74.8 | 76.0 | 77.1 | 77.5 | 77.3 | 77.8 | 77.2 | 76.8 | 74.8 |
| 2016 | 74.3 | 72.9 | 75.0 | 77.4 | 77.9 | 79.1 | 79.7 | 79.5 | 78.9 | 78.4 | 78.2 | 77.6 | 77.4 |
| 2017 | 74.8 | 74.8 | 75.3 | 76.5 | 77.9 | 79.7 | 80.1 | 80.5 | 80.0 | 79.9 | 80.0 | 80.1 | 78.3 |
| 2018 | 76.8 | 77.5 | 78.8 | 80.0 | 80.8 | 82.0 | 82.8 | 82.8 | 81.9 | 81.9 | 81.3 | 80.8 | 80.6 |
| 2019 | 79.0 | 78.4 | 79.5 | 80.0 | 80.8 | 82.3 | 83.2 | 83.3 | 82.4 | 83.5 | 82.8 | 82.7 | 81.5 |
| **Manufacturing** | | | | | | | | | | | | | |
| 2011 | 63.9 | 63.9 | 64.0 | 64.4 | 64.3 | 64.4 | 64.2 | 64.0 | 63.1 | 62.6 | 62.4 | 62.4 | 63.6 |
| 2012 | 62.1 | 61.7 | 61.6 | 61.4 | 61.3 | 61.9 | 61.9 | 61.7 | 60.1 | 59.8 | 59.8 | 59.8 | 61.1 |
| 2013 | 59.0 | 58.9 | 58.8 | 58.5 | 58.4 | 58.7 | 58.6 | 58.5 | 57.9 | 57.5 | 57.1 | 57.0 | 58.2 |
| 2014 | 56.0 | 55.8 | 55.9 | 56.2 | 56.2 | 56.5 | 56.3 | 56.3 | 56.0 | 56.0 | 56.0 | 55.9 | 56.1 |
| 2015 | 55.5 | 55.4 | 55.2 | 54.9 | 55.1 | 55.7 | 56.2 | 56.2 | 55.7 | 55.6 | 55.5 | 55.8 | 55.6 |
| 2016 | 55.1 | 55.0 | 55.1 | 55.6 | 55.8 | 56.2 | 56.3 | 56.5 | 56.1 | 56.0 | 56.0 | 56.1 | 55.8 |
| 2017 | 55.5 | 55.9 | 56.2 | 56.5 | 56.4 | 56.9 | 56.9 | 57.0 | 56.6 | 56.8 | 57.0 | 56.9 | 56.6 |
| 2018 | 56.6 | 56.5 | 56.5 | 57.1 | 57.1 | 57.7 | 58.2 | 58.6 | 58.3 | 58.5 | 58.4 | 58.6 | 57.7 |
| 2019 | 58.3 | 58.5 | 58.8 | 59.3 | 59.5 | 59.8 | 60.1 | 60.3 | 59.7 | 59.1 | 59.3 | 59.6 | 59.4 |

## Employment by Industry: Baltimore-Columbia-Towson, MD, 2011–2019—*Continued*

(Numbers in thousands, not seasonally adjusted)

| Industry and year | January | February | March | April | May | June | July | August | September | October | November | December | Annual average |
|---|---|---|---|---|---|---|---|---|---|---|---|---|---|
| **Trade, Transportation, and Utilities** | | | | | | | | | | | | | |
| 2011 | 225.5 | 223.6 | 225.1 | 227.8 | 229.1 | 229.9 | 228.8 | 229.4 | 229.5 | 230.9 | 236.2 | 239.8 | 229.6 |
| 2012 | 230.1 | 227.5 | 229.5 | 230.5 | 232.1 | 232.8 | 230.9 | 230.9 | 232.2 | 233.2 | 238.9 | 241.8 | 232.5 |
| 2013 | 233.8 | 231.1 | 232.2 | 232.7 | 234.7 | 235.5 | 233.9 | 233.7 | 234.0 | 234.9 | 240.4 | 243.7 | 235.1 |
| 2014 | 232.4 | 228.6 | 230.6 | 232.7 | 234.5 | 236.1 | 235.0 | 235.5 | 235.6 | 238.2 | 244.9 | 248.7 | 236.1 |
| 2015 | 237.1 | 234.9 | 235.3 | 238.9 | 240.9 | 243.3 | 242.8 | 242.4 | 242.6 | 246.9 | 251.7 | 255.2 | 242.7 |
| 2016 | 243.7 | 241.3 | 242.3 | 244.6 | 245.5 | 246.4 | 244.8 | 245.6 | 246.0 | 247.5 | 253.4 | 255.5 | 246.4 |
| 2017 | 244.8 | 241.4 | 241.3 | 243.2 | 244.6 | 246.3 | 245.6 | 246.0 | 246.1 | 248.6 | 257.2 | 257.7 | 246.9 |
| 2018 | 246.1 | 243.2 | 243.2 | 243.9 | 245.1 | 246.8 | 244.8 | 244.5 | 244.5 | 247.3 | 253.9 | 254.3 | 246.5 |
| 2019 | 247.5 | 243.3 | 242.4 | 243.3 | 244.6 | 246.5 | 246.1 | 246.1 | 246.1 | 250.4 | 255.4 | 258.1 | 247.5 |
| **Wholesale Trade** | | | | | | | | | | | | | |
| 2011 | 50.3 | 50.5 | 50.7 | 51.1 | 51.3 | 51.4 | 51.4 | 51.3 | 51.1 | 50.9 | 50.8 | 50.9 | 51.0 |
| 2012 | 50.5 | 50.5 | 50.9 | 51.5 | 51.9 | 52.2 | 52.0 | 51.9 | 51.7 | 51.7 | 51.7 | 51.9 | 51.5 |
| 2013 | 51.2 | 51.4 | 51.5 | 51.8 | 51.9 | 52.0 | 51.5 | 51.3 | 51.2 | 50.7 | 50.8 | 50.9 | 51.4 |
| 2014 | 50.1 | 50.0 | 50.0 | 50.5 | 50.8 | 51.0 | 51.1 | 51.0 | 50.7 | 51.3 | 51.4 | 52.0 | 50.8 |
| 2015 | 51.2 | 51.2 | 51.2 | 51.8 | 51.9 | 52.1 | 52.3 | 52.1 | 51.9 | 52.3 | 52.2 | 52.2 | 51.9 |
| 2016 | 51.8 | 51.7 | 51.7 | 52.4 | 52.4 | 52.4 | 51.9 | 52.1 | 51.7 | 51.6 | 51.5 | 51.7 | 51.9 |
| 2017 | 51.3 | 51.2 | 51.4 | 51.8 | 52.0 | 52.5 | 52.4 | 52.4 | 52.2 | 52.4 | 52.4 | 52.7 | 52.1 |
| 2018 | 51.9 | 52.0 | 51.8 | 52.3 | 52.4 | 52.8 | 52.9 | 53.0 | 52.9 | 52.8 | 52.7 | 53.0 | 52.5 |
| 2019 | 53.4 | 53.3 | 53.5 | 53.9 | 53.8 | 54.0 | 53.9 | 53.8 | 53.5 | 54.7 | 54.9 | 54.7 | 54.0 |
| **Retail Trade** | | | | | | | | | | | | | |
| 2011 | 132.4 | 130.5 | 131.6 | 132.5 | 133.5 | 134.2 | 133.4 | 134.0 | 133.3 | 135.4 | 140.1 | 143.0 | 134.5 |
| 2012 | 135.1 | 132.5 | 134.0 | 133.9 | 134.9 | 135.2 | 134.5 | 134.6 | 134.5 | 135.7 | 140.5 | 142.4 | 135.7 |
| 2013 | 137.1 | 134.9 | 135.5 | 135.7 | 136.9 | 137.7 | 137.7 | 137.9 | 136.7 | 137.8 | 142.6 | 144.6 | 137.9 |
| 2014 | 136.7 | 134.1 | 135.2 | 136.4 | 137.2 | 138.4 | 138.4 | 138.7 | 137.5 | 139.1 | 143.6 | 146.1 | 138.5 |
| 2015 | 137.9 | 135.6 | 136.3 | 137.8 | 138.9 | 140.3 | 139.8 | 139.7 | 138.4 | 140.6 | 144.6 | 146.6 | 139.7 |
| 2016 | 139.8 | 137.5 | 138.7 | 138.4 | 139.2 | 140.0 | 139.1 | 139.6 | 138.3 | 139.3 | 143.1 | 144.9 | 139.8 |
| 2017 | 137.8 | 135.3 | 135.3 | 136.0 | 136.6 | 137.1 | 136.8 | 136.8 | 135.7 | 137.0 | 142.4 | 143.1 | 137.5 |
| 2018 | 135.4 | 133.1 | 133.4 | 133.9 | 135.0 | 135.6 | 135.7 | 135.7 | 134.4 | 135.3 | 140.3 | 141.8 | 135.8 |
| 2019 | 134.1 | 131.0 | 131.3 | 130.8 | 131.1 | 131.6 | 131.5 | 131.9 | 130.2 | 132.4 | 137.0 | 137.9 | 132.6 |
| **Transportation and Utilities** | | | | | | | | | | | | | |
| 2011 | 42.8 | 42.6 | 42.8 | 44.2 | 44.3 | 44.3 | 44.0 | 44.1 | 45.1 | 44.6 | 45.3 | 45.9 | 44.2 |
| 2012 | 44.5 | 44.5 | 44.6 | 45.1 | 45.3 | 45.4 | 44.4 | 44.4 | 46.0 | 45.8 | 46.7 | 47.5 | 45.4 |
| 2013 | 45.5 | 44.8 | 45.2 | 45.2 | 45.9 | 45.8 | 44.7 | 44.5 | 46.1 | 46.4 | 47.0 | 48.2 | 45.8 |
| 2014 | 45.6 | 44.5 | 45.4 | 45.8 | 46.5 | 46.7 | 45.5 | 45.8 | 47.4 | 47.8 | 49.9 | 50.6 | 46.8 |
| 2015 | 48.0 | 48.1 | 47.8 | 49.3 | 50.1 | 50.9 | 50.7 | 50.6 | 52.3 | 54.0 | 54.9 | 56.4 | 51.1 |
| 2016 | 52.1 | 52.1 | 51.9 | 53.8 | 53.9 | 54.0 | 53.8 | 53.9 | 56.0 | 56.6 | 58.8 | 58.9 | 54.7 |
| 2017 | 55.7 | 54.9 | 54.6 | 55.4 | 56.0 | 56.7 | 56.4 | 56.8 | 58.2 | 59.2 | 62.4 | 61.9 | 57.4 |
| 2018 | 58.8 | 58.1 | 58.0 | 57.7 | 57.7 | 58.4 | 56.2 | 55.8 | 57.2 | 59.2 | 60.9 | 59.5 | 58.1 |
| 2019 | 60.0 | 59.0 | 57.6 | 58.6 | 59.7 | 60.9 | 60.7 | 60.4 | 62.4 | 63.3 | 63.5 | 65.5 | 61.0 |
| **Information** | | | | | | | | | | | | | |
| 2011 | 17.7 | 18.1 | 18.2 | 17.7 | 17.8 | 17.5 | 17.5 | 16.6 | 17.1 | 17.2 | 17.6 | 17.3 | 17.5 |
| 2012 | 17.1 | 17.1 | 17.1 | 16.7 | 16.7 | 17.2 | 17.2 | 17.2 | 17.1 | 16.8 | 16.9 | 17.6 | 17.1 |
| 2013 | 17.0 | 16.9 | 16.9 | 16.6 | 16.7 | 16.8 | 17.0 | 17.0 | 16.8 | 16.9 | 17.0 | 17.0 | 16.9 |
| 2014 | 16.8 | 16.3 | 16.4 | 16.2 | 16.5 | 16.2 | 16.5 | 16.8 | 16.2 | 16.6 | 16.4 | 16.4 | 16.4 |
| 2015 | 16.1 | 16.0 | 16.2 | 16.6 | 16.8 | 16.7 | 17.1 | 17.0 | 16.7 | 17.0 | 17.1 | 17.0 | 16.7 |
| 2016 | 16.3 | 16.5 | 16.6 | 17.3 | 16.7 | 17.7 | 17.6 | 17.5 | 17.2 | 17.2 | 17.3 | 17.5 | 17.1 |
| 2017 | 17.3 | 17.6 | 17.6 | 17.6 | 17.6 | 17.8 | 17.6 | 17.5 | 17.3 | 17.5 | 17.4 | 17.5 | 17.5 |
| 2018 | 17.0 | 17.2 | 17.1 | 17.3 | 17.4 | 17.5 | 17.5 | 17.4 | 16.9 | 17.3 | 17.3 | 17.2 | 17.3 |
| 2019 | 17.0 | 17.0 | 17.2 | 17.3 | 17.4 | 17.8 | 17.3 | 17.3 | 17.2 | 17.3 | 17.3 | 17.0 | 17.3 |
| **Financial Activities** | | | | | | | | | | | | | |
| 2011 | 73.1 | 73.1 | 73.5 | 73.7 | 73.6 | 73.8 | 73.9 | 73.6 | 73.2 | 73.2 | 73.2 | 73.1 | 73.4 |
| 2012 | 73.0 | 73.0 | 72.8 | 72.8 | 73.1 | 73.7 | 74.1 | 74.4 | 74.2 | 74.2 | 74.7 | 74.8 | 73.7 |
| 2013 | 74.4 | 74.4 | 74.5 | 74.9 | 75.2 | 75.9 | 76.2 | 76.1 | 75.8 | 75.6 | 75.8 | 75.8 | 75.4 |
| 2014 | 75.0 | 75.1 | 74.7 | 75.6 | 75.9 | 76.6 | 76.8 | 77.0 | 76.5 | 76.7 | 76.7 | 76.9 | 76.1 |
| 2015 | 76.3 | 76.5 | 76.4 | 76.7 | 77.0 | 77.8 | 78.2 | 78.5 | 77.5 | 77.9 | 78.2 | 78.6 | 77.5 |
| 2016 | 77.9 | 78.1 | 77.9 | 78.5 | 78.9 | 79.2 | 79.7 | 80.0 | 79.7 | 79.9 | 80.1 | 80.2 | 79.2 |
| 2017 | 79.8 | 80.0 | 80.3 | 80.4 | 80.7 | 81.8 | 83.1 | 83.3 | 82.6 | 82.3 | 80.8 | 80.7 | 81.3 |
| 2018 | 80.1 | 80.2 | 80.0 | 80.0 | 79.9 | 80.4 | 81.0 | 80.6 | 80.0 | 79.7 | 79.6 | 79.7 | 80.1 |
| 2019 | 79.4 | 79.5 | 79.3 | 79.2 | 79.0 | 79.4 | 80.0 | 79.7 | 79.2 | 79.2 | 78.5 | 78.1 | 79.2 |

## Employment by Industry: Baltimore-Columbia-Towson, MD, 2011–2019—*Continued*

(Numbers in thousands, not seasonally adjusted)

| Industry and year | January | February | March | April | May | June | July | August | September | October | November | December | Annual average |
|---|---|---|---|---|---|---|---|---|---|---|---|---|---|
| **Professional and Business Services** | | | | | | | | | | | | | |
| 2011 | 183.8 | 183.8 | 186.3 | 192.0 | 193.3 | 196.1 | 198.1 | 199.8 | 200.7 | 202.1 | 203.5 | 203.9 | 195.3 |
| 2012 | 199.5 | 199.4 | 201.7 | 203.9 | 206.5 | 208.3 | 207.9 | 211.3 | 211.6 | 211.7 | 213.4 | 212.4 | 207.3 |
| 2013 | 207.4 | 208.7 | 211.5 | 212.4 | 214.2 | 217.5 | 216.8 | 219.3 | 219.3 | 218.6 | 220.1 | 217.8 | 215.3 |
| 2014 | 212.5 | 213.4 | 215.4 | 220.0 | 221.9 | 223.5 | 223.6 | 224.7 | 223.5 | 223.8 | 223.7 | 223.2 | 220.8 |
| 2015 | 216.9 | 217.5 | 219.0 | 223.4 | 225.2 | 226.4 | 229.4 | 230.9 | 228.1 | 232.5 | 232.4 | 231.0 | 226.1 |
| 2016 | 225.7 | 225.3 | 226.6 | 230.4 | 231.8 | 233.7 | 234.2 | 236.5 | 235.1 | 235.4 | 236.5 | 234.5 | 232.1 |
| 2017 | 226.4 | 226.5 | 228.0 | 231.7 | 233.3 | 235.2 | 235.3 | 235.9 | 235.1 | 234.9 | 235.2 | 234.4 | 232.7 |
| 2018 | 230.8 | 231.4 | 233.3 | 236.3 | 238.4 | 240.6 | 242.5 | 244.0 | 242.6 | 242.5 | 244.3 | 240.8 | 239.0 |
| 2019 | 238.9 | 240.1 | 241.6 | 243.8 | 245.3 | 248.2 | 249.0 | 251.0 | 246.6 | 250.3 | 253.7 | 253.6 | 246.8 |
| **Education and Health Services** | | | | | | | | | | | | | |
| 2011 | 238.1 | 241.7 | 242.0 | 242.4 | 241.7 | 239.9 | 240.5 | 239.2 | 242.1 | 244.5 | 245.1 | 244.6 | 241.8 |
| 2012 | 243.0 | 245.5 | 246.3 | 247.2 | 246.5 | 246.0 | 245.4 | 244.4 | 247.1 | 249.6 | 249.9 | 251.4 | 246.9 |
| 2013 | 247.5 | 250.7 | 252.1 | 252.5 | 252.0 | 250.5 | 249.9 | 249.1 | 251.3 | 254.3 | 255.1 | 254.8 | 251.7 |
| 2014 | 250.0 | 252.0 | 253.3 | 254.1 | 253.9 | 253.0 | 252.2 | 251.9 | 254.7 | 256.2 | 257.5 | 257.9 | 253.9 |
| 2015 | 253.9 | 256.6 | 256.9 | 261.6 | 261.5 | 259.6 | 259.8 | 258.1 | 261.0 | 264.1 | 265.5 | 265.6 | 260.4 |
| 2016 | 260.1 | 262.5 | 264.0 | 265.6 | 265.2 | 262.0 | 264.7 | 262.7 | 266.3 | 269.7 | 270.8 | 270.9 | 265.4 |
| 2017 | 265.1 | 269.0 | 270.5 | 271.2 | 271.0 | 268.6 | 274.0 | 272.9 | 275.2 | 278.4 | 279.0 | 278.9 | 272.8 |
| 2018 | 275.5 | 278.6 | 279.8 | 279.1 | 278.7 | 277.0 | 277.0 | 275.3 | 277.4 | 280.3 | 281.0 | 280.1 | 278.3 |
| 2019 | 277.6 | 281.4 | 282.5 | 282.0 | 281.3 | 279.4 | 279.0 | 276.7 | 278.0 | 278.6 | 280.3 | 281.6 | 279.9 |
| **Leisure and Hospitality** | | | | | | | | | | | | | |
| 2011 | 104.5 | 105.0 | 108.8 | 113.4 | 118.1 | 121.1 | 121.9 | 121.1 | 118.5 | 113.7 | 113.0 | 112.4 | 114.3 |
| 2012 | 110.1 | 111.0 | 114.5 | 118.7 | 124.6 | 129.1 | 128.2 | 128.2 | 125.3 | 122.0 | 119.4 | 118.7 | 120.8 |
| 2013 | 115.5 | 115.8 | 119.1 | 123.5 | 129.0 | 133.0 | 133.4 | 133.0 | 128.6 | 126.5 | 124.3 | 123.4 | 125.4 |
| 2014 | 118.5 | 118.8 | 122.2 | 127.9 | 134.7 | 136.9 | 136.8 | 138.1 | 134.8 | 132.4 | 129.6 | 128.6 | 129.9 |
| 2015 | 124.8 | 125.2 | 127.7 | 132.3 | 139.4 | 141.1 | 142.0 | 141.4 | 137.1 | 133.8 | 132.1 | 132.3 | 134.1 |
| 2016 | 126.5 | 126.8 | 129.8 | 134.7 | 139.4 | 142.9 | 142.0 | 142.0 | 138.8 | 135.7 | 134.5 | 133.9 | 135.6 |
| 2017 | 129.7 | 130.3 | 132.9 | 136.9 | 142.4 | 146.1 | 144.9 | 144.5 | 140.1 | 137.3 | 135.2 | 133.6 | 137.8 |
| 2018 | 128.9 | 130.1 | 133.3 | 137.3 | 143.2 | 147.0 | 147.2 | 146.7 | 142.4 | 138.5 | 136.6 | 136.0 | 138.9 |
| 2019 | 130.1 | 130.8 | 133.8 | 138.8 | 144.0 | 147.5 | 147.0 | 146.1 | 139.5 | 136.7 | 136.8 | 137.6 | 139.1 |
| **Other Services** | | | | | | | | | | | | | |
| 2011 | 54.6 | 54.7 | 55.2 | 55.7 | 55.8 | 56.3 | 56.1 | 55.8 | 55.0 | 54.8 | 54.7 | 55.0 | 55.3 |
| 2012 | 54.3 | 54.3 | 54.7 | 55.4 | 55.4 | 56.1 | 56.0 | 55.4 | 55.2 | 54.9 | 54.6 | 54.8 | 55.1 |
| 2013 | 54.2 | 54.5 | 54.9 | 55.2 | 55.3 | 55.7 | 55.5 | 54.5 | 54.4 | 53.6 | 53.6 | 53.2 | 54.6 |
| 2014 | 52.2 | 52.0 | 52.3 | 53.4 | 53.4 | 53.9 | 53.7 | 53.1 | 53.1 | 52.6 | 52.4 | 52.3 | 52.9 |
| 2015 | 51.4 | 51.3 | 51.4 | 51.5 | 51.8 | 52.1 | 52.2 | 51.8 | 51.2 | 50.8 | 50.8 | 50.6 | 51.4 |
| 2016 | 50.3 | 50.1 | 50.2 | 50.5 | 50.8 | 51.1 | 51.4 | 51.0 | 50.9 | 50.9 | 51.0 | 50.7 | 50.7 |
| 2017 | 50.2 | 50.4 | 50.7 | 50.9 | 51.3 | 52.2 | 52.2 | 51.6 | 51.5 | 51.5 | 51.7 | 51.9 | 51.3 |
| 2018 | 51.4 | 51.5 | 51.9 | 52.2 | 52.4 | 52.8 | 52.7 | 52.2 | 51.5 | 51.8 | 52.0 | 51.7 | 52.0 |
| 2019 | 51.0 | 51.2 | 51.4 | 51.7 | 51.9 | 52.2 | 51.8 | 51.7 | 51.3 | 50.8 | 51.3 | 51.8 | 51.5 |
| **Government** | | | | | | | | | | | | | |
| 2011 | 229.6 | 235.7 | 239.2 | 240.2 | 238.3 | 233.5 | 224.0 | 224.7 | 232.1 | 239.9 | 238.7 | 239.1 | 234.6 |
| 2012 | 228.6 | 235.2 | 238.0 | 237.2 | 235.7 | 228.5 | 220.7 | 219.7 | 228.6 | 236.3 | 236.3 | 235.8 | 231.7 |
| 2013 | 228.0 | 233.6 | 235.9 | 235.5 | 235.0 | 229.5 | 219.7 | 218.8 | 227.2 | 232.0 | 234.0 | 232.5 | 230.1 |
| 2014 | 224.2 | 230.7 | 232.4 | 234.5 | 231.8 | 227.2 | 216.5 | 217.7 | 226.6 | 232.5 | 234.0 | 232.3 | 228.4 |
| 2015 | 223.7 | 229.2 | 231.5 | 231.7 | 231.3 | 225.5 | 217.1 | 217.1 | 224.1 | 230.5 | 231.6 | 231.6 | 227.1 |
| 2016 | 222.4 | 227.3 | 229.9 | 231.1 | 231.0 | 225.3 | 216.4 | 216.0 | 224.1 | 229.2 | 230.1 | 230.9 | 226.1 |
| 2017 | 223.0 | 227.9 | 229.1 | 230.0 | 230.1 | 225.4 | 215.3 | 214.6 | 222.6 | 228.5 | 229.9 | 229.3 | 225.5 |
| 2018 | 222.3 | 228.3 | 229.7 | 230.2 | 230.6 | 227.1 | 216.6 | 218.1 | 227.5 | 230.4 | 231.6 | 231.5 | 227.0 |
| 2019 | 223.0 | 228.0 | 229.1 | 229.2 | 229.5 | 224.4 | 212.6 | 213.4 | 221.6 | 226.3 | 227.8 | 226.2 | 224.3 |

# Employment by Industry: Charlotte-Concord-Gastonia, NC-SC, 2011–2019

(Numbers in thousands, not seasonally adjusted)

| Industry and year | January | February | March | April | May | June | July | August | September | October | November | December | Annual average |
|---|---|---|---|---|---|---|---|---|---|---|---|---|---|
| **Total Nonfarm** | | | | | | | | | | | | | |
| 2011 | 952.0 | 962.3 | 970.7 | 976.5 | 980.3 | 974.9 | 954.1 | 978.6 | 983.4 | 988.9 | 996.2 | 996.8 | 976.2 |
| 2012 | 981.6 | 987.1 | 998.1 | 1,001.6 | 1,010.9 | 999.5 | 981.6 | 1,002.9 | 1,009.1 | 1,019.7 | 1,025.8 | 1,027.4 | 1,003.8 |
| 2013 | 1,005.8 | 1,012.4 | 1,020.9 | 1,026.3 | 1,033.5 | 1,023.3 | 1,007.0 | 1,027.0 | 1,032.6 | 1,046.8 | 1,054.0 | 1,057.5 | 1,028.9 |
| 2014 | 1,040.3 | 1,038.8 | 1,053.0 | 1,061.7 | 1,071.3 | 1,064.2 | 1,046.4 | 1,065.0 | 1,071.8 | 1,087.6 | 1,093.9 | 1,099.1 | 1,066.1 |
| 2015 | 1,078.8 | 1,086.1 | 1,091.9 | 1,099.1 | 1,112.3 | 1,110.6 | 1,092.5 | 1,107.6 | 1,113.0 | 1,130.0 | 1,136.5 | 1,143.1 | 1,108.5 |
| 2016 | 1,120.3 | 1,125.5 | 1,134.9 | 1,144.8 | 1,149.8 | 1,146.9 | 1,134.0 | 1,147.1 | 1,157.6 | 1,165.9 | 1,171.0 | 1,172.9 | 1,147.6 |
| 2017 | 1,153.2 | 1,159.0 | 1,167.6 | 1,171.1 | 1,180.9 | 1,181.5 | 1,163.9 | 1,179.4 | 1,183.6 | 1,192.2 | 1,196.8 | 1,198.3 | 1,177.3 |
| 2018 | 1,179.4 | 1,187.0 | 1,194.5 | 1,198.6 | 1,207.4 | 1,208.0 | 1,194.6 | 1,209.0 | 1,209.6 | 1,223.6 | 1,228.3 | 1,227.4 | 1,205.6 |
| 2019 | 1,213.2 | 1,218.7 | 1,225.3 | 1,229.7 | 1,237.1 | 1,241.1 | 1,224.3 | 1,241.1 | 1,238.9 | 1,249.8 | 1,252.9 | 1,253.3 | 1,235.5 |
| **Total Private** | | | | | | | | | | | | | |
| 2011 | 808.7 | 817.8 | 825.3 | 830.5 | 834.2 | 839.1 | 838.9 | 842.2 | 843.1 | 844.5 | 848.8 | 849.8 | 835.2 |
| 2012 | 836.8 | 840.9 | 850.6 | 853.5 | 861.8 | 866.8 | 864.8 | 866.5 | 865.5 | 869.8 | 874.5 | 876.5 | 860.7 |
| 2013 | 857.1 | 862.7 | 869.9 | 875.2 | 881.9 | 888.0 | 887.6 | 891.0 | 889.3 | 895.2 | 901.3 | 905.2 | 883.7 |
| 2014 | 890.9 | 889.0 | 902.1 | 909.6 | 918.6 | 924.5 | 924.6 | 927.6 | 927.6 | 935.2 | 940.3 | 946.1 | 919.7 |
| 2015 | 928.7 | 934.8 | 939.8 | 946.6 | 959.3 | 966.6 | 968.1 | 968.4 | 967.2 | 976.9 | 982.2 | 988.4 | 960.6 |
| 2016 | 971.0 | 974.8 | 983.0 | 992.9 | 997.3 | 1,001.5 | 1,005.6 | 1,006.6 | 1,005.1 | 1,011.6 | 1,015.4 | 1,017.8 | 998.6 |
| 2017 | 1,000.3 | 1,004.7 | 1,012.3 | 1,015.1 | 1,024.9 | 1,032.7 | 1,032.7 | 1,036.1 | 1,028.6 | 1,036.2 | 1,040.3 | 1,041.8 | 1,025.5 |
| 2018 | 1,024.5 | 1,031.0 | 1,037.9 | 1,042.0 | 1,050.5 | 1,059.0 | 1,063.2 | 1,066.1 | 1,056.7 | 1,067.4 | 1,072.0 | 1,070.8 | 1,053.4 |
| 2019 | 1,058.8 | 1,063.3 | 1,068.8 | 1,072.8 | 1,079.9 | 1,090.2 | 1,090.0 | 1,093.3 | 1,083.4 | 1,090.9 | 1,094.2 | 1,094.2 | 1,081.7 |
| **Goods Producing** | | | | | | | | | | | | | |
| 2011 | 132.6 | 134.7 | 135.4 | 136.7 | 137.6 | 138.7 | 140.1 | 140.5 | 140.8 | 140.5 | 140.9 | 140.8 | 138.3 |
| 2012 | 140.6 | 141.6 | 143.1 | 143.5 | 144.7 | 145.8 | 145.7 | 145.7 | 145.5 | 144.3 | 145.8 | 146.3 | 144.4 |
| 2013 | 144.7 | 146.0 | 147.4 | 147.1 | 147.4 | 148.6 | 148.8 | 148.9 | 148.6 | 148.5 | 148.8 | 149.0 | 147.8 |
| 2014 | 147.5 | 147.6 | 149.6 | 150.3 | 151.9 | 152.9 | 153.5 | 154.1 | 154.4 | 155.1 | 156.0 | 156.8 | 152.5 |
| 2015 | 155.6 | 156.5 | 157.1 | 158.5 | 160.0 | 161.6 | 162.4 | 162.8 | 163.3 | 163.4 | 163.8 | 164.3 | 160.8 |
| 2016 | 163.8 | 164.8 | 165.5 | 166.5 | 165.6 | 165.8 | 166.7 | 166.1 | 166.0 | 165.8 | 165.8 | 166.3 | 165.7 |
| 2017 | 163.7 | 164.9 | 165.4 | 166.6 | 167.5 | 169.3 | 170.2 | 170.1 | 169.7 | 169.5 | 169.7 | 170.3 | 168.1 |
| 2018 | 169.1 | 170.4 | 171.7 | 172.6 | 173.7 | 175.6 | 176.5 | 176.7 | 176.3 | 176.3 | 176.1 | 176.4 | 174.3 |
| 2019 | 176.4 | 177.3 | 178.1 | 178.1 | 178.6 | 179.7 | 180.9 | 181.0 | 180.0 | 180.3 | 181.4 | 181.6 | 179.5 |
| **Service-Providing** | | | | | | | | | | | | | |
| 2011 | 819.4 | 827.6 | 835.3 | 839.8 | 842.7 | 836.2 | 814.0 | 838.1 | 842.6 | 848.4 | 855.3 | 856.0 | 838.0 |
| 2012 | 841.0 | 845.5 | 855.0 | 858.1 | 866.2 | 853.7 | 835.9 | 857.2 | 863.6 | 875.4 | 880.0 | 881.1 | 859.4 |
| 2013 | 861.1 | 866.4 | 873.5 | 879.2 | 886.1 | 874.7 | 858.2 | 878.1 | 884.0 | 898.3 | 905.2 | 908.5 | 881.1 |
| 2014 | 892.8 | 891.2 | 903.4 | 911.4 | 919.4 | 911.3 | 892.9 | 910.9 | 917.4 | 932.5 | 937.9 | 942.3 | 913.6 |
| 2015 | 923.2 | 929.6 | 934.8 | 940.6 | 952.3 | 949.0 | 930.1 | 944.8 | 949.7 | 966.6 | 972.7 | 978.8 | 947.7 |
| 2016 | 956.5 | 960.7 | 969.4 | 978.3 | 984.2 | 981.1 | 967.3 | 981.0 | 991.6 | 1,000.1 | 1,005.2 | 1,006.6 | 981.8 |
| 2017 | 989.5 | 994.1 | 1,002.2 | 1,004.5 | 1,013.4 | 1,012.2 | 993.7 | 1,009.3 | 1,013.9 | 1,022.7 | 1,027.1 | 1,028.0 | 1,009.2 |
| 2018 | 1,010.3 | 1,016.6 | 1,022.8 | 1,026.0 | 1,033.7 | 1,032.4 | 1,018.1 | 1,032.3 | 1,033.3 | 1,047.3 | 1,052.2 | 1,051.0 | 1,031.3 |
| 2019 | 1,036.8 | 1,041.4 | 1,047.2 | 1,051.6 | 1,058.5 | 1,061.4 | 1,043.4 | 1,060.1 | 1,058.9 | 1,069.5 | 1,071.5 | 1,071.7 | 1,056.0 |
| **Mining, Logging, and Construction** | | | | | | | | | | | | | |
| 2011 | 41.7 | 43.4 | 43.8 | 44.7 | 45.1 | 45.5 | 46.1 | 46.0 | 45.9 | 45.6 | 45.5 | 45.2 | 44.9 |
| 2012 | 44.7 | 45.0 | 46.0 | 46.2 | 46.7 | 47.4 | 47.2 | 47.1 | 46.9 | 46.9 | 47.1 | 47.2 | 46.5 |
| 2013 | 46.2 | 46.8 | 48.0 | 48.6 | 48.8 | 49.3 | 49.7 | 50.0 | 50.1 | 50.5 | 50.7 | 50.5 | 49.1 |
| 2014 | 49.4 | 49.5 | 50.9 | 51.2 | 52.1 | 52.6 | 53.0 | 53.3 | 53.4 | 54.0 | 54.2 | 54.3 | 52.3 |
| 2015 | 53.1 | 53.4 | 53.8 | 54.6 | 55.7 | 56.4 | 57.1 | 57.2 | 57.8 | 58.1 | 58.1 | 58.2 | 56.1 |
| 2016 | 57.8 | 58.6 | 59.8 | 60.7 | 60.9 | 61.3 | 61.5 | 61.5 | 61.5 | 61.7 | 61.6 | 61.4 | 60.7 |
| 2017 | 59.3 | 60.0 | 60.2 | 60.8 | 61.3 | 62.0 | 62.8 | 62.7 | 62.9 | 63.1 | 63.0 | 63.0 | 61.8 |
| 2018 | 62.2 | 62.7 | 63.3 | 63.7 | 64.3 | 65.0 | 65.6 | 66.0 | 65.8 | 66.2 | 65.9 | 65.8 | 64.7 |
| 2019 | 65.7 | 66.3 | 67.1 | 67.3 | 67.7 | 68.4 | 68.9 | 69.5 | 69.1 | 69.7 | 69.9 | 69.5 | 68.3 |
| **Manufacturing** | | | | | | | | | | | | | |
| 2011 | 90.9 | 91.3 | 91.6 | 92.0 | 92.5 | 93.2 | 94.0 | 94.5 | 94.9 | 94.9 | 95.4 | 95.6 | 93.4 |
| 2012 | 95.9 | 96.6 | 97.1 | 97.3 | 98.0 | 98.4 | 98.5 | 98.6 | 98.6 | 97.4 | 98.7 | 99.1 | 97.9 |
| 2013 | 98.5 | 99.2 | 99.4 | 98.5 | 98.6 | 99.3 | 99.1 | 98.9 | 98.5 | 98.0 | 98.1 | 98.5 | 98.7 |
| 2014 | 98.1 | 98.1 | 98.7 | 99.1 | 99.8 | 100.3 | 100.5 | 100.8 | 101.0 | 101.1 | 101.8 | 102.5 | 100.2 |
| 2015 | 102.5 | 103.1 | 103.3 | 103.9 | 104.3 | 105.2 | 105.3 | 105.6 | 105.5 | 105.3 | 105.7 | 106.1 | 104.7 |
| 2016 | 106.0 | 106.2 | 105.7 | 105.8 | 104.7 | 104.5 | 105.2 | 104.6 | 104.5 | 104.1 | 104.2 | 104.9 | 105.0 |
| 2017 | 104.4 | 104.9 | 105.2 | 105.8 | 106.2 | 107.3 | 107.4 | 107.4 | 106.8 | 106.4 | 106.7 | 107.3 | 106.3 |
| 2018 | 106.9 | 107.7 | 108.4 | 108.9 | 109.4 | 110.6 | 110.9 | 110.7 | 110.5 | 110.1 | 110.2 | 110.6 | 109.6 |
| 2019 | 110.7 | 111.0 | 111.0 | 110.8 | 110.9 | 111.3 | 112.0 | 111.5 | 110.9 | 110.6 | 111.5 | 112.1 | 111.2 |

## Employment by Industry: Charlotte-Concord-Gastonia, NC-SC, 2011–2019—*Continued*

(Numbers in thousands, not seasonally adjusted)

| Industry and year | January | February | March | April | May | June | July | August | September | October | November | December | Annual average |
|---|---|---|---|---|---|---|---|---|---|---|---|---|---|
| **Trade, Transportation, and Utilities** | | | | | | | | | | | | | |
| 2011 | 195.8 | 195.7 | 197.3 | 197.6 | 198.2 | 198.2 | 199.3 | 199.7 | 199.0 | 200.8 | 204.5 | 206.2 | 199.4 |
| 2012 | 200.9 | 200.0 | 201.6 | 202.5 | 203.8 | 204.9 | 205.1 | 205.3 | 205.3 | 206.9 | 211.8 | 213.2 | 205.1 |
| 2013 | 205.7 | 205.1 | 206.4 | 206.5 | 207.9 | 208.7 | 209.6 | 210.4 | 209.9 | 212.1 | 217.2 | 220.4 | 210.0 |
| 2014 | 213.2 | 211.4 | 213.7 | 213.7 | 215.2 | 216.8 | 216.3 | 216.9 | 217.3 | 220.3 | 225.9 | 228.9 | 217.5 |
| 2015 | 220.3 | 219.8 | 221.0 | 223.0 | 224.6 | 226.1 | 225.9 | 226.4 | 225.8 | 228.9 | 234.0 | 237.2 | 226.1 |
| 2016 | 229.5 | 229.2 | 229.8 | 230.5 | 231.7 | 231.7 | 233.6 | 234.2 | 234.1 | 236.6 | 242.4 | 246.6 | 234.2 |
| 2017 | 236.7 | 235.1 | 235.8 | 235.5 | 236.9 | 238.1 | 237.8 | 238.7 | 237.4 | 239.3 | 244.7 | 247.0 | 238.6 |
| 2018 | 239.0 | 238.6 | 239.5 | 239.7 | 241.2 | 241.9 | 243.3 | 243.2 | 242.0 | 245.1 | 251.9 | 253.7 | 243.3 |
| 2019 | 247.7 | 245.5 | 246.3 | 245.7 | 247.0 | 248.7 | 247.4 | 247.6 | 246.7 | 248.7 | 254.1 | 256.1 | 248.5 |
| **Wholesale Trade** | | | | | | | | | | | | | |
| 2011 | 47.7 | 48.0 | 48.2 | 47.8 | 47.9 | 47.9 | 48.2 | 48.3 | 48.3 | 48.5 | 48.6 | 48.8 | 48.2 |
| 2012 | 48.5 | 48.6 | 48.9 | 49.0 | 49.2 | 49.4 | 49.5 | 49.5 | 49.4 | 49.4 | 49.5 | 49.7 | 49.2 |
| 2013 | 49.1 | 49.5 | 49.7 | 49.6 | 49.7 | 49.9 | 50.2 | 50.4 | 50.3 | 50.8 | 51.0 | 51.3 | 50.1 |
| 2014 | 51.2 | 51.2 | 51.6 | 51.4 | 51.6 | 51.9 | 51.9 | 52.2 | 52.2 | 52.3 | 52.7 | 52.9 | 51.9 |
| 2015 | 52.3 | 52.6 | 53.0 | 53.0 | 53.4 | 53.7 | 53.8 | 53.9 | 53.9 | 54.2 | 54.4 | 54.8 | 53.6 |
| 2016 | 54.7 | 54.9 | 55.1 | 55.7 | 56.0 | 56.0 | 56.7 | 56.7 | 56.8 | 56.9 | 57.1 | 57.4 | 56.2 |
| 2017 | 56.5 | 57.1 | 57.2 | 57.1 | 57.3 | 57.5 | 56.5 | 56.4 | 56.1 | 55.8 | 56.0 | 56.0 | 56.6 |
| 2018 | 55.9 | 56.1 | 56.2 | 56.1 | 56.3 | 56.7 | 57.2 | 57.5 | 57.2 | 57.7 | 57.9 | 58.0 | 56.9 |
| 2019 | 58.1 | 58.1 | 58.3 | 58.2 | 58.4 | 58.8 | 58.6 | 58.7 | 58.4 | 58.9 | 59.5 | 58.9 | 58.6 |
| **Retail Trade** | | | | | | | | | | | | | |
| 2011 | 107.0 | 106.6 | 107.5 | 108.0 | 108.4 | 108.4 | 109.1 | 109.3 | 108.5 | 110.0 | 113.3 | 114.4 | 109.2 |
| 2012 | 110.4 | 109.4 | 110.4 | 111.1 | 112.2 | 112.7 | 112.8 | 112.9 | 112.8 | 114.4 | 118.8 | 119.4 | 113.1 |
| 2013 | 113.5 | 112.8 | 113.4 | 113.7 | 114.6 | 115.1 | 115.6 | 115.9 | 115.4 | 116.9 | 121.0 | 123.0 | 115.9 |
| 2014 | 116.7 | 115.3 | 116.6 | 116.8 | 117.4 | 118.2 | 117.9 | 118.1 | 117.7 | 120.2 | 124.6 | 126.3 | 118.8 |
| 2015 | 120.0 | 119.3 | 119.8 | 121.0 | 121.7 | 122.6 | 122.2 | 122.6 | 121.9 | 124.3 | 128.2 | 129.4 | 122.8 |
| 2016 | 123.2 | 123.2 | 123.5 | 124.1 | 124.7 | 124.5 | 125.3 | 125.7 | 125.4 | 127.4 | 130.9 | 132.0 | 125.8 |
| 2017 | 126.0 | 124.9 | 125.3 | 124.7 | 125.5 | 125.8 | 125.8 | 126.1 | 125.3 | 127.1 | 131.2 | 131.9 | 126.6 |
| 2018 | 126.4 | 125.8 | 126.5 | 126.7 | 127.6 | 127.8 | 127.8 | 127.3 | 126.1 | 127.9 | 132.7 | 133.3 | 128.0 |
| 2019 | 128.9 | 127.5 | 128.0 | 127.7 | 128.6 | 129.3 | 127.9 | 127.7 | 126.8 | 128.4 | 132.1 | 132.2 | 128.8 |
| **Transportation and Utilities** | | | | | | | | | | | | | |
| 2011 | 41.1 | 41.1 | 41.6 | 41.8 | 41.9 | 41.9 | 42.0 | 42.1 | 42.2 | 42.3 | 42.6 | 43.0 | 42.0 |
| 2012 | 42.0 | 42.0 | 42.3 | 42.4 | 42.4 | 42.8 | 42.8 | 42.9 | 43.1 | 43.1 | 43.5 | 44.1 | 42.8 |
| 2013 | 43.1 | 42.8 | 43.3 | 43.2 | 43.6 | 43.7 | 43.8 | 44.1 | 44.2 | 44.4 | 45.2 | 46.1 | 44.0 |
| 2014 | 45.3 | 44.9 | 45.5 | 45.5 | 46.2 | 46.7 | 46.5 | 46.6 | 47.4 | 47.8 | 48.6 | 49.7 | 46.7 |
| 2015 | 48.0 | 47.9 | 48.2 | 49.0 | 49.5 | 49.8 | 49.9 | 49.9 | 50.0 | 50.4 | 51.4 | 53.0 | 49.8 |
| 2016 | 51.6 | 51.1 | 51.2 | 50.7 | 51.0 | 51.2 | 51.6 | 51.8 | 51.9 | 52.3 | 54.4 | 57.2 | 52.2 |
| 2017 | 54.2 | 53.1 | 53.3 | 53.7 | 54.1 | 54.8 | 55.5 | 56.2 | 56.0 | 56.4 | 57.5 | 59.1 | 55.3 |
| 2018 | 56.7 | 56.7 | 56.8 | 56.9 | 57.3 | 57.4 | 58.3 | 58.4 | 58.7 | 59.5 | 61.3 | 62.4 | 58.4 |
| 2019 | 60.7 | 59.9 | 60.0 | 59.8 | 60.0 | 60.6 | 60.9 | 61.2 | 61.5 | 61.4 | 62.5 | 65.0 | 61.1 |
| **Information** | | | | | | | | | | | | | |
| 2011 | 20.2 | 20.2 | 20.3 | 20.3 | 20.1 | 20.3 | 20.3 | 20.2 | 20.0 | 19.9 | 19.9 | 19.9 | 20.1 |
| 2012 | 19.7 | 19.8 | 19.9 | 19.9 | 19.9 | 20.0 | 20.0 | 20.0 | 19.9 | 19.8 | 19.9 | 19.9 | 19.9 |
| 2013 | 20.0 | 20.0 | 20.0 | 20.0 | 20.4 | 20.4 | 20.4 | 20.6 | 20.5 | 20.7 | 20.9 | 21.1 | 20.4 |
| 2014 | 20.5 | 20.5 | 20.6 | 20.5 | 20.7 | 21.0 | 21.1 | 21.1 | 21.1 | 21.4 | 21.6 | 21.7 | 21.0 |
| 2015 | 21.8 | 21.8 | 21.8 | 21.7 | 22.1 | 22.2 | 22.6 | 22.6 | 22.4 | 22.5 | 22.7 | 22.8 | 22.3 |
| 2016 | 22.8 | 22.8 | 22.7 | 23.0 | 23.1 | 23.3 | 23.2 | 23.2 | 23.1 | 23.2 | 23.4 | 23.4 | 23.1 |
| 2017 | 23.2 | 23.1 | 23.3 | 22.7 | 23.0 | 23.2 | 23.4 | 23.5 | 23.5 | 23.9 | 24.1 | 24.3 | 23.4 |
| 2018 | 24.2 | 24.4 | 24.4 | 24.2 | 24.3 | 24.5 | 24.6 | 24.3 | 24.3 | 24.5 | 24.7 | 24.8 | 24.4 |
| 2019 | 24.5 | 24.7 | 24.5 | 24.0 | 24.1 | 24.2 | 24.3 | 24.2 | 24.1 | 24.2 | 24.4 | 24.6 | 24.3 |
| **Financial Activities** | | | | | | | | | | | | | |
| 2011 | 78.1 | 78.5 | 78.5 | 77.8 | 78.2 | 78.7 | 77.9 | 78.4 | 78.3 | 79.0 | 79.3 | 79.5 | 78.5 |
| 2012 | 79.1 | 79.5 | 79.7 | 79.2 | 79.5 | 80.0 | 79.9 | 79.9 | 79.8 | 80.2 | 80.5 | 80.8 | 79.8 |
| 2013 | 80.5 | 80.7 | 80.4 | 81.3 | 81.5 | 81.9 | 82.3 | 82.1 | 81.9 | 82.2 | 82.3 | 82.4 | 81.6 |
| 2014 | 82.9 | 82.8 | 83.1 | 83.3 | 83.6 | 84.2 | 84.8 | 84.9 | 84.9 | 85.4 | 85.8 | 86.2 | 84.3 |
| 2015 | 85.9 | 86.3 | 86.7 | 86.8 | 87.3 | 88.0 | 88.8 | 88.6 | 88.5 | 89.9 | 90.2 | 90.4 | 88.1 |
| 2016 | 90.6 | 90.9 | 91.3 | 91.6 | 91.8 | 92.5 | 93.4 | 93.7 | 93.2 | 93.7 | 93.8 | 94.2 | 92.6 |
| 2017 | 94.4 | 94.7 | 94.9 | 95.0 | 95.4 | 96.5 | 97.0 | 97.3 | 96.9 | 98.0 | 98.4 | 98.7 | 96.4 |
| 2018 | 98.4 | 98.8 | 99.3 | 98.9 | 99.2 | 100.0 | 100.5 | 100.8 | 100.3 | 100.9 | 100.8 | 100.7 | 99.9 |
| 2019 | 100.2 | 100.5 | 100.7 | 101.1 | 101.7 | 103.2 | 103.8 | 104.5 | 103.9 | 105.3 | 105.8 | 107.1 | 103.2 |

## Employment by Industry: Charlotte-Concord-Gastonia, NC-SC, 2011–2019—*Continued*

(Numbers in thousands, not seasonally adjusted)

| Industry and year | January | February | March | April | May | June | July | August | September | October | November | December | Annual average |
|---|---|---|---|---|---|---|---|---|---|---|---|---|---|
| **Professional and Business Services** | | | | | | | | | | | | | |
| 2011 | 149.3 | 153.6 | 155.1 | 157.1 | 156.4 | 157.4 | 156.9 | 157.5 | 159.4 | 159.2 | 159.6 | 159.1 | 156.7 |
| 2012 | 156.2 | 157.8 | 159.8 | 160.5 | 161.3 | 162.2 | 159.9 | 161.0 | 161.6 | 164.0 | 162.7 | 162.2 | 160.8 |
| 2013 | 157.3 | 159.3 | 160.8 | 163.5 | 164.0 | 165.2 | 165.8 | 167.6 | 168.3 | 171.4 | 172.1 | 171.5 | 165.6 |
| 2014 | 170.1 | 170.8 | 173.8 | 177.2 | 177.8 | 179.0 | 179.2 | 180.0 | 180.7 | 182.9 | 182.5 | 183.9 | 178.2 |
| 2015 | 179.9 | 182.6 | 183.0 | 183.7 | 185.6 | 186.5 | 187.2 | 188.3 | 189.8 | 192.0 | 192.9 | 193.0 | 187.0 |
| 2016 | 188.2 | 189.3 | 192.0 | 195.7 | 195.5 | 197.0 | 198.5 | 199.0 | 199.4 | 200.6 | 200.8 | 199.7 | 196.3 |
| 2017 | 197.0 | 198.9 | 201.7 | 202.0 | 202.3 | 203.2 | 203.5 | 203.9 | 202.0 | 204.2 | 204.9 | 202.9 | 202.2 |
| 2018 | 200.3 | 201.5 | 202.5 | 203.8 | 204.1 | 206.0 | 206.8 | 209.2 | 208.5 | 211.2 | 210.0 | 208.6 | 206.0 |
| 2019 | 205.8 | 208.1 | 209.4 | 211.3 | 211.2 | 213.5 | 213.3 | 215.0 | 213.8 | 215.3 | 214.0 | 210.6 | 211.8 |
| **Education and Health Services** | | | | | | | | | | | | | |
| 2011 | 103.3 | 104.4 | 104.5 | 104.3 | 103.8 | 103.0 | 102.8 | 103.7 | 104.9 | 105.7 | 106.2 | 106.6 | 104.4 |
| 2012 | 105.4 | 106.6 | 106.3 | 105.5 | 105.8 | 105.2 | 104.6 | 105.1 | 106.0 | 108.1 | 108.3 | 109.0 | 106.3 |
| 2013 | 106.2 | 107.7 | 107.2 | 107.4 | 107.8 | 107.3 | 106.2 | 107.1 | 108.4 | 108.6 | 109.4 | 110.0 | 107.8 |
| 2014 | 108.3 | 108.8 | 109.5 | 109.4 | 109.9 | 109.1 | 109.2 | 110.1 | 111.2 | 112.4 | 113.2 | 113.4 | 110.4 |
| 2015 | 112.4 | 113.5 | 113.6 | 113.7 | 114.6 | 113.5 | 113.0 | 112.7 | 113.7 | 116.0 | 116.4 | 116.6 | 114.1 |
| 2016 | 115.1 | 115.7 | 116.2 | 117.0 | 116.8 | 115.7 | 116.4 | 116.9 | 118.3 | 119.6 | 119.5 | 119.3 | 117.2 |
| 2017 | 119.3 | 120.5 | 120.1 | 120.2 | 120.6 | 120.1 | 119.0 | 120.0 | 121.7 | 123.0 | 122.6 | 122.9 | 120.8 |
| 2018 | 121.0 | 123.2 | 123.1 | 123.3 | 123.5 | 122.7 | 122.2 | 123.2 | 124.4 | 126.5 | 127.6 | 127.4 | 124.0 |
| 2019 | 127.3 | 128.5 | 128.4 | 128.8 | 128.7 | 127.8 | 126.4 | 128.1 | 128.7 | 130.1 | 129.8 | 128.1 | 128.4 |
| **Leisure and Hospitality** | | | | | | | | | | | | | |
| 2011 | 97.0 | 97.9 | 101.2 | 103.6 | 106.6 | 109.2 | 108.1 | 108.6 | 107.4 | 105.9 | 104.9 | 104.1 | 104.5 |
| 2012 | 101.6 | 102.2 | 106.4 | 108.4 | 112.4 | 114.2 | 114.6 | 114.4 | 112.2 | 111.3 | 110.1 | 109.5 | 109.8 |
| 2013 | 107.1 | 107.8 | 110.7 | 112.4 | 116.3 | 119.3 | 117.9 | 117.7 | 115.2 | 115.3 | 113.4 | 114.4 | 114.0 |
| 2014 | 112.3 | 111.2 | 115.1 | 118.1 | 122.3 | 124.3 | 123.1 | 123.0 | 120.7 | 120.3 | 118.0 | 117.7 | 118.8 |
| 2015 | 115.9 | 117.1 | 119.3 | 121.3 | 126.7 | 130.3 | 129.6 | 128.4 | 125.5 | 126.0 | 124.0 | 125.8 | 124.2 |
| 2016 | 122.9 | 123.9 | 127.1 | 130.0 | 133.7 | 136.5 | 134.7 | 134.5 | 132.0 | 132.9 | 130.6 | 129.3 | 130.7 |
| 2017 | 126.7 | 128.1 | 131.4 | 133.6 | 139.4 | 141.8 | 141.9 | 142.9 | 137.9 | 138.3 | 135.8 | 135.4 | 136.1 |
| 2018 | 132.4 | 133.9 | 137.0 | 138.8 | 143.3 | 146.8 | 148.0 | 147.3 | 140.0 | 141.4 | 139.5 | 137.6 | 140.5 |
| 2019 | 135.4 | 137.1 | 139.5 | 141.7 | 146.1 | 150.4 | 151.1 | 150.4 | 143.9 | 145.3 | 143.0 | 143.9 | 144.0 |
| **Other Services** | | | | | | | | | | | | | |
| 2011 | 32.4 | 32.8 | 33.0 | 33.1 | 33.3 | 33.6 | 33.5 | 33.6 | 33.3 | 33.5 | 33.5 | 33.6 | 33.3 |
| 2012 | 33.3 | 33.4 | 33.8 | 34.0 | 34.4 | 34.5 | 35.0 | 35.1 | 35.2 | 35.2 | 35.4 | 35.6 | 34.6 |
| 2013 | 35.6 | 36.1 | 37.0 | 37.0 | 36.6 | 36.6 | 36.6 | 36.6 | 36.5 | 36.4 | 37.2 | 36.4 | 36.6 |
| 2014 | 36.1 | 35.9 | 36.7 | 37.1 | 37.2 | 37.2 | 37.4 | 37.5 | 37.3 | 37.4 | 37.3 | 37.5 | 37.1 |
| 2015 | 36.9 | 37.2 | 37.3 | 37.9 | 38.4 | 38.4 | 38.6 | 38.6 | 38.2 | 38.2 | 38.2 | 38.3 | 38.0 |
| 2016 | 38.1 | 38.2 | 38.4 | 38.6 | 39.1 | 39.0 | 39.1 | 39.0 | 39.0 | 39.2 | 39.1 | 39.0 | 38.8 |
| 2017 | 39.3 | 39.4 | 39.7 | 39.5 | 39.8 | 40.5 | 39.9 | 39.7 | 39.5 | 40.0 | 40.1 | 40.3 | 39.8 |
| 2018 | 40.1 | 40.2 | 40.4 | 40.7 | 41.2 | 41.5 | 41.3 | 41.4 | 40.9 | 41.5 | 41.4 | 41.6 | 41.0 |
| 2019 | 41.5 | 41.6 | 41.9 | 42.1 | 42.5 | 42.7 | 42.8 | 42.5 | 42.3 | 41.7 | 41.7 | 42.2 | 42.1 |
| **Government** | | | | | | | | | | | | | |
| 2011 | 143.3 | 144.5 | 145.4 | 146.0 | 146.1 | 135.8 | 115.2 | 136.4 | 140.3 | 144.4 | 147.4 | 147.0 | 141.0 |
| 2012 | 144.8 | 146.2 | 147.5 | 148.1 | 149.1 | 132.7 | 116.8 | 136.4 | 143.6 | 149.9 | 151.3 | 150.9 | 143.1 |
| 2013 | 148.7 | 149.7 | 151.0 | 151.1 | 151.6 | 135.3 | 119.4 | 136.0 | 143.3 | 151.6 | 152.7 | 152.3 | 145.2 |
| 2014 | 149.4 | 149.8 | 150.9 | 152.1 | 152.7 | 139.7 | 121.8 | 137.4 | 144.2 | 152.4 | 153.6 | 153.0 | 146.4 |
| 2015 | 150.1 | 151.3 | 152.1 | 152.5 | 153.0 | 144.0 | 124.4 | 139.2 | 145.8 | 153.1 | 154.3 | 154.7 | 147.9 |
| 2016 | 149.3 | 150.7 | 151.9 | 151.9 | 152.5 | 145.4 | 128.4 | 140.5 | 152.5 | 154.3 | 155.6 | 155.1 | 149.0 |
| 2017 | 152.9 | 154.3 | 155.3 | 156.0 | 156.0 | 148.8 | 131.2 | 143.3 | 155.0 | 156.0 | 156.5 | 156.5 | 151.8 |
| 2018 | 154.9 | 156.0 | 156.6 | 156.6 | 156.9 | 149.0 | 131.4 | 142.9 | 152.9 | 156.2 | 156.3 | 156.6 | 152.2 |
| 2019 | 154.4 | 155.4 | 156.5 | 156.9 | 157.2 | 150.9 | 134.3 | 147.8 | 155.5 | 158.9 | 158.7 | 159.1 | 153.8 |

## Employment by Industry: Orlando-Kissimmee-Sanford, FL, 2011–2019

(Numbers in thousands, not seasonally adjusted)

| Industry and year | January | February | March | April | May | June | July | August | September | October | November | December | Annual average |
|---|---|---|---|---|---|---|---|---|---|---|---|---|---|
| **Total Nonfarm** | | | | | | | | | | | | | |
| 2011 | 989.5 | 996.2 | 1,002.5 | 1,007.5 | 1,007.0 | 995.5 | 993.8 | 1,004.3 | 1,009.7 | 1,012.2 | 1,022.8 | 1,025.0 | 1,005.5 |
| 2012 | 1,011.3 | 1,021.2 | 1,031.0 | 1,030.6 | 1,031.2 | 1,021.3 | 1,018.0 | 1,029.0 | 1,031.4 | 1,043.6 | 1,056.4 | 1,057.0 | 1,031.8 |
| 2013 | 1,037.1 | 1,051.3 | 1,059.1 | 1,059.6 | 1,063.7 | 1,056.9 | 1,054.0 | 1,069.4 | 1,069.4 | 1,079.0 | 1,092.9 | 1,094.7 | 1,065.6 |
| 2014 | 1,082.3 | 1,091.4 | 1,100.3 | 1,102.8 | 1,109.0 | 1,100.6 | 1,098.4 | 1,114.3 | 1,113.7 | 1,122.1 | 1,134.1 | 1,137.7 | 1,108.9 |
| 2015 | 1,122.4 | 1,135.0 | 1,142.0 | 1,150.0 | 1,156.2 | 1,148.8 | 1,148.5 | 1,162.2 | 1,164.2 | 1,177.9 | 1,190.7 | 1,196.3 | 1,157.9 |
| 2016 | 1,178.4 | 1,189.6 | 1,196.6 | 1,203.5 | 1,206.4 | 1,195.4 | 1,199.8 | 1,212.3 | 1,217.5 | 1,224.6 | 1,237.8 | 1,241.3 | 1,208.6 |
| 2017 | 1,226.6 | 1,237.0 | 1,242.0 | 1,245.4 | 1,248.1 | 1,239.7 | 1,235.4 | 1,248.5 | 1,234.4 | 1,267.3 | 1,282.1 | 1,286.9 | 1,249.5 |
| 2018 | 1,267.9 | 1,279.8 | 1,287.6 | 1,288.6 | 1,289.7 | 1,280.4 | 1,278.1 | 1,294.2 | 1,295.1 | 1,310.9 | 1,324.2 | 1,321.4 | 1,293.2 |
| 2019 | 1,303.8 | 1,320.0 | 1,324.8 | 1,327.7 | 1,326.7 | 1,314.5 | 1,314.2 | 1,330.0 | 1,325.2 | 1,337.4 | 1,347.7 | 1,353.3 | 1,327.1 |
| **Total Private** | | | | | | | | | | | | | |
| 2011 | 873.2 | 878.2 | 884.3 | 890.1 | 890.4 | 889.8 | 889.1 | 889.4 | 893.4 | 894.6 | 904.7 | 907.8 | 890.4 |
| 2012 | 893.7 | 901.8 | 911.1 | 912.4 | 914.0 | 914.8 | 912.0 | 911.9 | 914.2 | 925.0 | 937.0 | 938.6 | 915.5 |
| 2013 | 919.4 | 931.9 | 939.3 | 939.7 | 944.7 | 949.0 | 946.9 | 951.0 | 951.5 | 960.4 | 973.7 | 976.2 | 948.6 |
| 2014 | 963.4 | 972.2 | 980.9 | 982.4 | 989.3 | 991.8 | 990.1 | 994.8 | 994.5 | 1,000.8 | 1,012.6 | 1,016.3 | 990.8 |
| 2015 | 1,001.2 | 1,013.0 | 1,019.5 | 1,027.3 | 1,034.8 | 1,038.4 | 1,038.1 | 1,040.3 | 1,043.0 | 1,054.6 | 1,067.2 | 1,073.4 | 1,037.6 |
| 2016 | 1,054.9 | 1,065.7 | 1,072.0 | 1,078.4 | 1,081.6 | 1,081.0 | 1,085.2 | 1,087.1 | 1,092.6 | 1,098.7 | 1,110.8 | 1,115.1 | 1,085.3 |
| 2017 | 1,101.2 | 1,110.5 | 1,115.3 | 1,118.4 | 1,121.8 | 1,123.9 | 1,119.2 | 1,122.3 | 1,108.7 | 1,139.0 | 1,152.3 | 1,157.8 | 1,124.2 |
| 2018 | 1,139.1 | 1,150.6 | 1,157.9 | 1,159.3 | 1,161.9 | 1,163.1 | 1,160.2 | 1,165.5 | 1,167.1 | 1,180.0 | 1,191.9 | 1,190.5 | 1,165.6 |
| 2019 | 1,176.3 | 1,190.6 | 1,194.9 | 1,197.6 | 1,198.4 | 1,196.4 | 1,195.4 | 1,201.0 | 1,196.4 | 1,207.1 | 1,216.7 | 1,223.1 | 1,199.5 |
| **Goods Producing** | | | | | | | | | | | | | |
| 2011 | 83.1 | 83.3 | 83.1 | 83.0 | 83.1 | 83.0 | 83.3 | 83.4 | 83.8 | 83.3 | 83.5 | 83.5 | 83.3 |
| 2012 | 82.7 | 83.2 | 83.6 | 82.4 | 83.1 | 83.4 | 84.2 | 84.9 | 85.3 | 86.0 | 86.4 | 85.9 | 84.3 |
| 2013 | 85.1 | 86.2 | 87.0 | 87.9 | 88.7 | 89.4 | 90.0 | 91.0 | 91.4 | 91.7 | 92.2 | 92.3 | 89.4 |
| 2014 | 91.9 | 93.0 | 93.3 | 94.0 | 94.7 | 95.5 | 96.2 | 96.9 | 97.3 | 97.9 | 98.2 | 97.6 | 95.5 |
| 2015 | 97.1 | 98.1 | 98.8 | 99.7 | 100.8 | 101.9 | 102.7 | 103.0 | 103.5 | 105.5 | 106.0 | 106.5 | 102.0 |
| 2016 | 106.2 | 107.3 | 107.7 | 108.9 | 109.7 | 110.9 | 112.2 | 112.7 | 113.5 | 112.7 | 113.7 | 113.8 | 110.8 |
| 2017 | 113.7 | 115.5 | 116.7 | 116.4 | 117.6 | 119.2 | 119.5 | 120.1 | 117.9 | 121.2 | 122.4 | 123.1 | 118.6 |
| 2018 | 123.5 | 125.6 | 126.6 | 127.0 | 127.8 | 128.8 | 129.2 | 130.3 | 130.4 | 132.1 | 132.3 | 132.0 | 128.8 |
| 2019 | 132.1 | 133.6 | 134.5 | 134.8 | 135.5 | 135.9 | 136.1 | 136.8 | 136.6 | 137.5 | 138.3 | 137.9 | 135.8 |
| **Service-Providing** | | | | | | | | | | | | | |
| 2011 | 906.4 | 912.9 | 919.4 | 924.5 | 923.9 | 912.5 | 910.5 | 920.9 | 925.9 | 928.9 | 939.3 | 941.5 | 922.2 |
| 2012 | 928.6 | 938.0 | 947.4 | 948.2 | 948.1 | 937.9 | 933.8 | 944.1 | 946.1 | 957.6 | 970.0 | 971.1 | 947.6 |
| 2013 | 952.0 | 965.1 | 972.1 | 971.7 | 975.0 | 967.5 | 964.0 | 978.4 | 978.0 | 987.3 | 1,000.7 | 1,002.4 | 976.2 |
| 2014 | 990.4 | 998.4 | 1,007.0 | 1,008.8 | 1,014.3 | 1,005.1 | 1,002.2 | 1,017.4 | 1,016.4 | 1,024.2 | 1,035.9 | 1,040.1 | 1,013.4 |
| 2015 | 1,025.3 | 1,036.9 | 1,043.2 | 1,050.3 | 1,055.4 | 1,046.9 | 1,045.8 | 1,059.2 | 1,060.7 | 1,072.4 | 1,084.7 | 1,089.8 | 1,055.9 |
| 2016 | 1,072.2 | 1,082.3 | 1,088.9 | 1,094.6 | 1,096.7 | 1,084.5 | 1,087.6 | 1,099.6 | 1,104.0 | 1,111.9 | 1,124.1 | 1,127.5 | 1,097.8 |
| 2017 | 1,112.9 | 1,121.5 | 1,125.3 | 1,129.0 | 1,130.5 | 1,120.5 | 1,115.9 | 1,128.4 | 1,116.5 | 1,146.1 | 1,159.7 | 1,163.8 | 1,130.8 |
| 2018 | 1,144.4 | 1,154.2 | 1,161.0 | 1,161.6 | 1,161.9 | 1,151.6 | 1,148.9 | 1,163.9 | 1,164.7 | 1,178.8 | 1,191.9 | 1,189.4 | 1,164.4 |
| 2019 | 1,171.7 | 1,186.4 | 1,190.3 | 1,192.9 | 1,191.2 | 1,178.6 | 1,178.1 | 1,193.2 | 1,188.6 | 1,199.9 | 1,209.4 | 1,215.4 | 1,191.3 |
| **Mining, Logging, and Construction** | | | | | | | | | | | | | |
| 2011 | 44.9 | 45.0 | 44.9 | 44.7 | 44.9 | 45.0 | 45.4 | 45.5 | 45.9 | 45.6 | 45.7 | 45.7 | 45.3 |
| 2012 | 44.7 | 45.1 | 45.3 | 44.2 | 44.9 | 45.2 | 46.1 | 47.1 | 47.7 | 48.3 | 48.6 | 48.2 | 46.3 |
| 2013 | 47.7 | 48.6 | 49.4 | 49.8 | 50.5 | 51.1 | 51.7 | 52.7 | 52.9 | 53.2 | 53.5 | 53.6 | 51.2 |
| 2014 | 53.2 | 54.1 | 54.5 | 54.7 | 55.2 | 55.8 | 56.2 | 56.9 | 57.3 | 57.8 | 58.1 | 57.4 | 55.9 |
| 2015 | 57.1 | 57.9 | 58.4 | 59.0 | 60.0 | 60.9 | 61.6 | 62.1 | 62.5 | 63.6 | 64.2 | 64.6 | 61.0 |
| 2016 | 64.7 | 65.7 | 65.9 | 66.8 | 67.5 | 68.3 | 69.3 | 69.7 | 70.5 | 69.9 | 70.6 | 70.6 | 68.3 |
| 2017 | 70.6 | 71.9 | 72.9 | 72.7 | 73.7 | 74.7 | 74.6 | 75.2 | 73.6 | 76.3 | 77.2 | 77.6 | 74.3 |
| 2018 | 78.2 | 80.1 | 80.7 | 81.1 | 81.6 | 82.2 | 82.4 | 83.4 | 83.4 | 84.6 | 84.8 | 84.4 | 82.2 |
| 2019 | 83.8 | 84.9 | 85.4 | 85.7 | 86.0 | 86.2 | 86.6 | 87.4 | 87.3 | 87.8 | 88.3 | 88.7 | 86.5 |
| **Manufacturing** | | | | | | | | | | | | | |
| 2011 | 38.2 | 38.3 | 38.2 | 38.3 | 38.2 | 38.0 | 37.9 | 37.9 | 37.9 | 37.7 | 37.8 | 37.8 | 38.0 |
| 2012 | 38.0 | 38.1 | 38.3 | 38.2 | 38.2 | 38.2 | 38.1 | 37.8 | 37.6 | 37.7 | 37.8 | 37.7 | 38.0 |
| 2013 | 37.4 | 37.6 | 37.6 | 38.1 | 38.2 | 38.3 | 38.3 | 38.3 | 38.5 | 38.5 | 38.7 | 38.7 | 38.2 |
| 2014 | 38.7 | 38.9 | 38.8 | 39.3 | 39.5 | 39.7 | 40.0 | 40.0 | 40.0 | 40.1 | 40.1 | 40.2 | 39.6 |
| 2015 | 40.0 | 40.2 | 40.4 | 40.7 | 40.8 | 41.0 | 41.1 | 40.9 | 41.0 | 41.9 | 41.8 | 41.9 | 41.0 |
| 2016 | 41.5 | 41.6 | 41.8 | 42.1 | 42.2 | 42.6 | 42.9 | 43.0 | 43.0 | 42.8 | 43.1 | 43.2 | 42.5 |
| 2017 | 43.1 | 43.6 | 43.8 | 43.7 | 43.9 | 44.5 | 44.9 | 44.9 | 44.3 | 44.9 | 45.2 | 45.5 | 44.4 |
| 2018 | 45.3 | 45.5 | 45.9 | 45.9 | 46.2 | 46.6 | 46.8 | 46.9 | 47.0 | 47.5 | 47.5 | 47.6 | 46.6 |
| 2019 | 48.3 | 48.7 | 49.1 | 49.1 | 49.5 | 49.7 | 49.5 | 49.4 | 49.3 | 49.7 | 50.0 | 49.2 | 49.3 |

## Employment by Industry: Orlando-Kissimmee-Sanford, FL, 2011–2019—*Continued*

(Numbers in thousands, not seasonally adjusted)

| Industry and year | January | February | March | April | May | June | July | August | September | October | November | December | Annual average |
|---|---|---|---|---|---|---|---|---|---|---|---|---|---|
| **Trade, Transportation, and Utilities** | | | | | | | | | | | | | |
| 2011 | 188.7 | 188.3 | 188.5 | 189.2 | 189.5 | 189.4 | 190.3 | 191.3 | 191.2 | 193.3 | 199.7 | 201.8 | 191.8 |
| 2012 | 195.8 | 194.7 | 196.0 | 195.5 | 196.2 | 196.2 | 196.4 | 196.7 | 196.2 | 198.2 | 205.7 | 207.3 | 197.9 |
| 2013 | 199.9 | 199.4 | 199.9 | 199.9 | 201.1 | 202.2 | 203.1 | 204.0 | 204.4 | 206.1 | 214.0 | 216.6 | 204.2 |
| 2014 | 209.5 | 209.6 | 210.3 | 209.6 | 210.1 | 210.5 | 210.6 | 211.7 | 211.5 | 213.4 | 221.2 | 224.2 | 212.7 |
| 2015 | 216.3 | 216.2 | 216.5 | 217.3 | 218.1 | 219.5 | 219.7 | 221.1 | 220.7 | 222.4 | 229.6 | 233.5 | 220.9 |
| 2016 | 223.7 | 223.4 | 224.1 | 224.6 | 225.3 | 225.3 | 225.6 | 226.5 | 227.2 | 228.9 | 236.3 | 239.8 | 227.6 |
| 2017 | 231.4 | 229.8 | 230.1 | 230.8 | 231.0 | 231.0 | 230.7 | 231.3 | 228.6 | 233.7 | 243.2 | 245.1 | 233.1 |
| 2018 | 238.2 | 236.8 | 237.2 | 236.5 | 237.2 | 236.8 | 237.2 | 237.7 | 238.0 | 239.3 | 247.5 | 249.0 | 239.3 |
| 2019 | 242.9 | 241.2 | 240.3 | 239.5 | 239.7 | 239.7 | 241.0 | 241.4 | 240.0 | 242.7 | 248.5 | 252.1 | 242.4 |
| **Wholesale Trade** | | | | | | | | | | | | | |
| 2011 | 38.3 | 38.4 | 38.3 | 38.2 | 38.2 | 38.1 | 38.1 | 38.0 | 38.0 | 38.0 | 38.1 | 38.3 | 38.2 |
| 2012 | 38.2 | 38.2 | 38.5 | 38.6 | 38.5 | 38.7 | 38.8 | 39.0 | 38.9 | 39.1 | 39.4 | 39.3 | 38.8 |
| 2013 | 38.9 | 39.3 | 39.5 | 39.5 | 39.7 | 39.7 | 39.7 | 39.8 | 40.1 | 40.4 | 40.8 | 40.9 | 39.9 |
| 2014 | 40.5 | 40.9 | 41.1 | 41.2 | 41.6 | 41.7 | 41.9 | 42.1 | 42.2 | 42.4 | 42.5 | 42.7 | 41.7 |
| 2015 | 42.6 | 42.8 | 42.9 | 43.0 | 43.2 | 43.3 | 43.4 | 43.4 | 43.4 | 43.3 | 43.5 | 43.8 | 43.2 |
| 2016 | 43.3 | 43.6 | 43.6 | 43.9 | 44.0 | 43.8 | 43.4 | 43.5 | 43.8 | 43.5 | 43.8 | 44.0 | 43.7 |
| 2017 | 43.2 | 43.3 | 43.6 | 43.5 | 43.6 | 43.7 | 43.9 | 43.9 | 43.7 | 44.0 | 44.3 | 44.6 | 43.8 |
| 2018 | 44.3 | 44.4 | 44.4 | 44.3 | 44.4 | 44.5 | 44.6 | 44.8 | 44.9 | 45.2 | 45.6 | 45.6 | 44.8 |
| 2019 | 45.5 | 46.0 | 45.8 | 45.6 | 45.8 | 45.9 | 46.2 | 46.3 | 46.3 | 46.6 | 46.9 | 47.8 | 46.2 |
| **Retail Trade** | | | | | | | | | | | | | |
| 2011 | 120.9 | 120.4 | 120.3 | 121.0 | 121.3 | 121.3 | 122.2 | 123.2 | 123.0 | 124.7 | 130.6 | 131.8 | 123.4 |
| 2012 | 126.8 | 125.6 | 126.4 | 126.0 | 126.8 | 126.6 | 126.8 | 127.0 | 126.8 | 128.3 | 135.2 | 136.4 | 128.2 |
| 2013 | 130.4 | 129.5 | 129.6 | 129.5 | 130.1 | 131.0 | 132.2 | 132.8 | 132.7 | 134.2 | 141.1 | 143.4 | 133.0 |
| 2014 | 137.4 | 136.9 | 137.1 | 136.6 | 136.7 | 137.0 | 136.7 | 137.4 | 137.2 | 138.6 | 145.5 | 147.2 | 138.7 |
| 2015 | 140.4 | 140.2 | 140.4 | 140.7 | 140.8 | 141.5 | 141.4 | 142.5 | 142.1 | 143.3 | 149.2 | 151.2 | 142.8 |
| 2016 | 143.6 | 143.2 | 143.3 | 143.4 | 143.8 | 143.9 | 144.5 | 145.3 | 145.4 | 147.0 | 153.4 | 155.1 | 146.0 |
| 2017 | 149.0 | 147.7 | 147.2 | 147.9 | 147.7 | 147.6 | 147.0 | 147.4 | 145.1 | 148.7 | 156.4 | 157.2 | 149.1 |
| 2018 | 151.3 | 150.0 | 150.3 | 149.2 | 149.4 | 148.8 | 149.4 | 149.5 | 149.5 | 150.0 | 156.3 | 156.8 | 150.9 |
| 2019 | 151.3 | 149.7 | 149.3 | 148.8 | 148.8 | 148.9 | 149.7 | 149.9 | 148.5 | 150.8 | 155.2 | 156.3 | 150.6 |
| **Transportation and Utilities** | | | | | | | | | | | | | |
| 2011 | 29.5 | 29.5 | 29.9 | 30.0 | 30.0 | 30.0 | 30.0 | 30.1 | 30.2 | 30.6 | 31.0 | 31.7 | 30.2 |
| 2012 | 30.8 | 30.9 | 31.1 | 30.9 | 30.9 | 30.9 | 30.8 | 30.7 | 30.5 | 30.8 | 31.1 | 31.6 | 30.9 |
| 2013 | 30.6 | 30.6 | 30.8 | 30.9 | 31.3 | 31.5 | 31.2 | 31.4 | 31.6 | 31.5 | 32.1 | 32.3 | 31.3 |
| 2014 | 31.6 | 31.8 | 32.1 | 31.8 | 31.8 | 31.8 | 32.0 | 32.2 | 32.1 | 32.4 | 33.2 | 34.3 | 32.3 |
| 2015 | 33.3 | 33.2 | 33.2 | 33.6 | 34.1 | 34.7 | 34.9 | 35.2 | 35.2 | 35.8 | 36.9 | 38.5 | 34.9 |
| 2016 | 36.8 | 36.6 | 37.2 | 37.3 | 37.5 | 37.6 | 37.7 | 37.7 | 38.0 | 38.4 | 39.1 | 40.7 | 37.9 |
| 2017 | 39.2 | 38.8 | 39.3 | 39.4 | 39.7 | 39.7 | 39.8 | 40.0 | 39.8 | 41.0 | 42.5 | 43.3 | 40.2 |
| 2018 | 42.6 | 42.4 | 42.5 | 43.0 | 43.4 | 43.5 | 43.2 | 43.4 | 43.6 | 44.1 | 45.6 | 46.6 | 43.7 |
| 2019 | 46.1 | 45.5 | 45.2 | 45.1 | 45.1 | 44.9 | 45.1 | 45.2 | 45.2 | 45.3 | 46.4 | 48.0 | 45.6 |
| **Information** | | | | | | | | | | | | | |
| 2011 | 23.8 | 23.9 | 23.9 | 23.9 | 24.0 | 24.0 | 24.2 | 24.1 | 24.1 | 23.9 | 24.2 | 24.1 | 24.0 |
| 2012 | 23.9 | 23.9 | 23.8 | 23.6 | 23.5 | 23.5 | 23.5 | 23.6 | 23.5 | 23.3 | 23.6 | 23.5 | 23.6 |
| 2013 | 23.2 | 23.5 | 23.4 | 23.4 | 23.5 | 23.7 | 23.7 | 23.7 | 23.7 | 23.6 | 23.6 | 23.7 | 23.7 | 23.6 |
| 2014 | 23.7 | 23.6 | 23.8 | 23.7 | 23.9 | 24.1 | 23.9 | 23.8 | 23.7 | 23.8 | 24.2 | 24.2 | 23.9 |
| 2015 | 24.3 | 24.3 | 24.2 | 24.1 | 24.2 | 24.2 | 23.9 | 23.7 | 23.5 | 23.8 | 24.0 | 24.0 | 24.0 |
| 2016 | 24.0 | 24.0 | 23.9 | 24.0 | 24.1 | 24.0 | 24.3 | 24.3 | 24.0 | 24.1 | 24.4 | 24.3 | 24.1 |
| 2017 | 24.1 | 24.4 | 24.2 | 24.2 | 24.6 | 24.5 | 24.2 | 24.3 | 24.1 | 24.4 | 24.8 | 25.1 | 24.4 |
| 2018 | 25.1 | 25.9 | 25.4 | 25.0 | 25.3 | 25.2 | 25.2 | 25.1 | 25.0 | 25.2 | 25.7 | 25.4 | 25.3 |
| 2019 | 25.4 | 25.7 | 25.6 | 25.7 | 25.8 | 25.8 | 25.6 | 25.5 | 25.4 | 25.6 | 25.9 | 25.8 | 25.7 |
| **Financial Activities** | | | | | | | | | | | | | |
| 2011 | 65.5 | 65.8 | 66.1 | 65.7 | 65.7 | 65.5 | 65.9 | 65.9 | 66.1 | 65.8 | 66.0 | 66.2 | 65.9 |
| 2012 | 65.9 | 66.3 | 66.7 | 66.7 | 67.0 | 67.2 | 67.4 | 67.4 | 67.3 | 68.1 | 68.5 | 68.6 | 67.3 |
| 2013 | 68.0 | 68.5 | 68.9 | 69.1 | 69.3 | 69.9 | 69.8 | 70.2 | 70.1 | 70.8 | 71.2 | 71.1 | 69.7 |
| 2014 | 70.1 | 70.4 | 70.5 | 70.2 | 70.5 | 70.4 | 70.3 | 70.5 | 70.2 | 70.5 | 70.5 | 70.5 | 70.4 |
| 2015 | 70.0 | 70.2 | 70.5 | 70.5 | 70.9 | 71.0 | 71.2 | 71.4 | 71.3 | 72.0 | 72.5 | 72.7 | 71.2 |
| 2016 | 72.7 | 72.9 | 73.0 | 73.0 | 73.1 | 73.2 | 73.1 | 73.3 | 73.1 | 74.0 | 74.1 | 74.5 | 73.3 |
| 2017 | 73.3 | 73.6 | 73.7 | 74.0 | 74.3 | 74.5 | 74.2 | 74.3 | 74.1 | 74.7 | 74.9 | 75.2 | 74.2 |
| 2018 | 74.7 | 75.3 | 75.5 | 75.9 | 75.9 | 76.0 | 76.1 | 76.1 | 76.2 | 76.8 | 77.1 | 77.0 | 76.1 |
| 2019 | 76.6 | 76.9 | 77.1 | 77.5 | 77.6 | 78.2 | 78.4 | 78.7 | 78.5 | 79.2 | 79.6 | 80.0 | 78.2 |

## Employment by Industry: Orlando-Kissimmee-Sanford, FL, 2011–2019—*Continued*

(Numbers in thousands, not seasonally adjusted)

| Industry and year | January | February | March | April | May | June | July | August | September | October | November | December | Annual average |
|---|---|---|---|---|---|---|---|---|---|---|---|---|---|
| **Professional and Business Services** | | | | | | | | | | | | | |
| 2011 | 157.5 | 158.9 | 159.5 | 161.8 | 161.9 | 161.6 | 160.6 | 161.5 | 163.7 | 164.1 | 166.2 | 165.9 | 161.9 |
| 2012 | 164.8 | 167.9 | 169.9 | 169.8 | 170.4 | 168.9 | 166.2 | 167.0 | 168.2 | 172.1 | 173.7 | 173.3 | 169.4 |
| 2013 | 169.6 | 173.2 | 174.4 | 174.8 | 176.3 | 176.4 | 174.0 | 175.3 | 175.8 | 178.2 | 180.4 | 179.8 | 175.7 |
| 2014 | 179.5 | 180.8 | 182.2 | 182.0 | 184.7 | 184.1 | 183.0 | 184.7 | 183.8 | 185.3 | 186.8 | 185.7 | 183.6 |
| 2015 | 185.4 | 187.7 | 189.7 | 193.6 | 196.1 | 196.2 | 196.9 | 196.2 | 196.7 | 199.6 | 201.1 | 200.4 | 195.0 |
| 2016 | 198.4 | 200.4 | 203.0 | 205.3 | 205.6 | 206.3 | 208.9 | 209.4 | 210.5 | 213.6 | 214.8 | 214.5 | 207.6 |
| 2017 | 215.7 | 218.2 | 219.0 | 219.2 | 220.4 | 221.1 | 219.2 | 218.7 | 215.0 | 226.1 | 227.0 | 227.5 | 220.6 |
| 2018 | 224.0 | 225.6 | 228.1 | 229.0 | 229.4 | 230.6 | 228.5 | 229.7 | 229.1 | 234.3 | 235.4 | 234.0 | 229.8 |
| 2019 | 230.9 | 234.9 | 234.9 | 237.5 | 237.4 | 237.5 | 236.5 | 236.7 | 234.7 | 237.3 | 237.9 | 239.4 | 236.3 |
| **Education and Health Services** | | | | | | | | | | | | | |
| 2011 | 121.1 | 121.9 | 122.2 | 123.4 | 123.6 | 122.6 | 122.9 | 123.7 | 124.6 | 124.9 | 125.6 | 125.9 | 123.5 |
| 2012 | 124.3 | 125.1 | 125.8 | 128.4 | 128.5 | 127.9 | 127.6 | 128.3 | 129.3 | 130.5 | 130.9 | 131.1 | 128.1 |
| 2013 | 129.7 | 130.9 | 131.4 | 131.4 | 131.6 | 130.6 | 129.2 | 131.3 | 131.6 | 132.6 | 133.5 | 133.3 | 131.4 |
| 2014 | 132.3 | 133.5 | 134.2 | 135.1 | 136.0 | 134.7 | 133.5 | 135.8 | 136.8 | 138.2 | 139.2 | 139.8 | 135.8 |
| 2015 | 139.1 | 140.6 | 141.4 | 142.7 | 143.8 | 142.7 | 141.1 | 143.2 | 144.5 | 146.1 | 146.8 | 146.8 | 143.2 |
| 2016 | 145.7 | 146.9 | 147.1 | 148.6 | 148.7 | 146.9 | 146.4 | 147.6 | 149.2 | 150.2 | 150.9 | 151.4 | 148.3 |
| 2017 | 150.6 | 151.4 | 151.5 | 152.3 | 152.3 | 150.6 | 149.7 | 152.3 | 151.5 | 154.1 | 154.7 | 155.6 | 152.2 |
| 2018 | 153.8 | 155.1 | 155.7 | 155.7 | 155.7 | 153.5 | 152.5 | 155.1 | 155.8 | 157.0 | 157.6 | 158.0 | 155.5 |
| 2019 | 158.0 | 159.5 | 159.6 | 160.0 | 160.5 | 157.7 | 157.2 | 160.7 | 161.2 | 163.3 | 164.5 | 164.5 | 160.6 |
| **Leisure and Hospitality** | | | | | | | | | | | | | |
| 2011 | 195.7 | 198.2 | 202.8 | 205.1 | 204.9 | 206.5 | 205.4 | 203.7 | 204.5 | 204.2 | 204.8 | 206.1 | 203.5 |
| 2012 | 202.2 | 206.4 | 210.7 | 211.2 | 210.5 | 212.6 | 211.7 | 209.3 | 209.8 | 211.3 | 213.1 | 213.5 | 210.2 |
| 2013 | 208.7 | 214.9 | 218.8 | 217.4 | 218.3 | 220.7 | 221.1 | 219.5 | 218.5 | 221.1 | 222.1 | 222.6 | 218.6 |
| 2014 | 219.2 | 223.9 | 229.0 | 230.1 | 231.4 | 234.6 | 234.9 | 233.5 | 233.0 | 233.2 | 233.8 | 235.4 | 231.0 |
| 2015 | 229.8 | 236.3 | 238.6 | 239.0 | 240.0 | 242.0 | 241.6 | 240.3 | 241.2 | 243.1 | 244.6 | 246.6 | 240.3 |
| 2016 | 240.9 | 247.0 | 248.9 | 249.6 | 250.6 | 250.2 | 250.7 | 249.5 | 251.1 | 251.5 | 252.4 | 252.4 | 249.6 |
| 2017 | 248.5 | 253.6 | 256.4 | 257.6 | 257.7 | 259.1 | 258.0 | 257.6 | 254.5 | 261.0 | 261.3 | 261.9 | 257.3 |
| 2018 | 256.0 | 262.3 | 265.1 | 266.0 | 266.4 | 267.8 | 267.4 | 267.1 | 268.2 | 270.7 | 271.8 | 270.5 | 266.6 |
| 2019 | 266.1 | 274.1 | 277.8 | 277.6 | 276.8 | 276.5 | 275.8 | 276.4 | 275.5 | 277.3 | 277.5 | 278.2 | 275.8 |
| **Other Services** | | | | | | | | | | | | | |
| 2011 | 37.8 | 37.9 | 38.2 | 38.0 | 37.7 | 37.2 | 36.5 | 35.8 | 35.4 | 35.1 | 34.7 | 34.3 | 36.6 |
| 2012 | 34.1 | 34.3 | 34.6 | 34.8 | 34.8 | 35.1 | 34.9 | 34.8 | 34.8 | 35.2 | 35.2 | 35.4 | 34.8 |
| 2013 | 35.2 | 35.3 | 35.5 | 35.8 | 35.9 | 36.1 | 36.0 | 36.0 | 36.1 | 36.3 | 36.6 | 36.8 | 36.0 |
| 2014 | 37.2 | 37.4 | 37.6 | 37.7 | 38.0 | 37.9 | 37.7 | 37.9 | 38.2 | 38.5 | 38.7 | 38.9 | 38.0 |
| 2015 | 39.2 | 39.6 | 39.8 | 40.4 | 40.9 | 40.9 | 41.0 | 41.4 | 41.6 | 42.1 | 42.6 | 42.9 | 41.0 |
| 2016 | 43.3 | 43.8 | 44.3 | 44.4 | 44.5 | 44.2 | 44.0 | 43.8 | 44.0 | 43.7 | 44.2 | 44.4 | 44.1 |
| 2017 | 43.9 | 44.0 | 43.7 | 43.9 | 43.9 | 43.9 | 43.7 | 43.7 | 43.0 | 43.8 | 44.0 | 44.3 | 43.8 |
| 2018 | 43.8 | 44.0 | 44.3 | 44.2 | 44.2 | 44.4 | 44.1 | 44.4 | 44.4 | 44.6 | 44.5 | 44.6 | 44.3 |
| 2019 | 44.3 | 44.7 | 45.1 | 45.0 | 45.1 | 45.1 | 44.8 | 44.8 | 44.5 | 44.2 | 44.5 | 45.2 | 44.8 |
| **Government** | | | | | | | | | | | | | |
| 2011 | 116.3 | 118.0 | 118.2 | 117.4 | 116.6 | 105.7 | 104.7 | 114.9 | 116.3 | 117.6 | 118.1 | 117.2 | 115.1 |
| 2012 | 117.6 | 119.4 | 119.9 | 118.2 | 117.2 | 106.5 | 106.0 | 117.1 | 117.2 | 118.6 | 119.4 | 118.4 | 116.3 |
| 2013 | 117.7 | 119.4 | 119.8 | 119.9 | 119.0 | 107.9 | 107.1 | 118.4 | 117.9 | 118.6 | 119.2 | 118.5 | 117.0 |
| 2014 | 118.9 | 119.2 | 119.4 | 120.4 | 119.7 | 108.8 | 108.3 | 119.5 | 119.2 | 121.3 | 121.5 | 121.4 | 118.1 |
| 2015 | 121.2 | 122.0 | 122.5 | 122.7 | 121.4 | 110.4 | 110.4 | 121.9 | 121.2 | 123.3 | 123.5 | 122.9 | 120.3 |
| 2016 | 123.5 | 123.9 | 124.6 | 125.1 | 124.8 | 114.4 | 114.6 | 125.2 | 124.9 | 125.9 | 127.0 | 126.2 | 123.3 |
| 2017 | 125.4 | 126.5 | 126.7 | 127.0 | 126.3 | 115.8 | 116.2 | 126.2 | 125.7 | 128.3 | 129.8 | 129.1 | 125.3 |
| 2018 | 128.8 | 129.2 | 129.7 | 129.3 | 127.8 | 117.3 | 117.9 | 128.7 | 128.0 | 130.9 | 132.3 | 130.9 | 127.6 |
| 2019 | 127.5 | 129.4 | 129.9 | 130.1 | 128.3 | 118.1 | 118.8 | 129.0 | 128.8 | 130.3 | 131.0 | 130.2 | 127.6 |

## Employment by Industry: San Antonio-New Braunfels, TX, 2011–2019

(Numbers in thousands, not seasonally adjusted)

| Industry and year | January | February | March | April | May | June | July | August | September | October | November | December | Annual average |
|---|---|---|---|---|---|---|---|---|---|---|---|---|---|
| **Total Nonfarm** | | | | | | | | | | | | | |
| 2011 | 849.7 | 856.8 | 865.0 | 871.0 | 874.5 | 875.6 | 871.4 | 873.4 | 876.1 | 877.5 | 880.6 | 883.1 | 871.2 |
| 2012 | 867.8 | 876.2 | 883.4 | 888.4 | 894.0 | 898.8 | 891.5 | 898.5 | 899.8 | 903.9 | 909.1 | 912.2 | 893.6 |
| 2013 | 894.7 | 906.0 | 912.1 | 917.6 | 922.5 | 928.6 | 924.4 | 926.6 | 929.2 | 932.5 | 938.3 | 939.0 | 922.6 |
| 2014 | 923.6 | 932.5 | 940.2 | 948.3 | 955.2 | 960.6 | 955.7 | 958.0 | 959.6 | 969.5 | 974.8 | 976.1 | 954.5 |
| 2015 | 962.5 | 972.0 | 976.0 | 981.7 | 988.1 | 991.1 | 987.3 | 988.5 | 992.6 | 999.0 | 1,005.1 | 1,005.4 | 987.4 |
| 2016 | 993.4 | 1,001.6 | 1,006.0 | 1,012.0 | 1,015.6 | 1,018.0 | 1,016.4 | 1,019.0 | 1,023.6 | 1,026.5 | 1,033.8 | 1,035.1 | 1,016.8 |
| 2017 | 1,021.1 | 1,027.0 | 1,032.8 | 1,034.7 | 1,038.5 | 1,045.0 | 1,037.4 | 1,039.3 | 1,043.5 | 1,045.4 | 1,051.0 | 1,052.3 | 1,039.0 |
| 2018 | 1,034.8 | 1,043.6 | 1,049.9 | 1,055.8 | 1,059.4 | 1,066.0 | 1,059.0 | 1,063.0 | 1,062.7 | 1,067.4 | 1,073.8 | 1,074.9 | 1,059.2 |
| 2019 | 1,056.1 | 1,063.8 | 1,067.5 | 1,071.7 | 1,075.6 | 1,081.1 | 1,076.9 | 1,080.1 | 1,080.3 | 1,093.3 | 1,097.2 | 1,100.2 | 1,078.7 |
| **Total Private** | | | | | | | | | | | | | |
| 2011 | 686.5 | 691.1 | 699.8 | 705.6 | 709.0 | 712.7 | 714.9 | 717.1 | 714.8 | 713.6 | 717.0 | 719.4 | 708.5 |
| 2012 | 706.7 | 713.1 | 720.2 | 724.7 | 730.7 | 739.2 | 737.5 | 742.3 | 737.8 | 739.7 | 744.8 | 747.9 | 732.1 |
| 2013 | 732.8 | 741.8 | 747.9 | 752.7 | 757.9 | 766.3 | 766.6 | 768.8 | 766.1 | 766.5 | 772.1 | 773.3 | 759.4 |
| 2014 | 760.3 | 767.0 | 774.6 | 782.4 | 789.7 | 797.5 | 797.9 | 799.8 | 795.3 | 801.3 | 806.0 | 807.9 | 790.0 |
| 2015 | 795.7 | 803.4 | 807.6 | 812.8 | 819.1 | 825.7 | 826.8 | 827.6 | 824.1 | 829.1 | 833.5 | 834.1 | 820.0 |
| 2016 | 823.1 | 830.0 | 834.5 | 841.8 | 845.0 | 849.8 | 853.3 | 855.4 | 853.1 | 855.2 | 861.5 | 862.8 | 847.1 |
| 2017 | 849.9 | 854.1 | 859.5 | 862.1 | 865.7 | 875.1 | 873.0 | 874.5 | 872.7 | 873.5 | 877.8 | 879.1 | 868.1 |
| 2018 | 862.9 | 870.8 | 876.2 | 882.4 | 885.6 | 895.2 | 893.4 | 897.1 | 890.8 | 894.3 | 899.4 | 900.2 | 887.4 |
| 2019 | 883.1 | 889.4 | 892.5 | 897.5 | 900.7 | 909.2 | 910.0 | 912.4 | 906.1 | 917.8 | 920.3 | 923.4 | 905.2 |
| **Goods Producing** | | | | | | | | | | | | | |
| 2011 | 89.2 | 89.3 | 90.1 | 90.9 | 91.1 | 91.8 | 92.3 | 92.0 | 91.6 | 91.2 | 91.1 | 90.6 | 90.9 |
| 2012 | 90.2 | 90.5 | 90.9 | 91.7 | 92.1 | 93.3 | 93.5 | 94.0 | 93.5 | 93.9 | 94.2 | 94.2 | 92.7 |
| 2013 | 93.2 | 93.6 | 94.4 | 95.4 | 95.9 | 97.1 | 97.7 | 97.8 | 97.6 | 97.5 | 97.8 | 97.6 | 96.3 |
| 2014 | 97.0 | 97.8 | 98.4 | 99.4 | 100.3 | 101.4 | 102.0 | 102.6 | 102.7 | 104.2 | 104.7 | 105.1 | 101.3 |
| 2015 | 104.1 | 104.8 | 104.4 | 105.1 | 105.4 | 106.2 | 106.5 | 106.3 | 105.3 | 105.9 | 105.7 | 105.5 | 105.4 |
| 2016 | 104.7 | 105.3 | 105.0 | 104.9 | 104.7 | 104.9 | 105.9 | 105.8 | 105.9 | 105.4 | 105.3 | 105.5 | 105.3 |
| 2017 | 104.8 | 105.7 | 106.1 | 106.4 | 106.9 | 108.3 | 108.2 | 109.2 | 109.4 | 109.7 | 110.4 | 111.1 | 108.0 |
| 2018 | 110.7 | 111.9 | 112.2 | 112.8 | 113.4 | 114.8 | 115.0 | 115.3 | 114.4 | 115.0 | 115.5 | 115.8 | 113.9 |
| 2019 | 115.0 | 116.2 | 116.2 | 117.2 | 117.2 | 118.5 | 119.2 | 119.7 | 119.3 | 120.4 | 121.4 | 121.7 | 118.5 |
| **Service-Providing** | | | | | | | | | | | | | |
| 2011 | 760.5 | 767.5 | 774.9 | 780.1 | 783.4 | 783.8 | 779.1 | 781.4 | 784.5 | 786.3 | 789.5 | 792.5 | 780.3 |
| 2012 | 777.6 | 785.7 | 792.5 | 796.7 | 801.9 | 805.5 | 798.0 | 804.5 | 806.3 | 810.0 | 814.9 | 818.0 | 801.0 |
| 2013 | 801.5 | 812.4 | 817.7 | 822.2 | 826.6 | 831.5 | 826.7 | 828.8 | 831.6 | 835.0 | 840.5 | 841.4 | 826.3 |
| 2014 | 826.6 | 834.7 | 841.8 | 848.9 | 854.9 | 859.2 | 853.7 | 855.4 | 856.9 | 865.3 | 870.1 | 871.0 | 853.2 |
| 2015 | 858.4 | 867.2 | 871.6 | 876.6 | 882.7 | 884.9 | 880.8 | 882.2 | 887.3 | 893.1 | 899.4 | 899.9 | 882.0 |
| 2016 | 888.7 | 896.3 | 901.0 | 907.1 | 910.9 | 913.1 | 910.5 | 913.2 | 917.7 | 921.1 | 928.5 | 929.6 | 911.5 |
| 2017 | 916.3 | 921.3 | 926.7 | 928.3 | 931.6 | 936.7 | 929.2 | 930.1 | 934.1 | 935.7 | 940.6 | 941.2 | 931.0 |
| 2018 | 924.1 | 931.7 | 937.7 | 943.0 | 946.0 | 951.2 | 944.0 | 947.7 | 948.3 | 952.4 | 958.3 | 959.1 | 945.3 |
| 2019 | 941.1 | 947.6 | 951.3 | 954.5 | 958.4 | 962.6 | 957.7 | 960.4 | 961.0 | 972.9 | 975.8 | 978.5 | 960.2 |
| **Mining and Logging** | | | | | | | | | | | | | |
| 2011 | 2.9 | 2.9 | 2.9 | 3.0 | 3.0 | 3.1 | 3.3 | 3.3 | 3.3 | 3.4 | 3.4 | 3.5 | 3.2 |
| 2012 | 3.5 | 3.6 | 3.7 | 4.0 | 4.0 | 4.2 | 4.4 | 4.5 | 4.6 | 4.7 | 4.8 | 4.9 | 4.2 |
| 2013 | 5.0 | 5.1 | 5.2 | 5.5 | 5.7 | 5.8 | 6.3 | 6.3 | 6.3 | 6.8 | 6.8 | 6.9 | 6.0 |
| 2014 | 7.5 | 7.7 | 7.9 | 8.2 | 8.4 | 8.7 | 8.6 | 8.8 | 8.9 | 9.3 | 9.5 | 9.6 | 8.6 |
| 2015 | 9.4 | 9.4 | 8.9 | 8.8 | 8.6 | 8.6 | 8.6 | 8.4 | 8.0 | 7.9 | 7.8 | 7.8 | 8.5 |
| 2016 | 7.5 | 7.4 | 7.2 | 7.0 | 6.8 | 6.7 | 6.8 | 6.7 | 6.7 | 6.7 | 6.9 | 7.0 | 7.0 |
| 2017 | 6.8 | 7.0 | 7.1 | 7.3 | 7.5 | 7.9 | 8.0 | 8.1 | 8.1 | 8.4 | 8.6 | 8.8 | 7.8 |
| 2018 | 9.3 | 9.4 | 9.6 | 10.2 | 10.5 | 10.8 | 10.9 | 11.0 | 10.9 | 11.1 | 11.1 | 11.2 | 10.5 |
| 2019 | 11.1 | 11.2 | 11.2 | 11.0 | 10.9 | 10.8 | 10.9 | 10.8 | 10.6 | 10.6 | 10.5 | 10.2 | 10.8 |
| **Construction** | | | | | | | | | | | | | |
| 2011 | 41.0 | 41.1 | 42.0 | 42.3 | 42.4 | 42.6 | 42.8 | 42.6 | 42.1 | 41.6 | 41.3 | 40.6 | 41.9 |
| 2012 | 40.5 | 40.6 | 40.8 | 40.8 | 41.3 | 42.1 | 42.3 | 42.8 | 42.3 | 42.4 | 42.5 | 42.3 | 41.7 |
| 2013 | 41.7 | 42.1 | 43.1 | 43.5 | 43.9 | 44.8 | 44.9 | 45.1 | 44.8 | 44.7 | 44.7 | 44.3 | 44.0 |
| 2014 | 43.7 | 44.2 | 44.7 | 45.2 | 45.7 | 46.2 | 46.9 | 47.2 | 47.2 | 47.9 | 48.2 | 48.4 | 46.3 |
| 2015 | 48.0 | 48.5 | 48.7 | 49.3 | 49.8 | 50.3 | 51.0 | 51.2 | 50.6 | 50.7 | 50.5 | 50.2 | 49.9 |
| 2016 | 50.0 | 50.4 | 50.4 | 50.4 | 50.5 | 50.7 | 51.2 | 51.2 | 51.2 | 51.0 | 50.3 | 50.3 | 50.6 |
| 2017 | 50.1 | 50.5 | 50.8 | 50.8 | 51.2 | 51.7 | 51.4 | 51.9 | 52.0 | 51.7 | 51.8 | 52.0 | 51.3 |
| 2018 | 51.9 | 52.6 | 52.6 | 52.7 | 52.9 | 53.7 | 53.7 | 53.8 | 53.0 | 53.5 | 53.7 | 53.8 | 53.2 |
| 2019 | 53.5 | 54.4 | 54.5 | 55.2 | 55.3 | 56.3 | 56.9 | 57.4 | 57.2 | 57.5 | 58.0 | 58.4 | 56.2 |

## Employment by Industry: San Antonio-New Braunfels, TX, 2011–2019—*Continued*

(Numbers in thousands, not seasonally adjusted)

| Industry and year | January | February | March | April | May | June | July | August | September | October | November | December | Annual average |
|---|---|---|---|---|---|---|---|---|---|---|---|---|---|
| **Manufacturing** | | | | | | | | | | | | | |
| 2011 | 45.3 | 45.3 | 45.2 | 45.6 | 45.7 | 46.1 | 46.2 | 46.1 | 46.2 | 46.2 | 46.4 | 46.5 | 45.9 |
| 2012 | 46.2 | 46.3 | 46.4 | 46.9 | 46.8 | 47.0 | 46.8 | 46.7 | 46.6 | 46.8 | 46.9 | 47.0 | 46.7 |
| 2013 | 46.5 | 46.4 | 46.1 | 46.4 | 46.3 | 46.5 | 46.5 | 46.4 | 46.5 | 46.0 | 46.3 | 46.4 | 46.4 |
| 2014 | 45.8 | 45.9 | 45.8 | 46.0 | 46.2 | 46.5 | 46.5 | 46.6 | 46.6 | 47.0 | 47.0 | 47.1 | 46.4 |
| 2015 | 46.7 | 46.9 | 46.8 | 47.0 | 47.0 | 47.3 | 46.9 | 46.7 | 46.7 | 47.3 | 47.4 | 47.5 | 47.0 |
| 2016 | 47.2 | 47.5 | 47.4 | 47.5 | 47.4 | 47.5 | 47.9 | 47.9 | 48.0 | 47.7 | 48.1 | 48.2 | 47.7 |
| 2017 | 47.9 | 48.2 | 48.2 | 48.3 | 48.2 | 48.7 | 48.8 | 49.2 | 49.3 | 49.6 | 50.0 | 50.3 | 48.9 |
| 2018 | 49.5 | 49.9 | 50.0 | 49.9 | 50.0 | 50.3 | 50.4 | 50.5 | 50.5 | 50.4 | 50.7 | 50.8 | 50.2 |
| 2019 | 50.4 | 50.6 | 50.5 | 51.0 | 51.0 | 51.4 | 51.4 | 51.5 | 51.5 | 52.3 | 52.9 | 53.1 | 51.5 |
| **Trade, Transportation, and Utilities** | | | | | | | | | | | | | |
| 2011 | 144.8 | 143.6 | 144.4 | 145.4 | 145.6 | 146.0 | 146.5 | 147.8 | 147.2 | 148.6 | 151.5 | 153.2 | 147.1 |
| 2012 | 148.8 | 148.0 | 148.4 | 149.1 | 149.7 | 150.7 | 150.7 | 151.8 | 151.7 | 153.4 | 157.6 | 158.5 | 151.5 |
| 2013 | 153.6 | 153.5 | 153.6 | 154.6 | 155.5 | 156.3 | 156.8 | 158.6 | 158.6 | 160.5 | 164.1 | 166.3 | 157.7 |
| 2014 | 161.4 | 161.1 | 161.4 | 162.6 | 163.2 | 164.5 | 164.9 | 166.0 | 166.3 | 168.7 | 172.3 | 174.6 | 165.6 |
| 2015 | 169.2 | 168.4 | 168.8 | 170.0 | 171.1 | 172.2 | 172.9 | 173.8 | 174.3 | 176.2 | 179.1 | 180.8 | 173.1 |
| 2016 | 174.7 | 174.5 | 174.9 | 175.7 | 176.4 | 177.6 | 178.0 | 179.0 | 179.0 | 180.5 | 185.1 | 185.8 | 178.4 |
| 2017 | 180.7 | 179.0 | 178.7 | 179.2 | 179.6 | 180.1 | 179.6 | 181.0 | 180.2 | 181.4 | 185.9 | 186.7 | 181.0 |
| 2018 | 180.3 | 179.2 | 178.5 | 179.4 | 180.0 | 180.1 | 180.0 | 180.9 | 180.5 | 181.3 | 185.9 | 186.2 | 181.0 |
| 2019 | 180.8 | 179.7 | 179.6 | 180.5 | 180.4 | 181.5 | 182.3 | 183.2 | 182.9 | 185.3 | 188.8 | 190.3 | 182.9 |
| **Wholesale Trade** | | | | | | | | | | | | | |
| 2011 | 28.8 | 28.9 | 29.2 | 29.4 | 29.5 | 29.7 | 29.8 | 29.9 | 29.8 | 30.0 | 30.1 | 30.0 | 29.6 |
| 2012 | 30.1 | 30.2 | 30.4 | 30.5 | 30.6 | 30.9 | 30.9 | 31.1 | 30.8 | 31.1 | 31.0 | 31.0 | 30.7 |
| 2013 | 31.3 | 31.6 | 31.3 | 31.2 | 31.4 | 31.6 | 31.5 | 31.7 | 31.8 | 31.7 | 31.9 | 31.9 | 31.6 |
| 2014 | 31.7 | 32.1 | 32.2 | 32.2 | 32.3 | 32.6 | 32.7 | 32.8 | 33.0 | 33.3 | 33.6 | 33.7 | 32.7 |
| 2015 | 33.7 | 33.9 | 34.0 | 33.8 | 34.1 | 34.2 | 34.2 | 34.2 | 34.2 | 34.3 | 34.3 | 34.2 | 34.1 |
| 2016 | 34.3 | 34.4 | 34.4 | 34.5 | 34.5 | 34.6 | 34.8 | 34.8 | 34.9 | 34.8 | 34.8 | 34.9 | 34.6 |
| 2017 | 34.8 | 35.0 | 35.1 | 35.1 | 35.3 | 35.4 | 35.3 | 35.3 | 35.3 | 35.3 | 35.5 | 35.7 | 35.3 |
| 2018 | 35.5 | 35.7 | 35.7 | 35.9 | 36.0 | 36.1 | 36.1 | 36.3 | 36.3 | 36.4 | 36.3 | 36.4 | 36.1 |
| 2019 | 36.1 | 36.4 | 36.4 | 36.6 | 36.6 | 36.8 | 37.1 | 37.2 | 37.0 | 37.2 | 37.5 | 37.9 | 36.9 |
| **Retail Trade** | | | | | | | | | | | | | |
| 2011 | 95.6 | 94.3 | 94.7 | 95.4 | 95.4 | 95.5 | 95.8 | 96.8 | 96.0 | 97.2 | 99.9 | 101.2 | 96.5 |
| 2012 | 97.4 | 96.4 | 96.4 | 96.9 | 97.2 | 97.6 | 97.6 | 98.3 | 98.4 | 99.8 | 103.8 | 104.2 | 98.7 |
| 2013 | 99.3 | 99.0 | 99.3 | 100.1 | 100.6 | 100.9 | 101.6 | 102.9 | 102.7 | 104.5 | 107.3 | 108.9 | 102.3 |
| 2014 | 104.4 | 104.0 | 103.9 | 104.7 | 104.8 | 105.7 | 105.8 | 106.5 | 106.6 | 108.1 | 110.9 | 112.1 | 106.5 |
| 2015 | 107.4 | 106.8 | 106.9 | 108.3 | 108.9 | 109.6 | 110.1 | 110.9 | 111.3 | 113.0 | 115.2 | 116.1 | 110.4 |
| 2016 | 111.9 | 111.8 | 112.2 | 112.7 | 113.1 | 113.4 | 113.9 | 115.0 | 114.2 | 115.6 | 118.6 | 118.7 | 114.3 |
| 2017 | 115.0 | 113.6 | 113.5 | 114.1 | 114.1 | 114.0 | 114.0 | 114.8 | 113.7 | 114.8 | 117.7 | 118.1 | 114.8 |
| 2018 | 113.9 | 113.0 | 112.4 | 112.7 | 113.1 | 113.0 | 112.9 | 113.8 | 113.5 | 113.6 | 117.5 | 117.3 | 113.9 |
| 2019 | 113.1 | 112.2 | 112.2 | 112.7 | 112.5 | 112.7 | 112.8 | 113.4 | 113.1 | 114.9 | 116.7 | 117.1 | 113.6 |
| **Transportation and Utilities** | | | | | | | | | | | | | |
| 2011 | 20.4 | 20.4 | 20.5 | 20.6 | 20.7 | 20.8 | 20.9 | 21.1 | 21.4 | 21.4 | 21.5 | 22.0 | 21.0 |
| 2012 | 21.3 | 21.4 | 21.6 | 21.7 | 21.9 | 22.2 | 22.2 | 22.4 | 22.5 | 22.5 | 22.8 | 23.3 | 22.2 |
| 2013 | 23.0 | 22.9 | 23.0 | 23.3 | 23.5 | 23.8 | 23.7 | 24.0 | 24.1 | 24.3 | 24.9 | 25.5 | 23.8 |
| 2014 | 25.3 | 25.0 | 25.3 | 25.7 | 26.1 | 26.2 | 26.4 | 26.7 | 26.7 | 27.3 | 27.8 | 28.8 | 26.4 |
| 2015 | 28.1 | 27.7 | 27.9 | 27.9 | 28.1 | 28.4 | 28.6 | 28.7 | 28.8 | 28.9 | 29.6 | 30.5 | 28.6 |
| 2016 | 28.5 | 28.3 | 28.3 | 28.5 | 28.8 | 29.6 | 29.3 | 29.2 | 29.9 | 30.1 | 31.7 | 32.2 | 29.5 |
| 2017 | 30.9 | 30.4 | 30.1 | 30.0 | 30.2 | 30.7 | 30.3 | 30.9 | 31.2 | 31.3 | 32.7 | 32.9 | 31.0 |
| 2018 | 30.9 | 30.5 | 30.4 | 30.8 | 30.9 | 31.0 | 31.0 | 30.8 | 30.7 | 31.3 | 32.1 | 32.5 | 31.1 |
| 2019 | 31.6 | 31.1 | 31.0 | 31.2 | 31.3 | 32.0 | 32.4 | 32.6 | 32.8 | 33.2 | 34.6 | 35.3 | 32.4 |
| **Information** | | | | | | | | | | | | | |
| 2011 | 18.6 | 18.6 | 19.0 | 19.3 | 19.3 | 18.9 | 19.7 | 19.5 | 19.3 | 19.3 | 19.5 | 19.7 | 19.2 |
| 2012 | 19.7 | 19.7 | 20.1 | 20.3 | 20.3 | 20.3 | 20.3 | 20.4 | 20.3 | 20.2 | 20.6 | 20.5 | 20.2 |
| 2013 | 20.4 | 20.6 | 20.9 | 21.5 | 21.6 | 21.6 | 21.6 | 21.5 | 21.2 | 21.2 | 21.7 | 21.5 | 21.3 |
| 2014 | 20.8 | 20.8 | 21.0 | 21.6 | 21.7 | 21.5 | 21.6 | 21.4 | 21.4 | 21.4 | 21.5 | 21.8 | 21.4 |
| 2015 | 21.0 | 21.0 | 21.1 | 21.5 | 22.0 | 22.0 | 21.6 | 21.4 | 21.0 | 21.3 | 21.4 | 21.5 | 21.4 |
| 2016 | 21.1 | 21.2 | 21.1 | 21.4 | 21.5 | 21.3 | 21.3 | 20.9 | 20.7 | 21.0 | 20.8 | 21.1 | 21.1 |
| 2017 | 20.6 | 20.9 | 20.9 | 21.4 | 21.1 | 20.9 | 20.6 | 20.6 | 20.4 | 20.5 | 20.6 | 20.8 | 20.8 |
| 2018 | 20.6 | 20.8 | 20.9 | 21.3 | 21.3 | 21.2 | 20.8 | 20.6 | 20.5 | 20.2 | 20.2 | 20.4 | 20.7 |
| 2019 | 20.4 | 20.4 | 20.5 | 20.5 | 20.5 | 20.6 | 20.4 | 20.1 | 19.8 | 19.8 | 19.8 | 19.9 | 20.2 |

## Employment by Industry: San Antonio-New Braunfels, TX, 2011–2019—*Continued*

(Numbers in thousands, not seasonally adjusted)

| Industry and year | January | February | March | April | May | June | July | August | September | October | November | December | Annual average |
|---|---|---|---|---|---|---|---|---|---|---|---|---|---|
| **Financial Activities** | | | | | | | | | | | | | |
| 2011 | 69.2 | 70.0 | 70.4 | 70.6 | 70.8 | 71.2 | 71.9 | 71.5 | 71.2 | 71.5 | 71.5 | 71.9 | 71.0 |
| 2012 | 71.9 | 72.3 | 72.5 | 72.8 | 73.2 | 73.8 | 74.4 | 74.6 | 74.6 | 75.2 | 75.7 | 76.3 | 73.9 |
| 2013 | 75.7 | 76.6 | 77.0 | 77.2 | 77.4 | 78.0 | 78.4 | 78.3 | 78.1 | 78.1 | 78.6 | 78.6 | 77.7 |
| 2014 | 78.4 | 78.7 | 78.8 | 79.5 | 80.0 | 81.0 | 81.1 | 81.3 | 81.2 | 81.6 | 82.1 | 82.4 | 80.5 |
| 2015 | 82.5 | 82.7 | 82.7 | 83.1 | 83.6 | 84.4 | 84.8 | 84.8 | 84.7 | 85.5 | 85.9 | 86.2 | 84.2 |
| 2016 | 86.4 | 87.0 | 87.0 | 87.2 | 87.6 | 88.4 | 88.7 | 88.5 | 88.2 | 88.8 | 89.5 | 90.0 | 88.1 |
| 2017 | 89.8 | 90.4 | 90.3 | 89.9 | 90.0 | 90.8 | 90.8 | 90.6 | 90.3 | 90.5 | 90.8 | 90.8 | 90.4 |
| 2018 | 90.5 | 91.2 | 90.7 | 91.3 | 91.5 | 92.5 | 92.5 | 92.6 | 92.5 | 92.9 | 93.0 | 93.4 | 92.1 |
| 2019 | 92.9 | 93.2 | 93.2 | 93.5 | 94.1 | 94.8 | 94.6 | 94.6 | 94.3 | 95.1 | 95.4 | 95.9 | 94.3 |
| **Professional and Business Services** | | | | | | | | | | | | | |
| 2011 | 103.9 | 105.0 | 106.1 | 106.4 | 105.7 | 106.0 | 105.6 | 107.0 | 108.0 | 107.4 | 107.6 | 108.5 | 106.4 |
| 2012 | 106.3 | 107.7 | 108.5 | 109.0 | 109.3 | 110.1 | 110.3 | 112.6 | 112.6 | 112.4 | 113.2 | 114.4 | 110.5 |
| 2013 | 111.6 | 113.3 | 114.1 | 113.8 | 113.2 | 114.7 | 114.9 | 115.6 | 116.7 | 116.7 | 117.6 | 117.6 | 115.0 |
| 2014 | 115.6 | 117.5 | 118.4 | 120.7 | 120.7 | 121.5 | 121.6 | 122.8 | 122.4 | 123.8 | 124.2 | 123.0 | 121.0 |
| 2015 | 123.2 | 124.6 | 125.2 | 125.3 | 124.5 | 124.5 | 124.7 | 124.6 | 125.2 | 126.8 | 127.1 | 127.1 | 125.2 |
| 2016 | 127.5 | 127.7 | 128.5 | 130.2 | 128.7 | 128.9 | 130.7 | 132.1 | 133.3 | 134.2 | 134.4 | 134.0 | 130.9 |
| 2017 | 132.9 | 133.1 | 133.7 | 133.4 | 133.4 | 135.3 | 135.2 | 135.8 | 138.8 | 139.9 | 139.3 | 138.2 | 135.8 |
| 2018 | 136.1 | 137.5 | 139.0 | 140.1 | 139.1 | 140.6 | 140.8 | 142.3 | 141.9 | 143.2 | 144.2 | 143.3 | 140.7 |
| 2019 | 140.0 | 140.9 | 140.7 | 141.3 | 141.1 | 141.8 | 143.2 | 144.0 | 143.5 | 145.7 | 144.5 | 144.0 | 142.6 |
| **Education and Health Services** | | | | | | | | | | | | | |
| 2011 | 130.1 | 131.1 | 131.9 | 133.1 | 133.4 | 132.7 | 132.7 | 134.2 | 136.1 | 136.2 | 136.5 | 137.1 | 133.8 |
| 2012 | 134.7 | 136.3 | 137.1 | 136.8 | 137.6 | 137.7 | 135.3 | 137.0 | 137.2 | 137.7 | 138.2 | 138.7 | 137.0 |
| 2013 | 135.8 | 137.5 | 138.2 | 138.8 | 139.5 | 139.4 | 138.2 | 139.9 | 140.8 | 141.0 | 141.5 | 142.2 | 139.4 |
| 2014 | 140.5 | 142.0 | 142.9 | 143.1 | 144.4 | 144.5 | 144.3 | 145.4 | 145.9 | 146.9 | 147.1 | 147.4 | 144.5 |
| 2015 | 146.1 | 148.0 | 148.7 | 149.5 | 150.0 | 149.5 | 148.9 | 150.4 | 151.0 | 151.8 | 153.3 | 153.9 | 150.1 |
| 2016 | 152.1 | 153.6 | 154.8 | 155.4 | 156.3 | 155.1 | 155.2 | 157.0 | 158.5 | 159.5 | 160.9 | 161.3 | 156.6 |
| 2017 | 159.9 | 160.5 | 160.9 | 160.4 | 160.6 | 161.0 | 159.5 | 160.6 | 161.6 | 161.8 | 162.4 | 162.9 | 161.0 |
| 2018 | 161.2 | 162.5 | 163.3 | 162.9 | 163.7 | 164.7 | 163.2 | 164.8 | 165.8 | 166.9 | 167.3 | 167.7 | 164.5 |
| 2019 | 165.4 | 166.3 | 166.7 | 167.2 | 167.8 | 168.6 | 167.0 | 168.6 | 168.6 | 171.0 | 171.0 | 171.5 | 168.3 |
| **Leisure and Hospitality** | | | | | | | | | | | | | |
| 2011 | 98.9 | 101.3 | 105.6 | 107.3 | 110.2 | 112.2 | 112.1 | 111.3 | 108.1 | 106.4 | 106.0 | 105.6 | 107.1 |
| 2012 | 102.4 | 105.6 | 109.2 | 111.6 | 114.8 | 118.0 | 117.7 | 116.9 | 113.3 | 112.3 | 110.5 | 110.8 | 111.9 |
| 2013 | 108.4 | 112.0 | 114.8 | 116.4 | 119.3 | 122.5 | 122.0 | 120.6 | 117.2 | 115.6 | 114.8 | 114.2 | 116.5 |
| 2014 | 111.6 | 113.8 | 118.3 | 120.0 | 123.4 | 125.7 | 125.1 | 123.3 | 119.1 | 118.4 | 117.6 | 117.7 | 119.5 |
| 2015 | 114.1 | 117.9 | 120.6 | 122.8 | 126.4 | 129.4 | 130.1 | 129.2 | 126.2 | 125.2 | 124.3 | 123.0 | 124.1 |
| 2016 | 120.9 | 124.5 | 126.9 | 130.2 | 132.4 | 135.3 | 135.9 | 134.6 | 130.5 | 128.8 | 128.0 | 127.8 | 129.7 |
| 2017 | 124.7 | 127.4 | 131.7 | 133.6 | 136.0 | 139.6 | 140.5 | 138.4 | 133.9 | 131.8 | 130.0 | 130.8 | 133.2 |
| 2018 | 126.3 | 129.9 | 133.5 | 135.9 | 137.5 | 141.2 | 141.7 | 141.2 | 136.2 | 135.2 | 133.6 | 134.3 | 135.5 |
| 2019 | 130.3 | 133.9 | 136.6 | 138.1 | 139.8 | 142.9 | 143.1 | 142.0 | 138.0 | 140.7 | 139.3 | 140.4 | 138.8 |
| **Other Services** | | | | | | | | | | | | | |
| 2011 | 31.8 | 32.2 | 32.3 | 32.6 | 32.9 | 33.9 | 34.1 | 33.8 | 33.3 | 33.0 | 33.3 | 32.8 | 33.0 |
| 2012 | 32.7 | 33.0 | 33.5 | 33.4 | 33.7 | 35.3 | 35.3 | 35.0 | 34.6 | 34.6 | 34.8 | 34.5 | 34.2 |
| 2013 | 34.1 | 34.7 | 34.9 | 35.0 | 35.5 | 36.7 | 37.0 | 36.5 | 35.9 | 35.9 | 36.0 | 35.3 | 35.6 |
| 2014 | 35.0 | 35.3 | 35.4 | 35.5 | 36.0 | 37.4 | 37.3 | 37.0 | 36.3 | 36.3 | 36.5 | 35.9 | 36.2 |
| 2015 | 35.5 | 36.0 | 36.1 | 35.5 | 36.1 | 37.5 | 37.3 | 37.1 | 36.4 | 36.4 | 36.7 | 36.1 | 36.4 |
| 2016 | 35.7 | 36.2 | 36.3 | 36.8 | 37.4 | 38.3 | 37.6 | 37.5 | 37.0 | 37.0 | 37.5 | 37.3 | 37.1 |
| 2017 | 36.5 | 37.1 | 37.2 | 37.8 | 38.1 | 39.1 | 38.6 | 38.3 | 38.1 | 37.9 | 38.4 | 37.8 | 37.9 |
| 2018 | 37.2 | 37.8 | 38.1 | 38.7 | 39.1 | 40.1 | 39.4 | 39.4 | 39.0 | 39.6 | 39.7 | 39.1 | 38.9 |
| 2019 | 38.3 | 38.8 | 39.0 | 39.2 | 39.8 | 40.5 | 40.2 | 40.2 | 39.7 | 39.8 | 40.1 | 39.7 | 39.6 |
| **Government** | | | | | | | | | | | | | |
| 2011 | 163.2 | 165.7 | 165.2 | 165.4 | 165.5 | 162.9 | 156.5 | 156.3 | 161.3 | 163.9 | 163.6 | 163.7 | 162.8 |
| 2012 | 161.1 | 163.1 | 163.2 | 163.7 | 163.3 | 159.6 | 154.0 | 156.2 | 162.0 | 164.2 | 164.3 | 164.3 | 161.6 |
| 2013 | 161.9 | 164.2 | 164.2 | 164.9 | 164.6 | 162.3 | 157.8 | 157.8 | 163.1 | 166.0 | 166.2 | 165.7 | 163.2 |
| 2014 | 163.3 | 165.5 | 165.6 | 165.9 | 165.5 | 163.1 | 157.8 | 158.2 | 164.3 | 168.2 | 168.8 | 168.2 | 164.5 |
| 2015 | 166.8 | 168.6 | 168.4 | 168.9 | 169.0 | 165.4 | 160.5 | 160.9 | 168.5 | 169.9 | 171.6 | 171.3 | 167.5 |
| 2016 | 170.3 | 171.6 | 171.5 | 170.2 | 170.6 | 168.2 | 163.1 | 163.6 | 170.5 | 171.3 | 172.3 | 172.3 | 169.6 |
| 2017 | 171.2 | 172.9 | 173.3 | 172.6 | 172.8 | 169.9 | 164.4 | 164.8 | 170.8 | 171.9 | 173.2 | 173.2 | 170.9 |
| 2018 | 171.9 | 172.8 | 173.7 | 173.4 | 173.8 | 170.8 | 165.6 | 165.9 | 171.9 | 173.1 | 174.4 | 174.7 | 171.8 |
| 2019 | 173.0 | 174.4 | 175.0 | 174.2 | 174.9 | 171.9 | 166.9 | 167.7 | 174.2 | 175.5 | 176.9 | 176.8 | 173.5 |

## Employment by Industry: Portland-Vancouver-Hillsboro, OR-WA, 2011–2019

(Numbers in thousands, not seasonally adjusted)

| Industry and year | January | February | March | April | May | June | July | August | September | October | November | December | Annual average |
|---|---|---|---|---|---|---|---|---|---|---|---|---|---|
| **Total Nonfarm** | | | | | | | | | | | | | |
| 2011 | 977.5 | 984.4 | 988.1 | 998.3 | 1,000.3 | 1,001.2 | 995.3 | 995.9 | 1,002.0 | 1,012.2 | 1,016.9 | 1,016.9 | 999.1 |
| 2012 | 998.5 | 1,005.4 | 1,010.1 | 1,016.9 | 1,023.2 | 1,025.1 | 1,017.0 | 1,018.9 | 1,023.1 | 1,034.9 | 1,038.4 | 1,036.8 | 1,020.7 |
| 2013 | 1,014.6 | 1,024.6 | 1,029.1 | 1,039.1 | 1,046.1 | 1,048.7 | 1,040.8 | 1,046.2 | 1,052.5 | 1,063.2 | 1,069.5 | 1,067.8 | 1,045.2 |
| 2014 | 1,050.8 | 1,054.6 | 1,062.3 | 1,070.0 | 1,076.3 | 1,079.6 | 1,072.5 | 1,076.9 | 1,084.5 | 1,093.4 | 1,098.9 | 1,102.1 | 1,076.8 |
| 2015 | 1,084.0 | 1,092.9 | 1,098.1 | 1,105.8 | 1,110.4 | 1,114.2 | 1,111.2 | 1,114.8 | 1,120.1 | 1,131.9 | 1,135.1 | 1,138.2 | 1,113.1 |
| 2016 | 1,118.7 | 1,129.4 | 1,134.0 | 1,143.8 | 1,147.3 | 1,149.2 | 1,142.3 | 1,145.9 | 1,152.3 | 1,161.2 | 1,166.4 | 1,164.0 | 1,146.2 |
| 2017 | 1,139.2 | 1,156.9 | 1,164.4 | 1,173.1 | 1,177.6 | 1,183.6 | 1,175.1 | 1,177.3 | 1,182.4 | 1,189.7 | 1,195.4 | 1,196.7 | 1,176.0 |
| 2018 | 1,173.9 | 1,182.0 | 1,188.3 | 1,195.5 | 1,199.7 | 1,205.0 | 1,196.2 | 1,197.9 | 1,205.0 | 1,213.5 | 1,220.9 | 1,220.3 | 1,199.9 |
| 2019 | 1,203.7 | 1,206.4 | 1,213.2 | 1,218.7 | 1,222.4 | 1,225.1 | 1,218.9 | 1,222.9 | 1,224.5 | 1,231.0 | 1,232.5 | 1,235.6 | 1,221.2 |
| **Total Private** | | | | | | | | | | | | | |
| 2011 | 829.2 | 835.1 | 838.9 | 847.4 | 848.9 | 852.3 | 858.2 | 861.1 | 864.9 | 865.4 | 868.5 | 870.2 | 853.3 |
| 2012 | 852.0 | 857.4 | 862.1 | 869.0 | 874.0 | 876.7 | 880.2 | 884.2 | 885.9 | 888.6 | 890.6 | 890.5 | 875.9 |
| 2013 | 869.5 | 877.3 | 882.0 | 891.6 | 897.7 | 900.1 | 906.0 | 912.2 | 915.9 | 917.5 | 921.9 | 921.0 | 901.1 |
| 2014 | 904.5 | 907.1 | 914.2 | 920.9 | 925.9 | 930.4 | 935.4 | 939.6 | 943.9 | 943.9 | 947.4 | 951.2 | 930.4 |
| 2015 | 933.6 | 940.8 | 945.8 | 953.0 | 957.2 | 962.4 | 970.2 | 973.5 | 976.3 | 978.7 | 980.4 | 984.1 | 963.0 |
| 2016 | 965.9 | 974.6 | 978.5 | 987.4 | 989.5 | 992.5 | 997.1 | 1,002.0 | 1,004.4 | 1,005.3 | 1,008.9 | 1,007.3 | 992.8 |
| 2017 | 985.2 | 999.6 | 1,005.6 | 1,013.8 | 1,017.6 | 1,023.2 | 1,025.2 | 1,028.1 | 1,031.0 | 1,031.5 | 1,035.5 | 1,037.1 | 1,019.5 |
| 2018 | 1,024.0 | 1,030.2 | 1,036.1 | 1,042.3 | 1,046.1 | 1,051.5 | 1,053.2 | 1,056.9 | 1,058.1 | 1,061.1 | 1,066.1 | 1,066.3 | 1,049.3 |
| 2019 | 1,050.5 | 1,052.0 | 1,057.9 | 1,063.3 | 1,066.4 | 1,069.4 | 1,073.5 | 1,078.8 | 1,076.8 | 1,076.1 | 1,076.9 | 1,080.0 | 1,068.5 |
| **Goods Producing** | | | | | | | | | | | | | |
| 2011 | 151.9 | 153.2 | 154.5 | 156.5 | 158.0 | 160.3 | 163.1 | 164.2 | 163.8 | 163.4 | 162.0 | 161.6 | 159.4 |
| 2012 | 159.0 | 159.5 | 160.2 | 161.1 | 163.7 | 165.5 | 168.5 | 169.4 | 168.1 | 167.4 | 165.0 | 163.4 | 164.2 |
| 2013 | 161.3 | 162.3 | 163.3 | 165.6 | 167.0 | 170.0 | 172.3 | 173.8 | 173.5 | 173.8 | 172.6 | 171.2 | 169.0 |
| 2014 | 170.5 | 170.3 | 172.2 | 172.7 | 174.3 | 176.0 | 178.3 | 178.8 | 178.1 | 176.8 | 175.4 | 175.4 | 174.9 |
| 2015 | 174.1 | 174.7 | 175.7 | 176.6 | 178.1 | 180.4 | 183.2 | 183.8 | 183.3 | 183.8 | 182.1 | 182.2 | 179.8 |
| 2016 | 180.6 | 182.2 | 183.2 | 184.3 | 185.7 | 186.4 | 188.7 | 190.3 | 188.9 | 188.7 | 187.0 | 186.3 | 186.0 |
| 2017 | 183.0 | 185.7 | 187.2 | 189.1 | 191.4 | 194.2 | 196.1 | 196.9 | 196.4 | 196.7 | 195.7 | 196.2 | 192.4 |
| 2018 | 193.9 | 195.3 | 196.5 | 198.2 | 200.4 | 203.1 | 205.5 | 206.4 | 205.7 | 205.5 | 204.8 | 204.3 | 201.6 |
| 2019 | 202.0 | 202.1 | 204.0 | 204.5 | 206.2 | 207.8 | 209.9 | 210.4 | 209.0 | 206.6 | 206.7 | 205.5 | 206.2 |
| **Service-Providing** | | | | | | | | | | | | | |
| 2011 | 825.6 | 831.2 | 833.6 | 841.8 | 842.3 | 840.9 | 832.2 | 831.7 | 838.2 | 848.8 | 854.9 | 855.3 | 839.7 |
| 2012 | 839.5 | 845.9 | 849.9 | 855.8 | 859.5 | 859.6 | 848.5 | 849.5 | 855.0 | 867.5 | 873.4 | 873.4 | 856.5 |
| 2013 | 853.3 | 862.3 | 865.8 | 873.5 | 878.4 | 878.7 | 868.5 | 872.4 | 879.0 | 889.4 | 896.9 | 896.6 | 876.2 |
| 2014 | 880.3 | 884.3 | 890.1 | 897.3 | 902.0 | 903.6 | 894.2 | 898.1 | 906.4 | 916.6 | 923.5 | 926.7 | 901.9 |
| 2015 | 909.9 | 918.2 | 922.4 | 929.2 | 932.3 | 933.8 | 928.0 | 931.0 | 936.8 | 948.1 | 953.0 | 956.0 | 933.2 |
| 2016 | 938.1 | 947.2 | 950.8 | 959.5 | 961.6 | 962.8 | 953.6 | 955.6 | 963.4 | 972.5 | 979.4 | 977.7 | 960.2 |
| 2017 | 956.2 | 971.2 | 977.2 | 984.0 | 986.2 | 989.4 | 979.0 | 980.4 | 986.0 | 993.0 | 999.7 | 1,000.5 | 983.6 |
| 2018 | 980.0 | 986.7 | 991.8 | 997.3 | 999.3 | 1,001.9 | 990.7 | 991.5 | 999.3 | 1,008.0 | 1,016.1 | 1,016.0 | 998.2 |
| 2019 | 1,001.7 | 1,004.3 | 1,009.2 | 1,014.2 | 1,016.2 | 1,017.3 | 1,009.0 | 1,012.5 | 1,015.5 | 1,024.4 | 1,025.8 | 1,030.1 | 1,015.0 |
| **Mining and Logging** | | | | | | | | | | | | | |
| 2011 | 0.9 | 1.0 | 1.0 | 1.0 | 1.1 | 1.1 | 1.1 | 1.1 | 1.1 | 1.1 | 1.1 | 1.0 | 1.1 |
| 2012 | 0.9 | 0.9 | 0.9 | 0.9 | 1.0 | 1.0 | 1.0 | 1.0 | 1.0 | 1.0 | 1.0 | 1.0 | 1.0 |
| 2013 | 1.0 | 1.0 | 1.0 | 1.0 | 1.0 | 1.1 | 1.1 | 1.1 | 1.1 | 1.2 | 1.2 | 1.1 | 1.1 |
| 2014 | 1.1 | 1.1 | 1.1 | 1.2 | 1.2 | 1.2 | 1.2 | 1.3 | 1.3 | 1.2 | 1.2 | 1.2 | 1.2 |
| 2015 | 1.2 | 1.2 | 1.2 | 1.3 | 1.2 | 1.3 | 1.3 | 1.3 | 1.3 | 1.3 | 1.3 | 1.3 | 1.3 |
| 2016 | 1.3 | 1.3 | 1.3 | 1.3 | 1.3 | 1.3 | 1.4 | 1.4 | 1.3 | 1.4 | 1.3 | 1.3 | 1.3 |
| 2017 | 1.3 | 1.3 | 1.3 | 1.3 | 1.3 | 1.4 | 1.4 | 1.4 | 1.3 | 1.3 | 1.3 | 1.4 | 1.3 |
| 2018 | 1.3 | 1.3 | 1.3 | 1.4 | 1.4 | 1.4 | 1.4 | 1.4 | 1.4 | 1.4 | 1.4 | 1.4 | 1.4 |
| 2019 | 1.3 | 1.3 | 1.3 | 1.3 | 1.3 | 1.3 | 1.3 | 1.3 | 1.3 | 1.3 | 1.3 | 1.2 | 1.3 |
| **Construction** | | | | | | | | | | | | | |
| 2011 | 42.8 | 43.3 | 44.2 | 45.6 | 46.4 | 47.7 | 49.4 | 50.1 | 50.0 | 49.6 | 48.2 | 48.0 | 47.1 |
| 2012 | 46.2 | 46.3 | 46.7 | 47.3 | 49.0 | 49.7 | 51.3 | 52.5 | 51.4 | 50.8 | 48.8 | 47.7 | 49.0 |
| 2013 | 46.4 | 47.0 | 48.1 | 49.8 | 51.8 | 52.8 | 54.7 | 55.6 | 55.5 | 55.7 | 55.0 | 54.0 | 52.2 |
| 2014 | 53.6 | 53.2 | 54.7 | 54.9 | 55.8 | 56.7 | 57.7 | 58.0 | 57.2 | 55.8 | 54.8 | 54.3 | 55.6 |
| 2015 | 53.3 | 53.5 | 53.8 | 54.2 | 55.1 | 56.2 | 57.7 | 58.6 | 58.3 | 58.9 | 57.8 | 57.4 | 56.2 |
| 2016 | 56.6 | 57.9 | 58.5 | 60.0 | 61.1 | 61.9 | 63.9 | 65.0 | 64.9 | 64.4 | 63.7 | 63.1 | 61.8 |
| 2017 | 61.1 | 63.2 | 64.2 | 65.5 | 67.0 | 68.5 | 69.7 | 70.7 | 70.6 | 70.1 | 69.3 | 69.3 | 67.4 |
| 2018 | 67.8 | 68.7 | 69.4 | 70.6 | 72.2 | 73.6 | 75.1 | 76.1 | 75.5 | 75.3 | 74.6 | 73.8 | 72.7 |
| 2019 | 72.2 | 72.1 | 73.6 | 74.1 | 75.5 | 76.6 | 78.0 | 78.9 | 78.2 | 76.5 | 76.6 | 75.2 | 75.6 |

## Employment by Industry: Portland-Vancouver-Hillsboro, OR-WA, 2011–2019—*Continued*

(Numbers in thousands, not seasonally adjusted)

| Industry and year | January | February | March | April | May | June | July | August | September | October | November | December | Annual average |
|---|---|---|---|---|---|---|---|---|---|---|---|---|---|
| **Manufacturing** | | | | | | | | | | | | | |
| 2011 | 108.2 | 108.9 | 109.3 | 109.9 | 110.5 | 111.5 | 112.6 | 113.0 | 112.7 | 112.7 | 112.7 | 112.6 | 111.2 |
| 2012 | 111.9 | 112.3 | 112.6 | 112.9 | 113.7 | 114.8 | 116.2 | 115.9 | 115.7 | 115.6 | 115.2 | 114.7 | 114.3 |
| 2013 | 113.9 | 114.3 | 114.2 | 114.8 | 114.9 | 116.1 | 116.5 | 117.1 | 116.9 | 116.9 | 116.4 | 116.1 | 115.7 |
| 2014 | 115.8 | 116.0 | 116.4 | 116.6 | 117.3 | 118.1 | 119.4 | 119.5 | 119.6 | 119.8 | 119.4 | 119.9 | 118.2 |
| 2015 | 119.6 | 120.0 | 120.7 | 121.1 | 121.8 | 122.9 | 124.2 | 123.9 | 123.7 | 123.6 | 123.0 | 123.5 | 122.3 |
| 2016 | 122.7 | 123.0 | 123.4 | 123.0 | 123.3 | 123.2 | 123.4 | 123.9 | 122.7 | 122.9 | 122.0 | 121.9 | 123.0 |
| 2017 | 120.6 | 121.2 | 121.7 | 122.3 | 123.1 | 124.3 | 125.0 | 124.8 | 124.5 | 125.3 | 125.1 | 125.5 | 123.6 |
| 2018 | 124.8 | 125.3 | 125.8 | 126.2 | 126.8 | 128.1 | 129.0 | 128.9 | 128.8 | 128.8 | 128.8 | 129.1 | 127.5 |
| 2019 | 128.5 | 128.7 | 129.1 | 129.1 | 129.4 | 129.9 | 130.6 | 130.2 | 129.5 | 128.8 | 128.8 | 129.1 | 129.3 |
| **Trade, Transportation, and Utilities** | | | | | | | | | | | | | |
| 2011 | 184.7 | 183.5 | 183.4 | 184.7 | 185.9 | 186.8 | 187.9 | 187.7 | 188.0 | 188.5 | 192.4 | 194.1 | 187.3 |
| 2012 | 187.2 | 185.8 | 186.2 | 187.5 | 189.4 | 190.9 | 190.8 | 191.2 | 190.9 | 192.0 | 197.1 | 198.9 | 190.7 |
| 2013 | 191.3 | 191.0 | 191.2 | 192.2 | 193.9 | 194.6 | 196.0 | 196.8 | 197.0 | 197.3 | 201.7 | 203.4 | 195.5 |
| 2014 | 197.4 | 195.8 | 195.9 | 196.9 | 198.6 | 200.0 | 201.5 | 202.6 | 202.9 | 203.6 | 207.9 | 210.8 | 201.2 |
| 2015 | 203.8 | 202.7 | 203.1 | 203.8 | 205.1 | 206.6 | 207.7 | 208.7 | 208.9 | 209.5 | 212.6 | 215.1 | 207.3 |
| 2016 | 207.7 | 206.6 | 206.6 | 207.5 | 208.1 | 209.6 | 210.4 | 211.3 | 211.0 | 211.5 | 216.7 | 218.6 | 210.5 |
| 2017 | 212.5 | 212.1 | 212.2 | 212.6 | 213.7 | 214.5 | 215.3 | 216.1 | 216.1 | 216.9 | 221.6 | 223.9 | 215.6 |
| 2018 | 216.0 | 213.6 | 213.6 | 214.2 | 215.7 | 216.7 | 217.2 | 218.2 | 218.6 | 219.8 | 225.7 | 227.5 | 218.1 |
| 2019 | 221.3 | 217.6 | 217.5 | 218.0 | 218.8 | 219.3 | 221.1 | 222.1 | 221.5 | 223.3 | 224.7 | 228.2 | 221.1 |
| **Wholesale Trade** | | | | | | | | | | | | | |
| 2011 | 48.9 | 49.3 | 49.1 | 50.0 | 50.5 | 50.5 | 50.9 | 50.9 | 50.6 | 50.8 | 50.7 | 50.5 | 50.2 |
| 2012 | 50.1 | 50.4 | 50.5 | 51.5 | 52.0 | 51.9 | 52.3 | 52.3 | 52.0 | 52.1 | 52.4 | 52.4 | 51.7 |
| 2013 | 51.5 | 52.1 | 52.0 | 52.3 | 52.8 | 52.7 | 53.4 | 53.3 | 53.2 | 52.8 | 53.3 | 53.2 | 52.7 |
| 2014 | 52.5 | 52.7 | 52.5 | 52.6 | 52.8 | 52.9 | 53.4 | 53.5 | 53.4 | 53.2 | 53.4 | 53.6 | 53.0 |
| 2015 | 53.0 | 53.5 | 53.4 | 53.5 | 53.8 | 53.9 | 54.5 | 54.5 | 54.4 | 54.3 | 54.5 | 54.7 | 54.0 |
| 2016 | 53.7 | 54.1 | 54.0 | 54.4 | 54.3 | 54.6 | 54.9 | 55.1 | 54.8 | 54.8 | 55.2 | 55.5 | 54.6 |
| 2017 | 54.8 | 55.5 | 55.4 | 55.7 | 56.2 | 56.3 | 56.4 | 56.6 | 56.3 | 56.0 | 56.3 | 56.5 | 56.0 |
| 2018 | 55.7 | 56.1 | 56.0 | 56.3 | 56.6 | 56.8 | 57.1 | 57.3 | 57.2 | 56.9 | 57.1 | 57.4 | 56.7 |
| 2019 | 56.5 | 56.8 | 56.8 | 57.2 | 57.4 | 57.5 | 57.7 | 57.7 | 57.3 | 58.0 | 57.7 | 58.2 | 57.4 |
| **Retail Trade** | | | | | | | | | | | | | |
| 2011 | 102.2 | 100.9 | 100.9 | 101.2 | 101.7 | 102.6 | 103.6 | 103.5 | 103.1 | 103.8 | 107.4 | 108.8 | 103.3 |
| 2012 | 103.6 | 101.9 | 101.9 | 102.5 | 103.6 | 104.9 | 105.4 | 105.6 | 105.0 | 105.9 | 110.2 | 111.4 | 105.2 |
| 2013 | 106.1 | 105.1 | 105.2 | 105.8 | 107.0 | 107.7 | 109.0 | 109.7 | 109.2 | 109.9 | 113.4 | 114.6 | 108.6 |
| 2014 | 109.8 | 108.1 | 108.5 | 109.2 | 110.5 | 111.5 | 113.1 | 113.7 | 113.4 | 113.9 | 117.5 | 119.0 | 112.4 |
| 2015 | 113.6 | 112.3 | 112.7 | 113.7 | 114.5 | 115.1 | 116.6 | 117.3 | 116.9 | 117.3 | 119.7 | 120.8 | 115.9 |
| 2016 | 115.8 | 114.9 | 115.0 | 115.2 | 115.8 | 116.9 | 117.9 | 118.2 | 117.6 | 118.0 | 120.8 | 121.4 | 117.3 |
| 2017 | 117.5 | 116.9 | 117.1 | 117.4 | 117.6 | 118.1 | 119.4 | 119.7 | 119.3 | 119.9 | 123.0 | 123.8 | 119.1 |
| 2018 | 119.4 | 117.4 | 117.4 | 117.8 | 118.6 | 119.1 | 120.1 | 120.2 | 119.2 | 119.7 | 122.4 | 122.6 | 119.5 |
| 2019 | 118.9 | 116.4 | 116.4 | 116.6 | 116.9 | 116.8 | 118.1 | 118.2 | 117.5 | 118.0 | 119.4 | 121.2 | 117.9 |
| **Transportation and Utilities** | | | | | | | | | | | | | |
| 2011 | 33.6 | 33.3 | 33.4 | 33.5 | 33.7 | 33.7 | 33.4 | 33.3 | 34.3 | 33.9 | 34.3 | 34.8 | 33.8 |
| 2012 | 33.5 | 33.5 | 33.8 | 33.5 | 33.8 | 34.1 | 33.1 | 33.3 | 33.9 | 34.0 | 34.5 | 35.1 | 33.8 |
| 2013 | 33.7 | 33.8 | 34.0 | 34.1 | 34.1 | 34.2 | 33.6 | 33.8 | 34.6 | 34.6 | 35.0 | 35.6 | 34.3 |
| 2014 | 35.1 | 35.0 | 34.9 | 35.1 | 35.3 | 35.6 | 35.0 | 35.4 | 36.1 | 36.5 | 37.0 | 38.2 | 35.8 |
| 2015 | 37.2 | 36.9 | 37.0 | 36.6 | 36.8 | 37.6 | 36.6 | 36.9 | 37.6 | 37.9 | 38.4 | 39.6 | 37.4 |
| 2016 | 38.2 | 37.6 | 37.6 | 37.9 | 38.0 | 38.1 | 37.6 | 38.0 | 38.6 | 38.7 | 40.7 | 41.7 | 38.6 |
| 2017 | 40.2 | 39.7 | 39.7 | 39.5 | 39.9 | 40.1 | 39.5 | 39.8 | 40.5 | 41.0 | 42.3 | 43.6 | 40.5 |
| 2018 | 40.9 | 40.1 | 40.2 | 40.1 | 40.5 | 40.8 | 40.0 | 40.7 | 42.2 | 43.2 | 46.2 | 47.5 | 41.9 |
| 2019 | 45.9 | 44.4 | 44.3 | 44.2 | 44.5 | 45.0 | 45.3 | 46.2 | 46.7 | 47.3 | 47.6 | 48.8 | 45.9 |
| **Information** | | | | | | | | | | | | | |
| 2011 | 23.4 | 23.4 | 23.7 | 23.5 | 23.4 | 23.2 | 23.5 | 23.6 | 23.3 | 23.3 | 23.5 | 23.4 | 23.4 |
| 2012 | 23.1 | 23.4 | 23.8 | 24.0 | 23.9 | 24.2 | 24.4 | 24.1 | 24.0 | 24.4 | 24.5 | 24.3 | 24.0 |
| 2013 | 23.9 | 23.9 | 24.0 | 24.0 | 23.9 | 23.8 | 23.9 | 24.1 | 24.2 | 24.3 | 24.4 | 24.4 | 24.1 |
| 2014 | 23.6 | 23.7 | 24.0 | 24.1 | 24.0 | 24.3 | 24.7 | 24.7 | 24.7 | 24.6 | 24.7 | 24.8 | 24.3 |
| 2015 | 24.3 | 24.6 | 24.7 | 24.6 | 24.8 | 24.9 | 25.5 | 25.8 | 25.4 | 25.2 | 25.4 | 25.7 | 25.1 |
| 2016 | 25.2 | 25.5 | 25.6 | 25.7 | 26.1 | 26.1 | 25.9 | 26.2 | 27.1 | 26.7 | 26.5 | 26.4 | 26.1 |
| 2017 | 26.3 | 26.8 | 26.6 | 26.5 | 26.0 | 25.8 | 25.5 | 25.8 | 25.8 | 25.2 | 25.2 | 24.9 | 25.9 |
| 2018 | 24.7 | 25.1 | 25.4 | 25.4 | 25.1 | 25.3 | 25.8 | 25.6 | 25.5 | 25.9 | 26.2 | 26.0 | 25.5 |
| 2019 | 25.8 | 26.2 | 26.1 | 26.3 | 27.0 | 26.6 | 26.2 | 26.6 | 26.2 | 26.6 | 27.6 | 27.7 | 26.6 |

## Employment by Industry: Portland-Vancouver-Hillsboro, OR-WA, 2011–2019—*Continued*

(Numbers in thousands, not seasonally adjusted)

| Industry and year | January | February | March | April | May | June | July | August | September | October | November | December | Annual average |
|---|---|---|---|---|---|---|---|---|---|---|---|---|---|
| **Financial Activities** | | | | | | | | | | | | | |
| 2011 | 61.8 | 61.8 | 61.6 | 61.7 | 61.8 | 62.0 | 62.2 | 62.2 | 61.9 | 61.8 | 62.0 | 62.1 | 61.9 |
| 2012 | 61.8 | 61.9 | 61.9 | 62.2 | 62.2 | 62.4 | 63.0 | 63.1 | 62.8 | 62.9 | 62.9 | 63.2 | 62.5 |
| 2013 | 62.4 | 62.5 | 62.6 | 63.1 | 63.5 | 63.7 | 64.6 | 64.5 | 64.3 | 64.3 | 64.2 | 64.2 | 63.7 |
| 2014 | 63.3 | 63.2 | 63.2 | 63.5 | 63.8 | 64.2 | 64.8 | 65.1 | 65.0 | 65.2 | 65.2 | 65.4 | 64.3 |
| 2015 | 65.2 | 65.3 | 65.2 | 65.9 | 66.3 | 66.6 | 67.4 | 67.5 | 67.1 | 67.5 | 67.4 | 67.8 | 66.6 |
| 2016 | 66.8 | 66.7 | 66.6 | 67.5 | 67.8 | 68.3 | 69.1 | 69.5 | 69.1 | 69.5 | 69.8 | 69.8 | 68.4 |
| 2017 | 69.0 | 69.2 | 69.6 | 70.0 | 70.5 | 70.9 | 72.0 | 71.9 | 71.3 | 71.9 | 72.1 | 71.9 | 70.9 |
| 2018 | 71.2 | 71.3 | 71.6 | 72.0 | 72.3 | 72.5 | 73.3 | 73.3 | 72.7 | 72.8 | 72.7 | 72.6 | 72.4 |
| 2019 | 72.1 | 72.4 | 72.4 | 72.8 | 73.1 | 73.3 | 74.3 | 74.5 | 73.8 | 74.4 | 74.3 | 74.5 | 73.5 |
| **Professional and Business Services** | | | | | | | | | | | | | |
| 2011 | 136.6 | 138.1 | 139.2 | 141.5 | 141.4 | 142.3 | 144.7 | 145.4 | 145.8 | 145.9 | 146.1 | 146.4 | 142.8 |
| 2012 | 144.2 | 145.0 | 146.1 | 147.5 | 147.9 | 149.0 | 150.3 | 151.5 | 151.0 | 152.2 | 151.6 | 151.5 | 149.0 |
| 2013 | 148.4 | 149.8 | 151.7 | 154.1 | 154.8 | 156.1 | 158.5 | 160.1 | 159.9 | 160.7 | 160.7 | 160.7 | 156.3 |
| 2014 | 157.7 | 158.8 | 160.4 | 162.5 | 163.3 | 164.9 | 166.4 | 167.8 | 168.2 | 168.3 | 168.0 | 168.3 | 164.6 |
| 2015 | 164.9 | 166.5 | 168.2 | 170.6 | 171.2 | 172.2 | 174.2 | 175.0 | 174.7 | 175.4 | 174.8 | 174.9 | 171.9 |
| 2016 | 172.3 | 174.1 | 175.1 | 177.1 | 177.1 | 178.2 | 179.2 | 180.0 | 178.8 | 179.5 | 179.1 | 178.0 | 177.4 |
| 2017 | 175.1 | 178.1 | 179.3 | 181.6 | 182.0 | 183.8 | 183.3 | 183.8 | 183.7 | 183.5 | 183.1 | 182.9 | 181.7 |
| 2018 | 181.0 | 182.6 | 183.9 | 184.2 | 184.1 | 184.9 | 185.1 | 186.5 | 185.8 | 186.4 | 186.3 | 185.9 | 184.7 |
| 2019 | 184.7 | 185.6 | 186.8 | 188.1 | 188.7 | 189.6 | 190.4 | 191.6 | 190.6 | 192.0 | 191.7 | 190.8 | 189.2 |
| **Education and Health Services** | | | | | | | | | | | | | |
| 2011 | 144.5 | 147.3 | 147.8 | 148.1 | 146.3 | 143.4 | 140.9 | 141.2 | 146.2 | 149.3 | 150.2 | 149.8 | 146.3 |
| 2012 | 146.3 | 150.1 | 150.7 | 151.4 | 149.3 | 145.8 | 142.9 | 143.5 | 148.5 | 151.2 | 152.2 | 151.8 | 148.6 |
| 2013 | 147.7 | 151.8 | 151.9 | 153.3 | 152.2 | 148.3 | 145.4 | 146.6 | 151.6 | 155.3 | 156.4 | 155.8 | 151.4 |
| 2014 | 152.6 | 155.4 | 156.2 | 156.8 | 155.2 | 152.8 | 150.1 | 149.9 | 155.3 | 158.2 | 159.6 | 159.5 | 155.1 |
| 2015 | 156.3 | 160.3 | 160.6 | 161.3 | 159.2 | 156.9 | 155.0 | 154.9 | 160.3 | 163.1 | 164.2 | 163.8 | 159.7 |
| 2016 | 161.2 | 165.1 | 165.4 | 166.1 | 163.7 | 160.6 | 158.7 | 159.7 | 165.2 | 168.4 | 169.3 | 168.2 | 164.3 |
| 2017 | 164.1 | 169.9 | 170.9 | 171.2 | 169.4 | 166.3 | 163.8 | 164.8 | 170.6 | 173.0 | 174.0 | 173.4 | 169.3 |
| 2018 | 176.9 | 180.7 | 181.6 | 181.9 | 180.1 | 177.8 | 174.1 | 175.0 | 180.0 | 183.0 | 183.9 | 182.6 | 179.8 |
| 2019 | 180.6 | 184.3 | 185.2 | 185.2 | 182.3 | 179.8 | 177.4 | 179.1 | 183.8 | 184.9 | 186.0 | 185.7 | 182.9 |
| **Leisure and Hospitality** | | | | | | | | | | | | | |
| 2011 | 91.9 | 93.0 | 93.7 | 96.2 | 96.8 | 98.8 | 100.1 | 100.8 | 100.0 | 97.3 | 96.5 | 97.0 | 96.8 |
| 2012 | 94.7 | 95.6 | 97.0 | 98.7 | 100.4 | 101.9 | 103.3 | 104.4 | 103.8 | 101.5 | 100.7 | 101.0 | 100.3 |
| 2013 | 98.3 | 99.5 | 100.7 | 102.6 | 104.5 | 106.6 | 107.8 | 108.8 | 108.2 | 104.9 | 104.6 | 104.4 | 104.2 |
| 2014 | 102.5 | 102.9 | 104.9 | 106.9 | 108.5 | 109.6 | 111.0 | 112.0 | 111.1 | 108.7 | 108.2 | 108.6 | 107.9 |
| 2015 | 107.0 | 108.3 | 109.8 | 111.3 | 113.4 | 115.5 | 117.4 | 117.8 | 116.9 | 114.4 | 113.9 | 114.6 | 113.4 |
| 2016 | 112.1 | 113.8 | 115.1 | 117.6 | 119.1 | 121.2 | 123.1 | 122.8 | 122.0 | 119.0 | 118.6 | 118.6 | 118.6 |
| 2017 | 115.4 | 117.2 | 118.8 | 121.4 | 123.0 | 126.0 | 127.1 | 126.7 | 125.3 | 122.7 | 122.2 | 122.3 | 122.3 |
| 2018 | 119.4 | 120.3 | 121.8 | 124.2 | 125.8 | 128.3 | 129.2 | 129.2 | 127.5 | 125.2 | 124.1 | 125.2 | 125.0 |
| 2019 | 121.8 | 121.6 | 123.4 | 125.6 | 127.3 | 130.2 | 131.1 | 131.4 | 129.1 | 125.9 | 123.5 | 125.7 | 126.4 |
| **Other Services** | | | | | | | | | | | | | |
| 2011 | 34.4 | 34.8 | 35.0 | 35.2 | 35.3 | 35.5 | 35.8 | 36.0 | 35.9 | 35.9 | 35.8 | 35.8 | 35.5 |
| 2012 | 35.7 | 36.1 | 36.2 | 36.6 | 37.2 | 37.0 | 37.0 | 37.0 | 36.8 | 37.0 | 36.6 | 36.4 | 36.6 |
| 2013 | 36.2 | 36.5 | 36.6 | 36.7 | 37.2 | 37.0 | 37.5 | 37.5 | 37.2 | 36.9 | 37.3 | 36.9 | 37.0 |
| 2014 | 36.9 | 37.0 | 37.4 | 37.5 | 38.2 | 38.6 | 38.6 | 38.7 | 38.6 | 38.5 | 38.4 | 38.4 | 38.1 |
| 2015 | 38.0 | 38.4 | 38.5 | 38.9 | 39.1 | 39.3 | 39.8 | 40.0 | 39.7 | 39.8 | 40.0 | 40.0 | 39.3 |
| 2016 | 40.0 | 40.6 | 40.9 | 41.6 | 41.9 | 42.1 | 42.0 | 42.2 | 42.3 | 42.0 | 41.9 | 41.4 | 41.6 |
| 2017 | 39.8 | 40.6 | 41.0 | 41.4 | 41.6 | 41.7 | 42.1 | 42.1 | 41.8 | 41.6 | 41.6 | 41.6 | 41.4 |
| 2018 | 40.9 | 41.3 | 41.7 | 42.2 | 42.6 | 42.9 | 43.0 | 42.7 | 42.3 | 42.5 | 42.4 | 42.2 | 42.2 |
| 2019 | 42.2 | 42.2 | 42.5 | 42.8 | 43.0 | 42.8 | 43.1 | 43.1 | 42.8 | 42.4 | 42.4 | 41.9 | 42.6 |
| **Government** | | | | | | | | | | | | | |
| 2011 | 148.3 | 149.3 | 149.2 | 150.9 | 151.4 | 148.9 | 137.1 | 134.8 | 137.1 | 146.8 | 148.4 | 146.7 | 145.7 |
| 2012 | 146.5 | 148.0 | 148.0 | 147.9 | 149.2 | 148.4 | 136.8 | 134.7 | 137.2 | 146.3 | 147.8 | 146.3 | 144.8 |
| 2013 | 145.1 | 147.3 | 147.1 | 147.5 | 148.4 | 148.6 | 134.8 | 134.0 | 136.6 | 145.7 | 147.6 | 146.8 | 144.1 |
| 2014 | 146.3 | 147.5 | 148.1 | 149.1 | 150.4 | 149.2 | 137.1 | 137.3 | 140.6 | 149.5 | 151.5 | 150.9 | 146.5 |
| 2015 | 150.4 | 152.1 | 152.3 | 152.8 | 153.2 | 151.8 | 141.0 | 141.3 | 143.8 | 153.2 | 154.7 | 154.1 | 150.1 |
| 2016 | 152.8 | 154.8 | 155.5 | 156.4 | 157.8 | 156.7 | 145.2 | 143.9 | 147.9 | 155.9 | 157.5 | 156.7 | 153.4 |
| 2017 | 154.0 | 157.3 | 158.8 | 159.3 | 160.0 | 160.4 | 149.9 | 149.2 | 151.4 | 158.2 | 159.9 | 159.6 | 156.5 |
| 2018 | 149.9 | 151.8 | 152.2 | 153.2 | 153.6 | 153.5 | 143.0 | 141.0 | 146.9 | 152.4 | 154.8 | 154.0 | 150.5 |
| 2019 | 153.2 | 154.4 | 155.3 | 155.4 | 156.0 | 155.7 | 145.4 | 144.1 | 147.7 | 154.9 | 155.6 | 155.6 | 152.8 |

## Employment by Industry: Sacramento—Roseville—Arden-Arcade, CA, 2011–2019

(Numbers in thousands, not seasonally adjusted)

| Industry and year | January | February | March | April | May | June | July | August | September | October | November | December | Annual average |
|---|---|---|---|---|---|---|---|---|---|---|---|---|---|
| **Total Nonfarm** | | | | | | | | | | | | | |
| 2011 | 820.2 | 822.7 | 824.3 | 828.2 | 829.8 | 831.2 | 822.6 | 827.2 | 831.4 | 835.9 | 840.1 | 837.6 | 829.3 |
| 2012 | 826.2 | 831.7 | 835.6 | 845.9 | 851.1 | 859.0 | 845.1 | 848.4 | 848.6 | 854.1 | 860.8 | 858.4 | 847.1 |
| 2013 | 854.6 | 860.6 | 864.2 | 866.3 | 870.1 | 873.5 | 863.7 | 868.8 | 871.0 | 876.4 | 884.4 | 883.3 | 869.7 |
| 2014 | 872.6 | 876.0 | 880.5 | 885.7 | 891.4 | 898.0 | 885.2 | 891.0 | 892.6 | 899.6 | 906.3 | 903.3 | 890.2 |
| 2015 | 897.1 | 899.2 | 905.4 | 910.5 | 915.1 | 921.1 | 918.8 | 921.1 | 921.7 | 932.4 | 937.8 | 940.0 | 918.4 |
| 2016 | 930.2 | 936.3 | 937.0 | 945.9 | 949.4 | 953.0 | 950.6 | 953.8 | 953.2 | 958.2 | 963.1 | 963.9 | 949.6 |
| 2017 | 947.1 | 951.4 | 957.7 | 963.2 | 969.3 | 976.1 | 967.8 | 969.9 | 971.7 | 982.2 | 986.3 | 989.9 | 969.4 |
| 2018 | 977.9 | 983.7 | 985.4 | 991.0 | 997.2 | 1,003.8 | 996.8 | 1,002.2 | 1,001.7 | 1,009.3 | 1,014.4 | 1,016.0 | 998.3 |
| 2019 | 1,002.7 | 1,006.6 | 1,010.8 | 1,012.7 | 1,018.6 | 1,023.3 | 1,016.0 | 1,022.4 | 1,019.9 | 1,025.0 | 1,031.4 | 1,032.7 | 1,018.5 |
| **Total Private** | | | | | | | | | | | | | |
| 2011 | 592.9 | 593.6 | 594.0 | 597.3 | 600.3 | 602.9 | 608.5 | 612.2 | 612.2 | 610.7 | 614.9 | 616.6 | 604.7 |
| 2012 | 604.5 | 607.8 | 609.4 | 619.4 | 624.5 | 631.3 | 632.7 | 635.5 | 632.6 | 631.9 | 637.7 | 639.6 | 625.6 |
| 2013 | 633.9 | 638.1 | 639.5 | 641.5 | 644.1 | 647.1 | 648.9 | 652.7 | 651.6 | 652.3 | 657.1 | 659.6 | 647.2 |
| 2014 | 647.3 | 648.5 | 651.9 | 654.8 | 659.9 | 664.9 | 666.6 | 670.7 | 669.1 | 667.9 | 672.8 | 674.8 | 662.4 |
| 2015 | 666.2 | 667.6 | 672.0 | 676.3 | 681.3 | 686.0 | 694.1 | 695.2 | 693.3 | 697.3 | 701.1 | 706.2 | 686.4 |
| 2016 | 696.2 | 701.8 | 700.4 | 709.3 | 711.8 | 715.0 | 721.5 | 724.0 | 721.9 | 722.5 | 726.2 | 728.0 | 714.9 |
| 2017 | 712.4 | 716.3 | 720.4 | 726.1 | 731.2 | 737.9 | 739.3 | 741.9 | 740.5 | 744.9 | 747.8 | 752.1 | 734.2 |
| 2018 | 740.7 | 745.5 | 745.4 | 750.7 | 756.0 | 762.0 | 767.4 | 770.8 | 767.3 | 769.3 | 773.3 | 775.6 | 760.3 |
| 2019 | 762.5 | 765.5 | 767.4 | 769.1 | 773.6 | 778.0 | 782.7 | 785.9 | 781.8 | 780.9 | 787.7 | 789.8 | 777.1 |
| **Goods Producing** | | | | | | | | | | | | | |
| 2011 | 67.1 | 67.0 | 66.6 | 68.2 | 69.6 | 70.9 | 72.6 | 74.1 | 74.5 | 74.1 | 72.3 | 70.3 | 70.6 |
| 2012 | 68.3 | 68.2 | 67.4 | 69.2 | 71.8 | 73.9 | 75.7 | 77.0 | 77.0 | 76.1 | 74.8 | 73.9 | 72.8 |
| 2013 | 72.4 | 73.6 | 74.2 | 75.6 | 77.2 | 78.6 | 80.0 | 81.9 | 81.9 | 81.0 | 79.7 | 78.7 | 77.9 |
| 2014 | 76.8 | 77.2 | 77.4 | 78.6 | 80.9 | 82.3 | 83.7 | 85.1 | 85.0 | 84.2 | 83.7 | 81.3 | 81.4 |
| 2015 | 80.9 | 81.1 | 82.4 | 84.0 | 85.8 | 87.7 | 89.6 | 90.6 | 90.9 | 91.5 | 90.7 | 90.0 | 87.1 |
| 2016 | 86.9 | 87.9 | 87.3 | 90.2 | 91.6 | 92.6 | 94.8 | 95.6 | 95.5 | 93.9 | 92.9 | 90.5 | 91.6 |
| 2017 | 87.0 | 88.1 | 90.3 | 91.5 | 94.4 | 96.6 | 97.7 | 98.7 | 99.3 | 99.5 | 97.5 | 97.5 | 94.8 |
| 2018 | 94.1 | 95.8 | 94.5 | 96.6 | 99.1 | 102.4 | 104.3 | 105.8 | 106.0 | 105.3 | 104.1 | 103.2 | 100.9 |
| 2019 | 99.9 | 100.8 | 101.8 | 103.2 | 105.5 | 107.6 | 108.5 | 110.4 | 109.9 | 107.0 | 106.6 | 104.4 | 105.5 |
| **Service-Providing** | | | | | | | | | | | | | |
| 2011 | 753.1 | 755.7 | 757.7 | 760.0 | 760.2 | 760.3 | 750.0 | 753.1 | 756.9 | 761.8 | 767.8 | 767.3 | 758.7 |
| 2012 | 757.9 | 763.5 | 768.2 | 776.7 | 779.3 | 785.1 | 769.4 | 771.4 | 771.6 | 778.0 | 786.0 | 784.5 | 774.3 |
| 2013 | 782.2 | 787.0 | 790.0 | 790.7 | 792.9 | 794.9 | 783.7 | 786.9 | 789.1 | 795.4 | 804.7 | 804.6 | 791.8 |
| 2014 | 795.8 | 798.8 | 803.1 | 807.1 | 810.5 | 815.7 | 801.5 | 805.9 | 807.6 | 815.4 | 822.6 | 822.0 | 808.8 |
| 2015 | 816.2 | 818.1 | 823.0 | 826.5 | 829.3 | 833.4 | 829.2 | 830.5 | 830.8 | 840.9 | 847.1 | 850.0 | 831.3 |
| 2016 | 843.3 | 848.4 | 849.7 | 855.7 | 857.8 | 860.4 | 855.8 | 858.2 | 857.7 | 864.3 | 870.2 | 873.4 | 857.9 |
| 2017 | 860.1 | 863.3 | 867.4 | 871.7 | 874.9 | 879.5 | 870.1 | 871.2 | 872.4 | 882.7 | 888.8 | 892.4 | 874.5 |
| 2018 | 883.8 | 887.9 | 890.9 | 894.4 | 898.1 | 901.4 | 892.5 | 896.4 | 895.7 | 904.0 | 910.3 | 912.8 | 897.4 |
| 2019 | 902.8 | 905.8 | 909.0 | 909.5 | 913.1 | 915.7 | 907.5 | 912.0 | 910.0 | 918.0 | 924.8 | 928.3 | 913.0 |
| **Mining and Logging** | | | | | | | | | | | | | |
| 2011 | 0.4 | 0.4 | 0.4 | 0.4 | 0.4 | 0.4 | 0.4 | 0.5 | 0.5 | 0.5 | 0.5 | 0.4 | 0.4 |
| 2012 | 0.4 | 0.4 | 0.4 | 0.3 | 0.4 | 0.4 | 0.4 | 0.4 | 0.4 | 0.4 | 0.4 | 0.4 | 0.4 |
| 2013 | 0.3 | 0.3 | 0.3 | 0.3 | 0.4 | 0.4 | 0.4 | 0.4 | 0.4 | 0.4 | 0.4 | 0.4 | 0.4 |
| 2014 | 0.3 | 0.4 | 0.3 | 0.4 | 0.4 | 0.5 | 0.4 | 0.5 | 0.4 | 0.5 | 0.5 | 0.4 | 0.4 |
| 2015 | 0.4 | 0.4 | 0.4 | 0.4 | 0.4 | 0.4 | 0.5 | 0.5 | 0.5 | 0.5 | 0.4 | 0.4 | 0.4 |
| 2016 | 0.4 | 0.4 | 0.4 | 0.4 | 0.4 | 0.4 | 0.5 | 0.5 | 0.5 | 0.5 | 0.5 | 0.4 | 0.4 |
| 2017 | 0.4 | 0.4 | 0.4 | 0.4 | 0.4 | 0.5 | 0.5 | 0.5 | 0.5 | 0.5 | 0.4 | 0.4 | 0.4 |
| 2018 | 0.4 | 0.4 | 0.4 | 0.4 | 0.5 | 0.5 | 0.5 | 0.5 | 0.5 | 0.5 | 0.5 | 0.5 | 0.5 |
| 2019 | 0.5 | 0.5 | 0.5 | 0.5 | 0.5 | 0.5 | 0.6 | 0.6 | 0.5 | 0.5 | 0.6 | 0.5 | 0.5 |
| **Construction** | | | | | | | | | | | | | |
| 2011 | 34.4 | 34.2 | 33.6 | 35.1 | 36.3 | 37.3 | 39.3 | 39.6 | 39.6 | 39.3 | 38.5 | 36.4 | 37.0 |
| 2012 | 34.8 | 34.7 | 34.0 | 35.5 | 37.8 | 39.5 | 40.8 | 41.4 | 41.3 | 41.5 | 40.7 | 39.9 | 38.5 |
| 2013 | 38.8 | 39.8 | 40.6 | 41.6 | 43.0 | 44.3 | 45.4 | 46.4 | 46.2 | 46.1 | 44.9 | 43.7 | 43.4 |
| 2014 | 42.3 | 42.3 | 42.6 | 43.5 | 45.6 | 46.6 | 47.5 | 48.0 | 47.9 | 47.9 | 47.4 | 45.1 | 45.6 |
| 2015 | 45.0 | 45.2 | 46.2 | 47.6 | 49.3 | 50.9 | 52.2 | 52.8 | 52.9 | 54.4 | 53.9 | 53.2 | 50.3 |
| 2016 | 50.3 | 51.3 | 50.6 | 53.8 | 54.9 | 56.2 | 57.8 | 58.2 | 58.0 | 57.5 | 56.8 | 54.7 | 55.0 |
| 2017 | 51.5 | 52.5 | 55.2 | 56.0 | 58.5 | 60.5 | 61.3 | 61.9 | 62.1 | 62.7 | 61.1 | 61.0 | 58.7 |
| 2018 | 59.0 | 60.5 | 59.1 | 61.2 | 63.2 | 65.8 | 67.0 | 68.3 | 68.4 | 68.0 | 67.1 | 66.3 | 64.5 |
| 2019 | 63.3 | 64.2 | 65.4 | 66.6 | 68.8 | 70.8 | 72.0 | 72.8 | 72.1 | 69.5 | 68.8 | 66.8 | 68.4 |

## Employment by Industry: Sacramento—Roseville—Arden-Arcade, CA, 2011–2019—*Continued*

(Numbers in thousands, not seasonally adjusted)

| Industry and year | January | February | March | April | May | June | July | August | September | October | November | December | Annual average |
|---|---|---|---|---|---|---|---|---|---|---|---|---|---|
| **Manufacturing** | | | | | | | | | | | | | |
| 2011 | 32.3 | 32.4 | 32.6 | 32.7 | 32.9 | 33.2 | 32.9 | 34.0 | 34.4 | 34.3 | 33.3 | 33.5 | 33.2 |
| 2012 | 33.1 | 33.1 | 33.0 | 33.4 | 33.6 | 34.0 | 34.5 | 35.2 | 35.3 | 34.2 | 33.7 | 33.6 | 33.9 |
| 2013 | 33.3 | 33.5 | 33.3 | 33.7 | 33.8 | 33.9 | 34.2 | 35.1 | 35.3 | 34.5 | 34.4 | 34.6 | 34.1 |
| 2014 | 34.2 | 34.5 | 34.5 | 34.7 | 34.9 | 35.2 | 35.8 | 36.6 | 36.7 | 35.8 | 35.8 | 35.8 | 35.4 |
| 2015 | 35.5 | 35.5 | 35.8 | 36.0 | 36.1 | 36.4 | 36.9 | 37.3 | 37.5 | 36.6 | 36.4 | 36.4 | 36.4 |
| 2016 | 36.2 | 36.2 | 36.3 | 36.0 | 36.3 | 36.0 | 36.5 | 36.9 | 37.0 | 35.9 | 35.6 | 35.4 | 36.2 |
| 2017 | 35.1 | 35.2 | 34.7 | 35.1 | 35.5 | 35.6 | 35.9 | 36.3 | 36.7 | 36.3 | 36.0 | 36.1 | 35.7 |
| 2018 | 34.7 | 34.9 | 35.0 | 35.0 | 35.4 | 36.1 | 36.8 | 37.0 | 37.1 | 36.8 | 36.5 | 36.4 | 36.0 |
| 2019 | 36.1 | 36.1 | 35.9 | 36.1 | 36.2 | 36.3 | 35.9 | 37.0 | 37.3 | 37.0 | 37.2 | 37.1 | 36.5 |
| **Trade, Transportation, and Utilities** | | | | | | | | | | | | | |
| 2011 | 132.2 | 130.8 | 130.7 | 131.0 | 131.7 | 132.4 | 133.1 | 133.7 | 133.9 | 135.5 | 139.7 | 141.5 | 133.9 |
| 2012 | 135.5 | 133.9 | 134.3 | 136.4 | 137.3 | 138.4 | 138.5 | 139.1 | 139.3 | 140.0 | 144.6 | 146.0 | 138.6 |
| 2013 | 140.0 | 138.8 | 138.8 | 139.0 | 139.6 | 140.2 | 140.7 | 140.6 | 140.4 | 142.0 | 146.9 | 148.2 | 141.3 |
| 2014 | 141.7 | 140.3 | 140.4 | 140.4 | 140.9 | 141.8 | 142.4 | 143.2 | 142.7 | 143.7 | 148.3 | 150.3 | 143.0 |
| 2015 | 144.2 | 142.7 | 143.0 | 144.1 | 145.2 | 145.3 | 146.6 | 147.3 | 147.4 | 149.2 | 153.9 | 155.1 | 147.0 |
| 2016 | 149.5 | 148.5 | 148.2 | 149.6 | 150.3 | 150.5 | 151.9 | 152.6 | 151.9 | 153.1 | 158.0 | 158.5 | 151.9 |
| 2017 | 152.9 | 150.9 | 150.6 | 151.6 | 152.2 | 152.7 | 153.3 | 154.2 | 153.8 | 157.1 | 161.7 | 162.8 | 154.5 |
| 2018 | 157.8 | 156.3 | 156.2 | 157.0 | 157.7 | 158.3 | 160.3 | 160.5 | 160.1 | 161.6 | 166.5 | 166.9 | 159.9 |
| 2019 | 161.2 | 159.0 | 158.4 | 158.7 | 159.5 | 160.1 | 161.2 | 161.5 | 161.2 | 162.5 | 167.5 | 169.0 | 161.7 |
| **Wholesale Trade** | | | | | | | | | | | | | |
| 2011 | 22.5 | 22.4 | 22.5 | 23.0 | 23.2 | 23.4 | 23.4 | 23.4 | 23.6 | 24.0 | 24.3 | 24.5 | 23.4 |
| 2012 | 24.2 | 24.5 | 24.9 | 25.2 | 25.2 | 25.3 | 25.0 | 24.9 | 24.8 | 24.8 | 24.8 | 24.9 | 24.9 |
| 2013 | 24.5 | 24.5 | 24.5 | 24.6 | 24.5 | 24.6 | 24.7 | 24.4 | 24.4 | 24.6 | 24.7 | 24.6 | 24.6 |
| 2014 | 24.4 | 24.4 | 24.3 | 24.2 | 24.1 | 24.2 | 24.1 | 24.0 | 24.0 | 23.9 | 24.0 | 24.0 | 24.1 |
| 2015 | 24.1 | 24.0 | 23.9 | 24.2 | 24.3 | 24.3 | 24.5 | 24.4 | 24.4 | 24.9 | 25.0 | 25.0 | 24.4 |
| 2016 | 25.0 | 25.0 | 24.9 | 25.3 | 25.3 | 25.3 | 25.7 | 25.8 | 25.6 | 25.7 | 25.8 | 26.0 | 25.5 |
| 2017 | 25.8 | 26.0 | 25.9 | 26.1 | 26.2 | 26.5 | 26.6 | 26.6 | 26.6 | 26.8 | 27.1 | 27.4 | 26.5 |
| 2018 | 27.8 | 28.0 | 28.1 | 28.2 | 28.1 | 28.3 | 28.8 | 28.7 | 28.5 | 28.5 | 28.6 | 28.7 | 28.4 |
| 2019 | 28.9 | 29.1 | 28.9 | 28.8 | 28.8 | 29.0 | 28.8 | 28.6 | 28.4 | 28.1 | 28.6 | 28.2 | 28.7 |
| **Retail Trade** | | | | | | | | | | | | | |
| 2011 | 89.0 | 87.7 | 87.3 | 87.2 | 87.5 | 87.9 | 88.6 | 89.0 | 89.1 | 90.2 | 94.0 | 95.3 | 89.4 |
| 2012 | 90.7 | 88.7 | 88.8 | 89.7 | 90.3 | 90.9 | 91.2 | 91.8 | 91.9 | 92.6 | 97.0 | 97.8 | 91.8 |
| 2013 | 92.9 | 91.7 | 91.7 | 91.8 | 92.4 | 92.7 | 93.2 | 93.3 | 93.0 | 94.4 | 98.8 | 99.7 | 93.8 |
| 2014 | 94.5 | 93.2 | 93.4 | 93.3 | 93.6 | 94.2 | 94.7 | 95.2 | 94.7 | 95.8 | 99.8 | 101.1 | 95.3 |
| 2015 | 96.2 | 94.9 | 95.2 | 95.9 | 96.8 | 96.8 | 97.4 | 97.9 | 98.0 | 99.2 | 103.3 | 103.9 | 98.0 |
| 2016 | 99.5 | 98.7 | 98.4 | 99.0 | 99.2 | 99.1 | 99.9 | 100.4 | 99.9 | 101.1 | 105.1 | 105.1 | 100.5 |
| 2017 | 101.2 | 99.3 | 98.9 | 100.0 | 100.4 | 100.4 | 100.7 | 101.4 | 101.0 | 102.2 | 105.4 | 105.5 | 101.4 |
| 2018 | 101.6 | 100.1 | 99.9 | 100.3 | 100.8 | 100.9 | 102.2 | 102.3 | 101.8 | 102.4 | 105.9 | 105.9 | 102.0 |
| 2019 | 100.7 | 99.6 | 99.0 | 99.2 | 99.7 | 99.4 | 99.8 | 100.1 | 99.8 | 100.8 | 104.3 | 105.2 | 100.6 |
| **Transportation and Utilities** | | | | | | | | | | | | | |
| 2011 | 20.7 | 20.7 | 20.9 | 20.8 | 21.0 | 21.1 | 21.1 | 21.3 | 21.2 | 21.3 | 21.4 | 21.7 | 21.1 |
| 2012 | 20.6 | 20.7 | 20.6 | 21.5 | 21.8 | 22.2 | 22.3 | 22.4 | 22.6 | 22.6 | 22.8 | 23.3 | 22.0 |
| 2013 | 22.6 | 22.6 | 22.6 | 22.6 | 22.7 | 22.9 | 22.8 | 22.9 | 23.0 | 23.0 | 23.4 | 23.9 | 22.9 |
| 2014 | 22.8 | 22.7 | 22.7 | 22.9 | 23.2 | 23.4 | 23.6 | 24.0 | 24.0 | 24.0 | 24.5 | 25.2 | 23.6 |
| 2015 | 23.9 | 23.8 | 23.9 | 24.0 | 24.1 | 24.2 | 24.7 | 25.0 | 25.0 | 25.1 | 25.6 | 26.2 | 24.6 |
| 2016 | 25.0 | 24.8 | 24.9 | 25.3 | 25.8 | 26.1 | 26.3 | 26.4 | 26.4 | 26.3 | 27.1 | 27.4 | 26.0 |
| 2017 | 25.9 | 25.6 | 25.8 | 25.5 | 25.6 | 25.8 | 26.0 | 26.2 | 26.2 | 28.1 | 29.2 | 29.9 | 26.7 |
| 2018 | 28.4 | 28.2 | 28.2 | 28.5 | 28.8 | 29.1 | 29.3 | 29.5 | 29.8 | 30.7 | 32.0 | 32.3 | 29.6 |
| 2019 | 31.6 | 30.3 | 30.5 | 30.7 | 31.0 | 31.7 | 32.6 | 32.8 | 33.0 | 33.6 | 34.6 | 35.6 | 32.3 |
| **Information** | | | | | | | | | | | | | |
| 2011 | 16.9 | 16.8 | 16.8 | 16.7 | 16.6 | 16.5 | 16.4 | 16.2 | 15.9 | 15.9 | 15.7 | 15.6 | 16.3 |
| 2012 | 15.6 | 15.6 | 15.6 | 15.7 | 15.7 | 15.8 | 15.7 | 15.5 | 15.3 | 15.3 | 15.5 | 15.6 | 15.6 |
| 2013 | 15.3 | 15.3 | 15.0 | 15.1 | 15.1 | 15.0 | 14.9 | 14.7 | 14.4 | 14.2 | 14.2 | 14.2 | 14.8 |
| 2014 | 13.8 | 13.7 | 13.7 | 13.8 | 13.9 | 13.9 | 14.0 | 14.0 | 13.9 | 14.0 | 14.0 | 14.3 | 13.9 |
| 2015 | 14.2 | 14.2 | 14.1 | 14.2 | 14.3 | 14.3 | 14.3 | 14.2 | 14.1 | 14.1 | 14.0 | 14.2 | 14.2 |
| 2016 | 14.0 | 14.0 | 13.9 | 14.0 | 13.9 | 13.9 | 13.8 | 13.8 | 13.6 | 13.5 | 13.7 | 13.7 | 13.8 |
| 2017 | 13.5 | 12.8 | 12.7 | 12.4 | 12.4 | 12.4 | 12.5 | 12.5 | 12.3 | 12.3 | 12.4 | 12.6 | 12.6 |
| 2018 | 12.3 | 12.4 | 12.4 | 12.5 | 12.5 | 12.4 | 12.6 | 12.4 | 12.2 | 12.2 | 12.2 | 12.2 | 12.4 |
| 2019 | 12.1 | 12.1 | 12.0 | 11.9 | 11.9 | 11.9 | 12.0 | 11.8 | 11.6 | 11.6 | 11.7 | 11.7 | 11.9 |

## Employment by Industry: Sacramento—Roseville—Arden-Arcade, CA, 2011–2019—*Continued*

(Numbers in thousands, not seasonally adjusted)

| Industry and year | January | February | March | April | May | June | July | August | September | October | November | December | Annual average |
|---|---|---|---|---|---|---|---|---|---|---|---|---|---|
| **Financial Activities** | | | | | | | | | | | | | |
| 2011 | 46.5 | 46.2 | 46.3 | 46.6 | 46.8 | 46.8 | 47.2 | 47.4 | 47.2 | 46.9 | 46.8 | 46.8 | 46.8 |
| 2012 | 47.1 | 47.2 | 47.4 | 47.8 | 47.9 | 48.3 | 48.8 | 48.8 | 48.7 | 48.9 | 48.9 | 49.3 | 48.3 |
| 2013 | 49.1 | 49.3 | 49.3 | 49.6 | 49.6 | 49.8 | 50.2 | 50.1 | 49.6 | 49.2 | 48.9 | 49.1 | 49.5 |
| 2014 | 48.7 | 48.5 | 48.3 | 48.3 | 48.6 | 48.9 | 49.1 | 49.2 | 49.2 | 49.7 | 49.7 | 50.0 | 49.0 |
| 2015 | 49.9 | 50.1 | 50.4 | 50.4 | 50.7 | 51.0 | 51.8 | 51.4 | 51.0 | 51.3 | 51.4 | 51.4 | 50.9 |
| 2016 | 51.1 | 51.2 | 51.2 | 51.4 | 51.5 | 51.5 | 52.3 | 52.3 | 52.1 | 52.2 | 52.1 | 52.2 | 51.8 |
| 2017 | 51.9 | 52.0 | 52.0 | 51.9 | 52.1 | 52.3 | 52.9 | 52.9 | 52.5 | 52.7 | 52.6 | 52.8 | 52.4 |
| 2018 | 53.6 | 53.5 | 53.4 | 53.7 | 53.7 | 53.8 | 53.7 | 53.5 | 53.2 | 53.2 | 52.8 | 52.7 | 53.4 |
| 2019 | 52.2 | 52.3 | 52.0 | 51.8 | 52.0 | 52.4 | 52.7 | 52.7 | 52.4 | 52.9 | 53.2 | 53.7 | 52.5 |
| **Professional and Business Services** | | | | | | | | | | | | | |
| 2011 | 100.2 | 102.0 | 101.2 | 102.4 | 102.6 | 103.0 | 105.1 | 106.4 | 106.0 | 106.6 | 106.9 | 106.9 | 104.1 |
| 2012 | 103.7 | 106.1 | 105.6 | 109.6 | 111.3 | 112.8 | 113.8 | 114.4 | 112.2 | 113.9 | 113.7 | 112.8 | 110.8 |
| 2013 | 112.0 | 113.6 | 112.8 | 112.5 | 112.8 | 114.0 | 113.7 | 115.5 | 116.0 | 117.0 | 117.0 | 116.4 | 114.4 |
| 2014 | 114.2 | 116.4 | 116.9 | 117.6 | 118.1 | 118.6 | 118.5 | 119.6 | 119.6 | 118.8 | 119.2 | 119.1 | 118.1 |
| 2015 | 116.5 | 117.3 | 117.6 | 118.2 | 118.5 | 119.2 | 121.7 | 122.5 | 121.4 | 122.6 | 122.3 | 122.8 | 120.1 |
| 2016 | 123.4 | 125.4 | 124.7 | 127.2 | 127.4 | 127.6 | 128.8 | 130.1 | 128.9 | 130.5 | 130.0 | 129.9 | 127.8 |
| 2017 | 126.9 | 128.5 | 128.6 | 128.5 | 129.8 | 130.4 | 130.6 | 130.8 | 130.1 | 131.9 | 132.5 | 131.9 | 130.0 |
| 2018 | 129.8 | 131.5 | 131.5 | 132.6 | 133.8 | 133.6 | 133.8 | 135.3 | 135.1 | 135.8 | 135.0 | 134.2 | 133.5 |
| 2019 | 132.5 | 133.4 | 133.0 | 132.9 | 134.1 | 134.5 | 135.3 | 136.6 | 135.7 | 136.5 | 137.0 | 137.5 | 134.9 |
| **Education and Health Services** | | | | | | | | | | | | | |
| 2011 | 121.8 | 121.9 | 122.4 | 123.2 | 123.7 | 122.6 | 121.9 | 122.5 | 123.7 | 124.0 | 125.0 | 125.1 | 123.2 |
| 2012 | 125.3 | 126.0 | 127.3 | 127.0 | 127.7 | 126.9 | 124.5 | 124.9 | 126.4 | 125.8 | 127.4 | 127.0 | 126.4 |
| 2013 | 129.8 | 130.9 | 131.6 | 132.0 | 132.9 | 130.6 | 129.5 | 130.3 | 131.3 | 132.4 | 133.0 | 133.1 | 131.5 |
| 2014 | 133.1 | 132.5 | 133.7 | 134.3 | 135.9 | 134.5 | 133.6 | 134.8 | 136.0 | 136.9 | 137.5 | 137.7 | 135.0 |
| 2015 | 137.6 | 138.2 | 139.4 | 140.5 | 141.2 | 140.3 | 140.3 | 140.3 | 141.4 | 143.3 | 143.5 | 144.4 | 140.9 |
| 2016 | 143.4 | 145.1 | 144.9 | 145.7 | 146.5 | 146.0 | 145.0 | 145.3 | 147.1 | 148.8 | 149.3 | 150.5 | 146.5 |
| 2017 | 148.3 | 149.8 | 150.9 | 153.9 | 154.0 | 154.4 | 152.6 | 154.2 | 155.9 | 156.2 | 156.3 | 157.2 | 153.6 |
| 2018 | 156.8 | 158.0 | 158.6 | 158.4 | 159.3 | 158.9 | 158.5 | 160.0 | 160.2 | 162.3 | 162.9 | 164.0 | 159.8 |
| 2019 | 163.1 | 164.9 | 165.9 | 165.4 | 165.9 | 165.2 | 165.4 | 166.4 | 166.8 | 168.3 | 169.7 | 169.6 | 166.4 |
| **Leisure and Hospitality** | | | | | | | | | | | | | |
| 2011 | 80.5 | 81.2 | 82.2 | 80.9 | 80.9 | 82.3 | 83.6 | 83.4 | 82.4 | 79.7 | 80.6 | 82.5 | 81.7 |
| 2012 | 80.9 | 82.7 | 83.3 | 84.9 | 83.7 | 85.7 | 86.9 | 86.9 | 85.1 | 83.3 | 84.2 | 86.5 | 84.5 |
| 2013 | 87.0 | 87.9 | 88.8 | 88.7 | 87.7 | 89.6 | 90.7 | 90.3 | 88.6 | 87.1 | 88.0 | 90.5 | 88.7 |
| 2014 | 89.8 | 90.4 | 91.6 | 91.6 | 91.0 | 93.9 | 94.5 | 94.2 | 92.1 | 90.1 | 90.1 | 92.0 | 91.8 |
| 2015 | 93.1 | 94.0 | 94.8 | 93.9 | 94.4 | 96.9 | 98.2 | 97.5 | 95.8 | 94.1 | 94.3 | 97.4 | 95.4 |
| 2016 | 97.4 | 98.7 | 99.2 | 99.9 | 99.0 | 100.8 | 102.4 | 102.2 | 100.7 | 98.3 | 98.1 | 101.0 | 99.8 |
| 2017 | 100.6 | 102.3 | 103.1 | 103.6 | 103.2 | 105.5 | 106.3 | 105.1 | 102.8 | 101.6 | 101.5 | 104.1 | 103.3 |
| 2018 | 103.3 | 104.7 | 105.4 | 105.9 | 105.5 | 107.8 | 109.4 | 108.6 | 106.0 | 104.2 | 105.2 | 108.1 | 106.2 |
| 2019 | 107.6 | 108.6 | 109.5 | 110.0 | 109.4 | 110.8 | 112.0 | 110.8 | 108.5 | 106.7 | 107.0 | 109.0 | 109.2 |
| **Other Services** | | | | | | | | | | | | | |
| 2011 | 27.7 | 27.7 | 27.8 | 28.3 | 28.4 | 28.4 | 28.6 | 28.5 | 28.6 | 28.0 | 27.9 | 27.9 | 28.2 |
| 2012 | 28.1 | 28.1 | 28.5 | 28.8 | 29.1 | 29.5 | 28.8 | 28.9 | 28.6 | 28.6 | 28.6 | 28.5 | 28.7 |
| 2013 | 28.3 | 28.7 | 29.0 | 29.0 | 29.2 | 29.3 | 29.2 | 29.3 | 29.4 | 29.4 | 29.4 | 29.4 | 29.1 |
| 2014 | 29.2 | 29.5 | 29.9 | 30.2 | 30.6 | 31.0 | 30.8 | 30.6 | 30.6 | 30.5 | 30.3 | 30.1 | 30.3 |
| 2015 | 29.8 | 30.0 | 30.3 | 31.0 | 31.2 | 31.3 | 31.6 | 31.4 | 31.3 | 31.2 | 31.0 | 30.9 | 30.9 |
| 2016 | 30.5 | 31.0 | 31.0 | 31.3 | 31.6 | 32.1 | 32.5 | 32.1 | 32.1 | 32.2 | 32.1 | 31.7 | 31.7 |
| 2017 | 31.3 | 31.9 | 32.2 | 32.7 | 33.1 | 33.6 | 33.4 | 33.5 | 33.8 | 33.6 | 33.3 | 33.2 | 33.0 |
| 2018 | 33.0 | 33.3 | 33.4 | 34.0 | 34.4 | 34.8 | 34.8 | 34.7 | 34.5 | 34.7 | 34.6 | 34.3 | 34.2 |
| 2019 | 33.9 | 34.4 | 34.8 | 35.2 | 35.3 | 35.5 | 35.6 | 35.7 | 35.7 | 35.4 | 35.0 | 34.9 | 35.1 |
| **Government** | | | | | | | | | | | | | |
| 2011 | 227.3 | 229.1 | 230.3 | 230.9 | 229.5 | 228.3 | 214.1 | 215.0 | 219.2 | 225.2 | 225.2 | 221.0 | 224.6 |
| 2012 | 221.7 | 223.9 | 226.2 | 226.5 | 226.6 | 227.7 | 212.4 | 212.9 | 216.0 | 222.2 | 223.1 | 218.8 | 221.5 |
| 2013 | 220.7 | 222.5 | 224.7 | 224.8 | 226.0 | 226.4 | 214.8 | 216.1 | 219.4 | 224.1 | 227.3 | 223.7 | 222.5 |
| 2014 | 225.3 | 227.5 | 228.6 | 230.9 | 231.5 | 233.1 | 218.6 | 220.3 | 223.5 | 231.7 | 233.5 | 228.5 | 227.8 |
| 2015 | 230.9 | 231.6 | 233.4 | 234.2 | 233.8 | 235.1 | 224.7 | 225.9 | 228.4 | 235.1 | 236.7 | 233.8 | 232.0 |
| 2016 | 234.0 | 234.5 | 236.6 | 236.6 | 237.6 | 238.0 | 229.1 | 229.8 | 231.3 | 235.7 | 236.9 | 235.9 | 234.7 |
| 2017 | 234.7 | 235.1 | 237.3 | 237.1 | 238.1 | 238.2 | 228.5 | 228.0 | 231.2 | 237.3 | 238.5 | 237.8 | 235.2 |
| 2018 | 237.2 | 238.2 | 240.0 | 240.3 | 241.2 | 241.8 | 229.4 | 231.4 | 234.4 | 240.0 | 241.1 | 240.4 | 238.0 |
| 2019 | 240.2 | 241.1 | 243.4 | 243.6 | 245.0 | 245.3 | 233.3 | 236.5 | 238.1 | 244.1 | 243.7 | 242.9 | 241.4 |

## Employment by Industry: Pittsburgh, PA, 2011–2019

(Numbers in thousands, not seasonally adjusted)

| Industry and year | January | February | March | April | May | June | July | August | September | October | November | December | Annual average |
|---|---|---|---|---|---|---|---|---|---|---|---|---|---|
| **Total Nonfarm** | | | | | | | | | | | | | |
| 2011 | 1,116.5 | 1,118.4 | 1,128.4 | 1,143.1 | 1,153.0 | 1,160.7 | 1,144.3 | 1,140.4 | 1,153.6 | 1,160.6 | 1,163.2 | 1,160.0 | 1,145.2 |
| 2012 | 1,130.5 | 1,137.7 | 1,151.1 | 1,160.8 | 1,168.8 | 1,171.1 | 1,154.9 | 1,150.4 | 1,160.1 | 1,169.5 | 1,170.9 | 1,165.7 | 1,157.6 |
| 2013 | 1,133.7 | 1,140.9 | 1,148.1 | 1,158.5 | 1,168.1 | 1,170.0 | 1,157.1 | 1,152.7 | 1,161.7 | 1,167.8 | 1,168.0 | 1,164.3 | 1,157.6 |
| 2014 | 1,134.1 | 1,135.2 | 1,144.4 | 1,160.2 | 1,171.2 | 1,173.1 | 1,158.4 | 1,156.3 | 1,166.0 | 1,172.5 | 1,172.2 | 1,170.2 | 1,159.5 |
| 2015 | 1,139.7 | 1,139.7 | 1,146.1 | 1,161.9 | 1,172.3 | 1,171.8 | 1,161.9 | 1,160.5 | 1,167.4 | 1,172.6 | 1,175.4 | 1,169.6 | 1,161.6 |
| 2016 | 1,140.1 | 1,142.6 | 1,151.1 | 1,166.5 | 1,171.6 | 1,169.1 | 1,162.5 | 1,158.6 | 1,168.0 | 1,172.7 | 1,176.5 | 1,169.7 | 1,162.4 |
| 2017 | 1,143.4 | 1,150.9 | 1,157.3 | 1,172.9 | 1,181.7 | 1,180.4 | 1,171.9 | 1,170.9 | 1,183.1 | 1,189.3 | 1,190.7 | 1,186.4 | 1,173.2 |
| 2018 | 1,158.8 | 1,167.5 | 1,173.8 | 1,185.3 | 1,192.3 | 1,190.4 | 1,184.8 | 1,180.6 | 1,191.5 | 1,199.5 | 1,201.3 | 1,195.6 | 1,185.1 |
| 2019 | 1,170.9 | 1,175.4 | 1,182.0 | 1,194.5 | 1,200.3 | 1,199.3 | 1,193.3 | 1,192.0 | 1,201.0 | 1,206.7 | 1,208.2 | 1,204.0 | 1,194.0 |
| **Total Private** | | | | | | | | | | | | | |
| 2011 | 989.9 | 989.1 | 998.4 | 1,013.6 | 1,025.2 | 1,034.8 | 1,028.9 | 1,027.1 | 1,032.0 | 1,036.0 | 1,037.5 | 1,034.5 | 1,020.6 |
| 2012 | 1,011.0 | 1,013.5 | 1,026.6 | 1,036.5 | 1,044.6 | 1,049.9 | 1,042.3 | 1,038.7 | 1,040.1 | 1,046.9 | 1,047.2 | 1,042.4 | 1,036.6 |
| 2013 | 1,015.3 | 1,018.1 | 1,025.2 | 1,035.5 | 1,044.5 | 1,050.9 | 1,046.6 | 1,042.6 | 1,042.7 | 1,046.9 | 1,045.8 | 1,042.6 | 1,038.1 |
| 2014 | 1,016.1 | 1,014.9 | 1,023.9 | 1,039.1 | 1,049.9 | 1,055.2 | 1,049.0 | 1,047.7 | 1,048.4 | 1,052.5 | 1,051.3 | 1,049.5 | 1,041.5 |
| 2015 | 1,023.6 | 1,020.5 | 1,026.7 | 1,041.6 | 1,052.1 | 1,054.6 | 1,052.6 | 1,051.8 | 1,050.3 | 1,054.3 | 1,055.9 | 1,051.3 | 1,044.6 |
| 2016 | 1,025.2 | 1,024.7 | 1,032.3 | 1,047.8 | 1,052.5 | 1,053.2 | 1,052.7 | 1,050.4 | 1,050.9 | 1,054.3 | 1,057.4 | 1,051.0 | 1,046.0 |
| 2017 | 1,029.6 | 1,032.6 | 1,038.7 | 1,054.3 | 1,062.8 | 1,065.1 | 1,063.0 | 1,063.5 | 1,066.3 | 1,071.6 | 1,072.4 | 1,069.2 | 1,057.4 |
| 2018 | 1,045.9 | 1,050.4 | 1,056.3 | 1,067.8 | 1,076.0 | 1,075.6 | 1,076.5 | 1,074.3 | 1,075.9 | 1,082.8 | 1,083.3 | 1,078.9 | 1,070.3 |
| 2019 | 1,058.5 | 1,059.4 | 1,065.1 | 1,077.4 | 1,084.3 | 1,084.2 | 1,084.7 | 1,085.1 | 1,084.6 | 1,088.7 | 1,089.1 | 1,086.7 | 1,079.0 |
| **Goods Producing** | | | | | | | | | | | | | |
| 2011 | 137.9 | 137.8 | 141.7 | 146.0 | 149.3 | 152.1 | 153.6 | 154.1 | 154.3 | 154.7 | 153.3 | 150.5 | 148.8 |
| 2012 | 145.5 | 145.7 | 148.3 | 153.1 | 155.5 | 157.7 | 158.1 | 157.8 | 157.7 | 158.6 | 155.5 | 151.9 | 153.8 |
| 2013 | 146.2 | 146.4 | 148.7 | 152.5 | 155.3 | 157.0 | 157.6 | 157.4 | 156.7 | 156.5 | 153.9 | 150.1 | 153.2 |
| 2014 | 146.0 | 144.9 | 148.1 | 153.2 | 156.1 | 159.1 | 159.4 | 159.5 | 158.9 | 158.5 | 155.9 | 152.8 | 154.4 |
| 2015 | 147.4 | 145.9 | 148.0 | 152.8 | 155.5 | 157.7 | 158.9 | 158.8 | 157.5 | 155.7 | 153.5 | 150.1 | 153.5 |
| 2016 | 143.9 | 141.8 | 145.6 | 149.8 | 151.5 | 152.4 | 153.1 | 152.2 | 150.9 | 150.7 | 149.2 | 146.2 | 148.9 |
| 2017 | 142.0 | 142.4 | 144.7 | 150.3 | 153.7 | 156.6 | 157.8 | 157.9 | 157.7 | 157.8 | 156.0 | 153.6 | 152.5 |
| 2018 | 147.9 | 148.0 | 150.8 | 154.2 | 157.8 | 160.6 | 161.8 | 161.9 | 161.6 | 162.2 | 160.5 | 158.5 | 157.2 |
| 2019 | 154.2 | 153.9 | 156.9 | 161.4 | 164.5 | 165.8 | 166.9 | 166.9 | 165.6 | 164.6 | 164.2 | 161.3 | 162.2 |
| **Service-Providing** | | | | | | | | | | | | | |
| 2011 | 978.6 | 980.6 | 986.7 | 997.1 | 1,003.7 | 1,008.6 | 990.7 | 986.3 | 999.3 | 1,005.9 | 1,009.9 | 1,009.5 | 996.4 |
| 2012 | 985.0 | 992.0 | 1,002.8 | 1,007.7 | 1,013.3 | 1,013.4 | 996.8 | 992.6 | 1,002.4 | 1,010.9 | 1,015.4 | 1,013.8 | 1,003.8 |
| 2013 | 987.5 | 994.5 | 999.4 | 1,006.0 | 1,012.8 | 1,013.0 | 999.5 | 995.3 | 1,005.0 | 1,011.3 | 1,014.1 | 1,014.2 | 1,004.4 |
| 2014 | 988.1 | 990.3 | 996.3 | 1,007.0 | 1,015.1 | 1,014.0 | 999.0 | 996.8 | 1,007.1 | 1,014.0 | 1,016.3 | 1,017.4 | 1,005.1 |
| 2015 | 992.3 | 993.8 | 998.1 | 1,009.1 | 1,016.8 | 1,014.1 | 1,003.0 | 1,001.7 | 1,009.9 | 1,016.9 | 1,021.9 | 1,019.5 | 1,008.1 |
| 2016 | 996.2 | 1,000.8 | 1,005.5 | 1,016.7 | 1,020.1 | 1,016.7 | 1,009.4 | 1,006.4 | 1,017.1 | 1,022.0 | 1,027.3 | 1,023.5 | 1,013.5 |
| 2017 | 1,001.4 | 1,008.5 | 1,012.6 | 1,022.6 | 1,028.0 | 1,023.8 | 1,014.1 | 1,013.0 | 1,025.4 | 1,031.5 | 1,034.7 | 1,032.8 | 1,020.7 |
| 2018 | 1,010.9 | 1,019.5 | 1,023.0 | 1,031.1 | 1,034.5 | 1,029.8 | 1,023.0 | 1,018.7 | 1,029.9 | 1,037.3 | 1,040.8 | 1,037.1 | 1,028.0 |
| 2019 | 1,016.7 | 1,021.5 | 1,025.1 | 1,033.1 | 1,035.8 | 1,033.5 | 1,026.4 | 1,025.1 | 1,035.4 | 1,042.1 | 1,044.0 | 1,042.7 | 1,031.8 |
| **Mining and Logging** | | | | | | | | | | | | | |
| 2011 | 7.6 | 7.8 | 7.9 | 8.3 | 8.4 | 8.7 | 8.9 | 9.0 | 9.1 | 9.2 | 9.4 | 9.6 | 8.7 |
| 2012 | 9.6 | 9.7 | 9.7 | 9.8 | 9.9 | 10.1 | 10.1 | 10.1 | 10.1 | 10.1 | 10.1 | 10.1 | 10.0 |
| 2013 | 10.1 | 10.3 | 10.4 | 10.7 | 10.8 | 10.8 | 10.9 | 10.9 | 10.9 | 11.0 | 10.9 | 11.1 | 10.7 |
| 2014 | 11.2 | 11.1 | 11.3 | 11.5 | 11.7 | 11.9 | 12.0 | 12.1 | 12.1 | 12.2 | 12.3 | 12.3 | 11.8 |
| 2015 | 12.1 | 12.1 | 12 | 11.6 | 11.5 | 11.4 | 11.4 | 11.1 | 10.9 | 10.5 | 10.2 | 10.2 | 11.3 |
| 2016 | 9.9 | 9.4 | 9.1 | 8.8 | 8.8 | 8.6 | 8.5 | 8.5 | 8.5 | 8.6 | 8.8 | 8.9 | 8.9 |
| 2017 | 8.8 | 9.1 | 9.3 | 9.5 | 9.8 | 10.1 | 10.3 | 10.3 | 10.4 | 10.5 | 10.6 | 10.5 | 9.9 |
| 2018 | 10.4 | 10.5 | 10.5 | 10.8 | 11.0 | 11.2 | 11.3 | 11.3 | 11.4 | 11.8 | 11.7 | 11.8 | 11.1 |
| 2019 | 11.7 | 12.0 | 12.1 | 12.2 | 12.2 | 12.1 | 12.2 | 12.0 | 11.5 | 11.7 | 11.8 | 11.7 | 11.9 |
| **Construction** | | | | | | | | | | | | | |
| 2011 | 42.6 | 42.3 | 45.7 | 49.3 | 52.2 | 54.1 | 55.1 | 55.6 | 55.8 | 56.2 | 54.5 | 51.4 | 51.2 |
| 2012 | 47.1 | 47.2 | 49.6 | 54.1 | 55.8 | 57.1 | 57.4 | 57.0 | 57.4 | 58.3 | 55.1 | 51.8 | 54.0 |
| 2013 | 46.6 | 46.9 | 49.0 | 52.4 | 55.1 | 56.1 | 56.9 | 56.9 | 56.6 | 56.3 | 53.7 | 49.6 | 53.0 |
| 2014 | 46.5 | 45.6 | 48.1 | 53.2 | 55.9 | 58.0 | 58.5 | 58.2 | 58.2 | 57.9 | 55.1 | 51.7 | 53.9 |
| 2015 | 47.2 | 46.0 | 47.9 | 52.9 | 55.8 | 57.4 | 58.8 | 59.4 | 59.1 | 59.0 | 57.1 | 53.8 | 54.5 |
| 2016 | 48.6 | 47.4 | 50.6 | 55.2 | 56.7 | 57.3 | 57.9 | 57.4 | 56.9 | 56.7 | 55.0 | 51.5 | 54.3 |
| 2017 | 47.8 | 47.9 | 50.1 | 55.4 | 58.4 | 60.4 | 61.4 | 61.6 | 61.8 | 61.7 | 59.6 | 56.7 | 56.9 |
| 2018 | 51.8 | 51.9 | 54.3 | 57.4 | 60.4 | 62.1 | 63.1 | 63.0 | 63.3 | 63.5 | 61.4 | 59.0 | 59.3 |
| 2019 | 55.5 | 54.9 | 57.4 | 61.8 | 64.6 | 65.7 | 66.7 | 67.6 | 67.4 | 67.2 | 64.9 | 61.6 | 62.9 |

# Employment by Industry: Pittsburgh, PA, 2011–2019—*Continued*

(Numbers in thousands, not seasonally adjusted)

| Industry and year | January | February | March | April | May | June | July | August | September | October | November | December | Annual average |
|---|---|---|---|---|---|---|---|---|---|---|---|---|---|
| **Manufacturing** | | | | | | | | | | | | | |
| 2011 | 87.7 | 87.7 | 88.1 | 88.4 | 88.7 | 89.3 | 89.6 | 89.5 | 89.4 | 89.3 | 89.4 | 89.5 | 88.9 |
| 2012 | 88.8 | 88.8 | 89.0 | 89.2 | 89.8 | 90.5 | 90.6 | 90.7 | 90.2 | 90.2 | 90.3 | 90.0 | 89.8 |
| 2013 | 89.5 | 89.2 | 89.3 | 89.4 | 89.4 | 90.1 | 89.8 | 89.6 | 89.2 | 89.2 | 89.3 | 89.4 | 89.5 |
| 2014 | 88.3 | 88.2 | 88.7 | 88.5 | 88.5 | 89.2 | 88.9 | 89.2 | 88.6 | 88.4 | 88.5 | 88.8 | 88.7 |
| 2015 | 88.1 | 87.8 | 88.1 | 88.3 | 88.2 | 88.9 | 88.7 | 88.3 | 87.5 | 86.2 | 86.2 | 86.1 | 87.7 |
| 2016 | 85.4 | 85.0 | 85.9 | 85.8 | 86.0 | 86.5 | 86.7 | 86.3 | 85.5 | 85.4 | 85.4 | 85.8 | 85.8 |
| 2017 | 85.4 | 85.4 | 85.3 | 85.4 | 85.5 | 86.1 | 86.1 | 86.0 | 85.5 | 85.6 | 85.8 | 86.4 | 85.7 |
| 2018 | 85.7 | 85.6 | 86.0 | 86.0 | 86.4 | 87.3 | 87.4 | 87.6 | 86.9 | 86.9 | 87.4 | 87.7 | 86.7 |
| 2019 | 87.0 | 87.0 | 87.4 | 87.4 | 87.7 | 88.0 | 88.0 | 87.3 | 86.7 | 85.7 | 87.5 | 88.0 | 87.3 |
| **Trade, Transportation, and Utilities** | | | | | | | | | | | | | |
| 2011 | 214.9 | 212.7 | 213.3 | 215.2 | 217.0 | 216.7 | 214.0 | 214.0 | 215.8 | 217.6 | 222.1 | 224.8 | 216.5 |
| 2012 | 216.6 | 214.5 | 216.2 | 216.3 | 217.6 | 216.7 | 213.3 | 212.4 | 214.0 | 216.1 | 221.2 | 222.8 | 216.5 |
| 2013 | 213.7 | 211.1 | 211.8 | 211.9 | 214.2 | 214.2 | 211.6 | 212.2 | 213.2 | 215.0 | 219.9 | 222.9 | 214.3 |
| 2014 | 213.2 | 210.5 | 211.5 | 213.1 | 215.8 | 216.8 | 212.7 | 212.9 | 214.4 | 216.5 | 221.0 | 224.6 | 215.3 |
| 2015 | 215.7 | 212.0 | 212.4 | 213.2 | 216.1 | 216.3 | 213.2 | 213.0 | 213.2 | 215.3 | 219.7 | 222.9 | 215.3 |
| 2016 | 213.2 | 210.7 | 210.9 | 211.9 | 214.0 | 213.0 | 210.6 | 210.0 | 210.9 | 212.3 | 217.0 | 220.2 | 212.9 |
| 2017 | 211.7 | 209.3 | 209.3 | 210.5 | 211.8 | 210.8 | 208.8 | 208.3 | 210.3 | 211.8 | 216.7 | 218.8 | 211.5 |
| 2018 | 210.6 | 208.8 | 208.6 | 209.2 | 211.5 | 210.8 | 208.4 | 207.5 | 209.1 | 210.0 | 215.4 | 216.9 | 210.6 |
| 2019 | 210.1 | 206.0 | 205.9 | 206.0 | 208.2 | 207.3 | 205.6 | 205.2 | 206.1 | 207.2 | 210.0 | 212.5 | 207.5 |
| **Wholesale Trade** | | | | | | | | | | | | | |
| 2011 | 46.1 | 46.2 | 46.4 | 46.9 | 47.1 | 46.9 | 46.8 | 46.9 | 46.4 | 46.5 | 46.4 | 46.4 | 46.6 |
| 2012 | 46.0 | 46.2 | 46.5 | 46.6 | 46.4 | 46.4 | 46.1 | 45.8 | 45.4 | 45.4 | 45.2 | 45.2 | 45.9 |
| 2013 | 44.5 | 44.4 | 44.6 | 44.6 | 44.8 | 45.0 | 45.0 | 45.0 | 44.7 | 44.7 | 44.6 | 44.8 | 44.7 |
| 2014 | 44.4 | 44.3 | 44.3 | 44.3 | 44.7 | 45.0 | 45.1 | 44.8 | 44.6 | 44.8 | 44.8 | 44.9 | 44.7 |
| 2015 | 44.3 | 44.1 | 44.0 | 44.0 | 44.3 | 44.4 | 44.5 | 44.3 | 43.8 | 44.1 | 44.0 | 44.0 | 44.2 |
| 2016 | 43.3 | 43.3 | 43.2 | 43.2 | 43.3 | 43.3 | 43.2 | 43.0 | 42.6 | 42.5 | 42.4 | 42.4 | 43.0 |
| 2017 | 41.9 | 42.1 | 42.2 | 42.2 | 42.5 | 42.7 | 42.8 | 42.7 | 42.4 | 42.4 | 42.3 | 42.5 | 42.4 |
| 2018 | 41.9 | 42.0 | 41.9 | 42.1 | 42.4 | 42.7 | 42.8 | 42.7 | 42.3 | 42.6 | 42.5 | 42.5 | 42.4 |
| 2019 | 42.2 | 42.2 | 42.2 | 42.1 | 42.2 | 42.4 | 42.7 | 42.5 | 42.3 | 42.4 | 42.0 | 42.3 | 42.3 |
| **Retail Trade** | | | | | | | | | | | | | |
| 2011 | 126.0 | 123.7 | 124.1 | 125.2 | 126.7 | 127.3 | 127.5 | 127.9 | 126.1 | 127.5 | 131.6 | 133.5 | 127.3 |
| 2012 | 127.2 | 124.9 | 126.0 | 126.2 | 127.4 | 128.1 | 127.4 | 127.0 | 125.3 | 127.0 | 132.0 | 132.8 | 127.6 |
| 2013 | 125.9 | 123.7 | 124.0 | 124.2 | 125.9 | 127.0 | 126.6 | 126.9 | 124.9 | 126.5 | 130.7 | 132.7 | 126.6 |
| 2014 | 125.2 | 122.9 | 123.7 | 124.6 | 126.5 | 127.7 | 126.7 | 127.1 | 125.0 | 126.5 | 130.3 | 132.7 | 126.6 |
| 2015 | 125.9 | 123.0 | 123.4 | 124.0 | 126.0 | 126.9 | 126.6 | 126.6 | 124.2 | 125.9 | 129.7 | 131.8 | 126.2 |
| 2016 | 125.1 | 123.2 | 123.6 | 124.5 | 126.1 | 126.4 | 126.2 | 126.0 | 123.4 | 124.6 | 128.6 | 130.4 | 125.7 |
| 2017 | 124.9 | 122.3 | 122.2 | 123.1 | 123.6 | 124.2 | 123.8 | 123.4 | 121.6 | 122.9 | 127.0 | 127.8 | 123.9 |
| 2018 | 122.2 | 120.5 | 120.3 | 120.5 | 122.0 | 122.6 | 122.0 | 121.3 | 119.5 | 120.1 | 124.6 | 125.4 | 121.8 |
| 2019 | 120.4 | 117.3 | 117.3 | 117.4 | 119.0 | 119.2 | 118.9 | 118.7 | 116.7 | 117.3 | 119.8 | 120.5 | 118.5 |
| **Transportation and Utilities** | | | | | | | | | | | | | |
| 2011 | 42.8 | 42.8 | 42.8 | 43.1 | 43.2 | 42.5 | 39.7 | 39.2 | 43.3 | 43.6 | 44.1 | 44.9 | 42.7 |
| 2012 | 43.4 | 43.4 | 43.7 | 43.5 | 43.8 | 42.2 | 39.8 | 39.6 | 43.3 | 43.7 | 44.0 | 44.8 | 42.9 |
| 2013 | 43.3 | 43.0 | 43.2 | 43.1 | 43.5 | 42.2 | 40.0 | 40.3 | 43.6 | 43.8 | 44.6 | 45.4 | 43.0 |
| 2014 | 43.6 | 43.3 | 43.5 | 44.2 | 44.6 | 44.1 | 40.9 | 41.0 | 44.8 | 45.2 | 45.9 | 47.0 | 44.0 |
| 2015 | 45.5 | 44.9 | 45.0 | 45.2 | 45.8 | 45.0 | 42.1 | 42.1 | 45.2 | 45.3 | 46.0 | 47.1 | 44.9 |
| 2016 | 44.8 | 44.2 | 44.1 | 44.2 | 44.6 | 43.3 | 41.2 | 41.0 | 44.9 | 45.2 | 46.0 | 47.4 | 44.2 |
| 2017 | 44.9 | 44.9 | 44.9 | 45.2 | 45.7 | 43.9 | 42.2 | 42.2 | 46.3 | 46.5 | 47.4 | 48.5 | 45.2 |
| 2018 | 46.5 | 46.3 | 46.4 | 46.6 | 47.1 | 45.5 | 43.6 | 43.5 | 47.3 | 47.3 | 48.3 | 49.0 | 46.5 |
| 2019 | 47.5 | 46.5 | 46.4 | 46.5 | 47.0 | 45.7 | 44.0 | 44.0 | 47.1 | 47.5 | 48.2 | 49.7 | 46.7 |
| **Information** | | | | | | | | | | | | | |
| 2011 | 18.4 | 18.4 | 18.5 | 18.7 | 18.9 | 19.1 | 19.0 | 17.5 | 18.7 | 18.8 | 19.1 | 18.5 | 18.6 |
| 2012 | 18.4 | 18.4 | 18.7 | 18.7 | 19.8 | 19.2 | 19.1 | 19.1 | 18.9 | 18.9 | 18.9 | 18.7 | 18.9 |
| 2013 | 18.8 | 18.4 | 18.4 | 18.3 | 18.6 | 18.6 | 18.9 | 18.8 | 18.8 | 20.0 | 19.2 | 19.3 | 18.8 |
| 2014 | 18.3 | 18.3 | 18.4 | 19.1 | 18.6 | 18.6 | 18.7 | 18.7 | 18.6 | 18.4 | 18.4 | 18.4 | 18.5 |
| 2015 | 18.1 | 18.3 | 18.3 | 18.2 | 18.5 | 18.7 | 18.7 | 18.9 | 18.6 | 18.5 | 18.4 | 18.4 | 18.5 |
| 2016 | 18.0 | 18.0 | 18.0 | 18.4 | 17.4 | 18.9 | 19.0 | 19.1 | 18.8 | 18.9 | 18.8 | 18.5 | 18.5 |
| 2017 | 18.4 | 18.8 | 18.4 | 18.5 | 18.9 | 19.5 | 19.0 | 19.7 | 19.0 | 18.8 | 18.8 | 18.8 | 18.9 |
| 2018 | 18.5 | 19.3 | 19.1 | 19.4 | 19.3 | 19.5 | 19.3 | 19.2 | 19.4 | 19.6 | 19.6 | 19.3 | 19.3 |
| 2019 | 18.9 | 19.1 | 19.2 | 19.0 | 19.2 | 19.8 | 19.8 | 19.8 | 19.6 | 19.6 | 19.5 | 19.6 | 19.4 |

## Employment by Industry: Pittsburgh, PA, 2011–2019—*Continued*

(Numbers in thousands, not seasonally adjusted)

| Industry and year | January | February | March | April | May | June | July | August | September | October | November | December | Annual average |
|---|---|---|---|---|---|---|---|---|---|---|---|---|---|
| **Financial Activities** | | | | | | | | | | | | | |
| 2011 | 68.6 | 68.4 | 68.5 | 68.8 | 69.3 | 70.1 | 70.4 | 70.4 | 69.7 | 69.9 | 70.1 | 70.3 | 69.5 |
| 2012 | 69.9 | 70.0 | 70.3 | 70.3 | 70.7 | 71.7 | 71.8 | 71.8 | 71.0 | 71.1 | 71.3 | 71.3 | 70.9 |
| 2013 | 70.8 | 70.9 | 71.0 | 71.1 | 71.3 | 71.9 | 71.8 | 71.9 | 70.9 | 71.0 | 71.1 | 70.8 | 71.2 |
| 2014 | 70.9 | 70.7 | 70.5 | 70.3 | 70.8 | 71.2 | 71.3 | 71.0 | 69.9 | 70.0 | 70.2 | 70.1 | 70.6 |
| 2015 | 69.4 | 69.5 | 69.5 | 69.7 | 70.4 | 71.0 | 71.2 | 71.2 | 70.4 | 70.6 | 70.9 | 70.8 | 70.4 |
| 2016 | 70.3 | 70.5 | 70.4 | 70.7 | 71.2 | 71.9 | 72.3 | 72.5 | 71.9 | 72.0 | 72.2 | 72.4 | 71.5 |
| 2017 | 72.1 | 72.6 | 72.5 | 72.6 | 73.1 | 73.8 | 74.2 | 73.9 | 73.2 | 73.4 | 73.5 | 73.6 | 73.2 |
| 2018 | 73.4 | 73.7 | 73.7 | 74.0 | 74.5 | 75.5 | 75.9 | 75.8 | 75.1 | 75.4 | 75.6 | 75.4 | 74.8 |
| 2019 | 75.7 | 75.7 | 75.5 | 75.7 | 76.3 | 77.0 | 77.4 | 77.2 | 76.5 | 76.3 | 76.3 | 76.4 | 76.3 |
| **Professional and Business Services** | | | | | | | | | | | | | |
| 2011 | 160.1 | 160.4 | 161.5 | 164.6 | 166.1 | 167.4 | 167.7 | 167.8 | 167.9 | 169.8 | 169.7 | 168.5 | 166.0 |
| 2012 | 167.4 | 168.0 | 170.4 | 172.4 | 173.3 | 174.7 | 174.1 | 173.4 | 172.4 | 174.3 | 174.3 | 173.5 | 172.4 |
| 2013 | 171.0 | 172.6 | 174.1 | 175.8 | 176.9 | 177.8 | 177.9 | 177.1 | 175.5 | 176.1 | 175.5 | 174.2 | 175.4 |
| 2014 | 171.2 | 172.1 | 173.2 | 176.4 | 177.9 | 178.8 | 179.1 | 179.5 | 178.2 | 179.4 | 179.9 | 178.9 | 177.1 |
| 2015 | 176.5 | 176.9 | 177.8 | 180.5 | 181.7 | 182.2 | 182.8 | 182.2 | 181.2 | 183.5 | 183.7 | 182.3 | 180.9 |
| 2016 | 179.3 | 179.0 | 179.7 | 182.8 | 182.3 | 183.2 | 182.8 | 182.3 | 182.3 | 183.6 | 184.0 | 182.0 | 181.9 |
| 2017 | 179.0 | 178.9 | 179.6 | 182.2 | 182.7 | 183.4 | 183.0 | 182.8 | 182.3 | 183.2 | 182.7 | 181.0 | 181.7 |
| 2018 | 178.3 | 179.4 | 180.2 | 182.5 | 183.3 | 184.0 | 184.2 | 183.3 | 182.1 | 182.9 | 182.4 | 180.9 | 182.0 |
| 2019 | 179.4 | 180.1 | 180.0 | 183.8 | 184.3 | 184.6 | 185.7 | 186.0 | 184.9 | 186.4 | 185.3 | 185.5 | 183.8 |
| **Education and Health Services** | | | | | | | | | | | | | |
| 2011 | 238.2 | 240.1 | 240.6 | 240.6 | 238.6 | 239.1 | 235.9 | 234.4 | 240.3 | 243.2 | 244.1 | 243.2 | 239.9 |
| 2012 | 240.1 | 243.5 | 245.1 | 244.1 | 240.7 | 237.8 | 235.6 | 233.1 | 239.7 | 243.7 | 244.5 | 242.4 | 240.9 |
| 2013 | 239.6 | 243.4 | 243.3 | 243.4 | 238.5 | 237.1 | 235.2 | 231.9 | 239.4 | 242.9 | 244.0 | 242.7 | 240.1 |
| 2014 | 240.3 | 242.3 | 243.3 | 243.9 | 240.1 | 237.2 | 235.6 | 232.3 | 240.3 | 243.8 | 244.6 | 242.7 | 240.5 |
| 2015 | 239.7 | 241.0 | 241.3 | 242.6 | 238.6 | 234.1 | 233.5 | 232.3 | 239.6 | 243.6 | 244.4 | 241.8 | 239.4 |
| 2016 | 240.8 | 244.5 | 244.4 | 246.3 | 242.5 | 236.9 | 237.5 | 236.6 | 244.7 | 247.8 | 249.2 | 247.0 | 243.2 |
| 2017 | 245.8 | 249.7 | 250.4 | 251.5 | 248.4 | 242.4 | 242.9 | 242.2 | 251.3 | 255.7 | 256.7 | 255.6 | 249.4 |
| 2018 | 253.6 | 258.2 | 258.5 | 259.8 | 255.9 | 249.4 | 250.0 | 250.0 | 257.9 | 262.7 | 263.5 | 261.2 | 256.7 |
| 2019 | 258.2 | 262.3 | 262.6 | 263.2 | 258.8 | 252.5 | 252.5 | 252.6 | 260.2 | 262.4 | 263.3 | 261.3 | 259.2 |
| **Leisure and Hospitality** | | | | | | | | | | | | | |
| 2011 | 101.5 | 100.8 | 103.4 | 108.6 | 114.3 | 117.8 | 115.9 | 116.7 | 114.0 | 110.8 | 107.9 | 107.4 | 109.9 |
| 2012 | 102.4 | 102.5 | 106.1 | 109.9 | 115.0 | 119.0 | 117.4 | 118.9 | 114.8 | 112.9 | 110.5 | 110.8 | 111.7 |
| 2013 | 105.2 | 105.2 | 107.6 | 111.8 | 118.5 | 122.1 | 121.4 | 121.4 | 117.0 | 114.7 | 111.7 | 111.9 | 114.0 |
| 2014 | 106.3 | 106.1 | 108.5 | 112.8 | 119.8 | 121.9 | 120.0 | 121.8 | 117.2 | 115.2 | 110.9 | 111.4 | 114.3 |
| 2015 | 106.9 | 106.9 | 108.8 | 113.8 | 119.9 | 122.6 | 122.0 | 123.4 | 119.1 | 116.6 | 114.8 | 114.4 | 115.8 |
| 2016 | 109.5 | 110.0 | 112.6 | 116.9 | 122.3 | 124.8 | 125.2 | 126.1 | 120.9 | 118.2 | 116.7 | 114.5 | 118.1 |
| 2017 | 110.8 | 111.0 | 113.7 | 118.3 | 123.2 | 126.8 | 125.4 | 126.9 | 122.1 | 120.3 | 117.5 | 117.4 | 119.5 |
| 2018 | 113.9 | 113.3 | 115.5 | 118.7 | 123.5 | 125.0 | 125.6 | 125.8 | 121.0 | 120.2 | 116.9 | 117.5 | 119.7 |
| 2019 | 113.2 | 113.7 | 115.9 | 118.9 | 123.0 | 126.6 | 125.8 | 127.0 | 122.4 | 123.1 | 121.6 | 121.4 | 121.1 |
| **Other Services** | | | | | | | | | | | | | |
| 2011 | 50.3 | 50.5 | 50.9 | 51.1 | 51.7 | 52.5 | 52.4 | 52.2 | 51.3 | 51.2 | 51.2 | 51.3 | 51.4 |
| 2012 | 50.7 | 50.9 | 51.5 | 51.7 | 52.0 | 53.1 | 52.9 | 52.2 | 51.6 | 51.3 | 51.0 | 51.0 | 51.7 |
| 2013 | 50.0 | 50.1 | 50.3 | 50.7 | 51.2 | 52.2 | 52.2 | 51.9 | 51.2 | 50.7 | 50.5 | 50.7 | 51.0 |
| 2014 | 49.9 | 50.0 | 50.4 | 50.3 | 50.8 | 51.6 | 52.2 | 52.0 | 50.9 | 50.7 | 50.4 | 50.6 | 50.8 |
| 2015 | 49.9 | 50.0 | 50.6 | 50.8 | 51.4 | 52.0 | 52.3 | 52.0 | 50.7 | 50.5 | 50.5 | 50.6 | 50.9 |
| 2016 | 50.2 | 50.2 | 50.7 | 51.0 | 51.3 | 52.1 | 52.2 | 51.6 | 50.5 | 50.8 | 50.3 | 50.2 | 50.9 |
| 2017 | 49.8 | 49.9 | 50.1 | 50.4 | 51.0 | 51.8 | 51.9 | 51.8 | 50.4 | 50.6 | 50.5 | 50.4 | 50.7 |
| 2018 | 49.7 | 49.7 | 49.9 | 50.0 | 50.2 | 50.8 | 51.3 | 50.8 | 49.7 | 49.8 | 49.4 | 49.2 | 50.0 |
| 2019 | 48.8 | 48.6 | 49.1 | 49.4 | 50.0 | 50.6 | 51.0 | 50.4 | 49.3 | 49.1 | 48.9 | 48.7 | 49.5 |
| **Government** | | | | | | | | | | | | | |
| 2011 | 126.6 | 129.3 | 130.0 | 129.5 | 127.8 | 125.9 | 115.4 | 113.3 | 121.6 | 124.6 | 125.7 | 125.5 | 124.6 |
| 2012 | 119.5 | 124.2 | 124.5 | 124.3 | 124.2 | 121.2 | 112.6 | 111.7 | 120.0 | 122.6 | 123.7 | 123.3 | 121.0 |
| 2013 | 118.4 | 122.8 | 122.9 | 123.0 | 123.6 | 119.1 | 110.5 | 110.1 | 119.0 | 120.9 | 122.2 | 121.7 | 119.5 |
| 2014 | 118.0 | 120.3 | 120.5 | 121.1 | 121.3 | 117.9 | 109.4 | 108.6 | 117.6 | 120.0 | 120.9 | 120.7 | 118.0 |
| 2015 | 116.1 | 119.2 | 119.4 | 120.3 | 120.2 | 117.2 | 109.3 | 108.7 | 117.1 | 118.3 | 119.5 | 118.3 | 117.0 |
| 2016 | 114.9 | 117.9 | 118.8 | 118.7 | 119.1 | 115.9 | 109.8 | 108.2 | 117.1 | 118.4 | 119.1 | 118.7 | 116.4 |
| 2017 | 113.8 | 118.3 | 118.6 | 118.6 | 118.9 | 115.3 | 108.9 | 107.4 | 116.8 | 117.7 | 118.3 | 117.2 | 115.8 |
| 2018 | 112.9 | 117.1 | 117.5 | 117.5 | 116.3 | 114.8 | 108.3 | 106.3 | 115.6 | 116.7 | 118.0 | 116.7 | 114.8 |
| 2019 | 112.4 | 116.0 | 116.9 | 117.1 | 116.0 | 115.1 | 108.6 | 106.9 | 116.4 | 118.0 | 119.1 | 117.3 | 115.0 |

# Employment by Industry: Las Vegas-Henderson-Paradise, NV, 2011–2019

(Numbers in thousands, not seasonally adjusted)

| Industry and year | January | February | March | April | May | June | July | August | September | October | November | December | Annual average |
|---|---|---|---|---|---|---|---|---|---|---|---|---|---|
| **Total Nonfarm** | | | | | | | | | | | | | |
| 2011 | 797.2 | 797.2 | 803.5 | 810.3 | 811.3 | 807.5 | 804.5 | 803.8 | 811.5 | 817.6 | 818.4 | 816.5 | 808.3 |
| 2012 | 808.7 | 810.5 | 815.8 | 821.9 | 827.7 | 826.7 | 818.9 | 822.7 | 830.8 | 837.8 | 842.3 | 838.5 | 825.2 |
| 2013 | 831.1 | 832.4 | 839.5 | 846.7 | 850.5 | 851.0 | 845.1 | 849.3 | 853.8 | 861.7 | 867.8 | 865.6 | 849.5 |
| 2014 | 858.5 | 862.9 | 871.3 | 878.3 | 884.7 | 881.0 | 874.4 | 885.0 | 892.8 | 903.2 | 905.4 | 905.5 | 883.6 |
| 2015 | 898.1 | 900.4 | 908.1 | 915.3 | 919.3 | 915.4 | 910.0 | 918.1 | 924.7 | 935.3 | 941.4 | 941.8 | 919.0 |
| 2016 | 926.4 | 930.1 | 937.5 | 946.0 | 947.4 | 946.3 | 946.9 | 950.0 | 961.1 | 964.5 | 969.4 | 967.0 | 949.4 |
| 2017 | 959.5 | 961.9 | 972.8 | 968.5 | 976.5 | 972.1 | 971.0 | 975.1 | 985.0 | 992.2 | 997.4 | 997.3 | 977.4 |
| 2018 | 983.4 | 990.1 | 998.1 | 997.8 | 1,005.2 | 999.8 | 1,000.5 | 1,008.8 | 1,015.7 | 1,026.3 | 1,032.6 | 1,028.6 | 1,007.2 |
| 2019 | 1,016.3 | 1,022.7 | 1,028.4 | 1,031.6 | 1,036.6 | 1,028.2 | 1,028.4 | 1,034.8 | 1,040.8 | 1,044.7 | 1,050.9 | 1,045.6 | 1,034.1 |
| **Total Private** | | | | | | | | | | | | | |
| 2011 | 702.0 | 700.4 | 706.6 | 713.6 | 715.0 | 717.4 | 715.5 | 714.7 | 718.2 | 723.0 | 723.8 | 721.0 | 714.3 |
| 2012 | 716.1 | 716.0 | 720.1 | 726.3 | 731.9 | 735.3 | 729.6 | 734.0 | 736.4 | 742.4 | 746.0 | 741.3 | 731.3 |
| 2013 | 736.7 | 737.0 | 743.3 | 750.2 | 754.1 | 758.3 | 755.6 | 758.2 | 758.6 | 764.8 | 770.0 | 766.9 | 754.5 |
| 2014 | 762.7 | 765.6 | 772.9 | 780.4 | 786.5 | 788.4 | 783.5 | 793.1 | 795.9 | 805.0 | 806.7 | 806.0 | 787.2 |
| 2015 | 801.1 | 802.2 | 808.7 | 815.9 | 820.1 | 819.8 | 817.4 | 824.2 | 825.5 | 836.3 | 840.7 | 839.8 | 821.0 |
| 2016 | 827.3 | 829.5 | 835.5 | 844.9 | 846.3 | 850.9 | 852.0 | 854.6 | 859.7 | 863.3 | 866.8 | 863.4 | 849.5 |
| 2017 | 859.8 | 859.4 | 869.3 | 867.2 | 874.2 | 875.8 | 873.6 | 875.9 | 879.8 | 889.3 | 893.0 | 891.9 | 875.8 |
| 2018 | 882.7 | 886.0 | 893.0 | 895.1 | 901.3 | 901.7 | 903.0 | 909.5 | 909.7 | 920.0 | 924.4 | 919.8 | 903.9 |
| 2019 | 912.9 | 914.9 | 919.7 | 924.7 | 928.8 | 927.5 | 927.6 | 931.2 | 931.5 | 934.7 | 940.8 | 935.2 | 927.5 |
| **Goods Producing** | | | | | | | | | | | | | |
| 2011 | 57.7 | 57.5 | 57.2 | 57.6 | 57.1 | 57.2 | 57.9 | 58.6 | 58.0 | 58.0 | 57.2 | 57.0 | 57.6 |
| 2012 | 54.8 | 54.7 | 55.1 | 55.6 | 56.6 | 57.8 | 58.0 | 59.5 | 60.0 | 60.5 | 61.0 | 61.0 | 57.9 |
| 2013 | 59.3 | 59.8 | 60.4 | 61.2 | 61.1 | 61.9 | 62.0 | 63.4 | 63.3 | 64.2 | 64.4 | 64.1 | 62.1 |
| 2014 | 63.7 | 64.2 | 64.4 | 65.3 | 65.8 | 66.0 | 66.9 | 68.6 | 68.9 | 69.6 | 69.4 | 69.6 | 66.9 |
| 2015 | 69.8 | 70.3 | 70.4 | 70.9 | 72.1 | 72.7 | 72.6 | 74.0 | 74.3 | 76.0 | 76.4 | 77.0 | 73.0 |
| 2016 | 75.6 | 75.6 | 75.5 | 75.5 | 75.3 | 76.9 | 77.7 | 78.4 | 78.9 | 79.1 | 79.0 | 79.4 | 77.2 |
| 2017 | 79.4 | 80.1 | 81.9 | 81.5 | 81.9 | 83.0 | 82.5 | 82.4 | 83.5 | 84.2 | 84.0 | 84.0 | 82.4 |
| 2018 | 83.7 | 84.7 | 85.3 | 86.8 | 87.4 | 88.8 | 89.5 | 91.0 | 90.9 | 92.1 | 92.4 | 92.7 | 88.8 |
| 2019 | 92.1 | 93.2 | 94.7 | 94.8 | 95.4 | 96.0 | 96.8 | 97.5 | 97.7 | 99.1 | 100.2 | 100.2 | 96.5 |
| **Service-Providing** | | | | | | | | | | | | | |
| 2011 | 739.5 | 739.7 | 746.3 | 752.7 | 754.2 | 750.3 | 746.6 | 745.2 | 753.5 | 759.6 | 761.2 | 759.5 | 750.7 |
| 2012 | 753.9 | 755.8 | 760.7 | 766.3 | 771.1 | 768.9 | 760.9 | 763.2 | 770.8 | 777.3 | 781.3 | 777.5 | 767.3 |
| 2013 | 771.8 | 772.6 | 779.1 | 785.5 | 789.4 | 789.1 | 783.1 | 785.9 | 790.5 | 797.5 | 803.4 | 801.5 | 787.5 |
| 2014 | 794.8 | 798.7 | 806.9 | 813.0 | 818.9 | 815.0 | 807.5 | 816.4 | 823.9 | 833.6 | 836.0 | 835.9 | 816.7 |
| 2015 | 828.3 | 830.1 | 837.7 | 844.4 | 847.2 | 842.7 | 837.4 | 844.1 | 850.4 | 859.3 | 865.0 | 864.8 | 846.0 |
| 2016 | 850.8 | 854.5 | 862.0 | 870.5 | 872.1 | 869.4 | 869.2 | 871.6 | 882.2 | 885.4 | 890.4 | 887.6 | 872.1 |
| 2017 | 880.1 | 881.8 | 890.9 | 887.0 | 894.6 | 889.1 | 888.5 | 892.7 | 901.5 | 908.0 | 913.4 | 913.3 | 895.1 |
| 2018 | 899.7 | 905.4 | 912.8 | 911.0 | 917.8 | 911.0 | 911.0 | 917.8 | 924.8 | 934.2 | 940.2 | 935.9 | 918.5 |
| 2019 | 924.2 | 929.5 | 933.7 | 936.8 | 941.2 | 932.2 | 931.6 | 937.3 | 943.1 | 945.6 | 950.7 | 945.4 | 937.6 |
| **Mining, Logging, and Construction** | | | | | | | | | | | | | |
| 2011 | 38.3 | 38.1 | 37.7 | 38.0 | 37.6 | 37.5 | 38.2 | 38.6 | 38.0 | 37.9 | 37.2 | 36.9 | 37.8 |
| 2012 | 35.1 | 35.1 | 35.3 | 35.6 | 36.5 | 37.3 | 37.6 | 39.0 | 39.6 | 40.1 | 40.5 | 40.5 | 37.7 |
| 2013 | 39.1 | 39.5 | 40.0 | 40.6 | 40.3 | 41.0 | 41.1 | 42.5 | 42.5 | 43.3 | 43.4 | 42.9 | 41.4 |
| 2014 | 42.7 | 43.3 | 43.5 | 44.3 | 44.7 | 44.9 | 45.8 | 47.4 | 47.7 | 48.2 | 48.0 | 48.2 | 45.7 |
| 2015 | 48.5 | 49.0 | 48.9 | 49.5 | 50.5 | 50.9 | 51.0 | 52.5 | 52.7 | 54.3 | 54.5 | 55.1 | 51.5 |
| 2016 | 53.9 | 53.8 | 53.6 | 53.7 | 53.4 | 54.8 | 55.5 | 56.1 | 56.5 | 56.6 | 56.5 | 56.7 | 55.1 |
| 2017 | 56.9 | 57.5 | 59.1 | 58.5 | 58.9 | 59.8 | 59.2 | 59.2 | 60.2 | 60.8 | 60.4 | 60.3 | 59.2 |
| 2018 | 60.1 | 60.9 | 61.3 | 62.6 | 63.2 | 64.3 | 64.8 | 66.1 | 65.9 | 66.9 | 67.0 | 67.2 | 64.2 |
| 2019 | 66.9 | 67.9 | 69.1 | 69.2 | 69.8 | 70.2 | 70.8 | 71.6 | 71.8 | 72.9 | 74.2 | 74.0 | 70.7 |
| **Manufacturing** | | | | | | | | | | | | | |
| 2011 | 19.4 | 19.4 | 19.5 | 19.6 | 19.5 | 19.7 | 19.7 | 20.0 | 20.0 | 20.1 | 20.0 | 20.1 | 19.8 |
| 2012 | 19.7 | 19.6 | 19.8 | 20.0 | 20.1 | 20.5 | 20.4 | 20.5 | 20.4 | 20.4 | 20.5 | 20.5 | 20.2 |
| 2013 | 20.2 | 20.3 | 20.4 | 20.6 | 20.8 | 20.9 | 20.9 | 20.9 | 20.8 | 20.9 | 21.0 | 21.2 | 20.7 |
| 2014 | 21.0 | 20.9 | 20.9 | 21.0 | 21.1 | 21.1 | 21.1 | 21.2 | 21.2 | 21.4 | 21.4 | 21.4 | 21.1 |
| 2015 | 21.3 | 21.3 | 21.5 | 21.4 | 21.6 | 21.8 | 21.6 | 21.5 | 21.6 | 21.7 | 21.9 | 21.9 | 21.6 |
| 2016 | 21.7 | 21.8 | 21.9 | 21.8 | 21.9 | 22.1 | 22.2 | 22.3 | 22.4 | 22.5 | 22.5 | 22.7 | 22.2 |
| 2017 | 22.5 | 22.6 | 22.8 | 23.0 | 23.0 | 23.2 | 23.3 | 23.2 | 23.3 | 23.4 | 23.6 | 23.7 | 23.1 |
| 2018 | 23.6 | 23.8 | 24.0 | 24.2 | 24.2 | 24.5 | 24.7 | 24.9 | 25.0 | 25.2 | 25.4 | 25.5 | 24.6 |
| 2019 | 25.2 | 25.3 | 25.6 | 25.6 | 25.6 | 25.8 | 26.0 | 25.9 | 25.9 | 26.2 | 26.0 | 26.2 | 25.8 |

## Employment by Industry: Las Vegas-Henderson-Paradise, NV, 2011–2019—*Continued*

(Numbers in thousands, not seasonally adjusted)

| Industry and year | January | February | March | April | May | June | July | August | September | October | November | December | Annual average |
|---|---|---|---|---|---|---|---|---|---|---|---|---|---|
| **Trade, Transportation, and Utilities** | | | | | | | | | | | | | |
| 2011 | 147.0 | 145.5 | 146.1 | 147.4 | 147.7 | 148.3 | 149.0 | 149.5 | 149.6 | 151.9 | 156.1 | 156.6 | 149.6 |
| 2012 | 152.2 | 150.2 | 151.1 | 151.8 | 152.7 | 153.2 | 153.2 | 153.3 | 153.8 | 154.5 | 160.0 | 159.7 | 153.8 |
| 2013 | 154.6 | 152.5 | 151.6 | 152.3 | 154.6 | 155.4 | 156.1 | 156.7 | 157.2 | 158.9 | 163.9 | 165.3 | 156.6 |
| 2014 | 159.1 | 157.8 | 158.4 | 159.1 | 159.9 | 160.7 | 161.0 | 161.9 | 162.7 | 165.4 | 170.2 | 171.6 | 162.3 |
| 2015 | 166.0 | 164.4 | 165.6 | 166.4 | 167.4 | 167.6 | 167.7 | 168.4 | 168.9 | 170.7 | 175.1 | 175.5 | 168.6 |
| 2016 | 167.0 | 166.4 | 166.8 | 168.1 | 168.8 | 169.0 | 169.7 | 170.4 | 170.9 | 172.2 | 177.6 | 177.9 | 170.4 |
| 2017 | 172.2 | 170.6 | 170.5 | 170.5 | 171.7 | 172.3 | 172.8 | 174.4 | 175.0 | 177.4 | 183.9 | 185.5 | 174.7 |
| 2018 | 177.3 | 175.7 | 175.9 | 176.0 | 177.3 | 178.1 | 178.6 | 179.5 | 179.8 | 182.1 | 188.5 | 188.1 | 179.7 |
| 2019 | 183.2 | 180.5 | 180.0 | 180.2 | 182.2 | 183.1 | 183.5 | 184.3 | 184.7 | 185.9 | 190.8 | 190.5 | 184.1 |
| **Wholesale Trade** | | | | | | | | | | | | | |
| 2011 | 20.0 | 19.9 | 20.0 | 20.1 | 20.0 | 20.1 | 20.1 | 20.0 | 19.9 | 20.0 | 19.9 | 19.9 | 20.0 |
| 2012 | 19.7 | 19.7 | 19.8 | 19.8 | 19.9 | 20.0 | 20.0 | 20.0 | 20.0 | 20.0 | 20.0 | 20.1 | 19.9 |
| 2013 | 19.9 | 19.9 | 19.9 | 20.0 | 20.1 | 20.2 | 20.4 | 20.5 | 20.5 | 20.5 | 20.6 | 20.7 | 20.3 |
| 2014 | 20.5 | 20.7 | 20.7 | 20.7 | 20.7 | 20.7 | 20.9 | 20.9 | 20.9 | 21.0 | 21.0 | 21.1 | 20.8 |
| 2015 | 21.0 | 21.0 | 21.0 | 21.0 | 21.1 | 21.1 | 21.2 | 21.2 | 21.3 | 21.4 | 21.5 | 21.5 | 21.2 |
| 2016 | 21.0 | 21.1 | 20.9 | 21.1 | 21.2 | 21.2 | 21.4 | 21.4 | 21.5 | 21.5 | 21.6 | 21.7 | 21.3 |
| 2017 | 21.7 | 21.8 | 21.9 | 22.1 | 22.3 | 22.5 | 22.5 | 22.5 | 22.5 | 22.5 | 22.6 | 22.6 | 22.3 |
| 2018 | 22.5 | 22.5 | 22.7 | 23.0 | 23.2 | 23.4 | 23.6 | 23.7 | 23.7 | 24.0 | 24.1 | 24.2 | 23.4 |
| 2019 | 24.2 | 24.3 | 24.4 | 24.5 | 24.5 | 24.7 | 24.7 | 24.6 | 24.6 | 24.8 | 24.8 | 24.9 | 24.6 |
| **Retail Trade** | | | | | | | | | | | | | |
| 2011 | 92.7 | 91.3 | 91.6 | 92.2 | 92.7 | 93.0 | 93.4 | 94.1 | 94.2 | 95.9 | 100.1 | 100.6 | 94.3 |
| 2012 | 96.6 | 94.8 | 95.5 | 96.0 | 96.4 | 96.8 | 96.6 | 96.8 | 97.2 | 98.2 | 103.6 | 103.0 | 97.6 |
| 2013 | 98.1 | 96.4 | 96.4 | 96.8 | 97.9 | 98.4 | 98.9 | 99.5 | 99.7 | 101.1 | 105.8 | 106.9 | 99.7 |
| 2014 | 101.3 | 99.8 | 100.2 | 100.5 | 101.1 | 101.6 | 101.7 | 102.5 | 103.0 | 105.4 | 110.0 | 110.9 | 103.2 |
| 2015 | 105.3 | 104.0 | 104.8 | 105.4 | 105.9 | 106.0 | 105.9 | 106.6 | 106.5 | 108.2 | 112.1 | 112.1 | 106.9 |
| 2016 | 105.5 | 104.7 | 105.1 | 105.6 | 106.0 | 106.2 | 106.3 | 107.0 | 107.1 | 108.8 | 113.5 | 113.2 | 107.4 |
| 2017 | 107.7 | 106.3 | 106.1 | 106.0 | 106.8 | 106.8 | 106.8 | 107.2 | 107.5 | 109.3 | 114.6 | 114.9 | 108.3 |
| 2018 | 108.7 | 107.4 | 107.1 | 106.8 | 107.7 | 108.1 | 108.6 | 109.3 | 109.5 | 110.6 | 115.9 | 115.5 | 109.6 |
| 2019 | 110.5 | 108.5 | 108.1 | 107.9 | 108.3 | 108.3 | 108.3 | 108.7 | 108.6 | 109.2 | 113.2 | 112.4 | 109.3 |
| **Transportation and Utilities** | | | | | | | | | | | | | |
| 2011 | 34.3 | 34.3 | 34.5 | 35.1 | 35.0 | 35.2 | 35.5 | 35.4 | 35.5 | 36.0 | 36.1 | 36.1 | 35.3 |
| 2012 | 35.9 | 35.7 | 35.8 | 36.0 | 36.4 | 36.4 | 36.6 | 36.5 | 36.6 | 36.3 | 36.4 | 36.6 | 36.3 |
| 2013 | 36.6 | 36.2 | 35.3 | 35.5 | 36.6 | 36.8 | 36.8 | 36.7 | 37.0 | 37.3 | 37.5 | 37.7 | 36.7 |
| 2014 | 37.3 | 37.3 | 37.5 | 37.9 | 38.1 | 38.4 | 38.4 | 38.5 | 38.8 | 39.0 | 39.2 | 39.6 | 38.3 |
| 2015 | 39.7 | 39.4 | 39.8 | 40.0 | 40.4 | 40.5 | 40.6 | 40.6 | 41.1 | 41.1 | 41.5 | 41.9 | 40.6 |
| 2016 | 40.5 | 40.6 | 40.8 | 41.4 | 41.6 | 41.6 | 42.0 | 42.0 | 42.3 | 41.9 | 42.5 | 43.0 | 41.7 |
| 2017 | 42.8 | 42.5 | 42.5 | 42.4 | 42.6 | 43.0 | 43.5 | 44.7 | 45.0 | 45.6 | 46.7 | 48.0 | 44.1 |
| 2018 | 46.1 | 45.8 | 46.1 | 46.2 | 46.4 | 46.6 | 46.4 | 46.5 | 46.6 | 47.5 | 48.5 | 48.4 | 46.8 |
| 2019 | 48.5 | 47.7 | 47.5 | 47.8 | 49.4 | 50.1 | 50.5 | 51.0 | 51.5 | 51.9 | 52.8 | 53.2 | 50.2 |
| **Information** | | | | | | | | | | | | | |
| 2011 | 9.2 | 9.0 | 9.1 | 9.4 | 9.4 | 9.4 | 9.2 | 9.1 | 9.5 | 9.8 | 9.1 | 9.6 | 9.3 |
| 2012 | 9.1 | 9.2 | 9.4 | 9.4 | 9.5 | 9.5 | 9.2 | 9.5 | 9.6 | 10.2 | 11.3 | 9.9 | 9.7 |
| 2013 | 9.1 | 9.3 | 9.5 | 9.7 | 9.8 | 10.8 | 10.1 | 9.8 | 9.8 | 9.9 | 10.1 | 10.1 | 9.8 |
| 2014 | 9.8 | 9.9 | 9.7 | 10.9 | 11.7 | 12.2 | 10.3 | 10.1 | 10.4 | 10.5 | 10.9 | 10.7 | 10.6 |
| 2015 | 10.4 | 10.7 | 10.6 | 10.5 | 10.5 | 10.9 | 10.2 | 10.4 | 10.2 | 10.6 | 11.3 | 11.0 | 10.6 |
| 2016 | 11.0 | 11.1 | 10.7 | 11.6 | 11.4 | 11.5 | 11.1 | 10.7 | 10.8 | 11.0 | 10.8 | 10.6 | 11.0 |
| 2017 | 11.2 | 10.9 | 10.9 | 11.6 | 11.9 | 12.3 | 11.1 | 11.5 | 11.1 | 11.5 | 11.8 | 11.4 | 11.4 |
| 2018 | 11.1 | 11.3 | 11.2 | 12.3 | 12.8 | 12.2 | 11.2 | 11.3 | 11.1 | 11.3 | 11.8 | 11.3 | 11.6 |
| 2019 | 11.0 | 11.7 | 11.3 | 12.2 | 12.3 | 11.5 | 11.3 | 11.4 | 11.2 | 11.4 | 11.6 | 11.4 | 11.5 |
| **Financial Activities** | | | | | | | | | | | | | |
| 2011 | 39.8 | 39.6 | 39.8 | 40.0 | 39.9 | 40.0 | 39.9 | 39.7 | 40.0 | 40.2 | 40.2 | 40.5 | 40.0 |
| 2012 | 40.2 | 40.3 | 40.6 | 41.4 | 41.7 | 41.9 | 41.8 | 42.0 | 42.2 | 42.8 | 42.8 | 42.9 | 41.7 |
| 2013 | 42.5 | 42.9 | 43.6 | 43.3 | 43.7 | 43.5 | 43.0 | 43.0 | 42.9 | 43.4 | 43.6 | 43.8 | 43.3 |
| 2014 | 42.8 | 42.9 | 43.0 | 43.0 | 43.5 | 43.4 | 43.1 | 43.6 | 43.7 | 44.4 | 44.5 | 44.7 | 43.6 |
| 2015 | 44.3 | 44.8 | 45.0 | 45.5 | 46.1 | 45.7 | 46.1 | 46.1 | 46.3 | 47.3 | 47.3 | 47.9 | 46.0 |
| 2016 | 47.3 | 47.5 | 47.7 | 48.3 | 48.6 | 48.3 | 48.4 | 48.6 | 48.8 | 49.1 | 49.2 | 49.3 | 48.4 |
| 2017 | 49.1 | 49.7 | 49.5 | 50.0 | 50.8 | 50.6 | 51.3 | 51.3 | 51.4 | 51.9 | 51.9 | 52.0 | 50.8 |
| 2018 | 51.7 | 52.3 | 52.6 | 52.0 | 52.4 | 52.2 | 52.6 | 52.5 | 52.4 | 52.8 | 53.0 | 52.6 | 52.4 |
| 2019 | 52.1 | 52.5 | 53.0 | 53.3 | 53.9 | 53.7 | 53.7 | 54.1 | 54.2 | 54.7 | 54.9 | 55.2 | 53.8 |

# Employment by Industry: Las Vegas-Henderson-Paradise, NV, 2011–2019—*Continued*

(Numbers in thousands, not seasonally adjusted)

| Industry and year | January | February | March | April | May | June | July | August | September | October | November | December | Annual average |
|---|---|---|---|---|---|---|---|---|---|---|---|---|---|
| **Professional and Business Services** | | | | | | | | | | | | | |
| 2011 | 102.8 | 101.2 | 101.5 | 101.9 | 101.7 | 101.9 | 101.1 | 101.2 | 102.9 | 104.2 | 103.9 | 102.7 | 102.3 |
| 2012 | 107.3 | 106.6 | 105.2 | 106.1 | 106.2 | 106.7 | 103.5 | 107.0 | 108.0 | 109.7 | 108.5 | 106.9 | 106.8 |
| 2013 | 111.6 | 110.2 | 111.4 | 112.6 | 112.7 | 111.6 | 108.9 | 111.2 | 110.3 | 113.4 | 113.6 | 111.7 | 111.6 |
| 2014 | 115.5 | 115.6 | 116.5 | 116.8 | 116.9 | 116.9 | 113.6 | 117.5 | 118.3 | 123.1 | 121.8 | 120.6 | 117.8 |
| 2015 | 124.8 | 123.1 | 124.3 | 126.7 | 126.3 | 124.5 | 123.5 | 127.1 | 127.1 | 130.9 | 131.3 | 130.4 | 126.7 |
| 2016 | 130.9 | 129.5 | 131.4 | 133.3 | 132.4 | 134.2 | 133.2 | 134.0 | 136.6 | 138.3 | 137.9 | 135.3 | 133.9 |
| 2017 | 139.3 | 136.3 | 139.8 | 135.4 | 137.5 | 137.3 | 137.1 | 137.3 | 138.1 | 142.6 | 141.4 | 140.0 | 138.5 |
| 2018 | 142.3 | 141.4 | 141.7 | 142.5 | 143.5 | 142.6 | 143.8 | 147.4 | 146.7 | 151.7 | 150.2 | 148.1 | 145.2 |
| 2019 | 151.0 | 149.2 | 149.1 | 150.9 | 150.3 | 150.2 | 150.2 | 151.8 | 152.0 | 153.0 | 153.5 | 149.9 | 150.9 |
| **Education and Health Services** | | | | | | | | | | | | | |
| 2011 | 70.8 | 71.4 | 71.9 | 72.5 | 72.5 | 72.7 | 72.3 | 72.7 | 73.0 | 73.7 | 74.0 | 74.4 | 72.7 |
| 2012 | 73.9 | 74.6 | 74.6 | 75.2 | 75.8 | 75.4 | 74.9 | 76.0 | 75.9 | 76.8 | 76.8 | 77.2 | 75.6 |
| 2013 | 76.7 | 77.8 | 78.3 | 78.8 | 78.9 | 79.0 | 78.9 | 79.5 | 80.0 | 80.5 | 80.9 | 80.9 | 79.2 |
| 2014 | 80.2 | 80.9 | 81.4 | 81.5 | 81.8 | 82.0 | 81.8 | 82.5 | 82.8 | 83.9 | 84.1 | 84.3 | 82.3 |
| 2015 | 83.5 | 84.4 | 84.8 | 85.2 | 85.5 | 86.1 | 86.3 | 87.2 | 87.8 | 89.2 | 89.3 | 89.6 | 86.6 |
| 2016 | 88.6 | 89.6 | 89.8 | 90.2 | 90.7 | 90.8 | 91.2 | 92.1 | 92.7 | 94.5 | 94.5 | 94.9 | 91.6 |
| 2017 | 93.7 | 94.7 | 95.2 | 96.1 | 96.2 | 96.3 | 95.4 | 97.4 | 98.4 | 99.8 | 100.4 | 100.8 | 97.0 |
| 2018 | 100.3 | 101.4 | 102.0 | 101.7 | 102.2 | 102.0 | 101.3 | 102.9 | 103.7 | 104.4 | 104.7 | 104.7 | 102.6 |
| 2019 | 103.3 | 104.2 | 104.4 | 104.4 | 105.2 | 104.6 | 103.6 | 105.8 | 105.7 | 105.3 | 106.2 | 105.7 | 104.9 |
| **Leisure and Hospitality** | | | | | | | | | | | | | |
| 2011 | 252.0 | 253.2 | 257.8 | 261.4 | 263.2 | 264.2 | 262.4 | 260.3 | 261.8 | 261.9 | 260.1 | 256.9 | 259.6 |
| 2012 | 255.4 | 257.2 | 260.6 | 263.0 | 265.1 | 266.2 | 264.5 | 262.1 | 262.2 | 262.8 | 261.5 | 259.8 | 261.7 |
| 2013 | 259.2 | 260.6 | 264.3 | 267.7 | 268.5 | 271.2 | 271.7 | 269.8 | 270.5 | 269.9 | 268.9 | 266.4 | 267.4 |
| 2014 | 267.2 | 269.8 | 274.6 | 278.4 | 281.1 | 281.3 | 280.8 | 283.0 | 283.1 | 281.7 | 280.0 | 278.9 | 278.3 |
| 2015 | 276.9 | 278.9 | 282.1 | 284.4 | 285.5 | 285.1 | 283.7 | 283.5 | 283.4 | 283.9 | 282.1 | 280.1 | 282.5 |
| 2016 | 278.4 | 280.5 | 283.4 | 287.3 | 288.4 | 289.4 | 289.3 | 289.0 | 289.0 | 286.6 | 286.1 | 285.2 | 286.1 |
| 2017 | 284.2 | 286.4 | 290.6 | 290.8 | 292.9 | 292.5 | 291.5 | 289.8 | 290.5 | 290.1 | 287.9 | 286.6 | 289.5 |
| 2018 | 284.9 | 287.7 | 292.6 | 292.6 | 294.2 | 293.6 | 294.3 | 292.8 | 292.7 | 292.7 | 291.7 | 290.8 | 291.7 |
| 2019 | 289.4 | 292.5 | 295.9 | 297.1 | 297.5 | 296.5 | 296.6 | 294.0 | 294.0 | 293.1 | 291.8 | 290.7 | 294.1 |
| **Other Services** | | | | | | | | | | | | | |
| 2011 | 22.7 | 23.0 | 23.2 | 23.4 | 23.5 | 23.7 | 23.7 | 23.6 | 23.4 | 23.3 | 23.2 | 23.3 | 23.3 |
| 2012 | 23.2 | 23.2 | 23.5 | 23.8 | 24.3 | 24.6 | 24.5 | 24.6 | 24.7 | 25.1 | 24.1 | 23.9 | 24.1 |
| 2013 | 23.7 | 23.9 | 24.2 | 24.6 | 24.8 | 24.9 | 24.9 | 24.8 | 24.6 | 24.6 | 24.6 | 24.6 | 24.5 |
| 2014 | 24.4 | 24.5 | 24.9 | 25.4 | 25.8 | 25.9 | 26.0 | 25.9 | 26.0 | 26.4 | 25.8 | 25.6 | 25.6 |
| 2015 | 25.4 | 25.6 | 25.9 | 26.3 | 26.7 | 27.2 | 27.3 | 27.5 | 27.5 | 27.7 | 27.9 | 28.3 | 26.9 |
| 2016 | 28.5 | 29.3 | 30.2 | 30.6 | 30.7 | 30.8 | 31.4 | 31.4 | 32.0 | 32.5 | 31.7 | 30.8 | 30.8 |
| 2017 | 30.7 | 30.7 | 30.9 | 31.3 | 31.3 | 31.5 | 31.9 | 31.8 | 31.8 | 31.8 | 31.7 | 31.6 | 31.4 |
| 2018 | 31.4 | 31.5 | 31.7 | 31.2 | 31.5 | 32.2 | 31.7 | 32.1 | 32.4 | 32.9 | 32.1 | 31.5 | 31.9 |
| 2019 | 30.8 | 31.1 | 31.3 | 31.8 | 32.0 | 31.9 | 31.9 | 32.3 | 32.0 | 32.2 | 31.8 | 31.6 | 31.7 |
| **Government** | | | | | | | | | | | | | |
| 2011 | 95.2 | 96.8 | 96.9 | 96.7 | 96.3 | 90.1 | 89.0 | 89.1 | 93.3 | 94.6 | 94.6 | 95.5 | 94.0 |
| 2012 | 92.6 | 94.5 | 95.7 | 95.6 | 95.8 | 91.4 | 89.3 | 88.7 | 94.4 | 95.4 | 96.3 | 97.2 | 93.9 |
| 2013 | 94.4 | 95.4 | 96.2 | 96.5 | 96.4 | 92.7 | 89.5 | 91.1 | 95.2 | 96.9 | 97.8 | 98.7 | 95.1 |
| 2014 | 95.8 | 97.3 | 98.4 | 97.9 | 98.2 | 92.6 | 90.9 | 91.9 | 96.9 | 98.2 | 98.7 | 99.5 | 96.4 |
| 2015 | 97.0 | 98.2 | 99.4 | 99.4 | 99.2 | 95.6 | 92.6 | 93.9 | 99.2 | 99.0 | 100.7 | 102.0 | 98.0 |
| 2016 | 99.1 | 100.6 | 102.0 | 101.1 | 101.1 | 95.4 | 94.9 | 95.4 | 101.4 | 101.2 | 102.6 | 103.6 | 99.9 |
| 2017 | 99.7 | 102.5 | 103.5 | 101.3 | 102.3 | 96.3 | 97.4 | 99.2 | 105.2 | 102.9 | 104.4 | 105.4 | 101.7 |
| 2018 | 100.7 | 104.1 | 105.1 | 102.7 | 103.9 | 98.1 | 97.5 | 99.3 | 106.0 | 106.3 | 108.2 | 108.8 | 103.4 |
| 2019 | 103.4 | 107.8 | 108.7 | 106.9 | 107.8 | 100.7 | 100.8 | 103.6 | 109.3 | 110.0 | 110.1 | 110.4 | 106.6 |

## Employment by Industry: Austin-Round Rock, TX, 2011–2019

(Numbers in thousands, not seasonally adjusted)

| Industry and year | January | February | March | April | May | June | July | August | September | October | November | December | Annual average |
|---|---|---|---|---|---|---|---|---|---|---|---|---|---|
| **Total Nonfarm** | | | | | | | | | | | | | |
| 2011 | 789.3 | 797.4 | 804.6 | 812.8 | 814.2 | 815.7 | 804.5 | 809.2 | 818.3 | 820.9 | 827.2 | 828.5 | 811.9 |
| 2012 | 819.2 | 825.9 | 832.8 | 837.5 | 842.5 | 847.1 | 835.7 | 841.7 | 852.0 | 859.5 | 870.0 | 869.0 | 844.4 |
| 2013 | 855.3 | 864.9 | 871.7 | 878.5 | 883.7 | 888.8 | 878.6 | 881.7 | 892.1 | 897.9 | 908.3 | 907.3 | 884.1 |
| 2014 | 895.3 | 905.8 | 913.6 | 918.5 | 922.9 | 928.3 | 917.7 | 919.7 | 928.0 | 936.7 | 944.1 | 945.8 | 923.0 |
| 2015 | 933.4 | 943.5 | 949.9 | 955.8 | 962.2 | 969.1 | 960.6 | 962.5 | 970.6 | 979.7 | 985.6 | 987.0 | 963.3 |
| 2016 | 975.0 | 984.8 | 988.9 | 995.9 | 999.0 | 1,003.7 | 999.6 | 999.9 | 1,007.6 | 1,015.4 | 1,020.5 | 1,020.6 | 1,000.9 |
| 2017 | 1,009.1 | 1,018.5 | 1,024.7 | 1,029.9 | 1,035.9 | 1,040.5 | 1,030.9 | 1,031.3 | 1,037.7 | 1,049.6 | 1,054.7 | 1,055.9 | 1,034.9 |
| 2018 | 1,044.3 | 1,055.6 | 1,061.5 | 1,067.1 | 1,074.0 | 1,082.0 | 1,072.6 | 1,076.1 | 1,080.1 | 1,093.6 | 1,100.4 | 1,100.6 | 1,075.7 |
| 2019 | 1,087.2 | 1,099.9 | 1,103.8 | 1,109.2 | 1,113.9 | 1,119.3 | 1,114.7 | 1,117.6 | 1,118.1 | 1,130.7 | 1,136.1 | 1,142.0 | 1,116.0 |
| **Total Private** | | | | | | | | | | | | | |
| 2011 | 616.8 | 621.4 | 628.5 | 636.2 | 637.9 | 641.2 | 643.6 | 648.7 | 648.9 | 650.9 | 655.8 | 658.9 | 640.7 |
| 2012 | 648.5 | 653.2 | 659.9 | 664.1 | 669.0 | 675.7 | 675.6 | 682.5 | 682.5 | 688.0 | 696.0 | 697.3 | 674.4 |
| 2013 | 682.8 | 689.9 | 696.2 | 702.8 | 707.7 | 714.4 | 715.0 | 720.3 | 720.4 | 725.0 | 733.2 | 734.4 | 711.8 |
| 2014 | 721.7 | 729.9 | 737.1 | 742.5 | 746.3 | 753.5 | 753.5 | 757.6 | 755.7 | 761.6 | 768.1 | 770.1 | 749.8 |
| 2015 | 757.6 | 766.3 | 772.4 | 778.1 | 784.1 | 792.3 | 794.1 | 797.9 | 795.8 | 802.4 | 807.8 | 809.2 | 788.2 |
| 2016 | 797.7 | 806.3 | 808.4 | 816.0 | 818.1 | 823.8 | 829.2 | 831.7 | 830.4 | 835.0 | 838.6 | 838.7 | 822.8 |
| 2017 | 827.1 | 835.0 | 840.3 | 846.4 | 851.8 | 857.7 | 858.6 | 861.6 | 859.4 | 866.8 | 871.9 | 873.5 | 854.2 |
| 2018 | 861.9 | 871.4 | 876.1 | 882.2 | 887.9 | 896.1 | 897.1 | 901.9 | 897.7 | 908.3 | 915.5 | 915.5 | 892.6 |
| 2019 | 902.7 | 913.0 | 916.2 | 921.3 | 925.0 | 931.4 | 936.7 | 940.8 | 936.2 | 945.7 | 951.1 | 957.3 | 931.5 |
| **Goods Producing** | | | | | | | | | | | | | |
| 2011 | 93.3 | 93.6 | 94.3 | 94.3 | 94.5 | 95.5 | 96.0 | 96.2 | 95.9 | 96.0 | 95.9 | 96.0 | 95.1 |
| 2012 | 95.3 | 96.3 | 97.1 | 97.5 | 98.3 | 100.1 | 100.6 | 101.5 | 101.2 | 101.2 | 100.8 | 100.7 | 99.2 |
| 2013 | 99.7 | 100.3 | 101.1 | 102.2 | 103.0 | 103.9 | 104.1 | 104.6 | 104.4 | 104.7 | 105.3 | 105.6 | 103.2 |
| 2014 | 104.5 | 105.7 | 106.4 | 106.7 | 107.7 | 109.0 | 109.5 | 109.8 | 109.0 | 108.7 | 108.9 | 109.1 | 107.9 |
| 2015 | 108.7 | 109.6 | 109.9 | 109.7 | 110.0 | 111.5 | 112.3 | 112.5 | 111.3 | 111.7 | 111.7 | 111.7 | 110.9 |
| 2016 | 111.5 | 112.6 | 112.7 | 113.4 | 113.8 | 115.0 | 116.5 | 116.5 | 115.6 | 115.9 | 115.8 | 115.8 | 114.6 |
| 2017 | 114.6 | 115.7 | 116.6 | 117.8 | 119.0 | 120.8 | 121.4 | 121.6 | 120.9 | 121.5 | 121.9 | 122.1 | 119.5 |
| 2018 | 121.2 | 122.6 | 123.1 | 123.9 | 124.5 | 126.3 | 126.8 | 127.5 | 126.3 | 126.7 | 126.8 | 126.9 | 125.2 |
| 2019 | 126.8 | 128.4 | 129.1 | 129.6 | 130.5 | 132.2 | 132.7 | 132.9 | 132.2 | 133.0 | 135.3 | 135.1 | 131.5 |
| **Service-Providing** | | | | | | | | | | | | | |
| 2011 | 696.0 | 703.8 | 710.3 | 718.5 | 719.7 | 720.2 | 708.5 | 713.0 | 722.4 | 724.9 | 731.3 | 732.5 | 716.8 |
| 2012 | 723.9 | 729.6 | 735.7 | 740.0 | 744.2 | 747.0 | 735.1 | 740.2 | 750.8 | 758.3 | 769.2 | 768.3 | 745.2 |
| 2013 | 755.6 | 764.6 | 770.6 | 776.3 | 780.7 | 784.9 | 774.5 | 777.1 | 787.7 | 793.2 | 803.0 | 801.7 | 780.8 |
| 2014 | 790.8 | 800.1 | 807.2 | 811.8 | 815.2 | 819.3 | 808.2 | 809.9 | 819.0 | 828.0 | 835.2 | 836.7 | 815.1 |
| 2015 | 824.7 | 833.9 | 840.0 | 846.1 | 852.2 | 857.6 | 848.3 | 850.0 | 859.3 | 868.0 | 873.9 | 875.3 | 852.4 |
| 2016 | 863.5 | 872.2 | 876.2 | 882.5 | 885.2 | 888.7 | 883.1 | 883.4 | 892.0 | 899.5 | 904.7 | 904.8 | 886.3 |
| 2017 | 894.5 | 902.8 | 908.1 | 912.1 | 916.9 | 919.7 | 909.5 | 909.7 | 916.8 | 928.1 | 932.8 | 933.8 | 915.4 |
| 2018 | 923.1 | 933.0 | 938.4 | 943.2 | 949.5 | 955.7 | 945.8 | 948.6 | 953.8 | 966.9 | 973.6 | 973.7 | 950.4 |
| 2019 | 960.4 | 971.5 | 974.7 | 979.6 | 983.4 | 987.1 | 982.0 | 984.7 | 985.9 | 997.7 | 1,000.8 | 1,006.9 | 984.6 |
| **Mining, Logging, and Construction** | | | | | | | | | | | | | |
| 2011 | 39.8 | 39.8 | 40.1 | 39.7 | 39.6 | 40.2 | 40.3 | 40.4 | 40.4 | 40.1 | 40.0 | 40.1 | 40.0 |
| 2012 | 40.0 | 40.5 | 41.2 | 41.6 | 42.1 | 43.2 | 43.4 | 44.0 | 44.0 | 44.0 | 43.8 | 44.0 | 42.7 |
| 2013 | 43.4 | 44.1 | 44.9 | 45.4 | 46.1 | 46.3 | 46.4 | 46.8 | 46.9 | 47.0 | 47.2 | 47.4 | 46.0 |
| 2014 | 46.9 | 47.8 | 48.5 | 49.3 | 50.3 | 51.2 | 51.9 | 52.4 | 52.3 | 52.4 | 52.7 | 52.9 | 50.7 |
| 2015 | 52.9 | 53.8 | 54.1 | 54.2 | 54.6 | 55.4 | 56.1 | 56.4 | 56.0 | 56.5 | 56.6 | 56.8 | 55.3 |
| 2016 | 56.4 | 57.3 | 57.5 | 58.0 | 58.2 | 58.8 | 59.9 | 59.9 | 59.7 | 59.9 | 59.8 | 59.8 | 58.8 |
| 2017 | 58.9 | 59.7 | 60.4 | 61.1 | 62.1 | 63.1 | 63.4 | 63.3 | 63.0 | 63.3 | 63.3 | 63.3 | 62.1 |
| 2018 | 62.4 | 63.1 | 63.5 | 64.0 | 64.3 | 65.1 | 65.3 | 65.8 | 65.2 | 65.3 | 65.3 | 65.2 | 64.5 |
| 2019 | 65.2 | 66.3 | 66.9 | 67.4 | 68.1 | 69.3 | 69.6 | 69.7 | 69.7 | 70.9 | 72.7 | 72.1 | 69.0 |
| **Manufacturing** | | | | | | | | | | | | | |
| 2011 | 53.5 | 53.8 | 54.2 | 54.6 | 54.9 | 55.3 | 55.7 | 55.8 | 55.5 | 55.9 | 55.9 | 55.9 | 55.1 |
| 2012 | 55.3 | 55.8 | 55.9 | 55.9 | 56.2 | 56.9 | 57.2 | 57.5 | 57.2 | 57.2 | 57.0 | 56.7 | 56.6 |
| 2013 | 56.3 | 56.2 | 56.2 | 56.8 | 56.9 | 57.6 | 57.7 | 57.8 | 57.5 | 57.7 | 58.1 | 58.2 | 57.3 |
| 2014 | 57.6 | 57.9 | 57.9 | 57.4 | 57.4 | 57.8 | 57.6 | 57.4 | 56.7 | 56.3 | 56.2 | 56.2 | 57.2 |
| 2015 | 55.8 | 55.8 | 55.8 | 55.5 | 55.4 | 56.1 | 56.2 | 56.1 | 55.3 | 55.2 | 55.1 | 54.9 | 55.6 |
| 2016 | 55.1 | 55.3 | 55.2 | 55.4 | 55.6 | 56.2 | 56.6 | 56.6 | 55.9 | 56.0 | 56.0 | 56.0 | 55.8 |
| 2017 | 55.7 | 56.0 | 56.2 | 56.7 | 56.9 | 57.7 | 58.0 | 58.3 | 57.9 | 58.2 | 58.6 | 58.8 | 57.4 |
| 2018 | 58.8 | 59.5 | 59.6 | 59.9 | 60.2 | 61.2 | 61.5 | 61.7 | 61.1 | 61.4 | 61.5 | 61.7 | 60.7 |
| 2019 | 61.6 | 62.1 | 62.2 | 62.2 | 62.4 | 62.9 | 63.1 | 63.2 | 62.5 | 62.1 | 62.6 | 63.0 | 62.5 |

## Employment by Industry: Austin-Round Rock, TX, 2011–2019—*Continued*

(Numbers in thousands, not seasonally adjusted)

| Industry and year | January | February | March | April | May | June | July | August | September | October | November | December | Annual average |
|---|---|---|---|---|---|---|---|---|---|---|---|---|---|
| **Trade, Transportation, and Utilities** | | | | | | | | | | | | | |
| 2011 | 135.2 | 134.7 | 135.8 | 136.6 | 136.9 | 136.7 | 137.7 | 139.2 | 138.9 | 140.4 | 143.5 | 145.9 | 138.5 |
| 2012 | 141.0 | 140.4 | 140.9 | 141.7 | 142.4 | 143.0 | 143.1 | 144.9 | 144.1 | 145.7 | 150.4 | 151.8 | 144.1 |
| 2013 | 146.9 | 146.7 | 146.6 | 147.9 | 148.7 | 150.3 | 150.8 | 152.1 | 151.9 | 153.5 | 157.9 | 160.0 | 151.1 |
| 2014 | 155.0 | 154.4 | 154.4 | 154.8 | 154.9 | 156.0 | 156.0 | 156.9 | 156.6 | 158.3 | 162.1 | 164.3 | 157.0 |
| 2015 | 158.9 | 158.6 | 159.1 | 159.5 | 160.6 | 162.2 | 162.9 | 164.2 | 164.2 | 165.6 | 169.3 | 172.1 | 163.1 |
| 2016 | 166.7 | 166.6 | 166.9 | 167.4 | 167.5 | 168.4 | 169.7 | 170.9 | 170.7 | 172.3 | 175.9 | 178.0 | 170.1 |
| 2017 | 172.8 | 171.8 | 171.8 | 172.7 | 173.1 | 173.7 | 174.2 | 175.2 | 174.2 | 176.1 | 180.1 | 182.1 | 174.8 |
| 2018 | 176.7 | 176.3 | 176.5 | 176.9 | 177.5 | 178.6 | 179.2 | 180.2 | 180.0 | 181.2 | 186.0 | 187.6 | 179.7 |
| 2019 | 182.5 | 181.9 | 181.3 | 180.8 | 181.6 | 183.0 | 184.2 | 185.6 | 185.4 | 186.6 | 190.6 | 193.8 | 184.8 |
| **Wholesale Trade** | | | | | | | | | | | | | |
| 2011 | 37.5 | 37.8 | 38.1 | 38.3 | 38.5 | 38.7 | 39.0 | 39.1 | 39.5 | 40.1 | 40.3 | 40.5 | 39.0 |
| 2012 | 40.0 | 40.2 | 40.4 | 40.5 | 40.8 | 41.0 | 40.9 | 41.1 | 40.8 | 40.8 | 41.0 | 41.2 | 40.7 |
| 2013 | 41.4 | 41.7 | 41.9 | 41.9 | 41.8 | 42.5 | 42.6 | 42.8 | 42.6 | 43.0 | 43.1 | 43.3 | 42.4 |
| 2014 | 43.0 | 43.2 | 43.0 | 43.1 | 43.2 | 43.6 | 43.8 | 43.9 | 44.0 | 44.3 | 44.6 | 44.8 | 43.7 |
| 2015 | 45.1 | 45.3 | 45.4 | 45.4 | 45.6 | 46.1 | 46.5 | 47.0 | 46.9 | 47.0 | 47.4 | 47.6 | 46.3 |
| 2016 | 47.1 | 47.3 | 47.4 | 48.0 | 47.9 | 48.0 | 48.0 | 48.0 | 47.9 | 47.7 | 47.3 | 47.3 | 47.7 |
| 2017 | 47.6 | 47.6 | 47.8 | 48.1 | 48.1 | 48.3 | 48.7 | 48.8 | 48.8 | 48.6 | 48.7 | 48.7 | 48.3 |
| 2018 | 48.4 | 48.6 | 48.9 | 49.2 | 49.2 | 50.1 | 50.6 | 50.9 | 50.9 | 50.7 | 50.9 | 51.3 | 50.0 |
| 2019 | 50.9 | 51.2 | 51.3 | 51.3 | 51.5 | 52.2 | 52.5 | 52.7 | 52.5 | 52.0 | 52.6 | 53.2 | 52.0 |
| **Retail Trade** | | | | | | | | | | | | | |
| 2011 | 84.2 | 83.5 | 84.2 | 84.8 | 84.8 | 84.9 | 85.4 | 86.3 | 85.5 | 86.6 | 89.4 | 91.0 | 85.9 |
| 2012 | 87.1 | 86.2 | 86.5 | 87.3 | 87.7 | 88.2 | 88.5 | 89.6 | 89.0 | 90.7 | 94.9 | 95.7 | 89.3 |
| 2013 | 91.2 | 90.9 | 90.7 | 91.6 | 92.2 | 92.9 | 93.6 | 94.3 | 94.1 | 95.3 | 99.2 | 100.6 | 93.9 |
| 2014 | 96.4 | 95.9 | 96.0 | 96.2 | 96.2 | 96.8 | 97.1 | 97.6 | 96.9 | 98.2 | 101.5 | 102.7 | 97.6 |
| 2015 | 97.8 | 97.6 | 97.9 | 98.1 | 98.8 | 99.8 | 100.2 | 100.7 | 100.7 | 101.7 | 104.7 | 106.2 | 100.4 |
| 2016 | 102.0 | 102.0 | 102.3 | 102.4 | 102.4 | 103.0 | 103.4 | 104.1 | 103.8 | 105.0 | 108.4 | 109.6 | 104.0 |
| 2017 | 105.1 | 104.6 | 104.5 | 104.6 | 105.0 | 105.2 | 105.2 | 105.5 | 104.6 | 106.3 | 109.4 | 110.6 | 105.9 |
| 2018 | 106.6 | 106.1 | 105.9 | 106.2 | 106.6 | 106.7 | 107.0 | 107.4 | 107.1 | 107.9 | 111.8 | 112.3 | 107.6 |
| 2019 | 108.5 | 107.8 | 107.1 | 107.2 | 107.6 | 107.9 | 108.4 | 108.9 | 108.5 | 109.8 | 112.9 | 115.2 | 109.2 |
| **Transportation and Utilities** | | | | | | | | | | | | | |
| 2011 | 13.5 | 13.4 | 13.5 | 13.5 | 13.6 | 13.1 | 13.3 | 13.8 | 13.9 | 13.7 | 13.8 | 14.4 | 13.6 |
| 2012 | 13.9 | 14.0 | 14.0 | 13.9 | 13.9 | 13.8 | 13.7 | 14.2 | 14.3 | 14.2 | 14.5 | 14.9 | 14.1 |
| 2013 | 14.3 | 14.1 | 14.0 | 14.4 | 14.7 | 14.9 | 14.6 | 15.0 | 15.2 | 15.2 | 15.6 | 16.1 | 14.8 |
| 2014 | 15.6 | 15.3 | 15.4 | 15.5 | 15.5 | 15.6 | 15.1 | 15.4 | 15.7 | 15.8 | 16.0 | 16.8 | 15.6 |
| 2015 | 16.0 | 15.7 | 15.8 | 16.0 | 16.2 | 16.3 | 16.2 | 16.5 | 16.6 | 16.9 | 17.2 | 18.3 | 16.5 |
| 2016 | 17.6 | 17.3 | 17.2 | 17.0 | 17.2 | 17.4 | 18.3 | 18.8 | 19.0 | 19.6 | 20.2 | 21.1 | 18.4 |
| 2017 | 20.1 | 19.6 | 19.5 | 20.0 | 20.0 | 20.2 | 20.3 | 20.9 | 20.8 | 21.2 | 22.0 | 22.8 | 20.6 |
| 2018 | 21.7 | 21.6 | 21.7 | 21.5 | 21.7 | 21.8 | 21.6 | 21.9 | 22.0 | 22.6 | 23.3 | 24.0 | 22.1 |
| 2019 | 23.1 | 22.9 | 22.9 | 22.3 | 22.5 | 22.9 | 23.3 | 24.0 | 24.4 | 24.8 | 25.1 | 25.4 | 23.6 |
| **Information** | | | | | | | | | | | | | |
| 2011 | 20.1 | 20.2 | 20.3 | 20.4 | 20.6 | 20.8 | 21.2 | 21.3 | 21.4 | 21.4 | 21.8 | 21.9 | 21.0 |
| 2012 | 22.0 | 21.9 | 22.1 | 22.1 | 22.3 | 22.6 | 23.0 | 23.1 | 23.0 | 23.3 | 23.6 | 23.8 | 22.7 |
| 2013 | 23.1 | 23.2 | 23.7 | 23.4 | 23.4 | 23.9 | 24.1 | 24.3 | 24.1 | 24.1 | 24.7 | 25.0 | 23.9 |
| 2014 | 24.3 | 24.3 | 24.4 | 25.0 | 24.5 | 25.2 | 25.6 | 25.7 | 25.7 | 26.0 | 26.5 | 27.1 | 25.4 |
| 2015 | 26.7 | 26.7 | 26.9 | 27.3 | 27.5 | 28.0 | 27.8 | 28.0 | 28.0 | 28.2 | 28.8 | 28.9 | 27.7 |
| 2016 | 28.8 | 29.0 | 28.7 | 28.7 | 28.8 | 29.1 | 29.0 | 29.0 | 28.8 | 29.1 | 29.1 | 29.4 | 29.0 |
| 2017 | 29.4 | 29.5 | 29.8 | 29.8 | 30.0 | 30.5 | 30.9 | 30.8 | 31.1 | 32.3 | 32.3 | 32.7 | 30.8 |
| 2018 | 33.0 | 32.8 | 33.1 | 33.6 | 34.3 | 34.6 | 35.1 | 35.2 | 35.6 | 35.9 | 36.8 | 36.6 | 34.7 |
| 2019 | 36.5 | 37.0 | 37.8 | 38.4 | 38.7 | 38.9 | 38.6 | 38.7 | 38.6 | 38.9 | 39.0 | 39.3 | 38.4 |
| **Financial Activities** | | | | | | | | | | | | | |
| 2011 | 43.5 | 43.7 | 44.1 | 44.5 | 44.7 | 44.9 | 45.2 | 45.3 | 45.2 | 45.4 | 45.6 | 46.0 | 44.8 |
| 2012 | 45.7 | 45.9 | 46.2 | 46.3 | 46.7 | 47.1 | 47.0 | 47.4 | 47.4 | 48.0 | 48.1 | 48.3 | 47.0 |
| 2013 | 47.9 | 48.2 | 48.3 | 48.7 | 49.0 | 49.3 | 49.7 | 49.8 | 49.8 | 50.3 | 50.4 | 50.7 | 49.3 |
| 2014 | 50.7 | 51.1 | 51.3 | 51.4 | 51.7 | 52.1 | 52.0 | 52.2 | 51.9 | 52.4 | 52.5 | 53.0 | 51.9 |
| 2015 | 52.4 | 52.9 | 52.9 | 53.6 | 53.9 | 54.2 | 54.4 | 54.6 | 54.3 | 54.9 | 55.1 | 55.5 | 54.1 |
| 2016 | 55.1 | 55.5 | 55.8 | 56.1 | 56.3 | 56.9 | 57.5 | 57.9 | 57.6 | 58.0 | 58.1 | 58.7 | 57.0 |
| 2017 | 58.3 | 58.7 | 59.1 | 59.5 | 59.8 | 60.5 | 60.8 | 60.9 | 60.8 | 61.2 | 61.1 | 61.8 | 60.2 |
| 2018 | 61.2 | 61.7 | 61.9 | 62.0 | 62.5 | 63.2 | 63.8 | 64.3 | 63.7 | 64.2 | 64.1 | 64.2 | 63.1 |
| 2019 | 64.0 | 64.4 | 64.6 | 65.0 | 65.4 | 66.0 | 66.8 | 67.2 | 67.0 | 67.9 | 67.5 | 68.0 | 66.2 |

## Employment by Industry: Austin-Round Rock, TX, 2011–2019—*Continued*

(Numbers in thousands, not seasonally adjusted)

| Industry and year | January | February | March | April | May | June | July | August | September | October | November | December | Annual average |
|---|---|---|---|---|---|---|---|---|---|---|---|---|---|
| **Professional and Business Services** | | | | | | | | | | | | | |
| 2011 | 116.6 | 118.2 | 119.6 | 121.1 | 120.9 | 122.0 | 122.5 | 123.9 | 124.7 | 125.0 | 125.6 | 126.3 | 122.2 |
| 2012 | 124.8 | 125.9 | 127.7 | 127.8 | 128.5 | 129.8 | 130.9 | 132.9 | 133.3 | 134.7 | 136.0 | 135.3 | 130.6 |
| 2013 | 132.4 | 134.5 | 136.2 | 138.1 | 139.0 | 140.1 | 141.2 | 143.3 | 143.9 | 145.2 | 146.4 | 145.9 | 140.5 |
| 2014 | 143.8 | 146.5 | 149.1 | 150.4 | 150.9 | 151.8 | 152.4 | 153.9 | 153.7 | 156.1 | 156.7 | 156.5 | 151.8 |
| 2015 | 154.9 | 157.2 | 159.1 | 160.0 | 160.9 | 162.6 | 164.3 | 165.1 | 165.1 | 167.4 | 168.0 | 166.7 | 162.6 |
| 2016 | 165.0 | 167.4 | 167.8 | 169.9 | 169.9 | 171.1 | 172.6 | 173.2 | 172.7 | 174.0 | 174.7 | 173.2 | 171.0 |
| 2017 | 171.4 | 173.8 | 175.3 | 175.6 | 176.5 | 178.4 | 178.6 | 179.5 | 179.7 | 181.0 | 181.1 | 180.5 | 177.6 |
| 2018 | 179.4 | 182.4 | 183.0 | 184.5 | 185.7 | 188.0 | 188.2 | 189.5 | 189.5 | 193.3 | 194.6 | 193.9 | 187.7 |
| 2019 | 192.0 | 195.1 | 195.2 | 196.5 | 196.2 | 197.4 | 200.2 | 202.0 | 200.4 | 203.2 | 202.3 | 204.0 | 198.7 |
| **Education and Health Services** | | | | | | | | | | | | | |
| 2011 | 88.7 | 89.8 | 90.1 | 92.2 | 92.5 | 91.9 | 92.6 | 94.3 | 95.0 | 95.4 | 96.1 | 95.9 | 92.9 |
| 2012 | 95.0 | 96.4 | 97.0 | 97.2 | 97.7 | 97.5 | 96.8 | 98.3 | 99.4 | 100.1 | 100.7 | 100.6 | 98.1 |
| 2013 | 99.7 | 101.3 | 101.3 | 102.4 | 102.6 | 102.0 | 101.3 | 102.7 | 103.4 | 104.3 | 104.9 | 104.4 | 102.5 |
| 2014 | 102.9 | 104.6 | 104.9 | 106.2 | 106.7 | 106.1 | 105.3 | 106.5 | 107.0 | 108.5 | 109.5 | 109.1 | 106.4 |
| 2015 | 107.7 | 109.7 | 109.9 | 111.6 | 112.1 | 111.5 | 110.7 | 112.2 | 112.5 | 113.8 | 114.0 | 113.7 | 111.6 |
| 2016 | 113.4 | 114.9 | 114.2 | 114.6 | 114.7 | 113.6 | 115.0 | 116.4 | 116.9 | 118.1 | 117.6 | 117.4 | 115.6 |
| 2017 | 117.9 | 119.7 | 119.6 | 120.8 | 121.0 | 119.5 | 119.4 | 121.0 | 120.9 | 122.4 | 122.7 | 122.3 | 120.6 |
| 2018 | 122.1 | 124.4 | 123.7 | 125.2 | 124.8 | 123.8 | 124.5 | 126.3 | 125.6 | 127.7 | 128.1 | 127.5 | 125.3 |
| 2019 | 125.8 | 128.2 | 127.7 | 128.8 | 128.7 | 127.8 | 128.3 | 129.8 | 129.3 | 130.1 | 131.0 | 131.3 | 128.9 |
| **Leisure and Hospitality** | | | | | | | | | | | | | |
| 2011 | 84.8 | 86.2 | 88.6 | 91.3 | 91.9 | 92.2 | 90.9 | 91.5 | 91.7 | 91.0 | 91.1 | 90.6 | 90.2 |
| 2012 | 88.8 | 90.2 | 92.2 | 94.1 | 95.3 | 96.3 | 94.4 | 94.9 | 95.3 | 95.9 | 97.1 | 97.2 | 94.3 |
| 2013 | 94.5 | 96.5 | 99.2 | 100.1 | 101.6 | 103.1 | 101.7 | 101.9 | 102.3 | 102.1 | 102.4 | 101.6 | 100.6 |
| 2014 | 100.3 | 102.6 | 105.1 | 106.4 | 107.8 | 109.6 | 108.6 | 108.9 | 109.3 | 108.8 | 109.3 | 108.6 | 107.1 |
| 2015 | 106.8 | 109.7 | 112.2 | 114.8 | 117.0 | 118.5 | 117.6 | 117.5 | 117.8 | 118.0 | 118.2 | 118.1 | 115.5 |
| 2016 | 115.7 | 118.3 | 119.8 | 122.3 | 122.9 | 124.4 | 123.9 | 123.3 | 124.0 | 123.3 | 123.2 | 122.3 | 122.0 |
| 2017 | 119.5 | 121.9 | 123.8 | 125.4 | 127.3 | 127.9 | 127.3 | 127.0 | 126.7 | 127.1 | 127.2 | 126.9 | 125.7 |
| 2018 | 124.1 | 126.5 | 129.5 | 130.5 | 132.3 | 134.1 | 132.2 | 131.8 | 130.5 | 132.1 | 131.9 | 132.3 | 130.7 |
| 2019 | 129.3 | 131.7 | 134.0 | 135.3 | 136.6 | 137.8 | 137.6 | 136.5 | 135.8 | 138.0 | 137.1 | 137.2 | 135.6 |
| **Other Services** | | | | | | | | | | | | | |
| 2011 | 34.6 | 35.0 | 35.7 | 35.8 | 35.9 | 37.2 | 37.5 | 37.0 | 36.1 | 36.3 | 36.2 | 36.3 | 36.1 |
| 2012 | 35.9 | 36.2 | 36.7 | 37.4 | 37.8 | 39.3 | 39.8 | 39.5 | 38.8 | 39.1 | 39.3 | 39.6 | 38.3 |
| 2013 | 38.6 | 39.2 | 39.8 | 40.0 | 40.4 | 41.8 | 42.1 | 41.6 | 40.6 | 40.8 | 41.2 | 41.2 | 40.6 |
| 2014 | 40.2 | 40.7 | 41.5 | 41.6 | 42.1 | 43.7 | 44.1 | 43.7 | 42.5 | 42.8 | 42.6 | 42.4 | 42.3 |
| 2015 | 41.5 | 41.9 | 42.4 | 41.6 | 42.1 | 43.8 | 44.1 | 43.8 | 42.6 | 42.8 | 42.7 | 42.5 | 42.7 |
| 2016 | 41.5 | 42.0 | 42.5 | 43.6 | 44.2 | 45.3 | 45.0 | 44.5 | 44.1 | 44.3 | 44.2 | 43.9 | 43.8 |
| 2017 | 43.2 | 43.9 | 44.3 | 44.8 | 45.1 | 46.4 | 46.0 | 45.6 | 45.1 | 45.2 | 45.5 | 45.1 | 45.0 |
| 2018 | 44.2 | 44.7 | 45.3 | 45.6 | 46.3 | 47.5 | 47.3 | 47.1 | 46.5 | 47.2 | 47.2 | 46.5 | 46.3 |
| 2019 | 45.8 | 46.3 | 46.5 | 46.9 | 47.3 | 48.3 | 48.3 | 48.1 | 47.5 | 48.0 | 48.3 | 48.6 | 47.5 |
| **Government** | | | | | | | | | | | | | |
| 2011 | 172.5 | 176.0 | 176.1 | 176.6 | 176.3 | 174.5 | 160.9 | 160.5 | 169.4 | 170.0 | 171.4 | 169.6 | 171.2 |
| 2012 | 170.7 | 172.7 | 172.9 | 173.4 | 173.5 | 171.4 | 160.1 | 159.2 | 169.5 | 171.5 | 174.0 | 171.7 | 170.1 |
| 2013 | 172.5 | 175.0 | 175.5 | 175.7 | 176.0 | 174.4 | 163.6 | 161.4 | 171.7 | 172.9 | 175.1 | 172.9 | 172.2 |
| 2014 | 173.6 | 175.9 | 176.5 | 176.0 | 176.6 | 174.8 | 164.2 | 162.1 | 172.3 | 175.1 | 176.0 | 175.7 | 173.2 |
| 2015 | 175.8 | 177.2 | 177.5 | 177.7 | 178.1 | 176.8 | 166.5 | 164.6 | 174.8 | 177.3 | 177.8 | 177.8 | 175.2 |
| 2016 | 177.3 | 178.5 | 180.5 | 179.9 | 180.9 | 179.9 | 170.4 | 168.2 | 177.2 | 180.4 | 181.9 | 181.9 | 178.1 |
| 2017 | 182.0 | 183.5 | 184.4 | 183.5 | 184.1 | 182.8 | 172.3 | 169.7 | 178.3 | 182.8 | 182.8 | 182.4 | 180.7 |
| 2018 | 182.4 | 184.2 | 185.4 | 184.9 | 186.1 | 185.9 | 175.5 | 174.2 | 182.4 | 185.3 | 184.9 | 185.1 | 183.0 |
| 2019 | 184.5 | 186.9 | 187.6 | 187.9 | 188.9 | 187.9 | 178.0 | 176.8 | 181.9 | 185.0 | 185.0 | 184.7 | 184.6 |

# Employment by Industry: Cincinnati, OH-KY-IN, 2011–2019

(Numbers in thousands, not seasonally adjusted)

| Industry and year | January | February | March | April | May | June | July | August | September | October | November | December | Annual average |
|---|---|---|---|---|---|---|---|---|---|---|---|---|---|
| **Total Nonfarm** | | | | | | | | | | | | | |
| 2011 | 964.9 | 968.5 | 978.1 | 993.4 | 999.8 | 994.6 | 992.4 | 1,000.6 | 1,001.4 | 1,003.0 | 1,005.5 | 1,004.9 | 992.3 |
| 2012 | 979.5 | 986.6 | 996.5 | 1,008.5 | 1,019.3 | 1,016.5 | 1,006.5 | 1,012.9 | 1,016.9 | 1,021.9 | 1,021.0 | 1,018.1 | 1,008.7 |
| 2013 | 990.8 | 1,000.1 | 1,006.8 | 1,026.3 | 1,036.8 | 1,031.4 | 1,021.3 | 1,031.8 | 1,035.2 | 1,038.6 | 1,041.4 | 1,036.9 | 1,024.8 |
| 2014 | 1,009.1 | 1,015.2 | 1,027.6 | 1,042.0 | 1,054.7 | 1,047.6 | 1,040.5 | 1,049.0 | 1,048.7 | 1,053.4 | 1,057.5 | 1,058.8 | 1,042.0 |
| 2015 | 1,030.5 | 1,032.4 | 1,042.1 | 1,057.8 | 1,070.6 | 1,068.8 | 1,063.3 | 1,068.1 | 1,068.7 | 1,073.4 | 1,077.5 | 1,078.4 | 1,061.0 |
| 2016 | 1,051.7 | 1,055.1 | 1,066.5 | 1,079.3 | 1,088.4 | 1,083.2 | 1,082.2 | 1,085.0 | 1,087.8 | 1,091.5 | 1,094.7 | 1,094.3 | 1,080.0 |
| 2017 | 1,068.6 | 1,074.5 | 1,082.1 | 1,093.2 | 1,101.8 | 1,103.8 | 1,094.4 | 1,098.8 | 1,099.6 | 1,103.7 | 1,107.6 | 1,109.9 | 1,094.8 |
| 2018 | 1,081.6 | 1,086.9 | 1,093.8 | 1,103.2 | 1,111.9 | 1,116.2 | 1,109.9 | 1,112.3 | 1,114.7 | 1,118.4 | 1,124.3 | 1,121.9 | 1,107.9 |
| 2019 | 1,095.3 | 1,097.9 | 1,106.0 | 1,113.2 | 1,121.9 | 1,123.8 | 1,115.7 | 1,118.7 | 1,120.9 | 1,119.4 | 1,123.1 | 1,125.6 | 1,115.1 |
| **Total Private** | | | | | | | | | | | | | |
| 2011 | 834.4 | 835.6 | 844.3 | 859.3 | 866.9 | 870.6 | 874.1 | 875.5 | 871.1 | 870.1 | 873.0 | 875.3 | 862.5 |
| 2012 | 853.6 | 854.5 | 863.2 | 874.9 | 885.2 | 891.8 | 888.4 | 890.7 | 887.2 | 889.5 | 888.1 | 889.3 | 879.7 |
| 2013 | 864.4 | 867.7 | 874.8 | 891.1 | 902.5 | 907.2 | 904.9 | 906.6 | 903.2 | 905.3 | 907.8 | 908.0 | 895.3 |
| 2014 | 882.8 | 883.3 | 895.4 | 908.2 | 920.1 | 923.2 | 921.9 | 924.8 | 917.5 | 920.9 | 925.0 | 927.2 | 912.5 |
| 2015 | 902.7 | 901.5 | 910.1 | 925.3 | 937.1 | 943.5 | 943.0 | 943.0 | 938.3 | 941.6 | 945.3 | 946.9 | 931.5 |
| 2016 | 924.1 | 924.0 | 934.3 | 946.3 | 954.4 | 958.2 | 959.8 | 959.0 | 956.1 | 958.5 | 961.4 | 961.8 | 949.8 |
| 2017 | 939.6 | 942.2 | 948.7 | 959.3 | 968.3 | 976.3 | 972.9 | 973.8 | 967.7 | 970.3 | 973.8 | 977.0 | 964.2 |
| 2018 | 952.4 | 954.6 | 961.1 | 969.7 | 980.1 | 989.2 | 988.5 | 987.8 | 983.0 | 984.4 | 990.2 | 989.1 | 977.5 |
| 2019 | 966.9 | 966.0 | 971.7 | 980.4 | 990.9 | 999.5 | 996.7 | 996.6 | 990.4 | 988.1 | 991.5 | 996.0 | 986.2 |
| **Goods Producing** | | | | | | | | | | | | | |
| 2011 | 135.6 | 135.7 | 137.4 | 140.2 | 141.8 | 143.2 | 144.6 | 144.8 | 144.7 | 144.7 | 144.2 | 143.8 | 141.7 |
| 2012 | 139.7 | 139.4 | 140.8 | 142.7 | 144.2 | 146.1 | 146.2 | 146.1 | 145.4 | 144.9 | 144.4 | 143.7 | 143.6 |
| 2013 | 139.5 | 139.0 | 139.4 | 142.4 | 145.0 | 146.6 | 147.4 | 147.2 | 147.6 | 148.1 | 148.2 | 146.9 | 144.8 |
| 2014 | 143.6 | 143.7 | 146.6 | 149.5 | 152.2 | 153.6 | 153.7 | 154.4 | 153.8 | 154.5 | 154.5 | 153.8 | 151.2 |
| 2015 | 149.9 | 149.8 | 151.0 | 154.2 | 156.7 | 158.8 | 158.6 | 159.3 | 158.3 | 159.4 | 159.5 | 159.1 | 156.2 |
| 2016 | 155.1 | 154.9 | 157.0 | 159.2 | 160.5 | 162.0 | 162.7 | 162.4 | 162.0 | 161.6 | 161.8 | 161.2 | 160.0 |
| 2017 | 158.5 | 159.4 | 160.8 | 162.3 | 164.3 | 166.0 | 165.5 | 166.1 | 165.4 | 165.7 | 165.5 | 165.0 | 163.7 |
| 2018 | 160.2 | 161.5 | 163.4 | 165.2 | 166.9 | 168.5 | 169.1 | 168.7 | 168.5 | 168.7 | 168.1 | 167.4 | 166.4 |
| 2019 | 164.5 | 164.7 | 165.7 | 167.8 | 168.7 | 170.1 | 170.5 | 170.2 | 170.0 | 169.9 | 167.7 | 166.3 | 168.0 |
| **Service-Providing** | | | | | | | | | | | | | |
| 2011 | 829.3 | 832.8 | 840.7 | 853.2 | 858.0 | 851.4 | 847.8 | 855.8 | 856.7 | 858.3 | 861.3 | 861.1 | 850.5 |
| 2012 | 839.8 | 847.2 | 855.7 | 865.8 | 875.1 | 870.4 | 860.3 | 866.8 | 871.5 | 877.0 | 876.6 | 874.4 | 865.1 |
| 2013 | 851.3 | 861.1 | 867.4 | 883.9 | 891.8 | 884.8 | 873.9 | 884.6 | 887.6 | 890.5 | 893.2 | 890.0 | 880.0 |
| 2014 | 865.5 | 871.5 | 881.0 | 892.5 | 902.5 | 894.0 | 886.8 | 894.6 | 894.9 | 898.9 | 903.0 | 905.0 | 890.9 |
| 2015 | 880.6 | 882.6 | 891.1 | 903.6 | 913.9 | 910.0 | 904.7 | 908.8 | 910.4 | 914.0 | 918.0 | 919.3 | 904.8 |
| 2016 | 896.6 | 900.2 | 909.5 | 920.1 | 927.9 | 921.2 | 919.5 | 922.6 | 925.8 | 929.9 | 932.9 | 933.1 | 919.9 |
| 2017 | 910.1 | 915.1 | 921.3 | 930.9 | 937.5 | 937.8 | 928.9 | 932.7 | 934.2 | 938.0 | 942.1 | 944.9 | 931.1 |
| 2018 | 921.4 | 925.4 | 930.4 | 938.0 | 945.0 | 947.7 | 940.8 | 943.6 | 946.2 | 949.7 | 956.2 | 954.5 | 941.6 |
| 2019 | 930.8 | 933.2 | 940.3 | 945.4 | 953.2 | 953.7 | 945.2 | 948.5 | 950.9 | 949.5 | 955.4 | 959.3 | 947.1 |
| **Mining, Logging, and Construction** | | | | | | | | | | | | | |
| 2011 | 33.3 | 33.3 | 34.6 | 36.8 | 37.9 | 38.7 | 39.8 | 40.1 | 39.8 | 39.8 | 39.0 | 38.4 | 37.6 |
| 2012 | 35.4 | 34.9 | 36.1 | 37.9 | 38.8 | 39.6 | 39.7 | 39.9 | 39.8 | 39.4 | 39.0 | 38.0 | 38.2 |
| 2013 | 35.2 | 34.8 | 35.4 | 37.3 | 38.7 | 39.7 | 40.2 | 40.5 | 41.0 | 41.1 | 40.6 | 39.1 | 38.6 |
| 2014 | 36.5 | 36.0 | 38.0 | 40.2 | 42.0 | 42.5 | 42.8 | 43.3 | 43.1 | 43.2 | 42.9 | 41.8 | 41.0 |
| 2015 | 38.6 | 38.5 | 39.3 | 41.7 | 43.6 | 44.6 | 44.5 | 45.0 | 44.7 | 45.6 | 45.6 | 44.6 | 43.0 |
| 2016 | 41.4 | 41.2 | 43.3 | 45.2 | 45.9 | 46.7 | 47.1 | 47.0 | 47.0 | 47.0 | 46.9 | 45.9 | 45.4 |
| 2017 | 42.9 | 43.4 | 44.6 | 46.3 | 47.9 | 48.7 | 48.8 | 49.0 | 49.0 | 49.1 | 48.5 | 47.5 | 47.1 |
| 2018 | 43.2 | 44.2 | 45.8 | 47.7 | 49.0 | 49.5 | 49.6 | 49.3 | 49.3 | 49.3 | 48.4 | 47.3 | 47.7 |
| 2019 | 44.8 | 44.5 | 45.7 | 47.6 | 48.1 | 48.9 | 49.3 | 49.4 | 49.4 | 49.3 | 46.8 | 45.0 | 47.4 |
| **Manufacturing** | | | | | | | | | | | | | |
| 2011 | 102.3 | 102.4 | 102.8 | 103.4 | 103.9 | 104.5 | 104.8 | 104.7 | 104.9 | 104.9 | 105.2 | 105.4 | 104.1 |
| 2012 | 104.3 | 104.5 | 104.7 | 104.8 | 105.4 | 106.5 | 106.5 | 106.2 | 105.6 | 105.5 | 105.4 | 105.7 | 105.4 |
| 2013 | 104.3 | 104.2 | 104.0 | 105.1 | 106.3 | 106.9 | 107.2 | 106.7 | 106.6 | 107.0 | 107.6 | 107.8 | 106.1 |
| 2014 | 107.1 | 107.7 | 108.6 | 109.3 | 110.2 | 111.1 | 110.9 | 111.1 | 110.7 | 111.3 | 111.6 | 112.0 | 110.1 |
| 2015 | 111.3 | 111.3 | 111.7 | 112.5 | 113.1 | 114.2 | 114.1 | 114.3 | 113.6 | 113.8 | 113.9 | 114.5 | 113.2 |
| 2016 | 113.7 | 113.7 | 113.7 | 114.0 | 114.6 | 115.3 | 115.6 | 115.4 | 115.0 | 114.6 | 114.9 | 115.3 | 114.7 |
| 2017 | 115.6 | 116.0 | 116.2 | 116.0 | 116.4 | 117.3 | 116.7 | 117.1 | 116.4 | 116.6 | 117.0 | 117.5 | 116.6 |
| 2018 | 117.0 | 117.3 | 117.6 | 117.5 | 117.9 | 119.0 | 119.5 | 119.4 | 119.2 | 119.4 | 119.7 | 120.1 | 118.6 |
| 2019 | 119.7 | 120.2 | 120.0 | 120.2 | 120.6 | 121.2 | 121.2 | 120.8 | 120.6 | 120.6 | 120.9 | 121.3 | 120.6 |

## Employment by Industry: Cincinnati, OH-KY-IN, 2011–2019—*Continued*

(Numbers in thousands, not seasonally adjusted)

| Industry and year | January | February | March | April | May | June | July | August | September | October | November | December | Annual average |
|---|---|---|---|---|---|---|---|---|---|---|---|---|---|
| **Trade, Transportation, and Utilities** | | | | | | | | | | | | | |
| 2011 | 192.3 | 191.3 | 192.2 | 194.0 | 194.8 | 195.3 | 196.1 | 197.0 | 197.0 | 198.9 | 203.8 | 205.4 | 196.5 |
| 2012 | 196.2 | 194.9 | 196.4 | 197.4 | 199.6 | 199.7 | 198.6 | 199.4 | 199.3 | 201.0 | 204.7 | 205.4 | 199.4 |
| 2013 | 197.6 | 196.4 | 197.5 | 199.0 | 200.9 | 201.0 | 199.6 | 200.4 | 199.3 | 201.5 | 206.3 | 207.8 | 200.6 |
| 2014 | 199.0 | 198.2 | 199.1 | 200.6 | 202.0 | 202.6 | 201.8 | 203.3 | 201.8 | 205.3 | 209.2 | 211.1 | 202.8 |
| 2015 | 202.8 | 201.7 | 202.9 | 204.6 | 206.3 | 206.8 | 206.2 | 206.8 | 205.8 | 208.8 | 213.3 | 216.0 | 206.8 |
| 2016 | 207.6 | 206.5 | 207.2 | 208.3 | 209.5 | 209.1 | 209.6 | 210.7 | 210.3 | 212.8 | 216.5 | 218.5 | 210.6 |
| 2017 | 209.2 | 208.3 | 208.7 | 210.9 | 212.8 | 212.8 | 213.1 | 214.0 | 213.9 | 215.6 | 221.1 | 223.2 | 213.6 |
| 2018 | 218.1 | 215.3 | 215.3 | 216.2 | 218.1 | 218.7 | 219.1 | 218.7 | 218.8 | 221.0 | 227.6 | 227.7 | 219.6 |
| 2019 | 220.6 | 218.1 | 217.6 | 217.3 | 218.5 | 219.6 | 218.9 | 218.9 | 218.8 | 220.8 | 225.1 | 225.2 | 220.0 |
| **Wholesale Trade** | | | | | | | | | | | | | |
| 2011 | 54.3 | 54.4 | 54.7 | 55.1 | 55.3 | 55.4 | 55.7 | 55.8 | 55.9 | 55.7 | 55.8 | 55.8 | 55.3 |
| 2012 | 55.9 | 55.9 | 56.3 | 56.8 | 57.1 | 57.8 | 57.5 | 57.7 | 57.5 | 57.8 | 57.7 | 58.0 | 57.2 |
| 2013 | 58.1 | 58.3 | 58.5 | 58.7 | 59.0 | 59.1 | 59.0 | 58.9 | 58.8 | 58.6 | 58.8 | 58.9 | 58.7 |
| 2014 | 57.8 | 58.3 | 58.3 | 58.6 | 58.8 | 59.0 | 59.1 | 59.2 | 58.9 | 59.0 | 59.2 | 59.4 | 58.8 |
| 2015 | 58.8 | 59.0 | 59.2 | 59.3 | 59.8 | 60.1 | 59.8 | 59.9 | 59.3 | 59.6 | 59.9 | 60.1 | 59.6 |
| 2016 | 60.0 | 60.2 | 60.2 | 60.2 | 60.5 | 60.6 | 60.3 | 60.4 | 60.2 | 60.1 | 59.8 | 59.9 | 60.2 |
| 2017 | 58.9 | 58.7 | 58.6 | 58.9 | 59.2 | 59.6 | 59.5 | 59.5 | 59.1 | 59.0 | 59.2 | 59.6 | 59.2 |
| 2018 | 58.7 | 58.9 | 58.9 | 59.1 | 59.5 | 59.9 | 59.9 | 59.9 | 59.6 | 59.9 | 60.4 | 60.5 | 59.6 |
| 2019 | 60.3 | 60.5 | 60.6 | 60.3 | 60.4 | 60.7 | 60.3 | 60.1 | 59.9 | 60.2 | 60.3 | 59.9 | 60.3 |
| **Retail Trade** | | | | | | | | | | | | | |
| 2011 | 100.0 | 99.1 | 99.4 | 100.6 | 101.0 | 101.5 | 101.6 | 101.5 | 100.4 | 102.1 | 105.6 | 106.7 | 101.6 |
| 2012 | 100.3 | 99.0 | 100.1 | 100.9 | 102.3 | 102.2 | 101.8 | 101.7 | 101.5 | 103.3 | 107.0 | 107.3 | 102.3 |
| 2013 | 101.3 | 100.1 | 100.9 | 102.1 | 103.5 | 103.8 | 103.1 | 103.5 | 102.2 | 104.0 | 107.5 | 108.4 | 103.4 |
| 2014 | 102.3 | 101.2 | 101.7 | 103.1 | 104.0 | 104.4 | 103.9 | 104.5 | 103.3 | 105.9 | 109.1 | 110.1 | 104.5 |
| 2015 | 103.7 | 102.8 | 103.5 | 104.7 | 105.4 | 105.8 | 105.3 | 105.4 | 104.9 | 107.1 | 110.8 | 112.4 | 106.0 |
| 2016 | 106.0 | 104.9 | 105.5 | 106.4 | 107.0 | 106.7 | 107.3 | 107.7 | 107.1 | 109.3 | 112.3 | 113.0 | 107.8 |
| 2017 | 107.1 | 106.3 | 106.4 | 107.8 | 108.6 | 108.2 | 108.5 | 108.5 | 108.2 | 110.0 | 113.9 | 114.4 | 109.0 |
| 2018 | 110.0 | 107.7 | 107.3 | 107.6 | 108.8 | 108.4 | 108.9 | 108.0 | 108.1 | 109.1 | 113.4 | 112.5 | 109.2 |
| 2019 | 107.6 | 105.5 | 105.5 | 105.7 | 106.5 | 106.5 | 106.2 | 105.9 | 105.9 | 106.9 | 109.6 | 109.9 | 106.8 |
| **Transportation and Utilities** | | | | | | | | | | | | | |
| 2011 | 38.0 | 37.8 | 38.1 | 38.3 | 38.5 | 38.4 | 38.8 | 39.7 | 40.7 | 41.1 | 42.4 | 42.9 | 39.6 |
| 2012 | 40.0 | 40.0 | 40.0 | 39.7 | 40.2 | 39.7 | 39.3 | 40.0 | 40.3 | 39.9 | 40.0 | 40.1 | 39.9 |
| 2013 | 38.2 | 38.0 | 38.1 | 38.2 | 38.4 | 38.1 | 37.5 | 38.0 | 38.3 | 38.9 | 40.0 | 40.5 | 38.5 |
| 2014 | 38.9 | 38.7 | 39.1 | 38.9 | 39.2 | 39.2 | 38.8 | 39.6 | 39.6 | 40.4 | 40.9 | 41.6 | 39.6 |
| 2015 | 40.3 | 39.9 | 40.2 | 40.6 | 41.1 | 40.9 | 41.1 | 41.5 | 41.6 | 42.1 | 42.6 | 43.5 | 41.3 |
| 2016 | 41.6 | 41.4 | 41.5 | 41.7 | 42.0 | 41.8 | 42.0 | 42.6 | 43.0 | 43.4 | 44.4 | 45.6 | 42.6 |
| 2017 | 43.2 | 43.3 | 43.7 | 44.2 | 45.0 | 45.0 | 45.1 | 46.0 | 46.6 | 46.6 | 48.0 | 49.2 | 45.5 |
| 2018 | 49.4 | 48.7 | 49.1 | 49.5 | 49.8 | 50.4 | 50.3 | 50.8 | 51.1 | 52.0 | 53.8 | 54.7 | 50.8 |
| 2019 | 52.7 | 52.1 | 51.5 | 51.3 | 51.6 | 52.4 | 52.4 | 52.9 | 53.0 | 53.7 | 55.2 | 55.4 | 52.9 |
| **Information** | | | | | | | | | | | | | |
| 2011 | 13.9 | 13.9 | 13.8 | 13.8 | 13.9 | 14.0 | 14.0 | 14.1 | 14.0 | 13.8 | 14.0 | 13.9 | 13.9 |
| 2012 | 13.9 | 13.9 | 13.8 | 13.7 | 13.8 | 13.9 | 13.9 | 13.8 | 13.7 | 14.0 | 14.1 | 14.2 | 13.9 |
| 2013 | 14.1 | 14.2 | 14.1 | 14.1 | 14.1 | 14.1 | 14.0 | 13.9 | 13.6 | 13.5 | 13.5 | 13.5 | 13.9 |
| 2014 | 13.3 | 13.3 | 13.4 | 13.6 | 13.7 | 13.5 | 13.6 | 13.7 | 13.4 | 13.3 | 13.5 | 13.7 | 13.5 |
| 2015 | 13.5 | 13.5 | 13.6 | 13.6 | 13.5 | 13.7 | 13.5 | 13.8 | 13.5 | 13.9 | 14.0 | 14.2 | 13.7 |
| 2016 | 14.1 | 14.2 | 14.2 | 14.1 | 14.2 | 14.2 | 14.3 | 14.2 | 14.0 | 14.0 | 14.0 | 14.0 | 14.1 |
| 2017 | 13.9 | 14.1 | 13.9 | 13.9 | 14.0 | 14.1 | 14.2 | 14.0 | 13.8 | 13.6 | 13.8 | 13.7 | 13.9 |
| 2018 | 13.7 | 13.9 | 13.9 | 13.9 | 14.0 | 14.1 | 14.0 | 14.0 | 13.7 | 13.7 | 13.8 | 13.7 | 13.9 |
| 2019 | 13.5 | 13.5 | 13.5 | 13.6 | 13.7 | 13.8 | 13.5 | 13.4 | 13.3 | 13.3 | 13.4 | 13.4 | 13.5 |
| **Financial Activities** | | | | | | | | | | | | | |
| 2011 | 63.3 | 63.3 | 63.3 | 63.2 | 63.4 | 63.5 | 63.2 | 63.2 | 63.0 | 62.9 | 63.1 | 63.4 | 63.2 |
| 2012 | 63.4 | 63.3 | 63.4 | 63.6 | 64.0 | 64.5 | 64.6 | 64.5 | 64.5 | 64.5 | 64.7 | 65.2 | 64.2 |
| 2013 | 64.4 | 64.6 | 64.9 | 65.2 | 65.6 | 66.2 | 66.5 | 66.7 | 66.2 | 66.0 | 66.2 | 66.2 | 65.7 |
| 2014 | 65.6 | 65.7 | 65.8 | 66.1 | 66.8 | 67.4 | 67.8 | 67.8 | 67.2 | 67.2 | 67.9 | 67.8 | 66.9 |
| 2015 | 67.4 | 67.6 | 67.8 | 68.1 | 68.8 | 69.5 | 69.8 | 70.1 | 69.6 | 69.9 | 70.2 | 70.3 | 69.1 |
| 2016 | 70.4 | 70.8 | 70.8 | 71.3 | 71.8 | 72.4 | 73.2 | 73.3 | 72.9 | 73.2 | 73.5 | 73.9 | 72.3 |
| 2017 | 73.5 | 73.6 | 73.6 | 73.7 | 73.9 | 74.4 | 74.2 | 74.2 | 73.4 | 73.8 | 73.7 | 73.8 | 73.8 |
| 2018 | 73.2 | 73.5 | 73.2 | 73.7 | 73.9 | 74.4 | 74.7 | 74.4 | 73.4 | 73.7 | 73.7 | 73.8 | 73.8 |
| 2019 | 73.1 | 73.3 | 73.0 | 73.5 | 73.9 | 74.5 | 75.0 | 74.8 | 74.1 | 74.9 | 74.1 | 74.9 | 74.1 |

# Employment by Industry: Cincinnati, OH-KY-IN, 2011–2019—*Continued*

(Numbers in thousands, not seasonally adjusted)

| Industry and year | January | February | March | April | May | June | July | August | September | October | November | December | Annual average |
|---|---|---|---|---|---|---|---|---|---|---|---|---|---|
| **Professional and Business Services** | | | | | | | | | | | | | |
| 2011 | 149.0 | 149.4 | 151.2 | 154.1 | 153.2 | 153.6 | 156.2 | 157.0 | 156.9 | 157.6 | 158.7 | 158.8 | 154.6 |
| 2012 | 156.3 | 156.1 | 157.6 | 160.4 | 160.5 | 161.4 | 161.6 | 163.3 | 163.3 | 164.1 | 162.8 | 162.6 | 160.8 |
| 2013 | 157.1 | 158.0 | 159.3 | 162.9 | 163.0 | 164.1 | 164.0 | 165.6 | 166.0 | 166.4 | 166.9 | 167.8 | 163.4 |
| 2014 | 162.1 | 161.8 | 163.8 | 166.5 | 166.6 | 166.4 | 167.4 | 168.8 | 168.4 | 168.7 | 170.3 | 170.3 | 166.8 |
| 2015 | 165.2 | 164.2 | 164.9 | 168.0 | 167.7 | 169.2 | 169.6 | 169.9 | 168.9 | 169.9 | 170.0 | 169.6 | 168.1 |
| 2016 | 165.3 | 164.2 | 165.7 | 169.2 | 168.0 | 168.4 | 169.0 | 169.7 | 169.8 | 170.8 | 171.4 | 170.9 | 168.5 |
| 2017 | 166.2 | 165.1 | 165.5 | 168.6 | 167.5 | 169.7 | 169.5 | 169.8 | 168.4 | 170.5 | 172.1 | 171.4 | 168.7 |
| 2018 | 165.7 | 166.0 | 167.2 | 168.0 | 168.0 | 170.8 | 171.7 | 171.9 | 172.4 | 172.7 | 174.7 | 173.5 | 170.2 |
| 2019 | 168.3 | 166.7 | 168.2 | 170.3 | 171.4 | 173.9 | 173.7 | 173.8 | 173.8 | 175.3 | 178.1 | 180.5 | 172.8 |
| **Education and Health Services** | | | | | | | | | | | | | |
| 2011 | 146.4 | 147.6 | 148.2 | 150.1 | 151.2 | 149.4 | 148.6 | 148.8 | 150.0 | 150.7 | 151.0 | 151.2 | 149.4 |
| 2012 | 149.4 | 151.0 | 151.6 | 152.5 | 153.3 | 152.0 | 150.3 | 150.8 | 152.8 | 154.1 | 154.7 | 154.5 | 152.3 |
| 2013 | 152.4 | 154.1 | 154.7 | 156.3 | 157.5 | 156.1 | 155.2 | 155.5 | 157.1 | 158.0 | 159.6 | 158.9 | 156.3 |
| 2014 | 157.3 | 158.1 | 159.2 | 159.3 | 160.5 | 158.9 | 158.0 | 158.6 | 159.9 | 160.3 | 161.7 | 161.8 | 159.5 |
| 2015 | 159.4 | 159.7 | 160.9 | 161.7 | 162.6 | 160.8 | 159.7 | 160.2 | 161.7 | 163.2 | 164.4 | 163.9 | 161.5 |
| 2016 | 161.5 | 162.6 | 163.9 | 164.2 | 165.0 | 162.5 | 160.9 | 161.3 | 163.2 | 164.0 | 164.8 | 164.4 | 163.2 |
| 2017 | 163.2 | 164.4 | 165.1 | 165.3 | 166.4 | 165.1 | 162.7 | 162.8 | 164.4 | 165.6 | 166.1 | 166.6 | 164.8 |
| 2018 | 164.1 | 166.0 | 166.1 | 166.3 | 167.4 | 166.0 | 164.5 | 165.3 | 167.3 | 168.4 | 168.8 | 168.5 | 166.6 |
| 2019 | 167.7 | 169.2 | 169.6 | 170.3 | 171.3 | 170.4 | 168.7 | 169.6 | 170.5 | 171.9 | 172.2 | 173.7 | 170.4 |
| **Leisure and Hospitality** | | | | | | | | | | | | | |
| 2011 | 94.1 | 94.8 | 98.2 | 103.7 | 108.1 | 111.3 | 111.3 | 110.8 | 106.2 | 102.7 | 99.7 | 100.4 | 103.4 |
| 2012 | 96.9 | 98.3 | 101.7 | 106.1 | 110.9 | 114.6 | 113.7 | 113.3 | 109.0 | 107.5 | 103.3 | 104.1 | 106.6 |
| 2013 | 100.1 | 102.0 | 105.2 | 111.3 | 116.4 | 118.9 | 118.2 | 117.5 | 113.9 | 112.5 | 108.1 | 107.9 | 111.0 |
| 2014 | 103.6 | 104.2 | 108.8 | 113.6 | 119.0 | 121.3 | 120.3 | 119.0 | 114.6 | 112.8 | 109.2 | 109.9 | 113.0 |
| 2015 | 106.6 | 107.2 | 110.8 | 116.5 | 122.4 | 125.2 | 125.9 | 123.3 | 121.4 | 116.9 | 114.2 | 113.9 | 117.0 |
| 2016 | 110.4 | 110.9 | 115.2 | 119.1 | 124.2 | 128.5 | 128.6 | 126.1 | 122.7 | 120.2 | 117.5 | 116.8 | 120.0 |
| 2017 | 112.9 | 114.8 | 118.1 | 121.7 | 126.2 | 130.6 | 130.7 | 130.1 | 125.8 | 123.0 | 119.4 | 120.9 | 122.9 |
| 2018 | 115.7 | 116.5 | 119.8 | 124.4 | 129.7 | 134.4 | 133.4 | 133.0 | 127.4 | 124.8 | 122.3 | 123.2 | 125.4 |
| 2019 | 118.5 | 119.7 | 122.9 | 126.2 | 131.8 | 135.6 | 135.0 | 134.4 | 129.0 | 121.5 | 120.2 | 121.3 | 126.3 |
| **Other Services** | | | | | | | | | | | | | |
| 2011 | 39.8 | 39.6 | 40.0 | 40.2 | 40.5 | 40.3 | 40.1 | 39.8 | 39.3 | 38.8 | 38.5 | 38.4 | 39.6 |
| 2012 | 37.8 | 37.6 | 37.9 | 38.5 | 38.9 | 39.6 | 39.5 | 39.5 | 39.2 | 39.4 | 39.4 | 39.6 | 38.9 |
| 2013 | 39.2 | 39.4 | 39.7 | 39.9 | 40.0 | 40.2 | 40.0 | 39.8 | 39.5 | 39.3 | 39.0 | 39.0 | 39.6 |
| 2014 | 38.3 | 38.3 | 38.7 | 39.0 | 39.3 | 39.5 | 39.3 | 39.2 | 38.4 | 38.8 | 38.7 | 38.8 | 38.9 |
| 2015 | 37.9 | 37.8 | 38.2 | 38.6 | 39.1 | 39.5 | 39.7 | 39.6 | 39.1 | 39.6 | 39.7 | 39.9 | 39.1 |
| 2016 | 39.7 | 39.9 | 40.3 | 40.9 | 41.2 | 41.1 | 41.5 | 41.3 | 41.2 | 41.9 | 41.9 | 42.1 | 41.1 |
| 2017 | 42.2 | 42.5 | 43.0 | 42.9 | 43.2 | 43.6 | 43.0 | 42.8 | 42.6 | 42.5 | 42.1 | 42.4 | 42.7 |
| 2018 | 41.7 | 41.9 | 42.2 | 42.0 | 42.1 | 42.3 | 42.0 | 41.8 | 41.5 | 41.4 | 41.2 | 41.3 | 41.8 |
| 2019 | 40.7 | 40.8 | 41.2 | 41.4 | 41.6 | 41.6 | 41.4 | 41.5 | 40.9 | 40.5 | 40.7 | 40.7 | 41.1 |
| **Government** | | | | | | | | | | | | | |
| 2011 | 130.5 | 132.9 | 133.8 | 134.1 | 132.9 | 124.0 | 118.3 | 125.1 | 130.3 | 132.9 | 132.5 | 129.6 | 129.7 |
| 2012 | 125.9 | 132.1 | 133.3 | 133.6 | 134.1 | 124.7 | 118.1 | 122.2 | 129.7 | 132.4 | 132.9 | 128.8 | 129.0 |
| 2013 | 126.4 | 132.4 | 132.0 | 135.2 | 134.3 | 124.2 | 116.4 | 125.2 | 132.0 | 133.3 | 133.6 | 128.9 | 129.5 |
| 2014 | 126.3 | 131.9 | 132.2 | 133.8 | 134.6 | 124.4 | 118.6 | 124.2 | 131.2 | 132.5 | 132.5 | 131.6 | 129.5 |
| 2015 | 127.8 | 130.9 | 132.0 | 132.5 | 133.5 | 125.3 | 120.3 | 125.1 | 130.4 | 131.8 | 132.2 | 131.5 | 129.4 |
| 2016 | 127.6 | 131.1 | 132.2 | 133.0 | 134.0 | 125.0 | 122.4 | 126.0 | 131.7 | 133.0 | 133.3 | 132.5 | 130.2 |
| 2017 | 129.0 | 132.3 | 133.4 | 133.9 | 133.5 | 127.5 | 121.5 | 125.0 | 131.9 | 133.4 | 133.8 | 132.9 | 130.7 |
| 2018 | 129.2 | 132.3 | 132.7 | 133.5 | 131.8 | 127.0 | 121.4 | 124.5 | 131.7 | 134.0 | 134.1 | 132.8 | 130.4 |
| 2019 | 128.4 | 131.9 | 134.3 | 132.8 | 131.0 | 124.3 | 119.0 | 122.1 | 130.5 | 131.3 | 131.6 | 129.6 | 128.9 |

## Employment by Industry: Kansas City, MO-KS, 2011–2019

(Numbers in thousands, not seasonally adjusted)

| Industry and year | January | February | March | April | May | June | July | August | September | October | November | December | Annual average |
|---|---|---|---|---|---|---|---|---|---|---|---|---|---|
| **Total Nonfarm** | | | | | | | | | | | | | |
| 2011 | 950.5 | 953.4 | 966.0 | 976.6 | 981.9 | 982.3 | 972.0 | 971.7 | 981.2 | 985.6 | 990.3 | 989.2 | 975.1 |
| 2012 | 968.5 | 973.6 | 984.5 | 992.8 | 998.5 | 1,000.8 | 984.5 | 992.1 | 993.7 | 999.8 | 1,002.6 | 998.8 | 990.9 |
| 2013 | 977.8 | 981.2 | 987.9 | 1,000.9 | 1,007.6 | 1,011.9 | 996.3 | 1,002.9 | 1,009.9 | 1,014.7 | 1,014.8 | 1,014.4 | 1,001.7 |
| 2014 | 989.7 | 995.6 | 1,006.2 | 1,020.0 | 1,028.4 | 1,032.5 | 1,018.5 | 1,024.0 | 1,027.1 | 1,036.3 | 1,038.6 | 1,039.9 | 1,021.4 |
| 2015 | 1,017.0 | 1,023.9 | 1,032.2 | 1,042.3 | 1,050.9 | 1,055.3 | 1,045.0 | 1,045.2 | 1,051.2 | 1,060.3 | 1,060.0 | 1,061.9 | 1,045.4 |
| 2016 | 1,042.0 | 1,045.8 | 1,051.6 | 1,068.0 | 1,069.0 | 1,070.8 | 1,062.0 | 1,067.3 | 1,077.2 | 1,081.9 | 1,083.1 | 1,082.1 | 1,066.7 |
| 2017 | 1,058.2 | 1,064.2 | 1,070.8 | 1,081.0 | 1,084.4 | 1,089.4 | 1,079.5 | 1,081.8 | 1,090.1 | 1,091.2 | 1,096.5 | 1,096.3 | 1,082.0 |
| 2018 | 1,067.7 | 1,073.3 | 1,077.0 | 1,085.9 | 1,089.1 | 1,097.7 | 1,084.8 | 1,088.4 | 1,092.8 | 1,097.7 | 1,099.9 | 1,100.5 | 1,087.9 |
| 2019 | 1,078.3 | 1,077.4 | 1,080.9 | 1,096.1 | 1,101.4 | 1,104.0 | 1,089.6 | 1,098.2 | 1,101.0 | 1,106.5 | 1,110.2 | 1,109.1 | 1,096.1 |
| **Total Private** | | | | | | | | | | | | | |
| 2011 | 802.3 | 802.9 | 812.9 | 822.8 | 828.7 | 831.3 | 833.4 | 834.9 | 833.4 | 837.1 | 841.5 | 840.4 | 826.8 |
| 2012 | 822.9 | 824.3 | 834.0 | 841.6 | 846.9 | 853.1 | 848.9 | 852.9 | 846.4 | 851.0 | 853.8 | 850.4 | 843.9 |
| 2013 | 833.2 | 833.0 | 839.0 | 849.7 | 856.9 | 864.3 | 862.3 | 867.8 | 862.4 | 868.0 | 868.2 | 868.0 | 856.1 |
| 2014 | 846.2 | 849.0 | 858.6 | 872.0 | 879.3 | 885.5 | 883.8 | 889.8 | 880.2 | 888.9 | 891.3 | 893.6 | 876.5 |
| 2015 | 871.2 | 875.8 | 882.7 | 892.3 | 901.1 | 908.0 | 909.7 | 908.9 | 902.7 | 912.0 | 911.5 | 914.5 | 899.2 |
| 2016 | 894.5 | 896.3 | 901.7 | 916.7 | 919.0 | 923.0 | 925.3 | 929.1 | 926.3 | 931.6 | 933.0 | 933.0 | 919.1 |
| 2017 | 909.6 | 913.3 | 919.5 | 929.2 | 933.2 | 939.0 | 939.7 | 940.7 | 939.6 | 940.9 | 945.9 | 947.2 | 933.2 |
| 2018 | 919.0 | 922.4 | 925.6 | 936.2 | 939.4 | 949.1 | 947.4 | 950.1 | 944.6 | 948.6 | 950.9 | 951.5 | 940.4 |
| 2019 | 932.0 | 928.1 | 931.1 | 945.2 | 950.2 | 953.9 | 950.6 | 957.9 | 950.9 | 955.1 | 958.0 | 957.7 | 947.6 |
| **Goods Producing** | | | | | | | | | | | | | |
| 2011 | 102.5 | 101.6 | 104.6 | 107.1 | 108.0 | 109.2 | 109.2 | 107.4 | 108.9 | 108.9 | 108.8 | 107.9 | 107.0 |
| 2012 | 104.7 | 104.2 | 106.6 | 107.7 | 107.9 | 109.9 | 109.3 | 110.1 | 109.9 | 109.4 | 109.0 | 106.7 | 108.0 |
| 2013 | 105.3 | 104.8 | 106.9 | 108.5 | 110.7 | 112.6 | 110.4 | 112.5 | 113.0 | 113.0 | 113.0 | 111.4 | 110.2 |
| 2014 | 106.6 | 109.3 | 111.9 | 114.5 | 115.1 | 117.3 | 116.4 | 118.1 | 117.2 | 117.9 | 118.2 | 118.3 | 115.1 |
| 2015 | 113.2 | 115.6 | 118.0 | 117.1 | 120.5 | 122.2 | 121.7 | 121.6 | 122.4 | 123.3 | 122.5 | 122.2 | 120.0 |
| 2016 | 119.0 | 119.5 | 122.3 | 125.2 | 125.7 | 128.1 | 126.7 | 128.2 | 127.9 | 128.0 | 127.5 | 126.2 | 125.4 |
| 2017 | 122.1 | 123.3 | 124.8 | 126.0 | 126.6 | 129.2 | 129.1 | 126.5 | 127.9 | 124.8 | 126.4 | 126.3 | 126.1 |
| 2018 | 120.0 | 123.0 | 124.6 | 126.0 | 124.4 | 130.2 | 127.8 | 129.9 | 129.5 | 129.3 | 129.7 | 129.6 | 127.0 |
| 2019 | 126.3 | 125.5 | 126.9 | 130.1 | 130.9 | 133.2 | 128.2 | 133.3 | 132.7 | 131.4 | 133.8 | 134.2 | 130.5 |
| **Service-Providing** | | | | | | | | | | | | | |
| 2011 | 848.0 | 851.8 | 861.4 | 869.5 | 873.9 | 873.1 | 862.8 | 864.3 | 872.3 | 876.7 | 881.5 | 881.3 | 868.1 |
| 2012 | 863.8 | 869.4 | 877.9 | 885.1 | 890.6 | 890.9 | 875.2 | 882.0 | 883.8 | 890.4 | 893.6 | 892.1 | 882.9 |
| 2013 | 872.5 | 876.4 | 881.0 | 892.4 | 896.9 | 899.3 | 885.9 | 890.4 | 896.9 | 901.7 | 901.8 | 903.0 | 891.5 |
| 2014 | 883.1 | 886.3 | 894.3 | 905.5 | 913.3 | 915.2 | 902.1 | 905.9 | 909.9 | 918.4 | 920.4 | 921.6 | 906.3 |
| 2015 | 903.8 | 908.3 | 914.2 | 925.2 | 930.4 | 933.1 | 923.3 | 923.6 | 928.8 | 937.0 | 937.5 | 939.7 | 925.4 |
| 2016 | 923.0 | 926.3 | 929.3 | 942.8 | 943.3 | 942.7 | 935.3 | 939.1 | 949.3 | 953.9 | 955.6 | 955.9 | 941.4 |
| 2017 | 936.1 | 940.9 | 946.0 | 955.0 | 957.8 | 960.2 | 950.4 | 955.3 | 962.2 | 966.4 | 970.1 | 970.0 | 955.9 |
| 2018 | 947.7 | 950.3 | 952.4 | 959.9 | 964.7 | 967.5 | 957.0 | 958.5 | 963.3 | 968.4 | 970.2 | 970.9 | 960.9 |
| 2019 | 952.0 | 951.9 | 954.0 | 966.0 | 970.5 | 970.8 | 961.4 | 964.9 | 968.3 | 975.1 | 976.4 | 974.9 | 965.5 |
| **Mining, Logging, and Construction** | | | | | | | | | | | | | |
| 2011 | 33.1 | 32.4 | 35.1 | 37.4 | 38.1 | 38.9 | 39.4 | 39.2 | 38.9 | 38.7 | 38.6 | 37.6 | 37.3 |
| 2012 | 35.3 | 34.8 | 36.7 | 38.0 | 39.4 | 40.4 | 40.6 | 40.6 | 40.2 | 40.0 | 39.6 | 39.1 | 38.7 |
| 2013 | 36.6 | 37.2 | 37.9 | 39.7 | 41.6 | 42.8 | 43.7 | 43.4 | 43.0 | 43.2 | 42.7 | 41.1 | 41.1 |
| 2014 | 39.0 | 38.4 | 41.0 | 42.6 | 43.9 | 44.7 | 45.9 | 45.1 | 44.3 | 44.5 | 44.4 | 44.4 | 43.2 |
| 2015 | 42.1 | 42.3 | 43.5 | 45.3 | 45.5 | 46.4 | 47.2 | 47.1 | 46.6 | 47.0 | 46.1 | 45.6 | 45.4 |
| 2016 | 43.1 | 43.4 | 45.5 | 47.9 | 48.2 | 50.1 | 50.3 | 50.2 | 50.2 | 50.4 | 49.6 | 48.6 | 48.1 |
| 2017 | 46.3 | 46.9 | 47.9 | 48.9 | 49.6 | 51.4 | 51.5 | 50.9 | 50.5 | 50.9 | 50.3 | 49.6 | 49.6 |
| 2018 | 45.9 | 46.5 | 48.1 | 49.2 | 50.5 | 52.0 | 52.5 | 52.1 | 52.0 | 51.6 | 51.8 | 51.4 | 50.3 |
| 2019 | 48.9 | 47.9 | 49.7 | 52.1 | 52.8 | 54.8 | 55.3 | 55.1 | 54.6 | 54.6 | 54.5 | 54.5 | 52.9 |
| **Manufacturing** | | | | | | | | | | | | | |
| 2011 | 69.4 | 69.2 | 69.5 | 69.7 | 69.9 | 70.3 | 69.8 | 68.2 | 70.0 | 70.2 | 70.2 | 70.3 | 69.7 |
| 2012 | 69.4 | 69.4 | 69.9 | 69.7 | 68.5 | 69.5 | 68.7 | 69.5 | 69.7 | 69.4 | 69.4 | 67.6 | 69.2 |
| 2013 | 68.7 | 67.6 | 69.0 | 68.8 | 69.1 | 69.8 | 66.7 | 69.1 | 70.0 | 69.8 | 70.3 | 70.3 | 69.1 |
| 2014 | 67.6 | 70.9 | 70.9 | 71.9 | 71.2 | 72.6 | 70.5 | 73.0 | 72.9 | 73.4 | 73.8 | 73.9 | 71.9 |
| 2015 | 71.1 | 73.3 | 74.5 | 71.8 | 75.0 | 75.8 | 74.5 | 74.5 | 75.8 | 76.3 | 76.4 | 76.6 | 74.6 |
| 2016 | 75.9 | 76.1 | 76.8 | 77.3 | 77.5 | 78.0 | 76.4 | 78.0 | 77.7 | 77.6 | 77.9 | 77.6 | 77.2 |
| 2017 | 75.8 | 76.4 | 76.9 | 77.1 | 77.0 | 77.8 | 77.6 | 75.6 | 77.4 | 73.9 | 76.1 | 76.7 | 76.5 |
| 2018 | 74.1 | 76.5 | 76.5 | 76.8 | 73.9 | 78.2 | 75.3 | 77.8 | 77.5 | 77.7 | 77.9 | 78.2 | 76.7 |
| 2019 | 77.4 | 77.6 | 77.2 | 78.0 | 78.1 | 78.4 | 72.9 | 78.2 | 78.1 | 76.8 | 79.3 | 79.7 | 77.6 |

# Employment by Industry: Kansas City, MO-KS, 2011–2019—*Continued*

(Numbers in thousands, not seasonally adjusted)

| Industry and year | January | February | March | April | May | June | July | August | September | October | November | December | Annual average |
|---|---|---|---|---|---|---|---|---|---|---|---|---|---|
| **Trade, Transportation, and Utilities** | | | | | | | | | | | | | |
| 2011 | 189.0 | 187.7 | 189.1 | 191.1 | 192.0 | 191.7 | 191.8 | 192.5 | 192.1 | 193.3 | 197.2 | 198.2 | 192.1 |
| 2012 | 192.6 | 190.5 | 191.8 | 192.5 | 194.0 | 194.5 | 193.1 | 193.4 | 192.9 | 194.3 | 198.2 | 198.4 | 193.9 |
| 2013 | 191.9 | 190.5 | 191.1 | 192.8 | 193.8 | 194.9 | 195.1 | 195.8 | 195.0 | 197.6 | 201.5 | 202.9 | 195.2 |
| 2014 | 196.5 | 194.3 | 196.8 | 198.4 | 199.9 | 200.8 | 200.4 | 201.3 | 199.6 | 201.9 | 205.5 | 207.3 | 200.2 |
| 2015 | 201.2 | 199.9 | 200.4 | 202.0 | 204.0 | 205.5 | 204.6 | 204.6 | 203.6 | 206.2 | 209.4 | 211.5 | 204.4 |
| 2016 | 204.2 | 203.6 | 204.3 | 206.0 | 207.3 | 207.5 | 208.2 | 208.9 | 207.8 | 210.2 | 215.0 | 217.7 | 208.4 |
| 2017 | 209.7 | 208.6 | 208.6 | 209.8 | 210.9 | 211.3 | 211.7 | 214.0 | 213.7 | 215.4 | 222.0 | 223.2 | 213.2 |
| 2018 | 215.2 | 213.0 | 212.5 | 214.8 | 216.7 | 217.3 | 217.0 | 217.7 | 216.6 | 219.0 | 224.4 | 226.2 | 217.5 |
| 2019 | 219.3 | 215.8 | 215.6 | 216.9 | 217.8 | 217.8 | 217.5 | 218.6 | 217.4 | 219.4 | 222.8 | 224.3 | 218.6 |
| **Wholesale Trade** | | | | | | | | | | | | | |
| 2011 | 45.6 | 45.6 | 45.7 | 46.1 | 46.5 | 46.5 | 46.7 | 46.6 | 46.6 | 46.0 | 46.2 | 46.4 | 46.2 |
| 2012 | 46.4 | 46.3 | 46.6 | 46.6 | 46.8 | 47.1 | 47.1 | 47.0 | 46.7 | 46.7 | 46.7 | 46.7 | 46.7 |
| 2013 | 46.0 | 46.2 | 46.1 | 46.3 | 46.4 | 46.6 | 47.5 | 47.5 | 47.2 | 47.7 | 47.7 | 47.9 | 46.9 |
| 2014 | 47.5 | 47.3 | 48.2 | 48.2 | 48.5 | 48.8 | 48.7 | 48.6 | 48.3 | 48.7 | 48.5 | 48.6 | 48.3 |
| 2015 | 48.4 | 48.5 | 48.3 | 48.3 | 48.4 | 48.7 | 48.5 | 48.4 | 47.9 | 48.4 | 48.2 | 48.2 | 48.4 |
| 2016 | 47.7 | 47.7 | 47.8 | 48.4 | 48.7 | 48.6 | 49.1 | 49.0 | 48.9 | 49.1 | 49.1 | 49.3 | 48.6 |
| 2017 | 49.0 | 49.2 | 49.4 | 49.7 | 49.9 | 50.1 | 50.3 | 50.3 | 49.9 | 49.9 | 50.1 | 50.1 | 49.8 |
| 2018 | 49.8 | 49.8 | 50.0 | 50.4 | 50.5 | 51.0 | 51.2 | 51.3 | 51.2 | 51.2 | 51.4 | 51.6 | 50.8 |
| 2019 | 51.6 | 51.8 | 51.8 | 51.9 | 51.9 | 52.0 | 52.4 | 52.4 | 52.0 | 52.3 | 52.2 | 52.2 | 52.0 |
| **Retail Trade** | | | | | | | | | | | | | |
| 2011 | 101.5 | 100.1 | 101.2 | 102.5 | 103.1 | 103.4 | 103.4 | 103.6 | 102.7 | 104.0 | 107.5 | 107.9 | 103.4 |
| 2012 | 103.1 | 101.5 | 102.5 | 102.9 | 104.0 | 104.2 | 103.9 | 103.4 | 103.2 | 104.0 | 107.7 | 107.9 | 104.0 |
| 2013 | 102.8 | 101.3 | 102.0 | 103.2 | 103.9 | 104.9 | 104.8 | 104.7 | 104.1 | 105.6 | 108.8 | 110.1 | 104.7 |
| 2014 | 104.9 | 103.0 | 104.2 | 105.5 | 106.3 | 107.1 | 107.3 | 107.1 | 105.9 | 107.3 | 110.7 | 111.8 | 106.8 |
| 2015 | 106.5 | 105.2 | 105.9 | 107.4 | 108.9 | 110.4 | 110.0 | 109.6 | 108.4 | 110.3 | 113.1 | 114.1 | 109.2 |
| 2016 | 109.1 | 108.6 | 109.2 | 110.3 | 111.1 | 111.8 | 112.3 | 112.3 | 110.6 | 112.0 | 115.5 | 116.9 | 111.6 |
| 2017 | 111.8 | 110.5 | 110.6 | 111.3 | 111.9 | 112.4 | 112.4 | 112.2 | 110.4 | 111.8 | 115.7 | 116.4 | 112.3 |
| 2018 | 111.3 | 109.8 | 109.8 | 110.8 | 111.9 | 112.5 | 112.2 | 111.6 | 110.2 | 111.1 | 114.9 | 115.5 | 111.8 |
| 2019 | 110.9 | 108.2 | 108.4 | 109.2 | 110.0 | 110.5 | 110.0 | 109.4 | 108.4 | 109.5 | 112.3 | 113.3 | 110.0 |
| **Transportation and Utilities** | | | | | | | | | | | | | |
| 2011 | 189.0 | 187.7 | 189.1 | 191.1 | 192.0 | 191.7 | 191.8 | 192.5 | 192.1 | 193.3 | 197.2 | 198.2 | 192.1 |
| 2012 | 192.6 | 190.5 | 191.8 | 192.5 | 194.0 | 194.5 | 193.1 | 193.4 | 192.9 | 194.3 | 198.2 | 198.4 | 193.9 |
| 2013 | 191.9 | 190.5 | 191.1 | 192.8 | 193.8 | 194.9 | 195.1 | 195.8 | 195.0 | 197.6 | 201.5 | 202.9 | 195.2 |
| 2014 | 196.5 | 194.3 | 196.8 | 198.4 | 199.9 | 200.8 | 200.4 | 201.3 | 199.6 | 201.9 | 205.5 | 207.3 | 200.2 |
| 2015 | 201.2 | 199.9 | 200.4 | 202.0 | 204.0 | 205.5 | 204.6 | 204.6 | 203.6 | 206.2 | 209.4 | 211.5 | 204.4 |
| 2016 | 204.2 | 203.6 | 204.3 | 206.0 | 207.3 | 207.5 | 208.2 | 208.9 | 207.8 | 210.2 | 215.0 | 217.7 | 208.4 |
| 2017 | 209.7 | 208.6 | 208.6 | 209.8 | 210.9 | 211.3 | 211.7 | 214.0 | 213.7 | 215.4 | 222.0 | 223.2 | 213.2 |
| 2018 | 215.2 | 213.0 | 212.5 | 214.8 | 216.7 | 217.3 | 217.0 | 217.7 | 216.6 | 219.0 | 224.4 | 226.2 | 217.5 |
| 2019 | 219.3 | 215.8 | 215.6 | 216.9 | 217.8 | 217.8 | 217.5 | 218.6 | 217.4 | 219.4 | 222.8 | 224.3 | 218.6 |
| **Information** | | | | | | | | | | | | | |
| 2011 | 24.7 | 24.6 | 24.5 | 24.6 | 24.6 | 24.6 | 24.6 | 24.6 | 24.6 | 24.5 | 24.6 | 24.8 | 24.6 |
| 2012 | 24.7 | 24.6 | 24.6 | 24.7 | 24.7 | 24.8 | 24.6 | 24.8 | 24.4 | 24.7 | 24.7 | 24.8 | 24.7 |
| 2013 | 24.4 | 24.5 | 24.3 | 24.3 | 24.4 | 24.6 | 24.7 | 24.7 | 24.3 | 24.3 | 24.4 | 24.2 | 24.4 |
| 2014 | 24.2 | 24.1 | 23.9 | 23.3 | 23.1 | 23.1 | 22.8 | 22.4 | 21.8 | 21.5 | 21.4 | 21.3 | 22.7 |
| 2015 | 21.0 | 20.8 | 20.9 | 20.9 | 20.8 | 20.7 | 20.9 | 20.6 | 20.2 | 20.0 | 20.1 | 20.1 | 20.6 |
| 2016 | 19.9 | 19.9 | 19.7 | 18.8 | 18.8 | 18.8 | 18.9 | 18.8 | 18.5 | 18.5 | 18.6 | 18.7 | 19.0 |
| 2017 | 18.0 | 18.1 | 18.1 | 18.1 | 17.9 | 17.9 | 17.8 | 17.6 | 17.4 | 17.2 | 17.2 | 17.1 | 17.7 |
| 2018 | 17.3 | 17.2 | 17.2 | 17.3 | 17.2 | 17.1 | 16.9 | 16.6 | 16.4 | 16.3 | 16.4 | 16.3 | 16.9 |
| 2019 | 16.2 | 16.2 | 16.2 | 16.2 | 16.0 | 16.0 | 16.2 | 16.2 | 16.0 | 16.0 | 16.0 | 16.0 | 16.1 |
| **Financial Activities** | | | | | | | | | | | | | |
| 2011 | 72.5 | 72.7 | 72.8 | 73.2 | 73.9 | 73.9 | 73.9 | 73.9 | 73.5 | 75.0 | 75.1 | 75.0 | 73.8 |
| 2012 | 75.4 | 75.9 | 76.3 | 76.4 | 76.4 | 76.7 | 77.0 | 77.1 | 76.3 | 76.6 | 76.7 | 76.6 | 76.5 |
| 2013 | 76.9 | 77.2 | 76.8 | 76.5 | 76.6 | 77.3 | 77.6 | 77.2 | 76.6 | 76.1 | 76.2 | 76.0 | 76.8 |
| 2014 | 75.0 | 75.2 | 75.4 | 76.0 | 76.3 | 76.7 | 76.9 | 77.1 | 76.6 | 77.0 | 77.0 | 77.1 | 76.4 |
| 2015 | 76.8 | 77.2 | 77.4 | 77.7 | 77.9 | 78.4 | 79.1 | 79.0 | 78.0 | 78.5 | 78.6 | 78.6 | 78.1 |
| 2016 | 79.3 | 79.5 | 79.4 | 80.5 | 80.4 | 80.5 | 80.9 | 80.7 | 80.0 | 79.9 | 79.9 | 79.7 | 80.1 |
| 2017 | 79.2 | 79.4 | 79.4 | 80.0 | 80.4 | 81.0 | 80.7 | 80.3 | 79.7 | 80.2 | 80.0 | 79.9 | 80.0 |
| 2018 | 77.8 | 77.9 | 77.5 | 78.0 | 78.1 | 78.9 | 79.1 | 79.0 | 78.3 | 78.7 | 78.5 | 78.4 | 78.4 |
| 2019 | 77.7 | 77.9 | 77.7 | 78.3 | 78.6 | 79.1 | 79.5 | 79.7 | 79.0 | 79.4 | 79.1 | 78.9 | 78.7 |

## Employment by Industry: Kansas City, MO-KS, 2011–2019—*Continued*

(Numbers in thousands, not seasonally adjusted)

| Industry and year | January | February | March | April | May | June | July | August | September | October | November | December | Annual average |
|---|---|---|---|---|---|---|---|---|---|---|---|---|---|
| **Professional and Business Services** | | | | | | | | | | | | | |
| 2011 | 152.8 | 154.0 | 155.9 | 158.2 | 158.1 | 158.6 | 159.2 | 160.1 | 160.2 | 160.8 | 162.3 | 161.8 | 158.5 |
| 2012 | 158.6 | 160.0 | 162.0 | 164.5 | 164.7 | 166.5 | 166.4 | 166.8 | 167.1 | 169.9 | 169.8 | 169.2 | 165.5 |
| 2013 | 164.6 | 165.7 | 167.5 | 170.9 | 170.3 | 172.3 | 172.0 | 173.6 | 172.4 | 173.9 | 173.9 | 174.4 | 171.0 |
| 2014 | 169.4 | 170.6 | 171.6 | 174.8 | 174.8 | 177.3 | 178.6 | 180.2 | 178.5 | 181.5 | 183.1 | 184.2 | 177.1 |
| 2015 | 177.0 | 178.4 | 179.7 | 182.5 | 183.0 | 184.6 | 185.7 | 185.6 | 184.9 | 187.9 | 187.2 | 188.0 | 183.7 |
| 2016 | 182.0 | 183.1 | 183.2 | 186.2 | 185.0 | 186.5 | 189.2 | 190.7 | 191.3 | 192.1 | 192.0 | 191.3 | 187.7 |
| 2017 | 184.5 | 185.7 | 187.8 | 191.5 | 190.5 | 192.9 | 194.6 | 194.8 | 194.5 | 195.3 | 195.3 | 194.6 | 191.8 |
| 2018 | 188.3 | 189.5 | 190.7 | 193.5 | 193.2 | 194.5 | 195.9 | 195.2 | 194.0 | 194.0 | 193.4 | 192.2 | 192.9 |
| 2019 | 188.6 | 188.3 | 188.4 | 192.0 | 192.2 | 193.4 | 194.2 | 194.8 | 192.5 | 192.7 | 193.4 | 191.6 | 191.8 |
| **Education and Health Services** | | | | | | | | | | | | | |
| 2011 | 130.2 | 131.7 | 132.2 | 131.8 | 132.0 | 131.0 | 131.4 | 132.6 | 133.7 | 135.3 | 136.0 | 136.1 | 132.8 |
| 2012 | 133.1 | 134.3 | 134.7 | 134.7 | 135.3 | 134.9 | 133.6 | 134.8 | 134.4 | 136.0 | 136.8 | 137.3 | 135.0 |
| 2013 | 135.3 | 136.0 | 135.3 | 137.2 | 138.2 | 137.0 | 136.7 | 137.7 | 137.6 | 140.4 | 140.7 | 140.5 | 137.7 |
| 2014 | 138.6 | 139.6 | 139.3 | 142.3 | 143.2 | 142.6 | 142.3 | 142.7 | 142.9 | 144.9 | 145.3 | 145.3 | 142.4 |
| 2015 | 144.2 | 145.6 | 145.0 | 146.9 | 147.0 | 146.4 | 147.6 | 147.2 | 147.0 | 148.8 | 149.2 | 148.7 | 147.0 |
| 2016 | 147.2 | 147.8 | 147.5 | 149.3 | 149.1 | 146.5 | 147.3 | 147.1 | 149.3 | 151.2 | 151.2 | 150.5 | 148.7 |
| 2017 | 149.7 | 151.0 | 150.9 | 152.5 | 152.6 | 150.5 | 150.8 | 151.3 | 153.1 | 154.9 | 155.0 | 154.7 | 152.3 |
| 2018 | 153.3 | 154.5 | 154.1 | 154.1 | 154.3 | 153.0 | 153.2 | 153.4 | 154.8 | 157.3 | 157.2 | 157.0 | 154.7 |
| 2019 | 155.0 | 156.0 | 155.7 | 157.0 | 157.0 | 154.5 | 155.9 | 156.0 | 157.2 | 158.3 | 158.8 | 158.5 | 156.7 |
| **Leisure and Hospitality** | | | | | | | | | | | | | |
| 2011 | 86.9 | 87.0 | 89.9 | 92.7 | 95.9 | 97.9 | 98.8 | 99.4 | 96.3 | 95.0 | 93.3 | 92.4 | 93.8 |
| 2012 | 90.2 | 91.1 | 94.1 | 97.2 | 100.0 | 102.1 | 101.4 | 102.6 | 98.5 | 97.4 | 96.1 | 94.9 | 97.1 |
| 2013 | 92.7 | 92.3 | 95.0 | 97.7 | 100.9 | 103.4 | 103.5 | 103.9 | 101.4 | 100.8 | 96.7 | 96.7 | 98.8 |
| 2014 | 94.7 | 94.5 | 97.9 | 101.7 | 105.5 | 106.5 | 105.1 | 106.8 | 102.7 | 103.1 | 100.0 | 99.3 | 101.5 |
| 2015 | 97.1 | 97.6 | 100.3 | 103.9 | 106.4 | 108.5 | 108.3 | 108.4 | 105.2 | 105.3 | 102.7 | 103.6 | 103.9 |
| 2016 | 101.1 | 101.0 | 103.2 | 107.4 | 109.3 | 111.6 | 110.2 | 111.2 | 108.2 | 108.2 | 105.2 | 105.6 | 106.9 |
| 2017 | 103.4 | 104.2 | 106.9 | 108.9 | 111.6 | 113.4 | 112.3 | 113.6 | 110.8 | 110.1 | 107.2 | 108.7 | 109.3 |
| 2018 | 104.9 | 105.0 | 106.8 | 109.9 | 112.9 | 115.1 | 114.5 | 115.6 | 112.6 | 111.4 | 109.0 | 109.6 | 110.6 |
| 2019 | 106.9 | 106.2 | 108.2 | 111.6 | 114.6 | 116.6 | 115.6 | 116.3 | 113.4 | 114.9 | 111.3 | 111.5 | 112.3 |
| **Other Services** | | | | | | | | | | | | | |
| 2011 | 43.7 | 43.6 | 43.9 | 44.1 | 44.2 | 44.4 | 44.5 | 44.4 | 44.1 | 44.3 | 44.2 | 44.2 | 44.1 |
| 2012 | 43.6 | 43.7 | 43.9 | 43.9 | 43.9 | 43.7 | 43.5 | 43.3 | 42.9 | 42.7 | 42.5 | 42.5 | 43.3 |
| 2013 | 42.1 | 42.0 | 42.1 | 41.8 | 42.0 | 42.2 | 42.3 | 42.4 | 42.1 | 41.9 | 41.8 | 41.9 | 42.1 |
| 2014 | 41.2 | 41.4 | 41.8 | 41.0 | 41.4 | 41.2 | 41.3 | 41.2 | 40.9 | 41.1 | 40.8 | 40.8 | 41.2 |
| 2015 | 40.7 | 40.7 | 41.0 | 41.3 | 41.5 | 41.7 | 41.8 | 41.9 | 41.4 | 42.0 | 41.8 | 41.8 | 41.5 |
| 2016 | 41.8 | 41.9 | 42.1 | 43.3 | 43.4 | 43.5 | 43.9 | 43.5 | 43.3 | 43.5 | 43.6 | 43.3 | 43.1 |
| 2017 | 43.0 | 43.0 | 43.0 | 42.4 | 42.7 | 42.8 | 42.7 | 42.6 | 42.5 | 43.0 | 42.8 | 42.7 | 42.8 |
| 2018 | 42.2 | 42.3 | 42.2 | 42.6 | 42.6 | 43.0 | 43.0 | 42.7 | 42.4 | 42.6 | 42.3 | 42.2 | 42.5 |
| 2019 | 42.0 | 42.2 | 42.4 | 43.1 | 43.1 | 43.3 | 43.5 | 43.0 | 42.7 | 43.0 | 42.8 | 42.7 | 42.8 |
| **Government** | | | | | | | | | | | | | |
| 2011 | 148.2 | 150.5 | 153.1 | 153.8 | 153.2 | 151.0 | 138.6 | 136.8 | 147.8 | 148.5 | 148.8 | 148.8 | 148.3 |
| 2012 | 145.6 | 149.3 | 150.5 | 151.2 | 151.6 | 147.7 | 135.6 | 139.2 | 147.3 | 148.8 | 148.8 | 148.4 | 147.0 |
| 2013 | 144.6 | 148.2 | 148.9 | 151.2 | 150.7 | 147.6 | 134.0 | 135.1 | 147.5 | 146.7 | 146.6 | 146.4 | 145.6 |
| 2014 | 143.5 | 146.6 | 147.6 | 148.0 | 149.1 | 147.0 | 134.7 | 134.2 | 146.9 | 147.4 | 147.3 | 146.3 | 144.9 |
| 2015 | 145.8 | 148.1 | 149.5 | 150.0 | 149.8 | 147.3 | 135.3 | 136.3 | 148.5 | 148.3 | 148.5 | 147.4 | 146.2 |
| 2016 | 147.5 | 149.5 | 149.9 | 151.3 | 150.0 | 147.8 | 136.7 | 138.2 | 150.9 | 150.3 | 150.1 | 149.1 | 147.6 |
| 2017 | 148.6 | 150.9 | 151.3 | 151.8 | 151.2 | 150.4 | 139.8 | 141.1 | 150.5 | 150.3 | 150.6 | 149.1 | 148.8 |
| 2018 | 148.7 | 150.9 | 151.4 | 149.7 | 149.7 | 148.6 | 137.4 | 138.3 | 148.2 | 149.1 | 149.0 | 149.0 | 147.5 |
| 2019 | 146.3 | 149.3 | 149.8 | 150.9 | 151.2 | 150.1 | 139.0 | 140.3 | 150.1 | 151.4 | 152.2 | 151.4 | 148.5 |

# Employment by Industry: Columbus, OH, 2011–2019

(Numbers in thousands, not seasonally adjusted)

| Industry and year | January | February | March | April | May | June | July | August | September | October | November | December | Annual average |
|---|---|---|---|---|---|---|---|---|---|---|---|---|---|
| **Total Nonfarm** | | | | | | | | | | | | | |
| 2011 | 912.2 | 917.0 | 922.6 | 939.2 | 946.0 | 939.5 | 938.6 | 942.6 | 951.8 | 958.0 | 964.9 | 964.1 | 941.4 |
| 2012 | 940.9 | 947.7 | 953.1 | 961.8 | 971.6 | 968.9 | 960.5 | 963.6 | 973.1 | 987.3 | 994.7 | 993.1 | 968.0 |
| 2013 | 966.5 | 968.6 | 972.2 | 986.7 | 997.1 | 989.7 | 986.5 | 992.0 | 997.0 | 1,007.2 | 1,018.2 | 1,018.0 | 991.6 |
| 2014 | 987.5 | 990.0 | 993.8 | 1,009.8 | 1,021.3 | 1,013.8 | 1,012.4 | 1,020.2 | 1,025.5 | 1,034.8 | 1,044.9 | 1,045.3 | 1,016.6 |
| 2015 | 1,015.3 | 1,017.0 | 1,019.8 | 1,032.2 | 1,043.7 | 1,043.4 | 1,041.9 | 1,046.8 | 1,044.1 | 1,056.4 | 1,063.5 | 1,063.4 | 1,040.6 |
| 2016 | 1,039.2 | 1,042.1 | 1,047.4 | 1,056.3 | 1,065.4 | 1,063.4 | 1,063.0 | 1,067.9 | 1,070.1 | 1,080.3 | 1,090.2 | 1,086.7 | 1,064.3 |
| 2017 | 1,062.6 | 1,065.5 | 1,068.6 | 1,079.1 | 1,089.1 | 1,090.2 | 1,085.4 | 1,089.7 | 1,087.5 | 1,098.7 | 1,107.0 | 1,101.4 | 1,085.4 |
| 2018 | 1,078.0 | 1,081.3 | 1,082.4 | 1,090.9 | 1,102.7 | 1,104.8 | 1,103.6 | 1,107.0 | 1,104.4 | 1,114.7 | 1,120.1 | 1,114.9 | 1,100.4 |
| 2019 | 1,093.8 | 1,093.0 | 1,095.0 | 1,104.6 | 1,114.3 | 1,111.3 | 1,116.3 | 1,118.7 | 1,114.3 | 1,119.7 | 1,128.6 | 1,126.5 | 1,111.3 |
| **Total Private** | | | | | | | | | | | | | |
| 2011 | 747.9 | 750.5 | 755.0 | 768.7 | 774.5 | 776.0 | 781.6 | 784.8 | 784.9 | 789.4 | 795.0 | 795.7 | 775.3 |
| 2012 | 775.7 | 779.6 | 785.1 | 794.3 | 801.7 | 807.5 | 807.1 | 809.1 | 806.9 | 816.1 | 822.2 | 821.9 | 802.3 |
| 2013 | 800.9 | 800.9 | 804.6 | 817.1 | 826.2 | 830.4 | 831.7 | 834.9 | 831.3 | 837.4 | 846.2 | 846.6 | 825.7 |
| 2014 | 821.8 | 821.5 | 825.7 | 839.0 | 849.0 | 853.4 | 856.0 | 861.8 | 855.8 | 863.0 | 872.6 | 873.9 | 849.5 |
| 2015 | 846.6 | 845.7 | 848.6 | 859.9 | 870.4 | 876.2 | 879.5 | 881.5 | 873.1 | 882.3 | 888.8 | 889.0 | 870.1 |
| 2016 | 866.4 | 866.0 | 871.6 | 879.7 | 890.2 | 893.6 | 898.5 | 901.4 | 895.9 | 901.8 | 910.3 | 908.8 | 890.4 |
| 2017 | 885.1 | 886.1 | 889.5 | 898.9 | 909.6 | 915.8 | 916.7 | 918.0 | 909.3 | 917.7 | 924.7 | 921.3 | 907.7 |
| 2018 | 898.4 | 900.5 | 902.2 | 909.5 | 921.4 | 928.9 | 930.5 | 930.7 | 923.9 | 931.0 | 935.6 | 932.5 | 920.4 |
| 2019 | 911.7 | 909.4 | 911.4 | 920.8 | 929.2 | 934.3 | 940.1 | 940.2 | 931.3 | 932.6 | 940.8 | 939.0 | 928.4 |
| **Goods Producing** | | | | | | | | | | | | | |
| 2011 | 90.8 | 90.8 | 91.9 | 94.4 | 95.6 | 97.0 | 98.6 | 99.0 | 98.4 | 98.5 | 98.3 | 97.1 | 95.9 |
| 2012 | 94.3 | 94.7 | 95.7 | 97.5 | 99.0 | 100.3 | 101.2 | 101.3 | 100.8 | 100.7 | 100.5 | 99.5 | 98.8 |
| 2013 | 97.2 | 97.3 | 98.3 | 100.3 | 102.5 | 104.1 | 104.3 | 104.5 | 104.1 | 104.3 | 104.4 | 103.1 | 102.0 |
| 2014 | 99.5 | 99.3 | 100.7 | 102.9 | 104.9 | 106.1 | 106.8 | 107.0 | 106.5 | 106.4 | 107.1 | 105.2 | 104.4 |
| 2015 | 102.5 | 102.8 | 103.4 | 105.8 | 108.4 | 109.2 | 109.9 | 110.0 | 109.2 | 109.3 | 109.7 | 108.5 | 107.4 |
| 2016 | 104.9 | 105.3 | 107.1 | 108.6 | 110.0 | 111.1 | 111.2 | 111.1 | 110.2 | 110.3 | 110.5 | 109.0 | 109.1 |
| 2017 | 106.7 | 107.5 | 109.0 | 111.1 | 113.6 | 114.8 | 114.9 | 114.7 | 113.7 | 114.1 | 114.2 | 113.0 | 112.3 |
| 2018 | 110.0 | 110.6 | 111.5 | 113.3 | 116.2 | 117.7 | 118.2 | 118.4 | 117.5 | 117.7 | 117.7 | 116.4 | 115.4 |
| 2019 | 113.3 | 113.3 | 114.1 | 116.3 | 118.0 | 119.4 | 120.5 | 120.3 | 119.4 | 118.1 | 117.7 | 117.7 | 117.3 |
| **Service-Providing** | | | | | | | | | | | | | |
| 2011 | 821.4 | 826.2 | 830.7 | 844.8 | 850.4 | 842.5 | 840.0 | 843.6 | 853.4 | 859.5 | 866.6 | 867.0 | 845.5 |
| 2012 | 846.6 | 853.0 | 857.4 | 864.3 | 872.6 | 868.6 | 859.3 | 862.3 | 872.3 | 886.6 | 894.2 | 893.6 | 869.2 |
| 2013 | 869.3 | 871.3 | 873.9 | 886.4 | 894.6 | 885.6 | 882.2 | 887.5 | 892.9 | 902.9 | 913.8 | 914.9 | 889.6 |
| 2014 | 888.0 | 890.7 | 893.1 | 906.9 | 916.4 | 907.7 | 905.6 | 913.2 | 919.0 | 928.4 | 937.8 | 940.1 | 912.2 |
| 2015 | 912.8 | 914.2 | 916.4 | 926.4 | 935.3 | 934.2 | 932.0 | 936.8 | 934.9 | 947.1 | 953.8 | 954.9 | 933.2 |
| 2016 | 934.3 | 936.8 | 940.3 | 947.7 | 955.4 | 952.3 | 951.8 | 956.8 | 959.9 | 970.0 | 979.7 | 977.7 | 955.2 |
| 2017 | 955.9 | 958.0 | 959.6 | 968.0 | 975.5 | 975.4 | 970.5 | 975.0 | 973.8 | 984.6 | 992.8 | 988.4 | 973.1 |
| 2018 | 968.0 | 970.7 | 970.9 | 977.6 | 986.5 | 987.1 | 985.4 | 988.6 | 986.9 | 997.0 | 1,002.4 | 998.5 | 985.0 |
| 2019 | 980.5 | 979.7 | 980.9 | 988.3 | 996.3 | 991.9 | 995.8 | 998.4 | 994.9 | 1,001.6 | 1,010.9 | 1,008.8 | 994.0 |
| **Mining, Logging, and Construction** | | | | | | | | | | | | | |
| 2011 | 26.0 | 25.9 | 26.7 | 28.6 | 29.7 | 30.7 | 32.2 | 32.4 | 32.0 | 31.7 | 31.1 | 30.0 | 29.8 |
| 2012 | 27.8 | 27.8 | 28.6 | 30.0 | 31.2 | 32.0 | 32.7 | 32.8 | 32.4 | 32.3 | 31.5 | 30.5 | 30.8 |
| 2013 | 28.6 | 28.6 | 29.4 | 31.2 | 33.1 | 34.3 | 34.6 | 35.0 | 34.6 | 34.7 | 34.4 | 32.7 | 32.6 |
| 2014 | 30.5 | 30.2 | 31.7 | 33.5 | 35.1 | 36.3 | 36.5 | 36.6 | 36.2 | 36.1 | 35.6 | 34.3 | 34.4 |
| 2015 | 31.6 | 31.8 | 32.6 | 34.4 | 36.5 | 37.4 | 37.7 | 37.9 | 37.6 | 37.6 | 37.0 | 35.9 | 35.7 |
| 2016 | 33.4 | 33.5 | 35.1 | 37.1 | 38.4 | 39.5 | 39.6 | 39.6 | 39.0 | 38.9 | 38.4 | 37.1 | 37.5 |
| 2017 | 35.2 | 35.8 | 37.4 | 39.2 | 41.2 | 42.3 | 42.3 | 42.3 | 41.8 | 41.4 | 40.8 | 39.5 | 39.9 |
| 2018 | 37.2 | 37.8 | 39.0 | 40.9 | 43.3 | 44.5 | 44.7 | 44.7 | 44.4 | 44.1 | 43.5 | 42.1 | 42.2 |
| 2019 | 39.9 | 39.8 | 41.1 | 43.1 | 44.6 | 45.6 | 46.2 | 46.1 | 45.9 | 46.0 | 45.5 | 44.8 | 44.1 |
| **Manufacturing** | | | | | | | | | | | | | |
| 2011 | 64.8 | 64.9 | 65.2 | 65.8 | 65.9 | 66.3 | 66.4 | 66.6 | 66.4 | 66.8 | 67.2 | 67.1 | 66.1 |
| 2012 | 66.5 | 66.9 | 67.1 | 67.5 | 67.8 | 68.3 | 68.5 | 68.5 | 68.4 | 68.4 | 69.0 | 69.0 | 68.0 |
| 2013 | 68.6 | 68.7 | 68.9 | 69.1 | 69.4 | 69.8 | 69.7 | 69.5 | 69.5 | 69.6 | 70.0 | 70.4 | 69.4 |
| 2014 | 69.0 | 69.1 | 69.0 | 69.4 | 69.8 | 69.8 | 70.3 | 70.4 | 70.3 | 70.3 | 71.5 | 70.9 | 70.0 |
| 2015 | 70.9 | 71.0 | 70.8 | 71.4 | 71.9 | 71.8 | 72.2 | 72.1 | 71.6 | 71.7 | 72.7 | 72.6 | 71.7 |
| 2016 | 71.5 | 71.8 | 72.0 | 71.5 | 71.6 | 71.6 | 71.6 | 71.5 | 71.2 | 71.4 | 72.1 | 71.9 | 71.6 |
| 2017 | 71.5 | 71.7 | 71.6 | 71.9 | 72.4 | 72.5 | 72.6 | 72.4 | 71.9 | 72.7 | 73.4 | 73.5 | 72.3 |
| 2018 | 72.8 | 72.8 | 72.5 | 72.4 | 72.9 | 73.2 | 73.5 | 73.7 | 73.1 | 73.6 | 74.2 | 74.3 | 73.3 |
| 2019 | 73.4 | 73.5 | 73.0 | 73.2 | 73.4 | 73.8 | 74.3 | 74.2 | 73.5 | 72.1 | 72.2 | 72.9 | 73.3 |

## Employment by Industry: Columbus, OH, 2011–2019—*Continued*

(Numbers in thousands, not seasonally adjusted)

| Industry and year | January | February | March | April | May | June | July | August | September | October | November | December | Annual average |
|---|---|---|---|---|---|---|---|---|---|---|---|---|---|
| **Trade, Transportation, and Utilities** | | | | | | | | | | | | | |
| 2011 | 177.8 | 177.4 | 177.3 | 179.9 | 180.6 | 180.6 | 181.4 | 182.0 | 181.4 | 184.3 | 188.5 | 191.4 | 181.9 |
| 2012 | 182.9 | 181.3 | 181.4 | 182.0 | 183.7 | 184.1 | 183.9 | 184.0 | 183.8 | 187.1 | 192.2 | 193.8 | 185.0 |
| 2013 | 184.5 | 182.5 | 182.4 | 183.8 | 185.3 | 186.3 | 186.8 | 187.0 | 186.3 | 189.8 | 195.4 | 197.4 | 187.3 |
| 2014 | 187.1 | 185.2 | 185.1 | 187.3 | 189.3 | 190.3 | 190.8 | 192.2 | 191.9 | 195.9 | 202.2 | 205.2 | 191.9 |
| 2015 | 194.7 | 192.9 | 193.0 | 194.1 | 195.4 | 195.7 | 196.2 | 196.8 | 195.9 | 199.4 | 204.7 | 207.1 | 197.2 |
| 2016 | 198.6 | 196.7 | 196.4 | 196.6 | 198.8 | 198.6 | 199.9 | 200.5 | 201.1 | 205.2 | 212.5 | 217.3 | 201.9 |
| 2017 | 206.0 | 202.5 | 202.3 | 203.3 | 204.9 | 205.7 | 206.0 | 206.5 | 204.9 | 209.2 | 215.8 | 216.6 | 207.0 |
| 2018 | 207.2 | 204.9 | 204.1 | 204.6 | 206.5 | 207.3 | 207.9 | 207.7 | 207.4 | 210.9 | 216.9 | 218.0 | 208.6 |
| 2019 | 210.7 | 206.8 | 205.7 | 205.7 | 207.5 | 208.8 | 212.0 | 212.6 | 212.6 | 215.4 | 222.9 | 223.5 | 212.0 |
| **Wholesale Trade** | | | | | | | | | | | | | |
| 2011 | 36.9 | 37.0 | 37.0 | 37.3 | 37.5 | 37.4 | 37.4 | 37.5 | 37.2 | 37.4 | 37.4 | 37.5 | 37.3 |
| 2012 | 37.6 | 37.8 | 37.7 | 37.9 | 38.1 | 38.2 | 38.4 | 38.4 | 38.2 | 38.2 | 38.3 | 38.2 | 38.1 |
| 2013 | 38.0 | 38.1 | 38.1 | 38.5 | 38.7 | 38.6 | 38.8 | 39.1 | 38.8 | 39.2 | 39.4 | 39.4 | 38.7 |
| 2014 | 39.8 | 40.2 | 40.4 | 40.6 | 41.1 | 41.0 | 41.2 | 41.3 | 41.1 | 41.1 | 41.4 | 41.5 | 40.9 |
| 2015 | 40.8 | 40.9 | 41.1 | 41.2 | 41.4 | 41.2 | 41.3 | 41.4 | 41.0 | 41.3 | 41.5 | 41.7 | 41.2 |
| 2016 | 41.3 | 41.4 | 41.5 | 41.1 | 41.4 | 41.3 | 41.6 | 41.6 | 41.3 | 41.3 | 41.2 | 41.3 | 41.4 |
| 2017 | 40.9 | 40.9 | 40.6 | 40.7 | 41.0 | 41.2 | 41.1 | 41.1 | 40.7 | 40.7 | 40.8 | 40.6 | 40.9 |
| 2018 | 40.6 | 40.9 | 41.0 | 41.2 | 41.5 | 41.7 | 41.8 | 41.7 | 41.2 | 41.4 | 41.7 | 41.6 | 41.4 |
| 2019 | 41.3 | 41.6 | 41.7 | 41.9 | 42.2 | 42.3 | 42.3 | 42.3 | 41.9 | 42.9 | 42.9 | 42.5 | 42.2 |
| **Retail Trade** | | | | | | | | | | | | | |
| 2011 | 97.2 | 96.7 | 96.7 | 98.5 | 98.7 | 98.8 | 99.6 | 100.0 | 99.3 | 101.3 | 104.6 | 106.8 | 99.9 |
| 2012 | 99.7 | 98.3 | 98.5 | 99.2 | 100.2 | 100.1 | 99.6 | 99.8 | 99.4 | 101.7 | 105.7 | 106.4 | 100.7 |
| 2013 | 100.0 | 98.4 | 98.3 | 99.5 | 100.5 | 100.9 | 101.3 | 101.3 | 100.8 | 103.4 | 107.3 | 108.4 | 101.7 |
| 2014 | 100.3 | 99.0 | 98.5 | 100.4 | 100.8 | 101.5 | 101.6 | 102.4 | 101.5 | 104.2 | 108.2 | 109.4 | 102.3 |
| 2015 | 101.9 | 100.7 | 100.8 | 101.3 | 102.1 | 102.1 | 102.4 | 102.5 | 101.5 | 103.1 | 106.5 | 107.3 | 102.7 |
| 2016 | 102.6 | 101.4 | 101.0 | 101.7 | 102.8 | 102.7 | 103.4 | 103.7 | 102.8 | 104.2 | 107.4 | 108.6 | 103.5 |
| 2017 | 103.4 | 102.3 | 102.2 | 102.7 | 103.2 | 103.1 | 103.1 | 102.9 | 101.2 | 103.7 | 107.2 | 107.6 | 103.6 |
| 2018 | 102.9 | 101.6 | 101.3 | 101.4 | 103.0 | 102.5 | 103.1 | 102.8 | 101.9 | 103.2 | 106.6 | 107.1 | 103.1 |
| 2019 | 102.6 | 100.5 | 99.9 | 100.2 | 100.8 | 100.6 | 101.3 | 100.7 | 99.5 | 99.7 | 102.7 | 102.5 | 100.9 |
| **Transportation and Utilities** | | | | | | | | | | | | | |
| 2011 | 43.7 | 43.7 | 43.6 | 44.1 | 44.4 | 44.4 | 44.4 | 44.5 | 44.9 | 45.6 | 46.5 | 47.1 | 44.7 |
| 2012 | 45.6 | 45.2 | 45.2 | 44.9 | 45.4 | 45.8 | 45.9 | 45.8 | 46.2 | 47.2 | 48.2 | 49.2 | 46.2 |
| 2013 | 46.5 | 46.0 | 46.0 | 45.8 | 46.1 | 46.8 | 46.7 | 46.6 | 46.7 | 47.2 | 48.7 | 49.6 | 46.9 |
| 2014 | 47.0 | 46.0 | 46.2 | 46.3 | 47.4 | 47.8 | 48.0 | 48.5 | 49.3 | 50.6 | 52.6 | 54.3 | 48.7 |
| 2015 | 52.0 | 51.3 | 51.1 | 51.6 | 51.9 | 52.4 | 52.5 | 52.9 | 53.4 | 55.0 | 56.7 | 58.1 | 53.2 |
| 2016 | 54.7 | 53.9 | 53.9 | 53.8 | 54.6 | 54.6 | 54.9 | 55.2 | 57.0 | 59.7 | 63.9 | 67.4 | 57.0 |
| 2017 | 61.7 | 59.3 | 59.5 | 59.9 | 60.7 | 61.4 | 61.8 | 62.5 | 63.0 | 64.8 | 67.8 | 68.4 | 62.6 |
| 2018 | 63.7 | 62.4 | 61.8 | 62.0 | 62.0 | 63.1 | 63.0 | 63.2 | 64.3 | 66.3 | 68.6 | 69.3 | 64.1 |
| 2019 | 66.8 | 64.7 | 64.1 | 63.6 | 64.5 | 65.9 | 68.4 | 69.6 | 71.2 | 72.8 | 77.3 | 78.5 | 69.0 |
| **Information** | | | | | | | | | | | | | |
| 2011 | 16.7 | 16.7 | 16.6 | 16.9 | 17.0 | 17.0 | 17.1 | 17.1 | 16.8 | 16.9 | 16.9 | 17.0 | 16.9 |
| 2012 | 16.7 | 16.8 | 16.8 | 16.9 | 17.0 | 17.3 | 17.4 | 17.3 | 17.3 | 17.4 | 17.6 | 17.8 | 17.2 |
| 2013 | 18.0 | 18.3 | 18.5 | 18.7 | 18.6 | 18.7 | 18.8 | 18.8 | 18.6 | 18.5 | 18.5 | 18.5 | 18.5 |
| 2014 | 18.2 | 18.2 | 18.1 | 18.1 | 17.8 | 17.7 | 17.5 | 17.3 | 16.8 | 16.6 | 16.9 | 17.0 | 17.5 |
| 2015 | 16.6 | 16.8 | 16.8 | 17.1 | 17.0 | 17.2 | 17.0 | 16.9 | 16.8 | 16.8 | 17.0 | 17.0 | 16.9 |
| 2016 | 16.7 | 16.8 | 16.7 | 16.5 | 16.7 | 17.0 | 17.0 | 17.0 | 17.1 | 17.1 | 17.3 | 17.2 | 16.9 |
| 2017 | 17.0 | 17.3 | 17.2 | 17.5 | 17.6 | 17.5 | 17.6 | 17.7 | 17.5 | 17.3 | 17.5 | 17.5 | 17.4 |
| 2018 | 17.3 | 17.5 | 17.3 | 17.5 | 17.5 | 17.6 | 17.4 | 17.5 | 17.3 | 17.8 | 17.8 | 17.5 | 17.5 |
| 2019 | 17.4 | 17.5 | 17.4 | 17.4 | 17.4 | 17.4 | 17.6 | 17.4 | 17.1 | 17.2 | 17.3 | 17.3 | 17.4 |
| **Financial Activities** | | | | | | | | | | | | | |
| 2011 | 70.1 | 70.1 | 70.2 | 70.0 | 70.5 | 70.7 | 70.9 | 71.4 | 71.9 | 72.1 | 72.1 | 72.0 | 71.0 |
| 2012 | 72.3 | 72.5 | 72.9 | 72.9 | 73.5 | 74.0 | 74.2 | 74.3 | 74.0 | 74.3 | 74.8 | 74.9 | 73.7 |
| 2013 | 74.8 | 75.2 | 75.4 | 75.4 | 75.8 | 76.0 | 75.9 | 76.0 | 75.2 | 75.0 | 75.2 | 75.1 | 75.4 |
| 2014 | 75.2 | 75.3 | 75.2 | 75.3 | 76.1 | 76.5 | 77.0 | 77.5 | 77.1 | 77.6 | 78.1 | 78.1 | 76.6 |
| 2015 | 78.0 | 78.3 | 78.2 | 78.5 | 79.2 | 79.6 | 80.3 | 80.6 | 79.7 | 80.2 | 80.4 | 80.3 | 79.4 |
| 2016 | 81.2 | 81.6 | 81.6 | 82.2 | 82.7 | 82.7 | 83.2 | 83.4 | 83.0 | 83.6 | 83.9 | 84.3 | 82.8 |
| 2017 | 84.2 | 84.3 | 84.4 | 84.7 | 84.9 | 85.3 | 85.3 | 85.2 | 84.6 | 85.1 | 85.1 | 85.3 | 84.9 |
| 2018 | 85.2 | 85.7 | 85.2 | 85.5 | 86.1 | 86.5 | 86.8 | 86.7 | 86.1 | 86.6 | 86.6 | 86.6 | 86.1 |
| 2019 | 86.5 | 86.7 | 86.7 | 86.7 | 87.1 | 87.3 | 87.4 | 87.2 | 86.6 | 85.9 | 87.1 | 87.0 | 86.9 |

# Employment by Industry: Columbus, OH, 2011–2019—*Continued*

(Numbers in thousands, not seasonally adjusted)

| Industry and year | January | February | March | April | May | June | July | August | September | October | November | December | Annual average |
|---|---|---|---|---|---|---|---|---|---|---|---|---|---|
| **Professional and Business Services** | | | | | | | | | | | | | |
| 2011 | 146.2 | 146.6 | 148.0 | 150.4 | 149.9 | 150.7 | 152.8 | 153.7 | 154.2 | 155.5 | 157.2 | 157.5 | 151.9 |
| 2012 | 153.3 | 154.3 | 155.7 | 157.4 | 157.4 | 158.8 | 158.9 | 160.1 | 159.8 | 163.4 | 165.5 | 165.8 | 159.2 |
| 2013 | 160.0 | 159.4 | 159.8 | 163.0 | 164.1 | 165.3 | 166.3 | 167.4 | 167.3 | 170.1 | 173.0 | 174.3 | 165.8 |
| 2014 | 169.3 | 168.9 | 169.6 | 172.7 | 173.1 | 174.6 | 175.7 | 177.9 | 177.3 | 179.8 | 182.7 | 183.8 | 175.5 |
| 2015 | 173.7 | 171.5 | 171.8 | 174.5 | 175.1 | 177.0 | 178.4 | 179.0 | 176.6 | 181.0 | 182.3 | 181.3 | 176.9 |
| 2016 | 175.1 | 174.3 | 175.6 | 178.1 | 179.1 | 181.2 | 183.0 | 184.2 | 182.7 | 183.5 | 185.2 | 183.6 | 180.5 |
| 2017 | 177.1 | 176.6 | 176.5 | 177.4 | 179.1 | 181.1 | 180.5 | 181.0 | 180.4 | 182.5 | 184.7 | 183.3 | 180.0 |
| 2018 | 177.9 | 178.0 | 178.2 | 178.9 | 180.2 | 182.5 | 182.9 | 183.1 | 181.9 | 183.9 | 185.6 | 183.9 | 181.4 |
| 2019 | 178.3 | 178.1 | 178.2 | 181.4 | 181.9 | 183.6 | 183.7 | 183.3 | 181.5 | 183.4 | 184.5 | 181.0 | 181.6 |
| **Education and Health Services** | | | | | | | | | | | | | |
| 2011 | 127.4 | 129.0 | 129.2 | 131.5 | 132.0 | 129.0 | 129.7 | 130.4 | 133.5 | 134.4 | 135.1 | 135.1 | 131.4 |
| 2012 | 133.8 | 136.0 | 136.0 | 138.1 | 137.6 | 136.0 | 134.7 | 135.2 | 135.7 | 137.4 | 137.6 | 137.0 | 136.3 |
| 2013 | 136.3 | 137.3 | 136.6 | 138.9 | 139.0 | 137.2 | 137.4 | 138.9 | 139.5 | 140.9 | 141.9 | 141.8 | 138.8 |
| 2014 | 140.3 | 142.3 | 142.6 | 145.0 | 144.8 | 143.0 | 143.5 | 144.3 | 144.4 | 145.8 | 146.3 | 146.0 | 144.0 |
| 2015 | 145.5 | 146.9 | 146.8 | 148.2 | 149.2 | 149.0 | 149.7 | 149.9 | 149.2 | 150.2 | 150.7 | 151.1 | 148.9 |
| 2016 | 150.2 | 151.3 | 152.0 | 152.6 | 153.7 | 151.7 | 153.5 | 154.1 | 153.9 | 155.1 | 155.4 | 154.6 | 153.2 |
| 2017 | 154.5 | 156.0 | 156.4 | 158.5 | 159.0 | 158.2 | 159.3 | 159.9 | 159.3 | 160.8 | 160.9 | 159.8 | 158.6 |
| 2018 | 159.1 | 160.4 | 160.5 | 161.7 | 162.2 | 162.0 | 162.0 | 162.4 | 162.2 | 163.2 | 163.4 | 162.9 | 161.8 |
| 2019 | 161.4 | 162.4 | 163.2 | 163.9 | 163.8 | 162.7 | 163.2 | 164.2 | 163.4 | 164.1 | 163.4 | 163.2 | 163.2 |
| **Leisure and Hospitality** | | | | | | | | | | | | | |
| 2011 | 83.7 | 84.5 | 86.4 | 89.9 | 93.0 | 94.9 | 94.6 | 94.8 | 92.8 | 91.4 | 90.8 | 89.7 | 90.5 |
| 2012 | 86.6 | 87.9 | 90.3 | 92.7 | 96.4 | 99.1 | 98.4 | 99.0 | 97.6 | 96.7 | 95.6 | 94.8 | 94.6 |
| 2013 | 92.6 | 93.2 | 95.7 | 98.7 | 102.3 | 104.1 | 103.5 | 103.8 | 102.0 | 100.5 | 99.3 | 98.1 | 99.5 |
| 2014 | 93.9 | 93.9 | 95.7 | 98.8 | 103.6 | 105.3 | 104.5 | 105.2 | 101.8 | 100.7 | 99.3 | 98.8 | 100.1 |
| 2015 | 95.9 | 96.6 | 98.3 | 101.1 | 105.3 | 107.4 | 106.4 | 106.7 | 104.6 | 104.2 | 103.0 | 103.0 | 102.7 |
| 2016 | 99.3 | 99.5 | 101.5 | 103.9 | 107.7 | 109.3 | 109.0 | 109.0 | 106.3 | 105.0 | 103.8 | 102.4 | 104.7 |
| 2017 | 99.4 | 101.5 | 103.1 | 105.5 | 109.3 | 111.1 | 110.9 | 110.9 | 108.0 | 107.6 | 105.6 | 104.8 | 106.5 |
| 2018 | 101.0 | 102.5 | 104.4 | 106.7 | 111.2 | 112.8 | 112.7 | 112.6 | 109.7 | 108.6 | 105.8 | 105.7 | 107.8 |
| 2019 | 102.7 | 103.1 | 104.7 | 107.6 | 111.3 | 112.4 | 112.9 | 112.6 | 108.7 | 106.8 | 105.1 | 106.8 | 107.9 |
| **Other Services** | | | | | | | | | | | | | |
| 2011 | 35.2 | 35.4 | 35.4 | 35.7 | 35.9 | 36.1 | 36.5 | 36.4 | 35.9 | 36.3 | 36.1 | 35.9 | 35.9 |
| 2012 | 35.8 | 36.1 | 36.3 | 36.8 | 37.1 | 37.9 | 38.4 | 37.9 | 37.9 | 39.1 | 38.4 | 38.3 | 37.5 |
| 2013 | 37.5 | 37.7 | 37.9 | 38.3 | 38.6 | 38.7 | 38.7 | 38.5 | 38.3 | 38.3 | 38.5 | 38.3 | 38.3 |
| 2014 | 38.3 | 38.4 | 38.7 | 38.9 | 39.4 | 39.9 | 40.2 | 40.4 | 40.0 | 40.2 | 40.0 | 39.8 | 39.5 |
| 2015 | 39.7 | 39.9 | 40.3 | 40.6 | 40.8 | 41.1 | 41.6 | 41.6 | 41.1 | 41.2 | 41.0 | 40.7 | 40.8 |
| 2016 | 40.4 | 40.5 | 40.7 | 41.2 | 41.5 | 42.0 | 41.7 | 42.1 | 41.6 | 42.0 | 41.7 | 40.4 | 41.3 |
| 2017 | 40.2 | 40.4 | 40.6 | 40.9 | 41.2 | 42.1 | 42.2 | 42.1 | 40.9 | 41.1 | 40.9 | 41.0 | 41.1 |
| 2018 | 40.7 | 40.9 | 41.0 | 41.3 | 41.5 | 42.5 | 42.6 | 42.3 | 41.8 | 42.3 | 41.8 | 41.5 | 41.7 |
| 2019 | 41.4 | 41.5 | 41.4 | 41.8 | 42.2 | 42.7 | 42.8 | 42.6 | 42.0 | 41.7 | 42.8 | 42.5 | 42.1 |
| **Government** | | | | | | | | | | | | | |
| 2011 | 164.3 | 166.5 | 167.6 | 170.5 | 171.5 | 163.5 | 157.0 | 157.8 | 166.9 | 168.6 | 169.9 | 168.4 | 166.0 |
| 2012 | 165.2 | 168.1 | 168.0 | 167.5 | 169.9 | 161.4 | 153.4 | 154.5 | 166.2 | 171.2 | 172.5 | 171.2 | 165.8 |
| 2013 | 165.6 | 167.7 | 167.6 | 169.6 | 170.9 | 159.3 | 154.8 | 157.1 | 165.7 | 169.8 | 172.0 | 171.4 | 166.0 |
| 2014 | 165.7 | 168.5 | 168.1 | 170.8 | 172.3 | 160.4 | 156.4 | 158.4 | 169.7 | 171.8 | 172.3 | 171.4 | 167.2 |
| 2015 | 168.7 | 171.3 | 171.2 | 172.3 | 173.3 | 167.2 | 162.4 | 165.3 | 171.0 | 174.1 | 174.7 | 174.4 | 170.5 |
| 2016 | 172.8 | 176.1 | 175.8 | 176.6 | 175.2 | 169.8 | 164.5 | 166.5 | 174.2 | 178.5 | 179.9 | 177.9 | 174.0 |
| 2017 | 177.5 | 179.4 | 179.1 | 180.2 | 179.5 | 174.4 | 168.7 | 171.7 | 178.2 | 181.0 | 182.3 | 180.1 | 177.7 |
| 2018 | 179.6 | 180.8 | 180.2 | 181.4 | 181.3 | 175.9 | 173.1 | 176.3 | 180.5 | 183.7 | 184.5 | 182.4 | 180.0 |
| 2019 | 182.1 | 183.6 | 183.6 | 183.8 | 185.1 | 177.0 | 176.2 | 178.5 | 183.0 | 187.1 | 187.8 | 187.5 | 182.9 |

## Employment by Industry: Indianapolis-Carmel-Anderson, IN, 2011–2019

(Numbers in thousands, not seasonally adjusted)

| Industry and year | January | February | March | April | May | June | July | August | September | October | November | December | Annual average |
|---|---|---|---|---|---|---|---|---|---|---|---|---|---|
| **Total Nonfarm** | | | | | | | | | | | | | |
| 2011 | 901.3 | 903.0 | 913.5 | 926.2 | 934.0 | 925.0 | 925.4 | 936.7 | 943.7 | 946.5 | 948.7 | 950.9 | 929.6 |
| 2012 | 927.2 | 937.5 | 943.1 | 949.9 | 959.9 | 956.4 | 948.3 | 964.0 | 968.6 | 969.9 | 973.2 | 972.3 | 955.9 |
| 2013 | 945.0 | 952.3 | 959.7 | 967.4 | 976.1 | 973.5 | 965.4 | 985.1 | 987.4 | 990.6 | 1003.3 | 1000.8 | 975.6 |
| 2014 | 964.0 | 967.2 | 977.6 | 988.3 | 1001.1 | 996.6 | 985.7 | 1002.6 | 1001.9 | 1005.7 | 1018.0 | 1019.4 | 994.0 |
| 2015 | 987.5 | 991.0 | 1000.7 | 1012.2 | 1024.0 | 1022.7 | 1014.7 | 1029.8 | 1028.9 | 1034.7 | 1043.3 | 1045.9 | 1019.6 |
| 2016 | 1015.3 | 1020.8 | 1030.0 | 1038.5 | 1048.3 | 1043.0 | 1042.5 | 1055.0 | 1057.6 | 1053.4 | 1061.3 | 1058.5 | 1043.7 |
| 2017 | 1032.1 | 1036.3 | 1045.8 | 1054.4 | 1063.9 | 1065.3 | 1052.4 | 1066.9 | 1067.9 | 1069.3 | 1077.3 | 1078.4 | 1059.2 |
| 2018 | 1049.1 | 1052.5 | 1062.0 | 1064.7 | 1077.0 | 1078.3 | 1067.6 | 1083.4 | 1081.2 | 1083.4 | 1090.8 | 1088.1 | 1073.2 |
| 2019 | 1070.2 | 1074.4 | 1077.9 | 1083.5 | 1095.6 | 1090.6 | 1084.5 | 1096.7 | 1095.0 | 1097.4 | 1098.9 | 1093.3 | 1088.2 |
| **Total Private** | | | | | | | | | | | | | |
| 2011 | 771.9 | 772.8 | 782.9 | 795.6 | 803.0 | 803.1 | 808.4 | 813.3 | 815.6 | 817.4 | 819.5 | 821.3 | 802.1 |
| 2012 | 799.9 | 807.7 | 814.1 | 821.6 | 830.5 | 836.2 | 833.5 | 839.0 | 839.7 | 841.2 | 844.4 | 843.8 | 829.3 |
| 2013 | 820.1 | 823.6 | 830.5 | 838.7 | 847.1 | 853.6 | 853.3 | 859.0 | 859.0 | 862.0 | 873.5 | 871.2 | 849.3 |
| 2014 | 837.5 | 837.7 | 847.3 | 858.5 | 870.6 | 872.1 | 869.7 | 874.8 | 872.8 | 876.9 | 888.0 | 888.7 | 866.2 |
| 2015 | 858.6 | 861.0 | 870.3 | 882.0 | 893.0 | 898.0 | 897.4 | 901.6 | 897.8 | 904.8 | 912.0 | 913.7 | 890.9 |
| 2016 | 884.7 | 888.8 | 897.0 | 908.2 | 917.2 | 920.5 | 923.2 | 924.7 | 925.0 | 922.7 | 928.8 | 925.9 | 913.9 |
| 2017 | 900.5 | 903.9 | 912.9 | 922.4 | 930.5 | 938.9 | 932.7 | 935.3 | 934.1 | 936.4 | 942.6 | 943.5 | 927.8 |
| 2018 | 916.6 | 918.6 | 927.9 | 930.9 | 941.9 | 949.7 | 946.5 | 950.1 | 946.5 | 948.3 | 955.1 | 952.4 | 940.4 |
| 2019 | 935.0 | 938.8 | 941.9 | 949.7 | 960.2 | 961.6 | 962.3 | 962.2 | 958.4 | 960.8 | 961.5 | 956.0 | 954.0 |
| **Goods Producing** | | | | | | | | | | | | | |
| 2011 | 118.2 | 117.7 | 120.0 | 122.5 | 124.4 | 127.1 | 128.2 | 129.0 | 129.1 | 129.3 | 127.7 | 126.7 | 125.0 |
| 2012 | 124.1 | 123.9 | 125.8 | 128.3 | 130.1 | 132.7 | 133.1 | 133.1 | 133.5 | 131.8 | 131.4 | 129.6 | 128.7 | 129.4 |
| 2013 | 126.1 | 126.2 | 126.6 | 128.7 | 130.6 | 133.3 | 133.6 | 133.8 | 133.3 | 133.7 | 133.2 | 131.4 | 130.9 |
| 2014 | 126.6 | 126.1 | 128.3 | 130.4 | 132.0 | 134.6 | 135.7 | 135.7 | 134.9 | 134.4 | 134.1 | 133.3 | 132.2 |
| 2015 | 129.0 | 129.1 | 130.6 | 132.8 | 134.9 | 137.4 | 138.2 | 138.8 | 138.1 | 137.6 | 137.4 | 136.8 | 135.1 |
| 2016 | 132.6 | 132.7 | 134.9 | 137.6 | 139.7 | 142.3 | 142.8 | 142.7 | 142.3 | 142.0 | 141.7 | 140.9 | 139.4 |
| 2017 | 137.6 | 138.6 | 140.7 | 142.7 | 143.8 | 146.5 | 146.0 | 146.0 | 145.4 | 144.4 | 143.6 | 143.5 | 143.2 |
| 2018 | 139.2 | 138.3 | 139.5 | 141.3 | 142.9 | 146.3 | 146.7 | 147.4 | 146.3 | 146.5 | 145.9 | 145.5 | 143.8 |
| 2019 | 144.5 | 145.3 | 145.8 | 147.4 | 149.3 | 151.6 | 151.6 | 151.4 | 150.8 | 151.7 | 149.3 | 147.0 | 148.8 |
| **Service-Providing** | | | | | | | | | | | | | |
| 2011 | 783.1 | 785.3 | 793.5 | 803.7 | 809.6 | 797.9 | 797.2 | 807.7 | 814.6 | 817.2 | 821.0 | 824.2 | 804.6 |
| 2012 | 803.1 | 813.6 | 817.3 | 821.6 | 829.8 | 823.7 | 815.2 | 830.5 | 836.8 | 838.5 | 843.6 | 843.6 | 826.4 |
| 2013 | 818.9 | 826.1 | 833.1 | 838.7 | 845.5 | 840.2 | 831.8 | 851.3 | 854.1 | 856.9 | 870.1 | 869.4 | 844.7 |
| 2014 | 837.4 | 841.1 | 849.3 | 857.9 | 869.1 | 862.0 | 850.0 | 866.9 | 867.0 | 871.3 | 883.9 | 886.1 | 861.8 |
| 2015 | 858.5 | 861.9 | 870.1 | 879.4 | 889.1 | 885.3 | 876.5 | 891.0 | 890.8 | 897.1 | 905.9 | 909.1 | 884.6 |
| 2016 | 882.7 | 888.1 | 895.1 | 900.9 | 908.6 | 900.7 | 899.7 | 912.3 | 915.3 | 911.4 | 919.6 | 917.6 | 904.3 |
| 2017 | 894.5 | 897.7 | 905.1 | 911.7 | 920.1 | 918.8 | 906.4 | 920.9 | 922.5 | 924.9 | 933.7 | 934.9 | 915.9 |
| 2018 | 909.9 | 914.2 | 922.5 | 923.4 | 934.1 | 932.0 | 920.9 | 936.0 | 934.9 | 936.9 | 944.9 | 942.6 | 929.4 |
| 2019 | 925.7 | 929.1 | 932.1 | 936.1 | 946.3 | 939.0 | 932.9 | 945.3 | 944.2 | 945.7 | 949.6 | 946.3 | 939.4 |
| **Mining and Logging** | | | | | | | | | | | | | |
| 2011 | 0.5 | 0.5 | 0.6 | 0.6 | 0.7 | 0.7 | 0.7 | 0.7 | 0.6 | 0.6 | 0.6 | 0.6 | 0.6 |
| 2012 | 0.6 | 0.6 | 0.6 | 0.6 | 0.6 | 0.6 | 0.6 | 0.6 | 0.6 | 0.6 | 0.6 | 0.6 | 0.6 |
| 2013 | 0.6 | 0.6 | 0.6 | 0.6 | 0.6 | 0.6 | 0.6 | 0.6 | 0.6 | 0.6 | 0.6 | 0.6 | 0.6 |
| 2014 | 0.5 | 0.5 | 0.6 | 0.6 | 0.6 | 0.6 | 0.7 | 0.6 | 0.6 | 0.6 | 0.6 | 0.6 | 0.6 |
| 2015 | 0.6 | 0.6 | 0.6 | 0.6 | 0.6 | 0.7 | 0.6 | 0.6 | 0.6 | 0.7 | 0.7 | 0.6 | 0.6 |
| 2016 | 0.6 | 0.6 | 0.7 | 0.7 | 0.7 | 0.7 | 0.7 | 0.7 | 0.7 | 0.7 | 0.7 | 0.7 | 0.7 |
| 2017 | 0.6 | 0.7 | 0.7 | 0.7 | 0.7 | 0.7 | 0.7 | 0.7 | 0.7 | 0.7 | 0.7 | 0.7 | 0.7 |
| 2018 | 0.7 | 0.7 | 0.7 | 0.7 | 0.7 | 0.7 | 0.7 | 0.7 | 0.7 | 0.7 | 0.7 | 0.7 | 0.7 |
| 2019 | 0.7 | 0.7 | 0.7 | 0.7 | 0.7 | 0.7 | 0.7 | 0.7 | 0.7 | 0.7 | 0.7 | 0.7 | 0.7 |
| **Construction** | | | | | | | | | | | | | |
| 2011 | 35.3 | 34.9 | 36.6 | 38.9 | 40.5 | 42.5 | 43.6 | 44.1 | 44.2 | 44.3 | 43.6 | 42.3 | 40.9 |
| 2012 | 39.6 | 39.4 | 40.7 | 42.8 | 44.1 | 45.4 | 45.9 | 45.8 | 44.8 | 44.6 | 43.8 | 42.8 | 43.3 |
| 2013 | 39.7 | 39.7 | 40.1 | 42.1 | 43.9 | 45.8 | 46.3 | 46.1 | 46.0 | 46.7 | 46.4 | 44.3 | 43.9 |
| 2014 | 40.0 | 39.4 | 41.0 | 42.9 | 44.0 | 45.9 | 46.5 | 46.3 | 45.9 | 45.3 | 45.2 | 43.8 | 43.9 |
| 2015 | 40.2 | 40.1 | 41.3 | 43.6 | 45.6 | 47.1 | 47.8 | 48.1 | 47.9 | 48.0 | 47.8 | 46.9 | 45.4 |
| 2016 | 43.1 | 43.2 | 45.0 | 47.7 | 49.5 | 51.0 | 51.1 | 50.8 | 50.8 | 51.1 | 50.6 | 49.1 | 48.6 |
| 2017 | 45.8 | 46.5 | 48.3 | 50.4 | 51.1 | 52.9 | 52.9 | 53.0 | 52.7 | 51.8 | 51.0 | 50.3 | 50.6 |
| 2018 | 46.6 | 46.7 | 48.1 | 49.8 | 51.2 | 53.1 | 53.5 | 53.6 | 53.3 | 53.1 | 52.6 | 51.6 | 51.1 |
| 2019 | 50.1 | 50.1 | 50.9 | 53.1 | 54.6 | 55.5 | 55.7 | 55.8 | 55.9 | 56.7 | 55.7 | 53.6 | 54.0 |

# Employment by Industry: Indianapolis-Carmel-Anderson, IN, 2011–2019—*Continued*

(Numbers in thousands, not seasonally adjusted)

| Industry and year | January | February | March | April | May | June | July | August | September | October | November | December | Annual average |
|---|---|---|---|---|---|---|---|---|---|---|---|---|---|
| **Manufacturing** | | | | | | | | | | | | | |
| 2011 | 82.4 | 82.3 | 82.8 | 83.0 | 83.2 | 83.9 | 83.9 | 84.2 | 84.3 | 84.4 | 83.5 | 83.8 | 83.5 |
| 2012 | 83.9 | 83.9 | 84.5 | 84.9 | 85.4 | 86.7 | 86.6 | 87.1 | 86.4 | 86.2 | 85.2 | 85.3 | 85.5 |
| 2013 | 85.8 | 85.9 | 85.9 | 86.0 | 86.1 | 86.9 | 86.7 | 87.1 | 86.7 | 86.4 | 86.2 | 86.5 | 86.4 |
| 2014 | 86.1 | 86.2 | 86.7 | 86.9 | 87.4 | 88.1 | 88.5 | 88.8 | 88.4 | 88.5 | 88.3 | 88.9 | 87.7 |
| 2015 | 88.2 | 88.4 | 88.7 | 88.6 | 88.7 | 89.6 | 89.8 | 90.1 | 89.6 | 88.9 | 88.9 | 89.3 | 89.1 |
| 2016 | 88.9 | 88.9 | 89.2 | 89.2 | 89.5 | 90.6 | 91.0 | 91.2 | 90.8 | 90.2 | 90.4 | 91.1 | 90.1 |
| 2017 | 91.2 | 91.4 | 91.7 | 91.6 | 92.0 | 92.9 | 92.4 | 92.3 | 92.0 | 91.9 | 91.9 | 92.5 | 92.0 |
| 2018 | 91.9 | 90.9 | 90.7 | 90.8 | 91.0 | 92.5 | 92.5 | 93.1 | 92.3 | 92.7 | 92.6 | 93.2 | 92.0 |
| 2019 | 93.7 | 94.5 | 94.2 | 93.6 | 94.0 | 95.4 | 95.2 | 94.9 | 94.2 | 94.3 | 92.9 | 92.7 | 94.1 |
| **Trade, Transportation, and Utilities** | | | | | | | | | | | | | |
| 2011 | 192.5 | 191.6 | 192.3 | 194.7 | 196.6 | 197.2 | 197.5 | 198.0 | 196.7 | 199.0 | 202.6 | 203.8 | 196.9 |
| 2012 | 196.6 | 195.7 | 196.9 | 198.1 | 200.7 | 202.0 | 201.5 | 201.3 | 201.5 | 203.7 | 208.3 | 209.6 | 201.3 |
| 2013 | 201.1 | 200.9 | 201.7 | 203.5 | 205.7 | 207.3 | 206.2 | 206.8 | 207.0 | 208.8 | 213.6 | 214.8 | 206.5 |
| 2014 | 205.5 | 204.8 | 205.6 | 206.5 | 208.8 | 209.8 | 210.0 | 210.1 | 210.0 | 210.9 | 214.8 | 216.6 | 209.5 |
| 2015 | 208.5 | 207.8 | 209.0 | 210.5 | 213.2 | 214.6 | 215.6 | 216.7 | 215.8 | 218.4 | 222.7 | 225.8 | 214.9 |
| 2016 | 217.7 | 217.5 | 218.5 | 218.2 | 219.9 | 220.3 | 222.1 | 222.3 | 222.2 | 222.6 | 226.9 | 228.5 | 221.4 |
| 2017 | 220.7 | 219.4 | 220.0 | 220.8 | 222.2 | 224.2 | 222.6 | 223.1 | 222.6 | 224.2 | 229.3 | 230.7 | 223.3 |
| 2018 | 221.8 | 220.7 | 221.9 | 221.9 | 225.0 | 226.7 | 226.4 | 226.5 | 226.8 | 228.0 | 233.3 | 233.5 | 226.0 |
| 2019 | 226.7 | 225.3 | 224.9 | 225.8 | 227.8 | 228.3 | 228.1 | 227.7 | 227.0 | 227.3 | 230.9 | 232.1 | 227.7 |
| **Wholesale Trade** | | | | | | | | | | | | | |
| 2011 | 45.1 | 45.3 | 45.3 | 45.8 | 46.1 | 46.2 | 46.4 | 46.4 | 46.1 | 46.2 | 46.3 | 46.3 | 46.0 |
| 2012 | 45.7 | 45.7 | 45.8 | 46.1 | 46.4 | 46.5 | 46.7 | 46.4 | 46.3 | 46.4 | 46.2 | 46.3 | 46.2 |
| 2013 | 45.7 | 46.0 | 46.2 | 46.5 | 46.6 | 46.9 | 47.1 | 46.7 | 46.5 | 46.5 | 46.6 | 46.6 | 46.5 |
| 2014 | 46.1 | 46.1 | 46.3 | 46.4 | 46.7 | 46.9 | 47.1 | 46.9 | 46.7 | 46.7 | 46.7 | 46.8 | 46.6 |
| 2015 | 46.5 | 46.6 | 46.7 | 46.9 | 47.1 | 47.1 | 47.4 | 47.4 | 47.1 | 47.4 | 47.5 | 47.6 | 47.1 |
| 2016 | 47.7 | 47.7 | 47.9 | 48.1 | 48.4 | 48.5 | 48.8 | 48.4 | 48.2 | 48.1 | 48.3 | 48.4 | 48.2 |
| 2017 | 48.5 | 48.6 | 48.6 | 48.5 | 48.8 | 49.2 | 49.1 | 49.3 | 48.8 | 48.8 | 49.0 | 48.9 | 48.8 |
| 2018 | 48.7 | 48.8 | 49.1 | 49.2 | 49.5 | 49.8 | 50.2 | 50.0 | 49.9 | 50.4 | 50.5 | 50.7 | 49.7 |
| 2019 | 50.4 | 50.7 | 50.7 | 51.1 | 51.4 | 51.6 | 51.9 | 51.8 | 51.3 | 50.8 | 50.4 | 50.6 | 51.1 |
| **Retail Trade** | | | | | | | | | | | | | |
| 2011 | 93.4 | 92.1 | 92.7 | 93.9 | 95.2 | 95.3 | 95.3 | 95.6 | 94.4 | 95.7 | 98.4 | 99.3 | 95.1 |
| 2012 | 94.7 | 93.4 | 94.3 | 95.0 | 96.7 | 97.0 | 96.4 | 95.8 | 95.8 | 96.9 | 100.4 | 100.6 | 96.4 |
| 2013 | 94.9 | 94.3 | 94.6 | 95.8 | 97.3 | 98.2 | 97.4 | 97.7 | 97.5 | 98.7 | 101.5 | 102.1 | 97.5 |
| 2014 | 95.8 | 95.2 | 95.9 | 97.0 | 98.5 | 99.1 | 98.9 | 98.9 | 98.9 | 99.5 | 102.5 | 103.3 | 98.6 |
| 2015 | 98.0 | 97.4 | 98.0 | 99.1 | 100.6 | 101.2 | 101.4 | 101.7 | 100.9 | 102.4 | 105.1 | 106.1 | 101.0 |
| 2016 | 100.4 | 100.3 | 100.9 | 101.4 | 102.5 | 102.8 | 102.7 | 102.7 | 102.6 | 103.8 | 106.7 | 107.0 | 102.8 |
| 2017 | 103.1 | 102.1 | 102.7 | 104.1 | 105.1 | 105.4 | 104.0 | 103.8 | 103.2 | 104.2 | 107.4 | 107.7 | 104.4 |
| 2018 | 102.8 | 101.8 | 102.8 | 101.9 | 103.9 | 104.7 | 104.0 | 103.5 | 103.2 | 103.5 | 106.6 | 106.7 | 103.8 |
| 2019 | 102.6 | 101.4 | 101.4 | 101.3 | 102.7 | 102.5 | 101.5 | 100.9 | 99.7 | 101.5 | 103.8 | 104.3 | 102.0 |
| **Transportation and Utilities** | | | | | | | | | | | | | |
| 2011 | 54.0 | 54.2 | 54.3 | 55.0 | 55.3 | 55.7 | 55.8 | 56.0 | 56.2 | 57.1 | 57.9 | 58.2 | 55.8 |
| 2012 | 56.2 | 56.6 | 56.8 | 57.0 | 57.6 | 58.5 | 58.4 | 59.1 | 59.4 | 60.4 | 61.7 | 62.7 | 58.7 |
| 2013 | 60.5 | 60.6 | 60.9 | 61.2 | 61.8 | 62.2 | 61.7 | 62.4 | 63.0 | 63.6 | 65.5 | 66.1 | 62.5 |
| 2014 | 63.6 | 63.5 | 63.4 | 63.1 | 63.6 | 63.8 | 64.0 | 64.3 | 64.4 | 64.7 | 65.6 | 66.5 | 64.2 |
| 2015 | 64.0 | 63.8 | 64.3 | 64.5 | 65.5 | 66.3 | 66.8 | 67.6 | 67.8 | 68.6 | 70.1 | 72.1 | 66.8 |
| 2016 | 69.6 | 69.5 | 69.7 | 68.7 | 69.0 | 69.0 | 70.6 | 71.2 | 71.4 | 70.7 | 71.9 | 73.1 | 70.4 |
| 2017 | 69.1 | 68.7 | 68.7 | 68.2 | 68.3 | 69.6 | 69.5 | 70.0 | 70.6 | 71.2 | 72.9 | 74.1 | 70.1 |
| 2018 | 70.3 | 70.1 | 70.0 | 70.8 | 71.6 | 72.2 | 72.2 | 73.0 | 73.7 | 74.1 | 76.2 | 76.1 | 72.5 |
| 2019 | 73.7 | 73.2 | 72.8 | 73.4 | 73.7 | 74.2 | 74.7 | 75.0 | 76.0 | 75.0 | 76.7 | 77.2 | 74.6 |
| **Information** | | | | | | | | | | | | | |
| 2011 | 15.0 | 14.9 | 15.0 | 15.0 | 15.2 | 15.4 | 15.4 | 15.5 | 15.5 | 15.5 | 15.6 | 15.6 | 15.3 |
| 2012 | 16.0 | 16.1 | 16.1 | 16.1 | 16.2 | 16.5 | 16.4 | 16.4 | 16.3 | 16.6 | 16.6 | 16.5 | 16.3 |
| 2013 | 16.6 | 16.6 | 16.7 | 16.8 | 16.8 | 17.1 | 17.2 | 17.0 | 16.8 | 16.9 | 16.9 | 16.9 | 16.9 |
| 2014 | 16.8 | 16.8 | 16.9 | 17.0 | 17.2 | 17.4 | 17.5 | 17.2 | 16.9 | 16.7 | 16.7 | 16.7 | 17.0 |
| 2015 | 16.8 | 16.8 | 16.7 | 16.6 | 16.7 | 16.8 | 16.8 | 16.5 | 16.3 | 16.1 | 16.2 | 16.2 | 16.5 |
| 2016 | 16.1 | 16.1 | 16.1 | 16.0 | 16.1 | 16.2 | 16.0 | 15.9 | 15.8 | 15.9 | 15.7 | 15.7 | 16.0 |
| 2017 | 16.0 | 16.0 | 16.1 | 15.8 | 15.7 | 15.5 | 15.1 | 14.9 | 14.6 | 14.6 | 14.7 | 14.7 | 15.3 |
| 2018 | 14.2 | 14.1 | 14.1 | 13.9 | 13.8 | 13.8 | 13.5 | 13.4 | 13.3 | 13.3 | 13.2 | 13.3 | 13.7 |
| 2019 | 13.5 | 13.6 | 13.6 | 13.6 | 13.7 | 13.8 | 13.7 | 13.5 | 13.3 | 13.4 | 13.3 | 13.6 | 13.6 |

## Employment by Industry: Indianapolis-Carmel-Anderson, IN, 2011–2019—*Continued*

(Numbers in thousands, not seasonally adjusted)

| Industry and year | January | February | March | April | May | June | July | August | September | October | November | December | Annual average |
|---|---|---|---|---|---|---|---|---|---|---|---|---|---|
| **Financial Activities** | | | | | | | | | | | | | |
| 2011 | 59.8 | 59.9 | 60.1 | 60.0 | 60.3 | 60.7 | 60.8 | 60.5 | 60.2 | 60.3 | 60.2 | 60.4 | 60.3 |
| 2012 | 60.0 | 60.0 | 60.1 | 60.1 | 60.4 | 60.8 | 60.8 | 60.6 | 60.1 | 60.1 | 60.0 | 60.2 | 60.3 |
| 2013 | 59.7 | 59.6 | 59.6 | 59.9 | 60.4 | 61.1 | 61.1 | 61.0 | 60.6 | 60.7 | 60.8 | 61.0 | 60.5 |
| 2014 | 59.8 | 59.9 | 60.2 | 60.4 | 60.9 | 61.3 | 61.5 | 61.6 | 61.4 | 61.7 | 61.9 | 62.0 | 61.1 |
| 2015 | 61.6 | 61.9 | 62.2 | 62.5 | 63.1 | 63.7 | 63.9 | 64.2 | 63.9 | 64.3 | 64.5 | 64.7 | 63.4 |
| 2016 | 64.2 | 64.3 | 64.5 | 65.0 | 65.4 | 65.9 | 66.3 | 66.1 | 65.8 | 66.1 | 65.9 | 66.0 | 65.5 |
| 2017 | 65.4 | 65.6 | 65.6 | 66.0 | 66.3 | 67.2 | 67.5 | 67.7 | 67.6 | 67.9 | 68.2 | 68.6 | 67.0 |
| 2018 | 67.9 | 68.3 | 68.6 | 68.9 | 69.3 | 70.1 | 70.4 | 70.2 | 69.6 | 69.7 | 69.9 | 70.0 | 69.4 |
| 2019 | 69.6 | 69.8 | 69.9 | 70.6 | 71.0 | 71.4 | 71.5 | 71.3 | 70.6 | 71.3 | 71.2 | 70.7 | 70.7 |
| **Professional and Business Services** | | | | | | | | | | | | | |
| 2011 | 127.2 | 126.7 | 129.2 | 132.8 | 132.9 | 131.9 | 134.5 | 136.6 | 137.3 | 138.4 | 139.0 | 140.7 | 133.9 |
| 2012 | 133.5 | 137.2 | 137.5 | 139.1 | 140.5 | 143.5 | 142.9 | 145.4 | 145.1 | 145.7 | 146.8 | 145.7 | 141.9 |
| 2013 | 140.0 | 139.5 | 141.7 | 144.1 | 144.9 | 146.9 | 148.8 | 152.0 | 152.0 | 153.0 | 160.9 | 159.3 | 148.6 |
| 2014 | 150.3 | 147.5 | 150.0 | 154.7 | 157.3 | 156.3 | 154.8 | 158.6 | 158.7 | 162.2 | 169.8 | 168.9 | 157.4 |
| 2015 | 156.9 | 156.1 | 158.9 | 163.7 | 165.8 | 166.4 | 165.6 | 166.1 | 164.9 | 169.4 | 172.8 | 172.2 | 164.9 |
| 2016 | 162.1 | 161.7 | 163.1 | 167.2 | 168.2 | 168.3 | 169.4 | 170.1 | 170.0 | 169.7 | 172.1 | 170.6 | 167.7 |
| 2017 | 161.3 | 161.3 | 163.9 | 167.0 | 167.8 | 170.6 | 169.3 | 171.1 | 171.1 | 172.6 | 174.6 | 174.9 | 168.8 |
| 2018 | 167.8 | 167.5 | 169.8 | 169.1 | 170.3 | 172.1 | 171.5 | 174.1 | 172.9 | 173.8 | 176.5 | 174.3 | 171.6 |
| 2019 | 167.6 | 167.8 | 168.7 | 170.5 | 173.1 | 172.9 | 173.3 | 174.6 | 172.1 | 173.0 | 174.0 | 174.1 | 171.8 |
| **Education and Health Services** | | | | | | | | | | | | | |
| 2011 | 132.9 | 135.1 | 135.5 | 136.8 | 136.2 | 132.6 | 133.3 | 134.3 | 140.2 | 139.5 | 139.6 | 139.8 | 136.3 |
| 2012 | 138.1 | 141.3 | 141.7 | 141.3 | 140.2 | 136.7 | 135.9 | 137.6 | 143.6 | 143.4 | 143.7 | 144.0 | 140.6 |
| 2013 | 141.2 | 144.6 | 145.0 | 144.5 | 143.0 | 140.2 | 139.7 | 141.1 | 144.6 | 145.1 | 145.3 | 145.2 | 143.3 |
| 2014 | 141.5 | 144.2 | 144.7 | 144.7 | 144.2 | 140.9 | 140.0 | 140.6 | 143.8 | 144.2 | 144.7 | 145.0 | 143.2 |
| 2015 | 143.3 | 145.6 | 145.9 | 147.3 | 146.4 | 144.4 | 144.2 | 145.0 | 147.8 | 149.1 | 149.5 | 149.3 | 146.5 |
| 2016 | 147.7 | 150.4 | 150.8 | 152.2 | 152.0 | 150.0 | 149.8 | 150.8 | 154.1 | 153.7 | 154.5 | 153.6 | 151.6 |
| 2017 | 152.4 | 154.5 | 155.4 | 156.1 | 157.0 | 156.0 | 154.4 | 154.6 | 157.8 | 158.0 | 158.3 | 158.0 | 156.0 |
| 2018 | 157.2 | 159.7 | 160.9 | 161.0 | 161.2 | 159.9 | 157.9 | 158.6 | 161.8 | 161.8 | 162.3 | 161.9 | 160.4 |
| 2019 | 160.2 | 163.1 | 162.9 | 163.9 | 163.9 | 161.7 | 162.6 | 163.0 | 165.5 | 166.2 | 167.2 | 164.9 | 163.8 |
| **Leisure and Hospitality** | | | | | | | | | | | | | |
| 2011 | 86.7 | 87.2 | 90.5 | 93.4 | 96.8 | 97.0 | 97.1 | 97.9 | 95.6 | 94.6 | 93.9 | 93.5 | 93.7 |
| 2012 | 91.0 | 92.5 | 94.8 | 97.3 | 100.7 | 101.6 | 100.5 | 101.8 | 99.6 | 98.4 | 97.5 | 97.3 | 97.8 |
| 2013 | 93.8 | 94.1 | 96.5 | 99.2 | 103.1 | 103.9 | 103.0 | 103.8 | 101.7 | 100.5 | 99.3 | 98.8 | 99.8 |
| 2014 | 93.8 | 94.7 | 97.4 | 100.7 | 105.4 | 106.2 | 104.8 | 106.1 | 102.7 | 102.6 | 101.7 | 101.9 | 101.5 |
| 2015 | 98.5 | 99.4 | 102.3 | 104.6 | 108.3 | 109.4 | 107.7 | 109.2 | 106.4 | 105.5 | 104.1 | 104.0 | 105.0 |
| 2016 | 100.1 | 101.6 | 104.2 | 106.8 | 110.3 | 111.3 | 110.6 | 110.9 | 109.3 | 107.4 | 106.6 | 105.3 | 107.0 |
| 2017 | 102.4 | 103.6 | 105.8 | 108.5 | 111.6 | 112.1 | 111.4 | 112.2 | 109.7 | 109.3 | 108.4 | 107.5 | 108.5 |
| 2018 | 103.6 | 104.6 | 107.4 | 108.8 | 112.9 | 113.3 | 112.9 | 113.2 | 109.6 | 109.0 | 107.7 | 107.9 | 109.2 |
| 2019 | 106.7 | 107.7 | 109.5 | 111.3 | 114.3 | 114.4 | 113.8 | 113.6 | 112.0 | 111.8 | 109.7 | 108.2 | 111.1 |
| **Other Services** | | | | | | | | | | | | | |
| 2011 | 39.6 | 39.7 | 40.3 | 40.4 | 40.6 | 41.2 | 41.6 | 41.5 | 41.0 | 40.8 | 40.9 | 40.8 | 40.7 |
| 2012 | 40.6 | 41.0 | 41.2 | 41.3 | 41.7 | 42.4 | 42.4 | 42.4 | 41.7 | 41.9 | 41.9 | 41.8 | 41.7 |
| 2013 | 41.6 | 42.1 | 42.7 | 42.0 | 42.6 | 43.8 | 43.7 | 43.5 | 43.0 | 43.3 | 43.5 | 43.8 | 43.0 |
| 2014 | 43.2 | 43.7 | 44.2 | 44.1 | 44.8 | 45.6 | 45.4 | 44.9 | 44.4 | 44.2 | 44.3 | 44.3 | 44.4 |
| 2015 | 44.0 | 44.3 | 44.7 | 44.0 | 44.6 | 45.3 | 45.4 | 45.1 | 44.6 | 44.4 | 44.8 | 44.7 | 44.7 |
| 2016 | 44.2 | 44.5 | 44.9 | 45.2 | 45.6 | 46.2 | 46.2 | 45.9 | 45.5 | 45.3 | 45.4 | 45.3 | 45.4 |
| 2017 | 44.7 | 44.9 | 45.4 | 45.5 | 46.1 | 46.8 | 46.4 | 45.7 | 45.3 | 45.4 | 45.5 | 45.6 | 45.6 |
| 2018 | 44.9 | 45.4 | 45.7 | 46.0 | 46.5 | 47.5 | 47.2 | 46.7 | 46.2 | 46.2 | 46.3 | 46.0 | 46.2 |
| 2019 | 46.2 | 46.2 | 46.6 | 46.6 | 47.1 | 47.5 | 47.7 | 47.1 | 47.1 | 46.1 | 45.9 | 45.4 | 46.6 |
| **Government** | | | | | | | | | | | | | |
| 2011 | 129.4 | 130.2 | 130.6 | 130.6 | 131.0 | 121.9 | 117.0 | 123.4 | 128.1 | 129.1 | 129.2 | 129.6 | 127.5 |
| 2012 | 127.3 | 129.8 | 129.0 | 128.3 | 129.4 | 120.2 | 114.8 | 125.0 | 128.9 | 128.7 | 128.8 | 128.5 | 126.6 |
| 2013 | 124.9 | 128.7 | 129.2 | 128.7 | 129.0 | 119.9 | 112.1 | 126.1 | 128.4 | 128.6 | 129.8 | 129.6 | 126.3 |
| 2014 | 126.5 | 129.5 | 130.3 | 129.8 | 130.5 | 124.5 | 116.0 | 127.8 | 129.1 | 128.8 | 130.0 | 130.7 | 127.8 |
| 2015 | 128.9 | 130.0 | 130.4 | 130.2 | 131.0 | 124.7 | 117.3 | 128.2 | 131.1 | 129.9 | 131.3 | 132.2 | 128.8 |
| 2016 | 130.6 | 132.0 | 133.0 | 130.3 | 131.1 | 122.5 | 119.3 | 130.3 | 132.6 | 130.7 | 132.5 | 132.6 | 129.8 |
| 2017 | 131.6 | 132.4 | 132.9 | 132.0 | 133.4 | 126.4 | 119.7 | 131.6 | 133.8 | 132.9 | 134.7 | 134.9 | 131.4 |
| 2018 | 132.5 | 133.9 | 134.1 | 133.8 | 135.1 | 128.6 | 121.1 | 133.3 | 134.7 | 135.1 | 135.7 | 135.7 | 132.8 |
| 2019 | 135.2 | 135.6 | 136.0 | 133.8 | 135.4 | 129.0 | 122.2 | 134.5 | 136.6 | 136.6 | 137.4 | 137.3 | 134.1 |

# Employment by Industry: Cleveland-Elyria, OH, 2011–2019

(Numbers in thousands, not seasonally adjusted)

| Industry and year | January | February | March | April | May | June | July | August | September | October | November | December | Annual average |
|---|---|---|---|---|---|---|---|---|---|---|---|---|---|
| **Total Nonfarm** | | | | | | | | | | | | | |
| 2011 | 971.4 | 977.5 | 981.8 | 998.8 | 1,006.3 | 1,007.9 | 1,008.9 | 1,011.8 | 1,007.4 | 1,009.9 | 1,016.5 | 1,015.1 | 1,001.1 |
| 2012 | 987.1 | 994.5 | 1,002.9 | 1,016.2 | 1,027.3 | 1,032.9 | 1,025.8 | 1,025.5 | 1,023.8 | 1,031.4 | 1,034.9 | 1,032.0 | 1,019.5 |
| 2013 | 1,002.2 | 1,004.9 | 1,009.9 | 1,023.9 | 1,037.2 | 1,042.7 | 1,033.4 | 1,040.0 | 1,032.8 | 1,040.5 | 1,044.7 | 1,043.5 | 1,029.6 |
| 2014 | 1,011.0 | 1,012.1 | 1,017.7 | 1,031.5 | 1,044.9 | 1,048.8 | 1,039.6 | 1,044.8 | 1,039.3 | 1,047.9 | 1,050.4 | 1,051.3 | 1,036.6 |
| 2015 | 1,018.5 | 1,022.1 | 1,024.5 | 1,041.6 | 1,056.8 | 1,058.6 | 1,052.8 | 1,054.3 | 1,045.9 | 1,055.3 | 1,056.6 | 1,057.3 | 1,045.4 |
| 2016 | 1,033.6 | 1,036.0 | 1,040.8 | 1,053.3 | 1,063.6 | 1,064.2 | 1,063.6 | 1,064.3 | 1,056.1 | 1,062.6 | 1,065.0 | 1,060.6 | 1,055.3 |
| 2017 | 1,033.5 | 1,037.9 | 1,041.9 | 1,055.0 | 1,066.8 | 1,073.1 | 1,065.6 | 1,067.4 | 1,061.3 | 1,068.6 | 1,068.0 | 1,065.7 | 1,058.7 |
| 2018 | 1,042.2 | 1,047.4 | 1,051.6 | 1,063.4 | 1,076.3 | 1,083.5 | 1,079.4 | 1,081.8 | 1,072.1 | 1,081.2 | 1,083.1 | 1,080.2 | 1,070.2 |
| 2019 | 1,059.6 | 1,063.0 | 1,065.3 | 1,076.6 | 1,088.2 | 1,092.8 | 1,089.2 | 1,089.2 | 1,080.1 | 1,079.3 | 1,085.5 | 1,082.0 | 1,079.2 |
| **Total Private** | | | | | | | | | | | | | |
| 2011 | 838.8 | 840.5 | 844.3 | 860.4 | 868.2 | 870.6 | 877.4 | 881.7 | 874.1 | 875.1 | 880.3 | 879.2 | 865.9 |
| 2012 | 855.2 | 858.7 | 866.5 | 879.5 | 889.4 | 896.2 | 894.2 | 895.3 | 889.7 | 895.9 | 899.4 | 897.3 | 884.8 |
| 2013 | 868.9 | 870.8 | 876.2 | 889.3 | 900.8 | 908.1 | 904.8 | 909.7 | 900.4 | 906.2 | 909.7 | 908.8 | 896.1 |
| 2014 | 879.0 | 878.6 | 884.2 | 897.1 | 908.4 | 913.7 | 910.2 | 913.8 | 906.0 | 912.3 | 914.7 | 916.2 | 902.9 |
| 2015 | 885.7 | 888.0 | 891.8 | 906.4 | 919.5 | 922.2 | 922.6 | 921.9 | 912.1 | 918.7 | 920.0 | 920.7 | 910.8 |
| 2016 | 899.3 | 900.0 | 904.8 | 916.0 | 924.7 | 926.7 | 930.3 | 929.7 | 921.3 | 924.9 | 927.0 | 923.3 | 919.0 |
| 2017 | 898.1 | 901.0 | 905.3 | 917.8 | 928.0 | 934.9 | 933.1 | 933.1 | 925.5 | 930.4 | 929.9 | 928.3 | 922.1 |
| 2018 | 906.6 | 909.8 | 913.8 | 925.2 | 936.1 | 944.4 | 945.6 | 946.7 | 936.0 | 941.7 | 943.4 | 942.0 | 932.6 |
| 2019 | 923.1 | 924.6 | 926.6 | 937.2 | 946.4 | 952.9 | 953.3 | 953.7 | 943.9 | 941.5 | 946.9 | 944.8 | 941.2 |
| **Goods Producing** | | | | | | | | | | | | | |
| 2011 | 145.2 | 145.2 | 146.4 | 149.8 | 152.0 | 152.9 | 156.3 | 158.4 | 156.2 | 156.8 | 158.4 | 157.3 | 152.9 |
| 2012 | 150.4 | 151.6 | 153.4 | 156.1 | 158.1 | 160.2 | 159.4 | 160.0 | 159.4 | 158.5 | 159.5 | 158.5 | 157.1 |
| 2013 | 153.6 | 153.4 | 154.3 | 156.4 | 158.8 | 160.6 | 158.4 | 161.6 | 160.8 | 160.9 | 161.7 | 158.7 | 158.3 |
| 2014 | 154.1 | 153.6 | 155.2 | 157.6 | 160.2 | 162.4 | 161.0 | 163.3 | 162.6 | 163.0 | 162.9 | 161.6 | 159.8 |
| 2015 | 156.3 | 156.2 | 157.3 | 160.3 | 162.2 | 163.4 | 163.1 | 162.7 | 161.0 | 160.8 | 160.2 | 158.9 | 160.2 |
| 2016 | 155.3 | 154.3 | 155.1 | 157.0 | 158.2 | 159.1 | 159.1 | 158.9 | 157.3 | 157.4 | 157.3 | 155.3 | 157.0 |
| 2017 | 152.0 | 152.2 | 153.8 | 155.7 | 158.0 | 160.5 | 161.1 | 161.0 | 159.9 | 160.2 | 160.2 | 158.7 | 157.8 |
| 2018 | 155.3 | 156.2 | 157.2 | 159.5 | 162.6 | 165.2 | 165.6 | 165.7 | 164.1 | 164.3 | 163.7 | 162.6 | 161.8 |
| 2019 | 159.0 | 158.8 | 159.8 | 162.1 | 163.7 | 165.5 | 165.4 | 165.2 | 163.9 | 162.6 | 162.9 | 161.0 | 162.5 |
| **Service-Providing** | | | | | | | | | | | | | |
| 2011 | 826.2 | 832.3 | 835.4 | 849.0 | 854.3 | 855.0 | 852.6 | 853.4 | 851.2 | 853.1 | 858.1 | 857.8 | 848.2 |
| 2012 | 836.7 | 842.9 | 849.5 | 860.1 | 869.2 | 872.7 | 866.4 | 865.5 | 864.4 | 872.9 | 875.4 | 873.5 | 862.4 |
| 2013 | 848.6 | 851.5 | 855.6 | 867.5 | 878.4 | 882.1 | 875.0 | 878.4 | 872.0 | 879.6 | 883.0 | 884.8 | 871.4 |
| 2014 | 856.9 | 858.5 | 862.5 | 873.9 | 884.7 | 886.4 | 878.6 | 881.5 | 876.7 | 884.9 | 887.5 | 889.7 | 876.8 |
| 2015 | 862.2 | 865.9 | 867.2 | 881.3 | 894.6 | 895.2 | 889.7 | 891.6 | 884.9 | 894.5 | 896.4 | 898.4 | 885.2 |
| 2016 | 878.3 | 881.7 | 885.7 | 896.3 | 905.4 | 905.1 | 904.5 | 905.4 | 898.8 | 905.2 | 907.7 | 905.3 | 898.3 |
| 2017 | 881.5 | 885.7 | 888.1 | 899.3 | 908.8 | 912.6 | 904.5 | 906.4 | 901.4 | 908.4 | 907.8 | 907.0 | 901.0 |
| 2018 | 886.9 | 891.2 | 894.4 | 903.9 | 913.7 | 918.3 | 913.8 | 916.1 | 908.0 | 916.9 | 919.4 | 917.6 | 908.4 |
| 2019 | 900.6 | 904.2 | 905.5 | 914.5 | 924.5 | 927.3 | 923.8 | 924.0 | 916.2 | 916.7 | 922.6 | 921.0 | 916.7 |
| **Mining, Logging, and Construction** | | | | | | | | | | | | | |
| 2011 | 27.6 | 27.2 | 28.1 | 30.3 | 32.1 | 33.6 | 35.8 | 36.3 | 36.2 | 36.1 | 35.7 | 34.4 | 32.8 |
| 2012 | 30.0 | 29.3 | 30.4 | 32.6 | 34.4 | 35.4 | 36.1 | 35.7 | 35.0 | 35.5 | 35.2 | 33.9 | 33.6 |
| 2013 | 30.0 | 29.7 | 30.4 | 32.4 | 34.7 | 35.8 | 36.2 | 36.9 | 36.9 | 38.0 | 37.2 | 34.1 | 34.4 |
| 2014 | 30.3 | 30.2 | 31.5 | 33.9 | 36.1 | 37.4 | 38.0 | 38.4 | 38.1 | 38.4 | 37.7 | 35.9 | 35.5 |
| 2015 | 31.7 | 31.3 | 32.3 | 35.4 | 37.1 | 37.9 | 38.2 | 38.2 | 37.6 | 37.7 | 37.3 | 35.7 | 35.9 |
| 2016 | 32.9 | 32.5 | 33.6 | 35.7 | 36.9 | 37.7 | 37.9 | 37.8 | 37.2 | 37.2 | 36.7 | 34.6 | 35.9 |
| 2017 | 31.9 | 32.1 | 33.2 | 35.3 | 37.3 | 38.8 | 39.1 | 39.2 | 38.8 | 39.0 | 38.2 | 36.3 | 36.6 |
| 2018 | 33.3 | 33.6 | 34.5 | 36.6 | 39.1 | 40.6 | 41.1 | 41.0 | 40.5 | 40.5 | 39.4 | 37.8 | 38.2 |
| 2019 | 35.1 | 34.8 | 35.7 | 38.3 | 39.9 | 41.0 | 41.6 | 41.6 | 41.3 | 40.8 | 40.0 | 38.2 | 39.0 |
| **Manufacturing** | | | | | | | | | | | | | |
| 2011 | 117.6 | 118.0 | 118.3 | 119.5 | 119.9 | 119.3 | 120.5 | 122.1 | 120.0 | 120.7 | 122.7 | 122.9 | 120.1 |
| 2012 | 120.4 | 122.3 | 123.0 | 123.5 | 123.7 | 124.8 | 123.3 | 124.3 | 124.4 | 123.0 | 124.3 | 124.6 | 123.5 |
| 2013 | 123.6 | 123.7 | 123.9 | 124.0 | 124.1 | 124.8 | 122.2 | 124.7 | 123.9 | 122.9 | 124.5 | 124.6 | 123.9 |
| 2014 | 123.8 | 123.4 | 123.7 | 123.7 | 124.1 | 125.0 | 123.0 | 124.9 | 124.5 | 124.6 | 125.2 | 125.7 | 124.3 |
| 2015 | 124.6 | 124.9 | 125.0 | 124.9 | 125.1 | 125.5 | 124.9 | 124.5 | 123.4 | 123.1 | 122.9 | 123.2 | 124.3 |
| 2016 | 122.4 | 121.8 | 121.5 | 121.3 | 121.3 | 121.4 | 121.2 | 121.1 | 120.1 | 120.2 | 120.6 | 120.7 | 121.1 |
| 2017 | 120.1 | 120.1 | 120.6 | 120.4 | 120.7 | 121.7 | 122.0 | 121.8 | 121.1 | 121.2 | 122.0 | 122.4 | 121.2 |
| 2018 | 122.0 | 122.6 | 122.7 | 122.9 | 123.5 | 124.6 | 124.5 | 124.7 | 123.6 | 123.8 | 124.3 | 124.8 | 123.7 |
| 2019 | 123.9 | 124.0 | 124.1 | 123.8 | 123.8 | 124.5 | 123.8 | 123.6 | 122.6 | 121.8 | 122.9 | 122.8 | 123.5 |

## Employment by Industry: Cleveland-Elyria, OH, 2011–2019—*Continued*

(Numbers in thousands, not seasonally adjusted)

| Industry and year | January | February | March | April | May | June | July | August | September | October | November | December | Annual average |
|---|---|---|---|---|---|---|---|---|---|---|---|---|---|
| **Trade, Transportation, and Utilities** | | | | | | | | | | | | | |
| 2011 | 174.0 | 172.9 | 173.4 | 175.6 | 176.8 | 177.6 | 177.7 | 178.2 | 176.4 | 178.3 | 181.9 | 184.5 | 177.3 |
| 2012 | 177.8 | 176.4 | 177.8 | 179.0 | 181.1 | 181.7 | 181.1 | 180.7 | 179.7 | 181.5 | 185.5 | 187.1 | 180.8 |
| 2013 | 179.1 | 177.2 | 177.8 | 179.5 | 181.9 | 182.8 | 181.7 | 182.0 | 180.4 | 182.1 | 186.5 | 188.5 | 181.6 |
| 2014 | 180.3 | 178.7 | 178.8 | 180.7 | 183.1 | 183.8 | 182.4 | 182.9 | 180.7 | 182.7 | 186.7 | 189.2 | 182.5 |
| 2015 | 181.6 | 179.6 | 180.2 | 182.1 | 184.4 | 185.0 | 184.4 | 184.7 | 182.6 | 184.2 | 188.8 | 190.8 | 184.0 |
| 2016 | 184.5 | 182.9 | 183.4 | 183.6 | 185.2 | 185.3 | 184.7 | 185.1 | 182.4 | 183.3 | 186.8 | 189.0 | 184.7 |
| 2017 | 181.4 | 179.4 | 179.5 | 180.8 | 182.2 | 182.9 | 182.0 | 182.3 | 180.4 | 181.9 | 185.9 | 187.6 | 182.2 |
| 2018 | 180.4 | 178.6 | 178.9 | 179.7 | 181.7 | 182.4 | 182.1 | 182.4 | 180.4 | 183.1 | 187.2 | 189.6 | 182.2 |
| 2019 | 184.2 | 181.8 | 181.9 | 182.3 | 184.6 | 185.4 | 186.0 | 186.3 | 184.5 | 184.3 | 188.9 | 190.4 | 185.1 |
| **Wholesale Trade** | | | | | | | | | | | | | |
| 2011 | 47.1 | 47.1 | 47.1 | 47.5 | 47.8 | 48.0 | 48.3 | 48.3 | 47.9 | 48.3 | 48.4 | 48.7 | 47.9 |
| 2012 | 48.6 | 48.6 | 48.8 | 49.0 | 49.4 | 49.7 | 49.7 | 49.6 | 49.3 | 49.5 | 49.6 | 49.7 | 49.3 |
| 2013 | 48.9 | 48.8 | 49.0 | 49.2 | 49.5 | 49.8 | 49.5 | 49.5 | 49.2 | 49.9 | 50.1 | 50.3 | 49.5 |
| 2014 | 49.6 | 49.5 | 49.7 | 49.8 | 50.4 | 50.6 | 50.7 | 50.8 | 50.4 | 50.7 | 50.8 | 51.2 | 50.4 |
| 2015 | 50.3 | 50.4 | 50.6 | 50.6 | 50.9 | 51.2 | 51.3 | 51.2 | 50.7 | 50.9 | 51.1 | 51.0 | 50.9 |
| 2016 | 51.2 | 51.2 | 51.4 | 51.3 | 51.5 | 51.7 | 51.7 | 51.6 | 51.1 | 51.2 | 51.3 | 51.5 | 51.4 |
| 2017 | 50.8 | 50.6 | 50.6 | 50.7 | 51.0 | 51.5 | 51.6 | 51.6 | 51.3 | 51.5 | 51.6 | 51.8 | 51.2 |
| 2018 | 51.4 | 51.5 | 51.6 | 51.9 | 52.2 | 52.7 | 53.1 | 52.9 | 52.6 | 53.0 | 53.0 | 53.3 | 52.4 |
| 2019 | 52.6 | 52.6 | 52.6 | 52.6 | 53.1 | 53.3 | 53.4 | 53.1 | 52.7 | 52.5 | 53.0 | 53.0 | 52.9 |
| **Retail Trade** | | | | | | | | | | | | | |
| 2011 | 98.3 | 97.3 | 97.7 | 99.2 | 99.9 | 100.4 | 100.3 | 100.6 | 99.1 | 100.4 | 103.9 | 105.6 | 100.2 |
| 2012 | 100.2 | 98.7 | 99.8 | 100.5 | 101.8 | 102.0 | 101.4 | 100.8 | 100.1 | 101.6 | 105.0 | 106.0 | 101.5 |
| 2013 | 100.4 | 98.7 | 99.2 | 100.2 | 101.9 | 102.4 | 102.1 | 102.1 | 100.7 | 101.7 | 105.3 | 106.5 | 101.8 |
| 2014 | 100.3 | 99.0 | 99.1 | 100.4 | 101.8 | 102.3 | 101.4 | 101.6 | 99.9 | 101.4 | 104.7 | 105.9 | 101.5 |
| 2015 | 100.5 | 98.9 | 99.4 | 100.9 | 102.4 | 102.7 | 102.2 | 102.4 | 100.8 | 102.1 | 105.7 | 107.2 | 102.1 |
| 2016 | 102.3 | 100.9 | 101.3 | 101.4 | 102.5 | 102.5 | 102.1 | 102.3 | 100.1 | 101.1 | 104.1 | 105.6 | 102.2 |
| 2017 | 100.3 | 98.4 | 98.7 | 99.7 | 100.6 | 100.8 | 100.0 | 100.1 | 98.4 | 99.7 | 103.2 | 104.2 | 100.3 |
| 2018 | 99.1 | 97.2 | 97.5 | 97.8 | 99.1 | 99.2 | 98.8 | 98.9 | 97.1 | 97.9 | 101.0 | 102.0 | 98.8 |
| 2019 | 98.1 | 95.9 | 96.4 | 97.1 | 98.1 | 98.3 | 98.2 | 98.2 | 96.4 | 96.4 | 99.3 | 100.1 | 97.7 |
| **Transportation and Utilities** | | | | | | | | | | | | | |
| 2011 | 28.6 | 28.5 | 28.6 | 28.9 | 29.1 | 29.2 | 29.1 | 29.3 | 29.4 | 29.6 | 29.6 | 30.2 | 29.2 |
| 2012 | 29.0 | 29.1 | 29.2 | 29.5 | 29.9 | 30.0 | 30.0 | 30.3 | 30.3 | 30.4 | 30.9 | 31.4 | 30.0 |
| 2013 | 29.8 | 29.7 | 29.6 | 30.1 | 30.5 | 30.6 | 30.1 | 30.4 | 30.5 | 30.5 | 31.1 | 31.7 | 30.4 |
| 2014 | 30.4 | 30.2 | 30.0 | 30.5 | 30.9 | 30.9 | 30.3 | 30.5 | 30.4 | 30.6 | 31.2 | 32.1 | 30.7 |
| 2015 | 30.8 | 30.3 | 30.2 | 30.6 | 31.1 | 31.1 | 30.9 | 31.1 | 31.1 | 31.2 | 32.0 | 32.6 | 31.1 |
| 2016 | 31.0 | 30.8 | 30.7 | 30.9 | 31.2 | 31.1 | 30.9 | 31.2 | 31.2 | 31.0 | 31.4 | 31.9 | 31.1 |
| 2017 | 30.3 | 30.4 | 30.2 | 30.4 | 30.6 | 30.6 | 30.4 | 30.6 | 30.7 | 30.7 | 31.1 | 31.6 | 30.6 |
| 2018 | 29.9 | 29.9 | 29.8 | 30.0 | 30.4 | 30.5 | 30.2 | 30.6 | 30.7 | 32.2 | 33.2 | 34.3 | 31.0 |
| 2019 | 33.5 | 33.3 | 32.9 | 32.6 | 33.4 | 33.8 | 34.4 | 35.0 | 35.4 | 35.4 | 36.6 | 37.3 | 34.5 |
| **Information** | | | | | | | | | | | | | |
| 2011 | 15.4 | 15.3 | 15.2 | 15.3 | 15.4 | 15.4 | 15.5 | 15.5 | 15.5 | 15.4 | 15.5 | 15.5 | 15.4 |
| 2012 | 15.5 | 15.3 | 15.3 | 15.3 | 15.3 | 15.4 | 15.5 | 15.4 | 15.2 | 15.2 | 15.3 | 15.2 | 15.3 |
| 2013 | 14.9 | 15.0 | 15.0 | 15.0 | 15.1 | 15.3 | 15.4 | 15.3 | 15.2 | 15.1 | 15.0 | 15.3 | 15.1 |
| 2014 | 14.7 | 14.6 | 14.6 | 14.6 | 14.6 | 14.6 | 14.7 | 14.6 | 14.5 | 14.5 | 14.4 | 14.6 | 14.6 |
| 2015 | 14.3 | 14.3 | 14.3 | 14.4 | 14.3 | 14.3 | 14.4 | 14.3 | 14.1 | 14.1 | 14.2 | 14.3 | 14.3 |
| 2016 | 14.0 | 14.0 | 14.0 | 14.1 | 14.1 | 14.2 | 14.2 | 14.3 | 14.1 | 14.0 | 14.2 | 14.0 | 14.1 |
| 2017 | 13.9 | 13.8 | 13.8 | 13.9 | 13.9 | 14.1 | 14.0 | 14.1 | 14.0 | 13.8 | 13.9 | 13.9 | 13.9 |
| 2018 | 13.9 | 13.8 | 13.8 | 13.6 | 13.9 | 14.2 | 13.8 | 13.7 | 13.6 | 13.5 | 13.6 | 13.6 | 13.8 |
| 2019 | 13.5 | 13.7 | 13.5 | 13.2 | 13.4 | 13.5 | 13.5 | 13.4 | 13.2 | 13.2 | 13.2 | 13.3 | 13.4 |
| **Financial Activities** | | | | | | | | | | | | | |
| 2011 | 64.4 | 64.3 | 64.0 | 64.1 | 63.9 | 63.7 | 63.5 | 63.2 | 62.7 | 62.5 | 62.4 | 62.2 | 63.4 |
| 2012 | 61.8 | 61.8 | 61.9 | 62.2 | 62.5 | 62.7 | 63.1 | 63.1 | 62.6 | 62.9 | 63.0 | 63.0 | 62.6 |
| 2013 | 62.4 | 62.5 | 62.4 | 63.1 | 63.2 | 63.9 | 64.3 | 64.7 | 64.2 | 64.6 | 64.8 | 64.9 | 63.8 |
| 2014 | 64.0 | 64.3 | 64.5 | 64.5 | 64.7 | 65.2 | 64.9 | 64.9 | 64.2 | 64.5 | 64.8 | 64.9 | 64.6 |
| 2015 | 64.3 | 64.5 | 64.5 | 65.0 | 65.1 | 65.7 | 65.5 | 65.3 | 64.7 | 65.0 | 65.1 | 64.8 | 65.0 |
| 2016 | 64.5 | 64.5 | 64.4 | 64.8 | 65.0 | 65.5 | 66.0 | 66.0 | 65.6 | 66.0 | 66.2 | 66.3 | 65.4 |
| 2017 | 65.9 | 66.1 | 66.1 | 66.2 | 66.5 | 67.1 | 67.3 | 67.3 | 66.8 | 67.0 | 67.0 | 66.8 | 66.7 |
| 2018 | 66.6 | 66.9 | 66.6 | 66.8 | 67.2 | 67.8 | 68.0 | 68.0 | 67.1 | 67.3 | 67.4 | 67.2 | 67.2 |
| 2019 | 67.1 | 67.1 | 67.0 | 67.2 | 67.4 | 68.1 | 68.2 | 68.1 | 67.5 | 67.4 | 66.9 | 67.1 | 67.4 |

# Employment by Industry: Cleveland-Elyria, OH, 2011–2019—*Continued*

(Numbers in thousands, not seasonally adjusted)

| Industry and year | January | February | March | April | May | June | July | August | September | October | November | December | Annual average |
|---|---|---|---|---|---|---|---|---|---|---|---|---|---|
| **Professional and Business Services** | | | | | | | | | | | | | |
| 2011 | 132.9 | 134.3 | 135.4 | 140.3 | 141.0 | 142.3 | 144.9 | 146.2 | 144.8 | 144.9 | 144.8 | 143.7 | 141.3 |
| 2012 | 139.3 | 140.5 | 141.9 | 144.2 | 145.5 | 146.9 | 147.9 | 148.4 | 146.2 | 149.1 | 149.0 | 146.3 | 145.4 |
| 2013 | 140.2 | 141.7 | 143.3 | 147.3 | 149.3 | 151.2 | 150.8 | 152.5 | 149.1 | 151.7 | 151.4 | 150.6 | 148.3 |
| 2014 | 145.1 | 145.8 | 146.6 | 150.5 | 151.9 | 152.7 | 152.8 | 154.2 | 151.7 | 153.1 | 152.9 | 151.3 | 150.7 |
| 2015 | 145.8 | 146.6 | 146.9 | 149.6 | 152.8 | 153.3 | 154.3 | 154.3 | 150.6 | 153.6 | 151.9 | 150.2 | 150.8 |
| 2016 | 147.3 | 147.6 | 148.3 | 152.8 | 153.9 | 155.2 | 157.0 | 156.6 | 155.0 | 155.6 | 155.0 | 152.5 | 153.1 |
| 2017 | 149.3 | 150.4 | 150.5 | 154.5 | 156.0 | 158.5 | 158.3 | 159.0 | 156.6 | 158.1 | 156.5 | 154.5 | 155.2 |
| 2018 | 152.5 | 153.6 | 154.1 | 157.7 | 158.6 | 160.9 | 162.6 | 163.4 | 160.0 | 161.7 | 161.5 | 158.7 | 158.8 |
| 2019 | 156.4 | 157.5 | 156.7 | 161.7 | 162.5 | 163.7 | 165.3 | 166.0 | 162.5 | 162.6 | 162.2 | 158.6 | 161.3 |
| **Education and Health Services** | | | | | | | | | | | | | |
| 2011 | 185.2 | 187.0 | 186.8 | 188.2 | 188.4 | 185.7 | 184.9 | 184.9 | 187.5 | 189.3 | 189.8 | 189.6 | 187.3 |
| 2012 | 187.5 | 190.6 | 190.7 | 192.2 | 192.8 | 191.3 | 189.2 | 189.5 | 193.0 | 195.7 | 195.7 | 194.8 | 191.9 |
| 2013 | 191.5 | 193.9 | 193.9 | 193.8 | 193.3 | 192.6 | 192.1 | 192.4 | 193.7 | 195.9 | 196.8 | 196.7 | 193.9 |
| 2014 | 191.4 | 192.7 | 193.3 | 194.0 | 193.7 | 192.4 | 192.0 | 191.7 | 194.0 | 197.2 | 197.8 | 197.8 | 194.0 |
| 2015 | 193.1 | 195.5 | 195.7 | 197.1 | 197.4 | 195.6 | 195.6 | 195.4 | 197.9 | 200.7 | 201.1 | 202.2 | 197.3 |
| 2016 | 198.0 | 200.8 | 201.6 | 201.9 | 201.6 | 199.2 | 199.8 | 200.0 | 202.9 | 204.3 | 204.7 | 204.4 | 201.6 |
| 2017 | 198.9 | 201.6 | 202.2 | 203.0 | 203.1 | 201.4 | 200.2 | 200.2 | 202.7 | 204.2 | 204.6 | 204.2 | 202.2 |
| 2018 | 200.5 | 203.2 | 203.3 | 204.1 | 203.7 | 202.6 | 202.1 | 202.6 | 204.6 | 206.4 | 206.3 | 206.2 | 203.8 |
| 2019 | 203.3 | 206.4 | 206.4 | 206.8 | 206.5 | 205.4 | 203.5 | 204.2 | 206.6 | 207.4 | 208.1 | 207.5 | 206.0 |
| **Leisure and Hospitality** | | | | | | | | | | | | | |
| 2011 | 80.8 | 80.7 | 82.3 | 86.3 | 89.9 | 92.2 | 93.4 | 94.3 | 90.6 | 87.4 | 87.2 | 86.3 | 87.6 |
| 2012 | 83.2 | 82.7 | 85.4 | 90.4 | 93.8 | 97.2 | 97.3 | 97.7 | 93.7 | 93.2 | 91.7 | 92.6 | 91.6 |
| 2013 | 87.9 | 88.0 | 90.3 | 94.5 | 99.3 | 101.7 | 102.2 | 101.2 | 97.6 | 96.3 | 93.9 | 94.5 | 95.6 |
| 2014 | 90.2 | 89.7 | 91.9 | 95.7 | 100.2 | 102.6 | 102.5 | 103.3 | 99.0 | 97.6 | 95.6 | 96.9 | 97.0 |
| 2015 | 91.4 | 92.2 | 93.8 | 98.2 | 103.2 | 104.6 | 105.2 | 105.2 | 101.7 | 100.7 | 99.1 | 99.6 | 99.6 |
| 2016 | 95.9 | 96.1 | 98.1 | 101.7 | 106.3 | 107.8 | 108.8 | 108.5 | 104.3 | 104.4 | 103.1 | 102.2 | 103.1 |
| 2017 | 97.5 | 98.3 | 100.1 | 104.3 | 108.7 | 110.5 | 110.3 | 109.5 | 106.1 | 105.9 | 102.4 | 103.0 | 104.7 |
| 2018 | 98.3 | 98.2 | 100.5 | 104.1 | 108.5 | 111.2 | 111.2 | 110.8 | 106.7 | 105.9 | 104.0 | 104.3 | 105.3 |
| 2019 | 100.2 | 99.8 | 101.7 | 104.1 | 108.3 | 110.9 | 111.1 | 110.5 | 106.1 | 105.0 | 104.4 | 105.8 | 105.7 |
| **Other Services** | | | | | | | | | | | | | |
| 2011 | 40.9 | 40.8 | 40.8 | 40.8 | 40.8 | 40.8 | 41.2 | 41.0 | 40.4 | 40.5 | 40.3 | 40.1 | 40.7 |
| 2012 | 39.7 | 39.8 | 40.1 | 40.1 | 40.3 | 40.8 | 40.7 | 40.5 | 39.9 | 39.8 | 39.7 | 39.8 | 40.1 |
| 2013 | 39.3 | 39.1 | 39.2 | 39.7 | 39.9 | 40.0 | 39.9 | 40.0 | 39.4 | 39.6 | 39.6 | 39.6 | 39.6 |
| 2014 | 39.2 | 39.2 | 39.3 | 39.5 | 40.0 | 40.0 | 39.9 | 39.9 | 39.3 | 39.7 | 39.6 | 39.9 | 39.6 |
| 2015 | 38.9 | 39.1 | 39.1 | 39.7 | 40.1 | 40.3 | 40.1 | 40.0 | 39.5 | 39.6 | 39.6 | 39.9 | 39.7 |
| 2016 | 39.8 | 39.8 | 39.9 | 40.1 | 40.4 | 40.4 | 40.7 | 40.3 | 39.7 | 39.9 | 39.7 | 39.6 | 40.0 |
| 2017 | 39.2 | 39.2 | 39.3 | 39.4 | 39.6 | 39.9 | 39.9 | 39.7 | 39.0 | 39.3 | 39.4 | 39.6 | 39.5 |
| 2018 | 39.1 | 39.3 | 39.4 | 39.7 | 39.9 | 40.1 | 40.2 | 40.1 | 39.5 | 39.5 | 39.7 | 39.8 | 39.7 |
| 2019 | 39.4 | 39.5 | 39.6 | 39.8 | 40.0 | 40.4 | 40.3 | 40.0 | 39.6 | 39.0 | 40.3 | 41.1 | 39.9 |
| **Government** | | | | | | | | | | | | | |
| 2011 | 132.6 | 137.0 | 137.5 | 138.4 | 138.1 | 137.3 | 131.5 | 130.1 | 133.3 | 134.8 | 136.2 | 135.9 | 135.2 |
| 2012 | 131.9 | 135.8 | 136.4 | 136.7 | 137.9 | 136.7 | 131.6 | 130.2 | 134.1 | 135.5 | 135.5 | 134.7 | 134.8 |
| 2013 | 133.3 | 134.1 | 133.7 | 134.6 | 136.4 | 134.6 | 128.6 | 130.3 | 132.4 | 134.3 | 135.0 | 134.7 | 133.5 |
| 2014 | 132.0 | 133.5 | 133.5 | 134.4 | 136.5 | 135.1 | 129.4 | 131.0 | 133.3 | 135.6 | 135.7 | 135.1 | 133.8 |
| 2015 | 132.8 | 134.1 | 132.7 | 135.2 | 137.3 | 136.4 | 130.2 | 132.4 | 133.8 | 136.6 | 136.6 | 136.6 | 134.6 |
| 2016 | 134.3 | 136.0 | 136.0 | 137.3 | 138.9 | 137.5 | 133.3 | 134.6 | 134.8 | 137.7 | 138.0 | 137.3 | 136.3 |
| 2017 | 135.4 | 136.9 | 136.6 | 137.2 | 138.8 | 138.2 | 132.5 | 134.3 | 135.8 | 138.2 | 138.1 | 137.4 | 136.6 |
| 2018 | 135.6 | 137.6 | 137.8 | 138.2 | 140.2 | 139.1 | 133.8 | 135.1 | 136.1 | 139.5 | 139.7 | 138.2 | 137.6 |
| 2019 | 136.5 | 138.4 | 138.7 | 139.4 | 141.8 | 139.9 | 135.9 | 135.5 | 136.2 | 137.8 | 138.6 | 137.2 | 138.0 |

## Employment by Industry: San Jose-Sunnyvale-Santa Clara, CA, 2011–2019

(Numbers in thousands, not seasonally adjusted)

| Industry and year | January | February | March | April | May | June | July | August | September | October | November | December | Annual average |
|---|---|---|---|---|---|---|---|---|---|---|---|---|---|
| **Total Nonfarm** | | | | | | | | | | | | | |
| 2011 | 877.2 | 882.7 | 886.3 | 890.1 | 893.4 | 899.3 | 889.7 | 893.6 | 899.6 | 908.4 | 910.9 | 914.0 | 895.4 |
| 2012 | 901.4 | 907.7 | 914.3 | 923.0 | 928.9 | 937.3 | 926.8 | 932.4 | 936.1 | 946.0 | 951.7 | 954.5 | 930.0 |
| 2013 | 940.4 | 948.8 | 953.5 | 958.6 | 964.7 | 970.6 | 959.9 | 969.3 | 973.2 | 980.5 | 990.4 | 993.7 | 967.0 |
| 2014 | 981.7 | 989.4 | 994.4 | 1,000.0 | 1,005.8 | 1,011.6 | 1,002.2 | 1,011.5 | 1,014.9 | 1,022.7 | 1,027.5 | 1,030.1 | 1,007.7 |
| 2015 | 1,019.0 | 1,024.1 | 1,028.5 | 1,036.1 | 1,043.1 | 1,050.6 | 1,047.1 | 1,052.8 | 1,052.6 | 1,066.2 | 1,068.0 | 1,068.8 | 1,046.4 |
| 2016 | 1,058.4 | 1,064.3 | 1,064.9 | 1,076.1 | 1,080.7 | 1,086.8 | 1,082.7 | 1,085.5 | 1,082.9 | 1,090.9 | 1,096.7 | 1,098.2 | 1,080.7 |
| 2017 | 1,082.2 | 1,089.1 | 1,095.2 | 1,098.8 | 1,104.5 | 1,113.9 | 1,109.8 | 1,110.8 | 1,106.9 | 1,116.0 | 1,122.1 | 1,123.5 | 1,106.1 |
| 2018 | 1,102.0 | 1,111.1 | 1,114.2 | 1,117.6 | 1,123.8 | 1,134.2 | 1,128.1 | 1,130.8 | 1,126.4 | 1,138.7 | 1,145.7 | 1,145.9 | 1,126.5 |
| 2019 | 1,127.4 | 1,133.8 | 1,139.0 | 1,138.8 | 1,145.2 | 1,152.0 | 1,149.1 | 1,154.3 | 1,145.9 | 1,153.9 | 1,160.3 | 1,162.4 | 1,146.8 |
| **Total Private** | | | | | | | | | | | | | |
| 2011 | 782.6 | 787.4 | 790.6 | 793.6 | 796.6 | 803.1 | 808.4 | 811.2 | 808.7 | 814.6 | 816.5 | 819.6 | 802.7 |
| 2012 | 809.7 | 814.8 | 820.3 | 828.8 | 834.7 | 842.4 | 845.7 | 849.3 | 845.9 | 852.5 | 857.6 | 861.2 | 838.6 |
| 2013 | 847.8 | 854.8 | 860.4 | 864.3 | 869.0 | 876.2 | 881.3 | 885.9 | 881.9 | 886.4 | 895.0 | 899.5 | 875.2 |
| 2014 | 887.2 | 893.8 | 898.6 | 903.1 | 908.8 | 917.4 | 919.9 | 925.4 | 922.7 | 927.5 | 931.6 | 934.9 | 914.2 |
| 2015 | 925.2 | 929.5 | 934.4 | 941.3 | 947.9 | 955.9 | 963.4 | 965.5 | 961.0 | 971.4 | 972.5 | 973.6 | 953.5 |
| 2016 | 964.8 | 970.0 | 969.5 | 980.5 | 984.3 | 990.8 | 997.4 | 997.2 | 990.0 | 994.9 | 998.8 | 1,000.4 | 986.6 |
| 2017 | 986.4 | 993.3 | 998.4 | 1,001.3 | 1,006.5 | 1,017.2 | 1,021.8 | 1,021.2 | 1,012.9 | 1,018.4 | 1,023.5 | 1,025.5 | 1,010.5 |
| 2018 | 1,005.6 | 1,014.3 | 1,015.9 | 1,018.9 | 1,024.7 | 1,035.3 | 1,038.8 | 1,040.1 | 1,031.5 | 1,040.1 | 1,046.2 | 1,047.1 | 1,029.9 |
| 2019 | 1,031.5 | 1,037.4 | 1,039.9 | 1,039.6 | 1,045.4 | 1,053.6 | 1,058.8 | 1,061.5 | 1,049.8 | 1,055.2 | 1,060.5 | 1,062.8 | 1,049.7 |
| **Goods Producing** | | | | | | | | | | | | | |
| 2011 | 184.8 | 185.3 | 186.1 | 187.9 | 188.8 | 191.2 | 193.5 | 194.6 | 193.0 | 191.3 | 189.2 | 188.9 | 189.6 |
| 2012 | 188.1 | 188.4 | 189.1 | 190.9 | 193.1 | 196.4 | 197.1 | 197.9 | 196.4 | 195.0 | 194.3 | 194.0 | 193.4 |
| 2013 | 190.9 | 191.4 | 192.3 | 193.1 | 194.0 | 196.9 | 199.9 | 201.2 | 200.3 | 197.9 | 198.2 | 198.4 | 196.2 |
| 2014 | 196.2 | 197.2 | 198.0 | 198.2 | 200.0 | 202.6 | 204.1 | 206.6 | 206.1 | 203.6 | 203.8 | 204.1 | 201.7 |
| 2015 | 201.9 | 203.4 | 204.6 | 205.9 | 207.4 | 210.5 | 212.7 | 213.8 | 212.6 | 212.7 | 211.2 | 211.2 | 209.0 |
| 2016 | 210.1 | 211.0 | 211.1 | 213.3 | 214.3 | 216.8 | 220.1 | 220.1 | 218.2 | 216.5 | 216.0 | 215.5 | 215.3 |
| 2017 | 213.9 | 214.3 | 212.1 | 211.8 | 213.3 | 216.4 | 219.1 | 219.9 | 219.2 | 218.9 | 218.8 | 219.6 | 216.4 |
| 2018 | 217.2 | 218.6 | 218.9 | 219.8 | 220.4 | 223.4 | 224.9 | 225.3 | 224.4 | 224.8 | 224.2 | 224.2 | 222.2 |
| 2019 | 221.7 | 223.3 | 224.6 | 224.7 | 225.0 | 227.0 | 227.6 | 228.0 | 226.5 | 226.0 | 226.8 | 227.0 | 225.7 |
| **Service-Providing** | | | | | | | | | | | | | |
| 2011 | 692.4 | 697.4 | 700.2 | 702.2 | 704.6 | 708.1 | 696.2 | 699.0 | 706.6 | 717.1 | 721.7 | 725.1 | 705.9 |
| 2012 | 713.3 | 719.3 | 725.2 | 732.1 | 735.8 | 740.9 | 729.7 | 734.5 | 739.7 | 751.0 | 757.4 | 760.5 | 736.6 |
| 2013 | 749.5 | 757.4 | 761.2 | 765.5 | 770.7 | 773.7 | 760.0 | 768.1 | 772.9 | 782.6 | 792.2 | 795.3 | 770.8 |
| 2014 | 785.5 | 792.2 | 796.4 | 801.8 | 805.8 | 809.0 | 798.1 | 804.9 | 808.8 | 819.1 | 823.7 | 826.0 | 805.9 |
| 2015 | 817.1 | 820.7 | 823.9 | 830.2 | 835.7 | 840.1 | 834.4 | 839.0 | 840.0 | 853.5 | 856.8 | 857.6 | 837.4 |
| 2016 | 848.3 | 853.3 | 853.8 | 862.8 | 866.4 | 870.0 | 862.6 | 865.4 | 864.7 | 874.4 | 880.7 | 882.7 | 865.4 |
| 2017 | 868.3 | 874.8 | 883.1 | 887.0 | 891.2 | 897.5 | 890.7 | 890.9 | 887.7 | 897.1 | 903.3 | 903.9 | 889.6 |
| 2018 | 884.8 | 892.5 | 895.3 | 897.8 | 903.4 | 910.8 | 903.2 | 905.5 | 902.0 | 913.9 | 921.5 | 921.7 | 904.4 |
| 2019 | 905.7 | 910.5 | 914.4 | 914.1 | 920.2 | 925.0 | 921.5 | 926.3 | 919.4 | 927.9 | 933.5 | 935.4 | 921.2 |
| **Mining and Logging** | | | | | | | | | | | | | |
| 2011 | 0.2 | 0.2 | 0.2 | 0.2 | 0.2 | 0.2 | 0.2 | 0.2 | 0.2 | 0.2 | 0.2 | 0.2 | 0.2 |
| 2012 | 0.2 | 0.2 | 0.2 | 0.2 | 0.2 | 0.2 | 0.2 | 0.3 | 0.3 | 0.3 | 0.3 | 0.2 | 0.2 |
| 2013 | 0.2 | 0.2 | 0.2 | 0.2 | 0.3 | 0.3 | 0.3 | 0.3 | 0.3 | 0.3 | 0.3 | 0.3 | 0.3 |
| 2014 | 0.3 | 0.3 | 0.3 | 0.3 | 0.3 | 0.3 | 0.3 | 0.3 | 0.3 | 0.3 | 0.3 | 0.3 | 0.3 |
| 2015 | 0.2 | 0.2 | 0.2 | 0.2 | 0.2 | 0.2 | 0.3 | 0.3 | 0.3 | 0.2 | 0.2 | 0.2 | 0.2 |
| 2016 | 0.2 | 0.3 | 0.3 | 0.3 | 0.3 | 0.3 | 0.3 | 0.3 | 0.3 | 0.3 | 0.3 | 0.3 | 0.3 |
| 2017 | 0.2 | 0.2 | 0.2 | 0.2 | 0.2 | 0.2 | 0.2 | 0.2 | 0.2 | 0.2 | 0.2 | 0.2 | 0.2 |
| 2018 | 0.2 | 0.2 | 0.2 | 0.2 | 0.2 | 0.2 | 0.2 | 0.2 | 0.2 | 0.2 | 0.2 | 0.2 | 0.2 |
| 2019 | 0.2 | 0.2 | 0.2 | 0.2 | 0.2 | 0.2 | 0.2 | 0.2 | 0.2 | 0.2 | 0.2 | 0.2 | 0.2 |
| **Construction** | | | | | | | | | | | | | |
| 2011 | 30.0 | 29.9 | 30.3 | 30.3 | 30.6 | 31.3 | 33.0 | 33.3 | 33.6 | 33.2 | 33.0 | 32.8 | 31.8 |
| 2012 | 32.1 | 32.3 | 32.5 | 33.4 | 34.9 | 35.8 | 36.0 | 36.1 | 35.9 | 36.2 | 36.2 | 36.2 | 34.8 |
| 2013 | 35.1 | 35.6 | 35.9 | 36.1 | 36.5 | 37.4 | 39.0 | 39.4 | 38.8 | 38.7 | 38.6 | 38.8 | 37.5 |
| 2014 | 37.5 | 37.7 | 37.8 | 38.1 | 38.6 | 39.7 | 40.9 | 41.4 | 41.4 | 41.2 | 41.1 | 40.7 | 39.7 |
| 2015 | 40.4 | 41.1 | 41.8 | 42.8 | 43.1 | 44.2 | 45.1 | 45.9 | 45.5 | 46.4 | 45.7 | 45.3 | 43.9 |
| 2016 | 45.1 | 45.8 | 45.6 | 47.5 | 48.0 | 48.8 | 50.4 | 50.6 | 50.4 | 49.8 | 48.9 | 48.2 | 48.3 |
| 2017 | 47.1 | 47.2 | 48.2 | 48.6 | 49.0 | 49.9 | 50.6 | 50.8 | 50.4 | 50.5 | 50.1 | 49.7 | 49.3 |
| 2018 | 48.8 | 49.2 | 48.7 | 49.2 | 49.1 | 49.9 | 50.3 | 50.5 | 50.4 | 51.1 | 50.9 | 50.6 | 49.9 |
| 2019 | 49.6 | 50.3 | 51.4 | 52.1 | 52.9 | 53.7 | 54.1 | 54.3 | 54.0 | 53.2 | 52.9 | 51.9 | 52.5 |

## Employment by Industry: San Jose-Sunnyvale-Santa Clara, CA, 2011–2019—*Continued*

(Numbers in thousands, not seasonally adjusted)

| Industry and year | January | February | March | April | May | June | July | August | September | October | November | December | Annual average |
|---|---|---|---|---|---|---|---|---|---|---|---|---|---|
| **Trade, Transportation, and Utilities** | | | | | | | | | | | | | |
| 2011 | 125.1 | 123.9 | 123.4 | 123.9 | 124.2 | 125.0 | 125.9 | 126.5 | 126.4 | 127.9 | 132.1 | 134.4 | 126.6 |
| 2012 | 128.9 | 127.1 | 126.7 | 127.8 | 128.4 | 129.3 | 130.4 | 130.8 | 130.2 | 131.5 | 136.8 | 138.3 | 130.5 |
| 2013 | 132.4 | 131.2 | 131.0 | 131.1 | 131.3 | 132.5 | 133.3 | 133.5 | 132.8 | 133.7 | 138.3 | 140.3 | 133.5 |
| 2014 | 134.5 | 133.0 | 133.1 | 133.5 | 133.5 | 134.5 | 135.0 | 135.6 | 134.8 | 135.5 | 140.0 | 142.1 | 135.4 |
| 2015 | 136.8 | 134.8 | 134.5 | 134.3 | 134.7 | 135.4 | 136.5 | 137.1 | 136.6 | 138.5 | 141.8 | 143.4 | 137.0 |
| 2016 | 137.2 | 136.4 | 135.7 | 135.4 | 135.3 | 135.6 | 137.0 | 137.0 | 135.8 | 135.8 | 139.1 | 141.3 | 136.8 |
| 2017 | 135.1 | 133.6 | 133.3 | 133.5 | 133.7 | 134.5 | 134.6 | 134.9 | 133.8 | 133.6 | 137.2 | 138.9 | 134.7 |
| 2018 | 134.3 | 133.4 | 133.0 | 132.3 | 132.4 | 133.1 | 133.9 | 133.5 | 132.6 | 132.7 | 136.3 | 138.1 | 133.8 |
| 2019 | 132.7 | 130.9 | 130.3 | 129.3 | 129.9 | 129.9 | 130.9 | 131.5 | 130.1 | 130.8 | 134.8 | 136.6 | 131.5 |
| **Wholesale Trade** | | | | | | | | | | | | | |
| 2011 | 34.1 | 34.0 | 33.8 | 33.5 | 33.4 | 33.3 | 33.5 | 33.3 | 33.1 | 33.3 | 33.1 | 33.3 | 33.5 |
| 2012 | 33.5 | 33.8 | 33.5 | 33.9 | 34.0 | 34.2 | 34.8 | 34.9 | 34.7 | 35.4 | 35.4 | 35.4 | 34.5 |
| 2013 | 35.4 | 35.5 | 35.6 | 35.7 | 35.6 | 35.7 | 36.1 | 36.0 | 35.8 | 35.6 | 35.8 | 35.9 | 35.7 |
| 2014 | 35.8 | 35.7 | 35.8 | 35.7 | 35.5 | 35.7 | 35.9 | 35.9 | 35.7 | 35.8 | 36.0 | 36.0 | 35.8 |
| 2015 | 35.4 | 35.5 | 35.4 | 35.4 | 35.7 | 35.8 | 36.0 | 35.9 | 35.7 | 36.7 | 36.2 | 36.3 | 35.8 |
| 2016 | 35.8 | 35.9 | 35.9 | 36.0 | 35.8 | 35.7 | 35.8 | 35.8 | 35.3 | 34.8 | 34.6 | 34.7 | 35.5 |
| 2017 | 33.9 | 33.9 | 33.8 | 33.9 | 33.8 | 33.8 | 33.6 | 33.5 | 33.3 | 33.1 | 32.9 | 32.8 | 33.5 |
| 2018 | 32.7 | 32.7 | 32.5 | 32.5 | 32.5 | 32.5 | 32.3 | 32.0 | 31.7 | 31.8 | 31.8 | 31.9 | 32.2 |
| 2019 | 31.8 | 31.9 | 31.8 | 31.8 | 31.8 | 31.6 | 31.6 | 31.7 | 31.4 | 31.5 | 31.5 | 31.5 | 31.7 |
| **Retail Trade** | | | | | | | | | | | | | |
| 2011 | 79.2 | 78.0 | 77.7 | 78.4 | 78.7 | 79.5 | 80.2 | 81.1 | 81.1 | 82.5 | 86.8 | 88.5 | 81.0 |
| 2012 | 83.1 | 81.1 | 81.0 | 81.5 | 81.9 | 82.3 | 82.7 | 82.8 | 82.3 | 82.9 | 88.1 | 89.2 | 83.2 |
| 2013 | 83.8 | 82.3 | 82.0 | 82.0 | 82.3 | 83.2 | 83.4 | 83.7 | 83.0 | 83.8 | 87.9 | 89.2 | 83.9 |
| 2014 | 84.6 | 83.3 | 83.2 | 83.8 | 83.8 | 84.4 | 84.7 | 85.3 | 84.8 | 85.3 | 89.4 | 90.8 | 85.3 |
| 2015 | 86.5 | 85.2 | 85.0 | 84.7 | 84.8 | 85.3 | 86.0 | 86.6 | 86.3 | 87.1 | 90.4 | 91.2 | 86.6 |
| 2016 | 86.4 | 85.6 | 85.0 | 84.5 | 84.5 | 84.6 | 85.7 | 85.7 | 85.0 | 85.3 | 88.1 | 89.2 | 85.8 |
| 2017 | 85.7 | 84.4 | 84.3 | 84.4 | 84.7 | 85.3 | 85.8 | 86.0 | 85.1 | 85.3 | 88.9 | 89.8 | 85.8 |
| 2018 | 86.4 | 85.3 | 85.1 | 84.4 | 84.4 | 85.1 | 86.0 | 85.8 | 85.1 | 84.9 | 87.6 | 88.6 | 85.7 |
| 2019 | 84.7 | 83.3 | 82.9 | 82.0 | 82.5 | 82.6 | 83.3 | 83.4 | 82.3 | 82.7 | 86.2 | 87.4 | 83.6 |
| **Transportation and Utilities** | | | | | | | | | | | | | |
| 2011 | 11.8 | 11.9 | 11.9 | 12.0 | 12.1 | 12.2 | 12.2 | 12.1 | 12.2 | 12.1 | 12.2 | 12.6 | 12.1 |
| 2012 | 12.3 | 12.2 | 12.2 | 12.4 | 12.5 | 12.8 | 12.9 | 13.1 | 13.2 | 13.2 | 13.3 | 13.7 | 12.8 |
| 2013 | 13.2 | 13.4 | 13.4 | 13.4 | 13.4 | 13.6 | 13.8 | 13.8 | 14.0 | 14.3 | 14.6 | 15.2 | 13.8 |
| 2014 | 14.1 | 14.0 | 14.1 | 14.0 | 14.2 | 14.4 | 14.4 | 14.4 | 14.3 | 14.4 | 14.6 | 15.3 | 14.4 |
| 2015 | 14.9 | 14.1 | 14.1 | 14.2 | 14.2 | 14.3 | 14.5 | 14.6 | 14.6 | 14.7 | 15.2 | 15.9 | 14.6 |
| 2016 | 15.0 | 14.9 | 14.8 | 14.9 | 15.0 | 15.3 | 15.5 | 15.5 | 15.5 | 15.7 | 16.4 | 17.4 | 15.5 |
| 2017 | 15.5 | 15.3 | 15.2 | 15.2 | 15.2 | 15.4 | 15.2 | 15.4 | 15.4 | 15.2 | 15.4 | 16.3 | 15.4 |
| 2018 | 15.2 | 15.4 | 15.4 | 15.4 | 15.5 | 15.5 | 15.6 | 15.7 | 15.8 | 16.0 | 16.9 | 17.6 | 15.8 |
| 2019 | 16.2 | 15.7 | 15.6 | 15.5 | 15.6 | 15.7 | 16.0 | 16.4 | 16.4 | 16.6 | 17.1 | 17.7 | 16.2 |
| **Information** | | | | | | | | | | | | | |
| 2011 | 48.1 | 48.7 | 48.7 | 48.8 | 49.2 | 50.7 | 51.5 | 51.5 | 50.9 | 51.0 | 50.9 | 51.1 | 50.1 |
| 2012 | 50.8 | 51.2 | 51.4 | 52.0 | 52.2 | 53.1 | 54.1 | 53.9 | 53.5 | 53.6 | 53.7 | 54.0 | 52.8 |
| 2013 | 54.8 | 54.9 | 55.2 | 55.2 | 55.4 | 57.1 | 58.5 | 58.2 | 57.5 | 58.2 | 58.8 | 59.4 | 56.9 |
| 2014 | 59.5 | 60.4 | 61.2 | 61.5 | 62.2 | 64.4 | 66.5 | 65.9 | 65.2 | 65.6 | 65.8 | 66.2 | 63.7 |
| 2015 | 66.8 | 66.7 | 66.9 | 67.1 | 67.3 | 69.8 | 71.4 | 70.3 | 69.4 | 69.8 | 70.0 | 70.1 | 68.8 |
| 2016 | 72.8 | 72.9 | 72.5 | 72.9 | 73.7 | 76.4 | 76.5 | 76.1 | 75.4 | 76.9 | 78.2 | 78.6 | 75.2 |
| 2017 | 79.1 | 79.9 | 81.1 | 82.0 | 82.9 | 86.7 | 89.1 | 89.0 | 88.0 | 87.7 | 88.4 | 89.0 | 85.2 |
| 2018 | 87.5 | 87.9 | 88.5 | 88.9 | 89.9 | 93.5 | 95.4 | 95.1 | 93.9 | 94.7 | 95.5 | 96.0 | 92.2 |
| 2019 | 95.3 | 95.7 | 96.9 | 97.5 | 98.3 | 101.7 | 104.3 | 104.7 | 103.4 | 103.9 | 103.7 | 103.6 | 100.8 |
| **Financial Activities** | | | | | | | | | | | | | |
| 2011 | 31.6 | 31.7 | 31.7 | 31.9 | 32.0 | 32.3 | 32.5 | 32.5 | 32.5 | 32.8 | 33.1 | 33.2 | 32.3 |
| 2012 | 32.7 | 32.6 | 32.9 | 32.9 | 33.2 | 33.4 | 33.5 | 33.4 | 33.3 | 33.6 | 33.7 | 33.6 | 33.2 |
| 2013 | 32.6 | 32.9 | 33.3 | 33.5 | 33.8 | 33.8 | 33.9 | 33.9 | 33.7 | 34.1 | 34.2 | 34.2 | 33.7 |
| 2014 | 33.6 | 33.8 | 34.0 | 34.0 | 34.2 | 34.6 | 34.4 | 34.2 | 34.2 | 34.2 | 34.2 | 34.2 | 34.1 |
| 2015 | 34.0 | 34.0 | 33.8 | 34.1 | 34.4 | 34.7 | 34.9 | 34.9 | 34.7 | 35.3 | 35.3 | 35.0 | 34.6 |
| 2016 | 35.0 | 35.1 | 35.1 | 35.4 | 35.4 | 35.5 | 36.0 | 36.0 | 35.8 | 35.9 | 36.1 | 36.2 | 35.6 |
| 2017 | 35.8 | 35.9 | 35.9 | 36.3 | 36.2 | 36.4 | 36.4 | 36.2 | 35.8 | 36.1 | 36.1 | 36.1 | 36.1 |
| 2018 | 36.3 | 36.5 | 36.4 | 36.5 | 36.5 | 36.6 | 37.1 | 37.1 | 36.6 | 37.0 | 37.0 | 37.2 | 36.7 |
| 2019 | 36.9 | 37.0 | 36.8 | 37.1 | 37.3 | 37.4 | 38.4 | 38.5 | 38.0 | 38.6 | 38.3 | 38.6 | 37.7 |

## Employment by Industry: San Jose-Sunnyvale-Santa Clara, CA, 2011–2019—*Continued*

(Numbers in thousands, not seasonally adjusted)

| Industry and year | January | February | March | April | May | June | July | August | September | October | November | December | Annual average |
|---|---|---|---|---|---|---|---|---|---|---|---|---|---|
| **Professional and Business Services** | | | | | | | | | | | | | |
| 2011 | 167.5 | 168.7 | 169.9 | 170.2 | 169.8 | 171.5 | 174.2 | 174.9 | 174.1 | 174.5 | 174.3 | 174.9 | 172.0 |
| 2012 | 173.9 | 176.1 | 177.9 | 180.9 | 181.4 | 183.9 | 187.1 | 188.3 | 187.5 | 189.2 | 190.1 | 192.2 | 184.0 |
| 2013 | 190.0 | 192.5 | 194.0 | 193.7 | 194.1 | 196.4 | 199.9 | 202.0 | 200.4 | 200.9 | 203.2 | 204.8 | 197.7 |
| 2014 | 202.9 | 204.4 | 205.1 | 205.9 | 206.1 | 209.0 | 210.9 | 212.8 | 212.2 | 214.6 | 215.9 | 217.0 | 209.7 |
| 2015 | 215.1 | 216.3 | 217.5 | 220.1 | 221.2 | 222.9 | 227.1 | 228.0 | 226.8 | 229.2 | 230.2 | 230.5 | 223.7 |
| 2016 | 227.9 | 229.6 | 229.0 | 232.6 | 231.8 | 233.0 | 235.6 | 235.8 | 232.6 | 234.6 | 234.3 | 233.9 | 232.6 |
| 2017 | 229.9 | 231.8 | 235.8 | 236.9 | 236.2 | 238.3 | 240.4 | 239.9 | 236.8 | 237.7 | 237.7 | 237.4 | 236.6 |
| 2018 | 232.3 | 233.6 | 232.9 | 234.2 | 235.0 | 237.4 | 239.9 | 240.3 | 237.6 | 239.2 | 241.0 | 240.2 | 237.0 |
| 2019 | 238.5 | 239.8 | 240.1 | 240.5 | 241.8 | 244.5 | 246.0 | 246.7 | 243.8 | 243.9 | 244.9 | 244.1 | 242.9 |
| **Education and Health Services** | | | | | | | | | | | | | |
| 2011 | 128.7 | 130.5 | 130.9 | 129.7 | 130.2 | 129.3 | 126.1 | 126.7 | 127.0 | 132.0 | 133.7 | 134.0 | 129.9 |
| 2012 | 133.8 | 136.9 | 137.5 | 137.5 | 137.9 | 137.0 | 133.4 | 134.9 | 134.6 | 139.4 | 140.8 | 140.9 | 137.1 |
| 2013 | 140.7 | 142.9 | 143.7 | 144.4 | 145.3 | 144.0 | 140.7 | 142.1 | 142.1 | 146.3 | 148.2 | 147.9 | 144.0 |
| 2014 | 148.2 | 149.9 | 150.3 | 151.1 | 151.7 | 150.5 | 147.3 | 148.0 | 148.3 | 152.9 | 152.6 | 152.3 | 150.3 |
| 2015 | 153.4 | 155.0 | 155.9 | 156.4 | 157.3 | 156.5 | 154.7 | 155.2 | 155.0 | 159.7 | 160.2 | 160.0 | 156.6 |
| 2016 | 159.6 | 161.9 | 162.2 | 163.6 | 164.4 | 163.4 | 161.2 | 160.8 | 161.0 | 164.7 | 166.0 | 165.5 | 162.9 |
| 2017 | 166.6 | 169.3 | 170.2 | 169.1 | 170.2 | 169.7 | 167.2 | 166.8 | 166.1 | 170.7 | 172.0 | 172.3 | 169.2 |
| 2018 | 170.4 | 173.3 | 174.3 | 173.3 | 173.1 | 174.0 | 170.3 | 171.6 | 170.2 | 175.9 | 176.9 | 177.0 | 173.4 |
| 2019 | 176.2 | 179.0 | 177.7 | 174.7 | 176.1 | 175.5 | 171.6 | 172.5 | 171.3 | 176.1 | 177.3 | 177.8 | 175.5 |
| **Leisure and Hospitality** | | | | | | | | | | | | | |
| 2011 | 72.7 | 74.3 | 75.6 | 76.7 | 77.7 | 78.4 | 79.8 | 79.9 | 80.2 | 80.4 | 78.3 | 78.4 | 77.7 |
| 2012 | 77.4 | 78.3 | 80.4 | 82.0 | 83.5 | 84.1 | 84.9 | 85.2 | 85.6 | 85.3 | 83.4 | 83.5 | 82.8 |
| 2013 | 81.7 | 83.9 | 85.8 | 87.9 | 89.4 | 89.8 | 89.5 | 89.6 | 89.6 | 89.7 | 88.4 | 88.9 | 87.9 |
| 2014 | 86.8 | 89.3 | 90.9 | 92.4 | 94.4 | 94.9 | 95.1 | 95.7 | 95.4 | 94.4 | 92.6 | 92.6 | 92.9 |
| 2015 | 91.0 | 92.9 | 94.6 | 96.6 | 98.4 | 99.0 | 98.9 | 99.0 | 98.9 | 99.0 | 96.6 | 96.3 | 96.8 |
| 2016 | 95.6 | 96.1 | 97.0 | 99.9 | 101.7 | 102.4 | 103.0 | 103.4 | 103.3 | 102.3 | 101.0 | 101.4 | 100.6 |
| 2017 | 97.9 | 100.0 | 101.3 | 102.5 | 104.6 | 105.9 | 106.1 | 105.6 | 104.3 | 104.7 | 104.5 | 103.5 | 103.4 |
| 2018 | 99.5 | 102.2 | 103.1 | 104.9 | 108.1 | 108.0 | 108.1 | 108.3 | 107.4 | 106.8 | 106.3 | 105.6 | 105.7 |
| 2019 | 102.0 | 103.0 | 104.5 | 106.7 | 107.4 | 108.1 | 110.3 | 110.2 | 107.6 | 106.7 | 105.2 | 105.7 | 106.5 |
| **Other Services** | | | | | | | | | | | | | |
| 2011 | 24.1 | 24.3 | 24.3 | 24.5 | 24.7 | 24.7 | 24.9 | 24.6 | 24.6 | 24.7 | 24.9 | 24.7 | 24.6 |
| 2012 | 24.1 | 24.2 | 24.4 | 24.8 | 25.0 | 25.2 | 25.2 | 24.9 | 24.8 | 24.9 | 24.8 | 24.7 | 24.8 |
| 2013 | 24.7 | 25.1 | 25.1 | 25.4 | 25.7 | 25.7 | 25.6 | 25.4 | 25.5 | 25.6 | 25.7 | 25.6 | 25.4 |
| 2014 | 25.5 | 25.8 | 26.0 | 26.5 | 26.7 | 26.9 | 26.6 | 26.6 | 26.5 | 26.7 | 26.7 | 26.4 | 26.4 |
| 2015 | 26.2 | 26.4 | 26.6 | 26.8 | 27.2 | 27.1 | 27.2 | 27.2 | 27.0 | 27.2 | 27.2 | 27.1 | 26.9 |
| 2016 | 26.6 | 27.0 | 26.9 | 27.4 | 27.7 | 27.7 | 28.0 | 28.0 | 27.9 | 28.2 | 28.1 | 28.0 | 27.6 |
| 2017 | 28.1 | 28.5 | 28.7 | 29.2 | 29.4 | 29.3 | 28.9 | 28.9 | 28.9 | 29.0 | 28.8 | 28.7 | 28.9 |
| 2018 | 28.1 | 28.8 | 28.8 | 29.0 | 29.3 | 29.3 | 29.2 | 28.9 | 28.8 | 29.0 | 29.0 | 28.8 | 28.9 |
| 2019 | 28.2 | 28.7 | 29.0 | 29.1 | 29.6 | 29.5 | 29.7 | 29.4 | 29.1 | 29.2 | 29.5 | 29.4 | 29.2 |
| **Government** | | | | | | | | | | | | | |
| 2011 | 94.6 | 95.3 | 95.7 | 96.5 | 96.8 | 96.2 | 81.3 | 82.4 | 90.9 | 93.8 | 94.4 | 94.4 | 92.7 |
| 2012 | 91.7 | 92.9 | 94.0 | 94.2 | 94.2 | 94.9 | 81.1 | 83.1 | 90.2 | 93.5 | 94.1 | 93.3 | 91.4 |
| 2013 | 92.6 | 94.0 | 93.1 | 94.3 | 95.7 | 94.4 | 78.6 | 83.4 | 91.3 | 94.1 | 95.4 | 94.2 | 91.8 |
| 2014 | 94.5 | 95.6 | 95.8 | 96.9 | 97.0 | 94.2 | 82.3 | 86.1 | 92.2 | 95.2 | 95.9 | 95.2 | 93.4 |
| 2015 | 93.8 | 94.6 | 94.1 | 94.8 | 95.2 | 94.7 | 83.7 | 87.3 | 91.6 | 94.8 | 95.5 | 95.2 | 92.9 |
| 2016 | 93.6 | 94.3 | 95.4 | 95.6 | 96.4 | 96.0 | 85.3 | 88.3 | 92.9 | 96.0 | 97.9 | 97.8 | 94.1 |
| 2017 | 95.8 | 95.8 | 96.8 | 97.5 | 98.0 | 96.7 | 88.0 | 89.6 | 94.0 | 97.6 | 98.6 | 98.0 | 95.5 |
| 2018 | 96.4 | 96.8 | 98.3 | 98.7 | 99.1 | 98.9 | 89.3 | 90.7 | 94.9 | 98.6 | 99.5 | 98.8 | 96.7 |
| 2019 | 95.9 | 96.4 | 99.1 | 99.2 | 99.8 | 98.4 | 90.3 | 92.8 | 96.1 | 98.7 | 99.8 | 99.6 | 97.2 |

# Employment by Industry: Nashville-Davidson—Murfreesboro—Franklin, TN, 2011–2019

(Numbers in thousands, not seasonally adjusted)

| Industry and year | January | February | March | April | May | June | July | August | September | October | November | December | Annual average |
|---|---|---|---|---|---|---|---|---|---|---|---|---|---|
| **Total Nonfarm** | | | | | | | | | | | | | |
| 2011 | 759.8 | 765.8 | 773.1 | 781.5 | 785.6 | 779.5 | 780.8 | 790.4 | 796.4 | 801.5 | 808.6 | 810.5 | 786.1 |
| 2012 | 791.4 | 798.0 | 809.0 | 811.2 | 814.9 | 811.0 | 807.0 | 818.6 | 825.0 | 830.8 | 839.5 | 841.3 | 816.5 |
| 2013 | 817.6 | 827.1 | 833.1 | 841.0 | 845.1 | 840.9 | 837.1 | 849.7 | 855.0 | 863.0 | 871.4 | 872.4 | 846.1 |
| 2014 | 850.9 | 857.8 | 862.3 | 874.6 | 879.6 | 873.3 | 870.5 | 885.6 | 891.6 | 899.8 | 907.2 | 909.8 | 880.3 |
| 2015 | 886.4 | 891.9 | 896.7 | 907.0 | 913.1 | 908.8 | 907.6 | 917.8 | 925.0 | 934.6 | 941.3 | 945.0 | 914.6 |
| 2016 | 923.1 | 929.0 | 936.3 | 943.9 | 945.2 | 942.4 | 943.6 | 953.4 | 962.7 | 967.1 | 975.0 | 977.3 | 949.9 |
| 2017 | 955.3 | 964.6 | 969.3 | 976.2 | 978.0 | 977.2 | 976.0 | 986.1 | 994.7 | 1,000.1 | 1,010.5 | 1,008.4 | 983.0 |
| 2018 | 986.9 | 996.4 | 1,002.3 | 1,006.8 | 1,009.1 | 1,009.4 | 1,005.1 | 1,019.9 | 1,027.8 | 1,030.2 | 1,041.7 | 1,041.2 | 1,014.7 |
| 2019 | 1,022.3 | 1,030.8 | 1,034.6 | 1,042.4 | 1,045.2 | 1,043.3 | 1,038.9 | 1,051.8 | 1,058.0 | 1,063.3 | 1,073.7 | 1,070.5 | 1,047.9 |
| **Total Private** | | | | | | | | | | | | | |
| 2011 | 648.0 | 653.7 | 660.4 | 668.2 | 672.5 | 676.1 | 677.3 | 681.2 | 683.6 | 688.4 | 695.2 | 697.4 | 675.2 |
| 2012 | 680.5 | 685.2 | 695.4 | 698.6 | 703.9 | 709.7 | 706.6 | 711.7 | 714.2 | 719.0 | 726.8 | 728.7 | 706.7 |
| 2013 | 707.8 | 714.9 | 720.7 | 727.1 | 732.4 | 738.5 | 735.3 | 741.4 | 742.5 | 748.9 | 757.3 | 758.5 | 735.4 |
| 2014 | 739.5 | 743.8 | 748.2 | 760.6 | 765.5 | 770.0 | 767.8 | 776.3 | 777.9 | 784.7 | 790.2 | 794.3 | 768.2 |
| 2015 | 774.1 | 776.5 | 781.3 | 791.8 | 798.5 | 804.0 | 803.3 | 806.8 | 809.4 | 816.8 | 823.9 | 827.6 | 801.2 |
| 2016 | 809.4 | 812.9 | 818.1 | 827.1 | 830.2 | 836.5 | 837.7 | 840.2 | 844.7 | 849.3 | 856.3 | 858.7 | 835.1 |
| 2017 | 839.3 | 846.1 | 850.4 | 857.5 | 860.5 | 869.2 | 868.4 | 871.6 | 875.6 | 880.2 | 890.0 | 887.5 | 866.4 |
| 2018 | 868.9 | 875.9 | 881.6 | 886.2 | 889.9 | 899.5 | 896.0 | 904.1 | 907.3 | 908.2 | 918.8 | 918.4 | 896.2 |
| 2019 | 902.0 | 908.4 | 912.0 | 919.5 | 923.8 | 931.7 | 928.8 | 934.8 | 937.5 | 941.3 | 950.7 | 947.8 | 928.2 |
| **Goods Producing** | | | | | | | | | | | | | |
| 2011 | 93.5 | 94.4 | 95.9 | 97.8 | 98.0 | 99.0 | 99.2 | 99.5 | 100.1 | 100.7 | 100.7 | 101.1 | 98.3 |
| 2012 | 98.8 | 100.1 | 101.9 | 102.1 | 102.8 | 104.1 | 104.4 | 105.2 | 106.0 | 105.3 | 105.8 | 105.9 | 103.5 |
| 2013 | 104.2 | 105.2 | 106.0 | 106.5 | 107.6 | 108.8 | 108.9 | 109.7 | 110.0 | 110.6 | 110.6 | 110.9 | 108.3 |
| 2014 | 109.7 | 110.2 | 111.1 | 111.8 | 113.0 | 113.2 | 113.0 | 114.7 | 114.3 | 115.0 | 115.9 | 116.6 | 113.2 |
| 2015 | 114.8 | 115.7 | 115.7 | 117.6 | 118.9 | 119.5 | 118.8 | 119.5 | 120.0 | 119.7 | 119.7 | 119.4 | 118.3 |
| 2016 | 118.6 | 119.1 | 120.0 | 120.3 | 121.3 | 122.6 | 123.9 | 123.6 | 123.9 | 124.3 | 124.9 | 126.4 | 122.4 |
| 2017 | 125.0 | 126.0 | 126.3 | 127.5 | 127.5 | 128.6 | 128.7 | 128.4 | 128.6 | 127.9 | 128.5 | 128.1 | 127.6 |
| 2018 | 127.0 | 127.6 | 128.7 | 129.0 | 129.4 | 131.4 | 131.1 | 132.0 | 132.8 | 131.9 | 131.9 | 131.6 | 130.4 |
| 2019 | 130.7 | 131.9 | 132.0 | 133.6 | 134.3 | 135.6 | 135.5 | 135.0 | 135.2 | 132.5 | 134.3 | 134.3 | 133.7 |
| **Service-Providing** | | | | | | | | | | | | | |
| 2011 | 666.3 | 671.4 | 677.2 | 683.7 | 687.6 | 680.5 | 681.6 | 690.9 | 696.3 | 700.8 | 707.9 | 709.4 | 687.8 |
| 2012 | 692.6 | 697.9 | 707.1 | 709.1 | 712.1 | 706.9 | 702.6 | 713.4 | 719.0 | 725.5 | 733.7 | 735.4 | 712.9 |
| 2013 | 713.4 | 721.9 | 727.1 | 734.5 | 737.5 | 732.1 | 728.2 | 740.0 | 745.0 | 752.4 | 760.8 | 761.5 | 737.9 |
| 2014 | 741.2 | 747.6 | 751.2 | 762.8 | 766.6 | 760.1 | 757.5 | 770.9 | 777.3 | 784.8 | 791.3 | 793.2 | 767.0 |
| 2015 | 771.6 | 776.2 | 781.0 | 789.4 | 794.2 | 789.3 | 788.8 | 798.3 | 805.0 | 814.9 | 821.6 | 825.6 | 796.3 |
| 2016 | 804.5 | 809.9 | 816.3 | 823.6 | 823.9 | 819.8 | 819.7 | 829.8 | 838.8 | 842.8 | 850.1 | 850.9 | 827.5 |
| 2017 | 830.3 | 838.6 | 843.0 | 848.7 | 850.5 | 848.6 | 847.3 | 857.7 | 866.1 | 872.2 | 882.0 | 880.3 | 855.4 |
| 2018 | 859.9 | 868.8 | 873.6 | 877.8 | 879.7 | 878.0 | 874.0 | 887.9 | 895.0 | 898.3 | 909.8 | 909.6 | 884.4 |
| 2019 | 891.6 | 898.9 | 902.6 | 908.8 | 910.9 | 907.7 | 903.4 | 916.8 | 922.8 | 930.8 | 939.4 | 936.2 | 914.2 |
| **Mining, Logging, and Construction** | | | | | | | | | | | | | |
| 2011 | 29.5 | 30.1 | 31.3 | 32.8 | 32.9 | 33.8 | 33.7 | 33.9 | 34.2 | 33.8 | 33.5 | 33.1 | 32.7 |
| 2012 | 31.9 | 32.3 | 33.6 | 33.2 | 33.4 | 33.6 | 33.4 | 33.7 | 34.0 | 33.1 | 32.6 | 32.3 | 33.1 |
| 2013 | 31.0 | 31.8 | 32.5 | 33.0 | 33.7 | 34.3 | 34.2 | 34.2 | 34.2 | 34.2 | 33.4 | 33.3 | 33.3 |
| 2014 | 32.5 | 32.8 | 34.1 | 34.8 | 35.6 | 35.4 | 35.8 | 36.2 | 35.9 | 36.4 | 36.8 | 37.1 | 35.3 |
| 2015 | 36.2 | 36.8 | 37.2 | 38.7 | 39.7 | 40.1 | 40.4 | 40.0 | 40.3 | 40.3 | 40.1 | 39.3 | 39.1 |
| 2016 | 38.2 | 38.2 | 38.5 | 38.9 | 39.5 | 40.4 | 41.0 | 40.9 | 41.1 | 41.3 | 41.6 | 41.7 | 40.1 |
| 2017 | 40.4 | 41.1 | 41.9 | 42.8 | 43.3 | 43.9 | 43.9 | 44.1 | 44.1 | 43.8 | 44.3 | 44.1 | 43.1 |
| 2018 | 43.2 | 43.6 | 44.6 | 45.3 | 45.7 | 47.1 | 46.9 | 47.3 | 47.7 | 47.1 | 47.1 | 46.7 | 46.0 |
| 2019 | 46.3 | 47.0 | 47.3 | 48.7 | 49.3 | 50.1 | 50.0 | 49.9 | 49.9 | 50.4 | 49.1 | 48.8 | 48.9 |
| **Manufacturing** | | | | | | | | | | | | | |
| 2011 | 64.0 | 64.3 | 64.6 | 65.0 | 65.1 | 65.2 | 65.5 | 65.6 | 65.9 | 66.9 | 67.2 | 68.0 | 65.6 |
| 2012 | 66.9 | 67.8 | 68.3 | 68.9 | 69.4 | 70.5 | 71.0 | 71.5 | 72.0 | 72.2 | 73.2 | 73.6 | 70.4 |
| 2013 | 73.2 | 73.4 | 73.5 | 73.5 | 73.9 | 74.5 | 74.7 | 75.5 | 75.8 | 76.4 | 77.2 | 77.6 | 74.9 |
| 2014 | 77.2 | 77.4 | 77.0 | 77.0 | 77.4 | 77.8 | 77.2 | 78.5 | 78.4 | 78.6 | 79.1 | 79.5 | 77.9 |
| 2015 | 78.6 | 78.9 | 78.5 | 78.9 | 79.2 | 79.4 | 78.4 | 79.5 | 79.7 | 79.4 | 79.6 | 80.1 | 79.2 |
| 2016 | 80.4 | 80.9 | 81.5 | 81.4 | 81.8 | 82.2 | 82.9 | 82.7 | 82.8 | 83.0 | 83.3 | 84.7 | 82.3 |
| 2017 | 84.6 | 84.9 | 84.4 | 84.7 | 84.2 | 84.7 | 84.8 | 84.3 | 84.5 | 84.1 | 84.2 | 84.0 | 84.5 |
| 2018 | 83.8 | 84.0 | 84.1 | 83.7 | 83.7 | 84.3 | 84.2 | 84.7 | 85.1 | 84.8 | 84.8 | 84.9 | 84.3 |
| 2019 | 84.4 | 84.9 | 84.7 | 84.9 | 85.0 | 85.5 | 85.5 | 85.1 | 85.3 | 82.1 | 85.2 | 85.5 | 84.8 |

## Employment by Industry: Nashville-Davidson—Murfreesboro—Franklin, TN, 2011–2019—*Continued*

(Numbers in thousands, not seasonally adjusted)

| Industry and year | January | February | March | April | May | June | July | August | September | October | November | December | Annual average |
|---|---|---|---|---|---|---|---|---|---|---|---|---|---|
| **Trade, Transportation, and Utilities** | | | | | | | | | | | | | |
| 2011 | 152.8 | 152.9 | 154.1 | 155.6 | 156.2 | 156.5 | 156.8 | 157.1 | 157.5 | 159.6 | 163.4 | 164.8 | 157.3 |
| 2012 | 159.0 | 158.2 | 160.1 | 160.7 | 161.6 | 161.6 | 161.4 | 162.1 | 162.9 | 164.9 | 169.8 | 170.9 | 162.8 |
| 2013 | 162.6 | 162.4 | 163.1 | 165.0 | 165.9 | 166.9 | 166.3 | 167.3 | 167.0 | 169.2 | 174.5 | 177.1 | 167.3 |
| 2014 | 167.3 | 166.8 | 167.7 | 170.6 | 171.3 | 172.1 | 171.9 | 172.9 | 173.1 | 176.0 | 179.8 | 181.8 | 172.6 |
| 2015 | 173.1 | 171.6 | 172.0 | 173.4 | 174.4 | 175.0 | 175.0 | 175.9 | 175.9 | 178.6 | 182.9 | 185.1 | 176.1 |
| 2016 | 178.2 | 177.1 | 177.3 | 178.5 | 178.8 | 179.5 | 180.8 | 181.3 | 181.6 | 184.6 | 189.2 | 190.7 | 181.5 |
| 2017 | 182.6 | 182.2 | 182.6 | 183.7 | 184.2 | 185.6 | 186.0 | 187.4 | 188.1 | 190.8 | 196.5 | 197.2 | 187.2 |
| 2018 | 190.1 | 189.6 | 190.2 | 189.9 | 190.9 | 191.5 | 192.6 | 193.7 | 193.7 | 196.5 | 203.3 | 205.4 | 194.0 |
| 2019 | 198.4 | 197.9 | 197.8 | 198.0 | 198.5 | 199.7 | 200.3 | 201.5 | 201.9 | 205.8 | 211.2 | 213.6 | 202.1 |
| **Wholesale Trade** | | | | | | | | | | | | | |
| 2011 | 36.9 | 37.2 | 37.5 | 37.5 | 37.7 | 37.8 | 37.9 | 38.0 | 38.2 | 38.5 | 38.7 | 38.9 | 37.9 |
| 2012 | 38.6 | 38.8 | 39.0 | 39.1 | 39.4 | 39.5 | 39.7 | 40.0 | 40.0 | 40.2 | 40.4 | 40.5 | 39.6 |
| 2013 | 39.8 | 40.1 | 40.5 | 40.7 | 40.8 | 41.0 | 41.2 | 41.1 | 41.0 | 41.1 | 41.3 | 41.1 | 40.8 |
| 2014 | 40.2 | 40.1 | 40.3 | 40.3 | 40.4 | 40.4 | 40.4 | 40.4 | 40.5 | 40.6 | 40.5 | 40.6 | 40.4 |
| 2015 | 39.6 | 39.7 | 39.7 | 39.6 | 39.6 | 39.6 | 39.6 | 39.5 | 39.6 | 39.8 | 39.8 | 39.7 | 39.7 |
| 2016 | 38.8 | 38.7 | 38.6 | 38.6 | 38.7 | 38.8 | 39.2 | 39.5 | 39.7 | 40.0 | 40.1 | 40.3 | 39.3 |
| 2017 | 39.9 | 40.1 | 40.2 | 40.3 | 40.4 | 40.6 | 40.6 | 40.8 | 41.0 | 41.2 | 41.4 | 41.4 | 40.7 |
| 2018 | 41.2 | 41.3 | 41.4 | 41.3 | 41.5 | 41.8 | 41.8 | 42.1 | 42.2 | 42.2 | 42.2 | 42.6 | 41.8 |
| 2019 | 42.3 | 42.5 | 42.5 | 42.4 | 42.4 | 42.7 | 43.0 | 43.2 | 43.1 | 43.1 | 43.3 | 44.0 | 42.9 |
| **Retail Trade** | | | | | | | | | | | | | |
| 2011 | 86.6 | 86.5 | 87.1 | 88.1 | 88.2 | 88.5 | 88.5 | 88.5 | 88.4 | 89.1 | 91.9 | 93.0 | 88.7 |
| 2012 | 88.9 | 87.8 | 89.1 | 89.1 | 89.3 | 89.2 | 88.7 | 88.5 | 88.3 | 89.2 | 92.5 | 92.8 | 89.5 |
| 2013 | 88.0 | 87.1 | 87.4 | 88.7 | 89.4 | 89.7 | 89.4 | 89.8 | 89.4 | 90.7 | 93.5 | 94.6 | 89.8 |
| 2014 | 90.0 | 89.6 | 90.1 | 92.8 | 93.4 | 93.9 | 93.6 | 93.8 | 93.6 | 94.7 | 97.5 | 98.7 | 93.5 |
| 2015 | 94.0 | 93.0 | 93.3 | 94.1 | 94.8 | 95.1 | 95.0 | 95.0 | 94.4 | 95.6 | 98.5 | 99.6 | 95.2 |
| 2016 | 95.4 | 95.1 | 95.5 | 96.1 | 96.3 | 96.7 | 96.9 | 97.0 | 96.8 | 97.7 | 100.5 | 101.5 | 97.1 |
| 2017 | 97.7 | 97.2 | 97.3 | 98.1 | 98.4 | 99.0 | 99.3 | 99.4 | 99.0 | 99.7 | 103.3 | 104.1 | 99.4 |
| 2018 | 99.8 | 99.7 | 100.1 | 100.0 | 100.4 | 100.4 | 100.2 | 100.1 | 99.3 | 99.7 | 103.2 | 103.7 | 100.6 |
| 2019 | 101.7 | 101.0 | 100.7 | 100.6 | 100.8 | 101.2 | 101.1 | 101.5 | 100.8 | 102.9 | 106.0 | 106.5 | 102.1 |
| **Transportation and Utilities** | | | | | | | | | | | | | |
| 2011 | 29.3 | 29.2 | 29.5 | 30.0 | 30.3 | 30.2 | 30.4 | 30.6 | 30.9 | 32.0 | 32.8 | 32.9 | 30.7 |
| 2012 | 31.5 | 31.6 | 32.0 | 32.5 | 32.9 | 32.9 | 33.0 | 33.6 | 34.6 | 35.5 | 36.9 | 37.6 | 33.7 |
| 2013 | 34.8 | 35.2 | 35.2 | 35.6 | 35.7 | 36.2 | 35.7 | 36.4 | 36.6 | 37.4 | 39.7 | 41.4 | 36.7 |
| 2014 | 37.1 | 37.1 | 37.3 | 37.5 | 37.5 | 37.8 | 37.9 | 38.7 | 39.0 | 40.7 | 41.8 | 42.5 | 38.7 |
| 2015 | 39.5 | 38.9 | 39.0 | 39.7 | 40.0 | 40.3 | 40.4 | 41.4 | 41.9 | 43.2 | 44.6 | 45.8 | 41.2 |
| 2016 | 44.0 | 43.3 | 43.2 | 43.8 | 43.8 | 44.0 | 44.7 | 44.8 | 45.1 | 46.9 | 48.6 | 48.9 | 45.1 |
| 2017 | 45.0 | 44.9 | 45.1 | 45.3 | 45.4 | 46.0 | 46.1 | 47.2 | 48.1 | 49.9 | 51.8 | 51.7 | 47.2 |
| 2018 | 49.1 | 48.6 | 48.7 | 48.6 | 49.0 | 49.3 | 50.6 | 51.5 | 52.2 | 54.6 | 57.9 | 59.1 | 51.6 |
| 2019 | 54.4 | 54.4 | 54.6 | 55.0 | 55.3 | 55.8 | 56.2 | 56.8 | 58.0 | 59.8 | 61.9 | 63.1 | 57.1 |
| **Information** | | | | | | | | | | | | | |
| 2011 | 19.4 | 19.3 | 19.3 | 19.4 | 19.6 | 19.7 | 19.7 | 20.1 | 19.8 | 20.1 | 20.4 | 20.5 | 19.8 |
| 2012 | 20.3 | 20.5 | 20.4 | 20.5 | 21.3 | 21.5 | 20.4 | 20.6 | 20.4 | 20.6 | 20.6 | 20.7 | 20.7 |
| 2013 | 20.4 | 20.7 | 20.8 | 20.6 | 21.0 | 21.6 | 20.9 | 21.0 | 20.7 | 20.8 | 21.2 | 21.1 | 20.9 |
| 2014 | 20.5 | 20.5 | 20.6 | 20.6 | 20.7 | 20.8 | 20.6 | 20.6 | 20.4 | 20.6 | 20.6 | 20.5 | 20.6 |
| 2015 | 20.4 | 20.5 | 20.5 | 20.6 | 21.1 | 21.7 | 21.6 | 22.1 | 21.9 | 22.3 | 23.0 | 22.9 | 21.6 |
| 2016 | 22.7 | 22.9 | 22.4 | 22.4 | 22.4 | 23.8 | 22.2 | 22.3 | 23.1 | 23.1 | 23.9 | 22.8 | 22.8 |
| 2017 | 22.5 | 23.4 | 22.7 | 22.7 | 23.1 | 24.7 | 23.0 | 23.0 | 22.9 | 24.0 | 25.1 | 23.2 | 23.4 |
| 2018 | 23.1 | 23.4 | 23.2 | 23.2 | 23.0 | 25.0 | 22.6 | 23.1 | 23.6 | 23.5 | 24.1 | 23.3 | 23.4 |
| 2019 | 23.3 | 23.9 | 23.9 | 24.5 | 24.6 | 25.4 | 25.1 | 24.6 | 24.8 | 25.3 | 25.8 | 24.8 | 24.7 |
| **Financial Activities** | | | | | | | | | | | | | |
| 2011 | 48.4 | 48.5 | 48.5 | 49.3 | 49.8 | 49.5 | 49.7 | 50.0 | 50.0 | 50.2 | 50.5 | 50.4 | 49.6 |
| 2012 | 49.8 | 50.2 | 50.2 | 50.3 | 50.6 | 51.0 | 51.1 | 51.5 | 51.5 | 51.6 | 51.9 | 52.4 | 51.0 |
| 2013 | 52.1 | 52.4 | 52.8 | 53.4 | 53.7 | 53.7 | 54.4 | 54.2 | 54.0 | 54.4 | 54.7 | 54.7 | 53.7 |
| 2014 | 54.7 | 55.0 | 55.2 | 55.8 | 56.3 | 56.6 | 57.0 | 57.4 | 57.5 | 57.8 | 57.9 | 58.3 | 56.6 |
| 2015 | 57.9 | 58.3 | 58.6 | 58.9 | 59.2 | 59.6 | 59.9 | 60.0 | 59.9 | 60.5 | 60.7 | 61.1 | 59.6 |
| 2016 | 60.5 | 61.0 | 61.1 | 61.9 | 62.5 | 63.0 | 63.4 | 63.8 | 63.9 | 64.0 | 64.1 | 64.5 | 62.8 |
| 2017 | 63.9 | 64.7 | 65.2 | 65.5 | 65.9 | 66.5 | 66.6 | 66.9 | 66.7 | 67.9 | 67.1 | 67.0 | 66.2 |
| 2018 | 66.5 | 67.1 | 67.5 | 68.0 | 68.3 | 68.8 | 69.0 | 69.3 | 69.3 | 68.6 | 69.1 | 69.0 | 68.4 |
| 2019 | 69.4 | 69.8 | 69.8 | 70.5 | 70.9 | 71.6 | 72.1 | 72.2 | 72.3 | 72.6 | 72.8 | 72.8 | 71.4 |

## Employment by Industry: Nashville-Davidson—Murfreesboro—Franklin, TN, 2011–2019—*Continued*

(Numbers in thousands, not seasonally adjusted)

| Industry and year | January | February | March | April | May | June | July | August | September | October | November | December | Annual average |
|---|---|---|---|---|---|---|---|---|---|---|---|---|---|
| **Professional and Business Services** | | | | | | | | | | | | | |
| 2011 | 101.3 | 103.6 | 105.0 | 106.1 | 107.1 | 109.5 | 109.4 | 111.0 | 111.8 | 112.6 | 114.0 | 114.0 | 108.8 |
| 2012 | 109.8 | 111.5 | 114.6 | 114.8 | 116.1 | 118.5 | 118.0 | 119.8 | 120.9 | 122.4 | 124.0 | 123.7 | 117.8 |
| 2013 | 118.7 | 120.7 | 121.9 | 121.6 | 122.8 | 125.2 | 124.5 | 127.8 | 129.0 | 131.5 | 133.7 | 132.6 | 125.8 |
| 2014 | 129.2 | 130.3 | 129.8 | 133.4 | 134.6 | 137.0 | 135.4 | 139.8 | 140.3 | 142.4 | 142.9 | 144.3 | 136.6 |
| 2015 | 138.5 | 139.1 | 141.3 | 143.6 | 144.4 | 147.6 | 148.2 | 149.6 | 150.2 | 152.7 | 153.5 | 154.0 | 146.9 |
| 2016 | 150.0 | 150.6 | 151.8 | 154.7 | 154.7 | 156.5 | 155.8 | 156.8 | 157.3 | 158.8 | 158.5 | 158.5 | 155.3 |
| 2017 | 154.8 | 155.4 | 156.4 | 158.8 | 158.9 | 162.1 | 162.8 | 162.9 | 164.1 | 164.6 | 166.8 | 166.5 | 161.2 |
| 2018 | 162.5 | 164.3 | 164.9 | 166.1 | 166.7 | 169.6 | 167.7 | 170.8 | 171.8 | 172.4 | 174.9 | 174.8 | 168.9 |
| 2019 | 171.6 | 172.3 | 173.2 | 174.8 | 174.4 | 177.2 | 175.8 | 178.3 | 178.5 | 180.1 | 179.9 | 180.4 | 176.4 |
| **Education and Health Services** | | | | | | | | | | | | | |
| 2011 | 123.9 | 125.3 | 125.4 | 126.2 | 125.6 | 124.4 | 125.0 | 125.3 | 126.9 | 127.6 | 128.2 | 128.4 | 126.0 |
| 2012 | 127.6 | 128.8 | 129.3 | 129.6 | 128.5 | 128.3 | 127.9 | 128.8 | 130.9 | 131.1 | 131.7 | 131.4 | 129.5 |
| 2013 | 130.2 | 131.8 | 132.3 | 133.2 | 132.4 | 131.8 | 131.0 | 132.0 | 134.2 | 134.0 | 133.9 | 133.9 | 132.6 |
| 2014 | 133.2 | 134.2 | 134.8 | 136.0 | 135.3 | 134.4 | 134.5 | 135.4 | 137.7 | 138.5 | 138.5 | 138.8 | 135.9 |
| 2015 | 138.1 | 139.1 | 139.4 | 140.4 | 140.3 | 138.7 | 139.4 | 139.7 | 142.6 | 143.2 | 144.2 | 144.5 | 140.8 |
| 2016 | 142.1 | 143.7 | 144.5 | 144.9 | 144.8 | 143.2 | 144.3 | 145.3 | 148.2 | 148.3 | 148.9 | 148.8 | 145.6 |
| 2017 | 146.9 | 148.7 | 149.2 | 149.5 | 148.7 | 146.5 | 147.1 | 147.9 | 151.1 | 151.5 | 151.9 | 151.6 | 149.2 |
| 2018 | 150.2 | 152.1 | 152.6 | 153.1 | 151.9 | 150.3 | 150.6 | 151.9 | 154.4 | 154.4 | 154.8 | 153.9 | 152.5 |
| 2019 | 152.0 | 154.4 | 154.9 | 153.8 | 154.5 | 153.1 | 151.8 | 153.9 | 156.9 | 158.0 | 158.3 | 156.8 | 154.9 |
| **Leisure and Hospitality** | | | | | | | | | | | | | |
| 2011 | 75.9 | 76.4 | 78.6 | 80.5 | 82.5 | 83.0 | 83.2 | 84.1 | 83.7 | 83.8 | 83.9 | 84.1 | 81.6 |
| 2012 | 81.3 | 81.7 | 84.3 | 85.9 | 88.0 | 88.9 | 87.8 | 88.5 | 86.6 | 87.9 | 87.7 | 88.2 | 86.4 |
| 2013 | 84.3 | 85.9 | 87.7 | 90.4 | 92.3 | 93.3 | 92.4 | 92.7 | 91.2 | 92.0 | 92.1 | 91.9 | 90.5 |
| 2014 | 88.8 | 90.4 | 92.3 | 95.4 | 97.1 | 98.4 | 97.9 | 98.6 | 97.8 | 97.4 | 97.4 | 97.0 | 95.7 |
| 2015 | 94.5 | 95.4 | 96.8 | 100.0 | 102.3 | 103.5 | 102.3 | 102.4 | 101.2 | 102.0 | 102.0 | 102.4 | 100.4 |
| 2016 | 99.5 | 100.3 | 102.4 | 105.5 | 106.5 | 108.3 | 107.6 | 107.6 | 107.2 | 106.7 | 107.1 | 107.2 | 105.5 |
| 2017 | 104.2 | 105.9 | 107.9 | 109.5 | 111.5 | 113.7 | 113.0 | 113.9 | 112.9 | 112.3 | 112.8 | 112.4 | 110.8 |
| 2018 | 108.7 | 110.5 | 112.8 | 115.0 | 117.4 | 119.8 | 119.6 | 120.5 | 119.1 | 118.4 | 118.1 | 117.8 | 116.5 |
| 2019 | 114.4 | 115.7 | 117.6 | 121.1 | 122.9 | 125.0 | 124.3 | 125.7 | 124.3 | 124.1 | 124.5 | 122.4 | 121.8 |
| **Other Services** | | | | | | | | | | | | | |
| 2011 | 32.8 | 33.3 | 33.6 | 33.3 | 33.7 | 34.5 | 34.3 | 34.1 | 33.8 | 33.8 | 34.1 | 34.1 | 33.8 |
| 2012 | 33.9 | 34.2 | 34.6 | 34.7 | 35.0 | 35.8 | 35.6 | 35.2 | 35.0 | 35.2 | 35.3 | 35.5 | 35.0 |
| 2013 | 35.3 | 35.8 | 36.1 | 36.4 | 36.7 | 37.2 | 36.9 | 36.7 | 36.4 | 36.4 | 36.6 | 36.3 | 36.4 |
| 2014 | 36.1 | 36.4 | 36.7 | 37.0 | 37.2 | 37.5 | 37.5 | 36.9 | 36.8 | 37.0 | 37.2 | 37.0 | 36.9 |
| 2015 | 36.8 | 36.8 | 37.0 | 37.3 | 37.9 | 38.4 | 38.1 | 37.6 | 37.7 | 37.8 | 37.9 | 38.2 | 37.6 |
| 2016 | 37.8 | 38.2 | 38.6 | 38.9 | 39.2 | 39.6 | 39.7 | 39.5 | 39.5 | 39.5 | 39.7 | 39.8 | 39.2 |
| 2017 | 39.4 | 39.8 | 40.1 | 40.3 | 40.7 | 41.5 | 41.2 | 41.2 | 41.2 | 41.2 | 41.3 | 41.5 | 40.8 |
| 2018 | 40.8 | 41.3 | 41.7 | 41.9 | 42.3 | 43.1 | 42.8 | 42.8 | 42.6 | 42.5 | 42.6 | 42.6 | 42.3 |
| 2019 | 42.2 | 42.5 | 42.8 | 43.2 | 43.7 | 44.1 | 43.9 | 43.6 | 43.6 | 42.9 | 43.9 | 42.7 | 43.3 |
| **Government** | | | | | | | | | | | | | |
| 2011 | 111.8 | 112.1 | 112.7 | 113.3 | 113.1 | 103.4 | 103.5 | 109.2 | 112.8 | 113.1 | 113.4 | 113.1 | 111.0 |
| 2012 | 110.9 | 112.8 | 113.6 | 112.6 | 111.0 | 101.3 | 100.4 | 106.9 | 110.8 | 111.8 | 112.7 | 112.6 | 109.8 |
| 2013 | 109.8 | 112.2 | 112.4 | 113.9 | 112.7 | 102.4 | 101.8 | 108.3 | 112.5 | 114.1 | 114.1 | 113.9 | 110.7 |
| 2014 | 111.4 | 114.0 | 114.1 | 114.0 | 114.1 | 103.3 | 102.7 | 109.3 | 113.7 | 115.1 | 117.0 | 115.5 | 112.0 |
| 2015 | 112.3 | 115.4 | 115.4 | 115.2 | 114.6 | 104.8 | 104.3 | 111.0 | 115.6 | 117.8 | 117.4 | 117.4 | 113.4 |
| 2016 | 113.7 | 116.1 | 118.2 | 116.8 | 115.0 | 105.9 | 105.9 | 113.2 | 118.0 | 117.8 | 118.7 | 118.6 | 114.8 |
| 2017 | 116.0 | 118.5 | 118.9 | 118.7 | 117.5 | 108.0 | 107.6 | 114.5 | 119.1 | 119.9 | 120.5 | 120.9 | 116.7 |
| 2018 | 118.0 | 120.5 | 120.7 | 120.6 | 119.2 | 109.9 | 109.1 | 115.8 | 120.5 | 122.0 | 122.9 | 122.8 | 118.5 |
| 2019 | 120.3 | 122.4 | 122.6 | 122.9 | 121.4 | 111.6 | 110.1 | 117.0 | 120.5 | 122.0 | 123.0 | 122.7 | 119.7 |

## Employment by Industry: Virginia Beach-Norfolk-Newport News, VA-NC, 2011–2019

(Numbers in thousands, not seasonally adjusted)

| Industry and year | January | February | March | April | May | June | July | August | September | October | November | December | Annual average |
|---|---|---|---|---|---|---|---|---|---|---|---|---|---|
| **Total Nonfarm** | | | | | | | | | | | | | |
| 2011 | 720.8 | 722.5 | 730.7 | 739.8 | 743.3 | 751.0 | 749.4 | 749.0 | 745.5 | 742.9 | 743.4 | 743.5 | 740.2 |
| 2012 | 728.5 | 731.7 | 738.1 | 744.7 | 747.0 | 754.4 | 751.3 | 753.0 | 748.7 | 753.5 | 755.3 | 755.7 | 746.8 |
| 2013 | 740.2 | 742.6 | 748.6 | 755.0 | 758.4 | 765.1 | 763.6 | 765.4 | 758.6 | 758.7 | 760.2 | 760.2 | 756.4 |
| 2014 | 742.6 | 742.3 | 748.7 | 758.2 | 762.7 | 768.1 | 764.8 | 767.3 | 760.8 | 760.3 | 761.4 | 761.4 | 758.2 |
| | | | | | | | | | | | | | |
| 2015 | 747.9 | 748.4 | 752.1 | 763.5 | 767.7 | 773.7 | 774.9 | 776.4 | 771.4 | 774.1 | 775.5 | 775.2 | 766.7 |
| 2016 | 755.3 | 757.0 | 763.0 | 772.5 | 772.6 | 780.3 | 777.4 | 779.1 | 776.3 | 777.5 | 780.1 | 778.1 | 772.4 |
| 2017 | 760.8 | 768.4 | 773.5 | 782.2 | 784.0 | 792.7 | 788.6 | 788.9 | 785.0 | 786.5 | 789.7 | 791.4 | 782.6 |
| 2018 | 772.8 | 779.5 | 786.8 | 792.3 | 795.7 | 803.3 | 798.1 | 798.0 | 787.5 | 796.1 | 799.2 | 795.9 | 792.1 |
| 2019 | 781.3 | 785.3 | 790.5 | 795.0 | 797.3 | 806.0 | 800.2 | 800.4 | 794.2 | 795.3 | 798.8 | 799.2 | 795.3 |
| | | | | | | | | | | | | | |
| **Total Private** | | | | | | | | | | | | | |
| 2011 | 559.8 | 560.7 | 568.0 | 576.9 | 580.7 | 588.0 | 590.1 | 589.1 | 583.2 | 579.0 | 577.7 | 578.0 | 577.6 |
| 2012 | 565.5 | 567.6 | 574.5 | 581.0 | 583.6 | 590.7 | 592.4 | 593.8 | 587.4 | 590.1 | 590.4 | 591.6 | 584.1 |
| 2013 | 578.8 | 579.6 | 585.5 | 592.0 | 596.0 | 603.0 | 605.2 | 606.6 | 598.2 | 596.8 | 597.4 | 597.1 | 594.7 |
| 2014 | 582.6 | 581.5 | 587.5 | 596.7 | 602.1 | 608.1 | 608.0 | 609.6 | 601.8 | 600.7 | 600.6 | 600.4 | 598.3 |
| | | | | | | | | | | | | | |
| 2015 | 589.0 | 587.9 | 592.2 | 602.2 | 607.4 | 613.4 | 618.5 | 620.1 | 614.0 | 613.3 | 613.2 | 613.3 | 607.0 |
| 2016 | 596.7 | 596.6 | 601.7 | 611.3 | 612.3 | 619.9 | 621.2 | 622.5 | 617.3 | 616.4 | 617.7 | 615.8 | 612.5 |
| 2017 | 601.6 | 607.4 | 612.6 | 620.8 | 624.0 | 631.9 | 632.1 | 632.2 | 626.0 | 625.7 | 626.7 | 628.9 | 622.5 |
| 2018 | 613.8 | 618.4 | 625.2 | 630.8 | 634.7 | 642.0 | 642.4 | 642.5 | 629.1 | 634.9 | 635.9 | 633.1 | 631.9 |
| 2019 | 621.4 | 623.3 | 628.4 | 633.4 | 636.8 | 644.1 | 644.0 | 643.0 | 634.2 | 634.5 | 634.8 | 636.8 | 634.6 |
| | | | | | | | | | | | | | |
| **Goods Producing** | | | | | | | | | | | | | |
| 2011 | 85.7 | 85.7 | 86.7 | 86.6 | 87.3 | 87.6 | 88.3 | 88.3 | 87.8 | 86.9 | 86.8 | 86.7 | 87.0 |
| 2012 | 86.6 | 86.8 | 87.3 | 86.8 | 86.4 | 86.7 | 89.6 | 89.6 | 89.8 | 89.6 | 89.6 | 89.6 | 88.2 |
| 2013 | 88.2 | 88.6 | 88.8 | 89.0 | 89.2 | 89.8 | 90.4 | 90.4 | 90.1 | 89.5 | 89.7 | 89.8 | 89.5 |
| 2014 | 88.4 | 88.3 | 88.7 | 89.4 | 89.8 | 90.4 | 90.5 | 90.3 | 89.8 | 89.7 | 89.8 | 89.7 | 89.6 |
| | | | | | | | | | | | | | |
| 2015 | 88.5 | 88.2 | 88.6 | 89.9 | 90.0 | 90.6 | 91.4 | 91.0 | 90.5 | 90.7 | 90.2 | 90.0 | 90.0 |
| 2016 | 88.0 | 87.2 | 87.2 | 86.8 | 86.8 | 87.6 | 88.5 | 88.6 | 88.8 | 89.0 | 89.3 | 89.3 | 88.1 |
| 2017 | 88.3 | 88.9 | 89.4 | 89.8 | 90.2 | 90.8 | 90.8 | 91.0 | 90.9 | 91.5 | 92.0 | 92.5 | 90.5 |
| 2018 | 91.2 | 92.5 | 93.2 | 94.0 | 94.9 | 96.1 | 96.5 | 96.7 | 95.5 | 96.6 | 96.8 | 96.9 | 95.1 |
| 2019 | 96.1 | 96.5 | 96.9 | 97.0 | 97.3 | 98.1 | 98.3 | 98.1 | 97.8 | 98.9 | 99.4 | 99.6 | 97.8 |
| | | | | | | | | | | | | | |
| **Service-Providing** | | | | | | | | | | | | | |
| 2011 | 635.1 | 636.8 | 644.0 | 653.2 | 656.0 | 663.4 | 661.1 | 660.7 | 657.7 | 656.0 | 656.6 | 656.8 | 653.1 |
| 2012 | 641.9 | 644.9 | 650.8 | 657.9 | 660.6 | 667.7 | 661.7 | 663.4 | 658.9 | 663.9 | 665.7 | 666.1 | 658.6 |
| 2013 | 652.0 | 654.0 | 659.8 | 666.0 | 669.2 | 675.3 | 673.2 | 675.0 | 668.5 | 669.2 | 670.5 | 670.4 | 666.9 |
| 2014 | 654.2 | 654.0 | 660.0 | 668.8 | 672.9 | 677.7 | 674.3 | 677.0 | 671.0 | 670.6 | 671.6 | 671.7 | 668.7 |
| | | | | | | | | | | | | | |
| 2015 | 659.4 | 660.2 | 663.5 | 673.6 | 677.7 | 683.1 | 683.5 | 685.4 | 680.9 | 683.4 | 685.3 | 685.2 | 676.8 |
| 2016 | 667.3 | 669.8 | 675.8 | 685.7 | 685.8 | 692.7 | 688.9 | 690.5 | 687.5 | 688.5 | 690.8 | 688.8 | 684.3 |
| 2017 | 672.5 | 679.5 | 684.1 | 692.4 | 693.8 | 701.9 | 697.8 | 697.9 | 694.1 | 695.0 | 697.7 | 698.9 | 692.1 |
| 2018 | 681.6 | 687.0 | 693.6 | 698.3 | 700.8 | 707.2 | 701.6 | 701.3 | 692.0 | 699.5 | 702.4 | 699.0 | 697.0 |
| 2019 | 685.2 | 688.8 | 693.6 | 698.0 | 700.0 | 707.9 | 701.9 | 702.3 | 696.4 | 696.4 | 699.4 | 699.6 | 697.5 |
| | | | | | | | | | | | | | |
| **Mining, Logging, and Construction** | | | | | | | | | | | | | |
| 2011 | 34.8 | 34.9 | 35.1 | 35.5 | 35.6 | 35.7 | 35.6 | 35.5 | 35.0 | 34.6 | 34.5 | 34.4 | 35.1 |
| 2012 | 33.4 | 33.5 | 33.8 | 34.2 | 34.7 | 35.4 | 35.5 | 35.3 | 34.6 | 34.9 | 34.6 | 34.5 | 34.5 |
| 2013 | 33.9 | 34.1 | 34.4 | 34.4 | 34.7 | 35.2 | 35.4 | 35.4 | 35.1 | 34.6 | 34.7 | 34.5 | 34.7 |
| 2014 | 33.6 | 33.3 | 33.6 | 34.1 | 34.4 | 34.9 | 35.1 | 35.2 | 34.9 | 34.8 | 34.8 | 34.8 | 34.5 |
| | | | | | | | | | | | | | |
| 2015 | 34.1 | 34.1 | 34.4 | 35.6 | 36.0 | 36.4 | 37.1 | 37.0 | 36.6 | 36.9 | 36.8 | 36.8 | 36.0 |
| 2016 | 35.6 | 35.5 | 35.8 | 35.7 | 35.6 | 36.1 | 36.7 | 36.6 | 36.7 | 36.9 | 37.1 | 37.1 | 36.3 |
| 2017 | 36.3 | 36.7 | 37.0 | 37.2 | 37.6 | 38.1 | 37.8 | 38.0 | 37.6 | 37.8 | 37.9 | 38.0 | 37.5 |
| 2018 | 36.8 | 37.3 | 37.6 | 37.9 | 38.3 | 38.9 | 39.1 | 39.0 | 38.1 | 38.7 | 38.8 | 38.8 | 38.3 |
| 2019 | 38.2 | 38.3 | 38.4 | 38.5 | 38.8 | 39.2 | 39.4 | 39.2 | 39.0 | 40.0 | 40.1 | 40.1 | 39.1 |
| | | | | | | | | | | | | | |
| **Manufacturing** | | | | | | | | | | | | | |
| 2011 | 50.9 | 50.8 | 51.6 | 51.1 | 51.7 | 51.9 | 52.7 | 52.8 | 52.8 | 52.3 | 52.3 | 52.3 | 51.9 |
| 2012 | 53.2 | 53.3 | 53.5 | 52.6 | 51.7 | 51.3 | 54.1 | 54.3 | 55.2 | 54.7 | 55.0 | 55.1 | 53.7 |
| 2013 | 54.3 | 54.5 | 54.4 | 54.6 | 54.5 | 54.6 | 55.0 | 55.0 | 55.0 | 54.9 | 55.0 | 55.3 | 54.8 |
| 2014 | 54.8 | 55.0 | 55.1 | 55.3 | 55.4 | 55.5 | 55.4 | 55.1 | 54.9 | 54.9 | 55.0 | 54.9 | 55.1 |
| | | | | | | | | | | | | | |
| 2015 | 54.4 | 54.1 | 54.2 | 54.3 | 54.0 | 54.2 | 54.3 | 54.0 | 53.9 | 53.8 | 53.4 | 53.2 | 54.0 |
| 2016 | 52.4 | 51.7 | 51.4 | 51.1 | 51.2 | 51.5 | 51.8 | 52.0 | 52.1 | 52.1 | 52.2 | 52.2 | 51.8 |
| 2017 | 52.0 | 52.2 | 52.4 | 52.6 | 52.6 | 52.7 | 53.0 | 53.0 | 53.3 | 53.7 | 54.1 | 54.5 | 53.0 |
| 2018 | 54.4 | 55.2 | 55.6 | 56.1 | 56.6 | 57.2 | 57.4 | 57.7 | 57.4 | 57.9 | 58.0 | 58.1 | 56.8 |
| 2019 | 57.9 | 58.2 | 58.5 | 58.5 | 58.5 | 58.9 | 58.9 | 58.9 | 58.8 | 58.9 | 59.3 | 59.5 | 58.7 |

## Employment by Industry: Virginia Beach-Norfolk-Newport News, VA-NC, 2011–2019—*Continued*

(Numbers in thousands, not seasonally adjusted)

| Industry and year | January | February | March | April | May | June | July | August | September | October | November | December | Annual average |
|---|---|---|---|---|---|---|---|---|---|---|---|---|---|
| **Trade, Transportation, and Utilities** | | | | | | | | | | | | | |
| 2011 | 126.2 | 125.2 | 125.7 | 127.0 | 127.5 | 128.3 | 127.8 | 127.9 | 126.6 | 127.2 | 129.9 | 131.4 | 127.6 |
| 2012 | 125.5 | 124.3 | 125.2 | 126.0 | 127.2 | 128.0 | 127.5 | 126.9 | 125.6 | 127.4 | 130.6 | 131.6 | 127.2 |
| 2013 | 125.6 | 124.4 | 124.9 | 125.5 | 126.8 | 127.9 | 128.5 | 128.9 | 127.8 | 128.5 | 131.8 | 133.1 | 127.8 |
| 2014 | 126.4 | 125.3 | 125.6 | 126.7 | 127.7 | 128.8 | 129.0 | 129.5 | 128.8 | 129.9 | 133.6 | 134.7 | 128.8 |
| 2015 | 128.5 | 127.5 | 127.7 | 128.5 | 129.8 | 130.9 | 131.9 | 132.0 | 130.8 | 131.5 | 135.1 | 136.1 | 130.9 |
| 2016 | 130.0 | 129.2 | 129.8 | 131.3 | 132.8 | 133.8 | 133.4 | 133.8 | 133.3 | 134.1 | 137.6 | 137.6 | 133.1 |
| 2017 | 131.3 | 130.6 | 131.0 | 131.9 | 133.1 | 134.7 | 134.0 | 134.1 | 133.2 | 133.5 | 136.9 | 137.0 | 133.4 |
| 2018 | 130.1 | 129.4 | 129.6 | 129.6 | 131.4 | 131.3 | 131.1 | 131.2 | 129.3 | 130.7 | 134.0 | 133.7 | 131.0 |
| 2019 | 128.9 | 127.5 | 128.2 | 129.1 | 129.4 | 130.5 | 130.8 | 130.6 | 129.8 | 131.0 | 133.7 | 134.3 | 130.3 |
| **Wholesale Trade** | | | | | | | | | | | | | |
| 2011 | 20.6 | 20.5 | 20.6 | 20.6 | 20.7 | 20.7 | 20.6 | 20.5 | 20.3 | 20.2 | 20.1 | 20.3 | 20.5 |
| 2012 | 20.1 | 20.1 | 20.1 | 20.0 | 20.0 | 20.1 | 20.1 | 20.0 | 19.8 | 19.9 | 19.9 | 19.9 | 20.0 |
| 2013 | 19.4 | 19.4 | 19.4 | 19.3 | 19.4 | 19.4 | 19.5 | 19.6 | 19.5 | 19.5 | 19.5 | 19.6 | 19.5 |
| 2014 | 19.4 | 19.5 | 19.4 | 19.5 | 19.6 | 19.4 | 19.4 | 19.4 | 19.3 | 19.3 | 19.4 | 19.5 | 19.4 |
| 2015 | 19.2 | 19.2 | 19.1 | 19.2 | 19.2 | 19.3 | 19.4 | 19.3 | 19.3 | 19.3 | 19.3 | 19.4 | 19.3 |
| 2016 | 19.0 | 19.0 | 18.9 | 18.9 | 19.0 | 19.1 | 19.1 | 19.0 | 18.9 | 18.8 | 18.9 | 19.0 | 19.0 |
| 2017 | 18.9 | 18.8 | 18.8 | 19.0 | 19.0 | 19.1 | 19.0 | 18.9 | 18.8 | 18.9 | 18.8 | 19.0 | 18.9 |
| 2018 | 18.5 | 18.6 | 18.6 | 18.6 | 18.6 | 18.7 | 18.7 | 18.8 | 18.6 | 18.8 | 18.9 | 18.9 | 18.7 |
| 2019 | 18.6 | 18.8 | 18.9 | 18.9 | 18.9 | 19.0 | 18.9 | 18.8 | 18.6 | 18.6 | 18.7 | 18.7 | 18.8 |
| **Retail Trade** | | | | | | | | | | | | | |
| 2011 | 82.6 | 81.9 | 82.3 | 83.4 | 84.2 | 84.9 | 84.6 | 84.7 | 83.5 | 84.1 | 86.7 | 88.0 | 84.2 |
| 2012 | 83.3 | 81.9 | 82.8 | 83.4 | 84.3 | 84.8 | 84.4 | 84.0 | 82.9 | 84.3 | 87.6 | 88.4 | 84.3 |
| 2013 | 83.8 | 83.0 | 83.5 | 84.0 | 84.9 | 85.7 | 85.9 | 86.2 | 85.2 | 85.8 | 88.7 | 89.9 | 85.6 |
| 2014 | 84.1 | 83.1 | 83.4 | 84.4 | 85.1 | 86.1 | 86.2 | 86.7 | 86.0 | 87.2 | 90.1 | 90.8 | 86.1 |
| 2015 | 86.0 | 84.9 | 85.3 | 85.9 | 86.9 | 87.6 | 88.0 | 88.2 | 87.2 | 87.5 | 90.6 | 91.1 | 87.4 |
| 2016 | 86.6 | 86.0 | 86.6 | 87.7 | 88.6 | 89.2 | 88.8 | 89.2 | 88.7 | 89.3 | 92.0 | 91.7 | 88.7 |
| 2017 | 87.0 | 86.4 | 86.8 | 87.4 | 88.3 | 89.6 | 89.3 | 89.3 | 88.5 | 88.6 | 91.8 | 91.4 | 88.7 |
| 2018 | 86.5 | 85.7 | 85.9 | 86.0 | 87.5 | 87.0 | 86.6 | 86.4 | 85.1 | 86.0 | 88.9 | 88.1 | 86.6 |
| 2019 | 84.5 | 83.2 | 83.7 | 84.4 | 84.5 | 85.3 | 85.5 | 85.4 | 84.5 | 85.6 | 87.5 | 87.4 | 85.1 |
| **Transportation and Utilities** | | | | | | | | | | | | | |
| 2011 | 23.0 | 22.8 | 22.8 | 23.0 | 22.6 | 22.7 | 22.6 | 22.7 | 22.8 | 22.9 | 23.1 | 23.1 | 22.8 |
| 2012 | 22.1 | 22.3 | 22.3 | 22.6 | 22.9 | 23.1 | 23.0 | 22.9 | 22.9 | 23.2 | 23.1 | 23.3 | 22.8 |
| 2013 | 22.4 | 22.0 | 22.0 | 22.2 | 22.5 | 22.8 | 23.1 | 23.1 | 23.1 | 23.2 | 23.6 | 23.6 | 22.8 |
| 2014 | 22.9 | 22.7 | 22.8 | 22.8 | 23.0 | 23.3 | 23.4 | 23.4 | 23.5 | 23.4 | 24.1 | 24.4 | 23.3 |
| 2015 | 23.3 | 23.4 | 23.3 | 23.4 | 23.7 | 24.0 | 24.5 | 24.5 | 24.3 | 24.7 | 25.2 | 25.6 | 24.2 |
| 2016 | 24.4 | 24.2 | 24.3 | 24.7 | 25.2 | 25.5 | 25.5 | 25.6 | 25.7 | 26.0 | 26.7 | 26.9 | 25.4 |
| 2017 | 25.4 | 25.4 | 25.4 | 25.5 | 25.8 | 26.0 | 25.7 | 25.9 | 25.9 | 26.0 | 26.3 | 26.6 | 25.8 |
| 2018 | 25.1 | 25.1 | 25.1 | 25.0 | 25.3 | 25.6 | 25.8 | 26.0 | 25.6 | 25.9 | 26.2 | 26.7 | 25.6 |
| 2019 | 25.8 | 25.5 | 25.6 | 25.8 | 26.0 | 26.2 | 26.4 | 26.4 | 26.7 | 26.8 | 27.5 | 28.2 | 26.4 |
| **Information** | | | | | | | | | | | | | |
| 2011 | 11.6 | 11.5 | 11.6 | 11.6 | 11.7 | 11.8 | 11.9 | 10.9 | 11.6 | 11.4 | 11.4 | 11.6 | 11.6 |
| 2012 | 11.6 | 11.6 | 11.7 | 11.7 | 11.8 | 11.8 | 11.5 | 11.7 | 11.3 | 11.4 | 11.6 | 11.6 | 11.6 |
| 2013 | 11.5 | 11.6 | 11.6 | 11.4 | 11.6 | 11.6 | 11.6 | 11.6 | 11.3 | 11.3 | 11.4 | 11.2 | 11.5 |
| 2014 | 11.2 | 10.9 | 10.9 | 10.8 | 11.2 | 11.0 | 11.0 | 11.1 | 10.8 | 10.8 | 10.8 | 10.8 | 10.9 |
| 2015 | 10.8 | 10.7 | 10.7 | 10.8 | 11.0 | 11.0 | 11.2 | 11.0 | 10.8 | 11.0 | 11.1 | 11.1 | 10.9 |
| 2016 | 11.3 | 11.3 | 11.1 | 11.4 | 10.7 | 11.5 | 11.4 | 11.2 | 11.0 | 11.0 | 11.0 | 11.2 | 11.2 |
| 2017 | 11.2 | 11.3 | 11.2 | 11.2 | 11.3 | 11.4 | 11.4 | 11.2 | 11.0 | 10.9 | 11.0 | 11.2 | 11.2 |
| 2018 | 10.8 | 11.0 | 11.0 | 11.0 | 11.1 | 11.1 | 11.0 | 11.0 | 10.5 | 10.5 | 10.5 | 10.5 | 10.8 |
| 2019 | 10.4 | 10.5 | 10.6 | 10.5 | 10.7 | 10.6 | 10.5 | 10.5 | 10.2 | 10.2 | 10.3 | 10.2 | 10.4 |
| **Financial Activities** | | | | | | | | | | | | | |
| 2011 | 36.0 | 36.1 | 36.1 | 36.9 | 37.0 | 37.6 | 37.9 | 37.6 | 37.0 | 36.6 | 36.5 | 36.9 | 36.9 |
| 2012 | 36.4 | 36.7 | 36.8 | 37.3 | 37.1 | 37.9 | 38.3 | 38.2 | 37.8 | 37.7 | 37.6 | 37.7 | 37.5 |
| 2013 | 37.1 | 37.1 | 37.2 | 37.8 | 38.0 | 38.6 | 38.7 | 38.5 | 38.0 | 37.7 | 37.7 | 37.8 | 37.9 |
| 2014 | 36.9 | 37.0 | 37.2 | 37.5 | 37.9 | 38.4 | 38.6 | 38.5 | 38.2 | 37.7 | 37.6 | 37.8 | 37.8 |
| 2015 | 37.6 | 37.8 | 37.8 | 37.6 | 37.9 | 38.4 | 38.7 | 38.6 | 38.2 | 37.9 | 37.5 | 37.6 | 38.0 |
| 2016 | 37.0 | 36.8 | 37.0 | 37.5 | 37.8 | 38.5 | 38.6 | 38.5 | 38.0 | 37.9 | 37.7 | 37.8 | 37.8 |
| 2017 | 37.0 | 37.2 | 37.2 | 37.3 | 37.7 | 38.4 | 38.7 | 38.7 | 38.5 | 38.2 | 38.2 | 38.3 | 38.0 |
| 2018 | 38.4 | 38.4 | 38.6 | 38.7 | 39.1 | 39.7 | 39.6 | 39.6 | 39.1 | 39.0 | 39.0 | 39.1 | 39.0 |
| 2019 | 38.4 | 38.5 | 38.6 | 39.0 | 39.4 | 39.9 | 40.1 | 40.1 | 39.7 | 39.5 | 39.7 | 39.3 | 39.4 |

## Employment by Industry: Virginia Beach-Norfolk-Newport News, VA-NC, 2011–2019—*Continued*

(Numbers in thousands, not seasonally adjusted)

| Industry and year | January | February | March | April | May | June | July | August | September | October | November | December | Annual average |
|---|---|---|---|---|---|---|---|---|---|---|---|---|---|
| **Professional and Business Services** | | | | | | | | | | | | | |
| 2011 | 96.5 | 96.5 | 96.9 | 98.0 | 97.7 | 98.6 | 99.5 | 100.4 | 100.7 | 99.5 | 99.3 | 99.0 | 98.6 |
| 2012 | 97.6 | 98.2 | 98.6 | 99.3 | 98.7 | 99.7 | 99.6 | 100.4 | 99.9 | 101.5 | 101.4 | 101.7 | 99.7 |
| 2013 | 101.3 | 101.7 | 102.2 | 102.7 | 102.3 | 103.1 | 103.2 | 103.8 | 102.1 | 102.6 | 102.9 | 102.3 | 102.5 |
| 2014 | 101.6 | 102.1 | 103.1 | 104.9 | 104.5 | 105.5 | 105.5 | 106.1 | 104.9 | 105.5 | 104.9 | 104.3 | 104.4 |
| 2015 | 102.8 | 103.0 | 103.3 | 104.7 | 104.8 | 105.4 | 106.3 | 107.0 | 106.0 | 106.0 | 105.5 | 105.2 | 105.0 |
| 2016 | 102.2 | 102.9 | 102.5 | 104.1 | 103.1 | 104.5 | 105.4 | 105.9 | 105.4 | 105.6 | 105.8 | 105.3 | 104.4 |
| 2017 | 103.9 | 106.5 | 107.4 | 109.3 | 108.5 | 110.1 | 110.0 | 110.5 | 110.5 | 109.9 | 110.5 | 111.2 | 109.0 |
| 2018 | 109.4 | 111.7 | 113.0 | 114.5 | 113.6 | 115.0 | 114.7 | 115.1 | 112.7 | 114.3 | 114.1 | 113.6 | 113.5 |
| 2019 | 111.5 | 112.6 | 113.1 | 114.1 | 114.8 | 115.8 | 115.2 | 115.5 | 113.7 | 112.9 | 112.6 | 112.7 | 113.7 |
| **Education and Health Services** | | | | | | | | | | | | | |
| 2011 | 96.3 | 97.1 | 97.7 | 98.4 | 97.3 | 97.0 | 97.3 | 97.6 | 99.1 | 99.5 | 99.7 | 98.4 | 98.0 |
| 2012 | 98.8 | 99.6 | 99.9 | 100.4 | 99.1 | 99.2 | 98.6 | 99.6 | 101.2 | 102.9 | 103.3 | 102.5 | 100.4 |
| 2013 | 102.9 | 103.6 | 103.8 | 104.7 | 103.0 | 103.0 | 102.4 | 103.9 | 105.2 | 106.0 | 106.6 | 105.3 | 104.2 |
| 2014 | 105.1 | 105.3 | 105.3 | 106.2 | 104.7 | 104.1 | 103.8 | 105.0 | 106.0 | 106.4 | 106.4 | 105.3 | 105.3 |
| 2015 | 106.6 | 106.9 | 107.0 | 108.8 | 107.3 | 106.8 | 107.5 | 108.8 | 110.2 | 111.4 | 111.8 | 110.3 | 108.6 |
| 2016 | 110.3 | 110.7 | 111.1 | 112.2 | 110.2 | 109.3 | 108.8 | 110.0 | 111.6 | 112.3 | 112.4 | 110.7 | 110.8 |
| 2017 | 110.9 | 112.1 | 112.4 | 112.7 | 111.0 | 110.4 | 110.3 | 111.2 | 112.1 | 113.7 | 113.5 | 113.3 | 112.0 |
| 2018 | 113.0 | 114.3 | 114.8 | 114.5 | 112.3 | 112.3 | 112.2 | 113.0 | 113.8 | 115.0 | 115.1 | 113.5 | 113.7 |
| 2019 | 113.7 | 115.1 | 115.0 | 114.7 | 112.9 | 112.7 | 111.8 | 112.6 | 113.6 | 114.6 | 114.5 | 114.4 | 113.8 |
| **Leisure and Hospitality** | | | | | | | | | | | | | |
| 2011 | 74.0 | 74.9 | 79.1 | 83.6 | 87.2 | 91.8 | 92.0 | 91.0 | 85.3 | 82.9 | 79.3 | 79.3 | 83.4 |
| 2012 | 75.0 | 76.1 | 80.3 | 83.7 | 87.4 | 91.2 | 91.3 | 91.3 | 86.2 | 83.6 | 80.4 | 81.1 | 84.0 |
| 2013 | 76.8 | 77.0 | 81.2 | 84.7 | 88.7 | 92.3 | 93.6 | 93.0 | 87.6 | 85.3 | 81.5 | 81.9 | 85.3 |
| 2014 | 77.9 | 77.4 | 81.1 | 85.3 | 90.0 | 93.3 | 93.0 | 92.5 | 87.0 | 84.9 | 81.9 | 82.3 | 85.6 |
| 2015 | 78.9 | 78.5 | 81.5 | 86.3 | 90.6 | 94.0 | 95.2 | 95.4 | 91.6 | 88.8 | 86.0 | 87.0 | 87.8 |
| 2016 | 82.4 | 83.1 | 87.2 | 91.7 | 94.4 | 98.1 | 98.5 | 98.0 | 93.0 | 90.2 | 87.6 | 87.9 | 91.0 |
| 2017 | 83.2 | 84.9 | 87.8 | 92.7 | 96.1 | 99.6 | 100.3 | 99.2 | 93.8 | 92.1 | 88.9 | 89.7 | 92.4 |
| 2018 | 85.6 | 85.8 | 89.3 | 92.9 | 96.4 | 100.1 | 100.9 | 99.7 | 92.6 | 93.0 | 90.6 | 90.0 | 93.1 |
| 2019 | 86.7 | 86.7 | 89.8 | 92.5 | 95.5 | 99.2 | 99.9 | 98.5 | 92.8 | 90.8 | 88.1 | 89.9 | 92.5 |
| **Other Services** | | | | | | | | | | | | | |
| 2011 | 33.5 | 33.7 | 34.2 | 34.8 | 35.0 | 35.3 | 35.4 | 35.4 | 35.1 | 35.0 | 34.8 | 34.7 | 34.7 |
| 2012 | 34.0 | 34.3 | 34.7 | 35.8 | 35.9 | 36.2 | 36.0 | 36.1 | 35.6 | 36.0 | 35.9 | 35.8 | 35.5 |
| 2013 | 35.4 | 35.6 | 35.8 | 36.2 | 36.4 | 36.7 | 36.8 | 36.5 | 36.1 | 35.9 | 35.8 | 35.7 | 36.1 |
| 2014 | 35.1 | 35.2 | 35.6 | 35.9 | 36.3 | 36.6 | 36.6 | 36.6 | 36.3 | 35.8 | 35.6 | 35.5 | 35.9 |
| 2015 | 35.3 | 35.3 | 35.6 | 35.6 | 36.0 | 36.3 | 36.3 | 36.3 | 35.9 | 36.0 | 36.0 | 36.0 | 35.9 |
| 2016 | 35.5 | 35.4 | 35.8 | 36.3 | 36.5 | 36.6 | 36.6 | 36.5 | 36.2 | 36.3 | 36.3 | 36.0 | 36.2 |
| 2017 | 35.8 | 35.9 | 36.2 | 35.9 | 36.1 | 36.5 | 36.6 | 36.3 | 36.0 | 35.9 | 35.7 | 35.7 | 36.1 |
| 2018 | 35.3 | 35.3 | 35.7 | 35.6 | 35.9 | 36.4 | 36.4 | 36.2 | 35.6 | 35.8 | 35.8 | 35.8 | 35.8 |
| 2019 | 35.7 | 35.9 | 36.2 | 36.5 | 36.8 | 37.3 | 37.4 | 37.1 | 36.6 | 36.6 | 36.5 | 36.4 | 36.6 |
| **Government** | | | | | | | | | | | | | |
| 2011 | 161.0 | 161.8 | 162.7 | 162.9 | 162.6 | 163.0 | 159.3 | 159.9 | 162.3 | 163.9 | 165.7 | 165.5 | 162.6 |
| 2012 | 163.0 | 164.1 | 163.6 | 163.7 | 163.4 | 163.7 | 158.9 | 159.2 | 161.3 | 163.4 | 164.9 | 164.1 | 162.8 |
| 2013 | 161.4 | 163.0 | 163.1 | 163.0 | 162.4 | 162.1 | 158.4 | 158.8 | 160.4 | 161.9 | 162.8 | 163.1 | 161.7 |
| 2014 | 160.0 | 160.8 | 161.2 | 161.5 | 160.6 | 160.0 | 156.8 | 157.7 | 159.0 | 159.6 | 160.8 | 161.0 | 159.9 |
| 2015 | 158.9 | 160.5 | 159.9 | 161.3 | 160.3 | 160.3 | 156.4 | 156.3 | 157.4 | 160.8 | 162.3 | 161.9 | 159.7 |
| 2016 | 158.6 | 160.4 | 161.3 | 161.2 | 160.3 | 160.4 | 156.2 | 156.6 | 159.0 | 161.1 | 162.4 | 162.3 | 160.0 |
| 2017 | 159.2 | 161.0 | 160.9 | 161.4 | 160.0 | 160.8 | 156.5 | 156.7 | 159.0 | 160.8 | 163.0 | 162.5 | 160.2 |
| 2018 | 159.0 | 161.1 | 161.6 | 161.5 | 161.0 | 161.3 | 155.7 | 155.5 | 158.4 | 161.2 | 163.3 | 162.8 | 160.2 |
| 2019 | 159.9 | 162.0 | 162.1 | 161.6 | 160.5 | 161.9 | 156.2 | 157.4 | 160.0 | 160.8 | 164.0 | 162.4 | 160.7 |

# Employment by Industry: Providence-Warwick, RI-MA NECTA, 2011–2019

(Numbers in thousands, not seasonally adjusted)

| Industry and year | January | February | March | April | May | June | July | August | September | October | November | December | Annual average |
|---|---|---|---|---|---|---|---|---|---|---|---|---|---|
| **Total Nonfarm** | | | | | | | | | | | | | |
| 2011 | 531.6 | 534.8 | 537.3 | 548.7 | 554.5 | 554.5 | 546.1 | 545.3 | 555.0 | 556.7 | 556.8 | 554.2 | 548.0 |
| 2012 | 536.8 | 541.0 | 545.1 | 552.3 | 559.4 | 559.1 | 549.7 | 552.2 | 562.1 | 562.0 | 562.2 | 562.5 | 553.7 |
| 2013 | 543.8 | 545.2 | 549.4 | 558.8 | 567.2 | 568.9 | 559.6 | 560.5 | 570.1 | 572.8 | 572.4 | 570.5 | 561.6 |
| 2014 | 552.2 | 554.9 | 558.0 | 568.9 | 577.7 | 576.7 | 569.1 | 569.7 | 580.5 | 582.4 | 583.9 | 583.2 | 571.4 |
| 2015 | 562.5 | 560.4 | 564.9 | 577.1 | 586.4 | 585.7 | 579.6 | 577.6 | 586.9 | 590.8 | 592.2 | 591.6 | 579.6 |
| 2016 | 571.1 | 574.1 | 579.1 | 586.6 | 592.4 | 593.6 | 586.2 | 584.7 | 592.6 | 594.8 | 595.4 | 594.0 | 587.1 |
| 2017 | 575.7 | 578.0 | 580.9 | 590.1 | 597.6 | 599.4 | 591.7 | 592.7 | 598.4 | 600.9 | 601.8 | 600.9 | 592.3 |
| 2018 | 579.2 | 584.2 | 586.6 | 595.4 | 604.0 | 603.9 | 597.0 | 596.6 | 602.4 | 604.7 | 605.3 | 604.3 | 597.0 |
| 2019 | 585.4 | 588.6 | 589.1 | 597.6 | 604.1 | 604.6 | 597.2 | 597.6 | 603.8 | 607.0 | 609.1 | 607.3 | 599.3 |
| **Total Private** | | | | | | | | | | | | | |
| 2011 | 456.8 | 460.0 | 461.8 | 473.3 | 478.9 | 481.1 | 478.4 | 477.5 | 480.9 | 482.2 | 482.2 | 479.5 | 474.4 |
| 2012 | 462.6 | 466.4 | 470.4 | 477.5 | 483.9 | 487.0 | 482.2 | 484.4 | 487.9 | 487.3 | 487.0 | 487.5 | 480.3 |
| 2013 | 469.2 | 471.1 | 474.7 | 484.0 | 491.5 | 496.1 | 491.2 | 492.9 | 495.4 | 497.6 | 496.9 | 494.7 | 487.9 |
| 2014 | 477.4 | 479.9 | 482.9 | 493.5 | 501.2 | 503.2 | 500.6 | 501.8 | 505.1 | 506.9 | 507.7 | 507.4 | 497.3 |
| 2015 | 487.2 | 485.3 | 489.7 | 501.5 | 510.3 | 512.4 | 511.2 | 510.1 | 512.4 | 515.5 | 516.7 | 515.8 | 505.7 |
| 2016 | 495.8 | 498.8 | 503.2 | 511.1 | 516.3 | 519.8 | 517.2 | 516.2 | 517.2 | 519.0 | 519.1 | 517.9 | 512.6 |
| 2017 | 500.1 | 502.4 | 504.9 | 514.3 | 521.1 | 525.4 | 522.3 | 523.7 | 522.4 | 524.5 | 525.6 | 524.2 | 517.6 |
| 2018 | 503.0 | 508.0 | 510.3 | 519.2 | 526.4 | 528.9 | 526.8 | 526.9 | 525.1 | 527.8 | 528.2 | 527.3 | 521.5 |
| 2019 | 508.8 | 512.0 | 512.0 | 520.4 | 526.6 | 529.5 | 526.7 | 527.4 | 526.6 | 529.4 | 531.0 | 529.2 | 523.3 |
| **Goods Producing** | | | | | | | | | | | | | |
| 2011 | 67.2 | 66.6 | 67.1 | 69.5 | 70.7 | 71.8 | 71.3 | 72.1 | 71.8 | 71.7 | 71.4 | 70.4 | 70.1 |
| 2012 | 67.4 | 67.0 | 67.8 | 69.4 | 70.2 | 71.5 | 70.6 | 71.7 | 71.4 | 71.5 | 71.2 | 70.9 | 70.1 |
| 2013 | 67.5 | 66.7 | 67.9 | 69.6 | 71.3 | 72.3 | 71.1 | 72.6 | 72.6 | 72.5 | 72.6 | 71.7 | 70.7 |
| 2014 | 69.0 | 68.2 | 68.7 | 71.1 | 72.9 | 74.0 | 73.1 | 74.1 | 74.0 | 74.0 | 74.0 | 73.5 | 72.2 |
| 2015 | 70.3 | 69.1 | 69.7 | 72.0 | 73.8 | 74.7 | 74.7 | 75.3 | 74.9 | 75.1 | 75.3 | 74.8 | 73.3 |
| 2016 | 71.4 | 70.8 | 71.8 | 73.4 | 74.6 | 75.6 | 75.2 | 75.7 | 75.2 | 75.3 | 74.9 | 74.0 | 74.0 |
| 2017 | 71.2 | 70.7 | 71.0 | 73.5 | 74.7 | 76.0 | 75.6 | 76.3 | 75.8 | 76.1 | 76.0 | 75.5 | 74.4 |
| 2018 | 72.2 | 72.9 | 73.3 | 74.9 | 76.3 | 77.1 | 76.5 | 77.1 | 76.8 | 76.8 | 76.5 | 76.1 | 75.5 |
| 2019 | 73.5 | 73.0 | 73.3 | 75.4 | 76.3 | 77.2 | 76.6 | 77.5 | 76.9 | 77.0 | 76.5 | 76.2 | 75.8 |
| **Service-Providing** | | | | | | | | | | | | | |
| 2011 | 464.4 | 468.2 | 470.2 | 479.2 | 483.8 | 482.7 | 474.8 | 473.2 | 483.2 | 485.0 | 485.4 | 483.8 | 477.8 |
| 2012 | 469.4 | 474.0 | 477.3 | 482.9 | 489.2 | 487.6 | 479.1 | 480.5 | 490.7 | 490.5 | 491.0 | 491.6 | 483.7 |
| 2013 | 476.3 | 478.5 | 481.5 | 489.2 | 495.9 | 496.6 | 488.5 | 487.9 | 497.5 | 500.3 | 499.8 | 498.8 | 490.9 |
| 2014 | 483.2 | 486.7 | 489.3 | 497.8 | 504.8 | 502.7 | 496.0 | 495.6 | 506.5 | 508.4 | 509.9 | 509.7 | 499.2 |
| 2015 | 492.2 | 491.3 | 495.2 | 505.1 | 512.6 | 511.0 | 504.9 | 502.3 | 512.0 | 515.7 | 516.9 | 516.8 | 506.3 |
| 2016 | 499.7 | 503.3 | 507.3 | 513.2 | 517.8 | 518.0 | 511.0 | 509.0 | 517.4 | 519.5 | 520.5 | 520.0 | 513.1 |
| 2017 | 504.5 | 507.3 | 509.9 | 516.6 | 522.9 | 523.4 | 516.1 | 516.4 | 522.6 | 524.8 | 525.8 | 525.4 | 518.0 |
| 2018 | 507.0 | 511.3 | 513.3 | 520.5 | 527.7 | 526.8 | 520.5 | 519.5 | 525.6 | 527.9 | 528.8 | 528.2 | 521.4 |
| 2019 | 511.9 | 515.6 | 515.8 | 522.2 | 527.8 | 527.4 | 520.6 | 520.1 | 526.9 | 530.0 | 532.6 | 531.1 | 523.5 |
| **Mining and Logging** | | | | | | | | | | | | | |
| 2011 | 0.1 | 0.1 | 0.1 | 0.2 | 0.2 | 0.2 | 0.2 | 0.2 | 0.2 | 0.2 | 0.2 | 0.2 | 0.2 |
| 2012 | 0.2 | 0.2 | 0.2 | 0.2 | 0.2 | 0.2 | 0.2 | 0.2 | 0.2 | 0.2 | 0.2 | 0.2 | 0.2 |
| 2013 | 0.1 | 0.1 | 0.1 | 0.2 | 0.2 | 0.2 | 0.2 | 0.2 | 0.2 | 0.2 | 0.2 | 0.2 | 0.2 |
| 2014 | 0.2 | 0.2 | 0.2 | 0.2 | 0.2 | 0.3 | 0.3 | 0.3 | 0.3 | 0.3 | 0.3 | 0.3 | 0.3 |
| 2015 | 0.2 | 0.2 | 0.2 | 0.2 | 0.3 | 0.3 | 0.3 | 0.2 | 0.2 | 0.2 | 0.2 | 0.2 | 0.2 |
| 2016 | 0.2 | 0.2 | 0.2 | 0.2 | 0.2 | 0.3 | 0.3 | 0.3 | 0.3 | 0.3 | 0.2 | 0.2 | 0.2 |
| 2017 | 0.2 | 0.2 | 0.2 | 0.2 | 0.2 | 0.3 | 0.3 | 0.3 | 0.3 | 0.3 | 0.3 | 0.3 | 0.3 |
| 2018 | 0.2 | 0.2 | 0.2 | 0.2 | 0.3 | 0.3 | 0.3 | 0.3 | 0.3 | 0.2 | 0.3 | 0.3 | 0.3 |
| 2019 | 0.2 | 0.2 | 0.2 | 0.3 | 0.3 | 0.3 | 0.3 | 0.3 | 0.3 | 0.3 | 0.3 | 0.3 | 0.3 |
| **Construction** | | | | | | | | | | | | | |
| 2011 | 16.6 | 16.0 | 16.4 | 18.5 | 19.7 | 20.5 | 21.2 | 21.1 | 20.8 | 20.8 | 20.7 | 19.8 | 19.3 |
| 2012 | 17.6 | 17.0 | 17.8 | 19.3 | 19.9 | 20.8 | 21.2 | 21.1 | 20.8 | 20.8 | 20.5 | 20.1 | 19.7 |
| 2013 | 17.4 | 16.9 | 17.6 | 19.2 | 20.6 | 21.2 | 21.8 | 21.9 | 21.8 | 21.7 | 21.4 | 20.3 | 20.2 |
| 2014 | 18.2 | 17.5 | 17.9 | 20.0 | 21.4 | 22.0 | 22.4 | 22.3 | 22.2 | 22.2 | 22.0 | 21.3 | 20.8 |
| 2015 | 18.7 | 17.7 | 18.2 | 20.3 | 21.8 | 22.4 | 23.1 | 23.2 | 23.0 | 23.1 | 23.1 | 22.7 | 21.4 |
| 2016 | 20.2 | 19.6 | 20.4 | 22.2 | 23.4 | 23.9 | 24.4 | 24.5 | 24.3 | 24.3 | 23.9 | 22.9 | 22.8 |
| 2017 | 20.7 | 20.3 | 20.4 | 22.6 | 23.7 | 24.5 | 24.9 | 25.0 | 24.6 | 24.7 | 24.5 | 23.7 | 23.3 |
| 2018 | 21.0 | 21.6 | 21.8 | 23.6 | 24.9 | 25.6 | 25.8 | 25.8 | 25.7 | 25.8 | 25.4 | 24.8 | 24.3 |
| 2019 | 22.9 | 22.4 | 22.8 | 24.9 | 25.9 | 26.4 | 26.6 | 26.7 | 26.5 | 26.8 | 26.2 | 25.7 | 25.3 |

## Employment by Industry: Providence-Warwick, RI-MA NECTA, 2011–2019—*Continued*

(Numbers in thousands, not seasonally adjusted)

| Industry and year | January | February | March | April | May | June | July | August | September | October | November | December | Annual average |
|---|---|---|---|---|---|---|---|---|---|---|---|---|---|
| **Manufacturing** | | | | | | | | | | | | | |
| 2011 | 50.5 | 50.5 | 50.6 | 50.8 | 50.8 | 51.1 | 49.9 | 50.8 | 50.8 | 50.7 | 50.5 | 50.4 | 50.6 |
| 2012 | 49.6 | 49.8 | 49.8 | 49.9 | 50.1 | 50.5 | 49.2 | 50.4 | 50.4 | 50.5 | 50.5 | 50.6 | 50.1 |
| 2013 | 50.0 | 49.7 | 50.2 | 50.2 | 50.5 | 50.9 | 49.1 | 50.5 | 50.6 | 50.6 | 51.0 | 51.2 | 50.4 |
| 2014 | 50.6 | 50.5 | 50.6 | 50.9 | 51.3 | 51.7 | 50.4 | 51.5 | 51.5 | 51.5 | 51.7 | 51.9 | 51.2 |
| 2015 | 51.4 | 51.2 | 51.3 | 51.5 | 51.7 | 52.0 | 51.3 | 51.9 | 51.7 | 51.8 | 52.0 | 51.9 | 51.6 |
| 2016 | 51.0 | 51.0 | 51.2 | 51.0 | 51.0 | 51.4 | 50.5 | 50.9 | 50.6 | 50.7 | 50.8 | 50.9 | 50.9 |
| 2017 | 50.3 | 50.2 | 50.4 | 50.7 | 50.8 | 51.2 | 50.4 | 51.0 | 50.9 | 51.1 | 51.2 | 51.5 | 50.8 |
| 2018 | 51.0 | 51.1 | 51.3 | 51.1 | 51.1 | 51.2 | 50.4 | 51.0 | 50.8 | 50.8 | 50.8 | 51.0 | 51.0 |
| 2019 | 50.4 | 50.4 | 50.3 | 50.2 | 50.1 | 50.5 | 49.7 | 50.5 | 50.1 | 49.9 | 50.0 | 50.2 | 50.2 |
| **Trade, Transportation, and Utilities** | | | | | | | | | | | | | |
| 2011 | 93.6 | 93.0 | 92.7 | 94.0 | 94.9 | 95.5 | 94.2 | 94.3 | 95.5 | 96.5 | 98.5 | 99.7 | 95.2 |
| 2012 | 95.4 | 94.3 | 94.5 | 94.9 | 96.1 | 97.0 | 94.9 | 95.2 | 96.3 | 97.0 | 99.0 | 99.5 | 96.2 |
| 2013 | 94.5 | 93.7 | 93.6 | 94.5 | 95.7 | 96.6 | 95.0 | 95.3 | 96.2 | 97.2 | 99.0 | 100.3 | 96.0 |
| 2014 | 95.7 | 95.1 | 94.8 | 95.8 | 96.9 | 97.8 | 96.1 | 96.3 | 97.5 | 99.0 | 101.2 | 102.7 | 97.4 |
| 2015 | 98.1 | 96.8 | 96.6 | 97.8 | 98.8 | 99.9 | 98.3 | 98.4 | 99.3 | 100.0 | 102.4 | 103.7 | 99.2 |
| 2016 | 98.9 | 98.3 | 98.0 | 98.3 | 99.2 | 100.0 | 98.5 | 98.5 | 99.3 | 101.0 | 103.7 | 105.3 | 99.9 |
| 2017 | 100.4 | 99.2 | 99.0 | 99.7 | 101.0 | 101.8 | 100.6 | 100.6 | 101.6 | 103.1 | 105.5 | 106.7 | 101.6 |
| 2018 | 102.1 | 100.8 | 100.6 | 100.7 | 102.0 | 102.6 | 101.4 | 101.0 | 101.5 | 102.5 | 104.9 | 106.2 | 102.2 |
| 2019 | 101.5 | 100.0 | 99.0 | 99.3 | 100.5 | 101.5 | 99.9 | 100.0 | 101.0 | 101.6 | 105.3 | 107.2 | 101.4 |
| **Wholesale Trade** | | | | | | | | | | | | | |
| 2011 | 19.5 | 19.6 | 19.1 | 19.3 | 19.4 | 19.5 | 19.7 | 19.6 | 19.7 | 19.7 | 19.8 | 20.0 | 19.6 |
| 2012 | 19.8 | 19.9 | 20.0 | 20.0 | 20.1 | 20.3 | 20.2 | 20.2 | 20.1 | 20.1 | 20.1 | 20.0 | 20.1 |
| 2013 | 19.7 | 19.7 | 19.8 | 19.8 | 20.0 | 20.1 | 20.0 | 20.1 | 20.0 | 20.1 | 20.1 | 20.1 | 20.0 |
| 2014 | 19.8 | 19.9 | 19.8 | 19.8 | 20.0 | 20.0 | 20.1 | 20.2 | 20.1 | 20.2 | 20.3 | 20.3 | 20.0 |
| 2015 | 20.1 | 20.1 | 20.0 | 20.2 | 20.2 | 20.3 | 20.2 | 20.2 | 20.1 | 20.0 | 20.2 | 20.2 | 20.2 |
| 2016 | 19.7 | 19.8 | 19.7 | 20.0 | 20.0 | 20.0 | 19.9 | 20.0 | 19.9 | 19.8 | 19.8 | 19.9 | 19.9 |
| 2017 | 19.6 | 19.6 | 19.7 | 19.6 | 19.7 | 19.8 | 19.8 | 19.8 | 19.6 | 19.7 | 19.8 | 19.8 | 19.7 |
| 2018 | 19.6 | 19.6 | 19.6 | 19.7 | 19.6 | 19.7 | 19.7 | 19.7 | 19.5 | 19.7 | 19.8 | 19.8 | 19.7 |
| 2019 | 19.6 | 19.6 | 19.5 | 19.5 | 19.6 | 19.7 | 19.7 | 19.8 | 19.8 | 19.9 | 20.2 | 20.4 | 19.8 |
| **Retail Trade** | | | | | | | | | | | | | |
| 2011 | 61.6 | 60.9 | 61.1 | 61.8 | 62.4 | 62.7 | 62.4 | 62.8 | 62.4 | 63.4 | 65.3 | 65.9 | 62.7 |
| 2012 | 62.6 | 61.5 | 61.6 | 61.9 | 62.7 | 63.2 | 62.6 | 62.7 | 62.7 | 63.4 | 65.4 | 65.7 | 63.0 |
| 2013 | 62.1 | 61.2 | 61.0 | 61.6 | 62.4 | 63.0 | 62.7 | 62.8 | 62.6 | 63.5 | 65.2 | 66.0 | 62.8 |
| 2014 | 62.8 | 62.1 | 61.9 | 62.7 | 63.4 | 63.9 | 63.4 | 63.3 | 63.3 | 64.7 | 66.6 | 67.6 | 63.8 |
| 2015 | 64.2 | 63.0 | 63.1 | 63.7 | 64.4 | 65.3 | 65.0 | 65.1 | 64.8 | 65.5 | 67.6 | 68.4 | 65.0 |
| 2016 | 65.2 | 64.4 | 64.4 | 64.3 | 64.9 | 65.3 | 65.1 | 65.1 | 64.6 | 65.1 | 66.8 | 67.2 | 65.2 |
| 2017 | 64.2 | 63.1 | 62.9 | 63.9 | 64.7 | 65.0 | 64.7 | 64.8 | 64.4 | 65.4 | 67.1 | 67.4 | 64.8 |
| 2018 | 64.5 | 63.8 | 63.3 | 63.7 | 64.8 | 65.0 | 64.9 | 64.8 | 64.2 | 65.1 | 67.2 | 67.6 | 64.9 |
| 2019 | 64.6 | 63.3 | 63.1 | 63.1 | 63.8 | 64.3 | 64.0 | 63.9 | 63.7 | 64.1 | 66.4 | 67.0 | 64.3 |
| **Transportation and Utilities** | | | | | | | | | | | | | |
| 2011 | 12.5 | 12.5 | 12.5 | 12.9 | 13.1 | 13.3 | 12.1 | 11.9 | 13.4 | 13.4 | 13.4 | 13.8 | 12.9 |
| 2012 | 13.0 | 12.9 | 12.9 | 13.0 | 13.3 | 13.5 | 12.1 | 12.3 | 13.5 | 13.5 | 13.5 | 13.8 | 13.1 |
| 2013 | 12.7 | 12.8 | 12.8 | 13.1 | 13.3 | 13.5 | 12.3 | 12.4 | 13.6 | 13.6 | 13.7 | 14.2 | 13.2 |
| 2014 | 13.1 | 13.1 | 13.1 | 13.3 | 13.5 | 13.9 | 12.6 | 12.8 | 14.1 | 14.1 | 14.3 | 14.8 | 13.6 |
| 2015 | 13.8 | 13.7 | 13.5 | 13.9 | 14.2 | 14.3 | 13.1 | 13.1 | 14.4 | 14.5 | 14.6 | 15.1 | 14.0 |
| 2016 | 14.0 | 14.1 | 13.9 | 14.0 | 14.3 | 14.7 | 13.5 | 13.4 | 14.8 | 16.1 | 17.1 | 18.2 | 14.8 |
| 2017 | 16.6 | 16.5 | 16.4 | 16.2 | 16.6 | 17.0 | 16.1 | 16.0 | 17.6 | 18.0 | 18.6 | 19.5 | 17.1 |
| 2018 | 18.0 | 17.4 | 17.7 | 17.3 | 17.6 | 17.9 | 16.8 | 16.5 | 17.8 | 17.7 | 17.9 | 18.8 | 17.6 |
| 2019 | 17.3 | 17.1 | 16.4 | 16.7 | 17.1 | 17.5 | 16.2 | 16.3 | 17.5 | 17.6 | 18.7 | 19.8 | 17.4 |
| **Information** | | | | | | | | | | | | | |
| 2011 | 9.4 | 9.3 | 9.4 | 9.9 | 10.1 | 10.0 | 9.8 | 8.8 | 9.5 | 9.4 | 9.5 | 9.6 | 9.6 |
| 2012 | 9.3 | 9.3 | 9.4 | 9.2 | 9.0 | 9.2 | 8.9 | 9.0 | 8.8 | 8.8 | 8.8 | 8.8 | 9.0 |
| 2013 | 8.8 | 8.8 | 8.6 | 8.4 | 8.6 | 8.6 | 8.4 | 8.5 | 8.3 | 8.3 | 8.4 | 8.4 | 8.5 |
| 2014 | 8.5 | 8.3 | 8.3 | 8.3 | 8.4 | 8.3 | 8.4 | 8.5 | 8.3 | 8.2 | 8.2 | 8.3 | 8.3 |
| 2015 | 8.0 | 7.9 | 8.0 | 8.1 | 8.1 | 7.9 | 8.0 | 7.9 | 8.0 | 8.1 | 7.3 | 7.2 | 7.9 |
| 2016 | 7.2 | 7.3 | 7.2 | 7.4 | 6.5 | 7.4 | 7.5 | 7.3 | 7.4 | 7.3 | 7.3 | 7.3 | 7.3 |
| 2017 | 7.3 | 7.5 | 7.4 | 7.4 | 7.5 | 7.6 | 7.4 | 7.4 | 7.4 | 7.3 | 7.4 | 7.3 | 7.4 |
| 2018 | 7.1 | 7.2 | 7.2 | 7.1 | 7.0 | 7.1 | 7.0 | 7.2 | 7.2 | 7.3 | 7.4 | 7.2 | 7.2 |
| 2019 | 7.0 | 7.2 | 7.0 | 6.8 | 6.9 | 6.9 | 6.9 | 7.2 | 6.8 | 6.9 | 7.1 | 7.0 | 7.0 |

# Employment by Industry: Providence-Warwick, RI-MA NECTA, 2011–2019—*Continued*

(Numbers in thousands, not seasonally adjusted)

| Industry and year | January | February | March | April | May | June | July | August | September | October | November | December | Annual average |
|---|---|---|---|---|---|---|---|---|---|---|---|---|---|
| **Financial Activities** | | | | | | | | | | | | | |
| 2011 | 34.6 | 34.7 | 34.8 | 34.9 | 34.8 | 35.4 | 35.0 | 35.1 | 35.1 | 35.1 | 35.4 | 35.3 | 35.0 |
| 2012 | 35.1 | 35.3 | 35.5 | 35.6 | 35.9 | 36.1 | 36.1 | 36.0 | 36.1 | 36.1 | 36.2 | 36.2 | 35.9 |
| 2013 | 35.9 | 36.2 | 36.4 | 36.4 | 36.4 | 36.6 | 36.7 | 36.5 | 36.3 | 36.4 | 36.4 | 36.6 | 36.4 |
| 2014 | 36.2 | 36.1 | 36.2 | 36.6 | 36.7 | 36.9 | 37.0 | 36.8 | 36.7 | 36.7 | 36.7 | 36.7 | 36.6 |
| 2015 | 36.4 | 36.6 | 36.8 | 37.1 | 37.3 | 37.5 | 37.4 | 37.3 | 37.6 | 38.2 | 38.7 | 38.8 | 37.5 |
| 2016 | 37.9 | 38.1 | 38.2 | 38.0 | 38.0 | 38.4 | 38.4 | 38.4 | 38.3 | 38.3 | 38.4 | 38.4 | 38.2 |
| 2017 | 38.1 | 38.2 | 38.2 | 38.3 | 38.5 | 38.8 | 38.7 | 38.8 | 38.7 | 38.5 | 38.7 | 38.6 | 38.5 |
| 2018 | 38.1 | 38.2 | 38.1 | 38.1 | 38.0 | 38.3 | 38.3 | 38.2 | 37.8 | 38.0 | 37.9 | 37.9 | 38.1 |
| 2019 | 37.7 | 38.0 | 37.7 | 37.8 | 38.0 | 38.3 | 38.6 | 38.2 | 38.1 | 38.2 | 38.0 | 37.7 | 38.0 |
| **Professional and Business Services** | | | | | | | | | | | | | |
| 2011 | 56.9 | 57.4 | 57.6 | 59.7 | 60.0 | 60.4 | 60.2 | 60.7 | 61.4 | 61.4 | 61.1 | 59.7 | 59.7 |
| 2012 | 57.7 | 58.0 | 59.2 | 61.3 | 61.7 | 62.6 | 62.1 | 62.5 | 62.4 | 62.2 | 62.3 | 62.1 | 61.2 |
| 2013 | 59.9 | 60.5 | 60.8 | 63.5 | 64.3 | 65.8 | 64.9 | 65.6 | 65.7 | 66.7 | 66.3 | 65.5 | 64.1 |
| 2014 | 62.5 | 63.5 | 63.8 | 66.6 | 67.3 | 68.0 | 68.0 | 68.7 | 68.9 | 69.7 | 69.9 | 69.4 | 67.2 |
| 2015 | 64.9 | 65.1 | 65.6 | 69.0 | 70.2 | 70.5 | 70.7 | 70.6 | 70.4 | 71.1 | 71.5 | 71.0 | 69.2 |
| 2016 | 68.5 | 68.6 | 69.2 | 71.5 | 72.0 | 72.7 | 73.0 | 73.2 | 73.4 | 73.6 | 73.4 | 72.9 | 71.8 |
| 2017 | 70.3 | 71.0 | 71.1 | 73.6 | 74.0 | 75.2 | 75.7 | 75.9 | 75.6 | 76.0 | 75.7 | 75.0 | 74.1 |
| 2018 | 71.6 | 72.1 | 72.6 | 75.0 | 75.6 | 76.2 | 76.2 | 76.4 | 75.7 | 76.1 | 76.1 | 75.3 | 74.9 |
| 2019 | 72.2 | 72.6 | 72.2 | 74.6 | 75.0 | 75.6 | 75.8 | 76.2 | 75.6 | 76.7 | 76.2 | 75.5 | 74.9 |
| **Education and Health Services** | | | | | | | | | | | | | |
| 2011 | 116.9 | 120.2 | 120.7 | 121.8 | 121.8 | 117.2 | 116.0 | 115.2 | 119.0 | 122.1 | 122.1 | 121.4 | 119.5 |
| 2012 | 118.0 | 121.8 | 122.4 | 121.5 | 122.0 | 117.6 | 116.0 | 116.3 | 122.0 | 123.3 | 123.2 | 124.0 | 120.7 |
| 2013 | 120.9 | 123.2 | 123.8 | 123.9 | 123.6 | 120.4 | 119.1 | 118.8 | 123.3 | 125.7 | 125.9 | 124.4 | 122.8 |
| 2014 | 121.9 | 124.1 | 125.1 | 125.6 | 125.1 | 120.8 | 120.2 | 119.7 | 124.5 | 126.5 | 127.0 | 126.9 | 124.0 |
| 2015 | 123.4 | 124.6 | 126.0 | 126.6 | 126.1 | 122.6 | 121.8 | 120.8 | 125.3 | 127.7 | 128.2 | 127.5 | 125.1 |
| 2016 | 123.3 | 126.6 | 127.6 | 127.9 | 127.9 | 122.7 | 121.7 | 121.1 | 125.1 | 127.5 | 127.5 | 127.1 | 125.5 |
| 2017 | 124.0 | 126.3 | 127.9 | 128.5 | 128.2 | 123.6 | 122.3 | 122.4 | 125.4 | 127.2 | 128.0 | 127.7 | 126.0 |
| 2018 | 122.8 | 126.5 | 127.2 | 128.8 | 128.7 | 124.3 | 123.3 | 123.0 | 126.8 | 129.6 | 130.1 | 129.7 | 126.7 |
| 2019 | 125.6 | 129.4 | 130.6 | 131.0 | 130.4 | 125.7 | 124.4 | 124.5 | 128.7 | 131.2 | 132.9 | 131.9 | 128.9 |
| **Leisure and Hospitality** | | | | | | | | | | | | | |
| 2011 | 53.4 | 53.9 | 54.4 | 58.1 | 60.9 | 64.4 | 64.7 | 64.3 | 62.8 | 60.5 | 58.5 | 57.6 | 59.5 |
| 2012 | 54.6 | 55.5 | 56.3 | 59.7 | 62.9 | 66.2 | 66.4 | 66.4 | 64.4 | 62.3 | 60.1 | 59.6 | 61.2 |
| 2013 | 56.1 | 56.4 | 57.7 | 61.2 | 64.8 | 68.3 | 68.1 | 68.0 | 66.2 | 64.3 | 61.7 | 61.1 | 62.8 |
| 2014 | 57.6 | 58.4 | 59.5 | 62.9 | 66.8 | 69.5 | 69.4 | 69.4 | 68.0 | 65.9 | 63.7 | 62.8 | 64.5 |
| 2015 | 59.6 | 58.9 | 60.2 | 64.0 | 68.6 | 71.2 | 71.5 | 71.2 | 69.6 | 68.0 | 65.9 | 65.4 | 66.2 |
| 2016 | 61.7 | 62.2 | 64.0 | 67.1 | 70.3 | 74.2 | 73.6 | 73.0 | 71.0 | 68.7 | 66.5 | 65.4 | 68.1 |
| 2017 | 61.9 | 62.6 | 63.3 | 66.0 | 69.7 | 73.9 | 73.2 | 73.6 | 70.6 | 69.0 | 66.9 | 66.0 | 68.1 |
| 2018 | 62.6 | 63.6 | 64.4 | 67.7 | 71.6 | 75.1 | 75.3 | 75.2 | 71.9 | 70.2 | 68.1 | 67.5 | 69.4 |
| 2019 | 64.2 | 64.7 | 65.0 | 68.2 | 72.0 | 75.7 | 75.8 | 75.1 | 72.4 | 70.9 | 68.2 | 67.0 | 69.9 |
| **Other Services** | | | | | | | | | | | | | |
| 2011 | 24.8 | 24.9 | 25.1 | 25.4 | 25.7 | 26.4 | 27.2 | 27.0 | 25.8 | 25.5 | 25.7 | 25.8 | 25.8 |
| 2012 | 25.1 | 25.2 | 25.3 | 25.9 | 26.1 | 26.8 | 27.2 | 27.3 | 26.5 | 26.1 | 26.2 | 26.4 | 26.2 |
| 2013 | 25.6 | 25.6 | 25.9 | 26.5 | 26.8 | 27.5 | 27.9 | 27.6 | 26.8 | 26.5 | 26.6 | 26.7 | 26.7 |
| 2014 | 26.0 | 26.2 | 26.5 | 26.6 | 27.1 | 27.9 | 28.4 | 28.3 | 27.2 | 26.9 | 27.0 | 27.1 | 27.1 |
| 2015 | 26.5 | 26.3 | 26.8 | 26.9 | 27.4 | 28.1 | 28.8 | 28.6 | 27.3 | 27.3 | 27.4 | 27.4 | 27.4 |
| 2016 | 26.9 | 26.9 | 27.2 | 27.5 | 27.8 | 28.8 | 29.3 | 29.0 | 27.5 | 27.3 | 27.4 | 27.5 | 27.8 |
| 2017 | 26.9 | 26.9 | 27.0 | 27.3 | 27.5 | 28.5 | 28.8 | 28.7 | 27.3 | 27.3 | 27.4 | 27.4 | 27.6 |
| 2018 | 26.5 | 26.7 | 26.9 | 26.9 | 27.2 | 28.2 | 28.8 | 28.8 | 27.4 | 27.3 | 27.2 | 27.4 | 27.4 |
| 2019 | 27.1 | 27.1 | 27.2 | 27.3 | 27.5 | 28.6 | 28.7 | 28.7 | 27.1 | 26.9 | 26.8 | 26.7 | 27.5 |
| **Government** | | | | | | | | | | | | | |
| 2011 | 74.8 | 74.8 | 75.5 | 75.4 | 75.6 | 73.4 | 67.7 | 67.8 | 74.1 | 74.5 | 74.6 | 74.7 | 73.6 |
| 2012 | 74.2 | 74.6 | 74.7 | 74.8 | 75.5 | 72.1 | 67.5 | 67.8 | 74.2 | 74.7 | 75.2 | 75.0 | 73.4 |
| 2013 | 74.6 | 74.1 | 74.7 | 74.8 | 75.7 | 72.8 | 68.4 | 67.6 | 74.7 | 75.2 | 75.5 | 75.8 | 73.7 |
| 2014 | 74.8 | 75.0 | 75.1 | 75.4 | 76.5 | 73.5 | 68.5 | 67.9 | 75.4 | 75.5 | 76.2 | 75.8 | 74.1 |
| 2015 | 75.3 | 75.1 | 75.2 | 75.6 | 76.1 | 73.3 | 68.4 | 67.5 | 74.5 | 75.3 | 75.5 | 75.8 | 74.0 |
| 2016 | 75.3 | 75.3 | 75.9 | 75.5 | 76.1 | 73.8 | 69.0 | 68.5 | 75.4 | 75.8 | 76.3 | 76.1 | 74.4 |
| 2017 | 75.6 | 75.6 | 76.0 | 75.8 | 76.5 | 74.0 | 69.4 | 69.0 | 76.0 | 76.4 | 76.2 | 76.7 | 74.8 |
| 2018 | 76.2 | 76.2 | 76.3 | 76.2 | 77.6 | 75.0 | 70.2 | 69.7 | 77.3 | 76.9 | 77.1 | 77.0 | 75.5 |
| 2019 | 76.6 | 76.6 | 77.1 | 77.2 | 77.5 | 75.1 | 70.5 | 70.2 | 77.2 | 77.6 | 78.1 | 78.1 | 76.0 |

## Employment by Industry: Milwaukee-Waukesha-West Allis, WI, 2011–2019

(Numbers in thousands, not seasonally adjusted)

| Industry and year | January | February | March | April | May | June | July | August | September | October | November | December | Annual average |
|---|---|---|---|---|---|---|---|---|---|---|---|---|---|
| **Total Nonfarm** | | | | | | | | | | | | | |
| 2011 | 798.9 | 800.5 | 804.3 | 811.8 | 816.3 | 820.2 | 817.5 | 819.0 | 818.8 | 819.4 | 822.3 | 818.7 | 814.0 |
| 2012 | 799.8 | 803.0 | 809.8 | 815.2 | 825.1 | 829.5 | 822.8 | 825.8 | 826.0 | 830.3 | 834.8 | 832.0 | 821.2 |
| 2013 | 810.7 | 815.9 | 820.1 | 825.8 | 835.7 | 841.4 | 836.6 | 838.5 | 841.9 | 842.5 | 845.9 | 845.8 | 833.4 |
| 2014 | 824.1 | 828.3 | 830.1 | 836.7 | 843.8 | 853.0 | 847.2 | 854.7 | 852.3 | 853.2 | 859.1 | 857.8 | 845.0 |
| 2015 | 833.1 | 838.5 | 841.9 | 851.6 | 859.2 | 866.1 | 860.1 | 865.7 | 861.8 | 865.2 | 867.1 | 867.0 | 856.4 |
| 2016 | 847.6 | 851.9 | 853.6 | 863.4 | 865.9 | 870.9 | 866.6 | 871.8 | 867.7 | 868.4 | 870.7 | 868.5 | 863.9 |
| 2017 | 849.5 | 853.6 | 859.2 | 863.2 | 870.4 | 877.3 | 870.8 | 874.3 | 869.8 | 873.0 | 874.6 | 878.1 | 867.8 |
| 2018 | 859.4 | 863.3 | 866.7 | 870.2 | 876.3 | 884.1 | 877.5 | 881.2 | 875.9 | 878.3 | 881.9 | 881.3 | 874.7 |
| 2019 | 861.8 | 862.8 | 866.1 | 871.5 | 877.0 | 885.3 | 877.5 | 878.9 | 871.7 | 879.2 | 881.5 | 879.1 | 874.4 |
| **Total Private** | | | | | | | | | | | | | |
| 2011 | 710.0 | 707.7 | 712.0 | 720.2 | 725.3 | 729.5 | 730.3 | 732.4 | 730.9 | 732.9 | 733.8 | 729.9 | 724.6 |
| 2012 | 714.0 | 715.8 | 721.0 | 725.1 | 734.1 | 740.2 | 739.5 | 740.8 | 739.2 | 741.7 | 743.6 | 743.1 | 733.2 |
| 2013 | 726.0 | 727.8 | 732.0 | 737.8 | 748.0 | 754.1 | 754.8 | 755.1 | 754.5 | 754.8 | 758.0 | 758.2 | 746.8 |
| 2014 | 739.1 | 741.1 | 742.5 | 749.3 | 756.6 | 765.2 | 765.2 | 768.6 | 764.8 | 765.8 | 770.3 | 770.5 | 758.3 |
| 2015 | 750.0 | 751.0 | 754.6 | 763.3 | 771.6 | 779.3 | 777.8 | 781.8 | 774.9 | 778.1 | 780.1 | 779.6 | 770.2 |
| 2016 | 762.1 | 764.3 | 766.0 | 774.4 | 778.3 | 784.9 | 785.9 | 787.5 | 781.0 | 780.1 | 780.9 | 779.8 | 777.1 |
| 2017 | 764.8 | 765.9 | 771.5 | 774.9 | 782.6 | 791.7 | 790.2 | 791.1 | 784.3 | 785.8 | 787.2 | 790.5 | 781.7 |
| 2018 | 775.1 | 776.5 | 780.0 | 782.3 | 789.1 | 799.2 | 796.7 | 799.0 | 791.0 | 791.8 | 794.1 | 794.7 | 789.1 |
| 2019 | 778.4 | 777.3 | 780.4 | 784.9 | 791.2 | 800.6 | 797.0 | 797.6 | 787.5 | 792.1 | 794.1 | 791.9 | 789.4 |
| **Goods Producing** | | | | | | | | | | | | | |
| 2011 | 136.7 | 135.9 | 137.1 | 140.1 | 141.7 | 144.9 | 145.8 | 146.2 | 144.7 | 144.5 | 144.1 | 142.4 | 142.0 |
| 2012 | 139.8 | 139.1 | 140.1 | 142.4 | 143.7 | 146.6 | 147.5 | 147.0 | 145.5 | 145.3 | 144.7 | 143.7 | 143.8 |
| 2013 | 141.5 | 141.0 | 141.6 | 143.2 | 145.7 | 148.3 | 148.9 | 149.4 | 147.6 | 147.6 | 147.1 | 145.1 | 145.6 |
| 2014 | 142.6 | 142.4 | 143.5 | 145.4 | 147.7 | 149.9 | 151.9 | 152.4 | 150.8 | 149.9 | 149.9 | 148.7 | 147.9 |
| 2015 | 146.3 | 145.7 | 146.7 | 148.6 | 150.3 | 152.5 | 153.2 | 153.1 | 151.3 | 150.9 | 150.2 | 149.1 | 149.8 |
| 2016 | 146.3 | 146.0 | 146.5 | 148.2 | 149.2 | 151.4 | 152.0 | 152.0 | 150.0 | 149.5 | 149.0 | 147.5 | 149.0 |
| 2017 | 145.2 | 145.2 | 146.0 | 147.5 | 149.1 | 151.4 | 151.9 | 151.6 | 149.7 | 149.7 | 149.5 | 149.1 | 148.8 |
| 2018 | 146.7 | 146.7 | 147.7 | 149.2 | 151.0 | 154.0 | 154.9 | 155.1 | 153.5 | 153.3 | 153.1 | 152.7 | 151.5 |
| 2019 | 150.1 | 149.8 | 150.4 | 152.4 | 153.9 | 156.6 | 157.2 | 157.1 | 155.0 | 154.5 | 153.0 | 150.4 | 153.4 |
| **Service-Providing** | | | | | | | | | | | | | |
| 2011 | 662.2 | 664.6 | 667.2 | 671.7 | 674.6 | 675.3 | 671.7 | 672.8 | 674.1 | 674.9 | 678.2 | 676.3 | 672.0 |
| 2012 | 660.0 | 663.9 | 669.7 | 672.8 | 681.4 | 682.9 | 675.3 | 678.8 | 680.5 | 685.0 | 690.1 | 688.3 | 677.4 |
| 2013 | 669.2 | 674.9 | 678.5 | 682.6 | 690.0 | 693.1 | 687.7 | 689.1 | 694.3 | 694.9 | 698.8 | 700.7 | 687.8 |
| 2014 | 681.5 | 685.9 | 686.6 | 691.3 | 696.1 | 703.1 | 695.3 | 702.3 | 701.5 | 703.3 | 709.2 | 709.1 | 697.1 |
| 2015 | 686.8 | 692.8 | 695.2 | 703.0 | 708.9 | 713.6 | 706.9 | 712.6 | 710.5 | 714.3 | 716.9 | 717.9 | 706.6 |
| 2016 | 701.3 | 705.9 | 707.1 | 715.2 | 716.7 | 719.5 | 714.6 | 719.8 | 717.7 | 718.9 | 721.7 | 721.0 | 715.0 |
| 2017 | 704.3 | 708.4 | 713.2 | 715.7 | 721.3 | 725.9 | 718.9 | 722.7 | 720.1 | 723.3 | 725.1 | 729.0 | 719.0 |
| 2018 | 712.7 | 716.6 | 719.0 | 721.0 | 725.3 | 730.1 | 722.6 | 726.1 | 722.4 | 725.0 | 728.8 | 728.6 | 723.2 |
| 2019 | 711.7 | 713.0 | 715.7 | 719.1 | 723.1 | 728.7 | 720.3 | 721.8 | 716.7 | 724.7 | 728.5 | 728.7 | 721.0 |
| **Mining and Logging** | | | | | | | | | | | | | |
| 2011 | 0.3 | 0.3 | 0.3 | 0.3 | 0.3 | 0.4 | 0.4 | 0.4 | 0.4 | 0.4 | 0.4 | 0.3 | 0.4 |
| 2012 | 0.3 | 0.3 | 0.3 | 0.4 | 0.4 | 0.4 | 0.4 | 0.4 | 0.4 | 0.4 | 0.4 | 0.3 | 0.4 |
| 2013 | 0.3 | 0.3 | 0.3 | 0.4 | 0.4 | 0.4 | 0.4 | 0.4 | 0.4 | 0.4 | 0.4 | 0.4 | 0.4 |
| 2014 | 0.3 | 0.3 | 0.3 | 0.4 | 0.4 | 0.4 | 0.5 | 0.4 | 0.4 | 0.4 | 0.4 | 0.4 | 0.4 |
| 2015 | 0.4 | 0.4 | 0.4 | 0.4 | 0.5 | 0.5 | 0.5 | 0.5 | 0.5 | 0.5 | 0.5 | 0.4 | 0.5 |
| 2016 | 0.4 | 0.4 | 0.4 | 0.4 | 0.5 | 0.5 | 0.5 | 0.5 | 0.5 | 0.5 | 0.5 | 0.4 | 0.5 |
| 2017 | 0.4 | 0.4 | 0.4 | 0.4 | 0.4 | 0.5 | 0.5 | 0.5 | 0.5 | 0.4 | 0.4 | 0.4 | 0.4 |
| 2018 | 0.4 | 0.4 | 0.4 | 0.4 | 0.4 | 0.5 | 0.5 | 0.5 | 0.5 | 0.5 | 0.5 | 0.5 | 0.5 |
| 2019 | 0.4 | 0.4 | 0.4 | 0.4 | 0.5 | 0.5 | 0.5 | 0.5 | 0.5 | 0.5 | 0.5 | 0.4 | 0.5 |
| **Construction** | | | | | | | | | | | | | |
| 2011 | 21.6 | 21.0 | 21.6 | 23.8 | 25.2 | 26.4 | 26.7 | 26.8 | 26.4 | 26.2 | 25.6 | 23.6 | 24.6 |
| 2012 | 20.8 | 20.5 | 21.2 | 23.1 | 24.2 | 25.4 | 25.8 | 25.7 | 25.3 | 25.2 | 24.7 | 23.4 | 23.8 |
| 2013 | 21.6 | 21.6 | 22.1 | 23.1 | 25.8 | 26.9 | 27.8 | 28.3 | 27.7 | 27.7 | 27.2 | 25.2 | 25.4 |
| 2014 | 23.2 | 23.0 | 23.8 | 25.6 | 27.6 | 28.8 | 29.7 | 30.2 | 29.8 | 29.4 | 29.0 | 27.5 | 27.3 |
| 2015 | 25.3 | 25.0 | 25.7 | 27.7 | 29.3 | 30.4 | 30.9 | 30.9 | 30.2 | 30.2 | 29.7 | 28.6 | 28.7 |
| 2016 | 26.4 | 26.4 | 27.0 | 28.7 | 29.9 | 31.2 | 31.7 | 31.8 | 31.3 | 31.0 | 30.7 | 29.0 | 29.6 |
| 2017 | 27.4 | 27.4 | 28.0 | 29.7 | 31.4 | 32.5 | 33.1 | 33.0 | 32.3 | 32.4 | 31.9 | 30.8 | 30.8 |
| 2018 | 28.9 | 28.9 | 29.7 | 31.1 | 32.8 | 34.2 | 34.7 | 34.7 | 34.1 | 33.8 | 33.2 | 32.3 | 32.4 |
| 2019 | 30.2 | 29.7 | 30.1 | 32.0 | 33.3 | 34.5 | 34.9 | 35.1 | 34.5 | 34.9 | 33.8 | 31.5 | 32.9 |

## Employment by Industry: Milwaukee-Waukesha-West Allis, WI, 2011–2019—*Continued*

(Numbers in thousands, not seasonally adjusted)

| Industry and year | January | February | March | April | May | June | July | August | September | October | November | December | Annual average |
|---|---|---|---|---|---|---|---|---|---|---|---|---|---|
| **Manufacturing** | | | | | | | | | | | | | |
| 2011 | 114.8 | 114.6 | 115.2 | 116.0 | 116.2 | 118.1 | 118.7 | 119.0 | 117.9 | 117.9 | 118.1 | 118.5 | 117.1 |
| 2012 | 118.7 | 118.3 | 118.6 | 118.9 | 119.1 | 120.8 | 121.3 | 120.9 | 119.8 | 119.7 | 119.6 | 120.0 | 119.6 |
| 2013 | 119.6 | 119.1 | 119.2 | 119.7 | 119.5 | 121.0 | 120.7 | 120.7 | 119.5 | 119.5 | 119.5 | 119.5 | 119.8 |
| 2014 | 119.1 | 119.1 | 119.4 | 119.4 | 119.7 | 120.7 | 121.7 | 121.8 | 120.6 | 120.1 | 120.5 | 120.8 | 120.2 |
| 2015 | 120.6 | 120.3 | 120.6 | 120.5 | 120.5 | 121.6 | 121.8 | 121.7 | 120.6 | 120.2 | 120.0 | 120.1 | 120.7 |
| 2016 | 119.5 | 119.2 | 119.1 | 119.1 | 118.8 | 119.7 | 119.8 | 119.7 | 118.2 | 118.0 | 117.8 | 118.1 | 118.9 |
| 2017 | 117.4 | 117.4 | 117.6 | 117.4 | 117.3 | 118.4 | 118.3 | 118.1 | 116.9 | 116.9 | 117.2 | 117.9 | 117.6 |
| 2018 | 117.4 | 117.4 | 117.6 | 117.7 | 117.8 | 119.3 | 119.7 | 119.9 | 118.9 | 119.0 | 119.4 | 119.9 | 118.7 |
| 2019 | 119.5 | 119.7 | 119.9 | 120.0 | 120.1 | 121.6 | 121.8 | 121.5 | 120.0 | 119.1 | 118.7 | 118.5 | 120.0 |
| **Trade, Transportation, and Utilities** | | | | | | | | | | | | | |
| 2011 | 140.8 | 139.1 | 139.9 | 140.7 | 141.5 | 141.8 | 141.3 | 141.7 | 142.4 | 144.6 | 145.9 | 146.2 | 142.2 |
| 2012 | 141.9 | 140.2 | 140.5 | 139.6 | 142.2 | 142.8 | 141.7 | 142.3 | 142.4 | 144.0 | 146.7 | 147.3 | 142.6 |
| 2013 | 141.6 | 140.6 | 140.9 | 141.6 | 143.4 | 144.4 | 143.0 | 143.2 | 143.2 | 144.2 | 146.7 | 148.0 | 143.4 |
| 2014 | 142.2 | 141.3 | 141.9 | 142.9 | 144.0 | 145.4 | 143.8 | 144.2 | 143.3 | 144.3 | 147.2 | 148.1 | 144.1 |
| 2015 | 142.9 | 141.5 | 141.8 | 142.5 | 144.0 | 145.4 | 144.5 | 145.5 | 144.8 | 146.1 | 148.7 | 148.9 | 144.7 |
| 2016 | 144.2 | 143.5 | 143.7 | 144.8 | 145.4 | 146.0 | 145.9 | 146.3 | 144.9 | 146.3 | 148.5 | 149.3 | 145.7 |
| 2017 | 145.2 | 143.8 | 144.1 | 143.9 | 145.4 | 145.6 | 145.8 | 146.6 | 145.1 | 146.3 | 149.3 | 150.5 | 146.0 |
| 2018 | 146.9 | 145.4 | 146.0 | 145.9 | 147.1 | 147.0 | 147.3 | 147.9 | 145.7 | 146.4 | 149.3 | 150.8 | 147.1 |
| 2019 | 146.9 | 144.6 | 144.3 | 144.6 | 145.0 | 146.1 | 145.2 | 145.7 | 144.2 | 145.5 | 148.9 | 149.9 | 145.9 |
| **Wholesale Trade** | | | | | | | | | | | | | |
| 2011 | 37.2 | 37.1 | 37.3 | 37.5 | 37.7 | 37.9 | 38.4 | 38.4 | 38.1 | 38.6 | 38.5 | 38.3 | 37.9 |
| 2012 | 38.0 | 38.1 | 38.3 | 38.3 | 38.5 | 38.8 | 38.8 | 38.8 | 38.3 | 38.5 | 38.5 | 38.7 | 38.5 |
| 2013 | 38.0 | 38.0 | 38.0 | 38.1 | 38.2 | 38.5 | 38.4 | 38.5 | 38.1 | 38.0 | 37.9 | 38.0 | 38.1 |
| 2014 | 37.6 | 37.6 | 37.7 | 38.0 | 38.1 | 38.4 | 38.4 | 38.3 | 37.9 | 38.0 | 38.1 | 38.2 | 38.0 |
| 2015 | 38.0 | 37.9 | 38.1 | 38.3 | 38.5 | 38.9 | 39.0 | 39.1 | 38.5 | 38.6 | 38.6 | 38.7 | 38.5 |
| 2016 | 38.3 | 38.4 | 38.4 | 38.4 | 38.5 | 38.7 | 38.9 | 38.9 | 38.4 | 38.4 | 38.3 | 38.5 | 38.5 |
| 2017 | 38.3 | 38.2 | 38.3 | 38.2 | 38.3 | 38.7 | 38.7 | 38.8 | 38.3 | 38.3 | 38.3 | 38.6 | 38.4 |
| 2018 | 38.2 | 38.2 | 38.3 | 38.4 | 38.4 | 39.0 | 38.9 | 38.9 | 38.4 | 38.5 | 38.4 | 38.6 | 38.5 |
| 2019 | 38.3 | 38.3 | 38.2 | 38.3 | 38.3 | 38.7 | 38.9 | 38.7 | 38.3 | 38.4 | 38.1 | 39.0 | 38.5 |
| **Retail Trade** | | | | | | | | | | | | | |
| 2011 | 75.8 | 74.2 | 74.7 | 75.3 | 75.7 | 76.2 | 76.1 | 76.6 | 76.1 | 77.8 | 79.1 | 79.7 | 76.4 |
| 2012 | 76.4 | 74.6 | 74.8 | 74.8 | 75.9 | 76.6 | 76.5 | 77.0 | 76.6 | 77.9 | 80.5 | 80.7 | 76.9 |
| 2013 | 76.8 | 75.8 | 76.0 | 76.7 | 78.0 | 78.8 | 78.7 | 78.8 | 78.2 | 79.2 | 81.4 | 82.4 | 78.4 |
| 2014 | 78.3 | 77.3 | 77.8 | 78.3 | 79.0 | 80.0 | 79.7 | 79.9 | 78.4 | 79.0 | 81.6 | 82.1 | 79.3 |
| 2015 | 78.3 | 77.1 | 77.2 | 77.5 | 78.4 | 79.5 | 79.7 | 80.3 | 79.2 | 80.3 | 82.7 | 82.6 | 79.4 |
| 2016 | 79.7 | 78.9 | 79.1 | 79.8 | 80.3 | 81.1 | 81.5 | 81.6 | 79.8 | 80.9 | 82.9 | 83.2 | 80.7 |
| 2017 | 80.8 | 79.4 | 79.5 | 79.8 | 80.4 | 81.1 | 81.4 | 81.6 | 79.7 | 80.7 | 83.5 | 83.9 | 81.0 |
| 2018 | 80.4 | 79.0 | 79.3 | 79.1 | 80.1 | 80.3 | 80.7 | 80.6 | 78.1 | 78.6 | 81.0 | 81.7 | 79.9 |
| 2019 | 78.8 | 76.9 | 76.8 | 76.8 | 77.2 | 78.0 | 77.6 | 77.6 | 75.7 | 76.3 | 79.4 | 78.9 | 77.5 |
| **Transportation and Utilities** | | | | | | | | | | | | | |
| 2011 | 27.8 | 27.8 | 27.9 | 27.9 | 28.1 | 27.7 | 26.8 | 26.7 | 28.2 | 28.2 | 28.3 | 28.2 | 27.8 |
| 2012 | 27.5 | 27.5 | 27.4 | 26.5 | 27.8 | 27.4 | 26.4 | 26.5 | 27.5 | 27.6 | 27.7 | 27.9 | 27.3 |
| 2013 | 26.8 | 26.8 | 26.9 | 26.8 | 27.2 | 27.1 | 25.9 | 25.9 | 26.9 | 27.0 | 27.4 | 27.6 | 26.9 |
| 2014 | 26.3 | 26.4 | 26.4 | 26.6 | 26.9 | 27.0 | 25.7 | 26.0 | 27.0 | 27.3 | 27.5 | 27.8 | 26.7 |
| 2015 | 26.6 | 26.5 | 26.5 | 26.7 | 27.1 | 27.0 | 25.8 | 26.1 | 27.1 | 27.2 | 27.4 | 27.6 | 26.8 |
| 2016 | 26.2 | 26.2 | 26.2 | 26.6 | 26.6 | 26.2 | 25.5 | 25.8 | 26.7 | 27.0 | 27.3 | 27.6 | 26.5 |
| 2017 | 26.1 | 26.2 | 26.3 | 25.9 | 26.7 | 25.8 | 25.7 | 26.2 | 27.1 | 27.3 | 27.5 | 28.0 | 26.6 |
| 2018 | 28.3 | 28.2 | 28.4 | 28.4 | 28.6 | 27.7 | 27.7 | 28.4 | 29.2 | 29.3 | 29.9 | 30.5 | 28.7 |
| 2019 | 29.8 | 29.4 | 29.3 | 29.5 | 29.5 | 29.4 | 28.7 | 29.4 | 30.2 | 30.8 | 31.4 | 32.0 | 30.0 |
| **Information** | | | | | | | | | | | | | |
| 2011 | 15.7 | 15.7 | 15.6 | 15.6 | 15.6 | 15.6 | 15.5 | 15.6 | 15.5 | 15.4 | 15.4 | 15.3 | 15.5 |
| 2012 | 15.1 | 15.0 | 14.9 | 14.9 | 14.8 | 15.0 | 15.0 | 15.0 | 14.9 | 15.0 | 15.0 | 14.8 | 15.0 |
| 2013 | 14.8 | 14.7 | 14.6 | 14.9 | 15.0 | 15.0 | 15.0 | 15.0 | 14.9 | 14.7 | 14.8 | 14.6 | 14.8 |
| 2014 | 14.4 | 14.5 | 14.5 | 14.5 | 14.5 | 14.5 | 14.7 | 14.6 | 14.4 | 14.5 | 14.6 | 14.6 | 14.5 |
| 2015 | 14.4 | 14.3 | 14.2 | 14.2 | 14.3 | 14.4 | 14.3 | 14.4 | 14.3 | 14.5 | 14.6 | 14.6 | 14.4 |
| 2016 | 14.4 | 14.4 | 14.4 | 14.3 | 14.2 | 14.3 | 14.2 | 14.1 | 13.9 | 13.9 | 13.9 | 13.9 | 14.2 |
| 2017 | 14.0 | 14.0 | 13.9 | 13.7 | 13.7 | 13.8 | 13.7 | 13.6 | 13.4 | 13.3 | 13.4 | 13.5 | 13.7 |
| 2018 | 13.5 | 13.5 | 13.5 | 13.4 | 13.5 | 13.6 | 13.6 | 13.5 | 13.3 | 13.6 | 13.6 | 13.6 | 13.5 |
| 2019 | 13.6 | 13.5 | 13.5 | 13.4 | 13.4 | 13.7 | 13.7 | 13.5 | 13.2 | 13.3 | 13.3 | 13.3 | 13.5 |

## Employment by Industry: Milwaukee-Waukesha-West Allis, WI, 2011–2019—*Continued*

(Numbers in thousands, not seasonally adjusted)

| Industry and year | January | February | March | April | May | June | July | August | September | October | November | December | Annual average |
|---|---|---|---|---|---|---|---|---|---|---|---|---|---|
| **Financial Activities** | | | | | | | | | | | | | |
| 2011 | 52.9 | 52.8 | 52.9 | 52.9 | 52.9 | 53.3 | 53.2 | 52.9 | 52.7 | 52.5 | 52.5 | 51.9 | 52.8 |
| 2012 | 51.9 | 51.8 | 51.9 | 51.8 | 52.0 | 52.4 | 52.5 | 52.4 | 51.7 | 51.9 | 51.7 | 51.9 | 52.0 |
| 2013 | 51.4 | 51.4 | 51.4 | 51.8 | 52.0 | 52.5 | 53.0 | 52.5 | 52.1 | 52.1 | 51.9 | 52.1 | 52.0 |
| 2014 | 51.2 | 51.1 | 51.3 | 51.3 | 51.5 | 52.1 | 52.3 | 52.4 | 51.9 | 51.7 | 51.8 | 52.1 | 51.7 |
| 2015 | 51.7 | 51.5 | 51.7 | 51.9 | 52.1 | 52.7 | 53.0 | 52.7 | 51.7 | 51.5 | 51.3 | 51.6 | 52.0 |
| 2016 | 51.0 | 50.8 | 51.0 | 50.9 | 50.9 | 51.5 | 51.9 | 51.7 | 51.2 | 51.2 | 51.1 | 51.1 | 51.2 |
| 2017 | 51.2 | 51.2 | 51.5 | 51.4 | 51.4 | 51.9 | 51.8 | 51.8 | 51.0 | 50.8 | 50.6 | 50.8 | 51.3 |
| 2018 | 50.4 | 50.3 | 50.5 | 50.4 | 50.6 | 51.5 | 51.6 | 51.5 | 50.9 | 50.6 | 50.5 | 50.6 | 50.8 |
| 2019 | 50.1 | 49.9 | 50.1 | 50.1 | 50.2 | 50.9 | 51.2 | 51.0 | 50.3 | 50.3 | 50.3 | 50.4 | 50.4 |
| **Professional and Business Services** | | | | | | | | | | | | | |
| 2011 | 111.6 | 111.8 | 113.1 | 113.1 | 112.7 | 115.3 | 115.2 | 116.6 | 116.5 | 116.0 | 116.8 | 115.7 | 114.5 |
| 2012 | 114.0 | 114.8 | 116.4 | 116.7 | 117.6 | 119.8 | 119.2 | 120.1 | 121.1 | 121.5 | 122.0 | 121.0 | 118.7 |
| 2013 | 117.4 | 119.1 | 121.2 | 120.5 | 121.6 | 123.2 | 124.0 | 124.1 | 125.0 | 124.1 | 125.1 | 125.5 | 122.6 |
| 2014 | 120.7 | 121.9 | 121.3 | 121.5 | 123.0 | 124.4 | 124.5 | 126.3 | 126.1 | 126.9 | 127.4 | 126.4 | 124.2 |
| 2015 | 121.0 | 121.7 | 120.9 | 123.3 | 124.4 | 126.0 | 126.9 | 128.6 | 127.2 | 128.1 | 127.9 | 126.6 | 125.2 |
| 2016 | 124.1 | 124.9 | 124.4 | 126.2 | 125.8 | 127.4 | 128.4 | 129.1 | 128.5 | 127.6 | 127.5 | 127.2 | 126.8 |
| 2017 | 122.9 | 123.2 | 125.2 | 125.6 | 126.3 | 128.3 | 129.0 | 129.3 | 128.8 | 129.8 | 129.7 | 130.8 | 127.4 |
| 2018 | 125.7 | 127.2 | 126.5 | 127.0 | 127.3 | 129.3 | 128.4 | 129.1 | 127.2 | 127.3 | 127.6 | 126.1 | 127.4 |
| 2019 | 122.3 | 123.8 | 123.8 | 124.7 | 124.5 | 126.4 | 125.3 | 126.0 | 124.7 | 124.8 | 125.2 | 124.3 | 124.7 |
| **Education and Health Services** | | | | | | | | | | | | | |
| 2011 | 144.1 | 144.9 | 145.2 | 146.1 | 146.6 | 143.3 | 142.1 | 141.6 | 145.4 | 147.3 | 147.9 | 148.0 | 145.2 |
| 2012 | 143.1 | 146.4 | 147.9 | 148.2 | 148.8 | 147.0 | 145.2 | 146.2 | 148.8 | 151.2 | 151.6 | 152.1 | 148.0 |
| 2013 | 149.6 | 150.9 | 151.3 | 152.5 | 152.7 | 151.3 | 149.8 | 150.7 | 153.8 | 156.3 | 156.9 | 157.1 | 152.7 |
| 2014 | 155.0 | 156.3 | 156.7 | 157.5 | 157.3 | 156.5 | 155.0 | 156.2 | 158.9 | 160.4 | 161.8 | 162.3 | 157.8 |
| 2015 | 158.5 | 160.7 | 161.9 | 162.4 | 163.0 | 161.6 | 159.7 | 160.6 | 163.1 | 165.3 | 166.2 | 167.3 | 162.5 |
| 2016 | 163.7 | 165.8 | 166.4 | 167.4 | 167.2 | 165.9 | 164.4 | 164.7 | 167.7 | 168.5 | 169.2 | 168.9 | 166.7 |
| 2017 | 165.7 | 167.5 | 168.2 | 168.5 | 168.6 | 168.1 | 165.8 | 166.5 | 169.4 | 170.5 | 171.1 | 171.5 | 168.5 |
| 2018 | 168.7 | 170.4 | 171.3 | 171.4 | 171.5 | 170.9 | 167.9 | 168.9 | 171.6 | 172.9 | 173.9 | 174.1 | 171.1 |
| 2019 | 170.7 | 172.0 | 172.7 | 172.4 | 173.3 | 172.4 | 169.7 | 170.7 | 172.5 | 175.8 | 177.7 | 178.2 | 173.2 |
| **Leisure and Hospitality** | | | | | | | | | | | | | |
| 2011 | 65.0 | 64.5 | 65.1 | 68.2 | 70.7 | 71.6 | 73.3 | 74.0 | 70.7 | 69.4 | 68.3 | 67.4 | 69.0 |
| 2012 | 66.2 | 66.6 | 67.4 | 69.6 | 72.9 | 73.8 | 75.8 | 75.4 | 72.8 | 70.6 | 69.8 | 70.1 | 70.9 |
| 2013 | 68.2 | 68.6 | 69.3 | 71.1 | 75.2 | 76.5 | 78.1 | 77.4 | 75.2 | 73.4 | 73.0 | 73.1 | 73.3 |
| 2014 | 71.1 | 71.6 | 71.2 | 73.3 | 75.6 | 78.4 | 78.7 | 78.0 | 75.2 | 73.8 | 73.2 | 73.6 | 74.5 |
| 2015 | 70.8 | 71.0 | 72.3 | 75.0 | 77.9 | 80.7 | 79.8 | 80.6 | 76.8 | 76.2 | 75.8 | 75.7 | 76.1 |
| 2016 | 73.3 | 73.9 | 74.3 | 76.7 | 79.7 | 82.1 | 82.4 | 82.9 | 78.5 | 77.0 | 75.7 | 75.8 | 77.7 |
| 2017 | 74.8 | 75.1 | 76.5 | 77.7 | 81.3 | 85.0 | 84.8 | 84.3 | 79.9 | 78.7 | 77.1 | 77.6 | 79.4 |
| 2018 | 76.8 | 76.7 | 77.9 | 78.2 | 81.1 | 85.1 | 85.5 | 85.4 | 81.7 | 80.7 | 79.3 | 79.9 | 80.7 |
| 2019 | 78.1 | 77.4 | 78.9 | 80.3 | 83.7 | 86.8 | 87.2 | 86.1 | 80.9 | 81.3 | 79.3 | 78.8 | 81.6 |
| **Other Services** | | | | | | | | | | | | | |
| 2011 | 43.2 | 43.0 | 43.1 | 43.5 | 43.6 | 43.7 | 43.9 | 43.8 | 43.0 | 43.2 | 42.9 | 43.0 | 43.3 |
| 2012 | 42.0 | 41.9 | 41.9 | 41.9 | 42.1 | 42.8 | 42.6 | 42.4 | 42.0 | 42.2 | 42.1 | 42.2 | 42.2 |
| 2013 | 41.5 | 41.5 | 41.7 | 42.2 | 42.4 | 42.9 | 43.0 | 42.8 | 42.7 | 42.4 | 42.5 | 42.7 | 42.4 |
| 2014 | 41.9 | 42.0 | 42.1 | 42.9 | 43.0 | 44.0 | 44.3 | 44.5 | 44.2 | 44.3 | 44.4 | 44.7 | 43.5 |
| 2015 | 44.4 | 44.6 | 45.1 | 45.4 | 45.6 | 46.0 | 46.4 | 46.3 | 45.7 | 45.5 | 45.4 | 45.8 | 45.5 |
| 2016 | 45.1 | 45.0 | 45.3 | 45.9 | 45.9 | 46.3 | 46.7 | 46.7 | 46.3 | 46.1 | 46.0 | 46.1 | 46.0 |
| 2017 | 45.8 | 45.9 | 46.1 | 46.6 | 46.8 | 47.6 | 47.4 | 47.4 | 47.0 | 46.7 | 46.5 | 46.7 | 46.7 |
| 2018 | 46.4 | 46.3 | 46.6 | 46.8 | 47.0 | 47.8 | 47.5 | 47.6 | 47.1 | 47.0 | 46.8 | 46.9 | 47.0 |
| 2019 | 46.6 | 46.3 | 46.7 | 47.0 | 47.2 | 47.7 | 47.5 | 47.5 | 46.7 | 46.6 | 46.4 | 46.6 | 46.9 |
| **Government** | | | | | | | | | | | | | |
| 2011 | 88.9 | 92.8 | 92.3 | 91.6 | 91.0 | 90.7 | 87.2 | 86.6 | 87.9 | 86.5 | 88.5 | 88.8 | 89.4 |
| 2012 | 85.8 | 87.2 | 88.8 | 90.1 | 91.0 | 89.3 | 83.3 | 85.0 | 86.8 | 88.6 | 91.2 | 88.9 | 88.0 |
| 2013 | 84.7 | 88.1 | 88.1 | 88.0 | 87.7 | 87.3 | 81.8 | 83.4 | 87.4 | 87.7 | 87.9 | 87.6 | 86.6 |
| 2014 | 85.0 | 87.2 | 87.6 | 87.4 | 87.2 | 87.8 | 82.0 | 86.1 | 87.5 | 87.4 | 88.8 | 87.3 | 86.8 |
| 2015 | 83.1 | 87.5 | 87.3 | 88.3 | 87.6 | 86.8 | 82.3 | 83.9 | 86.9 | 87.1 | 87.0 | 87.4 | 86.3 |
| 2016 | 85.5 | 87.6 | 87.6 | 89.0 | 87.6 | 86.0 | 80.7 | 84.3 | 86.7 | 88.3 | 89.8 | 88.7 | 86.8 |
| 2017 | 84.7 | 87.7 | 87.7 | 88.3 | 87.8 | 85.6 | 80.6 | 83.2 | 85.5 | 87.2 | 87.4 | 87.6 | 86.1 |
| 2018 | 84.3 | 86.8 | 86.7 | 87.9 | 87.2 | 84.9 | 80.8 | 82.2 | 84.9 | 86.5 | 87.8 | 86.6 | 85.6 |
| 2019 | 83.4 | 85.5 | 85.7 | 86.6 | 85.8 | 84.7 | 80.5 | 81.3 | 84.2 | 87.1 | 87.4 | 87.2 | 85.0 |

# Employment by Industry: Jacksonville, FL, 2011–2019

(Numbers in thousands, not seasonally adjusted)

| Industry and year | January | February | March | April | May | June | July | August | September | October | November | December | Annual average |
|---|---|---|---|---|---|---|---|---|---|---|---|---|---|
| **Total Nonfarm** | | | | | | | | | | | | | |
| 2011 | 580.3 | 583.9 | 588.4 | 589.9 | 589.9 | 582.9 | 578.7 | 583.1 | 584.9 | 587.6 | 591.1 | 592.7 | 586.1 |
| 2012 | 584.2 | 588.9 | 593.3 | 595.5 | 597.9 | 592.8 | 588.3 | 593.6 | 594.0 | 598.4 | 602.7 | 604.1 | 594.5 |
| 2013 | 592.1 | 599.2 | 603.7 | 605.8 | 607.8 | 604.1 | 604.0 | 609.7 | 610.5 | 614.6 | 620.0 | 623.2 | 607.9 |
| 2014 | 608.7 | 613.7 | 617.4 | 621.4 | 624.1 | 619.2 | 617.4 | 624.8 | 624.2 | 634.0 | 638.8 | 643.6 | 623.9 |
| 2015 | 630.0 | 636.8 | 641.3 | 643.7 | 645.8 | 641.4 | 640.7 | 646.6 | 647.0 | 655.9 | 660.8 | 663.5 | 646.1 |
| 2016 | 651.0 | 656.3 | 660.5 | 666.4 | 668.3 | 662.4 | 665.0 | 671.1 | 673.5 | 676.2 | 684.4 | 685.1 | 668.4 |
| 2017 | 675.1 | 679.8 | 682.5 | 686.0 | 689.0 | 684.4 | 685.5 | 690.9 | 682.3 | 698.3 | 706.5 | 707.7 | 689.0 |
| 2018 | 698.2 | 702.3 | 705.4 | 704.9 | 708.0 | 703.5 | 701.7 | 710.2 | 710.9 | 713.7 | 723.9 | 725.9 | 709.1 |
| 2019 | 713.0 | 716.9 | 718.1 | 718.8 | 721.5 | 717.0 | 718.5 | 726.1 | 724.4 | 735.6 | 740.4 | 742.6 | 724.4 |
| **Total Private** | | | | | | | | | | | | | |
| 2011 | 502.5 | 505.7 | 510.2 | 511.7 | 511.9 | 509.5 | 506.5 | 507.4 | 509.0 | 511.1 | 514.4 | 516.0 | 509.7 |
| 2012 | 508.7 | 512.4 | 516.7 | 520.1 | 522.5 | 521.7 | 517.7 | 519.8 | 519.3 | 522.7 | 527.0 | 528.8 | 519.8 |
| 2013 | 518.1 | 523.8 | 528.3 | 530.4 | 532.5 | 533.7 | 534.5 | 536.8 | 536.8 | 540.3 | 545.1 | 548.2 | 534.0 |
| 2014 | 535.9 | 539.1 | 542.6 | 546.2 | 549.1 | 549.0 | 547.7 | 551.6 | 550.0 | 559.2 | 563.8 | 568.2 | 550.2 |
| 2015 | 556.9 | 561.5 | 565.7 | 568.1 | 570.5 | 570.8 | 570.5 | 572.7 | 572.2 | 580.1 | 584.6 | 587.1 | 571.7 |
| 2016 | 576.2 | 580.2 | 584.0 | 589.9 | 591.9 | 590.6 | 593.3 | 595.9 | 597.0 | 599.8 | 607.5 | 607.6 | 592.8 |
| 2017 | 599.6 | 602.6 | 604.9 | 608.7 | 611.4 | 611.4 | 613.2 | 615.2 | 605.7 | 621.2 | 628.8 | 630.0 | 612.7 |
| 2018 | 622.2 | 625.0 | 627.1 | 627.6 | 630.0 | 629.9 | 628.8 | 633.3 | 633.6 | 636.2 | 645.4 | 647.5 | 632.2 |
| 2019 | 636.2 | 638.5 | 639.8 | 640.4 | 642.9 | 642.8 | 644.7 | 648.3 | 646.2 | 656.7 | 661.1 | 663.3 | 646.7 |
| **Goods Producing** | | | | | | | | | | | | | |
| 2011 | 54.1 | 54.1 | 54.7 | 55.0 | 54.8 | 54.9 | 55.4 | 55.6 | 55.3 | 54.9 | 55.1 | 54.9 | 54.9 |
| 2012 | 54.1 | 54.2 | 54.6 | 55.2 | 55.3 | 55.9 | 55.9 | 56.0 | 56.2 | 56.4 | 56.6 | 56.5 | 55.6 |
| 2013 | 56.1 | 56.6 | 57.5 | 57.4 | 57.5 | 58.1 | 58.4 | 58.3 | 58.6 | 58.5 | 59.0 | 59.0 | 57.9 |
| 2014 | 58.4 | 58.8 | 59.1 | 59.5 | 60.1 | 60.6 | 60.9 | 61.3 | 61.3 | 62.0 | 62.4 | 62.5 | 60.6 |
| 2015 | 62.4 | 63.2 | 63.9 | 64.1 | 64.5 | 65.0 | 64.9 | 64.8 | 64.6 | 65.6 | 65.7 | 66.0 | 64.6 |
| 2016 | 66.0 | 66.5 | 67.0 | 68.0 | 68.5 | 69.3 | 69.6 | 69.2 | 69.8 | 69.9 | 70.7 | 71.0 | 68.8 |
| 2017 | 71.1 | 71.8 | 72.1 | 72.8 | 73.4 | 74.1 | 74.3 | 74.4 | 71.8 | 74.4 | 74.7 | 74.9 | 73.3 |
| 2018 | 74.6 | 75.7 | 76.2 | 76.3 | 76.4 | 76.9 | 76.4 | 77.1 | 76.9 | 77.1 | 77.4 | 77.2 | 76.5 |
| 2019 | 76.9 | 77.7 | 77.9 | 78.0 | 78.6 | 79.3 | 79.7 | 79.6 | 79.7 | 81.0 | 79.9 | 79.8 | 79.0 |
| **Service-Providing** | | | | | | | | | | | | | |
| 2011 | 526.2 | 529.8 | 533.7 | 534.9 | 535.1 | 528.0 | 523.3 | 527.5 | 529.6 | 532.7 | 536.0 | 537.8 | 531.2 |
| 2012 | 530.1 | 534.7 | 538.7 | 540.3 | 542.6 | 536.9 | 532.4 | 537.6 | 537.8 | 542.0 | 546.1 | 547.6 | 538.9 |
| 2013 | 536.0 | 542.6 | 546.2 | 548.4 | 550.3 | 546.0 | 545.6 | 551.4 | 551.9 | 556.1 | 561.0 | 564.2 | 550.0 |
| 2014 | 550.3 | 554.9 | 558.3 | 561.9 | 564.0 | 558.6 | 556.5 | 563.5 | 562.9 | 572.0 | 576.4 | 581.1 | 563.4 |
| 2015 | 567.6 | 573.6 | 577.4 | 579.6 | 581.3 | 576.4 | 575.8 | 581.8 | 582.4 | 590.3 | 595.1 | 597.5 | 581.6 |
| 2016 | 585.0 | 589.8 | 593.5 | 598.4 | 599.8 | 593.1 | 595.4 | 601.9 | 603.7 | 606.3 | 613.7 | 614.1 | 599.6 |
| 2017 | 604.0 | 608.0 | 610.4 | 613.2 | 615.6 | 610.3 | 611.2 | 616.5 | 610.5 | 623.9 | 631.8 | 632.8 | 615.7 |
| 2018 | 623.6 | 626.6 | 629.2 | 628.6 | 631.6 | 626.6 | 625.3 | 633.1 | 634.0 | 636.6 | 646.5 | 648.7 | 632.5 |
| 2019 | 636.1 | 639.2 | 640.2 | 640.8 | 642.9 | 637.7 | 638.8 | 646.5 | 644.7 | 654.6 | 660.5 | 662.8 | 645.4 |
| **Mining and Logging** | | | | | | | | | | | | | |
| 2011 | 0.3 | 0.3 | 0.3 | 0.3 | 0.3 | 0.3 | 0.3 | 0.3 | 0.3 | 0.3 | 0.3 | 0.3 | 0.3 |
| 2012 | 0.3 | 0.3 | 0.3 | 0.3 | 0.3 | 0.3 | 0.3 | 0.3 | 0.3 | 0.4 | 0.4 | 0.4 | 0.3 |
| 2013 | 0.4 | 0.4 | 0.4 | 0.4 | 0.4 | 0.4 | 0.4 | 0.4 | 0.4 | 0.4 | 0.4 | 0.4 | 0.4 |
| 2014 | 0.4 | 0.4 | 0.4 | 0.4 | 0.4 | 0.4 | 0.4 | 0.4 | 0.4 | 0.4 | 0.4 | 0.4 | 0.4 |
| 2015 | 0.4 | 0.4 | 0.4 | 0.4 | 0.4 | 0.4 | 0.4 | 0.4 | 0.4 | 0.4 | 0.4 | 0.4 | 0.4 |
| 2016 | 0.4 | 0.4 | 0.4 | 0.4 | 0.4 | 0.4 | 0.4 | 0.4 | 0.4 | 0.5 | 0.5 | 0.5 | 0.4 |
| 2017 | 0.5 | 0.5 | 0.5 | 0.5 | 0.5 | 0.5 | 0.5 | 0.5 | 0.5 | 0.5 | 0.5 | 0.5 | 0.5 |
| 2018 | 0.5 | 0.5 | 0.5 | 0.5 | 0.5 | 0.5 | 0.5 | 0.5 | 0.6 | 0.6 | 0.6 | 0.5 | 0.5 |
| 2019 | 0.5 | 0.5 | 0.5 | 0.5 | 0.5 | 0.5 | 0.5 | 0.5 | 0.5 | 0.5 | 0.5 | 0.5 | 0.5 |
| **Construction** | | | | | | | | | | | | | |
| 2011 | 26.4 | 26.4 | 27.0 | 27.2 | 27.0 | 27.2 | 27.6 | 27.7 | 27.6 | 27.2 | 27.3 | 27.0 | 27.1 |
| 2012 | 26.1 | 26.2 | 26.6 | 27.0 | 27.0 | 27.5 | 27.6 | 27.9 | 28.0 | 28.1 | 28.2 | 28.3 | 27.4 |
| 2013 | 27.7 | 28.3 | 29.1 | 29.1 | 29.2 | 29.7 | 30.1 | 30.2 | 30.5 | 30.6 | 31.0 | 30.9 | 29.7 |
| 2014 | 30.4 | 31.0 | 31.4 | 31.6 | 31.9 | 32.2 | 32.5 | 32.7 | 32.7 | 33.0 | 33.2 | 33.3 | 32.2 |
| 2015 | 33.1 | 33.8 | 34.4 | 34.5 | 34.9 | 35.3 | 35.3 | 35.3 | 35.3 | 36.3 | 36.6 | 36.9 | 35.1 |
| 2016 | 36.6 | 37.1 | 37.7 | 38.4 | 38.7 | 39.2 | 39.2 | 38.9 | 39.4 | 39.5 | 40.1 | 40.2 | 38.8 |
| 2017 | 40.1 | 40.4 | 40.7 | 41.2 | 41.7 | 42.1 | 42.5 | 42.7 | 41.3 | 42.9 | 43.1 | 43.2 | 41.8 |
| 2018 | 43.1 | 43.9 | 44.3 | 44.7 | 44.6 | 44.9 | 44.5 | 45.2 | 44.9 | 44.9 | 45.1 | 44.9 | 44.6 |
| 2019 | 44.7 | 45.2 | 45.4 | 45.5 | 45.9 | 46.3 | 46.6 | 46.6 | 46.6 | 47.8 | 46.6 | 46.5 | 46.1 |

## Employment by Industry: Jacksonville, FL, 2011–2019—*Continued*

(Numbers in thousands, not seasonally adjusted)

| Industry and year | January | February | March | April | May | June | July | August | September | October | November | December | Annual average |
|---|---|---|---|---|---|---|---|---|---|---|---|---|---|
| **Manufacturing** | | | | | | | | | | | | | |
| 2011 | 27.4 | 27.4 | 27.4 | 27.5 | 27.5 | 27.4 | 27.5 | 27.6 | 27.4 | 27.4 | 27.5 | 27.6 | 27.5 |
| 2012 | 27.7 | 27.7 | 27.7 | 27.9 | 28.0 | 28.1 | 28.0 | 27.8 | 27.9 | 27.9 | 28.0 | 27.8 | 27.9 |
| 2013 | 28.0 | 27.9 | 28.0 | 27.9 | 27.9 | 28.0 | 27.9 | 27.7 | 27.7 | 27.5 | 27.6 | 27.7 | 27.8 |
| 2014 | 27.6 | 27.4 | 27.3 | 27.5 | 27.8 | 28.0 | 28.0 | 28.2 | 28.2 | 28.6 | 28.8 | 28.8 | 28.0 |
| 2015 | 28.9 | 29.0 | 29.1 | 29.2 | 29.2 | 29.3 | 29.2 | 29.1 | 28.9 | 28.9 | 28.7 | 28.7 | 29.0 |
| 2016 | 29.0 | 29.0 | 28.9 | 29.2 | 29.4 | 29.7 | 30.0 | 29.9 | 30.0 | 29.9 | 30.1 | 30.3 | 29.6 |
| 2017 | 30.5 | 30.9 | 30.9 | 31.1 | 31.2 | 31.5 | 31.3 | 31.2 | 30.0 | 31.0 | 31.1 | 31.2 | 31.0 |
| 2018 | 31.0 | 31.3 | 31.4 | 31.1 | 31.3 | 31.5 | 31.4 | 31.4 | 31.5 | 31.6 | 31.7 | 31.7 | 31.4 |
| 2019 | 31.7 | 32.0 | 32.0 | 32.0 | 32.2 | 32.5 | 32.6 | 32.5 | 32.6 | 32.7 | 32.8 | 32.8 | 32.4 |
| **Trade, Transportation, and Utilities** | | | | | | | | | | | | | |
| 2011 | 122.5 | 122.7 | 123.3 | 123.7 | 123.1 | 123.2 | 123.2 | 123.3 | 122.9 | 122.9 | 125.3 | 126.2 | 123.5 |
| 2012 | 124.1 | 124.1 | 124.7 | 124.6 | 125.0 | 124.9 | 123.7 | 124.5 | 124.7 | 124.9 | 127.7 | 128.8 | 125.1 |
| 2013 | 125.1 | 125.1 | 125.8 | 126.7 | 126.8 | 126.6 | 126.8 | 127.2 | 126.8 | 128.4 | 131.1 | 133.2 | 127.5 |
| 2014 | 127.7 | 127.8 | 127.6 | 128.2 | 128.6 | 128.5 | 128.7 | 130.1 | 129.9 | 132.8 | 136.3 | 138.2 | 130.4 |
| 2015 | 133.1 | 133.1 | 133.0 | 132.9 | 133.5 | 133.5 | 133.7 | 135.1 | 135.0 | 135.7 | 138.9 | 140.1 | 134.8 |
| 2016 | 135.5 | 135.7 | 135.9 | 136.5 | 136.8 | 136.4 | 137.2 | 138.0 | 137.5 | 137.6 | 140.9 | 142.3 | 137.5 |
| 2017 | 139.3 | 138.9 | 138.7 | 139.3 | 139.3 | 139.2 | 139.5 | 140.1 | 140.0 | 143.5 | 149.4 | 150.8 | 141.5 |
| 2018 | 149.9 | 148.8 | 148.8 | 148.7 | 149.4 | 149.7 | 149.3 | 150.5 | 151.0 | 152.4 | 159.1 | 161.1 | 151.6 |
| 2019 | 156.9 | 155.1 | 154.6 | 154.3 | 154.8 | 154.8 | 156.0 | 156.3 | 156.8 | 158.7 | 163.5 | 163.7 | 157.1 |
| **Wholesale Trade** | | | | | | | | | | | | | |
| 2011 | 24.3 | 24.5 | 24.5 | 24.4 | 24.4 | 24.3 | 24.3 | 24.2 | 24.1 | 24.1 | 24.0 | 24.0 | 24.3 |
| 2012 | 24.1 | 24.2 | 24.5 | 24.4 | 24.5 | 24.4 | 24.6 | 24.5 | 24.4 | 24.4 | 24.4 | 24.5 | 24.4 |
| 2013 | 24.3 | 24.4 | 24.5 | 24.7 | 24.7 | 24.7 | 24.5 | 24.3 | 24.1 | 24.2 | 24.1 | 24.0 | 24.4 |
| 2014 | 23.7 | 23.8 | 23.7 | 23.5 | 23.7 | 23.7 | 23.6 | 23.7 | 23.6 | 23.9 | 23.9 | 23.9 | 23.7 |
| 2015 | 23.9 | 23.9 | 23.8 | 24.1 | 24.4 | 24.6 | 24.8 | 25.1 | 25.4 | 25.4 | 25.6 | 25.8 | 24.7 |
| 2016 | 25.3 | 25.7 | 25.8 | 25.4 | 25.5 | 25.3 | 25.5 | 25.6 | 25.4 | 25.2 | 25.2 | 25.2 | 25.4 |
| 2017 | 25.1 | 25.2 | 25.2 | 25.1 | 25.2 | 25.2 | 25.0 | 25.0 | 24.6 | 24.7 | 24.9 | 24.9 | 25.0 |
| 2018 | 25.2 | 25.2 | 25.1 | 25.4 | 25.6 | 25.6 | 25.7 | 25.9 | 26.1 | 26.1 | 26.6 | 26.7 | 25.8 |
| 2019 | 26.7 | 27.0 | 27.1 | 27.0 | 27.1 | 27.2 | 27.6 | 27.7 | 27.6 | 28.1 | 28.9 | 29.6 | 27.6 |
| **Retail Trade** | | | | | | | | | | | | | |
| 2011 | 67.9 | 67.8 | 68.3 | 68.4 | 68.5 | 68.8 | 68.7 | 68.9 | 68.7 | 69.0 | 71.3 | 71.8 | 69.0 |
| 2012 | 69.6 | 69.5 | 69.9 | 69.9 | 70.3 | 70.2 | 69.1 | 69.5 | 69.6 | 69.8 | 72.2 | 72.6 | 70.2 |
| 2013 | 70.1 | 69.8 | 70.2 | 70.5 | 70.8 | 71.1 | 71.5 | 71.4 | 71.0 | 72.2 | 75.0 | 75.5 | 71.6 |
| 2014 | 71.9 | 71.7 | 71.6 | 71.9 | 72.1 | 72.1 | 72.5 | 73.1 | 73.2 | 75.3 | 78.7 | 79.5 | 73.6 |
| 2015 | 75.4 | 75.3 | 75.3 | 74.6 | 75.0 | 75.2 | 75.3 | 75.8 | 75.2 | 75.7 | 78.3 | 78.8 | 75.8 |
| 2016 | 75.7 | 75.7 | 75.9 | 76.5 | 76.8 | 76.6 | 77.6 | 78.0 | 77.6 | 77.7 | 80.7 | 81.5 | 77.5 |
| 2017 | 79.0 | 78.6 | 78.2 | 78.7 | 78.8 | 78.8 | 78.8 | 79.2 | 77.6 | 79.6 | 83.7 | 83.7 | 79.6 |
| 2018 | 83.6 | 82.8 | 83.0 | 80.5 | 80.9 | 80.7 | 80.7 | 81.2 | 80.9 | 81.4 | 85.3 | 85.7 | 82.2 |
| 2019 | 82.7 | 81.9 | 81.8 | 81.0 | 81.2 | 81.0 | 81.3 | 81.4 | 81.1 | 82.0 | 85.2 | 83.2 | 82.0 |
| **Transportation and Utilities** | | | | | | | | | | | | | |
| 2011 | 30.3 | 30.4 | 30.5 | 30.9 | 30.2 | 30.1 | 30.2 | 30.2 | 30.1 | 29.8 | 30.0 | 30.4 | 30.3 |
| 2012 | 30.4 | 30.4 | 30.3 | 30.3 | 30.2 | 30.3 | 30.0 | 30.5 | 30.7 | 30.7 | 31.1 | 31.7 | 30.6 |
| 2013 | 30.7 | 30.9 | 31.1 | 31.5 | 31.3 | 30.8 | 30.8 | 31.5 | 31.7 | 32.0 | 32.0 | 33.7 | 31.5 |
| 2014 | 32.1 | 32.3 | 32.3 | 32.8 | 32.8 | 32.7 | 32.6 | 33.3 | 33.1 | 33.6 | 33.7 | 34.8 | 33.0 |
| 2015 | 33.8 | 33.9 | 33.9 | 34.2 | 34.1 | 33.7 | 33.6 | 34.2 | 34.4 | 34.6 | 35.0 | 35.5 | 34.2 |
| 2016 | 34.5 | 34.3 | 34.2 | 34.6 | 34.5 | 34.5 | 34.1 | 34.4 | 34.5 | 34.7 | 35.0 | 35.6 | 34.6 |
| 2017 | 35.2 | 35.1 | 35.3 | 35.5 | 35.3 | 35.2 | 35.7 | 35.9 | 37.8 | 39.2 | 40.8 | 42.2 | 36.9 |
| 2018 | 41.1 | 40.8 | 40.7 | 42.8 | 42.9 | 43.4 | 42.9 | 43.4 | 44.0 | 44.9 | 47.2 | 48.7 | 43.6 |
| 2019 | 47.5 | 46.2 | 45.7 | 46.3 | 46.5 | 46.6 | 47.1 | 47.2 | 48.1 | 48.6 | 49.4 | 50.9 | 47.5 |
| **Information** | | | | | | | | | | | | | |
| 2011 | 9.8 | 9.7 | 9.7 | 9.8 | 9.8 | 9.7 | 9.7 | 9.7 | 9.6 | 9.6 | 9.7 | 9.6 | 9.7 |
| 2012 | 9.4 | 9.4 | 9.3 | 9.4 | 9.4 | 9.3 | 9.3 | 9.2 | 9.0 | 9.2 | 9.2 | 9.2 | 9.3 |
| 2013 | 9.1 | 9.1 | 9.1 | 9.1 | 9.2 | 9.2 | 9.3 | 9.3 | 9.2 | 9.3 | 9.3 | 9.4 | 9.2 |
| 2014 | 9.3 | 9.3 | 9.3 | 9.3 | 9.3 | 9.3 | 9.3 | 9.3 | 9.2 | 9.1 | 9.2 | 9.2 | 9.3 |
| 2015 | 9.2 | 9.2 | 9.2 | 9.2 | 9.2 | 9.3 | 9.4 | 9.5 | 9.4 | 9.5 | 9.5 | 9.6 | 9.4 |
| 2016 | 9.3 | 9.4 | 9.4 | 9.5 | 9.6 | 9.5 | 9.5 | 9.5 | 9.5 | 9.4 | 9.5 | 9.5 | 9.5 |
| 2017 | 9.3 | 9.4 | 9.3 | 9.3 | 9.4 | 9.4 | 9.5 | 9.4 | 9.3 | 9.2 | 9.3 | 9.3 | 9.3 |
| 2018 | 9.2 | 9.3 | 9.3 | 9.4 | 9.5 | 9.4 | 9.3 | 9.2 | 9.1 | 9.2 | 9.2 | 9.1 | 9.3 |
| 2019 | 9.0 | 9.0 | 8.9 | 9.0 | 9.0 | 9.0 | 9.0 | 9.0 | 8.9 | 8.9 | 8.9 | 8.9 | 9.0 |

# Employment by Industry: Jacksonville, FL, 2011–2019—*Continued*

(Numbers in thousands, not seasonally adjusted)

| Industry and year | January | February | March | April | May | June | July | August | September | October | November | December | Annual average |
|---|---|---|---|---|---|---|---|---|---|---|---|---|---|
| **Financial Activities** | | | | | | | | | | | | | |
| 2011 | 57.0 | 57.3 | 57.8 | 57.8 | 57.7 | 58.0 | 57.9 | 58.0 | 58.5 | 58.4 | 58.3 | 59.0 | 58.0 |
| 2012 | 58.6 | 59.2 | 59.5 | 59.5 | 59.8 | 60.0 | 60.1 | 60.1 | 60.2 | 60.8 | 61.2 | 61.4 | 60.0 |
| 2013 | 60.8 | 61.1 | 61.1 | 61.2 | 61.2 | 61.6 | 61.7 | 61.7 | 61.6 | 61.7 | 61.9 | 62.0 | 61.5 |
| 2014 | 61.0 | 60.9 | 61.2 | 61.1 | 61.0 | 60.8 | 61.0 | 60.7 | 60.3 | 60.7 | 60.9 | 60.9 | 60.9 |
| 2015 | 61.2 | 61.2 | 61.3 | 61.0 | 61.0 | 61.1 | 61.0 | 61.2 | 61.4 | 62.3 | 62.5 | 62.5 | 61.5 |
| 2016 | 62.5 | 62.9 | 62.9 | 63.4 | 63.8 | 63.9 | 64.1 | 64.4 | 65.1 | 65.4 | 65.8 | 66.5 | 64.2 |
| 2017 | 66.2 | 66.4 | 66.8 | 67.0 | 67.1 | 67.2 | 67.0 | 67.2 | 66.9 | 67.5 | 67.8 | 67.8 | 67.1 |
| 2018 | 67.1 | 67.2 | 67.3 | 66.9 | 66.9 | 67.1 | 67.1 | 67.2 | 66.9 | 67.2 | 67.5 | 67.4 | 67.2 |
| 2019 | 66.5 | 66.7 | 66.7 | 67.0 | 66.8 | 67.0 | 66.9 | 67.2 | 67.1 | 67.7 | 67.9 | 68.6 | 67.2 |
| **Professional and Business Services** | | | | | | | | | | | | | |
| 2011 | 85.7 | 87.6 | 88.4 | 88.4 | 89.0 | 87.8 | 85.2 | 85.5 | 87.7 | 89.2 | 90.2 | 90.3 | 87.9 |
| 2012 | 89.2 | 90.4 | 90.9 | 92.5 | 93.4 | 92.3 | 89.8 | 90.6 | 90.3 | 91.6 | 92.0 | 91.7 | 91.2 |
| 2013 | 89.2 | 90.9 | 92.3 | 92.6 | 93.9 | 94.1 | 94.4 | 95.3 | 95.7 | 97.5 | 97.6 | 97.8 | 94.3 |
| 2014 | 95.1 | 95.5 | 95.9 | 97.1 | 98.3 | 97.8 | 97.4 | 98.7 | 99.1 | 101.3 | 102.3 | 103.2 | 98.5 |
| 2015 | 99.6 | 100.6 | 100.9 | 101.8 | 101.9 | 100.7 | 100.6 | 99.6 | 99.3 | 101.9 | 102.5 | 102.4 | 101.0 |
| 2016 | 99.4 | 99.5 | 100.6 | 102.3 | 102.1 | 101.2 | 102.5 | 102.9 | 102.9 | 106.1 | 106.9 | 105.7 | 102.7 |
| 2017 | 103.8 | 103.4 | 104.1 | 104.5 | 104.7 | 105.1 | 106.4 | 106.7 | 104.9 | 109.5 | 109.6 | 109.7 | 106.0 |
| 2018 | 106.4 | 107.1 | 107.1 | 106.9 | 107.7 | 107.9 | 108.3 | 108.8 | 108.6 | 109.1 | 109.6 | 110.1 | 108.1 |
| 2019 | 107.5 | 108.0 | 108.3 | 108.1 | 109.1 | 109.4 | 110.7 | 111.2 | 110.2 | 114.2 | 113.9 | 114.4 | 110.4 |
| **Education and Health Services** | | | | | | | | | | | | | |
| 2011 | 87.1 | 87.6 | 87.7 | 87.4 | 87.4 | 86.4 | 86.3 | 86.8 | 88.1 | 89.2 | 89.5 | 89.8 | 87.8 |
| 2012 | 87.6 | 88.4 | 88.7 | 88.7 | 89.0 | 88.6 | 88.2 | 88.9 | 90.0 | 90.5 | 90.8 | 91.3 | 89.2 |
| 2013 | 90.0 | 91.4 | 91.4 | 90.8 | 91.0 | 90.7 | 90.0 | 90.6 | 91.3 | 92.1 | 92.7 | 93.0 | 91.3 |
| 2014 | 91.4 | 92.5 | 92.8 | 93.4 | 93.3 | 92.4 | 92.2 | 93.2 | 93.7 | 95.1 | 95.3 | 96.0 | 93.4 |
| 2015 | 95.0 | 95.7 | 96.4 | 96.7 | 96.9 | 96.3 | 96.2 | 97.4 | 98.4 | 100.4 | 100.9 | 101.0 | 97.6 |
| 2016 | 99.7 | 100.9 | 101.2 | 102.4 | 102.7 | 101.7 | 101.9 | 103.0 | 103.7 | 104.6 | 104.8 | 104.6 | 102.6 |
| 2017 | 103.4 | 104.7 | 104.8 | 105.4 | 105.7 | 104.7 | 104.4 | 105.5 | 104.9 | 107.0 | 107.5 | 107.3 | 105.4 |
| 2018 | 106.1 | 107.0 | 107.4 | 107.4 | 107.1 | 106.3 | 105.3 | 106.7 | 108.0 | 109.1 | 109.6 | 109.5 | 107.5 |
| 2019 | 108.7 | 109.5 | 109.7 | 109.3 | 109.5 | 108.5 | 108.6 | 110.0 | 110.9 | 112.2 | 112.9 | 113.3 | 110.3 |
| **Leisure and Hospitality** | | | | | | | | | | | | | |
| 2011 | 63.8 | 64.1 | 65.8 | 67.1 | 68.0 | 67.7 | 67.1 | 67.2 | 66.0 | 66.3 | 66.1 | 66.3 | 66.3 |
| 2012 | 65.7 | 66.6 | 68.7 | 69.7 | 70.1 | 70.2 | 70.3 | 70.1 | 68.6 | 69.0 | 69.3 | 69.7 | 69.0 |
| 2013 | 67.8 | 69.5 | 70.9 | 72.2 | 72.4 | 72.7 | 73.1 | 73.5 | 72.9 | 71.9 | 72.4 | 72.7 | 71.8 |
| 2014 | 71.9 | 73.0 | 75.2 | 75.8 | 76.6 | 77.7 | 76.5 | 76.5 | 74.7 | 76.2 | 75.5 | 76.3 | 75.5 |
| 2015 | 74.5 | 76.4 | 78.7 | 80.0 | 80.7 | 81.8 | 81.3 | 81.6 | 80.6 | 80.9 | 80.7 | 81.4 | 79.9 |
| 2016 | 79.6 | 80.7 | 82.1 | 82.7 | 83.2 | 83.3 | 83.1 | 83.6 | 83.2 | 81.9 | 83.8 | 82.9 | 82.5 |
| 2017 | 81.8 | 83.0 | 84.0 | 85.4 | 86.4 | 86.1 | 86.4 | 86.4 | 82.8 | 84.6 | 84.9 | 84.4 | 84.7 |
| 2018 | 83.3 | 84.1 | 85.1 | 85.9 | 86.8 | 86.0 | 86.1 | 87.0 | 86.3 | 85.1 | 86.2 | 86.4 | 85.7 |
| 2019 | 84.2 | 85.7 | 86.7 | 87.8 | 88.0 | 87.4 | 86.6 | 87.9 | 85.6 | 86.9 | 86.9 | 87.4 | 86.8 |
| **Other Services** | | | | | | | | | | | | | |
| 2011 | 22.5 | 22.6 | 22.8 | 22.5 | 22.1 | 21.8 | 21.7 | 21.3 | 20.9 | 20.6 | 20.2 | 19.9 | 21.6 |
| 2012 | 20.0 | 20.1 | 20.3 | 20.5 | 20.5 | 20.5 | 20.4 | 20.4 | 20.3 | 20.3 | 20.2 | 20.2 | 20.3 |
| 2013 | 20.0 | 20.1 | 20.2 | 20.4 | 20.5 | 20.7 | 20.8 | 20.9 | 20.7 | 20.9 | 21.1 | 21.1 | 20.6 |
| 2014 | 21.1 | 21.3 | 21.5 | 21.8 | 21.9 | 21.9 | 21.7 | 21.8 | 21.8 | 22.0 | 21.9 | 21.9 | 21.7 |
| 2015 | 21.9 | 22.1 | 22.3 | 22.4 | 22.8 | 23.1 | 23.4 | 23.5 | 23.5 | 23.8 | 23.9 | 24.1 | 23.1 |
| 2016 | 24.2 | 24.6 | 24.9 | 25.1 | 25.2 | 25.3 | 25.4 | 25.3 | 25.3 | 24.9 | 25.1 | 25.1 | 25.0 |
| 2017 | 24.7 | 25.0 | 25.1 | 25.0 | 25.4 | 25.6 | 25.7 | 25.5 | 25.1 | 25.5 | 25.6 | 25.8 | 25.3 |
| 2018 | 25.6 | 25.8 | 25.9 | 26.1 | 26.2 | 26.6 | 27.0 | 26.8 | 26.8 | 27.0 | 26.8 | 26.7 | 26.4 |
| 2019 | 26.5 | 26.8 | 27.0 | 26.9 | 27.1 | 27.4 | 27.2 | 27.1 | 27.0 | 27.1 | 27.2 | 27.2 | 27.0 |
| **Government** | | | | | | | | | | | | | |
| 2011 | 77.8 | 78.2 | 78.2 | 78.2 | 78.0 | 73.4 | 72.2 | 75.7 | 75.9 | 76.5 | 76.7 | 76.7 | 76.5 |
| 2012 | 75.5 | 76.5 | 76.6 | 75.4 | 75.4 | 71.1 | 70.6 | 73.8 | 74.7 | 75.7 | 75.7 | 75.3 | 74.7 |
| 2013 | 74.0 | 75.4 | 75.4 | 75.4 | 75.3 | 70.4 | 69.5 | 72.9 | 73.7 | 74.3 | 74.9 | 75.0 | 73.9 |
| 2014 | 72.8 | 74.6 | 74.8 | 75.2 | 75.0 | 70.2 | 69.7 | 73.2 | 74.2 | 74.8 | 75.0 | 75.4 | 73.7 |
| 2015 | 73.1 | 75.3 | 75.6 | 75.6 | 75.3 | 70.6 | 70.2 | 73.9 | 74.8 | 75.8 | 76.2 | 76.4 | 74.4 |
| 2016 | 74.8 | 76.1 | 76.5 | 76.5 | 76.4 | 71.8 | 71.7 | 75.2 | 76.5 | 76.4 | 76.9 | 77.5 | 75.5 |
| 2017 | 75.5 | 77.2 | 77.6 | 77.3 | 77.6 | 73.0 | 72.3 | 75.7 | 76.6 | 77.1 | 77.7 | 77.7 | 76.3 |
| 2018 | 76.0 | 77.3 | 78.3 | 77.3 | 78.0 | 73.6 | 72.9 | 76.9 | 77.3 | 77.5 | 78.5 | 78.4 | 76.8 |
| 2019 | 76.8 | 78.4 | 78.3 | 78.4 | 78.6 | 74.2 | 73.8 | 77.8 | 78.2 | 78.9 | 79.3 | 79.3 | 77.7 |

## Employment by Industry: Oklahoma City, OK, 2011–2019

(Numbers in thousands, not seasonally adjusted)

| Industry and year | January | February | March | April | May | June | July | August | September | October | November | December | Annual average |
|---|---|---|---|---|---|---|---|---|---|---|---|---|---|
| **Total Nonfarm** | | | | | | | | | | | | | |
| 2011 | 564.6 | 567.7 | 575.5 | 582.0 | 582.2 | 579.0 | 574.4 | 577.7 | 586.6 | 587.4 | 590.8 | 593.7 | 580.1 |
| 2012 | 579.5 | 586.1 | 592.2 | 596.1 | 597.7 | 595.7 | 584.8 | 590.4 | 597.0 | 602.9 | 606.4 | 607.0 | 594.7 |
| 2013 | 593.2 | 600.2 | 604.7 | 607.7 | 611.7 | 608.4 | 602.2 | 607.4 | 612.4 | 615.9 | 621.6 | 619.1 | 608.7 |
| 2014 | 604.7 | 609.8 | 615.1 | 618.7 | 622.1 | 618.9 | 613.9 | 619.3 | 626.0 | 629.7 | 633.1 | 634.8 | 620.5 |
| 2015 | 621.5 | 626.5 | 627.7 | 630.1 | 631.8 | 629.8 | 625.0 | 628.6 | 632.9 | 635.1 | 637.5 | 638.0 | 630.4 |
| 2016 | 623.1 | 628.8 | 629.1 | 633.2 | 632.0 | 626.9 | 622.9 | 627.2 | 632.7 | 631.9 | 634.8 | 634.9 | 629.8 |
| 2017 | 617.4 | 624.6 | 629.8 | 634.1 | 635.1 | 636.0 | 631.7 | 635.3 | 643.0 | 644.1 | 648.3 | 649.1 | 635.7 |
| 2018 | 634.2 | 640.2 | 644.5 | 647.0 | 650.3 | 649.5 | 643.9 | 647.9 | 655.9 | 658.0 | 660.4 | 661.2 | 649.4 |
| 2019 | 647.8 | 654.1 | 656.3 | 658.7 | 659.6 | 654.3 | 650.3 | 653.9 | 664.5 | 670.4 | 670.3 | 669.1 | 659.1 |
| **Total Private** | | | | | | | | | | | | | |
| 2011 | 445.5 | 444.9 | 451.9 | 458.1 | 458.2 | 459.8 | 460.0 | 462.5 | 463.5 | 462.7 | 465.6 | 468.0 | 458.4 |
| 2012 | 459.4 | 462.6 | 467.7 | 471.1 | 472.8 | 475.8 | 471.3 | 474.3 | 473.9 | 476.6 | 479.5 | 480.9 | 472.2 |
| 2013 | 471.7 | 474.2 | 478.1 | 480.6 | 483.8 | 485.7 | 484.7 | 487.7 | 487.9 | 488.9 | 493.7 | 492.1 | 484.1 |
| 2014 | 483.2 | 483.9 | 488.8 | 492.3 | 494.7 | 496.5 | 496.8 | 499.8 | 500.3 | 501.6 | 504.6 | 506.9 | 495.8 |
| 2015 | 498.0 | 498.5 | 499.3 | 501.5 | 502.4 | 505.4 | 505.6 | 507.0 | 505.3 | 504.5 | 506.3 | 507.2 | 503.4 |
| 2016 | 496.7 | 498.1 | 497.8 | 501.2 | 500.3 | 500.2 | 501.1 | 502.9 | 502.5 | 501.1 | 503.7 | 504.5 | 500.8 |
| 2017 | 492.0 | 494.9 | 499.3 | 503.6 | 504.9 | 509.4 | 509.6 | 511.4 | 513.7 | 513.9 | 517.7 | 518.9 | 507.4 |
| 2018 | 508.3 | 510.5 | 514.3 | 517.2 | 520.0 | 523.1 | 522.6 | 524.2 | 525.6 | 526.1 | 527.9 | 529.4 | 520.8 |
| 2019 | 520.6 | 522.8 | 524.4 | 527.3 | 527.9 | 528.9 | 528.6 | 529.5 | 531.5 | 535.5 | 534.8 | 534.2 | 528.8 |
| **Goods Producing** | | | | | | | | | | | | | |
| 2011 | 72.3 | 72.2 | 73.5 | 74.9 | 75.3 | 76.3 | 77.0 | 77.1 | 77.2 | 77.4 | 77.7 | 78.7 | 75.8 |
| 2012 | 78.0 | 78.6 | 80.0 | 81.0 | 81.6 | 83.1 | 82.6 | 82.8 | 82.5 | 83.1 | 83.1 | 83.2 | 81.6 |
| 2013 | 82.7 | 82.9 | 83.4 | 83.7 | 84.3 | 85.4 | 85.2 | 85.2 | 84.9 | 85.2 | 85.5 | 85.4 | 84.5 |
| 2014 | 84.0 | 84.1 | 85.4 | 85.7 | 86.6 | 87.8 | 88.3 | 89.0 | 89.3 | 89.8 | 89.9 | 90.2 | 87.5 |
| 2015 | 89.8 | 89.1 | 88.1 | 86.7 | 86.2 | 86.4 | 87.3 | 87.1 | 86.2 | 85.0 | 84.1 | 83.6 | 86.6 |
| 2016 | 82.3 | 82.2 | 81.0 | 80.9 | 80.4 | 80.2 | 80.3 | 80.0 | 79.6 | 79.0 | 79.1 | 79.9 | 80.4 |
| 2017 | 78.1 | 79.0 | 79.5 | 79.9 | 80.5 | 81.9 | 82.3 | 82.7 | 83.4 | 83.2 | 83.8 | 84.3 | 81.6 |
| 2018 | 82.7 | 83.7 | 84.5 | 84.8 | 85.2 | 86.6 | 86.4 | 86.6 | 86.6 | 87.0 | 86.6 | 87.2 | 85.7 |
| 2019 | 86.4 | 86.9 | 86.5 | 86.2 | 85.9 | 86.4 | 85.9 | 85.3 | 84.8 | 84.8 | 83.5 | 83.5 | 85.5 |
| **Service-Providing** | | | | | | | | | | | | | |
| 2011 | 492.3 | 495.5 | 502.0 | 507.1 | 506.9 | 502.7 | 497.4 | 500.6 | 509.4 | 510.0 | 513.1 | 515.0 | 504.3 |
| 2012 | 501.5 | 507.5 | 512.2 | 515.1 | 516.1 | 512.6 | 502.2 | 507.6 | 514.5 | 519.8 | 523.3 | 523.8 | 513.0 |
| 2013 | 510.5 | 517.3 | 521.3 | 524.0 | 527.4 | 523.0 | 517.0 | 522.2 | 527.5 | 530.7 | 536.1 | 533.7 | 524.2 |
| 2014 | 520.7 | 525.7 | 529.7 | 533.0 | 535.5 | 531.1 | 525.6 | 530.3 | 536.7 | 539.9 | 543.2 | 544.6 | 533.0 |
| 2015 | 531.7 | 537.4 | 539.6 | 543.4 | 545.6 | 543.4 | 537.7 | 541.5 | 546.7 | 550.1 | 553.4 | 554.4 | 543.7 |
| 2016 | 540.8 | 546.6 | 548.1 | 552.3 | 551.6 | 546.7 | 542.6 | 547.2 | 553.1 | 552.9 | 555.7 | 555.0 | 549.4 |
| 2017 | 539.3 | 545.6 | 550.3 | 554.2 | 554.6 | 554.1 | 549.4 | 552.6 | 559.6 | 560.9 | 564.5 | 564.8 | 554.2 |
| 2018 | 551.5 | 556.5 | 560.0 | 562.2 | 565.1 | 562.9 | 557.5 | 561.3 | 569.3 | 571.0 | 573.8 | 574.0 | 563.8 |
| 2019 | 561.4 | 567.2 | 569.8 | 572.5 | 573.7 | 567.9 | 564.4 | 568.6 | 579.7 | 585.6 | 586.8 | 585.6 | 573.6 |
| **Mining, Logging, and Construction** | | | | | | | | | | | | | |
| 2011 | 40.9 | 40.6 | 41.6 | 42.4 | 42.7 | 43.5 | 43.9 | 43.7 | 43.7 | 43.7 | 43.8 | 44.4 | 42.9 |
| 2012 | 43.8 | 44.2 | 45.4 | 46.3 | 46.8 | 48.0 | 47.6 | 47.6 | 47.2 | 47.4 | 47.2 | 47.2 | 46.6 |
| 2013 | 46.9 | 47.0 | 47.4 | 47.5 | 47.9 | 48.8 | 48.5 | 48.5 | 48.4 | 48.3 | 48.4 | 48.3 | 48.0 |
| 2014 | 47.3 | 47.0 | 48.3 | 48.6 | 49.3 | 50.2 | 50.8 | 51.3 | 51.5 | 51.8 | 51.8 | 51.8 | 50.0 |
| 2015 | 51.3 | 50.6 | 49.9 | 48.9 | 48.6 | 49.0 | 49.8 | 49.7 | 49.1 | 48.3 | 47.8 | 47.3 | 49.2 |
| 2016 | 46.4 | 46.1 | 45.7 | 46.0 | 45.7 | 45.7 | 46.0 | 45.8 | 45.6 | 45.6 | 45.6 | 46.2 | 45.9 |
| 2017 | 45.2 | 45.9 | 46.6 | 46.8 | 47.3 | 48.4 | 48.8 | 49.1 | 49.7 | 49.5 | 49.9 | 50.3 | 48.1 |
| 2018 | 49.3 | 49.9 | 50.7 | 51.1 | 51.5 | 52.5 | 52.5 | 52.6 | 52.5 | 52.7 | 52.8 | 53.2 | 51.8 |
| 2019 | 52.2 | 52.4 | 52.2 | 51.9 | 51.7 | 52.2 | 51.6 | 51.2 | 50.9 | 50.9 | 49.5 | 49.6 | 51.4 |
| **Manufacturing** | | | | | | | | | | | | | |
| 2011 | 31.4 | 31.6 | 31.9 | 32.5 | 32.6 | 32.8 | 33.1 | 33.4 | 33.5 | 33.7 | 33.9 | 34.3 | 32.9 |
| 2012 | 34.2 | 34.4 | 34.6 | 34.7 | 34.8 | 35.1 | 35.0 | 35.2 | 35.3 | 35.7 | 35.9 | 36.0 | 35.1 |
| 2013 | 35.8 | 35.9 | 36.0 | 36.2 | 36.4 | 36.6 | 36.7 | 36.7 | 36.5 | 36.9 | 37.1 | 37.1 | 36.5 |
| 2014 | 36.7 | 37.1 | 37.1 | 37.1 | 37.3 | 37.6 | 37.5 | 37.7 | 37.8 | 38.0 | 38.1 | 38.4 | 37.5 |
| 2015 | 38.5 | 38.5 | 38.2 | 37.8 | 37.6 | 37.4 | 37.5 | 37.4 | 37.1 | 36.7 | 36.3 | 36.3 | 37.4 |
| 2016 | 35.9 | 36.1 | 35.3 | 34.9 | 34.7 | 34.5 | 34.3 | 34.2 | 34.0 | 33.4 | 33.5 | 33.7 | 34.5 |
| 2017 | 32.9 | 33.1 | 32.9 | 33.1 | 33.2 | 33.5 | 33.5 | 33.6 | 33.7 | 33.7 | 33.9 | 34.0 | 33.4 |
| 2018 | 33.4 | 33.8 | 33.8 | 33.7 | 33.7 | 34.1 | 33.9 | 34.0 | 34.1 | 34.3 | 33.8 | 34.0 | 33.9 |
| 2019 | 34.2 | 34.5 | 34.3 | 34.3 | 34.2 | 34.2 | 34.3 | 34.1 | 33.9 | 33.9 | 34.0 | 33.9 | 34.2 |

# Employment by Industry: Oklahoma City, OK, 2011–2019—*Continued*

(Numbers in thousands, not seasonally adjusted)

| Industry and year | January | February | March | April | May | June | July | August | September | October | November | December | Annual average |
|---|---|---|---|---|---|---|---|---|---|---|---|---|---|
| **Trade, Transportation, and Utilities** | | | | | | | | | | | | | |
| 2011 | 97.8 | 97.4 | 98.7 | 99.1 | 99.0 | 99.3 | 99.6 | 100.4 | 100.3 | 100.5 | 102.6 | 103.7 | 99.9 |
| 2012 | 100.3 | 100.1 | 100.8 | 101.4 | 102.1 | 102.4 | 102.2 | 102.6 | 102.9 | 104.0 | 106.7 | 107.8 | 102.8 |
| 2013 | 103.5 | 103.9 | 104.7 | 105.2 | 106.1 | 106.5 | 106.6 | 107.3 | 107.4 | 108.3 | 111.0 | 111.9 | 106.9 |
| 2014 | 108.1 | 107.3 | 107.8 | 107.7 | 108.2 | 108.9 | 108.8 | 109.4 | 109.6 | 110.3 | 112.6 | 114.3 | 109.4 |
| 2015 | 109.9 | 109.6 | 109.9 | 110.6 | 111.0 | 112.0 | 111.8 | 112.0 | 111.7 | 112.1 | 114.5 | 115.7 | 111.7 |
| 2016 | 110.9 | 110.7 | 111.1 | 111.6 | 111.7 | 111.5 | 111.5 | 111.8 | 111.7 | 111.9 | 114.6 | 114.7 | 112.0 |
| 2017 | 110.5 | 109.7 | 109.9 | 110.4 | 110.3 | 110.7 | 110.8 | 111.2 | 111.3 | 112.2 | 115.3 | 115.9 | 111.5 |
| 2018 | 111.8 | 110.6 | 110.8 | 111.1 | 111.8 | 112.1 | 112.3 | 112.6 | 113.1 | 113.7 | 116.5 | 116.8 | 112.8 |
| 2019 | 113.3 | 112.2 | 112.3 | 112.6 | 113.1 | 113.2 | 113.2 | 113.5 | 115.5 | 116.4 | 118.0 | 118.3 | 114.3 |
| **Wholesale Trade** | | | | | | | | | | | | | |
| 2011 | 21.0 | 21.0 | 21.2 | 21.3 | 21.3 | 21.5 | 21.5 | 21.4 | 21.5 | 21.6 | 21.6 | 21.8 | 21.4 |
| 2012 | 22.0 | 22.2 | 22.2 | 22.1 | 22.3 | 22.5 | 22.6 | 22.7 | 22.6 | 22.9 | 23.2 | 23.4 | 22.6 |
| 2013 | 23.4 | 23.5 | 23.6 | 23.5 | 23.7 | 23.9 | 23.7 | 23.7 | 23.8 | 23.9 | 24.1 | 24.1 | 23.7 |
| 2014 | 24.0 | 23.9 | 23.9 | 24.0 | 24.1 | 24.3 | 24.2 | 24.4 | 24.5 | 24.8 | 24.8 | 24.9 | 24.3 |
| 2015 | 24.7 | 24.7 | 24.6 | 24.4 | 24.4 | 24.5 | 24.5 | 24.4 | 24.4 | 24.3 | 24.3 | 24.3 | 24.5 |
| 2016 | 23.9 | 24.0 | 24.0 | 24.1 | 24.0 | 23.8 | 23.9 | 23.8 | 23.7 | 23.7 | 23.7 | 23.5 | 23.8 |
| 2017 | 23.4 | 23.5 | 23.6 | 23.7 | 23.8 | 23.9 | 23.8 | 23.9 | 23.9 | 24.5 | 24.5 | 24.6 | 23.9 |
| 2018 | 23.8 | 23.7 | 23.6 | 23.8 | 23.8 | 23.9 | 24.1 | 23.9 | 24.1 | 24.2 | 24.5 | 24.5 | 24.0 |
| 2019 | 24.1 | 24.1 | 24.1 | 24.1 | 24.3 | 24.3 | 24.2 | 24.1 | 23.9 | 23.8 | 23.8 | 23.5 | 24.0 |
| **Retail Trade** | | | | | | | | | | | | | |
| 2011 | 60.1 | 59.6 | 60.5 | 60.9 | 60.7 | 60.5 | 60.8 | 61.6 | 61.3 | 61.3 | 63.3 | 63.9 | 61.2 |
| 2012 | 60.9 | 60.5 | 61.2 | 61.8 | 62.0 | 62.1 | 61.6 | 61.9 | 62.2 | 63.0 | 65.3 | 66.0 | 62.4 |
| 2013 | 62.0 | 61.8 | 62.4 | 63.0 | 63.6 | 63.6 | 63.9 | 64.5 | 64.6 | 65.3 | 67.6 | 68.4 | 64.2 |
| 2014 | 65.0 | 64.6 | 64.8 | 65.0 | 65.1 | 65.5 | 65.6 | 65.9 | 66.0 | 66.3 | 68.4 | 69.4 | 66.0 |
| 2015 | 65.9 | 65.8 | 66.2 | 66.9 | 67.0 | 67.7 | 67.6 | 67.9 | 67.6 | 68.2 | 70.2 | 70.8 | 67.7 |
| 2016 | 67.2 | 67.1 | 67.5 | 67.9 | 68.0 | 67.9 | 67.8 | 68.2 | 68.2 | 68.4 | 70.5 | 70.1 | 68.2 |
| 2017 | 66.7 | 65.9 | 65.9 | 66.4 | 66.0 | 66.2 | 66.1 | 66.3 | 66.2 | 66.4 | 68.9 | 69.0 | 66.7 |
| 2018 | 66.3 | 65.4 | 65.5 | 65.6 | 65.9 | 65.7 | 65.6 | 65.9 | 66.1 | 66.3 | 68.4 | 68.1 | 66.2 |
| 2019 | 65.4 | 64.6 | 64.7 | 64.8 | 65.0 | 64.7 | 64.8 | 65.1 | 65.2 | 66.1 | 67.4 | 67.6 | 65.5 |
| **Transportation and Utilities** | | | | | | | | | | | | | |
| 2011 | 16.7 | 16.8 | 17.0 | 16.9 | 17.0 | 17.3 | 17.3 | 17.4 | 17.5 | 17.6 | 17.7 | 18.0 | 17.3 |
| 2012 | 17.4 | 17.4 | 17.4 | 17.5 | 17.8 | 17.8 | 18.0 | 18.0 | 18.1 | 18.1 | 18.2 | 18.4 | 17.8 |
| 2013 | 18.1 | 18.6 | 18.7 | 18.7 | 18.8 | 19.0 | 19.0 | 19.1 | 19.0 | 19.1 | 19.3 | 19.4 | 18.9 |
| 2014 | 19.1 | 18.8 | 19.1 | 18.7 | 19.0 | 19.1 | 19.0 | 19.1 | 19.1 | 19.2 | 19.4 | 20.0 | 19.1 |
| 2015 | 19.3 | 19.1 | 19.1 | 19.3 | 19.6 | 19.8 | 19.7 | 19.7 | 19.7 | 19.6 | 20.0 | 20.6 | 19.6 |
| 2016 | 19.8 | 19.6 | 19.6 | 19.6 | 19.7 | 19.8 | 19.8 | 19.8 | 19.8 | 19.8 | 20.4 | 21.1 | 19.9 |
| 2017 | 20.4 | 20.3 | 20.4 | 20.3 | 20.5 | 20.6 | 20.9 | 21.0 | 21.2 | 21.3 | 21.9 | 22.3 | 20.9 |
| 2018 | 21.7 | 21.5 | 21.7 | 21.7 | 22.1 | 22.5 | 22.6 | 22.8 | 22.9 | 23.2 | 23.6 | 24.2 | 22.5 |
| 2019 | 23.8 | 23.5 | 23.5 | 23.7 | 23.8 | 24.2 | 24.2 | 24.3 | 26.4 | 26.5 | 26.8 | 27.2 | 24.8 |
| **Information** | | | | | | | | | | | | | |
| 2011 | 9.2 | 9.1 | 8.9 | 9.0 | 9.0 | 9.0 | 9.0 | 8.9 | 8.9 | 9.0 | 9.0 | 9.0 | 9.0 |
| 2012 | 8.9 | 8.9 | 8.8 | 8.7 | 8.7 | 8.6 | 8.7 | 8.5 | 8.3 | 8.4 | 8.4 | 8.3 | 8.6 |
| 2013 | 8.1 | 8.1 | 8.0 | 8.2 | 8.2 | 8.2 | 8.2 | 8.2 | 8.2 | 8.2 | 8.4 | 8.3 | 8.2 |
| 2014 | 8.1 | 8.1 | 8.1 | 8.1 | 8.1 | 8.1 | 8.2 | 8.2 | 8.2 | 8.1 | 8.2 | 8.1 | 8.1 |
| 2015 | 8.1 | 8.0 | 8.1 | 8.1 | 8.3 | 8.3 | 8.3 | 8.3 | 8.3 | 8.4 | 8.4 | 8.5 | 8.3 |
| 2016 | 8.2 | 8.3 | 8.3 | 8.2 | 8.2 | 8.2 | 8.1 | 8.1 | 8.0 | 8.0 | 8.1 | 8.2 | 8.2 |
| 2017 | 7.8 | 7.8 | 7.8 | 7.8 | 7.8 | 7.7 | 7.7 | 7.6 | 7.5 | 7.5 | 7.5 | 7.5 | 7.7 |
| 2018 | 7.3 | 7.4 | 7.4 | 7.3 | 7.4 | 7.4 | 7.4 | 7.4 | 7.3 | 7.4 | 7.2 | 7.3 | 7.4 |
| 2019 | 7.1 | 7.1 | 7.1 | 7.1 | 7.1 | 7.1 | 7.1 | 7.1 | 6.9 | 6.9 | 7.0 | 7.1 | 7.1 |
| **Financial Activities** | | | | | | | | | | | | | |
| 2011 | 30.3 | 30.4 | 30.5 | 30.7 | 30.7 | 30.8 | 30.9 | 31.0 | 30.9 | 31.2 | 31.3 | 31.5 | 30.9 |
| 2012 | 31.2 | 31.4 | 31.5 | 31.6 | 31.8 | 32.0 | 31.8 | 31.9 | 31.7 | 31.9 | 32.1 | 32.4 | 31.8 |
| 2013 | 32.2 | 32.3 | 32.2 | 32.1 | 32.2 | 32.3 | 32.4 | 32.5 | 32.4 | 32.6 | 32.8 | 32.9 | 32.4 |
| 2014 | 32.5 | 32.7 | 32.9 | 32.9 | 33.1 | 33.2 | 33.3 | 33.4 | 33.2 | 33.3 | 33.5 | 33.9 | 33.2 |
| 2015 | 33.4 | 33.5 | 33.4 | 33.4 | 33.5 | 33.5 | 33.5 | 33.4 | 33.2 | 33.3 | 33.3 | 33.4 | 33.4 |
| 2016 | 32.8 | 33.0 | 32.9 | 32.9 | 32.9 | 33.0 | 33.4 | 33.4 | 33.3 | 33.4 | 33.4 | 33.6 | 33.2 |
| 2017 | 32.9 | 33.0 | 33.2 | 33.2 | 33.2 | 33.4 | 33.3 | 33.4 | 33.3 | 33.3 | 33.3 | 33.6 | 33.3 |
| 2018 | 32.9 | 32.9 | 33.1 | 33.1 | 33.3 | 33.5 | 33.6 | 33.6 | 33.6 | 33.5 | 33.5 | 33.8 | 33.4 |
| 2019 | 33.4 | 33.5 | 33.6 | 33.8 | 33.6 | 33.8 | 33.9 | 33.8 | 33.6 | 34.2 | 34.4 | 34.7 | 33.9 |

## Employment by Industry: Oklahoma City, OK, 2011–2019—*Continued*

(Numbers in thousands, not seasonally adjusted)

| Industry and year | January | February | March | April | May | June | July | August | September | October | November | December | Annual average |
|---|---|---|---|---|---|---|---|---|---|---|---|---|---|
| **Professional and Business Services** | | | | | | | | | | | | | |
| 2011 | 73.9 | 73.8 | 74.8 | 76.4 | 76.2 | 75.8 | 76.0 | 76.8 | 76.3 | 76.4 | 76.3 | 76.9 | 75.8 |
| 2012 | 75.4 | 76.5 | 77.0 | 77.1 | 76.4 | 77.6 | 76.3 | 77.3 | 76.3 | 77.5 | 77.4 | 76.8 | 76.8 |
| 2013 | 75.7 | 76.2 | 77.5 | 77.5 | 77.4 | 78.0 | 77.5 | 78.2 | 77.7 | 78.4 | 79.2 | 78.1 | 77.6 |
| 2014 | 76.9 | 77.0 | 77.8 | 78.2 | 78.2 | 78.3 | 78.9 | 79.7 | 79.1 | 79.9 | 80.5 | 80.1 | 78.7 |
| 2015 | 78.9 | 78.9 | 78.8 | 79.4 | 79.2 | 79.7 | 79.9 | 80.4 | 79.7 | 80.1 | 80.3 | 80.7 | 79.7 |
| 2016 | 79.2 | 79.3 | 79.0 | 79.7 | 79.2 | 79.3 | 79.3 | 80.1 | 80.4 | 80.5 | 79.9 | 79.8 | 79.6 |
| 2017 | 78.1 | 78.4 | 79.5 | 80.4 | 80.1 | 81.8 | 82.8 | 83.1 | 83.5 | 83.4 | 83.6 | 83.4 | 81.5 |
| 2018 | 82.7 | 83.4 | 84.0 | 84.8 | 84.6 | 86.0 | 86.0 | 86.1 | 86.6 | 87.6 | 87.5 | 87.6 | 85.6 |
| 2019 | 85.9 | 86.5 | 86.9 | 88.1 | 88.0 | 88.3 | 88.5 | 88.9 | 88.7 | 90.5 | 89.7 | 88.5 | 88.2 |
| **Education and Health Services** | | | | | | | | | | | | | |
| 2011 | 82.6 | 82.6 | 83.5 | 84.1 | 84.2 | 84.3 | 83.8 | 84.5 | 85.5 | 85.4 | 86.0 | 86.0 | 84.4 |
| 2012 | 84.5 | 85.2 | 85.8 | 86.4 | 86.6 | 86.5 | 85.4 | 86.5 | 87.3 | 87.4 | 87.7 | 88.0 | 86.4 |
| 2013 | 86.9 | 87.3 | 87.7 | 87.9 | 88.1 | 87.7 | 86.9 | 87.7 | 88.3 | 88.9 | 89.3 | 88.7 | 88.0 |
| 2014 | 87.7 | 88.1 | 88.6 | 89.4 | 89.3 | 88.8 | 88.2 | 88.5 | 89.1 | 89.5 | 89.6 | 89.9 | 88.9 |
| 2015 | 89.2 | 89.7 | 89.9 | 90.5 | 90.5 | 90.4 | 89.9 | 90.3 | 91.2 | 91.6 | 91.6 | 91.5 | 90.5 |
| 2016 | 90.7 | 91.0 | 90.9 | 91.3 | 91.0 | 90.3 | 90.9 | 91.3 | 91.8 | 91.3 | 91.7 | 91.7 | 91.2 |
| 2017 | 89.7 | 90.6 | 91.0 | 92.3 | 92.4 | 92.2 | 91.7 | 92.1 | 92.8 | 93.2 | 93.2 | 93.2 | 92.0 |
| 2018 | 91.9 | 92.6 | 92.7 | 92.9 | 93.1 | 92.4 | 93.1 | 93.8 | 94.2 | 94.7 | 94.5 | 94.6 | 93.4 |
| 2019 | 94.7 | 95.4 | 95.4 | 95.8 | 96.1 | 95.9 | 95.7 | 96.1 | 96.8 | 97.5 | 97.7 | 98.3 | 96.3 |
| **Leisure and Hospitality** | | | | | | | | | | | | | |
| 2011 | 57.0 | 57.0 | 59.5 | 61.2 | 60.8 | 61.3 | 60.9 | 61.1 | 61.6 | 60.1 | 59.9 | 59.6 | 60.0 |
| 2012 | 58.6 | 59.3 | 61.2 | 62.1 | 62.8 | 62.7 | 61.7 | 62.4 | 62.8 | 62.4 | 62.3 | 62.6 | 61.7 |
| 2013 | 60.9 | 61.7 | 62.8 | 64.0 | 65.3 | 65.1 | 65.2 | 65.9 | 66.3 | 64.6 | 64.6 | 63.8 | 64.2 |
| 2014 | 63.0 | 63.5 | 64.8 | 66.6 | 67.1 | 67.0 | 66.6 | 67.3 | 67.4 | 66.2 | 65.8 | 65.8 | 65.9 |
| 2015 | 64.2 | 65.0 | 66.0 | 67.6 | 68.4 | 69.5 | 69.3 | 70.0 | 69.5 | 68.7 | 68.8 | 68.5 | 68.0 |
| 2016 | 67.2 | 68.0 | 69.1 | 70.5 | 70.6 | 71.0 | 70.8 | 71.5 | 70.9 | 70.3 | 70.0 | 69.5 | 70.0 |
| 2017 | 68.0 | 69.1 | 70.7 | 71.8 | 72.5 | 73.1 | 72.5 | 72.9 | 73.2 | 72.5 | 72.3 | 72.2 | 71.7 |
| 2018 | 70.4 | 71.1 | 72.7 | 74.6 | 75.9 | 75.9 | 75.0 | 75.3 | 75.4 | 73.4 | 73.3 | 73.1 | 73.8 |
| 2019 | 71.2 | 72.3 | 73.7 | 74.8 | 75.0 | 74.8 | 74.9 | 75.5 | 75.9 | 76.0 | 75.2 | 74.5 | 74.5 |
| **Other Services** | | | | | | | | | | | | | |
| 2011 | 22.4 | 22.4 | 22.5 | 22.7 | 23.0 | 23.0 | 22.8 | 22.7 | 22.8 | 22.7 | 22.8 | 22.6 | 22.7 |
| 2012 | 22.5 | 22.6 | 22.6 | 22.8 | 22.8 | 22.9 | 22.6 | 22.3 | 22.1 | 21.9 | 21.8 | 21.8 | 22.4 |
| 2013 | 21.7 | 21.8 | 21.8 | 22.0 | 22.2 | 22.5 | 22.7 | 22.7 | 22.7 | 22.7 | 22.9 | 23.0 | 22.4 |
| 2014 | 22.9 | 23.1 | 23.4 | 23.7 | 24.1 | 24.4 | 24.5 | 24.3 | 24.4 | 24.5 | 24.5 | 24.6 | 24.0 |
| 2015 | 24.5 | 24.7 | 25.1 | 25.2 | 25.3 | 25.6 | 25.6 | 25.5 | 25.5 | 25.3 | 25.3 | 25.3 | 25.2 |
| 2016 | 25.4 | 25.6 | 25.5 | 26.1 | 26.3 | 26.7 | 26.8 | 26.7 | 26.8 | 26.7 | 26.9 | 27.1 | 26.4 |
| 2017 | 26.9 | 27.3 | 27.7 | 27.8 | 28.1 | 28.6 | 28.5 | 28.4 | 28.7 | 28.6 | 28.7 | 28.8 | 28.2 |
| 2018 | 28.6 | 28.8 | 29.1 | 28.6 | 28.7 | 29.2 | 28.8 | 28.8 | 28.8 | 28.8 | 28.8 | 29.0 | 28.8 |
| 2019 | 28.6 | 28.9 | 28.9 | 28.9 | 29.1 | 29.4 | 29.4 | 29.3 | 29.3 | 29.2 | 29.3 | 29.3 | 29.1 |
| **Government** | | | | | | | | | | | | | |
| 2011 | 119.1 | 122.8 | 123.6 | 123.9 | 124.0 | 119.2 | 114.4 | 115.2 | 123.1 | 124.7 | 125.2 | 125.7 | 121.7 |
| 2012 | 120.1 | 123.5 | 124.5 | 125.0 | 124.9 | 119.9 | 113.5 | 116.1 | 123.1 | 126.3 | 126.9 | 126.1 | 122.5 |
| 2013 | 121.5 | 126.0 | 126.6 | 127.1 | 127.9 | 122.7 | 117.5 | 119.7 | 124.5 | 127.0 | 127.9 | 127.0 | 124.6 |
| 2014 | 121.5 | 125.9 | 126.3 | 126.4 | 127.4 | 122.4 | 117.1 | 119.5 | 125.7 | 128.1 | 128.5 | 127.9 | 124.7 |
| 2015 | 123.5 | 128.0 | 128.4 | 128.6 | 129.4 | 124.4 | 119.4 | 121.6 | 127.6 | 130.6 | 131.2 | 130.8 | 127.0 |
| 2016 | 126.4 | 130.7 | 131.3 | 132.0 | 131.7 | 126.7 | 121.8 | 124.3 | 130.2 | 130.8 | 131.1 | 130.4 | 129.0 |
| 2017 | 125.4 | 129.7 | 130.5 | 130.5 | 130.2 | 126.6 | 122.1 | 123.9 | 129.3 | 130.2 | 130.6 | 130.2 | 128.3 |
| 2018 | 125.9 | 129.7 | 130.2 | 129.8 | 130.3 | 126.4 | 121.3 | 123.7 | 130.3 | 131.9 | 132.5 | 131.8 | 128.7 |
| 2019 | 127.2 | 131.3 | 131.9 | 131.4 | 131.7 | 125.4 | 121.7 | 124.4 | 133.0 | 134.9 | 135.5 | 134.9 | 130.3 |

# Employment by Industry: Raleigh, NC, 2011–2019

(Numbers in thousands, not seasonally adjusted)

| Industry and year | January | February | March | April | May | June | July | August | September | October | November | December | Annual average |
|---|---|---|---|---|---|---|---|---|---|---|---|---|---|
| **Total Nonfarm** | | | | | | | | | | | | | |
| 2011 | 499.0 | 502.9 | 505.9 | 508.4 | 510.2 | 506.8 | 505.5 | 508.3 | 512.2 | 515.4 | 517.8 | 517.3 | 509.1 |
| 2012 | 512.4 | 514.7 | 518.5 | 522.8 | 526.2 | 523.6 | 522.7 | 526.8 | 529.0 | 532.0 | 535.7 | 534.8 | 524.9 |
| 2013 | 525.8 | 530.5 | 533.8 | 535.5 | 538.1 | 535.1 | 534.3 | 542.1 | 548.0 | 550.1 | 554.2 | 554.0 | 540.1 |
| 2014 | 544.6 | 544.2 | 550.2 | 555.4 | 560.0 | 559.9 | 555.3 | 560.9 | 564.8 | 571.9 | 575.1 | 575.3 | 559.8 |
| 2015 | 564.1 | 567.7 | 570.4 | 575.9 | 579.7 | 579.5 | 576.1 | 581.7 | 585.3 | 590.9 | 594.5 | 595.2 | 580.1 |
| 2016 | 586.1 | 589.2 | 592.0 | 597.1 | 599.9 | 598.9 | 596.3 | 600.0 | 604.1 | 608.4 | 613.1 | 611.5 | 599.7 |
| 2017 | 599.8 | 605.7 | 608.3 | 609.7 | 615.4 | 614.8 | 614.8 | 620.9 | 621.2 | 626.3 | 630.8 | 630.6 | 616.5 |
| 2018 | 619.9 | 625.3 | 628.2 | 631.5 | 636.6 | 635.6 | 630.3 | 637.3 | 631.6 | 643.0 | 646.2 | 644.0 | 634.1 |
| 2019 | 638.8 | 642.2 | 644.2 | 646.6 | 650.8 | 651.0 | 647.4 | 653.2 | 652.3 | 658.3 | 659.4 | 656.9 | 650.1 |
| **Total Private** | | | | | | | | | | | | | |
| 2011 | 406.6 | 409.6 | 412.3 | 415.3 | 417.0 | 419.6 | 421.7 | 422.3 | 421.0 | 422.7 | 425.3 | 426.8 | 418.4 |
| 2012 | 421.4 | 422.4 | 426.2 | 431.0 | 434.8 | 436.7 | 439.2 | 440.5 | 437.6 | 439.4 | 442.9 | 443.8 | 434.7 |
| 2013 | 434.5 | 437.8 | 440.9 | 443.1 | 446.7 | 449.9 | 451.2 | 455.4 | 454.9 | 455.4 | 459.2 | 460.8 | 449.2 |
| 2014 | 451.7 | 450.8 | 456.3 | 460.8 | 466.1 | 470.2 | 470.3 | 473.1 | 470.5 | 475.0 | 477.9 | 480.1 | 466.9 |
| 2015 | 469.6 | 471.9 | 474.7 | 480.1 | 485.6 | 489.5 | 490.7 | 493.4 | 490.2 | 494.5 | 497.6 | 499.7 | 486.5 |
| 2016 | 491.4 | 492.6 | 495.3 | 500.7 | 505.1 | 507.9 | 510.5 | 511.6 | 508.7 | 511.2 | 514.9 | 515.3 | 505.4 |
| 2017 | 504.5 | 508.2 | 510.6 | 512.3 | 518.7 | 523.0 | 528.0 | 528.9 | 523.7 | 527.8 | 531.0 | 532.2 | 520.7 |
| 2018 | 522.7 | 526.3 | 528.9 | 532.5 | 537.9 | 542.3 | 541.8 | 544.5 | 534.0 | 543.3 | 546.0 | 545.0 | 537.1 |
| 2019 | 540.4 | 542.5 | 544.5 | 546.2 | 551.6 | 557.1 | 557.9 | 559.1 | 552.6 | 556.8 | 557.6 | 556.6 | 551.9 |
| **Goods Producing** | | | | | | | | | | | | | |
| 2011 | 57.4 | 58.1 | 58.7 | 58.7 | 59.0 | 59.5 | 59.9 | 59.6 | 59.3 | 59.0 | 59.0 | 59.2 | 59.0 |
| 2012 | 58.9 | 59.1 | 59.6 | 59.7 | 60.3 | 60.9 | 61.5 | 61.6 | 61.4 | 61.2 | 61.1 | 61.1 | 60.5 |
| 2013 | 59.8 | 60.1 | 60.5 | 60.5 | 60.9 | 61.6 | 61.9 | 62.3 | 62.2 | 62.4 | 62.6 | 62.9 | 61.5 |
| 2014 | 61.9 | 61.9 | 63.0 | 62.8 | 63.7 | 64.7 | 65.4 | 65.8 | 65.6 | 65.7 | 65.6 | 65.5 | 64.3 |
| 2015 | 65.2 | 65.7 | 65.9 | 66.5 | 67.4 | 68.2 | 68.4 | 68.4 | 67.9 | 68.2 | 68.0 | 68.3 | 67.3 |
| 2016 | 68.0 | 68.2 | 68.5 | 69.0 | 69.4 | 70.2 | 70.5 | 70.5 | 70.3 | 70.6 | 70.9 | 71.0 | 69.8 |
| 2017 | 70.4 | 71.3 | 71.7 | 71.7 | 72.1 | 73.2 | 74.0 | 74.0 | 73.8 | 74.1 | 74.0 | 74.3 | 72.9 |
| 2018 | 73.2 | 74.2 | 74.8 | 75.4 | 76.0 | 77.1 | 76.7 | 76.6 | 75.8 | 76.9 | 76.8 | 76.6 | 75.8 |
| 2019 | 76.4 | 76.8 | 77.0 | 76.9 | 77.5 | 78.8 | 78.5 | 78.3 | 78.0 | 78.0 | 77.7 | 77.6 | 77.6 |
| **Service-Providing** | | | | | | | | | | | | | |
| 2011 | 441.6 | 444.8 | 447.2 | 449.7 | 451.2 | 447.3 | 445.6 | 448.7 | 452.9 | 456.4 | 458.8 | 458.1 | 450.2 |
| 2012 | 453.5 | 455.6 | 458.9 | 463.1 | 465.9 | 462.7 | 461.2 | 465.2 | 467.6 | 470.8 | 474.6 | 473.7 | 464.4 |
| 2013 | 466.0 | 470.4 | 473.3 | 475.0 | 477.2 | 473.5 | 472.4 | 479.8 | 485.8 | 487.7 | 491.6 | 491.1 | 478.7 |
| 2014 | 482.7 | 482.3 | 487.2 | 492.6 | 496.3 | 495.2 | 489.9 | 495.1 | 499.2 | 506.2 | 509.5 | 509.8 | 495.5 |
| 2015 | 498.9 | 502.0 | 504.5 | 509.4 | 512.3 | 511.3 | 507.7 | 513.3 | 517.4 | 522.7 | 526.5 | 526.9 | 512.7 |
| 2016 | 518.1 | 521.0 | 523.5 | 528.1 | 530.5 | 528.7 | 525.8 | 529.5 | 533.8 | 537.8 | 542.2 | 540.5 | 530.0 |
| 2017 | 529.4 | 534.4 | 536.6 | 538.0 | 543.3 | 541.6 | 540.8 | 546.9 | 547.4 | 552.2 | 556.8 | 556.3 | 543.6 |
| 2018 | 546.7 | 551.1 | 553.4 | 556.1 | 560.6 | 558.5 | 553.6 | 560.7 | 555.8 | 566.1 | 569.4 | 567.4 | 558.3 |
| 2019 | 562.4 | 565.4 | 567.2 | 569.7 | 573.3 | 572.2 | 568.9 | 574.9 | 574.3 | 580.3 | 581.7 | 579.3 | 572.5 |
| **Mining, Logging, and Construction** | | | | | | | | | | | | | |
| 2011 | 27.2 | 27.8 | 28.2 | 28.0 | 28.3 | 28.8 | 29.3 | 29.1 | 28.9 | 28.7 | 28.6 | 28.6 | 28.5 |
| 2012 | 28.4 | 28.6 | 29.1 | 29.2 | 29.6 | 30.0 | 30.5 | 30.5 | 30.4 | 30.3 | 30.2 | 30.2 | 29.8 |
| 2013 | 29.0 | 29.3 | 29.6 | 29.6 | 30.1 | 30.4 | 30.4 | 30.6 | 30.5 | 30.9 | 30.9 | 30.8 | 30.2 |
| 2014 | 30.1 | 30.0 | 30.9 | 30.9 | 31.5 | 31.9 | 32.5 | 32.6 | 32.4 | 32.3 | 32.0 | 31.8 | 31.6 |
| 2015 | 31.6 | 31.8 | 32.1 | 32.7 | 33.4 | 33.8 | 34.3 | 34.1 | 33.8 | 34.1 | 34.0 | 34.1 | 33.3 |
| 2016 | 33.7 | 33.7 | 34.1 | 34.7 | 35.1 | 35.4 | 35.6 | 35.7 | 35.8 | 36.2 | 36.4 | 36.5 | 35.2 |
| 2017 | 35.7 | 36.4 | 36.8 | 37.0 | 37.4 | 38.2 | 38.8 | 38.7 | 38.6 | 38.7 | 38.9 | 38.9 | 37.8 |
| 2018 | 38.0 | 38.6 | 39.0 | 39.5 | 40.1 | 40.8 | 40.7 | 40.6 | 40.1 | 40.9 | 40.8 | 40.5 | 40.0 |
| 2019 | 40.3 | 40.4 | 40.6 | 40.5 | 40.9 | 41.7 | 41.4 | 41.4 | 41.4 | 41.4 | 41.2 | 41.5 | 41.1 |
| **Manufacturing** | | | | | | | | | | | | | |
| 2011 | 30.2 | 30.3 | 30.5 | 30.7 | 30.7 | 30.7 | 30.6 | 30.5 | 30.4 | 30.3 | 30.4 | 30.6 | 30.5 |
| 2012 | 30.5 | 30.5 | 30.5 | 30.5 | 30.7 | 30.9 | 31.0 | 31.1 | 31.0 | 30.9 | 30.9 | 30.9 | 30.8 |
| 2013 | 30.8 | 30.8 | 30.9 | 30.9 | 30.8 | 31.2 | 31.5 | 31.7 | 31.7 | 31.5 | 31.7 | 32.1 | 31.3 |
| 2014 | 31.8 | 31.9 | 32.1 | 31.9 | 32.2 | 32.8 | 32.9 | 33.2 | 33.2 | 33.4 | 33.6 | 33.7 | 32.7 |
| 2015 | 33.6 | 33.9 | 33.8 | 33.8 | 34.0 | 34.4 | 34.1 | 34.3 | 34.1 | 34.1 | 34.0 | 34.2 | 34.0 |
| 2016 | 34.3 | 34.5 | 34.4 | 34.3 | 34.3 | 34.8 | 34.9 | 34.8 | 34.5 | 34.4 | 34.5 | 34.5 | 34.5 |
| 2017 | 34.7 | 34.9 | 34.9 | 34.7 | 34.7 | 35.0 | 35.2 | 35.3 | 35.2 | 35.4 | 35.1 | 35.4 | 35.0 |
| 2018 | 35.2 | 35.6 | 35.8 | 35.9 | 35.9 | 36.3 | 36.0 | 36.0 | 35.7 | 36.0 | 36.0 | 36.1 | 35.9 |
| 2019 | 36.1 | 36.4 | 36.4 | 36.4 | 36.6 | 37.1 | 37.1 | 36.9 | 36.6 | 36.6 | 36.5 | 36.1 | 36.6 |

## Employment by Industry: Raleigh, NC, 2011–2019—*Continued*

(Numbers in thousands, not seasonally adjusted)

| Industry and year | January | February | March | April | May | June | July | August | September | October | November | December | Annual average |
|---|---|---|---|---|---|---|---|---|---|---|---|---|---|
| **Trade, Transportation, and Utilities** | | | | | | | | | | | | | |
| 2011 | 86.9 | 86.8 | 87.3 | 88.1 | 88.3 | 88.5 | 88.8 | 89.0 | 89.1 | 89.4 | 91.8 | 92.9 | 88.9 |
| 2012 | 90.6 | 89.8 | 90.6 | 90.4 | 91.3 | 91.5 | 91.6 | 91.4 | 91.3 | 91.8 | 94.3 | 94.8 | 91.6 |
| 2013 | 91.1 | 90.5 | 91.2 | 91.0 | 91.8 | 92.4 | 92.2 | 92.8 | 92.9 | 94.1 | 96.7 | 98.0 | 92.9 |
| 2014 | 95.1 | 94.5 | 95.4 | 96.2 | 96.9 | 97.4 | 97.4 | 98.0 | 97.8 | 99.2 | 102.2 | 104.0 | 97.8 |
| 2015 | 99.6 | 99.5 | 100.1 | 101.2 | 101.8 | 102.3 | 102.5 | 103.1 | 102.6 | 103.9 | 106.6 | 107.6 | 102.6 |
| 2016 | 103.7 | 103.6 | 104.4 | 105.4 | 106.3 | 106.5 | 106.6 | 106.8 | 106.5 | 107.2 | 109.6 | 111.5 | 106.5 |
| 2017 | 106.7 | 106.6 | 107.1 | 107.2 | 108.1 | 108.5 | 109.7 | 110.1 | 109.2 | 110.4 | 113.5 | 114.7 | 109.3 |
| 2018 | 110.6 | 110.3 | 110.4 | 110.3 | 110.8 | 110.8 | 110.8 | 111.1 | 109.3 | 111.0 | 114.4 | 115.1 | 111.2 |
| 2019 | 111.2 | 110.4 | 110.5 | 110.6 | 111.5 | 112.0 | 112.0 | 111.8 | 111.3 | 111.4 | 114.3 | 114.8 | 111.8 |
| **Wholesale Trade** | | | | | | | | | | | | | |
| 2011 | 20.1 | 20.2 | 20.2 | 20.6 | 20.7 | 20.7 | 21.1 | 21.2 | 21.5 | 21.2 | 21.4 | 21.5 | 20.9 |
| 2012 | 21.7 | 21.9 | 22.1 | 22.1 | 22.2 | 22.1 | 22.5 | 22.5 | 22.5 | 22.1 | 22.0 | 21.9 | 22.1 |
| 2013 | 21.6 | 21.7 | 21.7 | 21.4 | 21.5 | 21.7 | 21.4 | 21.5 | 21.5 | 21.5 | 21.5 | 21.5 | 21.5 |
| 2014 | 21.5 | 21.6 | 21.7 | 21.8 | 21.9 | 22.0 | 22.2 | 22.5 | 22.5 | 22.7 | 22.8 | 22.9 | 22.2 |
| 2015 | 22.8 | 22.9 | 22.9 | 23.0 | 23.0 | 23.1 | 23.3 | 23.4 | 23.3 | 23.3 | 23.4 | 23.4 | 23.2 |
| 2016 | 23.7 | 23.9 | 24.0 | 24.0 | 24.2 | 24.2 | 24.4 | 24.6 | 24.6 | 24.6 | 24.6 | 24.8 | 24.3 |
| 2017 | 24.5 | 24.7 | 24.8 | 25.0 | 25.2 | 25.3 | 26.2 | 26.3 | 26.2 | 26.2 | 26.1 | 26.3 | 25.6 |
| 2018 | 26.0 | 26.2 | 26.3 | 26.1 | 26.2 | 26.3 | 26.3 | 26.4 | 26.2 | 26.4 | 26.4 | 26.4 | 26.3 |
| 2019 | 26.3 | 26.4 | 26.3 | 26.4 | 26.5 | 26.7 | 26.8 | 27.0 | 26.9 | 26.1 | 26.2 | 25.8 | 26.5 |
| **Retail Trade** | | | | | | | | | | | | | |
| 2011 | 57.2 | 57.0 | 57.4 | 57.5 | 57.6 | 57.7 | 57.6 | 57.7 | 57.4 | 58.2 | 60.4 | 61.1 | 58.1 |
| 2012 | 58.8 | 57.9 | 58.4 | 58.3 | 58.9 | 59.1 | 58.9 | 58.8 | 58.7 | 59.6 | 62.1 | 62.4 | 59.3 |
| 2013 | 59.3 | 58.8 | 59.4 | 59.5 | 60.1 | 60.4 | 60.5 | 60.9 | 60.9 | 61.9 | 64.3 | 65.2 | 60.9 |
| 2014 | 62.0 | 61.5 | 62.1 | 62.9 | 63.3 | 63.7 | 63.6 | 63.8 | 63.5 | 64.8 | 67.4 | 68.5 | 63.9 |
| 2015 | 65.0 | 64.7 | 65.3 | 66.1 | 66.6 | 67.0 | 67.1 | 67.4 | 67.0 | 68.3 | 70.6 | 71.0 | 67.2 |
| 2016 | 67.5 | 67.3 | 67.9 | 68.9 | 69.4 | 69.5 | 69.5 | 69.5 | 69.0 | 69.8 | 72.0 | 73.0 | 69.4 |
| 2017 | 69.4 | 69.2 | 69.4 | 69.4 | 69.8 | 70.0 | 70.6 | 70.6 | 69.7 | 70.7 | 73.6 | 73.8 | 70.5 |
| 2018 | 70.8 | 70.3 | 70.3 | 70.3 | 70.6 | 70.4 | 70.7 | 70.7 | 69.0 | 70.1 | 72.9 | 73.0 | 70.8 |
| 2019 | 70.2 | 69.5 | 69.6 | 69.8 | 70.4 | 70.5 | 70.4 | 70.0 | 69.4 | 70.3 | 72.9 | 73.3 | 70.5 |
| **Transportation and Utilities** | | | | | | | | | | | | | |
| 2011 | 9.6 | 9.6 | 9.7 | 10.0 | 10.0 | 10.1 | 10.1 | 10.1 | 10.2 | 10.0 | 10.0 | 10.3 | 10.0 |
| 2012 | 10.1 | 10.0 | 10.1 | 10.0 | 10.2 | 10.3 | 10.2 | 10.1 | 10.1 | 10.1 | 10.2 | 10.5 | 10.2 |
| 2013 | 10.2 | 10.0 | 10.1 | 10.1 | 10.2 | 10.3 | 10.3 | 10.4 | 10.5 | 10.7 | 10.9 | 11.3 | 10.4 |
| 2014 | 11.6 | 11.4 | 11.6 | 11.5 | 11.7 | 11.7 | 11.6 | 11.7 | 11.8 | 11.7 | 12.0 | 12.6 | 11.7 |
| 2015 | 11.8 | 11.9 | 11.9 | 12.1 | 12.2 | 12.2 | 12.1 | 12.3 | 12.3 | 12.3 | 12.6 | 13.2 | 12.2 |
| 2016 | 12.5 | 12.4 | 12.5 | 12.5 | 12.7 | 12.8 | 12.7 | 12.7 | 12.9 | 12.8 | 13.0 | 13.7 | 12.8 |
| 2017 | 12.8 | 12.7 | 12.9 | 12.8 | 13.1 | 13.2 | 12.9 | 13.2 | 13.3 | 13.5 | 13.8 | 14.6 | 13.2 |
| 2018 | 13.8 | 13.8 | 13.8 | 13.9 | 14.0 | 14.1 | 13.8 | 14.0 | 14.1 | 14.5 | 15.1 | 15.7 | 14.2 |
| 2019 | 14.7 | 14.5 | 14.6 | 14.4 | 14.6 | 14.8 | 14.8 | 14.8 | 15.0 | 15.0 | 15.2 | 15.7 | 14.8 |
| **Information** | | | | | | | | | | | | | |
| 2011 | 16.9 | 17.0 | 17.0 | 17.1 | 17.1 | 17.4 | 17.5 | 17.7 | 17.5 | 17.6 | 17.8 | 17.8 | 17.4 |
| 2012 | 17.7 | 17.7 | 17.7 | 17.5 | 17.5 | 17.7 | 17.7 | 17.7 | 17.5 | 17.6 | 17.6 | 17.7 | 17.6 |
| 2013 | 17.7 | 17.8 | 17.8 | 17.8 | 17.9 | 18.0 | 18.2 | 18.2 | 18.0 | 17.9 | 18.1 | 18.2 | 18.0 |
| 2014 | 18.2 | 18.2 | 18.3 | 18.3 | 18.5 | 18.8 | 19.0 | 19.3 | 19.1 | 19.1 | 19.1 | 19.3 | 18.8 |
| 2015 | 19.2 | 19.3 | 19.3 | 19.3 | 19.4 | 19.7 | 19.9 | 20.0 | 20.0 | 20.2 | 20.3 | 20.4 | 19.8 |
| 2016 | 20.5 | 20.7 | 20.8 | 20.8 | 20.9 | 21.2 | 21.5 | 21.4 | 21.2 | 21.2 | 21.3 | 21.4 | 21.1 |
| 2017 | 21.2 | 21.4 | 21.4 | 21.5 | 21.6 | 21.8 | 22.0 | 21.9 | 21.7 | 21.5 | 21.6 | 21.7 | 21.6 |
| 2018 | 21.7 | 21.9 | 21.9 | 22.0 | 22.2 | 22.4 | 22.5 | 22.6 | 22.3 | 22.1 | 22.2 | 22.2 | 22.2 |
| 2019 | 22.6 | 22.6 | 22.6 | 22.5 | 22.7 | 22.8 | 22.8 | 22.8 | 22.3 | 22.3 | 22.4 | 22.6 | 22.6 |
| **Financial Activities** | | | | | | | | | | | | | |
| 2011 | 26.4 | 26.4 | 26.4 | 26.3 | 26.3 | 26.3 | 26.3 | 26.4 | 26.2 | 26.2 | 26.1 | 26.2 | 26.3 |
| 2012 | 25.8 | 26.1 | 26.2 | 26.4 | 26.4 | 26.5 | 26.4 | 26.3 | 26.2 | 26.7 | 26.6 | 26.7 | 26.4 |
| 2013 | 26.5 | 26.4 | 26.6 | 26.9 | 27.0 | 27.1 | 27.1 | 27.2 | 27.1 | 27.4 | 27.5 | 27.7 | 27.0 |
| 2014 | 27.2 | 27.3 | 27.3 | 27.5 | 27.7 | 27.9 | 27.9 | 28.0 | 27.9 | 28.2 | 28.2 | 28.5 | 27.8 |
| 2015 | 28.2 | 28.5 | 28.7 | 29.2 | 29.7 | 30.0 | 30.1 | 30.2 | 30.1 | 30.4 | 30.5 | 30.6 | 29.7 |
| 2016 | 30.5 | 30.6 | 30.5 | 30.7 | 30.7 | 30.8 | 31.1 | 31.1 | 30.9 | 31.0 | 31.0 | 30.9 | 30.8 |
| 2017 | 30.7 | 30.9 | 30.9 | 31.2 | 31.4 | 31.7 | 31.9 | 32.0 | 31.9 | 32.2 | 32.2 | 32.4 | 31.6 |
| 2018 | 32.2 | 32.2 | 32.2 | 32.6 | 32.7 | 33.0 | 33.2 | 33.3 | 33.0 | 33.0 | 33.0 | 33.0 | 32.8 |
| 2019 | 33.0 | 33.1 | 33.1 | 33.4 | 33.7 | 34.1 | 34.3 | 34.4 | 34.2 | 35.0 | 34.8 | 34.8 | 34.0 |

# Employment by Industry: Raleigh, NC, 2011–2019—*Continued*

(Numbers in thousands, not seasonally adjusted)

| Industry and year | January | February | March | April | May | June | July | August | September | October | November | December | Annual average |
|---|---|---|---|---|---|---|---|---|---|---|---|---|---|
| **Professional and Business Services** | | | | | | | | | | | | | |
| 2011 | 88.6 | 89.4 | 89.3 | 90.5 | 90.9 | 92.0 | 92.6 | 92.4 | 93.0 | 93.5 | 93.7 | 94.0 | 91.7 |
| 2012 | 93.0 | 93.0 | 93.5 | 96.5 | 96.7 | 97.7 | 99.4 | 99.6 | 98.9 | 99.5 | 100.4 | 100.4 | 97.4 |
| 2013 | 99.1 | 101.6 | 102.0 | 102.0 | 102.9 | 103.0 | 104.5 | 106.8 | 106.8 | 106.4 | 106.9 | 106.1 | 104.0 |
| 2014 | 104.2 | 103.6 | 104.8 | 106.5 | 107.7 | 108.6 | 108.7 | 109.6 | 108.8 | 110.3 | 110.1 | 110.1 | 107.8 |
| 2015 | 106.5 | 107.0 | 107.5 | 108.3 | 109.3 | 110.0 | 110.4 | 111.5 | 110.9 | 112.2 | 112.4 | 112.4 | 109.9 |
| 2016 | 110.0 | 109.8 | 109.8 | 110.5 | 111.8 | 112.7 | 113.8 | 114.0 | 114.2 | 114.8 | 114.6 | 113.5 | 112.5 |
| 2017 | 111.6 | 112.3 | 112.1 | 112.7 | 114.2 | 116.3 | 118.1 | 118.2 | 117.1 | 117.6 | 118.4 | 117.9 | 115.5 |
| 2018 | 116.1 | 117.1 | 117.7 | 118.7 | 119.4 | 121.0 | 122.5 | 123.0 | 120.1 | 122.6 | 123.0 | 122.1 | 120.3 |
| 2019 | 121.1 | 121.7 | 122.1 | 122.4 | 123.1 | 125.6 | 126.9 | 127.5 | 126.1 | 127.2 | 126.1 | 124.7 | 124.5 |
| **Education and Health Services** | | | | | | | | | | | | | |
| 2011 | 60.7 | 61.5 | 61.6 | 61.1 | 61.3 | 60.6 | 60.5 | 60.8 | 61.0 | 62.2 | 62.3 | 62.1 | 61.3 |
| 2012 | 62.1 | 62.8 | 63.4 | 63.2 | 63.8 | 62.9 | 62.7 | 63.3 | 63.7 | 64.5 | 64.7 | 64.8 | 63.5 |
| 2013 | 63.5 | 64.2 | 64.4 | 64.6 | 64.9 | 64.1 | 64.2 | 65.1 | 65.6 | 65.7 | 65.9 | 65.9 | 64.8 |
| 2014 | 64.9 | 65.5 | 66.0 | 66.1 | 66.7 | 65.8 | 66.0 | 66.8 | 66.9 | 67.9 | 68.3 | 68.2 | 66.6 |
| 2015 | 67.5 | 68.1 | 68.3 | 69.0 | 69.4 | 68.8 | 69.0 | 70.0 | 70.1 | 71.1 | 71.3 | 71.5 | 69.5 |
| 2016 | 71.0 | 71.7 | 72.2 | 72.6 | 73.0 | 71.9 | 72.2 | 73.1 | 73.1 | 74.1 | 74.5 | 74.5 | 72.8 |
| 2017 | 73.8 | 74.7 | 74.9 | 75.3 | 76.0 | 74.5 | 75.3 | 76.3 | 76.2 | 77.6 | 77.6 | 77.5 | 75.8 |
| 2018 | 76.9 | 77.6 | 77.8 | 78.5 | 79.0 | 78.3 | 78.1 | 79.2 | 78.7 | 80.8 | 80.7 | 80.4 | 78.8 |
| 2019 | 80.8 | 81.7 | 81.4 | 81.9 | 82.1 | 81.5 | 81.6 | 82.8 | 82.3 | 82.2 | 82.2 | 81.4 | 81.8 |
| **Leisure and Hospitality** | | | | | | | | | | | | | |
| 2011 | 49.5 | 50.2 | 51.5 | 53.1 | 53.6 | 54.3 | 55.1 | 55.4 | 54.2 | 53.8 | 53.7 | 53.9 | 53.2 |
| 2012 | 52.5 | 53.0 | 54.2 | 55.9 | 56.9 | 57.5 | 57.7 | 58.1 | 56.1 | 55.8 | 55.9 | 56.5 | 55.8 |
| 2013 | 55.1 | 55.2 | 56.1 | 57.8 | 58.5 | 60.5 | 60.4 | 60.5 | 59.9 | 59.1 | 59.2 | 59.8 | 58.5 |
| 2014 | 58.0 | 57.6 | 58.9 | 60.7 | 61.7 | 63.5 | 62.5 | 62.3 | 61.4 | 61.5 | 61.3 | 61.8 | 60.9 |
| 2015 | 61.0 | 61.3 | 62.2 | 63.5 | 65.2 | 66.9 | 66.6 | 66.6 | 65.2 | 65.1 | 65.1 | 65.5 | 64.5 |
| 2016 | 64.1 | 64.4 | 65.3 | 67.7 | 68.9 | 70.3 | 70.1 | 70.0 | 68.1 | 67.7 | 68.5 | 68.5 | 67.8 |
| 2017 | 66.5 | 67.4 | 68.6 | 68.7 | 71.1 | 72.5 | 72.5 | 72.1 | 69.8 | 69.9 | 69.4 | 69.4 | 69.8 |
| 2018 | 67.9 | 68.7 | 69.6 | 70.4 | 72.9 | 74.5 | 72.9 | 73.5 | 70.1 | 71.6 | 70.6 | 70.5 | 71.1 |
| 2019 | 70.3 | 70.9 | 72.2 | 72.8 | 75.2 | 76.3 | 75.9 | 75.6 | 72.7 | 74.7 | 74.1 | 74.8 | 73.8 |
| **Other Services** | | | | | | | | | | | | | |
| 2011 | 20.2 | 20.2 | 20.5 | 20.4 | 20.5 | 21.0 | 21.0 | 21.0 | 20.7 | 21.0 | 20.9 | 20.7 | 20.7 |
| 2012 | 20.8 | 20.9 | 21.0 | 21.4 | 21.9 | 22.0 | 22.2 | 22.5 | 22.5 | 22.3 | 22.3 | 21.8 | 21.8 |
| 2013 | 21.7 | 22.0 | 22.3 | 22.5 | 22.8 | 23.2 | 22.7 | 22.5 | 22.4 | 22.4 | 22.3 | 22.2 | 22.4 |
| 2014 | 22.2 | 22.2 | 22.6 | 22.7 | 23.2 | 23.5 | 23.4 | 23.3 | 23.0 | 23.1 | 23.1 | 22.7 | 22.9 |
| 2015 | 22.4 | 22.5 | 22.7 | 23.1 | 23.4 | 23.6 | 23.8 | 23.6 | 23.4 | 23.4 | 23.4 | 23.4 | 23.2 |
| 2016 | 23.6 | 23.6 | 23.8 | 24.0 | 24.1 | 24.3 | 24.7 | 24.7 | 24.4 | 24.6 | 24.5 | 24.0 | 24.2 |
| 2017 | 23.6 | 23.6 | 23.9 | 24.0 | 24.2 | 24.5 | 24.5 | 24.3 | 24.0 | 24.5 | 24.3 | 24.3 | 24.1 |
| 2018 | 24.1 | 24.3 | 24.5 | 24.6 | 24.9 | 25.2 | 25.1 | 25.2 | 24.7 | 25.3 | 25.3 | 25.1 | 24.9 |
| 2019 | 25.0 | 25.3 | 25.6 | 25.7 | 25.8 | 26.0 | 25.9 | 25.9 | 25.7 | 26.0 | 26.0 | 25.9 | 25.7 |
| **Government** | | | | | | | | | | | | | |
| 2011 | 92.4 | 93.3 | 93.6 | 93.1 | 93.2 | 87.2 | 83.8 | 86.0 | 91.2 | 92.7 | 92.5 | 90.5 | 90.8 |
| 2012 | 91.0 | 92.3 | 92.3 | 91.8 | 91.4 | 86.9 | 83.5 | 86.3 | 91.4 | 92.6 | 92.8 | 91.0 | 90.3 |
| 2013 | 91.3 | 92.7 | 92.9 | 92.4 | 91.4 | 85.2 | 83.1 | 86.7 | 93.1 | 94.7 | 95.0 | 93.2 | 91.0 |
| 2014 | 92.9 | 93.4 | 93.9 | 94.6 | 93.9 | 89.7 | 85.0 | 87.8 | 94.3 | 96.9 | 97.2 | 95.2 | 92.9 |
| 2015 | 94.5 | 95.8 | 95.7 | 95.8 | 94.1 | 90.0 | 85.4 | 88.3 | 95.1 | 96.4 | 96.9 | 95.5 | 93.6 |
| 2016 | 94.7 | 96.6 | 96.7 | 96.4 | 94.8 | 91.0 | 85.8 | 88.4 | 95.4 | 97.2 | 98.2 | 96.2 | 94.3 |
| 2017 | 95.3 | 97.5 | 97.7 | 97.4 | 96.7 | 91.8 | 86.8 | 92.0 | 97.5 | 98.5 | 99.8 | 98.4 | 95.8 |
| 2018 | 97.2 | 99.0 | 99.3 | 99.0 | 98.7 | 93.3 | 88.5 | 92.8 | 97.6 | 99.7 | 100.2 | 99.0 | 97.0 |
| 2019 | 98.4 | 99.7 | 99.7 | 100.4 | 99.2 | 93.9 | 89.5 | 94.1 | 99.7 | 101.5 | 101.8 | 100.3 | 98.2 |

## Employment by Industry: Memphis, TN-MS-AR, 2011–2019

(Numbers in thousands, not seasonally adjusted)

| Industry and year | January | February | March | April | May | June | July | August | September | October | November | December | Annual average |
|---|---|---|---|---|---|---|---|---|---|---|---|---|---|
| **Total Nonfarm** | | | | | | | | | | | | | |
| 2011 | 584.4 | 586.3 | 589.9 | 595.6 | 596.4 | 592.0 | 592.7 | 596.6 | 598.0 | 600.5 | 606.6 | 607.1 | 595.5 |
| 2012 | 590.6 | 595.0 | 598.5 | 600.4 | 603.1 | 600.8 | 598.7 | 603.9 | 605.5 | 609.4 | 618.1 | 618.8 | 603.6 |
| 2013 | 599.5 | 604.2 | 606.5 | 610.5 | 611.8 | 606.9 | 600.9 | 605.5 | 607.4 | 609.3 | 620.7 | 622.2 | 608.8 |
| 2014 | 604.0 | 605.4 | 609.0 | 617.5 | 617.5 | 614.0 | 609.9 | 616.8 | 617.8 | 622.3 | 630.5 | 632.9 | 616.5 |
| 2015 | 614.1 | 617.5 | 618.2 | 622.0 | 623.8 | 621.8 | 626.3 | 629.8 | 631.1 | 636.9 | 646.0 | 650.5 | 628.2 |
| 2016 | 628.8 | 631.4 | 633.1 | 637.4 | 636.0 | 632.3 | 633.6 | 638.4 | 641.4 | 643.9 | 650.7 | 652.0 | 638.3 |
| 2017 | 630.6 | 635.1 | 637.1 | 640.0 | 639.7 | 638.3 | 635.6 | 640.9 | 643.0 | 647.0 | 655.1 | 656.0 | 641.5 |
| 2018 | 634.8 | 639.8 | 642.7 | 644.1 | 646.8 | 644.7 | 642.1 | 648.9 | 650.5 | 655.4 | 664.6 | 663.2 | 648.1 |
| 2019 | 646.5 | 649.5 | 650.5 | 652.9 | 655.3 | 651.1 | 649.4 | 656.7 | 656.0 | 658.3 | 666.0 | 663.6 | 654.7 |
| **Total Private** | | | | | | | | | | | | | |
| 2011 | 499.0 | 499.4 | 503.2 | 508.7 | 510.7 | 512.4 | 513.4 | 513.6 | 513.2 | 515.2 | 520.9 | 522.4 | 511.0 |
| 2012 | 506.4 | 509.2 | 512.6 | 514.1 | 518.2 | 520.6 | 518.0 | 520.9 | 520.2 | 523.7 | 531.9 | 533.6 | 519.1 |
| 2013 | 515.6 | 518.0 | 520.6 | 523.7 | 527.3 | 528.1 | 522.8 | 524.6 | 524.3 | 525.8 | 536.6 | 539.7 | 525.6 |
| 2014 | 522.0 | 522.1 | 525.5 | 533.4 | 535.5 | 536.8 | 532.8 | 536.6 | 535.2 | 539.1 | 547.0 | 550.2 | 534.7 |
| 2015 | 532.4 | 533.3 | 534.1 | 538.7 | 542.9 | 545.7 | 550.2 | 550.7 | 548.9 | 553.5 | 562.5 | 568.4 | 546.8 |
| 2016 | 547.9 | 548.7 | 549.9 | 555.2 | 556.1 | 557.1 | 557.9 | 559.3 | 558.6 | 560.4 | 566.8 | 569.2 | 557.3 |
| 2017 | 548.7 | 551.3 | 553.4 | 556.0 | 557.7 | 560.8 | 557.8 | 560.1 | 558.0 | 562.3 | 569.8 | 572.1 | 559.0 |
| 2018 | 551.4 | 554.5 | 557.2 | 559.5 | 563.6 | 566.0 | 563.4 | 566.7 | 564.9 | 568.9 | 576.9 | 577.3 | 564.2 |
| 2019 | 562.5 | 563.7 | 564.5 | 568.1 | 572.1 | 572.3 | 570.6 | 574.4 | 570.1 | 572.0 | 579.3 | 577.5 | 570.6 |
| **Goods Producing** | | | | | | | | | | | | | |
| 2011 | 60.6 | 60.2 | 60.6 | 61.2 | 61.9 | 62.9 | 63.3 | 63.1 | 62.8 | 61.5 | 62.3 | 62.0 | 61.9 |
| 2012 | 61.0 | 61.0 | 61.7 | 62.3 | 63.0 | 63.8 | 63.7 | 64.0 | 62.8 | 62.2 | 63.0 | 62.5 | 62.6 |
| 2013 | 61.7 | 61.7 | 62.2 | 62.4 | 63.0 | 63.4 | 63.1 | 62.6 | 62.3 | 61.9 | 62.1 | 61.9 | 62.4 |
| 2014 | 62.0 | 61.9 | 61.8 | 62.8 | 63.4 | 63.3 | 63.7 | 63.8 | 63.5 | 63.5 | 63.6 | 63.9 | 63.1 |
| 2015 | 62.7 | 62.9 | 63.2 | 63.9 | 64.5 | 65.3 | 66.2 | 65.4 | 65.2 | 65.2 | 65.2 | 65.2 | 64.6 |
| 2016 | 64.2 | 64.0 | 63.8 | 64.9 | 65.1 | 65.5 | 66.1 | 65.4 | 65.0 | 64.5 | 64.6 | 64.8 | 64.8 |
| 2017 | 64.4 | 64.7 | 65.2 | 65.7 | 65.9 | 66.5 | 66.3 | 66.6 | 66.2 | 65.9 | 65.8 | 65.9 | 65.8 |
| 2018 | 64.7 | 65.2 | 65.6 | 66.4 | 67.0 | 68.0 | 68.1 | 68.2 | 68.0 | 67.5 | 67.7 | 67.7 | 67.0 |
| 2019 | 67.5 | 67.9 | 68.3 | 69.0 | 69.9 | 70.6 | 69.9 | 69.5 | 68.9 | 68.1 | 67.3 | 67.3 | 68.7 |
| **Service-Providing** | | | | | | | | | | | | | |
| 2011 | 523.8 | 526.1 | 529.3 | 534.4 | 534.5 | 529.1 | 529.4 | 533.5 | 535.2 | 539.0 | 544.3 | 545.1 | 533.6 |
| 2012 | 529.6 | 534.0 | 536.8 | 538.1 | 540.1 | 537.0 | 535.0 | 539.9 | 542.7 | 547.2 | 555.1 | 556.3 | 541.0 |
| 2013 | 537.8 | 542.5 | 544.3 | 548.1 | 548.8 | 543.5 | 537.8 | 542.9 | 545.1 | 547.4 | 558.6 | 560.3 | 546.4 |
| 2014 | 542.0 | 543.5 | 547.2 | 554.7 | 554.1 | 550.7 | 546.2 | 553.0 | 554.3 | 558.8 | 566.9 | 569.0 | 553.4 |
| 2015 | 551.4 | 554.6 | 555.0 | 558.1 | 559.3 | 556.5 | 560.1 | 564.4 | 565.9 | 571.7 | 580.8 | 585.3 | 563.6 |
| 2016 | 564.6 | 567.4 | 569.3 | 572.5 | 570.9 | 566.8 | 567.5 | 573.0 | 576.4 | 579.4 | 586.1 | 587.2 | 573.4 |
| 2017 | 566.2 | 570.4 | 571.9 | 574.3 | 573.8 | 571.8 | 569.3 | 574.3 | 576.8 | 581.1 | 589.3 | 590.1 | 575.8 |
| 2018 | 570.1 | 574.6 | 577.1 | 577.7 | 579.8 | 576.7 | 574.0 | 580.7 | 582.5 | 587.9 | 596.9 | 595.5 | 581.1 |
| 2019 | 579.0 | 581.6 | 582.2 | 583.9 | 585.4 | 580.5 | 579.5 | 587.2 | 587.1 | 590.2 | 598.7 | 596.3 | 586.0 |
| **Mining, Logging, and Construction** | | | | | | | | | | | | | |
| 2011 | 18.1 | 18.2 | 18.6 | 19.0 | 19.4 | 20.2 | 20.7 | 20.8 | 20.9 | 20.8 | 20.7 | 20.6 | 19.8 |
| 2012 | 19.6 | 19.5 | 20.0 | 20.4 | 20.9 | 21.4 | 21.3 | 21.5 | 21.3 | 20.8 | 20.7 | 20.6 | 20.7 |
| 2013 | 19.8 | 19.8 | 20.0 | 20.2 | 20.7 | 21.0 | 20.9 | 20.9 | 20.7 | 20.5 | 20.7 | 20.5 | 20.5 |
| 2014 | 20.5 | 20.3 | 19.9 | 21.0 | 21.4 | 21.1 | 21.1 | 21.2 | 21.1 | 21.4 | 21.5 | 21.4 | 21.0 |
| 2015 | 20.6 | 20.6 | 20.5 | 21.0 | 21.2 | 21.6 | 22.5 | 22.4 | 22.3 | 22.3 | 22.3 | 22.0 | 21.6 |
| 2016 | 21.2 | 21.0 | 20.9 | 21.5 | 21.5 | 21.8 | 22.4 | 22.0 | 22.1 | 21.9 | 22.0 | 21.9 | 21.7 |
| 2017 | 21.7 | 22.1 | 22.5 | 22.6 | 22.8 | 23.1 | 23.2 | 23.3 | 23.4 | 23.3 | 23.1 | 22.9 | 22.8 |
| 2018 | 21.8 | 22.3 | 22.6 | 22.8 | 23.2 | 23.8 | 23.8 | 23.9 | 24.2 | 23.7 | 23.6 | 23.3 | 23.3 |
| 2019 | 23.0 | 23.2 | 23.4 | 24.0 | 24.6 | 25.0 | 24.3 | 24.2 | 24.0 | 23.7 | 23.1 | 23.1 | 23.8 |
| **Manufacturing** | | | | | | | | | | | | | |
| 2011 | 42.5 | 42.0 | 42.0 | 42.2 | 42.5 | 42.7 | 42.6 | 42.3 | 41.9 | 40.7 | 41.6 | 41.4 | 42.0 |
| 2012 | 41.4 | 41.5 | 41.7 | 41.9 | 42.1 | 42.4 | 42.4 | 42.5 | 41.5 | 41.4 | 42.3 | 41.9 | 41.9 |
| 2013 | 41.9 | 41.9 | 42.2 | 42.2 | 42.3 | 42.4 | 42.2 | 41.7 | 41.6 | 41.4 | 41.4 | 41.4 | 41.9 |
| 2014 | 41.5 | 41.6 | 41.9 | 41.8 | 42.0 | 42.2 | 42.6 | 42.6 | 42.4 | 42.1 | 42.1 | 42.5 | 42.1 |
| 2015 | 42.1 | 42.3 | 42.7 | 42.9 | 43.3 | 43.7 | 43.7 | 43.0 | 42.9 | 42.9 | 42.9 | 43.2 | 43.0 |
| 2016 | 43.0 | 43.0 | 42.9 | 43.4 | 43.6 | 43.7 | 43.7 | 43.4 | 42.9 | 42.6 | 42.6 | 42.9 | 43.1 |
| 2017 | 42.7 | 42.6 | 42.7 | 43.1 | 43.1 | 43.4 | 43.1 | 43.3 | 42.8 | 42.6 | 42.7 | 43.0 | 42.9 |
| 2018 | 42.9 | 42.9 | 43.0 | 43.6 | 43.8 | 44.2 | 44.3 | 44.3 | 43.8 | 43.8 | 44.1 | 44.4 | 43.8 |
| 2019 | 44.5 | 44.7 | 44.9 | 45.0 | 45.3 | 45.6 | 45.6 | 45.3 | 44.9 | 44.4 | 44.2 | 44.2 | 44.9 |

# Employment by Industry: Memphis, TN-MS-AR, 2011–2019—*Continued*

(Numbers in thousands, not seasonally adjusted)

| Industry and year | January | February | March | April | May | June | July | August | September | October | November | December | Annual average |
|---|---|---|---|---|---|---|---|---|---|---|---|---|---|
| **Trade, Transportation, and Utilities** | | | | | | | | | | | | | |
| 2011 | 157.1 | 156.4 | 156.8 | 158.3 | 159.0 | 159.4 | 160.0 | 159.4 | 159.8 | 161.6 | 164.3 | 165.3 | 159.8 |
| 2012 | 160.2 | 159.4 | 160.1 | 160.1 | 161.2 | 161.5 | 161.4 | 161.4 | 161.6 | 162.3 | 166.2 | 167.5 | 161.9 |
| 2013 | 161.8 | 161.4 | 161.0 | 161.8 | 161.8 | 162.1 | 162.3 | 161.6 | 160.9 | 161.8 | 165.6 | 166.9 | 162.4 |
| 2014 | 160.9 | 160.8 | 161.7 | 163.2 | 163.1 | 163.9 | 163.8 | 163.9 | 164.1 | 166.1 | 169.9 | 170.5 | 164.3 |
| 2015 | 164.8 | 163.7 | 163.8 | 164.5 | 165.5 | 166.7 | 170.1 | 168.7 | 168.4 | 170.2 | 175.4 | 178.1 | 168.3 |
| 2016 | 171.0 | 170.6 | 170.7 | 172.0 | 172.3 | 173.7 | 174.7 | 173.9 | 173.7 | 176.0 | 179.3 | 180.6 | 174.0 |
| 2017 | 173.6 | 173.0 | 172.8 | 173.1 | 173.3 | 174.3 | 174.8 | 174.2 | 173.7 | 174.7 | 179.0 | 180.5 | 174.8 |
| 2018 | 173.7 | 172.6 | 172.8 | 172.5 | 173.5 | 174.5 | 174.7 | 174.4 | 174.3 | 175.8 | 180.2 | 180.9 | 175.0 |
| 2019 | 175.6 | 175.2 | 175.1 | 175.3 | 175.8 | 176.6 | 176.5 | 175.7 | 175.4 | 176.6 | 181.3 | 182.1 | 176.8 |
| **Wholesale Trade** | | | | | | | | | | | | | |
| 2011 | 32.4 | 32.4 | 32.4 | 32.6 | 32.7 | 32.8 | 32.9 | 32.9 | 32.9 | 32.9 | 33.0 | 32.8 | 32.7 |
| 2012 | 32.8 | 33.0 | 33.0 | 33.1 | 33.4 | 33.5 | 33.5 | 33.5 | 33.4 | 33.4 | 33.6 | 33.6 | 33.3 |
| 2013 | 33.1 | 33.2 | 33.3 | 33.5 | 33.5 | 33.6 | 33.5 | 33.6 | 33.6 | 33.3 | 33.3 | 33.4 | 33.4 |
| 2014 | 32.9 | 33.1 | 33.2 | 33.2 | 33.3 | 33.5 | 33.3 | 33.2 | 33.2 | 33.0 | 33.3 | 33.5 | 33.2 |
| 2015 | 33.3 | 33.3 | 33.2 | 33.5 | 33.7 | 33.8 | 34.3 | 34.5 | 34.7 | 34.8 | 35.2 | 35.5 | 34.2 |
| 2016 | 34.6 | 34.8 | 34.8 | 34.8 | 34.9 | 35.1 | 35.2 | 35.3 | 35.3 | 35.3 | 35.4 | 35.7 | 35.1 |
| 2017 | 35.7 | 35.8 | 35.9 | 35.4 | 35.5 | 35.6 | 35.5 | 35.4 | 35.3 | 35.2 | 35.2 | 35.1 | 35.5 |
| 2018 | 34.8 | 34.9 | 34.8 | 34.8 | 34.9 | 35.0 | 35.0 | 34.9 | 34.9 | 35.1 | 35.3 | 35.3 | 35.0 |
| 2019 | 35.0 | 35.0 | 34.9 | 35.2 | 35.3 | 35.5 | 34.9 | 34.7 | 34.7 | 35.0 | 35.1 | 35.3 | 35.1 |
| **Retail Trade** | | | | | | | | | | | | | |
| 2011 | 62.5 | 61.8 | 61.9 | 62.6 | 62.8 | 62.7 | 62.8 | 62.2 | 61.9 | 62.7 | 65.3 | 66.0 | 62.9 |
| 2012 | 62.7 | 62.0 | 62.6 | 62.7 | 63.2 | 63.3 | 63.2 | 62.6 | 62.3 | 63.1 | 66.0 | 66.3 | 63.3 |
| 2013 | 63.6 | 63.1 | 63.2 | 63.3 | 63.6 | 63.8 | 64.3 | 64.0 | 63.8 | 64.4 | 67.1 | 68.1 | 64.4 |
| 2014 | 64.4 | 63.9 | 64.2 | 65.2 | 65.4 | 65.6 | 65.6 | 65.2 | 65.0 | 65.7 | 68.1 | 68.7 | 65.6 |
| 2015 | 65.0 | 64.3 | 64.6 | 64.8 | 65.3 | 65.9 | 66.6 | 66.0 | 65.3 | 66.6 | 69.7 | 70.5 | 66.2 |
| 2016 | 66.9 | 66.8 | 67.0 | 67.8 | 67.7 | 67.8 | 68.5 | 67.6 | 67.4 | 69.0 | 70.3 | 70.9 | 68.1 |
| 2017 | 67.9 | 67.5 | 67.4 | 67.6 | 67.5 | 67.6 | 67.5 | 67.2 | 66.9 | 67.9 | 70.5 | 70.8 | 68.0 |
| 2018 | 67.4 | 66.7 | 66.6 | 66.4 | 66.8 | 66.6 | 66.5 | 66.1 | 65.6 | 65.9 | 67.8 | 68.0 | 66.7 |
| 2019 | 65.5 | 64.5 | 64.6 | 64.3 | 64.4 | 64.4 | 64.4 | 63.9 | 63.7 | 64.3 | 66.9 | 67.3 | 64.9 |
| **Transportation and Utilities** | | | | | | | | | | | | | |
| 2011 | 62.2 | 62.2 | 62.5 | 63.1 | 63.5 | 63.9 | 64.3 | 64.3 | 65.0 | 66.0 | 66.0 | 66.5 | 64.1 |
| 2012 | 64.7 | 64.4 | 64.5 | 64.3 | 64.6 | 64.7 | 64.7 | 65.3 | 65.9 | 65.8 | 66.6 | 67.6 | 65.3 |
| 2013 | 65.1 | 65.1 | 64.5 | 65.0 | 64.7 | 64.7 | 64.5 | 64.0 | 63.5 | 64.1 | 65.2 | 65.4 | 64.7 |
| 2014 | 63.6 | 63.8 | 64.3 | 64.8 | 64.4 | 64.8 | 64.9 | 65.5 | 65.9 | 67.4 | 68.5 | 68.3 | 65.5 |
| 2015 | 66.5 | 66.1 | 66.0 | 66.2 | 66.5 | 67.0 | 69.2 | 68.2 | 68.4 | 68.8 | 70.5 | 72.1 | 68.0 |
| 2016 | 69.5 | 69.0 | 68.9 | 69.4 | 69.7 | 70.8 | 71.0 | 71.0 | 71.0 | 71.7 | 73.6 | 74.0 | 70.8 |
| 2017 | 70.0 | 69.7 | 69.5 | 70.1 | 70.3 | 71.1 | 71.8 | 71.6 | 71.5 | 71.6 | 73.3 | 74.6 | 71.3 |
| 2018 | 71.5 | 71.0 | 71.4 | 71.3 | 71.8 | 72.9 | 73.2 | 73.4 | 73.8 | 74.8 | 77.1 | 77.6 | 73.3 |
| 2019 | 75.1 | 75.7 | 75.6 | 75.8 | 76.1 | 76.7 | 77.2 | 77.1 | 77.0 | 77.3 | 79.3 | 79.5 | 76.9 |
| **Information** | | | | | | | | | | | | | |
| 2011 | 6.2 | 6.1 | 6.1 | 6.1 | 6.2 | 6.1 | 6.1 | 6.1 | 6.0 | 6.0 | 6.0 | 6.0 | 6.1 |
| 2012 | 6.1 | 6.1 | 6.1 | 6.1 | 6.1 | 6.0 | 6.1 | 6.1 | 6.0 | 6.0 | 6.0 | 6.0 | 6.1 |
| 2013 | 5.9 | 5.9 | 5.9 | 5.9 | 6.0 | 6.1 | 6.0 | 6.0 | 6.0 | 6.0 | 6.1 | 6.1 | 6.0 |
| 2014 | 6.0 | 6.0 | 6.0 | 6.0 | 6.0 | 6.0 | 5.9 | 6.0 | 5.9 | 5.8 | 6.0 | 6.0 | 6.0 |
| 2015 | 5.8 | 5.8 | 5.8 | 5.9 | 5.9 | 5.9 | 5.8 | 5.8 | 5.7 | 5.7 | 5.8 | 5.9 | 5.8 |
| 2016 | 5.8 | 5.8 | 5.7 | 5.7 | 5.7 | 5.7 | 5.8 | 5.7 | 5.7 | 5.6 | 5.7 | 5.8 | 5.7 |
| 2017 | 5.7 | 5.7 | 5.7 | 5.6 | 5.7 | 5.7 | 5.8 | 5.8 | 5.7 | 5.7 | 5.8 | 5.9 | 5.7 |
| 2018 | 5.5 | 5.5 | 5.5 | 5.5 | 5.5 | 5.5 | 5.5 | 5.5 | 5.4 | 5.4 | 5.4 | 5.5 | 5.5 |
| 2019 | 5.5 | 5.5 | 5.5 | 5.6 | 5.6 | 5.6 | 5.6 | 5.6 | 5.5 | 5.5 | 5.6 | 5.6 | 5.6 |
| **Financial Activities** | | | | | | | | | | | | | |
| 2011 | 27.6 | 27.3 | 27.2 | 27.5 | 27.6 | 27.6 | 27.7 | 27.7 | 27.6 | 27.5 | 27.5 | 27.6 | 27.5 |
| 2012 | 27.4 | 27.4 | 27.4 | 27.3 | 27.5 | 27.3 | 27.5 | 27.4 | 27.1 | 27.3 | 27.4 | 27.4 | 27.4 |
| 2013 | 27.2 | 27.0 | 27.0 | 27.0 | 27.0 | 27.2 | 27.4 | 27.3 | 27.3 | 27.3 | 27.4 | 27.5 | 27.2 |
| 2014 | 27.1 | 27.1 | 27.1 | 27.4 | 27.6 | 27.6 | 27.6 | 27.6 | 27.4 | 27.5 | 27.5 | 27.5 | 27.4 |
| 2015 | 27.3 | 27.2 | 27.1 | 27.2 | 27.4 | 27.6 | 27.7 | 27.8 | 27.6 | 27.8 | 27.9 | 28.0 | 27.6 |
| 2016 | 27.7 | 27.8 | 27.6 | 27.8 | 27.9 | 28.0 | 28.2 | 28.2 | 28.1 | 28.1 | 28.2 | 28.3 | 28.0 |
| 2017 | 28.1 | 28.1 | 28.2 | 28.3 | 28.6 | 28.9 | 28.8 | 28.8 | 28.8 | 28.8 | 28.8 | 29.0 | 28.6 |
| 2018 | 28.9 | 29.2 | 29.4 | 29.4 | 29.6 | 29.6 | 29.7 | 29.6 | 29.8 | 29.8 | 29.8 | 29.8 | 29.6 |
| 2019 | 29.5 | 29.4 | 29.4 | 29.6 | 29.7 | 29.8 | 29.8 | 29.9 | 29.7 | 29.5 | 29.2 | 29.2 | 29.6 |

## Employment by Industry: Memphis, TN-MS-AR, 2011–2019—*Continued*

(Numbers in thousands, not seasonally adjusted)

| Industry and year | January | February | March | April | May | June | July | August | September | October | November | December | Annual average |
|---|---|---|---|---|---|---|---|---|---|---|---|---|---|
| **Professional and Business Services** | | | | | | | | | | | | | |
| 2011 | 79.6 | 80.7 | 81.8 | 82.8 | 82.8 | 82.5 | 82.9 | 84.0 | 84.3 | 87.5 | 89.4 | 90.2 | 84.0 |
| 2012 | 82.8 | 84.7 | 84.4 | 84.6 | 85.6 | 86.2 | 84.7 | 86.0 | 87.7 | 90.4 | 94.0 | 94.2 | 87.1 |
| 2013 | 86.4 | 87.8 | 88.9 | 89.3 | 90.7 | 90.4 | 86.8 | 89.7 | 90.9 | 91.7 | 97.7 | 100.0 | 90.9 |
| 2014 | 91.4 | 90.1 | 91.1 | 94.9 | 95.7 | 95.1 | 94.0 | 96.2 | 96.6 | 98.7 | 103.0 | 104.9 | 96.0 |
| 2015 | 97.4 | 97.4 | 97.7 | 98.0 | 99.1 | 99.2 | 99.4 | 101.0 | 101.1 | 102.8 | 106.0 | 107.8 | 100.6 |
| 2016 | 99.1 | 98.6 | 98.9 | 99.9 | 99.2 | 98.1 | 97.5 | 99.3 | 100.3 | 100.4 | 103.1 | 103.6 | 99.8 |
| 2017 | 93.8 | 94.3 | 94.3 | 95.0 | 95.0 | 95.7 | 94.5 | 95.4 | 95.4 | 98.5 | 101.7 | 102.1 | 96.3 |
| 2018 | 94.2 | 94.9 | 94.8 | 95.8 | 96.7 | 96.8 | 95.0 | 96.5 | 96.4 | 99.0 | 102.4 | 101.8 | 97.0 |
| 2019 | 94.9 | 94.9 | 94.1 | 95.1 | 96.2 | 95.2 | 94.9 | 97.2 | 95.3 | 94.4 | 97.0 | 96.6 | 95.5 |
| **Education and Health Services** | | | | | | | | | | | | | |
| 2011 | 82.5 | 83.0 | 83.5 | 84.3 | 84.1 | 83.6 | 83.8 | 84.5 | 85.6 | 85.8 | 86.2 | 86.1 | 84.4 |
| 2012 | 85.7 | 86.6 | 87.3 | 86.2 | 86.3 | 85.8 | 85.6 | 87.2 | 88.1 | 88.3 | 88.9 | 89.4 | 87.1 |
| 2013 | 88.1 | 89.3 | 89.5 | 89.3 | 89.4 | 88.4 | 87.4 | 88.1 | 89.2 | 89.6 | 90.1 | 90.1 | 89.0 |
| 2014 | 88.8 | 89.4 | 89.4 | 89.6 | 89.0 | 87.8 | 87.6 | 88.9 | 89.5 | 89.6 | 89.6 | 89.6 | 89.1 |
| 2015 | 88.3 | 89.5 | 89.6 | 89.7 | 89.2 | 88.4 | 89.1 | 90.5 | 91.3 | 91.7 | 92.2 | 92.6 | 90.2 |
| 2016 | 91.1 | 91.9 | 92.0 | 92.6 | 92.7 | 91.1 | 91.3 | 92.9 | 93.5 | 93.8 | 93.8 | 93.7 | 92.5 |
| 2017 | 92.2 | 93.4 | 93.8 | 93.8 | 93.7 | 92.6 | 91.8 | 93.5 | 94.2 | 94.6 | 94.7 | 94.6 | 93.6 |
| 2018 | 93.0 | 94.3 | 94.6 | 94.8 | 94.8 | 93.7 | 93.5 | 95.4 | 96.0 | 96.6 | 96.8 | 96.8 | 95.0 |
| 2019 | 96.1 | 97.3 | 97.4 | 97.2 | 98.1 | 97.2 | 97.0 | 98.7 | 98.7 | 100.0 | 100.9 | 99.2 | 98.2 |
| **Leisure and Hospitality** | | | | | | | | | | | | | |
| 2011 | 62.3 | 62.6 | 63.9 | 65.1 | 65.7 | 66.6 | 65.7 | 64.9 | 63.3 | 61.7 | 61.6 | 61.6 | 63.8 |
| 2012 | 59.7 | 60.4 | 61.7 | 63.4 | 64.2 | 65.4 | 64.6 | 64.6 | 62.8 | 63.1 | 62.4 | 62.6 | 62.9 |
| 2013 | 60.8 | 61.1 | 62.1 | 63.7 | 65.0 | 65.8 | 65.2 | 65.0 | 63.5 | 63.5 | 63.6 | 63.3 | 63.6 |
| 2014 | 62.1 | 62.9 | 64.4 | 65.5 | 66.6 | 68.6 | 65.9 | 66.1 | 64.1 | 63.9 | 63.6 | 63.9 | 64.8 |
| 2015 | 62.2 | 62.7 | 62.8 | 65.2 | 66.8 | 67.8 | 67.1 | 66.8 | 64.9 | 65.5 | 65.3 | 66.0 | 65.3 |
| 2016 | 64.3 | 65.2 | 66.2 | 67.3 | 68.1 | 69.5 | 68.8 | 68.5 | 66.9 | 66.8 | 66.8 | 67.1 | 67.1 |
| 2017 | 65.7 | 66.7 | 67.8 | 68.9 | 69.8 | 71.0 | 69.7 | 69.7 | 67.9 | 68.2 | 67.9 | 67.9 | 68.4 |
| 2018 | 65.5 | 66.4 | 67.9 | 68.5 | 69.7 | 70.5 | 69.4 | 69.7 | 67.7 | 67.4 | 67.5 | 67.7 | 68.2 |
| 2019 | 66.5 | 66.5 | 67.5 | 69.1 | 69.4 | 69.6 | 69.3 | 70.0 | 69.0 | 70.2 | 70.3 | 69.9 | 68.9 |
| **Other Services** | | | | | | | | | | | | | |
| 2011 | 23.1 | 23.1 | 23.3 | 23.4 | 23.4 | 23.7 | 23.9 | 23.9 | 23.8 | 23.6 | 23.6 | 23.6 | 23.5 |
| 2012 | 23.5 | 23.6 | 23.9 | 24.1 | 24.3 | 24.6 | 24.4 | 24.2 | 24.1 | 24.1 | 24.0 | 24.0 | 24.1 |
| 2013 | 23.7 | 23.8 | 24.0 | 24.3 | 24.4 | 24.7 | 24.6 | 24.3 | 24.2 | 24.0 | 24.0 | 23.9 | 24.2 |
| 2014 | 23.7 | 23.9 | 24.0 | 24.0 | 24.1 | 24.5 | 24.3 | 24.1 | 24.1 | 24.0 | 23.8 | 23.9 | 24.0 |
| 2015 | 23.9 | 24.1 | 24.1 | 24.3 | 24.5 | 24.8 | 24.8 | 24.7 | 24.7 | 24.6 | 24.7 | 24.8 | 24.5 |
| 2016 | 24.7 | 24.8 | 25.0 | 25.0 | 25.1 | 25.5 | 25.5 | 25.4 | 25.4 | 25.2 | 25.3 | 25.3 | 25.2 |
| 2017 | 25.2 | 25.4 | 25.6 | 25.6 | 25.7 | 26.1 | 26.1 | 26.1 | 26.1 | 25.9 | 26.1 | 26.2 | 25.8 |
| 2018 | 25.9 | 26.4 | 26.6 | 26.6 | 26.8 | 27.4 | 27.5 | 27.4 | 27.3 | 27.4 | 27.1 | 27.1 | 27.0 |
| 2019 | 26.9 | 27.0 | 27.2 | 27.2 | 27.4 | 27.7 | 27.6 | 27.8 | 27.6 | 27.7 | 27.7 | 27.6 | 27.5 |
| **Government** | | | | | | | | | | | | | |
| 2011 | 85.4 | 86.9 | 86.7 | 86.9 | 85.7 | 79.6 | 79.3 | 83.0 | 84.8 | 85.3 | 85.7 | 84.7 | 84.5 |
| 2012 | 84.2 | 85.8 | 85.9 | 86.3 | 84.9 | 80.2 | 80.7 | 83.0 | 85.3 | 85.7 | 86.2 | 85.2 | 84.5 |
| 2013 | 83.9 | 86.2 | 85.9 | 86.8 | 84.5 | 78.8 | 78.1 | 80.9 | 83.1 | 83.5 | 84.1 | 82.5 | 83.2 |
| 2014 | 82.0 | 83.3 | 83.5 | 84.1 | 82.0 | 77.2 | 77.1 | 80.2 | 82.6 | 83.2 | 83.5 | 82.7 | 81.8 |
| 2015 | 81.7 | 84.2 | 84.1 | 83.3 | 80.9 | 76.1 | 76.1 | 79.1 | 82.2 | 83.4 | 83.5 | 82.1 | 81.4 |
| 2016 | 80.9 | 82.7 | 83.2 | 82.2 | 79.9 | 75.2 | 75.7 | 79.1 | 82.8 | 83.5 | 83.9 | 82.8 | 81.0 |
| 2017 | 81.9 | 83.8 | 83.7 | 84.0 | 82.0 | 77.5 | 77.8 | 80.8 | 85.0 | 84.7 | 85.3 | 83.9 | 82.5 |
| 2018 | 83.4 | 85.3 | 85.5 | 84.6 | 83.2 | 78.7 | 78.7 | 82.2 | 85.6 | 86.5 | 87.7 | 85.9 | 83.9 |
| 2019 | 84.0 | 85.8 | 86.0 | 84.8 | 83.2 | 78.8 | 78.8 | 82.3 | 85.9 | 86.3 | 86.7 | 86.1 | 84.1 |

# Employment by Industry: Richmond, VA, 2011–2019

(Numbers in thousands, not seasonally adjusted)

| Industry and year | January | February | March | April | May | June | July | August | September | October | November | December | Annual average |
|---|---|---|---|---|---|---|---|---|---|---|---|---|---|
| **Total Nonfarm** | | | | | | | | | | | | | |
| 2011 | 586.8 | 589.0 | 593.4 | 600.1 | 600.7 | 602.6 | 601.4 | 598.6 | 601.3 | 607.4 | 610.8 | 609.3 | 600.1 |
| 2012 | 597.6 | 599.7 | 604.7 | 610.4 | 612.8 | 617.0 | 610.7 | 613.6 | 614.6 | 619.1 | 622.0 | 623.8 | 612.2 |
| 2013 | 608.6 | 611.3 | 615.7 | 620.9 | 621.1 | 624.2 | 622.0 | 622.9 | 622.9 | 625.1 | 634.1 | 631.9 | 621.7 |
| 2014 | 620.0 | 618.0 | 623.3 | 630.7 | 635.3 | 637.5 | 632.8 | 634.1 | 632.9 | 636.6 | 642.7 | 643.2 | 632.3 |
| 2015 | 632.6 | 632.9 | 635.5 | 644.0 | 649.1 | 652.0 | 651.2 | 652.2 | 655.0 | 662.2 | 668.2 | 666.9 | 650.2 |
| 2016 | 651.4 | 653.4 | 655.9 | 662.6 | 661.7 | 665.2 | 659.4 | 660.3 | 662.7 | 667.8 | 673.5 | 673.9 | 662.3 |
| 2017 | 656.4 | 662.1 | 664.9 | 667.5 | 669.7 | 674.9 | 670.3 | 670.4 | 671.3 | 674.3 | 678.3 | 677.8 | 669.8 |
| 2018 | 665.1 | 670.3 | 672.0 | 675.2 | 677.7 | 683.7 | 682.1 | 683.5 | 678.2 | 685.8 | 693.7 | 690.4 | 679.8 |
| 2019 | 676.4 | 679.0 | 680.4 | 684.9 | 685.9 | 691.7 | 686.7 | 686.3 | 684.7 | 689.8 | 697.9 | 696.2 | 686.7 |
| **Total Private** | | | | | | | | | | | | | |
| 2011 | 475.4 | 476.8 | 481.0 | 487.5 | 489.5 | 491.9 | 494.3 | 492.6 | 492.0 | 495.7 | 498.4 | 497.4 | 489.4 |
| 2012 | 486.0 | 486.9 | 491.6 | 498.5 | 502.0 | 506.4 | 505.1 | 507.9 | 506.6 | 509.2 | 510.6 | 512.6 | 502.0 |
| 2013 | 498.4 | 500.4 | 504.8 | 509.1 | 511.1 | 514.0 | 516.1 | 517.7 | 514.9 | 515.4 | 523.7 | 521.5 | 512.3 |
| 2014 | 509.9 | 507.7 | 512.5 | 520.0 | 525.3 | 527.5 | 526.3 | 527.2 | 523.6 | 526.1 | 531.5 | 532.0 | 522.5 |
| 2015 | 522.1 | 522.0 | 525.0 | 533.6 | 539.6 | 542.5 | 545.8 | 547.1 | 546.9 | 551.1 | 556.4 | 555.6 | 540.6 |
| 2016 | 541.3 | 541.6 | 543.7 | 550.1 | 551.1 | 554.4 | 552.6 | 554.0 | 552.9 | 556.3 | 561.0 | 561.4 | 551.7 |
| 2017 | 545.6 | 549.7 | 552.5 | 555.5 | 559.4 | 564.5 | 562.8 | 563.6 | 561.4 | 563.1 | 566.0 | 566.2 | 559.2 |
| 2018 | 554.4 | 558.1 | 559.6 | 563.2 | 567.0 | 572.9 | 573.2 | 573.8 | 567.3 | 573.6 | 579.8 | 577.5 | 568.4 |
| 2019 | 564.5 | 565.1 | 566.5 | 571.2 | 574.1 | 579.4 | 577.0 | 577.2 | 572.4 | 575.2 | 582.1 | 580.8 | 573.8 |
| **Goods Producing** | | | | | | | | | | | | | |
| 2011 | 61.3 | 61.5 | 62.0 | 62.4 | 62.6 | 62.7 | 63.0 | 62.8 | 62.6 | 63.2 | 63.1 | 63.0 | 62.5 |
| 2012 | 61.1 | 60.7 | 61.7 | 62.7 | 63.2 | 63.7 | 63.7 | 64.2 | 64.0 | 63.7 | 63.6 | 63.5 | 63.0 |
| 2013 | 61.9 | 62.5 | 63.3 | 64.0 | 64.3 | 65.1 | 65.2 | 65.2 | 64.8 | 64.2 | 64.1 | 63.6 | 64.0 |
| 2014 | 62.5 | 62.3 | 63.1 | 64.1 | 64.9 | 65.3 | 65.9 | 66.1 | 65.9 | 65.8 | 65.6 | 65.6 | 64.8 |
| 2015 | 64.2 | 64.3 | 65.2 | 66.8 | 67.5 | 67.6 | 68.5 | 68.7 | 68.5 | 68.2 | 67.8 | 67.5 | 67.1 |
| 2016 | 66.3 | 66.6 | 67.2 | 68.1 | 68.4 | 69.0 | 69.5 | 69.2 | 69.4 | 69.6 | 69.4 | 69.0 | 68.5 |
| 2017 | 67.2 | 68.0 | 68.8 | 69.5 | 70.0 | 71.1 | 71.5 | 71.6 | 71.5 | 71.1 | 70.6 | 70.5 | 70.1 |
| 2018 | 69.0 | 69.6 | 69.9 | 70.7 | 71.4 | 72.5 | 73.0 | 73.1 | 72.8 | 72.8 | 72.8 | 72.1 | 71.6 |
| 2019 | 70.7 | 70.9 | 71.3 | 71.7 | 72.3 | 72.5 | 72.7 | 72.5 | 72.1 | 72.2 | 72.4 | 72.3 | 72.0 |
| **Service-Providing** | | | | | | | | | | | | | |
| 2011 | 525.5 | 527.5 | 531.4 | 537.7 | 538.1 | 539.9 | 538.4 | 535.8 | 538.7 | 544.2 | 547.7 | 546.3 | 537.6 |
| 2012 | 536.5 | 539.0 | 543.0 | 547.7 | 549.6 | 553.3 | 547.0 | 549.4 | 550.6 | 555.4 | 558.4 | 560.3 | 549.2 |
| 2013 | 546.7 | 548.8 | 552.4 | 556.9 | 556.8 | 559.1 | 556.8 | 557.7 | 558.1 | 560.9 | 570.0 | 568.3 | 557.7 |
| 2014 | 557.5 | 555.7 | 560.2 | 566.6 | 570.4 | 572.2 | 566.9 | 568.0 | 567.0 | 570.8 | 577.1 | 577.6 | 567.5 |
| 2015 | 568.4 | 568.6 | 570.3 | 577.2 | 581.6 | 584.4 | 582.7 | 583.5 | 586.5 | 594.0 | 600.4 | 599.4 | 583.1 |
| 2016 | 585.1 | 586.8 | 588.7 | 594.5 | 593.3 | 596.2 | 589.9 | 591.1 | 593.3 | 598.2 | 604.1 | 604.9 | 593.8 |
| 2017 | 589.2 | 594.1 | 596.1 | 598.0 | 599.7 | 603.8 | 598.8 | 598.8 | 599.8 | 603.2 | 607.7 | 607.3 | 599.7 |
| 2018 | 596.1 | 600.7 | 602.1 | 604.5 | 606.3 | 611.2 | 609.1 | 610.4 | 605.4 | 613.0 | 620.9 | 618.3 | 608.2 |
| 2019 | 605.7 | 608.1 | 609.1 | 613.2 | 613.6 | 619.2 | 614.0 | 613.8 | 612.6 | 617.6 | 625.5 | 623.9 | 614.7 |
| **Mining, Logging, and Construction** | | | | | | | | | | | | | |
| 2011 | 30.7 | 30.7 | 31.2 | 31.7 | 31.9 | 31.9 | 32.3 | 32.1 | 31.9 | 32.4 | 32.4 | 32.3 | 31.8 |
| 2012 | 31.0 | 30.7 | 31.5 | 32.3 | 32.7 | 33.0 | 33.2 | 33.6 | 33.5 | 33.2 | 33.2 | 32.9 | 32.6 |
| 2013 | 31.6 | 31.9 | 32.7 | 33.3 | 33.4 | 34.0 | 34.1 | 34.2 | 33.9 | 33.3 | 33.2 | 32.7 | 33.2 |
| 2014 | 31.7 | 31.7 | 32.5 | 33.4 | 34.0 | 34.3 | 34.9 | 34.9 | 34.8 | 34.9 | 34.7 | 34.6 | 33.9 |
| 2015 | 33.6 | 33.8 | 34.6 | 36.2 | 36.7 | 36.6 | 37.5 | 37.7 | 37.5 | 37.2 | 36.7 | 36.3 | 36.2 |
| 2016 | 35.2 | 35.3 | 35.8 | 36.6 | 36.9 | 37.3 | 37.7 | 37.5 | 37.7 | 37.9 | 37.8 | 37.2 | 36.9 |
| 2017 | 35.7 | 36.2 | 36.9 | 37.3 | 37.8 | 38.7 | 39.0 | 39.1 | 39.1 | 39.0 | 38.6 | 38.5 | 38.0 |
| 2018 | 37.5 | 37.9 | 38.3 | 39.1 | 39.5 | 40.4 | 40.8 | 40.9 | 40.2 | 40.6 | 40.7 | 40.0 | 39.7 |
| 2019 | 38.8 | 38.9 | 39.5 | 39.7 | 40.2 | 40.3 | 40.9 | 41.0 | 40.7 | 41.0 | 41.2 | 41.1 | 40.3 |
| **Manufacturing** | | | | | | | | | | | | | |
| 2011 | 30.6 | 30.8 | 30.8 | 30.7 | 30.7 | 30.8 | 30.7 | 30.7 | 30.7 | 30.8 | 30.7 | 30.7 | 30.7 |
| 2012 | 30.1 | 30.0 | 30.2 | 30.4 | 30.5 | 30.7 | 30.5 | 30.6 | 30.5 | 30.5 | 30.4 | 30.6 | 30.4 |
| 2013 | 30.3 | 30.6 | 30.6 | 30.7 | 30.9 | 31.1 | 31.1 | 31.0 | 30.9 | 30.9 | 30.9 | 30.9 | 30.8 |
| 2014 | 30.8 | 30.6 | 30.6 | 30.7 | 30.9 | 31.0 | 31.0 | 31.2 | 31.1 | 30.9 | 30.9 | 31.0 | 30.9 |
| 2015 | 30.6 | 30.5 | 30.6 | 30.6 | 30.8 | 31.0 | 31.0 | 31.0 | 31.0 | 31.0 | 31.1 | 31.2 | 30.9 |
| 2016 | 31.1 | 31.3 | 31.4 | 31.5 | 31.5 | 31.7 | 31.8 | 31.7 | 31.7 | 31.7 | 31.6 | 31.8 | 31.6 |
| 2017 | 31.5 | 31.8 | 31.9 | 32.2 | 32.2 | 32.4 | 32.5 | 32.5 | 32.4 | 32.1 | 32.0 | 32.0 | 32.1 |
| 2018 | 31.5 | 31.7 | 31.6 | 31.6 | 31.9 | 32.1 | 32.2 | 32.2 | 32.6 | 32.2 | 32.1 | 32.1 | 32.0 |
| 2019 | 31.9 | 32.0 | 31.8 | 32.0 | 32.1 | 32.2 | 31.8 | 31.5 | 31.4 | 31.2 | 31.2 | 31.2 | 31.7 |

## Employment by Industry: Richmond, VA, 2011–2019—*Continued*

(Numbers in thousands, not seasonally adjusted)

| Industry and year | January | February | March | April | May | June | July | August | September | October | November | December | Annual average |
|---|---|---|---|---|---|---|---|---|---|---|---|---|---|
| **Trade, Transportation, and Utilities** | | | | | | | | | | | | | |
| 2011 | 107.3 | 106.5 | 107.0 | 108.5 | 108.8 | 109.3 | 109.3 | 109.5 | 108.6 | 110.0 | 112.6 | 114.2 | 109.3 |
| 2012 | 109.7 | 108.6 | 109.4 | 110.0 | 111.1 | 111.1 | 110.2 | 110.6 | 110.9 | 113.8 | 117.1 | 120.7 | 111.9 |
| 2013 | 112.9 | 111.8 | 112.0 | 112.6 | 113.3 | 113.7 | 114.0 | 114.3 | 113.9 | 115.3 | 118.5 | 120.0 | 114.4 |
| 2014 | 115.6 | 114.9 | 115.7 | 116.6 | 117.3 | 118.1 | 117.7 | 118.1 | 117.0 | 117.5 | 119.7 | 121.2 | 117.5 |
| 2015 | 116.9 | 116.0 | 116.1 | 117.4 | 118.1 | 119.1 | 120.8 | 120.9 | 120.6 | 121.5 | 124.2 | 125.7 | 119.8 |
| 2016 | 121.1 | 120.2 | 120.4 | 121.2 | 121.5 | 122.2 | 121.1 | 121.4 | 120.7 | 121.3 | 124.6 | 125.3 | 121.8 |
| 2017 | 120.3 | 119.0 | 119.0 | 120.2 | 121.0 | 122.1 | 121.6 | 121.6 | 122.4 | 123.0 | 126.3 | 127.1 | 122.0 |
| 2018 | 122.0 | 121.8 | 121.9 | 122.0 | 122.8 | 123.7 | 123.6 | 123.6 | 123.0 | 124.0 | 128.2 | 130.1 | 123.9 |
| 2019 | 122.0 | 120.5 | 120.5 | 120.7 | 121.6 | 122.0 | 121.6 | 121.7 | 121.0 | 121.2 | 123.2 | 125.2 | 121.8 |
| **Wholesale Trade** | | | | | | | | | | | | | |
| 2011 | 26.6 | 26.6 | 26.8 | 26.9 | 26.9 | 27.1 | 27.3 | 27.2 | 27.0 | 26.9 | 27.0 | 27.0 | 26.9 |
| 2012 | 26.8 | 26.9 | 27.2 | 27.6 | 27.8 | 28.0 | 27.8 | 28.0 | 27.9 | 27.9 | 28.0 | 28.0 | 27.7 |
| 2013 | 28.0 | 28.1 | 28.2 | 28.2 | 28.2 | 28.3 | 28.4 | 28.3 | 28.2 | 28.2 | 28.1 | 28.1 | 28.2 |
| 2014 | 27.7 | 27.7 | 27.8 | 27.9 | 28.1 | 28.3 | 28.3 | 28.4 | 28.2 | 28.0 | 28.1 | 28.2 | 28.1 |
| 2015 | 28.2 | 28.3 | 28.3 | 28.5 | 28.7 | 28.9 | 28.9 | 28.9 | 28.9 | 28.9 | 29.0 | 29.1 | 28.7 |
| 2016 | 28.6 | 28.5 | 28.6 | 28.6 | 28.6 | 28.5 | 28.5 | 28.5 | 28.4 | 28.4 | 28.5 | 28.6 | 28.5 |
| 2017 | 28.3 | 28.4 | 28.6 | 28.6 | 28.7 | 28.9 | 28.7 | 28.8 | 28.8 | 28.6 | 28.7 | 28.6 | 28.6 |
| 2018 | 28.4 | 28.4 | 28.4 | 28.3 | 28.2 | 28.4 | 28.4 | 28.4 | 28.2 | 28.0 | 27.8 | 27.8 | 28.2 |
| 2019 | 27.8 | 27.8 | 27.8 | 27.9 | 28.0 | 28.2 | 28.1 | 28.2 | 27.9 | 27.9 | 27.5 | 27.4 | 27.9 |
| **Retail Trade** | | | | | | | | | | | | | |
| 2011 | 63.3 | 62.5 | 62.7 | 63.4 | 63.6 | 63.7 | 63.3 | 63.6 | 62.9 | 64.3 | 66.6 | 67.8 | 64.0 |
| 2012 | 64.4 | 63.3 | 63.6 | 63.7 | 64.5 | 64.2 | 63.6 | 63.8 | 64.1 | 67.1 | 70.1 | 73.0 | 65.5 |
| 2013 | 65.6 | 64.5 | 64.4 | 64.9 | 65.5 | 65.6 | 65.7 | 65.9 | 65.5 | 66.9 | 69.7 | 70.3 | 66.2 |
| 2014 | 66.9 | 66.5 | 67.0 | 67.5 | 67.6 | 67.8 | 67.3 | 67.3 | 66.3 | 66.8 | 68.4 | 69.0 | 67.4 |
| 2015 | 65.4 | 64.5 | 64.5 | 65.1 | 65.5 | 66.0 | 66.1 | 66.0 | 65.5 | 66.1 | 68.0 | 68.5 | 65.9 |
| 2016 | 65.7 | 65.4 | 65.5 | 66.2 | 66.5 | 66.9 | 66.7 | 66.8 | 65.9 | 66.6 | 68.7 | 68.9 | 66.7 |
| 2017 | 66.2 | 65.3 | 65.5 | 65.9 | 66.4 | 67.1 | 67.2 | 66.6 | 66.0 | 66.8 | 68.9 | 69.3 | 66.8 |
| 2018 | 66.6 | 66.0 | 66.1 | 66.1 | 66.7 | 67.0 | 66.7 | 66.8 | 66.0 | 66.1 | 68.4 | 68.3 | 66.7 |
| 2019 | 66.1 | 65.4 | 65.6 | 65.8 | 66.3 | 66.3 | 65.9 | 65.8 | 65.2 | 65.4 | 67.4 | 68.3 | 66.1 |
| **Transportation and Utilities** | | | | | | | | | | | | | |
| 2011 | 17.4 | 17.4 | 17.5 | 18.2 | 18.3 | 18.5 | 18.7 | 18.7 | 18.7 | 18.8 | 19.0 | 19.4 | 18.4 |
| 2012 | 18.5 | 18.4 | 18.6 | 18.7 | 18.8 | 18.9 | 18.8 | 18.8 | 18.9 | 18.8 | 19.0 | 19.7 | 18.8 |
| 2013 | 19.3 | 19.2 | 19.4 | 19.5 | 19.6 | 19.8 | 19.9 | 20.1 | 20.2 | 20.2 | 20.7 | 21.6 | 20.0 |
| 2014 | 21.0 | 20.7 | 20.9 | 21.2 | 21.6 | 22.0 | 22.1 | 22.4 | 22.5 | 22.7 | 23.2 | 24.0 | 22.0 |
| 2015 | 23.3 | 23.2 | 23.3 | 23.8 | 23.9 | 24.2 | 25.8 | 26.0 | 26.2 | 26.5 | 27.2 | 28.1 | 25.1 |
| 2016 | 26.8 | 26.3 | 26.3 | 26.4 | 26.4 | 26.8 | 25.9 | 26.1 | 26.4 | 26.3 | 27.4 | 27.8 | 26.6 |
| 2017 | 25.8 | 25.3 | 24.9 | 25.7 | 25.9 | 26.1 | 25.7 | 26.2 | 27.6 | 27.6 | 28.7 | 29.2 | 26.6 |
| 2018 | 27.0 | 27.4 | 27.4 | 27.6 | 27.9 | 28.3 | 28.5 | 28.4 | 28.8 | 29.9 | 32.0 | 34.0 | 28.9 |
| 2019 | 28.1 | 27.3 | 27.1 | 27.0 | 27.3 | 27.5 | 27.6 | 27.7 | 27.9 | 27.9 | 28.3 | 29.5 | 27.8 |
| **Information** | | | | | | | | | | | | | |
| 2011 | 9.2 | 9.2 | 9.1 | 8.9 | 8.9 | 8.9 | 9.0 | 7.6 | 8.6 | 9.3 | 9.3 | 9.5 | 9.0 |
| 2012 | 8.1 | 8.1 | 8.2 | 8.1 | 8.1 | 8.2 | 8.1 | 8.3 | 7.7 | 7.7 | 8.0 | 8.0 | 8.1 |
| 2013 | 7.8 | 8.0 | 8.1 | 8.5 | 7.9 | 8.1 | 7.9 | 8.0 | 7.8 | 7.8 | 7.9 | 8.0 | 8.0 |
| 2014 | 8.3 | 7.9 | 7.9 | 7.9 | 8.1 | 7.6 | 7.9 | 8.1 | 7.7 | 7.8 | 7.6 | 7.6 | 7.9 |
| 2015 | 7.5 | 7.5 | 7.4 | 7.4 | 7.6 | 7.4 | 7.6 | 7.5 | 7.5 | 7.6 | 7.4 | 7.3 | 7.5 |
| 2016 | 7.3 | 7.4 | 7.2 | 7.5 | 6.8 | 7.6 | 7.5 | 7.5 | 7.7 | 7.3 | 7.2 | 7.4 | 7.4 |
| 2017 | 7.1 | 7.4 | 7.5 | 7.3 | 7.5 | 7.5 | 7.4 | 7.5 | 7.7 | 7.6 | 7.9 | 7.7 | 7.5 |
| 2018 | 7.4 | 7.5 | 7.4 | 7.2 | 7.5 | 7.4 | 7.4 | 7.1 | 6.9 | 7.0 | 7.2 | 6.8 | 7.2 |
| 2019 | 6.8 | 7.0 | 6.9 | 6.8 | 7.3 | 7.0 | 7.0 | 7.1 | 7.0 | 7.1 | 7.1 | 7.1 | 7.0 |
| **Financial Activities** | | | | | | | | | | | | | |
| 2011 | 42.2 | 42.3 | 42.6 | 42.8 | 43.1 | 43.4 | 44.0 | 44.2 | 44.0 | 44.3 | 44.7 | 45.1 | 43.6 |
| 2012 | 44.4 | 44.7 | 44.9 | 45.4 | 45.6 | 46.1 | 46.2 | 46.4 | 46.2 | 46.2 | 46.4 | 46.5 | 45.8 |
| 2013 | 46.0 | 46.1 | 46.3 | 46.6 | 46.7 | 47.0 | 47.5 | 47.6 | 47.3 | 47.3 | 47.4 | 47.3 | 46.9 |
| 2014 | 47.0 | 47.3 | 47.2 | 47.3 | 47.5 | 47.8 | 47.9 | 48.0 | 47.5 | 47.8 | 48.2 | 48.4 | 47.7 |
| 2015 | 48.4 | 48.8 | 48.8 | 49.0 | 49.0 | 49.2 | 49.4 | 49.5 | 49.1 | 49.2 | 49.2 | 49.1 | 49.1 |
| 2016 | 48.0 | 48.0 | 47.9 | 48.5 | 48.7 | 48.8 | 48.8 | 49.1 | 48.8 | 49.0 | 49.4 | 49.6 | 48.7 |
| 2017 | 48.7 | 49.1 | 49.0 | 49.0 | 49.3 | 49.8 | 50.0 | 50.0 | 49.4 | 49.6 | 49.6 | 49.6 | 49.4 |
| 2018 | 49.6 | 50.3 | 50.2 | 50.4 | 50.6 | 51.0 | 51.5 | 51.6 | 51.3 | 51.6 | 51.8 | 51.8 | 51.0 |
| 2019 | 51.8 | 52.0 | 52.0 | 52.3 | 52.8 | 53.6 | 53.7 | 53.5 | 53.2 | 53.1 | 54.1 | 53.3 | 53.0 |

# Employment by Industry: Richmond, VA, 2011–2019—*Continued*

(Numbers in thousands, not seasonally adjusted)

| Industry and year | January | February | March | April | May | June | July | August | September | October | November | December | Annual average |
|---|---|---|---|---|---|---|---|---|---|---|---|---|---|
| **Professional and Business Services** | | | | | | | | | | | | | |
| 2011 | 94.1 | 94.7 | 95.8 | 96.6 | 96.4 | 96.0 | 96.6 | 96.5 | 96.9 | 97.4 | 98.4 | 96.4 | 96.3 |
| 2012 | 95.9 | 96.8 | 96.9 | 98.1 | 98.5 | 99.3 | 99.5 | 100.0 | 100.5 | 101.0 | 100.0 | 99.7 | 98.9 |
| 2013 | 98.4 | 98.8 | 99.3 | 98.9 | 99.3 | 99.2 | 99.7 | 100.7 | 100.3 | 100.9 | 105.4 | 103.9 | 100.4 |
| 2014 | 100.7 | 99.1 | 99.6 | 101.2 | 102.7 | 102.6 | 101.6 | 101.5 | 101.8 | 103.6 | 108.3 | 108.1 | 102.6 |
| 2015 | 105.0 | 103.8 | 104.2 | 106.1 | 108.2 | 109.0 | 108.1 | 108.6 | 110.3 | 113.8 | 118.0 | 118.1 | 109.4 |
| 2016 | 111.8 | 111.0 | 110.6 | 111.9 | 112.0 | 111.8 | 110.8 | 111.0 | 112.7 | 114.6 | 116.9 | 119.0 | 112.8 |
| 2017 | 112.6 | 113.6 | 113.2 | 113.2 | 114.4 | 115.4 | 114.1 | 114.1 | 114.5 | 115.3 | 117.5 | 117.9 | 114.7 |
| 2018 | 114.7 | 115.2 | 114.6 | 114.9 | 116.0 | 116.9 | 116.6 | 117.2 | 116.0 | 119.2 | 121.3 | 119.8 | 116.9 |
| 2019 | 116.9 | 116.3 | 115.9 | 118.0 | 118.6 | 119.6 | 118.3 | 119.1 | 118.8 | 119.7 | 122.4 | 122.0 | 118.8 |
| **Education and Health Services** | | | | | | | | | | | | | |
| 2011 | 84.7 | 85.2 | 85.3 | 86.1 | 85.1 | 84.7 | 85.6 | 85.8 | 87.0 | 88.0 | 88.4 | 87.1 | 86.1 |
| 2012 | 87.0 | 87.5 | 87.7 | 88.9 | 87.7 | 87.7 | 87.8 | 88.7 | 90.2 | 90.7 | 90.9 | 90.0 | 88.7 |
| 2013 | 89.6 | 90.5 | 90.7 | 91.1 | 90.1 | 89.2 | 89.9 | 90.7 | 92.0 | 92.8 | 93.3 | 92.0 | 91.0 |
| 2014 | 92.0 | 92.4 | 92.8 | 94.1 | 93.0 | 92.5 | 92.4 | 93.0 | 93.6 | 94.7 | 94.8 | 93.6 | 93.2 |
| 2015 | 94.3 | 94.8 | 94.9 | 95.9 | 94.8 | 94.2 | 94.8 | 95.5 | 96.6 | 97.5 | 97.6 | 96.5 | 95.6 |
| 2016 | 96.9 | 97.4 | 97.3 | 97.7 | 96.4 | 95.7 | 95.0 | 96.4 | 97.1 | 98.9 | 99.0 | 97.5 | 97.1 |
| 2017 | 98.2 | 99.1 | 99.2 | 99.1 | 98.1 | 97.1 | 96.9 | 98.0 | 98.8 | 99.6 | 98.7 | 98.8 | 98.5 |
| 2018 | 99.1 | 99.7 | 99.8 | 100.0 | 98.3 | 98.2 | 98.5 | 99.2 | 100.0 | 101.1 | 101.2 | 100.0 | 99.6 |
| 2019 | 101.6 | 102.8 | 102.7 | 102.6 | 100.7 | 100.7 | 99.7 | 100.3 | 101.2 | 102.3 | 103.7 | 102.8 | 101.8 |
| **Leisure and Hospitality** | | | | | | | | | | | | | |
| 2011 | 47.4 | 48.1 | 49.8 | 52.4 | 54.9 | 56.9 | 56.9 | 56.4 | 54.9 | 54.0 | 52.4 | 52.5 | 53.1 |
| 2012 | 50.6 | 51.3 | 53.3 | 55.2 | 57.4 | 59.7 | 59.1 | 59.0 | 56.7 | 55.5 | 54.0 | 54.1 | 55.5 |
| 2013 | 52.3 | 53.0 | 55.1 | 57.1 | 58.9 | 60.8 | 60.8 | 60.1 | 58.0 | 56.3 | 56.4 | 56.1 | 57.1 |
| 2014 | 53.5 | 53.5 | 55.7 | 58.0 | 60.7 | 62.1 | 61.5 | 61.0 | 59.0 | 58.0 | 56.4 | 56.7 | 58.0 |
| 2015 | 55.2 | 56.0 | 57.4 | 60.1 | 63.0 | 64.4 | 64.9 | 64.6 | 62.9 | 61.7 | 60.6 | 60.0 | 60.9 |
| 2016 | 58.7 | 59.7 | 61.6 | 63.2 | 65.3 | 67.0 | 67.2 | 66.8 | 64.4 | 63.2 | 62.2 | 61.5 | 63.4 |
| 2017 | 59.6 | 61.5 | 63.5 | 65.3 | 67.1 | 69.2 | 68.8 | 68.5 | 64.9 | 64.6 | 63.3 | 62.7 | 64.9 |
| 2018 | 61.1 | 62.3 | 63.9 | 66.0 | 68.2 | 70.6 | 69.8 | 69.4 | 65.2 | 65.5 | 64.9 | 64.9 | 66.0 |
| 2019 | 63.0 | 63.6 | 64.9 | 66.8 | 68.3 | 71.1 | 70.8 | 70.0 | 66.6 | 67.0 | 66.6 | 65.6 | 67.0 |
| **Other Services** | | | | | | | | | | | | | |
| 2011 | 29.2 | 29.3 | 29.4 | 29.8 | 29.7 | 30.0 | 29.9 | 29.8 | 29.4 | 29.5 | 29.5 | 29.6 | 29.6 |
| 2012 | 29.2 | 29.2 | 29.5 | 30.1 | 30.4 | 30.6 | 30.5 | 30.7 | 30.4 | 30.6 | 30.6 | 30.1 | 30.2 |
| 2013 | 29.5 | 29.7 | 30.0 | 30.3 | 30.6 | 30.9 | 31.1 | 31.1 | 30.8 | 30.8 | 30.7 | 30.6 | 30.5 |
| 2014 | 30.3 | 30.3 | 30.5 | 30.8 | 31.1 | 31.5 | 31.4 | 31.4 | 31.1 | 30.9 | 30.9 | 30.8 | 30.9 |
| 2015 | 30.6 | 30.8 | 31.0 | 30.9 | 31.4 | 31.6 | 31.7 | 31.8 | 31.4 | 31.6 | 31.6 | 31.4 | 31.3 |
| 2016 | 31.2 | 31.3 | 31.5 | 32.0 | 32.0 | 32.3 | 32.7 | 32.6 | 32.1 | 32.4 | 32.3 | 32.1 | 32.0 |
| 2017 | 31.9 | 32.0 | 32.3 | 31.9 | 32.0 | 32.3 | 32.5 | 32.3 | 32.2 | 32.3 | 32.1 | 31.9 | 32.1 |
| 2018 | 31.5 | 31.7 | 31.9 | 32.0 | 32.2 | 32.6 | 32.8 | 32.6 | 32.1 | 32.4 | 32.4 | 32.0 | 32.2 |
| 2019 | 31.7 | 32.0 | 32.3 | 32.3 | 32.5 | 32.9 | 33.2 | 33.0 | 32.5 | 32.6 | 32.6 | 32.5 | 32.5 |
| **Government** | | | | | | | | | | | | | |
| 2011 | 111.4 | 112.2 | 112.4 | 112.6 | 111.2 | 110.7 | 107.1 | 106.0 | 109.3 | 111.7 | 112.4 | 111.9 | 110.7 |
| 2012 | 111.6 | 112.8 | 113.1 | 111.9 | 110.8 | 110.6 | 105.6 | 105.7 | 108.0 | 109.9 | 111.4 | 111.2 | 110.2 |
| 2013 | 110.2 | 110.9 | 110.9 | 111.8 | 110.0 | 110.2 | 105.9 | 105.2 | 108.0 | 109.7 | 110.4 | 110.4 | 109.5 |
| 2014 | 110.1 | 110.3 | 110.8 | 110.7 | 110.0 | 110.0 | 106.5 | 106.9 | 109.3 | 110.5 | 111.2 | 111.2 | 109.8 |
| 2015 | 110.5 | 110.9 | 110.5 | 110.4 | 109.5 | 109.5 | 105.4 | 105.1 | 108.1 | 111.1 | 111.8 | 111.3 | 109.5 |
| 2016 | 110.1 | 111.8 | 112.2 | 112.5 | 110.6 | 110.8 | 106.8 | 106.3 | 109.8 | 111.5 | 112.5 | 112.5 | 110.6 |
| 2017 | 110.8 | 112.4 | 112.4 | 112.0 | 110.3 | 110.4 | 107.5 | 106.8 | 109.9 | 111.2 | 112.3 | 111.6 | 110.6 |
| 2018 | 110.7 | 112.2 | 112.4 | 112.0 | 110.7 | 110.8 | 108.9 | 109.7 | 110.9 | 112.2 | 113.9 | 112.9 | 111.4 |
| 2019 | 111.9 | 113.9 | 113.9 | 113.7 | 111.8 | 112.3 | 109.7 | 109.1 | 112.3 | 114.6 | 115.8 | 115.4 | 112.9 |

## Employment by Industry: New Orleans-Metairie, LA, 2011–2019

(Numbers in thousands, not seasonally adjusted)

| Industry and year | January | February | March | April | May | June | July | August | September | October | November | December | Annual average |
|---|---|---|---|---|---|---|---|---|---|---|---|---|---|
| **Total Nonfarm** | | | | | | | | | | | | | |
| 2011 | 533.2 | 536.5 | 539.5 | 541.1 | 541.7 | 536.9 | 533.2 | 536.9 | 538.8 | 542.1 | 546.3 | 548.1 | 539.5 |
| 2012 | 537.1 | 540.5 | 543.0 | 549.4 | 550.8 | 545.1 | 541.0 | 543.5 | 539.7 | 546.8 | 552.0 | 554.0 | 545.2 |
| 2013 | 550.2 | 554.2 | 553.3 | 553.1 | 554.1 | 553.0 | 546.3 | 554.7 | 552.3 | 559.6 | 564.7 | 564.0 | 555.0 |
| 2014 | 554.4 | 559.7 | 563.3 | 563.4 | 565.3 | 567.2 | 562.7 | 567.1 | 564.8 | 571.1 | 578.1 | 578.3 | 566.3 |
| 2015 | 569.2 | 572.0 | 573.2 | 579.2 | 580.4 | 577.1 | 573.2 | 574.3 | 572.1 | 580.6 | 581.7 | 583.2 | 576.4 |
| 2016 | 572.8 | 572.8 | 573.8 | 579.1 | 580.8 | 575.8 | 572.4 | 574.5 | 576.2 | 577.7 | 580.4 | 578.0 | 576.2 |
| 2017 | 570.3 | 576.8 | 574.2 | 577.6 | 581.0 | 576.0 | 567.9 | 570.4 | 571.0 | 576.0 | 580.2 | 579.6 | 575.1 |
| 2018 | 572.3 | 574.3 | 576.4 | 580.9 | 581.8 | 577.9 | 570.8 | 575.4 | 575.6 | 582.9 | 585.4 | 583.1 | 578.1 |
| 2019 | 579.3 | 584.5 | 580.4 | 587.0 | 587.5 | 583.9 | 574.7 | 580.3 | 580.0 | 585.4 | 590.1 | 587.7 | 583.4 |
| **Total Private** | | | | | | | | | | | | | |
| 2011 | 450.8 | 454.1 | 457.4 | 458.8 | 459.6 | 456.8 | 454.8 | 457.1 | 457.5 | 461.3 | 465.4 | 467.6 | 458.4 |
| 2012 | 458.6 | 461.2 | 464.1 | 469.2 | 470.7 | 466.2 | 464.5 | 465.7 | 461.0 | 467.7 | 472.7 | 474.7 | 466.4 |
| 2013 | 472.6 | 476.1 | 475.2 | 475.3 | 476.0 | 476.0 | 472.5 | 481.2 | 477.8 | 484.8 | 489.6 | 488.7 | 478.8 |
| 2014 | 480.8 | 484.8 | 488.1 | 488.8 | 491.0 | 491.1 | 489.8 | 494.2 | 490.5 | 496.3 | 503.1 | 504.1 | 491.9 |
| 2015 | 496.0 | 497.6 | 499.4 | 505.0 | 506.3 | 504.0 | 502.7 | 503.0 | 499.1 | 508.3 | 509.2 | 511.1 | 503.5 |
| 2016 | 501.2 | 500.4 | 501.8 | 506.6 | 506.4 | 503.0 | 502.6 | 504.4 | 505.0 | 505.4 | 508.0 | 505.9 | 504.2 |
| 2017 | 499.1 | 504.4 | 502.1 | 503.5 | 506.7 | 503.1 | 497.9 | 500.0 | 499.4 | 503.0 | 506.7 | 506.4 | 502.7 |
| 2018 | 500.3 | 501.3 | 503.7 | 506.0 | 506.7 | 504.3 | 500.2 | 504.5 | 503.5 | 509.5 | 511.5 | 510.0 | 505.1 |
| 2019 | 506.8 | 510.6 | 507.2 | 511.6 | 512.2 | 510.1 | 503.9 | 509.1 | 507.7 | 511.6 | 516.1 | 514.6 | 510.1 |
| **Goods Producing** | | | | | | | | | | | | | |
| 2011 | 72.7 | 72.8 | 73.0 | 73.3 | 73.2 | 72.8 | 73.0 | 72.8 | 72.2 | 72.3 | 72.3 | 72.2 | 72.7 |
| 2012 | 71.2 | 71.3 | 71.5 | 71.0 | 71.6 | 72.0 | 72.2 | 72.1 | 71.9 | 72.0 | 72.1 | 71.4 | 71.7 |
| 2013 | 70.0 | 69.8 | 70.2 | 69.7 | 70.3 | 71.0 | 71.1 | 71.1 | 70.9 | 70.5 | 70.0 | 69.4 | 70.3 |
| 2014 | 68.7 | 69.1 | 69.6 | 69.3 | 69.9 | 69.7 | 69.9 | 69.7 | 69.4 | 69.7 | 69.7 | 70.1 | 69.6 |
| 2015 | 70.2 | 69.6 | 68.7 | 69.2 | 69.1 | 69.2 | 69.2 | 68.8 | 68.5 | 68.8 | 67.9 | 67.6 | 68.9 |
| 2016 | 65.5 | 65.1 | 64.9 | 64.8 | 64.4 | 64.5 | 65.0 | 64.4 | 64.6 | 63.9 | 63.7 | 63.3 | 64.5 |
| 2017 | 63.7 | 64.2 | 63.9 | 64.0 | 64.4 | 64.5 | 64.3 | 64.2 | 64.2 | 64.6 | 64.5 | 65.0 | 64.3 |
| 2018 | 64.4 | 64.1 | 64.7 | 64.5 | 64.7 | 65.4 | 65.0 | 64.7 | 64.6 | 64.6 | 64.0 | 64.0 | 64.6 |
| 2019 | 63.7 | 63.8 | 63.7 | 63.9 | 63.5 | 63.7 | 63.0 | 63.2 | 63.0 | 63.3 | 62.3 | 62.0 | 63.3 |
| **Service-Providing** | | | | | | | | | | | | | |
| 2011 | 460.5 | 463.7 | 466.5 | 467.8 | 468.5 | 464.1 | 460.2 | 464.1 | 466.6 | 469.8 | 474.0 | 475.9 | 466.8 |
| 2012 | 465.9 | 469.2 | 471.5 | 478.4 | 479.2 | 473.1 | 468.8 | 471.4 | 467.8 | 474.8 | 479.9 | 482.6 | 473.6 |
| 2013 | 480.2 | 484.4 | 483.1 | 483.4 | 483.8 | 482.0 | 475.2 | 483.6 | 481.4 | 489.1 | 494.7 | 494.6 | 484.6 |
| 2014 | 485.7 | 490.6 | 493.7 | 494.1 | 495.4 | 497.5 | 492.8 | 497.4 | 495.4 | 501.4 | 508.4 | 508.2 | 496.7 |
| 2015 | 499.0 | 502.4 | 504.5 | 510.0 | 511.3 | 507.9 | 504.0 | 505.5 | 503.6 | 511.8 | 513.8 | 515.6 | 507.5 |
| 2016 | 507.3 | 507.7 | 508.9 | 514.3 | 516.4 | 511.3 | 507.4 | 510.1 | 511.6 | 513.8 | 516.7 | 514.7 | 511.7 |
| 2017 | 506.6 | 512.6 | 510.3 | 513.6 | 516.6 | 511.5 | 503.6 | 506.2 | 506.8 | 511.4 | 515.7 | 514.6 | 510.8 |
| 2018 | 507.9 | 510.2 | 511.7 | 516.4 | 517.1 | 512.5 | 505.8 | 510.7 | 511.0 | 518.3 | 521.4 | 519.1 | 513.5 |
| 2019 | 515.6 | 520.7 | 516.7 | 523.1 | 524.0 | 520.2 | 511.7 | 517.1 | 517.0 | 522.1 | 527.8 | 525.7 | 520.1 |
| **Mining, Logging, and Construction** | | | | | | | | | | | | | |
| 2011 | 38.8 | 38.8 | 39.2 | 40.1 | 39.8 | 39.6 | 39.5 | 39.4 | 39.0 | 39.1 | 39.1 | 39.0 | 39.3 |
| 2012 | 38.4 | 38.7 | 39.1 | 38.8 | 39.2 | 39.5 | 39.6 | 39.6 | 39.8 | 39.9 | 39.9 | 39.2 | 39.3 |
| 2013 | 38.1 | 38.2 | 38.6 | 38.2 | 38.4 | 38.8 | 38.9 | 38.9 | 38.9 | 38.5 | 38.1 | 37.7 | 38.4 |
| 2014 | 37.2 | 37.7 | 38.2 | 38.2 | 38.4 | 38.4 | 38.7 | 38.6 | 38.6 | 38.9 | 39.1 | 39.4 | 38.5 |
| 2015 | 39.5 | 39.0 | 38.9 | 38.6 | 38.6 | 38.4 | 38.2 | 37.9 | 37.7 | 38.2 | 37.3 | 36.9 | 38.3 |
| 2016 | 35.5 | 35.0 | 34.9 | 34.6 | 34.2 | 34.3 | 34.8 | 34.4 | 34.5 | 34.0 | 33.8 | 33.1 | 34.4 |
| 2017 | 33.2 | 33.5 | 33.4 | 33.7 | 34.0 | 33.9 | 34.0 | 33.9 | 34.1 | 34.5 | 34.3 | 34.6 | 33.9 |
| 2018 | 34.3 | 34.2 | 35.0 | 34.9 | 35.0 | 35.4 | 35.1 | 34.7 | 34.7 | 34.6 | 34.1 | 33.9 | 34.7 |
| 2019 | 33.5 | 33.5 | 33.5 | 33.9 | 33.5 | 33.6 | 33.1 | 33.3 | 33.1 | 33.5 | 32.0 | 31.8 | 33.2 |
| **Manufacturing** | | | | | | | | | | | | | |
| 2011 | 33.9 | 34.0 | 33.8 | 33.2 | 33.4 | 33.2 | 33.5 | 33.4 | 33.2 | 33.2 | 33.2 | 33.2 | 33.4 |
| 2012 | 32.8 | 32.6 | 32.4 | 32.2 | 32.4 | 32.5 | 32.6 | 32.5 | 32.1 | 32.1 | 32.2 | 32.2 | 32.4 |
| 2013 | 31.9 | 31.6 | 31.6 | 31.5 | 31.9 | 32.2 | 32.2 | 32.2 | 32.0 | 32.0 | 31.9 | 31.7 | 31.9 |
| 2014 | 31.5 | 31.4 | 31.4 | 31.1 | 31.5 | 31.3 | 31.2 | 31.1 | 30.8 | 30.8 | 30.6 | 30.7 | 31.1 |
| 2015 | 30.7 | 30.6 | 29.8 | 30.6 | 30.5 | 30.8 | 31.0 | 30.9 | 30.8 | 30.6 | 30.6 | 30.7 | 30.6 |
| 2016 | 30.0 | 30.1 | 30.0 | 30.2 | 30.2 | 30.2 | 30.2 | 30.0 | 30.1 | 29.9 | 29.9 | 30.2 | 30.1 |
| 2017 | 30.5 | 30.7 | 30.5 | 30.3 | 30.4 | 30.6 | 30.3 | 30.3 | 30.1 | 30.1 | 30.2 | 30.4 | 30.4 |
| 2018 | 30.1 | 29.9 | 29.7 | 29.6 | 29.7 | 30.0 | 29.9 | 30.0 | 29.9 | 30.0 | 29.9 | 30.1 | 29.9 |
| 2019 | 30.2 | 30.3 | 30.2 | 30.0 | 30.0 | 30.1 | 29.9 | 29.9 | 29.9 | 29.8 | 30.3 | 30.2 | 30.1 |

# Employment by Industry: New Orleans-Metairie, LA, 2011–2019—*Continued*

(Numbers in thousands, not seasonally adjusted)

| Industry and year | January | February | March | April | May | June | July | August | September | October | November | December | Annual average |
|---|---|---|---|---|---|---|---|---|---|---|---|---|---|
| **Trade, Transportation, and Utilities** | | | | | | | | | | | | | |
| 2011 | 107.8 | 107.4 | 107.5 | 107.7 | 107.9 | 107.7 | 107.8 | 107.6 | 107.3 | 107.9 | 109.9 | 110.7 | 108.1 |
| 2012 | 108.0 | 107.4 | 107.8 | 108.1 | 108.3 | 108.2 | 107.8 | 107.8 | 107.3 | 109.3 | 112.3 | 113.2 | 108.8 |
| 2013 | 111.4 | 110.4 | 111.3 | 110.5 | 110.5 | 110.6 | 110.8 | 111.5 | 111.6 | 112.5 | 114.4 | 116.0 | 111.8 |
| 2014 | 112.6 | 112.1 | 112.7 | 112.8 | 113.6 | 114.2 | 114.6 | 115.2 | 114.8 | 115.5 | 118.1 | 120.2 | 114.7 |
| 2015 | 116.2 | 115.3 | 115.8 | 116.2 | 116.6 | 116.8 | 116.6 | 116.6 | 116.1 | 117.1 | 118.8 | 120.1 | 116.9 |
| 2016 | 116.4 | 115.5 | 115.8 | 115.9 | 115.8 | 115.6 | 115.5 | 115.7 | 115.0 | 115.6 | 117.4 | 118.7 | 116.1 |
| 2017 | 114.5 | 113.8 | 113.8 | 113.5 | 113.7 | 113.7 | 112.7 | 113.0 | 112.4 | 112.7 | 115.0 | 115.9 | 113.7 |
| 2018 | 113.2 | 112.6 | 112.6 | 112.7 | 113.0 | 112.9 | 112.7 | 113.1 | 112.3 | 113.3 | 115.6 | 116.2 | 113.4 |
| 2019 | 113.1 | 112.7 | 112.0 | 111.9 | 112.2 | 111.9 | 111.7 | 112.4 | 111.4 | 111.2 | 114.3 | 114.1 | 112.4 |
| **Wholesale Trade** | | | | | | | | | | | | | |
| 2011 | 23.0 | 23.2 | 23.1 | 22.6 | 22.8 | 22.9 | 22.8 | 22.8 | 22.7 | 22.8 | 22.8 | 22.8 | 22.9 |
| 2012 | 22.4 | 22.5 | 22.5 | 22.8 | 22.7 | 22.7 | 22.6 | 22.6 | 22.5 | 22.5 | 22.5 | 22.6 | 22.6 |
| 2013 | 23.1 | 23.2 | 23.3 | 23.1 | 23.1 | 23.2 | 23.2 | 23.3 | 23.3 | 23.4 | 23.4 | 23.5 | 23.3 |
| 2014 | 23.4 | 23.5 | 23.5 | 23.4 | 23.4 | 23.5 | 23.5 | 23.6 | 23.6 | 23.6 | 23.7 | 23.8 | 23.5 |
| 2015 | 23.3 | 23.3 | 23.4 | 23.4 | 23.5 | 23.5 | 23.4 | 23.4 | 23.2 | 23.4 | 23.3 | 23.4 | 23.4 |
| 2016 | 23.3 | 23.3 | 23.1 | 23.2 | 23.2 | 23.1 | 23.2 | 23.1 | 22.9 | 22.8 | 22.8 | 22.8 | 23.1 |
| 2017 | 22.3 | 22.3 | 22.4 | 22.5 | 22.6 | 22.6 | 22.5 | 22.5 | 22.4 | 22.4 | 22.4 | 22.4 | 22.4 |
| 2018 | 22.6 | 22.7 | 22.6 | 22.5 | 22.5 | 22.6 | 22.7 | 22.6 | 22.3 | 22.5 | 22.4 | 22.5 | 22.5 |
| 2019 | 22.1 | 22.2 | 22.1 | 22.1 | 22.2 | 22.2 | 22.2 | 22.2 | 22.0 | 22.1 | 22.2 | 22.2 | 22.2 |
| **Retail Trade** | | | | | | | | | | | | | |
| 2011 | 58.7 | 58.4 | 58.6 | 58.9 | 58.8 | 58.6 | 58.7 | 58.4 | 58.0 | 58.8 | 60.6 | 61.1 | 59.0 |
| 2012 | 59.2 | 58.4 | 58.5 | 58.5 | 58.7 | 58.6 | 58.6 | 58.3 | 57.9 | 59.5 | 62.1 | 62.6 | 59.2 |
| 2013 | 60.4 | 59.4 | 59.9 | 59.8 | 60.0 | 60.1 | 60.4 | 60.7 | 60.8 | 61.3 | 63.1 | 64.0 | 60.8 |
| 2014 | 61.3 | 60.9 | 61.1 | 61.2 | 61.7 | 62.4 | 62.8 | 62.9 | 62.4 | 63.0 | 65.1 | 66.5 | 62.6 |
| 2015 | 63.5 | 63.0 | 63.4 | 63.5 | 63.8 | 64.2 | 64.0 | 64.0 | 63.5 | 64.4 | 66.1 | 66.8 | 64.2 |
| 2016 | 64.1 | 63.6 | 63.9 | 64.1 | 64.1 | 64.3 | 64.1 | 64.1 | 63.6 | 64.4 | 66.1 | 66.8 | 64.4 |
| 2017 | 63.7 | 63.0 | 63.0 | 62.6 | 62.6 | 62.5 | 61.9 | 62.2 | 61.6 | 62.0 | 64.0 | 64.3 | 62.8 |
| 2018 | 62.0 | 61.1 | 61.2 | 61.1 | 61.4 | 61.1 | 60.9 | 61.0 | 60.5 | 61.0 | 63.0 | 63.1 | 61.5 |
| 2019 | 61.3 | 60.6 | 60.1 | 59.9 | 60.2 | 60.1 | 60.0 | 60.1 | 59.5 | 59.9 | 62.0 | 61.6 | 60.4 |
| **Transportation and Utilities** | | | | | | | | | | | | | |
| 2011 | 26.1 | 25.8 | 25.8 | 26.2 | 26.3 | 26.2 | 26.3 | 26.4 | 26.6 | 26.3 | 26.5 | 26.8 | 26.3 |
| 2012 | 26.4 | 26.5 | 26.8 | 26.8 | 26.9 | 26.9 | 26.6 | 26.9 | 26.9 | 27.3 | 27.7 | 28.0 | 27.0 |
| 2013 | 27.9 | 27.8 | 28.1 | 27.6 | 27.4 | 27.3 | 27.2 | 27.5 | 27.5 | 27.8 | 27.9 | 28.5 | 27.7 |
| 2014 | 27.9 | 27.7 | 28.1 | 28.2 | 28.5 | 28.3 | 28.3 | 28.7 | 28.8 | 28.9 | 29.3 | 29.9 | 28.6 |
| 2015 | 29.4 | 29.0 | 29.0 | 29.3 | 29.3 | 29.1 | 29.2 | 29.2 | 29.4 | 29.3 | 29.4 | 29.9 | 29.3 |
| 2016 | 29.0 | 28.6 | 28.8 | 28.6 | 28.5 | 28.2 | 28.2 | 28.5 | 28.5 | 28.4 | 28.5 | 29.1 | 28.6 |
| 2017 | 28.5 | 28.5 | 28.4 | 28.4 | 28.5 | 28.6 | 28.3 | 28.3 | 28.4 | 28.3 | 28.6 | 29.2 | 28.5 |
| 2018 | 28.6 | 28.8 | 28.8 | 29.1 | 29.1 | 29.2 | 29.1 | 29.5 | 29.5 | 29.8 | 30.2 | 30.6 | 29.4 |
| 2019 | 29.7 | 29.9 | 29.8 | 29.9 | 29.8 | 29.6 | 29.5 | 30.1 | 29.9 | 29.2 | 30.1 | 30.3 | 29.8 |
| **Information** | | | | | | | | | | | | | |
| 2011 | 6.9 | 6.8 | 8.4 | 7.6 | 8.5 | 8.0 | 6.9 | 6.9 | 7.1 | 7.4 | 7.4 | 8.0 | 7.5 |
| 2012 | 7.2 | 7.8 | 8.0 | 10.5 | 11.9 | 9.2 | 8.6 | 8.7 | 7.9 | 7.7 | 8.6 | 8.9 | 8.8 |
| 2013 | 9.1 | 10.1 | 9.2 | 9.6 | 10.2 | 10.5 | 7.6 | 8.3 | 8.0 | 9.6 | 10.6 | 9.1 | 9.3 |
| 2014 | 7.4 | 8.4 | 9.0 | 8.5 | 8.7 | 8.2 | 8.2 | 8.0 | 7.6 | 7.7 | 9.6 | 9.0 | 8.4 |
| 2015 | 6.8 | 8.4 | 8.5 | 9.8 | 10.3 | 9.7 | 9.2 | 8.6 | 8.1 | 9.0 | 9.6 | 9.8 | 9.0 |
| 2016 | 8.7 | 8.1 | 7.9 | 7.9 | 7.5 | 6.7 | 7.3 | 8.0 | 6.6 | 6.8 | 8.0 | 6.7 | 7.5 |
| 2017 | 6.5 | 8.3 | 7.6 | 8.2 | 8.7 | 6.7 | 6.4 | 7.2 | 7.0 | 7.1 | 7.2 | 7.0 | 7.3 |
| 2018 | 7.3 | 8.0 | 8.1 | 8.3 | 8.7 | 7.7 | 6.8 | 7.3 | 7.0 | 7.2 | 7.9 | 7.3 | 7.6 |
| 2019 | 7.0 | 9.0 | 8.1 | 8.7 | 8.9 | 7.4 | 7.1 | 8.0 | 7.2 | 6.9 | 7.2 | 6.8 | 7.7 |
| **Financial Activities** | | | | | | | | | | | | | |
| 2011 | 26.7 | 26.7 | 26.7 | 26.4 | 26.6 | 26.5 | 26.8 | 26.8 | 26.7 | 26.9 | 27.0 | 27.0 | 26.7 |
| 2012 | 26.7 | 26.8 | 26.8 | 26.8 | 26.9 | 27.0 | 26.9 | 26.9 | 26.8 | 27.0 | 27.1 | 27.1 | 26.9 |
| 2013 | 27.0 | 27.1 | 27.1 | 27.3 | 27.5 | 27.6 | 27.8 | 28.0 | 27.9 | 28.2 | 28.1 | 28.1 | 27.6 |
| 2014 | 28.0 | 28.2 | 28.3 | 28.6 | 28.7 | 28.9 | 29.0 | 29.1 | 28.9 | 29.1 | 29.3 | 29.3 | 28.8 |
| 2015 | 29.3 | 29.4 | 29.5 | 29.6 | 29.6 | 29.7 | 29.7 | 29.7 | 29.5 | 29.8 | 29.9 | 29.8 | 29.6 |
| 2016 | 29.6 | 29.6 | 29.6 | 30.0 | 30.2 | 30.1 | 30.3 | 30.3 | 30.5 | 30.5 | 30.3 | 30.2 | 30.1 |
| 2017 | 29.9 | 30.0 | 29.8 | 29.7 | 29.9 | 29.9 | 30.1 | 30.0 | 29.8 | 30.0 | 30.2 | 30.4 | 30.0 |
| 2018 | 30.0 | 30.2 | 30.3 | 30.3 | 30.3 | 30.2 | 30.2 | 30.2 | 30.0 | 30.3 | 30.3 | 30.3 | 30.2 |
| 2019 | 30.2 | 30.3 | 30.2 | 30.4 | 30.5 | 30.5 | 30.5 | 30.6 | 30.5 | 30.4 | 31.1 | 31.2 | 30.5 |

## Employment by Industry: New Orleans-Metairie, LA, 2011–2019—*Continued*

(Numbers in thousands, not seasonally adjusted)

| Industry and year | January | February | March | April | May | June | July | August | September | October | November | December | Annual average |
|---|---|---|---|---|---|---|---|---|---|---|---|---|---|
| **Professional and Business Services** | | | | | | | | | | | | | |
| 2011 | 67.1 | 68.6 | 68.3 | 68.8 | 68.5 | 68.1 | 67.4 | 68.0 | 68.0 | 69.7 | 69.8 | 69.9 | 68.5 |
| 2012 | 67.8 | 69.0 | 69.5 | 71.4 | 71.0 | 69.4 | 69.8 | 69.1 | 68.1 | 70.5 | 70.4 | 70.0 | 69.7 |
| 2013 | 70.3 | 73.6 | 71.7 | 72.0 | 71.7 | 71.6 | 72.2 | 72.6 | 71.9 | 74.0 | 74.1 | 74.4 | 72.5 |
| 2014 | 73.0 | 74.1 | 74.8 | 75.4 | 74.7 | 75.0 | 74.2 | 74.3 | 73.4 | 75.3 | 75.6 | 75.8 | 74.6 |
| | | | | | | | | | | | | | |
| 2015 | 74.1 | 74.5 | 75.4 | 77.0 | 76.4 | 75.5 | 75.3 | 75.3 | 73.7 | 75.8 | 75.3 | 75.2 | 75.3 |
| 2016 | 74.0 | 74.6 | 74.7 | 76.9 | 76.7 | 75.4 | 74.6 | 74.8 | 76.3 | 75.9 | 75.3 | 74.3 | 75.3 |
| 2017 | 74.4 | 76.4 | 75.5 | 74.7 | 75.5 | 74.6 | 74.6 | 74.1 | 74.3 | 76.2 | 77.3 | 75.1 | 75.2 |
| 2018 | 74.0 | 74.7 | 75.1 | 75.1 | 74.7 | 74.4 | 74.1 | 74.1 | 74.0 | 76.0 | 75.7 | 75.1 | 74.8 |
| 2019 | 75.3 | 76.0 | 76.0 | 77.0 | 76.6 | 76.6 | 76.0 | 75.8 | 75.9 | 78.4 | 79.4 | 78.3 | 76.8 |
| | | | | | | | | | | | | | |
| **Education and Health Services** | | | | | | | | | | | | | |
| 2011 | 77.5 | 78.6 | 79.1 | 79.8 | 79.1 | 77.4 | 77.5 | 78.6 | 80.2 | 81.4 | 82.1 | 81.7 | 79.4 |
| 2012 | 80.0 | 81.0 | 81.8 | 81.7 | 81.7 | 81.0 | 80.4 | 81.9 | 81.9 | 82.7 | 82.9 | 83.0 | 81.7 |
| 2013 | 84.4 | 84.9 | 84.5 | 84.0 | 83.6 | 82.2 | 81.5 | 85.9 | 86.6 | 88.3 | 88.4 | 88.2 | 85.2 |
| 2014 | 87.7 | 88.3 | 88.4 | 88.7 | 88.9 | 88.0 | 88.1 | 91.0 | 91.8 | 92.3 | 92.7 | 92.3 | 89.9 |
| | | | | | | | | | | | | | |
| 2015 | 92.3 | 92.7 | 92.9 | 94.2 | 94.4 | 93.3 | 93.2 | 95.1 | 95.7 | 97.8 | 97.7 | 97.8 | 94.8 |
| 2016 | 97.1 | 97.4 | 97.7 | 98.8 | 99.1 | 98.2 | 98.3 | 100.0 | 100.8 | 100.5 | 100.9 | 100.8 | 99.1 |
| 2017 | 99.0 | 99.6 | 99.2 | 100.0 | 100.0 | 99.4 | 96.6 | 98.6 | 99.6 | 99.3 | 99.5 | 99.1 | 99.2 |
| 2018 | 98.0 | 98.5 | 98.2 | 99.9 | 100.1 | 98.0 | 96.7 | 100.2 | 100.5 | 102.3 | 102.4 | 102.2 | 99.8 |
| 2019 | 101.7 | 102.5 | 101.7 | 103.5 | 103.5 | 102.6 | 101.0 | 103.6 | 104.0 | 105.8 | 105.0 | 104.1 | 103.3 |
| | | | | | | | | | | | | | |
| **Leisure and Hospitality** | | | | | | | | | | | | | |
| 2011 | 70.9 | 71.9 | 73.0 | 73.6 | 74.2 | 74.5 | 73.6 | 74.6 | 74.3 | 73.8 | 74.9 | 76.1 | 73.8 |
| 2012 | 75.8 | 75.9 | 76.5 | 77.4 | 76.9 | 76.9 | 76.3 | 76.8 | 74.8 | 76.1 | 76.9 | 78.6 | 76.6 |
| 2013 | 77.9 | 77.6 | 78.5 | 79.3 | 79.3 | 79.5 | 78.4 | 80.7 | 78.0 | 78.8 | 81.1 | 80.6 | 79.1 |
| 2014 | 80.4 | 81.7 | 82.3 | 82.5 | 83.3 | 83.9 | 82.6 | 83.7 | 81.6 | 83.5 | 84.9 | 84.0 | 82.9 |
| | | | | | | | | | | | | | |
| 2015 | 83.8 | 84.3 | 85.2 | 85.3 | 85.9 | 85.8 | 85.3 | 84.8 | 83.6 | 86.1 | 86.1 | 86.9 | 85.3 |
| 2016 | 86.1 | 86.4 | 87.4 | 87.9 | 88.4 | 88.2 | 87.2 | 86.8 | 87.0 | 88.0 | 88.1 | 87.8 | 87.4 |
| 2017 | 86.8 | 87.8 | 88.1 | 89.1 | 90.0 | 89.7 | 88.8 | 88.4 | 87.8 | 88.7 | 88.6 | 89.5 | 88.6 |
| 2018 | 88.9 | 88.8 | 90.3 | 90.8 | 90.7 | 91.2 | 90.2 | 90.4 | 90.8 | 91.3 | 91.3 | 90.5 | 90.4 |
| 2019 | 91.6 | 91.9 | 91.2 | 91.6 | 92.4 | 92.7 | 90.1 | 91.0 | 91.4 | 91.2 | 92.4 | 93.7 | 91.8 |
| | | | | | | | | | | | | | |
| **Other Services** | | | | | | | | | | | | | |
| 2011 | 21.2 | 21.3 | 21.4 | 21.6 | 21.6 | 21.8 | 21.8 | 21.8 | 21.7 | 21.9 | 22.0 | 22.0 | 21.7 |
| 2012 | 21.9 | 22.0 | 22.2 | 22.3 | 22.4 | 22.5 | 22.5 | 22.4 | 22.3 | 22.4 | 22.4 | 22.5 | 22.3 |
| 2013 | 22.5 | 22.6 | 22.7 | 22.9 | 22.9 | 23.0 | 23.1 | 23.1 | 22.9 | 22.9 | 22.9 | 22.9 | 22.9 |
| 2014 | 23.0 | 22.9 | 23.0 | 23.0 | 23.2 | 23.2 | 23.2 | 23.2 | 23.0 | 23.2 | 23.2 | 23.4 | 23.1 |
| | | | | | | | | | | | | | |
| 2015 | 23.3 | 23.4 | 23.4 | 23.7 | 24.0 | 24.0 | 24.2 | 24.1 | 23.9 | 23.9 | 23.9 | 23.9 | 23.8 |
| 2016 | 23.8 | 23.7 | 23.8 | 24.4 | 24.3 | 24.3 | 24.4 | 24.4 | 24.2 | 24.2 | 24.3 | 24.1 | 24.2 |
| 2017 | 24.3 | 24.3 | 24.2 | 24.3 | 24.5 | 24.6 | 24.4 | 24.5 | 24.3 | 24.4 | 24.4 | 24.4 | 24.4 |
| 2018 | 24.5 | 24.4 | 24.4 | 24.4 | 24.5 | 24.5 | 24.5 | 24.5 | 24.3 | 24.5 | 24.3 | 24.4 | 24.4 |
| 2019 | 24.2 | 24.4 | 24.3 | 24.6 | 24.6 | 24.7 | 24.5 | 24.5 | 24.3 | 24.4 | 24.4 | 24.4 | 24.4 |
| | | | | | | | | | | | | | |
| **Government** | | | | | | | | | | | | | |
| 2011 | 82.4 | 82.4 | 82.1 | 82.3 | 82.1 | 80.1 | 78.4 | 79.8 | 81.3 | 80.8 | 80.9 | 80.5 | 81.1 |
| 2012 | 78.5 | 79.3 | 78.9 | 80.2 | 80.1 | 78.9 | 76.5 | 77.8 | 78.7 | 79.1 | 79.3 | 79.3 | 78.9 |
| 2013 | 77.6 | 78.1 | 78.1 | 77.8 | 78.1 | 77.0 | 73.8 | 73.5 | 74.5 | 74.8 | 75.1 | 75.3 | 76.1 |
| 2014 | 73.6 | 74.9 | 75.2 | 74.6 | 74.3 | 76.1 | 72.9 | 72.9 | 74.3 | 74.8 | 75.0 | 74.2 | 74.4 |
| | | | | | | | | | | | | | |
| 2015 | 73.2 | 74.4 | 73.8 | 74.2 | 74.1 | 73.1 | 70.5 | 71.3 | 73.0 | 72.3 | 72.5 | 72.1 | 72.9 |
| 2016 | 71.6 | 72.4 | 72.0 | 72.5 | 74.4 | 72.8 | 69.8 | 70.1 | 71.2 | 72.3 | 72.4 | 72.1 | 72.0 |
| 2017 | 71.2 | 72.4 | 72.1 | 74.1 | 74.3 | 72.9 | 70.0 | 70.4 | 71.6 | 73.0 | 73.5 | 73.2 | 72.4 |
| 2018 | 72.0 | 73.0 | 72.7 | 74.9 | 75.1 | 73.6 | 70.6 | 70.9 | 72.1 | 73.4 | 73.9 | 73.1 | 72.9 |
| 2019 | 72.5 | 73.9 | 73.2 | 75.4 | 75.3 | 73.8 | 70.8 | 71.2 | 72.3 | 73.8 | 74.0 | 73.1 | 73.3 |

# Employment by Industry: Louisville/Jefferson County, KY-IN, 2011–2019

(Numbers in thousands, not seasonally adjusted)

| Industry and year | January | February | March | April | May | June | July | August | September | October | November | December | Annual average |
|---|---|---|---|---|---|---|---|---|---|---|---|---|---|
| **Total Nonfarm** | | | | | | | | | | | | | |
| 2011 | 573.1 | 575.5 | 580.4 | 586.1 | 588.6 | 590.9 | 581.7 | 588.5 | 590.0 | 591.1 | 596.1 | 594.4 | 586.4 |
| 2012 | 582.1 | 581.3 | 589.2 | 595.1 | 603.3 | 605.6 | 599.0 | 604.1 | 606.5 | 607.8 | 614.7 | 615.9 | 600.4 |
| 2013 | 599.6 | 600.4 | 605.3 | 611.9 | 615.6 | 616.6 | 609.0 | 618.7 | 618.5 | 619.6 | 625.4 | 626.0 | 613.9 |
| 2014 | 608.5 | 607.7 | 614.0 | 623.0 | 627.1 | 629.9 | 626.8 | 632.3 | 633.1 | 634.7 | 639.8 | 643.0 | 626.7 |
| 2015 | 628.3 | 627.7 | 631.8 | 635.8 | 645.5 | 647.6 | 638.2 | 646.4 | 646.9 | 651.0 | 658.1 | 661.1 | 643.2 |
| 2016 | 644.1 | 644.8 | 650.1 | 655.5 | 660.4 | 662.4 | 661.0 | 662.6 | 663.5 | 661.4 | 667.1 | 670.0 | 658.6 |
| 2017 | 653.2 | 653.2 | 657.2 | 662.7 | 667.2 | 671.0 | 667.3 | 669.1 | 671.1 | 671.3 | 677.6 | 677.6 | 666.5 |
| 2018 | 659.6 | 662.5 | 666.3 | 670.4 | 674.3 | 677.9 | 671.2 | 675.4 | 674.9 | 676.5 | 683.4 | 682.5 | 672.9 |
| 2019 | 666.0 | 666.9 | 670.0 | 671.9 | 677.4 | 678.2 | 673.3 | 677.2 | 677.9 | 679.0 | 680.6 | 683.5 | 675.2 |
| **Total Private** | | | | | | | | | | | | | |
| 2011 | 496.3 | 497.9 | 502.5 | 507.9 | 510.1 | 513.4 | 507.7 | 512.1 | 511.1 | 512.1 | 516.8 | 515.5 | 508.6 |
| 2012 | 503.8 | 502.7 | 510.1 | 516.0 | 524.1 | 527.3 | 524.8 | 527.6 | 527.8 | 528.7 | 535.7 | 537.1 | 522.1 |
| 2013 | 521.5 | 521.3 | 525.6 | 531.7 | 535.3 | 537.1 | 533.1 | 540.6 | 538.6 | 539.8 | 545.3 | 546.1 | 534.7 |
| 2014 | 529.7 | 528.9 | 534.6 | 543.4 | 547.7 | 551.0 | 551.1 | 554.3 | 553.3 | 554.8 | 560.1 | 563.6 | 547.7 |
| 2015 | 549.6 | 549.0 | 552.8 | 556.3 | 565.9 | 569.5 | 564.0 | 570.7 | 569.6 | 573.0 | 579.9 | 583.2 | 565.3 |
| 2016 | 566.9 | 567.7 | 571.8 | 578.0 | 583.1 | 586.1 | 587.2 | 587.6 | 586.8 | 585.6 | 591.1 | 594.3 | 582.2 |
| 2017 | 578.4 | 578.3 | 582.2 | 587.0 | 591.3 | 596.2 | 595.3 | 595.2 | 595.5 | 596.0 | 602.0 | 602.2 | 591.6 |
| 2018 | 585.6 | 587.3 | 590.8 | 594.9 | 598.5 | 602.4 | 598.9 | 601.1 | 598.8 | 599.9 | 607.3 | 606.7 | 597.7 |
| 2019 | 591.6 | 591.9 | 594.8 | 597.7 | 602.8 | 604.3 | 602.4 | 604.2 | 603.5 | 604.5 | 605.9 | 609.0 | 601.1 |
| **Goods Producing** | | | | | | | | | | | | | |
| 2011 | 83.2 | 83.4 | 84.1 | 85.6 | 86.0 | 87.4 | 84.6 | 88.0 | 88.3 | 88.1 | 88.7 | 87.9 | 86.3 |
| 2012 | 87.0 | 85.9 | 89.5 | 91.3 | 92.9 | 94.5 | 94.8 | 95.5 | 95.8 | 95.8 | 96.5 | 96.6 | 93.0 |
| 2013 | 94.4 | 94.3 | 94.8 | 95.8 | 96.5 | 97.5 | 95.0 | 98.6 | 98.4 | 98.2 | 98.4 | 98.3 | 96.7 |
| 2014 | 96.2 | 96.3 | 97.5 | 99.5 | 100.9 | 102.2 | 102.6 | 102.8 | 102.5 | 102.8 | 103.8 | 103.6 | 100.9 |
| 2015 | 102.1 | 101.9 | 102.3 | 101.0 | 105.3 | 106.6 | 103.8 | 107.4 | 107.3 | 107.3 | 107.5 | 107.7 | 105.0 |
| 2016 | 106.1 | 106.5 | 108.1 | 108.2 | 109.5 | 111.3 | 111.9 | 111.5 | 111.1 | 110.3 | 110.7 | 110.1 | 109.6 |
| 2017 | 107.7 | 107.8 | 108.5 | 109.5 | 110.3 | 111.3 | 112.6 | 112.2 | 112.2 | 111.4 | 112.4 | 111.8 | 110.6 |
| 2018 | 110.1 | 110.5 | 111.2 | 112.0 | 112.7 | 114.2 | 113.1 | 114.3 | 112.8 | 113.4 | 113.4 | 113.0 | 112.6 |
| 2019 | 111.9 | 111.5 | 112.2 | 112.3 | 112.7 | 113.8 | 114.1 | 114.8 | 113.6 | 112.1 | 111.1 | 112.2 | 112.7 |
| **Service-Providing** | | | | | | | | | | | | | |
| 2011 | 489.9 | 492.1 | 496.3 | 500.5 | 502.6 | 503.5 | 497.1 | 500.5 | 501.7 | 503.0 | 507.4 | 506.5 | 500.1 |
| 2012 | 495.1 | 495.4 | 499.7 | 503.8 | 510.4 | 511.1 | 504.2 | 508.6 | 510.7 | 512.0 | 518.2 | 519.3 | 507.4 |
| 2013 | 505.2 | 506.1 | 510.5 | 516.1 | 519.1 | 519.1 | 514.0 | 520.1 | 520.1 | 521.4 | 527.0 | 527.7 | 517.2 |
| 2014 | 512.3 | 511.4 | 516.5 | 523.5 | 526.2 | 527.7 | 524.2 | 529.5 | 530.6 | 531.9 | 536.0 | 539.4 | 525.8 |
| 2015 | 526.2 | 525.8 | 529.5 | 534.8 | 540.2 | 541.0 | 534.4 | 539.0 | 539.6 | 543.7 | 550.6 | 553.4 | 538.2 |
| 2016 | 538.0 | 538.3 | 542.0 | 547.3 | 550.9 | 551.1 | 549.1 | 551.1 | 552.4 | 551.1 | 556.4 | 559.9 | 549.0 |
| 2017 | 545.5 | 545.4 | 548.7 | 553.2 | 556.9 | 559.7 | 554.7 | 556.9 | 558.9 | 559.9 | 565.2 | 565.8 | 555.9 |
| 2018 | 549.5 | 552.0 | 555.1 | 558.4 | 561.6 | 563.7 | 558.1 | 561.1 | 562.1 | 563.1 | 570.0 | 569.5 | 560.4 |
| 2019 | 554.1 | 555.4 | 557.8 | 559.6 | 564.7 | 564.4 | 559.2 | 562.4 | 564.3 | 566.9 | 569.5 | 571.3 | 562.5 |
| **Mining, Logging, and Construction** | | | | | | | | | | | | | |
| 2011 | 21.9 | 21.9 | 22.9 | 23.9 | 24.2 | 25.1 | 25.5 | 25.4 | 25.2 | 24.8 | 24.7 | 24.2 | 24.1 |
| 2012 | 22.7 | 22.6 | 23.6 | 24.2 | 24.7 | 25.3 | 25.2 | 25.0 | 24.8 | 24.5 | 24.7 | 24.4 | 24.3 |
| 2013 | 22.7 | 22.5 | 23.2 | 24.1 | 24.7 | 25.4 | 26.1 | 26.1 | 26.0 | 25.7 | 25.7 | 25.4 | 24.8 |
| 2014 | 23.9 | 23.9 | 25.2 | 26.2 | 27.0 | 28.1 | 28.4 | 28.2 | 28.2 | 28.2 | 28.3 | 27.8 | 27.0 |
| 2015 | 26.3 | 26.4 | 26.6 | 27.7 | 28.7 | 29.4 | 30.4 | 29.6 | 29.3 | 29.2 | 28.9 | 28.7 | 28.4 |
| 2016 | 27.0 | 26.7 | 27.3 | 28.2 | 28.4 | 28.9 | 29.2 | 28.9 | 28.6 | 28.5 | 28.5 | 28.1 | 28.2 |
| 2017 | 26.6 | 26.8 | 27.5 | 28.1 | 28.6 | 29.4 | 30.4 | 29.9 | 29.7 | 29.6 | 29.6 | 29.2 | 28.8 |
| 2018 | 27.9 | 28.3 | 29.0 | 29.6 | 30.1 | 31.1 | 31.1 | 30.9 | 30.5 | 30.4 | 30.0 | 29.6 | 29.9 |
| 2019 | 28.7 | 28.4 | 29.2 | 29.5 | 29.9 | 30.5 | 30.7 | 31.0 | 30.4 | 29.7 | 29.5 | 29.4 | 29.7 |
| **Manufacturing** | | | | | | | | | | | | | |
| 2011 | 61.3 | 61.5 | 61.2 | 61.7 | 61.8 | 62.3 | 59.1 | 62.6 | 63.1 | 63.3 | 64.0 | 63.7 | 62.1 |
| 2012 | 64.3 | 63.3 | 65.9 | 67.1 | 68.2 | 69.2 | 69.6 | 70.5 | 71.0 | 71.3 | 71.8 | 72.2 | 68.7 |
| 2013 | 71.7 | 71.8 | 71.6 | 71.7 | 71.8 | 72.1 | 68.9 | 72.5 | 72.4 | 72.5 | 72.7 | 72.9 | 71.9 |
| 2014 | 72.3 | 72.4 | 72.3 | 73.3 | 73.9 | 74.1 | 74.2 | 74.6 | 74.3 | 74.6 | 75.5 | 75.8 | 73.9 |
| 2015 | 75.8 | 75.5 | 75.7 | 73.3 | 76.6 | 77.2 | 73.4 | 77.8 | 78.0 | 78.1 | 78.6 | 79.0 | 76.6 |
| 2016 | 79.1 | 79.8 | 80.8 | 80.0 | 81.1 | 82.4 | 82.7 | 82.6 | 82.5 | 81.8 | 82.2 | 82.0 | 81.4 |
| 2017 | 81.1 | 81.0 | 81.0 | 81.4 | 81.7 | 81.9 | 82.2 | 82.3 | 82.5 | 81.8 | 82.8 | 82.6 | 81.9 |
| 2018 | 82.2 | 82.2 | 82.2 | 82.4 | 82.6 | 83.1 | 82.0 | 83.4 | 82.3 | 83.0 | 83.4 | 83.4 | 82.7 |
| 2019 | 83.2 | 83.1 | 83.0 | 82.8 | 82.8 | 83.3 | 83.4 | 83.8 | 83.2 | 82.4 | 81.6 | 82.8 | 83.0 |

## Employment by Industry: Louisville/Jefferson County, KY-IN, 2011–2019—*Continued*

(Numbers in thousands, not seasonally adjusted)

| Industry and year | January | February | March | April | May | June | July | August | September | October | November | December | Annual average |
|---|---|---|---|---|---|---|---|---|---|---|---|---|---|
| **Trade, Transportation, and Utilities** | | | | | | | | | | | | | |
| 2011 | 128.3 | 127.7 | 128.7 | 129.3 | 129.5 | 130.2 | 129.4 | 129.5 | 129.0 | 129.6 | 132.9 | 134.4 | 129.9 |
| 2012 | 128.3 | 128.0 | 128.5 | 128.8 | 130.0 | 130.8 | 130.4 | 130.5 | 130.7 | 130.6 | 134.2 | 136.4 | 130.6 |
| 2013 | 129.9 | 129.5 | 130.3 | 130.2 | 131.0 | 131.6 | 131.4 | 132.5 | 132.3 | 132.7 | 136.3 | 139.2 | 132.2 |
| 2014 | 132.0 | 131.3 | 131.9 | 132.1 | 133.5 | 134.2 | 134.1 | 135.4 | 135.9 | 137.2 | 140.5 | 144.5 | 135.2 |
| 2015 | 137.7 | 136.8 | 137.3 | 137.3 | 138.5 | 139.6 | 139.0 | 140.7 | 140.4 | 141.8 | 145.1 | 147.4 | 140.1 |
| 2016 | 142.9 | 142.0 | 142.3 | 142.8 | 143.7 | 143.9 | 144.8 | 145.1 | 145.1 | 145.3 | 149.0 | 153.4 | 145.0 |
| 2017 | 145.5 | 144.4 | 144.5 | 144.7 | 145.3 | 146.6 | 146.2 | 147.0 | 146.9 | 147.6 | 152.2 | 154.9 | 147.2 |
| 2018 | 149.1 | 147.8 | 148.1 | 147.3 | 147.9 | 149.1 | 149.0 | 148.9 | 148.3 | 148.9 | 154.1 | 156.5 | 149.6 |
| 2019 | 151.1 | 149.0 | 148.3 | 147.9 | 148.6 | 149.7 | 150.1 | 150.0 | 149.9 | 150.1 | 152.2 | 153.6 | 150.0 |
| **Wholesale Trade** | | | | | | | | | | | | | |
| 2011 | 27.3 | 27.4 | 27.6 | 27.5 | 27.6 | 27.7 | 27.8 | 27.8 | 27.8 | 27.8 | 27.8 | 28.0 | 27.7 |
| 2012 | 27.6 | 27.7 | 27.7 | 27.8 | 28.0 | 28.1 | 28.3 | 28.3 | 28.4 | 28.4 | 28.5 | 28.5 | 28.1 |
| 2013 | 28.5 | 28.7 | 28.7 | 28.6 | 28.6 | 28.7 | 28.7 | 28.9 | 28.9 | 28.8 | 28.9 | 29.0 | 28.8 |
| 2014 | 28.7 | 28.8 | 28.8 | 28.7 | 28.8 | 28.7 | 28.8 | 28.8 | 28.8 | 28.7 | 28.6 | 28.7 | 28.7 |
| 2015 | 28.5 | 28.5 | 28.6 | 28.5 | 28.7 | 28.7 | 28.8 | 29.0 | 29.0 | 29.0 | 29.1 | 29.2 | 28.8 |
| 2016 | 28.8 | 28.8 | 28.9 | 28.9 | 29.0 | 29.0 | 29.1 | 28.8 | 28.8 | 28.8 | 29.0 | 29.2 | 28.9 |
| 2017 | 28.6 | 28.6 | 28.5 | 28.9 | 29.0 | 29.2 | 29.1 | 29.1 | 29.0 | 29.1 | 29.1 | 29.4 | 29.0 |
| 2018 | 29.1 | 29.2 | 29.4 | 29.3 | 29.1 | 29.3 | 29.3 | 29.2 | 29.1 | 29.3 | 29.4 | 29.5 | 29.3 |
| 2019 | 29.3 | 29.5 | 29.5 | 29.6 | 29.8 | 30.0 | 30.1 | 30.2 | 30.1 | 30.0 | 30.4 | 30.2 | 29.9 |
| **Retail Trade** | | | | | | | | | | | | | |
| 2011 | 58.9 | 58.2 | 58.9 | 59.5 | 59.6 | 59.6 | 59.3 | 59.3 | 58.7 | 59.6 | 61.6 | 62.2 | 59.6 |
| 2012 | 59.6 | 59.1 | 59.6 | 59.8 | 60.5 | 60.5 | 61.0 | 60.8 | 60.7 | 60.3 | 60.9 | 63.2 | 63.3 | 60.7 |
| 2013 | 60.0 | 59.6 | 60.0 | 60.2 | 60.8 | 61.1 | 61.0 | 61.3 | 61.0 | 61.4 | 63.6 | 64.3 | 61.2 |
| 2014 | 60.1 | 59.8 | 60.1 | 60.7 | 61.2 | 61.5 | 61.3 | 61.9 | 61.5 | 62.3 | 64.4 | 65.7 | 61.7 |
| 2015 | 62.4 | 61.9 | 62.2 | 62.6 | 63.3 | 63.7 | 63.2 | 63.6 | 62.9 | 63.8 | 65.8 | 66.7 | 63.5 |
| 2016 | 63.6 | 63.6 | 63.8 | 64.4 | 64.8 | 64.8 | 64.7 | 64.6 | 64.3 | 65.1 | 67.4 | 68.3 | 65.0 |
| 2017 | 65.8 | 65.2 | 65.4 | 65.6 | 65.9 | 66.1 | 66.1 | 66.1 | 65.7 | 66.2 | 68.7 | 69.0 | 66.3 |
| 2018 | 65.9 | 65.5 | 65.8 | 65.5 | 66.1 | 66.0 | 65.8 | 65.5 | 64.6 | 64.7 | 67.2 | 67.4 | 65.8 |
| 2019 | 64.9 | 63.8 | 63.8 | 63.6 | 64.1 | 63.9 | 63.7 | 63.4 | 62.8 | 63.1 | 63.5 | 63.7 | 63.7 |
| **Transportation and Utilities** | | | | | | | | | | | | | |
| 2011 | 42.1 | 42.1 | 42.2 | 42.3 | 42.3 | 42.9 | 42.3 | 42.4 | 42.5 | 42.2 | 43.5 | 44.2 | 42.6 |
| 2012 | 41.1 | 41.2 | 41.2 | 41.2 | 41.5 | 41.7 | 41.3 | 41.5 | 42.0 | 41.3 | 42.5 | 44.6 | 41.8 |
| 2013 | 41.4 | 41.2 | 41.6 | 41.4 | 41.6 | 41.8 | 41.7 | 42.3 | 42.4 | 42.5 | 43.8 | 45.9 | 42.3 |
| 2014 | 43.2 | 42.7 | 43.0 | 42.7 | 43.5 | 44.0 | 44.0 | 44.7 | 45.6 | 46.2 | 47.5 | 50.1 | 44.8 |
| 2015 | 46.8 | 46.4 | 46.5 | 46.2 | 46.5 | 47.2 | 47.0 | 48.1 | 48.5 | 49.0 | 50.2 | 51.5 | 47.8 |
| 2016 | 50.5 | 49.6 | 49.6 | 49.5 | 49.9 | 50.1 | 51.0 | 51.7 | 52.0 | 51.4 | 52.6 | 55.9 | 51.2 |
| 2017 | 51.1 | 50.6 | 50.6 | 50.2 | 50.4 | 51.3 | 51.0 | 51.8 | 52.2 | 52.3 | 54.4 | 56.5 | 51.9 |
| 2018 | 54.1 | 53.1 | 52.9 | 52.5 | 52.7 | 53.8 | 53.9 | 54.2 | 54.6 | 54.9 | 57.5 | 59.6 | 54.5 |
| 2019 | 56.9 | 55.7 | 55.0 | 54.7 | 54.7 | 55.8 | 56.3 | 56.4 | 57.0 | 57.0 | 58.3 | 59.7 | 56.5 |
| **Information** | | | | | | | | | | | | | |
| 2011 | 9.2 | 9.1 | 9.1 | 9.2 | 9.2 | 9.1 | 9.2 | 9.1 | 9.1 | 9.1 | 9.3 | 9.3 | 9.2 |
| 2012 | 9.2 | 9.2 | 9.5 | 9.6 | 9.6 | 9.6 | 9.5 | 9.5 | 9.3 | 9.2 | 9.3 | 9.3 | 9.4 |
| 2013 | 9.4 | 9.4 | 9.4 | 9.4 | 9.5 | 9.5 | 9.5 | 9.6 | 9.4 | 9.3 | 9.3 | 9.3 | 9.4 |
| 2014 | 9.4 | 9.4 | 9.5 | 9.4 | 9.4 | 9.4 | 9.3 | 9.3 | 9.1 | 9.2 | 9.3 | 9.2 | 9.3 |
| 2015 | 9.1 | 9.1 | 9.0 | 8.9 | 9.0 | 8.9 | 9.0 | 9.0 | 8.9 | 9.0 | 9.1 | 9.1 | 9.0 |
| 2016 | 9.1 | 9.2 | 9.1 | 9.1 | 9.2 | 9.2 | 9.2 | 9.3 | 9.3 | 9.3 | 9.4 | 9.4 | 9.2 |
| 2017 | 9.3 | 9.3 | 9.4 | 9.4 | 9.4 | 9.4 | 9.3 | 9.3 | 9.3 | 9.4 | 9.2 | 9.1 | 9.3 |
| 2018 | 9.1 | 9.1 | 9.1 | 9.2 | 9.3 | 9.2 | 9.1 | 9.2 | 9.1 | 9.1 | 9.3 | 9.2 | 9.2 |
| 2019 | 9.2 | 9.2 | 9.2 | 9.2 | 9.2 | 9.2 | 9.1 | 9.0 | 8.8 | 8.9 | 8.9 | 8.9 | 9.1 |
| **Financial Activities** | | | | | | | | | | | | | |
| 2011 | 40.2 | 40.4 | 40.4 | 39.8 | 39.9 | 40.2 | 40.1 | 40.3 | 40.6 | 40.6 | 40.7 | 40.8 | 40.3 |
| 2012 | 40.5 | 40.4 | 40.6 | 40.3 | 40.7 | 41.2 | 41.5 | 41.6 | 41.7 | 41.8 | 42.0 | 42.4 | 41.2 |
| 2013 | 42.1 | 42.2 | 42.4 | 42.4 | 42.6 | 43.0 | 43.2 | 43.4 | 43.5 | 43.7 | 43.9 | 44.1 | 43.0 |
| 2014 | 43.9 | 43.9 | 44.0 | 44.0 | 44.4 | 44.6 | 44.9 | 45.0 | 45.2 | 45.5 | 45.7 | 46.0 | 44.8 |
| 2015 | 45.6 | 45.6 | 45.8 | 45.4 | 45.7 | 46.1 | 46.1 | 46.1 | 46.0 | 46.2 | 46.3 | 46.6 | 46.0 |
| 2016 | 46.3 | 46.4 | 46.3 | 46.4 | 46.6 | 46.9 | 47.2 | 46.8 | 46.8 | 47.0 | 46.9 | 47.2 | 46.7 |
| 2017 | 46.6 | 46.4 | 46.3 | 46.3 | 46.5 | 46.9 | 46.7 | 46.6 | 46.7 | 46.8 | 46.8 | 46.9 | 46.6 |
| 2018 | 45.8 | 45.5 | 45.5 | 45.4 | 45.8 | 46.3 | 46.5 | 46.5 | 46.4 | 46.3 | 46.3 | 46.6 | 46.1 |
| 2019 | 46.3 | 46.3 | 46.2 | 46.3 | 46.7 | 47.0 | 47.1 | 47.2 | 47.0 | 47.5 | 47.2 | 47.3 | 46.8 |

## Employment by Industry: Louisville/Jefferson County, KY-IN, 2011–2019—*Continued*

(Numbers in thousands, not seasonally adjusted)

| Industry and year | January | February | March | April | May | June | July | August | September | October | November | December | Annual average |
|---|---|---|---|---|---|---|---|---|---|---|---|---|---|
| **Professional and Business Services** | | | | | | | | | | | | | |
| 2011 | 69.9 | 70.8 | 71.5 | 72.0 | 72.5 | 72.9 | 72.5 | 73.5 | 73.6 | 75.3 | 75.4 | 75.5 | 73.0 |
| 2012 | 72.1 | 71.4 | 72.1 | 73.5 | 74.7 | 74.6 | 73.9 | 75.4 | 76.3 | 77.5 | 79.0 | 78.9 | 75.0 |
| 2013 | 74.4 | 73.8 | 74.9 | 76.9 | 77.0 | 77.4 | 76.8 | 79.3 | 78.9 | 80.6 | 81.5 | 81.0 | 77.7 |
| 2014 | 77.4 | 76.3 | 77.9 | 80.1 | 80.9 | 81.1 | 81.3 | 82.9 | 82.5 | 83.6 | 84.6 | 85.1 | 81.1 |
| 2015 | 82.1 | 81.4 | 82.2 | 84.2 | 85.8 | 85.7 | 84.8 | 85.2 | 85.4 | 86.3 | 88.5 | 89.8 | 85.1 |
| 2016 | 83.9 | 83.2 | 83.1 | 84.8 | 85.7 | 85.7 | 85.2 | 85.8 | 86.3 | 86.8 | 88.5 | 89.0 | 85.7 |
| 2017 | 84.6 | 83.9 | 84.2 | 84.6 | 84.8 | 85.4 | 85.9 | 85.9 | 87.4 | 88.5 | 89.3 | 89.1 | 86.1 |
| 2018 | 84.9 | 85.4 | 85.9 | 87.1 | 86.8 | 87.2 | 86.6 | 87.4 | 87.7 | 88.8 | 90.9 | 89.5 | 87.4 |
| 2019 | 84.6 | 84.4 | 85.8 | 85.8 | 86.5 | 86.8 | 86.1 | 87.3 | 87.8 | 90.8 | 92.1 | 93.1 | 87.6 |
| **Education and Health Services** | | | | | | | | | | | | | |
| 2011 | 84.3 | 84.4 | 84.7 | 84.1 | 84.2 | 84.2 | 84.4 | 84.5 | 84.8 | 84.6 | 84.7 | 83.9 | 84.4 |
| 2012 | 84.6 | 84.8 | 84.9 | 85.3 | 85.6 | 85.8 | 85.4 | 85.7 | 86.0 | 86.6 | 86.9 | 87.1 | 85.7 |
| 2013 | 85.9 | 86.1 | 86.5 | 86.7 | 86.2 | 85.8 | 85.9 | 85.8 | 86.1 | 86.9 | 87.1 | 86.8 | 86.3 |
| 2014 | 85.8 | 86.0 | 86.4 | 86.7 | 86.1 | 85.6 | 85.6 | 86.2 | 87.1 | 87.6 | 86.7 | 87.5 | 86.4 |
| 2015 | 86.6 | 87.0 | 87.6 | 87.4 | 87.4 | 86.6 | 86.5 | 88.3 | 89.3 | 91.1 | 91.5 | 91.5 | 88.4 |
| 2016 | 90.2 | 90.7 | 91.1 | 90.6 | 90.7 | 90.1 | 90.7 | 91.3 | 92.2 | 92.6 | 92.8 | 92.9 | 91.3 |
| 2017 | 94.0 | 94.7 | 95.2 | 96.1 | 96.1 | 96.3 | 95.6 | 95.8 | 96.6 | 97.4 | 97.5 | 97.2 | 96.0 |
| 2018 | 96.5 | 97.3 | 97.5 | 98.1 | 98.0 | 97.1 | 95.7 | 96.2 | 98.1 | 98.4 | 98.7 | 98.7 | 97.5 |
| 2019 | 97.1 | 99.1 | 99.2 | 99.7 | 100.0 | 98.0 | 97.0 | 97.6 | 99.6 | 100.5 | 100.1 | 101.0 | 99.1 |
| **Leisure and Hospitality** | | | | | | | | | | | | | |
| 2011 | 55.8 | 56.5 | 58.2 | 62.1 | 63.0 | 63.3 | 61.3 | 61.3 | 60.0 | 59.3 | 59.6 | 58.0 | 59.9 |
| 2012 | 56.6 | 57.4 | 59.2 | 61.4 | 64.9 | 64.7 | 63.4 | 63.9 | 62.7 | 61.8 | 62.4 | 60.9 | 61.6 |
| 2013 | 59.8 | 60.3 | 61.5 | 64.4 | 66.6 | 66.3 | 65.5 | 65.6 | 64.5 | 63.2 | 63.7 | 62.3 | 63.6 |
| 2014 | 60.4 | 61.1 | 62.6 | 66.6 | 67.5 | 68.8 | 68.2 | 67.7 | 66.1 | 64.3 | 64.5 | 63.1 | 65.1 |
| 2015 | 62.0 | 62.6 | 63.8 | 67.5 | 69.3 | 70.6 | 69.5 | 68.6 | 67.2 | 66.0 | 66.3 | 65.6 | 66.6 |
| 2016 | 63.1 | 64.1 | 65.9 | 69.9 | 71.6 | 72.7 | 71.8 | 71.4 | 69.9 | 67.8 | 67.9 | 66.3 | 68.5 |
| 2017 | 65.0 | 65.9 | 67.8 | 69.9 | 72.2 | 73.6 | 72.3 | 71.7 | 70.0 | 68.6 | 68.4 | 67.0 | 69.4 |
| 2018 | 64.7 | 66.1 | 67.5 | 69.5 | 71.9 | 73.1 | 73.0 | 72.7 | 70.9 | 69.3 | 68.8 | 67.6 | 69.6 |
| 2019 | 66.2 | 67.2 | 68.4 | 71.1 | 73.6 | 74.0 | 73.4 | 72.8 | 71.4 | 69.2 | 68.9 | 67.6 | 70.3 |
| **Other Services** | | | | | | | | | | | | | |
| 2011 | 25.4 | 25.6 | 25.8 | 25.8 | 25.8 | 26.1 | 26.2 | 25.9 | 25.7 | 25.5 | 25.5 | 25.7 | 25.8 |
| 2012 | 25.5 | 25.6 | 25.8 | 25.8 | 25.7 | 26.1 | 25.9 | 25.5 | 25.3 | 25.4 | 25.4 | 25.5 | 25.6 |
| 2013 | 25.6 | 25.7 | 25.8 | 25.9 | 25.9 | 26.0 | 25.8 | 25.8 | 25.5 | 25.2 | 25.1 | 25.1 | 25.6 |
| 2014 | 24.6 | 24.6 | 24.8 | 25.0 | 25.0 | 25.1 | 25.1 | 25.0 | 24.9 | 24.6 | 25.0 | 24.6 | 24.9 |
| 2015 | 24.4 | 24.6 | 24.8 | 24.6 | 24.9 | 25.4 | 25.3 | 25.4 | 25.1 | 25.3 | 25.6 | 25.5 | 25.1 |
| 2016 | 25.3 | 25.6 | 25.9 | 26.2 | 26.1 | 26.3 | 26.4 | 26.4 | 26.1 | 26.5 | 25.9 | 26.0 | 26.1 |
| 2017 | 25.7 | 25.9 | 26.3 | 26.5 | 26.7 | 26.7 | 26.7 | 26.7 | 26.4 | 26.3 | 26.2 | 26.2 | 26.4 |
| 2018 | 25.4 | 25.6 | 26.0 | 26.3 | 26.1 | 26.2 | 25.9 | 25.9 | 25.5 | 25.7 | 25.8 | 25.6 | 25.8 |
| 2019 | 25.2 | 25.2 | 25.5 | 25.4 | 25.5 | 25.8 | 25.5 | 25.5 | 25.4 | 25.4 | 25.4 | 25.3 | 25.4 |
| **Government** | | | | | | | | | | | | | |
| 2011 | 76.8 | 77.6 | 77.9 | 78.2 | 78.5 | 77.5 | 74.0 | 76.4 | 78.9 | 79.0 | 79.3 | 78.9 | 77.8 |
| 2012 | 78.3 | 78.6 | 79.1 | 79.1 | 79.2 | 78.3 | 74.2 | 76.5 | 78.7 | 79.1 | 79.0 | 78.8 | 78.2 |
| 2013 | 78.1 | 79.1 | 79.7 | 80.2 | 80.3 | 79.5 | 75.9 | 78.1 | 79.9 | 79.8 | 80.1 | 79.9 | 79.2 |
| 2014 | 78.8 | 78.8 | 79.4 | 79.6 | 79.4 | 78.9 | 75.7 | 78.0 | 79.8 | 79.9 | 79.7 | 79.4 | 79.0 |
| 2015 | 78.7 | 78.7 | 79.0 | 79.5 | 79.6 | 78.1 | 74.2 | 75.7 | 77.3 | 78.0 | 78.2 | 77.9 | 77.9 |
| 2016 | 77.2 | 77.1 | 78.3 | 77.5 | 77.3 | 76.3 | 73.8 | 75.0 | 76.7 | 75.8 | 76.0 | 75.7 | 76.4 |
| 2017 | 74.8 | 74.9 | 75.0 | 75.7 | 75.9 | 74.8 | 72.0 | 73.9 | 75.6 | 75.3 | 75.6 | 75.4 | 74.9 |
| 2018 | 74.0 | 75.2 | 75.5 | 75.5 | 75.8 | 75.5 | 72.3 | 74.3 | 76.1 | 76.6 | 76.1 | 75.8 | 75.2 |
| 2019 | 74.4 | 75.0 | 75.2 | 74.2 | 74.6 | 73.9 | 70.9 | 73.0 | 74.4 | 74.5 | 74.7 | 74.5 | 74.1 |

## Employment by Industry: Salt Lake City, UT, 2011–2019

(Numbers in thousands, not seasonally adjusted)

| Industry and year | January | February | March | April | May | June | July | August | September | October | November | December | Annual average |
|---|---|---|---|---|---|---|---|---|---|---|---|---|---|
| **Total Nonfarm** | | | | | | | | | | | | | |
| 2011 | 585.3 | 586.9 | 589.9 | 594.6 | 595.0 | 597.7 | 596.1 | 600.2 | 603.5 | 604.7 | 609.1 | 610.4 | 597.8 |
| 2012 | 600.9 | 603.8 | 607.3 | 617.1 | 621.6 | 624.2 | 616.1 | 620.9 | 624.9 | 629.0 | 635.8 | 635.9 | 619.8 |
| 2013 | 624.7 | 628.5 | 631.9 | 636.3 | 637.6 | 639.2 | 634.4 | 637.8 | 640.8 | 647.8 | 653.6 | 654.7 | 638.9 |
| 2014 | 640.5 | 643.1 | 645.6 | 649.6 | 651.0 | 654.3 | 646.4 | 651.8 | 656.9 | 662.1 | 667.8 | 670.1 | 653.3 |
| 2015 | 659.3 | 662.5 | 667.1 | 668.7 | 672.9 | 674.6 | 672.7 | 675.9 | 680.4 | 687.3 | 691.5 | 694.5 | 675.6 |
| 2016 | 681.2 | 686.6 | 690.0 | 693.6 | 695.6 | 697.9 | 697.8 | 700.1 | 705.9 | 708.5 | 711.3 | 711.8 | 698.4 |
| 2017 | 701.2 | 704.6 | 707.4 | 709.3 | 712.1 | 715.8 | 709.9 | 713.9 | 719.3 | 724.6 | 730.4 | 732.6 | 715.1 |
| 2018 | 714.9 | 721.4 | 723.2 | 726.5 | 729.5 | 734.6 | 730.7 | 734.2 | 738.8 | 743.4 | 749.3 | 750.0 | 733.0 |
| 2019 | 734.8 | 739.1 | 741.9 | 751.1 | 754.7 | 755.5 | 750.0 | 756.5 | 758.9 | 766.3 | 770.3 | 772.4 | 754.3 |
| **Total Private** | | | | | | | | | | | | | |
| 2011 | 490.1 | 491.6 | 494.5 | 498.3 | 498.6 | 501.2 | 503.4 | 507.0 | 507.1 | 508.6 | 512.4 | 513.5 | 502.2 |
| 2012 | 504.1 | 506.6 | 510.0 | 518.5 | 523.4 | 526.0 | 522.5 | 527.4 | 527.2 | 530.0 | 537.0 | 537.8 | 522.5 |
| 2013 | 527.1 | 530.5 | 534.1 | 536.7 | 537.5 | 538.7 | 538.9 | 542.6 | 540.4 | 545.0 | 551.2 | 552.3 | 539.6 |
| 2014 | 538.3 | 540.1 | 542.4 | 545.1 | 546.1 | 549.1 | 548.4 | 554.5 | 554.3 | 558.5 | 564.1 | 566.2 | 550.6 |
| 2015 | 556.2 | 558.6 | 562.5 | 563.4 | 567.1 | 569.8 | 572.6 | 577.0 | 575.9 | 580.8 | 585.4 | 588.1 | 571.5 |
| 2016 | 576.7 | 580.7 | 583.6 | 585.6 | 587.3 | 590.0 | 595.7 | 599.4 | 598.5 | 599.2 | 602.3 | 602.5 | 591.8 |
| 2017 | 593.5 | 595.7 | 598.2 | 599.2 | 601.3 | 606.1 | 607.2 | 611.1 | 610.3 | 613.9 | 619.6 | 621.4 | 606.5 |
| 2018 | 606.3 | 611.8 | 613.4 | 615.3 | 618.3 | 622.0 | 625.6 | 630.6 | 629.0 | 632.7 | 638.7 | 639.5 | 623.6 |
| 2019 | 625.1 | 628.4 | 630.9 | 636.2 | 638.8 | 642.5 | 643.8 | 650.1 | 646.9 | 651.5 | 655.4 | 657.6 | 642.3 |
| **Goods Producing** | | | | | | | | | | | | | |
| 2011 | 83.0 | 82.8 | 83.4 | 84.4 | 85.3 | 86.6 | 88.6 | 89.5 | 89.0 | 88.7 | 88.5 | 87.5 | 86.4 |
| 2012 | 85.5 | 86.1 | 86.7 | 88.2 | 90.1 | 90.9 | 90.8 | 91.4 | 91.0 | 90.9 | 90.3 | 89.7 | 89.3 |
| 2013 | 87.5 | 87.3 | 88.1 | 89.3 | 89.8 | 90.2 | 90.1 | 90.9 | 90.2 | 89.7 | 89.3 | 88.5 | 89.2 |
| 2014 | 86.6 | 87.0 | 87.7 | 88.7 | 89.5 | 90.3 | 90.5 | 91.3 | 91.2 | 91.7 | 91.2 | 90.5 | 89.7 |
| 2015 | 88.7 | 89.0 | 90.1 | 90.9 | 91.9 | 92.9 | 93.7 | 93.8 | 93.6 | 94.4 | 94.1 | 94.1 | 92.3 |
| 2016 | 92.1 | 92.5 | 93.6 | 94.3 | 95.2 | 95.9 | 96.9 | 97.0 | 97.3 | 97.5 | 97.0 | 96.1 | 95.5 |
| 2017 | 94.8 | 95.5 | 97.1 | 96.8 | 98.3 | 99.7 | 100.2 | 100.4 | 100.4 | 100.6 | 100.7 | 100.4 | 98.7 |
| 2018 | 98.7 | 99.5 | 100.3 | 100.7 | 101.9 | 103.2 | 103.8 | 103.9 | 103.3 | 103.2 | 103.5 | 102.9 | 102.1 |
| 2019 | 101.3 | 102.1 | 103.2 | 104.2 | 105.7 | 107.2 | 107.6 | 108.2 | 108.1 | 109.0 | 109.6 | 109.2 | 106.3 |
| **Service-Providing** | | | | | | | | | | | | | |
| 2011 | 502.3 | 504.1 | 506.5 | 510.2 | 509.7 | 511.1 | 507.5 | 510.7 | 514.5 | 516.0 | 520.6 | 522.9 | 511.3 |
| 2012 | 515.4 | 517.7 | 520.6 | 528.9 | 531.5 | 533.3 | 525.3 | 529.5 | 533.9 | 538.1 | 545.5 | 546.2 | 530.5 |
| 2013 | 537.2 | 541.2 | 543.8 | 547.0 | 547.8 | 549.0 | 544.3 | 546.9 | 550.6 | 558.1 | 564.3 | 566.2 | 549.7 |
| 2014 | 553.9 | 556.1 | 557.9 | 560.9 | 561.5 | 564.0 | 555.9 | 560.5 | 565.7 | 570.4 | 576.6 | 579.6 | 563.6 |
| 2015 | 570.6 | 573.5 | 577.0 | 577.8 | 581.0 | 581.7 | 579.0 | 582.1 | 586.8 | 592.9 | 597.4 | 600.4 | 583.4 |
| 2016 | 589.1 | 594.1 | 596.4 | 599.3 | 600.4 | 602.0 | 600.9 | 603.1 | 608.6 | 611.0 | 614.3 | 615.7 | 602.9 |
| 2017 | 606.4 | 609.1 | 610.3 | 612.5 | 613.8 | 616.1 | 609.7 | 613.5 | 618.9 | 624.0 | 629.7 | 632.2 | 616.4 |
| 2018 | 616.2 | 621.9 | 622.9 | 625.8 | 627.6 | 631.4 | 626.9 | 630.3 | 635.5 | 640.2 | 645.8 | 647.1 | 631.0 |
| 2019 | 633.5 | 637.0 | 638.7 | 646.9 | 649.0 | 648.3 | 642.4 | 648.3 | 650.8 | 657.3 | 660.7 | 663.2 | 648.0 |
| **Mining, Logging, and Construction** | | | | | | | | | | | | | |
| 2011 | 31.1 | 30.8 | 31.4 | 32.1 | 32.8 | 33.8 | 35.2 | 35.7 | 35.3 | 35.1 | 34.8 | 33.7 | 33.5 |
| 2012 | 32.0 | 32.6 | 32.9 | 34.2 | 35.7 | 36.1 | 35.9 | 36.5 | 36.2 | 35.9 | 35.6 | 34.9 | 34.9 |
| 2013 | 33.1 | 33.0 | 33.7 | 34.8 | 35.3 | 35.6 | 35.5 | 36.3 | 35.8 | 35.3 | 35.1 | 34.1 | 34.8 |
| 2014 | 32.5 | 32.8 | 33.5 | 34.5 | 35.3 | 35.9 | 36.4 | 36.9 | 37.1 | 37.4 | 36.9 | 36.0 | 35.4 |
| 2015 | 34.3 | 34.6 | 35.4 | 36.0 | 36.6 | 37.3 | 38.0 | 38.0 | 38.1 | 38.5 | 38.3 | 38.1 | 36.9 |
| 2016 | 36.6 | 36.9 | 38.0 | 38.8 | 39.3 | 39.8 | 40.1 | 40.2 | 40.3 | 40.5 | 40.0 | 38.9 | 39.1 |
| 2017 | 37.7 | 38.2 | 39.6 | 39.8 | 41.3 | 42.5 | 42.9 | 43.1 | 43.3 | 43.3 | 43.1 | 42.6 | 41.5 |
| 2018 | 41.4 | 41.8 | 42.6 | 43.0 | 44.0 | 44.9 | 45.2 | 45.4 | 45.1 | 44.9 | 44.9 | 44.0 | 43.9 |
| 2019 | 42.7 | 43.3 | 44.2 | 45.1 | 46.3 | 47.3 | 47.9 | 48.4 | 48.4 | 49.3 | 50.1 | 49.2 | 46.9 |
| **Manufacturing** | | | | | | | | | | | | | |
| 2011 | 51.9 | 52.0 | 52.0 | 52.3 | 52.5 | 52.8 | 53.4 | 53.8 | 53.7 | 53.6 | 53.7 | 53.8 | 53.0 |
| 2012 | 53.5 | 53.5 | 53.8 | 54.0 | 54.4 | 54.8 | 54.9 | 54.9 | 54.8 | 55.0 | 54.7 | 54.8 | 54.4 |
| 2013 | 54.4 | 54.3 | 54.4 | 54.5 | 54.5 | 54.6 | 54.6 | 54.6 | 54.4 | 54.4 | 54.2 | 54.4 | 54.4 |
| 2014 | 54.1 | 54.2 | 54.2 | 54.2 | 54.2 | 54.4 | 54.1 | 54.4 | 54.1 | 54.3 | 54.3 | 54.5 | 54.3 |
| 2015 | 54.4 | 54.4 | 54.7 | 54.9 | 55.3 | 55.6 | 55.7 | 55.8 | 55.5 | 55.9 | 55.8 | 56.0 | 55.3 |
| 2016 | 55.5 | 55.6 | 55.6 | 55.5 | 55.9 | 56.1 | 56.8 | 56.8 | 57.0 | 57.0 | 57.0 | 57.2 | 56.3 |
| 2017 | 57.1 | 57.3 | 57.5 | 57.0 | 57.0 | 57.2 | 57.3 | 57.3 | 57.1 | 57.3 | 57.6 | 57.8 | 57.3 |
| 2018 | 57.3 | 57.7 | 57.7 | 57.7 | 57.9 | 58.3 | 58.6 | 58.5 | 58.2 | 58.3 | 58.6 | 58.9 | 58.1 |
| 2019 | 58.6 | 58.8 | 59.0 | 59.1 | 59.4 | 59.9 | 59.7 | 59.8 | 59.7 | 59.7 | 59.5 | 60.0 | 59.4 |

# Employment by Industry: Salt Lake City, UT, 2011–2019—*Continued*

(Numbers in thousands, not seasonally adjusted)

| Industry and year | January | February | March | April | May | June | July | August | September | October | November | December | Annual average |
|---|---|---|---|---|---|---|---|---|---|---|---|---|---|
| **Trade, Transportation, and Utilities** | | | | | | | | | | | | | |
| 2011 | 117.9 | 117.5 | 118.1 | 119.2 | 119.4 | 120.0 | 120.5 | 121.1 | 121.0 | 121.5 | 124.2 | 125.3 | 120.5 |
| 2012 | 122.2 | 121.8 | 122.8 | 123.9 | 124.7 | 125.5 | 124.8 | 125.5 | 126.0 | 126.7 | 129.8 | 130.1 | 125.3 |
| 2013 | 126.5 | 126.2 | 126.2 | 126.0 | 126.9 | 127.1 | 127.5 | 127.9 | 127.2 | 128.4 | 131.1 | 131.9 | 127.7 |
| 2014 | 127.1 | 126.7 | 127.0 | 127.4 | 128.0 | 128.6 | 128.2 | 129.1 | 129.5 | 131.2 | 134.2 | 135.4 | 129.4 |
| 2015 | 131.6 | 131.7 | 132.1 | 131.9 | 132.8 | 132.9 | 134.0 | 135.2 | 135.0 | 136.4 | 138.8 | 140.4 | 134.4 |
| 2016 | 136.3 | 136.6 | 137.2 | 136.8 | 137.4 | 137.3 | 138.3 | 139.0 | 139.2 | 139.0 | 141.8 | 143.4 | 138.5 |
| 2017 | 138.4 | 137.9 | 138.5 | 138.4 | 138.6 | 139.4 | 140.1 | 140.5 | 140.5 | 142.1 | 146.1 | 147.6 | 140.7 |
| 2018 | 141.7 | 141.7 | 142.2 | 141.9 | 142.8 | 143.7 | 145.2 | 146.0 | 146.8 | 148.7 | 153.4 | 154.5 | 145.7 |
| 2019 | 149.0 | 147.6 | 147.1 | 147.7 | 147.8 | 148.2 | 148.6 | 149.9 | 149.1 | 150.2 | 153.8 | 156.6 | 149.6 |
| **Wholesale Trade** | | | | | | | | | | | | | |
| 2011 | 28.5 | 28.7 | 29.0 | 29.1 | 29.2 | 29.5 | 29.6 | 29.7 | 29.7 | 29.7 | 29.8 | 29.9 | 29.4 |
| 2012 | 29.8 | 29.9 | 30.1 | 30.1 | 30.2 | 30.2 | 30.0 | 30.2 | 29.9 | 29.9 | 29.8 | 29.8 | 30.0 |
| 2013 | 30.1 | 30.1 | 30.0 | 30.0 | 30.2 | 30.1 | 30.1 | 30.2 | 29.9 | 29.9 | 30.0 | 30.0 | 30.1 |
| 2014 | 29.5 | 29.6 | 29.5 | 29.7 | 29.8 | 29.9 | 30.0 | 30.0 | 30.0 | 30.3 | 30.4 | 30.6 | 29.9 |
| 2015 | 30.1 | 30.4 | 30.5 | 30.7 | 31.0 | 31.1 | 31.2 | 31.3 | 31.1 | 31.1 | 31.2 | 31.3 | 30.9 |
| 2016 | 31.0 | 31.2 | 31.3 | 31.2 | 31.3 | 31.2 | 31.6 | 31.6 | 31.5 | 31.3 | 31.3 | 31.4 | 31.3 |
| 2017 | 31.0 | 31.1 | 31.2 | 31.3 | 31.5 | 31.6 | 31.7 | 31.7 | 31.6 | 31.8 | 32.0 | 32.1 | 31.6 |
| 2018 | 31.4 | 31.8 | 31.9 | 31.9 | 32.1 | 32.2 | 32.5 | 32.6 | 32.4 | 32.6 | 32.6 | 32.7 | 32.2 |
| 2019 | 32.5 | 32.6 | 32.6 | 32.7 | 32.7 | 32.6 | 33.3 | 33.5 | 33.2 | 32.8 | 32.9 | 33.2 | 32.9 |
| **Retail Trade** | | | | | | | | | | | | | |
| 2011 | 61.4 | 60.8 | 61.0 | 61.7 | 61.9 | 62.0 | 62.3 | 62.7 | 62.6 | 63.4 | 65.6 | 66.2 | 62.6 |
| 2012 | 63.5 | 62.9 | 63.5 | 64.1 | 64.7 | 65.3 | 65.6 | 65.8 | 66.3 | 67.0 | 69.9 | 69.9 | 65.7 |
| 2013 | 66.4 | 66.1 | 66.3 | 66.9 | 67.5 | 67.8 | 68.0 | 68.4 | 68.1 | 68.9 | 71.1 | 71.4 | 68.1 |
| 2014 | 67.5 | 67.2 | 67.5 | 67.7 | 68.2 | 68.4 | 68.7 | 69.3 | 69.4 | 70.4 | 72.6 | 73.3 | 69.2 |
| 2015 | 69.9 | 69.6 | 69.6 | 69.8 | 70.3 | 70.2 | 70.6 | 71.4 | 71.3 | 72.1 | 74.4 | 75.1 | 71.2 |
| 2016 | 72.0 | 72.2 | 72.6 | 72.4 | 72.8 | 73.0 | 73.2 | 73.7 | 73.7 | 74.0 | 76.1 | 76.7 | 73.5 |
| 2017 | 72.9 | 72.4 | 72.7 | 72.8 | 72.8 | 73.1 | 73.3 | 73.9 | 73.6 | 74.6 | 77.3 | 78.0 | 74.0 |
| 2018 | 74.5 | 73.9 | 74.1 | 74.3 | 74.8 | 75.1 | 76.0 | 76.5 | 76.0 | 76.8 | 79.0 | 79.5 | 75.9 |
| 2019 | 76.2 | 75.6 | 75.6 | 75.6 | 75.7 | 75.8 | 75.3 | 75.5 | 75.2 | 75.9 | 77.8 | 79.3 | 76.1 |
| **Transportation and Utilities** | | | | | | | | | | | | | |
| 2011 | 28.0 | 28.0 | 28.1 | 28.4 | 28.3 | 28.5 | 28.6 | 28.7 | 28.7 | 28.4 | 28.8 | 29.2 | 28.5 |
| 2012 | 28.9 | 29.0 | 29.2 | 29.7 | 29.8 | 30.0 | 29.2 | 29.5 | 29.8 | 29.8 | 30.1 | 30.4 | 29.6 |
| 2013 | 30.0 | 30.0 | 29.9 | 29.1 | 29.2 | 29.2 | 29.4 | 29.3 | 29.2 | 29.6 | 30.0 | 30.5 | 29.6 |
| 2014 | 30.1 | 29.9 | 30.0 | 30.0 | 30.0 | 30.3 | 29.5 | 29.8 | 30.1 | 30.5 | 31.2 | 31.5 | 30.2 |
| 2015 | 31.6 | 31.7 | 32.0 | 31.4 | 31.5 | 31.6 | 32.2 | 32.5 | 32.6 | 33.2 | 33.2 | 34.0 | 32.3 |
| 2016 | 33.3 | 33.2 | 33.3 | 33.2 | 33.3 | 33.1 | 33.5 | 33.7 | 34.0 | 33.7 | 34.4 | 35.3 | 33.7 |
| 2017 | 34.5 | 34.4 | 34.6 | 34.3 | 34.3 | 34.7 | 35.1 | 34.9 | 35.3 | 35.7 | 36.8 | 37.5 | 35.2 |
| 2018 | 35.8 | 36.0 | 36.2 | 35.7 | 35.9 | 36.4 | 36.7 | 36.9 | 38.4 | 39.3 | 41.8 | 42.3 | 37.6 |
| 2019 | 40.3 | 39.4 | 38.9 | 39.4 | 39.4 | 39.8 | 40.0 | 40.9 | 40.7 | 41.5 | 43.1 | 44.1 | 40.6 |
| **Information** | | | | | | | | | | | | | |
| 2011 | 16.0 | 16.3 | 16.4 | 16.0 | 16.1 | 16.2 | 16.1 | 16.3 | 16.1 | 16.1 | 16.5 | 16.5 | 16.2 |
| 2012 | 16.0 | 16.1 | 16.2 | 18.5 | 19.1 | 19.0 | 17.6 | 17.9 | 17.5 | 17.8 | 18.6 | 18.6 | 17.7 |
| 2013 | 19.3 | 19.4 | 19.4 | 18.0 | 18.1 | 18.1 | 18.0 | 18.2 | 17.8 | 17.8 | 18.5 | 18.6 | 18.4 |
| 2014 | 18.0 | 18.3 | 18.4 | 18.1 | 18.1 | 18.2 | 18.2 | 18.6 | 18.2 | 17.9 | 18.1 | 18.1 | 18.2 |
| 2015 | 17.6 | 17.8 | 17.8 | 17.6 | 17.9 | 17.8 | 18.2 | 18.6 | 18.4 | 18.6 | 19.2 | 19.0 | 18.2 |
| 2016 | 18.7 | 19.6 | 19.0 | 18.7 | 18.9 | 19.1 | 19.7 | 20.3 | 19.6 | 19.6 | 19.7 | 19.6 | 19.4 |
| 2017 | 19.8 | 20.5 | 20.0 | 19.9 | 20.0 | 20.5 | 20.9 | 21.4 | 21.2 | 21.7 | 21.5 | 20.9 | 20.7 |
| 2018 | 19.7 | 20.4 | 19.5 | 19.7 | 20.2 | 20.1 | 20.6 | 21.2 | 20.7 | 20.9 | 20.9 | 20.2 | 20.3 |
| 2019 | 19.8 | 20.4 | 20.1 | 20.4 | 21.3 | 21.0 | 21.4 | 21.7 | 21.4 | 21.6 | 22.1 | 22.5 | 21.1 |
| **Financial Activities** | | | | | | | | | | | | | |
| 2011 | 45.5 | 45.7 | 45.8 | 46.0 | 45.9 | 46.2 | 46.2 | 46.4 | 46.3 | 46.3 | 46.4 | 46.6 | 46.1 |
| 2012 | 45.9 | 46.0 | 46.1 | 46.4 | 46.5 | 46.8 | 47.0 | 47.6 | 47.4 | 47.5 | 47.9 | 48.4 | 47.0 |
| 2013 | 47.4 | 47.8 | 47.8 | 48.2 | 48.5 | 49.2 | 49.7 | 50.1 | 49.9 | 50.1 | 50.4 | 50.6 | 49.1 |
| 2014 | 49.4 | 49.7 | 49.5 | 49.6 | 49.9 | 50.4 | 50.8 | 51.4 | 51.0 | 51.5 | 51.9 | 52.1 | 50.6 |
| 2015 | 51.9 | 52.3 | 52.4 | 52.4 | 52.8 | 53.1 | 53.5 | 53.6 | 53.6 | 53.9 | 54.1 | 54.4 | 53.2 |
| 2016 | 54.2 | 54.7 | 54.7 | 54.8 | 55.3 | 55.7 | 56.3 | 56.7 | 56.2 | 56.6 | 56.9 | 57.0 | 55.8 |
| 2017 | 56.5 | 56.7 | 56.5 | 56.6 | 57.1 | 57.5 | 57.4 | 57.7 | 57.4 | 57.8 | 57.9 | 58.4 | 57.3 |
| 2018 | 57.9 | 58.4 | 58.3 | 58.2 | 58.7 | 59.3 | 59.8 | 60.2 | 59.5 | 59.2 | 59.2 | 59.5 | 59.0 |
| 2019 | 58.4 | 58.6 | 58.7 | 59.4 | 59.9 | 60.4 | 61.0 | 61.7 | 61.1 | 60.9 | 61.1 | 60.9 | 60.2 |

## Employment by Industry: Salt Lake City, UT, 2011–2019—*Continued*

(Numbers in thousands, not seasonally adjusted)

| Industry and year | January | February | March | April | May | June | July | August | September | October | November | December | Annual average |
|---|---|---|---|---|---|---|---|---|---|---|---|---|---|
| **Professional and Business Services** | | | | | | | | | | | | | |
| 2011 | 94.7 | 95.5 | 96.3 | 97.3 | 97.7 | 98.0 | 98.8 | 99.6 | 100.1 | 101.8 | 102.2 | 102.1 | 98.7 |
| 2012 | 99.5 | 100.5 | 101.2 | 101.4 | 102.5 | 103.5 | 103.7 | 105.0 | 105.1 | 106.7 | 107.7 | 107.2 | 103.7 |
| 2013 | 103.0 | 104.8 | 106.0 | 108.6 | 108.0 | 108.4 | 109.0 | 110.1 | 110.1 | 113.1 | 114.2 | 114.0 | 109.1 |
| 2014 | 110.7 | 110.6 | 111.0 | 111.9 | 112.4 | 113.3 | 112.8 | 114.5 | 115.1 | 116.5 | 117.2 | 117.8 | 113.7 |
| 2015 | 114.1 | 114.0 | 115.2 | 116.2 | 117.4 | 118.8 | 119.2 | 120.3 | 120.0 | 121.3 | 121.9 | 122.0 | 118.4 |
| 2016 | 119.0 | 119.1 | 119.9 | 120.8 | 121.5 | 122.3 | 124.1 | 124.8 | 124.1 | 124.4 | 124.1 | 123.0 | 122.3 |
| 2017 | 122.0 | 121.1 | 121.2 | 122.1 | 122.8 | 123.8 | 124.8 | 125.6 | 125.7 | 126.2 | 126.6 | 126.2 | 124.0 |
| 2018 | 121.9 | 123.4 | 124.5 | 125.8 | 126.6 | 127.6 | 128.5 | 129.0 | 129.1 | 130.2 | 130.7 | 130.0 | 127.3 |
| 2019 | 126.2 | 127.1 | 127.9 | 130.2 | 131.2 | 132.2 | 132.7 | 133.7 | 133.2 | 133.1 | 130.3 | 129.3 | 130.6 |
| **Education and Health Services** | | | | | | | | | | | | | |
| 2011 | 67.1 | 67.6 | 67.6 | 68.0 | 67.4 | 66.9 | 65.6 | 66.0 | 67.6 | 68.2 | 68.3 | 68.0 | 67.4 |
| 2012 | 67.7 | 68.1 | 68.1 | 70.7 | 70.6 | 70.3 | 68.4 | 69.2 | 70.3 | 71.2 | 71.9 | 71.9 | 69.9 |
| 2013 | 72.3 | 73.0 | 73.3 | 72.7 | 72.7 | 72.0 | 70.5 | 71.3 | 72.2 | 73.3 | 74.0 | 73.7 | 72.6 |
| 2014 | 72.3 | 72.9 | 73.3 | 73.1 | 73.4 | 72.5 | 71.8 | 73.0 | 73.6 | 74.3 | 75.3 | 75.2 | 73.4 |
| 2015 | 75.6 | 76.3 | 76.5 | 76.2 | 76.6 | 76.1 | 74.9 | 75.8 | 76.9 | 78.4 | 79.1 | 78.6 | 76.8 |
| 2016 | 78.2 | 79.1 | 79.3 | 80.0 | 79.6 | 78.9 | 78.7 | 79.6 | 81.1 | 81.7 | 82.5 | 82.1 | 80.1 |
| 2017 | 81.5 | 82.5 | 82.6 | 83.0 | 83.0 | 82.1 | 81.1 | 82.4 | 83.0 | 83.8 | 84.6 | 84.2 | 82.8 |
| 2018 | 83.9 | 84.6 | 84.6 | 84.7 | 83.9 | 83.0 | 82.5 | 83.7 | 84.6 | 85.9 | 86.2 | 85.9 | 84.5 |
| 2019 | 85.3 | 86.4 | 86.5 | 86.7 | 86.5 | 85.7 | 84.9 | 86.5 | 87.2 | 88.3 | 89.4 | 87.9 | 86.8 |
| **Leisure and Hospitality** | | | | | | | | | | | | | |
| 2011 | 48.2 | 48.4 | 49.0 | 49.4 | 48.5 | 48.9 | 48.9 | 49.3 | 48.6 | 47.7 | 48.1 | 49.3 | 48.7 |
| 2012 | 49.2 | 49.7 | 50.4 | 50.9 | 51.1 | 51.2 | 50.9 | 51.4 | 50.9 | 50.2 | 51.8 | 52.8 | 50.9 |
| 2013 | 52.1 | 52.7 | 53.6 | 53.8 | 53.1 | 53.8 | 53.8 | 53.8 | 53.2 | 53.0 | 53.9 | 55.2 | 53.5 |
| 2014 | 54.5 | 54.9 | 55.3 | 55.9 | 54.3 | 55.1 | 54.9 | 55.4 | 55.0 | 54.8 | 55.6 | 56.6 | 55.2 |
| 2015 | 55.6 | 56.2 | 57.0 | 57.2 | 56.7 | 57.0 | 57.5 | 58.1 | 57.3 | 56.8 | 57.1 | 58.5 | 57.1 |
| 2016 | 57.4 | 58.1 | 58.7 | 59.1 | 58.2 | 59.2 | 59.8 | 60.0 | 59.4 | 58.9 | 59.0 | 60.0 | 59.0 |
| 2017 | 59.2 | 60.1 | 60.7 | 60.8 | 59.8 | 61.0 | 60.4 | 60.9 | 60.5 | 60.1 | 60.6 | 62.0 | 60.5 |
| 2018 | 61.0 | 62.1 | 62.2 | 62.4 | 62.0 | 62.5 | 62.5 | 63.8 | 62.7 | 62.2 | 62.4 | 64.1 | 62.5 |
| 2019 | 62.9 | 63.9 | 64.9 | 65.1 | 63.7 | 64.7 | 64.5 | 65.1 | 64.0 | 65.6 | 66.4 | 68.6 | 65.0 |
| **Other Services** | | | | | | | | | | | | | |
| 2011 | 17.7 | 17.8 | 17.9 | 18.0 | 18.3 | 18.4 | 18.7 | 18.8 | 18.4 | 18.3 | 18.2 | 18.2 | 18.2 |
| 2012 | 18.1 | 18.3 | 18.5 | 18.5 | 18.8 | 18.8 | 19.3 | 19.4 | 19.0 | 19.0 | 19.0 | 19.1 | 18.8 |
| 2013 | 19.0 | 19.3 | 19.7 | 20.1 | 20.4 | 19.9 | 20.3 | 20.3 | 19.8 | 19.6 | 19.8 | 19.8 | 19.8 |
| 2014 | 19.7 | 20.0 | 20.2 | 20.4 | 20.5 | 20.7 | 21.2 | 21.2 | 20.7 | 20.6 | 20.6 | 20.5 | 20.5 |
| 2015 | 21.1 | 21.3 | 21.4 | 21.0 | 21.0 | 21.2 | 21.6 | 21.6 | 21.1 | 21.0 | 21.1 | 21.1 | 21.2 |
| 2016 | 20.8 | 21.0 | 21.2 | 21.1 | 21.2 | 21.6 | 21.9 | 22.0 | 21.6 | 21.5 | 21.3 | 21.3 | 21.4 |
| 2017 | 21.3 | 21.4 | 21.6 | 21.6 | 21.7 | 22.1 | 22.3 | 22.2 | 21.6 | 21.6 | 21.6 | 21.7 | 21.7 |
| 2018 | 21.5 | 21.7 | 21.8 | 21.9 | 22.2 | 22.6 | 22.7 | 22.8 | 22.3 | 22.4 | 22.4 | 22.4 | 22.2 |
| 2019 | 22.2 | 22.3 | 22.5 | 22.5 | 22.7 | 23.1 | 23.1 | 23.3 | 22.8 | 22.8 | 22.7 | 22.6 | 22.7 |
| **Government** | | | | | | | | | | | | | |
| 2011 | 95.2 | 95.3 | 95.4 | 96.3 | 96.4 | 96.5 | 92.7 | 93.2 | 96.4 | 96.1 | 96.7 | 96.9 | 95.6 |
| 2012 | 96.8 | 97.2 | 97.3 | 98.6 | 98.2 | 98.2 | 93.6 | 93.5 | 97.7 | 99.0 | 98.8 | 98.1 | 97.3 |
| 2013 | 97.6 | 98.0 | 97.8 | 99.6 | 100.1 | 100.5 | 95.5 | 95.2 | 100.4 | 102.8 | 102.4 | 102.4 | 99.4 |
| 2014 | 102.2 | 103.0 | 103.2 | 104.5 | 104.9 | 105.2 | 98.0 | 97.3 | 102.6 | 103.6 | 103.7 | 103.9 | 102.7 |
| 2015 | 103.1 | 103.9 | 104.6 | 105.3 | 105.8 | 104.8 | 100.1 | 98.9 | 104.5 | 106.5 | 106.1 | 106.4 | 104.2 |
| 2016 | 104.5 | 105.9 | 106.4 | 108.0 | 108.3 | 107.9 | 102.1 | 100.7 | 107.4 | 109.3 | 109.0 | 109.3 | 106.6 |
| 2017 | 107.7 | 108.9 | 109.2 | 110.1 | 110.8 | 109.7 | 102.7 | 102.8 | 109.0 | 110.7 | 110.8 | 111.2 | 108.6 |
| 2018 | 108.6 | 109.6 | 109.8 | 111.2 | 111.2 | 112.6 | 105.1 | 103.6 | 109.8 | 110.7 | 110.6 | 110.5 | 109.4 |
| 2019 | 109.7 | 110.7 | 111.0 | 114.9 | 115.9 | 113.0 | 106.2 | 106.4 | 112.0 | 114.8 | 114.9 | 114.8 | 112.0 |

# Employment by Industry: Hartford-West Hartford-East Hartford, CT NECTA, 2011–2019

(Numbers in thousands, not seasonally adjusted)

| Industry and year | January | February | March | April | May | June | July | August | September | October | November | December | Annual average |
|---|---|---|---|---|---|---|---|---|---|---|---|---|---|
| **Total Nonfarm** | | | | | | | | | | | | | |
| 2011 | 544.2 | 550.7 | 551.9 | 560.0 | 558.0 | 553.2 | 546.6 | 541.2 | 557.1 | 560.8 | 562.0 | 564.3 | 554.2 |
| 2012 | 545.8 | 553.3 | 556.0 | 560.1 | 559.9 | 558.2 | 550.6 | 546.8 | 562.5 | 569.1 | 572.8 | 572.1 | 558.9 |
| 2013 | 553.4 | 557.3 | 560.5 | 566.5 | 568.0 | 567.5 | 556.6 | 552.8 | 565.2 | 569.5 | 573.5 | 573.3 | 563.7 |
| 2014 | 557.2 | 560.2 | 563.0 | 571.5 | 573.7 | 571.7 | 561.4 | 558.3 | 571.7 | 578.3 | 581.0 | 581.3 | 569.1 |
| 2015 | 564.8 | 566.8 | 569.6 | 577.2 | 579.9 | 578.8 | 566.7 | 563.0 | 575.7 | 582.5 | 585.3 | 583.4 | 574.5 |
| 2016 | 568.1 | 570.2 | 573.0 | 576.9 | 580.4 | 578.1 | 569.9 | 565.2 | 577.0 | 581.9 | 585.5 | 584.7 | 575.9 |
| 2017 | 570.2 | 572.1 | 574.1 | 578.8 | 583.3 | 582.4 | 571.8 | 568.0 | 581.5 | 583.5 | 586.9 | 586.6 | 578.3 |
| 2018 | 572.7 | 575.1 | 576.2 | 580.1 | 585.7 | 586.2 | 576.2 | 574.0 | 584.8 | 589.3 | 591.6 | 591.0 | 581.9 |
| 2019 | 576.3 | 578.4 | 579.5 | 583.5 | 587.4 | 585.6 | 578.3 | 573.9 | 586.3 | 588.5 | 591.0 | 591.5 | 583.4 |
| **Total Private** | | | | | | | | | | | | | |
| 2011 | 452.0 | 452.3 | 453.3 | 460.1 | 463.0 | 465.8 | 464.0 | 461.2 | 462.3 | 461.6 | 462.2 | 464.8 | 460.2 |
| 2012 | 455.6 | 456.0 | 458.4 | 462.1 | 466.4 | 470.3 | 467.6 | 466.6 | 467.4 | 470.1 | 472.3 | 472.1 | 465.4 |
| 2013 | 461.3 | 460.4 | 463.1 | 468.3 | 472.8 | 476.7 | 472.3 | 471.5 | 471.9 | 471.8 | 474.9 | 474.8 | 470.0 |
| 2014 | 464.1 | 463.6 | 465.6 | 473.0 | 478.0 | 480.8 | 476.9 | 476.0 | 477.2 | 478.9 | 480.6 | 481.6 | 474.7 |
| 2015 | 470.6 | 469.9 | 472.2 | 478.4 | 484.1 | 488.5 | 482.9 | 481.5 | 481.6 | 484.0 | 485.5 | 485.3 | 480.4 |
| 2016 | 475.1 | 474.4 | 476.5 | 480.1 | 485.3 | 489.8 | 487.8 | 485.9 | 486.0 | 486.4 | 488.8 | 489.1 | 483.8 |
| 2017 | 478.9 | 478.0 | 479.5 | 484.0 | 490.1 | 493.6 | 488.4 | 486.9 | 489.4 | 489.9 | 492.5 | 493.0 | 487.0 |
| 2018 | 482.0 | 482.0 | 482.4 | 486.9 | 493.6 | 498.0 | 493.4 | 493.0 | 492.8 | 495.3 | 496.9 | 496.9 | 491.1 |
| 2019 | 484.3 | 484.1 | 484.8 | 489.1 | 494.1 | 497.4 | 495.2 | 492.7 | 493.6 | 494.1 | 495.6 | 496.7 | 491.8 |
| **Goods Producing** | | | | | | | | | | | | | |
| 2011 | 72.2 | 72.0 | 72.5 | 73.7 | 74.7 | 76.0 | 76.1 | 75.9 | 75.8 | 75.4 | 75.6 | 75.0 | 74.6 |
| 2012 | 73.1 | 72.7 | 73.0 | 74.1 | 74.7 | 75.7 | 76.1 | 75.9 | 75.3 | 75.5 | 75.4 | 75.1 | 74.7 |
| 2013 | 73.0 | 72.6 | 72.7 | 74.1 | 75.4 | 76.1 | 76.6 | 75.9 | 75.5 | 75.0 | 74.8 | 74.3 | 74.7 |
| 2014 | 71.9 | 71.6 | 71.7 | 73.5 | 74.5 | 75.3 | 75.9 | 75.9 | 75.6 | 75.6 | 75.4 | 75.0 | 74.3 |
| 2015 | 72.8 | 72.6 | 73.1 | 75.2 | 76.7 | 77.6 | 77.1 | 77.3 | 77.0 | 76.9 | 76.7 | 76.2 | 75.8 |
| 2016 | 74.2 | 73.5 | 74.2 | 75.8 | 76.8 | 77.8 | 78.3 | 78.2 | 77.5 | 77.5 | 77.3 | 76.9 | 76.5 |
| 2017 | 74.9 | 74.8 | 75.4 | 76.7 | 78.2 | 79.6 | 79.8 | 79.5 | 78.9 | 78.4 | 78.3 | 77.6 | 77.7 |
| 2018 | 75.5 | 75.9 | 76.2 | 77.8 | 79.2 | 80.6 | 80.7 | 80.8 | 80.1 | 80.6 | 80.5 | 80.2 | 79.0 |
| 2019 | 77.8 | 77.8 | 78.3 | 79.5 | 80.8 | 82.0 | 82.3 | 81.9 | 81.4 | 81.4 | 80.8 | 80.3 | 80.4 |
| **Service-Providing** | | | | | | | | | | | | | |
| 2011 | 472.0 | 478.7 | 479.4 | 486.3 | 483.3 | 477.2 | 470.5 | 465.3 | 481.3 | 485.4 | 486.4 | 489.3 | 479.6 |
| 2012 | 472.7 | 480.6 | 483.0 | 486.0 | 485.2 | 482.5 | 474.5 | 470.9 | 487.2 | 493.6 | 497.4 | 497.0 | 484.2 |
| 2013 | 480.4 | 484.7 | 487.8 | 492.4 | 492.6 | 491.4 | 480.0 | 476.9 | 489.7 | 494.5 | 498.7 | 499.0 | 489.0 |
| 2014 | 485.3 | 488.6 | 491.3 | 498.0 | 499.2 | 496.4 | 485.5 | 482.4 | 496.1 | 502.7 | 505.6 | 506.3 | 494.8 |
| 2015 | 492.0 | 494.2 | 496.5 | 502.0 | 503.2 | 501.2 | 489.6 | 485.7 | 498.7 | 505.6 | 508.6 | 507.2 | 498.7 |
| 2016 | 493.9 | 496.7 | 498.8 | 501.1 | 503.6 | 500.3 | 491.6 | 487.0 | 499.5 | 504.4 | 508.2 | 507.8 | 499.4 |
| 2017 | 495.3 | 497.3 | 498.7 | 502.1 | 505.1 | 502.8 | 492.0 | 488.5 | 502.6 | 505.1 | 508.6 | 509.0 | 500.6 |
| 2018 | 497.2 | 499.2 | 500.0 | 502.3 | 506.5 | 505.6 | 495.5 | 493.2 | 504.7 | 508.7 | 511.1 | 510.8 | 502.9 |
| 2019 | 498.5 | 500.6 | 501.2 | 504.0 | 506.6 | 503.6 | 496.0 | 492.0 | 504.9 | 507.1 | 510.2 | 511.2 | 503.0 |
| **Mining, Logging, and Construction** | | | | | | | | | | | | | |
| 2011 | 15.4 | 15.1 | 15.3 | 16.5 | 17.3 | 18.1 | 18.4 | 18.4 | 18.2 | 18.0 | 18.2 | 17.4 | 17.2 |
| 2012 | 15.8 | 15.3 | 15.7 | 16.8 | 17.2 | 17.7 | 18.2 | 18.3 | 18.1 | 18.2 | 18.1 | 17.6 | 17.3 |
| 2013 | 16.0 | 15.8 | 16.0 | 17.3 | 18.5 | 18.9 | 19.4 | 19.4 | 19.3 | 19.3 | 19.1 | 18.4 | 18.1 |
| 2014 | 16.8 | 16.5 | 16.6 | 18.3 | 19.4 | 19.7 | 20.4 | 20.5 | 20.4 | 20.2 | 20.0 | 19.4 | 19.0 |
| 2015 | 17.7 | 17.4 | 17.6 | 19.6 | 20.8 | 21.2 | 21.3 | 21.5 | 21.2 | 21.3 | 21.2 | 20.6 | 20.1 |
| 2016 | 19.0 | 18.3 | 19.0 | 20.4 | 21.3 | 21.7 | 21.9 | 21.9 | 21.4 | 21.2 | 20.9 | 20.0 | 20.6 |
| 2017 | 18.2 | 17.9 | 18.3 | 19.4 | 20.6 | 21.1 | 21.2 | 21.1 | 20.8 | 20.6 | 20.2 | 19.2 | 19.9 |
| 2018 | 17.4 | 17.6 | 17.9 | 19.3 | 20.3 | 20.8 | 21.0 | 21.1 | 20.9 | 21.2 | 20.9 | 20.3 | 19.9 |
| 2019 | 18.3 | 18.1 | 18.5 | 19.8 | 20.7 | 21.0 | 21.2 | 21.0 | 20.9 | 20.5 | 19.8 | 19.6 | 20.0 |
| **Manufacturing** | | | | | | | | | | | | | |
| 2011 | 56.8 | 56.9 | 57.2 | 57.2 | 57.4 | 57.9 | 57.7 | 57.5 | 57.6 | 57.4 | 57.4 | 57.6 | 57.4 |
| 2012 | 57.3 | 57.4 | 57.3 | 57.3 | 57.5 | 58.0 | 57.9 | 57.6 | 57.2 | 57.3 | 57.3 | 57.5 | 57.5 |
| 2013 | 57.0 | 56.8 | 56.7 | 56.8 | 56.9 | 57.2 | 57.2 | 56.5 | 56.2 | 55.7 | 55.7 | 55.9 | 56.6 |
| 2014 | 55.1 | 55.1 | 55.1 | 55.2 | 55.1 | 55.6 | 55.5 | 55.4 | 55.2 | 55.4 | 55.4 | 55.6 | 55.3 |
| 2015 | 55.1 | 55.2 | 55.5 | 55.6 | 55.9 | 56.4 | 55.8 | 55.8 | 55.8 | 55.6 | 55.5 | 55.6 | 55.7 |
| 2016 | 55.2 | 55.2 | 55.2 | 55.4 | 55.5 | 56.1 | 56.4 | 56.3 | 56.1 | 56.3 | 56.4 | 56.9 | 55.9 |
| 2017 | 56.7 | 56.9 | 57.1 | 57.3 | 57.6 | 58.5 | 58.6 | 58.4 | 58.1 | 57.8 | 58.1 | 58.4 | 57.8 |
| 2018 | 58.1 | 58.3 | 58.3 | 58.5 | 58.9 | 59.8 | 59.7 | 59.7 | 59.2 | 59.4 | 59.6 | 59.9 | 59.1 |
| 2019 | 59.5 | 59.7 | 59.8 | 59.7 | 60.1 | 61.0 | 61.1 | 60.9 | 60.5 | 60.9 | 61.0 | 60.7 | 60.4 |

## Employment by Industry: Hartford-West Hartford-East Hartford, CT NECTA, 2011–2019—*Continued*

(Numbers in thousands, not seasonally adjusted)

| Industry and year | January | February | March | April | May | June | July | August | September | October | November | December | Annual average |
|---|---|---|---|---|---|---|---|---|---|---|---|---|---|
| **Trade, Transportation, and Utilities** | | | | | | | | | | | | | |
| 2011 | 85.8 | 84.9 | 85.0 | 86.2 | 86.4 | 87.1 | 85.3 | 84.9 | 85.7 | 85.9 | 87.7 | 89.4 | 86.2 |
| 2012 | 86.2 | 85.0 | 85.6 | 85.7 | 86.9 | 87.3 | 85.3 | 85.2 | 86.5 | 87.4 | 89.4 | 90.2 | 86.7 |
| 2013 | 87.6 | 86.2 | 86.9 | 87.8 | 88.6 | 89.4 | 87.2 | 87.2 | 88.7 | 89.6 | 91.8 | 92.9 | 88.7 |
| 2014 | 89.2 | 87.9 | 88.0 | 88.9 | 89.7 | 90.2 | 87.7 | 87.3 | 89.2 | 90.0 | 91.6 | 92.7 | 89.4 |
| | | | | | | | | | | | | | |
| 2015 | 89.4 | 88.1 | 88.1 | 88.6 | 89.7 | 90.4 | 87.7 | 87.5 | 89.5 | 91.0 | 92.8 | 93.9 | 89.7 |
| 2016 | 90.8 | 89.5 | 89.8 | 89.3 | 90.6 | 90.5 | 88.7 | 88.0 | 89.4 | 90.3 | 92.4 | 94.0 | 90.3 |
| 2017 | 90.6 | 88.9 | 88.5 | 88.5 | 90.0 | 90.4 | 88.1 | 88.1 | 91.0 | 92.3 | 94.6 | 95.9 | 90.6 |
| 2018 | 92.7 | 91.1 | 90.7 | 90.1 | 92.4 | 92.9 | 90.5 | 90.0 | 91.7 | 92.9 | 95.2 | 95.6 | 92.2 |
| 2019 | 92.5 | 90.8 | 90.2 | 89.3 | 90.8 | 91.0 | 89.2 | 88.5 | 90.6 | 91.2 | 93.6 | 94.3 | 91.0 |
| | | | | | | | | | | | | | |
| **Wholesale Trade** | | | | | | | | | | | | | |
| 2011 | 18.0 | 17.9 | 18.0 | 18.2 | 18.3 | 18.4 | 18.3 | 18.3 | 18.1 | 18.0 | 17.9 | 17.9 | 18.1 |
| 2012 | 17.7 | 17.7 | 17.7 | 17.8 | 17.9 | 18.0 | 18.1 | 18.0 | 17.9 | 18.1 | 17.9 | 18.0 | 17.9 |
| 2013 | 17.8 | 17.8 | 17.8 | 17.9 | 18.0 | 18.1 | 18.0 | 18.0 | 17.9 | 17.9 | 17.9 | 18.0 | 17.9 |
| 2014 | 17.8 | 17.7 | 17.7 | 17.8 | 17.9 | 17.9 | 17.9 | 17.8 | 17.8 | 17.8 | 17.7 | 17.8 | 17.8 |
| | | | | | | | | | | | | | |
| 2015 | 17.7 | 17.6 | 17.6 | 17.8 | 17.9 | 18.0 | 17.9 | 18.0 | 17.9 | 17.8 | 17.8 | 17.8 | 17.8 |
| 2016 | 18.0 | 17.9 | 18.0 | 18.1 | 18.1 | 18.2 | 18.1 | 18.0 | 17.9 | 17.8 | 17.8 | 17.9 | 18.0 |
| 2017 | 17.9 | 17.8 | 17.8 | 17.9 | 18.1 | 18.1 | 18.0 | 17.9 | 17.9 | 17.9 | 17.8 | 18.0 | 17.9 |
| 2018 | 17.9 | 17.9 | 17.9 | 17.7 | 17.8 | 17.9 | 17.9 | 17.8 | 17.7 | 17.9 | 17.9 | 17.9 | 17.9 |
| 2019 | 17.7 | 17.7 | 17.7 | 17.8 | 17.8 | 17.9 | 17.9 | 17.7 | 17.6 | 17.6 | 17.5 | 17.6 | 17.7 |
| | | | | | | | | | | | | | |
| **Retail Trade** | | | | | | | | | | | | | |
| 2011 | 54.6 | 53.7 | 53.6 | 54.5 | 54.5 | 55.0 | 54.3 | 54.3 | 53.9 | 54.3 | 56.1 | 57.5 | 54.7 |
| 2012 | 55.2 | 54.0 | 54.4 | 54.5 | 55.2 | 55.4 | 54.6 | 54.7 | 54.3 | 55.0 | 57.1 | 57.5 | 55.2 |
| 2013 | 55.6 | 54.5 | 54.8 | 55.3 | 55.8 | 56.3 | 55.7 | 56.0 | 55.6 | 56.4 | 58.2 | 58.9 | 56.1 |
| 2014 | 56.4 | 55.2 | 55.3 | 55.9 | 56.5 | 56.9 | 55.9 | 55.8 | 55.7 | 56.3 | 58.0 | 58.6 | 56.4 |
| | | | | | | | | | | | | | |
| 2015 | 56.2 | 55.1 | 55.2 | 55.3 | 56.0 | 56.5 | 55.5 | 55.5 | 55.2 | 56.1 | 57.6 | 58.5 | 56.1 |
| 2016 | 55.8 | 54.7 | 55.0 | 54.8 | 55.5 | 55.9 | 55.4 | 55.2 | 54.6 | 55.4 | 57.0 | 57.5 | 55.6 |
| 2017 | 56.0 | 54.4 | 54.1 | 54.7 | 55.2 | 55.5 | 55.1 | 55.0 | 54.4 | 55.3 | 57.1 | 57.7 | 55.4 |
| 2018 | 55.6 | 54.3 | 54.0 | 54.2 | 55.0 | 55.2 | 54.6 | 54.5 | 53.9 | 54.5 | 56.2 | 56.6 | 54.9 |
| 2019 | 54.7 | 53.4 | 52.9 | 52.9 | 53.3 | 53.4 | 53.1 | 52.8 | 52.2 | 52.6 | 54.1 | 54.1 | 53.3 |
| | | | | | | | | | | | | | |
| **Transportation and Utilities** | | | | | | | | | | | | | |
| 2011 | 13.2 | 13.3 | 13.4 | 13.5 | 13.6 | 13.7 | 12.7 | 12.3 | 13.7 | 13.6 | 13.7 | 14.0 | 13.4 |
| 2012 | 13.3 | 13.3 | 13.5 | 13.4 | 13.8 | 13.9 | 12.6 | 12.5 | 14.3 | 14.3 | 14.4 | 14.7 | 13.7 |
| 2013 | 14.2 | 13.9 | 14.3 | 14.6 | 14.8 | 15.0 | 13.5 | 13.2 | 15.2 | 15.3 | 15.7 | 16.0 | 14.6 |
| 2014 | 15.0 | 15.0 | 15.0 | 15.2 | 15.3 | 15.4 | 13.9 | 13.7 | 15.7 | 15.9 | 15.9 | 16.3 | 15.2 |
| | | | | | | | | | | | | | |
| 2015 | 15.5 | 15.4 | 15.3 | 15.5 | 15.8 | 15.9 | 14.3 | 14.0 | 16.4 | 17.1 | 17.4 | 17.6 | 15.9 |
| 2016 | 17.0 | 16.9 | 16.8 | 16.4 | 17.0 | 16.4 | 15.2 | 14.8 | 16.9 | 17.1 | 17.6 | 18.6 | 16.7 |
| 2017 | 16.7 | 16.7 | 16.6 | 15.9 | 16.7 | 16.8 | 15.0 | 15.2 | 18.7 | 19.1 | 19.7 | 20.2 | 17.3 |
| 2018 | 19.2 | 18.9 | 18.8 | 18.2 | 19.6 | 19.8 | 18.0 | 17.7 | 20.1 | 20.5 | 21.1 | 21.1 | 19.4 |
| 2019 | 20.1 | 19.7 | 19.6 | 18.6 | 19.7 | 19.7 | 18.2 | 18.0 | 20.8 | 21.0 | 22.0 | 22.6 | 20.0 |
| | | | | | | | | | | | | | |
| **Information** | | | | | | | | | | | | | |
| 2011 | 11.5 | 11.4 | 11.4 | 11.3 | 11.3 | 11.3 | 11.3 | 11.3 | 11.2 | 11.1 | 11.1 | 11.0 | 11.3 |
| 2012 | 11.0 | 11.1 | 10.9 | 11.1 | 11.2 | 11.2 | 11.2 | 11.3 | 11.3 | 11.3 | 11.6 | 11.3 | 11.2 |
| 2013 | 11.5 | 11.7 | 11.7 | 11.4 | 11.5 | 11.6 | 11.5 | 11.6 | 11.2 | 11.2 | 11.3 | 11.3 | 11.5 |
| 2014 | 11.2 | 11.3 | 11.5 | 11.5 | 11.4 | 11.5 | 11.6 | 11.7 | 11.5 | 11.3 | 11.6 | 11.7 | 11.5 |
| | | | | | | | | | | | | | |
| 2015 | 11.5 | 11.6 | 11.6 | 11.8 | 11.8 | 11.9 | 11.9 | 12.0 | 11.9 | 11.9 | 12.0 | 12.0 | 11.8 |
| 2016 | 11.7 | 11.6 | 11.6 | 11.5 | 11.6 | 11.6 | 11.6 | 11.6 | 11.4 | 11.2 | 11.1 | 11.1 | 11.5 |
| 2017 | 10.7 | 10.6 | 10.6 | 10.6 | 10.5 | 10.6 | 10.6 | 10.6 | 10.5 | 10.3 | 10.4 | 10.3 | 10.5 |
| 2018 | 10.1 | 10.1 | 9.9 | 10.0 | 9.9 | 10.0 | 10.0 | 9.9 | 9.9 | 9.9 | 9.8 | 9.8 | 9.9 |
| 2019 | 9.5 | 9.5 | 9.7 | 9.7 | 9.6 | 9.8 | 9.9 | 9.9 | 9.9 | 9.9 | 9.8 | 9.9 | 9.8 |
| | | | | | | | | | | | | | |
| **Financial Activities** | | | | | | | | | | | | | |
| 2011 | 62.2 | 62.0 | 62.2 | 61.8 | 61.8 | 62.3 | 62.5 | 62.3 | 61.7 | 61.6 | 61.4 | 61.5 | 61.9 |
| 2012 | 61.1 | 61.1 | 61.3 | 60.7 | 60.7 | 61.6 | 61.6 | 61.1 | 60.5 | 60.3 | 60.1 | 60.1 | 60.9 |
| 2013 | 60.0 | 59.5 | 59.4 | 59.1 | 58.8 | 59.6 | 59.4 | 58.7 | 57.6 | 56.9 | 56.7 | 56.7 | 58.5 |
| 2014 | 57.0 | 56.6 | 56.4 | 56.3 | 56.5 | 57.1 | 57.4 | 57.1 | 56.6 | 56.7 | 56.7 | 56.8 | 56.8 |
| | | | | | | | | | | | | | |
| 2015 | 56.7 | 56.6 | 56.7 | 56.8 | 57.0 | 57.9 | 58.1 | 58.0 | 57.3 | 57.2 | 57.5 | 57.4 | 57.3 |
| 2016 | 57.2 | 57.0 | 57.2 | 57.3 | 57.3 | 58.2 | 58.1 | 58.0 | 57.3 | 57.1 | 57.1 | 57.0 | 57.4 |
| 2017 | 56.8 | 56.7 | 56.8 | 56.7 | 56.8 | 57.7 | 57.7 | 57.5 | 56.8 | 56.7 | 56.7 | 56.5 | 57.0 |
| 2018 | 56.2 | 56.2 | 56.3 | 56.2 | 56.2 | 57.3 | 57.4 | 57.0 | 56.5 | 56.4 | 56.3 | 56.1 | 56.5 |
| 2019 | 55.9 | 55.9 | 55.9 | 56.0 | 56.0 | 56.9 | 57.2 | 56.8 | 56.2 | 56.5 | 56.7 | 56.5 | 56.4 |

## Employment by Industry: Hartford-West Hartford-East Hartford, CT NECTA, 2011–2019—*Continued*

(Numbers in thousands, not seasonally adjusted)

| Industry and year | January | February | March | April | May | June | July | August | September | October | November | December | Annual average |
|---|---|---|---|---|---|---|---|---|---|---|---|---|---|
| **Professional and Business Services** | | | | | | | | | | | | | |
| 2011 | 60.6 | 60.9 | 60.5 | 62.4 | 62.6 | 63.2 | 63.4 | 63.1 | 63.2 | 63.8 | 63.5 | 64.2 | 62.6 |
| 2012 | 62.9 | 63.4 | 63.9 | 65.1 | 65.5 | 66.3 | 66.2 | 66.4 | 66.1 | 66.5 | 66.4 | 66.0 | 65.4 |
| 2013 | 63.7 | 64.5 | 64.5 | 66.0 | 66.6 | 67.6 | 67.5 | 68.1 | 68.5 | 68.5 | 68.9 | 68.9 | 66.9 |
| 2014 | 67.7 | 68.5 | 68.8 | 70.4 | 71.7 | 71.9 | 71.2 | 71.2 | 71.1 | 71.8 | 71.9 | 72.0 | 70.7 |
| 2015 | 70.8 | 71.5 | 72.0 | 72.8 | 73.6 | 74.9 | 73.8 | 73.4 | 72.9 | 73.1 | 73.3 | 72.7 | 72.9 |
| 2016 | 70.8 | 71.1 | 71.2 | 72.2 | 72.6 | 73.8 | 73.3 | 73.4 | 73.3 | 73.3 | 73.5 | 73.6 | 72.7 |
| 2017 | 71.8 | 72.0 | 72.3 | 73.8 | 74.3 | 74.9 | 74.7 | 74.4 | 74.2 | 74.0 | 74.5 | 74.3 | 73.8 |
| 2018 | 72.2 | 72.6 | 72.8 | 73.4 | 74.0 | 74.6 | 74.7 | 75.0 | 74.5 | 74.7 | 75.2 | 74.3 | 74.0 |
| 2019 | 71.7 | 72.0 | 71.7 | 73.4 | 73.7 | 74.4 | 74.6 | 74.6 | 74.5 | 73.8 | 73.7 | 75.2 | 73.6 |
| **Education and Health Services** | | | | | | | | | | | | | |
| 2011 | 100.4 | 101.0 | 101.5 | 102.0 | 101.4 | 100.0 | 99.2 | 98.4 | 100.2 | 100.0 | 99.8 | 100.3 | 100.4 |
| 2012 | 99.4 | 100.4 | 100.8 | 100.7 | 100.4 | 99.6 | 99.2 | 98.8 | 101.2 | 102.3 | 103.0 | 103.5 | 100.8 |
| 2013 | 101.5 | 102.1 | 103.0 | 103.1 | 102.5 | 102.0 | 100.6 | 100.8 | 103.2 | 103.5 | 104.3 | 103.9 | 102.5 |
| 2014 | 102.1 | 102.9 | 103.4 | 104.8 | 104.3 | 103.9 | 102.4 | 103.0 | 105.0 | 105.3 | 105.8 | 105.9 | 104.1 |
| 2015 | 103.8 | 104.2 | 104.4 | 105.4 | 105.0 | 104.9 | 103.7 | 103.1 | 104.5 | 105.2 | 105.5 | 105.6 | 104.6 |
| 2016 | 104.3 | 105.0 | 105.1 | 105.1 | 105.0 | 105.3 | 105.8 | 105.4 | 107.1 | 107.2 | 108.2 | 107.5 | 105.9 |
| 2017 | 106.9 | 107.7 | 107.8 | 107.9 | 108.4 | 106.9 | 105.2 | 105.4 | 107.5 | 107.8 | 108.2 | 108.8 | 107.4 |
| 2018 | 107.2 | 108.3 | 108.3 | 109.0 | 109.4 | 108.6 | 106.4 | 106.9 | 108.7 | 109.4 | 109.4 | 109.9 | 108.5 |
| 2019 | 108.5 | 109.6 | 109.9 | 110.4 | 110.3 | 109.5 | 108.1 | 108.5 | 110.5 | 111.3 | 112.7 | 113.0 | 110.2 |
| **Leisure and Hospitality** | | | | | | | | | | | | | |
| 2011 | 39.1 | 39.9 | 39.9 | 42.2 | 44.1 | 44.8 | 45.5 | 44.8 | 44.2 | 43.5 | 42.7 | 43.0 | 42.8 |
| 2012 | 41.4 | 41.8 | 42.6 | 44.2 | 46.2 | 47.4 | 46.8 | 46.6 | 45.3 | 45.2 | 44.6 | 44.8 | 44.7 |
| 2013 | 43.0 | 42.7 | 43.7 | 45.9 | 48.3 | 48.9 | 48.3 | 48.2 | 46.4 | 46.4 | 46.3 | 45.9 | 46.2 |
| 2014 | 44.2 | 44.0 | 44.9 | 46.5 | 48.6 | 49.3 | 49.1 | 48.4 | 46.8 | 46.7 | 46.1 | 46.1 | 46.7 |
| 2015 | 44.3 | 44.0 | 44.8 | 46.4 | 48.6 | 49.1 | 48.7 | 47.9 | 46.9 | 47.1 | 46.1 | 45.9 | 46.7 |
| 2016 | 44.5 | 45.1 | 45.7 | 47.2 | 49.5 | 50.4 | 49.8 | 49.2 | 48.2 | 47.9 | 47.4 | 47.1 | 47.7 |
| 2017 | 45.5 | 45.6 | 46.3 | 47.9 | 49.8 | 51.1 | 50.1 | 49.4 | 48.4 | 48.6 | 47.8 | 47.6 | 48.2 |
| 2018 | 45.9 | 45.6 | 45.7 | 47.6 | 49.7 | 50.8 | 50.6 | 50.4 | 48.7 | 48.8 | 47.8 | 48.3 | 48.3 |
| 2019 | 46.0 | 46.2 | 46.7 | 48.1 | 50.1 | 50.8 | 50.9 | 49.6 | 48.0 | 47.8 | 45.7 | 45.0 | 47.9 |
| **Other Services** | | | | | | | | | | | | | |
| 2011 | 20.2 | 20.2 | 20.3 | 20.5 | 20.7 | 21.1 | 20.7 | 20.5 | 20.3 | 20.3 | 20.4 | 20.4 | 20.5 |
| 2012 | 20.5 | 20.5 | 20.3 | 20.5 | 20.8 | 21.2 | 21.2 | 21.3 | 21.2 | 21.6 | 21.8 | 21.1 | 21.0 |
| 2013 | 21.0 | 21.1 | 21.2 | 20.9 | 21.1 | 21.5 | 21.2 | 21.0 | 20.8 | 20.7 | 20.8 | 20.9 | 21.0 |
| 2014 | 20.8 | 20.8 | 20.9 | 21.1 | 21.3 | 21.6 | 21.6 | 21.4 | 21.4 | 21.5 | 21.5 | 21.4 | 21.3 |
| 2015 | 21.3 | 21.3 | 21.5 | 21.4 | 21.7 | 21.8 | 21.9 | 22.3 | 21.6 | 21.6 | 21.6 | 21.6 | 21.6 |
| 2016 | 21.6 | 21.6 | 21.7 | 21.7 | 21.9 | 22.2 | 22.2 | 22.1 | 21.8 | 21.9 | 21.8 | 21.9 | 21.9 |
| 2017 | 21.7 | 21.7 | 21.8 | 21.9 | 22.1 | 22.4 | 22.2 | 22.0 | 22.1 | 21.8 | 22.0 | 22.0 | 22.0 |
| 2018 | 22.2 | 22.2 | 22.5 | 22.8 | 22.8 | 23.2 | 23.1 | 23.0 | 22.7 | 22.6 | 22.7 | 22.7 | 22.7 |
| 2019 | 22.4 | 22.3 | 22.4 | 22.7 | 22.8 | 23.0 | 23.0 | 22.9 | 22.5 | 22.2 | 22.6 | 22.5 | 22.6 |
| **Government** | | | | | | | | | | | | | |
| 2011 | 92.2 | 98.4 | 98.6 | 99.9 | 95.0 | 87.4 | 82.6 | 80.0 | 94.8 | 99.2 | 99.8 | 99.5 | 94.0 |
| 2012 | 90.2 | 97.3 | 97.6 | 98.0 | 93.5 | 87.9 | 83.0 | 80.2 | 95.1 | 99.0 | 100.5 | 100.0 | 93.5 |
| 2013 | 92.1 | 96.9 | 97.4 | 98.2 | 95.2 | 90.8 | 84.3 | 81.3 | 93.3 | 97.7 | 98.6 | 98.5 | 93.7 |
| 2014 | 93.1 | 96.6 | 97.4 | 98.5 | 95.7 | 90.9 | 84.5 | 82.3 | 94.5 | 99.4 | 100.4 | 99.7 | 94.4 |
| 2015 | 94.2 | 96.9 | 97.4 | 98.8 | 95.8 | 90.3 | 83.8 | 81.5 | 94.1 | 98.5 | 99.8 | 98.1 | 94.1 |
| 2016 | 93.0 | 95.8 | 96.5 | 96.8 | 95.1 | 88.3 | 82.1 | 79.3 | 91.0 | 95.5 | 96.7 | 95.6 | 92.1 |
| 2017 | 91.3 | 94.1 | 94.6 | 94.8 | 93.2 | 88.8 | 83.4 | 81.1 | 92.1 | 93.6 | 94.4 | 93.6 | 91.3 |
| 2018 | 90.7 | 93.1 | 93.8 | 93.2 | 92.1 | 88.2 | 82.8 | 81.0 | 92.0 | 94.0 | 94.7 | 94.1 | 90.8 |
| 2019 | 92.0 | 94.3 | 94.7 | 94.4 | 93.3 | 88.2 | 83.1 | 81.2 | 92.7 | 94.4 | 95.4 | 94.8 | 91.5 |

# Employment by Industry: Buffalo-Cheektowaga-Niagara Falls, NY, 2011–2019

(Numbers in thousands, not seasonally adjusted)

| Industry and year | January | February | March | April | May | June | July | August | September | October | November | December | Annual average |
|---|---|---|---|---|---|---|---|---|---|---|---|---|---|
| **Total Nonfarm** | | | | | | | | | | | | | |
| 2011 | 527.2 | 529.4 | 530.2 | 538.2 | 542.6 | 545.4 | 537.2 | 538.5 | 546.4 | 548.4 | 549.2 | 548.8 | 540.1 |
| 2012 | 530.7 | 534.9 | 536.8 | 539.3 | 546.3 | 548.4 | 539.7 | 542.4 | 545.4 | 551.4 | 551.1 | 551.2 | 543.1 |
| 2013 | 532.3 | 535.4 | 537.8 | 541.4 | 548.0 | 550.1 | 543.7 | 545.6 | 550.0 | 556.7 | 556.7 | 556.0 | 546.1 |
| 2014 | 535.1 | 538.8 | 540.7 | 547.0 | 552.5 | 555.3 | 549.0 | 550.2 | 553.5 | 559.6 | 558.2 | 559.4 | 549.9 |
| 2015 | 537.9 | 541.0 | 542.9 | 549.2 | 557.6 | 560.1 | 554.8 | 555.6 | 558.2 | 565.7 | 565.0 | 565.6 | 554.5 |
| 2016 | 544.0 | 548.1 | 550.0 | 557.4 | 561.4 | 563.4 | 558.9 | 559.2 | 562.7 | 567.8 | 567.6 | 565.6 | 558.8 |
| 2017 | 548.5 | 552.8 | 554.4 | 556.7 | 563.7 | 566.4 | 561.1 | 562.5 | 565.8 | 571.0 | 572.8 | 571.3 | 562.3 |
| 2018 | 550.0 | 554.4 | 556.3 | 560.1 | 567.8 | 569.8 | 564.6 | 566.4 | 568.7 | 574.0 | 572.0 | 571.8 | 564.7 |
| 2019 | 554.8 | 557.6 | 560.4 | 565.6 | 569.4 | 569.9 | 562.3 | 563.5 | 566.6 | 569.2 | 571.7 | 569.9 | 565.1 |
| **Total Private** | | | | | | | | | | | | | |
| 2011 | 434.0 | 435.1 | 436.3 | 443.8 | 448.7 | 452.9 | 449.4 | 450.6 | 456.4 | 455.7 | 456.2 | 455.9 | 447.9 |
| 2012 | 440.3 | 442.3 | 444.3 | 447.4 | 454.1 | 457.6 | 453.7 | 456.8 | 457.6 | 460.4 | 459.8 | 459.8 | 452.8 |
| 2013 | 443.6 | 444.5 | 446.8 | 451.2 | 458.0 | 461.1 | 459.0 | 460.8 | 463.2 | 466.5 | 466.5 | 466.1 | 457.3 |
| 2014 | 448.3 | 449.8 | 451.3 | 457.7 | 463.8 | 467.4 | 465.0 | 466.2 | 467.5 | 470.8 | 469.1 | 470.8 | 462.3 |
| 2015 | 451.0 | 452.6 | 454.4 | 460.9 | 469.0 | 472.0 | 470.5 | 471.1 | 471.6 | 476.6 | 475.7 | 476.0 | 466.8 |
| 2016 | 456.5 | 459.0 | 460.6 | 468.2 | 472.1 | 474.6 | 473.6 | 474.2 | 474.6 | 478.2 | 477.8 | 475.0 | 470.4 |
| 2017 | 458.8 | 462.3 | 463.9 | 466.3 | 473.1 | 476.5 | 474.6 | 476.5 | 477.3 | 480.4 | 481.6 | 479.8 | 472.6 |
| 2018 | 460.9 | 463.7 | 465.7 | 470.1 | 477.3 | 479.8 | 478.1 | 480.2 | 480.0 | 483.0 | 480.7 | 480.4 | 475.0 |
| 2019 | 465.3 | 467.0 | 469.5 | 474.6 | 478.9 | 479.7 | 475.6 | 477.0 | 477.3 | 477.5 | 479.8 | 477.6 | 475.0 |
| **Goods Producing** | | | | | | | | | | | | | |
| 2011 | 66.7 | 66.4 | 67.0 | 69.4 | 71.2 | 72.9 | 73.4 | 74.1 | 73.5 | 73.1 | 72.4 | 70.5 | 70.9 |
| 2012 | 68.0 | 67.5 | 68.3 | 69.8 | 71.6 | 72.9 | 73.1 | 73.4 | 72.6 | 72.4 | 71.3 | 70.2 | 70.9 |
| 2013 | 67.3 | 66.7 | 67.3 | 68.6 | 71.2 | 72.4 | 72.2 | 73.6 | 73.0 | 73.0 | 72.1 | 70.9 | 70.7 |
| 2014 | 68.3 | 68.3 | 68.7 | 70.8 | 73.2 | 74.7 | 74.3 | 75.6 | 75.1 | 74.7 | 73.1 | 72.2 | 72.4 |
| 2015 | 68.6 | 68.2 | 69.0 | 71.1 | 73.8 | 75.0 | 75.6 | 75.5 | 74.9 | 75.4 | 74.7 | 74.1 | 73.0 |
| 2016 | 70.8 | 70.2 | 70.8 | 72.5 | 74.3 | 75.5 | 75.9 | 75.9 | 75.3 | 75.0 | 74.5 | 72.2 | 73.6 |
| 2017 | 70.0 | 69.6 | 69.8 | 71.8 | 73.5 | 74.8 | 74.7 | 75.3 | 74.8 | 74.5 | 73.7 | 72.0 | 72.9 |
| 2018 | 69.2 | 69.5 | 69.8 | 71.5 | 73.8 | 75.2 | 75.8 | 76.0 | 75.2 | 75.1 | 73.9 | 73.0 | 73.2 |
| 2019 | 71.0 | 70.8 | 71.3 | 73.2 | 74.9 | 75.9 | 76.1 | 76.1 | 75.7 | 72.8 | 73.3 | 72.0 | 73.6 |
| **Service-Providing** | | | | | | | | | | | | | |
| 2011 | 460.5 | 463.0 | 463.2 | 468.8 | 471.4 | 472.5 | 463.8 | 464.4 | 472.9 | 475.3 | 476.8 | 478.3 | 469.2 |
| 2012 | 462.7 | 467.4 | 468.5 | 469.5 | 474.7 | 475.5 | 466.6 | 469.0 | 472.8 | 479.0 | 479.8 | 481.0 | 472.2 |
| 2013 | 465.0 | 468.7 | 470.5 | 472.8 | 476.8 | 477.7 | 471.5 | 472.0 | 477.0 | 483.7 | 484.6 | 485.1 | 475.5 |
| 2014 | 466.8 | 470.5 | 472.0 | 476.2 | 479.3 | 480.6 | 474.7 | 474.6 | 478.4 | 484.9 | 485.1 | 487.2 | 477.5 |
| 2015 | 469.3 | 472.8 | 473.9 | 478.1 | 483.8 | 485.1 | 479.2 | 480.1 | 483.3 | 490.3 | 490.3 | 491.5 | 481.5 |
| 2016 | 473.2 | 477.9 | 479.2 | 484.9 | 487.1 | 487.9 | 483.0 | 483.3 | 487.4 | 492.8 | 493.1 | 493.4 | 485.3 |
| 2017 | 478.5 | 483.2 | 484.6 | 484.9 | 490.2 | 491.6 | 486.4 | 487.2 | 491.0 | 496.5 | 499.1 | 499.3 | 489.4 |
| 2018 | 480.8 | 484.9 | 486.5 | 488.6 | 494.0 | 494.6 | 488.8 | 490.4 | 493.5 | 498.9 | 498.1 | 498.8 | 491.5 |
| 2019 | 483.8 | 486.8 | 489.1 | 492.4 | 494.5 | 494.0 | 486.2 | 487.4 | 490.9 | 496.4 | 498.4 | 497.9 | 491.5 |
| **Mining, Logging, and Construction** | | | | | | | | | | | | | |
| 2011 | 16.5 | 16.1 | 16.7 | 18.6 | 20.3 | 21.4 | 22.2 | 22.5 | 22.2 | 21.8 | 21.0 | 19.1 | 19.9 |
| 2012 | 17.1 | 16.6 | 17.4 | 18.9 | 20.3 | 21.3 | 21.5 | 21.7 | 21.1 | 20.8 | 19.9 | 18.7 | 19.6 |
| 2013 | 16.6 | 16.2 | 16.5 | 17.6 | 20.0 | 20.8 | 21.3 | 21.6 | 21.1 | 21.0 | 20.2 | 18.7 | 19.3 |
| 2014 | 16.5 | 16.3 | 16.8 | 18.6 | 20.9 | 22.1 | 22.6 | 23.0 | 22.7 | 22.4 | 20.8 | 19.6 | 20.2 |
| 2015 | 17.2 | 16.6 | 17.1 | 19.1 | 21.6 | 22.3 | 23.1 | 23.2 | 22.9 | 23.1 | 22.4 | 21.5 | 20.8 |
| 2016 | 18.8 | 18.5 | 19.0 | 20.7 | 22.5 | 23.3 | 23.7 | 23.7 | 23.3 | 22.9 | 22.3 | 20.2 | 21.6 |
| 2017 | 18.2 | 17.8 | 18.0 | 20.2 | 21.7 | 22.7 | 23.1 | 23.4 | 23.0 | 22.4 | 21.5 | 19.8 | 21.0 |
| 2018 | 17.8 | 17.8 | 18.1 | 19.7 | 21.8 | 22.8 | 23.2 | 23.4 | 22.7 | 22.4 | 21.2 | 20.1 | 20.9 |
| 2019 | 18.4 | 18.0 | 18.7 | 20.6 | 22.2 | 22.9 | 23.2 | 23.3 | 23.0 | 22.9 | 21.4 | 20.3 | 21.2 |
| **Manufacturing** | | | | | | | | | | | | | |
| 2011 | 50.2 | 50.3 | 50.3 | 50.8 | 50.9 | 51.5 | 51.2 | 51.6 | 51.3 | 51.3 | 51.4 | 51.4 | 51.0 |
| 2012 | 50.9 | 50.9 | 50.9 | 50.9 | 51.3 | 51.6 | 51.6 | 51.7 | 51.5 | 51.6 | 51.4 | 51.5 | 51.3 |
| 2013 | 50.7 | 50.5 | 50.8 | 51.0 | 51.2 | 51.6 | 50.9 | 52.0 | 51.9 | 52.0 | 51.9 | 52.2 | 51.4 |
| 2014 | 51.8 | 52.0 | 51.9 | 52.2 | 52.3 | 52.6 | 51.7 | 52.6 | 52.4 | 52.3 | 52.3 | 52.6 | 52.2 |
| 2015 | 51.4 | 51.6 | 51.9 | 52.0 | 52.2 | 52.7 | 52.5 | 52.3 | 52.0 | 52.3 | 52.3 | 52.6 | 52.2 |
| 2016 | 52.0 | 51.7 | 51.8 | 51.8 | 51.8 | 52.2 | 52.2 | 52.2 | 52.0 | 52.1 | 52.2 | 52.0 | 52.0 |
| 2017 | 51.8 | 51.8 | 51.8 | 51.6 | 51.8 | 52.1 | 51.6 | 51.9 | 51.8 | 52.1 | 52.2 | 52.2 | 51.9 |
| 2018 | 51.4 | 51.7 | 51.7 | 51.8 | 52.0 | 52.4 | 52.6 | 52.6 | 52.5 | 52.7 | 52.7 | 52.9 | 52.3 |
| 2019 | 52.6 | 52.8 | 52.6 | 52.6 | 52.7 | 53.0 | 52.9 | 52.8 | 52.7 | 49.9 | 51.9 | 51.7 | 52.4 |

# Employment by Industry: Buffalo-Cheektowaga-Niagara Falls, NY, 2011–2019—*Continued*

(Numbers in thousands, not seasonally adjusted)

| Industry and year | January | February | March | April | May | June | July | August | September | October | November | December | Annual average |
|---|---|---|---|---|---|---|---|---|---|---|---|---|---|
| **Trade, Transportation, and Utilities** | | | | | | | | | | | | | |
| 2011 | 97.3 | 95.8 | 95.9 | 97.0 | 98.2 | 99.6 | 98.2 | 99.1 | 99.9 | 100.7 | 103.1 | 103.9 | 99.1 |
| 2012 | 99.5 | 97.4 | 98.1 | 98.0 | 100.1 | 101.2 | 99.8 | 100.3 | 101.1 | 101.5 | 103.3 | 104.3 | 100.4 |
| 2013 | 99.2 | 97.5 | 97.9 | 98.2 | 99.7 | 101.0 | 99.9 | 99.8 | 100.9 | 101.4 | 104.0 | 105.7 | 100.4 |
| 2014 | 100.7 | 99.4 | 100.0 | 100.7 | 101.7 | 103.4 | 101.7 | 101.7 | 102.3 | 103.2 | 105.8 | 107.2 | 102.3 |
| 2015 | 102.0 | 100.9 | 100.9 | 101.6 | 103.3 | 104.4 | 103.1 | 103.0 | 103.5 | 104.4 | 106.4 | 107.7 | 103.4 |
| 2016 | 102.5 | 101.4 | 101.6 | 102.4 | 103.1 | 103.6 | 102.2 | 102.0 | 102.6 | 104.6 | 105.1 | 102.8 | 102.8 |
| 2017 | 100.9 | 99.1 | 99.6 | 98.9 | 100.5 | 101.4 | 99.9 | 99.8 | 100.8 | 101.7 | 103.9 | 104.7 | 100.9 |
| 2018 | 99.6 | 98.3 | 98.4 | 99.5 | 100.8 | 101.3 | 100.1 | 100.1 | 100.4 | 101.9 | 103.7 | 104.3 | 100.7 |
| 2019 | 99.6 | 98.0 | 98.2 | 98.3 | 99.3 | 99.8 | 98.1 | 98.0 | 98.9 | 100.4 | 102.5 | 103.1 | 99.5 |
| **Wholesale Trade** | | | | | | | | | | | | | |
| 2011 | 21.2 | 21.0 | 21.0 | 21.2 | 21.5 | 21.7 | 21.7 | 21.8 | 21.7 | 21.6 | 21.8 | 21.8 | 21.5 |
| 2012 | 21.6 | 21.5 | 21.6 | 21.5 | 21.7 | 21.9 | 21.8 | 22.0 | 21.8 | 21.9 | 21.8 | 21.9 | 21.8 |
| 2013 | 21.7 | 21.6 | 21.6 | 21.6 | 21.6 | 21.8 | 21.9 | 21.9 | 21.9 | 22.0 | 22.1 | 22.3 | 21.8 |
| 2014 | 22.2 | 22.0 | 22.0 | 22.2 | 22.4 | 22.5 | 22.2 | 22.3 | 22.2 | 22.3 | 22.3 | 22.4 | 22.3 |
| 2015 | 22.2 | 22.1 | 22.1 | 22.2 | 22.2 | 22.4 | 22.5 | 22.3 | 22.2 | 22.3 | 22.2 | 22.4 | 22.3 |
| 2016 | 22.0 | 21.9 | 21.8 | 21.9 | 22.0 | 21.9 | 21.9 | 21.7 | 21.3 | 21.5 | 21.6 | 21.6 | 21.8 |
| 2017 | 21.5 | 21.3 | 21.3 | 21.2 | 21.3 | 21.4 | 21.4 | 21.3 | 21.2 | 21.3 | 21.4 | 21.3 | 21.3 |
| 2018 | 20.9 | 20.8 | 20.8 | 20.9 | 20.9 | 21.0 | 21.0 | 20.9 | 20.9 | 20.9 | 20.9 | 21.0 | 20.9 |
| 2019 | 20.9 | 20.8 | 20.9 | 20.8 | 20.9 | 21.0 | 20.9 | 20.9 | 20.8 | 20.7 | 20.7 | 20.7 | 20.8 |
| **Retail Trade** | | | | | | | | | | | | | |
| 2011 | 60.4 | 59.3 | 59.5 | 60.3 | 60.8 | 61.7 | 61.4 | 62.3 | 62.0 | 62.9 | 65.0 | 65.5 | 61.8 |
| 2012 | 62.1 | 60.5 | 61.0 | 61.1 | 62.3 | 62.9 | 62.8 | 63.1 | 63.0 | 63.4 | 65.3 | 65.8 | 62.8 |
| 2013 | 61.7 | 60.3 | 60.6 | 60.9 | 61.9 | 62.8 | 62.5 | 62.5 | 62.3 | 62.7 | 65.0 | 66.1 | 62.4 |
| 2014 | 62.0 | 61.0 | 61.5 | 61.9 | 62.3 | 63.6 | 63.1 | 63.1 | 62.4 | 63.1 | 65.3 | 66.2 | 63.0 |
| 2015 | 62.5 | 61.7 | 61.7 | 62.3 | 63.2 | 63.8 | 63.6 | 63.8 | 63.3 | 64.0 | 65.9 | 66.6 | 63.5 |
| 2016 | 63.4 | 62.5 | 62.8 | 63.3 | 63.6 | 64.0 | 63.8 | 63.9 | 63.3 | 63.6 | 65.4 | 65.4 | 63.8 |
| 2017 | 62.4 | 60.9 | 61.4 | 61.1 | 61.8 | 62.3 | 61.5 | 61.9 | 61.4 | 62.3 | 64.3 | 64.5 | 62.2 |
| 2018 | 61.0 | 60.1 | 60.1 | 60.4 | 61.5 | 61.5 | 61.3 | 61.3 | 60.3 | 60.8 | 63.2 | 62.7 | 61.2 |
| 2019 | 59.8 | 58.5 | 58.6 | 58.8 | 59.4 | 59.7 | 59.2 | 59.1 | 58.8 | 59.7 | 61.4 | 61.4 | 59.5 |
| **Transportation and Utilities** | | | | | | | | | | | | | |
| 2011 | 15.7 | 15.5 | 15.4 | 15.5 | 15.9 | 16.2 | 15.1 | 15.0 | 16.2 | 16.2 | 16.3 | 16.6 | 15.8 |
| 2012 | 15.8 | 15.4 | 15.5 | 15.4 | 16.1 | 16.4 | 15.2 | 15.2 | 16.3 | 16.2 | 16.2 | 16.6 | 15.9 |
| 2013 | 15.8 | 15.6 | 15.7 | 15.7 | 16.2 | 16.4 | 15.5 | 15.4 | 16.7 | 16.7 | 16.9 | 17.3 | 16.2 |
| 2014 | 16.5 | 16.4 | 16.5 | 16.6 | 17.0 | 17.3 | 16.4 | 16.3 | 17.7 | 17.8 | 18.2 | 18.6 | 17.1 |
| 2015 | 17.3 | 17.1 | 17.1 | 17.1 | 17.9 | 18.2 | 17.0 | 16.9 | 18.0 | 18.1 | 18.3 | 18.7 | 17.6 |
| 2016 | 17.1 | 17.0 | 17.0 | 17.2 | 17.5 | 17.7 | 16.5 | 16.4 | 17.4 | 17.5 | 17.6 | 18.1 | 17.3 |
| 2017 | 17.0 | 16.9 | 16.9 | 16.6 | 17.4 | 17.7 | 17.0 | 16.6 | 18.2 | 18.1 | 18.2 | 18.9 | 17.5 |
| 2018 | 17.7 | 17.4 | 17.5 | 18.2 | 18.4 | 18.8 | 17.8 | 17.9 | 19.2 | 20.2 | 19.6 | 20.6 | 18.6 |
| 2019 | 18.9 | 18.7 | 18.7 | 18.7 | 19.0 | 19.1 | 18.0 | 18.0 | 19.3 | 20.0 | 20.4 | 21.0 | 19.2 |
| **Information** | | | | | | | | | | | | | |
| 2011 | 7.6 | 7.6 | 7.6 | 7.7 | 7.7 | 7.8 | 7.8 | 6.9 | 7.7 | 7.6 | 7.6 | 7.7 | 7.6 |
| 2012 | 7.6 | 7.6 | 7.6 | 7.6 | 7.7 | 7.8 | 7.7 | 7.6 | 7.6 | 7.5 | 7.6 | 7.6 | 7.6 |
| 2013 | 7.5 | 7.5 | 7.5 | 7.5 | 7.5 | 7.6 | 7.6 | 7.6 | 7.6 | 7.6 | 7.6 | 7.6 | 7.6 |
| 2014 | 7.6 | 7.6 | 7.6 | 7.6 | 7.6 | 7.7 | 7.6 | 7.6 | 7.6 | 7.6 | 7.6 | 7.6 | 7.6 |
| 2015 | 7.3 | 7.2 | 7.3 | 7.4 | 7.4 | 7.4 | 7.4 | 7.3 | 7.3 | 7.4 | 7.3 | 7.3 | 7.3 |
| 2016 | 7.1 | 7.1 | 7.0 | 7.1 | 6.5 | 7.2 | 7.1 | 7.1 | 7.1 | 7.0 | 7.0 | 7.1 | 7.0 |
| 2017 | 7.0 | 7.1 | 7.1 | 7.0 | 7.0 | 7.2 | 7.1 | 7.1 | 7.2 | 7.1 | 7.3 | 7.4 | 7.1 |
| 2018 | 7.2 | 7.4 | 7.5 | 7.5 | 7.5 | 7.6 | 7.4 | 7.4 | 7.2 | 7.2 | 7.2 | 7.1 | 7.4 |
| 2019 | 6.9 | 7.0 | 7.0 | 6.8 | 6.9 | 6.8 | 6.8 | 6.8 | 6.8 | 6.8 | 6.9 | 6.8 | 6.9 |
| **Financial Activities** | | | | | | | | | | | | | |
| 2011 | 31.1 | 31.1 | 31.2 | 31.5 | 31.1 | 31.4 | 31.4 | 31.7 | 31.5 | 31.4 | 31.5 | 32.2 | 31.4 |
| 2012 | 31.5 | 31.6 | 31.5 | 31.8 | 31.8 | 32.3 | 32.3 | 32.3 | 31.9 | 32.2 | 32.3 | 32.4 | 32.0 |
| 2013 | 31.9 | 31.9 | 32.0 | 31.9 | 31.9 | 32.2 | 32.8 | 32.1 | 31.7 | 32.0 | 32.1 | 32.6 | 32.1 |
| 2014 | 31.9 | 31.9 | 32.0 | 32.2 | 32.5 | 33.0 | 33.1 | 33.0 | 32.9 | 33.0 | 33.1 | 33.5 | 32.7 |
| 2015 | 32.9 | 32.9 | 33.0 | 33.3 | 33.7 | 34.0 | 34.3 | 34.4 | 34.1 | 34.2 | 34.4 | 34.6 | 33.8 |
| 2016 | 34.3 | 34.3 | 34.2 | 34.5 | 34.7 | 35.2 | 35.4 | 35.4 | 35.1 | 35.2 | 35.3 | 35.7 | 34.9 |
| 2017 | 36.4 | 36.6 | 36.7 | 36.5 | 36.6 | 37.1 | 37.4 | 37.2 | 36.9 | 36.7 | 36.9 | 37.1 | 36.8 |
| 2018 | 36.5 | 36.4 | 36.3 | 36.4 | 36.7 | 37.0 | 36.9 | 36.7 | 36.4 | 36.4 | 36.6 | 36.7 | 36.6 |
| 2019 | 36.4 | 36.5 | 36.4 | 36.3 | 36.5 | 36.8 | 36.8 | 36.7 | 36.4 | 37.0 | 36.8 | 36.4 | 36.6 |

## Employment by Industry: Buffalo-Cheektowaga-Niagara Falls, NY, 2011–2019—*Continued*

(Numbers in thousands, not seasonally adjusted)

| Industry and year | January | February | March | April | May | June | July | August | September | October | November | December | Annual average |
|---|---|---|---|---|---|---|---|---|---|---|---|---|---|
| **Professional and Business Services** | | | | | | | | | | | | | |
| 2011 | 70.1 | 70.3 | 70.1 | 72.0 | 72.5 | 73.7 | 74.4 | 74.0 | 73.8 | 73.7 | 72.9 | 72.6 | 72.5 |
| 2012 | 71.1 | 71.3 | 71.3 | 72.5 | 72.9 | 74.3 | 74.6 | 74.8 | 73.6 | 74.4 | 73.9 | 73.2 | 73.2 |
| 2013 | 71.3 | 71.6 | 72.0 | 73.1 | 73.7 | 75.0 | 75.1 | 75.0 | 74.8 | 74.0 | 73.4 | 72.6 | 73.5 |
| 2014 | 69.9 | 69.8 | 69.2 | 71.0 | 72.0 | 73.4 | 73.8 | 73.4 | 72.8 | 72.9 | 72.2 | 72.4 | 71.9 |
| 2015 | 69.5 | 69.9 | 69.5 | 71.3 | 72.7 | 73.7 | 73.8 | 73.7 | 72.9 | 73.2 | 71.9 | 71.6 | 72.0 |
| 2016 | 69.1 | 69.1 | 69.1 | 70.9 | 71.9 | 72.6 | 73.1 | 72.8 | 72.2 | 72.7 | 71.7 | 71.1 | 71.4 |
| 2017 | 68.5 | 69.0 | 69.2 | 70.4 | 70.9 | 72.0 | 72.7 | 73.0 | 72.2 | 73.1 | 72.8 | 72.2 | 71.3 |
| 2018 | 69.5 | 69.9 | 70.4 | 70.8 | 71.8 | 73.6 | 74.1 | 74.1 | 73.2 | 73.5 | 72.7 | 72.6 | 72.2 |
| 2019 | 70.4 | 70.7 | 71.1 | 73.2 | 73.5 | 74.2 | 74.0 | 74.3 | 73.2 | 72.5 | 73.6 | 72.8 | 72.8 |
| **Education and Health Services** | | | | | | | | | | | | | |
| 2011 | 88.7 | 90.7 | 90.8 | 91.2 | 90.6 | 88.2 | 86.1 | 86.0 | 89.5 | 90.9 | 91.4 | 91.4 | 89.6 |
| 2012 | 89.2 | 91.7 | 91.5 | 91.4 | 91.1 | 88.1 | 86.4 | 86.7 | 90.3 | 92.4 | 92.5 | 92.9 | 90.4 |
| 2013 | 90.3 | 92.3 | 92.7 | 93.1 | 92.4 | 89.9 | 88.7 | 88.9 | 92.6 | 94.7 | 95.0 | 95.0 | 92.1 |
| 2014 | 91.9 | 94.5 | 94.7 | 94.4 | 93.5 | 91.4 | 89.8 | 89.6 | 92.5 | 94.9 | 94.8 | 95.1 | 93.1 |
| 2015 | 92.1 | 94.1 | 94.5 | 94.4 | 93.9 | 91.8 | 90.3 | 90.8 | 93.4 | 96.1 | 96.6 | 96.7 | 93.7 |
| 2016 | 93.5 | 96.2 | 96.5 | 96.7 | 95.9 | 93.4 | 92.2 | 91.9 | 95.5 | 98.4 | 98.9 | 98.6 | 95.6 |
| 2017 | 95.5 | 98.4 | 98.4 | 98.4 | 97.9 | 95.5 | 94.1 | 94.5 | 97.2 | 99.7 | 99.9 | 99.9 | 97.5 |
| 2018 | 97.4 | 100.1 | 100.1 | 100.5 | 99.7 | 96.8 | 94.7 | 95.2 | 98.1 | 100.7 | 100.6 | 100.3 | 98.7 |
| 2019 | 98.6 | 101.1 | 101.4 | 101.1 | 100.0 | 97.6 | 95.7 | 96.0 | 99.3 | 101.6 | 102.2 | 102.3 | 99.7 |
| **Leisure and Hospitality** | | | | | | | | | | | | | |
| 2011 | 49.7 | 50.2 | 50.7 | 51.8 | 54.1 | 55.8 | 54.8 | 55.5 | 57.1 | 55.2 | 54.2 | 54.3 | 53.6 |
| 2012 | 50.4 | 52.2 | 52.8 | 53.1 | 55.4 | 57.3 | 56.3 | 58.2 | 57.2 | 56.5 | 55.4 | 55.6 | 55.0 |
| 2013 | 52.5 | 53.4 | 53.7 | 55.1 | 57.6 | 59.0 | 58.7 | 59.6 | 58.6 | 59.3 | 57.8 | 56.9 | 56.9 |
| 2014 | 53.7 | 53.9 | 54.4 | 56.5 | 58.6 | 59.2 | 59.9 | 60.5 | 60.0 | 59.8 | 57.9 | 58.1 | 57.7 |
| 2015 | 54.3 | 55.1 | 55.6 | 57.1 | 59.4 | 60.8 | 61.0 | 61.4 | 60.9 | 60.9 | 59.5 | 58.9 | 58.7 |
| 2016 | 54.9 | 56.2 | 56.8 | 59.2 | 60.6 | 62.2 | 62.5 | 63.8 | 62.6 | 62.2 | 60.6 | 60.3 | 60.2 |
| 2017 | 55.8 | 57.7 | 58.2 | 58.3 | 61.7 | 63.3 | 63.3 | 64.3 | 63.2 | 62.3 | 61.9 | 61.4 | 61.0 |
| 2018 | 56.9 | 57.4 | 58.3 | 58.9 | 61.8 | 63.0 | 63.3 | 65.0 | 64.0 | 62.5 | 60.3 | 60.6 | 61.0 |
| 2019 | 57.0 | 57.5 | 58.4 | 59.8 | 61.8 | 62.4 | 61.9 | 63.2 | 61.5 | 60.6 | 58.7 | 58.4 | 60.1 |
| **Other Services** | | | | | | | | | | | | | |
| 2011 | 22.8 | 23.0 | 23.0 | 23.2 | 23.3 | 23.5 | 23.3 | 23.3 | 23.4 | 23.1 | 23.1 | 23.3 | 23.2 |
| 2012 | 23.0 | 23.0 | 23.2 | 23.2 | 23.5 | 23.7 | 23.5 | 23.5 | 23.3 | 23.5 | 23.5 | 23.6 | 23.4 |
| 2013 | 23.6 | 23.6 | 23.7 | 23.7 | 24.0 | 24.0 | 24.0 | 24.2 | 24.0 | 24.5 | 24.5 | 24.8 | 24.1 |
| 2014 | 24.3 | 24.4 | 24.7 | 24.5 | 24.7 | 24.6 | 24.8 | 24.8 | 24.3 | 24.7 | 24.6 | 24.7 | 24.6 |
| 2015 | 24.3 | 24.3 | 24.6 | 24.7 | 24.8 | 24.9 | 25.0 | 25.0 | 24.6 | 25.0 | 24.9 | 25.1 | 24.8 |
| 2016 | 24.3 | 24.5 | 24.6 | 24.9 | 25.1 | 24.9 | 25.2 | 25.3 | 24.8 | 25.1 | 25.2 | 24.9 | 24.9 |
| 2017 | 24.7 | 24.8 | 24.9 | 25.0 | 25.0 | 25.2 | 25.4 | 25.3 | 25.0 | 25.3 | 25.2 | 25.1 | 25.1 |
| 2018 | 24.6 | 24.7 | 24.9 | 25.0 | 25.2 | 25.3 | 25.8 | 25.7 | 25.5 | 25.7 | 25.7 | 25.8 | 25.3 |
| 2019 | 25.4 | 25.4 | 25.7 | 25.9 | 26.0 | 26.2 | 26.2 | 25.9 | 25.5 | 25.8 | 25.8 | 25.8 | 25.8 |
| **Government** | | | | | | | | | | | | | |
| 2011 | 93.2 | 94.3 | 93.9 | 94.4 | 93.9 | 92.5 | 87.8 | 87.9 | 90.0 | 92.7 | 93.0 | 92.9 | 92.2 |
| 2012 | 90.4 | 92.6 | 92.5 | 91.9 | 92.2 | 90.8 | 86.0 | 85.6 | 87.8 | 91.0 | 91.3 | 91.4 | 90.3 |
| 2013 | 88.7 | 90.9 | 91.0 | 90.2 | 90.0 | 89.0 | 84.7 | 84.8 | 86.8 | 90.2 | 90.2 | 89.9 | 88.9 |
| 2014 | 86.8 | 89.0 | 89.4 | 89.3 | 88.7 | 87.9 | 84.0 | 84.0 | 86.0 | 88.8 | 89.1 | 88.6 | 87.6 |
| 2015 | 86.9 | 88.4 | 88.5 | 88.3 | 88.6 | 88.1 | 84.3 | 84.5 | 86.6 | 89.1 | 89.3 | 89.6 | 87.7 |
| 2016 | 87.5 | 89.1 | 89.4 | 89.2 | 89.3 | 88.8 | 85.3 | 85.0 | 88.1 | 89.6 | 89.8 | 90.6 | 88.5 |
| 2017 | 89.7 | 90.5 | 90.5 | 90.4 | 90.6 | 89.9 | 86.5 | 86.0 | 88.5 | 90.6 | 91.2 | 91.5 | 89.7 |
| 2018 | 89.1 | 90.7 | 90.6 | 90.0 | 90.5 | 90.0 | 86.5 | 86.2 | 88.7 | 91.0 | 91.3 | 91.4 | 89.7 |
| 2019 | 89.5 | 90.6 | 90.9 | 91.0 | 90.5 | 90.2 | 86.7 | 86.5 | 89.3 | 91.7 | 91.9 | 92.3 | 90.1 |

# Employment by Industry: Birmingham-Hoover, AL, 2011–2019

(Numbers in thousands, not seasonally adjusted)

| Industry and year | January | February | March | April | May | June | July | August | September | October | November | December | Annual average |
|---|---|---|---|---|---|---|---|---|---|---|---|---|---|
| **Total Nonfarm** | | | | | | | | | | | | | |
| 2011 | 489.7 | 492.1 | 495.2 | 497.1 | 498.8 | 501.1 | 498.1 | 498.5 | 501.1 | 500.8 | 504.3 | 505.5 | 498.5 |
| 2012 | 498.3 | 500.9 | 505.0 | 508.1 | 508.6 | 510.4 | 504.8 | 505.8 | 507.8 | 508.7 | 512.3 | 511.9 | 506.9 |
| 2013 | 502.9 | 506.3 | 508.4 | 512.0 | 514.0 | 515.4 | 511.3 | 512.0 | 513.8 | 514.5 | 518.2 | 520.1 | 512.4 |
| 2014 | 507.8 | 508.8 | 512.8 | 516.1 | 517.2 | 519.0 | 514.9 | 516.8 | 518.2 | 518.6 | 521.3 | 522.9 | 516.2 |
| 2015 | 512.4 | 515.1 | 516.6 | 520.4 | 523.2 | 524.6 | 522.8 | 523.2 | 523.2 | 525.5 | 527.9 | 528.4 | 521.9 |
| 2016 | 518.7 | 521.7 | 522.7 | 526.7 | 527.7 | 528.5 | 527.3 | 527.1 | 528.2 | 528.1 | 530.5 | 531.2 | 526.5 |
| 2017 | 522.4 | 525.9 | 527.8 | 528.6 | 530.9 | 533.6 | 532.0 | 533.0 | 533.6 | 534.9 | 538.7 | 538.3 | 531.6 |
| 2018 | 529.9 | 533.0 | 535.0 | 536.4 | 538.2 | 541.6 | 538.9 | 540.4 | 539.8 | 542.5 | 547.4 | 547.3 | 539.2 |
| 2019 | 537.7 | 541.3 | 542.8 | 544.5 | 545.3 | 547.1 | 547.1 | 547.9 | 545.7 | 548.4 | 551.0 | 553.6 | 546.0 |
| **Total Private** | | | | | | | | | | | | | |
| 2011 | 405.6 | 407.8 | 410.8 | 412.7 | 414.2 | 416.8 | 417.0 | 418.0 | 418.3 | 418.3 | 421.7 | 422.8 | 415.3 |
| 2012 | 416.3 | 418.2 | 421.9 | 425.2 | 425.7 | 428.1 | 425.9 | 426.7 | 426.8 | 426.5 | 429.9 | 429.4 | 425.1 |
| 2013 | 421.0 | 424.1 | 426.1 | 429.8 | 432.2 | 433.9 | 432.4 | 433.2 | 433.2 | 433.0 | 436.5 | 438.1 | 431.1 |
| 2014 | 426.6 | 427.4 | 431.2 | 434.2 | 434.9 | 436.8 | 435.1 | 436.5 | 436.4 | 436.4 | 438.8 | 440.3 | 434.6 |
| 2015 | 431.0 | 433.3 | 434.6 | 438.2 | 440.8 | 442.2 | 442.4 | 442.2 | 441.3 | 443.1 | 445.2 | 445.4 | 440.0 |
| 2016 | 436.4 | 439.1 | 440.0 | 443.7 | 444.6 | 445.4 | 445.5 | 445.0 | 445.0 | 444.8 | 446.8 | 447.3 | 443.6 |
| 2017 | 439.5 | 442.5 | 444.3 | 445.2 | 447.3 | 449.6 | 449.8 | 450.7 | 450.0 | 451.1 | 454.6 | 453.8 | 448.2 |
| 2018 | 446.5 | 449.5 | 451.2 | 452.5 | 454.0 | 456.8 | 456.1 | 457.1 | 455.2 | 457.4 | 461.9 | 461.5 | 455.0 |
| 2019 | 452.7 | 455.7 | 456.8 | 458.8 | 459.8 | 461.1 | 462.3 | 463.0 | 459.3 | 461.4 | 463.8 | 466.4 | 460.1 |
| **Goods Producing** | | | | | | | | | | | | | |
| 2011 | 60.3 | 60.8 | 61.8 | 61.9 | 62.6 | 63.3 | 62.9 | 63.3 | 63.8 | 63.9 | 64.3 | 64.8 | 62.8 |
| 2012 | 63.9 | 63.9 | 64.5 | 64.9 | 65.3 | 65.5 | 65.6 | 65.5 | 65.5 | 65.7 | 65.6 | 65.7 | 65.1 |
| 2013 | 65.2 | 64.8 | 65.6 | 66.0 | 66.3 | 66.5 | 66.4 | 66.6 | 66.4 | 66.4 | 66.3 | 66.9 | 66.1 |
| 2014 | 65.3 | 65.2 | 66.2 | 66.1 | 66.3 | 66.6 | 66.4 | 66.5 | 66.6 | 66.5 | 66.7 | 66.7 | 66.3 |
| 2015 | 66.1 | 66.4 | 66.1 | 65.7 | 66.0 | 66.4 | 66.7 | 66.7 | 66.4 | 66.6 | 66.6 | 66.5 | 66.4 |
| 2016 | 65.7 | 65.9 | 66.1 | 66.1 | 66.0 | 66.3 | 66.0 | 65.5 | 65.9 | 65.4 | 65.4 | 65.5 | 65.8 |
| 2017 | 64.7 | 64.8 | 65.4 | 65.1 | 65.8 | 66.4 | 66.5 | 66.8 | 67.4 | 67.6 | 67.4 | 67.8 | 66.3 |
| 2018 | 67.2 | 68.0 | 68.6 | 68.6 | 69.1 | 69.9 | 70.2 | 70.5 | 70.7 | 70.6 | 71.0 | 71.3 | 69.6 |
| 2019 | 70.5 | 71.0 | 71.3 | 71.5 | 71.9 | 72.1 | 72.4 | 72.5 | 72.3 | 71.6 | 70.9 | 72.1 | 71.7 |
| **Service-Providing** | | | | | | | | | | | | | |
| 2011 | 429.4 | 431.3 | 433.4 | 435.2 | 436.2 | 437.8 | 435.2 | 435.2 | 437.3 | 436.9 | 440.0 | 440.7 | 435.7 |
| 2012 | 434.4 | 437.0 | 440.5 | 443.2 | 443.3 | 444.9 | 439.2 | 440.3 | 442.3 | 443.0 | 446.7 | 446.2 | 441.8 |
| 2013 | 437.7 | 441.5 | 442.8 | 446.0 | 447.7 | 448.9 | 444.9 | 445.4 | 447.4 | 448.1 | 451.9 | 453.2 | 446.3 |
| 2014 | 442.5 | 443.6 | 446.6 | 450.0 | 450.9 | 452.4 | 448.5 | 450.3 | 451.6 | 452.1 | 454.6 | 456.2 | 449.9 |
| 2015 | 446.3 | 448.7 | 450.5 | 454.7 | 457.2 | 458.2 | 456.1 | 456.5 | 456.8 | 458.9 | 461.3 | 461.9 | 455.6 |
| 2016 | 453.0 | 455.8 | 456.6 | 460.6 | 461.7 | 462.2 | 461.3 | 461.6 | 462.3 | 462.7 | 465.1 | 465.7 | 460.7 |
| 2017 | 457.7 | 461.1 | 462.4 | 463.5 | 465.1 | 467.2 | 465.5 | 466.2 | 466.2 | 467.3 | 471.3 | 470.5 | 465.3 |
| 2018 | 462.7 | 465.0 | 466.4 | 467.8 | 469.1 | 471.7 | 468.7 | 469.9 | 469.1 | 471.9 | 476.4 | 476.0 | 469.6 |
| 2019 | 467.2 | 470.3 | 471.5 | 473.0 | 473.4 | 475.0 | 474.7 | 475.4 | 473.4 | 476.8 | 480.1 | 481.5 | 474.4 |
| **Mining, Logging, and Construction** | | | | | | | | | | | | | |
| 2011 | 25.9 | 26.3 | 27.1 | 27.3 | 27.7 | 28.1 | 27.9 | 28.0 | 28.5 | 28.3 | 28.5 | 28.8 | 27.7 |
| 2012 | 27.8 | 27.8 | 28.0 | 28.1 | 28.3 | 28.2 | 28.4 | 28.2 | 28.0 | 28.3 | 28.1 | 28.0 | 28.1 |
| 2013 | 27.6 | 27.1 | 27.9 | 28.0 | 28.2 | 28.2 | 28.3 | 28.4 | 28.0 | 28.0 | 27.7 | 28.1 | 28.0 |
| 2014 | 26.9 | 26.7 | 27.4 | 27.3 | 27.5 | 27.6 | 27.7 | 27.8 | 27.8 | 27.9 | 27.8 | 27.8 | 27.5 |
| 2015 | 27.2 | 27.5 | 27.3 | 27.6 | 28.0 | 28.3 | 28.6 | 28.8 | 28.7 | 28.9 | 28.9 | 28.8 | 28.2 |
| 2016 | 28.2 | 28.2 | 28.2 | 28.2 | 28.1 | 28.4 | 28.3 | 27.9 | 28.2 | 28.1 | 28.1 | 28.2 | 28.2 |
| 2017 | 27.5 | 27.5 | 27.8 | 27.6 | 28.3 | 28.6 | 28.8 | 29.1 | 29.5 | 29.6 | 29.1 | 29.3 | 28.6 |
| 2018 | 28.9 | 29.4 | 30.0 | 30.0 | 30.4 | 30.9 | 31.1 | 31.3 | 31.4 | 31.4 | 31.6 | 31.8 | 30.7 |
| 2019 | 31.0 | 31.5 | 31.9 | 32.1 | 32.3 | 32.6 | 32.9 | 33.1 | 33.1 | 33.0 | 32.4 | 33.0 | 32.4 |
| **Manufacturing** | | | | | | | | | | | | | |
| 2011 | 34.4 | 34.5 | 34.7 | 34.6 | 34.9 | 35.2 | 35.0 | 35.3 | 35.3 | 35.6 | 35.8 | 36.0 | 35.1 |
| 2012 | 36.1 | 36.1 | 36.5 | 36.8 | 37.0 | 37.3 | 37.2 | 37.3 | 37.5 | 37.4 | 37.5 | 37.7 | 37.0 |
| 2013 | 37.6 | 37.7 | 37.7 | 38.0 | 38.1 | 38.3 | 38.1 | 38.2 | 38.4 | 38.4 | 38.6 | 38.8 | 38.2 |
| 2014 | 38.4 | 38.5 | 38.8 | 38.8 | 38.8 | 39.0 | 38.7 | 38.7 | 38.8 | 38.6 | 38.9 | 38.9 | 38.7 |
| 2015 | 38.9 | 38.9 | 38.8 | 38.1 | 38.0 | 38.1 | 38.1 | 37.9 | 37.7 | 37.7 | 37.7 | 37.7 | 38.1 |
| 2016 | 37.5 | 37.7 | 37.9 | 37.9 | 37.9 | 37.9 | 37.7 | 37.6 | 37.7 | 37.3 | 37.3 | 37.3 | 37.6 |
| 2017 | 37.2 | 37.3 | 37.6 | 37.5 | 37.5 | 37.8 | 37.7 | 37.7 | 37.9 | 38.0 | 38.3 | 38.5 | 37.8 |
| 2018 | 38.3 | 38.6 | 38.6 | 38.6 | 38.7 | 39.0 | 39.1 | 39.2 | 39.3 | 39.2 | 39.4 | 39.5 | 39.0 |
| 2019 | 39.5 | 39.5 | 39.4 | 39.4 | 39.6 | 39.5 | 39.5 | 39.4 | 39.2 | 38.6 | 38.5 | 39.1 | 39.3 |

## Employment by Industry: Birmingham-Hoover, AL, 2011–2019—*Continued*

(Numbers in thousands, not seasonally adjusted)

| Industry and year | January | February | March | April | May | June | July | August | September | October | November | December | Annual average |
|---|---|---|---|---|---|---|---|---|---|---|---|---|---|
| **Trade, Transportation, and Utilities** | | | | | | | | | | | | | |
| 2011 | 104.7 | 104.6 | 105.0 | 104.7 | 104.9 | 105.1 | 105.2 | 105.6 | 105.5 | 106.1 | 107.9 | 109.0 | 105.7 |
| 2012 | 106.2 | 106.1 | 107.0 | 106.8 | 107.4 | 107.3 | 106.9 | 106.8 | 106.5 | 107.1 | 109.6 | 110.3 | 107.3 |
| 2013 | 106.6 | 106.8 | 107.4 | 107.2 | 107.7 | 108.0 | 108.2 | 108.3 | 108.1 | 108.6 | 111.0 | 112.4 | 108.4 |
| 2014 | 108.2 | 107.6 | 108.5 | 108.2 | 108.3 | 108.7 | 108.4 | 108.5 | 108.5 | 108.7 | 111.4 | 112.5 | 109.0 |
| 2015 | 108.2 | 108.1 | 108.8 | 109.5 | 110.1 | 110.4 | 110.3 | 110.2 | 109.7 | 110.4 | 112.5 | 113.3 | 110.1 |
| 2016 | 109.6 | 109.6 | 109.8 | 110.1 | 110.4 | 110.3 | 109.9 | 110.0 | 109.7 | 110.0 | 111.7 | 112.6 | 110.3 |
| 2017 | 109.2 | 109.0 | 109.1 | 108.8 | 109.0 | 109.0 | 108.8 | 108.8 | 108.5 | 109.1 | 111.1 | 111.5 | 109.3 |
| 2018 | 108.8 | 108.1 | 108.6 | 108.1 | 108.6 | 108.3 | 108.5 | 108.6 | 108.2 | 108.9 | 111.6 | 112.1 | 109.0 |
| 2019 | 108.4 | 107.9 | 108.0 | 107.7 | 107.6 | 107.5 | 107.8 | 107.7 | 107.3 | 108.4 | 109.7 | 112.5 | 108.4 |
| **Wholesale Trade** | | | | | | | | | | | | | |
| 2011 | 27.8 | 28.0 | 28.0 | 28.1 | 28.1 | 28.1 | 28.3 | 28.4 | 28.4 | 28.6 | 28.6 | 28.8 | 28.3 |
| 2012 | 28.5 | 28.8 | 28.9 | 28.8 | 29.1 | 29.0 | 29.0 | 29.0 | 28.9 | 29.0 | 29.1 | 29.2 | 28.9 |
| 2013 | 29.1 | 29.2 | 29.2 | 29.2 | 29.2 | 29.0 | 29.2 | 29.3 | 29.2 | 29.4 | 29.5 | 29.5 | 29.3 |
| 2014 | 28.9 | 29.0 | 29.0 | 28.9 | 29.0 | 29.0 | 29.1 | 29.2 | 29.3 | 29.3 | 29.4 | 29.5 | 29.1 |
| 2015 | 28.7 | 28.9 | 29.0 | 29.0 | 29.0 | 29.0 | 29.1 | 29.1 | 29.0 | 29.1 | 29.1 | 29.2 | 29.0 |
| 2016 | 28.8 | 28.9 | 28.9 | 28.9 | 29.0 | 29.0 | 28.9 | 28.9 | 28.7 | 28.9 | 28.8 | 28.9 | 28.9 |
| 2017 | 28.4 | 28.5 | 28.4 | 28.4 | 28.5 | 28.4 | 28.4 | 28.4 | 28.2 | 28.3 | 28.3 | 28.3 | 28.4 |
| 2018 | 28.0 | 28.1 | 28.1 | 27.9 | 28.0 | 28.0 | 28.1 | 28.1 | 28.0 | 28.1 | 28.2 | 28.1 | 28.1 |
| 2019 | 27.6 | 27.8 | 27.9 | 27.8 | 27.8 | 27.9 | 28.0 | 28.0 | 27.8 | 28.0 | 27.6 | 27.9 | 27.8 |
| **Retail Trade** | | | | | | | | | | | | | |
| 2011 | 56.0 | 55.5 | 55.8 | 56.0 | 56.1 | 56.3 | 56.1 | 56.4 | 56.2 | 56.6 | 58.4 | 59.1 | 56.5 |
| 2012 | 56.3 | 55.7 | 56.1 | 56.1 | 56.5 | 56.5 | 56.1 | 56.0 | 55.7 | 56.4 | 58.8 | 59.3 | 56.6 |
| 2013 | 55.3 | 55.3 | 55.7 | 55.7 | 56.1 | 56.5 | 56.5 | 56.4 | 56.2 | 56.9 | 59.2 | 60.3 | 56.7 |
| 2014 | 56.8 | 56.1 | 56.9 | 56.9 | 56.9 | 57.2 | 56.9 | 56.9 | 56.7 | 57.1 | 59.5 | 60.3 | 57.4 |
| 2015 | 56.9 | 56.8 | 57.3 | 57.9 | 58.5 | 58.7 | 58.3 | 58.2 | 57.9 | 58.4 | 60.4 | 60.9 | 58.4 |
| 2016 | 57.7 | 57.7 | 57.8 | 58.3 | 58.5 | 58.4 | 58.1 | 58.1 | 58.0 | 58.3 | 60.1 | 60.6 | 58.5 |
| 2017 | 57.7 | 57.4 | 57.5 | 57.5 | 57.7 | 57.8 | 57.7 | 57.5 | 57.3 | 57.9 | 59.7 | 59.7 | 58.0 |
| 2018 | 57.4 | 56.9 | 57.3 | 57.4 | 57.6 | 57.5 | 57.3 | 57.3 | 57.0 | 57.6 | 59.7 | 59.7 | 57.7 |
| 2019 | 57.4 | 56.8 | 56.8 | 56.9 | 56.9 | 56.8 | 56.6 | 56.4 | 56.3 | 56.5 | 58.0 | 59.7 | 57.1 |
| **Transportation and Utilities** | | | | | | | | | | | | | |
| 2011 | 20.9 | 21.1 | 21.2 | 20.6 | 20.7 | 20.7 | 20.8 | 20.8 | 20.9 | 20.9 | 20.9 | 21.1 | 20.9 |
| 2012 | 21.4 | 21.6 | 22.0 | 21.9 | 21.8 | 21.8 | 21.8 | 21.8 | 21.9 | 21.7 | 21.7 | 21.8 | 21.8 |
| 2013 | 22.2 | 22.3 | 22.5 | 22.3 | 22.4 | 22.5 | 22.5 | 22.6 | 22.7 | 22.3 | 22.3 | 22.6 | 22.4 |
| 2014 | 22.5 | 22.5 | 22.6 | 22.4 | 22.4 | 22.5 | 22.4 | 22.4 | 22.5 | 22.3 | 22.5 | 22.7 | 22.5 |
| 2015 | 22.6 | 22.4 | 22.5 | 22.6 | 22.6 | 22.7 | 22.9 | 22.9 | 22.8 | 22.9 | 23.0 | 23.2 | 22.8 |
| 2016 | 23.1 | 23.0 | 23.1 | 22.9 | 22.9 | 22.9 | 22.9 | 23.0 | 23.0 | 22.8 | 22.8 | 23.1 | 23.0 |
| 2017 | 23.1 | 23.1 | 23.2 | 22.9 | 22.8 | 22.8 | 22.7 | 22.9 | 23.0 | 22.9 | 23.1 | 23.5 | 23.0 |
| 2018 | 23.4 | 23.1 | 23.2 | 22.8 | 23.0 | 22.8 | 23.1 | 23.2 | 23.2 | 23.2 | 23.7 | 24.3 | 23.3 |
| 2019 | 23.4 | 23.3 | 23.3 | 23.0 | 22.9 | 22.8 | 23.2 | 23.3 | 23.2 | 23.9 | 24.1 | 24.9 | 23.4 |
| **Information** | | | | | | | | | | | | | |
| 2011 | 9.2 | 9.1 | 9.1 | 9.0 | 9.0 | 9.0 | 9.0 | 9.0 | 9.0 | 8.9 | 8.9 | 8.9 | 9.0 |
| 2012 | 8.9 | 8.9 | 9.0 | 8.8 | 8.8 | 8.9 | 8.9 | 8.9 | 8.9 | 8.8 | 8.8 | 8.9 | 8.9 |
| 2013 | 8.9 | 8.9 | 8.8 | 8.9 | 9.0 | 9.0 | 9.1 | 9.0 | 8.9 | 8.9 | 8.9 | 9.0 | 8.9 |
| 2014 | 8.8 | 8.7 | 8.7 | 8.6 | 8.6 | 8.5 | 8.3 | 8.3 | 8.2 | 8.3 | 8.4 | 8.4 | 8.5 |
| 2015 | 8.3 | 8.4 | 8.4 | 8.3 | 8.3 | 8.2 | 8.3 | 8.2 | 8.1 | 8.1 | 8.1 | 8.1 | 8.2 |
| 2016 | 8.0 | 8.0 | 8.0 | 8.0 | 7.9 | 8.0 | 7.9 | 7.9 | 7.8 | 7.9 | 8.0 | 7.9 | 7.9 |
| 2017 | 7.8 | 7.7 | 7.7 | 7.6 | 7.6 | 7.6 | 7.6 | 7.5 | 7.4 | 7.4 | 7.5 | 7.4 | 7.6 |
| 2018 | 7.4 | 7.6 | 7.6 | 7.7 | 7.5 | 7.7 | 7.5 | 7.5 | 7.5 | 7.4 | 7.4 | 7.4 | 7.5 |
| 2019 | 7.5 | 7.5 | 7.9 | 8.0 | 7.6 | 7.8 | 7.3 | 7.4 | 7.3 | 7.3 | 7.3 | 7.3 | 7.5 |
| **Financial Activities** | | | | | | | | | | | | | |
| 2011 | 40.0 | 40.1 | 40.0 | 40.2 | 40.1 | 39.7 | 40.1 | 39.9 | 39.8 | 39.8 | 39.9 | 40.0 | 40.0 |
| 2012 | 39.9 | 40.0 | 40.2 | 40.4 | 40.6 | 40.6 | 40.7 | 40.7 | 40.7 | 41.0 | 41.1 | 41.1 | 40.6 |
| 2013 | 40.6 | 40.8 | 40.8 | 41.0 | 41.3 | 41.5 | 41.8 | 42.1 | 42.1 | 42.4 | 42.8 | 42.9 | 41.7 |
| 2014 | 42.0 | 42.2 | 42.2 | 42.3 | 42.4 | 42.4 | 42.4 | 42.4 | 42.0 | 42.1 | 42.2 | 42.2 | 42.2 |
| 2015 | 42.1 | 42.1 | 42.2 | 42.2 | 42.3 | 42.3 | 42.4 | 42.4 | 42.2 | 42.3 | 42.3 | 42.3 | 42.3 |
| 2016 | 42.2 | 42.2 | 42.1 | 42.0 | 42.0 | 42.0 | 42.2 | 42.2 | 42.1 | 42.1 | 42.3 | 42.4 | 42.2 |
| 2017 | 42.3 | 42.4 | 42.4 | 42.2 | 42.3 | 42.5 | 42.4 | 42.4 | 42.2 | 42.4 | 42.5 | 42.4 | 42.4 |
| 2018 | 42.1 | 42.0 | 41.9 | 41.9 | 41.9 | 42.1 | 42.1 | 42.2 | 41.8 | 42.1 | 42.2 | 42.0 | 42.0 |
| 2019 | 41.5 | 41.6 | 41.6 | 41.6 | 41.8 | 42.0 | 42.4 | 42.5 | 42.4 | 42.3 | 42.5 | 42.5 | 42.1 |

# Employment by Industry: Birmingham-Hoover, AL, 2011–2019—*Continued*

(Numbers in thousands, not seasonally adjusted)

| Industry and year | January | February | March | April | May | June | July | August | September | October | November | December | Annual average |
|---|---|---|---|---|---|---|---|---|---|---|---|---|---|
| **Professional and Business Services** | | | | | | | | | | | | | |
| 2011 | 59.3 | 59.9 | 60.2 | 60.9 | 61.0 | 61.8 | 61.8 | 62.0 | 62.6 | 62.2 | 62.3 | 62.8 | 61.4 |
| 2012 | 61.7 | 62.5 | 63.1 | 64.0 | 63.5 | 64.4 | 64.1 | 64.6 | 64.4 | 64.1 | 63.8 | 63.1 | 63.6 |
| 2013 | 61.7 | 63.1 | 63.2 | 63.6 | 63.2 | 63.6 | 63.6 | 63.6 | 63.2 | 63.5 | 63.5 | 63.6 | 63.3 |
| 2014 | 61.5 | 62.2 | 62.5 | 63.6 | 63.6 | 63.7 | 63.7 | 64.6 | 64.5 | 64.8 | 64.3 | 64.4 | 63.6 |
| 2015 | 63.1 | 63.8 | 64.5 | 65.0 | 65.3 | 65.4 | 65.8 | 65.8 | 65.6 | 66.2 | 66.2 | 65.9 | 65.2 |
| 2016 | 64.9 | 65.4 | 65.3 | 66.0 | 66.1 | 66.1 | 66.4 | 66.4 | 65.9 | 66.1 | 66.3 | 66.0 | 65.9 |
| 2017 | 65.7 | 66.3 | 66.8 | 67.0 | 67.4 | 68.1 | 68.2 | 68.7 | 68.3 | 68.6 | 68.9 | 68.7 | 67.7 |
| 2018 | 67.8 | 68.7 | 69.0 | 69.2 | 68.6 | 69.3 | 68.6 | 69.0 | 68.9 | 70.3 | 70.9 | 70.5 | 69.2 |
| 2019 | 69.2 | 69.8 | 69.8 | 70.1 | 70.0 | 70.5 | 70.8 | 71.0 | 69.3 | 69.8 | 70.3 | 69.6 | 70.0 |
| **Education and Health Services** | | | | | | | | | | | | | |
| 2011 | 64.5 | 64.8 | 65.4 | 65.3 | 65.4 | 65.1 | 65.3 | 65.5 | 66.1 | 65.9 | 66.6 | 66.0 | 65.5 |
| 2012 | 65.8 | 66.1 | 66.4 | 67.0 | 66.4 | 66.7 | 66.2 | 66.9 | 67.7 | 67.4 | 68.3 | 68.3 | 66.9 |
| 2013 | 67.2 | 68.5 | 67.9 | 68.4 | 68.8 | 68.5 | 67.7 | 68.3 | 68.8 | 68.5 | 69.2 | 69.4 | 68.4 |
| 2014 | 67.8 | 68.4 | 68.5 | 69.1 | 68.6 | 68.7 | 68.3 | 68.8 | 69.4 | 69.9 | 69.4 | 69.8 | 68.9 |
| 2015 | 68.7 | 69.5 | 68.9 | 69.9 | 69.9 | 70.1 | 70.1 | 70.4 | 70.8 | 71.2 | 71.0 | 71.3 | 70.2 |
| 2016 | 69.9 | 70.8 | 70.4 | 71.2 | 71.1 | 70.9 | 71.3 | 71.7 | 72.8 | 72.9 | 72.5 | 72.9 | 71.5 |
| 2017 | 71.0 | 72.3 | 72.0 | 72.5 | 72.2 | 72.5 | 72.6 | 72.7 | 73.5 | 73.4 | 74.3 | 74.1 | 72.8 |
| 2018 | 72.4 | 73.5 | 73.1 | 73.7 | 73.6 | 74.0 | 73.8 | 74.1 | 74.5 | 74.6 | 75.4 | 75.2 | 74.0 |
| 2019 | 74.0 | 75.2 | 74.6 | 75.0 | 74.9 | 74.9 | 75.7 | 75.8 | 76.4 | 77.1 | 78.2 | 77.8 | 75.8 |
| **Leisure and Hospitality** | | | | | | | | | | | | | |
| 2011 | 40.7 | 41.3 | 42.1 | 43.3 | 43.7 | 45.0 | 44.8 | 45.0 | 44.1 | 44.0 | 44.1 | 43.8 | 43.5 |
| 2012 | 42.3 | 42.9 | 43.7 | 45.3 | 45.6 | 46.1 | 44.9 | 45.0 | 45.2 | 44.4 | 44.8 | 44.2 | 44.5 |
| 2013 | 43.1 | 43.5 | 44.5 | 46.7 | 47.8 | 48.2 | 47.1 | 46.8 | 47.3 | 46.6 | 46.7 | 45.8 | 46.2 |
| 2014 | 45.0 | 45.1 | 46.3 | 47.9 | 48.5 | 49.5 | 48.8 | 48.8 | 48.7 | 47.7 | 48.0 | 48.0 | 47.7 |
| 2015 | 46.3 | 46.7 | 47.3 | 48.9 | 50.0 | 50.4 | 49.9 | 49.7 | 49.7 | 49.6 | 49.6 | 49.2 | 48.9 |
| 2016 | 47.6 | 48.5 | 49.4 | 51.0 | 51.8 | 52.2 | 52.1 | 51.7 | 51.3 | 50.9 | 50.9 | 50.3 | 50.6 |
| 2017 | 49.1 | 50.0 | 50.8 | 51.7 | 52.6 | 53.0 | 53.1 | 53.2 | 52.1 | 52.0 | 52.2 | 51.4 | 51.8 |
| 2018 | 50.5 | 51.2 | 51.8 | 52.8 | 54.0 | 54.5 | 54.4 | 54.1 | 52.6 | 52.5 | 52.5 | 52.1 | 52.8 |
| 2019 | 50.5 | 51.4 | 52.3 | 53.6 | 54.6 | 54.7 | 54.4 | 54.5 | 52.8 | 53.3 | 53.7 | 53.7 | 53.3 |
| **Other Services** | | | | | | | | | | | | | |
| 2011 | 26.9 | 27.2 | 27.2 | 27.4 | 27.5 | 27.8 | 27.9 | 27.7 | 27.4 | 27.5 | 27.7 | 27.5 | 27.5 |
| 2012 | 27.6 | 27.8 | 28.0 | 28.0 | 28.1 | 28.6 | 28.6 | 28.3 | 27.9 | 28.0 | 27.9 | 27.8 | 28.1 |
| 2013 | 27.7 | 27.7 | 27.9 | 28.0 | 28.1 | 28.6 | 28.5 | 28.5 | 28.4 | 28.1 | 28.1 | 28.1 | 28.1 |
| 2014 | 28.0 | 28.0 | 28.3 | 28.4 | 28.6 | 28.7 | 28.8 | 28.6 | 28.5 | 28.4 | 28.4 | 28.3 | 28.4 |
| 2015 | 28.2 | 28.3 | 28.4 | 28.7 | 28.9 | 29.0 | 28.9 | 28.8 | 28.8 | 28.7 | 28.9 | 28.8 | 28.7 |
| 2016 | 28.5 | 28.7 | 28.9 | 29.3 | 29.3 | 29.6 | 29.7 | 29.6 | 29.5 | 29.5 | 29.7 | 29.7 | 29.3 |
| 2017 | 29.7 | 30.0 | 30.1 | 30.3 | 30.4 | 30.5 | 30.6 | 30.6 | 30.6 | 30.6 | 30.7 | 30.5 | 30.4 |
| 2018 | 30.3 | 30.4 | 30.6 | 30.5 | 30.7 | 31.0 | 31.0 | 31.1 | 31.0 | 31.0 | 30.9 | 30.9 | 30.8 |
| 2019 | 31.1 | 31.3 | 31.3 | 31.3 | 31.4 | 31.6 | 31.5 | 31.6 | 31.5 | 31.6 | 31.2 | 30.9 | 31.4 |
| **Government** | | | | | | | | | | | | | |
| 2011 | 84.1 | 84.3 | 84.4 | 84.4 | 84.6 | 84.3 | 81.1 | 80.5 | 82.8 | 82.5 | 82.6 | 82.7 | 83.2 |
| 2012 | 82.0 | 82.7 | 83.1 | 82.9 | 82.9 | 82.3 | 78.9 | 79.1 | 81.0 | 82.2 | 82.4 | 82.5 | 81.8 |
| 2013 | 81.9 | 82.2 | 82.3 | 82.2 | 81.8 | 81.5 | 78.9 | 78.8 | 80.6 | 81.5 | 81.7 | 82.0 | 81.3 |
| 2014 | 81.2 | 81.4 | 81.6 | 81.9 | 82.3 | 82.2 | 79.8 | 80.3 | 81.8 | 82.2 | 82.5 | 82.6 | 81.7 |
| 2015 | 81.4 | 81.8 | 82.0 | 82.2 | 82.4 | 82.4 | 80.4 | 81.0 | 81.9 | 82.4 | 82.7 | 83.0 | 82.0 |
| 2016 | 82.3 | 82.6 | 82.7 | 83.0 | 83.1 | 83.1 | 81.8 | 82.1 | 83.2 | 83.3 | 83.7 | 83.9 | 82.9 |
| 2017 | 82.9 | 83.4 | 83.5 | 83.4 | 83.6 | 84.0 | 82.2 | 82.3 | 83.6 | 83.8 | 84.1 | 84.5 | 83.4 |
| 2018 | 83.4 | 83.5 | 83.8 | 83.9 | 84.2 | 84.8 | 82.8 | 83.3 | 84.6 | 85.1 | 85.5 | 85.8 | 84.2 |
| 2019 | 85.0 | 85.6 | 86.0 | 85.7 | 85.5 | 86.0 | 84.8 | 84.9 | 86.4 | 87.0 | 87.2 | 87.2 | 85.9 |

## Employment by Industry: Grand Rapids-Wyoming, MI, 2011–2019

(Numbers in thousands, not seasonally adjusted)

| Industry and year | January | February | March | April | May | June | July | August | September | October | November | December | Annual average |
|---|---|---|---|---|---|---|---|---|---|---|---|---|---|
| **Total Nonfarm** | | | | | | | | | | | | | |
| 2011 | 452.8 | 455.0 | 457.6 | 465.9 | 470.4 | 470.6 | 467.1 | 468.9 | 476.8 | 476.7 | 479.4 | 479.7 | 468.4 |
| 2012 | 471.5 | 473.2 | 477.0 | 483.8 | 488.4 | 488.4 | 482.0 | 484.6 | 492.4 | 494.7 | 496.6 | 495.6 | 485.7 |
| 2013 | 487.2 | 490.1 | 492.7 | 495.0 | 501.8 | 503.4 | 497.4 | 502.0 | 508.1 | 509.4 | 511.7 | 513.0 | 501.0 |
| 2014 | 502.6 | 504.7 | 507.1 | 510.5 | 519.5 | 521.0 | 508.2 | 510.9 | 517.4 | 520.7 | 523.0 | 525.0 | 514.2 |
| 2015 | 514.3 | 516.6 | 519.2 | 523.8 | 531.2 | 532.4 | 525.8 | 524.5 | 533.9 | 538.1 | 539.9 | 542.2 | 528.5 |
| 2016 | 532.1 | 534.2 | 536.5 | 539.6 | 544.8 | 547.8 | 539.6 | 540.9 | 546.7 | 549.4 | 551.2 | 552.3 | 542.9 |
| 2017 | 543.9 | 545.9 | 548.4 | 550.3 | 556.7 | 559.6 | 548.0 | 549.8 | 555.0 | 559.8 | 561.3 | 562.4 | 553.4 |
| 2018 | 553.1 | 557.3 | 560.9 | 563.6 | 569.5 | 573.3 | 559.2 | 561.7 | 565.7 | 571.0 | 571.6 | 571.3 | 564.9 |
| 2019 | 561.3 | 563.4 | 565.8 | 566.9 | 571.9 | 574.3 | 562.2 | 565.6 | 567.7 | 569.3 | 569.1 | 567.0 | 567.0 |
| **Total Private** | | | | | | | | | | | | | |
| 2011 | 404.7 | 406.1 | 408.2 | 416.2 | 423.1 | 424.1 | 424.6 | 427.1 | 429.4 | 428.3 | 430.4 | 431.6 | 421.2 |
| 2012 | 423.4 | 424.7 | 428.4 | 435.6 | 441.4 | 443.9 | 440.7 | 443.2 | 444.8 | 446.2 | 447.8 | 448.0 | 439.0 |
| 2013 | 440.2 | 442.0 | 444.9 | 447.6 | 455.4 | 458.6 | 457.4 | 461.5 | 461.5 | 461.9 | 464.6 | 466.0 | 455.1 |
| 2014 | 455.9 | 457.2 | 459.5 | 463.3 | 473.6 | 476.1 | 468.2 | 470.6 | 470.9 | 472.7 | 474.9 | 477.6 | 468.4 |
| 2015 | 467.5 | 468.9 | 471.6 | 476.2 | 485.2 | 488.0 | 485.0 | 484.2 | 487.4 | 490.2 | 492.1 | 494.5 | 482.6 |
| 2016 | 485.2 | 486.4 | 488.6 | 491.9 | 498.4 | 502.0 | 498.6 | 499.7 | 499.7 | 501.1 | 502.6 | 503.9 | 496.5 |
| 2017 | 496.6 | 497.5 | 500.1 | 502.3 | 509.9 | 513.2 | 506.9 | 508.0 | 507.1 | 510.8 | 512.5 | 513.6 | 506.5 |
| 2018 | 505.8 | 508.0 | 512.0 | 515.0 | 522.4 | 527.5 | 517.6 | 518.5 | 516.9 | 521.6 | 521.9 | 521.9 | 517.4 |
| 2019 | 513.3 | 514.2 | 516.2 | 517.7 | 524.3 | 528.1 | 520.7 | 521.6 | 518.4 | 519.4 | 518.9 | 516.7 | 519.1 |
| **Goods Producing** | | | | | | | | | | | | | |
| 2011 | 100.8 | 101.0 | 101.7 | 103.9 | 106.0 | 107.9 | 108.2 | 109.0 | 108.6 | 108.6 | 108.9 | 109.1 | 106.1 |
| 2012 | 107.6 | 107.5 | 108.3 | 110.0 | 111.6 | 113.7 | 114.1 | 114.8 | 114.1 | 113.8 | 113.5 | 113.7 | 111.9 |
| 2013 | 112.5 | 112.6 | 113.5 | 114.6 | 116.9 | 118.9 | 119.4 | 120.1 | 119.5 | 119.4 | 119.8 | 119.8 | 117.3 |
| 2014 | 118.4 | 118.9 | 119.6 | 121.0 | 123.4 | 125.7 | 125.9 | 125.8 | 125.3 | 125.1 | 125.3 | 125.5 | 123.3 |
| 2015 | 123.6 | 124.0 | 124.7 | 126.3 | 128.4 | 130.8 | 131.3 | 131.4 | 130.9 | 131.5 | 131.3 | 131.7 | 128.8 |
| 2016 | 130.5 | 130.7 | 131.1 | 132.6 | 133.8 | 135.7 | 136.3 | 136.1 | 135.0 | 135.4 | 135.3 | 135.8 | 134.0 |
| 2017 | 135.1 | 135.3 | 135.8 | 137.4 | 139.0 | 141.4 | 141.0 | 141.3 | 139.8 | 139.4 | 139.2 | 139.6 | 138.7 |
| 2018 | 138.6 | 138.8 | 140.0 | 141.6 | 143.3 | 145.7 | 145.6 | 145.0 | 143.8 | 144.0 | 143.7 | 144.0 | 142.8 |
| 2019 | 143.0 | 142.8 | 143.2 | 144.1 | 145.2 | 147.7 | 147.7 | 146.7 | 145.2 | 144.7 | 144.7 | 144.0 | 144.9 |
| **Service-Providing** | | | | | | | | | | | | | |
| 2011 | 352.0 | 354.0 | 355.9 | 362.0 | 364.4 | 362.7 | 358.9 | 359.9 | 368.2 | 368.1 | 370.5 | 370.6 | 362.3 |
| 2012 | 363.9 | 365.7 | 368.7 | 373.8 | 376.8 | 374.7 | 367.9 | 369.8 | 378.3 | 380.9 | 383.1 | 381.9 | 373.8 |
| 2013 | 374.7 | 377.5 | 379.2 | 380.4 | 384.9 | 384.5 | 378.0 | 381.9 | 388.6 | 390.0 | 391.9 | 393.2 | 383.7 |
| 2014 | 384.2 | 385.8 | 387.5 | 389.5 | 396.1 | 395.3 | 382.3 | 385.1 | 392.1 | 395.6 | 397.7 | 399.5 | 390.9 |
| 2015 | 390.7 | 392.6 | 394.5 | 397.5 | 402.8 | 401.6 | 394.5 | 393.1 | 403.0 | 406.6 | 408.6 | 410.5 | 399.7 |
| 2016 | 401.6 | 403.5 | 405.4 | 407.0 | 411.0 | 412.1 | 403.3 | 404.8 | 411.7 | 414.0 | 415.9 | 416.5 | 408.9 |
| 2017 | 408.8 | 410.6 | 412.6 | 412.9 | 417.7 | 418.2 | 407.0 | 408.5 | 415.2 | 420.4 | 422.1 | 422.8 | 414.7 |
| 2018 | 414.5 | 418.5 | 420.9 | 422.0 | 426.2 | 427.6 | 413.6 | 416.7 | 421.9 | 427.0 | 427.9 | 427.3 | 422.0 |
| 2019 | 418.3 | 420.6 | 422.6 | 422.8 | 426.7 | 426.6 | 414.5 | 418.9 | 422.5 | 424.6 | 424.4 | 423.0 | 422.1 |
| **Mining, Logging, and Construction** | | | | | | | | | | | | | |
| 2011 | 14.7 | 14.5 | 14.8 | 15.9 | 17.0 | 17.7 | 18.3 | 18.2 | 17.9 | 17.6 | 17.3 | 16.8 | 16.7 |
| 2012 | 15.6 | 15.3 | 15.8 | 16.8 | 17.5 | 18.1 | 18.5 | 18.7 | 18.4 | 18.2 | 17.7 | 17.5 | 17.3 |
| 2013 | 16.6 | 16.4 | 16.7 | 17.3 | 18.7 | 19.5 | 20.0 | 20.2 | 19.9 | 19.8 | 19.5 | 18.9 | 18.6 |
| 2014 | 17.9 | 17.9 | 18.2 | 19.0 | 20.3 | 21.2 | 21.4 | 21.5 | 21.3 | 20.8 | 20.5 | 20.0 | 20.0 |
| 2015 | 18.7 | 18.6 | 19.0 | 20.1 | 21.2 | 22.0 | 22.2 | 22.2 | 21.9 | 21.7 | 21.3 | 20.8 | 20.8 |
| 2016 | 19.8 | 19.8 | 20.4 | 21.7 | 22.6 | 23.4 | 23.6 | 23.6 | 23.2 | 23.1 | 22.8 | 22.2 | 22.2 |
| 2017 | 21.4 | 21.4 | 21.8 | 23.1 | 23.9 | 24.9 | 25.0 | 25.0 | 24.4 | 24.2 | 23.8 | 23.4 | 23.5 |
| 2018 | 22.5 | 22.6 | 23.3 | 24.4 | 25.4 | 26.3 | 26.3 | 26.2 | 25.8 | 25.8 | 25.3 | 24.8 | 24.9 |
| 2019 | 24.1 | 23.7 | 24.2 | 25.0 | 26.1 | 27.1 | 27.3 | 27.1 | 26.6 | 27.0 | 26.8 | 25.8 | 25.9 |
| **Manufacturing** | | | | | | | | | | | | | |
| 2011 | 86.1 | 86.5 | 86.9 | 88.0 | 89.0 | 90.2 | 89.9 | 90.8 | 90.7 | 91.0 | 91.6 | 92.3 | 89.4 |
| 2012 | 92.0 | 92.2 | 92.5 | 93.2 | 94.1 | 95.6 | 95.6 | 96.1 | 95.7 | 95.6 | 95.8 | 96.2 | 94.6 |
| 2013 | 95.9 | 96.2 | 96.8 | 97.3 | 98.2 | 99.4 | 99.4 | 99.9 | 99.6 | 99.6 | 100.3 | 100.9 | 98.6 |
| 2014 | 100.5 | 101.0 | 101.4 | 102.0 | 103.1 | 104.5 | 104.5 | 104.3 | 104.0 | 104.3 | 104.8 | 105.5 | 103.3 |
| 2015 | 104.9 | 105.4 | 105.7 | 106.2 | 107.2 | 108.8 | 109.1 | 109.2 | 109.0 | 109.8 | 110.0 | 110.9 | 108.0 |
| 2016 | 110.7 | 110.9 | 110.7 | 110.9 | 111.2 | 112.3 | 112.7 | 112.5 | 111.8 | 112.3 | 112.5 | 113.6 | 111.8 |
| 2017 | 113.7 | 113.9 | 114.0 | 114.3 | 115.1 | 116.5 | 116.0 | 116.3 | 115.4 | 115.2 | 115.4 | 116.2 | 115.2 |
| 2018 | 116.1 | 116.2 | 116.7 | 117.2 | 117.9 | 119.4 | 119.3 | 118.8 | 118.0 | 118.2 | 118.4 | 119.2 | 118.0 |
| 2019 | 118.9 | 119.1 | 119.0 | 119.1 | 119.1 | 120.6 | 120.4 | 119.6 | 118.6 | 117.7 | 117.9 | 118.2 | 119.0 |

# Employment by Industry: Grand Rapids-Wyoming, MI, 2011–2019—*Continued*

(Numbers in thousands, not seasonally adjusted)

| Industry and year | January | February | March | April | May | June | July | August | September | October | November | December | Annual average |
|---|---|---|---|---|---|---|---|---|---|---|---|---|---|
| **Trade, Transportation, and Utilities** | | | | | | | | | | | | | |
| 2011 | 79.8 | 79.4 | 79.4 | 81.3 | 82.0 | 82.5 | 82.6 | 82.6 | 82.1 | 82.4 | 83.7 | 84.1 | 81.8 |
| 2012 | 81.0 | 80.4 | 81.1 | 82.7 | 83.8 | 84.1 | 83.9 | 84.1 | 83.8 | 84.7 | 86.3 | 86.6 | 83.5 |
| 2013 | 84.0 | 83.9 | 84.4 | 85.6 | 87.0 | 87.9 | 87.9 | 88.5 | 87.8 | 88.5 | 89.7 | 90.3 | 87.1 |
| 2014 | 86.5 | 86.3 | 86.7 | 88.0 | 89.5 | 90.4 | 90.4 | 90.5 | 90.1 | 91.1 | 92.8 | 93.6 | 89.7 |
| 2015 | 91.4 | 91.0 | 91.3 | 92.9 | 94.3 | 95.1 | 95.2 | 94.7 | 94.2 | 95.1 | 96.5 | 97.5 | 94.1 |
| 2016 | 94.2 | 93.9 | 93.9 | 95.3 | 96.5 | 96.9 | 96.7 | 96.6 | 95.3 | 96.0 | 97.7 | 97.9 | 95.9 |
| 2017 | 95.0 | 94.7 | 94.9 | 95.9 | 96.8 | 97.3 | 96.7 | 96.4 | 95.3 | 95.9 | 97.3 | 97.8 | 96.2 |
| 2018 | 95.5 | 95.1 | 95.4 | 96.2 | 98.0 | 98.7 | 98.7 | 98.6 | 97.2 | 97.8 | 99.1 | 99.5 | 97.5 |
| 2019 | 97.2 | 96.4 | 96.5 | 97.1 | 98.9 | 99.3 | 98.8 | 98.8 | 97.5 | 97.7 | 98.2 | 98.6 | 97.9 |
| **Wholesale Trade** | | | | | | | | | | | | | |
| 2011 | 24.3 | 24.3 | 24.3 | 24.9 | 25.1 | 25.4 | 25.5 | 25.6 | 25.3 | 25.3 | 25.4 | 25.4 | 25.1 |
| 2012 | 25.0 | 25.0 | 25.3 | 25.8 | 26.1 | 26.3 | 26.4 | 26.3 | 26.3 | 26.6 | 26.6 | 26.7 | 26.0 |
| 2013 | 26.3 | 26.3 | 26.4 | 26.8 | 27.2 | 27.6 | 27.8 | 28.0 | 27.9 | 28.1 | 28.2 | 28.5 | 27.4 |
| 2014 | 27.2 | 27.4 | 27.5 | 28.2 | 28.7 | 29.0 | 29.0 | 29.0 | 28.7 | 28.7 | 28.9 | 29.1 | 28.5 |
| 2015 | 28.9 | 29.0 | 29.1 | 29.6 | 29.9 | 30.2 | 30.4 | 30.4 | 30.2 | 30.4 | 30.7 | 30.9 | 30.0 |
| 2016 | 30.8 | 30.8 | 30.8 | 31.0 | 31.2 | 31.2 | 31.5 | 31.4 | 31.0 | 31.1 | 31.4 | 31.2 | 31.1 |
| 2017 | 30.7 | 30.9 | 31.1 | 31.4 | 31.7 | 31.8 | 31.9 | 31.7 | 31.4 | 31.2 | 31.3 | 31.5 | 31.4 |
| 2018 | 31.5 | 31.6 | 31.6 | 31.8 | 32.3 | 32.5 | 32.4 | 32.3 | 31.9 | 32.1 | 32.2 | 32.1 | 32.0 |
| 2019 | 32.0 | 32.2 | 32.1 | 32.2 | 32.8 | 32.9 | 32.9 | 32.8 | 32.5 | 32.6 | 32.4 | 32.6 | 32.5 |
| **Retail Trade** | | | | | | | | | | | | | |
| 2011 | 43.8 | 43.4 | 43.3 | 44.3 | 44.8 | 44.9 | 44.8 | 44.8 | 44.5 | 44.8 | 46.0 | 46.3 | 44.6 |
| 2012 | 44.0 | 43.3 | 43.7 | 44.5 | 45.2 | 45.2 | 45.0 | 45.2 | 44.9 | 45.4 | 46.9 | 46.8 | 45.0 |
| 2013 | 44.8 | 44.6 | 45.0 | 45.1 | 46.0 | 46.4 | 46.5 | 46.7 | 46.3 | 46.7 | 47.8 | 48.2 | 46.2 |
| 2014 | 45.8 | 45.5 | 45.7 | 46.2 | 47.1 | 47.5 | 47.5 | 47.6 | 47.3 | 48.3 | 49.6 | 49.8 | 47.3 |
| 2015 | 48.0 | 47.6 | 47.8 | 48.6 | 49.6 | 49.9 | 49.6 | 49.4 | 49.0 | 49.6 | 50.6 | 51.1 | 49.2 |
| 2016 | 48.7 | 48.6 | 48.5 | 49.4 | 50.3 | 50.5 | 50.1 | 50.1 | 49.3 | 49.8 | 51.0 | 51.1 | 49.8 |
| 2017 | 49.2 | 48.9 | 48.8 | 49.3 | 49.7 | 49.8 | 49.2 | 49.1 | 48.4 | 49.2 | 50.4 | 50.5 | 49.4 |
| 2018 | 48.6 | 48.2 | 48.4 | 49.0 | 50.1 | 50.4 | 50.3 | 50.2 | 49.2 | 49.5 | 50.4 | 50.6 | 49.6 |
| 2019 | 48.9 | 47.9 | 48.0 | 48.4 | 49.4 | 49.5 | 49.0 | 48.9 | 48.1 | 48.1 | 48.7 | 48.5 | 48.6 |
| **Transportation and Utilities** | | | | | | | | | | | | | |
| 2011 | 11.7 | 11.7 | 11.8 | 12.1 | 12.1 | 12.2 | 12.3 | 12.2 | 12.3 | 12.3 | 12.3 | 12.4 | 12.1 |
| 2012 | 12.0 | 12.1 | 12.1 | 12.4 | 12.5 | 12.6 | 12.5 | 12.6 | 12.6 | 12.7 | 12.8 | 13.1 | 12.5 |
| 2013 | 12.9 | 13.0 | 13.0 | 13.7 | 13.8 | 13.9 | 13.6 | 13.8 | 13.6 | 13.7 | 13.7 | 13.6 | 13.5 |
| 2014 | 13.5 | 13.4 | 13.5 | 13.6 | 13.7 | 13.9 | 13.9 | 13.9 | 14.1 | 14.1 | 14.3 | 14.7 | 13.9 |
| 2015 | 14.5 | 14.4 | 14.4 | 14.7 | 14.8 | 15.0 | 15.2 | 14.9 | 15.0 | 15.1 | 15.2 | 15.5 | 14.9 |
| 2016 | 14.7 | 14.5 | 14.6 | 14.9 | 15.0 | 15.2 | 15.1 | 15.1 | 15.0 | 15.1 | 15.3 | 15.6 | 15.0 |
| 2017 | 15.1 | 14.9 | 15.0 | 15.2 | 15.4 | 15.7 | 15.6 | 15.6 | 15.5 | 15.5 | 15.6 | 15.8 | 15.4 |
| 2018 | 15.4 | 15.3 | 15.4 | 15.4 | 15.6 | 15.8 | 16.0 | 16.1 | 16.1 | 16.2 | 16.5 | 16.8 | 15.9 |
| 2019 | 16.3 | 16.3 | 16.4 | 16.5 | 16.7 | 16.9 | 16.9 | 17.1 | 16.9 | 17.0 | 17.1 | 17.5 | 16.8 |
| **Information** | | | | | | | | | | | | | |
| 2011 | 5.4 | 5.4 | 5.4 | 5.3 | 5.4 | 5.4 | 5.4 | 5.5 | 5.3 | 5.4 | 5.4 | 5.5 | 5.4 |
| 2012 | 5.4 | 5.3 | 5.3 | 5.3 | 5.4 | 5.4 | 5.5 | 5.6 | 5.4 | 5.4 | 5.4 | 5.5 | 5.4 |
| 2013 | 5.5 | 5.5 | 5.5 | 5.6 | 5.6 | 5.7 | 5.6 | 5.6 | 5.5 | 5.5 | 5.6 | 5.6 | 5.6 |
| 2014 | 5.6 | 5.6 | 5.7 | 5.8 | 5.8 | 5.8 | 5.9 | 5.9 | 5.7 | 5.8 | 5.8 | 5.8 | 5.8 |
| 2015 | 5.5 | 5.5 | 5.6 | 5.5 | 5.6 | 5.6 | 5.6 | 5.5 | 5.4 | 5.5 | 5.5 | 5.6 | 5.5 |
| 2016 | 5.5 | 5.5 | 5.5 | 5.6 | 5.7 | 5.8 | 5.7 | 5.7 | 5.7 | 5.7 | 5.8 | 5.8 | 5.7 |
| 2017 | 6.0 | 6.0 | 6.0 | 6.1 | 6.2 | 6.2 | 6.1 | 6.1 | 6.0 | 6.0 | 6.1 | 6.2 | 6.1 |
| 2018 | 6.2 | 6.2 | 6.2 | 6.4 | 6.4 | 6.5 | 6.5 | 6.5 | 6.3 | 6.4 | 6.4 | 6.4 | 6.4 |
| 2019 | 6.3 | 6.4 | 6.4 | 6.3 | 6.4 | 6.3 | 6.5 | 6.5 | 6.3 | 6.3 | 6.4 | 6.4 | 6.4 |
| **Financial Activities** | | | | | | | | | | | | | |
| 2011 | 21.7 | 21.9 | 21.7 | 22.1 | 22.2 | 22.3 | 22.6 | 22.8 | 22.8 | 22.8 | 23.1 | 23.3 | 22.4 |
| 2012 | 22.8 | 22.9 | 23.0 | 23.2 | 23.4 | 23.4 | 23.6 | 23.3 | 23.3 | 23.7 | 23.8 | 23.7 | 23.3 |
| 2013 | 24.0 | 24.2 | 24.2 | 24.3 | 24.5 | 24.6 | 24.4 | 24.4 | 24.4 | 24.3 | 24.4 | 24.3 | 24.3 |
| 2014 | 24.6 | 24.3 | 24.3 | 24.5 | 24.7 | 24.8 | 24.9 | 25.1 | 25.0 | 24.7 | 24.8 | 24.9 | 24.7 |
| 2015 | 24.8 | 24.4 | 24.4 | 24.4 | 24.9 | 24.6 | 24.9 | 25.0 | 24.8 | 24.9 | 25.0 | 25.3 | 24.8 |
| 2016 | 25.4 | 25.0 | 25.1 | 25.5 | 25.8 | 25.7 | 25.8 | 25.8 | 25.6 | 25.7 | 25.7 | 25.9 | 25.6 |
| 2017 | 26.1 | 25.9 | 26.0 | 25.9 | 26.2 | 26.5 | 26.2 | 25.9 | 26.0 | 26.1 | 26.1 | 26.2 | 26.1 |
| 2018 | 26.1 | 26.1 | 26.3 | 26.3 | 26.4 | 26.8 | 26.5 | 26.5 | 26.4 | 26.7 | 26.4 | 26.6 | 26.4 |
| 2019 | 26.8 | 26.7 | 26.7 | 26.8 | 27.0 | 27.1 | 26.9 | 27.1 | 26.9 | 27.0 | 26.9 | 27.0 | 26.9 |

## Employment by Industry: Grand Rapids-Wyoming, MI, 2011–2019—*Continued*

(Numbers in thousands, not seasonally adjusted)

| Industry and year | January | February | March | April | May | June | July | August | September | October | November | December | Annual average |
|---|---|---|---|---|---|---|---|---|---|---|---|---|---|
| **Professional and Business Services** | | | | | | | | | | | | | |
| 2011 | 65.3 | 66.4 | 67.2 | 69.4 | 71.3 | 70.8 | 70.8 | 71.7 | 73.5 | 72.0 | 72.0 | 72.4 | 70.2 |
| 2012 | 71.9 | 72.4 | 73.0 | 74.8 | 75.7 | 75.7 | 73.0 | 73.7 | 74.7 | 75.0 | 74.9 | 74.3 | 74.1 |
| 2013 | 73.4 | 73.9 | 74.0 | 74.6 | 75.9 | 75.5 | 74.3 | 76.0 | 76.8 | 77.3 | 78.0 | 78.7 | 75.7 |
| 2014 | 76.3 | 76.3 | 76.0 | 77.9 | 80.8 | 79.6 | 72.9 | 74.1 | 74.6 | 76.3 | 76.3 | 76.7 | 76.5 |
| | | | | | | | | | | | | | |
| 2015 | 74.2 | 74.4 | 74.4 | 75.5 | 77.7 | 76.9 | 74.7 | 74.5 | 76.3 | 78.2 | 78.3 | 78.2 | 76.1 |
| 2016 | 77.2 | 77.0 | 77.7 | 76.7 | 77.4 | 78.4 | 75.9 | 76.6 | 79.0 | 79.7 | 79.6 | 79.5 | 77.9 |
| 2017 | 78.0 | 77.9 | 78.5 | 77.0 | 78.8 | 78.2 | 75.1 | 75.4 | 77.5 | 79.3 | 79.7 | 79.4 | 77.9 |
| 2018 | 77.5 | 78.2 | 79.2 | 80.0 | 80.9 | 81.6 | 75.5 | 76.6 | 77.9 | 80.8 | 81.2 | 79.7 | 79.1 |
| 2019 | 77.2 | 78.7 | 78.8 | 77.4 | 78.5 | 78.7 | 74.5 | 75.2 | 76.0 | 76.7 | 76.4 | 74.5 | 76.9 |
| | | | | | | | | | | | | | |
| **Education and Health Services** | | | | | | | | | | | | | |
| 2011 | 73.8 | 74.3 | 74.7 | 75.0 | 74.8 | 73.3 | 73.5 | 73.6 | 75.8 | 77.0 | 77.7 | 77.3 | 75.1 |
| 2012 | 75.8 | 77.1 | 77.7 | 78.1 | 78.1 | 76.9 | 76.5 | 77.1 | 79.1 | 80.1 | 80.9 | 80.8 | 78.2 |
| 2013 | 78.6 | 79.9 | 80.7 | 79.9 | 79.6 | 79.0 | 78.8 | 79.6 | 81.2 | 81.5 | 82.7 | 82.5 | 80.3 |
| 2014 | 81.4 | 82.7 | 83.2 | 82.1 | 82.4 | 81.6 | 80.6 | 81.3 | 83.3 | 83.4 | 84.3 | 84.9 | 82.6 |
| | | | | | | | | | | | | | |
| 2015 | 83.5 | 84.7 | 85.4 | 85.1 | 85.2 | 84.5 | 82.9 | 83.0 | 86.0 | 86.5 | 87.5 | 87.8 | 85.2 |
| 2016 | 85.9 | 87.2 | 87.6 | 87.5 | 88.0 | 87.0 | 86.0 | 86.7 | 88.4 | 88.6 | 89.2 | 89.9 | 87.7 |
| 2017 | 88.4 | 89.4 | 90.0 | 90.3 | 90.8 | 90.1 | 89.1 | 89.9 | 91.4 | 92.9 | 93.5 | 93.9 | 90.8 |
| 2018 | 92.6 | 93.7 | 94.5 | 93.9 | 94.0 | 93.4 | 90.2 | 91.0 | 93.0 | 93.6 | 94.1 | 94.3 | 93.2 |
| 2019 | 92.5 | 93.3 | 93.8 | 94.0 | 94.0 | 93.3 | 91.3 | 92.9 | 93.9 | 94.3 | 95.2 | 95.1 | 93.6 |
| | | | | | | | | | | | | | |
| **Leisure and Hospitality** | | | | | | | | | | | | | |
| 2011 | 37.5 | 37.5 | 37.9 | 39.1 | 41.1 | 41.7 | 41.4 | 41.6 | 41.3 | 40.2 | 39.8 | 40.0 | 39.9 |
| 2012 | 39.6 | 39.7 | 40.4 | 41.5 | 43.2 | 44.1 | 43.6 | 44.1 | 43.9 | 43.0 | 42.4 | 42.6 | 42.3 |
| 2013 | 41.3 | 41.2 | 41.7 | 42.3 | 45.0 | 45.9 | 45.7 | 46.0 | 45.1 | 44.3 | 43.3 | 43.6 | 43.8 |
| 2014 | 41.9 | 41.8 | 42.6 | 42.9 | 45.6 | 46.6 | 46.2 | 46.7 | 45.7 | 45.0 | 44.4 | 44.9 | 44.5 |
| | | | | | | | | | | | | | |
| 2015 | 43.4 | 43.8 | 44.5 | 45.1 | 47.6 | 48.6 | 48.6 | 48.6 | 48.1 | 47.0 | 46.5 | 46.6 | 46.5 |
| 2016 | 44.8 | 45.4 | 45.9 | 46.6 | 48.9 | 49.8 | 49.6 | 49.8 | 48.6 | 47.7 | 47.2 | 47.0 | 47.6 |
| 2017 | 46.0 | 46.3 | 46.7 | 47.7 | 49.9 | 51.1 | 50.4 | 50.8 | 49.0 | 49.0 | 48.3 | 48.2 | 48.6 |
| 2018 | 47.5 | 48.0 | 48.5 | 48.6 | 51.3 | 52.2 | 52.2 | 52.0 | 50.1 | 49.9 | 48.7 | 48.9 | 49.8 |
| 2019 | 47.9 | 47.6 | 48.3 | 49.2 | 51.3 | 52.5 | 52.0 | 51.5 | 50.0 | 50.0 | 48.4 | 48.4 | 49.8 |
| | | | | | | | | | | | | | |
| **Other Services** | | | | | | | | | | | | | |
| 2011 | 20.4 | 20.2 | 20.2 | 20.1 | 20.3 | 20.2 | 20.1 | 20.3 | 20.0 | 19.9 | 19.8 | 19.9 | 20.1 |
| 2012 | 19.3 | 19.4 | 19.6 | 20.0 | 20.2 | 20.6 | 20.5 | 20.5 | 20.5 | 20.5 | 20.6 | 20.8 | 20.2 |
| 2013 | 20.9 | 20.8 | 20.9 | 20.7 | 20.9 | 21.1 | 21.3 | 21.3 | 21.2 | 21.1 | 21.1 | 21.2 | 21.0 |
| 2014 | 21.2 | 21.3 | 21.4 | 21.1 | 21.4 | 21.6 | 21.4 | 21.2 | 21.2 | 21.3 | 21.2 | 21.3 | 21.3 |
| | | | | | | | | | | | | | |
| 2015 | 21.1 | 21.1 | 21.3 | 21.4 | 21.5 | 21.9 | 21.8 | 21.5 | 21.7 | 21.5 | 21.5 | 21.8 | 21.5 |
| 2016 | 21.7 | 21.7 | 21.8 | 22.1 | 22.3 | 22.7 | 22.6 | 22.4 | 22.1 | 22.3 | 22.1 | 22.1 | 22.2 |
| 2017 | 22.0 | 22.0 | 22.2 | 22.0 | 22.2 | 22.4 | 22.3 | 22.2 | 22.1 | 22.2 | 22.3 | 22.3 | 22.2 |
| 2018 | 21.8 | 21.9 | 21.9 | 22.1 | 22.1 | 22.6 | 22.4 | 22.3 | 22.2 | 22.4 | 22.3 | 22.5 | 22.2 |
| 2019 | 22.4 | 22.3 | 22.5 | 22.8 | 23.0 | 23.2 | 23.0 | 22.9 | 22.6 | 22.7 | 22.7 | 22.7 | 22.7 |
| | | | | | | | | | | | | | |
| **Government** | | | | | | | | | | | | | |
| 2011 | 48.1 | 48.9 | 49.4 | 49.7 | 47.3 | 46.5 | 42.5 | 41.8 | 47.4 | 48.4 | 49.0 | 48.1 | 47.3 |
| 2012 | 48.1 | 48.5 | 48.6 | 48.2 | 47.0 | 44.5 | 41.3 | 41.4 | 47.6 | 48.5 | 48.8 | 47.6 | 46.7 |
| 2013 | 47.0 | 48.1 | 47.8 | 47.4 | 46.4 | 44.8 | 40.0 | 40.5 | 46.6 | 47.5 | 47.1 | 47.0 | 45.9 |
| 2014 | 46.7 | 47.5 | 47.6 | 47.2 | 45.9 | 44.9 | 40.0 | 40.3 | 46.5 | 48.0 | 48.1 | 47.4 | 45.8 |
| | | | | | | | | | | | | | |
| 2015 | 46.8 | 47.7 | 47.6 | 47.6 | 46.0 | 44.4 | 40.8 | 40.3 | 46.5 | 47.9 | 47.8 | 47.7 | 45.9 |
| 2016 | 46.9 | 47.8 | 47.9 | 47.7 | 46.4 | 45.8 | 41.0 | 41.2 | 47.0 | 48.3 | 48.6 | 48.4 | 46.4 |
| 2017 | 47.3 | 48.4 | 48.3 | 48.0 | 46.8 | 46.4 | 41.1 | 41.8 | 47.9 | 49.0 | 48.8 | 48.8 | 46.9 |
| 2018 | 47.3 | 49.3 | 48.9 | 48.6 | 47.1 | 45.8 | 41.6 | 43.2 | 48.8 | 49.4 | 49.7 | 49.4 | 47.4 |
| 2019 | 48.0 | 49.2 | 49.6 | 49.2 | 47.6 | 46.2 | 41.5 | 44.0 | 49.3 | 49.9 | 50.2 | 50.3 | 47.9 |

# Employment by Industry: Rochester, NY, 2011–2019

(Numbers in thousands, not seasonally adjusted)

| Industry and year | January | February | March | April | May | June | July | August | September | October | November | December | Annual average |
|---|---|---|---|---|---|---|---|---|---|---|---|---|---|
| **Total Nonfarm** | | | | | | | | | | | | | |
| 2011 | 499.6 | 504.3 | 506.3 | 515.7 | 518.3 | 519.5 | 511.5 | 512.2 | 519.5 | 525.6 | 525.5 | 525.9 | 515.3 |
| 2012 | 505.9 | 512.2 | 514.7 | 517.0 | 523.7 | 523.3 | 513.9 | 512.7 | 519.8 | 527.7 | 527.8 | 528.2 | 518.9 |
| 2013 | 507.8 | 515.1 | 516.5 | 520.8 | 526.1 | 523.9 | 514.4 | 514.7 | 522.2 | 529.3 | 530.6 | 530.4 | 521.0 |
| 2014 | 510.1 | 517.8 | 519.1 | 522.2 | 527.2 | 527.1 | 517.7 | 518.0 | 524.4 | 532.3 | 532.9 | 532.9 | 523.5 |
| 2015 | 513.5 | 519.6 | 520.7 | 526.3 | 532.1 | 532.6 | 524.2 | 524.3 | 529.2 | 539.5 | 539.4 | 538.6 | 528.3 |
| 2016 | 522.3 | 527.3 | 529.8 | 536.4 | 537.9 | 536.9 | 528.1 | 526.5 | 532.3 | 541.6 | 541.1 | 540.0 | 533.4 |
| 2017 | 522.1 | 529.3 | 527.8 | 536.4 | 538.6 | 539.0 | 528.6 | 528.7 | 536.0 | 544.8 | 544.7 | 544.2 | 535.0 |
| 2018 | 525.3 | 532.9 | 533.9 | 539.0 | 543.4 | 543.6 | 534.6 | 534.9 | 541.5 | 549.3 | 548.5 | 547.5 | 539.5 |
| 2019 | 528.8 | 536.3 | 536.0 | 542.9 | 544.2 | 544.6 | 534.8 | 534.0 | 539.5 | 546.6 | 546.0 | 543.5 | 539.8 |
| **Total Private** | | | | | | | | | | | | | |
| 2011 | 418.2 | 420.2 | 422.2 | 431.2 | 434.1 | 436.1 | 436.5 | 437.2 | 439.3 | 442.3 | 441.5 | 441.3 | 433.3 |
| 2012 | 425.6 | 428.8 | 431.2 | 434.2 | 440.1 | 440.8 | 439.7 | 439.2 | 440.7 | 445.4 | 445.2 | 444.5 | 438.0 |
| 2013 | 428.0 | 432.6 | 433.7 | 438.0 | 442.9 | 442.1 | 440.9 | 441.5 | 443.5 | 448.2 | 448.7 | 448.1 | 440.7 |
| 2014 | 431.6 | 436.7 | 438.0 | 440.9 | 446.1 | 446.6 | 445.2 | 445.5 | 446.3 | 452.0 | 451.4 | 450.7 | 444.3 |
| 2015 | 435.1 | 438.6 | 439.8 | 445.7 | 450.4 | 451.9 | 451.9 | 452.2 | 451.7 | 459.2 | 458.3 | 457.4 | 449.4 |
| 2016 | 443.2 | 446.7 | 448.8 | 455.7 | 456.9 | 456.7 | 456.2 | 454.7 | 455.2 | 461.0 | 460.2 | 458.5 | 454.5 |
| 2017 | 443.2 | 448.3 | 447.2 | 455.1 | 457.5 | 458.8 | 456.4 | 456.5 | 457.8 | 464.2 | 463.5 | 462.9 | 456.0 |
| 2018 | 446.5 | 451.9 | 453.0 | 458.1 | 462.0 | 462.8 | 461.6 | 461.6 | 462.0 | 467.9 | 466.5 | 465.7 | 460.0 |
| 2019 | 449.7 | 454.8 | 454.6 | 460.8 | 462.6 | 463.8 | 461.9 | 461.0 | 460.8 | 465.5 | 464.3 | 462.0 | 460.2 |
| **Goods Producing** | | | | | | | | | | | | | |
| 2011 | 76.2 | 75.5 | 75.9 | 77.5 | 79.4 | 81.5 | 82.5 | 82.8 | 81.9 | 81.7 | 80.6 | 79.3 | 79.6 |
| 2012 | 77.2 | 76.5 | 76.7 | 78.0 | 79.6 | 81.6 | 82.2 | 82.1 | 80.9 | 80.6 | 79.4 | 78.7 | 79.5 |
| 2013 | 76.3 | 75.3 | 75.4 | 76.8 | 78.6 | 79.8 | 80.5 | 81.0 | 80.0 | 80.0 | 79.2 | 78.0 | 78.4 |
| 2014 | 75.7 | 74.9 | 75.4 | 76.3 | 78.5 | 80.2 | 81.3 | 81.5 | 80.5 | 80.7 | 79.5 | 78.2 | 78.6 |
| 2015 | 76.0 | 75.1 | 75.6 | 77.3 | 79.4 | 80.8 | 81.7 | 81.7 | 80.7 | 81.1 | 80.0 | 78.9 | 79.0 |
| 2016 | 76.5 | 76.1 | 76.5 | 77.5 | 79.0 | 80.4 | 80.9 | 80.7 | 79.8 | 79.5 | 78.5 | 77.1 | 78.5 |
| 2017 | 75.1 | 74.9 | 75.1 | 77.0 | 78.2 | 79.4 | 80.1 | 80.4 | 79.6 | 79.6 | 78.1 | 77.1 | 77.9 |
| 2018 | 75.0 | 75.0 | 75.2 | 76.3 | 78.3 | 80.1 | 80.8 | 81.3 | 80.8 | 80.8 | 79.7 | 78.8 | 78.5 |
| 2019 | 77.0 | 76.8 | 76.6 | 78.2 | 79.4 | 80.9 | 81.8 | 81.7 | 80.4 | 80.0 | 79.7 | 79.0 | 79.3 |
| **Service-Providing** | | | | | | | | | | | | | |
| 2011 | 423.4 | 428.8 | 430.4 | 438.2 | 438.9 | 438.0 | 429.0 | 429.4 | 437.6 | 443.9 | 444.9 | 446.6 | 435.8 |
| 2012 | 428.7 | 435.7 | 438.0 | 439.0 | 444.1 | 441.7 | 431.7 | 430.6 | 438.9 | 447.1 | 448.4 | 449.5 | 439.5 |
| 2013 | 431.5 | 439.8 | 441.1 | 444.0 | 447.5 | 444.1 | 433.9 | 433.7 | 442.2 | 449.3 | 451.4 | 452.4 | 442.6 |
| 2014 | 434.4 | 442.9 | 443.7 | 445.9 | 448.7 | 446.9 | 436.4 | 436.5 | 443.9 | 451.6 | 453.4 | 454.7 | 444.9 |
| 2015 | 437.5 | 444.5 | 445.1 | 449.0 | 452.7 | 451.8 | 442.5 | 442.6 | 448.5 | 458.4 | 459.4 | 459.7 | 449.3 |
| 2016 | 445.8 | 451.2 | 453.3 | 458.9 | 458.9 | 456.5 | 447.2 | 445.8 | 452.5 | 462.1 | 462.6 | 462.9 | 454.8 |
| 2017 | 447.0 | 454.4 | 452.7 | 459.4 | 460.4 | 459.6 | 448.5 | 448.3 | 456.4 | 465.2 | 466.6 | 467.1 | 457.1 |
| 2018 | 450.3 | 457.9 | 458.7 | 462.7 | 465.1 | 463.5 | 453.8 | 453.6 | 460.7 | 468.5 | 468.8 | 468.7 | 461.0 |
| 2019 | 451.8 | 459.5 | 459.4 | 464.7 | 464.8 | 463.7 | 453.0 | 452.3 | 459.1 | 466.6 | 466.3 | 464.5 | 460.5 |
| **Mining, Logging, and Construction** | | | | | | | | | | | | | |
| 2011 | 15.5 | 15.0 | 15.3 | 16.6 | 18.2 | 19.5 | 20.2 | 20.5 | 20.1 | 19.9 | 19.1 | 18.1 | 18.2 |
| 2012 | 16.4 | 16.0 | 16.4 | 17.7 | 19.0 | 20.3 | 20.9 | 21.0 | 20.4 | 20.1 | 19.3 | 18.5 | 18.8 |
| 2013 | 16.9 | 16.5 | 16.6 | 17.6 | 19.6 | 20.5 | 21.1 | 21.2 | 20.6 | 20.6 | 19.8 | 18.8 | 19.2 |
| 2014 | 17.0 | 16.6 | 16.9 | 18.0 | 20.0 | 21.1 | 21.7 | 21.8 | 21.2 | 21.4 | 20.6 | 19.3 | 19.6 |
| 2015 | 17.5 | 16.8 | 17.1 | 18.6 | 20.5 | 21.4 | 21.7 | 21.9 | 21.5 | 21.7 | 20.9 | 19.9 | 20.0 |
| 2016 | 18.0 | 17.7 | 18.1 | 19.3 | 20.8 | 21.7 | 22.3 | 22.3 | 21.8 | 21.8 | 21.3 | 20.1 | 20.4 |
| 2017 | 18.6 | 18.2 | 18.5 | 20.5 | 21.7 | 22.4 | 22.9 | 23.3 | 22.7 | 22.5 | 21.4 | 20.5 | 21.1 |
| 2018 | 19.1 | 19.0 | 19.3 | 20.4 | 22.1 | 23.3 | 23.6 | 23.8 | 23.5 | 23.6 | 22.6 | 21.9 | 21.9 |
| 2019 | 20.5 | 20.2 | 20.4 | 21.8 | 23.2 | 24.0 | 24.4 | 24.5 | 23.7 | 24.0 | 23.5 | 22.8 | 22.8 |
| **Manufacturing** | | | | | | | | | | | | | |
| 2011 | 60.7 | 60.5 | 60.6 | 60.9 | 61.2 | 62.0 | 62.3 | 62.3 | 61.8 | 61.8 | 61.5 | 61.2 | 61.4 |
| 2012 | 60.8 | 60.5 | 60.3 | 60.3 | 60.6 | 61.3 | 61.3 | 61.1 | 60.5 | 60.5 | 60.1 | 60.2 | 60.6 |
| 2013 | 59.4 | 58.8 | 58.8 | 59.2 | 59.0 | 59.3 | 59.4 | 59.8 | 59.4 | 59.4 | 59.4 | 59.2 | 59.3 |
| 2014 | 58.7 | 58.3 | 58.5 | 58.3 | 58.5 | 59.1 | 59.6 | 59.7 | 59.3 | 59.3 | 58.9 | 58.9 | 58.9 |
| 2015 | 58.5 | 58.3 | 58.5 | 58.7 | 58.9 | 59.4 | 60.0 | 59.8 | 59.2 | 59.4 | 59.1 | 59.0 | 59.1 |
| 2016 | 58.5 | 58.4 | 58.4 | 58.2 | 58.2 | 58.7 | 58.6 | 58.4 | 58.0 | 57.7 | 57.2 | 57.0 | 58.1 |
| 2017 | 56.5 | 56.7 | 56.6 | 56.5 | 56.5 | 57.0 | 57.2 | 57.1 | 56.9 | 57.1 | 56.7 | 56.6 | 56.8 |
| 2018 | 55.9 | 56.0 | 55.9 | 55.9 | 56.2 | 56.8 | 57.2 | 57.5 | 57.3 | 57.2 | 57.1 | 56.9 | 56.7 |
| 2019 | 56.5 | 56.6 | 56.2 | 56.4 | 56.2 | 56.9 | 57.4 | 57.2 | 56.7 | 56.0 | 56.2 | 56.2 | 56.5 |

## Employment by Industry: Rochester, NY, 2011–2019—*Continued*

(Numbers in thousands, not seasonally adjusted)

| Industry and year | January | February | March | April | May | June | July | August | September | October | November | December | Annual average |
|---|---|---|---|---|---|---|---|---|---|---|---|---|---|
| **Trade, Transportation, and Utilities** | | | | | | | | | | | | | |
| 2011 | 81.5 | 80.3 | 80.3 | 81.4 | 82.3 | 83.4 | 82.5 | 82.6 | 81.8 | 83.3 | 84.3 | 85.6 | 82.4 |
| 2012 | 82.2 | 80.3 | 80.7 | 80.8 | 83.1 | 84.3 | 83.4 | 83.2 | 82.6 | 83.9 | 85.0 | 85.7 | 82.9 |
| 2013 | 82.2 | 80.7 | 80.7 | 81.2 | 82.6 | 83.6 | 82.6 | 82.2 | 81.8 | 82.9 | 84.1 | 84.8 | 82.5 |
| 2014 | 81.8 | 80.8 | 80.5 | 81.3 | 82.7 | 83.7 | 82.6 | 82.7 | 82.2 | 83.1 | 84.2 | 85.1 | 82.6 |
| 2015 | 81.8 | 80.6 | 80.8 | 81.5 | 83.3 | 84.6 | 83.6 | 83.6 | 83.0 | 83.9 | 85.2 | 86.0 | 83.2 |
| 2016 | 82.9 | 81.9 | 81.9 | 82.9 | 83.6 | 84.5 | 83.9 | 83.8 | 83.7 | 84.5 | 85.7 | 86.0 | 83.8 |
| 2017 | 83.2 | 82.2 | 81.6 | 82.6 | 83.9 | 84.7 | 83.8 | 84.0 | 84.0 | 84.9 | 86.3 | 86.7 | 84.0 |
| 2018 | 83.6 | 82.8 | 82.6 | 83.7 | 84.5 | 85.1 | 84.3 | 84.0 | 83.8 | 84.2 | 85.3 | 85.6 | 84.1 |
| 2019 | 82.7 | 81.4 | 81.3 | 81.9 | 83.1 | 83.6 | 82.8 | 82.2 | 81.6 | 81.4 | 81.9 | 82.0 | 82.2 |
| **Wholesale Trade** | | | | | | | | | | | | | |
| 2011 | 16.2 | 16.2 | 16.3 | 16.5 | 16.6 | 16.8 | 16.8 | 16.7 | 16.6 | 17.0 | 16.9 | 16.9 | 16.6 |
| 2012 | 16.5 | 16.5 | 16.6 | 17.0 | 17.2 | 17.3 | 17.3 | 17.2 | 17.0 | 17.3 | 17.3 | 17.3 | 17.0 |
| 2013 | 17.2 | 17.1 | 17.1 | 17.2 | 17.3 | 17.4 | 17.4 | 17.3 | 17.3 | 17.2 | 17.1 | 17.2 | 17.2 |
| 2014 | 17.0 | 17.1 | 17.0 | 17.2 | 17.4 | 17.6 | 17.6 | 17.5 | 17.3 | 17.4 | 17.3 | 17.3 | 17.3 |
| 2015 | 17.1 | 17.0 | 17.1 | 17.1 | 17.2 | 17.4 | 17.4 | 17.4 | 17.1 | 17.3 | 17.3 | 17.3 | 17.2 |
| 2016 | 17.1 | 17.1 | 17.0 | 17.4 | 17.4 | 17.5 | 17.6 | 17.4 | 17.3 | 17.2 | 17.2 | 17.1 | 17.3 |
| 2017 | 17.1 | 17.1 | 17.1 | 17.2 | 17.3 | 17.4 | 17.2 | 17.4 | 17.4 | 17.4 | 17.4 | 17.3 | 17.3 |
| 2018 | 17.3 | 17.3 | 17.3 | 17.5 | 17.5 | 17.7 | 17.7 | 17.6 | 17.4 | 17.3 | 17.4 | 17.3 | 17.4 |
| 2019 | 16.9 | 16.8 | 17.0 | 17.0 | 17.2 | 17.2 | 17.2 | 17.1 | 17.0 | 16.8 | 16.8 | 16.8 | 17.0 |
| **Retail Trade** | | | | | | | | | | | | | |
| 2011 | 55.5 | 54.3 | 54.2 | 54.9 | 55.5 | 56.4 | 56.1 | 56.3 | 55.0 | 56.1 | 57.2 | 58.3 | 55.8 |
| 2012 | 55.8 | 54.0 | 54.3 | 54.1 | 55.8 | 56.7 | 56.5 | 56.4 | 55.4 | 56.4 | 57.6 | 57.9 | 55.9 |
| 2013 | 55.1 | 53.7 | 53.8 | 54.1 | 55.2 | 56.0 | 55.6 | 55.5 | 54.2 | 55.3 | 56.4 | 56.9 | 55.2 |
| 2014 | 54.5 | 53.5 | 53.3 | 53.9 | 54.9 | 55.7 | 55.2 | 55.5 | 54.5 | 55.2 | 56.3 | 57.0 | 55.0 |
| 2015 | 54.5 | 53.5 | 53.6 | 54.2 | 55.5 | 56.4 | 56.0 | 56.1 | 55.1 | 55.9 | 57.1 | 57.7 | 55.5 |
| 2016 | 55.5 | 54.5 | 54.5 | 55.0 | 55.6 | 56.3 | 56.1 | 56.2 | 55.4 | 56.3 | 57.3 | 57.5 | 55.9 |
| 2017 | 55.3 | 54.2 | 53.6 | 54.7 | 55.4 | 56.1 | 56.0 | 56.0 | 55.1 | 56.0 | 57.3 | 57.5 | 55.6 |
| 2018 | 55.2 | 54.4 | 54.1 | 54.6 | 55.4 | 55.7 | 55.4 | 55.3 | 54.8 | 55.0 | 56.3 | 56.0 | 55.2 |
| 2019 | 53.9 | 53.0 | 52.7 | 53.2 | 54.0 | 54.2 | 53.4 | 53.1 | 52.1 | 51.9 | 52.5 | 52.1 | 53.0 |
| **Transportation and Utilities** | | | | | | | | | | | | | |
| 2011 | 9.8 | 9.8 | 9.8 | 10.0 | 10.2 | 10.2 | 9.6 | 9.6 | 10.2 | 10.2 | 10.2 | 10.4 | 10.0 |
| 2012 | 9.9 | 9.8 | 9.8 | 9.7 | 10.1 | 10.3 | 9.6 | 9.6 | 10.2 | 10.2 | 10.1 | 10.5 | 10.0 |
| 2013 | 9.9 | 9.9 | 9.8 | 9.9 | 10.1 | 10.2 | 9.6 | 9.4 | 10.3 | 10.4 | 10.6 | 10.7 | 10.1 |
| 2014 | 10.3 | 10.2 | 10.2 | 10.2 | 10.4 | 10.4 | 9.8 | 9.7 | 10.4 | 10.5 | 10.6 | 10.8 | 10.3 |
| 2015 | 10.2 | 10.1 | 10.1 | 10.2 | 10.6 | 10.8 | 10.2 | 10.1 | 10.8 | 10.7 | 10.8 | 11.0 | 10.5 |
| 2016 | 10.3 | 10.3 | 10.4 | 10.5 | 10.6 | 10.7 | 10.2 | 10.2 | 11.0 | 11.0 | 11.2 | 11.4 | 10.7 |
| 2017 | 10.8 | 10.9 | 10.9 | 10.7 | 11.2 | 11.2 | 10.6 | 10.6 | 11.5 | 11.5 | 11.6 | 11.9 | 11.1 |
| 2018 | 11.1 | 11.1 | 11.2 | 11.6 | 11.6 | 11.7 | 11.2 | 11.1 | 11.6 | 11.9 | 11.6 | 12.3 | 11.5 |
| 2019 | 11.9 | 11.6 | 11.6 | 11.7 | 11.9 | 12.2 | 12.2 | 12.0 | 12.5 | 12.7 | 12.6 | 13.1 | 12.2 |
| **Information** | | | | | | | | | | | | | |
| 2011 | 9.3 | 9.2 | 9.1 | 9.1 | 9.1 | 9.1 | 9.2 | 9.2 | 9.1 | 9.1 | 9.0 | 9.0 | 9.1 |
| 2012 | 8.6 | 8.5 | 8.5 | 8.4 | 8.5 | 8.5 | 8.5 | 8.5 | 8.4 | 8.4 | 8.5 | 8.4 | 8.5 |
| 2013 | 8.3 | 8.2 | 8.2 | 8.3 | 8.3 | 8.3 | 8.4 | 8.4 | 8.1 | 8.1 | 8.2 | 8.2 | 8.3 |
| 2014 | 8.2 | 8.2 | 8.2 | 8.1 | 8.1 | 8.2 | 8.4 | 8.3 | 8.2 | 8.4 | 8.4 | 8.5 | 8.3 |
| 2015 | 8.4 | 8.4 | 8.3 | 8.4 | 8.4 | 8.4 | 8.4 | 8.3 | 8.2 | 8.3 | 8.3 | 8.4 | 8.4 |
| 2016 | 8.5 | 8.6 | 8.7 | 8.7 | 8.7 | 8.6 | 8.6 | 8.5 | 8.5 | 8.5 | 8.5 | 8.5 | 8.6 |
| 2017 | 8.2 | 8.1 | 8.1 | 8.1 | 8.1 | 8.1 | 8.1 | 8.1 | 8.0 | 8.0 | 8.0 | 8.1 | 8.1 |
| 2018 | 8.0 | 8.0 | 8.0 | 8.0 | 8.1 | 8.2 | 8.1 | 8.1 | 8.0 | 8.1 | 8.1 | 8.2 | 8.1 |
| 2019 | 7.9 | 8.0 | 7.9 | 7.9 | 7.9 | 7.9 | 7.9 | 7.9 | 7.7 | 7.7 | 7.9 | 7.9 | 7.9 |
| **Financial Activities** | | | | | | | | | | | | | |
| 2011 | 20.3 | 20.3 | 20.4 | 20.7 | 20.9 | 21.6 | 21.9 | 22.0 | 21.3 | 21.3 | 21.2 | 21.4 | 21.1 |
| 2012 | 21.3 | 21.3 | 21.2 | 21.3 | 21.5 | 22.2 | 22.3 | 22.4 | 21.6 | 21.6 | 21.5 | 21.7 | 21.7 |
| 2013 | 21.2 | 21.2 | 21.1 | 21.2 | 21.5 | 22.0 | 22.3 | 22.2 | 21.6 | 21.2 | 21.2 | 21.4 | 21.5 |
| 2014 | 21.0 | 20.9 | 21.1 | 21.0 | 21.4 | 22.0 | 22.2 | 22.2 | 21.7 | 21.7 | 21.6 | 21.9 | 21.6 |
| 2015 | 21.6 | 21.6 | 21.7 | 21.7 | 21.9 | 22.3 | 22.3 | 22.3 | 21.8 | 21.8 | 21.9 | 21.9 | 21.9 |
| 2016 | 21.8 | 21.9 | 21.9 | 22.1 | 22.3 | 22.7 | 23.1 | 23.1 | 22.4 | 22.4 | 22.2 | 22.4 | 22.4 |
| 2017 | 21.6 | 21.5 | 21.4 | 21.6 | 21.8 | 22.4 | 22.4 | 22.4 | 21.6 | 21.7 | 21.7 | 21.9 | 21.8 |
| 2018 | 21.9 | 21.8 | 21.8 | 21.9 | 22.2 | 22.7 | 22.6 | 22.6 | 22.0 | 22.3 | 22.2 | 22.3 | 22.2 |
| 2019 | 22.0 | 21.9 | 21.9 | 22.1 | 22.4 | 23.0 | 23.0 | 23.0 | 22.4 | 22.0 | 21.5 | 21.4 | 22.2 |

# Employment by Industry: Rochester, NY, 2011–2019—*Continued*

(Numbers in thousands, not seasonally adjusted)

| Industry and year | January | February | March | April | May | June | July | August | September | October | November | December | Annual average |
|---|---|---|---|---|---|---|---|---|---|---|---|---|---|
| **Professional and Business Services** | | | | | | | | | | | | | |
| 2011 | 60.4 | 60.4 | 61.1 | 63.5 | 63.5 | 65.2 | 65.7 | 66.1 | 66.3 | 65.6 | 65.9 | 65.8 | 64.1 |
| 2012 | 64.4 | 64.5 | 64.8 | 66.3 | 66.7 | 67.7 | 67.5 | 67.2 | 66.4 | 67.1 | 67.4 | 66.7 | 66.4 |
| 2013 | 65.4 | 65.4 | 65.4 | 66.2 | 66.5 | 68.0 | 68.0 | 68.0 | 67.3 | 67.6 | 68.2 | 67.8 | 67.0 |
| 2014 | 65.6 | 66.2 | 66.5 | 66.4 | 66.8 | 67.6 | 67.5 | 67.3 | 66.7 | 67.1 | 68.0 | 67.8 | 67.0 |
| 2015 | 66.5 | 67.0 | 66.6 | 68.0 | 68.5 | 70.1 | 70.8 | 70.9 | 69.9 | 70.5 | 69.8 | 69.5 | 69.0 |
| 2016 | 68.3 | 68.1 | 68.1 | 69.4 | 69.4 | 69.9 | 69.9 | 69.2 | 68.7 | 69.1 | 69.2 | 68.5 | 69.0 |
| 2017 | 67.2 | 67.9 | 67.6 | 68.5 | 69.1 | 70.3 | 70.1 | 70.0 | 69.8 | 69.9 | 69.9 | 69.9 | 69.2 |
| 2018 | 67.7 | 68.0 | 68.2 | 68.8 | 69.7 | 70.8 | 71.7 | 71.6 | 70.4 | 69.9 | 69.8 | 69.0 | 69.6 |
| 2019 | 67.3 | 67.7 | 67.2 | 68.7 | 68.8 | 69.9 | 69.9 | 70.1 | 69.1 | 69.8 | 69.9 | 69.0 | 69.0 |
| **Education and Health Services** | | | | | | | | | | | | | |
| 2011 | 111.2 | 115.1 | 115.4 | 116.8 | 114.3 | 108.9 | 107.7 | 107.5 | 114.5 | 117.4 | 117.7 | 117.8 | 113.7 |
| 2012 | 111.5 | 117.0 | 117.5 | 117.2 | 114.9 | 108.9 | 107.9 | 108.0 | 115.8 | 119.1 | 119.7 | 120.0 | 114.8 |
| 2013 | 113.3 | 119.8 | 120.3 | 120.2 | 117.9 | 111.2 | 109.6 | 110.3 | 118.5 | 122.0 | 122.7 | 122.7 | 117.4 |
| 2014 | 117.4 | 123.1 | 123.5 | 123.5 | 120.5 | 115.6 | 113.7 | 114.4 | 120.5 | 124.4 | 124.5 | 124.4 | 120.5 |
| 2015 | 118.7 | 123.5 | 123.8 | 124.0 | 120.5 | 116.2 | 115.3 | 115.7 | 120.8 | 126.9 | 127.5 | 127.0 | 121.7 |
| 2016 | 122.2 | 127.0 | 127.4 | 128.5 | 124.9 | 120.4 | 119.2 | 119.2 | 124.5 | 130.0 | 130.5 | 130.5 | 125.4 |
| 2017 | 124.9 | 130.6 | 130.2 | 131.4 | 128.6 | 123.5 | 121.4 | 121.4 | 127.5 | 133.0 | 133.9 | 133.8 | 128.4 |
| 2018 | 127.6 | 133.1 | 133.3 | 134.2 | 131.1 | 126.1 | 124.4 | 124.0 | 130.0 | 135.8 | 136.4 | 136.5 | 131.0 |
| 2019 | 129.8 | 135.7 | 136.1 | 136.8 | 133.1 | 129.0 | 127.3 | 127.1 | 133.0 | 138.5 | 138.9 | 138.3 | 133.6 |
| **Leisure and Hospitality** | | | | | | | | | | | | | |
| 2011 | 40.9 | 41.0 | 41.4 | 43.2 | 45.6 | 47.5 | 48.2 | 48.2 | 45.4 | 44.9 | 43.8 | 43.2 | 44.4 |
| 2012 | 41.3 | 41.6 | 42.5 | 42.8 | 46.2 | 48.0 | 48.7 | 48.7 | 45.9 | 45.6 | 44.5 | 44.1 | 45.0 |
| 2013 | 42.3 | 43.0 | 43.5 | 44.9 | 48.1 | 49.9 | 50.2 | 50.0 | 47.1 | 47.2 | 45.8 | 45.7 | 46.5 |
| 2014 | 42.8 | 43.4 | 43.6 | 45.0 | 48.5 | 49.9 | 50.3 | 50.0 | 47.3 | 47.2 | 45.8 | 45.4 | 46.6 |
| 2015 | 43.0 | 43.3 | 43.8 | 45.5 | 49.0 | 50.2 | 50.8 | 50.6 | 48.2 | 47.4 | 46.3 | 46.4 | 47.0 |
| 2016 | 44.0 | 44.2 | 45.3 | 47.2 | 49.5 | 50.8 | 51.5 | 51.2 | 48.5 | 47.7 | 46.4 | 46.2 | 47.7 |
| 2017 | 44.0 | 44.1 | 44.2 | 46.5 | 48.4 | 51.0 | 51.3 | 51.3 | 48.2 | 47.9 | 46.4 | 46.2 | 47.5 |
| 2018 | 43.7 | 44.2 | 44.8 | 46.0 | 48.8 | 50.5 | 50.7 | 51.1 | 47.9 | 47.6 | 45.8 | 46.1 | 47.3 |
| 2019 | 44.0 | 44.3 | 44.6 | 45.9 | 48.6 | 50.4 | 50.2 | 50.2 | 47.6 | 47.0 | 45.3 | 45.2 | 46.9 |
| **Other Services** | | | | | | | | | | | | | |
| 2011 | 18.4 | 18.4 | 18.6 | 19.0 | 19.0 | 18.9 | 18.8 | 18.8 | 19.0 | 19.0 | 19.0 | 19.2 | 18.8 |
| 2012 | 19.1 | 19.1 | 19.3 | 19.4 | 19.6 | 19.6 | 19.2 | 19.1 | 19.1 | 19.1 | 19.2 | 19.2 | 19.3 |
| 2013 | 19.0 | 19.0 | 19.1 | 19.2 | 19.4 | 19.3 | 19.3 | 19.4 | 19.1 | 19.2 | 19.3 | 19.5 | 19.2 |
| 2014 | 19.1 | 19.2 | 19.2 | 19.3 | 19.6 | 19.4 | 19.2 | 19.1 | 19.2 | 19.4 | 19.4 | 19.4 | 19.3 |
| 2015 | 19.1 | 19.1 | 19.2 | 19.3 | 19.4 | 19.3 | 19.0 | 19.1 | 19.1 | 19.3 | 19.3 | 19.3 | 19.2 |
| 2016 | 19.0 | 18.9 | 19.0 | 19.4 | 19.5 | 19.4 | 19.1 | 19.0 | 19.1 | 19.3 | 19.2 | 19.3 | 19.2 |
| 2017 | 19.0 | 19.0 | 19.0 | 19.4 | 19.4 | 19.4 | 19.2 | 18.9 | 19.1 | 19.2 | 19.2 | 19.2 | 19.2 |
| 2018 | 19.0 | 19.0 | 19.1 | 19.2 | 19.3 | 19.3 | 19.0 | 18.9 | 19.1 | 19.2 | 19.2 | 19.2 | 19.1 |
| 2019 | 19.0 | 19.0 | 19.0 | 19.3 | 19.3 | 19.1 | 19.0 | 18.8 | 19.0 | 19.1 | 19.2 | 19.2 | 19.1 |
| **Government** | | | | | | | | | | | | | |
| 2011 | 81.4 | 84.1 | 84.1 | 84.5 | 84.2 | 83.4 | 75.0 | 75.0 | 80.2 | 83.3 | 84.0 | 84.6 | 82.0 |
| 2012 | 80.3 | 83.4 | 83.5 | 82.8 | 83.6 | 82.5 | 74.2 | 73.5 | 79.1 | 82.3 | 82.6 | 83.7 | 81.0 |
| 2013 | 79.8 | 82.5 | 82.8 | 82.8 | 83.2 | 81.8 | 73.5 | 73.2 | 78.7 | 81.1 | 81.9 | 82.3 | 80.3 |
| 2014 | 78.5 | 81.1 | 81.1 | 81.3 | 81.1 | 80.5 | 72.5 | 72.5 | 78.1 | 80.3 | 81.5 | 82.2 | 79.2 |
| 2015 | 78.4 | 81.0 | 80.9 | 80.6 | 81.7 | 80.7 | 72.3 | 72.1 | 77.5 | 80.3 | 81.1 | 81.2 | 79.0 |
| 2016 | 79.1 | 80.6 | 81.0 | 80.7 | 81.0 | 80.2 | 71.9 | 71.8 | 77.1 | 80.6 | 80.9 | 81.5 | 78.9 |
| 2017 | 78.9 | 81.0 | 80.6 | 81.3 | 81.1 | 80.2 | 72.2 | 72.2 | 78.2 | 80.6 | 81.2 | 81.3 | 79.1 |
| 2018 | 78.8 | 81.0 | 80.9 | 80.9 | 81.4 | 80.8 | 73.0 | 73.3 | 79.5 | 81.4 | 82.0 | 81.8 | 79.6 |
| 2019 | 79.1 | 81.5 | 81.4 | 82.1 | 81.6 | 80.8 | 72.9 | 73.0 | 78.7 | 81.1 | 81.7 | 81.5 | 79.6 |

## Employment by Industry: Tucson, AZ, 2011–2019

(Numbers in thousands, not seasonally adjusted)

| Industry and year | January | February | March | April | May | June | July | August | September | October | November | December | Annual average |
|---|---|---|---|---|---|---|---|---|---|---|---|---|---|
| **Total Nonfarm** | | | | | | | | | | | | | |
| 2011 | 350.9 | 354.8 | 355.4 | 356.8 | 356.5 | 342.9 | 338.7 | 350.6 | 355.8 | 359.0 | 362.6 | 362.1 | 353.8 |
| 2012 | 357.3 | 361.1 | 362.6 | 362.7 | 362.2 | 351.0 | 344.5 | 355.3 | 360.9 | 363.5 | 367.3 | 368.1 | 359.7 |
| 2013 | 360.5 | 364.4 | 365.8 | 367.3 | 366.4 | 353.0 | 350.4 | 357.9 | 365.0 | 366.2 | 370.1 | 370.7 | 363.1 |
| 2014 | 363.9 | 366.9 | 366.7 | 367.9 | 366.3 | 356.6 | 353.5 | 357.5 | 366.1 | 369.5 | 373.1 | 374.0 | 365.2 |
| 2015 | 367.3 | 370.1 | 370.5 | 370.6 | 367.9 | 355.0 | 352.4 | 360.7 | 368.6 | 371.7 | 374.9 | 376.2 | 367.2 |
| 2016 | 369.2 | 372.2 | 373.3 | 375.7 | 373.0 | 362.0 | 360.0 | 364.8 | 374.5 | 377.9 | 380.7 | 382.2 | 372.1 |
| 2017 | 376.6 | 380.1 | 380.5 | 379.3 | 377.8 | 367.3 | 364.2 | 369.3 | 379.0 | 381.6 | 384.4 | 386.0 | 377.2 |
| 2018 | 378.6 | 382.8 | 383.1 | 383.5 | 381.9 | 372.0 | 369.8 | 375.5 | 385.8 | 388.3 | 392.4 | 394.3 | 382.3 |
| 2019 | 387.8 | 391.0 | 391.6 | 391.1 | 389.7 | 379.4 | 377.4 | 386.2 | 391.2 | 392.8 | 397.9 | 398.5 | 389.6 |
| **Total Private** | | | | | | | | | | | | | |
| 2011 | 274.3 | 275.5 | 276.5 | 277.5 | 277.7 | 276.3 | 274.3 | 276.7 | 277.2 | 279.3 | 282.5 | 283.9 | 277.6 |
| 2012 | 279.9 | 281.1 | 282.8 | 282.6 | 282.2 | 281.0 | 277.7 | 280.0 | 280.9 | 283.1 | 286.6 | 287.7 | 282.1 |
| 2013 | 282.6 | 284.0 | 285.5 | 286.8 | 286.6 | 284.1 | 282.6 | 285.4 | 286.0 | 286.6 | 290.3 | 291.0 | 286.0 |
| 2014 | 285.5 | 287.0 | 287.2 | 288.4 | 287.9 | 286.0 | 283.5 | 286.3 | 287.7 | 290.2 | 293.3 | 294.9 | 288.2 |
| 2015 | 289.7 | 291.0 | 291.4 | 291.3 | 290.0 | 287.9 | 287.0 | 289.6 | 289.7 | 292.4 | 294.4 | 296.1 | 290.9 |
| 2016 | 291.1 | 292.7 | 293.3 | 296.1 | 295.0 | 292.7 | 291.9 | 294.4 | 295.7 | 298.5 | 300.9 | 302.6 | 295.4 |
| 2017 | 299.2 | 300.7 | 300.8 | 299.6 | 298.9 | 298.5 | 295.6 | 297.9 | 299.1 | 301.6 | 304.2 | 305.9 | 300.2 |
| 2018 | 301.1 | 303.1 | 303.7 | 303.8 | 303.3 | 302.5 | 301.3 | 303.6 | 305.5 | 308.2 | 311.7 | 313.7 | 305.1 |
| 2019 | 308.9 | 310.5 | 310.8 | 310.1 | 309.3 | 308.5 | 307.3 | 308.6 | 309.3 | 310.6 | 314.8 | 315.9 | 310.4 |
| **Goods Producing** | | | | | | | | | | | | | |
| 2011 | 40.9 | 40.7 | 40.9 | 40.7 | 40.8 | 41.1 | 40.9 | 40.9 | 40.7 | 40.6 | 40.4 | 40.3 | 40.7 |
| 2012 | 40.0 | 39.8 | 40.2 | 40.3 | 40.5 | 41.2 | 41.3 | 41.4 | 41.2 | 41.4 | 41.8 | 42.0 | 40.9 |
| 2013 | 41.3 | 41.3 | 41.6 | 41.9 | 42.0 | 42.5 | 42.7 | 42.6 | 42.0 | 41.4 | 41.2 | 41.1 | 41.8 |
| 2014 | 40.7 | 40.6 | 40.5 | 40.4 | 40.4 | 40.7 | 40.8 | 41.2 | 41.0 | 40.9 | 40.5 | 40.4 | 40.7 |
| 2015 | 39.8 | 39.9 | 39.9 | 40.4 | 40.4 | 40.8 | 41.1 | 41.1 | 40.5 | 41.0 | 40.9 | 41.0 | 40.6 |
| 2016 | 40.4 | 40.6 | 40.6 | 40.9 | 41.0 | 41.3 | 41.6 | 41.7 | 41.4 | 41.7 | 41.8 | 41.9 | 41.2 |
| 2017 | 41.8 | 42.5 | 42.4 | 42.4 | 42.7 | 43.2 | 43.4 | 43.6 | 43.3 | 43.5 | 43.6 | 43.9 | 43.0 |
| 2018 | 43.6 | 43.9 | 44.4 | 44.5 | 44.7 | 45.4 | 45.6 | 45.7 | 45.9 | 46.4 | 46.7 | 47.0 | 45.3 |
| 2019 | 46.6 | 46.9 | 47.2 | 47.3 | 47.7 | 48.1 | 48.5 | 48.1 | 48.0 | 48.2 | 48.1 | 47.9 | 47.7 |
| **Service-Providing** | | | | | | | | | | | | | |
| 2011 | 310.0 | 314.1 | 314.5 | 316.1 | 315.7 | 301.8 | 297.8 | 309.7 | 315.1 | 318.4 | 322.2 | 321.8 | 313.1 |
| 2012 | 317.3 | 321.3 | 322.4 | 322.4 | 321.7 | 309.8 | 303.2 | 313.9 | 319.7 | 322.1 | 325.5 | 326.1 | 318.8 |
| 2013 | 319.2 | 323.1 | 324.2 | 325.4 | 324.4 | 310.5 | 307.7 | 315.3 | 323.0 | 324.8 | 328.9 | 329.6 | 321.3 |
| 2014 | 323.2 | 326.3 | 326.2 | 327.5 | 325.9 | 315.9 | 312.7 | 316.3 | 325.1 | 328.6 | 332.6 | 333.6 | 324.5 |
| 2015 | 327.5 | 330.2 | 330.6 | 330.2 | 327.5 | 314.2 | 311.3 | 319.6 | 328.1 | 330.7 | 334.0 | 335.2 | 326.6 |
| 2016 | 328.8 | 331.6 | 332.7 | 334.8 | 332.0 | 320.7 | 318.4 | 323.1 | 333.1 | 336.2 | 338.9 | 340.3 | 330.9 |
| 2017 | 334.8 | 337.6 | 338.1 | 336.9 | 335.1 | 324.1 | 320.8 | 325.7 | 335.7 | 338.1 | 340.8 | 342.1 | 334.2 |
| 2018 | 335.0 | 338.9 | 338.7 | 339.0 | 337.2 | 326.6 | 324.2 | 329.8 | 339.9 | 341.9 | 345.7 | 347.3 | 337.0 |
| 2019 | 341.2 | 344.1 | 344.4 | 343.8 | 342.0 | 331.3 | 328.9 | 338.1 | 343.2 | 344.6 | 349.8 | 350.6 | 341.8 |
| **Mining, Logging, and Construction** | | | | | | | | | | | | | |
| 2011 | 16.6 | 16.5 | 16.7 | 16.5 | 16.5 | 16.7 | 16.6 | 16.5 | 16.3 | 16.3 | 16.2 | 16.0 | 16.5 |
| 2012 | 15.7 | 15.5 | 15.8 | 15.9 | 16.1 | 16.7 | 16.8 | 16.9 | 16.8 | 17.0 | 17.3 | 17.5 | 16.5 |
| 2013 | 17.1 | 17.1 | 17.5 | 17.7 | 17.8 | 18.2 | 18.2 | 18.1 | 17.8 | 17.5 | 17.4 | 17.4 | 17.7 |
| 2014 | 17.0 | 17.0 | 17.0 | 17.0 | 16.9 | 17.0 | 17.1 | 17.6 | 17.4 | 17.5 | 17.1 | 16.8 | 17.1 |
| 2015 | 16.4 | 16.5 | 16.5 | 16.9 | 16.9 | 17.0 | 17.2 | 17.2 | 16.8 | 17.0 | 16.9 | 16.9 | 16.9 |
| 2016 | 16.4 | 16.5 | 16.4 | 16.5 | 16.6 | 16.7 | 16.6 | 16.6 | 16.6 | 16.8 | 16.9 | 16.9 | 16.6 |
| 2017 | 16.8 | 16.9 | 17.1 | 17.2 | 17.4 | 17.6 | 17.7 | 17.8 | 17.7 | 17.9 | 17.9 | 18.0 | 17.5 |
| 2018 | 17.9 | 18.0 | 18.4 | 18.4 | 18.6 | 18.8 | 18.9 | 18.9 | 19.0 | 19.3 | 19.4 | 19.5 | 18.8 |
| 2019 | 19.2 | 19.4 | 19.5 | 19.6 | 19.9 | 20.0 | 20.1 | 19.9 | 20.0 | 20.2 | 20.3 | 20.2 | 19.9 |
| **Manufacturing** | | | | | | | | | | | | | |
| 2011 | 24.3 | 24.2 | 24.2 | 24.2 | 24.3 | 24.4 | 24.3 | 24.4 | 24.4 | 24.3 | 24.2 | 24.3 | 24.3 |
| 2012 | 24.3 | 24.3 | 24.4 | 24.4 | 24.4 | 24.5 | 24.5 | 24.5 | 24.4 | 24.4 | 24.5 | 24.5 | 24.4 |
| 2013 | 24.2 | 24.2 | 24.1 | 24.2 | 24.2 | 24.3 | 24.5 | 24.5 | 24.2 | 23.9 | 23.8 | 23.7 | 24.2 |
| 2014 | 23.7 | 23.6 | 23.5 | 23.4 | 23.5 | 23.7 | 23.7 | 23.6 | 23.6 | 23.4 | 23.4 | 23.6 | 23.6 |
| 2015 | 23.4 | 23.4 | 23.4 | 23.5 | 23.5 | 23.8 | 23.9 | 23.9 | 23.7 | 24.0 | 24.0 | 24.1 | 23.7 |
| 2016 | 24.0 | 24.1 | 24.2 | 24.4 | 24.4 | 24.6 | 25.0 | 25.1 | 24.8 | 24.9 | 24.9 | 25.0 | 24.6 |
| 2017 | 25.0 | 25.6 | 25.3 | 25.2 | 25.3 | 25.6 | 25.7 | 25.8 | 25.6 | 25.6 | 25.7 | 25.9 | 25.5 |
| 2018 | 25.7 | 25.9 | 26.0 | 26.1 | 26.1 | 26.6 | 26.7 | 26.8 | 26.9 | 27.1 | 27.3 | 27.5 | 26.6 |
| 2019 | 27.4 | 27.5 | 27.7 | 27.7 | 27.8 | 28.1 | 28.4 | 28.2 | 28.0 | 28.0 | 27.8 | 27.7 | 27.9 |

# Employment by Industry: Tucson, AZ, 2011–2019—*Continued*

(Numbers in thousands, not seasonally adjusted)

| Industry and year | January | February | March | April | May | June | July | August | September | October | November | December | Annual average |
|---|---|---|---|---|---|---|---|---|---|---|---|---|---|
| **Trade, Transportation, and Utilities** | | | | | | | | | | | | | |
| 2011 | 57.5 | 57.1 | 57.1 | 57.3 | 57.6 | 57.5 | 57.2 | 58.1 | 57.4 | 58.1 | 60.0 | 60.5 | 58.0 |
| 2012 | 58.4 | 57.5 | 57.5 | 57.4 | 57.4 | 57.4 | 56.9 | 57.5 | 57.7 | 58.0 | 59.9 | 60.6 | 58.0 |
| 2013 | 58.5 | 57.9 | 58.1 | 58.2 | 58.6 | 58.4 | 58.5 | 59.5 | 59.5 | 59.6 | 61.5 | 62.6 | 59.2 |
| 2014 | 60.3 | 59.9 | 60.1 | 60.1 | 60.1 | 59.9 | 59.6 | 60.3 | 60.2 | 60.6 | 62.4 | 63.3 | 60.6 |
| 2015 | 60.7 | 59.8 | 59.8 | 59.6 | 59.8 | 59.4 | 59.5 | 60.4 | 60.5 | 60.8 | 62.3 | 62.8 | 60.5 |
| 2016 | 60.6 | 59.9 | 59.9 | 60.2 | 60.1 | 59.6 | 59.7 | 60.1 | 59.8 | 60.5 | 62.2 | 63.0 | 60.5 |
| 2017 | 61.4 | 61.1 | 60.7 | 60.9 | 60.8 | 60.6 | 60.4 | 60.9 | 60.8 | 61.4 | 63.0 | 63.6 | 61.3 |
| 2018 | 61.3 | 60.6 | 60.5 | 60.7 | 60.7 | 60.8 | 60.7 | 61.2 | 61.3 | 61.9 | 64.1 | 64.9 | 61.6 |
| 2019 | 63.2 | 62.5 | 62.6 | 62.3 | 62.5 | 62.5 | 62.4 | 62.6 | 62.6 | 62.7 | 64.0 | 64.4 | 62.9 |
| **Wholesale Trade** | | | | | | | | | | | | | |
| 2011 | 7.9 | 8.0 | 8.0 | 7.9 | 8.0 | 7.9 | 8.0 | 7.9 | 8.0 | 8.0 | 8.0 | 8.0 | 8.0 |
| 2012 | 7.8 | 7.8 | 7.9 | 7.9 | 8.0 | 8.0 | 8.0 | 8.0 | 8.1 | 8.0 | 8.0 | 8.1 | 8.0 |
| 2013 | 7.9 | 7.9 | 7.9 | 7.9 | 7.9 | 7.9 | 7.8 | 7.9 | 8.0 | 8.0 | 7.9 | 8.0 | 7.9 |
| 2014 | 7.8 | 7.8 | 7.9 | 7.9 | 7.9 | 7.9 | 7.9 | 7.8 | 7.9 | 7.8 | 7.8 | 7.8 | 7.9 |
| 2015 | 7.7 | 7.7 | 7.7 | 7.7 | 7.8 | 7.8 | 7.8 | 7.8 | 7.8 | 7.8 | 7.7 | 7.8 | 7.8 |
| 2016 | 7.7 | 7.8 | 7.7 | 7.7 | 7.8 | 7.7 | 7.8 | 7.8 | 7.7 | 7.8 | 7.8 | 7.8 | 7.8 |
| 2017 | 7.7 | 7.8 | 7.7 | 7.7 | 7.7 | 7.8 | 7.7 | 7.7 | 7.7 | 7.7 | 7.6 | 7.7 | 7.7 |
| 2018 | 7.5 | 7.5 | 7.5 | 7.6 | 7.5 | 7.6 | 7.4 | 7.3 | 7.3 | 7.2 | 7.1 | 7.3 | 7.4 |
| 2019 | 7.2 | 7.3 | 7.2 | 7.2 | 7.3 | 7.3 | 7.3 | 7.2 | 7.2 | 7.4 | 7.4 | 7.5 | 7.3 |
| **Retail Trade** | | | | | | | | | | | | | |
| 2011 | 39.9 | 39.4 | 39.4 | 39.6 | 39.7 | 39.7 | 39.4 | 40.2 | 39.4 | 40.1 | 41.9 | 42.2 | 40.1 |
| 2012 | 40.7 | 39.7 | 39.7 | 39.6 | 39.6 | 39.6 | 39.2 | 39.8 | 39.9 | 40.5 | 42.4 | 42.7 | 40.3 |
| 2013 | 41.2 | 40.6 | 40.9 | 41.1 | 41.3 | 41.2 | 41.2 | 41.9 | 41.8 | 41.9 | 43.8 | 44.5 | 41.8 |
| 2014 | 42.8 | 42.3 | 42.4 | 42.5 | 42.4 | 42.2 | 42.0 | 42.7 | 42.4 | 42.8 | 44.5 | 45.1 | 42.8 |
| 2015 | 42.8 | 41.9 | 41.9 | 41.8 | 41.8 | 41.5 | 41.6 | 42.4 | 42.3 | 42.6 | 43.9 | 44.2 | 42.4 |
| 2016 | 42.6 | 42.1 | 42.2 | 42.4 | 42.2 | 41.8 | 41.7 | 42.1 | 41.8 | 42.2 | 43.8 | 44.1 | 42.4 |
| 2017 | 42.9 | 42.3 | 42.2 | 42.3 | 42.1 | 41.8 | 41.7 | 42.1 | 41.8 | 42.2 | 43.7 | 43.9 | 42.4 |
| 2018 | 42.3 | 41.8 | 41.7 | 41.6 | 41.7 | 41.4 | 41.3 | 41.6 | 41.4 | 41.9 | 43.6 | 43.7 | 42.0 |
| 2019 | 42.4 | 41.8 | 41.7 | 41.5 | 41.6 | 41.5 | 41.4 | 41.4 | 41.3 | 41.0 | 42.1 | 42.1 | 41.7 |
| **Transportation and Utilities** | | | | | | | | | | | | | |
| 2011 | 9.7 | 9.7 | 9.7 | 9.8 | 9.9 | 9.9 | 9.8 | 10.0 | 10.0 | 10.0 | 10.1 | 10.3 | 9.9 |
| 2012 | 9.9 | 10.0 | 9.9 | 9.9 | 9.8 | 9.8 | 9.7 | 9.7 | 9.7 | 9.5 | 9.5 | 9.8 | 9.8 |
| 2013 | 9.4 | 9.4 | 9.3 | 9.2 | 9.4 | 9.3 | 9.5 | 9.7 | 9.7 | 9.7 | 9.8 | 10.1 | 9.5 |
| 2014 | 9.7 | 9.8 | 9.8 | 9.7 | 9.8 | 9.8 | 9.7 | 9.8 | 9.9 | 10.0 | 10.1 | 10.4 | 9.9 |
| 2015 | 10.2 | 10.2 | 10.2 | 10.1 | 10.2 | 10.1 | 10.1 | 10.2 | 10.4 | 10.4 | 10.7 | 10.8 | 10.3 |
| 2016 | 10.3 | 10.0 | 10.0 | 10.1 | 10.1 | 10.1 | 10.2 | 10.2 | 10.3 | 10.5 | 10.6 | 11.1 | 10.3 |
| 2017 | 10.8 | 11.0 | 10.8 | 10.9 | 11.0 | 11.0 | 11.0 | 11.1 | 11.3 | 11.5 | 11.7 | 12.0 | 11.2 |
| 2018 | 11.5 | 11.3 | 11.3 | 11.5 | 11.5 | 11.8 | 12.0 | 12.3 | 12.6 | 12.8 | 13.4 | 13.9 | 12.2 |
| 2019 | 13.6 | 13.4 | 13.7 | 13.6 | 13.6 | 13.7 | 13.7 | 14.0 | 14.1 | 14.3 | 14.5 | 14.8 | 13.9 |
| **Information** | | | | | | | | | | | | | |
| 2011 | 4.3 | 4.5 | 4.3 | 4.3 | 4.4 | 4.3 | 4.4 | 4.5 | 4.4 | 4.4 | 4.5 | 4.5 | 4.4 |
| 2012 | 4.4 | 4.6 | 4.5 | 4.5 | 4.6 | 4.4 | 4.4 | 4.5 | 4.3 | 4.4 | 4.5 | 4.4 | 4.5 |
| 2013 | 4.5 | 4.6 | 4.4 | 4.5 | 4.8 | 4.5 | 4.5 | 4.7 | 4.4 | 4.4 | 4.6 | 4.5 | 4.5 |
| 2014 | 4.5 | 4.6 | 4.4 | 4.4 | 4.5 | 4.4 | 4.4 | 4.4 | 4.3 | 4.4 | 4.5 | 4.5 | 4.4 |
| 2015 | 4.4 | 4.6 | 4.4 | 4.5 | 4.4 | 4.4 | 4.4 | 4.6 | 4.4 | 4.5 | 4.8 | 4.8 | 4.5 |
| 2016 | 4.8 | 5.0 | 5.0 | 5.1 | 5.1 | 5.0 | 5.0 | 5.1 | 5.1 | 5.1 | 5.3 | 5.3 | 5.1 |
| 2017 | 5.5 | 5.5 | 5.5 | 5.5 | 5.4 | 5.4 | 5.2 | 5.4 | 5.2 | 5.3 | 5.7 | 5.5 | 5.4 |
| 2018 | 5.6 | 6.1 | 5.6 | 5.7 | 5.6 | 5.6 | 5.5 | 5.4 | 5.4 | 5.6 | 5.6 | 5.6 | 5.6 |
| 2019 | 5.7 | 5.8 | 5.7 | 5.7 | 5.9 | 5.6 | 5.5 | 5.7 | 5.4 | 5.4 | 5.5 | 5.4 | 5.6 |
| **Financial Activities** | | | | | | | | | | | | | |
| 2011 | 17.0 | 17.0 | 17.0 | 16.9 | 16.8 | 16.8 | 16.9 | 16.8 | 16.8 | 16.8 | 16.8 | 17.0 | 16.9 |
| 2012 | 16.8 | 16.9 | 16.6 | 16.6 | 16.7 | 16.8 | 16.8 | 16.9 | 16.9 | 17.1 | 17.1 | 17.3 | 16.9 |
| 2013 | 17.0 | 17.1 | 17.2 | 17.0 | 17.1 | 17.3 | 17.2 | 17.2 | 17.2 | 17.5 | 17.5 | 17.7 | 17.3 |
| 2014 | 17.4 | 17.4 | 17.5 | 17.5 | 17.5 | 17.5 | 17.6 | 17.4 | 17.3 | 17.5 | 17.6 | 17.8 | 17.5 |
| 2015 | 17.3 | 17.4 | 17.4 | 17.3 | 17.3 | 17.2 | 17.1 | 17.1 | 17.0 | 17.2 | 17.2 | 17.2 | 17.2 |
| 2016 | 17.1 | 17.1 | 17.1 | 17.0 | 17.0 | 17.1 | 17.1 | 17.2 | 17.3 | 17.4 | 17.5 | 17.6 | 17.2 |
| 2017 | 17.4 | 17.4 | 17.5 | 17.4 | 17.4 | 17.7 | 17.6 | 17.6 | 17.6 | 17.9 | 17.9 | 18.0 | 17.6 |
| 2018 | 17.7 | 17.9 | 17.9 | 17.8 | 17.8 | 17.7 | 17.8 | 17.7 | 17.6 | 17.8 | 17.6 | 17.6 | 17.7 |
| 2019 | 17.0 | 17.0 | 17.0 | 17.0 | 17.1 | 17.2 | 17.2 | 17.1 | 17.2 | 17.4 | 17.3 | 17.3 | 17.2 |

## Employment by Industry: Tucson, AZ, 2011–2019—*Continued*

(Numbers in thousands, not seasonally adjusted)

| Industry and year | January | February | March | April | May | June | July | August | September | October | November | December | Annual average |
|---|---|---|---|---|---|---|---|---|---|---|---|---|---|
| **Professional and Business Services** | | | | | | | | | | | | | |
| 2011 | 45.0 | 45.3 | 45.7 | 45.7 | 45.4 | 45.6 | 45.3 | 45.5 | 46.5 | 47.3 | 47.7 | 48.3 | 46.1 |
| 2012 | 47.1 | 47.6 | 48.3 | 47.9 | 47.5 | 47.5 | 47.1 | 47.1 | 47.4 | 48.1 | 48.6 | 48.5 | 47.7 |
| 2013 | 48.3 | 48.7 | 49.1 | 49.6 | 49.1 | 48.0 | 47.7 | 47.9 | 48.4 | 48.7 | 49.7 | 49.6 | 48.7 |
| 2014 | 48.6 | 48.6 | 48.3 | 48.6 | 48.7 | 48.5 | 47.8 | 48.3 | 49.3 | 49.8 | 50.4 | 50.6 | 49.0 |
| 2015 | 49.8 | 50.0 | 49.6 | 49.4 | 48.6 | 48.2 | 48.4 | 48.7 | 49.3 | 49.8 | 50.1 | 50.4 | 49.4 |
| 2016 | 48.8 | 49.2 | 49.0 | 49.5 | 49.1 | 48.8 | 48.9 | 49.4 | 50.4 | 50.8 | 50.8 | 51.4 | 49.7 |
| 2017 | 50.7 | 50.7 | 50.5 | 50.0 | 49.6 | 50.0 | 49.8 | 49.8 | 50.0 | 50.0 | 50.2 | 50.7 | 50.2 |
| 2018 | 49.8 | 50.3 | 50.2 | 50.0 | 49.9 | 49.5 | 50.0 | 50.5 | 51.0 | 51.0 | 51.4 | 52.0 | 50.5 |
| 2019 | 50.8 | 51.3 | 50.9 | 50.7 | 49.4 | 49.5 | 50.2 | 49.9 | 50.1 | 49.7 | 51.4 | 52.2 | 50.5 |
| **Education and Health Services** | | | | | | | | | | | | | |
| 2011 | 58.7 | 59.2 | 59.1 | 59.8 | 59.9 | 59.4 | 59.2 | 60.1 | 60.4 | 60.5 | 60.9 | 61.2 | 59.9 |
| 2012 | 61.1 | 61.2 | 61.5 | 61.3 | 61.2 | 60.7 | 59.7 | 60.4 | 60.8 | 61.2 | 61.4 | 61.7 | 61.0 |
| 2013 | 60.6 | 61.1 | 61.3 | 61.5 | 61.4 | 60.8 | 61.0 | 61.9 | 62.1 | 62.2 | 62.6 | 62.6 | 61.6 |
| 2014 | 60.9 | 61.2 | 61.4 | 61.7 | 61.6 | 61.0 | 60.3 | 61.1 | 61.3 | 62.1 | 62.2 | 62.7 | 61.5 |
| 2015 | 61.9 | 62.0 | 62.3 | 62.4 | 62.6 | 61.9 | 62.0 | 62.9 | 63.0 | 63.8 | 63.7 | 64.2 | 62.7 |
| 2016 | 63.9 | 64.3 | 64.5 | 64.8 | 64.8 | 64.3 | 63.8 | 64.8 | 64.8 | 65.3 | 65.5 | 65.8 | 64.7 |
| 2017 | 65.1 | 65.5 | 65.6 | 65.3 | 65.3 | 64.9 | 64.0 | 64.9 | 65.4 | 65.5 | 65.8 | 66.1 | 65.3 |
| 2018 | 65.5 | 65.8 | 66.0 | 66.0 | 66.1 | 66.0 | 65.3 | 66.2 | 66.6 | 67.1 | 67.6 | 67.9 | 66.3 |
| 2019 | 67.2 | 67.6 | 67.8 | 67.6 | 67.6 | 67.6 | 67.2 | 68.2 | 68.3 | 69.0 | 69.8 | 70.1 | 68.2 |
| **Leisure and Hospitality** | | | | | | | | | | | | | |
| 2011 | 38.4 | 39.0 | 39.7 | 40.1 | 40.1 | 39.0 | 37.8 | 38.4 | 38.7 | 39.1 | 39.6 | 39.6 | 39.1 |
| 2012 | 39.7 | 40.9 | 41.4 | 41.8 | 41.4 | 40.0 | 38.6 | 39.3 | 39.8 | 40.0 | 40.4 | 40.4 | 40.3 |
| 2013 | 39.9 | 40.7 | 41.0 | 41.2 | 40.7 | 39.7 | 38.2 | 38.9 | 39.8 | 40.1 | 40.4 | 40.3 | 40.1 |
| 2014 | 40.6 | 42.1 | 42.3 | 43.1 | 42.4 | 41.1 | 40.0 | 40.6 | 41.3 | 41.7 | 42.3 | 42.1 | 41.6 |
| 2015 | 42.6 | 43.9 | 44.3 | 44.3 | 43.5 | 42.6 | 41.4 | 41.9 | 42.3 | 42.5 | 42.7 | 43.1 | 42.9 |
| 2016 | 42.6 | 43.7 | 44.2 | 45.6 | 44.9 | 43.5 | 42.7 | 43.1 | 43.9 | 44.7 | 44.9 | 44.7 | 44.0 |
| 2017 | 44.5 | 45.2 | 45.6 | 45.1 | 44.7 | 43.6 | 42.5 | 43.0 | 44.1 | 44.8 | 44.9 | 44.9 | 44.4 |
| 2018 | 44.5 | 45.3 | 45.7 | 45.8 | 45.1 | 44.0 | 43.1 | 43.6 | 44.3 | 45.0 | 45.2 | 45.2 | 44.7 |
| 2019 | 44.7 | 45.6 | 45.9 | 45.8 | 45.3 | 44.1 | 42.7 | 43.4 | 44.0 | 44.4 | 44.8 | 44.7 | 44.6 |
| **Other Services** | | | | | | | | | | | | | |
| 2011 | 12.5 | 12.7 | 12.7 | 12.7 | 12.7 | 12.6 | 12.6 | 12.4 | 12.3 | 12.5 | 12.6 | 12.5 | 12.6 |
| 2012 | 12.4 | 12.6 | 12.8 | 12.8 | 12.9 | 13.0 | 12.9 | 12.9 | 12.8 | 12.9 | 12.9 | 12.8 | 12.8 |
| 2013 | 12.5 | 12.6 | 12.8 | 12.9 | 12.9 | 12.9 | 12.8 | 12.7 | 12.6 | 12.7 | 12.8 | 12.6 | 12.7 |
| 2014 | 12.5 | 12.6 | 12.7 | 12.6 | 12.7 | 12.9 | 13.0 | 13.0 | 13.0 | 13.2 | 13.4 | 13.5 | 12.9 |
| 2015 | 13.2 | 13.4 | 13.7 | 13.4 | 13.4 | 13.4 | 13.1 | 12.9 | 12.7 | 12.8 | 12.7 | 12.6 | 13.1 |
| 2016 | 12.9 | 12.9 | 13.0 | 13.0 | 13.0 | 13.1 | 13.1 | 13.0 | 13.0 | 13.0 | 12.9 | 12.9 | 13.0 |
| 2017 | 12.8 | 12.8 | 13.0 | 13.0 | 13.0 | 13.1 | 12.7 | 12.7 | 12.7 | 13.2 | 13.1 | 13.2 | 12.9 |
| 2018 | 13.1 | 13.2 | 13.4 | 13.3 | 13.4 | 13.5 | 13.3 | 13.3 | 13.4 | 13.4 | 13.5 | 13.5 | 13.4 |
| 2019 | 13.7 | 13.8 | 13.7 | 13.7 | 13.8 | 13.9 | 13.6 | 13.6 | 13.7 | 13.8 | 13.9 | 13.9 | 13.8 |
| **Government** | | | | | | | | | | | | | |
| 2011 | 76.6 | 79.3 | 78.9 | 79.3 | 78.8 | 66.6 | 64.4 | 73.9 | 78.6 | 79.7 | 80.1 | 78.2 | 76.2 |
| 2012 | 77.4 | 80.0 | 79.8 | 80.1 | 80.0 | 70.0 | 66.8 | 75.3 | 80.0 | 80.4 | 80.7 | 80.4 | 77.6 |
| 2013 | 77.9 | 80.4 | 80.3 | 80.5 | 79.8 | 68.9 | 67.8 | 72.5 | 79.0 | 79.6 | 79.8 | 79.7 | 77.2 |
| 2014 | 78.4 | 79.9 | 79.5 | 79.5 | 78.4 | 70.6 | 70.0 | 71.2 | 78.4 | 79.3 | 79.8 | 79.1 | 77.0 |
| 2015 | 77.6 | 79.1 | 79.1 | 79.3 | 77.9 | 67.1 | 65.4 | 71.1 | 78.9 | 79.3 | 80.5 | 80.1 | 76.3 |
| 2016 | 78.1 | 79.5 | 80.0 | 79.6 | 78.0 | 69.3 | 68.1 | 70.4 | 78.8 | 79.4 | 79.8 | 79.6 | 76.7 |
| 2017 | 77.4 | 79.4 | 79.7 | 79.7 | 78.9 | 68.8 | 68.6 | 71.4 | 79.9 | 80.0 | 80.2 | 80.1 | 77.0 |
| 2018 | 77.5 | 79.7 | 79.4 | 79.7 | 78.6 | 69.5 | 68.5 | 71.9 | 80.3 | 80.1 | 80.7 | 80.6 | 77.2 |
| 2019 | 78.9 | 80.5 | 80.8 | 81.0 | 80.4 | 70.9 | 70.1 | 77.6 | 81.9 | 82.2 | 83.1 | 82.6 | 79.2 |

# Employment by Industry: Fresno, CA, 2011–2019

(Numbers in thousands, not seasonally adjusted)

| Industry and year | January | February | March | April | May | June | July | August | September | October | November | December | Annual average |
|---|---|---|---|---|---|---|---|---|---|---|---|---|---|
| **Total Nonfarm** | | | | | | | | | | | | | |
| 2011 | 285.4 | 289.7 | 292.0 | 293.8 | 294.7 | 292.7 | 289.5 | 289.4 | 292.6 | 293.3 | 292.4 | 290.4 | 291.3 |
| 2012 | 285.3 | 287.8 | 290.8 | 292.1 | 296.0 | 297.1 | 292.9 | 293.5 | 294.8 | 298.2 | 298.5 | 296.5 | 293.6 |
| 2013 | 292.6 | 297.2 | 300.0 | 300.8 | 303.2 | 303.7 | 299.9 | 302.4 | 305.1 | 307.2 | 307.7 | 307.2 | 302.3 |
| 2014 | 301.6 | 306.2 | 308.6 | 310.8 | 312.7 | 313.5 | 311.9 | 313.3 | 315.7 | 320.1 | 319.2 | 318.8 | 312.7 |
| 2015 | 313.7 | 317.2 | 320.0 | 322.3 | 324.2 | 325.7 | 323.2 | 324.4 | 328.0 | 332.3 | 331.7 | 331.3 | 324.5 |
| 2016 | 325.5 | 327.9 | 331.1 | 334.9 | 336.9 | 338.6 | 334.8 | 336.4 | 340.7 | 342.1 | 342.6 | 339.4 | 335.9 |
| 2017 | 333.4 | 337.5 | 340.5 | 343.3 | 345.0 | 345.6 | 340.2 | 342.7 | 346.5 | 346.9 | 348.6 | 347.1 | 343.1 |
| 2018 | 344.2 | 347.2 | 350.1 | 351.6 | 353.2 | 354.7 | 349.0 | 353.2 | 356.5 | 359.8 | 361.6 | 360.3 | 353.5 |
| 2019 | 353.0 | 354.9 | 357.2 | 360.6 | 362.5 | 362.9 | 356.8 | 361.7 | 364.9 | 366.4 | 368.3 | 367.5 | 361.4 |
| **Total Private** | | | | | | | | | | | | | |
| 2011 | 220.0 | 221.6 | 222.9 | 224.1 | 225.7 | 226.1 | 226.7 | 228.4 | 229.9 | 228.0 | 227.2 | 226.5 | 225.6 |
| 2012 | 221.8 | 222.5 | 224.6 | 225.7 | 229.6 | 231.4 | 231.3 | 233.9 | 233.2 | 233.4 | 234.1 | 232.9 | 229.5 |
| 2013 | 229.5 | 231.6 | 233.6 | 234.3 | 236.9 | 237.8 | 239.7 | 242.6 | 242.8 | 243.0 | 242.5 | 242.7 | 238.1 |
| 2014 | 237.1 | 239.4 | 240.9 | 242.9 | 244.2 | 245.3 | 248.0 | 251.5 | 251.5 | 253.0 | 251.8 | 251.7 | 246.4 |
| 2015 | 246.4 | 247.7 | 250.4 | 252.2 | 253.5 | 255.1 | 258.3 | 260.9 | 260.5 | 262.6 | 261.1 | 261.2 | 255.8 |
| 2016 | 255.4 | 257.0 | 258.9 | 262.1 | 263.7 | 265.4 | 268.7 | 270.7 | 270.4 | 270.0 | 269.7 | 267.4 | 265.0 |
| 2017 | 261.7 | 263.8 | 266.2 | 268.5 | 269.9 | 271.0 | 273.1 | 275.2 | 275.4 | 273.7 | 274.4 | 273.1 | 270.5 |
| 2018 | 269.8 | 271.5 | 272.4 | 274.1 | 276.1 | 278.3 | 280.9 | 284.4 | 284.2 | 284.9 | 285.5 | 284.9 | 278.9 |
| 2019 | 278.3 | 278.1 | 280.2 | 283.2 | 284.7 | 286.3 | 288.6 | 292.1 | 291.8 | 291.6 | 291.5 | 292.0 | 286.5 |
| **Goods Producing** | | | | | | | | | | | | | |
| 2011 | 34.0 | 34.0 | 34.1 | 34.4 | 35.5 | 36.3 | 36.9 | 37.5 | 37.8 | 36.5 | 34.9 | 34.6 | 35.5 |
| 2012 | 33.9 | 33.6 | 34.0 | 34.1 | 36.5 | 37.7 | 38.3 | 39.0 | 37.6 | 37.0 | 35.7 | 35.4 | 36.1 |
| 2013 | 34.6 | 34.5 | 34.8 | 34.9 | 36.0 | 36.9 | 38.2 | 39.0 | 38.6 | 37.7 | 36.4 | 36.3 | 36.5 |
| 2014 | 35.7 | 35.7 | 35.8 | 36.3 | 37.0 | 38.3 | 39.6 | 40.7 | 40.7 | 40.2 | 38.9 | 38.4 | 38.1 |
| 2015 | 37.9 | 38.1 | 39.0 | 39.3 | 39.7 | 41.1 | 42.9 | 43.4 | 43.3 | 42.6 | 40.6 | 40.2 | 40.7 |
| 2016 | 39.3 | 39.6 | 39.6 | 40.3 | 40.7 | 42.3 | 43.6 | 44.3 | 44.0 | 42.3 | 41.5 | 41.0 | 41.5 |
| 2017 | 40.0 | 40.8 | 41.6 | 42.3 | 43.6 | 43.8 | 44.6 | 45.4 | 45.6 | 44.3 | 43.9 | 43.4 | 43.3 |
| 2018 | 42.6 | 43.2 | 43.2 | 43.7 | 44.3 | 45.1 | 46.2 | 47.0 | 47.2 | 46.2 | 45.3 | 44.4 | 44.9 |
| 2019 | 43.3 | 43.1 | 43.7 | 44.3 | 44.8 | 45.6 | 46.3 | 47.8 | 47.8 | 47.1 | 46.1 | 45.6 | 45.5 |
| **Service-Providing** | | | | | | | | | | | | | |
| 2011 | 251.4 | 255.7 | 257.9 | 259.4 | 259.2 | 256.4 | 252.6 | 251.9 | 254.8 | 256.8 | 257.5 | 255.8 | 255.8 |
| 2012 | 251.4 | 254.2 | 256.8 | 258.0 | 259.5 | 259.4 | 254.6 | 254.5 | 257.2 | 261.2 | 262.8 | 261.1 | 257.6 |
| 2013 | 258.0 | 262.7 | 265.2 | 265.9 | 267.2 | 266.8 | 261.7 | 263.4 | 266.5 | 269.5 | 271.3 | 270.9 | 265.8 |
| 2014 | 265.9 | 270.5 | 272.8 | 274.5 | 275.7 | 275.2 | 272.3 | 272.6 | 275.0 | 279.9 | 280.3 | 280.4 | 274.6 |
| 2015 | 275.8 | 279.1 | 281.0 | 283.0 | 284.5 | 284.6 | 280.3 | 281.0 | 284.7 | 289.7 | 291.1 | 291.1 | 283.8 |
| 2016 | 286.2 | 288.3 | 291.5 | 294.6 | 296.2 | 296.3 | 291.2 | 292.1 | 296.7 | 299.8 | 301.1 | 298.4 | 294.4 |
| 2017 | 293.4 | 296.7 | 298.9 | 301.0 | 301.4 | 301.8 | 295.6 | 297.3 | 300.9 | 302.6 | 304.7 | 303.7 | 299.8 |
| 2018 | 301.6 | 304.0 | 306.9 | 307.9 | 308.9 | 309.6 | 302.8 | 306.2 | 309.3 | 313.6 | 316.3 | 315.9 | 308.6 |
| 2019 | 309.7 | 311.8 | 313.5 | 316.3 | 317.7 | 317.3 | 310.5 | 313.9 | 317.1 | 319.3 | 322.2 | 321.9 | 315.9 |
| **Mining, Logging, and Construction** | | | | | | | | | | | | | |
| 2011 | 11.2 | 11.3 | 11.6 | 11.6 | 11.7 | 11.9 | 12.3 | 12.3 | 12.2 | 11.8 | 11.4 | 11.5 | 11.7 |
| 2012 | 11.4 | 11.3 | 11.6 | 11.7 | 12.2 | 12.9 | 13.2 | 13.3 | 12.8 | 13.0 | 12.8 | 12.7 | 12.4 |
| 2013 | 12.4 | 12.4 | 12.8 | 13.0 | 13.5 | 13.8 | 14.1 | 14.2 | 14.0 | 13.7 | 13.6 | 13.5 | 13.4 |
| 2014 | 13.2 | 13.3 | 13.4 | 13.7 | 13.9 | 14.3 | 14.6 | 14.8 | 14.7 | 14.9 | 14.7 | 14.3 | 14.2 |
| 2015 | 14.0 | 14.1 | 14.6 | 15.0 | 15.2 | 15.7 | 16.1 | 16.0 | 15.7 | 15.9 | 15.8 | 15.8 | 15.3 |
| 2016 | 15.4 | 15.7 | 15.7 | 16.1 | 16.2 | 16.6 | 16.7 | 16.9 | 16.8 | 16.7 | 16.9 | 16.6 | 16.4 |
| 2017 | 15.8 | 16.3 | 16.9 | 17.4 | 17.7 | 18.2 | 18.4 | 18.4 | 18.4 | 18.4 | 18.4 | 18.3 | 17.7 |
| 2018 | 17.8 | 18.3 | 18.2 | 18.7 | 19.0 | 19.5 | 19.7 | 19.8 | 19.6 | 19.3 | 19.3 | 18.9 | 19.0 |
| 2019 | 18.2 | 18.0 | 18.4 | 18.9 | 19.2 | 19.7 | 19.8 | 20.1 | 19.9 | 19.8 | 19.4 | 19.3 | 19.2 |
| **Manufacturing** | | | | | | | | | | | | | |
| 2011 | 22.8 | 22.7 | 22.5 | 22.8 | 23.8 | 24.4 | 24.6 | 25.2 | 25.6 | 24.7 | 23.5 | 23.1 | 23.8 |
| 2012 | 22.5 | 22.3 | 22.4 | 22.4 | 24.3 | 24.8 | 25.1 | 25.7 | 24.8 | 24.0 | 22.9 | 22.7 | 23.7 |
| 2013 | 22.2 | 22.1 | 22.0 | 21.9 | 22.5 | 23.1 | 24.1 | 24.8 | 24.6 | 24.0 | 22.8 | 22.8 | 23.1 |
| 2014 | 22.5 | 22.4 | 22.4 | 22.6 | 23.1 | 24.0 | 25.0 | 25.9 | 26.0 | 25.3 | 24.2 | 24.1 | 24.0 |
| 2015 | 23.9 | 24.0 | 24.4 | 24.3 | 24.5 | 25.4 | 26.8 | 27.4 | 27.6 | 26.7 | 24.8 | 24.4 | 25.4 |
| 2016 | 23.9 | 23.9 | 23.9 | 24.2 | 24.5 | 25.7 | 26.9 | 27.4 | 27.2 | 25.6 | 24.6 | 24.4 | 25.2 |
| 2017 | 24.2 | 24.5 | 24.7 | 24.9 | 25.9 | 25.6 | 26.2 | 27.0 | 27.2 | 25.9 | 25.5 | 25.1 | 25.6 |
| 2018 | 24.8 | 24.9 | 25.0 | 25.0 | 25.3 | 25.6 | 26.5 | 27.2 | 27.6 | 26.9 | 26.0 | 25.5 | 25.9 |
| 2019 | 25.1 | 25.1 | 25.3 | 25.4 | 25.6 | 25.9 | 26.5 | 27.7 | 27.9 | 27.3 | 26.7 | 26.3 | 26.2 |

## Employment by Industry: Fresno, CA, 2011–2019—*Continued*

(Numbers in thousands, not seasonally adjusted)

| Industry and year | January | February | March | April | May | June | July | August | September | October | November | December | Annual average |
|---|---|---|---|---|---|---|---|---|---|---|---|---|---|
| **Trade, Transportation, and Utilities** | | | | | | | | | | | | | |
| 2011 | 55.6 | 55.5 | 55.2 | 55.9 | 56.2 | 56.4 | 57.4 | 57.9 | 58.7 | 59.1 | 60.2 | 60.0 | 57.3 |
| 2012 | 56.3 | 55.5 | 55.8 | 56.3 | 57.2 | 57.9 | 58.1 | 58.6 | 59.4 | 59.9 | 61.2 | 61.1 | 58.1 |
| 2013 | 58.1 | 58.7 | 59.1 | 59.2 | 60.3 | 60.0 | 60.7 | 61.7 | 61.9 | 61.8 | 63.0 | 63.2 | 60.6 |
| 2014 | 60.2 | 60.3 | 60.6 | 61.0 | 61.1 | 61.4 | 61.7 | 62.2 | 62.6 | 63.2 | 64.1 | 64.6 | 61.9 |
| 2015 | 61.5 | 61.3 | 61.4 | 61.6 | 62.0 | 62.3 | 63.2 | 64.1 | 64.6 | 65.7 | 66.2 | 66.4 | 63.4 |
| 2016 | 63.9 | 63.6 | 63.6 | 64.3 | 65.0 | 65.2 | 65.7 | 66.2 | 66.7 | 67.0 | 68.5 | 67.6 | 65.6 |
| 2017 | 65.5 | 64.9 | 64.6 | 64.9 | 65.0 | 65.4 | 65.6 | 66.3 | 66.6 | 67.0 | 68.3 | 68.3 | 66.0 |
| 2018 | 66.0 | 65.6 | 65.2 | 65.7 | 66.1 | 67.6 | 68.8 | 69.6 | 69.6 | 70.3 | 71.9 | 71.5 | 68.2 |
| 2019 | 69.5 | 67.7 | 67.8 | 68.1 | 69.1 | 69.3 | 70.0 | 70.4 | 70.6 | 70.8 | 72.1 | 72.5 | 69.8 |
| **Wholesale Trade** | | | | | | | | | | | | | |
| 2011 | 11.9 | 12.0 | 12.0 | 12.0 | 12.1 | 12.2 | 12.6 | 12.6 | 12.7 | 12.7 | 12.7 | 12.4 | 12.3 |
| 2012 | 12.1 | 12.1 | 12.2 | 12.2 | 12.5 | 12.8 | 12.9 | 13.0 | 13.0 | 13.0 | 12.9 | 12.8 | 12.6 |
| 2013 | 12.7 | 12.9 | 13.0 | 13.2 | 13.6 | 13.6 | 13.5 | 13.7 | 13.6 | 13.5 | 13.4 | 13.4 | 13.3 |
| 2014 | 13.4 | 13.5 | 13.5 | 13.3 | 13.3 | 13.5 | 13.6 | 13.7 | 13.6 | 13.6 | 13.4 | 13.3 | 13.5 |
| 2015 | 13.1 | 13.1 | 13.0 | 13.0 | 13.1 | 13.4 | 13.7 | 13.8 | 13.8 | 14.2 | 14.0 | 14.0 | 13.5 |
| 2016 | 13.8 | 13.7 | 13.7 | 13.7 | 13.9 | 14.1 | 14.3 | 14.2 | 14.3 | 14.3 | 14.3 | 14.1 | 14.0 |
| 2017 | 14.0 | 13.8 | 13.8 | 13.8 | 13.9 | 14.3 | 14.3 | 14.3 | 14.2 | 14.3 | 14.1 | 14.2 | 14.1 |
| 2018 | 13.9 | 14.0 | 13.9 | 14.1 | 14.2 | 14.4 | 14.7 | 15.0 | 14.6 | 14.7 | 14.6 | 14.6 | 14.4 |
| 2019 | 14.3 | 14.2 | 14.2 | 14.4 | 14.6 | 14.9 | 14.9 | 14.9 | 14.9 | 14.9 | 14.6 | 14.7 | 14.6 |
| **Retail Trade** | | | | | | | | | | | | | |
| 2011 | 32.9 | 32.7 | 32.4 | 32.9 | 33.0 | 33.0 | 33.2 | 33.4 | 33.9 | 34.2 | 35.5 | 35.9 | 33.6 |
| 2012 | 33.1 | 32.4 | 32.5 | 32.9 | 33.2 | 33.4 | 33.5 | 33.7 | 34.4 | 35.0 | 36.6 | 36.5 | 33.9 |
| 2013 | 34.1 | 34.2 | 34.4 | 34.4 | 34.7 | 34.6 | 34.9 | 35.5 | 35.7 | 36.0 | 37.6 | 37.8 | 35.3 |
| 2014 | 35.4 | 35.2 | 35.6 | 36.1 | 36.1 | 36.1 | 36.0 | 36.2 | 36.6 | 37.3 | 38.6 | 39.2 | 36.5 |
| 2015 | 36.7 | 36.5 | 36.7 | 36.6 | 36.8 | 36.8 | 37.2 | 37.8 | 38.1 | 38.7 | 39.5 | 39.6 | 37.6 |
| 2016 | 37.9 | 37.7 | 37.8 | 38.1 | 38.3 | 38.3 | 38.5 | 38.9 | 39.1 | 39.6 | 41.0 | 40.3 | 38.8 |
| 2017 | 38.9 | 38.5 | 38.2 | 38.3 | 38.1 | 38.1 | 38.3 | 38.7 | 38.7 | 39.3 | 40.5 | 40.6 | 38.9 |
| 2018 | 39.0 | 38.5 | 38.2 | 38.5 | 38.7 | 38.5 | 38.8 | 39.0 | 39.1 | 39.4 | 40.6 | 40.7 | 39.1 |
| 2019 | 38.5 | 38.1 | 38.0 | 37.8 | 38.0 | 37.9 | 38.3 | 38.5 | 38.4 | 38.7 | 40.1 | 40.5 | 38.6 |
| **Transportation and Utilities** | | | | | | | | | | | | | |
| 2011 | 10.8 | 10.8 | 10.8 | 11.0 | 11.1 | 11.2 | 11.6 | 11.9 | 12.1 | 12.2 | 12.0 | 11.7 | 11.4 |
| 2012 | 11.1 | 11.0 | 11.1 | 11.2 | 11.5 | 11.7 | 11.7 | 11.9 | 12.0 | 11.9 | 11.7 | 11.8 | 11.6 |
| 2013 | 11.3 | 11.6 | 11.7 | 11.6 | 12.0 | 11.8 | 12.3 | 12.5 | 12.6 | 12.3 | 12.0 | 12.0 | 12.0 |
| 2014 | 11.4 | 11.6 | 11.5 | 11.6 | 11.7 | 11.8 | 12.1 | 12.3 | 12.4 | 12.3 | 12.1 | 12.1 | 11.9 |
| 2015 | 11.7 | 11.7 | 11.7 | 12.0 | 12.1 | 12.1 | 12.3 | 12.5 | 12.7 | 12.8 | 12.7 | 12.8 | 12.3 |
| 2016 | 12.2 | 12.2 | 12.1 | 12.5 | 12.8 | 12.8 | 12.9 | 13.1 | 13.3 | 13.1 | 13.2 | 13.2 | 12.8 |
| 2017 | 12.6 | 12.6 | 12.6 | 12.8 | 13.0 | 13.0 | 13.0 | 13.3 | 13.7 | 13.4 | 13.7 | 13.5 | 13.1 |
| 2018 | 13.1 | 13.1 | 13.1 | 13.1 | 13.2 | 14.7 | 15.3 | 15.6 | 15.9 | 16.2 | 16.7 | 16.2 | 14.7 |
| 2019 | 16.7 | 15.4 | 15.6 | 15.9 | 16.5 | 16.5 | 16.8 | 17.0 | 17.3 | 17.2 | 17.4 | 17.3 | 16.6 |
| **Information** | | | | | | | | | | | | | |
| 2011 | 3.4 | 3.4 | 3.4 | 3.4 | 3.5 | 3.5 | 3.5 | 3.5 | 3.6 | 3.6 | 3.7 | 3.6 | 3.5 |
| 2012 | 3.8 | 3.7 | 3.7 | 3.8 | 3.8 | 3.9 | 3.8 | 3.8 | 3.8 | 3.8 | 3.8 | 3.8 | 3.8 |
| 2013 | 3.8 | 3.8 | 3.8 | 3.8 | 3.8 | 3.8 | 3.8 | 3.8 | 3.8 | 3.8 | 3.8 | 3.8 | 3.8 |
| 2014 | 3.8 | 3.8 | 3.8 | 3.8 | 3.8 | 3.8 | 3.9 | 3.9 | 3.9 | 3.9 | 3.9 | 4.0 | 3.9 |
| 2015 | 3.9 | 3.9 | 3.9 | 3.9 | 3.9 | 3.9 | 3.9 | 3.9 | 3.8 | 3.8 | 3.9 | 3.9 | 3.9 |
| 2016 | 3.8 | 3.8 | 3.8 | 3.8 | 3.8 | 3.8 | 3.8 | 3.7 | 3.7 | 3.7 | 3.7 | 3.6 | 3.8 |
| 2017 | 3.6 | 3.7 | 3.7 | 3.7 | 3.6 | 3.5 | 3.6 | 3.6 | 3.6 | 3.6 | 3.6 | 3.6 | 3.6 |
| 2018 | 3.6 | 3.6 | 3.5 | 3.6 | 3.6 | 3.6 | 3.6 | 3.6 | 3.6 | 3.5 | 3.5 | 3.5 | 3.6 |
| 2019 | 3.5 | 3.5 | 3.4 | 3.5 | 3.5 | 3.5 | 3.4 | 3.4 | 3.4 | 3.4 | 3.5 | 3.4 | 3.5 |
| **Financial Activities** | | | | | | | | | | | | | |
| 2011 | 13.2 | 13.3 | 13.2 | 13.2 | 13.1 | 13.1 | 13.0 | 13.0 | 12.8 | 12.6 | 12.6 | 12.6 | 13.0 |
| 2012 | 12.6 | 12.6 | 12.6 | 12.8 | 13.0 | 12.9 | 13.0 | 13.0 | 13.0 | 12.9 | 12.9 | 13.0 | 12.9 |
| 2013 | 12.9 | 12.9 | 13.0 | 13.0 | 12.9 | 12.9 | 13.0 | 13.0 | 12.9 | 12.9 | 12.8 | 12.7 | 12.9 |
| 2014 | 12.7 | 12.7 | 12.7 | 12.7 | 12.8 | 12.8 | 12.8 | 12.7 | 12.7 | 12.9 | 13.0 | 13.0 | 12.8 |
| 2015 | 12.8 | 12.8 | 13.0 | 13.0 | 13.1 | 13.1 | 13.3 | 13.3 | 13.2 | 13.3 | 13.3 | 13.2 | 13.1 |
| 2016 | 13.1 | 13.2 | 13.2 | 13.4 | 13.4 | 13.3 | 13.4 | 13.3 | 13.3 | 13.4 | 13.4 | 13.4 | 13.3 |
| 2017 | 13.5 | 13.5 | 13.6 | 13.6 | 13.7 | 13.7 | 13.8 | 13.8 | 13.7 | 14.0 | 14.1 | 14.1 | 13.8 |
| 2018 | 14.0 | 14.0 | 14.0 | 14.1 | 14.2 | 14.2 | 14.1 | 14.2 | 14.1 | 14.2 | 14.2 | 14.2 | 14.1 |
| 2019 | 14.3 | 14.3 | 14.3 | 14.5 | 14.5 | 14.5 | 14.4 | 14.5 | 14.4 | 14.8 | 14.9 | 14.8 | 14.5 |

# Employment by Industry: Fresno, CA, 2011–2019—*Continued*

(Numbers in thousands, not seasonally adjusted)

| Industry and year | January | February | March | April | May | June | July | August | September | October | November | December | Annual average |
|---|---|---|---|---|---|---|---|---|---|---|---|---|---|
| **Professional and Business Services** | | | | | | | | | | | | | |
| 2011 | 26.9 | 27.6 | 27.5 | 27.6 | 27.6 | 27.1 | 26.9 | 27.0 | 27.3 | 27.1 | 26.6 | 26.7 | 27.2 |
| 2012 | 26.7 | 27.0 | 27.4 | 27.0 | 26.5 | 26.4 | 26.4 | 26.7 | 26.9 | 27.6 | 28.7 | 27.4 | 27.1 |
| 2013 | 28.0 | 28.3 | 28.1 | 28.5 | 28.2 | 28.7 | 29.4 | 29.8 | 30.3 | 30.8 | 30.5 | 30.4 | 29.3 |
| 2014 | 29.3 | 30.4 | 30.6 | 30.2 | 30.6 | 30.4 | 31.6 | 32.4 | 32.6 | 33.3 | 32.1 | 31.9 | 31.3 |
| 2015 | 31.2 | 31.3 | 31.5 | 31.8 | 31.7 | 31.9 | 32.0 | 32.1 | 31.7 | 32.5 | 32.3 | 32.1 | 31.8 |
| 2016 | 31.5 | 31.5 | 31.8 | 32.2 | 32.3 | 32.2 | 33.0 | 32.8 | 33.0 | 33.3 | 32.7 | 31.9 | 32.4 |
| 2017 | 30.6 | 31.3 | 31.5 | 31.3 | 31.3 | 31.4 | 31.5 | 31.3 | 31.4 | 30.8 | 30.5 | 30.1 | 31.1 |
| 2018 | 31.2 | 31.8 | 31.6 | 31.8 | 32.0 | 31.9 | 32.4 | 33.2 | 33.5 | 33.5 | 33.3 | 34.0 | 32.5 |
| 2019 | 31.7 | 32.0 | 31.9 | 32.3 | 32.2 | 32.1 | 33.4 | 34.2 | 34.2 | 34.2 | 34.0 | 34.1 | 33.0 |
| **Education and Health Services** | | | | | | | | | | | | | |
| 2011 | 51.2 | 51.3 | 52.3 | 52.5 | 52.2 | 51.7 | 51.0 | 51.2 | 52.0 | 51.9 | 52.3 | 52.4 | 51.8 |
| 2012 | 51.9 | 52.9 | 53.3 | 53.3 | 53.2 | 52.9 | 52.2 | 52.8 | 53.3 | 53.4 | 53.4 | 53.7 | 53.0 |
| 2013 | 53.9 | 54.9 | 55.4 | 55.4 | 55.5 | 55.1 | 53.9 | 54.4 | 55.0 | 55.8 | 55.9 | 56.0 | 55.1 |
| 2014 | 55.2 | 55.6 | 56.4 | 57.2 | 56.5 | 56.2 | 55.8 | 56.6 | 57.0 | 57.7 | 57.9 | 58.2 | 56.7 |
| 2015 | 57.8 | 58.4 | 59.2 | 59.7 | 59.4 | 59.3 | 59.4 | 60.3 | 60.7 | 61.7 | 61.8 | 62.2 | 60.0 |
| 2016 | 61.6 | 62.5 | 63.5 | 64.0 | 63.7 | 63.6 | 63.4 | 64.1 | 64.6 | 64.9 | 65.1 | 65.5 | 63.9 |
| 2017 | 65.0 | 65.5 | 66.5 | 67.5 | 66.7 | 66.8 | 67.3 | 68.0 | 68.5 | 67.9 | 68.4 | 68.4 | 67.2 |
| 2018 | 67.8 | 68.3 | 69.3 | 68.7 | 68.7 | 68.7 | 68.7 | 69.3 | 69.5 | 70.3 | 71.0 | 71.0 | 69.3 |
| 2019 | 70.4 | 71.1 | 72.4 | 73.0 | 72.6 | 72.7 | 72.6 | 73.0 | 73.2 | 73.8 | 73.9 | 74.3 | 72.8 |
| **Leisure and Hospitality** | | | | | | | | | | | | | |
| 2011 | 26.0 | 26.6 | 27.3 | 27.1 | 27.6 | 27.9 | 27.9 | 28.0 | 27.3 | 26.8 | 26.5 | 26.3 | 27.1 |
| 2012 | 26.5 | 27.0 | 27.5 | 27.8 | 28.6 | 28.8 | 29.0 | 29.2 | 28.5 | 28.0 | 27.6 | 27.7 | 28.0 |
| 2013 | 27.5 | 27.6 | 28.4 | 28.5 | 29.2 | 29.6 | 30.0 | 29.9 | 29.3 | 29.3 | 29.1 | 29.3 | 29.0 |
| 2014 | 29.2 | 29.8 | 29.8 | 30.5 | 31.1 | 31.3 | 31.6 | 31.6 | 30.7 | 30.5 | 30.5 | 30.3 | 30.6 |
| 2015 | 30.1 | 30.5 | 31.0 | 31.3 | 32.1 | 32.1 | 32.2 | 32.2 | 31.5 | 31.3 | 31.3 | 31.5 | 31.4 |
| 2016 | 30.7 | 31.3 | 31.7 | 32.4 | 33.1 | 33.6 | 34.1 | 34.3 | 33.1 | 33.3 | 32.9 | 32.7 | 32.8 |
| 2017 | 32.2 | 32.6 | 33.1 | 33.5 | 34.0 | 34.7 | 35.1 | 34.9 | 34.1 | 34.1 | 33.6 | 33.3 | 33.8 |
| 2018 | 32.9 | 33.2 | 33.6 | 34.4 | 35.1 | 35.3 | 35.5 | 35.6 | 34.8 | 35.1 | 34.4 | 34.5 | 34.5 |
| 2019 | 34.0 | 34.7 | 34.9 | 35.6 | 36.0 | 36.9 | 36.8 | 36.6 | 36.1 | 35.3 | 34.9 | 35.2 | 35.6 |
| **Other Services** | | | | | | | | | | | | | |
| 2011 | 9.7 | 9.9 | 9.9 | 10.0 | 10.0 | 10.1 | 10.1 | 10.3 | 10.4 | 10.4 | 10.4 | 10.3 | 10.1 |
| 2012 | 10.1 | 10.2 | 10.3 | 10.6 | 10.8 | 10.9 | 10.5 | 10.8 | 10.7 | 10.8 | 10.8 | 10.8 | 10.6 |
| 2013 | 10.7 | 10.9 | 11.0 | 11.0 | 11.0 | 10.8 | 10.7 | 11.0 | 11.0 | 10.9 | 11.0 | 11.0 | 10.9 |
| 2014 | 11.0 | 11.1 | 11.2 | 11.2 | 11.3 | 11.1 | 11.0 | 11.4 | 11.3 | 11.3 | 11.4 | 11.3 | 11.2 |
| 2015 | 11.2 | 11.4 | 11.4 | 11.6 | 11.6 | 11.4 | 11.4 | 11.6 | 11.7 | 11.7 | 11.7 | 11.7 | 11.5 |
| 2016 | 11.5 | 11.5 | 11.7 | 11.7 | 11.7 | 11.4 | 11.7 | 12.0 | 12.0 | 12.1 | 11.9 | 11.7 | 11.7 |
| 2017 | 11.3 | 11.5 | 11.6 | 11.7 | 12.0 | 11.7 | 11.6 | 11.9 | 11.9 | 12.0 | 12.0 | 11.9 | 11.8 |
| 2018 | 11.7 | 11.8 | 12.0 | 12.1 | 12.1 | 11.9 | 11.6 | 11.9 | 11.9 | 11.8 | 11.9 | 11.8 | 11.9 |
| 2019 | 11.6 | 11.7 | 11.8 | 11.9 | 12.0 | 11.7 | 11.7 | 12.2 | 12.1 | 12.2 | 12.1 | 12.1 | 11.9 |
| **Government** | | | | | | | | | | | | | |
| 2011 | 65.4 | 68.1 | 69.1 | 69.7 | 69.0 | 66.6 | 62.8 | 61.0 | 62.7 | 65.3 | 65.2 | 63.9 | 65.7 |
| 2012 | 63.5 | 65.3 | 66.2 | 66.4 | 66.4 | 65.7 | 61.6 | 59.6 | 61.6 | 64.8 | 64.4 | 63.6 | 64.1 |
| 2013 | 63.1 | 65.6 | 66.4 | 66.5 | 66.3 | 65.9 | 60.2 | 59.8 | 62.3 | 64.2 | 65.2 | 64.5 | 64.2 |
| 2014 | 64.5 | 66.8 | 67.7 | 67.9 | 68.5 | 68.2 | 63.9 | 61.8 | 64.2 | 67.1 | 67.4 | 67.1 | 66.3 |
| 2015 | 67.3 | 69.5 | 69.6 | 70.1 | 70.7 | 70.6 | 64.9 | 63.5 | 67.5 | 69.7 | 70.6 | 70.1 | 68.7 |
| 2016 | 70.1 | 70.9 | 72.2 | 72.8 | 73.2 | 73.2 | 66.1 | 65.7 | 70.3 | 72.1 | 72.9 | 72.0 | 71.0 |
| 2017 | 71.7 | 73.7 | 74.3 | 74.8 | 75.1 | 74.6 | 67.1 | 67.5 | 71.1 | 73.2 | 74.2 | 74.0 | 72.6 |
| 2018 | 74.4 | 75.7 | 77.7 | 77.5 | 77.1 | 76.4 | 68.1 | 68.8 | 72.3 | 74.9 | 76.1 | 75.4 | 74.5 |
| 2019 | 74.7 | 76.8 | 77.0 | 77.4 | 77.8 | 76.6 | 68.2 | 69.6 | 73.1 | 74.8 | 76.8 | 75.5 | 74.9 |

## Employment by Industry: Tulsa, OK, 2011–2019

(Numbers in thousands, not seasonally adjusted)

| Industry and year | January | February | March | April | May | June | July | August | September | October | November | December | Annual average |
|---|---|---|---|---|---|---|---|---|---|---|---|---|---|
| **Total Nonfarm** | | | | | | | | | | | | | |
| 2011 | 407.7 | 405.2 | 411.7 | 414.8 | 416.0 | 415.7 | 414.3 | 414.4 | 418.1 | 421.9 | 422.8 | 423.8 | 415.5 |
| 2012 | 414.3 | 418.0 | 420.6 | 424.6 | 427.1 | 426.8 | 421.8 | 423.0 | 426.0 | 431.4 | 434.7 | 435.0 | 425.3 |
| 2013 | 423.1 | 425.8 | 428.7 | 431.4 | 433.6 | 433.8 | 430.9 | 432.4 | 434.3 | 437.2 | 438.6 | 438.0 | 432.3 |
| 2014 | 431.6 | 434.0 | 436.1 | 438.2 | 440.8 | 440.5 | 437.9 | 438.7 | 441.0 | 446.5 | 448.2 | 449.3 | 440.2 |
| 2015 | 442.7 | 444.2 | 445.1 | 448.0 | 449.2 | 448.2 | 445.9 | 444.4 | 446.4 | 451.4 | 453.6 | 452.9 | 447.7 |
| 2016 | 442.9 | 444.6 | 445.6 | 447.0 | 446.8 | 445.2 | 442.5 | 442.3 | 446.0 | 448.0 | 450.5 | 451.0 | 446.0 |
| 2017 | 437.9 | 440.9 | 445.0 | 446.8 | 448.8 | 450.5 | 446.5 | 447.2 | 450.6 | 452.1 | 454.5 | 456.5 | 448.1 |
| 2018 | 447.7 | 449.8 | 454.2 | 452.8 | 455.4 | 457.1 | 452.8 | 454.8 | 456.3 | 460.9 | 464.5 | 465.7 | 456.0 |
| 2019 | 453.1 | 456.3 | 460.0 | 460.8 | 462.1 | 461.9 | 458.8 | 460.3 | 464.4 | 466.8 | 466.9 | 465.7 | 461.4 |
| **Total Private** | | | | | | | | | | | | | |
| 2011 | 351.6 | 348.4 | 354.5 | 357.6 | 359.1 | 360.8 | 362.6 | 362.7 | 363.0 | 364.1 | 364.9 | 365.8 | 359.6 |
| 2012 | 358.8 | 360.9 | 362.9 | 367.2 | 369.4 | 372.0 | 371.1 | 372.0 | 370.1 | 373.3 | 376.3 | 376.7 | 369.2 |
| 2013 | 366.9 | 368.0 | 370.6 | 373.3 | 375.6 | 377.8 | 378.0 | 379.6 | 377.7 | 378.2 | 379.1 | 378.6 | 375.3 |
| 2014 | 374.3 | 374.9 | 376.7 | 379.1 | 381.4 | 384.0 | 384.6 | 385.0 | 383.6 | 386.5 | 387.8 | 389.3 | 382.3 |
| 2015 | 385.0 | 384.8 | 385.8 | 388.2 | 389.5 | 391.3 | 392.3 | 390.6 | 388.3 | 390.7 | 392.5 | 392.0 | 389.3 |
| 2016 | 384.4 | 384.4 | 385.1 | 387.0 | 387.2 | 388.4 | 388.8 | 388.5 | 387.9 | 389.2 | 391.4 | 391.2 | 387.8 |
| 2017 | 381.1 | 382.3 | 385.7 | 387.7 | 389.5 | 393.2 | 392.2 | 392.8 | 392.2 | 393.1 | 395.2 | 396.9 | 390.2 |
| 2018 | 390.1 | 391.2 | 395.3 | 394.6 | 396.7 | 401.0 | 400.5 | 401.8 | 400.9 | 401.7 | 404.8 | 405.7 | 398.7 |
| 2019 | 395.7 | 396.9 | 400.3 | 401.2 | 402.1 | 405.4 | 405.5 | 406.0 | 405.2 | 406.6 | 406.5 | 405.0 | 403.0 |
| **Goods Producing** | | | | | | | | | | | | | |
| 2011 | 77.1 | 76.4 | 78.1 | 79.0 | 79.4 | 80.3 | 80.8 | 80.7 | 81.0 | 81.8 | 82.1 | 82.3 | 79.9 |
| 2012 | 81.2 | 81.6 | 82.2 | 83.1 | 83.8 | 84.3 | 84.4 | 84.7 | 84.5 | 86.6 | 87.0 | 86.6 | 84.2 |
| 2013 | 84.2 | 84.5 | 84.9 | 85.2 | 85.5 | 86.2 | 85.8 | 86.3 | 85.6 | 85.9 | 85.3 | 85.1 | 85.4 |
| 2014 | 84.8 | 85.3 | 85.2 | 85.1 | 85.6 | 86.1 | 86.9 | 87.2 | 87.0 | 87.9 | 87.9 | 88.0 | 86.4 |
| 2015 | 87.3 | 87.8 | 87.0 | 86.4 | 85.9 | 86.0 | 85.6 | 84.8 | 84.4 | 84.2 | 84.0 | 83.9 | 85.6 |
| 2016 | 82.4 | 82.3 | 81.7 | 81.2 | 81.0 | 81.3 | 81.0 | 81.0 | 80.8 | 79.9 | 80.0 | 80.1 | 81.1 |
| 2017 | 78.4 | 78.9 | 79.4 | 79.4 | 80.3 | 81.7 | 81.7 | 82.0 | 82.4 | 82.5 | 82.5 | 83.4 | 81.1 |
| 2018 | 83.2 | 84.0 | 84.8 | 84.8 | 85.7 | 86.9 | 86.7 | 87.1 | 87.2 | 87.2 | 87.6 | 88.0 | 86.1 |
| 2019 | 87.0 | 88.0 | 88.7 | 87.9 | 87.8 | 88.8 | 88.4 | 88.1 | 88.2 | 86.8 | 87.0 | 86.3 | 87.8 |
| **Service-Providing** | | | | | | | | | | | | | |
| 2011 | 330.6 | 328.8 | 333.6 | 335.8 | 336.6 | 335.4 | 333.5 | 333.7 | 337.1 | 340.1 | 340.7 | 341.5 | 335.6 |
| 2012 | 333.1 | 336.4 | 338.4 | 341.5 | 343.3 | 342.5 | 337.4 | 338.3 | 341.5 | 344.8 | 347.7 | 348.4 | 341.1 |
| 2013 | 338.9 | 341.3 | 343.8 | 346.2 | 348.1 | 347.6 | 345.1 | 346.1 | 348.7 | 351.3 | 353.3 | 352.9 | 346.9 |
| 2014 | 346.8 | 348.7 | 350.9 | 353.1 | 355.2 | 354.4 | 351.0 | 351.5 | 354.0 | 358.6 | 360.3 | 361.3 | 353.8 |
| 2015 | 355.4 | 356.4 | 358.1 | 361.6 | 363.3 | 362.2 | 360.3 | 359.6 | 362.0 | 367.2 | 369.6 | 369.0 | 362.1 |
| 2016 | 360.5 | 362.3 | 363.9 | 365.8 | 365.8 | 363.9 | 361.5 | 361.3 | 365.2 | 368.1 | 370.5 | 370.9 | 365.0 |
| 2017 | 359.5 | 362.0 | 365.6 | 367.4 | 368.5 | 368.8 | 364.8 | 365.2 | 368.2 | 369.6 | 372.0 | 373.1 | 367.1 |
| 2018 | 364.5 | 365.8 | 369.4 | 368.0 | 369.7 | 370.2 | 366.1 | 367.7 | 369.1 | 373.7 | 376.9 | 377.7 | 369.9 |
| 2019 | 366.1 | 368.3 | 371.3 | 372.9 | 374.3 | 373.1 | 370.4 | 372.2 | 376.2 | 380.0 | 379.9 | 379.4 | 373.7 |
| **Mining, Logging, and Construction** | | | | | | | | | | | | | |
| 2011 | 26.2 | 25.6 | 26.7 | 27.0 | 27.1 | 27.4 | 27.3 | 27.3 | 27.3 | 27.6 | 27.5 | 27.4 | 27.0 |
| 2012 | 26.4 | 26.4 | 26.7 | 27.1 | 27.5 | 27.6 | 27.9 | 28.1 | 28.1 | 29.7 | 30.3 | 29.7 | 28.0 |
| 2013 | 27.7 | 27.9 | 28.5 | 29.1 | 29.5 | 30.0 | 29.8 | 30.4 | 30.0 | 30.7 | 30.1 | 29.8 | 29.5 |
| 2014 | 29.4 | 29.6 | 29.4 | 28.8 | 29.0 | 29.1 | 29.7 | 30.0 | 29.9 | 30.6 | 30.4 | 30.2 | 29.7 |
| 2015 | 29.5 | 30.0 | 29.7 | 29.8 | 29.8 | 30.1 | 30.3 | 30.1 | 30.0 | 30.2 | 30.0 | 29.9 | 30.0 |
| 2016 | 29.1 | 29.0 | 29.0 | 29.1 | 29.3 | 29.6 | 29.5 | 29.6 | 29.6 | 29.0 | 28.7 | 28.8 | 29.2 |
| 2017 | 27.9 | 28.0 | 28.4 | 28.4 | 28.9 | 29.7 | 29.7 | 29.9 | 30.2 | 30.2 | 30.0 | 30.3 | 29.3 |
| 2018 | 29.8 | 30.4 | 30.9 | 30.7 | 31.2 | 31.9 | 32.2 | 32.7 | 32.6 | 32.4 | 32.3 | 32.3 | 31.6 |
| 2019 | 31.7 | 32.4 | 32.8 | 32.2 | 32.0 | 32.6 | 32.7 | 32.6 | 32.8 | 32.0 | 31.9 | 32.0 | 32.3 |
| **Manufacturing** | | | | | | | | | | | | | |
| 2011 | 50.9 | 50.8 | 51.4 | 52.0 | 52.3 | 52.9 | 53.5 | 53.4 | 53.7 | 54.2 | 54.6 | 54.9 | 52.9 |
| 2012 | 54.8 | 55.2 | 55.5 | 56.0 | 56.3 | 56.7 | 56.5 | 56.6 | 56.4 | 56.9 | 56.7 | 56.9 | 56.2 |
| 2013 | 56.5 | 56.6 | 56.4 | 56.1 | 56.0 | 56.2 | 56.0 | 55.9 | 55.6 | 55.2 | 55.2 | 55.3 | 55.9 |
| 2014 | 55.4 | 55.7 | 55.8 | 56.3 | 56.6 | 57.0 | 57.2 | 57.2 | 57.1 | 57.3 | 57.5 | 57.8 | 56.7 |
| 2015 | 57.8 | 57.8 | 57.3 | 56.6 | 56.1 | 55.9 | 55.3 | 54.7 | 54.4 | 54.0 | 54.0 | 54.0 | 55.7 |
| 2016 | 53.3 | 53.3 | 52.7 | 52.1 | 51.7 | 51.7 | 51.5 | 51.4 | 51.2 | 50.9 | 51.3 | 51.3 | 51.9 |
| 2017 | 50.5 | 50.9 | 51.0 | 51.0 | 51.4 | 52.0 | 52.0 | 52.1 | 52.2 | 52.3 | 52.5 | 53.1 | 51.8 |
| 2018 | 53.4 | 53.6 | 53.9 | 54.1 | 54.5 | 55.0 | 54.5 | 54.4 | 54.6 | 54.8 | 55.3 | 55.7 | 54.5 |
| 2019 | 55.3 | 55.6 | 55.9 | 55.7 | 55.8 | 56.2 | 55.7 | 55.5 | 55.4 | 54.8 | 55.1 | 54.3 | 55.4 |

# Employment by Industry: Tulsa, OK, 2011–2019—*Continued*

(Numbers in thousands, not seasonally adjusted)

| Industry and year | January | February | March | April | May | June | July | August | September | October | November | December | Annual average |
|---|---|---|---|---|---|---|---|---|---|---|---|---|---|
| **Trade, Transportation, and Utilities** | | | | | | | | | | | | | |
| 2011 | 73.3 | 72.3 | 73.3 | 74.3 | 74.4 | 74.6 | 74.7 | 74.8 | 74.8 | 75.1 | 76.9 | 77.5 | 74.7 |
| 2012 | 74.9 | 74.5 | 75.0 | 75.4 | 75.9 | 76.5 | 76.1 | 75.9 | 75.6 | 76.6 | 78.8 | 79.3 | 76.2 |
| 2013 | 75.2 | 74.8 | 75.4 | 76.3 | 76.8 | 77.2 | 77.6 | 77.9 | 77.8 | 78.1 | 80.0 | 81.0 | 77.3 |
| 2014 | 78.7 | 78.2 | 78.5 | 78.8 | 79.4 | 80.3 | 80.3 | 80.5 | 80.3 | 81.1 | 82.7 | 83.8 | 80.2 |
| | | | | | | | | | | | | | |
| 2015 | 81.1 | 80.8 | 81.2 | 81.3 | 81.8 | 82.5 | 82.2 | 82.5 | 82.0 | 84.5 | 87.1 | 87.9 | 82.9 |
| 2016 | 83.4 | 82.5 | 82.8 | 83.3 | 83.3 | 83.2 | 82.8 | 83.2 | 82.8 | 84.7 | 87.7 | 87.2 | 83.9 |
| 2017 | 82.4 | 81.5 | 81.5 | 81.8 | 81.9 | 82.1 | 82.5 | 82.5 | 82.6 | 84.1 | 87.3 | 86.9 | 83.1 |
| 2018 | 83.5 | 82.3 | 82.9 | 82.8 | 83.0 | 83.1 | 83.4 | 83.9 | 84.1 | 85.1 | 88.2 | 88.6 | 84.2 |
| 2019 | 82.6 | 81.5 | 82.1 | 82.2 | 82.5 | 83.1 | 83.7 | 83.7 | 84.3 | 85.8 | 88.1 | 88.4 | 84.0 |
| | | | | | | | | | | | | | |
| **Wholesale Trade** | | | | | | | | | | | | | |
| 2011 | 14.9 | 14.9 | 15.0 | 15.1 | 15.0 | 15.1 | 15.3 | 15.2 | 15.2 | 15.1 | 15.1 | 15.1 | 15.1 |
| 2012 | 14.9 | 15.0 | 15.1 | 15.2 | 15.3 | 15.4 | 15.3 | 15.4 | 15.4 | 15.5 | 15.5 | 15.5 | 15.3 |
| 2013 | 15.2 | 15.2 | 15.2 | 15.4 | 15.4 | 15.4 | 15.5 | 15.6 | 15.6 | 15.5 | 15.5 | 15.5 | 15.4 |
| 2014 | 15.6 | 15.6 | 15.7 | 15.6 | 15.5 | 15.7 | 15.8 | 15.9 | 15.9 | 15.9 | 15.9 | 15.9 | 15.8 |
| | | | | | | | | | | | | | |
| 2015 | 15.8 | 15.8 | 15.8 | 15.7 | 15.7 | 15.8 | 15.8 | 15.8 | 15.6 | 15.8 | 15.7 | 15.8 | 15.8 |
| 2016 | 15.8 | 15.8 | 15.7 | 15.8 | 15.7 | 15.7 | 15.8 | 15.7 | 15.8 | 15.7 | 15.8 | 15.9 | 15.8 |
| 2017 | 15.8 | 15.9 | 16.0 | 16.2 | 16.2 | 16.3 | 16.2 | 16.3 | 16.2 | 16.3 | 16.3 | 16.4 | 16.2 |
| 2018 | 16.3 | 16.3 | 16.4 | 16.3 | 16.4 | 16.6 | 16.3 | 16.5 | 16.5 | 16.8 | 16.8 | 16.9 | 16.5 |
| 2019 | 16.5 | 16.5 | 16.6 | 16.6 | 16.6 | 16.7 | 17.3 | 17.2 | 17.2 | 17.2 | 17.2 | 17.2 | 16.9 |
| | | | | | | | | | | | | | |
| **Retail Trade** | | | | | | | | | | | | | |
| 2011 | 44.7 | 43.7 | 44.5 | 45.2 | 45.4 | 45.3 | 45.1 | 45.3 | 45.3 | 45.7 | 47.4 | 47.7 | 45.4 |
| 2012 | 45.5 | 44.8 | 45.3 | 45.5 | 45.8 | 46.2 | 45.9 | 45.6 | 45.4 | 46.3 | 48.4 | 48.7 | 46.1 |
| 2013 | 45.5 | 45.1 | 45.6 | 46.0 | 46.5 | 46.8 | 46.8 | 47.0 | 46.9 | 47.4 | 49.1 | 49.9 | 46.9 |
| 2014 | 47.4 | 47.0 | 47.2 | 47.5 | 48.1 | 48.6 | 48.4 | 48.5 | 48.3 | 48.9 | 50.2 | 51.2 | 48.4 |
| | | | | | | | | | | | | | |
| 2015 | 48.7 | 48.7 | 48.9 | 49.2 | 49.6 | 50.0 | 49.4 | 49.6 | 49.4 | 50.0 | 51.6 | 52.4 | 49.8 |
| 2016 | 49.8 | 49.6 | 50.1 | 50.3 | 50.4 | 50.4 | 50.0 | 50.0 | 49.3 | 49.9 | 51.7 | 51.7 | 50.3 |
| 2017 | 49.1 | 48.5 | 48.4 | 48.5 | 48.5 | 48.6 | 48.8 | 48.5 | 48.0 | 48.4 | 50.3 | 50.5 | 48.8 |
| 2018 | 48.8 | 48.0 | 48.3 | 48.4 | 48.5 | 48.3 | 48.2 | 48.3 | 47.9 | 47.9 | 49.5 | 49.6 | 48.5 |
| 2019 | 47.4 | 46.7 | 47.0 | 47.2 | 47.4 | 47.7 | 47.6 | 47.5 | 47.5 | 48.1 | 48.9 | 49.1 | 47.7 |
| | | | | | | | | | | | | | |
| **Transportation and Utilities** | | | | | | | | | | | | | |
| 2011 | 13.7 | 13.7 | 13.8 | 14.0 | 14.0 | 14.2 | 14.3 | 14.3 | 14.3 | 14.3 | 14.4 | 14.7 | 14.1 |
| 2012 | 14.5 | 14.7 | 14.6 | 14.7 | 14.8 | 14.9 | 14.9 | 14.9 | 14.8 | 14.8 | 14.9 | 15.1 | 14.8 |
| 2013 | 14.5 | 14.5 | 14.6 | 14.9 | 14.9 | 15.0 | 15.3 | 15.3 | 15.3 | 15.2 | 15.4 | 15.6 | 15.0 |
| 2014 | 15.7 | 15.6 | 15.6 | 15.7 | 15.8 | 16.0 | 16.1 | 16.1 | 16.1 | 16.3 | 16.6 | 16.7 | 16.0 |
| | | | | | | | | | | | | | |
| 2015 | 16.6 | 16.3 | 16.5 | 16.4 | 16.5 | 16.7 | 17.0 | 17.1 | 17.0 | 18.7 | 19.8 | 19.7 | 17.4 |
| 2016 | 17.8 | 17.1 | 17.0 | 17.2 | 17.2 | 17.1 | 17.0 | 17.5 | 17.7 | 19.1 | 20.2 | 19.6 | 17.9 |
| 2017 | 17.5 | 17.1 | 17.1 | 17.1 | 17.2 | 17.2 | 17.5 | 17.7 | 18.4 | 19.4 | 20.7 | 20.0 | 18.1 |
| 2018 | 18.4 | 18.0 | 18.2 | 18.1 | 18.1 | 18.2 | 18.9 | 19.1 | 19.7 | 20.4 | 21.9 | 22.1 | 19.3 |
| 2019 | 18.7 | 18.3 | 18.5 | 18.4 | 18.5 | 18.7 | 18.8 | 19.0 | 19.6 | 20.5 | 22.0 | 22.1 | 19.4 |
| | | | | | | | | | | | | | |
| **Information** | | | | | | | | | | | | | |
| 2011 | 8.3 | 8.2 | 8.2 | 8.1 | 8.2 | 8.2 | 8.3 | 8.3 | 8.2 | 8.2 | 8.1 | 8.2 | 8.2 |
| 2012 | 8.1 | 8.0 | 8.0 | 7.9 | 7.9 | 7.9 | 8.0 | 7.9 | 7.9 | 7.9 | 7.9 | 7.9 | 7.9 |
| 2013 | 7.8 | 7.8 | 7.8 | 7.9 | 7.9 | 7.9 | 7.9 | 7.8 | 7.7 | 7.7 | 7.6 | 7.6 | 7.8 |
| 2014 | 7.5 | 7.4 | 7.5 | 7.4 | 7.3 | 7.4 | 7.4 | 7.3 | 7.1 | 6.9 | 7.0 | 7.2 | 7.3 |
| | | | | | | | | | | | | | |
| 2015 | 7.1 | 7.1 | 7.1 | 7.1 | 7.2 | 7.2 | 7.2 | 7.2 | 7.1 | 7.2 | 7.3 | 7.4 | 7.2 |
| 2016 | 7.3 | 7.4 | 7.3 | 7.3 | 7.4 | 7.4 | 7.4 | 7.4 | 7.3 | 7.3 | 7.4 | 7.4 | 7.4 |
| 2017 | 7.4 | 7.4 | 7.4 | 7.4 | 7.4 | 7.3 | 7.3 | 7.1 | 7.0 | 7.0 | 7.0 | 7.2 | 7.2 |
| 2018 | 7.2 | 7.1 | 7.1 | 7.1 | 7.1 | 7.2 | 7.1 | 7.1 | 7.0 | 6.8 | 6.8 | 6.8 | 7.0 |
| 2019 | 6.7 | 6.7 | 6.7 | 6.6 | 6.6 | 6.7 | 6.7 | 6.6 | 6.6 | 6.6 | 6.6 | 6.6 | 6.6 |
| | | | | | | | | | | | | | |
| **Financial Activities** | | | | | | | | | | | | | |
| 2011 | 22.7 | 22.6 | 22.6 | 22.6 | 22.5 | 22.6 | 22.6 | 22.6 | 22.5 | 22.6 | 22.6 | 22.7 | 22.6 |
| 2012 | 22.4 | 22.5 | 22.4 | 22.2 | 22.3 | 22.4 | 22.5 | 22.5 | 22.4 | 22.6 | 22.6 | 22.7 | 22.5 |
| 2013 | 22.6 | 22.6 | 22.6 | 22.7 | 22.8 | 22.9 | 23.0 | 23.0 | 22.9 | 23.1 | 23.2 | 23.1 | 22.9 |
| 2014 | 22.8 | 22.8 | 22.8 | 22.9 | 22.8 | 22.8 | 22.9 | 22.9 | 22.8 | 22.9 | 23.0 | 23.0 | 22.9 |
| | | | | | | | | | | | | | |
| 2015 | 22.9 | 22.9 | 23.0 | 23.0 | 23.1 | 23.1 | 23.5 | 23.4 | 23.3 | 23.4 | 23.3 | 23.3 | 23.2 |
| 2016 | 23.2 | 23.2 | 23.1 | 23.1 | 23.2 | 23.2 | 23.3 | 23.2 | 23.1 | 23.2 | 23.1 | 23.3 | 23.2 |
| 2017 | 22.8 | 22.7 | 22.8 | 23.0 | 23.0 | 23.1 | 23.0 | 23.2 | 23.1 | 23.2 | 23.3 | 23.5 | 23.1 |
| 2018 | 23.3 | 23.3 | 23.4 | 23.3 | 23.2 | 23.4 | 23.3 | 23.3 | 23.2 | 23.1 | 23.2 | 23.2 | 23.3 |
| 2019 | 23.3 | 23.2 | 23.3 | 23.4 | 23.4 | 23.5 | 23.6 | 23.5 | 23.4 | 23.5 | 23.1 | 23.6 | 23.4 |

## Employment by Industry: Tulsa, OK, 2011–2019—*Continued*

(Numbers in thousands, not seasonally adjusted)

| Industry and year | January | February | March | April | May | June | July | August | September | October | November | December | Annual average |
|---|---|---|---|---|---|---|---|---|---|---|---|---|---|
| **Professional and Business Services** | | | | | | | | | | | | | |
| 2011 | 53.0 | 52.8 | 53.7 | 53.7 | 53.8 | 53.9 | 54.6 | 54.8 | 55.4 | 55.6 | 55.1 | 55.1 | 54.3 |
| 2012 | 53.3 | 54.6 | 54.8 | 55.9 | 56.1 | 56.8 | 56.9 | 57.5 | 57.0 | 57.3 | 57.5 | 56.9 | 56.2 |
| 2013 | 55.7 | 56.0 | 56.8 | 57.0 | 57.4 | 57.9 | 58.4 | 58.6 | 58.2 | 58.6 | 58.2 | 57.3 | 57.5 |
| 2014 | 56.8 | 57.0 | 57.6 | 58.3 | 58.8 | 59.3 | 59.0 | 58.7 | 58.4 | 60.0 | 59.6 | 59.3 | 58.6 |
| | | | | | | | | | | | | | |
| 2015 | 59.5 | 58.6 | 58.9 | 59.9 | 60.2 | 60.0 | 60.5 | 60.0 | 59.0 | 59.6 | 58.9 | 58.5 | 59.5 |
| 2016 | 57.8 | 57.9 | 57.7 | 58.7 | 58.7 | 59.2 | 59.3 | 59.0 | 59.2 | 59.5 | 59.0 | 58.9 | 58.7 |
| 2017 | 57.8 | 58.9 | 60.0 | 60.3 | 60.5 | 61.1 | 60.5 | 60.9 | 60.6 | 60.7 | 60.1 | 60.3 | 60.1 |
| 2018 | 58.2 | 59.2 | 60.0 | 59.4 | 59.8 | 61.4 | 61.4 | 61.6 | 61.2 | 61.4 | 61.4 | 60.9 | 60.5 |
| 2019 | 59.3 | 60.0 | 60.3 | 60.9 | 61.2 | 61.5 | 62.0 | 62.3 | 61.5 | 61.6 | 59.8 | 58.1 | 60.7 |
| **Education and Health Services** | | | | | | | | | | | | | |
| 2011 | 66.0 | 65.4 | 66.1 | 66.3 | 66.7 | 66.6 | 66.8 | 66.8 | 66.7 | 67.0 | 66.6 | 66.6 | 66.5 |
| 2012 | 66.1 | 66.1 | 65.9 | 66.6 | 66.8 | 66.8 | 66.5 | 66.9 | 67.1 | 67.4 | 67.6 | 68.0 | 66.8 |
| 2013 | 67.6 | 68.0 | 68.1 | 67.9 | 67.8 | 67.7 | 67.4 | 67.7 | 68.0 | 68.3 | 68.5 | 68.4 | 68.0 |
| 2014 | 67.8 | 68.0 | 68.2 | 68.4 | 68.4 | 68.3 | 68.1 | 68.5 | 68.8 | 69.1 | 69.2 | 69.4 | 68.5 |
| | | | | | | | | | | | | | |
| 2015 | 68.8 | 68.7 | 68.9 | 69.1 | 69.0 | 69.1 | 69.9 | 70.1 | 70.5 | 70.3 | 70.5 | 70.0 | 69.6 |
| 2016 | 70.2 | 70.4 | 70.6 | 70.3 | 70.0 | 69.8 | 70.2 | 70.4 | 70.8 | 71.3 | 71.1 | 71.2 | 70.5 |
| 2017 | 70.4 | 70.5 | 70.6 | 70.9 | 71.1 | 71.1 | 70.9 | 71.0 | 71.3 | 71.4 | 71.2 | 71.6 | 71.0 |
| 2018 | 71.3 | 71.4 | 71.9 | 71.5 | 71.6 | 71.5 | 71.4 | 71.5 | 72.0 | 72.4 | 72.2 | 72.7 | 71.8 |
| 2019 | 72.1 | 72.2 | 72.7 | 72.8 | 72.7 | 72.7 | 72.6 | 73.1 | 73.5 | 73.3 | 73.2 | 73.9 | 72.9 |
| **Leisure and Hospitality** | | | | | | | | | | | | | |
| 2011 | 34.9 | 34.4 | 36.0 | 37.1 | 37.5 | 37.7 | 37.9 | 38.1 | 37.8 | 37.2 | 36.8 | 36.7 | 36.8 |
| 2012 | 36.3 | 37.0 | 37.9 | 38.9 | 39.3 | 39.8 | 39.3 | 39.4 | 38.7 | 38.0 | 38.0 | 38.4 | 38.4 |
| 2013 | 37.2 | 37.6 | 38.4 | 39.3 | 40.3 | 40.4 | 40.4 | 40.9 | 40.3 | 39.5 | 39.3 | 39.2 | 39.4 |
| 2014 | 39.0 | 39.2 | 39.9 | 41.0 | 41.7 | 42.0 | 42.1 | 42.2 | 41.6 | 40.9 | 40.7 | 40.8 | 40.9 |
| | | | | | | | | | | | | | |
| 2015 | 40.5 | 41.0 | 41.6 | 43.4 | 44.1 | 44.9 | 44.3 | 44.2 | 43.8 | 43.3 | 43.2 | 42.9 | 43.1 |
| 2016 | 42.1 | 42.6 | 43.7 | 44.6 | 45.0 | 45.4 | 45.6 | 45.2 | 44.7 | 44.1 | 43.7 | 43.7 | 44.2 |
| 2017 | 42.5 | 42.8 | 44.2 | 45.3 | 45.5 | 46.4 | 45.8 | 45.9 | 45.0 | 43.9 | 43.5 | 43.6 | 44.5 |
| 2018 | 43.1 | 43.4 | 44.5 | 45.3 | 45.8 | 46.6 | 46.3 | 46.7 | 45.7 | 45.4 | 45.1 | 45.2 | 45.3 |
| 2019 | 44.5 | 45.0 | 46.0 | 46.9 | 47.4 | 48.1 | 47.6 | 47.9 | 47.0 | 48.3 | 48.0 | 47.4 | 47.0 |
| **Other Services** | | | | | | | | | | | | | |
| 2011 | 16.3 | 16.3 | 16.5 | 16.5 | 16.6 | 16.9 | 16.9 | 16.6 | 16.6 | 16.6 | 16.7 | 16.7 | 16.6 |
| 2012 | 16.5 | 16.6 | 16.7 | 17.2 | 17.3 | 17.5 | 17.4 | 17.2 | 16.9 | 16.9 | 16.9 | 16.9 | 17.0 |
| 2013 | 16.6 | 16.7 | 16.6 | 17.0 | 17.1 | 17.6 | 17.5 | 17.4 | 17.2 | 17.0 | 17.0 | 16.9 | 17.1 |
| 2014 | 16.9 | 17.0 | 17.0 | 17.2 | 17.4 | 17.8 | 17.9 | 17.7 | 17.6 | 17.7 | 17.7 | 17.8 | 17.5 |
| | | | | | | | | | | | | | |
| 2015 | 17.8 | 17.9 | 18.1 | 18.0 | 18.2 | 18.5 | 19.1 | 18.4 | 18.2 | 18.2 | 18.2 | 18.1 | 18.2 |
| 2016 | 18.0 | 18.1 | 18.2 | 18.5 | 18.6 | 18.9 | 19.2 | 19.1 | 19.2 | 19.2 | 19.4 | 19.4 | 18.8 |
| 2017 | 19.4 | 19.6 | 19.8 | 19.6 | 19.8 | 20.4 | 20.5 | 20.2 | 20.2 | 20.3 | 20.3 | 20.4 | 20.0 |
| 2018 | 20.3 | 20.5 | 20.7 | 20.4 | 20.5 | 20.9 | 20.9 | 20.6 | 20.5 | 20.3 | 20.3 | 20.3 | 20.5 |
| 2019 | 20.2 | 20.3 | 20.5 | 20.5 | 20.5 | 21.0 | 20.9 | 20.8 | 20.7 | 20.7 | 20.7 | 20.7 | 20.6 |
| **Government** | | | | | | | | | | | | | |
| 2011 | 56.1 | 56.8 | 57.2 | 57.2 | 56.9 | 54.9 | 51.7 | 51.7 | 55.1 | 57.8 | 57.9 | 58.0 | 55.9 |
| 2012 | 55.5 | 57.1 | 57.7 | 57.4 | 57.7 | 54.8 | 50.7 | 51.0 | 55.9 | 58.1 | 58.4 | 58.3 | 56.1 |
| 2013 | 56.2 | 57.8 | 58.1 | 58.1 | 58.0 | 56.0 | 52.9 | 52.8 | 56.6 | 59.0 | 59.5 | 59.4 | 57.0 |
| 2014 | 57.3 | 59.1 | 59.4 | 59.1 | 59.4 | 56.5 | 53.3 | 53.7 | 57.4 | 60.0 | 60.4 | 60.0 | 58.0 |
| | | | | | | | | | | | | | |
| 2015 | 57.7 | 59.4 | 59.3 | 59.8 | 59.7 | 56.9 | 53.6 | 53.8 | 58.1 | 60.7 | 61.1 | 60.9 | 58.4 |
| 2016 | 58.5 | 60.2 | 60.5 | 60.0 | 59.6 | 56.8 | 53.7 | 53.8 | 58.1 | 58.8 | 59.1 | 59.8 | 58.2 |
| 2017 | 56.8 | 58.6 | 59.3 | 59.1 | 59.3 | 57.3 | 54.3 | 54.4 | 58.4 | 59.0 | 59.3 | 59.6 | 58.0 |
| 2018 | 57.6 | 58.6 | 58.9 | 58.2 | 58.7 | 56.1 | 52.3 | 53.0 | 55.4 | 59.2 | 59.7 | 60.0 | 57.3 |
| 2019 | 57.4 | 59.4 | 59.7 | 59.6 | 60.0 | 56.5 | 53.3 | 54.3 | 59.2 | 60.2 | 60.4 | 60.7 | 58.4 |

# Employment by Industry: Urban Honolulu, HI, 2011–2019

(Numbers in thousands, not seasonally adjusted)

| Industry and year | January | February | March | April | May | June | July | August | September | October | November | December | Annual average |
|---|---|---|---|---|---|---|---|---|---|---|---|---|---|
| **Total Nonfarm** | | | | | | | | | | | | | |
| 2011 | 426.9 | 437.3 | 439.8 | 437.2 | 437.8 | 435.5 | 431.4 | 428.6 | 438.0 | 441.4 | 446.5 | 449.8 | 437.5 |
| 2012 | 428.3 | 442.5 | 444.5 | 445.3 | 448.0 | 446.3 | 438.9 | 443.8 | 447.0 | 450.8 | 458.9 | 459.1 | 446.1 |
| 2013 | 438.5 | 452.8 | 454.9 | 451.9 | 456.8 | 453.5 | 449.4 | 446.8 | 454.8 | 458.9 | 465.2 | 467.1 | 454.2 |
| 2014 | 453.8 | 458.0 | 460.9 | 458.9 | 461.7 | 458.0 | 451.5 | 452.7 | 459.1 | 461.9 | 468.2 | 467.4 | 459.3 |
| 2015 | 458.4 | 463.2 | 465.5 | 464.4 | 466.3 | 464.1 | 458.0 | 461.1 | 463.4 | 469.2 | 474.0 | 477.9 | 465.5 |
| 2016 | 461.4 | 468.5 | 470.1 | 467.6 | 470.7 | 467.2 | 462.9 | 464.4 | 470.7 | 471.1 | 477.3 | 475.1 | 468.9 |
| 2017 | 467.3 | 472.6 | 475.2 | 473.3 | 475.0 | 471.7 | 464.2 | 462.9 | 472.6 | 472.6 | 476.4 | 479.9 | 472.0 |
| 2018 | 466.7 | 472.9 | 475.1 | 473.6 | 475.5 | 473.8 | 464.0 | 466.8 | 471.8 | 474.7 | 481.0 | 483.7 | 473.3 |
| 2019 | 468.2 | 475.1 | 475.2 | 469.9 | 473.0 | 468.3 | 463.7 | 464.1 | 470.6 | 474.2 | 477.3 | 481.4 | 471.8 |
| **Total Private** | | | | | | | | | | | | | |
| 2011 | 332.9 | 336.8 | 338.8 | 336.5 | 336.4 | 336.5 | 337.8 | 339.1 | 341.7 | 342.2 | 345.6 | 348.4 | 339.4 |
| 2012 | 339.3 | 341.6 | 342.9 | 343.7 | 345.8 | 346.8 | 346.6 | 349.1 | 349.8 | 351.0 | 355.4 | 357.4 | 347.5 |
| 2013 | 349.4 | 351.6 | 353.4 | 353.5 | 354.7 | 355.3 | 357.2 | 357.1 | 357.8 | 359.1 | 364.3 | 365.7 | 356.6 |
| 2014 | 355.9 | 356.7 | 359.3 | 358.1 | 359.5 | 359.2 | 359.3 | 360.5 | 362.1 | 362.7 | 366.1 | 369.4 | 360.7 |
| 2015 | 361.3 | 362.9 | 364.9 | 364.1 | 365.2 | 365.8 | 367.0 | 367.3 | 366.9 | 370.0 | 374.1 | 377.0 | 367.2 |
| 2016 | 366.7 | 368.9 | 369.6 | 369.7 | 370.2 | 369.6 | 372.4 | 374.1 | 374.1 | 372.2 | 375.7 | 377.2 | 371.7 |
| 2017 | 371.4 | 372.5 | 375.2 | 373.7 | 375.0 | 375.0 | 374.5 | 375.6 | 376.1 | 374.4 | 377.0 | 379.9 | 375.0 |
| 2018 | 372.1 | 373.4 | 375.8 | 375.1 | 375.1 | 376.8 | 374.4 | 376.7 | 376.3 | 376.8 | 379.7 | 383.1 | 376.3 |
| 2019 | 373.1 | 375.6 | 376.0 | 371.5 | 373.0 | 371.3 | 372.5 | 373.9 | 373.7 | 375.4 | 377.5 | 381.4 | 374.6 |
| **Goods Producing** | | | | | | | | | | | | | |
| 2011 | 31.9 | 32.4 | 32.6 | 32.6 | 32.7 | 33.3 | 33.6 | 33.7 | 34.1 | 33.8 | 33.6 | 33.6 | 33.2 |
| 2012 | 32.8 | 32.7 | 32.7 | 32.6 | 32.7 | 33.0 | 33.4 | 33.6 | 33.9 | 34.0 | 34.2 | 34.1 | 33.3 |
| 2013 | 33.4 | 33.7 | 34.1 | 34.1 | 34.6 | 34.4 | 34.7 | 34.9 | 34.9 | 34.8 | 35.1 | 35.2 | 34.5 |
| 2014 | 34.3 | 34.5 | 34.7 | 34.6 | 35.0 | 35.5 | 36.0 | 36.3 | 36.3 | 36.5 | 36.5 | 36.4 | 35.6 |
| 2015 | 35.4 | 35.6 | 36.1 | 36.4 | 36.9 | 37.6 | 38.3 | 38.3 | 38.4 | 39.3 | 39.6 | 40.1 | 37.7 |
| 2016 | 39.4 | 40.0 | 40.4 | 40.2 | 40.4 | 40.5 | 40.8 | 40.8 | 40.3 | 39.7 | 39.7 | 39.5 | 40.1 |
| 2017 | 38.4 | 38.6 | 39.1 | 38.8 | 38.9 | 39.1 | 38.8 | 38.9 | 38.7 | 38.1 | 38.4 | 38.5 | 38.7 |
| 2018 | 37.8 | 37.9 | 38.3 | 38.4 | 38.3 | 38.7 | 38.9 | 38.8 | 38.6 | 38.8 | 38.6 | 38.5 | 38.5 |
| 2019 | 37.4 | 37.7 | 38.3 | 37.8 | 37.8 | 37.6 | 37.9 | 37.8 | 37.8 | 38.6 | 38.2 | 38.5 | 38.0 |
| **Service-Providing** | | | | | | | | | | | | | |
| 2011 | 395.0 | 404.9 | 407.2 | 404.6 | 405.1 | 402.2 | 397.8 | 394.9 | 403.9 | 407.6 | 412.9 | 416.2 | 404.4 |
| 2012 | 395.5 | 409.8 | 411.8 | 412.7 | 415.3 | 413.3 | 405.5 | 410.2 | 413.1 | 416.8 | 424.7 | 425.0 | 412.8 |
| 2013 | 405.1 | 419.1 | 420.8 | 417.8 | 422.2 | 419.1 | 414.7 | 411.9 | 419.9 | 424.1 | 430.1 | 431.9 | 419.7 |
| 2014 | 419.5 | 423.5 | 426.2 | 424.3 | 426.7 | 422.5 | 415.5 | 416.4 | 422.8 | 425.4 | 431.7 | 431.0 | 423.8 |
| 2015 | 423.0 | 427.6 | 429.4 | 428.0 | 429.4 | 426.5 | 419.7 | 422.8 | 425.0 | 429.9 | 434.4 | 437.8 | 427.8 |
| 2016 | 422.0 | 428.5 | 429.7 | 427.4 | 430.3 | 426.7 | 422.1 | 423.6 | 430.4 | 431.4 | 437.6 | 435.6 | 428.8 |
| 2017 | 428.9 | 434.0 | 436.1 | 434.5 | 436.1 | 432.6 | 425.4 | 424.0 | 433.9 | 434.5 | 438.0 | 441.4 | 433.3 |
| 2018 | 428.9 | 435.0 | 436.8 | 435.2 | 437.2 | 435.1 | 425.1 | 428.0 | 433.2 | 435.9 | 442.4 | 445.2 | 434.8 |
| 2019 | 430.8 | 437.4 | 436.9 | 432.1 | 435.2 | 430.7 | 425.8 | 426.3 | 432.8 | 435.6 | 439.1 | 442.9 | 433.8 |
| **Mining, Logging, and Construction** | | | | | | | | | | | | | |
| 2011 | 21.2 | 21.5 | 21.6 | 21.8 | 21.8 | 22.4 | 22.8 | 22.8 | 23.0 | 22.8 | 22.5 | 22.5 | 22.2 |
| 2012 | 21.9 | 21.8 | 21.9 | 21.9 | 22.1 | 22.3 | 22.6 | 22.7 | 22.9 | 23.1 | 23.1 | 23.0 | 22.4 |
| 2013 | 22.5 | 22.8 | 23.1 | 23.2 | 23.6 | 23.4 | 23.7 | 23.9 | 23.7 | 23.6 | 23.9 | 24.0 | 23.5 |
| 2014 | 23.3 | 23.5 | 23.7 | 23.6 | 24.0 | 24.3 | 24.6 | 24.8 | 25.0 | 25.1 | 25.1 | 24.9 | 24.3 |
| 2015 | 24.1 | 24.2 | 24.7 | 25.1 | 25.5 | 26.1 | 26.8 | 26.8 | 27.0 | 27.8 | 28.1 | 28.5 | 26.2 |
| 2016 | 28.1 | 28.5 | 28.9 | 28.7 | 28.9 | 28.9 | 29.2 | 29.1 | 28.7 | 28.1 | 28.1 | 27.9 | 28.6 |
| 2017 | 27.0 | 27.1 | 27.4 | 27.1 | 27.2 | 27.3 | 27.0 | 27.0 | 26.9 | 26.3 | 26.5 | 26.6 | 27.0 |
| 2018 | 26.0 | 26.2 | 26.6 | 26.7 | 26.8 | 27.3 | 27.5 | 27.4 | 27.4 | 27.5 | 27.3 | 27.2 | 27.0 |
| 2019 | 26.3 | 26.6 | 27.2 | 26.9 | 26.9 | 26.7 | 27.0 | 26.9 | 26.9 | 27.8 | 27.3 | 27.5 | 27.0 |
| **Manufacturing** | | | | | | | | | | | | | |
| 2011 | 10.7 | 10.9 | 11.0 | 10.8 | 10.9 | 10.9 | 10.8 | 10.9 | 11.1 | 11.0 | 11.1 | 11.1 | 10.9 |
| 2012 | 10.9 | 10.9 | 10.8 | 10.7 | 10.6 | 10.7 | 10.8 | 10.9 | 11.0 | 10.9 | 11.1 | 11.1 | 10.9 |
| 2013 | 10.9 | 10.9 | 11.0 | 10.9 | 11.0 | 11.0 | 11.0 | 11.0 | 11.2 | 11.2 | 11.2 | 11.2 | 11.0 |
| 2014 | 11.0 | 11.0 | 11.0 | 11.0 | 11.0 | 11.2 | 11.4 | 11.5 | 11.3 | 11.4 | 11.4 | 11.5 | 11.2 |
| 2015 | 11.3 | 11.4 | 11.4 | 11.3 | 11.4 | 11.5 | 11.5 | 11.5 | 11.4 | 11.5 | 11.5 | 11.6 | 11.4 |
| 2016 | 11.3 | 11.5 | 11.5 | 11.5 | 11.5 | 11.6 | 11.6 | 11.7 | 11.6 | 11.6 | 11.6 | 11.6 | 11.6 |
| 2017 | 11.4 | 11.5 | 11.7 | 11.7 | 11.7 | 11.8 | 11.8 | 11.9 | 11.8 | 11.8 | 11.9 | 11.9 | 11.7 |
| 2018 | 11.8 | 11.7 | 11.7 | 11.7 | 11.5 | 11.4 | 11.4 | 11.4 | 11.2 | 11.3 | 11.3 | 11.3 | 11.5 |
| 2019 | 11.1 | 11.1 | 11.1 | 10.9 | 10.9 | 10.9 | 10.9 | 10.9 | 10.9 | 10.8 | 10.9 | 11.0 | 11.0 |

## Employment by Industry: Urban Honolulu, HI, 2011–2019—*Continued*

(Numbers in thousands, not seasonally adjusted)

| Industry and year | January | February | March | April | May | June | July | August | September | October | November | December | Annual average |
|---|---|---|---|---|---|---|---|---|---|---|---|---|---|
| **Trade, Transportation, and Utilities** | | | | | | | | | | | | | |
| 2011 | 79.7 | 79.3 | 79.3 | 78.9 | 79.0 | 79.1 | 79.6 | 79.7 | 79.9 | 80.8 | 82.6 | 83.8 | 80.1 |
| 2012 | 81.6 | 81.1 | 81.3 | 81.1 | 81.8 | 82.3 | 82.5 | 82.5 | 82.9 | 83.4 | 86.0 | 86.8 | 82.8 |
| 2013 | 83.6 | 83.2 | 83.5 | 83.3 | 83.5 | 83.9 | 84.0 | 84.2 | 84.0 | 84.2 | 86.4 | 87.5 | 84.3 |
| 2014 | 84.2 | 83.4 | 83.6 | 83.4 | 83.4 | 83.8 | 84.2 | 83.8 | 84.0 | 84.4 | 86.6 | 88.4 | 84.4 |
| 2015 | 85.5 | 85.0 | 85.1 | 84.7 | 84.7 | 85.2 | 85.3 | 85.1 | 84.8 | 85.4 | 87.3 | 88.4 | 85.5 |
| 2016 | 85.3 | 84.8 | 84.5 | 84.0 | 84.2 | 84.1 | 84.8 | 85.0 | 85.3 | 86.0 | 87.5 | 89.1 | 85.4 |
| 2017 | 86.4 | 85.3 | 85.3 | 85.1 | 85.4 | 85.7 | 86.1 | 86.4 | 86.6 | 87.0 | 88.7 | 89.6 | 86.5 |
| 2018 | 87.2 | 86.2 | 86.2 | 86.5 | 86.6 | 86.8 | 87.0 | 87.1 | 87.0 | 87.0 | 88.9 | 89.6 | 87.2 |
| 2019 | 87.2 | 86.1 | 85.9 | 85.2 | 85.6 | 86.0 | 85.9 | 85.9 | 85.6 | 85.3 | 87.2 | 88.2 | 86.2 |
| **Wholesale Trade** | | | | | | | | | | | | | |
| 2011 | 14.3 | 14.3 | 14.2 | 14.3 | 14.3 | 14.3 | 14.4 | 14.4 | 14.4 | 14.5 | 14.5 | 14.6 | 14.4 |
| 2012 | 14.4 | 14.4 | 14.4 | 14.3 | 14.4 | 14.5 | 14.5 | 14.5 | 14.6 | 14.6 | 14.6 | 14.7 | 14.5 |
| 2013 | 14.5 | 14.4 | 14.5 | 14.5 | 14.5 | 14.5 | 14.5 | 14.5 | 14.5 | 14.4 | 14.5 | 14.5 | 14.5 |
| 2014 | 14.4 | 14.4 | 14.4 | 14.3 | 14.3 | 14.4 | 14.4 | 14.4 | 14.4 | 14.5 | 14.6 | 14.8 | 14.4 |
| 2015 | 14.5 | 14.6 | 14.6 | 14.6 | 14.6 | 14.6 | 14.7 | 14.7 | 14.6 | 14.6 | 14.6 | 14.6 | 14.6 |
| 2016 | 14.4 | 14.4 | 14.3 | 14.4 | 14.4 | 14.4 | 14.5 | 14.5 | 14.5 | 14.6 | 14.6 | 14.8 | 14.5 |
| 2017 | 14.6 | 14.5 | 14.5 | 14.5 | 14.5 | 14.5 | 14.5 | 14.5 | 14.6 | 14.5 | 14.6 | 14.7 | 14.5 |
| 2018 | 14.5 | 14.4 | 14.4 | 14.5 | 14.5 | 14.5 | 14.5 | 14.5 | 14.5 | 14.4 | 14.4 | 14.6 | 14.5 |
| 2019 | 14.5 | 14.5 | 14.5 | 14.3 | 14.4 | 14.4 | 14.3 | 14.3 | 14.2 | 14.3 | 14.2 | 14.3 | 14.4 |
| **Retail Trade** | | | | | | | | | | | | | |
| 2011 | 45.7 | 45.2 | 45.3 | 45.0 | 45.1 | 45.0 | 45.4 | 45.5 | 45.7 | 46.3 | 48.0 | 48.9 | 45.9 |
| 2012 | 47.1 | 46.7 | 46.7 | 46.6 | 47.0 | 47.2 | 47.3 | 47.2 | 47.3 | 47.7 | 50.1 | 50.7 | 47.6 |
| 2013 | 48.1 | 47.6 | 47.8 | 47.5 | 47.5 | 47.6 | 47.8 | 47.9 | 47.6 | 47.8 | 49.8 | 50.6 | 48.1 |
| 2014 | 47.8 | 47.0 | 47.1 | 47.0 | 47.0 | 47.4 | 47.7 | 47.5 | 47.7 | 47.9 | 49.7 | 50.9 | 47.9 |
| 2015 | 48.6 | 48.1 | 48.1 | 47.8 | 47.7 | 48.0 | 48.0 | 47.9 | 47.8 | 48.3 | 50.1 | 50.9 | 48.4 |
| 2016 | 48.4 | 47.9 | 47.7 | 47.0 | 46.9 | 46.8 | 47.4 | 47.5 | 47.9 | 48.3 | 49.6 | 50.6 | 48.0 |
| 2017 | 48.5 | 47.5 | 47.5 | 47.4 | 47.6 | 47.7 | 48.0 | 48.1 | 48.0 | 48.4 | 50.1 | 50.7 | 48.3 |
| 2018 | 48.9 | 48.0 | 47.8 | 47.9 | 48.0 | 48.1 | 48.3 | 48.4 | 48.3 | 48.5 | 50.2 | 50.5 | 48.6 |
| 2019 | 48.5 | 47.6 | 47.4 | 47.0 | 47.1 | 47.3 | 47.2 | 47.1 | 46.9 | 46.3 | 48.1 | 48.6 | 47.4 |
| **Transportation and Utilities** | | | | | | | | | | | | | |
| 2011 | 19.7 | 19.8 | 19.8 | 19.6 | 19.6 | 19.8 | 19.8 | 19.8 | 19.8 | 20.0 | 20.1 | 20.3 | 19.8 |
| 2012 | 20.1 | 20.0 | 20.2 | 20.2 | 20.4 | 20.6 | 20.7 | 20.8 | 21.0 | 21.1 | 21.3 | 21.4 | 20.7 |
| 2013 | 21.0 | 21.2 | 21.2 | 21.3 | 21.5 | 21.8 | 21.7 | 21.8 | 21.9 | 22.0 | 22.1 | 22.4 | 21.7 |
| 2014 | 22.0 | 22.0 | 22.1 | 22.1 | 22.1 | 22.0 | 22.1 | 21.9 | 21.9 | 22.0 | 22.3 | 22.7 | 22.1 |
| 2015 | 22.4 | 22.3 | 22.4 | 22.3 | 22.4 | 22.6 | 22.6 | 22.5 | 22.4 | 22.5 | 22.6 | 22.9 | 22.5 |
| 2016 | 22.5 | 22.5 | 22.5 | 22.6 | 22.9 | 22.9 | 22.9 | 23.0 | 22.9 | 23.1 | 23.3 | 23.7 | 22.9 |
| 2017 | 23.3 | 23.3 | 23.3 | 23.2 | 23.3 | 23.5 | 23.6 | 23.8 | 24.0 | 24.1 | 24.0 | 24.2 | 23.6 |
| 2018 | 23.8 | 23.8 | 24.0 | 24.1 | 24.1 | 24.2 | 24.2 | 24.2 | 24.2 | 24.1 | 24.3 | 24.5 | 24.1 |
| 2019 | 24.2 | 24.0 | 24.0 | 23.9 | 24.1 | 24.3 | 24.4 | 24.5 | 24.5 | 24.7 | 24.9 | 25.3 | 24.4 |
| **Information** | | | | | | | | | | | | | |
| 2011 | 7.0 | 8.0 | 8.7 | 6.7 | 6.6 | 6.4 | 6.9 | 6.8 | 6.8 | 6.9 | 7.2 | 7.3 | 7.1 |
| 2012 | 6.9 | 7.1 | 7.1 | 7.1 | 7.1 | 6.4 | 6.8 | 7.0 | 7.0 | 7.2 | 7.8 | 7.6 | 7.1 |
| 2013 | 7.0 | 7.1 | 7.2 | 7.1 | 6.7 | 6.6 | 8.3 | 7.0 | 7.4 | 8.1 | 8.4 | 8.6 | 7.5 |
| 2014 | 7.0 | 7.1 | 7.2 | 7.0 | 7.5 | 6.8 | 6.9 | 7.4 | 7.5 | 7.3 | 7.4 | 7.5 | 7.2 |
| 2015 | 7.2 | 7.3 | 7.3 | 7.1 | 7.0 | 6.9 | 7.3 | 7.3 | 7.2 | 7.4 | 8.3 | 8.4 | 7.4 |
| 2016 | 6.9 | 7.3 | 7.1 | 7.2 | 7.7 | 7.1 | 7.4 | 8.4 | 7.9 | 7.4 | 8.3 | 7.4 | 7.5 |
| 2017 | 7.6 | 7.8 | 7.9 | 7.8 | 8.5 | 7.6 | 7.7 | 8.7 | 7.9 | 7.0 | 7.1 | 7.3 | 7.7 |
| 2018 | 7.1 | 7.6 | 7.7 | 8.2 | 8.4 | 8.5 | 6.9 | 8.6 | 8.0 | 7.4 | 8.0 | 7.7 | 7.8 |
| 2019 | 7.5 | 8.7 | 7.3 | 6.7 | 7.6 | 6.4 | 6.7 | 7.8 | 7.4 | 7.2 | 7.5 | 7.4 | 7.4 |
| **Financial Activities** | | | | | | | | | | | | | |
| 2011 | 20.7 | 20.9 | 20.8 | 20.8 | 20.9 | 20.8 | 20.9 | 20.8 | 20.8 | 20.9 | 21.0 | 20.9 | 20.9 |
| 2012 | 20.5 | 20.6 | 20.7 | 20.6 | 20.7 | 21.0 | 20.9 | 20.9 | 20.9 | 20.9 | 21.0 | 21.0 | 20.8 |
| 2013 | 20.7 | 20.7 | 20.9 | 21.0 | 21.1 | 21.1 | 21.1 | 21.1 | 21.1 | 21.0 | 21.2 | 21.3 | 21.0 |
| 2014 | 21.0 | 21.1 | 21.3 | 21.2 | 21.4 | 21.4 | 21.5 | 21.4 | 21.4 | 21.5 | 21.4 | 21.8 | 21.4 |
| 2015 | 21.4 | 21.6 | 21.6 | 21.7 | 21.9 | 21.9 | 21.9 | 21.9 | 21.8 | 21.7 | 21.7 | 22.1 | 21.8 |
| 2016 | 22.0 | 22.1 | 22.1 | 22.1 | 22.2 | 22.3 | 22.6 | 22.6 | 22.4 | 22.4 | 22.5 | 22.6 | 22.3 |
| 2017 | 22.5 | 22.4 | 22.6 | 22.5 | 22.5 | 22.7 | 22.5 | 22.5 | 22.6 | 22.6 | 22.7 | 22.9 | 22.6 |
| 2018 | 22.5 | 22.5 | 22.7 | 22.7 | 22.6 | 22.6 | 22.7 | 22.6 | 22.6 | 22.7 | 22.8 | 22.9 | 22.7 |
| 2019 | 22.6 | 22.7 | 22.8 | 23.0 | 23.0 | 23.1 | 23.1 | 23.0 | 23.0 | 23.0 | 23.0 | 23.1 | 23.0 |

# Employment by Industry: Urban Honolulu, HI, 2011–2019—*Continued*

(Numbers in thousands, not seasonally adjusted)

| Industry and year | January | February | March | April | May | June | July | August | September | October | November | December | Annual average |
|---|---|---|---|---|---|---|---|---|---|---|---|---|---|
| **Professional and Business Services** | | | | | | | | | | | | | |
| 2011 | 52.9 | 53.9 | 54.3 | 54.3 | 53.8 | 53.9 | 53.7 | 54.5 | 54.8 | 54.6 | 55.1 | 56.1 | 54.3 |
| 2012 | 54.1 | 54.6 | 55.0 | 55.8 | 55.9 | 56.2 | 55.5 | 56.3 | 55.8 | 56.3 | 56.7 | 57.0 | 55.8 |
| 2013 | 56.1 | 56.7 | 57.0 | 56.8 | 56.6 | 56.8 | 57.3 | 57.5 | 57.4 | 58.2 | 58.9 | 59.0 | 57.4 |
| 2014 | 58.4 | 58.5 | 58.9 | 59.0 | 58.6 | 58.6 | 58.3 | 58.6 | 58.7 | 58.4 | 58.9 | 59.4 | 58.7 |
| 2015 | 58.3 | 58.4 | 58.9 | 58.6 | 58.3 | 58.4 | 58.4 | 58.0 | 57.7 | 58.2 | 58.3 | 58.2 | 58.3 |
| 2016 | 56.9 | 57.3 | 57.1 | 57.5 | 56.6 | 56.6 | 56.9 | 57.1 | 57.0 | 56.6 | 56.8 | 57.0 | 57.0 |
| 2017 | 56.1 | 56.3 | 56.5 | 56.3 | 56.0 | 56.7 | 56.7 | 56.5 | 56.3 | 56.3 | 56.6 | 56.6 | 56.4 |
| 2018 | 55.6 | 55.8 | 56.5 | 56.4 | 56.1 | 56.4 | 56.5 | 57.0 | 56.8 | 57.3 | 57.9 | 58.3 | 56.7 |
| 2019 | 57.1 | 57.4 | 57.7 | 56.6 | 56.6 | 56.4 | 56.7 | 57.2 | 56.7 | 57.6 | 57.5 | 58.4 | 57.2 |
| **Education and Health Services** | | | | | | | | | | | | | |
| 2011 | 58.8 | 60.2 | 60.4 | 60.3 | 60.5 | 59.8 | 60.0 | 59.7 | 60.7 | 60.8 | 61.5 | 61.7 | 60.4 |
| 2012 | 59.7 | 60.8 | 60.8 | 61.1 | 61.5 | 61.2 | 60.8 | 61.6 | 62.0 | 62.0 | 62.3 | 63.0 | 61.4 |
| 2013 | 61.6 | 62.5 | 62.8 | 62.8 | 63.0 | 62.9 | 62.1 | 62.4 | 63.0 | 62.6 | 63.8 | 63.4 | 62.7 |
| 2014 | 61.9 | 62.6 | 63.1 | 63.0 | 63.0 | 62.5 | 62.3 | 62.3 | 63.3 | 63.7 | 64.1 | 64.7 | 63.0 |
| 2015 | 63.7 | 64.8 | 65.3 | 65.2 | 65.4 | 64.7 | 64.5 | 64.7 | 65.4 | 66.0 | 66.3 | 66.7 | 65.2 |
| 2016 | 64.7 | 65.0 | 65.7 | 65.8 | 65.6 | 65.1 | 65.4 | 64.9 | 65.9 | 65.1 | 65.5 | 65.8 | 65.4 |
| 2017 | 65.4 | 65.9 | 66.4 | 66.4 | 66.4 | 65.4 | 65.0 | 64.3 | 66.0 | 65.7 | 65.9 | 66.6 | 65.8 |
| 2018 | 65.1 | 66.0 | 66.5 | 66.2 | 65.9 | 65.9 | 65.0 | 64.9 | 65.9 | 65.6 | 66.4 | 66.5 | 65.8 |
| 2019 | 64.5 | 65.9 | 66.1 | 65.3 | 65.2 | 64.3 | 64.6 | 64.5 | 65.6 | 66.4 | 66.9 | 67.0 | 65.5 |
| **Leisure and Hospitality** | | | | | | | | | | | | | |
| 2011 | 61.8 | 61.8 | 62.5 | 62.5 | 62.4 | 62.7 | 62.6 | 63.3 | 63.7 | 63.5 | 63.7 | 64.0 | 62.9 |
| 2012 | 63.3 | 64.0 | 64.5 | 64.6 | 65.1 | 65.8 | 65.9 | 66.2 | 66.3 | 66.2 | 66.4 | 66.9 | 65.4 |
| 2013 | 66.0 | 66.6 | 66.8 | 67.0 | 67.8 | 68.3 | 68.3 | 68.6 | 68.5 | 68.6 | 69.0 | 69.2 | 67.9 |
| 2014 | 67.9 | 68.3 | 69.0 | 68.7 | 69.3 | 69.3 | 69.0 | 69.4 | 69.5 | 69.5 | 69.7 | 69.6 | 69.1 |
| 2015 | 68.6 | 68.8 | 69.0 | 69.0 | 69.5 | 69.5 | 69.9 | 70.6 | 70.2 | 70.6 | 71.1 | 71.6 | 69.9 |
| 2016 | 70.1 | 70.9 | 71.1 | 71.2 | 71.8 | 72.2 | 72.8 | 73.6 | 73.5 | 73.3 | 73.5 | 74.0 | 72.3 |
| 2017 | 73.4 | 74.5 | 75.5 | 74.9 | 75.3 | 75.7 | 75.7 | 76.2 | 75.9 | 75.7 | 75.5 | 76.1 | 75.4 |
| 2018 | 75.1 | 75.5 | 75.8 | 74.8 | 75.3 | 75.9 | 75.5 | 75.9 | 75.5 | 76.2 | 75.2 | 77.7 | 75.7 |
| 2019 | 75.2 | 75.4 | 76.1 | 75.3 | 75.5 | 75.7 | 76.0 | 76.1 | 76.0 | 75.7 | 75.5 | 77.1 | 75.8 |
| **Other Services** | | | | | | | | | | | | | |
| 2011 | 20.1 | 20.3 | 20.2 | 20.4 | 20.5 | 20.5 | 20.5 | 20.6 | 20.9 | 20.9 | 20.9 | 21.0 | 20.6 |
| 2012 | 20.4 | 20.7 | 20.8 | 20.8 | 21.0 | 20.9 | 20.8 | 21.0 | 21.0 | 21.0 | 21.0 | 21.0 | 20.9 |
| 2013 | 21.0 | 21.1 | 21.1 | 21.4 | 21.4 | 21.3 | 21.4 | 21.4 | 21.5 | 21.6 | 21.5 | 21.5 | 21.4 |
| 2014 | 21.2 | 21.2 | 21.5 | 21.2 | 21.3 | 21.3 | 21.1 | 21.3 | 21.4 | 21.4 | 21.5 | 21.6 | 21.3 |
| 2015 | 21.2 | 21.4 | 21.6 | 21.4 | 21.5 | 21.6 | 21.4 | 21.4 | 21.4 | 21.4 | 21.5 | 21.5 | 21.4 |
| 2016 | 21.4 | 21.5 | 21.6 | 21.7 | 21.7 | 21.7 | 21.7 | 21.7 | 21.8 | 21.7 | 21.9 | 21.8 | 21.7 |
| 2017 | 21.6 | 21.7 | 21.9 | 21.9 | 22.0 | 22.1 | 22.0 | 22.1 | 22.1 | 22.0 | 22.1 | 22.3 | 22.0 |
| 2018 | 21.7 | 21.9 | 22.1 | 21.9 | 21.9 | 22.0 | 21.9 | 21.8 | 21.9 | 21.8 | 21.9 | 21.9 | 21.9 |
| 2019 | 21.6 | 21.7 | 21.8 | 21.6 | 21.7 | 21.8 | 21.6 | 21.6 | 21.6 | 21.6 | 21.7 | 21.7 | 21.7 |
| **Government** | | | | | | | | | | | | | |
| 2011 | 94.0 | 100.5 | 101.0 | 100.7 | 101.4 | 99.0 | 93.6 | 89.5 | 96.3 | 99.2 | 100.9 | 101.4 | 98.1 |
| 2012 | 89.0 | 100.9 | 101.6 | 101.6 | 102.2 | 99.5 | 92.3 | 94.7 | 97.2 | 99.8 | 103.5 | 101.7 | 98.7 |
| 2013 | 89.1 | 101.2 | 101.5 | 98.4 | 102.1 | 98.2 | 92.2 | 89.7 | 97.0 | 99.8 | 100.9 | 101.4 | 97.6 |
| 2014 | 97.9 | 101.3 | 101.6 | 100.8 | 102.2 | 98.8 | 92.2 | 92.2 | 97.0 | 99.2 | 102.1 | 98.0 | 98.6 |
| 2015 | 97.1 | 100.3 | 100.6 | 100.3 | 101.1 | 98.3 | 91.0 | 93.8 | 96.5 | 99.2 | 99.9 | 100.9 | 98.3 |
| 2016 | 94.7 | 99.6 | 100.5 | 97.9 | 100.5 | 97.6 | 90.5 | 90.3 | 96.6 | 98.9 | 101.6 | 97.9 | 97.2 |
| 2017 | 95.9 | 100.1 | 100.0 | 99.6 | 100.0 | 96.7 | 89.7 | 87.3 | 96.5 | 98.2 | 99.4 | 100.0 | 97.0 |
| 2018 | 94.6 | 99.5 | 99.3 | 98.5 | 100.4 | 97.0 | 89.6 | 90.1 | 95.5 | 97.9 | 101.3 | 100.6 | 97.0 |
| 2019 | 95.1 | 99.5 | 99.2 | 98.4 | 100.0 | 97.0 | 91.2 | 90.2 | 96.9 | 98.8 | 99.8 | 100.0 | 97.2 |

## Employment by Industry: Omaha-Council Bluffs, NE-IA, 2011–2019

(Numbers in thousands, not seasonally adjusted)

| Industry and year | January | February | March | April | May | June | July | August | September | October | November | December | Annual average |
|---|---|---|---|---|---|---|---|---|---|---|---|---|---|
| **Total Nonfarm** | | | | | | | | | | | | | |
| 2011 | 453.9 | 454.5 | 456.6 | 464.4 | 468.0 | 468.4 | 465.3 | 466.5 | 465.0 | 468.3 | 470.5 | 470.0 | 464.3 |
| 2012 | 460.3 | 460.2 | 464.2 | 469.2 | 474.0 | 473.1 | 471.7 | 471.8 | 470.7 | 474.4 | 477.2 | 476.5 | 470.3 |
| 2013 | 466.2 | 466.7 | 468.8 | 474.3 | 480.8 | 481.0 | 479.1 | 480.8 | 480.3 | 483.8 | 486.6 | 485.8 | 477.9 |
| 2014 | 475.1 | 476.8 | 478.7 | 483.2 | 488.2 | 487.7 | 484.6 | 486.7 | 485.8 | 489.6 | 491.4 | 492.4 | 485.0 |
| 2015 | 480.3 | 481.5 | 484.7 | 491.3 | 495.5 | 496.2 | 493.9 | 495.4 | 493.4 | 499.0 | 499.7 | 500.7 | 492.6 |
| 2016 | 486.2 | 487.3 | 491.6 | 497.1 | 500.7 | 500.8 | 499.9 | 499.2 | 500.1 | 502.5 | 502.1 | 502.1 | 497.5 |
| 2017 | 490.7 | 493.0 | 495.8 | 499.8 | 503.2 | 504.2 | 499.0 | 499.0 | 499.3 | 503.0 | 505.0 | 504.4 | 499.7 |
| 2018 | 492.1 | 493.9 | 496.7 | 501.6 | 507.4 | 507.8 | 502.6 | 503.3 | 502.9 | 506.5 | 509.7 | 508.2 | 502.7 |
| 2019 | 497.6 | 497.4 | 498.6 | 504.6 | 510.4 | 511.4 | 507.6 | 508.5 | 506.7 | 513.9 | 514.5 | 515.2 | 507.2 |
| **Total Private** | | | | | | | | | | | | | |
| 2011 | 388.5 | 388.5 | 391.2 | 397.6 | 401.0 | 403.2 | 402.2 | 402.7 | 400.4 | 401.8 | 403.8 | 404.1 | 398.8 |
| 2012 | 394.5 | 394.0 | 398.5 | 403.2 | 407.5 | 410.0 | 409.1 | 408.7 | 406.4 | 408.6 | 411.3 | 411.5 | 405.3 |
| 2013 | 401.4 | 401.3 | 403.7 | 408.6 | 414.4 | 416.2 | 416.0 | 417.4 | 415.9 | 418.1 | 420.7 | 420.8 | 412.9 |
| 2014 | 409.8 | 410.8 | 413.2 | 417.1 | 421.4 | 423.3 | 421.6 | 422.9 | 420.4 | 422.8 | 424.6 | 426.4 | 419.5 |
| 2015 | 414.6 | 415.4 | 418.9 | 424.5 | 428.2 | 430.7 | 430.3 | 431.2 | 428.4 | 432.1 | 432.6 | 434.0 | 426.7 |
| 2016 | 420.1 | 420.7 | 425.0 | 429.9 | 432.9 | 434.4 | 436.5 | 436.3 | 434.0 | 435.2 | 434.9 | 435.7 | 431.3 |
| 2017 | 424.5 | 426.4 | 429.5 | 432.6 | 435.6 | 437.8 | 436.5 | 436.5 | 433.2 | 435.5 | 437.6 | 437.8 | 433.6 |
| 2018 | 425.3 | 426.7 | 429.7 | 434.2 | 439.5 | 441.4 | 439.9 | 439.9 | 436.5 | 438.7 | 441.8 | 441.2 | 436.2 |
| 2019 | 430.5 | 430.1 | 431.6 | 436.9 | 442.3 | 444.2 | 443.7 | 444.2 | 440.1 | 445.8 | 445.9 | 447.3 | 440.2 |
| **Goods Producing** | | | | | | | | | | | | | |
| 2011 | 49.0 | 49.0 | 49.8 | 51.0 | 51.6 | 52.6 | 52.7 | 52.4 | 51.8 | 52.1 | 52.1 | 52.0 | 51.3 |
| 2012 | 49.9 | 49.5 | 50.6 | 51.7 | 52.5 | 53.3 | 53.6 | 53.5 | 53.4 | 53.6 | 53.7 | 53.5 | 52.4 |
| 2013 | 51.6 | 52.0 | 52.4 | 54.0 | 55.4 | 56.0 | 56.9 | 56.9 | 56.7 | 56.5 | 56.3 | 55.0 | 55.0 |
| 2014 | 53.3 | 53.4 | 53.9 | 56.2 | 56.9 | 57.9 | 58.3 | 58.5 | 58.3 | 58.4 | 58.1 | 57.8 | 56.8 |
| 2015 | 55.8 | 56.0 | 56.9 | 58.7 | 59.0 | 59.4 | 59.6 | 59.4 | 59.1 | 59.9 | 59.2 | 58.4 | 58.5 |
| 2016 | 56.2 | 56.1 | 57.5 | 58.9 | 59.5 | 60.2 | 60.6 | 60.6 | 60.2 | 60.2 | 59.8 | 59.0 | 59.1 |
| 2017 | 57.5 | 58.3 | 59.3 | 60.1 | 60.6 | 61.4 | 61.7 | 61.5 | 61.2 | 61.7 | 61.8 | 61.5 | 60.6 |
| 2018 | 59.0 | 59.4 | 60.6 | 62.3 | 63.3 | 64.2 | 64.4 | 64.4 | 63.8 | 63.8 | 63.9 | 63.0 | 62.7 |
| 2019 | 61.4 | 61.2 | 61.6 | 63.6 | 64.7 | 65.5 | 65.7 | 65.7 | 65.2 | 66.4 | 66.0 | 65.4 | 64.4 |
| **Service-Providing** | | | | | | | | | | | | | |
| 2011 | 404.9 | 405.5 | 406.8 | 413.4 | 416.4 | 415.8 | 412.6 | 414.1 | 413.2 | 416.2 | 418.4 | 418.0 | 412.9 |
| 2012 | 410.4 | 410.7 | 413.6 | 417.5 | 421.5 | 419.8 | 418.1 | 418.3 | 417.3 | 420.8 | 423.5 | 423.0 | 417.9 |
| 2013 | 414.6 | 414.7 | 416.4 | 420.3 | 425.4 | 425.0 | 422.2 | 423.9 | 423.6 | 427.3 | 430.3 | 430.8 | 422.9 |
| 2014 | 421.8 | 423.4 | 424.8 | 427.0 | 431.3 | 429.8 | 426.3 | 428.2 | 427.5 | 431.2 | 433.3 | 434.6 | 428.3 |
| 2015 | 424.5 | 425.5 | 427.8 | 432.6 | 436.5 | 436.8 | 434.3 | 436.0 | 434.3 | 439.1 | 440.5 | 442.3 | 434.2 |
| 2016 | 430.0 | 431.2 | 434.1 | 438.2 | 441.2 | 440.6 | 439.3 | 438.6 | 439.9 | 442.3 | 442.3 | 443.1 | 438.4 |
| 2017 | 433.2 | 434.7 | 436.5 | 439.7 | 442.6 | 442.8 | 437.3 | 437.5 | 438.1 | 441.3 | 443.2 | 442.9 | 439.2 |
| 2018 | 433.1 | 434.5 | 436.1 | 439.3 | 444.1 | 443.6 | 438.2 | 438.9 | 439.1 | 442.7 | 445.8 | 445.2 | 440.1 |
| 2019 | 436.2 | 436.2 | 437.0 | 441.0 | 445.7 | 445.9 | 441.9 | 442.8 | 441.5 | 447.5 | 448.5 | 449.8 | 442.8 |
| **Mining, Logging, and Construction** | | | | | | | | | | | | | |
| 2011 | 18.2 | 18.0 | 18.7 | 19.7 | 20.3 | 21.2 | 21.3 | 21.3 | 21.0 | 21.0 | 20.8 | 20.1 | 20.1 |
| 2012 | 19.0 | 18.6 | 19.5 | 20.6 | 21.3 | 21.8 | 22.0 | 22.1 | 22.0 | 22.4 | 22.2 | 21.9 | 21.1 |
| 2013 | 20.3 | 20.4 | 20.8 | 22.2 | 23.2 | 23.6 | 24.3 | 24.3 | 24.1 | 24.0 | 23.6 | 22.4 | 22.8 |
| 2014 | 21.1 | 21.0 | 21.6 | 23.7 | 24.4 | 25.3 | 25.5 | 25.8 | 25.7 | 25.8 | 25.4 | 25.0 | 24.2 |
| 2015 | 23.4 | 23.5 | 24.4 | 26.1 | 26.4 | 26.6 | 26.7 | 26.6 | 26.4 | 27.0 | 26.4 | 25.6 | 25.8 |
| 2016 | 23.8 | 23.7 | 24.9 | 26.2 | 26.8 | 27.5 | 27.9 | 27.9 | 27.6 | 27.5 | 27.3 | 26.3 | 26.5 |
| 2017 | 25.0 | 25.5 | 26.5 | 27.1 | 27.5 | 28.1 | 28.1 | 27.9 | 27.7 | 28.1 | 28.1 | 27.5 | 27.3 |
| 2018 | 25.5 | 25.6 | 26.7 | 28.5 | 29.3 | 30.1 | 30.3 | 30.2 | 29.9 | 29.8 | 29.9 | 29.1 | 28.7 |
| 2019 | 27.8 | 27.6 | 27.9 | 30.1 | 31.0 | 31.7 | 31.9 | 31.9 | 31.6 | 32.7 | 31.7 | 31.2 | 30.6 |
| **Manufacturing** | | | | | | | | | | | | | |
| 2011 | 30.8 | 31.0 | 31.1 | 31.3 | 31.3 | 31.4 | 31.4 | 31.1 | 30.8 | 31.1 | 31.3 | 31.9 | 31.2 |
| 2012 | 30.9 | 30.9 | 31.1 | 31.1 | 31.2 | 31.5 | 31.6 | 31.4 | 31.4 | 31.2 | 31.5 | 31.6 | 31.3 |
| 2013 | 31.3 | 31.6 | 31.6 | 31.8 | 32.2 | 32.4 | 32.6 | 32.6 | 32.6 | 32.5 | 32.7 | 32.6 | 32.2 |
| 2014 | 32.2 | 32.4 | 32.3 | 32.5 | 32.5 | 32.6 | 32.8 | 32.7 | 32.6 | 32.6 | 32.7 | 32.8 | 32.6 |
| 2015 | 32.4 | 32.5 | 32.5 | 32.6 | 32.6 | 32.8 | 32.9 | 32.8 | 32.7 | 32.9 | 32.8 | 32.8 | 32.7 |
| 2016 | 32.4 | 32.4 | 32.6 | 32.7 | 32.7 | 32.7 | 32.7 | 32.7 | 32.6 | 32.7 | 32.5 | 32.7 | 32.6 |
| 2017 | 32.5 | 32.8 | 32.8 | 33.0 | 33.1 | 33.3 | 33.6 | 33.6 | 33.5 | 33.6 | 33.7 | 34.0 | 33.3 |
| 2018 | 33.5 | 33.8 | 33.9 | 33.8 | 34.0 | 34.1 | 34.1 | 34.2 | 33.9 | 34.0 | 34.0 | 33.9 | 33.9 |
| 2019 | 33.6 | 33.6 | 33.7 | 33.5 | 33.7 | 33.8 | 33.8 | 33.8 | 33.6 | 33.7 | 34.3 | 34.2 | 33.8 |

# Employment by Industry: Omaha-Council Bluffs, NE-IA, 2011–2019—*Continued*

(Numbers in thousands, not seasonally adjusted)

| Industry and year | January | February | March | April | May | June | July | August | September | October | November | December | Annual average |
|---|---|---|---|---|---|---|---|---|---|---|---|---|---|
| **Trade, Transportation, and Utilities** | | | | | | | | | | | | | |
| 2011 | 93.0 | 92.3 | 92.8 | 93.5 | 94.1 | 93.7 | 93.4 | 94.0 | 93.9 | 94.4 | 97.0 | 97.9 | 94.2 |
| 2012 | 93.3 | 92.2 | 92.9 | 93.3 | 94.5 | 94.5 | 93.9 | 93.7 | 93.9 | 94.9 | 97.9 | 99.1 | 94.5 |
| 2013 | 94.2 | 92.9 | 93.3 | 93.5 | 94.9 | 95.1 | 94.9 | 95.5 | 95.4 | 96.3 | 99.5 | 101.2 | 95.6 |
| 2014 | 96.4 | 95.5 | 95.6 | 96.1 | 96.7 | 96.8 | 96.2 | 97.1 | 96.5 | 97.6 | 100.4 | 102.5 | 97.3 |
| 2015 | 96.3 | 95.6 | 96.1 | 97.1 | 97.9 | 98.5 | 97.8 | 98.4 | 97.7 | 98.8 | 101.3 | 102.9 | 98.2 |
| 2016 | 96.7 | 96.1 | 96.2 | 96.7 | 97.2 | 97.1 | 97.2 | 97.3 | 96.9 | 97.5 | 99.7 | 100.8 | 97.5 |
| 2017 | 96.3 | 95.9 | 96.2 | 96.8 | 97.5 | 97.2 | 96.9 | 97.1 | 96.6 | 97.1 | 100.4 | 101.1 | 97.4 |
| 2018 | 95.9 | 95.3 | 95.5 | 95.6 | 96.6 | 96.8 | 96.3 | 96.2 | 95.5 | 96.3 | 100.4 | 101.1 | 96.8 |
| 2019 | 96.2 | 94.9 | 95.0 | 95.4 | 95.8 | 95.9 | 95.7 | 95.8 | 95.0 | 96.1 | 98.4 | 99.4 | 96.1 |
| **Wholesale Trade** | | | | | | | | | | | | | |
| 2011 | 16.9 | 16.9 | 17.0 | 17.0 | 17.0 | 17.1 | 17.1 | 17.0 | 17.1 | 17.1 | 17.2 | 17.1 | 17.0 |
| 2012 | 16.7 | 16.7 | 16.8 | 16.8 | 16.9 | 16.9 | 16.9 | 16.8 | 16.7 | 16.7 | 16.8 | 16.8 | 16.8 |
| 2013 | 16.6 | 16.6 | 16.7 | 16.8 | 17.0 | 17.1 | 17.0 | 16.9 | 16.8 | 16.9 | 17.0 | 17.0 | 16.9 |
| 2014 | 16.9 | 16.9 | 17.0 | 17.1 | 17.1 | 17.2 | 17.2 | 17.1 | 17.0 | 16.9 | 17.0 | 17.0 | 17.0 |
| 2015 | 16.4 | 16.3 | 16.5 | 16.7 | 16.8 | 16.9 | 16.8 | 16.9 | 16.7 | 16.8 | 16.9 | 16.9 | 16.7 |
| 2016 | 16.7 | 16.6 | 16.7 | 16.7 | 16.7 | 16.8 | 16.9 | 16.9 | 16.6 | 16.6 | 16.7 | 16.6 | 16.7 |
| 2017 | 16.5 | 16.5 | 16.6 | 16.7 | 16.8 | 16.9 | 16.9 | 16.8 | 16.6 | 16.6 | 16.7 | 16.7 | 16.7 |
| 2018 | 16.5 | 16.5 | 16.6 | 16.6 | 16.8 | 17.0 | 16.8 | 16.7 | 16.5 | 16.6 | 16.6 | 16.7 | 16.7 |
| 2019 | 16.6 | 16.5 | 16.6 | 16.6 | 16.7 | 16.9 | 16.9 | 16.8 | 16.7 | 16.4 | 16.6 | 16.7 | 16.7 |
| **Retail Trade** | | | | | | | | | | | | | |
| 2011 | 49.3 | 48.7 | 49.0 | 49.6 | 50.1 | 49.9 | 49.7 | 49.9 | 49.6 | 50.3 | 52.7 | 53.4 | 50.2 |
| 2012 | 50.0 | 49.0 | 49.4 | 49.8 | 50.5 | 50.6 | 50.2 | 50.0 | 49.9 | 51.1 | 53.3 | 53.8 | 50.6 |
| 2013 | 50.2 | 49.4 | 49.7 | 50.1 | 50.7 | 50.9 | 51.0 | 51.0 | 51.0 | 52.0 | 54.6 | 55.5 | 51.3 |
| 2014 | 52.3 | 51.5 | 51.5 | 52.1 | 52.5 | 52.7 | 52.5 | 52.8 | 52.4 | 53.3 | 55.2 | 56.0 | 52.9 |
| 2015 | 52.7 | 52.3 | 52.5 | 52.9 | 53.3 | 53.8 | 53.3 | 53.4 | 52.9 | 53.8 | 55.7 | 56.4 | 53.6 |
| 2016 | 53.3 | 53.0 | 53.0 | 53.7 | 54.0 | 54.1 | 54.4 | 54.3 | 53.9 | 54.6 | 56.4 | 56.9 | 54.3 |
| 2017 | 53.7 | 53.3 | 53.5 | 54.0 | 54.3 | 54.1 | 54.0 | 54.0 | 53.4 | 54.2 | 56.8 | 57.0 | 54.4 |
| 2018 | 53.6 | 53.0 | 53.0 | 53.2 | 53.7 | 53.8 | 53.7 | 53.3 | 52.5 | 53.2 | 55.9 | 56.1 | 53.8 |
| 2019 | 52.8 | 51.9 | 51.9 | 52.2 | 52.5 | 52.5 | 52.3 | 52.2 | 51.6 | 52.6 | 53.9 | 53.7 | 52.5 |
| **Transportation and Utilities** | | | | | | | | | | | | | |
| 2011 | 26.8 | 26.7 | 26.8 | 26.9 | 27.0 | 26.7 | 26.6 | 27.1 | 27.2 | 27.0 | 27.1 | 27.4 | 26.9 |
| 2012 | 26.6 | 26.5 | 26.7 | 26.7 | 27.1 | 27.0 | 26.8 | 26.9 | 27.3 | 27.1 | 27.8 | 28.5 | 27.1 |
| 2013 | 27.4 | 26.9 | 26.9 | 26.6 | 27.2 | 27.1 | 26.9 | 27.6 | 27.6 | 27.4 | 27.9 | 28.7 | 27.4 |
| 2014 | 27.2 | 27.1 | 27.1 | 26.9 | 27.1 | 26.9 | 26.5 | 27.2 | 27.1 | 27.4 | 28.2 | 29.5 | 27.4 |
| 2015 | 27.2 | 27.0 | 27.1 | 27.5 | 27.8 | 27.8 | 27.7 | 28.1 | 28.1 | 28.2 | 28.7 | 29.6 | 27.9 |
| 2016 | 26.7 | 26.5 | 26.5 | 26.3 | 26.5 | 26.2 | 25.9 | 26.1 | 26.4 | 26.3 | 26.6 | 27.3 | 26.4 |
| 2017 | 26.1 | 26.1 | 26.1 | 26.1 | 26.4 | 26.2 | 26.0 | 26.3 | 26.6 | 26.3 | 26.9 | 27.4 | 26.4 |
| 2018 | 25.8 | 25.8 | 25.9 | 25.8 | 26.1 | 26.0 | 25.8 | 26.2 | 26.5 | 26.5 | 27.9 | 28.3 | 26.4 |
| 2019 | 26.8 | 26.5 | 26.5 | 26.6 | 26.6 | 26.5 | 26.5 | 26.8 | 26.7 | 27.1 | 27.9 | 29.0 | 27.0 |
| **Information** | | | | | | | | | | | | | |
| 2011 | 11.2 | 11.2 | 11.1 | 11.1 | 11.1 | 11.2 | 11.4 | 11.4 | 11.3 | 11.3 | 11.4 | 11.4 | 11.3 |
| 2012 | 11.3 | 11.4 | 11.4 | 11.4 | 11.3 | 11.3 | 11.3 | 11.2 | 11.2 | 11.1 | 11.1 | 11.1 | 11.3 |
| 2013 | 11.0 | 11.0 | 11.0 | 11.0 | 11.1 | 11.1 | 11.1 | 11.1 | 11.1 | 11.1 | 11.1 | 11.1 | 11.1 |
| 2014 | 11.1 | 11.0 | 11.0 | 11.0 | 11.1 | 11.1 | 11.2 | 11.2 | 11.2 | 11.2 | 11.3 | 11.4 | 11.2 |
| 2015 | 11.3 | 11.4 | 11.4 | 11.5 | 11.6 | 11.7 | 11.7 | 11.8 | 11.6 | 11.7 | 11.8 | 11.9 | 11.6 |
| 2016 | 11.8 | 11.8 | 11.8 | 11.8 | 11.8 | 11.8 | 11.8 | 11.8 | 11.8 | 11.8 | 11.8 | 11.9 | 11.8 |
| 2017 | 11.7 | 11.7 | 11.7 | 11.7 | 11.6 | 11.6 | 11.6 | 11.5 | 11.4 | 11.5 | 11.4 | 11.5 | 11.6 |
| 2018 | 11.4 | 11.3 | 11.3 | 11.3 | 11.2 | 11.2 | 11.2 | 11.1 | 11.0 | 11.0 | 10.9 | 10.9 | 11.2 |
| 2019 | 10.7 | 10.7 | 10.6 | 10.6 | 10.7 | 10.8 | 10.6 | 10.5 | 10.4 | 10.4 | 10.4 | 10.4 | 10.6 |
| **Financial Activities** | | | | | | | | | | | | | |
| 2011 | 40.9 | 40.9 | 41.0 | 41.2 | 41.4 | 41.4 | 41.4 | 41.3 | 41.3 | 41.3 | 41.5 | 41.7 | 41.3 |
| 2012 | 41.3 | 41.2 | 41.3 | 41.5 | 41.6 | 41.6 | 41.8 | 41.8 | 41.7 | 41.8 | 42.0 | 42.1 | 41.6 |
| 2013 | 41.8 | 41.9 | 41.9 | 42.0 | 42.1 | 42.2 | 42.2 | 42.1 | 42.0 | 42.1 | 42.2 | 42.2 | 42.1 |
| 2014 | 42.0 | 42.1 | 42.0 | 41.8 | 41.9 | 42.1 | 42.2 | 42.0 | 41.9 | 42.0 | 42.0 | 42.0 | 42.0 |
| 2015 | 41.5 | 41.6 | 41.5 | 41.7 | 42.0 | 42.3 | 42.4 | 42.4 | 42.3 | 42.6 | 42.7 | 43.1 | 42.2 |
| 2016 | 42.9 | 43.0 | 43.2 | 43.3 | 43.3 | 43.5 | 43.8 | 43.7 | 43.5 | 43.5 | 43.5 | 43.6 | 43.4 |
| 2017 | 43.3 | 43.3 | 43.3 | 43.4 | 43.4 | 43.8 | 43.9 | 43.9 | 43.9 | 44.2 | 44.1 | 44.3 | 43.7 |
| 2018 | 44.1 | 44.5 | 44.5 | 44.8 | 45.0 | 45.1 | 45.3 | 45.1 | 45.0 | 45.3 | 45.4 | 45.7 | 45.0 |
| 2019 | 45.4 | 45.5 | 45.6 | 45.5 | 45.9 | 46.1 | 46.2 | 46.1 | 45.9 | 46.2 | 46.4 | 46.6 | 46.0 |

## Employment by Industry: Omaha-Council Bluffs, NE-IA, 2011–2019—*Continued*

(Numbers in thousands, not seasonally adjusted)

| Industry and year | January | February | March | April | May | June | July | August | September | October | November | December | Annual average |
|---|---|---|---|---|---|---|---|---|---|---|---|---|---|
| **Professional and Business Services** | | | | | | | | | | | | | |
| 2011 | 63.3 | 63.4 | 63.7 | 65.3 | 65.3 | 66.1 | 66.8 | 67.0 | 67.0 | 66.6 | 66.6 | 66.4 | 65.6 |
| 2012 | 65.6 | 65.8 | 65.8 | 67.1 | 67.4 | 68.6 | 68.6 | 68.2 | 67.8 | 68.6 | 68.9 | 68.7 | 67.6 |
| 2013 | 67.6 | 67.7 | 67.9 | 69.3 | 69.8 | 70.5 | 70.4 | 70.5 | 70.7 | 72.1 | 72.4 | 73.0 | 70.2 |
| 2014 | 70.4 | 71.1 | 71.5 | 71.9 | 72.4 | 72.8 | 72.1 | 72.1 | 71.8 | 72.2 | 72.4 | 72.2 | 71.9 |
| 2015 | 71.7 | 71.9 | 72.5 | 73.7 | 73.8 | 74.4 | 74.3 | 74.1 | 73.8 | 74.4 | 74.2 | 74.2 | 73.6 |
| 2016 | 72.4 | 72.6 | 73.2 | 74.6 | 74.5 | 74.8 | 74.9 | 74.6 | 74.1 | 73.8 | 73.5 | 74.2 | 73.9 |
| 2017 | 72.0 | 72.1 | 72.6 | 73.0 | 72.9 | 73.2 | 73.0 | 72.6 | 72.0 | 72.1 | 72.5 | 72.4 | 72.5 |
| 2018 | 70.2 | 70.5 | 70.9 | 71.6 | 72.1 | 72.8 | 72.4 | 72.2 | 71.9 | 72.0 | 72.2 | 72.0 | 71.7 |
| 2019 | 70.7 | 70.8 | 70.8 | 72.4 | 72.6 | 73.1 | 73.2 | 73.1 | 72.6 | 73.7 | 73.4 | 73.1 | 72.5 |
| **Education and Health Services** | | | | | | | | | | | | | |
| 2011 | 72.0 | 72.5 | 72.5 | 73.0 | 73.2 | 72.8 | 72.1 | 72.6 | 72.8 | 73.9 | 74.2 | 74.2 | 73.0 |
| 2012 | 73.2 | 73.7 | 74.4 | 74.3 | 74.5 | 74.1 | 73.8 | 74.6 | 74.6 | 75.1 | 75.4 | 75.2 | 74.4 |
| 2013 | 74.2 | 74.8 | 74.7 | 74.8 | 74.9 | 74.4 | 73.9 | 74.3 | 74.5 | 75.0 | 75.2 | 75.0 | 74.6 |
| 2014 | 74.0 | 74.8 | 75.4 | 74.8 | 75.1 | 74.2 | 73.8 | 74.5 | 74.8 | 75.7 | 75.9 | 76.2 | 74.9 |
| 2015 | 74.9 | 75.2 | 75.5 | 75.5 | 75.6 | 74.8 | 75.5 | 76.1 | 76.6 | 77.8 | 77.9 | 77.8 | 76.1 |
| 2016 | 76.4 | 76.9 | 77.8 | 77.5 | 77.9 | 77.3 | 78.5 | 78.8 | 79.5 | 80.1 | 79.9 | 79.9 | 78.4 |
| 2017 | 78.4 | 79.2 | 79.6 | 79.3 | 79.7 | 79.0 | 78.7 | 79.0 | 79.3 | 80.1 | 80.2 | 80.0 | 79.4 |
| 2018 | 79.1 | 79.9 | 80.2 | 80.0 | 80.3 | 79.2 | 78.9 | 79.4 | 79.7 | 79.9 | 80.2 | 80.1 | 79.7 |
| 2019 | 78.9 | 79.7 | 79.7 | 79.6 | 80.3 | 79.2 | 79.4 | 79.8 | 79.9 | 80.8 | 80.4 | 81.1 | 79.9 |
| **Leisure and Hospitality** | | | | | | | | | | | | | |
| 2011 | 41.5 | 41.6 | 42.6 | 44.8 | 46.5 | 47.5 | 46.6 | 46.3 | 44.7 | 44.6 | 43.5 | 43.0 | 44.4 |
| 2012 | 42.4 | 42.8 | 44.5 | 46.1 | 47.6 | 48.4 | 48.0 | 47.6 | 45.9 | 45.7 | 44.6 | 44.1 | 45.6 |
| 2013 | 43.4 | 43.5 | 44.8 | 46.3 | 48.4 | 49.0 | 48.7 | 49.0 | 47.6 | 47.3 | 46.3 | 45.6 | 46.7 |
| 2014 | 44.9 | 45.2 | 46.0 | 47.2 | 49.1 | 49.9 | 49.5 | 49.3 | 47.7 | 47.6 | 46.3 | 46.2 | 47.4 |
| 2015 | 45.1 | 45.6 | 46.9 | 48.1 | 50.0 | 51.2 | 50.5 | 50.6 | 49.2 | 48.6 | 47.2 | 47.4 | 48.4 |
| 2016 | 45.8 | 46.2 | 47.3 | 49.0 | 50.6 | 51.4 | 51.3 | 51.3 | 49.9 | 50.1 | 48.5 | 48.1 | 49.1 |
| 2017 | 47.2 | 47.8 | 48.6 | 50.0 | 51.5 | 53.1 | 52.3 | 52.6 | 50.5 | 50.5 | 48.9 | 48.6 | 50.1 |
| 2018 | 47.4 | 47.5 | 48.4 | 50.2 | 52.5 | 53.5 | 52.8 | 53.0 | 51.2 | 51.7 | 50.2 | 50.0 | 50.7 |
| 2019 | 49.0 | 49.0 | 50.0 | 51.3 | 53.6 | 54.8 | 53.9 | 54.2 | 52.3 | 53.3 | 52.1 | 52.5 | 52.2 |
| **Other Services** | | | | | | | | | | | | | |
| 2011 | 17.6 | 17.6 | 17.7 | 17.7 | 17.8 | 17.9 | 17.8 | 17.7 | 17.6 | 17.6 | 17.5 | 17.5 | 17.7 |
| 2012 | 17.5 | 17.4 | 17.6 | 17.8 | 18.1 | 18.2 | 18.1 | 18.1 | 17.9 | 17.8 | 17.7 | 17.7 | 17.8 |
| 2013 | 17.6 | 17.5 | 17.7 | 17.7 | 17.8 | 17.9 | 17.9 | 18.0 | 17.9 | 17.7 | 17.7 | 17.7 | 17.8 |
| 2014 | 17.7 | 17.7 | 17.8 | 18.1 | 18.2 | 18.5 | 18.3 | 18.2 | 18.2 | 18.1 | 18.2 | 18.1 | 18.1 |
| 2015 | 18.0 | 18.1 | 18.1 | 18.2 | 18.3 | 18.4 | 18.5 | 18.4 | 18.1 | 18.3 | 18.3 | 18.3 | 18.3 |
| 2016 | 17.9 | 18.0 | 18.0 | 18.1 | 18.1 | 18.3 | 18.4 | 18.2 | 18.1 | 18.2 | 18.2 | 18.2 | 18.1 |
| 2017 | 18.1 | 18.1 | 18.2 | 18.3 | 18.4 | 18.5 | 18.4 | 18.3 | 18.3 | 18.3 | 18.3 | 18.4 | 18.3 |
| 2018 | 18.2 | 18.3 | 18.3 | 18.4 | 18.5 | 18.6 | 18.6 | 18.5 | 18.4 | 18.7 | 18.6 | 18.4 | 18.5 |
| 2019 | 18.2 | 18.3 | 18.3 | 18.5 | 18.7 | 18.8 | 19.0 | 19.0 | 18.8 | 18.9 | 18.8 | 18.8 | 18.7 |
| **Government** | | | | | | | | | | | | | |
| 2011 | 65.4 | 66.0 | 65.4 | 66.8 | 67.0 | 65.2 | 63.1 | 63.8 | 64.6 | 66.5 | 66.7 | 65.9 | 65.5 |
| 2012 | 65.8 | 66.2 | 65.7 | 66.0 | 66.5 | 63.1 | 62.6 | 63.1 | 64.3 | 65.8 | 65.9 | 65.0 | 65.0 |
| 2013 | 64.8 | 65.4 | 65.1 | 65.7 | 66.4 | 64.8 | 63.1 | 63.4 | 64.4 | 65.7 | 65.9 | 65.0 | 65.0 |
| 2014 | 65.3 | 66.0 | 65.5 | 66.1 | 66.8 | 64.4 | 63.0 | 63.8 | 65.4 | 66.8 | 66.8 | 66.0 | 65.5 |
| 2015 | 65.7 | 66.1 | 65.8 | 66.8 | 67.3 | 65.5 | 63.6 | 64.2 | 65.0 | 66.9 | 67.1 | 66.7 | 65.9 |
| 2016 | 66.1 | 66.6 | 66.6 | 67.2 | 67.8 | 66.4 | 63.4 | 62.9 | 66.1 | 67.3 | 67.2 | 66.4 | 66.2 |
| 2017 | 66.2 | 66.6 | 66.3 | 67.2 | 67.6 | 66.4 | 62.5 | 62.5 | 66.1 | 67.5 | 67.4 | 66.6 | 66.1 |
| 2018 | 66.8 | 67.2 | 67.0 | 67.4 | 67.9 | 66.4 | 62.7 | 63.4 | 66.4 | 67.8 | 67.9 | 67.0 | 66.5 |
| 2019 | 67.1 | 67.3 | 67.0 | 67.7 | 68.1 | 67.2 | 63.9 | 64.3 | 66.6 | 68.1 | 68.6 | 67.9 | 67.0 |

# Employment by Industry: Worcester, MA-CT, 2011–2019

(Numbers in thousands, not seasonally adjusted)

| Industry and year | January | February | March | April | May | June | July | August | September | October | November | December | Annual average |
|---|---|---|---|---|---|---|---|---|---|---|---|---|---|
| **Total Nonfarm** | | | | | | | | | | | | | |
| 2011 | 259.3 | 260.2 | 261.1 | 263.9 | 265.1 | 264.4 | 262.5 | 261.0 | 265.8 | 268.2 | 269.1 | 269.0 | 264.1 |
| 2012 | 261.7 | 261.9 | 264.3 | 265.1 | 266.7 | 268.5 | 264.7 | 264.6 | 268.4 | 270.6 | 271.1 | 270.2 | 266.5 |
| 2013 | 264.6 | 265.1 | 267.1 | 270.6 | 273.1 | 273.5 | 267.1 | 268.4 | 271.3 | 273.6 | 274.5 | 274.7 | 270.3 |
| 2014 | 268.1 | 269.8 | 271.8 | 275.8 | 277.4 | 277.3 | 272.5 | 272.8 | 276.8 | 280.2 | 281.2 | 281.0 | 275.4 |
| 2015 | 272.3 | 273.0 | 275.0 | 278.7 | 282.0 | 281.9 | 276.2 | 276.2 | 279.5 | 283.3 | 284.4 | 284.9 | 279.0 |
| 2016 | 275.6 | 277.8 | 279.4 | 283.7 | 285.8 | 286.0 | 282.4 | 281.7 | 285.8 | 286.8 | 288.4 | 287.7 | 283.4 |
| 2017 | 279.7 | 281.7 | 283.4 | 285.7 | 288.3 | 288.9 | 283.8 | 284.1 | 288.3 | 290.3 | 290.9 | 291.5 | 286.4 |
| 2018 | 281.9 | 284.8 | 285.7 | 288.0 | 290.4 | 290.7 | 285.5 | 285.7 | 289.1 | 292.3 | 294.0 | 293.9 | 288.5 |
| 2019 | 284.4 | 286.8 | 287.8 | 290.8 | 292.6 | 292.4 | 287.2 | 287.0 | 290.2 | 293.1 | 295.0 | 294.7 | 290.2 |
| **Total Private** | | | | | | | | | | | | | |
| 2011 | 218.4 | 218.6 | 219.3 | 222.1 | 223.1 | 223.3 | 224.6 | 223.8 | 225.1 | 226.7 | 227.6 | 227.4 | 223.3 |
| 2012 | 221.1 | 220.5 | 222.4 | 223.7 | 225.2 | 227.2 | 226.8 | 226.8 | 227.0 | 228.7 | 228.7 | 227.7 | 225.5 |
| 2013 | 223.5 | 222.6 | 224.5 | 226.8 | 229.5 | 231.8 | 229.2 | 230.1 | 229.1 | 230.3 | 230.6 | 230.5 | 228.2 |
| 2014 | 226.1 | 225.9 | 227.8 | 231.1 | 233.1 | 235.1 | 234.0 | 234.2 | 233.8 | 236.2 | 236.3 | 236.3 | 232.5 |
| 2015 | 230.3 | 229.1 | 230.6 | 234.0 | 237.5 | 238.6 | 237.6 | 238.0 | 237.0 | 239.3 | 239.9 | 240.3 | 236.0 |
| 2016 | 233.5 | 233.8 | 234.8 | 239.3 | 241.3 | 243.1 | 243.1 | 242.7 | 242.4 | 242.8 | 243.1 | 243.1 | 240.3 |
| 2017 | 237.0 | 237.5 | 239.1 | 241.2 | 243.6 | 245.9 | 244.8 | 245.2 | 244.6 | 245.4 | 245.6 | 245.9 | 243.0 |
| 2018 | 238.6 | 239.8 | 240.8 | 243.1 | 245.2 | 246.9 | 245.9 | 246.3 | 245.3 | 247.4 | 248.1 | 248.3 | 244.6 |
| 2019 | 241.3 | 241.4 | 242.3 | 245.1 | 246.6 | 248.1 | 247.3 | 247.2 | 246.0 | 247.9 | 248.8 | 248.8 | 245.9 |
| **Goods Producing** | | | | | | | | | | | | | |
| 2011 | 35.8 | 35.3 | 35.4 | 36.2 | 37.1 | 37.6 | 38.5 | 38.5 | 38.3 | 38.3 | 38.3 | 38.1 | 37.3 |
| 2012 | 36.0 | 35.6 | 35.9 | 36.4 | 36.6 | 37.0 | 37.1 | 37.1 | 36.9 | 37.0 | 36.7 | 35.9 | 36.5 |
| 2013 | 35.0 | 34.8 | 35.0 | 35.6 | 36.3 | 36.9 | 37.1 | 37.3 | 36.9 | 36.7 | 36.4 | 36.2 | 36.2 |
| 2014 | 35.5 | 35.1 | 35.4 | 35.9 | 36.6 | 37.2 | 37.5 | 37.4 | 37.2 | 37.7 | 37.6 | 37.1 | 36.7 |
| 2015 | 36.4 | 35.8 | 36.0 | 37.0 | 37.9 | 38.4 | 38.6 | 38.5 | 38.1 | 38.5 | 38.4 | 38.2 | 37.7 |
| 2016 | 37.2 | 36.9 | 37.3 | 38.0 | 38.5 | 39.3 | 39.3 | 39.3 | 39.0 | 38.7 | 38.7 | 38.7 | 38.4 |
| 2017 | 37.2 | 36.7 | 37.0 | 37.8 | 38.5 | 39.2 | 39.3 | 39.5 | 39.1 | 39.3 | 39.1 | 38.8 | 38.5 |
| 2018 | 37.9 | 37.8 | 38.0 | 38.8 | 39.4 | 40.1 | 40.4 | 40.2 | 39.9 | 39.8 | 39.7 | 39.7 | 39.3 |
| 2019 | 38.5 | 38.1 | 38.1 | 38.9 | 39.6 | 40.3 | 40.0 | 39.9 | 39.6 | 39.3 | 39.3 | 38.6 | 39.2 |
| **Service-Providing** | | | | | | | | | | | | | |
| 2011 | 223.5 | 224.9 | 225.7 | 227.7 | 228.0 | 226.8 | 224.0 | 222.5 | 227.5 | 229.9 | 230.8 | 230.9 | 226.9 |
| 2012 | 225.7 | 226.3 | 228.4 | 228.7 | 230.1 | 231.5 | 227.6 | 227.5 | 231.5 | 233.6 | 234.4 | 234.3 | 230.0 |
| 2013 | 229.6 | 230.3 | 232.1 | 235.0 | 236.8 | 236.6 | 230.0 | 231.1 | 234.4 | 236.9 | 238.1 | 238.5 | 234.1 |
| 2014 | 232.6 | 234.7 | 236.4 | 239.9 | 240.8 | 240.1 | 235.0 | 235.4 | 239.6 | 242.5 | 243.6 | 243.9 | 238.7 |
| 2015 | 235.9 | 237.2 | 239.0 | 241.7 | 244.1 | 243.5 | 237.6 | 237.7 | 241.4 | 244.8 | 246.0 | 246.7 | 241.3 |
| 2016 | 238.4 | 240.9 | 242.1 | 245.7 | 247.3 | 246.7 | 243.1 | 242.4 | 246.8 | 248.1 | 249.7 | 249.0 | 245.0 |
| 2017 | 242.5 | 245.0 | 246.4 | 247.9 | 249.8 | 249.7 | 244.5 | 244.6 | 249.2 | 251.0 | 251.8 | 252.7 | 247.9 |
| 2018 | 244.0 | 247.0 | 247.7 | 249.2 | 251.0 | 250.6 | 245.1 | 245.5 | 249.2 | 252.5 | 254.3 | 254.2 | 249.2 |
| 2019 | 245.9 | 248.7 | 249.7 | 251.9 | 253.0 | 252.1 | 247.2 | 247.1 | 250.6 | 253.8 | 255.7 | 256.1 | 251.0 |
| **Mining, Logging, and Construction** | | | | | | | | | | | | | |
| 2011 | 7.5 | 7.1 | 7.1 | 8.0 | 8.6 | 9.0 | 9.5 | 9.6 | 9.5 | 9.5 | 9.4 | 9.1 | 8.7 |
| 2012 | 8.2 | 7.8 | 8.1 | 8.7 | 8.9 | 9.2 | 9.5 | 9.6 | 9.4 | 9.3 | 9.2 | 8.9 | 8.9 |
| 2013 | 8.2 | 8.0 | 8.1 | 8.7 | 9.3 | 9.8 | 10.0 | 10.1 | 9.8 | 9.6 | 9.4 | 9.0 | 9.2 |
| 2014 | 8.3 | 8.1 | 8.2 | 8.9 | 9.5 | 10.0 | 10.3 | 10.3 | 10.2 | 10.3 | 10.2 | 9.7 | 9.5 |
| 2015 | 8.9 | 8.5 | 8.6 | 9.4 | 10.2 | 10.5 | 10.7 | 10.7 | 10.4 | 10.7 | 10.6 | 10.3 | 10.0 |
| 2016 | 9.5 | 9.2 | 9.5 | 10.1 | 10.6 | 11.0 | 11.3 | 11.3 | 11.2 | 11.3 | 11.1 | 11.0 | 10.6 |
| 2017 | 10.0 | 9.5 | 9.7 | 10.5 | 11.1 | 11.5 | 11.8 | 11.9 | 11.7 | 11.8 | 11.6 | 11.2 | 11.0 |
| 2018 | 10.4 | 10.3 | 10.4 | 11.1 | 11.6 | 11.9 | 12.2 | 12.1 | 12.0 | 11.7 | 11.5 | 11.2 | 11.4 |
| 2019 | 10.3 | 10.0 | 10.1 | 10.7 | 11.2 | 11.7 | 11.7 | 11.7 | 11.6 | 11.3 | 11.3 | 10.5 | 11.0 |
| **Manufacturing** | | | | | | | | | | | | | |
| 2011 | 28.3 | 28.2 | 28.3 | 28.2 | 28.5 | 28.6 | 29.0 | 28.9 | 28.8 | 28.8 | 28.9 | 29.0 | 28.6 |
| 2012 | 27.8 | 27.8 | 27.8 | 27.7 | 27.7 | 27.8 | 27.6 | 27.5 | 27.5 | 27.7 | 27.5 | 27.0 | 27.6 |
| 2013 | 26.8 | 26.8 | 26.9 | 26.9 | 27.0 | 27.1 | 27.1 | 27.2 | 27.1 | 27.1 | 27.0 | 27.2 | 27.0 |
| 2014 | 27.2 | 27.0 | 27.2 | 27.0 | 27.1 | 27.2 | 27.2 | 27.1 | 27.0 | 27.4 | 27.4 | 27.4 | 27.2 |
| 2015 | 27.5 | 27.3 | 27.4 | 27.6 | 27.7 | 27.9 | 27.9 | 27.8 | 27.7 | 27.8 | 27.8 | 27.9 | 27.7 |
| 2016 | 27.7 | 27.7 | 27.8 | 27.9 | 27.9 | 28.3 | 28.0 | 28.0 | 27.8 | 27.4 | 27.6 | 27.7 | 27.8 |
| 2017 | 27.2 | 27.2 | 27.3 | 27.3 | 27.4 | 27.7 | 27.5 | 27.6 | 27.4 | 27.5 | 27.5 | 27.6 | 27.4 |
| 2018 | 27.5 | 27.5 | 27.6 | 27.7 | 27.8 | 28.2 | 28.2 | 28.1 | 27.9 | 28.1 | 28.2 | 28.5 | 27.9 |
| 2019 | 28.2 | 28.1 | 28.0 | 28.2 | 28.4 | 28.6 | 28.3 | 28.2 | 28.0 | 28.0 | 28.0 | 28.1 | 28.2 |

## Employment by Industry: Worcester, MA-CT, 2011–2019—*Continued*

(Numbers in thousands, not seasonally adjusted)

| Industry and year | January | February | March | April | May | June | July | August | September | October | November | December | Annual average |
|---|---|---|---|---|---|---|---|---|---|---|---|---|---|
| **Trade, Transportation, and Utilities** | | | | | | | | | | | | | |
| 2011 | 49.2 | 48.7 | 48.8 | 49.0 | 49.3 | 49.3 | 48.8 | 48.8 | 49.4 | 50.5 | 51.2 | 51.9 | 49.6 |
| 2012 | 50.0 | 49.3 | 49.5 | 49.8 | 50.4 | 50.7 | 50.1 | 50.2 | 50.8 | 51.5 | 52.2 | 52.2 | 50.6 |
| 2013 | 50.5 | 49.8 | 50.1 | 50.9 | 51.8 | 52.4 | 51.3 | 51.4 | 51.7 | 52.2 | 53.3 | 53.7 | 51.6 |
| 2014 | 52.1 | 51.5 | 51.8 | 52.3 | 52.8 | 53.2 | 52.7 | 52.6 | 53.1 | 53.5 | 54.4 | 55.1 | 52.9 |
| 2015 | 52.2 | 51.3 | 51.6 | 52.1 | 52.7 | 53.1 | 52.4 | 52.6 | 52.6 | 53.2 | 54.1 | 54.7 | 52.7 |
| 2016 | 52.6 | 52.0 | 52.1 | 53.1 | 53.4 | 54.0 | 53.2 | 53.1 | 53.1 | 53.5 | 54.3 | 55.1 | 53.3 |
| 2017 | 53.4 | 52.7 | 52.7 | 53.0 | 53.5 | 54.0 | 53.3 | 53.4 | 53.2 | 53.6 | 54.3 | 54.8 | 53.5 |
| 2018 | 53.4 | 52.6 | 52.5 | 52.7 | 53.1 | 53.7 | 52.5 | 52.7 | 52.5 | 53.0 | 54.0 | 54.8 | 53.1 |
| 2019 | 52.6 | 51.8 | 51.9 | 52.2 | 52.6 | 53.1 | 52.4 | 52.4 | 52.5 | 53.0 | 53.9 | 54.3 | 52.7 |
| **Wholesale Trade** | | | | | | | | | | | | | |
| 2011 | 9.7 | 9.6 | 9.6 | 9.7 | 9.8 | 9.8 | 9.8 | 9.7 | 9.7 | 9.9 | 9.9 | 9.9 | 9.8 |
| 2012 | 9.9 | 9.8 | 9.9 | 10.0 | 10.1 | 10.2 | 10.2 | 10.2 | 10.2 | 10.5 | 10.5 | 10.3 | 10.2 |
| 2013 | 10.2 | 10.1 | 10.2 | 10.2 | 10.3 | 10.4 | 10.4 | 10.4 | 10.4 | 10.5 | 10.5 | 10.5 | 10.3 |
| 2014 | 10.4 | 10.3 | 10.4 | 10.5 | 10.6 | 10.7 | 10.7 | 10.7 | 10.6 | 10.6 | 10.6 | 10.5 | 10.6 |
| 2015 | 10.3 | 10.2 | 10.3 | 10.5 | 10.5 | 10.5 | 10.4 | 10.4 | 10.3 | 10.4 | 10.4 | 10.4 | 10.4 |
| 2016 | 10.2 | 10.2 | 10.2 | 10.4 | 10.4 | 10.5 | 10.5 | 10.5 | 10.4 | 10.5 | 10.4 | 10.4 | 10.4 |
| 2017 | 10.3 | 10.3 | 10.3 | 10.3 | 10.3 | 10.3 | 10.3 | 10.3 | 10.1 | 10.2 | 10.1 | 10.1 | 10.2 |
| 2018 | 10.1 | 10.0 | 10.0 | 10.0 | 10.0 | 10.0 | 9.7 | 9.7 | 9.5 | 9.6 | 9.6 | 9.6 | 9.8 |
| 2019 | 9.4 | 9.3 | 9.3 | 9.4 | 9.4 | 9.4 | 9.4 | 9.3 | 9.2 | 9.3 | 9.3 | 9.4 | 9.3 |
| **Retail Trade** | | | | | | | | | | | | | |
| 2011 | 29.0 | 28.5 | 28.5 | 28.8 | 28.9 | 29.0 | 28.9 | 29.0 | 29.1 | 29.8 | 30.4 | 30.9 | 29.2 |
| 2012 | 29.6 | 29.0 | 29.0 | 29.1 | 29.5 | 29.7 | 29.6 | 29.7 | 29.7 | 30.0 | 30.7 | 30.7 | 29.7 |
| 2013 | 29.5 | 28.9 | 29.0 | 29.6 | 30.3 | 30.5 | 30.0 | 30.1 | 29.9 | 30.3 | 31.1 | 31.3 | 30.0 |
| 2014 | 30.4 | 29.7 | 29.8 | 30.2 | 30.4 | 30.5 | 30.4 | 30.3 | 30.4 | 30.7 | 31.3 | 31.5 | 30.5 |
| 2015 | 30.2 | 29.4 | 29.5 | 29.8 | 30.3 | 30.6 | 30.3 | 30.5 | 30.0 | 30.5 | 31.1 | 31.3 | 30.3 |
| 2016 | 30.1 | 29.5 | 29.6 | 30.1 | 30.3 | 30.7 | 30.3 | 30.3 | 29.8 | 30.1 | 30.9 | 31.1 | 30.2 |
| 2017 | 30.1 | 29.5 | 29.5 | 29.8 | 30.1 | 30.5 | 30.2 | 30.3 | 29.8 | 30.1 | 30.7 | 30.9 | 30.1 |
| 2018 | 30.1 | 29.5 | 29.4 | 29.6 | 29.9 | 30.2 | 29.8 | 29.9 | 29.4 | 29.6 | 30.3 | 30.6 | 29.9 |
| 2019 | 29.6 | 28.9 | 29.0 | 29.0 | 29.3 | 29.6 | 29.4 | 29.5 | 29.2 | 29.5 | 30.0 | 30.1 | 29.4 |
| **Transportation and Utilities** | | | | | | | | | | | | | |
| 2011 | 10.5 | 10.6 | 10.7 | 10.5 | 10.6 | 10.5 | 10.1 | 10.1 | 10.6 | 10.8 | 10.9 | 11.1 | 10.6 |
| 2012 | 10.5 | 10.5 | 10.6 | 10.7 | 10.8 | 10.8 | 10.3 | 10.3 | 10.9 | 11.0 | 11.0 | 11.2 | 10.7 |
| 2013 | 10.8 | 10.8 | 10.9 | 11.1 | 11.2 | 11.5 | 10.9 | 10.9 | 11.4 | 11.4 | 11.7 | 11.9 | 11.2 |
| 2014 | 11.3 | 11.5 | 11.6 | 11.6 | 11.8 | 12.0 | 11.6 | 11.6 | 12.1 | 12.2 | 12.5 | 13.1 | 11.9 |
| 2015 | 11.7 | 11.7 | 11.8 | 11.8 | 11.9 | 12.0 | 11.7 | 11.7 | 12.3 | 12.3 | 12.6 | 13.0 | 12.0 |
| 2016 | 12.3 | 12.3 | 12.3 | 12.6 | 12.7 | 12.8 | 12.4 | 12.3 | 12.9 | 12.9 | 13.0 | 13.6 | 12.7 |
| 2017 | 13.0 | 12.9 | 12.9 | 12.9 | 13.1 | 13.2 | 12.8 | 12.8 | 13.3 | 13.3 | 13.5 | 13.8 | 13.1 |
| 2018 | 13.2 | 13.1 | 13.1 | 13.1 | 13.2 | 13.5 | 13.0 | 13.1 | 13.6 | 13.8 | 14.1 | 14.6 | 13.5 |
| 2019 | 13.6 | 13.6 | 13.6 | 13.8 | 13.9 | 14.1 | 13.6 | 13.6 | 14.1 | 14.2 | 14.6 | 14.8 | 14.0 |
| **Information** | | | | | | | | | | | | | |
| 2011 | 3.6 | 3.6 | 3.6 | 3.6 | 3.6 | 3.6 | 3.7 | 3.4 | 3.6 | 3.7 | 3.6 | 3.6 | 3.6 |
| 2012 | 3.6 | 3.6 | 3.6 | 3.6 | 3.7 | 3.7 | 3.7 | 3.8 | 3.7 | 3.6 | 3.7 | 3.7 | 3.7 |
| 2013 | 3.7 | 3.6 | 3.7 | 3.7 | 3.7 | 3.8 | 3.7 | 3.7 | 3.5 | 3.5 | 3.7 | 3.7 | 3.7 |
| 2014 | 3.7 | 3.7 | 3.7 | 3.6 | 3.7 | 3.8 | 3.8 | 3.8 | 3.7 | 3.7 | 3.7 | 3.8 | 3.7 |
| 2015 | 3.8 | 3.8 | 3.8 | 3.9 | 3.9 | 3.9 | 3.9 | 3.9 | 3.9 | 3.9 | 3.9 | 4.0 | 3.9 |
| 2016 | 4.0 | 4.0 | 3.9 | 3.9 | 3.7 | 4.0 | 4.0 | 3.9 | 3.8 | 3.8 | 3.7 | 3.7 | 3.9 |
| 2017 | 3.8 | 3.8 | 3.7 | 3.7 | 3.7 | 3.8 | 3.7 | 3.7 | 3.7 | 3.7 | 3.6 | 3.7 | 3.7 |
| 2018 | 3.6 | 3.6 | 3.6 | 3.6 | 3.6 | 3.7 | 3.6 | 3.6 | 3.4 | 3.5 | 3.5 | 3.6 | 3.6 |
| 2019 | 3.4 | 3.4 | 3.4 | 3.3 | 3.3 | 3.4 | 3.3 | 3.3 | 3.1 | 3.2 | 3.2 | 3.2 | 3.3 |
| **Financial Activities** | | | | | | | | | | | | | |
| 2011 | 14.7 | 14.7 | 14.7 | 14.7 | 14.7 | 14.7 | 14.9 | 14.9 | 14.9 | 15.0 | 15.0 | 15.0 | 14.8 |
| 2012 | 14.9 | 14.9 | 14.9 | 14.9 | 15.0 | 15.0 | 15.1 | 15.0 | 14.9 | 15.0 | 14.9 | 14.9 | 15.0 |
| 2013 | 14.8 | 14.8 | 14.8 | 14.8 | 14.8 | 15.0 | 14.9 | 14.9 | 14.8 | 14.8 | 14.8 | 14.8 | 14.8 |
| 2014 | 14.7 | 14.7 | 14.8 | 14.9 | 15.0 | 15.1 | 15.2 | 15.2 | 15.0 | 15.0 | 15.0 | 15.0 | 15.0 |
| 2015 | 14.8 | 14.8 | 14.8 | 14.9 | 15.0 | 15.0 | 15.2 | 15.2 | 14.9 | 15.0 | 14.9 | 14.9 | 15.0 |
| 2016 | 14.8 | 14.8 | 14.7 | 14.8 | 14.9 | 15.0 | 15.0 | 15.0 | 14.8 | 14.8 | 14.8 | 14.8 | 14.9 |
| 2017 | 14.7 | 14.7 | 14.6 | 14.8 | 14.9 | 15.1 | 14.9 | 14.9 | 14.7 | 14.7 | 14.6 | 14.6 | 14.8 |
| 2018 | 14.5 | 14.5 | 14.5 | 14.6 | 14.7 | 14.8 | 14.9 | 14.9 | 14.6 | 14.6 | 14.5 | 14.5 | 14.6 |
| 2019 | 14.4 | 14.4 | 14.4 | 14.4 | 14.4 | 14.5 | 14.5 | 14.5 | 14.3 | 14.3 | 14.4 | 14.4 | 14.4 |

# Employment by Industry: Worcester, MA-CT, 2011–2019—*Continued*

(Numbers in thousands, not seasonally adjusted)

| Industry and year | January | February | March | April | May | June | July | August | September | October | November | December | Annual average |
|---|---|---|---|---|---|---|---|---|---|---|---|---|---|
| **Professional and Business Services** | | | | | | | | | | | | | |
| 2011 | 26.9 | 27.0 | 26.7 | 27.9 | 27.5 | 27.6 | 27.7 | 27.3 | 27.3 | 27.1 | 27.9 | 26.8 | 27.3 |
| 2012 | 25.8 | 25.4 | 25.8 | 26.1 | 26.0 | 26.5 | 26.4 | 26.5 | 26.0 | 26.3 | 26.2 | 25.9 | 26.1 |
| 2013 | 25.3 | 25.3 | 25.6 | 26.1 | 26.4 | 26.5 | 26.2 | 26.4 | 26.0 | 26.1 | 25.9 | 25.5 | 25.9 |
| 2014 | 25.4 | 25.5 | 25.5 | 26.4 | 26.5 | 26.8 | 26.3 | 26.5 | 26.4 | 26.5 | 26.4 | 26.1 | 26.2 |
| 2015 | 25.8 | 25.8 | 25.6 | 26.0 | 26.3 | 26.6 | 26.8 | 27.0 | 26.9 | 27.0 | 27.2 | 27.2 | 26.5 |
| 2016 | 26.1 | 26.4 | 26.4 | 27.5 | 27.8 | 28.1 | 28.4 | 28.4 | 28.3 | 28.4 | 28.4 | 28.2 | 27.7 |
| 2017 | 27.1 | 27.6 | 27.8 | 27.9 | 27.9 | 28.4 | 28.8 | 28.9 | 29.1 | 28.5 | 28.6 | 28.5 | 28.3 |
| 2018 | 27.5 | 27.7 | 28.1 | 28.4 | 28.8 | 29.3 | 29.5 | 29.6 | 29.5 | 29.9 | 30.3 | 29.5 | 29.0 |
| 2019 | 27.8 | 28.2 | 28.1 | 28.8 | 28.9 | 29.1 | 29.2 | 29.5 | 29.1 | 29.1 | 29.0 | 28.8 | 28.8 |
| **Education and Health Services** | | | | | | | | | | | | | |
| 2011 | 58.5 | 59.5 | 59.9 | 59.4 | 59.0 | 57.9 | 58.4 | 58.4 | 59.8 | 60.4 | 60.6 | 60.7 | 59.4 |
| 2012 | 60.0 | 61.0 | 61.6 | 61.4 | 61.1 | 60.6 | 60.7 | 60.6 | 61.9 | 62.7 | 63.0 | 63.0 | 61.5 |
| 2013 | 62.3 | 62.9 | 63.4 | 62.7 | 62.6 | 62.1 | 61.3 | 61.5 | 62.2 | 62.9 | 63.1 | 63.4 | 62.5 |
| 2014 | 61.9 | 62.9 | 63.6 | 64.1 | 63.8 | 63.2 | 62.8 | 62.9 | 63.8 | 64.8 | 65.0 | 65.0 | 63.7 |
| 2015 | 63.6 | 64.5 | 65.0 | 65.4 | 65.7 | 65.0 | 64.2 | 64.1 | 65.5 | 66.7 | 67.0 | 66.9 | 65.3 |
| 2016 | 65.0 | 65.9 | 66.2 | 66.7 | 66.6 | 65.3 | 65.3 | 65.2 | 66.8 | 67.6 | 67.7 | 67.6 | 66.3 |
| 2017 | 66.1 | 67.6 | 68.1 | 68.4 | 68.4 | 67.3 | 66.8 | 66.7 | 68.2 | 68.7 | 68.9 | 69.1 | 67.9 |
| 2018 | 66.5 | 68.5 | 68.5 | 68.7 | 68.5 | 67.4 | 67.2 | 67.4 | 68.8 | 69.8 | 70.2 | 70.3 | 68.5 |
| 2019 | 69.3 | 70.5 | 71.0 | 71.1 | 70.7 | 69.8 | 69.8 | 69.8 | 71.0 | 72.3 | 72.6 | 72.2 | 70.8 |
| **Leisure and Hospitality** | | | | | | | | | | | | | |
| 2011 | 21.2 | 21.2 | 21.4 | 22.4 | 23.0 | 23.5 | 23.4 | 23.4 | 23.0 | 22.9 | 22.2 | 22.4 | 22.5 |
| 2012 | 22.0 | 21.9 | 22.3 | 22.5 | 23.3 | 24.3 | 24.1 | 24.0 | 23.5 | 23.1 | 22.4 | 22.4 | 23.0 |
| 2013 | 22.2 | 21.9 | 22.2 | 23.1 | 23.9 | 24.7 | 24.0 | 24.3 | 23.9 | 24.0 | 23.3 | 23.0 | 23.4 |
| 2014 | 22.8 | 22.5 | 22.9 | 23.6 | 24.3 | 25.1 | 24.8 | 24.9 | 24.3 | 24.7 | 23.9 | 23.8 | 24.0 |
| 2015 | 23.4 | 23.0 | 23.5 | 24.3 | 25.4 | 25.7 | 25.3 | 25.5 | 24.6 | 24.4 | 23.8 | 23.8 | 24.4 |
| 2016 | 23.4 | 23.4 | 23.5 | 24.5 | 25.5 | 26.1 | 26.5 | 26.4 | 25.8 | 25.3 | 24.7 | 24.2 | 24.9 |
| 2017 | 24.2 | 23.9 | 24.5 | 24.9 | 25.8 | 26.9 | 26.6 | 26.7 | 25.8 | 26.0 | 25.6 | 25.5 | 25.5 |
| 2018 | 24.7 | 24.6 | 24.9 | 25.5 | 26.2 | 26.7 | 26.4 | 26.5 | 25.8 | 25.9 | 25.0 | 25.0 | 25.6 |
| 2019 | 24.8 | 24.5 | 24.7 | 25.6 | 26.2 | 26.7 | 26.6 | 26.4 | 25.6 | 25.8 | 25.6 | 26.5 | 25.8 |
| **Other Services** | | | | | | | | | | | | | |
| 2011 | 8.5 | 8.6 | 8.8 | 8.9 | 8.9 | 9.1 | 9.2 | 9.1 | 8.8 | 8.8 | 8.8 | 8.9 | 8.9 |
| 2012 | 8.8 | 8.8 | 8.8 | 9.0 | 9.1 | 9.4 | 9.6 | 9.6 | 9.3 | 9.5 | 9.6 | 9.7 | 9.3 |
| 2013 | 9.7 | 9.5 | 9.7 | 9.9 | 10.0 | 10.4 | 10.7 | 10.6 | 10.1 | 10.1 | 10.1 | 10.2 | 10.1 |
| 2014 | 10.0 | 10.0 | 10.1 | 10.3 | 10.4 | 10.7 | 10.9 | 10.9 | 10.3 | 10.3 | 10.3 | 10.4 | 10.4 |
| 2015 | 10.3 | 10.1 | 10.3 | 10.4 | 10.6 | 10.9 | 11.2 | 11.2 | 10.5 | 10.6 | 10.6 | 10.6 | 10.6 |
| 2016 | 10.4 | 10.4 | 10.7 | 10.8 | 10.9 | 11.3 | 11.4 | 11.4 | 10.8 | 10.7 | 10.8 | 10.8 | 10.9 |
| 2017 | 10.5 | 10.5 | 10.7 | 10.7 | 10.9 | 11.2 | 11.4 | 11.4 | 10.8 | 10.9 | 10.9 | 10.9 | 10.9 |
| 2018 | 10.5 | 10.5 | 10.7 | 10.8 | 10.9 | 11.2 | 11.4 | 11.4 | 10.8 | 10.9 | 10.9 | 10.9 | 10.9 |
| 2019 | 10.5 | 10.5 | 10.7 | 10.8 | 10.9 | 11.2 | 11.5 | 11.4 | 10.8 | 10.9 | 10.8 | 10.8 | 10.9 |
| **Government** | | | | | | | | | | | | | |
| 2011 | 40.9 | 41.6 | 41.8 | 41.8 | 42.0 | 41.1 | 37.9 | 37.2 | 40.7 | 41.5 | 41.5 | 41.6 | 40.8 |
| 2012 | 40.6 | 41.4 | 41.9 | 41.4 | 41.5 | 41.3 | 37.9 | 37.8 | 41.4 | 41.9 | 42.4 | 42.5 | 41.0 |
| 2013 | 41.1 | 42.5 | 42.6 | 43.8 | 43.6 | 41.7 | 37.9 | 38.3 | 42.2 | 43.3 | 43.9 | 44.2 | 42.1 |
| 2014 | 42.0 | 43.9 | 44.0 | 44.7 | 44.3 | 42.2 | 38.5 | 38.6 | 43.0 | 44.0 | 44.9 | 44.7 | 42.9 |
| 2015 | 42.0 | 43.9 | 44.4 | 44.7 | 44.5 | 43.3 | 38.6 | 38.2 | 42.5 | 44.0 | 44.5 | 44.6 | 42.9 |
| 2016 | 42.1 | 44.0 | 44.6 | 44.4 | 44.5 | 42.9 | 39.3 | 39.0 | 43.4 | 44.0 | 45.3 | 44.6 | 43.2 |
| 2017 | 42.7 | 44.2 | 44.3 | 44.5 | 44.7 | 43.0 | 39.0 | 38.9 | 43.7 | 44.9 | 45.3 | 45.6 | 43.4 |
| 2018 | 43.3 | 45.0 | 44.9 | 44.9 | 45.2 | 43.8 | 39.6 | 39.4 | 43.8 | 44.9 | 45.9 | 45.6 | 43.9 |
| 2019 | 43.1 | 45.4 | 45.5 | 45.7 | 46.0 | 44.3 | 39.9 | 39.8 | 44.2 | 45.2 | 46.2 | 45.9 | 44.3 |

## Employment by Industry: Bridgeport-Stamford-Norwalk, CT NECTA, 2011–2019

(Numbers in thousands, not seasonally adjusted)

| Industry and year | January | February | March | April | May | June | July | August | September | October | November | December | Annual average |
|---|---|---|---|---|---|---|---|---|---|---|---|---|---|
| **Total Nonfarm** | | | | | | | | | | | | | |
| 2011 | 383.6 | 385.5 | 387.1 | 393.0 | 395.3 | 397.2 | 397.3 | 393.3 | 395.1 | 396.6 | 397.9 | 400.3 | 393.5 |
| 2012 | 389.4 | 389.8 | 393.3 | 396.0 | 399.3 | 403.6 | 402.1 | 398.5 | 399.2 | 400.4 | 402.2 | 405.0 | 398.2 |
| 2013 | 392.3 | 391.5 | 395.2 | 401.1 | 404.4 | 409.7 | 407.6 | 403.9 | 404.5 | 405.6 | 407.8 | 407.9 | 402.6 |
| 2014 | 396.1 | 395.0 | 398.2 | 404.1 | 408.0 | 410.7 | 409.4 | 407.1 | 407.2 | 409.7 | 412.8 | 414.2 | 406.0 |
| 2015 | 401.5 | 399.9 | 401.5 | 407.0 | 412.4 | 417.4 | 413.4 | 410.3 | 410.1 | 414.0 | 415.9 | 416.8 | 410.0 |
| 2016 | 404.0 | 402.9 | 406.1 | 409.0 | 412.9 | 418.0 | 415.8 | 411.6 | 411.2 | 412.1 | 413.3 | 412.8 | 410.8 |
| 2017 | 401.8 | 399.8 | 402.0 | 404.7 | 409.6 | 415.8 | 413.0 | 408.5 | 408.5 | 408.9 | 411.3 | 412.1 | 408.0 |
| 2018 | 400.4 | 400.8 | 402.2 | 404.6 | 410.1 | 416.5 | 412.7 | 408.4 | 408.9 | 410.1 | 412.4 | 413.3 | 408.4 |
| 2019 | 398.6 | 399.0 | 400.2 | 404.4 | 408.4 | 413.3 | 409.8 | 404.5 | 405.7 | 406.1 | 408.7 | 410.6 | 405.8 |
| **Total Private** | | | | | | | | | | | | | |
| 2011 | 339.8 | 340.0 | 341.5 | 346.8 | 349.6 | 353.2 | 355.8 | 353.2 | 350.3 | 350.9 | 352.1 | 354.4 | 349.0 |
| 2012 | 345.7 | 344.8 | 348.0 | 350.6 | 354.2 | 359.7 | 359.5 | 357.2 | 354.1 | 354.9 | 356.3 | 359.2 | 353.7 |
| 2013 | 348.1 | 346.1 | 349.6 | 355.5 | 359.2 | 364.6 | 364.4 | 362.2 | 359.5 | 359.8 | 361.6 | 362.0 | 357.7 |
| 2014 | 352.1 | 349.9 | 352.8 | 358.0 | 362.0 | 366.1 | 366.7 | 364.4 | 361.8 | 363.5 | 366.0 | 367.8 | 360.9 |
| 2015 | 357.1 | 354.8 | 356.1 | 361.1 | 366.8 | 371.6 | 370.3 | 368.0 | 364.7 | 368.2 | 369.7 | 371.0 | 365.0 |
| 2016 | 359.6 | 357.7 | 360.7 | 363.7 | 367.3 | 372.8 | 373.0 | 369.9 | 366.3 | 367.0 | 367.7 | 367.8 | 366.1 |
| 2017 | 357.7 | 354.9 | 356.8 | 360.1 | 364.4 | 370.9 | 370.7 | 367.0 | 364.1 | 364.0 | 366.3 | 367.7 | 363.7 |
| 2018 | 356.7 | 356.4 | 357.5 | 360.4 | 365.0 | 371.4 | 370.3 | 366.9 | 364.3 | 365.6 | 367.2 | 368.7 | 364.2 |
| 2019 | 354.9 | 354.6 | 355.8 | 360.3 | 363.6 | 368.9 | 367.9 | 363.4 | 360.9 | 361.3 | 363.3 | 365.8 | 361.7 |
| **Goods Producing** | | | | | | | | | | | | | |
| 2011 | 42.6 | 42.5 | 42.8 | 43.7 | 44.3 | 44.8 | 44.8 | 44.6 | 44.2 | 44.1 | 43.9 | 43.9 | 43.9 |
| 2012 | 42.6 | 42.5 | 42.4 | 42.6 | 42.9 | 43.7 | 43.6 | 43.4 | 42.9 | 42.8 | 42.8 | 42.8 | 42.9 |
| 2013 | 41.5 | 41.3 | 41.3 | 42.2 | 42.7 | 43.4 | 43.1 | 43.1 | 42.9 | 42.8 | 42.8 | 42.4 | 42.5 |
| 2014 | 41.1 | 40.9 | 41.0 | 41.8 | 42.2 | 42.6 | 42.6 | 42.5 | 42.1 | 42.5 | 42.3 | 41.9 | 42.0 |
| 2015 | 40.6 | 40.1 | 40.2 | 41.2 | 42.1 | 42.6 | 42.5 | 42.5 | 42.3 | 42.4 | 42.2 | 41.9 | 41.7 |
| 2016 | 40.7 | 40.5 | 40.8 | 41.5 | 42.0 | 42.5 | 42.6 | 42.5 | 42.0 | 42.0 | 41.8 | 41.4 | 41.7 |
| 2017 | 40.5 | 40.2 | 40.3 | 41.4 | 41.9 | 42.6 | 42.5 | 42.3 | 41.8 | 41.9 | 41.7 | 41.5 | 41.6 |
| 2018 | 39.8 | 39.9 | 39.9 | 40.9 | 41.6 | 42.3 | 42.5 | 42.4 | 41.9 | 42.0 | 42.1 | 41.9 | 41.4 |
| 2019 | 40.2 | 40.4 | 40.5 | 41.7 | 42.2 | 42.8 | 43.0 | 42.6 | 42.1 | 42.0 | 42.1 | 41.1 | 41.7 |
| **Service-Providing** | | | | | | | | | | | | | |
| 2011 | 341.0 | 343.0 | 344.3 | 349.3 | 351.0 | 352.4 | 352.5 | 348.7 | 350.9 | 352.5 | 354.0 | 356.4 | 349.7 |
| 2012 | 346.8 | 347.3 | 350.9 | 353.4 | 356.4 | 359.9 | 358.5 | 355.1 | 356.3 | 357.6 | 359.4 | 362.2 | 355.3 |
| 2013 | 350.8 | 350.2 | 353.9 | 358.9 | 361.7 | 366.3 | 364.5 | 360.8 | 361.6 | 362.8 | 365.0 | 365.5 | 360.2 |
| 2014 | 355.0 | 354.1 | 357.2 | 362.3 | 365.8 | 368.1 | 366.8 | 364.6 | 365.1 | 367.2 | 370.5 | 372.3 | 364.1 |
| 2015 | 360.9 | 359.8 | 361.3 | 365.8 | 370.3 | 374.8 | 370.9 | 367.8 | 367.8 | 371.6 | 373.7 | 374.9 | 368.3 |
| 2016 | 363.3 | 362.4 | 365.3 | 367.5 | 370.9 | 375.5 | 373.2 | 369.1 | 369.2 | 370.1 | 371.5 | 371.4 | 369.1 |
| 2017 | 361.3 | 359.6 | 361.7 | 363.3 | 367.7 | 373.2 | 370.5 | 366.2 | 366.7 | 367.0 | 369.6 | 370.6 | 366.5 |
| 2018 | 360.6 | 360.9 | 362.3 | 363.7 | 368.5 | 374.2 | 370.2 | 366.0 | 367.0 | 368.1 | 370.3 | 371.4 | 366.9 |
| 2019 | 358.4 | 358.6 | 359.7 | 362.7 | 366.2 | 370.5 | 366.8 | 361.9 | 363.6 | 364.1 | 366.6 | 369.5 | 364.1 |
| **Mining, Logging, and Construction** | | | | | | | | | | | | | |
| 2011 | 9.7 | 9.6 | 9.8 | 10.8 | 11.3 | 11.6 | 11.8 | 11.8 | 11.7 | 11.7 | 11.6 | 11.4 | 11.1 |
| 2012 | 10.4 | 10.3 | 10.5 | 11.2 | 11.5 | 11.9 | 12.1 | 11.9 | 11.7 | 11.6 | 11.6 | 11.5 | 11.4 |
| 2013 | 10.5 | 10.2 | 10.3 | 11.3 | 11.7 | 12.0 | 12.2 | 12.3 | 12.2 | 12.1 | 12.1 | 11.6 | 11.5 |
| 2014 | 10.4 | 10.2 | 10.5 | 11.6 | 12.2 | 12.5 | 12.7 | 12.7 | 12.6 | 12.7 | 12.6 | 12.2 | 11.9 |
| 2015 | 11.0 | 10.6 | 10.7 | 11.9 | 12.6 | 12.8 | 12.8 | 12.9 | 12.9 | 13.0 | 12.8 | 12.5 | 12.2 |
| 2016 | 11.4 | 11.1 | 11.5 | 12.3 | 12.7 | 12.9 | 13.0 | 13.0 | 12.9 | 12.9 | 12.7 | 12.2 | 12.4 |
| 2017 | 11.2 | 11.0 | 11.1 | 12.3 | 12.8 | 13.2 | 13.2 | 13.2 | 13.1 | 13.1 | 12.9 | 12.4 | 12.5 |
| 2018 | 11.1 | 11.1 | 11.3 | 12.2 | 12.8 | 13.2 | 13.2 | 13.3 | 13.2 | 13.2 | 13.2 | 12.9 | 12.6 |
| 2019 | 11.4 | 11.5 | 11.7 | 12.9 | 13.3 | 13.6 | 13.8 | 13.7 | 13.5 | 13.4 | 13.4 | 12.4 | 12.9 |
| **Manufacturing** | | | | | | | | | | | | | |
| 2011 | 32.9 | 32.9 | 33.0 | 32.9 | 33.0 | 33.2 | 33.0 | 32.8 | 32.5 | 32.4 | 32.3 | 32.5 | 32.8 |
| 2012 | 32.2 | 32.2 | 31.9 | 31.4 | 31.4 | 31.8 | 31.5 | 31.5 | 31.2 | 31.2 | 31.2 | 31.3 | 31.6 |
| 2013 | 31.0 | 31.1 | 31.0 | 30.9 | 31.0 | 31.4 | 30.9 | 30.8 | 30.7 | 30.7 | 30.7 | 30.8 | 30.9 |
| 2014 | 30.7 | 30.7 | 30.5 | 30.2 | 30.0 | 30.1 | 29.9 | 29.8 | 29.5 | 29.8 | 29.7 | 29.7 | 30.1 |
| 2015 | 29.6 | 29.5 | 29.5 | 29.3 | 29.5 | 29.8 | 29.7 | 29.6 | 29.4 | 29.4 | 29.4 | 29.4 | 29.5 |
| 2016 | 29.3 | 29.4 | 29.3 | 29.2 | 29.3 | 29.6 | 29.6 | 29.5 | 29.1 | 29.1 | 29.1 | 29.2 | 29.3 |
| 2017 | 29.3 | 29.2 | 29.2 | 29.1 | 29.1 | 29.4 | 29.3 | 29.1 | 28.7 | 28.8 | 28.8 | 29.1 | 29.1 |
| 2018 | 28.7 | 28.8 | 28.6 | 28.7 | 28.8 | 29.1 | 29.3 | 29.1 | 28.7 | 28.8 | 28.9 | 29.0 | 28.9 |
| 2019 | 28.8 | 28.9 | 28.8 | 28.8 | 28.9 | 29.2 | 29.2 | 28.9 | 28.6 | 28.6 | 28.7 | 28.7 | 28.8 |

# Employment by Industry: Bridgeport-Stamford-Norwalk, CT NECTA, 2011–2019—*Continued*

(Numbers in thousands, not seasonally adjusted)

| Industry and year | January | February | March | April | May | June | July | August | September | October | November | December | Annual average |
|---|---|---|---|---|---|---|---|---|---|---|---|---|---|
| **Trade, Transportation, and Utilities** | | | | | | | | | | | | | |
| 2011 | 69.0 | 68.0 | 67.8 | 68.7 | 69.2 | 69.9 | 69.0 | 68.6 | 68.4 | 69.0 | 70.7 | 72.6 | 69.2 |
| 2012 | 69.8 | 68.2 | 68.7 | 68.5 | 69.4 | 70.3 | 69.0 | 68.8 | 68.8 | 69.5 | 71.4 | 72.7 | 69.6 |
| 2013 | 70.0 | 68.5 | 69.1 | 69.4 | 69.9 | 70.7 | 69.7 | 69.6 | 69.7 | 70.3 | 72.1 | 73.6 | 70.2 |
| 2014 | 70.8 | 69.3 | 69.5 | 69.6 | 70.2 | 71.0 | 69.8 | 69.5 | 69.8 | 70.7 | 72.6 | 74.1 | 70.6 |
| 2015 | 70.9 | 69.4 | 69.6 | 69.5 | 70.6 | 71.5 | 70.0 | 69.8 | 70.3 | 71.4 | 73.3 | 74.8 | 70.9 |
| 2016 | 71.0 | 69.7 | 70.1 | 70.2 | 71.1 | 71.5 | 70.3 | 69.7 | 70.4 | 70.7 | 72.5 | 73.8 | 70.9 |
| 2017 | 71.1 | 69.5 | 69.4 | 69.4 | 70.3 | 71.1 | 69.8 | 69.2 | 69.7 | 70.2 | 72.4 | 73.7 | 70.5 |
| 2018 | 70.0 | 68.7 | 68.6 | 68.0 | 69.4 | 70.0 | 68.6 | 68.1 | 68.7 | 69.0 | 71.1 | 72.1 | 69.4 |
| 2019 | 68.3 | 66.8 | 66.5 | 66.6 | 67.0 | 67.4 | 66.4 | 66.0 | 66.2 | 66.7 | 68.7 | 70.4 | 67.3 |
| **Wholesale Trade** | | | | | | | | | | | | | |
| 2011 | 13.0 | 13.0 | 13.0 | 13.2 | 13.2 | 13.3 | 13.3 | 13.3 | 13.1 | 13.1 | 13.0 | 13.1 | 13.1 |
| 2012 | 12.9 | 12.9 | 13.0 | 12.9 | 12.9 | 13.1 | 13.1 | 13.1 | 13.0 | 13.1 | 13.1 | 13.1 | 13.0 |
| 2013 | 13.0 | 13.0 | 13.1 | 13.1 | 13.1 | 13.2 | 13.3 | 13.2 | 13.1 | 13.2 | 13.2 | 13.3 | 13.2 |
| 2014 | 13.2 | 13.2 | 13.2 | 13.2 | 13.2 | 13.3 | 13.2 | 13.2 | 13.1 | 13.1 | 13.1 | 13.2 | 13.2 |
| 2015 | 13.0 | 13.0 | 13.1 | 13.1 | 13.2 | 13.3 | 13.2 | 13.2 | 13.1 | 13.2 | 13.1 | 13.1 | 13.1 |
| 2016 | 12.8 | 12.8 | 12.9 | 13.0 | 13.2 | 13.3 | 13.3 | 13.2 | 13.1 | 13.1 | 13.1 | 13.2 | 13.1 |
| 2017 | 13.0 | 13.0 | 13.0 | 13.0 | 13.0 | 13.4 | 13.4 | 13.5 | 13.4 | 13.4 | 13.4 | 13.6 | 13.3 |
| 2018 | 13.3 | 13.4 | 13.5 | 13.4 | 13.4 | 13.5 | 13.4 | 13.4 | 13.2 | 13.2 | 13.1 | 13.2 | 13.3 |
| 2019 | 12.6 | 12.6 | 12.6 | 12.6 | 12.7 | 12.8 | 12.7 | 12.7 | 12.5 | 12.5 | 12.5 | 12.6 | 12.6 |
| **Retail Trade** | | | | | | | | | | | | | |
| 2011 | 46.4 | 45.4 | 45.2 | 45.8 | 46.2 | 46.7 | 46.4 | 46.2 | 45.6 | 46.2 | 47.9 | 49.3 | 46.4 |
| 2012 | 47.1 | 45.5 | 45.9 | 45.8 | 46.5 | 47.2 | 46.7 | 46.6 | 46.1 | 46.6 | 48.4 | 49.3 | 46.8 |
| 2013 | 47.3 | 46.0 | 46.3 | 46.5 | 47.0 | 47.6 | 47.2 | 47.3 | 46.6 | 47.2 | 48.9 | 50.0 | 47.3 |
| 2014 | 47.7 | 46.3 | 46.5 | 46.7 | 47.2 | 47.9 | 47.5 | 47.3 | 46.9 | 47.7 | 49.3 | 50.3 | 47.6 |
| 2015 | 47.9 | 46.7 | 46.8 | 46.7 | 47.5 | 48.2 | 47.4 | 47.5 | 47.1 | 48.0 | 49.8 | 50.8 | 47.9 |
| 2016 | 48.2 | 47.0 | 47.2 | 47.2 | 47.7 | 48.1 | 47.7 | 47.4 | 47.0 | 47.4 | 48.9 | 49.7 | 47.8 |
| 2017 | 48.1 | 46.7 | 46.6 | 46.8 | 47.4 | 47.8 | 47.6 | 47.2 | 46.6 | 47.1 | 49.0 | 49.6 | 47.5 |
| 2018 | 47.3 | 46.0 | 45.8 | 45.9 | 46.6 | 47.0 | 46.6 | 46.4 | 46.1 | 46.5 | 48.3 | 48.8 | 46.8 |
| 2019 | 46.5 | 45.2 | 44.9 | 45.0 | 45.2 | 45.5 | 45.2 | 45.1 | 44.6 | 45.0 | 46.5 | 47.1 | 45.5 |
| **Transportation and Utilities** | | | | | | | | | | | | | |
| 2011 | 9.6 | 9.6 | 9.6 | 9.7 | 9.8 | 9.9 | 9.3 | 9.1 | 9.7 | 9.7 | 9.8 | 10.2 | 9.7 |
| 2012 | 9.8 | 9.8 | 9.8 | 9.8 | 10.0 | 10.0 | 9.2 | 9.1 | 9.7 | 9.8 | 9.9 | 10.3 | 9.8 |
| 2013 | 9.7 | 9.5 | 9.7 | 9.8 | 9.8 | 9.9 | 9.2 | 9.1 | 10.0 | 9.9 | 10.0 | 10.3 | 9.7 |
| 2014 | 9.9 | 9.8 | 9.8 | 9.7 | 9.8 | 9.8 | 9.1 | 9.0 | 9.8 | 9.9 | 10.2 | 10.6 | 9.8 |
| 2015 | 10.0 | 9.7 | 9.7 | 9.7 | 9.9 | 10.0 | 9.4 | 9.1 | 10.1 | 10.2 | 10.4 | 10.9 | 9.9 |
| 2016 | 10.0 | 9.9 | 10.0 | 10.0 | 10.2 | 10.1 | 9.3 | 9.1 | 10.3 | 10.2 | 10.5 | 10.9 | 10.0 |
| 2017 | 10.0 | 9.8 | 9.8 | 9.6 | 9.9 | 9.9 | 8.8 | 8.5 | 9.7 | 9.7 | 10.0 | 10.5 | 9.7 |
| 2018 | 9.4 | 9.3 | 9.3 | 8.7 | 9.4 | 9.5 | 8.6 | 8.3 | 9.4 | 9.3 | 9.7 | 10.1 | 9.3 |
| 2019 | 9.2 | 9.0 | 9.0 | 9.0 | 9.1 | 9.1 | 8.5 | 8.2 | 9.1 | 9.2 | 9.7 | 10.7 | 9.2 |
| **Information** | | | | | | | | | | | | | |
| 2011 | 10.3 | 10.3 | 10.3 | 10.3 | 10.3 | 10.3 | 10.5 | 10.5 | 10.4 | 10.4 | 10.5 | 10.7 | 10.4 |
| 2012 | 10.6 | 10.6 | 10.5 | 10.6 | 10.5 | 10.6 | 10.6 | 10.7 | 10.6 | 10.6 | 10.7 | 10.8 | 10.6 |
| 2013 | 10.9 | 11.2 | 11.2 | 11.1 | 11.3 | 11.5 | 11.7 | 11.5 | 11.5 | 11.4 | 11.5 | 11.5 | 11.4 |
| 2014 | 11.4 | 11.4 | 11.5 | 11.5 | 11.5 | 11.5 | 11.6 | 11.6 | 11.5 | 11.4 | 12.1 | 12.2 | 11.6 |
| 2015 | 12.0 | 12.0 | 12.0 | 12.1 | 12.1 | 12.2 | 12.2 | 12.3 | 12.2 | 12.2 | 12.3 | 12.3 | 12.2 |
| 2016 | 12.4 | 12.4 | 12.4 | 12.5 | 12.5 | 12.6 | 12.8 | 13.2 | 12.8 | 12.8 | 12.8 | 12.4 | 12.6 |
| 2017 | 12.1 | 12.3 | 12.3 | 12.3 | 12.0 | 12.3 | 12.3 | 12.3 | 12.2 | 12.3 | 12.5 | 12.5 | 12.3 |
| 2018 | 12.8 | 12.9 | 12.8 | 12.8 | 12.7 | 12.8 | 12.7 | 12.8 | 12.8 | 12.9 | 13.0 | 13.0 | 12.8 |
| 2019 | 12.8 | 12.9 | 12.8 | 12.9 | 12.9 | 13.1 | 13.1 | 13.0 | 12.9 | 13.0 | 13.0 | 13.0 | 13.0 |
| **Financial Activities** | | | | | | | | | | | | | |
| 2011 | 42.4 | 42.4 | 42.4 | 42.4 | 42.3 | 42.3 | 43.2 | 43.0 | 42.1 | 42.1 | 42.1 | 42.1 | 42.4 |
| 2012 | 41.7 | 41.6 | 41.6 | 41.5 | 41.6 | 42.2 | 42.3 | 42.0 | 41.4 | 41.5 | 41.4 | 41.5 | 41.7 |
| 2013 | 41.4 | 41.2 | 41.2 | 41.1 | 41.3 | 41.9 | 42.1 | 41.9 | 41.4 | 41.3 | 41.4 | 41.5 | 41.5 |
| 2014 | 40.3 | 40.2 | 40.3 | 40.2 | 40.4 | 41.1 | 41.4 | 41.3 | 40.8 | 40.9 | 41.0 | 41.3 | 40.8 |
| 2015 | 40.9 | 40.9 | 41.0 | 41.0 | 41.1 | 41.8 | 41.9 | 41.7 | 41.0 | 41.1 | 41.1 | 41.2 | 41.2 |
| 2016 | 41.0 | 40.8 | 41.0 | 40.8 | 40.8 | 41.2 | 41.4 | 41.1 | 40.5 | 40.6 | 40.7 | 40.6 | 40.9 |
| 2017 | 40.2 | 39.9 | 39.9 | 39.8 | 39.9 | 40.4 | 40.6 | 40.3 | 39.6 | 39.6 | 39.4 | 39.6 | 39.9 |
| 2018 | 39.1 | 38.9 | 38.9 | 38.5 | 38.5 | 39.2 | 39.2 | 39.0 | 38.5 | 38.5 | 38.5 | 38.7 | 38.8 |
| 2019 | 37.7 | 37.6 | 37.5 | 37.2 | 37.4 | 37.7 | 38.1 | 38.0 | 37.3 | 37.3 | 37.3 | 37.8 | 37.6 |

## Employment by Industry: Bridgeport-Stamford-Norwalk, CT NECTA, 2011–2019—*Continued*

(Numbers in thousands, not seasonally adjusted)

| Industry and year | January | February | March | April | May | June | July | August | September | October | November | December | Annual average |
|---|---|---|---|---|---|---|---|---|---|---|---|---|---|
| **Professional and Business Services** | | | | | | | | | | | | | |
| 2011 | 63.9 | 64.6 | 65.1 | 66.6 | 66.9 | 67.4 | 68.0 | 67.6 | 67.3 | 67.5 | 67.4 | 67.2 | 66.6 |
| 2012 | 65.7 | 65.8 | 67.2 | 68.5 | 68.7 | 69.4 | 69.6 | 69.4 | 68.9 | 68.4 | 68.2 | 68.0 | 68.2 |
| 2013 | 65.3 | 65.5 | 66.0 | 68.1 | 68.6 | 69.5 | 69.6 | 69.8 | 69.0 | 68.9 | 68.5 | 67.9 | 68.1 |
| 2014 | 65.6 | 65.7 | 66.1 | 68.2 | 68.7 | 69.2 | 69.5 | 69.5 | 68.7 | 68.6 | 68.8 | 68.3 | 68.1 |
| 2015 | 66.2 | 66.2 | 66.1 | 68.1 | 68.8 | 69.3 | 69.5 | 69.6 | 68.6 | 69.9 | 69.9 | 69.4 | 68.5 |
| 2016 | 66.7 | 66.5 | 67.1 | 68.5 | 68.4 | 69.5 | 69.4 | 69.0 | 68.1 | 68.0 | 67.4 | 67.1 | 68.0 |
| 2017 | 64.1 | 63.8 | 64.2 | 65.0 | 65.3 | 66.3 | 66.4 | 66.4 | 65.9 | 65.9 | 66.0 | 65.8 | 65.4 |
| 2018 | 63.5 | 63.5 | 63.9 | 65.5 | 66.0 | 67.2 | 67.3 | 67.2 | 66.4 | 66.6 | 66.3 | 65.7 | 65.8 |
| 2019 | 63.7 | 64.0 | 64.3 | 66.5 | 66.7 | 67.6 | 67.7 | 67.3 | 66.4 | 66.8 | 67.4 | 68.0 | 66.4 |
| **Education and Health Services** | | | | | | | | | | | | | |
| 2011 | 65.2 | 65.7 | 65.9 | 66.2 | 66.1 | 65.6 | 65.6 | 64.9 | 65.9 | 66.3 | 66.9 | 67.1 | 66.0 |
| 2012 | 66.5 | 67.1 | 67.5 | 67.5 | 67.5 | 67.2 | 67.0 | 66.4 | 67.5 | 68.2 | 68.6 | 69.3 | 67.5 |
| 2013 | 67.6 | 67.7 | 68.4 | 69.3 | 69.3 | 69.0 | 68.4 | 67.5 | 68.6 | 69.4 | 69.9 | 69.4 | 68.7 |
| 2014 | 69.4 | 69.4 | 69.9 | 70.5 | 70.9 | 70.2 | 70.4 | 69.4 | 70.6 | 71.3 | 71.6 | 72.0 | 70.5 |
| 2015 | 71.3 | 71.3 | 71.5 | 71.7 | 72.2 | 71.9 | 71.1 | 70.3 | 70.9 | 72.2 | 72.5 | 72.4 | 71.6 |
| 2016 | 71.6 | 71.8 | 72.0 | 71.9 | 72.3 | 71.9 | 71.8 | 71.1 | 72.2 | 73.0 | 73.2 | 73.3 | 72.2 |
| 2017 | 72.7 | 72.9 | 73.1 | 73.7 | 74.2 | 73.9 | 73.6 | 72.7 | 74.0 | 73.8 | 74.3 | 74.4 | 73.6 |
| 2018 | 73.4 | 74.8 | 74.9 | 74.8 | 74.9 | 74.5 | 74.3 | 73.4 | 74.6 | 75.2 | 75.3 | 75.7 | 74.7 |
| 2019 | 74.1 | 75.2 | 75.2 | 75.1 | 75.3 | 74.8 | 73.7 | 72.5 | 74.5 | 74.9 | 75.0 | 75.6 | 74.7 |
| **Leisure and Hospitality** | | | | | | | | | | | | | |
| 2011 | 30.7 | 30.8 | 31.4 | 33.0 | 34.4 | 36.6 | 37.9 | 37.4 | 36.0 | 35.6 | 34.6 | 34.7 | 34.4 |
| 2012 | 32.8 | 32.9 | 34.0 | 35.2 | 37.2 | 39.5 | 40.3 | 39.6 | 37.7 | 37.5 | 36.8 | 37.6 | 36.8 |
| 2013 | 35.3 | 34.7 | 36.2 | 37.9 | 39.5 | 41.7 | 42.6 | 41.7 | 39.8 | 39.1 | 38.8 | 39.1 | 38.9 |
| 2014 | 37.1 | 36.7 | 38.0 | 39.6 | 41.2 | 43.4 | 44.0 | 43.3 | 41.5 | 41.2 | 40.6 | 40.8 | 40.6 |
| 2015 | 38.3 | 38.0 | 38.8 | 40.6 | 42.7 | 44.8 | 45.4 | 44.1 | 42.0 | 41.6 | 41.1 | 41.5 | 41.6 |
| 2016 | 39.0 | 38.8 | 40.0 | 40.9 | 42.6 | 45.3 | 46.2 | 45.1 | 42.7 | 42.3 | 41.7 | 41.6 | 42.2 |
| 2017 | 39.6 | 39.0 | 40.1 | 40.9 | 42.9 | 45.9 | 46.8 | 45.5 | 43.1 | 42.6 | 42.3 | 42.4 | 42.6 |
| 2018 | 40.7 | 40.4 | 41.1 | 42.2 | 44.0 | 47.0 | 47.2 | 45.8 | 43.8 | 43.7 | 43.0 | 43.6 | 43.5 |
| 2019 | 40.7 | 40.3 | 41.4 | 42.6 | 44.2 | 47.2 | 47.4 | 45.9 | 44.0 | 43.1 | 42.2 | 42.3 | 43.4 |
| **Other Services** | | | | | | | | | | | | | |
| 2011 | 15.7 | 15.7 | 15.8 | 15.9 | 16.1 | 16.3 | 16.8 | 16.6 | 16.0 | 15.9 | 16.0 | 16.1 | 16.1 |
| 2012 | 16.0 | 16.1 | 16.1 | 16.2 | 16.4 | 16.8 | 17.1 | 16.9 | 16.3 | 16.4 | 16.4 | 16.5 | 16.4 |
| 2013 | 16.1 | 16.0 | 16.2 | 16.4 | 16.6 | 16.9 | 17.2 | 17.1 | 16.6 | 16.6 | 16.6 | 16.6 | 16.6 |
| 2014 | 16.4 | 16.3 | 16.5 | 16.6 | 16.9 | 17.1 | 17.4 | 17.3 | 16.8 | 16.9 | 17.0 | 17.2 | 16.9 |
| 2015 | 16.9 | 16.9 | 16.9 | 16.9 | 17.2 | 17.5 | 17.7 | 17.7 | 17.4 | 17.4 | 17.3 | 17.5 | 17.3 |
| 2016 | 17.2 | 17.2 | 17.3 | 17.4 | 17.6 | 18.3 | 18.5 | 18.2 | 17.6 | 17.6 | 17.6 | 17.6 | 17.7 |
| 2017 | 17.4 | 17.3 | 17.5 | 17.6 | 17.9 | 18.4 | 18.7 | 18.3 | 17.8 | 17.7 | 17.7 | 17.8 | 17.8 |
| 2018 | 17.4 | 17.3 | 17.4 | 17.7 | 17.9 | 18.4 | 18.5 | 18.2 | 17.6 | 17.7 | 17.9 | 18.0 | 17.8 |
| 2019 | 17.4 | 17.4 | 17.6 | 17.7 | 17.9 | 18.3 | 18.5 | 18.1 | 17.5 | 17.5 | 17.6 | 17.6 | 17.8 |
| **Government** | | | | | | | | | | | | | |
| 2011 | 43.8 | 45.5 | 45.6 | 46.2 | 45.7 | 44.0 | 41.5 | 40.1 | 44.8 | 45.7 | 45.8 | 45.9 | 44.6 |
| 2012 | 43.7 | 45.0 | 45.3 | 45.4 | 45.1 | 43.9 | 42.6 | 41.3 | 45.1 | 45.5 | 45.9 | 45.8 | 44.6 |
| 2013 | 44.2 | 45.4 | 45.6 | 45.6 | 45.2 | 45.1 | 43.2 | 41.7 | 45.0 | 45.8 | 46.2 | 45.9 | 44.9 |
| 2014 | 44.0 | 45.1 | 45.4 | 46.1 | 46.0 | 44.6 | 42.7 | 42.7 | 45.4 | 46.2 | 46.8 | 46.4 | 45.1 |
| 2015 | 44.4 | 45.1 | 45.4 | 45.9 | 45.6 | 45.8 | 43.1 | 42.3 | 45.4 | 45.8 | 46.2 | 45.8 | 45.1 |
| 2016 | 44.4 | 45.2 | 45.4 | 45.3 | 45.6 | 45.2 | 42.8 | 41.7 | 44.9 | 45.1 | 45.6 | 45.0 | 44.7 |
| 2017 | 44.1 | 44.9 | 45.2 | 44.6 | 45.2 | 44.9 | 42.3 | 41.5 | 44.4 | 44.9 | 45.0 | 44.4 | 44.3 |
| 2018 | 43.7 | 44.4 | 44.7 | 44.2 | 45.1 | 45.1 | 42.4 | 41.5 | 44.6 | 44.5 | 45.2 | 44.6 | 44.2 |
| 2019 | 43.7 | 44.4 | 44.4 | 44.1 | 44.8 | 44.4 | 41.9 | 41.1 | 44.8 | 44.8 | 45.4 | 44.8 | 44.1 |

# Employment by Industry: Greenville-Anderson-Mauldin, SC, 2011–2019

(Numbers in thousands, not seasonally adjusted)

| Industry and year | January | February | March | April | May | June | July | August | September | October | November | December | Annual average |
|---|---|---|---|---|---|---|---|---|---|---|---|---|---|
| **Total Nonfarm** | | | | | | | | | | | | | |
| 2011 | 351.0 | 357.1 | 360.9 | 363.6 | 364.6 | 362.2 | 360.6 | 363.0 | 365.1 | 365.6 | 367.8 | 367.5 | 362.4 |
| 2012 | 360.8 | 363.6 | 366.8 | 367.5 | 370.8 | 369.8 | 364.9 | 367.5 | 370.3 | 370.6 | 374.8 | 375.1 | 368.5 |
| 2013 | 368.3 | 371.2 | 373.9 | 375.3 | 379.0 | 381.2 | 376.7 | 380.0 | 384.0 | 386.3 | 388.0 | 388.7 | 379.4 |
| 2014 | 378.6 | 380.3 | 385.2 | 386.8 | 389.5 | 389.4 | 384.3 | 387.7 | 390.7 | 393.8 | 397.1 | 398.6 | 388.5 |
| 2015 | 390.8 | 393.1 | 395.2 | 398.3 | 401.8 | 403.1 | 400.7 | 403.0 | 404.2 | 408.8 | 410.1 | 411.6 | 401.7 |
| 2016 | 401.3 | 404.3 | 406.4 | 409.4 | 410.4 | 409.3 | 407.3 | 409.4 | 410.7 | 412.7 | 415.1 | 415.5 | 409.3 |
| 2017 | 407.9 | 411.5 | 412.8 | 415.2 | 417.1 | 416.7 | 413.2 | 416.1 | 417.6 | 420.9 | 425.1 | 426.0 | 416.7 |
| 2018 | 419.5 | 422.5 | 424.4 | 427.9 | 428.8 | 429.4 | 425.2 | 427.8 | 428.0 | 432.5 | 435.8 | 435.7 | 428.1 |
| 2019 | 428.0 | 429.8 | 431.0 | 432.5 | 434.1 | 433.6 | 431.9 | 432.5 | 433.5 | 436.7 | 437.7 | 437.7 | 433.3 |
| **Total Private** | | | | | | | | | | | | | |
| 2011 | 295.7 | 301.5 | 305.3 | 307.7 | 308.6 | 307.1 | 307.0 | 309.8 | 309.8 | 309.6 | 311.6 | 311.4 | 307.1 |
| 2012 | 304.8 | 307.2 | 310.3 | 311.0 | 313.8 | 313.7 | 311.0 | 313.2 | 313.7 | 313.2 | 317.1 | 317.5 | 312.2 |
| 2013 | 311.0 | 313.7 | 316.0 | 317.2 | 321.1 | 323.6 | 321.7 | 324.6 | 326.5 | 327.9 | 329.7 | 330.3 | 321.9 |
| 2014 | 320.8 | 322.1 | 326.8 | 328.4 | 330.7 | 331.4 | 328.7 | 331.4 | 332.4 | 334.6 | 337.7 | 339.1 | 330.3 |
| 2015 | 332.1 | 333.8 | 335.6 | 338.6 | 341.9 | 343.8 | 343.9 | 345.5 | 344.7 | 348.4 | 349.7 | 350.9 | 342.4 |
| 2016 | 341.6 | 344.4 | 346.0 | 348.9 | 349.8 | 349.4 | 349.9 | 351.3 | 350.7 | 352.0 | 354.2 | 354.4 | 349.4 |
| 2017 | 347.8 | 351.1 | 352.0 | 354.1 | 355.8 | 356.1 | 354.8 | 356.8 | 356.4 | 359.0 | 362.9 | 363.7 | 355.9 |
| 2018 | 358.0 | 360.5 | 362.0 | 365.0 | 366.2 | 367.7 | 366.0 | 368.0 | 366.1 | 370.2 | 373.0 | 373.1 | 366.3 |
| 2019 | 365.6 | 366.9 | 367.9 | 368.8 | 370.7 | 370.7 | 370.8 | 370.7 | 369.6 | 372.4 | 372.9 | 373.0 | 370.0 |
| **Goods Producing** | | | | | | | | | | | | | |
| 2011 | 61.5 | 63.1 | 63.5 | 63.9 | 64.1 | 64.3 | 64.4 | 64.7 | 64.3 | 64.4 | 64.6 | 64.5 | 63.9 |
| 2012 | 64.0 | 64.3 | 64.8 | 64.9 | 65.4 | 65.3 | 65.1 | 65.6 | 65.6 | 66.0 | 66.3 | 66.4 | 65.3 |
| 2013 | 66.2 | 66.9 | 67.5 | 67.5 | 68.1 | 68.5 | 68.2 | 68.8 | 69.0 | 69.2 | 69.5 | 69.6 | 68.3 |
| 2014 | 68.8 | 69.0 | 69.7 | 69.9 | 70.5 | 70.9 | 70.3 | 70.7 | 70.6 | 70.6 | 70.9 | 71.2 | 70.3 |
| 2015 | 70.7 | 70.7 | 71.0 | 71.3 | 72.1 | 72.8 | 72.9 | 72.9 | 72.9 | 73.2 | 73.1 | 73.4 | 72.3 |
| 2016 | 73.3 | 73.5 | 73.9 | 74.5 | 75.0 | 75.3 | 76.0 | 76.0 | 75.6 | 75.6 | 76.1 | 76.4 | 75.1 |
| 2017 | 75.6 | 75.9 | 75.9 | 75.8 | 75.9 | 76.5 | 76.2 | 76.2 | 75.9 | 76.0 | 76.2 | 76.7 | 76.1 |
| 2018 | 76.3 | 76.7 | 76.7 | 77.2 | 77.3 | 78.0 | 77.7 | 77.6 | 77.3 | 77.4 | 77.4 | 77.7 | 77.3 |
| 2019 | 76.9 | 76.8 | 76.9 | 77.1 | 76.9 | 77.1 | 77.3 | 77.1 | 76.7 | 77.3 | 77.5 | 77.4 | 77.1 |
| **Service-Providing** | | | | | | | | | | | | | |
| 2011 | 289.5 | 294.0 | 297.4 | 299.7 | 300.5 | 297.9 | 296.2 | 298.3 | 300.8 | 301.2 | 303.2 | 303.0 | 298.5 |
| 2012 | 296.8 | 299.3 | 302.0 | 302.6 | 305.4 | 304.5 | 299.8 | 301.9 | 304.7 | 304.6 | 308.5 | 308.7 | 303.2 |
| 2013 | 302.1 | 304.3 | 306.4 | 307.8 | 310.9 | 312.7 | 308.5 | 311.2 | 315.0 | 317.1 | 318.5 | 319.1 | 311.1 |
| 2014 | 309.8 | 311.3 | 315.5 | 316.9 | 319.0 | 318.5 | 314.0 | 317.0 | 320.1 | 323.2 | 326.2 | 327.4 | 318.2 |
| 2015 | 320.1 | 322.4 | 324.2 | 327.0 | 329.7 | 330.3 | 327.8 | 330.1 | 331.3 | 335.6 | 337.0 | 338.2 | 329.5 |
| 2016 | 328.0 | 330.8 | 332.5 | 334.9 | 335.4 | 334.0 | 331.3 | 333.4 | 335.1 | 337.1 | 339.0 | 339.1 | 334.2 |
| 2017 | 332.3 | 335.6 | 336.9 | 339.4 | 341.2 | 340.2 | 337.0 | 339.9 | 341.7 | 344.9 | 348.9 | 349.3 | 340.6 |
| 2018 | 343.2 | 345.8 | 347.7 | 350.7 | 351.5 | 351.4 | 347.5 | 350.2 | 350.7 | 355.1 | 358.4 | 358.0 | 350.9 |
| 2019 | 351.1 | 353.0 | 354.1 | 355.4 | 357.2 | 356.5 | 354.6 | 355.4 | 356.8 | 359.4 | 360.2 | 360.3 | 356.2 |
| **Mining, Logging, and Construction** | | | | | | | | | | | | | |
| 2011 | 13.4 | 14.2 | 14.3 | 14.4 | 14.6 | 14.6 | 14.5 | 14.5 | 14.3 | 14.2 | 14.4 | 14.3 | 14.3 |
| 2012 | 14.1 | 14.3 | 14.6 | 14.4 | 14.7 | 14.7 | 14.6 | 14.7 | 14.6 | 14.8 | 14.9 | 14.9 | 14.6 |
| 2013 | 14.7 | 14.8 | 15.1 | 15.2 | 15.5 | 15.7 | 15.8 | 15.9 | 15.9 | 16.0 | 16.2 | 16.3 | 15.6 |
| 2014 | 15.7 | 15.7 | 16.1 | 16.1 | 16.3 | 16.5 | 16.1 | 16.4 | 16.3 | 16.3 | 16.5 | 16.6 | 16.2 |
| 2015 | 16.1 | 16.1 | 16.2 | 16.3 | 16.7 | 17.1 | 17.0 | 17.0 | 16.9 | 17.0 | 17.0 | 17.0 | 16.7 |
| 2016 | 17.0 | 17.2 | 17.5 | 17.8 | 18.2 | 18.4 | 18.7 | 18.6 | 18.3 | 18.2 | 18.3 | 18.3 | 18.0 |
| 2017 | 17.8 | 18.0 | 17.9 | 18.2 | 18.3 | 18.6 | 18.3 | 18.3 | 18.1 | 18.2 | 18.2 | 18.4 | 18.2 |
| 2018 | 18.4 | 18.6 | 18.7 | 18.9 | 18.9 | 19.1 | 19.0 | 18.9 | 18.8 | 18.8 | 18.8 | 18.9 | 18.8 |
| 2019 | 18.7 | 18.7 | 18.8 | 19.0 | 19.2 | 19.4 | 19.5 | 19.4 | 19.3 | 19.5 | 19.4 | 19.4 | 19.2 |
| **Manufacturing** | | | | | | | | | | | | | |
| 2011 | 48.1 | 48.9 | 49.2 | 49.5 | 49.5 | 49.7 | 49.9 | 50.2 | 50.0 | 50.2 | 50.2 | 50.2 | 49.6 |
| 2012 | 49.9 | 50.0 | 50.2 | 50.5 | 50.7 | 50.6 | 50.5 | 50.9 | 51.0 | 51.2 | 51.4 | 51.5 | 50.7 |
| 2013 | 51.5 | 52.1 | 52.4 | 52.3 | 52.6 | 52.8 | 52.4 | 52.9 | 53.1 | 53.2 | 53.3 | 53.3 | 52.7 |
| 2014 | 53.1 | 53.3 | 53.6 | 53.8 | 54.2 | 54.4 | 54.2 | 54.3 | 54.3 | 54.3 | 54.4 | 54.6 | 54.0 |
| 2015 | 54.6 | 54.6 | 54.8 | 55.0 | 55.4 | 55.7 | 55.9 | 55.9 | 56.0 | 56.2 | 56.1 | 56.4 | 55.6 |
| 2016 | 56.3 | 56.3 | 56.4 | 56.7 | 56.8 | 56.9 | 57.3 | 57.4 | 57.3 | 57.4 | 57.8 | 58.1 | 57.1 |
| 2017 | 57.8 | 57.9 | 58.0 | 57.6 | 57.6 | 57.9 | 57.9 | 57.9 | 57.8 | 57.8 | 58.0 | 58.3 | 57.9 |
| 2018 | 57.9 | 58.1 | 58.0 | 58.3 | 58.4 | 58.9 | 58.7 | 58.7 | 58.5 | 58.6 | 58.6 | 58.8 | 58.5 |
| 2019 | 58.2 | 58.1 | 58.1 | 58.1 | 57.7 | 57.7 | 57.8 | 57.7 | 57.4 | 57.8 | 58.1 | 58.0 | 57.9 |

## Employment by Industry: Greenville-Anderson-Mauldin, SC, 2011–2019—*Continued*

(Numbers in thousands, not seasonally adjusted)

| Industry and year | January | February | March | April | May | June | July | August | September | October | November | December | Annual average |
|---|---|---|---|---|---|---|---|---|---|---|---|---|---|
| **Trade, Transportation, and Utilities** | | | | | | | | | | | | | |
| 2011 | 67.6 | 68.2 | 68.8 | 69.0 | 69.2 | 69.3 | 69.3 | 69.4 | 69.0 | 69.2 | 70.4 | 70.9 | 69.2 |
| 2012 | 68.8 | 68.6 | 69.1 | 69.3 | 69.6 | 69.6 | 69.5 | 69.5 | 69.3 | 69.6 | 71.3 | 71.4 | 69.6 |
| 2013 | 68.5 | 68.5 | 69.3 | 69.6 | 70.2 | 70.7 | 70.6 | 71.2 | 70.8 | 71.5 | 72.9 | 73.6 | 70.6 |
| 2014 | 70.2 | 70.1 | 70.5 | 70.8 | 71.3 | 71.9 | 71.5 | 71.9 | 71.7 | 72.8 | 74.3 | 75.3 | 71.9 |
| 2015 | 73.1 | 72.9 | 73.5 | 74.2 | 74.6 | 74.7 | 74.9 | 75.1 | 74.6 | 75.6 | 77.2 | 77.6 | 74.8 |
| 2016 | 74.6 | 74.6 | 74.3 | 74.6 | 75.0 | 74.9 | 75.0 | 75.1 | 75.1 | 75.8 | 77.1 | 78.1 | 75.4 |
| 2017 | 75.6 | 75.7 | 75.5 | 75.2 | 75.3 | 75.3 | 75.4 | 75.7 | 75.1 | 75.8 | 77.8 | 78.8 | 75.9 |
| 2018 | 76.4 | 76.3 | 76.4 | 76.6 | 77.0 | 77.2 | 77.1 | 77.3 | 76.8 | 77.5 | 79.2 | 79.6 | 77.3 |
| 2019 | 77.0 | 76.7 | 76.8 | 76.6 | 77.3 | 77.6 | 77.8 | 77.5 | 77.3 | 78.6 | 79.7 | 79.9 | 77.7 |
| **Wholesale Trade** | | | | | | | | | | | | | |
| 2011 | 16.8 | 16.9 | 17.1 | 17.0 | 17.0 | 17.1 | 17.2 | 17.2 | 17.2 | 17.2 | 17.2 | 17.3 | 17.1 |
| 2012 | 17.1 | 17.1 | 17.2 | 17.3 | 17.3 | 17.4 | 17.4 | 17.5 | 17.2 | 17.3 | 17.3 | 17.4 | 17.3 |
| 2013 | 17.1 | 17.2 | 17.2 | 17.3 | 17.5 | 17.5 | 17.5 | 17.7 | 17.5 | 17.6 | 17.7 | 17.7 | 17.5 |
| 2014 | 17.1 | 17.1 | 17.1 | 17.2 | 17.4 | 17.6 | 17.6 | 17.7 | 17.7 | 18.2 | 18.3 | 18.4 | 17.6 |
| 2015 | 18.7 | 18.7 | 18.9 | 19.0 | 19.1 | 19.1 | 19.1 | 19.1 | 19.1 | 19.3 | 19.3 | 19.4 | 19.1 |
| 2016 | 19.0 | 19.0 | 18.9 | 18.9 | 18.8 | 18.9 | 18.8 | 18.8 | 18.7 | 18.8 | 18.9 | 19.0 | 18.9 |
| 2017 | 18.6 | 18.6 | 18.6 | 18.5 | 18.5 | 18.6 | 18.7 | 18.7 | 18.5 | 18.2 | 18.2 | 18.4 | 18.5 |
| 2018 | 17.9 | 18.0 | 17.9 | 18.3 | 18.3 | 18.5 | 18.4 | 18.5 | 18.4 | 18.6 | 18.6 | 18.8 | 18.4 |
| 2019 | 18.5 | 18.6 | 18.6 | 18.7 | 19.1 | 19.2 | 19.3 | 19.2 | 19.1 | 19.2 | 19.3 | 19.3 | 19.0 |
| **Retail Trade** | | | | | | | | | | | | | |
| 2011 | 40.0 | 40.3 | 40.7 | 40.9 | 40.9 | 40.8 | 40.9 | 41.0 | 40.7 | 40.9 | 42.0 | 42.4 | 41.0 |
| 2012 | 40.7 | 40.6 | 40.8 | 40.7 | 41.0 | 40.9 | 40.8 | 40.8 | 40.8 | 40.9 | 42.6 | 42.6 | 41.1 |
| 2013 | 40.4 | 40.2 | 41.0 | 41.2 | 41.5 | 41.9 | 41.9 | 42.2 | 42.1 | 42.6 | 43.9 | 44.3 | 41.9 |
| 2014 | 42.0 | 42.0 | 42.3 | 42.2 | 42.4 | 42.8 | 42.5 | 42.7 | 42.5 | 43.1 | 44.5 | 45.1 | 42.8 |
| 2015 | 43.2 | 43.0 | 43.3 | 43.9 | 44.1 | 44.2 | 44.3 | 44.6 | 44.2 | 44.9 | 46.3 | 46.5 | 44.4 |
| 2016 | 44.1 | 44.2 | 43.9 | 44.2 | 44.5 | 44.3 | 44.3 | 44.4 | 44.4 | 44.9 | 46.0 | 46.5 | 44.6 |
| 2017 | 44.6 | 44.7 | 44.6 | 44.5 | 44.5 | 44.4 | 44.5 | 44.8 | 44.4 | 45.2 | 46.9 | 47.2 | 45.0 |
| 2018 | 45.6 | 45.5 | 45.6 | 45.5 | 45.9 | 45.8 | 45.7 | 45.9 | 45.6 | 46.2 | 47.6 | 47.6 | 46.0 |
| 2019 | 45.9 | 45.7 | 45.7 | 45.4 | 45.6 | 45.6 | 45.7 | 45.5 | 45.3 | 46.5 | 47.4 | 47.3 | 46.0 |
| **Transportation and Utilities** | | | | | | | | | | | | | |
| 2011 | 10.8 | 11.0 | 11.0 | 11.1 | 11.3 | 11.4 | 11.2 | 11.2 | 11.1 | 11.1 | 11.2 | 11.2 | 11.1 |
| 2012 | 11.0 | 10.9 | 11.1 | 11.3 | 11.3 | 11.3 | 11.3 | 11.2 | 11.3 | 11.4 | 11.4 | 11.4 | 11.2 |
| 2013 | 11.0 | 11.1 | 11.1 | 11.1 | 11.2 | 11.3 | 11.2 | 11.3 | 11.2 | 11.3 | 11.3 | 11.6 | 11.2 |
| 2014 | 11.1 | 11.0 | 11.1 | 11.4 | 11.5 | 11.5 | 11.4 | 11.5 | 11.5 | 11.5 | 11.5 | 11.8 | 11.4 |
| 2015 | 11.2 | 11.2 | 11.3 | 11.3 | 11.4 | 11.4 | 11.5 | 11.4 | 11.3 | 11.4 | 11.6 | 11.7 | 11.4 |
| 2016 | 11.5 | 11.4 | 11.5 | 11.5 | 11.7 | 11.7 | 11.9 | 11.9 | 12.0 | 12.1 | 12.2 | 12.6 | 11.8 |
| 2017 | 12.4 | 12.4 | 12.3 | 12.2 | 12.3 | 12.3 | 12.2 | 12.2 | 12.2 | 12.4 | 12.7 | 13.2 | 12.4 |
| 2018 | 12.9 | 12.8 | 12.9 | 12.8 | 12.8 | 12.9 | 13.0 | 12.9 | 12.8 | 12.7 | 13.0 | 13.2 | 12.9 |
| 2019 | 12.6 | 12.4 | 12.5 | 12.5 | 12.6 | 12.8 | 12.8 | 12.8 | 12.9 | 12.9 | 13.0 | 13.3 | 12.8 |
| **Information** | | | | | | | | | | | | | |
| 2011 | 7.1 | 7.0 | 7.3 | 7.1 | 6.9 | 7.0 | 6.8 | 6.8 | 6.7 | 7.5 | 7.5 | 7.5 | 7.1 |
| 2012 | 7.3 | 7.6 | 7.5 | 7.6 | 7.8 | 7.8 | 7.2 | 7.1 | 7.1 | 7.0 | 7.1 | 7.3 | 7.4 |
| 2013 | 7.3 | 7.4 | 7.3 | 7.3 | 7.4 | 7.3 | 7.4 | 7.2 | 7.2 | 7.2 | 7.1 | 7.1 | 7.3 |
| 2014 | 7.0 | 6.9 | 6.9 | 6.9 | 7.1 | 7.1 | 7.2 | 7.1 | 7.1 | 7.1 | 7.3 | 7.3 | 7.1 |
| 2015 | 7.4 | 7.4 | 7.4 | 7.3 | 7.4 | 7.5 | 7.4 | 7.4 | 7.4 | 7.4 | 7.4 | 7.5 | 7.4 |
| 2016 | 7.3 | 7.3 | 7.2 | 7.2 | 7.2 | 7.1 | 7.1 | 7.0 | 7.1 | 7.1 | 7.0 | 7.1 | 7.1 |
| 2017 | 7.2 | 7.2 | 7.2 | 7.3 | 7.3 | 7.4 | 7.4 | 7.4 | 7.4 | 7.3 | 7.3 | 7.2 | 7.3 |
| 2018 | 7.2 | 7.3 | 7.3 | 7.3 | 7.3 | 7.4 | 7.5 | 7.4 | 7.3 | 7.2 | 7.1 | 7.1 | 7.3 |
| 2019 | 6.8 | 6.8 | 6.8 | 6.7 | 6.7 | 6.8 | 6.7 | 6.6 | 6.5 | 6.5 | 6.6 | 6.6 | 6.7 |
| **Financial Activities** | | | | | | | | | | | | | |
| 2011 | 15.0 | 15.0 | 15.0 | 15.1 | 15.1 | 14.9 | 15.1 | 15.1 | 15.1 | 15.1 | 15.1 | 15.1 | 15.1 |
| 2012 | 14.8 | 14.8 | 15.0 | 14.9 | 15.0 | 15.1 | 15.2 | 15.1 | 15.2 | 15.2 | 15.3 | 15.5 | 15.1 |
| 2013 | 15.5 | 15.6 | 15.7 | 15.9 | 16.0 | 16.1 | 16.0 | 16.0 | 16.0 | 16.1 | 16.2 | 16.2 | 15.9 |
| 2014 | 15.7 | 15.7 | 15.9 | 15.9 | 16.0 | 16.2 | 16.3 | 16.4 | 16.3 | 16.3 | 16.4 | 16.6 | 16.1 |
| 2015 | 16.2 | 16.2 | 16.3 | 16.4 | 16.5 | 16.8 | 16.8 | 16.8 | 16.8 | 17.1 | 17.1 | 17.4 | 16.7 |
| 2016 | 17.2 | 17.3 | 17.4 | 17.5 | 17.5 | 17.7 | 17.8 | 18.0 | 18.0 | 18.3 | 18.4 | 18.3 | 17.8 |
| 2017 | 18.1 | 18.2 | 18.3 | 18.3 | 18.4 | 18.4 | 18.6 | 18.6 | 18.5 | 18.5 | 18.7 | 18.8 | 18.5 |
| 2018 | 18.6 | 18.7 | 18.7 | 18.5 | 18.6 | 18.8 | 18.9 | 18.9 | 18.9 | 19.3 | 19.4 | 19.3 | 18.9 |
| 2019 | 19.0 | 19.0 | 19.0 | 19.1 | 19.2 | 19.4 | 19.7 | 19.6 | 19.6 | 19.3 | 18.9 | 18.8 | 19.2 |

## Employment by Industry: Greenville-Anderson-Mauldin, SC, 2011–2019—*Continued*

(Numbers in thousands, not seasonally adjusted)

| Industry and year | January | February | March | April | May | June | July | August | September | October | November | December | Annual average |
|---|---|---|---|---|---|---|---|---|---|---|---|---|---|
| **Professional and Business Services** | | | | | | | | | | | | | |
| 2011 | 56.4 | 58.2 | 59.3 | 60.4 | 60.5 | 60.4 | 61.0 | 62.6 | 63.1 | 62.4 | 62.5 | 62.4 | 60.8 |
| 2012 | 60.6 | 61.1 | 62.3 | 62.5 | 62.9 | 63.4 | 62.7 | 63.8 | 63.2 | 62.6 | 63.6 | 63.6 | 62.7 |
| 2013 | 62.0 | 62.8 | 63.3 | 62.9 | 64.1 | 65.4 | 64.4 | 65.3 | 66.4 | 66.7 | 66.9 | 66.6 | 64.7 |
| 2014 | 64.1 | 65.0 | 66.4 | 67.0 | 67.0 | 66.6 | 65.9 | 66.9 | 67.7 | 68.7 | 69.1 | 69.0 | 67.0 |
| 2015 | 67.0 | 67.6 | 67.4 | 68.6 | 69.7 | 70.0 | 70.5 | 70.9 | 71.2 | 71.8 | 71.5 | 71.6 | 69.8 |
| 2016 | 68.0 | 69.0 | 69.1 | 70.3 | 69.3 | 68.8 | 68.9 | 69.0 | 68.8 | 69.1 | 69.0 | 68.3 | 69.0 |
| 2017 | 67.3 | 68.1 | 68.1 | 69.9 | 70.2 | 70.1 | 69.5 | 70.1 | 71.1 | 72.5 | 73.4 | 73.4 | 70.3 |
| 2018 | 71.1 | 71.7 | 72.1 | 72.5 | 72.7 | 72.9 | 72.2 | 72.8 | 72.8 | 75.1 | 76.4 | 76.3 | 73.2 |
| 2019 | 74.7 | 75.1 | 74.8 | 75.0 | 75.4 | 75.3 | 74.6 | 74.5 | 74.5 | 74.5 | 75.6 | 74.6 | 74.9 |
| **Education and Health Services** | | | | | | | | | | | | | |
| 2011 | 41.5 | 42.3 | 42.5 | 42.0 | 42.1 | 41.9 | 41.5 | 41.6 | 41.6 | 41.4 | 41.6 | 41.6 | 41.8 |
| 2012 | 40.8 | 41.4 | 41.6 | 41.4 | 41.9 | 40.9 | 40.4 | 40.7 | 42.1 | 42.0 | 42.3 | 42.3 | 41.5 |
| 2013 | 41.5 | 42.0 | 42.2 | 42.3 | 42.9 | 42.6 | 42.3 | 42.9 | 43.5 | 43.9 | 44.2 | 44.5 | 42.9 |
| 2014 | 43.6 | 44.1 | 44.4 | 44.3 | 44.5 | 44.4 | 44.1 | 44.8 | 45.2 | 45.8 | 45.9 | 46.1 | 44.8 |
| 2015 | 45.1 | 45.8 | 46.1 | 46.3 | 46.4 | 46.6 | 46.0 | 47.1 | 47.1 | 47.6 | 47.9 | 48.0 | 46.7 |
| 2016 | 47.3 | 47.8 | 48.3 | 48.2 | 48.5 | 48.1 | 48.1 | 49.2 | 49.4 | 49.6 | 49.8 | 49.7 | 48.7 |
| 2017 | 48.6 | 49.5 | 49.6 | 49.7 | 50.0 | 49.5 | 49.3 | 50.1 | 50.4 | 50.9 | 50.9 | 50.8 | 49.9 |
| 2018 | 50.5 | 51.1 | 51.4 | 51.6 | 51.7 | 51.4 | 51.3 | 52.2 | 52.5 | 52.8 | 52.7 | 52.5 | 51.8 |
| 2019 | 51.5 | 52.2 | 52.5 | 52.1 | 52.3 | 51.8 | 51.6 | 52.3 | 52.4 | 53.1 | 52.5 | 52.5 | 52.2 |
| **Leisure and Hospitality** | | | | | | | | | | | | | |
| 2011 | 34.6 | 35.5 | 36.5 | 37.4 | 37.8 | 36.7 | 36.3 | 37.0 | 37.0 | 36.6 | 36.8 | 36.4 | 36.6 |
| 2012 | 35.1 | 35.6 | 36.4 | 36.6 | 37.4 | 37.8 | 37.2 | 37.8 | 37.6 | 37.1 | 37.4 | 37.2 | 36.9 |
| 2013 | 36.4 | 36.9 | 37.0 | 37.9 | 38.5 | 39.0 | 39.0 | 39.3 | 39.1 | 38.8 | 39.1 | 39.0 | 38.3 |
| 2014 | 38.0 | 37.9 | 39.3 | 39.9 | 40.5 | 40.5 | 39.8 | 40.1 | 40.3 | 39.8 | 40.2 | 40.1 | 39.7 |
| 2015 | 39.2 | 39.7 | 40.2 | 40.8 | 41.4 | 41.5 | 41.6 | 41.5 | 40.9 | 41.8 | 41.7 | 41.6 | 41.0 |
| 2016 | 40.2 | 41.0 | 41.8 | 42.5 | 43.2 | 43.3 | 42.8 | 42.8 | 42.4 | 42.3 | 42.6 | 42.3 | 42.3 |
| 2017 | 41.3 | 42.4 | 43.1 | 43.7 | 44.4 | 44.5 | 44.0 | 44.4 | 43.7 | 43.8 | 44.4 | 43.8 | 43.6 |
| 2018 | 43.6 | 44.3 | 44.9 | 46.5 | 46.8 | 47.1 | 46.4 | 47.0 | 45.8 | 46.2 | 46.1 | 45.8 | 45.9 |
| 2019 | 45.1 | 45.6 | 46.3 | 47.2 | 47.9 | 47.6 | 47.9 | 47.9 | 47.5 | 48.0 | 47.0 | 48.2 | 47.2 |
| **Other Services** | | | | | | | | | | | | | |
| 2011 | 12.0 | 12.2 | 12.4 | 12.8 | 12.9 | 12.6 | 12.6 | 12.6 | 13.0 | 13.0 | 13.1 | 13.0 | 12.7 |
| 2012 | 13.4 | 13.8 | 13.6 | 13.8 | 13.8 | 13.8 | 13.7 | 13.6 | 13.6 | 13.7 | 13.8 | 13.8 | 13.7 |
| 2013 | 13.6 | 13.6 | 13.7 | 13.8 | 13.9 | 14.0 | 13.8 | 13.9 | 14.5 | 14.5 | 13.8 | 13.7 | 13.9 |
| 2014 | 13.4 | 13.4 | 13.7 | 13.7 | 13.8 | 13.8 | 13.6 | 13.5 | 13.5 | 13.5 | 13.6 | 13.5 | 13.6 |
| 2015 | 13.4 | 13.5 | 13.7 | 13.7 | 13.8 | 13.9 | 13.8 | 13.8 | 13.8 | 13.9 | 13.8 | 13.8 | 13.7 |
| 2016 | 13.7 | 13.9 | 14.0 | 14.1 | 14.1 | 14.2 | 14.2 | 14.2 | 14.3 | 14.2 | 14.2 | 14.2 | 14.1 |
| 2017 | 14.1 | 14.1 | 14.3 | 14.2 | 14.3 | 14.4 | 14.4 | 14.3 | 14.3 | 14.2 | 14.2 | 14.2 | 14.3 |
| 2018 | 14.3 | 14.4 | 14.5 | 14.8 | 14.8 | 14.9 | 14.9 | 14.8 | 14.7 | 14.7 | 14.7 | 14.8 | 14.7 |
| 2019 | 14.6 | 14.7 | 14.8 | 15.0 | 15.0 | 15.1 | 15.2 | 15.2 | 15.1 | 15.1 | 15.1 | 15.0 | 15.0 |
| **Government** | | | | | | | | | | | | | |
| 2011 | 55.3 | 55.6 | 55.6 | 55.9 | 56.0 | 55.1 | 53.6 | 53.2 | 55.3 | 56.0 | 56.2 | 56.1 | 55.3 |
| 2012 | 56.0 | 56.4 | 56.5 | 56.5 | 57.0 | 56.1 | 53.9 | 54.3 | 56.6 | 57.4 | 57.7 | 57.6 | 56.3 |
| 2013 | 57.3 | 57.5 | 57.9 | 58.1 | 57.9 | 57.6 | 55.0 | 55.4 | 57.5 | 58.4 | 58.3 | 58.4 | 57.4 |
| 2014 | 57.8 | 58.2 | 58.4 | 58.4 | 58.8 | 58.0 | 55.6 | 56.3 | 58.3 | 59.2 | 59.4 | 59.5 | 58.2 |
| 2015 | 58.7 | 59.3 | 59.6 | 59.7 | 59.9 | 59.3 | 56.8 | 57.5 | 59.5 | 60.4 | 60.4 | 60.7 | 59.3 |
| 2016 | 59.7 | 59.9 | 60.4 | 60.5 | 60.6 | 59.9 | 57.4 | 58.1 | 60.0 | 60.7 | 60.9 | 61.1 | 59.9 |
| 2017 | 60.1 | 60.4 | 60.8 | 61.1 | 61.3 | 60.6 | 58.4 | 59.3 | 61.2 | 61.9 | 62.2 | 62.3 | 60.8 |
| 2018 | 61.5 | 62.0 | 62.4 | 62.9 | 62.6 | 61.7 | 59.2 | 59.8 | 61.9 | 62.3 | 62.8 | 62.6 | 61.8 |
| 2019 | 62.4 | 62.9 | 63.1 | 63.7 | 63.4 | 62.9 | 61.1 | 61.8 | 63.9 | 64.3 | 64.8 | 64.7 | 63.3 |

## Employment by Industry: Albuquerque, NM, 2011–2019

(Numbers in thousands, not seasonally adjusted)

| Industry and year | January | February | March | April | May | June | July | August | September | October | November | December | Annual average |
|---|---|---|---|---|---|---|---|---|---|---|---|---|---|
| **Total Nonfarm** | | | | | | | | | | | | | |
| 2011 | 367.7 | 371.7 | 372.3 | 375.8 | 375.3 | 373.2 | 370.3 | 370.4 | 373.6 | 373.8 | 372.9 | 371.7 | 372.4 |
| 2012 | 364.0 | 367.0 | 369.7 | 371.0 | 371.6 | 368.1 | 366.6 | 368.8 | 372.6 | 377.8 | 377.6 | 376.5 | 370.9 |
| 2013 | 368.9 | 371.9 | 372.6 | 376.3 | 377.2 | 373.7 | 372.4 | 374.2 | 375.1 | 377.8 | 378.8 | 378.8 | 374.8 |
| 2014 | 371.0 | 372.9 | 374.0 | 376.4 | 379.5 | 375.4 | 375.5 | 378.0 | 377.9 | 381.5 | 381.9 | 381.5 | 377.1 |
| 2015 | 373.5 | 376.5 | 377.0 | 380.9 | 381.6 | 379.6 | 378.6 | 380.4 | 381.6 | 385.7 | 388.2 | 386.0 | 380.8 |
| 2016 | 379.5 | 383.6 | 383.4 | 387.9 | 388.4 | 385.6 | 385.9 | 387.2 | 389.3 | 388.9 | 390.0 | 389.9 | 386.6 |
| 2017 | 382.9 | 385.9 | 386.8 | 389.8 | 388.5 | 389.9 | 387.1 | 388.3 | 390.8 | 392.0 | 393.3 | 393.5 | 389.1 |
| 2018 | 388.0 | 389.6 | 390.5 | 394.0 | 393.9 | 393.9 | 392.2 | 393.5 | 395.1 | 396.9 | 398.8 | 398.2 | 393.7 |
| 2019 | 391.6 | 395.5 | 395.5 | 399.4 | 399.5 | 397.9 | 397.9 | 400.3 | 401.2 | 402.4 | 403.7 | 401.7 | 398.9 |
| **Total Private** | | | | | | | | | | | | | |
| 2011 | 285.6 | 287.5 | 287.5 | 291.1 | 291.3 | 290.4 | 290.0 | 289.7 | 290.0 | 289.1 | 288.2 | 286.7 | 288.9 |
| 2012 | 282.8 | 283.5 | 285.7 | 287.8 | 288.6 | 289.4 | 288.4 | 289.0 | 289.7 | 293.6 | 293.2 | 291.9 | 288.6 |
| 2013 | 287.6 | 288.3 | 288.8 | 292.7 | 294.1 | 292.2 | 293.0 | 293.8 | 292.0 | 294.3 | 294.8 | 295.1 | 292.2 |
| 2014 | 290.1 | 289.9 | 290.4 | 294.2 | 296.6 | 295.2 | 296.3 | 298.0 | 295.9 | 298.9 | 299.0 | 298.5 | 295.3 |
| 2015 | 293.4 | 294.4 | 294.8 | 299.4 | 300.8 | 300.2 | 300.7 | 301.7 | 300.5 | 303.4 | 304.6 | 303.3 | 299.8 |
| 2016 | 298.9 | 300.3 | 299.8 | 304.8 | 305.9 | 304.6 | 306.9 | 307.5 | 306.9 | 306.2 | 306.4 | 306.7 | 304.6 |
| 2017 | 302.8 | 303.2 | 304.2 | 307.2 | 307.9 | 308.9 | 308.2 | 309.0 | 308.9 | 309.8 | 310.8 | 310.3 | 307.6 |
| 2018 | 307.2 | 307.3 | 307.9 | 311.7 | 313.0 | 313.0 | 312.7 | 313.7 | 312.4 | 313.9 | 315.3 | 315.3 | 312.0 |
| 2019 | 310.9 | 312.6 | 313.1 | 316.6 | 317.4 | 317.1 | 318.1 | 319.4 | 317.5 | 318.3 | 319.9 | 319.5 | 316.7 |
| **Goods Producing** | | | | | | | | | | | | | |
| 2011 | 37.6 | 37.3 | 38.0 | 38.4 | 38.5 | 38.8 | 39.0 | 38.6 | 37.9 | 37.7 | 37.1 | 36.6 | 38.0 |
| 2012 | 36.2 | 36.2 | 36.5 | 36.6 | 37.0 | 37.5 | 37.3 | 37.2 | 36.9 | 37.7 | 37.4 | 37.1 | 37.0 |
| 2013 | 36.3 | 36.4 | 36.7 | 37.2 | 37.6 | 37.9 | 38.0 | 37.8 | 37.4 | 37.8 | 37.2 | 36.8 | 37.3 |
| 2014 | 36.3 | 35.9 | 36.0 | 36.3 | 36.8 | 37.0 | 37.4 | 37.5 | 36.9 | 37.4 | 37.1 | 36.9 | 36.8 |
| 2015 | 36.4 | 36.2 | 36.2 | 36.9 | 37.0 | 37.3 | 37.5 | 37.4 | 37.0 | 37.6 | 37.4 | 37.3 | 37.0 |
| 2016 | 36.7 | 36.9 | 36.8 | 37.5 | 37.7 | 37.9 | 38.0 | 37.9 | 37.8 | 37.9 | 37.5 | 37.7 | 37.5 |
| 2017 | 37.3 | 37.2 | 37.6 | 38.1 | 38.3 | 38.9 | 39.2 | 39.4 | 39.4 | 39.6 | 39.6 | 39.7 | 38.7 |
| 2018 | 39.4 | 39.4 | 39.6 | 40.0 | 40.1 | 40.5 | 40.3 | 40.2 | 39.8 | 39.9 | 39.9 | 39.9 | 39.9 |
| 2019 | 39.4 | 39.7 | 39.8 | 40.4 | 41.2 | 41.8 | 42.2 | 42.2 | 41.7 | 42.2 | 42.4 | 42.9 | 41.3 |
| **Service-Providing** | | | | | | | | | | | | | |
| 2011 | 330.1 | 334.4 | 334.3 | 337.4 | 336.8 | 334.4 | 331.3 | 331.8 | 335.7 | 336.1 | 335.8 | 335.1 | 334.4 |
| 2012 | 327.8 | 330.8 | 333.2 | 334.4 | 334.6 | 330.6 | 329.3 | 331.6 | 335.7 | 340.1 | 340.2 | 339.4 | 334.0 |
| 2013 | 332.6 | 335.5 | 335.9 | 339.1 | 339.6 | 335.8 | 334.4 | 336.4 | 337.7 | 340.0 | 341.6 | 342.0 | 337.6 |
| 2014 | 334.7 | 337.0 | 338.0 | 340.1 | 342.7 | 338.4 | 338.1 | 340.5 | 341.0 | 344.1 | 344.8 | 344.6 | 340.3 |
| 2015 | 337.1 | 340.3 | 340.8 | 344.0 | 344.6 | 342.3 | 341.1 | 343.0 | 344.6 | 348.1 | 350.8 | 348.7 | 343.8 |
| 2016 | 342.8 | 346.7 | 346.6 | 350.4 | 350.7 | 347.7 | 347.9 | 349.3 | 351.5 | 351.0 | 352.5 | 352.2 | 349.1 |
| 2017 | 345.6 | 348.7 | 349.2 | 351.7 | 350.2 | 351.0 | 347.9 | 348.9 | 351.4 | 352.4 | 353.7 | 353.8 | 350.4 |
| 2018 | 348.6 | 350.2 | 350.9 | 354.0 | 353.8 | 353.4 | 351.9 | 353.3 | 355.3 | 357.0 | 358.9 | 358.3 | 353.8 |
| 2019 | 352.2 | 355.8 | 355.7 | 359.0 | 358.3 | 356.1 | 355.7 | 358.1 | 359.5 | 360.2 | 361.3 | 358.8 | 357.6 |
| **Mining, Logging, and Construction** | | | | | | | | | | | | | |
| 2011 | 20.1 | 19.9 | 20.5 | 20.7 | 20.8 | 21.0 | 21.1 | 20.6 | 20.1 | 19.8 | 19.4 | 18.9 | 20.2 |
| 2012 | 18.6 | 18.6 | 18.8 | 18.9 | 19.2 | 19.6 | 19.3 | 19.3 | 19.1 | 19.8 | 19.7 | 19.5 | 19.2 |
| 2013 | 18.8 | 19.0 | 19.4 | 19.8 | 20.2 | 20.4 | 20.5 | 20.3 | 20.1 | 20.5 | 20.2 | 19.8 | 19.9 |
| 2014 | 19.5 | 19.4 | 19.5 | 19.8 | 20.2 | 20.4 | 20.8 | 20.8 | 20.4 | 20.9 | 20.8 | 20.6 | 20.3 |
| 2015 | 20.1 | 19.8 | 19.8 | 20.6 | 20.5 | 20.7 | 20.9 | 20.7 | 20.6 | 20.9 | 20.8 | 20.7 | 20.5 |
| 2016 | 20.4 | 20.5 | 20.6 | 21.2 | 21.3 | 21.6 | 22.0 | 21.9 | 21.9 | 22.1 | 21.9 | 22.0 | 21.5 |
| 2017 | 21.7 | 21.7 | 22.1 | 22.6 | 22.8 | 23.3 | 23.5 | 23.7 | 23.7 | 23.8 | 23.8 | 23.8 | 23.0 |
| 2018 | 23.6 | 23.6 | 23.8 | 24.1 | 24.1 | 24.4 | 24.2 | 24.0 | 23.7 | 23.8 | 23.7 | 23.6 | 23.9 |
| 2019 | 23.3 | 23.5 | 23.6 | 24.0 | 24.6 | 25.1 | 25.3 | 25.3 | 24.9 | 25.3 | 25.4 | 25.6 | 24.7 |
| **Manufacturing** | | | | | | | | | | | | | |
| 2011 | 17.5 | 17.4 | 17.5 | 17.7 | 17.7 | 17.8 | 17.9 | 18.0 | 17.8 | 17.9 | 17.7 | 17.7 | 17.7 |
| 2012 | 17.6 | 17.6 | 17.7 | 17.7 | 17.8 | 17.9 | 18.0 | 17.9 | 17.8 | 17.9 | 17.7 | 17.6 | 17.8 |
| 2013 | 17.5 | 17.4 | 17.3 | 17.4 | 17.4 | 17.5 | 17.5 | 17.5 | 17.3 | 17.3 | 17.0 | 17.0 | 17.3 |
| 2014 | 16.8 | 16.5 | 16.5 | 16.5 | 16.6 | 16.6 | 16.6 | 16.7 | 16.5 | 16.5 | 16.3 | 16.3 | 16.5 |
| 2015 | 16.3 | 16.4 | 16.4 | 16.3 | 16.5 | 16.6 | 16.6 | 16.7 | 16.4 | 16.7 | 16.6 | 16.6 | 16.5 |
| 2016 | 16.3 | 16.4 | 16.2 | 16.3 | 16.4 | 16.3 | 16.0 | 16.0 | 15.9 | 15.8 | 15.6 | 15.7 | 16.1 |
| 2017 | 15.6 | 15.5 | 15.5 | 15.5 | 15.5 | 15.6 | 15.7 | 15.7 | 15.7 | 15.8 | 15.8 | 15.9 | 15.7 |
| 2018 | 15.8 | 15.8 | 15.8 | 15.9 | 16.0 | 16.1 | 16.1 | 16.2 | 16.1 | 16.1 | 16.2 | 16.3 | 16.0 |
| 2019 | 16.1 | 16.2 | 16.2 | 16.4 | 16.6 | 16.7 | 16.9 | 16.9 | 16.8 | 16.9 | 17.0 | 17.3 | 16.7 |

# Employment by Industry: Albuquerque, NM, 2011–2019—*Continued*

(Numbers in thousands, not seasonally adjusted)

| Industry and year | January | February | March | April | May | June | July | August | September | October | November | December | Annual average |
|---|---|---|---|---|---|---|---|---|---|---|---|---|---|
| **Trade, Transportation, and Utilities** | | | | | | | | | | | | | |
| 2011 | 61.9 | 61.5 | 61.4 | 62.1 | 62.3 | 61.7 | 61.2 | 61.4 | 61.4 | 61.9 | 63.2 | 63.5 | 62.0 |
| 2012 | 61.9 | 61.4 | 61.6 | 61.6 | 61.8 | 61.5 | 61.5 | 61.8 | 61.9 | 62.8 | 64.0 | 64.0 | 62.2 |
| 2013 | 62.0 | 61.4 | 61.4 | 62.0 | 62.1 | 62.0 | 62.6 | 62.9 | 62.4 | 63.2 | 64.7 | 65.3 | 62.7 |
| 2014 | 62.7 | 62.3 | 62.4 | 62.8 | 62.9 | 62.6 | 62.9 | 63.1 | 63.1 | 63.8 | 65.1 | 65.5 | 63.3 |
| 2015 | 63.5 | 63.1 | 62.9 | 63.3 | 63.7 | 63.3 | 63.5 | 63.8 | 63.7 | 64.3 | 65.6 | 65.9 | 63.9 |
| 2016 | 63.7 | 63.2 | 63.0 | 63.9 | 63.8 | 63.3 | 63.5 | 63.9 | 63.9 | 64.2 | 65.5 | 65.5 | 64.0 |
| 2017 | 63.4 | 62.7 | 62.6 | 62.6 | 62.5 | 62.6 | 62.6 | 62.9 | 62.8 | 63.5 | 64.9 | 65.3 | 63.2 |
| 2018 | 63.6 | 63.2 | 63.0 | 63.3 | 63.9 | 63.4 | 63.4 | 63.8 | 63.3 | 63.7 | 65.4 | 65.3 | 63.8 |
| 2019 | 63.5 | 63.1 | 62.8 | 63.0 | 63.1 | 62.8 | 62.7 | 62.9 | 62.7 | 63.2 | 64.3 | 64.8 | 63.2 |
| **Wholesale Trade** | | | | | | | | | | | | | |
| 2011 | 11.7 | 11.7 | 11.7 | 11.8 | 11.8 | 11.7 | 11.7 | 11.7 | 11.6 | 11.6 | 11.6 | 11.6 | 11.7 |
| 2012 | 11.6 | 11.7 | 11.8 | 11.8 | 11.9 | 11.8 | 11.9 | 11.9 | 11.8 | 11.9 | 11.9 | 11.9 | 11.8 |
| 2013 | 11.7 | 11.6 | 11.6 | 11.7 | 11.7 | 11.7 | 11.7 | 11.7 | 11.6 | 11.6 | 11.7 | 11.7 | 11.7 |
| 2014 | 11.7 | 11.8 | 11.8 | 11.9 | 12.0 | 11.9 | 11.9 | 11.9 | 11.9 | 11.9 | 11.9 | 11.9 | 11.9 |
| 2015 | 11.8 | 11.8 | 11.8 | 11.9 | 12.0 | 11.9 | 11.9 | 11.9 | 11.9 | 12.0 | 11.9 | 11.9 | 11.9 |
| 2016 | 12.0 | 12.0 | 11.9 | 12.1 | 12.0 | 11.9 | 11.9 | 11.9 | 11.9 | 11.8 | 11.7 | 11.7 | 11.9 |
| 2017 | 11.6 | 11.7 | 11.7 | 11.6 | 11.6 | 11.7 | 11.7 | 11.6 | 11.6 | 11.7 | 11.6 | 11.6 | 11.6 |
| 2018 | 11.7 | 11.7 | 11.6 | 11.7 | 11.8 | 11.8 | 11.8 | 11.8 | 11.7 | 11.7 | 11.7 | 11.8 | 11.7 |
| 2019 | 11.7 | 11.7 | 11.7 | 11.8 | 11.8 | 11.8 | 11.8 | 11.8 | 11.7 | 11.8 | 11.8 | 11.8 | 11.8 |
| **Retail Trade** | | | | | | | | | | | | | |
| 2011 | 40.6 | 40.2 | 40.3 | 40.8 | 41.0 | 40.6 | 40.2 | 40.4 | 40.3 | 40.7 | 42.0 | 42.1 | 40.8 |
| 2012 | 40.7 | 40.1 | 40.2 | 40.3 | 40.4 | 40.4 | 40.2 | 40.3 | 40.5 | 41.1 | 42.3 | 42.2 | 40.7 |
| 2013 | 40.5 | 40.1 | 40.1 | 40.6 | 40.7 | 40.7 | 41.2 | 41.4 | 41.0 | 41.8 | 43.2 | 43.5 | 41.2 |
| 2014 | 41.3 | 40.8 | 41.0 | 41.3 | 41.2 | 41.1 | 41.3 | 41.4 | 41.3 | 42.0 | 43.2 | 43.4 | 41.6 |
| 2015 | 41.6 | 41.2 | 41.1 | 41.4 | 41.7 | 41.5 | 41.8 | 42.0 | 41.9 | 42.4 | 43.6 | 43.7 | 42.0 |
| 2016 | 41.7 | 41.3 | 41.2 | 41.8 | 41.7 | 41.5 | 41.5 | 41.7 | 41.7 | 42.1 | 43.4 | 43.2 | 41.9 |
| 2017 | 41.6 | 40.9 | 40.8 | 41.0 | 40.9 | 41.0 | 41.0 | 41.2 | 41.0 | 41.5 | 43.0 | 43.1 | 41.4 |
| 2018 | 41.6 | 41.2 | 41.2 | 41.2 | 41.7 | 41.4 | 41.4 | 41.6 | 41.1 | 41.4 | 43.0 | 42.7 | 41.6 |
| 2019 | 41.3 | 40.9 | 40.7 | 40.8 | 40.8 | 40.6 | 40.6 | 40.6 | 40.5 | 40.9 | 41.9 | 42.2 | 41.0 |
| **Transportation and Utilities** | | | | | | | | | | | | | |
| 2011 | 9.6 | 9.6 | 9.4 | 9.5 | 9.5 | 9.4 | 9.3 | 9.3 | 9.5 | 9.6 | 9.6 | 9.8 | 9.5 |
| 2012 | 9.6 | 9.6 | 9.6 | 9.5 | 9.5 | 9.3 | 9.4 | 9.6 | 9.6 | 9.8 | 9.8 | 9.9 | 9.6 |
| 2013 | 9.8 | 9.7 | 9.7 | 9.7 | 9.7 | 9.6 | 9.7 | 9.8 | 9.8 | 9.8 | 9.8 | 10.1 | 9.8 |
| 2014 | 9.7 | 9.7 | 9.6 | 9.6 | 9.7 | 9.6 | 9.7 | 9.8 | 9.9 | 9.9 | 10.0 | 10.2 | 9.8 |
| 2015 | 10.1 | 10.1 | 10.0 | 10.0 | 10.0 | 9.9 | 9.8 | 9.9 | 9.9 | 9.9 | 10.1 | 10.3 | 10.0 |
| 2016 | 10.0 | 9.9 | 9.9 | 10.0 | 10.1 | 9.9 | 10.1 | 10.3 | 10.3 | 10.3 | 10.4 | 10.6 | 10.2 |
| 2017 | 10.2 | 10.1 | 10.1 | 10.0 | 10.0 | 9.9 | 9.9 | 10.1 | 10.2 | 10.3 | 10.3 | 10.6 | 10.1 |
| 2018 | 10.3 | 10.3 | 10.2 | 10.4 | 10.4 | 10.2 | 10.2 | 10.4 | 10.5 | 10.6 | 10.7 | 10.8 | 10.4 |
| 2019 | 10.5 | 10.5 | 10.4 | 10.4 | 10.5 | 10.4 | 10.3 | 10.5 | 10.5 | 10.5 | 10.6 | 10.8 | 10.5 |
| **Information** | | | | | | | | | | | | | |
| 2011 | 8.6 | 8.6 | 8.6 | 9.2 | 9.5 | 9.2 | 8.7 | 8.1 | 7.8 | 7.9 | 8.0 | 7.8 | 8.5 |
| 2012 | 8.1 | 8.4 | 8.8 | 8.8 | 8.1 | 8.0 | 8.3 | 8.4 | 8.6 | 8.4 | 8.5 | 8.4 | 8.4 |
| 2013 | 8.1 | 8.8 | 8.4 | 8.5 | 8.6 | 8.0 | 7.9 | 7.8 | 7.6 | 7.9 | 8.0 | 7.8 | 8.1 |
| 2014 | 7.4 | 7.7 | 7.9 | 7.7 | 8.2 | 8.1 | 8.0 | 8.2 | 7.5 | 7.8 | 8.2 | 8.1 | 7.9 |
| 2015 | 7.4 | 8.0 | 8.2 | 7.9 | 8.3 | 8.0 | 8.1 | 8.7 | 8.3 | 8.1 | 8.4 | 7.7 | 8.1 |
| 2016 | 7.5 | 7.4 | 7.4 | 7.8 | 7.6 | 7.4 | 7.8 | 7.9 | 7.8 | 7.4 | 8.1 | 7.8 | 7.7 |
| 2017 | 7.4 | 7.1 | 7.4 | 7.7 | 7.5 | 7.5 | 7.2 | 7.1 | 7.0 | 7.3 | 7.0 | 6.9 | 7.3 |
| 2018 | 6.6 | 6.6 | 6.7 | 6.7 | 6.7 | 6.6 | 6.6 | 6.2 | 6.3 | 6.3 | 6.4 | 6.4 | 6.5 |
| 2019 | 6.1 | 6.1 | 6.1 | 6.1 | 6.2 | 6.0 | 6.1 | 5.8 | 5.9 | 5.9 | 6.0 | 5.8 | 6.0 |
| **Financial Activities** | | | | | | | | | | | | | |
| 2011 | 17.4 | 17.4 | 17.4 | 17.6 | 17.5 | 17.6 | 17.7 | 17.7 | 17.7 | 17.7 | 17.6 | 17.7 | 17.6 |
| 2012 | 17.5 | 17.6 | 17.7 | 17.6 | 17.7 | 17.7 | 17.8 | 17.8 | 17.7 | 17.9 | 17.8 | 17.8 | 17.7 |
| 2013 | 17.8 | 17.7 | 17.6 | 17.7 | 17.9 | 17.8 | 17.9 | 18.0 | 17.9 | 18.0 | 18.2 | 18.2 | 17.9 |
| 2014 | 17.7 | 17.8 | 17.8 | 17.7 | 17.8 | 17.7 | 18.0 | 17.9 | 17.8 | 18.0 | 17.9 | 17.9 | 17.8 |
| 2015 | 17.7 | 17.8 | 17.9 | 18.0 | 18.1 | 18.1 | 18.2 | 18.1 | 17.9 | 18.1 | 18.1 | 18.2 | 18.0 |
| 2016 | 18.1 | 18.2 | 18.2 | 18.4 | 18.5 | 18.4 | 18.4 | 18.4 | 18.3 | 18.4 | 18.4 | 18.4 | 18.3 |
| 2017 | 18.5 | 18.5 | 18.4 | 18.5 | 18.5 | 18.6 | 18.7 | 18.7 | 18.6 | 18.7 | 18.7 | 18.7 | 18.6 |
| 2018 | 18.6 | 18.7 | 18.6 | 18.8 | 18.8 | 18.8 | 19.0 | 19.0 | 18.9 | 19.2 | 19.3 | 19.3 | 18.9 |
| 2019 | 19.3 | 19.3 | 19.3 | 19.4 | 19.3 | 19.3 | 19.3 | 19.4 | 19.3 | 19.3 | 19.5 | 19.9 | 19.4 |

## Employment by Industry: Albuquerque, NM, 2011–2019—*Continued*

(Numbers in thousands, not seasonally adjusted)

| Industry and year | January | February | March | April | May | June | July | August | September | October | November | December | Annual average |
|---|---|---|---|---|---|---|---|---|---|---|---|---|---|
| **Professional and Business Services** | | | | | | | | | | | | | |
| 2011 | 57.3 | 59.3 | 57.7 | 58.0 | 57.8 | 58.1 | 58.2 | 58.3 | 58.7 | 57.7 | 57.3 | 56.7 | 57.9 |
| 2012 | 55.2 | 55.2 | 55.6 | 55.9 | 56.0 | 56.8 | 56.4 | 56.4 | 56.5 | 57.2 | 57.3 | 56.6 | 56.3 |
| 2013 | 56.6 | 56.9 | 56.6 | 57.5 | 57.5 | 57.0 | 57.7 | 57.7 | 57.0 | 57.5 | 57.1 | 57.4 | 57.2 |
| 2014 | 56.7 | 56.8 | 56.3 | 57.7 | 57.7 | 57.1 | 57.8 | 58.0 | 56.8 | 57.5 | 57.2 | 57.3 | 57.2 |
| 2015 | 56.3 | 56.4 | 56.3 | 57.0 | 56.8 | 57.1 | 57.7 | 57.6 | 57.3 | 57.9 | 58.0 | 58.1 | 57.2 |
| 2016 | 57.2 | 57.5 | 57.2 | 58.0 | 58.0 | 58.5 | 59.6 | 59.3 | 59.3 | 59.2 | 58.8 | 59.0 | 58.5 |
| 2017 | 58.8 | 59.5 | 59.5 | 60.1 | 59.9 | 60.7 | 60.9 | 61.0 | 61.0 | 60.9 | 61.4 | 61.2 | 60.4 |
| 2018 | 60.4 | 60.4 | 60.3 | 61.4 | 61.2 | 62.0 | 62.0 | 62.5 | 62.4 | 62.7 | 62.7 | 63.1 | 61.8 |
| 2019 | 62.2 | 62.9 | 62.9 | 63.8 | 63.7 | 63.8 | 64.7 | 64.8 | 64.3 | 64.5 | 64.5 | 63.8 | 63.8 |
| **Education and Health Services** | | | | | | | | | | | | | |
| 2011 | 55.5 | 55.6 | 55.8 | 55.9 | 55.8 | 54.4 | 54.8 | 54.9 | 56.3 | 56.5 | 56.2 | 56.0 | 55.6 |
| 2012 | 56.1 | 56.3 | 56.3 | 56.7 | 56.6 | 55.7 | 55.4 | 55.3 | 56.9 | 57.7 | 57.7 | 57.8 | 56.5 |
| 2013 | 57.5 | 57.7 | 58.0 | 58.3 | 58.3 | 57.1 | 56.1 | 56.8 | 58.0 | 58.4 | 58.6 | 58.6 | 57.8 |
| 2014 | 58.7 | 58.8 | 59.0 | 59.5 | 59.7 | 58.8 | 58.2 | 58.8 | 60.2 | 60.8 | 60.8 | 60.5 | 59.5 |
| 2015 | 60.7 | 61.2 | 61.4 | 62.0 | 62.2 | 61.4 | 60.7 | 61.3 | 62.7 | 63.5 | 63.7 | 63.1 | 62.0 |
| 2016 | 63.7 | 64.2 | 64.1 | 64.6 | 64.7 | 63.5 | 63.0 | 63.6 | 64.4 | 64.4 | 64.1 | 64.6 | 64.1 |
| 2017 | 64.3 | 64.7 | 64.5 | 65.0 | 65.0 | 63.9 | 62.9 | 63.6 | 64.3 | 64.7 | 64.5 | 64.2 | 64.3 |
| 2018 | 64.5 | 64.6 | 64.6 | 65.3 | 65.3 | 64.3 | 63.4 | 64.3 | 65.2 | 65.7 | 65.7 | 65.8 | 64.9 |
| 2019 | 65.8 | 66.4 | 66.3 | 66.6 | 66.5 | 65.4 | 64.9 | 66.1 | 66.5 | 66.7 | 67.0 | 67.3 | 66.3 |
| **Leisure and Hospitality** | | | | | | | | | | | | | |
| 2011 | 35.8 | 36.1 | 36.8 | 38.1 | 38.2 | 38.4 | 38.2 | 38.6 | 38.5 | 38.1 | 37.3 | 36.9 | 37.6 |
| 2012 | 36.3 | 36.6 | 37.3 | 38.7 | 39.6 | 39.9 | 39.7 | 40.0 | 39.4 | 39.8 | 38.8 | 38.4 | 38.7 |
| 2013 | 37.8 | 37.8 | 38.5 | 39.8 | 40.5 | 40.6 | 40.9 | 41.0 | 40.2 | 39.9 | 39.4 | 39.4 | 39.7 |
| 2014 | 39.1 | 38.9 | 39.3 | 40.8 | 41.8 | 41.9 | 42.0 | 42.4 | 41.8 | 41.8 | 41.0 | 40.7 | 41.0 |
| 2015 | 40.1 | 40.2 | 40.4 | 42.7 | 43.1 | 43.1 | 43.0 | 42.9 | 42.0 | 42.3 | 41.8 | 41.5 | 41.9 |
| 2016 | 40.6 | 41.3 | 41.6 | 42.8 | 43.9 | 43.6 | 44.3 | 44.2 | 43.4 | 42.8 | 42.1 | 41.9 | 42.7 |
| 2017 | 41.6 | 41.8 | 42.5 | 43.3 | 44.2 | 44.3 | 44.3 | 44.2 | 43.9 | 43.3 | 42.9 | 42.5 | 43.2 |
| 2018 | 42.3 | 42.6 | 43.2 | 44.2 | 44.9 | 44.9 | 45.5 | 45.2 | 44.3 | 44.2 | 43.8 | 43.6 | 44.1 |
| 2019 | 42.7 | 43.1 | 43.8 | 45.2 | 45.3 | 45.5 | 45.7 | 45.8 | 45.0 | 44.4 | 44.1 | 43.0 | 44.5 |
| **Other Services** | | | | | | | | | | | | | |
| 2011 | 11.5 | 11.7 | 11.8 | 11.8 | 11.7 | 12.2 | 12.2 | 12.1 | 11.7 | 11.6 | 11.5 | 11.5 | 11.8 |
| 2012 | 11.5 | 11.8 | 11.9 | 11.9 | 11.8 | 12.3 | 12.0 | 12.1 | 11.8 | 12.1 | 11.7 | 11.8 | 11.9 |
| 2013 | 11.5 | 11.6 | 11.6 | 11.7 | 11.6 | 11.8 | 11.9 | 11.8 | 11.5 | 11.6 | 11.6 | 11.6 | 11.7 |
| 2014 | 11.5 | 11.7 | 11.7 | 11.7 | 11.7 | 12.0 | 12.0 | 12.1 | 11.8 | 11.8 | 11.7 | 11.6 | 11.8 |
| 2015 | 11.3 | 11.5 | 11.5 | 11.6 | 11.6 | 11.9 | 12.0 | 11.9 | 11.6 | 11.6 | 11.6 | 11.5 | 11.6 |
| 2016 | 11.4 | 11.6 | 11.5 | 11.8 | 11.7 | 12.0 | 12.3 | 12.3 | 12.0 | 11.9 | 11.9 | 11.8 | 11.9 |
| 2017 | 11.5 | 11.7 | 11.7 | 11.9 | 12.0 | 12.4 | 12.4 | 12.1 | 11.9 | 11.8 | 11.8 | 11.8 | 11.9 |
| 2018 | 11.8 | 11.8 | 11.9 | 12.0 | 12.1 | 12.5 | 12.5 | 12.5 | 12.2 | 12.2 | 12.1 | 11.9 | 12.1 |
| 2019 | 11.9 | 12.0 | 12.1 | 12.1 | 12.1 | 12.5 | 12.5 | 12.4 | 12.1 | 12.1 | 12.1 | 12.0 | 12.2 |
| **Government** | | | | | | | | | | | | | |
| 2011 | 82.1 | 84.2 | 84.8 | 84.7 | 84.0 | 82.8 | 80.3 | 80.7 | 83.6 | 84.7 | 84.7 | 85.0 | 83.5 |
| 2012 | 81.2 | 83.5 | 84.0 | 83.2 | 83.0 | 78.7 | 78.2 | 79.8 | 82.9 | 84.2 | 84.4 | 84.6 | 82.3 |
| 2013 | 81.3 | 83.6 | 83.8 | 83.6 | 83.1 | 81.5 | 79.4 | 80.4 | 83.1 | 83.5 | 84.0 | 83.7 | 82.6 |
| 2014 | 80.9 | 83.0 | 83.6 | 82.2 | 82.9 | 80.2 | 79.2 | 80.0 | 82.0 | 82.6 | 82.9 | 83.0 | 81.9 |
| 2015 | 80.1 | 82.1 | 82.2 | 81.5 | 80.8 | 79.4 | 77.9 | 78.7 | 81.1 | 82.3 | 83.6 | 82.7 | 81.0 |
| 2016 | 80.6 | 83.3 | 83.6 | 83.1 | 82.5 | 81.0 | 79.0 | 79.7 | 82.4 | 82.7 | 83.6 | 83.2 | 82.1 |
| 2017 | 80.1 | 82.7 | 82.6 | 82.6 | 80.6 | 81.0 | 78.9 | 79.3 | 81.9 | 82.2 | 82.5 | 83.2 | 81.5 |
| 2018 | 80.8 | 82.3 | 82.6 | 82.3 | 80.9 | 80.9 | 79.5 | 79.8 | 82.7 | 83.0 | 83.5 | 82.9 | 81.8 |
| 2019 | 80.7 | 82.9 | 82.4 | 82.8 | 82.1 | 80.8 | 79.8 | 80.9 | 83.7 | 84.1 | 83.8 | 82.2 | 82.2 |

# Employment by Industry: Bakersfield, CA, 2011–2019

(Numbers in thousands, not seasonally adjusted)

| Industry and year | January | February | March | April | May | June | July | August | September | October | November | December | Annual average |
|---|---|---|---|---|---|---|---|---|---|---|---|---|---|
| **Total Nonfarm** | | | | | | | | | | | | | |
| 2011 | 230.9 | 232.1 | 233.8 | 236.5 | 238.7 | 238.3 | 235.9 | 238.2 | 238.9 | 239.5 | 240.7 | 241.2 | 237.1 |
| 2012 | 238.8 | 240.7 | 243.7 | 245.6 | 248.2 | 249.0 | 243.6 | 245.3 | 247.4 | 249.8 | 250.8 | 250.5 | 246.1 |
| 2013 | 245.6 | 247.5 | 249.1 | 250.8 | 252.4 | 250.4 | 247.0 | 249.7 | 251.6 | 253.7 | 254.8 | 255.0 | 250.6 |
| 2014 | 250.8 | 252.3 | 254.4 | 256.4 | 258.2 | 255.9 | 252.3 | 256.3 | 258.9 | 259.3 | 261.7 | 261.8 | 256.5 |
| 2015 | 257.4 | 256.8 | 258.0 | 258.0 | 259.2 | 257.5 | 252.8 | 256.7 | 257.5 | 259.9 | 260.6 | 260.7 | 257.9 |
| 2016 | 256.1 | 256.0 | 255.6 | 257.2 | 256.5 | 256.1 | 250.1 | 253.0 | 256.1 | 258.7 | 261.0 | 259.9 | 256.4 |
| 2017 | 255.0 | 255.8 | 258.2 | 259.0 | 260.7 | 260.1 | 255.0 | 258.0 | 260.9 | 263.5 | 265.6 | 264.5 | 259.7 |
| 2018 | 262.2 | 263.1 | 264.6 | 265.5 | 266.9 | 267.6 | 261.3 | 266.5 | 269.1 | 272.5 | 274.6 | 273.8 | 267.3 |
| 2019 | 268.3 | 269.4 | 271.1 | 273.3 | 273.9 | 273.4 | 266.5 | 273.3 | 275.5 | 279.1 | 280.8 | 279.7 | 273.7 |
| **Total Private** | | | | | | | | | | | | | |
| 2011 | 170.4 | 171.0 | 172.0 | 174.8 | 176.9 | 176.7 | 179.1 | 180.5 | 180.8 | 179.5 | 180.3 | 180.9 | 176.9 |
| 2012 | 179.7 | 180.9 | 183.3 | 186.0 | 188.4 | 189.1 | 189.1 | 190.1 | 189.9 | 190.0 | 190.9 | 190.6 | 187.3 |
| 2013 | 187.1 | 188.2 | 189.3 | 191.1 | 193.1 | 193.0 | 192.6 | 194.4 | 193.8 | 194.1 | 194.8 | 194.8 | 192.2 |
| 2014 | 191.7 | 192.5 | 193.7 | 195.6 | 197.3 | 197.3 | 197.0 | 199.6 | 199.2 | 198.3 | 199.7 | 200.1 | 196.8 |
| 2015 | 196.2 | 195.5 | 195.9 | 195.6 | 196.4 | 196.2 | 196.5 | 197.6 | 196.3 | 196.5 | 197.2 | 197.1 | 196.4 |
| 2016 | 193.2 | 192.2 | 191.1 | 192.6 | 191.6 | 191.5 | 191.3 | 192.2 | 192.6 | 193.1 | 195.0 | 194.3 | 192.6 |
| 2017 | 189.8 | 190.2 | 191.8 | 193.0 | 194.8 | 194.2 | 195.0 | 196.0 | 196.5 | 196.6 | 198.1 | 197.5 | 194.5 |
| 2018 | 196.2 | 196.7 | 197.8 | 199.0 | 200.4 | 200.9 | 200.7 | 203.1 | 203.5 | 204.2 | 206.5 | 205.9 | 201.2 |
| 2019 | 201.4 | 201.7 | 202.8 | 204.6 | 205.0 | 205.8 | 206.1 | 208.5 | 207.8 | 208.8 | 210.1 | 209.3 | 206.0 |
| **Goods Producing** | | | | | | | | | | | | | |
| 2011 | 36.6 | 36.8 | 36.9 | 38.0 | 38.3 | 39.0 | 39.4 | 39.8 | 40.0 | 39.7 | 39.5 | 40.1 | 38.7 |
| 2012 | 40.5 | 41.0 | 41.7 | 42.5 | 42.8 | 43.5 | 44.0 | 44.4 | 44.5 | 44.0 | 44.0 | 43.3 | 43.0 |
| 2013 | 42.3 | 42.4 | 42.8 | 43.1 | 43.4 | 43.8 | 43.9 | 44.6 | 45.0 | 45.0 | 44.8 | 44.7 | 43.8 |
| 2014 | 44.3 | 44.4 | 44.6 | 45.2 | 45.5 | 45.9 | 46.2 | 46.8 | 46.7 | 46.3 | 46.1 | 45.8 | 45.7 |
| 2015 | 44.7 | 44.0 | 43.3 | 42.4 | 42.0 | 41.8 | 41.7 | 42.2 | 41.6 | 40.6 | 40.3 | 39.9 | 42.0 |
| 2016 | 38.8 | 38.0 | 37.0 | 36.6 | 36.3 | 36.3 | 36.7 | 36.9 | 37.5 | 36.9 | 37.0 | 36.8 | 37.1 |
| 2017 | 35.8 | 35.7 | 36.1 | 36.5 | 36.6 | 36.9 | 37.4 | 37.7 | 38.0 | 37.7 | 37.7 | 37.3 | 37.0 |
| 2018 | 37.6 | 37.8 | 37.7 | 37.5 | 38.0 | 38.2 | 38.7 | 39.2 | 39.2 | 39.2 | 38.9 | 38.8 | 38.4 |
| 2019 | 37.9 | 38.1 | 38.3 | 38.3 | 38.4 | 39.0 | 39.1 | 39.3 | 39.2 | 39.1 | 39.1 | 38.6 | 38.7 |
| **Service-Providing** | | | | | | | | | | | | | |
| 2011 | 194.3 | 195.3 | 196.9 | 198.5 | 200.4 | 199.3 | 196.5 | 198.4 | 198.9 | 199.8 | 201.2 | 201.1 | 198.4 |
| 2012 | 198.3 | 199.7 | 202.0 | 203.1 | 205.4 | 205.5 | 199.6 | 200.9 | 202.9 | 205.8 | 206.8 | 207.2 | 203.1 |
| 2013 | 203.3 | 205.1 | 206.3 | 207.7 | 209.0 | 206.6 | 203.1 | 205.1 | 206.6 | 208.7 | 210.0 | 210.3 | 206.8 |
| 2014 | 206.5 | 207.9 | 209.8 | 211.2 | 212.7 | 210.0 | 206.1 | 209.5 | 212.2 | 213.0 | 215.6 | 216.0 | 210.9 |
| 2015 | 212.7 | 212.8 | 214.7 | 215.6 | 217.2 | 215.7 | 211.1 | 214.5 | 215.9 | 219.3 | 220.3 | 220.8 | 215.9 |
| 2016 | 217.3 | 218.0 | 218.6 | 220.6 | 220.2 | 219.8 | 213.4 | 216.1 | 218.6 | 221.8 | 224.0 | 223.1 | 219.3 |
| 2017 | 219.2 | 220.1 | 222.1 | 222.5 | 224.1 | 223.2 | 217.6 | 220.3 | 222.9 | 225.8 | 227.9 | 227.2 | 222.7 |
| 2018 | 224.6 | 225.3 | 226.9 | 228.0 | 228.9 | 229.4 | 222.6 | 227.3 | 229.9 | 233.3 | 235.7 | 235.0 | 228.9 |
| 2019 | 230.4 | 231.3 | 232.8 | 235.0 | 235.5 | 234.4 | 227.4 | 234.0 | 236.3 | 240.0 | 241.7 | 241.1 | 235.0 |
| **Mining, Logging, and Construction** | | | | | | | | | | | | | |
| 2011 | 23.6 | 23.9 | 24.0 | 25.0 | 25.4 | 25.8 | 26.3 | 26.5 | 26.4 | 26.5 | 26.5 | 27.0 | 25.6 |
| 2012 | 27.7 | 28.1 | 28.7 | 29.4 | 29.7 | 30.0 | 30.3 | 30.5 | 30.2 | 30.1 | 30.2 | 29.6 | 29.5 |
| 2013 | 28.9 | 28.9 | 29.2 | 29.4 | 29.6 | 29.8 | 29.8 | 30.3 | 30.2 | 30.4 | 30.3 | 30.3 | 29.8 |
| 2014 | 30.1 | 30.2 | 30.3 | 30.6 | 31.0 | 31.2 | 31.6 | 31.8 | 31.6 | 31.5 | 31.6 | 31.4 | 31.1 |
| 2015 | 30.5 | 29.9 | 29.2 | 28.3 | 28.0 | 27.6 | 27.6 | 27.4 | 27.0 | 26.7 | 26.4 | 26.1 | 27.9 |
| 2016 | 25.4 | 24.6 | 23.6 | 23.3 | 23.0 | 22.9 | 23.1 | 23.1 | 23.2 | 23.2 | 23.5 | 23.4 | 23.5 |
| 2017 | 22.7 | 22.6 | 23.0 | 23.4 | 23.4 | 23.5 | 23.9 | 23.9 | 24.1 | 23.9 | 24.1 | 24.2 | 23.6 |
| 2018 | 24.4 | 24.5 | 24.5 | 24.7 | 25.0 | 25.1 | 25.7 | 25.9 | 25.8 | 25.7 | 25.6 | 25.9 | 25.2 |
| 2019 | 25.1 | 25.2 | 25.4 | 25.5 | 25.6 | 26.1 | 26.2 | 26.3 | 26.3 | 26.3 | 26.4 | 26.1 | 25.9 |
| **Manufacturing** | | | | | | | | | | | | | |
| 2011 | 13.0 | 12.9 | 12.9 | 13.0 | 12.9 | 13.2 | 13.1 | 13.3 | 13.6 | 13.2 | 13.0 | 13.1 | 13.1 |
| 2012 | 12.8 | 12.9 | 13.0 | 13.1 | 13.1 | 13.5 | 13.7 | 13.9 | 14.3 | 13.9 | 13.8 | 13.7 | 13.5 |
| 2013 | 13.4 | 13.5 | 13.6 | 13.7 | 13.8 | 14.0 | 14.1 | 14.3 | 14.8 | 14.6 | 14.5 | 14.4 | 14.1 |
| 2014 | 14.2 | 14.2 | 14.3 | 14.6 | 14.5 | 14.7 | 14.6 | 15.0 | 15.1 | 14.8 | 14.5 | 14.4 | 14.6 |
| 2015 | 14.2 | 14.1 | 14.1 | 14.1 | 14.0 | 14.2 | 14.1 | 14.8 | 14.6 | 13.9 | 13.9 | 13.8 | 14.2 |
| 2016 | 13.4 | 13.4 | 13.4 | 13.3 | 13.3 | 13.4 | 13.6 | 13.8 | 14.3 | 13.7 | 13.5 | 13.4 | 13.5 |
| 2017 | 13.1 | 13.1 | 13.1 | 13.1 | 13.2 | 13.4 | 13.5 | 13.8 | 13.9 | 13.8 | 13.6 | 13.1 | 13.4 |
| 2018 | 13.2 | 13.3 | 13.2 | 12.8 | 13.0 | 13.1 | 13.0 | 13.3 | 13.4 | 13.5 | 13.3 | 12.9 | 13.2 |
| 2019 | 12.8 | 12.9 | 12.9 | 12.8 | 12.8 | 12.9 | 12.9 | 13.0 | 12.9 | 12.8 | 12.7 | 12.5 | 12.8 |

## Employment by Industry: Bakersfield, CA, 2011–2019—*Continued*

(Numbers in thousands, not seasonally adjusted)

| Industry and year | January | February | March | April | May | June | July | August | September | October | November | December | Annual average |
|---|---|---|---|---|---|---|---|---|---|---|---|---|---|
| **Trade, Transportation, and Utilities** | | | | | | | | | | | | | |
| 2011 | 42.5 | 42.1 | 42.1 | 43.0 | 44.0 | 43.6 | 44.6 | 44.8 | 44.7 | 44.2 | 44.8 | 45.1 | 43.8 |
| 2012 | 43.7 | 43.3 | 43.6 | 44.7 | 45.4 | 45.7 | 45.8 | 45.8 | 45.6 | 46.0 | 47.3 | 47.8 | 45.4 |
| 2013 | 46.0 | 45.9 | 46.1 | 47.0 | 47.4 | 47.5 | 47.7 | 48.1 | 47.8 | 47.9 | 49.1 | 49.7 | 47.5 |
| 2014 | 47.7 | 47.7 | 48.0 | 48.7 | 49.3 | 49.3 | 49.4 | 50.5 | 50.4 | 49.7 | 50.9 | 51.6 | 49.4 |
| 2015 | 49.6 | 49.4 | 49.6 | 50.1 | 50.6 | 50.5 | 51.1 | 51.1 | 50.9 | 51.3 | 52.1 | 52.3 | 50.7 |
| 2016 | 50.5 | 50.2 | 50.2 | 50.8 | 51.3 | 51.0 | 51.0 | 51.1 | 50.9 | 51.3 | 52.8 | 52.6 | 51.1 |
| 2017 | 50.6 | 50.1 | 50.2 | 50.6 | 51.3 | 51.2 | 51.7 | 52.2 | 51.9 | 52.4 | 53.7 | 53.7 | 51.6 |
| 2018 | 52.7 | 52.3 | 52.7 | 53.1 | 53.5 | 53.4 | 53.1 | 53.5 | 53.1 | 53.2 | 54.5 | 54.4 | 53.3 |
| 2019 | 52.3 | 51.6 | 51.5 | 51.9 | 52.1 | 52.3 | 52.5 | 53.0 | 52.8 | 53.2 | 54.1 | 54.3 | 52.6 |
| **Wholesale Trade** | | | | | | | | | | | | | |
| 2011 | 7.2 | 7.1 | 6.9 | 7.3 | 7.4 | 7.5 | 8.4 | 8.3 | 8.3 | 7.9 | 7.5 | 7.3 | 7.6 |
| 2012 | 7.4 | 7.2 | 7.2 | 7.7 | 7.8 | 8.0 | 7.9 | 7.9 | 7.9 | 8.0 | 8.0 | 8.1 | 7.8 |
| 2013 | 8.3 | 8.4 | 8.4 | 8.4 | 8.4 | 8.5 | 8.6 | 8.6 | 8.6 | 8.5 | 8.5 | 8.5 | 8.5 |
| 2014 | 8.5 | 8.6 | 8.6 | 8.8 | 8.7 | 8.8 | 8.6 | 8.8 | 8.7 | 8.6 | 8.7 | 8.7 | 8.7 |
| 2015 | 8.6 | 8.6 | 8.4 | 8.2 | 8.3 | 8.3 | 8.4 | 8.4 | 8.3 | 8.2 | 8.2 | 8.2 | 8.3 |
| 2016 | 8.1 | 8.2 | 8.2 | 8.1 | 8.2 | 8.2 | 8.1 | 8.1 | 8.0 | 8.1 | 8.0 | 8.0 | 8.1 |
| 2017 | 7.9 | 7.9 | 8.0 | 8.0 | 8.1 | 8.1 | 8.5 | 8.6 | 8.5 | 8.4 | 8.4 | 8.3 | 8.2 |
| 2018 | 8.3 | 8.2 | 8.3 | 8.3 | 8.3 | 8.3 | 8.3 | 8.3 | 8.2 | 8.2 | 8.2 | 8.1 | 8.3 |
| 2019 | 7.9 | 7.9 | 7.9 | 7.9 | 7.9 | 8.0 | 8.0 | 8.0 | 8.0 | 8.0 | 8.0 | 8.0 | 8.0 |
| **Retail Trade** | | | | | | | | | | | | | |
| 2011 | 26.6 | 26.3 | 26.5 | 26.8 | 27.2 | 27.0 | 27.0 | 27.1 | 26.9 | 27.0 | 28.0 | 28.5 | 27.1 |
| 2012 | 27.4 | 27.0 | 27.3 | 27.7 | 27.9 | 27.8 | 27.8 | 27.8 | 27.6 | 27.9 | 29.3 | 29.6 | 27.9 |
| 2013 | 28.1 | 27.9 | 28.0 | 28.7 | 28.9 | 28.8 | 28.9 | 29.1 | 28.8 | 29.1 | 30.3 | 30.7 | 28.9 |
| 2014 | 29.2 | 29.1 | 29.2 | 29.8 | 30.2 | 30.0 | 30.1 | 30.8 | 30.8 | 30.6 | 31.7 | 32.1 | 30.3 |
| 2015 | 30.6 | 30.5 | 30.8 | 31.2 | 31.5 | 31.4 | 31.5 | 31.5 | 31.4 | 31.7 | 32.7 | 32.8 | 31.5 |
| 2016 | 31.6 | 31.4 | 31.5 | 32.0 | 32.1 | 31.8 | 31.9 | 31.9 | 31.7 | 32.0 | 33.5 | 33.5 | 32.1 |
| 2017 | 32.1 | 31.6 | 31.5 | 31.6 | 31.8 | 31.7 | 31.7 | 31.8 | 31.5 | 31.9 | 33.1 | 33.2 | 32.0 |
| 2018 | 32.0 | 31.6 | 31.6 | 31.7 | 31.9 | 31.7 | 31.6 | 31.6 | 31.2 | 31.3 | 32.7 | 32.8 | 31.8 |
| 2019 | 31.3 | 30.7 | 30.6 | 30.8 | 30.9 | 30.9 | 30.9 | 31.0 | 30.8 | 31.2 | 32.0 | 32.3 | 31.1 |
| **Transportation and Utilities** | | | | | | | | | | | | | |
| 2011 | 8.7 | 8.7 | 8.7 | 8.9 | 9.4 | 9.1 | 9.2 | 9.4 | 9.5 | 9.3 | 9.3 | 9.3 | 9.1 |
| 2012 | 8.9 | 9.1 | 9.1 | 9.3 | 9.7 | 9.9 | 10.1 | 10.1 | 10.1 | 10.1 | 10.0 | 10.1 | 9.7 |
| 2013 | 9.6 | 9.6 | 9.7 | 9.9 | 10.1 | 10.2 | 10.2 | 10.4 | 10.4 | 10.3 | 10.3 | 10.5 | 10.1 |
| 2014 | 10.0 | 10.0 | 10.2 | 10.1 | 10.4 | 10.5 | 10.7 | 10.9 | 10.9 | 10.5 | 10.5 | 10.8 | 10.5 |
| 2015 | 10.4 | 10.3 | 10.4 | 10.7 | 10.8 | 10.8 | 11.2 | 11.2 | 11.2 | 11.4 | 11.2 | 11.3 | 10.9 |
| 2016 | 10.8 | 10.6 | 10.5 | 10.7 | 11.0 | 11.0 | 11.0 | 11.1 | 11.2 | 11.2 | 11.3 | 11.1 | 11.0 |
| 2017 | 10.6 | 10.6 | 10.7 | 11.0 | 11.4 | 11.4 | 11.5 | 11.8 | 11.9 | 12.1 | 12.2 | 12.2 | 11.5 |
| 2018 | 12.4 | 12.5 | 12.8 | 13.1 | 13.3 | 13.4 | 13.2 | 13.6 | 13.7 | 13.7 | 13.6 | 13.5 | 13.2 |
| 2019 | 13.1 | 13.0 | 13.0 | 13.2 | 13.3 | 13.4 | 13.6 | 14.0 | 14.0 | 14.0 | 14.1 | 14.0 | 13.6 |
| **Information** | | | | | | | | | | | | | |
| 2011 | 2.7 | 2.6 | 2.6 | 2.6 | 2.6 | 2.6 | 2.7 | 2.6 | 2.6 | 2.6 | 2.6 | 2.6 | 2.6 |
| 2012 | 2.7 | 2.7 | 2.7 | 2.7 | 2.7 | 2.8 | 2.6 | 2.6 | 2.6 | 2.6 | 2.7 | 2.7 | 2.7 |
| 2013 | 2.7 | 2.6 | 2.6 | 2.6 | 2.6 | 2.6 | 2.5 | 2.5 | 2.5 | 2.4 | 2.5 | 2.4 | 2.5 |
| 2014 | 2.4 | 2.4 | 2.4 | 2.4 | 2.4 | 2.4 | 2.3 | 2.4 | 2.3 | 2.4 | 2.4 | 2.4 | 2.4 |
| 2015 | 2.4 | 2.4 | 2.4 | 2.4 | 2.4 | 2.8 | 2.8 | 3.0 | 3.0 | 2.9 | 2.8 | 2.9 | 2.7 |
| 2016 | 2.7 | 2.6 | 2.3 | 2.2 | 2.0 | 2.1 | 2.1 | 2.0 | 2.0 | 2.0 | 2.0 | 2.0 | 2.2 |
| 2017 | 2.0 | 2.0 | 2.0 | 2.1 | 2.1 | 2.1 | 2.0 | 2.0 | 2.0 | 2.0 | 2.0 | 2.1 | 2.0 |
| 2018 | 2.0 | 2.0 | 2.0 | 2.1 | 2.1 | 2.1 | 2.1 | 2.0 | 2.0 | 2.0 | 2.0 | 2.0 | 2.0 |
| 2019 | 2.0 | 2.0 | 2.0 | 2.0 | 2.0 | 2.0 | 1.9 | 1.9 | 1.9 | 1.9 | 1.9 | 1.9 | 2.0 |
| **Financial Activities** | | | | | | | | | | | | | |
| 2011 | 7.4 | 7.6 | 7.6 | 7.8 | 7.9 | 7.8 | 8.1 | 8.2 | 8.1 | 8.0 | 8.1 | 8.0 | 7.9 |
| 2012 | 8.0 | 8.1 | 8.1 | 8.4 | 8.6 | 8.4 | 8.4 | 8.4 | 8.4 | 8.4 | 8.3 | 8.3 | 8.3 |
| 2013 | 8.4 | 8.3 | 8.3 | 8.4 | 8.5 | 8.5 | 8.4 | 8.4 | 8.3 | 8.4 | 8.4 | 8.3 | 8.4 |
| 2014 | 8.3 | 8.2 | 8.2 | 8.2 | 8.3 | 8.2 | 8.2 | 8.2 | 8.1 | 8.3 | 8.1 | 8.2 | 8.2 |
| 2015 | 8.2 | 8.0 | 8.1 | 8.1 | 8.1 | 8.0 | 8.1 | 8.1 | 8.0 | 8.0 | 7.9 | 7.8 | 8.0 |
| 2016 | 7.9 | 7.8 | 7.8 | 8.0 | 7.9 | 7.9 | 7.8 | 7.8 | 7.7 | 7.7 | 7.7 | 7.6 | 7.8 |
| 2017 | 7.8 | 7.7 | 7.8 | 7.7 | 7.7 | 7.7 | 7.7 | 7.6 | 7.6 | 7.7 | 7.6 | 7.6 | 7.7 |
| 2018 | 7.5 | 7.5 | 7.5 | 7.6 | 7.6 | 7.6 | 7.6 | 7.5 | 7.6 | 7.6 | 7.6 | 7.5 | 7.6 |
| 2019 | 7.5 | 7.4 | 7.4 | 7.5 | 7.5 | 7.5 | 7.5 | 7.5 | 7.5 | 7.6 | 7.5 | 7.5 | 7.5 |

# Employment by Industry: Bakersfield, CA, 2011–2019—*Continued*

(Numbers in thousands, not seasonally adjusted)

| Industry and year | January | February | March | April | May | June | July | August | September | October | November | December | Annual average |
|---|---|---|---|---|---|---|---|---|---|---|---|---|---|
| **Professional and Business Services** | | | | | | | | | | | | | |
| 2011 | 25.4 | 25.7 | 26.1 | 26.1 | 26.1 | 25.9 | 26.5 | 26.7 | 27.1 | 26.7 | 26.9 | 26.5 | 26.3 |
| 2012 | 26.6 | 27.1 | 27.8 | 27.5 | 28.0 | 27.9 | 28.1 | 28.1 | 28.0 | 27.8 | 27.4 | 27.3 | 27.6 |
| 2013 | 26.9 | 27.6 | 27.6 | 27.4 | 27.8 | 27.8 | 27.5 | 27.7 | 27.4 | 27.3 | 26.9 | 26.7 | 27.4 |
| 2014 | 26.6 | 26.8 | 26.9 | 26.8 | 27.2 | 27.2 | 26.9 | 27.1 | 27.1 | 27.4 | 27.8 | 27.6 | 27.1 |
| 2015 | 27.0 | 26.9 | 27.0 | 26.6 | 26.7 | 26.8 | 26.7 | 26.5 | 26.1 | 26.8 | 27.1 | 27.2 | 26.8 |
| 2016 | 26.7 | 26.8 | 26.5 | 27.0 | 26.3 | 26.3 | 26.0 | 26.1 | 26.5 | 26.5 | 26.7 | 26.4 | 26.5 |
| 2017 | 25.9 | 26.1 | 26.4 | 26.1 | 26.4 | 26.2 | 26.2 | 26.2 | 26.4 | 25.9 | 26.0 | 25.9 | 26.1 |
| 2018 | 25.9 | 26.4 | 26.6 | 26.8 | 26.7 | 27.1 | 26.7 | 27.3 | 27.8 | 28.0 | 28.9 | 28.7 | 27.2 |
| 2019 | 27.6 | 27.7 | 27.9 | 28.9 | 28.3 | 28.5 | 28.2 | 29.2 | 29.1 | 29.2 | 29.5 | 29.4 | 28.6 |
| **Education and Health Services** | | | | | | | | | | | | | |
| 2011 | 29.5 | 29.6 | 29.7 | 29.9 | 30.1 | 29.9 | 30.1 | 30.4 | 30.6 | 30.5 | 30.5 | 30.8 | 30.1 |
| 2012 | 30.6 | 30.8 | 31.1 | 31.4 | 31.6 | 31.4 | 31.2 | 31.6 | 31.8 | 32.0 | 31.9 | 32.0 | 31.5 |
| 2013 | 31.6 | 32.0 | 32.1 | 32.4 | 32.6 | 32.1 | 32.1 | 32.4 | 32.3 | 32.5 | 32.6 | 32.5 | 32.3 |
| 2014 | 32.2 | 32.4 | 32.5 | 32.6 | 32.7 | 32.5 | 32.3 | 32.7 | 32.7 | 32.7 | 32.8 | 32.8 | 32.6 |
| 2015 | 32.5 | 32.7 | 32.9 | 33.3 | 33.5 | 33.5 | 33.2 | 33.7 | 33.7 | 34.0 | 34.1 | 34.1 | 33.4 |
| 2016 | 34.0 | 34.2 | 34.2 | 34.6 | 34.6 | 34.7 | 34.6 | 35.1 | 35.0 | 35.3 | 35.5 | 35.6 | 34.8 |
| 2017 | 35.3 | 35.9 | 36.1 | 36.5 | 36.7 | 36.1 | 36.2 | 36.5 | 36.6 | 37.0 | 37.2 | 37.1 | 36.4 |
| 2018 | 37.2 | 37.1 | 37.2 | 37.4 | 37.6 | 37.6 | 37.8 | 38.5 | 38.7 | 39.1 | 39.4 | 39.5 | 38.1 |
| 2019 | 39.3 | 39.7 | 40.0 | 40.0 | 40.3 | 40.5 | 41.1 | 41.5 | 41.4 | 41.7 | 41.8 | 41.6 | 40.7 |
| **Leisure and Hospitality** | | | | | | | | | | | | | |
| 2011 | 19.8 | 20.1 | 20.4 | 20.7 | 21.1 | 21.2 | 21.0 | 21.0 | 20.7 | 20.9 | 20.9 | 20.8 | 20.7 |
| 2012 | 20.6 | 20.8 | 21.2 | 21.6 | 22.0 | 22.2 | 22.0 | 21.9 | 21.7 | 21.8 | 21.9 | 21.9 | 21.6 |
| 2013 | 21.9 | 22.0 | 22.3 | 22.6 | 23.1 | 23.4 | 23.2 | 23.1 | 23.0 | 23.1 | 22.9 | 23.0 | 22.8 |
| 2014 | 22.6 | 22.9 | 23.4 | 23.8 | 24.0 | 24.1 | 24.1 | 24.0 | 24.0 | 23.6 | 23.8 | 24.0 | 23.7 |
| 2015 | 24.0 | 24.3 | 24.8 | 25.0 | 25.4 | 25.4 | 25.3 | 25.3 | 25.3 | 25.2 | 25.2 | 25.3 | 25.0 |
| 2016 | 25.2 | 25.2 | 25.5 | 25.8 | 25.7 | 25.8 | 25.6 | 25.3 | 25.2 | 25.4 | 25.4 | 25.4 | 25.5 |
| 2017 | 24.9 | 25.2 | 25.6 | 25.9 | 26.4 | 26.4 | 26.2 | 25.9 | 26.0 | 25.9 | 26.0 | 25.9 | 25.9 |
| 2018 | 25.8 | 26.1 | 26.5 | 26.8 | 27.2 | 27.2 | 27.0 | 26.7 | 26.7 | 26.7 | 27.0 | 26.8 | 26.7 |
| 2019 | 26.6 | 27.0 | 27.4 | 27.7 | 28.0 | 28.0 | 27.7 | 27.5 | 27.4 | 27.6 | 27.7 | 27.6 | 27.5 |
| **Other Services** | | | | | | | | | | | | | |
| 2011 | 6.5 | 6.5 | 6.6 | 6.7 | 6.8 | 6.7 | 6.7 | 7.0 | 7.0 | 6.9 | 7.0 | 7.0 | 6.8 |
| 2012 | 7.0 | 7.1 | 7.1 | 7.2 | 7.3 | 7.2 | 7.0 | 7.3 | 7.3 | 7.4 | 7.4 | 7.3 | 7.2 |
| 2013 | 7.3 | 7.4 | 7.5 | 7.6 | 7.7 | 7.3 | 7.3 | 7.6 | 7.5 | 7.5 | 7.6 | 7.5 | 7.5 |
| 2014 | 7.6 | 7.7 | 7.7 | 7.9 | 7.9 | 7.7 | 7.6 | 7.9 | 7.9 | 7.9 | 7.8 | 7.7 | 7.8 |
| 2015 | 7.8 | 7.8 | 7.8 | 7.7 | 7.7 | 7.4 | 7.6 | 7.7 | 7.7 | 7.7 | 7.7 | 7.6 | 7.7 |
| 2016 | 7.4 | 7.4 | 7.6 | 7.6 | 7.5 | 7.4 | 7.5 | 7.9 | 7.8 | 8.0 | 7.9 | 7.9 | 7.7 |
| 2017 | 7.5 | 7.5 | 7.6 | 7.6 | 7.6 | 7.6 | 7.6 | 7.9 | 8.0 | 8.0 | 7.9 | 7.9 | 7.7 |
| 2018 | 7.5 | 7.5 | 7.6 | 7.7 | 7.7 | 7.7 | 7.7 | 8.4 | 8.4 | 8.4 | 8.2 | 8.2 | 7.9 |
| 2019 | 8.2 | 8.2 | 8.3 | 8.3 | 8.4 | 8.0 | 8.1 | 8.6 | 8.5 | 8.5 | 8.5 | 8.4 | 8.3 |
| **Government** | | | | | | | | | | | | | |
| 2011 | 60.5 | 61.1 | 61.8 | 61.7 | 61.8 | 61.6 | 56.8 | 57.7 | 58.1 | 60.0 | 60.4 | 60.3 | 60.2 |
| 2012 | 59.1 | 59.8 | 60.4 | 59.6 | 59.8 | 59.9 | 54.5 | 55.2 | 57.5 | 59.8 | 59.9 | 59.9 | 58.8 |
| 2013 | 58.5 | 59.3 | 59.8 | 59.7 | 59.3 | 57.4 | 54.4 | 55.3 | 57.8 | 59.6 | 60.0 | 60.2 | 58.4 |
| 2014 | 59.1 | 59.8 | 60.7 | 60.8 | 60.9 | 58.6 | 55.3 | 56.7 | 59.7 | 61.0 | 62.0 | 61.7 | 59.7 |
| 2015 | 61.2 | 61.3 | 62.1 | 62.4 | 62.8 | 61.3 | 56.3 | 59.1 | 61.2 | 63.4 | 63.4 | 63.6 | 61.5 |
| 2016 | 62.9 | 63.8 | 64.5 | 64.6 | 64.9 | 64.6 | 58.8 | 60.8 | 63.5 | 65.6 | 66.0 | 65.6 | 63.8 |
| 2017 | 65.2 | 65.6 | 66.4 | 66.0 | 65.9 | 65.9 | 60.0 | 62.0 | 64.4 | 66.9 | 67.5 | 67.0 | 65.2 |
| 2018 | 66.0 | 66.4 | 66.8 | 66.5 | 66.5 | 66.7 | 60.6 | 63.4 | 65.6 | 68.3 | 68.1 | 67.9 | 66.1 |
| 2019 | 66.9 | 67.7 | 68.3 | 68.7 | 68.9 | 67.6 | 60.4 | 64.8 | 67.7 | 70.3 | 70.7 | 70.4 | 67.7 |

## Employment by Industry: Albany-Schenectady-Troy, NY, 2011–2019

(Numbers in thousands, not seasonally adjusted)

| Industry and year | January | February | March | April | May | June | July | August | September | October | November | December | Annual average |
|---|---|---|---|---|---|---|---|---|---|---|---|---|---|
| **Total Nonfarm** | | | | | | | | | | | | | |
| 2011 | 421.2 | 427.0 | 427.7 | 435.2 | 436.9 | 437.7 | 433.2 | 432.2 | 435.2 | 440.2 | 442.6 | 440.7 | 434.2 |
| 2012 | 428.0 | 433.8 | 434.9 | 441.2 | 444.9 | 446.0 | 437.9 | 438.3 | 440.8 | 447.2 | 450.0 | 447.0 | 440.8 |
| 2013 | 432.8 | 439.6 | 441.0 | 445.9 | 450.1 | 451.4 | 444.2 | 443.2 | 445.6 | 452.2 | 454.6 | 452.2 | 446.1 |
| 2014 | 435.5 | 442.7 | 444.2 | 449.2 | 453.0 | 454.8 | 447.8 | 447.6 | 449.0 | 458.5 | 459.0 | 457.0 | 449.9 |
| 2015 | 445.0 | 449.8 | 450.1 | 455.7 | 460.0 | 461.6 | 455.1 | 454.4 | 455.2 | 464.8 | 464.9 | 463.4 | 456.7 |
| 2016 | 450.4 | 456.7 | 458.4 | 465.1 | 465.0 | 467.6 | 463.0 | 463.3 | 464.1 | 472.8 | 472.1 | 470.6 | 464.1 |
| 2017 | 455.7 | 461.9 | 462.9 | 468.8 | 469.8 | 472.7 | 465.8 | 466.7 | 468.2 | 476.7 | 476.8 | 474.8 | 468.4 |
| 2018 | 458.4 | 465.6 | 466.3 | 471.2 | 474.6 | 477.6 | 470.0 | 469.7 | 471.0 | 479.2 | 479.5 | 476.5 | 471.6 |
| 2019 | 462.1 | 466.1 | 466.6 | 473.1 | 473.9 | 475.9 | 468.5 | 468.7 | 471.4 | 478.4 | 482.4 | 480.0 | 472.3 |
| **Total Private** | | | | | | | | | | | | | |
| 2011 | 320.5 | 323.7 | 324.6 | 330.9 | 332.3 | 333.4 | 334.4 | 334.8 | 335.7 | 337.3 | 339.3 | 337.3 | 332.0 |
| 2012 | 327.3 | 330.8 | 332.6 | 338.0 | 341.1 | 343.0 | 341.3 | 342.2 | 341.8 | 345.2 | 347.0 | 344.5 | 339.6 |
| 2013 | 332.1 | 336.1 | 337.9 | 342.9 | 346.5 | 347.8 | 346.6 | 346.8 | 347.2 | 350.6 | 351.8 | 349.9 | 344.7 |
| 2014 | 336.3 | 340.4 | 342.0 | 346.8 | 350.5 | 352.4 | 351.2 | 352.0 | 350.6 | 356.7 | 356.9 | 354.7 | 349.2 |
| 2015 | 345.0 | 347.8 | 348.2 | 353.6 | 357.3 | 359.1 | 358.6 | 359.0 | 357.0 | 362.9 | 362.9 | 361.3 | 356.1 |
| 2016 | 350.2 | 354.5 | 356.2 | 362.2 | 362.9 | 365.2 | 365.8 | 366.9 | 364.3 | 370.5 | 369.6 | 367.8 | 363.0 |
| 2017 | 354.6 | 358.9 | 359.9 | 365.4 | 367.2 | 369.8 | 368.3 | 370.0 | 368.5 | 373.9 | 373.7 | 371.5 | 366.8 |
| 2018 | 357.2 | 362.9 | 363.5 | 368.5 | 371.3 | 374.3 | 372.1 | 373.2 | 371.6 | 376.3 | 376.0 | 373.1 | 370.0 |
| 2019 | 360.3 | 362.4 | 363.4 | 369.2 | 370.3 | 372.1 | 370.2 | 370.9 | 370.6 | 374.9 | 378.4 | 376.0 | 369.9 |
| **Goods Producing** | | | | | | | | | | | | | |
| 2011 | 35.2 | 34.8 | 35.1 | 37.1 | 38.2 | 39.4 | 40.4 | 40.8 | 40.4 | 40.2 | 39.9 | 38.5 | 38.3 |
| 2012 | 37.0 | 36.4 | 37.0 | 39.0 | 40.1 | 41.3 | 41.8 | 42.0 | 41.6 | 41.3 | 40.9 | 40.3 | 39.9 |
| 2013 | 38.7 | 38.5 | 38.9 | 40.2 | 42.0 | 42.8 | 43.4 | 43.5 | 42.9 | 42.8 | 42.4 | 41.3 | 41.5 |
| 2014 | 39.5 | 39.0 | 39.3 | 40.9 | 43.2 | 44.4 | 44.8 | 45.3 | 44.7 | 44.7 | 44.4 | 43.6 | 42.8 |
| 2015 | 42.6 | 42.2 | 42.4 | 43.9 | 45.6 | 46.8 | 47.4 | 47.5 | 46.5 | 46.3 | 45.8 | 44.8 | 45.2 |
| 2016 | 43.1 | 42.6 | 43.0 | 44.6 | 46.0 | 46.9 | 47.6 | 47.7 | 47.1 | 47.2 | 46.0 | 45.0 | 45.6 |
| 2017 | 43.5 | 43.2 | 43.9 | 45.6 | 46.7 | 48.0 | 47.7 | 48.0 | 47.7 | 47.6 | 47.1 | 46.0 | 46.3 |
| 2018 | 43.9 | 43.6 | 44.3 | 45.6 | 46.9 | 48.3 | 48.7 | 48.5 | 47.5 | 47.6 | 46.8 | 45.6 | 46.4 |
| 2019 | 43.6 | 43.2 | 43.5 | 45.4 | 46.7 | 47.6 | 48.3 | 48.4 | 47.7 | 47.9 | 47.1 | 47.1 | 46.4 |
| **Service-Providing** | | | | | | | | | | | | | |
| 2011 | 386.0 | 392.2 | 392.6 | 398.1 | 398.7 | 398.3 | 392.8 | 391.4 | 394.8 | 400.0 | 402.7 | 402.2 | 395.8 |
| 2012 | 391.0 | 397.4 | 397.9 | 402.2 | 404.8 | 404.7 | 396.1 | 396.3 | 399.2 | 405.9 | 409.1 | 406.7 | 400.9 |
| 2013 | 394.1 | 401.1 | 402.1 | 405.7 | 408.1 | 408.6 | 400.8 | 399.7 | 402.7 | 409.4 | 412.2 | 410.9 | 404.6 |
| 2014 | 396.0 | 403.7 | 404.9 | 408.3 | 409.8 | 410.4 | 403.0 | 402.3 | 404.3 | 413.8 | 414.6 | 413.4 | 407.0 |
| 2015 | 402.4 | 407.6 | 407.7 | 411.8 | 414.4 | 414.8 | 407.7 | 406.9 | 408.7 | 418.5 | 419.1 | 418.6 | 411.5 |
| 2016 | 407.3 | 414.1 | 415.4 | 420.5 | 419.0 | 420.7 | 415.4 | 415.6 | 417.0 | 425.6 | 426.1 | 425.6 | 418.5 |
| 2017 | 412.2 | 418.7 | 419.0 | 423.2 | 423.1 | 424.7 | 418.1 | 418.7 | 420.5 | 429.1 | 429.7 | 428.8 | 422.2 |
| 2018 | 414.5 | 422.0 | 422.0 | 425.6 | 427.7 | 429.3 | 421.3 | 421.2 | 423.5 | 431.6 | 432.7 | 430.9 | 425.2 |
| 2019 | 418.5 | 422.9 | 423.1 | 427.7 | 427.2 | 428.3 | 420.2 | 420.3 | 423.7 | 430.5 | 435.3 | 432.9 | 425.9 |
| **Mining, Logging, and Construction** | | | | | | | | | | | | | |
| 2011 | 14.7 | 14.2 | 14.4 | 15.9 | 16.9 | 17.8 | 18.6 | 19.0 | 18.6 | 18.2 | 17.8 | 16.5 | 16.9 |
| 2012 | 15.2 | 14.5 | 14.8 | 16.7 | 17.6 | 18.5 | 18.8 | 18.9 | 18.5 | 18.2 | 17.7 | 17.1 | 17.2 |
| 2013 | 15.2 | 14.9 | 15.2 | 16.4 | 18.0 | 18.4 | 19.2 | 19.4 | 19.0 | 18.9 | 18.4 | 17.4 | 17.5 |
| 2014 | 15.9 | 15.6 | 15.8 | 17.2 | 19.3 | 20.0 | 20.3 | 20.7 | 20.3 | 20.3 | 19.9 | 19.0 | 18.7 |
| 2015 | 18.1 | 17.6 | 17.7 | 19.0 | 20.5 | 21.2 | 21.4 | 21.5 | 20.7 | 20.4 | 19.7 | 18.9 | 19.7 |
| 2016 | 17.2 | 16.7 | 17.1 | 18.5 | 19.8 | 20.4 | 20.9 | 21.0 | 20.6 | 20.5 | 19.8 | 18.8 | 19.3 |
| 2017 | 17.6 | 17.2 | 17.3 | 18.9 | 20.1 | 20.9 | 21.2 | 21.1 | 21.0 | 20.7 | 20.2 | 19.1 | 19.6 |
| 2018 | 17.4 | 17.2 | 17.6 | 18.9 | 20.1 | 21.0 | 21.4 | 21.4 | 21.0 | 20.9 | 20.2 | 19.4 | 19.7 |
| 2019 | 17.8 | 17.4 | 17.7 | 19.4 | 20.5 | 21.0 | 21.7 | 22.0 | 21.5 | 21.7 | 20.9 | 21.0 | 20.2 |
| **Manufacturing** | | | | | | | | | | | | | |
| 2011 | 20.5 | 20.6 | 20.7 | 21.2 | 21.3 | 21.6 | 21.8 | 21.8 | 21.8 | 22.0 | 22.1 | 22.0 | 21.5 |
| 2012 | 21.8 | 21.9 | 22.2 | 22.3 | 22.5 | 22.8 | 23.0 | 23.1 | 23.1 | 23.1 | 23.2 | 23.2 | 22.7 |
| 2013 | 23.5 | 23.6 | 23.7 | 23.8 | 24.0 | 24.4 | 24.2 | 24.1 | 23.9 | 23.9 | 24.0 | 23.9 | 23.9 |
| 2014 | 23.6 | 23.4 | 23.5 | 23.7 | 23.9 | 24.4 | 24.5 | 24.6 | 24.4 | 24.4 | 24.5 | 24.6 | 24.1 |
| 2015 | 24.5 | 24.6 | 24.7 | 24.9 | 25.1 | 25.6 | 26.0 | 26.0 | 25.8 | 25.9 | 26.1 | 25.9 | 25.4 |
| 2016 | 25.9 | 25.9 | 25.9 | 26.1 | 26.2 | 26.5 | 26.7 | 26.7 | 26.5 | 26.7 | 26.2 | 26.2 | 26.3 |
| 2017 | 25.9 | 26.0 | 26.6 | 26.7 | 26.6 | 27.1 | 26.5 | 26.9 | 26.7 | 26.9 | 26.9 | 26.9 | 26.6 |
| 2018 | 26.5 | 26.4 | 26.7 | 26.7 | 26.8 | 27.3 | 27.3 | 27.1 | 26.5 | 26.7 | 26.6 | 26.2 | 26.7 |
| 2019 | 25.8 | 25.8 | 25.8 | 26.0 | 26.2 | 26.6 | 26.6 | 26.4 | 26.2 | 26.2 | 26.2 | 26.1 | 26.2 |

## Employment by Industry: Albany-Schenectady-Troy, NY, 2011–2019—*Continued*

(Numbers in thousands, not seasonally adjusted)

| Industry and year | January | February | March | April | May | June | July | August | September | October | November | December | Annual average |
|---|---|---|---|---|---|---|---|---|---|---|---|---|---|
| **Trade, Transportation, and Utilities** | | | | | | | | | | | | | |
| 2011 | 71.3 | 70.2 | 70.4 | 71.2 | 71.7 | 72.5 | 72.0 | 72.5 | 72.1 | 72.6 | 74.5 | 75.9 | 72.2 |
| 2012 | 72.6 | 71.4 | 71.5 | 72.2 | 73.2 | 74.0 | 73.4 | 73.6 | 73.0 | 73.9 | 75.7 | 76.2 | 73.4 |
| 2013 | 72.3 | 71.4 | 71.6 | 72.2 | 73.2 | 74.4 | 73.9 | 73.9 | 73.7 | 74.8 | 76.4 | 77.1 | 73.7 |
| 2014 | 73.1 | 72.3 | 72.6 | 73.1 | 73.9 | 74.6 | 74.1 | 74.4 | 74.1 | 76.0 | 76.6 | 77.1 | 74.3 |
| 2015 | 73.9 | 72.7 | 72.8 | 73.4 | 74.2 | 75.0 | 74.6 | 74.8 | 74.5 | 76.0 | 77.1 | 77.8 | 74.7 |
| 2016 | 74.8 | 73.7 | 73.8 | 74.2 | 74.8 | 75.6 | 75.4 | 75.7 | 75.5 | 77.1 | 77.5 | 77.7 | 75.5 |
| 2017 | 74.4 | 73.1 | 72.9 | 73.5 | 73.9 | 74.5 | 74.4 | 74.6 | 74.4 | 75.7 | 76.6 | 76.8 | 74.6 |
| 2018 | 73.7 | 72.9 | 72.6 | 73.4 | 74.3 | 74.9 | 74.4 | 74.9 | 74.7 | 75.9 | 76.9 | 77.0 | 74.6 |
| 2019 | 73.9 | 72.8 | 72.8 | 73.4 | 73.8 | 74.4 | 73.5 | 74.0 | 74.5 | 74.9 | 77.4 | 77.7 | 74.4 |
| **Wholesale Trade** | | | | | | | | | | | | | |
| 2011 | 13.1 | 13.1 | 13.1 | 13.2 | 13.2 | 13.3 | 13.3 | 13.3 | 13.1 | 13.0 | 13.2 | 13.2 | 13.2 |
| 2012 | 13.1 | 13.1 | 13.2 | 13.4 | 13.5 | 13.7 | 13.7 | 13.7 | 13.5 | 13.6 | 13.6 | 13.5 | 13.5 |
| 2013 | 13.4 | 13.4 | 13.5 | 13.4 | 13.6 | 13.7 | 13.7 | 13.7 | 13.6 | 13.5 | 13.5 | 13.4 | 13.5 |
| 2014 | 13.4 | 13.4 | 13.4 | 13.7 | 13.8 | 13.9 | 13.9 | 14.0 | 13.8 | 13.9 | 13.8 | 13.8 | 13.7 |
| 2015 | 13.9 | 13.9 | 13.8 | 13.9 | 13.9 | 14.0 | 14.0 | 13.9 | 13.8 | 13.7 | 13.8 | 13.8 | 13.9 |
| 2016 | 13.7 | 13.6 | 13.7 | 13.6 | 13.7 | 13.8 | 13.8 | 13.8 | 13.7 | 13.7 | 13.6 | 13.6 | 13.7 |
| 2017 | 13.5 | 13.4 | 13.4 | 13.2 | 13.3 | 13.4 | 13.5 | 13.4 | 13.2 | 13.1 | 13.1 | 13.1 | 13.3 |
| 2018 | 12.9 | 12.9 | 12.9 | 12.9 | 13.0 | 13.2 | 13.3 | 13.3 | 13.2 | 13.4 | 13.6 | 13.6 | 13.2 |
| 2019 | 13.4 | 13.5 | 13.4 | 13.5 | 13.6 | 13.7 | 13.6 | 13.6 | 13.5 | 13.4 | 13.5 | 13.4 | 13.5 |
| **Retail Trade** | | | | | | | | | | | | | |
| 2011 | 46.1 | 45.0 | 45.3 | 45.9 | 46.2 | 46.9 | 46.5 | 46.9 | 46.5 | 47.1 | 48.7 | 49.8 | 46.7 |
| 2012 | 47.3 | 46.2 | 46.2 | 46.7 | 47.5 | 48.0 | 47.5 | 47.7 | 47.1 | 47.9 | 49.7 | 50.0 | 47.7 |
| 2013 | 47.0 | 45.9 | 46.1 | 46.6 | 47.2 | 48.1 | 47.8 | 47.8 | 47.5 | 48.5 | 49.8 | 50.3 | 47.7 |
| 2014 | 47.2 | 46.3 | 46.4 | 46.8 | 47.4 | 48.0 | 47.6 | 47.8 | 47.5 | 49.2 | 49.6 | 49.8 | 47.8 |
| 2015 | 47.1 | 46.0 | 46.1 | 46.5 | 47.2 | 47.9 | 47.6 | 47.9 | 47.6 | 48.9 | 49.6 | 50.0 | 47.7 |
| 2016 | 47.7 | 46.8 | 46.7 | 47.4 | 47.7 | 48.2 | 48.1 | 48.3 | 48.1 | 49.5 | 49.7 | 49.7 | 48.2 |
| 2017 | 47.3 | 46.2 | 46.0 | 46.7 | 46.9 | 47.4 | 47.4 | 47.5 | 47.3 | 48.7 | 49.3 | 49.2 | 47.5 |
| 2018 | 47.0 | 46.2 | 45.8 | 46.4 | 47.0 | 47.3 | 46.9 | 47.3 | 47.0 | 47.7 | 48.6 | 48.3 | 47.1 |
| 2019 | 46.4 | 45.2 | 45.2 | 45.7 | 46.0 | 46.4 | 45.9 | 46.4 | 46.5 | 47.0 | 49.0 | 48.9 | 46.6 |
| **Transportation and Utilities** | | | | | | | | | | | | | |
| 2011 | 12.1 | 12.1 | 12.0 | 12.1 | 12.3 | 12.3 | 12.2 | 12.3 | 12.5 | 12.5 | 12.6 | 12.9 | 12.3 |
| 2012 | 12.2 | 12.1 | 12.1 | 12.1 | 12.2 | 12.3 | 12.2 | 12.2 | 12.4 | 12.4 | 12.4 | 12.7 | 12.3 |
| 2013 | 11.9 | 12.1 | 12.0 | 12.2 | 12.4 | 12.6 | 12.4 | 12.4 | 12.6 | 12.8 | 13.1 | 13.4 | 12.5 |
| 2014 | 12.5 | 12.6 | 12.8 | 12.6 | 12.7 | 12.7 | 12.6 | 12.6 | 12.8 | 12.9 | 13.2 | 13.5 | 12.8 |
| 2015 | 12.9 | 12.8 | 12.9 | 13.0 | 13.1 | 13.1 | 13.0 | 13.0 | 13.1 | 13.4 | 13.7 | 14.0 | 13.2 |
| 2016 | 13.4 | 13.3 | 13.4 | 13.2 | 13.4 | 13.6 | 13.5 | 13.6 | 13.7 | 13.9 | 14.2 | 14.4 | 13.6 |
| 2017 | 13.6 | 13.5 | 13.5 | 13.6 | 13.7 | 13.7 | 13.5 | 13.7 | 13.9 | 13.9 | 14.2 | 14.5 | 13.8 |
| 2018 | 13.8 | 13.8 | 13.9 | 14.1 | 14.3 | 14.4 | 14.2 | 14.3 | 14.5 | 14.8 | 14.7 | 15.1 | 14.3 |
| 2019 | 14.1 | 14.1 | 14.2 | 14.2 | 14.2 | 14.3 | 14.0 | 14.0 | 14.5 | 14.5 | 14.9 | 15.4 | 14.4 |
| **Information** | | | | | | | | | | | | | |
| 2011 | 8.8 | 8.7 | 8.7 | 8.8 | 8.8 | 8.9 | 9.0 | 8.2 | 8.8 | 8.8 | 8.8 | 8.8 | 8.8 |
| 2012 | 8.7 | 8.7 | 8.7 | 8.7 | 8.7 | 8.7 | 8.7 | 8.6 | 8.5 | 8.6 | 8.6 | 8.5 | 8.6 |
| 2013 | 8.5 | 8.5 | 8.5 | 8.6 | 8.5 | 8.5 | 8.5 | 8.6 | 8.5 | 8.5 | 8.6 | 8.7 | 8.5 |
| 2014 | 8.6 | 8.7 | 8.7 | 8.7 | 8.7 | 8.8 | 8.5 | 8.5 | 8.4 | 8.4 | 8.4 | 8.4 | 8.6 |
| 2015 | 8.3 | 8.2 | 8.2 | 8.5 | 8.5 | 8.4 | 8.9 | 8.8 | 8.7 | 8.8 | 8.7 | 8.8 | 8.6 |
| 2016 | 8.7 | 8.7 | 8.7 | 8.8 | 8.2 | 8.8 | 8.9 | 8.8 | 8.8 | 8.7 | 8.6 | 8.7 | 8.7 |
| 2017 | 8.5 | 8.6 | 8.6 | 8.5 | 8.4 | 8.6 | 8.5 | 8.5 | 8.4 | 8.4 | 8.4 | 8.5 | 8.5 |
| 2018 | 8.6 | 8.7 | 8.7 | 8.6 | 8.7 | 8.7 | 8.6 | 8.7 | 8.5 | 8.3 | 8.3 | 8.3 | 8.6 |
| 2019 | 8.1 | 8.1 | 8.1 | 8.0 | 8.3 | 8.4 | 8.1 | 8.1 | 8.0 | 8.0 | 8.2 | 8.2 | 8.1 |
| **Financial Activities** | | | | | | | | | | | | | |
| 2011 | 24.3 | 24.3 | 24.3 | 24.4 | 24.4 | 24.8 | 25.0 | 25.1 | 24.7 | 24.6 | 24.6 | 24.7 | 24.6 |
| 2012 | 24.7 | 24.7 | 24.8 | 24.9 | 24.9 | 25.5 | 25.6 | 25.5 | 25.2 | 25.3 | 25.4 | 25.5 | 25.2 |
| 2013 | 25.0 | 25.0 | 25.1 | 25.2 | 25.3 | 25.7 | 25.7 | 25.6 | 25.2 | 25.3 | 25.2 | 25.3 | 25.3 |
| 2014 | 25.2 | 25.1 | 25.1 | 25.0 | 25.2 | 25.7 | 25.9 | 25.7 | 25.4 | 25.5 | 25.4 | 25.5 | 25.4 |
| 2015 | 25.5 | 25.5 | 25.5 | 25.7 | 25.7 | 26.1 | 26.3 | 26.3 | 25.9 | 25.9 | 25.9 | 26.1 | 25.9 |
| 2016 | 25.9 | 25.9 | 26.0 | 26.1 | 26.1 | 26.6 | 26.7 | 26.7 | 26.2 | 26.2 | 26.2 | 26.3 | 26.2 |
| 2017 | 25.9 | 25.8 | 25.8 | 25.9 | 26.2 | 26.7 | 26.6 | 26.6 | 26.3 | 26.3 | 26.3 | 26.4 | 26.2 |
| 2018 | 26.1 | 26.1 | 26.0 | 26.3 | 26.4 | 26.9 | 27.1 | 27.0 | 26.6 | 26.7 | 27.2 | 26.8 | 26.6 |
| 2019 | 26.9 | 26.8 | 26.7 | 27.0 | 27.0 | 27.4 | 27.5 | 27.3 | 26.7 | 26.8 | 26.9 | 26.7 | 27.0 |

## Employment by Industry: Albany-Schenectady-Troy, NY, 2011–2019—*Continued*

(Numbers in thousands, not seasonally adjusted)

| Industry and year | January | February | March | April | May | June | July | August | September | October | November | December | Annual average |
|---|---|---|---|---|---|---|---|---|---|---|---|---|---|
| **Professional and Business Services** | | | | | | | | | | | | | |
| 2011 | 50.1 | 50.2 | 50.3 | 51.5 | 51.2 | 51.8 | 52.2 | 51.8 | 51.7 | 51.8 | 52.5 | 51.7 | 51.4 |
| 2012 | 51.4 | 51.5 | 51.8 | 52.7 | 52.8 | 53.4 | 53.2 | 53.2 | 52.4 | 52.7 | 53.2 | 52.0 | 52.5 |
| 2013 | 51.8 | 51.8 | 52.0 | 53.0 | 53.1 | 53.7 | 53.6 | 53.3 | 52.8 | 52.4 | 52.4 | 51.8 | 52.6 |
| 2014 | 51.1 | 51.3 | 51.5 | 52.5 | 53.0 | 53.6 | 53.9 | 53.8 | 53.1 | 53.3 | 53.7 | 53.2 | 52.8 |
| 2015 | 53.3 | 53.2 | 53.0 | 54.0 | 54.3 | 55.1 | 54.7 | 54.7 | 53.8 | 54.5 | 54.4 | 54.1 | 54.1 |
| 2016 | 53.8 | 54.2 | 54.6 | 55.8 | 55.6 | 56.7 | 57.5 | 57.6 | 56.5 | 57.0 | 57.1 | 56.6 | 56.1 |
| 2017 | 55.4 | 55.6 | 55.5 | 56.1 | 56.2 | 57.1 | 57.1 | 57.2 | 55.9 | 56.1 | 56.1 | 55.7 | 56.2 |
| 2018 | 54.6 | 55.1 | 55.2 | 55.9 | 56.3 | 57.3 | 57.9 | 58.4 | 56.7 | 56.7 | 56.9 | 56.4 | 56.5 |
| 2019 | 55.2 | 55.5 | 55.7 | 56.5 | 56.7 | 57.7 | 58.0 | 58.9 | 56.9 | 57.7 | 58.7 | 57.5 | 57.1 |
| **Education and Health Services** | | | | | | | | | | | | | |
| 2011 | 81.4 | 85.4 | 85.4 | 85.9 | 84.7 | 81.9 | 80.5 | 79.9 | 83.6 | 86.1 | 86.5 | 85.4 | 83.9 |
| 2012 | 82.9 | 87.0 | 87.3 | 87.5 | 86.6 | 83.8 | 81.9 | 81.2 | 85.5 | 88.3 | 88.8 | 88.2 | 85.8 |
| 2013 | 85.0 | 89.1 | 89.1 | 89.9 | 88.4 | 84.8 | 83.6 | 83.0 | 87.6 | 90.6 | 91.3 | 90.6 | 87.8 |
| 2014 | 86.5 | 91.1 | 91.4 | 91.7 | 89.7 | 87.1 | 85.8 | 85.3 | 88.6 | 92.3 | 92.5 | 91.4 | 89.5 |
| 2015 | 87.8 | 92.0 | 92.1 | 92.2 | 90.6 | 88.5 | 86.8 | 86.2 | 89.7 | 93.3 | 93.6 | 92.5 | 90.4 |
| 2016 | 89.1 | 93.9 | 94.3 | 94.7 | 93.0 | 90.0 | 88.5 | 88.3 | 91.1 | 95.0 | 95.2 | 94.8 | 92.3 |
| 2017 | 90.6 | 95.3 | 95.7 | 96.6 | 94.7 | 92.5 | 90.8 | 90.8 | 94.8 | 98.0 | 98.6 | 97.8 | 94.7 |
| 2018 | 92.9 | 98.1 | 98.5 | 98.5 | 96.7 | 95.3 | 91.8 | 91.7 | 95.9 | 99.1 | 99.3 | 98.5 | 96.4 |
| 2019 | 95.1 | 98.4 | 98.5 | 98.9 | 96.6 | 94.0 | 91.9 | 90.9 | 96.1 | 99.3 | 99.3 | 99.0 | 96.5 |
| **Leisure and Hospitality** | | | | | | | | | | | | | |
| 2011 | 31.8 | 32.4 | 32.7 | 34.1 | 35.3 | 36.4 | 37.3 | 38.5 | 36.4 | 35.5 | 34.8 | 34.5 | 35.0 |
| 2012 | 32.5 | 33.5 | 33.6 | 35.1 | 36.9 | 38.3 | 38.7 | 40.2 | 37.8 | 37.2 | 36.5 | 36.0 | 36.4 |
| 2013 | 33.3 | 34.1 | 34.8 | 36.0 | 38.1 | 39.8 | 39.8 | 40.9 | 38.8 | 38.1 | 37.3 | 36.8 | 37.3 |
| 2014 | 34.3 | 34.8 | 35.2 | 36.6 | 38.6 | 40.2 | 39.9 | 40.7 | 38.2 | 38.2 | 37.4 | 37.0 | 37.6 |
| 2015 | 35.3 | 35.6 | 35.8 | 37.4 | 39.8 | 40.6 | 41.2 | 42.2 | 40.0 | 39.6 | 38.8 | 38.5 | 38.7 |
| 2016 | 36.2 | 36.9 | 37.2 | 39.1 | 40.4 | 41.8 | 42.3 | 43.4 | 40.6 | 40.5 | 40.2 | 39.8 | 39.9 |
| 2017 | 37.5 | 38.6 | 38.7 | 40.3 | 42.1 | 43.3 | 44.0 | 45.3 | 42.2 | 42.6 | 41.4 | 41.0 | 41.4 |
| 2018 | 38.3 | 39.1 | 38.9 | 40.8 | 42.5 | 43.5 | 44.0 | 44.6 | 42.7 | 42.5 | 41.1 | 41.1 | 41.6 |
| 2019 | 38.3 | 38.5 | 38.8 | 40.5 | 41.7 | 43.1 | 43.1 | 43.6 | 41.6 | 40.9 | 41.4 | 40.3 | 41.0 |
| **Other Services** | | | | | | | | | | | | | |
| 2011 | 17.6 | 17.7 | 17.7 | 17.9 | 18.0 | 17.7 | 18.0 | 18.0 | 18.0 | 17.7 | 17.7 | 17.8 | 17.8 |
| 2012 | 17.5 | 17.6 | 17.9 | 17.9 | 17.9 | 18.0 | 18.0 | 17.9 | 17.8 | 17.9 | 17.9 | 17.8 | 17.8 |
| 2013 | 17.5 | 17.7 | 17.9 | 17.8 | 17.9 | 18.1 | 18.1 | 18.0 | 17.7 | 18.1 | 18.2 | 18.3 | 17.9 |
| 2014 | 18.0 | 18.1 | 18.2 | 18.3 | 18.2 | 18.0 | 18.3 | 18.3 | 18.1 | 18.3 | 18.5 | 18.5 | 18.2 |
| 2015 | 18.3 | 18.4 | 18.4 | 18.5 | 18.6 | 18.6 | 18.7 | 18.5 | 17.9 | 18.5 | 18.6 | 18.7 | 18.5 |
| 2016 | 18.6 | 18.6 | 18.6 | 18.9 | 18.8 | 18.8 | 18.9 | 18.7 | 18.5 | 18.8 | 18.8 | 18.9 | 18.7 |
| 2017 | 18.8 | 18.7 | 18.8 | 18.9 | 19.0 | 19.1 | 19.2 | 19.0 | 18.8 | 19.2 | 19.2 | 19.3 | 19.0 |
| 2018 | 19.1 | 19.3 | 19.3 | 19.4 | 19.5 | 19.4 | 19.6 | 19.4 | 19.0 | 19.5 | 19.5 | 19.4 | 19.4 |
| 2019 | 19.2 | 19.1 | 19.3 | 19.5 | 19.5 | 19.5 | 19.8 | 19.7 | 19.1 | 19.4 | 19.4 | 19.5 | 19.4 |
| **Government** | | | | | | | | | | | | | |
| 2011 | 100.7 | 103.3 | 103.1 | 104.3 | 104.6 | 104.3 | 98.8 | 97.4 | 99.5 | 102.9 | 103.3 | 103.4 | 102.1 |
| 2012 | 100.7 | 103.0 | 102.3 | 103.2 | 103.8 | 103.0 | 96.6 | 96.1 | 99.0 | 102.0 | 103.0 | 102.5 | 101.3 |
| 2013 | 100.7 | 103.5 | 103.1 | 103.0 | 103.6 | 103.6 | 97.6 | 96.4 | 98.4 | 101.6 | 102.8 | 102.3 | 101.4 |
| 2014 | 99.2 | 102.3 | 102.2 | 102.4 | 102.5 | 102.4 | 96.6 | 95.6 | 98.4 | 101.8 | 102.1 | 102.3 | 100.7 |
| 2015 | 100.0 | 102.0 | 101.9 | 102.1 | 102.7 | 102.5 | 96.5 | 95.4 | 98.2 | 101.9 | 102.0 | 102.1 | 100.6 |
| 2016 | 100.2 | 102.2 | 102.2 | 102.9 | 102.1 | 102.4 | 97.2 | 96.4 | 99.8 | 102.3 | 102.5 | 102.8 | 101.1 |
| 2017 | 101.1 | 103.0 | 103.0 | 103.4 | 102.6 | 102.9 | 97.5 | 96.7 | 99.7 | 102.8 | 103.1 | 103.3 | 101.6 |
| 2018 | 101.2 | 102.7 | 102.8 | 102.7 | 103.3 | 103.3 | 97.9 | 96.5 | 99.4 | 102.9 | 103.5 | 103.4 | 101.6 |
| 2019 | 101.8 | 103.7 | 103.2 | 103.9 | 103.6 | 103.8 | 98.3 | 97.8 | 100.8 | 103.5 | 104.0 | 104.0 | 102.4 |

# Employment by Industry: Knoxville, TN, Selected Years, 2011–2019

(Numbers in thousands, not seasonally adjusted)

| Industry and year | January | February | March | April | May | June | July | August | September | October | November | December | Annual average |
|---|---|---|---|---|---|---|---|---|---|---|---|---|---|
| **Total Nonfarm** | | | | | | | | | | | | | |
| 2011 | 355.7 | 358.4 | 361.0 | 364.1 | 364.9 | 363.6 | 361.6 | 366.6 | 368.6 | 367.8 | 369.6 | 368.3 | 364.2 |
| 2012 | 361.2 | 362.7 | 365.9 | 367.7 | 368.7 | 366.7 | 364.6 | 368.6 | 369.6 | 370.4 | 372.2 | 372.0 | 367.5 |
| 2013 | 362.7 | 364.5 | 366.8 | 369.0 | 370.1 | 366.1 | 365.1 | 370.1 | 371.5 | 374.8 | 376.2 | 375.9 | 369.4 |
| 2014 | 367.9 | 369.2 | 371.9 | 374.8 | 376.7 | 372.2 | 372.5 | 377.7 | 380.8 | 382.6 | 386.3 | 385.1 | 376.5 |
| 2015 | 377.1 | 376.9 | 378.8 | 383.3 | 385.0 | 380.9 | 381.1 | 385.9 | 389.9 | 392.0 | 393.8 | 393.2 | 384.8 |
| 2016 | 383.7 | 386.1 | 389.6 | 393.2 | 393.3 | 390.2 | 388.6 | 392.6 | 397.0 | 397.4 | 399.6 | 397.6 | 392.4 |
| 2017 | 389.2 | 392.3 | 393.0 | 396.6 | 397.2 | 392.2 | 391.3 | 395.4 | 398.8 | 398.0 | 401.6 | 400.2 | 395.5 |
| 2018 | 391.8 | 394.4 | 396.3 | 399.3 | 401.7 | 396.5 | 395.0 | 399.8 | 402.5 | 403.8 | 407.0 | 405.6 | 399.5 |
| 2019 | 398.0 | 401.0 | 402.5 | 404.8 | 405.2 | 401.4 | 400.5 | 405.3 | 408.0 | 410.6 | 412.6 | 410.2 | 405.0 |
| **Total Private** | | | | | | | | | | | | | |
| 2011 | 296.5 | 298.9 | 301.5 | 304.3 | 305.1 | 306.6 | 306.5 | 308.0 | 308.8 | 308.0 | 309.2 | 308.3 | 305.1 |
| 2012 | 301.7 | 303.1 | 305.9 | 307.6 | 308.5 | 309.2 | 308.2 | 310.6 | 310.5 | 310.1 | 311.6 | 311.5 | 308.2 |
| 2013 | 303.7 | 305.1 | 307.4 | 308.2 | 309.5 | 309.5 | 309.3 | 312.1 | 312.1 | 312.7 | 315.0 | 314.4 | 309.9 |
| 2014 | 308.3 | 308.5 | 311.2 | 313.7 | 315.5 | 315.2 | 316.1 | 319.2 | 320.6 | 321.1 | 323.7 | 324.1 | 316.4 |
| 2015 | 316.9 | 316.7 | 318.8 | 322.7 | 324.8 | 324.5 | 325.0 | 327.5 | 328.7 | 330.2 | 331.1 | 331.8 | 324.9 |
| 2016 | 324.6 | 325.4 | 328.4 | 331.7 | 332.4 | 333.5 | 332.6 | 334.3 | 335.8 | 335.5 | 336.6 | 336.4 | 332.3 |
| 2017 | 330.3 | 331.5 | 332.6 | 335.6 | 336.5 | 335.7 | 335.2 | 337.2 | 338.1 | 336.7 | 339.8 | 339.3 | 335.7 |
| 2018 | 332.8 | 334.2 | 336.1 | 338.8 | 340.6 | 339.9 | 339.3 | 342.0 | 342.2 | 342.0 | 344.6 | 344.2 | 339.7 |
| 2019 | 339.1 | 340.3 | 342.1 | 344.0 | 344.8 | 345.5 | 346.1 | 348.3 | 347.8 | 349.2 | 351.0 | 350.2 | 345.7 |
| **Goods Producing** | | | | | | | | | | | | | |
| 2011 | 50.4 | 50.9 | 51.5 | 51.7 | 51.8 | 52.6 | 52.8 | 53.2 | 53.7 | 54.1 | 53.7 | 52.9 | 52.4 |
| 2012 | 51.3 | 51.6 | 51.7 | 51.7 | 52.0 | 52.5 | 52.6 | 52.9 | 53.0 | 52.9 | 52.7 | 52.3 | 52.3 |
| 2013 | 51.3 | 51.8 | 51.9 | 51.7 | 51.8 | 51.9 | 51.8 | 52.1 | 52.1 | 53.1 | 53.1 | 51.9 | 52.0 |
| 2014 | 50.8 | 51.2 | 51.6 | 51.7 | 51.6 | 51.7 | 52.1 | 52.6 | 52.9 | 53.3 | 53.8 | 53.4 | 52.2 |
| 2015 | 51.9 | 51.8 | 52.0 | 52.4 | 52.6 | 52.6 | 53.1 | 53.4 | 54.3 | 55.0 | 54.8 | 54.5 | 53.2 |
| 2016 | 54.2 | 54.3 | 55.4 | 55.9 | 55.7 | 56.1 | 56.1 | 56.4 | 56.9 | 57.0 | 56.9 | 56.5 | 56.0 |
| 2017 | 55.7 | 56.1 | 56.5 | 56.7 | 56.8 | 56.8 | 57.1 | 57.2 | 57.5 | 57.3 | 57.6 | 57.1 | 56.9 |
| 2018 | 56.6 | 56.7 | 57.3 | 57.6 | 58.0 | 58.2 | 58.7 | 59.0 | 59.2 | 59.5 | 60.0 | 59.3 | 58.3 |
| 2019 | 58.8 | 58.8 | 59.1 | 59.6 | 59.8 | 60.0 | 60.2 | 60.6 | 60.5 | 60.3 | 60.8 | 60.5 | 59.9 |
| **Service-Providing** | | | | | | | | | | | | | |
| 2011 | 305.3 | 307.5 | 309.5 | 312.4 | 313.1 | 311.0 | 308.8 | 313.4 | 314.9 | 313.7 | 315.9 | 315.4 | 311.7 |
| 2012 | 309.9 | 311.1 | 314.2 | 316.0 | 316.7 | 314.2 | 312.0 | 315.7 | 316.6 | 317.5 | 319.5 | 319.7 | 315.3 |
| 2013 | 311.4 | 312.7 | 314.9 | 317.3 | 318.3 | 314.2 | 313.3 | 318.0 | 319.4 | 321.7 | 323.1 | 324.0 | 317.4 |
| 2014 | 317.1 | 318.0 | 320.3 | 323.1 | 325.1 | 320.5 | 320.4 | 325.1 | 327.9 | 329.3 | 332.5 | 331.7 | 324.3 |
| 2015 | 325.2 | 325.1 | 326.8 | 330.9 | 332.4 | 328.3 | 328.0 | 332.5 | 335.6 | 337.0 | 339.0 | 338.7 | 331.6 |
| 2016 | 329.5 | 331.8 | 334.2 | 337.3 | 337.6 | 334.1 | 332.5 | 336.2 | 340.1 | 340.4 | 342.7 | 341.1 | 336.5 |
| 2017 | 333.5 | 336.2 | 336.5 | 339.9 | 340.4 | 335.4 | 334.2 | 338.2 | 341.3 | 340.7 | 344.0 | 343.1 | 338.6 |
| 2018 | 335.2 | 337.7 | 339.0 | 341.7 | 343.7 | 338.3 | 336.3 | 340.8 | 343.3 | 344.3 | 347.0 | 346.3 | 341.1 |
| 2019 | 339.2 | 342.2 | 343.4 | 345.2 | 345.4 | 341.4 | 340.3 | 344.7 | 347.5 | 350.3 | 351.8 | 349.7 | 345.1 |
| **Mining, Logging, and Construction** | | | | | | | | | | | | | |
| 2011 | 16.2 | 16.5 | 17.0 | 17.2 | 17.1 | 17.5 | 17.8 | 18.1 | 18.7 | 19.0 | 18.4 | 17.4 | 17.6 |
| 2012 | 15.9 | 16.1 | 16.4 | 16.3 | 16.6 | 17.0 | 17.0 | 17.4 | 17.5 | 17.4 | 17.2 | 16.9 | 16.8 |
| 2013 | 16.1 | 16.5 | 16.6 | 16.6 | 16.8 | 16.8 | 16.8 | 17.1 | 17.2 | 17.9 | 17.8 | 16.9 | 16.9 |
| 2014 | 15.9 | 16.2 | 16.5 | 16.7 | 16.7 | 16.7 | 17.0 | 17.3 | 17.6 | 17.9 | 18.2 | 17.8 | 17.0 |
| 2015 | 16.7 | 16.5 | 16.8 | 17.1 | 17.4 | 17.2 | 17.3 | 17.6 | 18.3 | 19.1 | 18.7 | 18.2 | 17.6 |
| 2016 | 16.9 | 16.7 | 17.5 | 17.8 | 17.4 | 17.7 | 17.8 | 17.9 | 18.5 | 18.3 | 18.1 | 17.8 | 17.7 |
| 2017 | 17.1 | 17.4 | 17.8 | 18.1 | 18.3 | 18.3 | 18.4 | 18.5 | 18.8 | 18.7 | 18.8 | 18.3 | 18.2 |
| 2018 | 17.7 | 17.7 | 18.2 | 18.2 | 18.4 | 18.6 | 18.5 | 18.5 | 18.7 | 18.9 | 19.3 | 18.9 | 18.5 |
| 2019 | 18.3 | 18.2 | 18.5 | 18.8 | 18.9 | 19.1 | 19.1 | 19.2 | 19.1 | 19.3 | 19.5 | 19.2 | 18.9 |
| **Manufacturing** | | | | | | | | | | | | | |
| 2011 | 34.2 | 34.4 | 34.5 | 34.5 | 34.7 | 35.1 | 35.0 | 35.1 | 35.0 | 35.1 | 35.3 | 35.5 | 34.9 |
| 2012 | 35.4 | 35.5 | 35.3 | 35.4 | 35.4 | 35.5 | 35.6 | 35.5 | 35.5 | 35.5 | 35.5 | 35.4 | 35.5 |
| 2013 | 35.2 | 35.3 | 35.3 | 35.1 | 35.0 | 35.1 | 35.0 | 35.0 | 34.9 | 35.2 | 35.3 | 35.0 | 35.1 |
| 2014 | 34.9 | 35.0 | 35.1 | 35.0 | 34.9 | 35.0 | 35.1 | 35.3 | 35.3 | 35.4 | 35.6 | 35.6 | 35.2 |
| 2015 | 35.2 | 35.3 | 35.2 | 35.3 | 35.2 | 35.4 | 35.8 | 35.8 | 36.0 | 35.9 | 36.1 | 36.3 | 35.6 |
| 2016 | 37.3 | 37.6 | 37.9 | 38.1 | 38.3 | 38.4 | 38.3 | 38.5 | 38.4 | 38.7 | 38.8 | 38.7 | 38.3 |
| 2017 | 38.6 | 38.7 | 38.7 | 38.6 | 38.5 | 38.5 | 38.7 | 38.7 | 38.7 | 38.6 | 38.8 | 38.8 | 38.7 |
| 2018 | 38.9 | 39.0 | 39.1 | 39.4 | 39.6 | 39.6 | 40.2 | 40.5 | 40.5 | 40.6 | 40.7 | 40.4 | 39.9 |
| 2019 | 40.5 | 40.6 | 40.6 | 40.8 | 40.9 | 40.9 | 41.1 | 41.4 | 41.4 | 41.0 | 41.3 | 41.3 | 41.0 |

## Employment by Industry: Knoxville, TN, Selected Years, 2011–2019—*Continued*

(Numbers in thousands, not seasonally adjusted)

| Industry and year | January | February | March | April | May | June | July | August | September | October | November | December | Annual average |
|---|---|---|---|---|---|---|---|---|---|---|---|---|---|
| **Trade, Transportation, and Utilities** | | | | | | | | | | | | | |
| 2011 | 71.2 | 71.0 | 71.5 | 72.1 | 72.4 | 72.6 | 72.6 | 72.6 | 72.6 | 73.0 | 74.6 | 75.2 | 72.6 |
| 2012 | 72.7 | 72.6 | 73.2 | 73.6 | 73.8 | 73.9 | 74.1 | 74.2 | 74.1 | 74.7 | 76.4 | 76.8 | 74.2 |
| 2013 | 73.8 | 73.7 | 74.1 | 74.1 | 74.2 | 74.2 | 74.4 | 74.5 | 74.3 | 74.8 | 76.5 | 77.1 | 74.6 |
| 2014 | 74.3 | 74.1 | 74.7 | 74.8 | 75.0 | 75.4 | 75.9 | 76.2 | 76.1 | 76.6 | 78.1 | 78.9 | 75.8 |
| 2015 | 76.1 | 75.3 | 75.8 | 76.7 | 77.0 | 77.1 | 77.4 | 78.0 | 78.0 | 78.6 | 80.0 | 81.0 | 77.6 |
| 2016 | 78.0 | 77.9 | 78.2 | 78.5 | 78.7 | 78.6 | 78.7 | 78.7 | 78.9 | 79.2 | 80.5 | 81.3 | 78.9 |
| 2017 | 77.9 | 77.3 | 77.1 | 77.3 | 77.2 | 77.2 | 77.0 | 77.4 | 77.3 | 77.6 | 79.4 | 80.0 | 77.7 |
| 2018 | 77.1 | 76.7 | 77.3 | 77.7 | 78.0 | 78.0 | 78.0 | 78.2 | 78.3 | 78.6 | 80.6 | 81.2 | 78.3 |
| 2019 | 78.5 | 78.5 | 78.6 | 78.3 | 78.6 | 78.6 | 78.6 | 78.9 | 78.7 | 79.6 | 81.2 | 81.1 | 79.1 |
| **Wholesale Trade** | | | | | | | | | | | | | |
| 2011 | 15.6 | 15.6 | 15.7 | 16.0 | 16.1 | 16.2 | 16.2 | 16.2 | 16.2 | 16.2 | 16.3 | 16.4 | 16.1 |
| 2012 | 16.3 | 16.4 | 16.4 | 16.5 | 16.5 | 16.6 | 16.4 | 16.5 | 16.6 | 16.5 | 16.5 | 16.4 | 16.5 |
| 2013 | 16.3 | 16.3 | 16.4 | 16.2 | 16.2 | 16.2 | 16.1 | 16.1 | 16.1 | 16.1 | 16.1 | 16.1 | 16.2 |
| 2014 | 16.0 | 16.0 | 16.0 | 16.0 | 16.1 | 16.0 | 15.9 | 16.1 | 16.1 | 16.1 | 16.1 | 16.2 | 16.1 |
| 2015 | 16.1 | 16.1 | 16.1 | 16.2 | 16.2 | 16.2 | 16.3 | 16.3 | 16.4 | 16.5 | 16.5 | 16.6 | 16.3 |
| 2016 | 16.4 | 16.4 | 16.4 | 16.4 | 16.4 | 16.5 | 16.4 | 16.4 | 16.5 | 16.5 | 16.4 | 16.5 | 16.4 |
| 2017 | 16.2 | 16.2 | 16.2 | 16.1 | 16.1 | 16.2 | 16.1 | 16.1 | 16.2 | 16.3 | 16.4 | 16.5 | 16.2 |
| 2018 | 16.0 | 16.1 | 16.2 | 16.1 | 16.2 | 16.2 | 16.3 | 16.3 | 16.3 | 16.4 | 16.5 | 16.6 | 16.3 |
| 2019 | 16.4 | 16.5 | 16.5 | 16.4 | 16.4 | 16.4 | 16.4 | 16.4 | 16.3 | 16.4 | 16.4 | 16.4 | 16.4 |
| **Retail Trade** | | | | | | | | | | | | | |
| 2011 | 44.0 | 43.6 | 43.9 | 44.1 | 44.2 | 44.4 | 44.4 | 44.3 | 44.2 | 44.7 | 46.1 | 46.4 | 44.5 |
| 2012 | 44.5 | 44.2 | 44.8 | 45.1 | 45.1 | 45.3 | 45.7 | 45.5 | 45.2 | 45.7 | 47.2 | 47.3 | 45.5 |
| 2013 | 45.0 | 44.8 | 45.0 | 45.0 | 45.0 | 45.0 | 45.4 | 45.2 | 44.9 | 45.4 | 47.0 | 47.3 | 45.4 |
| 2014 | 45.1 | 44.8 | 45.1 | 45.2 | 45.2 | 45.7 | 46.2 | 46.0 | 45.8 | 46.1 | 47.5 | 47.9 | 45.9 |
| 2015 | 45.6 | 45.0 | 45.4 | 46.1 | 46.2 | 46.4 | 46.6 | 46.9 | 46.7 | 47.2 | 48.4 | 49.0 | 46.6 |
| 2016 | 47.0 | 46.9 | 47.2 | 47.4 | 47.6 | 47.7 | 47.9 | 47.8 | 47.9 | 48.4 | 49.7 | 50.1 | 48.0 |
| 2017 | 48.1 | 47.7 | 47.6 | 48.0 | 47.9 | 48.0 | 47.9 | 47.9 | 47.7 | 47.9 | 49.4 | 49.6 | 48.1 |
| 2018 | 47.6 | 47.4 | 47.8 | 48.2 | 48.2 | 48.4 | 48.2 | 47.9 | 47.8 | 48.0 | 49.6 | 49.7 | 48.2 |
| 2019 | 48.1 | 47.8 | 47.8 | 47.6 | 47.8 | 48.0 | 48.0 | 47.9 | 47.6 | 48.4 | 49.8 | 49.5 | 48.2 |
| **Transportation and Utilities** | | | | | | | | | | | | | |
| 2011 | 11.6 | 11.8 | 11.9 | 12.0 | 12.1 | 12.0 | 12.0 | 12.1 | 12.2 | 12.1 | 12.2 | 12.4 | 12.0 |
| 2012 | 11.9 | 12.0 | 12.0 | 12.0 | 12.2 | 12.0 | 12.0 | 12.2 | 12.3 | 12.5 | 12.7 | 13.1 | 12.2 |
| 2013 | 12.5 | 12.6 | 12.7 | 12.9 | 13.0 | 13.0 | 12.9 | 13.2 | 13.3 | 13.3 | 13.4 | 13.7 | 13.0 |
| 2014 | 13.2 | 13.3 | 13.6 | 13.6 | 13.7 | 13.7 | 13.8 | 14.1 | 14.2 | 14.4 | 14.5 | 14.8 | 13.9 |
| 2015 | 14.4 | 14.2 | 14.3 | 14.4 | 14.6 | 14.5 | 14.5 | 14.8 | 14.9 | 14.9 | 15.1 | 15.4 | 14.7 |
| 2016 | 14.6 | 14.6 | 14.6 | 14.7 | 14.7 | 14.4 | 14.4 | 14.5 | 14.5 | 14.3 | 14.4 | 14.7 | 14.5 |
| 2017 | 13.6 | 13.4 | 13.3 | 13.2 | 13.2 | 13.0 | 13.0 | 13.4 | 13.4 | 13.4 | 13.6 | 13.9 | 13.4 |
| 2018 | 13.5 | 13.2 | 13.3 | 13.4 | 13.6 | 13.4 | 13.5 | 14.0 | 14.2 | 14.2 | 14.5 | 14.9 | 13.8 |
| 2019 | 14.0 | 14.2 | 14.3 | 14.3 | 14.4 | 14.2 | 14.2 | 14.6 | 14.8 | 14.8 | 15.0 | 15.2 | 14.5 |
| **Information** | | | | | | | | | | | | | |
| 2011 | 6.1 | 6.1 | 6.0 | 6.0 | 6.0 | 6.0 | 6.1 | 6.0 | 6.0 | 5.9 | 5.9 | 5.8 | 6.0 |
| 2012 | 5.8 | 5.9 | 5.8 | 5.9 | 5.9 | 5.9 | 6.0 | 6.0 | 5.8 | 6.0 | 5.9 | 6.0 | 5.9 |
| 2013 | 6.1 | 6.0 | 6.0 | 6.1 | 6.1 | 6.1 | 6.1 | 6.1 | 5.9 | 6.0 | 6.1 | 6.0 | 6.1 |
| 2014 | 6.1 | 6.0 | 6.0 | 6.1 | 6.0 | 6.1 | 6.1 | 6.1 | 6.0 | 5.9 | 6.0 | 6.0 | 6.0 |
| 2015 | 6.1 | 6.0 | 6.0 | 6.0 | 5.9 | 5.9 | 5.9 | 5.9 | 5.9 | 5.8 | 5.9 | 5.9 | 5.9 |
| 2016 | 5.9 | 5.9 | 5.9 | 5.9 | 5.9 | 5.9 | 6.0 | 5.9 | 5.9 | 5.8 | 5.8 | 5.9 | 5.9 |
| 2017 | 5.9 | 5.9 | 6.0 | 5.9 | 6.0 | 6.0 | 6.0 | 6.0 | 6.0 | 5.9 | 5.9 | 5.9 | 6.0 |
| 2018 | 5.9 | 5.9 | 5.9 | 6.0 | 6.0 | 6.0 | 6.0 | 6.0 | 6.0 | 5.9 | 5.9 | 5.9 | 6.0 |
| 2019 | 5.9 | 5.8 | 5.9 | 5.9 | 5.9 | 6.0 | 6.0 | 6.0 | 6.0 | 6.0 | 6.1 | 6.1 | 6.0 |
| **Financial Activities** | | | | | | | | | | | | | |
| 2011 | 17.5 | 17.5 | 17.5 | 17.6 | 17.6 | 17.8 | 17.7 | 17.8 | 17.7 | 17.8 | 17.8 | 17.9 | 17.7 |
| 2012 | 17.8 | 17.9 | 18.0 | 18.0 | 18.1 | 18.1 | 18.0 | 18.0 | 17.9 | 17.9 | 17.9 | 18.0 | 18.0 |
| 2013 | 17.7 | 17.6 | 17.9 | 17.9 | 18.0 | 18.1 | 18.1 | 18.1 | 18.1 | 18.0 | 18.0 | 18.1 | 18.0 |
| 2014 | 17.9 | 18.0 | 18.0 | 18.1 | 18.1 | 18.2 | 18.3 | 18.3 | 18.3 | 18.4 | 18.5 | 18.6 | 18.2 |
| 2015 | 18.5 | 18.6 | 18.6 | 18.6 | 18.6 | 18.8 | 18.8 | 18.8 | 18.7 | 18.8 | 18.9 | 19.0 | 18.7 |
| 2016 | 18.7 | 18.7 | 18.8 | 18.9 | 19.0 | 19.1 | 19.1 | 19.2 | 19.2 | 19.3 | 19.3 | 19.3 | 19.1 |
| 2017 | 19.2 | 19.2 | 19.2 | 19.4 | 19.4 | 19.5 | 19.5 | 19.6 | 19.5 | 19.6 | 19.6 | 19.7 | 19.5 |
| 2018 | 19.6 | 19.7 | 19.8 | 19.9 | 19.9 | 20.1 | 20.0 | 20.1 | 19.9 | 19.9 | 19.9 | 19.9 | 19.9 |
| 2019 | 19.6 | 19.6 | 19.6 | 19.7 | 19.8 | 19.9 | 20.0 | 19.9 | 19.9 | 19.7 | 19.8 | 19.8 | 19.8 |

# Employment by Industry: Knoxville, TN, Selected Years, 2011–2019—*Continued*

(Numbers in thousands, not seasonally adjusted)

| Industry and year | January | February | March | April | May | June | July | August | September | October | November | December | Annual average |
|---|---|---|---|---|---|---|---|---|---|---|---|---|---|
| **Professional and Business Services** | | | | | | | | | | | | | |
| 2011 | 54.6 | 55.6 | 56.1 | 56.2 | 56.0 | 55.4 | 55.6 | 56.3 | 56.5 | 56.4 | 56.6 | 56.3 | 56.0 |
| 2012 | 54.9 | 55.1 | 55.7 | 55.8 | 55.8 | 55.4 | 54.7 | 56.1 | 56.1 | 55.4 | 55.6 | 55.5 | 55.5 |
| 2013 | 54.5 | 55.0 | 55.3 | 55.4 | 55.7 | 55.5 | 55.4 | 57.0 | 57.2 | 57.2 | 57.6 | 57.8 | 56.1 |
| 2014 | 57.5 | 57.6 | 58.2 | 59.2 | 59.4 | 58.6 | 58.3 | 60.0 | 60.7 | 60.6 | 61.0 | 61.1 | 59.4 |
| 2015 | 60.0 | 59.9 | 60.3 | 61.4 | 62.4 | 61.5 | 61.2 | 62.6 | 63.0 | 63.4 | 62.9 | 63.2 | 61.8 |
| 2016 | 61.2 | 61.4 | 62.2 | 63.1 | 63.4 | 63.4 | 62.8 | 64.0 | 64.2 | 64.3 | 64.3 | 64.4 | 63.2 |
| 2017 | 63.5 | 64.1 | 64.6 | 65.5 | 65.6 | 64.8 | 64.2 | 65.0 | 65.5 | 64.6 | 65.2 | 65.1 | 64.8 |
| 2018 | 63.5 | 64.2 | 64.3 | 64.8 | 65.1 | 64.3 | 63.7 | 64.9 | 64.9 | 64.2 | 64.4 | 64.4 | 64.4 |
| 2019 | 63.8 | 64.3 | 64.9 | 65.3 | 65.1 | 64.9 | 65.1 | 66.1 | 66.0 | 66.4 | 65.8 | 65.4 | 65.3 |
| **Education and Health Services** | | | | | | | | | | | | | |
| 2011 | 48.7 | 49.1 | 49.4 | 50.1 | 50.1 | 50.3 | 50.3 | 50.5 | 50.8 | 50.2 | 50.0 | 49.9 | 50.0 |
| 2012 | 49.5 | 49.7 | 49.9 | 49.9 | 50.1 | 50.1 | 50.1 | 50.5 | 50.7 | 50.8 | 50.6 | 50.8 | 50.2 |
| 2013 | 49.6 | 50.0 | 50.2 | 50.2 | 50.2 | 49.6 | 49.5 | 49.8 | 50.1 | 50.1 | 50.4 | 50.6 | 50.0 |
| 2014 | 49.7 | 49.8 | 50.0 | 50.0 | 50.6 | 50.4 | 50.4 | 50.9 | 51.4 | 51.7 | 51.7 | 51.9 | 50.7 |
| 2015 | 51.4 | 51.6 | 52.0 | 51.8 | 52.1 | 52.0 | 51.8 | 52.1 | 52.2 | 52.4 | 52.5 | 52.6 | 52.0 |
| 2016 | 52.2 | 52.4 | 52.7 | 52.9 | 53.0 | 52.9 | 52.7 | 53.1 | 53.3 | 53.6 | 53.8 | 53.8 | 53.0 |
| 2017 | 53.8 | 54.1 | 54.1 | 54.1 | 54.2 | 53.8 | 53.8 | 54.1 | 54.1 | 54.3 | 54.5 | 54.4 | 54.1 |
| 2018 | 54.0 | 54.2 | 54.3 | 54.5 | 54.6 | 54.2 | 54.0 | 54.4 | 54.4 | 54.6 | 54.7 | 54.7 | 54.4 |
| 2019 | 54.4 | 54.7 | 54.8 | 54.8 | 54.8 | 54.6 | 54.6 | 55.2 | 55.5 | 55.5 | 55.9 | 56.1 | 55.1 |
| **Leisure and Hospitality** | | | | | | | | | | | | | |
| 2011 | 34.6 | 35.2 | 35.9 | 36.9 | 37.5 | 37.8 | 37.4 | 37.6 | 37.8 | 36.9 | 36.7 | 36.4 | 36.7 |
| 2012 | 35.8 | 36.4 | 37.6 | 38.4 | 38.5 | 38.8 | 38.3 | 38.6 | 38.6 | 38.3 | 38.5 | 38.2 | 38.0 |
| 2013 | 36.9 | 37.1 | 37.9 | 38.5 | 39.1 | 39.5 | 39.5 | 39.9 | 39.9 | 39.1 | 38.9 | 38.5 | 38.7 |
| 2014 | 37.8 | 37.5 | 38.2 | 39.5 | 40.4 | 40.4 | 40.6 | 40.7 | 40.8 | 40.4 | 40.2 | 39.8 | 39.7 |
| 2015 | 38.6 | 39.1 | 39.7 | 41.2 | 41.5 | 41.8 | 41.9 | 41.9 | 41.8 | 41.4 | 41.3 | 40.7 | 40.9 |
| 2016 | 39.7 | 40.0 | 40.4 | 41.5 | 41.9 | 42.6 | 42.3 | 42.2 | 42.6 | 41.5 | 41.2 | 40.4 | 41.4 |
| 2017 | 39.6 | 40.0 | 40.3 | 41.8 | 42.3 | 42.5 | 42.5 | 42.8 | 43.1 | 42.4 | 42.5 | 42.0 | 41.8 |
| 2018 | 41.1 | 41.6 | 41.9 | 43.0 | 43.6 | 43.6 | 43.4 | 43.8 | 43.8 | 43.7 | 43.5 | 43.1 | 43.0 |
| 2019 | 42.4 | 42.7 | 43.2 | 44.3 | 44.7 | 45.3 | 45.4 | 45.4 | 45.0 | 45.6 | 45.3 | 45.1 | 44.5 |
| **Other Services** | | | | | | | | | | | | | |
| 2011 | 13.4 | 13.5 | 13.6 | 13.7 | 13.7 | 14.1 | 14.0 | 14.0 | 13.7 | 13.7 | 13.9 | 13.9 | 13.8 |
| 2012 | 13.9 | 13.9 | 14.0 | 14.3 | 14.3 | 14.5 | 14.4 | 14.3 | 14.3 | 14.1 | 14.0 | 13.9 | 14.2 |
| 2013 | 13.8 | 13.9 | 14.1 | 14.3 | 14.4 | 14.6 | 14.5 | 14.6 | 14.5 | 14.4 | 14.4 | 14.4 | 14.3 |
| 2014 | 14.2 | 14.3 | 14.5 | 14.3 | 14.4 | 14.4 | 14.4 | 14.4 | 14.4 | 14.2 | 14.4 | 14.4 | 14.4 |
| 2015 | 14.3 | 14.4 | 14.4 | 14.6 | 14.7 | 14.8 | 14.9 | 14.8 | 14.8 | 14.8 | 14.8 | 14.9 | 14.7 |
| 2016 | 14.7 | 14.8 | 14.8 | 15.0 | 14.8 | 14.9 | 14.9 | 14.8 | 14.8 | 14.8 | 14.8 | 14.8 | 14.8 |
| 2017 | 14.7 | 14.8 | 14.8 | 14.9 | 15.0 | 15.1 | 15.1 | 15.1 | 15.1 | 15.0 | 15.1 | 15.1 | 15.0 |
| 2018 | 15.0 | 15.2 | 15.3 | 15.3 | 15.4 | 15.5 | 15.5 | 15.6 | 15.7 | 15.6 | 15.6 | 15.7 | 15.5 |
| 2019 | 15.7 | 15.9 | 16.0 | 16.1 | 16.1 | 16.2 | 16.2 | 16.2 | 16.2 | 16.1 | 16.1 | 16.1 | 16.1 |
| **Government** | | | | | | | | | | | | | |
| 2011 | 59.2 | 59.5 | 59.5 | 59.8 | 59.8 | 57.0 | 55.1 | 58.6 | 59.8 | 59.8 | 60.4 | 60.0 | 59.0 |
| 2012 | 59.5 | 59.6 | 60.0 | 60.1 | 60.2 | 57.5 | 56.4 | 58.0 | 59.1 | 60.3 | 60.6 | 60.5 | 59.3 |
| 2013 | 59.0 | 59.4 | 59.4 | 60.8 | 60.6 | 56.6 | 55.8 | 58.0 | 59.4 | 62.1 | 61.2 | 61.5 | 59.5 |
| 2014 | 59.6 | 60.7 | 60.7 | 61.1 | 61.2 | 57.0 | 56.4 | 58.5 | 60.2 | 61.5 | 62.6 | 61.0 | 60.0 |
| 2015 | 60.2 | 60.2 | 60.0 | 60.6 | 60.2 | 56.4 | 56.1 | 58.4 | 61.2 | 61.8 | 62.7 | 61.4 | 59.9 |
| 2016 | 59.1 | 60.7 | 61.2 | 61.5 | 60.9 | 56.7 | 56.0 | 58.3 | 61.2 | 61.9 | 63.0 | 61.2 | 60.1 |
| 2017 | 58.9 | 60.8 | 60.4 | 61.0 | 60.7 | 56.5 | 56.1 | 58.2 | 60.7 | 61.3 | 61.8 | 60.9 | 59.8 |
| 2018 | 59.0 | 60.2 | 60.2 | 60.5 | 61.1 | 56.6 | 55.7 | 57.8 | 60.3 | 61.8 | 62.4 | 61.4 | 59.8 |
| 2019 | 58.9 | 60.7 | 60.4 | 60.8 | 60.4 | 55.9 | 54.4 | 57.0 | 60.2 | 61.4 | 61.6 | 60.0 | 59.3 |

## Employment by Industry: McAllen-Edinburg-Mission, TX, 2011–2019

(Numbers in thousands, not seasonally adjusted)

| Industry and year | January | February | March | April | May | June | July | August | September | October | November | December | Annual average |
|---|---|---|---|---|---|---|---|---|---|---|---|---|---|
| **Total Nonfarm** | | | | | | | | | | | | | |
| 2011 | 224.2 | 225.2 | 226.5 | 227.4 | 228.0 | 226.8 | 220.6 | 224.1 | 225.6 | 226.5 | 229.9 | 231.1 | 226.3 |
| 2012 | 228.4 | 229.6 | 231.4 | 231.2 | 231.4 | 230.4 | 223.2 | 226.6 | 228.3 | 231.8 | 235.2 | 237.0 | 230.4 |
| 2013 | 232.3 | 234.6 | 236.2 | 236.5 | 237.2 | 236.7 | 229.5 | 233.8 | 235.1 | 238.1 | 241.8 | 243.7 | 236.3 |
| 2014 | 238.6 | 239.9 | 240.9 | 242.1 | 244.1 | 243.0 | 236.0 | 239.7 | 240.9 | 244.9 | 247.3 | 249.9 | 242.3 |
| 2015 | 245.7 | 247.4 | 248.4 | 248.1 | 250.4 | 249.0 | 242.9 | 245.4 | 246.3 | 248.9 | 251.8 | 253.1 | 248.1 |
| 2016 | 249.4 | 251.1 | 252.0 | 253.6 | 254.0 | 252.3 | 246.1 | 249.9 | 252.6 | 255.2 | 258.0 | 259.6 | 252.8 |
| 2017 | 255.9 | 256.2 | 257.7 | 259.0 | 260.3 | 259.0 | 251.1 | 253.7 | 256.7 | 260.1 | 263.6 | 265.6 | 258.2 |
| 2018 | 261.2 | 263.0 | 264.8 | 265.2 | 266.2 | 264.8 | 258.5 | 262.0 | 263.3 | 267.3 | 270.6 | 271.3 | 264.9 |
| 2019 | 267.1 | 269.1 | 270.3 | 271.4 | 271.6 | 270.8 | 264.5 | 269.1 | 270.4 | 274.5 | 275.5 | 276.8 | 270.9 |
| **Total Private** | | | | | | | | | | | | | |
| 2011 | 168.1 | 168.5 | 170.0 | 171.5 | 171.7 | 171.5 | 171.1 | 172.8 | 172.6 | 172.4 | 174.8 | 175.9 | 171.7 |
| 2012 | 173.6 | 174.2 | 175.6 | 176.0 | 176.0 | 175.6 | 174.0 | 175.8 | 175.3 | 176.7 | 179.4 | 181.0 | 176.1 |
| 2013 | 177.0 | 178.6 | 179.8 | 180.7 | 180.7 | 180.9 | 179.4 | 181.9 | 181.2 | 182.1 | 185.1 | 186.9 | 181.2 |
| 2014 | 181.9 | 182.8 | 183.5 | 185.4 | 186.1 | 186.0 | 185.0 | 187.1 | 186.6 | 188.2 | 190.0 | 192.2 | 186.2 |
| 2015 | 188.8 | 189.8 | 190.6 | 191.0 | 191.9 | 191.3 | 191.0 | 191.6 | 190.6 | 191.2 | 193.6 | 194.4 | 191.3 |
| 2016 | 191.4 | 192.3 | 193.0 | 194.2 | 194.0 | 193.0 | 192.5 | 194.5 | 194.6 | 195.6 | 198.1 | 199.1 | 194.4 |
| 2017 | 196.3 | 196.2 | 197.7 | 198.3 | 199.1 | 199.0 | 197.0 | 198.4 | 199.0 | 200.2 | 203.0 | 204.7 | 199.1 |
| 2018 | 201.8 | 202.3 | 203.6 | 204.1 | 204.5 | 204.1 | 203.6 | 205.5 | 205.5 | 206.9 | 209.6 | 210.0 | 205.1 |
| 2019 | 207.4 | 208.2 | 209.2 | 210.0 | 210.0 | 210.3 | 209.4 | 212.4 | 211.3 | 213.6 | 214.2 | 215.0 | 210.9 |
| **Goods Producing** | | | | | | | | | | | | | |
| 2011 | 14.7 | 14.7 | 14.8 | 14.5 | 14.6 | 14.7 | 14.7 | 15.0 | 15.0 | 15.1 | 15.4 | 15.3 | 14.9 |
| 2012 | 15.2 | 15.3 | 15.5 | 15.3 | 15.3 | 15.3 | 15.1 | 15.4 | 15.3 | 15.6 | 15.7 | 15.9 | 15.4 |
| 2013 | 15.6 | 15.8 | 15.9 | 16.0 | 16.0 | 16.1 | 15.9 | 16.2 | 16.0 | 16.2 | 16.3 | 16.4 | 16.0 |
| 2014 | 16.1 | 16.5 | 16.2 | 16.6 | 16.4 | 16.5 | 16.3 | 16.6 | 16.6 | 16.8 | 16.7 | 16.9 | 16.5 |
| 2015 | 16.5 | 16.7 | 16.4 | 16.4 | 16.2 | 16.2 | 15.9 | 15.5 | 15.3 | 15.2 | 15.1 | 15.1 | 15.9 |
| 2016 | 14.8 | 14.7 | 14.6 | 14.3 | 14.0 | 14.0 | 14.0 | 14.1 | 14.2 | 14.6 | 14.7 | 14.8 | 14.4 |
| 2017 | 14.9 | 14.9 | 14.9 | 14.8 | 15.1 | 15.3 | 15.2 | 15.4 | 15.2 | 15.2 | 15.6 | 15.7 | 15.2 |
| 2018 | 15.4 | 15.5 | 15.5 | 15.4 | 15.3 | 15.2 | 15.2 | 15.2 | 15.1 | 15.4 | 15.5 | 15.6 | 15.4 |
| 2019 | 15.5 | 15.6 | 15.6 | 15.4 | 15.4 | 15.5 | 15.3 | 15.5 | 15.4 | 15.5 | 15.6 | 15.4 | 15.5 |
| **Service-Providing** | | | | | | | | | | | | | |
| 2011 | 209.5 | 210.5 | 211.7 | 212.9 | 213.4 | 212.1 | 205.9 | 209.1 | 210.6 | 211.4 | 214.5 | 215.8 | 211.5 |
| 2012 | 213.2 | 214.3 | 215.9 | 215.9 | 216.1 | 215.1 | 208.1 | 211.2 | 213.0 | 216.2 | 219.5 | 221.1 | 215.0 |
| 2013 | 216.7 | 218.8 | 220.3 | 220.5 | 221.2 | 220.6 | 213.6 | 217.6 | 219.1 | 221.9 | 225.5 | 227.3 | 220.3 |
| 2014 | 222.5 | 223.4 | 224.7 | 225.5 | 227.7 | 226.5 | 219.7 | 223.1 | 224.3 | 228.1 | 230.6 | 233.0 | 225.8 |
| 2015 | 229.2 | 230.7 | 232.0 | 231.7 | 234.2 | 232.8 | 227.0 | 229.9 | 231.0 | 233.7 | 236.7 | 238.0 | 232.2 |
| 2016 | 234.6 | 236.4 | 237.4 | 239.3 | 240.0 | 238.3 | 232.1 | 235.8 | 238.4 | 240.6 | 243.3 | 244.8 | 238.4 |
| 2017 | 241.0 | 241.3 | 242.8 | 244.2 | 245.2 | 243.7 | 235.9 | 238.3 | 241.5 | 244.9 | 248.0 | 249.9 | 243.1 |
| 2018 | 245.8 | 247.5 | 249.3 | 249.8 | 250.9 | 249.6 | 243.3 | 246.8 | 248.2 | 251.9 | 255.1 | 255.7 | 249.5 |
| 2019 | 251.6 | 253.5 | 254.7 | 256.0 | 256.2 | 255.3 | 249.2 | 253.6 | 255.0 | 259.0 | 259.9 | 261.4 | 255.5 |
| **Mining, Logging, and Construction** | | | | | | | | | | | | | |
| 2011 | 8.5 | 8.6 | 8.7 | 8.6 | 8.7 | 8.8 | 8.9 | 9.1 | 9.1 | 9.0 | 9.1 | 9.0 | 8.8 |
| 2012 | 8.9 | 9.0 | 9.2 | 9.1 | 9.2 | 9.2 | 9.2 | 9.3 | 9.2 | 9.3 | 9.3 | 9.4 | 9.2 |
| 2013 | 9.0 | 9.1 | 9.3 | 9.5 | 9.6 | 9.8 | 9.7 | 9.9 | 9.8 | 9.8 | 9.8 | 9.9 | 9.6 |
| 2014 | 9.8 | 9.9 | 9.9 | 10.0 | 10.0 | 10.1 | 10.1 | 10.3 | 10.2 | 10.4 | 10.3 | 10.4 | 10.1 |
| 2015 | 10.0 | 9.8 | 9.7 | 9.6 | 9.6 | 9.7 | 9.3 | 9.1 | 9.0 | 8.8 | 8.5 | 8.4 | 9.3 |
| 2016 | 8.2 | 8.1 | 8.1 | 8.0 | 7.8 | 7.8 | 7.9 | 7.9 | 7.9 | 8.0 | 8.0 | 8.1 | 8.0 |
| 2017 | 8.1 | 8.1 | 8.2 | 8.2 | 8.4 | 8.6 | 8.6 | 8.7 | 8.5 | 8.5 | 8.5 | 8.5 | 8.4 |
| 2018 | 8.3 | 8.3 | 8.4 | 8.3 | 8.3 | 8.4 | 8.5 | 8.4 | 8.3 | 8.3 | 8.4 | 8.4 | 8.4 |
| 2019 | 8.3 | 8.4 | 8.5 | 8.5 | 8.6 | 8.7 | 8.6 | 8.7 | 8.6 | 8.6 | 8.5 | 8.3 | 8.5 |
| **Manufacturing** | | | | | | | | | | | | | |
| 2011 | 6.2 | 6.1 | 6.1 | 5.9 | 5.9 | 5.9 | 5.8 | 5.9 | 5.9 | 6.1 | 6.3 | 6.3 | 6.0 |
| 2012 | 6.3 | 6.3 | 6.3 | 6.2 | 6.1 | 6.1 | 5.9 | 6.1 | 6.1 | 6.3 | 6.4 | 6.5 | 6.2 |
| 2013 | 6.6 | 6.7 | 6.6 | 6.5 | 6.4 | 6.3 | 6.2 | 6.3 | 6.2 | 6.4 | 6.5 | 6.5 | 6.4 |
| 2014 | 6.3 | 6.6 | 6.3 | 6.6 | 6.4 | 6.4 | 6.2 | 6.3 | 6.4 | 6.4 | 6.4 | 6.5 | 6.4 |
| 2015 | 6.5 | 6.9 | 6.7 | 6.8 | 6.6 | 6.5 | 6.6 | 6.4 | 6.3 | 6.4 | 6.6 | 6.7 | 6.6 |
| 2016 | 6.6 | 6.6 | 6.5 | 6.3 | 6.2 | 6.2 | 6.1 | 6.2 | 6.3 | 6.6 | 6.7 | 6.7 | 6.4 |
| 2017 | 6.8 | 6.8 | 6.7 | 6.6 | 6.7 | 6.7 | 6.6 | 6.7 | 6.7 | 6.7 | 7.1 | 7.2 | 6.8 |
| 2018 | 7.1 | 7.2 | 7.1 | 7.1 | 7.0 | 6.8 | 6.7 | 6.8 | 6.8 | 7.1 | 7.1 | 7.2 | 7.0 |
| 2019 | 7.2 | 7.2 | 7.1 | 6.9 | 6.8 | 6.8 | 6.7 | 6.8 | 6.8 | 6.9 | 7.1 | 7.1 | 7.0 |

## Employment by Industry: McAllen-Edinburg-Mission, TX, 2011–2019—*Continued*
(Numbers in thousands, not seasonally adjusted)

| Industry and year | January | February | March | April | May | June | July | August | September | October | November | December | Annual average |
|---|---|---|---|---|---|---|---|---|---|---|---|---|---|
| **Trade, Transportation, and Utilities** | | | | | | | | | | | | | |
| 2011 | 46.8 | 46.3 | 46.7 | 47.4 | 47.4 | 47.3 | 47.3 | 47.9 | 47.3 | 47.7 | 49.3 | 50.1 | 47.6 |
| 2012 | 48.6 | 48.2 | 48.7 | 48.9 | 49.0 | 49.2 | 49.4 | 50.1 | 49.5 | 49.8 | 52.0 | 52.5 | 49.7 |
| 2013 | 50.7 | 50.3 | 50.5 | 50.8 | 50.8 | 51.1 | 50.7 | 51.1 | 50.8 | 51.0 | 53.1 | 54.1 | 51.3 |
| 2014 | 51.4 | 51.0 | 51.2 | 52.1 | 52.1 | 52.5 | 52.7 | 52.8 | 52.4 | 52.9 | 54.9 | 55.8 | 52.7 |
| 2015 | 53.6 | 53.4 | 53.8 | 54.1 | 54.4 | 54.3 | 54.3 | 54.8 | 54.2 | 54.4 | 55.9 | 56.4 | 54.5 |
| 2016 | 54.4 | 54.0 | 54.2 | 54.7 | 54.7 | 54.5 | 54.6 | 55.0 | 54.3 | 54.7 | 56.5 | 56.8 | 54.9 |
| 2017 | 54.6 | 53.9 | 54.0 | 53.7 | 53.8 | 53.7 | 53.6 | 53.7 | 53.4 | 53.3 | 54.8 | 55.2 | 54.0 |
| 2018 | 53.6 | 53.1 | 53.2 | 53.3 | 53.4 | 53.2 | 53.0 | 53.1 | 52.9 | 53.2 | 54.9 | 55.0 | 53.5 |
| 2019 | 53.6 | 53.0 | 53.1 | 53.5 | 53.4 | 53.5 | 53.2 | 53.8 | 53.3 | 53.9 | 55.4 | 55.9 | 53.8 |
| **Wholesale Trade** | | | | | | | | | | | | | |
| 2011 | 6.6 | 6.6 | 6.8 | 6.9 | 6.8 | 6.7 | 6.7 | 6.7 | 6.7 | 6.7 | 6.7 | 6.8 | 6.7 |
| 2012 | 6.9 | 6.9 | 7.0 | 7.2 | 7.2 | 7.1 | 7.0 | 7.1 | 7.2 | 7.3 | 7.3 | 7.4 | 7.1 |
| 2013 | 7.5 | 7.5 | 7.7 | 7.9 | 7.8 | 7.7 | 7.5 | 7.4 | 7.5 | 7.5 | 7.6 | 7.6 | 7.6 |
| 2014 | 7.5 | 7.6 | 7.7 | 8.1 | 8.1 | 7.9 | 7.7 | 7.7 | 7.8 | 7.9 | 7.9 | 8.0 | 7.8 |
| 2015 | 8.0 | 8.1 | 8.2 | 8.4 | 8.4 | 8.3 | 8.2 | 8.2 | 8.2 | 8.2 | 8.2 | 8.3 | 8.2 |
| 2016 | 8.1 | 8.2 | 8.2 | 8.5 | 8.5 | 8.4 | 8.2 | 8.2 | 8.2 | 8.3 | 8.3 | 8.4 | 8.3 |
| 2017 | 8.4 | 8.6 | 8.8 | 8.8 | 8.9 | 8.8 | 8.8 | 8.6 | 8.7 | 8.7 | 8.7 | 8.8 | 8.7 |
| 2018 | 8.8 | 8.9 | 9.1 | 9.3 | 9.3 | 9.2 | 8.8 | 8.8 | 8.9 | 8.9 | 8.9 | 8.9 | 9.0 |
| 2019 | 8.8 | 8.9 | 9.0 | 9.3 | 9.4 | 9.3 | 8.9 | 9.0 | 8.9 | 9.1 | 9.1 | 9.2 | 9.1 |
| **Retail Trade** | | | | | | | | | | | | | |
| 2011 | 33.3 | 32.7 | 32.8 | 33.3 | 33.3 | 33.3 | 33.3 | 33.8 | 33.3 | 33.6 | 35.2 | 35.8 | 33.6 |
| 2012 | 34.2 | 33.6 | 33.9 | 34.0 | 34.0 | 34.2 | 34.5 | 35.0 | 34.6 | 34.8 | 36.9 | 37.2 | 34.7 |
| 2013 | 35.4 | 35.0 | 35.0 | 35.0 | 35.0 | 35.3 | 35.2 | 35.6 | 35.2 | 35.4 | 37.4 | 38.3 | 35.7 |
| 2014 | 35.8 | 35.4 | 35.5 | 35.9 | 35.9 | 36.5 | 36.8 | 36.9 | 36.4 | 36.7 | 38.6 | 39.2 | 36.6 |
| 2015 | 37.0 | 36.8 | 37.0 | 37.3 | 37.4 | 37.4 | 37.4 | 37.8 | 37.3 | 37.6 | 39.0 | 39.3 | 37.6 |
| 2016 | 37.8 | 37.3 | 37.5 | 37.7 | 37.7 | 37.6 | 37.8 | 38.1 | 37.4 | 37.9 | 39.6 | 39.7 | 38.0 |
| 2017 | 37.8 | 37.0 | 36.9 | 36.6 | 36.5 | 36.4 | 36.3 | 36.7 | 36.2 | 36.5 | 38.0 | 38.0 | 36.9 |
| 2018 | 36.6 | 35.9 | 35.8 | 35.7 | 35.7 | 35.7 | 35.8 | 36.0 | 35.7 | 36.0 | 37.6 | 37.6 | 36.2 |
| 2019 | 36.3 | 35.7 | 35.7 | 35.8 | 35.6 | 35.6 | 35.7 | 36.1 | 35.7 | 36.2 | 37.5 | 37.8 | 36.1 |
| **Transportation and Utilities** | | | | | | | | | | | | | |
| 2011 | 6.9 | 7.0 | 7.1 | 7.2 | 7.3 | 7.3 | 7.3 | 7.4 | 7.3 | 7.4 | 7.4 | 7.5 | 7.3 |
| 2012 | 7.5 | 7.7 | 7.8 | 7.7 | 7.8 | 7.9 | 7.9 | 8.0 | 7.7 | 7.7 | 7.8 | 7.9 | 7.8 |
| 2013 | 7.8 | 7.8 | 7.8 | 7.9 | 8.0 | 8.1 | 8.0 | 8.1 | 8.1 | 8.1 | 8.1 | 8.2 | 8.0 |
| 2014 | 8.1 | 8.0 | 8.0 | 8.1 | 8.1 | 8.1 | 8.2 | 8.2 | 8.2 | 8.3 | 8.4 | 8.6 | 8.2 |
| 2015 | 8.6 | 8.5 | 8.6 | 8.4 | 8.6 | 8.6 | 8.7 | 8.8 | 8.7 | 8.6 | 8.7 | 8.8 | 8.6 |
| 2016 | 8.5 | 8.5 | 8.5 | 8.5 | 8.5 | 8.5 | 8.6 | 8.7 | 8.7 | 8.5 | 8.6 | 8.7 | 8.6 |
| 2017 | 8.4 | 8.3 | 8.3 | 8.3 | 8.4 | 8.5 | 8.5 | 8.4 | 8.5 | 8.1 | 8.1 | 8.4 | 8.4 |
| 2018 | 8.2 | 8.3 | 8.3 | 8.3 | 8.4 | 8.3 | 8.4 | 8.3 | 8.3 | 8.3 | 8.4 | 8.5 | 8.3 |
| 2019 | 8.5 | 8.4 | 8.4 | 8.4 | 8.4 | 8.6 | 8.6 | 8.7 | 8.7 | 8.6 | 8.8 | 8.9 | 8.6 |
| **Information** | | | | | | | | | | | | | |
| 2011 | 2.1 | 2.1 | 2.1 | 2.1 | 2.1 | 2.1 | 2.1 | 2.1 | 2.0 | 2.0 | 2.1 | 2.1 | 2.1 |
| 2012 | 2.1 | 2.0 | 2.0 | 2.0 | 2.0 | 2.0 | 2.0 | 2.0 | 1.9 | 2.1 | 2.1 | 2.2 | 2.0 |
| 2013 | 2.1 | 2.1 | 2.1 | 2.1 | 2.2 | 2.2 | 2.2 | 2.2 | 2.1 | 2.2 | 2.3 | 2.3 | 2.2 |
| 2014 | 2.2 | 2.2 | 2.2 | 2.2 | 2.2 | 2.2 | 2.2 | 2.2 | 2.1 | 2.2 | 2.3 | 2.3 | 2.2 |
| 2015 | 2.3 | 2.2 | 2.2 | 2.2 | 2.3 | 2.3 | 2.4 | 2.4 | 2.3 | 2.2 | 2.3 | 2.3 | 2.3 |
| 2016 | 2.2 | 2.2 | 2.2 | 2.3 | 2.3 | 2.3 | 2.3 | 2.3 | 2.2 | 2.2 | 2.3 | 2.3 | 2.3 |
| 2017 | 2.2 | 2.2 | 2.2 | 2.3 | 2.4 | 2.5 | 2.5 | 2.5 | 2.5 | 2.6 | 2.7 | 2.8 | 2.5 |
| 2018 | 2.8 | 2.9 | 2.9 | 2.9 | 2.9 | 3.0 | 3.0 | 2.9 | 2.8 | 2.8 | 2.8 | 2.9 | 2.9 |
| 2019 | 2.8 | 2.8 | 2.8 | 3.0 | 3.0 | 3.0 | 2.9 | 3.0 | 2.9 | 3.0 | 2.9 | 3.1 | 2.9 |
| **Financial Activities** | | | | | | | | | | | | | |
| 2011 | 8.4 | 8.4 | 8.5 | 8.5 | 8.5 | 8.6 | 8.6 | 8.6 | 8.7 | 8.7 | 8.6 | 8.7 | 8.6 |
| 2012 | 8.8 | 8.8 | 8.8 | 8.8 | 8.8 | 8.9 | 8.8 | 8.8 | 8.8 | 8.9 | 8.9 | 9.0 | 8.8 |
| 2013 | 8.8 | 8.9 | 8.9 | 8.9 | 8.9 | 8.9 | 8.9 | 9.0 | 8.9 | 9.0 | 9.0 | 9.0 | 8.9 |
| 2014 | 9.0 | 9.0 | 9.0 | 9.0 | 9.1 | 9.1 | 9.0 | 9.0 | 9.0 | 9.1 | 9.1 | 9.2 | 9.1 |
| 2015 | 9.0 | 9.0 | 9.1 | 8.9 | 9.0 | 9.0 | 9.0 | 9.0 | 9.0 | 9.0 | 9.0 | 9.1 | 9.0 |
| 2016 | 8.9 | 8.9 | 8.9 | 8.9 | 8.9 | 8.9 | 8.8 | 8.9 | 8.8 | 8.7 | 8.8 | 8.8 | 8.9 |
| 2017 | 8.8 | 8.7 | 8.7 | 8.9 | 8.9 | 8.8 | 8.9 | 8.8 | 8.8 | 8.9 | 8.9 | 9.0 | 8.8 |
| 2018 | 9.0 | 8.9 | 8.9 | 8.9 | 9.0 | 9.0 | 9.2 | 9.2 | 9.1 | 9.1 | 9.2 | 9.1 | 9.1 |
| 2019 | 9.0 | 9.0 | 9.0 | 8.8 | 8.8 | 8.8 | 8.8 | 8.9 | 8.9 | 8.9 | 8.9 | 8.9 | 8.9 |

## Employment by Industry: McAllen-Edinburg-Mission, TX, 2011–2019—*Continued*

(Numbers in thousands, not seasonally adjusted)

| Industry and year | January | February | March | April | May | June | July | August | September | October | November | December | Annual average |
|---|---|---|---|---|---|---|---|---|---|---|---|---|---|
| **Professional and Business Services** | | | | | | | | | | | | | |
| 2011 | 14.5 | 14.7 | 14.8 | 15.6 | 15.5 | 15.3 | 15.0 | 15.2 | 15.0 | 14.9 | 15.0 | 15.0 | 15.0 |
| 2012 | 15.3 | 15.4 | 15.3 | 15.7 | 15.5 | 15.0 | 15.0 | 15.0 | 15.1 | 15.2 | 14.8 | 14.9 | 15.2 |
| 2013 | 15.1 | 15.6 | 15.8 | 15.9 | 15.6 | 15.5 | 15.1 | 15.5 | 15.5 | 15.5 | 15.7 | 16.2 | 15.6 |
| 2014 | 15.5 | 15.7 | 16.0 | 16.1 | 15.9 | 15.7 | 15.3 | 15.8 | 15.6 | 16.1 | 15.5 | 15.8 | 15.8 |
| 2015 | 16.1 | 16.3 | 16.3 | 16.3 | 15.9 | 15.8 | 15.6 | 15.5 | 15.5 | 15.5 | 15.8 | 15.7 | 15.9 |
| 2016 | 15.9 | 16.3 | 16.7 | 16.7 | 16.2 | 16.0 | 16.1 | 16.2 | 16.4 | 16.8 | 16.9 | 16.9 | 16.4 |
| 2017 | 16.7 | 16.9 | 17.2 | 17.4 | 16.9 | 17.1 | 16.8 | 17.0 | 17.3 | 17.6 | 18.0 | 18.1 | 17.3 |
| 2018 | 17.9 | 17.9 | 18.1 | 18.0 | 17.6 | 17.5 | 17.2 | 17.2 | 17.3 | 17.8 | 17.9 | 18.2 | 17.7 |
| 2019 | 17.9 | 18.1 | 18.3 | 17.7 | 17.3 | 17.4 | 17.3 | 17.6 | 17.4 | 17.7 | 17.6 | 17.8 | 17.7 |
| **Education and Health Services** | | | | | | | | | | | | | |
| 2011 | 57.4 | 57.7 | 58.0 | 58.3 | 58.5 | 58.2 | 58.6 | 59.2 | 60.0 | 59.6 | 59.9 | 60.2 | 58.8 |
| 2012 | 59.4 | 59.9 | 60.1 | 59.9 | 60.0 | 59.6 | 58.6 | 59.2 | 59.5 | 59.8 | 60.2 | 60.4 | 59.7 |
| 2013 | 59.0 | 59.6 | 59.8 | 60.2 | 60.4 | 60.2 | 60.1 | 61.0 | 61.3 | 61.8 | 62.1 | 62.3 | 60.7 |
| 2014 | 61.2 | 61.6 | 61.6 | 61.9 | 62.5 | 62.0 | 62.0 | 62.8 | 63.1 | 63.4 | 63.9 | 64.2 | 62.5 |
| 2015 | 63.9 | 64.3 | 64.4 | 64.6 | 65.2 | 64.6 | 64.7 | 65.5 | 65.7 | 66.2 | 66.7 | 66.8 | 65.2 |
| 2016 | 66.2 | 66.9 | 66.8 | 67.8 | 68.2 | 67.4 | 67.0 | 68.2 | 69.0 | 69.0 | 69.4 | 70.0 | 68.0 |
| 2017 | 69.6 | 70.0 | 70.3 | 70.6 | 71.1 | 70.6 | 69.5 | 70.5 | 71.3 | 72.2 | 72.6 | 73.4 | 71.0 |
| 2018 | 72.9 | 73.4 | 73.6 | 74.5 | 74.9 | 74.7 | 75.0 | 76.3 | 76.3 | 77.3 | 78.0 | 77.9 | 75.4 |
| 2019 | 77.4 | 77.8 | 77.9 | 78.7 | 79.1 | 78.7 | 79.0 | 80.7 | 80.7 | 81.8 | 81.3 | 81.2 | 79.5 |
| **Leisure and Hospitality** | | | | | | | | | | | | | |
| 2011 | 19.2 | 19.5 | 20.0 | 20.0 | 19.9 | 20.1 | 19.6 | 19.6 | 19.5 | 19.2 | 19.4 | 19.4 | 19.6 |
| 2012 | 19.2 | 19.6 | 20.2 | 20.2 | 20.1 | 20.2 | 19.8 | 20.0 | 20.0 | 19.9 | 20.3 | 20.8 | 20.0 |
| 2013 | 20.5 | 21.0 | 21.5 | 21.4 | 21.3 | 21.3 | 20.9 | 21.3 | 21.2 | 20.9 | 21.1 | 21.2 | 21.1 |
| 2014 | 21.1 | 21.3 | 21.8 | 21.9 | 22.2 | 22.2 | 21.7 | 22.1 | 22.2 | 22.0 | 22.0 | 22.4 | 21.9 |
| 2015 | 21.9 | 22.3 | 22.8 | 22.9 | 23.2 | 23.3 | 23.3 | 23.1 | 23.0 | 23.1 | 23.2 | 23.5 | 23.0 |
| 2016 | 23.5 | 23.8 | 24.1 | 24.2 | 24.3 | 24.5 | 24.2 | 24.4 | 24.4 | 24.2 | 24.2 | 24.2 | 24.2 |
| 2017 | 24.2 | 24.3 | 25.0 | 25.2 | 25.5 | 25.5 | 25.1 | 25.1 | 25.1 | 24.9 | 24.9 | 25.0 | 25.0 |
| 2018 | 24.7 | 25.1 | 25.8 | 25.4 | 25.6 | 25.6 | 25.2 | 25.8 | 25.4 | 25.5 | 25.5 | 25.6 | 25.4 |
| 2019 | 25.6 | 26.2 | 26.8 | 27.2 | 27.2 | 27.5 | 27.0 | 27.0 | 26.9 | 26.9 | 26.7 | 26.9 | 26.8 |
| **Other Services** | | | | | | | | | | | | | |
| 2011 | 5.0 | 5.1 | 5.1 | 5.1 | 5.2 | 5.2 | 5.2 | 5.2 | 5.1 | 5.2 | 5.1 | 5.1 | 5.1 |
| 2012 | 5.0 | 5.0 | 5.0 | 5.2 | 5.3 | 5.4 | 5.3 | 5.3 | 5.2 | 5.4 | 5.4 | 5.3 | 5.2 |
| 2013 | 5.2 | 5.3 | 5.3 | 5.4 | 5.5 | 5.6 | 5.6 | 5.6 | 5.4 | 5.5 | 5.5 | 5.4 | 5.4 |
| 2014 | 5.4 | 5.5 | 5.5 | 5.6 | 5.7 | 5.8 | 5.8 | 5.8 | 5.6 | 5.7 | 5.6 | 5.6 | 5.6 |
| 2015 | 5.5 | 5.6 | 5.6 | 5.6 | 5.7 | 5.8 | 5.8 | 5.8 | 5.6 | 5.6 | 5.6 | 5.5 | 5.6 |
| 2016 | 5.5 | 5.5 | 5.5 | 5.3 | 5.4 | 5.4 | 5.5 | 5.4 | 5.3 | 5.4 | 5.3 | 5.3 | 5.4 |
| 2017 | 5.3 | 5.3 | 5.4 | 5.4 | 5.4 | 5.5 | 5.4 | 5.4 | 5.4 | 5.5 | 5.5 | 5.5 | 5.4 |
| 2018 | 5.5 | 5.5 | 5.6 | 5.7 | 5.8 | 5.9 | 5.8 | 5.8 | 5.8 | 5.8 | 5.8 | 5.7 | 5.7 |
| 2019 | 5.6 | 5.7 | 5.7 | 5.7 | 5.8 | 5.9 | 5.9 | 5.9 | 5.8 | 5.9 | 5.8 | 5.8 | 5.8 |
| **Government** | | | | | | | | | | | | | |
| 2011 | 56.1 | 56.7 | 56.5 | 55.9 | 56.3 | 55.3 | 49.5 | 51.3 | 53.0 | 54.1 | 55.1 | 55.2 | 54.6 |
| 2012 | 54.8 | 55.4 | 55.8 | 55.2 | 55.4 | 54.8 | 49.2 | 50.8 | 53.0 | 55.1 | 55.8 | 56.0 | 54.3 |
| 2013 | 55.3 | 56.0 | 56.4 | 55.8 | 56.5 | 55.8 | 50.1 | 51.9 | 53.9 | 56.0 | 56.7 | 56.8 | 55.1 |
| 2014 | 56.7 | 57.1 | 57.4 | 56.7 | 58.0 | 57.0 | 51.0 | 52.6 | 54.3 | 56.7 | 57.3 | 57.7 | 56.0 |
| 2015 | 56.9 | 57.6 | 57.8 | 57.1 | 58.5 | 57.7 | 51.9 | 53.8 | 55.7 | 57.7 | 58.2 | 58.7 | 56.8 |
| 2016 | 58.0 | 58.8 | 59.0 | 59.4 | 60.0 | 59.3 | 53.6 | 55.4 | 58.0 | 59.6 | 59.9 | 60.5 | 58.5 |
| 2017 | 59.6 | 60.0 | 60.0 | 60.7 | 61.2 | 60.0 | 54.1 | 55.3 | 57.7 | 59.9 | 60.6 | 60.9 | 59.2 |
| 2018 | 59.4 | 60.7 | 61.2 | 61.1 | 61.7 | 60.7 | 54.9 | 56.5 | 58.6 | 60.4 | 61.0 | 61.3 | 59.8 |
| 2019 | 59.7 | 60.9 | 61.1 | 61.4 | 61.6 | 60.5 | 55.1 | 56.7 | 59.1 | 60.9 | 61.3 | 61.8 | 60.0 |

# Employment by Industry: Baton Rouge, LA, 2011–2019

(Numbers in thousands, not seasonally adjusted)

| Industry and year | January | February | March | April | May | June | July | August | September | October | November | December | Annual average |
|---|---|---|---|---|---|---|---|---|---|---|---|---|---|
| **Total Nonfarm** | | | | | | | | | | | | | |
| 2011 | 364.6 | 368.5 | 370.4 | 372.1 | 371.4 | 368.0 | 365.9 | 366.4 | 371.9 | 374.5 | 374.5 | 373.8 | 370.2 |
| 2012 | 369.1 | 373.9 | 376.1 | 376.8 | 376.7 | 374.5 | 368.2 | 374.2 | 377.6 | 380.1 | 382.2 | 380.7 | 375.8 |
| 2013 | 375.0 | 381.0 | 383.8 | 385.6 | 386.6 | 384.8 | 381.7 | 386.3 | 389.3 | 392.4 | 393.2 | 389.5 | 385.8 |
| 2014 | 383.7 | 388.6 | 391.7 | 393.2 | 396.5 | 393.9 | 392.4 | 397.1 | 401.2 | 405.7 | 403.9 | 402.3 | 395.9 |
| 2015 | 397.8 | 401.0 | 401.7 | 402.2 | 405.5 | 403.4 | 402.8 | 405.5 | 407.2 | 411.5 | 411.5 | 408.6 | 404.9 |
| 2016 | 400.1 | 403.7 | 406.3 | 407.2 | 407.3 | 404.8 | 402.8 | 399.6 | 404.4 | 408.3 | 407.4 | 404.2 | 404.7 |
| 2017 | 401.7 | 408.1 | 408.1 | 407.5 | 408.3 | 405.3 | 401.6 | 405.1 | 406.1 | 409.7 | 410.5 | 407.9 | 406.7 |
| 2018 | 400.8 | 406.4 | 412.6 | 411.9 | 412.3 | 411.7 | 408.2 | 411.5 | 413.5 | 418.3 | 420.8 | 418.1 | 412.2 |
| 2019 | 412.5 | 417.2 | 418.0 | 415.3 | 414.4 | 410.3 | 403.4 | 408.5 | 409.4 | 411.7 | 414.2 | 413.3 | 412.4 |
| **Total Private** | | | | | | | | | | | | | |
| 2011 | 289.7 | 291.5 | 293.7 | 295.1 | 294.6 | 292.9 | 292.9 | 293.9 | 295.1 | 296.9 | 296.7 | 296.6 | 294.1 |
| 2012 | 294.2 | 297.9 | 300.5 | 301.5 | 301.8 | 301.3 | 298.1 | 301.7 | 303.0 | 305.7 | 307.6 | 306.7 | 301.7 |
| 2013 | 303.1 | 307.4 | 310.2 | 312.1 | 313.4 | 313.0 | 313.0 | 315.1 | 315.4 | 318.8 | 319.1 | 316.4 | 313.1 |
| 2014 | 312.4 | 315.8 | 318.8 | 320.7 | 324.3 | 322.9 | 323.7 | 326.2 | 327.9 | 332.5 | 330.2 | 329.3 | 323.7 |
| 2015 | 326.6 | 328.2 | 328.8 | 329.5 | 333.1 | 332.2 | 333.8 | 334.2 | 333.6 | 337.5 | 337.0 | 334.6 | 332.4 |
| 2016 | 327.8 | 329.6 | 332.0 | 333.2 | 333.3 | 332.2 | 332.5 | 327.2 | 329.7 | 334.2 | 332.7 | 329.6 | 331.2 |
| 2017 | 328.5 | 333.1 | 332.7 | 332.8 | 333.8 | 332.4 | 331.3 | 332.8 | 331.6 | 335.5 | 335.8 | 333.6 | 332.8 |
| 2018 | 328.1 | 331.8 | 337.8 | 337.4 | 338.0 | 338.7 | 337.5 | 338.4 | 337.9 | 342.9 | 345.0 | 342.0 | 338.0 |
| 2019 | 337.5 | 340.4 | 340.7 | 338.5 | 338.0 | 335.3 | 330.9 | 333.6 | 332.1 | 335.4 | 338.1 | 338.1 | 336.6 |
| **Goods Producing** | | | | | | | | | | | | | |
| 2011 | 64.5 | 65.7 | 66.5 | 66.4 | 65.6 | 64.8 | 64.8 | 64.6 | 65.6 | 66.5 | 65.1 | 64.4 | 65.4 |
| 2012 | 65.1 | 67.1 | 67.8 | 67.5 | 67.4 | 67.1 | 66.4 | 67.8 | 68.8 | 70.1 | 70.4 | 69.3 | 67.9 |
| 2013 | 68.9 | 71.3 | 72.4 | 72.2 | 72.7 | 72.9 | 72.6 | 73.2 | 74.0 | 76.8 | 75.7 | 73.7 | 73.0 |
| 2014 | 73.7 | 75.9 | 77.0 | 76.3 | 77.6 | 77.2 | 78.8 | 80.2 | 82.2 | 84.1 | 80.2 | 78.5 | 78.5 |
| 2015 | 77.5 | 78.4 | 79.0 | 78.1 | 78.9 | 80.1 | 81.7 | 82.0 | 82.3 | 85.3 | 83.4 | 81.3 | 80.7 |
| 2016 | 79.3 | 80.3 | 80.8 | 79.7 | 79.9 | 81.6 | 82.3 | 79.6 | 81.0 | 84.6 | 81.9 | 79.7 | 80.9 |
| 2017 | 81.5 | 83.9 | 82.9 | 82.1 | 82.5 | 81.4 | 81.4 | 81.4 | 80.5 | 83.1 | 81.6 | 81.0 | 81.9 |
| 2018 | 79.1 | 81.5 | 85.2 | 83.9 | 84.9 | 86.4 | 86.6 | 86.1 | 86.0 | 89.1 | 88.8 | 86.8 | 85.4 |
| 2019 | 85.1 | 86.1 | 85.8 | 82.4 | 81.5 | 79.6 | 77.5 | 78.0 | 77.3 | 78.2 | 79.6 | 79.4 | 80.9 |
| **Service-Providing** | | | | | | | | | | | | | |
| 2011 | 300.1 | 302.8 | 303.9 | 305.7 | 305.8 | 303.2 | 301.1 | 301.8 | 306.3 | 308.0 | 309.4 | 309.4 | 304.8 |
| 2012 | 304.0 | 306.8 | 308.3 | 309.3 | 309.3 | 307.4 | 301.8 | 306.4 | 308.8 | 310.0 | 311.8 | 311.4 | 307.9 |
| 2013 | 306.1 | 309.7 | 311.4 | 313.4 | 313.9 | 311.9 | 309.1 | 313.1 | 315.3 | 315.6 | 317.5 | 315.8 | 312.7 |
| 2014 | 310.0 | 312.7 | 314.7 | 316.9 | 318.9 | 316.7 | 313.6 | 316.9 | 319.0 | 321.6 | 323.7 | 323.8 | 317.4 |
| 2015 | 320.3 | 322.6 | 322.7 | 324.1 | 326.6 | 323.3 | 321.1 | 323.5 | 324.9 | 326.2 | 328.1 | 327.3 | 324.2 |
| 2016 | 320.8 | 323.4 | 325.5 | 327.5 | 327.4 | 323.2 | 320.5 | 320.0 | 323.4 | 323.7 | 325.5 | 324.5 | 323.8 |
| 2017 | 320.2 | 324.2 | 325.2 | 325.4 | 325.8 | 323.9 | 320.2 | 323.7 | 325.6 | 326.6 | 328.9 | 326.9 | 324.7 |
| 2018 | 321.7 | 324.9 | 327.4 | 328.0 | 327.4 | 325.3 | 321.6 | 325.4 | 327.5 | 329.2 | 332.0 | 331.3 | 326.8 |
| 2019 | 327.4 | 331.1 | 332.2 | 332.9 | 332.9 | 330.7 | 325.9 | 330.5 | 332.1 | 333.5 | 334.6 | 333.9 | 331.5 |
| **Mining, Logging, and Construction** | | | | | | | | | | | | | |
| 2011 | 39.3 | 40.5 | 41.3 | 41.2 | 40.2 | 39.4 | 38.9 | 38.4 | 39.2 | 40.0 | 38.7 | 37.9 | 39.6 |
| 2012 | 38.9 | 40.9 | 41.3 | 41.0 | 40.7 | 40.1 | 39.5 | 40.9 | 41.9 | 43.2 | 43.4 | 42.3 | 41.2 |
| 2013 | 42.1 | 44.5 | 45.5 | 45.3 | 45.6 | 45.5 | 45.1 | 45.4 | 46.0 | 48.7 | 47.6 | 45.6 | 45.6 |
| 2014 | 45.2 | 47.5 | 48.6 | 47.8 | 49.0 | 48.4 | 49.9 | 51.3 | 53.0 | 54.8 | 50.9 | 49.2 | 49.6 |
| 2015 | 48.7 | 49.4 | 50.0 | 49.0 | 49.7 | 50.7 | 52.1 | 52.3 | 52.7 | 55.4 | 53.7 | 51.7 | 51.3 |
| 2016 | 50.1 | 51.0 | 51.7 | 50.6 | 50.8 | 52.4 | 53.0 | 50.3 | 51.6 | 55.1 | 52.5 | 50.3 | 51.6 |
| 2017 | 52.3 | 54.6 | 53.6 | 52.8 | 53.2 | 52.0 | 52.1 | 52.0 | 51.3 | 53.7 | 52.4 | 51.7 | 52.6 |
| 2018 | 50.1 | 52.4 | 55.9 | 54.7 | 55.5 | 56.6 | 56.7 | 56.0 | 55.9 | 59.0 | 58.6 | 56.6 | 55.7 |
| 2019 | 54.9 | 55.8 | 55.6 | 52.5 | 51.7 | 49.7 | 47.6 | 48.0 | 47.3 | 48.2 | 49.6 | 49.3 | 50.9 |
| **Manufacturing** | | | | | | | | | | | | | |
| 2011 | 25.2 | 25.2 | 25.2 | 25.2 | 25.4 | 25.4 | 25.9 | 26.2 | 26.4 | 26.5 | 26.4 | 26.5 | 25.8 |
| 2012 | 26.2 | 26.2 | 26.5 | 26.5 | 26.7 | 27.0 | 26.9 | 26.9 | 26.9 | 26.9 | 27.0 | 27.0 | 26.7 |
| 2013 | 26.8 | 26.8 | 26.9 | 26.9 | 27.1 | 27.4 | 27.5 | 27.8 | 28.0 | 28.1 | 28.1 | 28.1 | 27.5 |
| 2014 | 28.5 | 28.4 | 28.4 | 28.5 | 28.6 | 28.8 | 28.9 | 28.9 | 29.2 | 29.3 | 29.3 | 29.3 | 28.8 |
| 2015 | 28.8 | 29.0 | 29.0 | 29.1 | 29.2 | 29.4 | 29.6 | 29.7 | 29.6 | 29.9 | 29.7 | 29.6 | 29.4 |
| 2016 | 29.2 | 29.3 | 29.1 | 29.1 | 29.1 | 29.2 | 29.3 | 29.3 | 29.4 | 29.5 | 29.4 | 29.4 | 29.3 |
| 2017 | 29.2 | 29.3 | 29.3 | 29.3 | 29.3 | 29.4 | 29.3 | 29.4 | 29.2 | 29.4 | 29.2 | 29.3 | 29.3 |
| 2018 | 29.0 | 29.1 | 29.3 | 29.2 | 29.4 | 29.8 | 29.9 | 30.1 | 30.1 | 30.1 | 30.2 | 30.2 | 29.7 |
| 2019 | 30.2 | 30.3 | 30.2 | 29.9 | 29.8 | 29.9 | 29.9 | 30.0 | 30.0 | 30.0 | 30.0 | 30.1 | 30.0 |

## Employment by Industry: Baton Rouge, LA, 2011–2019—*Continued*

(Numbers in thousands, not seasonally adjusted)

| Industry and year | January | February | March | April | May | June | July | August | September | October | November | December | Annual average |
|---|---|---|---|---|---|---|---|---|---|---|---|---|---|
| **Trade, Transportation, and Utilities** | | | | | | | | | | | | | |
| 2011 | 65.0 | 64.8 | 65.0 | 65.6 | 65.6 | 65.4 | 65.1 | 65.2 | 65.0 | 65.7 | 66.8 | 67.7 | 65.6 |
| 2012 | 65.9 | 65.8 | 66.4 | 66.5 | 66.7 | 66.4 | 66.0 | 66.3 | 65.8 | 66.8 | 68.7 | 69.1 | 66.7 |
| 2013 | 66.5 | 66.3 | 66.8 | 67.2 | 67.2 | 67.2 | 66.9 | 67.4 | 67.4 | 67.6 | 68.9 | 69.9 | 67.4 |
| 2014 | 67.7 | 67.2 | 67.7 | 67.7 | 67.8 | 67.8 | 67.7 | 67.9 | 67.8 | 68.5 | 70.4 | 71.3 | 68.3 |
| | | | | | | | | | | | | | |
| 2015 | 69.6 | 69.1 | 69.4 | 69.5 | 69.6 | 69.5 | 69.5 | 69.8 | 69.8 | 70.5 | 71.8 | 72.2 | 70.0 |
| 2016 | 70.3 | 69.8 | 70.4 | 70.2 | 70.2 | 69.5 | 69.8 | 69.5 | 69.5 | 70.4 | 72.0 | 72.6 | 70.4 |
| 2017 | 71.0 | 70.5 | 70.6 | 70.4 | 70.4 | 69.7 | 69.8 | 70.3 | 69.6 | 70.4 | 72.1 | 72.2 | 70.6 |
| 2018 | 70.6 | 70.0 | 70.5 | 70.7 | 70.7 | 69.9 | 70.0 | 70.6 | 70.3 | 70.7 | 73.0 | 73.1 | 70.8 |
| 2019 | 71.7 | 71.2 | 71.2 | 71.1 | 71.1 | 70.4 | 70.5 | 70.6 | 70.2 | 70.4 | 71.2 | 70.9 | 70.9 |
| | | | | | | | | | | | | | |
| **Wholesale Trade** | | | | | | | | | | | | | |
| 2011 | 12.7 | 12.7 | 12.7 | 12.8 | 12.9 | 12.9 | 12.9 | 12.9 | 12.9 | 13.0 | 13.0 | 13.0 | 12.9 |
| 2012 | 13.1 | 13.1 | 13.2 | 13.2 | 13.2 | 13.2 | 13.1 | 13.1 | 13.1 | 13.3 | 13.4 | 13.4 | 13.2 |
| 2013 | 13.6 | 13.6 | 13.8 | 13.9 | 13.8 | 13.7 | 13.6 | 13.6 | 13.5 | 13.6 | 13.5 | 13.5 | 13.6 |
| 2014 | 13.4 | 13.3 | 13.4 | 13.3 | 13.3 | 13.3 | 13.2 | 13.2 | 13.2 | 13.1 | 13.1 | 13.1 | 13.2 |
| | | | | | | | | | | | | | |
| 2015 | 13.2 | 13.2 | 13.3 | 13.2 | 13.2 | 13.2 | 13.1 | 13.1 | 13.1 | 13.3 | 13.3 | 13.3 | 13.2 |
| 2016 | 13.4 | 13.3 | 13.3 | 13.4 | 13.4 | 13.2 | 13.2 | 13.2 | 13.2 | 13.2 | 13.2 | 13.2 | 13.3 |
| 2017 | 13.0 | 13.1 | 13.1 | 13.1 | 13.1 | 13.1 | 13.1 | 13.3 | 13.2 | 13.3 | 13.3 | 13.3 | 13.2 |
| 2018 | 13.3 | 13.5 | 13.6 | 13.5 | 13.5 | 13.5 | 13.6 | 13.7 | 13.7 | 13.7 | 13.7 | 13.7 | 13.6 |
| 2019 | 13.6 | 13.8 | 13.9 | 13.8 | 13.8 | 13.7 | 13.7 | 13.7 | 13.8 | 13.8 | 13.8 | 13.8 | 13.8 |
| | | | | | | | | | | | | | |
| **Retail Trade** | | | | | | | | | | | | | |
| 2011 | 40.2 | 39.9 | 40.2 | 40.6 | 40.6 | 40.4 | 40.2 | 40.0 | 39.9 | 40.3 | 41.6 | 42.2 | 40.5 |
| 2012 | 40.5 | 40.5 | 40.9 | 41.0 | 41.0 | 41.0 | 40.9 | 40.8 | 40.5 | 41.3 | 43.0 | 43.2 | 41.2 |
| 2013 | 40.5 | 40.2 | 40.4 | 40.6 | 40.5 | 40.8 | 40.7 | 40.8 | 41.0 | 41.1 | 42.4 | 43.0 | 41.0 |
| 2014 | 40.9 | 40.6 | 40.8 | 40.9 | 40.9 | 41.2 | 41.2 | 41.0 | 41.0 | 41.7 | 43.5 | 44.1 | 41.5 |
| | | | | | | | | | | | | | |
| 2015 | 42.4 | 42.1 | 42.4 | 42.5 | 42.5 | 42.6 | 42.6 | 42.7 | 42.5 | 43.1 | 44.3 | 44.3 | 42.8 |
| 2016 | 42.8 | 42.7 | 43.1 | 42.9 | 42.8 | 42.9 | 43.0 | 42.5 | 42.5 | 43.5 | 45.0 | 45.7 | 43.3 |
| 2017 | 44.3 | 43.8 | 43.9 | 43.7 | 43.5 | 43.3 | 42.9 | 43.0 | 42.6 | 43.0 | 44.4 | 44.3 | 43.6 |
| 2018 | 42.7 | 41.9 | 42.2 | 42.3 | 42.2 | 41.9 | 41.8 | 41.8 | 41.6 | 41.7 | 43.4 | 43.1 | 42.2 |
| 2019 | 42.1 | 41.4 | 41.3 | 41.4 | 41.4 | 41.3 | 41.2 | 41.2 | 40.7 | 40.8 | 41.3 | 40.9 | 41.3 |
| | | | | | | | | | | | | | |
| **Transportation and Utilities** | | | | | | | | | | | | | |
| 2011 | 12.1 | 12.2 | 12.1 | 12.2 | 12.1 | 12.1 | 12.0 | 12.3 | 12.2 | 12.4 | 12.2 | 12.5 | 12.2 |
| 2012 | 12.3 | 12.2 | 12.3 | 12.3 | 12.5 | 12.2 | 12.0 | 12.4 | 12.2 | 12.2 | 12.3 | 12.5 | 12.3 |
| 2013 | 12.4 | 12.5 | 12.6 | 12.7 | 12.9 | 12.7 | 12.6 | 13.0 | 12.9 | 12.9 | 13.0 | 13.4 | 12.8 |
| 2014 | 13.4 | 13.3 | 13.5 | 13.5 | 13.6 | 13.3 | 13.3 | 13.7 | 13.6 | 13.7 | 13.8 | 14.1 | 13.6 |
| | | | | | | | | | | | | | |
| 2015 | 14.0 | 13.8 | 13.7 | 13.8 | 13.9 | 13.7 | 13.8 | 14.0 | 14.2 | 14.1 | 14.2 | 14.6 | 14.0 |
| 2016 | 14.1 | 13.8 | 14.0 | 13.9 | 14.0 | 13.4 | 13.6 | 13.8 | 13.8 | 13.7 | 13.8 | 13.7 | 13.8 |
| 2017 | 13.7 | 13.6 | 13.6 | 13.6 | 13.8 | 13.3 | 13.8 | 14.0 | 13.8 | 14.1 | 14.4 | 14.6 | 13.9 |
| 2018 | 14.6 | 14.6 | 14.7 | 14.9 | 15.0 | 14.5 | 14.6 | 15.1 | 15.0 | 15.3 | 15.9 | 16.3 | 15.0 |
| 2019 | 16.0 | 16.0 | 16.0 | 15.9 | 15.9 | 15.4 | 15.6 | 15.7 | 15.7 | 15.8 | 16.1 | 16.2 | 15.9 |
| | | | | | | | | | | | | | |
| **Information** | | | | | | | | | | | | | |
| 2011 | 4.8 | 4.9 | 4.8 | 4.9 | 4.8 | 4.8 | 4.8 | 4.9 | 4.8 | 5.0 | 4.9 | 5.0 | 4.9 |
| 2012 | 4.8 | 5.0 | 4.9 | 5.4 | 4.8 | 5.0 | 4.9 | 4.7 | 5.3 | 4.7 | 4.9 | 5.2 | 5.0 |
| 2013 | 5.5 | 5.9 | 6.3 | 6.7 | 6.7 | 6.7 | 7.2 | 6.4 | 5.8 | 5.9 | 6.1 | 5.6 | 6.2 |
| 2014 | 5.3 | 5.6 | 6.1 | 6.9 | 8.3 | 8.0 | 7.6 | 6.5 | 6.0 | 6.6 | 6.6 | 6.5 | 6.7 |
| | | | | | | | | | | | | | |
| 2015 | 7.0 | 7.2 | 6.1 | 6.9 | 8.0 | 7.5 | 7.7 | 6.9 | 6.2 | 5.6 | 5.7 | 5.8 | 6.7 |
| 2016 | 5.7 | 6.3 | 6.3 | 5.8 | 5.9 | 6.2 | 6.0 | 5.3 | 5.2 | 5.2 | 5.6 | 5.4 | 5.7 |
| 2017 | 4.9 | 5.4 | 5.6 | 5.9 | 6.0 | 5.9 | 5.5 | 5.0 | 5.0 | 5.0 | 5.1 | 5.1 | 5.4 |
| 2018 | 5.0 | 5.6 | 6.2 | 5.7 | 5.2 | 5.0 | 4.9 | 4.3 | 4.7 | 5.0 | 5.5 | 5.5 | 5.2 |
| 2019 | 5.1 | 5.1 | 5.3 | 5.3 | 5.0 | 5.3 | 5.5 | 5.1 | 4.8 | 4.8 | 5.4 | 5.1 | 5.2 |
| | | | | | | | | | | | | | |
| **Financial Activities** | | | | | | | | | | | | | |
| 2011 | 17.0 | 17.0 | 17.0 | 16.9 | 16.9 | 16.8 | 16.9 | 16.8 | 16.8 | 16.9 | 16.9 | 17.0 | 16.9 |
| 2012 | 16.9 | 16.9 | 17.0 | 17.0 | 17.0 | 17.0 | 16.9 | 17.1 | 16.9 | 17.1 | 17.3 | 17.3 | 17.0 |
| 2013 | 17.0 | 17.1 | 17.1 | 17.1 | 17.3 | 17.6 | 17.6 | 17.8 | 17.9 | 18.3 | 18.3 | 18.1 | 17.6 |
| 2014 | 17.5 | 17.4 | 17.4 | 17.5 | 17.6 | 17.7 | 18.0 | 18.2 | 18.3 | 18.5 | 18.5 | 18.5 | 17.9 |
| | | | | | | | | | | | | | |
| 2015 | 18.2 | 18.3 | 18.2 | 18.3 | 18.4 | 18.4 | 18.4 | 18.5 | 18.3 | 18.5 | 18.5 | 18.7 | 18.4 |
| 2016 | 18.5 | 18.5 | 18.5 | 18.5 | 18.8 | 18.7 | 19.0 | 18.9 | 19.0 | 19.0 | 18.9 | 18.8 | 18.8 |
| 2017 | 18.8 | 18.8 | 18.7 | 18.9 | 18.9 | 18.9 | 18.7 | 18.8 | 18.7 | 18.7 | 18.7 | 18.5 | 18.8 |
| 2018 | 18.3 | 18.3 | 18.4 | 18.4 | 18.4 | 18.6 | 18.7 | 18.6 | 18.4 | 18.5 | 18.5 | 18.5 | 18.5 |
| 2019 | 18.3 | 18.5 | 18.5 | 18.6 | 18.9 | 18.9 | 18.7 | 19.0 | 18.9 | 19.0 | 19.1 | 19.1 | 18.8 |

# Employment by Industry: Baton Rouge, LA, 2011–2019—*Continued*

(Numbers in thousands, not seasonally adjusted)

| Industry and year | January | February | March | April | May | June | July | August | September | October | November | December | Annual average |
|---|---|---|---|---|---|---|---|---|---|---|---|---|---|
| **Professional and Business Services** | | | | | | | | | | | | | |
| 2011 | 41.6 | 41.9 | 42.3 | 42.8 | 42.6 | 42.4 | 42.2 | 42.8 | 43.3 | 43.0 | 42.7 | 42.8 | 42.5 |
| 2012 | 42.9 | 43.4 | 43.9 | 44.8 | 45.0 | 44.7 | 43.6 | 43.9 | 44.4 | 44.8 | 44.3 | 44.0 | 44.1 |
| 2013 | 44.0 | 44.8 | 45.0 | 45.3 | 44.9 | 44.5 | 44.7 | 45.3 | 45.3 | 45.5 | 45.3 | 44.8 | 45.0 |
| 2014 | 44.8 | 45.4 | 45.7 | 46.2 | 46.1 | 45.6 | 45.8 | 46.0 | 46.3 | 47.2 | 47.9 | 48.0 | 46.3 |
| 2015 | 48.2 | 48.7 | 49.0 | 49.1 | 49.4 | 48.7 | 49.1 | 49.4 | 49.0 | 49.2 | 48.9 | 48.2 | 48.9 |
| 2016 | 47.6 | 47.7 | 48.1 | 49.3 | 48.4 | 46.9 | 46.8 | 46.3 | 48.0 | 47.6 | 47.4 | 46.3 | 47.5 |
| 2017 | 45.7 | 46.3 | 46.4 | 46.5 | 46.3 | 46.1 | 46.4 | 47.0 | 46.8 | 47.4 | 47.4 | 47.0 | 46.6 |
| 2018 | 46.9 | 47.3 | 47.6 | 48.0 | 47.8 | 47.7 | 47.6 | 47.8 | 47.4 | 48.3 | 48.3 | 47.5 | 47.7 |
| 2019 | 48.2 | 48.9 | 49.1 | 49.7 | 49.7 | 49.1 | 48.8 | 48.9 | 48.8 | 49.4 | 49.4 | 49.8 | 49.2 |
| **Education and Health Services** | | | | | | | | | | | | | |
| 2011 | 49.6 | 49.9 | 50.0 | 49.4 | 49.4 | 49.2 | 49.7 | 49.6 | 50.0 | 50.2 | 50.5 | 50.4 | 49.8 |
| 2012 | 49.9 | 50.6 | 50.8 | 50.3 | 50.3 | 50.4 | 49.9 | 50.6 | 50.5 | 51.1 | 51.1 | 51.2 | 50.6 |
| 2013 | 50.9 | 51.3 | 51.3 | 51.5 | 51.7 | 51.3 | 51.3 | 52.3 | 52.3 | 52.5 | 52.8 | 52.5 | 51.8 |
| 2014 | 52.4 | 52.6 | 52.8 | 52.7 | 52.7 | 52.3 | 51.9 | 53.1 | 53.4 | 53.7 | 53.5 | 53.4 | 52.9 |
| 2015 | 53.1 | 53.2 | 53.2 | 53.2 | 53.1 | 52.4 | 52.1 | 52.6 | 52.8 | 53.1 | 53.2 | 53.0 | 52.9 |
| 2016 | 51.9 | 52.0 | 51.9 | 52.6 | 52.6 | 52.2 | 52.2 | 52.4 | 52.2 | 52.4 | 52.2 | 52.5 | 52.3 |
| 2017 | 52.4 | 52.8 | 52.9 | 53.0 | 53.1 | 52.9 | 52.2 | 52.6 | 52.9 | 53.3 | 53.7 | 53.7 | 53.0 |
| 2018 | 53.0 | 53.3 | 53.3 | 53.6 | 53.7 | 53.3 | 52.9 | 53.8 | 53.7 | 54.1 | 54.1 | 54.1 | 53.6 |
| 2019 | 53.4 | 53.8 | 53.8 | 54.0 | 54.1 | 53.9 | 53.2 | 54.2 | 54.3 | 53.8 | 54.0 | 53.8 | 53.9 |
| **Leisure and Hospitality** | | | | | | | | | | | | | |
| 2011 | 32.5 | 32.6 | 33.3 | 34.1 | 34.8 | 34.4 | 34.1 | 34.6 | 34.3 | 34.4 | 34.5 | 34.2 | 34.0 |
| 2012 | 33.7 | 33.9 | 34.5 | 34.7 | 35.3 | 35.2 | 35.2 | 36.1 | 36.0 | 35.8 | 35.6 | 35.5 | 35.1 |
| 2013 | 35.1 | 35.3 | 35.7 | 36.6 | 37.3 | 37.1 | 37.2 | 37.1 | 37.1 | 36.7 | 36.5 | 36.3 | 36.5 |
| 2014 | 35.5 | 36.0 | 36.4 | 37.6 | 38.2 | 38.3 | 37.8 | 38.1 | 37.8 | 37.4 | 36.8 | 36.9 | 37.2 |
| 2015 | 36.7 | 37.0 | 37.5 | 38.0 | 39.0 | 39.0 | 38.7 | 38.5 | 38.6 | 38.5 | 38.8 | 38.7 | 38.3 |
| 2016 | 37.9 | 38.4 | 39.1 | 40.3 | 40.6 | 40.2 | 39.8 | 38.8 | 38.4 | 38.7 | 38.3 | 38.0 | 39.0 |
| 2017 | 37.8 | 38.8 | 39.0 | 39.4 | 40.1 | 40.7 | 40.6 | 41.0 | 41.5 | 40.9 | 40.6 | 39.8 | 40.0 |
| 2018 | 38.9 | 39.1 | 40.0 | 40.3 | 40.4 | 40.8 | 40.0 | 40.6 | 40.6 | 40.2 | 39.9 | 39.8 | 40.1 |
| 2019 | 38.8 | 39.7 | 39.8 | 40.5 | 40.6 | 41.1 | 39.8 | 40.8 | 40.7 | 42.6 | 42.3 | 43.0 | 40.8 |
| **Other Services** | | | | | | | | | | | | | |
| 2011 | 14.7 | 14.7 | 14.8 | 15.0 | 14.9 | 15.1 | 15.3 | 15.4 | 15.3 | 15.2 | 15.3 | 15.1 | 15.1 |
| 2012 | 15.0 | 15.2 | 15.2 | 15.3 | 15.3 | 15.5 | 15.2 | 15.2 | 15.3 | 15.3 | 15.3 | 15.1 | 15.2 |
| 2013 | 15.2 | 15.4 | 15.6 | 15.5 | 15.6 | 15.7 | 15.5 | 15.6 | 15.6 | 15.5 | 15.5 | 15.5 | 15.5 |
| 2014 | 15.5 | 15.7 | 15.7 | 15.8 | 16.0 | 16.0 | 16.1 | 16.2 | 16.1 | 16.5 | 16.3 | 16.2 | 16.0 |
| 2015 | 16.3 | 16.3 | 16.4 | 16.4 | 16.7 | 16.6 | 16.6 | 16.5 | 16.6 | 16.8 | 16.7 | 16.7 | 16.6 |
| 2016 | 16.6 | 16.6 | 16.9 | 16.8 | 16.9 | 16.9 | 16.6 | 16.4 | 16.4 | 16.3 | 16.4 | 16.3 | 16.6 |
| 2017 | 16.4 | 16.6 | 16.6 | 16.6 | 16.5 | 16.8 | 16.7 | 16.7 | 16.6 | 16.7 | 16.6 | 16.3 | 16.6 |
| 2018 | 16.3 | 16.7 | 16.6 | 16.8 | 16.9 | 17.0 | 16.8 | 16.6 | 16.8 | 17.0 | 16.9 | 16.7 | 16.8 |
| 2019 | 16.9 | 17.1 | 17.2 | 16.9 | 17.1 | 17.0 | 16.9 | 17.0 | 17.1 | 17.2 | 17.1 | 17.0 | 17.0 |
| **Government** | | | | | | | | | | | | | |
| 2011 | 74.9 | 77.0 | 76.7 | 77.0 | 76.8 | 75.1 | 73.0 | 72.5 | 76.8 | 77.6 | 77.8 | 77.2 | 76.0 |
| 2012 | 74.9 | 76.0 | 75.6 | 75.3 | 74.9 | 73.2 | 70.1 | 72.5 | 74.6 | 74.4 | 74.6 | 74.0 | 74.2 |
| 2013 | 71.9 | 73.6 | 73.6 | 73.5 | 73.2 | 71.8 | 68.7 | 71.2 | 73.9 | 73.6 | 74.1 | 73.1 | 72.7 |
| 2014 | 71.3 | 72.8 | 72.9 | 72.5 | 72.2 | 71.0 | 68.7 | 70.9 | 73.3 | 73.2 | 73.7 | 73.0 | 72.1 |
| 2015 | 71.2 | 72.8 | 72.9 | 72.7 | 72.4 | 71.2 | 69.0 | 71.3 | 73.6 | 74.0 | 74.5 | 74.0 | 72.5 |
| 2016 | 72.3 | 74.1 | 74.3 | 74.0 | 74.0 | 72.6 | 70.3 | 72.4 | 74.7 | 74.1 | 74.7 | 74.6 | 73.5 |
| 2017 | 73.2 | 75.0 | 75.4 | 74.7 | 74.5 | 72.9 | 70.3 | 72.3 | 74.5 | 74.2 | 74.7 | 74.3 | 73.8 |
| 2018 | 72.7 | 74.6 | 74.8 | 74.5 | 74.3 | 73.0 | 70.7 | 73.1 | 75.6 | 75.4 | 75.8 | 76.1 | 74.2 |
| 2019 | 75.0 | 76.8 | 77.3 | 76.8 | 76.4 | 75.0 | 72.5 | 74.9 | 77.3 | 76.3 | 76.1 | 75.2 | 75.8 |

## Employment by Industry: New Haven, CT, 2011–2019

(Numbers in thousands, not seasonally adjusted)

| Industry and year | January | February | March | April | May | June | July | August | September | October | November | December | Annual average |
|---|---|---|---|---|---|---|---|---|---|---|---|---|---|
| **Total Nonfarm** | | | | | | | | | | | | | |
| 2011 | 263.3 | 266.1 | 264.4 | 270.8 | 271.5 | 271.1 | 264.2 | 262.8 | 270.3 | 272.2 | 273.3 | 273.5 | 268.6 |
| 2012 | 266.6 | 271.0 | 270.4 | 274.6 | 276.5 | 275.9 | 268.5 | 266.7 | 274.4 | 276.3 | 278.3 | 279.6 | 273.2 |
| 2013 | 269.6 | 270.9 | 272.1 | 277.9 | 278.4 | 278.8 | 273.2 | 271.3 | 277.9 | 280.4 | 282.7 | 281.3 | 276.2 |
| 2014 | 274.1 | 275.2 | 274.7 | 280.6 | 280.7 | 280.6 | 275.0 | 273.0 | 281.0 | 282.5 | 284.9 | 285.2 | 279.0 |
| 2015 | 276.4 | 277.5 | 277.3 | 282.0 | 283.5 | 283.1 | 276.2 | 273.7 | 281.5 | 285.2 | 287.5 | 287.5 | 281.0 |
| 2016 | 276.6 | 279.4 | 281.2 | 284.0 | 285.8 | 285.8 | 278.8 | 277.0 | 284.8 | 287.5 | 289.0 | 290.2 | 283.3 |
| 2017 | 280.4 | 282.8 | 282.3 | 287.3 | 288.2 | 289.3 | 280.8 | 279.9 | 285.8 | 288.6 | 291.5 | 291.5 | 285.7 |
| 2018 | 280.5 | 284.4 | 283.1 | 287.9 | 289.3 | 290.0 | 284.4 | 282.8 | 288.5 | 291.2 | 293.6 | 294.6 | 287.5 |
| 2019 | 281.5 | 285.2 | 283.9 | 289.1 | 289.9 | 289.0 | 285.2 | 285.9 | 292.4 | 293.8 | 294.3 | 293.9 | 288.7 |
| **Total Private** | | | | | | | | | | | | | |
| 2011 | 227.5 | 228.8 | 227.9 | 233.0 | 234.5 | 235.0 | 232.9 | 232.4 | 234.3 | 235.2 | 236.0 | 236.2 | 232.8 |
| 2012 | 231.8 | 233.8 | 233.3 | 237.4 | 240.1 | 240.5 | 237.7 | 237.0 | 239.1 | 240.1 | 241.3 | 242.2 | 237.9 |
| 2013 | 234.0 | 234.5 | 235.5 | 240.2 | 241.2 | 241.8 | 241.1 | 240.7 | 241.8 | 244.1 | 245.3 | 244.6 | 240.4 |
| 2014 | 237.9 | 238.0 | 237.5 | 242.6 | 243.5 | 244.0 | 243.1 | 241.8 | 244.0 | 245.7 | 247.2 | 247.9 | 242.8 |
| 2015 | 240.2 | 239.9 | 239.6 | 244.0 | 245.7 | 246.5 | 244.1 | 242.4 | 244.5 | 247.5 | 249.3 | 249.8 | 244.5 |
| 2016 | 240.4 | 241.8 | 243.3 | 245.9 | 247.4 | 248.5 | 246.4 | 245.9 | 248.2 | 250.0 | 251.2 | 252.0 | 246.8 |
| 2017 | 244.4 | 245.3 | 245.0 | 249.7 | 250.7 | 252.6 | 249.1 | 248.8 | 249.7 | 251.3 | 254.2 | 254.0 | 249.6 |
| 2018 | 244.8 | 247.3 | 246.0 | 250.8 | 252.3 | 253.5 | 252.0 | 251.1 | 252.6 | 255.2 | 257.1 | 257.8 | 251.7 |
| 2019 | 246.3 | 248.7 | 247.4 | 252.9 | 253.5 | 254.1 | 253.3 | 254.2 | 256.5 | 257.4 | 257.5 | 257.1 | 253.2 |
| **Goods Producing** | | | | | | | | | | | | | |
| 2011 | 33.8 | 33.9 | 34.0 | 34.6 | 35.2 | 35.7 | 35.5 | 35.7 | 35.4 | 35.3 | 35.2 | 35.0 | 34.9 |
| 2012 | 34.1 | 34.1 | 34.1 | 34.5 | 35.1 | 35.4 | 35.4 | 35.4 | 35.2 | 34.9 | 34.8 | 34.6 | 34.8 |
| 2013 | 33.6 | 33.3 | 33.6 | 34.1 | 34.6 | 35.0 | 35.6 | 35.5 | 35.2 | 35.3 | 34.8 | 34.6 | 34.6 |
| 2014 | 33.5 | 33.3 | 33.4 | 34.3 | 34.9 | 35.2 | 35.7 | 35.6 | 35.4 | 35.2 | 34.8 | 34.6 | 34.7 |
| 2015 | 33.9 | 33.4 | 33.5 | 34.6 | 35.1 | 35.6 | 35.6 | 35.5 | 35.3 | 35.1 | 34.9 | 34.7 | 34.8 |
| 2016 | 33.6 | 33.3 | 33.5 | 34.0 | 34.4 | 34.9 | 35.0 | 35.0 | 34.7 | 34.5 | 34.4 | 34.0 | 34.3 |
| 2017 | 33.3 | 33.1 | 33.1 | 33.5 | 33.9 | 34.5 | 34.6 | 34.6 | 34.2 | 34.2 | 34.1 | 34.0 | 33.9 |
| 2018 | 32.7 | 32.9 | 33.2 | 33.7 | 34.5 | 35.2 | 35.6 | 35.5 | 35.0 | 35.2 | 35.1 | 34.9 | 34.5 |
| 2019 | 33.9 | 33.9 | 34.2 | 35.1 | 35.5 | 36.0 | 36.2 | 36.0 | 35.6 | 35.6 | 35.1 | 34.6 | 35.1 |
| **Service-Providing** | | | | | | | | | | | | | |
| 2011 | 229.5 | 232.2 | 230.4 | 236.2 | 236.3 | 235.4 | 228.7 | 227.1 | 234.9 | 236.9 | 238.1 | 238.5 | 233.7 |
| 2012 | 232.5 | 236.9 | 236.3 | 240.1 | 241.4 | 240.5 | 233.1 | 231.3 | 239.2 | 241.4 | 243.5 | 245.0 | 238.4 |
| 2013 | 236.0 | 237.6 | 238.5 | 243.8 | 243.8 | 243.8 | 237.6 | 235.8 | 242.7 | 245.1 | 247.9 | 246.7 | 241.6 |
| 2014 | 240.6 | 241.9 | 241.3 | 246.3 | 245.8 | 245.4 | 239.3 | 237.4 | 245.6 | 247.3 | 250.1 | 250.6 | 244.3 |
| 2015 | 242.5 | 244.1 | 243.8 | 247.4 | 248.4 | 247.5 | 240.6 | 238.2 | 246.2 | 250.1 | 252.6 | 252.8 | 246.2 |
| 2016 | 243.0 | 246.1 | 247.7 | 250.0 | 251.4 | 250.9 | 243.8 | 242.0 | 250.1 | 253.0 | 254.6 | 256.2 | 249.1 |
| 2017 | 247.1 | 249.7 | 249.2 | 253.8 | 254.3 | 254.8 | 246.2 | 245.3 | 251.6 | 254.4 | 257.4 | 257.5 | 251.8 |
| 2018 | 247.8 | 251.5 | 249.9 | 254.2 | 254.8 | 254.8 | 248.8 | 247.3 | 253.5 | 256.0 | 258.5 | 259.7 | 253.1 |
| 2019 | 247.6 | 251.3 | 249.7 | 254.0 | 254.4 | 253.0 | 249.0 | 249.9 | 256.8 | 258.2 | 259.2 | 259.3 | 253.5 |
| **Mining, Logging, and Construction** | | | | | | | | | | | | | |
| 2011 | 8.2 | 8.3 | 8.3 | 8.9 | 9.4 | 9.7 | 9.7 | 9.8 | 9.6 | 9.6 | 9.4 | 9.2 | 9.2 |
| 2012 | 8.5 | 8.5 | 8.5 | 8.9 | 9.3 | 9.5 | 9.7 | 9.8 | 9.7 | 9.5 | 9.5 | 9.2 | 9.2 |
| 2013 | 8.4 | 8.1 | 8.4 | 9.1 | 9.5 | 9.8 | 10.2 | 10.3 | 10.2 | 10.0 | 9.8 | 9.5 | 9.4 |
| 2014 | 8.6 | 8.5 | 8.7 | 9.6 | 10.1 | 10.3 | 10.6 | 10.7 | 10.6 | 10.4 | 10.3 | 10.1 | 9.9 |
| 2015 | 9.4 | 9.1 | 9.2 | 10.2 | 10.7 | 11.1 | 11.2 | 11.2 | 11.1 | 11.1 | 11.0 | 10.8 | 10.5 |
| 2016 | 9.9 | 9.7 | 10.0 | 10.6 | 11.0 | 11.3 | 11.4 | 11.4 | 11.3 | 11.1 | 11.0 | 10.5 | 10.8 |
| 2017 | 9.8 | 9.7 | 9.7 | 10.2 | 10.6 | 11.0 | 10.9 | 11.0 | 10.9 | 10.8 | 10.7 | 10.4 | 10.5 |
| 2018 | 9.4 | 9.6 | 9.9 | 10.4 | 11.0 | 11.5 | 11.8 | 11.7 | 11.4 | 11.5 | 11.3 | 10.9 | 10.9 |
| 2019 | 10.0 | 10.0 | 10.2 | 11.1 | 11.4 | 11.7 | 11.8 | 11.8 | 11.6 | 11.6 | 11.4 | 11.0 | 11.1 |
| **Manufacturing** | | | | | | | | | | | | | |
| 2011 | 25.6 | 25.6 | 25.7 | 25.7 | 25.8 | 26.0 | 25.8 | 25.9 | 25.8 | 25.7 | 25.8 | 25.8 | 25.8 |
| 2012 | 25.6 | 25.6 | 25.6 | 25.6 | 25.8 | 25.9 | 25.7 | 25.6 | 25.5 | 25.4 | 25.3 | 25.4 | 25.6 |
| 2013 | 25.2 | 25.2 | 25.2 | 25.0 | 25.1 | 25.2 | 25.4 | 25.2 | 25.0 | 25.3 | 25.0 | 25.1 | 25.2 |
| 2014 | 24.9 | 24.8 | 24.7 | 24.7 | 24.8 | 24.9 | 25.1 | 24.9 | 24.8 | 24.8 | 24.5 | 24.5 | 24.8 |
| 2015 | 24.5 | 24.3 | 24.3 | 24.4 | 24.4 | 24.5 | 24.4 | 24.3 | 24.2 | 24.0 | 23.9 | 23.9 | 24.3 |
| 2016 | 23.7 | 23.6 | 23.5 | 23.4 | 23.4 | 23.6 | 23.6 | 23.6 | 23.4 | 23.4 | 23.4 | 23.5 | 23.5 |
| 2017 | 23.5 | 23.4 | 23.4 | 23.3 | 23.3 | 23.5 | 23.7 | 23.6 | 23.3 | 23.4 | 23.4 | 23.6 | 23.5 |
| 2018 | 23.3 | 23.3 | 23.3 | 23.3 | 23.5 | 23.7 | 23.8 | 23.8 | 23.6 | 23.7 | 23.8 | 24.0 | 23.6 |
| 2019 | 23.9 | 23.9 | 24.0 | 24.0 | 24.1 | 24.3 | 24.4 | 24.2 | 24.0 | 24.0 | 23.7 | 23.6 | 24.0 |

# Employment by Industry: New Haven, CT, 2011–2019—*Continued*

(Numbers in thousands, not seasonally adjusted)

| Industry and year | January | February | March | April | May | June | July | August | September | October | November | December | Annual average |
|---|---|---|---|---|---|---|---|---|---|---|---|---|---|
| **Trade, Transportation, and Utilities** | | | | | | | | | | | | | |
| 2011 | 46.1 | 45.4 | 45.5 | 46.4 | 46.8 | 47.1 | 46.3 | 46.4 | 46.6 | 46.9 | 47.8 | 48.5 | 46.7 |
| 2012 | 47.2 | 46.5 | 46.7 | 46.8 | 47.8 | 48.3 | 47.6 | 47.4 | 47.6 | 48.3 | 49.8 | 50.1 | 47.8 |
| 2013 | 48.3 | 47.1 | 47.6 | 48.4 | 49.0 | 49.3 | 48.4 | 48.7 | 48.9 | 49.4 | 50.6 | 51.3 | 48.9 |
| 2014 | 48.8 | 48.2 | 48.4 | 49.0 | 49.6 | 49.9 | 49.3 | 49.3 | 49.5 | 50.1 | 51.5 | 52.1 | 49.6 |
| 2015 | 49.7 | 48.6 | 49.1 | 49.2 | 50.3 | 50.6 | 49.6 | 49.3 | 49.7 | 50.9 | 52.8 | 53.2 | 50.3 |
| 2016 | 50.6 | 49.6 | 50.2 | 50.6 | 51.2 | 51.3 | 50.7 | 50.8 | 51.1 | 52.0 | 53.3 | 53.9 | 51.3 |
| 2017 | 52.2 | 50.7 | 50.8 | 51.4 | 52.2 | 52.3 | 51.7 | 51.5 | 51.4 | 52.2 | 54.7 | 54.7 | 52.2 |
| 2018 | 52.0 | 50.7 | 50.9 | 50.9 | 51.5 | 52.0 | 51.3 | 51.1 | 51.1 | 52.4 | 54.9 | 54.9 | 52.0 |
| 2019 | 51.7 | 50.2 | 50.0 | 50.4 | 50.8 | 50.9 | 50.9 | 52.3 | 53.3 | 53.5 | 54.6 | 55.0 | 52.0 |
| **Wholesale Trade** | | | | | | | | | | | | | |
| 2011 | 11.3 | 11.2 | 11.2 | 11.3 | 11.3 | 11.4 | 11.4 | 11.4 | 11.3 | 11.2 | 11.2 | 11.2 | 11.3 |
| 2012 | 11.1 | 11.1 | 11.1 | 11.2 | 11.3 | 11.3 | 11.3 | 11.1 | 11.1 | 11.1 | 11.2 | 11.2 | 11.2 |
| 2013 | 11.0 | 10.9 | 11.0 | 11.1 | 11.2 | 11.2 | 11.2 | 11.2 | 11.1 | 11.1 | 11.1 | 11.1 | 11.1 |
| 2014 | 10.9 | 10.9 | 10.9 | 11.1 | 11.2 | 11.2 | 11.2 | 11.1 | 11.1 | 11.1 | 11.1 | 11.1 | 11.1 |
| 2015 | 11.0 | 11.0 | 11.0 | 11.1 | 11.3 | 11.3 | 11.4 | 11.3 | 11.2 | 11.3 | 11.3 | 11.4 | 11.2 |
| 2016 | 11.3 | 11.3 | 11.5 | 11.5 | 11.6 | 11.6 | 11.7 | 11.6 | 11.6 | 11.6 | 11.6 | 11.7 | 11.6 |
| 2017 | 11.6 | 11.5 | 11.5 | 11.6 | 11.7 | 11.8 | 11.7 | 11.6 | 11.5 | 11.5 | 11.6 | 11.6 | 11.6 |
| 2018 | 11.5 | 11.5 | 11.5 | 11.5 | 11.6 | 11.6 | 11.6 | 11.5 | 11.3 | 11.4 | 11.5 | 11.4 | 11.5 |
| 2019 | 11.1 | 11.1 | 11.1 | 11.3 | 11.4 | 11.4 | 11.4 | 11.3 | 11.2 | 11.2 | 11.2 | 11.2 | 11.2 |
| **Retail Trade** | | | | | | | | | | | | | |
| 2011 | 28.2 | 27.6 | 27.6 | 28.2 | 28.5 | 28.6 | 28.3 | 28.5 | 28.3 | 28.6 | 29.5 | 30.1 | 28.5 |
| 2012 | 29.1 | 28.4 | 28.5 | 28.4 | 29.1 | 29.4 | 28.9 | 28.9 | 28.5 | 29.0 | 30.4 | 30.6 | 29.1 |
| 2013 | 29.1 | 28.2 | 28.3 | 28.8 | 29.2 | 29.4 | 29.1 | 29.4 | 29.1 | 29.7 | 30.9 | 31.5 | 29.4 |
| 2014 | 29.5 | 28.9 | 29.0 | 29.2 | 29.6 | 29.9 | 29.8 | 29.9 | 29.5 | 30.0 | 31.3 | 31.8 | 29.9 |
| 2015 | 30.0 | 29.0 | 29.3 | 29.2 | 29.8 | 30.1 | 29.6 | 29.6 | 29.5 | 30.5 | 31.7 | 32.0 | 30.0 |
| 2016 | 30.2 | 29.3 | 29.5 | 29.7 | 30.0 | 30.2 | 30.0 | 30.2 | 29.9 | 30.6 | 31.9 | 32.1 | 30.3 |
| 2017 | 31.0 | 29.8 | 29.7 | 30.0 | 30.4 | 30.5 | 30.3 | 30.2 | 29.8 | 30.4 | 31.9 | 31.9 | 30.5 |
| 2018 | 30.3 | 29.2 | 29.3 | 29.4 | 29.6 | 29.9 | 29.7 | 29.6 | 29.2 | 29.9 | 31.6 | 31.8 | 30.0 |
| 2019 | 29.6 | 28.4 | 28.2 | 28.5 | 28.6 | 28.9 | 28.7 | 28.5 | 28.2 | 28.3 | 29.1 | 29.1 | 28.7 |
| **Transportation and Utilities** | | | | | | | | | | | | | |
| 2011 | 6.6 | 6.6 | 6.7 | 6.9 | 7.0 | 7.1 | 6.6 | 6.5 | 7.0 | 7.1 | 7.1 | 7.2 | 6.9 |
| 2012 | 7.0 | 7.0 | 7.1 | 7.2 | 7.4 | 7.6 | 7.4 | 7.4 | 8.0 | 8.2 | 8.2 | 8.3 | 7.6 |
| 2013 | 8.2 | 8.0 | 8.3 | 8.5 | 8.6 | 8.7 | 8.1 | 8.1 | 8.7 | 8.6 | 8.6 | 8.7 | 8.4 |
| 2014 | 8.4 | 8.4 | 8.5 | 8.7 | 8.8 | 8.8 | 8.3 | 8.3 | 8.9 | 9.0 | 9.1 | 9.2 | 8.7 |
| 2015 | 8.7 | 8.6 | 8.8 | 8.9 | 9.2 | 9.2 | 8.6 | 8.4 | 9.0 | 9.1 | 9.8 | 9.8 | 9.0 |
| 2016 | 9.1 | 9.0 | 9.2 | 9.4 | 9.6 | 9.5 | 9.0 | 9.0 | 9.6 | 9.8 | 9.8 | 10.1 | 9.4 |
| 2017 | 9.6 | 9.4 | 9.6 | 9.8 | 10.1 | 10.0 | 9.7 | 9.7 | 10.1 | 10.3 | 11.2 | 11.2 | 10.1 |
| 2018 | 10.2 | 10.0 | 10.1 | 10.0 | 10.3 | 10.5 | 10.0 | 10.0 | 10.6 | 11.1 | 11.8 | 11.7 | 10.5 |
| 2019 | 11.0 | 10.7 | 10.7 | 10.6 | 10.8 | 10.6 | 10.8 | 12.5 | 13.9 | 14.0 | 14.3 | 14.7 | 12.1 |
| **Information** | | | | | | | | | | | | | |
| 2011 | 4.8 | 4.8 | 4.8 | 4.7 | 4.7 | 4.7 | 4.6 | 4.5 | 4.5 | 4.6 | 4.6 | 4.6 | 4.7 |
| 2012 | 4.5 | 4.5 | 4.4 | 4.3 | 4.3 | 4.3 | 4.3 | 4.3 | 4.3 | 4.3 | 4.3 | 4.3 | 4.3 |
| 2013 | 4.3 | 4.3 | 4.3 | 4.2 | 4.2 | 4.2 | 4.2 | 4.2 | 4.1 | 4.2 | 4.2 | 4.3 | 4.2 |
| 2014 | 4.3 | 4.2 | 4.1 | 4.1 | 4.1 | 4.1 | 4.2 | 4.1 | 4.0 | 3.7 | 3.7 | 3.7 | 4.0 |
| 2015 | 3.6 | 3.6 | 3.6 | 3.5 | 3.5 | 3.5 | 3.4 | 3.4 | 3.4 | 3.4 | 3.4 | 3.4 | 3.5 |
| 2016 | 3.4 | 3.3 | 3.3 | 3.4 | 3.4 | 3.4 | 3.4 | 3.5 | 3.4 | 3.4 | 3.5 | 3.5 | 3.4 |
| 2017 | 3.7 | 3.7 | 3.7 | 3.7 | 3.8 | 3.7 | 3.7 | 3.7 | 3.6 | 3.6 | 3.6 | 3.6 | 3.7 |
| 2018 | 3.7 | 3.7 | 3.7 | 3.7 | 3.7 | 3.8 | 3.8 | 3.8 | 3.8 | 3.8 | 3.8 | 3.8 | 3.8 |
| 2019 | 3.8 | 3.8 | 3.8 | 3.7 | 3.7 | 3.7 | 3.7 | 3.7 | 3.6 | 3.7 | 3.6 | 3.7 | 3.7 |
| **Financial Activities** | | | | | | | | | | | | | |
| 2011 | 12.3 | 12.3 | 12.3 | 12.2 | 12.2 | 12.3 | 12.3 | 12.3 | 12.0 | 12.0 | 11.8 | 12.0 | 12.2 |
| 2012 | 12.1 | 12.0 | 12.1 | 12.1 | 12.1 | 12.3 | 12.3 | 12.2 | 12.1 | 12.0 | 12.0 | 12.1 | 12.1 |
| 2013 | 12.1 | 12.0 | 12.0 | 12.0 | 12.0 | 12.2 | 12.3 | 12.3 | 12.3 | 12.3 | 12.3 | 12.4 | 12.2 |
| 2014 | 12.3 | 12.3 | 12.3 | 12.4 | 12.5 | 12.6 | 12.7 | 12.7 | 12.6 | 12.5 | 12.5 | 12.6 | 12.5 |
| 2015 | 12.5 | 12.4 | 12.4 | 12.5 | 12.6 | 12.7 | 12.7 | 12.7 | 12.6 | 12.6 | 12.5 | 12.5 | 12.6 |
| 2016 | 12.4 | 12.4 | 12.4 | 12.5 | 12.5 | 12.7 | 12.7 | 12.6 | 12.4 | 12.4 | 12.3 | 12.4 | 12.5 |
| 2017 | 12.4 | 12.4 | 12.4 | 12.4 | 12.5 | 12.5 | 12.4 | 12.4 | 12.2 | 12.2 | 12.1 | 12.1 | 12.3 |
| 2018 | 12.1 | 12.1 | 12.0 | 12.1 | 12.1 | 12.2 | 12.2 | 12.2 | 12.0 | 11.9 | 11.9 | 12.0 | 12.1 |
| 2019 | 11.8 | 11.9 | 11.8 | 11.9 | 12.0 | 12.2 | 12.2 | 12.2 | 12.1 | 12.0 | 12.0 | 12.1 | 12.0 |

## Employment by Industry: New Haven, CT, 2011–2019—*Continued*

(Numbers in thousands, not seasonally adjusted)

| Industry and year | January | February | March | April | May | June | July | August | September | October | November | December | Annual average |
|---|---|---|---|---|---|---|---|---|---|---|---|---|---|
| **Professional and Business Services** | | | | | | | | | | | | | |
| 2011 | 25.8 | 26.1 | 25.8 | 26.8 | 26.7 | 27.2 | 27.2 | 27.2 | 27.1 | 27.1 | 27.4 | 27.6 | 26.8 |
| 2012 | 27.6 | 27.6 | 27.9 | 28.8 | 28.8 | 28.9 | 28.5 | 28.5 | 28.9 | 28.9 | 29.0 | 29.4 | 28.6 |
| 2013 | 28.8 | 29.0 | 29.0 | 29.2 | 29.4 | 29.8 | 29.9 | 29.8 | 29.3 | 29.6 | 29.9 | 29.9 | 29.5 |
| 2014 | 29.0 | 29.2 | 29.1 | 29.6 | 29.8 | 29.9 | 30.0 | 29.7 | 29.5 | 29.9 | 30.2 | 30.5 | 29.7 |
| 2015 | 29.7 | 30.0 | 29.9 | 30.5 | 30.6 | 30.8 | 30.5 | 30.2 | 30.2 | 30.5 | 30.6 | 30.6 | 30.3 |
| 2016 | 29.3 | 29.7 | 29.9 | 30.2 | 30.3 | 30.8 | 30.5 | 30.6 | 30.5 | 30.6 | 30.7 | 31.1 | 30.4 |
| 2017 | 30.2 | 30.2 | 30.6 | 31.4 | 31.0 | 31.7 | 31.6 | 31.4 | 31.1 | 31.1 | 31.4 | 31.4 | 31.1 |
| 2018 | 30.2 | 30.9 | 30.5 | 31.0 | 31.3 | 31.3 | 31.7 | 31.8 | 31.3 | 31.6 | 31.6 | 31.4 | 31.2 |
| 2019 | 29.2 | 29.7 | 29.6 | 30.5 | 30.6 | 31.0 | 31.3 | 31.3 | 30.7 | 30.5 | 30.5 | 31.0 | 30.5 |
| **Education and Health Services** | | | | | | | | | | | | | |
| 2011 | 74.8 | 75.9 | 74.7 | 76.0 | 75.6 | 73.6 | 72.8 | 72.2 | 75.4 | 76.5 | 76.8 | 75.7 | 75.0 |
| 2012 | 74.9 | 77.5 | 76.0 | 77.3 | 77.6 | 75.7 | 74.4 | 74.0 | 76.7 | 78.0 | 77.8 | 77.9 | 76.5 |
| 2013 | 75.4 | 77.7 | 76.7 | 78.5 | 77.2 | 75.4 | 75.1 | 74.8 | 77.6 | 79.3 | 79.7 | 78.6 | 77.2 |
| 2014 | 77.6 | 78.4 | 77.1 | 79.4 | 77.8 | 76.4 | 75.5 | 75.1 | 78.4 | 79.9 | 80.3 | 80.1 | 78.0 |
| 2015 | 78.0 | 79.2 | 77.7 | 79.6 | 78.3 | 76.8 | 76.3 | 75.7 | 78.4 | 80.4 | 80.8 | 80.9 | 78.5 |
| 2016 | 78.1 | 80.1 | 80.0 | 80.4 | 79.4 | 77.9 | 76.9 | 76.4 | 80.0 | 81.1 | 81.4 | 81.3 | 79.4 |
| 2017 | 78.0 | 80.4 | 79.4 | 81.2 | 80.1 | 79.2 | 76.8 | 77.0 | 80.2 | 81.2 | 81.5 | 81.8 | 79.7 |
| 2018 | 79.2 | 81.7 | 80.3 | 82.7 | 81.5 | 79.9 | 78.7 | 78.3 | 81.6 | 82.4 | 82.6 | 83.5 | 81.0 |
| 2019 | 80.9 | 83.4 | 82.0 | 84.0 | 82.4 | 81.1 | 80.2 | 80.1 | 83.6 | 84.6 | 84.4 | 83.7 | 82.5 |
| **Leisure and Hospitality** | | | | | | | | | | | | | |
| 2011 | 19.9 | 20.3 | 20.7 | 21.9 | 23.0 | 23.7 | 23.7 | 23.6 | 23.0 | 22.6 | 22.2 | 22.4 | 22.3 |
| 2012 | 21.0 | 21.2 | 21.7 | 22.9 | 23.8 | 24.9 | 24.5 | 24.5 | 23.8 | 23.1 | 23.0 | 23.2 | 23.1 |
| 2013 | 21.2 | 20.8 | 21.8 | 23.2 | 24.1 | 25.1 | 24.9 | 24.8 | 24.0 | 23.6 | 23.3 | 23.0 | 23.3 |
| 2014 | 22.0 | 22.0 | 22.6 | 23.2 | 24.1 | 25.0 | 24.8 | 24.5 | 24.0 | 23.6 | 23.5 | 23.5 | 23.6 |
| 2015 | 22.3 | 22.2 | 22.7 | 23.4 | 24.5 | 25.5 | 25.1 | 24.8 | 24.2 | 23.9 | 23.6 | 23.8 | 23.8 |
| 2016 | 22.4 | 22.8 | 23.2 | 24.0 | 25.3 | 26.4 | 26.2 | 26.1 | 25.2 | 25.1 | 24.8 | 24.8 | 24.7 |
| 2017 | 23.8 | 24.0 | 24.1 | 25.2 | 26.2 | 27.5 | 27.2 | 26.9 | 25.8 | 25.5 | 25.4 | 25.1 | 25.6 |
| 2018 | 23.9 | 24.2 | 24.4 | 25.4 | 26.3 | 27.5 | 27.2 | 27.0 | 26.4 | 26.5 | 25.7 | 25.9 | 25.9 |
| 2019 | 24.0 | 24.7 | 24.8 | 26.0 | 27.2 | 27.7 | 27.5 | 27.3 | 26.4 | 26.3 | 26.1 | 25.8 | 26.2 |
| **Other Services** | | | | | | | | | | | | | |
| 2011 | 10.0 | 10.1 | 10.1 | 10.4 | 10.3 | 10.7 | 10.5 | 10.5 | 10.3 | 10.2 | 10.2 | 10.4 | 10.3 |
| 2012 | 10.4 | 10.4 | 10.4 | 10.7 | 10.6 | 10.7 | 10.7 | 10.7 | 10.5 | 10.6 | 10.6 | 10.6 | 10.6 |
| 2013 | 10.3 | 10.3 | 10.5 | 10.6 | 10.7 | 10.8 | 10.7 | 10.6 | 10.4 | 10.4 | 10.5 | 10.5 | 10.5 |
| 2014 | 10.4 | 10.4 | 10.5 | 10.6 | 10.7 | 10.9 | 10.9 | 10.8 | 10.6 | 10.8 | 10.7 | 10.8 | 10.7 |
| 2015 | 10.5 | 10.5 | 10.7 | 10.7 | 10.8 | 11.0 | 10.9 | 10.8 | 10.7 | 10.7 | 10.7 | 10.7 | 10.7 |
| 2016 | 10.6 | 10.6 | 10.8 | 10.8 | 10.9 | 11.1 | 11.0 | 10.9 | 10.9 | 10.9 | 10.8 | 11.0 | 10.9 |
| 2017 | 10.8 | 10.8 | 10.9 | 10.9 | 11.0 | 11.2 | 11.1 | 11.3 | 11.2 | 11.3 | 11.4 | 11.3 | 11.1 |
| 2018 | 11.0 | 11.1 | 11.0 | 11.3 | 11.4 | 11.6 | 11.5 | 11.4 | 11.4 | 11.4 | 11.5 | 11.4 | 11.3 |
| 2019 | 11.0 | 11.1 | 11.2 | 11.3 | 11.3 | 11.5 | 11.3 | 11.3 | 11.2 | 11.2 | 11.2 | 11.2 | 11.2 |
| **Government** | | | | | | | | | | | | | |
| 2011 | 35.8 | 37.3 | 36.5 | 37.8 | 37.0 | 36.1 | 31.3 | 30.4 | 36.0 | 37.0 | 37.3 | 37.3 | 35.8 |
| 2012 | 34.8 | 37.2 | 37.1 | 37.2 | 36.4 | 35.4 | 30.8 | 29.7 | 35.3 | 36.2 | 37.0 | 37.4 | 35.4 |
| 2013 | 35.6 | 36.4 | 36.6 | 37.7 | 37.2 | 37.0 | 32.1 | 30.6 | 36.1 | 36.3 | 37.4 | 36.7 | 35.8 |
| 2014 | 36.2 | 37.2 | 37.2 | 38.0 | 37.2 | 36.6 | 31.9 | 31.2 | 37.0 | 36.8 | 37.7 | 37.3 | 36.2 |
| 2015 | 36.2 | 37.6 | 37.7 | 38.0 | 37.8 | 36.6 | 32.1 | 31.3 | 37.0 | 37.7 | 38.2 | 37.7 | 36.5 |
| 2016 | 36.2 | 37.6 | 37.9 | 38.1 | 38.4 | 37.3 | 32.4 | 31.1 | 36.6 | 37.5 | 37.8 | 38.2 | 36.6 |
| 2017 | 36.0 | 37.5 | 37.3 | 37.6 | 37.5 | 36.7 | 31.7 | 31.1 | 36.1 | 37.3 | 37.3 | 37.5 | 36.1 |
| 2018 | 35.7 | 37.1 | 37.1 | 37.1 | 37.0 | 36.5 | 32.4 | 31.7 | 35.9 | 36.0 | 36.5 | 36.8 | 35.8 |
| 2019 | 35.2 | 36.5 | 36.5 | 36.2 | 36.4 | 34.9 | 31.9 | 31.7 | 35.9 | 36.4 | 36.8 | 36.8 | 35.4 |

# Employment by Industry: Oxnard-Thousand Oaks-Ventura, CA, 2011–2019

(Numbers in thousands, not seasonally adjusted)

| Industry and year | January | February | March | April | May | June | July | August | September | October | November | December | Annual average |
|---|---|---|---|---|---|---|---|---|---|---|---|---|---|
| **Total Nonfarm** | | | | | | | | | | | | | |
| 2011 | 275.2 | 275.9 | 276.1 | 277.9 | 278.3 | 278.4 | 275.0 | 276.0 | 277.6 | 279.9 | 283.3 | 282.7 | 278.0 |
| 2012 | 278.6 | 280.2 | 281.1 | 281.7 | 283.7 | 284.4 | 279.1 | 280.2 | 281.6 | 285.7 | 289.2 | 290.1 | 283.0 |
| 2013 | 285.2 | 287.3 | 287.8 | 287.6 | 289.6 | 288.9 | 285.4 | 287.5 | 288.7 | 292.3 | 296.2 | 297.8 | 289.5 |
| 2014 | 290.7 | 291.5 | 292.8 | 293.7 | 294.6 | 294.6 | 290.0 | 291.6 | 292.3 | 296.1 | 298.3 | 298.6 | 293.7 |
| 2015 | 292.2 | 294.3 | 294.6 | 295.4 | 296.0 | 295.7 | 292.4 | 293.6 | 295.7 | 301.0 | 303.0 | 303.7 | 296.5 |
| 2016 | 295.8 | 298.0 | 298.2 | 300.0 | 301.1 | 301.2 | 297.9 | 298.4 | 299.9 | 303.7 | 305.1 | 305.8 | 300.4 |
| 2017 | 298.8 | 300.9 | 302.0 | 304.4 | 306.5 | 307.3 | 302.4 | 303.5 | 305.9 | 309.5 | 311.8 | 311.8 | 305.4 |
| 2018 | 304.4 | 307.2 | 307.7 | 309.0 | 310.0 | 308.9 | 305.9 | 307.5 | 308.2 | 312.1 | 313.8 | 314.4 | 309.1 |
| 2019 | 307.0 | 309.4 | 309.9 | 311.5 | 313.1 | 312.4 | 309.4 | 310.1 | 310.0 | 314.6 | 316.9 | 316.9 | 311.8 |
| **Total Private** | | | | | | | | | | | | | |
| 2011 | 230.4 | 230.6 | 230.6 | 232.5 | 233.1 | 232.7 | 233.9 | 234.1 | 234.3 | 235.2 | 237.7 | 238.4 | 233.6 |
| 2012 | 234.7 | 235.6 | 236.5 | 237.2 | 238.8 | 239.7 | 238.6 | 239.3 | 239.2 | 241.9 | 244.7 | 245.9 | 239.3 |
| 2013 | 241.4 | 242.9 | 243.2 | 243.2 | 244.7 | 244.2 | 244.9 | 246.4 | 246.2 | 248.4 | 251.9 | 253.5 | 245.9 |
| 2014 | 247.0 | 247.2 | 248.4 | 249.1 | 250.0 | 250.0 | 249.5 | 249.7 | 249.0 | 251.0 | 252.7 | 253.2 | 249.7 |
| 2015 | 247.1 | 248.2 | 248.6 | 249.2 | 249.1 | 249.2 | 251.3 | 251.4 | 250.9 | 254.7 | 256.3 | 256.8 | 251.1 |
| 2016 | 249.4 | 251.0 | 250.8 | 252.9 | 253.3 | 253.2 | 254.3 | 254.4 | 254.4 | 256.7 | 257.6 | 258.1 | 253.8 |
| 2017 | 251.8 | 253.2 | 254.2 | 256.5 | 258.4 | 259.9 | 258.6 | 259.1 | 259.7 | 262.4 | 263.8 | 264.3 | 258.5 |
| 2018 | 257.8 | 259.7 | 260.1 | 261.1 | 261.8 | 261.7 | 262.2 | 263.1 | 262.0 | 264.5 | 265.8 | 266.9 | 262.2 |
| 2019 | 260.0 | 261.4 | 262.0 | 263.6 | 265.0 | 264.9 | 265.1 | 265.2 | 264.1 | 266.6 | 268.4 | 268.5 | 264.6 |
| **Goods Producing** | | | | | | | | | | | | | |
| 2011 | 37.3 | 37.2 | 37.2 | 37.3 | 37.3 | 37.3 | 37.5 | 37.5 | 37.4 | 37.3 | 37.4 | 36.8 | 37.3 |
| 2012 | 36.5 | 36.6 | 37.0 | 36.8 | 37.0 | 37.4 | 37.4 | 37.6 | 37.7 | 37.6 | 37.6 | 37.7 | 37.2 |
| 2013 | 37.4 | 37.5 | 37.6 | 37.3 | 37.5 | 37.7 | 38.0 | 38.2 | 38.4 | 38.7 | 39.1 | 38.9 | 38.0 |
| 2014 | 38.8 | 39.1 | 39.7 | 39.3 | 39.8 | 39.9 | 40.3 | 40.7 | 40.7 | 40.7 | 40.6 | 40.4 | 40.0 |
| 2015 | 40.6 | 40.5 | 40.6 | 40.7 | 40.6 | 41.0 | 41.5 | 41.7 | 41.3 | 41.4 | 41.4 | 41.3 | 41.1 |
| 2016 | 40.4 | 40.7 | 40.7 | 41.1 | 41.1 | 41.3 | 41.8 | 41.7 | 41.7 | 41.6 | 41.3 | 41.1 | 41.2 |
| 2017 | 40.4 | 40.8 | 41.3 | 41.8 | 42.2 | 42.6 | 42.6 | 42.8 | 42.9 | 43.0 | 43.1 | 43.0 | 42.2 |
| 2018 | 42.8 | 43.2 | 42.9 | 43.3 | 43.5 | 43.9 | 44.4 | 44.4 | 44.6 | 44.6 | 44.7 | 44.4 | 43.9 |
| 2019 | 43.5 | 43.7 | 43.8 | 43.9 | 44.3 | 44.7 | 44.9 | 45.0 | 45.0 | 44.9 | 44.9 | 44.7 | 44.4 |
| **Service-Providing** | | | | | | | | | | | | | |
| 2011 | 237.9 | 238.7 | 238.9 | 240.6 | 241.0 | 241.1 | 237.5 | 238.5 | 240.2 | 242.6 | 245.9 | 245.9 | 240.7 |
| 2012 | 242.1 | 243.6 | 244.1 | 244.9 | 246.7 | 247.0 | 241.7 | 242.6 | 243.9 | 248.1 | 251.6 | 252.4 | 245.7 |
| 2013 | 247.8 | 249.8 | 250.2 | 250.3 | 252.1 | 251.2 | 247.4 | 249.3 | 250.3 | 253.6 | 257.1 | 258.9 | 251.5 |
| 2014 | 251.9 | 252.4 | 253.1 | 254.4 | 254.8 | 254.7 | 249.7 | 250.9 | 251.6 | 255.4 | 257.7 | 258.2 | 253.7 |
| 2015 | 251.6 | 253.8 | 254.0 | 254.7 | 255.4 | 254.7 | 250.9 | 251.9 | 254.4 | 259.6 | 261.6 | 262.4 | 255.4 |
| 2016 | 255.4 | 257.3 | 257.5 | 258.9 | 260.0 | 259.9 | 256.1 | 256.7 | 258.2 | 262.1 | 263.8 | 264.7 | 259.2 |
| 2017 | 258.4 | 260.1 | 260.7 | 262.6 | 264.3 | 264.7 | 259.8 | 260.7 | 263.0 | 266.5 | 268.7 | 268.8 | 263.2 |
| 2018 | 261.6 | 264.0 | 264.8 | 265.7 | 266.5 | 265.0 | 261.5 | 263.1 | 263.6 | 267.5 | 269.1 | 270.0 | 265.2 |
| 2019 | 263.5 | 265.7 | 266.1 | 267.6 | 268.8 | 267.7 | 264.5 | 265.1 | 265.0 | 269.7 | 272.0 | 272.2 | 267.3 |
| **Mining, Logging, and Construction** | | | | | | | | | | | | | |
| 2011 | 12.4 | 12.3 | 12.3 | 12.5 | 12.5 | 12.5 | 12.7 | 12.8 | 12.6 | 12.8 | 12.8 | 12.6 | 12.6 |
| 2012 | 12.5 | 12.6 | 12.8 | 12.7 | 12.9 | 13.1 | 13.1 | 13.2 | 13.3 | 13.3 | 13.5 | 13.6 | 13.1 |
| 2013 | 13.4 | 13.5 | 13.4 | 13.3 | 13.5 | 13.6 | 13.8 | 13.9 | 14.0 | 14.3 | 14.6 | 14.5 | 13.8 |
| 2014 | 14.4 | 14.6 | 14.9 | 14.7 | 15.0 | 15.0 | 15.2 | 15.4 | 15.4 | 15.3 | 15.2 | 15.0 | 15.0 |
| 2015 | 15.0 | 14.8 | 14.9 | 15.0 | 15.0 | 15.3 | 15.6 | 15.6 | 15.2 | 15.2 | 15.3 | 15.2 | 15.2 |
| 2016 | 14.8 | 15.0 | 15.0 | 15.5 | 15.6 | 15.5 | 15.8 | 15.8 | 15.8 | 15.9 | 15.8 | 15.7 | 15.5 |
| 2017 | 15.1 | 15.5 | 15.8 | 16.4 | 16.6 | 16.8 | 17.0 | 17.1 | 17.1 | 17.2 | 17.3 | 17.3 | 16.6 |
| 2018 | 17.0 | 17.3 | 16.8 | 17.5 | 17.5 | 17.7 | 18.1 | 18.0 | 18.1 | 18.1 | 18.2 | 17.9 | 17.7 |
| 2019 | 17.2 | 17.2 | 17.4 | 17.6 | 18.0 | 18.2 | 18.4 | 18.5 | 18.4 | 18.4 | 18.4 | 18.3 | 18.0 |
| **Manufacturing** | | | | | | | | | | | | | |
| 2011 | 24.9 | 24.9 | 24.9 | 24.8 | 24.8 | 24.8 | 24.8 | 24.7 | 24.8 | 24.5 | 24.6 | 24.2 | 24.7 |
| 2012 | 24.0 | 24.0 | 24.2 | 24.1 | 24.1 | 24.3 | 24.3 | 24.4 | 24.4 | 24.3 | 24.1 | 24.1 | 24.2 |
| 2013 | 24.0 | 24.0 | 24.2 | 24.0 | 24.0 | 24.1 | 24.2 | 24.3 | 24.4 | 24.4 | 24.5 | 24.4 | 24.2 |
| 2014 | 24.4 | 24.5 | 24.8 | 24.6 | 24.8 | 24.9 | 25.1 | 25.3 | 25.3 | 25.4 | 25.4 | 25.4 | 25.0 |
| 2015 | 25.6 | 25.7 | 25.7 | 25.7 | 25.6 | 25.7 | 25.9 | 26.1 | 26.1 | 26.2 | 26.1 | 26.1 | 25.9 |
| 2016 | 25.6 | 25.7 | 25.7 | 25.6 | 25.5 | 25.8 | 26.0 | 25.9 | 25.9 | 25.7 | 25.5 | 25.4 | 25.7 |
| 2017 | 25.3 | 25.3 | 25.5 | 25.4 | 25.6 | 25.8 | 25.6 | 25.7 | 25.8 | 25.8 | 25.8 | 25.7 | 25.6 |
| 2018 | 25.8 | 25.9 | 26.1 | 25.8 | 26.0 | 26.2 | 26.3 | 26.4 | 26.5 | 26.5 | 26.5 | 26.5 | 26.2 |
| 2019 | 26.3 | 26.5 | 26.4 | 26.3 | 26.3 | 26.5 | 26.5 | 26.5 | 26.6 | 26.5 | 26.5 | 26.4 | 26.4 |

## Employment by Industry: Oxnard-Thousand Oaks-Ventura, CA, 2011–2019—*Continued*

(Numbers in thousands, not seasonally adjusted)

| Industry and year | January | February | March | April | May | June | July | August | September | October | November | December | Annual average |
|---|---|---|---|---|---|---|---|---|---|---|---|---|---|
| **Trade, Transportation, and Utilities** | | | | | | | | | | | | | |
| 2011 | 53.4 | 52.9 | 52.9 | 53.7 | 53.7 | 53.9 | 54.1 | 54.2 | 53.9 | 54.4 | 56.6 | 57.4 | 54.3 |
| 2012 | 55.2 | 54.2 | 54.1 | 54.6 | 55.1 | 55.1 | 55.3 | 55.1 | 55.1 | 55.8 | 58.7 | 59.4 | 55.6 |
| 2013 | 56.6 | 56.4 | 55.9 | 56.0 | 56.5 | 56.6 | 56.7 | 56.9 | 56.5 | 57.1 | 60.0 | 61.0 | 57.2 |
| 2014 | 57.8 | 57.1 | 56.8 | 57.0 | 57.2 | 57.3 | 57.6 | 57.6 | 57.3 | 58.0 | 60.1 | 60.9 | 57.9 |
| 2015 | 58.1 | 57.8 | 57.3 | 57.3 | 57.5 | 57.7 | 58.4 | 58.2 | 57.9 | 59.2 | 60.9 | 61.4 | 58.5 |
| 2016 | 58.6 | 58.0 | 57.7 | 58.0 | 58.3 | 58.0 | 58.8 | 58.9 | 58.7 | 59.8 | 61.3 | 62.0 | 59.0 |
| 2017 | 59.3 | 58.4 | 58.2 | 58.8 | 58.9 | 58.9 | 59.1 | 59.2 | 58.8 | 60.0 | 61.7 | 62.1 | 59.5 |
| 2018 | 59.8 | 59.0 | 58.6 | 58.5 | 58.4 | 58.0 | 58.6 | 58.7 | 58.1 | 58.8 | 60.5 | 61.0 | 59.0 |
| 2019 | 58.4 | 57.8 | 57.5 | 57.6 | 57.6 | 57.5 | 58.0 | 57.9 | 57.3 | 57.7 | 59.2 | 59.7 | 58.0 |
| **Wholesale Trade** | | | | | | | | | | | | | |
| 2011 | 12.0 | 12.1 | 12.3 | 12.7 | 12.6 | 12.6 | 12.7 | 12.6 | 12.6 | 12.4 | 12.4 | 12.3 | 12.4 |
| 2012 | 12.3 | 12.3 | 12.4 | 12.6 | 12.7 | 12.7 | 12.7 | 12.7 | 12.7 | 12.5 | 12.6 | 12.7 | 12.6 |
| 2013 | 12.5 | 12.7 | 12.7 | 12.8 | 12.9 | 12.9 | 12.8 | 12.9 | 12.7 | 12.8 | 12.9 | 13.1 | 12.8 |
| 2014 | 12.8 | 12.8 | 12.8 | 12.8 | 12.8 | 12.8 | 12.7 | 12.7 | 12.5 | 12.6 | 12.6 | 12.7 | 12.7 |
| 2015 | 12.4 | 12.5 | 12.4 | 12.4 | 12.4 | 12.5 | 12.6 | 12.6 | 12.5 | 12.8 | 12.9 | 12.8 | 12.6 |
| 2016 | 12.7 | 12.8 | 12.7 | 12.8 | 12.9 | 12.9 | 13.1 | 13.1 | 13.1 | 13.1 | 13.2 | 13.3 | 13.0 |
| 2017 | 13.0 | 13.1 | 13.1 | 13.2 | 13.2 | 13.4 | 13.4 | 13.3 | 13.2 | 13.2 | 13.2 | 13.2 | 13.2 |
| 2018 | 13.1 | 13.2 | 13.1 | 13.1 | 13.1 | 13.1 | 13.2 | 13.2 | 13.0 | 13.1 | 13.1 | 13.2 | 13.1 |
| 2019 | 12.8 | 13.0 | 13.0 | 13.1 | 13.2 | 13.2 | 13.4 | 13.3 | 13.2 | 13.4 | 13.4 | 13.3 | 13.2 |
| **Retail Trade** | | | | | | | | | | | | | |
| 2011 | 36.1 | 35.5 | 35.3 | 35.6 | 35.6 | 35.8 | 35.8 | 36.0 | 35.8 | 36.5 | 38.5 | 39.3 | 36.3 |
| 2012 | 37.3 | 36.3 | 36.0 | 36.4 | 36.7 | 36.7 | 36.8 | 36.6 | 36.6 | 37.5 | 40.3 | 40.7 | 37.3 |
| 2013 | 38.4 | 37.9 | 37.5 | 37.4 | 37.8 | 37.9 | 38.0 | 38.1 | 37.9 | 38.4 | 41.1 | 41.7 | 38.5 |
| 2014 | 39.0 | 38.3 | 38.1 | 38.3 | 38.4 | 38.5 | 38.9 | 38.9 | 38.8 | 39.4 | 41.5 | 42.2 | 39.2 |
| 2015 | 39.8 | 39.3 | 39.0 | 38.9 | 39.1 | 39.2 | 39.7 | 39.6 | 39.5 | 40.5 | 42.0 | 42.5 | 39.9 |
| 2016 | 39.9 | 39.3 | 39.1 | 39.3 | 39.4 | 39.1 | 39.6 | 39.8 | 39.6 | 40.6 | 41.9 | 42.3 | 40.0 |
| 2017 | 40.2 | 39.3 | 39.1 | 39.5 | 39.6 | 39.4 | 39.6 | 39.8 | 39.5 | 40.6 | 42.2 | 42.4 | 40.1 |
| 2018 | 40.3 | 39.5 | 39.2 | 39.1 | 39.0 | 38.6 | 39.1 | 39.2 | 38.8 | 39.5 | 41.0 | 41.3 | 39.6 |
| 2019 | 39.2 | 38.5 | 38.2 | 38.2 | 38.1 | 38.0 | 38.3 | 38.3 | 37.8 | 38.0 | 39.5 | 39.9 | 38.5 |
| **Transportation and Utilities** | | | | | | | | | | | | | |
| 2011 | 5.3 | 5.3 | 5.3 | 5.4 | 5.5 | 5.5 | 5.6 | 5.6 | 5.5 | 5.5 | 5.7 | 5.8 | 5.5 |
| 2012 | 5.6 | 5.6 | 5.7 | 5.6 | 5.7 | 5.7 | 5.8 | 5.8 | 5.8 | 5.8 | 5.8 | 6.0 | 5.7 |
| 2013 | 5.7 | 5.8 | 5.7 | 5.8 | 5.8 | 5.8 | 5.9 | 5.9 | 5.9 | 5.9 | 6.0 | 6.2 | 5.9 |
| 2014 | 6.0 | 6.0 | 5.9 | 5.9 | 6.0 | 6.0 | 6.0 | 6.0 | 6.0 | 6.0 | 6.0 | 6.0 | 6.0 |
| 2015 | 5.9 | 6.0 | 5.9 | 6.0 | 6.0 | 6.0 | 6.1 | 6.0 | 5.9 | 5.9 | 6.0 | 6.1 | 6.0 |
| 2016 | 6.0 | 5.9 | 5.9 | 5.9 | 6.0 | 6.0 | 6.1 | 6.0 | 6.0 | 6.1 | 6.2 | 6.4 | 6.0 |
| 2017 | 6.1 | 6.0 | 6.0 | 6.1 | 6.1 | 6.1 | 6.1 | 6.1 | 6.1 | 6.2 | 6.3 | 6.5 | 6.1 |
| 2018 | 6.4 | 6.3 | 6.3 | 6.3 | 6.3 | 6.3 | 6.3 | 6.3 | 6.3 | 6.2 | 6.4 | 6.5 | 6.3 |
| 2019 | 6.4 | 6.3 | 6.3 | 6.3 | 6.3 | 6.3 | 6.3 | 6.3 | 6.3 | 6.3 | 6.3 | 6.5 | 6.3 |
| **Information** | | | | | | | | | | | | | |
| 2011 | 4.9 | 4.8 | 4.8 | 4.8 | 4.9 | 4.9 | 4.9 | 4.9 | 4.8 | 4.8 | 4.9 | 5.0 | 4.9 |
| 2012 | 5.0 | 5.0 | 5.1 | 5.0 | 5.1 | 5.2 | 5.2 | 5.2 | 5.1 | 5.3 | 5.3 | 5.3 | 5.2 |
| 2013 | 5.1 | 5.1 | 5.1 | 5.1 | 5.1 | 5.2 | 5.3 | 5.3 | 5.2 | 5.3 | 5.3 | 5.4 | 5.2 |
| 2014 | 5.4 | 5.4 | 5.4 | 5.4 | 5.4 | 5.5 | 5.4 | 5.3 | 5.2 | 5.2 | 5.2 | 5.3 | 5.3 |
| 2015 | 5.1 | 5.1 | 5.1 | 5.0 | 5.0 | 5.1 | 5.1 | 4.9 | 4.9 | 5.1 | 5.1 | 5.2 | 5.1 |
| 2016 | 4.9 | 4.9 | 4.9 | 4.9 | 5.0 | 5.1 | 5.0 | 5.1 | 5.0 | 4.9 | 5.0 | 5.0 | 5.0 |
| 2017 | 4.9 | 4.9 | 4.9 | 5.0 | 5.1 | 5.1 | 5.1 | 5.1 | 5.0 | 5.0 | 5.0 | 5.1 | 5.0 |
| 2018 | 5.0 | 5.0 | 4.9 | 5.0 | 5.1 | 5.1 | 5.1 | 5.0 | 4.9 | 4.9 | 5.1 | 5.1 | 5.0 |
| 2019 | 5.0 | 4.9 | 4.9 | 4.9 | 4.9 | 5.0 | 4.9 | 4.8 | 4.7 | 4.7 | 4.8 | 4.7 | 4.9 |
| **Financial Activities** | | | | | | | | | | | | | |
| 2011 | 20.6 | 20.6 | 20.8 | 20.7 | 20.7 | 20.7 | 20.7 | 20.3 | 20.1 | 20.0 | 19.6 | 19.9 | 20.4 |
| 2012 | 19.9 | 20.1 | 20.0 | 19.7 | 19.6 | 19.6 | 19.5 | 19.4 | 19.2 | 19.4 | 19.4 | 19.4 | 19.6 |
| 2013 | 19.1 | 19.1 | 19.2 | 18.8 | 18.8 | 18.7 | 18.8 | 18.9 | 18.9 | 18.9 | 18.9 | 18.9 | 18.9 |
| 2014 | 19.0 | 18.9 | 19.0 | 18.9 | 18.8 | 18.9 | 18.8 | 18.7 | 18.4 | 18.5 | 18.4 | 18.4 | 18.7 |
| 2015 | 18.0 | 17.8 | 17.8 | 17.9 | 17.9 | 17.6 | 17.8 | 17.7 | 17.6 | 17.7 | 17.6 | 17.5 | 17.7 |
| 2016 | 17.3 | 17.3 | 17.3 | 17.5 | 17.4 | 17.3 | 17.5 | 17.4 | 17.4 | 17.5 | 17.5 | 17.5 | 17.4 |
| 2017 | 17.1 | 17.1 | 17.0 | 16.9 | 17.0 | 16.9 | 16.9 | 16.8 | 16.8 | 16.9 | 16.9 | 16.7 | 16.9 |
| 2018 | 16.4 | 16.6 | 16.6 | 16.7 | 16.8 | 16.5 | 16.4 | 16.3 | 16.2 | 16.3 | 16.3 | 16.2 | 16.4 |
| 2019 | 15.8 | 15.9 | 15.8 | 15.8 | 15.9 | 15.8 | 15.7 | 15.7 | 15.7 | 16.1 | 16.3 | 16.0 | 15.9 |

## Employment by Industry: Oxnard-Thousand Oaks-Ventura, CA, 2011–2019—*Continued*

(Numbers in thousands, not seasonally adjusted)

| Industry and year | January | February | March | April | May | June | July | August | September | October | November | December | Annual average |
|---|---|---|---|---|---|---|---|---|---|---|---|---|---|
| **Professional and Business Services** | | | | | | | | | | | | | |
| 2011 | 39.3 | 39.3 | 39.3 | 39.6 | 39.6 | 39.6 | 40.4 | 40.2 | 40.1 | 40.2 | 40.3 | 40.5 | 39.9 |
| 2012 | 40.0 | 40.5 | 40.8 | 40.8 | 40.9 | 41.4 | 41.4 | 41.7 | 41.6 | 42.2 | 42.3 | 42.5 | 41.3 |
| 2013 | 42.1 | 42.2 | 42.6 | 42.5 | 42.5 | 42.5 | 43.0 | 43.0 | 43.0 | 43.3 | 43.3 | 43.6 | 42.8 |
| 2014 | 42.2 | 41.5 | 42.0 | 41.9 | 41.6 | 41.6 | 41.7 | 41.4 | 41.2 | 41.3 | 41.1 | 41.0 | 41.5 |
| 2015 | 39.4 | 39.7 | 40.4 | 40.4 | 39.7 | 39.9 | 40.5 | 40.6 | 40.4 | 41.6 | 41.4 | 41.6 | 40.5 |
| 2016 | 40.2 | 40.6 | 40.7 | 41.0 | 40.9 | 41.0 | 41.0 | 40.9 | 40.7 | 41.0 | 41.1 | 41.1 | 40.9 |
| 2017 | 40.8 | 41.2 | 41.4 | 41.8 | 41.9 | 42.4 | 42.7 | 42.4 | 42.4 | 42.9 | 42.9 | 43.0 | 42.2 |
| 2018 | 41.4 | 42.0 | 42.4 | 42.6 | 43.0 | 42.9 | 43.0 | 43.1 | 42.9 | 43.9 | 43.6 | 44.1 | 42.9 |
| 2019 | 42.9 | 43.2 | 43.6 | 44.0 | 44.3 | 44.4 | 44.7 | 44.7 | 44.5 | 45.3 | 45.5 | 45.7 | 44.4 |
| **Education and Health Services** | | | | | | | | | | | | | |
| 2011 | 35.6 | 36.2 | 35.9 | 36.3 | 36.3 | 35.6 | 35.3 | 35.8 | 36.7 | 37.2 | 37.5 | 37.6 | 36.3 |
| 2012 | 37.3 | 38.0 | 38.1 | 38.3 | 38.4 | 38.0 | 37.1 | 37.6 | 38.1 | 39.0 | 38.9 | 39.4 | 38.2 |
| 2013 | 39.3 | 40.2 | 40.3 | 40.5 | 40.6 | 39.8 | 39.1 | 39.9 | 40.3 | 41.2 | 41.5 | 41.6 | 40.4 |
| 2014 | 40.6 | 41.6 | 41.4 | 42.1 | 42.1 | 41.4 | 40.4 | 40.8 | 41.4 | 42.5 | 42.6 | 42.6 | 41.6 |
| 2015 | 41.8 | 42.7 | 42.6 | 42.8 | 43.0 | 42.4 | 42.2 | 42.3 | 43.0 | 43.9 | 44.1 | 44.2 | 42.9 |
| 2016 | 43.3 | 44.3 | 44.1 | 44.6 | 44.5 | 44.3 | 43.6 | 43.8 | 44.3 | 45.5 | 45.3 | 45.4 | 44.4 |
| 2017 | 44.1 | 45.1 | 45.3 | 45.5 | 45.9 | 46.3 | 44.9 | 45.6 | 46.6 | 47.1 | 46.9 | 47.3 | 45.9 |
| 2018 | 46.4 | 47.3 | 47.7 | 47.6 | 47.3 | 47.4 | 46.8 | 47.8 | 47.9 | 48.6 | 48.4 | 48.7 | 47.7 |
| 2019 | 48.0 | 49.2 | 49.2 | 49.4 | 49.6 | 49.1 | 47.7 | 48.2 | 48.4 | 49.3 | 49.6 | 50.0 | 49.0 |
| **Leisure and Hospitality** | | | | | | | | | | | | | |
| 2011 | 30.3 | 30.5 | 30.6 | 31.0 | 31.4 | 31.6 | 31.8 | 32.1 | 32.0 | 31.9 | 31.9 | 31.8 | 31.4 |
| 2012 | 31.6 | 31.8 | 32.1 | 32.6 | 33.1 | 33.3 | 33.2 | 33.3 | 33.0 | 33.1 | 33.2 | 32.9 | 32.8 |
| 2013 | 32.4 | 32.9 | 33.0 | 33.4 | 34.1 | 34.1 | 34.2 | 34.4 | 34.1 | 34.1 | 34.0 | 34.3 | 33.8 |
| 2014 | 33.5 | 33.8 | 34.2 | 34.6 | 35.1 | 35.5 | 35.5 | 35.5 | 35.2 | 35.0 | 34.9 | 34.9 | 34.8 |
| 2015 | 34.5 | 35.0 | 35.2 | 35.4 | 35.6 | 35.8 | 36.1 | 36.4 | 36.2 | 36.2 | 36.1 | 36.0 | 35.7 |
| 2016 | 35.2 | 35.6 | 35.8 | 36.1 | 36.5 | 36.6 | 37.0 | 37.0 | 36.9 | 36.7 | 36.6 | 36.5 | 36.4 |
| 2017 | 35.8 | 36.1 | 36.5 | 37.1 | 37.6 | 37.9 | 37.6 | 37.6 | 37.6 | 37.8 | 37.7 | 37.6 | 37.2 |
| 2018 | 36.7 | 37.2 | 37.7 | 37.9 | 38.2 | 38.4 | 38.4 | 38.3 | 37.8 | 37.8 | 37.5 | 37.8 | 37.8 |
| 2019 | 37.0 | 37.2 | 37.5 | 38.2 | 38.6 | 38.6 | 39.4 | 39.2 | 38.8 | 38.8 | 38.4 | 38.0 | 38.3 |
| **Other Services** | | | | | | | | | | | | | |
| 2011 | 9.0 | 9.1 | 9.1 | 9.1 | 9.2 | 9.1 | 9.2 | 9.1 | 9.3 | 9.4 | 9.5 | 9.4 | 9.2 |
| 2012 | 9.2 | 9.4 | 9.3 | 9.4 | 9.6 | 9.7 | 9.5 | 9.4 | 9.4 | 9.5 | 9.3 | 9.3 | 9.4 |
| 2013 | 9.4 | 9.5 | 9.5 | 9.6 | 9.6 | 9.6 | 9.8 | 9.8 | 9.8 | 9.8 | 9.8 | 9.8 | 9.7 |
| 2014 | 9.7 | 9.8 | 9.9 | 9.9 | 10.0 | 9.9 | 9.8 | 9.7 | 9.6 | 9.8 | 9.8 | 9.7 | 9.8 |
| 2015 | 9.6 | 9.6 | 9.6 | 9.7 | 9.8 | 9.7 | 9.7 | 9.6 | 9.6 | 9.6 | 9.7 | 9.6 | 9.7 |
| 2016 | 9.5 | 9.6 | 9.6 | 9.7 | 9.6 | 9.6 | 9.6 | 9.6 | 9.7 | 9.7 | 9.5 | 9.5 | 9.6 |
| 2017 | 9.4 | 9.6 | 9.6 | 9.6 | 9.8 | 9.8 | 9.7 | 9.6 | 9.6 | 9.7 | 9.6 | 9.5 | 9.6 |
| 2018 | 9.3 | 9.4 | 9.3 | 9.5 | 9.5 | 9.5 | 9.5 | 9.5 | 9.6 | 9.6 | 9.7 | 9.6 | 9.5 |
| 2019 | 9.4 | 9.5 | 9.7 | 9.8 | 9.8 | 9.8 | 9.8 | 9.7 | 9.7 | 9.8 | 9.7 | 9.7 | 9.7 |
| **Government** | | | | | | | | | | | | | |
| 2011 | 44.8 | 45.3 | 45.5 | 45.4 | 45.2 | 45.7 | 41.1 | 41.9 | 43.3 | 44.7 | 45.6 | 44.3 | 44.4 |
| 2012 | 43.9 | 44.6 | 44.6 | 44.5 | 44.9 | 44.7 | 40.5 | 40.9 | 42.4 | 43.8 | 44.5 | 44.2 | 43.6 |
| 2013 | 43.8 | 44.4 | 44.6 | 44.4 | 44.9 | 44.7 | 40.5 | 41.1 | 42.5 | 43.9 | 44.3 | 44.3 | 43.6 |
| 2014 | 43.7 | 44.3 | 44.4 | 44.6 | 44.6 | 44.6 | 40.5 | 41.9 | 43.3 | 45.1 | 45.6 | 45.4 | 44.0 |
| 2015 | 45.1 | 46.1 | 46.0 | 46.2 | 46.9 | 46.5 | 41.1 | 42.2 | 44.8 | 46.3 | 46.7 | 46.9 | 45.4 |
| 2016 | 46.4 | 47.0 | 47.4 | 47.1 | 47.8 | 48.0 | 43.6 | 44.0 | 45.5 | 47.0 | 47.5 | 47.7 | 46.6 |
| 2017 | 47.0 | 47.7 | 47.8 | 47.9 | 48.1 | 47.4 | 43.8 | 44.4 | 46.2 | 47.1 | 48.0 | 47.5 | 46.9 |
| 2018 | 46.6 | 47.5 | 47.6 | 47.9 | 48.2 | 47.2 | 43.7 | 44.4 | 46.2 | 47.6 | 48.0 | 47.5 | 46.9 |
| 2019 | 47.0 | 48.0 | 47.9 | 47.9 | 48.1 | 47.5 | 44.3 | 44.9 | 45.9 | 48.0 | 48.5 | 48.4 | 47.2 |

## Employment by Industry: El Paso, TX, 2011–2019

(Numbers in thousands, not seasonally adjusted)

| Industry and year | January | February | March | April | May | June | July | August | September | October | November | December | Annual average |
|---|---|---|---|---|---|---|---|---|---|---|---|---|---|
| **Total Nonfarm** | | | | | | | | | | | | | |
| 2011 | 281.1 | 281.6 | 283.0 | 284.2 | 284.4 | 282.7 | 280.6 | 281.9 | 285.6 | 283.0 | 285.4 | 286.8 | 283.4 |
| 2012 | 282.8 | 284.9 | 286.6 | 287.6 | 288.9 | 285.8 | 284.1 | 286.3 | 288.6 | 290.2 | 292.5 | 292.8 | 287.6 |
| 2013 | 287.0 | 289.3 | 290.4 | 291.1 | 292.3 | 289.1 | 287.5 | 290.5 | 293.3 | 294.6 | 297.5 | 297.6 | 291.7 |
| 2014 | 292.9 | 294.5 | 295.7 | 296.5 | 297.4 | 294.7 | 290.9 | 292.9 | 294.3 | 296.2 | 298.6 | 299.7 | 295.4 |
| 2015 | 296.2 | 297.9 | 298.8 | 300.2 | 302.2 | 300.8 | 298.0 | 300.2 | 302.3 | 305.5 | 307.6 | 307.6 | 301.4 |
| 2016 | 304.0 | 305.5 | 305.9 | 308.9 | 309.7 | 307.1 | 306.0 | 308.2 | 311.2 | 310.7 | 312.6 | 312.9 | 308.6 |
| 2017 | 309.6 | 311.8 | 312.0 | 313.4 | 314.4 | 311.3 | 307.3 | 309.2 | 312.9 | 314.6 | 317.5 | 317.9 | 312.7 |
| 2018 | 314.4 | 315.9 | 316.0 | 316.8 | 318.1 | 315.6 | 314.2 | 317.2 | 319.4 | 322.6 | 325.1 | 324.9 | 318.4 |
| 2019 | 319.8 | 322.4 | 322.6 | 323.1 | 324.0 | 321.1 | 320.4 | 323.0 | 325.3 | 327.9 | 329.5 | 329.5 | 324.1 |
| **Total Private** | | | | | | | | | | | | | |
| 2011 | 210.6 | 211.0 | 212.2 | 213.3 | 213.8 | 213.8 | 214.5 | 215.6 | 214.8 | 212.7 | 214.6 | 216.3 | 213.6 |
| 2012 | 212.2 | 214.2 | 215.8 | 217.0 | 218.1 | 218.7 | 218.1 | 220.1 | 219.1 | 219.3 | 221.1 | 221.6 | 217.9 |
| 2013 | 216.2 | 218.0 | 218.9 | 220.1 | 221.5 | 222.1 | 221.6 | 223.9 | 223.4 | 224.4 | 226.8 | 227.1 | 222.0 |
| 2014 | 223.5 | 224.6 | 225.8 | 226.1 | 226.9 | 227.1 | 225.4 | 227.0 | 225.3 | 225.9 | 227.8 | 229.0 | 226.2 |
| 2015 | 225.8 | 227.1 | 227.9 | 229.8 | 231.7 | 233.0 | 232.2 | 233.8 | 232.7 | 234.9 | 236.5 | 236.6 | 231.8 |
| 2016 | 233.3 | 234.4 | 234.6 | 237.2 | 237.8 | 238.0 | 239.0 | 240.6 | 239.6 | 238.3 | 240.1 | 240.6 | 237.8 |
| 2017 | 237.9 | 239.2 | 239.5 | 240.8 | 241.7 | 241.5 | 239.8 | 241.2 | 241.2 | 241.9 | 244.7 | 244.8 | 241.2 |
| 2018 | 241.9 | 242.8 | 242.9 | 243.6 | 244.9 | 245.3 | 246.0 | 248.4 | 247.3 | 249.7 | 252.0 | 251.7 | 246.4 |
| 2019 | 247.3 | 249.2 | 249.2 | 249.7 | 250.5 | 250.5 | 251.9 | 253.8 | 252.7 | 254.4 | 255.8 | 255.9 | 251.7 |
| **Goods Producing** | | | | | | | | | | | | | |
| 2011 | 31.2 | 31.1 | 31.3 | 31.3 | 31.4 | 31.2 | 31.1 | 31.9 | 31.6 | 30.7 | 30.7 | 30.5 | 31.2 |
| 2012 | 30.2 | 30.3 | 30.5 | 30.6 | 30.8 | 31.0 | 30.9 | 31.6 | 31.6 | 31.5 | 31.4 | 31.0 | 31.0 |
| 2013 | 30.4 | 30.9 | 30.8 | 30.9 | 31.0 | 31.0 | 30.9 | 31.6 | 31.5 | 31.3 | 31.1 | 30.9 | 31.0 |
| 2014 | 30.7 | 31.0 | 31.0 | 31.0 | 31.1 | 31.0 | 30.0 | 30.8 | 30.4 | 30.1 | 29.9 | 30.0 | 30.6 |
| 2015 | 29.7 | 30.2 | 30.3 | 30.6 | 31.2 | 31.1 | 31.1 | 31.4 | 31.6 | 31.9 | 31.7 | 31.7 | 31.0 |
| 2016 | 31.3 | 31.8 | 31.6 | 32.3 | 32.4 | 32.6 | 32.3 | 32.2 | 32.1 | 31.5 | 31.5 | 31.6 | 31.9 |
| 2017 | 31.6 | 32.1 | 32.5 | 32.6 | 32.8 | 33.0 | 32.2 | 32.1 | 32.1 | 32.1 | 32.1 | 32.0 | 32.3 |
| 2018 | 31.9 | 32.2 | 32.4 | 32.3 | 32.5 | 32.8 | 32.9 | 33.3 | 33.2 | 33.2 | 33.4 | 33.3 | 32.8 |
| 2019 | 32.9 | 33.6 | 33.6 | 33.6 | 33.9 | 34.2 | 34.0 | 34.3 | 34.3 | 34.1 | 34.2 | 34.1 | 33.9 |
| **Service-Providing** | | | | | | | | | | | | | |
| 2011 | 249.9 | 250.5 | 251.7 | 252.9 | 253.0 | 251.5 | 249.5 | 250.0 | 254.0 | 252.3 | 254.7 | 256.3 | 252.2 |
| 2012 | 252.6 | 254.6 | 256.1 | 257.0 | 258.1 | 254.8 | 253.2 | 254.7 | 257.0 | 258.7 | 261.1 | 261.8 | 256.6 |
| 2013 | 256.6 | 258.4 | 259.6 | 260.2 | 261.3 | 258.1 | 256.6 | 258.9 | 261.8 | 263.3 | 266.4 | 266.7 | 260.7 |
| 2014 | 262.2 | 263.5 | 264.7 | 265.5 | 266.3 | 263.7 | 260.9 | 262.1 | 263.9 | 266.1 | 268.7 | 269.7 | 264.8 |
| 2015 | 266.5 | 267.7 | 268.5 | 269.6 | 271.0 | 269.7 | 266.9 | 268.8 | 270.7 | 273.6 | 275.9 | 275.9 | 270.4 |
| 2016 | 272.7 | 273.7 | 274.3 | 276.6 | 277.3 | 274.5 | 273.7 | 276.0 | 279.1 | 279.2 | 281.1 | 281.3 | 276.6 |
| 2017 | 278.0 | 279.7 | 279.5 | 280.8 | 281.6 | 278.3 | 275.1 | 277.1 | 280.8 | 282.5 | 285.4 | 285.9 | 280.4 |
| 2018 | 282.5 | 283.7 | 283.6 | 284.5 | 285.6 | 282.8 | 281.3 | 283.9 | 286.2 | 289.4 | 291.7 | 291.6 | 285.6 |
| 2019 | 286.9 | 288.8 | 289.0 | 289.5 | 290.1 | 286.9 | 286.4 | 288.7 | 291.0 | 293.8 | 295.3 | 295.4 | 290.2 |
| **Mining, Logging, and Construction** | | | | | | | | | | | | | |
| 2011 | 14.2 | 14.0 | 14.1 | 14.0 | 14.0 | 13.7 | 13.8 | 14.1 | 13.9 | 13.2 | 13.2 | 13.0 | 13.8 |
| 2012 | 12.8 | 12.8 | 12.8 | 12.8 | 12.9 | 13.1 | 13.1 | 13.3 | 13.2 | 13.2 | 13.2 | 13.0 | 13.0 |
| 2013 | 12.5 | 12.8 | 12.7 | 12.7 | 12.9 | 13.0 | 13.1 | 13.4 | 13.4 | 13.5 | 13.4 | 13.3 | 13.1 |
| 2014 | 13.4 | 13.8 | 13.9 | 13.8 | 13.9 | 13.8 | 12.9 | 13.2 | 12.9 | 12.8 | 12.8 | 12.9 | 13.3 |
| 2015 | 12.8 | 13.1 | 13.2 | 13.5 | 14.0 | 14.0 | 14.1 | 14.3 | 14.5 | 14.7 | 14.6 | 14.6 | 14.0 |
| 2016 | 14.4 | 14.8 | 14.7 | 15.2 | 15.2 | 15.3 | 15.1 | 14.9 | 14.9 | 14.6 | 14.6 | 14.6 | 14.9 |
| 2017 | 14.7 | 15.0 | 15.4 | 15.5 | 15.8 | 16.0 | 15.5 | 15.5 | 15.5 | 15.4 | 15.4 | 15.5 | 15.4 |
| 2018 | 15.4 | 15.7 | 15.8 | 15.7 | 15.8 | 16.0 | 16.1 | 16.4 | 16.3 | 16.4 | 16.5 | 16.4 | 16.0 |
| 2019 | 16.1 | 16.6 | 16.5 | 16.6 | 16.9 | 17.2 | 17.0 | 17.3 | 17.4 | 17.3 | 17.3 | 17.3 | 17.0 |
| **Manufacturing** | | | | | | | | | | | | | |
| 2011 | 17.0 | 17.1 | 17.2 | 17.3 | 17.4 | 17.5 | 17.3 | 17.8 | 17.7 | 17.5 | 17.5 | 17.5 | 17.4 |
| 2012 | 17.4 | 17.5 | 17.7 | 17.8 | 17.9 | 17.9 | 17.8 | 18.3 | 18.4 | 18.3 | 18.2 | 18.0 | 17.9 |
| 2013 | 17.9 | 18.1 | 18.1 | 18.2 | 18.1 | 18.0 | 17.8 | 18.2 | 18.1 | 17.8 | 17.7 | 17.6 | 18.0 |
| 2014 | 17.3 | 17.2 | 17.1 | 17.2 | 17.2 | 17.2 | 17.1 | 17.6 | 17.5 | 17.3 | 17.1 | 17.1 | 17.2 |
| 2015 | 16.9 | 17.1 | 17.1 | 17.1 | 17.2 | 17.1 | 17.0 | 17.1 | 17.1 | 17.2 | 17.1 | 17.1 | 17.1 |
| 2016 | 16.9 | 17.0 | 16.9 | 17.1 | 17.2 | 17.3 | 17.2 | 17.3 | 17.2 | 16.9 | 16.9 | 17.0 | 17.1 |
| 2017 | 16.9 | 17.1 | 17.1 | 17.1 | 17.0 | 17.0 | 16.7 | 16.6 | 16.6 | 16.7 | 16.7 | 16.5 | 16.8 |
| 2018 | 16.5 | 16.5 | 16.6 | 16.6 | 16.7 | 16.8 | 16.8 | 16.9 | 16.9 | 16.8 | 16.9 | 16.9 | 16.7 |
| 2019 | 16.8 | 17.0 | 17.1 | 17.0 | 17.0 | 17.0 | 17.0 | 17.0 | 16.9 | 16.8 | 16.9 | 16.8 | 16.9 |

# Employment by Industry: El Paso, TX, 2011–2019—*Continued*

(Numbers in thousands, not seasonally adjusted)

| Industry and year | January | February | March | April | May | June | July | August | September | October | November | December | Annual average |
|---|---|---|---|---|---|---|---|---|---|---|---|---|---|
| **Trade, Transportation, and Utilities** | | | | | | | | | | | | | |
| 2011 | 57.2 | 56.7 | 57.0 | 57.7 | 57.9 | 57.8 | 58.2 | 58.6 | 58.1 | 58.3 | 59.9 | 60.9 | 58.2 |
| 2012 | 58.6 | 58.3 | 58.5 | 59.4 | 60.0 | 60.2 | 59.7 | 60.2 | 59.6 | 60.0 | 61.9 | 62.4 | 59.9 |
| 2013 | 59.9 | 59.8 | 60.2 | 61.1 | 61.6 | 61.8 | 61.6 | 62.2 | 61.8 | 62.8 | 64.7 | 65.5 | 61.9 |
| 2014 | 63.4 | 62.8 | 63.4 | 63.3 | 63.4 | 63.6 | 63.5 | 63.7 | 63.3 | 63.9 | 65.6 | 66.6 | 63.9 |
| 2015 | 64.2 | 63.8 | 64.3 | 64.7 | 65.1 | 65.3 | 65.2 | 65.5 | 65.1 | 66.3 | 67.4 | 67.7 | 65.4 |
| 2016 | 65.9 | 65.5 | 66.0 | 66.6 | 66.7 | 67.0 | 67.3 | 68.3 | 67.9 | 68.4 | 70.2 | 70.3 | 67.5 |
| 2017 | 68.0 | 67.5 | 67.5 | 67.2 | 67.2 | 67.5 | 67.1 | 67.8 | 67.6 | 67.9 | 70.0 | 70.0 | 67.9 |
| 2018 | 67.6 | 67.3 | 67.2 | 67.3 | 67.4 | 67.8 | 68.1 | 68.8 | 68.5 | 68.6 | 69.9 | 70.0 | 68.2 |
| 2019 | 68.2 | 67.8 | 67.6 | 67.7 | 67.7 | 67.7 | 67.9 | 68.0 | 67.9 | 68.5 | 70.0 | 70.6 | 68.3 |
| **Wholesale Trade** | | | | | | | | | | | | | |
| 2011 | 9.9 | 10.0 | 10.0 | 10.1 | 10.2 | 10.2 | 10.4 | 10.4 | 10.3 | 10.3 | 10.2 | 10.3 | 10.2 |
| 2012 | 10.1 | 10.3 | 10.3 | 10.4 | 10.4 | 10.4 | 10.3 | 10.3 | 10.2 | 10.3 | 10.4 | 10.4 | 10.3 |
| 2013 | 10.3 | 10.3 | 10.3 | 10.4 | 10.5 | 10.6 | 10.6 | 10.7 | 10.7 | 10.7 | 10.8 | 10.8 | 10.6 |
| 2014 | 10.6 | 10.7 | 10.8 | 10.8 | 10.8 | 10.9 | 10.9 | 10.9 | 10.9 | 10.9 | 10.9 | 10.9 | 10.8 |
| 2015 | 10.9 | 10.9 | 11.0 | 11.1 | 11.1 | 11.1 | 11.1 | 11.2 | 11.1 | 11.2 | 11.2 | 11.2 | 11.1 |
| 2016 | 11.2 | 11.2 | 11.3 | 11.3 | 11.4 | 11.4 | 11.4 | 11.4 | 11.4 | 11.4 | 11.4 | 11.5 | 11.4 |
| 2017 | 11.3 | 11.4 | 11.5 | 11.4 | 11.5 | 11.6 | 11.5 | 11.6 | 11.7 | 11.8 | 11.8 | 11.9 | 11.6 |
| 2018 | 11.9 | 11.9 | 12.0 | 11.9 | 11.9 | 12.0 | 12.0 | 12.1 | 12.1 | 12.2 | 12.2 | 12.3 | 12.0 |
| 2019 | 12.2 | 12.3 | 12.2 | 12.4 | 12.5 | 12.6 | 12.5 | 12.5 | 12.5 | 12.5 | 12.6 | 12.6 | 12.5 |
| **Retail Trade** | | | | | | | | | | | | | |
| 2011 | 34.7 | 34.1 | 34.3 | 35.0 | 35.1 | 35.1 | 35.0 | 35.3 | 34.9 | 35.2 | 36.8 | 37.5 | 35.3 |
| 2012 | 35.7 | 35.1 | 35.2 | 35.9 | 36.3 | 36.4 | 36.0 | 36.4 | 35.9 | 36.2 | 37.9 | 38.4 | 36.3 |
| 2013 | 36.2 | 36.1 | 36.2 | 36.9 | 37.2 | 37.2 | 37.2 | 37.6 | 37.3 | 38.2 | 40.0 | 40.7 | 37.6 |
| 2014 | 38.7 | 38.1 | 38.3 | 38.5 | 38.5 | 38.5 | 38.5 | 38.6 | 38.3 | 38.8 | 40.5 | 41.2 | 38.9 |
| 2015 | 38.9 | 38.5 | 38.6 | 38.8 | 39.1 | 39.2 | 38.9 | 39.1 | 38.8 | 39.7 | 40.7 | 40.9 | 39.3 |
| 2016 | 39.0 | 38.5 | 38.7 | 39.2 | 39.2 | 39.4 | 39.6 | 40.6 | 40.1 | 40.7 | 42.4 | 42.3 | 40.0 |
| 2017 | 40.5 | 40.0 | 39.8 | 39.6 | 39.5 | 39.5 | 39.4 | 39.9 | 39.6 | 39.8 | 41.8 | 41.7 | 40.1 |
| 2018 | 39.5 | 39.0 | 38.8 | 39.0 | 39.1 | 39.2 | 39.6 | 40.0 | 39.8 | 39.7 | 41.0 | 40.9 | 39.6 |
| 2019 | 39.2 | 38.7 | 38.6 | 38.5 | 38.3 | 38.1 | 38.3 | 38.4 | 38.3 | 38.7 | 40.0 | 40.6 | 38.8 |
| **Transportation and Utilities** | | | | | | | | | | | | | |
| 2011 | 12.6 | 12.6 | 12.7 | 12.6 | 12.6 | 12.5 | 12.8 | 12.9 | 12.9 | 12.8 | 12.9 | 13.1 | 12.8 |
| 2012 | 12.8 | 12.9 | 13.0 | 13.1 | 13.3 | 13.4 | 13.4 | 13.5 | 13.5 | 13.5 | 13.6 | 13.6 | 13.3 |
| 2013 | 13.4 | 13.4 | 13.7 | 13.8 | 13.9 | 14.0 | 13.8 | 13.9 | 13.8 | 13.9 | 13.9 | 14.0 | 13.8 |
| 2014 | 14.1 | 14.0 | 14.3 | 14.0 | 14.1 | 14.2 | 14.1 | 14.2 | 14.1 | 14.2 | 14.2 | 14.5 | 14.2 |
| 2015 | 14.4 | 14.4 | 14.7 | 14.8 | 14.9 | 15.0 | 15.2 | 15.2 | 15.2 | 15.4 | 15.5 | 15.6 | 15.0 |
| 2016 | 15.7 | 15.8 | 16.0 | 16.1 | 16.1 | 16.2 | 16.3 | 16.3 | 16.4 | 16.3 | 16.4 | 16.5 | 16.2 |
| 2017 | 16.2 | 16.1 | 16.2 | 16.2 | 16.2 | 16.4 | 16.2 | 16.3 | 16.3 | 16.3 | 16.4 | 16.4 | 16.3 |
| 2018 | 16.2 | 16.4 | 16.4 | 16.4 | 16.4 | 16.6 | 16.5 | 16.7 | 16.6 | 16.7 | 16.7 | 16.8 | 16.5 |
| 2019 | 16.8 | 16.8 | 16.8 | 16.8 | 16.9 | 17.0 | 17.1 | 17.1 | 17.1 | 17.3 | 17.4 | 17.4 | 17.0 |
| **Information** | | | | | | | | | | | | | |
| 2011 | 5.4 | 5.4 | 5.4 | 5.4 | 5.4 | 5.5 | 5.5 | 5.5 | 5.5 | 5.5 | 5.5 | 5.6 | 5.5 |
| 2012 | 5.7 | 5.7 | 5.8 | 5.7 | 5.8 | 5.8 | 5.9 | 5.9 | 5.9 | 6.0 | 6.0 | 6.1 | 5.9 |
| 2013 | 6.1 | 6.0 | 6.1 | 5.9 | 5.9 | 5.9 | 5.8 | 5.8 | 5.8 | 5.8 | 5.9 | 5.8 | 5.9 |
| 2014 | 5.7 | 5.7 | 5.5 | 5.5 | 5.5 | 5.4 | 5.4 | 5.3 | 5.3 | 5.5 | 5.5 | 5.6 | 5.5 |
| 2015 | 5.5 | 5.4 | 5.3 | 5.3 | 5.3 | 5.3 | 5.3 | 5.2 | 5.2 | 5.1 | 5.2 | 5.2 | 5.3 |
| 2016 | 5.1 | 5.0 | 5.0 | 5.1 | 5.1 | 5.1 | 5.1 | 5.1 | 5.0 | 4.9 | 5.0 | 5.0 | 5.0 |
| 2017 | 5.0 | 4.9 | 5.0 | 4.9 | 4.9 | 4.9 | 4.9 | 4.9 | 4.8 | 4.8 | 4.8 | 4.8 | 4.9 |
| 2018 | 4.6 | 4.4 | 4.4 | 4.5 | 4.5 | 4.6 | 4.6 | 4.5 | 4.5 | 4.5 | 4.5 | 4.6 | 4.5 |
| 2019 | 4.6 | 4.6 | 4.6 | 4.6 | 4.6 | 4.7 | 4.7 | 4.8 | 4.8 | 4.8 | 4.8 | 4.9 | 4.7 |
| **Financial Activities** | | | | | | | | | | | | | |
| 2011 | 12.1 | 12.1 | 12.2 | 12.3 | 12.4 | 12.5 | 12.5 | 12.4 | 12.4 | 12.5 | 12.4 | 12.6 | 12.4 |
| 2012 | 12.4 | 12.6 | 12.6 | 12.6 | 12.6 | 12.7 | 12.7 | 12.7 | 12.6 | 12.6 | 12.5 | 12.5 | 12.6 |
| 2013 | 12.3 | 12.3 | 12.3 | 12.4 | 12.4 | 12.4 | 12.1 | 12.1 | 12.1 | 12.1 | 12.1 | 12.1 | 12.2 |
| 2014 | 11.9 | 12.0 | 12.0 | 12.1 | 12.1 | 12.2 | 11.6 | 11.6 | 11.7 | 11.7 | 11.7 | 11.7 | 11.9 |
| 2015 | 11.9 | 12.0 | 12.0 | 12.0 | 12.1 | 12.2 | 12.2 | 12.3 | 12.2 | 12.4 | 12.4 | 12.5 | 12.2 |
| 2016 | 12.4 | 12.6 | 12.5 | 12.5 | 12.5 | 12.4 | 12.5 | 12.5 | 12.7 | 12.6 | 12.6 | 12.6 | 12.5 |
| 2017 | 12.5 | 12.6 | 12.6 | 12.6 | 12.6 | 12.5 | 12.6 | 12.7 | 12.7 | 12.7 | 12.6 | 12.7 | 12.6 |
| 2018 | 12.7 | 12.7 | 12.7 | 12.5 | 12.5 | 12.6 | 12.6 | 12.7 | 12.6 | 12.7 | 12.9 | 13.0 | 12.7 |
| 2019 | 13.0 | 13.1 | 13.1 | 13.0 | 13.1 | 13.1 | 13.4 | 13.5 | 13.5 | 13.5 | 13.5 | 13.6 | 13.3 |

## Employment by Industry: El Paso, TX, 2011–2019—*Continued*

(Numbers in thousands, not seasonally adjusted)

| Industry and year | January | February | March | April | May | June | July | August | September | October | November | December | Annual average |
|---|---|---|---|---|---|---|---|---|---|---|---|---|---|
| **Professional and Business Services** | | | | | | | | | | | | | |
| 2011 | 31.0 | 31.3 | 31.0 | 31.0 | 30.5 | 29.9 | 30.2 | 30.1 | 30.4 | 29.7 | 29.9 | 30.4 | 30.5 |
| 2012 | 29.9 | 30.1 | 30.5 | 30.5 | 30.1 | 29.8 | 30.0 | 30.3 | 30.3 | 30.5 | 30.4 | 30.6 | 30.3 |
| 2013 | 30.2 | 30.7 | 30.6 | 30.2 | 29.9 | 29.9 | 30.2 | 30.8 | 31.3 | 31.6 | 31.9 | 32.0 | 30.8 |
| 2014 | 31.4 | 31.5 | 31.5 | 31.6 | 31.4 | 31.1 | 31.3 | 31.5 | 31.1 | 31.7 | 31.7 | 31.5 | 31.4 |
| 2015 | 31.9 | 31.8 | 31.5 | 32.2 | 32.0 | 32.5 | 32.2 | 32.9 | 32.6 | 33.2 | 33.7 | 33.6 | 32.5 |
| 2016 | 33.5 | 33.4 | 32.9 | 33.4 | 33.0 | 32.7 | 33.6 | 33.7 | 33.8 | 33.5 | 33.5 | 33.9 | 33.4 |
| 2017 | 33.8 | 34.1 | 33.5 | 34.3 | 34.1 | 33.9 | 33.7 | 34.1 | 34.6 | 34.8 | 35.5 | 35.8 | 34.4 |
| 2018 | 35.5 | 36.0 | 35.4 | 35.2 | 35.1 | 34.9 | 35.2 | 35.6 | 36.0 | 36.8 | 37.1 | 37.8 | 35.9 |
| 2019 | 36.3 | 36.5 | 36.0 | 36.0 | 35.8 | 35.8 | 36.2 | 36.8 | 36.7 | 38.0 | 37.6 | 37.2 | 36.6 |
| **Education and Health Services** | | | | | | | | | | | | | |
| 2011 | 36.6 | 36.8 | 36.9 | 37.3 | 37.4 | 37.4 | 37.5 | 37.6 | 37.8 | 37.7 | 37.8 | 37.8 | 37.4 |
| 2012 | 37.5 | 38.3 | 38.6 | 38.4 | 38.5 | 38.5 | 38.3 | 38.7 | 38.8 | 39.3 | 39.4 | 39.4 | 38.6 |
| 2013 | 38.6 | 39.0 | 39.1 | 39.5 | 39.6 | 39.5 | 39.8 | 40.1 | 40.3 | 40.7 | 40.7 | 40.5 | 39.8 |
| 2014 | 40.3 | 40.9 | 40.9 | 40.9 | 41.1 | 41.0 | 41.0 | 41.2 | 41.1 | 41.5 | 41.8 | 42.0 | 41.1 |
| 2015 | 41.8 | 42.2 | 42.3 | 42.4 | 42.6 | 42.5 | 42.6 | 42.7 | 42.8 | 43.2 | 43.2 | 43.2 | 42.6 |
| 2016 | 43.0 | 43.2 | 43.1 | 43.4 | 43.6 | 43.3 | 43.7 | 44.0 | 44.0 | 44.1 | 44.1 | 44.1 | 43.6 |
| 2017 | 44.1 | 44.6 | 44.5 | 44.9 | 45.1 | 44.8 | 44.7 | 45.1 | 45.3 | 45.5 | 45.6 | 45.7 | 45.0 |
| 2018 | 45.6 | 45.8 | 45.7 | 46.1 | 46.4 | 46.2 | 46.1 | 46.7 | 46.6 | 46.8 | 47.1 | 46.8 | 46.3 |
| 2019 | 46.7 | 47.2 | 47.2 | 47.5 | 47.6 | 47.2 | 47.5 | 48.4 | 48.3 | 48.6 | 48.8 | 48.7 | 47.8 |
| **Leisure and Hospitality** | | | | | | | | | | | | | |
| 2011 | 28.0 | 28.3 | 29.1 | 29.1 | 29.6 | 29.9 | 29.9 | 29.8 | 29.5 | 28.9 | 29.0 | 29.1 | 29.2 |
| 2012 | 28.6 | 29.4 | 29.8 | 30.4 | 30.8 | 30.8 | 30.7 | 30.8 | 30.7 | 29.9 | 30.0 | 30.2 | 30.2 |
| 2013 | 29.5 | 29.9 | 30.5 | 30.9 | 31.7 | 31.8 | 31.4 | 31.5 | 31.0 | 30.8 | 30.9 | 31.0 | 30.9 |
| 2014 | 30.8 | 31.3 | 32.1 | 32.5 | 33.0 | 33.2 | 32.9 | 33.3 | 33.0 | 32.2 | 32.2 | 32.3 | 32.4 |
| 2015 | 31.5 | 32.2 | 32.7 | 33.3 | 34.1 | 34.4 | 33.9 | 34.2 | 33.8 | 33.4 | 33.5 | 33.3 | 33.4 |
| 2016 | 32.7 | 33.3 | 33.9 | 34.5 | 35.0 | 35.2 | 35.0 | 35.4 | 34.8 | 34.1 | 34.0 | 34.0 | 34.3 |
| 2017 | 33.8 | 34.3 | 34.7 | 35.3 | 35.9 | 35.7 | 35.4 | 35.4 | 35.1 | 35.0 | 35.0 | 34.8 | 35.0 |
| 2018 | 35.1 | 35.5 | 36.1 | 36.8 | 37.5 | 37.2 | 37.3 | 37.5 | 36.6 | 37.2 | 37.1 | 37.2 | 36.8 |
| 2019 | 36.7 | 37.5 | 38.1 | 38.3 | 38.7 | 38.5 | 38.9 | 38.7 | 38.1 | 37.8 | 37.7 | 37.7 | 38.1 |
| **Other Services** | | | | | | | | | | | | | |
| 2011 | 9.1 | 9.3 | 9.3 | 9.2 | 9.2 | 9.6 | 9.6 | 9.7 | 9.5 | 9.4 | 9.4 | 9.4 | 9.4 |
| 2012 | 9.3 | 9.5 | 9.5 | 9.4 | 9.5 | 9.9 | 9.9 | 9.9 | 9.6 | 9.5 | 9.5 | 9.4 | 9.6 |
| 2013 | 9.2 | 9.4 | 9.3 | 9.2 | 9.4 | 9.8 | 9.8 | 9.8 | 9.6 | 9.3 | 9.5 | 9.3 | 9.5 |
| 2014 | 9.3 | 9.4 | 9.4 | 9.2 | 9.3 | 9.6 | 9.7 | 9.6 | 9.4 | 9.3 | 9.4 | 9.3 | 9.4 |
| 2015 | 9.3 | 9.5 | 9.5 | 9.3 | 9.3 | 9.7 | 9.7 | 9.6 | 9.4 | 9.4 | 9.4 | 9.4 | 9.5 |
| 2016 | 9.4 | 9.6 | 9.6 | 9.4 | 9.5 | 9.7 | 9.5 | 9.4 | 9.3 | 9.2 | 9.2 | 9.1 | 9.4 |
| 2017 | 9.1 | 9.1 | 9.2 | 9.0 | 9.1 | 9.2 | 9.2 | 9.1 | 9.0 | 9.1 | 9.1 | 9.0 | 9.1 |
| 2018 | 8.9 | 8.9 | 9.0 | 8.9 | 9.0 | 9.2 | 9.2 | 9.3 | 9.3 | 9.9 | 10.0 | 9.0 | 9.2 |
| 2019 | 8.9 | 8.9 | 9.0 | 9.0 | 9.1 | 9.3 | 9.3 | 9.3 | 9.1 | 9.1 | 9.2 | 9.1 | 9.1 |
| **Government** | | | | | | | | | | | | | |
| 2011 | 70.5 | 70.6 | 70.8 | 70.9 | 70.6 | 68.9 | 66.1 | 66.3 | 70.8 | 70.3 | 70.8 | 70.5 | 69.8 |
| 2012 | 70.6 | 70.7 | 70.8 | 70.6 | 70.8 | 67.1 | 66.0 | 66.2 | 69.5 | 70.9 | 71.4 | 71.2 | 69.7 |
| 2013 | 70.8 | 71.3 | 71.5 | 71.0 | 70.8 | 67.0 | 65.9 | 66.6 | 69.9 | 70.2 | 70.7 | 70.5 | 69.7 |
| 2014 | 69.4 | 69.9 | 69.9 | 70.4 | 70.5 | 67.6 | 65.5 | 65.9 | 69.0 | 70.3 | 70.8 | 70.7 | 69.2 |
| 2015 | 70.4 | 70.8 | 70.9 | 70.4 | 70.5 | 67.8 | 65.8 | 66.4 | 69.6 | 70.6 | 71.1 | 71.0 | 69.6 |
| 2016 | 70.7 | 71.1 | 71.3 | 71.7 | 71.9 | 69.1 | 67.0 | 67.6 | 71.6 | 72.4 | 72.5 | 72.3 | 70.8 |
| 2017 | 71.7 | 72.6 | 72.5 | 72.6 | 72.7 | 69.8 | 67.5 | 68.0 | 71.7 | 72.7 | 72.8 | 73.1 | 71.5 |
| 2018 | 72.5 | 73.1 | 73.1 | 73.2 | 73.2 | 70.3 | 68.2 | 68.8 | 72.1 | 72.9 | 73.1 | 73.2 | 72.0 |
| 2019 | 72.5 | 73.2 | 73.4 | 73.4 | 73.5 | 70.6 | 68.5 | 69.2 | 72.6 | 73.5 | 73.7 | 73.6 | 72.3 |

## Employment by Industry: Allentown-Bethlehem-Easton, PA-NJ, 2011–2019

(Numbers in thousands, not seasonally adjusted)

| Industry and year | January | February | March | April | May | June | July | August | September | October | November | December | Annual average |
|---|---|---|---|---|---|---|---|---|---|---|---|---|---|
| **Total Nonfarm** | | | | | | | | | | | | | |
| 2011 | 328.8 | 330.9 | 334.7 | 339.8 | 343.8 | 344.9 | 337.7 | 337.9 | 342.7 | 344.2 | 345.1 | 346.5 | 339.8 |
| 2012 | 336.8 | 339.7 | 343.0 | 346.3 | 348.8 | 349.0 | 340.4 | 340.7 | 346.5 | 347.8 | 349.1 | 348.8 | 344.7 |
| 2013 | 340.2 | 341.3 | 343.8 | 347.6 | 351.1 | 352.3 | 344.8 | 345.6 | 350.4 | 351.5 | 353.8 | 352.7 | 347.9 |
| 2014 | 343.3 | 342.7 | 345.9 | 351.8 | 356.7 | 357.1 | 348.8 | 349.8 | 354.9 | 358.4 | 360.2 | 361.0 | 352.6 |
| 2015 | 348.9 | 348.7 | 351.0 | 355.6 | 360.8 | 360.7 | 355.6 | 356.0 | 360.7 | 365.1 | 367.4 | 367.7 | 358.2 |
| 2016 | 356.3 | 357.1 | 360.7 | 364.0 | 367.2 | 366.8 | 363.4 | 362.8 | 368.3 | 371.3 | 373.0 | 372.6 | 365.3 |
| 2017 | 362.7 | 363.3 | 364.9 | 368.2 | 372.2 | 372.2 | 366.5 | 366.0 | 372.3 | 374.2 | 376.8 | 376.4 | 369.6 |
| 2018 | 366.9 | 369.0 | 369.9 | 374.2 | 377.7 | 377.9 | 371.7 | 371.6 | 377.0 | 380.4 | 382.4 | 382.3 | 375.1 |
| 2019 | 374.0 | 374.8 | 377.2 | 379.6 | 383.0 | 382.5 | 377.9 | 378.2 | 381.6 | 386.5 | 388.5 | 387.3 | 380.9 |
| **Total Private** | | | | | | | | | | | | | |
| 2011 | 287.6 | 288.4 | 291.9 | 296.9 | 300.8 | 302.0 | 300.8 | 301.7 | 302.2 | 302.5 | 302.9 | 304.3 | 298.5 |
| 2012 | 295.8 | 297.9 | 301.2 | 304.2 | 306.2 | 307.8 | 305.0 | 305.6 | 306.4 | 306.4 | 307.6 | 307.0 | 304.3 |
| 2013 | 299.4 | 300.0 | 302.2 | 306.1 | 309.2 | 311.4 | 309.5 | 310.1 | 310.4 | 310.7 | 312.3 | 311.7 | 307.8 |
| 2014 | 303.0 | 302.0 | 305.0 | 310.7 | 315.3 | 316.4 | 314.0 | 314.6 | 315.2 | 317.8 | 319.2 | 319.9 | 312.8 |
| 2015 | 309.6 | 308.6 | 310.9 | 315.3 | 320.2 | 321.3 | 320.5 | 320.8 | 321.2 | 325.0 | 326.9 | 327.3 | 319.0 |
| 2016 | 317.1 | 317.0 | 320.3 | 323.5 | 326.5 | 327.2 | 327.8 | 327.9 | 328.8 | 331.1 | 332.4 | 331.9 | 326.0 |
| 2017 | 323.5 | 323.6 | 324.7 | 327.8 | 331.5 | 332.7 | 331.3 | 331.4 | 332.3 | 333.6 | 336.1 | 335.6 | 330.3 |
| 2018 | 327.5 | 328.5 | 329.4 | 333.4 | 336.7 | 337.7 | 336.4 | 336.4 | 336.8 | 339.5 | 341.1 | 341.0 | 335.4 |
| 2019 | 333.5 | 333.7 | 336.0 | 338.4 | 341.7 | 341.8 | 342.0 | 342.2 | 341.3 | 345.3 | 347.0 | 346.0 | 340.7 |
| **Goods Producing** | | | | | | | | | | | | | |
| 2011 | 45.7 | 45.3 | 46.3 | 47.1 | 48.0 | 48.7 | 48.5 | 48.9 | 48.5 | 47.9 | 47.5 | 47.0 | 47.5 |
| 2012 | 45.8 | 45.8 | 46.6 | 47.1 | 47.2 | 48.0 | 48.0 | 47.8 | 47.8 | 47.6 | 47.3 | 46.9 | 47.2 |
| 2013 | 45.8 | 45.5 | 46.0 | 46.8 | 47.5 | 48.0 | 48.1 | 48.2 | 48.1 | 48.3 | 48.1 | 47.6 | 47.3 |
| 2014 | 46.3 | 45.9 | 46.6 | 48.1 | 49.0 | 49.7 | 49.6 | 49.6 | 49.2 | 49.2 | 49.1 | 48.8 | 48.4 |
| 2015 | 47.3 | 46.8 | 47.4 | 48.5 | 49.5 | 49.9 | 50.0 | 50.1 | 49.7 | 50.3 | 50.0 | 49.4 | 49.1 |
| 2016 | 48.3 | 47.9 | 48.5 | 49.5 | 50.1 | 50.5 | 50.9 | 50.9 | 49.9 | 49.9 | 49.7 | 49.4 | 49.6 |
| 2017 | 48.2 | 48.4 | 48.9 | 49.8 | 50.7 | 51.4 | 51.4 | 51.6 | 51.2 | 51.3 | 51.4 | 51.2 | 50.5 |
| 2018 | 50.1 | 50.1 | 50.5 | 51.5 | 52.1 | 53.1 | 53.5 | 53.3 | 53.3 | 53.2 | 53.1 | 53.1 | 52.2 |
| 2019 | 52.2 | 52.2 | 52.6 | 53.5 | 53.9 | 54.4 | 54.4 | 54.0 | 53.7 | 53.5 | 53.1 | 53.0 | 53.4 |
| **Service-Providing** | | | | | | | | | | | | | |
| 2011 | 283.1 | 285.6 | 288.4 | 292.7 | 295.8 | 296.2 | 289.2 | 289.0 | 294.2 | 296.3 | 297.6 | 299.5 | 292.3 |
| 2012 | 291.0 | 293.9 | 296.4 | 299.2 | 301.6 | 301.0 | 292.4 | 292.9 | 298.7 | 300.2 | 301.8 | 301.9 | 297.6 |
| 2013 | 294.4 | 295.8 | 297.8 | 300.8 | 303.6 | 304.3 | 296.7 | 297.4 | 302.3 | 303.2 | 305.7 | 305.1 | 300.6 |
| 2014 | 297.0 | 296.8 | 299.3 | 303.7 | 307.7 | 307.4 | 299.2 | 300.2 | 305.7 | 309.2 | 311.1 | 312.2 | 304.1 |
| 2015 | 301.6 | 301.9 | 303.6 | 307.1 | 311.3 | 310.8 | 305.6 | 305.9 | 311.0 | 314.8 | 317.4 | 318.3 | 309.1 |
| 2016 | 308.0 | 309.2 | 312.2 | 314.5 | 317.1 | 316.3 | 312.5 | 311.9 | 318.4 | 321.4 | 323.3 | 323.2 | 315.7 |
| 2017 | 314.5 | 314.9 | 316.0 | 318.4 | 321.5 | 320.8 | 315.1 | 314.4 | 321.1 | 322.9 | 325.4 | 325.2 | 319.2 |
| 2018 | 316.8 | 318.9 | 319.4 | 322.7 | 325.6 | 324.8 | 318.2 | 318.3 | 323.7 | 327.2 | 329.3 | 329.2 | 322.8 |
| 2019 | 321.8 | 322.6 | 324.6 | 326.1 | 329.1 | 328.1 | 323.5 | 324.2 | 327.9 | 333.0 | 335.4 | 334.3 | 327.6 |
| **Mining, Logging, and Construction** | | | | | | | | | | | | | |
| 2011 | 10.9 | 10.7 | 11.4 | 12.2 | 12.8 | 13.1 | 13.2 | 13.2 | 13.2 | 13.0 | 12.8 | 12.2 | 12.4 |
| 2012 | 11.3 | 11.3 | 11.7 | 12.2 | 12.4 | 12.8 | 12.7 | 12.6 | 12.6 | 12.6 | 12.4 | 11.9 | 12.2 |
| 2013 | 11.1 | 10.9 | 11.4 | 12.1 | 12.7 | 12.9 | 13.0 | 13.1 | 13.3 | 13.4 | 13.1 | 12.5 | 12.5 |
| 2014 | 11.6 | 11.3 | 11.7 | 13.0 | 13.6 | 13.8 | 13.7 | 13.9 | 13.7 | 13.6 | 13.3 | 12.7 | 13.0 |
| 2015 | 11.6 | 11.1 | 11.5 | 12.6 | 13.3 | 13.4 | 13.5 | 13.6 | 13.5 | 14.0 | 13.6 | 13.0 | 12.9 |
| 2016 | 12.2 | 11.8 | 12.3 | 13.2 | 13.5 | 13.7 | 14.0 | 14.1 | 13.8 | 13.6 | 13.3 | 12.9 | 13.2 |
| 2017 | 12.0 | 12.1 | 12.5 | 13.1 | 13.7 | 14.0 | 14.0 | 14.2 | 13.9 | 13.9 | 13.8 | 13.3 | 13.4 |
| 2018 | 12.3 | 12.3 | 12.6 | 13.3 | 13.7 | 14.1 | 14.4 | 14.4 | 14.4 | 14.3 | 14.0 | 13.7 | 13.6 |
| 2019 | 13.0 | 12.8 | 13.0 | 13.8 | 14.2 | 14.3 | 14.2 | 14.2 | 13.9 | 13.8 | 13.5 | 13.2 | 13.7 |
| **Manufacturing** | | | | | | | | | | | | | |
| 2011 | 34.8 | 34.6 | 34.9 | 34.9 | 35.2 | 35.6 | 35.3 | 35.7 | 35.3 | 34.9 | 34.7 | 34.8 | 35.1 |
| 2012 | 34.5 | 34.5 | 34.9 | 34.9 | 34.8 | 35.2 | 35.3 | 35.2 | 35.2 | 35.0 | 34.9 | 35.0 | 35.0 |
| 2013 | 34.7 | 34.6 | 34.6 | 34.7 | 34.8 | 35.1 | 35.1 | 35.1 | 34.8 | 34.9 | 35.0 | 35.1 | 34.9 |
| 2014 | 34.7 | 34.6 | 34.9 | 35.1 | 35.4 | 35.9 | 35.9 | 35.7 | 35.5 | 35.6 | 35.8 | 36.1 | 35.4 |
| 2015 | 35.7 | 35.7 | 35.9 | 35.9 | 36.2 | 36.5 | 36.5 | 36.5 | 36.2 | 36.3 | 36.4 | 36.4 | 36.2 |
| 2016 | 36.1 | 36.1 | 36.2 | 36.3 | 36.6 | 36.8 | 36.9 | 36.8 | 36.1 | 36.3 | 36.4 | 36.5 | 36.4 |
| 2017 | 36.2 | 36.3 | 36.4 | 36.7 | 37.0 | 37.4 | 37.4 | 37.4 | 37.3 | 37.4 | 37.6 | 37.9 | 37.1 |
| 2018 | 37.8 | 37.8 | 37.9 | 38.2 | 38.4 | 39.0 | 39.1 | 38.9 | 38.9 | 38.9 | 39.1 | 39.4 | 38.6 |
| 2019 | 39.2 | 39.4 | 39.6 | 39.7 | 39.7 | 40.1 | 40.2 | 39.8 | 39.8 | 39.7 | 39.6 | 39.8 | 39.7 |

## Employment by Industry: Allentown-Bethlehem-Easton, PA-NJ, 2011–2019—*Continued*

(Numbers in thousands, not seasonally adjusted)

| Industry and year | January | February | March | April | May | June | July | August | September | October | November | December | Annual average |
|---|---|---|---|---|---|---|---|---|---|---|---|---|---|
| **Trade, Transportation, and Utilities** | | | | | | | | | | | | | |
| 2011 | 67.8 | 67.0 | 67.5 | 67.9 | 68.8 | 69.6 | 69.5 | 69.8 | 70.2 | 71.3 | 72.8 | 74.1 | 69.7 |
| 2012 | 71.6 | 71.0 | 71.6 | 71.7 | 71.9 | 72.3 | 71.7 | 71.8 | 72.0 | 72.6 | 74.3 | 75.0 | 72.3 |
| 2013 | 72.2 | 71.3 | 71.4 | 71.6 | 72.2 | 72.6 | 71.5 | 72.0 | 72.1 | 72.6 | 74.1 | 75.1 | 72.4 |
| 2014 | 72.5 | 71.4 | 72.1 | 72.8 | 73.6 | 74.2 | 73.8 | 74.1 | 74.4 | 75.2 | 77.0 | 78.3 | 74.1 |
| 2015 | 75.4 | 74.3 | 74.9 | 75.0 | 76.3 | 77.1 | 77.1 | 77.4 | 77.2 | 78.1 | 80.0 | 80.9 | 77.0 |
| 2016 | 77.9 | 77.3 | 77.9 | 78.4 | 79.3 | 79.8 | 79.9 | 80.4 | 81.1 | 82.6 | 85.1 | 85.7 | 80.5 |
| 2017 | 82.9 | 81.4 | 81.1 | 81.8 | 82.4 | 83.0 | 82.5 | 82.9 | 83.8 | 84.5 | 87.7 | 88.0 | 83.5 |
| 2018 | 84.6 | 83.5 | 83.5 | 84.0 | 84.7 | 85.1 | 84.5 | 84.5 | 84.9 | 85.7 | 88.7 | 89.8 | 85.3 |
| 2019 | 86.6 | 85.0 | 85.1 | 84.9 | 85.4 | 85.7 | 86.1 | 86.3 | 86.4 | 87.5 | 90.3 | 90.4 | 86.6 |
| **Wholesale Trade** | | | | | | | | | | | | | |
| 2011 | 12.9 | 12.9 | 13.1 | 13.1 | 13.3 | 13.3 | 13.5 | 13.5 | 13.4 | 13.6 | 13.5 | 13.5 | 13.3 |
| 2012 | 13.4 | 13.4 | 13.5 | 13.6 | 13.5 | 13.6 | 13.5 | 13.4 | 13.4 | 13.3 | 13.2 | 13.2 | 13.4 |
| 2013 | 12.9 | 12.9 | 12.9 | 12.9 | 13.0 | 13.1 | 13.0 | 13.0 | 13.0 | 12.9 | 12.9 | 12.9 | 13.0 |
| 2014 | 12.9 | 12.9 | 13.0 | 13.2 | 13.3 | 13.4 | 13.4 | 13.4 | 13.3 | 13.5 | 13.4 | 13.4 | 13.3 |
| 2015 | 13.2 | 13.2 | 13.2 | 13.1 | 13.2 | 13.3 | 13.5 | 13.5 | 13.3 | 13.4 | 13.4 | 13.4 | 13.3 |
| 2016 | 13.1 | 13.2 | 13.3 | 13.4 | 13.5 | 13.6 | 13.6 | 13.6 | 13.5 | 13.8 | 13.8 | 13.9 | 13.5 |
| 2017 | 13.6 | 13.6 | 13.7 | 13.8 | 13.8 | 14.0 | 14.1 | 14.1 | 14.1 | 14.2 | 14.1 | 14.1 | 13.9 |
| 2018 | 13.9 | 14.0 | 14.0 | 14.2 | 14.2 | 14.4 | 14.4 | 14.4 | 14.3 | 14.2 | 14.2 | 14.3 | 14.2 |
| 2019 | 14.1 | 14.1 | 14.2 | 14.2 | 14.3 | 14.4 | 14.8 | 14.8 | 14.7 | 14.8 | 14.7 | 14.8 | 14.5 |
| **Retail Trade** | | | | | | | | | | | | | |
| 2011 | 39.3 | 38.5 | 38.7 | 38.9 | 39.3 | 39.7 | 39.4 | 39.6 | 39.0 | 39.5 | 40.8 | 41.9 | 39.6 |
| 2012 | 39.9 | 39.1 | 39.3 | 39.4 | 39.7 | 40.0 | 39.8 | 40.0 | 39.4 | 40.0 | 41.6 | 42.0 | 40.0 |
| 2013 | 40.1 | 39.3 | 39.3 | 39.4 | 39.8 | 40.1 | 39.7 | 39.9 | 39.5 | 40.0 | 41.2 | 42.1 | 40.0 |
| 2014 | 39.9 | 38.9 | 39.3 | 39.8 | 40.4 | 40.7 | 40.4 | 40.4 | 40.0 | 40.3 | 41.8 | 42.6 | 40.4 |
| 2015 | 40.4 | 39.3 | 39.5 | 39.7 | 40.5 | 41.0 | 40.8 | 40.9 | 40.3 | 40.8 | 42.3 | 42.5 | 40.7 |
| 2016 | 40.6 | 39.9 | 40.0 | 40.3 | 40.7 | 41.0 | 40.9 | 41.1 | 40.6 | 41.1 | 42.4 | 42.8 | 41.0 |
| 2017 | 41.1 | 40.2 | 40.1 | 40.4 | 40.6 | 40.9 | 40.6 | 40.6 | 40.2 | 40.6 | 42.1 | 42.4 | 40.8 |
| 2018 | 40.6 | 40.0 | 40.1 | 40.2 | 40.5 | 40.7 | 40.5 | 40.4 | 39.8 | 40.2 | 41.6 | 41.9 | 40.5 |
| 2019 | 40.1 | 39.2 | 39.5 | 39.6 | 40.0 | 40.1 | 40.0 | 40.0 | 39.6 | 39.7 | 41.0 | 41.0 | 40.0 |
| **Transportation and Utilities** | | | | | | | | | | | | | |
| 2011 | 15.6 | 15.6 | 15.7 | 15.9 | 16.2 | 16.6 | 16.6 | 16.7 | 17.8 | 18.2 | 18.5 | 18.7 | 16.8 |
| 2012 | 18.3 | 18.5 | 18.8 | 18.7 | 18.7 | 18.7 | 18.4 | 18.4 | 19.2 | 19.3 | 19.5 | 19.8 | 18.9 |
| 2013 | 19.2 | 19.1 | 19.2 | 19.3 | 19.4 | 19.4 | 18.8 | 19.1 | 19.6 | 19.7 | 20.0 | 20.1 | 19.4 |
| 2014 | 19.7 | 19.6 | 19.8 | 19.8 | 19.9 | 20.1 | 20.0 | 20.3 | 21.1 | 21.4 | 21.8 | 22.3 | 20.5 |
| 2015 | 21.8 | 21.8 | 22.2 | 22.2 | 22.6 | 22.8 | 22.8 | 23.0 | 23.6 | 23.9 | 24.3 | 25.0 | 23.0 |
| 2016 | 24.2 | 24.2 | 24.6 | 24.7 | 25.1 | 25.2 | 25.4 | 25.7 | 27.0 | 27.7 | 28.9 | 29.0 | 26.0 |
| 2017 | 28.2 | 27.6 | 27.3 | 27.6 | 28.0 | 28.1 | 27.8 | 28.2 | 29.5 | 29.7 | 31.5 | 31.5 | 28.8 |
| 2018 | 30.1 | 29.5 | 29.4 | 29.6 | 30.0 | 30.0 | 29.6 | 29.7 | 30.8 | 31.3 | 32.9 | 33.6 | 30.5 |
| 2019 | 32.4 | 31.7 | 31.4 | 31.1 | 31.1 | 31.2 | 31.3 | 31.5 | 32.1 | 33.0 | 34.6 | 34.6 | 32.2 |
| **Information** | | | | | | | | | | | | | |
| 2011 | 5.5 | 5.6 | 5.6 | 5.7 | 5.8 | 5.8 | 5.9 | 5.7 | 5.8 | 5.8 | 5.9 | 5.8 | 5.7 |
| 2012 | 5.7 | 5.8 | 5.9 | 6.0 | 6.0 | 6.1 | 6.0 | 6.1 | 6.1 | 6.0 | 6.1 | 6.1 | 6.0 |
| 2013 | 6.1 | 6.2 | 6.2 | 6.1 | 6.2 | 6.2 | 6.2 | 6.2 | 6.1 | 6.1 | 6.1 | 6.1 | 6.2 |
| 2014 | 6.1 | 6.1 | 6.2 | 6.2 | 6.3 | 6.3 | 6.3 | 6.3 | 6.2 | 6.1 | 6.1 | 6.1 | 6.2 |
| 2015 | 6.0 | 6.1 | 6.1 | 6.1 | 6.2 | 6.2 | 6.2 | 6.2 | 6.1 | 6.0 | 6.0 | 6.0 | 6.1 |
| 2016 | 5.9 | 5.9 | 6.0 | 6.1 | 5.9 | 6.1 | 6.1 | 6.1 | 6.0 | 5.8 | 5.7 | 5.6 | 5.9 |
| 2017 | 5.6 | 5.7 | 5.6 | 5.6 | 5.6 | 5.7 | 5.7 | 5.7 | 5.5 | 5.5 | 5.6 | 5.3 | 5.6 |
| 2018 | 5.3 | 5.4 | 5.4 | 5.4 | 5.5 | 5.4 | 5.4 | 5.6 | 5.5 | 5.5 | 5.4 | 5.3 | 5.4 |
| 2019 | 5.3 | 5.3 | 5.3 | 5.3 | 5.3 | 5.4 | 5.4 | 5.5 | 5.4 | 5.3 | 5.3 | 5.3 | 5.3 |
| **Financial Activities** | | | | | | | | | | | | | |
| 2011 | 15.2 | 15.2 | 15.2 | 15.2 | 15.2 | 15.3 | 15.1 | 15.0 | 15.0 | 15.0 | 15.0 | 15.1 | 15.1 |
| 2012 | 15.2 | 15.2 | 15.2 | 15.1 | 15.1 | 15.1 | 15.1 | 15.1 | 14.9 | 14.8 | 14.8 | 14.9 | 15.0 |
| 2013 | 14.9 | 15.0 | 15.0 | 15.1 | 15.1 | 15.2 | 15.2 | 15.1 | 14.9 | 14.8 | 14.8 | 14.8 | 15.0 |
| 2014 | 14.5 | 14.6 | 14.6 | 14.7 | 14.9 | 15.1 | 15.2 | 15.1 | 14.9 | 14.9 | 14.9 | 15.0 | 14.9 |
| 2015 | 15.0 | 14.9 | 15.0 | 14.9 | 15.0 | 15.1 | 15.1 | 15.1 | 14.9 | 14.8 | 14.8 | 14.7 | 14.9 |
| 2016 | 14.6 | 14.5 | 14.6 | 14.5 | 14.6 | 14.8 | 14.7 | 14.7 | 14.6 | 14.3 | 14.3 | 14.3 | 14.5 |
| 2017 | 14.1 | 14.2 | 14.3 | 14.1 | 14.1 | 14.3 | 14.3 | 14.3 | 14.0 | 13.9 | 13.8 | 13.8 | 14.1 |
| 2018 | 13.8 | 13.8 | 13.8 | 13.9 | 13.9 | 14.0 | 14.1 | 14.0 | 13.8 | 13.8 | 13.8 | 13.8 | 13.9 |
| 2019 | 13.7 | 13.7 | 13.8 | 13.8 | 13.9 | 14.1 | 14.2 | 14.2 | 14.0 | 14.1 | 14.1 | 14.0 | 14.0 |

## Employment by Industry: Allentown-Bethlehem-Easton, PA-NJ, 2011–2019—*Continued*

(Numbers in thousands, not seasonally adjusted)

| Industry and year | January | February | March | April | May | June | July | August | September | October | November | December | Annual average |
|---|---|---|---|---|---|---|---|---|---|---|---|---|---|
| **Professional and Business Services** | | | | | | | | | | | | | |
| 2011 | 44.0 | 44.1 | 44.8 | 46.1 | 46.4 | 46.0 | 45.8 | 46.5 | 46.8 | 46.3 | 46.6 | 47.7 | 45.9 |
| 2012 | 45.3 | 45.2 | 45.5 | 46.2 | 46.2 | 46.5 | 45.8 | 46.0 | 46.5 | 46.8 | 47.2 | 47.5 | 46.2 |
| 2013 | 46.1 | 45.5 | 45.8 | 46.6 | 46.6 | 47.4 | 47.9 | 48.6 | 48.1 | 48.7 | 50.0 | 50.1 | 47.6 |
| 2014 | 48.1 | 47.2 | 47.1 | 48.4 | 48.8 | 49.0 | 48.3 | 48.9 | 49.0 | 49.6 | 51.0 | 51.2 | 48.9 |
| 2015 | 48.6 | 47.8 | 47.6 | 47.8 | 48.1 | 48.2 | 48.0 | 48.6 | 48.7 | 50.6 | 52.4 | 52.7 | 49.1 |
| 2016 | 48.9 | 47.9 | 47.8 | 49.2 | 49.2 | 49.6 | 49.8 | 50.0 | 50.6 | 51.7 | 51.9 | 51.8 | 49.9 |
| 2017 | 49.4 | 48.8 | 48.4 | 49.3 | 50.0 | 50.3 | 49.4 | 49.4 | 49.5 | 49.0 | 49.0 | 49.1 | 49.3 |
| 2018 | 48.4 | 48.1 | 47.4 | 48.4 | 48.7 | 49.0 | 48.5 | 48.3 | 48.6 | 49.0 | 49.8 | 49.2 | 48.6 |
| 2019 | 48.1 | 48.0 | 47.7 | 48.5 | 49.1 | 48.8 | 49.6 | 49.6 | 49.3 | 49.8 | 49.9 | 49.2 | 49.0 |
| **Education and Health Services** | | | | | | | | | | | | | |
| 2011 | 66.6 | 68.0 | 68.6 | 68.5 | 68.6 | 67.1 | 66.6 | 66.4 | 68.4 | 69.7 | 70.1 | 69.4 | 68.2 |
| 2012 | 67.9 | 70.2 | 71.1 | 71.1 | 70.6 | 69.1 | 68.2 | 68.0 | 70.7 | 71.5 | 71.6 | 71.0 | 70.1 |
| 2013 | 69.0 | 71.3 | 71.8 | 72.0 | 71.6 | 70.0 | 69.4 | 69.2 | 71.9 | 72.3 | 73.1 | 71.7 | 71.1 |
| 2014 | 69.9 | 71.6 | 72.2 | 72.8 | 72.5 | 70.6 | 69.8 | 69.4 | 72.3 | 73.9 | 74.2 | 73.7 | 71.9 |
| 2015 | 71.3 | 72.9 | 73.3 | 74.4 | 73.8 | 72.2 | 71.7 | 71.1 | 73.5 | 74.9 | 75.1 | 74.7 | 73.2 |
| 2016 | 72.6 | 74.4 | 75.3 | 75.5 | 74.8 | 72.5 | 72.3 | 71.6 | 74.3 | 75.3 | 75.6 | 74.8 | 74.1 |
| 2017 | 73.4 | 75.3 | 75.9 | 76.1 | 75.6 | 73.1 | 73.2 | 72.8 | 75.9 | 77.5 | 77.6 | 77.3 | 75.3 |
| 2018 | 75.5 | 77.9 | 78.5 | 78.8 | 78.3 | 75.9 | 75.5 | 75.9 | 78.4 | 80.1 | 79.8 | 79.4 | 77.8 |
| 2019 | 77.5 | 79.5 | 80.5 | 80.5 | 80.0 | 77.6 | 76.9 | 77.2 | 79.2 | 81.7 | 82.1 | 81.5 | 79.5 |
| **Leisure and Hospitality** | | | | | | | | | | | | | |
| 2011 | 29.0 | 29.4 | 30.0 | 32.3 | 33.8 | 35.0 | 34.9 | 35.1 | 33.5 | 32.5 | 30.9 | 31.0 | 32.3 |
| 2012 | 30.2 | 30.5 | 31.1 | 32.8 | 34.9 | 36.3 | 36.0 | 36.6 | 34.5 | 33.2 | 32.5 | 31.7 | 33.4 |
| 2013 | 31.7 | 31.6 | 32.3 | 34.1 | 36.1 | 37.9 | 37.2 | 36.9 | 35.6 | 34.3 | 32.5 | 32.7 | 34.4 |
| 2014 | 32.2 | 31.9 | 32.7 | 34.1 | 36.5 | 37.6 | 37.2 | 37.4 | 35.7 | 35.4 | 33.3 | 33.1 | 34.8 |
| 2015 | 32.5 | 32.4 | 33.0 | 34.8 | 37.3 | 38.6 | 38.4 | 38.4 | 37.4 | 36.5 | 34.8 | 34.9 | 35.8 |
| 2016 | 35.0 | 35.2 | 36.3 | 36.2 | 38.3 | 39.5 | 39.7 | 39.8 | 38.2 | 37.4 | 35.9 | 35.9 | 37.3 |
| 2017 | 35.7 | 35.5 | 36.2 | 36.7 | 38.5 | 40.1 | 40.0 | 40.1 | 38.1 | 37.6 | 36.7 | 36.5 | 37.6 |
| 2018 | 35.7 | 35.6 | 36.1 | 37.0 | 39.0 | 40.4 | 40.2 | 40.2 | 37.9 | 37.6 | 35.9 | 35.9 | 37.6 |
| 2019 | 35.8 | 35.6 | 36.6 | 37.4 | 39.4 | 40.8 | 40.6 | 40.5 | 38.6 | 38.6 | 37.4 | 37.9 | 38.3 |
| **Other Services** | | | | | | | | | | | | | |
| 2011 | 13.8 | 13.8 | 13.9 | 14.1 | 14.2 | 14.5 | 14.5 | 14.3 | 14.0 | 14.0 | 14.1 | 14.2 | 14.1 |
| 2012 | 14.1 | 14.2 | 14.2 | 14.2 | 14.3 | 14.4 | 14.2 | 14.2 | 13.9 | 13.9 | 13.8 | 13.9 | 14.1 |
| 2013 | 13.6 | 13.6 | 13.7 | 13.8 | 13.9 | 14.1 | 14.0 | 13.9 | 13.6 | 13.6 | 13.6 | 13.6 | 13.8 |
| 2014 | 13.4 | 13.3 | 13.5 | 13.6 | 13.7 | 13.9 | 13.8 | 13.8 | 13.5 | 13.5 | 13.6 | 13.7 | 13.6 |
| 2015 | 13.5 | 13.4 | 13.6 | 13.8 | 14.0 | 14.0 | 14.0 | 13.9 | 13.7 | 13.8 | 13.8 | 14.0 | 13.8 |
| 2016 | 13.9 | 13.9 | 13.9 | 14.1 | 14.3 | 14.4 | 14.4 | 14.4 | 14.1 | 14.1 | 14.2 | 14.4 | 14.2 |
| 2017 | 14.2 | 14.3 | 14.3 | 14.4 | 14.6 | 14.8 | 14.8 | 14.6 | 14.3 | 14.3 | 14.3 | 14.4 | 14.4 |
| 2018 | 14.1 | 14.1 | 14.2 | 14.4 | 14.5 | 14.8 | 14.7 | 14.6 | 14.4 | 14.6 | 14.6 | 14.5 | 14.5 |
| 2019 | 14.3 | 14.4 | 14.4 | 14.5 | 14.7 | 15.0 | 14.8 | 14.9 | 14.7 | 14.8 | 14.8 | 14.7 | 14.7 |
| **Government** | | | | | | | | | | | | | |
| 2011 | 41.2 | 42.5 | 42.8 | 42.9 | 43.0 | 42.9 | 36.9 | 36.2 | 40.5 | 41.7 | 42.2 | 42.2 | 41.3 |
| 2012 | 41.0 | 41.8 | 41.8 | 42.1 | 42.6 | 41.2 | 35.4 | 35.1 | 40.1 | 41.4 | 41.5 | 41.8 | 40.5 |
| 2013 | 40.8 | 41.3 | 41.6 | 41.5 | 41.9 | 40.9 | 35.3 | 35.5 | 40.0 | 40.8 | 41.5 | 41.0 | 40.2 |
| 2014 | 40.3 | 40.7 | 40.9 | 41.1 | 41.4 | 40.7 | 34.8 | 35.2 | 39.7 | 40.6 | 41.0 | 41.1 | 39.8 |
| 2015 | 39.3 | 40.1 | 40.1 | 40.3 | 40.6 | 39.4 | 35.1 | 35.2 | 39.5 | 40.1 | 40.5 | 40.4 | 39.2 |
| 2016 | 39.2 | 40.1 | 40.4 | 40.5 | 40.7 | 39.6 | 35.6 | 34.9 | 39.5 | 40.2 | 40.6 | 40.7 | 39.3 |
| 2017 | 39.2 | 39.7 | 40.2 | 40.4 | 40.7 | 39.5 | 35.2 | 34.6 | 40.0 | 40.6 | 40.7 | 40.8 | 39.3 |
| 2018 | 39.4 | 40.5 | 40.5 | 40.8 | 41.0 | 40.2 | 35.3 | 35.2 | 40.2 | 40.9 | 41.3 | 41.3 | 39.7 |
| 2019 | 40.5 | 41.1 | 41.2 | 41.2 | 41.3 | 40.7 | 35.9 | 36.0 | 40.3 | 41.2 | 41.5 | 41.3 | 40.2 |

## Employment by Industry: Columbia, SC, 2011–2019

(Numbers in thousands, not seasonally adjusted)

| Industry and year | January | February | March | April | May | June | July | August | September | October | November | December | Annual average |
|---|---|---|---|---|---|---|---|---|---|---|---|---|---|
| **Total Nonfarm** | | | | | | | | | | | | | |
| 2011 | 339.8 | 343.8 | 345.8 | 349.1 | 349.6 | 348.3 | 344.5 | 347.4 | 349.1 | 351.3 | 354.8 | 355.4 | 348.2 |
| 2012 | 349.6 | 351.6 | 353.9 | 353.9 | 355.9 | 354.6 | 352.4 | 355.0 | 356.4 | 359.5 | 366.5 | 366.3 | 356.3 |
| 2013 | 355.6 | 358.3 | 359.7 | 362.5 | 364.2 | 362.2 | 360.4 | 361.3 | 365.9 | 368.1 | 375.3 | 376.2 | 364.1 |
| 2014 | 367.2 | 366.9 | 371.7 | 373.4 | 375.2 | 372.2 | 369.9 | 373.6 | 375.8 | 380.1 | 385.7 | 386.8 | 374.9 |
| 2015 | 377.1 | 379.7 | 380.7 | 382.7 | 385.0 | 383.7 | 382.3 | 384.6 | 387.7 | 391.8 | 397.6 | 398.9 | 386.0 |
| 2016 | 387.1 | 390.4 | 391.1 | 394.0 | 396.2 | 393.5 | 392.2 | 394.6 | 397.2 | 399.1 | 403.9 | 403.3 | 395.2 |
| 2017 | 393.7 | 395.8 | 397.1 | 398.7 | 400.0 | 399.4 | 395.1 | 392.3 | 393.6 | 397.6 | 403.1 | 403.1 | 397.5 |
| 2018 | 395.7 | 398.3 | 399.6 | 401.0 | 401.0 | 400.1 | 396.6 | 397.6 | 398.6 | 400.8 | 404.4 | 403.4 | 399.8 |
| 2019 | 396.3 | 399.0 | 400.3 | 403.0 | 404.0 | 402.8 | 401.9 | 404.5 | 405.3 | 406.9 | 410.1 | 407.5 | 403.5 |
| **Total Private** | | | | | | | | | | | | | |
| 2011 | 259.3 | 262.6 | 264.3 | 268.1 | 269.2 | 269.1 | 267.8 | 269.4 | 268.9 | 270.6 | 273.9 | 274.7 | 268.2 |
| 2012 | 269.4 | 270.2 | 272.4 | 272.5 | 274.3 | 274.0 | 273.7 | 275.7 | 275.7 | 277.6 | 283.9 | 283.8 | 275.3 |
| 2013 | 274.4 | 275.8 | 277.0 | 280.2 | 282.1 | 282.1 | 282.6 | 284.6 | 285.1 | 286.3 | 292.8 | 294.1 | 283.1 |
| 2014 | 285.0 | 283.7 | 288.1 | 289.6 | 291.4 | 290.0 | 289.6 | 292.3 | 292.1 | 295.7 | 301.0 | 302.2 | 291.7 |
| 2015 | 293.0 | 294.7 | 295.5 | 297.2 | 299.7 | 300.4 | 300.3 | 301.5 | 302.4 | 306.4 | 311.8 | 312.8 | 301.3 |
| 2016 | 302.5 | 304.9 | 305.1 | 308.1 | 310.2 | 309.2 | 308.9 | 310.6 | 311.2 | 313.0 | 317.5 | 316.5 | 309.8 |
| 2017 | 308.2 | 309.6 | 310.5 | 311.8 | 313.1 | 313.9 | 312.0 | 308.9 | 307.7 | 311.2 | 316.2 | 316.2 | 311.6 |
| 2018 | 309.9 | 311.9 | 312.8 | 314.9 | 315.2 | 315.5 | 313.9 | 314.6 | 312.5 | 315.6 | 318.5 | 317.6 | 314.4 |
| 2019 | 311.6 | 313.9 | 314.7 | 317.7 | 318.8 | 319.2 | 319.4 | 321.2 | 319.4 | 320.9 | 323.7 | 320.9 | 318.5 |
| **Goods Producing** | | | | | | | | | | | | | |
| 2011 | 41.1 | 41.6 | 42.0 | 42.2 | 42.4 | 42.6 | 42.6 | 42.8 | 42.5 | 42.4 | 42.5 | 42.6 | 42.3 |
| 2012 | 41.9 | 42.1 | 42.5 | 41.9 | 42.2 | 42.5 | 42.7 | 42.7 | 42.6 | 42.9 | 42.9 | 42.7 | 42.5 |
| 2013 | 41.8 | 42.1 | 42.4 | 42.3 | 42.5 | 42.8 | 43.0 | 43.0 | 43.1 | 43.2 | 43.5 | 43.6 | 42.8 |
| 2014 | 43.5 | 43.5 | 44.0 | 44.4 | 44.6 | 44.5 | 44.9 | 45.0 | 45.1 | 45.3 | 45.5 | 45.9 | 44.7 |
| 2015 | 45.7 | 46.0 | 45.9 | 46.2 | 46.3 | 46.6 | 46.5 | 46.5 | 46.8 | 47.4 | 47.4 | 47.3 | 46.6 |
| 2016 | 46.7 | 46.8 | 46.9 | 46.7 | 47.0 | 47.5 | 48.0 | 48.3 | 48.2 | 48.4 | 48.6 | 48.8 | 47.7 |
| 2017 | 49.6 | 49.4 | 49.6 | 49.8 | 50.2 | 50.4 | 50.4 | 47.0 | 46.6 | 46.4 | 46.5 | 46.6 | 48.5 |
| 2018 | 46.7 | 47.2 | 47.3 | 47.2 | 47.4 | 47.9 | 48.0 | 47.9 | 47.8 | 47.7 | 47.6 | 47.8 | 47.5 |
| 2019 | 47.4 | 47.8 | 47.9 | 48.8 | 49.2 | 49.5 | 49.8 | 49.8 | 49.4 | 49.4 | 49.3 | 49.3 | 49.0 |
| **Service-Providing** | | | | | | | | | | | | | |
| 2011 | 298.7 | 302.2 | 303.8 | 306.9 | 307.2 | 305.7 | 301.9 | 304.6 | 306.6 | 308.9 | 312.3 | 312.8 | 306.0 |
| 2012 | 307.7 | 309.5 | 311.4 | 312.0 | 313.7 | 312.1 | 309.7 | 312.3 | 313.8 | 316.6 | 323.6 | 323.6 | 313.8 |
| 2013 | 313.8 | 316.2 | 317.3 | 320.2 | 321.7 | 319.4 | 317.4 | 318.3 | 322.8 | 324.9 | 331.8 | 332.6 | 321.4 |
| 2014 | 323.7 | 323.4 | 327.7 | 329.0 | 330.6 | 327.7 | 325.0 | 328.6 | 330.7 | 334.8 | 340.2 | 340.9 | 330.2 |
| 2015 | 331.4 | 333.7 | 334.8 | 336.5 | 338.7 | 337.1 | 335.8 | 338.1 | 340.9 | 344.4 | 350.2 | 351.6 | 339.4 |
| 2016 | 340.4 | 343.6 | 344.2 | 347.3 | 349.2 | 346.0 | 344.2 | 346.3 | 349.0 | 350.7 | 355.3 | 354.5 | 347.6 |
| 2017 | 344.1 | 346.4 | 347.5 | 348.9 | 349.8 | 349.0 | 344.7 | 345.3 | 347.0 | 351.2 | 356.6 | 356.5 | 348.9 |
| 2018 | 349.0 | 351.1 | 352.3 | 353.8 | 353.6 | 352.2 | 348.6 | 349.7 | 350.8 | 353.1 | 356.8 | 355.6 | 352.2 |
| 2019 | 348.9 | 351.2 | 352.4 | 354.2 | 354.8 | 353.3 | 352.1 | 354.7 | 355.9 | 357.5 | 360.8 | 358.2 | 354.5 |
| **Mining, Logging, and Construction** | | | | | | | | | | | | | |
| 2011 | 14.4 | 14.7 | 15.0 | 15.1 | 15.2 | 15.2 | 15.3 | 15.4 | 15.3 | 15.4 | 15.5 | 15.5 | 15.2 |
| 2012 | 14.9 | 15.0 | 15.3 | 14.8 | 15.1 | 15.3 | 15.5 | 15.6 | 15.6 | 15.6 | 15.7 | 15.7 | 15.3 |
| 2013 | 15.2 | 15.3 | 15.5 | 15.5 | 15.7 | 15.9 | 16.2 | 16.2 | 16.2 | 16.3 | 16.5 | 16.6 | 15.9 |
| 2014 | 16.6 | 16.4 | 16.5 | 16.6 | 16.7 | 16.8 | 17.0 | 17.1 | 17.0 | 17.2 | 17.2 | 17.3 | 16.9 |
| 2015 | 17.0 | 17.0 | 17.0 | 17.2 | 17.4 | 17.5 | 17.4 | 17.4 | 17.6 | 18.0 | 18.1 | 18.4 | 17.5 |
| 2016 | 18.2 | 18.4 | 18.7 | 18.8 | 19.0 | 19.4 | 19.7 | 20.0 | 20.1 | 20.3 | 20.6 | 20.7 | 19.5 |
| 2017 | 21.2 | 21.0 | 21.1 | 21.2 | 21.4 | 21.4 | 21.2 | 17.8 | 17.5 | 17.3 | 17.3 | 17.2 | 19.6 |
| 2018 | 17.3 | 17.5 | 17.5 | 17.5 | 17.5 | 17.6 | 17.5 | 17.5 | 17.4 | 17.2 | 17.2 | 17.1 | 17.4 |
| 2019 | 16.7 | 16.9 | 17.0 | 17.2 | 17.3 | 17.3 | 17.4 | 17.5 | 17.4 | 17.5 | 17.4 | 17.4 | 17.3 |
| **Manufacturing** | | | | | | | | | | | | | |
| 2011 | 26.7 | 26.9 | 27.0 | 27.1 | 27.2 | 27.4 | 27.3 | 27.4 | 27.2 | 27.0 | 27.0 | 27.1 | 27.1 |
| 2012 | 27.0 | 27.1 | 27.2 | 27.1 | 27.1 | 27.2 | 27.2 | 27.1 | 27.0 | 27.3 | 27.2 | 27.0 | 27.1 |
| 2013 | 26.6 | 26.8 | 26.9 | 26.8 | 26.8 | 26.9 | 26.8 | 26.8 | 26.9 | 26.9 | 27.0 | 27.0 | 26.9 |
| 2014 | 26.9 | 27.1 | 27.5 | 27.8 | 27.9 | 27.7 | 27.9 | 27.9 | 28.1 | 28.1 | 28.3 | 28.6 | 27.8 |
| 2015 | 28.7 | 29.0 | 28.9 | 29.0 | 28.9 | 29.1 | 29.1 | 29.1 | 29.2 | 29.4 | 29.3 | 28.9 | 29.1 |
| 2016 | 28.5 | 28.4 | 28.2 | 27.9 | 28.0 | 28.1 | 28.3 | 28.3 | 28.1 | 28.1 | 28.0 | 28.1 | 28.2 |
| 2017 | 28.4 | 28.4 | 28.5 | 28.6 | 28.8 | 29.0 | 29.2 | 29.2 | 29.1 | 29.1 | 29.2 | 29.4 | 28.9 |
| 2018 | 29.4 | 29.7 | 29.8 | 29.7 | 29.9 | 30.3 | 30.5 | 30.4 | 30.4 | 30.5 | 30.4 | 30.7 | 30.1 |
| 2019 | 30.7 | 30.9 | 30.9 | 31.6 | 31.9 | 32.2 | 32.4 | 32.3 | 32.0 | 31.9 | 31.9 | 31.9 | 31.7 |

# Employment by Industry: Columbia, SC, 2011–2019—*Continued*

(Numbers in thousands, not seasonally adjusted)

| Industry and year | January | February | March | April | May | June | July | August | September | October | November | December | Annual average |
|---|---|---|---|---|---|---|---|---|---|---|---|---|---|
| **Trade, Transportation, and Utilities** | | | | | | | | | | | | | |
| 2011 | 61.4 | 61.7 | 61.8 | 62.2 | 62.3 | 62.7 | 62.3 | 62.4 | 62.5 | 62.8 | 64.2 | 64.8 | 62.6 |
| 2012 | 63.0 | 62.4 | 62.9 | 62.7 | 63.2 | 63.0 | 63.1 | 63.9 | 63.9 | 64.5 | 66.3 | 66.7 | 63.8 |
| 2013 | 63.9 | 64.0 | 64.3 | 64.4 | 64.9 | 65.2 | 65.7 | 66.0 | 66.2 | 66.8 | 68.1 | 69.1 | 65.7 |
| 2014 | 66.9 | 66.7 | 67.4 | 67.1 | 67.6 | 67.7 | 67.7 | 68.3 | 68.1 | 68.8 | 70.2 | 71.4 | 68.2 |
| 2015 | 68.4 | 68.7 | 68.7 | 69.2 | 69.9 | 70.6 | 71.0 | 71.5 | 71.3 | 72.0 | 73.8 | 74.5 | 70.8 |
| 2016 | 72.1 | 72.4 | 72.3 | 73.0 | 73.7 | 73.7 | 74.1 | 74.0 | 73.6 | 74.0 | 75.6 | 75.6 | 73.7 |
| 2017 | 72.9 | 72.5 | 72.6 | 72.3 | 72.5 | 73.0 | 72.9 | 72.8 | 72.7 | 73.6 | 75.2 | 75.8 | 73.2 |
| 2018 | 72.7 | 72.7 | 73.1 | 72.8 | 72.7 | 72.7 | 72.3 | 72.1 | 71.8 | 72.8 | 74.6 | 74.8 | 72.9 |
| 2019 | 72.6 | 72.0 | 72.0 | 72.0 | 72.2 | 72.7 | 72.5 | 72.5 | 72.1 | 72.0 | 73.1 | 73.7 | 72.5 |
| **Wholesale Trade** | | | | | | | | | | | | | |
| 2011 | 13.5 | 13.6 | 13.6 | 13.6 | 13.6 | 13.6 | 13.6 | 13.5 | 13.6 | 13.4 | 13.5 | 13.5 | 13.6 |
| 2012 | 13.6 | 13.7 | 13.8 | 13.7 | 13.9 | 13.9 | 14.0 | 14.1 | 14.0 | 14.0 | 14.0 | 14.0 | 13.9 |
| 2013 | 13.8 | 13.9 | 14.0 | 14.0 | 14.2 | 14.3 | 14.3 | 14.3 | 14.4 | 14.4 | 14.6 | 14.7 | 14.2 |
| 2014 | 14.7 | 14.8 | 15.0 | 14.8 | 14.9 | 14.9 | 14.9 | 15.0 | 14.9 | 14.9 | 14.9 | 15.0 | 14.9 |
| 2015 | 14.8 | 14.8 | 14.8 | 14.9 | 15.0 | 15.1 | 15.0 | 15.1 | 15.1 | 15.2 | 15.3 | 15.4 | 15.0 |
| 2016 | 15.3 | 15.5 | 15.5 | 15.7 | 15.7 | 15.7 | 15.7 | 15.6 | 15.6 | 15.5 | 15.5 | 15.6 | 15.6 |
| 2017 | 15.5 | 15.5 | 15.5 | 15.3 | 15.3 | 15.4 | 15.3 | 15.3 | 15.2 | 15.2 | 15.2 | 15.2 | 15.3 |
| 2018 | 14.9 | 15.0 | 15.0 | 15.1 | 15.1 | 15.1 | 15.0 | 14.9 | 14.9 | 15.0 | 15.0 | 15.1 | 15.0 |
| 2019 | 15.0 | 15.0 | 15.1 | 15.0 | 15.1 | 15.2 | 15.2 | 15.1 | 14.9 | 14.9 | 14.9 | 14.9 | 15.0 |
| **Retail Trade** | | | | | | | | | | | | | |
| 2011 | 37.5 | 37.6 | 37.7 | 38.0 | 38.1 | 38.3 | 38.2 | 38.3 | 38.2 | 38.3 | 39.3 | 39.8 | 38.3 |
| 2012 | 38.2 | 37.6 | 38.0 | 37.8 | 38.0 | 37.7 | 37.7 | 38.0 | 37.9 | 38.2 | 39.6 | 39.8 | 38.2 |
| 2013 | 37.8 | 37.7 | 37.9 | 38.2 | 38.4 | 38.4 | 38.6 | 38.9 | 38.8 | 39.4 | 40.2 | 40.7 | 38.8 |
| 2014 | 38.9 | 38.5 | 38.8 | 38.7 | 38.9 | 38.9 | 38.9 | 39.2 | 39.0 | 39.5 | 40.6 | 41.2 | 39.3 |
| 2015 | 39.2 | 39.1 | 39.3 | 39.6 | 39.9 | 40.3 | 40.2 | 40.5 | 40.2 | 41.1 | 42.6 | 43.0 | 40.4 |
| 2016 | 41.0 | 41.1 | 41.2 | 41.5 | 41.8 | 41.8 | 41.9 | 42.1 | 41.9 | 42.0 | 43.4 | 43.3 | 41.9 |
| 2017 | 41.6 | 41.3 | 41.4 | 41.5 | 41.6 | 41.7 | 41.5 | 41.7 | 41.3 | 41.9 | 43.5 | 43.6 | 41.9 |
| 2018 | 41.6 | 41.5 | 41.8 | 42.0 | 42.0 | 41.9 | 41.7 | 41.6 | 41.3 | 41.9 | 43.4 | 43.2 | 42.0 |
| 2019 | 41.6 | 41.4 | 41.5 | 41.6 | 41.8 | 41.9 | 41.7 | 42.0 | 41.7 | 41.5 | 42.6 | 42.8 | 41.8 |
| **Transportation and Utilities** | | | | | | | | | | | | | |
| 2011 | 10.4 | 10.5 | 10.5 | 10.6 | 10.6 | 10.8 | 10.5 | 10.6 | 10.7 | 11.1 | 11.4 | 11.5 | 10.8 |
| 2012 | 11.2 | 11.1 | 11.1 | 11.2 | 11.3 | 11.4 | 11.4 | 11.8 | 12.0 | 12.3 | 12.7 | 12.9 | 11.7 |
| 2013 | 12.3 | 12.4 | 12.4 | 12.2 | 12.3 | 12.5 | 12.8 | 12.8 | 13.0 | 13.0 | 13.3 | 13.7 | 12.7 |
| 2014 | 13.3 | 13.4 | 13.6 | 13.6 | 13.8 | 13.9 | 13.9 | 14.1 | 14.2 | 14.4 | 14.7 | 15.2 | 14.0 |
| 2015 | 14.4 | 14.8 | 14.6 | 14.7 | 15.0 | 15.2 | 15.8 | 15.9 | 16.0 | 15.7 | 15.9 | 16.1 | 15.3 |
| 2016 | 15.8 | 15.8 | 15.6 | 15.8 | 16.2 | 16.2 | 16.5 | 16.3 | 16.1 | 16.5 | 16.7 | 16.7 | 16.2 |
| 2017 | 15.8 | 15.7 | 15.7 | 15.5 | 15.6 | 15.9 | 16.1 | 15.8 | 16.2 | 16.5 | 16.5 | 17.0 | 16.0 |
| 2018 | 16.2 | 16.2 | 16.3 | 15.7 | 15.6 | 15.7 | 15.6 | 15.6 | 15.6 | 15.9 | 16.2 | 16.5 | 15.9 |
| 2019 | 16.0 | 15.6 | 15.4 | 15.4 | 15.3 | 15.6 | 15.6 | 15.4 | 15.5 | 15.6 | 15.6 | 16.0 | 15.6 |
| **Information** | | | | | | | | | | | | | |
| 2011 | 5.4 | 5.4 | 5.4 | 5.3 | 5.4 | 5.4 | 5.4 | 5.4 | 5.3 | 5.3 | 5.4 | 5.4 | 5.4 |
| 2012 | 5.4 | 5.4 | 5.4 | 5.2 | 5.2 | 5.2 | 5.2 | 5.2 | 5.2 | 5.3 | 5.4 | 5.4 | 5.3 |
| 2013 | 5.5 | 5.8 | 5.8 | 5.9 | 5.6 | 5.4 | 5.5 | 5.5 | 5.5 | 5.6 | 5.7 | 5.7 | 5.6 |
| 2014 | 5.6 | 5.5 | 5.4 | 5.6 | 5.4 | 5.5 | 5.4 | 5.4 | 5.4 | 5.5 | 5.7 | 5.4 | 5.5 |
| 2015 | 5.5 | 5.5 | 5.4 | 5.5 | 5.6 | 5.4 | 5.4 | 5.4 | 5.4 | 5.4 | 5.5 | 5.6 | 5.5 |
| 2016 | 5.5 | 5.5 | 5.4 | 5.6 | 5.8 | 5.9 | 5.7 | 5.7 | 5.7 | 5.8 | 5.9 | 6.2 | 5.7 |
| 2017 | 5.6 | 5.9 | 5.9 | 5.7 | 5.9 | 5.6 | 5.4 | 5.3 | 5.2 | 5.2 | 5.3 | 5.2 | 5.5 |
| 2018 | 5.4 | 5.7 | 5.5 | 5.7 | 5.7 | 5.8 | 5.7 | 5.6 | 5.4 | 5.5 | 5.5 | 5.6 | 5.6 |
| 2019 | 5.5 | 5.8 | 6.1 | 6.6 | 6.6 | 6.6 | 6.0 | 6.1 | 5.8 | 5.8 | 5.9 | 5.9 | 6.1 |
| **Financial Activities** | | | | | | | | | | | | | |
| 2011 | 26.9 | 26.9 | 27.0 | 27.1 | 27.3 | 27.4 | 27.3 | 27.5 | 27.5 | 27.8 | 28.0 | 28.2 | 27.4 |
| 2012 | 28.2 | 28.3 | 28.4 | 28.4 | 28.6 | 28.7 | 28.8 | 28.9 | 29.0 | 29.1 | 29.3 | 29.3 | 28.8 |
| 2013 | 29.2 | 29.4 | 29.7 | 29.8 | 30.0 | 30.2 | 30.3 | 30.5 | 30.6 | 30.3 | 30.4 | 30.5 | 30.1 |
| 2014 | 30.1 | 30.1 | 30.1 | 30.1 | 30.2 | 30.2 | 30.1 | 30.2 | 30.2 | 30.1 | 30.1 | 30.2 | 30.1 |
| 2015 | 30.0 | 30.1 | 30.1 | 30.1 | 30.3 | 30.4 | 30.3 | 30.4 | 30.5 | 30.6 | 30.8 | 30.9 | 30.4 |
| 2016 | 30.5 | 30.6 | 30.6 | 30.6 | 30.7 | 30.9 | 30.8 | 31.0 | 31.1 | 31.3 | 31.5 | 31.4 | 30.9 |
| 2017 | 31.0 | 31.1 | 31.1 | 30.8 | 30.9 | 31.2 | 31.1 | 31.2 | 31.0 | 31.1 | 31.3 | 31.3 | 31.1 |
| 2018 | 31.2 | 31.2 | 31.2 | 31.0 | 31.1 | 31.1 | 30.9 | 31.0 | 30.9 | 31.2 | 31.3 | 31.2 | 31.1 |
| 2019 | 31.2 | 31.4 | 31.0 | 31.2 | 31.2 | 31.3 | 31.4 | 31.5 | 31.6 | 32.2 | 32.5 | 32.0 | 31.5 |

## Employment by Industry: Columbia, SC, 2011–2019—*Continued*

(Numbers in thousands, not seasonally adjusted)

| Industry and year | January | February | March | April | May | June | July | August | September | October | November | December | Annual average |
|---|---|---|---|---|---|---|---|---|---|---|---|---|---|
| **Professional and Business Services** | | | | | | | | | | | | | |
| 2011 | 40.1 | 41.1 | 41.3 | 42.4 | 42.3 | 42.2 | 42.0 | 42.5 | 42.1 | 42.5 | 43.3 | 44.1 | 42.2 |
| 2012 | 42.8 | 43.0 | 43.3 | 44.0 | 44.5 | 44.5 | 44.4 | 44.4 | 43.9 | 44.4 | 47.8 | 48.3 | 44.6 |
| 2013 | 45.0 | 44.0 | 43.8 | 44.8 | 45.2 | 45.2 | 45.2 | 45.6 | 45.7 | 45.9 | 49.9 | 50.8 | 45.9 |
| 2014 | 46.4 | 44.8 | 46.1 | 45.9 | 46.5 | 45.6 | 45.5 | 46.1 | 46.1 | 47.5 | 51.5 | 51.8 | 47.0 |
| 2015 | 47.7 | 47.4 | 47.3 | 47.2 | 47.6 | 47.9 | 47.9 | 47.8 | 48.5 | 51.0 | 53.0 | 54.0 | 48.9 |
| 2016 | 49.3 | 49.7 | 49.3 | 50.1 | 49.9 | 49.2 | 48.3 | 48.9 | 49.7 | 50.0 | 51.5 | 51.4 | 49.8 |
| 2017 | 47.8 | 47.8 | 47.9 | 48.9 | 49.2 | 49.9 | 49.1 | 48.7 | 48.8 | 50.5 | 53.4 | 53.5 | 49.6 |
| 2018 | 50.9 | 51.0 | 51.1 | 50.7 | 50.6 | 50.6 | 50.0 | 49.9 | 49.7 | 51.0 | 51.4 | 50.9 | 50.7 |
| 2019 | 49.7 | 50.3 | 50.5 | 50.8 | 51.2 | 51.0 | 50.7 | 51.6 | 51.6 | 51.9 | 52.0 | 50.8 | 51.0 |
| **Education and Health Services** | | | | | | | | | | | | | |
| 2011 | 42.2 | 42.8 | 42.8 | 43.9 | 43.8 | 43.5 | 43.3 | 43.0 | 43.3 | 43.6 | 43.7 | 43.4 | 43.3 |
| 2012 | 43.0 | 43.3 | 43.4 | 43.3 | 43.3 | 42.6 | 42.5 | 42.7 | 43.3 | 43.6 | 43.7 | 43.5 | 43.2 |
| 2013 | 42.6 | 43.2 | 43.2 | 43.7 | 44.0 | 43.7 | 43.8 | 44.1 | 44.4 | 44.8 | 45.0 | 45.0 | 44.0 |
| 2014 | 44.4 | 44.6 | 45.4 | 45.8 | 46.0 | 45.4 | 45.7 | 45.9 | 46.2 | 46.4 | 46.5 | 46.5 | 45.7 |
| 2015 | 45.9 | 46.4 | 46.6 | 46.7 | 47.2 | 47.0 | 46.9 | 46.8 | 46.9 | 47.0 | 47.4 | 47.3 | 46.8 |
| 2016 | 46.7 | 47.3 | 47.5 | 47.7 | 48.2 | 47.8 | 47.9 | 47.9 | 48.4 | 48.6 | 48.8 | 48.8 | 48.0 |
| 2017 | 48.0 | 48.7 | 48.8 | 48.8 | 48.7 | 48.5 | 48.2 | 48.2 | 48.2 | 48.6 | 48.4 | 48.4 | 48.5 |
| 2018 | 47.9 | 48.4 | 48.5 | 49.5 | 49.7 | 49.8 | 49.7 | 50.0 | 50.0 | 50.7 | 50.8 | 50.7 | 49.6 |
| 2019 | 50.4 | 50.9 | 51.1 | 50.9 | 50.9 | 51.1 | 50.9 | 51.2 | 51.0 | 52.1 | 52.4 | 51.3 | 51.2 |
| **Leisure and Hospitality** | | | | | | | | | | | | | |
| 2011 | 29.8 | 30.7 | 31.5 | 32.3 | 32.8 | 32.2 | 31.7 | 32.6 | 32.5 | 33.1 | 33.6 | 32.8 | 32.1 |
| 2012 | 31.4 | 31.9 | 32.5 | 33.0 | 33.2 | 33.1 | 32.7 | 33.6 | 33.5 | 33.5 | 34.1 | 33.4 | 33.0 |
| 2013 | 31.9 | 32.8 | 33.1 | 34.5 | 35.0 | 34.7 | 34.2 | 34.9 | 34.7 | 34.7 | 35.2 | 34.3 | 34.2 |
| 2014 | 33.2 | 33.5 | 34.6 | 35.4 | 35.7 | 35.6 | 35.0 | 35.9 | 35.7 | 36.7 | 36.1 | 35.6 | 35.3 |
| 2015 | 34.4 | 35.1 | 35.8 | 36.7 | 37.0 | 36.7 | 36.5 | 37.2 | 37.2 | 37.2 | 37.9 | 37.1 | 36.6 |
| 2016 | 35.7 | 36.6 | 36.9 | 38.2 | 38.7 | 38.0 | 38.0 | 38.7 | 38.4 | 38.7 | 39.3 | 38.1 | 37.9 |
| 2017 | 37.3 | 38.1 | 38.4 | 39.3 | 39.5 | 39.1 | 38.8 | 39.5 | 39.1 | 39.7 | 40.2 | 39.3 | 39.0 |
| 2018 | 38.9 | 39.4 | 39.8 | 41.4 | 41.5 | 41.1 | 40.7 | 41.5 | 40.5 | 40.3 | 40.9 | 40.2 | 40.5 |
| 2019 | 38.5 | 39.3 | 39.6 | 40.7 | 40.8 | 40.4 | 41.1 | 41.5 | 40.9 | 40.4 | 41.4 | 40.8 | 40.5 |
| **Other Services** | | | | | | | | | | | | | |
| 2011 | 12.4 | 12.4 | 12.5 | 12.7 | 12.9 | 13.1 | 13.2 | 13.2 | 13.2 | 13.1 | 13.2 | 13.4 | 12.9 |
| 2012 | 13.7 | 13.8 | 14.0 | 14.0 | 14.1 | 14.4 | 14.3 | 14.3 | 14.3 | 14.3 | 14.4 | 14.5 | 14.2 |
| 2013 | 14.5 | 14.5 | 14.7 | 14.8 | 14.9 | 14.9 | 14.9 | 15.0 | 14.9 | 15.0 | 15.0 | 15.1 | 14.9 |
| 2014 | 14.9 | 15.0 | 15.1 | 15.3 | 15.4 | 15.5 | 15.3 | 15.5 | 15.3 | 15.4 | 15.4 | 15.4 | 15.3 |
| 2015 | 15.4 | 15.5 | 15.7 | 15.6 | 15.8 | 15.8 | 15.8 | 15.9 | 15.8 | 15.8 | 16.0 | 16.1 | 15.8 |
| 2016 | 16.0 | 16.0 | 16.2 | 16.2 | 16.2 | 16.2 | 16.1 | 16.1 | 16.1 | 16.2 | 16.3 | 16.2 | 16.2 |
| 2017 | 16.0 | 16.1 | 16.2 | 16.2 | 16.2 | 16.2 | 16.1 | 16.2 | 16.1 | 16.2 | 16.1 | 16.1 | 16.1 |
| 2018 | 16.2 | 16.3 | 16.3 | 16.6 | 16.5 | 16.5 | 16.6 | 16.6 | 16.4 | 16.4 | 16.4 | 16.4 | 16.4 |
| 2019 | 16.3 | 16.4 | 16.5 | 16.7 | 16.7 | 16.6 | 17.0 | 17.0 | 17.0 | 17.1 | 17.1 | 17.1 | 16.8 |
| **Government** | | | | | | | | | | | | | |
| 2011 | 80.5 | 81.2 | 81.5 | 81.0 | 80.4 | 79.2 | 76.7 | 78.0 | 80.2 | 80.7 | 80.9 | 80.7 | 80.1 |
| 2012 | 80.2 | 81.4 | 81.5 | 81.4 | 81.6 | 80.6 | 78.7 | 79.3 | 80.7 | 81.9 | 82.6 | 82.5 | 81.0 |
| 2013 | 81.2 | 82.5 | 82.7 | 82.3 | 82.1 | 80.1 | 77.8 | 76.7 | 80.8 | 81.8 | 82.5 | 82.1 | 81.1 |
| 2014 | 82.2 | 83.2 | 83.6 | 83.8 | 83.8 | 82.2 | 80.3 | 81.3 | 83.7 | 84.4 | 84.7 | 84.6 | 83.2 |
| 2015 | 84.1 | 85.0 | 85.2 | 85.5 | 85.3 | 83.3 | 82.0 | 83.1 | 85.3 | 85.4 | 85.8 | 86.1 | 84.7 |
| 2016 | 84.6 | 85.5 | 86.0 | 85.9 | 86.0 | 84.3 | 83.3 | 84.0 | 86.0 | 86.1 | 86.4 | 86.8 | 85.4 |
| 2017 | 85.5 | 86.2 | 86.6 | 86.9 | 86.9 | 85.5 | 83.1 | 83.4 | 85.9 | 86.4 | 86.9 | 86.9 | 85.9 |
| 2018 | 85.8 | 86.4 | 86.8 | 86.1 | 85.8 | 84.6 | 82.7 | 83.0 | 86.1 | 85.2 | 85.9 | 85.8 | 85.4 |
| 2019 | 84.7 | 85.1 | 85.6 | 85.3 | 85.2 | 83.6 | 82.5 | 83.3 | 85.9 | 86.0 | 86.4 | 86.6 | 85.0 |

## Employment by Industry: North Port-Sarasota-Bradenton, FL, 2011–2019

(Numbers in thousands, not seasonally adjusted)

| Industry and year | January | February | March | April | May | June | July | August | September | October | November | December | Annual average |
|---|---|---|---|---|---|---|---|---|---|---|---|---|---|
| **Total Nonfarm** | | | | | | | | | | | | | |
| 2011 | 236.4 | 239.6 | 241.2 | 243.2 | 241.0 | 237.0 | 235.1 | 238.4 | 238.2 | 239.6 | 243.9 | 246.1 | 240.0 |
| 2012 | 243.1 | 245.1 | 248.2 | 247.6 | 246.9 | 242.9 | 240.0 | 242.7 | 243.4 | 246.9 | 252.2 | 253.9 | 246.1 |
| 2013 | 250.6 | 254.4 | 256.2 | 256.3 | 256.4 | 252.3 | 251.1 | 253.9 | 254.5 | 258.5 | 265.0 | 267.0 | 256.4 |
| 2014 | 263.1 | 266.3 | 268.9 | 269.0 | 268.7 | 265.1 | 263.9 | 267.5 | 268.3 | 273.8 | 278.6 | 282.0 | 269.6 |
| 2015 | 278.7 | 281.4 | 284.3 | 284.4 | 284.3 | 281.1 | 278.1 | 280.9 | 281.2 | 286.4 | 290.1 | 293.2 | 283.7 |
| 2016 | 290.1 | 293.2 | 295.0 | 294.9 | 293.6 | 289.3 | 289.0 | 291.5 | 292.2 | 296.7 | 300.7 | 302.6 | 294.1 |
| 2017 | 299.6 | 301.4 | 304.2 | 302.4 | 301.2 | 297.3 | 295.8 | 299.1 | 292.5 | 302.8 | 306.5 | 308.7 | 301.0 |
| 2018 | 305.8 | 309.4 | 311.4 | 309.5 | 308.3 | 304.3 | 302.2 | 307.7 | 305.4 | 311.0 | 314.7 | 314.1 | 308.7 |
| 2019 | 313.5 | 316.5 | 317.4 | 315.9 | 314.6 | 309.4 | 307.2 | 309.5 | 310.0 | 312.5 | 317.3 | 319.0 | 313.6 |
| **Total Private** | | | | | | | | | | | | | |
| 2011 | 209.0 | 212.0 | 213.5 | 215.5 | 213.8 | 212.7 | 211.1 | 211.2 | 211.3 | 212.3 | 216.4 | 218.8 | 213.1 |
| 2012 | 216.0 | 217.7 | 220.7 | 220.3 | 219.7 | 218.7 | 215.9 | 216.7 | 216.6 | 219.6 | 224.9 | 226.6 | 219.5 |
| 2013 | 223.5 | 227.1 | 228.8 | 229.1 | 229.4 | 228.2 | 227.1 | 228.1 | 227.9 | 231.2 | 237.4 | 239.5 | 229.8 |
| 2014 | 236.2 | 239.2 | 241.5 | 241.7 | 241.5 | 241.0 | 239.7 | 241.6 | 241.6 | 246.2 | 250.7 | 254.3 | 242.9 |
| 2015 | 251.1 | 253.7 | 256.4 | 256.6 | 256.6 | 256.5 | 253.5 | 254.6 | 254.2 | 258.7 | 262.3 | 265.4 | 256.6 |
| 2016 | 262.4 | 265.4 | 267.0 | 266.9 | 265.6 | 264.2 | 263.9 | 264.6 | 264.7 | 268.7 | 272.8 | 274.8 | 266.8 |
| 2017 | 271.7 | 273.3 | 276.0 | 274.8 | 273.2 | 272.1 | 270.7 | 272.5 | 264.9 | 274.6 | 278.2 | 280.2 | 273.5 |
| 2018 | 277.4 | 280.9 | 282.8 | 280.9 | 279.7 | 278.7 | 276.6 | 280.4 | 277.1 | 282.1 | 285.7 | 285.3 | 280.6 |
| 2019 | 284.6 | 287.2 | 288.1 | 286.6 | 285.4 | 282.8 | 281.7 | 282.7 | 280.7 | 283.0 | 287.5 | 289.6 | 285.0 |
| **Goods Producing** | | | | | | | | | | | | | |
| 2011 | 27.5 | 27.7 | 27.9 | 28.4 | 28.6 | 29.1 | 29.1 | 29.2 | 29.4 | 29.3 | 29.5 | 29.6 | 28.8 |
| 2012 | 29.3 | 29.4 | 29.6 | 29.6 | 29.9 | 30.0 | 29.9 | 30.3 | 30.3 | 30.5 | 30.8 | 30.8 | 30.0 |
| 2013 | 30.4 | 30.7 | 30.8 | 30.9 | 31.2 | 31.4 | 31.5 | 31.8 | 31.9 | 32.2 | 32.7 | 32.9 | 31.5 |
| 2014 | 32.8 | 33.0 | 33.2 | 33.6 | 34.1 | 34.3 | 34.5 | 34.8 | 35.3 | 35.4 | 35.5 | 35.8 | 34.4 |
| 2015 | 35.3 | 35.6 | 35.7 | 36.0 | 36.3 | 36.6 | 36.5 | 36.9 | 37.1 | 37.3 | 37.3 | 37.6 | 36.5 |
| 2016 | 37.4 | 37.7 | 37.9 | 38.2 | 38.2 | 38.5 | 38.8 | 38.8 | 39.0 | 39.3 | 39.7 | 40.0 | 38.6 |
| 2017 | 39.2 | 39.5 | 39.9 | 39.7 | 39.9 | 40.2 | 40.1 | 40.4 | 38.9 | 40.7 | 41.0 | 41.1 | 40.1 |
| 2018 | 40.6 | 41.3 | 41.6 | 41.8 | 41.9 | 42.4 | 42.1 | 42.4 | 42.4 | 42.8 | 42.9 | 43.1 | 42.1 |
| 2019 | 43.2 | 43.2 | 43.6 | 43.5 | 43.4 | 43.7 | 43.4 | 43.4 | 43.1 | 43.4 | 43.6 | 43.9 | 43.5 |
| **Service-Providing** | | | | | | | | | | | | | |
| 2011 | 208.9 | 211.9 | 213.3 | 214.8 | 212.4 | 207.9 | 206.0 | 209.2 | 208.8 | 210.3 | 214.4 | 216.5 | 211.2 |
| 2012 | 213.8 | 215.7 | 218.6 | 218.0 | 217.0 | 212.9 | 210.1 | 212.4 | 213.1 | 216.4 | 221.4 | 223.1 | 216.0 |
| 2013 | 220.2 | 223.7 | 225.4 | 225.4 | 225.2 | 220.9 | 219.6 | 222.1 | 222.6 | 226.3 | 232.3 | 234.1 | 224.8 |
| 2014 | 230.3 | 233.3 | 235.7 | 235.4 | 234.6 | 230.8 | 229.4 | 232.7 | 233.0 | 238.4 | 243.1 | 246.2 | 235.2 |
| 2015 | 243.4 | 245.8 | 248.6 | 248.4 | 248.0 | 244.5 | 241.6 | 244.0 | 244.1 | 249.1 | 252.8 | 255.6 | 247.2 |
| 2016 | 252.7 | 255.5 | 257.1 | 256.7 | 255.4 | 250.8 | 250.2 | 252.7 | 253.2 | 257.4 | 261.0 | 262.6 | 255.4 |
| 2017 | 260.4 | 261.9 | 264.3 | 262.7 | 261.3 | 257.1 | 255.7 | 258.7 | 253.6 | 262.1 | 265.5 | 267.6 | 260.9 |
| 2018 | 265.2 | 268.1 | 269.8 | 267.7 | 266.4 | 261.9 | 260.1 | 265.3 | 263.0 | 268.2 | 271.8 | 271.0 | 266.5 |
| 2019 | 270.3 | 273.3 | 273.8 | 272.4 | 271.2 | 265.7 | 263.8 | 266.1 | 266.9 | 269.1 | 273.7 | 275.1 | 270.1 |
| **Mining, Logging, and Construction** | | | | | | | | | | | | | |
| 2011 | 14.5 | 14.6 | 14.8 | 14.9 | 14.9 | 15.1 | 15.1 | 15.1 | 15.4 | 15.3 | 15.4 | 15.4 | 15.0 |
| 2012 | 14.9 | 15.0 | 15.1 | 15.2 | 15.3 | 15.5 | 15.5 | 15.7 | 15.7 | 16.0 | 16.1 | 16.1 | 15.5 |
| 2013 | 15.8 | 16.0 | 16.1 | 16.2 | 16.4 | 16.6 | 16.8 | 17.1 | 17.1 | 17.4 | 17.6 | 17.8 | 16.7 |
| 2014 | 17.7 | 17.8 | 18.1 | 18.4 | 18.7 | 18.9 | 19.1 | 19.3 | 19.6 | 19.7 | 19.6 | 19.7 | 18.9 |
| 2015 | 19.5 | 19.6 | 19.7 | 19.9 | 20.1 | 20.2 | 20.2 | 20.5 | 20.7 | 20.9 | 21.0 | 21.2 | 20.3 |
| 2016 | 20.9 | 21.2 | 21.4 | 21.7 | 21.7 | 21.9 | 22.1 | 22.2 | 22.4 | 22.6 | 22.9 | 23.1 | 22.0 |
| 2017 | 22.6 | 22.8 | 23.2 | 23.1 | 23.2 | 23.5 | 23.5 | 23.8 | 22.7 | 24.2 | 24.4 | 24.5 | 23.5 |
| 2018 | 24.0 | 24.7 | 24.9 | 25.1 | 25.2 | 25.6 | 25.4 | 25.7 | 25.7 | 25.9 | 26.0 | 26.1 | 25.4 |
| 2019 | 26.1 | 26.1 | 26.4 | 26.4 | 26.3 | 26.5 | 26.3 | 26.4 | 26.3 | 26.5 | 26.3 | 26.6 | 26.4 |
| **Manufacturing** | | | | | | | | | | | | | |
| 2011 | 13.0 | 13.1 | 13.1 | 13.5 | 13.7 | 14.0 | 14.0 | 14.1 | 14.0 | 14.0 | 14.1 | 14.2 | 13.7 |
| 2012 | 14.4 | 14.4 | 14.5 | 14.4 | 14.6 | 14.5 | 14.4 | 14.6 | 14.6 | 14.5 | 14.7 | 14.7 | 14.5 |
| 2013 | 14.6 | 14.7 | 14.7 | 14.7 | 14.8 | 14.8 | 14.7 | 14.7 | 14.8 | 14.8 | 15.1 | 15.1 | 14.8 |
| 2014 | 15.1 | 15.2 | 15.1 | 15.2 | 15.4 | 15.4 | 15.4 | 15.5 | 15.7 | 15.7 | 15.9 | 16.1 | 15.5 |
| 2015 | 15.8 | 16.0 | 16.0 | 16.1 | 16.2 | 16.4 | 16.3 | 16.4 | 16.4 | 16.4 | 16.3 | 16.4 | 16.2 |
| 2016 | 16.5 | 16.5 | 16.5 | 16.5 | 16.5 | 16.6 | 16.7 | 16.6 | 16.6 | 16.7 | 16.8 | 16.9 | 16.6 |
| 2017 | 16.6 | 16.7 | 16.7 | 16.6 | 16.7 | 16.7 | 16.6 | 16.6 | 16.2 | 16.5 | 16.6 | 16.6 | 16.6 |
| 2018 | 16.6 | 16.6 | 16.7 | 16.7 | 16.7 | 16.8 | 16.7 | 16.7 | 16.7 | 16.9 | 16.9 | 17.0 | 16.8 |
| 2019 | 17.1 | 17.1 | 17.2 | 17.1 | 17.1 | 17.2 | 17.1 | 17.0 | 16.8 | 16.9 | 17.3 | 17.3 | 17.1 |

## Employment by Industry: North Port-Sarasota-Bradenton, FL, 2011–2019—*Continued*

(Numbers in thousands, not seasonally adjusted)

| Industry and year | January | February | March | April | May | June | July | August | September | October | November | December | Annual average |
|---|---|---|---|---|---|---|---|---|---|---|---|---|---|
| **Trade, Transportation, and Utilities** | | | | | | | | | | | | | |
| 2011 | 46.2 | 46.2 | 46.4 | 46.8 | 46.3 | 46.0 | 45.8 | 45.9 | 46.2 | 46.6 | 48.3 | 49.1 | 46.7 |
| 2012 | 48.1 | 48.1 | 48.5 | 48.5 | 48.8 | 48.5 | 47.8 | 47.9 | 48.2 | 49.1 | 50.6 | 51.5 | 48.8 |
| 2013 | 49.8 | 50.2 | 50.1 | 50.4 | 50.4 | 50.3 | 50.2 | 50.3 | 50.3 | 51.2 | 53.2 | 54.0 | 50.9 |
| 2014 | 52.0 | 52.3 | 52.5 | 52.7 | 52.6 | 52.5 | 51.8 | 52.3 | 52.3 | 53.1 | 55.1 | 56.2 | 53.0 |
| 2015 | 54.4 | 54.5 | 54.8 | 54.6 | 54.6 | 54.7 | 54.3 | 54.6 | 54.7 | 55.3 | 57.2 | 58.0 | 55.1 |
| 2016 | 56.1 | 56.4 | 56.3 | 56.6 | 56.4 | 56.1 | 55.8 | 56.2 | 56.8 | 57.9 | 59.0 | 59.5 | 56.9 |
| 2017 | 57.5 | 57.2 | 57.3 | 57.0 | 56.4 | 56.2 | 55.9 | 56.6 | 55.5 | 58.0 | 59.6 | 59.9 | 57.3 |
| 2018 | 58.6 | 58.9 | 59.0 | 58.5 | 58.3 | 58.2 | 58.0 | 58.7 | 59.2 | 60.6 | 61.8 | 61.6 | 59.3 |
| 2019 | 60.6 | 60.2 | 60.3 | 59.8 | 59.6 | 59.0 | 58.6 | 58.9 | 58.6 | 59.1 | 60.7 | 61.1 | 59.7 |
| **Wholesale Trade** | | | | | | | | | | | | | |
| 2011 | 7.2 | 7.3 | 7.4 | 7.3 | 7.1 | 7.2 | 7.2 | 7.2 | 7.3 | 7.2 | 7.2 | 7.3 | 7.2 |
| 2012 | 7.3 | 7.3 | 7.4 | 7.4 | 7.5 | 7.5 | 7.3 | 7.3 | 7.3 | 7.5 | 7.5 | 7.5 | 7.4 |
| 2013 | 7.4 | 7.5 | 7.6 | 7.6 | 7.6 | 7.6 | 7.5 | 7.6 | 7.6 | 7.7 | 7.8 | 7.8 | 7.6 |
| 2014 | 7.6 | 7.7 | 7.7 | 7.8 | 7.9 | 7.9 | 7.9 | 8.0 | 8.0 | 8.1 | 8.2 | 8.3 | 7.9 |
| 2015 | 8.1 | 8.2 | 8.3 | 8.3 | 8.3 | 8.3 | 8.3 | 8.3 | 8.4 | 8.3 | 8.3 | 8.3 | 8.3 |
| 2016 | 8.3 | 8.3 | 8.2 | 8.3 | 8.3 | 8.4 | 8.4 | 8.4 | 8.4 | 8.4 | 8.4 | 8.4 | 8.4 |
| 2017 | 8.4 | 8.4 | 8.4 | 8.4 | 8.4 | 8.4 | 8.4 | 8.4 | 8.3 | 8.4 | 8.5 | 8.6 | 8.4 |
| 2018 | 8.4 | 8.6 | 8.6 | 8.6 | 8.6 | 8.6 | 8.7 | 8.7 | 8.7 | 8.7 | 8.8 | 8.8 | 8.7 |
| 2019 | 8.8 | 8.8 | 8.9 | 8.8 | 8.9 | 8.9 | 8.7 | 8.8 | 8.8 | 8.8 | 8.8 | 8.9 | 8.8 |
| **Retail Trade** | | | | | | | | | | | | | |
| 2011 | 34.7 | 34.7 | 34.8 | 35.2 | 35.0 | 34.6 | 34.4 | 34.5 | 34.7 | 35.2 | 36.8 | 37.3 | 35.2 |
| 2012 | 36.4 | 36.4 | 36.7 | 36.9 | 37.0 | 36.7 | 36.3 | 36.4 | 36.7 | 37.3 | 38.6 | 39.2 | 37.1 |
| 2013 | 37.9 | 38.1 | 37.9 | 38.2 | 38.2 | 38.2 | 38.1 | 38.1 | 38.1 | 38.8 | 40.5 | 41.2 | 38.6 |
| 2014 | 39.7 | 39.9 | 40.1 | 40.2 | 40.0 | 39.8 | 39.2 | 39.5 | 39.5 | 40.2 | 41.9 | 42.6 | 40.2 |
| 2015 | 41.4 | 41.4 | 41.5 | 41.5 | 41.4 | 41.5 | 41.2 | 41.5 | 41.5 | 42.2 | 43.8 | 44.4 | 41.9 |
| 2016 | 42.9 | 43.2 | 43.3 | 43.4 | 43.2 | 42.8 | 42.6 | 43.0 | 43.5 | 44.5 | 45.3 | 45.4 | 43.6 |
| 2017 | 43.9 | 43.7 | 43.7 | 43.4 | 43.0 | 42.6 | 42.4 | 42.9 | 42.1 | 44.4 | 45.4 | 45.2 | 43.6 |
| 2018 | 44.4 | 44.6 | 44.8 | 44.3 | 44.1 | 44.0 | 43.6 | 44.4 | 44.9 | 46.0 | 46.8 | 46.4 | 44.9 |
| 2019 | 45.4 | 45.3 | 45.3 | 44.9 | 44.6 | 44.0 | 43.7 | 43.8 | 43.6 | 44.0 | 45.5 | 45.6 | 44.6 |
| **Transportation and Utilities** | | | | | | | | | | | | | |
| 2011 | 46.2 | 46.2 | 46.4 | 46.8 | 46.3 | 46.0 | 45.8 | 45.9 | 46.2 | 46.6 | 48.3 | 49.1 | 46.7 |
| 2012 | 48.1 | 48.1 | 48.5 | 48.5 | 48.8 | 48.5 | 47.8 | 47.9 | 48.2 | 49.1 | 50.6 | 51.5 | 48.8 |
| 2013 | 49.8 | 50.2 | 50.1 | 50.4 | 50.4 | 50.3 | 50.2 | 50.3 | 50.3 | 51.2 | 53.2 | 54.0 | 50.9 |
| 2014 | 52.0 | 52.3 | 52.5 | 52.7 | 52.6 | 52.5 | 51.8 | 52.3 | 52.3 | 53.1 | 55.1 | 56.2 | 53.0 |
| 2015 | 54.4 | 54.5 | 54.8 | 54.6 | 54.6 | 54.7 | 54.3 | 54.6 | 54.7 | 55.3 | 57.2 | 58.0 | 55.1 |
| 2016 | 56.1 | 56.4 | 56.3 | 56.6 | 56.4 | 56.1 | 55.8 | 56.2 | 56.8 | 57.9 | 59.0 | 59.5 | 56.9 |
| 2017 | 57.5 | 57.2 | 57.3 | 57.0 | 56.4 | 56.2 | 55.9 | 56.6 | 55.5 | 58.0 | 59.6 | 59.9 | 57.3 |
| 2018 | 58.6 | 58.9 | 59.0 | 58.5 | 58.3 | 58.2 | 58.0 | 58.7 | 59.2 | 60.6 | 61.8 | 61.6 | 59.3 |
| 2019 | 60.6 | 60.2 | 60.3 | 59.8 | 59.6 | 59.0 | 58.6 | 58.9 | 58.6 | 59.1 | 60.7 | 61.1 | 59.7 |
| **Information** | | | | | | | | | | | | | |
| 2011 | 3.4 | 3.5 | 3.5 | 3.5 | 3.4 | 3.4 | 3.4 | 3.4 | 3.4 | 3.4 | 3.4 | 3.4 | 3.4 |
| 2012 | 3.5 | 3.4 | 3.4 | 3.4 | 3.4 | 3.3 | 3.3 | 3.3 | 3.3 | 3.3 | 3.3 | 3.4 | 3.4 |
| 2013 | 3.3 | 3.3 | 3.4 | 3.4 | 3.4 | 3.4 | 3.4 | 3.4 | 3.3 | 3.3 | 3.3 | 3.3 | 3.4 |
| 2014 | 3.3 | 3.3 | 3.3 | 3.4 | 3.4 | 3.4 | 3.4 | 3.4 | 3.4 | 3.4 | 3.4 | 3.5 | 3.4 |
| 2015 | 3.4 | 3.5 | 3.5 | 3.5 | 3.5 | 3.5 | 3.6 | 3.6 | 3.6 | 3.6 | 3.6 | 3.6 | 3.5 |
| 2016 | 3.6 | 3.6 | 3.5 | 3.5 | 3.5 | 3.5 | 3.6 | 3.5 | 3.5 | 3.5 | 3.5 | 3.5 | 3.5 |
| 2017 | 3.5 | 3.4 | 3.5 | 3.5 | 3.5 | 3.5 | 3.5 | 3.4 | 3.4 | 3.4 | 3.4 | 3.4 | 3.5 |
| 2018 | 3.5 | 3.5 | 3.5 | 3.4 | 3.4 | 3.4 | 3.4 | 3.4 | 3.4 | 3.4 | 3.4 | 3.3 | 3.4 |
| 2019 | 3.5 | 3.5 | 3.4 | 3.4 | 3.5 | 3.5 | 3.5 | 3.4 | 3.4 | 3.4 | 3.4 | 3.4 | 3.4 |
| **Financial Activities** | | | | | | | | | | | | | |
| 2011 | 13.8 | 13.9 | 14.0 | 13.9 | 14.0 | 14.0 | 14.1 | 14.1 | 14.0 | 14.1 | 14.2 | 14.3 | 14.0 |
| 2012 | 14.1 | 14.1 | 14.2 | 14.4 | 14.4 | 14.4 | 14.4 | 14.4 | 14.3 | 14.4 | 14.5 | 14.5 | 14.3 |
| 2013 | 14.3 | 14.3 | 14.3 | 14.5 | 14.4 | 14.4 | 14.5 | 14.5 | 14.5 | 14.5 | 14.6 | 14.7 | 14.5 |
| 2014 | 14.3 | 14.4 | 14.4 | 14.4 | 14.4 | 14.4 | 14.5 | 14.5 | 14.5 | 14.7 | 14.7 | 14.7 | 14.5 |
| 2015 | 14.5 | 14.5 | 14.7 | 14.7 | 14.7 | 14.7 | 14.7 | 14.7 | 14.6 | 14.8 | 14.6 | 14.9 | 14.7 |
| 2016 | 14.7 | 14.7 | 14.9 | 14.9 | 14.8 | 14.9 | 14.6 | 14.7 | 14.7 | 14.8 | 14.8 | 14.9 | 14.8 |
| 2017 | 14.9 | 14.9 | 15.0 | 14.8 | 14.8 | 15.0 | 14.9 | 14.8 | 14.7 | 14.9 | 14.9 | 15.1 | 14.9 |
| 2018 | 14.8 | 14.8 | 14.9 | 14.7 | 14.7 | 14.7 | 14.8 | 14.8 | 14.7 | 14.9 | 15.0 | 15.0 | 14.8 |
| 2019 | 14.9 | 15.0 | 15.0 | 15.2 | 15.3 | 15.3 | 15.4 | 15.4 | 15.4 | 15.5 | 15.6 | 15.5 | 15.3 |

## Employment by Industry: North Port-Sarasota-Bradenton, FL, 2011–2019—*Continued*

(Numbers in thousands, not seasonally adjusted)

| Industry and year | January | February | March | April | May | June | July | August | September | October | November | December | Annual average |
|---|---|---|---|---|---|---|---|---|---|---|---|---|---|
| **Professional and Business Services** | | | | | | | | | | | | | |
| 2011 | 28.5 | 29.8 | 29.9 | 31.0 | 30.9 | 31.0 | 30.6 | 30.6 | 30.3 | 30.3 | 31.0 | 31.4 | 30.4 |
| 2012 | 30.4 | 30.7 | 31.4 | 31.3 | 31.1 | 31.4 | 31.0 | 31.0 | 31.0 | 32.1 | 33.6 | 33.7 | 31.6 |
| 2013 | 33.1 | 33.9 | 34.6 | 34.6 | 35.2 | 35.2 | 35.0 | 35.3 | 35.4 | 36.1 | 37.1 | 37.4 | 35.2 |
| 2014 | 36.2 | 36.7 | 37.1 | 37.2 | 38.0 | 38.2 | 37.9 | 38.4 | 38.5 | 39.7 | 40.2 | 41.0 | 38.3 |
| 2015 | 39.7 | 40.5 | 40.9 | 41.4 | 42.3 | 42.9 | 41.4 | 41.4 | 41.3 | 42.5 | 43.0 | 43.6 | 41.7 |
| 2016 | 43.8 | 44.8 | 45.4 | 45.6 | 45.2 | 45.1 | 45.7 | 45.2 | 45.1 | 45.6 | 46.5 | 46.9 | 45.4 |
| 2017 | 46.0 | 46.6 | 47.4 | 47.3 | 47.1 | 47.4 | 47.8 | 48.0 | 46.7 | 47.2 | 47.5 | 47.8 | 47.2 |
| 2018 | 47.5 | 47.7 | 48.0 | 47.4 | 47.4 | 47.8 | 46.6 | 49.0 | 46.3 | 46.9 | 47.3 | 46.7 | 47.4 |
| 2019 | 46.3 | 46.8 | 46.6 | 46.4 | 46.4 | 46.3 | 46.0 | 46.3 | 46.0 | 46.9 | 48.6 | 49.4 | 46.8 |
| **Education and Health Services** | | | | | | | | | | | | | |
| 2011 | 44.1 | 44.5 | 44.7 | 44.8 | 44.7 | 44.3 | 44.1 | 44.3 | 44.4 | 44.7 | 44.9 | 45.3 | 44.6 |
| 2012 | 44.7 | 45.1 | 45.4 | 45.2 | 45.2 | 44.8 | 44.3 | 44.7 | 45.1 | 45.4 | 45.9 | 45.9 | 45.1 |
| 2013 | 45.6 | 46.1 | 46.1 | 46.2 | 46.2 | 45.6 | 45.4 | 45.8 | 46.0 | 46.6 | 47.0 | 47.2 | 46.2 |
| 2014 | 47.1 | 47.7 | 48.0 | 48.0 | 48.1 | 47.8 | 47.4 | 48.0 | 48.0 | 48.7 | 49.0 | 49.5 | 48.1 |
| 2015 | 49.3 | 49.6 | 49.8 | 49.8 | 49.9 | 49.7 | 49.5 | 49.9 | 49.9 | 50.7 | 51.0 | 51.3 | 50.0 |
| 2016 | 50.6 | 51.0 | 51.1 | 50.9 | 51.2 | 50.7 | 50.9 | 51.5 | 51.7 | 52.3 | 52.9 | 53.2 | 51.5 |
| 2017 | 52.6 | 53.0 | 52.9 | 53.1 | 53.0 | 52.6 | 52.0 | 52.7 | 52.0 | 53.5 | 53.6 | 54.0 | 52.9 |
| 2018 | 53.5 | 54.2 | 54.4 | 54.4 | 54.2 | 53.8 | 53.8 | 54.5 | 54.6 | 55.2 | 55.7 | 55.8 | 54.5 |
| 2019 | 55.5 | 56.1 | 56.0 | 56.0 | 55.9 | 55.1 | 55.6 | 56.3 | 56.2 | 56.1 | 56.0 | 56.2 | 55.9 |
| **Leisure and Hospitality** | | | | | | | | | | | | | |
| 2011 | 34.4 | 35.2 | 35.9 | 35.8 | 34.7 | 33.8 | 33.1 | 32.9 | 32.7 | 33.2 | 34.4 | 35.0 | 34.3 |
| 2012 | 35.4 | 36.3 | 37.5 | 37.1 | 36.2 | 35.6 | 34.7 | 34.6 | 33.8 | 34.3 | 35.6 | 36.0 | 35.6 |
| 2013 | 36.3 | 37.8 | 38.6 | 38.1 | 37.6 | 36.9 | 36.3 | 36.1 | 35.5 | 36.1 | 38.0 | 38.5 | 37.2 |
| 2014 | 38.8 | 39.9 | 41.0 | 40.4 | 39.0 | 38.6 | 38.5 | 38.4 | 37.8 | 39.2 | 40.6 | 41.4 | 39.5 |
| 2015 | 42.3 | 43.1 | 44.4 | 44.0 | 42.7 | 41.9 | 41.1 | 41.1 | 40.5 | 41.8 | 42.7 | 43.3 | 42.4 |
| 2016 | 43.1 | 44.0 | 44.6 | 44.0 | 43.1 | 42.3 | 41.6 | 41.8 | 41.0 | 42.4 | 43.4 | 43.8 | 42.9 |
| 2017 | 45.1 | 45.7 | 46.9 | 46.2 | 45.3 | 44.0 | 43.3 | 43.2 | 40.6 | 43.3 | 44.4 | 44.9 | 44.4 |
| 2018 | 45.1 | 46.4 | 47.1 | 46.4 | 45.5 | 44.2 | 43.9 | 43.5 | 42.4 | 43.9 | 45.1 | 45.2 | 44.9 |
| 2019 | 46.0 | 47.6 | 48.4 | 47.6 | 46.6 | 45.3 | 44.7 | 44.4 | 43.4 | 43.9 | 44.7 | 45.2 | 45.7 |
| **Other Services** | | | | | | | | | | | | | |
| 2011 | 11.1 | 11.2 | 11.2 | 11.3 | 11.2 | 11.1 | 10.9 | 10.8 | 10.9 | 10.7 | 10.7 | 10.7 | 11.0 |
| 2012 | 10.5 | 10.6 | 10.7 | 10.8 | 10.7 | 10.7 | 10.5 | 10.5 | 10.6 | 10.5 | 10.6 | 10.8 | 10.6 |
| 2013 | 10.7 | 10.8 | 10.9 | 11.0 | 11.0 | 11.0 | 10.8 | 10.9 | 11.0 | 11.2 | 11.5 | 11.5 | 11.0 |
| 2014 | 11.7 | 11.9 | 12.0 | 12.0 | 11.9 | 11.8 | 11.7 | 11.8 | 11.8 | 12.0 | 12.2 | 12.2 | 11.9 |
| 2015 | 12.2 | 12.4 | 12.6 | 12.6 | 12.6 | 12.5 | 12.4 | 12.4 | 12.5 | 12.7 | 12.9 | 13.1 | 12.6 |
| 2016 | 13.1 | 13.2 | 13.3 | 13.2 | 13.2 | 13.1 | 12.9 | 12.9 | 12.9 | 12.9 | 13.0 | 13.0 | 13.1 |
| 2017 | 12.9 | 13.0 | 13.1 | 13.2 | 13.2 | 13.2 | 13.2 | 13.4 | 13.1 | 13.6 | 13.8 | 14.0 | 13.3 |
| 2018 | 13.8 | 14.1 | 14.3 | 14.3 | 14.3 | 14.2 | 14.0 | 14.1 | 14.1 | 14.4 | 14.5 | 14.6 | 14.2 |
| 2019 | 14.6 | 14.8 | 14.8 | 14.7 | 14.7 | 14.6 | 14.5 | 14.6 | 14.6 | 14.7 | 14.9 | 14.9 | 14.7 |
| **Government** | | | | | | | | | | | | | |
| 2011 | 27.4 | 27.6 | 27.7 | 27.7 | 27.2 | 24.3 | 24.0 | 27.2 | 26.9 | 27.3 | 27.5 | 27.3 | 26.8 |
| 2012 | 27.1 | 27.4 | 27.5 | 27.3 | 27.2 | 24.2 | 24.1 | 26.0 | 26.8 | 27.3 | 27.3 | 27.3 | 26.6 |
| 2013 | 27.1 | 27.3 | 27.4 | 27.2 | 27.0 | 24.1 | 24.0 | 25.8 | 26.6 | 27.3 | 27.6 | 27.5 | 26.6 |
| 2014 | 26.9 | 27.1 | 27.4 | 27.3 | 27.2 | 24.1 | 24.2 | 25.9 | 26.7 | 27.6 | 27.9 | 27.7 | 26.7 |
| 2015 | 27.6 | 27.7 | 27.9 | 27.8 | 27.7 | 24.6 | 24.6 | 26.3 | 27.0 | 27.7 | 27.8 | 27.8 | 27.0 |
| 2016 | 27.7 | 27.8 | 28.0 | 28.0 | 28.0 | 25.1 | 25.1 | 26.9 | 27.5 | 28.0 | 27.9 | 27.8 | 27.3 |
| 2017 | 27.9 | 28.1 | 28.2 | 27.6 | 28.0 | 25.2 | 25.1 | 26.6 | 27.6 | 28.2 | 28.3 | 28.5 | 27.4 |
| 2018 | 28.4 | 28.5 | 28.6 | 28.6 | 28.6 | 25.6 | 25.6 | 27.3 | 28.3 | 28.9 | 29.0 | 28.8 | 28.0 |
| 2019 | 28.9 | 29.3 | 29.3 | 29.3 | 29.2 | 26.6 | 25.5 | 26.8 | 29.3 | 29.5 | 29.8 | 29.4 | 28.6 |

## Employment by Industry: Dayton, OH, 2011–2019

(Numbers in thousands, not seasonally adjusted)

| Industry and year | January | February | March | April | May | June | July | August | September | October | November | December | Annual average |
|---|---|---|---|---|---|---|---|---|---|---|---|---|---|
| **Total Nonfarm** | | | | | | | | | | | | | |
| 2011 | 358.0 | 359.4 | 362.3 | 366.7 | 367.8 | 366.3 | 362.3 | 363.2 | 368.0 | 369.4 | 371.3 | 370.5 | 365.4 |
| 2012 | 363.2 | 365.4 | 367.7 | 369.8 | 371.0 | 371.9 | 365.8 | 367.0 | 369.1 | 369.9 | 372.1 | 372.1 | 368.8 |
| 2013 | 360.9 | 363.7 | 365.2 | 367.9 | 371.2 | 370.4 | 366.0 | 367.8 | 369.1 | 370.4 | 374.1 | 373.1 | 368.3 |
| 2014 | 363.3 | 365.2 | 368.2 | 370.9 | 372.9 | 373.7 | 370.9 | 373.3 | 375.0 | 377.4 | 379.4 | 380.3 | 372.5 |
| 2015 | 370.3 | 371.9 | 373.5 | 378.1 | 380.7 | 380.5 | 380.4 | 381.4 | 380.9 | 384.7 | 387.0 | 388.1 | 379.8 |
| 2016 | 377.4 | 380.0 | 382.5 | 384.5 | 385.3 | 384.0 | 385.4 | 385.1 | 386.3 | 387.4 | 389.5 | 389.9 | 384.8 |
| 2017 | 380.5 | 382.5 | 383.9 | 388.3 | 389.3 | 388.6 | 389.0 | 389.6 | 389.3 | 391.4 | 393.9 | 393.0 | 388.3 |
| 2018 | 384.3 | 386.6 | 388.5 | 390.3 | 391.3 | 390.3 | 390.3 | 391.2 | 390.2 | 391.7 | 393.3 | 393.8 | 390.2 |
| 2019 | 386.3 | 386.3 | 388.7 | 391.5 | 394.1 | 392.2 | 392.4 | 393.1 | 392.2 | 395.3 | 395.3 | 395.4 | 391.9 |
| **Total Private** | | | | | | | | | | | | | |
| 2011 | 294.0 | 294.5 | 297.0 | 301.3 | 301.6 | 301.7 | 300.6 | 301.8 | 304.1 | 304.6 | 306.3 | 307.4 | 301.2 |
| 2012 | 300.7 | 301.3 | 303.4 | 305.4 | 306.3 | 308.0 | 305.9 | 306.3 | 305.8 | 306.0 | 308.0 | 308.2 | 305.4 |
| 2013 | 299.4 | 300.3 | 301.7 | 304.6 | 307.3 | 308.4 | 306.5 | 307.7 | 306.3 | 307.4 | 310.7 | 310.3 | 305.9 |
| 2014 | 302.5 | 302.4 | 305.1 | 308.7 | 310.7 | 312.6 | 312.3 | 313.7 | 312.2 | 314.1 | 315.8 | 317.0 | 310.6 |
| 2015 | 309.0 | 308.9 | 310.8 | 314.5 | 318.4 | 318.7 | 319.0 | 319.8 | 318.3 | 321.0 | 323.1 | 324.2 | 317.1 |
| 2016 | 316.0 | 316.7 | 319.2 | 320.5 | 322.8 | 321.6 | 323.8 | 323.4 | 322.5 | 323.5 | 325.3 | 325.8 | 321.8 |
| 2017 | 318.6 | 319.1 | 320.4 | 324.3 | 327.0 | 327.3 | 328.0 | 328.7 | 326.8 | 328.2 | 330.2 | 329.6 | 325.7 |
| 2018 | 323.0 | 323.7 | 325.5 | 327.3 | 329.7 | 329.6 | 330.2 | 330.6 | 328.1 | 328.8 | 330.3 | 331.0 | 328.2 |
| 2019 | 325.3 | 324.1 | 326.2 | 328.6 | 331.9 | 331.2 | 331.6 | 331.8 | 329.8 | 332.6 | 332.1 | 332.6 | 329.8 |
| **Goods Producing** | | | | | | | | | | | | | |
| 2011 | 46.4 | 46.4 | 47.2 | 47.7 | 48.5 | 49.0 | 49.4 | 49.6 | 49.6 | 49.6 | 49.7 | 49.6 | 48.6 |
| 2012 | 48.5 | 48.4 | 48.8 | 49.2 | 49.7 | 50.4 | 50.1 | 50.1 | 50.0 | 49.8 | 49.8 | 49.8 | 49.6 |
| 2013 | 48.4 | 48.5 | 48.9 | 48.9 | 49.8 | 50.3 | 50.0 | 49.9 | 49.6 | 49.7 | 49.9 | 49.7 | 49.5 |
| 2014 | 48.5 | 48.7 | 49.3 | 49.7 | 50.6 | 51.4 | 51.5 | 51.8 | 51.6 | 51.6 | 51.6 | 51.5 | 50.7 |
| 2015 | 50.5 | 50.6 | 50.7 | 51.5 | 52.2 | 52.5 | 52.8 | 53.1 | 52.9 | 53.3 | 53.0 | 53.2 | 52.2 |
| 2016 | 52.1 | 52.2 | 52.6 | 52.9 | 53.4 | 53.6 | 54.4 | 54.3 | 54.5 | 54.5 | 54.4 | 54.3 | 53.6 |
| 2017 | 53.3 | 53.2 | 53.4 | 53.9 | 54.5 | 55.3 | 55.4 | 55.5 | 55.2 | 55.3 | 55.2 | 55.2 | 54.6 |
| 2018 | 54.2 | 54.5 | 54.8 | 55.6 | 56.2 | 56.6 | 56.8 | 57.1 | 56.7 | 57.0 | 56.8 | 57.0 | 56.1 |
| 2019 | 56.3 | 56.3 | 56.7 | 57.0 | 57.3 | 57.9 | 58.1 | 57.9 | 57.5 | 57.9 | 57.8 | 57.8 | 57.4 |
| **Service-Providing** | | | | | | | | | | | | | |
| 2011 | 311.6 | 313.0 | 315.1 | 319.0 | 319.3 | 317.3 | 312.9 | 313.6 | 318.4 | 319.8 | 321.6 | 320.9 | 316.9 |
| 2012 | 314.7 | 317.0 | 318.9 | 320.6 | 321.3 | 321.5 | 315.7 | 316.9 | 319.1 | 320.1 | 322.3 | 322.3 | 319.2 |
| 2013 | 312.5 | 315.2 | 316.3 | 319.0 | 321.4 | 320.1 | 316.0 | 317.9 | 319.5 | 320.7 | 324.2 | 323.4 | 318.9 |
| 2014 | 314.8 | 316.5 | 318.9 | 321.2 | 322.3 | 322.3 | 319.4 | 321.5 | 323.4 | 325.8 | 327.8 | 328.8 | 321.9 |
| 2015 | 319.8 | 321.3 | 322.8 | 326.6 | 328.5 | 328.0 | 327.6 | 328.3 | 328.0 | 331.4 | 334.0 | 334.9 | 327.6 |
| 2016 | 325.3 | 327.8 | 329.9 | 331.6 | 331.9 | 330.4 | 331.0 | 330.8 | 331.8 | 332.9 | 335.1 | 335.6 | 331.2 |
| 2017 | 327.2 | 329.3 | 330.5 | 334.4 | 334.8 | 333.3 | 333.6 | 334.1 | 334.1 | 336.1 | 338.7 | 337.8 | 333.7 |
| 2018 | 330.1 | 332.1 | 333.7 | 334.7 | 335.1 | 333.7 | 333.5 | 334.1 | 333.5 | 334.7 | 336.5 | 336.8 | 334.0 |
| 2019 | 330.0 | 330.0 | 332.0 | 334.5 | 336.8 | 334.3 | 334.3 | 335.2 | 334.7 | 337.4 | 337.5 | 337.6 | 334.5 |
| **Mining, Logging, and Construction** | | | | | | | | | | | | | |
| 2011 | 9.5 | 9.5 | 9.8 | 10.4 | 11.1 | 11.5 | 11.8 | 11.8 | 11.7 | 11.4 | 11.4 | 11.0 | 10.9 |
| 2012 | 10.5 | 10.3 | 10.5 | 10.9 | 11.4 | 11.6 | 11.5 | 11.4 | 11.3 | 11.2 | 11.1 | 10.9 | 11.1 |
| 2013 | 10.1 | 10.2 | 10.6 | 10.8 | 11.5 | 11.8 | 11.7 | 11.7 | 11.6 | 11.6 | 11.6 | 11.2 | 11.2 |
| 2014 | 10.4 | 10.4 | 10.9 | 11.2 | 11.9 | 12.3 | 12.6 | 12.5 | 12.3 | 12.2 | 12.0 | 11.8 | 11.7 |
| 2015 | 11.1 | 11.0 | 11.2 | 12.0 | 12.4 | 12.6 | 12.8 | 12.8 | 12.8 | 12.9 | 12.7 | 12.6 | 12.2 |
| 2016 | 11.6 | 11.6 | 11.9 | 12.3 | 12.6 | 12.8 | 12.9 | 12.8 | 12.7 | 12.7 | 12.5 | 12.1 | 12.4 |
| 2017 | 11.5 | 11.6 | 11.8 | 12.3 | 12.7 | 13.1 | 13.2 | 13.3 | 13.1 | 13.0 | 12.9 | 12.7 | 12.6 |
| 2018 | 11.8 | 11.9 | 12.2 | 12.8 | 13.4 | 13.6 | 13.9 | 14.0 | 13.7 | 13.7 | 13.5 | 13.2 | 13.1 |
| 2019 | 12.7 | 12.5 | 12.9 | 13.3 | 13.6 | 13.9 | 14.1 | 14.2 | 14.0 | 14.0 | 13.8 | 13.5 | 13.5 |
| **Manufacturing** | | | | | | | | | | | | | |
| 2011 | 36.9 | 36.9 | 37.4 | 37.3 | 37.4 | 37.5 | 37.6 | 37.8 | 37.9 | 38.2 | 38.3 | 38.6 | 37.7 |
| 2012 | 38.0 | 38.1 | 38.3 | 38.3 | 38.3 | 38.8 | 38.6 | 38.7 | 38.7 | 38.6 | 38.7 | 38.9 | 38.5 |
| 2013 | 38.3 | 38.3 | 38.3 | 38.1 | 38.3 | 38.5 | 38.3 | 38.2 | 38.0 | 38.1 | 38.3 | 38.5 | 38.3 |
| 2014 | 38.1 | 38.3 | 38.4 | 38.5 | 38.7 | 39.1 | 38.9 | 39.3 | 39.3 | 39.4 | 39.6 | 39.7 | 38.9 |
| 2015 | 39.4 | 39.6 | 39.5 | 39.5 | 39.8 | 39.9 | 40.0 | 40.3 | 40.1 | 40.4 | 40.3 | 40.6 | 40.0 |
| 2016 | 40.5 | 40.6 | 40.7 | 40.6 | 40.8 | 40.8 | 41.5 | 41.5 | 41.8 | 41.8 | 41.9 | 42.2 | 41.2 |
| 2017 | 41.8 | 41.6 | 41.6 | 41.6 | 41.8 | 42.2 | 42.2 | 42.2 | 42.1 | 42.3 | 42.3 | 42.5 | 42.0 |
| 2018 | 42.4 | 42.6 | 42.6 | 42.8 | 42.8 | 43.0 | 42.9 | 43.1 | 43.0 | 43.3 | 43.3 | 43.8 | 43.0 |
| 2019 | 43.6 | 43.8 | 43.8 | 43.7 | 43.7 | 44.0 | 44.0 | 43.7 | 43.5 | 43.9 | 44.0 | 44.3 | 43.8 |

## Employment by Industry: Dayton, OH, 2011–2019—*Continued*

(Numbers in thousands, not seasonally adjusted)

| Industry and year | January | February | March | April | May | June | July | August | September | October | November | December | Annual average |
|---|---|---|---|---|---|---|---|---|---|---|---|---|---|
| **Trade, Transportation, and Utilities** | | | | | | | | | | | | | |
| 2011 | 60.1 | 59.3 | 59.7 | 60.5 | 60.9 | 61.1 | 60.9 | 61.1 | 61.1 | 62.1 | 63.7 | 64.7 | 61.3 |
| 2012 | 61.9 | 61.3 | 62.0 | 62.2 | 62.7 | 62.6 | 62.3 | 62.5 | 62.4 | 63.1 | 64.8 | 65.3 | 62.8 |
| 2013 | 62.2 | 61.8 | 62.0 | 62.5 | 63.0 | 63.1 | 63.0 | 63.1 | 62.9 | 63.6 | 65.8 | 66.5 | 63.3 |
| 2014 | 63.5 | 62.9 | 63.3 | 63.8 | 64.0 | 64.2 | 64.0 | 64.0 | 63.9 | 64.7 | 66.4 | 67.3 | 64.3 |
| 2015 | 64.7 | 64.4 | 64.5 | 64.9 | 65.7 | 65.7 | 65.5 | 65.5 | 65.0 | 65.6 | 67.2 | 68.1 | 65.6 |
| 2016 | 64.9 | 64.4 | 64.7 | 64.7 | 65.1 | 65.0 | 65.1 | 65.2 | 64.6 | 65.3 | 66.7 | 67.5 | 65.3 |
| 2017 | 64.9 | 64.4 | 64.3 | 64.7 | 65.2 | 65.3 | 65.7 | 65.7 | 65.0 | 65.9 | 67.8 | 68.2 | 65.6 |
| 2018 | 65.9 | 65.5 | 65.6 | 65.9 | 66.4 | 66.4 | 66.7 | 66.2 | 65.5 | 65.6 | 67.2 | 67.7 | 66.2 |
| 2019 | 66.0 | 64.7 | 64.8 | 64.8 | 65.4 | 65.3 | 65.1 | 65.3 | 65.0 | 65.0 | 66.1 | 66.6 | 65.3 |
| **Wholesale Trade** | | | | | | | | | | | | | |
| 2011 | 12.0 | 11.9 | 12.0 | 12.1 | 12.2 | 12.3 | 12.4 | 12.4 | 12.4 | 12.6 | 12.5 | 12.6 | 12.3 |
| 2012 | 12.7 | 12.8 | 12.9 | 12.6 | 12.7 | 12.7 | 12.9 | 12.9 | 12.8 | 12.9 | 12.8 | 12.9 | 12.8 |
| 2013 | 12.7 | 12.6 | 12.6 | 12.6 | 12.6 | 12.7 | 12.6 | 12.5 | 12.5 | 12.5 | 12.6 | 12.6 | 12.6 |
| 2014 | 12.6 | 12.6 | 12.6 | 12.7 | 12.8 | 12.9 | 12.8 | 12.7 | 12.8 | 12.8 | 12.8 | 12.9 | 12.8 |
| 2015 | 13.1 | 13.1 | 13.1 | 13.2 | 13.2 | 13.2 | 13.3 | 13.2 | 13.0 | 13.0 | 13.0 | 13.0 | 13.1 |
| 2016 | 12.9 | 12.9 | 12.9 | 12.8 | 12.9 | 12.9 | 12.9 | 12.9 | 12.8 | 12.8 | 12.8 | 12.9 | 12.9 |
| 2017 | 12.8 | 12.9 | 12.9 | 13.2 | 13.3 | 13.4 | 13.5 | 13.5 | 13.4 | 13.6 | 13.7 | 13.8 | 13.3 |
| 2018 | 13.8 | 13.9 | 14.0 | 14.0 | 14.1 | 14.2 | 14.2 | 14.1 | 14.0 | 14.0 | 14.0 | 14.0 | 14.0 |
| 2019 | 14.0 | 14.1 | 14.1 | 14.1 | 14.1 | 14.3 | 14.1 | 14.1 | 14.0 | 14.1 | 14.1 | 14.0 | 14.1 |
| **Retail Trade** | | | | | | | | | | | | | |
| 2011 | 37.4 | 36.8 | 37.1 | 37.7 | 37.9 | 38.0 | 37.7 | 37.8 | 37.7 | 38.6 | 40.2 | 40.8 | 38.1 |
| 2012 | 38.3 | 37.6 | 38.2 | 38.5 | 38.8 | 38.6 | 38.2 | 38.3 | 38.2 | 38.7 | 40.3 | 40.5 | 38.7 |
| 2013 | 38.2 | 37.8 | 38.1 | 38.6 | 39.0 | 38.9 | 38.8 | 38.9 | 38.6 | 39.2 | 40.9 | 41.3 | 39.0 |
| 2014 | 38.5 | 38.1 | 38.5 | 38.9 | 38.9 | 39.0 | 38.7 | 38.8 | 38.7 | 39.5 | 41.0 | 41.4 | 39.2 |
| 2015 | 38.7 | 38.5 | 38.6 | 38.9 | 39.4 | 39.5 | 39.2 | 39.3 | 39.0 | 39.5 | 40.9 | 41.5 | 39.4 |
| 2016 | 39.2 | 39.0 | 39.2 | 39.5 | 39.8 | 39.6 | 39.6 | 39.7 | 39.2 | 39.8 | 40.9 | 41.4 | 39.7 |
| 2017 | 39.5 | 38.9 | 38.9 | 39.1 | 39.4 | 39.4 | 39.6 | 39.6 | 39.1 | 39.8 | 41.4 | 41.4 | 39.7 |
| 2018 | 39.6 | 39.1 | 39.1 | 39.3 | 39.8 | 39.5 | 39.7 | 39.5 | 38.9 | 38.9 | 40.3 | 40.5 | 39.5 |
| 2019 | 38.8 | 37.7 | 37.9 | 38.0 | 38.4 | 38.2 | 38.3 | 38.4 | 38.3 | 38.2 | 39.4 | 39.5 | 38.4 |
| **Transportation and Utilities** | | | | | | | | | | | | | |
| 2011 | 10.7 | 10.6 | 10.6 | 10.7 | 10.8 | 10.8 | 10.8 | 10.9 | 11.0 | 10.9 | 11.0 | 11.3 | 10.8 |
| 2012 | 10.9 | 10.9 | 10.9 | 11.1 | 11.2 | 11.3 | 11.2 | 11.3 | 11.4 | 11.5 | 11.7 | 11.9 | 11.3 |
| 2013 | 11.3 | 11.4 | 11.3 | 11.3 | 11.4 | 11.5 | 11.6 | 11.7 | 11.8 | 11.9 | 12.3 | 12.6 | 11.7 |
| 2014 | 12.4 | 12.2 | 12.2 | 12.2 | 12.3 | 12.3 | 12.5 | 12.5 | 12.4 | 12.4 | 12.6 | 13.0 | 12.4 |
| 2015 | 12.9 | 12.8 | 12.8 | 12.8 | 13.1 | 13.0 | 13.0 | 13.0 | 13.0 | 13.1 | 13.3 | 13.6 | 13.0 |
| 2016 | 12.8 | 12.5 | 12.6 | 12.4 | 12.4 | 12.5 | 12.6 | 12.6 | 12.6 | 12.7 | 13.0 | 13.2 | 12.7 |
| 2017 | 12.6 | 12.6 | 12.5 | 12.4 | 12.5 | 12.5 | 12.6 | 12.6 | 12.5 | 12.5 | 12.7 | 13.0 | 12.6 |
| 2018 | 12.5 | 12.5 | 12.5 | 12.6 | 12.5 | 12.7 | 12.8 | 12.6 | 12.6 | 12.7 | 12.9 | 13.2 | 12.7 |
| 2019 | 13.2 | 12.9 | 12.8 | 12.7 | 12.9 | 12.8 | 12.7 | 12.8 | 12.7 | 12.7 | 12.6 | 13.1 | 12.8 |
| **Information** | | | | | | | | | | | | | |
| 2011 | 9.8 | 9.8 | 9.8 | 9.8 | 9.7 | 9.8 | 9.8 | 9.7 | 9.7 | 9.5 | 9.4 | 9.3 | 9.7 |
| 2012 | 9.2 | 9.1 | 9.0 | 9.0 | 8.9 | 8.9 | 9.0 | 8.8 | 8.8 | 8.7 | 8.7 | 8.7 | 8.9 |
| 2013 | 8.7 | 8.7 | 8.7 | 8.7 | 8.7 | 8.8 | 8.8 | 8.7 | 8.6 | 8.5 | 8.5 | 8.5 | 8.7 |
| 2014 | 8.4 | 8.4 | 8.4 | 8.5 | 8.5 | 8.6 | 8.6 | 8.5 | 8.4 | 8.4 | 8.4 | 8.5 | 8.5 |
| 2015 | 8.4 | 8.4 | 8.4 | 8.5 | 8.5 | 8.6 | 8.6 | 8.6 | 8.5 | 8.5 | 8.5 | 8.5 | 8.5 |
| 2016 | 8.4 | 8.5 | 8.5 | 8.5 | 8.5 | 8.5 | 8.5 | 8.4 | 8.3 | 8.4 | 8.4 | 8.4 | 8.4 |
| 2017 | 8.4 | 8.3 | 8.3 | 8.4 | 8.4 | 8.4 | 8.5 | 8.4 | 8.3 | 8.3 | 8.3 | 8.3 | 8.4 |
| 2018 | 8.3 | 8.3 | 8.3 | 8.3 | 8.2 | 8.3 | 8.2 | 8.1 | 8.0 | 7.9 | 7.9 | 7.9 | 8.1 |
| 2019 | 7.9 | 7.9 | 7.9 | 7.8 | 7.7 | 7.8 | 7.8 | 7.6 | 7.5 | 7.5 | 7.5 | 7.5 | 7.7 |
| **Financial Activities** | | | | | | | | | | | | | |
| 2011 | 16.3 | 16.3 | 16.3 | 16.4 | 16.4 | 16.5 | 16.5 | 16.5 | 16.4 | 16.4 | 16.5 | 16.6 | 16.4 |
| 2012 | 16.4 | 16.4 | 16.5 | 16.7 | 16.7 | 16.8 | 17.0 | 17.0 | 17.0 | 17.0 | 17.1 | 17.1 | 16.8 |
| 2013 | 16.8 | 16.9 | 16.8 | 16.9 | 17.1 | 17.1 | 17.1 | 17.1 | 17.0 | 17.0 | 17.1 | 17.1 | 17.0 |
| 2014 | 16.9 | 17.0 | 17.1 | 17.1 | 17.3 | 17.4 | 17.4 | 17.7 | 17.5 | 17.6 | 17.6 | 17.6 | 17.4 |
| 2015 | 17.3 | 17.2 | 17.3 | 17.3 | 17.5 | 17.6 | 17.6 | 17.7 | 17.5 | 17.8 | 17.8 | 17.8 | 17.5 |
| 2016 | 17.5 | 17.6 | 17.6 | 17.7 | 17.7 | 17.8 | 17.9 | 17.8 | 17.8 | 17.9 | 18.0 | 18.2 | 17.8 |
| 2017 | 17.8 | 17.9 | 17.8 | 18.0 | 18.0 | 18.2 | 18.2 | 18.2 | 18.2 | 18.2 | 18.1 | 18.2 | 18.1 |
| 2018 | 18.2 | 18.3 | 18.2 | 18.2 | 18.3 | 18.4 | 18.5 | 18.4 | 18.2 | 18.3 | 18.3 | 18.2 | 18.3 |
| 2019 | 18.1 | 18.1 | 18.2 | 18.1 | 18.3 | 18.3 | 18.4 | 18.5 | 18.4 | 18.2 | 18.2 | 18.2 | 18.3 |

## Employment by Industry: Dayton, OH, 2011–2019—*Continued*

(Numbers in thousands, not seasonally adjusted)

| Industry and year | January | February | March | April | May | June | July | August | September | October | November | December | Annual average |
|---|---|---|---|---|---|---|---|---|---|---|---|---|---|
| **Professional and Business Services** | | | | | | | | | | | | | |
| 2011 | 45.6 | 45.7 | 46.2 | 46.9 | 46.6 | 46.9 | 47.0 | 47.5 | 47.4 | 47.3 | 47.3 | 47.7 | 46.8 |
| 2012 | 46.9 | 47.1 | 47.1 | 47.4 | 47.4 | 47.7 | 47.8 | 47.8 | 47.3 | 47.7 | 47.4 | 47.4 | 47.4 |
| 2013 | 46.3 | 46.3 | 46.1 | 47.2 | 47.3 | 47.6 | 47.5 | 48.0 | 47.8 | 48.1 | 48.5 | 48.0 | 47.4 |
| 2014 | 47.2 | 47.0 | 47.4 | 48.5 | 48.6 | 49.2 | 49.6 | 49.8 | 49.2 | 49.9 | 50.0 | 49.9 | 48.9 |
| | | | | | | | | | | | | | |
| 2015 | 48.3 | 48.1 | 48.7 | 49.8 | 50.6 | 50.9 | 51.3 | 51.1 | 50.8 | 51.4 | 51.5 | 51.2 | 50.3 |
| 2016 | 50.1 | 50.2 | 51.0 | 50.8 | 51.0 | 50.7 | 51.2 | 50.9 | 50.6 | 50.9 | 51.1 | 50.8 | 50.8 |
| 2017 | 49.1 | 49.5 | 49.9 | 51.0 | 51.4 | 51.5 | 51.6 | 51.8 | 51.3 | 52.3 | 52.7 | 51.7 | 51.2 |
| 2018 | 51.1 | 51.2 | 51.8 | 52.2 | 52.3 | 52.6 | 52.4 | 52.5 | 52.3 | 52.8 | 53.4 | 53.0 | 52.3 |
| 2019 | 51.2 | 51.1 | 51.3 | 52.5 | 53.2 | 52.6 | 53.1 | 52.7 | 52.3 | 52.3 | 51.8 | 51.5 | 52.1 |
| | | | | | | | | | | | | | |
| **Education and Health Services** | | | | | | | | | | | | | |
| 2011 | 68.4 | 69.3 | 69.5 | 69.9 | 68.6 | 66.7 | 65.8 | 66.1 | 69.6 | 70.2 | 70.2 | 70.4 | 68.7 |
| 2012 | 69.2 | 70.2 | 70.1 | 69.9 | 68.9 | 68.6 | 67.3 | 67.7 | 69.1 | 69.5 | 69.9 | 69.6 | 69.2 |
| 2013 | 68.0 | 68.9 | 69.1 | 69.3 | 69.0 | 68.3 | 67.8 | 68.4 | 69.1 | 70.0 | 70.5 | 70.0 | 69.0 |
| 2014 | 68.6 | 69.2 | 69.6 | 69.9 | 69.6 | 68.7 | 68.4 | 69.1 | 70.3 | 70.9 | 71.1 | 71.5 | 69.7 |
| | | | | | | | | | | | | | |
| 2015 | 70.2 | 70.6 | 70.9 | 70.9 | 71.0 | 69.9 | 69.9 | 70.7 | 71.6 | 72.3 | 73.2 | 73.2 | 71.2 |
| 2016 | 71.9 | 72.6 | 73.0 | 72.8 | 73.0 | 71.6 | 72.0 | 72.4 | 73.4 | 73.5 | 73.8 | 73.6 | 72.8 |
| 2017 | 73.0 | 73.4 | 73.6 | 73.5 | 74.0 | 72.6 | 72.8 | 73.2 | 74.4 | 74.5 | 74.8 | 74.8 | 73.7 |
| 2018 | 74.1 | 74.4 | 74.5 | 74.2 | 74.1 | 72.4 | 72.7 | 73.3 | 74.1 | 74.4 | 74.6 | 74.8 | 74.0 |
| 2019 | 74.5 | 74.4 | 74.7 | 74.9 | 75.4 | 73.9 | 73.7 | 74.4 | 75.1 | 77.2 | 77.4 | 77.9 | 75.3 |
| | | | | | | | | | | | | | |
| **Leisure and Hospitality** | | | | | | | | | | | | | |
| 2011 | 33.3 | 33.5 | 34.1 | 35.7 | 36.4 | 37.1 | 36.7 | 36.9 | 36.0 | 35.4 | 35.3 | 35.0 | 35.5 |
| 2012 | 34.4 | 34.6 | 35.6 | 36.5 | 37.3 | 38.1 | 37.8 | 37.8 | 36.8 | 35.8 | 35.8 | 35.8 | 36.4 |
| 2013 | 34.7 | 34.7 | 35.5 | 36.3 | 37.5 | 38.3 | 37.7 | 37.9 | 36.9 | 36.2 | 36.2 | 36.3 | 36.5 |
| 2014 | 35.5 | 35.3 | 36.0 | 37.2 | 38.2 | 39.1 | 38.9 | 38.9 | 37.6 | 37.3 | 37.1 | 37.1 | 37.4 |
| | | | | | | | | | | | | | |
| 2015 | 36.0 | 36.0 | 36.7 | 37.9 | 38.9 | 39.5 | 39.1 | 39.0 | 38.0 | 38.1 | 38.0 | 38.2 | 38.0 |
| 2016 | 37.2 | 37.3 | 37.8 | 39.0 | 39.9 | 40.2 | 40.4 | 40.1 | 39.1 | 38.8 | 38.7 | 38.8 | 38.9 |
| 2017 | 37.9 | 38.2 | 38.8 | 40.4 | 41.1 | 41.5 | 41.4 | 41.5 | 40.3 | 39.7 | 39.4 | 39.3 | 40.0 |
| 2018 | 37.6 | 37.8 | 38.6 | 39.1 | 40.3 | 40.9 | 40.9 | 41.0 | 39.6 | 39.0 | 38.3 | 38.5 | 39.3 |
| 2019 | 37.7 | 37.9 | 38.8 | 39.6 | 40.6 | 41.3 | 41.3 | 41.3 | 40.1 | 40.6 | 39.4 | 39.2 | 39.8 |
| | | | | | | | | | | | | | |
| **Other Services** | | | | | | | | | | | | | |
| 2011 | 14.1 | 14.2 | 14.2 | 14.4 | 14.5 | 14.6 | 14.5 | 14.4 | 14.3 | 14.1 | 14.2 | 14.1 | 14.3 |
| 2012 | 14.2 | 14.2 | 14.3 | 14.5 | 14.7 | 14.9 | 14.6 | 14.6 | 14.4 | 14.4 | 14.5 | 14.5 | 14.5 |
| 2013 | 14.3 | 14.5 | 14.6 | 14.8 | 14.9 | 14.9 | 14.6 | 14.6 | 14.4 | 14.3 | 14.2 | 14.2 | 14.5 |
| 2014 | 13.9 | 13.9 | 14.0 | 14.0 | 13.9 | 14.0 | 13.9 | 13.9 | 13.7 | 13.7 | 13.6 | 13.6 | 13.8 |
| | | | | | | | | | | | | | |
| 2015 | 13.6 | 13.6 | 13.6 | 13.7 | 14.0 | 14.0 | 14.2 | 14.1 | 14.0 | 14.0 | 13.9 | 14.0 | 13.9 |
| 2016 | 13.9 | 13.9 | 14.0 | 14.1 | 14.2 | 14.2 | 14.3 | 14.3 | 14.2 | 14.2 | 14.2 | 14.2 | 14.1 |
| 2017 | 14.2 | 14.2 | 14.3 | 14.4 | 14.4 | 14.5 | 14.4 | 14.4 | 14.1 | 14.0 | 13.9 | 13.9 | 14.2 |
| 2018 | 13.6 | 13.7 | 13.7 | 13.8 | 13.9 | 14.0 | 14.0 | 14.0 | 13.7 | 13.8 | 13.8 | 13.9 | 13.8 |
| 2019 | 13.6 | 13.7 | 13.8 | 13.9 | 14.0 | 14.1 | 14.1 | 14.1 | 13.9 | 13.9 | 13.9 | 13.9 | 13.9 |
| | | | | | | | | | | | | | |
| **Government** | | | | | | | | | | | | | |
| 2011 | 64.0 | 64.9 | 65.3 | 65.4 | 66.2 | 64.6 | 61.7 | 61.4 | 63.9 | 64.8 | 65.0 | 63.1 | 64.2 |
| 2012 | 62.5 | 64.1 | 64.3 | 64.4 | 64.7 | 63.9 | 59.9 | 60.7 | 63.3 | 63.9 | 64.1 | 63.9 | 63.3 |
| 2013 | 61.5 | 63.4 | 63.5 | 63.3 | 63.9 | 62.0 | 59.5 | 60.1 | 62.8 | 63.0 | 63.4 | 62.8 | 62.4 |
| 2014 | 60.8 | 62.8 | 63.1 | 62.2 | 62.2 | 61.1 | 58.6 | 59.6 | 62.8 | 63.3 | 63.6 | 63.3 | 62.0 |
| | | | | | | | | | | | | | |
| 2015 | 61.3 | 63.0 | 62.7 | 63.6 | 62.3 | 61.8 | 61.4 | 61.6 | 62.6 | 63.7 | 63.9 | 63.9 | 62.7 |
| 2016 | 61.4 | 63.3 | 63.3 | 64.0 | 62.5 | 62.4 | 61.6 | 61.7 | 63.8 | 63.9 | 64.2 | 64.1 | 63.0 |
| 2017 | 61.9 | 63.4 | 63.5 | 64.0 | 62.3 | 61.3 | 61.0 | 60.9 | 62.5 | 63.2 | 63.7 | 63.4 | 62.6 |
| 2018 | 61.3 | 62.9 | 63.0 | 63.0 | 61.6 | 60.7 | 60.1 | 60.6 | 62.1 | 62.9 | 63.0 | 62.8 | 62.0 |
| 2019 | 61.0 | 62.2 | 62.5 | 62.9 | 62.2 | 61.0 | 60.8 | 61.3 | 62.4 | 62.7 | 63.2 | 62.8 | 62.1 |

# Employment by Industry: Charleston-North Charleston, SC, 2011–2019

(Numbers in thousands, not seasonally adjusted)

| Industry and year | January | February | March | April | May | June | July | August | September | October | November | December | Annual average |
|---|---|---|---|---|---|---|---|---|---|---|---|---|---|
| **Total Nonfarm** | | | | | | | | | | | | | |
| 2011 | 287.9 | 289.5 | 292.2 | 296.5 | 298.7 | 298.5 | 296.7 | 296.3 | 296.9 | 298.0 | 299.3 | 299.5 | 295.8 |
| 2012 | 295.6 | 298.9 | 302.1 | 306.2 | 307.7 | 308.1 | 305.2 | 306.7 | 306.4 | 307.6 | 311.3 | 309.9 | 305.5 |
| 2013 | 303.2 | 305.6 | 308.1 | 311.3 | 313.2 | 314.5 | 313.4 | 314.1 | 314.0 | 315.6 | 317.2 | 317.5 | 312.3 |
| 2014 | 311.1 | 313.9 | 316.9 | 322.5 | 325.4 | 325.6 | 322.8 | 324.3 | 324.3 | 326.5 | 328.6 | 328.7 | 322.6 |
| 2015 | 322.9 | 325.9 | 329.3 | 332.5 | 336.2 | 336.0 | 335.8 | 337.1 | 335.5 | 339.7 | 342.5 | 342.0 | 334.6 |
| 2016 | 336.1 | 338.8 | 341.3 | 345.2 | 347.1 | 348.1 | 347.5 | 346.9 | 347.1 | 345.4 | 349.8 | 349.4 | 345.2 |
| 2017 | 344.7 | 347.7 | 350.3 | 352.8 | 355.6 | 356.4 | 356.2 | 355.3 | 353.0 | 356.5 | 359.2 | 359.2 | 353.9 |
| 2018 | 356.5 | 360.5 | 361.7 | 367.3 | 370.1 | 371.1 | 369.2 | 369.0 | 363.8 | 369.4 | 372.2 | 372.9 | 367.0 |
| 2019 | 367.4 | 370.1 | 372.6 | 375.2 | 378.3 | 378.7 | 377.9 | 378.6 | 375.9 | 375.8 | 379.0 | 379.9 | 375.8 |
| **Total Private** | | | | | | | | | | | | | |
| 2011 | 226.8 | 228.1 | 230.7 | 234.5 | 236.7 | 237.4 | 236.8 | 237.0 | 235.6 | 236.7 | 237.8 | 237.9 | 234.7 |
| 2012 | 234.5 | 237.3 | 240.1 | 243.8 | 245.3 | 246.2 | 244.4 | 245.4 | 243.5 | 244.5 | 246.0 | 246.4 | 243.1 |
| 2013 | 240.9 | 242.8 | 245.1 | 247.8 | 250.1 | 251.9 | 252.0 | 252.8 | 251.0 | 253.2 | 254.4 | 254.9 | 249.7 |
| 2014 | 249.5 | 251.5 | 254.4 | 259.0 | 261.9 | 263.6 | 262.3 | 262.6 | 261.0 | 262.7 | 264.4 | 264.7 | 259.8 |
| 2015 | 260.1 | 262.1 | 265.2 | 268.3 | 272.0 | 273.1 | 273.2 | 274.2 | 271.2 | 274.8 | 277.1 | 276.6 | 270.7 |
| 2016 | 271.3 | 273.8 | 275.8 | 279.6 | 281.6 | 283.2 | 283.1 | 283.6 | 281.9 | 280.6 | 284.9 | 284.2 | 280.3 |
| 2017 | 280.4 | 283.2 | 285.4 | 287.8 | 290.7 | 292.2 | 292.2 | 291.6 | 287.6 | 290.7 | 293.0 | 293.0 | 289.0 |
| 2018 | 291.1 | 294.8 | 295.8 | 301.1 | 303.7 | 305.4 | 304.9 | 304.5 | 297.9 | 303.4 | 305.6 | 306.4 | 301.2 |
| 2019 | 301.4 | 303.5 | 305.7 | 308.1 | 310.9 | 311.9 | 312.1 | 312.3 | 308.3 | 308.0 | 310.9 | 311.7 | 308.7 |
| **Goods Producing** | | | | | | | | | | | | | |
| 2011 | 35.0 | 35.1 | 35.4 | 35.7 | 36.2 | 36.6 | 36.6 | 36.6 | 36.6 | 36.5 | 36.7 | 36.7 | 36.1 |
| 2012 | 36.4 | 36.5 | 36.9 | 37.1 | 37.3 | 37.5 | 37.5 | 37.5 | 37.4 | 37.4 | 37.6 | 37.8 | 37.2 |
| 2013 | 37.7 | 38.0 | 38.1 | 38.3 | 38.8 | 39.1 | 39.5 | 39.5 | 39.6 | 39.5 | 39.7 | 40.1 | 39.0 |
| 2014 | 39.8 | 39.9 | 40.1 | 40.4 | 40.9 | 41.5 | 41.4 | 41.4 | 41.3 | 41.7 | 41.9 | 42.1 | 41.0 |
| 2015 | 42.1 | 42.7 | 42.5 | 42.4 | 42.9 | 43.5 | 43.7 | 43.7 | 43.7 | 43.9 | 44.2 | 44.1 | 43.3 |
| 2016 | 44.1 | 44.6 | 44.6 | 44.7 | 44.8 | 45.3 | 45.4 | 45.4 | 45.5 | 45.2 | 45.4 | 45.7 | 45.1 |
| 2017 | 45.6 | 46.2 | 46.3 | 46.3 | 46.6 | 46.9 | 47.2 | 47.0 | 46.9 | 47.2 | 47.3 | 47.6 | 46.8 |
| 2018 | 47.9 | 48.6 | 48.4 | 49.2 | 49.7 | 50.2 | 50.5 | 50.6 | 50.3 | 50.8 | 51.1 | 51.4 | 49.9 |
| 2019 | 51.1 | 51.6 | 51.7 | 51.7 | 51.9 | 52.1 | 52.3 | 52.4 | 52.2 | 52.1 | 52.2 | 52.3 | 52.0 |
| **Service-Providing** | | | | | | | | | | | | | |
| 2011 | 252.9 | 254.4 | 256.8 | 260.8 | 262.5 | 261.9 | 260.1 | 259.7 | 260.3 | 261.5 | 262.6 | 262.8 | 259.7 |
| 2012 | 259.2 | 262.4 | 265.2 | 269.1 | 270.4 | 270.6 | 267.7 | 269.2 | 269.0 | 270.2 | 273.7 | 272.1 | 268.2 |
| 2013 | 265.5 | 267.6 | 270.0 | 273.0 | 274.4 | 275.4 | 273.9 | 274.6 | 274.4 | 276.1 | 277.5 | 277.4 | 273.3 |
| 2014 | 271.3 | 274.0 | 276.8 | 282.1 | 284.5 | 284.1 | 281.4 | 282.9 | 283.0 | 284.8 | 286.7 | 286.6 | 281.5 |
| 2015 | 280.8 | 283.2 | 286.8 | 290.1 | 293.3 | 292.5 | 292.1 | 293.4 | 291.8 | 295.8 | 298.3 | 297.9 | 291.3 |
| 2016 | 292.0 | 294.2 | 296.7 | 300.5 | 302.3 | 302.8 | 302.1 | 301.5 | 301.6 | 300.2 | 304.4 | 303.7 | 300.2 |
| 2017 | 299.1 | 301.5 | 304.0 | 306.5 | 309.0 | 309.5 | 309.0 | 308.3 | 306.1 | 309.3 | 311.9 | 311.6 | 307.2 |
| 2018 | 308.6 | 311.9 | 313.3 | 318.1 | 320.4 | 320.9 | 318.7 | 318.4 | 313.5 | 318.6 | 321.1 | 321.5 | 317.1 |
| 2019 | 316.3 | 318.5 | 320.9 | 323.5 | 326.4 | 326.6 | 325.6 | 326.2 | 323.7 | 323.7 | 326.8 | 327.6 | 323.8 |
| **Mining, Logging, and Construction** | | | | | | | | | | | | | |
| 2011 | 13.8 | 13.8 | 13.9 | 13.9 | 14.2 | 14.3 | 14.1 | 13.9 | 13.8 | 13.6 | 13.6 | 13.4 | 13.9 |
| 2012 | 13.0 | 13.1 | 13.3 | 13.5 | 13.7 | 13.9 | 14.0 | 14.0 | 13.9 | 13.7 | 13.8 | 13.9 | 13.7 |
| 2013 | 14.1 | 14.0 | 14.2 | 14.5 | 14.9 | 15.2 | 15.4 | 15.5 | 15.5 | 15.4 | 15.6 | 15.8 | 15.0 |
| 2014 | 15.5 | 15.6 | 15.7 | 15.9 | 16.3 | 16.7 | 16.5 | 16.5 | 16.4 | 16.7 | 16.8 | 16.9 | 16.3 |
| 2015 | 16.7 | 17.0 | 17.2 | 17.2 | 17.5 | 17.9 | 17.9 | 17.9 | 17.8 | 18.1 | 18.4 | 18.4 | 17.7 |
| 2016 | 18.4 | 18.5 | 18.7 | 18.8 | 19.0 | 19.3 | 19.4 | 19.4 | 19.4 | 19.3 | 19.5 | 19.7 | 19.1 |
| 2017 | 19.6 | 19.8 | 20.0 | 20.0 | 20.2 | 20.4 | 20.6 | 20.4 | 20.2 | 20.5 | 20.6 | 20.8 | 20.3 |
| 2018 | 21.3 | 21.5 | 21.6 | 21.7 | 22.0 | 22.1 | 22.1 | 22.0 | 21.6 | 21.7 | 21.7 | 21.7 | 21.8 |
| 2019 | 21.4 | 21.5 | 21.7 | 21.8 | 22.0 | 22.2 | 22.1 | 22.1 | 22.0 | 22.1 | 22.1 | 22.2 | 21.9 |
| **Manufacturing** | | | | | | | | | | | | | |
| 2011 | 21.2 | 21.3 | 21.5 | 21.8 | 22.0 | 22.3 | 22.5 | 22.7 | 22.8 | 22.9 | 23.1 | 23.3 | 22.3 |
| 2012 | 23.4 | 23.4 | 23.6 | 23.6 | 23.6 | 23.6 | 23.5 | 23.5 | 23.5 | 23.7 | 23.8 | 23.9 | 23.6 |
| 2013 | 23.6 | 24.0 | 23.9 | 23.8 | 23.9 | 23.9 | 24.1 | 24.0 | 24.1 | 24.1 | 24.1 | 24.3 | 24.0 |
| 2014 | 24.3 | 24.3 | 24.4 | 24.5 | 24.6 | 24.8 | 24.9 | 24.9 | 24.9 | 25.0 | 25.1 | 25.2 | 24.7 |
| 2015 | 25.4 | 25.7 | 25.3 | 25.2 | 25.4 | 25.6 | 25.8 | 25.8 | 25.9 | 25.8 | 25.8 | 25.7 | 25.6 |
| 2016 | 25.7 | 26.1 | 25.9 | 25.9 | 25.8 | 26.0 | 26.0 | 26.0 | 26.1 | 25.9 | 25.9 | 26.0 | 25.9 |
| 2017 | 26.0 | 26.4 | 26.3 | 26.3 | 26.4 | 26.5 | 26.6 | 26.6 | 26.7 | 26.7 | 26.7 | 26.8 | 26.5 |
| 2018 | 26.6 | 27.1 | 26.8 | 27.5 | 27.7 | 28.1 | 28.4 | 28.6 | 28.7 | 29.1 | 29.4 | 29.7 | 28.1 |
| 2019 | 29.7 | 30.1 | 30.0 | 29.9 | 29.9 | 29.9 | 30.2 | 30.3 | 30.2 | 30.0 | 30.1 | 30.1 | 30.0 |

## Employment by Industry: Charleston-North Charleston, SC, 2011–2019—*Continued*

(Numbers in thousands, not seasonally adjusted)

| Industry and year | January | February | March | April | May | June | July | August | September | October | November | December | Annual average |
|---|---|---|---|---|---|---|---|---|---|---|---|---|---|
| **Trade, Transportation, and Utilities** | | | | | | | | | | | | | |
| 2011 | 54.0 | 53.9 | 54.1 | 54.5 | 54.8 | 55.0 | 55.4 | 55.3 | 55.0 | 55.7 | 56.3 | 56.7 | 55.1 |
| 2012 | 55.3 | 55.5 | 56.0 | 56.5 | 56.9 | 57.1 | 57.1 | 57.1 | 56.7 | 57.4 | 58.9 | 59.3 | 57.0 |
| 2013 | 56.6 | 56.6 | 56.9 | 57.6 | 58.0 | 58.5 | 58.7 | 58.8 | 58.6 | 59.6 | 60.2 | 61.0 | 58.4 |
| 2014 | 58.6 | 58.5 | 58.6 | 59.4 | 59.9 | 60.8 | 60.2 | 60.2 | 59.8 | 60.2 | 61.5 | 61.9 | 60.0 |
| 2015 | 59.8 | 59.5 | 60.2 | 61.0 | 61.6 | 62.1 | 62.2 | 62.4 | 61.8 | 62.8 | 63.8 | 64.3 | 61.8 |
| 2016 | 62.0 | 62.2 | 62.4 | 63.3 | 63.7 | 63.9 | 63.8 | 63.8 | 63.6 | 63.4 | 65.2 | 65.8 | 63.6 |
| 2017 | 63.8 | 63.6 | 63.8 | 64.0 | 64.6 | 64.9 | 65.1 | 64.8 | 63.7 | 64.7 | 66.4 | 67.1 | 64.7 |
| 2018 | 65.2 | 65.4 | 65.6 | 65.8 | 66.6 | 67.3 | 67.1 | 67.1 | 65.9 | 67.1 | 69.1 | 69.8 | 66.8 |
| 2019 | 67.6 | 67.6 | 68.2 | 68.3 | 68.9 | 69.3 | 69.7 | 69.3 | 68.9 | 69.4 | 70.6 | 70.9 | 69.1 |
| **Wholesale Trade** | | | | | | | | | | | | | |
| 2011 | 8.0 | 8.0 | 8.0 | 8.1 | 8.1 | 8.0 | 8.1 | 8.0 | 7.9 | 7.9 | 7.9 | 7.9 | 8.0 |
| 2012 | 7.8 | 7.9 | 7.9 | 8.0 | 8.0 | 8.0 | 7.9 | 7.9 | 7.8 | 7.9 | 7.9 | 7.9 | 7.9 |
| 2013 | 7.7 | 7.7 | 7.8 | 7.9 | 7.9 | 8.0 | 8.0 | 8.0 | 8.0 | 8.0 | 7.9 | 8.0 | 7.9 |
| 2014 | 7.8 | 7.9 | 7.9 | 7.9 | 7.9 | 8.1 | 8.1 | 8.2 | 8.2 | 8.2 | 8.2 | 8.2 | 8.1 |
| 2015 | 8.2 | 8.3 | 8.3 | 8.4 | 8.5 | 8.4 | 8.5 | 8.5 | 8.5 | 8.8 | 8.8 | 8.8 | 8.5 |
| 2016 | 8.8 | 8.9 | 8.9 | 9.0 | 9.0 | 9.1 | 9.1 | 9.1 | 9.2 | 9.2 | 9.3 | 9.3 | 9.1 |
| 2017 | 9.3 | 9.4 | 9.4 | 9.4 | 9.5 | 9.6 | 9.6 | 9.6 | 9.5 | 9.5 | 9.6 | 9.6 | 9.5 |
| 2018 | 9.4 | 9.5 | 9.5 | 9.7 | 9.8 | 9.8 | 9.8 | 9.8 | 9.6 | 9.8 | 9.8 | 9.9 | 9.7 |
| 2019 | 10.0 | 10.0 | 10.1 | 10.3 | 10.3 | 10.4 | 10.5 | 10.5 | 10.4 | 10.5 | 10.5 | 10.5 | 10.3 |
| **Retail Trade** | | | | | | | | | | | | | |
| 2011 | 34.3 | 34.1 | 34.4 | 34.9 | 35.2 | 35.3 | 35.6 | 35.3 | 35.2 | 35.8 | 36.4 | 36.6 | 35.3 |
| 2012 | 34.9 | 34.9 | 35.3 | 35.5 | 35.8 | 36.0 | 36.1 | 36.1 | 35.8 | 36.2 | 37.6 | 37.7 | 36.0 |
| 2013 | 35.6 | 35.5 | 35.6 | 36.1 | 36.4 | 36.8 | 37.0 | 37.2 | 37.0 | 37.7 | 38.7 | 39.1 | 36.9 |
| 2014 | 37.0 | 36.9 | 37.3 | 37.7 | 38.0 | 38.5 | 38.4 | 38.2 | 37.9 | 38.1 | 39.4 | 39.8 | 38.1 |
| 2015 | 37.7 | 37.5 | 37.9 | 38.4 | 38.8 | 39.6 | 39.8 | 40.0 | 39.6 | 40.1 | 41.3 | 41.4 | 39.3 |
| 2016 | 39.5 | 39.6 | 39.7 | 40.3 | 40.7 | 40.7 | 40.7 | 40.6 | 40.3 | 40.0 | 41.5 | 41.8 | 40.5 |
| 2017 | 40.2 | 39.9 | 40.0 | 40.2 | 40.6 | 40.7 | 40.6 | 40.4 | 39.4 | 40.2 | 41.7 | 41.8 | 40.5 |
| 2018 | 40.7 | 40.8 | 40.9 | 41.0 | 41.4 | 41.9 | 41.9 | 41.9 | 41.1 | 42.0 | 43.4 | 43.5 | 41.7 |
| 2019 | 41.9 | 41.8 | 42.1 | 41.9 | 42.4 | 42.7 | 42.8 | 42.3 | 42.2 | 42.6 | 43.8 | 43.7 | 42.5 |
| **Transportation and Utilities** | | | | | | | | | | | | | |
| 2011 | 11.7 | 11.8 | 11.7 | 11.5 | 11.5 | 11.7 | 11.7 | 12.0 | 11.9 | 12.0 | 12.0 | 12.2 | 11.8 |
| 2012 | 12.6 | 12.7 | 12.8 | 13.0 | 13.1 | 13.1 | 13.1 | 13.1 | 13.1 | 13.3 | 13.4 | 13.7 | 13.1 |
| 2013 | 13.3 | 13.4 | 13.5 | 13.6 | 13.7 | 13.7 | 13.7 | 13.6 | 13.6 | 13.9 | 13.6 | 13.9 | 13.6 |
| 2014 | 13.8 | 13.7 | 13.4 | 13.8 | 14.0 | 14.2 | 13.7 | 13.8 | 13.7 | 13.9 | 13.9 | 13.9 | 13.8 |
| 2015 | 13.9 | 13.7 | 14.0 | 14.2 | 14.3 | 14.1 | 13.9 | 13.9 | 13.7 | 13.9 | 13.7 | 14.1 | 14.0 |
| 2016 | 13.7 | 13.7 | 13.8 | 14.0 | 14.0 | 14.1 | 14.0 | 14.1 | 14.1 | 14.2 | 14.4 | 14.7 | 14.1 |
| 2017 | 14.3 | 14.3 | 14.4 | 14.4 | 14.5 | 14.6 | 14.9 | 14.8 | 14.8 | 15.0 | 15.1 | 15.7 | 14.7 |
| 2018 | 15.1 | 15.1 | 15.2 | 15.1 | 15.4 | 15.6 | 15.4 | 15.4 | 15.2 | 15.3 | 15.9 | 16.4 | 15.4 |
| 2019 | 15.7 | 15.8 | 16.0 | 16.1 | 16.2 | 16.2 | 16.4 | 16.5 | 16.3 | 16.3 | 16.3 | 16.7 | 16.2 |
| **Information** | | | | | | | | | | | | | |
| 2011 | 5.0 | 4.9 | 4.9 | 5.0 | 5.0 | 5.0 | 5.0 | 5.0 | 4.9 | 4.8 | 4.8 | 4.8 | 4.9 |
| 2012 | 4.8 | 4.9 | 4.8 | 4.8 | 4.8 | 4.9 | 5.0 | 5.0 | 4.9 | 5.0 | 5.1 | 5.2 | 4.9 |
| 2013 | 5.0 | 5.0 | 5.0 | 5.1 | 5.0 | 5.1 | 5.1 | 5.0 | 5.0 | 5.0 | 5.0 | 5.1 | 5.0 |
| 2014 | 5.0 | 5.0 | 5.1 | 5.2 | 5.2 | 5.3 | 5.3 | 5.2 | 5.2 | 5.2 | 5.4 | 5.4 | 5.2 |
| 2015 | 5.3 | 5.3 | 5.3 | 5.3 | 5.3 | 5.3 | 5.4 | 5.4 | 5.4 | 5.4 | 6.2 | 5.6 | 5.4 |
| 2016 | 5.5 | 5.5 | 5.8 | 6.2 | 5.5 | 5.5 | 5.5 | 5.4 | 5.3 | 5.4 | 5.5 | 5.5 | 5.6 |
| 2017 | 5.4 | 5.4 | 5.4 | 5.4 | 5.5 | 5.8 | 5.5 | 5.5 | 5.7 | 5.5 | 5.5 | 5.8 | 5.5 |
| 2018 | 5.4 | 5.5 | 5.6 | 5.4 | 5.4 | 5.5 | 5.4 | 5.2 | 5.2 | 5.2 | 5.2 | 5.2 | 5.4 |
| 2019 | 5.3 | 5.3 | 5.2 | 5.3 | 5.4 | 5.4 | 5.4 | 5.4 | 5.3 | 5.3 | 5.3 | 5.4 | 5.3 |
| **Financial Activities** | | | | | | | | | | | | | |
| 2011 | 11.7 | 11.6 | 11.7 | 11.7 | 11.8 | 11.8 | 11.8 | 11.9 | 12.0 | 12.3 | 12.5 | 12.5 | 11.9 |
| 2012 | 12.4 | 12.6 | 12.5 | 12.4 | 12.4 | 12.6 | 12.4 | 12.6 | 12.5 | 12.6 | 12.7 | 12.9 | 12.6 |
| 2013 | 12.5 | 12.7 | 12.7 | 12.7 | 12.9 | 12.8 | 12.9 | 13.1 | 13.0 | 13.2 | 13.3 | 13.3 | 12.9 |
| 2014 | 12.9 | 13.2 | 13.1 | 13.1 | 13.3 | 13.3 | 13.3 | 13.4 | 13.5 | 13.7 | 13.7 | 13.9 | 13.4 |
| 2015 | 14.0 | 14.0 | 14.1 | 14.0 | 14.2 | 14.2 | 14.0 | 14.2 | 14.0 | 14.3 | 14.4 | 14.5 | 14.2 |
| 2016 | 14.3 | 14.4 | 14.1 | 14.4 | 14.5 | 14.5 | 14.5 | 14.6 | 14.5 | 14.7 | 14.8 | 14.7 | 14.5 |
| 2017 | 14.7 | 14.7 | 14.9 | 14.9 | 15.0 | 14.9 | 15.1 | 15.1 | 15.0 | 15.3 | 15.3 | 15.3 | 15.0 |
| 2018 | 15.4 | 15.5 | 15.8 | 15.8 | 15.8 | 15.7 | 15.7 | 15.7 | 15.4 | 15.7 | 15.9 | 15.9 | 15.7 |
| 2019 | 15.5 | 15.5 | 15.6 | 15.8 | 15.9 | 15.9 | 16.1 | 16.3 | 15.8 | 16.0 | 16.0 | 16.1 | 15.9 |

## Employment by Industry: Charleston-North Charleston, SC, 2011–2019—*Continued*

(Numbers in thousands, not seasonally adjusted)

| Industry and year | January | February | March | April | May | June | July | August | September | October | November | December | Annual average |
|---|---|---|---|---|---|---|---|---|---|---|---|---|---|
| **Professional and Business Services** | | | | | | | | | | | | | |
| 2011 | 42.9 | 43.4 | 43.9 | 44.7 | 44.8 | 44.3 | 44.1 | 44.6 | 44.2 | 44.9 | 44.9 | 44.8 | 44.3 |
| 2012 | 44.6 | 45.6 | 46.1 | 46.9 | 46.9 | 46.6 | 45.3 | 45.9 | 45.9 | 45.9 | 45.8 | 45.9 | 46.0 |
| 2013 | 45.3 | 46.0 | 46.5 | 46.4 | 46.5 | 46.4 | 46.1 | 46.4 | 46.6 | 47.4 | 47.6 | 47.5 | 46.6 |
| 2014 | 46.2 | 47.6 | 48.4 | 48.8 | 49.0 | 48.5 | 48.3 | 48.5 | 48.9 | 49.2 | 49.4 | 49.4 | 48.5 |
| 2015 | 48.1 | 49.0 | 49.5 | 50.2 | 50.6 | 50.7 | 50.2 | 50.8 | 50.6 | 51.8 | 51.9 | 52.0 | 50.5 |
| 2016 | 50.8 | 51.6 | 51.9 | 51.9 | 52.2 | 52.2 | 52.7 | 53.2 | 53.0 | 53.0 | 54.2 | 53.3 | 52.5 |
| 2017 | 53.2 | 54.2 | 54.6 | 55.3 | 55.5 | 55.5 | 55.4 | 55.5 | 55.6 | 56.2 | 56.7 | 56.2 | 55.3 |
| 2018 | 56.3 | 57.4 | 57.6 | 58.7 | 58.7 | 58.5 | 58.3 | 58.4 | 57.8 | 59.2 | 58.8 | 58.8 | 58.2 |
| 2019 | 57.7 | 58.3 | 58.6 | 58.8 | 58.9 | 58.5 | 57.5 | 58.1 | 58.0 | 58.1 | 59.2 | 58.7 | 58.4 |
| **Education and Health Services** | | | | | | | | | | | | | |
| 2011 | 34.5 | 35.1 | 35.2 | 35.1 | 35.0 | 34.7 | 34.4 | 34.5 | 34.8 | 34.6 | 34.7 | 34.6 | 34.8 |
| 2012 | 34.1 | 34.6 | 34.7 | 34.6 | 34.7 | 34.3 | 34.2 | 34.4 | 34.7 | 35.2 | 35.3 | 35.2 | 34.7 |
| 2013 | 34.8 | 35.2 | 35.2 | 35.0 | 35.1 | 34.9 | 35.0 | 35.3 | 35.1 | 35.7 | 35.9 | 35.8 | 35.3 |
| 2014 | 35.8 | 36.0 | 36.2 | 36.5 | 36.6 | 36.6 | 36.4 | 36.7 | 36.7 | 37.3 | 37.4 | 37.4 | 36.6 |
| 2015 | 37.1 | 37.4 | 37.5 | 37.6 | 37.9 | 37.4 | 37.7 | 38.1 | 38.1 | 38.6 | 38.8 | 38.5 | 37.9 |
| 2016 | 38.0 | 38.4 | 38.3 | 38.4 | 38.6 | 38.4 | 38.4 | 38.8 | 39.2 | 39.2 | 39.3 | 39.4 | 38.7 |
| 2017 | 39.3 | 39.9 | 39.8 | 39.8 | 39.7 | 39.5 | 39.7 | 40.0 | 39.9 | 40.5 | 40.8 | 40.8 | 40.0 |
| 2018 | 40.8 | 41.4 | 41.3 | 41.7 | 41.8 | 41.6 | 41.6 | 41.8 | 41.4 | 42.0 | 42.2 | 42.2 | 41.7 |
| 2019 | 41.7 | 42.2 | 42.2 | 42.3 | 42.5 | 42.4 | 42.7 | 43.1 | 42.9 | 42.9 | 43.0 | 43.0 | 42.6 |
| **Leisure and Hospitality** | | | | | | | | | | | | | |
| 2011 | 33.4 | 33.7 | 35.1 | 37.2 | 38.3 | 38.9 | 38.2 | 37.9 | 36.8 | 36.6 | 36.4 | 36.2 | 36.6 |
| 2012 | 35.2 | 35.7 | 37.0 | 39.0 | 39.6 | 40.3 | 39.9 | 40.0 | 38.7 | 38.3 | 37.8 | 37.3 | 38.2 |
| 2013 | 36.3 | 36.6 | 37.7 | 39.7 | 40.8 | 41.8 | 41.4 | 41.5 | 40.0 | 39.8 | 39.7 | 39.1 | 39.5 |
| 2014 | 38.2 | 38.3 | 39.8 | 42.3 | 43.5 | 43.9 | 43.6 | 43.5 | 42.0 | 41.8 | 41.5 | 41.0 | 41.6 |
| 2015 | 40.2 | 40.7 | 42.5 | 44.1 | 45.6 | 45.9 | 46.0 | 45.7 | 43.9 | 44.3 | 44.0 | 43.7 | 43.9 |
| 2016 | 43.1 | 43.5 | 45.1 | 46.9 | 48.4 | 49.4 | 48.8 | 48.5 | 47.0 | 46.0 | 46.6 | 46.0 | 46.6 |
| 2017 | 44.8 | 45.5 | 46.8 | 48.3 | 49.9 | 50.6 | 50.2 | 49.7 | 46.9 | 47.3 | 47.0 | 46.2 | 47.8 |
| 2018 | 46.0 | 46.7 | 47.2 | 50.0 | 51.1 | 51.8 | 51.7 | 51.2 | 47.7 | 48.8 | 48.7 | 48.5 | 49.1 |
| 2019 | 47.9 | 48.3 | 49.3 | 51.0 | 52.3 | 53.1 | 53.1 | 52.5 | 50.1 | 49.1 | 49.5 | 50.2 | 50.5 |
| **Other Services** | | | | | | | | | | | | | |
| 2011 | 10.3 | 10.4 | 10.4 | 10.6 | 10.8 | 11.1 | 11.3 | 11.2 | 11.3 | 11.3 | 11.5 | 11.6 | 11.0 |
| 2012 | 11.7 | 11.9 | 12.1 | 12.5 | 12.7 | 12.9 | 13.0 | 12.9 | 12.7 | 12.7 | 12.8 | 12.8 | 12.6 |
| 2013 | 12.7 | 12.7 | 13.0 | 13.0 | 13.0 | 13.3 | 13.3 | 13.2 | 13.1 | 13.0 | 13.0 | 13.0 | 13.0 |
| 2014 | 13.0 | 13.0 | 13.1 | 13.3 | 13.5 | 13.7 | 13.8 | 13.7 | 13.6 | 13.6 | 13.6 | 13.6 | 13.5 |
| 2015 | 13.5 | 13.5 | 13.6 | 13.7 | 13.9 | 14.0 | 14.0 | 13.9 | 13.7 | 13.7 | 13.8 | 13.9 | 13.8 |
| 2016 | 13.5 | 13.6 | 13.6 | 13.8 | 13.9 | 14.0 | 14.0 | 13.9 | 13.8 | 13.7 | 13.9 | 13.8 | 13.8 |
| 2017 | 13.6 | 13.7 | 13.8 | 13.8 | 13.9 | 14.1 | 14.0 | 14.0 | 13.9 | 14.0 | 14.0 | 14.0 | 13.9 |
| 2018 | 14.1 | 14.3 | 14.3 | 14.5 | 14.6 | 14.8 | 14.6 | 14.5 | 14.2 | 14.6 | 14.6 | 14.6 | 14.5 |
| 2019 | 14.6 | 14.7 | 14.9 | 14.9 | 15.1 | 15.2 | 15.3 | 15.2 | 15.1 | 15.1 | 15.1 | 15.1 | 15.0 |
| **Government** | | | | | | | | | | | | | |
| 2011 | 61.1 | 61.4 | 61.5 | 62.0 | 62.0 | 61.1 | 59.9 | 59.3 | 61.3 | 61.3 | 61.5 | 61.6 | 61.2 |
| 2012 | 61.1 | 61.6 | 62.0 | 62.4 | 62.4 | 61.9 | 60.8 | 61.3 | 62.9 | 63.1 | 65.3 | 63.5 | 62.4 |
| 2013 | 62.3 | 62.8 | 63.0 | 63.5 | 63.1 | 62.6 | 61.4 | 61.3 | 63.0 | 62.4 | 62.8 | 62.6 | 62.6 |
| 2014 | 61.6 | 62.4 | 62.5 | 63.5 | 63.5 | 62.0 | 60.5 | 61.7 | 63.3 | 63.8 | 64.2 | 64.0 | 62.8 |
| 2015 | 62.8 | 63.8 | 64.1 | 64.2 | 64.2 | 62.9 | 62.6 | 62.9 | 64.3 | 64.9 | 65.4 | 65.4 | 64.0 |
| 2016 | 64.8 | 65.0 | 65.5 | 65.6 | 65.5 | 64.9 | 64.4 | 63.3 | 65.2 | 64.8 | 64.9 | 65.2 | 64.9 |
| 2017 | 64.3 | 64.5 | 64.9 | 65.0 | 64.9 | 64.2 | 64.0 | 63.7 | 65.4 | 65.8 | 66.2 | 66.2 | 64.9 |
| 2018 | 65.4 | 65.7 | 65.9 | 66.2 | 66.4 | 65.7 | 64.3 | 64.5 | 65.9 | 66.0 | 66.6 | 66.5 | 65.8 |
| 2019 | 66.0 | 66.6 | 66.9 | 67.1 | 67.4 | 66.8 | 65.8 | 66.3 | 67.6 | 67.8 | 68.1 | 68.2 | 67.1 |

## Employment by Industry: Greensboro-High Point, NC, 2011–2019

(Numbers in thousands, not seasonally adjusted)

| Industry and year | January | February | March | April | May | June | July | August | September | October | November | December | Annual average |
|---|---|---|---|---|---|---|---|---|---|---|---|---|---|
| **Total Nonfarm** | | | | | | | | | | | | | |
| 2011 | 332.9 | 335.6 | 337.7 | 340.5 | 341.3 | 337.4 | 332.5 | 337.0 | 341.2 | 342.6 | 343.0 | 342.4 | 338.7 |
| 2012 | 337.1 | 339.5 | 341.0 | 342.5 | 343.9 | 337.8 | 329.4 | 338.9 | 342.4 | 345.5 | 347.4 | 347.7 | 341.1 |
| 2013 | 340.9 | 342.9 | 344.4 | 346.3 | 346.8 | 342.3 | 335.3 | 344.0 | 347.4 | 349.6 | 350.2 | 350.4 | 345.0 |
| 2014 | 342.6 | 342.5 | 345.6 | 349.0 | 350.5 | 345.0 | 338.7 | 346.0 | 349.9 | 353.5 | 354.6 | 354.7 | 347.7 |
| 2015 | 348.7 | 350.2 | 351.0 | 355.4 | 356.6 | 352.4 | 345.5 | 353.2 | 356.4 | 359.3 | 360.2 | 360.1 | 354.1 |
| 2016 | 352.6 | 354.6 | 356.3 | 358.8 | 358.7 | 354.1 | 349.8 | 355.4 | 359.0 | 362.2 | 365.3 | 363.8 | 357.6 |
| 2017 | 354.7 | 357.5 | 357.3 | 359.7 | 360.3 | 357.5 | 350.8 | 356.5 | 359.2 | 361.8 | 362.7 | 361.6 | 358.3 |
| 2018 | 356.7 | 358.8 | 360.3 | 361.6 | 362.5 | 359.2 | 352.7 | 358.7 | 361.4 | 365.2 | 367.2 | 364.7 | 360.8 |
| 2019 | 361.4 | 363.3 | 364.8 | 366.8 | 367.8 | 362.8 | 355.0 | 362.2 | 364.0 | 367.1 | 369.6 | 367.9 | 364.4 |
| **Total Private** | | | | | | | | | | | | | |
| 2011 | 286.6 | 289.0 | 290.8 | 293.7 | 294.4 | 295.5 | 295.0 | 296.2 | 295.7 | 296.0 | 296.1 | 295.7 | 293.7 |
| 2012 | 291.7 | 293.6 | 294.7 | 296.0 | 296.9 | 297.3 | 297.1 | 298.1 | 297.3 | 299.0 | 300.5 | 301.4 | 297.0 |
| 2013 | 295.0 | 296.7 | 297.7 | 299.9 | 300.2 | 301.0 | 300.9 | 303.1 | 302.3 | 303.8 | 304.0 | 304.4 | 300.8 |
| 2014 | 297.2 | 297.0 | 299.7 | 302.8 | 303.7 | 303.5 | 304.0 | 305.5 | 305.3 | 308.1 | 308.7 | 309.3 | 303.7 |
| 2015 | 303.8 | 305.2 | 306.0 | 310.1 | 311.0 | 311.1 | 311.0 | 313.2 | 312.2 | 314.7 | 315.3 | 315.3 | 310.7 |
| 2016 | 308.5 | 309.8 | 310.8 | 313.8 | 313.3 | 313.4 | 314.9 | 315.5 | 315.1 | 316.6 | 319.2 | 318.5 | 314.1 |
| 2017 | 310.2 | 312.5 | 312.2 | 314.4 | 315.0 | 316.8 | 315.7 | 316.3 | 314.8 | 316.9 | 317.8 | 317.0 | 315.0 |
| 2018 | 312.4 | 314.1 | 315.4 | 316.3 | 316.5 | 318.0 | 317.6 | 319.0 | 317.1 | 320.0 | 321.7 | 319.6 | 317.3 |
| 2019 | 317.3 | 318.6 | 320.0 | 321.7 | 322.4 | 323.1 | 321.8 | 322.5 | 319.6 | 321.8 | 324.2 | 323.0 | 321.3 |
| **Goods Producing** | | | | | | | | | | | | | |
| 2011 | 62.7 | 63.1 | 63.5 | 64.4 | 64.7 | 65.2 | 65.3 | 65.6 | 65.3 | 65.0 | 64.6 | 64.6 | 64.5 |
| 2012 | 64.6 | 64.9 | 64.9 | 64.5 | 64.8 | 64.9 | 64.9 | 64.8 | 65.1 | 65.1 | 65.2 | 65.7 | 65.0 |
| 2013 | 64.8 | 64.4 | 64.9 | 65.4 | 65.6 | 66.3 | 66.3 | 66.3 | 66.4 | 66.6 | 66.5 | 66.6 | 65.8 |
| 2014 | 65.7 | 65.7 | 66.2 | 66.3 | 66.6 | 67.0 | 66.9 | 66.9 | 67.1 | 67.0 | 67.1 | 67.4 | 66.7 |
| 2015 | 66.8 | 67.3 | 67.7 | 68.4 | 68.5 | 68.9 | 69.1 | 69.6 | 69.3 | 69.4 | 69.2 | 69.6 | 68.7 |
| 2016 | 68.9 | 69.1 | 69.5 | 69.5 | 69.7 | 70.1 | 71.0 | 71.0 | 70.9 | 70.8 | 70.9 | 71.2 | 70.2 |
| 2017 | 69.9 | 70.7 | 70.8 | 70.8 | 70.8 | 71.1 | 70.9 | 70.9 | 70.6 | 70.8 | 70.6 | 70.5 | 70.7 |
| 2018 | 70.1 | 70.4 | 70.5 | 70.2 | 70.2 | 70.8 | 70.5 | 70.2 | 69.9 | 69.6 | 69.6 | 69.7 | 70.1 |
| 2019 | 69.4 | 69.4 | 69.6 | 69.4 | 69.4 | 69.8 | 69.6 | 69.6 | 69.2 | 69.3 | 69.4 | 69.2 | 69.4 |
| **Service-Providing** | | | | | | | | | | | | | |
| 2011 | 270.2 | 272.5 | 274.2 | 276.1 | 276.6 | 272.2 | 267.2 | 271.4 | 275.9 | 277.6 | 278.4 | 277.8 | 274.2 |
| 2012 | 272.5 | 274.6 | 276.1 | 278.0 | 279.1 | 272.9 | 264.5 | 274.1 | 277.3 | 280.4 | 282.2 | 282.0 | 276.1 |
| 2013 | 276.1 | 278.5 | 279.5 | 280.9 | 281.2 | 276.0 | 269.0 | 277.7 | 281.0 | 283.0 | 283.7 | 283.8 | 279.2 |
| 2014 | 276.9 | 276.8 | 279.4 | 282.7 | 283.9 | 278.0 | 271.8 | 279.1 | 282.8 | 286.5 | 287.5 | 287.3 | 281.1 |
| 2015 | 281.9 | 282.9 | 283.3 | 287.0 | 288.1 | 283.5 | 276.4 | 283.6 | 287.1 | 289.9 | 291.0 | 290.5 | 285.4 |
| 2016 | 283.7 | 285.5 | 286.8 | 289.3 | 289.0 | 284.0 | 278.8 | 284.4 | 288.1 | 291.4 | 294.4 | 292.6 | 287.3 |
| 2017 | 284.8 | 286.8 | 286.5 | 288.9 | 289.5 | 286.4 | 279.9 | 285.6 | 288.6 | 291.0 | 292.1 | 291.1 | 287.6 |
| 2018 | 286.6 | 288.4 | 289.8 | 291.4 | 292.3 | 288.4 | 282.2 | 288.5 | 291.5 | 295.6 | 297.6 | 295.0 | 290.6 |
| 2019 | 292.0 | 293.9 | 295.2 | 297.4 | 298.4 | 293.0 | 285.4 | 292.6 | 294.8 | 297.8 | 300.2 | 298.7 | 295.0 |
| **Mining, Logging, and Construction** | | | | | | | | | | | | | |
| 2011 | 11.7 | 12.1 | 12.4 | 12.8 | 12.9 | 13.1 | 13.1 | 13.1 | 13.1 | 12.9 | 12.7 | 12.7 | 12.7 |
| 2012 | 12.5 | 12.4 | 12.5 | 12.2 | 12.2 | 12.3 | 12.4 | 12.4 | 12.3 | 12.3 | 12.2 | 12.2 | 12.3 |
| 2013 | 11.9 | 11.9 | 12.2 | 12.4 | 12.5 | 12.7 | 12.8 | 13.0 | 13.0 | 13.0 | 13.0 | 12.9 | 12.6 |
| 2014 | 12.6 | 12.6 | 12.9 | 12.9 | 13.1 | 13.3 | 13.3 | 13.3 | 13.4 | 13.4 | 13.4 | 13.4 | 13.1 |
| 2015 | 12.9 | 13.1 | 13.3 | 13.8 | 13.9 | 14.0 | 14.2 | 14.3 | 14.2 | 14.2 | 13.9 | 14.0 | 13.8 |
| 2016 | 13.8 | 13.8 | 14.0 | 14.3 | 14.3 | 14.4 | 14.9 | 14.9 | 15.0 | 14.9 | 14.8 | 14.8 | 14.5 |
| 2017 | 14.3 | 14.7 | 14.9 | 15.0 | 14.9 | 15.2 | 15.1 | 15.1 | 15.1 | 15.4 | 15.3 | 15.3 | 15.0 |
| 2018 | 15.0 | 15.2 | 15.5 | 15.4 | 15.4 | 15.8 | 15.8 | 15.6 | 15.5 | 15.5 | 15.5 | 15.5 | 15.5 |
| 2019 | 15.6 | 15.6 | 15.8 | 15.8 | 15.9 | 16.0 | 16.0 | 15.9 | 15.8 | 15.8 | 15.7 | 15.6 | 15.8 |
| **Manufacturing** | | | | | | | | | | | | | |
| 2011 | 51.0 | 51.0 | 51.1 | 51.6 | 51.8 | 52.1 | 52.2 | 52.5 | 52.2 | 52.1 | 51.9 | 51.9 | 51.8 |
| 2012 | 52.1 | 52.5 | 52.4 | 52.3 | 52.6 | 52.6 | 52.5 | 52.4 | 52.8 | 52.8 | 53.0 | 53.5 | 52.6 |
| 2013 | 52.9 | 52.5 | 52.7 | 53.0 | 53.1 | 53.6 | 53.5 | 53.3 | 53.4 | 53.6 | 53.5 | 53.7 | 53.2 |
| 2014 | 53.1 | 53.1 | 53.3 | 53.4 | 53.5 | 53.7 | 53.6 | 53.6 | 53.7 | 53.6 | 53.7 | 54.0 | 53.5 |
| 2015 | 53.9 | 54.2 | 54.4 | 54.6 | 54.6 | 54.9 | 54.9 | 55.3 | 55.1 | 55.2 | 55.3 | 55.6 | 54.8 |
| 2016 | 55.1 | 55.3 | 55.5 | 55.2 | 55.4 | 55.7 | 56.1 | 56.1 | 55.9 | 55.9 | 56.1 | 56.4 | 55.7 |
| 2017 | 55.6 | 56.0 | 55.9 | 55.8 | 55.9 | 55.9 | 55.8 | 55.8 | 55.5 | 55.4 | 55.3 | 55.2 | 55.7 |
| 2018 | 55.1 | 55.2 | 55.0 | 54.8 | 54.8 | 55.0 | 54.7 | 54.6 | 54.4 | 54.1 | 54.1 | 54.2 | 54.7 |
| 2019 | 53.8 | 53.8 | 53.8 | 53.6 | 53.5 | 53.8 | 53.6 | 53.7 | 53.4 | 53.5 | 53.7 | 53.6 | 53.7 |

## Employment by Industry: Greensboro-High Point, NC, 2011–2019—*Continued*

(Numbers in thousands, not seasonally adjusted)

| Industry and year | January | February | March | April | May | June | July | August | September | October | November | December | Annual average |
|---|---|---|---|---|---|---|---|---|---|---|---|---|---|
| **Trade, Transportation, and Utilities** | | | | | | | | | | | | | |
| 2011 | 67.8 | 68.1 | 68.3 | 68.7 | 68.9 | 68.8 | 68.7 | 68.8 | 68.6 | 69.0 | 69.9 | 70.5 | 68.8 |
| 2012 | 68.9 | 68.9 | 68.9 | 69.7 | 70.2 | 69.9 | 69.8 | 69.8 | 69.8 | 70.3 | 71.7 | 72.2 | 70.0 |
| 2013 | 69.8 | 69.9 | 70.0 | 70.6 | 70.7 | 70.5 | 70.7 | 70.9 | 70.8 | 72.0 | 72.7 | 73.5 | 71.0 |
| 2014 | 70.9 | 70.4 | 71.1 | 72.0 | 72.2 | 72.3 | 71.8 | 72.2 | 71.8 | 72.3 | 73.6 | 74.3 | 72.1 |
| 2015 | 71.7 | 71.6 | 71.8 | 72.7 | 72.5 | 72.5 | 72.3 | 72.8 | 72.8 | 73.8 | 74.6 | 75.7 | 72.9 |
| 2016 | 72.5 | 72.1 | 72.3 | 73.0 | 73.0 | 72.9 | 72.8 | 73.0 | 72.6 | 73.3 | 74.4 | 75.3 | 73.1 |
| 2017 | 73.3 | 72.8 | 72.5 | 73.5 | 73.7 | 74.3 | 74.2 | 74.3 | 73.9 | 75.0 | 76.4 | 76.9 | 74.2 |
| 2018 | 74.8 | 74.8 | 74.8 | 74.6 | 74.8 | 75.0 | 75.0 | 75.3 | 75.5 | 76.2 | 77.7 | 78.0 | 75.5 |
| 2019 | 76.8 | 76.7 | 76.8 | 77.3 | 77.6 | 77.6 | 77.6 | 77.7 | 77.5 | 77.8 | 78.6 | 79.1 | 77.6 |
| **Wholesale Trade** | | | | | | | | | | | | | |
| 2011 | 17.7 | 18.0 | 18.0 | 18.0 | 18.0 | 17.9 | 17.8 | 17.8 | 17.6 | 17.5 | 17.4 | 17.4 | 17.8 |
| 2012 | 17.4 | 17.6 | 17.7 | 17.9 | 18.0 | 18.0 | 17.9 | 18.0 | 18.0 | 18.1 | 18.2 | 18.4 | 17.9 |
| 2013 | 18.1 | 18.3 | 18.4 | 18.5 | 18.5 | 18.5 | 18.5 | 18.6 | 18.6 | 18.6 | 18.6 | 18.6 | 18.5 |
| 2014 | 18.4 | 18.4 | 18.6 | 19.0 | 19.1 | 19.0 | 18.9 | 18.9 | 18.8 | 18.6 | 18.6 | 18.7 | 18.8 |
| 2015 | 18.5 | 18.6 | 18.6 | 18.9 | 18.9 | 18.8 | 18.8 | 18.9 | 18.7 | 18.9 | 18.9 | 19.1 | 18.8 |
| 2016 | 18.9 | 18.8 | 19.0 | 19.3 | 19.4 | 19.3 | 19.2 | 19.2 | 19.0 | 19.1 | 18.9 | 19.0 | 19.1 |
| 2017 | 18.8 | 18.9 | 18.9 | 19.0 | 19.0 | 19.2 | 19.2 | 19.3 | 19.1 | 19.3 | 19.3 | 19.5 | 19.1 |
| 2018 | 19.3 | 19.4 | 19.5 | 19.6 | 19.6 | 19.7 | 19.7 | 19.8 | 19.7 | 19.9 | 19.6 | 19.6 | 19.6 |
| 2019 | 19.5 | 19.7 | 19.7 | 19.8 | 19.8 | 19.9 | 19.8 | 19.8 | 19.7 | 19.8 | 19.8 | 19.8 | 19.8 |
| **Retail Trade** | | | | | | | | | | | | | |
| 2011 | 34.6 | 34.5 | 34.7 | 34.9 | 35.1 | 35.1 | 35.1 | 35.2 | 35.0 | 35.4 | 36.4 | 36.8 | 35.2 |
| 2012 | 35.6 | 35.4 | 35.2 | 35.7 | 36.1 | 35.9 | 36.0 | 35.8 | 35.8 | 36.0 | 37.4 | 37.5 | 36.0 |
| 2013 | 35.8 | 35.8 | 35.9 | 36.2 | 36.4 | 36.2 | 36.4 | 36.3 | 36.2 | 37.1 | 38.0 | 38.5 | 36.6 |
| 2014 | 36.6 | 36.2 | 36.5 | 36.8 | 36.9 | 37.0 | 36.7 | 37.0 | 36.6 | 37.1 | 38.2 | 38.4 | 37.0 |
| 2015 | 36.7 | 36.5 | 36.6 | 36.9 | 37.0 | 37.1 | 37.0 | 37.3 | 37.3 | 37.9 | 38.9 | 39.4 | 37.4 |
| 2016 | 37.4 | 37.3 | 37.3 | 37.7 | 37.7 | 37.7 | 37.7 | 37.8 | 37.7 | 38.3 | 39.4 | 39.7 | 38.0 |
| 2017 | 37.8 | 37.6 | 37.3 | 37.5 | 37.5 | 37.6 | 37.7 | 37.6 | 37.1 | 37.6 | 38.8 | 38.8 | 37.7 |
| 2018 | 37.2 | 37.1 | 37.0 | 37.1 | 37.3 | 37.2 | 37.3 | 37.3 | 37.2 | 37.6 | 38.9 | 38.9 | 37.5 |
| 2019 | 37.7 | 37.5 | 37.5 | 37.8 | 37.9 | 37.6 | 37.8 | 37.8 | 37.7 | 37.9 | 38.6 | 38.8 | 37.9 |
| **Transportation and Utilities** | | | | | | | | | | | | | |
| 2011 | 15.5 | 15.6 | 15.6 | 15.8 | 15.8 | 15.8 | 15.8 | 15.8 | 16.0 | 16.1 | 16.1 | 16.3 | 15.9 |
| 2012 | 15.9 | 15.9 | 16.0 | 16.1 | 16.1 | 16.0 | 15.9 | 16.0 | 16.0 | 16.2 | 16.1 | 16.3 | 16.0 |
| 2013 | 15.9 | 15.8 | 15.7 | 15.9 | 15.8 | 15.8 | 15.8 | 16.0 | 16.0 | 16.3 | 16.1 | 16.4 | 16.0 |
| 2014 | 15.9 | 15.8 | 16.0 | 16.2 | 16.2 | 16.3 | 16.2 | 16.3 | 16.4 | 16.6 | 16.8 | 17.2 | 16.3 |
| 2015 | 16.5 | 16.5 | 16.6 | 16.9 | 16.6 | 16.6 | 16.5 | 16.6 | 16.8 | 17.0 | 16.8 | 17.2 | 16.7 |
| 2016 | 16.2 | 16.0 | 16.0 | 16.0 | 15.9 | 15.9 | 15.9 | 16.0 | 15.9 | 15.9 | 16.1 | 16.6 | 16.0 |
| 2017 | 16.7 | 16.3 | 16.3 | 17.0 | 17.2 | 17.5 | 17.3 | 17.4 | 17.7 | 18.1 | 18.3 | 18.6 | 17.4 |
| 2018 | 18.3 | 18.3 | 18.3 | 17.9 | 17.9 | 18.1 | 18.0 | 18.2 | 18.6 | 18.7 | 19.2 | 19.5 | 18.4 |
| 2019 | 19.6 | 19.5 | 19.6 | 19.7 | 19.9 | 20.1 | 20.0 | 20.1 | 20.1 | 20.1 | 20.2 | 20.5 | 20.0 |
| **Information** | | | | | | | | | | | | | |
| 2011 | 5.5 | 5.5 | 5.5 | 5.5 | 5.5 | 5.5 | 5.5 | 5.5 | 5.5 | 5.5 | 5.4 | 5.4 | 5.5 |
| 2012 | 5.4 | 5.5 | 5.4 | 5.4 | 5.4 | 5.4 | 5.4 | 5.3 | 5.3 | 5.3 | 5.3 | 5.3 | 5.4 |
| 2013 | 5.2 | 5.2 | 5.1 | 5.0 | 5.0 | 5.0 | 5.0 | 4.9 | 4.9 | 4.9 | 4.9 | 5.0 | 5.0 |
| 2014 | 4.9 | 4.9 | 4.9 | 4.9 | 4.9 | 5.0 | 5.0 | 5.0 | 5.0 | 5.1 | 5.1 | 5.1 | 5.0 |
| 2015 | 5.1 | 5.1 | 5.1 | 5.0 | 5.1 | 5.1 | 5.1 | 5.0 | 4.9 | 4.9 | 4.9 | 4.9 | 5.0 |
| 2016 | 4.9 | 5.0 | 5.0 | 4.8 | 4.8 | 4.8 | 4.9 | 4.9 | 4.8 | 4.8 | 4.8 | 4.8 | 4.9 |
| 2017 | 4.7 | 4.8 | 4.8 | 4.6 | 4.6 | 4.6 | 4.7 | 4.7 | 4.7 | 4.7 | 4.8 | 4.8 | 4.7 |
| 2018 | 4.7 | 4.6 | 4.6 | 4.6 | 4.6 | 4.6 | 4.6 | 4.6 | 4.5 | 4.6 | 4.5 | 4.6 | 4.6 |
| 2019 | 4.7 | 4.6 | 4.6 | 4.6 | 4.6 | 4.7 | 4.7 | 4.6 | 4.6 | 4.6 | 4.7 | 4.7 | 4.6 |
| **Financial Activities** | | | | | | | | | | | | | |
| 2011 | 19.6 | 19.6 | 19.7 | 19.7 | 19.6 | 19.6 | 19.6 | 19.5 | 19.4 | 19.0 | 18.9 | 18.8 | 19.4 |
| 2012 | 18.3 | 18.4 | 18.4 | 18.4 | 18.3 | 18.4 | 18.4 | 18.4 | 18.5 | 18.5 | 18.7 | 18.8 | 18.5 |
| 2013 | 18.3 | 18.4 | 18.4 | 18.4 | 18.4 | 18.5 | 18.3 | 18.4 | 18.1 | 18.1 | 18.2 | 18.2 | 18.3 |
| 2014 | 18.2 | 18.1 | 18.1 | 17.8 | 17.8 | 17.7 | 17.8 | 17.7 | 17.6 | 17.6 | 17.6 | 17.6 | 17.8 |
| 2015 | 17.6 | 17.5 | 17.5 | 17.6 | 17.8 | 18.0 | 18.1 | 18.1 | 18.0 | 18.1 | 18.2 | 18.3 | 17.9 |
| 2016 | 18.2 | 18.2 | 18.2 | 18.1 | 18.0 | 18.0 | 18.2 | 18.1 | 18.0 | 18.0 | 18.2 | 18.2 | 18.1 |
| 2017 | 17.9 | 17.9 | 17.7 | 17.6 | 17.6 | 17.7 | 17.8 | 17.7 | 17.7 | 17.8 | 17.9 | 18.0 | 17.8 |
| 2018 | 18.2 | 18.3 | 18.4 | 18.4 | 18.5 | 18.7 | 18.6 | 18.6 | 18.6 | 18.6 | 18.7 | 18.7 | 18.5 |
| 2019 | 18.5 | 18.7 | 18.6 | 18.8 | 18.8 | 18.9 | 19.0 | 19.1 | 19.0 | 19.2 | 19.2 | 19.4 | 18.9 |

## Employment by Industry: Greensboro-High Point, NC, 2011–2019—*Continued*

(Numbers in thousands, not seasonally adjusted)

| Industry and year | January | February | March | April | May | June | July | August | September | October | November | December | Annual average |
|---|---|---|---|---|---|---|---|---|---|---|---|---|---|
| **Professional and Business Services** | | | | | | | | | | | | | |
| 2011 | 44.2 | 45.1 | 45.7 | 46.1 | 45.9 | 46.1 | 46.4 | 46.7 | 47.3 | 47.6 | 47.6 | 47.1 | 46.3 |
| 2012 | 46.6 | 47.0 | 47.7 | 47.5 | 47.1 | 47.1 | 46.6 | 47.2 | 46.8 | 47.4 | 47.6 | 47.6 | 47.2 |
| 2013 | 46.2 | 47.0 | 46.9 | 47.4 | 47.0 | 47.0 | 47.0 | 48.1 | 48.5 | 49.0 | 48.6 | 48.3 | 47.6 |
| 2014 | 47.0 | 47.0 | 47.7 | 48.4 | 48.0 | 47.7 | 48.7 | 49.4 | 50.0 | 51.7 | 51.1 | 51.0 | 49.0 |
| 2015 | 49.5 | 49.7 | 49.4 | 50.4 | 50.1 | 49.8 | 50.0 | 50.9 | 50.5 | 51.7 | 51.6 | 50.5 | 50.3 |
| 2016 | 49.0 | 49.4 | 49.1 | 50.1 | 48.7 | 48.7 | 49.5 | 49.6 | 50.3 | 50.8 | 51.7 | 50.6 | 49.8 |
| 2017 | 48.1 | 48.8 | 48.6 | 49.2 | 49.0 | 49.3 | 49.0 | 49.2 | 49.2 | 49.5 | 49.1 | 48.6 | 49.0 |
| 2018 | 47.4 | 47.5 | 47.8 | 48.7 | 48.0 | 48.1 | 48.2 | 48.8 | 48.7 | 50.1 | 49.7 | 48.5 | 48.5 |
| 2019 | 48.3 | 48.6 | 48.7 | 48.7 | 48.3 | 47.9 | 47.7 | 48.0 | 47.2 | 47.5 | 48.7 | 47.7 | 48.1 |
| **Education and Health Services** | | | | | | | | | | | | | |
| 2011 | 46.1 | 46.4 | 46.3 | 46.7 | 46.6 | 46.4 | 45.9 | 46.3 | 46.7 | 47.4 | 47.5 | 47.3 | 46.6 |
| 2012 | 46.6 | 47.2 | 47.0 | 47.3 | 47.1 | 46.7 | 47.0 | 47.4 | 48.0 | 48.2 | 48.5 | 48.4 | 47.5 |
| 2013 | 47.9 | 48.5 | 48.6 | 48.5 | 48.4 | 47.8 | 47.7 | 48.3 | 48.7 | 48.5 | 48.5 | 48.4 | 48.3 |
| 2014 | 47.3 | 47.7 | 47.6 | 48.0 | 48.0 | 47.4 | 47.3 | 47.5 | 48.2 | 48.6 | 48.8 | 48.6 | 47.9 |
| 2015 | 48.9 | 49.4 | 49.3 | 49.7 | 49.7 | 49.3 | 49.1 | 49.4 | 50.1 | 50.2 | 50.5 | 50.4 | 49.7 |
| 2016 | 49.8 | 50.6 | 50.7 | 51.0 | 50.9 | 50.4 | 50.3 | 50.8 | 50.9 | 51.2 | 51.2 | 51.0 | 50.7 |
| 2017 | 50.0 | 50.5 | 50.2 | 50.5 | 50.5 | 50.1 | 49.7 | 50.1 | 50.3 | 51.1 | 51.1 | 50.9 | 50.4 |
| 2018 | 50.4 | 51.1 | 51.2 | 51.3 | 51.3 | 50.8 | 50.6 | 51.4 | 51.2 | 51.8 | 52.1 | 51.7 | 51.2 |
| 2019 | 51.3 | 51.8 | 51.9 | 52.4 | 52.7 | 52.3 | 51.7 | 52.1 | 51.9 | 52.2 | 52.8 | 52.6 | 52.1 |
| **Leisure and Hospitality** | | | | | | | | | | | | | |
| 2011 | 28.8 | 29.3 | 30.0 | 30.7 | 31.3 | 31.8 | 31.5 | 31.8 | 31.0 | 30.6 | 30.3 | 30.0 | 30.6 |
| 2012 | 29.4 | 29.8 | 30.5 | 31.1 | 31.7 | 32.3 | 32.5 | 32.7 | 31.6 | 31.7 | 31.2 | 31.0 | 31.3 |
| 2013 | 30.5 | 30.9 | 31.4 | 32.3 | 32.7 | 33.2 | 33.2 | 33.6 | 32.5 | 32.3 | 32.1 | 32.0 | 32.2 |
| 2014 | 30.9 | 30.9 | 31.7 | 32.8 | 33.5 | 33.5 | 33.6 | 34.0 | 33.1 | 33.2 | 32.9 | 32.8 | 32.7 |
| 2015 | 31.8 | 32.2 | 32.8 | 33.8 | 34.7 | 34.9 | 34.4 | 34.8 | 34.3 | 34.1 | 33.9 | 33.5 | 33.8 |
| 2016 | 33.0 | 33.2 | 33.7 | 34.9 | 35.7 | 35.9 | 35.6 | 35.7 | 35.2 | 35.1 | 35.5 | 35.0 | 34.9 |
| 2017 | 34.1 | 34.7 | 35.3 | 35.8 | 36.3 | 37.0 | 36.7 | 37.0 | 36.1 | 35.7 | 35.6 | 35.0 | 35.8 |
| 2018 | 34.6 | 35.1 | 35.8 | 36.2 | 36.8 | 37.3 | 37.6 | 37.7 | 36.4 | 36.7 | 37.0 | 36.0 | 36.4 |
| 2019 | 36.0 | 36.4 | 37.3 | 38.1 | 38.6 | 39.2 | 38.7 | 38.9 | 37.8 | 38.7 | 38.4 | 37.8 | 38.0 |
| **Other Services** | | | | | | | | | | | | | |
| 2011 | 11.9 | 11.9 | 11.8 | 11.9 | 11.9 | 12.1 | 12.1 | 12.0 | 11.9 | 11.9 | 11.9 | 12.0 | 11.9 |
| 2012 | 11.9 | 11.9 | 11.9 | 12.1 | 12.3 | 12.6 | 12.5 | 12.4 | 12.2 | 12.3 | 12.3 | 12.4 | 12.2 |
| 2013 | 12.3 | 12.4 | 12.4 | 12.3 | 12.4 | 12.7 | 12.7 | 12.6 | 12.4 | 12.4 | 12.5 | 12.4 | 12.5 |
| 2014 | 12.3 | 12.3 | 12.4 | 12.6 | 12.7 | 12.9 | 12.9 | 12.8 | 12.5 | 12.6 | 12.5 | 12.5 | 12.6 |
| 2015 | 12.4 | 12.4 | 12.4 | 12.5 | 12.6 | 12.6 | 12.9 | 12.6 | 12.3 | 12.5 | 12.4 | 12.4 | 12.5 |
| 2016 | 12.2 | 12.2 | 12.3 | 12.4 | 12.5 | 12.6 | 12.6 | 12.4 | 12.4 | 12.6 | 12.5 | 12.4 | 12.4 |
| 2017 | 12.2 | 12.3 | 12.3 | 12.4 | 12.5 | 12.7 | 12.7 | 12.4 | 12.3 | 12.3 | 12.3 | 12.3 | 12.4 |
| 2018 | 12.2 | 12.3 | 12.3 | 12.3 | 12.3 | 12.7 | 12.5 | 12.4 | 12.3 | 12.4 | 12.4 | 12.4 | 12.4 |
| 2019 | 12.3 | 12.4 | 12.5 | 12.4 | 12.4 | 12.7 | 12.8 | 12.5 | 12.4 | 12.5 | 12.4 | 12.5 | 12.5 |
| **Government** | | | | | | | | | | | | | |
| 2011 | 46.3 | 46.6 | 46.9 | 46.8 | 46.9 | 41.9 | 37.5 | 40.8 | 45.5 | 46.6 | 46.9 | 46.7 | 45.0 |
| 2012 | 45.4 | 45.9 | 46.3 | 46.5 | 47.0 | 40.5 | 32.3 | 40.8 | 45.1 | 46.5 | 46.9 | 46.3 | 44.1 |
| 2013 | 45.9 | 46.2 | 46.7 | 46.4 | 46.6 | 41.3 | 34.4 | 40.9 | 45.1 | 45.8 | 46.2 | 46.0 | 44.3 |
| 2014 | 45.4 | 45.5 | 45.9 | 46.2 | 46.8 | 41.5 | 34.7 | 40.5 | 44.6 | 45.4 | 45.9 | 45.4 | 44.0 |
| 2015 | 44.9 | 45.0 | 45.0 | 45.3 | 45.6 | 41.3 | 34.5 | 40.0 | 44.2 | 44.6 | 44.9 | 44.8 | 43.3 |
| 2016 | 44.1 | 44.8 | 45.5 | 45.0 | 45.4 | 40.7 | 34.9 | 39.9 | 43.9 | 45.6 | 46.1 | 45.3 | 43.4 |
| 2017 | 44.5 | 45.0 | 45.1 | 45.3 | 45.3 | 40.7 | 35.1 | 40.2 | 44.4 | 44.9 | 44.9 | 44.6 | 43.3 |
| 2018 | 44.3 | 44.7 | 44.9 | 45.3 | 46.0 | 41.2 | 35.1 | 39.7 | 44.3 | 45.2 | 45.5 | 45.1 | 43.4 |
| 2019 | 44.1 | 44.7 | 44.8 | 45.1 | 45.4 | 39.7 | 33.2 | 39.7 | 44.4 | 45.3 | 45.4 | 44.9 | 43.1 |

# APPENDIX

# CORE BASED STATISTICAL AREAS (CBSAs), METROPOLITAN DIVISIONS, AND COMBINED STATISTICAL AREAS (CSAs), MARCH 2020

| CBSA Code | Metropolitan Division Code | CBSA Title | County/County Equivalent | State Name | FIPS State Code |
|-----------|---------------------------|------------|--------------------------|------------|-----------------|
| 35620 | 35004 | New York-Newark-Jersey City, NY-NJ-PA | Nassau County | New York | 36 |
|  | 35004 |  | Suffolk County | New York | 36 |
|  | 35084 |  | Essex County | New Jersey | 34 |
|  | 35084 |  | Hunterdon County | New Jersey | 34 |
|  | 35084 |  | Morris County | New Jersey | 34 |
|  | 35084 |  | Sussex County | New Jersey | 34 |
|  | 35084 |  | Union County | New Jersey | 34 |
|  | 35084 |  | Pike County | Pennsylvania | 42 |
|  | 35154 |  | Middlesex County | New Jersey | 34 |
|  | 35154 |  | Monmouth County | New Jersey | 34 |
|  | 35154 |  | Ocean County | New Jersey | 34 |
|  | 35154 |  | Somerset County | New Jersey | 34 |
|  | 35614 |  | Bergen County | New Jersey | 34 |
|  | 35614 |  | Hudson County | New Jersey | 34 |
|  | 35614 |  | Passaic County | New Jersey | 34 |
|  | 35614 |  | Bronx County | New York | 36 |
|  | 35614 |  | Kings County | New York | 36 |
|  | 35614 |  | New York County | New York | 36 |
|  | 35614 |  | Putnam County | New York | 36 |
|  | 35614 |  | Queens County | New York | 36 |
|  | 35614 |  | Richmond County | New York | 36 |
|  | 35614 |  | Rockland County | New York | 36 |
|  | 35614 |  | Westchester County | New York | 36 |
| 31080 | 11244 | Los Angeles-Long Beach-Anaheim, CA | Orange County | California | 06 |
|  | 31084 |  | Los Angeles County | California | 06 |
| 16980 | 16984 | Chicago-Naperville-Elgin, IL-IN-WI | Cook County | Illinois | 17 |
|  | 16984 |  | DuPage County | Illinois | 17 |
|  | 16984 |  | Grundy County | Illinois | 17 |
|  | 16984 |  | McHenry County | Illinois | 17 |
|  | 16984 |  | Will County | Illinois | 17 |
|  | 20994 |  | DeKalb County | Illinois | 17 |
|  | 20994 |  | Kane County | Illinois | 17 |
|  | 20994 |  | Kendall County | Illinois | 17 |
|  | 23844 |  | Jasper County | Indiana | 18 |
|  | 23844 |  | Lake County | Indiana | 18 |
|  | 23844 |  | Newton County | Indiana | 18 |
|  | 23844 |  | Porter County | Indiana | 18 |
|  | 29404 |  | Lake County | Illinois | 17 |
|  | 29404 |  |  |  |  |
| 19100 | 19124 | Dallas-Fort Worth-Arlington, TX | Collin County | Texas | 48 |
|  | 19124 |  | Dallas County | Texas | 48 |
|  | 19124 |  | Denton County | Texas | 48 |
|  | 19124 |  | Ellis County | Texas | 48 |
|  | 19124 |  | Hunt County | Texas | 48 |
|  | 19124 |  | Kaufman County | Texas | 48 |
|  | 19124 |  | Rockwall County | Texas | 48 |
|  | 23104 |  | Johnson County | Texas | 48 |
|  | 23104 |  | Parker County | Texas | 48 |
|  | 23104 |  | Tarrant County | Texas | 48 |
|  | 23104 |  | Wise County | Texas | 48 |
| 26420 |  | Houston-The Woodlands-Sugar Land, TX | Austin County | Texas | 48 |
|  |  |  | Brazoria County | Texas | 48 |
|  |  |  | Chambers County | Texas | 48 |
|  |  |  | Fort Bend County | Texas | 48 |
|  |  |  | Galveston County | Texas | 48 |
|  |  |  | Harris County | Texas | 48 |
|  |  |  | Liberty County | Texas | 48 |
|  |  |  | Montgomery County | Texas | 48 |
|  |  |  | Waller County | Texas | 48 |
| 47900 | 23224 | Washington-Arlington-Alexandria, DC-VA-MD-WV | Frederick County | Maryland | 24 |
|  | 23224 |  | Montgomery County | Maryland | 24 |
|  | 47894 |  | District of Columbia | District of Columbia | 11 |
|  | 47894 |  | Calvert County | Maryland | 24 |
|  | 47894 |  | Charles County | Maryland | 24 |
|  | 47894 |  | Prince George's County | Maryland | 24 |
|  | 47894 |  | Arlington County | Virginia | 51 |
|  | 47894 |  | Clarke County | Virginia | 51 |
|  | 47894 |  | Culpeper County | Virginia | 51 |
|  | 47894 |  | Fairfax County | Virginia | 51 |

| CBSA Code | Metropolitan Division Code | CBSA Title | County/County Equivalent | State Name | FIPS State Code |
|---|---|---|---|---|---|
| | 47894 | | Fauquier County | Virginia | 51 |
| | 47894 | | Loudoun County | Virginia | 51 |
| | 47894 | | Madison County | Virginia | 51 |
| | 47894 | | Prince William County | Virginia | 51 |
| | 47894 | | Rappahannock County | Virginia | 51 |
| | 47894 | | Spotsylvania County | Virginia | 51 |
| | 47894 | | Stafford County | Virginia | 51 |
| | 47894 | | Warren County | Virginia | 51 |
| | 47894 | | Alexandria city | Virginia | 51 |
| | 47894 | | Fairfax city | Virginia | 51 |
| | 47894 | | Falls Church city | Virginia | 51 |
| | 47894 | | Fredericksburg city | Virginia | 51 |
| | 47894 | | Manassas city | Virginia | 51 |
| | 47894 | | Manassas Park city | Virginia | 51 |
| | 47894 | | Jefferson County | West Virginia | 54 |
| 33100 | 22744 | Miami-Fort Lauderdale-Pompano Beach, FL Metro Area | Broward County | Florida | 12 |
| | 33124 | | Miami-Dade County | Florida | 12 |
| | 48424 | | Palm Beach County | Florida | 12 |
| 37980 | 15804 | Philadelphia-Camden-Wilmington, PA-NJ-DE-MD | Burlington County | New Jersey | 34 |
| | 15804 | | Camden County | New Jersey | 34 |
| | 15804 | | Gloucester County | New Jersey | 34 |
| | 33874 | | Bucks County | Pennsylvania | 42 |
| | 33874 | | Chester County | Pennsylvania | 42 |
| | 33874 | | Montgomery County | Pennsylvania | 42 |
| | 37964 | | Delaware County | Pennsylvania | 42 |
| | 37964 | | Philadelphia County | Pennsylvania | 42 |
| | 48864 | | New Castle County | Delaware | 10 |
| | 48864 | | Cecil County | Maryland | 24 |
| | 48864 | | Salem County | New Jersey | 34 |
| 12060 | | Atlanta-Sandy Springs-Alpharetta, GA | Barrow County | Georgia | 13 |
| 12060 | | | Bartow County | Georgia | 13 |
| 12060 | | | Butts County | Georgia | 13 |
| 12060 | | | Carroll County | Georgia | 13 |
| 12060 | | | Cherokee County | Georgia | 13 |
| 12060 | | | Clayton County | Georgia | 13 |
| 12060 | | | Cobb County | Georgia | 13 |
| 12060 | | | Coweta County | Georgia | 13 |
| 12060 | | | Dawson County | Georgia | 13 |
| 12060 | | | DeKalb County | Georgia | 13 |
| 12060 | | | Douglas County | Georgia | 13 |
| 12060 | | | Fayette County | Georgia | 13 |
| 12060 | | | Forsyth County | Georgia | 13 |
| 12060 | | | Fulton County | Georgia | 13 |
| 12060 | | | Gwinnett County | Georgia | 13 |
| 12060 | | | Haralson County | Georgia | 13 |
| 12060 | | | Heard County | Georgia | 13 |
| 12060 | | | Henry County | Georgia | 13 |
| 12060 | | | Jasper County | Georgia | 13 |
| 12060 | | | Lamar County | Georgia | 13 |
| 12060 | | | Meriwether County | Georgia | 13 |
| 12060 | | | Morgan County | Georgia | 13 |
| 12060 | | | Newton County | Georgia | 13 |
| 12060 | | | Paulding County | Georgia | 13 |
| 12060 | | | Pickens County | Georgia | 13 |
| 12060 | | | Pike County | Georgia | 13 |
| 12060 | | | Rockdale County | Georgia | 13 |
| 12060 | | | Spalding County | Georgia | 13 |
| 12060 | | | Walton County | Georgia | 13 |
| 38060 | | Phoenix-Mesa-Chandler, AZ | Maricopa County | Arizona | 04 |
| 38060 | | | Pinal County | Arizona | 04 |
| 14460 | 14454 | Boston-Cambridge-Newton, MA-NH | Norfolk County | Massachusetts | 25 |
| 14460 | 14454 | | Plymouth County | Massachusetts | 25 |
| 14460 | 14454 | | Suffolk County | Massachusetts | 25 |
| 14460 | 15764 | | Essex County | Massachusetts | 25 |
| 14460 | 15764 | | Middlesex County | Massachusetts | 25 |
| 14460 | 40484 | | Rockingham County | New Hampshire | 33 |
| 14460 | 40484 | | Strafford County | New Hampshire | 33 |
| 41860 | 36084 | San Francisco-Oakland-Berkeley, CA | Alameda County | California | 06 |
| 41860 | 36084 | | Contra Costa County | California | 06 |
| 41860 | 41884 | | San Francisco County | California | 06 |
| 41860 | 41884 | | San Mateo County | California | 06 |
| 41860 | 42034 | | Marin County | California | 06 |
| 40140 | | Riverside-San Bernardino-Ontario, CA | Riverside County | California | 06 |
| 40140 | | | San Bernardino County | California | 06 |
| 19820 | 19804 | Detroit-Warren-Dearborn, MI | Wayne County | Michigan | 26 |
| 19820 | 47664 | | Lapeer County | Michigan | 26 |
| 19820 | 47664 | | Livingston County | Michigan | 26 |
| 19820 | 47664 | | Macomb County | Michigan | 26 |
| 19820 | 47664 | | Oakland County | Michigan | 26 |

| CBSA Code | Metropolitan Division Code | CBSA Title | County/County Equivalent | State Name | FIPS State Code |
|---|---|---|---|---|---|
| 42660 | 42644 | Seattle-Tacoma-Bellevue, WA | King County | Washington | 53 |
| 42660 | 42644 | | Snohomish County | Washington | 53 |
| 42660 | 45104 | | Pierce County | Washington | 53 |
| 33460 | | Minneapolis-St. Paul-Bloomington, MN-WI | Anoka County | Minnesota | 27 |
| 33460 | | | Carver County | Minnesota | 27 |
| 33460 | | | Chisago County | Minnesota | 27 |
| 33460 | | | Dakota County | Minnesota | 27 |
| 33460 | | | Hennepin County | Minnesota | 27 |
| 33460 | | | Isanti County | Minnesota | 27 |
| 33460 | | | Le Sueur County | Minnesota | 27 |
| 33460 | | | Mille Lacs County | Minnesota | 27 |
| 33460 | | | Ramsey County | Minnesota | 27 |
| 33460 | | | Scott County | Minnesota | 27 |
| 33460 | | | Sherburne County | Minnesota | 27 |
| 33460 | | | Washington County | Minnesota | 27 |
| 33460 | | | Wright County | Minnesota | 27 |
| 33460 | | | Pierce County | Wisconsin | 55 |
| 33460 | | | St. Croix County | Wisconsin | 55 |
| 41740 | | San Diego-Chula Vista-Carlsbad, CA | San Diego County | California | 06 |
| 45300 | | Tampa-St. Petersburg-Clearwater, FL | Hernando County | Florida | 12 |
| 45300 | | | Hillsborough County | Florida | 12 |
| 45300 | | | Pasco County | Florida | 12 |
| 45300 | | | Pinellas County | Florida | 12 |
| 19740 | | Denver-Aurora-Lakewood, CO | Adams County | Colorado | 08 |
| 19740 | | | Arapahoe County | Colorado | 08 |
| 19740 | | | Broomfield County | Colorado | 08 |
| 19740 | | | Clear Creek County | Colorado | 08 |
| 19740 | | | Denver County | Colorado | 08 |
| 19740 | | | Douglas County | Colorado | 08 |
| 19740 | | | Elbert County | Colorado | 08 |
| 19740 | | | Gilpin County | Colorado | 08 |
| 19740 | | | Jefferson County | Colorado | 08 |
| 19740 | | | Park County | Colorado | 08 |
| 41180 | | St. Louis, MO-IL | Bond County | Illinois | 17 |
| 41180 | | | Calhoun County | Illinois | 17 |
| 41180 | | | Clinton County | Illinois | 17 |
| 41180 | | | Jersey County | Illinois | 17 |
| 41180 | | | Macoupin County | Illinois | 17 |
| 41180 | | | Madison County | Illinois | 17 |
| 41180 | | | Monroe County | Illinois | 17 |
| 41180 | | | St. Clair County | Illinois | 17 |
| 41180 | | | Franklin County | Missouri | 29 |
| 41180 | | | Jefferson County | Missouri | 29 |
| 41180 | | | Lincoln County | Missouri | 29 |
| 41180 | | | St. Charles County | Missouri | 29 |
| 41180 | | | St. Louis County | Missouri | 29 |
| 41180 | | | Warren County | Missouri | 29 |
| 41180 | | | St. Louis city | Missouri | 29 |
| 12580 | | Baltimore-Columbia-Towson, MD | Anne Arundel County | Maryland | 24 |
| 12580 | | | Baltimore County | Maryland | 24 |
| 12580 | | | Carroll County | Maryland | 24 |
| 12580 | | | Harford County | Maryland | 24 |
| 12580 | | | Howard County | Maryland | 24 |
| 12580 | | | Queen Anne's County | Maryland | 24 |
| 12580 | | | Baltimore city | Maryland | 24 |
| 16740 | | Charlotte-Concord-Gastonia, NC-SC | Anson County | North Carolina | 37 |
| 16740 | | | Cabarrus County | North Carolina | 37 |
| 16740 | | | Gaston County | North Carolina | 37 |
| 16740 | | | Iredell County | North Carolina | 37 |
| 16740 | | | Lincoln County | North Carolina | 37 |
| 16740 | | | Mecklenburg County | North Carolina | 37 |
| 16740 | | | Rowan County | North Carolina | 37 |
| 16740 | | | Union County | North Carolina | 37 |
| 16740 | | | Chester County | South Carolina | 45 |
| 16740 | | | Lancaster County | South Carolina | 45 |
| 16740 | | | York County | South Carolina | 45 |
| 36740 | | Orlando-Kissimmee-Sanford, FL | Lake County | Florida | 12 |
| 36740 | | | Orange County | Florida | 12 |
| 36740 | | | Osceola County | Florida | 12 |
| 36740 | | | Seminole County | Florida | 12 |
| 41700 | | San Antonio-New Braunfels, TX | Atascosa County | Texas | 48 |
| 41700 | | | Bandera County | Texas | 48 |
| 41700 | | | Bexar County | Texas | 48 |
| 41700 | | | Comal County | Texas | 48 |
| 41700 | | | Guadalupe County | Texas | 48 |
| 41700 | | | Kendall County | Texas | 48 |
| 41700 | | | Medina County | Texas | 48 |
| 41700 | | | Wilson County | Texas | 48 |

| CBSA Code | Metropolitan Division Code | CBSA Title | County/County Equivalent | State Name | FIPS State Code |
|---|---|---|---|---|---|
| | | Portland-Vancouver-Hillsboro, OR-WA | | | |
| 38900 | | | Clackamas County | Oregon | 41 |
| 38900 | | | Columbia County | Oregon | 41 |
| 38900 | | | Multnomah County | Oregon | 41 |
| 38900 | | | Washington County | Oregon | 41 |
| 38900 | | | Yamhill County | Oregon | 41 |
| 38900 | | | Clark County | Washington | 53 |
| 38900 | | | Skamania County | Washington | 53 |
| | | Sacramento-Roseville-Folsom, CA | | | |
| 40900 | | | El Dorado County | California | 06 |
| 40900 | | | Placer County | California | 06 |
| 40900 | | | Sacramento County | California | 06 |
| 40900 | | | Yolo County | California | 06 |
| | | Pittsburgh, PA | | | |
| 38300 | | | Allegheny County | Pennsylvania | 42 |
| 38300 | | | Armstrong County | Pennsylvania | 42 |
| 38300 | | | Beaver County | Pennsylvania | 42 |
| 38300 | | | Butler County | Pennsylvania | 42 |
| 38300 | | | Fayette County | Pennsylvania | 42 |
| 38300 | | | Washington County | Pennsylvania | 42 |
| 38300 | | | Westmoreland County | Pennsylvania | 42 |
| 29820 | | Las Vegas-Henderson-Paradise, NV | Clark County | Nevada | 32 |
| 12420 | | Austin-Round Rock-Georgetown, TX | Bastrop County | Texas | 48 |
| 12420 | | | Caldwell County | Texas | 48 |
| 12420 | | | Hays County | Texas | 48 |
| 12420 | | | Travis County | Texas | 48 |
| 12420 | | | Williamson County | Texas | 48 |
| 17140 | | Cincinnati, OH-KY-IN | Dearborn County | Indiana | 18 |
| 17140 | | | Franklin County | Indiana | 18 |
| 17140 | | | Ohio County | Indiana | 18 |
| 17140 | | | Union County | Indiana | 18 |
| 17140 | | | Boone County | Kentucky | 21 |
| 17140 | | | Bracken County | Kentucky | 21 |
| 17140 | | | Campbell County | Kentucky | 21 |
| 17140 | | | Gallatin County | Kentucky | 21 |
| 17140 | | | Grant County | Kentucky | 21 |
| 17140 | | | Kenton County | Kentucky | 21 |
| 17140 | | | Pendleton County | Kentucky | 21 |
| 17140 | | | Brown County | Ohio | 39 |
| 17140 | | | Butler County | Ohio | 39 |
| 17140 | | | Clermont County | Ohio | 39 |
| 17140 | | | Hamilton County | Ohio | 39 |
| 17140 | | | Warren County | Ohio | 39 |
| 28140 | | Kansas City, MO-KS | Johnson County | Kansas | 20 |
| 28140 | | | Leavenworth County | Kansas | 20 |
| 28140 | | | Linn County | Kansas | 20 |
| 28140 | | | Miami County | Kansas | 20 |
| 28140 | | | Wyandotte County | Kansas | 20 |
| 28140 | | | Bates County | Missouri | 29 |
| 28140 | | | Caldwell County | Missouri | 29 |
| 28140 | | | Cass County | Missouri | 29 |
| 28140 | | | Clay County | Missouri | 29 |
| 28140 | | | Clinton County | Missouri | 29 |
| 28140 | | | Jackson County | Missouri | 29 |
| 28140 | | | Lafayette County | Missouri | 29 |
| 28140 | | | Platte County | Missouri | 29 |
| 28140 | | | Ray County | Missouri | 29 |
| 18140 | | Columbus, OH | Delaware County | Ohio | 39 |
| 18140 | | | Fairfield County | Ohio | 39 |
| 18140 | | | Franklin County | Ohio | 39 |
| 18140 | | | Hocking County | Ohio | 39 |
| 18140 | | | Licking County | Ohio | 39 |
| 18140 | | | Madison County | Ohio | 39 |
| 18140 | | | Morrow County | Ohio | 39 |
| 18140 | | | Perry County | Ohio | 39 |
| 18140 | | | Pickaway County | Ohio | 39 |
| 18140 | | | Union County | Ohio | 39 |
| 26900 | | Indianapolis-Carmel-Anderson, IN | Boone County | Indiana | 18 |
| 26900 | | | Brown County | Indiana | 18 |
| 26900 | | | Hamilton County | Indiana | 18 |
| 26900 | | | Hancock County | Indiana | 18 |
| 26900 | | | Hendricks County | Indiana | 18 |
| 26900 | | | Johnson County | Indiana | 18 |
| 26900 | | | Madison County | Indiana | 18 |
| 26900 | | | Marion County | Indiana | 18 |
| 26900 | | | Morgan County | Indiana | 18 |
| 26900 | | | Putnam County | Indiana | 18 |
| 26900 | | | Shelby County | Indiana | 18 |
| 17460 | | Cleveland-Elyria, OH | Cuyahoga County | Ohio | 39 |
| 17460 | | | Geauga County | Ohio | 39 |

| CBSA Code | Metropolitan Division Code | CBSA Title | County/County Equivalent | State Name | FIPS State Code |
|---|---|---|---|---|---|
| 17460 | | | Lake County | Ohio | 39 |
| 17460 | | | Lorain County | Ohio | 39 |
| 17460 | | | Medina County | Ohio | 39 |
| 41940 | | San Jose-Sunnyvale-Santa Clara, CA | San Benito County | California | 06 |
| 41940 | | | Santa Clara County | California | 06 |
| 34980 | | Nashville-Davidson--Murfreesboro--Franklin, TN | Cannon County | Tennessee | 47 |
| 34980 | | | Cheatham County | Tennessee | 47 |
| 34980 | | | Davidson County | Tennessee | 47 |
| 34980 | | | Dickson County | Tennessee | 47 |
| 34980 | | | Macon County | Tennessee | 47 |
| 34980 | | | Maury County | Tennessee | 47 |
| 34980 | | | Robertson County | Tennessee | 47 |
| 34980 | | | Rutherford County | Tennessee | 47 |
| 34980 | | | Smith County | Tennessee | 47 |
| 34980 | | | Sumner County | Tennessee | 47 |
| 34980 | | | Trousdale County | Tennessee | 47 |
| 34980 | | | Williamson County | Tennessee | 47 |
| 34980 | | | Wilson County | Tennessee | 47 |
| 47260 | | Virginia Beach-Norfolk-Newport News, VA-NC | Camden County | North Carolina | 37 |
| 47260 | | | Currituck County | North Carolina | 37 |
| 47260 | | | Gates County | North Carolina | 37 |
| 47260 | | | Gloucester County | Virginia | 51 |
| 47260 | | | Isle of Wight County | Virginia | 51 |
| 47260 | | | James City County | Virginia | 51 |
| 47260 | | | Mathews County | Virginia | 51 |
| 47260 | | | Southampton County | Virginia | 51 |
| 47260 | | | York County | Virginia | 51 |
| 47260 | | | Chesapeake city | Virginia | 51 |
| 47260 | | | Franklin city | Virginia | 51 |
| 47260 | | | Hampton city | Virginia | 51 |
| 47260 | | | Newport News city | Virginia | 51 |
| 47260 | | | Norfolk city | Virginia | 51 |
| 47260 | | | Poquoson city | Virginia | 51 |
| 47260 | | | Portsmouth city | Virginia | 51 |
| 47260 | | | Suffolk city | Virginia | 51 |
| 47260 | | | Virginia Beach city | Virginia | 51 |
| 47260 | | | Williamsburg city | Virginia | 51 |
| 39300 | | Providence-Warwick, RI-MA | Bristol County | Massachusetts | 25 |
| 39300 | | | Bristol County | Rhode Island | 44 |
| 39300 | | | Kent County | Rhode Island | 44 |
| 39300 | | | Newport County | Rhode Island | 44 |
| 39300 | | | Providence County | Rhode Island | 44 |
| 39300 | | | Washington County | Rhode Island | 44 |
| 33340 | | Milwaukee-Waukesha, WI | Milwaukee County | Wisconsin | 55 |
| 33340 | | | Ozaukee County | Wisconsin | 55 |
| 33340 | | | Washington County | Wisconsin | 55 |
| 33340 | | | Waukesha County | Wisconsin | 55 |
| 27260 | | Jacksonville, FL | Baker County | Florida | 12 |
| 27260 | | | Clay County | Florida | 12 |
| 27260 | | | Duval County | Florida | 12 |
| 27260 | | | Nassau County | Florida | 12 |
| 27260 | | | St. Johns County | Florida | 12 |
| 27300 | | | Morgan County | Illinois | 17 |
| 27300 | | | Scott County | Illinois | 17 |
| 27340 | | | Onslow County | North Carolina | 37 |
| 27380 | | | Cherokee County | Texas | 48 |
| 36420 | | Oklahoma City, OK | Canadian County | Oklahoma | 40 |
| 36420 | | | Cleveland County | Oklahoma | 40 |
| 36420 | | | Grady County | Oklahoma | 40 |
| 36420 | | | Lincoln County | Oklahoma | 40 |
| 36420 | | | Logan County | Oklahoma | 40 |
| 36420 | | | McClain County | Oklahoma | 40 |
| 36420 | | | Oklahoma County | Oklahoma | 40 |
| 39580 | | Raleigh-Cary, NC | Franklin County | North Carolina | 37 |
| 39580 | | | Johnston County | North Carolina | 37 |
| 39580 | | | Wake County | North Carolina | 37 |
| 32820 | | Memphis, TN-MS-AR | Crittenden County | Arkansas | 05 |
| 32820 | | | DeSoto County | Mississippi | 28 |
| 32820 | | | Marshall County | Mississippi | 28 |
| 32820 | | | Tate County | Mississippi | 28 |
| 32820 | | | Tunica County | Mississippi | 28 |
| 32820 | | | Fayette County | Tennessee | 47 |
| 32820 | | | Shelby County | Tennessee | 47 |
| 32820 | | | Tipton County | Tennessee | 47 |
| 40060 | | Richmond, VA | Amelia County | Virginia | 51 |
| 40060 | | | Charles City County | Virginia | 51 |
| 40060 | | | Chesterfield County | Virginia | 51 |
| 40060 | | | Dinwiddie County | Virginia | 51 |
| 40060 | | | Goochland County | Virginia | 51 |

| CBSA Code | Metropolitan Division Code | CBSA Title | County/County Equivalent | State Name | FIPS State Code |
|---|---|---|---|---|---|
| 40060 | | | Hanover County | Virginia | 51 |
| 40060 | | | Henrico County | Virginia | 51 |
| 40060 | | | King and Queen County | Virginia | 51 |
| 40060 | | | King William County | Virginia | 51 |
| 40060 | | | New Kent County | Virginia | 51 |
| 40060 | | | Powhatan County | Virginia | 51 |
| 40060 | | | Prince George County | Virginia | 51 |
| 40060 | | | Sussex County | Virginia | 51 |
| 40060 | | | Colonial Heights city | Virginia | 51 |
| 40060 | | | Hopewell city | Virginia | 51 |
| 40060 | | | Petersburg city | Virginia | 51 |
| 40060 | | | Richmond city | Virginia | 51 |
| 35380 | | New Orleans-Metairie, LA | Jefferson Parish | Louisiana | 22 |
| 35380 | | | Orleans Parish | Louisiana | 22 |
| 35380 | | | Plaquemines Parish | Louisiana | 22 |
| 35380 | | | St. Bernard Parish | Louisiana | 22 |
| 35380 | | | St. Charles Parish | Louisiana | 22 |
| 35380 | | | St. James Parish | Louisiana | 22 |
| 35380 | | | St. John the Baptist Parish | Louisiana | 22 |
| 35380 | | | St. Tammany Parish | Louisiana | 22 |
| 31140 | | Louisville/Jefferson County, KY-IN | Clark County | Indiana | 18 |
| 31140 | | | Floyd County | Indiana | 18 |
| 31140 | | | Harrison County | Indiana | 18 |
| 31140 | | | Washington County | Indiana | 18 |
| 31140 | | | Bullitt County | Kentucky | 21 |
| 31140 | | | Henry County | Kentucky | 21 |
| 31140 | | | Jefferson County | Kentucky | 21 |
| 31140 | | | Oldham County | Kentucky | 21 |
| 31140 | | | Shelby County | Kentucky | 21 |
| 31140 | | | Spencer County | Kentucky | 21 |
| 41620 | | Salt Lake City, UT | Salt Lake County | Utah | 49 |
| 41620 | | | Tooele County | Utah | 49 |
| 25540 | | Hartford-East Hartford-Middletown, CT | Hartford County | Connecticut | 09 |
| 25540 | | | Middlesex County | Connecticut | 09 |
| 25540 | | | Tolland County | Connecticut | 09 |
| 15380 | | Buffalo-Cheektowaga, NY | Erie County | New York | 36 |
| 15380 | | | Niagara County | New York | 36 |
| 13820 | | Birmingham-Hoover, AL | Bibb County | Alabama | 01 |
| 13820 | | | Blount County | Alabama | 01 |
| 13820 | | | Chilton County | Alabama | 01 |
| 13820 | | | Jefferson County | Alabama | 01 |
| 13820 | | | St. Clair County | Alabama | 01 |
| 13820 | | | Shelby County | Alabama | 01 |
| 24340 | | Grand Rapids-Kentwood, MI | Ionia County | Michigan | 26 |
| 24340 | | | Kent County | Michigan | 26 |
| 24340 | | | Montcalm County | Michigan | 26 |
| 40380 | | Rochester, NY | Livingston County | New York | 36 |
| 40380 | | | Monroe County | New York | 36 |
| 40380 | | | Ontario County | New York | 36 |
| 40380 | | | Orleans County | New York | 36 |
| 40380 | | | Wayne County | New York | 36 |
| 40380 | | | Yates County | New York | 36 |
| 46060 | | Tucson, AZ | Pima County | Arizona | 04 |
| 23420 | | Fresno, CA | Fresno County | California | 06 |
| 46140 | | Tulsa, OK | Creek County | Oklahoma | 40 |
| 46140 | | | Okmulgee County | Oklahoma | 40 |
| 46140 | | | Osage County | Oklahoma | 40 |
| 46140 | | | Pawnee County | Oklahoma | 40 |
| 46140 | | | Rogers County | Oklahoma | 40 |
| 46140 | | | Tulsa County | Oklahoma | 40 |
| 46140 | | | Wagoner County | Oklahoma | 40 |
| 46520 | | Urban Honolulu, HI | Honolulu County | Hawaii | 15 |
| 36540 | | Omaha-Council Bluffs, NE-IA | Harrison County | Iowa | 19 |
| 36540 | | | Mills County | Iowa | 19 |
| 36540 | | | Pottawattamie County | Iowa | 19 |
| 36540 | | | Cass County | Nebraska | 31 |
| 36540 | | | Douglas County | Nebraska | 31 |
| 36540 | | | Sarpy County | Nebraska | 31 |
| 36540 | | | Saunders County | Nebraska | 31 |
| 36540 | | | Washington County | Nebraska | 31 |
| 49340 | | Worcester, MA-CT | Windham County | Connecticut | 09 |
| 49340 | | | Worcester County | Massachusetts | 25 |
| 14860 | | Bridgeport-Stamford-Norwalk, CT | Fairfield County | Connecticut | 09 |

| CBSA Code | Metropolitan Division Code | CBSA Title | County/County Equivalent | State Name | FIPS State Code |
|---|---|---|---|---|---|
| 24860 | | Greenville-Anderson, SC | Anderson County | South Carolina | 45 |
| 24860 | | | Greenville County | South Carolina | 45 |
| 24860 | | | Laurens County | South Carolina | 45 |
| 24860 | | | Pickens County | South Carolina | 45 |
| 10740 | | Albuquerque, NM | Bernalillo County | New Mexico | 35 |
| 10740 | | | Sandoval County | New Mexico | 35 |
| 10740 | | | Torrance County | New Mexico | 35 |
| 10740 | | | Valencia County | New Mexico | 35 |
| 12540 | | Bakersfield, CA | Kern County | California | 06 |
| 10580 | | Albany-Schenectady-Troy, NY | Albany County | New York | 36 |
| 10580 | | | Rensselaer County | New York | 36 |
| 10580 | | | Saratoga County | New York | 36 |
| 10580 | | | Schenectady County | New York | 36 |
| 10580 | | | Schoharie County | New York | 36 |
| 28940 | | Knoxville, TN | Anderson County | Tennessee | 47 |
| 28940 | | | Blount County | Tennessee | 47 |
| 28940 | | | Campbell County | Tennessee | 47 |
| 28940 | | | Knox County | Tennessee | 47 |
| 28940 | | | Loudon County | Tennessee | 47 |
| 28940 | | | Morgan County | Tennessee | 47 |
| 28940 | | | Roane County | Tennessee | 47 |
| 28940 | | | Union County | Tennessee | 47 |
| 32580 | | McAllen-Edinburg-Mission, TX | Hidalgo County | Texas | 48 |
| 12940 | | Baton Rouge, LA | Ascension Parish | Louisiana | 22 |
| 12940 | | | Assumption Parish | Louisiana | 22 |
| 12940 | | | East Baton Rouge Parish | Louisiana | 22 |
| 12940 | | | East Feliciana Parish | Louisiana | 22 |
| 12940 | | | Iberville Parish | Louisiana | 22 |
| 12940 | | | Livingston Parish | Louisiana | 22 |
| 12940 | | | Pointe Coupee Parish | Louisiana | 22 |
| 12940 | | | St. Helena Parish | Louisiana | 22 |
| 12940 | | | West Baton Rouge Parish | Louisiana | 22 |
| 12940 | | | West Feliciana Parish | Louisiana | 22 |
| 35300 | | New Haven-Milford, CT | New Haven County | Connecticut | 09 |
| 37100 | | Oxnard-Thousand Oaks-Ventura, CA | Ventura County | California | 06 |
| 21340 | | El Paso, TX | El Paso County | Texas | 48 |
| 10900 | | Allentown-Bethlehem-Easton, PA-NJ | Warren County | New Jersey | 34 |
| 10900 | | | Carbon County | Pennsylvania | 42 |
| 10900 | | | Lehigh County | Pennsylvania | 42 |
| 10900 | | | Northampton County | Pennsylvania | 42 |
| 17900 | | Columbia, SC | Fairfield County | South Carolina | 45 |
| 17900 | | | Kershaw County | South Carolina | 45 |
| 17900 | | | Lexington County | South Carolina | 45 |
| 17900 | | | Richland County | South Carolina | 45 |
| 17900 | | | Saluda County | South Carolina | 45 |
| 35840 | | North Port-Sarasota-Bradenton, FL | Manatee County | Florida | 12 |
| 19430 | | Dayton-Kettering, OH | Greene County | Ohio | 39 |
| 19430 | | | Miami County | Ohio | 39 |
| 19430 | | | Montgomery County | Ohio | 39 |
| 16700 | | Charleston-North Charleston, SC | Berkeley County | South Carolina | 45 |
| 16700 | | | Charleston County | South Carolina | 45 |
| 16700 | | | Dorchester County | South Carolina | 45 |
| 24660 | | Greensboro-High Point, NC | Guilford County | North Carolina | 37 |
| 24660 | | | Randolph County | North Carolina | 37 |
| 24660 | | | Rockingham County | North Carolina | 37 |

Note: The 2010 OMB Standards for Delineating Metropolitan and Micropolitan Statistical Areas are at <https://www.gpo.gov/fdsys/pkg/FR-2010-06-28/pdf/2010-15605.pdf> and <https://www.gpo.gov/fdsys/pkg/FR-2010-07-07/pdf/2010-16368.pdf>.
Source: File prepared by U.S. Census Bureau, Population Division, based on Office of Management and Budget, March 2020 delineations <https://www.whitehouse.gov/wp-content/uploads/2020/03/Bulletin-20-01.pdf>.
Internet Release Date: April 2020